2001

Gift to the Library of
Vermont College
and The Union Institute,
from the chief Editor, Handbook of
Marriage and The Family

Marvin B. Sussman

Handbook of
Marriage and the Family

SECOND EDITION

Handbook of
Marriage and the Family

SECOND EDITION

Edited by

Marvin B. Sussman

Union Institute
Cincinnati, Ohio

Suzanne K. Steinmetz

Indiana University — Purdue University at Indianapolis
Indianapolis, Indiana

and

Gary W. Peterson

Arizona State University
Tempe, Arizona

PLENUM PRESS • NEW YORK AND LONDON

Library of Congress Cataloging-in-Publication Data

Handbook of marriage and the family / edited by Marvin B. Sussman,
  Suzanne K. Steinmetz, and Gary W. Peterson. -- 2nd. ed.
       p.   cm.
    Includes bibliographical references and index.
    ISBN 0-306-45754-7
    1. Family--Handbooks, manuals, etc. 2. Life cycle, Human-
-Handbooks, manuals, etc. 3. Marriage--Handbooks, manuals, etc.
I. Sussman, Marvin B. II. Steinmetz, Suzanne K. III. Peterson,
Gary W.
  HQ518.H154 1999
  306.8--dc21   98-45465
                                                           CIP

ISBN 0-306-45754-7

© 1999, 1987 Plenum Press, New York
A Division of Plenum Publishing Corporation
233 Spring Street, New York, N.Y. 10013

http://www.plenum.com

10 9 8 7 6 5 4 3 2 1

Printed in the United States of America

Contributors

Alan C. Acock
Department of Human Development and Family Sciences
Oregon State University
Corvallis, Oregon 97331-5102

Bert N. Adams
Department of Sociology
University of Wisconsin–Madison
Madison, Wisconsin 53176

Robert Aponte
Department of Sociology
Indiana University–Purdue University at Indianapolis
Indianapolis, Indiana, 46202

Hector Balcazar
Department of Family Resources and Human Development
Arizona State University
Tempe, Arizona 85287-2502

Paul S. Carlin
Department of Economics
Indiana University–Purdue University at Indianapolis
Indianapolis, Indiana 46202

Sheila McIsaac Cooper
Associate Dean of the Graduate School
Indiana University
Indianapolis, Indiana 46202

Douglas E. Crews
Department of Anthropology and School of Public Health
The Ohio State University
Columbus, Ohio 43210

John DeFrain
Department of Family and Consumer Sciences
University of Nebraska
Lincoln, Nebraska 68583-0801

Fran C. Dickson
Department of Human Communication Studies
University of Denver
Denver, Colorado 80208

William J. Doherty
Family Social Science Department
University of Minnesota
St. Paul, Minnesota 55108

Eugene W. Farber
Department of Psychiatry and Behavioral Sciences
Emory University
Atlanta, Georgia 30335-3801

Kimberly A. Faust
Department of Behavioral Science
Fitchburg State College
Fitchburg, Massachusetts 01420-2697

Kay B. Forest
Department of Sociology
Northern Illinois State University
DeKalb, Illinois 60115

Robert T. Francoeur
Biology and Allied Health Sciences
Fairleigh Dickinson University
Madison, New Jersey 07940

Jane F. Gilgun
School of Social Work
University of Minnesota, Twin Cities
St. Paul, Minnesota 55108

Linda Haas
Department of Sociology
Indiana University–Purdue University at
    Indianapolis
Indianapolis, Indiana 46202

Della Hann
National Institute of Mental Health
Rockville, Maryland 20857

Karla K. Hemesath
Department of Family and Community Medicine
College of Medicine at Rockford
Rockford, Illinois 61107-1897

Linda L. Hendrixson
Department of Health
East Stroudsburg University
East Stroudsburg, Pennsylvania 18301

Florence W. Kaslow
Florida Couples and Family Institute
Palm Beach Gardens, Florida 33418
Department of Medical Psychology in Psychiatry
Duke University
Durham, North Carolina 77708-0001
School of Professional Psychology
Florida Institute of Technology
Melbourne, Florida 32901-6988

Nadine J. Kaslow
Departments of Psychiatry and Behavioral
    Sciences and Pediatrics and Psychology
Emory University and Grady Health System
Atlanta, Georgia 30335-3801

Dean D. Knudsen
Department of Sociology and Anthropology
Purdue University
West Lafayette, Indiana 47907

Leora Lawton
TechSociety Research
2342 Shattuck Avenue, #362
Berkeley, California 94704

Gary R. Lee
Department of Sociology
Bowling Green State University
Bowling Green, Ohio 43403-0231

Jerome N. McKibben
Department of Behavioral Science
Fitchburg State College
Fitchburg, Massachusetts 01420-2697

JoAnn Langley Miller
Department of Sociology and Anthropology
Purdue University
West Lafayette, Indiana 47907

Phyllis Moen
Bronfenbrenner Life Course Center
Cornell University
Ithaca, New York 14850-4401

David H. Olson
Department of Family Social Sciences
University of Minnesota
St. Paul, Minnesota 55108

Gary W. Peterson
Department of Sociology
Arizona State University
Tempe, Arizona 85287-2502

Karen A. Polonko
Department of Sociology
Old Dominion University
Norfolk, Virginia 23529

David M. Rosen
Department of Social Sciences and History
Fairleigh Dickinson University
Madison, New Jersey 07940

John Scanzoni
Department of Sociology
University of Florida
Gainesville, Florida 23611

Walter R. Schumm
School of Family Studies and Human Services
College of Human Ecology
Kansas State University
Manhattan, Kansas 66506-1403

Barbara H. Settles
Individual and Family Studies
University of Delaware
Newark, Delaware 19716

Jetse Sprey
Department of Sociology
Case Western Reserve University
Cleveland, Ohio 44106

Suzanne K. Steinmetz
Department of Sociology
Indiana University–Purdue University at
    Indianapolis
Indianapolis, Indiana 46236

Jay D. Teachman
Department of Sociology
Western Washington University
Bellingham, Washington 98225-9081

Judith Treas
Department of Social Sciences
University of California, Irvine
Irvine, California 92717

Brian S. Vargus
Department of Political Science and Indiana
    University Public Opinion Laboratory
Indiana University–Purdue University at
    Indianapolis
Indianapolis, Indiana 46202

Alexis J. Walker
Human Development and Family Services
Oregon State University
Corvallis, Oregon 97331-5102

Gail G. Whitchurch
Department of Communication Studies
Indiana University–Purdue University at
    Indianapolis
Indianapolis, Indiana 46202

Patricia Wittberg
Department of Sociology
Indiana University–Purdue University at
    Indianapolis
Indianapolis, Indiana 46202

Preface

To know where we are going as scholars, educators, and practitioners in the field of marriage and family life, we first need to know where we have been. A perusal of early texts on marriage and family life provides some thought-provoking insights into the accuracy of the saying "what goes around, comes around."

It is interesting to note who has been considered to be in a position to provide information on marriage and family life. Included in the eclectic collection of texts we reviewed were ministers whose focus was on spirituality, doctors who emphasized medical aspects of child and adult health, and public health professionals and home economists concerned with fighting disease, who emphasized cleanliness, order, fighting germs, and eliminating rodents and insects. There are also philosophers who drew from ancient texts when discussing family life and a count who assembled a group of German intellectual elites to address various topics. An insightful essay of this type is by Marta Karlweis (1926), in which she notes:

> There is no other fetish that society holds to so firmly as the conception "woman," with all its usual associations of infantilism and dependence.... The child requires protection, is a minor and consequently a serf, but above all it possesses no spiritual existence. Neither doctorates or other distinctions nor the right to vote have as yet been able to dispel this sweet idea of the childishness of woman, which man cherishes. (p. 209)

Academic Treatment of Marriage and Family

This Preface, however, concentrates on a brief review of the academic treatment of marriage and family in earlier times. Since the publication of Alex Haley's *Roots* (1976), there has been considerable interest generated over finding one's ancestors. In a similar way, learning about our academic roots and about the research and theory legacy provided by those who preceeded us helps us to understand how similar are the problems addressed by academics throughout this century. A select few texts are discussed to provide some insights into the topics our academic predecessors considered to be family problems and their suggestions for solutions. This Preface does not pretend to be either comprehensive or representative in the coverage of the materials but rather seeks to provide some insights on problems that have appeared to trouble those who studied and provided services to families in earlier times.

Charles Franklin and Carrie F. Butler Thwing

The Family, A Historical and Social Study (1886, revised in 1913) was written by Charles Franklin Thwing, president of Western Reserve University, and his wife, Carrie F. Butler Thwing. This book examines family life among the prehistoric family; the Greeks, Romans, and Jews; the family in the Middle Ages; and the "contemporary family." Of interest is that one of the editors of this *Handbook*, Marvin Sussman, was chair of the Department of Sociology at Western Reserve University and another editor, Suzanne Steinmetz, was his student—although by then the university had merged with Case Institute to become Case Western Reserve University. The legacy thus continues, transferred across the academic lineage.

In a chapter entitled "The Family Destroyed," the Thwings use U.S. Census data to demonstrate that "the rate of increase in divorce is far greater than the rate of increase in population" (p. 188). They report that between 1871 and 1880, the rate of increase for the population was 30.1%; for divorce, 79.4%. Desertion accounted for 38.9% of divorces granted between 1887 and 1906. Between 1867 and 1906, adultery became a less prominent cause (38.6% vs. 27.0%), while cruelty increased (4.2% vs. 12.5%). The authors lamented, "The last seventy-five years have apparently changed the marriage relations from a permanent and lifelong state to a union existing during the pleasure of the parties" (p. 197). The authors also observed that marriage changed from a status or sacred arrangement created by God or by large political/economic entities to a civil contract entered into by two consenting parties. With this change, the wife and children were no longer under the domination of the father/husband/patriarch, but under the control of society's rules. We also learn from this text that Roman law, similar to a law currently being proposed in Louisana, had several forms of marriage. Those couples joined by *comemptio* or *usus* could obtain a divorce rather easily; those couples joined by *confarreatio*, a sacred binding, found it quite difficult to obtain a divorce.

Anne Garlin Spencer

Many of the topics covered in Spencer's volume, *Women's Share in Social Culture*, written in 1912 and revised in 1925, are remarkably similar to those covered in contemporary texts: women's rights, women and family, divorce, sex and family, and controlling children. The dedication of the book reads:

> To the memory of Lucretia Mott, who prophesied in life and in work the Womanhood of the Future, not neglectful of least or oldest duty, not loath to assume the largest and newest service, linking the past and present to coming ideal.

Spencer notes that women had performed midwifery and child health duties until the medical profession in the United States was influenced by and began to take training in "obstetrics" in England. Dr. James Lloyd, in 1762, after 2 years' training in England, became the first such doctor to practice this specialty in the United States (p. 72). However, it was not until 1848 that Dr. Samuel Gregory established the first medical training school for women in Boston. He defended himself from the onslaught of male doctors who believed that the value of their degree would be lessened if women could also obtain that degree by noting that women could perform midwifery duties at a cost of about one-third that charged by men. This would enable poor women to obtain medical care. With formal medical training, women were again able to enter the work that throughout history had been their calling, that of midwifery.

According to Spencer, marriage in Western cultures had become a contract, with each party having the power to break the contract. This has provided women with power, which is why, according to Spencer,

> ultra opponents of "Women's Rights" always and instinctively related the greater freedom of women to domestic disaster; and this is also the reason why the ultra proponents of "Women's Rights" as instinctively begin their demands for a larger share of the powers and obligations of social life by women with some radical attack upon that family order which rests upon the legal despotism of the husband and father. (p. 254)

Ernest Groves

The tracing of one's academic lineage is not only limited to the materials covered in textbooks but also can be traced through the leaders in the field—who taught whom and who influenced whom. As we read through one of the early texts, *Social Problems of the Family* (1927) by Ernest Groves, we reflected on two points: First, that we are privileged to be a member of Groves (Conference on Marriage and Family), and second, that Suzanne Steinmetz has a copy of Groves' book inscribed: "This was the textbook for a course on the family that I took at Michigan State College in 1932 under E. Mumford. Signed, Wm. H. Sewell."

In the preface of his book Groves notes: "A scientific study of the family is not an ignoring of the values and ideals attached to the home, but an effort to put aside all subjective attitudes in order to understand the family as it actually is." In lamenting the lack of current, scientific data on family life, he suggests that "the intimacies and reticence of family life create difficulty in its investigation and hamper scientific analysis. This explains in part why literature has attempted to interpret modern family life more often than has science" (p. viii).

The topics explored are most enlightening. In a chapter entitled, "History of the American Family," Groves discusses the advantages expected and evils prophesied from women's suffrage (it would ruin the home and unsex women). Groves concludes that the number of people who were voting had increased and that women's issues such as prohibition as a national policy had gained attention. It appeared to Groves that the major change in family life after the passage of women's suffrage was to make the family more democratic.

A chapter on the "Arrested Family" discusses the term "companionate marriage" and notes that it first appeared in an article in *Journal of Social Hygiene* in May 1924. This term referred to those couples who chose to marry so as to enjoy "a program of pleasure and mutual advantage" but one that sought to avoid "all possible social responsibilities, particularly those connected with having and rearing children" (p. 89). The term was an attempt to provide a more socially desirable one for those who could not, or chose not, to have children and replaced the previous terms "defective," "misfortunate," or what Groves called the "arrested" family.

Divorce and desertion were given a very contemporary treatment, with statistics provided by state and region. Upon examining a 36-year period (1887–1922), Groves found that less than one-third of the divorces granted were obtained by husbands and that the grounds on which divorce could be obtained (nonsupport, neglect, cruelty, adultery) appeared to be a more common offense among men. He also noted that the masculine "social code" demanded that the man assume the burden of guilt as far as legal procedures are concerned so that this wife remained entirely innocent. Groves believed that other states should follow Wisconsin's law requiring a medical examination prior to marriage to screen for venereal diseases, which were incurable at this time. He also recommended abolishing common law marriages since by definition of the law (consent and consummation of the relationship via sexual intercourse) meant that one entered a common law marriage via fornication.

Abolishing alimony was also suggested as a needed reform. Groves provided a quote from an Appellate Court judge of the New York Supreme Court: "Everything considered, I believe alimony should be discontinued because it keeps certain women lazy, gratifies their revenge, makes men miserable and serves no good ends" (p. 156). Groves believed that a woman's right to lifelong financial support when she divorced her husband had been taken for granted for such a long period of time that it had become an assumed matter of justice, which was no longer needed since women were now able to provide for themselves.

The influence of broken homes on delinquency was explored and, in a manner similar to current practices, it was shown, using data from 36 states, that 51.8% of youth in a correctional facility had not lived with both biological parents in an intact family. The summary statement was that "the broken home contributed to delinquency in fully one-half of the cases." Groves reported the findings of another study regarding conditions in New York institutions for delinquent boys that indicated that 45% of these youth came from homes with "abnormal marital relations." Unfortunately, we are left to ponder the reasons for delinquency in the more than half of the residents who came from intact families or families with "normal" marital relations.

Groves believed that the family provided a continuous socializing process—the home not only begins the process of socialization for the child who experience normal family life but also continues the process for a long period, for most persons throughout life. Social problems related to family life, according to Groves, included poverty, housing, roomers, illegitimacy, prostitution, intemperance, leisure (commercialized recreation not within the family), health, and mental hygiene. Under the topic of conservation of the family, Groves examined child labor laws, protection of women, and eugenic marriage laws (laws requiring a physical exam for venereal disease before a marriage license is granted). He reported that as of 1925 only Alabama, Indiana, North Carolina, North Dakota, Oregon, Wyoming, and Wisconsin had laws that required males to be tested and to present a certificate in order to receive a license to marry. Eugenical sterilization to eliminate inferior (mental) stock was first passed by Indiana in 1907, but was later declared unconstitutional in 1921 because it violated the 14th Amendment—the right to privacy. How interesting that the 14th Amendment, used in 1921 to grant all women the right to reproduce, was used again a half-century later in *Roe v. Wade* (1973) to grant women the right to terminate a pregnancy—thus establishing women's right to control all aspects of their reproductive choices. Groves also advocated the reform of child marriage laws, noting that in 1925 the minimum age of marriage was 12 for girls in 14 states; in an additional nine states it was only 14. Thus, the legal age for females to marry, bear and raise children, and live independently of their parents in about half of the states in the United States as late as 1925 was 12 to 14 years of age. Perhaps it is not the behavior of young teenage girls that has changed over the past century but the contemporary interpretation of the meaning of early partnering and parenting.

Family allowance, defined as a living wage, was typically based on the amount needed to support a family of five (two adults and three dependent children). Groves states that computing a family's allowance by this means would result in an income that was inadequate for about 10%–15% of American workers, but in excess of the actual needs for about 70%–80% of the workers. A rather novel solution was suggested, one that would base the minimum-wage scale on the actual needs of the worker who has the responsibility of maintaining a family. On this basis, a single man would not need the same income as a fellow worker who was the father of several children. Groves does note that this would be impractical because employers would give preference to single men since they would work for less. He suggests that a more practical solution might be to adopt the European system of family allowance in which men are paid a single wage and an allowance for wife and children is derived from a common government fund to which all employers contribute. Pensions for mothers was another way to help families; in 1911, Missouri passed the first law in the United States to provide a regular allowance for mothers to assist them in providing care to their own children. By 1921, most states had passed similar legislation. Mothers' allowances, Groves warns, should not be confused with public relief or private charity, which carry a stigma. (As an aside, the price marked on this over 300-page book indicated that it sold for $2.20 in 1932.)

Willystine Goodsell

In *Problems of the Family* by Goodsell (1928), 24 chapters cover historical influences, social conditions (family instability, immigrant family public aid, prostitution, working mothers, illegitimacy), and individualism and the family (the women's movement, married women and careers, birth control, divorce, and freedom in love). A final section includes a chapter on the renaissance of family education and the family in the future. As in other texts written during this era, mandatory testing for venereal disease to obtain a marriage license was a controversial issue. On one side of this controversy were the devastating effects on women if they contracted venereal disease, which had already been associated with pelvic inflammatory disease and sterility, or of making the "innocent baby suffer from the sins of the father." On the other side of the controversy was the issue of confidentiality and considerable stigma if the doctor must tell the male that he may not be granted a marriage license. Goodsell suggests that the issue of medical secrecy may be defended "when no other life is endangered." However, when the wife and child will be endangered, the role of the physician can easily become one of an accomplice in crime because of the likelihood of injury or death of the wife and child resulting from venereal disease.

It is amazing how similar this is to the current controversy regarding AIDS testing and the dilemma that health-care workers face today; without consent, they are prohibited by law from sharing information regarding a person's HIV status. Without consent, physicians and other health-care professionals may not inform the partner or spouse and thus are condemning the partner to a high risk of contracting HIV and eventual death.

Ruth Lindquist

Lindquist (1931), in *The Family in the Present Social Order: A Study of Needs of American Families*, uses the results of her study of 306 homes as the basis for discussions throughout the text. This volume has a fairly comprehensive chapter on research methodology, or the "scientific study" of the family. She discusses the limitation in her study, that is, that most of the information comes from mothers and wives, with only one brief section from husbands and fathers and none from children. Lindquist did request, however, that fathers complete this brief section, thus avoiding, in part, the problems later noted by Safilios-Rothschild (1969) and Steinmetz (1974). This text also has a chapter on trends in college training from marriage and parenthood. Among these trends are specialization with specific sets of courses and gaining the best knowledge to prepare for marriage and parenthood at the same time that one gains job skills. An interesting observation was that a general sociology and a general psychology course was required in all institutions comprising the study; however, child development was only required in six of the nine institutions and family health in four of the nine institutions. The author also laments that only six of the nine institutions required residence in a home management house, and in only three was there the presence of an infant or young child to enable the teaching of childcare and development under conditions approximating those in a home.

A comparison of these curricula with needs noted in the survey revealed that more than 75% of mothers wanted more information on children and their care and development. All institutions required courses in food preparation, yet only two-thirds required a course in child development. Lindquist summarizes her finding:

> Training of the past has been primarily in the techniques of homemaking with emphasis upon good standards in the routine processes carried on in the home; that at the present time a transition from process to persons, particularly the young child, is occurring; and that in the future one may anticipate more emphasis upon philosophy, perspective, personnel of the family, factors promoting successful marriage and family life, the use of leisure, and the role of home managers as citizens and community builders.

Una Bernard Sait

The format of Sait's *New Horizons for the Family*, published in 1938, appears to be quite modern in its coverage of marriage and family life. After an introductory chapter on social change and the family, a section entitled "The Family in Historical Perspective" examines the family and trends of social change, social organization, religion, economics, sex, and education. A section on "The Modern Family," contains chapters addressing education in the century of the child, reciprocal functions of home and school, public responsibility for child welfare, children in need of special care and protection, changes in status of women, and occupations of women in America. Sait also addresses conflicting values in women's lives such as population and birth control and instability, which is defined as a revolt against traditional morality (i.e., prostitution, venereal disease, divorce, and reform of marriage and divorce laws).

In the epilogue, "New Horizons for the Family," Sait discusses her fear of the coercive control that goes under the name of fascism in Europe and reflects a growing concern with dictatorships throughout Europe. She decries fanatical idealism, the ruthless cruelty killing of human lives, suppression of freedom of speech, and terrorism as a means of imposing conformity and compliance on a society. She notes that these ideologies offer the citizens an escape from futility and bring meaning into their lives—a new religion in which youth are sinisterly indoctrinated into the symbols of the dictatorship, which focus on hating the enemy. Sait raises the question, "What will all these marching children, bred to violence and hatred, mean to the future of humanity?" (p. 737). As we have learned from the Holocaust, those bred to violence and hatred went on to commit the most heinous crimes of the century—the systematic genocide of millions of Jews, gypsies, and others in the name of purifying the race.

Willard Waller

In the early decades of the twentieth century, research was difficult and the topics covered had to fall within that which was considered appropriate, for example, mate selection or the characteristics that predict a happy marriage. This was noted by Jesse Bernard (1987) in her Foreword to the first edition of this *Handbook*. She reported that Willard Waller, in his family text published in 1938, stated: "[F]ifty years or more ago about 1890, most people had the greatest respect for the institution called the family and wished to learn nothing whatever about it.... Everything that concerned the life of men and women and their children was shrouded from the light" (pp. 3–4).

Harold Christiensen

The end of World War II saw not only considerable growth in educational, employment, and housing opportunities for families but also an interest in how they were adjusting to the end of the war, the expanding economy, and the new technology. Research grew and the large body of accumulated knowledge was presented in Christiansen's *Handbook of Marriage and Family* (1964). Consisting of 24 chapters, the volume largely dealt with the positive aspects of marriage and family. Only one chapter, "Families under Stress," gave an indication that families might have problems. Divorce was included in a chapter entitled "Legal and Procedural Aspects of Marriage and Divorce." In the chapter on "Marital and Nonmarital Sexual Behavior," the author only hints at premarital sexual behavior being a problem.

> The premarital relation of males and females has become institutionalized, that is, established in socially accepted and expected patterns of behavior running over several stages of increasingly involved commitments in interpersonal relations. (Ehrmann, 1964, p. 601)

Where do we go from here?

The first edition of this *Handbook* (Sussman & Steinmetz, 1987) featured chapters on voluntary childlessness, singlehood, remarried and reconstituted families, and single-parent families as well as chapters on family violence, power, and gender roles. This coverage indicated that not only had social science scholars addressed changes in the family structure, but that they also had a more realistic view of family processes. The *Handbook* also reflected the large body of research that was conducted during an era characterized by the reaction to the Vietnam War, a questioning of all values and authority, and attempts to find new ways to solve old family problems.

After more than a decade of Lyndon Johnson's Great Society and the expansion of welfare programs, a conservative backlash occurred, which, along with changes occurring in technology, public policy, education, health care, and employment, has resulted in some fairly extensive changes in family life. Most of these are extensively documented in the various chapters in this *Handbook*, but some are still in their infancy.

For example, we have not yet measured the long-term impact of corporate downsizing on families. The computer age is upon us. The impact of a widening gap between the knowledge base and experience of middle-class children entering school and those families living in poverty is just being recognized. We have not yet measured the outcome of the new welfare reforms. While the concept of work rather than welfare is a noble one and most welfare recipients report wanting a job, the reality is that relatively few jobs are available for those with emotional or mental problems, as well as those with limited education, training, and employment experience.

Much research demonstrates the negative outcomes for families on welfare. However, we do not know whether it is living on welfare, that is, not being in the paid labor force, that results in these negative outcomes, or if collecting welfare is but one of a series of negative factors such as marginality, a lower standard of living, and family and environmental circumstance. It may be that for many families, rather than a mother's employment being a pathway out of poverty, a mother in the paid labor force may compound the problems faced by these families. In the next decade, we may witness a plethora of research evaluating the effects of mother absence as an compounding factor resulting in increased dysfunction and delinquency among lower income children living in female-headed families. Clearly, new paradigms must be created to balance the needs of families with the needs of society in a way that will best preserve our future—our children.

MARVIN B. SUSSMAN
SUZANNE K. STEINMETZ
GARY W. PETERSON

References

Bernard, J. (1987). Foreword. In M. B. Sussman & S. K. Steinmetz (Eds.), *Handbook of marriage and the family* (pp. ix–xi). New York: Plenum.

Christensen, H. T. (Ed.) (1964). *Handbook of marriage and the family*. Chicago: Rand McNally.

Ehrmann, W. (1964). Marital and nonmarital sexual behavior. In H. T. Christensen (Ed.), *Handbook of marriage and the family* (pp. 585–622). Chicago: Rand McNally.

Goodsell, W. (1928). *Problems of the family*. New York: The Century Co.

Groves, E. (1927). *Social problems of the family*. Philadelphia: Lippincott.

Haley, A. (1976). *Roots*. Garden City, NY: Doubleday.

Karlweis, M. (1926). Marriage and the changing woman. In Count H. Keyserling (Ed.), *The book of marriage*. New York: Harcourt, Brace & Company.

Lindquist, R. (1931). *The family in the present social order: A study of needs of American families*. Chapel Hill: University of North Carolina Press.

Safilios-Rothschild, C. (1969). Family sociology of wives' family sociology: A cross cultural examination of decision-making. *Journal of Marriage and the Family, 31*, 190–301.

Sait, U. B. (1938). *New horizons for the family*. New York: Macmillan.

Spencer, A. G. (1925). *Women's share in social culture*. Philadelphia: Lippincott (Original work published 1912).

Steinmetz, S. K. (1974). The sexual context of social research. *The American Sociologist, 9*(3), 111–116.

Thwing, C. F., & Thwing, C. F. B. (1886). *The family, a historical and social study*. Boston: Lothrop, Lee & Shepard.

Waller, W. (1938). *The family: A dynamic interpretation*. New York: Dryden Press.

Contents

Introduction

Perspectives on Families as We Approach the Twenty-First Century—Challenges for Future Handbook Authors

Gary W. Peterson and Suzanne K. Steinmetz

Coediting a handbook is filled with joy and excitement, as well as sorrow and disappointment. The joy and excitement comes not only at the point when the book is finally on your bookshelf, but also when you read a truly exciting chapter that you have seen emerge from an outline. Excitement also results from discovering that a colleague who has been asked to join the project at a late date is able to quickly shoulder the task, do considerable rewriting, and deliver a remarkably polished product in a very short period of time.

The sorrow comes when you lose a valued friend like Marie Osmond, who was initially scheduled to coauthor one of the theory chapters. Her death was a great loss to all of us who study families and to this project. We also experienced, of course, the disappointment resulting from unfulfilled promises to deliver a chapter. Along these lines, astute wisdom provided by one chapter author pretty much summarizes the dilemma experienced during the progress of such major projects:

> Big handbooks are held hostage by the slowest writer, whose chapter you often fantasize about canceling, but know you can't afford to—plus a multitude of life's foibles that just happen to authors along the way!

An additional predicament is that slow authors (often of irreplaceable chapters) appear to be clever enough to figure out that you're only bluffing about "fail-safe" deadlines and that you really can't afford to cancel their chapter! On the whole, however, we have found this experience to be both an exciting and rewarding learning experience.

As in the first edition of the *Handbook of Marriage and the Family*, the chapter authors herein represent the combined talents of scholars and practitioners from the diverse fields of sociology, psychology, demography, political science, economics, social work, family therapy, history, child and family studies, medicine, and law. Another similarity with the first edition is our conceptualization of a handbook as a compendium of concepts, ideas, and reviews of research and theoretical essays. Nevertheless, because of rapidly growing bodies of family research, chapter authors were encouraged to focus their reviews of the literature on developments since the publication of the first edition.

Despite many similarities with the first edition, however, substantial differences exist between the first and second editions of this *Handbook*. Many of these distinctive qualities result from both pragmatic workload considerations and significant developments in the study of families. As a result, the second edition is now a product of an expanded editorial team and an effort to provide current trends and

Gary W. Peterson • Department of Sociology, Arizona State University, Tempe, Arizona 85287. **Suzanne K. Steinmetz** • Department of Sociology, Indiana University–Purdue University at Indianapolis, Indianapolis, Indiana 46202.

Handbook of Marriage and the Family, 2nd edition, edited by Marvin Sussman, Suzanne K. Steinmetz, and Gary W. Peterson. Plenum Press, New York, 1999.

analyses of the contemporary research, theory, and intervention strategies that contribute to our understanding of families.

The first such change was the addition of Gary (Pete) Peterson of Arizona State University as an editor. His background in child and family studies has provided additional knowledge and insights into this project. His addition also provided geographic representation within the continental United States. A second event that influenced the substance of this volume resulted from the fact that Sue Steinmetz obtained her M.S.W. and certification in civil and family mediation. Conducting family therapy and mediation has provided her with new insights into the complexity of family relationships, especially the effect of conflict, violence, and trauma within families. This is reflected in various chapters.

A third change is conveyed both in the topics presented and in the authorship of chapters included in this second edition. In many instances we sought new authors for chapters, while in other cases we invited authors of a first edition chapter to conceptualize and write on a different topic. Our decisions should not be interpreted as reflecting dissatisfaction with the quality of any chapter in the first edition, but rather as an attempt to provide new perspectives on previously dealt with, but essential, topics. Continuity between the two editions also is maintained through numerous references to chapters included in the first edition.

Further changes involved the addition of new topics to the second edition, including chapters on family communication (Whitechurch & Dickson, Chapter 25), adolescence (Steinmetz, Chapter 14), and health (Crews & Balcazar, Chapter 22) that reflect growing interest in and increased research on these topics. In other instances, however, chapters concerned with stress and power were combined into a single chapter on dynamics (Sprey, Chapter 24). We also have broadened some of the topics included in various chapters. An example of this approach is found in the current chapter on marital dissolution, which now examines annulment, separation, and widowhood as well as divorce, a strategy reflecting the variety of ways in which marital relationships can be discontinued (Faust & McKibben, Chapter 17).

Family Diversity as the Norm

The first edition of the *Handbook* included separate chapters on nontraditional families, singlehood, voluntary childlessness, and single-parent families, as well as remarriage and reconstituted families. Such an approach reflected the growing interest in these family forms during the 1980s. This edition has combined these areas into a single chapter that examines contemporary families (DeFrain & Olson, Chapter 12). As we enter the twenty-first century, however,

variant family structures are no longer considered unique or viewed as contrary to the dominant norms of our society. This is strongly reinforced by the fact that nuclear families consisting of two heterosexual parents, biologically related children, fathers who are in the paid labor force, and mothers who are homemakers have declined to the point of being a minority circumstance in our society (Teachman, Polonko, & Scanzoni, Chapter 2). Recognizing this reality does not diminish the value of nuclear families, but simply acknowledges the current generality and dominance of diversity.

Social historians have demonstrated that current nostalgia for nuclear families, often expressed by conservative interests, may hearken back to idealized conceptions of family life that either became a reality only for a minority of families or was dominant only for a brief period in our past (Coontz, 1997; Currie, 1988, Hareven, 1987). Nuclear families with dads who are sole breadwinners and stay-at-home moms who are able to focus almost exclusively on children's emotional well-being are a recent development, even in Western societies (O'Barr, Pope, & Wyer, 1990). This idealized family form was and remains largely a culturally privileged circumstance rooted largely in white populations and Western conceptions of family life. Most women, for example, but especially those from low-income, ethnic minority backgrounds, have never attained the ideal of total investment in motherhood, a circumstance that has again waned in America, even among middle-class and higher income women (see Aponte, Chapter 5).

The stance taken here, therefore, reflects the growing realization that it no longer makes sense to use nuclear families as the standard against which various forms of the family (e.g., divorced families, single-parent families, and stepfamilies) are measured (Peterson, Bodman, Bush, & Madden-Derdich, in press). Such comparisons fail to recognize the reality of family pluralism in contemporary American society and reify an unattainable, even mythological, standard for most families. Simply stated, it makes no sense to continually "normalize" a form of the family that is attainable only by a minority and may have been dominant only briefly in our history. Feminist scholars remind us, for example, that comparisons between mother-headed and nuclear families involve inherent gender biases and fail to adjust for the reality that families with a single female parent are at a distinct socioeconomic disadvantage compared to many two-parent families (Osmond & Thorne, 1993; Thompson & Walker, 1995). That is, women continue to be treated inequitably in the workplace and are less capable of providing economic resources for children than either two-parent or single-parent families headed by males (see Walker, Chapter 16).

Diversity in family structure, therefore, is not synonymous with being dysfunctional or deviant, but has simply become part of a broader normative range. Current research on various family structures suggests that members of diverse family forms share many goals, face similar challenges, and demonstrate common processes. Similar to the biologist's view that complex ecosystems are viable precisely because they adapt, social change and transformations in the structure and relationships of families are viewed as inevitable, necessary, and important to recognize (Brubaker & Kimberly, 1993).

The fact that no single family form predominates as we stand on the threshold of a new millennium does not suggest, as some observers have claimed, that "the family" or family relationships are endangered (Popenoe, 1993). A more defensible position is that families are constantly changing and adapting to meet the current and emerging demands of a dynamic society (Coontz, 1997). Changes in fundamental arenas of everyday life, however, are often difficult to adjust to. As the award-winning novelist John Updike proposes: "An old world is collapsing and a new world arising, we have better eyes for the collapse than the rise, for the old is the one we know" (Carnegie Endowment for Peace, 1992).

Like nuclear families, families of diverse structure are often vital emotional units, based primarily on love and affection, that provide psychological security and nurturance to their members. Increasingly, families in Western societies cannot be described in terms of specific structural definitions. They exist largely because individuals subjectively define themselves as members of intimate groups to which they assign primary significance in shaping their everyday lives. Specific structural definitions have become increasingly inadequate to encompass the wide array of variable family forms that include dual-earner, single-parent, divorced, step-, and lesbian and gay families.

Even a cursory examination of contemporary American families reveals that social change and diversity are the norm. A major aspect of this malleability in family life has been high rates of divorce-related transitions that, in turn, have contributed to growing numbers of single-parent households, stepfamilies, and shared custody arrangements (Hines, 1997). Although divorce rates fluctuate somewhat from year to year, estimates continue to indicate that nearly half of all couples who are currently married will eventually become divorced (Centers for Disease Control, 1995). The pervasiveness of this pattern is further supported by the fact that divorce rates remain high across all racial and ethnic groups in American society (U.S. Department of Commerce, Bureau of the Census, 1996).

A related trend is that a majority of divorcing individuals who are parents will eventually remarry after divorce, which means that many children will grow up in stepfamilies. Recent data indicate, for example, that 13% of white children, 15% of Hispanic children, and 31% of African American children are currently living with a biological mother and a stepparent (see Teachman, Polonko, & Scanzoni, Chapter 2). Because second marriages with children result in divorce more frequently than first marriages, many children are likely to experience divorce-related transitions more than once before they reach the age of 18.

A closely related trend is the dramatic growth of single-parent families due not to divorce, but as a result of childbearing outside of marriage or the death of a parent. Recent estimates indicate that 25% of white children, 35% of Hispanic children, and 57% of African-American children are currently living in single-parent households (see Faust & McKibben, Chapter 17; Hines, 1997; U.S. Department of Commerce, Bureau of the Census, 1996).

The most rapidly increasing source of growth in single-parent families is the tendency for women who have children to remain single. Considerable differences exist, however, across ethnic groups in the tendency for mothers to refrain from marriage. Recent data comparing the numbers of never-married mothers in 1970 with the corresponding figures for 1994 indicates that increases occurred from 1% to 4% for white mothers and 4% to 30% for African American mothers during the 24-year period. Data were not available in 1970 for Hispanic mothers, but in 1994 11% remained single (Hines, 1997; U.S. Bureau of the Census, 1996).

Another major change in family life during the last several decades has been the increased number of mothers who are employed outside the home. More than 75% of mothers with children work outside the home, with the percentage being over 80% for women who are single parents (Bryant & Zick, 1996; Gottfried, Gottfried, & Bathurst, 1995; Haas, Chapter 21). The common assumption, of course, is that many children are left unsupervised, receive less parental attention, and are at risk for adverse social consequences. Although these fears about adverse child outcomes have been largely unrealized (Gottfried et al., 1995; Hoffman, 1989; Lerner, 1994; Menaghan & Parcells, 1990), women's employment outside the home has extensively redefined what is expected in marriage; gendered divisions of labor and power and decision-making within family life (Thompson & Walker, 1995; Walker, Chapter 16).

Based on such observations about the normality of change and diversity, we requested that chapter authors examine a wider variety of families and lifestyles within each chapter, rather than devoting specific chapters to a specific diversity topic. We believe that this position more accurately reflects the contemporary view that families with diverse structures are more similar than dissimilar. As a result, we have included only one chapter that specifically focuses on diverse family structures (DeFrain & Olson, Chapter 12), although a number of chapters examine issues of family diversity, such as race and ethnicity (Aponte, Chapter 5), demography (Teachman, Polonko, & Scanzoni, Chapter 2), family dissolution (Faust & McKibbin, Chapter 17), gender (Walker, Chapter 16), and human sexuality (Francoeur & Hendrixson, Chapter 27).

As our theoretical and methodological sophistication grows, new tools become available for collecting, analyzing, and explaining family phenomena. There is a need for alternative types of data (see Gilgun, Chapter 9) as well as new ways to measure family phenomena (see Acock, Chapter 10; Schumm & Hemesath, Chapter 11). As Gilgun notes in Chapter 9, we need to expand the metaphor of a "lens" into that of a "kaleidoscope"—just turn it ever so slightly and a new way to view phenomena comes into play. Many family problems that have become mainstream topics began as a whisper from clinicians, social workers, teachers, or the police.

We need to ask what it means when we are told by the experts that no problem existed because "official" government, police, or agency reports were not available for documentation. One of the early researchers in the field of domestic violence, Richard Gelles, has written that, since there are no documented cases of satanic abuse in the official records, it does not exist (see Miller, Knudsen, & Copenhaver, Chapter 26). However, prior to the early 1960s, there were no documented studies of child abuse, and a similar problem existed regarding the presence of wife abuse and elder abuse until the mid-1970s.

If one were to ask therapists who work with clients who present with a history of severe molestation, addictions, eating disorders, countless suicide attempts, memory loss, and ritual (including satanic) abuse, a very different finding would occur. Furthermore, there are a number of major agencies, and numerous smaller ones, nationwide that work exclusively with victims of ritual abuse. Most of these agencies will only work with an individual who already has considerable knowledge about his or her alter-system and abuse history to avoid the problems associated with the false memory syndrome. How is it possible that so many individuals separated by time, space, age, and gender could be reporting similar histories to a variety of clinicians (social workers, marriage and family therapists, ministers), stories that are virtually identical? Is it because we do not want to acknowledge that extremely cruel and violent side of human behavior? Is it because quantitative, official documents are not available? Or is it that we are reluctant to give credence to qualitative, oral histories?

The Influence of Macro-Level Trends

The second edition of the *Handbook of Marriage and the Family*, as with any project of this scope, has been influenced by political, economic, and mass communication trends that are reshaping the larger society. Several economic and political trends suggest, for example, that twenty-first-century families may need to find innovative ways to solve old problems. First, postindustrial societies place increased value on cutting-edge technology, not loyalty. Children who have been socialized to be hard-working, obedient, and loyal may not be prepared to work and pursue careers in companies that are bought and sold without regard to their job security. Moreover, surviving companies often demonstrate substantial risk-taking attributes as well as ruthless entrepreneurial practices. An increasingly important question, therefore, is "how will parents need to respond so that the young can be adequately prepared for a society characterized by diminished loyalty and greater insecurity in the workplace?"

During the second half of the twentieth century, cohorts were identified by various catch phrases that characterized their attitudes, beliefs, lifestyles, and decision-making. The "Silent Generation," for example, are those who were born before 1933 and experienced World War II (the "good war") as young adults. Veterans returned to the states to enjoy a rapidly expanding economy, increasing educational opportunities, and readily available low-cost financing for a home. Most important, however, was that they experienced a lifetime of economic security. The masses had returned home from the war with the promise of the middle-class standard of living that was pictured in the movies and later on television. Mitchell (1995) suggests that the returning GIs or those who were part of the Silent Generation consciously or unconsciously raised their children, the "Baby Boomers," to rebel and to question values. Members of this generation are currently retired and cherishing their golden years.

The Baby Boomers, children of the Silent Generation, consist of those born between 1946 and 1964 who are currently in their latter 30s to early 50s. The older members of this cohort reached adulthood during the turbulent 1960s, when all values and symbols of authority were questioned. In the 1980s, however, this independence resulted in increased entrepreneurialism, the self-help movement, and the rise of New Age spiritualism. Boomers are currently on the cusp of retirement in some instances because of the early retirement options offered by large companies when they are downsizing.

Members of "Generation X," who were born between 1965 and 1976, are well educated, media savvy, and self-centered. Mitchell (1995) notes that although they have been defined as "slackers," they are no less ambitious than were the Baby Boomers during their youth. The one major difference is that they reached adulthood during difficult economic times. Members of this generation, who range in age from late teens to early 30s, found that they were not necessarily successful in obtaining the lifetime security promised to them if they followed traditional middle-class paths. Unlike their Baby Boom parents (especially the older ones), who anticipated a lifetime of employment security, members of the Gen X cohort entered a workplace that was experiencing downsizing, company buyouts, and company relocations to Mexico, Asia, and a variety of Third World countries.

Generation X will soon to be replaced by a new generation—the "Millennials" (Celente, 1997; Mitchell, 1995). These are the youth who were born between 1977 and 1997. The oldest members are just entering adulthood. According to Susan Mitchell (1995), the Millennials, who were raised with computers, the Internet, and unfettered communication via the World Wide Web, will be less worried about nuclear war and unencumbered by guilt over Vietnam, but more concerned with AIDS, pollution, street violence, and terrorism. They will be realistic, independent, and more civic-minded. Moreover, Millennials have been raised within the context of job market insecurity and will increasingly come to view downsizing as the norm. They will expect even such mundane activities as shopping to be increasingly accomplished via home computers. A possible result of such trends, in turn, will be a declining need for lower-paid service workers such as sales clerks, thus increasing the gap between the "haves" and "have nots."

America's current and perhaps future family members face a growing awareness that disparities between rich and poor have been exacerbated by what has been referred to recently as our "winner-take-all society" (Frank & Cook, 1995). Despite persistent beliefs that poor families have unfairly profited from public assistance and welfare programs, in reality, other interests have been at work and have redefined subtly what is considered to be a reasonable (or "fair") profit. An important result, therefore, is that a substantial redistribution of wealth has occurred.

According to recent social observers (Coontz, 1997) and statistics from the U.S. Census Bureau (U.S. Department of Commerce, Bureau of the Census, 1997), our society's wealth is increasingly being concentrated in the hands of the upper 20% (and especially the upper 5%) of the population. Increasingly, a few individuals who begin with only a relatively small advantage in terms of luck, capital, and skill now appear capable of gaining increasingly disproportionate rewards with modest investments (Frank & Cook, 1995).

Some of these "excessive winnings," of course, simply result for those who are better educated and better adapted to the demands of a newer "information" society, rather than the waning "industrial" culture. A growing proportion of this reallocated wealth, however, is a consequence of only small initial advantages that, in the end, are translated into disproportionate rewards (Coontz, 1997). Thus, the average corporate CEO who earned 41 times the amount paid to an average factory worker in the early 1960s (which is still four times the current average paid to CEOs in Japan and Germany) now, in the last half of 1990s, earns 200 times as much (Coontz, 1997; Harrison, 1995)!

A further irony has been the emergence of these disparities during times when many of the same CEO were advocating (1) that workers be laid-off to downsize companies, (2) that workers be hired who would not receive health and retirement benefits, (3) that highly paid union jobs ought to be eliminated, (4) that jobs be sent to foreign countries for cheap labor, and (5) that "family-friendly" policies, such as paid parental leave, be opposed. Tomorrow's families will likely continue to face these challenges, especially if and when a downward trend emerges in the ever-present economic cycle (i.e., "what goes up, must come down!")). Consequently, despite conservative protests about how the much maligned welfare system "redistributes wealth" to the poor, the true reallocations of wealth appear to be favoring those individuals who already have the largest piece of the American pie.

As a result, the complex world faced by new generations of youth and families appears to be one in which considerable insecurity will be the norm. Despite recent economic prosperity for a significant percentage of middle-class, upper-middle-class, and wealthy families, current research has indicated that the likelihood of experiencing poverty has actually demonstrated a long-term pattern of increase since the early 1970s. This trend appears to be especially prominent among age groups born after the Baby Boomers generation (Browne, 1995) and may be a chronic issue for families in the twenty-first century.

According to recent assessments, the odds that white heads of households will face poverty has increased by five times when compared to the same data for members of the Baby Boom generation (Browne, 1995). Disturbing patterns include long-term trends for a widening gap between rich and poor families and strikingly high rates of poverty among children, the inheritors of the twenty-first century. Recent estimates, based on Census Bureau data, indicate that 20.8% (more than 14 million) of U.S. children live in poverty, compared with only 15% in the early 1970s (Baugher & Lamison-White, 1996). A continuing ironic aspect of American life, therefore, is the persistent growth of poverty and economic inequality in a society characterized by rapid economic growth and extreme accumulation of wealth by a few.

Education, race, and age are factors that strongly affect the likelihood that family members will experience poverty. Families headed by adults who are members of minority groups, the relatively young, and the poorly educated are often several times more likely to experience poverty. A slow growth in the real value of wages (due, in part, to intense worldwide economic competition) and increased inequality of earnings among adult family members over the past 30 years have led to higher poverty rates, especially among families with relatively low levels of educational attainment (i.e., the underclass) (Betson & Michael, 1997; Coontz, 1997). For two-parent families, this trend has been somewhat offset by the dramatic growth in the number of women entering the labor force during the same period. Many families, therefore, have only tenuously retained their middle-class status, simply by sending two rather than only one adult into the labor market.

Another primary factor in the growth of family poverty and the increased disparity between rich and poor has been the rapid rise in the numbers of single-parent, mother-only families. High divorce rates and growing numbers of non-marital births within poor families have contributed to a decline in the number of adults per child (Danziger & Gottschalk, 1995). Poverty is even more likely to occur in households headed by single mothers, with 35% of white, 68% of Puerto Rican, 55% of Mexican American, and 57% of African American single-parent homes falling below the poverty line. Moreover, divorce contributes to poverty, but most dramatically within single-parent families headed by mothers. During the first year of life after divorce, for example, the family income of single mothers appears to fall about 50% (Ambert, 1997; Lichter & Lansdale, 1995).

The presence of fewer adults per child within families has meant, in turn, that a family's earning potential is reduced, which increases the likelihood that both the adults and the children involved will experience poverty. A recent estimate, for example, indicates that children and adolescents in mother-only families are five times more likely to be poor than are comparable youngsters in two-parent families (Betson & Michael, 1997).

Thus, slow growth in the real value of wages, an expanding disparity between rich and poor, and growth in the proportion of mother-only families continue to redefine the circumstances of American families and perhaps the well-being of future generations in the next century (Danziger & Gottschalk, 1995). A compelling issue, in turn, is the extent to which these trends will continue to shape the nature of family life and define important issues for chapter authors of future *Handbooks*. Increased poverty and the gap between rich and poor families may become even more prevalent, especially if economic expansion slows and recession sets in.

Individualism versus Collectivism in Current Family Social Policies

The current circumstances faced by American families, therefore, include the following challenges: (1) a reallocation of wealth to the "haves," (2) growing rates of family poverty, (3) inadequate health care and retirement for many family members, (4) the increased necessity for two parents to work outside the home, (5) inadequate daycare for children, (6) rapidly growing numbers of single-parent (and single-earner) families, (7) the high rates of domestic violence and crime on the streets, and (8) the lack of adequate, accessible mental health care. In the face of such challenges,

current changes in family social policy are clearly being guided by a return to the historic commitment by Americans to individualistic values (Bellah, Madsen, Sullivan, Swidler, & Tipton, 1985; Peterson, 1995a).

The revival of these core values, in turn, has been coupled with a corresponding rejection of earlier efforts to counterbalance this traditional emphasis with moderate amounts of collectivistic interventions. Consequently, authors of future *Handbook* chapters will most likely be faced with the task of assessing the consequences that are brought about by reasserting our traditional cultural values.

The message conveyed by recent changes in national and state policies, therefore, is that family members should reduce their reliance on government assistance as a means of dealing with the rapid changes and diverse circumstances of American family life. Instead, families (especially adult family members) are increasingly expected to pull themselves up by their bootstraps, accept personal responsibility for their circumstances, and become more self-reliant in solving their own problems (Heclo, 1997). Against a backdrop of complex social, political, and economic forces that are now shaping the society of the twenty-first century, conservative interests often encourage family members to assume personal responsibility for family well-being by: (1) reviving traditional marriages, (2) reducing tendencies to divorce easily, (3) saying "no" to sexual relations prior to marriage, (4) refraining from giving birth to children outside of marriage, and (5) reestablishing parents (especially those experiencing poverty) as role models of productive work for their children (Coontz, 1997; Heclo, 1997).

Individualism has a long history in Western civilization, with its modern form emerging in England and America from the seventeenth through nineteenth centuries in the writings of such thinkers as Thomas Hobbes, Adam Smith, John Locke, Thomas Jefferson, and Thomas Paine. An individualistic cultural orientation places emphasis on being person-centered, with one's self-interest and personal goals taking precedence over the interest of social groups. Individualism includes the ideas that society is best served by allowing all members to maximize their freedoms (profits), accept responsibility for choosing their own objectives, and acquire the means to pursue their own interests (Adams & Steinmetz, 1993; Baumeister, 1987; Kim, 1994; Perloff, 1987; Peterson, 1995a).

In contrast, the modern form of collectivism first emerged in the eighteenth- and nineteenth-century writings of such thinkers as Jean-Jacques Rousseau, G. W. F. Hegel, and Karl Marx (see Vargus, Chapter 7). As a response to individualism, collectivism emphasized the community and its right, rather than the rights of isolated persons. A collectivistic cultural orientation underscores the importance of relationships based on trust, cooperation, harmony, common ownership, loyalty, and social planning (Kagitcibasi, 1994; Kim, 1994). Individuals are often viewed as being encouraged to place the interests of other people, the group, and the general social welfare before their own priorities (Kim, 1994; Peterson, 1995a).

As contemporary social scientists have frequently emphasized (Kagitcibasi, 1994; Kim, 1994; Spence, 1985; Triandis, 1994), every society must deal with these fundamental aspects of the human experience—individualism and collectivism. The particular balance established between these forces, however, varies widely across societies and among various ethnic subcultures within a particular nation. In the United States, for example, a frequent observation has been that the particular balance between these two cultural values has been resolved decidedly in favor of individualism (Bellah et al., 1985; Peterson, 1995a). Whether we speak of individual rights enshrined by America's founding fathers, the rugged individualism required to tame and settle the Western frontier, the economic autonomy enshrined in laissez-faire capitalism, the supply-side economics of the Reagan–Bush era, or the anti-big government sentiments of the "Contract with America" promoted by the 1994 Republican Congress, our society has a long history of promoting more individualistic, decentralized values.

Largely in the twentieth century, collectivism as a general guide for social policy has provided a moderate challenge to the dominate force of individualism in American life. Most notably since the 1930s. governmental assistance programs initiated by Franklin Roosevelt's New Deal and Lyndon Johnson's Great Society provided the largest impetus for collectivistic policies toward families and family members (e.g., Social Security and Aid to Families with Dependent Children). Beginning in the late 1960s, however, collectivistic solutions to the nation's social issues have declined consistently in the face of a rising crescendo of criticism from conservative forces that is deeply rooted in a revival of individualistic values.

The strong reascendance of individualistic values and the corresponding decline of collectivism has encouraged beliefs that adult family members should avoid dependency and seek self-sufficiency. Such beliefs are often associated with anti-government sentiments and beliefs that social mobility should result only from equal opportunity and risk, not through public assistance, social guarantees, government subsidies, or safety nets (Helco, 1997). This enhanced emphasis on individualism and rejection of collectivistic solutions have become increasingly evident through many positions taken by conservative interests in reference to family social policies. Individualistic values orientations serve as partial justifications for opposing many proposals designed to help families such as national health care, welfare subsidies, paid parental leave, government funding for childcare,

and gun control legislation as a means of diminishing family violence. Instead of collectivistic solutions to family issues, advocates of individualism often seek to revive traditional nuclear families by moralizing about the need to accept personal responsibility and stop having divorces, to discontinue sexual relations outside of marriage, to refrain from having children outside of wedlock, and to refuse to diminish the sanctity of marriage between heterosexual partners.

The primary strategy appears to involve efforts by conservative interests to roll back powerful social-historical trends toward family diversity and reinstate traditional nuclear families (sometimes referred to as the "family values" agenda by the mass media). Frequent ways to implement this strategy involve systematic cheerleading efforts on behalf of nuclear families and opposition to "family-friendly" programs based in collectivistic values, but few if any real incentives that might provide a genuine basis for reversing these major patterns of change.

Of particular concern as the second edition of the *Handbook* goes to press is the application of greater individualistic orientations to the circumstances of low-income, single-parent families. Despite original beliefs that children would benefit from having single-parent mothers remain at home to care for children (a much-idealized strength of nuclear families), recent welfare reforms clearly convey the message that these women must now become role models of self-sufficiency and productive work for their children (Heclo, 1997). The potential adverse consequences of such policies may be that many of these women will soon be entering a labor market during a time when little provision exists for quality childcare. Moreover, entry-level jobs for these women often provide low pay and deficient (if any) benefits, with the possible result being that many of these mothers (and especially their children) will end up even more impoverished as members of the "working poor."

Much of this renewed emphasis on individual responsibility in policies toward families is not consistent with other aspects of American life. The federal government, for example, has been involved in financing and regulating many areas of our social and economic life for a long time. Examples of such government investment abound in the form of funding for public highways, aviation safety standards, meat inspection standards, disease control, tax incentives for corporations, import protections for corporations against unfair foreign competition, and the enforcement of fair investment practices.

Even such apostles of individualism and free markets as Adam Smith once argued strongly for public investment in areas of social welfare that were too expensive for private interests to expect a reasonable profit (Smith, 1976). Other social observers, such as Garret Hardin (1968), for example, have challenged the central assumption of individualism by posing the moral dilemma concerning what he referred to as the "tragedy of the commons." In raising this issue, he questioned the extent to which decisions and interests pursued individually will adequately contribute to the general welfare in particular areas of social interest. The message here, of course, is that certain areas of social life have always existed that both require and deserve public investment. The follow-up to this message, in turn, should be the question: What could possibly be assigned a higher priority for public investment than the welfare of families and children, our most valuable capital for the twenty-first century?

For a complex society such as ours, characterized by extensive diversity, the consequence of extreme devotion to individualistic social policies solutions may indeed be to experience the "tragedy of the commons." Specifically, in a society characterized by what some observers describe as the increased "Balkanization" of American life (Schlesinger, 1992), a major risk is that we will fail to develop common solutions that hold our society together and prevent fragmentation. In anticipation of such consequences, social observers (Bellah et al., 1985) have been cautioning us for some time that America's preoccupation with personal individualism "may have grown cancerous" to the point of endangering the essential forces of integration that serve to moderate trends toward social disintegration (Peterson, 1995b).

The most comprehensive expression of concern about excessive individualism, however, is by sociologist Amitai Etzioini (1993). Specifically, he concludes that America is indeed continuing to experience: (1) a lack of sufficient consensus about critical institutions, (2) a family system that is stressed by change and deficient support systems, and (3) inner cities that remain in ruins, despite a long period of economic prosperity that has benefitted many individuals.

The primary source of such problems, Etzioni proposes, is our current preoccupation with individual rights and the divisive demands of ever-growing numbers of special interest groups. The price of such fragmentation, he argues, is a society that no longer fosters the welfare of the larger collective and diminishes the tendencies for individuals and various subgroups to accept responsibilities for encouraging societal integration.

The proper response, Etzioni (1993) proposes, is for responsible members of society to commit themselves to a new social contract that serves the interest of society by reestablishing a balance between the interest of individuals and the larger collective. He argues further that building social responsibility will require at least some sacrifice on the part of individual and specialized interests. This is necessary, however, to strengthen the nation's families, place absolute value on the welfare of children, and identify and teach a common set of values that transcend (as much as possible) the disparate interests of individuals and specialized groups.

Such principles must become key elements of our national social policies and prevention strategies aimed at individual, family, neighborhood, community, and societal levels of analysis.

The common theme here, of course, is the recognition that our society's problems are rooted, in part, within the macro system level and require programs that foster a balance between the interests of collectivism and individualism. Effective solutions to the complicated problems of children and families will continue to require at least some changes in the larger infrastructure of our society. Correspondingly, it does not seem reasonable to expect that disproportionate reliance on a renewal of individualism will be the best strategy for responding to all of our social issues pertaining to families.

In fact, a portion of the problems facing families today can be traced to society giving up its collective responsibility under the guise of the rights of the individual to make choices. How many drug-addicted babies should a mother be permitted to give birth to before birth control and long-term drug treatment are mandated? How many babies can a father "make" when he has made no attempt to provide emotional or financial support before he has the choice of mandatory incarcerated or sterilization? It is not unusual for female clients to report that the father of her child has 10, 15, or, in one case, 27 other children—none that he supports, few that he visits. And when will children truly get rights? How many times can a parent sexually or physically abuse a child before all children in the family are removed? Whose rights are being protected when each child in the family must experience the trauma of sexual and physical abuse? Obviously, the ideal would be to have programs in place that would prevent these situations, but in their absence, must we continue to allow children to be harmed by parents who are not equipped to appropriately discharge their duties appropriately (see Miller, Knudsen, & Copenhaver, Chapter 26)?

Problems such as the need to control access to lethal weapons and the trafficking of illegal drugs, for example, must be addressed by individual, community, state, and national interests. Failure to do so will create "evasion loopholes" stemming from individual/community variability and the absence of societal continuity in prevention and enforcement policies. The recalcitrant problem of growing poverty among families and children, perhaps the root of the many risks our youth face (see Peterson & Hann, Chapter 13; Steinmetz, Chapter 14), will probably require at least some restructuring of major social institutions, not just simple reliance on reinstilling individual incentives to climb out of poverty.

Although renewed emphasis on individualism may provide some assistance, a broader perspective will likely be needed to address aspects of our most persistent problems. Effective measures to prevent and treat the roots of poverty will require social policies that provide meaningful job-training programs, a welfare system that provides an effective safety net without fostering long-term dependency, a wage/salary and benefits system that provides incentives to reenter the labor market profitably (and discontinue welfare), government funding for daycare, paid parental leave to care for children, and a system of universally accessible health care (Edelman & Solow, 1994; Moen & Forest, Chapter 23).

These policies will probably be necessary because recent periods of economic growth (often alleged to be a simple function of individual incentives and entrepreneurial activities) have not reduced and may have even accentuated some of the current problems faced by families (e.g., growing levels of family poverty and the gap between the "haves" and "have nots"). A central lesson of U.S. history prior to the 1930s, in turn, was that extensive reliance on individualism and local wisdom to deal with major social and economic problems often resulted in substantial inequities that did not benefit the social welfare (e.g., no Social Security, segregated schools, and Jim Crow laws) (Burns, 1985, 1987). Much of the twentieth-century experience has involved the recognition that some of these inequalities could only be addressed through the concerted efforts of an "activist" central or federal government that had the "interest of the commons at heart." Authors of chapters for future *Handbooks* will have a better standpoint from which to assess our most recent experiment with "individualism" as well as the cautions that we have provided here.

References

Adams, B. N., & Steinmetz, S. K. (1993). Family theory and method in the classics. In P. G. Boss, W. J. Doherty, R. LaRossa, W. R. Schumm, & S. K. Steinmetz (Eds.), *Sourcebook of family theory and methods: A contextual approach* (pp. 71–94). New York: Plenum.

Ambert, A. (1997). *Parents, children, and adolescents: Interactive relationships and development in context.* Binghamton, NY: Haworth.

Baugher, E., & Lamison-White, L. (1996). *Poverty in the United States: 1995* (U.S. Bureau of the Census, Current Population Reports, P-60, 194). Washington, DC: U.S. Government Printing Office.

Baumeister, R. F. (1987). How the self became a problem: A psychological review of historical research. *Journal of Personality and Social Psychology, 6*, 226–244.

Bellah, R. N., Madsen, R., Sullivan, W. M., Swidler, A., & Tipton, L. M. (1985). *Habits of the heart: Individualism and commitment in American life.* New York: Harper & Row.

Betson, D. M., & Michael, R. T. (1997). Why so many children are poor. *Children and Poverty, 7*(2), 25–39.

Browne, I. (1995). The baby and trends in poverty, 1967–1987. *Social Forces, 73*, 1072–1086.

Brubaker, T. H., & Kimberly, J. A. (1993). Challenges to the American family. In T. H. Brubaker (Ed.), *Family relations: Challenges for the future* (Vol. 1, pp. 4–15). Newbury Park, CA: Sage.

Bryant, W. K., & Zick, C. D. (1996). An examination of parent–child shared household work. *Journal of Marriage and the Family, 58*(1), 227–238.

Burns, J. M. (1985). *The workshop of democracy: From the Emancipation Proclamation to the era of the New Deal.* New York: Vintage.

Burns, J. M. (1987). *The crosswinds of freedom: From Roosevelt to Reagan: America in the last half century.* New York: Vintage.

Carnegie Endowment for Peace, *Changing our way: America and the new World.* Washington, DC: Author.

Celente, G. (1997). *Trends 2000.* New York: Warner Books.

Centers for Disease Control and Prevention/National Center for Health Statistics. (1995). *Monthly Vital Statistics* (Report 43, No. 13). Washington, DC: U.S. Department of Health and Human Services, Public Health Service.

Coontz, S. (1997). *The way we really are.* New York: Basic Books.

Currie, D. (1988). Re-thinking what we do and how we do it: A study of reproductive decisions. *Canadian Review of Sociology and Anthropology, 25*(2), 231–252.

Danziger, S., & Gottschalk, P. (1995). *America unequal.* Cambridge, MA: Harvard University Press.

Edelman, M. W., & Solow, R. M. (1994). *Wasting America's future: Children's defense fund report on the costs of child poverty.* Boston: Beacon.

Etzioni, A. (1993). *The spirit of community: The reinvention of American society.* New York: Simon & Schuster.

Frank, P., & Cook, P. (1995). *The winner-take-all society: How more and more Americans compete for fewer and bigger prizes, encouraging economic waste, income inequality, and an impoverished cultural life.* New York: Free Press.

Gottfried, A. E., Gottfried, A. W., & Bathurst, K. (1995). Maternal and dual-earner employment status and parenting. In M. H. Bornstein (Ed.), *Handbook of parenting: Vol. 4. Biology and ecology of parenting* (pp. 139–161). Hillsdale, NJ: Erlbaum.

Hardin, G. (1968). The tragedy of the commons. *Science, 162*, 1243–1248.

Hareven, T. K. (1987). Historical analysis of the family. In M. B. Sussman & S. K. Steinmetz (Eds.), *Handbook of marriage and the family* (pp. 37–58). New York: Plenum.

Harrison, B. (1995). *Lean and mean: The changing landscape of corporate power in the age of flexibility.* New York: Basic Books.

Heclo, H. H. (1997). Values underpinning poverty programs for children. *Children and Poverty, 7*(2), 141–148.

Hines, A. M. (1997). Divorce-related transitions, adolescent development, and the role of the parent–child relationship: A review of the literature. *Journal of Marriage and the Family, 59*, 375–388.

Huston, A. C. (1983). Sex typing. In E. M. Hethington (Ed.), *Handbook of child psychology, socialization, personality, and social development* (Vol. 4, pp. 387–467). New York: Wiley.

Kagitcibasi, C. (1994). A critical appraisal of individuation and collectivism: Toward new formulation. In U. Kim, H. C. Triandis, C. Kagitcibasi, S. Choi, & G. Yoon (Eds.), *Individualism and collectivism: Theory, method, and applications* (pp. 52–65). Thousand Oaks, CA: Sage.

Kim, U. (1994). Individualism and connectedness: Conceptual clarification and elaboration. In U. Kim, H. C. Triandis, C. Kagitcibasi, S. Choi, & G. Yoon (Eds.), *Individualism and collectivism: Theory, method, and applications* (pp. 19–40). Thousand Oaks, CA: Sage.

Lerner, J. V. (1994). *Employed mothers and their families.* Newbury Park, CA: Sage.

Lichter, D. T., & Lansdale, N. S. (1995). Parental work, family structure, and poverty among Latino children. *Journal of Marriage and the Family, 57*, 346–354.

Menaghan, E. G., & Parcel, T. L. (1990). Parental employment and family life: Research in the 1980s. *Journal of Marriage and the Family, 52*, 1079–1098.

Mitchell, S. (1995). *The official guide to the generations.* Ithaca, NY: New Strategist Publications.

O'Barr, J., Pope, D., & Wyer, M. (1990). Introduction. In J. O'Barr, D. Pope,

& M. Wyer (Eds.), *Ties that bind: Essays on mothering* (pp. 1–14). Chicago: University of Chicago Press.

Osmond, M. W., & Thorne, B. (1993). Feminist theories: The social construction of gender in families and society. In P. G. Boss, W. J. Doherty, R. W. LaRossa, W. R. Schumm, & S. K. Steinmetz (Eds.), *Sourcebook of families and methods: A contextual approach* (pp. 591–623). New York: Plenum.

Perloff, R. (1987). Self-interest and personal responsibility redux. *American Psychologist, 42*, 3–11.

Peterson, G. W. (1995a). Autonomy and connectedness in families. In R. D. Day, K. R. Gilbert, B. H. Settles, & W. R. Burr (Eds.), *Research and theory in family science* (pp. 20–41). Pacific Grove, CA: Brooks/Cole.

Peterson, G. W. (1995b). The need for common principles in prevention programs for children, adolescents, and families. *Journal of Adolescent Research, 10*(4), 470–485.

Peterson, G., Bodman, D. A., Bush, K. A., & Madden-Derdich, D. (in press). In D. H. Demo, K. R. Allen, & M. A. Fine (Eds.), *Handbook of family diversity*. London: Oxford University Press.

Popenoe, D. (1993). American family in decline, 1960–1990. A review and appraisal. *Journal of Marriage and the Family, 49*, 527–555.

Schlesinger, A., Jr. (1992). *The disuniting of America: Reflections on a multicultural society*. New York: Norton.

Smith, A. (1976). *An inquiry into the nature and causes of the wealth of nations* (Vol. 2). Chicago: University of Chicago Press.

Spence, J. (1985). Achievement American style: The rewards and costs of individualism. *American Psychologist, 40*, 1285–1295.

Thompson, L., & Walker, A. J. (1995). The place of feminism in family studies. *Journal of Marriage and the Family, 57*(4), 847–866.

Triandis, H. C. (1994). Theoretical and methodological approaches to the study of collectivism and individualism. In U. Kim, H. C. Triandis, C. Kagcibasi, S. Choi, & G. Yoon (Eds.), *Individualism and collectivism: Theory, method, and applications* (pp. 66–79). Thousand Oaks, CA: Sage.

U.S. Department of Commerce, U.S. Bureau of the Census. (1995). *Statistical Abstract of the United States: 1995* (115th Edition). Washington, DC: U.S. Government Printing Office.

U.S. Bureau of the Census. (1997). *Income inequality 1947–1994*, Table 1, Washington, DC: US Government Printing Office, Internet access.

U.S. Department of Commerce, Bureau of the Census. (1996). *Current Population Series P-20: Households and family characteristics, various years, marital status and living arrangements* (Nos. 443, 445, 450). Washington, DC: U.S. Government Printing Office, Internet access.

Family Diversity

Past, Present, and Future

Part I consists of six chapters that explore the ethnic, cross-national, and structural variety of contemporary families in the past, present, and future. Particular attention is devoted to capturing the idea that diversity and social change are the dominant themes for understanding both the substance of family life and the methods that social scientists use to study these fundamental social relationships.

Chapter 1, "Historical Analysis of the Family," by Sheila McIsaac Cooper, provides a historical analysis of the emergence of family in Europe. Cooper recognizes the work of Febvre and Bloch and other French scholars who investigated how social systems and groups functioned in economic, cultural, temporal, and spatial dimensions. She notes that Lacombe's work on the Roman family, Engels' Marxist writings on the family, Namier's work in England, and Morgan's historical studies of family in the United States were early applications of historical methodologies to the study of family. However, it was not until the theoretical work of Parsons and Smelser that historians were provided with the impetus to study families utilizing a perspective that went beyond economic or political concerns. Cooper applies these contemporary and historical methodologies to explore marriage patterns, household and family forms, the economy, kin, and various stages in the life course.

Teachman, Polonko, and Scanzoni's comprehensive review of the literature, Chapter 2, "Demography and Families," presents two aims: first, to summarize the major empirical themes, and second, to place these themes within a conceptual and explanatory framework. The authors note that family demography, which has historical roots in the general field of demography, seeks to describe the size and distribution of aggregate groups (i.e., race, sex, age, ethnicity), as well as to document change over time. Structural or macro-type analysis overlooks the dynamic character of the family and the pluralism evident in contemporary families. Therefore, a more appropriate focus is one in which action is intertwined with structure and is based on the premise that individuals act, behave, and make choices in a manner that either maintains or changes the status quo. The authors also examine other trends, such as female labor force participation, marriage and nonmarital cohabitation, fertility, marital disruption, remarriage, and household size and composition.

In Chapter 3, "Cross-Cultural and U.S. Kinship," Bert Adams notes the importance that kinship plays, especially in agricultural societies, in terms of economic, political, and religious roles. Adams suggests that the function of kin units include property-holding and inheritance, housing, need-obligations, and affective or emotional ties. Kinship functions that are evident in agricultural societies are less central in U.S. society, although need-obligation, and to a lesser extent housing and inheritance, are still present. Adams explores such issues as kin terms, descent and inheritance, kin as persons, kinship analysis, categories of U.S. kin, and specific characteristics of American kinship relationships.

Chapter 4, "Comparative Perspectives," by Gary Lee, provides a description of the methodology of comparative research, or the study of families and family relations within two or more societies. Lee describes the history of family scholarship prevalent in the mid- to late 1800s as not only comparative but also as strongly influenced by Social Darwinist (Eurocentric) logic, which traced the evolution of the family from original promiscuity to the monogamous, nuclear family common in Europe. Using the antecedents of family structure as an example, Lee examines the method of comparative research (which includes cross-cultural, cross-societal, cross-national, and historical), as well as the structure and composition of families with emphasis on the historical context. Lee concludes with the note that comparative research in not a distinct or unique field of study, but rather a method, or set or related methods, for the study of human behavior that becomes even more useful when combined with other methods.

In Chapter 5, "Ethnic Diversity in Families," Robert Aponte notes that the range of variation within groups on any particular variable is usually greater than is commonly observed between different groups. He suggests that much of what passes for cultural differences actually stems from factors such as social class, rather than ethnicity. He notes that there is a trend toward convergence on key family attributes such as family size. He also proposes, however, that some lack of convergence among ethnic groups can be sustained by extraordinary circumstance. Moreover, many changes occurring within American ethnic communities frequently are prevalent within the original societies from which members of these groups have immigrated. Aponte illustrates these points by examining six American ethnic groups: Chinese Americans, Japanese Americans, Mexican Americans, Puerto Rican Americans, African Americans, and the Amish.

The final chapter in this part, "The Future of Families," by Barbara Settles, is an outgrowth of a similar chapter prepared for the first edition of the *Handbook*. Settles suggests that families are shaped by three factors: the legacies or histories of their past, the currencies of the moment, and their theories of the future. The chapter provides a theoretical-based concept of the future and its relationship to families. A key aspect of this chapter is the models Settles develops for describing families' futures under specific conditions. Settles concludes with a series of predicted trends, derived from various literatures, under the influences of conservatism, continuity, substitution, and change.

CHAPTER 1

Historical Analysis of the Family

Sheila McIsaac Cooper

Introduction

The family, like other social groups, is both subject to change over time and also retains characteristics from the past in its present form. It is a sum of its beginning plus the changes that have occurred along the way to the present. As a consequence, part of understanding the family and its social, political, and economic importance depends on understanding the family in history. For many years scholars, historians among them, made assumptions about the historical configuration and dynamic aspects of families on evidence that often was quite slim. The putative rise of the nuclear family, for example, fitted various theories of modernization, urbanization, and industrialization well enough to obscure the haziness about its birth. In the past 3 decades, however, assumptions about the family have been reconsidered as historical analysis of the family became an important component of history and other academic disciplines that study families.

In examining the family in the past, the historian has had to consider its milieu or context. Not only is the family subject to change, but so too are the components of the society, place, and tradition in which the family is located. Government, education, economy, religion, demography, and climate, among other institutions and factors, are all liable to flux, which in turn affects family form and function in a myriad of ways. In addition to the changes generated in interactions between the family and external forces, much change in the family is internal, caused by the development of its individual members. Influenced in part by biology as well as by events within and outside of the family, these individual histories intertwine to produce the history of a particular family and of families generically in an ever-changing context.

Although historians as a group came relatively late to the study of marriage and family, they brought with them the special expertise of their discipline. Recognition of time as an important consideration and as an ordering principle, along with recognition that every group or process has a temporal milieu, distinguishes historians from other scholars. Those who practice historical analysis of the family transcribe, interpret, and correct the record when and where it needs correcting. This last task was one of the first that the "new" family historians undertook as they dealt with the myth of the extended preindustrial family and that they continue to address in their approach to the myth of the prototypical and ubiquitous modern nuclear family.

Like their fellow social scientists, historians often employ theoretical models, but they are less likely to construct overarching theories, preferring midlevel theorizing and empirical research. They examine a process, event, or organization in light of its earlier or later state or compare it to processes, events, or organizations from another era. Believing that the roots of the present lie in the past, historians have helped to bring a much needed longitudinal dimension to family research.

Time also affects historians through the realization that academic disciplines do not stand apart from contemporary trends. The field of family history can be seen as a product of the present and the immediate past. It results from a confluence of theoretical developments within the field of history and associated disciplines, of technological advances, and of pressing social concerns within the wider society, among other trends. This confluence has not only encouraged historical analysis of the family but has also helped to enlarge the vision of the family historian.

The field of the family now attracts historians in great numbers throughout the world, but especially in North America and Europe. As historical study of the family has devel-

Sheila McIsaac Cooper • Associate Dean of the Graduate School, Indiana University, Indianapolis, Indiana 46202.

Handbook of Marriage and the Family, 2nd edition, edited by Marvin Sussman, Suzanne K. Steinmetz, and Gary W. Peterson. Plenum Press, New York, 1999.

oped and the number of its practitioners has surged, analysis has moved in a widening gyre. Research on the family group has expanded from coresident family and household to include nonresident kin. Work on the family dynamic has branched out from families at a given moment to the family cycle and the individual life course, while subfields have multiplied. The productivity of family historians has been so extensive during the last few decades, however, that a brief review cannot cover all aspects of the field.

This chapter will review the development of family history primarily in the United States, Britain, and western Europe. It will then address three major areas that have surfaced as the field has matured: demographically based family history, including marriage patterns, household and family forms, and kin; the family cycle and the relationship of the individual life course to it; and the family and the economy. Finally, the chapter will briefly consider future directions the field of family history might take.

Background of the Historical Analysis of the Family

Traditionally, political and economic considerations gave the historical discipline its basic shape, determining its periodization and the questions that the discipline tackled. While historians acknowledged the underlying importance of the family to more complex organizations like the state, few studied the family. When need arose, historians relied on the work of their social science colleagues, especially anthropologists and sociologists, who had studied the family since the birth of their disciplines.

Wedded to a particular time and a given place, especially place defined as nation-state, historians in the West, predominantly white males, have framed their questions out of their own experience and within the established practice of their discipline. Appropriate sources took the form of written records, largely in the public sphere, which were usually produced by men of power for themselves and for other men of power—whether local or national. For most, the historical record consisted of statutes, pamphlets, tracts, newspapers, treatises, essays, and similar documents generally intended for public consumption. The product of an educated elite, these sources helped define the major concerns of historians—political, economic, constitutional, religious, and intellectual. Other sources like journals and letters augmented the historical economic picture and provided a vision of private life, a vision that usually framed society's more affluent, educated, and politically significant members.

A heavy emphasis on accumulation of material from original sources marked the German School of historical scholarship, which dominated the discipline for over a cen-

tury. But like the more literary and exemplary history it replaced in the nineteenth century, the German School assumed a developmental framework of a progressive nature. And like their predecessors, these historians generally found social history peripheral to the political and economic milestones that seemingly marked human progress. However, other nineteenth-century scholars increasingly examined social structure for underlying patterns akin to scientific laws, establishing a spate of new disciplines that included anthropology, economics, political science, psychology, and sociology.

In France, philosophers, sociologists, geographers, economists, and other historians joined with Lucien Febvre and Marc Bloch in their move toward a new history of broader scope, which *Annales d'histoire économique et sociale* heralded in 1929. Their colleague, Georges Duby, believes that in the struggle to advance economic and social history *Annales* has led the fight against positivist traditions, against history as a series of battles, against an isolated political history, and against history shorn of ideas (1994, p. 194). The French scholars investigated how social systems and groups functioned in a variety of dimensions—economic, cultural, temporal, spatial, etc. Casting their nets more widely than their German colleagues and seeking alternatives to narrative history, the French found sources like tax and census data, which captured a more diverse population. They also used aggregative and serial techniques that later became part of the methodology of "quantitative" history.

In the immediate post-World War II period, most historians still considered historical analysis of the family—compared to study of politics or economics—peripheral to the discipline. But increasing interest in social processes and social structures emerged with other signs of shift (D. Smith, 1991). Some of the few early histories of the family received favorable, if belated, attention, such as that bestowed in France on Paul Lacombe's work on the Roman family (1889). And the prominence of Marxist intellectuals in the postwar era, especially in Europe, elicited new interest in Marxist writing on the family, notably that of Friedrich Engels (1884/1972). English historians, in the wake of the increasingly influential Sir Lewis Namier (1929/1957, 1930/1963), studied family connections in conjunction with political alliances. And in the United States, historians read Edmund Morgan (1944/1966), who had applied traditional historical techniques to a solid study of the Puritan family.

Meanwhile, interest in new theoretical perspectives was growing among historians. Sociologist Talcott Parsons (1951; and Parsons & Bales, 1955), who had applied structuralist and functionalist theory to illuminate family relations in democratic industrial society, inspired both sociologists and historians in postwar North America and subsequently abroad. Parsons' theoretical model suffered telling criticism for being too static and therefore not helpful for explaining instability or change. Still, its emphasis on the smaller unit as part of larger society, on the utility of each part of society to the whole, has had an important and lasting effect on history as well as other disciplines. Influenced by Parsons, Neil J. Smelser (1959) applied structural-functionalist theory to a sociological analysis of structural change in examining the cotton industry and family life in late-eighteenth- and nineteenth-century Lancashire. Such studies of the historical family were rare, and even Smelser focused more on economy and class, especially the working class, than on family. Students of the family applying theory to an unexplored past, not surprisingly, felt the lack of historical analysis of the family. William J. Goode, for example, hoped his sociological work on family patterns would stimulate historical studies of the family, a field that historians, "far more concerned with economic or political processes," had neglected (1963, p. 367).

The cumulative effect of the *Annales* paradigm (Stoianovich, 1976), social scientific theory, and social issues began to tell by the 1960s, when historical researchers in large numbers started to study the family. *Annales** inspired British and American, as well as Continental, scholars to investigate new sources, methods, and theoretical frameworks. Public concern about issues of social policy such as divorce, dysfunctional families, and poverty fostered a climate favorable for historical analysis of the family. International awareness and planning encouraged historians to examine population and family issues (e.g., Banks, 1954). Moreover, the nascent women's movement, notably in the United States, forced a new look at what many had traditionally viewed as woman's arena—the family.

Establishment by Peter Laslett and E. A. Wrigley in 1964 of the Cambridge Group for the History of Population and Social Structure gave visibility to the family and household as important components of historical studies. Informed by French historical demography, the Cambridge Group also emulated to some extent the Sixième Section de l'École des Hautes Études, the research base for Fernand Braudel and others of the *Annalistes*. Like those associated with *Annales*, scholars affiliated with or influenced by the Cambridge Group came from a number of different disciplines—anthropology, demography, economics, geography, history, political science, among others—but they viewed their work as primarily historical in nature. Questioning dependence on literary sources, the Cambridge Group collected and used sources covering long periods of time—notably parish registers and nominal household lists—which lent themselves to quantification and comparison. In the past 30 years many scholars of family and demography have found their way to Cam-

bridge for study or collaboration so that the Cambridge Group has become the Cambridge School.

These events and effects of the 1960s converged with rapidly advancing computer technology, which fostered a new kind of historical analysis of the family. Historians began to employ aggregative techniques with family, household, or demographic events such as age of first marriage as the unit of analysis. Computers and software packages that could handle large databases increasingly made possible investigation of quantitative sources and bulky records, in which non-elites had been hidden. The social historian who studied non-elites could more readily reconstruct their history from previously difficult sources—tax lists, muster rolls, assessments of the poor, and the like. History "from the bottom up" became acceptable, indeed fashionable, and growing numbers of historians undertook research on the family and related topics.

Much work on the history of the family undertaken in the 1960s and 1970s featured quantification, and like other new social historians, scholars working on the family often attempted to wed quantitative and qualitative techniques. The quantifiers became known as *cliometricians* for coupling Clio, the muse of history, to a statistical approach, a marriage of dubious legitimacy to some of the more traditional of Clio's devotees (Fogel & Elton, 1983). This marriage and that between Clio and social science theory introduced new subfields. For that reason and because social science historians were not always understood or welcomed by their more traditional breathren, the "new" historians sought different outlets for their work.

With their emphasis on journal articles, their rising productivity, and the proliferation of subfields, social historians and historical demographers established one new journal after another both in the United States—*Demography*, (1964), *Journal of Social History* (1967), *Journal of Interdisciplinary History* (1970), *Journal of Family History* (1976), *Social Science History* (1976), etc.—and in Britain—*Population Studies* (1947), *Local Population Studies* (1968), *Social History* (1976), *Continuity and Change* (1986), and *Social History of Medicine* (1988), among others. Although as in traditional history the monograph and the large synthetic work form the milestones of family history, these journals, along with French ones such as *Annales*, *Population* (1946), and *Annales de démographie historique* (1965), contain the articles that mark the direction the field is taking.

The new family historians emphasized comparative study. Because relatively little published work was available, scholars used studies from widely disparate times and locations for comparative purposes, with the earliest work focusing on the preindustrial family or, more often in western Europe, the household (Laslett & Wall, 1972). As more studies emerged, family historians had more appropriate

---

*From 1946 on, *Annales: Économies, sociétés, civilisations*.

comparative contexts for their work in terms of time and place, and the tendency to indulge in wide-ranging comparisons ebbed. In the 1970s a number of large syntheses was published, mostly by the "sentiments" school discussed later in this chapter, some of whose theoretical structures have been heavily criticized (Shorter, 1975; Stone, 1977). Although more synthetic works may lie in the future, the current norm is research leading to papers and articles, often either expanded at a later time into monographs or collected for anthologies focused on a single theme.

Demographically Based History of the Family

Current historical research on the family as an institution began largely with work that had its roots in historical demography, the study of those events that both define the family cycle—marriage, birth, migration, death—and determine population size. Historical demographers analyze the impact of population events on economic and political developments in the past as well as the impact of those developments on population. Demographers who examine modern populations often use census data, but reliable censuses generally do not exist before the modern period, with large areas of the world still lacking minimally complete population surveys. The absence of accurate censuses, in turn, has motivated demographers to make imaginative use of data available to them in parish registers, tax surveys, and the like (Hollingsworth, 1969; Willigan & Lynch, 1982). Demographic techniques, especially family reconstitution, record linkage, and development of large databases, underlie much historical analysis of the family.

Historical Demography

As World War II was ending, Meuvret (1946) and Goubert (1952) undertook demographic research in France using early modern parish registers. Independently, Henry (1953, 1956) along with Fleury (Fleury & Henry, 1956) and Gautier (Gautier & Henry, 1958) were using parish registers to analyze demographic trends.* The French demographers, in their separate research efforts, developed family reconstitution, a technique for reconstructing families by linking individual marriage, baptismal, and burial entries from parish registers or, in some cases, from genealogies.

Using vital statistics and family reconstitution, historical demographers have provided information on age at marriage, duration of marriage, remarriage, reproduction rates, birth intervals, number of children within marriage, illegitimacy, life expectancy, mortality (including neonatal and

*Somewhat earlier, scholars in Germany and elsewhere had undertaken similar research, but their work was not widely known.

maternal mortality), and other family issues. Where sources are good enough, these statistics can be calculated by occupational group as well as by gender, although demographers using parish registers have to be mindful of the settled nature of the register population, among other problems. Some results have been surprising. For example, Louis Henry (1956), in examining birth intervals, concluded that Genevan bourgeois families were attempting family limitation by the early eighteenth century.

Historical demographers in England also used parish registers and family reconstitution, initiating a major revision in the understanding of the English past. Their studies generally remained well within the Malthusian tradition (Malthus, 1798/1986), both in analysis of demographic events and in connecting demography and economics. Perhaps foremost among this group, Wrigley (1966a,b) employed parish registers and family reconstitution to look initially at the demographic histories of individual communities, most notably Colyton in Devon, and the relationship of fertility, nuptiality, and mortality to the economy. American historians also adopted family reconstitution techniques, especially to illuminate the history of the colonial family (e.g., Greven, 1970; Lockridge, 1970).

While much historical demography has been community based and has provided insights into family and kin networks on a local level, Wrigley and Schofield (1981) have used aggregative analysis and back projection to estimate the size and age structure of population in the past. Aggregating demographic data from selected parishes over 3 centuries, they have projected the size of the English population backward from the 1871 census to the mid-sixteenth century. They argue that late age of first marriage limited fertility, which in turn limited population. This late initial age of marriage could readily adjust to changing economic circumstances as could the mobility of the nuclear family and single adults. A fall in age at first marriage as a response to improved economic conditions would and did increase fertility. Current work on an extended series of family reconstitutions should further illuminate population and family behavior in the past and allow Wrigley and Schofield to reexamine questions about their earlier work, such as the impact on fertility levels of the proportion of the population who never married (Schofield, 1985; Weir, 1984).

While demographers address demographic transition (the fall in fertility and mortality from the end of the nineteenth century) and other population issues, many historians use demography as a keen tool in the study of the family. Demographic events are closely related to family and household form and size, inheritance, and the family economy. But such events can be used to inform many other aspects of family life as well—from simulations that provide a missing universe for kinship research, to event analysis.

Marriage Patterns

Peter Laslett's seminal study, *The World We Have Lost* (1965), summarized contemporary research on the preindustrial English family, household, and marriage patterns including that of the demographers and of John Hajnal. Laslett depicted a surprisingly mobile preindustrial English population fitting a northwest European pattern of late-marrying couples with concomitant low fertility. These couples headed simple households containing small, nuclear families, often with young, unmarried servants. *The World We Have Lost* had an immediate and wide-ranging effect on historians in much of the Anglophone world as well as in Europe and beyond.

In a highly influential study Hajnal (1965) outlined two ideal types of marriage patterns. The northwest European pattern, prevalent north and west of an imaginary line stretching from Trieste to St. Petersburg, featured a late age of first marriage for both spouses and a relatively large proportion of adults who never married. It customarily resulted in neolocalism, that is, establishment of their own household by the newly married couple. The southern and eastern European pattern, characterized by early age of first marriage with relatively few adults remaining unmarried, often ended with the couple's residing with parents or other relatives. Both Hajnal and Laslett acknowledged that a prevalent pattern did not mean an exclusive one. Laslett (1983) had tried, for example, to encompass some of the variation within geographical area by dividing the West European family form into northwest and southeast European categories with two subcategories each. Further investigation, however, especially on the Mediterranean subcategory (Benigno, 1989), has led historians including Laslett to abandon the typology. Hajnal by 1983 divided areas where simple households predominated (i.e., northwest Europe) from areas, still under study, where joint households (of at least two married couples) seem to have been common.

Hajnal's work, which historians have used as a tool of analysis for both European and non-European populations, has been widely explored and applied. Herlihy (1987), for example, has argued that exogamy fostered by the Catholic Church led to the western European marriage pattern. His work augments that of Goody (1983). The Church's emphasis on monogamy and its definition and prohibition of incest resulted in more commensurable households and a more even distribution of women across these units than in earlier Europe. Although historians hold cultural influences to be important to marriage patterns, they also find economic factors crucial. Hajnal's marriage patterns, Seccombe (1990) believes, reflect changes in economic organization in the aftermath of feudal crises in the later medieval period.

While some historians attempt to explain Hajnal's patterns, others are modifying them. Kertzer and Hogan (1991) find central Italian sharecroppers living in joint households in the early twentieth century, yet marrying late despite the absence of neolocality. Kaser (1994), writing on the joint family in eastern Europe, endorses Hajnal's "bifurcated" European marriage and household patterns, but presses the significance of intraregional diversity. Moreover, regions have modified patterns over time, with Tuscany changing by the mid-nineteenth century from a Mediterranean to a classic northwestern European marriage pattern having high celibacy rates (Viazzo, 1994). Similarly, complex households in southwest Finland gave way to simple ones with a change in the law to allow partible inheritance and as fishing became less labor intensive (Moring, 1994).

American historians, using Hajnal's typology, have found that age of first marriage was on average many years lower among the English in colonial America than among those in the old country, with celibacy rare unless sex ratios necessitated it (Wells, 1992). Although age of first marriage and practice of lifetime celibacy were subject to changing economic and cultural conditions, neolocalism remained a constant. In that respect, the northwest European marriage pattern held among colonial Americans (Smith, 1993). Despite some major exceptions, especially in the case of the black family and a significant portion of post-1960s families in general, most scholars have considered the northwest European marriage pattern the basic American form.*

Lynch (1991) restates the cultural importance of the western European marriage pattern, although she points out that the difficulty of capturing migrants (who could be early marrying) might bias the interpretation of that pattern. The desire to strike a balance between reproduction and material resources, Lynch finds, has been a western European value for several centuries, which presaged the early adoption of modern family limitation in western Europe. A more general point emerging from the assessment of Hajnal's work is that while variation appears to have been greater in European marriage patterns than he once thought, the basic contours remain. The European marriage patterns typology has become a standard measure of analysis for historians of the family.

Household and Family Forms

Work on marriage patterns readily connects with scholarship on the character of households and families. The Cambridge Group conducted much early research on the

*Ann Patton Malone (1992) finds Louisiana slave families had three basic household types (simple, female-headed, solitary), which permitted necessary adaptability to forces well beyond family control. The seminal work on African American history of the family is Herbert G. Gutman, *The Black Family in Slavery and Freedom* (1976).

shape and size of the household and family and attempted to standardize definitions of household form (Laslett & Wall, 1972; see also Nettig, Wilk, & Arnould, 1984). Cambridge research on preindustrial family and household types and size has largely rested on surviving lists of households from relatively small communities in the English past, for which little longitudinal household data exist. Although these cross-sectional lists are complete, dated, and meet high standards of accuracy, they do not represent a random sample of the English preindustrial population. However, from some rare repetitive lists Laslett and Harrison (1963) ascertained that the nuclear household was a common form across preindustrial England and proceeded to examine household and family form comparatively across countries and centuries.

Historians, especially in Europe, have often placed work on family forms into the context of the studies of Frédéric LePlay, one of several nineteenth-century social scientists (along with Lewis Henry Morgan and Friedrich Engels) who theorized about the family. LePlay (1855–1878, especially 1871) had distinguished three familial types: the patriarchal, the stem, and the unstable. The patriarchal family featured continuity, lineage, authority, and tradition. The stem family was a particular, and to LePlay common, version of the patriarchal, differing only in that just one child and his (occasionally her) family would coreside with his parents and inherit their real property. The stem family is a three-generational family whose authority resides in the oldest generation (Mitterauer & Sieder, 1982, p. 33), but the stem-family form also implies eventual inheritance by one child in the second generation. For that reason historians find that stem families often coexist with primogeniture.

LePlay's third model, the unstable (or nuclear) family, was created when two individuals married and often dissolved when one or the other of them died. Its duration was fleeting—generally the married lifetime of the two original partners—unlike the continuing stability of the multigenerational patriarchal or stem-family system. LePlay thought the unstable or nuclear family to be an aberration that those repairing to the city and the rural proletarian laborers tended to adopt. Conversely, Laslett would find the nuclear form standard in preindustrial England. He and others successfully challenged what Goode (1970, p. 6) has derisively called "the classical family of Western nostalgia"—the three-generational group surrounded by lateral kin, who presumably worked and played together in the past within a mutually sustaining environment. Laslett (1972) also suggested that the nuclear family might have been the predominant family type for centuries throughout western Europe if not farther afield.

Not all historians of the family accepted the possible ubiquity of the preindustrial nuclear family. Using age data from eighteenth-century Austrian peasant households, Berkner (1972, 1975) questioned the heavy reliance on household

lists, which reflect family form at the time each list was drawn. Household lists do not indicate the proportion of families which at some point in their cycle might have taken a different form. Berkner found that a stem-family pattern emerged as parents aged and children married. Many of his nuclear families, he concluded, were stem families in embryo, with their simple households being complex households in waiting.

In a subsequent early computer simulation Wachter, Hammel, and Laslett (1978) used English household data to argue that, given age of marriage and other demographic variables, a stem-family pattern—even of short duration—could not have been a significant part of the English experience. Fitch (1980) has in turn questioned the assumptions built into that simulation. Nonetheless, historians generally acknowledge that demographic constraints—age of marriage, number of surviving children, and longevity—would have made the stem family attainable for only a small proportion of families for a limited time. Thus, "the nuclear family may be regarded as a structural given whether or not it is also a social construct" (Douglass, 1991, pp. 301–302).

Berkner's argument for family-cycle studies or cohort analysis had been anticipated to some extent by the demographically based community studies of early America. Greven (1970), for example, linked age at marriage and household form to inheritance as he assessed the power of the colonial Andover, Massachusetts, patriarchy over four generations in their "modified extended" families. In the fourth generation, however, migration by these families in search of new opportunity considerably weakened familial ties. Much of North America and northwest Europe in the preindustrial period featured households that were usually simple in form, single- or two-generational, and headed by a married couple or a single parent. Few, if any, kin other than children or stepchildren resided in the household, although youthful servants were often present. That pattern seemingly held for colonial America and the period of the early republic.

Ruggles (1987) argues that the family in Europe and in European North America has not remained constant to the nuclear family model. Rather, reversing the traditional perception of the historically extended family's giving way to the modern nuclear one, he maintains that the typical nuclear family of the early modern period often gave way to a form of the stem family in the Victorian period, especially among the upper classes. This development was fueled by ideology as much as, if not more than, by economics or demography. Definition is crucial to the analysis of family form, and Ruggles' definition of stem family may be more inclusive than that commonly used by other scholars.

Ruggles (1994) decries the "crippling effect" that the belief that family structure has been stable for centuries has had on the historical analysis of the family. The old orthodoxy of the extended family, he claims, has fallen victim to a new orthodoxy of the nuclear family—at least for northwest Europe and North America. Early and widespread acceptance of the new orthodoxy, especially in relation to families in the past century, has in Ruggles' mind aborted further quantitative study of household and family form as historians of the family have moved on to other areas, especially relationships among kin. The recent work of Ruggles, Smith (1993), and others may help fuel a revival of interest in household and family form if such interest has indeed waned.

Within demographic constraints, the stem family appears to have been relatively common to parts of central Europe in addition to Austria (Mitterauer & Sieder, 1982). However, it has also emerged as a norm in regions of France—in Haute-Provence in the seventeenth and eighteenth centuries (Collomp, 1983), elsewhere in southern France in the eighteenth and nineteenth centuries (Darrow, 1989), and in the French Pyrenees from at least the early seventeenth century (Fauve-Chamoux, 1987). Also a "strict norm" of primogeniture seemingly ensured the primacy of the stem family in rural Catalonia until very recently (González, 1990).

Families in regions of southwestern and west central Europe frequently lived in complex households considered more typical of eastern Europe. Shaffer (1982) has found joint households—usually married siblings and their families sharing a home—persisting from the sixteenth to the twentieth centuries in the Nivernais in France. Complex households have appeared with frequency during the past few centuries in central Italy, where sharecropping was common (Kertzer, 1984; Viazzo, in press). The Florentine *catasto* of 1427 reveals a multiplicity of family forms in medieval Tuscany (Herlihy & Klapisch-Zuber, 1985). There the group solidarity of the wealthy and of landed peasants emerged in complex households, while the masses of small peasants and renters lived in families with a simple structure. In the rural quarter of Santo Spirito, Florence, responsibility for a complete farm—whether as a proprietor, leaseholder, or sharecropper—was key to household size (Herlihy, 1985). These studies exemplify the importance of economic circumstances and social class to analysis of household and family structure.

Discussion of household and family forms has underscored the need for demographically based family history to consider longitudinal as well as cross-sectional analysis, to look at the history or life cycle of individual families, and to consider regional and temporal variation as well as economic class and social stratum. As history of the family has matured, household and family forms have emerged as more varied and complex in the past than historians initially thought, thus demanding a multifaceted approach.

Family and Kin

Concern of demographically based historians with marriage and family formation led naturally to the examination of marriage patterns as historians began to look beyond the coresident group to kin and related issues like inheritance. As Benigno, citing patrivirilocality or "kinship areas," notes, household walls might not have coincided "with the boundaries of mutual rights and duties, of solidarity and of affection" (1989, p. 186). In undertaking work in fields like kinship, long tended by anthropologists, historical scholars routinely employ the explanatory power of theoretical perspective. Fortes' early articulation (1949) of a developmental concept, common to biology and used by many other disciplines, including psychology (e.g., Erikson, 1950), influenced study of kin by other anthropologists (e.g., Goody, 1971) and in turn became important to historians (e.g., Demos, 1970). The writings of Lévi-Strauss (1949, 1963) and other anthropologists on alliance systems also contributed to historical analysis, while Goody's work on inheritance (1976a) has proved particularly influential.

Although Fortes, Lévi-Strauss, and other structuralists later came under attack for their legalism, in this case belief that decisions about marriage follow a set of underlying rules rather than emanating from conscious choice (Bourdieu, 1976), structuralism still provides theoretical underpinning for some historians working on kin. Others, however, have relied more on alternative theories like network analysis (Smith, 1979; Wheaton, 1987) or exchange theory (Anderson, 1971).

Other social science disciplines have traditionally focused more on theory-building than has history. Each of the set of interlinked propositions, which Plakans notes that theory produces, states a relationship that should hold in a wide range of societies and historical time (1984, p. 251). Possibly because historians tend to be more empirically particularistic in their work, more reluctant to apply findings from one period or place to another, they have forced consideration of time as a significant variable in the study of kinship. Smith, for example, believes that identification of a pattern of kin interaction in late-thirteenth-century Suffolk gives us "no sound reason for supposing" that the pattern was either typical of England at the time or of Suffolk earlier or later (1979, p. 249). Yet although historians are often leery of wide-ranging generalizations, theory is an important tool in their analysis of kinship.

Reliable data, never abundant for historians studying earlier centuries, become scarcer as historians include wider circles or greater degrees of kinship in their studies, and identification of kin is often a problem. Family-reconstitution techniques are most feasible for small populations, especially units like parishes or manors. In such locations, a continuous set of records may survive that can be linked to other contemporary records such as wills, deeds, or debt records and can help to identify kin networks. The resulting community studies possess an immediacy difficult to attain for large populations. Studies of preindustrial England and America such as that of Terling, Essex (Wrightson & Levine, 1979), or that of Plymouth (Demos, 1970) or Andover, Massachusetts (Greven, 1970), have generally not been replicated for large, urban areas. Boulton (1987) has explored early modern kin and family in London south of the Thames, but his work concentrates on one district within St. Saviour's parish, Southwark, and is in effect a community study. Censuses and city directories of the nineteenth and twentieth centuries, which allow family historians to study larger populations with greater facility, are often of limited help in capturing kin (Katz, 1975; Thernstrom, 1964) in part because urban populations have high rates of transiency.

Some historians with access to lengthy genealogical records employ computerized analysis to understand the importance of kinship in the past, as Segalen (1991) did in examining marriage and inheritance across fifteen generations in Brittany (1720–1980). Canada's Research Project on Regional Societies (SOREP) uses the Saguenay, Quebec, population register (1842–1911) to reconstitute families and to analyze kin clusters (Bouchard, 1991; Bouchard & du Pourbaix, 1987). Other large databases helpful to kinship research include those of the University of Montreal's Programme de recherche en démographie historique (PRDH), the Swedish Demographic Data Base at the University of Umeå, and the Utah Population Data Base at the University of Utah (Bean, Minean, & Anderton, 1990). PRDH contains French Canadian population, parish, and mission registers prior to 1730; the Umeå project links comprehensive church books to other kinds of nineteenth-century records; and the Utah data are a subset of Mormon genealogical records, predating vital registration. For the most part, however, long series of records useful to study of kinship historically are generally difficult to locate or to build for many times and places.

Recapturing the richness of kin interaction is also difficult for historians, who unlike most anthropologists and sociologists can usually neither observe nor question their subjects. Sociologists Peter Willmott and Michael Young (1960; Young & Willmott, 1957), for example, used interviews to determine the impact of class and gender on the relationships among close kin in the 1950s, when they traced interaction in a working-class London neighborhood and in a middle-class suburban one. Historians do encounter some rich sources besides the more usual wills, diaries, and letters, such as the Inquisition records that informed Ladurie's study of Montaillou (1979). Generally, however, historians must depend on more indirect indicators for assessing the quality of the interaction taking place and for determining to what extent physical proximity mattered to the quality of kin relationships. A tendency to infer cultural or emotional attributes on the basis of sparse or absent evidence is an occupational hazard for historians. Theoretical explanations are thus a great asset.

Applying exchange theory to explore relationships in nineteenth-century Lancashire, Anderson (1971) has found that even relatively distant kin played an important role in critical life situations for most families except the very poor, who had little with which to bargain. Hareven (1982) echoes that conclusion in her investigations of nineteenth-century New Hampshire female factory workers whose kin aided their migration and acculturation. But Ruggles (1987) believes that, among the less wealthy, nineteenth-century kin were not of great help in critical life situations. He finds no evidence, for example, that extended-family living arrangements were a strategy for assistance. The poor could not usually afford to help unemployed kin although, Ruggles asserts, cultural values encouraged those who could afford such help to provide it.

Some studies that examine the nuclear family's relationship to its kin have not been demographically based. Analysis of sets of family letters (Cressy, 1987; Erickson, 1972) disclose the continuity of familial relationships across large expanses of time and water as well as the qualitative nature of those relationships. Understandably the proportion of immigrants who did not retain contact with kin has forever escaped us, and letters to nonkin are not so likely to survive for comparative use. However, computer simulation systems like CAMSIM (Laslett, 1988) or MOMSIM (Ruggles, 1987) provide estimates of numbers and types of kin for given groups at given times, allowing a vision, albeit cloudy, of the universe of kinship.

Macfarlane (1970) has applied structuralist techniques to investigate the importance of family and kin to Ralph Josselin, a seventeenth-century diarist. Josselin had much closer ties to one uncle and one sibling than to others, but his sporadic, selective interchanges with kin other than his wife and children help to underline the primacy of the early modern nuclear family, a position Macfarlane furthers in his work on English individualism (1979). Macfarlane's case study of Josselin explores many facets of his life—demographic, economic, political, emotional—in effect, a "total history" of the man within his nuclear family. Josselin's interactions with his kin illustrate one pattern of relationships. Similarly rich case studies from Josselin's time and locale might substitute for a sample and depict a range of plausible relationships, but the necessary sources are rare and historians' approaches to such material differ (MacDonald, 1981; Seaver, 1985; Slater, 1984). Nonetheless, conclusions about typicality and universality necessarily depend upon a representative sample of family groups. For that reason, and because diarists like Josselin are few, most historical studies of kin have been community-wide and demographically based rather than focused on case studies.

More work will have to be done on families in varying historical, geographic, and economic settings before a clear idea emerges of roles played by kin generally. Some analytical consensus on which relatives are family members and which are kin would also help. Historians will likely divide, nonetheless, on locational issues—whether nonresident family and kin in relatively close proximity could be as important as those in residence and, if so, when, how, and why.

Demographically based analysis has been crucially important in opening up the field of family history. Some early work claimed too much and some early methods embraced too little, but they provided a base upon which to build. Historians of the family have become consistently more sophisticated over time, increasing the scope of their studies geographically, longitudinally, and in the number and types of variables considered such as gender, class, and occupation.

Family Cycle and the Life Course

As family historians moved increasingly from cross-sectional to longitudinal analysis or a combination of the two, the concept of family cycle—of a developmental pattern in the life of the family—gained prominence. That idea, which can be traced at least to Rowntree (1901), surfaced again after World War II among anthropologists like Fortes, Goody, and others and sociologists like Goode or Hill and Rodgers (1964). But it was Berkner's call (1972) for consideration of the family as a process, not a series of snapshots—reinforced by others (Cuisenier & Segalen, 1977; Hareven, 1977)—that focused the attention of historians on the idea of a family cycle.

Stages of the family cycle in the West have corresponded to a major extent with stages in parenting or in a marriage's history. Rowntree (1901) recognized three stages—family poverty when children are young, increasing prosperity as they either contribute wages or live on their own, and poverty again in the parents' old age. These economically defined stages feature changes in the ratio of wage earners to dependents (Rodgers, 1977).*) Stages in the family cycle can also be demographically defined. The simple or nuclear family in the West historically began with marriage, lasted through birth and rearing of children if any, and ended with the death of one or both spouses. (For a discussion of endpoints of families and households, see Janssens, 1993). Stem-family

cycles are necessarily demographically defined, for the possibility of a stem-family phase depended on demographic events. Contemporary scholars divide the family cycle into varying numbers of stages, most of which center on entry into marriage, children's births, children's schooling or leaving home, and parental retirement or death.

Family cycle and individual life course interact importantly with each other and with society at large. A cluster of social, economic, geographical, health, and other factors influences the timing both of family and of individual life stages, which in turn influences the cluster. But family and individual life-course stages are not coterminous, for while the family usually begins with marriage, the individual life course starts at birth, and over the life span a person might be a resident member of several families.

In life-course studies the unit of analysis has shifted from the household and its head featured in early family and demographic studies to individuals in the family and the timing of crucial events or transitions in their lives. Modell (1989) examines four such transitions centering on mating—dating, sexual intimacy, marriage, and parenthood. Other events, retirement, for example, also lend themselves well to life-course study. Cohort analysis is particularly helpful in life-course research, as Elder's model study, *Children of the Great Depression* (1974), has shown. Data on historical age cohorts are difficult to find, but Elder reconfigured data from the Oakland Growth Study of 1932 and from later studies on the same population to address the cohort's life experiences.

Most life-course researchers seek a data source and adapt their questions to that source. Like household lists and censuses, the materials—often early surveys or population registers—have not been framed with the historian in mind. Researchers who study the past, like Elder, must find innovative ways to tease information from such sources. Other researchers apply newer methodologies such as event-course analysis (Alter, 1988) to censuslike sources. As a general rule, the earlier the period of the study, the more difficult life-course analysis is with historians framing questions and painstakingly putting several sources together to address these issues as part of life-course analysis. Lacking surveys, censuses, population registers, city directories, or their equivalent, scholars examining preindustrial periods usually will construct their own universes of biographies and genealogies and relatively few will be able to undertake cohort analysis.

Psychological theory would seem particularly suited for application to life-course studies, of which some historians have made use (DeMause, 1974a,b; Trumbach, 1978). But psychoanalytical theory does not come easily to terms with traditional historical evidence, a difficulty that may explain why most psychoanalytically oriented historians have chosen to write historical psychobiographies. Nonetheless, the concept of a psychologically based, life-course approach, in

---

*A. V. Chayanov (1927) found a similar cyclical ratio of earners to dependents determining expansion and contraction of Russian peasant farms (Smith, 1984a).

particular the theoretical work of Erikson (1950), has reached a broad group of readers and popularized the developmental concept from a psychoanalytical perspective. Among others, Hunt (1970) and Demos (1970) have applied the Eriksonian model, the latter wedding family reconstitution and individual development to address transitional stages and the life course of family members in colonial Plymouth. More recently, Elder, Modell, and Parke (1993a) have issued a call for collaboration between social historians and developmental psychologists, among others interested in the life cycle.

In sum, as the field of family history has matured, especially with investigation of the life course, historians have increasingly studied family members other than the household head, traditionally a productive male adult around whom the family has been defined. In doing so, they address broad life-course stages—infancy, childhood, adolescence or youth, adulthood, and older age—as well as transitions that mark individual and family stages, like leaving home, marriage, parenthood, and retirement. Relatively little work other than household studies and studies of parenting and employment has been done on middle age, but the marital transition, as well as childhood, adolescence, and older age, have become important topics to historians. While some early life-course studies embodied the perspective of adult society, more recent work is beginning to view life stages from the perspective of the individuals involved in them.

Marriage

Marriage studies, so central to historical analysis of the Western family, have loomed large in major theoretical syntheses by that group of scholars writing in the 1960s and 1970s whom Anderson (1980) has called the "sentiments" school. The group, which includes Philippe Ariès, Jean-Louis Flandrin, Edward Shorter, and Lawrence Stone, suggests that a major change in family relationships occurred in modern times between husbands and wives and between parents and children. They posit a move from a calculating to a more affective behavior sometime between the late seventeenth and early twentieth centuries. These synthetic works of broad sweep often provide a backdrop for discrete studies of family cycle or life course. Ariès and Stone in particular have been much relied upon by American scholars of the American family for their material on preindustrial relationships as well as for theoretical perspective (e.g., Degler, 1980). But the "sentiments" volumes have been roundly attacked, notably by colleagues—both European and American—who write on the European family, especially the medieval and early modern family.

Shorter (1975) claims that during the past 2 centuries "romantic love unseated material considerations," children shifted from being one of their mothers' priorities to their major concern, and the family's ties to the outside world became weakened. "The traditional family …, much more a productive and a reproductive unit than an emotional [one]," was dislodged by a "surge of sentiment," driven by advancing industrialism, which resulted in the modern family (p. 5). Mates were selected for romantic, not dynastic, reasons while privacy and intimacy increased. Shorter argues that this sentimental egoism surfaced as a subculture of the oppressed, possibly in the eighteenth century, and progressed rapidly thereafter. He attributes an increased illegitimacy rate to a freeing of young people, especially young women, from traditional moral codes. Migration and industrialization made this freedom possible by allowing affective behavior to emerge.

Although some historians (e.g., Traer, 1980) have embraced Shorter's thesis, others have strongly questioned his work. Tilly, Scott, and Cohen (1976) argue that women were not necessarily emancipated from family controls. Rather, the rise in nineteenth-century European illegitimacy represents aborted marriages: Geographic and occupational mobility allowed men to abandon women whom they had seduced and would in earlier times have married. *Declarations de grossessen*, interrogations of unmarried French women late in their pregnancies, show that sexual encounters leading to illegitimate births were most often forced, very seldom romantic, and represented instrumental, not affective, behavior—in short, "date rape." Increase in bastardy rates thus reflected male, not female, emancipation from village control in a mobile and none too romantic society (Fairchilds, 1978).

Stone (1977) also posits change in the nineteenth century in the nature of the family. Members of traditional open-lineage, patriarchal English families, he argues, were responsive to their kin groups and communities but had weak emotional ties to close family members. Dominant loyalties to lineage, kin, patron, and community began to recede in the mid-sixteenth century, with the closed nuclear family's emergence among the upper bourgeoisie and squirearchy by the late seventeenth century. Late in the nineteenth century after some reversals, this affective model had spread both upward to the court aristocracy and downward to the masses of artisans and "respectable wage-earners," with all classes loving their spouses, cherishing their children, and desiring privacy.

Most historians of the medieval and early modern family—Continental and English—seriously disagree with Stone's evidence and his interpretation. The most telling criticism, which Stone himself recognized in the 1979 abridged version of *Family, Sex, and Marriage*, was that his evidence came from the elite (some 4% of seventeenth-century English society*) and should not have been generalized to other social strata (e.g., Anderson, 1980; Houl-

*See Gregory King's contemporary analysis of 1688 data in Laslett (1965, pp. 36–37).

brooke, 1984). Herlihy in 1985 found that Stone's thesis had "little left in it" (1985, p. 207), but his work continues to have widespread currency among historians of other periods (Davidoff & Hall, 1987) and in general summaries (Skolnick, 1991).

A major critic of the sentiments school, Macfarlane finds that Stone's and Shorter's assumptions about the affective family's evolution from a brutish, loveless group echoes nineteenth-century anthropologists, whose writing depicted "early modern men and women replacing the unenlightened 'savages'" (1979, p. 192n). Macfarlane holds that since the fourteenth century, partially because of late age at marriage, English young people generally made their own marriage choices. They chose on the basis of romantic love, an example of that English individualism that Macfarlane finds pervasive over 7 centuries (1979; O'Hara, 1991, suggests a modification of Macfarlane).

The medieval Roman Catholic Church had institutionalized acceptable alternatives to marriage like celibacy (Goody, 1983; Watkins, 1984). Indeed, the medieval Catholic Church bolstered romantic love by emphasizing the union of hearts, especially the consent of the two principals, and insisting that promises to marry were binding, a position reaffirmed by the Council of Trent in the sixteenth century. Courts and aristocrats, not the Church, promoted arranged marriages, which provided a means to preserve and expand titles and estates (Duby, 1978). In medieval Florence, dynastic considerations drove marriages, and a wide disparity in ages existed between spouses. By "exert[ing] a powerful influence on behavior and mentalities within the family and on images of authority," the disparity sustained the patriarchy of the medieval family (Herlihy & Klapisch-Zuber, 1985, p. 362). Marriages in medieval and early modern England, where spouses were very close in age, may have resulted in a considerably less dominant patriarchy, although Anderson (1980) cautions against drawing such a conclusion.

Indicators of emotional involvement in a largely illiterate society are difficult to find, but emotional ties between medieval family members in England were probably much like modern ones (Hanawalt, 1986). Ozment (1983), using a wealth of largely German material from household accounts to catechisms, believes that the patriarchal family in Reformation Europe commonly incorporated companionate marriage and deeply affectionate relationships between parents and children and was not a society where the father's rights over his children outweighed his duties to them (as Flandrin, 1979, had suggested).

Among the doctrinal innovations that draw historians of the family to study the Protestant Reformation is acceptance of divorce. The introduction of divorce into sixteenth-century Germany changed traditional values only slowly (Safley, 1984), and until about the middle of the twentieth century formal divorce was relatively uncommon across Europe. Death usually terminated marriages, although divorce was not the only other option. Gillis (1985), Menefee (1981), O'Hara (1991), Phillips (1991), Quaife (1979), and Stone (1990, 1992, 1993), among others, have contributed to a growing body of historical analysis of how marriage partners have chosen each other and how they have separated, legally and otherwise. Much, too, has been written about marriage partnerships in the past, with some, like Segalen (1983), arguing for the historical partnership of husband and wife—in this case the French peasant. Others, however, find full partnership not only missing frequently in the past (Hammerton, 1992), but also problematic in the present (Pahl, 1989; Scanzoni, 1982).

Historical reconstructions may overlook the often mixed nature of human decision. The continuum of decisions on marriage in any period may stretch between totally calculating and totally romantic behavioral poles. Even in England, where a national consensus on questions of marriage and the family that allowed for romantic espousals seemingly developed early (Macfarlane, 1979, 1986), marital decisions must often have reflected mixed views. The ideal at all times and places may have been a romantic choice who also met socially appropriate economic and other criteria.

Two problems for the historian looking at marriage in the past are problems for all historians. First, recapturing the feelings of historical actors, most of them illiterate, is extraordinarily difficult despite increased sensitivity of historians to *mentalités* since the advent of the *Annalistes*. Second, while historians are sensitive to the sweep of time, their identification with particular periods predisposes them to find important change in the periods they study, sometimes overlooking the roots of that change in earlier periods.

Childhood

Some historical studies that have analyzed children in the context of the family since 1960 are direct descendants of investigative reports that led to nineteenth- and twentieth-century legislation (Walvin, 1982). Other studies have used traditional sources and methods to address the relationship between the child, the family, and the state (Brenner, 1970–1974; Pinchbeck & Hewitt, 1969–1973; Wishy, 1968). They have helped encourage an important and sizeable literature, more often considered intellectual or political than social history.

Historical cohort studies such as Elder's (1974) *Children of the Great Depression*, on the other hand, are few and largely produced by sociologists, economists, or statisticians under the aegis of government. Hernandez (1993) has used census and survey data from 1940 to 1990 to examine the economic, familial, and societal revolutions that American children have undergone, arguing for public policies to ameliorate the negative consequences of social and economic change. British investigators are following a cohort comprising virtually every British baby born between March 3 and 9, 1958, and to some extent their families (Fogelman, 1983). Such sociological and economic studies of contemporary populations both inform and become fodder for historians of family and childhood.

In the past few decades, social historians of childhood have tended to spread themselves along a continuum on each of two issues—whether a concept of childhood existed in the past and whether children were important to their parents historically. Those who believe that a concept of childhood as a life stage existed in the early modern period or before also generally think that early modern and medieval parents loved their children. Sentiments scholars, on the other hand, argue that a concept of childhood did not generally tend to exist until an important change occurred in parental attitude. They generally date this recognition of childhood to the late seventeenth and eighteenth centuries, although Shorter (1975) finds it beginning with the sixteenth-century elite. Before that change, whatever its actual timing, they assume that emotional ties between parents and children were very weak.

For many scholars, Ariès' *Centuries of Childhood* (1962) opened the field of history of childhood. His work, which electrified family historians with its innovative use of sources, especially art, asserts that preindustrial children were viewed as miniature adults, not as persons at a special stage in life with special needs. Denying that a concept of childhood existed in medieval and early modern Europe, Ariès dated progressive change to the seventeenth and eighteenth centuries, when, he suggests, the idea of childhood as a recognizable stage began to take root. Many other social historians seemed to confirm Ariès' general thesis while differing in regard to the timing of the change. Stone (1977) has argued that English families underwent "remarkable change" in attitudes toward children, moving from uncaring parenting of miniature adults to affective parent–child relationships once childhood as a concept was emerging. These changes, he contends, trickled between 1660 and 1800 from the upper to the lower classes. Trumbach (1978), who like Stone depends on sources featuring elites, claims that patrilineal inheritance and ideology weakened the family in the early Middle Ages. Echoing Plumb (1975), Trumbach sees an attitudinal change at the end of the seventeenth century with more egalitarian relationships emerging between parents and children as well as between spouses in eighteenth-century England.

American historians often concur with the general attitude of the sentiments writers, believing that lack of sentiment in England transferred to colonial North America but finding New World conditions modifying an earlier starkness. Wishy (1968) sees a modern concept of childhood emerging in America by the mid-eighteenth century and gathering

momentum thereafter. Other American historians of childhood view the preindustrial period less negatively. Bremner (1970–1974) identifies changing perceptions of children over 2 centuries but accepts Bailyn's progressive or "Whig" economic thesis (1960) that ready availability of land ultimately liberated the American child from parental control. And Greven (1977) claims that diverse views of childhood and parent–child relationships coexisted from the seventeenth to the nineteenth centuries.

Psychoanalytically influenced writers who examine key stages in the life of the growing child, such as weaning and toilet training, view the past darkly. Hunt (1970) found the cynical upbringing of Louis XIII exemplary of the dismal, contemporary thought on elite childrearing. DeMause (1974a) judged the period before the Enlightenment brutal for children but concurred with Walzer's view (1974) that their harsh world improved in eighteenth-century America. And Demos (1970) concluded that childhood, except perhaps before the age of 7, was not a recognizable stage in the life cycle of those living in Plymouth Colony. However, he finds redeeming elements in Plymouth parenting, which often did not reflect that society's ideology, a point Morgan (1944) had made years before and a good example of the discrepancy between proscriptive and descriptive sources.

While a strong body of historical opinion had originally supported the evolution-of-childhood thesis, more recent scholarly work has modified the idea of linearly progressive change. Heywood (1988) argues that for the French masses 50 years of worsening conditions in attitudes toward children preceded major improvements in the middle of the nineteenth century. But beginning for the most part in the late 1970s, what might be called the optimistic school has attacked the work of Ariès and others who have seen the past as devaluing children. Medievalists have found that both French and English parents recognized childhood in the Middle Ages as a separate stage of life (Hanawalt, 1986; Paterson, 1993). And early modernists, notably Pollock (1983, 1987), assert that a concept of childhood existed in the preindustrial West, with parents emotionally attached to their children. Indeed, Wheaton (1980, p. 21), surveying French research, finds no conformity between Ariès' basic themes and the history of the French family.

In her review of the history of childhood literature, Pollock (1983, p. 12) criticizes those who think that ideas about childhood and parenting have changed fundamentally over time. She believes that societies in the past always had elements that held enlightened ideas about childhood but that use of proscriptive materials like sermons, advice books, and art instead of descriptive materials like diaries, memoirs, and letters helps camouflage the reality. Like Pollock, more and more historians of the family are discounting the alleged change in parental attitudes and especially in parental behavior in the seventeenth and eighteenth centuries that sentiments scholars have identified. Even Ariès himself came to believe that greater familiarity with medieval sources might have modified his position (Hareven, 1991). Macfarlane's (1970) study of the Josselin family, MacDonald's (1981) work on the patient records of the physician-astrologer Napier, and Seaver's (1985) research on the Wallington diary exemplify the use of English descriptive materials that support the belief that affective attitudes were present in all historical periods. Bremner (1970–1974), among others, provides descriptive American sources.

Two problems confront the sentiments theorists. The first is whether the conditions they identify in the past—negative parental attitudes, lack of affection, the inflated expectations of miniature adulthood as opposed to the comfort of childhood, etc.—were prevalent. The second is whether positive parental attitudes—affection, cossetting of children, and the like—of later periods actually existed in relatively greater proportion than they had previously. A growing understanding of the silence that still accompanies abuse and denigration of children and openness to new methods of evaluating their status may help provide better data on children's position and may give us a clearer idea about childhood in the past.

One of the ways historians have attempted to assess parents' affection for their children is by examining inheritance patterns, although inheritance patterns also reflect tradition and economic imperatives. While families with large landholdings seemingly tried to pass their lands intact—early modern Dutch gentry heavily favored sons (Marshall, 1987)—the aristocratic model should not be generalized. Removed to colonial New York, the Dutch were egalitarian in inheritance practice, while colonial Englishmen there were not (Narrett, 1992). However, in early modern England many substantial families treated their children with equality to the extent that such treatment was possible. Eldest sons may have disproportionately received land that had been long in the family, but parents routinely acquired equivalent amounts of land for their other children or provided them with comparable amounts of money and arranged for special needs like those of a deaf mute (Cooper, 1992). Such transactions frequently occurred in *inter vivos* or other nontestamentary arrangements often missed in studies heavily based on wills. Interpreting the behavior involved in these transactions also has its risks. One may suspect a strong affective bond between parents and children, but evidence that speaks largely to the former's concern for the latter's education and training is not conclusive (Marshall, 1987). Moreover, inheritance may be driven by community norms. In Württemberg partible inheritance meant that every child, regardless of gender, received not only a legacy of equal value but one consisting of the same kinds of property (Sabean, 1990).

As in marriage choice, historical views about children may have fallen between poles of economic calculation and sentimental affection. Zelizer (1985) has identified a sacralization of the American child in the late nineteenth century, the separation of the child from economic valuation as the child's sentimental value grew. Finding that cultural values shaped economic choices, Zelizer questions Becker's economic model (1976). Without a family wage, however, when everyone's survival depended on everyone's work, the useless child might have been loved but might not have been viable.

Historians have published a number of studies on the abandonment and reclamation of infants and children. Parental abandonment occurred commonly in Imperial Rome and earlier, although how commonly is not known, and it continued until very recent times (Boswell, 1988). Reviewing much of the limited extant data on abandonment from the classical period onward, Boswell argues that abandonment did not indicate a "general absence of tender feelings for children as special beings among any premodern European peoples" (1988, p. 37). Rather, abandonment was a mechanism for family limitation under economic duress. He sees a low point in abandonment in the eleventh and twelfth centuries when oblation peaked, followed by the founding in the fourteenth century of hospitals for abandoned children in Italy, France, and Germany and a growth in abandonment to an eighteenth-century zenith. Estimates of abandonment vary from one time and place to another: from about 3% of all baptisms in nineteenth-century Bologna to about 40% in Milan, from 6% in fifteenth-century Florence to 38% there 4 centuries later (Henderson & Wall, 1994a; see also Kertzer, 1993).

Among eighteenth- and nineteenth-century foundlings, the great majority of surviving legitimate babies, largely abandoned when bread prices were high, were reclaimed (Hunecke, 1987; Sherwood, 1988). Distressed families used the foundling hospitals as temporary relief. Although the social stigma attached to illegitimacy and migration for employment were also crucially important to abandonment practices, the economic necessity of keeping their domestic jobs led single mothers to give up their children (Fuchs, 1984; Ransell, 1978; Sherwood, 1988). For many parents a priceless child was not an option, but parental indifference may have played a role in child abandonment, as did the willingness of state and society to protect fathers of illegitimate offspring (Kertzer, 1993).

Interaction among the family, the economy, and the environment has had a crucial impact on children. West (1989) has shown that children in the western United States a century ago shaped their own experience thanks to limited parental supervision, freedom of movement outdoors for both boys and girls, and early economic independence. On the other hand, child rearing in isolated, wealthier white families on what Cashin (1991) calls the Southern frontier resulted in extremes of wild independence for the growing male child and increased dependence for his sister.

However controversial, the history of childhood and its place in the history of the family are by now well established, and life-course studies may be useful in changing the perspective of historians about children. West and Petrik (1992) note that the outpouring of children's history over the last 25 years represents adults' perceptions of children and childhood, not the children's view. Emerging concern for the child's perspective (Pelling, 1988; Thomas, 1989) may mark the natural evolution of a field that has increasingly given voice to the hitherto voiceless.

Youth

Despite the contention that adolescence is a recent development, historical analysis of adolescence or youth as a life-cycle stage is a subfield coming into its own (see *Journal of Family History*, Volume 17, 1992, and *Continuity and Change*, Volume 6, 1991). While the term adolescence emerged in our family vocabulary with Hall (1904), the stage known as youth was commonly recognized earlier, especially by the evangelicals of the nineteenth century (Kett, 1977). Although government and public recognition of adolescence, accompanied by guidance books, may have been an early twentieth-century phenomenon in the United States, the idea of adolescence or youth is at least as old as the Greeks. Some like Modell (1989) assert, however, that this stage of the life cycle may have assumed greater importance in the twentieth century than in previous eras.

The definition of adolescence is key to its discussion by historians, for to some extent how one defines adolescence determines whether it exists (Katz & Davey, 1978). Important to that discussion is the differentiation between childhood and adolescence, which Elder et al. (1993a) addressed. By physical definition, adolescence starts at puberty—a clearer marker for girls, who undergo menarche, than for boys. In many cultures puberty marks the end of childhood and the beginning of adulthood and is often celebrated by particular rituals, which, some have pointed out, were socially more than physically determined (Gillis, 1974; Hendrick, 1990; Kett, 1977). This sociological aspect is not surprising, for physical growth and sexual maturation in the past were spread out over a much longer period of time than they are today.

Puberty rituals generally do not exist in the West, nor is there any single ceremonial occasion to mark either the physical or the psychological end of adolescence. For Hall (1904) adolescence ran from puberty to the end of individuals' physical growth, generally in their early 20s, and was marked by certain kinds of psychological and moral develop-

ment. Mitterauer (1993) opts for a more purely sociological and psychological definition, not for the biological one of puberty. He finds that adolescence, the time during which young people prepare for marriage and develop autonomous personalities, varies historically and geographically. Because of the marriage pattern, adolescence has been especially extended in the West until legal definitions of age of majority have become widespread.

Adolescence may be defined sociologically not only by its progression in the life cycle or by attainment of a certain age, but also by dependency (Katz & Davey, 1978). Such a definition is not totally satisfactory because dependency may end well beyond the point of that physical maturity that helps mark the end of youth. An adult child, even a middle-aged one, may remain with and be dependent on the parent or may stay in domestic or other service. Yet, there is no one age at which adolescence clearly ends. Marriage marks a definitive upper threshold but one that excludes those who remain single or marry late in life (Mitterauer, 1993). Thus, for historians the end of adolescence depends on an unwritten general consensus about the balance between an individual's age and his or her dependent status. In the end a useful definition of adolescence should probably embrace physical, psychological, social, and legal attributes.

For a long historical period in the West children left their families to live in other households as dependents—as apprentices, servants, or students—between puberty and marriage. In the late nineteenth- and early twentieth-centuries, however, young people began to spend that period of the life cycle in prolonged dependency on parents while attending age-specialized schools. But the change may not have been stark. In both preindustrial and nineteenth-century England children did not leave home at one particular age but gradually, as family circumstances and the nature of the local labor market influenced their departures (Wall, 1978). Indeed, modern perceptions of events such as leaving home are possibly inappropriate when analyzing the past, when overlapping events occurring over longer periods of time blurred the sequence of the typology (Young, 1992).

The life-course perspective, which looks at age-graded groups, addresses transitions, many of which occur in youth and early adulthood—leaving school, leaving home, entering employment, courtship, etc. Availability of data makes cohort studies easier to carry out on modern populations. But historical analysis of past youthful populations such as Kussmaul's work (1981) on early modern agricultural servants can use age-graded data from diverse communities and populations very effectively to enlarge our understanding not only of service in husbandry but also of transition points like entry and exit.

Some of the controversy that attends the history of childhood also attaches to the history of adolescence. Those who believe that societies in the past saw children as miniature adults and did not conceptualize childhood as a separate stage tend to believe that adolescence was not perceived as such either. Those who have found a discrete childhood tend to find a separate adolescence; Hanawalt (1992, 1993), for example, finds adolescence a well-recognized life stage in the Middle Ages. Struggles between adults and youth over entry to and exit from adolescence and for control during that life stage have been occurring since at least the thirteenth century. In late medieval and sixteenth-century France, as well as elsewhere in Europe, youth enjoyed a special license at carnival and other periods of misrule (Davis, 1971). In a kind of brotherhood, young men assumed the lead in mocking those who violated village mores, undertaking charivaris and other demonstrations. Davis challenges Ariès' beliefs that there was no distinction between childhood and adolescence.

Youth in the past, especially apprentices and servants, have received a good bit of attention, but much work remains to be done on adolescence in relationship to the family. We know little about how the position of youths within the family shifted as they became physically stronger and better able to command wages in a society that depended on manpower while their elders became less able physically. Besides questions of shifting power within the family, historians of adolescence need to address questions of gender. As Dyhouse (1981) has pointed out, most of what has been written about the history of adolescence focuses on males.

Age

The history of the elderly is now attracting the kind of attention that the history of childhood was receiving 2 decades ago. Yet while the changing demographics of Western populations and governmental concern have encouraged much research on the elderly, studies by social scientists have often addressed contemporary conditions, and historians before the mid-1970s had not contributed greatly to the debate. A growing group of historians has since undertaken research on the aged, although the history of aging does not have an Ariès, someone with a sweeping and engaging, if imperfect, theoretical perspective. However, in the wake of the increase of the elderly in modern populations, Laslett (1991) has issued a call for action that is informed by historical English data over the last 450 years, including material on life expectancies, retirement, family support, and attitudes toward the aged. Almost by definition the history of the aged is importantly connected to the history of the family, although much of the current historical scholarship concentrates on the relationship of the elderly to the state, to employment, to medical practice, or, in France, to the history of the concept of aging (Bourdelais, 1993).

Like adolescence, old age has had no agreed-upon clear beginning other than noticeable physical deterioration, especially in motor or intellectual performance of a person beyond the threshold of adulthood. Life-cycle stages were often loosely defined in the past, for age-grading in years was limited in importance and approximate birthdates were largely acceptable until the rise of regular registration of vital data. The idea that old age is a functional rather than a chronological condition is supported by markers like loss of employment, death of spouse and friends, dependence, decrepitude, etc. (Bulder, 1993; Laslett, 1991). Yet from the medieval period to the twentieth century, recurring illustrations of life stages have depicted a 50-year-old on a plateau with those younger on ascending steps and those older descending (Hazelzet, c.1994).* Life stages have proceeded in chronological order even if they have not begun at a given age. And in the twentieth century, government pensions and social security insurance have become effective at specific ages, a widely accepted signal of the start of old age.

Most social scientists recognize retirement as a pivotal transition in the family life cycle as well as in the individual life course. The widely held belief that in the past all men without private income worked as long as they were physically able has undergone revision. Demos (1970) has found, for example, that although older people cut back on work in colonial America, only a germ of modern retirement existed. Complete retirement, however, was not unusual in nineteenth- and early twentieth-century America, and the lessening of the workload of elderly men allowed semiretirement while they retained an income (Ransom & Sutch, 1986). Women's retirement status was obscured by their involvement in domestic roles while they came and went in the labor market (Chudacoff & Hareven, 1978). Retirement contracts exist in some number for medieval and early modern Europe, often stipulating lodging and care in exchange for land and usually drawn while the retiree appeared in good health (Smith, 1991). Where the contract was between parent and child, questions of inheritance, independence, and relationship to other members of the family arise. But many arrangements were with nonkin, and these too could secure independence for the elderly (Gaunt, 1983). The persistence of independent living can be found through the nineteenth and into the twentieth centuries (Thomson, 1991) and suggests that independence was a value cherished over time, cherished perhaps by children and kin as well as by the elderly.

The nuclear-hardship hypothesis formulated by Laslett (1984, 1988) suggests that, in areas of the West where nuclear families and simple households predominated and where celibacy was widespread, the community needed to cooperate with the household and kin to maintain the elderly and

*I am grateful to Richard Wall for sharing this exhibition catalogue with me.

other dependent persons. The Elizabethan Poor Law of 1601, which endured for over 2 centuries and forms to this day the basis of local welfare programs in the Anglophone world, is the classic example of support from the collectivity. Such legislation lessened the need for family help, obviated the need for support from kin, and made extended families less desirable (J. E. Smith, 1984).

Early and continued independence of the elderly and the nuclear-hardship hypothesis support the idea of persistence of an independent or limited dependent relationship between the elderly and their Western families over time. In contrast, modernization theory, articulated notably by Tönnies (1957) and Simmons (1945), views the status of the elderly as at its height in patriarchally based agricultural societies, where older people continue to work and where their property confers both power over the young as well as rank. Presumably held in high regard, the aged are seen as repositories of wisdom. Yet in the last 2 decades explanations based on structural differences between traditional and modern societies have come under increasing attack (Gratton, 1986a,b). Stearns (1976) has denounced the "facile generalizations" of nonhistorians who, unable to keep their hands off history, claim that modern society has displaced the elderly from the "patriarchal eminence of the respectful village" (p. 8). Discovery of the historical importance of the nuclear family in the West as well as evidence from some early societies that the elderly were not revered has dealt significant blows to modernization theory.

Much historical analysis of the aged has focused on attitudes toward the old both within and outside the family. In general, American historians interpret positively attitudes toward the aged in the early period, finding the elderly at least respected and often revered (Achenbaum, 1978; Demos, 1970). David Hackett Fischer (1977) traces "the exaltation of age" in early America, which succumbed to a revolution in age relations coinciding with American independence and ended in a cult of youth prevalent into our own time. Some could see in Fischer and others support for modernization theory since pre-Revolution America was a preindustrial, if not a primitive, society (Haber & Gratton, 1994; R. M. Smith, 1984c).

Most Americanists, like modernization theorists, do find that darker days followed the halcyon ones, but although disagreeing about its timing, American historians do not generally relate this attitudinal change to industrialization. Achenbaum believes that pre-Civil War Americans revered their elders. From then until World War I, the growth of organizations and bureaucracy, not industrialization, obviated the need for the wisdom of the aged and "accentuated their handicaps." This new cultural and intellectual position did not reflect any major change in the socioeconomic or demographic conditions of the elderly, although cultural

beliefs and economic realities neared convergence prior to the Social Security Act of 1935, which introduced wide-scale retirement. Haber (1983) also finds the late nineteenth century a watershed, when, among other things, old age was seen as an illness. She argues, however, for more attention to eighteenth-century thought. The colonial period may have featured cultural veneration of the aged, but their position may in fact have been more precarious than such veneration would seem to imply.

American studies differ fundamentally from what little work has been done on England in the early modern period. Thomas (1976) finds that power resided with the middle-aged and that contemporary literature that praised the elderly misleads historians. With their bodies decaying, the ageds' wealth was the only source of respect, and old age was viewed "as a wretched time of physical deterioration" (p. 244). In the nineteenth century, "the repetitive circularity of welfare debates and practices" and the community's willingness to underwrite a considerable part of an individual's welfare, depending on the circumstances, has meant that the family has had to play only a minor role in England in support of the aged (Thomson, 1991, p. 213). R. M. Smith, identifying repetitive welfare cycles since medieval times, argues for understanding welfare processes within the context of a perduring cultural tradition "that can only in a very strained fashion been [sic] seen as the product of a specific mode of production" (1984c, p. 425).

French attitudes about aging and the elderly shift from ridicule and neglect in the seventeenth century, when the aged were presumed to be preparing for an edifying death, to respect and care in the eighteenth century (Troyansky, 1989). Yet as the French population aged in succeeding centuries, old people had an unwelcome visibility that fostered resentment. The eighteenth-century hiatus tempers Stearns' (1976) view that the "overall history of French aging went from a "foul" preindustrial period "to difficult, to better" (p. 158). Troyansky's emphasis on the impact of demographic fluctuation upon contemporary thought about the aged fits R. M. Smith's (1984c) belief that "demographically induced difficulties" have had repercussions upon community support for the aged (p. 423).

Modernization theory, while it has received some telling blows, is not yet dead. Mitterauer and Sieder (1982) find industrialization and urbanization, which some consider synonymous with modernization, responsible for the isolation of the elderly, replacing integration of aged parents into the families of their children. Quadagno (1982) suggests that the early stages of modernization negatively affected the aged although that impact diminished as industrial societies matured. She sees industrial advance demanding younger workers and pushing older men into casual labor in late life, what Haber (1983) has called the industrial scrapheap. Industrialization and other modern developments may have had differential impacts on different societies, some of which had long-standing traditions concerning the aged that modernization did not sweep away. As Bulder (1993) notes about the Netherlands, the collectivity's part in individuals' welfare predates industrialization. The elderly often appear to have supported themselves from a variety of sources, some private and some public, by what is known as "income packaging" but with considerable individual and national variation. While the elderly contributed both labor and savings, the collectivity provided some outdoor relief as well as pensions, which were seen as deserved for previous service and not as charity (R. M. Smith, 1984c). The family probably provided some assistance as well; that help, however, is very difficult to document.

Much work of a major nature remains to be done on the history of aging. There is no strong consensus about timing of attitudinal changes. And aside from the relative position of the aged, the role of the elderly within the family in the past has not been systematically studied. Works by Robin (1980), Chudacoff and Hareven (1978), and Mitterauer and Seider (1982) place the elderly within the family context. But the more prominent studies focused on the history of the aging generally address societal attitudes and mention family and kin tangentially. Some cohort studies have been undertaken, like that of Robin (1984) on Colyton, which shows that the elderly who do live with kin live most frequently with daughters. As study of the elderly in the past increases, questions about economic issues (occupation, wealth, retirement), social concerns (affective and instrumental relationships, religion, power, isolation), and physical well-being (health, sexuality) will receive more attention, and more cohort studies will be undertaken.

* * *

While more and more scholars are looking at individual parts of the life course, relatively few have followed it from birth to old age. Modell (1989), however, uses a life-course approach with successive American birth cohorts from 1920 to 1975 to examine a series of life transitions from youth to adulthood—leaving school, male military service, starting employment, premarital sexual relations, marriage, parenthood, and divorce. Recognizing variation within and among groups, Modell has examined gender, class, and racial differences, finding that women's experience has become more akin to men's and that the importance of youth has grown over time. The historical study of children is the most explored area of life-course history, followed by that of adolescence and youth. The history of age and aging has just begun to be written, and the history of adulthood and middle-age outside of marriage and parenting is largely unexplored. The emergence of research on the life course has drawn attention to large areas for historians of the family to analyze.

Family and Economy

From its inception, the new family history has addressed the connection between family and economy, especially the family's role in regional and national economies. Historians were influenced by sociologists like Parsons and Bales (1955), who viewed the extended family as the production unit of the preindustrial age, which industrialization with its need for a mobile labor force necessarily and probably beneficially transfigured. On the other hand, modernization theorists like Tönnies, who saw the negative impact of industrialization on the extended family, also shaped historical analysis. Such theorists argued that the increased mobility and individualism that came with industrialism hastened the loss of traditional community values while lessening the utility and weakening the position of the elderly. The discovery of the preindustrial nuclear family, which undercut both structural-functionalist and modernization theoretical analysis, encouraged new thought on industrialization and the family.

Influenced by Marxism, Braun (1990), Mendels (1972), and others argued that proto-industrial households were units of production for employers who supplied the capital, frequently the means of production along with raw materials, and generally the markets. These historians depicted a progression from peasantry through cottage industry or proto-industrialism to industrialism as capitalistic demands for labor encouraged the transformation of peasants into proletarians. Material factors shaped family size and domestic arrangements, age at marriage declined, and fertility rose. Proto-industrial opportunity for wage labor thus led to earlier marriages, which in turn resulted in increased fertility and ultimately a loss of ties to the land, with important consequences for family life (Braun, 1989; Levine, 1977).

The work of the historical demographers informed Levine (1984a,b) and others who accommodated "Marxist and Malthusian hypotheses on proletarianization and population growth within a single framework" (p. 87). They found that the traditional peasant economy in northwest Europe, which had featured variable mortality and fertility controlled by a late age of marriage, fell victim in the early modern period to a proletarianization that capitalist agriculture and proto-industrialization induced. However, the idea that peasants abandoned agriculture for manufacture and assumed a new role as a demoralized proletariat has been widely questioned. Such studies of the family and economy of the working class have been criticized for being based "on a conceptual separation between family and economy using an 'essentialist' view of the family, often seen as a pre-industrial enclave or survival" (Davidoff & Hall, 1987, p. 31). A stark dichotomy between agricultural and nonagricultural work seems overdrawn when seasonality in agriculture and desire for supplemental income had for centuries encouraged cottage industries without necessarily affecting social structures. For example, unlike Braun's spinners, peasants in nineteenth-century Normandy engaged in by-employment in textiles, maintained earlier social patterns, and continued to marry late (Gullickson, 1986).

Demographic behavior across societies was not uniform but differed according to environment and the nature of economic change. In nineteenth-century Belgium patterns of land ownership, inheritance, and social structure affected the impact of economic change while late age of marriage continued (Gutmann & Leboutte, 1984). Change in economic organization contributed to change in social organization and change in the sense of community (Accampo, 1989). But traditional patterns of behavior, local imperatives, and demographic structures helped shape the economy as well. Historians need to consider a wide range of possible variables, including the sexual division of labor and wages and employment levels for people at varying ages, as suggested by Gullickson (1986), before an accurate picture of proto-industrialization can emerge.

Most historians of the family have considered industrialization an important historical divide for the domestic group. In the past 2 decades, however, as modernization theory was expiring and proto-industrial analysis beginning to limp, historians have found the move to the factory, which often entailed migration to an urban area, relatively benign (Hareven, 1991). Economic and social disruption could lead to strengthening family ties and building kinship alliances (Sabean, 1990). But evidence that industrial migration often was disruptive and that the presence of children in factories broke family bonds (Lynch, 1988) serves as a caution to historians not to romanticize the changes that occurred with industrialization.

Smelser (1959) used a model of structural differentiation to study what he labelled the family economy, "those organized roles which govern production and consumption in the family" (p. 3). The family-economy concept, which to some extent viewed the family as the basic, small economic unit, became popular with the new home economists (e.g., Becker, 1976, 1991) among other scholars. By focusing on the family unit, historians began to see that the family was not always a reactive agent but could and often did act assertively. While sometimes acknowledging the importance of individual decisions, many viewed the family as a unit with a single economy, frequently shaped by "family strategies" (Chayanov, 1927; Hill, 1989; Tilly, 1979; Tilly & Scott, 1978; Tilly, Scott, & Cohen, 1976).

Family strategy, largely directed toward economic matters, has featured widely in the historical literature in the past 20 years and even earlier in that of anthropology (see, e.g., Bourdieu, 1976, on marriage strategies, and Goody, 1976a, on inheritance strategies). Scholars have disagreed about what family strategy is, when it became possible, who has employed it, and to what ends. Debate has addressed whether a strategy must be perceived as such by the actors, whether strategy implies rational decision making, and whether historians infer strategic behavior based on outcomes rather than intentions. The last are difficult to identify in individuals and groups long dead. (For discussion of family strategy from differing perspectives see Moch, Folbre, Smith, Cornell, & Tilly, 1987).

Some historians who employ family strategy see a change in the past from the family economy, where the family was both the unit of production and consumption and the household with its common pool of labor its locus, and the family wage economy, where the household was a unit of consumption and increase in its members meant increased wages in the common pool (Tilly & Scott, 1989). In the preindustrial period, therefore, the family economy represented a common pool of labor; after industrialization, the family wage economy meant a common pool of wages, and women performed their essential work within the context of the family wage economy. The idea, however, that industrialism brought with it a relatively abrupt change in the locus of production may fail to reflect historical reality, for diversity of employment and payment of wages had existed in the preindustrial period. Families operating within a multi-faceted local economy may have valued flexibility and used an adaptive family economy that allowed them to maximize their economic well-being by diversifying employment of their members (Wall, 1986).

The use of family strategy as a tool of analysis may obscure the importance of the strategy of individuals. As the field of family history has increasingly extended its view from the group to its members, debate has mounted about the application of the family-strategy approach (Moch et al., 1987). Alter (1988) has used event analysis to assess the influence of the family on decisions young Belgian women were making in the latter part of the nineteenth century. Defining an event as "any kind of demographic change that affects some analytically interesting characteristic of a person in the sample" (p. 31), he considers both transition between and duration of events including migration, employment, marriage, and fertility. His finding that parental control was not economic but normative challenges the importance of women's economic emancipation, which Anderson (1971) and Shorter (1975) emphasize. Recapturing the interplay between individual and group strategies will challenge historians for some time to come.

As research on the family and the economy has expanded, historians have become increasingly sensitive to the systems nature of the interconnections between the two. Inheritance patterns provide a prime example of such interaction, as Goody (1976b) recognized when he found modes of inheritance linked to particular socioeconomic systems. Modification in one part of the system, such as property transmission, produces modification in other parts, such as kin alliances (Delille, 1985). The relationship between property and family has a "pile of elements that intrude between any simple conceptualization of the family-land bond" as R. M. Smith notes, "and one could add between the family's form and its economy" (1984b, p. 86).

The Future of Historical Analysis of the Family

Historical analysis of the family, a trickle in the 1960s, has reached full flood. Born in reaction to a traditional history that often seemed too uncritically dependent on qualitative sources, history of the family has become a diverse field not merely as a result of its methodology and interdisciplinary nature but also because of the excitement of discovery that an emerging field promises. One new interpretation after another has increased knowledge and understanding of the once obscure historical family and has in turn been refined, revised, and used as a block for further building.

Much early historical analysis of the family viewed the family and household in isolation. Sentiments historians in particular saw a division between public and private spheres as the modern family turned inward to become the "haven in a heartless world" that Lasch (1977) saw as continually assaulted by modern business and government. The result has been, Lynch (1994) argues, 2 decades of a depoliticized analysis. She calls for placing the family and its members in its political and institutional setting, which her study of the nineteenth-century connections between French bourgeois social policy and working-class families (1988) has done. In a development that some might find ironic, historical analysis of the family is returning with new methodological and theoretical sophistication and richer insight to address issues and sources, some of which historical inquiry has traditionally embraced—the role of legislation and the state, the impact of culture and religion, the effects of *mentalité*, as well as questions of class and gender.

The development of the family as a subfield within history has been accompanied by growth in the historical analysis of women. While some historians have been studying women's roles in the public arena, however, those who view the modern family as a self-contained unit have been encapsulating women within the private sphere of life (Folbre in Moch et al., 1987; Tilly, 1987). As the feminist debate on public and private spheres has increased awareness on the part of those who study the family, emphasis on gender analysis and individual life course should realign these two streams of history (e.g., Alter, 1988; Davidoff & Hall, 1987; Folbre, 1994; Rose, 1992).

Historians, still engaged with household and family form and actively studying kinship, are enlarging their studies to include those traditionally outside or on the margins of the Western family—fictive kin, steprelations, adoptees, illegitimates, the abandoned, the abused, the divorced, lodgers, and servants. Some of these groups have been investigated but generally not in the context of the family. Others have been examined within a family setting but not from the perspective of the subjects themselves. Several historians (e.g., Alter, 1988; Laslett, 1977; Laslett, Oosterveen, & Smith, 1980) have addressed illegitimacy, and others have studied illegitimates among foundlings. But history and family life from the perspective of the illegitimate remains to be undertaken. Similarly, historical studies of divorce also tend to overlook the subsequent family life of divorcés. In the wake of modern social concerns, historians are also beginning to study those for whom the family is a Hades, not a haven (Gordon, 1988). The divide between the affectionless family and the affective one is not primarily or even particularly chronological.

Most historians of the family are wary of too great a dependence on qualitative sources, a dependence that has often narrowed, if not blighted, historical analysis. The future of historical analysis of the family will, however, continue to utilize qualitative and quantitative sources. Over time the methodologies and theories of that analysis may change, but the anchoring of historians in their own chronology will remain. The growth of family history has paralleled post-War public concern with population and industrialization, moved with it through Marxist developments, responded to the emphasis on women and minorities, and now is beginning to explore family values, looking at the dispossessed but also at the impact of culture and religion on the family. Historians of the family will examine these issues, however, from the perspective of a mature field.

ACKNOWLEDGMENTS. The author wishes to thank Richard Wall of the Cambridge Group for the History of Population and Social Structure for conversations that have informed this chapter. She is also grateful to George Alter and James Riley of Indiana University and James L. Cooper of DePauw University for helpful comments on an earlier version of the chapter.

References

Accampo, E. A. (1989). *Industrialization, family life, and class relations: Saint Chamond, 1815–1914.* Berkeley: University of California Press.
Achenbaum, W. A. (1978). *Old age in the new land: The American experience since 1790.* New York: Oxford University Press.
Alter, G. (1988). *Family and the female life course: The women of Verviers, Belgium, 1849–1880.* Madison: University of Wisconsin press.

Anderson, M. (1971). *Family structure in nineteenth-century Lancashire.* Cambridge: Cambridge University Press.

Anderson, M. (1980). *Approaches to the history of the Western family, 1500–1914.* London: Macmillan.

Ariès, P. (1962). *Centuries of childhood: A social history of family life.* New York: Knopf. First published as *L'enfant et la vie familiale sous l'Ancien Regime.* Paris: Librarie Plon, 1960.

Avery, G., & Briggs, J. (Eds.), (1989). *Children and their books: A celebration of the work of Iona and Peter Opie.* Oxford: Clarendon.

Bailyn, B. (1960). *Education in the forming of American society: Needs and opportunities for study.* Chapel Hill: University of North Carolina Press.

Banks, J. A. (1954). *Prosperity and parenthood: A study of family planning in the Victorian middle classes.* London: Routledge & Kegan Paul.

Bean, L. L., Mineau, G. P., & Anderton, D. L. (1990). *Fertility change on the American frontier: Adaptation and innovation.* Berkeley: University of California Press.

Becker, G. S. (1976). *The economic approach to human behavior.* Chicago: University of Chicago Press.

Becker, G. S. (1991). *A treatise on the family.* Cambridge, MA: Harvard University Press.

Bell, H. E., & Ollard, R. L. (Eds.). (1963). *Historical essays, 1600–1750, presented to David Ogg.* New York: Barnes and Noble.

Benigno, F. (1989). The Southern Italian family in the early modern period: A discussion of coresidential patterns. *Continuity and Change, 4,* 165–194.

Berkner, L. K. (1972). The stem family and the developmental cycle of a peasant household: An eighteenth-century Austrian example. *American Historical Review, 77,* 398–418.

Berkner, L. K. (1975). The use and misuse of census data for the historical analysis of family structure. *Journal of Interdisciplinary History, 5,* 721–738.

Berquó, E., & Xenos, P. (Eds.). (1992). *Family systems and cultural change.* New York: Clarendon.

Bonfield, L., Smith, R. M., & Wrightson, K. (Eds.). (1986). *The world we have gained: Histories of population and social structures.* Oxford: Basil Blackwell.

Boswell, J. (1988). *The kindness of strangers: The abandonment of children in western Europe from late antiquity to the Renaissance.* New York: Pantheon.

Bouchard, G. (1991). Mobile populations, stable communities: Social and demographic processes in the rural parishes of the Saguenay, 1840–1911. *Continuity and Change, 6,* 59–86.

Bouchard, G., & du Pourbaix, I. (1987). Individual and family life courses in the Saguenay region, Quebec, 1842–1911. *Journal of Family History, 12,* 225–242.

Boulton, J. (1987). *Neighbourhood and society: A London suburb in the seventeenth century.* Cambridge: Cambridge University Press.

Bourdelais, P. (1993). *Le nouvel âge de la vieillesse: Histoire du vieillissement de la population.* Paris: Éditions Odile Jacob.

Bourdieu, P. (1976). Marriage strategies as strategies of social reproduction. In R. Forster & O. Ranum (Eds.), *Family and society: Selections from the Annales: Économies, Sociétés, Civilisations* (pp. 117–144). Baltimore: Johns Hopkins University Press.

Braun, R. (1990). *Industrialisation and everyday life.* Cambridge: Cambridge University Press. First published as *Industrialisierung und Volksleben.* Göttingen: Vandenhoeck & Ruprecht, 1960.

Bremner, R. H. (Ed.). (1970–1974). *Children and youth in America: A documentary history* (3 vols.). Cambridge, MA: Harvard University Press.

Bulder, E. (1993). *The social economics of old age: Strategies to maintain income in later life in the Netherlands, 1880–1940.* Rotterdam, The Netherlands: Tinbergen Institute Research Series, Erasmus University.

Cashin, J. E. (1991). *A family venture: Men and women on the southern frontier.* New York: Oxford University Press.

Chayanov, A. V. (1986). *The theory of peasant economy.* Madison: University of Wisconsin Press. First published as *Organizatsiia krest' ianskogo khoziaistva,* 1927.

Christensen, H. (Ed.). (1964). *Handbook of marriage and the family.* Chicago: Rand McNally.

Chudacoff, H. P., & Hareven, T. K. (1978). Family transitions into old age. In T. K. Hareven (Ed.), *Transitions: The family and the life course in historical perspective* (pp. 217–243). New York: Academic Press.

Collomp, A. (1983). *La Maison du père: Famille et village en Haute-Provence aux XVIIe et XVIIIe siècles.* Paris: Presses Universitaires de France.

Cooper, S. M. (1992). Intergenerational social mobility in late seventeenth- and early eighteenth-century England. *Continuity and Change, 7,* 283–301.

Cressy, D. (1987). *Coming over: Migration and communication between England and New England in the seventeenth century.* Cambridge: Cambridge University Press.

Cuisenier, J., & Segalen, M. (Eds.). (1977). *The family life cycle in European societies.* The Hague: Mouton.

Darrow, M. H. (1989). *Revolution in the house: Family, class, and inheritance in southern France, 1775–1825.* Princeton, NJ: Princeton University Press.

Davidoff, L., & Hall, C. (1987). *Family fortunes: Men and women of the English middle class, 1780–1850.* Chicago: University of Chicago Press.

Davis, N. Z. (1971). The reasons of misrule: Youth groups and charivaris in 16th century France. *Past and Present, 50,* 41–45.

Degler, C. N. (1980). *At odds: Women and the family in America from the Revolution to the present.* New York: Oxford University Press.

Delille, G. (1985). *Famille et propriété dans le royaume de Naples (XVe–XIXe siècle).* Paris: École Française de Rome.

DeMause, L. (1974a). The evolution of childhood. In L. DeMause (Ed.), *The history of childhood* (pp. 1–73). New York: Psychohistory Press.

DeMause, L. (Ed.). (1974b). *The history of childhood.* New York: Psychohistory Press.

Demos, J. (1970). *A little commonwealth: Family life in Plymouth Colony.* New York: Oxford University Press.

Demos, J., & Boocock, S. S. (Eds.). (1978). *Turning points: Historical and sociological essays on the family.* Chicago: University of Chicago Press.

Douglas, W. A. (1991). The joint-family household in eighteenth-century southern Italian society. In D. I. Kertzer & R. P. Saller (Eds.), *The family in Italy from Antiquity to the present* (pp. 286–303). New Haven, CT: Yale University Press.

Duby, G. (1978). *Medieval marriage: Two models from twelfth-century France.* Baltimore: Johns Hopkins University Press.

Duby, G. (1994). *Love and marriage in the Middle Ages.* Chicago: University of Chicago Press.

Dyhouse, C. (1981). *Girls growing up in late Victorian and Edwardian England.* London: Routledge & Kegan Paul.

Elder, G. H., Jr. (1974). *Children of the Great Depression: Social change in life experience.* Chicago: University of Chicago Press.

Elder, G. H.,Jr., Modell, J., & Parke, R. D. (Eds.). (1993a). *Children in time and place: Development and historical insights.* Cambridge: Cambridge University Press.

Elder, G. H., Jr., Modell, J., & Parke, R. D. (1993b). Studying children in a changing world. In G. H. Elder, Jr., J. Modell, & R. D. Parke (Eds.), *Children in time and place: Development and historical insights* (pp. 3–21). Cambridge: Cambridge University Press.

Engels, F. (1884/1972). *The origin of the family, private property, and the state in light of the researchers of Lewis H. Morgan.* New York: International Publishers.

Erickson, C. (1972). *Invisible immigrants: The adaptation of English and Scottish immigrants in nineteenth-century America.* Coral Gables, FL: University of Miami Press.

Erikson, E. H. (1950/1963). *Childhood and society.* New York: Norton.

Eversley, D. E. C., Laslett, P., & Wrigley, E. A. (Eds.). (1966). *An introduction to English historical demography.* London: Weidenfield and Nicolson.

Fairchilds, C. (1978). Female sexual attitudes and the rise of illegitimacy: A case study. *Journal of Interdisciplinary History, 8,* 627–667.

Fauve-Chamoux, A. (1987). Le fonctionnement de la famille-souch dans les baronnies des Pyrenees avant 1914. *Annales de Démographie Historique,* 241–262.

Fischer, D. H. (1977). *Growing old in America.* New York: Oxford University Press.

Fitch, N. (1980). The household and the computer: A review. *Historical Methods, 13,* 127–137.

Flandrin, J.-L. (1979). *Families in former times: Kinship, household, and sexuality.* Cambridge: Cambridge University Press.

Fleury, M., & Henry, L. (1956). *Des Registres paroissieux l'histoire de la population: Manuel de dépouillement et d'exploitation de l'état civil ancien.* Paris: Institut National des Études Démographiques.

Fogel, R. W., & Elton, G. (1983). *Which road to the past? Two views of history.* New Haven, CT: Yale University Press.

Fogelman, K. (Ed.). (1983). *Growing up in Great Britain: Papers from the National Child Development Study.* London: Macmillan.

Folbre, N. (1994). *Who pays for the kids? Gender and the structures of constraint.* London: Routledge.

Forster, R., & Ranum, O. (Eds.). (1976). *Family and society: Selections from the Annales: Économies, Sociétés, Civilisations.* Baltimore: Johns Hopkins University Press.

Fortes, M. (1949). *The web of kinship among the Tallensi.* London: Oxford University Press.

Fuchs, R. G. (1984). *Abandoned children: Foundlings and child welfare in nineteenth-century France.* Albany: State University of New York Press.

Gaunt, D. (1983). The property and kin relationships of retired farmers in northern and central Europe. In R. Wall, J. Robin, & P. Laslett (Eds.), *Family forms in historic Europe* (pp. 249–279). Cambridge: Cambridge University Press.

Gautier, E., & Henry, L. (1958). *La population de Crulai, paroisse normande. Étude historique.* Paris: Institut National des Études Démographiques.

Gillis, J. R. (1974). *Youth and history: Tradition and change in European age relations, 1770–present.* New York: Academic Press.

Gillis, J. R. (1985). *For better, for worse: British marriages, 1600 to the present.* New York: Oxford University Press.

Glass, D. V., & Eversley, D. E. C. (Eds.). (1965). *Population in history: Essays in historical demography.* London: E. Arnold.

González, A. B. (1990). *Casa, herenica y familia en la Cataluña rural (Logica de la razon doméstica).* Madrid: Alianza Editorial.

Goode, W. J. (1963/1970). *World revolution and family patterns.* New York: Free Press of Glencoe.

Goody, J. (Ed.). (1971). *The development cycle in domestic groups.* Cambridge: Cambridge University Press. First published as *Cambridge papers in social anthropology,* No. 1, 1958. Cambridge, England: Published for the Department of Archaeology and Anthropology at the University Press.

Goody, J. (1976a). Inheritance property and women: Some comparative considerations. In J. Goody, J. Thirsk, & E. P. Thompson (Eds.), *Family and inheritance: Rural society in western Europe 1200–1800* (pp. 10–36). Cambridge: Cambridge University Press.

Goody, J. (1976b). *Production and reproduction: A comparative study of the domestic domain.* Cambridge: Cambridge University Press.

Goody, J. (1983). *The development of the family and marriage in Europe.* Cambridge: Cambridge University Press.

Goody, J., Thirsk, J., & Thompson, E. P. (Eds.). (1976). *Family and inheritance: Rural society in western Europe, 1200–1800.* Cambridge: Cambridge University Press.

Gordon, L. (1988). *Heroes of their own lives: The politics and history of family violence, Boston 1880–1960.* New York: Viking.

Goubert, P. (1952). En Beauvaisis: Problèmes démographiques du XVIIe siècle. *Annales: Économies, Sociétés, Civilisations, 7,* 453–468.

Gratton, B. (1986a). A new history of the aged: A critique. In D. Van Tassel & P. N. Stearns (Eds.), *Old age in a bureaucratic society: The elderly, the experts, and the state in American history* (pp. 3–29). New York: Greenwood Press.

Gratton, B. (1986b). *Urban elders: Family, work, and welfare among Boston's aged, 1890–1950.* Philadelphia: Temple University Press.

Greven, P. J. (1970). *Four generations: Population, land, and family in colonial Andover, Massachusetts.* Ithaca, NY: Cornell University Press.

Greven, P. J. (1977). *The Protestant temperament: Patterns of child-rearing, religious experience, and the self in early America.* New York: Knopf.

Gullickson, G. L. (1986). *Spinners and weavers of Auffay: Rural industry and the sexual division of labor in a French village, 1750–1850.* Cambridge: Cambridge University Press.

Gutman, H. G. (1976). *The black family in slavery and freedom.* New York: Pantheon.

Gutmann, M. P., & Leboutte, R. (1984). Rethinking protoindustrialization and the family. *Journal of Family History, 14,* 587–607.

Haber, C. (1983). *Beyond sixty-five: The dilemma of old age in America's past.* Cambridge: Cambridge University Press.

Haber, C., & Gratton, B. (1994). *Old age and the search for security: An American social history.* Bloomington: Indiana University Press.

Hajnal, J. (1965). European marriage patterns in perspective. In D. V. Glass & D. E. C. Eversley (Eds.), *Population in history: Essays in historical demography* (pp. 101–143). London: E. Arnold.

Hajnal, J. (1983). Two kinds of pre-industrial household formation system. In R. Wall, J. Robin, & P. Laslett (Eds.), *Family forms in historic Europe* (pp. 65–104). Cambridge: Cambridge University Press.

Hall, G. S. (1904/1969). *Adolescence.* New York: Arno Press.

Hammerton, A. J. (1992). *Cruelty and companionship: Conflict in nineteenth-century married life.* London: Routledge.

Hanawalt, B. A. (1986). *The ties that bound: Peasant families in medieval England.* New York: Oxford University Press.

Hanawalt, B. A. (1992). Historical descriptions and prescriptions for adolescence. *Journal of Family History, 17,* 341–351.

Hanawalt, B. A. (1993). *Growing up in medieval London.* New York: Oxford University Press.

Hareven, T. K. (1977). The family cycle in historical perspective: A proposal for a developmental approach. In J. Cuisenier & M. Segalen (Eds.), *The family life cycle in European societies* (339–352). The Hague: Mouton.

Hareven, T. K. (Ed.). (1978). *Transitions: The family and the life course in historical perspective.* New York: Academic Press.

Hareven, T. K. (1982). *Family time and industrial time: The relationship between the family and work in a New England industrial community.* Cambridge: Cambridge University Press.

Hareven, T. K. (1991). The history of the family and the complexity of social change. *American Historical Review, 96,* 95–124.

Hazelzet, K. (c.1994). *De levenstrap.* Zwolle: Uitgeverij Catena.

Henderson, J., & Wall, R. (1994a). Introduction. In J. Henderson & R. Wall (Eds.), *Poor women and children in the European past* (pp. 1–28). London: Routledge.

Henderson, J., & Wall, R. (Eds.). (1994b). *Poor women and children in the European past*. London: Routledge.

Hendrick, H. (1990). *Images of youth: Age, class and the male youth problem, 1880–1920*. Oxford: Clarendon.

Henry, L. (1953). Une richesse démographique en fiche. Les registres paroissiaux. *Population, 8*, 281–290.

Henry, L. (1956). *Anciennes familles genevoises: Étude démographique: XVIe–XXe siècle*. Paris: Institut National des Études Démographiques.

Herlihy, D. (1985). *Medieval households*. Cambridge, MA: Harvard University Press.

Herlihy, D. (1987). The family and religious ideologies in medieval Europe. *Journal of Family History, 12*, 3–17.

Herlihy, D., & Klapisch-Zuber, C. (1985). *Tuscans and their families: A study of the Florentine catasto of 1427*. New Haven, CT: Yale University Press.

Hernandez, D. J. (1993). *America's children: Resources from family, government, and the economy*. New York: Russell Sage Foundation.

Heywood, C. (1988). *Childhood in nineteenth-century France: Work, health, and education among the classes populaires*. Cambridge: Cambridge University Press.

Hill, B. (1989). *Women, work, and sexual politics in eighteenth-century England*. Oxford: Basil Blackwell.

Hill, R., & Rodgers, R. H. (1964). The developmental approach. In H. Christensen (Ed.), *Handbook of marriage and the family* (pp. 171–211). Chicago: Rand McNally.

Hollingsworth, T. H. (1969). *Historical demography*. London: The Sources of History Limited.

Houlbrooke, R. A. (1984). *The English family, 1450–1750*. London: Longman.

Hunecke, V. (1987). *Die Findelkinder von Mailand: Kindaussetzung und aussetzende Eltern vom 17, bis zum 19. Jahrhundert*. Stuttgart, Germany: Klett-Cotta.

Hunt, D. (1970). *Parents and children in history: The psychology of family life in early modern France*. New York: Basic Books.

Janssens, A. (1993). *Family and social change: The household as a process in an industrializing community*. Cambridge: Cambridge University Press.

Kaser, K. (1994). The Balkan joint family: Redefining a problem. *Social Science History, 18*, 243–269.

Katz, M. B. (1975). *The people of Hamilton, Canada West: Family and class in a mid-nineteenth-century city*. Cambridge, MA: Harvard University Press.

Katz, M. B., & Davey, I. E. (1978). Youth and early industrialization in a Canadian city. In J. Demos & S. S. Boocock (Eds.), *Turning points: Historical and sociological essays on the family* (pp. S81–S119). Chicago: University of Chicago Press.

Kertzer, D. I. (1984). *Family life in central Italy, 1880–1910: Sharecropping, wage labor, and coresidence*. New Brunswick, NJ: Rutgers University Press.

Kertzer, D. I. (1993). *Sacrificed for honor: Italian infant abandonment and the politics of reproductive control*. Boston: Beacon.

Kertzer, D. I., & Hogan, D. P. (1991). Reflections on the European marriage pattern: Sharecropping and proletarianization in Casalecchio, Italy, 1861–1921. *Journal of Family History, 16*, 31–45.

Kertzer, D. I., & Saller, R. P. (Eds.). (1991). *The family in Italy from Antiquity to the present*. New Haven, CT: Yale University Press.

Kett, J. F. (1977). *Rites of passage: Adolescence in America, 1790 to the present*. New York: Basic Books.

Kussmaul, A. (1981). *Servants in husbandry in early modern England*. Cambridge: Cambridge University Press.

Lacombe, P. (1889). *La famille dans la société romaine: Étude de moralité comparée*. Paris: Lecrosnier et Babe.

Ladurie, E. L. (1979). *Montaillou: The promised land of error*. New York: Vintage.

Lasch, C. (1977). *Haven in a heartless world: The family besieged*. New York: Basic Books.

Laslett, P. (1965). *The world we have lost*. New York: Charles Scribner's Sons.

Laslett, P. (1972). Introduction. In P. Laslett & R. Wall (Eds.), *Household and family in past time: Comparative studies in the size and structure of the domestic group over the past three centuries in England, France, Serbia, Japan and colonial North America, with further materials from Western Europe* (pp. 1–89). Cambridge: Cambridge University Press.

Laslett, P. (1977). *Family life and illicit love in earlier generations*. Cambridge: Cambridge University Press.

Laslett, P. (1983). Family and household as workgroup and kin group: Areas of traditional Europe compared. In R. Wall, J. Robin, & P. Laslett (Eds.), *Family forms in historic Europe* (pp. 513–563). Cambridge: Cambridge University Press.

Laslett, P. (1984). The significance of the past in the study of ageing: Introduction to the special issue on history and ageing. *Ageing and Society, 4*, 429–499.

Laslett, P. (1988). Family, kinship and the collectivity. *Continuity and Change, 3*, 153–175.

Laslett, P. (1991). *A fresh map of life: The emergence of the Third Age*. Cambridge, MA: Harvard University Press.

Laslett, P., & Harrison, J. (1963). Clayworth and Cogenhoe. In H. E. Bell and R. L. Ollard (Eds.), *Historical essays, 1600–1750, presented to David Ogg* (pp. 157–184). New York: Barnes and Noble.

Laslett, P., Oosterveen, K., & Smith, R. M. (1980). *Bastardy and its comparative history*. Cambridge, MA: Harvard University Press.

Laslett, P., & Wall, R. (Eds.). (1972). *Household and family in past time: Comparative studies in the size and structure of the domestic group over the last three centuries in England, France, Serbia, Japan and colonial North America, with further materials from Western Europe*. Cambridge: Cambridge University Press.

LePlay, F. (1877–1879). *Les ouvriers européens: Études sur les travaux, la vie domestique et la condition morale des populations ouvrières de L'Europe, précédées d'un exposé de la methode d'observation* (2nd ed), Tours: Alfred Moore. (Original edition published 1855–1878).

Lévi-Strauss, C. (1967). *Les structure élémentaires de la parente* (2nd ed). Paris: Mouton & Co. Published in English as *The Elementary Structure of Kinship*. Boston: Beacon Press, 1969.

Lévi-Strauss, C. (1963). *Structural anthropology*. Garden City, NY: Doubleday.

Levine, D. (1977). *Family formation in an age of nascent capitalism*. New York: Academic Press.

Levine, D. (1984a). Production, reproduction, and the proletarian family in England, 1500–1851. In D. Levine (Ed.), *Proletarianization and family history* (pp. 87–127). Orlando, FL: Academic Press.

Levine, D. (Ed.). (1984b). *Proletarianization and family history*. Orlando, FL: Academic Press.

Lockridge, K. A. (1970). *A New England town: The first hundred years, Dedham, Massachusetts, 1639–1736*. New York: W. W. Norton.

Lynch, K. A. (1988). *Family, class, and ideology in early industrial France: Social policy and the working-class family, 1825–1848*. Madison: University of Wisconsin Press.

Lynch, K. A. (1991). European marriage pattern in the cities: Variations on a theme by Hajnal. *Journal of Family History, 16*, 79–86.

Lynch, K. A. (1994). The family and the history of public life. *Journal of Interdisciplinary History, 24*, 665–684.

MacDonald, M. (1981). *Mystical Bedlam: Madness, anxiety, and healing in seventeenth-century England*. Cambridge: Cambridge University Press.

Macfarlane, A. (1970). *The family life of Ralph Josselin, a seventeenth-*

century clergyman: An essay in historical anthropology. Cambridge: Cambridge University Press.

Macfarlane, A. (1979). *The origins of English individualism: The family, property and social transition.* Oxford: Basil Blackwell.

Macfarlane, A. (1986). *Marriage and love in England: Modes of reproduction, 1300–1840.* Oxford: Basil Blackwell.

Malone, A. P. (1992). *Sweet chariot: Slave family and household structure in nineteenth-century Louisiana.* Chapel Hill: University of North Carolina Press.

Malthus, T. R. (1986). An essay on the principle of population. In E. A. Wrigley & D. Souden (Eds.), *The works of Thomas Robert Malthus*, Vol. 1, London: W. Pickering. (Originally published in 1798)

Marshall, S. (1987). *The Dutch gentry, 1500–1650: Family, faith, and fortune.* New York: Greenwood.

Mendels, F. (1972). Proto-industrialization: The first phase of the industrialization process. *Journal of Economic History, 32,* 241–261.

Menefee, S. P. (1981). *Wives for sale: An ethnographic study of British popular divorce.* New York: St. Martin's.

Meuvret, J. (1946). Les crises de subsistances de la démographie de la France de l'Ancien Régime. *Population, 1,* 643–650. Reprinted under the title Demographic crisis in France from the sixteenth to the eighteenth century in D. V. Glass and D. E. C. Eversley (Eds.), *Population in history: Essays in historical demography* (pp. 507–522). London: E. Arnold, 1965.

Mitterauer, M. (1993). *A history of youth.* Oxford: Basil Blackwell.

Mitterauer, M., & Sieder, R. (1982). *The European family: Patriarchy to partnership from the Middle Ages to the present.* Chicago: University of Chicago Press.

Moch, L. P., Folbre, N., Smith, D. S., Cornell, L. T., & Tilly, L. A. (1987). Family strategy: A dialogue. *Historical Methods, 20,* 113–125.

Modell, J. (1989). *Into one's own: From youth to adulthood in the United States, 1920–1975.* Berkeley: University of California Press.

Morgan, E. (1944/1966). *The Puritan family: Religion and domestic relations in seventeenth-century New England.* New York: Harper & Row.

Moring, B. (1994). *Skärgårdshor: Hushåll, familj och demografi i finländsk kustbygd på 1600-, 1700- och 1800-talen.* Helsingfors (Helsinki): Ekenäs Trykeri Ab.

Namier, L. B. (1929/1957). *The structure of politics at the accession of George III.* London: Macmillan.

Namier, L. B. (1930/1963). *England in the age of the American Revolution.* London: Macmillan.

Narrett, D. E. (1992). *Inheritance and family life in colonial New York City.* Ithaca, NY: Cornell University Press.

Netting, R. McC., Wilk, R. R., & Arnould, E. J. (Eds.). (1984). *Households: Comparative and historical studies of the domestic group.* Berkeley: University of California Press.

O'Hara, D. (1991). 'Ruled by my friends': Aspects of marriage in the diocese of Canterbury, c. 1540–1570. *Continuity and Change, 6,* 9–41.

Ozment, S. (1983). *When fathers ruled: Family life in Reformation Europe.* Cambridge, MA: Harvard University Press.

Pahl, J. (1989). *Money & marriage.* London: Macmillan.

Parsons, T. (1951). *The social system.* Glencoe, IL: Free Press.

Parsons, T., & Bales, R. F. (1955). *Family socialization and interaction process.* Glencoe, IL: Free Press.

Paterson, L. (1993). *The world of the troubadours: Medieval Occitan society, c1100–c1300.* Cambridge: Cambridge University Press.

Pelling, M. (1988). Child health as a social value in early-modern England. *Social History of Medicine, 1,* 135–164.

Pelling, M., & Smith, R. M. (Eds.). (1991). *Life, death, and the elderly: Historical perspectives.* London: Routledge.

Phillips, R. (1991). *Untying the knot: A short history of divorce.* Cambridge: Cambridge University Press.

Pinchbeck, I., & Hewitt, M. (1969–1973). *Children in English society* (2 Vols.). London: Routledge & Kegan Paul.

Plakans, A. (1984). *Kinship in the past: An anthropology of European family life, 1500–1800.* Oxford: Basil Blackwell.

Plumb, J. H. (1975). The new world of children in the 18th century. *Past and Present, 67,* 64–95.

Pollock, L. A. (1983). *Forgotten children: Parent-child relations from 1500–1900.* Cambridge: Cambridge University Press.

Pollock, L. A. (Ed.). (1987). *A lasting relationship: Parents and children over three centuries.* Hanover, NH: University Press of New England.

Quaife, G. R. (1979). *Wanton wenches and wayward wives.* London: Croom Helm.

Quadagno, J. S. (1982). *Aging in early industrial society: Work, family, and social policy in nineteenth-century England.* New York: Academic Press.

Ransell, D. (1978). *Mothers of misery: Child abandonment in Russia.* Princeton, NJ: Princeton University Press.

Ransom, R. L., and Sutch, R. (1986). The labor of older Americans: Retirement of men on and off the job, 1870–1937. *Journal of Economic History, 46,* 1–30.

Robin, J. (1980). *Elmdon: Continuity and change in a north-west Essex village, 1861–1964.* Cambridge: Cambridge University Press.

Robin, J. (1984). Family care of the elderly in a nineteenth-century Devonshire parish. *Ageing and Society, 4,* 505–516.

Rodgers, R. H. (1977). The family cycle concept: Past, present, and future. In J. Cuisenier & M. Segalen (Eds.), *The family life cycle in European studies* (pp. 39–57). The Hague: Mouton.

Rose, S. O. (1992). *Limited livelihoods: Gender and class in nineteenth-century England.* Berkeley: University of California Press.

Rowntree, B. S. (1901/1980). *Poverty: A study of town life.* New York: Garland.

Ruggles, S. (1987). *Prolonged connections: The rise of the extended family in nineteenth-century England and America.* Madison: University of Wisconsin Press.

Ruggles, S. (1994). The transformation of American family structure. *American Historical Review, 99,* 103–128.

Sabean, D. W. (1990). *Property, production, and family in Neckarhausen, 1700–1870.* Cambridge: Cambridge University Press.

Safley, T. M. (1984). *Let no man put asunder: The control of marriage in the German southwest, a comparative study, 1550–1600.* Kirksville, MO: Sixteenth Century Journal Publishers.

Scanzoni, J. (1982). *Sexual bargaining: Power politics in the American marriage.* Chicago: University of Chicago Press.

Schofield, R. (1985). English marriage patterns revisited. *Journal of Family History, 10,* 2–33.

Seaver, P. S. (1985). *Wallington's world: A Puritan artisan in seventeenth-century London.* Stanford, CA: Stanford University Pres.

Seccombe, W. (1990). The Western European marriage pattern in historical perspective: A response to David Levine. *Journal of Historical Sociology, 3,* 50–74.

Segalen, M. (1983). *Love and power in the peasant family: Rural France in the nineteenth century.* Oxford: Basil Blackwell.

Segalen, M. (1991). *Fifteen generations of Bretons: Kinship and society in lower Brittany 1720–1980.* Cambridge: Cambridge University Press.

Shaffer, J. W. (1982). *Family and fare: Agrarian change and household organization in the Loire Valley, 1500–1900.* Albany: State University of New York Press.

Sherwood, J. (1988). *Poverty in eighteenth-century Spain: The women and children of the Inclusa.* Toronto: University of Toronto Press.

Shorter, E. (1975). *The making of the modern family.* New York: Basic Books.

Simmons, L. W. (1945/1970). *The role of the aged in primitive society.* Hamden, CT: Archon Books.

Skolnick, A. (1991). *Embattled paradise: The American family in an age of uncertainty.* New York: Basic Books.

Slater, M. (1984). *Family life in the seventeenth century: The Verneys of Claydon House.* London: Routledge & Kegan Paul.

Smelser, N. J. (1959). *Social change in the industrial revolution: An application of theory to the British cotton industry.* Chicago: University of Chicago Press.

Smith, D. (1991). *The rise of historical sociology.* Cambridge, England: Polity Press.

Smith, D. S. (1993). American family and demographic patterns and the northwest European model. *Continuity and Change, 8,* 389–415.

Smith, J. E. (1984). Widowhood and ageing in traditional society. *Ageing and Society, 4,* 429–449.

Smith, R. M. (1979). Kin and neighbors in a thirteenth-century Suffolk community. *Journal of Family History, 4,* 219–256.

Smith, R. M. (Ed.). (1984a). *Land, kinship and life-cycle.* Cambridge: Cambridge University Press.

Smith, R. M. (1984b). Some issues concerning families and their property in rural England 1250–1800. In R. M. Smith (Ed.), *Land, kinship and life-cycle* (pp. 1–86). Cambridge: Cambridge University Press.

Smith, R. M. (1984c). The structured dependence of the elderly as a recent development: Some skeptical historical thoughts. *Ageing and Society, 4,* 409–428.

Smith, R. M. (1991). The manorial court and the elderly tenant in late medieval England. In M. Pelling & R. M. Smith (Eds.), *Life, death and the elderly: Historical perspectives* (pp. 39–61). London: Routledge.

Stearns, P. N. (1976). *Old age in European society: The case of France.* New York: Holmes & Meier.

Stoianovich, T. (1976). *French historical method: The Annales paradigm.* Ithaca, NY: Cornell University Press.

Stone, L. (1977). *The family, sex and marriage in England, 1500–1800.* New York: Harper & Row. Abridged edition (1979), Harmondsworth, England: Penguin.

Stone, L. (1990). *Road to divorce: England, 1530–1987.* Oxford: Oxford University Press.

Stone, L. (1992). *Uncertain unions: Marriage in England, 1660–1753.* Oxford: Oxford University Press.

Stone, L. (1993). *Broken lives: Separation and divorce in England, 1660–1857.* Oxford: Oxford University Press.

Thernstrom, S. (1964). *Poverty and progress: Social mobility in a nineteenth-century city.* Cambridge, MA: Harvard University press.

Thomas, K. (1976). Age and authority in early modern England. *Proceedings of the British Academy, 62,* 205–248.

Thomas, K. (1989). Children in early modern England. In G. Avery & J. Briggs (Eds.), *Children and their books: A celebration of the work of Iona and Peter Opie* (pp. 45–77). Oxford: Clarendon.

Thomson, D. (1991). The welfare of the elderly in the past: A family or community responsibility? In M. Pelling & R. M. Smith (Eds.), *Life, death, and the elderly: Historical perspectives* (pp. 194–221). London: Routledge.

Tilly, L. A. (1979). Individual lives and family strategies in the French proletariat. *Journal of Family History, 4,* 137–152.

Tilly, L. A. (1987). Women's history and family history: Fruitful collaboration or missed connection? *Journal of Family History, 12,* 303–315.

Tilly, L. A., & Scott, J. W. (1978/1989). *Women, work, and family.* New York: Routledge.

Tilly, L. A., Scott, J. W., & Cohen, M. (1976). Women's work and European fertility patterns. *Journal of Interdisciplinary History, 6,* 447–476.

Tönnies, F. (1957). *Community and society.* East Lansing: The Michigan State University Press. First published in Germany as *Gemeinschaft und Gesellschaft,* 1887.

Traer, J. F. (1980). *Marriage and the family in eighteenth-century France.* Ithaca, NY: Cornell University Press.

Troyansky, D. (1989). *Old age in the Old Regime: Image and experience in eighteenth century France.* Ithaca, NY: Cornell University Press.

Trumbach, R. (1978). *The rise of the egalitarian family: Aristocratic kinship and domestic relations in eighteenth-century England.* New York: Academic Press.

Van Tassel, D., & Stearns, P. N. (Eds.). (1986). *Old age in a bureaucratic society: The elderly, the experts, and the state in American history.* New York: Greenwood Press.

Viazzo, P. P. (1994). Anthropology, family history and the concept of 'strategy.' In J. Henderson and R. Wall (Eds.), *Poor women and children in the European past* (pp. 31–50). London: Routledge.

Viazzo, P. P. (in press). Family structures and the early phase in the individual life cycle. In R. Wall and O. Saito (Eds.), *Economic and social aspects of the family life cycle.* Cambridge: Cambridge University Press.

Wachter, K. W., Hammel, E. A., & Laslett, P. (1978). *Statistical studies of historical social structure.* New York: Academic Press.

Wall, R. (1978). The age at leaving home. *Journal of Family History, 3,* 181–202.

Wall, R. (1986). Work, welfare and the family: An illustration of the adaptive family economy. In L. Bonfield, R. M. Smith, & K. Wrightson (Eds.), *The world we have gained: Histories of population and social structure* (pp. 261–294). Oxford: Basil Blackwell.

Wall, R., Robin, J., & Laslett, P. (Eds.). (1983). *Family forms in historic Europe.* Cambridge: Cambridge University Press.

Wall, R., & Saito, O. (Eds.). (in press). *Economic and social aspects of the family life cycle.* Cambridge: Cambridge University Press.

Walvin, J. (1982). *A child's world: A social history of English childhood, 1800–1914.* Harmondsworth, England: Penguin.

Walzer, J. F. (1974). A period of ambivalence: Eighteenth-century American childhood. In L. DeMause (Ed.), *The History of childhood* (pp. 351–382). New York: Psychohistory Press.

Watkins, S. C. (1984). Spinsters. *Journal of Family History, 9,* 310–325.

Weir, D. R. (1984). Rather never than late: Celibacy and age at marriage in English cohort fertility, 1541–1871. *Journal of Family History, 9,* 340–354.

Wells, R. V. (1992). The population of England's colonies in America: Old English or new Americans? *Population Studies, 46,* 85–102.

West, E. (1989). *Growing up with the country: Childhood on the far-western frontier.* Albuquerque: University of New Mexico Press.

West, E., & Petrik, P. (Eds.). (1992). *Small worlds: Children and adolescents in America, 1850–1950.* Lawrence: University Press of Kansas.

Wheaton, R. (1980). Introduction: Recent trends in the historical study of the French family. In R. Wheaton & T. Hareven (Eds.), *Family and sexuality in French history* (pp. 3–26). Philadelphia: University of Pennsylvania Press.

Wheaton, R. (1987). Observations on the development of kinship history. *Journal of Family History, 12,* 285–301.

Wheaton, R., & Hareven, T. (Eds.). (1980). *Family and sexuality in French history.* Philadelphia: University of Pennsylvania Press.

Willigan, J. D., & Lynch, K. A. (1982). *Sources and methods of historical demography.* New York: Academic Press.

Willmott, P., & Young, M. (1960). *Family and class in a London suburb.* London: Routledge & Kegan Paul.

Wishy, B. W. (1968). *The child and the Republic: The dawn of modern American child nurture* (Vols. 1–3). Philadelphia: University of Pennsylvania Press.

Wrightson, K., & Levine, D. (1979). *Poverty and piety in an English village: Terling, 1525–1700*. New York: Academic Press.

Wrigley, E. A. (1966a). Family limitation in pre-industrial England. *Economic History Review, 19*, 82–109.

Wrigley, E. A. (1966b). Family reconstitution. In D. E. C. Eversley, P. Laslett, & E. A. Wrigley (Eds.), *An introduction to English historical demography* (pp. 96–159). London: Weidenfeld and Nicolson.

Wrigley, E. A., & Schofield, R. S. (1981). *The population history of England, 1541–1871: A reconstruction*. Cambridge: Cambridge University Press.

Wrigley, E. A., & Souden, D. (Eds.). (1986). *The works of Thomas Robert Malthus* (Vol. 1). London: W. Pickering.

Young, M. L. (1992). Analysing household histories. In E. Berquó & P. Xenos (Eds.), *Family systems and cultural change* (pp. 176–200). New York: Clarendon.

Young, M., & Willmott, P. (1957). *Family and kinship in East London*. London: Routledge & Kegan Paul.

Zelizer, V. A. (1985). *Pricing the priceless child: The changing social value of children*. New York: Basic Books.

CHAPTER 2

Demography and Families

Jay D. Teachman, Karen A. Polonko, and John Scanzoni

Introduction

In recent years, the demography of families has drawn increasing attention from a number of disciplines, including sociology, history, anthropology, economics, psychology, and family studies. This chapter aims, first, to summarize the major empirical themes of family demography. Second, it aims to place these themes within a conceptual and explanatory framework.

The demography of families has some of its historical roots in the broader field of general demography, as seen in Bogue's (1969) description:

> Demography is the statistical and mathematical study of the size, composition, and spatial distribution of human population (structure), and of changes over time in these aspects through the operation of the five processes of fertility, mortality, marriage, migration, and social mobility. Although it maintains a continuous descriptive and comparative analysis of trends in each of these processes and in their net result, its long-run goal is to develop a body of theory to explain the events that it charts and compares. (pp. 1–2)

In effect, general demography may seek to describe first, the size of an entire population (e.g., the United States or Canada); second, the distribution of aggregates of persons within the total population (e.g., women, racial and ethnic categories); and third, changes over time (called "trends") in the characteristics of those aggregates (e.g., shifting proportions of women in the labor force). In the past, those foci have meant that demography has been identified as a *macro*-level

specialty. Its concerns have been with broad, large-scale phenomena (e.g., trends in birth rates or divorce rates) as opposed to *micro*-level phenomena (e.g., decision making between partners regarding sexual intercourse and contraception).

As Bogue suggests, demography has sought "to develop a body of theory to explain the [macro-level] events that it charts and compares." Until recently, those explanations existed almost exclusively at the *structural* level. To say that one is concerned entirely with structural issues is to say that one focuses solely on the macro level. Chafetz (1984), for instance, contends that structural variables can be explained by other structural variables, quite apart from resorting to micro-level variables. As an example, Smith and Cutright (1988) recently accounted for the variable, "trends in increases over time in female-headed families," by variables such as "increase in divorces" and "increases in illegitimacy."

More recently, however, demographers interested in families have begun to view preoccupation with macro-type analyses as excessively parochial. In part, this view stems from the dynamic character of the empirical phenomena under consideration. Aldous (1991) captures the mood by suggesting that "we are now dealing with the sociology of *families* rather than family sociology" (p. 660, italics added). Because empirical "facts" are sharply divergent today from what they were during the 1960s, it tends to be misleading to speak of "the family" in its singular form. Instead it becomes more valid to talk about "families" in their plural form. Bumpass (1990) raised similar kinds of issues in a presidential address delivered to the Population Association of America.

Alongside shifting empirical realities, major theoretical currents spreading throughout the social sciences represent a second reason why some demographers are forsaking explanations focused exclusively on the structural, or macro, level. Alexander (1988) organizes those currents under the head of

Jay D. Teachman • Department of Sociology, Western Washington University, Bellingham, Washington 98225-9081. **Karen A. Polonko** • Department of Sociology, Old Dominion University, Norfolk, Virginia 25329. **John Scanzoni** • Department of Sociology, University of Florida, Gainesville, Florida 23611.

Handbook of Marriage and the Family, 2nd edition, edited by Marvin Sussman, Suzanne K. Steinmetz, and Gary W. Peterson. Plenum Press, New York, 1999.

the "new theoretical movement" (e.g., see also Giddens, 1976; Turner, 1988). Although this "movement" has facets too numerous to be detailed here, perhaps its core element is the growing realization by social scientists across a range of disciplines that "action and structure must now be intertwined" (Alexander, 1988, p. 77). Given that explanations focused exclusively at the micro level are no more valid than uniquely macro analyses, the goal is to synthesize the two levels as part of what Alexander calls *new action theory*. Certain elements of "new" action theory are at least as "old" as Simmel, a German sociologist writing during the early twentieth century (Levine, Carter, & Gorman, 1976). Simmel heavily influenced the Chicago School of sociology that predated the rise of demographers' attempts to account for macro phenomena apart from micro-level action.

The intertwining of structure and action begins with the premise that persons act, behave, and make choices either to continue the status quo or to change it. Importantly, persons' choices are either constrained or enhanced by the structural conditions and the cultural milieu in which they live. Often, both constraint and enhancement occur simultaneously. The historical demographer Modell (1989), for instance, shows that although the Great Depression (an obvious macro event) prevented engaged couples from marrying, it nevertheless facilitated their choices to have sexual intercourse. Time has always been a central variable for demographers, and Modell demonstrates that over time the choices of American youth have brought about certain changes in both structural conditions and the cultural milieu. The dynamics of this model lie at the heart of new action theory and are central to our understanding of contemporary families: Micro-level behaviors are indeed significantly influenced by macro conditions. However, over time, micro patterns bring about changes in subsequent structural and cultural environments: Persons/groups are "making choices within a structure of constraints that then modify that structure" (Mullins, 1987; cited in Smith, 1989, p. 335). In turn, that modified structure influences micro behaviors, and so forth.

Life-Course Analyses

This shift away from exclusively structural analyses in favor of more complex conceptual models can be seen by the growing preference among demographers for the construct *life course* and the corresponding decline of interest in the construct "family life cycle."

As early as Rowntree's (1906) analysis of poverty over the life cycle, the family life cycle has been associated with family demography (Sweet, 1977). The family life cycle has generally been constructed as a varying number of predetermined stages—based on marriage, childbearing, child rear-

ing, and dissolution through the death of a spouse—that characterize the development of family units (Aldous, 1978; Baltes & Brim, 1980; Davids, 1980; Duvall, 1963; Glick, 1947, 1955, 1957).

This framework has provided a scheme into which families can be sorted and has also been used as an independent variable predicting some other element of the social world (Sandefur & Scott, 1981; Stolzenberg, Blair-Loy, & Waite, 1995; Waite, 1980; White, 1982). When combined with the concept of birth cohort or marriage cohort (Ryder, 1965), the family life cycle has also served as a convenient mechanism for studying changes in family structure and process (see especially Spanier & Glick, 1980a; Uhlenberg, 1974, 1978). More recent research in this area has expanded to include information on the interrelationships between the family life cycle and a variety of related life cycle processes, such as schooling and employment (Elder, 1974, 1977, 1978, 1981; Furstenberg, 1979; Hogan, 1978b, 1980) or other outcomes (Anderson, Russell, & Schumm, 1983; Peterson, 1990).

The life-cycle notion rested on a combination of biological elements and cultural norms that were said to determine the sequencing of persons' behaviors into particular "stages" over time. Simultaneously, those norms were structurally reinforced by kin, friends, and community. Virtually no attention was paid to the idea of persons' choices nor to the possibilities of variation from the externally imposed cultural script. Furthermore, persons violating traditional norms stating, for example, that the "proper" sequence is marriage *prior* to children (not afterwards) were labeled as "deviant" (White, 1991, pp. 189ff). This tendency to label nonconformity as deviance rather than choice (i.e., *action*) indicates the long-standing influence of structural-functionalism on the life-cycle literature (Kingsbury & Scanzoni, 1993).

Beginning with Elder (1974, 1977, 1981), analysts began to concentrate on the development of persons (adults as well as children and youth) throughout their entire life course. The conceptual focus became the choices persons make, along with their consequences, within an ever-shifting structural and cultural context (Buchmann, 1989; Swidler, 1980). In response to criticisms (e.g., Aldous, 1978, p. 331) that a life-course approach is "individualistic" and thus ignores families as social, that is, *group*, realities, analysts have focused on the ongoing construction of families qua groups over time (e.g., Scanzoni, Polonko, Teachman, & Thompson, 1989).

From one perspective, construction of family emerges because two partners are participating in what Gravenhorst (1988) calls an "erotic friendship," thus merging their life courses for an indefinite period of time. Their attempts at creating what Gubrium and Holstein (1990) call "being in family" is marked by numerous elements, including (if they are heterosexuals) gender-based struggle (Scanzoni & Marsiglio, 1993). From a second perspective, construction of family may emerge (or dissipate) among persons linked by blood and economic interdependence (Wilson & Pahl, 1988). Similarly, persons linked by economic interdependence and often friendship may also construct family, as has been the case among African Americans for generations (Stack, 1974). Throughout this second perspective (as well as the first), persons' own life-course development is influenced by, as well as influences, the life-course development of other persons with whom they are "in family."

Regardless of which of the two perspectives is in view, the construct of life course *transition* is pivotal. Cowan (1991) defines transition as a long-term process that reorganizes "both inner life and external behavior" (p. 5). Cowan draws a crucial distinction between what he calls a "life-marker" and a genuine lifecourse transition (p. 5). A male senior executive passes marker when his wife bears a child even though his own behaviors barely change in terms of caregiving or household chores. Objectively, he is a father, but compared to his wife he has experienced no "transition to parenthood." By contrast she has made a transition first, because her own behaviors change drastically. Second, her own view of herself—her identity ("I am a mother")—shifts dramatically, and, third, so does her perception of how others view her. She perceives that now others view her very differently (and usually more positively) than before. Conversely, not only does her husband's own identity *not* alter significantly, but his perception is that neither his wife, colleagues, nor friends view him any differently than they did prior to the child's birth.

Because students of the family life cycle believed that transitions often generate stress, that construct, along with *coping*, became central to their analyses. Families learning to cope effectively with unexpected and unforeseen transitions (layoffs caused by job disappearance, plant/business closings, technological upheavals, natural disasters, sudden death, dread disease) or with anticipated transitions (e.g., to parenthood) were said to experience less stress (Boss, 1987). The construct of coping is a natural outgrowth of viewing life-cycle events as part of a larger schema that concentrates, first, on phenomena external to persons and, second, on the ways in which those external phenomena constrain action.

More recently, as analysts focus on persons' ongoing reconstruction of their life course over time, increased attention is being paid to the construct of *control* (Buchmann, 1989). Coping asks, "How do I/we deal with the changes that have happened to me/us?" Control asks, "How do I/we make changes happen?" Rodin (1990) suggests that "the desire to make decisions and affect outcomes, that is to exercise control, is a basic feature of human behavior" (p. 1). The anthology edited by Rodin, Schooler, and Shaie (1990) wrestles with the issue of conceptualizing the life course in these

terms. How do persons continually *re*construct their lives, their relationships, and their families so as to achieve a sense of control? Control within the sphere of one's primary groups, as well as within the occupational realm, is viewed as a means to achieve *well-being* (Mirowsky & Ross, 1989). Well-being is defined as mental and emotional health (including fewer stress symptoms) and also as physical health (Cohen, 1990; Syme, 1990).

The issues of control and well-being throughout the life course are critical to the demographic understanding of contemporary families. Throughout this chapter, we empirically document the dramatic changes occurring in phenomena such as median age at first marriage, marriage rates, percentage of women in paid labor, fertility rates, divorce and cohabitation patterns, and so forth. How should we account for those and many other connected changes? One means is to follow the conventional demographic mode by arguing that "the properties of systems themselves become the agents of historical change" (Smith, 1989, p. 354). An alternative is to argue that "It is the wants and needs of people that continuously modify the material and symbolic environments in which we live" (Smith, 1989, pp. 354–355). Following the latter premise, we argue that the ongoing changes in families documented herein can in large measure be viewed in terms of what Smith (1989) calls "human agency ... as a medium as well as an outcome of social structure" (p. 355). Persons, based on their wants and needs regarding their primary groups—their relationships and families—are making choices in hopes of exercising control over their lives, aspiring thereby to make their lives better, that is, to achieve well-being.

Fox (1986) illustrates this perspective in the context of what many observers call the "feminization of poverty." He first cites the sharp rises in the proportions of *white* women living in their own households with children and having incomes "near or below poverty level" (p. 237). There are several conventional structural "explanations" for these increases: "absence of a male breadwinner," "inability to work at full capacity due to childcare demands," and "differentials in pay between men and women" (p. 237). We might add inadequate job training, childcare, and public assistance strategies, as well as inequitable divorce settlements among women married prior to their childbearing. Fox comments that "In crude jargon, white women have been taking on the role of 'welfare mother' long considered primarily a black cultural phenomenon resulting from weakening of the black family by three centuries of slavery and racial oppression" (p. 237).

But Fox demurs from that logic and instead raises issues stimulated by new action theory: "To accept these [structural and cultural] factors as explanations ... would be to cast the women entirely as victims and fail to recognize their aspirations to be independent and self-supporting" (p. 237). Provocatively, he asserts that "the many white single women with children who end up having to survive on poverty incomes have not come into their poverty status because the 'white family' is disintegrating, but as the result of their own struggles to escape dependence on marriage for economic support" (p. 237). He adds that "It is far more appropriate to consider these white women, together with black and minority women supporting their children on their own, as a potential labor force with tremendous energy and determination" (p. 238).

There is no doubt that conventional demographers and feminists alike could pose numerous objections to Fox's reasoning. What about, for example, those persons who have not chosen their life circumstances, but instead have had their circumstances inflicted upon them, for example, a person whose partner leaves him/her against his/her wishes? What about dependent children who do not participate in the adult choices that children perceive as having negative impacts for their lives? What about persons making choices in the hopes of increasing their control, only to find their lives are far more chaotic and stressful than before?

Nevertheless, despite these and other objections, Fox's ideas seem to have merit in at least two respects. First, the notion of women (and men) seeking to exercise choice and control throughout their life course within structural and cultural contexts forever in flux provides an intriguing and stimulating means to interpret the mass of data that follow. Second, Fox's reasoning generates researchable hypotheses that can be explored by future empirical efforts. Among other things, a major research goal would be to address the potential shortcomings of new action theory highlighted by these and other conceptual difficulties.

Data

Data from the decennial census and the vital statistics registration system provided the basis for most early demographic research on the family. An important supplement to these data is the Current Population Survey, especially the periodic birth and marital histories that have been gathered. These data sources constitute a reasonably representative sample of the U.S. population and contain a large number of cases. In combination, they provide information on levels, trends, and differentials with respect to marriage, divorce, remarriage, and fertility, as well as family or household structure.

These data suffer from several limitations, however. First, the detail of information pertaining to social, economic, and other characteristics of individuals experiencing family-related events is limited. Second, most of the information on

such characteristics refers to the time of enumeration, therefore opening up the issue of causality, as various transitions themselves affect the social and economic characteristics of individuals. Third, the continuity of data collected over time with respect to topical coverage, definitions used, and so on is often low. Such a circumstance leads to considerable difficulties in constructing a picture of long-term trends and plagues researchers who attempt to perform historical analyses (see Hareven, 1978).

A full understanding of family structure and process, including explanations for the processes themselves, requires what Tuma et al. (1979) have called event-history data, or data that contain the dates at which events occur in time. Along with information on social, economic, and other characteristics, such data can provide a very detailed description and explanation of family composition and change. The appropriate data may be gathered in longitudinal studies or by asking a series of retrospective questions in a cross-sectional investigation. Retrospective surveys, however, may suffer from problems of recall as well as misreporting. Panel studies are also useful but pose analysis problems not found when the data of events are recorded (see Tuma, Hannan, & Groeneveld, 1979). Some of the more widely used longitudinal survey efforts include the Panel Study on Income Dynamics (Hill, 1991), the National Longitudinal Surveys of Labor Market Experience (Center for Human Resource Research, 1990), the Survey of Income and Program Participation (David, 1985), the National Longitudinal Study of the High School Class of 1972 (U.S. Department of Education, 1987a), the High School and Beyond Study (U.S. Department of Education, 1987b), the National Educational Longitudinal Study (U.S. Department of Education, 1990), and the National Survey of Families and Households (Center for Demography and Ecology, 1988).

Methods

Because family demographers deal with discrete, observable variables, their methods are mainly quantitative, making use of the descriptive and inferential statistics commonly found in the social science literature. Some demographic analyses of family-related events have also relied heavily on mathematical models to illuminate underlying regularities and associations in family structure and process (Bongaarts, Burch, & Wachter, 1987; Coale, 1971; Hernes, 1972; Namboodiri & Suchindran, 1987).

Family demographers also rely on specific concepts and methodological tools to study population structure and process. A central concept is that of a rate, or the number of events during an interval relative to some population exposed to the risk of that event (e.g., divorces per 1000 married couples). The body of literature surrounding the concept of a rate also includes procedures for separating changes due to rates from changes due to shifts in composition (Althauser & Wigler, 1972; Kitagawa, 1955, 1964). For example, such procedures can determine whether the increase in the number of marriages over recent decades can be attributed to the decline in the number of available spouses or a decline in the proclivity to marry irrespective of available alternatives (Qian & Preston, 1993). Similarly, the growth of families headed by women can be disaggregated into components such as out-of-wedlock childbearing and marital disruption (Wojtkiewicz, McLanahan, & Garfinkel, 1990).

Rates are also the main component underlying life-table analysis. Although originally developed to study mortality, life tables are useful in studying the number and timing of family-related events (Elandt-Johnson & Johnson, 1980; Gehan, 1969; Gross & Clark, 1975; Namboodiri & Suchindran, 1987). Thus, life tables focus on the incidence of events as they occur in a population of individuals exposed to the risk of experiencing the event. This emphasis is distinct from an emphasis on prevalence, which considers the number or percentage of individuals characterized by having experienced the event in question at some point in time. For instance, the prevalence of divorced persons in a population can be distinguished from the incidence of new divorces taking place. Recent advances have also enabled the multivariate analysis of life tables in a regressionlike fashion (Allison, 1982; Blossfeld, Hamerle, & Mayer, 1989; Kalbfleisch & Prentice, 1980; Tuma et al., 1979; Yamaguchi, 1991).

In the remainder of this chapter, six major substantive areas are covered: female labor force participation, marriage and cohabitation, fertility, divorce, remarriage, and household size and composition. Emphasis is placed on an update of trends, differentials, and explanations that have occurred since 1960, and attention is also limited to the United States. The discussion of each substantive area begins with a general overview of trends in the recent past. Attention is then focused on differentials and explanations that have been covered in the literature. The review of previous work is selective, stressing what we perceive to be the most salient findings from the most representative studies.

Female Labor Force Participation

In 1950, about 34% of women ages 16 and older were in the labor force, comprising approximately 29% of all workers. By 1994, the percentage of women working or looking for work rose to nearly 59%, constituting 46% of the labor force. In contrast, over the same period, male labor force participation dropped from 84% to 75%, and the male

percentage of all workers declined from 71% to 54%. This trend is detailed in Table 1, which shows increased female labor force participation rates for all marital statuses between 1970 and 1994. Since 1970, single women have increased their employment by 10 percentage points, married women by 20 percentage points. Thus, the rapid increase in female labor force participation rates cannot be explained by the increase in the proportion of single women in the population.

A shift in the age structure of the population of women is also an insufficient explanation for the increase, as there has been an increase in labor force participation for each age group under age 65 between 1960 and 1994 (see Table 2). The increase in female labor force participation has been strongest at the younger ages, when women have traditionally married, started childbearing and childrearing, and dropped out of the labor force. Over the 34-year period, employment increased approximately 15 percentage points for women ages 20–34 and 14 percentage points for women ages 35–44. Conversely, at the older ages, when children are older or have left home, labor force participation increased much less, including a drop of 5 percentage points between 1960 and 1994 for women ages 65 and over.

Regarding age patterns of female employment over the past century (see Bianchi & Spain, 1986; Oppenheimer, 1970, 1973; Smith, 1980; Sweet, 1973b; Waite, 1981), women born before the turn of the century generally had their highest rates of labor force participation at the youngest ages, leaving the labor force after marriage and not returning unless forced to support themselves or their family. Women born after the turn of the century (until recent cohorts) have generally been characterized by an M-shaped pattern of labor force participation, with each successive cohort experiencing higher

Table 1. Percentage of Women in the Labor Force by Marital Status: 1970–1994

	Percentage[a] by marital status		
Year	Single	Married	Widowed, divorced, and married (spouse absent)
1994	66.7	60.7	47.5
1992	66.4	59.2	47.0
1990	66.9	58.4	47.2
1989	68.0	57.8	47.0
1985	66.8	53.8	45.1
1980	64.4	49.8	43.6
1975	59.8	44.3	40.1
1970	56.8	40.5	40.3

[a]Age 16 and over.
Sources: U.S. Bureau of the Census (1991). *Statistical Abstract of United States, 1991*, Table No. 641. Washington D.C.: US Government Printing Office. U.S. Bureau of the Census (1995). *Statistical Abstract of the United States, 1995*, Table No. 637. Washington, D.C.: US Government Printing Office.

**Table 2. Percentage of Women in the Labor Force
by Age: 1960–1994**

Year	Percentage in labor force					
	20–24	25–34	35–44	45–54	55–65	65 and over
1994	71.1	74.0	77.1	74.6	48.9	9.2
1990	71.6	73.6	76.5	71.2	45.3	8.7
1980	68.9	65.5	65.5	59.9	41.3	8.1
1970	57.7	45.0	51.1	54.4	43.0	9.7
1960	55.6	58.4	63.4	58.6[a]	—	14.1

[a]Includes women ages 45–64.
Source: U.S. Bureau of the Census, (1995) *Statistical Abstract of the United States: 1995*. Table no. 627. Washington, D.C.: US Government Printing Office.

peaks on both sides of the M. However, although their employment histories are truncated, women born after World War II appear to be generating a new profile of employment across their life course. Women in these more recent birth cohorts have increased their employment at all ages, with a flattening of the M-shaped pattern, leading to the possibility that the shape of the curve as well as the levels of labor force participation for women will approach for those men (Bianchi & Spain, 1986; Masnick & Bane, 1980).

Falling fertility may help explain why more recent cohorts of women have been more likely to enter and stay in the labor force. However, labor force participation rates for married women with children, especially preschool children, have increased faster than for other women (see Table 3). In 1960, only about 19% of married women with children under 6 years old were in the labor force, a figure that increased to almost 62% by 1994. The increase in labor force participation was also much greater for married women compared to divorced women, although women without a spouse are still more likely to be working.

**Table 3. Percentage of Women in the Labor Force
by Marital Status and Age of Children: 1960–1994**

Subject	Percentage in labor force				
	1994	1989	1980	1970	1960
Married husband present	60.6	57.8	50.1	40.8	30.5
No children under age 18	53.2	75.5	46.0	42.2	34.7
Children ages 6–17 only	76.0	73.2	61.7	49.2	39.0
Children under age 6	61.7	58.4	45.1	30.3	18.6
Divorced	a	75.5	74.5	71.5	—
No children under age 18	a	72.5	71.4	67.7	—
Children ages 6–17 only	a	85.0	82.3	82.4	—
Children under age 6	a	70.5	68.3	63.3	—

[a]Data no longer presented separately for divorced persons.
Sources: U.S. Bureau of the Census (1991). *Statistical Abstract of the United States: 1991*. Table 643. U.S. Bureau of the Census (1995). *Statistical Abstract of the United STates: 1995*, Table 638. Washington, D.C.: US Government Printing Office.

Even though married women with young children have increased their labor force participation the greatest, they are the least likely to be working full time, followed by married women with older children. This finding underscores the point made by Masnick and Bane (1980) that participation in the labor force does not necessarily imply full-time or continuous employment and that high participation rates "can mask wide fluctuations in work schedules to accommodate childcare" (p. 65). Historically, only a minority of women have been employed full-time for 50 or more weeks per year. For mothers with young children, the percentages have been particularly small, although they have increased dramatically over time (Bianchi & Spain, 1986; Presser, 1989). Women often cite "taking care of home responsibilities" as the most common reason for being employed only part of the year (Barrett, 1979; Presser, 1989; Presser & Bladwin, 1980). Several studies have also shown that childcare costs are a significant constraint on the employment of mothers (Blau & Robins, 1988a, 1988b, 1991; Michalopoulas, Robins, & Garfinkel, 1992; Ribar, 1992). The most recent research, however, finds that later cohorts of women have been much less likely to interrupt their work careers to stay at home with their children (Klerman & Leibowitz, 1994).

Research using a variety of approaches has reached opposite conclusions on the degree to which female employment is sequential (involving movement in and out of the labor force) or bipolar (involving women who remain either employed or not employed) (Bianchi & Spain, 1986; Blau & Robins, 1991; Cramer, 1980; Ewer, Crimmins, & Oliver, 1979; Heckman & Willis, 1977; Masnick & Bane, 1980; Smith, 1982). For example, Heckman and Willis (1977) argued that there is consistency over time in the percentage continuously employed versus the percentage continuously not employed. Based on a question about whether the wife did any work for money in a particular year, they found that 27% had worked 5 out of 5 years, 35% had not been employed in any of the 5 years, and 38% had moved in and out of the labor force. Other research has found significant increases over time in the proportion of years women have worked since leaving school (Smith, 1982) and the proportion of women who worked every year during a 10-year period (Mallan, 1982). Similar findings have been reported by Nakamura and Nakamura (1994), Shapiro and Mott (1994) and Shaw (1994).

However, using the same data analyzed by Heckman and Willis, but for a 10-year period and defining work as earning more than $100 in a year, Masnick and Bane (1980) stressed the continuing sequential nature of female employment in response to family demands, as only 20% of wives were in the labor force all 10 years, 18% never participated, and 62% moved in and out. The youngest wives were the most likely to have ever been employed, but the least likely to have worked all 10 years. Also, if earnings greater than 20% of the family income or greater than 33% of the family income, respectively, are used as a crude proxy for being employed, the same data suggest that between 2% and 7% of the wives were fully employed for all 10 years (Masnick & Bane, 1980). Thus, the minimal definition of paid employment most commonly used (i.e., having worked for pay in a particular year) allows for substantial shifts from full- to part-time employment as family needs dictate. More recent studies (Blau & Robins, 1991; Moen, 1985) have found similar volatility in the labor supply of young women over time.

Conclusions regarding consistency in the labor market activity of women are dependent on time frame and methods used. Also, to more fully understand the nature and implications of consistency or continuity in light of the increasing age at marriage, the postponement of having children, and the greater percentage remaining permanently childless, there is a need to examine employment patterns in relation to the presence or absence of children (Shapiro & Mott, 1994). Cramer's results (1980), for example, suggest that, in the short run, there is evidence of the bipolar, "mover–stayer" model of employment, but that "the effect of employment before birth on subsequent employment clearly diminishes over time as intervening events and contingencies become more common and more important" (p. 181).

Female Labor: Demand and Supply

Oppenheimer (1970, 1973, 1976, 1982) has provided an attractive framework that helps to explain the large influx of married women into the labor force over this century. Starting with the point that occupations are typed by sex, she showed that females have traditionally monopolized several occupations that have expanded tremendously over this century (e.g., teachers, nurses, and secretaries). At first, this demand could be met by the supply of young single women preferred by employers and supported by prevailing norms. Over time, however, the supply of young, single women declined, leaving the demand unmet. To meet the demand, older women first moved into the labor force, followed by younger married women with children. Therefore, at least part of the reason for the increase in female employment, particularly for married women, has been a structural transformation involving economic and demographic components: an economic component in the increasing demand for female labor and a demographic component in the changing relative supply of female labor by age and marital status.

Economic Necessity

In addition to structural changes, there have been economic pressures to work because of recessions, male unemployment, and inflation (Bianchi & Spain, 1986; Bowen & Finegan, 1969; Levy, 1987; Smith, 1979; Waite, 1981). The majority of female workers still are unmarried or are married to men with low incomes and thus may be working out of economic necessity (Barrett, 1979; Bianchi & Spain, 1986; Levy, 1987; Waite, 1981). Even though women earn only about 65% of what men earn for the same full-time full-year employment (U.S. Bureau of the Census, 1992), their contribution to the family income can be significant. Currently, husband–wife families with both spouses employed have incomes roughly $12,000 greater than families in which the wife remains at home, and on average, working wives contribute about one-fourth of total family income (U.S. Bureau of the Census, 1992).

Oppenheimer (1979) and Levy (1987) have noted that the economic position of men ages 20–34 vis-à-vis men ages 45–54 has declined since World War II, a period when consumption standards and aspirations rose. To meet consumption demands and to offset the relative economic deprivation of young males, more married women in their childbearing years have moved into the labor force. Once in the labor force, particularly given the rising educational levels of women and their own increasing taste for employment outside the home, they are not as likely to leave permanently. Recent research has found that female labor force participation is increasingly sensitive to economic opportunities available to women and less sensitive to the economic characteristics of men (Leibowitz & Klerman, 1995).

Occupations and Income

Occupational segregation has not decreased over this century and may even have increased, especially in heavily female occupations like nursing and secretarial work. Half of all women in the labor force work in jobs where men constitute 20% or less of their coworkers (Waite, 1981). Since 1960, there has been a slight reversal, but even this trend is far from a random assignment of new employees to jobs (Bianchi & Spain, 1986; Blau & Hendricks, 1979; Jacobs, 1989).

Segregation may be attributable to at least three factors: (1) the lower educational attainment of women (although this is rapidly changing); (2) discrimination on the part of employers; and (3) preferences on the part of women. Brown, Moon, and Zoloth (1980) found that the occupational attainments of women highly committed to the labor force are less than those of males, controlling for the effects of age, experience, and education (see also Barrett, 1979; Bergmann, 1971; Bianchi & Spain, 1986). However, data show that many women, even among the more highly educated, desire traditionally female jobs (Barrett, 1979) and are less committed to the labor market (Bielby & Bielby, 1989; Loscocco, 1989; Moen & Smith, 1986). Undoubtedly, all three factors interact, so that even highly educated women may misperceive their chances for occupational success, limited partially by discrimination practices, and therefore aspire to a career dominated by females.

One consequence of this occupational segregation is that women earn less than men, as female occupations are traditionally low-paying (Barrett, 1979; Bergman, 1971; Bianchi & Spain, 1986; Peterson & Morgan, 1995). While many researchers have noted that women are paid less than men even within the same occupations (Bianchi & Spain, 1986; Waite, 1981), a recent study by Peterson and Morgan (1995) indicates that occupational segregation is by far the most important determinant of the lower wages received by women. Furthermore, the male–female gap in earnings has only closed slowly over time (Bianchi & Spain, 1986), although it has closed more rapidly for younger, more educated women. Bernhardt, Morris, and Handcock (1995) find evidence that some of the convergence in male–female earnings is due to the growing inequality in men's wages, rather than rapid growth in women's wages.

Differentials in Female Labor Force Participation

Research on the correlates of female labor force participation has mainly focused on married, husband-present women, likely because single and divorced women have historically witnessed substantially higher rates of labor market participation. As this literature is extensive, only a few of the major studies and findings are reviewed here. Married women are more likely to be in the labor force if they are black, highly educated, their potential wage rate is high, the local labor market provides greater opportunity for employment, and their husbands have lower incomes (Bianchi & Spain, 1986; Bowen & Finegan, 1969; Cain, 1966; Cramer, 1980; Greenstein, 1989; Heckman & Willis, 1977; Mincer, 1963; Mott, 1972; Peterson, 1989; Smith-Lovin & Tickamyer, 1978; Waite, 1980; Waite & Stolzenberg, 1976). In addition, fewer and older children are associated with increased female employment (Blau & Robins, 1991; Cain, 1966; Sweet, 1973b; Waite, 1980; Waite, Haggstrom, & Kanouse, 1985). Employment plans and attitudes of both husbands and wives also affect the labor market activity of women, although they are largely dependent on the woman's past employment behavior (Cramer, 1980; Ferber, 1982; Spitze & Waite, 1981; Waite et al., 1985).

The effects of these variables have also been found to vary according to factors such as the race and education of women (Leibowitz, 1974; Oppenheimer, 1982; Sweet, 1973b). Moreover, the labor force participation of married women has been found to respond differentially according to the presence of children, their age and spacing, and expected future fertility (Clifford & Tobin, 1977; Mott, 1972; Nakamura & Nakamura, 1994; National Center for Health Statistics, 1980b; Oppenheimer, 1979, 1982; Shapiro & Mott, 1979, 1994; Waite, 1980).

Consequences

One of the most cited consequences of female employment is that of reduction in fertility. Considerable effort has been expended in trying to determine the nature of the relationship between female employment and fertility, and much of the recent research focuses on a reciprocal relationship between these two variables. Waite and Stolzenberg (1976) found a strong effect of employment plans on reducing fertility expectations but only a weak effect of fertility expectations on reducing plans for employment. Smith-Lovin and Tickamyer (1978), on the other hand, found that actual fertility (number of live births) has a much greater effect on years in the labor market. Such divergent findings could be due to the use of plans versus behavior or to the use of different control variables. However, Cramer (1980), noting that both studies used structural equation models to estimate the reciprocal relationship, estimated a series of dynamic models and concluded that, "in the short run, fertility has a strong effect on employment, but, in the longer run, the effect of employment on fertility may be stronger" (p. 165). Similar conclusions are reached by Greenstein (1989) and McLaughlin (1982). It may also be the case that increased female employment reduces the likelihood of marriage or at least delays entry into marriage, and delayed marriage is related to lower fertility (Rindfuss & Bumpass, 1978).

Once in a marriage, a wife's employment does little to change the household division of labor (Coverman & Sheley, 1986; Geerken & Gove, 1983; Gershuny & Robinson, 1988; Vanek, 1980), as men whose wives have paid employment outside the home do not appreciably increase the amount of household labor they perform. However, most of these wives do not state a preference for extra household help from their husbands. Rather, working wives have reduced their total weekly labor input, mainly by cutting down on the amount of housework they perform (Stafford, 1980). Results from a study of faculty women similarly indicate that, even among dual-career couples, the traditional division of labor exists (Yogev, 1981).

Female employment may influence household structure by affecting rates of marital dissolution and remarriage. A growing body of literature indicates that working wives are more likely to dissolve their marriages than housewives (Becker, Landes, & Michael, 1977; Bishop, 1980; Cherlin, 1977, 1979; Hannan, Tuma, & Groenveld, 1978; Moore & Waite, 1981; Morgan & Rindfuss, 1985; Mott & Moore, 1979; Ross & Sawhill, 1975; South & Spitze, 1986; Spitze & South, 1985). In addition, divorced and widowed women who work are less likely to remarry (Smock, 1990; Teachman & Heckert, 1985; Wolf & MacDonald, 1979). The net result is that increasing labor force participation of women is tied to the increasing proportion of female-headed households.

Marriage and Nonmarital Cohabitation

From the turn of the century through the Baby Boom, age at marriage in the United States declined; a particularly steep decline occurred during the 1940s and 1950s. Since the mid-1960s, however, the trend has reversed. As shown in Table 4, between 1970 and 1988, the median age at first marriage rose from 22.5 to 25.5 for men, and from 20.6 to 23.7 for women. Also, the age difference between males and females at first marriage has declined from about 4 years at the beginning of this century to 2.5 years in 1960 and 1.8 years in 1988, because of the more rapid increase in recent years in the age of females at first marriage compared to that of males.

Period marriage rates, also shown in Table 4, are seemingly inconsistent with the rise in median age at first marriage, as they indicate that the number of marriages per 1000 total population did not decline until after 1970. However, the number of marriages per 1000 unmarried women ages 15 and older has declined consistently. Shifts in the U.S. age structure were responsible for the delay in the decrease in the crude marriage rate before 1980. Because of the Baby Boom, an increasing proportion of the population moved into the most common marriage ages, keeping the crude marriage from declining. But among those eligible to marry, the marriage rate has declined.

Another view of this phenomenon is shown in Table 5. Between 1960 and 1994, the percentage of never-married women ages 20–24 rose from 28% to 66%. Similarly, the percentage of never-married women ages 25–29 nearly tripled, increasing from 11% to 35%. The delay in marriage, therefore, is particularly sharp for women reaching their 20s during the 1970s and 1980s, primarily for women born after 1945 (i.e., Baby Boomers). The percentages of those never

Table 5. Percentage of Women Never Married by Age: 1960–1994

Age	Percentage by year				
	1994	1989	1980	1970	1960
20–24	66.0	62.5	50.2	35.8	28.4
25–29	35.3	29.4	20.9	10.5	10.5
30–34	19.9	16.9	9.5	6.2	6.9
35–39	12.8	9.9	6.2	5.4	6.1

Source: U.S. Bureau of the Census (1994). "Marital Status and Living Arrangements: March 1994," *Current Population Reports*, Series P-20. No. 484, Table 1. Washington, D.C.: Government Printing Office.

married of women ages 20–29 are now consistent with pre-1940 levels, and as Masnick and Bane (1980) pointed out, "the rate of increase in the proportion single for specific age groups [has been] greater than ever before experienced by any successive cohorts born in the twentieth century" (p. 27). The decrease in the percentage of those never married between 1960 and 1970 for women over age 30 and the lower rate of increase between 1970 and 1994 for this age group mainly involve women who reached marriageable ages during the Baby Boom years, when marriage and birth rates were high.

Another element of changing marriage statistics is shown in Table 4. The percentage of marriages that are first marriages has declined over the 1970s from 76% to 65% for both men and women. In part, this shift is due to the increasing delay in first marriages as well as a consistent rise in divorce rates, which has increased the proportion of once-married persons in the pool of eligible partners. Further, divorce has been occurring at younger ages, increasing the probability of remarriage.

An adequate model of historical shifts in marriage age has not appeared in the literature. About all that can be generalized from the efforts of formal modeling is that marriage is heavily age-stratified (Coale, 1971; Schoen, Utron, Woodrow, & Baj, 1985; Trussel, 1976b) and that marriage markets are inherently unstable. One element in the instability of marriage markets has been imbalances in the sex ratio (i.e., the imbalance in the number of eligible persons of each sex) that may occur, for instance, when war losses reduce the number of marriageable men relative to the number of eligible women (Guttentag & Secord, 1983). More common are marriage squeezes caused by shifts in fertility. The escalating number of births in the United States during the late 1940s and through the 1950s has meant that females born during these periods have faced a relative shortage of slightly older men, perhaps as much as 10%. Recently, attention has focused on imbalances associated with deficits of educated, employed men (Lichter, LeClere, & McLaughlin,

Table 4. Median Age at First Marriage, Marriage Rates, and Percentage of Marriages That Are First Marriages: 1970–1988

Year	Median age at first marriage		Marriage rate		Percentage first marriages	
	Male	Female	Crude[a]	General[b]	Male	Female
1988	25.5	23.7	9.7	54.6		
1987	25.3	23.6	9.9	55.7	65.2	65.2
1985	24.4	23.0	10.1	57.0	65.1	65.7
1980	23.6	21.8	10.6	61.4	64.3[c]	65.9[c]
1975	22.7	20.8	10.0	66.9	68.7	70.1
1970	22.5	20.6	10.6	76.5	75.8	76.2

[a]Rate per 1000 total population.
[b]Rate per 1000 unmarried women age 15 and over.
[c]1979 data.
Sources: Various issues of *Monthly Vital Statistics Reports*, National Center for Health Statistics; U.S. Bureau of the Census (1995). *Statistical Abstract of the United States: 1995*, Table No. 145. Washington, D.C.: US Government Printing Office.

1991; Mare & Winship, 1991; South & Lloyd, 1992; Wilson, 1987; Wood, 1995).

Adaption to imbalances can occur in several ways: (1) women may marry later or remain permanently single; (2) they may shift the preferred age range of potential spouses to include younger men; or (3) they may marry men who previously would not have been selected in the marriage market (Guttentag & Secord, 1983; Sweet, 1977). It would also be expected that marriage rates for men would increase to meet the age-induced shift in demand. However, shifts in age differences between spouses have not coincided with the recent marriage squeeze (Presser, 1975). Further, age at first marriage for men has risen along with that for women, a trend opposite to what would be expected if only sex ratio imbalances were in operation.

Some researchers have argued that increases in economic uncertainty have slowed the rate at which individuals enter marriage (Becker, 1991; Oppenheimer, 1988; Teachman, Polonko, & Leigh, 1987). Modell (1980; see also Modell, Furstenberg, & Stong, 1978) has argued that economic opportunity during the Baby Boom years allowed individuals to achieve early marriage ideals and that poor economic times during the Great Depression kept individuals from achieving these goals. As discussed by Espenshade (1985), other potential explanations for the rise in age at first marriage following the 1960s include the greater availability of contraception and abortion, rising levels of educational attainment, the increasing labor force participation of women, and changing ideology consistent with the women's movement—in short, increases over time in the status of women.

Another factor related to the formation of marital unions has been the substantial increase in nonmarital cohabitation over the past 2 decades. Although no official government statistics on such unions are kept, a number of recent survey efforts have documented the prevalence of nonmarital unions. By the early 1990s, nearly one-quarter of 25–29-year-old men and women who were not married were living in consensual unions (Waite, 1995). Bumpass and Sweet (1989) estimate that nearly one-half of recent marriages involve a couple that cohabited prior to marriage. The prevalence of cohabitation is so high that while the average age at marriage has increased substantially over the past 2 decades, the average age at union formation has remained relatively constant (Manning & Smock, 1995). Bumpass, Raley, and Sweet (1995) estimate that national estimates of stepparent households would have to be adjusted upward by 25% if cohabiting unions were counted. The available evidence suggests that marital and nonmarital cohabitation on the part of young adults is closely linked to parental marital behavior and attitudes (Axinn & Thornton, 1996) and that nonmarital cohabitation, if not serving as an alternative to marriage, is related to less commitment to traditional behavior and values

(Clarkberg, Stolzenberg, & Waite, 1995; Manning & Smock, 1995).

Differentials in Marital Timing

A number of early studies focused on factors associated with marital timing, but many used small, nonrepresentative samples. Research using census data is limited in the range of variables available for examination, and seldom do these variables tap the circumstances or the characteristics of individuals at the time they decide to marry. Thus, the differentials considered here are those examined in larger, more representative survey efforts, many of which are quite recent.

Of all background variables, parental socioeconomic status (SES) has received the most attention. Multivariate studies have failed to find strong direct effects of parental SES on marital timing. This is particularly true for males (Hogan, 1978a) and blacks (McLanahan & Bumpass, 1988), although Waite and Spitze (1981) found that the socioeconomic status of parents does have a direct effect on reducing the chances of marriage for young teenage women, a finding suggesting that parents use their resources in a more direct fashion to prevent their daughters from marrying too early. Overall, research suggests that the effects of parental SES on marital timing are primarily indirect, through such variables as high educational aspirations and achievement (Teachman et al., 1987).

Recent studies investigating other characteristics of the parental household have found that factors that may serve to increase the costs associated with the adolescent role hasten marriage. For example, research has linked lower parental resources and household amenities to an increased rate at which adolescents and young adults leave home (Aquilino, 1991; Avery, Goldscheider, & Speare, 1992). Other research has linked parental divorce and remarriage to higher rates of union formation, both marital and nonmarital (Michael & Tuma, 1985; Thornton, 1991).

In summary, it appears that early background variables do not play an important direct role in creating differentials in age at marriage. Rather, the findings suggest influences that are primarily indirect, particularly as they impact on norms, values, preferences, and life-course plans and experiences that are formed in young adulthood, before marriage. Moreover, there appears to be a substantial intergenerational linkage between the marital behavior of parents and the values and attitudes of their children that, in turn, affects the rate at which they form marital and nonmarital unions (Axinn & Thornton, 1993, 1996). Children who experience divorce and remarriage are more likely to form early nonmarital unions.

Experiences during the high school years have a more substantial impact on marital timing than earlier family background factors. Research suggests that high grades or academic success, parental encouragement, and educational expectations and goals delay marriage, operating primarily through educational attainment (Teachman et al., 1987). Overall, it appears that expectations and events that lead to the development of achievement (vs. familistic) orientations, combined with academic success, delay marriage, especially for females.

A consistent finding in the literature is that education delays marriage, although most individuals marry shortly after completing their education (Blossfeld & Huinink, 1991; Davis & Bumpass, 1976; Goldscheider & Waite, 1986; Hogan, 1978a; Keeley, 1977; MacDonald & Rindfuss, 1981; Preston & Richards, 1975; Teachman et al., 1987; Thornton, Axinn, & Teachman, 1995). Research has also explored possible reciprocal effects by estimating structural equation models allowing for a simultaneous relationship between age at marriage and education. It is generally found that, for women, education delays marriage; in turn, early marriage has a negative, but much smaller, impact on educational attainment (Marini, 1978; Marini & Hodson, 1981). For men, education also acts to delay marriage, but less so than for women, and marital timing has no significant impact on educational attainment (Marini, 1978).

Alexander and Reilly (1981) have criticized these efforts for a number of methodological and substantive reasons and have suggested dynamic models as an alternative to structural equation models. Using such models, they concluded that previous studies are biased in overestimating the effect of marital timing on education. However, their substantive conclusion is not different from previous research: Early marriage reduces further educational attainment for females, but not for males.

Overall, the stronger relationships for women than for men point to the differential salience of socioeconomic achievements. In contrast to men, most women are socialized to view marriage and childbearing as primary goals and means of status attainment, thus allowing marriage to interfere with their educational attainments (Marini, 1978). However, among women, higher education does serve to increase the attractiveness of alternatives to the wife role and to increase the costs of marriage. Both of these outcomes are a products, in part, of the more egalitarian preferences or tastes of more educated women and the more rewarding occupational and income potentials that this education affords them.

Research findings show the proportion of never-married women in their early 20s is higher in urban areas where the industrial structure provides more opportunities for female employment and in areas where female earnings are higher (Preston & Richards, 1975; White, 1985). Research on individual-level data (Keeley, 1977) also finds that higher-income women delay marriage longer. More recently, Lich-

ter, McLaughlin, Kephart, and Landry (1992) report that income increases the likelihood that a woman will marry.

Findings on women's premarital employment are more complex. For example, Waite and Spitze (1981) found that premarital employment acts to hasten marriage, and they reasoned that employment may increase contact with potential spouses and make women more attractive in the marriage market (see also Lichter et al., 1992). However, Cherlin (1981) found that prior employment had little effect on marriage 2 years later. In contrast, however, both Cherlin (1981) and Waite and Spitze (1981) found that women who planned to be in the labor force at age 35 were more likely to delay marriage. Thus, it appears that commitment to the labor force (e.g., full-time employment and plans for employment) and actual career success (e.g., higher income) are key variables that serve to increase the costs of assuming the wife role. In contrast, more traditional women, who are not committed to the labor force, may use their paid employment as a resource to marry earlier.

With respect to males, the results are generally opposite to those for females, as higher earnings are associated with earlier marriage for men who have entered a career (Cooney & Hogan, 1991; Keeley, 1977; MacDonald & Rindfuss, 1981). The study by MacDonald and Rindfuss (1981) also found that current male income relative to parental income had no effect on marital timing. This finding is contrary to Easterlin's relative income hypothesis (1980), which predicts that men who experience greater financial success than their parental household when they were growing up will marry earlier. Current employment and a first full-time job are related to earlier marriage for men (MacDonald & Rindfuss, 1981), although men with higher-status jobs are slightly more likely to delay marriage (Hogan, 1978a). Service in the military has also been found to delay marriage (Hogan, 1978a; MacDonald & Rindfuss, 1981).

These different effects for males and females are most likely due to the difficulty that women have in combining attractive nonfamilial roles with marriage (Marini, 1978; Waite & Spitze, 1981). As women typically must make their occupational achievements secondary to their husband's career and to their responsibilities for housekeeping and childcare, the women who are most committed to their careers and who are the most successful have the most to gain from delaying marriage. Conversely, as men typically assume the primary provider role, marriage does not hold the same costs in terms of expected career sacrifices, and higher socioeconomic resources increase the male's attractiveness as a future wage earner.

Early heterosexual involvement and sexual experimentation are related to early union formation, either marital or nonmarital. Among teenage females, premarital sex is associated with more traditional sex-role preferences, which would reduce the perceived costs of a premarital pregnancy. Thus, it is not surprising that many early marriages are accompanied by a premarital pregnancy, and this proportion has been growing over time (Glick & Norton, 1977; Teachman, 1985). Cherlin, Kiernan, and Chase-Lansdale (1995) argue that conflict in the parental home often leads to sexual activity, which in turn leads to early union formation.

The aggregate impact of premarital conceptions on marital timing depends not only on the frequency of conception but also on the availability of and willingness to obtain an abortion and the propensity to legitimize the pregnancy. Some evidence suggests that the advent of legal abortion may be one factor in the rising age at marriage as premarital pregnancies are increasingly terminated (Bauman, Koch, Udry, & Freedman, 1975). Over time, a lower proportion of premarital pregnancies have been legitimized (Bennett, Bloom, & Miller, 1995; O'Connell & Moore, 1980; Zelnik et al., 1981). Although the impact of a premarital birth on marital timing varies by age at birth (Teachman &Polonko, 1984; Waite & Spitze, 1981), Bennett, Kanter, and Ford (1995; see also Ryder & Westoff, 1971) report that women with a premarital birth marry, on average, later than women without a premarital birth. This finding indicates that women who do not choose abortion or legitimize the pregnancy operate differently in the marriage market. Research on blacks, for example, has found an increasing disassociation between legal marriage and childbearing (Teachman, 1985).

Controlling for other variables, blacks still marry later than whites (Bennett, Bloom, & Craig, 1989; Carter & Glick, 1976; Lichter et al., 1991, 1992; Marini, 1978; Preston & Richards, 1975; Schoen & Kluegel, 1988; South & Lloyd, 1992; Waite & Spitze, 1981). However, it may be inappropriate to assume that the same variables influence marital timing for each race. For instance, highly educated white women are less likely to have married than highly educated black women. High educational attainments thus appear to be more incompatible with marriage for white women than for black women, perhaps because of the greater importance of female income and labor force participation to the economic viability of marriages among blacks (Lichter et al., 1992; Teachman et al., 1987).

Black women, however, were actually more likely to marry when median female earnings were higher. The black–white differential in marital timing is also likely to be affected by variations in premarital fertility, abortion, and legitimization. Unmarried black women are more likely than white women to become pregnant but are less likely to seek an abortion (although, overall, black women are more likely than white women to obtain an abortion) and are less likely to marry to legitimize a pregnancy (O'Connell & Moore, 1980; Zelnik & Kantner, 1980). But, when both contextual and individual-level factors are taken into account, race differ-

ences in marriage are diminished but remain significant (Lichter et al., 1992).

For both men and women, age at marriage is consistently higher in larger cities and in the Northeast (especially compared to the South). These differentials cannot be explained by compositional differences on a number of variables, such as race and education (Carter & Glick, 1976; Hogan, 1978a; Preston & Richards, 1975; Waite & Spitze, 1981). Similarly, shifts in age at marriage by birth cohorts of individuals remain after controlling for numerous control variables (Cooney & Hogan, 1991; Hogan, 1978a; Rodgers & Thornton, 1985; Schoen et al., 1985). It remains for future research to identify the factors responsible for geographic and birth cohort variations in marital timing.

Waite and Spitze (1981) have found that the effects of many variables on marital timing vary by the age of the woman, with most serving to enhance or decrease the probability of marriage at young and old ages. This age grading may help to explain the failure of earlier research to find significant effects for some variables, as they operate differentially across age groups. Recent research has generally considered the impact of predictor variables specific to age of respondent. However, no one has developed and tested an adequate rationale for explaining why the effects of predictor variables should vary according to age.

Consequences

Marriage is a life-course transition with long-term consequences. Marrying at a young age, especially for women, can define the nature, content, and structure of future roles, often truncating the development of preferences for and participation in alternative roles (e.g., education, postmarital employment, and earnings) in which tastes competing with familial activities are generated and reinforced (Bianchi & Spain, 1986; Gerson, 1985; Goldscheider & Waite, 1991; Presser, 1971; Waite, 1995).

Age at marriage also has implications for fertility. For instance, Gibson (1976) attributed about one-fifth of the decline in U.S. fertility rates between 1971 and 1975 to increased age at marriage. On the individual level, an early marriage is associated with higher completed parity and rapid birth spacing (Bumpass, Rindfuss, & Janosik, 1978; Marini & Hodson, 1981; Tsui, 1982; Westoff & Ryder, 1977a; Wilkie, 1981), although this relationship has weakened over time (Teachman & Heckert, 1985a). In part, the association between early fertility and subsequent childbearing may reflect the greater amount of reproductive time available to couples who marry earlier, as well as their less efficient contraceptive use. It may also be that couples with higher fertility ideals may marry younger (Modell, 1980) or, more important, that younger married couples are less likely to participate in activities competing with childbearing (Bianchi & Spain, 1986; Gerson, 1985; Goldscheider & Waite, 1991; Presser, 1971).

Studies have also linked early marriage to higher levels of marital instability, for both males and females and blacks and whites (Becker et al., 1977; DeMaris & Rao, 1992; Kahn & London, 1991; Morgan & Rindfuss, 1985; South & Spitze, 1986; Teachman, 1983; Teachman, Thomas, & Paasch, 1991). Weed (1974) found that age at marriage is a factor in explaining differentials in divorce rates by state. Marriage timing also has an impact on family and household structure (Bongaarts et al., 1987; Cherlin, 1981; Masnick & Bane, 1980; Santi, 1988). With an older age at marriage, fewer children are born. Delayed marriage, in conjunction with an increased propensity to leave the parental household, has also contributed to the rise in the number of individuals living alone (Goldscheider & DaVanzo, 1989).

Fertility

Fertility is covered extensively in the decennial census, the Current Population Surveys, and vital statistics (Cho, Grabill, & Bogue, 1970; Rindfuss & Sweet, 1977). In addition, much work has been done on documenting trends and differentials in childbearing (Grabill, Kiser, & Whelpton, 1958; Rindfuss & Sweet, 1977; Ryder & Westoff, 1971; Westoff, Potter, Sagi, & Mushler, 1961; Westoff & Ryder, 1977a; Whelpton, Campbell, & Patterson, 1966); identifying and modeling the complex biosocial process by which childbearing varies across time and individuals (Bongaarts, 1978; Davis & Blake, 1956; Potter, 1963; Ryder, 1980, 1981; Sheps & Menken, 1973); examining socioeconomic differentials in fertility, offering theoretical orientations (see Andorka, 1978; Bagozzi & Van Loo, 1978; Cherlin, 1990; Hawthorne, 1970; Kasarda, Billy, & West, 1986); and measuring fertility, recognizing that different views of the same phenomenon can suggest different explanations (Hendershot & Placek, 1981; Rindfuss & Sweet, 1977; Ryder, 1975).

Given the richness of detail concerning fertility, only very broad trends on general fertility trends in number and timing, illegitimacy, planning status, and contraception are covered here.

Trends in Number

Between 1917 and 1935, the nation's total fertility rate, a period measure, dropped from 3333 to 2145 per 1000 women, or an average decline of over 1 child per woman. By 1957, the total fertility rate had risen to 3682, or an average increase of over 1½ children per woman. Between 1957 and 1975, fertility levels dropped precipitously, with the 1975 total fertility rate being 1774, or about one-half the 1957 level. Since 1975, the total fertility rate has risen slightly, to about 1932 in 1988. The increase in fertility during the Baby Boom years and its subsequent decline occurred among virtually every major subgroup of the U.S. population, although with variation in the magnitude of rise and decline (Rindfuss & Sweet, 1977).

The upward shift in completed fertility for cohorts of women producing the Baby Boom was largely due to fewer women remaining childless or having only one birth compared to women passing through their childbearing years during the Great Depression (Cutright & Shorter, 1979; Ryder, 1969). Thus, the Baby Boom was not the result of more women having very large families. In addition, Ryder (1969, 1980, 1981) has shown that period fertility rates for Baby Boom years were inflated because of the rapid tempo in childbearing. Thus, the Baby Boom represented a convergence around the two- to three-child family, with early marriage and closely spaced births.

Explanations for the Baby Boom are still subject to debate and focus on a variety of factors, including the pro-marriage and pronatalist norms of the period (Blake & Das Gupta, 1975; Bouvier, 1980; Gibson, 1976) and the privileged economic position of young adults in the 1950s compared to that of their parents (Easterlin, 1973, 1980). It may be the case that, after a decade of depression and 4 years or war, as well as a postwar economic boom, Americans were especially anxious to enjoy the perceived security of a strong family life (Cherlin, 1981, 1990; Modell, 1980). Other explanations include shifts in the timing of births in reaction to anticipated female wages and labor force participation (Butz & Ward, 1977, 1978) and to high levels of unwanted births, with later fertility declines due to reductions in unwanted births via improved contraceptive technology (Westoff & Ryder, 1977a). Masnick and McFalls (1978) showed, however, that the fertility decline since the Baby Boom is due less to changes in contraceptive technology than to changes in the rigor of contraceptive use once sexual activity is begun. This is an important point, because modern contraceptive innovations cannot explain the low fertility of the Depression years.

Table 6 shows the change in fertility between 1970 and 1992, accompanied by changes in expected lifetime fertility for wives ages 18–34. As fertility has dropped, so has expected fertility. Although fertility expectations are not always a sure indicator of future childbearing (Hendershot & Placek, 1981), the magnitude of the declines indicates a substantial downward revision in preferences, both within and across cohorts of women. Indeed, 1975 and later levels of expected lifetime fertility imply replacement levels of childbearing.

In addition, part of the fertility decline following the Baby Boom reflects increases in the proportion of women at each age who are childless (Bloom & Pebley, 1982; Chen &

Table 6. Total Fertility Rates and Expected Lifetime Births per 1000 Married Women Ages 18–24, 25–29, and 30–34: 1970–1992

Year	Total fertility rate[a]	Lifetime births expected by age[b]		
		18–24	25–29	30–34
1992	2065	2279	2271	2218
1990	2081	2244	2285	2277
1988	1932	2128	2260	2175
1985	1843	2183	2236	2167
1980	1840	2134	2160	2248
1975	1774	2173	2260	2610
1970	2480	2375[c]	2619[c]	2989[c]

[a]Births per 1000 women ages 15–49 over their lifetime under current fertility levels.
[b]Per 1000 married women.
[c]1971 data.
Sources: U.S. Bureau of the Census (1992). *Statistical Abstract of the United States : 1991*, Table 99. Washington, D.C.: US Government Printing Office. U.S. Bureau of the Census (1995). *Statistical Abstract of the United States: 1995*, Tables 91 & 103. Washington, D.C.: US Government Printing Office.

Morgan, 1991; Rindfuss, Morgan, & Swicegood, 1988). Between 1967 and 1976, the percentage of all wives ages 14–39 intending to remain childless increased from 3.1% to 5.4%. The increase was more pronounced for white women and highly educated women (i.e., 4.5% of white wives ages 14–39 with one or more years of college intended to remain childless in 1971 vs. 8.7% in 1976; the corresponding figures for white women with less than a high school education were 3.1% and 3.4%). As of 1990, about 9% of all women ages 18–34 expected to remain childless. There have also been substantial increases in the percentage of women expecting to have one child. Numerous researchers have noted a trend toward increased childlessness and the one-child family over that experienced by Baby Boom mothers (Blake, 1981; Cutright & Polonko, 1977; DeJong & Sell, 1977; Freshnock & Cutright, 1978; Hastings & Robinson, 1974; Houseknecht, 1978; Poston & Gotard, 1977; Veevers, 1979).

Trends in Timing

Significant differentials exist with respect to nonmarital fertility and child spacing. Most important, perhaps, blacks are much more likely to experience nonmarital fertility and a rapid first birth than are whites (Rindfuss & Parnell, 1989; Teachman, 1985; U.S. Bureau of the Census, 1976a). Rapid first childbirth is also more likely to occur among women who marry early, have less education, are Catholic, and do not participate in the labor force (Bloom & Trussell, 1984; Davidson, 1970; Hastings, 1971; Hastings & Robinson, 1975; Namboodiri, 1964; National Center for Health Statistics,

1981; Teachman & Polonko, 1985; Tsui, 1982; Whelpton, 1964; Wilkie, 1981).

For subsequent births, however, these differentials in birth spacing are considerably diminished. The spacing of second and subsequent births has not changed as significantly over time as that of first births (National Center for Health Statistics, 1981; Tsui, 1982; Wineberg & McCarthy, 1989). Rather, a major determinant of subsequent birth timing is the spacing of the first birth (Bumpass et al., 1978; Marini & Hodson, 1981; Millman & Hendershot, 1980; Presser, 1971; Tsui, 1982), although this differential has also declined across time (Teachman & Heckert, 1985a).

Another way to look at the timing of fertility is to consider the percentage of women who have remained childless to particular ages. Table 7 shows that the percentage childless at various ages has been increasing since 1970. In 1970, about 24% of all women ages 25–29 were childless. By 1994, this figure had increased to almost 44%. This delay in childbearing is also evident in the proportions childless at ages 30–34 and 35–39. The figures for never-married women follow the same general pattern as for all women, showing that the trend toward delaying childbearing cannot be fully explained by the concurrent rise in age at first marriage.

Bloom (1981) showed that the mean age at first birth for women age 14 and over increased from 22.1 in the early 1950s to 22.9 in the late 1960s. For white women, the change was from 22.4 years to 23.4 years. Among black women, however, there was actually a decrease, from 20.7 to 20.3 years. Bloom also found that, although the overall mean age at first birth had been going up in recent years, there had been a drop in the age at which appreciable numbers of women had first births. This finding indicates an increasing tendency toward bifurcation in the childbearing experience of women: fertility

Table 7. Percentage of All Women and Ever-Married Women Who Were Childless at Selected Ages: 1970–1994

Year	Percentage of all women			Percentage of ever-married women		
	25–29	30–34	35–39	25–29	30–34	35–39
1994	43.6	26.3	19.6	28.9	17.5	13.3
1990	42.1	25.7	17.7	29.3	16.8	12.2
1986	40.7	23.9	16.6	27.3	15.1	11.5
1980	36.8	19.8	12.1	25.3	13.7	8.0
1975	31.1	15.2	9.6	21.1	8.8	5.3
1970	24.4	11.8	9.4	15.8	8.3	7.3

Sources: Various issues of Series P-20, *Current Population Reports*. U.S. Bureau of Census. *Fertility of American Women*, June 1994. *Current Population Reports P-20*, No. 482. Tables F & 1. Washington, D.C.: US Government Printing Office.

increasingly either occurs at a young age or is delayed. Also, as discussed earlier, the analyses by Bloom and others indicate increases in the proportion who will remain childless permanently, representing another example of the apparently increasing tendency to disassociate childbearing from marriage. Thus, women are more likely to be entering the parent role either early, late, or never. The bifurcation of childbearing experiences reflects not only more varied alternatives to family life but also a greater consistency between gender-role preferences and fertility behavior: Egalitarian women delay or forgo childbearing, and women with a familistic orientation become young parents.

Contraception and Birth Planning

Table 8 shows changes in contraceptive use patterns among married women. Overall contraceptive use has increased 18 percentage points from 1965 to 1990. The distribution of methods among users has shifted considerably, with increases in the proportion of women relying on sterilization and increases followed by decreases in use of the intrauterine device (IUD) and the pill. By far the most dramatic change was in increased reliance on sterilization, an upward shift of nearly 40 percentage points. Since 1976 pill use has dropped over 18 percentage points, while use of the IUD has dropped about 8 percentage points. The net effect of these changes, especially given the substantial increase in the use of sterilization, is greater overall contraceptive efficiency. Still, very low fertility was achieved by women living their childbearing years during the Depression through the use of methods

Table 8. Percentage of Married Women Using Contraception by Method and Abortion Rate: 1965–1990

Method	Percentage by Year				
	1990	1988	1982	1976	1965
Contraception[a]	79.7	82.1	81.0	68.8	64.1
Sterilization	46.0	44.0	40.9	13.9	6.5
Pill	14.5	15.1	13.4	32.9	24.0
IUD	1.0	1.5	4.8	9.2	1.1
Other methods	18.2	21.5	21.9	12.8	32.5
Nonusers[b]	6.6	4.8	5.0	—	—
Abortion rate[c]	27.4	27.1[d]	28.8	24.2	13.2[e]

[a]Among currently married women ages 15–44.
[b]Excludes those noncontractively sterile, pregnant, postpartum, or seeking pregnancy.
[c]Abortions per 1000 women ages 16–44.
[d]1987 data.
[e]1972 data.
Sources: U.S. Bureau of the Census (1991). *Statistical Abstract of the United States: 1991.* Washington, D.C.: US Government Printing Office. U.S. Bureau of the Census (1995). *Statistical Abstract of the United States: 1995.* Washington, D.C.: US Government Printing Office.

currently believed to be "unattractive and inefficient" (Dawson, Meny, & Ridley, 1980), leaving open the question about the extent to which shifts in contraceptive technology can themselves explain shifts in fertility behavior (see also Blake & Das Gupta, 1975).

The trends in legal abortion between 1972, the year preceding the U.S. Supreme Court decision, and 1990 are also presented in Table 8. In 1972, there were 13.2 abortions per 1000 women ages 15–44, rising to 28.8 in 1982 and declining slightly to 27.4 in 1990. Increases in abortion have slowed because of problems with geographic location, cutbacks in Medicaid funding, increased use of parental notification and consent, and restrictions placed on abortions by clinics that perform them (Forrest, Tietze, & Sullivan, 1978; Henshaw, 1991; Henshaw, Forrest, Sullivan, & Thietze, 1982).

Nonmarital Fertility

As overall fertility dropped during the years following the Baby Boom, rates of nonmarital fertility continued their historical upward trend (Bumpass & McLanahan, 1989; Cutright, 1972a). In 1940, there were 7.1 nonmarital births per 1000 unmarried women ages 15–44, and by 1992, the figure had increased to 38.6. Although a decrease in the rate of nonmarital fertility occurred between 1970 and 1975, the upward trend resumed thereafter (see Table 9). For a historical view on nonmarital fertility, see Cutright (1971a, 1972a,b) and Smith and Hendus (1975). Illegitimacy rates for nonwhites are much higher than for whites, although the rate for whites has risen consistently while the rate for nonwhites decreased consistently until the mid-1980s. However, the percentage of all live births occurring outside of marriage has increased for both races. Only 2% of all white births were nonmarital in 1960, rising to 18% in 1988. For nonwhites, the jump was from about 22% to 64%. Part of this increase, especially among whites, can be explained by rising non-

Table 9. Birth Rates of Unmarried Women by Race: 1970–1992

Year	Rate[a]			Year	Rate[a]		
	Total	White	Nonwhite		Total	White	Nonwhite
1992	45.2	35.2	86.5[b]	1980	28.4	16.2	78.0
1990	43.8	31.8	93.9[b]	1975	24.5	12.4	79.0
1988	38.6	26.6	81.8	1970	26.4	13.9	89.9
1985	32.8	21.8	73.2				

[a]Rate are live births to unmarried women per 1000 unmarried women ages 15–44.
[b]Birth rates for black women.
Sources: Various issues of *Monthly Vital Statistics Reports*, National Center for Health Statistics. U.S. Bureau of the Census (1995). *Statistical Abstract of the United States: 1995*, Table 94. Washington, D.C.: US Government Printing Office.

marital fertility rates, but the major determinant for both races has been the substantial decline in marital fertility.

Nonmarital fertility has been increasingly concentrated among teenage women and thus has been more likely to involve first, premarital births (O'Connell, 1980; see also Bumpass & McLanahan, 1989, and Smith & Cutright, 1988). Focusing on premarital births among young women under age 24, O'Connell and Moore (1980) reported findings confirming those listed for nonmarital fertility in general, documenting a strong differential between blacks and whites. They also found that, since 1970, premarital fertility had changed little for women ages 20–24, whereas premarital fertility for women under age 20 had risen substantially. Recent research has noted a strong positive link between nonmarital cohabitation and nonmarital fertility, especially for black women (Loomis & Landale, 1995).

With respect to contraceptive use, the 1970s and 1980s witnessed more sexually active young women having ever used a contraceptive method prior to a pregnancy and declines in those who never used (Mosher & McNally, 1991; Zelnik & Kantner, 1974, 1977, 1978, 1980; Zelnik, Kim, & Kantner, 1979; Zelnick et al., 1981). Yet the level of premarital pregnancy among women ages 15–19 increased consistently over these 2 decades, as increased levels of premarital sexual activity more than offset the increased use of contraception. Pregnancy levels also rose among ever-users of contraception as there was a shift away from the most efficient methods. This increase in premarital pregnancies was translated into more premarital births, despite an increased propensity to abort, because a decline occurred in the likelihood of marriage before the birth.

Static versus Dynamic Perspectives on Fertility

Although there are several competing perspectives with respect to fertility (see Bagozzi & Van Loo, 1978), an emerging distinction has been made between a static versus a dynamic approach. To the static approach (Becker, 1960, 1991; Becker & Lewis, 1979; Mincer, 1963; Willis, 1974), fertility represents an economic choice, made at the time of marriage, between fertility and competing goods and services, depending on income, prices, and opportunity costs. The assumption of a static family-size decision made at marriage has received much criticism, and a dynamic perspective has been formed as an alternative (Cherlin, 1990; Hagestad, 1988; Namboodiri, 1972, 1981; Pillai, 1987). Several studies have shown the variability of fertility expectations and desire of individuals over time, especially downward revisions during the 1960s and 1970s (Butz & Ward, 1978; Coombs, 1979; Freedman, Freedman, & Thornton, 1980; Westoff & Ryder, 1977b). Attitudes toward and actual timing of births have also changed (Pebley, 1981; Tsui, 1982).

Morgan (1981) illustrated the considerable indecision characterizing fertility decisions after minimal acceptable family size has been reached. Rindfuss and Bumpass (1978) argued that fertility interacts with the age of the woman, as norms exist about the appropriate ages for parity-specific births.

A dynamic perspective views fertility as an ongoing, decision-making process. Not only do the social and economic conditions of women and couples change over time, and in directions that cannot always be anticipated, but they are also affected by the birth of a child. These changing conditions make it unlikely that fertility decisions made at marriage, if they are made at this time, will not be questioned or modified in the future.

Consequences

Basically, two sets of consequences of fertility can be identified: those for parents and those for children. Consequences for parents involve the number of children, as well as their timing and spacing. Children are expensive in terms of time and monetary costs (Espenshade, 1977, 1984; Kasarda et al., 1986) and in terms of cost due to the wife's leaving the labor force or reducing her hours of paid employment (Calhoun & Espenshade, 1988; Cramer, 1979; Goldscheider & Waite, 1991; Nakamura & Nakamura, 1994; Smith & Ward, 1980). Aside from constraints on consumption patterns, the presence of children, particularly preschool children, also affects the marital relationship by shifting it toward a more traditional sex-role ideology; a decrease in the wife's labor force participation; an increase in the number of household chores she performs and a decrease in the husband's participation; and an increase in the husband's power (Goldscheider & Waite, 1991; Hoffman & Manis, 1978; LaRossa & LaRossa, 1981; Lloyd, 1975; Rossi, 1968). Other effects of the presence and/or number of children on the marital relationship include decreased spouse companionship and marital satisfaction (Figley, 1973; Glenn & Weaver, 1978; Houseknecht, 1979; Miller, 1976; Polonko, Scanzoni, & Teachman, 1982; Rollins & Galligan, 1978) and decreased parental satisfaction (Marini, 1980; Nye, Carlson, & Farrett, 1970). Although marital satisfaction declines with the advent of children, research suggests that the vast majority of mothers view "being a parent" as a source of high satisfaction (Hoffman & Manis, 1978).

Timing or spacing of children has also been related to consequences for parents, especially with respect to the first birth. Early fertility and premarital fertility have been associated with reduced education for women (Bacon, 1974; Garfinkel & McLanahan, 1986; Pohlman, 1968; Presser, 1971; Upchurch & McCarthy, 1990; Waite & Moore, 1978); rapid subsequent childbearing and higher levels of fertility (Bumpass et al., 1978; Marini & Hodson, 1981; Millman & Hendershot, 1980; Teachman & Heckert, 1985a); economic deprivation and reduced asset accumulation relative to those who delay childbearing (Baldwin, 1976; Coombs & Freedman, 1970; Coombs, Freedman, Freedman, & Pratt, 1970; Freedman & Coombs, 1966a,b; Garfinkel & McLanahan, 1986; Smith & Ward, 1980; Trussell, 1976a); and subsequent marital dissolution (Teachman, 1983; Waite et al., 1985; Waite & Lillard, 1991).

Concerning the consequences of fertility for children, Menken (1972) documented that children of young mothers are more likely to be premature, to have low birth weight, and to have higher rates of mortality. Card (1981) found that children of teenage parents are likely to show relative decrements in academic achievement, are more likely to live in single-parent or stepparent homes, and are more likely to repeat the early marriage, early parent, high-fertility tendencies of their parent or parents.

A useful summary of this research (through the mid-1980s) is provided by Garfinkel and McLanahan (1986). More recent studies and reviews have continued to show a negative relationship between early childbearing a wide range of outcomes for both children and parents (Dubow & Luster, 1990; Furstenberg, 1991; Furstenberg, Brooks-Gunn, & Morgan, 1987; Geronimous, 1991; Moore & Burt, 1987; Moore & Snyder, 1991).

Marital Disruption

The long-term trend in marital disruption in the United States has been upward, whether measured by the number of divorces, by period divorce rates, or by marriage-cohort-specific divorce rates (Preston & McDonald, 1979). With the exception of a brief "divorce boom" following World War II, the upward trend in divorce was gradual until the mid-1960s, when a very steep increase in the divorce rate was observed. The 1950s were a period of relative stability with respect to marital dissolution, with lower than expected divorce rates based on the long-term upward trend, serving to heighten the magnitude of increase observed over the 1960s and 1970s.

Table 10 presents various period indicators of the trend in divorce between 1965 and 1990, showing that divorces went up from approximately 480,000 in 1965 to well over 1 million after 1975. The crude divorce rate increased from 2.5 in 1965 to 5.2 in 1980 and declined slightly to 4.7 in 1990. Relating the number of divorces to the exposed population, estimated by the number of married women age 15 and over, the divorce rate increased from 10.6 in 1965 to 22.6 in 1980, with a slight decline to 20.9 in 1990.

Because marital disruption occurs most often in the early years of marriage, period measures are dependent on

Table 10. Number of Divorces and Divorce Rates per 1000 Married Persons: 1965–1990

Year	Number	Divorce rate	
		Crude[a]	General[b]
1990	1,182,000	4.7	20.9
1988	1,167,000	4.7	20.7
1980	1,189,000	5.2	22.6
1975	1,036,000	4.9	20.3
1970	708,000	3.5	14.9
1965	479,000	2.5	10.6

[a]Rate per 1000 total population.
[b]Rate per 1000 married women ages 15 and over.
Sources: National Center for Health Statistics, 1988. "Advance Report of Final Divorce Statistics, 1991." *Monthly Vital Statistics Reports*, Vol. 40, No. 2 (Supplement), Table 2; U.S. Bureau of the Census (1980). "Marital Status and Living Arrangements: March 1979." *Current Population Reports*, Series P-20, No. 349, Table C. *Statistical Abstract of the United States: 1995*, Table 142. Washington, D.C.: US Government Printing Office.

the distribution of current marriages by duration. Therefore, the steep rise in divorce rates after 1965 could be explained, in part, by the influx of Baby Boom cohorts into marriage, tipping the distribution of marriages toward those with short durations. Components analyses by Michael (1978) and Horiuchi (1979), however, indicate that this was not the case. Also, certain compositional changes have occurred, such as an upward shift in the educational distribution and a rise in age at marriage, which should operate to lower divorce rates as more highly educated individuals and those who marry older are less likely to experience marital dissolution (see the discussion that follows).

Changes have occurred, on the other hand, that could explain increased divorce rates. Although no estimate of their effects is available, a number of factors have been discussed in the literature, including the negative impact of the war in Vietnam on family life (Glick & Norton, 1977; Preston & Richards, 1975); the impact of the welfare system (Bishop, 1980; Cain & Wissoker, 1990; Hannan et al., 1978; Moffitt, 1990; Norton & Glick, 1976; Schultz, 1994); and an increase in the proportion of marriages involving premarital births. However, lower fertility overall has been cited as a contributor to increased divorce rates, as smaller families are associated with greater labor force participation among wives, and hence, financial independence. As sex roles have become more egalitarian and labor force participation rates have risen, women have increased their bargaining power in marriage, including the ultimate threat to dissolve the relationship (Cherlin, 1981; Hannan, Tuma, & Groeneveld, 1977; Hannan et al., 1978; Norton & Glick, 1976; Waite & Lillard, 1991).

Table 11. Percentage of First Marriages Disrupted within 5 Years, by Marriage Cohort: 1960–1985

Marriage/Cohort	Percentage divorced within 5 years
1980–1985[a]	23
1975–1979[a]	22
1970–1974[a]	18
1965–1969[a]	14
1960–1964[a]	11

Sources: [a]Martin and Bumpass (1988), Table 1. National Center for Health Statistics, 1979, "Divorces by Marriage Cohort." Series 21, No. 34, Table 4; [b]National Center for Health Statistics (1980a), "National Estimates of Marriage Dissolution and Survivorship: United States." Series 3, No. 19, Table A.

Another way to measure the trend in marital disruption, one in which a control for marital duration can be made, is to compare the incidence of divorce in successive marriage cohorts (Carlson, 1979; National Center for Health Statistics, 1979, 1980a; Preston & McDonald, 1979; Schoen & Nelson, 1974; Schoen, Greenblatt, & Mielke, 1975). Table 11 presents the percentage of marriage cohorts, married between 1960 and 1985, divorcing within the first year of marriage. Later cohorts show a consistently greater percentage divorced. As suggested by the figures in Table 10, however, the rate at which marital disruption has increased has slowed in the 1980s (and subsequent cohorts may even show a slight decline in the risk of marital dissolution).

The data presented in Tables 10 and 11 refer to divorce alone, as separations are not counted in the national reporting system. However, separations plus divorces constitute a better indicator of marital disruption than does divorce alone (Norton & Glick, 1976; Sweet, 1977), and most analyses based on survey data include separation as a form of marital disruption. Blacks, for instance, are more likely to terminate a marriage through separation than divorce and to take longer to divorce once separated, compared to other groups (Teachman, 1983). Failure to recognize this point and subsequent reliance on divorce statistics alone can lead to incorrect conclusions about differential levels of marital disruption. Upward shifts in marital disruption may also be underestimated by divorces alone, as separations may occur more rapidly than divorces. Liberalized divorce laws, however, may increase divorce rates by shortening the period between separation and divorce and by encouraging divorces among separated couples who might not have otherwise divorced (Schoen et al., 1975), although this effect is likely to be short-lived.

Differentials in Marital Disruption

The notion that there is a modest intergenerational transmission of marital instability has received some attention in the literature (McLanahan, 1988; McLanahan & Bumpass, 1988; Moore & Waite, 1981; Mott & Moore, 1979; Mueller & Pope, 1977; Pope & Mueller, 1976). Axinn & Thornton (1993, 1996) find that most of the intergenerational effects can be traced to the impact of parental marital dissolution on values and attitudes toward marriage and divorce. Children who experience the dissolution of their parent's marriage are more likely to accept divorce as a possible outcome of marriage.

Individuals with less than a high school education experience the highest level of marital dissolution, whereas the lowest level occurs at 4 years of college for women and at 5 years of college for men (Martin & Bumpass, 1989; U.S. Bureau of the Census, 1976b, 1977). Both men and women with 6 or more years of college experience increased rates, although the increase is greatest and the pattern more clear for women, because highly educated women are more likely to have a career and are less financially dependent on their husbands (Houseknecht & Spanier, 1980). Over time, differentials in marital instability according to education level have increased (Martin & Bumpass, 1989).

In multivariate models, the effects of education for either blacks or whites, or for men or women, are generally attenuated or nonsignificant (Becker et al., 1977; Cherlin, 1977; Cutright, 1971b; Hannan et al., 1977; McCarthy, 1978; Mott & Moore, 1979), although stronger among more recent cohorts (Martin & Bumpass, 1989; Teachman, 1986). Individuals with less than a high school education appear to run an exceptionally high risk of marital disruption.

Premarital fertility has been consistently associated with an increased risk of marital disruption (Billy, Landale, & McLaughlin, 1986; Furstenberg, 1976a,b; Martin & Bumpass, 1989; McCarthy & Menken, 1979; Morgan & Rindfuss, 1985; Teachman, 1983; U.S. Bureau of the Census, 1976c). An early marriage combined with a premarital birth represents a set of characteristics related to very high levels of marital instability (Teachman, 1983).

The risk of marital disruption declines sharply from marriage during the teen years to marriages in the early 20s and thereafter tends to level off (Martin & Bumpass, 1989; South & Spitze, 1986; Teachman, 1983, 1986; Thornton & Rodgers, 1987). This general pattern appears to be true for both males and females and blacks and whites. Carter and Glick (1976), however, noted that the risk of marital disruption for women marrying after age 30 is greater than that for women marrying in their early to mid-20s. This difference reflects the greater likelihood that women who marry at an older age will have some postgraduate education and therefore a career (Glick & Norton, 1977). Results from multivariate analyses indicate that the extent to which early marriage increases marital disruption is greater for white women than for blacks or for men (Becker et al., 1977; Teachman, 1983, 1986).

Evidence suggests that Catholics, controlling for other factors, are slightly less likely to divorce or separate than are Protestants (Teachman, 1983, 1986), although the difference is small in comparison to differences observed for other variables. In addition, religiosity, measured as the frequency of church attendance or communion, has been related to marital disruption. If one controls for religious affiliation and other variables, more religious individuals are less likely to divorce or separate (Ross & Sawhill, 1975; Teachman, 1983, 1986).

Blacks experience the highest rate of marital dissolution, followed by whites, and then other racial/ethnic groups. In multivariate analyses, the black–white difference in marital instability is reduced slightly but remains considerable (Billy et al., 1986; Houseknecht & Spanier, 1980; Martin & Bumpass, 1989; Moore & Waite, 1981; Ross & Sawhill, 1975; Teachman, 1983, 1986). A full accounting of racial and ethnic differences is complex, however, as the same factors do not always affect marital dissolution for each racial or ethnic group, and common factors are often of varying importance (McCarthy & Menken, 1979; Moore & Waite, 1981; Mott & Moore, 1979; Pope & Mueller, 1976; Teachman, 1983, 1986).

Heterogamous marriages are more likely to experience marital dissolution than homogamous marriages (Becker, 1977; Cherlin, 1977; Norton & Glick, 1976; Teachman, 1983). Differences with the largest effects include interfaith marriages where one spouse is Catholic; marriages involving considerable age differences between spouses, especially if the wife is older; and interracial marriages. Heterogamy raises the likelihood of marital disruption more among whites than among blacks (Teachman, 1983, 1986). The reason is not clear, but it may be that problems associated with heterogamy are less salient in a population where rates of marital disruption are high because of low education and unstable financial conditions. Huber and Spitze (1980), looking at the probability of having ever thought about divorce, also found that heterogamy has little effect on wives but is much more likely to spur husbands to consider divorce.

Greater income of the husband has been related to greater marital stability (Becker et al., 1977; Cutright, 1971b; Martin & Bumpass, 1989; Mott & Moore, 1979; South & Spitze, 1986), although at least one study has reported no significant effect (Ross & Sawhill, 1975). A more important factor appears to be the husband's history of unemployment or earnings trajectory. Husbands with a history of unemployment or earnings that are below those for men with comparable market resources are the most likely to experience marital dissolution (Cherlin, 1979; Ross & Sawhill, 1975; Teachman et al., 1991). For women, higher earnings and labor force participation have been related to greater marital instability, as their greater economic resources make them less financially dependent on their husbands (Cherlin, 1977, 1978; Mott & Moore, 1979; Ross & Sawhill, 1975; Spitze & South,

1985). This has been called the independence effect. Other research has found that labor force participation by itself often acts to reduce the risk of divorce, likely because the additional income reduces financial stress experienced by the family (Greenstein, 1989; South & Spitze, 1986). This has been called the income effect. Hannan et al. (1977, 1978) provide a good discussion of the potentially offsetting nature of income and independence effects.

Overall, the evidence suggests that economic factors are most important when a family's financial condition varies across time. Even at low income levels, marital disruption is not higher than expected if consistent financial and employment conditions have been maintained (Cherlin, 1979; Ross & Sawhill, 1975). The failure to measure economic changes within the family in an adequate fashion may explain why income measures have traditionally explained less variance in marital stability than have factors such as age at marriage and premarital fertility (Mott & Moore, 1979).

Studies using census data to study the effects of level of public assistance benefits on marital dissolution have had contradictory results, with some studies finding a positive association (Hannan et al., 1977, 1978; Honig, 1973; Moles, 1976; Ross & Sawhill, 1975) and others finding no relationship (Cain & Wissoker, 1990; Cutright & Scanzoni, 1973). A recent study by Schultz (1994) finds that welfare programs reduce the likelihood of marriage. However, the size of the effect, while statistically significant, is modest. A review of many of these findings is provided by Bishop (1980) and Moffitt (1990).

Analyses of separation ratios or proportions of women who head families may be biased because public assistance payments may influence such measures not by inducing separation or divorce, but by slowing the process of remarriage. For example, Bane (1975) found no association between average welfare payments per recipient and ever having been divorced. However, she did find that higher welfare payments were related to a lower probability that divorced or widowed men and women had remarried. Moffitt (1994) finds that welfare benefits are negatively related to female headship when a model is estimated that allows for geographic-specific effects.

Though several studies have used longitudinal data to focus on the probability of separation or divorce over some period of time, consistent findings have not appeared, as several studies have reached different conclusions about the existence of an association, even using the same data (see the debate between Cain & Wissoker, 1990, and Hannan & Tuma, 1990, based on separate analyses of data from the Seattle–Denver Income Maintenance Experiment).

Moles (1979) and Bishop (1980) have argued that the evidence is not sufficient to support a relationship between public assistance programs and marital disruption, especially a strong relationship. However, he also noted that no study has been conducted using a set of data specifically designed to test the hypothesis of a direct relationship. In addition, no study has adequately addressed the potential reciprocal relationship between public assistance programs and marital disruption.

Becker et al. (1977) present what appear to be the first estimates of the impact of marital fertility on marital stability. Their results suggest that both younger children and fewer children act to inhibit marital dissolution, whereas greater numbers of children may act to increase marital instability. Similar results are presented by Waite et al. (1989). In perhaps the most definitive work on the subject, Waite and Lillard (1991) find that firstborn children decrease marital instability at least until they begin school. Subsequent children decrease marital stability only when they are very young. Older children actually seem to increase the risk of marital dissolution. The net result of having children, when balancing the opposite effects of having young versus older children, appears to decrease slightly the risk of marital disruption when compared to childless couples.

The influence of previous life-course events on marital disruption is visible from the importance of differences observed by age at marriage and premarital fertility. For instance, women who marry young or who have a premarital birth are subject to an increased risk of marital disruption. Preston and McDonald (1979) also found that divorce within a marriage cohort is greater than expected following periods of armed service mobilization, an event that typically alters the life course of males. A similar finding is reported by Pavalko and Elder (1990). Hogan (1978b, 1980) reported that men who have nonnormative sequencing of major life-course events (schooling, then job, then marriage as a normative sequence) are more likely to experience marital dissolution, as societal institutions are not geared to nonnormative sequencing patterns, and a variety of role conflicts may therefore occur among those who deviate from the norm. Similar arguments can be constructed to apply to individuals who follow normative sequencing but who time or space events in a nonnormative fashion.

One of the more recent and strongest findings is that premarital cohabitation is related to an increased risk of union dissolution. That is, nonmarital unions are more likely to dissolve than marital unions (Teachman et al., 1991) and marital unions preceded by a spell of nonmarital cohabitation are more likely to end than marital unions not preceded by nonmarital cohabitation (Axinn & Thornton, 1992; Bennett, Blanc, & Bloom, 1988; Schoen, 1992; Teachman et al., 1991; Thomson & Colella, 1992). There is some evidence to suggest, however, that the negative impact of premarital cohabitation on marital stability may be declining in more recent marriage cohorts (DeMaris & Rao, 1992; Schoen, 1992; Teachman & Polonko, 1990).

A variety of additional factors have also been found to influence marital disruption. For instance, whites who experience multiple marriages are more likely to divorce than couples in their first marriages (Becker et al., 1977; Cherlin, 1977; Martin & Bumpass, 1989; McCarthy, 1978; Teachman, 1986; U.S. Bureau of the Census, 1976b, 1977), but the converse is less likely to be true for blacks (McCarthy, 1978; Teachman, 1986). Moreover, the factors associated with the disruption of first marriages do not appear to be the same as those associated with the disruption of subsequent marriages (McCarthy, 1978; Teachman, 1986). Cherlin (1978) noted that second and subsequent marriages may involve problems of childrearing and kinship interaction that produce stress not found in first marriages. Overall, blacks are less likely to remarry than are whites; however, this may indicate a greater selectivity in spouses or greater difficulty in finding an acceptable spouse.

Rates of marital dissolution also vary according to urban–rural, farm–nonfarm, and regional residence (Carter & Glick, 1976; Glenn & Shelton, 1985; Houseknecht & Spanier, 1980; Moore & Waite, 1981; Mott & Moore, 1979; Ross & Sawhill, 1975). In general, urban residence, a nonfarm background, and residence in a western state are all related to higher rates of marital instability. Commonly, the differentials by geographic location are not large but remain significant.

Research in the past decade has linked a variety of additional factors to marital instability. Factors found to increase the risk of marital disruption include aggregate economic conditions (South, 1985), sex ratios indicating an abundance of women (Trent & South, 1989), lack of social integration (Glenn & Shelton, 1985), and the availability of potential spouses (South & Lloyd, 1995).

Consequences

As discussed elsewhere in this chapter, marital instability has played a significant role in changing the structure of U.S. households over time (Cherlin, 1991; Masnick & Bane, 1980; Sweet & Bumpass, 1988), in conjunction with other processes such as the availability and choice of housing alternatives and remarriage. Marital disruption and changes in household structure are also reshaping the socialization experiences of American youth. Bumpass and Rindfuss (1979), using data from the 1973 National Survey of Family Growth, indicated that one-third of all children spent a portion of their lives in a single-parent home, with an average duration of 4½ years. For blacks, the numbers involved are even greater. Using more recent data (1980 Current Population Survey), Bumpass (1984) estimated that 40% of all children would experience the divorce of their parents, and when premarital fertility is considered, 50% of all children will spend part of their lives in a single parent family. Numerous studies have documented the negative consequences of marital dissolution on both the short-term and long-term well-being of children (Amato & Keith, 1991; Amato, Spencer, & Booth, 1995; Astone & McLanahan, 1991; Axinn & Thornton, 1996; Cherlin, 1991; Cherlin et al., 1995; Goldscheider & Waite, 1991; Furstenberg, Hoffman, & Shrestha, 1995; McLanahan & Sandefur, 1994; Thomson, Hanson, & McLanahan, 1994).

Marital disruption is also closely related to the economic status of women. Separated and divorced women suffer a considerable drop in income from married levels (Burkhauser, Duncan, Hauser, & Berntsen, 1991; Duncan & Hoffman, 1985; Hoffman, 1977; Holden & Smock, 1991; Smock, 1994). A similar drop in income is not observed for men. This drop in income and the relative disadvantage experienced by women in the labor force may help to explain the usually high rates of remarriage and the higher labor force participation rates of separated and divorced women. A growing body of literature has implicated marital disruption in the poverty experienced by women and children (Bane, 1986; Bane & Ellwood, 1989; Cherlin, 1988; Duncan & Rodgers, 1988, 1991; Eggebeen & Lichter, 1991; Garfinkel & McLanahan, 1986; McLanahan, 1985; McLanahan & Garfinkel, 1989; Wilson & Neckerman, 1986).

Many studies have also noted the lower fertility of ever-divorced compared to continuously married women. Thornton (1978) showed that this deficit in fertility for ever-divorced women is not found at the time of separation and therefore results from lower fertility after separation and during the period between divorce and remarriage. Cohen and Sweet (1974) also attributed the fertility deficit of ever-divorced women to time lost in the married state. Levin and O'Hara (1978) expanded on these results by showing that the fertility of remarried women depends on the prior fertility history of the second husband, with higher fertility occurring if the woman marries a man with no children of his own. Rindfuss and Bumpass (1977) also showed that fertility between marriages varies according to the social and economic characteristics of the women; that is, women who are less educated, are of lower parity, are younger, and are black are more likely to have children between marriages.

Remarriage

The trend in remarriage, while upward over the 1960s, has been downward since 1970. As shown in Table 12, the rate of remarriage (remarriage per 1000 widowed and divorced women age 14 and over) declined from 66.8 in 1970 to 43.1 in 1987. Glick and Norton (1977) estimated that, in the recent past, about 80% of people ever divorced remarried,

Table 12. Median Age at Remarriage, Difference between Median Age at First Marriage and Remarriage and Remarriage Rates: 1970–1988

Year	Median age at remarriage		Difference[a]		Rate[b]
	Male	Female	Male	Female	
1987	37.7	34.1	12.4	10.5	43.1
1980	35.2	32.0	11.6	10.2	49.0
1975	35.5	32.0	12.8	11.2	62.8
1970	37.5	33.3	12.0	12.7	66.8

[a]Calculated as difference between median age at first marriage and median age at remarriage.
[b]Remarriages per 1000 widowed and divorced women ages 15 and over.
Source: Various issues of *Monthly Vital Statistics Reports*, National Center for Health Statistics. Washington, D.C.: Government Printing Office.

although this figure may be now closer to 70–75% and varies according to sociodemographic characteristics (Sweet, 1973a; Sweet & Bumpass, 1988; Thornton, 1975). Given high levels of disruption of first marriages, however, over 50% of marriages in the United States now involve at least one partner that was previously married (Sweet & Bumpass, 1988).

Other indicators of change in remarriage are also presented in Table 12. The median age at remarriage declined between 1970 and 1980, to 35.2 years for males and 32.0 years for females. After 1980, the trend reversed, with the median age at remarriage increasing to 37.7 for males and 34.1 for females. These values are greater than those observed for 1970 and reflect the continuing decline in the likelihood of remarriage over the 1980s.

Between 1970 and 1980, the difference between median age at remarriage and median age at first marriage also declined, from 15.0 to 11.6 years for males and from 12.7 to 10.2 years for females. Once again, though, this trend reversed in the 1980s as rates of remarriage declined. By 1987 the difference between median age at remarriage and median age at remarriage increased to 12.4 for males and 10.5 for females.

Differentials in Remarriage

Unlike marital disruption, remarriage has received relatively little attention in the literature, despite the growing numbers of those eligible to remarry (Glick & Lin, 1986; Norton & Moorman, 1987). Therefore, differentials with respect to remarriage are not as well documented, especially when examined in a multivariate framework. In part, this lack of research stems from less adequate data (Sweet, 1977). Census data, for instance, provide no information on the timing of remarriage after separation or divorce or on characteristics of individuals at the time of marital disruption and remarriage. Basically, the same limitations apply to data gathered in the vital statistics registration system. Most of the information on remarriage differentials thus comes from surveys.

Males tend to remarry more than women (Glick & Norton, 1977; Sweet, 1973a; Sweet & Bumpass, 1988), although the remarriage probabilities of women are strongly affected by the presence or absence of children (Spanier & Glick, 1980b). Becker et al. (1977) found that women without children are actually more likely to remarry than men, suggesting that the customary awarding of child custody to wives plays a role in affecting their remarriage probabilities. Research by Koo and Suchindran (1980) and Teachman and Heckert (1985a) also indicates that the effects of the presence of children on remarriage are dependent on the woman's age at divorce, with childless women being more likely to remarry if they divorce before age 25 and less likely to remarry if they divorce after age 35. The presence or absence of children appears to have little effect on the remarriage chances of women who divorce between ages 25 and 34. Remarriage among women is also affected by their age at marital disruption and widowhood, with younger women and women who divorce being more likely to remarry (Becker et al., 1977; Smock, 1990; Spanier & Glick, 1980b; Sweet, 1973a; Teachman & Heckert, 1985a).

Hispanics are the most likely to remarry and to do so quickly, followed by whites and then blacks (National Center for Health Statistics, 1980c; Sweet & Bumpass, 1988). Blacks especially are more likely to remain separated, lowering their remarriage probability and increasing the length of time between marriages. Even controlling for the greater reliance on separation versus divorce for marital disruption, blacks are less likely to remarry and take longer to do so (Hannan et al., 1977; McCarthy & Menken, 1979; Spanier & Glick, 1980b). Furthermore, Hannan and colleagues (1977) noted significant differences in the impact of income maintenance on the probabilities of remarriage. Specifically, income transfers significantly delay remarriage among Hispanics, act to hasten remarriage among blacks, and have no significant pattern among whites.

Men with higher incomes are more likely to remarry than men with less income (Becker et al., 1977; Sweet, 1973a), although Wolf and MacDonald (1979), considering several indicators of male income, including current earnings, earnings stability, income relative to other men, and permanent income, found that only permanent income has a significant net positive effect on the probability of remarriage. Most of the discussion has centered on the income of males, although some concern about the effects of income transfers focuses on women (Hannan et al., 1977).

Census data indicate that men with higher education, income, and job status are more likely to remarry after divorce, whereas the converse is true for women (Carter & Glick, 1976). Among women, those with an early age at first marriage, an early first birth, and no illegitimate births have a greater likelihood of remarriage (McCarthy & Menken, 1979; Spanier & Glick, 1980b; Teachman & Heckert, 1985a). Education generally shows little association with the rate of remarriage for women, with the exception that divorced black women with less than a high school degree are particularly unlikely to remarry (Smock, 1990).

Consequences

As a demographic event, remarriage plays an important role in altering households and families. It acts to combine households—often separate families—into a single unit. As mentioned in the section on marital disruption, remarriage plays an important role in determining the size and the growth of the separated and divorced population. Remarriage also acts to change the economic situation and the living conditions of husbands, wives, and children (Bane, 1986; Duncan & Rodgers, 1988, 1991). Depending on its timing and earlier life-course transitions, remarriage can affect fertility and child spacing. Cherlin (1978, 1981) and Furstenberg (1979) have noted that remarriage implies consequences for patterns of kinship terminology, childrearing responsibilities, and the structure of interaction across split families. As noted earlier, these factors may be related to the higher rate of marital disruption among second and subsequent marriages than among first marriages.

Recent research has documented that remarriage does not provide the same level of well-being for children as does living with both biological parents (Astone & McLanahan, 1991; McLanahan & Sandefur, 1994; Sandefur, McLanahan, & Wojtkiewicz, 1992). For example, children in stepfamilies are less likely to graduate from high school and are more likely to experience a premarital birth. What is not clear is whether remarriage causes such reductions in child well-being or is simply an indicator of preexisting problems.

Household Size and Composition

Over time, the United States has experienced considerable variation in household and family structure. To some extent, changes in household and family structure can be predicted by changes in the age-sex-marital status structure, which, in turn, is a product of change in fertility and mortality. Much of the long-term decline in household size is due to the fertility and mortality declines occurring since the early nineteenth century. On the other hand, discretionary shifts in living arrangements, such as those associated with divorce or remarriage, have also had an impact, especially after World War II.

Kobrin (1973, 1976a,b) has outlined the historical decline in size of households. Fertility decline has reduced household size by decreasing the proportion of large units, and falling mortality has meant that more husband–wife couples survive past their childbearing years, increasing the proportion of small units. Fertility and mortality declines have also acted together to increase the proportion of small units by lowering the age at which the couples bear their last child and by lengthening the "empty-nest" stage in the life course. Over time, separated and divorced persons have been less likely to return to their parents' home and have been more likely to set up separate households. Smaller units have also increased because of the upward trend in marital disruption and have increased in periods during which there is greater delay in marriage. Since about 1950, another trend has emerged, the rise of primary individuals (most of whom live alone), leading to an increase in the proportion of single-member households (Kobrin, 1976a; Pampel, 1983).

Table 13 illustrates the fall in household size between 1960 and 1994. Both the number of children and the number of adults per household and per family have declined since 1960. The decline in the number of children per household is particularly dramatic, falling from an average of 1.2 to an average of about 0.7. This is the result of two processes: the continuing decline in fertility since the Baby Boom and the increasing proportion of nonfamily households. The decline in the number of adults per household largely reflects the increasing propensity for living alone among those who are single, separated, divorced, or widowed.

Table 13 also shows the change in family size between 1960 and 1994. The mean number of adults per family has remained constant from 1960 to 1994 at approximately 2.2 persons. However, the mean number of children per family has declined from 1.4 to slightly less than 1.0.

Treas (1981) also found that changes in mean family size have varied according to family type, age of family head, and race. Husband–wife families are larger than female-headed families, which, in turn, are larger than male-headed families. Since about 1950, however, female-headed families have been converging with the average husband–wife family size, while diverging from the average male-headed family size. This shift has occurred as declines in adult members in female-headed families have been largely offset by increases in children. Families characterized by the age of the head have also varied differentially, with younger-headed families being more affected by trends in fertility and older-headed families being more affected by the consistent decline in adult members. Black families have begun to converge with mean white family size because of their greater fertility decline in recent years. This decline was preceded by a period of divergence during the Baby Boom, however, as blacks increased their fertility more than whites. Racial differences in family size have not been strongly affected by the decline in adult members.

As mentioned earlier, household size has been affected by changes in household type (see Table 14). In 1970, over 81% of households were family households, and about 70% were husband–wife households. By 1994, about 71% of households were family households, and only about 55% were husband–wife households, as single-parent families and nonfamily households gained an increased share of the total number of households. Over these 2 decades, the absolute number of family households increased 33%, husband–wife families 19%, and all other categories over 100%. Of the growth in new households over the decade, about 50% were family households, but only 25% were husband–wife families. In other words, nearly 80% of the increase in households between 1970 and 1994 were due to nontraditional family and nonfamily units. Almost 20% of the increment in households was attributable to newly formed female-headed families. The largest proportion of the increase in new households, however, stemmed from the creation of nonfamily households, most of which involved persons living alone.

The growth in female-headed families over the past 2 decades is particularly noteworthy. As just noted, nearly one in five new households formed since 1970 was headed by a single woman. Increasingly, female headship also involves younger women and children (Garfinkel & McLanahan, 1986; Ross & Sawhill, 1975; Wojtkiewicz et al., 1990). Female-headed families containing children have been growing half again as fast as all families headed by women. Furthermore, nonwhite female-headed families have grown more rapidly than white families headed by women (Bianchi, 1980, 1981; Bianchi & Spain, 1986).

The economic position of families headed by women has consistently declined, relative to husband–wife families,

Table 13. Average Number of Persons per Household and per Family, by Age: 1960–1994

	Households			Families		
Year	All ages	Age < 18	Age ≥ 18	All ages	Age < 18	Age ≥ 18
1994	2.67	0.72	1.95	3.20	0.99	2.21
1990	2.63	0.69	1.94	3.17	0.96	2.21
1980	2.76	0.79	1.97	3.28	1.05	2.23
1970	3.14	1.09	2.05	3.58	1.34	2.25
1960	3.33	1.21	2.12	3.67	1.41	2.26

Source: U.S. Bureau of the Census (1994). "Households and Families by Type: March 1994." *Current Population Reports*, Series P-20, No. 483, Table A-1. Washington, D.C.: US Government Printing Office.

Table 14. Change in Households by Type: 1970–1994

Household type	Percentage by year			Percentage change[a]	Percentage of total increase[b]
	1994	1980	1970		
Family households	70.5	73.7	81.2	33.1	50.5
Married couple	54.8	60.8	70.5	18.9	25.0
Male head, spouse absent	3.0	2.1	1.9	137.2	5.0
Female head, spouse absent	12.8	10.8	8.7	120.1	20.5
Nonfamily households	29.5	26.3	18.8	139.6	49.5
Male householder	12.8	10.9	6.4	206.7	24.9
Female householder	16.6	15.4	12.4	105.0	24.5
Persons living alone	24.3	22.7	17.1	117.6	37.9

[a]Percentage change in household type between 1970 and 1994.
[b]Percentage of total increase in households between 1970 and 1994 according to household type.
Sources: U.S. Bureau of the Census (1991). "Households and Family Characteristics: March 1991." *Current Population Reports*, Series P-20, No. 458, Tables B. "Households and Family Characteristics: March 1994." Current Population Reports P-20, No. 483, Table A.

for both blacks and whites (Bianchi, 1980; Garfinkel & McLanahan, 1986; McLanahan & Garfinkel, 1989). Table 15 illustrates the economically disadvantaged status associated with female headship in a comparison with all other families from 1975 to 1990. Female-headed families are more likely to exist in poverty, irrespective of age of head, presence or absence of children, and employment status. In 1990, families headed by females were over five times as likely to be under the poverty line as all other families. In 1959, this ratio was just under three times, reflecting the more rapid exodus from poverty by families not headed by women. Table 15 also indicates that female headship accompanied by children is a particularly disadvantaged status.

Controlling for population growth alone, the major contributor to the increase in female-headed families with children was increased marital separation and divorce involving children, followed by illegitimacy (Garfinkel & McLanahan, 1986; Wojtkiewicz et al., 1990). More specifically, increased marital dissolution has increased the proportion of female-headed families, a process not matched by remarriage or other factors. Although widows make up a large (but declining) proportion of female-headed families, widowhood has declined over time as an important growth mechanism. Similarly, changes in the propensity for spouse-absent women to create new households has not been an important factor in the growth of female-headed families. Although these conclusions on female-headed families hold for both blacks and whites, illegitimacy is a significant difference between the races, as illegitimacy is a more important source of female headship among blacks.

Primary Individuals

Even more dramatic than the growth in female headship of families has been the growth in nonfamily households (see Table 14). Persons living alone accounted for over 85% of nonfamily households in 1994 and were responsible for some 42% of the growth in households over the past 2 decades. Females are more likely to head a nonfamily household than are males, but male-headed nonfamily households have been the most rapidly growing category of households in recent years.

Nonfamily households are created by several processes. Although a detailed components analysis of the relative effects of each of these processes has not been conducted, it is known that headship rates among those eligible to form nonfamily households have increased over time, and therefore,

Table 15. Percentage of Families under the Poverty Line by Household Type: 1975–1992

Household type	Percentage by year		
	1990[a]	1985[b]	1975[c]
Headed by female	33.4	34.0	32.5
Ages 25–44	39.0	40.5	40.8
Age 65 and over	13.3	13.3	12.7
No children	9.6	10.3	7.5
With children	44.5	45.4	44.0
All other families	6.0	7.0	6.2
Ages 25–44	6.6	7.3	5.3
Age 65 and over	5.0	6.0	8.3
No children	3.8	4.8	4.9
With children	8.4	9.2	7.3

[a]U.S. Bureau of the Census (1991). "Poverty in the U.S. 1990." Series P-60, No. 175, Table 18.
[b]U.S. Bureau of the Census (1987). "Poverty in the U.S. 1985." Series P-60, No. 158, Table 15.
[c]U.S. Bureau of the Census (1977). "Poverty in the U.S. 1975." Series P-60, No. 106, Table 20. Washington, D.C.: US Government Printing Office.

the growth in these units cannot be explained by changes in age-sex-marital status structure alone (Kobrin, 1976a; Masnick & Bane, 1980; Santi, 1988).

Studies of the socioeconomic determinants of living alone suggest shifts in either income or tastes as reasonable explanations for the growth in single living (Beresford & Rivin, 1966; Carlinger, 1975; Chevan & Korson, 1972; Goldscheider & Waite, 1991; Kobrin, 1981; Leppel, 1987; Michael, Fuchs, & Scott, 1980; Pampel, 1983; Santi, 1988; Troll, 1971). In an analysis of the proportions of persons living alone among never-married males and females ages 25–34 and widows age 65 and over, using 1970 state-level data, Michael et al. (1980) found income to be an important predictor. Using results from their cross-sectional model, they also found changes in the propensity to live alone between 1950 and 1976 could be largely explained by changes in income. A similar analysis by Pampel (1983), using individual-level data from the 1960 and 1970 U.S. Censuses and the 1976 Current Population Survey, supports the notion that income shifts have allowed or prompted more persons to live alone, controlling for other factors like age, education, labor force participation, and race. Pampel's study, however, which was not restricted by age and used a series of cross-sections, found a significant upward shift in single living between 1960 and 1976 that could not be explained by income shifts or shifts in any of the other variables considered, possibly reflecting an increased taste for living alone.

A third study, by Kobrin (1981), used 1970 U.S. Census data to determine factors associated with living with non-family members (including living alone) as opposed to living in a family. Consistent with the research described earlier, greater income was related to a greater propensity to live away from family members, even when controls for other variables were introduced. Additional findings from this study include: (1) never-married persons were more likely to live with kin with ever-married persons; (2) males were more likely to live with unrelated household members or by themselves than were females; (3) males and females "aged" differently with respect to living arrangements, as males moved away from kin more abruptly; (4) the availability of kin reduced the propensity to live alone or with unrelated individuals; and (5) the effects of marital status and income on the propensity to live away from kin did not vary by age.

A more recent study has documented the positive effect of income on the formation of independent households, including living alone (Santi, 1988). Consistent with Pampel's (1983) results, however, Santi found that changes in income could not fully explain the rise in the propensity to form independent households over the 1970–1980 period. After 1980, however, net of income and other factors, rates of headship have actually declined. While these results are consistent with first an increase and then a decrease in tastes for independent living, Santi suggested other factors, such as

increased costs of housing, that have been responsible for the decline in rates of headship after 1980. In the past few years, a number of the researchers have documented a wide range of factors individuals take into account when making decisions about living arrangements (Aquilino, 1991; Avery et al., 1992; Goldscheider & DaVanzo, 1985, 1989). These factors include income, personal tastes, housing costs, employment opportunities, parental resources, and contemporaneous roles.

Living Arrangements of Children

The 1970s and 1980s was a period of change in children's living arrangements, as shown in Table 16. The percentage of children living with two parents dropped by 16 percentage points, from 85.2% to 69.2%. For black children, the figures are even more striking, with less than half living with two parents (Garfinkel & McLanahan, 1986; Glick & Norton, 1977; Sweet & Bumpass, 1988). An increasing percentage of children are therefore living with one parent, usually the mother. In 1994, over one-fifth of all children lived with their mother only.

The changing living arrangements of children is a result of the changing living arrangements of adults. Marital disruption, remarriage, and nonmarital fertility are all factors involved in this process. Since 1960, marital disruption, operating at a rate greater than that of remarriage, has been the most important contributor to shifting children out of two-parent families (Garfinkel & McLanahan, 1986; Ross & Sawhill, 1975; Wojtkiewicz et al., 1990). Among blacks, however, nonmarital fertility has also played an important role (Bumpass & McLanahan, 1989).

Cohabitation

Although they represent a small percentage of all households (see Table 17), cohabiting couples are an increasingly common occurrence (Bumpass & Sweet, 1989, 1991; Cherlin,

Table 16. Living Arrangements of Children (Age < 18): 1970–1994

Living with	Percentage by year				
	1994	1990	1989	1980	1970
Two parents	69.2	72.5	73.1	76.7	85.2
One parent	26.7	24.7	24.3	19.7	11.9
Mother only	23.5	21.6	21.5	18.0	10.8
Father only	3.2	3.1	2.8	1.7	1.1
Other relatives	3.1	2.2	2.1	3.1	2.2
Nonrelatives	1.0	0.5	0.4	0.6	0.7

Sources: U.S. Bureau of Census (1990). "Marital Status and Living Arrangements: March 1989." *Current Population Reports*, Series P-20, No. 445 Table C. *Current Population Reports*, Series P-20, No. 484, Table A-5. Washington, D.C.: US Government Printing Office.

Table 17. Adults Living as Unmarried Couples: 1970–1994

Subject	Year			
	1994	1989[a]	1979[b]	1970[b]
Percentage of all households	3.8	4.2	1.7	0.8
Percentage unmarried couples with children present	34.7	31.0	26.7	37.5
Percentage unmarried couples with male householder	56.2	60.3	63.5	50.9
Percentage unmarried couples with female householder	43.8	39.7	36.5	49.1

[a]U.S. Bureau of the Census, 1990. "Marital Status and Living Arrangements: March 1989." Current Population Reports, Series P-20, No. 445, Table 8.

[b]U.S. Bureau of the Census, 1980. "Marital Status and Living Arrangements: March 1979." Current Population Reports, Series P-20, No. 349, Table E. Washington, D.C.: U.S. Government Printing Office.

1981; Glick & Spanier, 1980; Macklin, 1978; Sweet & Bumpass, 1988; Thornton, 1988). In 1970, unmarried heterosexual couples made up less than 1% of all households. By 1994, approximately 4% of all households were unmarried heterosexual couples, a quadrupling of the 1970 percentage. The percentage of such couples with children has declined over time, from about 38% in 1970 to 35% in 1994, although the figure for 1994 is well above that for 1979, indicating a reversal in the trend toward young, never-married couples in the cohabiting population.

These figures, because they represent proportions at two points in time, considerably underestimate the proportion of individuals who ever experience cohabitation. In a national study of men ages 20–30 in 1975, for instance, Clayton and Voss (1977) found that 18% had lived with a woman to whom they were not married. More recently, using data from the National Survey of Families and Households, Bumpass and Sweet (1989) found that about 50% of respondents in their early 30s and 50% of recent marriage cohorts have cohabited. Indeed, the growth in cohabitation has been so great that it has largely offset the sharp decline in marriage that has occurred over the past 2 decades. That is, young persons are entering into intimate, coresidential unions at about the same rate as 2 decades ago—the difference being that the first union is today more likely to be nonmarital (Bumpass & Sweet, 1989, 1991; Thornton, 1988).

Knowledge about cohabitation before 1970 is virtually nonexistent, but Glick and Spanier's (1980) data for the 1970s suggest that it involves at least two distinct groups of couples. The first group consists of better-educated, younger, and never-married couples who apparently try cohabitation as a temporary alternative to marriage or as a transitional stage before marriage. A second group is made up of less well-educated, older couples in which at least one of the partners has been previously married. Bumpass and Sweet

(1989) report that the second group is the most prevalent. While popular opinion may suggest cohabitation is a trend set by college students, Bumpass and Sweet report that cohabitation is greater for individuals with less education whose family received welfare while growing up and who did not grow up in an intact family.

Consequences

The changes in household size and composition considered here—as well as others not given specific attention, such as the timing of the move of younger adults out of the parental household (Carter & Glick, 1976; Duncan & Morgan, 1976; Goldscheider & DaVanzo, 1985, 1989; Goldscheider & Waite, 1991; Hill & Hill, 1976; Kobrin & Goldscheider, 1978; Sweet, 1971)—imply a variety of different consequences. Most obvious is that if present trends continue, individuals will continue to experience increasingly different household and family environments during their lifetimes. This experience will serve to further distinguish various birth cohorts of individuals, as each has tended to experience these changes in household and family-living arrangements differently, and it will therefore acts to exacerbate existing forms of age segregation (Masnick & Bane, 1980). These different family environments may also serve to alter the role of families in providing satisfying personal relationships, and thus may enhance the importance of nonfamily relationships (Cherlin, 1981; Goldscheider & Waite, 1991). It is probable that completely new lifestyles will continue to emerge as alternatives to the traditional husband–wife family.

Changes in household size and composition also mean changes in the demand for housing and other goods and services. Over the past few decades, the number of households has grown much more rapidly than the total population, spurring the demand for housing. Shifts in household type and declines in household size have also altered the type of housing that is in demand. In addition, greater pressure may be put on government to supply various services, such as childcare, medical care, welfare, and other forms of support traditionally supplied by families.

There is emerging evidence that household structure is closely related to income and housing inequality (Bianchi, 1981; Kuznets, 1976, 1978). Research has also indicated a link between the living arrangements of individuals and their mental and physical health status, as well as levels of mortality (Hughes & Gove, 1981; Kobrin & Hendershot, 1977; McLanahan & Sorenson, 1985; Pearlin & Johnson, 1977). Increasingly, differences in household size and composition are being related to cross-national differences in culture, development, and modernization processes (Burch, 1980; Kuznets, 1976, 1978; Young, 1975). Other research has documented intergenerational consequences of the living arrangements of parents for children's overall well-being and the decisions they make about household living arrangements (Axinn & Thornton, 1996; Garfinkel & McLanahan, 1986; McLanahan, 1988; McLanahan & Bumpass, 1988).

Conclusion

The past several decades have witnessed a substantial change in the demography of the family. Following an all-time low, the 1970s saw a tremendous increase in age at marriage and the percentage never married, primarily involving cohorts born after 1945. These increases have placed the percentage never married among younger women consistent with pre-1940 levels and have occurred at rates greater than ever before experienced in this century (Masnick & Bane, 1980). Similarly impressive increases have occurred in the labor force participation of women of all marital statuses and ages, but particularly among women during their prime childbearing years. These changes have been characterized as a "revolution" in female labor market activity and point to women's growing commitment to paid employment.

Not surprisingly, given the strong interconnections between employment and fertility, significant declines in actual and expected fertility have also taken place, with significant increases in the proportion of women expecting to have one child or to remain childless permanently. There have also been notable increases in the postponement of childbearing, in the use of more effective methods of birth control, and in the percentage of births planned. Congruent with the greater bipolar tendency for women to remain either in or out of the labor force, at least in the short run, there is also tentative evidence of an increasing bipolar tendency among women either to engage in lengthier postponement and have fewer children or to have premarital births or pregnancies. Overall, the events of marriage and childbearing are becoming increasingly disassociated (Modell et al., 1978).

Although the changes in these areas have been considerable, the upsurge in divorce as well as in remarriage has been even more widespread during this period. Also, in contrast to other areas, such as age at marriage, increases in divorce over the past several decades have been greater than long-term historical trends would predict (Cherlin, 1981). Projected estimates for the marriage cohorts of the early 1970s to the mid-1970s indicate that close to 50% of marriages will end in divorce, with most individuals also remarrying. Moreover, changes in the timing of divorce and remarriage imply an increasing concentration of marital life-course events.

Finally, to a large extent, changes in all of these areas are reflected in changes in household composition. As Masnick and Bane (1980) stated, "the once typical household—

two parents and children, with a husband-breadwinner and a wife-homemaker—has faded in prominence" (p. 95). The increase in nonfamily households—including, for instance, the growing number of cohabitators, unrelated individuals living together, and never-married and divorced persons living alone—has been significant. Likewise, increases in divorce as well as in illegitimacy have resulted in substantial increases in female-headed households and in the proportion of children not living in the traditional husband–wife structure. Overall, the evidence is not only for growth in nontraditional family and nonfamilial living arrangements, but also for a more fluid set of arrangements, with a greater likelihood of experiencing several different household environments over one's lifetime (Cherlin, 1981).

An additional example of this fluidity may be the evolution of "dual households." Persons in such households maintain separate living quarters but spend days and nights per week at a "friend's" residence. This type of arrangement may be as socially significant as cohabitation but would be classified as living alone. As a consequence, increases in living alone since the 1950s may involve not only a quantitative shift but also a qualitative shift in the lifestyle arrangements of singles and, hence, in the social meaning of "singleness." The development of "dual-household" arrangements could be an additional reason for the trend in delayed marriage reported in this chapter.

Numerous factors have been cited in attempts to explain historical shifts in the areas reviewed in this chapter. On one level are the more straightforward demographic factors that "explain" change, at least partially, as the result of shifts in population structure (e.g., the marriage squeeze in relationship to marital timing). On another, deeper level are factors that appear as more general explanations across areas, two of which are changes in the economic structure and changes in women's roles. The former, for example, stresses the importance of changing economic conditions as a causal agent in determining marital timing, female labor participation, fertility, divorce, and remarriage (Becker, 1991; Cherlin, 1981, 1991; Easterlin, 1978, 1980). The latter emphasizes the importance of shifts in sex-role ideology and behavioral changes on the part of women, reflecting a general decline in familism and a growth of individualism and alternative opportunities outside the family (Cherlin, 1981, 1991; Modell, 1980; Sweet, 1977; White, 1979). Because we lack research to provide solid estimates of the impact of these factors on historical changes in the six areas covered, attention was focused on the research and theory on predictors/differentials to provide some preliminary insight. What was reviewed under changes in women's roles can be drawn on in an illustrative fashion to provide just one example of how family sociology and family demography can work in concert.

Beginning with the findings reviewed in this chapter on

marital timing, women who delay marriage are, on average, more likely to come from a high SES family background where there is a greater emphasis on developing egalitarian preferences and achievement orientations. These, in turn, facilitate higher educational and occupational aspirations and, bolstered by actual successful academic performance, are likely to increase the cost inherent in early heterosexual involvement and experimentation, which might interfere with highly valued goals concerning future attainments. Subsequent achievements in line with these preferences (i.e., higher education, career commitment, and economic success) then serve to further delay both marriage and children, as the attractiveness of alternatives to marriage increases— as do the costs of trying to combine a career and a family.

These same types of factors are related not only to marital timing but also to the likelihood of adolescent childbearing. As Chilman's (1980) intensive review of the literature indicates, lower SES, poor academic performance, low educational goals, and traditional sex-role preferences are related to one or more of the following: increased likelihood of adolescent coitus, failure to use birth control, and unwillingness to abort. In turn, premarital fertility and early marriage tend to truncate further the female's educational attainment and participation in nonfamilial roles.

The changes that have occurred in labor force participation and fertility suggest that, once married, sex role-egalitarian women are more likely to minimize incursions into nonfamilial roles. They evidence greater commitment to employment and, to facilitate it, use more effective birth control, plan and postpone childbearing, and have fewer children. Thus, trends in fertility, labor force participation, and labor market continuity point to an intensification of the "deferral syndrome" characterizing sex role-egalitarian preferences and behaviors consistent with the attainment of individualistic goals. However, the preliminary evidence concerning the increasing tendency for women to stay in or out of the labor force and to have children very early or to engage in postponement, also suggests that links between traditional preferences and behaviors consistent with familistic goals (e.g., early childbearing and nonparticipation in the labor force) are becoming more distinct for a subset of women.

Currently, it appears that women are increasingly unwilling to accommodate traditional demands in an extreme fashion. Instead, they are attempting to minimize the amount of time spent out of the labor force by shifting between various part- and full-time employment schedules. If such is the case, women would not only be accruing benefits in the labor market but also might be minimizing many of the changes in marriage typically associated with the interrelated events of dropping out of the labor force and lower marital satisfaction. Expecting that greater changes have occurred is

not, at this time, supported by extant data on the family. First, although women are postponing having children and are having fewer children, with increases in the percentage voluntarily remaining childless, the majority of wives still have at least two children. Second, the traditional division of labor still prevails in most marriages today. Women continue to assume responsibilities for childcare and housework because of little recourse to large-scale, quality daycare centers and/or equal husband participation in household and childcare.

Thus, it is reasonable that increasing preferences for a commitment to labor market activity among women take the form of minimizing costly prolonged stays out of the labor force. The result is high labor force participation rates, primarily part-time for women in the peak years of family demands, and shifts in work "attachment" as subsequent events demand or permit. The findings for women can also be viewed as further evidence of the incompatibility of marriage with significant achievement and career success for women. An equal partnership, for women desiring one, is difficult to find, as it implies that the careers of both spouses will be given equal weight and that housework and childcare will be equally shared.

The shifts in the areas reviewed in this chapter, although impressive, certainly do not indicate a large-scale rejection of marriage and childbearing; rather, they suggest changes in the direction of making family life more compatible with women's individualistic achievements. Consequently, although people's (gender-role) preferences are indeed shifting, the outcomes are not unrecognizable compared to those of the past.

Concepts regarding women's roles and family structures suggest ways in which the articulation between family demography and family sociology can and should be occurring not only with respect to women's roles, but also with respect to changing economic conditions and other factors. Consequently, the task of family sociology and family demography, working in concert, will be to identify the array of newly developing predictors that will enable us to understand and accurately predict variations, as well as trends, in lifecourse patterns. Ideally, the emphasis will be on understanding changes over time in family structure and process.

References

Aldous, J. (1978). *Family careers*. New York: Wiley.

Aldous, J. (1991). In the families' ways. *Contemporary Sociology*, *20*, 660–662.

Alexander, J. (1988). The new theoretical movement. In N. J. Smelser (Ed.), *Handbook of sociology* (pp. 77–101). Newbury Park, CA: Sage.

Alexander, K., & Reilly, T. (1981). Estimating the effects of marriage timing on educational attainment: Some procedural issues and substantive clarifications. *American Journal of Sociology*, *87*, 143–156.

Allison, P. (1982). Discrete-time methods for the analysis of event histories. In S. Leinhardt (Ed.), *Sociological methodology, 1982* (pp. 61–98). San Francisco: Jossey-Bass.

Althauser, R., & Wigler, M. (1972). Standardization and component analysis. *Sociological Methods and Research, 1,* 97–135.

Amato, P., & Keith, B. (1991). Parental divorce and the well-being of children. *Psychological Bulletin, 110,* 26–46.

Amato, P., Spencer, L., & Booth, A. (1995). Parental divorce, marital conflict and offspring well-being during early adulthood. *Social Forces, 73,* 895–915.

Anderson, S., Russell, C., & Schumm, W. (1983). Perceived marital quality and family life-cycle categories: A further analysis. *Journal of Marriage and the Family, 45,* 127–139.

Andorka, R. (1978). *Determinants of fertility in advanced societies.* New York: Free Press.

Aquilino, W. (1991). Family structure and home leaving: A further specification of the relationship. *Journal of Marriage and the Family, 53,* 999–1010.

Astone, N., & McLanahan, S. (1991). Family structure, parental practices and high school completion. *American Sociological Review, 56,* 309–320.

Avery, R., Goldscheider, F., & Speare, A. (1992). Living arrangements and the transition to adulthood. *Demography, 29,* 375–388.

Axinn, W., & Thornton, A. (1992). The relationship between cohabitation and divorce: Selectivity of causal influence? *Demography, 29,* 357–374.

Axinn, W., & Thornton, A. (1993). Mothers, children and cohabitation: The intergenerational effects of attitudes and behavior. *American Sociological Review, 58,* 233–246.

Axinn, W., & Thornton, A. (1996). The influence of parent's marital dissolution on children's attitudes toward family formation. *Demography, 33,* 66–81.

Bacon, L. (1974). Early motherhood, accelerated role transition, and social pathologies. *Social Forces, 52,* 333–341.

Bagozzi, R., & Van Loo, M. (1978). Fertility as consumption: Theories from behavioral sciences. *Journal of Consumer Research, 4,* 199–220.

Baldwin, W. (1976). Adolescent pregnancy and childbearing—growing concerns for Americans. *Population Bulletin, 31*(2).

Baltes, P., & Brim, O. (1980). *Life span development and behavior* (Vol. 3). New York: Academic.

Bane, M. (1975). *Economic influences on divorce and remarriage.* Cambridge, MA: Center for the Study of Public Policy, Harvard University.

Bane, M. (1986). Household composition and poverty. In S. Danziger & D. Weinberg (Eds.), *Fighting poverty: What works and what doesn't* (pp. 281–303). Cambridge, MA: Harvard University Press.

Bane, M., & Ellwood, D. (1989). One fifth of the nation's children: Why are they poor? *Science, 212,* 1047–1053.

Barrett, N. (1979). Women in the job market: Occupations, earnings, and career opportunities. In R. Smith (Ed.), *The subtle revolution: Women at work* (pp. 102–135). Washington, DC: Urban Institute.

Bauman, K., Koch, G., Udry, R., & Freedman, J. (1975). The relationship between legal abortion and marriage. *Social Biology, 22,* 117–124.

Becker, G. (1960). An economic analysis of fertility. In National Bureau of Economic Research (Ed.), *Demographic and economic change in developed countries* (pp. 45–81). Princeton, NJ: Princeton University Press.

Becker, G. (1991). *A treatise on the family.* Cambridge, MA: Harvard University Press.

Becker, G., & Lewis, H. (1979). Interaction between quantity and quality of children. In T. Schultz (Ed.), *Economics of the family* (pp. 19–32). Chicago: University of Chicago.

Becker, G., Landes, E., & Michael, R. (1977). An economic analysis of marital instability. *Journal of Political Economy, 85,* 1141–1187.

Bennett, N., Blanc, A., & Bloom, . (1988). Commitment and the modern union: Assessing the link between premarital cohabitation and subsequent marital stability. *American Sociological Review, 53,* 127–138.

Bennett, N., Bloom, D., & Craig, P. (1989). The divergence of black and white marriage patterns. *American Journal of Sociology, 95,* 692–722.

Bennett, N., Bloom, D., & Miller, C. (1995). The influence of nonmarital childbearing on the formation of first marriages. *Demography, 32,* 47–62.

Beresford, J., & Rivin, A. (1966). Privacy, poverty and old age. *Demography, 3,* 247–258.

Bergman, B. (1971). The effects on white incomes of discrimination in employment. *Journal of Political Economy, 79,* 294–313.

Bernhardt, A., Morris, M., & Handcock, M. (1995). Women's gains or men's losses: A closer look at the shrinking gender gap in earnings. *American Journal of Sociology, 101,* 302–328.

Bianchi, S. (1980). Racial differences in per capita income, 1960–1976: The importance of household size, headship, and labor force participation. *Demography, 17,* 129–143.

Bianchi, S. (1981). *Household composition and racial inequality.* New Brunswick, NJ: Rutgers University Press.

Bianchi, S., & Spain, D. (1986). *American women in transition.* Newbury Park, CA: Sage.

Bielby, W., & Bielby, D. (1989). Family ties: Balancing commitments to work and family in dual earner households. *American Sociological Review, 54,* 76–89.

Billy, J., Landale, N., & McLaughlin, S. (1986). The effect of marital status at first birth on marital dissolution among adolescent mothers. *Demography, 23,* 329–349.

Bishop, J. (1980). Jobs, cash transfers and marital instability: A review and synthesis of the evidence. *Journal of Human Resources, 15,* 301–334.

Blake, J. (1981). The only child in America: Perjudice versus performance. *Population and Development Review, 7,* 43–54.

Blake, J., & Das Gupta, P. (1975). Reproductive motivation versus contraceptive technology: Is recent American experience an exception? *Population and Development Review, 1,* 229–247.

Blau, F., & Hendricks, W. (1979). Occupational segregation by sex: Trends and prospects. *The Journal of Human Resources, 24,* 197–210.

Blau, D., & Robins, P. (1988a). Child care costs and family labor supply. *Review of Economics and Statistics, 70,* 374–381.

Blau, D., & Robins, P. (1988b). Fertility, employment and child care costs. *Demography, 26,* 287–299.

Blau, D., & Robins, P. (1991). Child care demand and labor supply of women over time. *Demography. 28,* 333–351.

Bloom, D. *What's happening to the age at first birth in the United States? A study of recent white and nonwhite cohorts.* Paper presented at the Annual Meeting of the Population Association of America, Washington, DC.

Bloom, D., & Pebley, A. (1982). Voluntary childlessness: A review of the evidence and implications. *Population Research and Policy Review, 3,* 203–224.

Bloom, D., & Trussell, J. (1984). What are the determinants of delayed childbearing and permanent childlessness in the United States? *Demography, 21,* 591–611.

Blossfeld, H., & Huinink, J. (1991). Human capital investments or norms of role transition? How women's schooling and career affect the process of family formation. *American Journal of Sociology, 97,* 143–168.

Blossfeld, H., Hamerle, A., & Mayer, K. (1989). *Event history analysis.* Hillsdale, NJ: Erlbaum.

Bogue, D. (1969). *Principles of demography.* New York: Wiley.

Bongaarts, J. (1978). A framework for analyzing the proximate determinants of fertility. *Population and Development Review, 1,* 105–132.

Bongaarts, J., Burch, T., & Wachter, K. (1987). *Family demography: Methods and their application.* Oxford: Clarendon.

Boss, P. (1987). Family stress. In M. B. Sussman & S. K. Steinmetz (Eds.), *Handbook of marriage and the family* (pp. 695–765). New York: Plenum.

Bouvier, L. (1980). America's baby boom generation: The fateful bulge. *Population Bulletin, 35*(1).

Bowen, W., & Finegan, T. (1969). *The economics of labor force participation.* Princeton, NJ: Princeton University Press.

Brown, R., Moon, M., & Zoloth, B. (1980). Occupational attainment and segregation by sex. *Industrial and Labor Relations Review, 33,* 506–517.

Buchmann, M. (1989). *The script of life in modern society: Entry into adulthood in a changing world.* Chicago: University of Chicago Press.

Bumpass, L. (1984). Children and marital disruption: A replication and update. *Demography, 21,* 71–82.

Bumpass, L. (1990). What's happening to the family? Interactions between demographic and institutional change. *Demography, 27,* 483–498.

Bumpass, L., & McLanahan, S. (1989). Unmarried motherhood: Recent trends, composition and black–white differences. *Demography, 26,* 279–286.

Bumpass, L., & Rindfuss, R. (1979). Children's experience of marital disruption. *American Journal of Sociology, 85,* 49–65.

Bumpass, L., & Sweet, J. (1989). National estimates of cohabitation. *Demography, 26,* 615–626.

Bumpass, L., & Sweet, J. (1991). Cohabitation and declining rates of marriage. *Journal of Marriage and the Family, 53,* 913–927.

Bumpass, L., Raley, R., & Sweet, J. (1995). The changing character of stepfamilies: Implications of cohabitation and nonmarital childbearing. *Demography, 32,* 425–436.

Bumpass, L., Rindfuss, R., & Janosik, R. (1978). Age and marital status at first birth and the pace of subsequent fertility. *Demography, 15,* 75–86.

Burkhauser, R., Duncan, G., Hauser, R., & Berntsen, R. (1991). Wife or frau, women do worse: A comparison of men and women in the United States and Germany following marital disruption. *Demography, 28,* 353–360.

Butz, W., & Ward, M. (1977). *The emergence of counter-cyclical U.S. fertility.* Santa Monica, CA: Rand.

Butz, W., & Ward, M. (1978). *Completed fertility and its timing: An economic analysis of U.S. experience since World War II.* Santa Monica, CA: Rand.

Cain, G. (1966). *Married women in the labor force.* Chicago: University of Chicago Press.

Cain, G., & Wissoker, D. (1990). A reanalysis of marital stability in the Seattle–Denver income maintenance experiment. *American Journal of Sociology, 85,* 1235–1269.

Calhoun, C., & Espenshade, T. (1988). Childbearing and wives' foregone earnings. *Population Studies, 42,* 5–37.

Card, J. (1981). Long-term consequences for children of teenage parents. *Demography, 18,* 137–156.

Carlinger, G. (1975). Determinants of household headship. *Journal of Marriage and the Family, 37,* 28–38.

Carlson, E. (1979). Divorce rate fluctuation as a cohort phenomenon. *Population Studies, 33,* 523–536.

Carter, H., & Glick, P. (1976). *Marriage and divorce: A social and economic study.* Cambridge, MA: Harvard University Press.

Chafetz, J. (1984). *Sex and advantage: A comparative, macro-structural theory of sex-stratification.* Totowa, NJ: Rowman & Allanheld.

Center for Demography and Ecology. (1988). *National survey of families and households: Codebook and documentation, survey design and content.* Madison: Center for Demography and Ecology, University of Wisconsin.

Center for Human Resource Research. (1990). *NLS handbook, 1990.* Columbus: Ohio State University Press.

Chen, R., & Morgan, P. (1991). Recent trends in the timing of first births in the United States. *Demography, 28,* 513–533.

Cherlin, A. (1977). The effect of children on marital instability. *Demography, 14,* 165–172.

Cherlin, A. (1978). Remarriage as an incomplete institution. *American Journal of Sociology, 83,* 634–650.

Cherlin, A. (1979). Work life and marital dissolution. In G. Levinter & O. Moles (Eds.), *Divorce and separation* (pp. 151–166). New York: Basic Books.

Cherlin, A. (1981). *Marriage, divorce, remarriage.* Cambridge, MA: Harvard University Press.

Cherlin, A. (1988). *The changing American family and public policy.* Washington, DC: Urban Institute.

Cherlin, A. (1990). Recent changes in American fertility, marriage and divorce. *Annals of the American Academy of Political and Social Science, 510,* 145–154.

Cherlin, A. (1991). *Divided families: What happens to children when parents part.* Cambridge, MA: Harvard University Press.

Cherlin, A., Kiernan, K., & Chase-Lansdale, P. L. (1995). Parental divorce in childhood and demographic outcomes in young adulthood. *Demography, 32,* 299–318.

Chevan, A., & Korson, J. (1972). The widowed who live alone: An examination of social and demographic factors. *Social Forces, 51,* 45–53.

Chilman, C. (1980). Social and psychological research concerning adolescent child-bearing: 1970–1980. *Journal of Marriage and the Family, 42,* 793–805.

Cho, L., Grabill, W., & Bogue, D. (1970). *Differential current fertility in the United States.* Chicago: Community and Family Study Center.

Clarkberg, M., Stolzenberg, R., & Waite, L. (1995). Attitudes, values and entrance into cohabitational versus marital unions. *Social Forces, 74,* 609–634.

Clifford, W., & Tobin, P. (1977). Labor force participation of working mothers and family formation: Some further evidence. *Demography, 14,* 273–284.

Coale, A. (1971). Age patterns of marriage. *Population Studies, 25,* 193–214.

Cohen, S. (1990). Control and the epidemiology of physical health: Where do we go from here?" In J. Rodin, C. Schooler, & K. Warner Schaie (Eds.), *Self-directedness: Cause and effects throughout the life course* (pp. 189–201). Hillsdale, NJ: Erlbaum.

Cohen, S., & Sweet, J. (1974). The impact of marital disruption and remarriage on fertility. *Journal of Marriage and the Family, 36,* 87–96.

Coombs, L. (1979). Reproductive goals and achieved fertility: A fifteen-year perspective. *Demography, 16,* 523–534.

Coombs, L., & Freedman, R. (1970). Premarital pregnancy, child spacing and later economic achievement. *Population Studies, 24,* 389–412.

Coombs, L., Freedman, R., Freedman, J., & Pratt, W. (1970). Premarital pregnancy and status before and after marriage. *American Journal of Sociology, 75,* 800–820.

Cooney, T., & Hogan, D. (1991). Marriage in an institutionalized life course: First marriage among American men in the twentieth century. *Journal of Marriage and the Family, 53,* 178–190.

Coverman, S., & Sheley, J. (1986). Change in men's housework and child-care time, 1965–1975. *Journal of Marriage and the Family, 48,* 413–422.

Cowan, P. (1991). Individual and family life transitions: A proposal for a new definition. In P. Cowan & M. Hetherington (Eds.), *Family transitions* (pp. 62–89). Hillsdale, NJ: Erlbaum.

Cramer, J. (1979). Employment trends of young mothers and the opportunity cost of babies in the United States. *Demography, 16,* 177–197.

Cramer, J. (1980). Fertility and female employment: Problems of causal direction. *American Sociologial Review, 45,* 397–432.

Cutright, P. (1971a). Illegitimacy: Myths, causes, and cures. *Family Planning Perspectives, 3,* 26–48.

Cutright, P. (1971b). Income and family events: Marital stability. *Journal of Marriage and the Family, 33,* 291–306.

Cutright, P. (1972a). Illegitimacy in the United States: 1920–1968. In C. Westoff & R. Parke (Eds.), *Social and demographic aspects of population growth* (pp. 106–124). Washington, DC: U.S. Government Printing Office.

Cutright, P. (1972b). The teenage sexual revolution and the myth of an abstinent past. *Family Planning Perspectives, 4,* 24–31.

Cutright, P., & Polonko, K. (1977). Areal structure and rates of childlessness among American wives in 1970. *Social Biology, 24,* 52–61.

Cutright, P., & Scanzoni, J. (1973). Income supplements and the American family. In Joint Economic Committee (Ed.), *The family, poverty, and welfare programs: Factors influencing family instability* (pp. 212–231). Washington, DC: U.S. Government Printing Office.

Cutright, P., & Shorter, F. (1979). The effects of health on the completed fertility of nonwhite and white U.S. women born between 1867 and 1935. *Journal of Social History, 13,* 191–217.

David, M. (1985). Survey of Income and Program Participation (special issue on SIPP). *Journal of Economic and Social Measurement, 13.*

Davids, L. (1980). Family change in Canada, 1971–1976. *Journal of Marriage and the Family, 42,* 177–183.

Davidson, M. (1970). Social and economic variations in child spacing. *Social Biology, 17,* 107–113.

Davis, K., & Blake, J. (1956). Social structure and fertility: An analytic framework. *Economic Development and Cultural Change, 4,* 211–235.

Davis, N., & Bumpass, L. (1976). The continuation of education after marriage among women in the United States. *Demography, 13,* 161–174.

Dawson, D., Meny, D., & Ridley, J. (1980). Fertility control in the United States before the contraceptive revolution. *Family Planning Perspectives, 12,* 76–86.

DeJong, G., & Sell, R. (1977). Changes in childlessness in the United States: A demographic path analysis. *Population Studies, 31,* 129–141.

DeMaris, A., & Rao, K. (1992). Premarital cohabitation and subsequent marital stability in the United States: A reassessment. *Journal of Marriage and the Family, 54,* 178–190.

Dubow, E., & Luster, T. (1990). Adjustment of children born to teenage mothers: The contribution of risk and protective factors. *Journal of Marriage and the Family, 52,* 393–404.

Duncan, G., & Hoffman, S. (1985). A reconsideration of the economic consequences of divorce. *Demography, 22,* 485–498.

Duncan, G., & Morgan, J. (1976). Young children and "other" family members. In G. Duncan & J. Morgan (Eds.), *Five thousand American families: Patterns of economic progress* (pp. 152–182). Ann Arbor: Institute for Social Research, University of Michigan.

Duncan, G., & Rodgers, W. (1988). Longitudinal aspects of childhood poverty. *Journal of Marriage and the Family, 50,* 1007–1022.

Duncan, G., & Rodgers, W. (1991). Has children's poverty become more persistent? *American Sociological Review, 56,* 538–550.

Duvall, E. (1963). *Family development.* New York: Lippincott.

Easterlin, R. (1973). Relative economic status and the American fertility swing. In E. B. Sheldon (Ed.), *Family economic behavior: Problems and prospects* (p. 170–223). Philadelphia: Lippincott.

Easterlin, R. (1978). What will 1984 be like? Socioeconomic implications of recent twists in age structure, *Demography, 15,* 397–432.

Easterlin, R. (1980). *Birth and fortune: The impact of numbers of personal welfare.* New York: Basic Books.

Eggebeen, D., & Lichter, D. (1994). Race, family structure and changing poverty among American children. *American Sociological Review, 56,* 801–817.

Elandt-Johnson, R., & Johnson, N. (1980). *Survival models and data analysis.* New York: Wiley.

Elder, G. (1974). Age differentiations in the life course. In A. Inkeles, J. Coleman & N. Smelser (Eds.), *Annual review of sociology* (Vol. 1, pp. 165–190). Palo Alto, CA: Annual Reviews.

Elder, G. (1977). Family history and the life course. *Journal of Family History, 2,* 279–304.

Elder, G. (1978). Family history and the life course. In T. Hareven (Ed.), *Transitions: The family and the life course in historical perspective* (pp. 17–64). New York: Academic Press.

Elder, G. (1981). History and the family: The discovery of complexity. *Journal of Marriage and the Family, 43,* 489–519.

Elder, G. (1985). *Life course dynamics: Trajectories and transitions, 1968–1980.* Ithaca, NY: Cornell University Press.

Espenshade, T. (1977). The value and cost of children. *Population Bulletin, 32*(1).

Espenshade, T. (1984). *Investing in children: New estimates of parental expenditures.* Baltimore: Urban Institute.

Espenshade, T. (1985). Marriage trends in America: Estimates, implications and underlying causes. *Population and Development Review, 11,* 193–245.

Ewer, P., Crimmins, E., & Oliver, R. (1979). An analysis of the relationship between husband's income, family size and wife's employment in the early stages of marriage. *Journal of Marriage and the Family, 41,* 727–738.

Ferber, M. (1982). Labor-market participation of young married women: Causes and effects. *Journal of Marriage and the Family, 44,* 457–468.

Figley, C. (1973). Child density and the marital relationship. *Journal of Marriage and the Family, 35,* 272–282.

Forrest, J., Tietze, C., & Sullivan, E. (1978). Abortion in the U.S., 1976–1977. *Family Planning Perspective, 10,* 271–279.

Fox, K. (1986). *Metropolitan America: Urban life and urban policy in the U.S.—1940–1980.* Jackson: University of Mississippi Press.

Freedman, R., & Coombs, L. (1966a). Child spacing and family economic positions. *American Sociological Review, 31,* 631–648.

Freedman, R., & Coombs, L. (1966b). Economic considerations in family growth decisions. *Population Studies, 20,* 197–222.

Freedman, R., Freedman, D., & Thornton, A. (1980). Changes in fertility expectations and preferences between 1962 and 1977: Their relation to final parity. *Demography, 17,* 365–378.

Freshnock, L., & Cutright, P. (1978). Structural determinants of childlessness: A nonrecursive analysis of 1970 U.S. rates. *Social Biology, 25,* 169–178.

Furstenberg, F. (1976a). Premarital pregnancy and marital instability. *Journal of Social Issues, 32,* 67–86.

Furstenberg, F. (1976b). *Unplanned parenthood: The social consequences of teenage childbearing.* New York: Free Press.

Furstenberg, F. (1979). Recycling the family: Perspectives for a neglected family form. *Marriage and Family Review, 2,* 11–22.

Furstenberg, F. (1991). As the pendulum swings: Teenage childbearing and social concern. *Family Relations, 40,* 127–138.

Furstenberg, F., Brooks-Gunn, J., & Morgan, S. (1987). *Adolescent mothers in later life.* Cambridge: Cambridge University Press.

Furstenberg, F., Hoffman, S., & Shrestha, L. (1995). The effect of divorce on intergenerational transfers: New evidence. *Demography, 32,* 319–333.

Garfinkel, I., & McLanahan, S. (1986). *Single mothers and their children: A new American dilemma.* Washington, DC: Urban Institute.

Geerken, M., & Gove, W. (1983). *At home and at work: The family's allocation of labor.* Beverly Hills, CA: Sage.

Gehan, E. (1969). Estimating survivor functions from the life table. *Journal of Chronic Diseases, 21,* 629–644.

Geronimus, A. (1991). Teenage childbearing and social and reproductive disadvantage: The evolution of complex questions and the demise of simple answers. *Family Relations, 40,* 463–471.

Gershuny, J., & Robinson, J. (1988). Historical changes in the household division of labor. *Demography, 25,* 537–552.

Gerson, K. (1985). *Hard choices: How women decide about work, career and motherhood.* Berkeley: University of California Press.

Gibson, C. (1976). The U.S. fertility decline, 1961–1975: The contribution of changes in marital status and marital fertility. *Family Planning Perspectives, 8,* 249–252.

Giddens, A. (1976). *New rules of sociological methods.* New York: Basic Books.

Glenn, N., & Shelton, B. (1985). Regional differences in divorce in the United States. *Journal of Marriage and the Family, 47,* 641–652.

Glenn, N., & Weaver, C. (1978). A multivariate, multi-survey study of marital happiness, *Journal of Marriage and the Family, 40,* 269–282.

Glick, P. (1947). The family cycle. *American Sociological Review, 12,* 164–174.

Glick, P. (1955). The life cycle of the family. *Marriage and Family Living, 18,* 2–9.

Glick, P. (1957). *American families.* New York: Wiley.

Glick, P., & Lin, S. (1986). Recent changes in divorce and remarriage. *Journal of Marriage and the Family, 48,* 737–747.

Glick, P., & Norton, A. (1977). Marrying, divorcing, and living together in the U.S. today. *Population Bulletin, 32*(5).

Glick, P., & Spanier, G. (1980). Married and unmarried cohabitation in the United States. *Journal of Marriage and the Family, 42,* 19–20.

Goldscheider, F., & DaVanzo, J. (1985). Living arrangements and the transition to adulthood. *Demography, 22,* 545–563.

Goldscheider, F., & DaVanzo, J. (1989). Pathways to independent living in early adulthood: Marriage, semiautonomy and premarital residential independence. *Demography, 26,* 597–614.

Goldscheider, F., & Waite, L. (1986). Sex differences in the entry into marriage. *American Journal of Sociology, 92,* 91–109.

Goldscheider, F., & Waite, L. (1991). *New families, no families? The transition of the American home.* Berkeley: University of California Press.

Grabill, W., Kiser, C., & Whelpton, P. (1958). *The fertility of American women.* New York: Wiley.

Gravenhorst, L. (1988). A feminist look at family development theory. In D. Klein & J. Aldous (Eds.), *Social stress and family development* (pp. 79–101). New York: Guilford.

Greenstein, T. (1989). Human capital, marital and birth timing and the postnatal labor force participation of married women. *Journal of Family Issues, 10* 359–382.

Gross, A., & Clark, V. (1975). *Survival distributions: Reliability applications in the biomedical sciences.* New York: Wiley.

Gubrium, J., & Holstein, J. (1990). *What is family?* Mountain View, CA: Mayfield.

Guttentag, M., & Secord, P. (1983). *Too many women?* Beverly Hills, CA: Sage.

Hagestad, G. (1988). Demographic change and the life course: Some emerging trends in the family realm. *Family Relations, 37,* 405–410.

Hannan, M., & Tuma, N. (1990). A reassessment of the effect of income maintenance on marital dissolution in the Seattle–Denver experiment. *American Journal of Sociology, 95,* 1270–1298.

Hannan, M., Tuma, N., & Groeneveld, L. (1977). Income and marital events: Evidence from an income maintenance experiment. *American Journal of Sociology, 82,* 1186–1211.

Hannan, M., Tuma, N., & Groeneveld, L. (1978). Income and independence effects on marital dissolution. *American Journal of Sociology, 84,* 611–633.

Hareven, T. (1978). *Transitions: The family and the life course in historical perspective.* New York: Academic Press.

Hastings, D. (1971). Child-spacing differentials for white and non-white couples according to educational level of attainment for the 1/1000 samples of the United States population in 1960. *Population Studies, 25,* 105–116.

Hastings, D., & Robinson, J. (1974). Incidence of childlessness for United States women: Cohorts born 1891–1945. *Social Biology, 21,* 178–184.

Hastings, D., & Robinson, W. (1975). Open and closed birth intervals for once-married spouse-present white women. *Demography, 12,* 455–466.

Hawthorne, G. (1970). *The sociology of fertility.* New York: Macmillan.

Heckman, J., & Willis, R. (1977). A beta-logistic model for the analysis of sequential labor force participation by married women. *Journal of Political Economy, 85,* 27–58.

Hendershot, G., & Placek, P. (1981). *Predicting fertility.* Lexington, MA: Lexington Books.

Henshaw, S. (1991). The accessibility of abortion services in the United States. *Family Planning Perspectives, 23,* 246–252.

Henshaw, S., Forrest, J., Sullivan, E., & Tietze, C. (1982). Abortion services in the United States, 1979 and 1980. *Family Planning Perspectives, 19,* 5–15.

Hernes, G. (1972). The process of entry into first marriage. *American Sociological Review, 37,* 173–182.

Hill, M. (1991). *The Panel Study of Income Dynamics.* Newbury Park, CA: Sage.

Hill, D., & Hill, M. (1976). Older children and splitting off. In G. Duncan & J. Morgan (Eds.), *Five thousand American families: Patterns of economic progress* (pp. 117–151). Ann Arbor: Institute for Social Research, University of Michigan.

Hoffman, L., & Manis, J. (1978). Influences of children on marital interaction and parental satisfactions and dissatisfactions. In R. Lerner & G. Spanier (Eds.), *Child influences on marital and family interaction: A life-span perspective* (pp. 165–213). New York: Academic Press.

Hoffman, S. (1977). Marital instability and the economic status of women. *Demography, 14,* 67–76.

Hogan, D. (1978a). The effects of demographic factors, family background, and job achievement on age at marriage. *Demography, 15,* 155–175.

Hogan, D. (1978b). The variable order of events in the life course. *American Sociological Review, 43,* 573–586.

Hogan, D. (1980). The transition to adulthood as a career contingency. *American Sociological Review, 45,* 261–276.

Holden, K., & Smock, P. (1991). The economic costs of marital dissolution: Why do women bear a disproportionate cost? *Annual Review of Sociology, 17,* 51–78.

Honig, M. (1973). The impact of welfare payment levels on family stability. In Joint Economic Committee (Ed.), *The family, poverty, and welfare programs: Factors influencing family instability* (pp. 62–91). Washington, DC: U.S. Government Printing Office.

Horiuchi, S. (1979). Decomposition of the rise in divorce rates: A note on Michael's results. *Demography, 16,* 549–551.

Houseknecht, S. (1978). Voluntary childlessness: A social psychological model. *Alternative Lifestyles, 1,* 379–402.

Houseknecht, S. (1979). Childlessness and marital adjustment. *Journal of Marriage and the Family, 41,* 259–265.

Houseknecht, S., & Spanier, G. (1980). Marital disruption and higher education among women in the United States. *Sociological Quarterly, 21,* 375–389.

Huber, J., & Spitze, G. (1980). Considering divorce: An expansion of Becker's theory of marital instability. *American Journal of Sociology, 86,* 75–89.

Hughes, M., & Gove, W. (1981). Living alone, social integration, and mental health. *American Journal of Sociology, 87,* 48–74.

Jacobs, J. (1989). Long-term trends in occupational segregation by sex. *American Journal of Sociology, 95,* 160–173.

Kahn, J., & London, K. (1991). Premarital sex and the risk of divorce. *Journal of Marriage and the Family, 53*, 845–855.

Kalbfleisch, J., & Prentice, R. (1980). *The statistical analysis of failure time data.* New York: Wiley.

Kasarda, J., Billy, J., & West, K. (1986). *Status enhancement and fertility: Reproductive responses to social mobility and educational opportunity.* New York: Academic Press.

Keeley, M. (1977). The economics of family formation. *Economic Inquiry, 15*, 238–250.

Kingsbury, N., & Scanzoni, J. (1993). Structural-functionalism. In P. Boss, W. Doherty, R. LaRoossa, W. Shumm, & S. Steinmetz (Eds.), *Sourcebook of theories and methods about families* (pp. 195–217). New York: Plenum.

Kitagawa, E. (1955). Components of a difference between two rates. *Journal of the American Statistical Association, 50*, 1168–1194.

Kitagawa, E. (1964). Standardized comparisons in demographic research. *Demography, 1*, 296–513.

Klerman, J., & Leibowitz, A. (1994). The work-employment distinction among new mothers. *Journal of Human Resources, 29*, 277–303.

Kobrin, F. (1973). Household headship and its changes in the United States, 1940–1960, 1970. *Journal of the American Statistical Association, 68*, 793–800.

Kobrin, F. (1976a). The fall of household size and the rise of the primary individual in the United States. *Demography, 13*, 127–139.

Kobrin, F. (1976b). The primary individual and the family: Changes in living arrangements in the United States since 1940. *Journal of Marriage and the Family, 38*, 233–239.

Kobrin, F. (1981). Family extension and the elderly: Economic, demographic and family cycle factors. *Journal of Gerontology, 36*, 307–377.

Kobrin, F., & Goldscheider, C. (1978). *The ethnic factor in family structure and mobility.* Cambridge, MA: Ballinger.

Kobrin, F., & Hendershot, G. (1977). Do family ties reduce mortality: Evidence from the United States, 1966–1968. *Journal of Marriage and the Family, 39*, 373–380.

Koo, H., & Suchindran, C. (1980). Effects of children on women's remarriage prospects. *Journal of Family Issues, 1*, 497–515.

Kuznets, S. (1976). Demographic aspects of the size distribution of income: An exploratory essay. *Economic Development and Cultural Change, 25*, 1–94.

Kuznets, S. (1978). Size and age structure of family households: Exploratory comparisons. *Population and Development Review, 4*, 187–223.

LaRossa, R., & LaRossa, M. (1981). *Transition to parenthood: How infants change families.* Beverly Hills, CA: Sage.

Leibowitz, A. (1974). Education and the allocation of women's time. In F. Juster (Ed.), *Education, income and human behavior* (pp. 171–197). New York: McGraw-Hill.

Leibowitz, A., & Klerman, J. (1995). Explaining changes in married mothers' employment over time. *Demography, 32*, 365–378.

Leppel, K. (1987). An examination of the effects of income on household composition choice, i.e., marriage vs. living alone or with unrelated individuals, with focus on gender differences. *Social Science Research, 16*, 138–153.

Levin, M., & O'Hara, C. (1978). The impact of marital history of current husbands on the fertility of remarried white women in the U.S. *Journal of Marriage and the family, 40*, 95–102.

Levine, D. N., Carter, E. B., & Gormon, E. M. (1976). Simmel's influence on American sociology. *American Journal of Sociology, 81*, 813–845.

Levy, F. (1987). *Dollars and dreams: The changing American income distribution.* Beverly Hills, CA: Sage.

Lichter, D., LeClere, F., & McLaughlin, D. (1991). Local marriage markets and the marital behavior of black and white women. *American Journal of Sociology, 96*, 843–867.

Lichter, D., McLaughlin, D., Kephart, G., & Landry, D. (1992). Race and the retreat from marriage: A shortage of marriageable men. *American Sociological Review, 57*, 781–799.

Lloyd, C. (1975). The division of labor between the sexes: A review. In C. Lloyd (Ed.), *Sex, discrimination and the division of labor* (pp. 1–24). New York: Columbia University Press.

Loomis, L., & Landale, N. (1995). Nonmarital cohabitation and childbearing among black and white American women. *Journal of Marriage and the Family, 57*, 949–962.

Loscocco, K. (1989). The interplay of personal and job characteristics in determining work commitment. *Social Science Research, 18*, 70–94.

MacDonald, M., & Rindfuss, R. (1981). Earnings, relative income, and family formation. *Demography, 18*, 123–136.

Macklin, E. (1978). Non-marital heterosexual cohabitation: A review of the recent literature. *Marriage and Family Review, 1*, 1–12.

Mallan, L. (1982). Labor force participation, work experience and the pay gap between men and women. *Journal of Human Resources, 17*, 437–448.

Manning, W., & Smock, P. (1995). Why marry? Race and the transition to marriage among cohabitors. *Demography, 32*, 509–520.

Mare, R., & Winship, C. (1991). Socioeconomic change and the decline of marriage in for blacks and whites. In C. Jencks & P. Peterson (eds.), *The urban underclass* (pp. 175–202). Washington, DC: The Brookings Institution.

Marini, M. (1978). The transition to adulthood: Sex differences in educational attainment and age at marriage. *American Sociological Review, 433*, 483–507.

Marini, M. (1980). Effects of the number and spacing of children on marital and parental satisfaction. *Demography, 17*, 225–242.

Marini, M., & Hodson, P. (1981). Effects of the timing of marriage and the first birth on the spacing of subsequent births. *Demography, 18*, 529–548.

Martin, T., & Bumpass, L. (1989). Recent trend in marital disruption. *Demography, 26*, 37–51.

Masnick, G., & Bane, M. (1980). *The nation's families: 1960–1990.* Boston: Auburn House.

Masnick, G., & McFalls, J. (1978). *Those perplexing U.S. fertility swings: A new perspective on a 20th century puzzle.* Washington, DC: Population Reference Bureau.

McCarthy, J. (1978). A comparison of the probability of the dissolution of first and second marriage. *Demography, 15*, 345–360.

McCarthy, J., & Menken, J. (1979). Marriage, remarriage, marital disruption, and age at first birth. *Family Planning Perspectives, 11*, 21–30.

McLanahan, S. (1985). Family structure and the reproduction of poverty. *American Journal of Sociology, 90*, 873–901.

McLanahan, S. (1988). Family structure and dependency: Early transitions to female household headship. *Demography, 25*, 1–16.

McLanahan, S., & Bumpass, L. (1988). Intergenerational consequences of marital disruption. *American Journal of Sociology, 94*, 130–152.

McLanahan, S., & Garfinkel, I. (1989). Single mothers, the underclass and social policy. *Annals of the American Academy of Political and Social Science, 501*, 91–104.

McLanahan, S., & Sandefur, G. (1994). *Growing up with a single parent.* Cambridge, MA: Harvard University Press.

McLanahan, S., & Sorenson, A. (1985). Life events and psychological well-being over the life course. In G. Elder (Ed.), *Life course dynamics: Trajectories and transitions, 1968–180* (pp. 217–238). Ithaca, NY: Cornell University Press.

McLaughlin, S. (1982). Differential patterns of female labor force participation surrounding the first birth. *Journal of Marriage and the Family, 44*, 407–420.

Menken, J. (1972). Teenage childbearing: Its medical aspects and implications for the United States population. In C. Westoff & R. Parke (Eds.), *Demographic and social aspects of population growth* (Vol. 1, pp. 78–96). Washington, DC: U.S. Government Printing Office.

Michael, R. (1978). The rise in divorce rates, 1960–1974: Age-specific components. *Demography, 15,* 177–182.

Michael, R., & Tuma, N. (1985). Entry into marriage and parenthood by young men and women. *Demography, 22,* 515–523.

Michael, R., Fuchs, V., & Scott, S. (1980). Changes in the propensity to live alone: 1950–1976. *Demography, 17,* 39–53.

Michalopoulos, C., Robins, P., & Garfinkel, I. (1992). A structural model of labor supply and child care demand. *Journal of Human Resources, 27,* 166–203.

Miller, B. (1976). A multivariate development model of marital satisfaction. *Journal of Marriage and the Family, 38,* 643–657.

Millman, S., & Hendershot, G. (1980). Early fertility and lifetime fertility. *Family Planning Perspectives, 12,* 139–149.

Mincer, J. (1963). Market prices, opportunity costs, and income effects. In C. Christ (Ed.), *Measurement in economics: Studies in mathematical economics and economics in memory of Yehuda Grunfeld* (pp. 67–102). Stanford, CA: Stanford University Press.

Mirwosky, J., & Ross, C. (1989). *Social causes of psychological distress.* New York: Aldine de Gruyter.

Modell, J. (1980). Normative aspects of American marriage timing since World War II. *Journal of Family History, 5,* 210–234.

Modell, J. (1989). *Into one's own: From youth to adulthood in the United States, 1920–1975.* Berkeley: University of California Press.

Modell, J., Furstenberg, F., & Strong, D. (1978). The timing of marriage in the transition to adulthood: Continuity and change, 1860–1975. In J. Demos & S. Boocock (Eds.), *Turning points: Historical and sociological essays on the family* (pp. 5120–5150). Chicago: University of Chicago Press.

Moen, P. (1985). Continuities and discontinuities in women's labor force activity. In G. Elder (Ed.), *Life course dynamics: Trajectories and transitions, 1968–1980* (pp. 113–155). Ithaca, NY: Cornell University Press.

Moen, P., & Smith, K. (1986). Women at work: Commitment and behavior over the life course. *Sociological Forum, 3,* 450–475.

Moffitt, R. (1990). The effect of the U.S. welfare system on marital status. *Journal of Public Economics, 41,* 101–124.

Moffitt, R. (1994). Welfare effects on female headship with area effects. *Journal of Human Resources, 29,* 621–636.

Moles, O. (1976). Marital dissolution and public assistance programs: Variations among American states, *Journal of Social Issues, 32,* 87–101.

Moles, O. (1979). Public welfare payments and marital dissolutions: A review of recent studies. In G. Levinger & O. Moles (Eds.), *Divorce and separation* (pp. 118–139). New York: Basic Books.

Moore, K., & Burt, M. (1987). *Private crisis, public cost: Policy perspectives on teenage childbearing.* Washington, DC: Urban Institute.

Moore, K., & Snyder, N. (1991). Cognitive attainment among firstborn children of adolescent mothers. *American Sociological Review, 55,* 122–136.

Moore, K., & Waite, L. (1981). Marital dissolution, early motherhood, and early marriage. *Social Forces, 60,* 20–40.

Morgan, S. (1981). Intentions and uncertainty at later stages of childbearing: The United States 1965 and 1970. *Demography, 18,* 267–285.

Morgan, S., & Rindfuss, R. (1985). Marital disruption: Structural and temporal dimensions. *American Journal of Sociology, 90,* 1055–1077.

Mosher, W., & McNally, J. (1991). Contraceptive use at first premarital intercourse: United States, 1965–1988. *Family Planning Perspectives, 23,* 108–116.

Mott, F. (1972). Fertility, life cycle stage, and female labor force participation in Rhode Island: A retrospective overview. *Demography, 9,* 173–185.

Mott, F., & Moore, S. (1979). The causes of marital disruption among young American women: An interdisciplinary perspective. *Journal of Marriage and the Family, 41,* 355–365.

Mueller, C., & Pope, H. (1977). Marital instability: A study of its transmission between generations. *Journal of Marriage and the Family, 39,* 83–93.

Mullins, L. (Ed.). (1987). *Cities of the United States.* New York: Columbia University Press.

Nakamura, A., & Nakamura, M. (1994). Predicting female labor supply: Effects of children on women's work. *Journal of Human Resources, 29,* 304–327.

Namboodiri, N. (1964). The wife's work experience and child spacing. *Milbank Memorial Fund Quarterly, 42,* 65–77.

Namboodiri, N. (1972). Some observations on the economic framework for fertility analysis. *Population Studies, 26,* 185–206.

Namboodiri, N. (1981). On factors affecting fertility at different stages in the reproductive history: An exercise in cohort fertility. *Social Forces, 59,* 1114–1129.

Namboodiri, N., & Suchindran, C. (1987). *Life table techniques and their applications.* New York: Academic Press.

National Center for Health Statistics. (1979). *Divorce by marriage cohort* (Series 21, No. 34). Washington DC: U.S. Government Printing Office.

National Center for Health Statistics. (1980a). *National estimates of marriage dissolution and survivorship: United States* (Series 3, No. 19).

National Center for Health Statistics. (1980b). *Patterns of employment before and after childbirth* (Series 23, No. 4). Washington DC: U.S. Government Printing Office.

National Center for Health Statistics. (1980c). *Remarriages of women 15–44 years of age whose first marriage ended in divorce: United States, 1976* (Advance Data, No. 58). Washington DC: U.S. Government Printing Office.

National Center for Health Statistics. (1981). *Socioeconomic differentials and trends in the timing of births* (Series 23, No. 6). Washington DC: U.S. Government Printing Office.

Norton, A., & Glick, P. (1976). Marital instability: Past, present, and future. *Journal of Social Issues, 34,* 5–20.

Norton, A., & Moorman, J. (1987). Current trends in marriage and divorce among American women. *Journal of Marriage and the Family, 49,* 3–14.

Nye, F., Carlson, J., & Farrett, G. (1970). Family size, interaction, affect, and stress. *Journal of Marriage and the Family, 32,* 216–226.

O'Connell, M. (1980). Comparative estimates of teenage illegitimacy in the United States, 1940–1944 to 1970–1974. *Demography, 17,* 13–23.

O'Connell, M., & Moore, M. (1980). The legitimacy status of first births to U.S. women aged 15–24, 1939–1978. *Family Planning Perspectives, 12,* 16–25.

Oppenheimer, V. (1970). *The female labor force in the United States: Demographic and economic factors governing its growth and changing composition* (Population Monograph Series, No. 5). Berkeley: University of California Press.

Oppenheimer, V. (1973). Demographic influences on female employment and the status of women. *American Journal of Sociology, 78,* 946–961.

Oppenheimer, V. (1976). The Easterlin hypothesis: Another aspect of the echo to consider. *Population and Development Review, 2,* 433–437.

Oppenheimer, V. (1979). Structural sources of economic pressure for wives to work: An analytical framework. *Journal of Family History, 4,* 177–197.

Oppenheimer, V. (1982). *Work and the family: A study in social demography.* New York: Academic Press.

Oppenheimer, V. (1988). A theory of marriage timing. *American Journal of Sociology, 94,* 563–591.

Pampel, F. (1983). Changes in the propensity to live alone: Evidence from consecutive cross-sectional surveys, 1960–1976. *Demography, 20,* 433–448.

Pavalko, E., & Elder, G. (1990). World War II and divorce: A life-course perspective. *American Journal of Sociology, 95,* 1213–1234.

Pearlin, L., & Johnson, J. (1977). Marital status, life strains, and depression. *American Sociological Review, 42,* 704–715.

Pebley, A. (1981). Changing attitudes toward the timing of first births. *Family Planning Perspectives, 13,* 171–175.

Peterson, C. (1990). Husbands' and wives' perceptions of marital fairness across the family life cycle. *International Journal of Aging and Human Development, 31,* 179–188.

Peterson, R. (1989). *Women, work and divorce.* Albany: State University of New York.

Peterson, T., & Morgan, L. (1995). Separate and unequal: Occupation-establishment sex segregation and the gender wage gap. *American Journal of Sociology, 101,* 329–365.

Pillai, V. (1987). The postwar rise and decline of American fertility: The pace of transition to motherhood among 1950–1969 marital cohorts of white women. *Journal of Family History, 12,* 421–436.

Pohlman, E. (1968). The timing of first births: A review of effects. *Eugenics Quarterly, 15,* 252–263.

Polonko, K., Scanzoni, J., & Teachman, J. (1982). Assessing the implications of childlessness for marital satisfaction. *Journal of Family Issues, 3,* 545–573.

Pope, H., & Mueller, C. (1976). The inter-generational transmission of marital instability: Comparisons by race and sex. *Journal of Social Issues, 32,* 49–66.

Poston, D., & Gotard, E. (1977). Trends in childlessness in the United States: 1910–1975. *Social Biology, 24,* 212–224.

Potter, R. (1963). Birth intervals: Structure and change. *Population Studies, 18,* 155–166.

Presser, H. (1971). The timing of the first birth, female roles, and black fertility. *Milbank Memorial Fund Quarterly, 49,* 329–361.

Presser, H. (1975). Age differences between spouses: Trends, patterns, and social implications. *American Behavioral Scientist, 19,* 190–205.

Presser, H. (1989). Can we make time for children? The economy, work schedules and child care. *Demography, 26,* 523–543.

Presser, H., & Baldwin, W. (1980). Child care as a constraint on employment: Prevalence, correlates, and bearing on the work and fertility nexus. *American Journal of Sociology, 85,* 1202–1213.

Preston, S., & McDonald, J. (1979). The incidence of divorce within cohorts of American marriages contracted since the Civil War. *Demography, 16,* 1–25.

Preston, S., & Richards, A. (1975). The influence of women's work opportunities on marriage rates. *Demography, 12,* 209–222.

Qian, Z., & Preston, S. (1993). Changes in American marriage, 1972–1987: Availability and forces of attraction by age and education. *American Sociological Review, 58,* 482–495.

Ribar, D. (1992). Child care and the labor supply of married women. *Journal of Human Resources, 27,* 134–165.

Rindfuss, R., & Bumpass, L. (1977). Fertility during marital disruption. *Journal of Marriage and the Family, 39,* 517–528.

Rindfuss, R., & Bumpass, L. (1978). Age and the sociology of fertility: How old is too old? In K. Taeuber, L. Bumpass, & J. Sweet (Eds.), *Social demography* (pp. 37–61). New York: Academic Press.

Rindfuss, R., & Parnell, A. (1989). The varying connection between marital status and childbearing in the United States. *Population and Development Review, 15,* 447–470.

Rindfuss, R., & Sweet, J. (1977). *Postwar fertility trends and differentials in the United States.* New York: Academic Press.

Rindfuss, R., Morgan, S., & Swicegood, G. (1988). *First births in America: Changes in the timing of parenthood.* Berkeley: University of California Press.

Rodin, J. (1990). Control by any other name: Definitions, concepts and processes. In J. Rodin, C. Schooler, & K. Warner Shaie (Eds.), *Self-directedness: Cause and effects throughout the life course* (pp. 118–131). Hillsdale, NJ: Erlbaum.

Rodin, J., Schooler, C., & Schaie, K. W. (Eds.) (1990). *Self-directedness: Cause and effects throughout the life course.* Hillsdale, NJ: Erlbaum.

Rodgers, W., & Thornton, A. (1985). Changing patterns of first marriage in the United States. *Demography, 22,* 265–279.

Rollins, B., & Galligan, R. (1978). The developing child and marital satisfaction of parents. In R. Lerner & G. Spanier (Eds.), *Child influences on marital and family interaction: A life-span perspective* (pp. 45–68). New York: Academic Press.

Ross, H., & Sawhill, L. (1975). *Time of transition: The growth of families headed by women.* Washington, DC: Urban Institute.

Rossi, A. (1968). Transition to parenthood. *Journal of Marriage and the Family, 30,* 26–39.

Rowntree, B. (1906). *Poverty: A study of town life.* London: Macmillan.

Ryder, N. (1965). The cohort as a concept in the study of social change. *American Sociological Review, 30,* 843–861.

Ryder, N. (1969). The emergence of a modern fertility pattern: United States, 1917–1966. In Behrman, L. Corsa, & R. Freedman (Eds.), *Fertility and family planning: A world view* (pp. 132–148). Ann Arbor: University of Michigan Press.

Ryder, N. (1975). Fertility measurement through cross-sectional surveys. *Social Forces, 54,* 7–35.

Ryder, N. (1980). Components of temporal variations in American fertility. In R. Hiorns (Ed.), *Demographic patterns in developed societies* (pp. 67–89). London: Taylor & Francis.

Ryder, N. (1981). A time series of instrumental fertility variables. *Demography, 18,* 487–509.

Ryder, N., & Westoff, C. (1971). *Reproduction in the United States,* 1965. Princeton, NJ: Princeton University Press.

Sandefur, G., & Scott, W. (1981). A dynamic analysis of migration: An assessment of the effects of family and career variables. *Demography, 18,* 355–368.

Sandefur, G., McLanahan, S., & Wojtkiewicz, R. (1992). The effects of parental marital status during adolescence on high school graduation. *Social Forces, 71,* 103–121.

Santi, L. (1988). The demographic context of recent changes in the structure of American households. *Demography, 25,* 509–520.

Scanzoni, J. (1980). Contemporary marriage types: A research note. *Journal of Family Issues, 1,* 125–140.

Scanzoni, J. (1983). *Is family possible: theory and policy for the 21st century.* Beverly Hills, CA: Sage.

Scanzoni, J. (in press). *Contemporary families and relationships.* New York: McGraw-Hill.

Scanzoni, J., & Marsiglio, W. (1993). New action theory and contemporary families. *Journal of Family Issues, 14,* 105–132.

Scanzoni, J., Polonko, K., Teachman, J., & Thompson, L. (1989). *The sexual bond: Rethinking families and close relationships.* Newbury Park, CA: Sage.

Schoen, R. (1992). First unions and the stability of first marriages. *Journal of Marriage and the Family, 54,* 281–284.

Schoen, R., & Kluegel, J. (1988). The widening gap in black and white marriage rates: The impact of population composition and different marriage propensities. *American Sociological Review, 53,* 895–907.

Schoen, R., & Nelson, V. (1974). Marriage, divorce, and mortality: A life table analysis. *Demography, 11,* 267–290.

Schoen, R., Greenblatt, H., & Mielke, R. (1975). California's experience with non-adversary divorce. *Demography, 12,* 223–243.

Schoen, R., Utron, W., Woodrow, K., & Baj, J. (1985). Marriage and divorce in twentieth century American cohorts. *Demography, 22,* 101–114.

Schultz, T. (1994). Marital status and fertility in the United States: Welfare and labor market effects. *Journal of Human Resources, 29,* 637–669.

Shapiro, D., & Mott, F. (1979). Labor supply behavior of prospective and new mothers. *Demography, 16,* 199–208.

Shapiro, D., & Mott, F. (1994). Long-term employment and earnings of women in relation to employment behavior surrounding the first birth. *Journal of Human Resources, 29,* 248–276.

Shaw, K. (1994). The persistence of female labor supply: Empirical evidence and implications. *Journal of Human Resources, 29,* 348–378.

Sheps, M., & Menken, J. (1973). *Mathematical models of conception and birth.* Chicago: University of Chicago Press.

Smith, D., & Hendus, M. (1975). Premarital pregnancy in America, 1640–1971: An overview and interpretation. *Journal of Interdisciplinary History, 5,* 537–570.

Smith, H., & Cutright, P. (1988). Thinking about change in illegitimacy ratios: United States, 1963–1983. *Demography, 25,* 235–248.

Smith, J. (1980). *Female labor supply.* Princeton, NJ: Princeton University Press.

Smith, J., & Ward, M. (1980). Asset accumulation and family size. *Demography, 17,* 243–260.

Smith, M. (1989). Urbanism—Medium or outcome of human agency? *Urban Affairs Quarterly, 24,* 353–358.

Smith, R. (1979). *The subtle revolution: Women at work.* Washington, DC: Urban Institute.

Smith, S. (1982). New worklife estimates reflect changing profile of labor force. *Monthly Labor Review, 105,* 15–20.

Smith-Lovin, L., & Tickamyer, A. (1978). Non-recursive models of labor force participation, fertility behavior, and sex role attitudes. *American Sociological Review, 43,* 541–557.

Smock, P. (1990). Remarriage patterns of black and white women: Reassessing the role of educational attainment. *Demography, 27,* 467–473.

Smock, P. (1994). Gender and the short-run consequences of marital disruption. *Social Forces, 73,* 243–262.

South, S. (1985). Economic conditions and the divorce rate. *Journal of Marriage and the Family, 47,* 31–41.

South, S., & Lloyd, K. (1992). Marriage opportunities and family formation: Further implications of imbalanced sex ratios. *Journal of Marriage and the Family, 54,* 440–451.

South, S., & Lloyd, K. (1995). Spousal alternatives and marital dissolution. *American Sociological Review, 60,* 21–35.

South, S., & Spitze, G. (1986). Determinants of divorce over the life course. *American Sociological Review, 51,* 583–590.

Spanier, G., & Glick, P. (1980a). The life cycle of American families: An expanded analysis. *Journal of Family History, 5,* 97–111.

Spanier, G., & Glick, P. (1980b). Paths to remarriage. *Journal of Divorce, 3,* 283–298.

Spanier, G., Sauer, W., & Larzelere, R. (1979). An empirical evaluation of the family life cycle. *Journal of Marriage and the Family, 41,* 27–38.

Spitze, G., & South, S. (1985). Women's employment, time expenditure and divorce. *Journal of Family Issues, 6,* 307–329.

Spitze, G., & Waite, L. (1981). Wives' employment: The role of husbands' perceived attitudes. *Journal of Marriage and the Family, 43,* 117–124.

Stack, C. (1974). *All our kin—strategies for survival in a black community.* New York: Harper & Row.

Stafford, F. (1980). Women's use of time converging with men's. *Monthly Labor Review, 103,* 57–59.

Stolzenberg, R., Blair-Loy, M., & Waite, L. (1995). Religious participation in early adulthood: Age and family life cycle effects on church membership. *American Sociological Review, 60,* 84–103.

Stone, L. (1977). *The family, sex, and marriage: England 1500–1800.* New York: Harper & Row.

Sweet, J. (1972). The living arrangements of separated, widowed, and divorced mothers. *Demography, 9,* 143–157.

Sweet, J. (1973a). *Differentials in remarriage probabilities.* Madison: Center for Demography and Ecology, University of Wisconsin.

Sweet, J. (1973b). *Women in the labor force.* New York: Academic Press.

Sweet, J. (1977). Demography and the family. In A. Inkeles, J. Coleman, & N. Smelser (Eds.), *Annual review of sociology* (Vol. 3, pp. 87–108). Palo Alto, CA: Annual Reviews.

Sweet, J., & Bumpass, L. (1988). *American families and households.* New York: Russell Sage Foundation.

Swidler, A. (1980). Love and adulthood in American culture. In N. Smelser & E. Erikson (Eds.), *Themes of love and work in adulthood* (pp. 106–125). Cambridge, MA: Harvard University Press.

Syme, S. (1990). Control and health: An epidemiological perspective. In J. Rodin, C. Schooler, & K. Warner Schaie (Eds.), *Self-directedness: Cause and effects throughout the life course* (pp. 201–222). Hillsdale, NJ: Erlbaum.

Teachman, J. (1983). Early marriage, premarital fertility, and marital dissolution: Results for blacks and white. *Journal of Family Issues, 4,* 105–126.

Teachman, J. (1985). Historical and subgroup differences in the association between marriage and first childbirth. *Journal of Family History, 10,* 379–401.

Teachman, J. (1986). First and second marital dissolution: A decomposition exercise for whites and blacks. *Sociological Quarterly, 27,* 571–590.

Teachman, J., & Heckert, A. (1985a). The declining significance of first birth timing. *Demography, 22,* 185–198.

Teachman, J., & Heckert, A. (1985b). The impact of age and children on remarriage. *Journal of Family Issues, 6,* 185–203.

Teachman, J., & Polonko, K. (1984). Out of sequence: The timing of marriage following a premarital birth. *Social Forces, 63,* 245–260.

Teachman, J., & Polonko, K. (1985). Timing of the transition to parenthood: A multidimensional birth-interval approach. *Journal of Marriage and the Family, 47,* 867–879.

Teachman, J., & Polonko, K. (1990). Cohabitation and marital stability in the United States. *Social Forces, 69,* 185–203.

Teachman, J., Polonko, K., & Leigh, G. (1987). Marital timing: Race and sex comparisons. *Social Forces, 66,* 239–268.

Teachman, J., Thomas, J., & Paasch, K. (1991). Legal status and the stability of coresidential unions. *Demography, 28,* 571–586.

Thomson, E., & Colella, U. (1992). Cohabitation and marital stability: Quality or commitment? *Journal of Marriage and the Family, 54,* 259–267.

Thomson, E., Hanson, T., & McLanahan, S. (1994). Family structure and child well-being: Economic resources vs. parental behaviors. *Social Forces, 73,* 221–242.

Thornton, A. (1975). *Marital instability and fertility.* Ph.D. thesis. University of Michigan, Ann Arbor.

Thornton, A. (1978). Marital dissolution, remarriage, and childbearing. *Demography, 15,* 361–380.

Thornton, A. (1988). Cohabitation and marriage in the 1980s. *Demography, 25,* 497–508.

Thornton, A. (1991). Influence of the marital history of parents on the marital and cohabitational experiences of children. *American Journal of Sociology, 96*, 868–894.

Thornton, A., & Rodgers, W. (1987). The influence of individual and historical time on marital dissolution. *Demography, 24*, 1–22.

Thornton, A., Axinn, W., & Teachman, J. (1995). The influence of school enrollment and accumulation on cohabitation and marriage in early adulthood. *American Sociological Review, 70*, 762–774.

Treas, J. (1981). Postwar trends in family size. *Demography, 18*, 321–334.

Trent, K., & South, S. (1989). Structural determinants of the divorce rate: A cross-national analysis. *Journal of Marriage and the Family, 51*, 391–404.

Troll, L. (1971). The family and labor life: A decade review. *Journal of Marriage and the Family, 33*, 263–290.

Trussel, T. (1976a). Economic consequences of teenage childbearing. *Family Planning Perspective, 8*, 184–190.

Trussel, T. (1976b). A refined estimator of measures of location of the age at first marriage. *Demography, 13*, 225–234.

Tsui, A. (1982). The family formation process among U.S. marriage cohorts. *Demography, 19*, 1–27.

Tuma, N., Hannan, M., & Groeneveld, L. (1979). Dynamic analysis of event histories. *American Journal of Sociology, 81*, 820–851.

Turner, J. (1988). *A theory of social interaction.* Stanford, CA: Stanford University Press.

Uhlenberg, P. (1974). Cohort variations in family life cycle experiences of U.S. females. *Journal of Marriage and the Family, 36*, 281–292.

Uhlenberg, P. (1978). Changing configurations in the life course. In T. Harevan (Ed.), *Transitions: The family and life course in historical perspective* (pp. 65–97). New York: Academic Press.

Upchurch, D., & McCarthy, J. (1990). The timing of a first birth and high school completion. *American Sociological Review, 55*, 224–234.

U.S. Bureau of the Census. (1976a). *Fertility history and prospects of American women: June 1975* (Current Population Reports, Series P-20, No. 288). Washington, DC: U.S. Government Printing Office.

U.S. Bureau of the Census. (1976b). *Number, timing, and duration of marriages and divorces in the United States: June 1975* (Current Population Reports, Series P-20, No. 297). Washington, DC: U.S. Government Printing Office.

U.S. Bureau of the Census. (1976c). *Premarital fertility* (Current Population Reports, Series P-23, No. 63). Washington, D.C.: U.S. Government Printing Office.

U.S. Bureau of the Census. (1977). *Marriage, divorce, widowhood, and remarriage by family characteristics: June 1975* (Current Population Reports, Series P-20, No. 312). Washington, D.C.: U.S. Government Printing Office.

U.S. Bureau of the Census. (1992). *Statistical abstract of the United States: 1992* (112th Ed.). Washington, D.C.: U.S. Government Printing Office.

U.S. Bureau of Education. (1987a). *The National Longitudinal Study of the High School Class of 1972 (NLS-72) fifth follow-up data file user's manual.* Washington, D.C.: National Center for Education Statistics.

U.S. Department of Education. (1987b). *High School and Beyond 1980 senior cohort third follow-up (1986) data file user's manual.* National Center for Education Statistics.

U.S. Department of Education. (1990). *National Education Longitudinal Study of 1988: Base year sample design report.* National Center for Education Statistics.

Vanek, J. (1980). Household work, wage work, and sexual equality. In S. Berk (Ed.), *Women and household labor* (pp. 275–291). Beverly Hills, CA: Sage.

Veevers, J. (1979). Voluntary childlessness: A review of issues and evidence. *Marriage and Family Review, 2*, 1–26.

Waite, L. (1980). Working wives and the family life cycle. *American Journal of Sociology, 86*, 272–294.

Waite, L. (1981). Women at work. *Population Bulletin, 36*(2).

Waite, L. (1995). Does marriage matter? *Demography, 32*, 483–508.

Waite, L., & Lillard, L. (1991). Children and marital disruption. *American Journal of Sociology, 96*, 930–953.

Waite, L., & Moore, K. (1978). The impact of an early first birth on young women's educational attainment. *Social Forces, 56*, 845–865.

Waite, L., & Spitze, G. (1981). Young women's transition to marriage. *Demography, 18*, 681–694.

Waite, L., & Stolzenberg, R. (1976). Intended childbearing and labor force participation of young women: Insights from non-recursive models. *American Sociological Review, 41*, 235–252.

Waite, L., Haggstrom, G., & Kanouse, J. (1985). The consequences of parenthood for the marital stability of young adults. *American Sociological Review, 50*, 850–857.

Weed, J. (1974). Age at marriage as a factor in state divorce rate differentials. *Demography, 11*, 361–375.

Westoff, C., & Ryder, N. (1977a). *The contraceptive revolution.* Princeton, NJ: Princeton University Press.

Westoff, C., & Ryder, N. (1977b). The predictive validity of reproductive intentions. *Demography, 14*, 431–453.

Westoff, C., Potter, R., Sagi, R., & Mishler, E. (1961). *Family growth in metropolitan America.* Princeton, NJ: Princeton University Press.

Whelpton, P. (1964). Trends and differentials in the spacing of births. *Demography, I*, 83–93.

Whelpton, P., Campbell, A., & Patterson, J. (1966). *Fertility and family planning in the United States.* Princeton, NJ: Princeton University Press.

White, J. (1991). *Dynamics of family development: A theoretical perspective.* New York: Guilford.

White, L. (1979). The correlates of urban illegitimacy in the United States, 1960–1970. *Journal of Marriage and the Family, 41*, 715–726.

White, L. (1981). A note on racial differences in the effect of female economic opportunity on marriage rates. *Demography, 18*, 349–354.

White, R. (1982). Family size composition differentials between central city–suburb and metropolitan–non-metropolitan migration streams. *Demography, 19*, 29–36.

Wilkie, J. (1981). The trend toward delayed parenthood. *Journal of Marriage and the Family, 43*, 583–591.

Willis, R. (1974). A new approach to the economic theory of fertility behavior. In T. Schultz (Eds.), *Economics of the family* (pp. 25–75). Chicago: University of Chicago Press.

Wilson, P., & Pahl, R. (1988). The changing sociological construct of the family. *Sociological Review, 36*, 233–272.

Wilson, W. (1987). *The truly disadvantaged.* Chicago: University of Chicago.

Wilson, W., & Neckerman, K. (1986). Poverty and family structure: The widening gap between evidence and public policy issues. In S. Danziger & D. Weinberg (Eds.), *Fighting poverty: What works and what doesn't* (pp. 232–259). Cambridge, MA: Harvard University Press.

Wineberg, H., & McCarthy, J. (1989). Child spacing in the United States: Recent trends and differentials. *Journal of Marriage and the Family, 51*, 213–228.

Wolf, W., & MacDonald, M. (1979). The earnings of men and remarriage. *Demography, 16*, 389–399.

Wojtkiewicz, R., McLanahan, S., & Garfinkel, I. (1990). The growth of families headed by women: 1950–1980. *Demography, 27*, 19–30.

Wood, R. (1995). Marriage rates and marriageable men: A test of the Wilson hypothesis. *Journal of Human Resources, 30*, 163–193.

Yamaguchi, K. (1991). *Event history analysis.* Newbury Park, CA: Sage.

Yogev, S. (1981). Do professional women have egalitarian marital relationships? *Journal of Marriage and the Family, 43,* 865–872.

Young, C. (1975). Factors associated with the timing and duration of the leaving home stage of the family life cycle. *Population Studies, 29,* 61–73.

Zelnik, M., & Kantner, J. (1974). The revolution of teenage first pregnancies. *Family Planning Perspectives, 6,* 74–80.

Zelnik, M., & Kantner, J. (1977). Sexual and contraceptive experience of young unmarried women in the U.S., 1976 and 1971. *Family Planning Perspectives, 9,* 55–71.

Zelnik, M., & Kantner, J. (1978). Contraceptive patterns and premarital pregnancy among women aged 15–19 in 1976. *Family Planning Perspectives, 10,* 135–142.

Zelnik, M., & Kantner, J. (1980). Sexual activity, contraceptive use and pregnancy among metropolitan area teenagers: 1971–1979. *Family Planning Perspectives, 12,* 230–237.

Zelnik, M., Kim, Y., & Kantner, J. (1979). Probabilities of intercourse and conception among U.S. Teenage women, 1971–1976. *Family Planning Perspectives, 11,* 177–183.

Zelnik, M., Kantner, J., & Ford, K. (1981). *Sex and pregnancy in adolescence.* Beverly Hills, CA: Sage.

CHAPTER 3

Cross-Cultural and U.S. Kinship

Bert N. Adams

Introduction

Kinship units in certain societies, especially agricultural, play economic, political, religious, and other institutional roles. Additional characteristics of kin units in some societies include property-holding and inheritance, housing, need-obligation, and affective or emotional ties. There is, however, no simple linear disappearance of these characteristics as one moves from the kin-based society to the "originally solidary" or differentiated modern industrial state. Yet, compared to agricultural societies, kin units of the United States are less central to society's operation, fulfilling an affective function to differing degrees and a need-obligation function to some extent and performing idiosyncratically in the areas of housing and inheritance. In the middle section of this chapter the significance of kin terms, the relative as a person, and the meanings of kin "distance" are considered. The last section of the chapter is given to a characterization of relationships among the following kin: parents and adult offspring, siblings and grandparents, secondary kin, and in-laws, with some attention to kin-keeping and to gender and ethnic differences in the United States.

Kin Characteristics in Cross-Cultural Perspective

In traditional agricultural societies, institutions and individuals alike are embedded within the larger kin unit, so that most of the activities and interactions that occur are predicated upon kin ties of one sort or another. Schneider (1968) characterizes the difference between kinship in such societies and kinship in Western societies today:

> The kinship systems of modern, western societies are relatively differentiated as compared with the kinship systems

Bert N. Adams • Department of Sociology, University of Wisconsin–Madison, Madison, Wisconsin, 53176.

Handbook of Marriage and the Family, 2nd edition, edited by Marvin Sussman, Suzanne K. Steinmetz, and Gary W. Peterson. Plenum Press, New York, 1999.

found in many primitive and peasant societies. By "differentiated" I mean simply that kinship is clearly and sharply distinguished from all other kinds of social institutions and relationships. In many primitive and peasant societies a large number of kinds of institutions are organized and built as *parts of the kinship system itself*. Thus the major social units of the society may be kin groups—lineages perhaps. These same kin groups may be property-owning units, the political units, the religious units, and so on. Thus, whatever a man does in such a society he does *as a kinsman of one kind or another*. (p. v, italics added)

The Papago of northern Mexico, for example, have no political institutions beyond the village council, which consists of the elders in the various family units. These same elders perform the major religious rituals on behalf of their kin. Even the economic division of labor is coterminous with the kin networks, there being no separate traders or market functionaries.

What are the major characteristics of kin in various societies? These include:

- Property-holding and inheritance
- Housing and maintenance of residential proximity
- Obligation, or helping in time of need
- Affection, emotional ties, or primary relationships

The first of these, descent/inheritance, is clearly basic to societies with corporate or property-holding kin units. So let us look in some detail at descent and inheritance in settled agricultural societies.

Descent and Inheritance

Descent and inheritance are closely related, but not synonymous. Descent has to do with the formal manner in which the individual is related to kin. Inheritance involves the property, goods, and obligations that are passed along through specified kin. The four most prevalent types of descent groups are *patrilineal* and *matrilineal* (unilineal) systems and *bilateral*—as practiced in Western societies—and, to a lesser extent, *bilineal* systems. All determine property-holding and inheritance, as well as performing

Matrilineal System

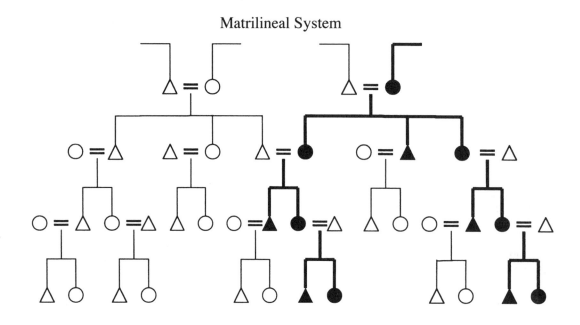

Patrilineal System

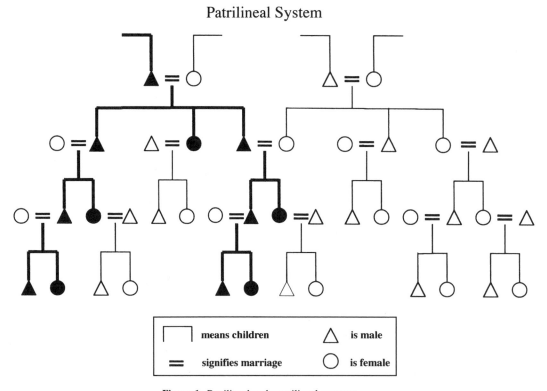

⌐ means children	△ is male
= signifies marriage	○ is female

Figure 1. Patrilineal and matrilineal systems.

other functions. As seen in Figure 1, in the patrilineage each time a female is born, she is part of her father's patrilineage. But the line stops with her; it does not continue through her children. However, when a male child is born the patriline continues through him to his children. The role of a woman in a patrilineal system, then, is to provide offspring for her husband's line and productive labor for his patrilineage.

In the matrilineage precisely the opposite principle is at work; that is, each time a male is born the line stops with him, whereas each time a female is born the line continues through her to her children. The role of the man is, therefore, to provide offspring for his wife's lineage. Notice another aspect of these unilineal systems. In Figure 1 those on both sides of the equal sign are *never* in the same lineage. This means that, compared to blood ties, marital ties are secondary. Being in a Western family system where marriage is the central fact, it is difficult to put ourselves inside a system where the wife may be sent back to her kin for not providing children for her husband's lineage. It is also striking that in the patrilineage one's own mother is an outsider: She is part of the lineage into which she was born. It is not that she is not intimately related to her children; she is imply not part of her husband's and children's kin group.

As for inheritance, there are three possibilities in the patrilineage. First, first-born or the last-born son may inherit all the property, with the others having to make their own way, though often with some help from the kin line. These are known, respectively, as *primogeniture* and *ultimogeniture*. Or the inheritance may be partible, so that each son is given a separate share. Or the inheritance may be nonpartible, so that the sons collectively inherit an "undivided interest" in it. This is most frequent and occurs in agrarian societies, as described by Harris (1983): "If the property concerned is a farm whose economic viability depends on its *size*, then, in order to inherit, the children of the owner of that farm will have to stay together to work on it" (pp. 20–21).

Another aspect of unilineal systems concerns genealogical relationships. While I was living in Uganda, our neighbor, a Muganda, invited us to the wedding of his brother. At the close of the wedding we were introduced not only to this brother, but to 23 other siblings. Noting our interest, he indicated that he also had 7 fathers, so the number of brothers should not be all that unusual. What he meant, of course, was that all those of the same sex and generation are related to the next generation the same way. So, instead of a father and 6 uncles, he had, sociologically speaking, 7 fathers. Likewise, instead of 3 brothers and 20 male cousins on his father's side, he had 23 brothers.

Every system works once an individual is inside it, and every system has stresses and tensions inherent in it. The tensions in the patrilineage are likely to be between mother-in-law and daughter-in-law, since both are outsiders to the lineage and have low status until it is gained with age. In fact, the daughter-in-law's position in the family is lower than that of her sons, and it borders on servitude. She can, however, comfort herself with the thought that her son will eventually bring her a daughter-in-law to dominate in the household. Another point of tension in the patrilineage occurs among brothers, when they are due to inherit the family property jointly. The greatest point of tension in the matrilineage occurs between the man and his wife's brother because the man is in fact raising sons who will inherit not from him but from his wife's line. One must remember that matrilineage does not mean matriarchy, or women running society. In fact, the brothers tend to control the property that will eventually pass through the female line and to play the dominant political role in the clan/community. The husband can console himself in the matrilineage with the thought that his sister is raising children for him.

Bilaterality signifies normativie equality in affiliation with both the mother's and the father's kin, although in actuality kin ties in a bilateral system tend to be overbalanced in favor of the preferred kin. Inheritance follows the same types of patterns, but is generally more complex than the determination of descent because multiple items tend to be inherited, as we shall see later. The U.S. family is basically bilateral in descent; that is, American's trace descent through, and consider themselves equally related to, both parental kin groups. Only in the practice of adding the husband's family name to the wife's at marriage, a practice also showing signs of changing, does the U.S. family retain a vestige of patrilineal inheritance.

Although unilineal descent lines tend to be relatively clear-cut, neither descent nor inheritance ordinarily operates in either–or terms. Patrilineal descent does not mean that an individual is related to her/his father's male kin to the exclusion of interaction, obligation, and intimacy with his/her mother's kin. In fact, intimacy in a patrilineal society is often greater between an individual and the mother's family simply because there are "no strings attached." In the case of inheritance, even more than in the case of descent, involvement with the two kin groups tends to be a matter of degree or kind rather than of exclusiveness. For example, Christensen (1954) reports that, among the Fanti of West Africa, along with membership in a matrilineal clan (matrilineal descent) goes the right of property inheritance, the use of clan land, succession to a position of political authority, and a proper funeral and burial. Thus, the Fanti might easily be considered a matrilineal society. Yet the father's line among the Fanti is also a source of certain types of inheritance. From the patriline, individuals receive their military allegiance, their fathers' deity, and their souls; physically, they regard their fathers as the primary sources of their blood. Christensen concludes that the Fanti are, in fact, characterized by double descent (from our perspective, "double inheritance"), receiving certain benefits and obligations from each of the two kin lines. While inheritance is not always as equally divided as it is among the Fanti, many unilineal, that is, either patrilineal or matrilineal, systems are characterized by a secondary inheritance and by close relationships with members of the opposing kin group or line.

What factors favor unilineal descent in a society, and what factors lead to the disintegration of these systems? According to E. Kathleen Gough, as quoted by Robert Winch (1979), factors favoring unilineal descent include

> scarcity of land and the heritability of valuable immovable property (buildings, trees, etc.) and a mode of organization whereby the leaders of the descent group control distribution to its members of the fruits of production. Conversely she found that the rise of a market system, access to jobs, and the opportunity to acquire personal property were factors leading to the disintegration of the descent group. (p. 165)

Majid al-Haj (1995) adds that individual modernity in the hamula, or kin group of the Arabs in Israel, does not result in a weakening of the political or social network connections of kinship. However, kin economics change away from kin ownership and inheritance to a pooling of resources for individual mobility. That is, the change is from lineal property concerns to individual careers and success.

Several authors have noted that matrilineages are more fragile than patrilineages under the pressure of modern urban life, the tendency being to reverse inheritance rules from the mother's brother to the father (see Nsamenang, 1987, p. 290) or to change to bilaterality.

In the United States, since colonial times the wife can hold property separately from her husband and can distribute it to her offspring separately if she so desires. In U.S. society, as Farber (1971) has noted, high status groups have much to gain by working out mutually beneficial marriage alliances and by stressing not only the economic family estate but also what he calls the "symbolic family estate." Inheritance, then, includes both property and "name," or a significant ancestry, and these forms of inheritance serve to separate or differentiate those of higher status from the rest of society (pp. 6, 115).

Offspring desiring to inherit property when a parent dies may be obliged to help care for that property while the parent is alive. For this and other socioeconomic reasons, it is not surprising that a fairly high correlation exists between residential clustering and descent-inheritance patterns: patrilocality with patriliny, matrilocality with matriliny, and neolocality with bilaterality. These correlations are, however, far from perfect. Under certain conditions, matrilocal residence may occur in combination with bilateral or patrilineal descent. To understand the bases for the relation between residential clustering and descent-inheritance in a particular society, one must understand its economy, polity, and geography, not just its kin norms, as real behavior is always more varied and complicated than a society's rules or norms.

Other Kin Characteristics

The *housing-residential proximity* function noted in the last section has two factors and is most difficult to place on a change continuum. For one thing, household sharing may assume various forms. In one society the form may be the "long-house," in which the men live apart from the women and children. In another it may be a joint family of brothers and their wives and children. In a third, aged parents may live with one of their married offspring. In a fourth, the family compound includes a man, his wives, and their children. Furthermore, although the norms of certain societies include household sharing, residence may actually be *proximate* rather than shared—with the kin group acting as a unit. Finally, housing may be temporarily shared with kin in virtually any society, including the contemporary United States. Beck and Beck (1989) call this the "intermittent extended family," occurring as one or more family members pass through a transition or crisis. Thus, if the issue is simply kin proximity, one might argue that there is a progressive change toward greater dispersion from the small, undifferentiated society to the modern industrial society. But if the issue is stated as the provision by kin of housing for one another, this is about as likely in rural-to-urban migrant groups in the United States as it is in the Hindu joint family of India. The difference is that, in the former case, the relatives with whom one *should* share residence are not specified, and permanent sharing is not expected.

The *obligatory* factor, based on the expectation that one will help kin under certain circumstances, also varies greatly. In one society, the strongest obligation may be to the mother's brother; in another, to the grandfather; and in still another, to one's own parents. Also, the obligations range from warrior allegiance and a proper burial to financial assistance or simply keeping in touch. In the United States, according to Rossi and Rossi (1990), the "obligation to provide financial aid moves in a more restricted network than the obligation to provide comfort" (p. 207). A good example of the kind of help kin may provide in U.S. society is job recruitment and migration. That is, employees tell kin about opportunities where they work or help them migrate to where work is available (Grieco, 1982). The strongest sense of mutual obligation in contemporary U.S. kinship seems to be between aging parents and their adult offspring, but even this is mitigated by the equally powerful societal value of nuclear family independence and self-sufficiency.

Unlike the U.S. upper class, in which the inheritance-differentiating function is still strong, the working and lower classes are characterized by proximity and strong obligation.

"Domestic aspects of kinship," notes Farber (1971), "are those which emerge in the course of living together.... The domestic level predominates in the lower class and represents the use of kindred as an aggregate by a population at the mercy of economic uncertainties" (pp. 114–115).

The final function of a kinship system, providing affection or *emotional* ties for the individual, operates as a matter of choice in most systems. Although each society has an expectation that certain kin will provide such ties, the actual strength of affectional relationships is extremely varied. In societies in which institutions are embedded in the kin network, so that one kin line has jural and economic power over the individual, his or her closest ties are often with members of the other line. For example, in some patrilineal societies, the individual's closest feelings are toward members of his or her mother's kin group. Perhaps the most outstanding examples in U.S. kinship of the blocking of affect by functional ties are those instances when children and their parents work in the same business and, as a result, seek leisure interaction and emotional gratifications elsewhere among their kin. Farber (1981) goes so far as to say that modern society actually discourages nonbureaucratic personal commitments, such as kinship "(a) by emphasizing personal freedom in nonwork affairs and (b) by defining traditional family and kinship institutions as coercive, as ineffective loci of socialization, and as interfering with self-realization" (p. 16). Jarrett (1985) adds that affection is simply not necessary for kin obligation to be carried out. The "affection myth" may need to be dispelled, "so that caregiving is done from motives of kinship obligations which, historically, have formed the basis for family aid" (p. 5). In an important paper, Collier, Rosaldo, and Yanagisako (1982) remind us that even in the nuclear family of parents and children affection is not universal, but is a modern expectation that has become part of family ideology and a key factor in forming families and holding them together.

One can say that the greatest difference in kinship between, for example, Papago society and contemporary U.S. society is the meeting of institutional needs outside the family, so that the kin network in and of itself seldom performs economic-productive, political, religious, or "formal" educational functions. Apart from that, however, it is difficult to summarize briefly the differences in specific characteristics of kinship in different societies. For example, patriarchy exists in both kin-based societies and those in which the small nuclear family is normative. However, there are subtle gender differences between the two. Warner, Lee, and Lee (1986) note that wives have more power in nuclear family societies than in extended kin societies because the wife is more essential and less replaceable in the former. This, however, is negated when she is restricted to the domestic sphere and is thus economically dependent on the husband. Also, women

gradually played an increasingly central kin role as industry and economic life were differentiated from the kin network. Oliker (1989) describes this change:

> Histories of the daily lives of women and men in early industrial society suggest that bonds among female kin and neighbors were less affected by encroaching industry than were bonds among males. Indeed, as women continued to exchange child care, sick care, domestic production, and kinship ritual, kinship bonds remained critical through the vicissitudes of daily family survival. Even though the man's new provider role required less daily exchange among kin, the woman's domestic responsibilities continued to rely on—indeed, in periods of market contraction, relied increasingly on—nonmarket exchange among friends and kin. (p. 23)

Perhaps we should move ahead with the assertion that, in the contemporary United States affection is an expectation that is extremely varied in reality. Kin perform certain specific obligations and operate differentially by class in the areas of inheritance and housing, yet this summary only hints at many crucial issues that must be confronted before kinship in the United States can be understood fully.

Some Issues in Kinship Analysis

Of the many issues regarding kinship that could be reviewed in this chapter, five are the most essential to understanding kin relations in the United States: the significance of *kin terms*, the idea of the *relative as a person*, the meaning of kin "*distance*," and the issues of kin *unimportance* and nuclear family *isolation* in urban-industrial society.

Kin Terms

For many years, the significance of kin terms has been debated in the literature on kinship. Do the terms used—such as *mother's brother*, *parallel cousin*, or *aunt*—have direct behavioral connotations, so that the compilation and comparison of terminological systems can be used to symbolize the kinship systems of different societies? Are the terms psychologically grounded cultural constructs only indirectly related, at best, to behavioral patterns? Or are the terms anachronistic survivals only partially correlated with actual kinship norms, behaviors, and roles in a given society? Lewis Henry Morgan, notes Fox (1967), "saw in the study of terminology the royal road to the understanding of kinship systems" (p. 240). Eggan (1950) states bluntly that "the verbal behavior symbolizes the socially defined relationships" (p. 295). Radcliffe-Brown (1941) shows that Choctaw and Omaha kin terms are as reasonable for their kinship systems as are our terms for our system. Likewise, Davies (1949) points out that the kin-based Syrian Arabs employ terms that distinguish among five generations. This stress on the sociological significance of terminology is epitomized in Murdock's book *Social Structure* (1949), in which various types of kinship systems are classified and distinguished from one another primarily on the basis of terms.

On the other side of the question are scholars such as Kroeber (1952), who claimed that kinship terms reflect psychology, not sociology. In fact, says Kroeber, kinship systems are "linguistic patterns of logic, and their uncritical and unrestrained use as if they were uncontaminated reflectors of past or present institutions" is unsound and dangerous (pp. 172, 181). And, as Fox (1967) notes, Bronislaw Malinowski had little use for the study of kin terms, arguing that the study of norms and actual relationships would be more productive.

While the debate has not been completely resolved, it seems that Fox's (1967) conclusion is valid. Kinship systems, he says, are many-sided, and terminology may not reflect every side. What a system of terms may tell us

> is *how the people themselves* see their world of kin. Who do they distinguish from whom and on what basis? It is often the case that they regard a certain distinction as crucial which has no meaning for us in terms of our analysis of the system of groups, alliances, etc. (p. 243)

There is, then, a correlation between terminology and behavior, but it is simply not perfect.

Part of the discussion of kin terms has concerned the European-American system and its peculiarities. Fox (1967), for example, points out that in this system "the terms for members of the nuclear family (father, mother, son, daughter, brother, sister) are *not used for anyone outside the family* without being marked as "grand" or "in-law." This is very different from the terminological systems of societies in which the nuclear family receives little or no stress (p. 258). Among the Papago Indians of southern Arizona and northern Mexico, for example, "all cousins of every degree, on both sides, are called brothers and sisters," although the Papago can, if need be, use words that mean a "near brother" (one's own) and a "far brother" (a cousin) (Underhill, 1965, p. 150). The European-American terminological system (which Murdock classifies with the "Eskimo") manifests both the bilateral nature of our kin relations—that is, our normatively equal relation to both mother's and father's kin—and the special importance attached to members of the nuclear family.

The previously mentioned studies are concerned with comparative differences in kin terms. A few authors have tried to determine the significance of American kin terms. Schneider and Homans (1955) assert that one of the more fundamental and interesting characteristics of American terminology is the wide variety of alternatives for the same individual:

> Mother may be called "mother," "mom," "ma," "mummy," "mamma," by her first name, nickname, diminutive, "old woman," and a variety of other less commonly used designations.

> Father may be called "father," "pop," "pa," "dad," "daddy," by his first name, diminutive, "old man," "boss," and a variety of less commonly used designations. Uncles may be addressed or referred to as uncle-plus-first name, first name alone, or uncle alone. Similarly for aunts. (p. 1195)

Schneider and Homans then proceed to report the relationship between terms and behavior. Among their findings are the following:

1. On the assumption that parental terms can be ranged on a continuum from most formal, *father* and *mother*, to least formal, first name only, there is a tendency for both sexes to become relatively more formal with their same-sex parent.
2. Use of the terms *father* and *mother* for one's parents symbolizes a more formal and less close relationship with them.
3. Females use a wider variety of terms for their parents than do males for theirs.
4. The tendency is "for more first-name-alone designations to be applied to aunts and uncles on the mother's side than on the father's."
5. Males are more likely than females to address aunts and uncles by first name alone. In cases of either strong positive or strong negative sentiment the formal terms *aunt* and *uncle* are dropped and first name only is used (p. 1195).

Since Schneider and Homans' article appeared, attempts at replication have verified only findings 3, 4, and 5. Hagstrom and Hadden (1965) interpret these findings to mean that females are generally more involved in kinship and that people tend to be somewhat closer to maternal kin. They also found that, with the exception of females and their fathers' siblings, aunt and uncle terminology and sentiment is unilinear rather than curvilinear; that is, the closer one feels to an aunt or uncle the more likely one is to use first name only.

That there may be more than one kinship system in the United States is made clear by Farber (1971) in his reconciliation of the views of Goodenough (1965) and Schneider (1965) on terminology. Goodenough, after working with a New England sample, reported that affines (kin-by-marriage) as well as blood kin are considered to be relatives. However, first cousins "have no ascribed lifelong obligations other than a show of cordiality" (p. 281). Schneider, on the other hand, having investigated kin terms in the Midwest, concluded that kinship is primarily a matter of blood ties. Thus, the first cousin is in the inner circle of kin, while affines are not truly kin at all. Moreover, he finds that terminological distinctions exist that express the structural distinctions he is reporting.

Farber's (1971) response is that they are both right. There is the old New England kinship system, with its emphasis upon marriage as linking two kin groups, and there is the Midwestern type, with its emphasis upon blood kin. He goes on to conclude that in present-day U.S. society the former is more prevalent in higher status groups, the latter in lower status groups. Suppose, then, one felt close to one's parents-in-law. This would probably be expressed at the higher statuses, says Farber, by the use of the terms mother and father, and at the lower statuses by the use of first names—to indicate friendship, not kinship. Farber further generalizes this distinction to speak to the issue raised by Hagstrom and Hadden (1965): In high-status families affection is generally expressed by using the appropriate kin term; in low-status families, by using first names.

In addition to cross-cultural comparisons and analysis of the significance of kin terms in the United States, the study of kin terms includes the naming of children. In a sample of 384 primarily middle-class women in the Chicago area, Rossi (1965) noted that between 1920 and 1950 there was a tendency away from naming offspring for mother's mother and father's father and toward naming them for mother's father and especially father's mother. This, she feels, may indicate a greater equalitarianism within the family and the lessening role segregation between males and females and between maternal and paternal kin. Rossi's article has, of course, only scratched the surface of what might be discovered from a study of names and naming. In fact, as can be seen from the sources used in this discussion, Little has been done recently—although much could be done—in the analysis of kinship terms in a single society such as the United States. Farber's (1971) discoveries are a step in the right direction.

The Relative as a Person

The kinship network does not consist of terminological distinctions or of roles and functions, but of people. These people have various personalities, behave in various ways, and view their social worlds from various perspectives. The kinship component of a relationship gives it an enduring quality, as distinct from the contingent solidarity of friendship; but, within this difference, the unique character of a kin relationship results from the involvement of kinfolk with one another. There are, as Schneider (1968) points out, "Famous Relatives" who hold a particularly honored place among their kin (p.67) and whether dead or alive, are referred to with pride. A cousin with whom one enjoys doing things may be described as "more a friend than a relative," the implication of the expression being that the term cousin ordinarily connotes little affection or interaction, while this particular cousin is of greater significance than that. On the other side of this coin are the friends one refers to as "Uncle Ronald" and "Aunt Maruine," though they are actually not relatives at all. The kin terms indicate a relationship that is based on more than the fleeting interests and activities of the typical friend-

ship and is enduring and intimate to a degree usually present in relationships with certain kin.

It is very likely that the fuzziness of kinship designations in the United States, and the flexibility with which kin ties are interpreted by specific people, are related to the great emphasis that is placed on personal achievement rather than on ascription. This emphasis is related both to the restricted terminological system referred to here and to the great variability in the actual relations between people holding the same structural positions within the kinship system, such as mother-son or uncle-niece. This variability is made clearer by examining the three meanings of "distance" in kinship, especially as these pertain to U.S. kin relations.

Kin "Distance"

Distance, says Schneider, means three things in U.S. kinship. First, it signifies *genealogical* distance, so that we may speak of a second cousin as being a more distant kinsman than an uncle. Some have tried to delineate the various circles of relatives in U.S. society according to genealogical distance. Thus, the inner circle of relatives includes only those from one's own families of procreation and orientation—parents and children, brothers and sisters. The outer circle of relatives includes those from one's parents' family or orientation, including aunts, uncles, and grandparents. Finally, beyond this outer circle are cousins, great aunts, and so on. The respondents in the Rossi and Rossi (1990) study actually put the following numerical ranking on obligation to categories of relatives:

> What mattered most for obligation level was not a specific type of kinperson, but the degree of relatedness of ego to the various kintypes. Grandparents, grandchildren, and siblings—all related to ego through one connecting link—evoked comparable levels of felt obligation (between 6 and 7 on a 10-point scale); aunts and uncles, nieces and nephews—related to ego through two connecting links—showed similar levels of obligation (between 4 and 5 on the scale); while the lowest obligation level was to cousins—related through a minimum of three connecting links (a mean of 3.2 on the scale).

The terms *closeness* and *distance* immediately elicit a second interpretation that Schneider calls *socioemotional* distance (1968, p.73). Feelings toward kin may or may not be governed by genealogical distance. In fact, Johnson (1988) claims that people "most often use the subjective notions of closeness and distance rather than genealogical distance to identify their relatives" (p. 166). Emotional closeness is governed as much by the interactions and experiences shared or not shared with certain relatives as by genealogical distance. On this point, Weston (1991) notes the way in which discourse and culture have "denied lesbians and gays access to kinship" by treating them as outcasts (p. 21).

The third type of distance that pertains to kinship is *physical* or residential distance. Intense interaction clearly requires proximity, and proximity in U.S. society is broadly related to genealogical closeness. However, the association among the three types of closeness or distance is far from perfect. Proximity is simply not a sufficient condition for intimacy or socioemotional closeness. Parents, on the one hand, are considered intimate relatives even when not physically accessible. Aunts, uncles, and cousins, on the other hand, may be quite proximate, yet not be objects of great affection or frequent interaction. As Schneider (1968) points out: "A person who is genealogically close may be physically distant and neutral on the socioemotional dimension. Or a person may be close socioemotionally and physically but distant genealogically" (p. 73). The same functional character of U.S. kinship that gives rise to a terminological system stressing the nuclear family and that allows for fuzzy boundaries and idiosyncratic personal relationships within the kin network also makes for a relatively low correlation among the three types of closeness or distance in U.S. kinship. But, although hinted at here, what precisely does kinship *do* in the United States?

Unimportance, Isolation, and Consistency

Fifty years ago, Parsons' (1943) article on kinship in the United States made three major points. First, compared with kinship in many other societies, kinship in the United States is relatively unimportant to the ongoing of the society. With the parceling out of institutional functions to other settings—institutional differentiation—the kinship network has little role to play in societal maintenance, particularly compared with the role it played in the past (and which it still plays in other cultures). Second, the normal household unit is the nuclear, conjugal family, living "in a home segregated from those of both pairs of parents (if living) and … economically independent of both. In a very large proportion of cases the geographical separation is considerable" (p. 27). Third, this isolated, open, bilateral kinship system with nuclear household units is most functional for, or best suited to, the U.S. occupational system and urban living. It makes residential mobility in pursuit of occupational opportunities much easier than if one's corporate kin group have to be carried along on each move.

This article and its conclusions have been a favorite target of kinship researchers since the 1950s. Among other things, researchers discovered that adult offspring are more likely to live close to their parents and other kin than "considerably separated" from them. Cancian (1987), reviewing much of the research, states that 60% of Americans visit a relative at least once a week, with the parent–adult offspring bond being especially strong. Noting that Parsons was writ-

ing about the middle class, specifically excluding farmers, matrilocal lower-class families, and the upper class, several researchers found that even among middle-class families the separation from kin is not likely to be great.

Even more important, researchers noted that the kin network does "function" in several ways: providing affectional ties, help when needed, and even supports for or deterrents to residential mobility. The functionality of the kin network, demonstrated in study after study, led Sussman (1965) to conclude that

> the evidence on the viability of an existing kinship structure carrying on extensive activities among kin is so convincing that we find it unnecessary to continue further descriptive work in order to establish the existence of the kin network in modern urban society. (p. 63)

Some lower-class individuals and families may be isolated, and some highly residentially and socially mobile middle-class families may pay little attention to kin, although Darroch (1981) notes that in the nineteenth century families migrated along kin lines. Osborn and Williams (1976) report that "younger people and people of high social status not only move more frequently but their moves are more likely to result in reduced propinquity" (p. 205). This means two things: first, higher status families tend to follow the job market, regardless of the location of kin, and second, young marrieds are moving away from their families, although later in life they may close the residential distance again.

The pattern is for working-class people to have a cluster of kin close at hand and for high-status individuals to be very much concerned about their kin links—the symbolic family estate. It is worth noting at this point that at present both the domestic and the symbolic estate function can be found among the black population of the United States. For example, Parish, Hao, and Hogan (1991) found that young black mothers are more likely to live near kin and to receive childcare assistance from them than are whites. Taylor (1986) finds that "familial relationships, proximity to relatives, and family contact all play a crucial role in the informal social support networks of blacks" (p. 74). These bonds include both residential distance and affective closeness. In addition, one aspect of the increasing ethnic solidarity of the black community is what Alex Haley calls the search for "roots" (1974). In Farber's (1971) terms, these roots are the black individual's symbolic family estate.

Therefore, although Parsons (1943) claimed that kinship is *relatively* unimportant in U.S. society and that this is consistent with the economic-industrial structure of this society, his critics responded that nuclear families are not isolated, kin networks do function, and many of their functions are perfectly consistent with the economic structure of the society. Where kinship and economics seem at odds is ordinarily when kin relations and the economic-productive function are linked directly, as in a family-run business. Twenty years after the original article, Parsons (1943) sought to reemphasize his comparative perspective, while at the same time acknowledging the findings of his critics. The view of the "isolated nuclear family" and that of its critics, Parsons claims (1965),

> are not contradictory but complementary. The concept of isolation applies in the first instance to kinship structure as seen in the perspective of anthropological studies in that field. In this context our system represents an extreme type, which is well described by that term. It does not, however, follow that all relations to kin outside the nuclear family are broken. Indeed, the very psychological importance for the individual of the nuclear family in which he was born and brought up would make any such conception impossible. (p. 35)

Adams (1968a) and Lee (1980) call the isolation of the nuclear family in the United States a "relative" matter, meaning that it is isolated compared to most other times and places.

Thus, it may be concluded that neither institutions nor individuals are as embedded in the kin networks of the United States as they have been in many other societies. This is not to say, however, that kinship performs no functions in the United States. Nor is it to say that its performance of certain functions is inconsistent with the achievement-based institutions of that society. Nor, finally, is it to say that the absence of individual embeddedness in a household and solidarity sense means that kin are isolated from one another, either interactionally or emotionally. It does mean that the volitional element, the flexibility and variety that come with choice, is heightened in U.S. kinship. It also means that generalizations about kin are risky; when based simply on "the kin network," are clearly *over*generalizations. Likewise, when generalizations are about "the family" and kin they are also incorrect, since females are much more embedded in the kin network than are males, as we will see in the discussion of parents and offspring in the following section. One much instead speak of the relations between specific categories of kin—parents and offspring, siblings, in-laws, and so on.

Categories of U.S. Kin and Their Characteristics

Kin might be subdivided into a large number of genealogical categories, including cousins, grandparents, grandchildren, mothers-in-law, and many others. We will, however, discuss four major divisions: parents and their adult offspring, siblings and grandparents, secondary kin (i.e., all blood kin and their affines connected to one by more than one link), and in-laws.

Parents and Adult Offspring

In 1971 I wrote that "the relations between young adults and their aging parents are ordinarily the closest kin tie attitudinally and residentially" (Adams, 1971, p 177). The relations between parents and adult offspring can be characterized by the phrase *position concern*. This positive, or active, concern is manifested in several ways. First, there is extremely frequent contact between these intergenerational kin. When they live close to one another, weekly or more frequent contact is the rule. However, "to bridge the distances separating the residences of parents and children takes both time and money," and communication by telephone or travel cannot be as frequent as in cases of proximity (Rossi & Rossi, 1990, p. 387; Fischer, 1982, pp. 370–372). The gender difference is pointed out by the Rossis, who find that distance represents:

> *the* major factor affecting the frequency of interaction between mothers and adult children in all parent-child dyads.... In contact with fathers, however, the quality of the relationship has even more of an influence than sheer opportunity as indexed by geographic distance. (p. 387)

A second manifestation of positive concern between adult offspring and their parents is the strong affectional tie, which, according to the Rossis, increases over the adult years regardless of who rates it. However, as in the case of residential distance, this varies from family to family and by gender. Of the four possible parent–offspring relationships—mother–daughter, mother–son, father–daughter, father–son—the closest, both affectionally and interactionally, is that between mother and daughter. I will say more about this bond later. The third aspect of positive concern is obligation, which includes both being "on call" and regular forms of aid. The help pattern, say the Rossis, "tends to be reciprocal in nature for two or more decades, when children are in their mid-twenties to mid-forties and parents in their mid-forties to mid-sixties" (p. 498). At the beginning of that period of time, most of the aid flows downward, from parents to children, while later it flows both ways. Finally, if the parents live long enough, it may flow mostly from offspring to parents, and "women kin evoke more obligation than men, especially if they are unmarried or widowed" (p. 206). This, then, is the nature of positive concern between parents and adult offspring.

Several qualifications must be mentioned regarding this contact–affection–obligation configuration. First, the obligatory element does not stand in the way of affectional closeness unless it becomes the primary factor in continued contact. An example of such a situation is the young adult male who has few interests in common with his widowed mother, but is obliged to help her anyway (Adams, 1968b). The issue of "interests in common" raises a second qualification: "The Rossis note that they were unprepared "to find that dissensus in core values (religion, politics, general outlook on life) would depress the emotional closeness of parents and adult children" (Rossi & Rossi, 1990, p. 361). The third qualification is that obligation to aging parents may be greatly affected by a divorce, and this has been reported in a paper by Spitze, Logan, Deane, & Zenger (1994). They report that divorced daughters with custody have more contact with their aging parents, receive more help from the parents (especially aging mothers), and give less help to them. However, the authors note that the differences are small, indicating more continuity than change after divorce. It would not be surprising that all aspects of relationship with the noncustodial parent are affected by a divorce while the child is still at home. In fact, a divorce on the part of either generation may have a weakening effect on the parent–adult offspring relationship. The final qualification is that social mobility, meaning the movement of the offspring to a different occupational level, "influences feelings and perceptions but not behavior" (Kulis, 1987, pp. 429–430). That is, mobility is related to neither visiting nor aid, except when a son has been downwardly mobile.

The mother–daughter bond is one of, as Lucy Fischer (1986) puts it, "linked lives." This linking, says Fischer, is not merely one of forced labor due to patriarchy. It is one predicated on the "kinkeeping" function performed by women in this society. It is also a result of what Willmott and Young (1960) a generation ago called "female role convergence." Based on the traditional norm of women as mothers and wives, this argument simply said that while men assume a variety of occupations, mothers and daughters are more likely to assume the same role in adulthood. While women's occupational liberation has begun to change this, the fact remains that the motherhood role (not marriage) coupled with that of kinkeeper links women more strongly than men to kin.

Additional specifics of mother–daughter relations include the fact that adult daughters are the principle caregivers for the elderly, one result being a feeling of strain and constraint (Brody, 1985; Roff & Klemner, 1986). (As was noted previously, obligation and affection are not always positively related.) Jill Suitor (1987) finds that when a married daughter returns to school this meets with the approval of a well-educated mother, but with disapproval by a less-educated mother. The reasons for this seem to be that the more-educated mother holds more liberal gender role attitudes, and the daughter's further education will make hers and her mother's education closer together. However, while the mother–daughter relationship is the closest, we should repeat that all four parent–offspring relationships tend to be closer than relationships between any other two relatives in U.S. kin networks. Most of the exceptions to this are found among siblings and with grandparents.

Adult Sibling Relations and Grandparents

When the emphasis in kinship is upon lineage, the tie between grandparents and grandchildren tends to be the second most intense, after parent–child. However, in the standard American model siblings take precedence (Farber, 1981, p. 46). These are the two relationships, as Rossi and Rossi (1990) note, that have only one connecting link.

The terms that seem to summarize best the relations between adult siblings are *interest* and *comparison/identification*. Interest simply means a general feeling that one should keep up with one's siblings, keep posted on their activities, but that except in extreme circumstances there is no need for contact to be as frequent or mutual aid to be as great as that with parents. In fact, apart from the exchange of babysitting between proximate sisters, the sharing of financial or other forms of aid between siblings is likely to become a bone of contention or even a basis for alienation. Interest, then, is just that: The individual is "interested" in how brothers and sisters are getting along.

This notion of sibling rivalry has been a topic of discussion for some time in the socialization literature. It must now be added that when brothers and sisters leave home such rivalry does not end, but is transformed into *comparison* or *identification*. In a success- and achievement-oriented society, with substantial emphasis on individualism within the family, brothers and sisters are the comparative reference group par excellence. That is, the question "How am I doing?" can well be answered by noting how one's achievements compare with those of one's siblings. Siblings, unlike friends, are "givens" in the individual's social network. We cannot (as we can with friends) drop them if we become dissatisfied with them. And when the kin of orientation (adult offspring and their parents) get together, conversation is likely to turn—sometimes subtly, sometimes openly—to how well brother George or sister Susan is doing professionally or to how their marriages are going. There can be considerable emotional alienation between brothers whose occupations diverge greatly in prestige. In other sibling combinations, a prestige divergence generally results in a one-way, or unreciprocated, identification. That is, the lower-status sibling expresses affection for (and sometimes jealousy of) and wants to be like the higher-status sibling, but the feelings are not reciprocated. This, then, is one point at which the economic success values of the society impinge upon and help to determine the social psychology of kin involvement. It is noteworthy, however, that such variations in feeling are not very evident in the area of interaction. Females especially seem to have little control over the frequency of their contact with siblings and are thus unable, due to obligation, to bring that frequency into line with their feelings. This is, of course, another indication of the greater obligatory burden that females bear in kinship relations.

Ann Goetting (1986) has summarized the work of Cicirelli (1985), Lamb and Sutton-Smith (1982), and others on sibling relations across the life cycle. Her summary of adult sibling relations includes the issues of interest and comparison just described, but goes further. The relations between *young adult* siblings, says Goetting, include the following: (1) companionship; (2) emotional support; (3) cooperation in care for the elderly; and (4) aid and services (Goetting, 1986). The relations between siblings in *old age* include (1) and (4) from the previous list, but (2) is reminiscence or shared memory, and (3) is the resolution of rivalry. Several comments on her list are in order. First, it is possible that care for the elderly may be a matter of strain and even bitter disagreement rather than cooperation, although the latter is clearly the goal. Second, aid occurs when there is proximity, but even then not as often as between the siblings and their parents. Third, the resolution of rivalry means laying to rest whatever remnants exist of the comparisons noted earlier.

Some pairs of brothers and sisters evolve activity patterns that make them extremely close friends in adulthood. "Best friend" status for a sibling is, however, the exception rather than the rule. Activity-based relationships are even less prevalent between secondary kin, such as cousins, however.

Grandparents are in the second circle of kin along with siblings, being connected through one intervening link. In fact, aging grandparents, along with females, form the hub of kin activity and involvement. Cherlin and Furstenberg's (1986) important study of grandparents in the United States distinguishes three styles of grandparents: 55% of the respondents are compassionate, 29% are remote, and 16% are involved. Compassionate grandparents report frequent enough contact, but without either services or much parenting behavior. Grandparents who are most likely to indicate spending a lot less time with grandchildren than they would like are, of course, remote. Involved grandparents (i.e., those that provide parenting and services) meet three conditions: proximity, being younger then old grandparents, and need (such as a divorce).

An important point in the Cherlin and Furstenberg (1986) study is that grandparents believe there is a greater need now for warmth, understanding, and love in the relationship between grandchildren and grandparents than when their grandparents were alive. These grandparents indicated that they feel that the more unstable family life is, the greater the supportive role needed for and from grandparents. However, Cherlin and Furstenberg note that the increasing strength of the grandparent–grandchild relationship is overstated by their respondents. After all, the harsh reality of death rates 50 years ago and high rates of immigration early this century meant that one-fourth of the current grandparents never knew a grandparent themselves.

Other research has found that grandparents—especially in the higher social classes—often pass monetary gifts to younger generations (Caplow, 1982). Also, grandfathers may be particularly helpful to the single mother with a small child (Gershenson, 1983). But by the time the young person reaches adulthood, some grandparents are no longer alive.

Another issue is coresidence, or the sharing of housing with elderly parents. It has been found that the elderly are often more opposed to such sharing than are the offspring. Suitor and Pillemer (1991) note that more conflict occurs when the adult offspring are younger and when their marital status is different from that of their elderly parent(s). Health, gender, and length of coresidence seem to have no relation to conflict.

One further point: The "kinkeeping" function often performed by women was discussed earlier. This role is often played by a grandmother, who is the hub of kin activity; in fact, her death frequently means the fragmenting of the kin network. Another potential kinkeeper is an elderly lifelong single woman (Allen & Pickett, 1987). Still another is a sibling who takes over when the grandmother dies (Rosenthal, 1985). But the fact that it is women rather than men, and older rather than younger women, who most often do the "work" of kin contact, means a central figure is likely to be a grandmother—as long as she is alive. Women play this kinkeeping role, we should add, for several reasons. One is their greater embeddedness in the family through socialization. Another is the male avoidance of the task, an indication of the delegatory power that goes with patriarchy.

Secondary Kinship

Secondary kin are all those relatives (aunts, uncles, cousins, and so on) who are connected to an individual through contacts best described in U.S. society as *circumstantial* and *incidental*. Secondary kin relations seldom involve frequent contact, common interests, mutual aid, or strong affectional and obligatory concern. Yearly contact—the Christmas card, for example, or perhaps kin reunion at holidays or during a vacation—frequently suffices. The incidental nature of such kin relations may be seen in those instances in which an aunt and uncle drop in while one is visiting parents or in which one goes to see a cousin while on a trip home for the purpose of visiting parents and siblings. The circumstantial side of secondary kin contact is well depicted in the "wakes and weddings" relatives of whom Schneider (1968) speaks. These are kin brought together by such circumstances as the marriage or death of a mutual kinsman. Interestingly enough, Rosenblatt, Johnson, and Anderson (1981) find that, in general, kin visits involving "family trouble" (death, illness, etc.) are characterized by less tension and a greater feeling that the visit was "a good one."

The notion of incidental and circumstantial contact is opposed to that of intentional or volitional contact and fits quite well the character of most secondary kin in the United States. In the Greensboro study (Adams, 1968a), a few respondents were troubled by the weakness of secondary kin ties. The wife of a clerk explained: "It is distressing that distance is pulling families apart so. Seeing relatives was very important when I was young, and I miss it now. It bothers me that my children don't know their cousins and play with them like I did" (p. 167). However, a much greater proportion of respondents made this sort of comment: "My parents and sister mean a lot to me, but I simply don't have time to spend keeping up with a lot of kinsfolk that don't mean anything to me anyway." Or even more pointedly: "I have an aunt and one cousin besides my mother and brothers that mean a lot to me. As for the others—phooey!" (Quoted from interviews.)

The primary exception to circumstantiality is the activity pattern and mutual concern of secondary kin in many ethnic groups. Rossi and Rossi (1990) note the obligation to secondary kin among Irish and blacks who had close childhood relations especially to aunts and uncles. The activities that indicate closeness—originally meant for ensuring mutual survival—are now more likely to be a means for achieving individual success. Leichter and Mitchell (1967) report a phenomenon that was somewhat prevalent among the Jewish families they studied in New York City:

> Family circles and cousin clubs may also support occupational achievement by giving instrumental help as an organization: the group's loan fund may help to support children's education, or special collections may be taken up when there is particular need on the part of one member. (p. 156)

Such secondary kin support has not automatically disappeared as the various ethnic groups have been incorporated into the dominant structures of U.S. society. Yet these exceptions do not alter the overriding generalization that, even in the lower and working classes, secondary kin ordinarily play a relatively minor role in the individual's social network.

In-Law Relations

The discussion of in-laws, relatives one gains by marriage, requires that several distinctions be made. First, it should be—but is not always—made clear whether one is referring to the spouses' relations with their in-laws or with the influence of the in-laws upon relations between the spouses. This section will attempt to deal with both. Second, investigations of in-law relationships should distinguish between specific in-laws, such as the husband's mother and the wife's mother, sisters-in-law, and so on. Such specification is as necessary here as it is in the discussion of blood kin. Third, the focus of in-law studies should be not only on the roots of trouble or conflict—which is the case for most such studies—but also on the conditions that make for satisfactory relationships.

According to Goetting (1990) in-law relationships are, for the most part, without intensity. The reasons for this include: (1) the partial replacement of kin functions by formal organizations; (2) the increase in individualistic over familistic values; (3) geographic mobility; and (4) feminism, which may serve to weaken ties between women and their in-laws, especially if the in-laws are more conservative.

This last point reminds us that in her classic article on sex roles, Komarovsky (1950) hypothesized that as a result of the female's close ties to her parents, in-law troubles would more often involve the husband and the wife's parents than the wife and the husband's parents. Several later studies also found substantial conflict between the husband and the wife's parents. Yet, despite these studies, the majority of studies since Komarovsky's hypothesis was formulated have found in-law troubles to be generally more frequent between the wife and the husband's mother. This is the case despite the tendency of married couples to interact somewhat more often with the wife's parents than with the husband's.

The factors that give rise to in-law conflict or peace have not all been specified, but several have been tentatively isolated. Older women have less in-law trouble than *younger* ones. The presence of offspring in the home is likely to improve relations, particularly between the two mothers. Thus, the fact that younger marrieds appear to have more in-law troubles than older marrieds can be explained partially by the independence struggle that is completed during the early years of marriage and partially by in-law stresses that result from the birth of the grandchild. Fischer (1983) puts this very succinctly: "The birth of the child increases the importance of both the mother–daughter and the mother-in-law–daughter-in-law bonds, while accentuating the asymmetry between these relationships" (p. 192).

The second and third necessary, but not sufficient, conditions for in-law trouble are *proximity* and *dependence*. There is simply less likely to be trouble with in-laws when they are at a distance than when they are close by and interaction is frequent. Dependence, though not entirely separate from age and proximity, is a third factor. Young adult wives are more likely to be somewhat emotionally dependent on their parents than are husbands on theirs, but the latter situation, when it occurs, is more likely to cause trouble between his wife and his parents.

Several researchers have found that after marriage the husband's allegiance may actually transfer to his wife's family (Goetting, 1990). But treating a daughter-in-law or, more often, son-in-law as family or as one's own offspring is not the only mechanism for avoiding in-law conflict, especially with the mother-in-law. The myth of mother-in-law trouble has itself caused many women to resolve *not* to be that way, but to do everything possible not to meddle. Even gender equality may have helped to smooth out in-law relations and to improve their quality in recent years.

Over a generation ago, Landis and Landis (1963) found a close relation between marital happiness and good in-law relations. But a simple relationship may be causatively interpreted only with great caution. Although it is easy to jump to the conclusion that in-law trouble causes marital difficulties, an equally plausible interpretation would be that marital difficulties also disrupt the relations of couples with other members of their social network—including in-laws. Still, however one explains it, there is a relationship between in-law trouble and marital conflict. A final point on the asymmetry in-laws relations comes from Rossi and Rossi (1990), who believe, although they cannot cite any supportive evidence, that parents tend to feel more comfortable and "at home" literally and figuratively with their daughter and their daughter's spouse than with their sons and daughters-in-law, precisely because women largely determine the cuisine, childbearing values, and social activities of a household. And, again, feeling comfortable is a likely conflict reducer.

The Complicating Factor: Divorce

Most of the discussion thus far assumes that couples get married, stay married, and deal with two sets of kin. Of course, in the United States today (and many other societies) it is not that simple. As noted briefly earlier, the rising divorce rate has complicated kinship and has not yet given rise to uniform expectations or norms for dealing with the relationships produced by either divorce or remarriage. In 1978 Andrew Cherlin called remarriage an "incomplete institution," meaning that the rules were not spelled out. When it comes to kin relations, the incompleteness is true of both divorce and remarriage. How does one relate to ex-in-laws, or does one? Clearly, the presence or absence of grandchildren is crucial to the continuation of or change in in-law links, as Spitze et al. have noted (1994). However, the variety of postdivorce kin relations is as great as the number of couples experiencing it, meaning that each divorcing couple has to work out its own resolution.

Colleen Johnson, in *Ex Familia* (1988), points out that distance from kin and in-laws is likely to be greater for the man, since he is ordinarily less involved in kin relations when the couple is together. McLanahan, Wedenmeyer, and Adelberg (1981) have also found that divorced women, while having financial difficulties, are much more likely than men

to be reabsorbed into their own kin network as a means of social support.

With remarriage the complications increase, as the individual takes on new in-laws to go with the ex-in-laws. How long it will take for the process of institutionalization or norm emergence to be completed in the area of kinship and divorce is unclear at this point.

Conclusions

The least disrupted marriages, in terms of kin relationships, are those in which there are children and in which the couple live at least 4 or 5 hours away from the two sets of close kin. Moreover, these relationships often involve little emotional dependence upon kin, so that their attention is focused on their own family of procreation, rather than on their kin of orientation or other relatives. Such a conclusion assumes, however, that a great amount of value is placed upon simply avoiding conflict, with the positive functions of kinship involvement considered insignificant. However, the literature on kinship in the United States seems to show that most people disagree with Moore's (1958) assertion that kinship is nothing more than a barbaric "obligation to give affection as a duty to a particular set of persons on account of the accident of birth" (p. 163). Despite the emphasis U.S. society places on individualism and independence—which makes the relations of couples with their parents, in-laws, and other kin tenuous at times—most people seem to prefer the sense of identity, emotional support, visiting, and emergency help that genealogically close kin provide, rather than the total independence and isolation that might be achieved in a totally individualized society.

Compared with those of many other societies, cross-culturally and historically, kinship ties in the United States appear insignificant and weak. There is little institutional embeddedness in the kin network, and individual solidarity with kin exists more among women and only with the inner circle of kin in most middle-class and some working- and lower-class families. While kin relations are not voluntary, how one relates to kin certainly has an element of choice in it in the United States, and increasingly in the rest of the world. Despite such limitations, however, U.S. kin ties have a form of viability that is positively valued by most.

Having drawn these conclusions, it is well to be reminded of the issues still unresolved. Worldwide, more needs to be known about the relations between kinship, households, and urban life. Second, increasing intermarriage—racial, religious, etc.—leaves us wanting to know more about the effects of such differences on kin ties, both to one's own kin and to in-laws. Finally, births outside of marriage may eventually have almost as much effect on kinship as divorce, and so far little is known about this. Change, then, continues to make conclusions tentative at best.

ACKNOWLEDGMENTS. The author wishes to thank Bernard Farber and Gary Peterson for their suggestions and encouragement in the writing of this chapter.

References

Adams, B. N. (1968a). *Kinship in an urban setting.* Chicago: Markham.

Adams, B. N. (1968b). The middle class adult and his widowed or still-married mother. *Social Problems, 16,* 50–59.

Adams, B. N. (1968–1969). Kinship systems and adaptation to modernization. *Studies in Comparative International Development, 4.*

Adams, B. N. (1971). Isolation, function, and beyond: American kinship in the 1960s. In G. F. Broderick (Ed.), *A decade of family research and action* (pp. 163–186). Minneapolis: National Council on Family Relations.

al-Haj, M. (1995). Kinship and modernization in developing societies: The emergence of instrumentalized kinship. *Journal of Comparative Family Studies, 26,* 311–328.

Allen, K. R., & Pickett, R. (1987). Forgotten streams in the family life course: Utilization of qualitative retrospective interviews in the analysis of lifelong single women's family careers. *Journal of Marriage and the Family, 49,* 517–526.

Beck, R. W., & Beck, S. H. (1989). The incidence of extended household among middle-aged black and white women: Estimates from a 15-year panel study. *Journal of Family Issues, 10,* 147–168.

Brody, E. M. (1985). Parent care as a normative family stress. *Gerontologist, 25,* 19–29.

Caplow, T. (1982). Christmas gifts and kin networks. *American Sociological Review, 47,* 383–392.

Cherlin, A. (1978). Remarriage as an incomplete institution. *American Journal of Sociology, 84,* 634–650.

Cherlin, A. J., & Furstenberg, F. F. (1986). *The new American grandparent.* New York: Basic Books.

Christensen, J. B. (1954). *Double descent among the Fanti.* New Haven, CT: Human Relations Area Files.

Cicirelli, V. G. (1985). Sibling relationships throughout the life cycle. In L. L'Abate (Ed), *The handbook of family psychology and therapy* (pp. 177–214). Homewood, IL: Dorsey.

Collier, J., Rosaldo, M. Z., & Yanagisako, S. (1982). Is there a family? New Anthropological views. In B. Thorne & M. Yalem (Eds.), *Rethinking the family: Some feminist questions* (pp. 25–39). New York: Longman.

Darroch, A. G. (1981). Migrants in the nineteenth century: Fugitives or families in motion. *Journal of Family History, 6,* 257–277.

Davies, R. P. (1949). Syrian Arabic kinship terms. *Southwestern Journal of Anthropology, 5,* 244–252.

Eggan, F. (1950). *Social organization of the western Pueblos.* Chicago: University of Chicago Press.

Farber, B. (1971). *Kinship and class: A midwestern study.* New York: Basic Books.

Farber, B. (1981). *Conceptions of kinship.* New York: Elsevier North Holland.

Fischer, C. S. (1982). The dispersion of kinship ties in modern society: Contemporary data and historical speculation. *Journal of Family History, 7,* 353–375.

Fischer, L. R. (1983). Mothers and mothers-in-law. *Journal of Marriage and the Family, 45,* 187–192.

Fischer, L. R. (1986). *Linked lives: Adult daughters and their mothers.* New York: Harper and Row.

Fox, J. R. (1967). *Kinship and marriage.* Baltimore: Penguin.

Gershenson, H. P. (1983). Redefining fatherhood in families with white adolescent mothers. *Journal of Marriage and the Family, 45,* 591–599.

Goetting, A. (1986). The developmental tasks of siblingship over the life cycle. *Journal of Marriage and the Family, 48,* 703–714.

Goetting, A. (1990). Patterns of support among in-laws in the United States: A review of research. *Journal of Family Issues, 11,* 67–90.

Goodenough, W. H. (1965). Yankee kinship terminology: A problem in componential analysis. *American Anthropologist, 67,* 259–287.

Grieco, M. S. (1982). Family structure and industrial employment: The role of information and migration. *Journal of Marriage and the Family, 44,* 701–707.

Hagstrom, W. O., & Hadden, J. K. (1965). Sentiment and kinship terminology in American society. *Journal of Marriage and the Family, 27,* 324–332.

Harris, C. C. (1983). *The family and industrial society.* London: George Allen and Unwin.

Haley, Alex (1974). *Roots.* Garden City, NY: Doubleday.

Jarrett, W. H. (1985). Caregiving within kinship systems: Is affection really necessary? *Gerontologist, 25,* 5–10.

Johnson, C. L. (1988). *Ex familia: Grandparents, parents, and children adjust to divorce.* New Brunswick, NJ: Rutgers University Press.

Komarovsky, M. (1950). Functional analysis of sex roles. *American Sociological Review, 47,* 383–392.

Kroeber, A. L. (1952). *The nature of culture.* Chicago: The University of Chicago Press.

Kulis, S. (1987). Socially mobile daughters and sons of the elderly: Mobility effects within the family revisited. *Journal of Marriage and the Family, 49,* 421–433.

Lamb, M. & Sutton-Smith, B. (1982). *Sibling relationships: Their nature and significance across the life span.* Hillsdale, NJ: Erlbaum.

Landis, J. T., & Landis, M. G. (1963). *Building a successful marriage.* Englewood Cliffs, NJ: Prentice-Hall.

Lee, G. (1980). Kinship in the seventies: A decade review of research and theory. *Journal of Marriage and the Family, 42,* 923–934.

Leichter, H. J., & Mitchell, W. E. (1967). *Kinship and casework.* New York: Russell Sage Foundation.

McLanahan, S., Wedenmeyer, N. V., & Adelberg, T. (1981). Network structure, social support, and psychological well-being in the single-parent family. *Journal of Marriage and the Family, 43,* 601–612.

Moore, B. (1958). *political power and social theory.* Cambridge, MA: Harvard University Press.

Murdock, G. P. (1949). *Social structure.* New York: Macmillan.

Murdock, G. P. (1957). World ethnographic sample. *American anthropologist, 59,* 647–687.

Nsamenang, A. B. (1987). A West African perspective, in M. Lamb (Ed.), *The father's role—cross cultural perspectives.* Hillsdale, NJ: Erlbaum.

Oliker, S. J. (1989). *Best friends and marriage: Exchange among women.* Berkeley: University of California Press.

Osborn, R. W., & Williams, J. I. (1976). Determining patterns of exchange and expanded family relationships. *International Journal of Sociology of the Family, 6,* 197–210.

Parish, W. L., Hao, L., & Hogan, D. (1991). Support networks, welfare and work among young mothers. *Journal of Marriage and the Family, 53,* 203–215.

Parsons, T. (1943). The kinship system of the contemporary United States. *American Anthropologist, 45,* 22–38.

Parsons, T. (1965). The normal American family. In B. Farber (Ed.), *Man and civilization.* New York: McGraw-Hill.

Radcliffe-Brown, A. R. (1941). The study of kinship systems. *Journal of the Royal Anthropological Institute, 71.*

Roff, L. L., & Klemmeck, D. L. (1986). Norms for employed daughters' and sons' behavior toward frail older parents, *Sex Roles, 14,* 363–368.

Rosenblatt, P. C., Johnson, P. A., & Anderson, R. M. (1981). When out-of-town relatives visit. *Family Relations, 30,* 403–409.

Rosenthal, C. J. (1985). Kinkeeping in the familial division of labor. *Journal of Marriage and the Family, 47,* 965–974.

Rossi, A. S. (1965). Naming children in middle class families. *American Sociological Review, 30,* 499–513.

Rossi, A. S., & Rossi, D. H. (1990). *Of human bonding: Parent–child relations across the life course.* New York: Aldine de Gruyter.

Schneider, D. M. (1965). American kin terms for kinsman: A critique of Goodenough's componential analysis of Yankee kinship terminology. *American Anthropologist, 67,* 292–294.

Schneider, D. M. (1968). *American kinship: A cultural account.* Englewood Cliffs, NJ: Prentice-Hall.

Schneider, D. M., & Homans, G. C. (1955). Kinship terminology and the American kinship system. *American Anthropologist, 57,* 1194–1208.

Spitze, G., Logan, J. R., Deane, G., & Zenger, S. (1994). Adult children's divorce and intergenerational relationships. *Journal of Marriage and the Family, 56,* 279–293.

Suitor, J. J. (1987). Mother-daughter relations when married daughter returns to school: Effects of status similarity. *Journal of Marriage and the Family, 49,* 435–444.

Suitor, J. J., & Pillemer, K. (1991). Family conflict when adult children and elderly parents share a home. In K. Pillemer & K. McCartney (Eds.), *Parent–child relations throughout life* (pp. 163–178). Hillsdale, NJ: Erlbaum.

Sussman, M. B. (1965). Relationships of adult children with their parents in the United States. In E. Shanas & G. Streib (Eds.), *Social structure and the family* (pp. 62–92). Englewood Cliffs, NJ: Prentice-Hall.

Taylor, R. J. (1986). Receipt of support from family among black Americans: Demographic and familial differences. *Journal of Marriage and the Family, 48,* 67–77.

Underhill, R. M. (1965). The Papago family. In M. F. Nimkoff (Ed.), *Comparative family systems* (pp. 147–163). Boston: Houghton-Mifflin.

Warner, R. I., Lee, G. R., & Lee, J. (1986). Social organization, spousal resources, and marital power: A cross-cultural study. *Journal of Marriage and the Family, 48,* 121–128.

Weston, K. (1991). *Families we choose—lesbians, gays, kinship.* New York: Columbia University Press.

Willmott, P., & Young, M. (1960). *Family and class in a London suburb.* London: Routledge & Kegan Paul.

Winch, R. F. (1979). Toward a model of familial organization. In W. Burr, R. Hill, F. I. Nye, and I. Reiss (Eds.), *Contemporary theories about the family* (Vol. 2, pp. 162–179). New York: Free Press.

CHAPTER 4

Comparative Perspectives

Gary R. Lee

Introduction

The objective of this chapter is to apply the method of comparative research to the study of families and family relations. The phrase *comparative research*, in the social sciences, is literally a redundancy. Research is inherently comparative (Kohn, 1987; Lee, 1982, 1984; Lee & Haas, 1993; Swanson, 1971). Any assessment of covariation or correlation between two variables is in fact a comparative statement: Cases that differ in terms of values of an independent variable are compared to ascertain whether they tend to be similar or different on a dependent variable. In this literal sense, all scientific knowledge is comparative.

However, from its inception social science has reserved the term *comparative* for research in which two or more societies or social systems are compared. In other words, *society* is a unit of analysis in comparative generalizations. It may be the only unit or one of multiple units of analysis, but comparisons between societies are essential components of comparative social research.

Comparative research has played a central role in the study of the family for well over a century. Family scholarship in the latter part of the nineteenth century was almost exclusively comparative, but based heavily on Social Darwinist evolutionary logic (Bachofen, 1861; Maine, 1861; Morgan, 1877; Westermarck, 1891). These scholars posited a series of invariant stages in the evolution of the family, differing from author to author but always beginning in "original promiscuity" and culminating in the monogamous nuclear family common to Europe at the time.

Gary R. Lee • Department of Sociology, Bowling Green State University, Bowling Green, Ohio 43403-0231.

Handbook of Marriage and the Family, 2nd edition, edited by Marvin Sussman, Suzanne K. Steinmetz, and Gary W. Peterson. Plenum Press, New York, 1999.

Near the end of the nineteenth century, anthropologists such as Boas (1896) argued against comparative methods based on the assumption that all cultures are unique, and hence incomparable. This led to the development of the *historicist* school of anthropology, which saw the ethnography (the intensive study of a single society or culture) as the ultimate form of knowledge about human behavior (e.g., Malinowski, 1929). Boas' differences with the comparative method are more accurately viewed as disagreements with the evolutionary logic that dominated comparative research at the time (Lee, 1984). Nonetheless, comparison fell out of favor among family scholars, and the first half of the twentieth century was dominated by social reform and social psychological approaches (Reiss & Lee, 1988) in which the comparison of multiple societies played almost no part.

Comparative family research has enjoyed something of a revival in the second half of the twentieth century. To oversimplify a bit, this is for two reasons. First, although comparative research is still a difficult, methodologically hazardous, and often expensive means of generating knowledge, our methods have improved; we can do a better job of multisociety comparison now, and, perhaps more importantly, we understand better what we have done and how it is useful. Second, scholars have come to understand that the only way to apprehend the effects of the characteristics of social systems on the behavior of individuals or other units that comprise these systems is to compare systems with different characteristics. We no longer search for the "correct" invariant sequence of stages that describes the evolution of "the" human family. Instead, we ask how the properties of families and family relations vary according to the characteristics of the societies in which they occur. In short, we are asking relevant, and to some degree answerable, questions.

Any issue that can be addressed by empirical social research can be addressed comparatively, although there are often good reasons not to do so (see Kohn, 1987, 1989; and Lee & Haas, 1993 for appropriate qualifications to the utility of the method). For example, divorce may be studied in terms of its antecedents (White, 1990) and consequences (Kitson & Morgan, 1990) on the individual level, and variation in divorce *rates* across societies may be examined for clues to their macro-level antecedents (Goode, 1993; Trent & South, 1989). We can ask whether polygynous marriages are more or less likely than monogamous marriages to end in divorce in a society where polygyny is practiced (e.g., Gage-Brandon, 1992, for Nigeria), and we can ascertain the kinds of societies in which polygyny is likely to be practiced by comparative analyses (e.g., Lee & Whitbeck, 1990).

The plan of this chapter is to analyze one major substantive issue in family scholarship that has been addressed by comparative research as an example of how the method has been applied and employed. The issue involves the antecedents of family structural complexity. It is a useful example because it has been the subject of all major types of comparative research, and interest in the issue spans the entire history of family scholarship.

Several decades ago there was widespread consensus that "nuclear" family systems, consisting only of parents and their dependent children, are produced by industrialization, and that more complex "extended" family systems predominated prior to industry; this was termed the *modernization theory* of family structure. More comprehensive comparative methods and data, however, showed that nuclear family systems were quite common in many nonindustrial societies, casting doubt on the causal role of industrialization. Subsequently, even more sophisticated comparative and historical research showed that nuclear families may appear under a great variety of economic circumstances; the entire modernization theory was called into question because historical data showed little evidence of extended families at any point in time. Today we have discovered that extended family systems do indeed occur under certain circumstances where demographic parameters permit them and they maximize the economic well-being of their members.

These advances in our knowledge of variation in family structure were made possible by improvements in the methodology of comparative research. Different methods produced different types of evidence, leading in turn to different conclusions. To understand how this happened, and how some apparently contradictory conclusions have been reconciled, one needs to understand some principles of the methods of comparative research.

Many more detailed treatments of comparative methods are available (e.g., Kohn, 1987. 1989; Lee, 1984, 1995; Lee & Haas, 1993; Przeworski & Teune, 1971; Ragin, 1987), so our discussion here will be quite general. The objective is to establish a common universe of discourse and a frame of reference for understanding the potentials and limitations of the comparative study of the family.

The Method of Comparative Sociology

Kohn (1987) defines *cross-national research* (I prefer the term *comparative* for the generic usage) as "studies that utilize systematically comparable data from two or more nations" (p. 714). I have previously (Lee, 1982) introduced a typology of comparative research based on the kinds of data that are used in comparisons, and will briefly review that typology here. The terms that designate each type are arbitrary, but the types themselves are substantially different. They vary according to the nature of the data that are employed.

Cross-Cultural

The first type of comparative research is termed *cross-cultural*. The raw data for cross-cultural comparisons are ethnographies that describe the culture or way of life of the members of a society, usually done by cultural anthropologists (see Barnard & Good, 1984, and Bernard, 1994, for a discussion of the ethnographic method). To make the cultural descriptions that comprise ethnographies useful in multicultural comparisons, the descriptions must be content-analyzed and coded, a very difficult and demanding process. Fortunately several ethnographic data banks consisting of coded data for large numbers of societies have been compiled by ethnologists. These include the Ethnographic Atlas (Murdock, 1967); the Standard Cross-Cultural Sample (Barry & Schlegel, 1980; Murdock & White, 1969), and the Atlas of World Cultures (Murdock, 1981), among others. In these data sets, each society constitutes a case just as an individual does in a survey. Values are recorded for each variable based on ethnologists' judgments of the contents of ethnographic reports.

One advantage of cross-cultural research is that relatively large samples of societies may be studied. The most recent version of the Ethnographic Atlas, for example, contains data on over 1200 distinct societies. However, there are two major disadvantages. One is that no modern contemporary societies are contained in ethnographic data banks. The ethnographic method is not effective in describing the cultures of large, heterogeneous, complex societies, although small subunits within such societies may certainly be studied ethnographically. In consequence, the United States is not described in any ethnographic data set; however, many early Native American cultures do appear. This restricts the utility of cross-cultural research for descriptive and some explanatory purposes.

Second, cross-cultural data permit the researcher to make comparisons between, but not within, societies or cultures. In other words, we may learn from ethnographic data that polygyny is practiced in a particular society, but no information is available on differences between polygynous and monogamous marriages within that society. Comparisons are restricted to the societal level: How do societies that practice polygyny differ from those that are exclusively monogamous?

Cross-Societal

This disadvantage is shared by the second type of comparative research, termed *cross-societal*. Here the raw data consist of quantitative information on numbers, rates, proportions, averages, etc., of the populations of contemporary nation-states. For example, Trent and South (1989) studied variation in divorce rates across contemporary societies; they correlated the rate of divorce per 1000 population with other variables such as the proportion of adult women in the labor force.

In one sense, cross-societal research is like cross-cultural research translated to a contemporary context. The cross-societal researcher has data *on* societies, but does not have information on intrasocietal variation. This means that comparisons can be made only on the societal level. Trent and South (1989), for instance, could compare divorce rates in societies where female labor force participation is high with divorce rates in other societies where female labor force participation is low, but they could not compare marriages in which the wife is employed with marriages in which she is not, either within or across societies. However, cross-societal researchers may often obtain data on upward of 100 different societies, allowing some statistical analyses.

Cross-National

The third type of comparative research, *cross-national*, is the only type that allows intrasocietal comparisons; indeed, that is its defining characteristic. The cross-national researcher conducts, or makes use of, comparable studies in multiple societies—surveys, experiments, or whatever—and compares the results. This is potentially the most powerful form of comparative analysis because it allows the researcher to observe correspondences between the properties of societies and the behaviors or characteristics of units within those societies—usually, but not always, individuals. Barber, Chadwick, and Oerter (1992), for example, found a positive relation between parental support and self-esteem among adolescent boys in the United States, but not in Germany. This sort of finding provides fertile ground for theoretical development: What is it about the context of parenting that varies between these two societies in a manner that might produce such a difference?

The major disadvantage of cross-national research is that it is logistically impossible to examine large numbers of societies by this method. Samples of 100 societies, for example, are simply not possible when comparable data must be collected independently in each one. Although there are some exceptions, most cross-national comparisons are based on data from two societies.

The most obvious problem this creates for cross-national research is termed *overidentification*. Any difference between two societies is perfectly correlated with any other difference between those societies, so statistical methods cannot be employed to assess the merits of competing explanations. Note that this is true regardless of the sizes of the samples from within the nations in question. There is no magical solution. The cross-national researcher must place less reliance on statistical analyses and more on *theory* in pursuing his or her research agenda. That is, when a cross-national comparison is made it should be made for a specifiable reason, in anticipation (based on theory) of a certain outcome. If that outcome is in fact observed, the theory gains in credibility. If the expected outcome is not observed (i.e., the hypothesis is not supported), the theory loses credibility and should be modified or discarded. In any comparison, societies should be chosen for their utility in testing a theory (Kohn, 1987, 1989; Lee & Haas, 1993).

Historical

A fourth type of research that is similar in some respects to the other three, and may be used for many of the same purposes, is *historical*. The field of family history has enjoyed a remarkable rate of growth in the past several decades. This is due in large part to the development and refinement of the methods of historical demography, pioneered most prominently by Peter Laslett (1970, 1971, 1977a,b; Laslett & Wall, 1978). Family history can address many of the same issues as comparative family research and can also provide a longitudinal perspective that is lacking in the other types. Comparative scholars have warned for generations that it is not necessarily the case that today's "less-developed" societies are anything like societies of the past and that, in consequence, we cannot infer patterns of change over time from contemporary differences between less- and more-developed societies.

Family history provides the opportunity to see what changes have occurred, how and at what rate they have occurred, and most importantly how changes in family behaviors and relations correspond with changes in other social institutions. This is particularly crucial since many of our theories involve the effects of change.

A disadvantage of historical research on the family is that most of the available data come from Europe and the United States. However, this fills an important gap in the ethnographic database; anthropologists, who are and have been mainly European and American, rarely study themselves.

We turn now to the application of comparative research to the study of variation in family structure. Of all the issues examined by comparative and historical family scholars, the question of the determinants of family structure has perhaps generated the most controversy. This is somewhat surprising because, not too many decades ago, there was widespread consensus about the nature and causes of variation in family structure. Advances in the methodology of comparative research created controversy when they generated new data that seemed to be at variance with accepted wisdom. Further advances in comparative methods have helped to resolve some of the controversy and replace it with a more sophisticated consensus.

Family Structure and Composition

By *family structure* I mean the composition of the coresidential family unit. There are several typologies of family structure, but all begin with the *nuclear* family (consisting of parents and dependent children) as the simplest category. Families consisting of only the adult couple, or one parent with child(ren), are sometimes termed *subnuclear*, but regardless of the term are nuclear families. More complex variations on the nuclear family depend on what children do when they become adults.

Murdock (1949) refers to all more complex family types as *extended* and classifies extended families into three subtypes. The *stem* family occurs when one and only one child remains in the parents' household after marriage, raising his/ her own children there and ultimately inheriting the family property. All other children leave, either to marry into other stem families or to begin their own nuclear families. The *lineal* family is more complex, occurring when all children of one gender remain in the parental home after their own marriages; however, the lineal family breaks up into its component nuclear family units, with an appropriate division of property, at some point in its life cycle, usually at or near the death of the elderly parent(s). When this division does not occur (i.e., when the families of siblings remain together in perpetuity) we have the *fully extended* family.

Laslett and Wall (1978) note a simpler classification scheme, again taking the nuclear family as the basic unit. For them, an *extended* family is a nuclear family with any other relative(s) coresiding. The family is *multiple* if it contains more than one *conjugal unit* (married couple or widowed person).

In this chapter I will rely primarily on Murdock's (1949) scheme, as it is frequently useful to differentiate stem families from more complex forms. These types produce different patterns in the data, and the failure to distinguish among them can result in misinterpretation. In Laslett and Wall's (1978) typology, stem, lineal, and fully extended families are all multiple, and thus cannot be differentiated.

There is no dispute that the contemporary United States and similar societies are characterized by nuclear families. According to the U.S. Bureau of the Census (1995, Table 65), only 2% of all married couples lacked their own household in 1994, and 4.1% of all families were classified as *related subfamilies*—a married couple or single parent with children living with a related householder. Clearly the nuclear family (including the subnuclear or single-parent family) is the predominant family type in the contemporary United States, although, as we will document later in the chapter, other family types occur with some frequency.

In the middle of this century there was a high degree of consensus among scholars that the nuclear family represented a new and "modern" family form, whose arrival coincided with the development of industry (Burgess & Locke, 1960; Ogburn & Nimkoff, 1955; Parsons, 1943). In the most thorough and sophisticated analysis of that time, Goode (1963) traced the rise of the *conjugal* family (defined as nuclear in structure) coincident with industrialization and explained how and why the conjugal family came to supplant extended family systems common to preindustrial economies.

Goode's (1963) logic, often termed the modernization theory of family structure, consisted of four essential points. First, an industrial economy requires geographic mobility as workers move in pursuit of jobs. Because workers must be free to pursue employment, the most adaptive family type contains the smallest possible number of potential workers so that the mobility needs of multiple workers do not conflict. And because there are few workers per family, these workers can support only a limited number of dependents. In contrast, in societies with economies based on agriculture (or at least those sufficiently advanced to have developed the plow), the primary requirement for economic success is access to land. Since the land doesn't move, it is in the self-interests of workers to remain on the land, and a high degree of residential stability results (Huber & Spitze, 1988). If young adult workers do not leave the family land in pursuit of economic opportunity, they also do not leave the family. Not incidentally, this produces a larger and more differentiated family work group, which is highly adaptive in many circumstances in agricultural economies (Lee, 1982; Rudolph, 1992). The residential compounding of generations on the land produces extended families.

Second, an industrial economy also produces high rates of social mobility. As industry develops, more positions (proportionally as well as numerically) are created for administrative, technical, and managerial workers and the need for unskilled and semiskilled labor decreases. This creates high rates of upward social mobility, meaning that parents and their adult children may have markedly different socio-economic characteristics. This often produces generational differences in values, attitudes, interests, and lifestyles. While this does not make extended family living logistically impossible, it may make it less desirable; independent residences also allow independence in other ways. In agricultural societies, most children inherit their occupations from their parents, along with access to land. Social mobility is rare or nonexistent.

Third, in industrial economic systems occupational positions are achieved rather than ascribed. That is, workers obtain positions in the labor force based on training, qualifications, and experience rather than because of kinship connections. While family resources have a great deal to do with an individual's opportunities to develop qualifications for occupational positions, the individual is not entirely dependent on his or her family of orientation for access to the productive economy. In agricultural societies, occupations are inherited along with land. Young adults who do not inherit land often have apprenticeships or other occupational opportunities arranged for them by their parents (Gottlieb, 1993; O'Day, 1994). Family connections are essential for economic success in such societies; they are helpful, but are not determinative, in industrial societies.

Fourth, industrialization creates greater differentiation and functional specialization in the social structure. The most important aspect of this differentiation, which underlies the previous three points, is that work and family are separated. In most nonindustrial types of economies, the family is the unit of production as well as the unit of consumption. Families attempt to maximize their economic well-being by structuring themselves in such a way as to maximize productive efficiency given the available land, technology, etc., to which they have access (Ermisch, 1988; Gaunt, 1977, 1978; Mitterauer, 1992; Rudolph, 1992). Under some circumstances (to be reviewed later), families are more effective units of production if they are larger and more differentiated. This is rarely the case in industrial societies, where families are units of consumption. The principles of productive efficiency do not apply to the composition of families that are not units of production.

For these reasons, nuclear families predominate in industrial societies both normatively and behaviorally. This is not in dispute. What *is* in dispute is the theory that argues that the nuclear family is a consequence of industrialization. Two kinds of evidence have been brought to bear on this issue that challenge the theory in many ways and that are certainly cause for major refinements in the theory, if not its outright rejection. One challenge to the theory comes from cross-cultural research, the other from historical demography. We will deal with each in turn.

Cross-Cultural Variation in Family Structure

The earliest, and most naive, view of the relation between economic systems and family systems held that nuclear families emerged coincident with the development of industry, and extended family systems predominated in nonindustrial societies. This is not the case, as was demonstrated many years ago by Nimkoff and Middleton (1960). Using the World Ethnographic Sample (Murdock, 1957), a precursor of Murdock's (1967) Ethnographic Atlas, Nimkoff and Middleton found a positive relationship between *societal complexity* (defined primarily as economic development) and family structural complexity: Societies with more complex economic systems were more likely to have extended family systems.

While this appears to contradict Goode's (1963) hypothesis of decreasing family complexity with increasing technological development, in fact the two studies are entirely consistent. Nimkoff and Middleton employed cross-cultural data to show that extended family systems are more common in agricultural than foraging economies. Goode used cross-societal data to show that extended families were more common in agricultural than industrial economies. The studies agree that there is an association between agriculture as a mode of subsistence and the occurrence of extended family systems. Nimkoff and Middleton's contribution was to show that nuclear family systems characterize not only industrial but also foraging economies. The nuclear family was not invented subsequent to industrialization.

In fact, the predominance of nuclear family systems in hunting-and-gathering economies makes sense in the context of Goode's (1963) theory. Hunters and gatherers must move in pursuit of game and vegetation; when the supplies in a given area are consumed, workers have no way of replenishing them. Hunting and gathering as modes of subsistence can support only small concentrations of people (Huber & Spitze, 1988). There is no land or other property to pass down to succeeding generations, and individuals do not depend on access to land controlled by their families for a livelihood, but rather on their own efforts in wresting subsistence from the environment. Under these circumstances, small, mobile families are adaptive. Larger, more differentiated family groups carry little benefit and considerable cost: They consume available food in a given location more rapidly and thus would occasion more frequent mobility.

According to these studies, extended family systems are not caused by the simple absence of industry, but rather make their appearance in the more specific economic circumstance of an agricultural economy. In particular, agricultural economies sufficiently developed to allow the cultivation of permanent fields, which then become family property and are passed down to succeeding generations, are most likely to be characterized by extended family systems (Huber & Spitze, 1988; Lee, 1982; Mitterauer, 1992; Rudolph, 1992).

Somewhat later, Blumberg and Winch (1972; see also Winch, 1977, 1979) brought together these research streams under the heading of the *curvilinear hypothesis*. They argued that, if one thinks of "societal complexity" as ranging from low complexity in foraging economies to high complexity in industrial economies, with agricultural subsistence types intermediate, then the relation between societal complexity and family complexity is curvilinear, with the most complex (i.e., extended) family systems occurring at intermediate ranges of societal complexity and simple (nuclear) families at the extremes. They marshalled both cross-cultural and cross-societal evidence to show that, indeed, this curvilinear pattern appeared when family complexity was related to a variety of measures of societal complexity (involving community size, permanence of residence, and political, stratification, as well as economic systems). With their cross-cultural evidence (the Ethnographic Atlas), they found an *inflection point* (where the proportional occurrence of complex family systems began to decrease) approximating the development of irrigation; agricultural societies with irrigation were slightly less likely to have complex family systems than those without. But complex family systems characterized about 80% of all societies with economies based on intensive agriculture on permanent fields.

For some time, the question of the relation between economic complexity and family complexity was treated as settled, at least by those working with cross-cultural data (e.g., Lee, 1982). However, a reexamination of the ethnographic evidence (Lee, 1996) suggests that this may not be the case. Blumberg and Winch (1972) did not distinguish precisely between nuclear and extended family systems, but rather between family systems of "low" and "high" complexity. They defined these categories as follows:

> A society is classified as having familism of low complexity if its system is the independent nuclear family with either (a) monogamy or (b) only limited or occasional polygyny (less than 20% of all unions). All other family forms as coded in the EA [Ethnographic Atlas] are classified a showing familism of high complexity. *This category includes independent families in which polygyny covers more than 20% of all unions.* Also classified as having high complexity are all types of extended familism (e.g., joint, stem, etc.), irrespective of form of marriage. (p. 905, italics added)

So Blumberg and Winch (1972) defined their categories by combining marital types with familial types; a society was classified as having a family system of high complexity if it

evinced frequent polygyny, even if the associated *family* structure was nuclear. While it is reasonable to argue that families with multiple wives and their children are "complex," it may be problematic in the sense that the theory being evaluated is about family structure, not marital structure. Indeed, the only point at which Blumberg and Winch mention polygynous marriage in their article is in the measurement section, quoted here.

In fact, if marital and family types are defined independently, there is very little correlation between them (see Table 1). Frequent polygyny is almost as likely to occur in conjunction with nuclear (45.1%) as extended family systems (53.3% summing across the subtypes). Exclusive monogamy is practiced most frequently in stem-family systems (35.7%), but societies with nuclear families (14.7%) are indistinguishable from those with either lineal (11.9%) or fully extended family systems (14.3%) on this criterion. Extended families and frequent polygyny are empirically different kinds of complexity.

This would matter little if polygynous marital systems and extended family systems were related in the same way to indicators of societal complexity. Unfortunately they are not. Table 2 shows the relationship between economic complexity, in the categories employed by Blumberg and Winch (1972), and three measures of marital and/or family structure. The first column, taken directly from Blumberg and Winch, shows the distribution of "high familial complexity" as they defined it. The second column documents the relationship between economic complexity and the occurrence of extended family systems (stem, lineal, or fully extended) regardless of marital structure. Column three shows the proportional occurrence of frequent polygyny across types of economy. The three distributions are quite dissimilar.

The column labelled "high familial complexity" shows the clear curvilinear relation reported by Blumberg and

Table 1. The Relationship between Marital and Family Structure

Marital structure	Type of family structure				
	Nuclear	Stem	Small extended	Large extended	Total
Monogamy	86 (14.7%)	15 (35.7%)	35 (11.9%)	32 (14.3%)	168 (14.6%)
Occasional polygyny	236 (40.2%)	16 (38.1%)	110 (37.3%)	54 (24.1%)	416 (36.2%)
Frequent polygyny	265 (45.1%)	11 (26.2%)	150 (50.8%)	138 (61.6%)	564 (49.1%)
Total %	100.0%	100.0%	100.0%	100.0%	99.9%
n	507	42	295	224	1148

Source: Adapted from Lee (1996, p. 360). Reprinted by permission of the *Journal of Comparative Family Studies*.

**Table 2. Family Structure
and Type of Subsistance Economy**

Subsistence economy	Indicator of family structure		
	High familial complexity	Extended family system	Frequent polygyny
Hunting and gathering	53.9 (180)	39.4 (180)	31.1 (180)
Incipient agriculture	65.1 (86)	54.7 (86)	29.9 (87)
Extensive agriculture	79.5 (415)	46.6 (414)	66.2 (417)
Intensive agriculture	80.4 (163)	52.1 (163)	53.3 (165)
Intensive with irrigation	65.2 (89)	58.4 (89)	16.7 (90)
n	933	932	939

Source: Adapted from Lee (1996, p. 364.) Reprinted by permission of the *Journal of Comparative Family Studies*.

Winch (1972). However, this pattern is virtually indetectable in the distribution of extended family systems. The best that can be said here is that extended family systems are slightly more common among agricultural societies (almost regardless of the type of agriculture) than among those with foraging economies. The factor that drives familial complexity is clearly the occurrence of frequent polygyny, which evinces a strong curvilinear relation with economic complexity. Frequent polygyny is most common among societies with moderately complex agricultural economies and most rare in societies at both extremes of economic complexity, particularly the most complex. But it is in these "most complex" economies, those based on intensive agriculture with irrigation, where extended family systems are marginally *most* common.

We have here a theory of family structure that happens to predict the occurrence of polygynous marriage quite well, but unfortunately predicts variation in family structure rather poorly. However, the data do have three very important implications for our further discussion. First, although variation in family structure among agricultural societies does not conform to the curvilinear pattern Blumberg and Winch (1972) reported, it is important to note that extended family systems are more common in agricultural than hunting-and-gathering societies. This is a critical point in assessing the overall merits of the theory; in fact, the theory explains variation among types of agricultural societies much less clearly than it explains differences between agricultural and foraging economies.

Second, regardless of type of economy, nearly half (actually 48.9%) of all societies in the Ethnographic Atlas are characterized has having some form of extended family system. This may seem like a minor point, but in the next section we will evaluate an argument, based on good demographic evidence, to the effect that extended families have never really existed on any large scale. This evidence sug-

gests otherwise. Ethnographic and demographic data are not directly comparable, but each type of evidence does have something to contribute to this debate.

Third, there is no doubt that extended family systems are much more common among the societies comprising the Ethnographic Atlas than they are among contemporary industrial societies. Goode's (1963) modernization theory argues that, as industrialization proceeds, the family systems of societies around the world have converged, or are converging, on a conjugal family model that is based on the nuclear family structure. This argument does not require that the "inflection point" in the curve relating societal complexity to extended family systems occur among societies practicing intensive agriculture. Instead, it predicts that extended family systems become less common as industry replaces agriculture as the primary mode of subsistence. The data shown in Table 2 are in no way inconsistent with this prediction. Of course there are no comparable ethnographic data on contemporary industrialized societies, but we know from demographic and other evidence to be reviewed later in this chapter that extended families are fairly uncommon within such societies and are unlikely to be regarded as normative. If we could calculate the proportion of contemporary industrial societies that are characterized by extended family *systems* (i.e., where extended families are normative), it undoubtedly would be much closer to zero than is the case for the societies in the Ethnographic Atlas.

But this conclusion comes from comparisons of different societies with different types of economies. The theory we are evaluating really pertains to the coincidence of multiple trends over time: industrialization, urbanization, and concomitant decreases in family structural complexity. Do families really become less complex—that is, extended families less common and nuclear families more common—as economic systems change from agricultural to industrial? There is considerable evidence both for and against this proposition. We now turn to an evaluation of this evidence and accompanying theoretical arguments.

Historical Variation in Family Structure

The application of historical demography to the study of the family has experienced enormous growth, in both volume of research and influence, over the past few decades. This is due largely to the pioneering efforts of Peter Laslett and his colleagues in the Cambridge Group for the History of Population and Social Structure (Laslett, 1965, 1977a, 1983; Laslett & Wall, 1978; Wall, Robin, & Laslett, 1983). Laslett's research on population records of various sorts from many centuries of English and western European history led him to conclude that extended families were very uncommon prior to industrialization, and in fact probably less common in preindustrial times than contemporarily. He argued that "It is simply untrue as far as we can yet tell that there ever was a time or place when the complex family was the universal background to the ordinary lives of ordinary people" (Laslett, 1977a, p. 90).

Many other scholars writing in the 1960s and 1970s found evidence that, in both Europe and America, the nuclear family had been the statistically predominant residential unit for many centuries; it certainly had not suddenly appeared to supplant an extended family system during or subsequent to industrialization (e.g., Anderson, 1973; Demos, 1970; Furstenberg, 1966; Greven, 1970; B. Laslett, 1975, 1977; Netting, 1979; E. Smith, 1978). In fact, some evidence suggested that industrialization and urbanization might act to *increase* the proportion of extended families. Anderson (1973) found that extended family households were proportionally more common in an English city during a period of rapid industrialization than in either a comparable rural area or in a broader sample of England for the previous 2 centuries. A number of other studies (Burch, 1967; Conklin, 1976; DeVos, 1993; Stinner, 1977, 1979) have observed higher proportions of extended family households in urban than rural areas both historically and contemporarily, although they still constituted a small minority of all families.

In one of the strongest arguments against the supposed link between industrialization and the nuclear family system, Seward (1978) analyzed U.S. census data for the decennial years from 1850 to 1880. This was a period of rapid industrialization, sparked to some degree by the Civil War and the need for factories to produce war materials. In 1850, when the American economy was primarily agricultural, Seward (1978, p. 86) found that only 2.4% of all family households contained three-generation extended families, a remarkably low proportion if one postulates that extended family systems coincide with agricultural economies. But even worse (from the perspective of modernization theory), by 1880 the proportion of extended family households had increased to 7.3%. Ruggles (1987), in a subsequent detailed analysis of changes in household and family structure in England and the United States, found increases in the proportions of extended family households in both countries during the latter half of the nineteenth century. If industrialization is a cause of the emergence of nuclear family systems and the demise of extended family systems, it is difficult to reconcile the theory with an increasing prevalence of extended families coincident with industrialization.

Difficult perhaps, but not impossible. There are several reasons why the evidence marshalled by Laslett and his colleagues does not disconfirm the theory relating industrialization to family structure, although this evidence has led to important modifications and refinements of the theory. These reasons include (1) the failure of early historical demographers to recognize that extended family systems are not caused simply by the absence of industry; (2) the use of static data that could not capture life-cycle variations in family structure; and (3) the consequent failure to recognize that demographic parameters such as life expectancies influence the frequency of extended families.

Many authors (e.g., Alderson & Sanderson, 1991; Anderson, 1980) have noted that the approach of the early historical demographers to the issue of the antecedents of family structure was rather atheoretical. The hypothesis they tested was that increases in industrialization and urbanization are associated with decreases in family structural complexity—that is, with increasing prevalence of nuclear families. This hypothesis is based on the assumption that families were generally extended prior to industrialization; the research of Laslett and others cited here found no evidence that this was the case. leading to the rejection of the hypothesis. However, the modernization theory of family structure does not assume that families were extended under any and all preindustrial conditions.

Goode (1963), Winch (1977, 1979), and others actually posited that extended families occur under a specific set of conditions that are not likely to appear in industrial economies; this does not imply that these conditions automatically obtain in all nonindustrial economies. We have already seen that extended family systems are more prevalent in agricultural than foraging economies (Nimkoff & Middleton, 1960; Table 2, this chapter). It is not necessarily the case that all agricultural economic systems foster the conditions that promote extended family households either.

Many scholars have recently argued, in various forms, that the composition of the family household should be viewed as a strategy that people devise to maximize their well-being (Anderson, 1980; Ermisch, 1988; Ogawa & Retherford, 1993; Rudolph, 1992; Wallerstein, 1974, 1980). It follows that different strategies may be appropriate under different circumstances. We have learned that such circumstances may vary *within* broad categories of economic systems as well as between them. Both historical demography and contemporary survey research have documented wide variation in family structure according to several parameters that vary within societies and time periods as well as across them.

Huber and Spitze (1988) argued that extended families are likely to occur only when family elders control valuable resources. This principle helps make sense of the differences between hunting-and-gathering and agricultural economies: It is only in agricultural economies that land is a valued family resource and that land ownership, on an individual or family basis, makes economic sense. But in many agricultural economies, particularly in historic Europe, those who did the farming did not control the land, but instead either rented it from absentee landlords who received a percentage of the crop or worked for wages. Many recent studies have shown that, where peasants actually owned their farms, extended families were quite common, much more common than in places and times where peasants did not own the land (Alderson & Sanderson, 1991; Gunnlaugsson & Guttormsson, 1993; Moring, 1993; Rogers & Tedebrand, 1993; Rudolph, 1992; K. Wall, 1994). This makes sense with respect to Huber and Spitze's (1988) principle, because if land is not owned by farming families then family elders do not control a resource needed by younger generations, and there is correspondingly less reason for young adults to remain in their parents' households.

Many of these same studies also show that, among those societies where peasants owned their farms, extended families are more likely to appear under conditions of impartible inheritance. This means that land is passed intact to one child (usually a son in the European case) rather than subdivided among all children or all sons. Noninheriting children would generally receive some form of compensation other than land and would be encouraged to seek their fortunes elsewhere or, occasionally, remain on their inheriting brother's farm to contribute to the family labor force (Kertzer & Hogan, 1989; Moring, 1993; O'Day, 1994; Rogers & Tedebrand, 1993; Rudolph, 1992; Segalen, 1986). If inheritance of land was partible—divided among multiple children—farms would become too small over the generations to support the families. Further, the families of inheriting children would have separate residences on their own lands. Extended families seem to have occurred not just where agriculture was the dominant mode of subsistence, but where agricultural subsistence was combined with land ownership by peasants and impartible inheritance customs. Where these conditions did not coincide, families tended to be nuclear in structure.

In addition, many scholars have shown that under these circumstances wealthier peasant households were more likely to be extended than were poorer households (Gottlieb, 1993; O'Day, 1994; K. Wall, 1994). Wealthier families owned more land, and thus needed more labor to maximize the productive utility of the land. Also, the resources of wealthier families provided a stronger inducement to young adults to remain as members of their parents' households after their own marriages. Poorer families could not support multiple generations as easily and had less need for family labor because they had less (or less productive) land.

Variation in these conditions produced substantial variation in family structure across the societies of preindustrial Europe. Extended families were quite rare in England, the Netherlands, and many other areas of northern Europe (where the data analyzed by Laslett and his colleagues came from), but were much more common in southern and eastern Europe (Alderson & Sanderson, 1991; Gottlieb, 1993; Kertzer & Hogan, 1989; Rudolph, 1992; Segalen, 1986; R. Wall et al.,

1983). Even within the same society at the same time, the conditions producing different family structures could vary. Gunnlaugsson and Guttormsson (1993), for example, found that in Iceland between 1880 and 1930 nuclear families predominated in coastal fishing villages, but extended families were more common in inland communities where agriculture and animal husbandry were the primary means of subsistence. Families who engaged in both farming and fishing were very likely to be extended because these activities require intensive male labor at the same times of the year, so a larger family labor force was necessary. Moring (1993) found a similar pattern in seventeenth-century Finland, where many families were engaged in multiple economic pursuits (farming, fishing, and animal husbandry) and so needed multiple workers. When the development of fishing technology permitted families to be supported by fishing alone, thus removing the need to own land or engage in several subsistence activities at the same time, the family households of fishermen became overwhelmingly nuclear.

In summary, the economic conditions prevalent in preindustrial Europe produced extended family systems in some times and places but not others. Much of the evidence on family structure analyzed by historical demographers in the 1960s and 1970s came from populations in which extended families were rare because the conditions causing them did not exist. But they were much more common elsewhere for reasons that are consistent with the theory we are evaluating.

There is another major reason why the methods of historical demography may have detected very low incidences of extended family households in preindustrial Europe. As documented earlier, throughout Europe extended families appear to have occurred where the inheritance of land was impartible. This produces extended families because the family can remain on the land generation after generation without exceeding the carrying capacity of the land. However, impartible inheritance, in which the land is passed on to one and only one child, produces a particular type of extended family—in Murdock's (1949) terminology, the *stem family*. The stem family consists of one nuclear family of the senior generation and one of the junior generation—the family of the inheriting child (usually a son) and his spouse. All other children leave the household when they become adults, which usually coincides with marriage. The stem family is not a distinctive category in Laslett's typology (Laslett & Wall, 1978), which distinguishes only between nuclear, extended (containing any nonnuclear kin), and multiple (two or more conjugal units). Nonetheless, this type of family has certain properties that differentiate it from more complex family forms in several important ways.

One of these properties is that children who leave the parental household when they marry generally form their own nuclear families (the exception to this is the children who become spouses of inheriting children in other stem families). Thus, in a stem-family *system*, a high proportion of actual families is necessarily nuclear. This proportion varies directly with the fertility rate; since all noninheriting children leave the stem family at adulthood, the more children there are the more nuclear families there will be.

In addition, the stem family itself is actually extended for only a fraction of its life cycle—the time between the marriage of the inheriting child and the death of the parent(s). In many cases this period may be brief or even nonexistent. This is particularly true in demographic regimes with low life expectancies and relatively late ages at marriage, conditions that characterized most of preindustrial Europe for many centuries (Gottlieb, 1993; O'Day, 1994; Ruggles, 1987). Demographic profiles of populations at a single point in time provide a static picture of family structure: What proportion of family households contain extended families *at that point in time*? But in a stem-family system, coresidence of multiple generations in the same household is only one stage, possibly a short one, in the life cycle of the family. It is entirely possible that virtually all families may go through a stage in which they are extended, but very few are extended at any given time. Any "snapshot" count of the frequency of various family types is likely to seriously underrepresent the proportional occurrence of extended families over the course of the life cycle.

Some years ago, Levy (1965) argued that, in cultures with extended family norms, there is inevitably a gap between the ideals reflected in those norms and the realities of actual family households. Under the nutritional and medical conditions that prevail in most nonindustrial societies, where the norms are most likely to conform to extended family models, it is unlikely that a substantial proportion of parents will long survive the marriages of their children. Thus, he contended, most families are likely to be nuclear at any given time regardless of the family system stipulated by the norms. This is especially likely to be the case in stem-family systems, where most young adults form nuclear families under the best of circumstances. This highlights an important difference between the ethnographic and demographic methods of measuring family structure. Ethnographers focus on cultural norms and characterize cultures according to the way families are "supposed" to be; demographers count the actual frequencies of each family type in the population. It is entirely possible that, in a society an ethnographer would correctly characterize as having a stem-family system, the proportion of actual extended family households may be no higher, and possibly lower, than may be observed in a contemporary industrial society with nuclear family norms.

There are many examples of this in the research literature; a few will suffice here. Ring (1979) studied family structure in a ninth-century Italian village and discovered that only about 5% of all family households contained extended families. However, using reasonable assumptions about demographic parameters in that population (life expectancy, fertility, age at marriage, etc.). Ring estimated that only about 5.5% of all households could *possibly* have been extended at that time. Because the actual proportion of extended family households approached the theoretically possible limit, Ring argued that this village had an extended family system even though the proportion of extended family households was quite low.

In contemporary India, Ram and Wong (1994) reported high frequencies of extended-family households among young married couples and older parents, who often lived together. Middle-aged couples were rarely members of such households, however, because their parents were deceased and their children not yet of marriageable age.

Even the United States provides historical evidence of the effects of demographic processes on family structure. In an analysis of census data from 1900, Daniel Smith (1979) observed that only about 7% of all family households contained extended families, a fact that would appear to be strong evidence for a nuclear family system. However, at the same time, nearly two-thirds of all elderly parents lived with a child; this compares to less than 20% in the latter part of the century (Coward, Cutler, & Schmidt, 1989). This was possible because (1) life expectancies were still quite low (under 50 at birth) by modern standards, so there were relatively few older parents; (2) these parents had had relatively large numbers of children who had lived to adulthood; and (3) since adult children almost never lived together, each parent lived with only one. Thus most elderly parents could live with a child, while at the same time extended family households were quite rare. But they were rare not because they were nonnormative, but because most people did not have the *opportunity* to live in them. It is unlikely, in a family system that is normatively nuclear, that two-thirds of all elderly parents would live with a child.

We are now in a position to explain one of the most difficult empirical facts for the modernization theory of family structure to accommodate: the increase in the proportion of extended family households in the latter part of the nineteenth century. As noted earlier, Seward (1978) found that extended family households constituted a higher proportion of all family households in 1880 (7.3%) than in 1850 (2.4%) in the United States. Ruggles (1987) subsequently supported this pattern of increase with a more sophisticated methodology, and showed that it also occurred in England during the same period. How is this possible if industrialization promotes nuclear families?

The answer, provided most definitively by Ruggles (1987), is largely demographic. Because improved standards of living and medical and nutritional conditions accompanied industrialization, the latter part of the nineteenth century saw a rapid increase in the proportion of the population living to advanced ages. Lower mortality rates increased the odds of three generations of the same family being alive simultaneously, and thus allowed the formation of more extended families than was the case in earlier decades. Furthermore, the increase in the proportion of extended family households was much greater among families of the higher socioeconomic strata; this was also the segment of society among which life expectancies increased the earliest and most rapidly. More people lived in extended family households because demographic parameters allowed them to do so.

Some scholars argue that extended family households can indeed occur with some frequency when life expectancies are low, and therefore that their absence in many areas of preindustrial Europe is indeed strong evidence against the modernization theory of family structure. Kertzer (1989), for example, found high frequencies of extended families despite low life expectancies in an area of Italy in the late nineteenth century. However, it appears that these extended families consisted primarily of adult brothers, their wives, and children—the type that Murdock (1949) called the *fully extended family*. While such families are certainly extended, they require only two generations for this extension. The coresidence of adult siblings (particularly married siblings) has never been normative or widespread in the United States, and was undoubtedly very rare in most of Europe. Three-generation extended families are bound to be unusual if the life spans of nonadjacent generations rarely overlap. It was the extension of the life span in the later decades of the nineteenth century that was the primary driving force behind the increase in extended family households.

However, as Ruggles (1987, 1994) and many others have shown, the proportional frequency of extended family households declined rapidly after the turn of the century, despite the fact that life expectancies continued to increase. Also, age at marriage declined substantially from the early to the middle part of the century; other things being equal, this would allow more extended family households because of closer generational spacing. The factors that precipitated the increase in extended family households in the latter part of the nineteenth century did not continue to do so in the twentieth century. Something clearly changed.

Ruggles (1987) hypothesized that the change was in residential preferences—in effect, the culture of family structure. In order for the increased life expectancies of the later nineteenth century to precipitate increases in the proportion of extended families, it is necessary to posit that some substantial proportion of the population *wanted* to live in such families. Extended families require a coincidence of demographic possibilities and supportive norms. Ruggles posits a widespread stem-family system in England and

America at the cultural or normative level prior to 1900, but it was only in the later decades of the nineteenth century that the demographic realities of these societies allowed a significant proportion of the population to realize these norms. Ironically, the processes of modernization that produced the demographic changes that allowed increased frequencies of extended families eventually produced cultural changes that decreased the *preferences* for extended family living, for the reasons enumerated by Goode (1963). Family structures and associated norms were not immediately altered by the onset of industrialization. The decrease in the prevalence of extended family households in the United States was particularly marked after 1940 (Ruggles, 1994), which is the year in which the Social Security system made its first payments to beneficiaries. This is no coincidence; the increasing financial resources of older persons allowed the generations to maintain independent households (Kobrin, 1976).

The naive version of the modernization theory we have been discussing asserts that family systems change from extended to nuclear in response to industrialization. While there is an element of truth to this generalization, in many ways it obscures more than it illuminates. There are multiple problems with this interpretation. First, it assumes that the emergence of nuclear families is the phenomenon that must be explained. It makes much more sense to assume that family systems are likely to be nuclear unless the causes of extended family systems are present. Extended family households are strategies that people devise to maximize their economic well-being under circumstances where such strategies are likely to be effective. These circumstances include subsistence agricultural economies (alone or in combination with activities such as animal husbandry or fishing) with family-owned farms and impartible inheritance. In effect, this means circumstances under which family elders control valuable resources (e.g., land in an agricultural economy) to which younger generations require access (Huber & Spitze, 1988) and where a large and differentiated work group is beneficial for productivity. Note that this implies that the family and the work group are contiguous. If individuals work for wages, as in an industrial economy, there is no need to structure families to be efficient work groups; they become units of consumption rather than production.

Second, the naive version of the theory is ambiguous about what constitutes a family "system." Ethnographers and demographers can easily agree on what constitutes an extended *family*, but how many of them does it take to constitute an extended family *system*? Ethnographers don't count the number of such families, but rather inquire into the cultural norms regarding how families are supposed to be structured; the proportional frequency of extended family households is one relevant item of information, but it is not determinative. Demographers do count the number of extended families, of course, but how many of them it takes to make a system (in proportional terms) is an open, and very difficult, question.

Third, in its simple form the theory fails to account for demographic constraints on family structure. High proportional frequencies of three-generation households simply cannot occur when life expectancies are low, particularly when low life expectancies coincide with relatively late ages at marriage and correspondingly late ages at inception of childbearing. Grandparents and grandchildren cannot live *together* if they do not live *simultaneously*. This is a major reason why the search for extended family households in preindustrial Europe and America often came up empty, or nearly so. Relatedly, the stem family does not provide obvious demographic evidence of its existence in "snapshot" counts of family types in a population.

Historical family demography has shown us that extended families were far from universal in the preindustrial era of Europe and America, but nonetheless did occur with some frequency where demography allowed them and economic factors favored them. In the next section we will briefly examine some evidence on variation in family structure in the contemporary United States and other societies that sheds some light on why extended families are relatively rare despite the fact that demographic parameters would allow a very high proportion of the population to live in them.

Evidence from Contemporary Societies

Much of the evidence regarding extended family households in the contemporary United States and similar societies is to be found in the literature on coresidence between aging parents and their adult children. Alwin (1996) introduces a recent article on attitudes about coresidence by arguing that "Coresidence with extended kin, while often thought to be more prevalent in early America, is a form of household living that is virtually extinct in contemporary society" (p. 393). There is no doubt that the prevalence of intergenerational coresidence has decreased dramatically in the United States since the turn of the century (Ruggles, 1994), but the term "extinct" is an overstatement. In fact, Glick, Bean, and Van Hook (1997) have shown that a modest increase in extended family households occurred between 1980 and 1990.

In this section, I argue that even in contemporary societies such as the United States, extended family households appear when they help to resolve problems experienced by family members. These problems do not normally involve economic production, since the family is not the unit of production in contemporary economies, but instead involve some form of support. Either young adults or aging parents may be in need of such support.

As noted earlier, Smith (1979) estimated that nearly two-thirds of all elderly (65 and over) parents lived with a child in the United States in 1990. Ruggles (1994) estimates that 60.7% of all elderly whites (nonparents as well as parents) and 48.5% of all elderly blacks lived with a child in 1880. Crimmins and Ingegneri (1990) used three survey data sets from 1962, 1975, and 1984 to produce comparable estimates, and found 28% of older parents living with a child in 1962; this percentage dropped to 18 by 1975, but remained constant at 18 in 1984. Coward et al. (1989) found approximately 19% of elderly parents living with a child according to the 1980 census data. Ruggles (1994) estimated that 16.4% of all elderly whites (including those with no children) and 25.6% of elderly blacks lived with a child in 1980. There seems to be some consensus that slightly less than one in five elderly parents live with a child in the United States in the latter part of the twentieth century. This is certainly a substantial reduction from 1900; Ruggles (1994) shows that most of this reduction has occurred since 1940. However, it is not a trivial portion, and it may be increasing (Glick et al., 1997).

These estimates all come from single points in time. Beck and Beck (1989) followed a sample of middle-aged American women over a 15-year period ending in 1984. In 1984, about 8% of married white women and 20% of unmarried white women lived in households containing nonnuclear kin. But over the preceding 15 years, 24% of the continuously married and 57% of the continuously unmarried had lived in an extended family household at some point. The percentages were consistently higher for comparable black women. Beck and Beck concluded that, overall, about one-third of white women and two-thirds of black women lived with extended kin for some period during the 15-year study. And the part of the life cycle covered by the study did not include either young adulthood or very old age, where the probabilities of coresidence with kin are higher. So extended family living is not an entirely unfamiliar situation for contemporary Americans.

Not all elderly parents who live with a child are living in an extended family household. Many of these instances involve adult children living in their parents' homes, and the great majority of adult children who live with parents are unmarried (Aquilino, 1990; Ward, Logan, & Spitze, 1992). In the past few decades there has been a small but observable increase in the proportion of young adults living with their parents (Aquilino, 1991; Buck & Scott, 1993; Glick & Lin, 1986; Goldscheider & DaVanzo, 1989). This is important because age at leaving home had been declining for most of the century in the United States (Goldscheider & LeBourdais, 1986) and in other Western societies (Kiernan, 1989). Some of the young adults who live with parents have left home but returned again, following divorces or difficulties entering the labor force (Avery, Goldscheider, & Speare,

1992; Glick & Lin, 1986). This phenomenon also is not restricted to the United States. Young (1984) found that, in Australia, about half of all young men and 40% of young women who left their parents' homes later returned. Other young adults are simply remaining in their parents' households longer than their predecessors did. This is connected to some extent to increases in average ages at marriage since 1970 (Buck & Scott, 1993), although young adults who leave their parents' homes are doing so increasingly for independent living rather than marriage (Buck & Scott, 1993; Goldscheider & DaVanzo, 1989).

These instances of intergenerational coresidence do not result in extended family households unless the young adults in question are either married or have children from a prior marriage or nonmarital relationship. Neither of these situations is typical. Instead, the evidence suggests that parents are providing homes for their young adult children for somewhat longer periods of the children's lives, on average, than was the case 20 or 30 years ago. Aquilino (1990) showed that the odds of living with a child are significantly higher for parents who have an unemployed child. Other studies (Avery et al. 1992; Goldscheider & Goldscheider, 1993) report that young adults from families of higher socioeconomic status leave the parental home for marriage at later ages. These findings suggest that parents are helping their children by providing a home and the support that goes with it.

However, delayed nest-leaving or returns to the nest tend to occur among young adults whose parents are in late middle-age. As these parents age, their children gradually make the transition to independent households; the lowest proportion of parents living with adult children is found among those between the ages of 70 and 75 (Coward et al., 1989). Beyond that age, the incidence of coresidence increases directly with age (Lee & Dwyer, 1996); Coward et al. (1989) found 41% of parents age 90 and over lived with children in 1980. In many of these cases the adult children are themselves married and have children of their own, so the presence of the aging parent in the household does create an extended family. In these cases, parental dependency characteristics such as widowhood and poor health, along with advanced age, predict coresidence (Crimmins & Ingegneri, 1990; Glick et al., 1997; Lee & Dwyer, 1996).

Coresidence between older parents and adult children in the contemporary United States and similar societies appears to be a strategy families use to resolve or deal with specifiable problems. It is not normative in the sense that people expect to live in multigenerational households when children reach adulthood. But it is a means families employ to deal with difficulties experienced by one generation or the other. In the case of young adults living with their middle-aged parents, coresidence seems to be due in large part to problems experienced by the young adults either with marriages or

gaining entry into the labor force. For very old parents who live with their middle-aged children, it appears to be the parents' problems (poor health, usually in combination with widowhood) that trigger coresidence.

This relates clearly to our earlier argument that, in preindustrial societies, families adopt the strategy of extended family households when such households are useful in improving their standards of living by helping to maximize production, and thus consumption. Ram and Wong (1994) argue that "The optimal choice of household structure is the one that provides maximum level of consumption for its members" (p. 855). Thus we find extended families in societies with agricultural economic bases, particularly where agriculture is combined with other modes of subsistence that require larger, more differentiated work groups. When farming families own their own land and pass it on intact to the next generation to maintain farm size, the extended family produces this larger work group that simultaneously maximizes production and allows more people access to the land.

In contemporary societies it is not the maximization of family productivity that is important, because families are generally not work groups and do not have to be structured to maximize productive efficiency. Instead, the extended family household (or intergenerational coresidence more generally) is a strategy that may be adopted to provide support, economic and otherwise, for one generation or the other in the face of the exigencies of either young adulthood (unemployment, divorce) or old age (widowhood, declining health). As Beck and Beck (1989) have shown, individuals move in and out of extended family households as their circumstances change (see Ram & Wong, 1994, for India and DeVos, 1993, for Latin America).

The proportional frequency of coresidence between aging parents and their adult children is substantially higher today in Asian societies than in the United States or western Europe (see, e.g., Ogawa & Retherford, 1993, for Japan, Ram & Wong, 1994, for India, Won & Lee, in press, for Korea, and Zang, 1993, for China), although these frequencies have been decreasing in recent years. Kamo and Zhou (1994) have shown that elderly Chinese and Japanese parents in the United States are substantially more likely to live with their adult children, and correspondingly less likely to live alone, than are elderly American parents of European ancestry.

Most analysts attribute this difference to the strong tradition of filial piety in many Asian societies, based largely on Confucian norms, and the recent decrease in intergenerational coresidence to a weakening of these norms coincident with the progress of industrialization and urbanization. Kamo and Zhou (1994), for example, show that differences between elders of Asian and European descent in the United States persist after controlling for a variety of indicators of "modernization" such as urban residence, employment status, age, and income. They find that measures of acculturation (length of residence in the United States, having been born in the United States, speaking English at home) are related to the maintenance of separate residences among Chinese and Japanese elders. Ogawa and Retherford (1993) found decreases in the endorsement of norms of support for aging parents in Japan that parallel decreases in the prevalence of coresidence between 1960 and 1990. Cultural expectations have a great deal to do with intergenerational coresidence, and changes in culture appear to effect changes in coresidential behavior.

However, it is overly simplistic to attribute cross-national differences in intergenerational coresidence, or changes over time within nations, solely to culture. Morgan and Hirosima (1983), in a study of the families of Japanese schoolchildren, found that those who had grandparents living in their homes had higher standards of living than those from nuclear families. They interpreted extended family households as strategies for dealing with the high cost of housing and the relatively early age at retirement (generally around 55) in Japan. Coresident grandparents allowed both parents to work by providing a source of childcare and allowed the generations to combine their resources to purchase larger and better-quality housing. And Zang (1993) reported that the frequency of patrilocal postmarital residence in China, after decreasing from the turn of the century to the mid-1960s, has gradually increased since then, probably in response to a tight housing supply and decreased job availability. These findings point to structural causes of extended family households.

Glick et al. (1997) show that, in the United States, the proportional frequency of extended family households is higher among recent immigrants from Latin American as well as Asian countries than among households headed by persons born in the United States. Among Latin American immigrants, measures of acculturation (length of time in the United States) and sociodemographic characteristics (age, marital status, poverty status) are related to household extension: Extended family households are more likely to contain poor subunits and to include older and unmarried adults. Extended family households are more common in the Latin American countries from which these people immigrated (DeVos, 1995), but at the same time their circumstances in the United States influence the formation and maintenance of extended family households.

There is no necessary opposition or conflict between cultural and structural explanations. Both household production theory (Ermisch, 1988) and modernization theory (Goode, 1963) suggest that family households are structured in such a way as to maximize the standard of living of the individuals and families involved according to the circumstances they face. When, because of variation in these structural circumstances, one or another form of family household has demonstrable economic advantages, this form is likely to be institutionalized in cultural norms. When structural changes are rapid, or where the circumstances of individuals are changed rapidly by factors such as migration to a new society, culture is likely to change much more slowly than are structural factors, producing differences between cultural groups such as those observed by Kamo and Zhou (1994). But this does not mean that cultural explanations are superior to structural explanations.

Interestingly, there is evidence of change in majority culture in the United States in the opposite direction to the change observed in Asian societies. Alwin (1996) and Glenn (1987) found increases over time in the proportion of Americans who endorse norms supportive of intergenerational coresidence. Alwin (1996) decomposed this increase into effects of intracohort change and effects of cohort replacement, and found that both are occurring. Younger cohorts of Americans are more supportive of intergenerational coresidence than their older counterparts, and have also become more supportive over time. Alwin suggests that the cohort difference is due to the increasing need of younger adults for economic and other support, and the fact that aging parents are more likely to support adult children than the reverse (Aquilino, 1990).

However, cohort differences in this direction have been observed for some time (e.g., Brody, Johnsen, & Fulcomer, 1983, 1984). In the United States, aging parents are very concerned about "being a burden" on their children (Lee, 1985). It is possible that older persons are less favorable toward intergenerational coresidence because it would imply not only an imposition on their children, but also a loss of their own independence. In Japan older persons are more supportive of intergenerational coresidence than are members of younger cohorts (Ogawa & Retherford, 1993), perhaps because in Japanese culture it has long been a mark of distinction or success for parents to have raised children who are willing and able to support them in old age.

The secular decrease in support for norms of coresidence in Japan and the increase in the United States mean that the norms of these two historically different cultures are converging. At the same time the frequencies of coresidence are also becoming more similar. As noted, coresidence is declining in frequency in Japan (Ogawa & Retherford, 1993). In the United States, Glick et al. (1997) have recently shown that the percentage of households containing extended kin increased marginally (from roughly 10% to 12%) between 1980 and 1990, reversing at least a century of decline (Ruggles, 1994). Glick et al. (1997) tested the hypothesis that this increase was due to increasing immigration and the higher frequencies of extended family households among immigrants, but found that this was not the case; instead, they argue that the increase stems from socioeconomic and demographic causes. These causes are likely to involve (1) the increasing difficulties young adults faced gaining entry into the labor force, combined with stagnating wages; and (2) the increasing frequency with which older persons are living to very advanced ages and experiencing the physical and mental infirmities associated with these ages (Lee & Dwyer, 1996). It does not appear to be the case that extended family households are disappearing from the American scene. While they still constitute a small proportion of all households, the reversal of the long-term downward trend during the 1980s may be a harbinger of higher frequencies in the future.

Neither norms nor realities of family structure are static, but instead change with changing circumstances. Family structure is best conceptualized as a set of alternatives from among which families choose in attempts to maximize their well-being and resolve problems, whether these problems involve productive efficiency or the support of young adults or aging parents. In the contemporary United States, extended family households occur fairly rarely because the need for this degree of intergenerational support is relatively rare and usually temporary. But it is an option that families select when the circumstances require and are selecting more frequently today than in the recent past.

Conclusions

In this chapter we have examined only one major issue that has been addressed by comparative research, the antecedents of family structure. This is, however, a good example of the kinds of contributions that comparative research can make to the development of explanatory theory for several reasons. First, virtually all types of comparative research have contributed to the current state of knowledge on this question. Second, there is a clear progression in the scholarly consensus on the antecedents of family structural complexity that corresponds with the introduction of new types of evidence to the debate; the increasing sophistication of both research and theory over time is clear. Third, there are obvious connections between comparative and intrasystemic research on this issue. This shows that comparative research doesn't exist in a vacuum. It is instead a valuable tool for addressing issues that are common to the study of the family by whatever method.

The progression of comparative research on family structure over the past several decades mirrors the increasing sophistication of comparative research in general. Early versions of the modernization theory ran into difficulty when research became sufficiently refined to enable us to go be-

yond the characterization of the family structures of entire societies to examine directly the composition of individual families in historical societies. Initially these examinations did not support the theory, causing many scholars to reject the theory entirely. But subsequent studies made it clear that the theory needed refinement, not rejection.

We have moved beyond sweeping generalizations to the effect that, for example, extended family systems appear in agricultural economies, to an understanding that the specific circumstances that make extended family households more useful to their members are more likely to occur in agricultural than industrial economies. We also apprehend much more clearly that there are demographic constraints on the formation and maintenance of extended family households that make them difficult to detect with synchronic data, particularly in stem-family systems. This has allowed the application of the theory to the level of individual families, where we now recognize that extended family households are strategies that families adopt to optimize their standards of living and/or resolve specifiable problems. The circumstances under which this strategy is effective vary across types of societies depending on whether the family is a unit of production or a unit of consumption exclusively, but the underlying principles are very similar.

Comparative research may contribute, and has contributed, to the study of a virtually infinite number of other family-related issues in a similar fashion. It is not a distinct or unique field of study in itself, but a method (or rather a set of related methods) of approaching the study of human behavior that is most useful when it is combined with other methods. It is a source of insights into the ways in which the characteristics of societies influence the behavior of individuals and families. The only way in which the effects of societal characteristics may be apprehended is to compare societies with different characteristics. Comparative research therefore does play a unique and irreplaceable role in the testing and development of explanatory theory, but one that should not stand on its own. Many hypotheses that may be tested in a comparative context may also be tested, although perhaps in different forms, in other contexts as well (Kohn, 1987, 1989; Lee, 1982). And more general theories of human behavior should give rise to both comparative and noncomparative hypotheses. The parallels between the comparative literature on family structure and the intrasocietal research on intergenerational coresidence testify to this.

Perhaps most importantly, comparative research shows that families in the contemporary United States are not entirely new and different, but instead are the products of circumstances that have counterparts in other societies and at earlier points in human history. Scholars who study American families in isolation from those of other times and places are likely to overlook the common principles that make family behavior understandable.

References

Alderson, A. S., & Sanderson, S. K. (1991). Historic European household structures and the capitalist world economy. *Journal of Family History, 16*, 419–432.

Alwin, D. F. (1996). Coresidence beliefs in American society—1973 to 1991. *Journal of Marriage and the Family, 58*, 393–403.

Anderson, M. (1973). Family, household, and the industrial revolution. In M. Gordon (Ed.), *The American family in social-historical perspective* (pp. 59–75). New York: St. Martin's.

Anderson, M. (1980). *Approaches to the history of the western family.* London: Macmillan.

Aquilino, W. S. (1990). The likelihood of parent–adult child coresidence: Effects of family structure and parental characteristics. *Journal of Marriage and the Family, 52*, 405–419.

Aquilino, W. S. (1991). Family structure and home leaving: A further specification of the relationship. *Journal of Marriage and the Family, 53*, 999–1010.

Avery, R., Goldscheider, F., & Speare, A., Jr. (1992). Feathered nest/gilded cage: Parental income and leaving home in the transition to adulthood. *Demography, 29*, 375–388.

Bachofen, J. J. (1861). *Das mutterecht.* Basel, Switzerland: Benno Schwabe.

Barber, B. K., Chadwick, B. A., & Oerter, R. (1992). Parental behaviors and adolescent self-esteem in the United States and Germany. *Journal of Marriage and the Family, 54*, 128–141.

Barnard, A., & Good, A. (1984). *Research practices in the study of kinship.* New York: Academic Press.

Barry, H., III, & Schlegel, A. (Eds.). (1980). *Cross-cultural samples and codes.* Pittsburgh, PA: University of Pittsburgh Press.

Beck, R. W., & Beck, S. H. (1989). The incidence of extended households among middle-aged black and white women: Estimates from a fifteen-year panel study. *Journal of Family Issues, 10*, 147–168.

Bernard, H. R. (1994). *Research methods in anthropology* (2nd ed.). Walnut Creek, CA: Altamira Press.

Blumberg, R. L., & Winch, R. F. (1972). Societal complexity and familial complexity: Evidence for the curvilinear hypothesis. *American Journal of Sociology, 77*, 898–920.

Boas, F. (1896). The limitations of the comparative method in anthropology. *Science, 4*, 901–908.

Brody, E. M., Johnsen, P. T., & Fulcomer, M. C. (1984). What should adult children do for elderly parents? Opinions and preferences of three generations of women. *Journal of Gerontology, 39*, 736–746.

Brody, E. M., Johnsen, P. T., Fulcomer, M. C., & Lang, A. M. (1983). Women's changing roles and help to elderly parents: Attitudes of three generations of women. *Journal of Gerontology, 38*, 597–607.

Buck, N., & Scott, J. (1993). She's leaving home: But why? An analysis of young people leaving the parental home. *Journal of Marriage and the Family, 55*, 863–874.

Burch, T. K. (1967). The size and structure of families: A comparative analysis of census data. *American Sociological Review, 32*, 347–363.

Burgess, E. W., & Locke, H. S. (1960). *The family: From institution to companionship.* New York: American Book Co.

Conklin, G. H. (1976). The household in urban India. *Journal of Marriage and the Family, 38*, 771–779.

Coward, R. T., Cutler, S. J., & Schmidt, F. (1989). Differences in the household composition of elders by age, gender, and area of residence. *The Gerontologist, 29*, 814–821.

Crimmins, E. M., & Ingegneri, D. G. (1990). Interaction and living arrangements of older parents and their children: Past trends, present determinants, future implications. *Research on Aging, 12*, 3–35.

Demos, J. (1970). *A little commonwealth.* New York: Oxford University Press.

DeVos, S. M. (1993). Is there a socioeconomic dimension to household extension in Latin America? *Journal of Comparative Family Studies, 24*, 21–34.

DeVos, S. M. (1995). *Household composition in Latin America.* New York: Plenum.

Ermisch, J. (1988). An economic perspective on household modelling. In N. Kielman, A. Kuijsten, & A. Vossen (Eds.), *Modelling household formation and dissolution* (pp. 23–39). New York: Oxford University Press.

Furstenberg, F. F. (1966). Industrialization and the American family: A look backward. *American Sociological Review, 31*, 326–337.

Gage-Brandon, A. J. (1992). The polygyny-divorce relationship: A case study of Nigeria. *Journal of Marriage and the Family, 54*, 285–292.

Gaunt, D. (1977). Preindustrial economy and population structure: The elements of variance in early modern Sweden. *Scandinavian Journal of History, 2*, 183–210.

Glenn, N. D. (1987). Social trends in the U.S. *Public Opinion Quarterly, 51*, S109–S126.

Glick, J. E., Bean, F. D., & Van Hook, J. V. W. (1997). Immigration and changing patterns of extended household structure in the United States: 1970–1990. *Journal of Marriage and the Family, 59*, 177–191.

Glick, P., & Lin, S. L. (1986). More young adults are living with their parents: Who are they? *Journal of Marriage and the Family, 48*, 105–112.

Goldscheider, F., & DaVanzo, J. (1989). Pathways to independent living in early adulthood: Marriage, semi-autonomy, and premarital residential independence. *Demography, 26*, 278–285.

Goldscheider, F., & Goldscheider, C. (1993). Whose nest? A two-generational view of leaving home during the 1980s. *Journal of Marriage and the Family, 55*, 851–862.

Goldscheider, F., & LeBourdais, C. (1986). The falling age at leaving home, 1920–1979. *Sociology and Social Research, 70*, 99–102.

Goode, W. J. (1963). *World revolution and family patterns.* New York: Free Press.

Goode, W. J. (1993). *World changes in divorce patterns.* New Haven, CT: Yale University Press.

Gottlieb, B. (1993). *The family in the western world: From the black death to the industrial age.* New York: Oxford University Press.

Greven, P. (1970). *Four generations: Population, land, and family in colonial Andover.* Ithaca, NY: Cornell University Press.

Gunnlaugsson, G. A., & Guttormsson, L. (1993). Household structure and urbanization in three icelandic fishing districts, 1880–1930. *Journal of Family History, 18*, 315–340.

Huber, J., & Spitze, G. (1988). Trends in family sociology. In N. J. Smelser (Ed.), *Handbook of sociology* (pp. 425–448). Newbury Park, CA: Sage.

Kamo, Y., & Zhou, M. (1994). Living arrangements of elderly Chinese and Japanese in the United States. *Journal of Marriage and the Family, 56*, 544–588.

Kertzer, D. I. (1989). The joint family household revisited: Demographic constraints and household complexity in the European past. *Journal of Family History, 14*, 1–15.

Kertzer, D. I., & Hogan, D. P. (1965). *Family, political economy, and demographic change: The transformation of life in Casalecchio, Italy, 1861–1921.* Madison: University of Wisconsin Press.

Kiernan, K. (1989). The departure of children. In E. Grebenik, C. Hohn, & R. Mackensen (Eds.), *Later phases of the family cycle* (pp. 120–144). Oxford: Oxford University Press.

Kitson, G. C., & Morgan, L. A. (1990). The multiple consequences of divorce: A decade review. *Journal of Marriage and the Family, 52,* 913–924.

Kobrin, F. E. (1976). The fall in household size and the rise of the primary individual in the United States. *Demography, 13,* 127–138.

Kohn, M. L. (1987). Cross-national research as an analytic strategy. *American Sociological Review, 52,* 713–731.

Kohn, M. L. (Ed.) (1989). *Cross-national research in sociology.* Newbury Park, CA: Sage.

Laslett, B. (1975). Household structure on an American frontier: Los Angeles, California in 1850. *American Journal of Sociology, 81,* 109–128.

Laslett, B. (1977). Social change and the family: Los Angeles, California, 1850–1870. *American Sociological Review, 42,* 268–291.

Laslett, P. (1965). *The world we have lost.* London: Methuen.

Laslett, P. (1970). The comparative history of household and family. *Journal of Social History, 4,* 75–87.

Laslett, P. (1971). *The world we have lost* (2nd ed.). London: University Paperbacks.

Laslett, P. (1977a). Characteristics of the western family considered over time. *Journal of Family History, 2,* 89–115.

Laslett, P. (1977b). *Family life and illicit love in earlier generations.* Cambridge: Cambridge University Press.

Laslett, P. (1983). Family and household as work group and as kin group: Areas of traditional Europe compared. In R. Wall, J. Robin, & P. Laslett (Eds.), *Family forms in historic Europe* (pp. 513–563). Cambridge: Cambridge University Press.

Laslett, P., & Wall, R. (Eds.). (1978). *Household and family in past time* (3rd ed.). Cambridge: Cambridge University Press.

Lee, G. R. (1982). *Family structure and interaction: A comparative analysis* (2nd ed.). Minneapolis: University of Minnesota Press.

Lee, G. R. (1984). The utility of cross-cultural data: Potentials and limitations for family sociology. *Journal of Family Issues, 5,* 519–541.

Lee, G. R. (1985). Kinship and social support of the elderly: The case of the United States. *Ageing and Society, 5,* 19–38.

Lee, G. R. (1995). Comparative research methodology. In B. B. Ingoldsby & S. Smith (Eds.), *Families in multicultural perspective* (pp. 59–77). New York: Guilford.

Lee, G. R. (1996). Economies and families: A further investigation of the curvilinear hypothesis. *Journal of Comparative Family Studies, 27,* 353–372.

Lee, G. R., & Dwyer, J. W. (1996). Aging parent–adult child coresidence: Further evidence on the role of parental characteristics. *Journal of Family Issues, 17,* 46–59.

Lee, G. R., & Haas, L. (1993). Comparative methods in family research. In P. G. Boss, W. J. Doherty, R. LaRossa, W. R. Schumm, & S. K. Steinmetz (Eds.), *Sourcebook of family theories and methods: A contextual approach* (pp. 117–131). New York: Plenum.

Lee, G. R., & Whitbeck, L. B. (1990). Economic systems and rates of polygyny. *Journal of Comparative Family Studies, 21,* 13–24.

Levy, M. J., Jr. (1965). Aspects of the analysis of family structure. In A. J. Cole, L. A. Fallers, M. J. Levy, D. M. Schneider, & S. S. Thompkins (Eds.), *Aspects of the analysis of family structure* (pp. 1–63). Princeton, NJ: Princeton University Press.

Maine, H. S. (1861). *Ancient law.* London: Murray.

Malinowski, B. (1929). *The sexual life of savages in north-western Melanesia.* New York: Harvest Books.

Mitterauer, M. (1992). Peasant and non-peasant family forms in relation to the physical environment and the local economy. *Journal of Family History, 17,* 139–159.

Morgan, L. H. (1877). *Ancient society.* Chicago: Charles S. Kerr.

Morgan, S. P., & Hirosima, K. (1983). The persistence of extended family residence in Japan: Anachronism or alternative strategy? *American Sociological Review, 48,* 269–281.

Moring, B. (1993). Household and family in Finnish coastal societies. *Journal of Family History, 18,* 395–414.

Murdock, G. P. (1949). *Social structure.* New York: Free Press.

Murdock, G. P. (1957). World ethnographic sample. *American Anthropologist, 59,* 664–687.

Murdock, G. P. (1967). Ethnographic Atlas: A summary. *Ethnology, 6,* 109–236.

Murdock, G. P. (1981). *Atlas of world cultures.* Pittsburgh, PA: University of Pittsburgh Press.

Murdock, G. P., & White, D. R. (1969). Standard Cross-Cultural Sample. *Ethnology, 8,* 329–369.

Netting, R. M. (1979). Household dynamics in a nineteenth century Swiss village. *Journal of Family History, 4,* 39–58.

Nimkoff, M. F., & Middleton, R. (1960). Type of family and type of economy. *American Journal of Sociology, 66,* 215–225.

O'Day, R. (1994). *The family and family relationships, 1500–1900: England, France, and the United States of America.* New York: St. Martin's.

Ogawa, N., & Retherford, R. D. (1993). Care of the elderly in Japan: Changing norms and expectations. *Journal of Marriage and the Family, 55,* 585–597.

Ogburn, W. F., & Nimkoff, M. F. (1955). *Technology and the changing family.* Boston: Houghton Mifflin.

Parsons, T. (1943). The kinship system of the contemporary United States. *American Anthropologist, 45,* 22–38.

Przeworski, A., & Teune, H. (1971). *The logic of comparative social inquiry.* New York: Wiley-Interscience.

Ragin, C. C. (1987). *The comparative method: Moving beyond qualitative and quantitative strategies.* Berkeley: University of California Press.

Ram, M., & Wong, R. (1994). Covariates of household extension in rural India: Change over time. *Journal of Marriage and the Family, 56,* 853–864.

Reiss, I. L., & Lee, G. R. (1988). *Family systems in America* (4th ed.). New York: Holt, Rinehart and Winston.

Ring, R. R. (1979). Early medieval peasant households in central Italy. *Journal of Family History, 4,* 2–25.

Rogers, J., & Tedebrand, L.-G. (1993). Living by the sea: Farming and fishing in Sweden from the late eighteenth to the early twentieth century. *Journal of Family History, 18,* 369–393.

Rudolph, R. L. (1992). The European family and economy: Central themes and issues. *Journal of Family History, 17,* 119–138.

Ruggles, S. (1987). *Prolonged connections: The rise of the extended family in nineteenth-century England and America.* Madison: University of Wisconsin Press.

Ruggles, S. (1994). The origins of African-American family structure. *American Sociological Review, 59,* 136–151.

Segalen, M. (1986). *Historical anthropology of the family.* Cambridge: Cambridge University Press.

Seward, R. R. (1978). *The American family: A demographic history.* Beverly Hills, CA: Sage.

Smith, D. S. (1979). Life course, norms, and the family system of older Americans in 1900. *Journal of Family History, 4,* 285–298.

Smith, E. C. (1978). Family structure and complexity. *Journal of Comparative Family Studies, 9,* 299–310.

Stinner, W. F. (1977). Urbanization and household structure in the Philippines. *Journal of Marriage and the Family, 39,* 377–385.

Stinner, W. F. (1979). Modernization and family extension in the Philippines: A social demographic analysis. *Journal of Marriage and the Family, 41,* 161–168.

Swanson, G. (1971). Frameworks for comparative research: Structural anthropology and the theory of action. In I. Vallier (Ed.), *Comparative methods in sociology: Essays on trends and applications* (pp. 141–122). Berkeley: University of California Press.

Trent, K., & South, S. J. (1989). Structural determinants of the divorce rate:

A cross-societal analysis. *Journal of Marriage and the Family, 51,* 391–404.

U.S. Bureau of the Census. (1995). *Statistical abstract of the United States, 1995.* Washington, DC: U.S. Department of Commerce.

Wall, K. (1994). Peasant stem families in northwestern Portugal: Life transitions and changing family dynamics. *Journal of Family History, 19,* 237–259.

Wall, R., Robin, J., & Laslett, P. (Eds.). (1983). *Family forms in historic Europe.* Cambridge: Cambridge University Press.

Wallerstein, I. (1974). *The modern world-system: Capitalist agriculture and the origins of the European world economy in the sixteenth century.* New York: Academic Press.

Wallerstein, I. (1980). *The modern world-system II: Mercantilism and the consolidation of the European world economy, 1600–1750.* New York: Academic Press.

Ward, R., Logan, J., & Spitze, G. (1992). The influence of parent and child needs on coresidence in middle and later life. *Journal of Marriage and the Family, 54,* 209–221.

Westermarck, E. (1891). *The history of human marriage* (5th ed.). New York: Allerton Book Co.

White, L. K. (1990). Determinants of divorce: A review of research in the eighties. *Journal of Marriage and the Family, 52,* 904–912.

Winch, R. F. (1977). *Familial organization: A quest for determinants.* New York: Free Press.

Winch, R. F. (1979). Toward a model of familial organization. In W. R. Burr, R. Hill, F. I. Nye, & I. L. Reiss (Eds.), *Contemporary theories about the family, vol. 1: Research-based theories* (pp. 162–179). New York: Free Press.

Won, Y. H., & Lee, G. R. (in press). Living arrangements of older parents in Korea. *Journal of Comparative Family Studies.*

Young, C. M. (1984). *Young people leaving home in Australia: The trend towards independence* (Australian Family Formation Project Monograph No. 9). Melbourne: Australian Institute of Family Studies.

Zang, X. (1993). Household structure and marriage in urban China: 1900–1982. *Journal of Comparative Family Studies, 24,* 35–44.

CHAPTER 5

Ethnic Variation in the Family

The Elusive Trend toward Convergence

Robert Aponte

with Bruce A. Beal and Michelle E. Jiles

Introduction

A recurring theme in the literature on "the family" is the idea that the functions, forms, "values," or lifestyles of families will vary strongly by ethnic background. However, in sharp contrast with earlier times, latterday family diversity is more likely to be celebrated than castigated. The shift in perspective has doubtlessly elicited great satisfaction among those—usually minority—scholars whose efforts helped bring forth the change (Mirande, 1977; Staples & Mirande, 1980). In addition, representatives of the "helping professions" (e.g., social workers) often welcome the shift because it facilitates the incorporation of more appropriately varied modalities for "servicing" their increasingly multicultural clientele (e.g., Devore & Schlesinger, 1987; McDade, 1995).

However, some of the celebratory discourse about family diversity (e.g., Gonzales, 1994; McAdoo, 1993) may overstate its true salience. For one thing, the range of variation *within* groups on any specific item (e.g., family size), is usually far greater than the gap *separating* groups on the item (difference in average size). Additionally, it is well known that many differences between groups actually reflect socioeconomic standing, or more simply "class," rather than "culture" or "ethnicity," even though we often cannot show this for lack of data or technique (Goldscheider & Goldscheider, 1989; Staples & Mirande, 1980). Beyond that, the

Robert Aponte • Department of Sociology, Indiana University–Purdue University at Indianapolis, Indianapolis, Indiana 46202.

Handbook of Marriage and the Family, 2nd edition, edited by Marvin Sussman, Suzanne K. Steinmetz, and Gary W. Peterson. Plenum Press, New York, 1999.

comparative dimension in much of the relevant discourse is often "static" or "cross-sectional" in nature (differences at a given time), rather than "dynamic" or "longitudinal" (trends over time). Since families of all varieties have experienced, or are experiencing, significant change (Baca Zinn & Eitzen, 1996; Demos, 1986; Ross & Sawhill, 1975; Skolnick & Skolnick, 1989), a static comparison necessarily provides limited insights. Such an approach cannot reveal, for example, whether the *direction* of change is toward convergence or divergence—an issue of obvious significance.

This chapter advances the following ideas. First, we propose that much of what passes for cultural differences among families actually stems from factors other than "ethnicity" per se (e.g., class). Second, and most importantly, we suggest the trend over time for all major groups is toward convergence on key family attributes (e.g., family size), although not necessarily toward a specific model (e.g., four-person nuclear family), but rather toward a variegated model with a variety of lifestlyes. Third, we contend that exceptions to this pattern constitute truly exceptional cases where the lack of such convergence is sustained by extraordinary circumstances. Finally, we note that the trend toward convergence is hardly limited to the ethnic variation in the United States; rather, families in societies from which U.S. minorities hail are also changing in ways consistent with our convergence perspective, albeit to varying degrees.

The central idea suggested here is that virtually all distinct groups in contemporary U.S. society will tend, over time, toward similarity on a particular set of characteristics, although not necessarily toward identical configurations of them. Indeed, more options for individuals and greater variation of family types constitute, broadly put, one such characteristic. In more specific terms, we hold that all groups will—as compared with their traditional patterns—tend toward lower fertility and smaller family size, later ages at marriage, less parental influence on marital partnering, less endogamy, increased marital dissolution (and consequently, more single-parent families), less interdependence with extended kin, decreased male dominance, and so forth (Goode, 1963).*

In addition, these changes are held to stem from the changing conditions that all contemporary families face in the United States (and other modern societies), rather than from an inevitable process of assimilation. Indeed, we hold that such convergence *need not* (although it can) entail full-fledged "assimilation," since the opportunities and constraints posed by modern society—which bring forth the changes—are not conditional on either allegiance to, or alienation from, the lifestyles of the larger (i.e., "European American") groupings. Consistent with this, as we show here, families in other modern (or modernizing) societies have experienced (or are experiencing) remarkably similar changes without benefit of U.S. cultural domination.

It is worth stressing that we do not here predict an end to family diversity. On the contrary, we expect diversity among families to remain formidable or even to increase. For one thing, a major source of contemporary diversity, immigration from societies at different levels of development (e.g., Mexico), shows little sign of abating as we approach the twenty-first century. Moreover, large numbers of such migrants often spring from the least developed sectors or areas (agricultural-rural, urban slums) of their originating societies, thereby exacerbating differences between them and the typical families of the host society.

Beyond that, there are at least two additional underlying items that will ensure a continuation of many forms of diversity. First, the impact of class—a key influence on family organization—will continue to differentiate families significantly, as it has in the past (e.g., Baca Zinn & Eitzen, 1996; Farber, 1973). Since clusters of ethnics often share class standings at lower levels than societal averages, the resulting class-based differences will remain linked to both "group" and "class." Second, since at least *some* of the

changes underway in family organization appear to reflect the *increasing array* of *options* more readily available to individuals and couples in modern societies (Baca Zinn & Eitzen, 1996), diversity *within groups* will almost surely increase. In short, diversity among families in unlikely to diminish, but we hypothesize that it will increasingly reflect exigencies and choices rather than "ethnicity" or tradition.*

The basic thrust of the general argument is supported on the basis of the experiences of five ethnic minorities—African Americans, Japanese, Mexicans, Chinese, and Puerto Ricans (living in the United States)—and one religious minority (Amish), as documented in the literature. Our focus is on objective indicators, although attitudinal items receive some attention. Four of the subject groups—Japanese, Mexicans, Chinese, and mainland Puerto Ricans—are largely twentieth century immigrants, although the latter are technically a migrant group since the United States has fully incorporated their homeland, Puerto Rico, after first taking it as a colony. Still, in most "cultural" respects (e.g., language, customs), mainland-resident Puerto Ricans are very much like other immigrants. The remaining two groups, the Amish and African Americans, are clearly not twentieth-century immigrants. Ironically, it is these last groups that seemingly least conform to the convergence argument advanced here, a finding we explain in a manner consistent with our central ideas. Special attention is paid to the plight of African American families not only because they are the largest and most senior of the minority groups, but also because of the particularly harsh and long-standing oppression they have endured and its implications for their current conditions.

It is worth noting that the social designations utilized here under the general banner of "ethnicity" are not necessarily consistent with those used by other analysts because, unfortunately, usage will sometimes vary (cf. Farley, 1995; Marger, 1991). As Steinmetz, Claven, and Stein (1990) have noted, the dictionary definition indicates that ethnicity is "of or relating to races or large groups of people classified according to common traits and customs" (p. 55). They go on to note that in the social sciences, the designation can refer to people from a particular nation, of a particular religion, or of a particular race. Indeed, the central defining feature of an ethnic group, according to ethnic relations specialists, is that the so-designated group recognizes itself as such and is so recognized by others (Farley, 1995; Marger, 1991). Hence, our categorizations here fit well within the broad patterns of accepted usage.

The Changing Family

The first critical item to be noted in a comparative review of families is that change is ubiquitous (Boh et al., 1989; Das & Jesser, 1980; Maddock, Hogan, Antonov, & Matskov-

---

*The arguments made here have much in common with the classic work by William Goode (1963). However, whereas Goode advanced the idea that increasing modernization across nations should lead to increasing convergence of family types across such nations, a notion we find agreeable, the core proposition here is simply that this should be so for all groups *within a single society*, where the economic, social, and legal infrastructures are necessarily the same. Thus, any dispositions toward convergence should be stronger. Moreover, we endeavor here to delineate conditions that facilitate or impede such processes, thereby generating differential outcomes, but without violating the general logic of the causal relationships. We note that Alex Inkeles (1980) revisited Goode's global thesis and found considerable support for it, although he concluded that it was still too early to draw final conclusions and that there were at least some items on which dissimilar outcomes appeared in evidence.

sky, 1994; Weisner, Bradley, & Kilbridge, 1997). Thus, not only does the change among ethnic minority families have to be accounted for, but the change among the base or comparative reference group must also be taken into consideration. In this study, the referent is variously (as available) the total U.S. population or non-Hispanic whites (European Americans)—the latter still accounting for over three-quarters of the total U.S. population in the 1990 census. The trend among both groupings has been similar: The family is known to have experienced significant change since the nation's founding, especially over the last few decades (Demos, 1986; Ellwood, 1988; Ross & Sawhill, 1975; Scott & Wishby, 1982; Skolnick & Skolnick, 1989). Key changes include decreased fertility and family size, decreased parental influence on marital choices, increased age at marriage, increased marital dissolution, increased authority of women within the family, increased labor force participation by wives/mothers, and an especially significant increase—recently—in single-parent families led by women.

What has brought forth these changes? Reduced to a single word, the source is generally labeled "modernization," a term or concept that refers primarily to such interwoven societal shifts as urbanization and industrialization (Goode, 1963; Inkeles, 1980). In brief, we may note that in modern, highly urban and industrial societies, traditional family arrangements encounter increasing ecological or economic constraints. Over time, newer arrangements, more compatible with the modern exigencies, tend to emerge. For example, large families may be more compatible with rural than urban living because on farms, children may constitute assets (child labor), while in urban settings, they are more likely to constitute liabilities (no labor/higher costs).

In modern societies (socialist and capitalist alike), the state assumes responsibilities that were previously the domain of the family, such as providing schooling and various forms of financial security. This lessens the obligations of kin and diffuses the socialization process; elders' and kin's traditionalist influence on the young is thereby necessarily diminished. The sheer exposure to masses of people, often of varying lifestyles, which is common in *urban* (as opposed to rural) places, may reinforce this.

The greater occupational differentiation of modern society, moreover, generally stimulates expanded schooling and increased economic (including geographical) mobility. The latter may attenuate kin ties while the former may introduce nontraditionalist ideals along with inducing the postponement of marriage and fertility (outcomes facilitated by *modern* techniques of fertility control). Finally, the emergence of economic opportunities for women, characteristic of modern society, can have two effects. First, as a large body of research shows (Baca Zinn & Eitzen, 1996), married women with earnings tend to have more household authority than nonearning ones. Second, such earnings (and guarantees for

support from the modern state) can facilitate marital dissolution or nonmarriage, since women (and their children) will be less reliant on the earnings of men than they would otherwise be. In addition to disrupting the influence of tradition, such changes contribute to an increase in the array of options individuals can pursue.

In short, many of the changes in marriage and the family that were earlier described can easily be linked to the exigencies of modern society. We may hypothesize that just as modernization appears to be eliciting change on the mainstream societal family, so too will it elicit similar changes on any incoming grouping of families that is subjected to the same societal milieu. However, we hasten to add, not all groups are truly exposed to precisely the same societal milieu. That is, groups are seldom afforded precisely the same set of opportunities, constraints, or possibilities, for a variety of reasons. For example, regional differences in economic growth or decline, along with varying public services (e.g., educational quality) by place, provide differing opportunity structures for members of different communities. In addition, some groups are forced to shoulder extensive discriminatory treatment, irrespective of place. Such varying conditions will foster varying levels of social or economic success, which, in turn, may stimulate differing strategies of family organization (including dissolution or disintegration).

Consider, for example, the effects of unemployment on families. A passage in Baca Zinn and Eitzen (1996) expertly captures the issues:

> Family changes result when a breadwinner loses a job. Younger families may delay having children during such a crisis.... [Others] may move in with other family members—adult children with parents or parents with adult children. A common coping strategy ... is for the spouse to enter the work force. Although it helps solve the economic problem, this strategy has some possible negative outcomes.... For one, it increases the burden on women who work for wages and who continue to do most of the housework. Also, many tradition-minded husbands find the loss of their breadwinner status intolerable, especially when that role is taken over by their wives. These men lose self-esteem. They may react by ... drinking and physically and mentally abusing their spouses and children. A ... [recent study found] cases of child abuse increased an average of 123 percent ... where unemployment had increased.... In contrast, those counties in which unemployment declined tended to have reduced reports of child abuse. (p. 109)

This strongly indicates that family characteristics are affected by the broader influences of society, such as economic conditions. Such influences are sometimes experientially group-specific (e.g., discrimination), and sometimes not (e.g., recession). The former will tend to accentuate "group" differences, the latter will not. That neither of the resulting differences should be seen as culturally based, although they often are, is the subject we next consider.

Interpreting Diversity

Slightly over three-quarters (75.7%) of the nation's population was classified as non-Hispanic white in the 1990 census, down from nearly 80% 10 years earlier; by halfway into the next century, assuming a continuation of current trends, the proportion is expected to dip below half. The projection was widely publicized in a *TIME* magazine feature entitled "Beyond the Melting Pot," which, among other things, popularized the phrase "the Browning of America" (Henry, 1990). The ramifications of the potential population shift, in turn, have been the subject of all manner of speculation about commensurate changes in society, including family diversity. However, we suggest that comprehending what may be on the horizon for ethnic families is likely to require a better understanding of family diversity at present.

Literature directly examining family diversity in the United States has a relatively short, and initially sordid, history. Drawing on the classic overview of Staples and Mirande (1980), we may divide this short history into at least two or three broad stages. Briefly put, the first stage was a period in which scholarship was limited to Anglo (non-Hispanic white) researchers, was focused almost solely on blacks and Latinos (generally just of Mexican origin or "Chicanos"), and was often fantastically pejorative of minorities.* The emphasis was on the alleged pathological nature of minority family life. A second stage can be described as one where minority scholars entered the fray and advanced more flattering perspectives on minority families, along with ferreting out many of the analytically unfounded and pejorative stereotypes. However, many of these authors (especially writers on the Chicano family) took things too far, advancing overly romanticized views (Mirande, 1977). A final stage—which largely survives to the present—is one where more balanced views, inclusive of widely varying perspectives, prevail.

At the risk of further oversimplification, it appears that recent family studies have encompassed a multiculturalist outlook. Despite differences in emphasis, this body of work (e.g., Baca Zinn & Eitzen, 1996; Goldscheider & Goldscheider, 1989; Gonzales, 1994; Jacobson, 1995; Taylor, 1994) values, rather than denigrates, diverse cultural styles.

It also recognizes the multiplicity of influences directly bearing on family life (e.g., class, racism), but maintains that ethnic or cultural background factors still exert considerable influence (e.g., McAdoo, 1993).

However, as noted at the outset, we find some fundamental problems with much of the current work. First, because of the difficulties of truly "controlling" extraneous influences in statistical modeling techniques, we believe that the influence of "ethnicity" remains overstated in analytic studies. Second, we believe that even differences that exist, net of extraneous factors, are not necessarily useful indicators of varying group *values*, a position we illustrate later. Finally, we find that an important dimension of ethnic differences, that is, the trend over time, is either ignored or underplayed in this literature. However, failing to account for trends will exaggerate existing ethnic differences if the trend is actually toward convergence, since the lack of a context of attenuation implies a measure of permanence.

The point to be stressed is not that differences by group are nonexistent. Rather, it is (1) that many of the differences are diminishing and (2) that ideas about the underlying basis for the differences often rest on slippery ground. While our understanding of the differences may remain incomplete, indications are that the bulk of the differences stem from sources other than "ethnicity," although this is often difficult to show. For example, in an overview of research on differential living arrangements by ethnicity, Goldscheider and Goldscheider (1989) note a vast array of influences on residential patterns beyond ethnicity (e.g., demographic feasibility—adults cannot coreside with elders if the latter are abroad or deceased), many of which could nevertheless be confounded with ethnicity (varying mortality or immigration patterns by group) and be difficult to untangle (i.e., "control for").

Goldscheider and Goldscheider (1989) note the especially vexing difficulties in separating class from ethnicity:

> A major challenge in disentangling ethnic effects is that ethnic groups are often different in ways that lead to economic deprivation, whether they are new entrants into a society, and hence have not yet acquired the skills to function successfully in it, or because their "difference" leads to discrimination ... [etc., such that] what are often interpreted as ethnic differences may simply be the result of differences in resources. (p. 192)

Indeed, the numerous difficulties with attempts to "control for class" include problems beyond the capacity of even the most sophisticated analyses. For example, income figures, even when accurate, do not convey differentials in living costs or accumulated wealth that could easily vary by group (e.g., Oliver & Shapiro, 1995). Furthermore, since income is generally tabulated for only one point in time (as opposed to income averaging over many years), families of

---

*Examples of fantastically pejorative characterizations are numerous (Mirande, 1977; Staples and Mirande, 1980). For example, as recently as 1971, Rudoff (1971) offered the following absurdity about Mexican males "The Mexican American has little concern for the future, perceives himself as predestined to be poor and subordinate, is still influenced by magic, is gangminded, distrusts women, sees authority as arbitrary, tends to be passive and dependent, and is alienated from Anglo culture" (pp. 236–237, cited in Mirande, 1977; p. 749). Likewise, and even more recently, Madsen (1973) characterized Mexican males as upholding the notion that, "The better man is the one who can drink more, defend himself best, have more sex relations, and have more sons borne by his wife" (cited in Staples and Mirande, 1980; p. 893).

modest backgrounds that only recently achieved middle-level incomes, for example, may be compared with families long accustomed to middle incomes (or previously higher ones) and far more accumulated wealth. This can also result in inappropriate comparisons.

Finally, there are "class" background factors that reflect neither income nor ethnicity, but may nevertheless underlie differences mistakenly taken to reflect ethnic culture. For example, it is often noted that the fertility among Mexicans is higher than that among others. However, it is also the case that all groups exhibit higher rural than urban fertility at the same time that Mexicans in the United States are disproportionately rural-origin persons; this alone could account for much of the gap, but is seldom accounted for in observations of Mexicans' "remarkable fertility."*

Even where group differences cannot be tied to extraneous causes, interpreting them as indicative of varying group *values* is problematic. For example, differences in family size (or fertility) across groups are often interpreted as reflecting cultural differences. However, such averages actually reflect *varying proportions* of families with very large (and very small) numbers within both groups. Unless we assume that all such deviations from the group averages stem from faulty family planning (or other biological/social constraints), the tendencies cannot logically be said to reflect "group values."

An alternative interpretation, better suited to these circumstances, is simply that a *higher proportion* of the larger group than of the smaller group form large families, and vice versa. Posing the "finding" this way stays closer to the truth and more readily stimulates further inquiry focusing on differences rather than the blanket, group membership interpretation, which inherently "writes it off" as a property of the group (i.e., culture).

Another related problem with the cultural interpretation concerns "choice." For example, if by ethnic or cultural influences we really mean "values," then those following the prescribed traditions should be doing so *voluntarily*, thereby pursuing strongly held values. But as often as not, the charac-

teristics alleged to separate people culturally are hardly freely chosen. For example, much has made about the disproportionately high percentage of female-headed African American families, but a significant proportion of these entered single parenthood via widowhood, abandonment, and other essentially *involuntary* means. Moreover, even those single mothers who truly exercised "choice" on the road to family headship can hardly be said to be reflecting their "traditional" culture if their "choices" have likewise been exercised by only a limited proportion of their ethnic/racial counterparts. Finally, even if (as in the African American community) the relative numbers of such family types have mushroomed into a substantial minority within a group, the outcome can hardly be pinned on "tradition" if it is largely a new development (post World War II), as is the case among all U.S. groups for whom we have systematic information (including African Americans).

Finally, some of the very ethnic categories themselves (e.g., "Mexican" families, "Japanese" families, etc.) are problematic units for cultural explanations because of the substantial variation within these groups, not only with regard to class background, current socioeconomic status (SES), and so forth, but even more fundamentally with respect to the extent the various parties can truly be said to represent their "traditional" cultures. This is because such parties necessarily represent *varying amounts of exposure* to U.S. society, in terms of both tenure and intensity of immersion. The socialization of second-generation immigrants, for example, will necessarily include significant "Americanized" influences totally absent in their parents' corresponding upbringing.

Despite much rhetoric to the contrary, virtually all incoming groups change rapidly after entering this society. Thus, recent studies of post-World War II immigration show that by the second generation, English is the preferred language, and by the third, relatively few can even speak the language of their forbearers (Rumbaut, 1994), a situation not unlike that among early twentieth-century immigrants from Europe (Steinberg, 1989). Moreover, rates of intermarriage generally rise with time as well, creating multiethnic and multiracial offspring (Stephan & Stephan, 1989). Many of the latter do not identify with either of their parental groups, but prefer the multicategory label (if any at all). Indeed, recent media reports (McLeod, 1997; El Nassar, 1997) have shown that growing concerns on the issue has caused the Census Bureau to seriously consider formulating multiethnic/racial categories for use in the year 2000 census.

In summary, we offer here an interpretation of ethnic-based differences among families today, and by extension among those of the future, that is somewhat at odds with much of the literature (e.g., Gonzales, 1994; McAdoo, 1993). We contend that the differences that exist are unlikely to

---

*There are numerous additional examples of varying indicators across groups in which the causal item is unlikely to be "culturally" based, but nevertheless tied to the "group." A useful example is the minority group status hypothesis (e.g., Johnson, 1979; Johnson & Burton, 1987). While a number of versions of the idea have been advanced, a consideration of Johnson's (1979) alone will suffice to make the point. In that instance, the idea was that whereas black Americans showed considerably higher fertility than whites on average, within the middle classes, the relationship reversed. The interpretation was that middle-class blacks, as members of a stigmatized minority group, were less secure in their status than others and thus were more cautious in their reproductive behavior. If those ideas are correct, they provide an example of an existing "group" difference not originating in culture that might well be interpreted that way since its true source will not be readily apparent.

stem from cultural values or traditions, as they often appear to. Rather, we believe that the immersion in a common social milieu sets the stage for a convergence of family organizational strategies among the various groups, but that total convergence is seldom realized because as the traditional sources of diversity wane (for all groups, newcomers and veterans alike), the exigencies of contemporary society (*differentials* in opportunities and constraints, *increases* in options and possibilities) give rise to still more varied family forms, functions, or lifestyles. The next sections attempt to support the ideas presented here on the basis of brief overviews of the relevant experiences of several ethnic (and one religious) minority groups.

Family Diversity and the Dynamics of Change

Chinese and Japanese Americans, and by extension, their families, have an interesting history in the United States; both were extremely vilified at various periods and both now share the designation of "model minority" as a result of establishing solid reputations for economic success, minimal involvement in welfare or crime, and a legacy of strong family values. More importantly for our purposes, each is thoroughly believed to maintain strong "traditional" cultural orientations that, in turn, are believed to underlie their success (Glenn, 1983; Glenn & Yap, 1994; O'Brien & Fugita, 1991; Takagi, 1994; Wong, 1988).

To be sure, these groups have achieved, on average, substantially higher social and economic levels than the general population has. Table 1 provides a selected scattering of 1990 data that underscore the point. In 1989, median incomes for the nation's Chinese and Japanese families ($41,300 and $51,600, respectively, 1989 dollars) were substantially higher than that for the total population ($35,200). However, we argue that whatever underlies their relative successes, each of these groups has long departed from their traditional ways here in the United States—not unlike their compatriots back home.

Chinese Families in the United States

The nation's Chinese families, as illustrated here, provide a clear example of this. The Chinese are currently the largest Asian-origin nationality group, numbering over 1.6 million as of the 1990 census (see Table 1). Largely situated in West Coast cities, where they first entered the United States, they have an established presence in midwestern and northeastern cities as well. Their numbers have been rising rapidly in recent years; just 20 years previously they numbered less than .5 million, a figure lower than that registered by Japanese Americans at the time. Indeed, as shown in Table

2 (data for 1980), the Chinese were only half as numerous in 1980 as in 1990) (see Table 1). Thus, they have doubled in size within a scant decade. Their recent brisk growth largely results from increases in U.S.-bound migration, a process that received a hefty boost from the nation's immigration reforms of 1965 (Glenn & Yap, 1994). However, neither the recent arrivals nor the longtime residents truly typify the traditional Chinese family type.

In fact, it is difficult to pinpoint the best representative model of the traditional Chinese American family. For one thing, the Chinese American family has taken various distinct forms during its tenure in the United States, each of which can be related to specific "structural" conditions it encountered, rather than differing regions of origin or other "cultural" background distinctions (Glenn, 1983; Gonzales, 1994; Wong, 1988). These include the "split household" family, which refers to families split across the Pacific Ocean as a result of immigration restrictions, and the "small producer family," which consists of families immersed in small family businesses, usually in Chinatowns. The differences in these types were significant: In the former, husband/fathers were separated from families for long periods; in the latter, they and their family members were totally united at both home and "work," since the latter was a collective enterprise. This strategy became popular, at least in part, because of the dearth of alternative opportunities (due to reasons such as discrimination) and because the families of "merchants" were provided exceptions to the general ban on Chinese immigration. Finally, a third type is the dual-earner family. This designation, which more or less survives to the present, represents poor and working-class families where both parents work outside the home, often for Chinese employers.

At present, the Chinese American family is still seen as roughly divisible into two main types, the "ghetto or Chinatown Chinese"—small business owners, working-class families, disadvantaged immigrants—and the "middle-class" or professional Chinese who reside outside of Chinatowns, often in well-to-do suburbs (cf. Gonzales, 1994; Wong, 1985, 1988). Many of the latter are also recent immigrants. Not surprisingly, these components experience varying conditions and lifestyles. Whereas the Chinatown residents are tightly clustered, more likely to be poor or struggling, and appear to receive many working-class immigrants, the better-off group includes many highly educated and trained persons, both native born and immigrants. In fact, 1990 census microdata amassed by Farley (1996) show that among recent Chinese immigrants ages 25–54, less than 20% of the men (and 30% of the women) lack at least 12 years of schooling, while fully 60% of the men and 40% of the women were college graduates. Further, in contrast to the idea that strong traditional values propel success among Asians, the more

**Table 1. Selected Descriptive Indicators of Persons and Families
in the United States by Selected Racial/Ethnic Groups, 1989–1990**

Characteristic	Group						
	Total population	Non-Hispanic white	Chinese American	Japanese American	Mexican American	Puerto Rican	African American
Persons							
Totals (in hundreds of thousands)	248.7	188.1	1.6	0.8	13.5	2.7	30.0
Percent Foreign born	7.9	NA	69.3	32.4	33.4	NA	NA
Median Age	33.0	34.9	32.3	36.5	23.8	25.5	28.3
Ages 0–17							
With two parents (%)	71.8	80.4	86.8	85.2	67.5	45.1	36.8
Percent female	48.7	48.6	47.8	49.0	48.8	48.7	49.3
Ages 5–17							
Percent English Only	NA	NA	22.3	65.3	33.4	29.9	NA
Ages 20–64							
LFPR, male[a]	86.6	87.2	83.6	86.6	87.8	78.6	76.6
LFPR, female[a]	69.7	70.4	68.1	64.3	61.3	55.4	70.5
Ages 25 and over							
HSG/+ male (%)[b]	75.7	79.6	79.5	89.9	43.9	53.1	62.2
Female	74.8	78.5	68.0	85.6	44.5	53.5	63.8
BA/+ Male (%)[b]	23.3	25.6	46.7	42.6	6.8	9.5	11.0
Female	17.6	18.8	35.0	28.2	5.6	9.4	11.7
Women 15 and over							
Divorce ratio[c]	12.2	11.8	4.6	8.5	10.7	17.4	18.5
Native/Foreign[d]	NA	NA	9.5/3.9	9.3/7.6	14.3/6.1	NA	NA
Women 35–44							
Percent ever married	90.2	92.1	90.8	88.4	90.8	83.8	78.2
Children ever born	2.0	1.8	1.7	1.5	2.8	2.5	2.3
Native/foreign[d]	NA	NA	1.4/1.8	1.6/1.3	2.5/3.3	NA	NA
Families[e]							
Average size	3.2	3.0	3.6	3.1	4.1	3.5	3.5
Lone-women headed (%)	18.7	13.6	6.7	9.7	18.0	40.8	47.7
Native/foreign[d]	NA	NA	8.7/6.4	10.0/9.4	22.8/13.1	NA	NA
Median income (in thousands of $)	35.2	37.6	41.3	51.6	24.1	21.9	22.4
Per capita income (in thousands of $)	14.4	16.1	14.9	19.4	7.4	8.4	8.9
Percent in poverty	10.0	7.0	11.2	3.4	23.4	29.6	26.3

[a]LFPR, labor force participation rate.
[b]HSG/+, denotes high school completion (or more); BA/+, BA degree (or more).
[c]Divorce ratio denotes *currently* divorced per 100 *ever married* without regard to divorcees *currently* remarried widowed, etc.
[d]Figures separated for native born/foreign born. NA, not applicable.
[e]Average size not available by nativity; female headship rate is for families with *own* children.
Source: U.S. Bureau of the Census (1992; 1993a,b,c; 1994). Note where census data vary across reports (e.g., sampling variation), maximizing consistency guided choices; thus, U.S. Bureau of the Census (1992) utilized only for non-Hispanic white divorce ratio (only available there). Income and poverty data, 1989; all other, 1990.

successful of the Chinese groups is also the more assimilated of the two. Indeed, the idea that the Chinese are marked by economic bipolarity is supported by Table 1: Despite a *substantially* higher than average median family income, the group also has a *slightly* higher than average poverty rate (11.2% vs. 10.0% for the total population).

It might be expected that traditionalist practices, even if not pillars of economic success, might still flourish within the Chinatowns (particularly among newer immigrants), as suggested in the research literature (cf. Glenn & Yap, 1994; Wong, 1985, 1988). Some of the more pertinent ones are large family size, male domination, filiel piety (devotion to family, especially elders), a strong preference for male offspring, a form of primogeniture, strict sex roles, family extension

**Table 2. Selected Descriptive Indicators of Persons and Families
in the United States by Selected Racial/Ethnic Groups, 1979–1980**

Characteristic	Group						
	Total population	Non-Hispanic white	Chinese American	Japanese American	Mexican American	Puerto Rican	African American
Persons							
Totals (in hundreds of thousands)	226.5	180.6	0.8	0.7	8.7	2.0	26.5
Percent foreign born	6.2	NA	63.3	28.4	25.7	NA	NA
Ages 0–17							
With two parents (%)	76.7	83.5	88.2	87.3	74.8	50.9	45.4
Women 15 and over							
Divorce ratio[a]	9.3	8.8	3.8	6.8	8.9	13.0	13.8
Native/foreign[b]	NA	NA	7.7/2.9	7.0/6.6	na	NA	NA
Women 35–44							
Children ever born	2.6	2.5	2.2	1.9	3.6	3.2	3.2
Native/foreign[b]	NA	NA	2.0/2.3	1.9/1.8	na	NA	NA
Families[c]							
Average size	3.3	3.2	3.7	3.6	4.1	3.7	3.7
Lone-women headed (%)	16.2	11.9	6.5	12.0	15.8	39.3	41.8
Native/foreign[c]	NA	NA	9.6/5.7	8.6/19.6	na	NA	NA
Percent in poverty	9.6	6.6	10.5	4.2	20.6	34.9	26.5

[a]Divorce ratio denotes *currently* divorced per 100 *ever married* without regard to divorcees *currently* remarried widowed, etc.
[b]Figures separated for native born/foreign born. NA, not applicable, na, not available.
[c]Average size not available by nativity; female headship rate is for families with *own* children.
Source: U.S. Bureau of the Census (1983a,b; 1988) various tables. Note, where census data vary across reports maximizing consistency guided choices. Poverty data, 1979; all other, 1980.

(usually parents of husband), and by implication, endogamy. However, many of these seem clearly to have waned. For example, the continued exercising of the traditional preference for male offspring (believed to underlie much female infanticide in China) is unsupported by the data on the sex balance of children shown in Table 1. Indeed, there is little difference in the percent of female children among all the groups shown (just under 50%). In addition, there are few indications that arranged marriages or primogeniture continue to be practiced, contrary to tradition and despite continuing and brisk immigration.

Although many of the remaining traditional practices that might persist, such as attitudinal items, cannot be judged here (beyond indirect evidence, such as noting increasing female education and exogamy), trends in Chinese family size can be culled from the literature. Wong (1988) notes, for example, that in the early post-World War II period, the families of New York's Chinatown averaged 4.4 children, versus 2.9 among the city's whites. However, he also notes, "[I]f both parents were born in China, the median number of children ... was 6.2; if both were American born, the median number was 3.2," adding, "As the Chinese became more Americanized and acculturated, the number of children in the Chinese family declined" (p. 243).

Data in Table 1 indicate a continuation of the implied trend. For example, children ever born among Chinese women ages 35–44 (1.7) is shown as significantly lower than the corresponding national average (2.0). The group's average family size, however, is shown as somewhat larger (3.6 vs. 3.2 persons, respectively). The juxtaposition of these two indicators suggests that Chinese families practice more extension than do other groups, a practice in keeping with tradition and that has been detected in research on living arrangements among the elderly (Kamo & Zhou, 1994). However, despite extensive and ongoing immigration, the 1990 family size average of the Chinese is actually *down* from their 1980 figure of 3.7, as shown in Table 2 (see also Glenn & Yap, 1994). This suggests an attentuation of the practice, particularly in view of the brisk migration of late (which would be expected to raise, rather than lower, its extent).

Another generalization about the Chinese concerns their aversion to divorce and their strong sense of familism (Wong, 1988). Data in Table 1 provide some support to these ideas. Only 6.7% of Chinese families are headed by a lone women, and only 13.2% of their children reside with less than two parents, as compared with national averages of 16.0% and 28.2%, respectively. Here again, however, the figures are up from 10 years earlier (6.5% and 11.8%, respectively), as shown in Table 2. In addition, consistent with our general points, native born Chinese in 1990 show a higher rate of female headship (8.7%) than do foreign born (6.4%). Finally, as Table 1 shows, the Chinese exhibit the lowest divorce ratio of all included groups, exhibiting a 4.6 ratio, versus 12.2 for the total population. Here too, however, their ratio is up from 1980 (3.8), and it is substantially higher among the native born (9.5) than among the foreign born (3.9), as was true in 1980 (see Table 2).

On a related note, a substantial body of research has shown a significant rise in the rate of Chinese intermarriage with others, particularly whites and other Asians (cf. Fong & Young, 1995; Kitano & Yeung, 1982; Kitano et al., 1984; Sung, 1990). For example, Kitano et al. (1984) showed that third-generation females in Los Angeles registered an astounding 74.0% rate of out-marriage in 1979. Overall rates for the year were 43.7% for males and 56.3% for females, with U.S. nativity and membership in still higher order generations (e.g., third generation immigrant) key predisposing factors.

In addition, retention of Chinese language skills is clearly faltering. As data in Table 1 show, over one-fifth (22.3%) of Chinese children were *English monolingual* in 1990, despite the fact that nearly 70% of all Chinese are *foreign born.* (As recently as 1960, a majority of the nation's Chinese were U.S. born.) The data also show that a substantial portion of Chinese women are highly educated—over one-third hold bachelors degrees, more than any other group, including non-Hispanic whites and Japanese (who show the second-highest proportion). It is difficult to imagine that such highly educated women would embrace many of the male-centered traditional ways.

Before concluding that all of this stems from "assimilation," it is worth noting that substantial and similar changes have also occurred in China. Aside from the changes already taking place under prior regimes (Goode, 1963), the Chinese Revolution of 1949 promoted its own reforms. For example, the "Marriage Law of 1950 abolished arranged marriages, restricted payments for brides ... and provided greater access to divorce" (Meredith & Abbott, 1995, p. 216). Follow-up legislation in 1980 promoted additional reforms, including further liberalization of divorce (Eshleman, 1997). Perhaps more importantly, Meredith and Abbott (1993) note:

> Of course, as one looks at the Chinese family in historical perspective, it is important to keep in mind that ... [the traditional model] represents the ideal; reality was not always so generous. Much depended on one's class and economic resources. The Confucian ideal of the extended family ... [etc.] was possible only for wealthier families.... [poor families] often broke down under the stress of ... famine or poverty. Sometimes children had to be sold and old people left to fend for themselves. Much peasant folklore centers around the often tragic and futile efforts of the poor to live up to filial piety. (pp. 215–216)

Several of the essays in the collected edition edited by Lin et al. (1994) provide additionally relevant observations.

For example, Li (1994, p. 46) notes that while some 170,000 divorces were granted in 1978 in mainland China, the corresponding number in 1985 was 458,000. The 1990 figure, according to Eshleman (1997), was 800,000. Moreover, according to survey data cited by this author, the percentage of arranged marriages dropped markedly just from the mid 1940s to the late 1950s, although both Eshleman (1997) and Li (1994) note that many of the reforms are far less likely to be enforced (or practiced) in rural, versus urban, areas. In a similar vein, Marsh and Hsu (1994) show substantial changes in outlook (with respect to perceived obligations to extended kinfolk) within Taiwan, where the more conservative government had not pursued a sweeping reform agenda like that of the mainland.

In short, changes in the family among Chinese in the United States are not unlike those back home. Thus, despite brisk immigration, the Chinese American community of the present—with all its internal diversity—is likely to continue along its current, unambiguously nontraditionalist, path.

Japanese Families in the United States

The nation's Japanese offer an interesting contrast to the Chinese. As shown in Table 1, the former group's 1990 U.S. population was just under 850,000. Thus, they were the third largest Asian origin group in the country, following both Chinese Americans and Filipino Americans. However, only 20 years previously, the Japanese were the largest of the groups, when their numbers approaches 600,000 (Wilkinson, 1987). Thus, their growth has been slow due to both scant migration and modest natural increase. Like the Chinese, they are primarily settled in the West Coast (and Hawaii), where they initially entered the United States. Unlike the Chinese, Japanese Americans largely remain in their traditional areas of settlement.

A far more important point of contrast, however, concerns their society of origin. Unlike China, Japan is a thoroughly modern society, similar to the United States or the modern European states. One implication of this for our purposes is that we should expect less of a gap in our indicators of relevance when comparing Japanese immigrants with those born in the United States. As noted later, this is precisely the case. And, in both instances, the indicators are different from those the "traditional" Japanese should have exhibited.

It is difficult to say precisely what the traditional Japanese family is supposed to be like because there have been important changes over time, particularly after the onset of the so-called Meiji Restoration (Kitano, 1988; Nozomu, 1989). Occurring toward the end of the nineteenth century, the Meiji period marks both the onset of modernization and the start of migration to the United States. For this period, at least, the literature suggests that several key elements have been present in Japanese families. These include extreme devotion one's family and family line (within a system called *ie*), male dominance in the household (and beyond), extended families (mainly via inclusion of elders), virtually universal adherence to the practice of arranged marriages, a preference for male offspring, patrilineal descent including primogeniture, low divorce rates, and near universal marriage by adults, particularly women (cf. Gonzales, 1994; Iwao, 1993; Kitano, 1988; Kumagai, 1996). In addition, fertility and family size were both relatively high and exogamy was both extremely rare and strongly proscribed.

During this period, the U.S.-based Japanese family experienced difficulties not unlike those visited upon the Chinese. For example, immigration patterns initially fostered skewed sex ratios and delayed the formation of many families. Since antimiscegenation laws and related racist practices (no doubt including the men's own preference for endogamy) precluded intermarriage, the men inclined to marriage in the United States turned to importing brides (mainly via "arranged" marriages) from Japan. Aside from imported brides, much of the subsequent migration in the early years consisted of relatives of the pioneers. One result of this, according to Kitano (1988), is that the settlers had a stronger basis for reproducing traditional-like communities than might otherwise have been the case (see O'Brien & Fugita, 1991, for a slightly different interpretation with similar conclusions). Thus, as noted by Kitano (1988):

> [F]amily life and marriages were from the beginning a continuity of family life in Japan. Family and kin were intimately involved in all stages of the marriage; it was the rare Issei [first-generation Japanese] who married without the approval of parents. (p. 263)

Given this kind of continuity, it would appear that in the beginning, the earlier noted characteristics about Japanese families were in operation here in the United States, as well as in Japan.

However traditionalist in structure and outlook during the early days, Japanese families have undergone overwhelming change since then. Numerous notable changes have been chronicled in the literature, just between the immigrant generation (*Issei*) and their offspring, the *Nisei* generation. The latter have been generally described as less traditionalist, more English-speaking than Japanese-speaking, experiencing reduced fertility (roughly half), and being far less likely to rely on parental choices for marital mates, among other things (Gonzales, 1994; Kitano, 1988; O'Brien & Fugita, 1991; Takagi, 1994). A number of writers further suggest that declining parental influence was facilitated by life in the concentration camps, where most West Coast Japanese were interned during much of World War II. This was mainly deemed to result from the more general usurpa-

tion of authority over most facets of the inmates' lives by camp managers (Gonzales, 1994; Kitano, 1988; O'Brien & Fugita, 1991).

A shift in attention to the present makes clear that Japanese families have experienced continuing marked changes in the United States. For example, Table 1 reveals that the number of children ever born for women ages 35–44 (the oldest age bracket for which data are consistently available) is, at 1.5, the lowest of all groups. This is down from the estimated 4.3 (for completed fertility) of the immigrant generation (Gonzales, 1994). In addition, the data reveal that nearly two-thirds (65.3%) of all Japanese children are English monolingual, by far the highest rate among the immigrant groups, despite the fact that nearly a full third of all Japanese (32.4%) are foreign born.

Data on average family size in Table 1 for the Japanese are consistent with their showing on fertility: Their 3.1 figure is second lowest among the groups. However, in 1980 (see Table 2), the Japanese showed higher than average family size despite lower than average fertility. This suggests that the Japanese, like the Chinese, were practicing some form of family extension. The likeliest scenario, of course, is that elderly parents tended to live with their married children, a circumstance well supported in the literature for both the United States (Kamo & Zhou, 1994) and Japan (Morgan & Hirosima, 1983; Ogawa & Ermisch, 1996). However, as noted earlier and consistent with the perspective advanced here, the practice appears to have abated considerably by 1990 when the indicators on fertility and family size were more balanced. In addition, no preference for male children is in evidence in Table 1, as all groups show similarly balanced sex ratios.

On the additional proxy measures for family solidarity shown in Table 1, the story is much the same. The percentage of Japanese children with two parents, 85.2, is higher by nearly five percentage points than that for whites (80.4), but it is also down from the group's corresponding 1980 figure of 87.3%, a shift consistent with trends among all groups. The figures on divorce, a status considered anathema to the Japanese, also support the argument here. Some 8.5% of Japanese ever-married women are currently divorced, nearly twice the proportion for the Chinese and nearly three-quarters the proportion among whites. Moreover, the figure is up from the group's 1980 statistic (see Table 2) and it understates the true prevalence of divorcees in the group because those who have divorced and remarried (including if subsequently widowed) are excluded from the calculation, for methodological reasons (a point true for the others as well). And, as Table 1 notes, the proportion of Japanese women ages 35–44 who are married is less than that for whites and the other immigrant groups. Finally, it is also likely that separation and divorce are more prevalent among younger couples, as suggested in the literature (cf. Kitano, 1988; Takagi, 1994). However, because of the age structure of the group favoring older adults over younger ones, youthful couples do not make as dramatic an impact on aggregated statistics as is true within other groups. Indeed, as shown in Table 1, the Japanese exhibit the oldest median age of all the groups.

On the measure for female family headship, the data in Table 1 also provide support to the views advanced here (although with some complications stemming from the data in Table 2). Some 9.7% of Japanese families with their own children in residence were headed by a single woman in 1990, a figure 3 percentage points higher than that for the Chinese and within 4 percentage points of the higher figure for whites. But contrary to expectations, the group's corresponding figure for 1980 is higher still (12.0%), exceeding even the figure for whites that year. The figure suggests that parity has already been reached between whites and the Japanese on the formation of such families, but the reduction in the rate since 1980 among the Japanese (while all others experience increases), along with the fact that the main source for the outlier appears to be the contribution of the foreign born, suggests the earlier year's data should be interpreted cautiously.*

The indicator providing the strongest support to the ideas in this chapter, however, is intermarriage. Here, there is no mistaking the trend noted in the literature: From very low rates among the early settlers, outmarriage among the Japanese has mushroomed to astoundingly high rates (e.g., Gonzales, 1994; Kitano et al., 1984; Takagi, 1994). For example, in Los Angeles County alone, where the largest concentration of Japanese Americans can be found, the group's outmarriage rate went from a mere 2% in 1924 to 11% in 1950 to 63% in 1977! (Kitano, 1988). The high rate of intermarriage has led many to question the future integrity of the very concept of "Japanese Americans":

> If current projections of out-marriage continue, we will not be able to speak much longer of the Japanese American family in the singular. Rather, we will have to consider whether Japanese Americans married to other races constitute a "Japanese American" family. (Takagi, 1994, p. 157)

---

*The view here is that the discrepancy in Japanese headship figures necessarily stems from an error somewhere in the compilation process. The figures shown here were rigorously checked and rechecked, but no mistakes could be detected. In view of the facts that all other statistics are consistent with the perspective that rates should have *increased* over the 1980–1990 period, rather than *decreased*, and absolutely no literature on Japan, whatsoever, indicates higher female headship rates for Japanese families (or outmigrant ones) than for American ones, no other explanation appears possible. Because the census in question dates back over 15 years, retracing census errata has not been pursued. Thus, readers must exercise their own judgment on the matter.

Once again, it is worth emphasizing that many of the family changes experienced by Japanese Americans have also occurred in Japan itself. For one thing, as earlier suggested, the data in Tables 1 and 2 that are disaggregated by nativity show relatively few differences for the Japanese, in contrast to the other immigrant groups. Likewise, the literature on families in Japan is fairly consistent with the generalizations offered here. For example, average family size is down by over two persons since the pre-World War II period, while the total fertility rate has fallen from greater than five births in the 1920s to about 1.5 in the early 1990s (Kumagai, 1996; Ogawa & Retherford, 1993).

In a related vein, the average age at first marriage is up significantly, and it appears that an increasing number of individuals will remain single. Indeed, it is estimated that the percentage of never-married above age 30 has doubled (for both sexes) over the last 20 years. As earlier noted, despite the traditional pressure toward universal marriage (especially for women), the proportion married among 35- to 44-year-old Japanese women in the United States is *less* than 9 out of 10 (see Table 1), a figure even lower than for that all other groups (except blacks and Puerto Ricans). Significant increases have also occurred in the rates of divorce and single parenting in Japan, while the prevalence of arranged marriages is sharply down (cf. Applbaum, 1995; Hendry, 1989; Itoi & Powell, 1992; Iwao, 1993; Kumagai, 1996).

Whereas some 70% of marriages during the World War II period are estimated to have been "arranged," the estimated proportion for the 1990s is well below 20%, especially in urban areas. By contrast, family extension, consisting largely of elders living with their grown children, remains prevalent in Japan. Research on the practice, however, strongly indicates that rather than representing an "anachronism" of the filial piety tradition, it is best interpreted as a strategy for coping with modern-day demands. The idea is that the in-laws' presence allows for the increased labor force participation of wives via the provision of childcare and related assistance. Indeed, the women in such households spend more time in paid employment and simultaneously have more children (Morgan & Hirosima, 1983; Ogawa & Ermisch, 1996). Moreover, many of the wives express a preference, rather than a sense of duty, for the arrangement. As Morgan and Hirosima (1983) put it, "Extended residence is not an anachronism. Rather, it offers an appealing alternative to some of the most modern segments of contemporary Japanese society" (p. 269).

In summary, Japanese families in both Japan and the United States have clearly shed or reduced many of their traditional ways. Because this has transpired on both sides of the Pacific, it cannot easily be pinned on Japanese American "assimilation" or related ideas. Indeed, as suggested later, other groups are experiencing similar changes.

Mexican Families in the United States

In sharp contrast to the comparatively affluent Asian groups, the two Hispanic-origin groups, Mexicans and Puerto Ricans, each sustain family incomes well below average and each endure substantially higher rates of poverty (see Table 1). Indeed, it is subsequently argued here that these circumstances are key factors in interpreting the deviations from average values exhibited by the Latino (Hispanic) groups on many of the remaining indicators. Moreover, the groups' profiles clash particularly strongly when compared with the Asians'. However, despite these and an additional array of differences, there is at least one potentially meaningful similarity between them. Specifically, as we will see, it is interesting how some of the Hispanic groups' imputed traditional ways so closely resemble those of the Asians.

The Mexican origin population of the United States is, by far, the largest of the immigrant groups considered here. Their 13.5 million population count for 1990 (see Table 1) is at least eight times that of the Chinese and nearly 15 times that of the Japanese. Their rapid growth owes much to immigration and, as can be seen from comparing Tables 1 and 2, they have added nearly 5 million persons to their ranks since 1980. They have traditionally resided in the southwestern part of the United States, mainly in the four states bordering Mexico (California, Arizona, New Mexico, and Texas) and Colorado. Not coincidentally, this area was a part of the republic of Mexico until taken by the force in the early to mid-nineteenth century. To this day, about four-fifths of the group continue to reside in the area, although large numbers can also be found in the Midwest (primarily Chicago) and elsewhere.*

Like the Japanese and Chinese, Mexicans in the United States have experienced much exploitation and discrimination. Table 1 shows that the group sustains a substantial rate of poverty (23.4%) and shows the lowest educational attainment among the groups. They are the only group depicted among whom majorities of both men and women lack at least 12 years of schooling. Worse still, Mexicans' per capita income is the absolute lowest of the groups shown. Relatedly, their nation of origin is properly considered a third world (or newly developing) nation with rampant joblessness and widespread impoverishment. As recently as 1960, over half the population was rural and less than 20% lived in places with more than 20,000 residents (Bridges, 1980). Not surprisingly, low-skilled labor migrants account for most of Mexico's rapid immigration to the United States (Aponte, in press; Aponte & Siles, 1997; Portes & Rumbaut, 1996).

*It should be noted that some Americans of Mexican origin can trace their ancestry to a time when much of the Southwest was a part of Mexico. However, it has long been clear that the proportion so descended can only account for a minute portion of the overall group (cf. Bean & Swicegood, 1982; Grebler et al., 1970).

Indeed, Farley's (1996) review of 1990 data shows that among recent Mexican immigrants ages 25–54, less than 5% hold college degrees, while over three-quarters have less than 12 years of schooling. In view of these facts, we should expect larger differences between U.S. born Mexicans and foreign-born ones on those indicators delineating traditionalist orientations.

As noted earlier, it is only with some difficulty that one can even delineate what various groups' traditional families are supposed to be like, and this holds for Mexicans as well. As noted in a thorough review by Bridges (1980):

> Perhaps the greatest error which could be made concerning the Mexican family would be to make broad generalizations. Mexican culture is no more monolithic than that of the United States, India, or any other populous society of the world. For one thing, about 200 different indigenous dialects are spoken in Mexico. Obviously, this fact alone has contributed to distinct forms of family organization.
>
> There is wide divergence between the family patterns of rural and urban residents; of upper, middle and lower classes; of Catholics, Protestants, and Jews; of native-born Mexicans and those who have immigrated from … [abroad] … [etc.]. (p. 303)

Despite this, there are numerous cultural traits widely noted in the literature that are believed to characterize Mexican families of the early to middle twentieth century (Alvirez & Bean, 1976; Baca Zinn, 1994; Becerra, 1988; Bridges, 1980; Eshleman, 1997; Gelles, 1995). The key ones, in very general terms, are familism and machismo. The first of these refers to devotion to family, the latter to male domination. Despite differences in terminology, it is clear that these ideas bear more than a passing resemblance to the traditional ways of the Asians noted earlier.

A number of more specific features about the traditional Mexican family deriving from these broader traits are more straightforward and can be examined for changes over time. These include larger family size, rigid sex roles (women in the home with the children), low age at marriage, low rates of divorce, and endogamy (cf. Alvirez & Bean, 1976; Baca Zinn, 1994; Grebler, Moore, & Guzman, 1970). It is easily seen that fertility in Mexico has been exceptionally high throughout this century because of that nation's tremendous rate of growth. It is estimated that from 1940 to 1970 fertility levels in Mexico "remained high," maintaining a crude birth rate of over 43 per 1000 at the latter time, "the highest in the world among nations of at least 50 million in population" (Bridges, 1980; p. 325). Likewise, the record clearly shows that even in recent decades (1960s–1970s), Mexican Americans married young, produced big families, rarely divorced, and generated low rates of female labor force activity (cf. Baca Zinn, 1994; Bean & Tienda, 1987; Grebler et al., 1970; Rindfuss & Sweet, 1977).

Yet, irrespective of how strongly held such traits might

have been, the literature strongly indicates that they have been receding and that the direction of change is similar to that among mainstream U.S. families. In addition, U.S. nativity and tenure heightens the evident convergence. Further, the group's internal variation on those indicators for which we have data are patterned very much like that of other groups (e.g., higher status, lower fertility). In summary, fertility and family size are falling, with status and U.S. tenure (or nativity) predisposing factors, while marriage and endogamy are down and female labor force activity, intermarriage, marital dissolution, and single parenting are all up (Alvirez & Bean, 1976; Bean & Tienda, 1987; Frisbie & Bean, 1995; Rindfuss & Sweet, 1977).

An especially thorough and comparative fertility analysis (Rindfuss & Sweet, 1977) found that Mexican Americans and several other minorities uniformly experienced fertility declines from the mid-1950s to the late 1960s, as did whites. Moreover, when data was disaggregated by education levels, the pattern still held for all groups, and it did so with the expected inverse relationship between higher status and lower fertility clearly in evidence. Thus, their estimates show that from a peak total fertility rate of about 4.7 children in the late 1950s, the Mexican group's figure declined to about 3.2 per woman at the latter time. Bean and Swicegood (1982) also found, on the basis of 1976 special survey results, that while Mexicans showed higher fertility than whites, rising levels of education and U.S. nativity decreased the group's fertility and brought it closer to the levels among whites. A detailed analysis of 1970 census data by Bean, Cullen, Stephen, and Swicegood (1984) provided similar results.

The most comprehensive demographic analysis of Hispanics in the United States, one of a series of census monographs (Bean & Tienda, 1987), also provides evidence of convergence on some key indicators. For example, it showed that Mexican women ages 35–44 experienced a reduction in children ever born from 4.2 births per women in 1970 to 3.6 in 1980 (see also Table 2). As Table 1 shows, the corresponding 1990 figure is 2.8 children per women, signaling a continuation of the trend. But Bean and Tienda also analyzed raw census data that allowed for controlling background factors and concluded that much, although not all, of the fertility gap between Mexican and non-Hispanic white women was a function of standard background factors (age, schooling, etc.), most especially education, that separated the groups more generally.

Bean and Tienda's (1987) study also found consistent decreases in Mexican family size from 1960 to 1980, paralleling a similar decrease among whites. Likewise, they documented steady decreases in the proportion of ever-married Mexican-origin women over the same period, along with corresponding rises in the median age at first marriage similar

to trends observed among white women. Moreover, the authors also found a sharp drop in the proportion of Mexican origin households headed by a married couple, along with a corresponding rise in "other family" types (primarily female headed), which very closely matched the similarly declining figures for whites. Finally, the authors noted that Mexican-origin women experienced steady increases in labor force participation over the 1960–1980 period, running parallel to a similar trend among whites. Moreover, participation was higher among U.S.-born Mexican women than among foreign-born women throughout the period.

The data assembled here tell a similar story (see also Frisbie & Bean, 1995). As noted earlier, fertility among Mexicans fell from 1980 to 1990 (see Tables 1 and 2). But, just as significantly, fertility is considerably lower for native-born women than for foreign-born ones in 1990 (disaggregated data not available for 1980), consistent with the argument here. However, the average family size is unchanged across the period. Although this seems inconsistent with the trend through 1980, there are two factors that help explain the deviation. First, the 4.1 figure for 1990 represents upward rounding (from 4.08), while the 1980 figure represents downward rounding (from 4.14), as shown in census publications (U.S. Bureau of the Census, 1983b, 1993a). Second, there is the critically important immigrant factor noted earlier.

The number of Mexicans in the United States increased by nearly 5 million between those census years (see Tables 1 and 2), and migration was clearly a major, if not the key, factor (Rumbaut, 1994). Whereas only about one-quarter (25.7%) of the Mexican-origin population was foreign born in 1980, over one-third (33.4%) of the 1990 group were so born (see Tables 1 and 2). In turn, it stands to reason that the immigrants' presence accounts for the *slowing* of the family size reduction because on all other indicators, the figures are in line with the expected change. This is observed wherever the data are displayed by nativity, the native-born/foreign-born differences are sizable in the expected direction, that is, the native born show the more "modernized" profile. Thus, the rapid infusion of numerous less "modernized" profiles dampens the ongoing shift.

The figures on divorce in Table 1, for example, show that despite their reputed deeply held familism, over 1 out every 10 ever-married Mexican origin women ages 35–44 (10.7%) is currently divorced, a figure that is similar to that for white women (11.8%). However, the overall Mexican figure masks a sizable gap within the group by nativity. In fact, only 6.1% of the foreign born are divorced, whereas fully 14.3% of the native born are divorced, the latter figure being over 2½ percentage points greater than that for whites.

Table 1 also shows the effect of nativity. Although 18% of the Mexicans' families are female headed, a figure roughly 5 percentage points greater than that for whites (13.6%), only

13.1% of the foreign-born family heads are women, while some 22.8% of the native-born Mexican women head families. Moreover, both the white and Mexican figures are up from their respective 1980 proportions (see Table 2). Further, the data show that the percentage of children with two parents dropped significantly for both groups over the period, with one out of five white and one out of three Mexican children living in single-parent households in 1990. And, despite the fact that, as Table 1 shows, 9 out of 10 mexican women are married, over 6 out of 10 (between 20 and 64 years old) are labor force participants.

Still more evidence of significant change away from traditional ways among Mexican Americans is found in the data in Table 1 on language use. There, fully one-third of Mexican children are shown to be English monolingual, a proportion larger than that for all but the Japanese among the immigrant groups (including Puerto Ricans). In addition, scattered evidence on intermarriage (Alvirez & Bean, 1976; Anderson & Saenz, 1994; Becerra, 1988; Gonzales, 1994; Murguia, 1982) shows rates have varied wildly across places and time periods, but that the frequency of exogamy is likely increasing and that, on average, it is at least moderate in scope (although lower overall than for Asians). An ironic example is provided by Gonzales (1994), who notes that over a century ago, New Mexico cities showed rates or intermarriage that exceeded 50%. However, these rates resulted from highly unbalanced sex ratios among "Anglos" (i.e., non-Hispanic whites) in areas where few white women, but an abundance of white men, were found.

In more recent times, according to Gonzales' (1994) review, Mexican intermarriage rates have averaged around 20%, although with continued wide variation from place to place. On the other hand, the classic study by Murguia (1982) showed significantly higher rates, particularly in New Mexico and California, where rates approached or surpassed 50%. Despite the wide variation in findings, this research uniformly points to a similar set of predisposing factors on exogamy. Not surprisingly, these are higher educational attainment, U.S. nativity (especially higher order generations), higher income, and exposure to more "contact opportunities" (e.g., residence in an integrated area vs. an ethnic enclave).

Finally, participant observation and in-depth interviews conducted by Williams (1990) led her to conclude that many traditionalist practices were indeed diminishing among Mexican American families in the South Texas area of her study. She found that such traditional practices as the *compadragzo* (bonding) rituals and lifestyles organized around the extended family have faded considerably at the same time that spousal relations have become *more* egalitarian than in the past (although not completely so). Relatedly, Suro (1992) has noted increasing generational conflicts characterizing

numerous Mexican families in the Houston, Texas, area, often language based. In one instance, he notes:

> [E]ven though her children are still young, ages 3 to 9, she is already worried that she is losing touch. "My oldest boy is totally American," she said in Spanish. "His culture is American. His food is American. He speaks English, reads English, writes English." (p. A16)

Suro also notes divisions among the young themselves, pitting the long-time residents against the more recently arrived.

It is worth noting that even in Mexico itself, some change is apparently in the air. For example, in a recent issue of *American Demographics* (Fost, 1992), a story points out that upwardly mobile, *young urban Mexicans* have been dubbed "Yummies" because of the striking resemblance they bear to the United States' "Yuppies" of the 1980s. The group is alleged to be leading the charge of change. Among the changes are a rising middle class, more women professionals, more women in the labor force generally, and a decreased annual rate of population growth. For example, in 1979, the Mexican total fertility rate registered at about 5.0, at the same time that some 21.5% of women were in the labor force. By 1993, the fertility rate had dropped to 3.4 and the proportion of women in the labor force had risen to 31.4% (Fleck & Sorrentino, 1994). Additionally, Fost (1992) notes that the proportion of Mexicans with educations beyond the elementary grades rose from only 13% in 1970 to around 45% in 1990. This, in turn, has led to shifts in other spheres of life, including a slowly but gradually emerging shift in the role of women. Taken together, these indicators suggest that many traditional practices may well be faltering, at least among the more advantaged segments of society, even in Mexico itself.

Puerto Rican Families on the U.S. Mainland

Sharing much with those of Mexican origin are the nation's Puerto Ricans. Like the former group, the latter are Spanish speaking, and they also share numerous background characteristics with Mexicans. Like the Mexicans, Puerto Ricans experienced U.S. imperialism firsthand, only their nation was completely, rather than only partially, taken. As previously noted, they also currently endure much material deprivation. In fact, their poverty rate (29.6%) is the highest of all groups noted in Table 1, exceeding even that for African Americans (26.3%), traditionally the poorest of the nation's people. While Puerto Ricans show a slightly higher per capita income than that of the Mexicans, their median family income is quite a bit lower than the Mexicans' and slightly lower than that of the African Americans. Furthermore, they are the most segregated ethnic group of all, after blacks (Massey & Bitterman, 1985). Indeed, it has often been noted that Puerto Ricans "look" a lot more like African Americans than they "look" like other Latinos, in terms of economic and social indicators.

Puerto Ricans in the mainland number nearly 3 million (see Table 1) and have long been concentrated in the Northeast, particularly the New York City area. As recent as 1970, well over half of the group could be found there. Settlement patterns have broadened since then, but the group remains settled mainly in the northeast section of the country. Their migration to the mainland did not begin in earnest until after World War II, when direct flights were instituted and the U.S. and Puerto Rican governments began a development campaign for the island that included encouraging migration to the mainland. A major instigator of that part of the effort was the fear of impending overpopulation on the island, which was then experiencing rapid growth. While the migrations undoubtedly provided social mobility for many, Puerto Ricans have consistently shown very high poverty rates, at least since data have become available, but probably from the very start of their tenure in the United States (Aponte, 1991).

Any study of the Puerto Rican family would do well to heed the opening remarks in a section of a recent such essay (Carrasquillo, 1994):

> It must be immediately acknowledged that to write of the "traditional" Puerto Rican family is to engage in a deep oversimplification. Even when the island culture was relatively uninfluenced by migration, many variations in form could be found in accordance with a family's social status, wealth, geographical location, race, or age-cohort group. (p. 83)

Nevertheless, there are many items that are commonly understood to characterize traditional Puerto Rican families (cf. Carrasquillo, 1994; Gonzales, 1994; Fitzpatrick, 1987; Hill et al., 1959; Sanchez-Ayendez, 1988). As might be anticipated, the composite model is very close to that described earlier as characterizing Mexicans, including use of the very same terminology. Thus, in place of the *ie* and filial piety of the Asians, Puerto Ricans have familism and machismo (male domination) along with such corollaries as strict sex roles and the less related *compradragzo*, which together amount to similarly held norms of patriarchy and devotion to "family," both nuclear and extended. Indeed, the only major difference seems to be that neither Mexicans nor Puerto Ricans show a recent (i.e., twentieth century) legacy of arranged marriages or variations on primogeniture.

Following the broad categories noted here, a number of the more objective traits characterizing traditional Puerto Rican families can be delineated for comparison with trends among the group's contemporary families. These include high fertility, large families, women confined to homemaking, family extension, young ages at marriage (especially for females), little marital dissolution, and endogamy. However, despite strongly held orientations toward paired procreation,

formal marriage was not universally practiced in Puerto Rico. But this was only because "consensual union" pairings (particularly in rural areas) were often preferred and largely accepted among the poor (probably as a hedge against expenses). Moreover, their incidence had been steadily declining since 1899 (Fitzpatrick, 1987; Gonzales, 1994; Hill et al., 1959).

Perhaps the most clearly visible, striking, and consistent manifestation of traditional Puerto Rican family characteristics was high fertility. As noted by Hill et al. (1959), whereas the average U.S. woman in 1950 had borne some 2.8 children by age 50, the corresponding average on the island was 5.7 for women age 45 and over and 6.8 for those age 55 and older. However, even then, it was apparent that such averages masked significant differences between urban and rural populations and even sharper differences between women with varying levels of education. Thus, while rural women age 45 and older with no formal schooling exhibited an average of slightly higher than 7.0 children ever born, similarly aged urban women with some college averaged less than 2.0 children, while their similarly educated rural counterparts only showed a slightly higher average number (2.1) of births.

On the more subjective factors of family organization, mainland Puerto Ricans began to experience change almost from the very beginning of their arrival in large numbers, according to the literature. Virtually every single manuscript on Puerto Rican families on the mainland stresses how Puerto Ricans have been beset by changing values, behaviors, and levels of solidarity (Cortés, 1995; Fitzpatrick, 1987; Rogler & Procidano, 1989; Rogler & Santana Cooney, 1984; Sanchez Ayendez, 1988). Descriptive material in Sanchez Ayendez (1988), for example, notes perceived losses of the old traditional ways by *both* immigrants and their mainland-born/raised offspring. In particular, she notes lessening use of Spanish and lessening acceptance of traditional sex roles (by females) among those born or reared on the mainland. Consistent with part of this, data in Table 1 show that nearly 3 out of 10 Puerto Rican children were English monolingual in 1990.

Additional descriptive material on Puerto Rican family change includes observations of weakening extended kinship ties and, especially, the rise of intergenerational conflicts (Fitzpatrick, 1987). Likewise, Carrasquillo (1994) reviews literature that underscores the shifting of sex roles among Puerto Ricans, contrary to tradition, which partly arose as a result of the sharp increase in female-headed families. And finally, Rogler and Procidano (1989) find both immigrant and second-generation wives exhibiting increased marital satisfaction in more egalitarian households. However, the pace of change is far better represented by the notable shifts in objective indicators elaborated below.

Perhaps the strongest example of the changing Puerto

Rican family concerns fertility, as shown by Bean and Tienda (1987). First, these authors show that in 1960, the number of children ever born among mainland Puerto Rican women ages 35–44 was far below the earlier noted levels for older women on the island. Only some 2.9 children were ever born by such mainland women at the time. This compares with a 2.4 rate among whites that year. In keeping with the Baby Boom phenomena of U.S. families, the number rose to 3.5 children for such women in 1970 (Sullivan, 1976), after which it dropped to 3.2 in 1980 and 2.5 in 1990 (see Tables 1 and 2). Likewise, whites experienced increased fertility on this measure for 1970 (2.9), after which they showed reduced rates for 1980 (2.5) and 1990 (1.8) (Bean & Tienda, 1987; Tables 1 and 2). Thus the Puerto Ricans' 1990 rate is equal to that of whites in 1980, and both groups are shifting in concert toward smaller families.

Bean and Tienda's (1987) analysis also disaggregated the fertility rates of Puerto Rican and other women by education levels and nativity for 1980. They found that the mainland-born minority women consistently showed lower fertility than their first-generation (island-born) counterparts at all categories of educational attainment, with fertility falling as attainment rose for both nativity categories. Indeed, the authors held that if Puerto Ricans had the same educational profile as whites, the groups' fertility levels would have been quite close (although not identical), even in 1980.

Stronger evidence of change was found by Bean and Tienda (1987) in data on marriage and household size from 1960 to 1990. Examining Puerto Rican women age exactly 25 at the 3 census years, they found the proportion of ever married dropped steadily across the period, falling from 80% to 67%. A similar shift, but in the opposite direction, was in evidence for the women's median age at marriage (from 19.1 to 21.4 years of age). Further, in both cases, similar shifts of nearly identical magnitudes occurred among white women. Correspondingly, consistent decreases in mean household size of comparable magnitude transpired over the 20-year period for both groups.

Following this, Tables 1 and 2 show that for the slightly different measure of average family size (most, but not all, households are family households) Puerto Ricans and whites each experienced exactly the same (.2 persons) reduction from 1980 to 1990. While the groups' family size averages remain separated by .5 persons, as we have seen, fertility and education are inversely related for both groups. If fertility is increasingly the major determinant of family size (as extension declines), then the substantial differences in educational attainment separating whites from Puerto Ricans (see Table 1) alone might well account for much or all of the family size gap.

Turning to the remaining indicators in Table 1 (see also Table 2), we are confronted with a number of interesting twists in the data. For example, the percentage of families headed by a lone woman among Puerto Ricans increased by 1.5 percentage points over the 1980–1990 interim (39.3% to 40.8%), a rise very similar to the 1.7 percentage point rise among whites (11.9% to 13.6%). However, the gap between the two is enormous—over 27 percentage points! How this can signify a form of convergence is a legitimate question. Likewise, the divorce ratio is considerably higher among Puerto Rican women ages 35–44 (17.4) than among their white counterparts (11.8), despite both experiencing similarly sized increases over the period. Alternatively, the percent ever married among Puerto Rican women (83.8) is a good bit lower than that for whites (92.1), and the percentage of Puerto Rican children with two parents (45.1) is well below the comparable white percentage (80.4). Combined with the earlier showing that both whites and Puerto Ricans are experiencing later (or reduced) marriage, it is clear that both groups are experiencing family fragmentation, but with Puerto Ricans well in the lead.

In contrast to their showing on family fragmentation, Puerto Ricans exhibit (see Table 1) substantially lower female labor force participation than whites. Indeed, theirs is the lowest of all figures (55.4%) shown, and it registers a full 15 percentage points lower than the rate for whites (70.4%). However, it should be noted that both white and Puerto Rican women have exhibited increases in labor force participation since 1960. For example, Bean and Tienda (1987) found that 1960, female labor force participation rates among those ages 16–64 were 39.5 for whites and 40.3 for Puerto Ricans, while at 1980 they were, respectively, 57.9 and 41.7. Thus the 55.4% rate of the slightly older (ages 20–64) Puerto Rican women in 1990 is likely to result from increased activity.

Nevertheless, to the extent that females' increased earnings, commensurate with increased labor force activity, largely underlie declines in marriage, then Puerto Ricans do not fully fit the pattern. Indeed, subsequently it is argued that the complex dynamic underlying Puerto Rican women's decreasing likelihood of marrying differs appreciably from that operating among whites. Because a similar dynamic appears to fit African Americans, the discussion of these issues is combined for both groups and pursued afterward. It is clear, however, that mainland Puerto Ricans' demographic characteristics are changing markedly from the imputed traditional model. Not surprisingly, similar changes are apparent on the island as well, as noted subsequently.

Finally, we note that while the best available data suggest that rates of intermarriage among Puerto Ricans are relatively low, the pattern is strikingly similar to that among other groups. That is, their intermarriage is selective of the more educated and the U.S.-born, as well as of those residing away from concentrations of fellow ethnics. Thus, their low rates may perhaps be seen as a function of the lower levels of educational attainment among the group at large, as well as their relative segregation, factors undoubtedly related to Puerto Ricans' relative economic impoverishment.

Sources of data on Puerto Rican outmarriage are varied across time and scope of coverage. Still, the basic patterning is deducible. The most comprehensive coverage was provided by Jaffe et al. (1980), although their findings entailed some qualifications. First, they only looked at native-born women who were still with their husbands at the time of the 1970 census. Thus, the island-born were omitted as were those who had divorced, been widowed, or were separated. Second, their outmarriage data ignore marriage to other Spanish-speaking people. Thus, Puerto Ricans marrying Dominicans, for example, were not distinguished from those marrying endogamously. Still, their findings were straightforward enough. Overall, one-third of all U.S.-born and married (but not separated) females of Puerto Rican descent in 1970 had outmarried. However, those with at least 12 years of schooling were twice as likely (44% vs. 21%) to outmarry as those with fewer than 12 years of schooling.

However, findings on New York City, long the residential center of gravity for mainland Puerto Ricans, show substantially less exogamy than those at the national level. For example, based on marital records for the 2 years under study, Fitzpatrick (1987) showed that among island-born Puerto Rican women, outmarriage increased from 8.5% in 1949 to 12.9% in 1975. However, within second-generation women, the shift was downward—from 30.0% to 20.7% across the period. Yet, Fitzpatrick attributes the downturn to the density of Puerto Rican settlement in New York at the later time because national level data (noted earlier) showed substantially higher rates just for 1970. The idea is that in 1949, second-generation Puerto Rican females of marriageable ages, being very few in number, confronted scant options for endogamy, as compared with their counterparts in 1975. Such a pattern has been noted in the literature for other groups (Gilbertson et al., 1996).

However, a serious shortcoming in Fitzpatrick's (1987) findings is made apparent by a 1991 study on intermarriage among several Latino groups in New York City (Gilbertson, Fitzpatrick & Yang, 1996). The problem concerns Puerto Rican outmarriage with other Latinos. Most earlier studies of Puerto Rican intermarriage tended to exclude such marriages from both the numerator and the denominator when calculating rates. The 1991 study, however, encompassed, and provided figures on, both types of outmarriages. The results showed that among 1991 New York City marriages where the female party was a first- or second-generation Puerto Rican, about half were outmarriages. However, the vast majority of such intermarriages united the brides with other Hispanics, and within that group, the bulk were with Dominicans, an impoverished Caribbean-origin group with long-standing

and strong social ties to Puerto Ricans. Only 6.5% of all such island-born Puerto Rican brides, and 14.9% of second-generation brides, married non-Hispanic grooms. Thus, the kind of intermarriage that is most likely to signal integration remains spotty among Puerto Ricans in New York, in contrast to those elsewhere.*

Changes in the family among mainland Puerto Ricans have been more than matched by their fellow ethnics on the island. Indeed, the enormous changes in family organization in Puerto Rico are striking for both their sweep and their rapidity (Rivera-Batiz & Santiago, 1996). As recently as 1950, for example, the crude birth rate in Puerto Rico was approximately 40 per 1000. In the succeeding 4 decades, the rate fell to 18.8 per 1000, ending nearly as low as the rate for the U.S. (16.7) that year. Between 1980 and 1990 alone, the average number of children ever born among island women ages 35–44 declined from 3.3 to 2.5, figures comparable to those among their mainland counterparts (see Tables 1 and 2). Indeed, the 1990 figure for the island's women is as low as that for mainland white women in 1980 (see Table 2). As expected, fertility varied by educational attainment. Thus, among island women with less than 8 years of schooling, the average number of children ever born was 4.2 in 1990, but among those with at least a college degree, the corresponding figure was 1.6.

Rivera-Batiz and Santiago (1996) also show that the proportion of Puerto Rican women on the island ages 30–39 that had ever married decreased from 92.8% in 1960 to 87.1% in 1990. An even sharper drop, from 76.0% to 60.4% occurred among 20- to 29-year-olds. Relatedly, the median age at first marriage rose from 24.6 to 28.5 among island women, from 1980 to 1990. Likewise, the percentage of families headed by women rose from 15.6% in 1970 to 23.2% in 1990. Finally, Rivera-Batiz and Santiago noted that divorce rose substantially and average household size plummeted during this general period. Whereas the average island household contained around five persons in 1950, by 1990, the average was closer to 3⅓. Between 1970 and 1990, the proportion of women age 15 and over who were currently divorced rose from 3.8% to 9.2%.

In short, Puerto Rican families, both on the mainland and on the island, have shifted markedly away from earlier

---

*It should be noted that some methodological difficulties in Gilbertson et al. (1996) downwardly bias their intermarriage findings slightly. Fist, since only marriages registered in New York City (but not its suburbs) are considered, marriages among higher-status Puerto Ricans in the metropolitan area will be underrepresented because proportionately more of the latter can be expected to occur in the suburbs (and outmarriages will almost surely occur in greater proportions among the latter group). Beyond that, the authors only considered first- and second-generation Puerto Ricans because marriage records only permitted as much. However, third-generation Puerto Ricans are also likelier to outmarry non-Hispanics than their first- (and perhaps even second-) generation counterparts.

prevalent patterns. The shaping of change, moreover, bears much in common with family shifts in the United States. In this instance, it would perhaps seem reasonable to advance the claim that the apparent similarities in the changes across places result from U.S. hegemony on the island. However, that interpretation falls short of explaining the earlier reviewed remarkably similar changes occurring in other nations where far less U.S. influence was apparent. Moreover, while it is true that the U.S.-dominated post-war occupation of Japan witnessed many of that nation's societal changes noted here, in fact, much of Japan's rapid modernization and accompanying changes long preceded the war (Hane, 1982). Indeed, it is clear that many similar changes transpired in revolutionary China during a period when that society could only be characterized as strongly anti-Western (and most especially so with respect to the United States), rather than the opposite.

African American Families: A Special Case

African Americans clearly constitute a special case. African Americans have endured intense forms of oppression from the very start of their arrival in the United States. Indeed, it has only been some 3 odd decades since they were finally granted equal citizenship throughout the nation. In addition, it is clear that despite reductions in the overt oppression visited upon them, African Americans' average economic position remains precarious and that various forms of discrimination remain implicated in this. Discrimination, whether direct or indirect, continues to take a toll in housing (Massy & Denton, 1993), employment (Turner, Fix, & Struyk, 1991), public education (Kozol, 1991) and public accommodations (Feagin & Vera, 1995). Still, it also clear that a large and growing segment of the group has achieved considerable success, at the same time that an equally sizable (or larger) group has sustained downward mobility or prolonged destitution (cf. Wilson, 1980, 1987, 1996).

Numbering some 30 million in 1990, African Americans are the largest of the nation's minority groups (Table 1). As Table 1 further reveals, African American families showed a substantial rate of poverty (26.3%) in 1990, nearly four times that among white families, and a per capita income ($8900) only about half of whites' ($16,100). Indeed, only the deeply impoverished Mexicans and Puerto Ricans exhibit deprivation rivaling African Americans', despite the latter's "seniority" in the United States. Blacks are also the most highly segregated of all the minority groups (Massey & Denton, 1993), a factor of some significance to issues subsequently examined. Moreover, on such indirect measures of hardship as families led by single women and children without two parents, black Americans are unquestionably the worst off (see Table 1).

African Americans were predominately settled in the

rural South through the early part of the twentieth century, but this has subsequently changed. A series of major migrations from the rural South to the urban North, triggered primarily by the two World Wars, significantly transformed the population (Hamilton, 1964; Marks, 1989). Although about half the group remains in the South, they are found in significant numbers in the Northeast and Midwest, especially in large cities, and their presence in the largest cities of the West is well established (although their overall presence in that region is low). Indeed, over the course of the twentieth century, the group has shifted from being substantially more rural than the general population to being substantially more urban (Wilson, 1980).

Clearly, African American families have sustained more than their fair share of social science scrutiny and mythology, and they have been the subject of much vociferous disagreement. From the controversial "Moynihan Report" of the mid 1960s (Moynihan, 1965) to the present, scores of studies, publications, and opinions (both expert and lay) have joined the fray (cf. Bennett, 1992; Demos, 1990; Rainwater & Yancy, 1967; Staples & Mirande, 1980; Taylor, Cutters, Tucker, & Lewis, 1990). While some of the earlier heated controversies have died down, it would be premature to claim that a consensus has emerged. Notwithstanding that state of affairs, our concerns here are limited to showing in which respects African American families are converging with those of whites and in which respects they are not and to advancing a credible explanation for any resulting discrepancy.

Perhaps the most difficult aspect of our purposes here is providing a prototypical "traditional black family" for baseline purposes. Such a model is not readily available for many reasons. First, the ancestral homes of the group are too far removed chronologically to realistically derive models from—very few (if any) African Americans have contacts or known kin extensions in Africa. In addition, the major portion of the group experienced slavery over several generations, and their conditions and practices under slavery remain the subject of some dispute (Eshleman, 1997).*

What is clear on this issue is that the mid-twentieth-century conventional wisdom (Frazier, 1966; Moynihan, 1965) that slavery destroyed black families (with particular regard to the decline of two-parent and rise of single parent families) has been effectively refuted (cf. Furstenberg, Hershberg, & Modell, 1975; Gutman, 1976; Wilson & Neckerman, 1986). The revisionist view, based on scattered records throughout the nation from the late nineteenth and early

---

*It should be noted that a fair number of writers do indeed hold that latter-day African American family practices retain significant aspects of African-based cultures (cf. Nobles, 1974, 1978, 1988; Sudarkasa 1988, 1993). While we do not subscribe to that perspective, we note that recent research clearly shows that changes in the family, resembling those in the United States, are also occurring in many African nations (Weisner et al., 1997).

twentieth centuries, along with census returns from 1940 to 1960, is that African American families were predominately "intact" (two parent) for the greater part of the century following slavery. Thus, the view holds that whatever the basis for the increasing fragmentation of blacks families, it is of modern (post-World War II) vintage.*

In fact, the main features of the African American family that are currently suggested as culturally distinctive are related to their disproportionate numbers of one-parent configurations, and thus are not easily tied to heritage. These include low rates of marriage, including prolonged singlehood and high rates of marital dissolution, and a relatively high incidence of out-of-wedlock births (Farley & Allen, 1987). Additionally distinct characteristics of African American families, which do appear to predate the modern (post-World War II) period, concern fertility and family extension (Ruggles, 1994). Black families have long been noted for having larger families on the basis of these two items. Thus, in looking for convergence between black and white families, we should look to recent trends in fertility, family size and composition, and the set of items related to female headship.

Converging Indicators. On the question of black–white convergence, the indicators provide an admittedly mixed portrait. Whereas virtually all changes experienced by African American families in recent decades have been paralleled by similar shifts among whites, long-standing differences remain, and some have widened considerably. Still, the logic of the convergence hypothesis retains support even from the mixed record of African Americans.

*Ruggles (1994) has suggested that the revisionist perspective itself needs revising. Specifically, on the basis of newly processed nineteenth-century census returns, he claims that the gap separating blacks and whites on the proportion of children residing without both parents has been so persistent that it is likely to reflect African (or slavery-based) cultural practices. We find his suggestions unconvincing on numerous grounds. First, a finding that *nearly*, but less than, 30% of children reside without both parents present (from 1880 to 1940) hardly qualifies as evidence of a cultural practice since, by definition, most persons in the category (over 70%) are unaffected. Further, since children seldom determine their own living arrangements, the critical variable is what percent of living, noninstitutionalized black parents were "absent," and *why* this was so. Ruggles' less than definitive discussion of those issues includes the suggestion that higher than average black mortality fails to account for the gap. However, as he himself notes, "our knowledge of race differences in mortality in the late nineteenth century is inexact" (p. 142), and varying interpretations of black mortality for the period abound (e.g., Farley & Allen, 1987; pp. 22–28). Finally, Ruggles' rejection of the "economic stress" hypothesis (for his 1880 figures) is mainly based on the finding that the proportion of white children so "semi-orphaned" varied inversely with the overall per capita wealth of their counties of residence, the precise opposite of the pattern for blacks. However, it is quite feasible that blacks' conditions varied inversely with whites' to the extent that much of the latter's wealth rested precisely on the extreme exploitation of the former slaves—a truly defining feature of the emerging Jim Crow society.

Trends in fertility and family size are cases in point. On these indicators, blacks and whites have experienced similar trends throughout the entire post-World War II period. Each experienced something of a baby boom in the immediate post-war years, and each has experienced substantial declines thereafter. As the landmark study by Rindfuss and Sweet (1977) makes clear, the post-war trends were pervasive across major groups: "[I]t should be emphasized that for virtually every education, racial, and age group, fertility rates increased during the 1950s and decreased during the 1960s. There are differences in the levels, the slopes, the timing of the peaks; but the dominant picture is that of a rise followed by a decline" (p. 38).

For example, Farley and Allen (1987) note that the 1960 total fertility rates for whites and blacks registered at 3.5 and 4.5 births, respectively, whereas the corresponding rates were down to 1.7 and 2.2 by 1984. Bean and Tienda (1987) also show racial comparisons in fertility over time. They found that the number of children ever born by women ages 15–44 fell from 1.7 to 1.2 for whites between 1960 and 1980 with a matching decrease among blacks from 2.0 to 1.6. Corresponding figures for 1990 on this measure were 1.2 for whites and 1.5 for (non-Hispanic) blacks, according to census microdata amassed by Frisbie and Bean (1995). Further, data on children ever born among women ages 35–44 show consistent declines for both racial groups from 1970 through 1990. For whites, the number dropped from 2.9 in 1970 to 2.5 in 1980 and 1.7 in 1990, while the corresponding decline among African Americans was from 3.8 to 3.2 to 2.3 (Tables 1 and 2; U.S. Bureau of the Census, 1983b). Thus, racial differences in fertility have converged substantially and, as shown later, socioeconomic differentials can account for much of the remaining fertility gap.

Trends in family size, not surprisingly, run parallel to those noted for fertility. Data for 1970 on family size for blacks and whites provided by Sweet (1978) were presented separately by family type. However, estimates for all family types combined are easily derived by weighting the varying family types on the basis of their corresponding proportions in the population that year (provided in Bean & Tienda, 1987). On that basis, 1970 average family size for whites was approximately 3.5, whereas for blacks, the figure was approximately 4.2. As Tables 1 and 2 show, the respective figures uniformly show continued decline thereafter. From 1980 to 1990, average family size among whites fell from 3.2 to 3.0, while among blacks, the decline was from 3.7 to 3.5 persons per family.*

Much of the remaining gap in fertility is easily ac-

*It would, of course, be best to provide data on family size separately by headship. Unfortunately, however, such data are not published and only researchers able to access and analyze microdata can provide such figures. Still, the limitation appears to introduce no significant bias here.

counted for by the racial variation in characteristics. For example, Farley and Allen (1987) disaggregated fertility by educational attainment among women ages 35–49 and found the familiar pattern of lower fertility among the more educated. Not only did completed fertility drop uniformly as education rose for both blacks and whites, but the gaps separating the groups narrowed significantly. For example, among women with only an elementary education, blacks had borne 4.3 children, as compared with 3.3 births among whites, whereas among those with 5 or more years of college, the figures were 1.9 and 1.7, respectively. As the figures in Table 1 show, the gap in levels of educational attainment of African American and white women remains formidable and could account for much of the remaining gap in fertility.

Family extension is another item on which black and white families have differed over time, but have begun to converge (Ruggles, 1994). Moreover, the gaps in this indicator are easily explained. For example, on the basis of 1980 census microdata, Farley and Allen (1987) have shown that, for both races, the socially vulnerable (the widowed, elderly, divorced, single, or separated) were more likely to be members of extended families than were others. Thus, to the extent that one finds proportionately more such individuals among blacks, as is true for single-parent families, it accounts for much of the racial gap in extension. Moreover, despite not finding income to be a causal factor, the authors found higher levels of education (and higher-status occupations) to be associated with lower levels of family extension among both blacks and whites (more for the former than the latter). This also would help explain the higher rates of family extension among African Americans since their average educational and occupational profiles are significantly less privileged than those among whites.

Similar findings have been reported by other researchers (Angel & Tienda, 1982; Tienda & Angel, 1982). For example, Angel and Tienda (1982) found that single-female family heads were more likely to lead extended families than others. In addition, they found that the earnings of nonnuclear adults in extended families contributed significantly to total household income among minority families, but not white ones, suggesting that income needs among minorities are important predisposing factors.

Finally, a more recent study (Ruggles, 1994) traced the incidence of extended families among blacks and whites back a full century (1880–1980). He found that historically, the rates of family extension were actually quite close during two early census years (1880, 1910), but began widening thereafter mainly as a result of an earlier onset in family extension declines among whites. Among blacks, a substantial decline in family extension didn't materialize until after 1960, after which the falling rate began closing the racial gap. By 1980, the remaining differential was actually smaller than the corresponding gap of 1960, although larger than had been the case historically. Further, he found that over half the difference in the 1980 gap was accounted for by the higher rates of female-headed families and parentless children among blacks relative to whites.

Ruggles (1994) found a similar pattern among multigenerational extended families:

> The current race differential in multigenerational living arrangements is therefore of recent origin and did not result from change among black families, but from an extremely rapid change among white families.... [Thus] any explanation for why blacks reside with relatives comparatively more often than whites should actually focus on the reasons for the extraordinary decline in white co-residence over the past century. (p. 147)

Taken as a whole, the cited research suggests that family extension differentials across race are strongly related to differences in levels of well-being between the races. Moreover, such gaps are narrowing and the portion of the differences that remain after accounting for standard background variables appear sufficiently small as to preclude any additional major influences.

Diverging Indicators: Marriage and Mother-Only Families. Clearly the most significant racially based family differentials concern marriage and female headship. Specifically, there is an enormous gap in the relative proportions of married adults and single-parent families between African Americans and whites. African Americans appear to marry less frequently, divorce or separate more readily, experience more out-of-wedlock childbearing, and, as a result of those factors, exhibit the largest portion of mother-only families among those groups for which we have statistics. As shown in Table 1, for example, less than 80% of black women ages 35–44 were ever married in 1990, as compared with well over 90% of comparable white women. At the same time, some 18% of such women were divorced, versus 12% of comparable white women. Likewise, some 48% of black families with children were headed by a lone female, as compared with only 14% of white ones. Finally, and most remarkably, only 37% of black children resided with both parents, as compared with 80% of white children.

Since marital status is the most crucial indicator of family fragmentation, it merits the strongest examination. First, when we consider age at marriage over the full course of the century, the *recency* of the marked divergence by racial group becomes even more apparent. As Cherlin (1981) has noted, from 1890 to 1950, black women (proxied by nonwhites) ages 20–24 showed significantly higher rates of marriage than did white women. Whereas from 1890 to 1940, roughly half or slightly more white females in that age category were never married, less than 40% of such blacks were still single. Only in 1950 did the groups' respective rates converge (at around one-third single), and only afterward did the reversal settle in. Thus, by 1979, the last year for which Cherlin assembled data, the gap had fully reversed. At that time, nearly half of whites, but almost two-thirds of blacks, were still single. The 1990 figures were 62.5% and 79.4%, respectively (U.S. Bureau of the Census 1992, 1994), an even wider gap. A remarkably similar reversal also holds at higher ages (see Table 1).

Cherlin (1981) also shows that the declines in marriage among African American females, while permeating the full spectrum of "class" categories (proxied by educational attainment), were far more extensive among the lower classes than among others. For example, he shows that the decline in the percentage of women ages 25–44 who were married with husbands present between 1940 and 1979 was only 5 percentage points for black women with some college, while it was 28 percentage points for those with less than 12 years of schooling. Likewise, the increase in "never marrieds" over the same period by comparably aged black women with less than high school was 12 percentage points, while among those with some college, the rate actually decreased slightly (by 1 percentage point), although remaining slightly higher than that for the other groups. He thus concludes, "[I]t is clear from the evidence received that a substantial part of the current differences between black and white family patterns are of recent origin" (pp. 103–104) and that "the changes were greatest for those with less education" (p. 108).

The issues surrounding the decline in marriage and the rise in female headship, particularly among less well-off African Americans, began receiving systematic reviews and penetrating analyses in the 1980s (cf. Joe, 1984; Staples, 1985; Wilson, 1987; Wilson & Neckerman, 1986), although pertinent works appeared even earlier (e.g., Farley, 1971) and an even wider array have subsequently emerged (e.g., Fossett & Kiecolt, 1993; Lichter et al., 1991, 1992; Raley, 1996; Schoen & Kluegel, 1988; Smock, 1990; South & Lloyd, 1992; Wilson, 1996; Wojtkiewicz, McLanahan, & Garfinkel, 1990; Wood, 1995). Although a consensus on the issues has yet to materialize, the essential conclusion in this body of work reduces to a simple proposition: Blacks' orientation to marriage appears not to have shifted dramatically, whereas their marital prospects clearly have.

The key components of the hypothesized marriage squeeze is a steadily declining sex ratio of eligible black men to black women, fostered by such factors as increasing joblessness, incarceration, premature mortality, and addiction among African American men (Staples, 1985; Wilson & Neckerman, 1986). However, these factors should be seen as operating *in conjunction with* the factors that have brought about declining marriage rates, more generally (i.e., among whites and others), such as increasing labor force participation and earnings among women (which provide alternative forms of support for women beyond the earnings of men) and rising rates of cohabitation and premarital intercourse (which provide some of the major benefits of marriage in its absence) (cf. Ellwood, 1988; Raley, 1996; Rosos & Sawhill, 1975).

Clearly, the most influential of the many systematic at-

tempts to interpret rising female headship among African Americans was that by Wilson and Neckerman (1986; see also Neckerman, Aponte, & Wilson, 1988; Wilson, 1987). These authors first showed the paucity of explanatory power offered by the then-popular "welfare as cause" hypothesis (Murray, 1984). Briefly put, they showed that studies have consistently found that female headship rates do not correlate closely with welfare benefits, despite the logic or popularity of the alleged close relationship. Indeed, high benefit states generate no significantly higher rates of divorce, out-of-wedlock births, or female-headed families (Ellwood, 1988; Wilson & Neckerman, 1986) than do low benefit states, at the same time that declining benefit levels throughout the nation in the late 1970s and 1980s (and lower caseloads) were accompanied by soaring rates of female headship.

In fact, the major effect on family structure of welfare is that higher benefits facilitate the formation of independent households by single mothers who, in lower benefit areas, will tend to live within other households (Ellwood & Bane, 1985). Indeed, as Table 1 shows, despite exhibiting the absolute highest rate of single parenthood and higher than average fertility, black women also show the highest labor force participation of all groups, thus clearly negating the welfare stereotype.

In place of the welfare hypothesis, Wilson and Neckerman (1986) argued that the real source of the phenomenal rise of female headship among poor blacks was declining employment among men. This, in turn, stemmed from the deindustrialization process that had its first, and most severe, impact in older central cities of the North where blacks were heavily concentrated. Based on the idea that men needed to be employed to be eligible for marriage, Wilson and Neckerman constructed several series where the number of "marriageable" (employed) men were compared with the total number of women in comparable age categories, separately for whites and blacks. Termed the "male marriageable pool index" (MMPI), the measure showed a solid fit between the downward trends in male employment and rising rates of female headship among blacks, but not whites. White male employment hardly changed at all over the periods in question (roughly 1960 to the early 1980s), and female headship among whites grew slowly. Neckerman et al. (1988) provided figures for census years 1960–1980, by region, and provided further support to the MMPI interpretation, as have numerous works since (e.g., Fossett & Kiecolt, 1993; Lichter et al., 1991; South & Lloyd, 1992; Testa, Astone, Krogh, & Neckerman, 1989).

The MMPI hypothesis, however, primarily applies to women among the black poor, since it is mainly their male social counterparts that are likely to be plagued by increasing joblessness. However, the college-educated African American woman has long since confronted a shortage of socially matched male counterparts. As Staples (1985) showed some time ago, many more black women than men ever graduate from college. He notes, for example, that in 1980, there were some 133,000 more black women enrolled in college than there were black men, while some 60% of all bachelor's degrees awarded to blacks in 1981 went to women.

An update of the figures reveals that the situation has worsened considerably. Taking the MMPI figures for 1990 first, whereas for every 100 non-Hispanic white women ages 25–54, some 87.5 comparably aged white men were employed, only 59.6 black men were employed for every 100 comparably aged black women—a spread of nearly 30 percentage points (U.S. Bureau of the Census 1993c). Moreover, the situation is likely to be worse than these numbers imply, since more black workers than white workers labor at low wage or unstable jobs. For example, Aponte (1996) recently compared employment profiles of a sample of inner-city men that included whites, blacks, and Hispanics. Among the employed men with less than 12 years of education, only Mexican immigrants earned as little per hour as did African Americans, and the latter had the least time on the job of all groups (less than one-third the time of others), a fact indicating less stable work histories among them.

The marriage market for educated African American women, likewise, appears bleaker than ever and the contrast between their situation and that faced by white women is nothing short of incredible. For example, as Table 1 shows, among adults age 25 and over in 1990, some 11.7% of black women hold at least a bachelor's degree, while only 11.0% of the black men do so. No other group shown exhibits such a sex based ranking, though Puerto Ricans come close with a showing of near sexual parity. Among Whites, the respective figure are 25.6% and 18.8%, favoring males. However, the figures do not reveal the raw numbers from which the percentages derive. In most such instances, this is inconsequential, but not in the case of African Americans.

When ratios between female and male graduates are made on the basis of absolute numbers, the true nature of the widening sex gap among African Americans is made clearer. For example, simple calculations of 1990 data reveal that for every 100 college-educated white males age 25 and over, there are only 81.2 comparably aged college-educated white women, while among blacks, the corresponding number is an incredible 131. Considering only 25- to 34-year-olds brings the whites to near parity–96.7 women per 100 men with college degrees (still a favorable ratio for females' marriage prospects). Among blacks, the figure rises still further to 138 college educated black women for every 100 college educated black males (U.S. Bureau of the Census, 1993c). Moreover, interracial marriages involving African Americans have generally been skewed to unions among black males and white females, rather than the reverse, and they have tended to involve higher-status males—precisely the ones considered the social counterparts of educated African American women (Kalmijn, 1993; Staples, 1985).

Parenthetically, it was earlier noted that Puerto Ricans show rates of female headship rivaling those of African Americans and that their situation bore much in common with that of blacks. In fact, the Puerto Rican MMPI is very likely to resemble that among African Americans and to operate the same way. As Table 1 shows, Puerto Rican male labor force participation is virtually tied with that among black men, Puerto Rican families are poorer than black families, and the incidence of female headship among Puerto Ricans is very close to that among blacks. In addition, Puerto Ricans are even more tied to older central cities than are African Americans (where deindustrialization had its strongest initial impact), and their trends in joblessness and female headship closely parallel those of blacks (Aponte, 1991, 1993; Tienda, 1989). In short, the interpretation that the formation of intact African American families is constrained by the deficits in the pool of "eligible" men stemming from men's employment problems appears eminently applicable to Puerto Ricans as well.

One point where African Americans and Puerto Ricans significantly diverge, noted in Table 1, is in female labor force participation. Whereas black women show the highest rate (70.5%), Puerto Rican women show the lowest rate (55.4%). An explanation for this disjunct is not readily available in the literature; still, a potentially viable explanation may be found in three overlapping points. First, Puerto Rican single mothers may receive more welfare than black single mothers because the former group happen to be clustered in areas of relatively more liberal programs (Aponte, 1991). Second, as Table 1 shows, Puerto Rican women are generally less educated than black women, thus their employability and earning's potentials are likely to be lower; such factors could easily suppress their employment. Finally, and most importantly, proportionately more Puerto Rican families have children than do black families, irrespective of family type. For example, as of 1990, 62% of Puerto Rican married couple families, but only 53% of African American ones, had children at home, whereas 73% of Puerto Rican lone-mother families had children at home, versus only 62% of such black families (U.S. Bureau of the Census, 1993c).*

A final source of support for the general idea that the more rapidly falling rates of marriage among blacks, relative

---

*It is worth noting here that Mexican women also exhibit higher labor force participation than Puerto Rican women, despite higher fertility and lower educational attainment (see Table 1). However, their participation is only modestly higher than that of the Puerto Rican women. Beyond that, two other factors help explain the gap. First, many needy Mexican women and their families are not eligible for assistance (due to their immigrant status), a potentially important alternative source of support for the group's poor single parents. Second, Mexican families are generally settled in areas of less liberal benefits, but higher employment prospects for the less skilled and educated, than the areas where Puerto Ricans are settled (Aponte, 1991, 1993). Each of these items may independently influence the noted outcome.

to whites, reflect race-specific constraints more than race-specific changing orientations stems from attitudinal research. Briefly put, such studies (Ball & Robbins, 1986; Broman, 1993; Bulcroft & Bulcroft, 1993; Hatchett, 1991) tell the following story: Younger blacks are actually more oriented to marriage than whites, but advancing years and, especially, marital experiences tend to reverse things. For example, based on a subsample (never-married and never-cohabitated) of the 1987–1988 National Survey of Families and Households, Bulcroft and Bulcroft (1993) found that younger black women were the most oriented to marriage of all groupings, with black and white men equally oriented once background factors were controlled. Indeed, the authors note, "Rather than propensity to marry factors working to suppress marriage rates, they may be keeping the marital institution alive among blacks. Never-married black women continue to see marriage as preferable state despite the economic nonviability of many such unions and the high risks involved as a result" (p. 352).

The findings from the National Survey of Black Americans echo and buttress those noted here. Hatchett's (1991) analysis of these data found that while over 40% of all African Americans surveyed were wary of marriage, at least half were positively inclined, irrespective of gender. Moreover, clear majorities of the never-married and those still currently married were positively inclined, with the formerly married the least oriented. However, large local area samples (Ball & Robbins, 1986) and national ones (Broman, 1993) consistently find relatively low satisfaction in marriage among blacks, particularly among men. These findings are believed to stem from the disproportionate stress endured by black families in countless ways. For example, a large proportion live in segregated, impoverished areas where daily life is hampered by poor schools, drugs, and crime. Those enduring such conditions are likely to experience great strains in marital life.

Other marital unions are likely to be marred by the difficulty of providing adequately for their families, a factor that may especially affect men, the traditional providers. As Ball and Robbins (1986) state, "Difficulty in the provider role often leads to difficulty in spousal relationships" (p. 393). Another source of strain involves the tendency for higher-status African American women to marry less educated men because of the extreme "marriage squeeze." This reversal of the more traditional status match-up can also undermine marital satisfaction for *both* partners. Finally, the often extreme sex ratios favoring men at all levels, as reviewed earlier, may also undermine some men's commitment to marriage, since under those conditions, many men are likely to find an excess of "more rewarding and less demanding relationships outside of marriage," as some researchers have speculated (Ball & Robbins, 1986, p. 393). In short, there is ample reason to believe that markedly poor conditions, rather

than markedly shifting orientations, underlie the drop in African American marital formations.

Out-of-wedlock childbearing is a final area where a racial gap has long endured (Farley & Allen, 1987). However, here again, the gap appears to result from differentials in levels of living across the racial divide, rather than from purely race-specific factors. Indeed, as we note later, black women are hardly alone in generating high rates of out-of-wedlock childbearing. As Bumpass and McLanahan (1989) put it some time ago, "There is no monolithic culture that leads to high rates of unmarried childbearing among Blacks" (p. 284). Rather, as Duncan and Hoffman (1990) have noted, with reference to teens (whose births are overwhelming outside marriage), "Women with the least to lose are the most likely to have children during their teen years" (p. 532). These statements rest on a set of simple findings: Out-of-wedlock births, particularly to youthful women, primarily occur to females in "high-risk" (impoverished) circumstances, irrespective of whether they are black or white. The latter, however, are far less likely to find themselves in such high-risk circumstances.

It is instructive in reviewing trends in illegitimacy to first distinguish illegitimacy rates from illegitimacy ratios. Illegitimacy rates refer to the number of such births borne by a population of unmarried women, whereas illegitimacy ratios denote what percentage of the total births to a population (in and out of wedlock, combined) occur outside marriage. As is well known, illegitimacy rates have been generally falling among black women while generally rising among whites, despite the wide gap favoring the former. Moreover, the rates for women over 25 are not really very far apart—the major gap resides among the young. The indicator showing an increasing gap, the illegitimacy ratio, is actually rising among both groups, although rising faster among African Americans. Thus, while only 8.6% of *unmarried* African American women gave birth in 1992, versus 3.5% of such Whites, fully 68.4% of black births that year, versus 18.6% of white births, were out of wedlock (National Center for Health Statistics [NCHS], 1996).

In fact, the main component of the rapidly rising ratios is not any increasing illegitimacy among either group, but the earlier noted decline in marriage, on the one hand, and the overlapping phenomenon of falling marital fertility, on the other. Because the general fall in fertility has had its greatest impact within marriage, and women are spending far fewer of their fertile years in marriage, marital fertility has plummeted. This, in turn, has led to unprecedentedly higher proportions of births occurring to the unmarried, despite relatively little change in out-of-wedlock rates.

Explanations for the racial gap in nonmarital childbirth have, not surprisingly, focused on the young and have produced consistent findings (cf. Bumpass & McLanahan, 1989; Duncan & Hoffman, 1990; Hogan & Kitagawa, 1985). First, on the basis of a large sample in Chicago, Hogan and Kitagawa (1985) showed that black female adolescents from "low-risk" backgrounds (high-status families and neighborhoods) bore relatively few births outside marriage, as compared with girls from impoverished families and neighborhoods (where such births were prevalent). This strongly undermines the notion of a cultural cause. Similar findings emerged from Bumpass and McLanahan's (1989) national-level study. Their study examined both black and white women and showed that the effect of a "high-risk" background was even stronger for whites than for blacks (although the latter showed higher rates in both background circumstances). Finally, on the basis of yet another national sample, Duncan and Hoffman (1990) tested the competing hypotheses of "welfare benefits" versus "blocked opportunities" (similar to " high-risk" or impoverished backgrounds) as the cause of unmarried childbearing among black teenagers. They found no support for the first hypothesis but substantial support for the latter.

There are numerous other sources of reinforcement for the general points made here. In 1992, for example, women ages 25–34 who didn't complete high school generated some 73,100 out-of-wedlock births, whereas their college-educated counterparts generated only about 14,000 such births (NCHS, 1996). Using the 1990 census estimates for women in these categories as a basis for calculation indicates that the former group generated around *eight times* as many such births per woman (without regard to marital status) as did the latter (U.S. Bureau of the Census, 1993c). Perhaps more to the point, it is also the case that young Puerto Rican and, to a lesser extent, young Mexican women show out-of-wedlock birth rates quite comparable to those of American Americans.

These cross-group similarities in nonmarital birth rates have not received much attention because no direct data on them exist—however, they can easily be inferred. Thus, while 68.4% of black births in 1992 and 18.6% of white births occurred outside of marriage, so too did 57.5% of births to Puerto Ricans and 36.3% of births to Mexicans (NCHS, 1996). Moreover, differential rates of marriage between young black and Hispanic women likely account for much of the gap separating them on the illegitimacy ratio measure. Whereas only 11.7% of African American women ages 15–24 had ever married in 1990, some 22.7% of such Puerto Ricans, and 29.2% of such Mexicans, had ever married (U.S. Bureau of the Census, 1993c). Hence, many more births to young women among the latter two groups would have occurred in marriage, thereby lowering their group ratios, even as their illegitimacy rates (certainly the Puerto Ricans') are probably close to blacks'. In short, the high rates of illegitimacy among blacks are far from unique and are undoubtedly a product of the group's widespread deprivation.

Intermarriage: The Final Hurdle. Black–white intermarriages clearly occur less frequently than do marriages linking whites to the others, but they are nevertheless increasingly occurring. Porterfield's (1982) review showed that over the last century, such marriages were rare, although apparently unevenly so across time and place, and they tended to pair black men with white women more so than the converse (a pattern that continues). Prior to the 1960s, such marriages met near universal disapproval and were illegal in many states. Often, they were conducted with some secrecy, particularly toward the white partner's families. Since the Civil Rights era, legal prohibitions have ended, acceptance and frequency of occurrence have increased, and the aura of secrecy has declined.

Subsequent research on interracial marriage has reinforced Porterfield's (1982) major findings while adding crucial items. First, such marriages have continued to grow in frequency; second, they continue to be skewed to Black male outmarriers; and third, as was true among the others, such marriages continue to be skewed to higher-status persons (Holmes, 1997; Kalmijn, 1993; Tucker & Mitchell-Kernan, 1990). However, an important recent finding concerns variation in intermarriage across space.

First, Tucker and Mitchell-Kernan (1990) found that of *existing* marriages in 1980 at the national level, the highest proportions of interracial ones were found in the west region (where the fewest blacks reside) and the lowest proportion in the south region (where the largest number of blacks reside). Next, Kalmijn (1993) reviewed marriage license data for 33 states from 1968, the first full year since the Supreme Court overturned the antimiscegenation statues of several states, to 1986 (the last year for which data were then available). His review showed that both within and outside the South, the percentage of yearly black marriages that included a white was inversely related to the percentage of the state's population that was African American. Hence, southern states with low black percentages experienced higher intermarriage than those with high black perentages, just as occurred outside the South, even as the frequency of such marriages increased across the board. Thus, while the proportion of black men's marriages that paired them with white women outside the South rose from 3.9% to 10.1% over the period, inside the South (where states average high black proportions) there was a comparable, albeit lower, rise from .24% to 4.2%. The corresponding intermarriage increases for black women was from 0.7% to 1.7% in the South and from 1.2% to 3.7% outside it.

A similar compositional factor was apparent in the analysis by Tucker and Mitchell-Kernan (1990). Their study closely examined existing intermarriages in Los Angeles County, which holds the largest concentration of blacks in the West (and accounts for nearly a third of the region's total) and found that while interracial marriages there accounted for a higher proportion of all existing black marriages than was true for the nation at large, the percentage was considerably higher (over twice as many) within the balance of the western region. It is also possible, however, that places of low African American concentration are also places where blacks' average status is relatively high, thereby confounding the two predisposing factors. It is likewise possible that the extremely high levels of segregation endured by blacks contribute significantly to the group's low propensity toward intermarriage by maximizing in-group concentration and minimizing contacts and interactions with others.

Finally, a study reviewed by Holmes (1997) provides the most recent national-level numbers on intermarriages. It suggests that while 6.6% of all 1980 marriages that included at least one black spouse also included a white partner, the corresponding percentage had grown to 10.6% in 1990 and 12.1% in 1993. While the proportion of all *existing* marriages that represents those linking blacks to whites is much lower, since it is weighted toward the cumulative outcome of earlier patterns, the study's figures suggest that after a long delay, such intermarriages are finally increasing to nontrivial levels. Taken as a whole, then, trends in intermarriage among African Americans are similar to trends among the other groups: They are rising in frequency and are skewed toward higher-status persons and those residing away from higher concentrations of their own group. In contrast to the other groups, however, African Americans exhibit more male than female outmarriers. The reasons for this last factor remain clouded, although various hypotheses may be found in Porterfield (1982) and Tucker and Mitchell-Kernan (1990).

In summary, we conclude this section noting that while significant convergence between blacks and whites is in evidence on only a number of family organization characteristics, where convergence is absent or occurring slowly relative to the existing gap, it appears to stem not from cultural sources, but from vast differentials in living conditions favoring whites. Moreover, the large gaps in indicators between blacks and whites are not unique. Rather, other impoverished groups—such as Puerto Ricans—exhibit indicators comparably at odds with those of whites, although these similarities are not widely recognized. Finally, on the most salient form of family convergence of all, intermarriage, the trends for blacks parallel those of others' in terms of direction and composition, although currently at lower levels.

Amish Families: An Extraordinary Group

Our final and briefest case study group, the Amish, unquestionably constitute an extraordinary group. Brevity in their case is justified not only because their numbers are low and systematic information on them scarce, but also because

we readily concede at the outset that the group has largely maintained their traditional ways. Indeed, they have clearly resisted virtually all of the changes elucidated in this chapter as having been experienced by our other groups.* Just as was true a century or so ago, their fertility is high, their sex roles are rigid, and they continue to show tight, extended kinship lines. In addition, their version of male domination remains securely in place, virtually all their adults marry, and they successfully resist both exogamy and marital dissolution (Hostetler, 1993; Huntington, 1988; Kephart & Zellner, 1994). Despite all of this, their example actually supports the argument here.

The Amish experience supports our case because their extraordinary outcomes have been achieved only by the expenditure of likewise extraordinary, if not Herculean, efforts. These efforts rest precisely on tightly controlled avoidance of all manner of modernization itself, including urban living, higher education, all modern gadgetry (including electricity, indoor plumbing, and telephones in most circumstances), and, most especially, sustained interactions with all non-Amish (modern?) people, whom they dub "the English." In short, they have deliberately and systematically sought to avoid or keep at bay the very influences that are credited here with modifying the strictures of traditionalism among the other groups. Yet, for all their efforts, there are faint but growing indications that change is gradually transforming them in very small ways toward some of the very outcomes that others have long since embraced.

A product of sixteenth-century European religious fractures, the Amish came to North America largely to escape relentless persecution in the eighteenth and nineteenth centuries (Hostetler, 1993; Huntington, 1988; Wasao & Donnermeyer, 1996). They remain a religious-based collectivity and retain their native tongue, a German dialect sometimes called Pennsylvania Dutch (though they also speak fluent English). In particular, the old order Amish are well known for their numerous distinctive characteristics, including a devotion to an agrarian lifestyle and avoidance of outsiders, government schools and institutions, and manmade technology such as telephones, cars, electrical farm equipment, and household appliances (gas-run equipment is permitted). They till their lands with horse-drawn plows and sport a style of dress similar to that worn by 18th-century European peasantry. And, like farm families of our own not-so-distant past, Amish families are large, their sex-roles are rigid, their divorce rates

---

*It is important to note that the Amish are not the only group that have been able to avoid or minimize experiencing the kinds of transformations examined here. For additional examples (e.g., Hasidic Jews, Hutterites) see Kephart and Zellner (1994) and Belcove-Shalin (1995). Such groups tend, like the Amish, to be tightly knit, religious-based collectivities that engage in such practices as limiting contact with outsiders and stressing religious over secular education, etc.

are near zero, and they exhibit numerous additional "traditional" attributes (Hostetler, 1993; Huntington, 1988; Kephart & Zellner, 1994).

The Amish generally live in isolated farmland clusters or settlements, organized along the lines of "church districts," and the number of such settlements has grown considerably over time. Originally settled in Pennsylvania, the group's rapid growth fostered continual outmigration that generally scattered toward cheaper and more isolated lands. By the early 1990s, when their population was estimated at well over 100,000 (by this writing, perhaps 150,000), settlements could be found in some 20 states, although 75% of the group resided in their core areas of residence, the states of Pennsylvania, Ohio, and Indiana (Hostetler, 1993; Kephart & Zellner, 1994). Still, precise figures on the Amish are not available as no hard data exist on the group. In addition, no apparent overarching organizational or authority structure unites Amish settlements, save a steering committee formed to deal with government bureaucracies (Olshan, 1990). Accordingly, differences in lifestyles among their settlements do exist, but these are of limited significance to our purposes.

The Amish have been described as "an ethnoreligious group that has had great success in preserving its traditions and preventing wholesale assimilation" (Huntington, 1988, p. 367), and few would challenge the description. However, this raises at least two questions: Why do they so, and how do they succeed? Briefly put, their spartan lifestyles are strongly prescribed by their deeply held religious convictions, while their success at resisting change rests on their relentless and extraordinary efforts at minimizing outside influences, especially as they might have an impact on the very young. To the extent that parents and elders can control it, socialization among the Amish is strongly geared to producing faithful and obedient followers, a process reinforced by the often severe sanctioning of members straying from the prescribed lifestyles.

For example, by all accounts, obedience is the key trait parents strive to teach their young children (Huntington, 1988; Kephart & Zellner, 1994), who are "kept away from the outside world as much as possible" and "not usually introduced to non-Amish people" (Hostetler, 1993, p. 173), along with being subjected to a fair amount of corporal punishment. In addition, most school-aged children are required to attend Amish schools, with the remaining few attending only very small rural public schools. The Amish schools, however, utilize Amish teachers who, like all Amish, were limited to an elementary education. The schools' curriculum and materials are very carefully chosen with an eye toward inculcating Amish traits. Moreover, *no children* are allowed to advance beyond the 8th grade, under any circumstances, because as noted by an author of several books on the group, "the child who continues formal schooling will not remain Amish"

(Hostetler, 1993, p. 189). Indeed, the ban on high school attendance is one of the most deeply held by the group. As Hostetler (1993) explains:

> High school comes at a time in the life of an Amish young person when cultural isolation is most important for the development of personality.... If he acquires competence in the "English" culture at this stage, he will likely be lost to the Amish fellowship.... The "way of life" of the high school is feared perhaps even more than the curriculum itself. If the child is removed from the community for most of the working hours of the day, there is virtually no chance that he will learn to *enjoy the Amish way of life*. (pp. 261–261; emphasis added)

Their success at "keeping them down on the farm" has been formidable, but not complete. It is variously estimated that approximately 20% leave, one way or another, including by way of expulsion (Hostetler, 1993; Huntington, 1988; Kreps et al., 1994). Moreover, many leavers of both varieties depart deeply embittered. The relentless pressure toward conformity is a recurring theme in their testimonials (American Broadcasting Companies [ABC], 1997. Hostetler, 1993). Youthful leavers, many of whom run away, claim the corporal punishment they frequently endured was often brutal, while a former Amish Bishop, the highest ranking in the community, called the Amish way of life nothing short of "bondage" (ABC, 1997, pp. 5–8). Still another former member, now a psychologist who has treated other former members for some 2 odd decades, claims that clinical depression is their "number-one problem" (ABC, 1997, p. 7). While there may be reason to question the objectivity of former members, it appears almost certain that the struggle to maintain the Amish way of life is fraught with hardship for many.

The future will undoubtedly present even greater challenges to the Amish way of life. While they currently feel besieged by many modern-day pressures, the most critical one by all accounts concerns the Amish's inability to continue to eke out a living on farms and related agricultural trades. Their access to sufficient land for these purposes has markedly dwindled under the related pressures of encroaching urban areas, rapid population growth, and rising land prices. Like so many others before them, their response has been to turn to other pursuits, particularly cottage industries. However, the growing diversity of their enterprises, the increasing commercial pressures, and the necessarily heightened scale of interaction with "the English" under these circumstances has begun to take a serious toll on their ability to resist change (cf. Huntington, 1988; Janofsky, 1997; Kephart & Zellner, 1994; Kreps et al., 1994; Olshan, 1991).

Among the problems emanating from the shift in occupational structure is the fact that many families experience difficulty eking out a living outside of farming. Research has shown that nonfarm Amish families generate more leavers than farm ones, at least partly due to financial strains, although possibly due to lifestyle differences. Huntington (1988) notes, "Among a sample of Lancaster [Pennsylvania] Amish it was observed that the likelihood of leaving ... was five times as great for children of nonfarmers as for children of farmers" (p.394). Perhaps more worrisome than the leavers, however, are the lifestyle changes that may engulf the stayers. One veteran Amish watcher, Olshan (1991), refers to the rise of cottage industries among them as a "trojan horse." Consistent with this, there are increasing reports of the Amish engaging in limited use of telephones (including cell phones), electricity, automobile driving, and so forth, primarily in Amish businesses (Janofsky, 1997; Kreps et al., 1994).

As the *New York Times* recently reported, one Amishman was quoted as stating, "Its unbelievable what's happening.... We're now using color advertising in our catalogues. When we started, all we did was open the front door" (Janofsky, 1997, p. A8). In addition, demographers in at least two studies have detected clear differences in fertility patterns among varying Amish family types (after controlling for age and other variables) that led them to conclude that *some* type of family planning was being practiced by *some* Amish, despite their strict prohibition on any form of birth control (Waseo & Donnermeyer, 1996), while another set of researchers reported that informants have verified the secretive use of family planning among some younger couples (Kreps et al., 1994).

Finally, a passage by Huntington (1988) captures the plight from yet another vantage point:

> The trend from farming to non-farming occupations may have a profound effect on the Amish culture. The Amish family and Amish patterns of childrearing are built on the concept of shared responsibility, on the expectation that both parents work together caring for the farm and the children, that both parents are almost always in the home.... For example, family devotions are led by the father, but it is difficult to have these when the father has to punch a clock rather than being able to adjust his farm chores to the sleeping patterns of his growing family. The authority patterns within the family change when the father is absent most of the day.... On an Amish farm the boys spend most of the time, when they are awake and not in school, working with or under the direction of their father. In *no other occupation* can the father so *consistently teach, instruct, admonish,* and *correct* his children. (pp. 394–395; emphasis added)

Relatedly, Olshan (1991) concludes his review with noting that while the shift from agriculture "does not inexorably lead to the dissolution of Amish culture," it remains to be seen "how successful the Amish will be in perpetuating the values of an agrarian society once agriculture is no longer the foundation of economic life" (p. 383).

Conclusion

The argument advanced here was that all of the groups immersed in the modernized socioeconomic (and political) order of the United States will tend, over time, toward convergence on such key family attributes as family size (smaller, relative to traditional norms), although not necessarily to the same model because an expanded array of options is part and parcel of the modern model. We further held that exceptions to this would only be possible in the face of extraordinary circumstances. We have attempted to show this on the basis of the experiences of six groups, four immigrant groups and two domestic minorities.

In fact, we have shown this to be the case in five of the six examples. In the major outlier case, that of the Amish, we have shown the presence of truly extraordinary circumstances. Until recently, the group has managed to limit its economic activities to farming and related pursuits in rural areas, taking great pains to isolate itself from the remainder of society. Conformity to group norms is strenuously inculcated within the membership, and serious deviations are heavily sanctioned. Even with that, about one in five leave the fold, and an additional number are expelled. In addition, minute changes are starting to occur among the group for reasons similar to those that have affected the other groups.

We note here that change among the others was hardly even. In particular, African Americans, who have the most in common with the majority or baseline group (whites), in terms of longevity in the United States, mother tongue, and average years of schooling, conformed the least. We explain this on the basis of an additional set of extraordinary circumstances that appear to have little to do with culture or group-specific traditions. We argue that it is the group's intense deprivation reinforced by their high levels of segregation—both of which undoubtedly rest strongly upon the high levels of discrimination visited upon them—that underlie their nonconformity. These circumstances create formidable barriers to the group's ability to fulfill their family aspirations, which do not appear to differ substantially from those of the majority. Moreover and contrary to popular knowledge, attributes believed unique to this group are found among others, notably Puerto Ricans, a group with a vastly different cultural background.

Even the most cursory examination of Table 1 shows that, as a whole, deviation from average values on an array of family characteristics are highly related to deprivation. Thus, the groups with the highest rates of poverty and the lowest figures on income and education (African Americans, Hispanics) show the lowest degree of conformity, while those with the opposite patterns (Asians, whites) show the highest degree of conformity. This is so despite the fact that, in general, the conforming minority groups (the Asians) are more likely to be immigrants and to originate in societies considered more culturally different (non-Christian, non-Western) than our own, relative to the others. Furthermore, changes over time for all groups (except the Amish) appear consistent with our key ideas, especially over the long haul, and literature reviewed here indicates that similar changes are occurring in all of our immigrant groups' societies of origin. This latter point serves to underscore the fact that the shifts noted here are not merely signs of assimilation. Most emphatically of all, the findings here indicate that *inequality* among groups, far more than the diversity in the groups' traditional origins, underlies the differential tendencies in family organization among them.

References

Alvirez, D., & Bean, F. D. (1976). The Mexican American family. In C. H. Mindel & R. W. Haberstein (Eds.), *Ethnic families in America: Patterns and variations* (2nd ed., pp. 271–292). New York: Elsevier.

American Broadcasting Companies (ABC). The Secret Life of the Amish. On Television Broadcast Program *20/20*, July 25, 1997. ABC Transcript #1731.

Anderson, R. N., & Saenz, R. (1994). Structural determinants of Mexican American intermarriage, 1975–1980. *Social Science Quarterly, 75*(2), 414–430.

Angel, R., & Tienda, M. (1982). Determinants of extended household structure: Cultural pattern or economic need. *American Journal of Sociology, 87*(6), 1360–1383.

Aponte, R. (1991). Urban Hispanic poverty: Disaggregations and explanations. *Social Problems, 38*(4), 516–528.

Aponte, R. (1993, November). Hispanic families in poverty: Diversity, context, and interpretation. *The Journal of Contemporary Human Services*, 527–536.

Aponte, R. (1996). Urban unemployment and the mismatch dilemma: Accounting for the immigrant exception. *Social Problems, 43*(3), 268–283.

Aponte, R. (in press). Latinos in the U.S. and century's end and beyond. *Latino Studies Journal, 9.*

Aponte, R., & Siles, M. (1997). Winds of change: Latinos in the heartland and the nation. CIFRAS No. 5, Julian Samora Research Institute, Michigan State University.

Applbaum, K. D. (1995). Marriage with the proper stranger: Arranged marriage in metropolitan Japan. *Ethnology, 34*(1), 37–51.

Baca Zinn, M. (1994). Adaptation and continuity in Mexican-origin families. In R. L. Taylor (Ed.), *Minority families in the United States: A multicultural perspective* (pp. 64–81). Englewood Cliffs, NJ: Prentice-Hall.

Baca Zinn, M., & Eitzen, D. S. (1996). *Diversity in families* (4th ed.). New York: HarperCollins.

Ball, R. E., & Robbins, L. (1986). Marital status and life satisfaction among black Americans. *Journal of Marriage and the Family, 48*(May), 389–394.

Bean, F. D., & Swicegood, G. (1982). Generation, female education and Mexican American fertility. *Social Science Quarterly, 63*(1), 131–144.

Bean, F. D., & Tienda, M. (1987). *The Hispanic population of the United States.* New York: Russell Sage Foundation.

Bean, F. D., Cullen, R. M., Stephen, E. H., & Swicegood, C. G. (1984). Generational differences in fertility among Mexican Americans: Impli-

cations for assessing the effects of immigration. *Social Science Quarterly, 65*(2), 572–582.

Becerra, R. M. (1988). The Mexican-American family. In C. H. Mindel, R. W. Haberstein & R. Wright, Jr. (Eds.), *Ethnic families in America: Patterns and variations* (3rd ed., pp. 141–159). New York: Elsevier.

Belcove-Shalin, J. S. (Ed.). (1995). *New World Hasidim: Ethnographic studies of Hasidic Jews in America.* Albany: State University of New York Press.

Bennett, L. Jr. (1992, November). The 10 biggest myths about the black family. *Ebony*, 118–124.

Boh, K., Bak, M., Clason, C., Pankratova, M., Qvortrup, J., Sgritta, G. B., & Waerness, K. (1989). *Changing patterns of European family life: A comparative analysis of 14 European countries.* New York: Routledge.

Bridges, J. C. (1980). The Mexican family. In M. Das & C. J. Jesser (Eds.), *The family in Latin America* (pp. 295–334). New Delhi, India: Vikas.

Broman, C. L. (1993). Racial differences in marital well-being. *Journal of Marriage and the Family, 55*(Feb.), 724–732.

Bulcroft, R. A., & Bulcroft, K. A. (1993). Race differences in attitudinal and motivational factors in the decision to marry. *Journal of Marriage and the Family, 55*(May), 338–355.

Bumpass, L., & McLanahan, S. (1989). Unmarried motherhood: Recent trends, composition, and black–white differences. *Demography, 26*(2), 269–286.

Carrasquillo, H. (1994). The Puerto Rican family. In R. L. Taylor (ed.), *Minority families in the United States: A multicultural perspective* (pp. 82–94). Englewood Cliffs, NJ: Prentice-Hall.

Cherlin, A. J. (1981). *Marriage divorce remarriage.* Cambridge, MA: Harvard University Press.

Cortés, D. E. (1995). Variations in familism in two generations of Puerto Ricans. *Hispanic Journal of Behavioral Sciences, 17*(2), 249–255.

Das, M., & Jesser, C. J. (Eds.). (1980). *The Family in Latin America.* New Delhi, India: Vikas.

Demos, J. (1986). *Past, present, and personal: The family and life course in American history.* New York: Oxford University Press.

Demos, V. (1990). Black family studies in the *Journal of Marriage and the Family* and the issue of Distortion: A trend analysis. *Journal of Marriage and the Family, 52*, 603–612.

Devore, W., & Schlesinger, E. G. (1987). *Ethnic sensitive social work practice* (2nd ed.). Columbus, OH: Merrill.

Duncan, G. J., & Hoffman, S. D. (1990). Welfare benefits, economic opportunities, and out-of-wedlock births among teenage black girls. *Demography, 27*(4), 519–535.

El Nassar, H. (1997, May 8). Measuring race: Multi-ethnics balk at "Pick-One" forms. *USA Today*, 1A–2A.

Ellwood, D. T. (1988). *Poor support: Poverty in the American family.* New York: Basic Books.

Ellwood, D. T., & Bane, M. J. (1985). The impact of AFDC on family structure and living arrangement. *Research in Labor Economics, 7*, 137–207.

Eshleman, J. R. (1997). *The family: An introduction* (7th ed.). Boston: Allyn and Bacon.

Farber, B. (1973). *Family & kinship in modern society.* Glenview, IL: Scott Foresman.

Farley, J. E. (1995). *Majority–minority relations* (3rd ed.). Englewood Cliffs, NJ: Prentice-Hall.

Farley, R. (1971). Family types and family headship: A comparison of trends among blacks and whites. *The Journal of Human Resources, VI*(3), 275–296.

Farley, R. (1996). *The new American reality: Who we are, how we got here, where we are going.* New York: Russell Sage Foundation.

Farley, R., & Allen, W. R. (1987). *The color line and the quality of life in America.* New York: Russell Sage Foundation.

Feagin, J. R. & Vera, H. (1995). *White racism: The basics*. New York: Routledge.

Fitzpatrick, J. P. (1987). *Puerto Rican Americans: The meaning of migration to the mainland* (2nd ed.). Englewood Cliffs, NJ: Prentice-Hall.

Fleck, S., & Sorrentino, C. (1994). Employment and unemployment in Mexico's labor force. *Monthly Labor Review*, *117*(11), 3–31.

Fong, C., & Young, J. (1995). In search of the right spouse: Interracial marriage among Chinese and Japanese Americans. *Amerasia Journal*, *21*(3), 77–98.

Fossett, M. A., & Kiecolt, K. J. (1993). Mate availability and family structure among African Americans in U.S. metropolitan areas. *Journal of Marriage and the Family*, *5*(May), 288–302.

Fost, D. (1992, September). Mexico's middle class is Yummie. *American Demographics*, 9–10.

Frazier, E. F. (1966). *The Negro family in the United States* (rev. ed.). Chicago: University of Chicago Press.

Frisbie, W. P., & Bean, F. D. (1995). The Latino family in comparative perspectives: Trends and current conditions. In C. K. Jacobson (Ed.), *American families: Issues in race and ethnicity* (pp. 29–71). New York: Garland.

Furstenberg, F. F., Jr., Hershberg, T., & Modell, J. (1975). The origins of the female-headed black family: The impact of the urban experience. *Journal of Interdisciplinary History*, *6*(2), 211–233.

Gelles, R. J. (1995). *Contemporary families: A sociological view*. Thousand Oaks, CA: Sage.

Gilbertson, G. A., Fitzpatrick, J. P., & Yang, L. (1996). Hispanic intermarriage in New York City: New evidence from 1991. *International Migration Review*, *30*(2), 4.

Glenn, E. N. (1983, February). Split household, small producer and dual wage earner: An analysis of Chinese-American family strategies. *Journal of Marriage and the Family*, 35–46.

Glenn, E. N., & Yap, S. G. H. (1994). Chinese American families. In R. L. Taylor (Ed.), *Minority families in the United States: A multicultural perspective* (pp. 115–145). Englewood Cliffs, NJ: Prentice-Hall.

Goldscheider, F. K., & Goldscheider, C. (1985). Ethnicity and the new family economy: Synthesis and research findings. In F. K. Goldscheider & C. Goldscheider (Eds.), *Ethnicity and the family economy: Living arrangements and intergenerational financial flows* (pp. 185–197). Boulder, CO: Westview.

Gonzales, J. L., Jr. (1994). *Racial and ethnic families in America* (2nd ed.). Dubuque, IA: Kendall Hunt.

Goode, W. (1963). *World revolution and family patterns*. New York: Free Press.

Grebler, L., Moore, J. W., & Guzman, R. C. (1970). *The Mexican-American people: The Nation's second largest minority*. New York: Free Press.

Gutman, H. G. (1976). *The family in slavery and freedom, 1750–1925*. New York: Pantheon Books.

Hatchett, S. (1991). Women and men. In J. Jackson (Ed.), *Life in black America* (pp. 84–104). Newbury Park, CA: Sage.

Hamilton, C. H. (1964). The Negro leaves the South. *Demography*, *1*, 273–295.

Hane, M. (1982). *Peasants, rebels, and outcasts: The underside of modern Japan* (1st ed.). New York: Pantheon.

Hendry, J. (1993). *Understanding Japanese Society*. New York: Routledge.

Henry, W., III. (1990, April 9). Beyond the melting pot. *Time*, *135*, 28–31.

Hill, R., Stycos, J. M., & Back, K. W. (1966). *The family and population control: A Puerto Rican experiment in social change*. Chapel Hill: University of North Carolina Press.

Hogan, D., & Kitagawa, E. (1985). The impact of social status, family structure, and neighborhood on the fertility of black adolescents. *American Journal of Sociology*, *90*, 825–855.

Holmes, S. (1997, July 3). Study finds rising number of black-white marriages. *New York Times*, A10.

Hostetler, J. A. (1993). *Amish society* (4th ed.). Baltimore: Johns Hopkins University Press.

Huntington, G. E. (1988). The Amish family. In C. H. Mindel, R. W. Habenstein, & R. Wright, Jr. (Eds.), *Ethnic families in America: Patterns and variations* (3rd ed., pp. 367–399). New York: Elsevier.

Inkeles, A. (1980). Modernization and family patterns: A test of convergence theory. *Conspectus of History*, *1*(6), 31–63.

Itoi, K., & Powell, B. (1992, August 10). Take a hike, Hirosho. *Newsweek*, 38–39.

Iwao, S. (1993). *The Japanese woman: Traditional image and changing reality*. New York: Free Press.

Jaffe, A. J., Cullen, R. M., & Boswell, T. D. (1980). *The changing demography of Spanish Americans*. New York: Academic Press.

Janofsky, M. (1997, July 6). Rustic life of Amish is slowly changing. *The New York Times*, p. A8.

Joe, T. (1984). *The "flip-side" of black families headed by women: The economic status of men*. Washington, DC: Center for the Study of Social Policy.

Johnson, N. E. (1979). Minority group status and the fertility of black Americans: A new look. *American Journal of Sociology*, *84*(May), 1386–1400.

Johnson, N. E., Burton, L. (1987). Religion and reproduction in Philippine society: A new test of the minority group status hypothesis. *Sociological Analysis*, *48*, 217–233.

Kalmijn, M. (1993). Trends in black/white intermarriage. *Social Forces*, *72*(1), 119–146.

Kamo, Y., & Zhou, M. (1994). Living arrangements of elderly Chinese and Japanese in the United States. *Journal of Marriage and Family Review*, *56*, 544–558.

Kephart, W. M., & Zellner, W. W. (1994). *Extraordinary groups: An examination of unconventional life-styles* (5th ed.). New York: St. Martin's.

Kitano, H. H. L. (1988). The Japanese American family. In C. H. Mindel, R. W. Habenstein, & R. Wright, Jr. (Eds.), *Ethnic families in America: patterns and variations* (3rd ed., pp. 258–274). New York: Elsevier.

Kitano, H., & Yeung, W. (1982). Chinese interracial marriage. *Marriage and Family Review*, *5*(1), 35–48.

Kitano, H., Yeung, W., Chai, L., & Hatanka, H. (1984, February). Asian-American interracial marriage. *Journal of Marriage and the Family*, 179–190.

Kozol, J. (1991). *Savage inequalities: Children in America's schools*. New York: Crown.

Kumagai, F. (1996). *Unmasking Japan today: The impact of traditional values on modern Japanese society*. Westport, CT: Praeger.

Li, E. B. C. (1994). Modernization: Its impacts on families in China. In P. L. Lin, K. Mei, & H. Peng (Eds.), *Marriage and the family in Chinese societies: Selected readings* (pp. 39–52). Indianapolis, IN: University of Indianapolis Press.

Lichter, D. T., LeClere, F. B., & McLaughlin, D. K. (1991). Local marriage markets and the marital behavior of black and white women. *American Journal of Sociology*, *96*(4), 843–867.

Lichter, D. T., McLaughlin, D. K., Kephart, G., & Landry, D. J. (1992). Race and the retreat from marriage: A shortage of marriageable men? *American Sociological Review*, *57*(6), 781–799.

Maddock, J. W., Hogan, M. J., Antonov, A. I., & Matskovsky, M. S. (Eds). (1994). *Families before and after perestroika: Russian and U.S. perspectives*. New York: Guilford.

Madsen, W. (1973). *The Mexican-Americans of South Texas* (2nd ed.). New York: Holt, Rinehart and Winston.

Marger, M. N. (1991). *Race and ethnic relations: American and global perspectives* (4th ed.). Belmont, CA: Wadsworth.

Marks, C. (1989). *Farewell—We're good and gone: The great black migration*. Bloomington: Indiana University Press.

Marsh, R. M., & Hsu, C. (1994). Modernization and changes in extended kinship in Taipei, Taiwan, 1963–1991. In P. L. Lin, K. Mei, & H. Peng (Eds.), *Marriage and the family in Chinese societies: Selected readings* (pp. 53–78). Indianapolis, IN: University of Indianapolis Press.

Massey, D. S., & Bitterman, B. (1985). Explaining the paradox of Puerto Rican segregation. *Social Forces, 64,* 306–331.

Massey, D. S., & Denton, N. A. (1993). *American apartheid: Segregation and the making of the underclass.* Cambridge, MA: Harvard University Press.

McAdoo, H. P. (1993). Ethnic families: Strengths that are found in diversity. In H. P. McAdoo (Ed.), *Family ethnicity: Strength in diversity* (pp. 3–14). Newbury Park, CA: Sage.

McDade, K. (1995). How we parent: Race and ethnic differences. In C. K. Jacobson (Ed.), *American families: Issues in race and ethnicity* (pp. 283–300). New York: Garland.

McLeod, R. G. (1997, July 9). Mixed-race people cheer census proposal. *San Francisco Chronicle,* p. A3.

Meredith, W. H., & Abbott, D. A. (1995). Chinese families in later life. In B. B. Ingoldsby & S. Smith (Eds.), *Families in multicultural perspectives* (pp. 213–230). New York: Guilford.

Mirande, A. (1977). The Chicano family: A reanalysis of conflicting views. *Journal of Marriage and the Family, 42,* 747–756.

Morgan, S. P., & Hirosima, K. (1983). The persistence of extended family residence in Japan: Anachronism or alternative strategy? *American Sociological Review, 48,* 269–281.

Moynihan, D. (1965). *The Negro family: The case for national action.* Washington, DC: U.S. Government Printing Office.

Murguia, E. (1982). *Chicano intermarriage: A theoretical and empirical study.* San Antonio, TX: Trinity University Press.

Murray, C. (1984). *Losing ground: American social policy 1950–1980.* New York: Basic Books.

National Center for Health Statistics (NCHS). (1996). *Vital statistics of the United States: 1992. Volume 1—natality.* Washington, DC: US Department of Health and Human Services.

Neckerman, K. M., Aponte, R., & Wilson, W. J. (1988). Family structure, black unemployment, and American social policy. In M. Weir, A. S. Orloff, & T. Skocpol (Eds.), *The politics of social policy* (pp. 397–419). Princeton, NJ: Princeton University Press.

Nobles, W. (1974). African root and American fruit: The black family. *Journal of Social and Behavioral Sciences, 20,* 52–64.

Nobles, W. (1978). Toward an empirical and theoretical framework for defining black families. *Journal of Marriage and the Family, 40,* 679–688.

Nobles, W. (1988). African-American family life: An instrument of culture. In H. P. McAdoo (Ed.), *Black families* (2nd ed., pp. 3–14). Newbury Park, CA: Sage.

Nozomu, K. (1989). The transition of the household system in Japan's modernization. In Y. Sugimoto & R. E. Mouer (Eds.), *Constructs for understanding Japan* (pp. 202–227). Kegan Paul International.

O'Brien, D. J., & Fugita, S. S. (1991). *The Japanese American experience.* Bloomington: Indiana University Press.

Ogawa, N., & Ermisch, J. F. (1996). Family structure, home time demands, and the employment patterns of Japanese married women. *Journal of Labor Economics, 14*(4), 177–196.

Ogawa, N., & Retherford, R. D. (1993). The resumption of fertility decline in Japan: 1973–92. *Population and Development Review, 19*(4), 703–741.

Oliver, M. L., & Shapiro, T. M. (1995). *Black wealth/white wealth: A new perspective on racial inequality.* New York: Routledge.

Olshan, M. A. (1990). The old order Amish Steering committee: A case study in organizational evolution. *Social Forces, 69*(2), 603–616.

Olshan, M. A. (1991). The opening of Amish society: Cottage industry as trojan horse. *Human Organization, 50*(4), 378–384.

Porterfield, E. (1982). Black-American intermarriage in the United States. *Marriage and Family Review, 5*(1), 17–34.

Portes, A., & Rumbuat, R. G. (1996). *Immigrant America: A portrait* (2nd ed.). Berkeley: University of California Press.

Rainwater, L., & Yancey, W. L. (1967). *The Moynihan Report and the politics of controversy.* Cambridge, MA: M.I.T. Press.

Raley, R. K. (1996). A shortage of marriageable men? A note on the role of cohabitation in black–white differences in marriage rates. *American Sociological Review, 61,* 973–983.

Rindfuss, R. R., & Sweet, J. A. (1977). *Postwar fertility trends and differentials in the United States.* New York: Academic Press.

Rivera-Batiz, F. L., & Santiago, C. E. (1996). *Island paradox: Puerto Rico in the 1990s.* New York: Russell Sage Foundation.

Rogler, L. H., & Procidano, M. A. (1989). Egalitarian spouse relations and wives' marital satisfaction in intergenerationally linked Puerto Rican families. *Journal of Marriage and the Family, 51,* 37–39.

Rogler, L. H., & Santana Cooney, R. (1984). *Puerto Rican families in New York City: Intergenerational processes.* Maplewood, NJ: Waterfront Press.

Ross, H., & Sawhill, I. (1975). *Time of transition: The growth of families headed by women.* Washington, DC: Urban Institute.

Rudoff, A. (1971). The incarcerated Mexican-American delinquent. *Journal of Criminal Law, 62*(June), 224–238.

Ruggles, S. (1994). The origins of African-American family structure. *American Sociological Review, 59,* 136–151.

Rumbaut, R. G. (1994). Origins and destinies: Immigration to the United States since World War II. *Sociological Forum, 9*(4), 583–621.

Sanchez-Ayendez, M. (1988). The Puerto Rican American family. In C. H. Mindel, R. W. Haberstein, & R. Wright (Eds.), *In ethnic families in America: Patterns and variations* (3rd ed., pp. 173–195). New York: Elsevier.

Schoen, R., & Kluegel, J. R. (1988). The widening gap in black and white marriage rates: The impact of population composition and differential marriage propensities. *American Sociological Review, 53*(Dec), 895–907.

Scott, D. M., & Wishy, B. (Eds.). (1982). *America's families: A documentary history.* New York: Harper & Row.

Skolnick, A. S., & Skolnick, J. H. (1989). *Family in transition* (6th ed.). New York: Longman.

Smock, P. (1990). Remarriage patterns of black and white women: Reassessing the role of educational attainment. *Demography, 27*(3), 467–473.

South, J. S., & Lloyd, K. M. (1992). Marriage opportunities and family formation: Further implications of unbalanced sex ratios. *Journal of Marriage and the Family, 54*(May), 440–451.

Staples, R. (1985). Changes in black family structure: The conflict between family ideology and structural conditions. *Journal of Marriage and the Family, 47*(4), 1005–1013.

Staples, R., & Mirandé, A. (1980). Racial and cultural variations among American families: A decennial review of the literature on minority families. *Journal of Marriage and the Family, 42,* 887–903.

Steinberg, S. (1989). *The ethnic myth: Race, ethnicity, and class in America.* Boston: Beacon.

Steinmetz, S. K., Claven, S., & Stein, K. F. (1990). *Marriage and family realities: Historical and contemporary perspectives.* New York: Harper & Row.

Stephan, C. W., & Stephan, W. G. (1989). After intermarriage: Ethnic identity among mixed-heritage Japanese-Americans and Hispanics. *Journal of Marriage and the Family, 51,* 507–519.

Sudarkasa, N. (1988). Interpreting the African heritage in Afro-American family organization. In H. P. McAdoo (Ed.), *Black families* (2nd ed., pp. 81–89). Newbury Park, CA: Sage.

Sudarkasa, N. (1993). Female-headed African American households: Some neglected dimensions. In H. P. McAdoo (Ed.), *Family ethnicity: Strength in diversity* (pp. 81–89). Newbury Park, CA: Sage.

Sullivan, T. A. (1978). Racial-ethnic differences in labor force participation: An ethnic stratification perspective. In F. D. Bean & W. P. Frisbie (Eds), *The demography of racial and ethnic groups* (pp. 165–187). New York: Academic Press.

Sung, B. L. (1990). *Chinese American intermarriage.* New York: Center for Migration Studies.

Suro, R. (1992, January 20). Generational chasm leads to cultural turmoil for young Mexicans in U.S. *New York Times,* A16.

Sweet, J. A. (1978). Indicators of family and household structure of racial and ethnic minorities in The United States. In F. D. Bean & W. P. Frisbie (Eds.), *The demography of racial and ethnic groups* (pp. 221–259). New York: Academic Press.

Takagi, D. Y. (1994). Japanese American families. In R. L. Taylor (Ed.), *Minority families in the United States: A multicultural perspective* (pp. 146–163). Englewood Cliffs, NJ: Prentice-Hall.

Taylor, R. L. (Ed.). (1994). *Minority families in the United States: A multicultural perspective.* Englewood Cliffs, NJ: Prentice-Hall.

Taylor, R. L., Catters, L. M., Tucker, M. B., & Lewis, E. (1990). Developments in research on black families: A decade review. *Journal of Marriage and the Family, 52,* 993–1014.

Testa, M., Astone, N. M., Krogh, M., & Neckerman, K. M. (1989). Employment and marriage among inner city fathers. *Annals of the American Academy of Social and Political Sciences, 501,* 79–91.

Tienda, M. (1989). Puerto Ricans and the underclass debate. *Annals of the American Academy of Social and Political Sciences, 501,* 105–119.

Tienda, M., & Angel, R. (1982). Headship and household composition among blacks, Hispanics, and other whites. *Social Forces, 61*(2), 508–531.

Tucker, M. B., & Mitchell-Kernan, C. (1990). New trends in black American interracial marriage: The social structural context. *Journal of Marriage and the Family, 52*(1), 209–218.

Turner, M. A., Fix, M., & Struyk, R. J. (1991). *Opportunities denied, opportunities dismissed: Racial discrimination in hiring.* Washington, DC: Urban Institute Press.

U.S. Bureau of the Census. (1983a). *Census of the Population, 1980. General Population Characteristics: United States Summary* (PC80(1)-B1). Washington, DC: U.S. Government Printing Office.

U.S. Bureau of the Census. (1983b). *Census of the Population, 1980. General Social and Economic Characteristics: United States Summary* (PC80(1)-C1). Washington, DC: U.S. Government Printing Office.

U.S. Bureau of the Census. (1988). *Census of the Population, 1980. Asian and Pacific Islander Population in the United States: 1980* (PC80(2)-1E). Washington, DC: U.S. Government Printing Office.

U.S. Bureau of the Census. (1992). *Census of the Population, 1990. General Population Characteristics: United States* (CP-1-1). Washington, DC: U.S. Government Printing Office.

U.S. Bureau of the Census. (1993a). *Census of the Population, 1990. Persons of Hispanic Origin in the United States* (CP-3-3). Washington, DC: U.S. Government Printing Office.

U.S. Bureau of the Census. (1993b). *Census of the Population, 1990. Asian and Pacific Islanders in the United States* (CP-3-5). Washington, DC: U.S. Government Printing Office.

U.S. Bureau of the Census. (1993c). *Census of the Population, 1990. General Social and Economic Characteristics: United States Summary* (CP-2-1). Washington, DC: U.S. Government Printing Office.

U.S. Bureau of the Census. (1994). *Census of the Population, 1990. Characteristics of the Black Population* (CP-3-6). Washington, DC: U.S. Government Printing Office.

Wasao, S. W., & Donnermeyer, J. F. (1996). An analysis of factors related to parity among the Amish in northeast Ohio. *Population Studies, 50,* 235–246.

Weisner, T. S., Bradley, C., & Kilbride, P. L. (Eds.). (1997). *African families and the crisis of social change.* Westport, CT: Bergin & Garvey.

Wilkinson, D. (1987). Ethnicity. In M. B. Sussman & S. K. Steinmetz (Eds.), *Handbook of marriage and the family* (pp. 183– 210). New York: Plenum.

Williams, N. (1990). *The Mexican American family: Transition and change.* Dix Hills, NY: General Hall.

Wilson, W. J. (1980). *The declining significance of race: Blacks and changing American institutions.* Chicago: University of Chicago Press.

Wilson, W. J. (1987). *The truly disadvantaged: The inner city, the underclass, and public policy.* Chicago: University of Chicago Press.

Wilson, W. J. (1996). *When work disappears: The world of the new urban poor.* New York: Knopf.

Wilson, W. J., & Neckerman, K. M. (1986). Poverty and family structure: The widening gap between evidence and public policy issues. In S. H. Danzinger & D. H. Weinberg (Eds.), *Fighting poverty: What works and what doesn't* (pp. 232–259). Cambridge, MA: Harvard University Press.

Wojtkiewicz, R. A., McLanahan, S. S., & Garfinkel, I. (1990). The growth of families headed by women: 1950–1980. *Demography, 27*(1), 19–20.

Wong, B. (1985). Family, kinship, and ethnic identity of the Chinese in New York City, with comparative remarks on the Chinese in Lima, Peru and Manila, Philippines. *Journal of Comparative Family Studies, 2,* 231–254.

Wong, M. G. (1988). The Chinese American family. In C. H. Mindel, R. W. Habenstein, & R. Wright, Jr. (Eds.), *Ethnic families in America: Patterns and variations* (3rd ed., pp. 230–257). New York: Elsevier.

Wood, R. G. (1995). Marriage rates and marriageable men: A test of the Wilson hypothesis. *The Journal of Human Resources, 30*(1), 163–193.

CHAPTER 6

The Future of Families

Barbara H. Settles

Introduction

The purpose of this chapter is to examine ideas about families in the future from the viewpoints of both what is likely and what may be possible. Families are shaped by the legacies of their past, the currencies of the moment, and their theories of the future. They live with the outcomes of past decisions and commitments and have long-term investments in the future. The roles that families have in shaping the greater destinies of the society as a whole are often acknowledged in the various political uses of family as a concept and references to family values. The use of family as a building block of social order is another indication of its potential influence. However, in most studies of families or family policy the families themselves are treated as a dependent variable affected by greater social and economic forces. Therefore, families are not seen as even an interactive variable. In contrast, this chapter examines how families may influence outcomes in the larger social context, relevant to their own lives. Perception is itself a powerful force both in behavior and in forming future perceptions. Beliefs held about the future are important determinants of outcomes. To make a plan may increase its probable likelihood of happening. To care about the future for as yet unborn generations is a particularly familistic outlook.

The variety of current family lifestyles is seen in both historical and present cultural themes. Current issues that affect prediction for the future are (1) the impact of technological change, (2) the visions that we have developed of the future, (3) the incomplete integration of new technologies and concepts into current societies, (4) the incomplete and unsophisticated understanding of the past as an influence on today's and tomorrow's family choices, and (5) the inability and lack of opportunity of individuals to separate their destiny from that of their families.

In this chapter, I will discuss the difficulties of assessing the potential for changing the aspects about the ways families are defined within the framework of some of the common paradigms about the present and future. Next, the future as the setting for substantive areas of family life is considered. The potentials for change, imagination, ideologies, invention, and technological and demographic facts that are played out over time are discussed and contrasted with the prevalence and durability of family types and individual lifestyles, primarily from the American perspective. Family dynamics, in the areas of intimacy, involvement, and conflict, are discussed for potential change in relationships and future orientations.

Futuristic literature is helpful in forming a critique of current practice, but it is not the only tool for prediction and articulation of trends. The task for this chapter is defined as extracting from a variety of sources some of the more relevant ideas and issues that will be shaping the future for families instead of just being limited to the review of the literature of the future of the family.

Theory-building and model development have been important efforts in family science in recent years. The utility of general family theory to long-term planning and decision-making models has been central to the ideas presented in this chapter. Development of a model to include choice in planning and decision making for individual and family futures is included in this chapter. I conclude this chapter with my own positive assessment of the future and durability of families. The family is a source of action that will change to provide for its members.

Barbara H. Settles • Individual and Family Studies, University of Delaware, Newark, Delaware 19716.

Handbook of Marriage and the Family, 2nd edition, edited by Marvin Sussman, Suzanne K. Steinmetz, and Gary W. Peterson. Plenum Press, New York, 1999.

Aspects of Defining the Family Now and for the Future

The struggles over definition of family for theory, research, practice, and social policy have become more heated in recent years. No longer can the definition be thought of as a student or scholarly exercise of no particular interest to those outside the field of family science. Instead, it is a matter for grave concern in people's everyday lives and in the benefits given and limits developed around the concept of family. Several approaches to definition are suggestive of the range and force of some of the available ideas that are driving policy debates. They are of special interest to families because these concepts will be incorporated into family policies, programs, and opportunities that will be faced in their future. The choice of definitions and criteria for evaluating families is a highly political decision both in the greater society and within family science. Several of these definitions were explored in Settles (1987); however, more have emerged as important in scholarship (Settles, Sussman, Trost, & Levin, in press) and political discourse. The many ways of defining the family suggest different outcomes in futurist speculations. A few of these perspectives illustrate this point.

Ideological Abstraction. Definitions based on ideological abstractions have considerable power in social movements. Traditional definitions are being used by the pro-family coalitions in America and by religious groups throughout the world to promote more restrictive family public policy for a single approved type of family. A more clearly articulated statement of egalitarian family organization could have a similar utility for the women's movement. Wisensale (1991), in reviewing the ways the major political think tanks address family issues, notes that the line between "research and political lobbying is increasingly blurred" (p. 206). Conservative groups have become more active and liberal groups have suffered decreased funding and influence. Other family definitions may become important in shaping social change to the extent an ideology could be framed and promoted to sympathetic audiences.

Romantic Image. Romanticizing families continues to have great impact. Although this view is generally rejected in family and women's studies literature and teaching, the fact that media must be countered suggests a tenacity in the concept. Because romantic ideas seem not to be important other than as entertainment, their influence on political struggles may be underestimated. The future of a romantic view of a family is likely to continue to be emphasized by advertising and individuals because it simplifies the complexity of life for the moment. It is not appropriate for scholars and educators to allow these images to shape their vision and programs (Arcus, 1992).

Household. Most of our large data files on families really reflect data collection at the household level. This overlap is particularly troublesome when international and intercultural comparisons are being made (Kain, 1993). For some purposes the household is the relevant unit. Economic and social role flexibility is best examined in terms of household maintenance, household tasks, and expenditures shared within a living space. Analysis of data on homemaking assumes this overlap is appropriate for analytic purposes. However, blended families and other families that have permeable boundaries may not be captured accurately in a household survey. Similarly, being homeless is destructive to maintaining family because the interventions to assist do not restore a home and housing to the family as a group (Dail, 1993). Defining a lifestyle, a status, and a way of life through housing (Axelson & Dail, 1988) is linked to defining boundaries and privacy and establishing spheres of responsibility and influence. When one is unable to maintain the preferred household arrangement family relationships are altered as well.

Comparative and Cross-National Views. There are usually detailed examinations of types of families by number of spouses of each sex, locale of residence of the generations, and functions performed in the family in the classic textbook cross-cultural comparisons of family life. A typology of classification is often made and some evaluation is given of the practical and long-term effect of societies emphasizing one type of family over another (Ingoldsby, 1995; Stanton, 1995). New concepts would be helpful in prospective family research and practice in an ever more linked international scene. Comparative study and rapid social change requires knowledge be less parochial when immigration, employment, and technological communication create a worldwide mix of cultural and familial heritage. Language differences intensify difficulties in clear communication and comparability. Shared meanings about family cross-culturally are fundamental to understanding families and trends for the future.

Process. Attention to definitions based on process have become important both for research and for therapeutic practice. Since Burgess and Locke (1945, 1953) presented the rationale of a contemporary "modern" family based on companionship, the interest has shifted to analyzing how such a family may operate. Families are strategic hunting grounds for potentially rich relationships. In contrast to work, school, and leisure settings, where temporary relationships and direct exchange are built into the institutions, families provide an opportunity for stability and indirect exchange as normative options. When families break up these ties, those memories and moments still influence current relationships. Many of the formerly married have contact and turn to each other for response (Kitson & Morgan, 1990). Having fewer people in whom we have higher investments sets the stage for crisis when such relationships are attenuated or severed. The importance of focusing on the content of relationships is critical. All process is not equal. Not every unit that would be a family is committed to wholesome and fair process.

Networks. Both kin and friends are receiving scholarly attention and public policy notice. Divorce and remarriage are adding great complexity to the potential for kin and family support systems (Kent, 1980). Grandparents' rights are still limited, and those rights that have been established often are not implemented (Kivett, 1991; Purnell & Bagby, 1993). The price paid in loss of continuity may be regained in the intimacy and specialty of such relationships. Connectedness and emotional support do not happen in the moment of creating the new unit (Pill, 1990). Coleman and Ganong (1990) note a neglect of the complexity of stepfamilies in much of the research. Maintaining networks over the life course and family development is more formidable in today's demographic outlook.

Set of Dyads. Trost (in press) has suggested that families are built from a number of dyads with the specific pairs open to change and movement over time. The history of overlap of these dyadic relationships at different points in the life course could also be related to such concepts as the familial career or family life cycle. As White (1991) has noted, the life cycle of families can be addressed as things really happen, if one develops a notation for tracing the boundaries of families over time and interaction. Trost's notion has added utility when one is attempting to describe families in different places, times, and contexts and in making some comparisons. Many years ago, Bossard and Boll (1956) pointed out that families are not simply additive, but geometric in complexity when they are expanded by the addition of member(s). The complex computer-based data analysis techniques make dyadic analysis possible and are equally useful for qualitative analysis where the specific dynamics of each dyad can be elaborated.

Use of Personal Experience. A relatively new approach to family definition is emphasizing the personal experience. The new definition includes how the individual conceptualizes the future of the group that he or she sees as family and how that is communicated among those who share some of the same views. The power of this approach illuminates talk about family and the person's perspective in shaping their family relationships. It does not focus on the objective reality but upon the controlling reality. Levin and Trost (1992a) describe a set of techniques for use in the classroom to illustrate this approach. Personal definitions enhance the diversity that is fundamental to having a multicultural, open educational process (Abbey, Brindis, & Casas, 1990). In research work with younger adolescents, Liprie (1993) used a simple personal perspective question listing family ties within the household. In today's schools, the pressure of ideologies in the community and the requirements for parental permission for research studies have limited research on families with students. The approach of allowing the student to define his or her family was quite helpful in gaining cooperative and forthcoming responses in today's politically charged atmosphere. Personalizing the family to the extreme can mean that it is only a structure in one's thoughts, and not a functioning group at all. The construction of this personal reality is under constant revision. Sampling opinions over time and changing perception might explore the dynamics of the family moving through time and space.

Social Construction. Social construction is based on whether a group functioning as a family negotiates the interchange between the "family" members and the greater society to be recognized. Gubrium and Holstein (1990) illustrate how social workers' and case managers' discussion of their clients affected the potentiality for the family to be helped. Frequently, the decision to place a child away from his home is made after the team reaches a consensus that the family is not behaving as a family. Indicators such as housekeeping, food availability and preparation, underlying order, personal grooming of the children and parents, and indicators of marginal behavior like drug or alcohol use are discussed as measures of and prerequisites to family functioning.

Complex families illustrate other aspects of negotiation and construction. Blended families have many points of negotiation for family status especially when they do not have custody or have not cross-adopted children (Duran-Aydintug & Ihinger-Tallman, 1995). From the perspective of lesbian couples, there is concern about discrimination for children raised in their homes and lack of social and community support (Koepke, Hare, & Moran, 1992; Macklin & Van Antwerp, 1996). Families are required to have skills in representing themselves as families when they face institutions.

Eligibility to receive difficult and stressful major medical treatments may be influenced by the availability of family members to provide support both at the hospital and later at home. The patient's access is jeopardized if the immediate family is unable to perform these tasks. Another medical setting requiring negotiation is the visitors' list for intensive care. People in alternative family forms have difficulty in dealing with the conventional family ties that may evidence themselves at this time. An estranged sister may take precedence over a cohabitant. Families will need new ways of presenting themselves and advocating for their members in the future.

Legal Entity. Family law within the nation differs markedly at the state levels. Regulation of the family through legal definitions and processes is an important source of structure. Fineman (1994) notes, "while one may 'chose' to live out side the conventional norms, one does not escape them totally" (p. 28). The concept of private family includes a carryover from the relationship of property law to husband domination of wife. It creates problems in addressing such issues as domestic violence (Olsen, 1994; Schneider, 1994).

In the study of inheritance, Sussman (1983) found much symmetry between individuals' desires for transfers to follow legal guidance in the state laws. However, in many areas, such as visitation, child support, and filial responsibility, legal regulations vary from state to state. The "bench law" of different judges provides wide latitude in the interpretation of the laws regarding family. Questions of equity are more difficult to resolve, as the population has become more mobile, crossing state and national lines. While states have the primary scope in family law, Erickson and Babcock (1995) suggest that the entry of supreme court findings and the spread of similar reforms in the states is leading to a nationalization of family law. Legal rights may conflict when extended families are located in different jurisdictions. Legal standing for the person, as a potential guardian of children's or elder's care, is limited by whether their residence is within the jurisdiction of a particular court. Local judges and state legislators are reluctant to grant custody and financial guardianship of children and elders to those outside their community.

Legal definition of family and familial rights and responsibilities are complex internationally. Reforms in Europe have been undertaken in divorce, by easing the grounds and procedures, although France still has more lengthy process and considerable judicial control (Fine & Fine, 1994). While we have turned to Europe for models of pro-family child-friendly policy (Kamerman & Kahn, 1991), the European Community is becoming aware of how much economic unity brings the questions of families' legal, residential, and citizenship status to the fore (Dumon & Nuelant, 1994).

Legal foundations of family, now a complex of local, state, national, and international codes and enforcement, create confusion and controversy. The increasingly mobile national and world population is greatly inconvenienced and confused by the localized legal regulation of family matters. However, there is great reluctance for governments to move toward a more integrated legal system because of local cultural differences and perceived local individual needs.

Unit of Treatment. The family, as a unit of treatment, is the "cornerstone" of the professional conceptualization of family. In Rosenblatt's (1994) critical analysis of common theory in therapy, he shows that examining thinking and imagining about families can help show what is obscured by a metaphor. Techniques may not relate well to either treatment or outcome, but in the future, it may be possible to evaluate these approaches for relative quality. Gubrium and Holstein (1993) note family therapy is moving away from negatively described family dynamics that are to be treated by the therapist to a conception that the therapist is in conversation with the family constructing solutions. Sporakowski (1992) sees the future challenges to the therapist in being inclusive and evolving with families to emphasize wellness. Sprenkle and Piercy (1991) suggest therapists should be building on the "needs and strengths" of families and resisting "negative narratives" about the state of families in order to be useful to families (p. 407). Fish and Osborn (1992) found practicing therapists in agreement with this perspective of inclusiveness and supportiveness.

Some "family" problems may later be understood more fundamentally as medical, individual, or social. Many physical and mental illnesses formerly thought of psychosomatic or familial based are no longer treated as such. Nichols and Schwartz (1991) suggest in coping situations "the family's structural flaws are construed as the *result* of rather than the *cause* of the presenting problem" (p. 491). Well-accepted studies of children held in psychosomatic patterns because of excessive family involvement and difficulty with conflict management are currently being reassessed (Doherty & Baptiste, 1993). Helping the family to adjust to the medical therapies will continue to be necessary even if the problems are redefined.

Last Resort. Both conservative political groups and more liberal professional social-welfare service groups agree that a residual or last resort role for families is critical in understanding individuals and their resources. A person with few family ties may become lost in the institutional settings that replace the family support; hence, he or she may be or remain institutionalized long after the need has passed because no advocate asks questions (Goldman, 1993; Shanas & Sussman, 1981). Stein (1981) suggested that the crucial issue may not be marriage versus singlehood, but the strength of the support network. The problems that AIDS patients have had in getting their supportive relationships recognized as family for the purposes of caregiving and decision making is but one illustration of the many challenges in arranging for help when there is need (Anderson, 1989; Tibler, Walker, & Rolland, 1989).

The availability of family members and the concern and care of extended kin are crucial to the life course of elderly people. One can outlive one's family or caregiver. The younger person in the caregiving dyad may only be younger in relationship to the elder, but may qualify as an older citizen also in need of care or support (Sanborn & Bould, 1991). Threats to the Social Security and Medicare system, awareness of the fragility of private pension arrangements, coupled with trends in longevity, emphasize the salient role of the family in making its own arrangements to deal with the life course (Cooney, 1993; Doolittle & Wiggens, 1993; Foulke, Alford-Cooper, & Butler, 1993). Whether the policy debate about caregiving becomes one of intergenerational conflict or integration depends on how the arguments are framed and how the family is understood (Hirshorn, 1991; Sussman, 1991). There is a possibility of overwhelming systems and individuals. Families may be destroyed by those who would give to the family everything that the rest of society cannot manage.

The Future of Family Definitions

The fluid quality of the word "family" makes it especially useful for political propagandizing and as a residual variable in societal studies. It is not likely that specifying what is meant by family will progress rapidly. Consensus would be costly for politicians and improbable for scholars. Scholarly interpretation and analysis may be used to shape the opportunities for families. Research may have the consequence of limiting the recognition, support, and access to the goods and benefits of the society for families. Attention is directed to Settles and colleagues (in press), which details developments in the discourse on families and the theoretical understanding of the concept of family.

The issues surrounding both the scientific and practical implications of the choices of the theoretical definitions of family are immensely important for the future of families. What is known about the dynamics of families and treatment of perceived problems of families is highly influenced by the theoretical lens through which they are viewed. Families will be acknowledged or forgotten as they are accorded family status. Evaluation of the health and well-being of family is influenced by what is seen as family. The presence, or lack, of social support for individuals is found in the context of whether those whom the individual sees as family are also recognized by the larger society and other institutions.

The Concept of the Future and Its Relationship to Families over Time

Imagination and Images

The future is a dry and uninteresting place because of the failure in the content of our imagination (Ornaurer, Wiberg, Sicinski, & Galtung, 1976). We see it as only more of what we have now or the loss of everything we hold dear. The storylines shown on television or in movies are borrowed either from Greek myth or medieval legend. These images may be as good as any, for they have durability. Space fiction and games such as Traveler and other fantasy role-playing games integrate the images taken from the real and the fictional past and give them new life. King Arthur's legendary sword in the stone becomes a laser, while the dragon becomes hundreds of specialized characters. Thus, we tend to expect new technology to support old ideology.

The ideological and theoretical changes of the twentieth century have been as interesting as the accompanying technological innovations. The technological inventions are the material evidence of changed thinking and innovations. The thinking is far more revolutionary because the view of the reality and the possibilities is altered so completely. Physics has given us arguments about the universe that shake our sense of time, physical space, and knowledge. Biology has begun to specify the mechanics of the life process at a much more fundamental level, which leaves us wondering what is the "nature" we have so often used as an explanation for our ideology. Cybernetics has overloaded our sense of what must be included in our systematic examination of knowledge. Even architecture has become an expression not just of technological possibilities but also of the ideology in fashion at the moment. Images of future cities and environments emphasize the manufactured interior, not the vista. Buckminster Fuller's geodesic dome is an expression not just of the technological possibilities, but also of the controlled environment as an ideal.

If there is an increasingly responsive world, where products can be made to order by computer and fitted to individual requirements and where resources are allocated without waste and confusion, then resources available to humanity may expand as needed (Rosen, 1982; Toffler, 1980). Current day families' investments in a worldview may predict their approaches to making choices and accepting strategies. Families today have as windows to the future the media, government, religious organizations, political and social organizations, and informal social networks. Their ability to see opportunity is sometimes overwhelmed by their concern about the problems change makes in life. Choices are desired, but consequences are seen as uncertain (Groller, 1990).

The twentieth-century fantasy of the future has invested heavily in technological innovation, rapid duplication and dissemination of information, symmetry of solutions, and reduction of human energy by replacement with other energy sources. The classic futurist description places a forever young population on a moving sidewalk dressed in sequined long underwear with a communicator-light ray gadget in hand. Pickett (1977) suggested that these artists' conceptions may indeed be sharper and closer to the truth than some of the more academic models. He sees utopian thinking as rediscovering personal alternatives that have always existed. A vision of the future and its incorporation into the meaning of everyday life is part of the process of shaping the future. Individuals and their families look to their futures in the context of societal values, institutions, opportunities, and constraints. Larger institutions control resources and incentives and constrain the choices at the micro level of the family. Families are active participants who "respond to, rework, or reframe external constraints and opportunities" (Moen & Firebaugh, 1993, p. 22). Community resources are essentially latent until a family accesses them or until the community intervenes in the family's life. What services, environmental opportunities, and networks are present may be quite different from the family's knowledge and perception of their availability (Pilisuk & Parks, 1983; Unger & Powell, 1980).

A community is defined as an interactive process, and whether or not a locality is considered a community may vary as different actors see it. The access that families have to regional, national, and even international resources is highly variable (Settles, 1990). The boundary between family and the surrounding economic and societal institutions is negotiated continuously (Schwartzman, 1982). Individuals and families have partial control over social and economic policies and programs that they depend on for long-term resources and support. They must deal with many elements outside their manageable interest, either by trying to build relationships, contracts, and expectations or by developing alternatives and fallback positions. Increased opportunity for nondiscrimination in jobs, housing, education, public accommodation, and mobility are social changes that have opened choices and allowed more families to shape their own lives (Bolger, Moen, & Downey, 1985).

Progress and Change

The idea of progress itself has its own history and is linked to a view of time as linear, flowing, and cumulative (Nisbit, 1980). Historical accuracy can help us to avoid trying to explain trends that never were and can keep us from seeing present and future situations as stranger than they are. Hare-

ven (1994) notes that not only were there no ideal three-generation families as a rule in America, but also states, "Nor was there a 'golden age' in the family relations of older people in the American or European past" (p. 442). Currently, we must deal with time as a variable that can be shaped and with a growing sense that progress is not inevitable.

Change in any society includes a process of innovation, adoption, and conservative challenge. When the transitions are rapid, these processes overlap, and predicting the future is especially difficult. Incorporating the new reality of technological change into the philosophical foundations of thought is often much slower than adopting the technology itself. Bell's (1973) thesis of a postindustrial society suggested that the society is moving is away from the family as the dominant power and the direct access system. However, the family still has considerable influence on the child's opportunities to utilize other access routes.

Individual families, who are on the front edge of social change, are often adaptable and flexible. In contrast to this flexibility, the family in philosophy and religion is usually seen as conservative and traditional (Elshtain, 1982, 1990). Rights, duties, and mobility opportunities are especially important in predicting family change. Equity, as the ideal of the twentieth century, has made great progress in infiltrating ideology and practice. The opinions expressed in public polls suggest that such issues as equal pay, equal opportunity, personal credit, and freedom to choose or reject childbearing are established American values for men and women and in all racial groups (Harris & Associates, 1981; Thornton, 1989; Yankelovich, 1981).

The industrial revolution's effect had been stabilized for most of the twentieth century by the individual's sense of commitment to an industry, a corporation, a profession, or trade (Hanks, 1990). However, in the worldwide economy, it is as simple now to move capital, through incentives, as it was to move labor, through immigration. Families are uncertain that loyalty in the workplace and extra effort will assure them their futures (Piotrakowski, Rapoport, & Rapoport, 1987; Voydanoff, 1990). Billingsley (1988) suggests that the employment and opportunity structures of new industrial technology have had a particularly negative impact on black families. More recently middle managers and seasoned professionals have been affected by downsizing and reorganizing workplaces.

In response to this uncertainty, families have made major changes in workforce participation. More adults and now youth have entered or reentered the workplace and paid employment. In more than half of the U.S. families in the workforce, the wife is employed (Glick, 1989b). Employment is the central foundation for the quality of life and financial preparedness for most families (Kilty & Behling,

1986) and dual employment creates discretionary resources and potential choices (Van Name, 1991). Working or middle-class lifestyle for many families depends on these jobs. In poor families maintaining the households is central to women's work.

Although much of the developed world augments and organizes the resources for health and retirement through state programs, in the United States these benefits are firmly linked to specific employers. Employers have great power over the long-term prospects of families, and a medical problem can mean limited employment mobility (Rock, 1992). Employment of women has helped maintain family economic strength as the Baby Boom generation matured, but there are disturbing trends toward lower-paid, part-time jobs and fewer middle managers (Russell, 1982). Employers use fewer full-time or permanent employees and more part-time, contract, or temporary employees who do not create overhead benefit expenses (Winnick, 1988).

Incentives for early retirement have caused disruptions in family plans and personal careers (Hanks, 1990). The impact of the workplace on family life and uncertainty of employment has concerned families across the nation (Cornfield, 1990; Voydanoff, 1990). Legal changes, such as affirmative action, have had some impact in recent years in moderating the work environment and policies. As these policies have been attacked, the likelihood is reduced that minority families and women can depend upon access to the workplace (Lemann, 1995).

Balancing work and family demands and developing workplace policies that are friendly to families both in the short and long term are of interest to both men and women (Menaghan & Parcel, 1990; Mortimer & London, 1984; Piotrakowski et al., 1987; Spitze, 1990). Although resources created by individuals and families outside of wage and salary work are important alternatives and supplements to the larger economic picture, nonwage productivity in the home has not been carefully examined and in our societal bookkeeping is not given a value (Culley, Settles, & Van Name, 1976; Vanek, 1974; Walker & Woods, 1976). Most dual-employment families report rather high amounts of household labor being performed (Demo & Acock, 1993). Simple ideas of continued progress do not capture what families are experiencing as they deal with macro-level changes in everyday life.

Pluralism versus Single Ideologies

In reviewing research on nontraditional family forms, Macklin (1980) saw continued pluralism and emphasis on individual choices as trends. Now in the 1990s, some scholars predict some return to earlier social structures and traditions.

Among the fastest growing religious groups in the Third World are those with more traditional doctrines on family structure and class/race status. Secular humanism and science are under attack by conservative religious groups in both the Western and the Eastern worlds.

Many Americans say that both biblical and evolutionary theories should be covered in public school classes on science, thereby equating information obtained by religious belief with information obtained by scientific examination. Legislative efforts to ensure this practice have not been effective, but scholars are concerned about the limits on academic decision making (Creationism, 1982). Other scholars and political figures believe that the momentum for change is so strong that the organized groups working for equity in family policy will continue the fight (Aldous & Dumon, 1980).

Cohabitation has become more common and more accepted in the past 3 decades as a form of family, not just as a household. Axinn & Thornton (1993) suggest that the interaction about cohabitation between parents and young adult children may run in both directions about cohabitation and that the shaping of behavior and attitudes concerning cohabitation continues over time. Cohabitation has moved from an innovation to a commonplace event across the life course. It may be impossible for those who have experienced freedom and equity to return to traditional forms and practices.

While there has been a lack of political support for diverse family forms, in actual practice there are many types of family and household structural arrangements. In examining the variety of family arrangements in the African American community, Staples (1994) discusses the "dissonance between Black family ideology and actual family arrangements" (p. 16). He focuses on structural conditions that limit the achievement of the idealized form. Scott (1994) sees the way some young women adapt to the lack of good marriage opportunities and social structural situations by sharing married men as a type of polygamy in the black community. McAdoo (1992), in exploring the situation for a sample of African American single mothers, found high levels of stress, but also many different configurations of support patterns and histories. This difference between actual practice and public discourse may continue, and diverse family forms may have an uncertain future.

Invention and Innovation

Technologies are always being developed. At some times and places the populous becomes aware that changes are happening rapidly, and they must find ways to accommodate the changes. At other times generations may not handle new technologies on a daily basis or may feel great stability in both the techniques and meanings associated with the accepted technologies. Marciano (1993) states that "All cultures possess technologies," but she notes that the use and meaning of the technology are a dialogue of valuing and questioning and recognizing that the adoption of "change is piecemeal and tends to serve first those who already have power" (pp. 126, 133).

Although a writer in an article on the future of the family cannot anticipate the nature of continued invention and innovation in the technical world, surely new technologies will invalidate old adjustments and will require further change in individual and family lifestyles. Some families will incorporate changes into their relationships and lifestyles. Others may not be able to accommodate to these stresses with appropriate changes and may want to hold on to old ways and relationships that will cause the family to regroup in different configurations. Family stability in the face of these technological changes can be achieved by adapting to the innovations.

In 1980, Toffler emphasized that computer wizardry, video display, telephone interface, and automation could create opportunities for flexibility in the workplace and could return to the home many tasks currently carried on outside. The opportunity to work in one's home may appeal to men who are not expected to balance the demands and conflicts of both homemaking and career, but it may be viewed by women as a narrowing of the choice between work inside or outside the home. The virtual workplace that does not require an office and has no boundaries of time or place has become a reality for many workers. One can order from the catalog in the middle of the night or talk to one's computer support consultant half way across the country to rebuild his or her machine. A major international network can be run by a family from their home as easily as from a large office building.

Over the years, differences in gender access and preferences have been observed in home-based technology and education for high technology. Coleman (1994) saw isolation as a problem with home-based computers for both men and women. Gates (1995) suggests that educators need to pay attention to gender imbalance in access and experience. Constantine (1995) is urging the program developers of today to work for the ordinary consumer by simplifying the interface and carefully choosing the analogs and models from life to work well in the mind. The range and availability of reasonably priced, friendly desktop publishing and data management tools have put the controllable interest in the hands of many individual entrepreneurs and consultants.

Much as the Guttenberg press with movable type overturned traditional power bases in Renaissance Europe, this new access to quality publication may also change power distribution. The Internet opens to the public an international set of direct communication techniques at relatively low or no direct cost. The forces of censorship of information regulation are undone. As Gates (1995) maintains, "The major benefit of the PC revolution has been the way it has empowered people" (p. 111).

Another promising area of continued innovation is found in biological research and health care applications, which bring even more areas of life into the realm of choice and decision making (Doolittle & Wiggens, 1993; Pines, 1976). Intervention in the early development of the fetus, the prevention of anomalies, and the understanding of brain function all appear to be within this generation's grasp. The family is faced with major changes in responsibility for participation in these biological and medical opportunities. Providing informed consent for dependents such as elders and children is a burden for family members when consequences are as yet unknown (Crutchfield, 1981a,b; Rodman, 1981; Zimmerman, 1981). Legal relationships, responsibility, and control of "minor" children are controversial policies. Basic questions about the beginning or cessation of life have not yet been thoroughly addressed by philosophy or religion in light of the current technical innovations that stretch the boundary of life itself.

In Western religious traditions, medical decisions made by families and practitioners have been guided by the principle that "reasonable means" should be used to preserve life and functioning. This concept has not adapted well to the changing technological situation. One year's dramatic intervention is next year's standard practice. The expectation of new scientific breakthroughs allows families to hold on to hope for a possible discovery and a new miracle. Simple necessities such as good food, shelter, and a healthy emotional climate have not been available for all persons in society, but kidney machines and open heart surgery are potentially available. Families cannot know all the consequences of their decisions; therefore, when their decisions are evaluated later in terms of newly discovered knowledge, they may experience unwarranted guilt or remorse.

Information processing and biological understanding are relatively well-known technical areas that have affected families. Families' predictions of the future are limited by at least two factors: their willingness to use an innovation and the adoption by society of the infrastructure to support changing technologies and theories.

Family Substitutes, Alternatives, and Varieties

The literature on the family in the 1970s focused on flexible definitions of familial ties and studying the varieties of personal lifestyles that had familial qualities. Textbooks devoted chapters to alternative lifestyles, single parents, living-together arrangements, communal groups, and group marriages. A greater diversity of the population was presented as representing normal family life. It was more important to view the arrangements as alternatives rather than as problems (Sussman, 1980). The numbers of cohabitants and single-headed and blended families have continued to increase, but the lack of acceptance of these common family forms is recognized in the contemporary family policy debate.

Reports on many planned alternatives to classical families became available, and evaluation of the outcomes and patterns of group marriage (Constantine, 1973), communal life (Berger, 1981), and utopian or reform communities (Kephart, 1976, 1982) could be made. At the same time the likelihood of major shifts in personal living arrangements is quite modest as the turn of the century approaches. The toleration of these small minorities, when openly recognized, is less certain now than formerly when these ideas were seen as signals indicating positive social change. However, documentation of other kinds of diversity in meeting of familial needs is far more common and suggests that the family is a more flexible concept than public discourse usually allows.

Three categories of substitutes, varieties, and alternatives are presented to illustrate this range of alternatives: (1) deinstitutionalization versus institutionalization, (2) blood versus emotional ties, and (3) regional and ethnic subcultural variations versus national cultural uniformity.

Deinstitutionalization versus Institutional Substitutes. The rise of the institutional household for living arrangements and as a substitute for the family seems to have reached its crest. However, in this area of criminal justice and perhaps for children at risk due to poverty or welfare status, there has been a rebound of plans to build institutions. Community- and family-based alternatives are more effective than orphanages and long-term-care hospitals for the disabled, the deficient, and the mentally and physically ill (Cook & Wright, 1995). Advocacy of these excellent programs in child and family welfare by the professional family service community has not been as effective as the evaluation data would support (Woolf, 1990). When the institutional household in the early twentieth century grew in complexity and specialization, it was seen as part of modernization.

The problems that these institutions created outweighed their benefits. The creation of smaller, less complex, and less specialized facilities that are mainstreamed into ordinary residential neighborhoods has been found to be beneficial to those in need of care and to provide opportunity for families to maintain connections. Small-scale group homes are particularly useful when ongoing treatment is needed (Woolf,

1990). For adolescents some form of congregate care may be more practical than foster care even though more expensive (Van Biema, 1994). Although fewer young mothers terminate parental rights and seek adoption at their child's birth, the use of foster care with children under 1 year of age is the fastest-growing category of foster care (Young, 1994). As the child grows older, the pile-up of stress and failure of informal support systems to handle problems leads to the need for foster care that is treatment oriented and has a continuum of care (Woolf, 1990).

Cost-benefit analysis has proven favorable to these smaller-scale programs compared to large institutions, although the cost of residential group care is still about $36,500, compared to about $4800 in foster care homes or $2644 in welfare support, according to the Child Welfare League of America (Van Biema, 1994). Even in institutional settings, least restrictive alternatives have been implemented. This trend toward downscaling institutions and turning to in-home care significantly affects family lifestyles and choices. There has been investment in policy implementation to preserve or reunite families who are problematic (Theiman & Dail, 1992). In theory these programs should be both cost effective and reduce long-term dependency and placement. Evaluation of these programs has proven to be difficult and elusive. Traditional control groups and comparisons are not easy to create. Methods of measuring at-risk to placement status and family functioning over time have not developed into comparable databases across programs and regions (Theiman & Dail, 1992). When a mistake is made in estimating risk, the likelihood of injuring or even murdering a child or spouse is so grave that the consequences do not fit into a conventional cost-benefit analysis. One real case of abuse and murder on the cover of a national magazine, no matter what the circumstances, puts the program of family preservation in jeopardy (Van Biema, 1995).

The often overworked and undertrained case workers are making tough calls and may not have available the full range of model preservation and prevention services suggested for the child welfare system (Hornblower, 1995; Smolowe, 1995). There have been some calls to bring back orphanages and other formal institutional solutions to social programs. The political rationale seems to advocate breaking up the welfare system's support of "undesirable" family forms, especially among teenagers who have had children. The evaluation of such programs would have different assumptions about the appropriate values and the benefits in the family service sector since the moneys would be directed to private contractors.

Quality care in institutional settings is evaluated by comparison to home and family care alternatives. Professional and expert-based institutional care that characterized health care in the earlier years of the twentieth century has been challenged by both by a declining confidence in institutions and the dynamic process of long-term care and cost over the life course (Pescosolido & Kronenfeld, 1995). Transitions back and forth between the formal care system and informal care are mediated by a number of social processes, perceptions, and information sources (Haug, 1990).

One of the major forces in promoting deinstitutionalization in medicine has been the availability of drugs that control "acting-out" and aggressive behavior and medical regimens adapted to the less trained paraprofessional's or lay person's skills (Bassick & Gerson, 1978). According to Cook and Wright (1995), "Large numbers of persons with mental illness who formerly lived in state-funded psychiatric institutions now reside in the community for most of their life times, interspersed with short hospital stays. The lives they lead in unwelcoming and/or threatening neighborhoods are often difficult, stressful and unrewarding" (p. 97). The widespread use of mood and anxiety drugs on an outpatient basis has removed them from hospitalization. Counselor supervision is lacking for many who remain dysfunctional (Begley, 1994). The failure of the communities to develop support systems for day-to-day care leaves many individuals with few people they can count upon as they proceed through a mental illness treatment over time (Pescosolido & Kronenfeld, 1995).

The supporting technology for smaller care facilities and home-care alternatives is characterized by throwaway syringes, premeasured medicine, paper goods, disposal thermometer tips, and prepared dietetic foods. An important part of the medical personnel's job is training of family members to provide medical care in the home that was previously only found in hospitals and clinics. Most medical treatments and care can be adapted for an in-home alternative. Even chemotherapy and kidney dialysis appear to be adaptable to home care. Outpatient and clinic treatment and surgery have become commonplace for problems that once required days of hospitalization. As home computers and assessment devices become more common and more cost effective, further decentralization and long distance supervision of substitute care may be possible. New models of professional and patient interaction are needed as "patients and their families will be required to assume a participatory role in their health care across the life span" (Cogswell, 1988, p. 254).

Some change is driven by findings that indicate lower risk factors at home and improved care and support, but transfer of care is a cost-control initiative by insurance companies and workplaces. Several state legislatures have regulated dismissal time for mothers giving birth because of concerns about endangering child and mother outcomes. In the case of outpatient surgery the dismissal may come very quickly because of advances in anesthesia and monitoring,

if the patient has transportation available. In the case of a woman having a mastectomy, there is not sufficient inquiry over "whether there is anyone to care for the women following surgery" (Pescosolido & Kronenfeld, 1995, p. 20).

Understanding the patterns and content of intergenerational relationships prior to needs for care may be helpful (Aldous & Klein, 1991). Choices made by both the younger and older generations may affect involvement. Geographic distance does attenuate contact. Motivations to care for parents may be found in the relationships and perceptions held across adult life and may be different by gender on the relative importance of affection and expectations (Silverstein, Parrott, & Bengston, 1995). Hirsch (1993), in a small qualitative study of men who were direct caregivers, found that the caregivers saw caregiving as stemming from affection. The skills of counseling and diagnosing problems from a long distance are necessary for both generations. The fluid processes of care demands, elder preferences, and available resources suggest the utility of a decision-making analytic support group in the future. The many choices but limited resources of frail elderly in our society require a more sophisticated view of elder care alternatives and choices.

Within schools least restrictive options have brought a wide range of children together in common classrooms. Sheltered living arrangements have given many families the security of knowing their adult dependent "child" will be protected even as the parents age and die. For other dependent adults and special needs children the changes in institutional arrangements have opened a range of opportunities to deal with dependent care issues.

Several general problems with deinstitutionalization and least restrictive options have been identified that are not part of a political agenda: (1) role overload and the stereotyping of the homemaker as caregiver, (2) an extension of the dependency phase of the family life cycle, (3) failure to serve some individuals whose families reject the responsibility for special needs care, (4) conflict between family and institutional expectations, and (5) increased alternative costs to family members. The usual benefits include (1) improved individualized care of the individual in the family setting, (2) some economies in costs to larger social institutions and transfer from the government to the family of caregiving costs, and (3) greater family control of and responsibility for quality of life.

Institutionalization as a substitute for family support and care has continued to be seen as essential in criminal control, but it has fallen out of favor for the handicapped, the mentally ill, the elderly, and children. With the present medical and household technology, it has been assumed that these latter groups can be handled at home, usually by women. Policy makers have assumed that women can be encouraged to care for persons with special needs in the family setting. However, the resources and community support for this solution have not been forthcoming. Financial and emotional incentives are needed to alter the competition with the marketplace for women's time. The complexity of long-term planning and appropriate intervention in families over the life course remains a major challenge. The need for replanning and refocusing options as needs change and new approaches become available are important for elder care alternatives.

Blood versus Emotional Ties: Variations in Family Structure. Defining one's family as those people who function for one in familistic ways puts the emphasis on emotional and social support and networks. Recent theoretical discussion of family definition from the perspective of the individual has emphasized the fragility of blood and marital ties as fundamental definers of the functioning family (Levin & Trost, 1992b). However, in the legal arena there has been an intense scrutiny on blood and legal ties in determining custody, support, and responsibility.

Examining the genealogies of families is simpler because of computer software. Kinship charting itself has residual meaning in the American view of the family. When Alex Haley's (1976) romantic novel *Roots* took hold of America's imagination, part of the interest aroused was in individuals who had not functioned directly in their close family. The story's broad appeal and wide audience inspired action in searching for ties (Lieberson & Mikelson, 1995). Latent ties were thought to give meaning to today's experiences, and many resources are available to help individuals in this quest. The Church of Jesus Christ of the Latter Day Saints has assembled an immense library that has as its primary purpose searching for ties so that members may bring these ancestors into the church's system (Kephart, 1976, 1982). Local historical societies are making available their archives for computers searches and are teaching families how to assemble family records.

Although psychological theory and research have tended to emphasize the parent figure as most important, the current movement is toward identifying kin even when these kin have expressed the wish to be unknown. Adoption agencies are torn between their belief that ethically they owe clients of the past the confidentiality that they were promised and the reality of grown adoptees demanding to meet, to know, and to have records about their parents and other "lost kin" (Simpson, Timm, & McCubbin, 1981). Foster parents now commonly seek to adopt and to continue their ties with foster children despite being originally oriented toward acknowledging foster parenthood as a temporary tie. The termination of parent rights to free children for adoption is still a difficult process demanding great skill of agency workers and law-

yers, as public attitudes about permanently breaking blood ties are so negative. The primacy of blood ties is so strong that adoptive parents may indeed be troubled by social interaction that devalues adoption as second best or different or not a real bond (Miall, 1987).

Many alternatives to blood ties both in reproductive technologies and approaches to adoption are more common (Miall, 1995). In this last decade several legal cases have returned adopted children to blood parents. A high level of proof is required to substantiate informed consent by the putative fathers, as well as the mothers. Legal action is common due to confusion over surrogacy contracts, *in vitro* fertilization, artificial insemination, and the meaning of parenthood. In both the courts and the media, assumptions about confidentiality and commitment to severing rights are being examined.

Separated, divorced, never-married, and widowed single-parent homes may deal with relationships in a multitude of ways (Verazo & Hermon, 1980). They may become indebted in their families of orientation and bring grandparents into the household. Remarriage, cohabitation, and friendship patterns add to the complexity of the alternatives. Fictive kin, neighbors, and colleagues have become more important to many families as the need and utility for support networks has become identified.

Research on resources for the nuclear family has drawn attention to how these patterns of additional relationships can be encouraged and developed. Confusion over the functioning and meaning of emotional and kinship ties apparently will continue in the next few years. Tests in the courts and confrontations among vested interests are likely to become more frequent until a consensus is reached.

Regional and Ethnic Subcultural Variations versus National Cultural Uniformity. Ethnic and regional pride has reasserted itself both in America and in the world at large (Mendel & Habenstein, 1976). Fragmentation into smaller and more specific heritage groups has been encouraged both by scholarship and by public policy. Nationally, demands for representation are being solidified, and rationales and doctrines are being developed. Scholarship has encouraged a historic reexamination of earlier images and perceptions. The discovery of "unremembered" events, people, and data has enlarged the view of the past family as a part of one's subcultural and ethnic experience. Individual families have been encouraged to develop rituals and a greater expression of their relationship to older generations and distant cultural ties.

Among the indicators of these more positive attitudes toward cultural separatism has been the development of folk festivals, gourmet food magazines featuring ethnic foods, associations and organizations for ethnic groups, genealogical services, language instruction in so-called minor languages, and bilingualism in the schools (Naisbitt, 1982). The adoption of distinctive African American names for children has been an important innovation that has become more frequent in the past 25 years. Analyzing the linguistic structure of the names chosen suggests some continuity with the general American perceptions of appropriate gender endings for names (Lieberson & Mikelson, 1995). Some searches for a connection to past immigration have led young people to change their names back to more clearly identified forms of the name (e.g., authors Wallace to Wallachinsky, or actors Sheen to Estevez).

Native American, Hispanic, and black organizations have particularly demonstrated the power of identity to shape public policy toward families (Taylor, Chatters, Tucker, & Lewis, 1990; Vega, 1990). Nagel (1995) notes that the huge increase in people identified as American Indian cannot be accounted for by the usual explanations of population growth. She proposes that individual and collective identities are routinely revised and even invented and that ethnic renewal may build on political activism and pride. Ethnicity is the result of a process that continues to unfold (Yancey, Eriksen, & Juliani, 1976).

The major changes that these sectors of the population have made in access to American society and in tempering of public discrimination have been one of the most dramatic changes ever made in a few decades within any large country. These official changes have made a great deal of difference to many families in their interaction, their aspirations, and their actual quality of life. Negative stereotypes have been undermined, although many problems of discrimination remain untouched.

Maintaining separate cultural heritage, identity, and free access to a larger society presents a difficult problem of social balance. In many countries today, major conflicts are being fought in the streets over perceived inequities (e.g., in Southeast Asia, Ireland, Iran, South Africa, South and Central America, and the Middle East); less dramatic but as strongly felt differences appear in other countries (e.g., Canada, Belgium, India, and Pakistan). There are many possibilities for conflict in this country. A Mexican immigrant in the Southwest United States, a Haitian landing in Florida, or a Cuban or Vietnamese arriving in the Northeast is definitely not in a secure situation in which to preserve her or his cultural background. Tensions continue for families in reference to their identity vis-à-vis their subculture and social mobility.

How cultural and racial background contributes to mobility options is thought to be a complex interaction with larger economic trends. The life-course trajectory of black women varies more than that of white women (Spanier & Glick, 1980), including a greater range in the timing of life events such as marriage, children, employment, divorce, and

remarriage. Staples (1976) noted many upwardly mobile blacks want to preserve some of their cultural traditions that are usually associated with a lower-class status. If the opportunity for social mobility becomes more limited in the future, then ethnic support systems may be more valuable. In contrast, if economic recovery is successful and mobility opens up again, families may have less time and energy for investment in these subcultures as they learn the ways of their new occupations.

Yancey et al. (1976) suggested that ethnicity, as it now operates, is embedded in the larger social structures and occupational patterns and merges with regionality. Regional differences in family lifestyles reflect migration patterns of ethnic groups. Family decisions about economic and recreational opportunities within a locale shape daily life and interest. Regions often are dominated by a central set of activities. Themes built around an industry (e.g., chemical, automobile, mining, or high technology); an enterprise (e.g., farming, ranching, or fishing); or a service (e.g., government, fast foods, or education) give a common meaning and destiny to families in a community. Family and individual tastes vary in potential for an outlet in the regional scene. Sailing, hiking, hunting, music, theater, dance, organized sports, and other hobbies are not evenly distributed across society. Participation in activities may replace the support of kin strength of a subcultural experience.

National and multinational efforts to develop a common set of expectations and tastes pull against ethnic and regional differentiation. Both governments and corporations seek some standardization. Brand names, quality standards, and media campaigns are organized to bring some symmetry to the vision and opportunities that families have in their lives. Continued interest in the variety and complexity of ethnic and regional subcultures is likely, but the movement toward national and international shared perspectives and artifacts is strong.

Prevalence and Durability of Various Family Types and Individual Lifestyles

Families are the most stable sources of long-term relationships in comparison to other personal relationships. Modernization and improved medical and health practices have resulted in a worldwide extension of the life span. These demographic changes have meant that individuals are confronted with new choices and possibilities (Rossi, 1993). More families are able to enjoy the generations over an expanded time frame (Glick, 1989b). The concept of four- and five-generation extended families are not only an idea but are also more often a reality (Pitts, 1986). Although these ties are important, household composition has tended to reflect the smaller nuclear family, and the horizontal dimension of lateral kinship ties with siblings and cousins may be reduced (Glick, 1989b; Hareven, 1996).

Later first marriage is more common, and marriage rates are depressed (Norton & Moorman, 1987). Cherlin (1990) suggests that, if cohabitation is included, then the about two-thirds decline in marriage among young people is compensated. He sees many adults moving in and out of different unions over the life course. Most men and women will live alone several times during their adult lives. As Glick (1980) noted, the ideal of marriage is still highly regarded, but satisfaction often requires the second attempt.

Women should expect to spend a major portion of their lives in a postmarriage period (Lopata, 1973). Guttentag and Second (1983) detailed many implications of the larger ratio of women to men in some cohorts today. The dramatic increase of women's life span and lowered morbidity in early adult childbearing years has been an engine in rapid social change. Currently, a number of studies are focusing on critical pathways in adult life that modify personal decisions. Moen (1992) points out that women continue to have opportunities to reshape their multiple roles to improve life chances.

The concepts of replanning and shifting goals and action are particularly useful for women in contemporary society. The real dividend for women in longer life expectancy is not simply in the childbearing period, but in the whole new era in which they may see their great-grandchildren and have new careers and avocations. No easy recipe for responding to the costs and benefits of timing events with family and careers has been found. Barriers to education and career development created for those having children early in their adolescence are not easy to overcome (Aldous, 1990). In addition, young parents may find it increasingly difficult to provide for the needs of the child and meet their own needs. Because many of these children often have special needs due to poor outcomes in pregnancy and prenatal care, there is increased strain on limited resources (Adolescent pregnancy, 1986). Single parenthood is becoming a "normal" not a deviant phenomenon, but it is still associated with poverty (Glick, 1979, 1990). The sector of families and single women not in cohabiting relationships that have more likelihood of giving birth includes teenage mothers as a major component (Cherlin, 1990).

Within these generic trends, there are many differences for African American families. Some trends appear to be led by African Americans. Their life expectancies remain lower than the general population. Some rates do not differ from the larger population in direction. However, single and teen parenting, lower marriage rates, increased divorce rates, and lower remarriage rates are more extreme (Cherlin, 1990; Dickson, L., 1993).

The search for explanations varies from seeing these data as an indication of pathology in the group to looking for structural and cultural differences. Certainly, opportunity patterns have been limited for the large numbers of African Americans males in poverty (Taylor et al., 1990). Demographic shifts have increased the unequal sex ratios at usual age at marriage across the board, and some social differences in gender role expectations and stereotypes are reported (Dickson, L., 1993). Although African American men are often ignored in the study of family, in a small exploratory study, Lawson and Thompson (1995) found that men reported financial strain, differences in spending priorities, personal clashes, and religious differences to be important marital themes. While these factors are more commonly applied to African Americans in the general population, the trends are amplified as other groups face similar problems. Many young men do not earn enough to support a family (Riche, 1991). Young people's jobs frequently do not provide health insurance and other benefits needed for new families, and women provide more support to families at all stages of the life course.

Some authors saw reasons for a decline in divorce rate (Kemper, 1983); however, the slight decline in the 1980s appears to end an upward trend (Norton & Moorman, 1987). The high rates of divorce and remarriage appear to be stabilizing (Glick, 1979, 1990) but are met with concern for the potentiality of second and third divorces rates being similar in remarriage (Counts, 1992).

Clarke and Wilson (1994), in examining divorce rates for remarriages, looked at both partners' histories and age and were impressed with the offsetting effects. They see the likelihood of second divorce as overexaggerated. Longer life expectancies make it possible for people to survive several marriages, each of which is as long as many lifetime marriages were in colonial days. In addition, those committed to long-term marriages have the potential for records in length and durability of relationships (Bane, 1976). Adults can expect longer periods of childfree older married life (Glick, 1979). He notes that a lifelong marriage at the turn of the century would have lasted a little over 30 years; now a lifelong marriage lasts 45 years (Glick, 1990).

The effects on children as consequences of divorce and remarriage across the life course are difficult to assess. Immediate effects on children have been of great concern. The consequences of divorce and remarriage across the life course are difficult to assess. Family disruption appears to have some long-term effects. McLanahan and Bumpass (1988) suggest that living as a child in a single female-headed household increases the likelihood of having similar experiences as an adult, attributable simply to economic factors. Children have a continuing challenge in their relationships to their divorced parents and in initiating new relationships. If the divorce occurs when the children are adults, the cultural belief is that there is less of a problem. However, the stresses in relationships with parents appear significant to young adults, especially when parents have had major problems with drinking or personal adjustment, or when financial vulnerability of young adults is relevant (Cooney, Hutchinson, & Leather, 1995).

Glick (1989b, 1993) has documented the prevalence of the preference for familial arrangements over other lifestyles. Plans made as a family may continue to influence lifestyles as families experience launching of children, separation, divorce, remarriage, and death. The outcomes of previous plans and approaches can be seen in the content of property settlements, child support, and spousal rehabilitation agreements. Some will cite earlier informal agreements as the basis for the new replanning (Rettig, Christensen, & Dahl, 1991; Salt, 1991). Stepfamilies can be highly adaptive groups when the separate households cooperate and new bonds and rituals are established (Ganong, Coleman, & Fine, 1994).

Continuity in family life provides the context for current events. One of the tragedies of divorce is the need to forget the good with the bad. Family continuity provides recurring opportunities for people to do out-of-character and cross-generational activities that provide materials for further elaboration. Taking the children or the grandparents to the fair or on a picnic reinforces the texture of the relationship. Second chances for families and individuals are more likely in future. Families have opportunities to drift apart and pull together over several decades (Bengtson, 1996).

Family Dynamics: Intimacy, Involvement, and Conflict

Twentieth-century social psychology promoted the study of intimacy and the expression of emotions. Instead of viewing affection and sexuality as by-products of a marital union that were simply outcomes of other processes making the marriage viable, these items have become for many the primary rationale for marriage. Sexuality as related to a loving relationship or a separate process has been of great interest. However, in documenting the everyday activities, style and substance of communication of positive affect in the intimacy of couples, the study of families and households has lagged behind (Vangelisti, 1991; Vangelisti & Banski, 1993). The accumulation of daily events may be fundamental to conceptualizing affection and positive functioning (Settles, 1995). Burr and Christensen (1992) suggest attention be given to "ways to create enabling, enduring, emotional connections between people" (p. 464). Vannoy (1993) has argued that only within a marriage of equals could love be a main engine of relationships in family. She sees the reduction of hierarchy as opening the door to real intimacy. Quality of life in intimate personal relationships has become the stan-

dard for measuring marital success and continued commitment, at least in Western industrialized societies (Campbell, Converse, & Rodgers, 1976).

The expression of affection between generations has become more prevalent. Fathers find it easier to express warmth and support to children of both sexes, both as infants and as young adults. The "new fatherhood," as Levine (1982) characterized these changes, has important benefits for the parent as well as the child. Expressiveness has also been attached to the process of having children, enriching fathers' and mothers' roles in the birth of their babies and the subsequent childcare. Birth and parent education classes have grown rapidly and have affected the style and content of the medical regimen (Block, Norr, Meyering, Norr & Charles, 1981). The success of these programs suggests that families perceived the need for such support at the transition to parental status and were open to the forum in which it was given.

Involvement in close family interaction provides an opportunity not only for the expression of affection, but also for displaying negative emotions and actions. In addition to the positive aspects of increased expressiveness within the family, the opportunities for sexual assault, incest, and mental and physical violence occur in this same private setting (Steinmetz, 1987, 1988). Wives who have been abused by their husbands or male companions report men apologizing or taking other aligning actions to mend the relationship, which suggests that linking of emotionally polar affect is common (Wolf-Smith & La Rossa, 1992). It is only as the women begin to reject or fail to honor these apologies that they are able to leave the relationship. Gelles and Maynard (1987) point out that in the larger world of family relationships, many situations are not so clear or extreme as the situations upon which the abuse literature has focused our attention. They believe that family therapy may be useful in dealing with some cases of family violence.

Violence in courtship has met with more attention (Billingham, 1987), and a model for analyzing the socialization of the couple into seeing violence as a component of intimate relationships has been proposed (Flynn, 1987). Strategies of resolving conflicts in premarital relationships do appear to be linked with the quality of the developing relationships and may have considerable carryover into marriage (Barnes, Greenwood, & Sommer, 1991; Billingham, 1987; Lloyd, 1987; Mayseless, 1991). Interpretation of courtship violence as jealousy or love contains a real risk for continued violence. Romance may mask the evaluation of the negative behavior (Lloyd, 1991). Continuity in dating behavior suggests that couple interaction must be studied, in addition to parental and peer tolerance of aggressive behavior (Gwartney-Gibbs, Stockard, & Bohmer, 1987). Reciprocity of violence and aggressive acts from both men and women in dating are often heightened by drinking and verbal abuse (Barnes et al., 1991; Stets & Henderson, 1991).

Conflicts require family ties to mature in complexity, scope, and impact. Families can cling to incidents over time and organize current life around them. Lesser groups give up too soon, and only "world" powers have more weapons to throw into disputes. Case studies from family therapy (Minuchin, 1974; Walsh, 1993) and stage plays illustrate the intrigue and power of family conflicts across generations and eras.

Perceptions of conflicts in the outside world influence the internal dynamics of family life. Families live in a context of crisis in which they are not assured that there is a generational continuity or even continuity of life in general (Ptacek, 1988). For young people, who never knew a world without the potential for nuclear war and total devastation, it is hard to imagine how many of their elders do not see a flaming holocaust as a possible future. For parents and grandparents there has been a norm of silence about these issues (Jacobs, 1988). Living closer to the present in imagination is a protection against the unthinkable. A potential force for change is the role of family in giving meaning to life and increasing communication (Ptacek, 1988). Political and social action groups are actively seeking to draw attention to these critical decisions and to involve families in socialization and social action. Cole and Rueter (1993) see families as a force in developing a peaceful world. Their model of connection between the interactions at a familial level and linking these processes to world change is ambitious, but it speaks to the importance of conflict resolution at all levels in society.

The interest in "strong" families and marriages has primarily produced a list of characteristics rather than a dynamic theory (Robinson & Blanton, 1993). Measurement of intimacy is often self-reported as a state or overall perception, and current work to conceptualize and to build connections is needed (Van den Broucke, Vertommen, & Vandereycken, 1995). Peterson (1995), when exploring autonomy and connectedness in families, explained that families have the unequaled opportunity to express the intensity, variety, and continuity of emotions, both positive and negative. We should not confuse the greater quantity of research and discussion about dysfunction and negative emotional expression with the relative importance of these issues to families. It is a reflection of society's higher standards for positive family interaction and discourse that directs us to the problematic aspects of family interaction.

Models for Describing the Futures of Families

To this point this chapter has identified the controversies in understanding the concept of family and the use of defini-

tions for political and scientific purposes. A selection of stresses, challenges, and opportunities facing families today was examined to illustrate what the menu of choices is for families and what the dynamics are of facing these issues for families. Given the complexity of the environment and options available, how is it possible to think we could develop a model of the futures of families? One of the commonalities all individuals and families have is that they try to deal with their environment. They attempt to make sense out of their lives and find meaning and purpose. Whether or not their efforts are rewarded with meeting their expectations, the actions taken to affect future outcomes are an important component of creating meaning and direction for their families.

Predictive models for describing the future of families are still in the process of development. The codification, explication, and integration of theories applied to families were a major scholarly enterprise of the 1970s. Five major theoretical schemes were examined in detail in Burr, Hill, Nye, and Reiss (1979): choice exchange and the family (Nye, 1979); symbolic interaction and the family (Burr, Leigh, Day, & Constantine, 1979); a general systems approach to the family (Broderick & Smith, 1979); conflict theory and the study of marriage and the family (Sprey, 1979); and the phenomenological sociology of the family (McLain & Weigart, 1979).

Each approach has some mechanisms for understanding change and stability in families and presents some specific comments about the future. Sprey (1979) noted in his conclusion on conflict theory that the deep structure of families limits the potential for orderly change. McLain and Weigart (1979) suggested that the family is likely to remain a universal form of human organization and experience because it balances objective and subjective experience for the individual.

Revisiting the major statements of current theory, Doherty, Boss, LaRossa, Schumm, and Steinmetz (1993) directly addressed the issues of relating theory to method and application. In their search for future prospects they see a "synthesis of new and old theories and methods" (p. 27) and find the dialogue between those scholars who emphasize context of family action and those who hold on to the "best elements of scholarly rigor and creativity from our social science tradition" as a productive interchange. The outcome in terms of developing models that anticipate the future may be found in this dialogue, but no one theoretical view has begun to dominate the future.

Family scholars have pursued the integrative and application tasks related to family theories. In black and women's studies, there has been interest in enhancing a potential for change. These scholars have seen politics as part of the issues in the understanding of family processes. Recognition of human ecology theory (Bubolz & Sontag, 1993; Westney, 1993), feminist criticism (Goldner, 1993; Osmond & Thorne,

1993), and ethnic minority criticism (Dilworth-Anderson, Burton, & Johnson, 1993; Hardy, 1993) has contributed to viewing families as active agents in their futures.

Both gender and ethnic scholars have examined domestic life for higher-level theoretical propositions. While housekeeping encompasses the most mundane and unfashionable activities of everyday life, issues in role flexibility, balancing work and family, child and elder caregiving, and community resources require understanding the strategies involved in homemaking. The house is now a major crossroads of social and cultural values and requirements because of its theoretical importance to the relationships of the family, the political economy, and change (Blair & Johnson, 1992; Broman, 1988; Coltrane & Ishii-Kuntz, 1992; Hardesty & Bokemeier, 1989; Malos, 1980; Millet, 1970; Oakley, 1974; Piña & Bengston, 1993; Spitz & Ward, 1995; Strasser, 1982). Egalitarian roles between spouses are at issue in housework and caregiving and are resistant to amelioration.

The aspects of family life that reflect social change and dynamic models of family process are not well specified in family theories. Kantor and Lehr (1975) noted the importance of the family's future-orienting behavior in the way family strategies operate. Doherty and Baptiste (1993) focus on issues of epistemology and philosophic issues in construction of reality in reviewing family therapy theories. The vast growth of practice and the need for theoretical underpinnings for professional education in family therapy has been a driving force for both therapeutic theories and more fundamental understanding of family processes. Two areas in which there have been substantial contributions that affect understanding how families manage their futures are communication (Dickson & Markman, 1993; Fitzpatrick & Ritchie, 1993) and family discourse (Gubrium & Holstein, 1993).

Models for Planning and Decision Making

Families as decision makers and actors in social and economic change have been studied primarily around substantive topics and at times of crisis and transition. The use of theoretical concepts and explanations has been modest.

Decision Making and Planning Situations. The primary areas of family decision making that have been studied in detail are consumer preferences and family planning of fertility. Consumer research has emphasized demographic factors to predict consumer interests by residential and occupational sectors. These findings have been primarily used by marketing specialists to target advertising and to plan merchandising strategies. Some academics and consumer advocates use information to assist families in comparative shopping or in choosing more personally rewarding decisions.

Studies include the role parents play in their children's consumption patterns in clothing and fast foods and their continuing influence on adolescents in the areas of educational aspirations, drug use, career choices, and peer groups (Lewis, Dyer, & Moran, 1995; Reynolds, Kennon, & Palakurthi, 1995). Long-term consumption patterns and the impact of repeated consumer decisions on families are addressed primarily at the macro level in economic modeling.

In fertility research, questions of spouses' relative power, outside resources, and availability of information and family planning technologies have been minutely studied in many cultures and within societies' subcultures. Families have more confidence in knowing they will spend more time with their children as independent grown-ups than as dependent youngsters (Keyfitz, 1989). Demographic models of the shift to smaller families emphasized the variables of education, women's employment, and availability of contraceptive and abortion technologies (Miller, 1987; Thompson, 1989).

Information about birth control and access to contraceptives has been a major element in declining birth rates worldwide (Keyfitz, 1989). Education and employment may be seen as indicators of women's power in decision making related to achieved family size or as an investment in women's personal development because of greater value being given to the adult roles outside of parenting (Teachman, Polonko, & Scanzoni, 1987). Regulation and mandates have not been necessary to create major changes in family size in most of the world. However, China's single child family policy, dictating the age of marriage and the practice of contraception and induced abortion, which is accompanied by organized social pressure and emphasizes sanctions for those who do not conform, is an example of extreme regulation (Coale, Feng, Riley, & De, 1991; Sun, 1993).

Any model of family planning decisions must at some point go beyond the macro social context to the micro level of how couples act on a daily basis in their own most private moments. The intervening or mediating variables are still primarily discussed around reports couples make rationalizing their past histories. As fathers assume a greater role in parenting, rather than simply procreating, they are found to support family planning efforts worldwide (Fox, 1993). A consistent finding across many studies is that women gain control in limiting fertility and in lowering their desired number of children with access to education, paid employment, and availability of technologies.

Understanding the dynamics of problem solving in family study requires a more abstract analysis. Even developing a taxonomy of problems has been an important step toward better theoretical understanding of how families are challenged by different tasks and requirements in decision making and implementation (Tallman, 1993). Family problem-solving and decision-making research in other domains has asked couples how they see each other deciding specific issues (Blood & Wolfe, 1960; Kingsbury & Scanzoni, 1989; Safilios-Rothchild, 1970). Dyadic processes are examined and then used to explain the larger family and social system. Family problem-solving and decision-making research has identified the importance of education, access to monetary and technological resources, and family dynamics in planning and action.

Decision Opportunities with Crisis. The use of crisis points in capturing the dynamics of change and family adaptation has been a useful strategy for researchers seeking to understand how families solve problems. Family science research has been particularly rich in medical crisis investigations. Due to the nature of funding and interest in medicine these studies are scattered and tend to be focused by disease and anomaly rather than organized around commonalties. Better health over a lifetime does not mean escape from illness. Medical care and support create the environment for longer and more intense chronic illness and disability due to accidents and genetic conditions, resulting in a greater need for caregivers and long-term plans (Doolittle & Wiggens, 1993; Strauss, 1984). Prevention and lifestyle alterations may alleviate some of the problems and certainly help with cost and quality of life issues. Greater personal and family responsibility in planning and action are required for quality outcomes. Planning for long-term life activities and caregiving becomes central when life expectancy is suddenly extended, as in cystic fibrosis and Down's syndrome (Mount, 1988; Settles, MacRostie, & Lucca, 1986). In reviewing a number of books written by parents of exceptional children, Mullins (1987) found parents had decision-making and planning challenges in finding a realistic assessment and appraisal of the disability, in handling the everyday demands and interface with institutions, and in dealing with the recurrent emotional stress of the child's uncertain future and changed life trajectory. Investigations of families with chronic illnesses have been particularly helpful in illustrating the salience of families' management of the relationship with the formal supportive services in decisions and action (Hauser, 1990). These crises provide the researcher with a window of opportunity to follow families' handling of high-demand problems, changing conditions, and outcomes. One of the interesting findings about these families is that compliance with recommendations from the medical community does not always produce a better outcome. Reiss (1991) found that highly compliant patients in hemodialysis, whose families were supportive of that approach, were actually less likely to survive in advanced disease stages.

Decision Opportunities with Life-Course Transitions. Normal life-span transitions provide occasions to look at problem solving and planning. Old age has now developed new transitions with two periods of retirement: the first period of active independent living and the second period of frailty and appropriate support. The elderly over 80 years of age commonly have outlived both close friends and family (Sanborn & Bould, 1991). Their plans and provisions that once were adequate now do not handle their situations (Settles, 1993a). They may be able to manage because have hardy constitutions and have survived well all along (Angier, 1995). This new transition of frailty provides an opportunity to examine continuity and disjuncture in problem solving and planning.

Intergenerational transfers are one of the indicators of this process of interdependence (Sussman, 1983). Filial responsibility laws are in place in most of the states in the United States and the expectation is that more vigorous enforcement will be tried as the number of caregivers compared to the number of aged becomes smaller (Sussman, 1993). Hareven (1996) and her colleagues have found that uneasy and unstable intergenerational relationships were found in both traditional and changing communities all over Europe and the new world. The understanding of duties, responsibilities, and exchanges in families was much less dependable and trustworthy than has been assumed. As social and economic change met with traditional arrangements, there was dislocation. Often the younger members simply were no longer closely proximate to the older ones.

Current demographic, social, and technological trends have created not only the opportunity but also the necessity for looking at the relationships among generations in a different way (Hanks, 1991). Assumptions about generational interaction and strategic planning must be reexamined and clarified to be realistic about options for any family. The study of planning and decision making is complicated by diversity from conventional family structure and process. Individuals may participate in a variety of family and household arrangements. New families may be the result of action taken to meet changing needs and resources. The balance between individual and group process and equity is especially challenging.

Changing family forms over the life course require a more refined calculation of individual and family plans. Life-course trajectories are changed by these arrangements. Many children, within their childhood experience, live in a classic nuclear family, a single-parent family, a dual-earner family, a blended family, or an intergenerational household. Despite frequent criticism of such diversity in family life and household arrangements, there is likely to be continuing individual choice and great flexibility in family circumstance (Skolnick, 1993). Blended families are increasing in number and are challenging relationships among stepparents, stepchildren, and other relatives (Glick, 1989a; Spanier & Furstenberg,

1987). The political conflicts over family forms become the background against which plans are made and implemented (Levin & Trost, 1992b; Rettig, 1987, 1993; Settles, 1987).

Equity and Fair Representation in Planning and Decisions. Determining whose interests must be represented in problem solving and planning has become a concern. Children, dependent or handicapped adults, and elders are more likely to be considered as members of the decision-making and planning team today. Parents and adolescents may have quite different perceptions of each other's role in the decision-making process (Brown & Mann, 1989, 1990; Liprie, 1993). Representing the interests of dependents of all ages when they cannot participate actively is an ethical challenge to both the family and community (Clavan, 1985; Hanks & Settles, 1990; Schulz, 1985). Knowing when to intervene and how to handle changed relationships is a challenge in dealing either with elders or youth in cross-generational planning and problem solving (Hansson et al., 1990; Liprie, Hanks, & Berke, 1992).

Jackson (1988) found in her study of young adults whose parents had taken early retirement that they were unaware of any later consequences in their own lives from this act and saw only the advantages of their parents presently enjoying their lives. In a study of how parents and an adolescent reacted to potentially problematic situations, Aldous and Ganey (1989) noted that gender and affect were important to the processes of defining problems, but that the tendency was to shortcut the discussion and use implicit situational definitions rather than exploration and explicit definitions. While planning and implementation of a wide diversity of family issues are part of everyday life in families, it is difficult to link the processes to studies that in laboratories or questionnaires measure how people represent their interaction in shaping of their futures.

Interactive Planning Model: Expansion and Choice

Since no one approach has suggested a strong explanation of how families take action to affect their future lives, my own thinking about models of family change tends toward an eclectic perspective borrowing from several of these views. The model developed presents an integration of processes that describes how there can be expansion of choice within personal, family, work, and community domains. This approach builds on the decision-making and planning literature and has used information and risk assessment findings produced by research in large-scale government and corporate planning. The model for interactive planning in the area of choice provides a summary of some of the major dimensions of the mental, social, and material space that affect what choices, plans, and strategies individuals and groups

have within their grasp (Settles, 1974, 1987). It focuses on the processes that families may use in relating current actions to future outcomes and challenges.

The model assumes that all choices are made in a milieu of conflicting perceptions, limited information, unclear problem definitions, differential power and resource allocations, and only partially rational thinking. Even when an individual or familial group does not do anything, the inaction may in this model be viewed as a choice. The model pays attention to how individuals interact to form a future for their families. It does not mean that the individual is not also able to monitor how his or her own life is affected or changed by commitment to the group. In this model those interactions and resultant actions that raise or lower commitment may be seen as elements in the evaluation of the choices and plans. It may be that opting out of a family or household is an important survival mechanism for an individual.

This model speaks to some of the processes that operate to expand or limit actual efforts to take action for both present and future goals. Some of them are malleable, such as education and training; others are less open to change, such as personality. The model assumes that actors are not knowledgeable in all important respects. It notes there are many choices that can be made even when they are highly affected by events, dispositions, limits, and resources. In addition, the habits, rituals, and paradigms that the familial group has established may shape perceptions and problem definitions. Feelings and structured behavior can be included in the scope of the outreach to the family when these aspects are addressed by families.

When groups like families have common destinies they may find that choice is actually more limited because of certain individuals' characteristics or decision-making approaches. Family members make sacrifices in the near term for long-range outcomes or to sponsor members. Some family members may have personal limitations or talents that shape everyone's daily life. The added skills and knowledge of several people being involved in planning and action may offset the individual limits. Because of power deferentials or family histories, some new information may not be readily received by the family as a whole.

Boundary of Area of Choice. The area of choice available is dynamic over the life course. During one's youth a person often has great energy, few monetary resources, and limited experience, so one may borrow for education, work two jobs, and attend every concert that comes to town. In contrast, families at other life-course stages may be able to spend savings to renovate a home for handicapped access or use experiences to enrich current activities. One needs to revisit issues and choices in new circumstances over the life course. Changed importance in costs and benefits as well as

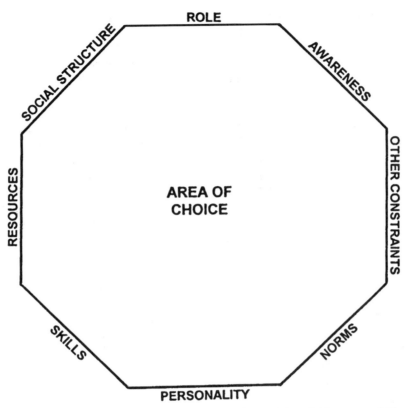

Figure 1. Area of choice in decision making for individuals and families. This area is bounded by many variables; only some are shown.

investments in implementing plans may require families to revisit issues and choices again and again over the life course. Areas of choice in lifestyle are influenced by awareness, roles, social structure, resources, skills, personality, norms, and other constraints. While these concepts are widely used in a similar fashion in family social science, some attention is given to the way they are used in the context of this model.

The area of choice that individuals and families have is influenced by these variables. Figure 1 shows how these variables surround the area of choice. They form a boundary, which can be expanded or contracted. It would appear that a symmetry exists. However, in reality these variables are not equally limiting or expansive for a specific family.

Awareness. The development of awareness is a crucial resource for choice; it is not costly, but it requires exposure and time to develop a sense of what options and choices are possible. In terms of such items as family patterns, work choices, recreational activities, and group associations, awareness may be a continuing process. One cannot use this information in making decisions or judgments unless one is aware of an issue or experience. Once you are aware, it is difficult to forget it. Increasing awareness can help one im-

prove extent and diversity of social networks, information sources, values and worldviews, flexibility, understanding, and skills. Both education and individual and/or family therapy are effective in helping change perspectives and enlarging the prospects for personal and familial growth.

Roles. Many roles are important in our lives: friend, spouse, parent, sibling, employee, athlete, etc. Role-playing meshes individual preferences and styles with expectations of others about how we should act. Some are complementary, for example, parent–child, student–teacher, doctor–patient. Participation in a number of groups allows a person to demonstrate a wider range of interests, styles, and approaches to problem solving. With membership in multiple groups, one becomes aware of the multiplicity of roles one can play.

Some roles are more formal and standardized with clear penalties for failure to carry through the expected behavior and rewards for conformity. Roles are often flexible with a wide range of acceptable behavior and reflect personal choice and preference. Much of the turmoil and excitement in social and family life has resulted from the need to work out what expectations will govern each family. Communication is critical in negotiating complementary roles and opening up choices for individuals. Where there are multiple roles, the individual has to answer questions of personal integrity and choice of a "master" or priority role.

Social Structure. The social structure of contemporary society offers many individuals and families the flexible opportunities for many kinds of mobility. Immigrants, such as Hispanic, Asian, and African groups, are cultural agents of change. Migrants move geographically for occupational, educational, and vocational opportunity. Social class influences our perceptions of opportunity and stability. Each cohort has its own critical events. These events affect what opportunities are available. Stability has its comforts because we can plan more easily, but most families hope for some mobility opportunities (Settles, 1993b). In family decision making and long-term planning, early experiences influence how we understand the life cycle and society.

Resources. A wide variety of resources come to bear on planning and strategies for implementation. Time, energy, money, material goods, expert advice, and social and physical support are some of the important variables, and they may be limited by many factors such as health, job opportunities, critical economic events, and government tax and incentive programs. Expansion of one resource may be at a cost to other resources. Many families do not have an understanding of the range of available resources. Individual and family dimensions of material and supportive resources can be drawn upon to accomplish an individual's choice. Within this ideal situation, affection and concern are powerful resources, as are financial and housing investments. Friends and relatives can provide not only expert advice, but social and physical support as well.

Skill. The development of skill is based on an investment of resources by an individual, family, or a social group and represents their beliefs about what abilities will have long-term utility. Some skills are more general, such as reading and mathematics, and open many resources to the person. Others are much narrower and more specific, such as athletics and arts, which often require much practice and refinement to be helpful to the person. Everyone has the same 24-hour day and must choose where and when to invest in building skills. Mental and physical gifts are not equally available to all and some skills are outside of one's grasp. Choices must be made as to which skills should be acquired for whom and at what level the skill should be polished. Skills provide possibilities of better resource use and efficiency of problem solving and action.

Personality. The integration of a person's experience and the social context is found in those aspects of the indi-

vidual usually referred to as personality. This understanding of a person's predispositions, inclinations, and sense of the self is useful for identifying choices that a person will be comfortable in examining. Not all areas of choice will be actually available to individuals because of his or her own experience and perception of the meaning of those choices in his or her own social situation.

A personal phobia may limit one's choices of housing, vacation, or participation in the community. Although personality is assumed to be one of the less easily affected aspects of one's predispositions, adult resocialization and change are quite common in institutions such as higher education, the military, and religion. Increasing self-esteem and self-efficacy by interventions that include social support and achievement experiences has been shown to increase individual's abilities to use new opportunities despite personality constraints. Early experience is both a conscious awareness and a forgotten but present influence in how one sees the world now. In specific situations one's personal style and perception may have an excellent or poor fit with reality. Understanding one's own personality can open options not previously considered. Understanding others' personalities and style can give one a more realistic idea of what can be expected from them in cooperative and competitive situations.

Norms. Expectations of appropriate behavior in specific situations and for different roles form the norms. These norms may be manifest in legal codes, regulations, and policies, or they may be informal understandings about the context of behavior and its style and substance. When a society is stable, norms change relatively slowly and expectations learned in childhood will serve one well throughout life. When society is experiencing rapid change, more communication and learning are required. Individuals and families are not just passive reactors to change; they may directly seek to change what is expected of them in some situations. Diffuse norms may lead to misunderstanding or discomfort if the parties do not anticipate a wider range of response.

Other Constraints. At any one time there may be events that precipitate decision making or planning or that limit individuals and their families from assuming control over their life course. Wars and famines are dramatic versions of this phenomenon. Economic shifts, plant closings, and the weather may be equally overwhelming to families. Opportunities such as unexpected property appreciation or discovery of an innovation may produce an expansion of choice to some families.

Process Affecting the Area of Choice. The decision making and choices that individuals and families have are influenced by a number of processes that affect the area of choice available at any one time and place. These processes, which can help to increase or decrease the area of choice are simple socialization versus complex socialization, training versus education, naiveté versus sophistication, stability versus social change, tradition versus technology and discovery, group (as in family) loyalty versus multigroup participation, conformity versus deviance, and isolation versus consciousness-raising or psychological treatment.

This multidimensionality, presented as spokes radiating outward and inward on Figure 2, illustrates the processes that influence the area of choice for family decision making by enlarging or collapsing the boundaries. As it becomes possible to move toward more complex choices, changes, and new options through these processes, individuals and their families must deal with whether to use all their options as these boundaries are expanded. They can also choose to move to simplify their choices by simply restricting their area of choice by closing in the boundaries. In Figure 2 the processes that are particularly salient for an aspect of choice are placed next to that sector. While the other processes may contribute more to other parts of the model, they do contribute throughout to all sectors in some respects.

Decision making can be used as a tool to enlarge, retain,

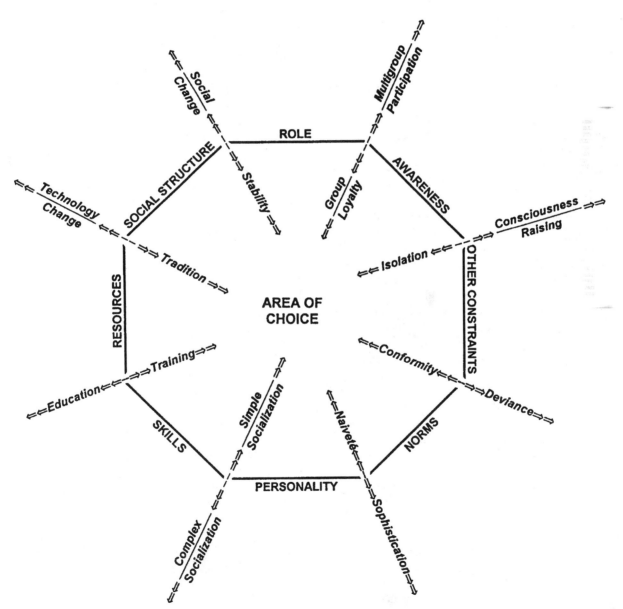

Figure 2. Area of choice in decision making for individuals and families. This area can be expanded or contracted by many processes; only some are shown.

or restrict the area of choice. An individual may decide to use the processes of education, technological change, social change, consciousness raising, nonconformity, sophistication, or complexity resulting in enlarging the area of choice. A decision to maintain stability, tradition, group loyalty, isolation, conformity, naiveté, simplicity, or to use training could result in retaining or restricting the area of choice.

Choice is found in the part of decision making in which a person is operating at a level of knowledge and judgment that is not at the habitual or unconscious level. It is possible to change what is in the area of choice by intervention. At any one time, there are specific conceptual and resource limitations.

Simple versus Complex Socialization. In less complex societies or societies that are not undergoing extensive change, individuals and families are able to use the knowledge gained during childhood and young adult socialization throughout their lives. In more complex societies, or those undergoing rapid change, knowledge and skills obtained during our young adult years may no longer suffice for making the best decisions. While enmeshed in day-to-day life, we may not take advantage of what we know about the future. We fail to anticipate or plan for the changes that are inevitable because of our lifestyles and our place in the life-cycle continuum.

We go to school, choose careers, marry, reach mid-life, plan for retirement, reach the end of our work lives or choose early retirement and a second career, and settle into our later years. Moving from decade to decade across the life span, we face different questions and problems that require maturity, creativity, productivity, nurturance, and acceptance. The resources, perceptions, and experiences we bring into each decade will expand or constrain the choices that we can make at each stage. Some of the common influences in expanding or constricting choice are found in processes of involvement in the community surrounding the family. Learning, tolerance, and a common sense of shared destiny energize the family unit for change.

Training versus Education. Training and education represent two ends of a continuum of approaches to developing skills and resources. Training focuses on specific skills and relevant information and is quicker and less expensive in the immediate time period. It usually has a short shelf life in a rapidly changing world and retraining must be anticipated as part of the process.

Educational experience that focuses on basic principles, goal setting, and decision making may require more investment up front but often has a long-term payoff in a continued utility. Educational opportunities introduce many people to awareness, exposure, and an increase in choices. Education increases a person's contact with the diversity of cultural,

religious, and recreational choices. For most people, this exposure first comes at the time in their lives when they have the most flexibility to explore personal selections from the options that are available to them. The choice of employment or a profession offers opportunities for developing new ideas. As careers are more open and less restrictive than they have been in the past, the selection of a field in which to work offers another chance to move beyond single group identification to more diverse loyalties.

Retraining and adult education have become important trends in our society. Both sorts of learning experiences are more common in a lifelong process when individuals have multiple careers and changing circumstances and needs. Opening up educational and training opportunities to women, the handicapped, the elderly, and special needs populations has been a force in opening up choice and providing hope for a better quality of life.

Naiveté versus Sophistication. One of the most difficult prerequisites to increasing choice in life is a sophisticated tolerance for complexity and loose ends. Many plans and decisions must be continuously reevaluated and altered if the goals desired are to be reached. Simple solutions and commitments may feel good, but are usually not effective in the long run. The push for any action may lead us to unsophisticated and naive responses. Naiveté allows the conflicts to be ignored or kept in separate compartments of reality in the person. Helpful problem-solving skills include being able to handle conflict, selecting appropriate expectations and norms, giving attention to priorities, focusing on issues, tolerating uncertainty, and integrating specific activities with long-term outcomes.

Problem solving requires knowledge of trend, causalities, and probabilities. Connecting all the important factors requires careful study and analysis and an openness to new ideas and opinions. The realization of unexpected consequences requires revising plans and implementing them. One can be sure that many unexpected events will influence the future, the maintaining options provides good insurance to back up plans.

Stability versus Social Change. Families have more stability than most other social groups today, with longer-term and more involved relationships than other friendships and organizational memberships. Families often stay together over the life course and reap the benefits and rewards or consequences of earlier plans. Rituals and recall of earlier experiences bind families together. The recurrent activities of everyday life provide continuity. Shared artifacts, years of living together, and establishing a lifestyle provide a sense of shared meaning. The common household and its environment links together experiences and processes of family life. Continuity is a sounder goal for families than stability itself.

The normal development of individuals and families requires change for the family to operate in everyday life.

The costs and benefits of social change affect families differently, but often provide more choice and opportunity to make decisions for the family's future. In contemporary society some roles have become decoupled from age grading and symmetry with family and occupational status. The returning student in higher or technical education may now be any age. A mother or grandmother may be doing homework beside their children. A displaced homemaker or bread-winner may be retrained beside a teenage apprentice. While social class is a powerful predictor of taste, style, and activity, there is more room for individuals to have friends and groups whose status is different from their own. Avocations and interests bring diverse people into contact with each other, contributing to broader awareness of opportunities.

Tradition versus Technological Change. Fascination with the possibilities of technological discovery and innovation has dominated our understanding of the future. The tremendous impact of electronic communication, automation, biomedical advances, and new products for everyday life has been felt around the world, even in isolated communities. We expect to have more change, but our imaginations are often not creative. To handle the impact of new technologies on families, individuals need to become aware of how innovations are adopted, to realize the costs and benefits of early adoption, and to develop a tolerance of relearning the consequences of that which cannot be anticipated.

Families need to find ways to accommodate the ordinary chaos of change within their current reality. Individual families are often flexible and adaptable, but finding the social support necessary may be more difficult. Organizations and institutions lag behind the implications of innovations and discoveries in their policies. Each technological change produces the opportunity for application and creates a challenge to traditional knowledge and ways of life. Early adoption of new technologies can provide the individual with windfall profits yet also carries risks of major failure. Not all technologies are equally meaningful or easy to incorporate into ongoing patterns. Enhancing flexibility of roles by multigroup participation, learning new skills, developing individuality and sophistication, and openness to new information and recognition of error can enhance choice in a technologically changing society.

Group Loyalty versus Multigroup Participation. When loyalty is a major social control mechanism, rigidity in roles might be expected since flexible roles are less common within groups that seek total loyalty of their members. A religious or subcultural group such as the Amish or the Nation of Islam may seek to define and enforce clearly defined roles and to limit individuals from developing dyadic relationships based on personal definitions of role. One of the reasons such groups may seek to channel youth into or away from educational experiences is the likelihood that broadened perspectives may loosen the hold of their doctrines.

Conformity versus Deviance. While choice has many benefits, there is comfort and security in more structured social arrangements. People may choose to forego personal choices to be associated with others who would make their decisions for them, even when these behaviors are not considered appropriated by society at large. Knowing what is expected and how the other will react can be a relief. However, there is a potential for abuse when allowing a group to make the choice in place of the individual's choice. Even within a family, one cannot be certain that everyone's interests will be equitably served. When there is dysfunction in a family, the case worker may find that someone is being pressed to accept an unwholesome role in an attempt to stabilize the family.

Isolation versus Consciousness Raising. The experience of living in a remote area, urban enclave, or close-knit primary group can limit the individual's choices by screening out information, social and technical change, and alternative lifestyles. Subcultures such as the Amish and Hutterites have norms and sanctions to limit the impact of outside influences (Kephart, 1982). The social and economic support of tightly organized groups can easily shape the worldview of their members to accept ideas and actions that are quite narrow in scope. Schisms and cults that have charismatic leadership have been in the headlines again as millennial predictions and apostolic thought lead to rigid group practices and even suicide pacts. Within American society, the lure of the frontier, the family farm or homestead, or life as a lone drifter has had some appeal. Somehow a deserted island or a mountain sanctuary is seen as offering freedom by its very limitations.

At the other extreme, there are experiences that produce the ability to take in new information and schemas. *Consciousness raising* became a common term to describe what happened to people in the civil rights and women's movements when they had a sudden insight as to the new equity paradigms. Not only was there an emphasis on having many sources and types of information, but there is also an attempt to help the person relate to new options in a meaningful way. In consciousness-raising experiences a person has an opportunity to reframe and incorporate new ideas and theories into his or her perspective. Real shifts in options occur because they now seem plausible. The form these experiences take can range from simply becoming friends or colleagues with a new group to an informal support group to a planned therapeutic intervention. While the model shows these processes as linear, in this process it is easy to see that one might have a transformation that would create a new isolation. A religious vocation, an escape from addiction, a reformation of character, professional training for career, or a new love could all result in narrowing of future options as the commitment might produce some isolation in future.

Choices and Change in Gender Roles: An Application of the Model. Role is an interesting concept to examine considering social change in the last 2 centuries. Increasing access for individuals to political and legal freedoms has provided more choices in lifestyle. There has been increased flexibility in how one enacts or defines these gender roles. As women have had more opportunity to participate in a variety of groups outside the family they too have had the option of trying on a variety of roles that are not integrated into a master family role. The range of options has grown, although discrimination and opposition to social change and more flexible gender roles have not been overcome.

Men are also attempting to integrate new options with family roles. Earlier in this century, contributing financially to the family's support and not abusing family members were the only roles that constrained men. Less attention was given to their presence and behavior within the family group. Now men feel challenged to have early interaction with their children and to maintain emotionally satisfying relationships with their spouses. The fatherhood movement continues to secure the economic support of fathers for families, but also emphasizes social and emotional support as essential.

Two of the processes of change that greatly affect the gender roles boundary are stability versus social change and group loyalty versus multigroup participation. These are illustrated in Figure 2. It is possible to perform a simple cost-benefit analysis to show how and why the gender roles might be expanded or contracted for an individual.

Stability and group loyalty can be associated with rigid gender roles, while social change and multigroup participation can be associated with flexible gender roles. Flexible gender role benefits include personal growth, opportunity for individuality, self-actualization, and responsibility. Rigid gender role benefits include simplicity, predictability, ease of relating within the structure, and group support. Costs of expanding the barrier to increase the area of choice toward more flexibility via social change and multigroup participation include anomie, generational communication problems, insecurity, and complexity. Moving the barrier to more rigid gender roles via stability and group loyalty can result in loss of freedom, loss of mobility, and boredom.

Future of Families Outlook

This chapter has attempted to link the research and theory on families that suggest trends and issues for the future

of families with the actions that families can take to shape their own futures in the current demographic, social, economic, and technological situation. While it is usual to see families as the dependent variable in research or the client in intervention, this analysis seeks to note the ways in which families are active, independent agents for their own futures. While there are many processes that one could use to group trends for the future, four will be described in this summary: conservatism, continuity, substitution, and change.

Conservatism

Throughout this analysis a long-term consistent swing in the direction of conservative and restrictive social and familial policy options has continued to be evident. The four summary points made in the first edition of this *Handbook* (Settles, 1987) seem to have been sturdy survivors over time. Unless a new invigorated progressive political movement finds a strong plan and works at creating a political foundation for support, it is likely that these trends will continue to be influential in our national and state discourse on family.

1. Conservative trends in defining and regulating the family still have sufficient energy to be important in both industrial and developing nations.
2. The search for a middle ground in family policy and programs will continue to erode more liberal views of family adjustment and functioning in response to conservative political organization.
3. However, individual families will bridge the two approaches with a variety of evasions and compartmental thinking. Families and fictive kin may be able to find a new paradigm for maintaining continuity and handling change.
4. Relating secular and sacred views of the family will continue to frustrate philosophers, theologians, and family scholars dealing with new realities about choice and decision making in the context of changing demographics, needs, and opportunities.

Continuity

Newer documentation of the trends in continuity for families provides support for the trends earlier identified:

1. Images of historical and cross-cultural descriptions of family life will continue to be revised as scholarship becomes more intense and refined.
2. The classic tie of technological change and family change will be redefined to include more individual solutions because of more flexible, diffuse technologies.
3. The trend toward employment outside the home for

men, women, and older children will continue even in developing nations, although some tasks can be done in the high-tech home "workshop."

4. Women and children will continue to bear most of the costs of technological and family change in the near future.

5. Redefinition of family roles toward equity will continue despite the pressure to maintain or revert to conventional roles.

6. Providing continuity for individual life transitions will continue to be an important function of life in the family.

7. Family life will continue to be the major opportunity to have intense relationships of long-term endurance that express both affection and conflict.

8. Adult dyadic relationships resulting in marriage or domestic partnership will continue to be long-term, but they are also likely not to be lifelong or monogamous.

9. The primary tie between parents and children will continue to be the most enduring of familial relationships. The debate over whether the adopted and the foster child or the child of reproductive intervention are really included in their new families has become intense. Whether or not these socially constructed families take precedence in the law or are always vulnerable to claims from the genetic parents is not settled. The outcome seems not necessarily to be based on the child's best interest, but more likely to be an extension of property rights law.

10. Single-parent families will continue to be a common experience for many children, at least for a portion of their childhood. Remarriage and other family reconstitution are likely to mean that single parenting is often a transition experience.

11. Complexity in family arrangements will continue to increase. Available options are increasing with former spouses' recurrent presence at times of stress and change and with longer lifetimes, through rearrangements contributing to the larger range of potential interactive people.

12. Continuity and functionality of kinship ties will be further refined, accounting for divorce, remarriage, and more surviving generations.

13. Small family size in the nuclear family appears likely in the next few years as the result of decisions already made by the present childbearing cohort, including teenagers.

14. Families, defined broadly, will continue to be the most convenient and cost-effective living arrangement across the life span, but not the exclusive choice for all people at all stages of their lives.

Substitution

Institutionalization has lost support in most interventions that substitute for family living. However, the hope that the large-scale expansion of prisons would be short-lived and that they would be seen as obsolete and impractical has been eroded. If anything has changed, it is more punitive attitudes toward individuals and their families. In fact, it is more acceptable to recommend punitive action against families in trouble. Diversity is at great risk of being eliminated. The fine evaluations of exemplary intervention programs are not widely known and do not enter into policy formation effectively.

The defeat of a universally available health care access in this country has strengthened the private sector's domination and regulation of health-care options. While managed health care may give some short-term cost savings to employers and increases profits for insurance companies, it may be a means of limiting family and individual participation in selecting and understanding options. Families may be forced to pick up the pieces when bureaucratic policies provide less than adequate care. A trend toward excluding families and primary care medical professionals from decision making seems to be underway in HMO medical delivery.

Newer documentation of the trends for family substitutes and alternatives provides support for the trends earlier identified:

1. Family substitutes are more likely to be designed as small-scale informal "families" than as major formal institutions such as schools, hospitals, and day-care centers.

2. The current practice of building large-scale prisons will result in large capital and personnel investments. Data supports alternative interventions, however, even though in the present political climate policy makers seek to punish and reject rehabilitation as a strategy. Although there is technology available for home confinement, there will not be a major shift in the direction of family-centered care for deviant behavior.

3. Families will be expected to provide or enhance treatment in-home settings in more areas of intervention in health care, education, and rehabilitation.

4. The family will continue to be the institution that handles the leftover problems of society and the advocate for individuals with special needs and deficits. Brokerage skills and knowledge of institutions and new information and technologies will be even more important. The divide separating sophisticated consumers from those who are less knowing is likely to become even greater.

5. Cohabitation, communal arrangements, and other

group-oriented alternatives to traditional marriage and family will continue to serve the needs of selected groups for portions of the life course.

6. Single lifestyles will be a major part of most people's lives. Family ties, not households, and fictive kin will be more important over the life course.

Change

Among the changes anticipated in the first edition of this *Handbook* that have begun to be realized are:

- The return to the states of even more of the program responsibilities for family support and legal action for regulation.
- The downsizing and reorganization of the workforce continues with more early retirement, part-time jobs and multiple careers.
- Pioneering work in developing better outreach to families over the life course has been the focus of many developmental, experimental, and innovative programs.
- The widespread availability of home-based high-tech communication and computer access has given some sectors of the society much greater access and power to handle information and develop networks for decision support. Others have been left even more disadvantaged.

Many of the ideas presented for change in 1987 remain interesting ideas that have not been developed:

1. The present concern with ethnicity and regional differences in family lifestyles will be less pervasive when and if economic mobility opportunities reopen and the barriers to migration are relaxed.
2. Families will have more opportunity to choose therapeutic and support strategies with a more precise knowledge of their efficacy and results.
3. A major redrafting of family law and practice will be needed to incorporate the family's increasingly sophisticated responsibilities toward one another and over the life cycle. International family legal issues will be more important as international companies continue to involve families in moving and international crises push families to immigrate.
4. Coordinated social action for narrowly defined humanitarian goals will become more common among nation-states, bringing improved quality of life to families. An understanding of legal and human rights as more than a local option could improve the choices and options families have.
5. Families will be organized not around the concept of

dependency but around interdependency. Intergenerational transfers and support will be reorganized to acknowledge changing life expectancies and economic leverage at different points in the life course. Conventional inheritance transfers may be revised to emphasize earlier exchanges.

6. Living arrangements may be more closely related to current family needs, with investment in housing as a lifetime home-place less critical to family definition. Homelessness will continue to be a major problem unless community planning and a shared sense of destiny become more influential.
7. Early retirement, lower wage rates throughout work careers, and unprotected retirement investments threaten the financial stability of the retirement years, especially the later years of greater frailty. Changing government programs and regulations continue to require families to adjust to different cost-benefit ratios and reevaluate strategies constantly.
8. Making new friends and seeking new information will be fundamental to family well-being over the life course

The Family as a Source of Action and Change

Families of the future will no doubt be more inventive and interesting than this discussion has suggested. If we can catch up to their decisions in our research as they happen, we will indeed be fortunate. Turning the paradigm around and seeing families as a source of influence on the future can be an interesting theoretical and practical exercise. Informed choices and preferences may be more available to families. In institutions such as education and medicine the process that includes families in decisions and support for treatment, intervention, and education has already begun.

In retail and consumer businesses there is a wide recognition that high technology can make more individual selection possible. The client, as designer and refiner of consumer goods and services, is well within the picture of the immediate future as one can specify features and products. The ecological setting of families as linked to a global set of options may be increasingly realized, not simply an ideal in the academic's schema of potentiality. An active view of families and individuals across the life course could radically change our way of doing research and comparison. Explaining variability and enhancing variability are quite different ventures. Families may want more information about themselves and their possibilities.

Surrendering the expert role for the resource role may be difficult for professionals, but it may have many new and exciting insights. Whatever the professional community that family studies embraces, it is important for them to recognize that the theories, data, and interpretations they bring to advancing the field may have far-reaching influence. An ethical commitment needs to be made not just to disseminating what is easy to grasp but also to making the complex findings available. Translating and adapting the concepts with clarity and setting appropriate limits of application is needed. To be of service to families will require much more refined and involved commitment to their point of view.

The accepted belief today is that the family is in trouble, that it is often dysfunctional and unable to care for its members. This message is repeated so often in our media, by our institutions, in our houses of worship, in our schools, and by our political and business leaders. It has become accepted as fact. When one looks at reality, scientific data, and history, we find that it is not the family that is fragile, but that our institutions are fragile. Only the family takes responsibilities for an individual over her or his lifetime. Our multinational free enterprise system has discarded the myth of providing for its employees. Governments change policies and benefits many times over an individual's lifetime, putting some in place, then taking away some. The only institution that has survived the total existence of mankind is the family. It has been and will continue to be more flexible, stronger, and more adaptable than the multinational free enterprise system and political policy! If history has taught us anything, it is that businesses and governments will fail and the family will thrive. We as family scientists should be assisting families to grow, change, adapt, and become different.

ACKNOWLEDGMENTS. This paper is a revision and expansion of "A Perspective on Tomorrow's Family" (Settles, 1987). It draws upon the research and program development materials supported by several grants. From 1986 to 1990, funding was provided by the Administration on Aging U.S.H.H.S. Grant #0090AM0219, "Interactive Planning for Family Futures." Additional research and program materials were supported from 1993 to 1995 by the Department of Public Instruction, State of Delaware Grants #RFPIII B-4-93 and 95, "Family Life and Parenthood Education for Underserved Youth." Barbara H. Settles was principal investigator for all grants. Working papers and reports are available from the author at the University of Delaware, Newark, Delaware 19716.

References

Abbey, N., Brindis, C., & Cassas, M. (1990). *Family life education in multicultural classrooms*. Santa Cruz, CA: ETR Associates.

Adolescent pregnancy: Testing prevention strategies. (1986). *Carnegie Quarterly*, *31*(3&4), 1–7.

Aldous, J. (1990). Family development and the life course: Two perspectives on family change. *Journal of Marriage and the Family*, *52*(3), 571–583.

Aldous, J., & Dumon, W. (1980). *The politics and programs of family policy*. South Bend, IN: University of Notre Dame and Leuvan University Press.

Aldous, J., & Ganey, R. (1989). Families' definitional behavior of problematic situations. *Social Forces*, *67*(4), 871–897.

Aldous, J., & Klein, D. M. (1991). Sentiment and services: Models of intergenerational relationships in mid-life. *Journal of Marriage and the Family*, *53*(3), 595–608.

Anderson, E. A. (1989). Implications for public policy: Towards a pro-family AIDS social policy. In E. D. Macklin (Ed.), *AIDS and the family* (pp. 187–228). Binghamton, NY: Haworth Press.

Angier, N. (1995, June 11). The rise of the "Oldest Old": If you're really ancient, you might be better off. *New York Times*, D1–D5.

Arcus, M. E. (1992). Family life education: Toward the 21st century. *Family Relations*, *41*(4), 390–393.

Arcus, M. E., & Thomas, J. (1993). The nature and practice of family life education. In M. E. Arcus, J. D. Schvaneveldt, & J. J. Moss (Eds.), *Handbook of family life education* (Vol. 2, pp. 1–32). Newbury Park, CA: Sage.

Auerbach, J. D., & Figert, A. E. (1995, extra issue). Women's health research: Public policy and sociology. *Health and Social Behavior* 115–131.

Axelson, L. J., & Dail, P. W. (1988). The changing character of homelessness in the United States. *Family Relations*, *37*(4), 463–469.

Axinn, W. G., & Thornton, A. (1993). Mothers, children, and cohabitation: The intergenerational effects of attitudes and behavior. *American Sociological Review*, *58*(2), 233–246.

Bane, M. J. (1976). *Here to stay: American families in the twentieth century*. New York: Basic Books.

Barnes, G. E., Greenwood, L., & Sommer, R. (1991). Courtship violence in a Canadian sample of male college students. *Family Relations*, *40*(1), 37–44.

Bassick, E. L., & Gerson, S. (1978). Deinstitutionalization and mental health services. *Scientific American*, *238*(2), 46, 33.

Begley, S. (1994, February 7). One pill makes you larger, one pill makes you small. *Newsweek*, *CXXIII*(6), 36–40.

Bell, D. (1973). *The coming of the post industrial society*. New York: Basic Books.

Bengtson, V. L. (1996, March). *Families, aging, and social change: Intergenerational relationships in the future*. Paper presented at the Groves Conference on Marriage and the Family, San Diego, CA.

Berger, B. (1981). *The survival of a counter culture*. Berkeley: University of California Press.

Billingham, R. E. (1987). Courtship violence: The patterns of conflict resolution strategies across seven levels of emotional commitment. *Family Relations*, *36*(3), 283–289.

Billingsley, A. (1988). The impact of technology on Afro-American families. *Family Relations*, *37*(4), 420–425.

Blair, S. L., & Johnson, M. P. (1992). Wives' perceptions of the fairness of household work: The intersection of housework and ideology. *Journal of Marriage and the Family*, *54*(3), 570–581.

Block, C. R., Norr, K. L., Meyering, S., Norr, J. I., & Charles, A. G. (1981). Husband gatekeeping at birth. *Family Relations*, *30*(2), 197–204.

Blood, R. O., Jr., & Wolfe, D. M. (1960). *Husbands and wives*. Glencoe, IL: Free Press.

Bolger, N., Moen, P., & Downey, G. (1985). *Family transitions and work decisions: A life course analysis of labor force reentry for mature married women*. Washington, DC: American Sociological Association.

Bossard, J. H., & Boll, E. (1956). *The large family system*. Philadelphia: University of Pennsylvania Press.

Broderick, C., & Smith, J. (1979). The general systems approach to the family. In W. R. Burr, R. Hill, F. I. Nye, & I. L. Reiss (Eds.), *Contemporary theories about the family* (Vol. 2, pp. 112–129). New York: Free Press.

Broman, C. L. (1988). Household work and the family life satisfaction of blacks. *Journal of Marriage and the Family, 50*(3), 743–748.

Brown, J. E., & Mann, L. (1989). Parents and adolescents' perceptions of participation in family decisions. *Australian Journal of Sex, Marriage, & Family, 10*(2), 65–73.

Brown, J. E., & Mann, L. (1990). The relationship between family structure and process variables and adolescent decision making. *Journal of Adolescence, 13*, 25–37.

Bubolz, M. M., & Sontag, M. S. (1993). Human ecology theory. In P. G. Boss, W. J. Doherty, R. LaRossa, W. R. Schumm, & S. K. Steinmetz (Eds.), *Sourcebook of family theories and methods: A contextual approach* (pp. 419–447). New York: Plenum.

Burgess, E. W., & Locke, H. J. (1945). *The family: From institution to companionship.* New York: American Book Co.

Burgess, E. W., & Locke, H. J. (1953). *The family: From institution to companionship* (2nd ed.). New York: American Book Co.

Burr, W. R., & Christensen, C. (1992). Undesirable side effects of enhancing self esteem. *Family Relations, 41*(4), 460–465.

Burr, W. R., Hill, R., Nye, E. I., & Reiss, I. L. (Eds.). (1979). *Contemporary theories about the family* (Vols. 1 & 2). New York: Free Press.

Burr, W. R., Leigh, G. K., Day, R. D., & Constantine, J. (1979). Symbolic interaction and the family. In W. R. Burr, R. Hill, F. I. Nye, & I. L. Reiss (Eds.), *Contemporary theories about the family* (Vol. 2, pp. 42–111). New York: Free Press.

Campbell, A., Converse, P. E., & Rodgers, W. L. (1976). *The quality of American life: Perceptions, evaluations and satisfaction.* New York: Russell Sage Foundation.

Cherlin, A. (1990, July). Recent changes in American fertility, marriage and divorce. *Annals of the American Academy of Political and Social Science, 520*, 145–154.

Clarke, S. C., & Wilson, B. F. (1994). The relative stability of remarriages: A cohort approach using vital statistics. *Family Relations, 43*(3), 305–310.

Clavan, S. (1985). Even if a deformed baby or a person in a long term coma is unable to make a decision for him or herself to remove life support systems, the family has no right to make the decision. In H. Feldman & M. Feldman (Eds.), *Current controversies in marriage and the family* (pp. 333–344). Newbury Park, CA: Sage.

Coale, A. J., Feng, W., Riley, N. E., & De, L. F. (1991, January 25). Recent trends in fertility and nuptiality in China. *Science, 251*, 389–393.

Cogswell, B. E. (1988). The walking patient and the revolt of the client: Impetus to develop new models of physician-patient roles. In S. K. Steinmetz (Ed.), *Family and support systems across the life span* (pp. 243–256). New York: Plenum.

Cole, C. L., & Rueter, M. A. (1993). The family-peace connection: Implications for constructing the reality of the future. In B. H. Settles, R. S. Hanks, & M. B. Sussman (Eds.), *American families and the future: Analyses of possible destinies* (pp. 263–278). Binghamton, NY: Haworth Press.

Coleman, C. (1994, October 14). Home alone: For many home-based entrepreneurs, the biggest obstacles may be overcoming the feeling of isolation. *Wall Street Journal*, R20.

Coleman, M., & Ganong, L. H. (1990). Remarriage and stepparenting. *Journal of Marriage and the Family, 52*(4), 925–940.

Collingridge, D. (1983). Hedging and flexing: Two ways of choosing under ignorance. *Technology Forecasting and Social Change, 23*, 161–172.

Coltrane, S., & Ishii-Kuntz, M. (1992). Men's housework: A life course perspective. *Journal of Marriage and the Family, 54*(2), 43–57.

Constantine, L. L. (1973). *Group marriage: A study of contemporary multilateral marriage.* New York: Macmillan.

Constantine, L. L. (1995). *Constantine on Peopleware.* Englewood Cliffs, NJ: Yourdon Press.

Cook, J. D., & Wright, E. R. (1995). Medical sociology and the study of severe mental illness: Reflections on past accomplishments and directions for future research. *Health and Social Behavior* (extra issue), 95–114.

Cooney, T. M. (1993). Recent demographic change: Implications for families planning for the future. In B. H. Settles, R. S. Hanks, & M. B. Sussman (Eds.), *American families and the future: Analyses of possible destinies* (pp. 37–56). New York: Haworth Press.

Cooney, T. M., Hutchinson, M. K., & Leather, D. M. (1995). Surviving the breakup? Predictors of parent–adult child relations after parental divorce. *Family Relations, 44*(2), 153–161.

Cornfield, D. B. (1990). Labor unions, corporations and families: Institutions competition in the provision of social welfare. *Marriage and Family Review, 15*(3–4), 37–58.

Counts, R. M. (1992). Second and third divorces: The flood to come. *Journal of Divorce and Remarriage, 17*(1/2), 193–200.

Creationism. (1982). *Academe, 68*(2), 10.

Crutchfield, C. F. (1981a). Medical treatment for minor children: The roles of parents, the state, the child and the Supreme Court of the United States. *Family Relations, 30*(2), 165–178.

Crutchfield, C. F. (1981b). Medical treatment for minor children: Replies to Zimmerman and Rodman. *Family Relations, 30*(2), 185–186.

Culley, J. D., Settles, B. H., & Van Name, J. B. (1976). *Understanding and measuring the cost of foster care.* Newark: Bureau of Economic and Business Research, University of Delaware.

Dail, P. W. (1993). Homelessness in America: Involuntary family migration. In B. H. Settles, D. E. Hanks III, & M. B. Sussman (Eds.), *Families on the move: Migration, immigration, emigration, and mobility* (pp. 55–76). Binghamton, NY: Haworth Press.

Demo, D. H., & Acock, A. C. (1993). Family diversity and the division of domestic labor: How much have things really changed? *Family Relations, 42*(3), 323–331.

Dickson, F. C., & Markman, H. J. (1993). The benefits of communication research: Intervention programs for couples and families. In P. G. Boss, W. J. Doherty, R. LaRossa, W. R. Schumm, & S. K. Steinmetz (Eds.), *Sourcebook of family theories and methods: A contextual approach* (pp. 586–590). New York: Plenum.

Dickson, L. (1993). The future of marriage and family in black America. *Journal of Black Studies, 23*(4), 472–491.

Dilworth-Anderson, P., Burton, L. M., & Johnson, L. B. (1993). Reframing theories for understanding race, ethnicity and families. In P. G. Boss, W. J. Doherty, R. LaRossa, W. R. Schumm, & S. K. Steinmetz (Eds.), *Sourcebook of family theories and methods: A contextual approach* (pp. 627–645). New York: Plenum.

Doherty, W. J., & Baptiste, Jr., D. A. (1993). Theories emerging from family therapy. In P. G. Boss, W. J. Doherty, R. LaRossa, W. R. Schumm, & S. K. Steinmetz (Eds.), *Sourcebook of family theories and methods: A contextual approach* (pp. 505–524). New York: Plenum.

Doherty, W. J., Boss, P. G., LaRossa, R., Schumm, W. R., & Steinmetz, S. K. (1993). Family theories and methods: A contextual approach. In P. G. Boss, W. J. Doherty, R. LaRossa, W. R. Schumm, & S. K. Steinmetz (Eds.), *Sourcebook of family theories and methods: A contextual approach* (pp. 3–30). New York: Plenum.

Doolittle, N. O., & Wiggens, S. D. (1993). Present and future health care for an aging society. In B. H. Settles, R. S. Hanks, & M. B. Sussman (Eds.), *American families and the future: Analyses of possible destinies* (pp. 57–72). Binghamton, NY: Haworth Press.

Dumon, W., & Nuelant, T. (1994). *National family policies in the member states of the European Union in 1992 and 1993.* Leuven, Belgium: European Observatory on National Family Policies, European Commission, Directorate General V, Employment, Industrial Relations and Social Affairs.

Duran-Aydintug, C., & Ihinger-Tallman, M. (1995). Law and stepfamilies. *Marriage and Family Review, 21*(3/4), 169–192.

Elshtain, J. B. (1982). *The family in political thought.* Amherst: University of Massachusetts Press.

Elshtain, J. B. (1990). The family and civic life. In D. Blakenhorn, S. Bayme, & J. B. Elshtain (Eds.), *Rebuilding the nest: A new commitment to the American family* (pp. 119–132). Milwaukee, WI: Family Service America.

Erickson, R. J., & Babcock, G. M. (1995). Men and family law: From patriarchy to partnership. In L. J. McIntyre & M. B. Sussman (Eds.), *Families and law* (pp. 31–54). Binghamton, NY: Haworth Press.

Fine, M. A., & Fine, D. R. (1994). An examination and evaluation of recent changes in divorce laws in five western countries: The critical role of values. *Journal of Marriage and the Family, 56*(2), 249–264.

Fineman, M. (1994). The end of family law? Intimacy in the twenty-first century. In S. Ingber (Ed.), *Changing perspectives of the family* (pp. 23–32). Proceedings of the fifth annual symposium of the constitutional law resource center, April 16, 1994. Des Moines, IA: Drake University Law School.

Fish, L. S., & Osborn, J. L. (1992). Therapists' views of family life: A Delphi study. *Family Relations, 41*(4), 409–416.

Fitzpatrick, M. A., & Ritchie, L. D. (1993). Communication theory and the family. In P. G. Boss, W. J. Doherty, R. LaRossa, W. R. Schumm, & S. K. Steinmetz (Eds.), *Sourcebook of family theories and methods: A contextual approach* (pp. 565–585). New York: Plenum.

Flynn, C. P. (1987). Relationship violence: A model for family professionals. *Family Relations, 36*(3), 295–299.

Foulke, S. R., Alford-Cooper, F., & Butler, S. (1993). Intergenerational issues in long term planning. In B. H. Settles, R. S. Hanks, & M. B. Sussman (Eds.), *American families and the future: Analyses of possible destinies* (pp. 73–96). Binghamton, NY: Haworth Press.

Fox, G. L. (1993). A child is born: Conception, fertility and childbearing. In K. Altergott (Ed.), *One world, many families* (pp. 27–31). Minneapolis, MN: National Council on Family Relations.

Ganong, L., Coleman, M., & Fine, M. A. (1994). Remarriage and stepfamilies. In R. D. Day, K. R. Gilbert, B. H. Settles, & W. R. Burr (Eds.), *Research and theory in family science* (pp. 287–303). Pacific Grove, CA: Brooks/Cole.

Gates, B., with Myhrvold, N., & Rinearson, P. (1995). *The road ahead.* New York: Viking.

Gelles, R. J., & Maynard, P. E. (1987). Structural family systems approach to intervention in cases of family violence. *Family Relations, 36*(3), 270–275.

Glick, P. C. (1979, January). *The future of the American family.* Current Population Reports: Special Studies, Series D-23, No. 78. Washington, D.C.: U.S. Government Printing Office.

Glick, P. C. (1980). Remarriage: Some recent changes and variations. *Journal of Family Issues, 1*(4), 453–478.

Glick, P. C. (1989a). Remarried families, stepfamilies, and stepchildren: A brief demographic profile. *Family Relations, 38*(1), 24–27.

Glick, P. C. (1989b). The family life cycle and social change. *Family Relations, 38*(2), 123–129.

Glick, P. C. (1990). American families; as they are and were. *Sociology and Social Research, 74*(3), 139–145.

Glick, P. C. (1993). The impact of geographic mobility on individuals and families. In B. H. Settles, D. E. Hanks III, & M. B. Sussman (Eds.), *Families on the move: Migration, immigration, emigration, and mobility* (pp. 31–54). Binghamton, NY: Haworth Press.

Goldman, N. (1993). The perils of single life in contemporary Japan. *Journal of Marriage and the Family, 55*(1), 191–204.

Goldner, V. (1993). Feminist theories. In P. G. Boss, W. J. Doherty, R. LaRossa, W. R. Schumm, & S. K. Steinmetz (Eds.), *Sourcebook of family theories and methods: A contextual approach* (pp. 623–626). New York: Plenum.

Groller, I. (1990). The future of the family. *Parents' Magazine, 65*(1), 31.

Gubrium, J. F., & Holstein, J. A. (1990). *What is family?* Mountain View, CA: Mayfield.

Gubrium, J. F., & Holstein, J. A. (1993). Phenomenology, ethnomethodology, and family discourse. In P. G. Boss, W. J. Doherty, R. LaRossa, W. R. Schumm, & S. K. Steinmetz (Eds.), *Sourcebook of family theories and methods: A contextual approach* (pp. 651–672). New York: Plenum.

Guttentag, M., & Secord, P. F. (1983). *Too many women?* Beverly Hills, CA: Sage.

Gwartney-Gibbs, P. A., Stockard, J., & Bohmer, S. (1987). Learning courtship aggression: The influence of parents, peers and personal experiences. *Family Relations, 36*(3), 276– 283.

Haley, A. (1976). *Roots.* Garden City, NY: Doubleday.

Hanks, R. S. (1990). *Family and corporation linkage in timing and control of incentive based early retirement.* Unpublished doctoral dissertation, University of Delaware, Newark, DE.

Hanks, R. S. (1991). An intergenerational perspective on family ethical dilemmas. *Marriage and Family Review, 16*(1–2), 161–174.

Hanks, R. S., & Settles, B. H. (1990). Theoretical questions and ethical issues in a family caregiving relationship. In D. E. Biegal & A. Blum (Eds.), *Aging and caregiving: Theory, research, and policy* (pp. 98–120). Newbury Park, CA: Sage.

Hansson, R. O., Nelson, R. E., Carver, M. D., NeeSmith, D. H., Dowling, E. M., Fletcher, W. L., & Suhr, P. (1990). Adult children will frail elderly parents: When to intervene? *Family Relations, 3*(2), 153–158.

Hardesty, C., & Bokemeier, J. (1989). Finding time and making do: Distribution of household labor in nonmetropolitan marriages. *Journal of Marriage and the Family, 51*(1), 253–267.

Hardy, K. V. (1993). Implications for practice with ethnic minority families. In P. G. Boss, W. J. Doherty, R. LaRossa, W. R. Schumm, & S. K. Steinmetz (Eds.), *Sourcebook of family theories and methods: A contextual approach* (pp. 646–650). New York: Plenum.

Hareven, T. (1994). Aging and generational relations: A historical and life course perspective. *Annual Reviews Sociology, 20,* 437–461.

Hareven, T. (Ed.). (1996). *Aging and generational relations over the life course: A historical and cross-cultural perspective.* Berlin: Walter de Gruyter.

Harris, L., & Associates, Inc. (1981). *The General Mills, American Family Report, 1980–81: Families at work, strength and strains.* Minneapolis, MN: General Mills.

Haug, M. R. (1990). The interplay of formal and informal health care: Theoretical issues and research needs. *Advances in Medical Sociology, 1,* 207–231.

Hauser, S. T. (1990). The study of families and chronic illness: Ways of coping and interacting. In G. H. Brody & I. E. Sigel (Eds.), *Methods of family research* (Vol. 2, pp. 63–86). Hillsdale, NJ: Erlbaum.

Hirsch, C. (1993). Microstructural and gender role influences on male caregivers. Paper presented at the 30th Seminar of the Committee on Family Research of the International Sociological Association, Annapolis, MD.

Hirshorn, B. (1991). Sharing or competition: Multiple views of the intergenerational flow of society's resources. In S. K. Pfeifer & M. B. Sussman (Eds.), *Families: Intergenerational and generational connections* (pp. 175–193). Binghamton, NY: Haworth Press.

Hornblower, M. (1995, December 11). Fixing the system. *Time, 146*(24), 44–45.

Ingoldsby, B. B. (1995). Marital structure. In B. B. Ingoldsby & S. Smith (Eds.), *Families in multicultural perspective* (pp. 117–138). New York: Guilford.

Jackson, M. A. (1988). *Filial responsibility attitudes of adult children toward early retired parents.* Unpublished master's thesis, University of Delaware, Newark, DE.

Jacobs, J. B. (1988). Families facing the nuclear taboo. *Family Relations, 37*(4), 432–436.

Kain, E. I. (1993). Patterns and change in women's education and labor force participation: Contrasts between the developed and the developing world. Paper presented at the 30th Seminar of the Committee on Family Research of the International Sociological Association, Annapolis, MD.

Kamerman, S. B., & Kahn, A. J. (1991). A U.S. policy change. In S. B. Kamerman & A. J. Kahn (Eds.), *Child care, parental leave, and the under 3s* (pp. 1–22). New York: Auburn House.

Kantor, D., & Lehr, W. (1975). *Inside the family.* San Francisco: Jossey-Bass.

Kemper, T. D. (1993). Predicting the divorce rate, down? *Journal of Family Issues, 4*(3), 507–524.

Kent, O. (1980). Remarriage: A family systems perspective. *Social Casework, 61,* 146–154.

Kephart, W. M. (1976). *Extraordinary groups: The sociology of unconventional lifestyles.* New York: St. Martin's.

Kephart, W. M. (1982). *Extraordinary groups: The sociology of unconventional life-styles* (2nd ed.). New York: St. Martin's.

Keyfitz, N. (1989). The growing human population. *Scientific American, 261*(9), 119–126.

Kilty, K. M., & Behling, J. H. (1986). Retirement financial planning among professional workers. *The Gerontologist, 26*(5), 525–530.

Kingsbury, N. M., & Scanzoni, J. H. (1989). Process power and decision outcomes among dual career couples. *Journal of Comparative Family Studies, 20*(2), 231–246.

Kitson, G. C., & Morgan, L. A. (1990). The multiple consequences of divorce: A decade review. *Journal of Marriage and the Family, 52*(4), 913–924.

Kivett, V. R. (1991). The grandparent–grandchild connection. In S. K. Pfeifer & M. B. Sussman (Eds.), *Families: Intergenerational and generational connections* (pp. 267–290). Binghamton, NY: Haworth Press.

Koepke, L., Hare, J., & Moran, P. M. (1992). Relationship quality in a sample of lesbian couples with children and child-free lesbian couples. *Family Relations, 41*(2), 224–229.

Lawson, E. J., & Thompson, A. (1995). Black men make sense of marital distress and divorce: An exploratory study. *Family Relations, 44*(2), 211–218.

Lemann, N. (1995, June 11). Taking affirmative action apart. *The New York Times Magazine,* 36–42, 52–54.

Levin, I., & Trost, J. (1992a). Understanding the concept of family. *Family Relations, 41*(3), 348–351.

Levin, I., & Trost, J. (1992b). *Women and the concept of family.* (Family Reports, 21). Uppsala, Sweden: Uppsala University.

Levine, J. (1982, June). *The new fatherhood.* Paper presented at the Groves Conference, Ocean City, MD.

Lewis, M. A., Dyer, C. L., & Moran, J. D. (1995). Parental and peer influences on the clothing purchases of female adolescent consumers as a function of discretionary income. *Journal of Family Consumer Sciences, 87*(1), 15–20.

Lieberson, S., & Mikelson, K. S. (1995). Distinctive African American names: An experimental, historical, and linguistic analysis of innovation. *American Sociological Review, 60*(6), 928–946.

Liprie, M. L. (1993). Adolescents' contributions to family decision making. In B. H. Settles, R. S. Hanks, & M. B. Sussman (Eds.), *American families and the future: Analysis of possible destinies* (pp. 241–254). Binghamton, NY: Haworth Press.

Liprie, M. L., Hanks, R. S., & Berke, D. (1992). *Teen pregnancy: Decision making, critical thinking and locus of control.* Newark: Delaware Department of Public Instruction and University of Delaware.

Lloyd, S. A. (1987). Conflict in premarital relationships: Differential perceptions of males and females. *Family Relations, 36*(3), 290–294.

Lloyd, S. A. (1991). The darkside of courtship: Violence and sexual exploitation. *Family Relations, 40*(1), 14–20.

Lopata, H. Z. (1973). *Widowhood in an American city.* Cambridge, MA: Schenkman.

Macklin, E. D. (1980). Nontraditional family forms: A decade of research. *Journal of Marriage and the Family, 42,* 905–922.

Macklin, E. D., & Van Antwerp, G. (1996, March 6–10). *Gay and lesbian families: Intergenerational issues.* Workshop presented at Groves Conference on Marriage and the Family, San Diego, CA.

Malos, E. (1980). *The politics at housework.* London: Allison & Bushy.

Marciano, T. D. (1993). Issues of technology's possible futures. In B. H. Settles, R. S. Hanks, & M. B. Sussman (Eds.), *American families and the future: Analyses of possible destinies* (pp. 125–134). Binghamton, NY: Haworth Press.

Mayseless, O. (1991). Adult attachment patterns and courtship violence. *Family Relations, 40*(1), 21–28.

McAdoo, H. P. (1992). Stress levels, family help patterns, and religiosity in middle and working class African-American single mothers. In J. L. McAdoo (Ed.), *Proceedings of Empirical Research on Black Psychology Conference, XIII* (pp. 212–309). East Lansing: MSU Foundation, College of Human Ecology, Michigan State University.

McLain, R., & Weigart, A. (1979). Toward a phenomenological sociology of family: A programmatic essay. In W. R. Burr, R. Hill, F. I. Nye, & I. L. Reiss (Eds.), *Contemporary theories about the family* (Vol, 2, pp. 160–205). New York: Free Press.

McLanahan, S., & Bumpass, L. (1988). Intergenerational consequences of family disruption. *American Journal of Sociology, 94*(1), 130–152.

Menaghan, E. C., & Parcel, T. L. (1990). Parental employment and family life research in 1980s. *Journal of Marriage and the Family, 52*(4), 1079–1098.

Mendel, C. H., & Habenstein, R. W. (1976). *Ethnic families in America.* New York: Elsevier.

Miall, C. E. (1987). The stigma of adoptive parent status: Perception of community attitudes toward adoption and the experience of informal social sanction. *Family Relations, 36*(1), 34–39.

Miall, C. E. (1995, August). *The social construction of adoption: Clinical and community perspectives.* Paper presented at the American Sociological Association annual meeting. Washington, DC.

Miller, B. C. (1987). Marriage, family, and fertility. In M. B. Sussman & S. K. Steinmetz (Eds.), *Handbook of marriage and the family* (pp. 565–590). New York: Plenum.

Millet, K. (1970). *Sexual politics.* Garden City, NY: Doubleday.

Minuchin, S. (1974). *Families and family therapy.* Cambridge, MA: Harvard University Press.

Moen, P. (1992, March). A life course approach to women's multiple roles, health and well-being. *The Sociology of Aging Newsletter,* 8–12.

Moen, P., & Firebaugh, F. M. (1993). Life course issues and family resources: Preparing for an uncertain future. In K. Altergott (Ed.), *One world, many families* (pp. 21–26). Minneapolis, MN: National Council on Family Relations.

Mortimer, J. T., & London, J. (1984). The varying linkages of work and family. In P. Voyandoff (Ed.), *Changing roles of men and women* (pp. 20–22). Palo Alto, CA: Mayfield.

Mount, B. (1988, November 2). *Personal futures planning: A person centered approach to service delivery.* Unpublished paper delivered at the Conference on The Rights of Passage, Coordinating Council for the

Handicapped Child of Delaware, Alfred I. DuPont Institute, Wilmington, DE.

Mullins, J. B. (1987). Authentic voices from parents of exceptional children. *Family Relations, 36*(1), 30–33.

Nagel, J. (1995). American Indian ethnic renewal: Politics and the resurgence of identity. *American Sociological Review, 60*(6), 947–965.

Naisbitt, J. (1982). *Megatrends: Ten new directions transforming our lives.* New York: Warner Books.

Nichols, M. P., & Schwartz, R. C. (1991). *Family therapy: Concepts and methods* (2nd ed.). Boston: Allyn & Bacon.

Nisbit, R. (1980). *History of the idea of progress.* New York: Basic Books.

Norton, A. J., & Moorman, J. E. (1987). Current trends in marriage and divorce among American women. *Journal of Marriage and the Family, 49*(1), 3–14.

Nye, F. I. (1979). Choice, exchange, and the family. In W. R. Burr, R. Hill, F. I. Nye & I. L. Reiss (Eds.), *Contemporary theories about the family* (Vol. 2, pp. 1–41). New York: Free Press.

Oakley, A. (1974). *The sociology of housework.* New York: Pantheon.

Olsen, F. (1994). Gender, intimate relationships, and state authority. In S. Ingber (Ed.), *Changing perspectives of the family* (pp. 45–53). Proceedings of the fifth annual symposium of the constitutional law resource center. Des Moines, IA: Drake University Law School.

Ornauer, H., Wiberg, H., Sicinski, A., & Galtung, J. (Eds.). (1976). *Images of the world in the year 2000: A comparative ten nation study.* Atlantic Highlands, NJ: Humanities Press.

Osmond, M. W., & Thorne, B. (1993). Feminist theories: The social construction of gender in families and society. In P. G. Boss, W. J. Doherty, R. LaRossa, W. R. Schumm, & S. K. Steinmetz (Eds.), *Sourcebook of family theories and methods: A contextual approach* (pp. 591–623). New York: Plenum.

Pescosolido, B. A., & Kronenfeld, J. J. (1995). Health, illness, and healing in an uncertain era: Challenges from and for medical sociology. *Health and Social Behavior* (extra issue), 5–33.

Peterson, G. W. (1995). Autonomy and connectedness in families. In R. D. Day, K. R. Gilbert, B. H. Settles, & W. R. Burr (Eds.), *Research and theory in family science* (pp. 20–41). Pacific Grove, CA: Brooks/Cole.

Pickett, R. S. (1977, April). Tomorrow's family. *Intellect, 105,* 330–332.

Pilisuk, M., & Parks, S. H. (1983). Social support and family stress. *Marriage and Family Review, 6*(1–2), 137–156.

Pill, C. J. (1990). Stepfamilies: Redefining the family. *Family Relations, 39*(2), 186–193.

Pines, M. (1976). Genetic profile will put our health in our own hands. *Smithsonian, 4,* 86–90.

Piña, D. L., & Bengston, V. (1993). The division of household labor and wives' happiness: Ideology, employment, and perceptions of support. *Journal of Marriage and the Family, 55*(4), 901–912.

Piotrakowski, C. S., Rapoport, R. N., & Rapoport, R. (1987). Families and work. In M. B. Sussman & S. K. Steimmetz (Eds.), *Handbook of marriage and the family* (pp. 251–283). New York: Plenum.

Pitts, J. M. (1986, October 4). Planning for tomorrow's elderly. *Economics Review,* 17–20.

Ptacek, C. (1988). The nuclear age: Context for family interaction. *Family Relations, 37*(4), 437–443.

Purnell, M., & Bagby, B. R. (1993). Grandparents' rights: Implications for family specialists. *Family Relations, 42*(2), 173–178.

Reiss, D. (1991, November). *Realignments in families of chronically ill patients: The death of the patient and the survival of the family.* Paper presented at the National Council on Family Relations Annual Meeting, Denver, CO.

Rettig, K. D. (1987). *A cognitive conceptual family decision making framework* (Tech. Rep. No. NCR116). MN: Family Resource Management Research Reporting Technical Group.

Rettig, K. D. (1993). Problem-solving and decision-making as central processes of family life: An ecological framework for family relations and family resource management. In B. H. Settles, R. S. Hanks, & M. B. Sussman (Eds.), *American families and the future: Analyses of possible destinies* (pp. 187–222). Binghamton, NY: Haworth Press.

Reynolds, J. S., Kennon, L. R., & Palakurthi, R. (1995). Parents' perceptions of fast food consumption by children. *Journal of Family and Consumer Sciences, 87*(4), 39–44.

Riche, M. F. (1991). The future of the family. *American Demographics, 13*(3), 44–46.

Riessman, F., & Carroll, D. (1995). *Redefining self-help: Policy and practice.* San Francisco, CA: Jossey-Bass.

Robinson, L., & Blanton, P. W. (1993). Marital strengths in enduring marriages. *Family Relations, 42*(1), 38–45.

Rock, M. S. (1992). *Analysis of variables affecting concern for future health planning in families.* Unpublished doctoral dissertation, University of Delaware, Newark, DE.

Rodman, H. (1981). Understanding the United States Supreme Court's position on parental consent requirements: In defense of Danforth and Bellotte, A response to Butchfield. *Family Relations, 40*(2), 182–184.

Rosen, M. (1982). The family of the future. *Parents' Magazine, 57,* 65–68, 117–118.

Rosenblatt, R. C. (1994). *Metaphors of family systems theory: Toward new constructions.* New York: Guilford.

Rossi, A. S. (1993). The future in the making: Recent trends in work–family interface. *American Journal of Orthopsychiatry, 63*(2), 66–177.

Russell, L. B. (1982). *The baby boom generation and the economy.* Washington, DC: Brookings Institution.

Safilios-Rothchild, C. (1970). The study of family power structure: A review of 1960–1969. *Journal of Marriage and the Family, 32,* 239–352.

Salt, R. (1991). Child support in context: Comments on Rettig, Christensen & Dahl. *Family Relations, 40*(2), 175–178.

Sanborn, B., & Bould, S. (1991). Intergenerational caregivers of the oldest old. In S. K. Pfeifer & M. B. Sussman (Eds.), *Families: Intergenerational and generational connections* (pp. 125–142). Binghamton, NY: Haworth Press.

Schneider, E. (1994). Response to S. Ingber, Gender, intimate relationships, and state authority. In S. Ingber (Ed.), *Changing perspectives of the family* (pp. 56–57). Proceedings of the fifth annual symposium of the constitutional law resource center, April 16, 1994. Des Moines, IA: Drake University Law School.

Schulz, D. A. (1985). The family has the right to make the decision to remove life-support systems if the affected individual is unable to do so. In H. Feldman & M. Feldman (Eds.), *Current controversies in marriage and the family* (pp. 345–352). Newbury Park, CA: Sage.

Schwartzman, J. (1982). Normality from a cross-cultural perspective. In F. Walsh (Ed.), *Family process* (pp. 383–398). New York: Guilford.

Scott, J. W. (1994). From teenage parenthood to polygamy: Case studies in black polygamous family formation. In R. Staples (Ed.), *The black family: Essays and studies* (pp. 300–310). Belmont, CA: Wadsworth.

Settles, B. (1974, October). *Demonstration of teaching of family theory.* Paper presented at the National Council on Family Relations, St. Louis, MO.

Settles, B. H. (1987). A perspective on tomorrow's families. In M. B. Sussman & S. K. Steinmetz (Eds.), *Handbook of marriage and the family* (pp. 157–180). New York: Plenum.

Settles, B. H. (1990). *Interactive planning for family futures* (Final report Grant #0090AM0219, United States Department of Health and Human Services, Administration on Aging). Newark: University of Delaware.

Settles, B. H. (1993a). Expanding choice in long term planning for family futures. In B. H. Settles, R. S. Hanks, & M. B. Sussman (Eds.), *American families and the future: Analyses of possible destinies* (pp. 1–36). Binghamton, NY: Haworth Press.

Settles, B. H. (1993b). The illusion of stability in family life: The reality of change and mobility. In B. H. Settles, D. E. Hanks III, & M. B. Sussman (Eds.), *Families on the move: Migration, immigration, emigration, and mobility* (pp. 5–30). Binghamton, NY: Haworth Press.

Settles, B. H. (1995). Families in everyday life. In R. D. Day, K. R. Gilbert, B. H. Settles, & W. R. Burr (Eds.). *Research and theory in family science* (pp. 154–170). Pacific Grove, CA: Brooks/Cole.

Settles, B. H., MacRostie, L., & Lucca, J. (1986, March). *Parental coping strategies in the management of cystic fibrosis.* Paper presented at the Second Annual Parenting Symposium, Philadelphia, PA.

Settles, B. H., Sussman, M. B., Trost, J., & Levin, I. (in press). Concepts and definitions of family: Dialogue between theory and practice. *Marriage and Family Review.*

Shanas, E., & Sussman, M. R. (1981). *Aging: Stability and change in the family.* New York: Academic Press.

Silverstein, M., Parrott, T. M., & Bengston, V. L. (1995). Factors that predispose sons and daughters to provide social support to older parents. *Journal of Marriage and the Family, 57*(2), 465–476.

Simpson, M., Timm, H., & McCubbin, H. L. (1981). Adoptees in search of their past: Policy induced strain on adoptive families and birth parents. *Family Relations, 30*(3), 427–434.

Skolnick, A. (1993). Families in transition: America's and the world's. In K. Altergott (Ed.), *One world, many families* (pp. 3–7). Minneapolis, MN: National Council on Family Relations.

Smolowe, J. (1995, December 11). Making the tough calls. *Time, 146*(24), 40–44.

Spanier, G. B., & Furstenberg, Jr., F. F. (1987). Remarriage and reconstituted families. In M. B. Sussman & S. K. Steinmetz (Eds.), *Handbook of marriage and the family* (pp. 419–434). New York: Plenum.

Spanier, G. B., & Glick, P. C. (1980). The life cycle of American families. *Journal of Family History, 15*(1), 97–111.

Spitze, G. (1990). Women's employment and family relations: A review. *Journal of Marriage and the Family, 52*, 595–618.

Spitze, G., & Ward, R. (1995). Household labor in intergenerational households. *Journal of Marriage and the Family, 57*(2), 355–361.

Sporakowski, M. J. (1992). Enhancing family life in the future: A potential for family therapists. *Family Relations, 41*(4), 394–397.

Sprenkle, D. H., & Piercy, F. P. (1992). A family therapy informed view of the current state of the family in the United States. *Family Relations, 41*(4), 404–408.

Sprey, J. (1979). Conflict theory and the study of marriage and the family. In W. R. Burr, R. Hill, F. I. Nye & I. L. Reiss (Eds.), *Contemporary theories about the family* (Vol. 2, pp. 130–159). New York: Free Press.

Stanton, M. E. (1995). Patterns of kinship and residence. In B. B. Ingoldsby & S. Smith (Eds.), *Families in multicultural perspective* (pp. 117–138). New York: Guilford.

Staples, R. (1976). *Introduction to black sociology.* New York: McGraw-Hill.

Staples, R. (1994). Changes in black family structure: The conflict between family ideology and structural conditions. In R. Staples (Ed.), *The black family: Essays and studies* (pp. 11–19). Belmont, CA: Wadsworth.

Stein, P. J. (1981, May). *Singlehood.* Paper presented at the Groves Conference on Marriage and the Family, Mt. Pocono, PA.

Steinmetz, S. K. (1987). Family violence: Past, present and future. In M. B. Sussman & S. K. Steinmetz (Eds.), *Handbook of marriage and the family* (pp. 725–766). New York: Plenum.

Steinmetz, S. K. (1988). *Duty bound: Elder abuse and family care.* Newbury Park, CA: Sage.

Stets, J. E., & Henderson, D. A. (1991). Contextual factors surrounding conflict resolution while dating: Results from a national study. *Family Relations, 40*(1), 29–36.

Strasser, S. (1982). *Never done.* New York: Pantheon.

Strauss, A. L. (1984). *Chronic illness and the quality of life.* St. Louis, MO: Mosby.

Sun, L. H. (1993). *A great leap backward. Third world, second class: The burden of womanhood. Washington Post* reprint. Washington, DC: Washington Post Corp.

Sussman, M. B. (1980). Future trends in society and social services. In *National Conference on Social Welfare.* New York: Columbia University Press.

Sussman, M. B. (1983). Law and legal systems: The family connection. *Journal of Marriage and the Family, 45*(1), 11–34.

Sussman, M. B. (1991). Reflection on intergenerational and kin connections. In S. K. Pfeifer & M. B. Sussman (Eds.), *Families: Intergenerational and generational connections* (pp. 3–9). Binghamton, NY: Haworth Press.

Sussman, M. B. (1993). Families in the time to come: Taking a position on trends and issues. In B. H. Settles, R. S. Hanks, & M. B. Sussman (Eds.), *American families and the future: Analyses of possible destinies* (pp. 303–313). Binghamton, NY: Haworth Press.

Tallman, I. (1993). Theoretical issues in researching problem solving in families. In B. H. Settles, R. S. Hanks, & M. B. Sussman (Eds.), *American families and the future: Analyses of possible destinies* (pp. 155–186). Binghamton, NY: Haworth Press.

Taylor, R., Chatters, L. M., Tucker, M. B., & Lewis, E. (1990). Developments in research on black families: a decade review. *Journal of Marriage and the Family, 52*(4), 993–1014.

Teachman, J. D., Polonko, K. A., & Scanzoni, J. H. (1987). Demography of the family. In M. B. Sussman & S. K. Steinmetz (Eds.), *Handbook of marriage and the family* (pp. 3–36). New York: Plenum.

Theiman, A. A., & Dail, P. W. (1992). Family preservation services: Problems of measurement and assessment of risk. *Family Relations, 41*(2), 185–191.

Thompson, E. (1989). Dyadic models of contraceptive choice 1957 and 1975. In D. Brinberg & J. Jaccard (Eds.), *Decision making* (pp. 268–285). New York: Springer-Verlag.

Thornton, A. (1989). Changing attitudes toward family issues in the United States. *Journal of Marriage and the Family, 51*(4), 873–893.

Tibler, K. B., Walker, G., & Rolland, J. S. (1989). Therapeutic issues when working with families of persons with AIDS. In E. D. Macklin (Ed.), *AIDS and the family* (pp. 187–228). Binghamton, NY: Haworth Press.

Toffler, A. (1980). *The third wave.* New York: William Morrow.

Trost, J. (in press). Family as a set of dyads. In B. H. Settles, M. B. Sussman, J. Trost, & I. Levin (Eds.), Concepts and definitions of family: Dialogue between theory and practice. *Marriage and Family Review.*

Unger, D. & Powell, D. (1980). Supporting families under stress: The role of social networks. *Family Relations, 29*(4), 566–574.

Van Biema, D. (1994, December 12). The storm over orphanages. *Time, 144*(24), 58–62.

Van Biema, D. (1995, December 11). Abandoned to her fate. *Time, 146*(24), 32–36.

Van den Broucke, S., Vertommen, H., & Vandereycken, W. (1995). Assessing change with preventive interventions: The reliable change index. *Family Relations, 44*(3), 285–290.

Van Name, J. A. (1991). *Financial management practices of married single earner and dual earner families in Delaware.* Unpublished doctoral dissertation, Virginia Polytechnic Institute and State University, Blacksburg, VA.

Vanek, J. (1974). Time spent in housework. *Scientific American, 231*(5), 116–120.

Vangelisti, A. L. (1991). Communication in the family: The influence of time relational prototypes, and irrationality. *Communication Monographs, 60*(March), 42–54.

Vangelisti, A. L., & Banski, M. A. (1993). Couples' debriefing conservations: The impact of gender, occupation, and demographic characteristics. *Family Relations, 42*(3), 149–157.

Vannoy, D. (1993). Love and marriage: The horseless carriage. Paper presented at the 30th Seminar on the Committee on Family Research of the International Sociological Association, Annapolis, MD.

Vega, W. A. (1990). Hispanic families in the 1980's: A decade of research. *Journal of Marriage and the Family, 52*(4), 1015–1024.

Verazo, M., & Hermon, C. B. (1980). Single parent families: Myth and reality. *Journal of Home Economics, 72*(3), 31–33.

Voydanoff, P. (1990). Economic distress and family relations: A review of the eighties. *Journal of Marriage and the Family, 52,* 1099–1115.

Walker, K. Z., & Woods, M. E. (1976). *Time use: A measure of household production of family goods and services.* Paper presented at the American Home Economics Association meeting, Washington, DC.

Walsh, F. (1993). *Normal family process* (2nd ed.). New York: Guilford.

Westney, O. E. (1993). Human ecology theory: Implications for education, research, and practice. In P. G. Boss, W. J. Doherty, R. LaRossa, W. R. Schumm, & S. K. Steinmetz (Eds.), *Sourcebook of family theories and methods: A contextual approach* (pp. 448–450). New York: Plenum.

White, J. M. (1991). *Dynamics of family development: A theoretical perspective.* New York: Guilford.

Winnick, A. J. (1988). The changing distribution of income and wealth in the United States 1960–1985: An examination of the movement toward two societies, "Separate and Unequal." In P. Voydanoff & L. C. Majka (Eds.), *Families and economic distress: Coping strategies and social policy* (pp. 232–260). Newbury Park, CA: Sage.

Wisensale, S. K. (1991). The family in the think tank. *Family Relations, 40*(2), 199–207.

Wolf-Smith, J. H., & LaRossa, R. (1992). After he hits her. *Family Relations, 41*(3), 324–329.

Woolf, G. D. (1990). An outlook for foster care in the United States. *Child Welfare, LXIX*(1), 75–81.

Yancey, W. L., Eriksen, E. R., & Juliani, R. N. (1976). Emergent ethnicity: A review and reformation. *American Sociological Review, 41*(3), 391–401.

Yankelovich, D. (1981, April). New rules in American life: Searching for self fulfillment in a world turned upside down. *Psychology Today, 15,* 35–91.

Young, K. T. (1994). To create a culture of responsibility toward young children. *Carnegie Quarterly, 39*(2), 14–15.

Zimmerman, S. L. (1981). More than a matter of parent's versus children's rights: Response to Crutchfield. *Family Relations, 30*(2), 179–181.

The Family

Theory and Methods

Part II is devoted to chapters on theoretical ideas that are used to describe and explain family structures and processes. An even more extensive focus of these chapters concerns the methodologies used to measure, collect, and analyze data acquired from families. Important themes are the assessment of current theory and research issues as well as perceptive critiques of standard assumptions about families and how this knowledge is created. These chapters also illustrate and evaluate a representative variety of strategies that are used in contemporary family research.

The first chapter in this part, "Classical Social Theory and Family Studies: The Triumph of Reactionary Thought in Contemporary Family Studies," by Brian Vargus, illuminates three basic positions. First, the family is ultimately defined consistent with basic Judeo-Christian concepts in both classical scholarship and modern ideological debates. Second, the rejection of the dominant organic model of the family and society, which resulted from "consciousness of kind" thinking, only serves to reiterate, under new labels (gender, ethnic, gay views of family), the same error of endorsing group repression in the family. Third, these themes produce a denial of the role of individual choice in negotiating reproductive and socialization relations. According to Vargus, contemporary family studies have not dealt with the issues raised by Aristotle, Plato, Kant, Hume, and Rousseau, namely, "Do we think as individuals or are we merely the product of that which has come before?"

In Chapter 8, "Postmodernism and Family Theory," William Doherty describes the emerging developments in family theory during the last decades of the twentieth century. Doherty argues that the recent movement from modernism to postmodern thought in culture, philosophy, and social science is a principal force influencing developments within contemporary family theory. He notes that postmodern thinking has forced us to reconsider the commonly held assumption of positivistic thinking that values and moral beliefs are irrelevant to social science, education, therapy, and public policy. Consistent with this idea, he challenges family scholars to articulate the ethical and values assumptions that underlie their work and address the issue of accountability in research.

Chapter 9, "Methodological Pluralism and Qualitative Family Research," by Jane Gilgun, demonstrates that methodological stasis (or the positivistic style of doing science) is a relatively recent and quickly diminishing phenomena in family research. She elaborates these ideas by exploring the European and U.S. heritage of qualitative research and expands the metaphor of a "lens" into that of a "kaleidoscope" in showing how theoretical perspectives shape our views of both society and family. From this perspective, researchers can simply turn the "kaleidoscope" slightly and a new vision of family life suddenly appears. Although only limited opportunities continue to exist for in-depth training and the publication of qualitative research, the intellectual foundation for pluralism in qualitative methodologies offers an exciting future.

Chapter 10, "Quantitative Methodology for Studying Families," by Alan Acock, begins by noting the various ways in which family scholars and their research topics are both diverse and overlapping. An important result of this diversity, Acock proposes, is that no single research paradigm is currently established, a circumstance that should encourage family scholars to use multiple methodologies. He further discusses the importance of selecting an appropriate time frame for specific research issues (e.g., cross-sectional, longitudinal, time series) and a research strategy for data collection that fits a particular research issue (survey designs, experimental and quasi-experimental, observation, and in-depth interviews). Subsequently, he considers measurement alternatives (e.g., self-report items and scales, questionnaires and interviews, and missing data) and issues relating to statistical significance, measures of association, imperfect models, and interaction effects. Finally, he explores the concept of ethics and the potential risks to the individuals we study as a reminder that family researchers study sensitive issues that concern people above all and thus have the potential to enhance or harm the well-being of family members.

In the final chapter in this part, "Measurement in Family Studies," Walter Schumm and Karla Hemesath note that measurement in research is the process of linking theoretical ideas to empirical indicators (i.e., linking concepts to variables). Topics addressed include issues about reliability, analysis of covariance structures, development of global measures, physiological assessment, and multiple perspectives. Schumm and Hemesath also address the limitation of measurement techniques and the need to consider diversity, social desirability, and practitioner interest. They note that although contemporary scholars are blessed with an abundance of readily available measures, new approaches to measurement and analysis, and large, nationally representative data sets, one must base the selection or construction of family measures on theory.

CHAPTER 7

Classical Social Theory and Family Studies

The Triumph of Reactionary Thought in Contemporary Family Studies

Brian S. Vargus

Introduction

The world of social theory, particularly as it is applied to family and gender issues, has become a tangle of claims and counterclaims regarding ideological predisposition and the sheer impossibility of understanding the world without the appropriate perspective. Therefore, it seems important to review the myriad threads of classical social theory that have the origins and impact of familial, blood, and marital ties as part of their concern.

The turn of the discipline of sociology (from whence family studies sprang) to almost total concern with issues such as family and gender appears a result of modern developments. Critics have attributed it to things such as the need for political correctness or even the movement to the forefront of many scholars who are not white males. Proponents have seen the renewed emphasis on familial issues as a reflection of simple population and moral concerns and of attaching significance to normal social practices that have been devalued.

Brian S. Vargus • Department of Political Science and Indiana University Public Opinion Laboratory, Indiana University–Purdue University at Indianapolis, Indianapolis, Indiana 46202.

Handbook of Marriage and the Family, 2nd edition, edited by Marvin Sussman, Suzanne K. Steinmetz, and Gary W. Peterson. Plenum Press, New York, 1999.

It is the contention of this somewhat arbitrary review of the place of the family in the development of social theory that a concern for family as one of several "blood" or "natural" ties has been at the core of most social theory. Further, it is a corollary of that position that the concern for the family reflects the conservatism of social thought. Developed to explain social change, social theory since about 1850 has always identified the family or the "blood" group as key and all groups as dominant in social action. Far from liberating the numerous groups that lead the rediscovered concerns— women, children, gays, and ultimately a host of "everyday" minorities—it seems much of the development of social theory regarding the family does more to advance specialties in social science and interests of particularistic groups than it does to illuminate social life. At many points, from the Greek society onward, social theory has returned to issues of consciousness of kind and explanations based on the traditional family. Today this is at the height of classical theory in modern family studies. Despite an apparent diversity of perspectives, such as feminist thought, exchange theory, critical theory, etc., each can be shown to be derivative from either traditional views of the family anchored in Christian thought, functionalism, or variations of consciousness of kind perspectives. Social theory, becoming an elite enterprise when applied to families, is part of a repressive social discourse and modern ideology that denies the dignity of the individual and the value of scholarship. Its purpose is to reinforce an idealized family or special group that removes the individual and reason from consideration. Despite appearances of diversity and liberating perspectives, family studies has not lost its fundamental traditional, functional, and group-dominant perspective.

The Beginnings

The earliest concerns in social theory turned on a very simple issue: blood versus association. These simple divisions are behind most modern explanations of the family. The ancient Greeks had a strong concern for family/clan linkages and relied often on them to explain what happened in their tiny but important social structure. Fusel de Coulanges (1864/1956) shows the import that Greek society gave to the linkages of family in most of what they did. The early philosophers showed that concern also.

Aristotle begins his *Politics* with a concern for the household as the primary tie in power relationships.

> The first result of these two elementary associations [of male and female, and of master and slave] is the household or family.... The next form of association, which is also the *first* to be formed from more households than one, and for the satisfaction of something more than daily recurrent needs— is the village.... When we come to the final and perfect association, formed from a number of villages, we have already reached the polis—an association which may be said to have reached the height of full self-sufficiency; or rather ... we may say that while it *grows* for the sake of mere life, ... it exists for the sake of a good life. (pp. 4–5)

> It is clear ... that the business of household management is concerned more with human beings than it is with inanimate property; that it is concerned more with the good condition of human beings ... it is concerned more with the goodness of the free members of the household. (1946 edition, pp. 33–34)

Early on, Aristotle has made a distinction between what we might call the "economic"—the management of property— and the creation of a just or "moral" household/family. Following his famous defense of slavery, he spends considerable effort discussing arrangements that must exist in the household to justify the creation of a "good society." He follows his teacher Plato in discussions of the "guardians" and their families. It is only later that Aristotle begins to consider the role of other relationships, especially forms of the polis. Plato had shown in *The Republic* a concern for the just society but devoted special attention to the communal nature of familial relationship for his "guardians" and seemed to advocate a primitive communism for them in family ties. This special case of the guardians, however, is acknowledged by Plato and seems not to have been meant for the rest of Greek society, who would abide by "normal" rules of kinship and other social ties.

While much of Western thought seems to have been on hold for many centuries after these two giants drew their re-

spective boundaries, the early Christian scholastics certainly did not miss the important role of family or blood ties in their explanations of society. Saint Augustine, in *City of God Against the Pagans* (410/1950), saw everything as an interpretation of God's will on earth as revealed by the Catholic Church, but he acknowledged the role of the Church in supporting traditional blood ties and the family. St. Thomas Aquinas saw much the same thing, though in a more sophisticated manner. In his works he returns, again and again, to the need to discover God's will in forging a society that is the revealed word of God on earth. He attributes nothing to the individual that is not rooted in the family as defined by the Holy Writ. For him the problem is one of interpreting or "discovering" the word of God.

By the late medieval period, it is for Machiavelli, as the most prominent spokesperson for "realism" in matters social and political, to start to raise the issue of the importance of individuals (rather than families) in interpreting the power that is the social web. When he wrote in his *The Discourses on the First Ten Books of Titus Livy* (1513/1983) that a republic was superior to a "Prince," he made special recognition of the problem of conspiracies and factions; many of these are attributable to disagreements based in gender, family, or other group/blood ties. Old Nick may not be everyone's favorite, but he saw the importance of appearance over reality and the role of individuals. In doing so for the Prince, he is laying the framework for an individualist and realist interpretation of both the social bond and family ties that is ignored, as we shall see, by most subsequent thinkers. *Virtú* was the unfolding of *both* a common concern and an individual's ability to understand the intersection of individual and collective interests. It was Machiavelli who saw the role of practical wisdom as superior to that of hereditary right/ divine right or to the ties of blood, family, and tradition. Thus, far from the setting developed by most textbooks in intellectual history, the main debate was not between explanations based on superstition/religion versus reason/science. Machiavelli had framed a middle way, between group ideology and individual rights. However, most seem to have missed his point about the use of "prudence" (see Garver, 1987) in individual decision making as a factor in developing social encounters. The sections that follow attempt to illustrate the group/blood-based notion of most classical theory and the important role family played in the explanations. This, in turn, lays the foundation for contemporary family theory.

The Discovery of Society

The discovery of society, and ultimately social theory, is not a routine historical event. The notion that people could subject their surroundings, especially their social surrounding, to any kind of analysis took a special intellectual step. While Bacon and Newton had established the role of "science" as a useful tool to understand the nonhuman world, it took early modern social philosophy to get to the root of what was to become social theory.

Two figures stand out in this process—Thomas Hobbes and John Locke. Each had a distinct reason for taking the step of calling into question the ability of humans to understand what we call their "social" surrounding. Hobbes (1588–1679) was uprooted and disturbed by the English Revolution. The attendant disorder, which influenced not only his residence but also his view of proper and essential patterns in life, led to his concern for the problem of order. He saw a life that was "nasty, brutish and short" as a distinct pattern developing for everyone. The bastion to prevent disorder was the monarch, who would restore order by his own definition. Most of this thought was decidedly antisocial in that Hobbes saw human beings, and human nature, as highly individual. There are independent individuals that attempt to realize their interests—self-preservation, etc. Thus, there are inherent presocial qualities carried by individuals. The specific nature of the state, or society, is dependent upon the inherent human nature Hobbes attributes to people. Clearly, these assumptions impact conceptions of family behavior. Locke (1632–1704), on the other hand, had a much more "hopeful" view of human potential. He saw humans as capable of reason, but governed by natural laws. He could support the right to oppose a monarch, but only within the existing rules of nature—God's Laws. The human being was "written upon" by society, but was capable only of expanding by experiencing more of the world. Thus, two sources impact human beings: their sensations and the functions of their minds. For Locke there is an objective world, but it is somewhat problematic as to how we come to know it. This foundation for positivism was advanced broadly in early social thought and the essence of human nature was debated. Interestingly, concerns for family, gender, blood ties, etc. were far removed in this discussion because the fight was too often framed as the individual versus the group. The nature of groups or the processes involved remained unspecified. Still, Locke laid the foundation for an explanation of how it might be possible for ideas to originate in something other than natural law or the deity's revealed wisdom. Thus, the lines for family theory were drawn early—an assumption of innate traditional social/family ties on the one hand and an assumption of individuals as creating social ties through interaction on the other.

The entire period of thought, of which these two are but small portions, is an exercise in defending the individual in the name of something else—generally religion versus human nature. It is fair to assert, as Cassier (1932/1968) has shown,

the fundamental tendency and the main endeavor of the philosophy of the Enlightenment are not to observe life and to portray it in terms of reflective thought. This philosophy believes rather in an original spontaneity of thought; it attributes to thought not merely an imitative function but the power and task of shaping life itself. (p. viii)

Thus, the philosophy of the Enlightenment was one based upon a new respect for the individual. Science was an exalted task, albeit in the service of "someone," and it would free the individual from the superstitions of religion and the tyranny of the king. Though Hume and Kant* would add to this discussion in important ways, for social thinkers, the debate seemed closed at the apparent dichotomy of the group-based ideological "superstitions" of things such as religion and the innate truth to be found in the experience of nature through "scientific reasoning." Hume demonstrated that natural law could not be substantiated by analysis of human experience. Thus, all knowledge "degenerates into probability," in his words. Knowledge is a "custom," built largely on a primitive stimulus–response pattern of a very special cause and effect. But, Hume laid the groundwork for establishing something that later "classicists" in family studies still assume—the notion that natural law cannot be taken for granted. Hume built upon Locke in such a way that nothing could be taken as "given," including the divine inspiration or tradition of familial or blood relations. Few saw the connections between family and society at the time. It was for the Philosphes to clarify this problem of the role of the family in social relations.

Two of the Philosophes stand tall in general, but maybe not as deservedly as elementary textbooks frequently suggest.† Voltaire (1694–1778), who persisted in expressing freedoms from the repression of *his* speech and so forth, did so only when it did not stop his patrons—see his fawning in letters over "the greats," Catherine and Frederick, idolized account of Charles XII, etc.—or his personal interests. Voltaire was no friend of the individual and no democrat. In a letter of 1761 he shows his preferences early: "(T)here are truths which are not for all men, nor for all times" (Besterman, 1962, p. 112). While he was willing to denounce both religion and government, it is not clear he was at home with a government that was centered in the people. The individual was worth something, but not all were equal to the tasks of reason. More than any other thinker, it is Voltaire who set up a dichotomy of thought between superstition (religion) and reason (science).‡ Yet Voltaire's science was an attempt to uncover the universal law of progress that would liberate reason to understand the innate nature of man, not a totally

*Hume (1711–1776) felt that human experience was of a real word that, in turn, was interpreted in terms as subjective ideas of cause and effect; thus, it was not from reason, but "impressions." Kant (1724–1804) argued that knowledge of an "orderly world" is only possible through our senses and that its "form" is contributed by the actions of the mind. In particular, it is not until "sociobiology" achieved a modicum of respect that anyone acknowledged the progressive diminution of attention to blood ties in social thought.
†This debate is probably fruitless and irrelevant since scholars cannot even agree on when the period began and ended.
‡Peter Gay has produced the best exposition of the movement known as the Enlightenment and its important divisions between superstition and reason (see Gay, 1966, esp. pp. 72–88, and 1969).

individuated pattern in any way. Voltaire objected to Locke's *tabula rasa*, more for its denial of a constant human nature that might be discovered than for anything else. This led many social thinkers into a consistency of error that does not serve analysis of family dynamics well to this day. Instead of seeing the division of family and tradition from reason and science, they have amplified science without seeing its clear ties to traditional family views and styles.

Rousseau (1712–1778), at his best a worthy opponent to Voltaire and a too often overlooked social theorist of great brilliance, saw the problem. In formulating the social contract, he allowed for something that came outside the individual. "The General Will" is left virtually undefined, although modern scholars insist it was something akin to what we call "public opinion." Modern scholars have overlooked this essential contribution to social thought, and more apropos of this discussion, this contribution to sociology of the family and family studies. Rousseau was hardly one for ties, as his treatment of his own children attests (see Cranston, 1982, 1991). He saw the duality of his life and the existence he craved in Geneva. Community was to him a place where individuals could flourish, against the wishes of groups of all sorts, including one's family—of origin or of creation. The natural man he carved in his thought was both a song of praise for individuality and purity of the individual against society and a repudiation of the notion that traditional/ biological categories, ties and family, were important to social development.

This duality of the individual and his relation to society found its origins in the Reformation, but achieved nontheological currency during the French Revolution. One cannot deny Rousseau's seeming *Confessions* (1936) as an attempt to reassert his theological "acceptance." It is as a "fox hole" Christian (he was facing death) that we find this written and one can hardly defend it as repudiation of much of Rousseau's actions, or "seductions by society," as he would have it. Indeed, it might be interpreted as a "see what I did" self-advertisement on some terms. Thus, duality—the individual versus the group/society (in this case as represented by the Church)—was at the heart of Rousseau's social thought. The duality, however, was posed as one between the Church and the "rational" individual, with a turn away from the family. On the surface the family seemed unimportant; for example, witness the planned socialization experiences of *Emile* (1762/1986). Again, as with many predecessors in the Enlightenment tradition, Rousseau and his contemporaries overlooked the importance of Machiavelli's assertion of "practical wisdom"—a prudence that rejected familial, blood-based, or doctrinal boundaries and asserted the dignity of individual action in changing circumstances.

The reaction to Rousseau's *Emile*—a defense of many kinds of privilege—is best seen in Mary Wollstonecraft's *Vindication of the Rights of Women* (1929). Not satisfied with Rousseau's picture of a woman as a "servant" for the virtually Godlike Emile, Wollstonecraft assumed a strong position against him. It is somewhat ironic, as she praised his writings in most places and found his picture of natural man—with "natural woman" as his servant—an abomination, for her commitment was to Enlightenment-based equality. The family was suspect to her: "Parental affection ... is but a pretext to tyrannize where it can be done with impunity, for only good and wise men are content with the respect that will bear discussion" (p. 165). Note that she saw society as a union of strong-willed individuals, not a family-based or theologically based set of rights.*

The French Revolution may have been carried out in the name of liberty, equality, and brotherhood, but the latter was an afterthought. Virtually all sides in the French Revolution could find something in both Voltaire and Rousseau to support them and their positions. However, it is the individualistic, and Enlightenment-inspired, economists (the physiocrats) such as Turgot, Robiespierre, revolutionaries such as Bebeuf, and the "encylopedists" such as Diderot that had more to do with the shape of events of the revolution and its aftermath. Napoleon may have been elected by plebiscite, but he never turned his back on the Church. One must remember even Robiespierre saw the Church and its doctrine—he especially admired Rousseau's *Confessions*—as the defense against "the terror" (see Jordan, 1985). That crucial tie that bound the state and the Church is never lost, except in more modern readings. The family at the time was reasserted and worthy of study within Church doctrine—within natural law.

Reactionaries such as Bonald and DeMaistre reasserted the primary sources of the Church as the "true answer" to the chaos that Napoleon let loose upon Western Europe. This reasserted the importance of belief and the Holy See, or its equivalent, in men's thought. However, they were naive, narrowminded, and not effective. The individual's role was only valid within the Church and through a Church-sanctioned version of the family. By the 1820s, Church doctrine was unlikely to convince any of the intellectuals that the individual should submit to the Church. Yet the dichotomy of individual versus group (reason versus religion) did address the family by implication. The family and traditional gender roles were defined only at the religious end of the continuum.

No single thinker shows this better than Alexis de Tocqueville (1805–1859). Although an aristocrat, he was nervous about what had happened in France. Napoleon's centralization seemed to represent the substitution of real tyranny for a softer tyranny rooted in natural law and God's will. His observations of the American experience with

---

*The exception with Wollstonecraft, as with many others during the Enlightenment, was race, for she saw distinct inequalities by race (see Shapiro, 1992, pp. 108–111), although she was not satisfied, apparently, with accepting inequalities as natural.

equality still exert immense influence on social and political thought and, by implication, on the family and related matters. For de Tocqueville, the strength of the American experience was the "science of association." Equality meant some changes in family matters including the end of the importance of inherited property and primogeniture. This was a decline in the authority of the old family in the face of the democratizing movement in America. He saw the intermediate groups between the state and the family as the ultimate buffer in his early pluralism. They formed an economic/political barrier that prevented tyranny, but also asserted a new level of "community." Certainly the "tyranny of the majority" had to be resisted in America: "[T]he same equality which renders him independent of each of his fellow-citizens, taken severally, exposes him alone and unprotected to the influence of the greater number" (de Tocqueville, 1956, p. 148). But de Tocqueville was interested in the political, rather than the cultural/social, changes and implications of equality. When he wrote "I know of no country in which there is so little independence of mind and real freedom of discussion as in America" (1956, p. 117), he was reacting to the impact of equality as it changed the expected role for traditional "cultured" aristocrats and institutions.

But this was more than a simple hope. de Tocqueville had "seen" that the "science of association" worked in the Jacksonian United States. It was much later, in his stronger book *The Old Regime and the French Revolution* (1856/1955), that de Tocqueville showed his concern for what might have been and reasserted the importance of traditional institutions—the aristocracy and its "other half," the family. de Tocqueville did not hold the monarchy blameless, and he showed their contribution to the great inequalities that sowed revolution, especially in France. However, he still saw the value of the old system and that the removal of feudalism had a large price:

> [T]hese old feudal institutions had still entered into and shaped the religious and political institutions of Europe and had, in addition, given rise to a host of ideas, sentiments, manners and morals that admitted to them. Thus a frightfully violent convulsion was required in order to excise these institutions from the social organism and to destroy them. (quoted in Zeitlin, 1971, p. 152)

His long discussion of the character and meaning of "gentleman" from England to France shows an almost wistful recognition of the consequence of equality, but his preference for the familial "honor" of aristocracy. Remember that de Tocqueville was an aristocrat, and he never got away from the aristocratic orientation toward the individual. There was a destruction of "noblesse oblige"—in many ways—that produced the egalitarian move that bred the revolution:

> This contrast between theory and practice, between good intentions and acts of savage violence, which was a salient feature of the French Revolution, becomes less startling when we remember that the Revolution, though sponsored by the most civilized classes of the nation, was carried out by its least educated and most unruly elements. For, since the members of the cultured elite had formed a habit of keeping to themselves, were unused to acting together, and had no hold on the masses. (1856/1955, pp. 206–207)

And the Old Regime wasn't that bad, according to de Tocqueville, since many liberties were enjoyed. It was the error of centralized nobility, in the apparently inevitable march to equality, to destroy the restraints of the traditional paternalistic and familial ties.

Clearly, de Tocqueville was no modern liberal. He ignored the roots of industrial change in America, acknowledged but dismissed the importance of economic *inequalities* (see Zeitlin, 1971). Although a relentless crusader to end slavery in French colonies, de Tocqueville seems not to have attributed great significance to the institution in America. His analysis is careful and contains important insights into the development of new institutions that restricted the individual under more modern organization. Equality bred centralization and that, inevitably, seemed to produce "modern" tyranny. de Tocqueville produced a methodological masterpiece in *The Old Regime* that showed both understanding and a strange appreciation for the duality of modern institutions and the decline of the individual in the face of modern equality.

One of the ironies of history occurred with de Tocqueville's brief stint as Minister of Foreign Affairs in France (1849). His personal secretary was the Count de Gobineau. This is the same de Gobineau (1915) that argued vigorously for racial inequalities in a work that would later be referred to often by Adolf Hitler. de Tocqueville was no racist, but seemed to see no real significance for that factor as a variable in his explanations of the inevitability of equality.* Thus, in distinction to other thinkers in this area he ignored blood ties or what would become any concern for "consciousness of kind."

---

*Thus, in a letter to his friend Beaumont, de Tocqueville says of Gobineau's "thick book," "I do not believe a word of it, and yet I think that there is in every nation, whether in consequence of race *or of an education which has lasted for centuries*, some peculiarity, tenacious if not permanent, which combines with all the events that befall it, and is seen both in good and in bad fortune, in every period of history" (Pope, 1986, p. 36, emphasis added). Note the strong concern, even as late as 1862 (the date given for this letter), for a cultural elite. On the matter of race in America, it is important to reassert de Tocqueville's extensive thoughts on the matter as expressed in *Democracy in America*: "As soon as it is admitted that the whites and the emancipated blacks are placed upon the same territory in the situation of two alien communities, it will be readily understood that there are but two alternatives for the future; the negroes and the whites must either wholly part or wholly mingle.... I do not imagine that the white and black races will ever live in any country upon an equal footing.... The danger of a conflict between the white and the black inhabitants ... is inevitable" (1980, pp. 333ff). As with most of his Enlightenment contemporaries, de Tocqueville had difficulty imaging races comingling without the buttress of tradition and historical/cultural support. The individual was not as important as familial/biological ties.

At this point we must skip back in our time line to show the impact on social thought from the emerging school of political economy. We have seen the development by Enlightenment thinkers of a false dichotomy of superstition and reason, based on the group represented by the Church/state or natural law and the individual represented by science. While the family had receded from the role it held as early as Aristotle, it was not gone altogether. It was early sociology and political economy that reasserted the important role of the family in all social life.

Socialism and Sociology

Some Early Sociology

Henri Saint Simon (1760–1825) is frequently overlooked by social theorists. Most of this is the result of the misrepresentation of his ideas, but much can be attributed to the supposed socialism he embraced that was repudiated by his intellectual progeny. Remarkably similar to the reactionaries before him, Saint Simon, who witnessed both the American and French Revolutions, attributed stability in prerevolutionary times to religion. However, he saw the changes, including the turmoil after the revolution, as both caused by the ideas of the Enlightenment and solved by them. For Saint Simon, there was to be a new religion of science. He admired those that went before–especially Newton—and saw a scientific elite and the "functional equivalent" of religion under his version of modern circumstances. The hope was to lie with "positive philosophy"—a system of thought based upon the unification of knowledge on a scientific and positivist base. Even his intellectual descendent, Emile Durkheim, admits that this founding and the resultant development of what was to be called sociology belongs to the mind of Saint Simon, and not the person who claimed most of the credit—Auguste Comte.* Saint Simon could never get beyond a society governed by an intellectual elite, almost acknowledging the tradition of Plato. For him society was to be governed by "brotherly love." Thus, in his thought he incorporates the transition from religion to modern society, but ultimately falls back on the role of a religion that is international and led by a scientific elite. He neglected the family in the face of the embryonic industrialism that inspired his followers, but the groundwork was laid for a reassertion of the role of the family, and it came in direct connection from Saint Simon to Comte and Durkheim.

Some 8 years before his death Saint Simon engaged a private secretary, Auguste Comte (1798–1857). Comte, famous to all introductory sociology students as the "Father of Sociology,"* has his portrait in virtually every introductory sociology text. The fact that most of his central ideas came from Saint Simon seems unimportant to most students of the family. Yet in fairness, Comte admits that his basic principle, the three stages of knowledge—or what he called the "great discovery of the year 1822"—was established at a time when he was still employed by the originator of this principle, Saint Simon.

Comte's ideas are as utopian as those of Saint Simon, although considerably more influential. His law of the three stages of knowledge—from theological through metaphysical to positive—leaves no real room for the individual. Note that the missing link of psychology was a conscious omission by Comte. The individual psyche was a religious tool in Comtean thought and thus outside the realm of science, much less "positive science." Comtean thought is, therefore, the first conscious break with the Enlightenment's scientific tradition of the dignity of the individual. Society is a cumulative enterprise, beyond the individual. In turn, the new religion that found the unique laws of the collective, by the use of positive science, was to be sociology.

The rejection of methodological individualism, a cornerstone of Comte's sociology, promotes the family into a key position as the "indispensable unit" linking the individual to society: "The whole human race might be conceived as the gradual development of a single family" (1896, vol. 1, p. 145). Comte had written in admiration of Bonald and wanted no part of making individual reason and consequent claims to rights any part of positive science. Thus, the system at the end of the three stages was given a religious quality. Inequality was part of that system (religion?) and, as sociology, it needed to be taught to all the citizens. All this was science of the highest order, and Comte's followers embraced it as such. Here, at last, was a system that placed the social, and its familial origins, above and separate from the individual. Finally, thinkers had cause to release themselves from concerns for original nature. This laid groundwork for the science of association, with the "sociologist" being the elite who will show the limits of intervention. As a scientific utopian, but a reactionary, Comte has no parallel in social thought. He was to find, however removed from his intent, support in a parallel tradition of intellectual development in England.

*In the tradition of Sorokin's marvelous analysis of sociology, *Fads and Foibles in Modern Sociology* (1956), one is led to assert that the first, "new Columbus" was Comte. Thus, we should not be surprised that social theory is more a history of derived ideas than a history of anything terribly original.

*There is ample reason to hold that title for either of the ancient Greeks—Aristotle or Plato. or, if one insists on a more modern "father," the Baron de Montesquieu or the Marquis de Condorcet seem to be sound candidates for the title.

The Scots, Spencer, and Evolution

The Scottish Moralists, as they are dubbed by most intellectual historians, had noted the problematic relation between the group and the individual. More significant, they also noted implications for the family and for the economy. Central to the thought of these often overlooked intellectual giants was a distinction between two categories of social relations—the more "natural" familial type of relations and the artificial relations produced by a changing and industrializing wider society. Anticipating later developments, they seemed to have not downplayed reason in the face of "passion," but to have located reason in an emerging form of social life—economic interaction.

Hume had discussed the problem of what humans do to social interactions. His work laid a fertile plot for the development of "interactionist" perspectives in American in the twentieth century, although few saw the implications. Hume, concentrating on human nature in an empiricist fashion, saw interaction as resulting from the fact that "the minds of all men are similar in their feelings and operations" (1949, pp. 575–576). However, these bonds of sympathy are limited to those matters that are "near at hand" or more personal in terms of interaction. Distant, or less familial and more social, reactions are artificial for Hume, and they acquire a much more utilitarian cast to most of their operation. As Stewart (1963) suggests, Hume makes a clear break between familial relationships on one side and the "newer" civil relationship of a developing industrial or, at least, postfeudal society:

> The former are the direct results of the feelings men have for others, and therefore they can be called "natural." The latter are artificial: when men are seeking scarce economic goods, when the natural relation among them is competition, and society and state are the framework within which this competition can go on with results most satisfactory to all. (p. 302)

In this manner, Hume laid a foundation for positivistic social science, though few readers saw that implication.

As early as 1759, Adam Smith (1723–1790) produced a now seldom read but very influential work, *The Theory of Moral Sentiments* (1759/1976). The book raised several issues some 16 years before he produced the "Bible" of capitalism, *An Inquiry into the Nature and Causes of the Wealth of Nations* (1776). Most of the 1759 manuscript is an inquiry into moral philosophy. The task, as Smith saw it at that time—and there is ample reason to hold it changed by the time of his more famous work—was to find how moral judgments are formed. He raised the issue of relations between humans by focusing on sympathy (this is absent in the 1776 volume) as the basis for judging things as moral. Thus, our passions are restrained by an internal moral voice that guides each to self-command, which Smith called "a great virtue, but from it all other virtues seem to derive their

principle lustre" (1759, p. 112). The source and manifestation of "sympathy" lay with the family. Smith raised natural law to an even greater supra-individual level. Duty will overcome some of the "natural deceits" such as wealthy, but the way this nature works remained invisible. The moral sense comes not, then, from natural law, but from some acquired social sense—sympathy. Smith, in distinction to Hume, does not see this as utilitarian. Indeed, it is a sense that is acquired in a manner that presages American pragmatism. Human are not brutes, but they find that their common affections are the basis for moral connection. There is an anticipation here of the family and its product, the self, as conscious of the context of interaction: "We sometimes feel for another, a passion of which he himself seems to be altogether incapable" (Smith, 1971, p. 7).*

This is the time at which social thought seems to divide into two strains, one that asserts the importance of the sympathy/moral bond (family) between men, and one that relies on simple utility to explain the division of labor. The rise of the liberal market society called for reactions and explanation. Utility is advanced by both Hume and Smith as the explanation for the dominance of the new division of labor. The individual is reasserted as a calculating and rational figure. Smith writes at some length about the "corrupting" influence of this division of individuals (see 1963, Vol. 2, pp. 284–285). Jeremy Bentham (1748–1832) becomes one of the most influential of thinkers by casting all this into a general theory of utility—human beings are motivated by the desire to gain pleasure and avoid pain. This utilitarianism is the basis for understanding the rational side of the division of labor. David Ricardo (1772–1823) saw everything in the activity used in production (labor) as producing value that could be rationally evaluated and exchanged. This, however, must be restrained by the sympathies raised within a family to avoid destruction of the social network. Both Smith—who devotes large portions of *Wealth of Nations* to education's influence on developing sentiment—and Ricardo place strong emphasis on the family's role in mitigating the destructive influences of the division of labor. It is with this subtle movement in interpretation that an essential dichotomy is established between the rational and the moral. Unfortunately for social thought and family studies, few people recognized the break between two related strains of thought.

Charles Darwin (1809–1882) had produced his arguments for evolution in their full statements in 1859. They were an instant success but not produced in isolation. An

---

*The contrast here, between a fleeting self as proposed by Hume and a more enduring self as advanced by Smith, is a particularly modern conception, and it is to our loss that many of the nineteenth- and twentieth-century social thinkers—including founding fathers such as Durkheim and Weber—did not follow this strain of thought. It seemed to promise an answer to the paradox of the individual and the family in society.

important forerunner to these ideas, beyond the population theories of Thomas Malthus, was the writings of Herbert Spencer. Spencer is the person thanked in Darwin's Preface to *On the Origin of Species* (1936) for the phrase and concept of the "survival of the fittest." It is also Spencer who reasserts the rational/scientific strain into the study of social life. This was to have important implications for how social theorists evaluated the family.

Herbert Spencer (1820–1903) was a giant among giants. His works span topics from philosophy to biology and psychology to social policy. His discussion of things such as the rights of women, comparative social systems, and forms of marriage and family are all decidedly modern in emphasis and tone, although totally misinformed by his reluctance to retreat from his principle thesis: The law of evolution is a philosophical generalization capable of explaining all phenomena. Central to this thesis was a formulation of evolution as creating pressures for differentiation of function. In all this, Spencer had accepted the idea advanced by Comte in viewing society and biology as operating in tandem—with similar structure and functions. The breadth of his work, and its enormous influence on social and political thought, cannot be overlooked, although by the end of his life Spencer saw his main ideas rejected.

Spencer's friends, including both John Stuart Mill and the novelist George Eliot (Mary Ann Evans) were the intellectual elite of his time. He conversed with world intellectual leaders, including Comte. His research and publications were financed by people such as Mill and Thomas Huxley. His ideas and books, especially in America, became the basis for much instruction and were hailed as the height of the new application of science to the development of social systems.

Spencer's work emerged, as shown by Turner, Beeghley, & Powers (1995, pp. 47ff), from a marriage of biological thought and developments in physics. Spencer had read Comte, and although consciously rejecting several aspects of Comte's thought, Spencer stayed in the "Scottish-English" tradition by insisting on applying science to the human condition. He realized that the social world consisted of both that currently studied as science and that currently compartmentalized in areas such as psychology and biology, and they were equally worthy of consideration. Spencer was a generalist of the highest order at a time when specialization was advancing unabated; that, ultimately, lead to his repudiation.

Working within his overall commitment to a first principle of evolution, but still holding to principles of the Enlightenment (ignorance versus faith but now faced with a scientific principle to support the process) and trying to solve the "Adam Smith" problem—that is, reconciling the egocentric rational (selfish/economic) behavior with the sentiments (emotions/moral nature or family aspects) of social behavior, Spencer published a variety and amount of work that is virtually unimaginable by contemporary standards. His work in the area of "moral sentiments" fell squarely into the developing sociological tradition. However, he rejected Comte on a simple methodological approach. Spencer was a methodological individualist. Having embraced Lamarck's* ideas concerning the adaptation and development of traits—an erroneous concept as it turns out—Spencer was forced to consider that psychological development followed those same evolutionary laws and that individuals went through the same stages as the total organism (in Spencer's case, society). Thus, human nature will adapt. As he states in a letter to John Stuart Mill included in one of his last works, *The Principles of Ethics* (1904/1978):

> [C]orresponding to the fundamental oppositions of a developed Moral Science, thee have been, and still are, developing in the race, certain fundamental moral intuitions; and that, though these moral intuitions are the results of accumulated experiences of Utility, gradually organized and inherited, they have come to be quite independent of conscious experience.... I believe that the experiences ... have been producing corresponding nervous modifications ... which have no apparent basis in the individual experiences of utility. (Vol. 1, p. 157)

Whereas Comte allowed only for human manifestations of nature to be changed, Spencer formulated a pattern for the progressive change of human nature, all in the name of evolutionary progress. There is a general connection between structural development and function. This is seen in many ways, and particularly in family and gender roles.

The young Spencer, probably due to the influence of his friend Evans, had issued a ringing defense of women's rights. In his works of the 1850s he rejected any a priori inborn differences between men and women. In *Social Statics* (1857) he specifically asserted that gender differences may be learned. This position, however, was rejected in later writings such as *Principles of Psychology* (1874) and *The Study of Sociology* (1873) when he reasserted female inferiority due to "a somewhat earlier arrest of individual evolution in women; necessitated by the reservation of vital power to meet the cost of reproduction" (1873/1961, p. 75).† All his work follows three essential positions: (1) the truth of Lamarck's notions regarding inheritance of acquired traits; (2) the dominance of sentiments over rationality; and (3) the necessity of a fit between individual and societal forms. It is in the latter case that we see his development of a "typology" of societies that sees an implied evolutionary development from militant to industrial societies, coupled with his development of a sys-

---

*For two contrasting but comprehensive summaries of Spencerian thought, see Turner et al. (1995) and Ashely and Orenstein (1995). The summary here simply cannot do justice to the scope and details of the thought system Spencer developed.

†See also *The Principles of Ethics*, Spencer's final formulation of the Synthetic Philosophy.

tematic concern for a typology of phases for all societies at any particular stage of evolution. This becomes the outline for Spencer's structural and functional analysis of society and its institutions. He has special notions about the family and related institutions. In his *Principles of Sociology* (1898) he argued that kinship "emerged" to meet a basic need, reproduction. Anticipating many modern students of family systems, Spencer asserted that kinship would be the principle means of integrating a society, and it would become more elaborate as a society grew. Conflict-based societies were asserted to be patrilineal and more likely to promote inequality by gender. Thus, his grand evolutionary scheme saw society as moving toward a functional integration of sentiments, based in part on kinship. Despite his acceptance of conflict, as is befitting a Darwinian, he failed to see class conflicts. He simply missed part of the point of Adam Smith's analysis and that "problem." As Ashley and Orenstein (1995; pp. 178–179) point out, much of modern sociology has simply adopted Spencer's fundamental paradigm, mostly without acknowledgment. Still, many of those that followed him did not and do not see the importance he gave to moral consensus and family issues at the same time he saw no real hope of a "utilitarian" balance that would hold society together. That position, the centrality of moral consensus based on blood or family, within the division of labor was left to be developed by Emile Durkheim.

Durkheim's Blend

The work of Emile Durkheim (1855–1917) lies at the center of modern social thought and also has important implications for family studies. Durkheim's doctoral dissertation—often revised and reprinted over his career—*The Division of Labor in Society* (1893; references are to Halls 1984 translation) took society's essential characteristic to be its social solidarity. A student of Coulanges and Comte, Durkheim followed in their footsteps. Thus, he rejects any individualism as at best "pathological." While asserting the importance of a collective consciousness to social solidarity, he also finds "excessive" individualism as pathological. These pathological states, and the biological metaphor in intended by Durkheim since he was familiar with both Spencer and Comte, are variously cast as anomie or force.

Durkheim's contribution was to place social thought back into a consideration of the sources of "sentiments" or morality, principally the family, that were supra-individual. This was certainly in the Comtean tradition, but it contrasts strongly with Spencer and, in many ways, with how Spencer has been interpreted since Durkheim. Durkheim accepted liberalism's assumptions, while rejecting the "statist" solutions of Comte. He accepted that Adam Smith was correct about the contributions of division of labor, but he saw a

scientific way to solve Smith's "problem" of the sources of sentiments or morality from the family. Durkheim saw the evolutionary progress advanced by Spencer and Comte as incorrect in a world he saw as increasingly troubled. The advance was neither unilineal, nor was it necessarily positive. His project, and insight, was to search for a manner to advance the structure/function formulation to cover the less optimistic evidence of instability and war that contrasted with the organic/biological models' predictions about the inevitability of progress. In all this, the family was to loom large.

The first task Durkheim set for himself was to detail the nature of social solidarity and its "cause." Initially Durkheim begins by assessing the impact of the division of labor. It is its function that concerns him most, and its function is more than that ascribed to it by Smith and the utilitarians:

> We are therefore led to consider the division of labor in a new light.... [T]he economic services that it can render are insignificant compared with the moral effect that it produces, and its true function is to create between two or more people a feeling of solidarity. However this result is accomplished, it is this that gives rise to these associations of friends and sets its mark upon them. The history of marital relationships affords an even more striking example of the same phenomenon. (1984; p. 17)

The choice of the familial bond as the "functional equivalent" of the solidarity Durkheim wishes to explain is a conscious one and has implications to this day for family studies. Much as did Spencer, Durkheim describes an ever more complex relation between society and marriage/kinship as society develops a more complex division of labor. Indeed, the biological underpinnings/causes are surpassed quickly as the marital "tie that binds" acquires functions such that "it goes very considerably beyond the sphere of purely economic interests, for it constitutes the establishment of a social and moral order *sui generis*" (1984; p. 21). For Durkheim the problem was a relatively simple one: How are individuals made to feel part of a system that is increasingly complex? His answer was also simple—the development of a collective consciousness. This is the equivalent to the development of the familial bond from primitive to modern developments. It is the "totality of beliefs and sentiments common to the average citizen"—here the parallels to Rousseau's General Will are both obvious and intended—that form Durkheim's supra-individual set of social facts (see *Rules of the Sociological Method*, 1895/1964). As with Spencer and Tonnies, Durkheim has a general typology of development from mechanical to organic solidarity. The typology finds its expression in the collective reaction of law, repressive in the former case and "restitutive" in the latter case. These collective representations are the manifestations, as one reads Durkheim's tortured defense of his "theory," of the underlying collective consciousness that form the "social facts." These social facts are derived from social structure and one can read Durkheim's entire body of work as an attempt to derive both group and individual "representations" of the collective consciousness from changing social structures. There is a distinct tendency for Durkheim to ignore the economic or "nonmoral" aspects of the division of labor. That, in turn, creates fertile ground for him to deny, essentially, the insights of many others as to the benefits and deficits of an economic nature.

Durkheim's work, as read by sociologists and family studies experts, is frequently cited as a "model" for positivistic functionalism. His work in *Suicide* (1897/1966) is cited, virtually universally, as a model of social methodology. Somewhat ironically, it is also in that work that we see the fullest development of Durkheim's notions of "abnormality." In the discussion of abnormal social solidarity—*Division of Labor*—Durkheim mentions three "abnormal forms" of the division of labor: anomic, forced, and "another abnormal form" that can best be described as lack of coordination. The last is left out of the manifestations of the decrease of social solidarity evidenced by the types of suicide—egoistic, altruistic, anomic, and "fatalistic."* The four types are reduced to two, in many ways, since the examples used show one having to do with too little (or footnoted too much) regulation and the other having to do with too little or too much social solidarity. In each case, the fundamental problem for Durkheim is when the individual acts as an individual—in contravention of the collective consciousness that binds society. While aware of the Marxist criticisms of the rational side of the division of labor, even with his empirical "proof" for the force of social solidarity in *Suicide*, Durkheim cannot get beyond the moral aspects of the division and its function to cement the group. Repression of an individual is abnormal too, but it is simply not as important to Durkheim. When he moved from his first book to the *Rules*, Durkheim was attempting to establish the legitimacy of what he had done. The elevation of the group, particularly as manifested by the family, over the individual seems complete in that work:

> [S]ociety is not a mere sum of individuals. Rather, the system formed by their association represents a specific reality which has its own characteristics. Of course, nothing collective can be produced if individual consciousnesses are not assumed; but this necessary condition is by itself insufficient. These consciousnesses must be combined in a certain way; social life results from this combination and is, consequently, explained by it. (1895/1964, p. 103)

At this point the individual stands little hope as either being responsible for his/her acts or for even initiating action that is not abnormal.

*This last type is based solely on Durkheim's (1897/1966) famous footnote.

Durkheim had longed viewed his work as one in the tradition of Spencer in the sense that he wanted to found a science of morality. Thus, early in his career, while still modifying *The Division of Labor*, he was giving lectures and writing on issues of morality and family. For example, in 1888–1889, while still lecturing in Bourdeavux, Durkheim (cited in Lukes, 1972) gave his second public "lecture-course" on the family. Along with his courses on morality, which were to become his ultimate goal, he considered his family work among his most cherished. In this work he built upon the comparative and anthropological approaches of Westermarck, Bachofen, Maine, and others: "His starting point was a firm assertion ... that the family and marriage are social institutions, and that there is a definite relation between these and other forms of social organization" (Lukes, 1972, p. 181). Thus, Durkheim was to cast the family as an institution in transition, much like society, that would "lose" some of its functions to other groups—especially the occupational or professional group. Still, as Lukes notes, "the family, though it 'plays a smaller role in life,' would continue to be an important centre of morality, a basis for moral education" (p. 185). Much as Saint Simon and Comte had called for a new "secular religion," Durkheim held forth for a new secular morality. This was not to be far removed from the family, for Durkheim's intent, which remained unfulfilled, was to write a formal work on morality. His early work on the family laid the groundwork for that, but it was his work on religion that was the first concrete step in his incomplete journey.

The Elementary Forms of the Religious Life (1912/1947) was his first chance to bring together his previous thoughts on morality and to sequence the steps from the family to religion to the essence of social solidarity. Durkheim saw society as advancing in such a manner that the specialized and moral functions of groups such as the family would be stripped. The importance of moral education was understood by looking to religion because it was the institution that provided the symbolic system allowing individuals to be tied into collective units and form the collective consciousness. The work on religion was an attempt to specify, in many respects, the fundamental sources of human social and moral integration. It was religiosity that emerged as humans formed into larger groups and it came to be the force over and above them, which they felt as a "moral" constraint. It was Durkheim's intent, in this most complex of his works, to examine the elementary forms of this social bond in order to understand the function of religion in more complex societies. Durkheim had defined religion, after several arguments eliminating other definitions for quite specific reasons (see Jones, 1986, pp. 115–124),

> A religion is a unified system of beliefs and practices relative to sacred things, that is to say, things set apart and forbidden—beliefs and practices which unite into one single

moral community called a Church, all those who adhere to them. (1947, p. 47)

To explain religion in this form, Durkheim had to eliminate existing theories that explained primitive animism and naturism. With the emergence of groups beyond the "horde" and forming the first permanent "clans" (see Durkheim, 1984, pp. 132ff), there was a need to develop some representation for the group. This led to the first primitive religious symbol, the totem, and its attendant form, totemism. Clearly, this is an important recognition of family ties in society. These "collective representations" are remarkable because "we arrive at the remarkable conclusion that the images of totemic beings are more scared than the beings themselves" (1912/1947, p. 133). In a real sense, society is worshipping itself and in doing so is creating the sentiments in individuals that make social solidarity possible. Durkheim is rejecting both Hume and Kant, the former because he wanted a simple transfer of experience to the mind and the latter because the mind was active in categorization of experience. For Durkheim, all thinking and reflective mental activity are imposed on individuals by the structure and the morality of society. While the family is poorly developed in the "collective representations" of religion, Durkheim never gave up on the role the family ought to play in developing morality in the individual. The family is always, for Durkheim, "a school of life which cannot lose its role" (quoted in Lukes, 1972, p. 186). In this sense then, Durkheim locates the structure and function of the family in a broader morality that is supra-individual and outside rational explanations of individual development. Even the inequalities denounced by Rousseau and considered by Marx could not be seen as anything but abnormal forms of solidarity from Durkheim's view. The implications for considerations of the family should be clear to all who read Durkheim's work. The family is the basis for society and, under modern conditions, can produce abnormalities. Clearly the traditional family is preferred.

The Marxist Challenge

There is no bigger champion of the Enlightenment than Karl Marx. He acknowledges as such in his famous summary in *A Contribution to the Critique of Political Economy* (1859/1978a) when he writes of his 1840s intellectual development in Paris. As Oakley (1984/1985) has shown, this adventurous intellectual exploration by Marx was the essence of what he was to be as a scholar and thinker. He did not see the faults of his historicism (or bad economics), but he saw the price paid by the domination of the individual by social groups, including the family. Indeed, the Paris manuscripts (1844/1978b) show a concern for the price extracted from individuals by a new form of social organization. This

"alienation," or "exploitation" as it becomes much later in his work, must be dealt with by new social developments. The only alternative is a kind of Hegelian triumph of the state on the political level, or on the personal level, the tyranny of the family. Marx, perhaps more than any of the classical thinkers, has a clear connection to Rousseau, and much of his concept of the human being owes its origins to Rousseauian concepts.

In *The Communist Manifesto* (1848/1978d) Marx and Engels are positively eloquent in their praise of the triumphs of the bourgeoisie. They also paint a bleak picture of the destruction of the family, as traditionally conceived, by the new capitalist system. Part of this is a product of Marx's analysis of historical change in *The German Ideology* (1845–1846/1932/1978c), but it also shows his romantic concern for the flowering of the individual and sensitivity to the impact of the new industrial capitalist system. Problems can be solved, but Marx and Engels do acknowledge the role of the family. From there Marx turns to other concerns and the important later work *Capital* (1906) mentions little about the family.

Thus, it is later, in one of the more important, although often overlooked, works of Engels, *The Origin of the Family, Private Property, and the State*, (1891) that Marxism's concerns for the family return to consideration. Engels' 1884 Preface presents the work as Marx's interpretation of recent (Morgan's [1877] *Ancient Society*) anthropological findings "in the light of ... his own ... materialistic examination of history" (1884, reprinted 1945, p. 5). According to Engel's self-proclaimed "extension" of his and Marx's work, the society was an extension of the interfaced "forces of labor" and the family—"tools necessary for ... the propagation of the species." By 1891, Engels could recount historical and anthropological researches on the family back to Bachofen (1967), Tylor (1883), and McLennan (1970). He sees them as a preface to his own argument for the confirmation of the Marxist view of the evolution of social organization. In particular, Engels' work becomes an application of *German Ideology* to the development of the family. Stages of the family and marriage are matched to Marx's stages of historical development:

> We thus have three principal forms of marriage which correspond broadly to the three principal stages of human development. For the period of savagery, group marriage; for barbarianism, pairing marriage; for civilization, monogamy, supplemented by adultery and prostitution. (1945, p.66)

For Engels, the history of the family is a mirror image of Marx's history of the development of the contradictions of capitalism. Sexual relations and procreation with any freedom is impossible under capitalism. The "economic considerations" of modern society must be torn asunder if human beings are to escape the chains of their newfound industrial system's influence on the family. The division of labor's advance is always, in Engels' view, at the expense of the individual's choices in matters of family and marriage:

> The stage of commodity production with which civilization begins is distinguished by the introduction of (1) metal money, and with it money capital, interest and usury; (2) merchants, as the class of intermediaries between the producers; (3) private ownership of land, and the mortgage system; (4) slave labor as the dominant form of production. The form of the family corresponding to civilization and coming to definite supremacy with it is monogamy, the domination of the man over the woman, and the single family as the economic unit of society. The central link in civilized society is the state, which ... is without exception the state of the ruling class, and in all cases continues to be essentially a machine for holding down the oppressed, exploited class. (1945, pp. 160–161)

In *The Origin of the Family* (1891) Engels, and the ghost of Marx, develop an interesting explanation for the essence of the family as they see it under modern or capitalist circumstances. It is a bleak picture that is directly descended from the Enlightenment. Obviously, the jump from Rousseau's "Man is born free; and everywhere he is in chains" (1762/1978, p. 154) to "The proletarians have nothing to lose but their chains" (1978, p. 500) is not very far. It keeps alive the notion that any group domination diminishes the individual, and that includes the domination built in by the gender and social demands of family.

The Inward Turn and Romantic Responses

While the Scots and the French had enhanced Enlightenment assumptions, although not faring well in dealing with Marxist critiques, they seemed "blissfully ignorant" of the nonrational aspects of human social life. Even allowing for the Adam Smith problem of sentiments versus rationality, they showed little acquaintance with early anthropological philosophy that formed early family studies.

Beginning with Johann von Herder (1744–1803) there was significant thought among German scholars that raised a different view of the social bond.* Herder seemed intent on fusing elements of Christianity with the Enlightenment. In doing so, he anticipated people such as Comte and presaged what would become the concept of culture. However, he became a precursor for romantic thought that acknowledged human beings as formed by association and their thought, thus, less rational. Herder writes, "Reason the creation of man, nothing more than something formed by experience ... an aggregate of the experiences and observations of the mind" (quoted in Westby, 1991, p. 111). Because human experience is unique, Herder rejects the separation of the ra-

tional from the emotional. Thus, human nature and the family, as assumed by most Enlightenment thinkers, no longer causes society.

Herder carries this to its fullest as he develops his notion of the *Volk* and related concepts:

> Every *Volk* forms a society at the core of which is its "Seele" or "Geist," its "inner spirit." The culture of a Volk represents its special genius and is an entity sui generis. Although they may be in some indeterminate sense comparable, cultures are incommensurable with one another, at least in terms of value judgments about their progress.... Herder has in mind a unity supposedly manifest in the common understandings held to underlie the literature, music, art, and science of a people. (Westby, 1991, pp. 110–111)

Thus, for any real understanding of the "culture" of a society, one must penetrate to the inner spirit.

Herder had quite specific and negative judgments of "modern" society. A culturally unified "community" is seen as under attack by the modernizing process. The *Volk* will not stand against the forms of life imposed by the state and the military necessities of a money economy. As with many others, the inequalities Herder sees being born here— referred to as the "master–slave relationship"*—needed to understand anything about human relationships, could be found only if you penetrate to the "inner spirit" of a group. While the Scottish Moralists had elaborated a society dichotomized by sympathy and primary relations on one side and the rational calculations of utilitarian capitalism on the other, Herder had gone them "one better" with his location of collective products of association as central. As Westby indicates, " the *collective products* of association rather than the technical qualities of associational forms themselves, the *culture* rather than the *social structure*" (1991, p. 117), formulated by Herder, becomes the core of German Idealism and forms the basis for the creation of a social form, sui generis, and superior to anything the individual might do. Clearly, this culture was to be carried by blood ties, and the family was the implied and ultimate repository for the *Geist*.

A more complex version of this concern, although little tied to the family, can be seen in Hegel's work. However, a version with more direct ties to family social theory comes from the philosophical anthropology of Friedrich Nietzsche (1844–1900). Though not often noted, Nietzsche's thought is, at the first at any rate, part of the birth of modern anthropology. People such as Maine, Bachofen, and Durkheim's teacher de Coulanges had embarked on an elaborate cataloging project of diverse kinship systems. All these developments, about the 1860s, resulted in a new concern to include these "primitives" as somehow part of human social development. Nietszche started by noting the famous distinction

---

*This discussion owes much of its substance to Westby's insightful discussion in his 1991 volume.

*This reference is made by Herder long before the phrase so frequently identified with Hegel was used by the later thinker.

between Apollonian and Dionysian cultures and the war with Christianity—the supposed tie of all values in Western culture. This created an instability that results, in Nietzsche's view, from a misplaced notion of human social life. Nietzche, along with several others, including Freud (discussed later), Hume, and Kant, had at least responded to the existence, if not the primary role, of the irrational side of human action as an antidote to the rationalism of the Enlightenment.

From this point of view real human nature is not consciousness or logical or even mentally constructed categories (cf. Plato, Kant, and others). Rather, Nietzsche places his explanation as relying on the individual human *will*. Human essence is will or the untrammeled selfish ego as expressed freely, but encountering obstacles that cause self-reflection and a creative civilization. Conscience became the repressed primal, egotistical will represented by the triumph of the "slave" mentality as expressed in Christianity. Life becomes, from Nietzsche's view, worthwhile only as a clear, unobstructed expression of will. This is possible when humans free themselves as *Ubermensch* or the superman. This strange doctrine of individuality has part of its source, obviously, in the socialization experience provided by the family and religious institutions. From Nietzsche's perspective, everything is destined to recur. It is in this vein that Nietzsche's contribution needs to be assessed, for he laid the groundwork for the ultimate "inward" theorist of the family, Freud. In addition, the consciousness of kind thinking in Herder, Hegel, and Nietzsche laid a foundation for interpreting gender and family ties as based on shared "emotional" categories.

Sigmund Freud (1856–1939) is the thinker that is most responsible for giving content to this unfulfilled strain of social thought covering the irrational—by constructing a usable concept, the unconscious. It is unnecessary to recount here the complex theory of psychosexual developmental stages that he crafted because it has become such a staple to many family theorists and some practitioners. While the work may be controversial on several grounds, from its validity to its sexist underpinnings, it has been used heavily by family practitioners. Setting that aside for the time being, Freud's ultimate contribution to family studies probably comes from his later work. While we will discuss his tie to modern structural functional analysis of the family later (especially as it relates to the work of Talcott Parsons), we must acknowledge his introduction of the libidinal tie as an explanation for group/individual relations. The importance of this development lies with both its timing—the three-part division of the unconscious predates and lays the foundation for the important work *Group Psychology and The Analysis of the Ego* (1922)—and the development, for the first time, of a reasonable position regarding the importance of psychological characteristics to social ties—placing libidinal ties as

predominant over communities of interest. No matter how it is reformulated—Freud's basic assertion was that social arrangements are based upon sexual organization—it follows that a libidinal bond, rather than a set of shared interests, will provide social cohesion. This bond is a matter of individual characteristics and beyond human control. It allowed Freud to develop an image of society as a giant family, with the father figure or superego as a "cultural superego." This achieves its grandest design in Jung's work (1875–1961) in which there is an innate collective nature to the unconsciousness. Thus, ultimately, Freud's work returns to the nest built by people as diverse as Comte, Durkheim, and Spencer with society preceding the individual and the "culture" or family ending as a key influence in how the individual expresses his situation in time and social organization. The key tie is always familial in the sense that the tie between the individual and the unconscious was a tie between the individual, the family, and the unconscious. As late as his 1935 autobiography, Freud was explaining how he came to understand larger cultural processes as a reflection of psychic conflict and familial tension. By the 1960s, Freud's major impact came through Marcuse (1966) with an assertion that reason had to be rejected to free people from the natural repression of family and its bigger form, society.

However, all this steps over two important and strangely related works in German social thought. Thus, we are lead to reconsider the development of both a style or methodology to handle the individual/family conflict and a second "theory" that rejects a real individual role at all. We must look at the contributions of Weber, on the one hand, and at a related strain in the consciousness of kind works of Gumplowicz.

Weber and Verstehen as a Method

Max Weber's status as a thinker is high, but people persistently resist the idea that "Weberism" is not a theory. This interpretation, not without some controversy, has its roots in the status of German thought at Weber's time. Max Weber (1864–1920) was squarely within a major dispute in German social thought—the *Methodenstriet*. That dispute has it impact on modern social thought and in modern family studies. Few see his direct influence on family studies, because there is not much of one. His own familial experiences, as recounted by people as diverse as Collins (1986) and Mitzman (1970), display considerable turmoil and a strange detachment from connecting his work with the implications it might hold for the family as an institution. Weber began as an economist—where the *Methodenstriet* was strongest. The debate, essentially, was over whether human or "cultural" matters could be studied scientifically.

The *Methodenstreit* stresses a conflict between historicism—the notion that unique and historically specific emergent cultural units vary (such as the family)—and the anti-Enlightenment notion that the essential nature of all entities is organic in the sense that their authenticity or value springs from their "inner nature." The opposition was, in overly simple terms, the "objective" versus the "subjective." This parallels a dichotomy in contemporary family studies between individual and group interpretations. The early work of the German historian Dilthey, with its concern for *Verstehen*, argues that it is only what we create that we can understand. Fundamentally, individual understanding is tied back to Hegel and Herder and the importance of the *Volk*, because all things derive from the "spirit" as opposed to reason. Thus, there may be patterns to human development and the family, but there are no laws. Weber, embracing this importance of the subjective, is a direct heir to Herder, Hegel, and Kant.

For Weber, the essence of the individual is the ability to construct meaning in the world. Weber needed a concept of individuals and meaning because the world was constructed as irreducibly diverse and without a universal human history, although replete with value conflicts. There are no universal or basic natural laws, interests, instincts, or human nature. Personality emerges, grows, and is modified through struggles in which there is a constant forming of the individual in the family and society. This struggle is never elaborated, but as in Nietzsche, there is a rather tragic flowering individuality in conflict with an objective reality. Indeed, Weber suggests the need for "balance" in his essay on politics (1974a,b). Weber's main intellectual task was to find a method that allowed consideration of constraints within which human actions occur. That, in turn, would allow him to reveal the facts of history, but to do it in the context of understanding those facts as "objectifications" created by humans reflecting their "ideals." While not directly, this obviously influenced how subsequent thinkers conceptualized the family.

Weber, in his constant debate with the "ghost of Marx," sees values as more than a "superstructure," but as "meanings" that may or may not involve Marx's notion of material interests. For Weber, there is a clash of interests in the ideal (subjective) realm as well as in the material (objective) realm. In that sense, Weber rejects Marx's famous dictum from *Theses on Feuerbach*: "The Philosophers have only interpreted the world, in various ways; the point, however, is to change it" (Marx, 1845/1978a, p. 145). Weber sees the omission of either as unacceptable to the advance of understanding the dynamics of culture. He solves this by relying on the ideas of Rickert. This German historian saw objects as brought into being by a selective process of "value-relevance" or our personal interest in constructing objects of scientific interest. Thus, we select from the constant flux of experience through some criterion of value and that is how we form concepts, or subjective interpretations concerning

the objective realities of cultural and family life. Weber saw this ideal as valuable because it acknowledged the limits of scientific truth. Historical ideal types allow an investigator to represent the "infinite multiplicity" of the world with the investigator's subjective understanding of the world. Thus, in his main empirical case, capitalism has "meaning" to actors and the historical "ideal type" allows a link between the "subjective" and the "objective." It is through

> one sided accentuation of one or more points of view and by the synthesis of a great many diffuse, discrete, more or less present and occasionally absent concrete individual phenomena, which are arranged according to those one-sidedly emphasized viewpoints into a unified analytical construct. (quoted in Westby, 1991, p. 343)

that we can understand the operation of any specific historical/cultural development.

However, the methodological advance is not complete until Weber acknowledges unanticipated consequences. This is at the root of family in Weber's work. Weber rejects Dilthey's universal *Verstehen*, rooted as it is in a common "psychic chain" or *Volk*, to admit the ability of individuals to interpret social action. Thus he advances four types—and they are "pure" or ideal types—of social action: instrumentally rational (*zweckrational*), value rational (*wertrational*), emotional (*affektuel*), or traditional action. Interestingly, it is the last category that constitutes most action, although contemporary thinkers and followers of Weber seem to overlook this point. Weber's concern with formal rationality has much to do with his recognition of the price to be paid by a routinized society following capitalism and its impact on traditional structures, such as the family, similar to Adam Smith's problem. For example, Weber acknowledges the role of tradition in the face of capitalism in his discussion of topics such as households and kinship in *Economy and Society* (1978, pp. 356–384). For Weber, there is a diabolical trade-off here between the family and society, and it lies at the root of the individual/family/social bond.

Meaning for Weber is only sensible within a context of norms, or simple rules of culturally sanctioned behavior. While shared meanings cannot be reduced to individuals, thereby rejecting methodological individualism, Weber also rejects the individual psychology of meanings because they are constructed by individuals but not *de nova*. Weber's actors do concentrate on traditional actions, such as patrimonialism, because there are things that simply are outside the subject of Weber's study—they are "devoid of subjective meaning." Thus Weber made a great methodological advance for macro subjects such as the state, but the family and more mundane matters are left to habit, in his categories, traditional social action.

Weber was not the evolutionist so many want to make him out to be. Rationalization was problematic for him, though it was a tendency in history he deplored. Weber saw the critical feature of Western development as dominance by a conscience-laced personality that objectified everything and removed it from its roots in conceptions of religion and natural law. Weber's individual is trivialized in a social and historical progression that debases the individualism from which it has sprung. Again, this is not far removed from Adam Smith's concerns for the fate of moral sentiments in the face of capitalist development. For Weber, as shown throughout his work, ideas are important and he turns to religion for their source. However, at the same time, he allows for the continued power of traditional familial forces as being antagonistic to the economic activity forcing interaction with outsiders on members of the family, clan, and village. This was outside the more utopian schemes of the Enlightenment and the understanding common during this period of history about the development of modern capitalism. For Weber, the consideration of the ends of action had supplanted the means of action. Weber asserted the understanding of human society, based upon rationality, was simply not enough to advance the "cultural sciences," unless there was room for human irrationality. He gives no reason why understanding of the latter would be any advance over the established understanding of the former. Obviously, this development implies drastic reevaluation of the family and its ties. Weber has given us insights beyond many others, but still allows room for an ultimate reality that resides above, and external to, the individual to which he must adjust or decay into Weber's "iron cage of rationality"—a disenchanted world of petty squabbles and emotional desiccation.

Gumplowicz, the "Consciousness of Kind" Theme, and American Reactions

The historical memory of social theorists is a political agenda. For that reason, perhaps more than any other, there is a set of thinkers that related important insights into the development of social theory and its application to family studies that are essentially ignored by contemporary practitioners. Most of these thinkers are portrayed, variously, as biological determinists, racists, or simply dated. While the labels fit in many cases, where they do not they cause students of the family to neglect links that display the degree to which family theory has been deadlocked for virtually 200 years. It is these thinkers that laid the groundwork for many of the new (conflict, gender, gay, etc.) paradigms to interpret the family. One of the most important of these thinkers, with much to say about the family, is Ludwig Gumplowicz (1838–1909).

By the late nineteenth century there were several writers dabbling in theory that derived from Herder's affirmation of the importance of the *Volk*. This strain in theory, combined with Darwin's evolutionism and Spencer's adaptations of

those ideas to society, led many to consider biological bases for human social action. Lombroso in Italy, for example, attributed criminal behavior to biological characteristics. The aforementioned de Gobineau and less blameless thinkers, such as Chamberlain and Stoddard, embraced racial determinism. Frequently dismissed with these types is the Polish thinker Gumplowicz, and his colleague and Austrian friend, Gustav Ratzenhofer (1842–1904). Both are worthy of consideration because they understood, as few did before them, the importance of conflict in human social relationships. In that sense they stand as useful antidotes to the influences of functionalism and consciousness of kind in all social thought since Spencer.

What follows concentrates on Gumplowicz, mostly because he is available in English and much of Ratzenhofer remains untranslated. The two agree in several ways, especially in their interpretations of the biological analogy of Spencer and what it meant for a positivistic sociology.* The contribution of Gumplowicz to positivistic social science is his assertion of the primacy of group phenomena. While he acknowledged that others preceded him in basing human society in interaction, it was Gumplowicz who conceptualized the context of social interaction as paramount and showed the relationship of the context of interpersonal interaction to the individual personality. He rejected both the neo-Hegelians in Germany and the unequivocal acceptance of Spencerian applications of biology to society. For him, French sociology, particularly Comte and Quetelet, were the correct path—with a healthy respect for the Cartesian spirit of rational description based upon mathematics. He was skeptical of the idea that positivistic sociology would lead to a humanistic religion or that statistical proofs were available for social laws. However, he saw sociology as the study of groups interacting and argued that thought is a product of group life—positions that set the scope of modern social thought. Of greatest importance in this reassertion of French thought was the unique way in which Gumplowicz moved from human association and differentiation *within* a group—certainly a traditional approach shared by Spencer and Durkheim—to a concern for association and differentiation *between* groups. All this was based on an acknowledgment of the primary role of the family.

Gumplowicz attempted a theory of class evolution based upon class membership and separated from romantic notions of *Geist*, on the one hand, and material interest on the other. Individual conscience or morality have little to do with the conflicts of society. Individuals have conscience and moral sentiments, but societies and social groupings do not. Human beings are not what ought to be, but what they are:

*Ratzenhofer is available by reading the work of his principal American disciple, Albion Small.

By social phenomena we mean phenomena which appear through the operation of groups and aggregates of men on one another. The aggregates are the social elements. We must assume that the simplest and original social elements were primitive hordes, of which ... there must have been a great number in remote antiquity. (1980, p. 158)

Thus, the ultimate origins of groups lie outside the scope of Gumplowicz's concept of sociology. It is culture and the family that account for the psychic types embraced by others of his time. While Gumplowicz appreciated Tonnies' classic division between *Gemeinshaft* and *Gesellschaft* social organizations, he did not idealize the *Gemeinshaft* society, as did Tonnies. He sought to accentuate those factors that contributed to strife between groups having different customs and habits.

The central agency in human interaction spins on two poles: consanguinity, local association, and common interests—a kind of horizontal connection—and, on a "vertical pole," material, economic and secondary associations. Thus, the structure of a group is determined by the quality of its cohesion and discipline, the number of cohesion-producing factors, and homogeneity among the group. Society becomes the formation and reformulation, in constant conflict, of group life. Thus, as Horowitz (1980) notes: "[I]f Spencer can be said to be the first sociological functionalist, Gumplowicz can ... be said to be the earliest critic of functionalism" (p. 23). For him, change and development are not Spencerian adaptations, but a succession of effective and ineffective conflicts. Thus, in Gumplowicz's world there were laws for change, rather than laws for persistence. Consequently, he turned to forms of social conflict and the substitution of fatalism for causality. A dynamic of equilibrium and revolution is the centerpiece of change, and that change is external rather than internal:

Rights are always due to contact of unlike social elements and every right bears evidence of such an origin. There is not one that does not express inequality, for each is the mediation between unlike social elements, the reconciliation of conflicting interests which was originally enforced by compulsion but has through usage and familiarity acquired the sanction of a new custom. (1980, p. 262).

Again, the law of unintended consequences looms large because ideals sought are rarely ideals gained. Problems of class, race, and ethnicity are special conditions of the general laws of social evolution through conflict. At the root of all of this is the essential group, the "consanguineous social group"—the family—which has an elemental power in social life. However, the inevitability of conflict means that people and groups will change as they come in contact with those that are different:

Man tries also with his whole being to preserve "forever" all the social institutions which he, the blind instrument and

means of natural impulses and inclinations, creates; along with cultural products for making life tolerable, beautiful and noble—while natural and necessary decay labors to overthrow them, undermines them, gnaws at and devours them. We would preserve the social community in which we are well off; but it must end as surely as the life of the individual. We would preserve our language, religion, customs, nationality and do not notice how they daily waste away like rocks under dripping water. (1980, p. 274)

Society forms everything, and the individual is but a "prism." In their actions, once in a group, individuals are sheeplike. It is intergroup conflict that leads to rights, a state or intergroup union of different elements as a concept. This is opposed to morals—a simple group/individual phenomenon that is implanted through natural development of simple, familylike groups.

The importance of the Gumplowicz stream of thought is its impact on early American social science and especially family studies. There are several thinkers that stand at the forefront of early American social science: Lester Ward, Albion Small, Franklin H. Giddings, Edward A. Ross, and William Graham Summer. Of these, Ward and Small probably had more influence on the development of sociology in the United States than the others, both because of the time their work was conducted and their positions in academic circles. Ward's *Dynamic Sociology* (1883) reflected the influence of Gumplowicz and was possibly the first important work in the developing field of sociology in the United States.* Small's text with Vincent—*An Introduction to the Study of Sociology* (1894)—was probably the first American text in the field and reflected Small's affection for the ideas of Ratzenhofer and Spencer. Both scholars had immense influence because Ward was the first president of the American Sociological Society (ASS, as it was then called), and Small chaired the first American Department of Sociology (1892) at the University of Chicago. Ward had been in direct correspondence with Gumplowicz for several years and is acknowledged in the latter's work many times, while Small studied in Germany and chose to place conflict theory at the forefront of his investigations of social phenomena. All these individuals were classical liberals—embracing both evolutionary thought from Spencer and social reform. The overriding concerns of each of these moralistic individuals—many were sons of ministers or had careers at one time in the ministry—were social problems and how to justify intervention, given the laissez-faire stance of Spencerian evolutionary thought. Their position, advanced by Ward as the "principle of social

---

*Ward's attempt (see Schwendinger & Schwendinger, 1974) was to bridge Spencer's social Darwinism with a reform approach involving things such as universal education. This did not prevent Ward and his intellectual progeny at Chicago, W. I. Thomas, however, from advocating gender roles that were clearly an adjustment to dominant norms. The family was modeled on tradition and, from many perspectives, oppression.

telesis," was that it was a natural evolution of people to assist the evolutionary process because of their "consciousness" and choice. Thus, while social problems were charted in many college courses and social scientists searched for "laws" governing behavior, these thinkers searched for justifications to "correct" these social problems.

The list of problems absorbing interest at the time is both enlightening and tell a tale of the drive to seek consensus on values in the society. Traditional institutions, in all forms, were to be maintained. In that regard, William Graham Sumner is perhaps most interesting. As with his contemporaries, Sumner accepted progress through evolution. He also believed interfering with the "scientific progress" of society was wrong. Sumner embraced Social Darwinism as no social theorist has since. Sumner defended theories as diverse as the continued existence of extreme poverty and the "Gospel of Wealth" because he thought to do otherwise was a perversion of society's natural order. The traditional family, for example, was sacrosanct. Many social thinkers of the early twentieth century, with backgrounds in theology, rural environments, and small towns, saw the problems of society as associated with the growth of the city.* The city, as it developed in the early twentieth century, fostered all the pathologies that churched, middle-class, law and order citizens of small-town communities deplored: crime, drunkenness, illegitimacy, divorce, unemployment, and, almost parenthetically because it was rarely confronted in these terms, the weakening of family ties so treasured by traditionalists. As a result of influences from the progressive political movement of early twentieth-century America, therefore, social thinkers turned to two areas to address the problems: social work and education.

As Collins and Makowsky (1993) propose, "[N]either the theorizing nor the research of the early sociologists produced any real advancement in knowledge (p. 91). Because they were politically naive and insisted on environmental amelioration as the answer to the problems of the city, their reforms were spectacularly unsuccessful. Their long catalogues of "social problems" are either still with us or have been defined away. For example, divorce, a "horror" to these "objective scientific investigators," is still with us, but has been stripped of its moral definitions as individuals have been liberated from collective definitions of morality. Sumner's acceptance of the power of norms to make anything right was perhaps more accurate than the progressive opponents realized. Although his primary achievement was to defend the role of wealth and continuation of systems of great inequality, he understood traditional forces in American society reflected a dominant value consensus that was the result of scientific evolutionary development. Though he accepted

Gumplowicz's "in-group/out-group" distinction he never got much beyond a defense of the status quo. His concepts of folkways and their operation were as standard an explanation of the lack of importance to the individual as was anything else written in the ear following Spencer's dominance in American thought. However, it must be remembered that Sumner's defense of the traditional family was part of the foundation of all his work.

The center of reaction to all this was the Sociology Department at the University of Chicago. There, somewhat by happenstance, three trends joined: the growth of the modern city of Chicago around the university, the progressive political reaction—at least by intellectuals—to it, and the development of a school of philosophy that attempted a uniquely modern interpretation of society, American Pragmatism.

Pragmatism,* Chicago Sociology, and the Supremacy of the Family

As Chicago grew and intellectuals such as Jane Addams (1860–1935) founded the ameliorative attempts at work to restore the family, several thinkers began to explore the higher-level meanings of all these developments. Much of this had its roots at other places and times, particularly Harvard and Michigan and in the work of William James and Charles Horton Cooley.

William James is probably best remembered in social science as a psychologist, but his impact on other disciplines, particularly through his essays and the 1907 work *Pragmatism* must never be underemphasized. James' impact on family studies was to be indirect—largely through his student George Herbert Mead and, in turn, Mead's impact on others. James advanced a philosophical doctrine, pragmatism, that was both a means for determining meaning and a theory about truth. Acknowledging his debt to one of the remarkably overlooked founders of this school of thought, Charles Sanders Pierce, James argued that truth or falsity of a judgment or its consonance with reality depends upon obtaining corroboration (consequences) expected from any such judgment. Meaning is revealed by examining the practical consequences of a concept, theory, or action. Thus, James calls into question the completely static nature of truth assumed by thinkers in sociology such as Comte and Durkheim, and he equates truth with ideas such as usefulness, expediency, and workability.

Mead, whose good fortune it was to be hired by James as a tutor for James' children, spent many hours in unrecorded conversations with the populizer of pragmatism. He

---

*Here Mills' (1943) classic work on their ideologies is of particular interest.

*For a one-sided but comprehensive review of this American school of thought, see Diggins (1994).

found in some of James' ideas and those of another Harvard philosopher, Josiah Royce, a "home" for his developing ideas about the evolutionary and Hegelian idea of the developing self. By the early 1890s, and after study in Europe, Mead traveled to Michigan as an instructor of philosophy. Here he fell under the influence of two key figures in the development of modern thought in family studies—Charles Horton Cooley and John Dewey. Dewey was to Mead a role model on how to combine academic life with social and educational reform, while Cooley offered a more immediate plan for a method of studying the world.

Cooley (1864–1929) is best remembered in family studies for his two major works, *Human Nature and Social Order* (1964) and *Social Organization* (1962). These works, which provide concepts to social thought such as the primary group and the "looking glass self," also provided Mead with an example of the need to study the socialization of children in order to understand the development of adult behavior and relations. For Cooley, the images people have of one another are the facts of society, so that "[S]ociety exists in my mind as the concept and reciprocal influence of certain ideas named 'I.' … It exists in your mind as a similar group, and so in every mind" (1902, p. 84). Since the family is the foremost primary group, basic experiences of social unity occur within that arena first. Ideas are created in this primary social environment that expand to the entire social unit if the basic values of good faith and justice are to prevail. Moreover, it is obvious that such a perspective places tremendous weight on subjective impressions, rather than objective reality. While Cooley is frequently cast as secondary to George Herbert Mead (see later)—his emphasis was the nature of children as they developed the self as a process—his work was probably superior to Mead's, whose dominant emphasis was upon the genesis of the self.

John Dewey, the most systematic of the pragmatists, is remembered for the assemblage of philosophers he created at the University of Chicago—including George Herbert Mead—more than he is for his influence on family studies. Building on James, and in certain respects Weber, Dewey saw his task as reconciling science and values. For Dewey, the scientific method is part of the quest for "certainty," and that quest is realizable by reconnection of practical activity with philosophical inquiry. From a decidedly marked agenda for social reform, Dewey fashioned an argument for the primacy of inquiry as a skill, rather than factual accumulation. Thus, knowledge is uncertain from time one to time two, but the act of inquiry is a constant and will provide its practitioner with skills to continue to adjust and unravel the facts of life. For Dewey, nothing seems to overshadow the importance of education and socialization in the development of the skills needed to survive modern society. After

founding his laboratory school in Chicago, he moved on to Columbia University to continue his efforts for social reform and a liberal political agenda. In doing so, he also argued for education as the instrument of social and moral reconstruction. This marriage of science and idealism led him to emphasize the entire socialization process and the family as important to any understanding of the modern situation.

Dewey had invited Mead to join him at Chicago and Mead remained there the rest of his life. It was at Chicago that Mead had his major impact on the first graduate sociology department, in part through his influence on the first generation of sociologists and family studies specialists trained in the United States. Although Mead was to write little (most work attributed to him is based on lectures and articles published by others), his ideas still exert strong influence in family studies.

Mead, by his own admission, was Hegelian in that he asserted humans had to be social to impact the environment. Thus, individual achievement was meaningless because it had to follow a selfhood based upon being part of an identified social whole or group. He rejected the Kantian notion of ideas coming from fixed categories of the mind. Combining this with a Darwinian emphasis on adaptation, Mead argued for the importance of gestures, as did Darwin, in the development of mind, self, and society. He also acknowledged Rousseau's concept of the community's spirit in his own concept of the "generalized other." For Mead, the generalized other involves the self's ability to develop collective rules and culture through acquisition of a group's orientation. This is acquired by a child, according to Mead, as he/she goes through a series of stages of socialization from an individual, primary orientation to an acceptance of the "generalized other" that encompassed a unified society of humanity. Yet Mead also saw the importance of the Adam Smith problem and attributed considerable significance to the positive aspects of exchange learned in decision making that is required by capitalist development. Unlike Marx and others who reacted to the deleterious impact of capitalism as mentioned by Smith, mead regarded exchange as an important socializing force for human beings.

Because of William James' influence and that of other pragmatists, Mead was supported in his interest in adaptation and emergence. Adhering to pragmatist principles, Mead saw meaning as a social construction—an adaptive mechanism that allows an individual to manipulate the environment in goal-oriented activity. In Mead's construction, individuals emerge from society but society emerges from individuals' adaptations. While this may seem a conundrum to some thinkers, Mead avoided the circularity implied by hypothesizing that human beings lived in social groupings before they achieved their current biological form. Since individuals grow up in society first, and they are children first, it is within the primary familial unit that society, ultimately, is formed. Still, as shown in his *The Philosophy of the Act* (1972), while society has priority, the individual emerges from behavior in a series of "social acts" that are the basic unit of social analysis.

The family was the most fundamental unit for Mead in several ways. First, as a structure it was a fundamental unit for reproduction. Second, it was the unit that allowed the development of larger units and, therefore, societal development. This is clear in his major work, *Mind, Self and Society* (1962), in which he writes: "[L]arger units or forms of human social organization such as the clan or the state are ultimately based upon, and … are developments from or extensions of, the family" (p. 229). The self, for Mead a process more than a structure, was the result of continuous adaptations to day-to-day existence, with the earliest of these behaviors arising in the family.

Making a distinction between "play"—a beginning, almost imitative state of learning a role in infantile development—and "the game"—an advanced stage in which self-reflection is accomplished and the child can take the roles of others into account—Mead develops a model of human socialization. This "game stage" is the first instance of the "generalized other"—the fully developed social self or socialized adult. It is through his study and his students' promulgation of these stages that family studies became aware of and was heavily influenced by Mead's ideas. The self emerges in these stages through Mead's treatment of a kind of generalizable biography of a child. Virtually all mainstream texts mention Mead's work on socialization. His concepts and stages are used extensively in teaching child socialization, but are frequently confounded with ideas such as those of Freud. In that sense, few practitioners in family studies see the fundamental difference between Mead's notions of the self as a "process" rather than "conflicting" parts as in Freud's concepts of superego and the ego. Mead's "generalized other" was part of his "reformist" political agenda and had more to do with an idealized form of Rousseau's "General Will" and a unified society of mankind than it did with simpler stages of interaction. For this use of the generalized other, family studies was distorted to fit notions of a conservative view and collective consciousness as the source of the truth of individual existence.

As indicated, Mead's influence upon graduate students at Chicago was immense. It is seen first in the work of W. I. Thomas, a colleague and friend, along with Jane Addams. Thomas was among the more committed social reform advocates on the Chicago sociology faculty. His classic work—some refer to it as the most important work in sociology in the twentieth century—with Florian Znaniecki, *The Polish Peasant in Europe and America* (1927) is an exhaustive study

of the adaptation of working-class immigrants to American culture. It is distinctive for its time in that it attempts to meld theory with method to achieve reformist goals. The work is a conscious attempt to break with the Social Gospel movement* and the entire biological imperative carried by Darwinism and Spencer. It also tries, conspicuously, to build on the symbolic as central to understanding human social interaction. At the heart of the work is a realization that family holds a key to understanding modern social life.

The work has four distinct aspects—a study of one "ethnic" group, a theoretical attitudes–values framework, a historical, but process-oriented account of a group's life, and a work that is self-consciously attuned to methodological advancement and sophistication. Within the conceptual framework—which conditions the entire enterprise—Thomas and Znaniecki use social values as "objective cultural elements" and social attitudes as "subjective characteristics of … the social group." The interplay between these two concepts provide a social technique (methodological tool) to understand the interplay between the codependence of the individual and society. Reference to any meaningful activity requires that actors draw upon one or the other, and the investigator must assess the relative importance of one over the other in the situation. Their empirical case is one that is rooted in an ethnic group that is, in turn, rooted in a familial-based culture.

Following the Polish immigrants from a traditional village in which the peasant family is depicted as a traditional solidary group, the Roman Catholic Church provides meaning and support to their tradition. Change occurs as individualistic values penetrate the culture, first in the village as industrialization occurs, but most forcefully as peasants immigrate to urban Poland and, ultimately, the urban United States. The main institutions of traditional Polish social control—family, community, and church—become much weaker in the United States, and the authors note the rise of new institutions—various kinds of benevolent or mutual aid societies—that serve the functional equivalent (to use a phrase from later developments in sociology) for the traditional organizations of peasant Polish life. However, the conditions of peasant life transplanted to America are prone to disorganization because primary group ties, especially those of the family, cannot restore themselves to their former

*Christian impacts and "uplift" were strong at this time. While socialism had been pushed aside over debates regarding World War I and pacifist reactions to the conflict (see Fried, 1992, esp. 504ff) some of the "intellectual" socialists, including Jane Addams and Clarence Darrow, embraced a conscious Christian application to change society. The foremost exponent of this entire movement was probably Walter Rauschenbusch (1912). Earlier discussion of Christian socialism can be found in Dombrowski (1977).

primacy. The cure for this personal and social disorganization, according to the authors, is to restore the family values lost in the immigration and adaptation. Although remaining vague as to the implementation of this solution, the work laid groundwork for a tradition at the University of Chicago that has impact on family studies to this day.

This tradition was "highjacked" by the change in methodology at Chicago from Mead's concern for hypothesis testing to Robert Ezra Park's concern for observational studies without any notion of generalizability or problem solving. The concern became much more "sensitizing" and interpretive research, with results that are not without merit, running as they do from classic works such as Anderson's *The Hobo* (1923) to Thrasher's *The Gang* (1927). Such a concern becomes one of fitting the "socially disorganized" case back into the dominant ideology of the time. There is little concern with the strength of the adaptations made by the groups, and park's concerns, therefore, were very idiosyncratic. For example, as Fisher and Strauss (1978) point out, Park's notion of reform was limited because of his fondness for Sumnerian analysis: "The basic processes of social change were beyond legislation. People would handle the problems of conflict and accommodation far better than would unrealistic legislation" (p. 467).

The Chicago School was definitely to be a transitional point in the development of family studies. It represented the key themes of the late reform mentality with an emphasis on scientific explanations for social problems, the application of Darwinian explanations including Park's ecological/urban models of problems and change, and an acceptance of problems as the inevitable outgrowth of an age of transition. Increasingly, as the studies at Chicago proliferated, they tended to identify the values and interests of middle- and upper-class groups with those of society as a whole. Indeed, the most graphic example of this is the treatment of the family in Chicago-inspired work. The middle-class family, and traditional gender roles, was equated with normality, and the problem in dealing with transition was to simply reassert the dominant and "good" that was known (see Heiskanen, 1971). The family and adjustment to it can be seen as important objectives to achieve social control in the 1920s and 1930s in American social thought:

> Improvident behavior, extreme selfishness, prejudicial attitudes, and the lack of personal ambition were being defined as the *causes* of social *unrest, crime, racism, war,* and *poverty.* Consequently, the family was considered important precisely because it was eventually regarded as the prime institutional means for achieving social stability and order. The family could be expected to eliminate the causes of outstanding social problems through the proper socialization of individual moral values, self-control, status attitudes, and ethnic or racial tolerance. (Schwendinger & Schwendinger, 1974, p. 330)

This philosophy is seen in the work of Park's (and Thomas'*) students such as Janowitz, Blumer, Everett Hughes, and Howard S. Becker.

In 1917, Albion Small published Harry Elmer Barnes' first work on the history of social thought. For 30 years, Barnes continued his contribution and summarized the Chicago School's role with his 1948 volume, *An Introduction to the History of Sociology.* In his preface Barnes acknowledges the reformist efforts of "sociologists from … Comte and … Ward to Sorokin" as the chief justification for the discipline that had become American sociology. The book, dedicated to Small, is a compendium of articles summarizing the neo-Darwinian aspects of social thought, with some deference to Gumplowicz and his "ilk," but it contains two articles more remarkable for their historical interest than anything else—an article by C. Wright Mills on family theory and a piece by the emerging superstar of mid-twentieth-century sociology, Talcott Parsons, on Max Weber. It was this second individual, and his earlier manuscript designed to reassert both Weber and Durkheim, that forever changed both social thought and family studies in America.

Functionalism, Parsons on Family, and the New Consciousness of Kind

In 1937, Parsons had presented his attempt to unit social science into a general stream of thought of structure. *The Structure of Social Action* was the beginning of Parsons' lifelong attempt to provide sociology with a theoretical framework that would serve to synthesize accumulated work in the social sciences. The major message in this seminal work is that the "greats" of social thought, Durkheim, Weber, Marshall, and Pareto, had developed a middle ground between positivism, as it had developed, and idealism, as Parsons understood it. Some of this is based on common themes in the works of those cited, but much is based on the creative readings of each by Parsons. Moore, in a 1978 summary of the functionalist perspective, summarized it as follows:

> Human social aggregates involve differentiated units which are interdependent. These units may be individuals, families and kinship structures, villages, or such analytical structures as age-sex categories or broader status groups.... The combination of differentiation and interdependence permits asking two related questions: how is the interdependence of units

---

*Thomas' early "retirement" limited his contact with students, although he and Park shared many. The controversial nature of his "dismissal" from Chicago probably says more about how much he infuriated dominant political powers than it does about family studies. Still, he turned attention to "unadjusted girls" in work that suggested traditional morality could be questioned, and his subsequent treatment is another in a series of tragic rejections by elites of ideologies that sought alternative explanations of family and gender roles.

effected? what contribution do parts make to the whole? (Moore, 1978, pp. 323–324)

Naturally, Moore begins the exposition with the work of Durkheim, but he is quick to move to the Spencerian biological analogies so characteristic of early American sociology. Moore points out that Parsons had begun with a concern for the famous problem of order, and central to that was the entire issue of integration. However, if one reads Parsons' 1937 work, there are two important qualifiers to Moore's interpretation: Durkheim is virtually ignored in Parsons' work until almost half of the work is completed and, more importantly, Parsons begins with the infamous question, "[W]ho now reads Spencer?" (Parsons, 1937, p. 3). Ironically, it is Parsons that provides the basis for a variety of Spencer's functionalism as an answer to the issue of integration and in so doing elevates the study of the family to the central focus of sociology in the 1940s through the 1960s. Just as Durkheim held that the family was the central unit in his "conscience collective," Parson's was to place the family squarely at the center of his theory of social action.

Because Parsons embraced the "problem of order" stated by Hobbes, he also accepted Durkheim's collective conscience as a source of social solidarity. Much of this was taken from anthropology and its functionalism and rather simply renamed the "value system"—something that was passed as cultural values to all the members of a society. The issue for Parsons now became how to explain the manner through which this value system exerted "power" or social control over the individuals in the group/society. Rejecting the rather crude, almost group, psychology of Durkheim, Parsons substituted Freud and his collective unconscious as discussed earlier. This had several merits from Parsons' view, including the value of being able to assert that the collective consciousness (superego?) could be found in all individuals. In a series of subsequent publications, Parsons simply elaborated this fundamental set of assertions. The differentiation of society—following Comte, Spencer, and Durkheim—was to amplify itself in all manners and parts of society. The foundation of society, in turn, if social order was to be maintained, was a strong family system, adequate socialization, and, consequently, value consensus.

Parsons had posed the problem as one based upon a dichotomy of positivist action and idealist action. The solution was what he eventually called voluntaristic order—the actor reacts to the interplay of positivistic and idealistic factors that must be balanced against each other. This is resolved, in Parsons' mind, by the Freudian conflict of ego, id, and superego and the acceptance of "norms" by the actor. It is this process that promotes socialization, and the family, to the forefront in Parsons' scheme. This "theory of action" was given its first statement in Parsons' 1937 work, but it was

to change and be modified by a collective enterprise that resulted in the 1951 coedited volume with Edward Shils,* *Toward a General Theory of Action* (1951).

This work moved Parsons, and most of sociology, away from a theory of action and toward concern for theory that depended upon analysis of systems. Parsons had developed his initial work in terms of an actor's orientation toward social, cultural, and physical objects. His interactions with the multidisciplinary team that produced the 1951 volume—they began their collaboration in 1948—convinced him that the orientations that he wanted to understand were coordinated through three different systems that were "above" the actor: the social, cultural, and personality systems. Thus, in the section "A General Statement," (Parsons, Shils, et al., 1951, esp. pp. 8–20) describing underlying psychological "need-dispositions," the authors attribute explicit import to "learning and interactive experience" as the things that integrate the systems (1951, pp. 8–20). The systems are interrelated by institutionalization, internalization, and socialization—which binds the individual to norms, roles, and, therefore, the social system. This is based, in large part, on Parsons' conception of "pattern variables" or basic choices for action faced by all actors. These choices apply to "the *normative* or ideal aspects of the structure of systems of action" (1951, p. 79) and they become integrated into an actor's personality system. At this point Parsons turns his elaborate conceptual apparatus into a study of the entire personality system and eventually produces his definite analysis of *The Social System* (1951).

A crucial link forged in all this work is the work of the small group psychologist Robert F. Bales. Bales had begun, in 1946, to develop an instrument to measure interaction. By July 1949, Bales was able to produce a manual for his analysis of interaction, *Interaction Process Analysis: A Method for the Study of Small Groups* (1950). In this document he makes an important distinction concerning the time frame of reference for actors during problem solving—whether they are instrumental or expressive. The implications for this distinction become important for both Parsonian theory and the study of the family. As early as the 1951 *Toward a General Theory of Action*, Bales was credited with coauthorship of the principle paper and showed influence in the section on "The Social System." In discussing the content of roles, three sets of problems are mentioned: instrumental interaction, expressive interaction, and integration (1951, p. 209). The accompanying footnote is crucial to understanding the role these distinctions make in the theory and, ultimately, in family studies:

> So far as problems of instrumental and affective interaction are concerned, it seems fair to treat complex societies and

*This marks an important "cross-pollination" in thought, since Shils visited the "working group" at Harvard from his academic home at Chicago.

smaller units (e.g., conjugal families of which it is composed as homologous. They will differ ... with respect to their structural integration. (1951, p. 209)

Subsequent work—first, *Working Papers in the Theory of Action* (1953), coauthored by Parsons, Shils, and Bales, and, second, Parsons and Bales' (1955) *Family, Socialization and Interaction Process*—establishes both the "systems problems" or functional problems aspects of Parsonian behavior (Adaptation–Goal Attainment–Integration–Latency) based on Bales' work and the importance of Freud's conflicting aspects of personality systems. Generalizations were made from Bales' work on small groups and combined with Freudian interpretations to reassert the socialization impact of the family. Parsons (1961), on his own, was to craft a system that placed all behavior at the end point of effective socialization. Thus, when Bales' categories were applied to families, socialization and existing values combining with traditional gender roles implied by the instrumental versus expressive categories served as an important pattern for the "effective" or functional family.* The status of that interpretation remained unchallenged for most of the rest of the twentieth century in family studies and family sociology. One perceptive student of Parsonian functionalism summarized the pattern as follows:

> [T]he human personality emerges as an autonomous system from the interpenetration of the organic needs, drives, desires, and instincts of the individual with the factual, social, and cultural environment. This gives rise to a personality that is composed of four subsystems: Id, Ego, Superego, and Ego identity (Ego ideal). The interaction between socialize and socializing agents shapes the character and development of all these aspects of the personality. (Munch, 1994, vol. 2, p. 88)

Combining this with the "systems problems" of small groups from Bales, one gets the prescriptive family of current family studies and family practitioners.

There is the continuation of a tradition in sociology here that cannot be overlooked. Since Franklin Giddings at Columbia at the turn of the century, many sociologists embraced versions of Gumplowicz's consciousness of kind thinking. Spencer's evolutionary theories, with their biological analogies, did little to counter such tendencies because they included an emergent and evolutionary development of a universal human facility that made human social life possible. Indeed, it is useful to recall the degree to which social thinkers and students of the family relied on images of the

primal hoard or primitive clan from early anthropology to justify many of the explanations. The degree to which contemporary family studies follows that tradition, when examined in light of all that has gone before, should not be discounted.

Volumes such as Bell and Vogel's (1960) reader, *A Modern Introduction to the Family*, contained numerous references to the necessity of the family and its indispensable role in socialization. William Goode in several works, justifies ideas as diverse as romantic love and the "dysfunctional" nature of divorce. These also are tied to the Bell and Vogel volume—which can be characterized as a contemporary justification for the family—and family studies, which is based on traditional family structures and norms. The issue, at least from this writer's viewpoint, is whether the diverse theories family studies now uses are relevant for modern society, or more broadly, for nonsanguine groups. While that is not easily answered in its entirety, it seems important that people in family studies acknowledge the lack of innovation in family theory and its roots in conservative defenses of privilege and tradition.

Certainly there are numerous criticisms of "functionalist traditionalism" represented by some family theory and studies. However, in some ways, they are less heard now than at any time since the turn of the last century. Many of these criticisms are of the Spencerian model. Gumplowicz made several of these in his work, including the inevitability of conflict, which did not allow him to accept labeling "dysfunctional elements" in society. Natural adaptation or equilibrium were foreign to him also because he took change as a cyclical constant. The empiricism of traditional functionalism asserted, according to Gumplowicz's critique, an adaptive survival that was superior, whereas he could se it as merely an explanation that defended the powerful and the established. For him, forms of conflict were normal and the consensual acceptance demanded by traditional functionalism was simply incorrect. Change occurred because there are diverse interests and no "value system" or family system is better than any other. Thus, there is a strong need to reassert the notion that Adam Smith had at the outset: "Moral sentiments" may be disrupted by "capitalist development," but neither need be dismissed as "dysfunctional." As Machiavelli noted, the values actors hold need to be pushed into the background, since purity of intention is no sign of justice or guarantee for success. Since fortune makes success unpredictable, the truest test is the connections between causes and effects and principles and consequences. This type of argument for a pragmatic, in the American sense, judgment of the family and its organization has been brushed aside in modern work.

One classical theorist we have "left out" to this point, who seems to have understood the "pragmatic" basis to the

---

*Schwendinger and Schwendinger (1974, esp. pp. 335–382) show the earlier pattern of the use of Freud by sociologists in a political agenda. While one is tempted to place the same onus on Parsons, it is probably not accurate, since he was mostly concerned with abstract theory and not any applications. Indeed, he probably missed even Durkheim's and Weber's concern for dysfunctional developments.

modern family, is the German social philosopher Georg Simmel, who stated, "Society is merely the name for a number of individuals connected by interaction.... society is certainly not a 'substance,' nothing concrete, but an event" (1950, p. 11). Thus, Simmel saw the individual and society as interdependent and society as nothing but *living, experiencing*. For him, it was the dialectical relation mandated between the two that was the defining characteristic of social life. Simmel saw conflicts or "contradictions" between the society and individuals as harmful to both. Thus, he developed a theme of the strain between "objective culture," for example, technology, environment, and "subjective culture," for example, individuals' inner worlds or interpretations. Donald Levine (1971) has framed this as Simmel's devotion to a Kantian view of the world.

Although persuasive since Simmel wrote his dissertations on Kant, this alleged devotion neglects the degree to which Simmel accepted Hegel's conception of the dialectic. Therefore he saw a constant tension between individuals and society. For Simmel, tensions, as well as conflict and competition, were inevitable. Indeed, it was such tension, created as a solution to the dynamic between objective and subjective, between the unlimited objective culture and the limits to an individual's ability to understand these "forms," that created the ability to play the many parts in modern society. In his most important work, *The Philosophy of Money* (1990)* Simmel acknowledged that the division of labor is strong and imposes a fragmented self, but he developed a model that, while seeing life as tragic, saw the money economy as providing liberating opportunities for the "practical" individual. Thus as modern culture multiplies and overwhelms an individual's subjective world, it also allows for an enhanced potential for the creative synthesis of individual abilities and interests. The development of the monetary form of exchange allowed for a certain excitement for life, as individuals do adapt to forms that allow them creativity. Money, rationalization, and all that goes with modern development have both positive and negative characteristics.

This is reflected in the family because, as Simmel describes it (see, for example, 1950, pp. 190–223, 326–329), the relationship between men and women is based upon reciprocal orientations of dominance and submission. This form or framework of "sociation" which appears to be imposed allows ways through which personal subjectivity can be expressed. The issue is much less the dominance of the group than it is the perpetual ability of individuals to negotiate their reality in an ever-changing, and not always hostile or

*This work is seldom read by modern thinkers since its first translation in 1978. It seems, to this writer at least, to provide some important insights for social thinkers and, especially, for current students of familial change. Some theorists turned to this work in the 1980s.

friendly, social framework. Thus, Simmel has gone beyond Kant by searching for sociological priorities that bind individuals, but also allows them freedom in their subjective adaptation. Human life becomes an unfolding process of growth that shapes the forms of existence—such as the family—and, more importantly, allows creative responses from individuals to the societal forms. Exchange theorists such as George Homans and Peter Blau, in particular, took the model of interpersonal exchange as the basis for social life.

In many respects this development is not surprising. After all, Adam Smith began with a concern for the rational actions required by the new, "modern" systems of exchange required by developing capitalism. As Horowitz points out (1993, pp. 103–129), work by those such as Homans, Blau, March, and Simon, and especially James Coleman (*Foundations of Social Theory*, 1990) shows how the corporate structure displaces the family network:

> Nothing less than human culture as such is dissolved in formal sociological subsystems of corporate life: actors receiving benefits—marginal and total, acting and not acting, contributors and noncontributors....
>
> *Foundations of Social Theory* tells us much about ... the research world of economists and psychologists but precious little about the state of affairs in the messy world of ordinary men and women. (1993, p. 115)

Again, the dominance of the group is so total that little is left for individual adaptation and sentiment. The dilemma of Adam Smith comes full circle in this set of work as it completely removes the individual, even with Homans' cries about "bringing men back in," from its equations. The model cannot accept basic conflicts in human life and, therefore, removes itself to a periphery self-defined as "from other fields." The study of human social behavior and family studies is rendered even less possible when reduced to institutional "exchange."

The reader may, at this point if not long ago, have dismissed this as another critique of functionalism that is irrelevant. I hope not because it is an attempt to acknowledge the degree to which family studies are rooted in a popular culture receptive to repression. The conservative foundation of modern family studies is writ large and loudly in that popular culture. It was not long ago that former Vice President Quayle was able to evoke a, first hostile and then sympathetic, response about a fictional character who had an illegitimate birth. Discussions of illegitimacy, especially "teenage pregnancy" in popular sources, decry this "decline of family values," while they blithely ignore the fact that the illegitimacy rate in this society has not changed markedly in virtually a century. Family scholars such as Popenoe (1988) feed the frenzy with scholarly analyses of the decline of "family values" (sources of values unspecified) and their implications for the demise of American society. Lipset (1996) has taken such superficial analyses of the family, divorce, and sexual mores to task. As Lipset shows, there is no value crisis in America, merely an individuated interpretation of values. While republican theorists (in the tradition of de Tocqueville) keep rediscovering community, the American public remains liberal in its commitment to individualism. Indeed, Brent Staples (1996), reviewing Michael Lind's (1996) diatribe remarks that "to blame the right wing for resurgent racism and hostility toward the poor is to miss powerful forces at work in the culture," and "Middlebrow moral corruption is the air in which we swim" (p. 5), argues that the best part of Lind's attack is on family matters when he focuses on mass illegitimacy. Lind ends his assessment by showing that "scholars" who assess the modern situation are, somehow, unaware of the national mood that allows attribution of moral inferiority to the poor and accepts a conservative notion that the traditional family is in decline. Obviously, such an assessment is contradicted by most scientific evidence.

Conclusion

It seems clear the intellectual elites that "practice" sociology of the family and family studies are divorced from ideas of individual liberation. Their concepts are rooted in a stream of very conservative social thought that roots most social action in biological categories and biological needs. It rejects the "practical wisdom" of the average person. The hoi polloi are not too glamorous and seem not to operate the way ideologues, dogmatists, and, especially, social theorists want. They are "emotional," unpredictable, individualistic, violent, "self-destructive," and repressive in ways that elites neither understand nor tolerate (see Lasch, 1995). In that sense, as shown in the choices classical theorists applied, family social theory is neither liberating to individuals nor without a political/religious agenda. Family and gender studies are repressive and concentrate on the biological need or group as defining the individual. They follow Durkheim, Spencer, and Herder more than contemporary practitioners realize. Some would say that is at the root of the problems with a discipline—sociology—that many such as Horowitz (1993) see as having lost its way. There is a place for Machiavelli's "practical wisdom" in understanding human social grouping, and it is not there in modern family studies with its insistence on the primacy of traditionally defined biological/familial categories. Marriage and family theorists seem, when considered in relation to classical theory, to be those leading a "wander into the wilderness"—a wilderness rooted in biological categories and no concern for individual processes that transcend those categories. Further, the practitioners are wandering with them, without a Moses.

It may be appropriate to reconsider the cultural tyranny suggested by the paradigms of contemporary adaptations of classical theory. It is as if cultural categories, of various kinds, are viewed as the defining aspects of social relations, while the label of "dysfunctional" is applied with abandon—without its deeply conservative nature. As one contemporary poet put it:

> In our longing for some assurance that we're behaving O.K. inside fairly isolated families, personal experience has assumed some new power.... I came to believe that our families are working, albeit in new forms. People go on birthing babies and burying dead and loving those with whom they've shared deeply wretched patches of history. We do this partly by telling stories, in voices that seek neither to deny family struggles nor to make demons of our beloveds. (Karr, 1996, p. 70)

The relation between the individual and society is problematic—as scholars have recognized from time immemorial. It is worth remembering that the ultimate product is an individual, albeit a thinking one. To escape the tyranny of the group advanced by classical theory, it is necessary to understand that the "dysfunctional" family is as likely to work and as likely to produce a healthy, thinking, feeling individual as is any other form. While recognizing that few family scholars consciously embrace functionalism, we must recognize that the roots of the variety of so-called new approaches are still rooted either in functionalism or, more insidiously, in modern variations of consciousness of kind thinking. To hold otherwise is to assert that values determined by family theorists are superior to anyone else's values. That is an untenable position for something that claims the objectivity of science as a mantle for its therapeutic activities:

> The truth, of course, is that liberalism was conceived as a way to *preserve* some form of livable peaceful community. Perhaps it takes living in a 17th-century theocracy or a 20th-century dictatorship to appreciate how a forced community is, in fact, no community at all. And to see that contemporary attempts at a more binding politics—from Robert Putnam's to Amitai Etzioni's—can be cloying, and ultimately irrelevant, diversions from the rigors of constructing life together in modernity. (Sullivan, 1996, p. 6)

This gets to the crux of the issue of family theory derived from the classics.

Contemporary sociology and family studies have not dealt with the issues raised by Aristotle, Plato, Kant, and Hume. Rousseau's major contributions have gone largely unread and ignored. Do we think as individuals or are we merely the product of the community that comes before? The creative individual is real, in my mind at least, and those who operate in the name of science, and therapy, deriving from the "sociological tradition," are denying the creative dignifying aspects of individual human life. That is a mistake, the product of the conservatism of most family and social theorists and/or the specialization Lasch deplored.

ACKNOWLEDGMENTS. My thanks to Sue Steinmetz, Bill Blomquist, the editors, and an anonymous reviewer for helpful comments. Further special thanks to Rachel McIntosh and Lana Bandy for typing and editing in the face of my ability to break my hand before a deadline.

References

Anderson, N. (1923). *The hobo.* Chicago: University of Chicago Press.

Aristotle. (1946). *Politics.* London: Oxford University Press.

Ashley, D., & Orenstein, D. M. (1995). *Sociological theory* (3rd ed.). Boston: Allyn & Bacon.

Augustine, Saint. (1950). *City of God against the pagans.* New York: Random House. (Date of original work, AD. 410)

Bachofen, J. (1967). *Muth, religion, and mother right.* Princeton, NJ: Princeton University Press.

Bales, R. (1950). *Interaction process analysis: A method for the study of small groups.* Ann Arbor, MI: University Microfilms.

Barnes, H. E. (1948). *An introduction to the history of sociology.* Chicago: University of Chicago Press.

Bell, N. W., & Vogel, E. (Eds.). (1960). *A modern introduction to the family.* Glencoe, IL: Free Press.

Cassier, E. (1968). *The philosophy of the enlightenment.* Princeton, NJ: Princeton University Press. (Original work published 1932)

Coleman, J. (1990). *Foundations of social theory.* Cambridge, MA: Harvard University Press.

Collins, R. (1986). *Max Weber: A skeleton key.* Beverly Hills, CA: Sage.

Collins, R., & Makowsky, M. (1993). *The discovery of society* (5th ed.). New York: McGraw-Hill.

Comte, A. (1896). *The positive philosophy* (3 Vols.). London: George Bell.

Cooley, C. H. (1964). *Human nature and social order.* New York: Schocken Books.

Coulanges, F. de (1956). *The ancient city.* New York: Doubleday. (Original work published 1864)

Cranston, M. (1982). *Jean-Jacques.* Chicago: University of Chicago Press.

Cranston, M. (1991). *The noble savage.* Chicago: University of Chicago Press.

Darwin, C. (1936). *The origin of species and the descent of man.* New York: Modern Library.

Davis, K. (1937). The sociology of prostitution. *American Sociological Review, 2,* 744–755.

Davis, K., & Moore, W. M. (1945). Some principles of stratification. *American Sociological Review, 10,* 243–249.

Diggins, J. P. (1994). *The promise of pragmatism.* Chicago: University of Chicago Press.

Dombrowski, J. (1977). *The early days of Christian socialism in America.* New York: Farrar, Straus, and Giroux.

Durkheim, E. (1947). *The elementary forms of the religious life.* New York: Free Press. (Original work published 1912.)

Durkheim. E. (1962). *Social organization.* New York: Schocken Books.

Durkheim. E. (1964). *Rules of the sociological method.* New York: Free Press. (Original work published 1895)

Durkheim, E. (1966). *Suicide.* New York: Free Press. (Original work published 1897)

Durkheim, E. (1984). *The division of labor in society.* W. D. Halls (Trans.). New York: Free Press. (Original work published 1893)

Engels, F. (1945). *The origin of the family, private property, and the state.* New York: International. (Original work published 1891)

Fisher, B., & Strauss, A. (1978). Interactionism. In T. Bottomore & R. Nisbet (Eds.), *A history of sociological analysis.* New York: Basic Books.

Freud, S. (1922). *Group psychology and the analysis of the ego.* London: International Psychoanalytical Press.

Fried, A. (Ed.). (1992). *Socialism in America: From the Shakers to the Third International.* New York: Columbia University Press.

Garver, E. (1987). *Machiavelli and the history of prudence.* Madison: University of Wisconsin Press.

Gay, P. (1966). *The Enlightenment: The rise of modern paganism.* New York: Norton.

Gay, P. (1969). *The Enlightenment: The science of freedom.* New York: Norton.

Gobineau, J. A. de. (1915). *The inequality of human races.* New York: Putnam.

Gumplowicz, L. (1980). *Outlines of sociology.* New Brunswick, NJ: Transaction Books.

Hegel, G. W. F. (1967). *Philosophy of right.* Oxford: Clarendon Press.

Heiskanen, V. (1971). The myth of the middle-class family in American family sociology. *American Sociologist, 6,* 14–18.

Horowitz, I. L. (1980). Introduction. L. Gumplowicz (Eds.), *Outlines of sociology* (pp. 3–85). New Brunswick, NJ: Transaction Books.

Horowitz, I. L. (1993). *The decomposition of sociology.* New York: Oxford University Press.

Hume, D. (1949). *A treatise of human nature.* Oxford: Clarendon Press.

James, W. (1907). *Pragmatism.* New York: Meridian Books.

Jones, R. A. (1986). *Emile Durkheim: An introduction to four major works.* Beverly Hills, CA: Sage.

Jordan, D. P. (1985). *The revolutionary career of Maximilien Robespierre.* Chicago: University of Chicago Press.

Kant, I. (1993). *The philosophy of Kant.* New York: Modern Library.

Karr, M. (1996, May 12). Dysfunctional nation. *New York Times Magazine,* 70.

Lasch, C. (1995). *The revolt of the elites and the betrayal of democracy.* New York: Norton.

Levine, D. (1971). *Georg Simmel on individuality and social forms.* Chicago: University of Chicago Press.

Lind, M. (1996). *Up from conservatism.* New York: Free Press.

Lipset, S. M. (1996). *American exceptionalism: A double-edged sword.* New York: Norton.

Lukes, S. (1972). *Emile Durkheim: His life and work.* New York: Harper and Row.

Machiavelli, N. (1983). *The discourses on the first ten books of Titus Livy.* London: Penguin Books. (Original work published 1513)

Marcuse, H. (1966). *Eros and civilization.* Boston: Beacon Press.

Marx, K. (1906). *Capital: A critique of political economy.* New York: Modern Library.

Marx, K. (1978a). *A contribution to the critique of political economy.* In R. C. Tucker (Ed.), *The Marx–Engels reader* (2nd ed., pp. 3–6). New York: Norton. (Original work published 1859)

Marx, K. (1978b). *The economic and philosophic manuscripts of 1844.* In R. C. Tucker (Ed.), *The Marx–Engels reader* (2nd ed., pp. 66–125). New York: Norton. (Original work published 1844)

Marx, K. (1978c). *The German ideology,* Part I. In R. C. Tucker (Ed.), *The Marx–Engels reader* (2nd ed., pp. 146–200). New York: Norton. (Original work written 1845–1846, published 1932)

Marx, K. (1978d). *Manifesto of the Communist Party.* In R. C. Tucker (Ed.), *The Marx–Engles reader* (2nd ed., pp. 469–500). New York: Norton. (Original work published 1848)

Marx, K. (1978e). *Theses on Feuerbach.* In R. C. Tucker (Ed.), *The Marx—*

Engels Reader (2nd ed., pp. 143–145). New York: Norton. (Original work published 1845)

McLennan, J. F. (1970). *Primitive marriage.* Chicago: University of Chicago Press.

Mead, G. H. (1962). *Mind, self and society.* Chicago: University of Chicago Press.

Mead, G. H. (1972). *The philosophy of the act.* Chicago: University of Chicago Press.

Mill, J. S. (1859). *On liberty.* London: John W. Parker and Son.

Mill, J. S. (1909). *Principles of political economy.* London: Longmans, Green.

Mills, C. W. (1943). The professional ideology of social pathologists. *American Journal of Sociology, 49,* 165–180.

Mitzman, A. (1970). *The iron cage.* New York: Knopf.

Moore, W. E. (1978). Functionalism. In T. Bottomore & R. Nisbet (Eds.), *A history of sociological analysis* (pp. 321–361). New York: Basic Books.

Morgan, L. (1877). *Ancient society.* London: Macmillan.

Munch, R. (1994). *sociological theory: From the 1920s to the 1960s* (Vol. 2). Chicago: Nelson Hall.

Oakley, A. (1984/1985). *Marx's critique of political economy* (2 Vols.). London: Routledge & Kegan Paul.

Parsons, T. (1937). *The structure of social action.* Glencoe, IL: Free Press.

Parsons, T. (1951). *The social system.* Glencoe, IL: Free Press.

Parsons, T. (1961). Introduction to Culture and the Social System. In T. Parsons, E. Shils, K. Naegele, & J. Pitts, *Theories of society* (pp. 963–993). New York: Free Press.

Parsons, T., & Bales, R. (1955). *Family, socialization and interaction process.* Glencoe, IL: Free Press.

Parsons, T., & Shils, E. (1951). *Toward a general theory of action.* New York: Harper & Row.

Parsons, T., Shils, E., & Bales, R. B. (1953). *Working papers in the theory of action.* Glencoe, IL: Free Press.

Parsons, T., Shils, E., et al. (1951). *Toward a general theory of action.* Cambridge, MA: Harvard University Press.

Plato. (1937). *The Republic.* New York: Dutton.

Pope, W. (1986). *Alexis de Tocqueville: His social and political theory.* Beverly Hills, CA: Sage.

Popenoe, D. (1988). *Disturbing the nest: Family change and decline in modern societies.* New York: Aldine de Gruyter.

Rauschenbusch, W. (1912). *Christianizing the social order.* New York: Macmillan.

Rousseau. J.-J. (1936). *The confessions of Jean-Jacques Rousseau.* New York: Tudor.

Rousseau, J.-J. (1979). The social contract. In J. J. Mason (Ed.), *The indispensable Rousseau* (pp. 147–178). London: Quartet. (Original work published 1762)

Rousseau, J.-J. (1986). *Emile.* London: Everyman's Library. (Original work published 1762)

Schwendinger, H., & Schwendinger, J. (1974). *The sociologists of the chair.* New York: Basic Books.

Shapiro, V. (1992). *A vindication of political virtue: The political theory of Mary Wollstonecraft,* Chicago: University of Chicago Press.

Simmel, G. (1950). *The sociology of George Simmel.* Glencoe, IL: Free Press.

Simmel, G. (1990). *The philosophy of money.* London: Routledge.

Small, A., & Vincent, G. (1894). *An introduction to the study of sociology.* New York: American Book Co.

Smith, A. (1776). *An inquiry into the nature and causes of the wealth of nations* (2 Vols.). London: W. Strahan.

Smith, A. (1976). *The theory of moral sentiments.* Crawfordsville, IN: R. R. Donnelley. (Original work published 1759)

Sorokin, P. A. (1956). *Fads and foibles in modern sociology.* Chicago: Henry Regnery.

Spencer, H. (1898). *Principles of psychology* (3 Vols.). New York: D. Appleton.

Spencer, H. (1897). *Social statics.* New York: D. Appleton.

Spencer, H. (1961). *The study of sociology.* Ann Arbor: University of Michigan. (Original work published 1873)

Spencer, H. (1978). *The principles of ethics* (2 Vols.). Indianapolis: Liberty Fund. (Original work published 1904)

Staples, B. (1996, August 4). Zeal of a convert. *New York Times Book Review,* 5.

Stewart, J. B. (1963). *The moral and political philosophy of David Hume.* Westport, CT: Greenwood Press.

Sullivan, A. (1996, May 19). Review of M. J. Sandel's *Democracy's discontent. New York Times Book Review,* 6.

Thomas, W. I., & Znaniecki, F. (1927). *The Polish peasant in Europe and America* (2 Vols.). New York: Knopf.

Tocqueville, Alexis de. (1955). *The old regime and the French Revolution.* Garden City, NY: Doubleday. (Original work published 1856)

Tocqueville, Alexis de. (1956). *Democracy in America.* New York: New American Library.

Tocqueville, Alexis de. (1980). *On democracy, revolution, and society.* Chicago: University of Chicago Press.

Thrasher, F. (1927). *The gang.* Chicago: University of Chicago Press.

Turner, J., Beeghley, L., & Powers, C. (1995). *The emergence of sociological theory* (3rd ed.). Belmont, CA: Wadsworth.

Tylor, E. (1883). *Primitive culture* (2 Vols.). New York: Henry Holt.

Voltaire, F. M. A. de. (1962). *Letter to Cardinal de Bernis.* In T. Besterman (Ed.), *Voltaire's correspondence* (Vol. 87, p. 112).

Ward, L. F. (1883). *Dynamic sociology* (2 Vols.). New York: D. Appleton.

Weber, M. (1978). *Economy and society* (2 Vols.). Berkeley: University of California Press.

Weber, M. (1974a). Politics as a Vocation. In H. Gerth & C. W. Mills (Eds.), *From Max Weber: Essays in sociology* (pp. 77–128). New York: Oxford University Press. (Original work published 1918)

Weber, M. (1974b). Science as a vocation. In H. Gerth & G. W. Mills (Eds.), *From Max Weber: Essays in sociology* (pp. 129–156). New York: Oxford University Press. (Original work published 1918)

Westby, D. L. (1991). *The growth of sociological theory: Human nature, knowledge, and social change.* Englewood Cliffs, NJ: Prentice-Hall.

Westermarck, E. (1921). *The history of human marriage* (3 Vols.). London: Macmillan.

Wollstonecraft, M. (1929). *The vindication of rights of women.* London: Dent and Sons.

Zeitlin, I. (1971). *Liberty, equality, and revolution in Alexis de Tocqueville.* Boston: Little, Brown.

CHAPTER 8

Postmodernism and Family Theory

William J. Doherty

This chapter describes emerging developments in family theory in the last decade of the twentieth century. This task is at once easier and more difficult because it follows the 1993 publication of the comprehensive *Sourcebook of Family Theories and Methods: A Contextual Approach* (Boss, Doherty, LaRossa, Schumm, & Steinmetz, 1993). It is easier to catalog emerging theories about the family because a major section of the *Sourcebook* was devoted to newly emerging theories. But it is more difficult to say something new about the specific emerging theories that were covered in depth: phenomenology, feminism, biosocial, and race and ethnicity theories. Furthermore, the opening chapter of the *Sourcebook* put these emerging theories into the contexts of prior theories, developments in philosophy of science, and larger social and cultural developments (Doherty, Boss, LaRossa, Schumm, & Steinmetz, 1993).

Rather than retrace ground well covered in these prior writings, this chapter will describe what I believe is the overarching theoretical paradigm influencing new developments in family theory in the late twentieth century: the movement from modernism to postmodernism in culture, philosophy, and social science. I am not suggesting that postmodernism has won hegemony in the family field, only that it is the principal force shaping newly emerging theories—for better or for worse, depending on one's philosophy of science, values, and theoretical predilections.

A note of caution is necessary. The analysis in this chapter must perforce be quite general and sweeping. I will refer to exceptions and countertrends, but inevitably the argument will be broadly drawn. In addition, efforts to describe current trends and influences are particularly fraught with peril, like a fish describing the stream in which it swims. What postmodernists have taught us is that there are no "privileged positions" of observation, no piece of writing that does not reflect the ideology of the author and his or her personal and historical context. In that light, it might be helpful for the reader to know that I am neither a full advocate for postmodern family theory nor a critical skeptic. I am a sympathetic observer more than a partisan promoter of the movement I will describe in this chapter.

This chapter on emerging theories assumes that the reader is familiar with the major conceptual frameworks that have guided family theory and research in this century. It also assumes familiarity with basic metatheoretical issues such as the distinction between positivism and postpositivism in social science. Readers who require more background on these topics are referred to Boss et al. (1993) and Thomas and Wilcox (1987).

Since 1990 there has been a growing stream of writing on postmodernism and the family field. The case for viewing new developments in family theory as reflecting postmodernism was made most strongly by David Cheal in his 1991 book *Family and the State of Theory*. In family therapy, Doherty (1991) demonstrated how the origins of the field reflected cultural modernism in the mid-twentieth century and took a postmodern turn in the late 1980s. Doherty and colleagues (1993), in the *Sourcebook* overview chapter, also pointed to the emerging influence of postmodernism on the family science field. The *Sourcebook* chapter on feminist theories about families, by Osmond and Thorne (1993), explicitly took up the issue of postmodernism and feminism. A 1993 special issue of the *Journal of Family Issues* offered a number of explicitly postmodern perspectives on the theme "Rethinking Family as a Social Form" (Gubrium, 1993). And Baber and Allen (1992) used a postmodernist feminist framework in their book *Women and Families: Feminist Reconstructions*. Postmodern thinking clearly has become a strong influence on family theory in the 1990s.

William J. Doherty • Family Social Science Department, University of Minnesota, St. Paul, Minnesota 55108.

Handbook of Marriage and the Family, 2nd edition, edited by Marvin Sussman, Suzanne K. Steinmetz, and Gary W. Peterson. Plenum Press, New York, 1999.

The first section of the chapter will define and describe the terms *modernity* and *modernism* and will show how family theory until the past decade was predominantly shaped by modernist assumptions. The next section will define and describe the murky terms *postmodernity* and *postmodernism* and will discuss how this recent cultural movement has emerged into prominence in a number of areas. Then I will document how recent trends in family theory reflected a shift from modernism to postmodernism. In the last section, I will evaluate these developments and discuss countertrends that are colliding with postmodern family theory.

Modernism and Family Theory

Modernity as conceptualized by social theorists from the time of Marx and Weber is the period of Western history following the Middle Ages and the breakdown of feudalism, in which societies based on tradition and communalism were transformed by the processes of "individualization, secularization, industrialization, cultural differentiation, commodification, urbanization, bureaucratization, and rationalization which together have constituted the modern world" (Best & Kellner, 1991, p. 3; see also Cheal, 1991, and Giddens, 1990). The process of *modernization* is occurring in many non-Western regions of the world at the end of the twentieth century. Modernity represents a decisive break with traditional, premodern forms of social organization.

Modernism is a term often used to describe the worldview, philosophy, and aesthetics of Western modernity (Best & Kellner, 1991; Cheal, 1991). Formulated following the Enlightenment of the eighteenth century, philosophical modernism emphasized several major new themes:

1. The idea of change and progress in human affairs— in social structures, economy, science, and every other domain
2. Dedication to rational planning
3. Rejection of history and tradition
4. Emphasis on individual rights and individual experience

Aesthetic modernism was a cultural movement primarily of the first half of the twentieth century in art, literature, and architecture (Cantor, 1988; Karl, 1988). It emerged from a rebellion against Victorian constraints and the alienating experience of urbanization and industrialization. Aesthetic modernism emphasized the following elements in addition to philosophical modernism's rejection of history and emphasis on individualism:

1. The dense analysis of personal experience and the micro environment (as seen in the novels of James Joyce and the plays of Samuel Beckett)

2. The discontinuous or fragmented nature of reality (as seen in Cubist painters and Abstract Expressionists)
3. The search for universals that transcend culture and time (as seen in the "international style" of architecture that featured the clean, unadorned lines of skyscrapers)

The social sciences were born out of both philosophical and aesthetic modernism (Cantor, 1988; Cheal, 1991). They are based on a search for rational explanatory theories, on a belief in human change and adaptability, on assumptions about individualism, on a rejection of religious and moral traditions as the basis for understanding human behavior, and on a search for universals. Functionalism, perhaps the dominant theoretical model for sociology and anthropology for much of the twentieth century, is a quintessentially modernist theory: It focuses on the current internal dynamics of a social system, on how the parts and whole fit together, and on the search for universal processes. Social exchange theory, although the mirror opposite of structural functionalism in scope and method, nevertheless is clearly modernist in orientation, with its focus on rationality and micro interactions (Nye, 1979; Sabatelli & Shehan, 1993).

Social science of the family was also born out of modernism in the twentieth century. Its pioneers sought to apply rational, value-free scientific principles and procedures to the study of families in specific circumstances, rather than employing the global theoretical and historical approaches that dominated nineteenth-century family scholarship (Adams & Steinmetz, 1993; Christensen, 1984; Howard, 1981). Most family theories focused on the careful analysis of the micro world of family experience, with a particular emphasis on the subjective perceptions and experiences of individual family members. Indeed, marital satisfaction has been the most extensively studied construct in the field. Although structural functional family theory examined the family's connections with the wider society, its approach was ahistorical: Current social structures were the "given" to which families should adjust, as opposed to being viewed as the result of historically contested and malleable processes (Kingsbury & Scanzoni, 1993). Furthermore, structural-functionalism was used by most family scholars primarily as a model for studying intrafamily adjustment.

Other traditional family theories were equally modernist in perspective. Symbolic interactionism was used to examine the psychosocial interior of the family through careful analysis of cognitive and interactional elements (Blumer, 1969; LaRossa & Reitzes, 1993). Although not given to the grand theorizing of Talcott Parsons and the structural functionalists, symbolic interactionists nevertheless believed in the rationalization of family processes through the scientific enterprise and had a high degree of optimism about the pursuit of knowledge and the potential of this knowledge to help families shape their lives (Cheal, 1991). Early symbolic interactionists such as sociologists Ernest W. Burgess and Leonard Cottrell (1939), for example, were eager to apply their scientific work to the improvement of marital adjustment and the prevention of divorce. Furthermore, symbolic interactionism's focus on individual identity and role performance marks it as modernist in contrast to premodern family and postmodern family theory, neither of which has emphasized individual identity.

Family systems theory avoided the modernist focus on the individual, but it nonetheless has emphasized intrafamilial interactions outside of historical and larger ecological contexts. It has also embraced modernist beliefs in the power of change and progress in human affairs, as seen particularly in the development of family therapy, along with the pursuit of universal theories that transcend culture (Doherty & Baptiste, 1993).

Although an important alternative to individually oriented and macro-oriented theories, family systems theory in its origins in the 1950s and 1960s nevertheless mirrored the dominant modernist model of literary criticism in the United States in the mid-twentieth century: the New Criticism. The New Criticism posited that a literary critic should provide a close analysis of the interactions among parts of a literary text, without regard for the intentions of the author, the historical context, or the emotional response of the reader (Cantor, 1988). This literary theory is strikingly similar to early family systems theories stemming from cybernetics (Broderick & Smith, 1979; Whitchurch & Constantine, 1993).

Modernism in family science has generally been associated with positivist social science and quantitative methods, although qualitative methods can also be used with positivist, modernist assumptions. Positivism applies the standards of natural science to the study of social phenomena, with an emphasis on objective observation and verification and the inductive method of deriving laws from observation and experimentation (Klein & Jurich, 1993; Thomas & Wilcox, 1987). Positivism fits hand in glove with the Enlightenment Project's belief in the progress of human knowledge through rational methods. Until a reevaluation of positivism set in during the 1980s, the field of family science was predominantly positivist in orientation (Doherty et al., 1993; Thomas & Wilcox, 1987).

Finally, the modernist influence in family theory can be seen in the quest for universal and value-free scientific principles. Christensen (1964) explicitly endorsed modernist assumptions in his classic overview of the development of the family field: "Essentially, therefore, the attitude of science is that of value-free truth-seeking; the method is that of objective analysis of empirical data; and the aim is that of predictive theory" (p. 11). The apex of modernist family theory came with the efforts of authors of the *Contemporary Theories About the Family* volumes (Burr, Hill, Nye, & Reiss,

1979a,b) to construct family theories based on objective, value-free, quantitative scientific data and rigorous scientific reasoning. But by then the seeds of the decline of modernist social science had already been sown, and the postmodern era had dawned outside the family field.

The social sciences, like all human enterprises, are products of the social organization and mores of their era. Family theory in the middle decades of the twentieth century was an effort by family theorists to understand the organization and mores of the family in their world through modernist theoretical lenses—the only lenses available to them. Because the scholarly community was less diverse in terms of gender, race, ethnicity, and sexual orientation, there were additional limitations on the kinds of issues and problems that researchers and theorists could perceive and define. The late-twentieth-century social and cultural world, however, has been shifting markedly from modernity to postmodernity, and family theory is accordingly being transformed.

The Emergence of Postmodernism

The late 1970s brought on what Cheal (1991) called "The Big Bang" in family theory. A wave of internal criticism swept the field, ushered in by feminists, racial and ethnic minority scholars, phenomenologists, and reinvigorated symbolic interactionists. The family field entered "a pluralistic and self-questioning world of the late twentieth century that has been termed postmodern" (Doherty et al., 1993, p. 15). What is postmodernism? There is no universal consensus on the meaning and usefulness of the terms *postmodernity* and *postmodernism*. However, the following discussion focuses on elements consistently used to characterize these movements.

Postmodernity refers to the historical period beginning in the 1970s that is characterized by "cultural fragmentation, changes in the experience of space and time, and new modes of experience, subjectivity, and culture" (Best & Kellner, 1991, p. 3). The postmodern era was born partly out of the failed social revolutions of the 1960s and the growing dominance of new technologies such as television and computers, which transformed modes of communication. Postmodern social organization is fluid and ambiguous and postmodern economies are postindustrial and international, as opposed to industrial and regional.

Postmodernism refers to the philosophical and aesthetic movement of the late twentieth century that rejects Enlightenment philosophy and modernist art and culture. Reflecting the social conditions of postmodernity and the disenchantment of intellectual elites with Marxism and other grand theories such as structuralism, postmodernism involves the following elements, which combine the philosophical and the aesthetic domains:

1. Skepticism about the idea of progress (Cheal, 1991)
2. Skepticism about rationality, universal theories, and great authors (Cantor, 1988)
3. Abandonment of the goal of broad knowledge consensus as illusory and even dangerous (Connor, 1989)
4. Emphasis on the social construction of knowledge and on knowledge as potentially oppressive (Foucault, 1980)
5. Deemphasis on the centrality of the individual, as seen in both literary theory (Derrida, 1976) and in social psychology (the illusion of the automous self; Gergen, 1991)
6. Focus on language as a swirl of internal contradictions as opposed to fixed meanings, as seen in poststructuralist or deconstructionist literary theory (Derrida, 1976)
7. Reappropriation of the past and acceptance of eclecticism, as seen in the postmodern architecture with its varying historical styles and in postmodern art with the multimedia works that defy definition as "painting" or "sculpture" (Cantor, 1988)

Postmodernism attempts to sweep away the few certainties that remained in modernism after the demise of traditional societies. While modernism offered an aesthetic of purity, order, clarity, and analytical abstraction, postmodernism offers an aesthetic of elaboration, eclecticism, ornamentation, and inclusiveness. Hegel, with his soaring philosophical abstractions, gives way to Richard Rorty (1987), who declines to distinguish philosophy from "culture criticism." Mondrian, with his pure artistic lines in painting, gives way to Frank Stella, who uses a variety of media in a continuing experimentation with random objects. Postmodern artists continually disrupt time-honored distinctions between art and life, as seen in the pop art paintings of Andy Warhol, the blurring of journalism and fiction in the writings of Tom Wolfe, and the juxtaposition of realism and fantasy in the late 1980s movies of Woody Allen.

Until recently, many social scientists dismissed the idea of a postmodern era as trendy and empty rhetoric, and some cultural critics continue to believe that postmodernism is merely modernism in its latest permutation (Connor, 1989; Huyysen, 1990; Karl, 1988). However, in the mid-1990s there is a growing acceptance that there is enduring intellectual and historical substance behind postmodernism. Indeed, most fields of the social sciences and humanities—and even the natural sciences through development such as chaos theory— came under the influence of postmodern thinking during the 1980s (Best & Kellner, 1991; Rosenau, 1992; Doherty, Graham, & Malek, 1992). In this chapter, I assume that postmodernism represents a distinctly new cultural phenomenon that differs substantively from its modernist roots, while at

the same time inevitably being influenced by its cultural predecessor.

In the social sciences, postmodernism's influence has been most clearly seen in the new emphasis on "deconstruction" and "discourse analysis." Based on the work of French philosopher Derrida (1976) and other "poststructuralists," deconstruction is used to critically examine the internal contradictions in hallowed concepts such as "the self" (Sampson, 1989) and "gender differences" (Hare-Mustin & Marecek, 1988). For example, when "autonomous" is used to define a uniquely male way of being, and "relational" a uniquely female way of being, a deconstructionist analysis shows that autonomous and relational can only be defined in terms of one another. Each of these concepts involves a necessary element of the other, and the apparent dichotomy is misleading and dangerous (Hare-Mustin & Marecek, 1990). Similarly, postmodern social scientists deconstruct every attempt to advance a general, universal theory through an examination of how the theory's basic concepts and explanations inevitably reveal the particular social and historical situation of the author (Seidman & Wagner, 1992). Perhaps the most obvious example, Sigmund Freud's theory, reflected both Victorian European culture at the turn of the twentieth century and aspects of his personal life experience (Gay, 1988).

Discourse analysis is the "description of recurrently used words, phrases and linguistic devices which categorize and reproduce the social world" (Parker, 1992, p. 83). Discourse analysis focuses on language in written or oral forms, in public or private settings, but not primarily as a guide to subjective states such as feelings and highly personal meanings—postmodernists are not much concerned with individual psychological issues. Rather, it is a way of connecting modes of communication to broader social practices and modes of power and meaning. An important strand of discourse analysis in the social sciences follows Foucault's (1980) work on the "archaeology" of discourses of surveillance and power in modern societies.

At the level of theory, postmodern social science abandons the attempt to establish disciplinary or interdisciplinary consensus through analytical means. All meanings are, and should be, contested. Rather than being concerned with grand theory or "meta-narratives," postmodern social science concentrates on provisional understandings based on small stories. In the introduction to their book *Postmodernism and Social Theory*, Seidman and Wagner (1992), after noting that critique and reconstruction have been an enduring feature of social science since the beginning, offer this summary of the postmodern critique:

> The postmodern critique is perhaps unique in that it challenges a project of social science shared by virtually all rival schools or paradigms. Postmodernism criticizes the modernist notion that science itself, not this or that theory or para-

digm, is a privileged form of reason or the medium of truth. It disputes the scientist's claim that only scientific knowledge can be securely grounded. It takes issue with the unifying consensus-building agenda of science. It contests the modernist idea that social theory has as its chief role the securing of the conceptual grounds for social research. And postmodernism criticizes the modernist notion that science is or should be value-neutral; postmodernism underlines the practical and moral meaning of science. (p. 60)

Social science theory, then becomes a discursive practice or a conversation that takes place over time and through different media of communication. It becomes a more modest enterprise than in the past (Ryder, 1987), more aware of how context shapes theory, less concerned with achieving consensus, and more accountable to the broader society for how it functions and what it contributes (Brown, 1992).

Postmodernism and postmodern social science are not without their critics. I will raise a number of these criticisms in a later section of the chapter, after describing the influences of postmodernism on emerging family theories.

Postmodern Influences on Family Theories

The most striking indicator of postmodern infiltrations into family theories has been the contesting of the idea of "family" as an entity for study and intervention. Just as deconstructionists celebrated the "death of the Author" of literary works, family scholars, led by feminists such as Barrie Thorne in the early 1980s, attacked the essentialist assumptions behind the use of the term "family" as a standard heterosexually based, gender-normed, two-generational unit headed by a married couple (Thorne & Yalom, 1982). Indeed, the White House Conference on the Family in 1980 foundered on the question of how to define a family in rapidly changing American social landscape. Judith Stacey (1990) explicitly tied changes in American families to modernity and postmodernity:

> We are living, I believe, through a transitional and contested period of family history, a period *after* the modern family order, but before what we cannot foretell. Precisely because it is not possible to characterize with a single term the competing sets of family cultures that coexist at present, I identify this family regime as postmodern. *The* postmodern family is not a new model of family life, not the next stage in an orderly progression of family history, but the stage when the belief in a logical progression of stages breaks down. Rupturing evolutionary models of family history and incorporating both experimental and nostalgic elements, "the" postmodern family lurches forward and backward into an uncertain future. (p. 18)

Tying developments toward pluralism in American families to the history of family science, Cheal (1993) argues that the standard approach to family structure and family process, ushered in by Burgess' notion of the family as "a

unity of interacting personalities," emphasized the highly integrated family over the loosely integrated family. This emphasis fit what Stacey (1990) termed the "modern" family based on a two-parent nuclear model. Cheal maintains that changes in the direction of pluralistic family forms, coupled with broader social shifts toward postmodernity, pushed family science in the 1980s and 1990s toward a greater attention to concepts of "divergence and difference." The same case was made by Doherty et al. (1993), who observed how the dramatic changes in family demographics between 1965 and 1980 (such as rapid increase in divorce and employed mothers) were part of larger historical and cultural trends that "washed over the [family] field" in the 1980s and early 1990s.

The second major area in which postmodernism has influenced family theory in the 1980s and 1990s is the critique of positivist family science and the emergence of writing about postpositivist family science. Thomas and Wilcox (1987), in their chapter "The Rise of Family Theory" in the first edition of this *Handbook* (Sussman & Steinmetz, 1987), offered the most thorough critique of traditional family theories for their assumptions of objective, value-free descriptions of family realities. The heart of the postpositivist paradigm is that theory precedes observation, that there are not facts without theories to interpret them, and that all theories are socially constructed (Doherty et al., 1993; Thomas & Wilcox, 1987). An indication that postpositivism was part of postmodernist developments in the field is Thomas and Roghaar's (1990) explicit statement that they view the two terms as "almost synonymous." In the *Sourcebook of Family Theories and Methods* (Boss et al., 1993), the index heading for postmodernism is "see postpositivism."

The blending of postmodernism and postpositivism reflected uncertainty on the part of the editors of the *Sourcebook*, in 1989 and 1990, about whether postmodernism was a passing fad, whether it should be highlighted as a movement, or whether it should be folded into postpositivism as a philosophy of science. In this chapter, I argue that postmodernism has emerged in its own right and that postpositivism is best viewed as a philosophy of science that fits well with postmodernism.

The third major incursion of postmodernism in family science is evident in the growing use of discourse analysis in family research. This approach, stemming from phenomenology and ethnomethodology, is exemplified by the work of Gubrium and his colleagues (see especially Gubrium & Holstein, 1990) and formed the basis of Sprey's (1990) analysis of "theoretical practice" as a form of discourse. Gubrium and Holstein (1993a) describe the bases for understanding families in terms of language and meaning in everyday life:

> The study of family discourse highlights how language serves to assign meaning to objects and social conditions. Regarding the familial, we can ask how the social organiza-

tion of family discourse—the family terms and family theories available to people, the social distribution of the terms and theories, their organizational links, and their social borders—comes to reveal family in the way it does. (p. 655).

Although the idea of the social construction of family realities is by no means original with postmodern perspectives (e.g., Berger & Kellner, 1964; LaRossa & Reitzes, 1993; Reiss, 1981), what is distinctive about the "new," postmodern social constructionism is: (1) the explicitly postpositivist assumptions about social science, (2) the lack of interest in broader theories or explanatory models, and (3) the emphasis on the connections between family narratives and organizational narratives—in other words, the idea that home life is inextricably embedded in organizational activities and institutional images. The family/larger system connection, of course, has been a major concern of sociologists since early in this century. What is different in postmodern analysis is the emphases not on social structural factors such as social class, but on the interweaving of family and organization meanings.

In applying discourse analysis to family life, Gubrium (1987, 1992) has examined how the families and systems they interact with construe such central family domains as order versus disorder (in the case of troubled children in institutional treatment) and caregiving (in the case of Alzheimer's disease). Professionals' constructions of family realities are communicated to family members, who also bring their own understandings to create shared family narratives and family processes. Gubrium and Holstein (1993b) give the following example:

> A mother who participates in parent effectiveness classes encounters general understandings of what families are like, how they work, what makes them break up, and how to effectively intervene to help them—that is, local culture. Yet it is never precisely indicated how these understandings apply to particular parenting experiences, hers included. We can analyze how this is clarified by orienting to the mother's and others' practical reasoning, which, like local culture, reveals itself in family discourse. (p. 73)

Gubrium (1992) himself carves out a position between modernism and postmodernism. He is postmodernist in his emphasis on indeterminacy, on the social construction of reality, and on the power of institutional discourse to shape family discourse. But he also posits that the practical reality of domestic issues such as violence and alcoholism is fully real and not to be relegated simply to simple "constructions" of reality. I will address this issue later in discussing critiques of postmodernism.

The fourth important postmodernist influence on emerging family theories is the blend of feminism and postmodernism. Osmond and Thorne (1993) took an open but cautious stance toward postmodernism in their chapter on feminist theories about families. After describing the deconstructionist ideas of Derrida and Foucault, they write:

> In criticizing bodies of knowledge that claim universality but in fact are derived from the experiences of privileged men, feminists have themselves embarked on a postmodern path. This attention to suppressed realities, and to connections between knowledge and power, has deepened as feminists have become more attuned to other lines of difference—social class, race, ethnicity, sexual orientation, age—that undermine any unitary notion of "woman." And by closely attending to the varieties of women's experiences, feminists have helped deconstruct the unitary and ideological notion of "The Family" (heterosexual, nuclear, bounded in space and time) that has been central to various kinds of oppression. (p. 596)

Osmond and Thorne (1993), however, express the same reservations with postmodern theories that some other feminists have noted (see Nicholson, 1990). Postmodern feminists are willing to deconstruct the concepts of gender and patriarchy, ideas that are central to traditional feminist theories and that many feminists are loathe to see turned into theoretical sand. Furthermore, many feminists worry that the process of continually shifting meanings and contextualizing every position can impede effective political action. In reply, postmodern feminists assert that feminist theories themselves risk becoming "totalizing and discriminating against the experiences and realities of some" (Nicholson, 1990, p. 15).

Baber and Allen (1992) take up the challenge of creating a postmodern feminist analysis of women's experiences in families. Although aware of the danger of slipping into stultifying relativism, Baber and Allen propose that postmodern thinking can avoid the ethnocentrism and classism that plagued the first 2 decades of the feminist movement when the experiences of heterosexual, white, middle-class, Western women dominated theory and action. Drawing on the work of Flax and Harding, Baber and Allen describe three models of feminist epistemology. *Feminist empiricism* uses traditional scientific methods to correct biases and omissions in the understanding of women's experiences. *Feminist standpoint theories* emphasize the fundamental similarity of women as an oppressed group who have "a unique and privileged vantage point for understanding social experience." Men, as members of the oppressor group, have less adequate perceptions of the social world than women and less adequate ways of being and doing. Both types of feminist epistemology assume a universal experience for women and tend to emphasize gender differences as fundamental.

From a *postmodern feminist perspective*, gender is seen as one of a number of socially constructed "differences." Being oppressed does not give women a uniquely privileged perspective on the social world. Baber and Allen (1992) write:

From a postmodern feminist perspective, gender is not a natural fact, rooted in anatomical sex differences. Gender alone does not determine a woman's experiences, identity, or status; the way a woman constructs her understanding of reality is mediated by factors such as her age, class, race, physical attractiveness, sexual orientation, and family status. There is no single standpoint that captures women's experiences, nor is there a single mode of feminism or path to a feminist consciousness. (p. 10)

In their groundbreaking postmodernist deconstruction of gender dualism, Hare-Mustin and Marecek (1988, 1990) view gender as a form of social relation shaped particularly by power and status. From this relational, social constructionist position, the traditional emphasis on gender "differences" reifies either essential similarities (alpha bias) or essential differences (beta bias) between women and men. As the deconstructionists point out, dichotomies inevitably lead to better/worse thinking; turning the tables to put women in the superior position simply perpetuates the underlying dynamics of gender inequality.

Neither Hare-Mustin and Marecek (1990) nor Baber and Allen (1992) believe that gender becomes less important in postmodern feminism, as some critics fear, but it becomes more fluid and more contextualized in a broader series of aspects of social relations. And postmodernism gives feminism a self-corrective lens with which to examine its own blind spots and distortions in the continuing process of "dialectic, contradiction, paradox, debate, and difference" (Baber & Allen, 1992, p. 12).

The fifth influence of postmodernism on family theories may be termed the "new historicism" in family science. The historical study of the family itself was a well-established field for many decades before postmodernism, and life-course theorists such as Elder have focused extensively on the historical and social contexts of families (Bengtson & Allen, 1993; Elder, 1974). What is distinctively postmodern about the new family historicism is that it applies an understanding of social and cultural history to the thinking and behavior of family scholars and family practitioners themselves. Postmodern family historicism turns the social and historical spotlight not only on the families we study, but also on ourselves and why we study what we study.

Although Howard (1981) had done this kind of historical analysis in his groundbreaking dissertation, mainstream family science did not pick up on his lead until the 1990s. As in most mainstream disciplines, analysis of the social context of family science previously had been conducted primarily by those whose work or reference group had been marginalized, such as feminists (Bernard, 1972) and African Americans (Allen, 1978). These scholars could not understand their experience and their marginalization within the field without examining the broad social context (see reviews by Dilworth-

Anderson, Burton, & Johnson, 1993, and Osmond & Thorne, 1993). Until the onset of postmodern influences, most mainstream scholars in family science and other fields were not forced to engage in self-reflexive social history to do their theories and research.

Attempting to bring historical criticism into the mainstream of the family field and using Howard and other sources in social history, Doherty and colleagues (1993) described how many of the varieties of family theories were products of their era in American history: for example, the focus on marital adjustment during the "inward-looking" 1920s and 1930s; the focus on traditional family and gender norms during the war and postwar years of "stability" and fear of Communism; the emergence of conflict theory and social exchange theory during the 1960s' "breakdown of the Post-war consensus" (Alexander, 1987); and more recent development in feminist theories and racial and ethnic minority theories stemming from the social revolutions of the 1960s and 1970s.

In a similar historicist vein, LaRossa and Reitzes (1993) showed how the prescriptive element of family studies in the 1920s and 1930s fit well with the American culture's love affair with science and technology, coupled with a new emphasis on personal satisfaction in relationships. Doherty and Baptiste (1993) described how family therapy brought together scientific and cultural movements of the 1950s to create a quintessential American approach to psychotherapy. Likewise, Cheal (1991) demonstrated how family scholars in the midtwentieth century looked at families through modernist lenses.

Prior histories of the family field, and other social science fields as well, focused almost exclusively on professional leaders and professional developments—the history of great thinkers or great ideas or great methodologies. The new family historicism, also termed a "contextual approach" (Boss et al., 1993), has brought a self-reflexive quality to the field. Not only must families be studied in their social and historical contexts, but the study of the family and applied work with families must also be studied in their social and historical contexts.

There is a remarkable convergence between developments in literary theory and developments in family science and other social sciences. The newest mode of literary theory during the late 1980s and early 1990s in the English-speaking world was the "New Historicism" (Montrose, 1992). The New Historicism emerged out of postmodernism and deconstruction in the work of Stephen Greenblatt and others who believed that the deconstructionist method was too text-oriented and did not go far enough in examining the mutual influences between texts and historical conditions (Thomas, 1991). For example, Greenblatt (1980) analyzed the connections between Renaissance culture and the theme of "self-fashioning" of social identity in Elizabethan literature. The New Historicism has put history and culture back into literary studies after the modernist New Critics of the midtwentieth century removed it, but with the social and political awareness of the postmodern deconstructionists or poststructuralists. My point in this excursion into literary theory is to highlight the cultural soil out of which family science, and all social sciences, grow.

Countercurrents to Postmodernism in Family Theory

Just as in contemporary medicine, where there are contradictory movements toward humanistic medicine and extreme forms of biological medicine, in family theory postmodern influences have been occurring side by side with the emergence of a theory from the other end of the epistemological continuum: biosocial theories (Filsinger, 1988; Troost & Filsinger, 1993). Theories of the family that derive concepts from genetics and physiology come from the opposite perspective from postmodernism's emphasis on the sociocultural level. Moreover, biosocial theories of the family like those espoused by Troost and Filsinger (1993), while probabilistic and not deterministic in orientation and integrative rather than reductionistic, are unabashedly positivist and modernist. They set out to discover more or less accurate explanations for human behavior in families, and they often use the most rigorous quantifiable methods available. They aspire to objectivity and assume that scientific data can lead to a consensus among open-minded individuals. These traditional canons of science are reflections of the Enlightenment Project so roundly criticized by postmodernists.

From another perspective, however, postmodernism itself can embrace the contradictions described here. A few scholars even combine elements of postmodernism and biosocial theories. Family sociologist Sprey (1988, 1990) espouses postmodern discourse analysis for family theory construction along with some elements of an evolutionary biological model for understanding family conflict. And family psychiatrist David Reiss, a pioneer in social constructionist views of the family, has recently focused on how genes affect family interaction (Bussell & Reiss, 1993). Such integrative scholars, however, are at risk for being seen as traitors from both sides of the biological/sociocultural divide.

Another countercurrent to postmodernism can be seen in the growing use of sophisticated quantitative statistical methods to analyze complex data on families (Teachman & Neustadtl, 1993). Structural equations models (such as LISREL), for example, allow the testing of theory-based relationships between composite variables while controlling for measurement error. The very concept of controlling for measurement error is quite foreign to postmodern sensibilities because it assumes that indeterminacy and bias can be determined objectively and controlled statistically. Closer to postmodern theory are the emerging qualitative methods for studying families, methods that assume the possibility of multiple valid perspectives and the fluidity of research findings (Gilgun, Daly, & Handel, 1992; Rosenblatt & Fischer, 1993). As Rosenau (1992) observed:

> Postmodernism is oriented toward methods that apply to a broad range of phenomena, focus on the margins, highlight uniqueness, concentrate on the enigmatic, and appreciate the unrepeatable.... Postmodern social science presumes methods that multiply paradox, inventing ever more elaborate repertoires of questions, each of which encourages an infinity of answers, rather than methods that settle on solutions. (p. 117)

A truly consistent postmodern perspective on research methods, however, would support the existence of diverse and sometimes contradictory research methods, as long as neither claims to provide the ultimate grounding for knowledge about families. In other words, postmodernists do not necessarily dismiss sophisticated quantitative methods, only the assumption that such methods yield "privileged" data about social life.

The ideological gulf between biology and postmodernism, then, may not be so wide after all, and the two movements may be helpful to each other: Postmodernism can help biosocial theorists to constantly examine the biases in their assumptions about human behavior, and biosocial data can help postmodernists be grounded in certain biological "realities" that are not socially constructed. An example is neoteny, the prolonged dependence of human children before reaching biological maturity. This dependence of children on parents and other adults is one of the "domestic realities" that Gubrium (1992) wishes to incorporate into a phenomenological theoretical lens on the family and that Baber and Allen (1992) wish to maintain in a feminist theory of family life.

Critiques and Defense of Postmodern Family Theories

An interesting feature of the emerging postmodern influences on family theory is that all of the proponents are careful to point out dangers in postmodern theory as it applies to the family. None of the authors cited in this chapter is a "true-believing" postmodernist who dismisses concerns and cautions. The following criticisms are more or less consensually agreed upon by postmodern family theorists. Moreover, the ways that postmodern theorists defend their positions in reference to these criticisms is described.

The two most important criticisms of postmodern theory for social science are (a) that its focus on language, discourse, meaning, and constructivism can blind scholars to the "objective" social forces affecting families (such as gender-linked injustice and child abuse), and (b) that such relativism about truth leads to the demise of any meaningful standards for judging the merits of theories or research findings (Baber & Allen, 1992; Best & Kellner, 1991; Rosenau, 1992). I will address these criticisms in turn and discuss how postmodern family theorists respond.

Critics of postmodernism emphasize that societal structures of oppression are not reducible to discourse, and they believe that such linguistic reductionism undermines political motivation to bring about change. For example, although wife-battering involves a major element of socially constructed meaning and social discourse, it is grounded in certain nonlinguistic and noninterpretive realities such as economic dependence and physical harm. It seems inappropriate to use concepts that could ultimately be used to "deconstruct" wife-battering into a narrative that can be "restoried" (to use the expression of postmodern family therapists White & Epston, 1990), into something other than wrongful violence.

Postmodern family theorists are not unaware of this potential pitfall of postmodern thinking. Gubrium (1992, 1993) explicitly discusses the danger of defining "social disorder" into a nether world that has no practical significance outside of forms of discourse. Postmodern feminists such as Hare-Mustin and Marecek (1990) and Baber and Allen (1992) unambiguously assert the independent existence of forms of oppression, whether or not individuals construe their situation as oppressive. As a former student of mine once said, turning W. I. Thomas' famous dictum on its head, "What people do not define as real can be real in its consequences."

Even postmodern family therapists like White and Epston (1990) suspend their deconstructionist method of dialogue when there is a severe family crisis that warrants an emergency response. The problem for postmodern family theorists, then, is not that they philosophically dismiss "objective" realities for families, but that they may not be theoretically consistent in allowing notions of objectivity into their thinking (Holstein & Gubrium, 1994). Are they being wishy-washing postmodernists who want to have it both ways? Are they unreconverted modernists who are appropriating postmodernist ideas into their old paradigm?

The second critique, concerning the lack of standards, is also one that postmodern family theorists take seriously. With its emphasis on the endlessly contested and fluid nature of "truth," postmodernism can provide a shaky underpinning for social science theory and research. How would one decide which theory was more adequate or which set of

findings was better justified? Is every view of family life equally valid? The paradox, of course, is that a rigorously relativistic standpoint allows equal footing for the narrow and totalizing theories that postmodernism abhors. None of the postmodern family scientists embraces such full-throttle relativism. Baber and Allen (1992) write: "All truth claims do not carry the same justificatory force. Feminists can use critical reflection and rational argument to illuminate the problems in social relations and identify the inaccuracies in opposing accounts" (p. 11). And Gubrium's (1992) research clearly assumes that more careful attention to discourses of families and larger systems can lead to more adequate understandings of how families live in their world. The problem, as I see it, is not that postmodern family theorists posit no standards, but whether they are being inconsistent with postmodern assumptions.

Let me frame the conundrum for postmodern family theorists in broader terms. Is it theoretically consistent to embrace postmodernism's constructivism, relativism, and pluralism while at the same time allowing for objective realities and standards for good and bad theory and research? Clearly the postmodern family theorists reflect implicit and explicit concerns about how families are being treated in the world beyond discourse, and clearly they feel free to extol and excoriate other family theorists and researchers through careful rational analysis and documentation. For example, they certainly don't view Talcott Parsons' ideas about families as having equal merit with their own. Although postmodern family theorists reject formal theory-building, they nevertheless justify this rejection on carefully articulated theoretical grounds. Are they being truly postmodernist, or just modernists with the trappings of postmodernism?

In her book *Postmodernism and the Social Sciences*, Rosenau (1992) makes a distinction that can help resolve these concerns about postmodern family theory. She distinguishes between "affirmative postmodernists" and "skeptical postmodernists." Affirmative postmodernists are optimistic about the potential contributions of social science, are willing to posit an objective world outside of discourse, and in general are willing to forego tight consistency with postmodern assumptions in order to move social science and political action forward:

> The absence of truth for the affirmatives yields intellectual humility and tolerance. They see truth as personal and community-specific: although it may be relative, it is not arbitrary. For the affirmatives theory is unsystematic, decentered, heterological, and makes no claim to a privileged voice. (p. 23)

The postmodern skeptics, who dismiss truth standards and even the idea of a unified, coherent human subject, present a far greater challenge to social science. They are "pure" postmodernists in the sense that they maintain as tight a consistency as they can with the assumptions of postmodern constructivism, relativism, and pluralism:

> Skeptical postmodernists deny the possibility of truth or merely state their indifference to all projects designed to discover truth. As they see it, truth is either meaningless or arbitrary.... For the skeptics, truth claims are a form of terrorism. They threaten and provoke.... Only traces of the past, reminiscences, myths, all of which must "must lie," make up postmodern truth. (pp. 78–79)

Rosenau (1992) continues:

> If skeptics were to rewrite social science ... [it] would have to do without representation, without objects or subjects who represent and are represented; research as now known would be rendered improbable.... The skeptics' logic ... results in their limiting the role of any postmodern social science to that of critique (via deconstruction). (pp. 171–172)

In the concluding chapter of their book on postmodern theory, Best and Kellner (1991) make a distinction essentially similar to Rosenau's. They contrast "extreme postmodern theories" with "reconstructive postmodern theories." Examples of the former, which attempt to start all over in creating theories and politics, include the theories of Lyotard and Foucault. Examples of the latter, which combine modern and postmodern positions on theory and politics, include the work of Flax and other postmodern feminists.

Based on these analyses of postmodern theories, it seems clear that postmodern family theories thus far could be considered "affirmative" or "reconstructivist." It is also clear that skeptical or extreme postmodernism is what is feared by those who view postmodern developments warily or antagonistically. The affirmatives criticize modern social science epistemology and methods in order to revise them and make them more useful for the postmodern world. Baber and Allen (1992), after discussing the problem of relativism and their commitment to the use of standards and critical reflection, summarize their form of affirmative postmodernism:

> We see this central paradox, rather than serving as an impediment to our work in this book, as a *corrective* for the blinders imposed by our own private experiences. To begin with a belief in the limitations of our own perspective requires us to explore critically and systematically existing social relations, contradictory viewpoints, and accepted explanations. Such an approach offers emancipatory potential without the expectation that we abandon our own experiences and constructions of reality. (p. 11).

Conclusion

Under the influence of postmodernism, along with feminism and the movement for social justice by racial and ethnic minorities, the family field in the United States has become more diverse and eclectic in the last 2 decades of the twentieth century. The diversity shows itself in the wide range of theories and methods described in Boss et al. (1993). The eclecticism shows itself in the blurring of traditional disciplinary boundaries, especially between psychological and family science theories (Crosbie-Burnett & Lewis, 1993) and between biosocial theories and family science theories (Troost & Filsinger, 1993). And unlike earlier periods of family scholarship, there is no discernible movement to integrate these diverse, eclectic theories into an overarching grand theory of the family.

Family theories influenced by postmodernism have the potential for bridging family and societal levels of analysis and understanding. Discourse analysis, for example, can shed light on the complex interweaving of family and larger cultural and social meanings. Postmodern feminist theories combine the trenchant analysis of oppressive social structures with an understanding of gender-linked family interactions and beliefs. And the new historicism in family science can open up rich new veins of understanding of how the study of the family interacts with larger social and cultural movements.

As a fledgling movement, postmodern family science also has a number of blind spots and trouble spots. First, although affirmative postmodern family theorists do not exclude quantitative methods as sources of understanding, so far postmodern family research has been largely qualitative in method. A major challenge is to learn whether quantitative research methods, still overwhelmingly represented in family science journals, can be used to generate knowledge that is seen as useful by postmodern theorists. If this merger does not occur, then postmodernism may further split the field into quantitative and qualitative researchers, the former holding on dearly to modernist assumptions about knowledge and scientific consensus, and the latter skating farther out on the ice toward skeptical or extreme postmodernism.

A second area of concern has to do with the place of the individual in the family. Postmodern philosophy grew out of a rejection of the humanist ideal of the individual actor. To postmodernist psychologists like Gergen (1991), the individual is a "saturated self," a repository of the myriad social and media-generated forces of the late twentieth century. The individual has evaporated into a social sea. This kind of reductionism does not appear to leave room for the study of individual development within the family or for the consideration of how biological and psychological factors interact with family and larger social factors. Affirmative postmodernists may retort that they do not see any reason to give up on the idea of a boundaried individual (e.g., Baber & Allen, 1992, describing women's individual development), but I believe it is hard for postmodernists to transcend the fundamental antiindividual orientation of postmodern philosophy.

As philosopher Alasdair MacIntyre (1990) has argued, there appears to be a self-contradiction in postmodern writing about the dissolved self: These authors write with their own unique voices about ideas they have come to believe and espouse—in other words, they seem to regard themselves as individual persons! MacIntyre (1990) asks whether skeptical postmodernists like Foucault and de Man are not "self-indulgently engaged in exempting [their own] utterances from the treatment to which everyone else's is subjected" (p. 210).

Which brings me to my final concern about postmodern family theory, even in its affirmative or reconstructive forms. Postmodern theories have persuasively undermined the moral neutrality of modernist social science, but they have not replaced it with anything except moral relativism, at least at a theoretical level. It is not enough for individual postmodernist scholars to maintain that, of course, they oppose violence and oppression in families and in society, when they do not articulate the moral and ethical ground upon which they make these judgments.

The issue of morality reveals a paradox at the heart of the postmodern critique of metanarratives and universal principles. Postmodernism has served fundamentally as a movement of liberation from post-Enlightenment systems of knowledge that claimed universal validity but actually served the goals of the knowledge makers—most often privileged, white European and American males. The implicit ethic of postmodernism, then, involves freedom from oppression and equality of diverse peoples to shape their own meanings. These appear to be universal values, but the central figures in postmodernism, such as Lyotard (1984), explicitly reject the possibility of universal values. In an incisive commentary on this issue, Connor (1989) writes:

> Indeed, when inspected closely, it becomes apparent that the postmodern critique of unjust and oppressive systems of universality implicitly depends for its force upon the assumption of the universal right of all not to be treated unjustly and oppressively—otherwise, who would care whether metanarratives were false or not, oppressive or not, and what reason might there be for their abandonment when they no longer compelled assent. Seen in these terms, the very "incredulity towards metanarratives" that Lyotard writes about is not a symptom of the collapse of general or collective ethical principles, but a testimony to their continuing corrective force. (p. 243)

Postmodern feminism has been more forthcoming about the moral dimensions of its work, perhaps because there is a clear underlying ethic of justice in feminist theory. The ethic of care, however, has been written about mostly by feminists who do not identify with postmodernism (see Larrabee, 1993), with some exceptions, such as Baber and Allen (1992). Like other postmodernists, feminists postmodernists by and large focus on issues of justice and freedom from oppression,

but do not systematically articulate a broader set of moral assumptions about other family-related issues such as care, commitment, and honesty.

Postmodernists may argue that I am assuming that there is one best ethical system that can underlie family theories—a premodernist position. In fact, I am assuming the opposite, namely, that we will continue to have "rival versions of moral inquiry," to use MacIntyre's (1990) phrase. Now that postmodern thinking has stripped us of the naive belief that values and moral beliefs are irrelevant to social science, education, therapy, and public policy, it is not enough to be quiet on the subject. The challenge for family scholars—postmodernist or not—is to articulate the ethical and values assumptions that underlie their work. Is wife-battering only "dysfunctional," or is it morally wrong—and if so, why? When fathers abandon their children, is this only an issue of establishing whether there are long-term effects on children's psychosocial well-being, or is it also a matter of a moral mandate of parental commitment? Rather than construct elaborate moral theories, which is outside the competence of social scientists anyway, I am suggesting that family scholars begin by articulating the ethical values and principles that are already present in their work and by suggesting how these values and principles are connected with a particular location in social and historical space. Such articulations can allow us to dialogue and dispute with one another about moral issues, and thereby hopefully refine our ideas and beliefs.

I also believe that postmodernist scholars should address the issue of accountability in research. Anti-postmodernists' worst nightmare is that, since for extreme postmodernists research is merely a form of rhetorical persuasion, there will be no standards for good scholarship—and perhaps even a license to make things up. How does one practice ethical research in a world without certainties, in which truth is a form of social consensus, in which there are no privileged perspectives? Postmodernist family scholars owe their colleagues reassurance on these issues.

I suggest that an answer lies in the idea of certain "virtues" that researchers should be held accountable to practice, even in the face of uncertainty and indeterminism. Virtues for social science researchers would include honesty in reporting what one sees and hears, fairness in acknowledging the contributions of other scholars, justice and sensitivity to participants in research, open-mindedness about the limits of one's work, and responsibility for influencing the public use to which one's research is put. Whatever our theoretical orientation—modernist, postmodernist, positivist, postpositivist, sick of all these distinctions—are these not among the traits we wish to encourage in our graduate students? Are these not the foundations for the possibility of meaningful debate about research and theory? I suggest that it would be helpful in a postmodern world for theorists and researchers to articulate the values and virtues underlying their scholarship, while acknowledging the historically contingent nature of the understanding and the practice of these values and virtues.

It is clearly too soon to tell how much the postmodern movement in family theory will influence the rest of the field, particularly research in mainstream journals. However, more so than any of other development in family theory in this century, postmodern perspectives offer a new paradigm for the field. In my view, the challenge for the next decade will be to winnow out the nihilistic forms of postmodern thinking from those that encourage creative, self-reflexive, pluralistic, accountable, and ethically informed family scholarship. We will have no common standard for the winnowing, but that comes with the postmodern territory that we all will have to live with, like it or not, until the next cultural movement sweeps on stage to transform our consciousness in ways we cannot now imagine.

References

Adams, B. N., & Steinmetz, S. K. (1993). Family theory and methods in the classics. In P. G. Boss, W. J. Doherty, R. LaRossa, W. R. Schumm, & S. K. Steinmetz (Eds.), *Sourcebook of family theories and methods: A contextual approach* (pp. 71–94). New York: Plenum.

Alexander, J. C. (1987). *Twenty lectures: Sociological theory since World War II*. New York: Columbia University Press.

Allen, W. (1978). The search for applicable theories of black family life. *Journal of Marriage and the Family, 40*, 117–131.

Baber, K. M., & Allen, K. R. (1992). *Women and families: Feminist reconstructions*. New York: Guilford.

Bengston, V. L., & Allen, K. R. (1993). The life course perspective applied to families over time. In P. G. Boss, W. J. Doherty, R. LaRossa, W. R. Schumm, & S. K. Steinmetz (Eds.), *Sourcebook of family theories and methods: A contextual approach* (pp. 505–524). New York: Plenum.

Berger, P. I., & Kellner, H. (1964). Marriage and the construction of reality: An exercise in microsociology of knowledge. *Diogenes, 46*, 1–25.

Bernard, J. (1972). *The future of marriage*. New York: Word Publishing.

Best, S., & Kellner, H. (1991). *Postmodern theory*. New York: Guilford.

Blumer, H. (1969). *Symbolic interactionism: Perspective and method*. Englewood Cliffs, NJ: Prentice-Hall.

Boss, P. G., Doherty, W. J., LaRossa, R., Schumm, W. R., & Steinmetz, S. K. (Eds.) (1993). *Sourcebook of family theories and methods: A contextual approach*. New York: Plenum.

Broderick, C., & Smith, J. (1979). The general systems approach to the family. In W. R. Burr, R. Hill, F. I. Nye, & I. L. Reiss (Eds.), *Contemporary theories about the family* (Vol. 2, pp. 112–129). New York: Free Press.

Brown, R. H. (1992). Social science and society as discourse: Toward a sociology for civic competence. In S. Seidman & D. G. Wagner (Eds.), *Postmodernism and social theory*. Cambridge, MA: Blackwell.

Burgess, W. E., & Cottrell, L. (1930). *Predicting success and failure in marriage*. Englewood Cliffs, NJ: Prentice-Hall.

Burr, W. R., Hill, R., Nye, F. I., & Reiss, I. L. (Eds.). (1979a). *Contemporary theories about the family* (Vol. 1). New York: Free Press.

Burr, W. R., Hill, R., Nye, F. I., & Reiss, I. L. (Eds.). (1979b). *Contemporary theories about the family* (Vol. 2). New York: Free Press.

Bussell, D. A., & Reiss, D. (1993). Genetic influences on family process: The emergence of a new framework for family research. In F. Walsh (Ed.), *Normal family processes* (2nd edition, pp. 161–181). New York: Guilford.

Cantor, N. F. (1988). *Twentieth-century culture: Modernism to deconstruction*. New York: Peter Lang.

Cheal, D. (1991). *Family and the state of theory*. New York: Harvester Wheatsheaf.

Cheal, D. (1993). Unity and difference in postmodern families. *Journal of Family Issues, 14*, 5–19.

Christensen, H. T. (1964). Development of the family field of study. In H. T. Christensen (Ed.), *Handbook of marriage and the family* (pp. 3–22). Chicago: Rand McNally.

Connor, S. (1989). *Postmodernist culture: An introduction to theories of the contemporary*. New York: Basil Blackwell.

Crosbie-Burnett, M., & Lewis, E. A. (1993). Theoretical contributions from social and cognitive-behavioral psychology. In P. G. Boss, W. J. Doherty, R. LaRossa, W. R. Schumm, & S. K. Steinmetz (Eds.), *Sourcebook of family theories and methods: A contextual approach* (pp. 531–558). New York: Plenum.

Derrida, J. (1976). *Of grammatology*. Baltimore: Johns Hopkins University Press.

Dilworth-Anderson, P., Burton, L. M., & Johnson, L. B. (1993). Reframing theories for understanding race, ethnicity, and families. In P. G. Boss, W. J. Doherty, R. LaRossa, W. R. Schumm, & S. K. Steinmetz (Eds.), *Sourcebook of family theories and methods: A contextual approach* (pp. 627–646). New York: Plenum.

Doherty, J., Graham, E., & Malek, M. (1992). *Postmodernism and the social sciences*. New York: St. Martin's.

Doherty, W. J. (1991). Postmodern family therapy. *The Family Therapy Networker, 15*, 36–42.

Doherty, W. J., & Baptiste, D. A. (1993). Theories emerging from family therapy. In P. G. Boss, W. J. Doherty, R. LaRossa, W. R. Schumm, & S. K. Steinmetz (Eds.), *Sourcebook of family theories and methods: A contextual approach* (pp. 505–524). New York: Plenum.

Doherty, W. J., Boss, P. G., LaRossa, R., Schumm, W. R., & Steinmetz, S. K. (1993). Family theories and methods: A contextual approach. In P. G. Boss, W. J. Doherty, R. LaRossa, W. R. Schumm, & S. K. Steinmetz (Eds.), *Sourcebook of family theories and methods: A contextual approach* (pp. 3–30). New York: Plenum.

Elder, G. H., Jr. (1974). *Children of the Great Depression: Social change in life experience*. Chicago: University of Chicago Press.

Filsinger, E. E. (Ed.). (1988) *Biosocial perspectives on the family*. Newbury Park, CA: Sage.

Foucault, M. (1980). *Power/knowledge*. (C. Gordon, Ed.). New York: Pantheon.

Gay. P. (1988). *Freud: A life for our time*. New York: Norton.

Gergen, K. J. (1991). *The saturated self*. New York: Basic Books.

Giddens, A. (1990). *The consequences of modernity*. Stanford, CA: Stanford University Press.

Gilgun, J. F., Daly, K., & Handel, G. (Eds.). (1992). *Qualitative methods in family research*. Newbury Park, CA: Sage.

Greenblatt, S. (1980). *Renaissance self-fashioning*. Chicago: University of Chicago Press.

Gubrium, J. F. (1987). Organizational embeddedness and family life. In T. Brubaker (Ed.), *Aging, health and family* (pp. 23–41). Newbury Park, CA: Sage.

Gubrium, J. F. (1988). Family responsibility and caregiving in the qualitative analysis of the Alzheimer's disease experience. *Journal of Marriage and the Family, 50*, 197–207.

Gubrium, J. F. (1992). *Out of control: Family therapy and domestic disorder*. Newbury Park, CA: Sage.

Gubrium, J. F. (Ed.). (1993). *Rethinking the family as a social form*. Special issue of *Journal of Family Issues, 14*.

Gubrium, J. F., & Holstein, J. A. (1990). *What is family?* Mountain View, CA: Mayfield.

Gubrium, J. F., & Holstein, J. A. (1993a). Phenomenology, ethnomethodology, and family discourse. In P. G. Boss, W. J. Doherty, R. LaRossa, W. R. Schumm, & S. K. Steinmetz (Eds.), *Sourcebook of family theories and methods: A contextual approach* (pp. 651–672). New York: Plenum.

Gubrium, J. F., & Holstein, J. A. (1993b). Family discourse, organizational embeddedness, and local enactment. *Journal of Family Issues, 14*, 66–81.

Hare-Mustin, R. T., & Marecek, J. (1988). The meaning of difference: Gender theory, postmodernism, and psychology. *American Psychologist, 43*, 455–464.

Hare-Mustin, R. T., & Marecek, J. (Eds.) (1990). *Making a difference: psychology and the construction of gender.* New Haven, CT: Yale University Press.

Holstein, J. A., & Gubrium, J. F. (1994). Phenomenology, ethnomethodology, and interpretive practice. In N. Denzin & Y. Lincoln (Eds.), *Handbook of qualitative research* (pp. 262–272). Newbury Park, CA: Sage.

Howard, R. L. (1981). *A social history of American family sociology, 1865–1940.* Westport, CT: Greenwood Press.

Huyssen, A. (1990). Mapping the postmodern. In L. J. Nicholson (Ed.), *Feminism/postmodernism* (p. 234–277). New York: Routledge.

Karl, F. R. (1988). *Modern and modernism.* New York: Atheneum.

Klein, D. M., & Jurich, J. A. (1993). Metatheory and family studies. In P. G. Boss, W. J. Doherty, R. LaRossa, W. R. Schumm, & S. K. Steinmetz (Eds.), *Sourcebook of family theories and methods: A contextual approach* (pp. 31–67). New York: Plenum.

Kingsbury, N., & Scanzoni, J. (1993). Structural-functionalism. In P. G. Boss, W. J. Doherty, R. LaRossa, W. R. Schumm, & S. K. Steinmetz (Eds.), *Sourcebook of family theories and methods: A contextual approach* (pp. 195–217). New York: Plenum.

LaRossa, R., & Reitzes, D. C. (1993). Symbolic interactionism and family studies. In P. G. Boss, W. J. Doherty, R. LaRossa, W. R. Schumm, & S. K. Steinmetz (Eds.), *Sourcebook of family theories and methods: A contextual approach* (pp. 135–163). New York: Plenum.

Larrabee, M. J. (Ed.). (1993). *An ethic of care: Feminist and interdisciplinary perspectives.* New York: Routledge.

Lyotard, J. F. (1984). *The postmodern condition: A report on knowledge.* (Trans. G. Bennington & B. Massumi). Manchester, England: Manchester University Press. (Original work published 1979)

MacIntyre, A. (1990). *Three rival versions of moral inquiry.* South Bend, IN: University of Notre Dame Press.

Montrose, L. (1992). New historicisms. In S. Greenblatt & G. Gunn (Eds.), *Redrawing the boundaries: The transformation of English and American literary studies* (pp. 392–418). New York: Modern Language Association of America.

Nicholson, L. J. (Ed.). (1990) *Feminism/postmodernism.* New York: Routledge.

Nye, F. I. (1979). Choice, exchange, and the family. In W. R. Burr, R. Hill, F. I. Nye, & I. L. Reiss (Eds.), *Contemporary theories about the family.* (Vol. 2, pp. 1–41). New York: Free Press.

Osmond, M. W. (1987). Radical-critical theories. In M. B. Sussman & S. K. Steinmetz (Eds.), *Handbook of marriage and the family* (pp. 103–124). New York: Plenum.

Osmond, M. W., & Thorne, B. (1993). Feminist theories: The social construction of gender in families and society. In P. G. Boss, W. J. Doherty, R. LaRossa, W. R. Schumm, & S. K. Steinmetz (Eds.), *Sourcebook of family theories and methods: A contextual approach* (pp. 591–623). New York: Plenum.

Parker, I. (1992). Social psychology and postmodernity. in J. Doherty, E. Graham, & M. Malek (Eds.). (1992). *Postmodernism and the social sciences* (pp. 80–94). New York: St. Martin's.

Reiss, D. (1981). *The family's construction of reality.* Cambridge, MA: Harvard University Press.

Rorty, R. (1987). Pragmatism and philosophy. In K. Baynes, J. Bohman, & T. McCarthy (Eds.), *Philosophy: End or transformation?* (pp. 26–66). Cambridge, MA: MIT Press.

Rosenblatt, P. C., & Fischer, L. R. (1993). Qualitative family research. In P. G. Boss, W. J. Doherty, R. LaRossa, W. R. Schumm, & S. K. Steinmetz (Eds.), *Sourcebook of family theories and methods: A contextual approach* (pp. 167–177). New York: Plenum.

Rosenau, P. M. (1992). *Postmodernism and the social sciences.* Princeton, NJ: Princeton University Press.

Ryder, R. G. (1987). *The realistic therapist: Modesty and relativism in therapy and research.* Newbury Park, CA: Sage.

Sabatelli, R. M., & Shehan, C. L. (1993). Exchange and resource theories. In P. G. Boss, W. J. Doherty, R. LaRossa, W. R. Schumm, & S. K. Steinmetz (Eds.), *Sourcebook of family theories and methods: A contextual approach* (pp. 385–411). New York: Plenum.

Sampson, E. E. (1989). The challenge of social change for psychology: Globalization and psychology's theory of the person. *American Psychologist, 44*, 914–921.

Seidman, S., & Wagner, D. G. (1992). Introduction. In S. Seidman & D. G. Wagner (Eds.), *Postmodernism and social theory* (p. 1–14). Cambridge, MA: Blackwell.

Sprey, J. (1988). Sociobiology and the study of family conflict. In E. E. Filsinger (Ed.), *Biosocial perspectives on the family* (pp. 137–158). Newbury Park, CA: Sage.

Sprey, J. (1990). Theoretical practice in family studies. In J. Sprey (Ed.), *Fashioning family theory: new approaches* (pp. 9–33). Newbury Park, CA: Sage.

Stacey, J. (1990). *Brave new families: Stories of domestic upheaval in late twentieth century America.* New York: Basic Books.

Sussman, M. B., & Steinmetz, S. K. (Eds.) (1987). *Handbook of marriage and the family.* New York: Plenum.

Teachman, J. D., & Neustadtl, A. (1993). Emerging methods. In P. G. Boss, W. J. Doherty, R. LaRossa, W. R. Schumm, & S. K. Steinmetz (Eds.), *Sourcebook of family theories and methods: A contextual approach* (pp. 715–727). New York: Plenum.

Thomas, B. (1991). *The new historicism and other old-fashioned topics.* Princeton, NJ: Princeton University Press.

Thomas, D. L. & Roghaar, H. B. (1990). Postpositivist theorizing: The case of religion and the family. In J. Sprey (Ed.), *Fashioning family theory: New approaches* (pp. 136–170). Newbury Park, CA: Sage.

Thomas, D. L., & Wilcox, J. E. (1987). The rise of family theory: A historical and critical analysis. In M. B. Sussman & S. K. Steinmetz (Eds.), *Handbook of Marriage and the Family* (pp. 81–102). New York: Plenum.

Thorne, B., with Yalom, M. (Eds.). (1982). *Rethinking the family: Some feminist questions.* New York: Longman.

Troost, K. M., & Filsinger, E. (1993). Emerging biosocial perspectives on the family. In P. G. Boss, W. J. Doherty, R. LaRossa, W. R. Schumm, & S. K. Steinmetz (Eds.), *Sourcebook of family theories and methods: A contextual approach* (pp. 715–727). New York: Plenum.

Whitchurch, G. G., & Constantine, L. L. (1993). Systems theory. In P. G. Boss, W. J. Doherty, R. LaRossa, W. R. Schumm, & S. K. Steinmetz (Eds.), *Sourcebook of family theories and methods: A contextual approach* (pp. 325–352). New York: Plenum.

White, M., & Epston, D. (1990). *Narrative means to therapeutic ends.* New York: Norton.

CHAPTER 9

Methodological Pluralism and Qualitative Family Research

Jane F. Gilgun

Introduction

Methodological pluralism is the hallmark of contemporary research on families. Such pluralism is not likely to go away because it is firmly embedded in tradition and in the methodological transformations current in the social and human sciences. Practicing in a wide array of disciplines, family scholars are being swept up in —and helping to create—the exciting possibilities these transformations present. Such possibilities are so recent that the words of LaRossa and Reitzes (1993), written not long ago, although compelling, soon will be outdated. They wrote, "family research is for the most part dominated by relatively static models and methodologies" (p. 158), an observation other family scholars have articulated (e.g., Osmond, 1987; Thomas & Wilcox, 1987). The exploration of methodological stasis in family research will provide a context in which to interpret the state of contemporary qualitative family research methods. As I will show, methodological stasis is a relatively recent phenomenon. Research on families stands on a tradition of methodological pluralism.

In the not so distant past in most training institutions and funding agencies, one approach to research was taken for granted and not named. Students had virtually no choice as to the philosophy of science to which they were exposed and the kinds of research that professors and others in authority expected them to do. Researchers seeking funding, publica-

Jane F. Gilgun • School of Social Work, University of Minnesota, Twin Cities, St. Paul, Minnesota 55108.

Handbook of Marriage and the Family, 2nd edition, edited by Marvin Sussman, Suzanne K. Steinmetz, and Gary W. Peterson. Plenum Press, New York, 1999.

tion, and tenure were restricted in how they could approach research questions. The dominance of a particular type of research was so entrenched that those who taught it, wrote about it, and practiced it rarely reflected on this hegemony and its impact. There was a single, hallowed term for this type of research: science. A positivistic style of doing science, the general approach was based on the measurement of observables and on deduction; that is, on theories that already had been created. To some extent, this positivistic, deductive hegemony still exists. Many young scholars wait until after they attain tenure before then embark upon the great methodological adventures offered by qualitative approaches to studies of families. These pursuits are also part of science, but a form of science usually based on approaches that are inductive and interpretive in nature. In these interpretive versions of science, unobservables, such as experience, perceptions, and memories, are of interest, and the goals are understandings, concepts, and theories.

What accounts for the creation of the hegemony of positivistic, deductive science and what accounts for its breaking apart is not clear. One term, however, sums up what is happening: postmodernism (see Doherty in Chapter 8 of this volume for an extended discussion of postmodernism). More than anything else, a sense that researchers can say and do whatever they want characterizes postmodernism in social and human sciences. The only constraint on absolute freedom that I see in contemporary research is self-imposed and perhaps based on common sense; that is, if I want to communicate with others, I have to use language and approaches that others can understand, or, if my approaches and my language are not intelligible to my audiences of interest, I must explain in terms that are familiar. In my teaching and research, I have found, however, that even the clearest exposition possible of a research project that departs from positivistic, deductive approaches may not be well understood because the ideas behind the project are unfamiliar.

The task of writing about qualitative family research in today's postmodern contexts involves the impossible task of imposing order on the near chaos that characterizes contemporary research on families. A kaleidoscope is a metaphor that helps me think about what is happening at the moment. Turn it just a bit, and new visions open up. Keep turning and additional forms appear. Each turn creates new possibilities, representing the yet unexplored vistas of qualitative family research.

Methods as a Starting Point

Methods as a starting point is an unusual approach in family scholarship. Other appraisals of the state of the scholarship, particularly since the 1950s, have focused almost exclusively on theory and sometimes on methodologies. Sadly, appraisal after appraisal is characterized by despair over the state of family theory (Adams, 1988; Larzelere & Klein, 1987; Lavee & Dollahite, 1991; Nye, 1988; Osmond, 1987; Thomas & Wilcox, 1987). When scholars discuss methodologies that are promising in terms of generating theory, they stop short of making links to the procedures that will actualize methodological principles. This, of course, is understandable because of the challenges inherent in in-depth methodological analyses. Nonetheless, somehow we as a scholarly community need to encourage each other to push ourselves toward the actualization that methodologies encourage. For example, in an exemplary review of radical-critical theories, Osmond (1987) critiqued positivism in family studies and called for research methods that are "true to the nature of the phenomena being studied" (p. 121). Although she provided a multilayered and potentially generative basis for the development of research procedures that could lead the field into a postpositivistic future, she did not suggest methods that might do so.

Larzelere and Klein (1987) also were concerned with methods that fit family research and would help generate theory. In their exploration of the possibilities, they discussed qualitative methods, the one set of methods that I believe has the most promise of generating theory. Unfortunately, they did not do an in-depth analysis, assuming perhaps that other scholars would pick up on this important insight. Books that might have greatly advanced the development of family theory include Glaser's (1978) neglected classic, *Theoretical Sensitivity*, whose purpose is to offer "a rigorous, orderly guide to theory development" (p. 2) and Glaser and Strauss' (1967) *The Discovery of Grounded Theory*. Both volumes lay out in clear language methods and methodologies of systematically generating theory from either qualitative or quantitative data.

In this chapter, I want to bring attention to the potential significance of qualitative methods for advancing family theory and for deepening and broadening our understanding of the often hidden and private realms of meaning related to experiences of family life. Although my experience suggests that starting with methods will be an improvement over a focus on theory and methodologies, I am not certain. This chapter will explore the possibilities.

The proof of the value of qualitative methods is in their products. The necessity of showing the products of qualitative research is pressing. Although some of the classic studies of families are based on qualitative methods, contemporary qualitative researchers must make their cases anew that this style of research has something important to offer, such as adding to knowledge and understanding and in promoting the common good. Otherwise, the research community, policy makers, program planners, practitioners, journal editors, and funders would not take qualitative research seriously. More than 130 years ago, LePlay (1866) made a similar point when he said that social scientists justify their methods by the results.

Principles Guiding This Chapter

I am deeply challenged personally and intellectually as I attempt to understand and do qualitative family research. In my roles as professor, researcher, and editor of other scholars' qualitative family research (e.g., Gilgun & Sussman, 1996; Gilgun, Daly, & Handel, 1992) I have observed the grit and intellect that other scholars have displayed as they, too, struggle to learn how to do and to present qualitative family research.

There are many sources of the challenges of doing this kind of research, but the most important for the present chapter is intellectual. Inductive methods are the basis of most qualitative research. LePlay (1855, 1879), one of the first, if not the first, qualitative family researchers, used a form of induction, and its procedures remain fundamental to the analysis of qualitative data. Induction has more than one guise, and in whatever form researchers use it, it helps us analyze the massively detailed data that we gather. What do we do with all that data? How do we organize our data and our findings? How do we demonstrate the bases of our findings? When we learn so much from qualitative inquiry and want others to know what we know, how do we decide what to include in our research reports and what to leave out? The procedures of analytic induction help us respond to these questions.

Such considerations demand sharp analytic skills and immersion in procedures that can help us see what is in the data and can help think even more deeply about the data. Bob Bogdan (Bogdan & Biklen, 1992), who through his teaching and writing has guided many family researchers in their qualitative analysis, pointed out that qualitative research is about thinking conceptually. He said about his training with Blanche Geer (Becker, Geer, & Hughes, 1968; Becker, Geer, Hughes, & Strauss, 1961) on qualitative methods: "Blanche modeled how to think conceptually. What I got out of her seminar was not the content. She was teaching a way of thinking" (Gilgun, 1992c, p. 9). Glaser (1978) emphasized the centrality of ideas in qualitative research and for sociology in general: "Good ideas contribute the most to the science of sociology" (p. 8). The power of qualitative methods resides in the ideas that guide the research and in the ideas that the methods help develop.

Our personal biographies, however, are intertwined with the intellectual demands of qualitative family research. Often involving close contact with research informants and thus engagement in their hurts and joys, qualitative family research can be emotionally evocative for researchers, stirring up memories and emotions related to our own experiences in our families of origin and our struggles to create our own families. Researchers thus can learn about themselves and be changed by the research (Allen, 1994; Hall & Zvonkovic, 1996). In addition, our personal biographies can play a part in the selection of topics we study and in how we interpret data. LePlay (1879) was clear that his personal history was the impetus for his decades-long research on European working class families. Our social status—gender, race, and class—are becoming increasingly obvious mediators of how we conduct our research and how we interpret findings. The role of personal experience and social location, then, is a theme of this chapter, and I will trace it from the time of LePlay to today.

In this chapter, I also will deal with how qualitative researchers deal with issues of social change and being social change agents themselves. Do researchers let the data speak for themselves, or do researchers become advocates and social reformists on behalf of the persons researched? That is, do we seek to change the difficult human situations that we encounter? These issues have a long history in qualitative family research and are contested today.

These three issues—induction, subjectivity, and social reform—then, are the main methodological foci of this chapter. I will trace these themes from the mid-nineteenth century to the present. I will begin with a discussion of how these themes appeared in the work of University of Chicago sociologists, anthropologists, and social workers; move to an examination of the European origins of social research; and then trace the legacy of the Chicago School of Sociology to the present. Examination of the early years demonstrates the continuities and discontinuities between early, middle, and contemporary family research. Our heritage is a source of generative ideas that will help us shape the future of qualita-

tive family research. Even some of the methodological puzzles of the early years continue to challenge us to this day, despite changes in historical contexts. All three sections illustrate a point Small (1916) made when writing about the first 50 years of sociology, namely, that the history of science is not only "the record of discovery of absolutely new facts or truths" but also the reconsideration and recombinations of "ideas long more or less familiar" (p. 723).

In the spirit of the history of qualitative family research, I wrote this chapter in the first person. First-person research accounts were usual during the early years. In his first-person essay, Small (1916) recommended it as means of providing contexts in terms of which future scholars may understand historically situated research. Many scholars in the Chicago tradition followed his lead.

In this essay, I leave out the important contributions of psychiatry and psychology to the life history (Cohler, 1988; Runyan, 1984), although I emphasize sociology's contributions to life history research, which is an important approach in the Chicago School of Sociology. While this chapter is not an intellectual history of feminist qualitative family research, much of the material I cover is relevant to contemporary feminist thought.

The Heritage of Qualitative Family Research

The history of qualitative family research is difficult to disentangle from the history of qualitative research in general, particularly qualitative sociology. Family researchers until fairly recently were primarily sociologists, and they often were trained in research methods by professors who did not specialize in families. Qualitative family research might not exist at all were if not for the cross-fertilization provided by researchers and methodologists in allied disciplines not necessarily doing research on families. In my version of the heritage of qualitative research, I move back and forth between researchers whose specialty is families and researchers who sometimes did family research and often did other kinds of research, but who influenced qualitative family researchers profoundly or still could potentially.

Since the origins of qualitative family research in the mid-1800s until at least the 1940s, methodological pluralism was the norm. The philosophies of science underlying this pluralism continue to be influential today, although symbolic interactionism and its precursors may be the theoretical orientation that has been most prominent in research on families since the early part of the twentieth century (LaRossa & Reitzes, 1993). Starting perhaps in the late 1940s and 1950s, choices of method appear to have become restricted, a state that only began breaking apart in the last few years.

The Roots of Methodological Pluralism

During the first third or so of the twentieth century, the generative cross-disciplinary thought of many persons closely linked to the University of Chicago came together to produce a flourish of sociological thought and method (Bulmer, 1984). Founded in 1892, the University of Chicago was well funded with Rockefeller money and contributions from other wealthy patrons. Resources located in the city of Chicago and the vision of William Rainey Harper, the first president, attracted some of the most creative and productive academics of the time. Harper's goal was to establish a center of basic research and graduate training (Bulmer, 1984). For Harper, research was primary, and his faculty had far fewer teaching responsibilities than professors at most other institutions. To disseminate research findings, Harper established The University of Chicago Press, which developed series for the academic disciplines, including the *Sociological Series*, and encouraged the founding of scholarly journals. In the 1890s, Harper recruited John Dewey, George Herbert Mead, and other pragmatist philosophers whose ideas influenced Chicago's social science departments as they were developing during the early part of the twentieth century.

Harper hired Albion Small from his presidency at Colby College in Maine. Small chaired the department of sociology and anthropology for more than 30 years, retiring in 1924 at age 70. At that time, sociology as a discipline was in a formative stage, and Chicago's department was the first. Ruth Cavan (1983), a Ph.D. student in the 1920s, wrote with some hyperbole, "the task fell to this department to define the field of sociology and its methods of study" (p. 409). Within a year, other departments of sociology were founded at Michigan, Kansas, and Columbia. Other universities and colleges soon had their own departments (Faris, 1967). By 1929, sociology became a separate department, but during those decades of association, there was a great deal of crossover between anthropological research methods and Chicago sociology.

With resources, support from the university administration, and generative ideas current at the university, Small had a major impact on sociology and research methods. From the beginning Small "cultivated an eclectic attitude toward current American and European approaches to sociology" (Hammersley, 1989, p. 67). He fostered the view that probing deeply into human actions was more fruitful than the current philosophically based theorizing (Small, 1916). He encouraged his students to do research in the city of Chicago, whose ongoing social transformations formed a naturalistic setting for the urban research that became characteristic of Chicago sociology in later years (Faris, 1967). His thinking meshed with the general pragmatist tenor of the university, and his views were influential not only in his overseeing of the sociology department but also in his many other pioneering efforts. Upon Harper's suggestion, he founded the *American Journal of Sociology* in 1895 and was editor until 1924. He was one of the founders of the American Sociological Society, which became the American Sociological Association.

W. I. Thomas, who joined the sociology faculty in 1895, a year before he received his Ph.D. there, expanded the legacies of Small and other Chicago pragmatists. In particular, his work with Florian Znaniecki on *The Polish Peasant in Europe and America*, published between 1918 and 1920, brought to fruition many ideas current at the time. Widely recognized as a landmark in sociological research in general and qualitative family research in particular (Blumer, 1939/1969; Bulmer, 1984; Faris, 1967; Handel, 1992; LaRossa & Wolf, 1985; Rosenblatt & Fischer, 1993), *The Polish Peasant* was based upon personal documents, such as letters, diaries, and life histories; newspaper accounts; and public records. Thomas and Znaniecki (1918–1920/1927) sought to develop "social theory" that "takes into account the whole life of a given society" (Vol. 1, p. 18). This holistic perspective includes the personal meanings that individuals give to their social situations, but also encompasses less personal accounts in newspapers and official documents.

Emphasis on Meaning. Emphases on understanding and meanings were prevalent at Chicago at the time. Many of the Chicago faculty, including Robert Park, a major figure in Chicago sociology, received their Ph.D.s in German universities, and many others studied there, such as Small, Mead, and Thomas. They undoubtedly came into contact with the ideas of Simmel, Kant, and Dilthey, progenitors of many of the ideas underlying Chicago sociology, ideas that are still influential today in interpretive, phenomenological research and the human sciences in general (see Dreyfus, 1991; Palmer, 1969; Polkinghorne, 1983; and Van Manen, 1990 for a discussion of the human sciences).

Building upon Kant's subjectivist, relativist, and perspectivalist thinking, Dilthey (1976) developed the notion of *Erlebnis*, translated as "lived experience," which he saw as the subject of scientific investigations. For Dilthey, human experience—composed of such intangibles as hopes, emotions, and thoughts—was subject to empirical investigation. The experiences of individuals compose human social and cultural life, and, conversely, human beings cannot be understood apart from their social and cultural lives. Dilthey agreed with the positivist emphasis on a rigorous empirical basis for research (Palmer, 1969; Polkinghorne, 1983).

The ideas of Kant and Dilthey also centered research efforts on *verstehen*, or understanding—an understanding situated in social, cultural, and historical context, in contrast to Cartesian emphases on explanation, objectivity, and mathematics (Hamilton, 1994). Bulmer (1984) speculated that

Thomas and Znaniecki's (1918–1920/1927) emphases on life histories and personal meanings had a "theoretical origin" related to Dilthey, whom he quoted: "Autobiography is the highest and most instructive form in which the understanding of life comes before us" (p. 53, citing Hodges, 1994, p. 29).

Life history accounts not only conveyed personal meanings, but, for Thomas and Znaniecki (1918–1920/1927), they contributed to the science of sociology. They believed that the purpose of science was to reach "generally applicable conclusions." This could be done through studying "each datum ... in its concrete particularity." This, from their view, is the basis of science. They emphasized induction, or drawing general statements from careful analysis of particular situations:

> The original subject matter of every science is constituted by particular data existing in a certain place, at a certain time, in certain special conditions, and it is the very task of science to reach, by a proper analysis of these data, generally applicable conclusions. And the degree of reliability of these general conclusions is directly dependent on the carefulness with which each datum has been studied in its concrete particularity. (p. 1191)

This is no less true for the study of the individual who must be understood "in connection with his [sic] particular social milieu before we try to find in him [sic] features of a general human interest" (Thomas & Znaniecki, 1918–1920/1927, Vol. 2, p. 1911). Although, as this excerpt suggests, they valued scientific generalization, they stated that they do not consider their work as giving "any definitive and universally valid sociological truths" (pp. 340–341). Rather, their work is suggestive and prepares the ground for further research.

The following excerpt from a life history demonstrates how a single case can exemplify major social themes. The speaker is a young Polish man in conflict with his parents over their joint business and values relative to the meaning of marriage:

> First they [his parents] wanted me to marry any girl whatever provided she had money, and after receiving the dowry they wanted me to give them 300 rubles; then they would go somewhere else and establish a shop and leave me my own bakery. And in leaving they were to take all the contents of the shop. It was well planned, but I was not so stupid as to agree to everything my father wanted. I was rather too good a son, and allowed everything to be done with me, but in the matter of marriage I opposed them positively. I wanted to marry only a girl whom I could really love and in whom I should have a good companion of life. As to giving money to my parents, I thought that we would talk about it when the time came. (Thomas & Znaniecki, 1918–1920/1927, Vol. 2, p. 2174)

Economics versus companionship as a basis for marriage, parental prerogatives, duties of children, and rebellion against parental expectations are themes in this particular life history, taken at a particular time, in a particular place, from the point of view of a particular individual. Yet, these themes appear throughout decades of family research, a strong argument for their general applicability. These themes also exemplify the young man's lived experience as taking place in a historical, cultural context.

Although Thomas left the university in 1918, his legacy lived on. Almost 60 years later, Cavan (1983) acknowledged not only the contributions of Thomas but those of Ernest Burgess and Robert Park. She wrote of the importance of two books that gave shape to subsequent Chicago sociological research: *The Polish Peasant* and *Introduction to the Science of Sociology*, a textbook written by Park and Burgess (1921), who both joined the faculty in the second decade of the twentieth century. Thomas had a Ph.D. in philosophy from Heidelberg, while Burgess received his Ph.D. in sociology at Chicago (Bulmer, 1984; Faris, 1967).

Research and Lived Experience. Consistent with nineteenth-century German philosophy within a human sciences tradition, Park and Burgess (1921) encouraged the development of findings that incorporated the experience of researchers and the points of view of informants, leading their students toward understanding and not toward axiomatic explanatory frameworks. In their textbook (1921), they stated that they wanted the text to "appeal to the experience of the student" (p. v), and they advised students to use "their own experience" in recording their observations and in the reading they did for their research (p. vi). Park, in particular, was articulate about the centrality of understanding "the meaning of other people's lives" (quoted in Bulmer, 1984, p. 93). This is done not solely through intellectual processes, but through imaginative participation in the lives of others. According to Matthews (1977), Park frequently quoted William James: "the most real thing is a thing that is most keenly felt rather than the thing that is most clearly conceived" (p. 33).

Park applied these ideas to his work with students. For example, he advised Pauline Young (1928, 1932) to "think and feel" like the residents of Russian Town, the subject of her dissertation, published in 1932 (Faris, 1967). At the same time, both Burgess and Park emphasized the science and objectivity of the styles of research they were shaping. For us today, emphasizing personal experience and the meanings of other persons' lives while considering them part and parcel of an objective science appears to be contradictory. Yet for Park and his colleagues, subjective accounts are proper subjects of scientific research. Researchers become objective insofar as they do not distort findings to serve a reformist agenda. For Park, the disinterested researcher who assembled subjective findings without distortion was displaying objectivity and doing science.

No One Predominant School of Thought. Symbolic interactionism, which through Blumer (1969/1986) draws upon Pierce, Dewey, Mead, and Cooley, is the enduring legacy of the Chicago School of Sociology. Bulmer (1984) pointed out that in the first quarter of the twentieth century no one school of thought was predominant; rather, the emphasis in Chicago Sociology was the "blending of firsthand inquiry with general ideas" and "the integration of research and theory as part of an organized program" (p. 3). Park had a pungent and direct way of instructing his students to combine firsthand experience with library research and document analysis. Not only did he endorse research that included library research that led to "a mass of notes," but he also advised his students "to choose problems wherever you can find musty stacks of routine records based on trivial schedules prepared by tired bureaucrats and filled out by reluctant applicants of aid or fussy do-gooders or indifferent clerks" (McKinney, 1966, p. 71). Noting the dust involved in these enterprises, he told his students that this is "getting your hands dirty in research." He didn't stop here, however:

> But one more thing is needful: first hand observation. Go and sit in the lounges of the luxury hotels and on the doorsteps of the flophouses; sit on the Gold Coast settees and on the slum shakedowns; sit in the Orchestra Hall and in the Star and Garter Burlesk. In short, gentlemen [sic], go get the seat of your pants dirty. (McKinney, 1966, p. 71)

Not only does this quote reveal much about Chicago methodology, but it also demonstrates Park's command of the language. Writing well is a legacy of the Chicago School of Sociology. Writing in cogent, evocative terms supports the credibility of qualitative studies. The department held seminars on the use of literature in research, and Park and Burgess encouraged students to read autobiographies and novels (Bulmer, 1984). The research on families done by Chicago sociologists during this time closely followed these approaches, using observation, interviews, and personal document analysis, all of which brings researchers into close contact with social worlds.

Multiple Methods. Park and Burgess encouraged the use of multiple methods and statistics. A typical study used interviewing, observations, document analysis, census data, social mapping, and, in the later years, statistical analysis. Social mapping involved locating on maps of Chicago not only distributions of social problems but also locations of residential, undeveloped, and business areas. Students used to joke that they couldn't get their degrees without doing a social map. As Bulmer (1984) documented, Vivien Palmer, who was a senior researcher in the sociology department from 1924 to 1930, also worked closely with the Chicago graduate students, amassed archival material that provided contexts for their urban ethnographies, and wrote the second book on field methods (Palmer, 1928). Examples abound of the plurality of methods used to capture the multiple ecologies of social life in the city. The following sections discuss some of them.

The Hobo. Nels Anderson's (1925) *The Hobo*, written for a master's thesis, was the first in the *Sociological Series* (Faris, 1967). Because of poverty, as a graduate student Anderson lived among hobos—today's counterpart of homeless men—and observed and interacted with them in their daily lives, talked with professionals who worked with them, and elicited life histories. From these sources, both oral and written, he wrote his thesis, arranging his materials in piles on the floor "without misplacing any pages" (Anderson, 1983, p. 404). The result was a classic of sociological research, embodying the principles characteristic of the Chicago School of Sociology.

The Gold Coast and the Slum. At about the same time, Harvey Zorbaugh (1929) was gathering data for *The Gold Coast and the Slum*, a study of juxtaposed, contrasting economic lifestyles of two Chicago neighborhoods. He used reports from government and social agencies; maps; historical documents; informal contacts with business leaders, nurses in hospitals, officials at night court, and newspaper reporters; and door-to-door neighborhood surveys on incomes, rent, and related topics. He organized his findings through social mapping, case studies of members of the social groups he identified, statistical analysis of the financial data, and a social history of the neighborhoods.

Family Disorganization and *Domestic Discord.* Mowrer's (1927) *Family Disorganization*, based on his 1924 dissertation, and his *Domestic Discord* (Mowrer & Mowrer, 1928), written in collaboration with his wife Harriet Rosenthal Mowrer, used statistics, social mapping, and written documents such as diaries, newspapers, and case study materials taken from records of social workers. In addition, Mowrer and Mowrer linked their findings with previous research and theory and created a theoretical analysis of families under stress.

The Negro Family in Chicago. The methods and methodologies of Frazier's (1932) dissertation *The Negro Family in Chicago* and his later work, *The Negro Family in the United States* (Frazier, 1939), evolved from those in *The Polish Peasant*. Both of these studies used personal documents such as written life histories, agency case records, interviews, and demographic data. In his Chicago study, Frazier developed a typology: the migrant, the old settler, and the *nouveau riche*. Frazier's purposes in the Chicago study were to find "insight into the meaning of the world" to the members of these three groups, to gain a "picture of the social and cultural world in which the Negro lives," and "to see the development of the Negro family in relationship to social organization and social control" (p. 258). In brief, he sought to place the "Negro" in a "definite cultural context," so that "he [sic] no longer remains an abstraction in a vacuum as most studies have presented him" [sic] (p. 258). Burgess (1932), in the editor's preface of the Chicago study, noted that Frazier's work exemplified and forecast "a new approach to the more intimate aspects of family and social life" (p. ix). This field study, like others done at about the same time, marked a change from studies of families that were in an institutional and social organizational framework (p. ix).

In *The Negro Family in the United States*, Frazier (1939) used court and archival material, letters, and published autobiographies, in addition to other documents mentioned earlier, to give an account of 150 years of family history within social contexts that included slavery, emancipation, caste-like social status, and migration from rural to urban areas. In the editor's preface, Burgess (1932) called this work "the most valuable contribution to the literature on the family" (p. ix) since the publication more than 20 years earlier of *The Polish Peasant*.

Many other research projects modeled themselves on the methodological diversity characteristic of Chicago research. Charles S. Johnson's (1922) masterful study *The Negro in Chicago: A Study of Race Relations and a Race Riot in 1919* and Warner and Lunt's (1941) widely recognized *The Social Life of a Modern Community* are just two of many examples of studies that were within the Chicago tradition but not conducted by Chicago graduates.

Some Methodological Issues and Dilemmas. Not only were multiple methods, inductive approaches, social processes, urban ecologies, social dislocation, social change, and subjective points of view characteristic of the Chicago School of Sociology, but many researchers were eloquent about methodological dilemmas and issues that are widely discussed today. Mowrer (1932), Dollard (1937), and Anderson (1983) are examples. Mowrer was interested in the relationships between observations and theory, a theme he addressed repeatedly. This is the regularly debated issue of the difficulties—some say, the impossibility—of induction: how researchers go from concrete observations to concepts and ideas. In *The Family*, yet another volume in the *Sociological Series*, Mowrer (1932) observed:

> But facts are not born full bloom to be plucked by anyone. In every perceptive experience there is an infinite number of observations which might be made but which are not. What the individual sees is determined in part, at least, by what he [sic] is trained to observe.... Abstraction thus takes the form of replacing of the actual experiences of the individual by

symbols which serve as carriers of what he [sic] considers to be the essential elements of his [sic] experience. Events and objects are grouped by observed regularities or similarities in them. In this third step in scientific method there is always a certain amount of arbitrariness in the selection of what is considered essential, growing out of the training and experience of the researcher. (pp. 281–286)

This early formulation of issues related to induction has been a theme in symbolic interactionism and the social sciences in general for generations (Becker, 1988; Blumer, 1939/1969; Hammersley, 1989; Wolcott, 1994). These and other difficulties with induction are bases for those who argue for the superiority of deduction.

John Dollard, in his *Caste and Class in a Southern Town* (1937), gave a first-person account that demonstrates that reflexivity in research was an issue then as it is today. For example, Dollard described the social awkwardness of being white in a southern town whose mores forbade treating "Negroes" as equals. Fearing that other white persons were watching as he talked to "Negroes" on his front porch, when he knew their "proper" place was at the back door, he wrote:

> My Negro friend brought still another Negro up on the porch to meet me. Should we shake hands? Would he be insulted if I did not, or would he accept the situation? I kept my hands in pockets and did not do it, a device that was often useful in resolving such a situation. (p. 7)

This description is a poignant verbal picture of a pivotal moment in Dollard's fieldwork, and it is full of connotations about the racist social practices of the time. This excerpt from Dollard illustrates a methodological point Small (1916) made in his essay on the first 50 years of sociological research in the United States, namely, the importance of going beyond "technical treatises" and providing first-person "frank judgments" that can help future generations interpret sociology. Without such contexts, "the historical significance of treatises will be misunderstood" (p. 722). Throughout his essay, Small used the first person and provided his views—or frank judgments—on the events he narrated.

Dollard undoubtedly was building on Small's ideas. In a footnote, Dollard (1937) commented on his use of "I," which he said he used reluctantly but did so because "it will show the researcher as separate from his data ... and it will give the reader a more vivid sense of the research experience" (p. 2). These concerns anticipate contemporary methodological discussions of the role of reflexivity in research.

As shown by the story about not shaking hands with the "Negro," Dollard had an additional reason for using the first person: He wanted to bring issues to life. The use of "I" became outmoded for decades and, ironically, Chicago graduate William Foote Whyte's (1943) first-person account of "slum sex codes," except for the use of the term *slum*, sounds as if it could have been written today, not only in terms of the information it provides but in terms of its writing style, which is lively and in the first person.

Concern about bias, an issue then and now, also appeared in Dollard's writing. He wrote a chapter on his own biases regarding his study, including a detailed analysis of how an informant, who was a well-known white southern writer, angered him but ultimately helped him become aware of his biases toward white southerners. Subsequent early sociologists have been concerned as well. Waller (1934), for instance, pointed out that prior concepts can help researchers see things they might not have seen but can also blind them to what could be there. Webb and Webb (1932) developed procedures for dealing with researchers' bias, including writing down all of one's ideas, preconceptions, and favorite theories prior to designing the research. They assured researchers if they put aside even their favorite questions and hypotheses, they would find that the processes of direct involvement in the field results in both answers to questions and to testing and verification of hypotheses. Today's qualitative researchers recommend these procedures as well (Bogdan & Biklen, 1992).

In their concern for bias and the place of researchers in research, they were addressing major themes in contemporary epistemological discussions of reflexivity. For instance, Harding (1991), among many others, argues that situating researchers as part of research processes creates a "stronger" and more objective science. Rather than presenting the research through an anonymous narrator whose standpoint is not known, researchers tell much more about their findings when the context the researcher provides is included in research reports.

Concerns about Method. Chicago-trained sociologists made other cogent methodological points. Concerns about methods training and the place of previous research and theory in the conduct of fieldwork plagued Anderson (1925), who presented himself as knowing nothing about method. He kept away from other graduate students because of his felt ignorance. Even after his master's thesis became the first in Chicago's *Sociological Series*, he characterized himself as a poor researcher and, tongue-in-cheek perhaps, noted that "the book contained not a single sociological concept" (p. 403). His book contains concepts, of course, but not highly abstract concepts and hypotheses; rather, his ideas were embedded in the meanings of the words in his text. Anderson appeared to be making fun of sociologists who may have made a bigger deal over concepts than Anderson thought was necessary for field research.

Dollard (1937) also had concerns about the place of concepts and previous research in his field research. He reported that he did not review pertinent literature until after he finished his study. He deemed it "advisable to try for the

advantage which lies in naivete and a freshened perception of the local scene," rather than risk "repeating the well-documented findings of others" (p. 31). In addition, he preferred "to give the reader as deep a sense of participation as may be in what I have heard, seen, and sensed" (pp. 31–32), a theme I discussed earlier and one characteristic of Chicago sociology. Unlike Anderson, then, he found research and theory useful, but only after he completed his research, and, like Waller, he was concerned that his openness to data might be affected by knowledge of the literature. How and when to involve previous research and theory in qualitative studies are of interest in contemporary discussions of qualitative research in general and qualitative family research in particular.

The Seeking of a Statistician. While there was a richness of thought related to field methods and to the methodological challenges that such methods engender, the faculty in sociology did not lose sight of the importance of quantification and statistics. By the mid-1920s, the members of the sociology department saw their lack of expertise in statistics as a weakness and a threat to the national and international stature of their department. They voted unanimously to invite William Ogburn, a leading quantitative sociologist, to join the faculty (Bulmer, 1984). In the late 1920s, there was a flurry of controversy that pitted statistics against case study methods, but within a few years, after many colloquia, journal articles, and long discussions, both professors and students came to view the two approaches as complementary (Faris, 1967). Burgess (1927) and Blumer (1928) made major contributions to this rapprochement. In a 1927 paper on statistics and the case study, for instance, Burgess wrote that statistics and case studies are complementary. Statistics provide correlations and indices, while case studies can reveal social processes and the meanings persons attribute to processes and events that will help "build more adequate statistical indices" (p. 120). The tradition of methodological pluralism most likely created an openness to the new discipline of statistics, and subsequent Chicago-style research usually made ample use of them.

While the Chicago sociologists may have been open to multiple methods, this openness did not maintain itself in sociology in general over the decades. By the 1950s, for instance, even Burgess, identified earlier with field research, was involved almost exclusively in quantitative family research. Other Chicago researchers, however, such as Waller (1934), staunchly maintained that qualitative insight is the basis of knowledge, saw a central place for nonobservables such as the imagination and perception, and continued the tradition of inductive methodologies. Waller wrote, "Quantification is not the touchstone of scientific method. Insight is the touchstone" (p. 288), a view that Cook and Campbell

(1979) echoed several decades later when they noted that qualitative knowing underlies all research. Statistics, Waller said, as did Cook and Campbell, serves insight, and experimentation serves the testing and verification of insight.

Waller's (1934) description of the scientific method is similar to later descriptions of analytic induction (Znaniecki, 1934) and grounded theory (Glaser & Strauss, 1967). Waller wrote that the scientific method was primarily inductive, based on "direct study of human and interhuman behavior.... in an attempt to discover recurrent patterns, and, if possible, to make out the entire configuration of events" (p. 289). He assigned a central role to imagination, something few positivists would do given their emphasis on observables and knowledge based on the senses. Concepts for Waller were "transposable perceptual patterns to which we give names" (p. 289). These ideas are current today.

Imagination and the Scientific Method. Waller (1934), like Park, saw a role for imagination in scientific methods and processes, and he compared processes of science to artistic processes:

> The application of insight as the touchstone of method enables us to evaluate properly the role of imagination in scientific method. The scientific process is akin to the artistic process; it is a process of selecting out those elements of experience which fit together and recombining them in the mind. Much of this kind of research is simply ceaseless mulling over, and even the physical scientist has considerable need of an armchair. (p. 290)

Waller is reminiscent of Kant and Dilthey, who recognized the centrality of reflection and the power of thought. Conceptualizations of scientific processes as similar to artistic processes have made many social scientists uncomfortable, but I have found through my own qualitative research that development of ideas depends upon imagination and probably are developed through creative processes similar to artistic creativity.

Waller's (1934) thought was consistent with Cooley (1930), when he observed that "our knowledge of human beings is internally as well as externally derived" (p. 294) and called "imagining what it would be like to be somebody else" a form of "the scientific method" (p. 295). This, of course, is akin to what Blumer (1969/1986) called taking "each other's roles" (p. 9) and is an elaboration of Park's views. Sympathetic understanding as part of the scientific method is very different from the idea of scientific detachment.

The Immediate Context of the Sociology Department

Links between academic settings and the community characterized the early years of Chicago sociology. For ex-

ample, faculty members such as Dewey, Mead, and Thomas were close associates of Jane Addams, whose Hull House provided a setting and an intellectual atmosphere for the further development of pragmatist thought and methods. The reciprocal influence between academicians and community activists is chronicled in Deegan (1990). According to Deegan, Addams and her associates contributed to Chicago's research methods. Building on the example of Booth's research on the city of London, she and her colleagues at Hull House did detailed studies of the city of Chicago (*Hull-House Maps and Papers*, 1895). These methods of the Hull House group included many subsequently used in Chicago's sociology department.

Addams' ideas of social reform and those of her activist colleagues were compatible with the reformist ideas of the early Chicago pragmatists, who also sought to improve social conditions. Dewey, for example, set up a series of laboratory elementary schools, where he could try out the ideas being developed in the philosophy department (Bulmer, 1984). Addams linked poverty and exploitation of workers with oppressive social and economic conditions, and she was a key figure in such reform movements as standards for occupational safety, the establishment of unions and the support of strikes, and various federal legislation on child labor and family social welfare (Deegan, 1990). Not only was the work of Addams enriched by her association with University of Chicago faculty, but her ideas influenced subsequent developments in sociological research. In addition, Chicago faculty frequently taught courses at Hull House, and residents of Hull House, such as Sophonisba Breckinridge and Edith Abbott (Abbott, 1910; Abbott & Breckinridge, 1916), taught in the sociology department.

Reformist ideas, however, came under heavy criticism for what was seen as their moralistic and paternalistic underpinnings (Bulmer, 1984; Deegan, 1990; Faris, 1967). Sociologists, among them Park and Burgess, disassociated themselves from what they considered "do-gooder" ideologies and the persons whom they viewed as embodying them. Park, showing obvious disrespect for social workers, discouraged his students from taking courses with Abbott and Breckinridge, and he told students in a seminar that "women reformers" had done great damage to the city of Chicago (Bulmer, 1984, p. 68). Abbott and Breckenridge brought the independent School of Civics and Philanthropy to the University in 1920, renaming it the School of Social Service Administration. By the close of the second decade of the twentieth century, there was limited contact between social work reformists and the sociology faculty.

Without the influence of social reformers, Chicago sociology might have taken a different turn (Bulmer, 1984). Under the leadership of Burgess and Park, Chicago sociology was concerned with social problems and the social forces bringing about human oppression and suffering. Their response to social problems was to emphasize the importance of enlightening public opinion, a stance quite different from the social policy, action-oriented research of social workers. Ironically, Park was a social reformer of highest repute. He worked for almost a decade as Booker T. Washington's secretary. He nurtured some major research on African American social problems, such as Charles S. Johnson's (1922) *The Negro in Chicago: A Study of Race Relations and a Race Riot in 1919* and Frazier's work discussed earlier. He chaired Chicago's Urban League and spent the last 7 years of his life at Fiske University in Atlanta, a traditional black institution (Bulmer, 1984). Like LePlay, who will be discussed later, Park kept his reformist ideas separate from his research and research advising.

The European Origins of Research on Families

Addams and her associates contributed to Chicago sociology, as did other early social reformists, including Charles Booth, Beatrice and Sidney Webb, and E. S. Rowntree in England and Frederic LePlay, a French metallurgist and social scientist who did research on families and their economic status throughout Europe in the second quarter of the nineteenth century. They developed a multimethods approach that later characterized Chicago sociology, such as social surveys, in-depth interviews, participant observation, document analysis, analysis of demographic data, and social mapping. Booth (1903), for example, pinpointed taverns and churches on a detailed map of the city of London to facilitate understanding of the relationships between "drunkenness," religion, and family poverty. Wax (1971), a Chicago-trained anthropologist, reported that Burgess and Park used Webb and Webb's (1932) *Methods of Social Study* in their field methods seminar. In this book, the authors, who worked closely with Booth and shared his reformist ideals, describe participant observation, methods of dealing with researcher bias, and inductive methods of data analysis and interpretation.

A typical method was participant observation, which did not have that name yet. A tactic of the research was to tap into a wide variety of points of view. Booth (1903) described a participant observation: His researchers took "long walks in all parts of London day after day with picked police officers who were permitted to assist us during the revision of our maps" (p. 61). He sought "diversities of opinion affected by the point of view of the observer, as well as by the class observed." He therefore presented his findings as "a patchwork of quotations … drawn from the clergy, ministers of religion, and missionaries, from schoolmasters and others" (p. 60). Park frequently took his students on long walking tours of Chicago neighborhoods and, as

discussed earlier, emulated methods based on diverse sources of data.

Booth (1903), however, freely labeled social conditions "evil," tried to identify sources of responsibility, and sought to change conditions, qualities that may have offended later researchers who valued a more detached stance. The following illustrates his perspectives: "In considering this subject [housing] I shall first enumerate the evils and try to allocate responsibility, and then indicate the efforts that are being made to improve matters, and their results" (p. 158). Then and now, researchers with a social reform—or critical, emancipatory—stance may find his language quaint but essentially agree with him. Here again is a contrast between reform-minded researchers on the one hand and basic researchers on the other. Park and Burgess (1921), however, praised Booth's work as an example of "disinterested investigation" (p. 44) that threw "great light, not only upon poverty in London, but upon human nature in general" (p. 45). Approvingly, they noted that this mammoth study "raised more questions than it settled," and they agreed with Booth when he said that the problems need to be better stated (Booth, 1889). They apparently did not see his reformist ideas affecting his objectivity.

First Use of Field Methods in Sociology. Frederic LePlay, the earliest of the social reformists and the first to employ field methods in sociology, did the most extensive research on families and social conditions that has ever been done. His field research began in 1829 and ended in the 1850s, with the 1855 publication of *Les ouvriers europeens*. His contributions to sociology are monumental and well documented by Silver (1982), who also noted that, in later years, LePlay's contributions eventually were discounted, not only because of the dominance of statistical methods but also because of the general distaste for his reformist ideas and possibly a mistrust of inductive methods. By the 1930s, academics such as philosopher Mortimer Adler were advocating deductive methodologies and condemning induction as "bad science" (Bulmer, 1984, p. 203).

LePlay was driven by his concern for human suffering, but he did not present his reformist ideas in *Les ouvriers europeens*. Like Park several decades later, he assumed that his ideas and findings would speak for themselves and lead to social reform. When he saw that this didn't happen, he devoted the last decades of his life to social activism, seeking ways to apply his ideas to social interventions. In the course of doing so, he wrote several other books and produced a new edition of *Les ouvriers* (LePlay, 1879). His fieldwork, however, ended by the 1850s, and he died about 30 years later in 1882.

Trained as an engineer and metallurgist, LePlay applied the scientific methods of his day to the study of families during times of great social and economic changes. The methods of his research, like the research that succeeded his, continue to be viable today. These include inductive reasoning based on direct and prolonged contact with the empirical world and the centrality of his personal history to his choice of topic and method. Institutional support for his research enabled him to do his decades-long fieldwork.

Induction as Scientific Method. LePlay deliberately based his social research methods on his training as an engineer and metallurgist, or "the scientific method." In LePlay's terms, this was an method of observation and reasoning that leads "to the truth" (in French, *au vrai*). He noted that "the method is as old as the human species and practiced by eminent men [sic] long before Descartes, Bacon, and Aristotle recommended it to philosophers" (LePlay, 1866, p. 3). He held up the practice of the chemist as a model for doing research, and it was this type of research in which he had confidence.

This, of course, is the method of induction. His inductive, observational methods contrasted with the speculative, deductive methods prevalent in his time (Silver, 1982). In his own words, LePlay was repelled by the "blind propaganda of the salons" (LePlay, 1879, Vol. 1, p. 47) and the unverified moral precepts of the social reformists (Silver, 1982). He wrote, "In scientific matters, only direct observation of facts can lead to rigorous conclusions and to their acceptance" (LePlay, 1879, Vol. 6, translated by Silver, 1982, p. 179). For LePlay, observations are verified many times. For instance, after almost 20 years of research, he went back into the field for 7 more years to check and revise his findings in preparation for the publication of *Les ouvriers* (Silver, 1982). Through observation, classification, and induction, he sought "the principles of social science" (Zimmermann & Frampton, 1935, p. 567).

His approach in social research was to do in-depth studies of families in many countries before he came to any conclusions. He completed about 300 studies of families, which he called monographs, with the assistance of 100 other researchers. The methods were observation—including living with families from a week to a month at a time, interviewing family members, and then interviewing a variety of public officials who knew the family members.

His initial efforts were marked by confusion. Unfamiliarity with languages and the "complexity and variety of facts" with which he was confronted unsettled him (Silver, 1982, p. 160), but he eventually managed and made sense of his observations. He lived with families "to understand their language and their life" (Zimmerman & Frampton, 1935, p. 473). He learned to speak several languages in the course of his studies. To organize data collection, he developed a framework consisting of 16 topics, such as description of the setting in which the family lived, family demographics, family history, family social status, food and meals, health and hygiene, and family economics.

The framework is a prior conceptualization, against which he railed. Pragmatically, however, he needed it to organize his unruly findings. His discussions of interviewing suggest a middle road between imposing ideas on social life and an entirely inductive method:

> Questioning should be conducted in the order indicated by the method. Nevertheless, this order must not be followed too rigorously. The workingman [sic] will naturally tend to elaborate on certain subjects: he [sic] will enjoy related memories of his [sic] youth and telling his [sic] family history. It is important not to interrupt him [sic], so that useful information will not be lost.... It is much better to listen than to ask questions. (LePlay, 1862, translated by Silver, 1982, p. 182)

In his procedures, then, he allowed new material to emerge. Yet, the framework was probably indispensable in guiding the research. It also provided the organizational structure for the presentation of the findings. LePlay was in tune with a principle that methodologists since at least the time of Durkheim (1966) have recognized, namely, the importance of general principles to guide data collection and interpretation.

Trust in Research Processes. Giving much thought to the influence of preconceived ideas on his own research, LePlay expressed confidence that research processes would take care of this problem. He stated that it is common for observers to begin their studies seeking to find facts that fit their "erroneous" principles, but the method itself will lead to correct conclusions (Silver, 1982, p. 181). In addition, working with other researchers "removed ... error arising from preconceived ideas" (Zimmerman & Frampton, 1935, p. 377). How exactly these processes work was not spelled out.

This reticence about research procedures is characteristic of the work of our predecessors. Leonard Schatzman (Schatzman, 1991; Schatzman & Strauss, 1973), who taught grounded theory, a form of qualitative research for more than 30 years, said in an interview:

> In the history of qualitative research, most professors couldn't articulate the method. A student would ask a prof, "Where did you get that concept?" The prof would mumble something and then add, "Hang around a few years, and you'll see." Sure enough, the student would hang around for a couple of years and would see. The student becomes a professor and her student asks "Where did you get that concept?" The prof mumbles something and then says, "Hang around a few years. You'll see." (Gilgun, 1993a, p. 1)

This reticence began to change in 1967 with the publication of Glaser and Strauss' *The Discovery of Grounded Theory*, and today researchers are much more articulate about research procedures. Nonetheless, the essential ambiguity of induction may be intractable.

Faith in—or the trustworthiness of—the processes of induction may be increased by repeated observations, multiple interpreters, and the interplay between hypothesis generation and testing. For example, 15 years into his research, LePlay came to believe that he had developed some "principles of social science drawn by inductions from the facts observed." He concluded that "there was no longer any occasion to add anything to them by observing new facts" (Zimmerman & Frampton, 1935, p. 573). Glaser and Strauss (1967) would call this theoretical saturation. Few researchers take 15 years to reach saturation. The scope of LePlay's project was so broad that it took a decade and a half. Few researchers undertake such far-ranging projects.

LePlay noted that he was not able to formulate the social science principles he sought with the "clearness which I am now able to give them" (Zimmerman & Frampton, 1935, p. 573). This statement, from a man who was in the field for more than 20 years and was brilliant enough to finish 4 years of study at the *Ecole des mines* in 2 years, clearly articulates the difficulties of formulating principles derived from inductive research. Interpretation of qualitative data requires much thought, as discussed earlier, and time in which to reflect.

Personal History. LePlay wrote an autobiography published as the first chapter in the first volume of the second edition of *Les ouvriers* (LePlay, 1879). He did so to demonstrate that his method was not based on preconceived ideas, arguing instead that his ideas arose from his life experiences. In this sense, he saw living his life as personal fieldwork, an inductive process through which he developed his own guiding ideas, primary among which was the relief of human suffering. In the autobiography, LePlay discussed the effect on him of economic depressions, social upheavals, and revolutions that characterized France in the eighteenth and nineteenth centuries. During LePlay's childhood, his uncle and friends of his uncle instructed him on the social and political history of France, and they were strongly on the side of the common people. In 1830, disabled by a laboratory accident, he listened to his friends discuss the Napoleonic revolutions and heard and saw the turmoil from his window. He wrote, "When I saw the blood spilled by the July Revolution [of 1830], I dedicated my life to the restoration of social harmony in my country" (LePlay, 1879, Vol. 1, p. vii). The more remote influences were the childhood years that he spent in the countryside among French working families, times he recalled with great warmth. He affectionately recalled his mother, who read books with him during his childhood. LePlay, then, is part of a long tradition of using autobiographical material to generate ideas for research.

Silver (1982) saw contradictions between LePlay's view that his research did not reflect preconceived ideas and his stance that his personal experiences influenced him profoundly. How much of an issue this actually is may be hard to pin down. Today, it is generally assumed that personal experiences influence research processes (Sollie & Leslie, 1994). Researchers have standpoints, as do readers (Allen, 1994). The meanings of texts do not depend solely upon the intentions and methods of the writers of texts (Barthes, 1974). Readers, however, often appreciate knowing writers' personal experiences to aid in interpretive processes. For today's poststructuralists, the interpretations of readers take precedence over the intentions of writers (Barthes, 1974; Gilgun, 1995a; Noth, 1995). While LePlay appeared to believe that the truth is out in the world waiting to be discovered, more contemporary qualitative researchers take a social constructivist, poststructuralist view that we as well as "what is out there" are forms of texts to which we give meaning (Barthes, 1974; Manning & Cullum-Swan, 1994).

Institutional Support. LePlay enjoyed institutional support for his research. For 25 years, the French Ministry of Public Works gave him 6 months of paid leave from his professorship at the *Ecole des mines* to do his social science research. Harper's release of the University of Chicago faculty from teaching to allow them to do research is another example of institutional support that had great dividends. Today, released time for research remains a boon for academic researchers.

The Early Years: A Summary

In its origins, family research methods were primarily but not exclusively inductive. The methods engaged researchers in the worlds of informants through personal documents, participant observation, and interviewing, and they were respectful of quantification, which often provided some of the context in which to interpret findings. They often used official documents and demographic data to flesh out their understandings. That persons interact with their social environments in terms of mutually influential processes was assumed. Earlier researchers sought the points of view of informants, although some, such as LePlay, did not include other "voices" in their research but instead were omniscient and detached narrators much in the manner of most of today's positivistic research reports. Thomas, at the end of the nineteenth century and into the twentieth, was one of the earliest to demonstrate the significance of personal meanings of informants, a perspective based on nineteenth-century German philosophy.

Scores of subsequent Chicago sociological researchers took up these views, and they eventually became part of symbolic interactionism and other interpretive methodologists, including those who consider themselves part of a human sciences tradition. The early sociologists discussed enduring methodological dilemmas and sometimes consciously attempted to invite readers into the experience of these dilemmas, such as the meanings of doing research in an unfamiliar culture, the place of concepts in research, confronting and managing bias, and the place of social reform sentiments, the latter appearing today in emancipatory, critical stances. Chicago sociologists are part of a human sciences tradition, although further scholarship is necessary to see whether these researchers so situated themselves.

The Chicago sociologists did not consider their theories to be universal and applicable independent of time, place, and person. Rather, they were aware of the situational boundedness of ideas, and, indeed, were probably influenced by historicist theories that made that very point. As Thomas and Znaniecki (1918–1920/1927) pointed out in their methodological note, their findings are not universal but simply prepare the ground for further inquiry. They were interested in understanding persons in historical situations, and their theories were meant to illuminate social processes.

Many contemporary qualitative researchers are doing their work without knowing the richness of their own heritage. The roots of qualitative family research go deep, to the origins of empirical research. This review of the early history of qualitative family research hopefully will help establish for qualitative family researchers that not only do we have a rich tradition on which to build but also, as qualitative researchers, we have a central place in family studies.

The Tradition Endures: The "Middle Years"

Although other methods and methodologies eventually became ascendant, sociologists and members of other disciplines trained at Chicago from the 1920s to the 1960s carried on the tradition. For instance, the writings of Glaser and Strauss (Glaser, 1978; Glaser & Strauss, 1967; Strauss, 1997; Strauss & Corbin, 1990) are replete with statements about the importance of methodological pluralism and the self-evident nature of researchers' subjective engagements with informants and the meanings of their data. Glaser (1978), for instance, stated about methodological pluralism: "*Our perspective is but a piece of a myriad of action in Sociology, not the only right action....* The division of labor in sociology needs *all* perspectives on styles of both theoretical and empirical renderings of research data" (p. 3, emphasis in original). Glaser (1978) stressed the centrality of the "social psychology of the analyst" and noted that "Generating theory is done by a human being who is at times intimately involved with and other times quite distant from the data—and who is surely plagued by other conditions in his [sic] life" (p. 2). This is a clear statement on the role of reflexivity in research. Glasser and Strauss, whose primary work was medical soci-

ology, assume that the results of their research will be applied and used to ameliorate personal and social ills.

Other researchers, too, made such assumptions. Much of the work of researchers in the Chicago tradition focused on research for social amelioration and social change, a thrust similar to their European and American predecessors. Examples of research related to families and social change are Cavan and Ranck's (1938) *The Family and the Depression*; Rainwater, Coleman, and Handel's (1959) *Workingman's Wife*; Hess and Handel's (1959) *Family Worlds*; Komarovsky's *The Unemployed Man and his Family* (1940) and *Blue Collar Marriage* (1962); and Lopata's series of studies on women's occupations (1971, 1973, 1979, 1984, 1985, 1992a, 1996).

During these middle years from the late 1930s to the mid-1980s, Chicago continued to have an interdisciplinary faculty and graduate students who were drawn to its traditional styles of research. The writing of Rosalie Wax (1971), a Chicago graduate with a Ph.D. in anthropology, demonstrates how methodological ideas espoused by Park, Thomas, and others of the Chicago school earlier in the twentieth century continued to be developed. The work of English anthropologist Elizabeth Bott (1957) on couples' social network shared methodologies with the Chicago tradition, and she later became a faculty member at Chicago. Bott, with Znaniecki (1934), Lindesmith (1947), Cressey (1953), and Glaser and Strauss (1967), played a major role in the ongoing articulation of inductive procedures characteristic of qualitative research.

Chicago graduates and former Chicago faculty fanned out across the United States to create small pockets of graduate students and professors who sustained the tradition. For instance, Anselm Strauss went to the University of California–San Francisco in 1968 to form the department of social and behavioral sciences. There he recruited like-minded faculty, such as Barney Glaser, Leonard Schatzman, Fred Davis, and Virginia Olesen. This faculty trained generations of nursing and sociology students, with Strauss, Glaser, and Schatzman having decades-long responsibility for training in research methods and methodologies. As will be shown in the next section of this chapter, nursing researchers today are among the most productive qualitative family scholars. Chicago graduates Howard Becker spent most of his career at Northwestern, Blanche Geer had several academic jobs including at Syracuse University where she was Bob Bogdan's (Bogdan & Biklen, 1992) advisor, and Erving Goffman was at Berkeley. Jacqueline Wiseman (1979, 1981, 1991), a qualitative family researcher, is one of Goffman's students. Blumer also was at Berkeley for many years.

Nursing and sociology students at the University of California–San Francisco routinely took courses at Berkeley with Blumer, Goffman, and such phenomenologically oriented philosophers as Hubert Dreyfus (1991), Jane Rubin (1988), and Martin Packer (Packer, 1985; Packer & Addison, 1989), all of whom have had a major influence. In some ways, the Berkeley area during these middle years and into contemporary times replicated the intellectual atmosphere of the University of Chicago in the early part of this century.

Helena Lopata's Graduate School Years

A sense of the continuities and transformations of Chicago traditions are part of the life history accounts of Helena Lopata (1992b), who was a student at Chicago from 1945 to 1954, and Gerald Handel (Gilgun, 1992a), who received his Ph.D. in human development in 1962. Lopata emphasized theoretical issues such as role theory and sensitizing concepts and appeared less focused on method, as if her method is self-evident, which it undoubtedly was to her and the tradition in which she learned and practiced research. From her Chicago sociology professors, she received the same directives that Park gave his students decades earlier. An immigrant from Poland, she wanted to study Polish immigrant family life in the United States. She said her professors "told [me] to go to Polonia—and actually talk with the people, attend meetings, and even collect questionnaires? I went" (Lopata, 1992b, p. 1).

She was open about her "reformist" attitude—that is, her interest in social change, aroused while she was at the University of Chicago. She stated in her life history her concern about the response to Nazism in the midwestern United States:

> Speeches given around the midwest about Nazism and the crucial need for clothing and money for medicine to send back to Europe met with total indifference and ignorance. I ended up doing a master's thesis on "International Cooperation in Medicine," probably to convince myself that cooperation is possible in the world. (Lopata, 1992b, p. 1)

She showed no trace of self-consciousness about the personal meanings of this and subsequent research projects. Lopata had no courses on research methods, but learned methods of procedure through course lectures, reading theory and research reports, and field experience.

Gerald Handel and Creative, Independent Thinking

When Handel was a student at Chicago, he, too, had no formal training in research methods, but he was enchanted by the Chicago emphasis on interpretation. Like Lopata, he found that students were expected to be independent scholars in close contact with informants and the worlds in which they lived. Handel's work is embedded in interactionism and his interest is in the meanings that informants attribute to their situations.

My account of Gerald Handel's experiences as a student at the University of Chicago is based on an interview (Gilgun, 1992a). Besides the works cited earlier, Handel is coeditor with Kerry Daly and me of *Qualitative Methods in Family Research*. His other publications include the study of whole families (Handel, 1965, 1996; Hess & Handel, 1959), the psychosocial interior of the family (Handel, 1967; Handel & Whitchurch, 1993), childhood socialization (Handel, 1988), and case studies (Handel, 1991).

Handel studied with Carl Rogers, Bruno Bettelheim, Lloyd Warner, and Elizabeth Bott in an exemplary interdisciplinary program. He said he regrets not taking Everett Hughes' research course in which each student was assigned a census tract and had to find out everything possible about that tract: qualitative and quantitative data, the subcultures, the institutions, and demographics. This, of course, is part of the Chicago methodological tradition of social mapping. For Handel, the environment at Chicago was demanding and creative, and students were surrounded by faculty who were at the height of their careers, creating new insights through interpretive activities. He was immersed in exciting new ideas that inspired him in his own research:

> Each of us had to come to our own interpretation of the material. No one would do it for us. Bettelheim was developing his own ideas, Carl Rogers was doing his thing, and Warner was developing his ideas about American communities. Individuals as rooted in society was a core idea at Chicago.... The act of interpretation was a central activity. Interpreting symbols—that's what Freud did. That's what G. H. Mean said was important. Warner's course based on his studies of Yankee City was subtitled *The Symbolic Life of America*. He had an analysis of the symbolic organization of a Memorial Day parade in Yankee City—what kind of floats people produced and who was allowed to do what. He interpreted the symbolic meaning of the floats. This was an extraordinary analysis.
>
> Another was on the social organization of the cemetery— who's buried where and how. It was amazing stuff to us. These ideas were very, very innovative. One way or another, among the work we studied, the intellectual activity was interpreting human behavior: Freud, Erikson, G. H. Mean, Piaget, and Warner. (Gilgun, 1992a, p. 5)

Handel struggled with the notion that the ideas being presented in class and encountered through reading often did not match up with what was called research: "Here I was reading [and studying with] those magnificent, insightful thinkers," he said, "and then there was this other kind of [quantitative] literature which was smaller in scale." Handel said, "Students who did quantitative work puzzled me. My question was, Why were they doing that?" Excited by ideas and the inductive processes of working with ideas, Handel could not connect with the thinking behind quantitative studies. Handel did not take courses on qualitative interviewing, which was his main method of data collection. "I was not explicitly trained," he said. "It's a mystery how I absorbed it. Somehow I absorbed it, probably through the notion of whose ideas were important to me—G. H. Mead, Freud, M. Mead, Erikson, Piaget" (Gilgun, 1992a, p. 5).

As students together in human development, Hess and Handel cowrote a proposal to the National Institute of Mental Health, which was funded. That research was written up as *Family Worlds* (Hess & Handel, 1959), based on in-depth qualitative interviews with each member of 35 families. They also used the projective Thematic Apperception Test. This work blended Burgess' (1926) notion of family interaction with Chicago's emphasis on multiple methods and personal meanings in interpretations of situations. Through primarily inductive analysis, they formulated five processes of family interaction and functioning: patterns of separation and connectedness, notions of individual and family images, family themes, family boundaries, and the meanings of age and gender to each family member. These ideas have been applied in a wide range of theoretical and applied settings (Handel, 1996; LaRossa & Reitzes, 1993; Rosenblatt & Fischer, 1993).

Other Excellent Qualitative Research

Many other well-known qualitative studies were published during these middle years. Some were based on large-scale surveys, were concerned with representativeness and generalizability, and had much in common with quantified surveys (e.g., Rainwater et al., 1959), demonstrating once more the methodological pluralism that has characterized family research almost from the beginning. Other classic family research at that time includes Komarovsky's (1962) studies of families and class, in which she documented the centrality of mother–daughter ties, and Lillian Rubin's (1976) profoundly emotive accounts of the pain of living at the edge of poverty. Rubin's background as a psychotherapist, her clinical interviewing skills, and her experience growing up in a poor family contributed to the depth of her study, which was unique for the time, but was consistent with the methodological perspectives of the early Chicago School of Sociology. Anthropologists studying the family also had great impact. Among them are Lewis (1962, 1963, 1964, 1965) on Mexican families and Stack (1974) on African American kinship systems. These studies and others continued to remind the research community of the value of qualitative research methods.

The theory developed during these middle years continues to be influential to our day. Boss' (1987) account of the history of the concept *family stress* is an example of how major family theories rest on the bedrock of inductive research conducted during these middle years. According to Boss (1987) contemporary notions of family stress were based

on the work of Cavan and Ranck (1938) and Angell (1936) on families and the Depression. Both used inductive case study methods. Angell identified and defined the concepts of family integration and adaptability as being important to how families respond to the stress of a sudden loss of income. His analysis, according to Boss "remains unchallenged today" (p. 696) and is recognized as relevant in current deductive research.

Cavan and Ranck (1938) supported Angell's conclusions. They found that well-organized families under economic stress "continued to be organized, whereas disorganized families became further disorganized" (Boss, 1987, p. 696). Other researchers over time successfully build on this seminal work. Boss lists the qualitative research of Komarovsky (1940), Koos (1946), Angell (1936), and Cavan and Ranck (1936) as the foundation of Hill's (1949) model of family stress, which he elaborated using case study and survey methods. In addition, Hill incorporated the notion of meaning into his theory of family stress; that is, the meanings and significance that events have to family members are central to whether or not an event is experienced as stressful.

For many of today's family researchers, Reuben Hill is an icon, and his early work rests solidly on Chicago-based researchers with its methodological pluralism and the centrality of meaning. Boss' own work (Boss, 1988; Fravel & Boss, 1992) and that of McCubbin (McCubbin & Thompson, 1989; McCubbin, Cauble, & Patterson, 1984; McCubbin, Thompson, Thompson, & Fromer, 1994), both well-known for research and theory on family stress, have built on the research of the middle years, including Hill's work. As Boss (1987) pointed out, however, research on meaning requires qualitative methods, and the reluctance of researchers to use these methods may be a reason why we know so little about the meanings family members attribute to events that could be stressful. Undoubtedly, there are many generative family theories originating from inductive, case study methods. Boss' (1987) analysis provides one example.

Continual Mutual Influences in Sociology and Anthropology

Mutual influences between anthropology and sociology continued in these middle years. The work of Rosalie Wax, a Chicago Ph.D. in anthropology, and English social anthropologist Elizabeth Bott (1957) illustrate this point. Wax continued Chicago's tradition of reflecting on methodological issues related to subjectivity, particularly in her classic fieldwork text (Wax, 1971) that embodies many of the ideas circulating at the University of Chicago. In her preface, she thanked, among others, the Chicago sociologist Everett Hughes. In her presentation of fieldwork, she incorporated her biography, which is a traditional Chicago approach, as shown earlier. Her stated purpose was pedagogical: to train "future generations of fieldworkers" (p. x). This view is solidly in the Chicago tradition of speaking in the first person to provide historical contexts that aid in interpretation, articulated by Small (1916) early in the twentieth century and sustained over the ensuing decades. She shared her "precollege life experiences," such as how she earned a living during the Depression, how she managed her life as a junior college student, and how she learned about cultural variations as a child. These and other autobiographical details situated Wax within her text and helped in its interpretation.

Wax was concerned with "*shared* meanings" (p. 11), which she saw as preconditions for understanding, her view of the purpose of fieldwork. This, of course, is within the human sciences tradition and fits well with Chicago traditions. For Wax, researchers attain understanding through personal experience, that is, a resocialization into the culture under consideration, a stance Park imparted to his students and probably based on his training in German philosophy. Wax gave many examples of resocialization but noted that researchers remain outsiders.

Wax (1971) recognized that resocialization may entail personal transformations, an insight she attributed to Malinowski. In other words, participation in research processes can change researchers. In some cases, researchers become social reformists, a theme in the early qualitative family research of such persons as LePlay and Booth. Wax noted that as a result of their fieldwork, she and her anthropologist husband Murray "became moral protagonists of Indian communities" (p. 41). Likewise Alfred Lindesmith became an opponent of harsh narcotic laws after his research on opium addicts, and many other social researchers found that fieldwork "undermined" the "pretence of moral neutrality" (p. 41). Wax acknowledged that these transformations met with approval by some but "antagonized" those who "defined science as pure" (p. 41). She built upon some major themes within the Chicago tradition and transformed others, such as her frank statement of advocacy as an outcome of research. Some contemporary phenomenological nursing researchers view her work as influential on their own, as SmithBattle attested (L. SmithBattle, personal communication, 1996). In contemporary work, there also is an awareness of the effect of research on researchers, not only in terms of methodological and often feminist discussions of reflexivity (Sollie & Leslie, 1994), but also in databased research reports (cf. Gilgun, 1995a,b; Hall & Zvonkovic, 1996; Stacey, 1990).

Elizabeth Bott and Inductive Research Processes. The work of English anthropologist Elizabeth Bott (1957) on couples' social networks was quite different from that of Wax. While Wax emphasized shared meanings and researchers' resocialization, Bott's focus was on theory development. In her work, she illustrated the interplay between

induction and deduction in the conduct of qualitative family research. Her work anticipates many of today's research methods, particularly grounded theory (Glaser & Strauss, 1967), a form of induction. Terming her research *exploratory*, Bott did not begin her study with "well-formed hypotheses" but had the general goal of "psychological understanding of some ordinary urban families" (Bott, 1957, p. 8). She said she and her team "succumbed to the confusion" of open-ended research "in the hope that constant careful comparisons would eventually lead to a formulation of specific problems" (p. 9). Bott not only anticipated the methods of grounded theory, but she even used the term *constant comparison*, a term Glaser and Strauss later used.

Having no hypotheses does not mean that the research was atheoretical and unguided by concepts. Bott's theoretical framework was Lewin's field theory (1935, 1936), which holds that behavior is a function of person and environment. This, of course, is a variation of ecological theory and is consistent with the interactionist perspectives that characterized the Chicago School of Sociology from its inception. Lewin's concepts undoubtedly were sensitizing (Blumer, 1954/1969), helping Bott and her team to identify and name processes they might never have noticed otherwise. For Blumer, sensitizing concepts give researchers "a general sense of reference and guidance in approaching empirical instances" (p. 148). In other words, sensitizing concepts orient researchers to the analysis and interpretation of data, as Lopata showed in her intellectual life history and as is routine for most researchers within Chicago traditions.

Doing her research during a time when probability theory and deductive research were in ascendence, Bott (1957) made important methodological points about the generalizability of her findings and the nature of the hypotheses that result from studies such as hers. Her sample of 20 urban families, Bott noted, was neither representative nor random. Whether any facts that such research uncovers were typical was not her concern. What was of concern were hypotheses, which she saw as possibly "generalizable to other families but require further testing" (p. 10), not only on English families but on families in other societies. In short, she saw the kind of research she did as a way of developing viable, testable theory. She pointed out that such hypotheses are written in general terms so as to permit testing. Thomas and Znaniecki (1918–1920/1927), Lindesmith (1946), and Znaniecki (1934), among others, articulated similar views on the generalizability of inductive research.

As unorthodox for the times as her research was, Bott's results were well received and set off a series of studies and papers that Bott (1959/1971) chronicled in a long chapter at the end of the second edition of *Family and Social Network*. Her work continues to be quoted in contemporary research on social networks. Bott was aware of how different her research was and conceded that some would find it difficult to accept. When Bott presented her preliminary analyses to Max Gluckman's seminar on social anthropology at the University of Manchester, England, and asked the seminar participants what to do with her material, Gluckman and one participant said simultaneously, "Write a novel about it" (Gluckman, 1971, p. xiv). Gluckman later admitted he was wrong and called her work "one of the most illuminating analyses ever to emerge from social anthropology" (p. xiv).

Blending Induction and Deduction

The place of preconceived ideas in inductive procedures has intrigued qualitative researchers over the decades. Bott (1957) was not clear about when sensitizing concepts entered her research. Others are very clear, such as Schatzman's (1991) account of the discovery of the theory of "negotiated order" discussed above and Lindesmith's (1947) use of hypotheses in his study of opium addiction. In an interview (Gilgun, 1993a), Schatzman demonstrated the use of sensitizing concepts and showed that they do not preclude discoveries of new theories:

> "The theory of negotiated order (Strauss, Schatzman, Bucher, Ehrlich, & Sabshin, 1964) grew out of our Chicago psychiatric study," he said. "We applied sensitizing concepts, the usual stuff of the social organization of a hospital, having to do with rule and norms. Strauss, in discussion with Schatzman, Rue Bucher, and other members of the research team, was saying, 'Yeah, yeah, there are rules and norms in this hospital. What else is going on here?' We came up with the negotiation concept. There are rules, but rules are negotiated, rules are bent, broken, ignored, argued over, all within the negotiation process. We literally declared that modern organizations are better regarded as negotiated processes where rules are constantly being negotiated and re-negotiated. It isn't that the rules are not there or not fair—it is rather that rules and norms are in flux.
>
> "We looked at each other, and we gasped and said, 'Gee, that's a theory.' Put in your thumb and pull out a plum and say what a good boy am I. We dared publish it that way, and it rang a bell. Terrific. I know there are rules. We set that aside and said rules are not central. What is central is how these people deal with each other and negotiate problems day to day." (p. 5)

In this description of inductive processes that led to a new concept and theory, Schatzman is clear that the research team used "prior conceptualizations," which were concepts taken from symbolic interactism and role theory. Schatzman called these concepts *sensitizing*, using the term as Blumer (1954/1969) recommended. Although Strauss' research team used sensitizing concepts, they did not have a clue at the onset of their research that they would discover the concept of negotiated order. Schatzman conveyed the astonishment and joy the team experienced in their discovery. As Schatzman's account shows, the use of sensitizing concepts and hypotheses does not preclude the discovery of new ideas

(Gilgun, 1995b), or what Glaser and Strauss (1967) have termed *emergence* of theory grounded in data that are gathered inductively.

Grounded Theory Analysis. As conceptualized by Strauss, Glaser, and Corbin (Glaser, 1978, 1992; Glaser & Strauss, 1967; Strauss, 1987; Strauss & Corbin, 1990), the procedures of grounded theory analysis involve sensitizing concepts that guide researchers in a conscious effort to discover what can be considered latent, or core, variables that underlie descriptions of social phenomena. The notion of "negotiated order" is an example of a core variable. These core variables are identified, the possibility of multidimensionality is explored, the consequences of these processes are investigated, and, finally, the conditions, or the social contexts, under which these processes occur are identified (Strauss & Corbin, 1990). Grounded theory, as developed over the years by Strauss and his associates, then, is a set of procedures designed to build substantive, or middle-range, theories. To build a more generally applicable theory, Glaser and Strauss (1967) suggest constructing theory inductively across substantive areas.

Glaser and Strauss have been interpreted as eschewing any use of preconceived ideas. Yet, in their 1967 text, they instruct researchers in Lazarfeld's elaboration theory, which involves investigating "conditions, consequences, dimensions, types, processes" as well as causes when applicable (p. 104) over the course of data analysis and interpretation. In 1978, Glaser carefully presented procedures of becoming sensitive to basic social processes (BSPs), which are present in some grounded theory research but not all. BSPs "are fundamental, patterned processes in the organization of social behaviors which occur over time and go on irrespective of the conditional variation of place" (p. 100) and to which Glaser instructs researchers to be sensitive. Such instructions direct researchers to use preconceived categories and ideas. At the same time, they advise other researchers "to maintain a sensitivity to all possible theoretical relevances" (p. 194). Strauss and Corbin (1990) further developed elaboration theory and also alerted researchers to the social ecologies of the phenomena they study. "Preconceived" ideas held lightly are sensitizing concepts, and without sensitizing concepts researchers have no way of making sense of their data. Strauss and Glaser (1970) made a similar point in their commentary on a case history of a woman dying of cancer in a hospital setting, among many other works.

Hypothesis Testing in Analytic Induction. Analytic induction goes beyond the use of sensitizing concepts and tests explicit hypotheses for the purpose of modifying hypotheses to fit data. Similar to the procedures of grounded theory, analytic induction begins with explicit hypotheses, and the goal is to modify these hypotheses to fit emerging understandings of the data (Gilgun, 1995b). Researchers using analytic induction have goals similar to those of grounded theorists: to develop relevant hypotheses that are modifiable, work, and fit the data. Lindesmith (1947) developed his hypothesis on opium addiction not from a literature review but from observations and conversations with addicts. He tested the hypothesis by interviewing more than 60 addicts, seeking to disconfirm the hypothesis so as to modify it to fit his emerging findings. Only after some ideas "crystallized" through these primarily inductive procedures did he consult previous research and theory. Lindesmith reviewed the theory many times over the course of the interviews, and this led him to conclude that the theory would be revised continuously in response to new information. Like those who came before him, therefore, Lindesmith discussed the open-ended nature of inductively derived theory.

Methodologists such as Znaniecki (1934) support and amplify Lindesmith's conclusions about the nature of inductively developed theory. Znaniecki wrote that the challenge in analytic induction is to find general principles that will guide the analysis and help identify the central features of cases. Centrality is not dependent upon how often it appears. Out of comparisons and general principles, researchers formulate hypotheses. Znaniecki (1934) saw contradictory evidence as reason to develop competing hypotheses and to continue the analysis out of which "emerges new hypotheses and new problems" (p. 282). Later methodologists have names for two of these processes: constant comparison (Glaser & Strauss, 1967), which was foreshadowed by Bott's use of the term, and negative case analysis (Cressey, 1953, among others), which is a deliberate seeking out of cases that will disconfirm the emerging theory. Besides Lindesmith's (1947) research, there are a few other examples (Becker, 1953; Cressey, 1953; Gilgun, 1995b; Nosek et al., 1995; Olesen, Heading, Shadick, & Bistodeau, 1994).

Given the emphasis during these middle years on generalizability and the hope for theory that was universal and deterministically causal, it is not surprising that some researchers dismissed the hypotheses produced by inductive procedures. Manning (1982), for example, misinterpreted analytic induction, evaluating it in terms of its ability to produce universal, deterministically causal hypotheses, and found it lacking in these regards, a view that Vidich and Lyman (1994) echoed. As the earlier discussion shows, a careful reading of the originators of inductive research processes illustrates that they did not intend analytic induction to produce such hypotheses. Rather, researcher after researcher, such as Bott (1957/1971), Lindesmith (1947), Znaniecki (1934), Thomas and Znaniecki (1918–1920/1927), and Glaser and Strauss (1967) stated that their hypotheses were situated, bounded by space, time, and persons, and that any relationships they discovered were tentative, subject to revision when held up to a new case. Such hypotheses illuminate other similar situations but were not presumed automatically to be generalizable to any other situation (Alasuutari, 1996; Gilgun, 1994a,b; Stake, 1995). Instead, these hypotheses were deliberately flexible to allow their application to particular settings. Furthermore, deterministic causality was not the style of causality in which they were interested, when and if they were interested in causation at all. Rather, they were interested in interactions between persons and environments and how larger social forces affect individuals and groups.

Applied Research and Inductive Methods. Glaser and Strauss (1967) assumed that inductively derived grounded theories sometimes would be used to ameliorate social conditions, a social reform orientation that harkens to the originators of qualitative family research, such as the pragmatist philosophers discussed earlier. Extending the principle of modifiability, they wrote that persons who want to apply grounded theories "can bend, adjust or quickly reformulate" them when fitting them to "situational realities that he [sic] wishes to improve" (p. 242). They pointed out that nurses use grounded theories to guide their work with dying patients.

The assumption that grounded theory is flexible can be extended to any inductively derived theory. Such perspectives invite clinical researchers such as nurses, social workers, family therapists, clinical psychologists, and psychiatrists to use inductive methods in their research. This is exactly what began happening during these middle years as Strauss, Glaser, and Schatzman educated generations of nurses at the University of California–San Francisco. As will be discussed in the next section of this chapter, nursing researchers have been highly productive in furthering the development of inductive, qualitative research methods. Other clinical disciplines are becoming aware of the usefulness of these methods.

Credibility of Inductive Research. During these middle years, the epistemological concerns of reliability and validity were the standards by which the quality of research was judged. Although much of qualitative research is concerned with ontological issues, such as what it means to be human in particular situations, qualitative researchers could and sometimes did justify their research in the epistemological terms of their day (e.g., Jick, 1979; Kidder, 1981; LeCompte & Goetz, 1982; Rosenblatt, 1983). Most qualitative approaches, however, represented more than what could be accounted for in these other epistemologies.

Glaser and Strauss (1967) were concerned that qualitative research be taken seriously. Building on Chicago traditions, they developed guidelines for evaluating qualitative research that were quite different from the prevailing ideas of the time. As they pointed out, the immersion of researchers in the field became a fundamental argument for the strength of qualitative research. By the time researchers are ready to publish, they are so intimate with their material that they have great confidence in its credibility.

Researchers' confidence and the demonstration of credibility, however, are not the same thing, as Glaser and Strauss demonstrated. Researchers have the responsibility to convey the bases on which others may conclude that the findings are credible. They can do so in several ways. Credibility rests on conveying findings in understandable terms. The first strategy that Glaser and Strauss (1967) suggested is for researchers to present their theoretical frameworks using conventional "abstract social science terminology" (p. 228). The presentation should be extensive, and, since the terms are familiar, the framework should be readily understood.

The second strategy that Glaser and Strauss (1967) discussed is to present findings in such a way that the reader is "sufficiently caught up in the description so that he [sic] feels vicariously that he [sic] was also in the field" (p. 230). Glaser (1978) later called this quality "grab." This connects to the methodological stances of the Chicago School of Sociology, especially as represented by Robert Park and others. Denzin, who worked for several years with Lindesmith and Strauss on a social psychology textbook (Lindesmith, Strauss, & Denzin, 1975), reworked this idea for contemporary times and saw its relevance to policy research. He wrote, *"The perspectives and experiences of those persons who are served by applied programs must be grasped, interpreted, and understood, if solid, effective applied programs are to be created"* (p. 12, emphasis in original). A third strategy is to convey how researchers analyzed the data so that readers can understand how researchers arrived at their conclusions. Constantly comparing emerging findings across and within cases and searching for "negative cases" and "alternative hypotheses" (p. 230) all are important to delineate. Above all, integrating the theoretical statements with evidence helps in conveying credibility.

Finally, Glaser and Strauss (1967) recognize the mutual responsibilities of researchers and their audiences. Researchers have the responsibility to convey findings as clearly as they can, including specifying how they arrived at their theoretical statements. Readers have the responsibility not only of demanding such evidence but also of making "the necessary corrections, adjustments, invalidations and inapplications when thinking about or using the theory" (p. 232). These researchers, therefore, made modest claims for their theories, seeing them as provisional and subject to interpretations and applications by others.

In *Theoretical Sensitivity*, Glaser (1978) again discussed the evaluation of grounded theory, which he said is to be judged on fit, relevance, modifiability, and whether it works. Fit means whether or not abstract statements and concepts are congruent with the evidence. Refitting the theory to ever-emerging understandings as the research continues is part of the assessment. Thus, concepts and theory are not borrowed, but they "earn" a place in the emerging theory (p. 4). Findings become relevant when researchers allow emergence to happen and do not impose preconceived ideas onto them or do not shape findings to fit preformulations. Like other qualitative methodologists, such as Thomas and Znaniecki (1918–1920/1927), discussed earlier, Glaser viewed all findings as modifiable as new understandings emerge. Modifiability, in fact, is a standard by which Glaser believes theory could fruitfully be evaluated. Theory that has fit, relevance, and modifiability will also "work;" that is, it "should be able to explain what happened, predict what will happen and interpret what is happening" (p. 4).

Guidelines for evaluating the theory generated by qualitative methods, then, were important to Glaser and to Strauss. Their views are based on grounded theory, which has much in common with other methods and methodologies, but there also are differences between approaches. These variations in approaches are to be taken into account if the many kinds of qualitative research are to be evaluated fairly. I will discuss some of these other guidelines for evaluation later in this chapter.

Other Influences on Qualitative Family Researchers

As important as analytic induction and the legacies of Strauss and Glaser may be, there are strands of qualitative family research that may not have been directly influenced by the Chicago School of Sociology. These include ethnomethodology (Holstein & Gubrium, 1994), critical theory (Comstock, 1982; Lather, 1991; Morrow, 1994; Osmond, 1987), qualitative family therapy research (Sprenkle & Moon, 1996), narrative theory (Bruner, 1990; Riessman, 1993; Rosenwald & Ochberg, 1992; Smith, 1993; Stivers, 1993), and some forms of feminist research (Reinharz, 1992). Many of the foundational ideas for these approaches to qualitative family research were developed during these middle years and are only now beginning to be actualized in qualitative family research. An exception is some feminist qualitative family research reminiscent of the Chicago School that flourished during these middle years in studies already cited (e.g., Komarovsky, 1940, 1962; Lopata, 1971, 1973, 1979, 1984, 1985, 1992a, 1996; Rubin, 1976; Stack, 1974) and is flourishing today. These approaches to qualitative family research will be discussed in more detail later in this chapter.

A classic naturalistic study that has had a major influence on family therapy research is Kantor and Lehr's (1975) analysis of family processes. This is one of the few databased research projects where the qualitative methods used are named and delineated. Kantor and Lehr did participant observation with 19 families, aiming for as much detail as possible with a limited number of families. They used multiple qualitative methods for gathering data, including, other than participant observation, interviews, tape recording, videotapes, and self-reports of thoughts, perceptions, and feelings of family members while they were engaged in behaviors observed by researchers. They also used the Thematic Apperception Test. This qualitative study of the family resulted in a theory of family process that was quickly integrated into the theory and practice of family therapy. The concepts of open, closed, and random family types and the family's use of space, time, and energy, and distance regulation models, all developed through qualitative methods, have become fundamental concepts in the understanding of families. The use of more than one method of data collection enhanced the quality of the findings. This study is a model study of qualitative research on families; it is a model because of its thoroughness, use of multiple methods, and the quality and generativity of the theory it produced. This research is in the spirit of the Chicago School of Sociology.

The End of an Era and the Beginning of Another

I date the end of the middle years and the beginning of a new era as happening in 1985 with the publication of LaRossa and Wolf's 5(1985) "On Qualitative Family Research." This article is significant in the history of qualitative family research and may have signaled the influence of the postmodernist methodological pluralism that was emerging in other disciplines. After examining articles appearing in *Journal of Marriage and the Family* (*JMF*) spanning almost 20 years (1965–1983), LaRossa and Wolf (1985) concluded that "qualitative family research is not taken seriously by [contemporary] family researchers" while, historically, they noted, it was "central" to the development of family studies (p. 538).

The article was a revision of a paper LaRossa and Wolf had presented the year before at the Pre-Conference Workshop on Theory Construction and Research Methodology at the National Council on Family Relations (NCFR). The warm reception this paper received indicated the high interest qualitative methods held for family scholars. Encouraged by such a reception, LaRossa founded the Qualitative Family Research Network, which meets yearly at NCFR conferences as a focus group of the Research and Theory Section. Interdisciplinary from the start, within 7 years the Network had about 400 members with no advertisment of its existence, but developing through word of mouth. Members keep in touch through a newsletter called *Qualitative Family Research*, through phone calls and letters, and, in the 1990s, through e-mail.

Encouraging each other and gaining enthusiasm for their research goals and the methods that helped them to reach their goals, members planned symposia and paper presentations for the Pre-Conference Workshop and during the regular conference program. The book *Qualitative Methods in Family Research*, which I edited with Kerry Daly and Gerald Handel (1992), was a project of the Network, financed with seed money from the Network, and which to date receives a portion of the book's royalties.

There were other direct outcomes of LaRossa and Wolf's (1985) article. LaRossa (1988) edited a special issue of *The Journal of Contemporary Ethnography* on qualitative family research, a collection of research reports based on observations, interviews, and written documents using a variety of perspectives. In his introductory article, LaRossa noted that Form (1987), editor of the *American Sociological Review* (*ASR*), had invited submissions of qualitative manuscripts and stated that they "would be taken seriously and given a fair review" (p. 243). Although, to date, few qualitative pieces appear in *ASR*, such a situation has many possible causes, including lack of training opportunities for both reviewers and researchers; an underappreciation of research that emphasizes meaning, understanding, and experience; and the relatively small number of qualitative research projects compared to positivistic, qualitative projects.

Demos (1990) followed up on LaRossa and Wolf's (1985) assessment of qualitative pieces and shifted perspectives to examine *JMF* from 1939 to 1987 for its studies of African American families. He found what he labeled "underrepresentation of qualitative approaches" (p. 609), which reflected the overall underrepresentation of qualitative pieces in family journals. Coincidental or not with the scarcity of qualitative studies, Nye (1988) noted little use of theory in empirical research appearing in 50 years of *JMF*. As is evident, many forms of qualitative research have as their main purpose the generation of theory, and they use theory to guide research procedures.

The Middle Years: A Summary

During these middle years when qualitative methods were eclipsed by deductive, positivistic research based on probability theory and statistics, a relatively small group of sociologists, anthropologists, and methodologists carried on the traditions begun in the earlier part of the century at the University of Chicago. Not only did they produce work that is the foundation for many contemporary theories, but these researchers continued to develop the methods and methodologies that originated in the early years. They elaborated upon inductive methods, explicitly recognized the role of researchers' subjectivities and the centrality of the subjective aspects of informants' experiences, and were characteristically emancipatory in intent. Some, like Wax (1971) and Lindesmith (1947), became advocates for social causes as a result of their investigations.

Many were strong proponents of methodological pluralism, although some, like Handel, were puzzled by the relatively small scope of some of the quantitative research of his contemporaries. Many were explicitly devoted to the development of theory that fit data, that was relevant and modifiable, and that did what theory has some usefulness for—explanation and prediction. Universalistic causal theory was not the goal of these researchers; rather, they recognized the bounded nature of human understanding and often encouraged the modification of theory to fit and illuminate particular situations.

Glaser and Strauss (1967) are among the best-known methodologists to emerge from that period, possibly because they and their colleagues presented a way of analyzing qualitative data and of making theoretical sense of it. Other researchers, although less explicit about their methods and methodologies, continued to do inductive family research. During the middle years and earlier, like today, researchers must have access to procedures that help them to apply ideas to research projects. The work of Glaser and Strauss has been a major source of guidance for contemporary qualitative family research. Had there been more widespread attention to the 1967 book and to Glaser's (1978) *Theoretical Sensitivity*, contemporary family theory would be much different. Glaser and Strauss built upon a long tradition stemming from and filtering through the Chicago School of Sociology.

Finally, when researchers such as LaRossa and Wolf (1985) pointed out the neglect of qualitative methods in family research, the responses of the scholarly community were strongly positive. Encouragement abounded. As I will show in the next section, training continues to lag but is gaining ground.

The Postmodern Pastiche

In our own day, the whirlwind of discussions of methodological, epistemological, ethical, and ontological aspects of research are harbingers that qualitative family research again is in the ascendence. Accompanying these spectacular philosophical and methodological changes is the ongoing use of interviewing, observation, and document analysis practices that have been with us since the origins of sociological research, as discussed earlier. In fact, these methods and the procedures of data analysis and interpretation are the nuts and bolts of qualitative research. Ontologies, ethics, and epistemologies give research direction, scope, and perspectives, but methods bring these philosophical issues to life.

The guiding principle for this part of the chapter is the centrality of the *doing* of qualitative research. Subjectivity, induction, and emancipation continue to be issues in contemporary qualitative research. Given the diversity of qualitative approaches now available, even within critical and interpretive paradigms (Schwandt, 1994), methodological pluralism is characteristic of contemporary times.

No More Ignorance about Philosophical Underpinnigs of Method

Today it is nearly impossible to remain naive about the philosophical and methodological underpinnings of the various qualitative research methods. There are far too many relevant texts raising our consciousness about ontologies, ethics, epistemologies, and methodologies for any researcher to ignore them. For example, the best-selling *Handbook of Qualitative Research* (Denzin & Lincoln, 1994) says practically nothing about research methods but bulges with chapters on ontologies, epistemologies, and methodologies relevant to qualitative research. Particularly compelling chapters for raising awareness of the philosophical contexts of contemporary qualitative research are Olesen's (1994) chapter on feminism; Guba and Lincoln (1994) on competing paradigms; Schwandt (1994) on constructivist, interpretivist approaches; and Holstein and Gubrium (1994) on ethnomethodology.

Other texts that are raising awareness include Dreyfus (1991) on Heidegerrian hermeneutics, Polkinghorne (1983) on methodologies for human sciences, Harding (1987, 1991) and Fine (1992, 1994) on feminist methodologies and epistemologies, Lather (1991) on feminist postmodernism and critical theory, Baber and Allen (1992) on feminist postmodernism and families, Rosenau (1992) on postmodernism, and Morrow (1994) on the methodology of critical theory. Although focused on ethnography, the edited volume of Clifford and Marcus (1986), *Writing Culture*, has had a major transdisciplinary influence, centered as it is on the writing of texts: who writes them, who and what the text represents, and the methods of writing. This is only a sampling of the outpouring of texts that challenge conventional thinking about approaches to research. Many others are noteworthy. A range of journals have had an impact on thinking about philosophical issues and will continue to do so. A few of them are *Signs*, *Symbolic Interactionism*, *Qualitative Health Research*, and *Qualitative Inquiry*.

Transformed forever, I hope, is the style of research training that avoided discussing the philosophical underpinnings of research methods and methodologies. There is far too much being written to allow such narrowness of vision. Hopefully today's students are learning the differences between induction and deduction, probabilistic and analytic generalizability, interpretive and positivistic research, critical emancipatory research, and "pure" research. It is more likely now than ever that students are exposed to choices about how they might conduct their research. Given the current philosophical discussions, it may be routine a few years hence to ask Ph.D. students about the paradigms in which they are operating, not only when students are doing qualitative work, but also when they are doing large-scale surveys or experimental or quasi-experimental designs. Perhaps this will be routine in journal articles, books, and public and private presentations of research as well.

Disconnections. As significant as this outpouring of new ways to think about research may be, there is a serious downside. Researchers who do not already know something about the procedures of qualitative research can become confused about what to do with these generative ideas. Few of the aforementioned texts and few journals articles link their philosophical discussions with specific procedures on how to do research. The connections between methods, methodologies, epistemologies, ethics, and ontologies, for many of today's researchers, may be experienced as fragments. The fragments are elusive, like flocks of butterflies. How explicitly to connect methods with ontologies, epistemologies, and methodologies is a major challenge facing many of today's researchers.

Making sense of this unruly flock of terms related to qualitative methods is daunting. Some, but certainly not all, of the terms currently attached to styles of qualitative research include grounded theory, phenomenology, ethnography, ethnoscience, cultural studies, semiotics, discourse analysis, conversation analysis, analytic induction, social constructionism, constructivism, symbolic constructivism, interpretive phenomenology, interpretivism, feminist empiricism, deconstructionism, postmodernism, poststructuralism, postpositivism, feminist standpointism, feminist postmodernism, heremeneutics, critical theory, reflexivity, participant observation, domain analysis, interpretive interactionism, sensitizing concepts, ehtnomethodology, praxis, emancipation, constant comparative method, negative case analysis, theoretical sampling, axial coding, open coding, dimensional analysis, subjectivism, new objectivity, cultural analysis, genealogy, methods, methodologies, ontologies, ethics, epistemologies, narrative analysis, *in vivo* codes, *in situ* codes, human sciences, historical realism, relativism, pragmatism, *verstehen*, meaning-making, positivism, induction, deduction, lived experience, and paradigm cases. This is chaos. Chaos is a defining quality of postmodernism. Organizing and making sense of all these terms will take the lifetimes of several scholars.

Given time, effort, and study, this flock of terms possibly could be rounded up and organized under relatively few rubrics, such as postpositivism, social constructivism, and

critical theory, three orientations to social research, or paradigms of social research. Social scientists Yvonna Lincoln and Egon Guba (Guba, 1990; Guba & Lincoln, 1994; Denzin & Lincoln, 1994; Lincoln & Guba, 1985) and feminist philosophers and methodologists (Baber & Allen, 1992; Fine, 1992, 1994; Harding, 1987; Lather, 1991; Thompson, 1992), among others, have popularized these terms and in so doing have taken leadership in discussing paradigm issues in social research. They have alerted research communities to the centrality of ontologies, epistemologies, ethics, and methodologies to social research.

Making the Connections: Interpretive Phenomenology. A few texts on qualitative family research are meeting the challenge of encompassing the intellectual contexts of the conduct of research; that is, they are successful in discussing method, methodologies, epistemologies, ethics, and ontologies. Exemplary in this regard is the work of Benner (1994) and her students on interpretive phenomenology. Benner appears to have made the connections between her practical interest in promoting the health and well-being of nursing patients and the massive project of delineating not only a philosophical base for interpretive phenomenology but also the specific methods and methodologies that will actualize interpretive phenomenology.

Benner, a professor of nursing at the University of California–San Francisco, has developed an approach that is different from grounded theory (personal communication, 1992). Benner's interpretive phenomenology seeks to convey lived experience and what it means to be human, presented in research reports through straightforward categories and theoretical statements that are inductively derived. She sees interpretive phenomenology as a scholarly discipline that provides perspectives that can promote understanding of everyday practices and meanings. The research enterprises of such disciplines as nursing, clinical psychology, family therapy, and social work, guided by ethics of caring and responsiveness, may find philosophical homes in the ontologically oriented interpretive phenomenology. Benner's students are beginning their research careers, and among them are qualitative family researchers SmithBattle (1993, 1994, 1995, 1996), Plager (1994), and Chesla (Chesla, 1994, 1995).

Lee SmithBattle's brief history of her career as a student summarizes a great deal of information about training in interpretive phenomenology, underlying principles, and their implications for the practice of this type of research:

> I studied with Pat Benner (1994) at the University of California, San Francisco, School of Nursing. Pat had several classes on interpretive phenomenology. We had some classes where we read and discussed the philosophical background and issues of interpretive phenomenology, and we had other classes that were devoted to analysis of data. I as well as

many of her other students had the opportunity to be research assistants on research she was conducting. These experiences were invaluable.

We also had quite a bit of course work at University of California at Berkeley with Hubert Dreyfus (1991) on early and late Heidegger, with Jane Rubin (1988) whose work on Kierkegaard was relevant to my work, and also with Martin Packer (Packer, 1985; Packer & Addison, 1989). So Pat's students had incredibly rich resources for studying the philosophical underpinnigs of interpretive research and doing analysis as well (SmithBattle, personal communication, 1996).

Being an Interpretive Phenomenologist.   In much of my work, I am an interpretive phenomenologist (distinctive from Husserlian phenomenologists). Interpretive phenomenologists seek to understand lives, events, situations, or texts as lived out or as always situated by our concerns and by meanings available to us in the practices and social customs we learn by virtue of being members and participants of families, communities, nations, and epochs.

The point of interpretive work is to understand the lives, events, situations, or texts that are studied, which requires understanding the background conditions and meanings that situate activities and contextualize the self. I particularly like Wax's (1971) definition of understanding:

> Understanding … does not refer to a mysterious empathy between human beings. Nor does it refer to an intuitive or rationalistic ascription of motivations. instead, it is a social phenomenon—a phenomenon of shared meanings. Thus, a fieldworker who approaches a strange people soon perceives that these people are saying and doing things which they understand but he does not understand. One of the strangers may make a particular gesture, whereupon all the other strangers laugh. They share in the understanding of what the gesture means, but the fieldworker does not. When he does share it, he begins to "understand." He possesses a part of the "insider's" view. (p. 11)

Getting insiders' perspectives is what interpretive researchers strive for and is just as relevant to studying families, communities, practices (e.g., nursing, teaching, mothering, etc.), or different epochs, as well as different cultures. So the goal is to understand people's lives or actions as they themselves understand their lives and actions, rather than imposing an "outsider" perspective that misconstrues and obscures (SmithBattle, personal communication, 1996).

SmithBattle's description of interpretive phenomenology shows its roots in human sciences traditions and thus its kinship with the origins of qualitative family research. What she does not say is that she is in an applied discipline and that the information she is gathering is not being done simply because it is interesting or because it contributes to theory, both of which are good reasons to do research and are true for hers. In her own case, she also has the goal of improving the lives of adolescent mothers, their children, and the mothers of the adolescent mothers. Within interpretive phenomenology, therefore, there is an emancipatory thrust.

Discussions of the philosophical groundings of research methods in general and those used in family research in particular are so new that except for researchers trained in a particular paradigms, such as Benner's students, trained in a type of interpretive phenomenology, most qualitative family researchers are inching their way toward more integrated research. Even the ongoing use of the term *qualitative* in this essay suggests that I and many of my contemporaries are equating styles of research with a term that designates the kind of data we gather. At some future time, the term *qualitative* may become outmoded and be replaced by other terms. Presently, the term *qualitative* has many possible meanings, such as interpretive, phenomenological, social constructivist, and critical. Positivist qualitative research also is possible. The term *qualitative* may be here to stay because it is a blanket term that covers so many possible ways of doing research that involve language and that do not involve quantification.

Ongoing Elaborations of Qualitative Approaches

Benner's (1994) interpretive phenomenology is one of many examples of contemporary, ongoing elaborations of qualitative approaches. Some of the other styles of research that family scholars currently use are elaborations are grounded theory and analytic induction, ethnomethodology, feminist theory, critical theory, family therapy research, and textual analysis. These styles of research often are overlapping, but each has its own distinctive qualities that contribute unique perspectives. Some are connected to Chicago Sociology while others are not. As Glaser (1978) stated more than 2 decades ago, we need all possible perspectives in our research quests.

Grounded Theory.   From the middle 1960s to the present, students of Glaser, Strauss, and Schatzman, among others, joined the effort to define grounded theory (e.g., Charmaz, 1975, 1990; Daly, 1995; Fagerhaugh, 1975; Gilgun, 1992b,d; 1994d; Quint, 1966, 1967; Reif, 1975; Stern, 1980, 1985; Strauss & Corbin, 1990; Wiener, 1975, among many others). Some responded to the perception of an underrepresentation of "lived experience" (Wilson & Hutchinson, 1991), constructivist perspectives (Charmaz, 1990), and feminist perspectives (Wuest, 1995) in grounded theory and proposed modifications. Daly (1995) made the cogent point that although theory is the expected product of grounded theory research, a full accounting of the development of theory may require a depiction of the roles of researchers' selves in theory development. Grounded theory, then, is robust today and is influencing the conduct of qualitative family research.

Scholarly journals publishing nursing research are particularly receptive to many forms of qualitative research, including grounded theory, while other disciplines apparently are lagging. From 1990 to 1995, for example, the database CINAHL, which tracks nursing and allied health journals, logged a range of 74 to 106 articles using grounded theory methods. This represents a tripling of the number of articles using grounded theory during the 1980s. In contrast, Sociofile, a database logging articles in sociologically oriented journals, listed a range of 7 to 17 articles for each year of the 1990s. Some of the journals indexed in Sociofile also are indexed in CINAHL; the Sociofile numbers, then, are conflated with those of CINAHL. Sociologically oriented disciplines, then, are lagging behind nursing researchers in their use of grounded theory methods.

Analytic Induction. Analytic induction, a form of qualitative analysis that is linked to and predates grounded theory, as the earlier discussion demonstrates, appears only rarely as a method of social research, possibly because it has been overshadowed by the work of Strauss and his colleagues on grounded theory (e.g., Glaser, 1992; Glaser & Strauss, 1967; Strauss, 1987; Strauss & Corbin, 1990, 1994). For example, during the 11 years between 1974 and 1995, Sociofile recorded 10 instances of the use of analytic induction as a method; all but a few were on methodological issues, and none were on family issues. This database, however, did not record subsequently published contemporary uses of analytic induction of which I am aware. Subsequently published were my article on incest perpetrators (Gilgun, 1995b) and the work of Rettig, Tam, and Magistad (1996), who used a form of analytic induction in their study of justice principles in child support guidelines.

Transcendental Phenomenology. Moustakas (1994) explicated transcendental phenomenological research based on Husserl's (1931, 1977) transcendental phenomenology. The three volumes of *The Duquense Studies in Phenomenological Psychology* (Giorgi, Fischer, & von Eckartsberg, 1971; Giorgi, Fischer, & Murray, 1975; Giorgi, Knowles, & Smith, 1979) contain a series of examples of this kind of research. Practitioners of interpretive phenomenology see their work as quite different from transcendental phenomenology. According to Moustakas, transcendental phenomenology "emphasizes subjectivity" and seeks to discover "the essences of experience and provides a systematic and disciplined methodology for derivation of knowledge" (p. 45). "Transcendental" refers to the possibility of "a completely unbiased and presuppositionless state" (p. 60). Associated terms include intentionality, *noema, noesis, epoche*, bracketing, phenomenological reduction, imaginative variation, and textual-structural synthesis.

The process of doing transcendental phenomenological research involves in-depth interviewing as the primary method, analyzing data in clusters that have meanings in common, identification of variations on themes, portraying the themes through excerpts from the interviews, and creating a structural synthesis, which involves searching for the core meanings or essence of the experience (Patton, 1990). When the abstract terms of transcendental phenomenology are broken down into research operations, transcendental phenomenology has some procedures in common with both interpretive phenomenology and grounded theory. Regarding the claims of lack of bias and prior conceptualizations, Glaser (1978) remarked, in *Theoretical Sensitivity*, that "immaculate conceptions are not necessary" (p. 8), a stance that has echoed over the ages among interpretive researchers. The term "transcendent," however, might appeal to Glaser, as he used it himself to describe how grounded theory transcends data.

Ethnomethodology. Ethnomethodology (Atkinson, 1988; Garfinkel, 1967) originated during the middle years and is achieving prominence today as a method of qualitative family research. Ethnomethodology's focus is on persons' interpretations of how they apply, bend, or disregard social values, rules, and sanctions in their explanations of their behaviors and decisions. According to Holstein and Gubrium (1994), the data of ethnomethodology are talk, or human discourse. Variable in terms of how ethnomethodology includes context in its analysis, the range is from ethnographic studies that look at the situated nature of discourse to forms of conversational analysis that often involves micro-analyses whose links to context may be unarticulated.

Garfinkel (1967), the originator of ethnomethodology, was termed "a renegade student" of Talcott Parsons by Lynch and Peyrot (1992, p. 113). Garfinkel developed ethnomethodology as an alternative to Parsons' theory of social action. For Garfinkel, Parsons' action theory was inadequate in that it assumed that human beings responded to "external forces" and were "motivated by internalized directives and imperatives" (Holstein & Gubrium, 1994, p.264). Garfinkel, on the other hand, saw human beings as engaged in ongoing interpretive process, actively creating social institutions and the social order in particular contexts, a point similar to that of Strauss et al. (1964) in their theory of negotiated order. Ethnomethodological researchers suspend "all commitments to an a priori or privileged version of social structure, focusing instead on how members accomplish, manage, and reproduce a *sense* of social structure" (Holstein & Gubrium, 1994, p. 264). In sum, ethnomethodological research seeks to describe how human beings "account for the order in their everyday lives" (p. 264).

Gubrium and Holstein have taken the lead in applying

enthnomethodology to family discourse in a variety of settings, while Gale and Chenail have taken creative approaches to the study of family discourse in clinical settings. Among the studies of Gubrium and Holstein is *Where Is Family?* (Gubrium & Holstein, 1990), which examines how family is enacted through language in a variety of organizational settings, such as nursing homes, caregiver support groups, and courtrooms. In a review article, they demonstrate in several ways how ethnomethodology can be applied to family discourse (Gubrium & Holstein, 1993). Gale analyzes the discourse of family therapy (Gale, 1991; Gale & Newfield, 1992), as does family therapist Chenail and his colleagues (Chenail, 1991; Chenail & Fortugno, 1995; Chenail et al., 1990, 1993; Morris & Chenail, 1995).

Ethnomethodology does not appear to have a specific method of how to do research; it, instead, is more a methodology that includes a sketchy ontology and epistemology. Data are analyzed and interpreted through primarily inductive processes. The ideas of constructed realities and the centrality of processes of human interpretation appear to be driving principles in ethnomethodological research. Researchers within the ethnomethodological tradition are creating methods that are consistent with the philosophical principles of ethnomethodology.

Feminist Methodologies. Feminist qualitative family research, like interpretive phenomenology and ethnomethodology, is undergoing rapid development in contemporary times. Underpinning contemporary discussions are generative ideas present in articles published in feminist journals founded during the middle years—such as *Signs, Feminist Studies, Gender & Society, Psychology of Women Quarterly,* and *Women's Studies International Quarterly*—and in major feminist books such as Bernard (1981), Bleier (1984), Chodorow (1978), Dobash and Dobash (1979), Gilligan (1982), Hochschild (1983), Hooks (1981, 1984), Komarovsky (1940, 1962), Lipman-Blumen (1984), Oakley (1974), Rossi and Calderwood (1973), Stanley and Wise (1983), and Thorne and Yalom (1982). These writings focus on the meanings of gender and its relationship to power, seek the points of view of women, and intend that their research be emancipatory, that is, to change social conditions, so that women can participate more fully in social life. Fine pointed out that many of today's feminist researchers attempt to avoid a stance of dominance toward informants, and she elaborated upon the challenges, contradictions, and compromises involved in doing so.

Feminist research is part of a reformist tradition, and many feminist researchers claim Jane Addams as their forbear (Deegan, 1990). Feminist social work researchers also claim reformists Edith Abbott and Sophinisba Breckinridge (Abbott, 1910, 1950; Abbott & Breckinridge, 1916), who were associates of Jane Addams and whose work was in the Chicago style. The origins of feminism and an ongoing source of its energy and vision are reformist, working at grassroots levels on behalf of women and social change.

There is a considerable range of thought on which methods might best fit a feminist agenda (Osmond & Thorne, 1993; Reinharz, 1992; Thompson, 1992). Like ethnomethodology, feminist methodologies do not have a specific set of procedures for data collection and interpretation, and the general consensus is that there is nothing inherently feminist about the method; rather, researchers' ontologies, epistemologies, and methodologies create the *feminism* in feminist research. Feminist research enjoys methodological pluralism, although feminist postmodernism (Baber & Allen, 1992) most likely will be articulated in research methods that are flexible, allow researchers to be in close contact with informants, and permit analyses that show the intersection of individual lives with cultural themes and practices. Reflexivity is a major issue in contemporary feminist qualitative family research (Gilgun, 1995; Hall & Zvonkovic, 1996; Sollie & Leslie, 1994; Stacey, 1990). Many feminist researchers situate themselves within a critical theory perspective (cf. Fine, 1988, 1992, 1994; Lather, 1991).

Although contemporary journals that are not specifically feminist, such as *JMF*, have published some qualitative feminist research (e.g., Blaisure & Allen, 1995; Gilgun, 1995), feminist journals, such as *Gender & Society*, have offered space to many contemporary examples of qualitative feminist family research. Typical recent issues contain two or more qualitative pieces out of an average of five featured articles. Some of the more recent articles include topics such as men in childcare (Murray, 1996), meanings of childcare (Uttal, 1996), and women's multiple work strategies (Wright, 1996).

The collection I edited with Marvin Sussman (Gilgun & Sussman, 1996) contains several different types of feminist qualitative family research, including Walker's (1996) interpretive study of letters 18 women wrote to each other annually for 25 years. The stories in these letters connect the private and public worlds; they communicate the events experienced, things hoped for, and things not done. Other feminist reports in the collection include Farnsworth's (1996) reflexive account of maternal bereavement, Holbrook's (1996) emancipatory study of the journal of a welfare mother, Hall and Zvonkovic (1996) on the effects of research on researchers, Hanawalt (1996) on a composite biography of a woman in medieval London, and Olsen's (1996) interviews of middle-class African American adolescent young women.

Contemporary book-length qualitative feminist research receives wide recognition. For example, Martha McMahon's (1995) study of women's perspectives on engendering motherhood recently won two awards: one from the

National Council on Family Relations and the other from the Sex and Gender Section of the American Sociological Association. Judith Stacey's (1990) work on late twentieth century families is foundational in contemporary feminist family studies. Feminist research based on numbers and statistical analysis not only can be done but is important (cf. Reinharz, 1992). In the future, however, it is highly likely that we will see an exponential increase in the numbers of feminist studies using qualitative methods.

Critical Theory. Critical theory originated in the early decades of this century and is developing rapidly today. The analysis of social power and the necessity of social change are core ideas in critical theory (Morrow, 1994; Osmond, 1987). Not only can feminism, with its focus on gender, power, and social change, be linked to critical theory (Lanther, 1991; Osmond & Thorne, 1993), but so can social work with its core idea of social change.

The practitioners of critical theory seek both to understand and to change social conditions, and they specifically analyze structures and processes of social power from the points of view of those who are oppressed (Comstock, 1982; Lather, 1991; Morgaine, 1992a, 1994; Morrow, 1994). Robert Park might have approved of some of the tenets of the unabashedly reformist critical theory. Park, as discussed earlier, criticized "do-gooders" for their paternalism, but he sought to understand persons in situations from their points of view, and he saw knowledge as the pathway to human liberation.

Critical theorists attempt to be on the same plane as oppressed individuals and, through dialogue, in the words of Morrow (1994), to "construct a coherent account of the understandings" individuals have of "their world" (p. 380). Dialogue also plays a part in the action-oriented aspects of critical theory, where critical theorists educate individuals about the social conditions under which they live. Social reform comes not from critical theorists but from the actions of oppressed persons (Morgaine, 1994).

The origins of critical theory is associated with the Frankfurt Institute for Social Research, founded in 1923. Nine years later Hitler forced its theorists into exile. While contemporary critical theory claims a wide range of roots, from neo-Weberian conflict theory to neo-Marxist theory, critical theory is Marxist in origin (Morrow, 1994). In the 1960s and 1970s, influenced by Weber, phenomenology, and hermeneutics, Habermas (1971) and Giddens (1971)—neither of whom consider themselves within a Marxian tradition—revised critical theory (Morrow, 1994, p. 110). Reflexivity—that is, reflection—on social forces, ideologies, and institutions that are oppressive is a fundamental idea in critical methodology and fits well with phenomenological methodologies as they are discussed today.

Dollard's (1937) reflections on his experience researching for *Caste and Class in a Southern Town* is a precursor of the type of reflexivity that is part of critical theory's method. Osmond (1987) cited Lasch (1977), Zaretsky (1976), Donzelot (1977), the Red Collective (1978), Gordon (1977), Barry (1979), Carmody (1979), Laws (1979), and Janeway (1980) as examples of critical theory. For the most part, these researchers depended a great deal on interviews, document analysis, and reflections on the social order.

The influence of critical theory in contemporary qualitative family research is in its beginning stages, appearing, for example, in Fine's (1988) evaluation of a sex education program and in the work of Morgaine (1992a,b; 1994) on family life education. Osmond (1987), as discussed earlier, critiqued family studies for its normative focus and offers radical-critical theory as a road map toward looking at all aspects of family life in terms of power relations, both within the family and between the family and other social institutions.

The research methods of critical theory are largely undelineated, with Barton (1971), Comstock (1982), Eichler (1981), Morgaine (1994), and Morrow (1994) offering some guidance. Morrow stated that the methods most strongly associated with critical theory involve comparative analysis, the application of general theories of history, and the "analysis of causal regularities" (p. 253). Comparative analyses of a small number of cases in contrast to large samples analyzed through statistics is emerging as an approach compatible with critical theory.

Morgaine (1994) used reflective, critical inquiry (Comstock, 1982; Friere, 1968/1986; Lather, 1991) as a method of developing a theory of self-formation. A method that involves inquiring into and reflecting upon the situations of others and of the self, critical inquiry as Morgaine practiced it followed Comstock's recommendations for the procedures of the research. The first step is the identification of an oppressed group or a group whose self-interest was being undercut by their own ideologies. In Morgaine's case, the group of interest was her own students, and her focus was their ideologies, which she viewed as interfering with their effectiveness in working with children and families. The second step is developing an understanding of the circumstances and perspectives of the group chosen. Dialogue and ongoing reflection on all aspects of the engagement with subjects characterize the process. Through reflection and dialogue, the critical theorist begins to identify emergent themes, and then examines the historical context of these themes, which is the third step. In Morgaine's study, she found power and saving face to be major themes among her students, and she consequently read widely about social power and subordination. Still following Comstock, she took the fourth step of creating an explanation for the belief systems of her students. Finally, she offered the explanations to her students, who began to change their views of themselves. Morgaine's identification of themes is similar to procedures in grounded theory analysis (Glaser & Strauss, 1967; Strauss, 1987; Strauss & Corbin, 1990).

Qualitative methods that seek insider perspectives are well suited to critical research, especially interviews, in light on the emphasis on dialogue. Document analysis, observation, and critical reflection are other methods that further the goals of critical theory. The *critical* in critical research comes from its philosophical base: Methods actualize the ideas, and the same methods can be used in other types of research whose purposes are quite different from those of critical theory.

Family Therapy. Qualitative methods are the unacknowledged underpinnings of theory development in family therapy. The theoretical foundation of contemporary family therapy is based on the formulations of gifted therapists who were in direct interaction with clients. A look at the writings of some of the major family therapy theorists, however, shows they did not discuss how they arrived at their formulations. Given the nature of the practice of family therapy, it is safe to state that these therapists developed their theories through participant observation, often supplemented by audiotapes and videotapes. What kind of observation, how long, how many families, and how data are collected and analyzed remained unstated and, undoubtedly, were not recorded systematically.

Several contemporary researchers have noted the congruence of many family therapy theories with methodologies associated with qualitative research (e.g., Gilgun, 1990b; Moon, Dillon, & Sprenkle, 1990; Sells, Smith, & Sprenkle, 1995). Although originating from many theoretical and methodological roots (Newmark & Beels, 1994), much of the theory of family therapy is broadly based on the work of anthropologist Gregory Bateson (1972) and systems theorist Bertalanffy (1968). Notions such as the significance of context, circular causality, the nonexistence of reality independent of the observer, and the reciprocal relationship of client and therapist (Gurman, Kniskern, & Pinsof, 1986) characterize family therapy.

This congruence is widely recognized and is likely to result in a great increase in the use of qualitative methods for research on family therapy. Doherty (Chapter 8, this volume) pointed out that family therapy moved toward postmodernism in the late 1980s, leading to an open field in terms of how to conduct qualitative family therapy research. To provide another perspective on contemporary qualitative family therapy, I invited Cynthia Franklin (Franklin, 1995, 1996a,b; Franklin & Jordan, 1995), a family therapist and an associate professor of social work at the University of Texas at Austin, to write a short overview especially for this chapter. This is what she wrote:

> The field of family therapy has endorsed both qualitative and quantitative methods of research. In the past decade, family

therapy researchers have increasingly called for an acceptance of qualitative research as well as an integration of qualitative and quantitative methods (Moon et al., 1990; Sells et al., 1995; Sprenkle & Bischoff, 1995). Half of a recent textbook on family therapy research (Sprenkle & Moon, 1996) is devoted to qualitative methods, although there are only a few examples of how it actually is done.

> Studies using qualitative methods are appearing in greater frequency in family therapy literature, and the approaches are diverse, including ethnographies (e.g., Newfield, Kuehl, Joanning, & Quinn, 1990; Sells, Smith, Coe, Yoshioka, & Robbins, 1994; Smith, Winston, & Yoshioka, 1992; Smith, Yoshioka, & Winston, 1993; Smith, Sells, & Clevenger, 1994), discourse and conversation analysis borrowing from ethnomethodology (e.g., Buttny, 1990; Buttny & Jensen, 1995; Chenail & Fortugno, 1995; Gale & Newfield, 1992), case studies using dialectical analysis (e.g., Franklin, 1996a; Keeney & Ross, 1985), Recursive Frame Analysis (e.g., Keeney, 1990; Keeney & Bobele, 1989), focus groups (e.g., Polson & Piercy, 1993), and phenomenology (Pollner & McDonald-Wilker, 1985, Stamp, 1991).

> Many family therapy researchers draw from a wide range of methodologies, epistemologies, and ontologies. Typical of this trend is the research of Newfield et al. (1990), who used ethnographic interviews (Spradley, 1979) to explore the perceptions of adolescent clients who participated in systemic family therapy in the context of substance abuse treatment. Systemic family therapies propose that reciprocity between therapists and clients is key to the therapy process. Attention to feedback from clients, however, is a neglected aspect of research on family therapy. The researchers based their interpretations on postmodern anthropology and radical constructivism, both of which consider "reality" more imagined than real. The scientist who believes he/she is objective actually confuses his/her own perceptions with what the client "really" feels.

> Another recent development is the growth of family therapy educational programs that emphasize qualitative research methods. Most programs teach qualitative as well as quantitative research, and some programs specialize in qualitative methods. Nova Southeastern University in Florida and the University of Iowa, for example, have research programs that prepare their Ph.D. students to be qualitative researchers.

Family therapy by nature is applied, and it can be considered emancipatory in that it seeks to liberate persons from oppressive patterns of interaction. Within family therapy research, there is recognition of subjectivist, constructivist dimensions of the experiences of both clients and practitioners, and the research often is based on inductive methods.

The Analysis of Texts. Much of the work currently being done in qualitative family research can be viewed as forms of textual analysis, a term associated with postmodernism. In the broadest sense, all qualitative research is an analysis of texts, when texts are defined as they usually are in postmodern writing; that is, as anything that can be interpreted, such as clothing, the fins of cars, cathedrals, radio towers, and mass media such as television, computer games, and radio programs (Barthes, 1974; Fiske, 1994; Gilgun,

1995a; Manning & Cullum-Swan, 1994; Noth, 1995). In general, however, textual analysis usually refers to studies of various types of written texts meant to deconstruct their significance. Synonyms for deconstruction include "unpacking" and "decoding," that is, the breaking down of texts to explore meanings, contradictions, connotations, relationships of images, and connotations to culture.

This inclusive definition is applicable to most forms of textual analysis, and there appear to be unlimited numbers of ways to analyze texts. I think of textual analysis as a huge and open field strewn with countless tools, objects, and other materials, metaphors for the plethora of methods, methodologies, epistemologies, and ontologies now available to researchers, as discussed earlier. Researchers can chose among these items and use them to construct their particular ways of conducting analyses of texts. For example, when talk comprises the text, then the method can be termed *discourse analysis*. Enthnomethodology, discussed earlier, is a form of discourse analysis. Textual analysis can be termed *narrative analysis* when the data can be construed as being composed of a story or story line. Cultural studies (Alasuutari, 1996; Denzin, 1995; Fiske, 1994; Schwartz, 1994) is another form of textual analysis that looks at how persons enact and create culture in particular settings and times.

There are a myriad of other choices within textual analysis. The purposes of textual analysis can be multiple, such as human emancipation, or expository so as to inform or to create new understandings through formulation of concepts and theories. In addition, researchers can choose from a range of ways to use concepts and theory in the analysis: the use of codes formulated by others (Barthes, 1974), grounded theory, analytic induction, and phenomenology. Researchers can share their responses to the text and disclose their relationships to informants, or they may not. Examples of family research that is unabashedly reflexive, that uses principles from cultural analysis, and that is based on narrative accounts are Steedman's (1991) biography of Margaret McMillan, a pioneer in nursery education, and Hamabata's (1993) reflexive, postmodern ethnography of wealthy Japanese families.

Understandably, practitioners generally avoid defining textual analysis, possibly because of the range of types and the overlapping and amorphous boundaries of types. For instance, researchers can do a discourse analysis of a story that involves linking the particularities of the story to wider cultural themes and practices. This at once is narrative, discourse, and cultural analysis. If researchers break the text into units and then analyze the units for the connotations of words and particularizations of the wider culture, this can be considered a narrative, semiotic, deconstructionist, postmodern discourse analysis. Finally, if the researcher's purpose is to bring about some kind of social reform, then *emancipatory* is yet another term that can accurately describe some aspects of the research.

Textual analysis, like feminist research, critical theory, and ethnomethodology, can be infused with many combinations of methodologies, epistemologies, and ontologies. The *textuality* of a piece of research arises from the perspectives researchers impose on their subject matter.

Narrative Analysis. Narrative analysis is increasingly discussed in the social sciences; it also is receiving a great deal of attention as an approach to family therapy (Freedman & Combs, 1996; Gilligan & Price, 1993; White & Epston, 1990), but less so as a form of family therapy research. Story is the central metaphor in narrative theory, but the approach is composed of diverse traditions, from the near atheoretical and practical approaches of oral histories to the methodologically dense discussions in feminist writings (Smith, 1993; Stivers, 1993) to the constructivist versions of psychologists and philosophers (Bruner, 1990; Manning & Cullum-Swan, 1994; McCabe & Peterson, 1991; Mischler, 1990; Singer & Salovey, 1993) and the social constructivist, emancipatory versions of Riessman (1990, 1993, 1994) and McLaughlin and Tierney (1993).

Martin's (1995) oral history project on African American families of the rural south provides an example of applications of narrative analysis to the understanding of family life over time. Oral history in particular, but other many forms of narrative research as well, offer opportunities to give voice to the "voiceless," that is, to persons whose experiences and interests are not well represented in social science, such as poor rural African Americans or women with HIV/AIDS. Some researchers who are proponents of narrative analysis are frankly emancipatory in intent. LeCompte (1993), for instance, stated that giving voice to the voiceless is important because silenced persons provide views that are "counter-hegemonic" (p. 10). Emancipation in narrative research can be personal as well. Jago's (1996) personal account of her father's abandonment, in her words, "helped me confront my personal demons and transform my family story" (p. 514), although she also demonstrated the methodological point of how stories can be revised over time.

The semiotic, poststructuralist analytic approach of Roland Barthes (1974), whose method I replicated in a study of family murder (Gilgun, 1995a), discussed earlier, is a form of narrative analysis, where the text is broken and deconstructed. Semiotics, a form of textual analysis, is a study of signs and what signs signify. Signs constitute texts. I chose the written text that I analyzed from transcripts of several months' worth of interviewing. I guided my choice of text partially by how the pieces of a man's account contributed to the temporal, narrative flow of a story, with a beginning, middle, and end. Barthes' five codes, which provide a fluid structure to the analysis, guided me toward an analysis of how culture, individual behavior, and experience intersect on the connotations of language and on the bounded actions of narrators. Semiotics, however, ranges far more widely than focusing on written texts and includes the study of anything that can be interpreted, including the fins of cars, paintings, and music (Noth, 1995). Narrative analysis, then, like textual analysis more generally, can be created in any number of guises, depending upon the researchers' philosophical and methodological approaches.

Cultural Studies. The focus of cultural studies is on how persons create or enact particularized cultural themes and practices (Denzin, 1995). Human beings are assumed to have various degrees of agency. An additional assumption is that the particularized meanings are ever-shifting and conflictual (Fiske, 1994). Fiske and others view the term *cultural studies* as "contested and currently trendy" (p. 189) and do not define it. Although there are many styles of doing cultural studies (Schwartz, 1994), practitioners generally view human beings as not passive recipients of culture but as persons who actively shape, interpret, give meaning to, repress, and transcend their experiences and socialization. Texts that contain stories are the usual focus of analysis. Theory can be but is not necessarily a product of cultural studies (Alasuutari, 1996). Conceptual frameworks associated with cultural studies include feminist poststructuralism, neo-Marxism, feminist materialism (Bogdan & Biklen, 1992), and interpretive cultural studies (Denzin, 1995). Thus interest could be in power—who has it and how it manifests itself—and in the meanings persons draw from other persons, emotions, acts, consequences, and objects.

Families as depicted in the media have been subjects of cultural studies. Fiske (1994), for example, "told a story" about the television show "Married ... With Children" and located his analysis within such considerations as "the market economy," "new information technologies," and the depiction of teenagers in the media (p. 190). Fiske linked the specifics of the television show to cultural themes and practices, within a type of critical, emancipatory perspective. Denzin's (1995) version of cultural studies includes the analysis of the meanings of films and the search for "storied" lives.

Ethnography. Cultural studies and ethnographies focus on culture, but anthropological ethnographies have come under severe criticism, considered by some to be products of a colonial mentality where ethnographers view informants as the Other and where researchers think of themselves as neutral, when in fact they have standpoints conditioned by gender, race, class, nationality, and self-interest (Clifford & Marcus, 1986; Fine, 1994). Those who practice cultural studies want to divest themselves of such baggage, and there is an effort in ethnographies to do so as well. Writing is a major concern for contemporary ethnographers, sparked by the work represented in Clifford and other postmodern ef-

forts. The subtitle of Clifford and Marcus book, *The Poetics and Politics of Ethnography*, suggests both a literary nature and the interest in power dynamics in personal/cultural intersections.

Recently, *The Journal of Contemporary Ethnography* and *Symbolic Interactionism* have given considerable attention to examining the possibilities for ethnography, which has been challenged by "postmodernist and poststructuralist perspectives on truth, neutrality, objectivity, and language" (Bochner & Ellis, 1996, p. 3). Mitchell and Charmaz (1996) provide a enlightening dialogue that shows some of the implications for ethnography of the postmodern emphasis on writing. Some examples of contemporary experimental ethnographies that connect to family studies are Ellis' (1995a) *Final Negotiations* and Brown's (1996) study of a Jewish family resort area. The intersection of feminism, cultural studies, ethnography, autobiography, and postcolonialism is the topic of a recent book by Visweswaran (1994). Methodological discussions of feminist ethnographies (Reinharz, 1992) have many generative ideas for the conduct of research that is continually reflexive about the meanings of gender and power in a wide range of social contexts.

There also continue to be less "postmodernist" trends in ethnography. For instance, Lofland and Lofland (1995) have published their third edition of *Analyzing Social Settings* to critical acclaim (Charmaz & Preissle, 1996), primarily for its accessibility to beginning researchers. The terms *ethnography* and *ethnographic* travel across disciplines; they are widely used, being found, among other places, in some ethnomethodological studies and in family therapy research. Like any other kind of qualitative family research, ethnographic family research is an open field.

Rich Tradition of Book-Length Studies. These postmodern times have opened unprecedented opportunities for the deployment and development of qualitative research methods. Researchers can pick and chose among ontologies, epistemologies, methodologies, and methods. Pluralism applies not only to qualitative approaches but also to any number of mathematically based approaches. Despite these developments within family research and in the larger context provided by contemporary discussions, overall there are still few articles on qualitative family research compared to quantitative reports. Ambert, Adler, Adler, and Detzner (1995) pointed out that four of 527 articles published in *JMF* between 1989 to 1994 were entirely qualitative. In addition, one was partly qualitative and five others used a combination of qualitative and quantitative approaches, for a total of 1.9%.

The rarity of journal articles contrasts with a tradition of qualitative family research published in books, which often use a variety of sources of data and whose authors are trained in a variety of disciplines, as Rosenblatt and Fischer's (1993) review of qualitative family research demonstrates. Among the classics Rosenblatt and Fischer cited are Bossard and Boll's (1950) study of family ritual, Waller's (1930) case studies of divorce, Hunt (1969) on marital infidelity, and Rainwater's (1970) study of families in federal housing projects. These books generally are esteemed in family studies.

Today, book-length studies based on historical documents are fairly easy to find, and they include historian Barbara Hanawalt's (1986, 1993) studies of medieval families, social psychologist Paul Rosenblatt's (1983) analysis of nineteenth-century diaries and twentieth-century grief theories, historian Drew Gilpin Faust's (1996) study of women in the slaveholding southern states during the American Civil War, ethnographer Hamabata's (1993) study of Japanese business families, Curry's (1996) account of a southern African American family's courage in creating opportunities for their children's education, and social worker Howard Goldstein's (1996) study of the life course of Jewish children who grew up in an orphanage from the 1920s to the 1940s. The interdisciplinary team of Bell-Scott, Guy-Sheftall, Royster, Sims-Wood, DeCosta-Willis, & Fultz (1991) assembled a major collection of documents portraying mother–daughter relationships in black families.

Book-length studies based on interviews and observations often win wide recognition. As mentioned earlier, McMahon's (1995) book has won two awards. The last three books, including McMahon's, that received the Student/New Professional Book Award sponsored by the National Council on Family Relations and Sage Publications, were based on qualitative methods (Dienhart [1996] and Nadeau [1997]).

Encouragement Abounds. Like those on other editorial boards, *JMF* editors and commentators during the last few decades have been favorable to qualitative family research. Wiseman (1981) predicted that family researchers "will move toward qualitative, naturalistic approaches," given what she saw as a "burgeoning interest" in micro-interactions within families (p. 264). In the same issue, Hill (1981) discussed the projected limited resources for social science research and predicted that researchers may do more exploratory and descriptive studies, which generate "more discoveries per hour expended than large scale quantitative verification or experimentally designed studies in laboratories" (p. 256). The next year, Sprey (1982), as editor of *JMF*, said he would like to see more qualitative articles in the journal. Marilyn Coleman, editor from 1990 to 1995, encouraged the submission of articles based on qualitative methods. *Family Relations*, the applied journal of NCFR, *Families in Society*, published by Family Service America, and *Journal of Family Issues* have also displayed an openness to qualitative family research, as have other journals less strongly associated with family studies, including *Qualitative Inquiry*, *Qualitative Sociology*, and *Journal of Contemporary Eth-*

nography. For several decades, then, editors and other gatekeepers could hardly have been more encouraging.

Learning to Be a Qualitative Researcher. Although not a lot has changed in terms of quantities of qualitative family research published in scholarly journals since LaRossa and Wolf (1985) published their essay, the intellectual context has been transformed, as the earlier discussion demonstrated. The lag between intellectual context, encouragement, and actual publications is likely due to many factors. Lack of training in qualitative methods is a primary reason. Not only does the quality of research suffer because of lack of training, but often the quality of the reviews of manuscripts is compromised by undertrained reviewers. Among the many reviewer-related issues that Ambert et al. (1995) identified are bias against the so-called "softness" of qualitative research, an insistence upon documentation of qualitative work when such documentation is not required in quantitative approaches, the epistemology-specific training of some qualitative researchers who are unable to appreciate ways of qualitative research that run counter to their own training, and a lack of appreciation of research that seeks to raise new questions rather than formulate new theory.

Lack of training shows itself in the quality of some of the manuscripts submitted for publication. Marilyn Coleman, former editor of *JMF*, found that reviewers who were qualitative researchers often rejected manuscripts as not good examples of qualitative research. She and the reviewers often worked with authors through revision after revision in order to get a piece in shape for publication (Coleman, personal communication, 1996). In coediting two volumes of qualitative family research (Gilgun & Sussman, 1996; Gilgun et al., 1992) and in reading manuscripts for several journals, I found that some researchers could analyze and write up their material in exemplary ways, but others needed much editorial guidance, not because they were unintelligent but because they simply did not know how to do it.

Although there now is more training available than ever before, there are few programs whose primary emphasis is on qualitative approaches. Higher education rarely offers students the in-depth training that competency in these methods requires. Those who want to learn how to do qualitative analysis and who do not have teachers readily available—and their numbers are not known—learn by trial and error, a difficult route, since most texts are sketchy about procedures of data analysis (Schatzman, 1991; Strauss, 1987).

Ralph LaRossa (LaRossa, 1983; LaRossa & LaRossa, 1981) tells a story that stands for the experiences of many contemporary qualitative researchers. He described how he learned to do qualitative analysis when he was a Ph.D. student in sociology at the University of New Hampshire: "I did what Richard Gelles (1974) had done two years before me. I had my interviews transcribed. I read them several times. I cut them up in strips. I wrote memos. Then I got to the point where I wanted to know what to do next. I put the piles on the floor next to me, and I read the chapter in Glaser and Strauss (1967) on the constant comparative method. They told me I was supposed to look for concepts" (Gilgun, 1993a, pp. 6–7). Opportunities to learn how to do qualitative analysis, then, have been limited in the past and, although more available now, rarely are available in the depth required for competency.

Training through Seminars. One of the few opportunities for intensive academic training in qualitative methods has been at the University of California–San Francisco. As discussed earlier, with the arrival of Strauss in the late 1960s to found the department of social and behavioral sciences, nursing doctoral students for decades took a sequence of research courses that Strauss, Schatzman, and Glaser taught. They also took philosophy of science courses at the University of California–Berkeley. Not only did many of these graduates go on to teach qualitative methods at other schools of nursing, but other nursing research professors taught additional forms of qualitative research, such as Newman's method of understanding health as expanding consciousness (Lamendola & Newman, 1994; Newman, 1986, 1989) and transcultural nursing and ethnoscience (Leininger, 1969, 1978, 1985). As a result, nursing qualitative research is more advanced than the research of most other disciplines.

Learning how to do qualitative research can involve years of training in interactive seminars, based on group analysis of data. These seminars appear to be the most effective way to learn (Gilgun, 1992b,c; Schatzman, 1991; Strauss, 1987; Strauss & Corbin, 1990). Traditional in qualitative research, group analysis of data for teaching purposes was used by Robert Park, Ernest Burgess, and Vivian Palmer at the University of Chicago during the 1920s and early 1930s (Bulmer, 1984) and were similar to the group data analysis sessions that Booth conducted when he did studies of the London poor (Webb & Webb, 1932). A contemporary example of this approach to data analysis is described in Olesen, Droes, Hatton, Chico, and Schatzman (1994). In seminars, the usual method is for students to provide copies of their fieldnotes a week or so ahead of time to other seminar participants. Each week participants discuss fieldnotes in detail. Beginning researchers learn analysis through doing it, an action-oriented approach that may have received some of its rationale from Dewey (1922, 1938), whose ideas were highly influential at the University of Chicago earlier in this century, as discussed earlier.

Syracuse University is another locale where in-depth training in qualitative methods has been available for more than 30 years. Bogdan (Gilgun, 1992c) provided a sense of what it was like for him to be a student in the 1960s in a seminar with Blanche Geer (Becker, Geer, Hughes, & Strauss, 1961; Becker, Geer, & Hughes, 1968):

> In the seminar, we talked about what was happening in our own studies. A lot of it was sharing stories and problems. There was no text book. I recall there were no readings, except that Blanche would refer you to things you could read to help illuminate some problem or some conceptual area she thought your study was about. We were required to do an observation with a corresponding set of notes each week. It was a lot of work. In really got into it. Part of the enjoyment was feeling and working in a way I had never worked before. I like what the process produced. I arranged my week so I could do the work for the seminar. (Gilgun, 1992c, p. 9)

Although some students thrived in these seminars, others were not so responsive. Susan O'Connor, who received her doctoral research training at Syracuse University in the 1990s, showed how she and several of her student colleagues were taken by the methods, while other students were repelled by their ambiguity. O'Connor wrote the following especially for this chapter.

> My formal exposure to qualitative methods was a first semester course in the Ph.D. program. This was a year-long research methodology course. The first six weeks were devoted to qualitative research. Sari Knopp Biklen (Bogdan & Biklen, 1992) was our instructor. She was strong and clear about the method and her dissemination of information. We were immediately required to begin our research. I remember thinking that I didn't have enough knowledge of the process and had so many questions that should be answered. I came to find rather quickly that this was the nature of the research and that my learning was a process as well as a product.
>
> The most striking memory I have from that class was how we as students separated ourselves out. There were those students who just did not connect with the process. It was too unclear. Those unknowns, I began learning, was that I loved and what connoted the difference between the paradigms. I understood what Sari was explaining, and I liked and understood the ambiguity, the inquiry, the discovery. The handful of us who went on with the qualitative process began to sit on the same side of the room talking among ourselves and feeling very engaged in the process. Other classmates were frustrated.
>
> This cadre of students went on and were clear after just one semester that qualitative research met our needs. We were then together in the year-long qualitative strand taught by Bob Bogdan. For the most part, I remember most of us really looking forward to the course. It was a world of ideas. Bob pushed us to question and, without giving in-depth feedback, would ask questions that forced us to re-conceptualize and inquire in a variety of ways. The joy of inquiry is consistent in the experience of qualitative researchers.

Long Apprenticeships. Students of Strauss, Schatzman, and Glaser often struggled with learning-grounded theory analysis (Schatzman, 1991), and my experience suggests that other forms of qualitative research are equally challenging to learn. Schatzman wrote that grounded theory analysis does not have a clearly recognizable "research paradigm" and does not portray "how the operations [of grounded theory analysis] link together concretely as a system" (p. 306). Although the writings of Schatzman, Strauss, and Corbin have sought to redress this situation, the challenges of learning and doing exemplary qualitative research may be enduring because of its very nature. Corbin (1991) tells a story about Strauss that illustrates the difficulty of learning and doing qualitative data analysis: During the mid- to late-1940s Strauss left qualitative data from two studies unanalyzed "because he did not really know how to analyze them" (pp. 24–25). LePlay, as discussed earlier, struggled to learn to manage and analyze his data.

As primarily inductive in their approaches, the procedures of almost all qualitative research require that researchers set aside their own theories as much as possible and open themselves to the perspectives of the persons in the situations in which they are conducting their research. Even when using procedures that use preestablished codes and sensitizing concepts, or in forms of analytic induction, researchers put aside preformulations in an attempt to understand informants and their situations. Such preformulations do not stymie emergence; sometimes they are of great help in aiding researchers in understanding what informants are saying (Gilgun, 1995b) or in sensitizing them to the theoretical implications of their data (Glaser, 1978). Like Glaser, Schatzman (1991) observed that students commonly tended to prematurely bring closure to the analysis by the imposition of "received theory" or they would impose the "received method" of grounded theory analysis before they had carefully analyzed the dimensions of their own data (Schatzman, 1991, pp. 304–305).

Once students trained through seminars graduate and go on to their own professorships, they can become isolated. For example, Marianne McCarthy studied extensively with Strauss, and she and several other students did a group independent study over several quarters with Schatzman to analyze their data for their dissertation research. "The group independent study was wonderful," she said in an interview. "We worked as a group, critiqued each others' fieldnotes and each others memos" (Gilgun, 1993a, p. 6). When she completed her dissertation and left San Francisco to become a professor, she found herself searching unsuccessfully for another group with whom to do analysis. "Doing analysis is an interactional process," she said, "and I didn't have anyone to interact with" (p. 6).

Who Constructs Findings. The isolation that many qualitatively oriented scholars experience is an additional issue in the ongoing development of skills. Analysis is complex and often requires long discussions with other re-searchers, a process that the seminars heed. Yet, qualitative researchers frequently have few if any like-minded scholars with whom to analyze data. Funding is important in the building of such groups, but funding remains problematic for most qualitative researchers. Many researchers work closely with graduate students on projects, so that at least there is a group of two involved in the analysis. My work has benefitted from interaction with a series of research assistants, who have helped me in my formulation of ideas as I work with data. I've also found paper presentations to be important in fostering my understandings, and I seek opportunities to do presentations and workshops to professional colleagues in the human services. Correspondence through e-mail has linked me more closely with other qualitative researchers. I also teach courses in which I can present my developing ideas. Finally, I convene a qualitative research interest group composed of graduate students and professors that meet regularly to discuss our research. I incorporate feedback from these venues into my analysis.

Group analysis of data, however, might not suit every situation. Some researchers, for example, find spending time alone to work with and think about their data an important part of their analytic process. The act of writing helps in the clarification and delineation of ideas. Doing the analysis with others who have not been in the field and who are not able to connect with fieldworkers' experiences, especially if there are status and power differences, can be counterproductive. For group analysis to be generative, there appears to be a requirement that the perspectives of the group members be compatible and complementary.

Informants can facilitate data analysis. Barry (1996) developed a continuum of collaboration, from the more "soloist" to the more "coproduced" research (p. 421). In my own long-term research on how persons overcome childhood adversities (Gilgun, 1990a; 1991; 1996a,b; in press), which involves multiple interviews, I gradually share with informants my understandings of their lives in order to check whether or not I am in tune with their own meanings. Often I am not, and my informants then add nuances to their perspectives that I had not previously been able to grasp. Before submitting articles for publication, I usually share them with one or more informants, again to test whether I am close to their meanings. Other researchers, such as Bloom (1996), provide transcripts of interviews to informants. Bloom based her decision on Harding's (1987) idea that an important contribution of feminist research is that it responds to questions women have about their own lives. In some instances, she found, as I did, that such sharing stimulated deeper reflection into personal experience.

The doing of qualitative research, then, ideally involves collaborative work. As researchers conduct their analyses, they may use computer programs to help in data management and to support processes of theorizing and discovery (Richards & Richards, 1994). Researchers also may develop lists, tables, matrices, and diagrams such as those described in Miles and Huberman (1994) as they work with data. This level of data analysis is guided by ideas. Thus, the basic skills in qualitative analysis center around interpreting the meanings of the data, not in the technicalities of data management.

Ethics and Emotional Impact. Under ideal conditions, students learning to do qualitative research are well prepared to deal with the multiple possible happenstances that characterize fieldwork. Although beginners can, without much harm to themselves and others, do informal observations, library research, and simple brief interviews on non-controversial topics, fieldwork is potentially full of risks. Simple and well-supervised tasks probably are sufficient for getting started. Many qualitative studies involve in-depth investigations into sensitive topics. Under these conditions, students require a great deal of supervision in handling their own responses to fieldwork and in interpreting the responses of others. Inexperienced researchers who stride confidently into field settings can, as Punch (1994) noted, be unprepared for the ethical and political dilemmas inherent in fieldwork and may cause a great deal of damage to themselves and to others.

Ethical considerations, then, are yet another reason to view the learning of qualitative methods as ongoing processes that require frequent meeting with others to process the gamut of field experiences, including the analysis and interpretation of informants' data and not excluding informants' subjective responses and concerns about field relations.

The development of research teams composed of experienced qualitative researchers and students is an alternative to the seminar format when such seminars are not available and a supplement when they are. Through such teams, students may process a range of responses and interpretations of their field experiences, and the more experienced researchers can also model ways of doing so. The research team discussed in Hall and Zvonkovic (1996) is an example of this style of apprenticeship in research on marriage. Other family researchers (e.g., Gilbert, 1996; Kitson et al., 1996) have developed methods of acknowledging and processing emotional aspects of doing qualitative research. Brown (1996) uses a range of approaches to prepare researchers for the subjective dimensions of fieldwork, including using students' research journals in class discussions and role-playing as informants and researchers. It is important to note that Brown, like many other methodologists, views education about the uses of subjectivity in research as an acknowledgment of the interconnections of the affective and cognitive domains.

Paying careful attention to the emotional responses of informants, as well as the intellectual content of their words, is an ethical and humane stance that requires the attention of both students and experienced researchers. Informing respondents of the pitfalls and opportunities of participating in the research, stating that respondents are free not to respond, and checking in to see how informants are doing are ways of dealing with informants' emotions (Gilgun, 1994c; Kitson et al., 1996). Such sensitivity to informants requires a great deal of awareness that experienced and new researchers best cultivate in group analysis of field experiences.

Funding and Getting Published. Funding is an issue for qualitative researchers. Although the situation may change in the future, far too often proposals based on qualitative approaches are not funded because they are judged by criteria developed for the evaluation of quantitative work. As discussed earlier, most quantitative work roughly can be categorized as positivistic and Cartesian, while most qualitative work is interpretive and often phenomenological. Qualitative work centers around meanings in a variety of situations from a variety of perspectives. The focus in quantitative work, then, is epistemological, while much qualitative work is ontologically oriented. These two foci are not the same. To judge one by the procedures of the other makes little sense. Much has been written about how to write proposals for funding qualitative research (Marshall & Rossman, 1995; Morse, 1991, 1994). Hopefully within a few years there will be a widespread acceptance of methodological pluralism. From that will come an understanding of the wisdom of funding a range of types of research. Science can be done under a variety of kinds of methods, methodologies, epistemologies, and ontologies.

Guidelines for Evaluation. By now I hope it is clear that there is no one way to do qualitative research. The very richness of these possibilities, however, can render evaluation of qualitative research problematic. Many persons have written about judging quality (cf. among others, Altheide & Johnson, 1994; Ambert et al., 1995; Gilgun, 1993b; Lincoln, 1995; Reason & Rowan, 1981; Smith, 1993; Schwandt, 1996; Van Maanen, 1988). From the point of view of common sense, a research report perhaps could best be evaluated in terms of what it purports to be (Gilgun, 1993b). After all, we judge apples by their appleness and oranges by their orangeness. We do not fault an apple because it is not an orange. For example, a report that considers itself phenomenological should present results that represent informants' lived experience. If such a report does not, then it should be revised until the purpose and the intellectual context of the research line up with findings. If authors state their research is based on grounded theory or analytic induction, then the finding must contain a theory. In the case of analytic induction, an initial hypothesis also must be present. If a report states that it is experimental and is pushing the boundaries, say, of ethnography to create, perhaps, a personal ethnography, then this report can be evaluated as to whether or not cultural themes and practices are part of the report as well as whether the report is a narrative about the personal meanings of the author.

To facilitate evaluation of qualitative pieces, authors routinely, but not always, state the type of research they are doing and provide citations. Reviewers not familiar with the style of qualitative research can use the references to educate themselves or send the article back to the journal editor who would find a more knowledgeable reviewer. Some articles using qualitative methods do not state the type of research they are doing. As a reviewer, I would fault the authors and ask them to situate themselves in a research tradition. In some experimental work, the tradition may be identified in the article's abstract, but it is there somewhere, if for no other reason than to orient those not familiar with that style of research.

Besides these general guidelines, the views of Glaser and Strauss (1967) and Glaser (1978) continue to be relevant: "grab," modifiability to fit particular situations, an account of procedures that led to the results, and the situating of findings within social science traditions. The idea of ongoing emergence implies the idea that there always is more to learn about the phenomena; thus, Glaser and Strauss—and the Chicago School of Sociology tradition on which they have built—have modest goals for the universality of findings. Perhaps because they were concerned that methods and the findings could be misunderstood they also recommended that researchers present their theoretical frameworks in conventional social science language. Using language familiar to audiences of interest to describe methods and findings helps bridge research traditions.

Depending upon the type of research, many of the desirable qualities Lincoln (1995) identified may be relevant: researchers being clear about their own stances regarding their topics; findings that are relevant not only to other researchers and policy makers but also to communities that have a stake in findings; attention to voice so that multiple points of views—or voices—are represented in research reports, not simply those who have traditionally spoken for others; and accounts of reflexivity that show a deep understanding of the positions of others while staying in touch with one's own experiences, including any transformation that researchers may experience as a result of the research. This long yet incomplete list is suggestive; some and not all of these desired qualities are relevant to any particular research report. I think most qualitative researchers would agree on the overall importance of presenting evidence of researchers' immersion in the field, conveyed through rich and deep descriptions that evoke new understandings.

Although researchers from within an interpretive tradition would accept these qualities as desirable, there are some who consider themselves qualitative researchers who would not. As one example, Clavarino, Najman, and Silverman (1995), concerned with the ambiguity of analysis, argued forcefully that inter-rater reliabilities must be established in the analysis of qualitative data. They urged other researchers to resist "methodological anarchy" (p. 224). They don't specify what constitutes this "anarchy," but it could be such tradition-bound procedures as group analysis of data that does not involve mathematical inter-rater reliability. Miles and Huberman (1994) also recommend doing inter-rater reliabilities. They use the term *check coding*. They note as an issue in this regard that persons from one social science tradition may not see the same things in data as persons from others. Their discussion suggests that the coders should ultimately agree on the names of the codes and the meanings of the data. Such a stance could be consistent with some philosophies of science, but a viable alternative is to code the same chunk of data in more than one way and to heed the idea that multiple interpretations are not only possible but desirable.

Not all qualitative data must be subjected to inter-rater reliability studies. By the time well-done qualitative research is presented in a research report, researchers and the coresearchers with whom they have analyzed data are so immersed in the data that not only is the analog of inter-rater reliability already present, but there is also a depth and breadth made possible through prolonged discussion and reflection that goes far beyond what highly focused inter-rater reliability studies can offer. Similarly, no one of any of the described desirable qualities must be in any one study. The paradigm underlying the research guides in making decisions about procedures and interpretive processes. To insist that all qualitative studies must do a quantified assessment of inter-rater reliability or must use other procedures that are inconsistent with the research paradigm would be akin to insisting that the only good apples are those whose juice tastes like the liquid that comes from oranges.

Qualitative interview data are sometimes subjected to inter-rater reliability studies, as Mendenhall, Grotevant, and McRoy (1996) did in their study of couples' movement and nonmovement to openness in adoption. They were interested in relatively focused phenomena, and the use of inter-rater reliabilities in the context of their research goals made sense. Given the methodological sophistication that is emerging in these postmodern times, the perspective that one set of criteria fits all research is not operative. Each type of qualitative research productively can be evaluated in terms of what it purports to be doing.

Some qualities are desirable regardless of the paradigms in which they are embedded. Coherent organization of ideas, ideas supported by data, and clarity in the presentation of ideas are some of them. Sussman (1993) identified "heart" as an important quality in any kind of research. By heart, he meant a sense that the authors conveyed something meaningful and in which they believe.

Summary

In our own time, the array of possibilities for the design of research points to a methodologically pluralistic future for research on families. More than 2 decades ago, Glaser (1978) stated that grounded theory is one of many styles of sociological research and that the field "needs *all* perspectives" (p. 3, emphasis in original). Today, there is much more of an intellectual foundation for the pluralism for which Glaser made a case. For many family scholars, the future is exciting because of these possibilities.

There still is limited opportunity for in-depth training in qualitative research, despite the plethora of research approaches now available in these postmodern times. Learning to do qualitative research requires a long apprenticeship. The philosophical underpinnings of qualitative methods are challenging and quite different from how most of today's researchers have been trained. Qualitative research may most effectively be done in teams, where more than one person becomes deeply immersed in data and therefore can contribute to interpretation. Variety and challenge characterize contemporary qualitative family research. Some researchers learn on their own by trial and error and produce exemplary qualitative research. Others are doing the best they can, but struggle to reach the level of skill required for publication. Once researchers have attained some facility in the doing of qualitative research, finding colleagues with whom to analyze data can be problematic. Processing of field experiences is most effectively done in interaction with others. Technical skills are important, but working with ideas is foundational to qualitative analysis.

The range of types of qualitative research has expanded in contemporary times. Researchers can do tightly controlled qualitative studies that carry on a positivistic tradition or they can attempt to actualize the challenges of postmodernist thinking, as many working within cultural studies are doing. Some approaches are more explicitly emancipatory than others. Some are emancipatory in terms of changing social structures, while others, such as family therapy, focus on interpersonal change. Procedures of induction characterize contemporary approaches, although by now I hope it is clear that deduction and induction are probably present in all research. In qualitative research, however, the emphasis is on induction. Reflexivity, too, is an issue within qualitative family research, with a range of emphases and an open field in terms of how subjectivity can be represented in our research. Contemporary qualitative research not only is caught up in the postmodern methodological transformations we are now undergoing, but the history of qualitative research also shows that today's methodological concerns have roots in the origins of qualitative research and social research in general.

Discussion

Social research originated with qualitative family research. From the beginning, qualitative researchers immersed themselves in the worlds they studied, used inductive methods to study social problems in need of amelioration, and recognized the importance of their own subjectivities and the subjectivities of those being researched. Their methods were pluralistic. In tune with pragmatist views, they used whichever methods fit their research goals: participant observation, interviewing, document analysis, surveys, and use of demographic data. Philosophically, their methods were based on the notions of lived experience and *verstehen*, or understanding situated in social, cultural, and historical context, in contrast to Cartesian emphases on explanation, objectivity, and mathematics (Hamilton, 1994).

During the recent past, few scholars were aware of the possibilities represented in inductive, experiential, reflexive, and emancipatory research. From about the 1940s to the late 1980s and beyond, Cartesian philosophies eclipsed the human sciences approaches characteristic of the Chicago School of Sociology. When contemporary scholars brought attention back to human experience and understanding as important in social research, the response was immediate and widespread. Countless graduate students began pursuing qualitatively based research for their dissertations. Editors began searching for qualitative family research for their journals. There was an outpouring of books that support the development of qualitative methods. Graduate training is becoming more available.

Family scholars are ready to claim their heritage. As we learn more about the traditions in which such research is situated, we can gain confidence in our approaches because we are learning that we have a galaxy of scholars who prepared the philosophical and methodological bases for our work today. Research that is inductive, focuses on human experience, that recognizes researchers' subjectivities and that is emancipatory is solidly within a long tradition. Feminist perspectives, too, are part of this heritage. The work of Jane Addams and her colleagues at Hull House influenced the intellectual milieu of the Chicago School of Sociology.

How we conduct our research today and the philosophical assumptions that we make are not identical with those of our forebears. On the other hand, many of the ideas of the nineteenth and early part of the twentieth century that undergirded early family research are the ideas that are influencing us today. Glaser's words (1978) on the need for all perspectives are becoming self-evident in contemporary family scholarship and in the social and human sciences in general.

ACKNOWLEDGMENTS. The author thanks reviewers Katherine Allen, Kerry Daly, and one anonymous reviewer for their helpful comments and editors Sue Steinmetz, Marv Sussman, and Gary "Pete" Peterson for cheering me on and for offering valuable suggestions.

References

Abbott, E. (1910). *Women in industry*. New York: Appleton.

Abbott, E. (1950). Grace Abbott and Hull-House, 1908–1921. Part 1. *Social Service Review, 24,* 374–394.

Abbott, E., & Breckinridge, S. P. (1916). *The tenements of Chicago, 1908–1935*. Chicago: University of Chicago Press.

Ackerman, N. (1958). *The psychodynamics of family life*. New York: Basic Books.

Adams, B. N. (1988). Fifty years of family research: What does it mean? *Journal of Marriage and the Family, 50,* 5–17.

Alasuutari, P. (1996). Theorizing in qualitative research: A cultural studies perspective. *Qualitative Inquiry, 2,* 371–384.

Allen, K. R. (1989). *Single women/family ties: Life histories of older women.* Newbury Park, CA: Sage.

Allen, K. R. (1994). Feminist reflections on lifelong single women. In Donna L. Sollie & Leigh A. Leslie (Eds.), *Gender, families, and close relationships: Feminist research journeys* (pp. 97–119). Thousand Oaks, CA: Sage.

Allen, K. R., & Pickett, R. S. (1987). Forgotten streams in the family life course: Utilization of qualitative retrospective interviews in the analysis of lifelong single women's family careers. *Journal of Marriage and the Family, 49,* 517–526.

Altheide, D. L., & Johnson, J. M. (1994). Criteria for assessing interpretive validity in qualitative research. In N. K. Denzin & Y. S. Lincoln (Eds.), *Handbook of qualitative research* (pp. 485–499). Thousand Oaks, CA: Sage.

Ambert, A. M., Adler, P. A., Adler, P., & Detzner, D. F. (1995). Understanding and evaluating qualitative research. *Journal of Marriage and the Family, 57,* 879–893.

Anderson, N. (1925). *The hobo*. Chicago: University of Chicago Press.

Anderson, N. (1983). A stranger at the gate: Reflections on the Chicago School of Sociology. *Urban Life, 11,* 396–406.

Angell, R. C. (1936). *The family encounters the depression*. New York: Scribner.

Atkinson, P. A. (1988). Ethnomethodology: A critical review. *Annual Review of Sociology, 14,* 441–465.

Baber, K. M., & Allen, K. R. (1992). *Women and families: Feminist reconstructions*. New York: Guilford.

Bailey, K. D. (1984). On integrating theory and method. *Current Perspectives in Social Theory, 6,* 21–44.

Barry, K. (1979). *Female sexual slavery*. Englewood Cliffs, NJ: Prentice-Hall.

Barry, D. (1996). Artful inquiry: A symbolic constructivist approach to social science research. *Qualitative Inquiry, 2,* 411–438.

Barthes, R. (1974). *S/Z: An essay*. (R. Miller, Trans.). New York: Hill and Wang. (Original work published 1970 by Editions du Seuil, Paris)

Barton, A. H. (1971). Empirical methods and radical sociology: A liberal critique. In J. D. Colfax & J. L. Road (Eds.), *Radical sociology*. New York: Basic Books.

Bateson, G. (1972). *Steps to an ecology of mind*. New York: Ballentine.

Becker, H. S. (1953). Becoming a marihuana user. *American Journal of Sociology, 59,* 235–242.

Becker, H. S. (1988). Blumer's conceptual impact. *Symbolic Interaction, 11,* 13–20.

Becker, H. S., Geer, B., Hughes, E., & Strauss, A. L. (1961). *Boys in white.* Chicago: University of Chicago Press.

Becker, H. S., Geer, B., & Hughes, E. (1968). *Making the grade*. New York: Wiley.

Bell-Scott, P., Guy-Sheftall, B., Royster, J. J., Sims-Wood, J., DeCosta-Willis, M., & Fultz, L. (Eds.). (1991). *Double stitch: Black women write about mothers & daughters*. Boston: Beacon.

Benner, P. (Ed.). (1994). *Interpretive phenomenology*. Thousand Oaks, CA: Sage.

Berger, P., & Luckmann, T. (1966). *The social construction of reality*. New York: Doubleday.

Bernard, J. (1981). *The female world*. New York: Free Press.

Bertalanffy, L. von. (1968). *General systems theory: Foundations, development, applications*. New York: Braziller.

Blaisure, K. R., & Allen, K. R. (1995). Feminism and the ideology and practice of marital equality. *Journal of Marriage and the Family, 57,* 5–19.

Bleier, R. (Ed.). (1984). *Science and gender: A critique of biology and its theories on women*. New York: Pergamon.

Bloom, L. R. (1996). Stories of one's own: Nonunitary subjectivity in narrative representation. *Qualitative Inquiry, 2,* 176–197.

Blumer, H. (1928). *Method in social psychology*. Ph.D. dissertation, University of Chicago.

Blumer, H. (1969). An appraisal of Thomas and Znaniecki's *The Polish peasant in Europe and America* (pp. 117–126). (Original work published in 1939)

Blumer, H. (1986). What is wrong with social theory? In H. Blumer (Ed.), *Symbolic interactionism: Perspective and method* (pp. 140–152). Berkeley: University of California Press. (Original work published in 1969)

Blumer, H. (1986). The methodological position of symbolic interactionism. In H. Blumer (Ed.), *Symbolic interactionism: Perspective and method* (pp. 1–60). Berkeley: University of California Press. (Original work published in 1969)

Bochner, A. P., & Ellis, C. (1996). Taking ethnography into the twenty-first century. *Journal of Contemporary Ethnography, 25,* 3–5.

Bogdan, R., & Biklen, S. K. (1992). *Qualitative research methods for education* (2nd ed.). Boston: Allyn & Bacon.

Booth, C. (1889). *Life and labour of the people* (Vol. 1). London: Macmillan.

Booth, C. (1903). *Life and labour of the people in London*. Final volume. London and New York: Macmillan.

Boss, P. G. (1987). Family stress. In M. B. Sussman & S. K. Steinmetz (Eds.), *Handbook of marriage and the family* (pp. 695–723). New York: Plenum.

Boss, P. G. (1988). *Family stress management*. Newbury Park, CA: Sage.

Boss, P. G. (1993). The reconstruction of family life with Alzheimer's disease: Generating theory to lower family stress from ambiguous loss. In P. G. Boss, W. J. Doherty, R. LaRoussa, W. R. Schummn, & S. K. Steinmetz (Eds.), *Sourcebook of family theories and methods: A contextual approach* (pp. 163–166). New York: Plenum.

Bossard, J. H. S., & Boll, E. S. (1950). *Ritual in family living*. Philadelphia: University of Pennsylvania Press.

Bott, E. (1957). *Family and social network*. New York: Free Press.

Bott, E. (1971). *Family and social network* (2nd ed.). New York: Free Press.

Bowen, M. (1978). *Family therapy in clinical practice*. New York: Aronson.

Brown, J. R. (1996). *The I in science: Training to utilize subjectivity in research*. Oslo, Norway: Scandinavian University Press.

Brown, P. (1996). Catskill culture: The rise and fall of a Jewish resort area seen through personal narrative and ethnography. *Journal of Contemporary Ethnography, 24*, 83–119.

Bruner, J. (1990). *Acts of meaning.* Cambridge, MA: Harvard University Press.

Bulmer, M. (1984). *The Chicago School of Sociology: Institutionalization, diversity, and the rise of sociological research.* Chicago: University of Chicago Press.

Burgess, E. W. (1926). The family as a unity of interacting personalities. *Family, 7*, 3–9.

Burgess, E. W. (1927). Statistics and case studies as methods of sociological research. *Sociology and Social Research, 12*, 103–120.

Burgess, E. W. (1932). Editor's preface. In E. Franklin Frazier, *The Negro family in Chicago* (pp. ix–xii). Chicago: University of Chicago Press.

Buttny, R. (1990). Blame-accounts sequences in therapy: The negotiation of relational meanings. *Semiotica, 78*, 219–248.

Buttny, R., & Jensen, A. D. (1995). Telling problems in an initial family therapy session: The hierarchical organization of problem-talk. In G. H. Morris & R. J. Chenail (Eds.), *The talk of the clinic: Explorations in the analysis of medical and therapeutic discourse* (pp. 19–47). Hillsdale, NJ: Erlbaum.

Cavan, R. S. (1983). The Chicago School of Sociology, 1918–1933. *Urban Life*, 407–420.

Cavan, R. S., & Ranck, K. H. (1936). *The family and the depression: A study of one hundred Chicago families.* Chicago: University of Chicago Press.

Charmaz, K. (1975). The coroners' strategies for announcing death. *Urban Life, 4*, 296–316.

Charmaz, K. (1990). "Discovering" chronic illness: Using grounded theory. *Social Science in Medicine, 30*, 1161–1172.

Charmaz, K., & Preissle, J. (1996). New ethnographies: Review Symposium. *Journal of Contemporary Ethnography, 25*, 390–396.

Chenail, R. (1991). *Medical discourse and systemic frames of comprehension.* Norwood, NJ: Ablex.

Chenail, R. J., & Fortugno, L. (1995). Resourceful figures in therapeutic conversations. In G. H. Morris & R. J. Chenail (Eds.), *The talk of the clinic: Explorations in the analysis of medical and therapeutic discourse* (pp. 71–88). Hillsdale, NJ: Erlbaum.

Chenail, R. J., Douthit, P., Gale, J., Stormberg, J., Morris, G. H., Park, J., Sridaromont, S., & Schmer, V. (1990). "It's probably nothing serious, but ..." Parents' interpretation of referral to pediatric cardiologists. *Health Communication, 2*, 165–188.

Chenail, R. J., Itkin, P., Bonneau, M., & Andriacchi, C. (1993, October). *Managing solutions in divorce mediation: A discourse analysis.* Paper presented at the Twenty-first Annual Society of Professionals in Dispute Resolution International Conference, Toronto, Canada.

Chesla, C. A. (1994). Parents' caring practices with schizophrenic offspring. In P. Benner (Ed.), *Interpretive phenomenology* (pp. 167–183). Thousand Oaks, CA: Sage.

Chesla, C. A. (1995). Hermeneutic phenomenology: An approach to understanding families. *Journal of Family Nursing, 1*, 68–78.

Chesla, C. A. (1996). Early beginnings of the Qualitative Family Research Network: Interview with Ralph LaRossa. *Qualitative Family Research, 10*(1), 3–9.

Chesla, C., Martinson, A. I., & Muswaswes, M. (1994). Continuities and discontinuities in family relations with Alzheimer's patients. *Family Relations, 43*, 3–14.

Chodorow, N. (1978). *The reproduction of mothering: Psychoanalysis and the sociology of gender.* Berkeley, CA: University of California Press.

Clavarino, A. M., Najman, J. M., & Silverman, D. (1995). The quality of qualitative data: Two strategies for analyzing medical interviews. *Qualitative Inquiry, 1*, 223–242.

Clifford, J., & Marcus, G. E. (Eds.). (1986). *Writing culture: The poetics and politics of ethnography.* Berkeley: University of California Press.

Cohler, B. J. (1988). The human studies and the life history: The Social Service Review Lecture. *Social Service Review, 62*, 552–577.

Comstock, D. E. (1982). A method for critical research. In E. Bredo & W. Feinberg (Eds.), *Knowledge and values in social and educational research* (pp. 370–390). Philadelphia, PA: Temple University Press.

Cook, T. D., & Campbell, D. T. (1979). *Quasi-experimentation: Design and analysis for field settings.* Boston: Houghton Mifflin.

Cooley, C. H. (1930). *Sociological theory and social research.* New York: Holt.

Corbin, J. (1991). Anselm Strauss: An intellectual biography. In D. R. Maines (Ed.), *Social organization and social process: Essays in honor of Anselm Strauss* (pp. 17–42). New York: Aldine de Gruyter.

Cressey, D. (1953). *Other people's money.* Glencoe, IL: Free Press.

Curry, C. (1996). *Silver rights.* New York: Algonquin.

Daly, K. (1995, November). *How persons generate theory: Second order stories.* Paper presented at the Symposium on Interpreting Qualitative Data, Annual Conference, National Council on Family Relations, Portland, OR.

Deegan, M. J. (1990). *Jane Addams and the men of the Chicago School, 1892–1918.* New Brunswick, NJ: Transaction.

Demos, V. (1990). Black family studies in the *Journal of Marriage and the Family* and the issue of distortion: A trend analysis. *Journal of Marriage and the Family, 52*, 603–612.

Denzin, N. K. (1989). *Interpretative interactionism.* Newbury Park, CA: Sage.

Denzin, N. K. (1995). On the shoulders of Anselm. *Mind, Culture, and Activity, 2*, 39–47.

Denzin, N. K., & Lincoln, Y. S. (Eds.). (1994). *Handbook of qualitative research.* Thousand Oaks, CA: Sage.

Dewey, J. (1922). *Human nature and conduct.* New York: Holt.

Dewey, J. (1938). *Logic: The theory of inquiry.* New York: Holt.

Dienhart, A. (1986). *Men and women co-constructing fatherhood through shared parenting: Beyond the dominant discourse.* Thousand Oaks, CA: Sage.

Dilthey, W. (1976). *Selected writings* (H. P. Rickman, Ed. & Trans.). Cambridge: Cambridge University Press.

Dobash, E. E., & Dobash, R. P. (1979). *Violence against wives: A case against the patriarchy.* New York: Free Press.

Dollard, J. (1937). *Caste and class in a southern town.* New Haven, CT: Yale University Press.

Donzolet, J. (1977). *The policing of families.* New York: Pantheon.

Dreyfus, H. L. (1991). *Being in the world: A commentary on Heidegger's Being and Time, Division I.* Cambridge, MA: MIT Press.

Durkheim, E. (1966). *Rules of sociological method.* (S. A. Soloway & J. H. Mueller, Trans.; G. E. Catlin, Ed.). Glencoe: Free Press.

Eichler, M. (1981). Monolithic model of the family. *The Canadian Journal of Sociology, 6*, 367–388.

Ellis, C. (1995a). *Final negotiations: A story of love, loss, and chronic illness.* Philadelphia, PA: Temple University Press.

Fagerhaugh, S. (1975). Getting around with emphysema. In A. L. Strauss (Ed.), *Chronic illness and the quality of life* (pp. 99–197). St. Louis, MO: Mosby.

Faris, R. E. L. (1967). *Chicago sociology 1920–1932.* Chicago: University of Chicago Press.

Farnsworth, E. B. (1996). Reflexivity and qualitative family research: An insider's perspectives in bereaving the loss of a child. In J. F. Gilgun & M. B. Sussman (Eds.), *The methods and methodologies of qualitative family research* (pp. 399–415). Binghamton, NY: Haworth.

Faust, D. G. (1996). *Mothers of invention: Women of the slaveholding south in the American Civil War.* Chapel Hill: University of North Carolina Press.

Fine, M. (1988). Sexuality, schooling, and adolescent females: The missing discourse of desire. *Harvard Educational Review, 58*, 29–53.

Fine, M. (1992). *Disruptive voices: The possibilities of feminist research.* Ann Arbor: University of Michigan Press.

Fine, M. (1994). Working the hyphens: Reinventing self and other in qualitative research: In N. K. Denzin & Y. S. Lincoln (Eds.), *Handbook of qualitative research* (pp. 70–82). Thousand Oaks, CA: Sage.

Fiske, J. (1994). Audiencing: Cultural practice and cultural studies. In N. K. Denzin & Y. S. Lincoln (Eds.), *Handbook of qualitative research* (pp. 189–198). Thousand Oaks, CA: Sage.

Form, W. (1987). Two issues: Documentation and nonstatistical manuscripts. *American Sociological Review, 52,* vi.

Franklin, C. (1995). Expanding the vision of the social constructionist debates: Creating relevance for practitioners. *Families in Society, 76,* 395–407.

Franklin, C. (1996a). Solution-focused therapy: A marital case study using recursive dialectic analysis. *Journal of Family Psychotherapy, 7*(1), 31–51.

Franklin, C. (1996b). Learning to teach qualitative research: Reflections of a quantitative research. In J. F. Gilgun & M. B. Sussman (Eds.), *The methods and methodologies of qualitative family research* (pp. 241–274). New York: Haworth.

Franklin, C., & Jordan, C. (1995). Qualitative assessment: A methodological review. *Families in Society, 78,* 281–295.

Fravel, D. L., & Boss, P. G. (1992). An in-depth interview with the parents of missing children. In J. F. Gilgun, K. Daly, & G. Handel (Eds.), *Qualitative methods in family research* (pp. 126–145). Newbury Park, CA: Sage.

Frazier, E. F. (1932). *The Negro family in Chicago.* Chicago: University of Chicago Press.

Frazier, E. F. (1939). *The Negro family in the United States.* Chicago: University of Chicago Press.

Freedman, J., & Combs, G. (1996). *Narrative therapy: The social construction of preferred realities.* New York: Norton.

Freire, P. (1986). *Pedagogy of the oppressed* (M. B. Ramos, Trans.). New York: Continuum. (Original work published in 1968).

Gale, J. E. (1991). *Conversation analysis of therapeutic discourse.* Hillsdale, NJ: Erlbaum.

Gale, J. (1996). Conversation analysis: Studying the construction of therapeutic realities. In D. H. Sprenkle & S. M. Moon (Eds.), *Research methods in family therapy* (pp. 107–124). New York: Guilford.

Gale, J., & Newfield, N. (1992). A conversation analysis of a solution-focused marital therapy session. *Journal of Marital and Family Therapy, 18,* 153–165.

Garfinkel, H. (1967). *Studies in ethnomethodology.* Englewood Cliffs, NJ: Prentice-Hall.

Gelles, R. J. (1974). *The violent home: A study of physical aggression between husbands and wives.* Beverly Hills, CA: Sage.

Giddens, A. (1971). *Capitalism and modern social theory.* Cambridge: Cambridge University Press.

Gilbert, K. (1996, July). *Collateral damage? Indirect exposure to emotions among students and staff.* Paper presented at Essex '96 the Fourth International Social Science Methodology Conference, University of Essex, Essex, England.

Gilgun, J. F. (1990a). The sexual development of men sexually abused as children. In M. Hunter (Ed.), *The sexually abused male: Prevalence, impact, and treatment* (pp. 177–190). Lexington, MA: Lexington Books.

Gilgun, J. F. (1990b, November). *The place of qualitative methods in the study of the family.* A paper presented on the Pre-Conference Workshop on Theory Construction and Research Methodology, National Council on Family Relations Annual Meeting, Seattle, WA.

Gilgun, J. F. (1991). Resilience and the intergenerational transmission of child sexual abuse. In M. Q. Patton (Ed.), *Family sexual abuse:*

Frontline research and evaluation (pp. 93–105). Newbury Park, CA: Sage.

Gilgun, J. F. (1992a). Chicago days: Handel, Lopata, and Strauss tell stories of their lives as students at Chicago. *Qualitative Family Research, 6*(2), 3–6.

Gilgun, J. F. (1992b). Definitions, methods, and methodologies in qualitative family research. In J. F. Gilgun, K. Daly, & G. Handel (Eds.), *Qualitative methods in family research* (pp. 22–41). Newbury Park, CA: Sage.

Gilgun, J. F. (1992c). Field methods training in the Chicago School traditions: The early career of Bob Bogdan. *Qualitative Family Research, 6*(1), 8–11.

Gilgun, J. F. (1992d). Hypothesis generation in social work research. *Journal of Social Service Research, 15,* 113–135.

Gilgun, J. F. (1993a). Dimensional analysis and grounded theory: Interviews with Leonard Schatzman. *Qualitative Family Research, 7*(1–2), 1–2, 4–7.

Gilgun, J. F. (1993b). Publishing research reports based on qualitative methods. *Marriage & Family Review, 18,* 177–180.

Gilgun, J. F. (1994a). A case for case studies in social work research. *Social Work, 39,* 371–380.

Gilgun, J. F. (1994b). Avengers, conquerors, playmates, and lovers: A continuum of roles played by perpetrator of child sexual abuse. *Families in Society, 75,* 467–480.

Gilgun, J. F. (1994c). Freedom of choice and research interviewing in child sexual abuse. In B. G. Compton & B. Galaway (Eds.), *Social work processes* (5th ed., pp. 358–368). Chicago: Dorsey.

Gilgun, J. F. (1994d). Hand into glove: Grounded theory and social work practice research. In W. Reid & E. Sherman (Eds.), *Qualitative methods and social work practice research* (pp. 115–125). New York: Columbia University Press.

Gilgun, J. F. (1995a, November). *Fingernails painted red: A reflexive, semiotic analysis of a case of family murder.* Paper presented at the symposium on Interpreting Qualitative Data at the annual meeting of the National Council on Family Relations, Portland, OR.

Gilgun, J. F. (1995b). We shared something special: The moral discourse of incest perpetrators. *Journal of Marriage and the Family, 57,* 265–281.

Gilgun, J. F. (1996a). Human development and adversity in ecological perspective: Part 1: A conceptual framework. *Families in Society, 77,* 395–402.

Gilgun, J. F. (1996b). Human development and adversity in ecological perspective: Part 2: Three patterns. *Families in Society, 77*(2), 459–476.

Gilgun, J. F. (in press). Mapping resilience as process among adults with childhood adversities. In H. McCubbin, J. Futrell, & A. Thompson (Eds.), *Resilience in families: Qualitative approaches.* Madison, WI: Center for Excellence in Family Studies.

Gilgun, J. F., & Sussman, M. B. (Eds.). (1996). *The methods and methodologies of qualitative family research.* Binghamton, NY: Haworth.

Gilgun, J. F., Daly, K., & Handel, G. (Eds.). (1992). *Qualitative methods in family research.* Newbury Park, CA: Sage.

Gilligan, C. (1982). *In a different voice: Psychological theory and women's development.* Cambridge, MA: Harvard University Press.

Gilligan, S., & Price, R. (1993). *Therapeutic conversations.* New York: Norton.

Giorgi, A., Fischer, W. F., & von Eckartsberg, R. (Eds.). (1971). *Duquesne studies in phenomenological psychology* (Vol. 1). Pittsburgh, PA: Duquesne University Press.

Giorgi, A., Fischer, W. F., & Murray, E. (Eds.). (1975). *Duquesne studies in phenomenological psychology* (Vol. 2). Pittsburgh, PA: Duquesne University Press.

Giorgi, A., Knowles, R., & Smith, D. L. (1979). *Duquesne studies in phenomenological psychology* (Vol. 3). Pittsburgh, PA: Duquesne University Press.

Glaser, B. (1978). *Theoretical sensitivity*. Mill Valley, CA: Sociology Press.

Glaser, B. (1992). *Basics of grounded theory analysis*. Mill Valley, CA: Sociology Press.

Glaser, B., & Strauss, A. (1967). *The discovery of grounded theory*. Chicago: Aldine.

Gluckman, M. (1971). Preface. In E. Bott (Ed.), *Family and social network* (2nd ed., pp. xiii–xxx). New York: Free Press.

Goldstein, H. (1996). *The home on Gorham Street and the voices of its children*. Tuscaloosa: University of Alabama Press.

Gordon, L. (1977). *Women's body, women's right: A social history of birth control in America*. New York: Penguin.

Guba, E. (Ed.). (1990). *The paradigm dialogue*. Newbury Park, CA: Sage.

Guba, E., & Lincoln, Y. S. (1994). Competing paradigms in qualitative research. In N. K. Denzin & Y. S. Lincoln (Eds.), *Handbook of qualitative research* (pp. 105–117). Thousand Oaks, CA: Sage.

Gubrium, J. F., & Holstein, J. A. (1990). *Where is family?* Mountain View, CA: Mayfield.

Gubrium, J. F., & Holstein, J. A. (1993). Family discourse, organizational embeddedness, and local enactment. *Journal of Family Issues, 14*, 66–81.

Gurman, A., Kniskern, D., & Pinsof, W. (1986). Research on the process and outcome of marital and family therapy. In S. Bergin & A. Garfield (Eds.), *Handbook of psychotherapy and behavior change* (3rd ed., pp. 565–624). New York: Wiley.

Habermas, J. (1971). *Knowledge and human interests*. (J. J. Shapiro, Trans.). Boston: Beacon.

Haley, J. (1987). *Family problem solving* (2nd ed.). San Francisco: Jossey-Bass.

Hall, L., & Zvonkovic, A. (1996). Egalitarianism and oppression in marriage: The effects of research on researchers. In J. F. Gilgun & M. B. Sussman (Eds.), *The methods and methodologies of qualitative family research* (pp. 89–104). Binghamton, NY: Haworth.

Hamabata, M. M. (1993). *Crested kimono: Power and love in the Japanese business family*. Ithaca, NY: Cornell University Press.

Hamilton, D. (1994). Traditions, preferences, and postures in applied qualitative research. In N. K. Denzin & Y. S. Lincoln (Eds.), *Handbook of qualitative research* (pp. 60–69). Thousand Oaks, CA: Sage.

Hamilton, G. V. (1929). *A research in marriage*. New York: Albert & Charles Boni.

Hammersley, M. (1989). *The dilemma of qualitative method: Herbert Blumer and the Chicago tradition*. London: Routledge.

Hanawalt, B. (1996). The composite biography as a methodological tool for the study of childhood in history. In J. F. Gilgun & M. B. Sussman (Eds.), *The methods and methodologies of qualitative family research* (pp. 323–334). Binghamton, NY: Haworth.

Hanawalt, B. A. (1986). *The ties that bound: Peasant families in medieval England*. New York: Oxford University Press.

Hanawalt, B. A. (1993). *Growing up in medieval London*. New York: Oxford University Press.

Handel, G. (1965). Psychological study of whole families. *Psychological Bulletin, 63*, 19–41.

Handel, G. (Ed.). (1967). *The psychosocial interior of the family*. Chicago: Aldine.

Handel, G. (Ed.). (1988). *Childhood socialization*. New York: Aldine.

Handel, G. (1991). Case study in family research. In J. R. Geagin, A. M. Orum, & G. Sjoberg (Eds.), *A case for the case study* (pp. 244–268). Chapel Hill: University of North Carolina Press.

Handel, G. (1992). The qualitative tradition in family research. In J. F. Gilgun, K. Daly, & G. Handel (Eds.), *Qualitative methods in family research* (pp. 12–21). Newbury Park, CA: Sage.

Handel, G. (1996). *Family Worlds* and qualitative family research. In J. F. Gilgun & M. B. Sussman (Eds.), *The methods and methodologies of qualitative family research* (pp. 335–348). Binghamton, NY: Haworth.

Handel, G., & Whitchurch, G. G. (Eds.). (1993). *The psychosocial interior of the family* (4th ed., pp. 69–85). New York: Aldine.

Harding, S. (Ed.). (1987). *Feminism and methodology*. Bloomington: Indiana University Press.

Harding, S. (1991). *Whose science? Whose knowledge? Thinking from women's lives*. Ithaca, NY: Cornell University Press.

Heidegger, M. (1962). *Being and time* (J. Macquarried & E. Robinson, Trans.). New York: Harper & Row. (Original work published 1927)

Hess, R. D., & Handel, G. (1959). *Family worlds: A psychosocial approach to family life*. Chicago: University of Chicago Press.

Hill, R. (1941). *Families under stress*. New York: Harper & Row.

Hill, R. (1981). Whither family research in the 1980s: Continuities, emergence, constraints, and new horizons. *Journal of Marriage and the Family, 43*, 255–257.

Hochschild, A. R. (1983). *The managed heart: Commercialization of human feeling*. Berkeley: University of California Press.

Hodges, H. A. (1994). *William Dilthey: An introduction*. London: Routledge.

Hoffman, L. (1981). *Foundations of family therapy: A conceptual framework for systems change*. New York: Basic Books.

Holbrook, T. L. (1996). Document analysis: Contrasts between official case records and the journal of a woman on welfare. In J. F. Gilgun & M. B. Sussman (Eds.), *The methods and methodologies of qualitative family research* (pp. 41–56). Binghamton, NY: Haworth.

Holstein, J. A., & Gubrium, J. F. (1994). Phenomenology, ethnomethodology, and interpretive practice. In N. K. Denzin & Y. S. Lincoln (Eds.), *Handbook of qualitative research* (pp. 262–272). Thousand Oaks, CA: Sage.

Hooks, B. (1981). *Aint I a Woman? Black women and feminism*. Boston: South End Press.

Hooks, B. (1984). *Feminist theory: From margin to center*. Boston: South End Press.

Hunt, M. (1969). *The affair*. New York: World.

Hull-House maps and papers, by residents of Hull-House, a social settlement. A presentation of nationalities and wages in a congested district of Chicago, together with comments and essays on problems growing out of the social conditions. (1895). New York: Crowell.

Husserl, E. (1931). *Ideas* (W. R. Boyce Gibson, Trans.) London: Allen & Unwin.

Husserl, E. (1977). *Basic writings* (D. Krell, Ed.). New York: Harper & Row.

Jago, B. J. (1996). Postcards, ghosts, and fathers: Revising family stories. *Qualitative Inquiry, 2*, 495–516.

Janeway, E. (1980). Who is Sylvia? On the loss of sexual paradigms. *Signs, 5*, 573–589.

Jick, T. D. (1979). Mixing qualitative and quantitative methods: Triangulation in action. *Administration Science Quarterly, 24*, 602–611.

Johnson, C. S. (1922). *The Negro in Chicago: A study of race relations and a race riot in 1919*. Chicago: University of Chicago Press.

Kanton, D., & Lehr, W. (1975). *Inside the family: Toward a theory of family process*. New York: Harper & Row.

Keeney, B. P. (1990). *Improvisational therapy*. St. Paul, MN: Systemic Therapy Press.

Keeney, B. P., & Bobele, M. (1989). A brief note on family violence. *Australian and New Zealand Journal of Family Therapy, 10*(2), 93–95.

Keeney, B. P., & Ross, J. M. (1985). *Mind in therapy: Constructing systemic family therapies*. New York: Basic Books.

Kidder, L. H. (1981). Qualitative research and quasi-experimental frameworks. In M. B. Brewer & B. E. Collins (Eds.), *Scientific inquiry and the social sciences* (pp. 226–256). San Francisco: Jossey-Bass.

Kitson, G. C., Clark, R. D., Rushforth, N. B., Brinich, P. M., Sudak, H. S., & Zyzanski, J. (1996). Research on difficult family topics: Helping new and experienced researchers cope with research on loss. *Family Relations, 45*, 183–188.

Komarovsky, M. (1940). *The unemployed man and his family*. New York: Dryden.

Komarovsky, M. (1962). *Blue-collar marriage*. New York: Random House.

Koss, E. L. (1946). *Families in trouble*. New York: King's Crown Press.

Lamendola, F. P., & Newman, M. A. (1994). The paradox of HIV/AIDS as expanding consciousness. *Advances in Nursing Science, 16*(3), 13–21.

LaRossa, R. (1983). The transition to parenthood and the social reality of time. *Journal of Marriage and the Family, 45,* 579–589.

LaRossa, R. (1988). Renewing our faith in qualitative family research. *Journal of Contemporary Ethnography, 17,* 243–260.

LaRossa, R., & LaRossa, M. M. (1981). *The transition to parenthood: How infants change families*. Beverly Hills, CA: Sage.

LaRossa, R., & Reitzes, D. C. (1993). Symbolic interactionism and family studies. In P. G. Boss, W. J. Doherty, R. LaRossa, W. R. Schumm, & S. K. Steinmetz (Eds.), *Sourcebook of family theories and methods: A contextual approach* (pp. 135–163). New York: Plenum.

LaRossa, R., & Wolf, J. (1985). On qualitative family research. *Journal of Marriage and the Family, 47,* 531–541.

Larzelere, R. E., & Klein, D. M. (1987). Methodology. In M. B. Sussman & S. K. Steinmetz (Eds.), *Handbook of marriage and the family* (pp. 125–155). New York: Plenum.

Lasch, C. (1977). *Haven in a heartless world: The family besieged*. New York: Basic Books.

Lather, P. (1991). *Getting smart: Feminist research and pedagogy with/in the postmodern*. New York: Routledge.

Lavee, Y., & Dollahite, D. C. (1991). The linkage between theory and research in family science. *Journal of Marriage and the Family, 53,* 361–373.

Laws, J. L. (1979). *The second X: Sex role and social role*. New York: Elsevier.

LeCompte, M. D. (1993). A framework for hearing silence: What does telling stories mean when we are supposed to be doing science? In D. McLaughlin & W. G. Tierney (Eds.), *Naming silenced lives: Personal narratives and the process of educational change* (pp. 2–9). New York: Routledge.

LeCompte, M. D., & Goetz, J. P. (1982). Problems of reliability and validity in ethnographic research. *Review of Educational Research, 52,* 31–60.

Leininger, M. (1969). Ethnoscience: A new and promising research approach for the health sciences. *Images, 3*(1), 2–8.

Leininger, M. (1978). *Transcultural nursing: Concepts, theories and practices*. New York: Wiley.

Leininger, M. (1985). *Qualitative research methods in nursing*. Orlando, FL: Grune & Stratton.

Leonard, V. W. (1994). In P. Benner (Ed.), *Interpretive phenomenology* (pp. 43–63). Thousand Oaks, CA: Sage.

LePlay, F. (1855). *Les ouvriers europeens*. Tours: Alfred Mame.

LePlay, F. E. (1866). *La reforme social en France*. Paris: Dentu.

LePlay, F. (1879). *Les ouvriers europeens* (2nd ed.). Paris: Alfred Mame et fils.

Lewin, K. (1935). *A dynamic theory of personality*. New York: McGraw-Hill.

Lewin, K. (1936). *Principles of topological psychology*. New York: McGraw-Hill.

Lewis, O. (1962). *Five families*. New York: Wiley.

Lewis, O. (1963). *The children of Sanchez*. New York: Vintage.

Lewis, O. (1964). *Pedro Martinez*. New York: Random House.

Lewis, O. (1965). *La vida*. New York: Vintage.

Lincoln, Y. (1995). Emerging criteria for quality in qualitative and interpretive research. *Qualitative Inquiry, 1,* 275–289.

Lincoln, Y. S., & Guba, E. G. (1985). *Naturalistic inquiry*. Newbury Park, CA: Sage.

Lindesmith, A. R. (1947). *Opiate addiction*. Bloomington, IN: Principia.

Lindesmith, A. R., Strauss, A. L., & Denzin, N. K. (1975). *Social psychology* (5th ed.). New York: Holt, Rinehart and Winston.

Lipman-Blumen, J. (1984). *Gender roles and power*. Englewood Cliffs, NJ: Prentice-Hall.

Lofland, J., & Lofland, L. H. (1995). *Analyzing social settings: A guide to qualitative observation and analysis* (3rd ed.). Belmont, CA: Wadsworth.

Lopata, H. Z. (1971). *Occupation: Housewife*. Oxford: Oxford University Press.

Lopata, H. Z. (1973). *Widowhood in an American city*. Cambridge, MA: Schenkman.

Lopata, H. Z. (1979). *Women as widows: Support systems*. New York: Elsevier.

Lopata, H. Z. (1992a). *Circles and settings: Role changes of American women*. Philadelphia, PA: Temple University Press.

Lopata, H. Z. (1992b). Sensitizing concepts, historical analysis, and role theory. *Qualitative Family Research, 6*(1), 1–2, 13.

Lopata, H. Z. (1996). *Current widowhood*. Thousand Oaks, CA: Sage.

Lopata, H. Z., with Miller, C. A., & Barnewolt, D. (1984). *City women: Work, jobs, occupations, careers. Volume 1: America*. New York: Praeger.

Lopata, H. Z., with Barnewolt, D., & Miller, C. A. (1985). *City women: Work, jobs, occupations, careers. Volume 2: Chicago*. New York: Praeger.

Lynch, M., & Peyrot, M. (1992). Introduction: A reader's guide to ethnomethodology. *Qualitative Sociology, 15,* 113–122.

Manning, P. K. (1982). Analytic induction. In R. B. Smith & P. K. Manning (Eds.), *Qualitative methods, Vol. II, Handbook of Social Sciences* (pp. 273–302). Cambridge, MA: Ballinger.

Manning, P. K., & Cullum-Swan, B. (1994). Narrative, content, and semiotic analysis. In N. K. Denzin & Y. S. Lincoln (Eds.), *Handbook of qualitative research* (pp. 463–477). Thousand Oaks, CA: Sage.

Marshall, C., & Rossman, G. B. (1995). *Designing qualitative research* (2nd ed.), Newbury Park, CA: Sage.

Martin, R. R. (1995). *Oral history in social work: Research, assessment, and intervention*. Thousand Oaks, CA: Sage.

Matthews, F. H. (1977). *Quest for an American sociology: Robert E. Park and the Chicago School*. Montreal: McGill-Queens University Press.

McCabe, A., & Peterson, C. (1991). *Developing narrative structure*. Hillsdale, NJ: Erlbaum.

McCubbin, H. I., & Thompson, A. I. (1989). *Balancing work and family life on Wall Street: Stockbrokers and families coping with economic instability*. Edina, MN: Burgess International.

McCubbin, H. I., & Cauble, E., & Patterson, J. M. (Eds.). (1984). *Family stress, coping and social support*. Springfield, IL: Thomas.

McCubbin, H. I., Thompson, E. A., Thompson, A. I., & Fromer, J. E. (Eds.). (1994). *Sense of coherence and resiliency: Stress, coping, and health*. Madison, WI: Center for Excellence in Family Studies.

McKinney, J. C. (1966). *Constructive typology and social theory*. New York: Appleton-Century-Crofts.

McLaughlin, D., & Tierney, W. G. (Eds.). (1993). *Naming silenced lives: Personal narratives and the process of educational change*. New York: Routledge.

McMahon, M. (1995). *Engendering motherhood: Identity and transformation in women's lives*. New York: Guilford.

Mendenhall, T. J., Grotevant, H. D., & McRoy, R. G. (1996). Adoptive couples: communication and changes made in openness levels. *Family Relations, 45,* 223–229.

Merleau-Ponty, M. (1962). *Phenomenology of perception* (C. Smith, Trans.). London: Routledge & Kegan Paul.

Miles, M. B., & Huberman, A. M. (1994). *Qualitative data analysis* (2nd ed.). Thousand Oaks, CA: Sage.

Minuchin, S., & Fishman, H. C. (1981). *Family therapy techniques.* Cambridge, MA: Harvard University Press.

Mitchell, R. G., Jr., & Charmaz, K. (1996). Telling tales, writing stories: Postmodernist visions and realist images in ethnographic writing. *Journal of Contemporary Ethnography, 25,* 144–166.

Moon, S. M., Dillon, D. R., & Sprenkle, D. H. (1990). Family therapy and qualitative research. *Journal of Marital and Family Therapy, 16,* 357–373.

Morgaine, C. A. (1992a). Alternative paradigms in family life education. *Family Relations, 41,* 12–17.

Morgaine, C. A. (1992b). Beyond prevention: A program for empowering parents and professionals. *Family Science Review, 5,* 65–84.

Morgaine, C. A. (1994). Enlightenment for emancipation: A critical theory of self-formation. *Family Relations, 43,* 325–335.

Morris, G. H., & Chenail, R. J. (Eds.). (1995). *The talk of the clinic: Explorations in the analysis of medical and therapeutic discourse.* Hillsdale, NJ: Erlbaum.

Morrow, R. A., with Brown, D. D. (1994). *Critical theory and methodology.* Thousand Oaks, CA: Sage.

Morse, J. M. (1991). On the evaluation of qualitative proposals. *Qualitative Health Research, 1,* 147–151.

Morse, J. M. (1994). Designing funded qualitative research. In N. K. Denzin & Y. S. Lincoln (Eds.), *Handbook of qualitative research* (pp. 220–235). Thousand Oaks, CA: Sage.

Moustakas, C. (1994). *Phenomenological research methods.* Thousand Oaks, CA: Sage.

Mowrer, E. R. (1927). *Family disorganization: An introduction to a sociological analysis.* Chicago: University of Chicago Press.

Mowrer, E. R. (1932). *The family.* Chicago: University of Chicago Press.

Mowrer, E. R., with Mowrer, H. R. (1928). *Domestic discord: Its analysis and treatment.* Chicago: University of Chicago Press.

Murray, S. B. (1996). "We all love Charles:" Men in child care and the social construction of gender. *Gender & Society, 10,* 368–387.

Nadeau, J. (1997). *Families making sense of death: Meaning-making in bereavement.* Thousand Oaks, CA: Sage.

Newfield, N. A., Kuehl, B. P., Joanning, H. P., & Quinn, W. H. (1990). A mini ethnography of the family therapy of adolescent drug abuse: The ambiguous experience. *Alcoholism Treatment Quarterly, 7,* 57–79.

Newfield, N. A., Joanning, H. P., Kuehl, B. P., & Quinn, W. H. (1991). We can tell you about "psychos" and "shrinks": An ethnography of the family therapy of adolescent drug abuse. In T. C. Todd & M. D. Selekman (Eds.), *Family therapy approaches with adolescent substance abuse* (pp. 277–310). Boston: Allyn & Bacon.

Newman, M. A. (1986). *Health as expanding consciousness.* St. Louis, MO: Mosby.

Newman, M. A. (1989). The spirit of nursing. *Holistic Nursing Practice, 3*(3), 1–6.

Newmark, M., & Beels, C. (1994). The misuse and use of science in family therapy. *Family Process, 33,* 3–17.

Nosek, M. A., Young, M. E., Rintala, D. H., Howland, C. A., Foley, C. C., & Bennett, J. L. (1995). Barriers to reproductive health maintenance among women with physical disabilities. *Journal of Women's Health, 4,* 505–518.

Noth, W. (1995). *Handbook of semiotics.* Bloomington: Indiana University.

Nye, F. I. (1988). Fifty years of family research, 1937–1987. *Journal of Marriage and the Family, 50,* 305–316.

Oakley, A. (1974). *The sociology of housework.* New York: Pantheon.

Olesen, M., Heading, C., Shadick, K. M., & Bistodeau, J. A. (1994). Quality of life in long-stay institutions in England: Nurse and resident perceptions. *Journal of Advanced Nursing, 20,* 23–32.

Olesen, V. (1994). Feminisms and models of qualitative research. In N. K. Denzin & Y. S. Lincoln (Eds.), *Handbook of qualitative research* (pp. 158–174). Thousand Oaks, CA: Sage.

Olesen, V., Droes, N., Hatton, D., Chico, N., & Schatzman, L. (1994). Analyzing together: Recollections of a team approach. In A. Bryman & R. G. Burgess (Eds.), *Analyzing qualitative data* (pp. 111–128). London: Routledge.

Olsen, C. S. (1996). African-American adolescent women: Perceptions of gender, race, and class. In J. F. Gilgun & M. B. Sussman (Eds.), *The methods and methodologies of qualitative family research* (pp. 105–121). Binghamton, NY: Haworth.

Osmond, M. W. (1987). Radical-critical theories. In M. B. Sussman & S. K. Steinmetz (Eds.), *Handbook of marriage and the family* (pp. 103–124). New York: Plenum.

Osmond, M. W., & Thorne, B. (1993). Feminist theories: The social construction of gender in families and society. In P. G. Boss, W. J. Doherty, R. LaRossa, W. R. Schumm, & S. K. Steinmetz (Eds.), *Sourcebook of family theories and methods: A contextual approach* (pp. 591–623). New York: Plenum.

Packer, M. (1985). Hermeneutic inquiry in the study of human conduct. *American Psychologist, 40,* 1081–1093.

Packer, M. J., & Addison, R. B. (Eds.). (1989). *Entering the circle: Hermeneutic investigation in psychology.* Albany: State University of New York Press.

Palmer, R. E. (1969). *Hermeneutics: Interpretive theory in Schleiermacher, Dilthey, Heidegger, and Gadamer.* Evanston, IL: Northwestern University Press.

Palmer, V. (1928). *Field methods in sociology.* Chicago: University of Chicago Press.

Park, R. E., & Burgess, E. W. (Eds.). (1921). *Introduction to the science of sociology.* Chicago: University of Chicago Press.

Patton, M. Q. (1990). *Qualitative evaluation and research methods* (2nd ed.). Newbury Park, CA: Sage.

Plager, K. A. (1994). Hermeneutic phenomenology: A methodology for family health and health promotion study in nursing. In P. Benner (Ed.), *Interpretive phenomenology* (pp. 65–83). Thousand Oaks, CA: Sage.

Polkinghorne, D. (1983). *Methodology for the human sciences: Systems of inquiry.* Albany: State University of New York at Albany.

Pollner, M., & McDonald-Wilker, L. (1985). The social construction of unreality: A case study of a family's attribution of competence to a severely retarded child. *Family Process, 28,* 241–254.

Polson, M., & Piercy, F. P. (1993). The impact of training stress on married family therapy trainees and their families: A focus group study. *Journal of Marital and Family Therapy, 4,* 69–92.

Punch, M. (1994). Politics and ethics in qualitative research. In N. K. Denzin & Y. S. Lincoln (Eds.), *Handbook of qualitative research* (pp. 83–97). Thousand Oaks, CA: Sage.

Quint, J. C. (1966). Awareness of death and the nurses' composure. *Nursing Research, 15,* 49–55.

Quint, J. C. (1967). *The nurse and the dying patient.* New York: Macmillan.

Rainwater, L. (1970). *Behind ghetto walls.* Chicago: Aldine.

Rainwater, L., Coleman, R., & Handel, G. (1959). *Workingman's wife.* New York: Oceana.

Reason, P., & Rowan, J. (Eds.). (1981). *Human inquiry: A sourcebook of new paradigm inquiry.* New York: Wiley.

Red Collective. (1978). *The politics of sexuality in capitalism.* London: Publications Distribution Cooperative.

Reif, L. (1975). Ulcerative colitis: Strategies for managing life. In A. Strauss (Ed.), *Chronic illness and the quality of life* (pp. 81–88). St. Louis, MO: Mosby.

Reinharz, S. (1992). *Feminist methods in social research.* New York: Oxford University Press.

Rettig, K. D., Tam, V. C.-W., & Magistad, B. M. (1996). Using pattern matching and modified analytic induction in examining justice principles in child support guidelines. In J. F. Gilgun & M. B. Sussman (Eds.), *The methods and methodologies of qualitative family research* (pp. 193–222). Binghamton, NY: Haworth.

Richards, T. J., & Richards, L. (1994). Using computers in qualitative research. In N. K. Denzin & Y. S. Lincoln (Eds.), *Handbook of qualitative research* (pp. 445–462). Thousand Oaks, CA: Sage.

Riessman, C. K. (1990). *Divorce talk: Women and men make sense of personal relationships.* New Brunswick, NJ: Rutgers University Press.

Riessman, C. K. (1993). *Narrative analysis.* Newbury Park, CA: Sage.

Riessman, C. K. (Ed.). (1994). *Qualitative studies in social work research.* Thousand Oaks, CA: Sage.

Rosenau, P. M. (1992). *Post-modernism and the social sciences.* Princeton, NJ: Princeton University Press.

Rosenblatt, P. C. (1983). *Bitter, bitter tears: Nineteenth century diarists and twentieth century grief theories.* Minneapolis: University of Minnesota Press.

Rosenblatt, P. C., & Fischer, L. R. (1993). Qualitative family research. In P. G. Boss, W. J. Doherty, R. LaRossa, W. R. Schumm, & S. K. Steinmetz (Eds.), *Sourcebook of family theories and methods: A contextual approach* (pp. 167–177). New York: Plenum.

Rosenwald, G. C., & Ochberg, R. (Eds.). (1992). *Storied lives: The cultural politics of self-understanding.* New Haven, CT: Yale University Press.

Rossi, A., Calderwood, A. (1973). *Academic women on the move.* New York: Russell Sage.

Rubin, J. (1988, January). *Ethics and the concept of the person.* Lecture series at the University of California, San Francisco.

Rubin, L. B. (1976). *Worlds of pain: Life in the working-class family.* New York: Basic Books.

Runyan, W. M. (1984). *Life histories and psychobiography: Explorations in theory and method.* New York: Oxford University Press.

Satir, V. (1967). *Conjoint family therapy.* Palo Alto, CA: Science and Behavior Books.

Schatzman, L. (1991). Dimensional analysis: Notes on an alternative approach to the grounding of theory in qualitative research. In D. R. Maines (Ed.), *Social organization and social process: Essays in honor of Anselm Strauss* (pp. 303–314). New York: Aldine.

Schatzman, L., & Strauss, A. (1973). *Field research: Strategies for a natural sociology.* Englewood Cliffs, NJ: Prentice-Hall.

Schwandt, T. A. (1994). Constructivist, interpretivist approaches to human inquiry. In N. K. Denzin & Y. S. Lincoln (Eds.), *Handbook of qualitative research* (pp. 118–137). Thousand Oaks, CA: Sage.

Schwandt, T. A. (1996). Farewell to criteriology. *Qualitative Inquiry, 2,* 58–72.

Schwartz, B. (1994). Where is cultural studies? *Cultural Studies, 8,* 377–393.

Sells, S. P., Smith, T. E., Coe, M. J., Yoshioka, M., & Robbins, J. (1994). An ethnography of couple and therapist experiences in reflecting team practice. *Journal of Marital and Family Therapy, 20*(3), 247–266.

Sells, S. P., Smith, T. E., & Sprenkle, D. H. (1995). Integrating qualitative and quantitative research methods: A research model. *Family Process, 34,* 199–218.

Selvini-Palazzoli, M., Cecchin, G., Prata, G., & Boscolo, L. (1978). *Paradox and counterparadox.* New York: Aronson.

Shaw, C. (1930). *The jack roller.* Chicago: University of Chicago Press.

Silver, C. B. (1982). (Ed., Trans. and with an introduction by C. B. Silver). *Frederic LePlay: On family, work, and social change.* Chicago: University of Chicago Press.

Singer, J., & Salovey, P. (1993). *The remembered self.* New York: Free press.

Small, A. W. (1916). Fifty years of sociology in the United States, 1865–1915. *American Journal of Sociology, 21,* 712–864.

Smith, K. (1993). *After the demise of empiricism: The problem of judging social and education inquiry.* Norwood, NJ: Ablex.

Smith, S. (1993). Who's talking/Who's talking back? *Signs, 18,* 392–407.

Smith, T. E., Winston, M., & Yoshioka, M. (1992). A qualitative understanding of reflective-teams II: Therapists' perspectives. *Contemporary Family Therapy, 14,* 419–432.

Smith, T. E., Yoshioka, M., & Winston, M. (1993). A qualitative understanding of Reflecting teams I: Clients' perspectives. *Journal of Systemic Therapies, 12,* 29–45.

Smith, T. E., Sells, S. P., & Clevenger, T. (1994). Ethnographic content analysis of couple and therapist perceptions in a reflecting team setting. *Journal of Marital and Family Therapy, 20,* 267–286.

SmithBattle, L. (1993). Mothering in the midst of danger. In S. L. Feetham, S. B. Meister, J. M. Bell, & C. L. Gilliss (Eds.), *The nursing of families* (pp. 141–166). Newbury Park, CA: Sage.

SmithBattle, L. (1994). Beyond normalizing: The role of narrative in understanding teenage mothers' transition to mothering. In P. Benner (Ed.), *Interpretive phenomenology* (pp. 141–166). Thousand Oaks, CA: Sage.

SmithBattle, L. (1995). Teenage mothers' narratives of self: An examination of risking the future. *Advances in Nursing Science, 17,* 22–36.

SmithBattle, L. (1996). Intergenerational ethics of caring for adolescent mothers and their children. *Family Relations, 45,* 56–64.

Sollie, D. L., & Leslie, L. A. (Eds.). (1994). *Gender, families, and close relationships: Feminist research journeys.* Thousand Oaks, CA: Sage.

Spradley, J. (1979). *The ethnographic interview.* New York: Holt, Rinehart and Winston.

Sprenkle, D. H., & Moon, S. M. (Eds.). (1996). *Research methods in family therapy.* New York: Guilford.

Sprey, J. (1982). Editorial comments. *Journal of Marriage and the Family, 44,* 5.

Stacey, J. (1990). *Brave new families: Stories of domestic upheaval in late twentieth century America.* New York: Basic Books.

Stack, C. B. (1974). *All our kin: Strategies for survival in a black community.* New York: Harper.

Stake, R. (1996). *The art of case study research.* Thousand Oaks, CA: Sage.

Stamp, G. H. (1991). Family conversation: Description and interpretation. *Family Process, 30,* 251–263.

Stanley, L., & Wise, S. (1983). *Breaking out: Feminist consciousness and feminist research.* London: Routledge & Kegan Paul.

Steedman, C. (1990). *Childhood, culture and class in Britain: Margaret McMillan, 1860–1931.* New Brunswick, NJ: Rutgers University Press.

Stern, P. N. (1980). Grounded theory methodology: Its uses and processes. *Image, 12,* 29–33.

Stern, P. N. (1985). Using grounded theory method in nursing research. In M. Leininger (Ed.), *Qualitative research methods in nursing* (pp. 149–160). Orlando, FL: Grune & Stratton.

Stivers, C. (1993). Reflections on the role of personal narrative in social science. *Signs, 18,* 408–425.

Strauss, A. (1987). *Qualitative analysis for social scientists.* New York: Cambridge University Press.

Strauss, A., & Corbin, J. (1990). *Basics of qualitative research: Grounded theory procedures and techniques.* Newbury Park, CA: Sage.

Strauss, A. L., & Glaser, B. G. (1970). *Anguish: A case history of a dying trajectory.* Mill Valley, CA: Sociology Press.

Strauss, A., Schatzman, L., Bucher, R., Ehrlich, D., & Sabshin, M. (1964). *Psychiatric ideologies and institutions.* New York: Free Press.

Sussman, M. B. (1993). Commentary on publishing. *Marriage & Family Review, 18,* 109–117.

Taylor, C. (1985). *Human agency and language: Philosophical papers I.* Cambridge, MA: Harvard University Press.

Taylor, C. (1989). *Sources of the self: The making of the modern identity.* Cambridge, MA: Harvard University Press.

Taylor, C. (1991). *The ethics of authenticity.* Cambridge, MA: Harvard University Press.

Thomas, D. L., & Wilcox, J. E. (1987). The rise of family theory: A historical and critical analysis. In M. B. Sussman & S. K. Steinmetz (Eds.), *Handbook of marriage and the family* (pp. 81–102). New York: Plenum.

Thomas, W. I., & Znaniecki, F. (1927). *The Polish peasant in Europe and America,* Vol. 1–2. New York: Knopf. (Original work published 1918–1920)

Thompson, L. (1992). Feminist methodology for family studies. *Journal of Marriage and the Family, 54,* 3–18.

Thorne, B., with Yalom, M. (1982). *Rethinking the family: Some feminist questions.* New York: Longman.

Uttal, L. (1996). Custodial care, surrogate care, and coordinated care: Employed mothers and the meaning of child care. *Gender & Society, 10,* 291–311.

Van Maanen, J. (1988). *Tales of the field: On writing ethnography.* Chicago: University of Chicago Press.

Van Manen, M. (1990). *Researching lived experience: Human science for an action sensitive pedagogy.* Albany: State University of New York.

Vidich, A. J., & Lyman, S. M. (1994). Qualitative methods: Their history in sociology and anthropology. In N. K. Denzin & Y. S. Lincoln (Eds.), *Handbook of qualitative research* (pp. 23–59). Thousand Oaks, CA: Sage.

Visweswaran, K. (1994). *Fictions of feminist ethnography.* Minneapolis: University of Minnesota Press.

Walker, J. A. (1996). Letters in the attic: Private reflections of women, wives, and mothers. In J. F. Gilgun & M. B. Sussman (Eds.), *The methods and methodologies of qualitative family research* (pp. 9–40). Binghamton, NY: Haworth.

Waller, W. (1930). *The old love and the new.* New York: Liveright.

Waller, W. (1934). Insight and the scientific method. *American Journal of Sociology, XL,* 285–297.

Warner, W. L., & Lunt, P. S. (1941). *The social life of a modern community* (Vol. 1 of *The Yankee City Series*). New Haven: Yale University Press.

Wax, R. H. (1971). *Doing fieldwork: Warnings and advice.* Chicago: University of Chicago Press.

Webb, S., & Webb, B. (1932). *Methods of social study.* London: Longman, Green.

White, M., & Epston, D. (1990). *Narrative means to therapeutic ends.* New York: Norton.

Whyte, W. F. (1943). A slum sex code. *American Journal of Sociology, XLIX,* 24–31.

Wiener, C. L. (1975). The burden of rheumatoid arthritis. In A. Strauss (Ed.), *Chronic illness and the quality of life* (pp. 71–80). St. Louis, MO: Mosby.

Wilson, H. A., & Hutchinson, S. A. (1991). Triangulation of qualitative methods: Heideggerian hermeneutics and grounded theory. *Qualitative Health Research, 1,* 263–276.

Wiseman, J. E. (1979). *Stations of the lost: The treatment of Skid Row alcoholics.* Chicago: University of Chicago Press.

Wiseman, J. E. (1981). The family and its researcher in the eighties: Retrenching, renewing, and revitalizing. *Journal of Marriage and the Family, 43,* 263–266.

Wiseman, J. E. (1991). *The other half: Wives of alcoholics and their social-psychological situation.* New York: Aldine.

Wittgenstein, L. (1980). *Remarks on the philosophy of psychology* (2 Vols.). Chicago: University of Chicago Press.

Wolcott, H. F. (1994). *Transforming qualitative data: Description, analysis, and interpretation.* Thousand Oaks, CA: Sage.

Wolf, M. (1968). *The house of Lim: A study of a Chinese farm family.* New York: Appleton-Century-Crofts.

Wright, M. M. (1995). "I never did any fieldwork, but I milked an awful lot of cows!" Using rural women's experience to reconceptualize models of work. *Gender & Society, 9,* 216–235.

Wuest, J. (1995). Feminist grounded theory: An exploration of the congruency and tensions between two traditions in knowledge discovery. *Qualitative Health Research, 5,* 125–137.

Young, P. V. (1928). The reorganization of Jewish family life in America. *Social Forces, VII,* 238–243.

Young, P. V. (1932). *The Pilgrims of Russian Town.* Chicago: University of Chicago Press.

Zaretsky, E. (1976). *Capitalism, the family, and personal life.* New York: Harper & Row.

Zimmerman, C. C., & Frampton, M. E. (1935). *Family and society: A study of the sociology of reconstruction.* New York: Van Nostrand Reinhold.

Znaniecki, F. (1934). *The method of sociology.* New York: Farrar & Rinehart.

Zorbaugh, H. (1929). *The Gold Coast and the slum.* Chicago: University of Chicago Press.

CHAPTER 10

Quantitative Methodology for Studying Families

Alan C. Acock

Quantitative Research Methods for Study of Families

Many characteristics shape the research methods of family scholars. First, families have a shared past and future (Copeland & White, 1991). Other fields study groups that have history, but few areas involve a history that is so persistently salient to everyday decisions. Second, families are both sacred and profane. The reverence we have for families challenges researchers who seek to objectify and measure them, while also recognizing the levels of violence, dishonesty, and abuse in families that expressions like "dirty linen" fail to capture. Being both sacred and profane introduces a level of privacy that is difficult to unravel.

Third, family scholars come from a variety of disciplines including anthropology, communications, counseling, demography, economics, family and consumer science, gerontology, history, human ecology, nursing, political science, psychology, social work, and sociology. Each field has its own questions, ideas, standards of proof, and methodologies. Fourth, family scholars utilize a plethora of theories and frameworks including hedonistic and exchange theories, developmental theories, critical theory, hermeneutics, self theory, role theory, symbolic interaction, systems theory, structural-functional theory, therapeutic systems theory, feminist theory, conflict theory, psychoanalytic theory, humanistic theories, and ecological theories (see, e.g., Burr,

1995). These theories point to different questions, offer different explanations, and require different standards of proof.

Fifth, family topics overlap with many content specialties. As an example, adolescent well-being overlaps with juvenile delinquency research. Family subject matter may overlap with such content areas as adolescence, counseling, deviance, drug abuse, health, nutrition, and women's studies. Each content area has a distinct literature, related theories, and methodologies for doing research. However, the theory, substantive content, and methodologies for family topics versus other related areas are difficult to separate (Bailey, 1984; Gilgun, 1992).

Sixth, although other fields of study focus on isolated individuals, family scholars study individuals embedded in family systems. Unfortunately, most methodologies available to family scholars are designed to study isolated individuals. Seventh, there is no consensus about what constitutes a family, and this chapter will not provide a new definition. The difference between traditional definitions based on legal or religious codes and more inclusive definitions based on what members do for each other is noted as a factor that influences research.

There is no single paradigm for doing research, with the result being that family scholars must be versed in multiple methodologies. Some fields have specialists in research methods, per se, who select, apply, and interpret the results of the appropriate procedures. This is rarely possible, except through collaboration, in studying families because researchers must select the most appropriate method, know how to apply procedures, and interpret results within the context of the theory, literature, and research traditions of family scholarship. Thus, all family scholars must be methodologists, and it is impossible to be a good family methodologist without being a family scholar.

Alan C. Acock • Department of Human Development and Family Sciences, Oregon State University, Corvallis, Oregon 97331-5102.

Handbook of Marriage and the Family, 2nd edition, edited by Marvin Sussman, Suzanne K. Steinmetz, and Gary W. Peterson. Plenum Press, New York, 1999.

Miller, Rollins, and Thomas (1982) addressed the methodological complexity of studying families. By referring to some of the characteristics we have discussed, they sought to explain the extraordinary amalgam of quantitative and qualitative methods, direct and indirect observation, experimental and survey methods, and cross-sectional and longitudinal methods. Although insufficient space is available here to detail the intricate relationship between root disciplines or specialty areas and the research methodologies used by groups of scholars, an exposition of these issues is provided by Larzelere and Klein (1987).

The unit of analysis, that is, the smallest unit about which a family scholar draws a conclusion, may be an individual (child, mother, nonresident father), a dyad (husband and wife, siblings), a family (nuclear, stem), a kinship system, a social network, a culture (Cuban immigrants to the United States), a historical cohort (Generation X, post-World War II Baby Boomers), or a historical period (colonial American family values). The outcome variable (dependent variable) in one study may be the predictor variable (cause or independent variable) in another study. For example, a researcher may want to explain how a hyperactive child influences outcomes for the family such as marital conflict, although another investigator may explain hyperactivity in children with family factors including conflict. For the first researcher the child's hyperactivity is the independent variable (predictor), but for the second researcher it is the dependent variable (outcome).

A recurrent problem is that researchers collect data on one level of analysis and then act as if they have data on another level. Thompson and Walker (1982) illustrated this in their discussion of confusing individual data with relationship data. Although an individual (unit) may be happy about his or her marital relationship, such data are limited to the isolated individual and require information about the dyadic unit to measure relationship quality. A husband who exploits his wife may feel very good about "his" marital relationship quality, but an objective observer might describe the marital relationship quality as extremely imbalanced. Miller et al. (1982) point out that mixing levels of analysis is an area where methodology lags behind theory. Many theories conceptualize variables at the family level, or at least the dyad, but researchers often measure variables at the level of a single individual by interviewing or observing single persons within families.

The *ecological fallacy* involves drawing conclusions about a relationship at one level of analysis (say, the individual) level from observing a relationship at a different level of analysis (say, the family or the state). Carver and Teachman (1995) give an example of a correlation between the percentage of children in a school district from single-parent families and the percentage of children who repeat a grade. Assuming

the correlation is 0.4, this means the higher the proportion of children in a school district who come from a single-parent family, the higher the proportion of children in the district who repeat a grade (see Figure 1).

It might be tempting to conclude from such a relationship that divorce leads to school problems such as repeating grades. Although this is an enticing conclusion for many conservative political activists, the data provides no evidence about who is repeating grades. It may be that school districts with a high rate of single parents have low property values and hence less is spent on the schools. Because such districts lack economic resources, there is a higher rate of school failure among all children, regardless of whether the child is from a divorced family or not.

The agenda for some scholars is understanding and providing descriptions of families as an inherently interesting topic of study. They are not especially interested in whether their research leads to improving the well-being of individuals, families, or societies. Still others seek to solve current social ills or have an ideological agenda. For example, many feminists seek to do research that can benefit people generally, the participants in a study directly, and can facilitate social change. A researcher's agenda has major implications for research strategies and influences how participants are selected, what they are told about the study (informed consent), and how they are measured.

The Appropriate Time Frame

Data is the empirical information researchers use for drawing conclusions. For an observational study, empirical information may be the number of times a child has eye contact with a parent in a family decision meeting, while for a survey it may be self-reported depression or marital satisfaction. Research methodologies vary greatly in the time frame they use for data collection. At one end, *cross-sectional designs* collect data at a single point, providing snapshots of how things are at the particular moment of collection. In a 100-meter race between Joan, Ann, and Tasha, for example, one cross-sectional measurement might be 2 seconds into the race when Joan is the momentary leader. Another cross-sectional measurement might occur when the first person crosses the finish line, with Ann being the winner. A single cross-sectional measurement tells us little about the process of the race.

A *longitudinal design* (sometimes called a panel design) collects data at two or more points in time. In experimental and quasi-experimental designs, it is common for data to be collected twice—just before and just after an intervention. Sometimes data are collected at three points: before the intervention, shortly after the intervention, and at several months

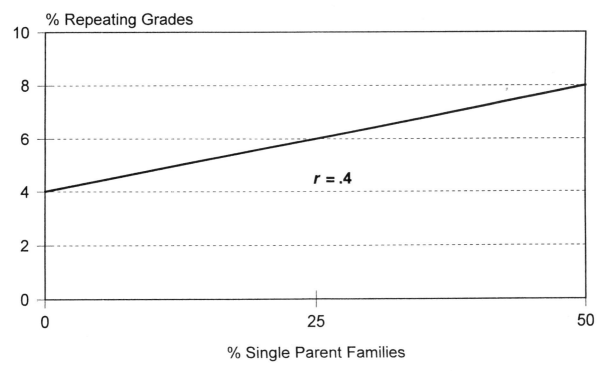

Figure 1. Percent single-parent households and percent repeating grades.

later to check for long-term effects. Although each collection point provides a snapshot, it is also possible to make inferences about changes. It is possible to make stronger inferences about causation in a longitudinal rather than in a cross-sectional design. Where data is collected at many time points (often 30 or more), the design is referred to as *time-series analysis*. Generally, more data collection points create the potential for stronger causal inferences, but the disadvantage of more data collection points is that they require more complex data management and analysis. This dilemma is illustrated by a study of caregiving daughters and care-receiving mothers that involved numerous contacts with the daughters and mothers (Walker, Acock, Bowman, & Li, 1996). Each interview asked parents and adult daughters a series of questions about various types of care given or received. The result was that many assessment points, types of care issues, and questions about each type of care produced over 20,000 variables requiring complex data management.

Cross-sectional, longitudinal, and time-series designs for data collection will be compared using a single example. We assume that the researcher is interested in the influence of marital conflict on the school performance of the child. The hypothesis is that the higher the level of parental conflict (independent variable or predictor), the worse the child performs in school (dependent variable or outcome). This hypothesis and two alternative models are presented in Figure

2. At the top of Figure 2 is the most simple model with the level of parental conflict having a direct effect on children's grades (hypothesis A). This model suggests that interventions focused on lowering parental conflict will improve school performance. In the center of Figure 2 is a model in which the relationship between parental conflict and school grades is spurious (no direct effect) because both of them are caused by a common antecedent variable, family income (hypothesis B). This model implies that a program designed to lower parental conflict will have no effect on school grades with the real problem being inadequate economic resources. That is, when families have limited economic resources they are more likely to have both parental conflict and children who are more likely to have poor grades. At the bottom of Figure 2 is a model in which part of the relationship between parental conflict and the school grades is spurious and part of it is direct (hypothesis C). This model suggests that a program aimed at lowering parental conflict will lead to some improvement in school grades, but that improving income is also important.

Cross-Sectional Time Frame

A cross-sectional design gathers data at one point through a survey, experiment, in-depth interview, or observational study. This is the most widely used design in family

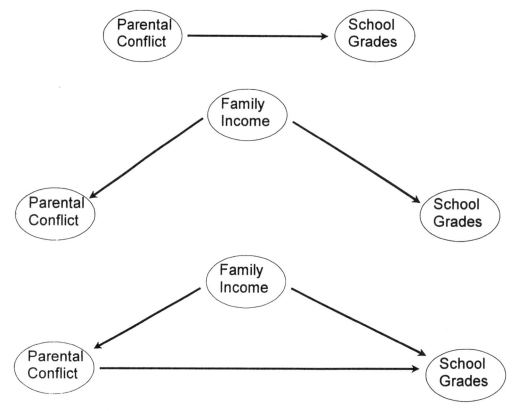

Figure 2. Three simple models of parental conflict–school performance.

scholarship, with the usual justifications being cost or that no other design is possible.

Application—Cross-Sectional Time Frame. A cross-sectional design could interview a large sample of two-parent families with at least one child in which the mother–father–child triad is the unit of analysis. The conflict between the parents could be measured by interviewing either or both parents or observing them in a family decision meeting. The child's school performance could be measured by interviewing the child's teacher, either parent, or the child. The researcher could then correlate the level of parental conflict with the school performance of the child. The hypothesis would be supported if the correlation were negative, substantial, and statistically significant.

Although cross-sectional research can be consistent with the hypothesis, it is difficult to exclude alternative explanations. Cross-sectional analysis can use covariates (control variables) to minimize the effects of some alternatives, such as family income, as seen in the bottom of Figure 2. If the partial correlation (or partial regression coefficient) between parental conflict and school grades is negative, significant, and substantial

when the researcher controls for family income, then hypotheses A and C are supported—hypothesis B can be eliminated.

Importantly, you never know if you have controlled for all the important covariates. Because of this, the best cross-sectional designs are those that involve a well-developed theory that points to all the important covariates that need to be controlled. The weaker the theory in a given area, therefore, the less confident the researcher can be that alternative explanations have been eliminated. Unfortunately, the weakest theoretical development is most likely to occur in research areas dominated by cross-sectional designs.

Another persistent problem with cross-sectional designs is that they cannot establish the direction of a causal relationship. It is possible, for example, that children who perform poorly at school create a great source of concern for their parents. Poor grades become a source of parental conflict and may be such a family problem that other areas of family life (e.g., work performance) may be adversely affected—thus reducing family income. This is an example of one type of a *specification error*. A specification error is a mistake in the model such as having the direction of influence misspecified or excluding an important covariate.

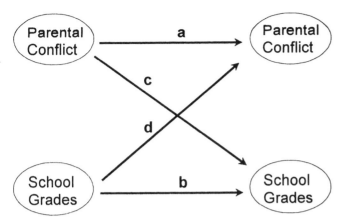

Figure 3. Panel design of relationship between parental conflict and school grades.

Longitudinal Time Frame

Longitudinal data collection is used much less frequently by family scholars than cross-sectional data collection. With longitudinal data the variables measured at *time one* (T1) can cause the variables at *time two* (T2), but the reverse is not the case. This is the primary strength of longitudinal designs.

Application—Longitudinal Time Frame. Figure 3 shows how a longitudinal design could test the effects of parental conflict on school grades. It illustrates the key strength of longitudinal designs in their ability to demonstrate causal direction. In Figure 3 the effects labeled a and b should be strong, indicating that in most families the more parents fight at time one (T1), the more they fight at time two (T2) and the better their child's grades at T1 the better their child's grades at T2. The effect labeled c and d are used to test the causal order of the relationship between the two variables with the expectation being that if c is negative, significant, and strong, then higher parental conflict at T1 may worsen their child's grades at T2. The longitudinal design eliminates questions about causal order, with the result supporting both hypotheses a and b. Correspondingly, if the effects are as modeled in the top of Figure 1 (hypothesis a), then the value of d in Figure 3 should be relatively small and insignificant.

Although longitudinal designs are appealing, problems remain. First, these designs also require adjustment for covariates. Second, other variables such as maturation may occur between the first and second time periods. If T1 and T2 are 5 years apart, for example, this is a long time in the life of a child. If the child was 10 at T1, she or he will be 15 at T2. An obvious problem is that many developmental experiences can account for changes in the school performance of a 10-year-old and a 15-year-old. It is often difficult to determine an appropriate time lag. Should the lag between T1 and T2 be 1 week, 1 month, 1 year, 1 decade, or some other interval? An effect may be highly significant in the short term but be mitigated by time. Studies of the effect of divorce on children, for example, are more severe when T2 is a short time after the divorce than they are when T2 is 5 years or more after the divorce (Acock & Demo, 1994). Moreover, when variables are measured imperfectly (see later), the errors in the first wave are often correlated with the errors in the second and third waves. Statistical analyses of longitudinal data are typically very complex. Although statistical procedures are very complex, substantial progress has been made over the last decade (Kasprzyk, Duncan, Kalton, & Singh, 1989).

Attrition. A major problem for family researchers is that it is difficult to track the same people at the two time periods. When a participant cannot be interviewed at T2, this is referred to as sample attrition or participant mortality. Loss of participants occurs for various reasons: (1) loss of participants by death, (2) inability to participate, (3) refusal, and (4) failure to locate. The National Survey of Families and Households (NSFH) (Sweet, Bumpass, & Call, 1988) is one of the most carefully administered national surveys used by family scholars. In 1987 and 1988, interviews were completed in 13,008 households (referred to as NSFH1), while efforts to recontact the same respondents in 1993–1994 resulted in 10,008 completed interviews (referred to as NSFH2). Researchers were able to track and interview 77% of the original respondents; when people who died were excluded from the calculation, the retention rate was 82%. The special problem of longitudinal research, therefore, is that the people not interviewed at T2 might be very different from the people who were tracked. A preliminary analysis by NSFH staff (NSFH Staff, 1995) examined the NSFH1 characteristics of nonrespondents at NSFH2 to gauge the potential problem of attrition. The retention rate for people who were 45–54 years old at NSFH1 was 86%, compared to 77% for people under 25. Thus, if the NSFH1 data were representative of U.S. households, the NSFH2 data would overrepresent older people because (1) everybody in the sample would be 5–7 years older than they were in NSFH1, and (2) younger people were more difficult to t ack and are underrepresented at NSFH2. The preliminary analysis also noted that (1) the retention rate for non-Hispanic whites was 85% compared to 68% for Puerto Rican respondents and (2) the retention rate ranged from 71% for those with 0–8 years of education to 89% for those with a college degree.

Table 1 presents a logistic regression of missing data on NSFH2 that was estimated for this chapter. The outcome variable is whether the individual was retained. Included in Table 1 are only a few of the variables that might be related to

**Table 1. Logistic Regression of Missing Data on NSFH2
by Selected Respondent Characteristics at NSFH1**

Variables[a]	Unstandardized	Standardized	Wald χ^2	Probability >	Odds ratio
Intercept	0.090	—	.561	.454	—
Male, 1; female, 0	0.390	.105	57.419	.001	1.477
Non-Hispanic white, 1; other, 0	−0.250	−.060	18.042	.001	0.779
Church attendance 0–90	−0.053	−.082	13.409	.001	0.948
Education, years	−0.122	−.214	197.814	.001	0.885
Family income ($10,000)	−0.062	−.138	29.757	.001	0.940
Percent urban	0.001	.085	32.207	.001	1.005

[a]Education and family income are measured using NSFH computed variables EDUCAT and IHTOT2, respectively. Percent urban is the percentage of the population of the respondent's county that is urban. Although NSFH2 has 10,008 respondents, because of missing data on some of the predictors, this table is based on 9739 respondents. Of these, 2119 did not complete NSFH2 and 7620 did.

missingness. The table shows that being male and from an urbanized county increased the odds of the person being missing in NSFH2. In contrast, being non-Hispanic white, attending church regularly, having more years of education, and lower family income all reduced the odds of the person being missing in NSFH2. Some results are dramatic, with the odds of a man being missing at NSFH2 being 1.477 times the odds of a woman being missing. Miller and Wright (1995) review alternative methods of evaluating attrition bias.

A survey that has a response rate of 70% at each wave has an expected response rate of 49% for two waves and 33% for three waves. Following this pattern, a five-wave longitudinal survey would have an expected response rate of 18%, and the 18% of respondents who complete all five waves are very likely to be dramatically different from the 82% who did not (cf. Miller & Wright, 1995). We can speculate that the 18% will be more stable, more conventional, and more educated, while the 82% who are missing will have higher levels of conflict, children with more adjustment problems, and associated differences.

Longitudinal designs introduce other complications, one of which is the problem that family variables are typically measured imperfectly. Sometimes this error may be random and other times it may be systematic. We might expect, for example, that many parents will systematically underreport parental conflict, while other parents considering a divorce might overreport parental conflict in a systematic manner. When variables are measured imperfectly, the systematic errors in the first wave are correlated with the errors in subsequent waves. If the parents had an argument just before the interview, on the other hand, they might report a higher level of conflict than if they had a pleasant dinner engagement just prior to the interview. This sort of error is usually thought of as random.

The statistical analyses of longitudinal data are typically very complex, primarily because of problems with correlated measurement error. An assumption of ordinary least squares

(OLS) regression is that there is no error in the predictor variables. With longitudinal analysis there are measurement errors in variables, and these errors are likely to be correlated over time. When errors are correlated over time, procedures such as OLS regression are inappropriate. Because OLS regression cannot incorporate correlated errors, these procedures are misspecified and produce biased estimates. Structural equation modeling procedures are an example of a statistical strategy that makes it possible to correlate measurement error over time. These procedures use a full information approach to identify correlated errors, incorporate correlated errors into the model, and make it possible to obtain unbiased estimates of parameters.

One approach to correcting for attrition bias is based on the work of Heckman (1976, 1979). This approach was designed for sample selection bias, but applies equally to attrition bias (Campbell, Roberts, & Rubenfeld, 1986; Miller & Wright, 1995). The approach involves a two-step process, the first of which involves a logistic or probit analysis to regress the odds of having missing data at T2 on relevant T1 characteristics. This regression is used to produce an estimated probability of inclusion at T2 for each respondent, called lambda (λ), with each participant having his or her own value. In step two, the λ variable is added to all the analyses. The purpose of λ is to control all the individual characteristics that are related to attrition.

There are many ways researchers minimize attrition. When interviewing the participant it is common to request the name and address of a relative or close friend who will know where the participant is in case he or she moves. Where there is a substantial interval between interviews, researchers will call or send a postcard one or more times. Other strategies include sending greeting cards, a newsletter, or a summary of results. Such contacts help keep participants motivated to continue with the project and alert researchers of possible relocations through mailings returned by the post office when they cannot be delivered.

Alternative Approaches to Longitudinal Modeling. There are a wide variety of statistical procedures family scholars can use with longitudinal models. Researchers can (1) use regression employing lagged dependent variables (Rogosa, 1988; Willet, 1988), (2) use structural equation modeling that can identify both lagged and reciprocal effects as well as handle correlated measurement error (Acock & Schumm, 1992), (3) use repeated measures (ANOVA) (e.g., Johnson, Amoloza, & Booth, 1992), (4) change scores (Allison, 1990), (5) use latent growth curve models (Karney & Bradbury, 1995; Willet & Sayer, 1994), and (6) use hierarchical linear models (Bryk & Raudenbush, 1992).

Time Series Framework

Time series data involve an extension of longitudinal analysis to numerous measurement points, usually 30 times or more, which focus on the process of change. For example, parental conflict may increase during the first month after a child's birth and then decrease during the second month. By tracking the respondents over time, changes are attributed to what is happening in their lives.

Application—Time Series Framework. Using the example of the effects of divorce on children, a researcher may be interested in how effects vary over time. Perhaps there is an initial negative effect on children, but the effect diminishes over time. Alternatively, initial adverse effects may abate over time for girls but increase for boys. Time series data is much more powerful than other longitudinal data. Numerous measurements allow researchers to plot complex "growth curves." These can help the researcher unearth possible alternative explanations.

Time series models may work nicely for research where measurements can be taken at short intervals, such as when marital conflict is measured during each of the 12 weeks before the birth of the first child and the 12 weeks after the birth. Even in this case, maintaining the cooperation of participants through 24 weekly interviews is difficult because subjects may drop out, be unable to participate, or be influenced by 24 measurement sessions over a 6-month interval. There are special problems when the same or parallel information is collected at each time point. It is difficult to convince participants that each measurement is an important and independent part of the data.

Other areas where time series models would seem ideal are impractical to implement because they would take too long. It would be ideal to follow children from birth to age 18 with measurements taken every 3 months, but few researchers can afford the cost of such a study or wait 18 years for the data to be collected. Participant attrition would be an enormous problem for such a study design. Over an 18-year period, children may move several times and to several different regions, which makes the tracking of participants extremely difficult and costly. The issues that were identified as important early in the study may be supplanted by different issues. Since the new issues have been unanticipated, the early surveys will not have the necessary baseline data.

A variety of statistical approaches can be used with time series data. Where the outcome variable is discrete (becoming divorced versus remaining married, having a second child versus not having a second child), event history or hazard models are appropriate (Heaton & Call, 1995; Teachman, 1982). Frequently, when the outcome variable is conceptualized as continuous (marital satisfaction, perceived likelihood of divorce), the appropriate choice is pooled time-series analysis with either a fixed-effects or a random-effects model (Johnson, 1995; see also Allison, 1994). This approach is especially promising because it can be applied to longitudinal data that runs from a two-wave panel to a true time series analysis with numerous points of measurement.

The underlying logic of the pooled time-series design can be illustrated for the fixed-effects model. The basic equation where there are just two waves and n cases is:

$$(Y_{i2} - Y_{i1}) = a + b(X_{i2} - X_{i1}) + e_i, \quad i = 1, \ldots n \quad (1)$$

and the basic equation where there may be any number of waves (t) and n observations is:

$$(Y_{it} - Y_{i.}) = b(X_{it} - X_{i.}) + e_{it}, \quad i = 1, \ldots, n \quad (2)$$

In this equation Y_{it} is the score of the ith individual at time t, and $Y_{i.}$ is the mean of the ith individual over all measurements. For example, suppose Kareem had scores on marital satisfaction measured at 10 times (5, 6, 6,6, 3, 5, 2, 3, 2, 2). Then his $Y_{i.}$ is $(5 + 6 + 6 + 6 + 3 + 5 + 2 + 3 + 2 + 2)/10 = 4.1$. The X values are defined similarly. This model allows us to measure the effect of changes in the predictor variable (X) on changes in the outcome variable (Y). Equation (2) can be generalized to include multiple predictors.

Approaches to Collecting Data

There are many approaches to collecting quantitative data, including surveys, experimental and quasi-experimental designs, observations, and in-depth interviews. Each of these approaches has strengths, weaknesses, and scientific standards.

Survey Designs

The most common data collection strategy is the survey, which may be as simple as passing out questionnaires to classes or as complicated as administering the NSFH. For most quantitative research, there is a desire for surveys to represent a large population. In the United States, the NSFH is a probability survey, that is, the probability of selection of each respondent can be specified. Such surveys allow researchers to generalize their findings from sample results to a larger population, such as households in the United States. These large-scale surveys allow us to answer many questions: Does marital conflict harm children? Do stepfamilies have more parental conflict than first marriages? Because these surveys are large, researchers can identify special populations such as cohabiting partners, marriages where spouses are unhappy but do not become divorced, or single-parent families headed by fathers. Surveys like the NSFH are "general purpose" surveys. Literally hundreds of independent scholars who had nothing to do with the data collection analyze the results. Indeed, the independent scholars' work may involve research questions never imagined by the people who collected the original data.

A second type of survey focuses on a special population and a small set of variables. Researchers with a particular interest, for example, middle-aged daughters caring for aged mothers (e.g., Walker et al., 1996), focus all of their resources on collecting data about a small set of variables for a special group. In many cases, these surveys are not national probability samples that would cost more than the researchers can afford, so they use other means. Credibility for generalizing from nonprobability samples comes from three sources. First, if a relationship between variables is assumed to apply to all segments of a population, then finding a relationship in one segment of the population can be generalized. Assume that any correlation between the personal efficacy of care-receiving mothers and their relationship with their caregiving daughters applies regardless of education, income, race, region, and so on. If this assumption is reasonable, then we can show the relationship using a sample of highly educated, all white, mother–daughter dyads taken from one region of the country. Another researcher can show this relationship using a sample of low-income, Native American, mother–daughter dyads taken from a different region of the country. This is the rationale underlying the numerous surveys of convenience samples such as students in a handful of college classes, parents in five daycare centers, or single-parent fathers volunteering for a study. It is common to find this nonrepresentative sampling being conducted in a variety of fields. An important example is medical researchers who use convenience samples in drug tests and assume that these apply universally to all people.

A second source of credibility for nonprobability samples comes from identifying important covariates of a relationship. If the correlation between the mother's efficacy and her relationship quality with her daughter is related to income, education, and race, these variables can be included as

statistical controls. Controlling for such variables can minimize the concern about the sample. This assumes that the sample has sufficient variation on these variables to make the controls meaningful and that the researcher has identified the critical controls. Although it is important to incorporate these statistical controls, there is always the risk that important variables are missed. In this example, both the mothers' efficacy and the relationship quality may be dependent on the mothers' health. That is, very ill mothers or cognitively impaired mothers may have both a low sense of efficacy and a difficult relationship with their daughter. Since very ill mothers and cognitively impaired mothers are most likely to be excluded from a survey because they cannot or will not participate, there is no way to control for extreme levels of these variables. Up to the 1980s, many medical studies were done on samples of men, a practice commonly justified because men are biologically less complicated than women. It is not always reasonable, however, to assume that the determination of drug effects on a sample of men will generalize to a sample of women. Today, most federally funded studies are required to include women unless there is a compelling reason not to do so.

A final source of credibility derives from efforts to select a nonprobability sample that is as broadly representative as possible so that researchers can compare their sample to national or regional data using demographic information. If their sample is similar on education, racial distribution, age, and income to national or regional demographic information, then it may be easier to trust generalizations that are made on this basis.

A great deal of important analysis has been done using nonprobability samples. At the very least, careful analysis of nonprobability samples can provide information that can be compared to other studies. If the results for a study that is limited to prosperous, white, single-parent fathers, for example, are subsequently replicated in another study that is limited to poor minority, single-parent fathers, the corresponding confidence in the initial finding is strengthened. A key to using nonprobability surveys is having replications across diverse groups, but a problem is that most replications are conducted on similar groups.

There is a class of conclusions from nonprobability samples that are not helped by these strategies. Although relationships can be investigated using nonprobability surveys, it is not practical to estimate central tendencies for individual variables. Prime examples of this are the various surveys of magazine subscribers who complete a questionnaire posted in the magazine and then mail it to the company. Several studies of extramarital sexual relationships of women have been based on this type of survey. Married women who have never had an extramarital sexual relationship are unlikely to complete a detailed questionnaire about this topic and pay to mail it, while married women who have had several such relationships are more likely to complete the detailed questionnaire. Misinformation, therefore, is the likely result of generalizations about the frequency of extramarital relationships from this type of sample.

A probability sample has enormous advantages over even the best nonprobability sample. Probability surveys can answer the questions the researcher wants to ask. A large and nationally representative sample of single-parent fathers would allow us to expand our knowledge of this type of family, as would a representative survey of same-sex parents.

The field of family studies has few national probability samples, but as more large-scale probability samples are conducted, the study of families will be strengthened. At the same time, there is a risk of exaggerating the strength of national probability samples. The NSFH is an example in that researchers tend to describe this as a nationally representative sample when many potential respondents refused to participate and others refused to answer key questions. If you have a survey that 30% of the potential respondents refused to complete and in which another 25% refused to report their income, then generalization about the income of different types of families is suspect. A second problem is that many studies using national probability samples are doing secondary data analysis where the survey questions are not a close match to the research objectives. When performing secondary data analysis, it is common for researchers to use single items or just a few items to measure complex family processes and relationships. The resulting inadequate reliability and validity may negate the advantages of a national probability sample.

Limitations of Probability Samples. Although probability samples have clear advantages, we need to understand how these samples are obtained and what this means for statistical inference procedures. A random sampling procedure, where every individual has the same probability of being selected, is rarely used. The problem with obtaining a random sample is that it requires a complete enumeration of the population with participants randomly selected from this list. For most research situations, it is not possible to obtain a complete enumeration, and for large-scale studies by the time the enumeration were completed it would be out of date because of deaths, births, and migration.

Surveys that most closely match the conditions of a random sample often are done by telephone (Dillman, 1978). In the past many people did not have a telephone, but today nearly all households have one. By using a modified random digit dialing system, it is possible to include virtually all households that have telephones, including those with unlisted numbers. Thus, one of the least expensive data collection procedures may be closest to meeting the conditions of a random sample. Telephone surveys fall short of a random sample to the extent that some numbers are more likely to be called than others, some households are more likely to answer the phone than others, and some people are more likely to complete the questionnaire than others.

Sometimes a *stratified* design is used, in which the population is divided into strata and a random sample is selected from each stratum. This is efficient where it is practical to identify strata that are very homogeneous on the outcome variable and obtain a list of everyone in each stratum. If you were estimating the attitudes of employees of a large firm toward an onsite daycare program, you might divide your population into males with no custodial children under 18, females with no custodial children under 18, males with custodial children under 18, and females with custodial children under 18. Because we might expect each stratum to differ on their attitude but be homogeneous among themselves (e.g., females with custodial children might be generally very supportive and males with no custodial children might be least supportive), this would be an efficient sampling design. In general, the more variation between strata and the more homogeneity within strata, the more efficient a stratified sample design is (Scheaffer, Mendenhall, & Ott, 1979). When stratified sampling is used, conventional inferential procedures are problematic. There are ways to adjust standard errors to obtain valid statistical inferences for such population parameters as means and proportions. These adjustments are rarely used in family research. If the appropriate conditions for doing a stratified sample exist, however, the bias is conservative. That is, results will be more statistically significant than conventional inferential procedures suggest. Stratified sampling designs are uncommon in family studies because it is unusual for the special circumstances to occur in cases where a list of everyone in each stratum can be obtained.

Cluster designs are used to reduce the cost of a survey, especially where a face-to-face interview is required. If you were selecting a probability sample of people in a small city of 100,000 people, you would divide the city into blocks using census definitions. You would then interview every individual in the blocks you selected. This would save a great deal of time and travel. When your interviewer got to Block A, she or he could go from house to house to find somebody who was home. After completing that interview the interviewer could look for somebody else who was at home. This would be much more efficient than driving all over a city between interviews.

Although cluster samples are often efficient in terms of costs per interview, they are less efficient in terms of the sample size needed to have statistically reliable results. Cluster designs are less efficient than random samples because people in each block tend to be homogenous. As a result, each interview gives you less "independent" information than would a randomly selected person. Cluster designs have the opposite conditions of stratified designs. A cluster sample will be less efficient than a random sample when individual clusters are more homogeneous than the general population (Scheaffer et al., 1979), and people living on the same block are usually homogeneous on important variables such as income and education. There are standard statistical procedures for handling statistical inference (estimating the standard errors) with cluster samples when estimating population parameters such as means and proportions. These procedures are rarely used in family research. Replicate sampling procedures for adjusting standard errors in complex designs such as structural equation modeling or time-series analysis are not yet used in family studies. Although not using the corresponding adjustments with a stratified design has a conservative bias, just the opposite is likely with cluster designs. Rules of thumb suggest that standard errors can be multiplied by a factor of 1.2 to 1.4 and if the results are still statistically significant, then greater confidence in the findings are merited (Davis & Smith, 1992).

Most large-scale surveys use extremely complex sampling designs that combine area probability sampling with oversampling of certain categories of people. When a household is selected, an eligible respondent within the household is randomly selected. Because that person may not be at home at the time of the interview, return visits are often necessary. Even with the best national surveys based on probability sampling designs, these steps may compromise the representation of the sample. The NSFH presents itself as a probability sample of 13,017 participants. The survey includes a main sample of 9643 participants who "represent the noninstitutional United States population age 19 and older." The other participants are from groups that were "double sampled" (double sampling involves interviewing twice as many people from the group as you would include in a probability sample), including minority groups, single parents, persons with stepchildren, cohabiting partners, and those who were recently married. A self-administered questionnaire was given to the spouse or cohabiting partner where appropriate. A 5- to 7-year follow-up survey was conducted that included interviews with the original primary respondent and the current spouse or partner. The follow-up had just over 10,000 primary participants left from the original survey. Additional interviews were obtained from former spouses and partners at T2, one randomly selected child, and a randomly selected parent of the primary respondent.

With such extremely complex data sets, relying on standard inferential procedures is problematic. An illustration of this is the effects of oversampling. The groups that were oversampled would have occurred too infrequently to support statistically sound inferences. By double sampling these groups we have sufficient data to make meaningful state-ments about groups such as cohabiting couples, recently married people, stepfamilies, and certain minorities. When making inferences about the United States population age 19 and over, oversampling means that some groups will be over represented. We will have, for example, more stepfamilies than a random sample would have. One way to minimize this problem is to use *weighted data*. Indeed, the NSFH provides various weighting variables that make adjustments for over sampling of certain groups. The variable WEIGHT is designed to reproduce the distribution of the United States individuals age 19 and above by age, race, and sex to match the Current Population Survey. The variable SPWEIGHT is designed to reproduce the population of married persons by age, sex, and race/ethnicity. This is for analyzing the spouse data that has a lot of missing values. Although such variables are extremely valuable for the specific purpose for which they were designed, they are not a general solution. For example, using the WEIGHT variable with a study comparing stepfamilies to first marriages would raise the problem of individual age and race data, as stepfamilies normally have older adults and are disproportionately white.

Although it is possible to use probability samples to obtain excellent estimates of certain population parameters, it should be clear that even the best probability surveys are problematic when doing complex analyses involving many variables. Conventional statistical tests and inferential procedures provide a useful check on findings, but they do not offer the precision that many authors assume. Specialized software such as Sudan and WesVar (SPSS) can be used.

Experimental and Quasi-Experimental Designs

Experimental and quasi-experimental designs provide much stronger evidence of causal effects than do surveys. The ability to demonstrate that one variable such as parental conflict causes another variable such as the child's grades is known as *internal validity*. Experimental designs are used when internal validity is critical (Brown & Melamed, 1990), the random assignment of participants to groups is possible, and the manipulation of the independent variable by the researcher is desired. For the types of variables that family scholars study, random assignment is often out of the question. An example would be the unethical circumstance of randomly assigning parents to a high-conflict condition.

For all their strength with internal validity, experimental designs often are lacking in terms of external validity. Because locating participants who will volunteer to be randomly assigned to groups is difficult, many experiments are based on "captive" populations such as college students. Captive populations are typically homogeneous with regards to age, education, race, and socioeconomic status, making it difficult to generalize (external validity). Experiments that involve putting homogeneous strangers together for a short experience provide a qualitatively different group than do naturally occurring families (Copeland & White, 1991). For many family investigations the defining characteristics involve intimate relationships that extend over a long time.

Quasi-Experimental Designs Balance Internal and External Validity. A researcher interested in the effect of an outreach program for young parents who are at risk may not be able to assign randomly young parents so that half of them are exposed to the treatment (the outreach program) and the other half are not. However, the program may be introduced in one city and not in an adjoining city that is similar in socioeconomic characteristics. The adjoining city provides a comparison group. If it is possible to identify young parents at risk in the adjoining city, their parenting skills can be compared to the young parents who are exposed to the outreach program.

Observation and In-Depth Interview Designs

Both qualitative and quantitative researchers use observation and in-depth interviews in a deliberately unstructured way. For instance, a researcher may observe the interaction between African American mothers and their child when the child is dropped off at a childcare facility and compare this to the mother–child interaction for other ethnic and racial groups. A crucial standard for this approach is a deliberate and continuous attempt to revise understandings (Blumer, 1969), with the goal of this approach being to build theory from observations. In this sense, observation is used as an inductive strategy to induce theoretical concepts and explanations from observed data. For example, Homans (1974) developed much of what is called social exchange theory based on his own research, which was grounded in observational studies that were highly inductive and began without any hypotheses. Those who use this strategy, however, often contrast it with traditional quantitative research that they see as purely deductive in the sense that hypotheses are deduced from theories. Modern science suggests that this is a false dichotomy, with both induction and deduction often being used at different stages of research using the scientific method.

The observations may be structured around specific aspects of interaction. Whether identified deductively before the data collection or inductively after spending considerable time observing behavior, they are often highly quantifiable. Do parents from different groups vary in how much they say to the child? This could be quantified using the number of words spoken or amount of time they talk with the child. The research could develop a coding scheme measuring the character of what is said as positive, negative, directive, and so on. How much they touch the child could be measured as yes or no, or there could be a count of tactile contact.

Some observational researchers use elaborate coding systems that may involve video recording of either ordinary or contrived situations. For example, a researcher interested in family decision making might give each family a task such as what they would do with $1000. Alternatively, the researcher might record family interaction at home over the family's dinner table. The videotape would be using multiple observers and a prearranged system, with observers recording how often each family member spoke, how often each member suggested a solution, how often each member tried to relieve tension, and how often each family member solicited opinions from others (cf. Bales, 1950).

It is important that observational studies sample time in a systematic or random way. For example, studies of young children in a daycare setting should be done at a variety of times. If they were all done just after a nap, for example, the results might be quite different from if they were all done just before a nap. Sampling time at a fixed interval or selecting times randomly will minimize this problem (Bronson, 1994).

Observational studies often focus on nonverbal behavior. Several researchers have shown that social desirability and reactivity are more likely with verbal behavior than they are with nonverbal behavior. Because participants often try to please the researcher, observational studies that focus on nonverbal behavior may be less biased by social desirability and reactivity (Vincent, Friedman, Nugent, & Messerly, 1979).

An effective way of examining how family relationships work is the unstructured, in-depth interview as a means of studying everyday family processes and making comparisons across family members and across families. Interviewers using an unstructured, in-depth strategy hope to understand how meaning is created, habituated, and modified. A white researcher with limited experience in interracial settings may want to understand the relationship between mothers-in-law and their daughters-in-law in interracial marriages. Instead of using a structured interview that presumes the researcher knows what to ask a priori, a researcher would gain much from a less structured, in-depth interview strategy. Such interviews can provide knowledge to replace assumptions and stereotypes and may require a series of extended and unstructured interviews before the researcher can develop a structured interview, much less design a survey or experiment.

Unstructured, in-depth interviews and observational studies are not restricted to areas where knowledge is limited. These designs can open new perspectives for research precisely where survey or experimental researchers naively believe they have detailed knowledge. By grounding research in the social constructions, behaviors, and interactions of ordinary people, we are less likely to impose preexisting assumptions and stereotypes.

Observational and in-depth interviews have two major problems. First, if a large sample is needed, these approaches are extremely costly. Second, there are dangers that researchers will lose their objectivity. When a researcher spends months with a group as an observer or participant-observer, the danger exists that identification with the group will occur and objectivity will be lost. Another problem is that the researcher's multiple roles may conflict to an extent that family members may not differentiate the role of researcher from other roles such as mediator, counselor, and friend. Insofar, as the researcher becomes a mediator, counselor, or friend, the family hierarchy, structure, and everyday processes are inextricably altered.

In-depth interviews and observations are an excellent way to tap into the areas of family life that are private, especially those areas that are subject to stigma, such as family conflict and violence. Although the survey researcher is in and out of the family in a matter of minutes, the qualitative researcher has the advantage of taking the time necessary to gain the confidence, trust, and access to the private aspects of family life.

Selected Other Strategies

Because family scholars have training in so many different disciplines, a wide variety of other approaches from these disciplines are used to study families. Case studies are used for studying populations that are rare, such as families in which a parent has AIDS. Content analysis can identify such emergent themes as the role of single-parent mothers in popular novels of the 1930s, 1960s, and 1990s, which, in turn, may tell us much about the changing gender ideology of America. Over the last 3 decades there has been a considerable growth in historical analysis (Elder, 1981), as evidenced by the scholarship found in the *Journal of Family History*. Demographic analysis is used to provide background information (e.g., a profile of continuously single-parent families; see Acock & Demo, 1994), document trends (e.g., increase in the frequency of continuously single families; see Teachman, Polonko, & Scanzoni, 1987), and comparative studies (e.g., the division of household chores in Japan and the United States; see Kamo, 1988). Increasingly, studies are using multiple approaches: quantitative, qualitative, historical, and so on (Allen & Walker, 1993), with the term "triangulation" being used to refer to the use of a variety of methodological strategies within a study to show convergence on common conclusions.

Measurement

The scientific advancement of many disciplines is built on progress in measurement (Draper & Marcos, 1990). The complexity of the variables being measured in family studies makes good measurement critical. Family concepts have multiple dimensions, perspectives, and subjective components. The difficulty of measuring a "good marriage" illustrates these problems. How, for example, does a marriage that is mediocre for both the husband and the wife compare to one that is good for the husband and bad for the wife? How do you measure a good marriage in which the husband and wife are happy, but the children are miserable?

Whenever we attempt to measure an individual or family, the fact that participants know that we are measuring them may influence their behavior. The Hawthorne Effect was derived from a series of studies conducted in the 1920s and 1930s at the Hawthorne plant for the Western Electric Company in which working conditions were manipulated and measured to determine how this influenced performance. Since the workers knew their performance was being measured, they worked harder and harder. When working conditions were made worse, the workers took this as a challenge and redoubled their work rate (French, 1950). Regardless of how data is collected, when people know researchers are going to measure them, there may be a tendency for participants to "put their best foot forward."

Self-Report Items and Scales

A problem with large, comprehensive national probability surveys is that so many variables are measured that many of them are measured poorly. The NSFH uses a single item to measure marital happiness: How would you rate your marital happiness? Would you say you are: (a) very happy, (b) somewhat happy, (c) somewhat unhappy, or (d) very unhappy? A global response to a single item masks areas of concern ("my husband does no housework"), of satisfaction ("my wife is an excellent sexual partner"), and personality issues (the respondent is clinically depressed).

The most common approach to measurement is to develop a scale by giving the respondent a series of statements about a concept. The respondent checks whether she or he strongly agrees, agrees, disagrees, or strongly disagrees with each of the statements. Enough items are used in such a Likert scale in a way that is supposed to represent the full domain of the idea. Thus, for measuring marital happiness, several items are needed to represent various aspects of the marriage. Other types of scales are the Bogardus Social Distance Scale, Thurstone Scales, Semantic Differential Scales, and Guttman Scales (Babbie, 1995).

Family Studies Emerging Standards for Evaluating a Scale. Researchers are expected to have several items for each scale and to select items in a way that represents the full domain of the idea. A pilot test is often conducted on a small sample and this is statistically analyzed. First, a factor analysis is conducted to see if the several items converge on a single concept. When measuring adolescent alienation from the family, for instance, a factor analysis of 10 items may reveal a single dimension with all the items loading (correlated) strongly on the dimension. However, sometimes factor analysis reveals that there are multiple dimensions, with a few items tapping concepts such as feelings of powerlessness and a few items representing feelings of value-isolation. When a factor analysis is based on an orthogonal rotation, this means these dimensions are unrelated to each other. Although some researchers simply combine them, the fact that items may be unrelated to each other makes this equivalent to combining apples and oranges. A better solution is to either include both types of alienation, powerlessness, and value-isolation as separate variables (dimensions) or to select the type that is most important theoretically.

Although orthogonal rotation is conventional, there are alternatives. Some researchers may use an oblique rotation that allows the factors to be correlated. This is more reasonable if the items are all supposed to be tapping the same underlying construct. A limitation of oblique rotations in factor analysis is that the correlation between the factors is unidentified unless arbitrary assumptions are made. Statistical programs typically set the assumptions by default. A

superior solution is to perform a confirmatory factor analysis whereby the dimensions are theoretically specified and all the parameters can be identified. An extension of this that is rarely used in family studies is second-order confirmatory factor analysis (See Acock & Schumm, 1992; Teachman, Carver, & Day, 1995). For the present example, the construct of alienation is defined as a second-order factor in which powerlessness, value-isolation, and other specific aspects of alienation are first-order factors.

A second step is to assess the reliability of the scale or the extent to which a measure will produce a consistent result when administered again. Reliability is illustrated in Figure 4, where the center of each circle represents the true score of each participant on the variable. The stars represent the measurements we obtained on each of several replications for a particular participant, say Juan. Figure 4a shows a moderate degree of reliability, as the repeated measurements of Juan produced results that are generally not too far apart. Figure 4b represents a very high level of reliability, as each time we measured Juan we got virtually identical results. Figure 4c shows a low degree of reliability because we got very different results each time we measured Juan. Figures 4d and 4e, however, are both very reliable, since the dispersion is so small and very biased, with 4d being particularly problem-

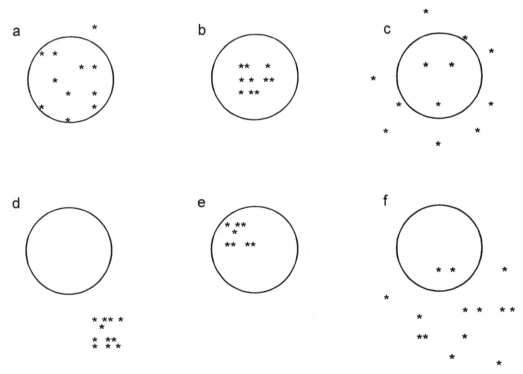

Figure 4. Reliability and validity.

atic. Finally, 4f has considerable dispersion and would not be considered reliable.

The reliability of a scale is estimated by using the scale twice (or more often) on the same people and seeing if their answers are consistent or by using the alpha coefficient (a) as a measure of reliability. Although $\alpha > .80$ is recognized as a reliable scale, a review of articles in the November 1983 issue of the *Journal of Marriage and the Family* (selection of the issue was arbitrary) found reliability coefficients reported in only 5 of 22 articles. A review of the articles in the November 1992 issue, however, found reliability coefficients reported in 11 of 22 articles in which scales were used.

The reliability of a scale is functionally related to the number of items used in the scale, with scales that include many items typically reporting very high reliability (Parker, Hanson, & Hunsley, 1988). Unfortunately, scales developed from large-scale surveys often have only a few items and tend to have low reliability. It is not unusual to find published articles based on secondary data analysis that have α's in the .6 to .7 range. One interpretation of the value $1 - \alpha$ is that of the error variance in the scale, or, for example, that where $\alpha = .6$, $1 - .60$ or 40% of the variance in the scale is measurement error. If a researcher is using one variable with an $\alpha = .60$ to predict another variable with an $\alpha = .60$, then the correlation will be greatly attenuated. It should be noted that measurement error in X or Y has a conservative effect and attenuates the bivariate correlation between them.

However, the effect of low reliabilities is not always conservative. Consider the case of regressing Y on X and Z. Assume that $r_{YX} = .5$, $r_{YZ} = .4$, and $r_{XZ} = .6$. Suppose we have measurement error only in the Z variable such that with the measurement error $r_{YZ'} = .2$ and $r_{XZ''} = .3$, where Z' is the Z variable measured with error. The partial relationship between Y and X need not be attenuated but can be exaggerated when Z is measured with error. The slope $B_{Y.X} = (r_{yx} - r_{yz}r_{xz})/(1 - r_{XZ}^2)(Sy/Sx)$. Assuming the variables have been standardized so $S_y S_z = 1.0$, when we have no measurement error we estimate the slope to be .416, indicating a moderate relationship. Assuming we are using Z' to measure Z, then $B_{yx} = .88$, indicating a very strong relationship between X and Y. The conclusion is that measurement error in one predictor can bias the estimated effects of other variables and that the bias can be in either direction.

The validity of a scale is its ability to measure the variable without any bias (DeVellis, 1991). A scale of marital conflict based on the decibel level of dinner conversation might sound like an appealing idea. If this scale were developed using an upper-income Swedish sample, it might give biased results if it were applied to a lower-income Italian sample. In the Swedish sample a high decibel level might be a reasonable indicator of conflict, but in the Italian sample, the silence reflected by a low decibel level might indicate high conflict (i.e., family members were too mad to talk). Thus, a scale may be valid on one group or class of people and invalid on another.

Figure 4 illustrates validity and its relationship to reliability. Parts a, b, and c are equally valid because there is no clear bias—they are on target. Parts d, e, and f are not valid because they are off target. Clearly part b represents the best of all cases since it is both reliable (consistent) and valid (on target). Part a is probably the second choice because it is valid and reasonably reliable. What is the third best case? Some researchers might prefer part e over c because e is giving a better estimate even though it is slightly biased.

The validity of the scales is assessed using a variety of procedures (Carmines & McIver, 1979; DeVellis, 1991). A common approach is to correlate a new scale with a well-established scale. The established scale serves as the *criterion*. If many researchers have used a 100-item scale to measure marital adjustment and you have a 10-item scale that is highly correlated with the 100-item scale, then this is evidence of your new scale's criterion validity.

A more elaborate approach is known as *construct validity*, whereby the scale of interest should be positively correlated with some constructs and negatively correlated with others in a manner consistent with existing theory. Our marital adjustment scale should be positively correlated with such variables as existing marital adjustment scales and the reported likelihood of divorce. Our scale of marital adjustment should be negatively correlated with marital conflict as expected according to existing research.

Family scholars are paying increasing attention to measurement. There are now several books that provide scales that are intended to measure key concepts. In varying degrees, these sources provide information on the reliability and validity of the scales (e.g., see McCubbin & Thompson, 1991), and greater attention is devoted to demonstrating the reliability and validity of these measures. A persistent problem is that these demonstrations are often based on fairly narrow samples of people. Each time an established scale is applied to a specialized population, it is important to evaluate the scale's reliability and validity on that population. A scale of dyadic adjustment may be reliable and valid on a sample of couples in the first few years of their marriage. This does not mean the same scale will be reliable on a sample of couples who have been married for 25 or more years. Nor does it mean it will be adequate for a study of stepfamilies. Whenever a researcher uses a scale on a new population, the researcher is responsible for assessing the scales' reliability and validity. Despite this potential problem, many researchers continue to report the reliability and validity of a scale based on applications of the scale to other samples and fail to report the reliability and validity of the scale on their own sample.

Not all variables are measured by scales. Some variables, such as age, are adequately measured with a single question. Researchers doing observational studies often measure variables as "counts" of behavior such as the number of times a child interrupts a parent, the number of times a person went to church in the last month, and how often the family had meals together in the last week. Observations are typically done by two or more judges and the interrelated reliability is reported.

Measuring Socioeconomic Variables Family researchers frequently use some measure of socioeconomic stratification as a predictor or as a covariate. Too often, measuring class as a variable is accomplished without sensitivity to the theoretical rationale for the variable (Smith & Graham, 1995). Marxist theory emphasizes a dichotomous class system based on differential relationships to the means of production. One class owns the means of production and the other class is exploited by the owners. Other theoretical orientations suggest a continuous measure of stratification. The functionalist view (e.g., see Davis & Moore, 1945) emphasizes the value of an occupation to society as determining its location in the stratification system. Dahrendorf (1969) adds to this the market explanation based on supply and demand with higher locations in stratification systems being based on providing valued services that are scarce. Weber (1921/1968) differentiated groups of people based upon class or economic resources, status based on prestige, and power. Smith and Graham (1995) note that Haller (1982) added information to Weber's typology in which some groups of people are high on some bases (economics and power) and low on others (prestige). For example, *Time* magazine selected the Speaker of the House Newt Gingrich as the "man of the year" in 1995; at the same time, he was being investigated for corrupt practices and had negative voter ratings of over 60%.

Currently, family scholars rely on using income and education along with some index of occupation, with the most common being Duncan's Socioeconomic Index (1961), known as the SEI. This is based on the income, education, and prestige of occupations. The relationship between current measures such as income and education and the theoretical orientations toward stratification are typically ambiguous or missing all together. Indeed, it could be argued that components such as income and education should be used as resource variables, without using the rhetoric of socioeconomic status. Simply, the more income a person/family has or the more education the parents have, the better the person/family can respond to issues.

Much of the theory and conceptualization of socioeconomic status was developed before women played a significant role in the family's socioeconomic position, and

most attempts at measuring family socioeconomic status have been incomplete. In the case of single-parent families headed by mothers, the mother's role is the determining factor in the family's socioeconomic position. Although it is possible to use the characteristics of the person with the strongest relationship to the labor force to measure family socioeconomic status, this becomes increasingly misleading as both women and men have essential relationships to the labor force. An individualized approach measures the characteristics of each adult in the family, a strategy with the advantage of including the contributions of both women and men, but it minimizes the family level effect in family socioeconomic status. This approach would locate a family where both the husband and wife have 14 years of education and are bookkeepers making $40,000 each as equivalent to another family where the husband and wife both have a college degree, the husband is a senior accountant making $80,000, and the wife is a homemaker.

Smith and Graham (1995) make the following recommendations. First, family researchers should include a variety of measures that fall under the broad categories of occupation, education, income, physical possessions, and area of residence. Second, measures should be obtained for both men and women so that different combinations (male only, female only, both) can be evaluated. Third, measures should be as precise as possible, and when variables are measured continuously, they should not be collapsed into broad classes without a strong theoretical rationale.

Censoring Effects—Ceilings and Floors. A major limitation of many items and scales is that the wording creates a ceiling or floor effect. Items are worded in a way that censors the full variance among the participants. This is extremely common where yes/no answers are required. Consider the question: "Is your marriage happy?" If the only response options are "yes" or "no," a likely result is censoring. Some of the people who say yes are somewhat happy, some are moderately happy, some are very happy, and others may be ecstatic. Yet, because all these people have the same response, that is, yes, meaningful variation in the data is destroyed.

The NSFH (wave one) asked married people: "How do you feel about the fairness in your relationship in each of the following areas?" In the area of household chores 245 people said the relationship was "very unfair to me," 967 said it was "somewhat unfair to me," 4642 said it was "fair to both," 703 said it was "somewhat unfair to her/him," and 101 said it was "very unfair to her/him." An alternative way of asking this question might be to ask if the relationship is "unfair to me" or "not unfair to me." If this had been done, there would have been 1212 people who said it was unfair and 5446 people who would have said it was "not unfair to me." This alternative would have censored the variance at both ends of the distribution because the 1212 people who said it was unfair varied in how unfair it was and would be censored from below. Censoring from above occurred among the 5446 who would not say it was not unfair. They would vary all the way from seeing the relationship as equitable to seeing themselves as exploiting their partners.

Censoring occurs not only from poor item design, but also when researchers collapse categories of responses to simplify their analysis. For example, an investigator might replace income measured in dollars with three categories: poor, middle-level, and high-level income. A result of this approach is that everybody making from $100,000 to the richest person in the world would be classified as identical under the high income level. Although problematic in many instances, it is also recognized that reducing quantitative variables to a few categories or merging categories is justified at times. For example, if a person feels that having less than a high school degree, regardless of how much less, is going to lead to an equally high divorce rate, then it would make sense to treat all years of education below 12 as a single category.

Censoring is a serious problem in before/after experimental designs or in longitudinal surveys. When the censoring masks real variation, as in the aforementioned example of marital happiness, then no room exists for improvement in the item. When no improvement is found between the pretest and posttest, this may mean that there is no change or that a ceiling effect has occurred.

Measuring Dyadic and Family Level Variables. When the unit of analysis moves beyond the individual, special measurement problems occur. In a study of reports of marital violence Scinovacz and Egley (1995) looked at differences in the reports of husbands and wives. They found that one-partner reports would need to be increased by 50%–80% to match rates based on couple data. Scinovacz and Egley contend that studies of marital violence need independent reports from both partners.

Complexity of dyadic data is illustrated by considering how to measure marital quality. Various alternatives have been used (1) the mean couple score, (2) the discrepancy score (i.e., wife's score − husband's score), (3) the absolute discrepancy score (i.e., |wife's score − husband's score|), (4) the maximum or minimum score, (5) the couple ratio score (i.e., wife's score/husband's score), and (6) the percentage agreement between partners on a series of items (Larsen & Olson, 1990). Although each approach has strengths, they also have limitations. The mean couple score, for example, does not differentiate between a couple where both individuals are average in quality from a couple where the husband is very happy and the wife is miserable. The discrepancy and ratio measures deal with this problem by focusing on discrep-

ancy or balance, but they tell us nothing about the couple's relative location. Spouses who are both very happy or both very unhappy will have a difference score of 0.0 and a ratio of 1.0. Although no discrepancy or imbalance exists in either couple, the two couples differ greatly in the quality of their marriages.

There are often unanticipated statistical complexities introduced by couple measures of predictor variables. These problems occur when researchers try to use both measures of location (the score of the wife and the score of the husband) and measures of difference (the wife's score − the husband's score). For example,

$$Y' = \beta_0 + \beta_1 X_1 + \beta_2 X_2 + \beta_3(X_1 - X_2) \qquad (3)$$

where Y' is the estimated marital stability, X_1 is the wife's marital satisfaction, X_2 is the husband's marital satisfaction, and $X_1 - X_2$ is the difference. In this equation, the estimated marital stability is a function of the wife's marital satisfaction, the husband's marital satisfaction, and the discrepancy score. This is appealing because having both X_1 and X_2 in the equation measures the location of their satisfaction (similar to what is done by a couple mean score), and having $X_1 - X_2$ identifies the effects of discrepancy. The researcher may hypothesize that both β_1 and β_2 will be positive because higher satisfaction leads to higher stability, and β_3 will be negative because the greater the discrepancy between the wife and husband, the less stable the marriage.

Although appealing, this equation cannot be estimated because of multicolinearity. If we call $X'' = X_1 - X_2$, then the equation

$$X'' = \beta_0 + \beta_1 X_1 + \beta_2 X_2 \qquad (4)$$

will have a multiple correlation of 1.0. This is because $\beta_0 = 0$, $\beta_1 = 1$, and $\beta_2 = -1$ will necessarily predict X'' perfectly. Thus, there is no variance in $X_1 - X_2$, that is independent of the values of X_1 and X_2, indicating that a difference score cannot be an independent variable if it has no independent variance. It is possible to obtain identification of equation (4) by transforming the difference score. One way of doing this is to use $(X_1 - X_2)^2$ rather than $X_1 - X_2$. Such transformations make the interpretation more complex and may still involve a sufficiently high level of multicolinearity to drastically limit the statistical power of the model.

Even where a discrepancy score is theoretically appropriate, it is rarely the best solution from an empirical estimation standpoint. Suppose a researcher felt that stability was dependent only on the discrepancy. One way to describe this is:

$$Y' = \beta_0 + \beta_1 X_1 + \beta_2 X_2 \qquad (5)$$

and another way is:

$$Y' = \beta_0 + \beta_1'(X_1 - X_2). \qquad (6)$$

Equation (5) is a simple additive model where the wife and husband each have a β and most likely both will be positive. The only way the discrepancy model in equation (6) can do as well as the additive model is $\beta_1 = -\beta_2 = \beta_1'$. To make things worse, there is no circumstance under which the discrepancy model in (6) will do better than the simple additive model in (5). Thus, while discrepancy scores may be conceptually appealing as independent variables, they bring forward serious methodological problems.

Structural equation modeling offers an alternative method to measuring dyadic and family variables. Although it is beyond the scope of this chapter to explicate this approach, the objective is to identify both within- and between-family variation of patterns of effects (Acock & Schumm, 1992; Teachman et al., 1995). This is done by deriving first-order factors to represent the views of individual family members and second-order factors to represent the "family" view. Both individual variables (first-order factors) and family variables (second-order factors) can then be used to predict some outcome. If the family level variable plays the pivotal role, then the individual level variables should have no direct effects on outcomes. Although these structural equation models have great potential to represent family level variables, they are typically difficult to identify mathematically, complicated to estimate statistically, and produce ambiguous results (see, for example, Teachman et al., 1995).

Questionnaires and Interviews

Questionnaires are the most common method of measuring the variables used in a study. Some questionnaires may be designed to be self-administered, others so they can be asked in face-to-face interviews, and still others for telephone interviews. Computer-assisted interviews are used for all three collection procedures. Self-administered questionnaires can use computer-assisted technology by putting the respondent in front of a computer. After a question is answered, the computer automatically goes to the next appropriate question, which allows each respondent to have an individually tailored questionnaire. This saves much time because entire series of questions are skipped for each individual. For instance, men and young women are not asked questions about their experience with menopause. The drawback of this system is that some people refuse to work on a computer and others experience anxiety that may bias their responses. One solution is to have an interviewer use the computer and enter the responses. This will mitigate the participant's computer anxiety, but will increase the cost of the interview.

Computer-assisted interviews are becoming the standard for telephone surveys. Some organizations run telephone surveys continuously, which are especially helpful in locating rare populations such as single-parent fathers, gay couples who have children, or cohabiting partners (with each other for at least 12 years) who have adolescent children. Each time a person who falls into the targeted population is identified, they are asked the appropriate series of questions, a feature that allows the telephone lab to conduct many different surveys simultaneously. An advantage of computer-assisted interviews is that when the responses are entered, the software will create a data file that statistical software can analyze. When paper and pencil interviews are used, transferring the responses to a data file is time-consuming and can introduce errors.

In the past, researchers believed that face-to-face interviews were uniformly superior to self-administered questionnaires and telephone surveys. It remains true, however, that face-to-face interviews have some clear advantages. For example, researchers can ask more complex questions such as when an interviewer wants to ask parents the importance of 10 outcomes for their children (completing college, having children, having a good income, being a good spouse, being a good parent, etc.). In a face-to-face interview the investigator could show the parent the 10 items on a card and make sure the items are ranked from 1 to 10, whereas, in a telephone survey, the parent can forget some of the outcomes before the interviewer finished reading the list. Face-to-face interviews also provide a measure of quality control because the interviewer will know when the respondents are distracted. Face-to-face interviews often include better opportunities for the interviewer to rate the quality of the interview in terms of the participant's attention, distractions, understanding, and factors that might bias responses. For example, wave two of the NSFH had interviewers report if somebody was close enough to hear the participant's answers; how long the spouse, partner, relative, or nonrelative was present; whether the respondent could understand questions; whether the respondent was cooperative; and whether the respondent was interested.

Telephone interviews also have advantages. Face-to-face interviews are highly reactive environments for which interviewers are chosen to match the characteristics of the respondents (sex and race) as much as practical and are trained to minimize explanations that bias responses. In contrast to this is a telephone interview, which is much less reactive than a face-to-face interview.

In the past, face-to-face interviews had higher response rates than telephone interviews. This is changing for several reasons, one of which is that people are more fearful of letting an interviewer into their home than was the case 20 years ago. This is particularly problematic in urban areas and areas with high crime rates, making it increasingly difficult to schedule face-to-face interviews. A telephone surveyor can arrange to call back and make repeated attempts when the participant misses an appointment, whereas "no-shows" in face-to-face interviews incur much greater logistical costs. For example, in wave two of the NSFH, 1388 of the 10,008 interviews required the interviewer to travel over 125 miles for the interview. Over 70% of the interviews required the interviewer to travel 25 or more miles.

Missing Data

Regardless of the methodological approach, missing data is a critical issue. Although attrition in longitudinal analysis was discussed previously, this section focuses on missing data caused by refusals to participate or to answer specific items. It is not unusual for cross-sectional survey studies to have 20%–50% or more of the cases missing. This missing data may occur because the person refuses to participate, has a cognitive limitation, or is subject to hearing difficulty. Although researchers in the United States may have a Spanish version of questionnaires and interview schedules, respondents who speak other languages are typically dropped. It may also be impossible to schedule a meeting or telephone interview with the person because they are sick or on an extended vacation.

To minimize bias caused by missing data, some researchers compare the distribution of their sample to census data on important variables such as race, gender, marital status, and age. By doing this, a weighting variable can be computed that counts the respondents from underrepresented groups (in terms of race, gender, marital status, and age) more than participants in the overrepresented groups. Through such means generalizations can be made that reproduce population values on whatever criteria the researchers use in computing the weights. There is no magic response rate that ensures the quality of generalizations from studies, and if those who drop out of a study are different from participants, then the generalizability of the study must be questioned. Although statistical procedures can be used to adjust for variations in a sampling design, they cannot compensate for unspecified systematic differences between the respondents and the nonrespondents.

Many researchers go to considerable lengths to maximize the response rate. At first glance it would seem that anything that increases the response rate will make the sample more representative, a practice that assumes that additional participants are not biased. For example, paying participants $20 to answer a questionnaire may recruit additional participants who place greater value on this incentive and change the sample composition in ways that make it less representative (Jones & Lang, 1980; Karney et al., 1995). People who are economically motivated and for whom $20 is a sufficient incentive may differ from people who are not motivated economically or for whom $20 is an insufficient incentive. For some people a $20 incentive will raise questions about the legitimacy of the study: Why do they have to pay participants? A result may be that these people will be underrepresented in the survey because some will refuse to participate.

Missing Values on Specific Variables. One type of missing value involves participants who have missing values that are limited to particular variables. It is likely that 20%–30% of respondents will not report their income in an interview. If a wife is asked how many hours her husband spends doing a series of 10 household chores, she may simply leave the answers blank. Why? Perhaps he spends so little time and this irritates her so much that she does not want to think about it. Perhaps she answers the first few items and then skips to the next section because her husband does so few household chores that she does not think it matters. Alternatively, it may be that her husband does work that she believes she should do, and it would embarrass her to report how much he does.

Call, Sprecher, and Schwartz (1995) examined NSFH respondents who refused to report whether they had sex in the last month by looking at the response their spouse gave to the same question. They found that older respondents were much more likely to have missing data, indicating that answering the question was strongly related to the age of the respondent. For younger respondents who refused to answer, their spouses frequently reported having intercourse in the last month. For older respondents who refused to answer, their spouses frequently reported having no sex. Consequently, missing data for older respondents probably means they did not have intercourse, whereas the opposite tends to be true for younger respondents.

Since many people refuse to report their income, it is important to understand how not reporting income is related to other variables. Using the NSFH, wave one, we computed a variable called "MISSING" that was coded 1 if the respondent answered the questions used to determine total household income and 2 if the respondent did not answer these questions. We then regressed this variable on the respondent's race, years of education, number of children under 5, and age. We also included whether anybody in the household had a drug problem and whether the respondent was in a specially oversampled group. This is done for illustrative purposes only and other variables should be included in a complete model of missing data. The results appear in Table 2.

Table 2 shows that all the predictor variables are significant in ways that tend to support the general expectations of survey researchers. White, non-Hispanics are significantly less likely to have skipped the income items, with their odds being a little over half as likely as others to have missing data on income. Each year of additional education reduces the odds of not reporting income, with a surprising result being

**Table 2. Logistic Regression of Missing Data
for Total Household Income on Selected Variables Using NSFH1 Data**

Variables[a]	Unstandardized	Standardized	Wald χ^2	Probability >	Odds ratio
Intercept	−0.019	—	0.881	.881	—
Race: Non-Hispanic white, 1; other, 0	−0.372	−.091	51.477	.001	0.689
Education, years	−0.047	−.084	40.332	.001	0.954
Main sample, 1; oversample, 0	0.178	.043	10.851	.001	1.195
Drug problem in home: yes, 1; no, 0	0.273	.034	8.531	.004	1.314
Number of children under 5	−.478	−.153	98.017	.001	0.620
Respondent's age	−.008	−.075	29.376	.001	0.992

[a]e was coded 1 if it was missing 2 if it was present. The model predicts the odds of income missing. Weight was computed by the NSFH staff to reproduce Current Population Statistics characteristics. Education was measured using the EDUCAT variable computed by NSFH staff. Sample was coded 1 if the respondent was in the main sample and 0 if the respondent was in an oversampled group. Drug or alcohol problem was coded 1 if any household member had a problem and 0 if none had a problem. Although NSFH has 13,008 respondents, because of missing data on some of the predictors, this table is based on 11,473 respondents. Of these, 2744 did not report income and 8729 did.

that those in the main sample are somewhat more likely to skip the income questions than those who were deliberately oversampled. Those households with a member who has a drug or alcohol problem are more likely to be missing the income variable, while those that have several young children are less likely to be missing it. Finally, older respondents are more likely to report their income than are younger respondents.

These analyses demonstrate that missing data is a problem in many aspects of family research. We not only have so many cases with missing data that generalizations are called into question, but we also have systematically missing data. That is, certain types of people are significantly more likely to have missing data on some variables than other types of people, and the underlying motivation for data being missing may vary across different types of people.

Although no simple solution exists for dealing with missing data, the default in some statistical packages is to use listwise deletion. That is, any participant who does not have a score on every variable is simply dropped from the analysis. In our example of wives' reports of household work we might speculate that wives' whose husbands do nearly no household work are likely to skip one or more of these items. If we eliminate all cases with missing data on any of the items, then we are likely to overestimate the amount of work done by the typical husband because many of the husbands who do little or no work are eliminated.

When doing complex analyses, researchers sometimes use what is called pairwise deletion. All participants who answered both items for a given correlation are included in estimating the correlation. The matrix of correlations calculated in this fashion is then used to perform multiple regression or other types of analysis. Because different people fail to answer different items, it is likely that each correlation is based on a different sample. The resulting correlation matrix does not represent a single population, and each element of

the matrix is based on a different subset of participants. This is a dubious solution to problems of missing data. Since the resulting matrix does not refer to any specific population, it is not a "real" matrix. At the very least, pairwise deletion compromises the statistical estimation process, and at the extreme, the correlation matrix may not even be positive definite.

Researchers can impute a value for missing cases. For example, if 20% of the respondents did not report their income, the researcher might substitute the median income of those who did report their income. The problem with this strategy is that those not reporting their income may not be represented very well by the median income. For example, poor people may feel embarrassed to report their income, while rich people may want to conceal their income. Since we do not know the proportions missing for either rich or poor, using the median value is a poor way of imputing the true income for these people. A better imputation procedure is to substitute the median income for a homogeneous subgroup. The researcher might substitute a different median income for respondents who have high education than for those who have low education. Gender could also be used so that males with high education would have a much higher imputed income than females with limited education. An extension of this type of imputation uses multiple regression to impute missing values. For example, income is predicted from all available variables with the resulting equation used to compute an estimated income for participants who have income missing. One limitation of this approach is that if the other variables in the model are used to predict income, then the imputed value will be perfectly predicted by these values. If a researcher uses education, race, and gender to predict income for those with missing data on income, then any model that includes education, race, and gender will predict the imputed cases perfectly.

There have been major advances in the treatment of

missing data that are just now being introduced to family studies (Graham, Hofer, & Piccinin, 1994; McArdle & Hamagami,1992; Walker et al., 1996). A procedure that is relatively easy to implement is known as expectation maximization (EM) (see Schafer [1997] for a discussion of multiple imputation). Where a particular score is missing, it is imputed using multiple regression (other imputation methods can be used for non-normal distributions). Then, a random error is added to the imputation, with the size of this term being based on the strength of prediction. Adding the error term is critical, otherwise the process would impute a value that would subsequently be perfectly predicted (cf. multiple regression imputation). The conclusion of step one occurs, therefore, when all missing values are computed and covariance matrix is estimated.

The second step repeats the first step but now with more information. For example, if Damon skipped 3 items out of the set of 20, the first time around each missing value would be imputed based on knowing Damon's score on 17 variables. However, the second step now can use 19 variables for each imputation. A covariance matrix is computed and compared to the covariance matrix from step one. If there is a substantial difference, the process is repeated a third time. The EM process is repeated until the difference between two covariance matrices is tiny (Rubin, 1987). This approach has substantial advantages over the other approaches that have been used in marriage and family research.

Imputation based on an EM algorithm (Graham et al., 1994) is straightforward, but the benefits may be limited. The procedure is most useful for cases where there is substantial missing data on covariates such as income but not on the dependent variable or any of the primary independent variables. The imputation allows the researcher to keep all the data that is available on the independent and dependent variables. When the missing data is on the dependent variable or on primary independent variables, no power or precision is added to estimating slopes (Darlington, 1990).

Quantitative Analysis

The variety of statistical analysis techniques seems endless. To get some notion of the range of analysis procedures used, a review of a single year of the *Journal of Marriage and the Family* was conducted. The 1992 volume was selected. The following list of procedures is shown to demonstrate the range of procedures.

- Univariate: means, standard deviations, percentages
- Bivariate: Chi-square on contingency tables, ANOVA (analysis of variance), correlations, repeated measures ANOVA, paired t-test
- Multivariate: MANOVA (multivariate analysis of variance), repeated measures MANOVA, ANCOVA (analysis of covariance), logistic regression, probit regression, ordered probit regression, proportional hazard models with covariates, hazard rate modeling, hierarchical analysis of variance, factor analysis, principal components analysis, confirmatory factor analysis, structural equation modeling, path analysis, OLS regression, trend analysis, event history analysis, Chow test, interaction analysis

Few academic disciplines use such a broad range of quantitative procedures. Importantly, this list is based on a single volume of a single journal. Some commonalities in analysis strategies need to be noted, with most involving several independent variables. OLS regression is widely used as a basic statistical model because it includes multiple independent variables (predictors) and systematically controls for important covariates. Many of the procedures are either special cases of OLS regression (for example, ANOVA, ANCOVA) or extensions of OLS that can handle limited variables such as categorical dependent variables (for example, logistic regression). Factor analysis procedures and their extensions such as confirmatory factor analysis play a major role. Two areas that are important but have limited coverage in most graduate programs are time series analysis procedures and structural equation modeling.

As the variety of procedures used by family scholars have mushroomed, the statistical software has done the same. Up to the 1980s most family scholars used SPSS and occasionally SAS or BMDP. Since then, SAS has been used increasingly. Many specialized packages have emerged. GAUSS and S are two high level programming languages oriented toward statistical applications. Structural equation models are estimated using various packages, including LISREL, EQS, and AMOS. Although LISREL has been used in over 90% of the SEM papers in the *Journal of Marriage and the Family* since the 1980s, EQS and AMOS have special features and simplified user interfaces. GLIM is a generalized linear modeling program and LIMDEP is an economicetric package that is designed for models with limited dependent variables such as variables that are highly skewed, censored, and counts. Information about these and other statistical packages is available at a home page on the World Wide Web:

http://asa.ugl.lib.umich.edu/chdocs/statistics/mailing.html#3

The rapid development of technical skills by family scholars has been facilitated by the growth in statistical software. This software is not only more powerful than earlier versions, but it is also more accessible. Programs that once required hundreds of lines of arcane code can now be done in a graphic environment by clicking on variables, types of models, and options.

Overreliance on Statistical Significance

A systematic limitation of quantitative analysis is an overreliance on results being statistically significant. Researchers state a null hypothesis (there is no difference in means, there is no relationship between the variables, etc.). This null hypothesis or absence of a relation is usually the opposite of the research hypothesis. A statistically significant result is one that would be extremely unlikely to happen by chance if the null hypothesis were true. Importantly, statistical significance is only one aspect of substantive significance, which consists of being (1) statistically significant, (2) in the direction predicted, (3) of a substantial size, and (4) able to explain a substantial portion of the variation in the outcome variable. The fact that a result is statistically significant means only that it differs from zero, but not that it differs from zero by very much.

Statistical significance can be misused in two circumstances. First, when the sample is small and many variables are being examined, there may not be enough statistical power to detect a result that is substantial. Cohen (1988) provides procedures for deciding when this is a problem. Second, when the sample is very large, even substantively critical results can be statistically significant. As family scholars utilize large, national surveys this second circumstance is becoming highly problematic.

Deal and Anderson (1995) illustrate how both of these circumstances apply to family research. They point out that with just 50 cases an r must be .27 or greater to be significant at the .05 level. With 10,000 cases, an $r = .02$ is statistically significant. In the first case, if the true correlation in the population is $\rho = .20$, then we may not have the power to obtain significant results in our sample of 50 cases. In multivariate analysis, having sufficient power on small samples requires the population parameters to be extremely large. In the second case, because of the large sample, we are very confident that the population correlation, ρ, is not zero, but we are also very confident that it is less than .04! One way of interpreting a statistically significant correlation of .02 is to recognize that we are nearly certain that we are *not* explaining over 99% of the variance in the outcome variable [the explained variation is $(1 - r^2) \times 100$].

A problem with the overemphasis on statistical significance can be illustrated with an applied evaluation example. Suppose a researcher tests whether a teen program reduces parent–child conflict by comparing 1500 teens from a particular high school who went through the program to 1500 teens in a neighboring high school that did not have the class. We will assume that she found a statistically significant difference in parent–child conflict. Some researchers would jump from this result to the conclusion that the program is effective and should be implemented. Before doing this, however, she needs to address the other conditions of substantive significance. First, she needs to make sure which group had lower parent–child conflict. Let's say the program group had a mean of 69 on a 100-point scale and the control group, who did not get the program, had a mean of 66.

Next, she needs to see if the difference is substantial. With a total of 3000 high school girls in her study, even a tiny difference might be statistically significant. One way to evaluate the difference is with the standard deviations of the two groups. If the standard deviation for both groups is about 2, this means that the majority of the teens who did not get the program will be between 64 and 68 and the majority of those who got the program will be between 67 and 71. There is some overlap, but the teens who got the program seem to be substantially higher as a group. If the standard deviation for both groups is about 20, this means the majority of the teens who did not get the program will be between 46 and 86, while the majority of teens who got the program will be between 49 and 89. These two distributions seem to overlap a great deal. In this case, although the program produced a statistically significant difference and it was in the predicted direction, there does not appear to be a substantial difference. Finally, she needs to consider how much of the variation in parent–child conflict is explained by the difference between the treatment and control groups. Procedures for estimating the effect size for several widely used statistical procedures are provided by Cohen (1988).

Excessive reliance on statistical significance can have harmful consequences. For example, suppose a research study found that boys do significantly worse than girls at music. Although the difference may be statistically significant, it may also be very small (difference between the mean for girls and the mean for boys), and there may huge individual variance for both boys and girls. Treating boys differently because of a significant but small difference is harmful. Even though boys may do worse than girls on average, an individual boy may do better than an individual girl. Despite such individual variability, however, significant differences between groups have been used as rationales for discriminating against individuals. For example, some have suggested that girls or African Americans should not receive advanced training in mathematics because girls, on average, do significantly worse than boys, and African Americans, on average, do significantly worse than other racial or ethnic groups on standardized tests.

Overreliance on Standardized Measures of Association

Family researchers rely more on standardized than on unstandardized measures of association. A standardized measure such as a correlation, partial correlation, multiple correlation, or beta weight are standardized by forcing all the variables to have the same variance (1.0) and mean (0.0).

These transformations produce coefficients than range from −1.0 to 1.0, where −1.0 is a perfect negative relationship and 1.0 is a perfect positive relationship. Within a single population where the effects of several variables are being compared it is often useful to display standardized coefficients. If the beta weight (standardized partial regression coefficient) between education and attitude toward abortion is .26 and the beta weight between income and attitude toward abortion is .03, we can say that education is the better predictor.

There are several cases where we should be using unstandardized coefficients. Where the scales are measured in units that are meaningful, then the unstandardized coefficients offer a more informative interpretation. A unit of measurement is meaningful when a culture has a shared understanding of it, for example, income measured in dollars, education measured in years, number of times a family eats together per week, or the number of times a woman has been married. These are qualitatively different from many scales that are created by researchers using an arbitrary range, say attitude toward divorce measured on a scale ranging from 9 to 25. If the correlation, a standardized coefficient, between education and income is .4 this suggests the relationship is moderate. However, if the unstandardized regression coefficient, B, is .5, education is measured in years, and income is measured in $1000s, then each year of education yields an expected increase in income of $500 per year. This is far more useful information than knowing that the correlation is .4.

Although scales often do not have as clear a meaning as income, it is still possible to identify a substantively important change in the dependent variable. Using the relationship between education (in years) and attitude toward abortion (1, strongly disagree; 2, disagree; 3, agree; 4, strongly agree), we might agree that a one unit change would be substantively important as a person moves from disagree to agree or from agree to strongly agree. If the correlation is .4 we know the relationship is moderate, whereas an unstandardized regression coefficient of .2 would indicate that 5 additional years of education would be required to change the attitude toward abortion by one unit. If the unstandardized regression coefficient were 1.0, then it would take just 1 additional year of education to cause a substantively significant change in attitude toward abortion.

Standardized coefficients are sensitive to differences in the variance of the independent variable. This can be illustrated with hypothetical data generated from 160 cases under two conditions. In condition one the sample is 50% white and 50% non-white, while in condition two the sample is 6% white and 94% non-white. For both samples, the difference in education between whites and non-whites is identical, with whites being expected to attain 3.2 years more education. Although this is hypothetical data, if such a difference were true, it would be a dramatic race difference. A regression

equation yields the following unstandardized results for both hypothetical samples:

$$y' = 10.60 + 3.20(\text{Race}) \qquad (7)$$

Thus, unstandardized regression is not influenced by the variance in the independent variable, race (race has a standard deviation of .50 for the first sample and .24 for the second sample due solely to differences in the percentage of the sample that is white), but the standardized coefficients are. For the first sample the $R^2 = .28$ and the $\beta = .53$, a very strong result. In the second sample the $R^2 = .09$ with the $\beta = .30$, only a moderate relationship.

Although this example is hypothetical, this problem can occur for a number of reasons. Suppose one research study examined the relationship between race and education in North Dakota and another in Louisiana. Despite unstandardized difference being identical in both states (3.2 years), North Dakota has a much higher percentage of whites and will, therefore, have a much weaker R^2. Although tempting to use the difference in the R^2 as evidence of greater discrimination in Louisiana, this would be inappropriate. After all, both states have an average of 3.2 more years of education for whites.

When comparing across two or more groups, the use of standardized coefficients is incorrect. Many researchers have compared correlations across groups as evidence of group differences. For example, if they argue that the correlation between education and income is stronger for men than for women and if the genders differ in their variance on the independent variable, education, then comparison among the correlations is inappropriate. Instead, the appropriate comparisons would involve the unstandardized effects (e.g., differences in the unstandardized regression coefficients).

Models Are Not Perfect

Researchers develop models that represent sets of related hypotheses. These are widely used in path analysis (Pedhazur, 1982) and structural equation modeling. When dealing with a set of related hypotheses, models have clear advantages. Consider a simple, abstract model containing the following set of hypotheses: (a) the greater X_1 the greater X_2, (b) the greater X_1 the greater X_3, (c) the greater X_1 the greater X_4, (d) the greater X_2 the greater X_3, (e) the greater X_2 the greater X_4, (f) the greater X_3 the greater X_4. The six hypotheses are represented in Figure 5 as an integrated model. Each straight line ending with an arrow represents one of the hypotheses. Such models can clarify our thinking by showing places where we may have omitted a relationship. Models allow us to decompose relationships into parts consisting of a direct effect (shown by the lines ending in arrows in Figures 5, a, b, c, d, e, and f, indirect effects (relationship

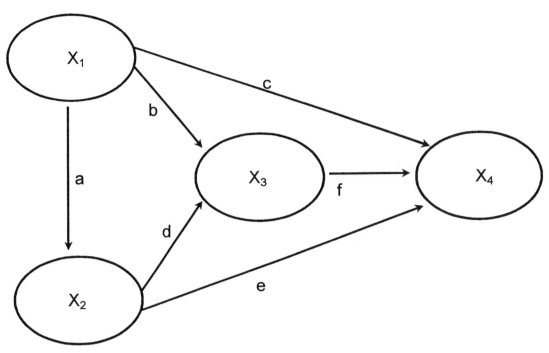

Figure 5. Hypothetical model.

between X_1 and X_3 includes an indirect linkage, ad, as well as a direct link, b), and spurious effects (part of the relationship between X_3 and X_4 is because they both have a common cause in X_1, bc).

Although these models are useful, it is often easy to criticize them for not being perfect. A model may leave out one or more potentially relevant variables and the model may even ignore possible feedback. Such limitations of a model are called specification errors and can result in biased estimates. It is important to consider these limitations, but it is also important to recognize that any model is going to be imperfect. These are called models precisely because they are simplifications of reality. A model that included all possible variables and relations would be so complex that it would not be very useful and probably could not be estimated.

Statistical Interaction

Many theories involve the interaction of two or more variables. Statistical interaction has a very limited meaning. If the effect of X on Y is conditional on the level of a third variable, say Z, then we say that X and Y interact. Imagine that a researcher believes that there is a negative relationship between adverse effects of divorce on children and the time since the divorce was finalized. The idea is that the adverse effects of divorce are greatest right after the divorce is finalized and then gradually diminish over time. Imagine further that a researcher believes this is a much stronger relationship for girls than it is for boys. Figure 6 illustrates these hypothetical relationships. Immediately after the divorce is finalized, both boys and girls have substantial adjustment problems. However, over time the girls' problems are diminished at a much greater rate than the boys problems. This is a classic example of statistical interaction. Time since the divorce and gender interact because the relationship between time since divorce and adjustment problems has a different slope for girls than it has for boys.

A model such as the one in Figure 6 is estimated using a single regression equation:

$$Y' = B_0 + B_1 D + B_2 X + B_3 DX \tag{8}$$

where: Y = adjustment problems, D = gender coded 0 for boys and 1 for girls, X = months since divorce was finalized, and DX = interaction between gender and months.

For Figure 6 the estimated equation will be $Y' = 10 + 0D - 1X - 2DX$. This equation actually contains an separate implicit equations for girls and boys. For boys, the value of D is 0.0, so the equation becomes $Y' = 10 - 1X$. For girls, the value of D is 1.0, so the equation becomes $Y' = 10 - 3X$. Assuming B_2 and B_3 are statistically significant, we can say that boys and girls do not differ in the immediate adjustment

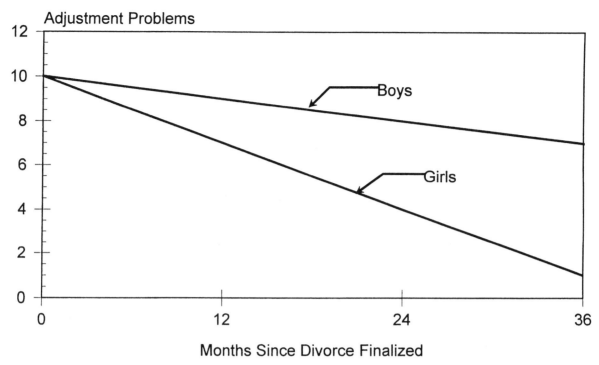

Figure 6. Adjustment problems of adolescents and time since divorce was finalized (hypothetical data).

problems after a divorce ($B_0 = 0$), boys' problems diminish significantly with time ($B_2 = -1$), and girls' problems diminish significantly more quickly than boys ($B_3 = -2$). Statistical interaction is sometimes confused with joint effects or additive effects. In reality, statistical interaction means that the slopes differ depending on the level of a third variable (Aiken & West, 1991).

There are many ways to perform interaction analysis, and some of them are extremely complex. Structural equation modeling allows a researcher to estimate complex models simultaneously across groups. For example, a model of factors influencing marital happiness could be estimated simultaneously in a sample of husbands and wives. This strategy can identify any interactions that exist by testing which effects are stronger or weaker for husbands than they are for wives.

The example illustrates interaction in the special case of one dichotomous variable (gender) and one continuous variable (time since divorce). It is possible to extend this to other combinations of levels of measurement. When continuous variables interact, the analysis requires centering of all the predictors. This is done by computing new variables that subtract the mean from each existing variable. When this is done, the new variables have a mean of 0.0 without changing their standard deviations (Aiken & West, 1991).

Special Problem and Ethical Issues

Family researchers study the issues that concern people the most—factors that enhance or harm the well-being of people and families. This often involves asking sensitive questions. We ask whether people are happy or depressed. A number of studies involve people who are at risk such as women who are being physically abused or children who are not performing at their optimum level.

What happens when we ask these people to answer sensitive questions? Will they refuse to participate? Are the answers truthful? Most studies have a high compliance rate, with 80%–90% of the people answering most questions (income is a notable exception). When studies begin by asking questions that respondents are willing to answer, the respondents "buy into their role" as respondents and report intimate information. In the last 2 decades, researchers have moved from calling people subjects to calling them participants or respondents. This reflects the respect researchers must have for these people, but it also helps the people appreciate the importance of what they are doing. The reality is that participants will tell a stranger personal data they would never share with members of their own family.

Although researchers are able to get people to cooperate with studies, a crucial question is how we should limit ourselves in what we ask people to do. All universities have "human subjects" committees that review proposals involving human participants where researchers must show that the results of their study are sufficiently promising to justify any risks to their participants. Researchers need to take precautions to minimize risks, sometimes involving anonymity (no name or identification associated with participants) or confidentiality (name or identification known only to the project's staff) for the participants.

"Informed consent" is also involved, whereby participants agree to be involved after they are told what the study involves, as well as what the procedures and potential risks are. Informed consent is an issue for many studies. We have seen how the Hawthorne Effect shows that when people know they are being observed and their performance measured, they react to this knowledge. When informed consent is provided, it is important that the hypothesis not be provided since this may serve as a "demand characteristic" (Orne, 1959, 1962). By demand characteristics we mean that participants guess the purpose of a study and they "help" the scientist find it. These issues are difficult for experimental studies where there is a single hypothesis and informed consent may communicate this hypothesis. This is less of a problem in surveys that measure many variables. Informed consent should describe the type of variables that are being measured but not specify what the researcher is trying to prove. Informed consent is also a special problem with some observational research. The design of some observational research is emergent and the researcher may not know exactly what is being tested before going into the field. Consequently, it is difficult to have meaningful informed consent.

Another problem occurs with studies of school-age children. Parents need to give informed consent for their children to participate in studies. Some researchers rely on "passive consent," where children take notes home to their parents and the parents are assumed to approve unless the note is returned saying the parents disapprove. Other researchers require active consent, where the parents must return the approval form before the child can participate. Although active consent has fewer ethical dilemmas, the return rate on forms sent home is so low that the external validity of the study is questionable. When notes are sent home for parents' signature it is common for fewer than 50% of them to be returned. This creates such a low response rate that we cannot generate national norms. As this is written, a law is being considered that will require active consent of parents. If this law passes, it will be difficult to obtain reliable information about many youth-related issues such as use of alcohol, other drugs, and sexual activity.

Even the most ethically sensitive scholar will put participants at some at risk. Asking children how often they see their nonresident father may bring back problems that had been put to rest. In some cases the effect of this can be positive; in some cases it can be negative. Observational studies and participant observation studies are especially prone to risks for participants. A scholar interested in the roles of family members and physicians when a dying family member is on a life support system is dealing with very important questions: Who decides to turn off the machine? What are the roles of family members? Of the physician? The presence of the researcher may be intrusive and influence the decision-making process. Yet, the researcher has neither the medical expertise nor the family role that would justify his or her influence.

Another special risk for observational work is unanticipated self-exposure (LaRossa, Bennett, & Gelles, 1985). A study of the relationship between parents and adult children who are gay or lesbian illustrates this problem. What happens when the adult child indicates they have a drug habit or when a parent reports sexually abusing the child? The participants may reveal information about themselves that goes beyond the original informed consent agreement. Such problems are not limited to observational studies.

Feminist methodology is not a particular research design method, nor a data collection method (Nielsen, 1990). It is distinguished by (1) directly stating the researchers' values, (2) recognizing the influence doing research has on the researcher and participant, (3) sensitivity to how families are sources of both support and oppression for women, and (4) the intention of doing research that benefits women rather than simply being about women (Allen & Walker, 1993). Given this worldview, feminist methodology presents complex ethical issues to researchers and demands all family scholars to be sensitive to these concerns.

Conclusions

There are a wide variety of strategies, designs, and methods of analysis used by marriage and family researchers. This diversity reflects the equally diverse root discipline and content areas that overlap the study of marriage and the family. Cross-sectional surveys remain the most widely used strategy, and quantitative analysis is dominant in the major journals. However, experiments and longitudinal, time series, and observational strategies are all crucial tools for research.

The future of family scholarship will benefit greatly by the rapid progress in computer and the computer interface. This applies to all styles of research but most strongly to the multivariate quantitative studies and to observational research. Procedures that were computationally prohibitive in the 1970s are now done on desktop computers. Software that was difficult to understand and tedious to apply has been replaced with software that is much more accessible. Datasets in the public domain can now be obtained by computer transfers.

There have been many advances in the treatment of missing data, with family studies lagging behind in implementing these. As more complex data collection procedures become common, improved treatment of missing data is critical. This is a serious issue with longitudinal designs where even the best efforts typically result in 50% or more of the cases having at least some missing data.

Although a great variety exists in statistical procedures, a review of major journals in the field of family studies such as *The Journal of Marriage and the Family* reveals less diversity of methods of data collection. Studies of single individuals based on cross-sectional surveys remain predominate for most issues. Where information on family systems is incorporated into studies, the response is often obtained from a single individual from each family. It is hoped that new datasets will be used in ways that involve multiple family members, direct observations, and longitudinal designs, but such studies are in the minority at the time of this writing.

ACKNOWLEDGMENT. I would like to thank Aphra Katzev for assistance reviewing journals to identify the types of quantitative methodology that is employed.

References

Acock, A. C., & Demo, D. (1994). *Family diversity and well-being*. Newbury Park, CA: Sage.

Acock, A. C., & Schumm, W. (1992). Analysis of covariance structures applied to family research and theory. In P. Boss, W. Doherty, R. LaRossa, W. Schumm, & S. Steinmetz (Eds.), *Sourcebook of family theories and methods* (pp. 451–468). New York: Plenum.

Aiken, L. S., & West, S. G. (1991). *Multiple regression: Testing and interpreting interactions*. Newbury Park, CA: Sage.

Allen, K. R., & Walker, A. J. (1993). A feminist analysis of interviews with elderly mothers and their daughters. In J. F. Gilgun, K. Daly, & G. Handel (Eds.), *Qualitative methods in family research* (pp. 198–214). Newbury Park, CA: Sage.

Allison, P. D. (1990). Change scores ad dependent variables in regression analysis. In C. Clogg (Ed.), *Sociological methodology* (Vol. 20, pp. 93–114). Oxford: Basil Blackwell.

Allison, P. D. (1994). Using panel data to estimate the effects of events. *Sociological Methods and Research*, 23, 174–199.

Babbie, E. (1995). *The practice of social research* (7th ed.). Belmont, CA: Wadsworth.

Bailey, K. D. (1984). On integrating theory and method. *Current Perspectives in Social Theory*, 6, 21–44.

Bales, R. F. (1950). *Interaction process analysis: A method for the study of small groups*. Cambridge, MA: Addison-Wesley Press.

Blumer, H. (1969). *Symbolic interactionism: Perspectives and method*. Englewood Cliffs, NJ: Prentice-Hall.

Bronson, G. W. (1994). Infants' transitions toward adult-like scanning. *Child Development*, 5, 1243–1261.

Brown, S. R., & Melamed, L. E. (1990). *Experimental design and analysis*. Newbury Park, CA: Sage.

Bryk, A. S., & Raudenbush, S. W. (1992). *Hierachical linear models: Applications and data analysis techniques*. Newbury Park, CA: Sage.

Burr, W. R. (1995). Using theories in family science. In R. D. Day, K. R. Gilbert, B. H. Settles, & W. R. Burr (Eds.), *Research and theory in family science* (pp. 73–90). Pacific Grove, CA: Brooks/Cole.

Call V., Sprecher, S., & Schwartz, P. (1995). The incidence and frequency of marital sex in a national sample. *Journal of Marriage and the Family*, 57, 639–652.

Campbell, M. L., Roberts, R. E. L., & Rubenfeld, L. A. (1986, November). *Selective attrition thirteen years later: Implications for the study of change in marital satisfaction*. Paper presented at the annual meeting of the Gerontology Society of America, Chicago, IL.

Carmines, E. G., & McIver, J. P. (1979). *Reliability and validity assessment*. Beverly Hills, CA: Sage.

Carver, K. P., & Teachman, J. D. (1995). The science of family science. In R. D. Day, K. R. Gilbert, B. H. Settles, & W. R. Burr (Eds.), *Research and theory in family science* (pp. 113–127). Pacific Grove, CA: Brooks/ Cole.

Cohen, J. (1988). *Statistical power analysis for the behavioral sciences* (2nd ed.). Hillsdale, NJ: Erlbaum.

Copeland, A. P., & White, K. M. (1991). *Studying families*. Newbury Park, CA: Sage.

Dahrendorf, R. (1969). On the origins of inequality among men. In A. Beteile (Ed.), *Social inequality: Selected readings* (pp. 16–44). New York: Harmondsworth/Penguin.

Darlington, R. B. (1990). *Regression and linear models*. New York: McGraw-Hill.

Davis, K., & Moore, W. (1945). Some principles of stratification. *American Sociological Review*, 10, 242–249.

Davis, J. A., & Smith, T. W. (1992). *The NORC general social survey: A user's guide*. Newbury Park, CA: Sage.

Deal, J. E., & Anderson, E. R. (1995). Reporting and interpreting results in family research. *Journal of Marriage and the Family*, 57, 1040–1048.

DeVellis, R. F. (1991). *Scale development: Theory and application*. Newbury Park, CA: Sage.

Dillman, D. A. (1978). *Mail and telephone surveys: The total design method*. New York: Wiley.

Draper, T. W., & Marcos, A. C. (1990). *Family variables: Conceptualization, measurement and use*. Newbury Park, CA: Sage.

Duncan, O. D. (1961). A socioeconomic index for all occupations. In A. J. Reiss, Jr. (Ed.), *Occupations and social status* (pp. 109–138). New York: Free Press.

Elder, G. H., Jr. (1981). History and the family: The discovery of complexity. *Journal of Marriage and the Family*, 43, 489–514.

French, J. R. P. (1950). Field experiments: Changing group productivity. In J. G. Miller (Ed.), *Experiments in social process: A symposium on social psychology* (pp. 79–96). New York: McGraw-Hill.

Gilgun, J. F. (1992). Definitions, methodologies, and methods. In J. F. Gilgun, K. Daly, & G. Handel (Eds.), *Qualitative methods in family research* (pp. 22–49). Newbury Park, CA: Sage.

Gilgun, J. F., Daly, K., & Handel, G. (Eds.). (1992). *Qualitative methods in family research*. Newbury Park, CA: Sage.

Graham, J. W., Hofer, S. M., & Piccinin, A. M. (1994). Analysis with missing data in drug prevention research. In L. M. Collins & L. A. Seitz (Eds.), *Advances in data analysis for prevention intervention research* (National Institute on Drug Abuse Research Monograph Series no. 142), Washington, DC: National Institute on Drug Abuse.

Haller, A. (1982). *Social structure and behavior*. New York: Academic Press.

Heaton, T. B., & Call, V. R. A. (1995). Modeling family dynamics with event history techniques. *Journal of Marriage and the Family*, 57, 1078–1090.

Heckman, J. J. (1976). The common structure of statistical models of truncation, sample selection, and limited dependent variables, and a simple estimator for such models. *Annals of Economic and Social Measurement, 5,* 475–492.

Heckman, J. J. (1979). Sample selection bias as a specification error. *Econometrica, 47,* 153–161.

Homans, G. (1974). *Elementary forms of human behavior* (rev. ed.). New York: Harcourt Brace.

Johnson, D. R. (1995). Alternative methods for the quantitative analysis of panel data in family research: Pooled time-series models. *Journal of Marriage and the Family, 57,* 1065–1077.

Johnson, D. R., Amoloza, T. O., & Booth, A. (1992). Stability and developmental change in marital quality: A three-wave panel analysis. *Journal of Marriage and the Family, 64,* 582–594.

Jones, W. H., & Lang, J. R. (1980). Sample composition bias and response bias in a mail survey: A comparison of inducement methods. *Journal of Marketing Research, 17,* 69–76.

Kamo, Y. (1988). Determinants of the household division of labor: Resources, power, and ideology. *Journal of Family Issues, 9,* 177–200.

Karney, B. R., & Bradbury, T. N. (1995). Assessing longitudinal change in marriage: An introduction to the analysis of growth curves. *Journal of Marriage and the Family, 57,* 1091–1108.

Karney, B. R., Davila, J., Cohan, C. L., Sullivan, K. T., Johnson, M. D., & Bradbury, T. H. (1995). An empirical investigation of sampling strategies in marital research. *Journal of Marriage and the Family, 57,* 909–920.

Kasprzyk, D., Duncan, G., Kalton, G., Singh, M. P. (Eds.). (1989). *Panel surveys.* New York: Wiley.

LaRossa, R., Bennett, L. A., & Gelles, R. (1985). Ethical dilemmas in qualitative family research. In G. Handel (Ed.), *The psychosocial interior of the family* (pp. 95–111). New York: Aldine.

Larsen, A., & Olson, D. H. (1990). Capturing the complexity of family systems: Integrating family theory, family scores, and family analysis. In T. W. Draper & A. C. Marcos (Eds.), *Family variables: Conceptualization, measurement, and use* (pp. 19–47). Newbury Park, CA: Sage.

Larzelere, R. E., & Klein, D. M. (1987). Methodology. In M. B. Sussman & S. K. Steinmetz (Eds.), *Handbook of marriage and the family* (pp. 125–156). New York: Plenum.

McArdle, J. J., & Hamagami, F. (1992). Modeling incomplete longitudinal and cross-sectional data using latent growth structural models. *Experimental Aging Research, 18,* 145–166.

McCubbin, H. I., & Thompson, A. I. (Eds.). (1991). *Family assessment inventories for research and practice.* Madison: University of Wisconsin Press.

Miller, B. C., Rollins, B. C., & Thomas, D. L. (1982). On methods of studying marriages and families. *Journal of Marriage and the Family, 44,* 851–873.

Miller, R. B., & Wright, D. W. (1995). Detecting and correcting attrition bias in longitudinal family research. *Journal of Marriage and the Family, 57,* 921–929.

Nielsen, J. M. (1990). Introduction. In J. M. Nielsen (Ed.), *Feminist research methods* (pp. 1–37). Boulder, CO: Westview.

NSFH Staff. (1995). *Preliminary differential response rates of main respondent by characteristics at NSFH 1* (December 24 release as response. rep.ftlp://elaine.ssc.wisc.edu/pub/nsfh).

Orne, M. T. (1959). The nature of hypnosis: Artifact and essense. *Journal of Abnormal and Social Psychology, 58,* 277–299.

Orne, M. T. (1962). On the social psychology of the psychological experiment: With particular reference to demand characteristics and their implications. *American Psychologist, 17,* 776–783.

Parker, K. C., Hanson, R. K., & Hunsley, J. (1988). MMPI, Rorschach, and WAIS: A meta-analytic comparison of reliability, stability, and validity. *Psychological Bulletin, 103,* 367–373.

Pedhazur, E. (1982). *Multiple regression in behavioral research: Explanation and prediction.* New York: Holt, Rinehart and Winston.

Rogosa, D. (1988). Myths about longitudinal research. In K. W. Schaie (Ed.), *Methodological issues in aging research* (pp. 171–209). New York: Springer.

Rubin, D. B. (1987). *Multiple imputation for nonresponse in surveys.* New York: Wiley.

Schafer, J. L. (1997). Analysis of incomplete multivariate data. London: Chapman & Hall.

Scheaffer, R. L., Mendenhall, W., & Ott, L. (1979). *Elementary survey sampling* (2nd ed.). North Scituate, MA: Duxbury Press.

Scinovacz, M. E., & Egley, L. C. (1995). Comparing one-partner and couple data on sensitive marital behaviors: The case of marital violence. *Journal of Marriage and the Family, 57,* 995–1010.

Smith, T. E., & Graham, P. B. (1995). Socioeconomic stratification in family research. *Journal of Marriage and the Family, 57,* 930–940.

Sweet, J., Bumpass, L., & Call, V. (1988). *The design and content of the national survey of families and households* (Working paper NSFH1). Madison: Center for Demography and Ecology, University of Wisconsin–Madison.

Teachman, J. D. (1982). Methodological issues in the analysis of family formation and dissolution. *Journal of Marriage and the Family, 44,* 1037–1053.

Teachman, J. D., Polonko, K. A., & Scanzoni, J. (1987). Demography of the family. In M. B. Sussman & S. K. Steinmetz (Eds.), *Handbook of marriage and the family* (pp. 3–36). New York: Plenum.

Teachman, J. D., Carver, K., & Day, R. (1995). A model for the analysis of paired data. *Journal of Marriage and the Family, 57,* 1011–1024.

Thompson, L., & Walker, A. J. (1982). The dyad as the unit of analysis: Conceptual and methodological issues. *Journal of Marriage and the Family, 44,* 999–1008.

Vincent, J. P., Friedman, L. S., Nugent, J., & Messerly, L. (1979). Demand characteristics in observations of marital interaction. *Journal of Consulting and Clinical Psychology, 47,* 557–566.

Walker, A., Acock, A. C., Bowman, S., & Li, F. (1996). Amount of caregiven and caregiving satisfaction: A latent growth curve analysis. *Journal of Gerontology: Psychological Sciences, 51B,* P130–P142.

Weber, M. (1968). *Classes.* London: Verso. (Original work published 1921)

Willet, J. B. (1988). Questions and answers in the measurement of change. In E. Z. Rothkopf (Ed.), *Review of research in education: 1988–89* (pp. 345–422). Washington, DC: American Educational Research Association.

Willet, J. B., & Sayer, A. G. (1994). Using covariance structure analysis to detect correlates and predictors of individual change over time. *Psychological Bulletin, 116,* 363–381.

CHAPTER 11

Measurement in Family Studies

Walter R. Schumm and Karla K. Hemesath

Introduction

Measurement is the process of linking theoretical ideas—concepts—to empirical indicators—variables (Miller, 1986, p. 49). More specifically, it has been defined as "the assignment of numbers to objects or events according to rules" (Stevens, 1951, p. 22) or "the process of assigning numerals to units of analysis in order to represent conceptual properties" (Singleton, Straits, & Straits, 1988, p. 124). We believe that the traditional goal of measurement has been to allow us to operationally define concepts as variables in ways that permit the application of mathematical operations among the created variables. Mathematics as a powerful language allows us to assess variable interrelationships in creative ways. However, important information may be lost in the translation, a concern that underlies the skepticism regarding the validity of much quantitative research and the use of multivariate analyses for understanding families (Miller, 1986).

There are important risks in translating concepts into numbers and in interpreting mathematical relationships among those numbers as representing anything meaningful about family relationships. Even positivists have long admitted that poor theory and invalid measurement can put the most sophisticated statistical analyses at risk (Schumm, 1982). Postpositivist or radical critical scholars (Osmond, 1987) might question the validity of the process itself, deeming it intrinsically and hopelessly flawed.

Walter R. Schumm • School of Family Studies and Human Services, College of Human Ecology, Kansas State University, Manhattan, Kansas 66506-1403. **Karla K. Hemesath** • Department of Family and Community Medicine, College of Medicine at Rockford, Rockford, Illinois 61107-1897.

Handbook of Marriage and the Family, 2nd edition, edited by Marvin Sussman, Suzanne K. Steinmetz, and Gary W. Peterson. Plenum Press, New York, 1999.

If advances in science—and family social science in particular—depend in part on improving measurement (Jackson & Borgatta, 1981, pp. 6–7), then where are we in family measurement? If measurement is as important to social science as is widely acknowledged (Sabatelli & Bartle, 1995; Sabatelli & Waldron, 1995), then where we are in family measurement *is* important. Klein and Jurich (1993) interpreted Schumm (1990) as suggesting that the answer still might be "not far along" (p. 40). However, we, as well as others (Bray, 1995, p. 475), think that family scholars can legitimately take credit for *some* major progress in the past decade.

Progress

Availability of Measures

Whereas about one major family measurement compendium used to be produced each decade (Straus, 1969; Straus & Brown, 1978), the past decade has witnessed a virtual explosion in compendia from those that discuss thousands of measures more briefly to those that discuss dozens of measures in more depth (Fischer & Corcoran, 1994; Fredman & Sherman, 1987; Grotevant & Carlson, 1989; Jacob & Tennenbaum, 1988; L'Abate & Bagarozzi, 1993; O'Leary, 1987; Touliatos, Perlmutter, & Straus, 1990). Entire surveys are available in some compilations (Card, 1993). A number of articles have also addressed the validity of various sets of family measures (Burnett, 1987; Fowers, 1990; Sabatelli & Waldron, 1995; Tutty, 1995). Among these sourcebooks one can even find measures cataloged by number of items and date of development, as well as by concept. Most of these reference texts contain data on the reliability and validity of their measures, which may help prevent the use of scales simply because they exist, regardless of their validity; many contain copies of the actual instruments. The total effort represents a tremendous labor of love by a few dedicated family scholars, to whom the field owes a substantial debt of gratitude.

Whereas Straus (1964) discussed only 263 instruments, then 319 (1969) and later 813 (Straus & Brown, 1978), the more recent compendia discuss well over 1000 marriage and family instruments. Lindholm & Touliatos (1993) found that, for the most part, measurement work has grown steadily since 1928 in the family field. We would be negligent if we did not also mention the progress represented by reviews of various measurement instruments that have become standard features of some journals (e.g., Bagarozzi's Family Measurement Techniques section in *The American Journal of Family Therapy*, that was a significant contribution to the measurement literature from 1984 to 1992 as well as a special issue on family measurement in 1990 [Bagarozzi, 1990]). Journals have begun to publish detailed research and clinical assessments of specific scales (e.g., the Family Adaptability and Cohesion Evaluation Scales (FACES) in Gaughan [1995] and Ben-David & Jurich [1993]). Boughner, Hayes, Bubenzer, and West (1994) noted that *The Journal of Marital and Family Therapy* published over two dozen articles on measurement between 1981 and 1991. *Family Relations* devoted most of a recent issue to measurement issues, including articles on the Dyadic Adjustment Scale (Hunsley, Pinsent, Lefebvre, James-Tanner, & Vito, 1995), the Marital Problems Questionnaire (Douglass & Douglass, 1995), a variety of premarital assessment questionnaires (Larson et al., 1995), the Gendergram (White & Tyson-Rawson, 1995), the Multiple Determinants of Relationship Commitment Inventory (Kurdek, 1995), the Behavioral and Emotional Reactivity Index (Bartle & Sabatelli, 1995), and the Marital Intimacy Questionnaire (Van den Broucke, Vertommen, & Vandereycken, 1995). The *Journal of Family Issues* recently published a detailed assessment of a revised version of the Conflict Tactics Scales (Straus, Hamby, Boney-McCoy, & Sugarman, 1996).

Assessment of Reliability

A second area of substantial progress is that more and more family measures have been assessed for and have yielded adequate estimates of internal consistency reliability, often at the .70 or .80 levels recommended (Nunnally, 1978, p. 245; Spector, 1992; Carmines & Zeller, 1979; Zeller & Carmines, 1980). Some measures have been assessed for test-retest reliability (McGuire & Earls, 1993). Most research articles in leading journals now report reliability estimates for their measures; for example, of the articles in the November 1993 issue of *Journal of Marriage and the Family* that included measures (for which reliability could have been assessed) over 78% reported reliability estimates for at least some of their measures.

Analysis of Covariance Structures

A third area of at least some progress is the growing use of analysis of covariance structures (ACS) to integrate measurement and analysis more precisely. In particular, some recent authors have described the use of Linear Structural Relations (LISREL) and related methods to assess dyadic or family level variables (Acock & Schumm, 1993; Bray, Maxwell, & Cole, 1995; Sabatelli & Bartle, 1995; Teachman, Carver, & Day, 1995; Thompson & Walker, 1982). One unfortunate by-product of success, however, has been a tendency to omit reliability information altogether (e.g., Shagle & Barber, 1993) or to only report reliability information from previous (rather than the current) research (e.g., MacEwen & Barling, 1993). Another risk is that researchers will fail to use theory in setting up their ACS measurement models and therefore produce structural models of questionable value (Lavee, 1988). Other multivariate approaches, such as Q factor analysis (Deal, 1995), advances in the analysis of dyadic data (Kenny, 1996), and hazards modeling (Heaton & Call, 1995) are also being used to improve family measurement.

Development of Global Evaluative Measures

A fourth area of progress has been the development of highly reliable and probably valid global measures of life and family satisfaction. For example, in his review of marital satisfaction measures, Sabatelli (1988) found that most measures were reliable and at least some offered considerable evidence for their validity. Some of these measures appear to be reliable and valid despite their brevity, consisting of only a few items; Bradbury (1995, p. 462), for example, recommends Norton's (1983) Quality Marriage Index (QMI) (6 items) and Schumm et al's (1986) Kansas Marital Satisfaction Scale (KMSS) (3 items) over Spanier's (1976) 32-item Dyadic Adjustment Scale, for certain purposes. In fact, Johnson (1993) has argued that even some single-item global satisfaction measures may have adequate reliability and validity, although Sabatelli and Waldron (1995) are more critical of single-item measures since, in their opinion, the reliability and validity of global satisfaction items are almost intrinsically doubtful. Even though some sniping still occurs about which of these measures is most valid, many of the measures are so highly correlated with each other (concurrent validity) that there simply isn't much room for one to be much better than the other. For example, while some scholars—including myself—would like to think that Norton's (1983) 6-item QMI has more face validity than the 3-item KMSS, studies that have correlated the KMSS and the QMI have found zero-order correlations between .89 and .94 (Calahan, 1997; Karney, Bradbury, Finchan, & Sullivan,

1994; Schumm et al., 1986; Symonds-Mueth, personal communication).

Physiological Assessment

A fifth area of progress has been the development of ways to assess biological or physiological variables as important family factors, as in Gottman's work on marital stability and adjustment (Gottman, 1994; Gottman & Levenson, 1992; Jacobsen et al., 1994; Levenson, Carstensen, & Gottman, 1994) and recent work on testosterone and marital success (Booth & Dabbs, 1993; Julian & McKenry, 1989). Booth and Dabbs (1993) found that testosterone level in males was positively related to nonmarried status and marital instability and was negatively related to every aspect of marital quality used in their study. Men with higher levels of testosterone also reported a poorer quality of marital interaction than men with lower levels of testosterone. They argue that the traits associated with higher levels of testosterone, including aggressiveness, dominance behavior, and sensation seeking directly interfere with many types of intimate behaviors necessary for successful marriages. Booth and Dabbs (1993) assert that an awareness of the effects of testosterone as demonstrated in this study should be considered when trying to understand marital success and quality. Even though the use of biological measures is still very novel, it was seldom, if ever, done until recently (Bradbury & Finchman, 1990, p. 57).

In addition to Gottman and colleagues' (Gottman, 1994; Gottman & Levenson, 1992; Jacobson et al.,1994; Levenson et al., 1994) seminal work in this area, several other research groups are investigating the links between marital conflict and physiological variables such as endocrine function (Kiecolt-Glaser et al., 1995; Malarkey, Kiecolt-Glaser, Pearl, & Glaser, 1994) and blood pressure levels (Ewart, Taylor, Kraemer, & Agras, 1991).

Another area in which the measurement of biological variables has gained importance in family measurement is Plomin, McCearn, Pedersen, Nesselroae, and Bergeman's (1989) work merging behavioral genetics and family measurement. Plomin and colleagues' work investigated the genetic influences on adults' perception of family environment as measured by the Family Environment Scale (FES). They found that genetic factors significantly influenced how twins reared apart and together rated their families of origin, finding that approximately 25% of the variance in adults' responses on the FES was due to genetic differences among individuals (Plomin et al.,1989, p. 800). This work represents a virtually unexplored area of family measurement.

The questions raised by this area of endeavor are important for the other aspects of family measurement and assessment. How do we as family researchers capture this important component of perception of family life? How much of

what we measure is due to inherited features of our personality rather than the actual climate of family life? Of additional importance is the interpretation and use of measurement in clinical work. If perceptions of family life have a significant component that is inherited, how much will we be able to work with as clinicians?

Multiple Perspectives

A sixth area of progress is the growing recognition that multiple measures are needed for a full understanding of family life. Whereas we once debated the superiority of observational versus self-report measures, most family scholars now recognize the usefulness of both insider and outsider reports (Grotevant & Carlson, 1989), although both are vulnerable to subjectivity (Tutty, 1995). Discrepancies among different methods or between family members are even seen as a useful source of information rather than as an inherent problem. Many of the best family research articles report self-report, observer, and physiological measures integrated in the same analysis. Furthermore, there is at least a recognition that there are multiple conceptual levels in family research. Level of construct refers to whether we are defining concepts at the individual, dyadic, or family level; level of assessment refers to how we actually measure the concept (Copeland & White, 1991, p. 23). Copeland & White (1991, p. 24) add the idea of the level of variable formation, the level at which the measures are handled statistically. Perhaps our most common continuing problem is attempting to measure a family construct using individual self-reports that are combined statistically into a "family" latent variable.

Assessment of Elusive Concepts

We also find a growing recognition of the importance of theory to the field of measurement (Gottman, 1989; Grotevant, 1989). Related to that recognition we find a seventh area of progress: the gradual development of measures for concepts that have in the past proven elusive to operationalize. For example, measures have been developed recently to measure the concepts of forgiveness (accommodation) (Rusbult & Verette, 1991; Rusbult, Verette, Whitney, Slovik, et al., 1991; Yovetich & Rusbult, 1994), commitment (Kurdek, 1995; Lund, 1985; Stanley & Markman, 1992; Sternberg, 1988), marital stability (Booth, Johnson, & Edwards, 1983; Weiss & Cerreto, 1980), relationships beliefs (Eidelson & Epstein, 1982); marital attributions (Fincham & Bradbury, 1992), detailed marital interaction processes (Bowen, 1991; Sullaway & Christensen, 1989; Kurdek, 1994), emotional reactivity (Bartle & Sabatelli, 1995), and family emotional work (Erickson, 1993). We particularly like the scales that provide spouses with situations and ask for their most likely response, especially when the responses are balanced in terms of apparent social desirability (e.g., the Assertiveness Scale for Adolescents, in Fischer & Corcoran, 1994, pp. 407–416). Bradbury (1995) has discussed in detail improved measures in other areas, such as daily hassles, life stress, and family violence. However, the area of family power appears to remain elusive (Piotrikowski, Rapoport, & Rapoport, 1987, p. 264; Shehan & Lee, 1990; Szinovacz, 1987). While Fisher, Kokes, Ransom, Phillips, and Rudd (1985) suggested the use of transactional measures that assess the entire family system, an outstanding idea, relatively little work appears to have been advanced along those lines.

Problems and Prospects

Therefore, much progress has been and is being made in family measurement. Of course, substantial problems remain. Some of these problems parallel the previous indications of progress, representing their limitations.

Integration Lag

One interesting, if minor, problem is an apparent time lag between the publishing of technical reports on a measure and the integration of those reports into summary reviews of such measures. The problem is surprising, given the widespread availability of computer search technology and the easy availability of compendia on measures, which should make tracking down references on specific instruments relatively easy. For example, in a recent report, Sabatelli and Waldron (1995) discuss the validity of the Kansas Parental Satisfaction Scale (KPSS) but base their entire conclusions on a single, decade-old report (James, Schumm, Kennedy, Grigsby, & Schectman, 1985), overlooking more recent results (Canfield, Schumm, Swihart, & Eggerichs, 1990; Chang, Schumm, Coulson, Bollman, & Jurich, 1994; James, Kennedy, & Schumm, 1986; Jeong & Schumm, 1990). Likewise, Heyman, Sayers, and Bellack (1994) complain about the KMSS being used primarily by its original authors (Schumm, Bollman, & Jurich, 1997) rather than by independent researchers—somehow overlooking the fact that most of the recent publications using the KMSS have been by independent researchers (Bowen, 1991; Domenico & Windle, 1993; Finkel & Hansen, 1992; Fowers, 1991; Green, Harris, Forte, & Robinson, 1991; Hendrix & Anelli, 1993; Herman, 1991; Hunsley et al., 1995; Karney et al., 1994; Kurdek, 1994, 1995; Kurdek & Fine, 1991; Lee & Rittenhouse, 1992; Morris & Blanton, 1994; Russell & Wells, 1992; Sanderson & Kurdek, 1993; Shek & Tsang, 1993; Shek, Lam, Tsoi, & Lam, 1993; Tubman, 1991, 1993; Tucker & O'Grady, 1991; Wasielewski, 1991; White, Stahmann, & Furrow, 1994) rather than the original authors. One wonders how many other instru-

ments have been or are being evaluated without the benefit, for example, of the most current reliability and validity data.

Limitations of ACS Techniques

While analysis of covariance techniques appear very promising, their results can be misleading if not used properly. First, there is always a danger of reifying results obtained from complex procedures so that we end up describing families in "SPSS [Statistical Package for the Social Sciences] computer language" (Osmond, 1987, p. 121) or perhaps "ACS [analysis of covariance structures] computer language" today. Furthermore, it can be very tempting to try to salvage poor measurement with such sophisticated statistical analyses (Schumm, 1982). In particular, ACS can be misused to "magic" away poor reliability. For example, items may be so weakly correlated as to represent chance results—yet ACS techniques can be used to create what appear to be highly reliable measures, as discussed elsewhere (Schumm, 1993). Measurement error may vary as a functional of psychological construct availability (Beach, Etherton, & Whitaker, 1995, p. 22), yet we are not aware of any ACS modeling by family researchers that has taken that issue into account. ACS, as popularly used, tends to minimize the effects of differences between family members (Hobfoll & Spielberger, 1992, p. 109; Osmond, 1987, p. 119); it may therefore lead to bias against theories that highlight differences, such as gender differences, among family members. Even though Teachman, Carver, and Day (1995) successfully illustrate the use of ACS techniques to model paired dyadic data, they stop short of discussing how to explain mean differences in such analyses. Lorenz, Conger, Simons, and Whitbeck (1995) have demonstrated how ACS parameters can be biased by unequal measurement reliabilities or different degrees of stability over time for key measures; they also admit that aspects of ACS analyses, such as reciprocal effects within contemporaneous models, may seem like a mystery to many other researchers. Perhaps the most challenging criticism of ACS techniques has been by Sabatelli and Waldron (1995), who point out that items can appear to be good indicators of a single underlying construct when in fact their intercorrelations represent causal relationships between distinct (although interrelated) constructs, a problem that has plagued factor analysis for a long time (Schumm, 1982).

For small samples, on the other hand, using even ACS techniques can be self-defeating from a measurement perspective. For example, Schafer, Wickrama, and Keith 1996) used LISREL in a situation in which they had an 11-item measure of depression and a 7-item measure of efficacy, both of which probably had at least adequate reliability (though they failed to report the alphas). But they converted the items into two subscales for use as indicators of a latent construct rather than using the items as separate indicators, probably to avoid an overidentification problem. It seems ironic to have to collapse good sets of several items into two sets just to be able to run your analysis. Aside from the model testing features of ACS techniques, ordinary regression analysis using the scale items summed into a single scale would have been as useful and, in my opinion, simpler and less "forced." Otherwise, it seems that analysis limitations are driving the measurement process, rather than measurement driving the analysis procedures.

A related problem, perhaps, is the increasing popularity and availability of national data sets, which have often assessed their constructs with single items or scales with very few items. For example, the National Survey of Families and Households (over 13,000 cases) is becoming more accessible to a broad range of scholars—but some of its popular measures, such as self-esteem (Demo & Acock, 1996) and perceived qualities of housework (Sanchez & Kane, 1996) feature marginal to inadequate Cronbach alphas. There may be a temptation for scholars to "settle for" measures with inadequate reliability (and validity) as the price of working with large, national data sets. If journal editors or reviewers weigh the value of such data sets too highly, the state of family measurement might be, inadvertently, set back rather than pushed forward, a situation that could be compounded by overreliance upon ACS techniques such as LISREL that give the appearance of solving the (low) reliability problem in the analysis stage. In more colloquial parlance, without careful attention, major "fixes" *can* sometimes yield *worse* endstates.

Social Desirability

Another problem area is found with respect to response bias. While controlling for response bias in terms of social desirability has been recognized as important for a long time (DeMaio, 1984; Edmonds, 1967; Hansen, 1981; Straus, 1964, p. 369), we do not think we really understand why subjects respond in socially desirable ways. Fowers and his colleagues (Fowers & Applegate, 1995; Fowers, Applegate, Olson, & Pomerantz, 1994) have conducted confirmatory factor analyses with marital satisfaction and social desirability items, finding that items from Edmonds' (1967) Marital Conventionalization Scale (MCS) are not distinct from marital satisfaction although they correlate with both self- and other deception measures of individual social desirability. Fowers and Applegate (1995) prefer to label the marital social desirability construct as idealistic distortion, even though we don't really know if subjects are responding because of idealism or if they are consciously distorting their answers. However, Fowers overlooked previous research (Schumm, Hess, Bollman, & Jurich, 1981) on the MCS in which it was shown that at lower levels of conventionalization (or marital adjustment), the MCS probably is nothing other than a marital adjustment measure and that the greater

validity of the MCS as a marital social desirability measure probably occurs at higher levels of marital adjustment.

It does appear that eliminating subjects who respond in socially desirable ways can improve one's results—in one unpublished analysis, I found that the correlation between locus of control and marital satisfaction increased from $r = 0.17$ for all subjects to $r = 0.50$ for only those subjects scoring low on marital social desirability. But it remains unclear if such improvements are an artifact of methodology (eliminating subjects whose scores do not contribute much variance to the analysis) or of genuine clarity of measurement. It appears that social desirability response bias may affect certain content domains more than others (Szinovacz & Egley, 1995). It is also possible that less socially desirable responses may be obtained by asking questions about more recent time frames, such as last week as opposed to the previous year (Jacob, 1995).*

Overlooked Methodologies

Some methodologies are being overlooked by many family scholars. For example, family scholars rarely use item response theory (IRT) to assess their measures, even though it is gaining wider acceptance within psychology (Nosofsky,

*In our unpublished research on marital social desirability, understanding has proven elusive. In one study, we had developed parallel measures of marital social desirability (MSD), one set using true/false response categories and the other set using Likert-type responses (strongly agree, agree, ?, disagree, strongly disagree). A significant cubic relationship was found between the measures, with those subjects who answered in the middle on the Likert items tending to split their answers on the true/false items. We interpreted that result as reflecting confusion over the intent of the items. Even those subjects who endorsed most of the true/false items in a socially desirable direction failed to strongly agree with the Likert-type items, suggesting they were not strongly committed to social desirability. In the same data we found that MSD was correlated with being Catholic, being older, and being retired. Our best hunch was that MSD reflected one's lack of alternatives—if you are much older, just having a spouse may be so much better than the alternative of being a widow or dead that a "socially desirable" response seems more reasonable. In another study, we attempted to find correlates of MSD such as a desire for privacy, fear of exposure, etc., but the best correlation was for the item, "My marriage isn't perfect, but it's closer to perfection than to the opposite." Perhaps our subjects interpreted the items as clumsy marital adjustment items rather than tests of their conceptual clarity; perhaps they were thinking "Wow, these researchers sure write some stupid questions" even while we were thinking, "Wow, it's amazing how many respondents provide socially desirable answers." We think that only qualitative research will help us out of our box here. Very preliminary work suggests highly idiosyncratic reasons for giving socially desirable responses. One wife who reported that her husband was perfect admitted that she answered that way only to demonstrate her loyalty to him; one husband said that his wife was a perfect match because her shortcomings challenged him in necessary ways for his own character development (apparently that viewpoint has limitations, as the couple later divorced despite the "character development" opportunities they shared). In any event, we doubt that many subjects are responding to the questions as intended by Edmonds (1967).

1992; Thissen & Sternberg, 1988; Torangeau and Raskinski, 1988). Nosofsky found that if one placed a global life satisfaction measure after a marital satisfaction measure, one received lower global life satisfaction scores, as if the subjects read the meaning of the second item, as "aside from your marital satisfaction which you just mentioned, how is your overall life satisfaction?" Combined with qualitative work, IRT could prove to be a very powerful tool for improving family measurement. Likewise, family scholars have only begun (e.g., Fincham, Garnier, Gano-Phillips, & Osborne, 1995) to take advantage of the insights of social cognition research and theory (Wyer & Srull, 1994) for understanding how individuals cognitively process (both consciously and unconsciously) relationship information. We think that a complete assessment of interpersonal cognitions will not occur until perceptions of the other, interpretations of those perceptions, emotional reaction to the interpretations, perceived norms about appropriate responses, and intended/actual responses are studied simultaneously.*

Q factor analysis is another promising technique (Deal, 1995), although it requires at least three, preferably four, family member participants; many items; and more intensive statistical analysis. Amidst the many arguments about summing/averaging individual family member scores versus looking at their differences, it is often forgotten that such questions actually concern three-dimensional models that can be represented by mathematical equations. For example, Schumm, Milliken, Jurich, Bollman, Jeong, and Hawkinson (1990) demonstrated how data from two family members could be tested as a three-dimensional model without using either difference scores or averaged family member scores. From a three-dimensional perspective, knowing how two family members' scores predict a third outcome variable yields a picture of a flat surface or plane in space. Basically, what most researchers hope to capture in a difference score can better be assessed as an interaction effect between variables, an effect that can be portrayed as a variety of possible nonplanar shapes in three-dimensional space. Deviations of the actual data from the flat, planar surface have the potential to represent interaction or perhaps dyadic effects.

Bollman, Schumm, Jurich, and Yoon (1997) saw marital satisfaction as a function of ideal versus actual sex roles (modern versus traditional roles) as seen by mothers and fathers. The result yielded the equivalent of a roof gable that was steeper on one side than the other; in other words, similarity of ideal and actual roles was the ridge line or the gable (higher values), with discrepancies in roles associated with reduced marital satisfaction on either side of the ridge line. The steeper slope on one side was keyed to the result that the ideal = modern versus actual = traditional discrepancy

was associated with lower satisfaction than the ideal = traditional versus actual = modern discrepancy (probably because many husbands in this sample expected their wives to work outside the home and were disappointed if they were not so employed and contributing hard currency to the total family income).

Researchers continue, however, to struggle with family differences. Schafer et al. (1996, p. 171) state, "In order to capture the effect of a difference score (nonlinear relationship to the dependent variable) as an approximate linear effect that can be included in the analysis, we created disconfirmation scores by taking absolute differences between defining variables." By their own admission, they appear to have selected the absolute difference model for methodological reasons (to create nonlinearity) rather than for theoretical reasons (i.e., determining that the absolute difference score model was the best theoretical model of several possible theoretical models).

Practitioner Interest

Another frustrating concern is the relative lack of interest in assessment by applied practitioners, despite proclamations to the contrary (McPhatter, 1991). Both Bray (1995) and Bradbury (1995) cite Boughner, Hayes, Bubenzer, and West's (1994) survey of 598 clinical members of the American Association for Marriage and Family Therapy in which they found that over two-thirds of their respondents found standardized assessment to be unimportant, with only one-third using any at all. However, Bray (1995) suggests that the lack of use may reflect the fact that most instruments are not designed for easy clinical use. Carlson (1989) argues that the criteria for family assessment are different for researchers and clinicians, making useful linkages between the two groups more difficult. Furthermore, few instruments, even of the short, global measures of marital adjustment or distress, have been evaluated for their sensitivity (the chances of correctly detecting severe marital distress) or their specificity (correctly rejecting a diagnosis of marital distress) in a wide range of subpopulations. Perhaps the best recent example of evaluating an important instrument for both sensitivity and specificity is a study by Eddy, Heyman, and Weiss (1991) on the Dyadic Adjustment Scale. More work similar to that of Crane, Allgood, Larson, and Griffin (1990), White et al. (1994), Whisman and Jacobson (1991), and Gondoli and Jacob (1993) needs to be done to enable accurate comparisons across different measures of similar constructs—that is, what score on one test is equivalent to a distress cutoff score on another test? Work continues on the refinement of some traditional instruments—for example, Bubsy, Christensen, Crane, and Larson's (1995) recent attempt to develop a valid shorter version of the Dyadic Adjustment Scale that might be

---

*Many of the ideas are derived directly from the awareness wheel model (Miller, Nunnally, & Wackman, 1976).

more useful for clinicians and the latest revision of the Conflict Tactics Scales (Straus et al., 1996).

Lack of Attention to Diversity

Issues of family diversity are often overlooked in the area of family measurement. Many assessment tools are based upon and validated with white, middle-class families and may completely overlook the variations in form, organizations, roles, rules, and composition that are presented by families of diverse cultural and ethnic backgrounds (Bray, 1995). Assessment tools have not been validated with families from diverse cultural and ethnic backgrounds and with nontraditional family structures (Hampson, Beavers, & Hulgus, 1990; Morris, 1990).

Norms of family functioning vary across cultures and ethnic groups. Measures based on white, middle-class norms of family functioning are often inappropriate to use when assessing families of differing ethnic and cultural backgrounds. Morris (1990) used the Family Assessment Device (FAD) to assess family functioning in Hawaiian American and Japanese American families, both known to have different cultural norms family roles, communication, affective involvement, and problem solving. Hawaiian Americans' assessments of their families using the FAD described very "healthy" family functioning in all aspects of family functioning assessed (Morris, 1990). Conversely, Morris reported that the Japanese American participants reported significantly "unhealthy" assessments on the affective responsiveness and behavior control dimensions of the FAD. Use of an unmodified FAD in assessing these families would lead to insensitive and erroneous conclusions about a family's "normal" functioning. Based on this work, Morris offers suggestions for improvement of the FAD for use with families of these cultural backgrounds. While this study was limited to using the FAD in cross-cultural family functioning assessment, similar issues could arise in cross-cultural family assessment using other structured measures.

Hampson, Beavers, and Hulgus (1990) used the Beavers Interactional Competence Scale (Beavers, 1981; Lewis, Beavers, Gossett, & Phillips, 1976) and the Beavers-Interactional Style Scale (Kelsey-Smith & Beavers, 1981) to rate interactions in Caucasian, African American and Mexican American families with a developmentally disabled child. Hampson and colleagues (1990) did not find significant differences on global family competence ratings and global ratings of family style across the ethnic groups. They did find slight trends of difference in competence and style subscale scores across the groups. Hampson and colleagues assert that the lack of difference between the ethnic groups on competence and global style scores indicates the "cultural fairness" of these assessment tools. The trends toward difference noted between the ethnic groups was attributed to differences in style of structure and interaction rather than differences in family health or competence between the ethnic groups.

Another example of the use of standardized marital and family assessment measures in cross-cultural research is Jeong and Schumm's (1990) investigation of the perceptions of family satisfaction of Korean women married to American men. Jeong and Schumm (1990) used the KMSS (Schumm et al., 1986), the Parental Satisfaction Scale (James et al., 1986) and the Family Life Satisfaction Scale (McCollum, Schumm, & Russell, 1988), all translated into Korean, to assess the wives' perceptions of satisfaction with marriage and family life with an American spouse. Jeong and Schumm (1990) found that the scales used in this research maintained their internal consistency reliability when translated to and used in Korean. Limited work has also been done using the KMSS in other cross-cultural research endeavors, including Chinese (Shek, 1998; Shek & Tsang, 1993; Shek, Lam, Tsoi, & Lam, 1993), Arab immigrants to the United States (Faragallah, Schumm, & Webb, 1997), and Greek–American couples (Wasieliwski, 1991). Overall, the factor structure and internal consistency reliability of the KMSS appears to have been maintained across a variety of cultures.

The KMSS has also been used in situations of diversity within the American culture. It has been translated to American Sign Language (ASL) for use in research with couples with a hearing-impaired spouse (Mikol, 1995) and has been used in research with diverse samples of couples. Kurdek (1994) has used the KMSS in research of relationship satisfaction with gay and lesbian couples, and Morris and Blanton (1994) used the KMSS in research with traditional clergy couples.

Language is significant problem in cross-cultural family assessment. Recently, attempts have been made to develop uniform translation schemes to translate traditional assessment tools to different languages for use in cross-cultural research and assessment (Herrera, DelCampo, & Ames, 1993). Herrera and colleagues (1993) developed a "serial approach" for translation of standard assessment instruments for use with non-English-speaking populations. This serial approach consists of six steps: translation, assessment of clarity and equivalence in the translated language, back translation to English, field testing of both the original and translated instruments, reliability assessment of the translated measure, and interpretation. Herrera et al. (1993) further expressed the need to assess the construct validity of the translated instrument, in addition to its reliability.

Child and Family Assessment

An important area not adequately addressed in the current family assessment literature is the inclusion of children's points of view and the assessment of children in a family context. Self-report measures of family functioning usually do not include young children because of their inability to understand and complete these measures of family dynamics and functioning. One interesting exception to this situation is the Family Cohesion Index developed by Cooper, Holman, and Brainthwaite (1983), which employs pictorial representations of family structure with circles representing various family members to measure from the child's perception and the degree of acceptance and support experienced by the child. When using this assessment tool, the children use the arrangements of circles to describe the structure of their own family system. Young children have been able to accurately use this assessment tool to describe their family environment, particularly aspects of marital discord and triangulation, in research settings (Kerig, 1995). Kerig (1995) also recommends use of the Family Cohesion Index in clinical settings to gain children and adults' perspectives of family structure.

Several measures exist that tap children's perception of parental marital conflict (Emery, 1988). Emery and O'Leary's Personal Data Form (1982) assesses, from a child's perspective, the frequency of parental marital conflict. Grych, Seid, and Fincham's (1992) Children's Perception of Interparental Conflict Scale not only assesses the child's perception of frequency of parental marital conflict, but also his or her perceptions of intensity, resolution, and content as well as appraisals of perceived threat, coping efficacy, self-blame, and causal stability. The scale developers purport that this measure is a reliable and valid measure of children's perceptions of parental marital conflict (Grych et al., 1992).

Observational assessment methods exist for assessing family dynamics, particularly parenting styles, in families with young children. Milner and Murphy (1995), in a review of assessment methods of child abuse offenders, recommend the Dyadic Parent–Child Interactional Coding System (Robinson & Eyberg, 1981), the Home Observation for Measurement of the Environment (HOME) (Caldwell & Bradley, 1978), the Maternal Observation Matrix (Tutuer, Ewigman, Peterson, & Hosokawa, 1995), and the Mother–Child Interaction Scale (Tutuer, Ewigman, Peterson, & Hosokawa, 1995) as tools for assessment of parent–child dynamics in suspected child abuse cases. While these methods have been suggested for use in serious clinical circumstances, further inquiry is necessary to determine their utility in less serious clinical families and in nonclinical settings.

Inadequate Theory

Our primary concern in the area of measurement, however, is inadequate use of family theory. The importance of family theory has been recognized more explicitly in recent years (Bradbury & Fincham, 1990; Cowan, 1987; Gottman, 1989; Grotevant, 1989; Sabatelli & Bartle, 1995; Sabatelli & Waldron, 1995), but the importance is *not* reflected properly, as seen in the poor attention often given to conceptualization in the measurement process (Sabatelli & Bartle, 1995; Sabatelli & Waldron, 1995). We may have many measures but nevertheless poor conceptualization and, therefore, great difficulty in integrating results across studies (Grotevant, 1989). Sabatelli and Bartle (1995) barely hide their frustration at the fact that some measures continue to be very popular despite years of accurate criticism of their construct validity and that some researchers continue to select their measures more on the basis of availability than demonstrated validity. The field continues to be a battleground over the validity of brief, global, evaluative measures such as for marital or parental satisfaction; some argue for their usefulness and validity (Bradbury & Fincham, 1988; Fincham & Bradbury, 1987), while others doubt that there are any such meaningful, general dimensions, at least that can be assessed briefly (Donohue & Ryder, 1982; Sabatelli & Waldron, 1995).

Furthermore, we have not examined the philosophical aspects of explaining individuals and families on the basis of numbers. Hanson (1993, pp.186–187) has "tested" IQ testing, for example, and finds that so much weight is given to intelligence tests that they can ruin the lives and futures of children who happen—for a variety of reasons other than poor intelligence—to do poorly on them. Hanson challenges the notion that a single numerical score can capture anything truly meaningful about a human, persons being so complex that such simplifications amount to nothing more than gross distortions that can be very destructive. Hanson also notes that measurement can actually cause the problems it was designed to solve; for example, employee integrity tests can reduce trust and lead to employee dishonesty rather than preventing it. Hanson believes that measuring people on narrow dimensions leads us to believe that we understand the whole person when in fact that false belief may make us worse informed (pp. 296–297). The possible racist or sexist bias of measures is well known. But what if our basic concepts such as those of marital adjustment are flawed? A good case can be made that they are.

First, some of the items in the tests are outdated at best, if not outright biased. For example, many scholars continue to use the Locke–Wallace (Locke–Wallace, 1959) marital adjustment test even though its items assume that certain types of more traditional marriages will be better. It ought not to be surprising if studies with the MAT (Locke & Wallace, 1959) find that more traditional marriages are happier—but such results are an artifact of the instrument, not of valid research. Even the improved Dyadic Adjustment Scale (DAS) (Spanier, 1976) has items that are questionable. One item relates frequency of kissing to higher adjustment, but in one study we had a Japanese wife tell us that kissing (on the mouth) was not a relevant affective behavior in her culture and thus it was rare in her marriage. Was that a sign of poor adjustment or just a cultural difference? Another DAS item credits people with better adjustment if they say that they "desperately want their relationship to succeed and will go to almost any length to see that it does." From a feminist perspective at least, agreement with that statement might reflect excessive dependency or codependency rather than responsible commitment or mature adjustment—yet such respondents are treated as if they are better adjusted.

Even the concept of marital adjustment or satisfaction may be dysfunctional for families. In some cultures, spouses consider marriage a duty for which personal satisfaction is largely irrelevant. In such cultures, evaluating one's marriage for happiness would be like evaluating your elbow for satisfaction—you could try it, but why? Perhaps our cultural concern with deriving satisfaction from relationships is counterproductive, at least for relationship stability. If we make marital satisfaction the primary dependent variable in much of our research, do we not run the risk of reaffirming (subtly) what might be only a cultural dysfunction? Why is it we don't at least ask questions about how one is succeeding at making one's spouse happier? Or better yet, why don't we ask about marital quality from the point of view of what one is doing for other family members rather than what those members are doing for oneself?

Even within the old paradigm, it is possible that our marital adjustment/marital stability research is totally flawed because of theoretical misunderstanding. In particular, we are aware that individuals may report variations in both marital satisfaction and stability. However, we usually analyze only one of those variables at a time as a dependent variable; for example, Karney and Bradbury (1995) found that of the 115 longitudinal studies on either marital quality or marital stability, only 16% assessed both of those variables. Yet this practice inherently confounds our analysis. If the dependent variable is satisfaction alone, then we confound stable unhappy marriages with unstable unhappy marriages, as if those were the same type of relationship. If the dependent variable is stability, then we confound happy and unhappy marriages at the stable end of the continuum. A similar problem may exist with other typologies such as those for physical and verbal violence.

Failure to consider theory may render useless much of our statistical gymnastics by which many family scholars (Fisher et al., 1985; Ball, McKenry & Bonham, 1983; Schumm et al., 1985) have attempted to assess "family" or "dyadic" components of responses from individual family members. The mere existence of a difference in scores between two

family members may mean nothing if we do not understand the context. An unresolved difference might reflect a marriage with a distressing unresolved power struggle, or it might reflect a nondistressed marriage in which the partners were both mature enough to feel free to disagree on some matters. The meaning of differences can vary across developmental changes in the family life cycle—enmeshment and disengagement might both be functional, depending on whether an adult parent's relationship was with an infant or with an older adolescent (Tutty, 1995). Sometimes it amazes us that we think we can come up with dyadic or family characteristics represented by just one or two numbers when it is questionable if that can even be done with the much less complex arena of individual intelligence.

We question whether our theory has allowed us to measure what may be important concepts such as what we call "the logic of the illogical." From certain perspectives it is not logical to delay gratification, to respond calmly to an insult, to care about those less fortunate than yourself, to not take advantage of less powerful or weaker persons, to try to help the poor get fair justice, to raise children, or to think of others' needs as much as your own.* However, we would submit that many things that might seem illogical are more beneficial to family relationships than things that might seem more logical. In a similar vein, random acts of kindness and senseless acts of beauty may not be logical, but they may improve a society's quality of life.

Likewise, in an intimate relationship, doing nice things with or for one's partner for their own sake rather than for what one can get out of it may not be logical, but it may nevertheless improve the quality of the relationship. Even sexual infidelity can be analyzed from the "logic versus illogic" perspective. If you were confronted by an offer to engage in sex with someone else, you might reject the offer because (1) the cost/reward ratio didn't look promising at the time or (2) because you considered infidelity to be out of the question as a matter of principle. The end result in terms of behavior would be the same. The second reason might be very illogical; after all, might not you someday meet someone who could give you a lifetime of better sex than your current partner? Yet, consider which reason would foster the

---

*If you want to have a roaring class discussion, toss out the hypothesis that gay relationships are much more logical than heterosexual ones. It is an easy argument to make. For example, suppose that half the world's people had backs and half didn't. If you wanted a good backrub, to which group would you go? Having the same physiology is a long step, according to this sort of argument, to more accurate communication and understanding, which are essential to effective interaction. From such a perspective, asking, "Why is anyone heterosexual?" may seem more logical than asking "Why is anyone gay?" Space does not permit me to address the counterarguments to the hypothesis.

highest level of relationship quality (an outcome, of course, that might depend on the type of relationship involved).*

Some religions may feature norms that encourage compliance with principles rather than mere responsiveness to the immediate logic of one's changing circumstances and needs. Attention to such norms may capture the value of (nontoxic) religion to interpersonal relationships far better than items on church attendance, scripture reading, prayer, etc., as commonly used in current research (e.g., Booth, Johnson, Branaman, & Sica, 1995).† We must add that research on religion and family life will probably continue to find weak results until both beneficial and toxic effects of various types of religiosity are taken into account (see Schumm, Jeong, & Silliman, 1990, for a possible example of an effect of toxic religion on marital communication).

Furthermore, the challenges of assessing family dynamics or change are well articulated (Galligan, 1989; Powers, 1989). Advances in the development of systems theory may be critical to improved measurement in our field (Grotevant, 1989). Sabatelli and Bartle (1995) have presented one of the more detailed attempts to conceptualize various system concepts and relate those constructs to current measurement instruments; however, it is clear that a great deal of work remains to be done in that area. We think that more efforts would be useful if we deliberately developed self-report and observational measures based on similar conceptualizations. Eggeman, Moxley, and Schumm (1991) once developed a self-report measure of Gottman's (1982) temporal form typology, for example, but it has remained untested to the best of our knowledge. Gottman has challenged the underlying theories of much of family therapy (1998a) and

family life education or marriage enrichment (1998b). It remains to be seen whether all of his new ideas on the factors critical to marital success should be or can be measured effectively by individual spouse self-report or can be measured with equal effectiveness in terms of observational assessments in the laboratories of other investigators. However, the difficulty and costs of the observational measurement of his important concepts have probably discouraged many family researchers from attempting to replicate Gottman's (1998a) measurement work.

One largely untapped resource for such work in family studies may be feminist theory (Thompson & Walker, 1995). One recent feminist methods text, for example, discussed many aspects of research methods brilliantly, but gave very little attention per se to potential feminist contributions to improving measurement in the social sciences (Reinharz, 1992).* We have concluded that the development of creative typologies, perhaps based on good qualitative, feminist research, may be the best available approach for resolving the levels of analysis problem that we constantly fight as we try to turn data from individuals into data on couples or families, even though feminist researchers would be among the first to recognize the limitations of "objective" observers (Osmond, 1987, p. 109). A recent study along such typological lines was one in which four types of premarital couples were evaluated in terms of marital satisfaction and marital stability over 3 years (Fowers, Montel, & Olson, 1996). Feminist research and theory would also help to keep raising the issue of the validity of contemporary measures in nontraditional, minority, or oppressed populations, an issue often mentioned (Osmond, 1987; Sabatelli & Bartle, 1995; Tutty, 1995) but seldom worked. It may be easier if we build such typologies on dyadic relationship models before we try to create models for triads or larger groups (Sabatelli & Bartle, 1995).

Recommendations

Rather than rehashing our previous comments, we would like to make some personal recommendations regarding the avenues that we think might be most fruitful in improving measurement in family studies in the future. If we consider theory as the most important foundation of measurement, we think that the most productive work will come either from feminist thought or possibly from a careful reanalysis of scriptural theory. For example, in the latter we do not find much discussion of how to be a happy person but more of what kind of person one should seek to become. That might suggest a different sort of dependent variable, perhaps

---

*Of course, the issues may be even more complex. For example, some individuals might prefer someone who would abide by the first reason, figuring that keeping you around was a magnificent reflection of their own sexual prowess ("I'm better than anyone else could ever be"). Fidelity for its own sake would say more about your partner's character than it would about your own attractiveness, which could be interpreted as a put-down of sorts. Many individuals may feel better about "earning" fidelity from their partner than receiving it as a matter of their partner's principles.

†The first author's own view, not widely accepted in religious circles, is that decisions can have consequences over a range of time (zero to eternity) and over a range of persons (self, partner, neighbor, community, world, deity). Morality can be defined as the extent to which one does what is logical given the time frame, "person frame," and domain of personal satisfaction (physical, emotional, spiritual) considered. If one is making decisions based on the next 10 minutes, solely for one's own personal benefit and solely in terms of physical gratification, then it might be logical to do some things that were very hurtful to other people. On the other hand, if one was thinking about long-term consequences, for a wide range of other people, over a wide range of domains of personal outcomes, then entirely different decisions—maybe even dying to save someone's life—might be logical. The critical factor would not be one's apparent logic but the ranges actually considered in making the decision. Moral education might consist of broadening time frames, person frames, and domains of personal outcomes as much as teaching proper "rules" of moral behavior.

*The first person to write a book on feminism and family measurement will probably have a hit and be able to retire with fame and wealth (we hope).

along the lines of "striving to become an excellent father to one's children" or "striving to be an egalitarian husband," rather than mere parental or marital satisfaction or adjustment. Other variables might be something like "spiritual connectedness," "ability to respond graciously to criticism," or the "ability to think of and implement creative ways of showing love for one's friends." It would probably be necessary to conduct detailed interviews with couples about exactly how they process their interactions and strive to improve their relationship in order to develop such measures.

While we think that use of ACS techniques can make some incremental progress in family measurement, we think that we must catch up with our technology and adapt our instruments to contemporary methods. Rather than try to describe issues with words or still photographs and elicit responses from subjects, why not show videotapes of targeted interactions (perhaps with comments from the role-players about their inner perceptions) and elicit responses from subjects? Subjects might even be shown a variety of follow-up actions and discuss which were most likely, most beneficial, most harmful, etc. From such research might emerge typologies of dyads or families that would lead to entirely new paradigms or ways of thinking about families as opposed to creating incremental knowledge only. Ideally, such typologies would have predictive value and allow couples to have a better idea of how they might want to change, depending on what sort of relationship outcomes were desired. Of course, any such typologies would need to be assessed with a diverse variety of populations lest they reflect only the experiences of a narrow segment of all individuals or families. At this point, we think that typologies are the better approach for conceptualizing something of "family" or "group" effects rather than trying to combine individual family or group member reports in some sophisticated manner.

In the area of assessing the effects of differences among family members, theory must be placed before methodology. Instead of using difference scores automatically in this area, we should consider how the partners' perceptions might interact in their possible effect on another variable. Three-dimensional diagrams are available that reflect different theoretical hypotheses; from those diagrams, one can select the most appropriate regression equation for testing one's hypotheses (Schumm et al., 1990). Even the renowned circumplex model can be visualized three-dimensionally and analyzed with an appropriate equation.

Today, scholars are blessed with an abundance of readily available measures from a variety of compendia, a variety of new statistical approaches to measurement and analysis, more choices other than self-report for types of instruments, and readily accessible, large, nationally representative data sets, among other advantages. The constant temptation will be to charge ahead with whatever is cheap, available, and

superficially valid. However, like the military logistician who may have to remind the gung-ho general that "you don't have the resources to do it," we find that most of our recommendations and worries center on the proper use of family theory when selecting or constructing family measures. We must always be willing to challenge the extent to which a project's measurement is adequately based on theory or to which its measures are adequate for testing the model's theory. That may be becoming more difficult than it might seem. The senior author recently read a news clip that claimed that some educators are now calling spelling errors "personal spellings," as if such errors no longer require comment. Such logic applied to the family theory/measurement linkage might lead us further away from rigorous theoretical thinking into a "whatever-seems-interesting" approach to all aspects of family research, including measurement. Nevertheless, we continue to believe that the credibility of our research depends upon improving the quality of the theory/measurement linkage, regardless of the challenges or inconveniences that might be involved.

References

Acock, A., & Schumm, W. R. (1992). Analysis of covariance structures applied to family research and theory. In P. Boss, W. Doherty, R. LaRossa, W. Schumm, & S. Steinmetz (Eds.), *Sourcebook of family theories and methods* (pp. 451–468). New York: Plenum.

Acock, A. C., & Schumm, W. R. (1993). Analysis of covariance structures applied to family research and theory. In P. G. Boss, W. Doherty, R. LaRossa, W. R. Schumm, & S. Steinmetz (Eds.), *Sourcebook of family theories and methods: A contextual approach* (pp. 451–468). New York: Plenum.

Bagarozzi, D. A. (1990). Special issue on marital and family measurements: Preface. *American Journal of Family Therapy, 18*, 3–4.

Ball, D., McKenry, P. C., & Price-Bonham, S. (1983). Use of repeated measures designs in family research. *Journal of Marriage and the Family, 45*, 885–896.

Bartle, S. E., & Sabatelli, R. M. (1995). The Behavioral and Emotional Reactivity Index: preliminary evidence for construct validity from three studies. *Family Relations, 44*, 267–277.

Beach, S. R. H., Etherton, J., & Whitaker, D. (1995). Cognitive accessibility and sentiment override—starting a revolution: Comment on Fincham et al. (1995). *Journal of Family Psychology, 9*(1), 19–23.

Beavers, W. R. (1981). A systems model of family for family therapists. *Journal of Marital and Family Therapy, 7*, 299–307.

Ben-David, A., & Jurich, J. (1993). A test of adaptability: Examining the curvilinear assumption. *Journal of Family Psychology, 7*(3), 370–375.

Bharat, S. (1993). Psychological assessment in family studies. Special issue: Psychoeducation assessment. *Psychological Studies, 38*(3), 114–118.

Bollman, S. R., Schumm, W. R., Jurich, A. P., & Yoon, G. J. (1997). Predicting marital satisfaction from ideal and actual maternal roles. *Psychological Reports, 80*, 99–106.

Booth, A., & Dabbs, J. (1993). Testosterone and men's marriages. *Social Forces, 47*, 334–355.

Booth, A., Johnson, D. R., & Edwards, J. N. (1983). Measuring marital instability. *Journal of Marriage and the Family, 45*, 387–393.

Booth, A., Johnson, D. R., Branaman, A., & Sica, A. (1995). Belief and behavior: Does religion matter in today's marriage? *Journal of Marriage and the Family, 57*(3), 661–671.

Boughner, S. R., Hayes, S. F., Bubenzer, D. L., & West, J. D. (1994). Use of standardized assessment instruments by marital family therapists: A survey. *Journal of Marital and Family Therapy, 20*(1), 69–75.

Bowen, G. L. (1991). *Navigating the marital journey: MAP, a corporate support program for couples.* New York: Praeger.

Bradbury, T. N. (1995). Assessing the four fundamental domains of marriage. *Family Relations, 44,* 459–468.

Bradbury, T. N., & Fincham, F. D. (1988). Individual difference variables in close relationships: a contextual model of marriage as an integrative framework. *Journal of Personality and Social Psychology, 54,* 713–721.

Bradbury, T. N., & Fincham, F. D. (1990). Attributions in marriage: Review and critique. *Psychological Bulletin, 107,* 3–33.

Bray, J. H. (1995). Family assessment: Current issues in evaluating families. *Family Relations, 44,* 469–477.

Bray, J. H., Maxwell, S. E., & Cole, D. (1995). Multivariate statistics for family psychology research. *Journal of Family Psychology, 9,* 144–160.

Burnett, P. (1987). Assessing marital adjustment and satisfaction: A review. *Measurement and Evaluation in Counseling and Development, 20*(3), 113–121.

Busby, D. M., Christensen, C., Crane, D. R., & Larson, J. H. (1995). A revision of the Dyadic Adjustment Scale for use with distressed and nondistressed couples: Construct hierarchy and multidimensional scales. *Journal of Marital and Family Therapy, 21,* 289–308.

Calahan, C. (1997). Internal consistency, reliability, and concurrent validity of the Kansas Marital Satisfaction Scale and the Quality Marriage Index. *Psychological Reports, 80,* 49–50.

Caldwell, B. M., & Bradley, R. H. (1978). *Home observation for measurement of the environment.* Little Rock: University of Arkansas.

Canfield, K. R., Schumm, W. R., Swihart, J. J., & Eggerichs, E. E. (1990). Factorial validity of brief satisfaction scales in surveys of Mormon, Roman Catholic, and Protestant fathers. *Psychological Reports, 67,* 1319–1322.

Card, J. J. (1993). *Handbook of adolescent sexuality and pregnancy: Research and evaluation instruments.* Newbury Park, CA: Sage.

Carlson, C. I. (1989). Criteria for family assessment in research and intervention contexts. *Journal of Family Psychology, 3,* 158–176.

Carmines, E. G., & Zeller, R. A. (1979). *Reliability and validity assessment.* Beverly Hills, CA: Sage.

Chang, L., Schumm, W. R., Coulson, L. A., Bollman, S. R., & Jurich, A. P. (1994). Dimensionality of brief family interaction and satisfaction scales among couples from eight western and midwestern states. *Psychological Reports, 74,* 131–144.

Cooper, J. E., Holman, J., & Braithwaite, V. A. (1983). Self-esteem and family cohesion: The child's perspective of adjustment. *Journal of Marriage and the Family, 45,* 153–159.

Copeland, A. P., & White, K. M. (1991). *Studying families.* Newbury Park, CA: Sage.

Cowan, P. A. (1987). The need for theoretical and methodological integrations in family research. *Journal of Family Psychology, 1*(1), 48–50.

Crane, D. R., Allgood, S. M., Larson, J. H., & Griffin, W. (1990). Assessing marital quality with distressed and nondistressed couples: A comparison and equivalency table for three frequently used measures. *Journal of Marriage and the Family, 52,* 87–93.

Deal, J. E. (1995). Utilizing data from multiple family members: A within family approach. *Journal of Marriage and the Family, 57,* 1109–1121.

DeMaio, T. J. (1984). Social desirability and survey measurement: A review. In C. F. Turner & E. Martin (Eds.), *Surveying subjective phenomena* (Volume 2, pp. 257–282). New York: Russell Sage.

Demo, D. H., & Acock, A. C. (1996). Singlehood, marriage, and remarriage: The effects of family structure and family relationships on mothers' well-being. *Journal of Family Issues, 17,* 388–407.

Domenico, D., & Windle, M. (1993). Intrapersonal and interpersonal functioning among middle-aged female adult children of alcoholics. *Journal of Consulting and Clinical Psychology, 61,* 659–666.

Donohue, K. C., & Ryder, R. G. (1982). A methodological note on marital satisfaction and social variables. *Journal of Marriage and the Family, 44*(3), 743–747.

Douglass, F. M., & Douglass, R. (1995). The marital problems questionnaire: A short screening instrument for marital therapy. *Family Relations, 44*(3), 238–244.

Eddy, J. M., Heyman, R. E., & Weiss, R. L. (1991). An empirical evaluation of the Dyadic Adjustment Scale: Exploring the differences between marital "satisfaction" and "adjustment." *Behavioral Assessment, 13,* 199–220.

Edmonds, V. H. (1967). Marital conventionalization: Definition and measurement. *Journal of Marriage and the Family, 29,* 681–688.

Eggeman, K., Moxley, V., & Schumm, W. R. (1985). Assessing spouses' perceptions of Gottman's temporal form in marital conflict. *Psychological Reports, 57,* 171–181.

Emery, R. E. (1988). *Marriage, divorce, and children's adjustment.* Newbury Park, CA: Sage.

Emery, R. E., & O'Leary, K. D. (1982). Children's perceptions of marital discord and behavior problems of boys and girls. *Journal of Abnormal Child Psychology, 10,* 11–24.

Emery, R. E., & O'Leary, K. D. (1984). Marital discord and child behavior problems in a non-clinic sample. *Journal of Abnormal Child Psychology, 12,* 411–420.

Ewart, C. K., Taylor, C. B., Kraemer, H. C., & Agras, W. S. (1991). High school pressure and marital discord: Not being nasty matters more than being nice. *Health Psychology, 10,* 155–163.

Faragallah, M. H., Schumm, W. R., & Webb, F. J. (1997). Acculturation of Arab-American immigrants: An exploratory study. *Journal of Comparative Family Studies, 28,* 182–203.

Finchman, F. D., & Bradbury, T. N. (1987). The assessment of marital quality: a reevaluation. *Journal of Marriage and the Family, 49,* 797–809.

Fincham, F. D., & Bradbury, T. N. (1993). Marital satisfaction, depression, and attributions: A longitudinal analysis. *Journal of Personality and Social Psychology, 64,* 442–452.

Fincham, F. D., Bradbury, T. N., & Scott, C. K. (1990). Cognition in marriage. In F. D. Fincham & T. N. Bradbury (Eds.), *The psychology of marriage* (pp. 118–149). New York: Guilford.

Fincham, F. D., Garnier, P. C., Gano-Phillips, S., & Osborne, L. N. (1995). Preinteraction expectations, marital satisfaction, and accessibility: A new look at sentiment override. *Journal of Family Psychology, 9,* 3–14.

Finkel, J. S., & Hansen, F. J. (1992). Correlates of retrospective marital satisfaction in long-lived marriages: A social constructivist perspective. *Family Therapy, 19,* 1–16.

Fischer, J., & Corcoran, K. (1994). *Measures for clinical practice: A sourcebook, Volume 1: Couples, families, and children* (2nd ed.). New York: Free Press.

Fisher, L., Kokes, R., Ransom, D., Phillips, S., & Rudd, P. (1985). Alternative strategies for creating relational family data. *Family Process, 24,* 213–224.

Fowers, B. J. (1990). An interactional approach to standardized marital assessment: A literature review. *Family Relations, 39,* 369–377.

Fowers, B. J., & Applegate, B. (1995). Do marital conventionalization scales measure a social desirability response bias? A confirmatory factor analysis. *Journal of Marriage and the Family, 57,* 237–241.

Fowers, B. J., Applegate, B., Olson, D. H., & Pomerantz, B. (1994). Marital conventionalization as a measure of marital satisfaction: a confirmatory factor analysis. *Journal of Family Psychology, 8,* 98–103.

Fowers, B. J., Montel, K., & Olson, D. H. (1996). Predicting marital success for premarital couples types based on PREPARE. *Journal of Marital and Family Therapy, 22*(1), 103–119.

Fredman, N., & Sherman, R. (1987). *Handbook of measurements for marriage and family therapy.* New York: Brunner/Mazel.

Galligan, R. J. (1989). Theory has arrived, will real dynamic variables be far behind? *Journal of Family Psychology, 3*(2), 206–210.

Gaughan, E. (1995). Family assessment in psychoeducational evaluations: Case studies with the Family Adaptability and Cohesion Scales. *Journal of School Psychology, 33*(1), 7–28.

Gondoli, D. M., & Jacob, T. (1993). Factor structure within and across three family assessment procedures. *Journal of Family Psychology, 6*(3), 278–289.

Gottman, J. M. (1982). Temporal form: Toward a new language for describing relationships. *Journal of Marriage and the Family, 44,* 943–962.

Gottman, J. M. (1989). Toward programmatic research in family psychology. *Journal of Family Psychology, 3*(2), 211–214.

Gottman, J. M. (1994). *What predicts divorce: The relationship between marital processes and marital outcomes.* Hillsdale, NJ: Erlbaum.

Gottman, J. M. (1998a). Psychology and the study of marital processes. In J. T. Spence, J. M. Darley, & D. J. Foss (Eds.), *Annual Review of Psychology* (pp. 169–197). Palo Alto, CA: Annual Reviews.

Gottman, J. M. (1998b). Predicting marital happiness and stability from newlywed interactions. *Journal of Marriage and the Family, 60,* 5–22.

Gottman, J. M., & Levenson, R. W. (1992). Marital processes predictive of later dissolution: Behavior, physiology, and health. *Journal of Personality and Social Psychology, 63,* 221–233.

Green, R. G., Harris, R. N., Forte, J. A., & Robinson, M. (1991). Evaluating FACES III and the Circumplex model: 2,440 families. *Family Process, 30,* 55–73.

Grotevant, H. D. (1989). The role of theory in guiding family assessment. *Journal of Family Psychology, 3*(2), 104–117.

Grotevant, H. D., & Carlson, C. I. (1989). *Family assessment: A guide to methods and measures.* New York: Guilford.

Grych, J. H., Seid, M., & Fincham, F. D. (1992). Assessing marital conflict from the child's perspective: The children's perception of interparental conflict scale. *Child Development, 63,* 558–572.

Hampson, R. B., Beavers, W. R., & Hulgus, Y. (1990). Cross ethnic family differences: Interactional assessment of white, black, and Mexican-American families. *Journal of Marital and Family Therapy, 16,* 307–319.

Hansen, G. L. (1981). Marital adjustment and conventionalization: A Re-examination. *Journal of Marriage and the Family, 43,* 855–863.

Hanson, F. A. (1993). *Testing testing: Social consequences of the examined life.* Berkeley: University of California Press.

Heaton, T. B., & Call, V. R. A. (1995). Modeling family dynamics with event history techniques. *Journal of Marriage and the Family, 57*(4), 1078–1090.

Hendrix, C. C., & Anelli, L. M. (1993). Impact of Vietnam War service on veterans' perceptions of family life. *Family Relations, 42,* 87–92.

Herman, S. M. (1991). A psychometric evaluation of the marital satisfaction questionnaire: A demonstration of reliability and validity. *Psychotherapy in Private Practice, 9*(4), 85–94.

Herrera, R. S., DelCampo, R. L., & Ames, M. H. (1993). A serial approach for translating family science instrumentation. *Family Relations, 42,* 357–360.

Heyman, R. E., Sayers, S. L., & Bellack, A. S. (1994). Global marital satisfaction versus marital adjustment: An empirical comparison of three measures. *Journal of Family Psychology, 8,* 432–446.

Hobfoll, S. E., & Spielberger, C. D. (1992). Family stress: Integrating theory and measurement. *Journal of Family Psychology, 6*(2), 99–112.

Hunsley, J., Pinsent, C., Lefebvre, M., James-Tanner, S., & Vito, D. (1995). Constructive validity of the short forms of the Dyadic Adjustment Scale. *Family Relations, 44,* 231–237.

Jackson, D. J., & Borgatta, E. F. (1981). Introduction: Measurement in sociological research. In D. J. Jackson & E. F. Borgatta (Eds.), *Factor analysis and measurement in sociological research: A multidimensional perspective* (pp. 3–7). Beverly Hills, CA: Sage.

Jacob, T. (1995). The role of time frame in the assessment of family functioning. *Journal of Marital and Family Therapy, 21*(3), 281–288.

Jacob, T., & Tennenbaum, D. L. (1988). *Family assessment: Rationale, methods, and future directions.* New York: Plenum.

Jacobson, N. S., Gottman, J. M., Waltz, J., Rushe, R., Babcock, J., & Holtzworth-Munroe, A. (1994). Affect, verbal content, and psychophysiology in the arguments of couples with a violent husband. *Journal of Consulting and Clinical Psychology, 62,* 982–988.

James, D. E., Schumm, W. R., Kennedy, C. E., Grigsby, C. C., Shectman, K. L., & Nichols, C. W. (1985). Characteristics of the Kansas Parental Satisfaction Scale among two samples of married parents. *Psychological Reports, 57,* 163–169.

James, D. E., Kennedy, C. E., & Schumm, W. R. (1986). Changes in parental attitudes and practices following a religiously oriented parent education program. *Family Perspective, 20*(1), 45–59.

Jeong, G. J., & Schumm, W. R. (1990). Family satisfaction in Korean/American marriages: An exploratory study of the perceptions of Korean wives. *Journal of Comparative Family Studies, XXI,* 325–336.

Johnson, D. R. (1993, November). *Are single-item measures of marital quality valid: The case of marital happiness?* Paper presented at the Theory Construction and Research Methodology Preconference Workshop, National Council on Family Relations, Baltimore.

Julian, T., & McKenry, P. (1989). Relationship of testosterone to men's family functioning at mid-life: A research note. *Aggressive Behavior, 15,* 281–289.

Karney, B. R., & Bradbury, T. N. (1995). The longitudinal course of marital quality and stability: A review of theory, method, and research. *Psychological Bulletin, 118,* 3–34.

Karney, B. R., Bradbury, T. N., Fincham, F. D., & Sullivan, K. T. (1994). The role of negative affectivity in the association between attributions and marital satisfaction. *Journal of Personality and Social Psychology, 66,* 413–424.

Kelsey-Smith, M., & Beavers, W. R. (1981). Family assessment: Centripetal and centrifugal family systems. *American Journal of Family Therapy, 9,* 3–13.

Kenny, D. A. (1996). Models of non-independence in dyadic research. *Journal of Social and Personal Relationships, 13,* 279–294.

Kiecolt-Glaser, J. K., Newton, T., Cacioppo, J. T., MacCullum, R. C., Glaser, R., & Marlarky, W. B. (1995). Marital conflict and endocrine function: Are men really more physiologically affected than women? *Journal of Consulting and Clinical Psychology, 64*(2), 324–332.

Kerig, P. K. (1995). Triangles in the family circle: Effects of family structure on marriage, parenting and child adjustment. *Journal of Family Psychology, 9*(1), 28–43.

Klein, D. M., & Jurich, J. A. (1993). Metatheory and family studies. In P. G. Boss, W. J. Doherty, R. La Rossa, W. R. Schumm, & S. K. Steinmetz (Eds.), *Sourcebook of family theories and methods: A contextual approach* (pp. 31–67). New York: Plenum.

Kurdek, L. A. (1994). Conflict resolution styles in gay, lesbian, heterosexual nonparent, and heterosexual parent couples. *Journal of Marriage and the Family, 56,* 705–722.

Kurdek, L. A. (1995). Predicting change in marital satisfaction from husbands' and wives' conflict resolution styles. *Journal of Marriage and the Family, 57,* 153–164.

Kurdek, L. A., & Fine, M. A. (1991). Cognitive correlates of satisfaction for mothers and stepfathers in stepfather families. *Journal of Marriage and the Family, 53,* 565–572.

L'Abate, L., & Bagarozzi, D. A. (1993). *Sourcebook of marriage and family evaluation.* New York: Brunner/Mazel.

Larson, J. H., Holman, T. B., Klein, D. M., Busby, D. M., Stahann, R. F., & Peterson, D. (1995). A review of comprehensive questionnaires used in premarital education and counseling. *Family Relations, 44*(3), 245–252.

Lavee, Y. (1988). Linear structural relationships (LISREL) in family research. *Journal of Marriage and the Family, 50,* 937–948.

Lee, K. A., & Rittenhouse, C. A. (1992). Health and perimenstrual symptoms: Health outcomes for employed women who experience perimenstrual symptoms. *Women and Health, 19,* 65–78.

Levenson, R. W., Carstensen, L. L., & Gottman, J. M. (1994). Influence of age and gender on affect, physiology, and their interrelations: A study of long-term marriages. *Journal of Personality and Social Psychology, 67*(1), 56–68.

Lewis, J. M., Beavers, W. R., Gossett, J. T., & Phillips, V. A. (1976). *No single thread: Psychological health in family systems.* New York: Brunner/Mazel.

Lindholm, B. W., & Touliatos, J. (1993). Measurement trends in family research. *Psychological Reports, 72,* 1265–1266.

Locke, H. J., & Wallace, K. L. (1959). Short marital adjustment and prediction tests: Their reliability and validity. *Marriage and Family Living, 21,* 251–255.

Lorenz, F. O., Conger, R. D., Simons, R. L., & Whitbeck, L. B. (1995). The effect of unequal covariances and reliabilities on contemporaneous inference: The case of hostility and marital happiness. *Journal of Marriage and the Family, 57*(4), 1049–1064.

Lund, M. (1985). The development of investment and commitment scales for predicting continuity of personal relationships. *Journal of Social and Personal Relationships, 2,* 3–23.

MacEwen, K., & Barling, J. (1993). Type A behavior and marital satisfaction: Differential effects of achievement striving and impatience/irritability. *Journal of Marriage and the Family, 55,* 1001–1010.

Malarkey, W., Kiecolt-Glaser, J. K., Pearl, D., & Glaser, R. (1994). Hostile behavior during marital conflict alters pituitary and adrenal hormones. *Psychosomatic Medicine, 56,* 41–51.

McCollum, E. E., Schumm, W. R., & Russell, C. S. (1988). Reliability and validity of the Kansas Family Life Satisfaction scale in a predominantly middle-aged sample. *Psychological Reports, 62,* 95–98.

McGuire, J., & Earls, F. (1993). Exploring the reliability of measures of family relations, parental attitudes, and parent-child relations in a disadvantaged minority population. *Journal of Marriage and the Family, 55,* 1042–1046.

McPhatter, A. R. (1991). Assessment revisited: A comprehensive approach to understanding family dynamics. *Families in Society, 72*(1), 11–22.

Mikol, L. L. (1995). *Intimacy, loneliness, communication, and marital satisfaction: Comparisons between deaf, non-deaf, and mixed couples.* Unpublished clinical research project report, Psy. D. program, Illinois School of Professional Psychology, Chicago, IL.

Miller, B. C. (1986). *Family research methods.* Beverly Hills, CA: Sage.

Miller, S., Nunnally, E. W., & Wackman, D. (1976). Minnesota Couples Communication Program (MCCP): Premarital and marital group. In D. H. L. Olson (Ed.), *Treating relationships* (pp. 21–39). Lake Mills, IA: Graphic Publishing.

Milner, J. S., & Murphy, W. D. (1995). Assessment of child physical and sexual abuse offenders. *Family Relations, 44,* 478–488.

Morris, M. L., & Blanton, P. W. (1994). The influence of work-related stressors on clergy-husbands and their wives. *Family Relations, 43,* 189–195.

Morris, T. M. (1990). Culturally sensitive family assessment: An evaluation

of the Family Assessment Device used with Hawaiian-American and Japanese-American families. *Family Process, 29,* 105–116.

Norton, R. (1983). Measuring marital quality: A critical look at the dependent variable. *Journal of Marriage and the Family, 45,* 141–151.

Nosofsky, R. M. (1992). Similarity scaling and cognitive process models. In M. R. Rosenzweig & L. W. Porter (Eds.), *Annual review of psychology, 43* (pp. 25–53). Palo Alto, CA: Annual Reviews Inc.

Nunnally, J. C. (1978). Psychometric theory. (2nd ed.). New York: McGraw-Hill.

O'Leary, K. D. (Ed.). (1987). *Assessment of marital discord.* Hillsdale, NJ: Erlbaum.

Osmond, M. W. (1987). Radical-critical theories. In M. B. Sussman & S. K. Steinmetz (Eds.), *Handbook of marriage and the family* (pp. 103–124). New York: Plenum.

Piotrikowski, C. S., Rapoport, R. N., & Rapoport, R. (1987). Families and work. In M. B. Sussman & S. K. Steinmetz (Eds.), *Handbook of marriage and the family* (pp. 251–283). New York: Plenum.

Plomin, R., McLearn, G. E., Pedersen, N. L., Nesselroad, J. R., Bergeman, C. S. (1989). Genetic influence on adults' ratings of their current family environment. *Journal of Marriage and the Family, 51,* 791–803.

Powers, S. I. (1989). Theory and assessment in family psychology: Weak links. *Journal of Family Psychology, 3*(2), 222–228.

Reinharz, S. (1992). *Feminist methods in social research.* New York: Oxford University Press.

Rho, J. J., & Schumm, W. R. (1989). The factorial validity of brief satisfaction scales in a survey of 58 Korean-American interracial couples. *Psychological Reports, 65,* 1347–1350.

Robinson, E. A., & Eyberg, S. M. (1981). The dyadic parent–child interactional coding system: Standardization and validation. *American Journal of Psychiatry, 143,* 760–763.

Rusbult, C. E., Verette, J., Whitney, G. A., Slovik, L. F., & Lipkus, I. (1991). Accommodation processes in close relationships: theory and preliminary empirical evidence. *Journal of Personality and Social Psychology, 60,* 53–78.

Rusbult, C. E., & Verette, J. (1991). An interdependence analysis of accommodation processes in close relationships. *Representative Research in Social Psychology, 19,* 3–33.

Russell, R. J. H., & Wells, P. A. (1992). Social desirability and quality of marriage. *Personality and Individual Differences, 13,* 787–791.

Sabatelli, R. M. (1988). Measurement issues in marital research. *Journal of Marriage and the Family, 50*(4), 891–916.

Sabatelli, R. M., & Bartle, S. E. (1995). Survey approaches to the assessment of family functioning: Conceptual, operational, and analytic issues. *Journal of Marriage and the Family, 57*(4), 1025–1039.

Sabatelli, R. M., & Waldron, R. J. (1995). Measurement issues in the assessment of the experiences of parenthood. *Journal of Marriage and the Family, 57*(4), 969–980.

Sanchez, L., & Kane, E. W. (1996). Women's and men's constructions of perception of housework fairness. *Journal of Family Issues, 17,* 358–387.

Sanderson, B., & Kurdek, L. A. (1993). Race and gender as moderator variables in predicting relationship satisfaction and relationship commitment in a sample of dating heterosexual couples. *Family Relations, 42,* 263–267.

Schafer, R. B., Wickrama, K. A. S., & Keith, P. M. (1996). Self-concept disconfirmation, psychological distress, and marital happiness. *Journal of Marriage and the Family, 58,* 167–177.

Schumm, W. R. (1982). Can marital conventionalization explain away relationships between religiosity and marital satisfaction? *Journal of Psychology and Christianity, 1*(2), 16–21.

Schumm, W. R. (1993). On publishing family research using "sophisticated" quantitative methodologies. *Marriage and Family Review*, *18*(1–2), 171–175.

Schumm, W. R., Bollman, S. R., & Jurich, A. P. (1997). Gender and marital satisfaction: A replication using a seven-point item response version of the Kansas Marital Satisfaction Scale. *Psychological Reports*, *81*, 1004–1006.

Schumm, W. R., Hess, J. L., Bollman, S. R., & Jurich, A. P. (1981). Marital conventionalization revisited. *Psychological Reports*, *59*, 391–394.

Schumm, W. R., Barnes, H. L., Bollman, S. R., Jurich, A. P., & Milliken, G. A. (1985). Approaches to the statistical analysis of family data. *Home Economics Research Journal*, *14*, 112–122.

Schumm, W. R., Paff-Bergen, L. A., Hatch, R. C., Obiorah, F. C., Copeland, J. M., Meens, L. D., & Bugaighis, M. A. (1986). Concurrent and discriminant validity of the Kansas Marital Satisfaction Scale. *Journal of Marriage and the Family*, *48*, 381–387.

Schumm, W. R., Jeong, G. J., & Silliman, B. (1990). Protestant fundamentalism and marital success revisited. *Psychological Reports*, *66*, 905–906.

Schumm, W. R., Milliken, G., Jurich, A. P., Bollman, S. R., Jeong, G. J., & Hawkinson, D. P. (1990). Mobility effect models: A comment on Glenn, McRae, and Brody. *Social Forces*, *69*, 617–620.

Shagle, S. C., & Barber, B. K. (1993). Effects of family, marital and parent-child conflict on adolescent self-derogation and suicidal ideation. *Journal of Marriage and the Family*, *55*, 964–974.

Shehan, C. L., & Lee, G. R. (1990). Roles and power. In J. Touliatos, B. F. Perlmutter, & M. A. Straus (Eds.), *Handbook of family measurement techniques* (pp. 420–441). Newbury Park, CA: Sage.

Shek, D. T. L. (1998). Reliability and validity of the Kansas Marital Satisfaction Scale for Chinese parents. *Psychological Reports*, *83*, 81–82.

Shek, D. T. L., & Tsang, S. K. (1993). The Chinese version of the Kansas Marital Satisfaction scale: Some psychometric and normative data. *Social Behavior and Personality*, *21*, 205–214.

Shek, D. T. L., Lam, M. C., Tsoi, K. W., & Lam, C. M. (1993). Psychometric properties of the Chinese version of the Kansas Marital Satisfaction Scale. *Social Behavior and Personality*, *21*, 241–249.

Singleton, R. A., Jr., Straits, B. C., & Straits, M. M. (1988). *Approaches to social research*. New York: Oxford University Press.

Spanier, G. B. (1976). Measuring dyadic adjustment: New scales for assessing the quality of marriage and similar dyads. *Journal of Marriage and the Family*, *38*, 15–28.

Spector, P. E. (1992). *Summated Rating Scale Construction: An introduction*. (Sage University Paper series on Quantitative Applications in the Social Sciences, no. 07-082). Newbury Park, CA: Sage.

Stanley, S. M., & Markman, H. J. (1992). Assessing commitment in personal relationships. *Journal of Marriage and the Family*, *54*, 595–608.

Stevens, S. S. (1951). Mathematics, measurement, and psychophysics. In S. S. Stevens (Ed.), *Handbook of experimental psychology* (pp. 1–49). New York: Wiley.

Straus, M. A. (1964). Measuring families. In H. T. Christensen (Ed.), *Handbook of marriage and the family* (pp. 335–400). Chicago: Rand McNally.

Straus, M. A. (1969). *Family Measurement Techniques: Abstracts of Published Instruments, 1935–1965*. Minneapolis: University of Minnesota.

Straus, M. A., & Brown, B. W. (1978). *Family measurement techniques: abstracts of published instruments, 1935–1974* (Rev. ed.). Minneapolis: University of Minnesota.

Straus, M. A., Hamby, S. L., Boney-McCoy, S., & Sugarman, D. B. (1996). The Revised Conflict Tactics Scales (CTS2): Development and preliminary psychometric data. *Journal of Family Issues*, *17*, 283–316.

Sullaway, M., & Christensen, A. (1983). Assessment of dysfunctional inter-action patterns in couples. *Journal of Marriage and the Family*, *45*, 656–660.

Szinovacz, M. E. (1987). Family power. In M. B. Sussman & S. K. Steinmetz (Eds.), *Handbook of marriage and the family* (pp. 651–693). New York: Plenum.

Szinovacz, M. E., & Egley, L. C. (1995). Comparing one-partner and couple data on sensitive marital behaviors: The case of marital violence. *Journal of Marriage and the Family*, *57*(4), 995–1010.

Teachman, J. D., Carver, K., & Day, R. (1995). A model for the analysis of paired data. *Journal of Marriage and the Family*, *57*(4), 1011–1024.

Thissen, D., & Steinberg, L. (1988). Data analysis using item response theory. *Psychological Bulletin*, *104*, 299–314.

Thompson, L., & Walker, A. (1982). The dyad as the unit of analysis: Conceptual and methodological issues. *Journal of Marriage and the Family*, *44*, 889–900.

Thompson, L., & Walker, A. (1995). The place of feminism in family studies. *Journal of Marriage and the Family*, *57*(4), 847–865.

Touliatos, J., Perlmutter, B. F., & Straus, M. A. (Eds.). (1990). *Handbook of family measurement techniques*. Newbury Park, CA: Sage.

Tourangeau, R., & Rasinski, K. A. (1988). Cognitive processes underlying context effects in attitude measurement. *Psychological Bulletin*, *103*, 299–314.

Tubman, J. G. (1991). A pilot study of family life among school-age children of problem drinking men: Child, mother, and family comparisons. *Family Dynamics of Addiction Quarterly*, *1*, 10–20.

Tubman, J. G. (1993). Family risk factors, parental alcohol use, and problem behavior among school age children. *Family Relations*, *42*, 81–86.

Tucker, M. W., & O'Grady, K. E. (1991). Effects of physical attractiveness, intelligence, age at marriage, and cohabitation on the perception of marital satisfaction. *Journal of Social Psychology*, *131*, 253–269.

Tutty, L. M. (1995). Theoretical and practical issues in selecting a measure of family functioning. *Research on Social Work Practice*, *5*(1), 80–106.

Tutuer, J. M., Ewigman, B. E., Peterson, L., & Hosokawa, M. C. (1995). The Maternal Observation Matrix and Mother–Child Interaction Scale: Brief observational screening instruments for physically abusive mothers. *Journal of Clinical Child Psychology*, *24*(1), 55–62.

Van den Broucke, S., Vertommen, H., & Vandereycken, W. (1995). Construction and validation of a marital intimacy questionnaire. *Family Relations*, *44*(3), 285–290.

Wasielewski, M. C. (1991). *Marital adjustment in bicultural and monocultural marriages*. Master's Abstracts International, 29, 2, 232, AAC 1341240.

Weiss, R., & Cerreto, M. C. (1980). The marital status inventory: Development of a measure of dissolution potential. *American Journal of Family Therapy*, *8*, 80–86.

Whisman, M. A., & Jacobson, N. S. (1992). Change in marital adjustment following marital therapy: A comparison of two outcome measures. *Psychological Assessment*, *4*(2), 219–223.

White, M. B., & Tyson-Rawson, K. J. (1995). Assessing the dynamics of gender in couples and families. *Family Relations*, *44*(3), 253–260.

White, M. B., Stahmann, R. F., & Furrow, J. L. (1994). Shorter may be better: A comparison of the Kansas Marital Satisfaction scale and the Locke-Wallace Marital Adjustment test. *Family Perspective*, *28*(1), 53–66.

Wyer, R. S., Jr., & Srull, T. K. (1994). *Handbook of social cognition*. Hillsdale, NJ: Erlbaum.

Yovetich, N. A., & Rusbult, C. E. (1994). Accommodative behavior in close relationships. *Journal of Experimental Social Psychology*, *30*, 138–164.

Zeller, R. A., & Carmines, E. G. (1980). *Measurement in the social sciences: The link between theory and data*. New York: Cambridge University Press.

PART III

Changing Family Patterns and Roles

The third part of the *Handbook* considers several topics related to microlevel structural and developmental changes within families. Of particular concern is the manner in which age (i.e., the developmental stage of individual or families) and gender have important structural and relationship implications for families. Another topic is the importance of structural and relationship changes that have redefined diverse family forms as being within the normative range. Also explored in this part are the family structural and relationship issues involved in the various ways that marriages become dissolved.

In Chapter 12, "Contemporary Family Patterns and Relationships," John DeFrain and David Olson challenge some traditional assumptions: (1) being married is better than being single or living together, (2) having children is better than not having children, (3) two parents are better than one, (4) biological parents are preferred over other types of parental arrangements, and (5) being a stay-at-home mother is better than being employed. The authors prefer the term "contemporary" families to avoid the negative or deviant connotations associated with labels such as variant, nontraditional, or alternative. This strategy seeks to avoid reinforcing tendencies to define diverse family forms as being somewhat less acceptable than traditional two-parent (nuclear) families. Family diversity, the authors propose, should be viewed by social scientists much like biologists have come to view ecosystems in nature as constantly changing, diversifying, and adapting.

Gary Peterson and Della Hann, in Chapter 13, "Socializing Children and Parents in Families," describe three major transformations that have reshaped the research and theory on socializing children in families. First, researchers are no longer limited to classical scientific approaches for understanding parent–child relations based on unidirectional socialization models, with parents being portrayed as "molding" their children's development. Second, parent–child relationships are increasingly recognized as complex, transactional processes involving reciprocal or simultaneous exchanges. Third, the parent–child relationship has been reconceptualized extensively in terms of connections that families have with the surrounding systemic ecology. The authors then review the current scholarship within the parent effects, child effects, reciprocal, and systemic-ecological perspectives.

Addressing the young at a later stage of development, Suzanne Steinmetz in Chapter 14, "Adolescence in Contemporary Families," explores several theories of adolescent socialization. She also describes the major developmental tasks of adolescence and contemporary adolescents' ability to fulfill these developmental challenges. The author discusses variables that impact on adolescents' decision making and can result in risky behavior and negative outcomes. The chapter explores some of the more prominent adolescent problems, such as alcohol and drugs, risky sexual behavior, crime and delinquency, emotional and mental illness, and dropping out of school. Another focus addresses the positive accomplishments of adolescents, including the increasing number who are attending postsecondary education, engaging in volunteer activities, helping at home, and working part-time.

Judith Treas and Leora Lawton note in Chapter 15, "Family Relations in Adulthood," that, until recently, research on adulthood had been focused on the family of procreation, not the family of origin. Some refocusing of the scholarship was required because recent cohorts tend to marry later, which means that parents and siblings continued to be central features of family relationships during both the early and middle years of adulthood. Consistent with this objective, the authors address recent trends on (1) co-residence or renesting, (2) social support in parent–adult relationships, (3) the effects of divorce on parent–child relationships, and (4) the consequences of intergenerational exchange and careers for siblings. An important conclusion is that siblings are a major source of support, especially when a spouse of children is not available.

In Chapter 16, "Gender and Family Relationships," Alexis Walker demonstrates that early research on gender tended to portray sex roles within families as lacking malleability, even to the point of being unchangeable. A large amount of this early work was based on the pervasive view in society regarding the biological basis of women's roles. Feminist perspectives, however, rejected these earlier views, partly because of the biological assumptions involved and the failure of early perspectives to recognize the importance of social structure. Contemporary feminist researchers have revised traditional scientific methodologies to enable them to address issues that are important to women. In her review of current scholarship on partnership, parenthood, family work, and kinship, Walker challenges current biases and commonly held assumptions that prevent a more accurate understanding of reality.

Kimberly Faust and Jerome McKibben, in Chapter 17, "Marital Dissolution: Divorce, Separation, Annulment, and Widowhood," note that while most marriages in previous eras ended through death, most are now terminated by divorce. Important contributions of their chapter include the historical and theoretical perspectives provided about divorce. The authors also examine the societal factors (e.g., the economy, cultural attitudes, legal issues, and health status) that influence marital dissolution. Other topics explored include issues relating to marital separation, annulments, and widowhood. In a final section, the authors conclude that future research on marital dissolution should focus on such issues as (1) the sequential decision-making process of multiple marriages, (2) the positive outcomes of ending unhappy marriages, and (3) family changes brought about when a spouse, exspouse, parent, or stepparent dies.

CHAPTER 12

Contemporary Family Patterns and Relationships

John DeFrain and David H. Olson

When Americans refer to traditional family values and dynamics, they commonly extol the virtues of lifelong marriage with children. Tradition in our culture holds that (1) being married is better than being single; (2) being married is better than living together; (3) having children is better than not having children; (4) two parents are better than one; (5) blood is thicker than water (i.e., especially when applied to distinctions between biological parents and stepparents); and (6) a mother at home is better than a mother at work, which is father's domain.

Cultural values, because they are often the glue of a society that gives meaning and guidance for individuals, must be seriously considered. However, over the past 30 years or more, it has become increasingly clear that vast changes are occurring in American society. Although some would argue that tradition is being tossed in the dustbin of cultural history (Popenoe, 1993), it is more likely that old norms are being amended to be more inclusive, taking into account changing economic, social, and political realities (Kain, 1990).

Although we still have many families in the United States who would define themselves as quite traditional, we also have an increasing number of individuals and families who live happily and successfully outside the traditional norms. Researchers and professionals in the field of family studies have experimented with terminology for years with respect to such relationships: variant, nontraditional, and

John DeFrain • Department of Family and Consumer Sciences, University of Nebraska, Lincoln, Nebraska 68583-0801. **David H. Olson** • Department of Family Social Sciences, University of Minnesota, St. Paul, Minnesota 55108.

Handbook of Marriage and the Family, 2nd edition, edited by Marvin Sussman, Suzanne K. Steinmetz, and Gary W. Peterson. Plenum Press, New York, 1999.

alternative family forms are three terms used widely in the past (Kain, 1990; Skolnick, 1991).

In keeping with the creative and experimental nature of the families themselves, we choose the terminology "contemporary family patterns and relationships" as preferable to the labels variant, nontraditional, or alternative, which seem to imply something a bit less than sound, less than normal, or even deviant.

This approach is both more humane and scientifically sound, not only because it describes these families in a more positive light, but also because it examines their own unique qualities. These families are not offshoots of the traditional norm; thus it is not meaningful to evaluate them in reference to the traditional norm any more than it would be to learn about African American families only through comparing them with Euro-American families. Likewise, a stepfamily is a unique family with unique qualities; labeling these families as nontraditional does not capture this uniqueness. These relatively new developments in family patterns and dynamics have proven to be workable for many people, and a more positive terminology reflecting this fact is needed.

For this chapter, therefore, we examine singlehood, cohabitation, the childfree family, single-parent families, stepfamilies, changing gender roles, dual-career families, and coparenting. These family forms or issues, in many ways, have become more "normative" in recent decades, as demonstrated by what could be designated as their "staying power." They have survived the test of time and are continuing to develop. A reasonable proposal, therefore, is that several different "normative" family relationships are currently in existence, not just the classical nuclear family as described by Talcott Parsons (Parsons & Bales, 1955).

We are not arguing, however, that traditional nuclear family patterns and relationships in the Parsonian sense should be dismantled. Rather, we are proposing that the wide variety of contemporary and traditional family patterns in American culture can be seen as a sign of health, just as diversity in an ecosystem is judged by biologists to indicate strength and adaptability within a complex web of life forms (Kain, 1990; Skolnick, 1991).

Families face a myriad of challenges today, and many contemporary families exhibit creative responses to their unique challenges. Not all contemporary families work effectively, of course, but seldom has the need arisen for traditional families to be defended by showing that all are successful.

Singlehood

Seligmann (1993) suggests that there are both good and bad reasons for getting married as well as good and bad reasons for remaining single. Today, marriage is a personal choice, not a social dictate. In fact, more people are remaining single, and this choice is increasingly regarded as an acceptable alternative to marriage (Seccombe & Ishii-Kuntz, 1994).

Approximately 90% of young Americans expect to marry at some point in their lives—a proportion that has remained relatively stable for the past quarter of a century. Despite high levels of divorce, most young people expect their marriages to last. Despite such expectations, recent demographic studies indicate that young people are staying single longer and getting married at a slightly older age. In 1993, for example, there were more men and an even greater number of women who had never been married than there were in 1960 (Table 1). Government figures indicate that 40.8% of women and 36.6% of men over age 18 are single (U.S. Bureau of the Census, 1994, p. 57).

Many factors contribute to the increase in singlehood today. The first of these involves the fact that educational plans and career involvement are delaying the age at which young people are marrying. Associated with this trend is an

increasing recognition that in our society singlehood can be a legitimate, healthy, and happy alternative to marriage. Shostak (1987) found, for example, that most young people interviewed said they would be "a little" bothered if they failed to marry. Relatively few said they would be "greatly bothered" by failing to marry at some point during their lives. Moreover, the mothers of these young people generally acknowledged that marriage was not a "must" for their children.

Shostak (1987) also concluded that marriage continues to be more important to young women than to young men. Although more and more young women are seeking jobs and careers, they still tend to value marriage and parenthood to a greater extent than do young men. This is the case even though there are greater educational and occupational opportunities for women in recent decades; if they choose to, women can make it on their own more easily than in the past. Shostak also noted that individuals who have experienced divorce in their families are also more likely to have both negative attitudes about marriage and positive attitudes about singlehood.

Some singles have been married before but are now in transition. About three-fourths of divorced people remarry, usually 2 to 3 years after they divorce. But researchers are finding that even though most people remarry after a divorce, the rate of remarriage has dropped by more than 25% (Cherlin & Furstenberg, 1994; Coleman & Ganong, 1991).

Historical Considerations

Singlehood is being viewed increasingly as a legitimate alternative to marriage by more and more people in our society (Janus & Janus, 1993), a view that represents a major shift in attitudes. Throughout most of American history, the failure to marry (note how even the terminology is loaded) was considered undesirable. Not everyone, of course, married in eighteenth- and nineteenth-century America, and many married in their late 20s or their 30s. Marriage was highly valued; social circumstances and economic deficiencies probably discouraged marriage more than did personal desires. "Old maid" and "spinster" were certainly not flattering descriptions for unmarried women (Degler, 1980).

In colonial times (the seventeenth and eighteenth centuries), virtually all unmarried individuals lived in a family environment of some type—either in their parents' home or as servants in another's home. Unmarried people of all ages usually stayed dependent on the families with whom they lived and were not considered fully independent members of society until they married (Degler, 1980; Hareven, 1987).

In the nineteenth century, the position of unmarried people began to change. They increasingly became involved in wage labor outside the family and often lived in boarding

Table 1. Women and Men Remaining Single

	1960 (%)	1970 (%)	1980 (%)	1993 (%)
Women remaining single				
Ages 20–24	28.4	35.8	50.2	66.8
Ages 25–29	10.5	10.5	20.8	33.1
Men remaining single				
Ages 20–24	53.1	54.7	68.6	81.0
Ages 25–29	20.8	19.1	32.4	48.4

Source: U.S. Bureau of the Census (1994).

houses. With the rise of the industrial system, many young people were needed to work in factories, which were often located a considerable distance from their rural family's home. Although attitudes toward singlehood may have improved in the nineteenth and early twentieth centuries, social custom held that marriage was by far the preferable state, and those who remained single continued to be stigmatized (Veroff, Douvan, & Kulka, 1981).

Reasons for the Trend

Today, an increasing number of single people live with their parents. In 1993, 60% of 20- to 24-year-old males and 52% of females of that age group lived with their families of origin (see Table 2). In 1960, only 10% of 25- to 34-year-olds lived with their parents, as compared with 23% of 25- to 34-year-olds who lived with their parents in 1993. Consequently, such data underscore the current trend for young adults to live with their parents more frequently now than was the case in the 1960s.

There are a number of reasons for this trend. Some young people postpone marriage until they are older and live at home until the wedding. College costs force many to stay at home to save money. Unemployment or divorce causes financial troubles for some. Single mothers often must stay at home with their parents for financial aid and help with their infant (Glick & Lin, 1986).

The lifestyles of single individuals have clearly changed in recent decades. Singlehood is increasingly being viewed as a viable option to marriage, with more people remaining single longer and choosing to live together without being married; they are enjoying some of the benefits of marriage without the legal or religious commitments and with less stigmatization. There is at least one positive result of this

Table 2. Living Arrangements of People Ages 15 and Older (1993)

	Males (%)			Females (%)		
	15–19	20–24	25–34	15–19	20–24	25–34
Living alone	1	7	11	1	5	7
Living with spouses	1	17	52	4	28	60
Living with family of origin	95	60	23	91	52	25
Living with nonrelatives	3	17	14	4	15	8
Total	100	100	100	100	100	100

Source: U.S. Bureau of the Census (1994).

trend toward longer singlehood and later marriage: Those individuals who marry in their teens or early 20s are more likely to divorce than those who marry later. Delaying marriage until one has completed one's education and found satisfying work contributes to marital stability (Martin & Bumpass, 1989; White, 1991). However, those who wait until their mid-30s or older before marrying are also more likely to seek a divorce because they may be less tolerant of differences and more likely to recognize that they are capable of living alone (Eshleman, 1997).

Olson and DeFrain (1997) suggest that some forces or factors attract individuals to marriage, but some less-than-ideal reasons for marriage, such as pressure from parents, the desire to leave home, fear of independence, loneliness, and not having a sense of the alternatives, are likely to predict an unstable marriage. They note, on the other hand, that there are factors that have been found to contribute to marital stability, including the desire for a family, emotional attachment and love for one another, as well as security, social status, and prestige. Some of the negative forces that impel individuals toward singlehood are poor communication with one's partner; boredom, unhappiness, and anger; and the feeling of being trapped in a relationship. Some of the positive reasons for choosing singlehood are career opportunities, the desire for self-sufficiency, the desire for mobility, and the freedom to change (Olson & DeFrain, 1997).

Successful Singles

The adult single population today includes people who are single for a variety of reasons. One large group of singles are professional and career-oriented individuals. These people tend to be highly educated and achievement-oriented and prefer to remain unattached in life. Although common in the past for employers to believe that single professionals were less desirable employees (thinking perhaps that they could not adjust to marriage or were unstable or undependable), they are now apparently beginning to appreciate the flexibility of "unattached" employees. Single individuals can transfer to new locations more efficiently than whole families, and they usually have fewer outside commitments, which can complicate a married employee's adjustment to a new locale. Single employees are free to devote more extra hours to their careers and they are as highly trained and capable as married employees (Olson & DeFrain, 1997).

Although single women have been subject to discrimination in salary and promotions (often due to employer expectations that they might marry and resign), firms are increasingly adopting affirmative action policies to provide more equitable treatment of female employees. As a result, singlehood is losing much of its negative stigma within professional groups (Olson & DeFrain, 1997).

Recent research on the attitudes of single workers indicates discontent, however. A survey of single/childless workers revealed that 80% said their needs were not receiving as much attention from management as those of employees with spouses and children. Moreover, 81% felt they were carrying a greater burden than their married-with-children coworkers. These employees felt that they are getting a larger share of work and making more sacrifices, while getting a smaller share of the benefits. Such results suggest that the business world could expect a backlash from singles in the future (Flynn, 1996).

Women who remain single are likely to be high achievers with above-average intelligence, making it difficult for these women to find an unattached man of equal status. This is especially a problem for African American women. First-born girls (who are often achievement-oriented) and "only children" are somewhat more likely to remain single than other children (Macklin, 1980, p. 906). To overcome one of the biggest problems that singles face, that of developing a network of friends and associates with whom to share social activities, a variety of churches, synagogues, and social organizations (as well as resort lodges and nightclubs) have created "singles' nights."

Sexuality

Single people have many of the same problems coping with their sex life as married people. Although they have the same basic desire to be sexually intimate and to be loved by someone, they have to use different approaches to fulfill their needs. Perhaps the greatest change in the sexual behavior of singles in recent years has been the increased sexual activity of females. During the past 3 decades, much of the stigma of women engaging in premarital sex has been eliminated, and research has indicated that approximately 90% of adult females who are single have experienced premarital intercourse (Miller & Moore, 1991).

Although the "swinging singles" stereotype provides good movie material, few singles have the inclination or motivation to "swing" for any length of time. Most seem to prefer that sexual intimacy be tied to some degree of affection or companionship, with one-night stands being of limited appeal (Masters, Johnson, & Kolodny, 1988). This has become even more true with the growing risk of contracting sexually transmissible diseases (STDs) and HIV (Janus & Janus, 1993). One study provides some evidence that single individuals engage in sexual relations less often than married individuals, but with a greater variety of partners (Michael, Liagnon, Laumann, & Kolata, 1994). Singles also report that satisfaction with their sexual encounters varies a great deal, depending on the identity of the particular partner.

Loneliness

One societal stereotype about single individuals is that they are lonely. Rollins insists that being alone is not synonymous with loneliness, noting, "Ninety percent of the singles in my study are not what I call lonely, they are alone" (cited in Peterson & Lee, 1985). In fact, Rollins found that of 99 singles between the ages of 21 and 66 who were surveyed, 65% were moderately happy or happier. Rollins argued that the problem is not with singlehood but with society: "The sad part is that 33% of Americans 20–55 are single at any given time. The message we're giving them is you're lonely and atypical, and they begin to believe it." It's conceivable, therefore, that the social stereotype of the distressed and lonely single might push an individual into a marriage that he or she really doesn't want or need because of social conformity.

A nationally representative sample of 3600 adults found that individuals who live alone are not socially isolated but actually have a more active social life with more social contacts outside the home than married individuals and that if singles are unhappy, they don't view living alone as being the primary reason (Alwin, cited in Elias, 1985). Alwin found that married couples did report a somewhat greater sense of well-being than unmarried people, but having children tended to lower these couples' happiness scores.

Alwin reported that, as a group, only single parents (90% of whom are women) experienced painful isolation and significantly poorer mental health as a result of living alone. He explained, "It's having the children that limits their friendship network; they have a limited ability to get away from the kids." Alwin concluded, "Our changing lifestyles don't necessarily bring negative consequences" (cited in Elias, 1985, p. 6).

In a similar vein, Hughes' study of 2248 individuals revealed that singles who live with another person give up privacy and have to adjust to the demands of roommates. "When you live with others, you must interact with them. If you live alone, you can choose to either interact or not to interact with others or not. Roommates drive some individuals crazy.... Living alone is no worse and in many circumstances better for non-marrieds than living with others" (cited in Peterson & Lee, 1985, pp. 8, 9).

Fulfillment

Margaret Adams (1976) argued in her classic study, *Single Blessedness: Observations on the Single Status in Married Society*, that there are three essential criteria for a successful single life: the capacity and opportunity to be economically self-sufficient, the capacity and opportunity to be socially and psychologically autonomous, and a clearly thought-out intent to remain single by choice rather than by default.

Singles by choice enjoy the opportunities for solitude and for developing a wide network of friendships. Singles by choice enjoy the freedom to invest as much time in their careers as they want and the freedom to spend money as they wish (Adams, 1976; Barkas, 1980).

Cohabitation

For many people, marriage is no longer considered a prerequisite for living with a romantic partner. In fact, by the time they reach their early 30s, almost one-half of the U.S. population has cohabited at some time (Nock, 1995). Cohabitation is defined by the federal government as two unrelated adults of the "opposite" sex sharing the same living quarters. A broader definition would include same-sex couples who have an emotional and sexual relationship. Between 1980 and 1993, the number of couples cohabiting doubled, to 3,510,000 (U.S. Bureau of the Census, 1994). Among cohabiting couples, about half of the partners (54%) had never been married before, and one-third (37%) had been divorced, and the rest were widowed.

Although cohabitation is becoming more common in America, is also has sparked a good deal of controversy. Numerous studies have been conducted to evaluate this phenomenon, but the results are somewhat difficult to interpret. Marriage is a risky proposition, with conflict being inevitable and the likelihood of divorce currently more than 50%. For these and numerous other reasons, more people are deciding to live together rather than marry.

Types of Cohabitation

People cohabit for many reasons and have various types of cohabitation arrangements. In a classic review of research and the observations of counselors, Ridley, Peterman, and Avery (1978) identified four common patterns of cohabitation:

1. Linus blanket: Named for the character in the comic strip *Peanuts* who carries a security blanket with him, the Linus blanket-type of cohabiting relationship occurs when one partner is so dependent or insecure that he or she prefers a relationship with anyone to being alone. The insecure partner often finds the open communication on which a successful relationship thrives to be difficult; the stronger partner does not feel that he or she can criticize the more "fragile" partner.

2. Emancipation: Cohabitation is one way to break free from one's parents' values and influence. Females who grew up in very conservative religious traditions often seek sexual emancipation not permitted by their parents or their faith through cohabitation.

3. Convenience: Relationships in which one person is the giver and the other is the taker are often relationships of convenience. Typically, the woman supplies loving care and domestic labor—and hopes, but dares not ask, for marriage; the man gains domestic labor and sex without a commitment.

4. Testing: Cohabitation can be a true testing ground for marriage if the partners are relatively mature and clearly committed to trying out their already mutually satisfying relationship in a situation more closely resembling marriage. However, because it is not truly a marriage, some argue, it cannot serve as a test of marriage and is only "playing house" (Kurdek, 1994; Kurdek & Schmitt, 1986).

Many couples report that cohabitation is a test of future marital compatibility. Eleanor Macklin (1980) found, for example, that the majority of the participants in her study would not consider marriage without first having lived with the potential mate. Similarly, the majority of cohabitants in another study stated that the arrangement was primarily preparation for marriage (Lewis, Spanier, Atkinson, & Lehecka, 1977). Some research views the growing prevalence of cohabitation among middle-class youth as a new step within the mate-selection process. Other research, however, found that cohabitation was not necessarily a positive experience (Stets, 1993; Stewart & Olson, 1990; Thomson & Colella, 1992), and Kaczmarek, Backlund, and Biemer (1990) note that dealing with the pain of a broken cohabiting relationship can be as difficult as the circumstances of ending a legal marriage.

In a study of 4271 engaged couples Stewart and Olson (1990) found that cohabiting couples had the lowest level of premarital satisfaction, whereas premarital couples in which both persons lived alone had the highest level of premarital satisfaction. While about two-thirds of the cohabiting couples fell into the low-satisfaction group, about two-thirds of the couples in which both individuals lived alone fell into the high-satisfaction group (Stewart & Olson, 1990). Other studies also have reported that cohabiting couples tend to be at a disadvantage for attaining satisfying intimate relationships (Stets, 1991, 1993).

Watson (1983) studied 87 Canadian couples in an effort to find out if cohabitation is, indeed, "a new stage of courtship which, in replacing dating, may provide a more realistic basis for the selection of a mate" (p. 139). He found that about two-thirds (64%) of the couples studied had engaged in some form of cohabitation before marriage and found that noncohabitors were better adjusted during the first year of marriage than those who had previously cohabited. Perhaps this was a post hoc justification; however, 94% of those who cohabited reported that they had no regrets and 90% of those who had not cohabited before marriage stated that they did the right thing.

Cohabitation and Divorce

Researchers have found that cohabitation is associated with a greater hazard of dissolution than noncohabitation (DeMaris & Rao, 1992; Hall & Zhao, 1995; Lillard, Brien, & Waite, 1995; Schoen, 1992; Teachman & Polonko, 1990). A comparison of couples who did and did not cohabit before marriage found that those who had cohabited reported lower quality marriages, a lower commitment to the institution of marriage, more individualistic views of marriage (wives only), and greater likelihood of divorce than those who had not (Thomson & Callously, 1992).

Two decades ago, Ridley et al. (1978) noted, "It would seem unfortunate to conclude that cohabitation is an inherently good or bad preparation for marriage, but rather it should be viewed as having the potential for both" (p. 134). Little evidence exists, however, that cohabitation yields substantial benefits for most participants in terms of preparation for marriage (Stets, 1991, 1993), and Hall (1996) suggests that the attitudes regarding intimacy that each person brings to the relationship may be more germane to marital and family stability.

A study of 231 college-aged Boston couples found that most college students who cohabit expect to marry at some time in the future. Another finding was that no significant differences existed between couples who were "going together" and those who were cohabiting as to whether they broke up or got married (Risman, Hill, Rubin, & Peplau, 1981).

Legal Issues

Although to some the most important aspect of marriage is the spiritual and religious dimension, and to others the psychological and emotional aspects are the most important aspect of an intimate relationship, the legal aspect, which is complex, is also important. Monica Seff (1995) reminds us that, "Since state laws have not established cohabitation as a legal relationship, the rights of cohabitors have been established through court decisions. Consequently, cohabitors are likely to find themselves in a position of uncertainty with respect to their legal rights" (p. 3).

For younger people who don't have a lot of money or property to fight over after a relationship has broken up,

this advice may sound a bit curious. However, the much-publicized 1976 court ruling in *Marvin v. Marvin* (Bernstein, 1977), changed this uncomplicated circumstance. Movie actor Lee Marvin and Michelle Triola had lived together from 1964 to 1970, during which time she had adopted his last name, calling herself Michelle Marvin. When the couple separated, the actor supported her for a period of 2 years. When the support ceased, Michelle Marvin sued Lee Marvin on the grounds that he had broken his verbal promise to her that if she would live with him and abandon her career as an actress, he would support her for life, sharing his earnings. She argued that she had kept her part of the bargain, but he had not kept his. The California Supreme Court made a landmark decision in the case, since clear legal guidelines did not exist upon which a judgment could be based. The court set a value on Michelle Marvin's services in the relationship in order to make a property settlement. In 1979 the court awarded Ms. Marvin $104,000 and thus she became the first unmarried women to obtain "equitable relief" under a new label, palimony. This money was to compensate her for the lost years of her career, and part of the money was to help her reestablish herself in the working world (Olson & DeFrain, 1997).

In one legal arrangement called contract cohabitation, one cohabitant in essence hires the other as a live-in companion. The agreement specifies each partner's rights and obligations and is especially useful for middle-aged couples with considerable financial assets. The contract cohabitation agreement may be canceled at any time. The "employer" is thus protected from having to pay palimony or having to divide up her or his property, as might be required without such contract.

Gays and Lesbians

Same-gender cohabitants (both gay men and lesbians) often feel stigmatized by society, and as cohabitants, their legal status is murky (Demo & Allen, 1996). As homosexuals, they are stigmatized for their sexual orientation, and their relationship may cause great discomfort to their parents, other family members, and friends. Consequently, they may choose not to divulge the secret of their sexual preference to people who would disapprove.

Commitment, essential to a sound and long-lasting relationship, is especially difficult to build in an "invisible" relationship, as is noted by one gay male who is in a committed relationship:

> Right, they [gays] don't have the externals imposed by the institution of marriage. They don't have the in-laws; they don't have the children; they don't have the PTA; they don't have the office parties.... All of these things, you know, are great supports for couples, those straight couples, to try to keep their marriage together. You know, gay people don't

have that, none of those institutional supports to back them up. So it's got to come out of some real need, some real commitment to each other to try to keep it together and to try to remain allies against what is ultimately a hostile world to them. (Denneny, 1979, p. 72)

A study investigating the level of commitment among homosexual couples (32 lesbian and 50 gay males) who had lived together for at least 6 months found that about 25% of gay males reported that they had known each other for less than 1 year, compared with 50% of lesbians reporting that they had known each other for 1–2 years (Lewis, Kozac, Milardo, & Grosnick, 1981). However, 48% of the males reported that they had developed a "long-term commitment" to each other; 38% of the lesbians reported similar long-term commitments. Furthermore, 62% of the gay males and 31% of the lesbians reported that their relationship "will probably result in a formal, recognized commitment," such as a "holy union."

In general, the research indicates that the similarities in the qualities of gay male and lesbian cohabiting relationships were much more noteworthy than the few differences observed (Blumstein & Schwartz, 1983; Kurdek & Schmitt, 1986).

The Child-Free Family

The terms applied to couples who choose not to have children, such as nonparenthood, voluntary childlessness, or the childfree family, are all emotionally laden terms, and all seem to ask whether a person can be happy and fulfilled in life without having children. Government figures indicate that 9.3% of U.S. wives between the ages of 18 and 34 do not expect to have children (U.S. Bureau of the Census, 1994, p. 83). Reviews of research literature in the area of voluntary childlessness focus on four key questions:

1. *What long-term effects does voluntary childlessness have?* Although adult children are often very important to their parents in old age, older people without children also do quite well by developing a network of friends and relatives to help meet their needs as well as by learning how to cope with isolation if necessary (Rempel, 1985). Researchers investigating whether aging childless couples might regret their earlier decision to remain childfree found few social, economic, or psychological differences between couples with children and those who remained child free (Beckman & Houser, 1982; Keith, 1983; Singh & Williams, 1981). Most nonparents create alternate sources of life satisfaction (Bell & Eisenberg, 1985; Kivett & Learner, 1980). The presence or absence of children does not appear to alter their quality of life in an appreciable manner.

2. *Is there something wrong with people who don't wish to have children?* Jean Veevers (1983) found that the majority of studies on this topic concluded that nonparents exhibit no more psychopathology or deviance than a control group of randomly sampled parents. Other researchers have found that when compared to parents, those without children are more likely to be from urban areas (Rhee, 1973); to have delayed their first marriage (Ritchey & Stokes, 1974); to have been previously married (Rhee, 1973); to be college-educated or hold graduate degrees (Crispell, 1993; Gustavus & Itenley, 1971; Krishnan, 1993; Magarick, 1975; Mommsen, 1973); to report "no religion" (almost all studies); to have both spouses employed in relatively high-paying positions (Ramu, 1985; Rhee, 1973; Ritchey & Stokes, 1974); to be disproportionately first-born (Barnett & MacDonald, 1976; Ory, 1978; Thoen, 1977), last-born (Pupo, 1980), or only children (Baum & Cope, 1980); to report that the advent of children negatively affected their parents' lives (Lichtman, 1976; Toomey, 1977); to be in good mental health (Magarick & Brown, 1981; Malmquist & Kaij, 1971; Teicholz, 1977); to be more androgynous (Teicholz, 1977); and to be less conventional (Bram, 1985; Magarick, 1975).

3. *Do people without children do better in their careers?* Apparently, many people without children do very well. Veevers (1983) noted that voluntary childlessness leaves people with time and energy that can be focused on career goals; among women of eminence, a disproportionate number are childless. Childfree persons, in general, tend to be more successful professionally, and academics of both sexes have a stronger publication record (Hargens, McCann, & Reskin, 1978).

4. *Is the quality of a childfree marriage as good as that of a marriage with children?* Recent studies have found more vital and happy relationships among childfree couples than among those with children (Olson et al., 1989; Somers, 1993). This is, in part, because childfree couples can devote more time to their marriages, but also because those who do not have a good relationship are more likely to divorce if they do not have children. Researchers have documented that voluntarily childless couples experience some degree of disapproval from others (Callan, 1985; Cooper, Cumber, & Hartner, 1978; Magarick, 1975; Marcks, 1976; Ory, 1978), indicating that a pronatalist bias still exists in our society. To date, researchers have not created a sophisticated way of

measuring whether the pressure to have children is abating, or to what degree.

Single-Parent Families

Nearly one-third of all American families were headed by a single parent in 1994, a number that represents a considerable increase over the last 2 decades. The percentage of one-parent families was about 13% in 1970, rising to 22% in 1980. By 1990, the number had increased to 28%, and it reached 30.8% in 1994 (U.S. Bureau of the Census, 1995).

By far the majority of single-parent households are headed by females. There were almost 10 million single mothers heading households in 1994 compared to 1.6 million single fathers. Single fathers were twice as common in white families as compared with black families—16% and 8%, respectively.

During the last several years, the number of single-parent households increased most dramatically for families of color. In 1994, 25% of Caucasian households were single parent; the rate was 34% for Mexican American and 65% for African American families.

Although single parents must deal with challenges that include loneliness and isolation, economic problems, and work overload, many single parents develop healthy and functional families. Meanwhile, the parent who is not living with the children is also struggling to establish a new identity and to maintain a relationship with the children he or she has "lost."

Single-parent families have been described as one-parent, lone-parent, or solo-parent families (Weinraub & Gringlas, 1995). Some have suggested that single-parent families are often problem families, but this is an inaccurate picture confounded by the level of poverty experienced by female-headed families. Of all single-parent families, the most common group is divorced mothers (36.8%), followed by never-married mothers (24.4%) and separated mothers (18.5%). Other single-parent family categories are widows (6.8%), divorced fathers (5.8%), separated fathers (2.4%), spouse-absent mothers (2.4%), never-married fathers (1.5%), and widowers (0.9%) (Glick & Lin, 1986; Weinraub & Gringlas, 1995).

Family Terminology

The changing nature of the family in our society has made new vocabulary necessary. Constance Ahrons and Morton Perlmutter (1982) have suggested the term *binuclear family* to reflect the fact that divorce is "a process that results in family reorganization rather than disintegration" (p. 35), establishing two households, the mother's and father's, which interrelate with each other (DeFrain, Fricke, & Elmen, 1987).

Ahrons and Rodgers (1987) provide four types of relationship behaviors between ex-spouses in binuclear families: "perfect pals," "cooperative colleagues," "angry associates," and "fiery foes," with the "dissolved duo" referring to a relationship that is completely over.

Mothers with Custody

Divorced mothers who head single-parent families must cope with many sources of stress. One of the major problems for mothers with sole custody is limited economic resources, often made worse by lack of child support from the father. In a study of 492 court records, Rettig, Christensen, and Dahl (1991) found that the court-ordered awards met only 58% of the children's income needs when measured against poverty-level support. As expected, the custodial (residential) parent spent a much higher proportion of her (or his) income to support the children than did the noncustodial (nonresidential) parent. This is a serious problem nationally and is made worse by the fact that only about half (48%) of the noncustodial parents make full child support payments, 26% make partial payments, and 26% make no payments at all (Rettig, Christensen, & Dahl, 1991; Weinraub & Gringlas, 1993).

Loneliness is also a common problem for most single parents. One mother commented, "The only real sorrow we feel about the arrangement [single parenthood] is that her father isn't with us to share in the daily goings on of family life" (Olson & DeFrain, 1997, p. 539). The other parent is not there to share the child's artwork, the loss of the first tooth, or the birthday parties—in short, the everyday experiences of childrearing. Some divorced mothers with custody also lamented the loss of positive grandparent relationships as these ties are severed in many families after divorce. "I bleed for my children when I see their loneliness in being away from Dad and former friends. I regret seeking more conversation and support from them in my own loneliness than they can give me," a mother said (Olson & DeFrain, 1997, p. 539). Some mothers worry that the day may come when the children will no longer know their father (Hetherington & Stanley-Hagan, 1997).

For some single parents, battles with the ex-spouse continue for years, with many custodial mothers dreading continued contact with the ex-partner (Amato, 1993). These parents are not the "perfect pals" and "cooperative colleague" that Ahrons and Rodgers (1987) talked about, but the "angry associates" and "fiery foes" who often square off against each other.

Olson and DeFrain (1997, p. 540) conclude that strong, single-parent families share the same constellation of qualities that strong, two-parent families share: appreciation and affection for each of the family members; commitment to the family; open, honest, and straightforward communication patterns; adequate amounts of time together; spiritual well-being; and the ability to cope creatively with stress and crisis. Besides reporting many challenges, mothers with sole custody report a number of specific joys inherent in their situations. These include the freedom to make decisions about their own lives and the lives of their children without interference or harassment from hostile fathers.

For some mothers with custody, the burden of almost total responsibility for the children is nearly unbearable, but others thrive on the responsibility: "The joy that is unique to being a single parent is the all-engulfing satisfaction when things are going well. You not only take all of the responsibility, but you receive all of the joy from the growth and new discovery that the child is experiencing" (Olson & DeFrain, 1997, p. 540).

Mothers with sole custody are appreciative of fathers who stay involved with their children after the divorce, and some former spouses remain friends, or at least neutral colleagues, in the challenge of rearing children after divorce (Hetherington & Stanley-Hagan, 1995; Weinraub & Gringlas, 1995). This contributes to the health, happiness, and adjustment of the children.

Fathers with Custody

Many family researchers have found that fathers can do a good job rearing children after a divorce, just as mothers who formerly were full-time homemakers can successfully work outside the home after a divorce (Grief, 1995; Hetherington & Stanley-Hagan, 1997; Meyer & Garasky, 1993; Richards & Schmiege, 1993). For example, DeFrain and Eirick (1981) compared divorced single fathers and divorced single mothers on six major areas of adjustment to divorce: the process of divorce, the stresses of single parenthood, childrearing philosophies and behaviors, children's behaviors, relationships with the ex-spouse, and forming new social relationships. For most of these variables, the researchers found no significant statistical differences between the single-parent fathers and the mothers.

Most studies indicate that the answer to the question, "Can fathers be good single parents?" is yes. It also appears that the sorrows and joys of solo parenting for fathers are very similar to those related by mothers with custody (Hetherington & Stanley-Hagan, 1997; Parke, 1996).

Single-parent fathers, like single mothers, often feel sorrow over the fact that the family unit has been broken up, suffer loneliness, and experience time and money constraints. Single fathers, similar to single mothers, report the joy of watching their children grow up, the convenience of having control over the situation, as well as becoming closer to their children. Fathers with custody often have to adjust their priorities so that children take precedence over their job, but in return they have the opportunity to really enjoy their children in a more natural environment (Hetherington & Stanley-Hagan, 1997).

Some fathers do get along with their ex-spouse. One 54-year-old father who was caring for nine children said he was especially pleased that "my ex-wife and I get along. If there is a problem—and we do have some—I get on the phone, and we talk it out and resolve it. Something we didn't do too well when we were married" (Olson & DeFrain, 1997, p. 542). Although the marriage is over, ex-spouses can sometimes build a solid partnership for the good of their children (Meyer & Garasky, 1993).

Split Custody

Split custody is a child custody arrangement that involves both divorced parents separately (DeFrain et al., 1987). Each parent has responsibility for at least one of their children and thus has all the stresses, strains, and joys of solo parenting. In many families split custody is a family decision, involving input from all involved.

Split custody is apparently the least common of all parenting options after divorce, but it works quite well for many of the parents involved in it. A number of fathers said that their sons wanted to live with them, especially during adolescence when children became difficult to handle (Olson & DeFrain, 1997, p. 542). Some "switching" of households may almost be inevitable after divorce, adolescents need to balance their fantasies about life in the other home with the other parent and reality. They may find that the other home is no better than the home in which they currently live.

Joint Custody

In their study of 738 families in 45 states, DeFrain et al. (1987) concluded that no one particular custody arrangement is best for all families. Rather, each divorce is unique, and what is best for the children has to be decided on the basis of answers to numerous questions, including: (1) Do the children and both parents feel it best that both parents continue contact with the children after the divorce? (2) Do both parents have the capabilities to maintain an adequate home for the children? (3) Can the parents get along with each other well enough to manage a joint-custody arrangement after a divorce? If all members of the family can honestly answer yes to all three questions and can manage the innumerable details that have to be worked out, then joint custody might be a feasible solution (Hetherington & Stanley-Hagan, 1995).

Parents who have arranged joint custody report less stress than single-custody parents and have more time to pursue their own interests because the ex-spouse assumes a major share of the childcare responsibilities.

Joint-custody parents are also more likely to come from a burned-out marriage. They are likely to neither love nor hate their ex-spouse but to be able to detail rationally with her or him. Parents who fight for sole custody are more likely to dislike or hate their ex-spouse (DeFrain, Fricke, & Elmen, 1987).

Divorce and Children

There have been numerous studies on the effects of divorce on children (Amato, 1993; Demo & Acock, 1991; Hetherington & Stanley-Hagan, 1995; Wallerstein & Blakeslee, 1989). These studies suggest three conclusions regarding the effects of divorce on children. First, divorce is a very difficult crisis in the lives of the vast majority of children who experience it. Most children grieve over the divorce and wish it were not happening. This is especially true in the case of marriage devitalization or burn-out, in which the divorce may have come as a complete surprise to the children (Hetherington & Stanley-Hagan, 1995; Wallerstein & Blakeslee, 1989).

Second, many are angry at their parents, and many are angry at themselves. One 11-year-old girl we know told this story:

> My best friend's parents got a divorce, and I felt so sorry for her. I imagined once what it would be like if my parents got a divorce, I did this so I could understand what my friend was going through. Then when my parents got a divorce, I felt so guilty. I thought they got a divorce because I had imagined they got one.

When parents break up, children often feel responsible. It takes sensitive parents to help guide the children through their grief. Some parents, overburdened with their own anger and sadness, are of little help to their children (Wallerstein & Blakeslee, 1989).

Third, although divorce is difficult for almost all children, subjection to long-term marital hostilities is even worse (Amato, 1993; Amato & Keith, 1991). After reviewing many studies of the effects of divorce on children, White (1991) concluded that family discord has more of a negative impact on children than the type of marital structure in which they live. In essence, a stable one-parent family is better than an unstable two-parent family. A tension-filled home can have negative consequences for all living there. Children respond to this type of environment with depression, anger, troubles in school, and various physiological symptoms (Hetherington & Stanley-Hagan, 1995; see also Peterson & Hann, Chapter 13, Faust & McKibben, Chapter 17, and Steinmetz, Chapter 14, this volume).

Stepfamilies

The stepfamily, in which one or both of the married adults have children from a previous union with primary residence in the household, is not a new family pattern. We have chosen to use the term stepfamily in this chapter, rather than blended family, agreeing with the reasons provided by Emily Visher and John Visher (1992). First and foremost, the label fosters unrealistic expectations that the new family will quickly and easily blend together into a harmonious family. Second, the term assumes a homogeneous unit without previous history or background.

The terms stepfamily and stepparent, on the other hand, have suffered from a number of stereotypes, often bringing to mind childhood fairy-tale visions of "wicked stepmothers." Most stepparent–stepchild relationships, however, function relatively well (Coleman & Ganong, 1991; Ganong & Coleman, 1994).

Before the dramatic increase of divorce in American society, however, stepfamilies traditionally followed the widowhood of one or both spouses. Today the great majority of those who divorce marry again and many of these remarriages involve children (Cherlin & Furstenberg, 1994). Bumpass, Raley, and Sweet (1995) argue that if researchers broaden the definition of stepfamilies to include single parents who are cohabitating for a long time but do not marry, then they will find stepfamilies are "extremely common in the U.S. at this time. About 40% of all women and 30% of all children will spend some time in a stepfamily situation" (p. 425).

Few people marry with the expectation that they will divorce, but the odds are reasonably good that this will happen (see Faust & McKibben, Chapter 17, this volume, for a discussion of divorce). Despite the prevalence of divorce, which may be a positive change for a particular family, our society still sees it as a tragedy and as a sign of the breakdown of the American family (Popenoe, 1993). However, divorce can also be viewed by some as the first step in a journey of healing and growth that has led to satisfying single life or, perhaps, a successful marriage to a new partner. In the words of Paul Bohannan (1970), "Divorcees are people who have not achieved a good marriage. They are also people who would not settle for a bad one" (p. 54).

Although marriage continues to be popular, with up to 90% of adults marrying at least once, the likelihood of these marriages being successful is only about 50%. Some researchers argue that the 50% rate may be too conservative for future estimates, predicting that two-thirds of all marriages in the United States today will end in divorce (Martin & Bumpass, 1989); for second marriages (about 75% of divorced individuals remarry), the divorce rate is even higher

(Glick & Lin, 1986). As research has indicated, single parents who marry again must subsequently face the challenge of developing a stepfamily system that works (Cherlin & Furstenberg, 1994; Ganong & Coleman, 1994).

Phases in the Formation of a Stepfamily

People whose marriage has unraveled are often quite careful about entering into another marriage. Divorced individuals are likely to be skeptical about the institution of marriage and are often more open to premarital and marital counseling. As one remarried man put it, "I take my car in for a tune-up every year, and I know our relationship could use some help at times also" (Olson & DeFrain, 1997, p. 543).

People go through three steps in the process of forming a new family through remarriage: (1) entering a new relationship, (2) planning the new marriage and family, and (3) remarriage and reconstitution of the family (Carter & McGoldrick, 1988; McGoldrick & Carter, 1980).

Phase 1, Entering the New Relationship. Before beginning this stage, divorced individuals should feel that they have recovered from the loss of the first marriage. A full recovery from a crisis like divorce can take a long time, and many people remarry before they have completely recovered from their divorce. If bonding to the second partner is to succeed, however, one must be divorced both "emotionally" as well as legally from the initial partner.

The major developmental issue during this step of the process is a recommitment to the institution of marriage and to the idea of forming a new partnership and family. Before marrying again, individuals need to decide whether they want a new intimate relationship that requires closeness and personal commitment.

Phase 2, Planning the New Marriage and Family. In the second step of the remarrying process, individuals must learn to accept their own fears, the fears of the spouse-to-be, and the concerns of all the children involved about the new marriage and formation of a stepfamily. This step also requires acceptance of the fact that it takes a good deal of time and patience for people to adjust to the complexity and ambiguities of a new family (Ganong & Coleman, 1994).

One difficulty during this phase is dealing with multiple new roles: that of being a new spouse, a new stepparent, and a new member of a new extended family. Other complexities include adjustments that will need to be made in terms of space, time, membership, and authority. Further complexities and ambiguities that must be dealt with in the affective area include feelings of guilt, loyalty conflicts, the desire for mutuality, and unresolvable past hurts (Ganong & Coleman,

1994). Individuals planning to marry again often feel guilty because they must spend time and energy developing relationships with members of their soon-to-be family, often at the expense of time spent with the "old" family. This was acknowledged by one new stepfather, who stated, "By spending so much time, money, and energy on my new spouse and stepchildren, I am neglecting my biological children" (Olson & DeFrain, 1997, p. 543).

In this second step of planning the new marriage and family, a number of developmental issues or tasks must be addressed. All members of the new family must work to build open, honest, straightforward communication patterns in order to avoid pseudomutuality—a false sense of togetherness. Other issues include building and planning to maintain cooperative coparenting relationships with ex-spouses, for the benefit of all parents and the children. It is also necessary to realign relationships with both extended families so that there is a place for the new spouse. If family members can manage to do all these things relatively well, the remarriage will have a better chance of succeeding.

Phase 3, Marriage and Reconstitution of the Family. In the third step of the process of forming a new family, the newly married partners need to strengthen their couple relationship so that they can function as coparents. Family members need to see that the new marriage is genuine and that the stepfamily initiated by a couple is becoming "a good family" in its own right.

There are a number of developmental issues or tasks in this third step of the remarriage process. Family boundaries must be restructured to include the new spouse/stepparent. Relationships throughout the different subsystems of the "old" families may need to change to permit the interweaving of this new family system. In short, there must be room in the family for stepchildren, half-siblings, new sets of grandparents, and extended kin. It is also important to make room for relationships between all the children and their biological (noncustodial) parents, grandparents, and other extended family members. Sharing memories and histories of each side of the new stepfamily can enhance integration.

"Blending" or "reconstituting" or "reorganizing" families with children after divorce and remarriage is very difficult. Stepparents face many challenges in dealing with the offspring of their new spouse (Ahrons & Rodgers, 1987; Burt, 1989; Cherlin & Furstenberg, 1994; Ganong & Coleman, 1994; LeMasters & DeFrain, 1989; Visher & Visher, 1988).

Stepparents, by assuming many of the childrearing responsibilities formerly held by a biological parent, can find themselves either overidealized by their stepchildren or the victims of displaced hostility (Visher & Visher, 1979, 1988,

1992). Because our culture considers biological family ties to be special, as the adage "Blood is thicker than water" connotes, biological bonds, even when dysfunctional, are difficult to break (Hetherington & Henderson, 1997; Hetherington & Stanley-Hagan, 1995; Visher & Visher, 1988, 1992). Since it is not unusual for children of divorced parents to hope that their parents will reunite, the remarriage of one of the parents can produce despair and bitterness toward the stepparent, who has become the villain in the child's mind (Visher & Visher, 1988, 1992).

Greif (1995) notes that daughters may develop an almost "wifelike" relationship, serving as confidant and household manager for her father during the single-parent period. When the father remarries, the daughter loses her privileged status and may view the stepmother as competitor (Hetherington & Stanley-Hagan, 1995). Attempting to replace the former parent (Ganong & Coleman, 1994; Hetherington & Stanley-Hagan, 1995) or trying to be "superparent" (Hetherington & Henderson, 1997; Hetherington & Stanley-Hagan, 1995) are problematic ways to approach stepparenthood. Stepparents in families with both biological and stepchildren have the additional challenge of avoiding favoritism when dealing with "his," "hers," and "their" children (Visher & Visher, 1988, 1992).

In stepfamilies, financial problems can arise when former spouses or partners do not comply with child support arrangements, placing additional financial burdens on the new family (Ihinger-Tallman & Pasley, 1987). Ganong and Coleman (1994) note that loyalty issues can develop, particularly with adolescents, when there is greater loyalty to the biological parent than the stepparent who may have the day-to-day responsibility for the child.

One study compared 24 stepfamilies and 24 first-marriage families on the three dimensions of family cohesion, flexibility, and communication from the Circumplex Model (Pink & Wampler, 1985) using the Family Adaptability and Cohesion Evaluation Scales (FACES II) (Olson, Portner, & Bell, 1986). Family communication was assessed using the Parent–Adolescent Communication Scale (Barnes & Olson, 1986). All stepfamily members reported lower family cohesion and lower flexibility than did the members of first-marriage families.

Poorer father–adolescent communication was prevalent in stepfamilies compared to first-marriage families as rated by the fathers from both of these family types. There were no differences, however, when the adolescents' communication ratings were used. There were no significant differences in mother–adolescent communication between the stepfamilies and the first-marriage families. The reason could be, in part, that the mother was the biological parent in both types of families, whereas that was not the case with the fathers.

MacDonald and DeMaris (1995) assessed marital conflict in a nationally representative sample of 2655 married couples representing both biological and stepfamilies and found that remarried couple's stepchildren do not report more frequent marital conflict, and in some cases are less inclined to do so, than children in biological families.

Despite limitations in the research including failure to account for the complexity in terms of extra "family" members, the use of small samples, and relying on self-report questionnaires typically from only one member of the family (Cherlin & Furstenberg, 1994; Coleman & Ganong, 1991; Ganong & Coleman, 1994; Hetherington & Stanley-Hagan, 1995), Coleman and Ganong (1991) concluded that there is little reported evidence that children in stepfamilies differ significantly from children in other family structures in terms of self-image, psychosomatic illness, or personality characteristics. They also report that stepchildren also are comparable to children in nuclear families in regard to school grades, academic achievement scores, and IQ. Stepchildren do not have more problems in the area of social behavior than do children in nuclear families. Finally, although close emotional bonds between stepparents and stepchildren tended to be less close than bonds between biologically related parents and children, most stepchildren indicate that they like their stepparents and get along well with them.

Changing Gender Roles, Dual-Career Families, and Coparenting

One final striking change among contemporary American families is the increasing proportion of families with mothers in the labor force. By the year 2000, an estimated 61.6% of all women in the United States will be working outside the home, an increase from 57.5% in 1990 and 43.3% in 1970 (U.S. Bureau of the Census, 1994, p. 395).

An examination of changing employment patterns among "traditional" families in which the father works full-time and the mother is at home full-time was found to be a common but not particularly dominant family type represented by 33% of families. A larger number of families, 45%, have fathers working full-time outside the home and mothers working full-time or part-time. The remainder consist of employed single mothers (17%), employed single fathers (2%), and families in which neither parent is employed (3%).

There are differing viewpoints on the advantages and disadvantages of the trend of mothers in the labor force. Although the added stress of two jobs or careers within families can lead to problems in marital and parent–child relations and an increased likelihood of divorce, a second income helps stabilize the family economically, increases the self-esteem of the mother, and helps balance power more equitably. In a similar vein, while some individuals focus on the inability or resistance of many fathers to become actively involved in childcare and housework, others point out how many fathers have risen to the challenge, developing excellent relationships with their children (Gottfried, Gottfried, & Bathurst, 1995).

Parsons' (1965; Parsons & Bales, 1955) dichotomy of men fulfilling "instrumental" roles and women fulfilling the "expressive" has been attacked by numerous critics, and it is no longer a dominant theory of the family (Kingsbury & Scanzoni, 1993). Today, it is more commonly assumed that both genders are capable and can be successful in a variety of roles at home and at work. Not only can women be independent, strong, logical, and task-oriented, but men can be nurturing, sensitive, cooperative, and detail-oriented. Perhaps most importantly, however, men and women can both benefit by learning from each other and by becoming more interdependent (Beal, 1994; Lipman-Blumen, 1984; Maccoby, 1990).

Androgyny

Androgyny, which refers to a blending of traditional masculinity and traditional femininity in the same individual, is a "newly discovered old concept," according to Ellen Piel Cook (1985, p. 18). (See Table 3 for a listing of androgynous, masculine and feminine characteristics.) Jung believed the integration of masculinity and femininity was essential to the development of personal wholeness (Olds, 1981).

Diana Safilios-Rothschild (1976) speculated that gender-typed men and women tend to see members of the other gender as people to be manipulated rather than as partners in give-and-take relationships. To maintain control, macho men learn not to express their feelings or to let themselves become dependent on others. Highly feminine women, on the other hand, often believe that the only way to relate successfully with men is to flirt, tease, and use other so-called feminine wiles to gain power.

Sandra Bem (1974; 1981a,b), a pioneer in the development of an instrument to measure psychological androgyny, suggested in her book *The Lenses of Gender: Transforming the Debate on Sexuality Inequality* (1993) that the concepts of masculinity and femininity be dropped altogether because they are cultural constructs rather than biological realities. Bem's perspective is inconsistent with some contemporary feminist thought (Osmond & Thorne, 1993; Thompson & Walker, 1989, 1995) that advocates the "woman-centered voice" (Bem, 1993, p. 192).

Studies have found that people who had a good balance of both masculine and feminine characteristics were more loving than those who were stereotypically "macho" or feminine (Stark, 1985). An androgynous parent, for example, would be one who could be both expressive-affectional when the situation demanded it and instrumental-adaptive at other times (DeFrain, 1975, 1979; Parke, 1996).

Many feminists have called for men to become more active in childrearing (Olson & DeFrain, 1997; Osmond & Thorne, 1993; Thompson & Walker, 1989, 1995). Influenced by these voices, a number of men responded with criticisms of conventional American fatherhood (Parke, 1996). They argued that fathers suffer from the inattention and emotional sterility of a life consumed by "careerism" at the expense of family and described the dreariness of the working world for fathers.

Egalitarian Roles

Research indicates that younger couples are more egalitarian than older couples in their beliefs, feelings, and attitudes about marital and family roles. Olson and colleagues (1989) examined egalitarian versus traditional values and

Table 3. Characteristics of Androgynous, Masculine, and Feminine People

Androgynous (both male and female)	Masculine
High on friendly-dominance	High on hostile-dominance
Outgoing, social, high in leadership, responsible, mature, high achieving, concerned about others	Low on dependency
Attribute generally positive characteristics to themselves	Leadership-oriented, domineering, egotistical, demanding, temperamental
Highest on self-esteem measure	Lowest on self-reported anxiety
Rated by others as most likable and well-adjusted	Low on nurturant behaviors
Seen as highly attractive (especially by women)	Feminine
High rating in assertion skills	High on friendly-submissiveness
More self-disclosing to a variety of people	Conforming, nonassertive, question ability to handle themselves
Prefer egalitarian marriages and having an androgynous spouse	Less independent
	Indirect approach to influencing others

Source: Adapted by permission from Cook (1985), pp. 99–101. Copyright 1985 by E. P. Cook.

roles with a sample of 1000 couples at seven stages in the family life cycle. They found that young couples without children were the most egalitarian in their views, with these views decreasing steadily thereafter and reaching the lowest point among retired couples.

Despite many changes in gender roles, old patterns persist. American couples still tend to exhibit highly gender-segregated family work patterns. In the home, men tend to do "men's work," and women tend to do "women's work." One research team found that, for families to achieve gender equality in the division of labor, "American males would have to reallocate 60 percent of their family work time to other tasks" (Blair & Lichter, 1991, p. 91). In a similar vein, other researchers have found that women carry a larger share of the responsibility for the children and childcare than do men (Leslie, Anderson, & Branson, 1991).

In many families, however, both fathers and mothers take a major responsibility for rearing children. In a *USA Today* poll 56% of the males and 46% of the females said both parents take primary responsibility for the children (Ehrlich, 1984). *USA Today* found that financial management was divided relatively equally, according to husbands but not according to wives. Thirty-nine percent of the husbands said they took primary responsibility for money matters in the family, 41% said their wives took primary responsibility, and 19% said both spouses shared this responsibility. When the wives were questioned, 25% said their husbands took primary responsibility for money matters, 53% said they themselves took responsibility, and 22% said the responsibility was shared.

Household chores—cooking, washing, and cleaning—were the most clearly gender-segregated tasks for families in the *USA Today* study. Fourteen percent of the men said they did the most household chores, 86% of the men said their wives did, and no men said the division of labor was equal. Similarly, 7% of the women said their husbands did most of the household chores, 93% said they themselves did most of the chores, and no women said the division of labor was equal. Twenty-two percent of the women in the study felt their husbands should do more housework, and 9% of the husbands felt their wives should do more housework (Ehrlich, 1984).

Blumstein and Schwartz (1983), in a survey of nearly 3000 couples, found that even among couples where the wives were employed women still bear almost all the responsibility for the housework. Although husbands of women who are employed did help out more around the house than husbands of homemakers, the contribution was minimal. And even if a husband was unemployed, he still did much less housework than a wife who was working a 40-hour week (Blumstein & Schwartz, 1983).

Although attitudes are changing, housework may be the last bastion of tradition in American families (Perry-Jenkins & Folk, 1994). Blumstein and Schwartz (1983) found that even among couples who professed egalitarian ideals, the reality was that the women did most of the housework. Working-class husbands, in particular, did not believe they should be equal partners in domestic activities, and thus did little housework. Among middle-class and upper-middle-class couples, Blumstein and Schwartz found two common patterns: In two-career couples in which the husband encourages the wife to work outside the home to contribute to the family income, husbands share some of the housework. When only the husband works outside the home, however, the wife does most of the housework herself.

Arlie Hochschild (1989) interviewed 50 two-job couples and found that most men do not really do much child-rearing, cooking, cleaning, food shopping, or enough other chores. In her book, *The Second Shift*, she described wives who plan domestic schedules and activities for their children while driving home from the office. Upon arrival at home, the women begin a second shift of work. Hochschild notes that these women looked so exhausted that "at least for two-career couples who are trying to raise children ... the information should be withheld from the young, or the race may not reproduce" (p. 62). Men shared housework equally with their wives in only 20% of the two-job families. Women who "do it all" tend to suffer chronic exhaustion, low sex drive, and more frequent illness, with the result being that both partners forfeit their health, happiness, and often the vitality of their marriage.

Ongoing polls by the Roper Organization over the past 20-plus years have indicated that women's anger at men has risen steadily. Relationships between the sexes have become more combative as more women have begun working outside the home. In 1970, 70% of women surveyed believed that "most men are basically kind, gentle, and thoughtful." In 1989, only 50% of the women believed that statement to be true (Gallup, 1989).

In gay and lesbian couples, equality may be somewhat easier. Because both partners are the same gender, they do not have to contend with traditional gender-role stereotypes and thus may be more free to create a fair and equal division of labor in the home (Blumstein & Schwartz, 1983; Demo & Allen, 1996).

Coparenting

A growing number of parents have adopted a cooperative approach to parenting. Traditional family roles, in which father was the provider and mother the nurturer and in which father was "tough" and mother "tender" are changing. More mothers are working outside the home, while more men are sharing in parenting tasks. An increasing number of mothers are providing income for their families and enjoying the connection to the world outside the home, and an increasing number of fathers are experiencing the joy of watching their children grow and learn (Olson & DeFrain, 1997, p. 405).

Researchers have found a number of advantages to the shared-parenting model. Parents in these situations maintain that they are quite satisfied with their marriages and family lives, arguing that they get along better with their spouses than they did before they adopted the approach and that their relationships with their children have improved. Adopting attitudes favoring coparenting has had a positive effect on marriages because it frees men to spend more time relating to, caring for, and relaxing with their children and at the same time frees women to pursue outside interests. Both parents have much to gain from active involvement in their children's growth (DeFrain, 1979; Schwartz, 1994). In one father's words, "Parenthood is too important and too much fun to be left up to one person" (Olson & DeFrain, 1997, p. 405).

Another important benefit of this approach is that it brings fathers into the family on an emotional level. Some observers have concluded that fathers often "draw on their life at home to take care of their emotional needs, but ... distance themselves from the emotional needs of other family members" (Larson & Richards, 1994).

Conclusion

Each moment of our lives within the most intimate of environments, the family, can be a creative act. Living with our loved ones gives us countless opportunities to exercise our artistic capacities as we weave the tapestry of our journey together.

Sometimes our creations seem to work for us, causing pleasure and a sense of connection. Sometimes our creations seem to flop, causing pain and feelings of alienation. All of our efforts can be seen as important features of the overall tapestry. Although we may not choose to try a particular approach in our intimate relationships again, given a less-than-fruitful result, it is difficult to argue that the experience was not valuable, because we usually have learned important lessons about ourselves and our loved ones. In essence, we say about these experiments in human relations, "I wouldn't take a million dollars for that experience, and I wouldn't do it again for a million dollars either."

Much of the writing on families over the years has taken a different approach. Rather than using metaphors of art, experiment, and creation, the metaphors have often been framed in more stark, simplistic, and often apocalyptic terms: Is the family doomed? Is the family dying? What is the *best* way to live in a family? What is the *best* kind of family?

and so forth. Frankly, we find these questions and their shrill negative implications quite tiresome. They don't evoke in us much curiosity, even as they leap out at us in large newsstand type or television glare. They may sell magazines, but they miss the point.

In this chapter we have focused on six important developments affecting many families today: (1) singlehood as a viable alternative to marriage; (2) cohabitation becoming commonplace and being seen as a normative stage in the dating and mate-selection processes; (3) the increase in voluntary childlessness; (4) the rapid increase in single-parent families; (5) the rapid increase in stepfamilies; and (6) changing gender roles, reflected in the rapid increase in dual-career families and coparenting.

We see these developments as potentially creative and positive acts by countless individuals and families who are trying to live their lives in meaningful and creative ways. In the final analysis, whether or not these individual experiments "work" can only be decided by the creators themselves. And although it is currently popular to comment that we are developing new, diverse forms of families, it is probably more likely that we have always had a good measure of diversity in our culture. The difference is that the diversity is more visible, and we seem to be moving slowly but steadily toward broader acceptance of these contemporary families. Instead of one accepted family pattern, the Parsonian family of tradition, we are becoming a society in which multiple patterns of family living are gaining credibility. Because many types of families have proven their viability over time, it is now possible to argue that these examples of diversity have "staying power." We may be entering a long overdue historical period in which variety in family patterns and relationships has gained substantial acceptance in our society.

References

Adams, M. (1976). *Single blessedness: Observations on the single status in married society*. New York: Basic Books.

Ahrons, C., & Perlmutter, M. (1982). The relationship between former spouses: A fundamental subsystem in the remarriage family. In J. C. Hanson & L. Messinger (Eds.), *Therapy with remarriage families* (pp. 31–46). Rockville, MD: Aspen.

Ahrons, C., & Rodgers, R. H. (1987). *Divorced families: A multidisciplinary view*. New York: Norton.

Amato, P. R. (1993). Children's adjustment to divorce: Theories, hypothesis, and empirical support. *Journal of Marriage and the Family, 55*, 23–38.

Amato, P. R., & Keith, B. (1991). Parental divorce and adult well-being: A meta-analysis. *Journal of Marriage and the Family, 53*, 43–58.

Barkas, J. L. (1980) *Single in America*. New York: Atheneum.

Barnett, L. D., & MacDonald, R. H. (1976, Winter). A study of the membership of the National Organization for Non-Parents. *Sociology Biology, 23*, 297–310.

Barnes, H., & Olson, D. H. (1986). Parent-adolescent communication. In D. H. Olson, H. I. McCubbin, H. Barnes, A. Larsen, M. Muxen, & M.

Wilson (Eds.), *Family inventories* (pp. 51–67). St. Paul: University of Minnesota, Family Social Science.

Baum, F., & Cope, D. R. (1980). Some characteristics of intentionally childless wives in Britain. *Journal of Biosocial Science, 12*(3), 287–299.

Beal, C. R. (1994). *Boys and girls: The development of gender roles.* New York: McGraw-Hill.

Beckman, L. F., & Houser, B. B. (1982). Consequences of childlessness on the social-psychological well-being of older women. *Journal of Gerontology, 37,* 243–250.

Bell, J. E., & Eisenberg, N. (1985). Life satisfaction in midlife childless and empty-nest men and women. *Lifestyles, 7*(3), 146–155.

Bem, S. L. (1974). The measurement of psychological androgyny. *Journal of Consulting and Clinical Psychology, 42*(2), 155–162.

Bem, S. L. (1981a). The BSRI and gender schema theory: A reply to Spence and Helmreich. *Psychological Review, 88,* 369–371.

Bem, S. L. (1981b). Gender schema theory: A cognitive account of sex typing. *Psychological Review, 88,* 354–364.

Bem, S. L. (1993). *The lenses of gender: Transforming the debate on sexual inequality.* New Haven, CT: Yale University Press.

Bernstein, B. E. (1977, October). Legal problems of cohabitation. *The Family Coordinator,* 361–366.

Blair, S. L., & Lichter, D. T. (1991). Measuring the division of household labor: Gender segregation of housework among American couples. *Journal of Family Issues, 12*(1), 91–113.

Blumstein, P. W., & Schwartz, P. (1983). *American couples.* New York: Morrow.

Bohannan, P. (1970). The six stations of divorce. In P. Bohannan (Ed.), *Divorce and after* (pp. 29–55). New York: Doubleday.

Bram, S. (1985). Childlessness revisited: A longitudinal study of voluntarily childless couples, delayed parents, and parents. *Lifestyles, 8*(1), 46–66.

Bumpass, L. L., Raley, R. K., & Sweet, J. A. (1995). The changing character of stepfamilies: Implications of cohabitation and nonmarital childbearing. *Demography, 32,* 425–437.

Burt, M. (Ed.). (1989). *Stepfamilies stepping ahead* (3rd ed.). Lincoln, NE: Stepfamilies Press.

Callan, V. J. (1985). Perceptions of parents, the voluntarily and involuntarily childless: A multidimensional scaling analysis. *Journal of Marriage and the Family, 47*(4), 1045–1050.

Carter, B., & McGoldrick, M. (Eds.). (1988). *The changing family life cycle: A framework for family therapy* (2nd ed.). New York: Gardner.

Cherlin, A. J., & Furstenberg, F. F. (1994). Stepfamilies in the United States: A reconsideration. *Annual Review of Sociology, 20,* 359–381.

Coleman, M., & Ganong, L. H. (1991). Remarriage and stepfamily research in the 1980s: Increased interest in an old family form. In A. Booth (Ed.), *Contemporary families: Looking forward, looking back* (pp. 192–207). Minneapolis: National Council of Family Relations.

Cook, E. P. (1985). *Psychological androgyny.* New York: Pergamon.

Cooper, P. E., Cumber, B., & Hartner, R. (1978). Decision-making patterns and postdecision adjustment of childfree husbands and wives. *Alternative Lifestyles, 1*(2), 71–94.

Crispell, D. (1993, October). Planning no family, now or ever. *American Demographics, 15*(10), 23–25.

DeFrain, J. (1974, October 26). *A father's guide to parent guides: Review and assessment of the paternal role as conceived in the popular literature.* Paper presented at the annual meeting of the National Council on Family Relations.

DeFrain, J. (1975). *The nature and meaning of parenthood.* Unpublished doctoral dissertation, University of Wisconsin, Madison.

DeFrain, J. (1979, April). Androgynous parents outline their needs. *The Family Coordinator,* 237–243.

DeFrain, J., & Eirick, R. (1981). Coping as divorced single parents: A comparative study of fathers and mothers. *Family Relations, 29,* 264–273.

DeFrain, J., Fricke, J., & Elmen, J. (1987). *On our own: A single parent's survival guide.* Lexington, MA: Lexington Books/Simon & Schuster.

DeFrain, J., Fricke, J., & Elmen, J. (1987). *On our own: A single parent's survival guide.* Lexington, MA: D.C. Heath/Lexington Books.

Degler, C. N. (1980). *At odds.* New York: Oxford University Press.

DeMaris, A., & Rao, K. V. (1992). Premarital cohabitation and marital stability. *Journal of Marriage and the Family, 54,* 178–190.

Demo, D. H., & Acock, A. C. (1991). The impact of divorce on children. In A. Booth (Ed.), *Contemporary families: Looking forward, looking back* (pp. 162–191). Minneapolis: National Council on Family Relations.

Demo, D., & Allen, K. P. (1996). Sincerity within lesbian and gay families: Challenges and implication for family and research. *Journal of Personal and Social Issues, 3*(3), 415–434.

Denneny, M. (1979). *Lovers: The story of two men.* New York: Avon.

Ehrlich, H. (1984, December 31). Double duty for moms: Keeping house and a job is a strain. *USA Today,* p. 1.

Elias, J. (1985, February 7). Most singles are enjoying life to fullest. *USA Today,* p. D1.

Eshleman, J. R. (1997). *The family.* Boston: Allyn and Bacon.

Flynn, G. (1996). Backlash: Why single employees are angry. *Personnel Journal, 75*(9), 58–66.

Gallup, Inc. (1989). *Love and marriage.* Lincoln, NE: Author.

Ganong, L. H., & Coleman, M. (1994). *Remarried family relationships.* Thousand Oaks, CA: Sage.

Glick, P., & Lin, S. L. (1986). More young adults are living with their parents: Who are they? *Journal of Marriage and the Family, 48,* 107–112.

Greif, G. L. (1995). Single fathers with custody following separation and divorce. *Marriage and Family Review, 20*(1/2), 213–232.

Gustavus, S. O., & Henley, J. R. (1971). Correlates of voluntary childlessness in a select population. *Social Biology, 18,* 277–284.

Hall, D. R. (1996). Marriage as a pure relationship: Exploring the link between premarital cohabitation and divorce in Canada. *Journal of Comparative Family Studies, 27,* 1–12.

Hall, D. R., & Zhao, J. Z. (1995). Cohabitation and divorce in Canada: Testing the selectivity hypothesis. *Journal of Marriage and the Family, 57,* 421–427.

Hareven, T. (1987). Historical analysis of the family. In M. B. Sussman & S. K. Steinmetz (Eds.), *Handbook of marriage and the family* (pp. 37–57). New York: Plenum.

Hargens, L. L., McCann, J. C., & Reskin, B. R. (1978). Productivity and reproductivity: Fertility and professional achievement among research scientists. *Social Forces, 57,* 154–163.

Hetherington, M. E., & Henderson, L. H. (1997). Fathers in stepfamilies. In M. E. Lamb (Ed.), *The role of the father in child development* (3rd ed., pp. 212–226). New York: Wiley.

Hetherington, M. E., & Stanley-Hagan, M. (1995). Parenting in divorced and remarried families. In M. H. Bornstein (Ed.), *Handbook of parenting: Vol. 3, Status and social conditions of parenting* (pp. 233–254). Hillsdale, NJ: Erlbaum.

Hetherington, M. E., & Stanley-Hagan, M. (1997). The effects of divorce on fathers and their children. In M. E. Lamb (Ed.), *The role of the father in child development* (3rd ed., pp. 191–211). New York: Wiley.

Hochschild, A. (1989). *The second shift.* New York: Viking.

Hunt, M. (1974). *Sexual behavior in the 1970's.* Chicago: Playboy Press.

Ihinger-Tallman, M., & Pasley, K. (1987). *Remarriage.* Newbury Park, CA: Sage.

Janus, S. S, & Janus, C. L. (1993). *The Janus report on sexual behavior.* New York: Wiley.

Kain, E. L. (1990). *The myth of family decline.* Lexington, MA: D.C. Heath.

Keith, P. M. (1983). A comparison of resources of parents and childless men and women in very old age. *Family Relations, 32*(3), 403–409.

Kingsbury, N., & Scanzoni, J. (1993). Structural-functionalism. In P. G. Boss, W. J. Doherty, R. W. LaRossa, W. R. Schumum, & S. K. Steinmetz (Eds.), *Sourcebook of family theories and methods: A contextual approach* (pp. 195–217). New York: Plenum.

Kivett, V. R., & Learner, R. M. (1980). Perspectives of the childless rural elderly: A comparative analysis. *The Gerontologist, 20,* 708–716.

Krishnan, V. (1993). Religious homogamy and voluntary childlessness in Canada. *Sociological Perspectives, 36*(1), 83–94.

Kurdek, L. A. (1994). Areas of conflict among gay, lesbian, and heterosexual couples: What couples argue about influences marital satisfaction. *Journal of Marriage and the Family, 56,* 923–934.

Kurdek, L. A., & Schmitt, J. P. (1986). Early development of relationship quality in heterosexual married, heterosexual cohabiting, gay, and lesbian couples. *Developmental Psychology, 22,* 305–309.

Larson, R., & Richards, M. H. (1994). *Divergent realities: The emotional lives of mothers, fathers, and adolescents.* New York: Basic Books.

LeMasters, E. E., & DeFrain, J. (1989). *Parents in contemporary America: A sympathetic view.* Belmont, CA: Wadsworth.

Leslie, L. A., Anderson, E. A., & Branson, M. P. (1991). Responsibility for children: The role of gender and employment. *Journal of Family Issues, 12*(2), 197–210.

Lewis, R. A., Kozac, E. B., Milardo, R. M., & Grosnick, W. A. (1981). Commitment in same-sex love relationships. *Alternative Lifestyles, 4*(1), 22–42.

Lewis, R., Spanier, G., Atkinson, V. L. S., & Lehecka, C. F. (1977). Commitment in married and unmarried cohabitation. *Sociological Focus, 10*(4), 367–374.

Lichtman, C. H. (1976). *Voluntary childlessness: A thematic analysis of the person and the process.* Unpublished doctoral dissertation, Columbia University Teacher's College, New York.

Lillard, L. A., Brien, M. J., & Waite, L. J. (1995). Premarital cohabitation and subsequent marital dissolution: A matter of self-selection. *Demography, 32*(3), 437–458.

Lipman-Blumen, J. (1984). *Gender roles and power.* Englewood Cliffs, NJ: Prentice-Hall.

MacDonald, W. L., & DeMaris, A. (1995). Remarriage, stepchildren, and marital conflict: Challenges to the incomplete institutionalization hypothesis. *Journal of Marriage and the Family, 57,* 387–398.

Maccoby, E. E. (1990). Gender and relationships: A developmental account. *American Psychologist, 28,* 745–753.

Macklin, E. D. (1980). Nontraditional family forms: A decade of research. *Journal of Marriage and the Family, 42,* 905–922.

Macklin, E. D. (1987). Nontraditional family forms. In M. B. Sussman & S. Steinmetz (Eds.), *Handbook of marriage and the family* (pp. 317–353). New York: Plenum.

Magarick, R. H. (1975). *Social and emotional aspects of voluntary childlessness in vasectomized childless men.* Unpublished doctoral dissertation, University of Maryland, College Park.

Magarick, R. H., & Brown, R. A. (1981). Social and emotional aspects of voluntary childlessness in vasectomized childless men. *Journal of Biosocial Science, 13,* 157–167.

Malmquist, A., & Kaij, L. (1971). Motherhood and childlessness in monozygous twins. Part 2: The influence of motherhood on health. *British Journal of Psychiatry, 118,* 22–28.

Marcks, B. R. (1976). *Voluntary childless couples: An exploratory study.* Unpublished master's thesis, Syracuse University, Syracuse, New York.

Martin, T. C., & Bumpass, L. L. (1989). Recent trends in marital disruption. *Demography, 26,* 37–51.

Masters, W. H., Johnson, V., & Kolodny, R. C. (1988). *Human sexuality* (4th ed.). New York: HarperCollins.

McGoldrick, M., & Carter, E. A. (1980). Forming a re-married family. In E. A. Carter & M. McGoldrick (Eds.), *The family life cycle: A framework for family therapy* (pp. 265–294). New York: Gardner.

Meyer, D. R., & Garasky, S. (1993). Custodial father: Myths, realities, and child support policy. *Journal of Marriage and the Family, 55,* 73–89.

Michael, R. T., Gagnon, J. H., Laumann, E. O., & Kolata, G. (1994). *Sex in America: A definitive survey.* Boston: Little, Brown.

Miller, B. C, & Moore, K. A. (1991). Adolescent sexual behavior, pregnancy, and parenting: Research through the 1980s. In A. Booth (Ed.), *Contemporary families: Looking forward, looking back* (pp. 307–326). Minneapolis: National Council on Family Relations.

Mommsen, K. G. (1973). Differentials in fertility among black doctorates. *Social Biology, 10,* 20–29.

Nason, E. M., & Poloma, M. M. (1976). *Voluntarily childless couples: The emergence of a variant lifestyle.* Beverly Hills, CA: Sage.

Nock, S. L. (1995). A comparison of marriages and cohabiting relationships. *Journal of Family Issues, 17,* 53–76.

Olds, L. (1981). *Fully human.* Englewood Cliffs, NJ: Prentice-Hall.

Olson, D. H., & DeFrain, J. D. (1997). *Marriage and the family: Diversity and strengths* (2nd ed.). Mountain View, CA: Mayfield.

Olson, D. H., Portner, J., & Bell, R. (1986). *FACES II.* St. Paul: University of Minnesota, Family Social Science.

Olson, D. H., McCubbin, H. I., Barnes, H., Larsen, A., Muxen, M., & Wilson, M. (1989). *Families: What makes them work* (2nd ed.). Los Angeles, CA: Sage.

Ory, M. G. (1978). The decision to parent or not: Normative and structural components. *Journal of Marriage and the Family, 40*(3), 531–539.

Osmond, M. W., & Thorne, B. (1993). Feminist theories: The social construction of gender in families and society. In P. G. Boss, W. J. Doherty, R. W. LaRossa, W. R. Schuum, & S. K. Steinmetz (Eds.), *Sourcebook of family theories and methods: A contextual approach* (pp. 591–623). New York: Plenum.

Parke, R. (1996). *Fatherhood.* Cambridge, MA: Harvard University Press.

Parsons, T. (1965). The normal American family. In S. M. Farber, P. Mustacchi, & R. H. L. Wilson (Eds.), *Man and civilization: The family's search for survival* (pp. 31–50). New York: McGraw-Hill.

Parsons, T., & Bales, R. F. (1955). *Family socialization and interaction process.* Glencoe, IL: Free Press.

Perry-Jenkins, M., & Folk, K. (1994). Class, couples, and conflict: Effects of the division of labor on assessments of marriage in dual-earner families. *Journal of Marriage and the Family, 56,* 165–180.

Peterson, K. S., & Lee, F. (1985, March 17). Most find the single life isn't lonely. *USA Today,* p. 1B.

Pink, J. E. T., & Wampler, K. S. (1985). Problem areas in stepfamilies: Cohesion, adaptability and the stepfather–adolescent relationship. *Family Relations, 34,* 327–335.

Popenoe, D. (1993). American family decline, 1960–1990: A review and appraisal. *Journal of Marriage and the Family, 55,* 527–555.

Pupo, A. M. (1980). *A study of voluntary childless couples.* Unpublished doctoral dissertation, U. S. International University, Washington DC.

Ramu, G. N. (1985). Voluntarily childless and parental couples: A comparison of their lifestyle characteristics. *Lifestyles, 7*(3), 131–145.

Rempel, J. (1985). Childless elderly: What are they missing? *Journal of Marriage and the Family, 47*(2), 343–348.

Rettig, K. D., Christensen, D. H., & Dahl, C. M. (1991). Impact of child support guidelines on the economic well-being of children. *Family Relations, 40,* 167–175.

Rhee, J. M. (1973). *Trends and variations in childlessness in the United States.* Unpublished doctoral dissertation, University of Georgia, Athens.

Richards, L. N., & Schmiege, C. J. (1993). Problems and strengths of single-parent families: Implications for practice and policy. *Family Relations, 42,* 277–285.

Ridley, C. A., Peterman, D. J., & Avery, A. W. (1978, April). Cohabitation: Does it make for a better marriage? *The Family Coordinator*, 129–136.

Risman, B. J., Hill, C. T., Rubin, Z., & Peplau, A. (1981). Living together in college: Implications for courtship. *Journal of Marriage and the Family*, 77–83.

Ritchey, P. N., & Stokes, C. S. (1974). Correlates of childlessness and expectations to remain childless. *Social Forces, 52*, 349–356.

Rosenstein, H. (1973, May), On androgyny. *Ms.*, p. 38.

Safilios-Rothschild, D. (1976). A macro- and micro-examination of family power and love: An exchange model. *Journal of Marriage and the Family, 37*, 355–362.

Schoen, R. (1992). First unions and the stability of first marriages. *Journal of Marriage and the Family, 54*, 281–284.

Schwartz, P. (1994, September/October). Peer marriage: What does it take to create a truly egalitarian relationship? *The Family Therapy Networker*, 57–61, 92.

Seccombe, K., & Ishii-Kuntz, M. (1994). Gender and social relationships among the never-married. *Sex Roles, 30*(7–8), 585–604.

Seff, M. (1995). Cohabitation and the law. *Marriage & Family Review, 21*, 3–4.

Seligmann, J. (1993, March 1). The art of flying solo. *Newsweek, 121*(9), 70–73.

Seltzer, K. A. (1994). Consequences of marital dissolution for children. *Annual Review of Sociology, 20*, 235–266.

Shostak, A. (1987). Singlehood. In M. Sussman & S. Steinmetz (Eds.), *Handbook of marriage and the family* (pp. 355–368). New York: Plenum.

Singh, B. K., & Williams, J. S. (1981). Childlessness and family satisfaction. *Research on Aging, 3*, 218–277.

Skolnick, A. (1991). *Embattled paradise: The American family in an age of uncertainty.* New York: Basic Books.

Somers, M. S. (1993). A comparison of voluntarily childfree adults and parents. *Journal of Marriage and the Family, 55*, 643–650.

Stark, E. (1985, June). Androgyny makes better lovers. *Psychology Today*, p. 19.

Stets, J. E. (1991). Cohabiting and marital aggression: The role of social isolation. *Journal of Marriage and the Family, 53*, 669–680.

Stets, J. E. (1993). The link between past and present intimate relationships. *Journal of Family Issues, 14*, 236–260.

Stewart, K. L., & Olson, D. H. (1990). *Predicting premarital satisfaction on PREPARE using background factors.* Unpublished manuscript, PREPARE/ENRICH, Inc., Minneapolis, MN.

Stinnett, N., Stinnett, N., DeFrain, J., & DeFrain, N. (1999). *Creating a strong family.* Lafayette, LA: Howard.

Teachman, J. D., & Polonko, K. A. (1990). Cohabitation and marital stability in the United States. *Social Forces, 69*, 207–220.

Teicholz, J. G. (1977). *A preliminary search for psychological correlates of voluntary childlessness in married women.* Unpublished doctoral dissertation, Boston University School of Education, Boston, MA.

Thoen, G. A. (1977). *Commitment among voluntary childless couples to a variant lifestyle.* Unpublished doctoral dissertation, University of Minnesota, Minneapolis.

Thomson, E., & Colella, U. (1992). Cohabitation and marital stability: Quality of commitment? *Journal of Marriage and the Family, 54*, 259–267.

Thompson, L., & Walker, A. J. (1989). Gender in families. *Journal of Marriage and the Family, 51*, 845–871.

Thompson, L., & Walker, A. J. (1995). The place of feminism in family studies. *Journal of Marriage and the Family, 57*, 847–866.

Toomey, B. G. (1977). *College women and voluntary childlessness: A comparative study of women indicating they want to have children and those indicating they do not want to have children.* Unpublished doctoral dissertation, Ohio State University, Columbus.

U. S. Bureau of the Census. (1992). *Statistical abstract of the United States* (112th ed.). Washington, DC: U.S. Government Printing Office.

U. S. Bureau of the Census. (1994). *Statistical abstract of the United States* (114th ed.). Washington, DC: U.S. Government Printing Office.

U. S. Bureau of the Census. (1995). *Statistical abstract of the United States* (115th ed.). Washington, DC: U.S. Government Printing Office.

Veevers, J. E. (1983). Voluntary childlessness. A critical assessment of the research. In E. E. Macklin & R. Rubin (Eds.), *Contemporary families and alternative lifestyles: Handbook of research and theory* (pp. 48–68). Beverly Hills, CA: Sage.

Veroff, J., Douvan, E., & Kulka, R. A. (1981). *The inner American: A self portrait from 1957 to 1976.* New York: Basic Books.

Visher, E. B. (1989). The Stepping Ahead Program. In M. Burt (Ed.), *Stepfamilies stepping ahead* (3rd ed., pp. 57–89). Lincoln, NE: Stepfamilies Press.

Visher, E. B., & Visher, J. S. (1988). *Old loyalties: New ties.* New York: Brunner/Mazel.

Visher, E. B., & Visher, J. S. (1992). *How to win as a stepfamily* (2nd ed.) New York: Brunner/Mazel.

Wallerstein, J. S., & Blakeslee, S. (1989). *Second chances: Men, women and children a decade after divorce.* New York: Ticknor & Fields.

Watson, R. E. L. (1983). Premarital cohabitation vs. traditional courtship: Their effects on subsequent marital adjustment. *Family Relations, 32*, 139–147.

Weinraub, M., & Gringlas, M. B. (1995). Single parenthood. In M. H. Bornstein (Ed.), *Handbook of parenting: Vol., 3, status and social conditions of parenting* (pp. 66–88). Mahwah, NJ: Erlbaum.

White, L. K. (1991). Determinants of divorce: A review of research in the eighties. In A. Booth (Ed.), *Contemporary families: Looking forward, looking back* (pp. 141–149). Minneapolis: National Council on Family Relations.

CHAPTER 13

Socializing Children and Parents in Families

Gary W. Peterson and Della Hann

Introduction

The classical scientific approach for understanding human social development has been to isolate particular phenomena, examine their components, and identify cause–effect patterns. This tradition, often referred to as positivism, has dominated the study of parent–child relationships in recent decades (Peterson & Rollins, 1987; Stafford & Bayer, 1993). Until quite recently, research on this fundamental aspect of family life was conceptualized largely in isolation from its social context, with parents being viewed as the "socializers and shapers" of the young (Arnett, 1995; Baumrind, 1978; Collins & Repinski, 1994; Maccoby & Martin, 1983; Rollins & Thomas, 1979; Stafford & Bayer, 1993). During the past 2 decades, however, more comprehensive models of the parent–child relationship have received substantial attention (Maccoby, 1992; Peterson & Rollins, 1987).

The first complication for the classical view was the recognition that a unidirectional model with parents viewed as "molding" the development of children was much too limited. Instead, children from infancy to adolescence were increasingly portrayed as active socializers of their parents in complex ways (Ambert, 1992, 1997; Bell & Harper, 1977). The second deviation from "normal science" was the realization that parent–child relationships are complex transactional processes involving reciprocal or simultaneous exchanges of behavior (Peterson & Rollins, 1987; Tronick,

Gary W. Peterson • Department of Sociology, Arizona State University, Tempe, Arizona 85287-2502. **Della Hann** • National Institute of Mental Health, Rockville, Maryland 20857.

Handbook of Marriage and the Family, 2nd edition, edited by Marvin Sussman, Suzanne K. Steinmetz, and Gary W. Peterson. Plenum Press, New York, 1999.

1989). Finally, a third transformation involved rethinking parent–child relationships in terms of connections with larger family systems (Belsky, Rovine, & Fish, 1989; Stafford & Bayer, 1993) and social contexts beyond family boundaries (Bronfenbrenner, 1979; Peterson & Rollins, 1987).

The purpose of this chapter, therefore, is to review and integrate the current research and scholarship on parent–child relationships. Conceptually, the extensive work on this topic has been described earlier in terms of four primary research traditions: (1) parent effects, (2) child effects, (3) reciprocal socialization, and (4) systemic-ecological theory (Peterson & Rollins, 1987). Prior to in-depth considerations of these traditions, this chapter examines the goals of socialization that motivate parents' childrearing strategies, with particular focus on the desire to foster social competence in children, a multidimensional collection of valued psychosocial attributes.

The Parent Effects Perspective

The oldest tradition of parent–child research, the *parent effects perspective*, explores the extent to which parental styles, behaviors, and characteristics contribute to various social and psychological qualities in children (Maccoby & Martin, 1983; Peterson & Rollins, 1987; Rollins & Thomas, 1979). From this unidirectional perspective, parents are conveyers of social reality who "mold" or "shape" the young into either functional or deviant participants in society. Parents serve as social agents who are teachers of social norms, models of behavior, managers of conduct, and providers of children's emotional support (Clarke-Stewart, 1988). Despite frequent criticisms about the limits of parent effects approaches, adherents of this perspective continue to offer compelling ideas that remain prominent in much of the parent–child research. A common justification for this approach is that parents have greater control than children over environmental contingencies and that socialization is primarily an adult-initiated process (Baumrind, 1980; Stafford & Bayer, 1993). Specifically, parents tend to have greater power and to possess socialization goals that are more intentionally focused than their offspring (especially compared to infants and younger children). Another reason is that "parent training," a strategy that assumes a parent effects model, remains that most feasible means of intervening within the parent–child relationship and improving how children are socialized (Clarke-Stewart, 1988). Thus, this section discusses the influence of parent behavior, modeling, and authority as antecedents of social competence in children.

Parental Goals

Before describing how parents influence their offspring, however, it is important to consider how parents' conscious or unconscious goals, beliefs, and expectations function to shape the influence strategies that are chosen to achieve their purposes (Dix, 1991, in press; Okagaki & Divecha, 1993). In the following, three parental goals are described: socialization concerns, parental self-interest, and child-focused concerns.

Socialization Concerns: The First Parental Goal

Perhaps the most important parental goal, *socialization concerns*, are child-centered objectives intended to benefit the young, without necessarily pleasing children as individuals (Dix, in press). Specifically, parents often impose expectations that reflect the normative patterns of society and seek to make children more adaptive to their social environments. That is, children are often expected to cooperate, help, share, and function autonomously, even when they prefer other alternatives. Parents of different societies vary in the extent to which they promote independence, individualism, and self-expression on the one hand, and conformity, connectedness, and collectivism on the other (Arnett, 1995).

An important goal of socialization that governs the behavior of many parents is the intention to foster valued qualities in children that adults believe are adaptive within a particular social context (Arnett, 1995; Baumrind, 1972, 1991; Peterson & Leigh, 1990; Peterson & Rollins, 1987; Rollins & Thomas, 1979). Consequently, many contemporary U.S. parents who value *social competence* in children are more likely to use childrearing behaviors such as firm, rational control combined with nurturance, while deemphasizing arbitrary, punitive, rejecting, and neglectful strategies. Parents who are viewed by the young as having valued resources and "parental competence" (i.e., power) (Peterson & Leigh, 1990) also tend to facilitate the development of social competence in the young.

Although many parents seek to promote social competence, it is a mistake to assume that all parents and families either achieve this goal or are the exclusive cradles of such outcomes in the young. In fact, many families may accomplish just the opposite by serving as the primary wellsprings for "social incompetence" in the form of debilitating dependencies, alienation, violent behavior, substance abuse, conduct disorders, and antisocial behavior (Barber, 1992; Jessor, 1992; Patterson, 1986). While parents vary in their abilities to foster valued social outcomes in children, most have good intentions to encourage socially "competent" rather than socially "incompetent" qualities through their selected parenting strategies. Consequently, social competence is used in this chapter both as a possible socialization goal that parents seek to instill in the young and as a means of conceptualizing many important outcomes of the socialization process (i.e., social competence or incompetence).

Issues in Defining Social Competence. Although an important goal of the social sciences is to develop precise definitions of phenomena that are measurable, the concept of social competence is sufficiently complex so that very general definitions have often been used that are lacking in scientific rigor. Consequently, the failure to develop precise "operational" definitions in favor of more "global" ideas has clouded the meaning of this construct (Peterson & Leigh, 1990). Such general definitions include that of Inkeles (1968), who described "competence" as becoming reasonably responsive to patterns of the social order and the personal requirements of others with whom a person is in contact (i.e., social conformity). Contrasting with this viewpoint is the broader proposal by Zigler and Trickett (1978) that social competence consists of both meeting societal expectations and the extent to which a person experiences self-actualization. Foote and Cottrell (1955), in turn, described *interpersonal competence* as the ability to engage in and control the outcomes of interactive episodes, while White (1959) defines a similar construct as the capacity of organisms to interact effectively with their environment as a product of intrinsic motivation. Finally, Waters and Sroufe (1983) refer to competent individuals as those who make use of environmental and personal resources to achieve good developmental outcomes.

An alternative strategy is the identification of specific components of social competence, without benefit of general integrative definitions. In extreme cases, this "reductionistic approach" has been manifested through such specific indicators of children's social competence as "knowing how and when to follow directions" or "knowing when to share a toy" in interpersonal settings (Burns & Farina, 1984). Consequently this focus on specific components without an overall construct brings to mind the metaphor of "not being able to see the forest for the trees." Perhaps the best approach for understanding social competence, however, is to recognize that the many components of this concept, when considered together, take on a larger meaning (Felner, Lease, & Phillips, 1990). Social competence may be a useful concept precisely because it illuminates important dimensions of children's social development, but it does so only by defying the social scientist's desire for parsimony through its complexity.

General Definitions of Social Competence. As indicated, most conceptions of competence consist of qualities that include, but go well beyond, simply "fitting in" with one's social environment. That is, children and adolescents who are socially competent must also demonstrate adaptive functioning that draws on less predictable responses that are required within interpersonal situations (Waters & Sroufe, 1983). As children develop, therefore, they are increasingly expected to be creative in assessing circumstances, enacting behavior that is socially meaningful, and making constant readjustments to changing interpersonal circumstances. Consequently, social competence is defined as a multidimensional construct consisting of qualities that children and youth demonstrate for (1) successfully meeting the clearer expectations of their social environments (i.e., structured situations) and (2) successively coping with social situations in which the norms and expectations are not well defined (i.e., ambiguous or flexible situations).

Specific Subdimensions of Social Competence. Because such general definitions sketch only the broad parameters of social competence, greater clarity is provided by describing key subdimensions of this concept within "mainstream" Euro-American societies. Specifically, the major components of social competence are: (1) internal or cognitive resources, (2) a balance between sociability and autonomy, and (3) social skills necessary for effective relationships with parents, other adults, and peers (Peterson & Leigh, 1990).

Internal and Cognitive Capacities. Internal and cognitive capacities encompass several attributes that serve as underlying bases for social skills that are needed for effective interpersonal relationships. First, important internal capacities consist of problem-solving or decision-making abilities that become increasingly more sophisticated as the young mature. Children and adolescents who gradually become more socially competent increasingly are capable of (1) being sensitive to interpersonal problem situations, (2) generating alternative solutions, (3) planning to attain

interpersonal goals, (4) weighing consequences in terms of their effectiveness and social acceptability, (5) developing workable courses of action, and (6) making midcourse corrections by using interpersonal feedback to refine goals and strategies (Felner et al., 1990). The effectiveness of children in dealing with problematic interpersonal circumstances is also partially dependent on such internal or cognitive abilities as the development of a positive self-esteem, social perspective-taking, an internal locus of control, and moral development. Specifically, a positive self-esteem provides children with sufficient self-confidence to engage in and expand their social relationships (Baumrind, 1972; Openshaw & Thomas, 1986; Rollins & Thomas, 1979). An internal locus of control, or the feeling of exercising control over one's life, is an internal resource that encourages self-initiative and leadership skills in interpersonal settings (Baumrind, 1972; Stafford & Bayer, 1993). Social perspective-taking (i.e., social role-taking and empathy), on the other hand, is a third resource for social competence by representing the capacity of children to understand and become sensitive to the feelings, intentions, and abilities of others (Baumrind, 1972; Grotevant & Cooper, 1986; Peterson & Leigh, 1990). Closely associated with social perspective-taking is a fourth internal resource— moral development, which promotes an awareness of other's needs, an understanding of the impact of one's actions on others, and a willingness to accommodate one's behavior accordingly (Hoffman, 1982, 1994).

The Balance between Sociability and Autonomy. A second major component of social competence is the seemingly paradoxical but necessary balance between sociability (or togetherness) and autonomy (or individuality) (Arnett, 1995; Peterson, 1995a). Although cultures vary in the precise mix of this balance (Arnett, 1995), these apparently contradictory aspects of the human experience are actually complementary functions that contribute to interpersonal competence during the human life course. Sociability functions, on the one hand, involve the process of connecting with or conforming to significant others—or tendencies toward "communion" in relationships. Examples of sociability include the early formation of an attachment bond during infancy (Ainsworth, 1989; Bowlby, 1988; Bretherton, 1990; Sroufe & Fleeson, 1986) and the continued close ties that older children and adolescents maintain with parents, despite increased pressures for autonomy (Peterson, 1995a; Steinberg, 1990).

The autonomy (or individuality) function, on the other hand, designates the process of becoming unique, differentiated, and having freedom of action from others. Such developments are illustrated by (1) the infant's exploratory behavior through which parents are used as "secure bases" from which they expand into the environment, (2) the obstinate behavior of toddlers who seek greater independence from parents, and (3) the movement during adolescence toward greater autonomy (Ainsworth, 1989; Bowlby, 1988; Bretherton, 1990; Sroufe & Fleeson, 1986). A critical aspect of competence, therefore, is the recognition that social adaptability involves the gradual emergence of an identifiable "self" through emancipation and individuation. This is a form of individuality, however, that is most adaptive when it emerges within social relationships characterized by at least moderate connectedness.

Social Skills. The third major component of social competence, the social skills of children, refers to the extent to which children actually perform interpersonal roles effectively in relation to various significant others. This aspect of social competence focuses on the behavioral repertoires and social skills that the young acquire in relation to peers, parents, and other adults. Consequently, a child's total complement and degree fo flexibility in specific "role-making" skills are involved, such as asking and answering questions, expressing opinions, showing interest in others, joining conversations, and avoiding conflict. Children's social relations with opposite-sex peers, same-sex peers, siblings, parents, and other key adults require increasingly more effective interpersonal capabilities as they develop. A key development is the extent to which children develop interpersonal abilities that enhance their acceptance and status within social groups.

Much of this work, in turn, results from the concern that many children acquire inadequate interpersonal abilities and require intervention for such circumstances as play activities, classroom behavior, excessive aggression, and either ineffective relationships with prosocial peers or growing associations with deviant peers (Brown, Mounts, Lambom, & Steinberg, 1993; Jones, Freeman, & Goswick, 1981; Jones, Hobbs, & Hockenbury, 1982; Parker et al., 1989; Patterson, 1982; Patterson, DeBaryshe, & Ramsey, 1989). Socially withdrawn children also manifest social skill deficits that prevent them from establishing and maintaining effective interpersonal relationships. Finally, youngsters with social skill deficits spend less time in social situations with contemporaries and receive more diminished peer acceptance than their better adjusted counterparts (Patterson et al., 1989). The inverse of these qualities, of course, suggests that socially competent children will engage in effective conversations, play activities, and situational interactions with others, while spending considerable amounts of time with peers.

Variability in Social Competence. Before assuming that the elusive nature of social competence has been captured with these general and specific definitions, several precautions underscore the variability and complexity of this concept. The first source of variability in social competence, situational variability, involves the recognition that the definition of social competence will vary because the requirements for adaptive qualities in one situation will often fail to meet (at least exactly) the expectations of another setting (Goldfried & d'Zurrilla, 1969; Schwartz & Gottman, 1976). Although some continuity in interpersonal skills is needed across situations, almost every setting has at least some features that are idiosyncratic, are subject to interpretations, and require adjustment to changing circumstances. Judgments about social competence must be made, at least partially, in terms of the specific circumstances occurring within distinctive contexts. During both routine or nonroutine activities, the young may misunderstand others, commit faux pas, behave in unpredictable ways, disagree with one another, seek goals in conflict with others, and introduce novelty into situations. Consequently, children and adolescents who are defined as "competent" are those who are adept at reading cues in various social situations, ascertaining the expectations of others, and being open to reinterpretations of situations as circumstances change.

A second source of variability in social competence concerns the idea that particular qualities considered adaptive at one age may change substantially in content by a subsequent time period, yet remain the same concept (Kobak & Sceery, 1988). This idea, referred to as developmental variability, can be illustrated with the concepts "sociability and autonomy," or aspects of social competence referred to earlier. During infancy, for example, the primary form of sociability is the young child's attachment to parents, largely in the form of behavior that seeks proximity and physical contact with their elders. Although attachment persists across time and continues to exist during adolescence and adulthood, it differs extensively from infant attachment by emphasizing less direct means involving diminished physical proximity and contact comfort. That is, attachment during adolescence or early adulthood may be less obvious as the young only intermittently seek security and personal contact (i.e., advice) from parents when facing stressful circumstances through long distance telephone calls (while away at college). In a similar manner, autonomy also retains its meaning at a general level, but changes fundamentally in terms of specific indicators across different developmental periods. Specifically, a toddler may demonstrate autonomy by playing just beyond the parent's view in the next room, while an adolescent may demonstrate independence by engaging in peer activities when "cruising" many miles from home. The overall idea, once again, is that dimensions of social competence retain their general validity, but change substantially over time in terms of their specific indicators. (Other sources of variability in social competence resulting from socioeconomic status [SES], ethnicity, and family structure are discussed throughout this chapter.)

Parental Self-Interest and Child-Focused Goals

Besides the parental goal of fostering social competence, two goals that guide childrearing behavior or influence strategies are (1) parental self-interest and (2) child-focused concerns (Dix, in press). The first of these goals, parental self-interest, reflects the desire of parents to give priority to their own wants, needs, and objectives over those of children. That is, parents are often involved in various endeavors to which they assign considerable value, but, in many cases, are of much less interest to children. For example, mothers and fathers often spend a great deal of time pursuing their career endeavors, dealing with stressful circumstances in their lives, cleaning house, conversing with friends, reading newspapers, and getting children to bed early so they can relax.

Although nothing is inherently wrong with pursuing self-interest in moderation, parents who disproportionately emphasize their own concerns over those of children are more likely to demonstrate a lack of attention to the needs of the young through the childrearing strategies they choose (Dix, 1991, in press). Specifically, parents who are excessively self-interested (or self-oriented) might be more inclined to devote less time to providing nurturance and support to children. Moreover, during conflictual episodes, parents who are preoccupied with their own agendas might devote less energy to the time-consuming process of reasoning with children, while being more inclined to use coercive (or punitive) strategies for dealing with children's behavior as "efficiently" as possible." Other parents who excessively emphasize their own needs might be more inclined to be unresponsive to children, fail to monitor the young adequately, and be neglectful of their offspring's needs. Consequently, because children's wants and needs are inadequately represented in the goal structure of such parents, it is less likely that children will be exposed to parental influence attempts and behaviors that foster beneficial outcomes in the young. Self-interested parents, then, often govern their childrearing behavior with the intention of satisfying their own needs first, rather than those of their children.

Contrasting with self-interested parents, however, are parents whose primary childrearing goal can be characterized as child-focused (Dix, in press); these are parents who organize much of their daily activities around the wants and needs of the young. Child-focused parents seek to make children happy and foster their development by placing high priority on teaching, spending quality time, and engaging in playful activities with the young. These parents devote considerable energy to the process of empathizing with children by attuning themselves to the needs, feelings, and viewpoints of the young (Dix, 1991, in press). Parents who give priority to child-focused goals might be expected to demonstrate childrearing behavior that is more likely to encourage competent development in children. For example, child-oriented parents would be more likely to respond immediately to children's needs through the frequent use of support (nurturance), praise, and encouragement. These parents would be more likely to take sufficient time to reason with and listen to the young, while being less inclined to treat children insensitively through the use of punitive or coercive behavior. Consequently, child-oriented parents govern their socialization behavior with the intention of placing first priority on their children's, not their own, interests.

A balanced position for long-term parental competence, however, is likely to be one involving neither an extreme self-focus nor an extreme child orientation. That is, parents may find it as equally unacceptable to repeatedly sacrifice and frustrate their own needs as to be self-interested and neglectful in reference to the young. Instead, parents who fall somewhere in between these two extremes, with perhaps some leaning toward the child-focused direction, are probably the most effective over the long-term process of raising children. We suspect, then, that parents who focus on their children's welfare, without neglecting their own needs, are likely to experience a balanced sense of well-being in their lives, feelings of satisfaction with parenting, and greater competence in childrearing.

Parental Typologies or Styles

Given that many parents seek to foster socially competent outcomes in children, researchers have devised several means to examine how parents either foster or inhibit these qualities in the young. A common means of conceptualizing parents as socializing agents for the young is through the identification of parental "styles" or "typologies." This school of thought has examined complex collections or blends of controlling, nurturant, and communication behavior (Darling & Steinberg, 1993; Peterson & Rollins, 1987; Smetana & Asquith, 1994; Stafford & Bayer, 1993). One orientation within this tradition has sought to develop configurational or circumplex models that provide classification schemes of various childrearing styles that are formed through combinations of parental behavior (Becker, 1964; Schaefer, 1959, 1965). Consistent with this tradition, Symonds (1939) was perhaps the first to develop such a model with the dimensions of parental acceptance/rejection and dominance/submission (see Maccoby & Martin, 1983; Peterson & Rollins, 1987; Stafford & Bayer, 1993), while other investigators attempted to extend circumplex models from two to three dimensions of parental behavior. Schaefer (1965), for example, identified acceptance/rejection, firm control/lax control, and psychological autonomy/psychological control, whereas Siegelman (1965) preferred the dimensions of loving, demanding, and punishing behaviors for another conception.

One of the most prominent three-dimensional models was Becker's (1964) extension of Symond's (1939) model in which warmth/hostility, restrictiveness/permissiveness, and anxious involvement/calm detachment were identified as aspects of parental childrearing.

Perhaps the most widely known set of parental typologies, however, was developed by Baumrind (1978, 1980, 1991) through her identification of permissive, authoritarian, harmonious, and authoritative patterns of childrearing (Darling & Steinberg, 1993; Stafford & Bayer, 1993). The authoritarian style, for example, refers to the frequent imposition of parental authority through arbitrary or punitive means in combination with low amounts of nurturance. Specific behavioral components of this style consist of high amounts of coercive control, but limited if any use of communication, reasoning (i.e., rational control), and supportive behavior. Permissiveness, on the other hand, designates an approach to childrearing in which the parent serves as a nurturant resource for the young, but refrains from the use of control (either rational or punitive) to shape either the present or future behavior of children. The harmonious parent, in turn, acquires influence without actually seeking to impose his or her will, but rather through exercising egalitarian techniques. Parents who use this style tend to employ substantial amounts of communication and support, but refrain from either rational or punitive control. Finally, the authoritative style involves the application of parental influence in a rational, issue-oriented manner in which verbal give-and-take is encouraged. This approach to parenting provides an atmosphere that favors individual interests of the young, while simultaneously offering considerable nurturance. Authoritative parents tend to communicate effectively and to use high-levels of firm, rational control, while minimizing the use of coercion with the young (Baumrind, 1978, 1991).

Although all of Baumrind's typologies have received considerable attention, the most prominent has been the authoritative style. According to Baumrind (1978, 1991), this style fosters a particular kind of youthful social competence that is associated with success in Western societies. Specifically, social or instrumental competence is defined by such attributes as social responsibility, vitality, independence, achievement, friendliness, and cooperativeness with others. Moreover, in recent articles, Baumrind (1991) has placed substantial emphasis on *interdependence*, or the balance between agency and communion as a crucial aspect of social competence, the hallmark of adaptive children and adolescents.

More research that examines the consequences of parental styles on a greater variety of child and adolescent outcomes is certainly needed. Although operationalized differently from Baumrind's work, for example, current re-

search indicates that parental involvement in schooling and authoritative parenting seem to foster more effective school performance by adolescents (Dornbusch, Ritter, Leiderman, Roberts, & Fraleigh, 1987; Steinberg, Lambom, Dornbusch, & Darling, 1992). Other positive outcomes of authoritative parenting include greater competence, autonomy, and self-esteem (Baumrind, 1989; 1991; Semtana & Asquith, 1994; Steinberg, Mounts, Lamborn, & Dornbush, 1991), less deviance (Baumrind, 1991) and a more well-rounded peer orientation (Durbin, Darling, Steinberg, & Brown, 1993). Recent work has also demonstrated that the problematic consequences of authoritarian parenting for school performance seem to hold up across socioeconomic and family structural variations (Dornbusch et al., 1987). It is important to recognize, however, that while American ideals seem compatible with authoritative parenting but incompatible with authoritarian childrearing, it remains problematic (without further research) to generalize these results beyond American middle- and upper-middle-class parents. Special caution is required when we attempt to transcend the boundaries of SES, ethnicity, and family structure in assessing the adaptiveness of specific parental styles (Darling & Steinberg, 1993) (see the section on the "Systemic-Ecological Perspective").

A serious problem with parental typologies is that none of the models incorporate all of the identified dimensions of parental behavior that are possible, and as such, styles are often unsystematic collections of behavior. Consequently, the existing typologies fail to adequately represent the many childrearing styles that are conceptually possible in the overall population of parents (Peterson & Rollins, 1987; Rollins & Thomas, 1979).

Parental Behavior

Although the study of parental behavior is similar to the work on parental styles, important conceptual distinctions exist between these two traditions of research. Parental typologies or styles, on the one hand, consist of unsystematic collections of parental behavior in which primary concern is devoted to the combined efficacy of several childrearing dimensions in fostering or inhibiting psychosocial outcomes in the young (Maccoby & Martin, 1983; Peterson & Rollins, 1987; Rollins & Thomas, 1979). Other observers take an even broader perspective by defining parental styles as constellations of attitudes communicated to children that create an overall emotional climate within which specific parental behaviors are expressed (Darling & Steinberg, 1993). In contrast, the study of specific parental behavior seeks to examine the extent to which precisely defined childrearing practices are predictors of socially competent (or socially incompetent) outcomes in a manner that distinguishes them from other childrearing behaviors (Darling & Steinberg, 1993).

Since the 1940s, numerous studies and reviews have identified two generic dimensions of parental behavior, support and control, which predict dimensions of youthful social competence or incompetence. The first of these dimensions, parental support, has received such labels as warmth, verbal affection, physical affection, nurturance, and acceptance (Becker, 1964; Rohner, 1986; Rollins & Thomas, 1979; Schaefer, 1959; Siegelman, 1965; Stafford & Bayer, 1993). Although parental support has been studied most often as a unitary dimension, recent investigators are beginning to identify several subdimensions of this variable, including companionship, physical affection, rejection, and general support. As yet, however, only a few studies have compared the relative predictive capacity of these subdimensions on various aspects of youthful social competence or incompetence (Barber & Thomas, 1986; Felson & Zielinski, 1989; Rohner, 1986; Young, Miller, Norton, & Hill, 1995).

The second childrearing dimension, parental control, has been conceptualized in a variety of ways—a tendency that has often contributed to conceptual confusion. For example, parental control has been defined as (1) a specific outcome or characteristic of children that indicates whether or not particular control attempts by parents have been successful (i.e., whether control of the child's behavior is actually achieved), and (2) a general controlling atmosphere or climate (i.e., or overall rule structure) for children's behavior that parents establish (Darling & Steinberg, 1993; Maccoby & Martin, 1983; Peterson & Rollins, 1987; Rollins & Thomas, 1979). The most common definition of control, however, refers to (3) actions used by parents (i.e., control attempts) while attempting to modify the behavior and internal states of children (Peterson & Rollins, 1987). The concern here is with specific behavioral efforts used by parents to influence the young that may or may not be successful.

Partly due to such conceptual confusion, a continual problem has been the large number of inconsistent findings for parental control as a predictor of several dimensions of adolescent social competence (Peterson & Rollins, 1987; Rollins & Thomas, 1979). Consequently, replication problems have stimulated efforts to reconceptualize the control dimension by identifying different kinds of parental influence attempts and the manner in which they predict various aspects of youthful social competence and incompetence (Barber, Olsen, & Shagle, 1994; Hoffman, 1994; Maccoby & Martin, 1983; Peterson & Rollins, 1987; Rollins & Thomas, 1979; Smith, 1983). The most frequently identified subdimensions of parental control have been two types of firm control referred to as induction and monitoring and two types

of excessive control identified as punitiveness and psychological overcontrol.

Firm Control

A key component of childrearing behavior identified during the last 3 decades involves the exercise of influence that teaches self-discipline through firmness, places reasonable demands on children, and eschews the use of autocratic techniques. Today, experts on childrearing and child development often take the view that parents should exercise authority in a manner that provides guidance and sets limits without being punitive. Perhaps the most appropriate basis for the exercise of authority is the superior wisdom, knowledge, and skill of the parent compared to the inexperience of the young. Although a focus of several investigators (Hoffman, 1980; Peterson & Rollins, 1987; Rollins & Thomas, 1979), the most prominent advocate of firm control as a childrearing strategy has been Baumrind (1971, 1978, 1980, 1991), who defines this form of parental influence as the "firm enforcement of rules, effective resistance to the child's coercive demands, and willingness to guide the child by regime and structured interventions" (1971, p. 87).

Several observers (Baumrind, 1978, 1991; Peterson & Leigh, 1990; Peterson & Rollins, 1987; Rollins & Thomas, 1979; Stafford & Bayer, 1993) have argued that firm control is partially responsible for encouraging such aspects of childhood social competence as social responsibility, self-control, autonomy, and self-esteem. For example, two of these dimensions, social responsibility and self-control, are facilitated by parents who use firm control with the young to encourage both external compliance and internalized conformity to the expectations of others (Baumrind, 1978; Higgins, 1991; Peterson, Rollins & Thomas, 1985; Putallaz & Heflin, 1990).

Another feature of social competence, the self-esteem of children, is also viewed as being enhanced by parents who use firm control through the enforcement of clearly defined limits (Coopersmith, 1967). The young seem to gain a clearer concept of themselves when faced with forms of parental control that are viewed as being clear, consistent, and legitimate (Coopersmith, 1967; Felson & Reed, 1986; Openshaw & Thomas, 1986). Parental authority of this kind facilitates self-esteem by contributing to the internalization of values and expectations that, in turn, lead to greater confidence in one's definition of the situation and standards for judging success and failure.

Standard interpretations of parental firm control and its effects on youthful social competence, however, have been challenged from the perspective of attribution theory (Grusec & Goodnow, 1994; Lepper, 1981; Lewis, 1981). Advocates of this position believe that firm control may apply excessive pressure (i.e., functionally superfluous pressure) that is more likely to induce external compliance to authority, rather than encouraging the young to internalize norms and become self-responsible. In contrast, children and adolescents who are exposed to pressure that is "just sufficient" are likely to comply based on internal resources (i.e., the willingness of the child to comply) rather than external inducements (i.e., external control by parents) and, therefore, are less likely to deviate in the absence of external surveillance (Lepper, 1981). Consequently, Lewis (1981) reinterprets much of Baumrind's (Baumrind, 1971) early research as being measures of child compliance that result from the internal responsiveness of the young rather than from the firm control of parents. She further proposes that reciprocal communication rather than the firm control used by authoritative parents is the primary mechanism that fosters social competence in children. Lewis also argues that firm control may not be a necessary antecedent of social competence because many of these outcomes also result from styles of parenting (e.g., the harmonious style) that do not include this form of demanding influence.

Perhaps one means of reconciling such differing viewpoints on parental behavior is to clearly distinguish between the specific kind of control attempt that is used, rather than simply the magnitude of control applied (Baumrind, 1991; Rollins & Thomas, 1979; Stafford & Bayer, 1993). Two dimensions of childrearing behavior that are commonly classified as firm control and seem to foster social competence in children are parental induction and monitoring.

Parental Induction. Parental induction is a type of firm control used by parents in which reason is applied to communicate expectations or rules as a means of influencing the behavior and psychological characteristics of children. Parental control, expressed with a rational component, is intended to help children understand (1) why rules are necessary, (2) why their misbehavior is unacceptable, (3) how their behavior impacts others, and (4) how they might make their behavior more acceptable and make amends for any harm they have done. Frequently, the use of induction may begin as early as the toddler years (Kuczynski, Kochanska, Radke-Yarrow, & Girnius-Brown, 1987) and become increasingly important during late childhood and adolescence (Baumrind, 1991).

Induction is a psychological form of firm control used by parents to explain how a child's actions have either positive or negative consequences for both themselves and others (Hoffman, 1980, 1994; Maccoby & Martin, 1983; Rollins & Thomas, 1979). This behavior is "psychological" in nature as a result of operating on the internal monitors of children as a means of fostering internalization and (eventually) voluntary commitment to expectations from parents and the larger society. Induction is distinguished from punitiveness through the lack of imposing arbitrary authority so that children have opportunities to engage in two-way communication and express viewpoints that differ from their parents' perspectives (Peterson & Rollins, 1987). Contrary to authoritarian behaviors, induction elicits fewer feelings of hostility and resistance from the young. Inductive techniques are more likely to be viewed as "minimally sufficient" control, rather than the "functionally superfluous pressure" communicated through punitive influence attempts (Peterson & Leigh, 1990; Smith, 1986). Correspondingly, parental induction is often viewed as fostering dimensions of social competence that involve expressing concern for others. Prosocial behavior and moral development, for example, are especially facilitated by the use of inductive reasoning that focuses on the consequences of adolescents' actions for others (Higgins, 1991; Hoffman, 1970, 1980, 1994; Stafford & Bayer, 1993). Moral development and prosocial behavior are fostered through inductive explanations that sensitize the young to the internal experiences of others and by helping to "internalize" the parents' rationale (Hoffman, 1980). Consequently, an inductive control attempt is primarily an attempt by parents to persuade or convince the young by calling upon such internal psychological resources of children as rationality, empathy, and pride.

Current research also suggests that parental induction may foster a higher self-esteem in children, an important cognitive resource for social competence (Coopersmith, 1967; Openshaw & Thomas, 1986; Openshaw, Thomas & Rollins, 1983). The use of induction as a childrearing behavior often transmits to the young a recognition of their ability (1) to engage in dialogues with parents, (2) to be treated with respect (i.e., not arbitrarily), (3) to evaluate the consequences of their own behavior for others and themselves, and (4) to make decisions based on these judgments. In short, induction enhances adolescent self-esteem by communicating parental confidence in youthful abilities to understand and cope successfully with the social environment (Peterson & Rollins, 1987; Stafford & Bayer, 1993).

Parental induction also may be an important contributor to the balance that many youngsters establish between autonomy and conformity in reference to parents (Baumrind, 1978, 1980; Peterson & Leigh, 1990; Stafford & Bayer, 1993). Induction may enhance autonomy through influence efforts that refrain from imposing the arbitrary will of parents, while allowing children to assert their own wills and offer perspectives that contrast with parents' viewpoints. Moreover, induction also encourages conformity to parents by communicating behavioral expectations to the young (Rollins & Thomas, 1979). Investigators have reported that youth whose parents use rational control are often both externally compliant when parents are present and internally responsive to parent's expectations for various attitudes and behaviors (Peterson et al., 1985; Putallaz & Heflin, 1990; Stafford & Bayer, 1993).

Parental Monitoring or Supervision. Another aspect of firm control, parental supervision and monitoring (or behavioral control), refers to influence attempts that reflect the extent to which parents are aware of and seek to manage their children's schedules, peer associations, activities, and physical whereabouts (Barber, 1992; Barber et al., 1994; Patterson & Capaldi, 1991; Small, 1990). Early in the parent–child relationship, for example, adults monitor young children by confining them to playpens, keeping them away from dangerous household appliances, and restricting their activities while shopping in department stores. Several years later, parents monitor adolescents by supervising their dating activities, preventing deviant peer associations, being aware of drug use symptoms, and overseeing the kinds of popular media observed by the young (e.g., movies, television programs, and books).

Parental supervision or monitoring (behavioral control) requires that parents maintain a clear set of rules about the time that children should be home from school, when they must return from peer activities, with whom they may associate, and places where youth are forbidden to venture. Effective monitoring also requires that parents verify their children's compliance by "checking up" on them and by implementing discipline when rules are violated. Because the young spend less time with parents and other adults during later childhood and adolescence, monitoring becomes more complicated, but continues to play a critical role in keeping the behavior of children within a normal range (Small, 1990). Although monitoring is an important dimension of firm control that parents use to foster social competence, much of the research has been focused on the contribution of insufficient supervision to higher frequencies of antisocial, delinquent, and externalizing problems (Barber et al., 1994; Patterson & Dishion, 1985). Specifically, deficient monitoring has been associated with fighting, lying, stealing, fire-setting (Patterson, 1982), delinquent behavior (McCord, 1990; Patterson & Bank, 1989), deviant peer associations (Elliot, Huizinga, & Ageton, 1985), sexual precocity (Miller, McCoy, Olson, & Wallace, 1986), and drug use (Dishion & Loeber, 1985). Although not well established in the existing research literature, growing evidence indicates that parental monitoring is related to lower rates of sexual activity, drug and alcohol use, truancy, running away, and delinquency (Barber et al., 1994; Small, 1990). It would appear, therefore, that parents who effectively monitor the young help to foster social competence and prevent the drift of youth into problematic peer associations, troubled involvements, and deviant behavior.

Excessive Parental Control

Besides components of firm control that foster social competence, other forms of parental behavior referred to as *excessive control* appear to inhibit the development of adaptive prosocial qualities in children. These controlling efforts can be viewed as "functionally superfluous pressure" that either places heavy responsibility on parents to control their children's behavior through external compliance or intrudes upon and impedes the individuation process (Barber et al., 1994; Lepper, 1981; Lewis, 1981). Dimensions of excessive control often have intrusive, arbitrary, or irrational qualities that are aimed most often at the needs of the parent rather than those of the child. Two dimensions of excessive control are psychological overcontrol and punitiveness.

Psychological Overcontrol. The first type of excessive control, referred to as psychological overcontrol, is behavior used by parents that is psychologically intrusive, manipulates children's emotional experiences, and impairs the individuation process. Parental control of this kind has long been examined within the parent–child literature as the central component of overprotectiveness, anxious involvement, and related forms of intrusive psychological influence (Barber et al., 1994; Becker, 1964; Schaefer, 1959, 1965; Symonds, 1939). The excessive use of control in this manner often functions to inhibit children's social competence by fostering "internalized problems" that are manifested privately against the "self," including depression, suicide, eating disorders, and failures to achieve emotional autonomy in adulthood (Barber, 1992; Barber et al., 1994).

The psychologically controlling nature of this parenting strategy also is represented in the work of Stierlin (1974) and Hauser, Powers, Noam, and Jacobson (1984). These scholars have identified a type of control in disturbed families that interferes with the autonomy of children through "binding interactions." Such problematic interactions have cognitive dimensions that involve the use of distractions, withholding of information, and the expression of indifference in conjunction with affective components such as judging, devaluing, and excessive gratification.

Another form of psychological overcontrol is the frequent use of love withdrawal, a parental behavior receiving considerable research attention in previous years (Hoffman, 1970; Maccoby & Martin, 1983; Rollins & Thomas, 1979; Smith, 1983; Stafford & Bayer, 1993). Love withdrawal techniques such as inducing guilt, turning one's back, and refusing to speak to the young are often used to manipulate children's fears and dependency needs about loss of parental affection. Withdrawal of love is a parental technique that is experienced as punishment or threatened punishment by the young through its intent to foster feelings of blame. Frequently, it is used to keep children responsive to parental perspectives, inhibit movements toward autonomy, and discourage youthful tendencies to deviate from parental expectations (Maccoby & Martin, 1983; Smith, 1983). Despite such results, love withdrawal has produced inconclusive findings as a predictor of child outcomes (Hoffman, 1970; Peterson & Rollins, 1987; Rollins & Thomas, 1979). An overall view, however, is that scholars continue to suspect that love withdrawal and other forms of psychological (or manipulative) control will hinder the development of children's social competence by restricting their autonomy, inhibiting their individuality, and manipulating their emotions.

Punitiveness. Although a common strategy used by parents, there is little evidence that coercive or punitive behaviors facilitate the development of socially competent qualities in the young (Straus, 1994). Punitive or coercive behavior is a form of excessive control that consists of either verbal or physical attempts to apply control, without the benefit of rational explanations (Hoffman, 1980; Peterson et al., 1985). Childrearing behaviors of this kind involve the application of arbitrary force that often elicits hostility and resistance to parental influence from the young (Rollins & Thomas, 1975, 1979; Turner & Finkelhor, 1996). More severe forms of punitiveness can be characterized as corporal punishment or violence within the parent–child relationship (Strauss, 1994).

Although parents may use this strategy to change youthful behavior in the short term, there is mounting evidence that coercive strategies are counterproductive for encouraging long-term features of social competence (Hoffman, 1980; Peterson et al., 1985). Moreover, the efficacy of parental punitiveness diminishes considerably as cultural norms increasingly delegitimize its use with older children and adolescents (Smith, 1986), although many parents continue being punitive even toward teenagers (Straus, 1994). At best, parental coercion appears to achieve only external compliance to parents when children are closely monitored, but may actually discourage the "internalization" of (or commitment to) parents' perspectives and the tendency to become self-responsible for their own actions (Lepper, 1981; Peterson et al., 1985; Stafford & Bayer, 1993). Because other research indicates that the young often respond to parental coercion by "counterattacking" their elders, it is apparent that even external compliance to punitive parents may become increasingly problematic (Patterson, 1986).

Although research indicates that coercive parents may predispose the young to be less responsive and more resistant, this does not mean that punitiveness promotes the kind of autonomy from parents that is part of social competence (Peterson, 1986; Peterson & Leigh, 1990). Instead, the use of coercive behavior often promotes a "separation process" in which the desirable balance between autonomy and continued connectedness with parents is not maintained (Peterson & Leigh, 1990). Parents who make consistent use of punitiveness often elicit feelings of rejection from children. Moreover, parental punitiveness inhibits the development of self-esteem in the young, probably because the behavior of parents communicates rejection and a lack of respect for children (Eckenrode, Laird, & Doris, 1993; Oppenshaw & Thomas, 1986). Additional findings indicate that parental coercion or punitiveness impairs the development of moral internalization and behavior (Eisenberg, 1989; Hoffman, 1980), while placing youth at risk for substance abuse and delinquent activities (Eckenrode et al., 1993; Straus, 1994). Although some research disputes the inevitability of adverse outcomes (Simons, Johnson, & Conger, 1994), the pattern of results indicates that several dimensions of social competence are adversely effected by parental punitiveness.

Support and Affection

Perhaps the closest thing to a general law of parenting is that supportive, warm, sensitive, and responsive childrearing is associated with the development of social competence in the young. Parental support, whether conceptualized as general support, physical affection, acceptance, or companionship, is a diverse category of behaviors communicating warmth, affection, rapport, and feelings of being valued (Barber & Thomas, 1986; Becker, 1964; Rollins & Thomas, 1979; Rohner, 1986). Early in the parent–child relationship, for example, support is conveyed through the array of behaviors that parents express in being sensitive and responsive to infants as secure attachment is fostered (Ainsworth, Blehar, Waters, & Wall, 1978; Clarke-Stewart, 1988). During later periods of development, support has been conceptualized as hugging, touching, praising, approving, encouraging, helping, expressing terms of endearment, and spending positive time with children (Barber & Thomas, 1986; Rohner, 1986; Young et al., 1995).

Demo (1992), on the other hand, takes a more general perspective on support (or nurturance) and argues for a reconceptualization that recognizes that parents in modern society are faced with diminished abilities to spend face-to-face time with the young. Although parents typically provide considerable nurturance and financial support for children, the competing demands of daycare settings, work involvements, school environments, before and after school care, peer associations, and the mass media all suggest that parental nurturance is being redefined in contemporary times as "supportive detachment." Demo (1992) further suggests that the increased role of supportive detachment in parenting does not necessarily lead to the conclusion that such newer means of providing support are negative, nor should we view parents in terms of their extreme qualities—either as being emotionally responsive, or as being detached and uncaring. Instead, parental support has simply been redefined in modern society so that nurturance is communicated in a newer, more systemic manner that differs from face-to-face relationships.

Regardless how support is defined, an interesting paradox is that nurturance is an aspect of childrearing that seems to foster a balance between connectedness within the parent–child relationship and individuality through the assertion of sufficient autonomy. Several studies have reported that supportive childrearing behavior is predictive of children's connectedness to parents in several ways. For example, because parental support communicates that children are valued and accepted, the young often seek to increase the frequency of this behavior by conforming to parents' expectations (Henry, Wilson, & Peterson, 1989; Peterson et al., 1985; Rollins & Thomas, 1975). Nurturant or emotionally supportive relationships also encourage the young to identify with parents and incorporate their attitudes, values, and role expectations. Consequently, parental support often contributes to moral internalization and voluntary responsiveness to parental expectations (e.g., internalized conformity) (Henry et al., 1989; Hoffman, 1980; Peterson et al., 1985).

Besides eliciting continued responsiveness to parents, parental support paradoxically provides the basis for a seemingly opposite development—the progress of children toward autonomy. Specifically, parent–child relationships characterized by considerable nurturance appear to provide a secure base from which children can explore and meet challenges that exist beyond family boundaries (Bowlby, 1988; Peterson & Leigh, 1990; Peterson & Stivers, 1986). For many children, therefore, parental support is an important feature of the social environment that contributes to a balance between continued ties with parents and gradual progress toward autonomy. Failure to receive sufficient levels of support, however, hinders the development of socially competent autonomy by contributing to feelings of separation, the expression of hostility and aggression, diminished self-confidence, emotional unresponsiveness, and disturbed peer relations (Becker, 1964; Rohner, 1985; Rollins & Thomas, 1979).

Parental support also plays a key role in the development of self-esteem in children, another aspect of social competence (Felson & Zielinski, 1989). Because support conveys information to the young about the extent to which they have inherent worth, the self-esteem of children is fostered by the use of this behavior. Supportive actions by parents also suggest that parents trust and consider the young to be responsible parents. The communication of such confidence and warmth by parents, in turn, often has favorable consequences for the self-esteem and life satisfaction of children

(Bachman, O'Malley, & Johnson, 1978; Coopersmith, 1967; Felson & Zielinski, 1989; Gecas & Schwalbe, 1986; Openshaw & Thomas, 1986; Openshaw et al., 1983; Young et al., 1995).

Probably an overall assessment, therefore, is that parental support connects the young to their parents in a positive and often lasting way. One of its most important contributions is that of "preparing the way" for children to become more receptive to parental guidance and control attempts. That is, children who receive affection from and feel close to parents are often inclined to be more receptive to parental influence without the need for authoritarian approaches. The frequent use of support, therefore, seems to foster social competence in two ways, directly through the diverse psychological influences of affection and indirectly by mediating and enhancing the efficacy of parental control attempts.

Observational Learning and Parental Authority

Other forms of parent socialization influence, referred to as observational learning (or modeling) and authority (or power), account for the inclination of children to be influenced by the attributes and behaviors of parents in the absence of deliberate efforts by mothers and fathers to do so (Bandura, 1976). The first of these, observational learning, occurs on a moment-to-moment basis as models teach prosocial and antisocial qualities to the young, while simply pursuing their own interests and frequently without being aware of intending to teach anything in particular (Bandura, 1976; Peterson & Rollins, 1987; Smith, 1986). The fundamental importance of modeling, then, may be that parents who are perceived as exhibiting socially competent (or incompetent) qualities are likely to foster these attributes in the young without the intention to do so.

The work on imitation modeling, a tradition most closely identified with Bandura and associates (Bandura, 1976), conceptualizes a process through which observations of parents' (and other models') behaviors are vicariously learned and reproduced by the young. Children and adolescents are active mediators who view the actions of others, construct symbolic representations of these activities, and develop the skills to reproduce the model's behavior. Specifically, the young acquire these characteristics by (1) attending to and being reinforced vicariously by the positive consequences that befall others (i.e., vicarious reinforcement), (2) defining situations in a positive manner (i.e., self-reinforcement), and (3) anticipating that certain circumstances will occur in the future. Such cognitive processes allow the young either to be reinforced by the consequences experienced by others or by the anticipation of reinforcement during similar circumstances in the future. Thus, incentives that are anticipated beforehand may subsequently lead to reproduction (or learning) of the model's behavior. Rather than learning responses exclusively through external reinforcement mechanisms, therefore, much of human behavior is believed to be self-regulated by consequences that are self-produced or self-reinforced. That is, children and adolescents set their own performance standards and, in many cases, respond to their own accomplishments either positively or negatively in accordance with these self-imposed demands.

Various aspects of social competence or incompetence, such as aggression, moral behavior, prosocial behavior, and self-esteem, are acquired through socialization processes that Bandura has described (Bandura, Ross, & Ross, 1963; Peterson & Leigh, 1990; Peterson & Rollins, 1987; Radke-Yarrow, Zahn-Waxler, & Chapman, 1983). The learning of these characteristics has been found to be enhanced when models (e.g., parents) are perceived as having the attributes of power and nurturance. That is, children and adolescents are active, thinking beings who contribute in many ways to their own development by actively attending to, encoding, and retaining the behaviors displayed by social models.

Research on "power" or authority in the parent–child relationship, on the other hand, reminds us again that perceptions by the young of their parents' influence may be as consequential for the young as overt efforts to provide affection, guidance, and discipline. The term perceived "authority" is used (and preferred) here (instead of perceived "power") to distinguish this concept from other conceptions of "power" that have greatly confused the meaningful use of this construct (e.g., power as a process or outcome). Although parental behavior and observational learning deal with influence that is actualized through overt behavior, research on perceived parental authority (power) is concerned with *perceptions* by the young of their parents' *potential abilities* to influence them. As such, parental authority is the subjective assessment by children and adolescents that parents have abilities or competencies to exercise influence, but may or may not actually enact this potential. The important difference between potential influence and actual parental behavior, therefore, is that parental authority does not have to be used for the behavior and internal states of the young to be affected. Conceptualized as interpersonal resources that a person is perceived as being capable of using, authority refers to distinctive social bases of influence that one person attributes to another. Parental authority is the perception by the young, therefore, that their elders have resources or abilities of considerable importance within the parent–youth relationship (Peterson, 1986; Peterson & Rollins, 1987). The authority of a parent in relation to a child is a product of the young person's perception of their elder's interpersonal resources. That is, the parent's authority resides in the "eyes of the beholder"—or the child's subjective assessment of the parent's ability to exercise influence. Because authority is based on subjective interpretations of the

parents' abilities, a very different assessment of a particular parent's interpersonal resources may be held by a third party (e.g., another child and/or sibling) outside a specific parent–child dyad and may differ from one relationship to another.

Besides its subjective nature, authority is also a multidimensional concept with several dimensions or forms being identified as follows: (1) reward authority, the perceived ability to supply gratifications; (2) *coercive authority*, the perceived ability to administer punishments or adverse consequences; (3) *legitimate authority*, the perceived right to exercise influence based on social norms; (4) *expert authority*, the perceived potential to provide useful information; and (5) *referent authority*, the potential to function as an identification object or significant other (Henry et al., 1989; Henry & Peterson, 1995; Peterson, Bush, & Supple, in press; Peterson et al., 1985; Smith, 1983, 1986). These dimensions of parental authority have been reported to predict such dimensions of youthful social competence as conformity to parents, identification with parents, and autonomy in reference to parents (Henry et al., 1989; McDonald, 1977, 1979, 1980; Peterson, 1986; Peterson & Day, 1994; Peterson, Bush, & Supple, in press; Peterson & Leigh, 1990; Peterson et al., 1985; Smith, 1983, 1986). Thus, children and adolescents are likely to develop many positive psychosocial qualities when their parents are perceived as having the potential to function as referents (referent authority), provide useful information (expert authority), offer gratifications (reward authority), inflict adverse consequences (coercive authority), and exercise authority based on social norms (legitimate authority) (Henry et al., 1989; Peterson, 1986; Peterson, Bush, & Supple, in press; Peterson et al., 1985; Smith, 1983, 1986). A general way of conceptualizing such results is that parents who are perceived as having "authority" tend to foster social competence in their young.

While only limited empirical support exists, there is some evidence that legitimate, expert, and referent authority are more likely to foster conformity by children and adolescents based on internal commitments to parental expectations. Reward and coercive authority, on the other hand, seem to be more relevant to circumstances involving the external mechanisms of parental surveillance and monitoring of youthful behavior—that is, forms of parental influence that encourage "external compliance" to their elders, but not commitment to parental values (Peterson, 1986; Peterson et al., 1985; Smith, 1983).

Although appearing contradictory, the same dimensions of perceived parental authority that contribute to conformity may also foster the development of autonomy in adolescents. Specifically, adolescents are likely to become autonomous within the context of continued ties with parents (i.e., the young will not separate from parents) when they perceive their elders as having expert, legitimate, referent, and reward authority. Coercive authority, on the other hand, is the only dimension of potential influence that appears to inhibit youthful autonomy within the parent–adolescent relationship (Peterson, 1986; Peterson, Bush, & Supple, in press).

Recent research and scholarship also has indicated that authority may be examined bidirectionally as a "child effect" as well as a "parent effect" within the parent–youth relationship (Henry & Peterson, 1995; Peterson, 1986; Peterson, Bush, & Supple, in press; Peterson & Day, 1994; Peterson & Rollins, 1987; Smith, 1983, 1986). Specifically, one study has indicated that parents viewed their adolescents as having reward, coercive, expert, legitimate, and referent authority (perhaps perceived dimensions of adolescent social competence). Such results indicated, in turn, that potential influence is a "two-way street," with both adolescents *and* parents viewing each other as having interpersonal resources (Peterson, 1986). Moreover, those adolescents who were perceived by parents as high in expert, legitimate, reward, and referent authority also were viewed by their parents as functioning in an autonomous manner (Peterson, 1986).

Combinations of Parental Behavior and Attributes

Although the quest to determine the consequences of specific features of the parent–child relationship is important, we must recognize that the social world shared by the young and their elders is probably a great deal more complicated than much of the existing research. In fact, although there is very limited evidence about such complexities, it is useful to speculate how specific features of the parent–youth relationship (e.g., parental behavior, parental authority, and modeling) may operate together or "interact" to predict dimensions of social competence. The proposal here is to explore combined influences among specific dimensions of the parent–youth relationship through precise statistical or multiplicative interactions, rather than through unsystematically organized collections of parental behavior (i.e., parental typologies—see Peterson & Rollins, 1987; Rollins & Thomas, 1979). Despite the identified need for such research during more than 2 decades (Peterson & Rollins, 1987; Rollins & Thomas, 1975, 1979), researchers have continued to examine the influences of separate dimensions of childrearing or unsystematic typologies on aspects of children's social competence.

The most common example of interaction among parent–child dimensions are those that are supposed to transpire between various parental behaviors such as control and support (Rollins & Thomas, 1975). One of the most prominent predictions has been that parents can enhance the efficacy of such controlling efforts as induction by also using supportive or nurturant behavior with the young (Hoffman, 1970). Parental support is thought to encourage greater closeness to parents in a manner that makes the young more receptive or responsive to the controlling efforts of parents,

with the efficacy of induction being enhanced when parents also use high levels of support.

Another type of interaction might occur between dimensions of parental authority and parental behavior (Peterson & Rollins, 1987; Smith, 1983). It seems likely, for example, that parents who use inductive techniques to gain compliance from the young will be more likely to be successful when children also view them as having legitimate and expert authority. Such a conception indicates that being perceived as having the "right" to exercise influence (i.e., legitimate authority) and as having knowledge in a particular area (i.e., expert authority) will increase the likelihood that children will listen to the reasoning efforts (i.e., induction) of parents and respond appropriately. A final example, in turn, indicates that youthful modeling of parental attributes may interact with specific childrearing behavior and the competence or authority that parents are perceived to have. In support of this idea, research has indicated that the young are more likely to model an adult when they also view this person as being warm (or supportive) and a source of "authority" or "power" (Bandura, 1976; Bandura & Huston, 1961).

Any effort to conceptualize a "general parent effects model," therefore, must account for the separate influences of several parental characteristics as well as the interactions among these dimensions. Specifically, the primary predictors of children's characteristics would consist of parental behavior, perceived authority, and modeled attributes, plus the possible interactions among these parental qualities. Such a comprehensive model recognizes that children are influenced by the separate effects of their parents' intentional efforts to socialize them (i.e., parental behavior), the extent to which parents are perceived as competent authority figures (i.e., parental authority), as well as behavior that parents are not necessarily intent on directing at the young (i.e., parental modeling). This model also recognizes that interactions among the parental behavior, authority, and modeling dimensions are likely to have consequences for the socialization of children that go beyond the degree of prediction provided by each parental characteristic considered separately.

Critique of the Parent Effects Tradition

Although research based on parent effects models has made major contributions to our understanding of parent–child relationships, the portrayal of socialization as a unidirectional process has been the subject of growing criticisms. Specifically, 2 decades of research documenting alternative approaches such as the child effects, reciprocal, and systemic perspectives (see later sections of this chapter) (Ambert, 1992; Bell & Harper, 1977; Bronfenbrenner, 1979; Peterson & Rollins, 1987; Stafford & Bayer, 1993) has provided numerous reasons why a parent effects orientation seems too limited. Of special importance has been criticism that parent effects research is excessively dominated by the use of one-sided summary variables (e.g., summary scores of parental support or induction) or cumulative scores of perceived or observed behavior across situations, rather through moment-to-moment recordings of interaction sequences.

Another confusing aspect of the parent effects literature has been the use of many diverse methodologies (in different studies) to operationalize the same concepts in a manner that contributes to inconsistent results. The vast body of research on parent effects includes almost every kind of methodology that is common in the social sciences. Despite simplistic conclusions by some observers that certain methods are virtually always better than others (Holden & Edwards, 1989), probably the best position is that different research strategies or methodologies have respective strengths that can complement each other (Sabatelli & Waldron, 1995). For example, the acquisition of survey data through self-report questionnaires is best designed to assess the subjective reality of parents and children that may, in turn, influence their actual behavior. Such perceptions of parent–child phenomena convey an "insider's" view of the knowledge, attitudes, perceptions, expectations, self-concepts, personality dimensions, evaluations of others, meaning of various actions, and subjective assessments about the quality of relationships (Copeland & White, 1991; Larzelere & Klein, 1987; Sigafoos, Reiss, Rich, & Douglas, 1985). In contrast, observational research is ostensibly more appropriate for measuring "objective" reality about parents and children, including overt actions, interaction processes, and nonverbal communication. Research that involves direct observation is best designed to assess an "outsider's" view of parent–child interaction that develops over a brief period of time (Copeland & White, 1991; Larzelere & Klein, 1987). The assumption here (and a considerable leap it is) is that "outsider observers" can somehow truly see what is going on, simply because they are not immediately involved. Perhaps a more accurate view, however, is that different methodologies simply impose some form of alternative "reality." Given these much trumpeted differential strengths, perhaps a sound strategy for parent–child researchers is to choose from among the various approaches based on the nature of a topic, the state of the existing literature on a topic, and the resources available to conduct the research (Larzelere & Klein, 1987).

One of the real dilemmas of parent–child research is that each method of measurement will inherently have its limitations and bends the empirical world to its premises by evoking different meanings for individual research participants. That is, operational methods, by their very nature, function to create their own reality and meaning for those who participate in research. We should not expect, for example, that parents will be highly coercive toward children in situations where they are aware of being watched and re-

corded (i.e., the typical behavioral observation situation) as compared to their reports on a confidential paper-and-pencil instrument (i.e., the typical self-report questionnaire) about their private inclinations. This is not a new idea, but one having a long history stretching back to W. I. Thomas, who argued that any situation (including a research situation) involves (1) the objective conditions under which the individual acts; (2) the preexisting attitudes of the individual, which at any given moment influences his or her behavior; and (3) the person's perception or "definition of the situation" about a particular set of circumstances (Thomas & Thomas, 1928).

Although distinct methods (e.g., behavioral observation versus self-report) have such inherent tendencies to measure something different, this is not an argument to abandon the use of multiple methodologies in parent–child research. Instead, investigators can learn much about the respective strengths and weaknesses of various methods from studies that use multiple methodologies to examine the convergent and discriminate validity of various measures. In fact, analysis strategies that combine the multitrait-multimethod matrix (Campbell & Fiske, 1959) with confirmatory factor analysis (Schmitt & Stults, 1986; Widaman, 1985) can be used to measure the degree of trait variance, method variance, and unique factors in different parent–child research methods.

Because change is a central aspect of families and the parent–child relationship, there is great need to expand the use of longitudinal designs to trace the alternations in parental behavior, authority, and modeling as sources of influence on the development of social competence and incompetence among adolescents (Mattesich & Hill, 1987; Rodgers & White, 1993). Although expensive, complicated, time-consuming, and labor intensive, longitudinal research provides better insight into assumptions about temporal and causal issues than cross-sectional research (Larzelere & Klein, 1987; Menaghan & Godwin, 1993). Studies that examine change over time are increasingly productive because of new analytical tools referred to as maximum likelihood linear structural equations. Such programs as LISREL and EQS allow investigators to (1) develop measurement models of unmeasured constructs, (2) provide better estimates about the stability of the unmeasured constructs, and (3) construct complex simultaneous linear structural equations that can be applied to theoretically based predictions across time (Acock & Schumm, 1993; Joreskog & Sorbom, 1988).

Despite obvious shortcomings and the need to rejuvenate parent effects research with newer methodological, design, and analytical strategies, compelling reasons remain for investigators to continue work based in this perspective. Specifically, it is difficult to deny that parents certainly have (1) greater control over environmental contingencies, (2) intentions to socialize children in ways that the young do not share, and (3) attributes, behaviors, and characteristics that children do not possess. In some areas of socialization, it is difficult to argue with the assumption that adults are social agents who have greater insight than children into the expectations, attitudes, and behaviors of their culture (Baumrind, 1980; Peterson & Rollins, 1987; Stafford & Bayer, 1993).

Child Effects

A commonsense idea for most parents, but one that many social scientists have been somewhat reluctant to accept, is the conception that children "socialize" or "influence" their parents (Ambert, 1992, 1997; Bell & Chapman, 1986; Bell & Harper, 1977; Lytton & Romney, 1991). This approach, referred to as the *child effects perspective*, examines how children influence the attitudes, values, behaviors, experiences, and circumstances of parents (Bell & Harper, 1977; Maccoby & Martin, 1983; Peterson & Rollins, 1987). By underscoring the fundamental impact of children on the lives of mothers and fathers, this orientation functions as the "mirror-reverse orientation" for the premise that socialization occurs unilaterally from parent to child (i.e., the social mold perspective) (Ambert, 1992; Stafford & Bayer, 1993). Research on the influence of infants illustrates, for example, that even very young children socialize their parents simply by their presence, without the intention to do so. The many consequences of the infant's presence include the possibilities that a mother may leave the labor market, that new economic pressures confront the family, and that adults must assume the new identity of "parent" (with all its incumbent rewards and responsibilities) (Ambert, 1992; Peterson & Rollins, 1987).

Infant Effects

Of considerable importance in defining the child effects perspective is earlier work indicating that different infant states and behaviors evoke varied forms of responsiveness from parents (Ambert, 1992; Stafford & Bayer, 1993). Specifically, earlier investigators examined the different ways that parents responded to the alert states, smiling, sighs, helplessness, irritability, and crying of infants (Bell & Harper, 1977; Brazelton, Koslowski, & Main, 1974; Clarke-Stewart, 1973; Korner, 1974; Maccoby & Martin, 1983; Peterson & Rollins, 1987; Schaffer, 1977). Child characteristics also were being implicated as factors that elicit the abuse of the young by parents (Belsky, 1980; Thomas & Chess, 1977). Specifically, irritable children, infants who cry extensively, or youngsters with abnormalities in appearance seemed more likely to experience parental abuse than children who were viewed as more placid or normal in physical attributes (Bates, 1987; Pettit & Bates, 1989).

Earlier research also documented that parents tended to respond differently to the young based on the gender of infants. Mothers tended to stimulate male infants through physical means to engage in gross motor activity, whereas female infants received less encouragement for physical activity, but greater emphasis on visual and auditory stimulation. Moreover, the gender of infants has been found to shape the expectations of parents, which, in turn, may influence different caregiving responses that parents make in reference to male and female infants. Specifically, infant daughters are often described by parents in terms of such traditional gender attributions as more beautiful, softer, smaller, less attentive, weaker, and cuter than infant sons. In contrast, male infants were viewed as better coordinated, more alert, stronger, and hardier than daughters (Korner, 1974; Lamb, 1977; Maccoby & Martin, 1983; Moss, 1974; Parke & O'Leary, 1975; Peterson & Rollins, 1987; Rubin, Provenzano, & Luria, 1974; Schaffer, 1977).

More recent research also indicates that parents respond to the child's gender by structuring the play environment of young children according to gender stereotypes. Because parents believe that boys and girls have different sex-typed toy preferences at an early age (as early as 5 months old), they often are influenced by their offsprings' gender to select different toys for them, even before children can express their own preferences (Fagot & Leinbach, 1989; O'Brien & Huston, 1985). Parents also assign chores to children according to gender-role stereotypes and encourage gender-typed play activities (Bloch, 1987; Block, 1979; Caldera, Huston, & O'Brien, 1989; Lackey, 1989; Lytton & Romney, 1991; O'Brien & Huston, 1985; Pomerleau, Bolduc, Malcuit, & Cossette, 1990). Other research also indicates that parents of sons are more sex-typed than parents of daughters. Specifically, fathers with sons appear to be significantly less feminine than fathers with daughters, while mothers with sons seem more feminine than mothers of daughters (Ganong & Coleman, 1987). A possible explanation for these findings is that parents place greater emphasis on socializing male rather than female children for sex-typed behavior.

Infant Temperament as a Child Effect

The child effects perspective during infancy can be effectively illustrated through a growing body of scholarship dealing with infant temperament. Broadly speaking, temperament refers to individual styles of behaving or reacting to environmental events. In defining temperament, a number of behavioral dimensions have been identified, including mood, rhythmicity, adaptability, intensity, emotionality, activity, sociability, irritability, and impulsivity (Bates, 1987; Emde et al., 1992; Frodi & Senchak, 1990; Goldsmith & Campos, 1986; Kagan, Reznick, & Snidman, 1989; Lerner, 1993; Plomin & Dunn, 1986). Although controversy exists in specifying the dimensions of temperament (Bates, 1987), research concerning the concept of "difficult" temperament has resulted in a body of work that is especially relevant to the study of parent–infant interaction (Kagan, Reznick, & Snidman, 1989). Difficult temperament, as defined by Thomas et al. (1968), refers to a constellation of affect, poor adaptability to new situations, and poorly regulated sleep and feeding cycles. Longitudinal research on the impact of difficult temperament in infancy has indicated that difficult temperament may increase the risk for developing behavior problems during childhood and adolescence (Bates, 1987; Kagan, 1989; Sanson, Oberklaid, Pedlow, & Prior, 1991; Thomas, Chess, & Korn, 1982).

One of the primary ways by which difficult temperament may impact later child development is through its effects on parent–infant and parent–child interactions. Early research indicated that mothers of difficult infants were less responsive to infant cues than mothers of less difficult infants (Bates, 1987). Later work, however, has indicated that mothers of difficult infants were more involved with their infants and exhibited more positive caretaking behaviors. Moreover, difficult toddlers appear more likely to approach troublesome situations and are more likely to resist parental control attempts. Mothers of difficult toddlers, in turn, were more likely to use reactive forms of control, such as warnings and restraints (Bates, 1989).

Overall, however, research examining the effects of temperament on parent–infant and parent–child interactions has failed to provide clear and consistent findings to date. This body of work reveals that temperament differences in children may have important effects on parent–child relations, but in a form of influence that may be more indirect than direct. Specifically, this means that infant temperament may influence parent–child relations in a more complicated manner than originally expected through the "goodness-of-fit" between child temperament, parental characteristics, and environmental demands (Lerner, 1993; Lerner & Lerner, 1986). Moreover, caregiver perceptions may help foster difficult temperament attributes because they lead adults to treat children more negatively. From this perspective, a more complete understanding of temperament effects requires that the context in which children are developing be considered, including the characteristics of parents as well as the strengths and risks that are prevalent in the environment.

Child Effects after Infancy

Although the research literature on child effects by older children and adolescents is more scarce than the comparable

scholarship for infants and toddlers, there is a small but growing body of evidence that youth influence their parents in a variety of ways after the earliest periods of development (Stafford & Bayer, 1993). For example, one body of literature indicates that children with emotional and attention-deficit problems contribute to several adverse consequences for parents, including discouragement, demoralization, and depression (Ambert, 1992; Brown, Borden, Clingerman, & Jenkins, 1988). Moreover, parents of children with emotional problems are more likely to become less affectionate, less interested, and less communicative (Loeber & Stouthamer-Loeber, 1986).

Closely related to research on children with emotional problems is the growing evidence that children who are viewed as oppositional, hostile, and as manifesting conduct disorders often have such adverse consequences as the loss of parents' abilities to discipline and control them (Ambert, 1997; Farrington, 1986; Kazdin, 1987; Loeber & Stouthamer-Loeber, 1986; Patterson, 1982; Patterson & Capaldi, 1991). Because certain types of problematic behaviors in children are quite stable over time (Farrington, 1986; Fishbein, 1990), there is increased speculation that delinquent behavior by adolescents may evoke hostile, punitive, inconsistent, and withdrawing behavior from parents (Ambert, 1992). Other research indicates that parents experience greater satisfaction with childrearing when they perceive their adolescents as demonstrating socially competent attributes (Henry & Peterson, 1995). Moreover, parents who perceived their adolescent offspring as becoming more interpersonally competent (i.e., as having interpersonal power or resources) seem more likely to foster and allow greater autonomy by their teenage sons and daughters (Peterson, 1986; Peterson, Bush, & Supple, in press).

Evidence also exists that adolescent physical development may act as a stimulus for parents and lead to changes in the parent–youth relationship. Specifically, pubertal development in the young appears to foster a period of temporary disruption in the parent–youth relationship, involving increased conflict, ineffective attempts at control and discipline, increased tension, decreased expressions of warmth, and less involvement by parents (Steinberg, 1989). Such alterations in parent–youth relationships appear more characteristic of mother–son relationships than father–youth dyads, with the possible exception that fathers seem to increase flirtatious expressions of warmth toward daughters who are experiencing pubertal change. Such alterations in parental responses involve the possibility that adolescent pubertal changes provide meaningful social cues for parents that, in turn, elicit new responses from them (Steinberg, 1989).

Another potential source of evidence for youthful influence results from the likelihood that much of the social mold research on older children and adolescents can be reinterpreted as child rather than parent effects (Bell & Chapman, 1986; Bell & Harper, 1977; Peterson & Leigh, 1990). Specifically, the frequent use of both cross-sectional methodologies and correlational statistics in the parent effects research fails to establish the direction of influence within the parent–child relationship. As a result, instead of assuming that various aspects of social competence are fostered by certain parental behaviors (e.g., support), it could just as easily be argued that parents are more likely to respond with (or be "influenced" by the attributes of children) certain positive behaviors (e.g., support) when they view their offspring as behaving in a socially competent manner (Bell & Chapman, 1986; Bell & Harper, 1977; Peterson & Leigh, 1990; Peterson & Rollins, 1987). Children who demonstrate social competence, then, tend to elicit more competent parenting from their elders, whereas socially incompetent youth are likely to be the recipients of less competent parenting (Henry & Peterson, 1995).

In a more general sense, however, older children and adolescents increasingly become sources of socialization experiences for parents that result simply from the presence of youth. The young serve, for example, as the catalysts for parents to initiate contacts with a wide variety of professionals, school authorities, community agencies, youthful peers, and social networks resulting from children's activities. Many of these connections provide mothers and fathers with socialization experiences that can occur only with the assumption of complex parenting roles (Ambert, 1992, 1997).

Conceptualizing Child Effects

Although systematic theorizing about child effects remains quite limited, scholars are beginning to make initial steps toward conceptualizing how children influence their parents. For example, while viewing children as the socializers of parents is becoming more widely acknowledged (Bell & Chapman, 1986; Maccoby & Martin, 1983), it has become clear only recently that both the parents' "subjective" interpretations of children's qualities and the objective qualities of the young play important roles in the socialization of mothers and fathers (Bell & Chapman, 1986; Dix & Grusec, 1985; McGillicudy-De Lisi, 1985; Okagaki & Divecha, 1993). Of special importance in the area of subjectively constructed child effects is the idea that parental beliefs, values, attitudes, expectations, and "developmental scenarios" have important psychological consequences for mothers and fathers as well as their children. Because parents often impose subjective definitions on children (or subjectively assign "attributes" to them), these interpretations also help shape how mothers and fathers respond to their young (Dix, 1991, in press; Dix & Grusec, 1985; Dix, Ruble, & Zambarano, 1989; Peterson & Rollins, 1987).

One of the most prominent sources of subjective interpretations of children (and the resulting child effects) are the implicit theories of discipline that parents bring to their interactions with the young (Dix et al., 1989; Maccoby & Martin, 1983). Specifically, childrearing behaviors appear to vary from one child to another based on (1) parents' attributions about why children act as they do and (2) parents' conceptions of the appropriate childrearing practices that are needed (Dix et al., 1989). Faced with what they view as undesirable child behavior, therefore, mothers and fathers appear to adjust their socialization practices on the basis of interpretations they make about children's moods, motives, intentions, conscious responsibilities, and competencies. Mothers and fathers who hold their children responsible for negative behavior, therefore, seem to believe that children foresee, intend, and are competent to prevent what occurs as a result of youthful behavior. Consequently, these parents are more likely to use more punitive behaviors with youngsters, whom they view as "competent" (i.e., the assumption being that these children should "know better"), as a means of altering the negative motives and intentions that are assumed to be prevalent in these children. In contrast, parents who believe that children are not fully competent, volitional, or responsible for their actions would be less inclined to condemn children's behavior and more likely to moderate their responses with rational and inductive control attempts. The use of explanation and reasoning, in this case, is intended to impart knowledge and skill that parents have assumed is either absent or deficient in the young (Dix & Grusec, 1985; Dix et al., 1989).

A closely related means of conceptualizing child effects deals with the number and extent to which children's characteristics are viewed as deviating from parents' expectations for socially competent attributes (Ambert, 1992). According to this idea, parents often define children as deviating from their expectations in either positive or negative directions, with greater deviations from the subjectively accepted "norm" producing greater child effects on parents. A negative deviation, on the one hand, is an adversely viewed characteristic that is deficient compared to both the perceived social norms and the prevalent conception of social competence (Ambert, 1992). The most frequent parental responses to such negative deviations are (1) adverse subjective experiences for parents and (2) feedback to children that represents either the parents' negative feelings or their efforts to cope with problematic circumstances. Correspondingly, a child effect representing a negative deviation can be illustrated by a mother who feels incompetent and depressed, in part, because she feels unable to control the aggressive behavior (i.e., a dimension of social incompetence) that she views as being too prevalent in her 8-year-old son.

Positive deviations, on the other hand, are favorably

viewed characteristics, in part because parents have come to view these attributes as dimensions of social competence that either meet or surpass existing social norms (Ambert, 1992). The most common positive deviations that function as child effects are those attributes and behaviors that parents view as (1) enhancing the quality of their childrearing experiences and (2) evoking feedback to the young that reflects the positive feelings of parents and seeks to maintain the valued child attributes (Henry, Wilson, & Peterson, 1989). An illustration of such child effects representing positive deviations would be a father who experiences satisfaction that is based on perceiving his 10-year-old daughter as academically successful (being in the top 1% of her class at school) and well-behaved. Frequent consequences for the parent, therefore, will be (1) favorable subjective experiences and (2) feedback (behavior) that conveys such positive interpretations to children.

A further complication in conceptualizing discrepancies between children's perceived qualities and societal norms is the distinction between deviations that are perceived to be avoidable versus those viewed as unavoidable (Ambert, 1992). In the first case, an avoidable child effect is based on child characteristics that are believed to be fostered by the social environment and for which parents might feel at least some, if not considerable, responsibility (i.e., social incompetence). Examples of attributes that contribute to avoidable child effects include the influence of children's conduct disorders and adolescent delinquent activities on parents. In contrast, unavoidable child effects are those attributes of the young and circumstances within the parent–child relationship that seem inevitable and not subject to parental control. Examples of such unavoidable child effects include the extensive demands faced by parents in dealing with the helplessness of newborns or the psychological consequences associated with being the parents of a Down's syndrome child. Because it is believed that parents are more inclined to view "avoidable child effects" as something they might have prevented, these "discretionary effects" carry greater potential for being defined as negative deviations than those attributes or circumstances classified as "unavoidable" child effects (Ambert, 1992).

Besides the predictors of child effects, one means of conceptualizing how parents both interpret and respond to children's attributes and behaviors involves the concepts upper and lower limit control (Bell & Chapman, 1986; Bell & Harper, 1977). Upper limit control refers to parental behavior that is intended to reduce or redirect children's behavior that exceeds parental expectations in intensity and frequency (e.g., social incompetence in the form of hostile or noncompliant behavior). Upper limit control often involves the use of verbal or physical punitiveness by parents to respond to children who are behaving in a noisy, intense, or uncontrol-

lable manner. In contrast, lower limit control refers to parental behavior that seeks to foster children's behavior that falls below parental expectations in frequency and quality (e.g., social incompetence in the form of withdrawn or overly dependent behavior) (Bell & Chapman, 1986; Bell & Harper, 1987). Lower limit control often consists of parental support, encouragement, urging, prompting, reasoning, helping, and modeling in reference to children who demonstrate low activity, inhibition, low assertiveness, and deficient performance. The overall objective, of course, is to foster children's attributes that fall somewhere in between these upper and lower extremes and meets the parents' expectations for desirable attributes and socially competent behavior.

Regardless how child effects are conceptualized, however, observers also caution that youthful influence on adults is often a product of other factors besides the objective and subjectively assigned qualities of children. Mothers and fathers, for example, vary extensively in their vulnerability (or susceptibility) to different child characteristics and behavior. Because of their own characteristics, certain parents are likely to experience gratification from children, while other parents are more inclined to be adversely effected (Ambert, 1992). Moreover, parental attributes such as the quality of marital relationships, personality qualities, coping skills, parenting skills, and economic resources function as either potential resources or possible deficiencies that greatly influence the impact of various child characteristics on adults (Okagaki & Divecha, 1993). The effects of children on their elders, therefore, are greatly modified by aspects of the surrounding social context such as the availability and quality of daycare, the supportive nature of work environments, income supplements for impoverished families, and the acceptance of minority values and lifeways by the dominant culture (Ambert, 1992; Bronfenbrenner, 1979; Okagaki & Divecha, 1993) (see the "Systemic-Ecological Perspective" section in this chapter).

Critique of the Child Effects Perspective

Although investigators of child effects research have "turned the tables" on the parent effects models, the work in this tradition suffers from the same limitations as the approach it was designed to correct. Despite claims to the contrary (Ambert, 1992; Bell & Harper, 1977; Stafford & Bayer, 1993), the child effects orientation does not deal with reciprocal causation as much as it does with an inverted one-way model. Consequently, it seems just as problematic to argue that socialization influence flows primarily from child to parent as it does in the opposite direction. A more complete picture emerges when both the child and parent effects perspectives are considered simultaneously.

The child effects research would, of course, benefit from

continuing efforts to expand the use of longitudinal research and multivariate tests of hypotheses. Child effects research has also been plagued by a lack of theoretical models that systematically provide interpretations about the nature of youthful influence on parents. As a result, there is little understanding about child effects issues that parallel the topics in the parent effects literature. For example, although a substantial amount of work exists on the control attempts, supportive behavior, modeling influences, and the perceived competence of parents, we know very little about the kinds of influence strategies used, the dimensions of nurturance provided, and how perceived competence is acquired by children as development proceeds. Moreover, very limited knowledge exists about the consequences of these child variables on the socialization and well-being of parents (see Henry & Peterson, 1995). Perhaps one way to address some of these deficiencies would be through the application of qualitative research, which is especially useful for probing areas that have not been well studied and require exploratory efforts. Qualitative research can also be a very powerful tool for examining theoretical questions about the meanings, understandings, perceptions, and subjective aspects of the parent–child relationship (Rosenblatt & Fischer, 1993).

Reciprocal Socialization

Rather than choosing whether socialization originates either with parents or children, the perspective that considers *reciprocal socialization* accounts for both sides of the parent–child equation simultaneously. From this perspective, socialization is a mutual process through which parents and children serve as active social agents who influence both each other's and their own development (Peterson & Rollins, 1987; Stafford & Bayer, 1993). Although both sides of the parent–youth relationship are considered in reciprocal models, this does not mean, however, that children and parents necessarily affect each other in the same way, with equal strength, or in all areas. Instead, reciprocity simply means that two actors have some manner of mutual influence on each other, with great variability existing in (1) the relative strength of each actor's influence, (2) the specific behaviors exchanged, and (3) the diversity of areas that are affected. Other sources of variability, of course, are the fundamental changes in the nature of reciprocity that occur as the parent–child relationship progresses through infancy, toddlerhood, and later childhood.

Parent–Infant Reciprocity

One tradition of research on reciprocal socialization is that which examines dynamic processes of synchrony or reciprocity between parents and infants (Beebe, Alson, Jaffe, Feldstein, & Crown, 1988; Brazelton et al., 1974; Field, Healy, & LeBlanc, 1989; Field, Healy, Goldstein, & Gutherz, 1990; Koester, Papousek, & Popousek, 1989; Lester, Hoffman, & Brazelton, 1985; Peterson & Rollins, 1987; Stafford & Bayer, 1993; Schaffer, 1977; Tronick, 1989). Investigators who conduct such research often use sophisticated microanalyses of interactive or sequential behavior in search of patterns and organization between infants and caretakers. An important aspect of mother–infant reciprocity is the mutuality or "synchrony" that occurs between the two participants in interaction (Beebe et al., 1988; Field et al., 1990; Peterson & Rollins, 1987; Schaffer, 1977). Synchrony, as a type of interaction, indexes each participant's capacity to maintain a mutual or shared focus in their dyadic relationship. For mothers, synchronous behavior reflects their capacity to remain available to the young, while from the child's perspective, this mutuality may indicate the ability to fill the role of relationship partner in initial ways. Synchronous interactions often involve approach rhythms composed of mutual gazes, facial displays, "en face" positions, and vocalizations as well as changes in head and neck orientations. Such reciprocal interactions have been characterized variously as either a "waltz" (Schaffer, 1977) or as the beginnings of a "conversation of gestures" (Peterson & Rollins, 1987) that leads to social competence between parent and infant in its most elementary form.

Besides synchrony, a variety of more specific concepts are used to describe different kinds of mutuality that occur between mothers and infants. Some observers have characterized such interactions as "turn-taking," or rapidly repeating episodes in which one partner is initially active while the other is quiet. Such cyclical episodes are coupled with role reversals that rapidly redefine who initiates synchronous activity and who is quiet (Brazelton et al., 1974; Schaffer, 1977; Tronick, 1989). Others have examined reciprocity in terms of "behavior state matching," in which the percentage of time that mothers and infants spend in the same state (i.e., mutual gazing) is the focus (F. Field et al., 1992; T. Field et al., 1989, 1990), while "coherence" refers to circumstances where one behavioral sequence (e.g., mother's vocalization) is predicted by another behavioral sequence (e.g., infant crying).

An important concept in the literature on reciprocity or synchrony is the idea that mothers should "follow in order to lead" (Schaffer, 1977). That is, responsive mothers seem to be those who monitor and fetch items that have caught their infants' interests as a means of initiating bouts of mutual gazing and vocalization. Moreover, when infants choose to discontinue face-to-face interaction, sensitive mothers are those who allow these periodic withdrawals to occur. As a result, it appears that competent reciprocity is demonstrated

by those mothers who both provide for moderate levels of stimulation and allow for periods of withdrawal by the infant. The assumption here is that substantial amounts of redundancy are necessary, tempered with sufficient novelty to encourage further development within the mother–infant relationship (Peterson & Rollins, 1987).

The concept that parents follow in order to lead has also been applied to research on mother–child synchrony as a predictor of compliance by toddlers (Rocissano, Slade, & Lynch, 1987). Specifically, these results indicate that mothers who frequently gain the compliance of toddlers are those who allow the young some control of their own activities by using their children's current involvement states to guide their requests. Such synchronous patterns of responding, as manifested by a mother's respect for a child's initiatives, would appear to be one aspect of sensitive maternal responding. Another way of viewing such processes is through the concept of "intuitive parenting" (Papousek & Papousek, 1991a,b). Specifically, intuitive parenting consists of behaviors that parents regularly enact in a nonconscious fashion that are sensitive to the development of children, and thus have the goal of enhancing adaptation. This capacity of mothers to follow the child's lead seems to foster compliance by the young, a sense of connectedness between mother and child, and mutual communication, as well as self-directing behavior by infants and toddlers (i.e., early evidence of social competence by both parent and infant within their relationship).

In general, reciprocal or synchronous interaction between mothers, infants, and toddlers seems to develop early as their behavioral systems become attuned to each other and form basic elements of a competent relationship. Each partner provides stimulation for the other and has a modulating influence on the other's arousal level. As social interactions become more rhythmically structured, investigators have often suggested that the participants feel more effectively responsive and connected to each other. Although substantial disputes exist about the implications of synchronous interactions, some observers have proposed that such rhythmic interdependencies may be important precursors of both language development in infants and attachment relationships between infants and parents (Brazelton et al., 1974; T. Field et al., 1989, 1990; Peterson & Rollins, 1987; Stafford & Bayer, 1993).

Infant–Caregiver Attachment

As just suggested, an area of parent–child research that increasingly has taken a bidirectional (or reciprocal) perspective is the extensive work on infant-to-parent attachment (Pederson & Moran, 1995; Seifer & Schiller, 1995). Specifically, attachment refers to the close emotional bond that is formed between an infant and caregiver (or parent) and endures over time (Ainsworth et al., 1978; Bowlby, 1988). From an observer's perspective, infant attachment is represented by behaviors that function to maintain proximity to the caregiver (e.g., crying, clinging, separation anxiety, approaching) and are particularly evident during conditions of threat. Early attachment relationships are also believed to become internalized and serve as basic prototypes or "internal working models" for subsequent development and interpersonal relationships (Bowlby, 1988; Bretherton, 1990; Waters, Vaughn, Posada, & Kondo-Ikemura, 1995).

The primary purpose of attachment is believed to be rooted in human evolutionary history, with the intent being to enhance the likelihood of infant survival by maintaining the caregiver's proximity. More recently, the functional aspect of attachment has been expanded to include the extent to which infants demonstrate exploratory behavior and learn from ever-expanding environmental experiences (Bowlby, 1988; Sroufe & Fleeson, 1986). According to this perspective, infant exploratory behavior has its origins in the bonds of attachment and the abilities of the young to use caregivers as "secure bases" from which to expand their activities. Recent evidence also indicates that secure base behavior has considerable cross-cultural generality (Posada et al., 1995). The attachment of infants to parents, therefore, is a major developmental milestone having relevance for the survival of infants and implications for the emotional, social, and cognitive development of children (Posada et al., 1995; Sroufe & Fleeson, 1986).

The core of infant attachment is the affectional tie or bond that develops between the young and their caregivers. Part of this relationship is influenced by the maturational capabilities of infants (i.e., physical, cognitive, and emotional abilities) during the first year of life that assist them in discriminating caregivers from less familiar people (Bretherton, 1990). Of more direct relevance for the issue of reciprocity, however, are daily patterns of interaction concerned with the development of security in infant attachment relationships. Besides the fact that infants monitor parents and become distressed upon separation, parents also keep watchful eyes on their infants and become alarmed when their whereabouts are not known and danger is prevalent. Subsequently, parents appear to feel relieved when the infant is found and the danger is past (Bretherton, Biringen, & Ridgeway, 1991; Seifer & Schiller, 1995).

A key to understanding the parents' side of bidirectional attachment relationships, therefore, is the idea that maternal responsiveness, sensitivity, and warmth seem to be reciprocated by the most adaptive forms of attachment behavior (i.e., proximity seeking and exploratory behaviors) by infants (Ainsworth, 1985; Goldberg et al., 1986; Pederson & Moran, 1995; Seifer & Schiller, 1995). Longitudinal research on the

development of attachment has indicated that the degree of responsivity, sensitivity, and warmth by mothers is important in fostering secure attachment in infants (Ainsworth et al., 1978; Egeland & Farber, 1984; Isabella & Belsky, 1991; Isabella, Belsky, & Von Eye, 1989). Specifically, caregivers in secure relationships are actively sought as sources of comfort during periods of threat and serve as secure bases from which to explore the environment during less stressful circumstances.

Reciprocity between mother and child also appears to be apparent in relationships in which the quality of maternal behavior and infant attachment is less adaptive. Specifically, maternal–infant interactions characterized by low levels of sensitivity, greater hostility, and inept caretaking have been associated with infants who display one of three forms of less well-developed forms of attachment. In the first of these, insecure-avoidant attachment, infants appear indifferent to caregivers and may avoid interaction during both stressful and nonstressful conditions. Maternal behaviors characterized by lower sensitivity, diminished warmth, and higher hostility are associated with the insecure-avoidant type of attachment (Cassidy, 1994; Goldberg et al., 1986; Pederson & Moran, 1995). The second insecure form, resistant attachment, is characterized by high levels of anger and ambivalence toward caregivers during periods of stress, but limited exploration of the environment when stress is diminished. Early inept forms of parenting (i.e., unresponsive, rejecting, and inconsistent) appear to be associated with this form of insecure attachment (Cassidy & Berlin, 1993; Egeland & Farber, 1984; Isabella, 1993; Peterson & Moran, 1995).

A third pattern of problematic infant–caregiver relationship, disorganized attachment (Main & Solomon, 1991), is characterized by infants who demonstrate contradictory, apprehensive, or misdirected behaviors in reference to caregivers during stressful conditions. Such attributes suggest that disorganized infants lack an organized strategy for dealing with caregivers and may be related to earlier maternal–caregiver interactions that either frighten or communicate a sense of fear to infants (Main & Hesse, 1990b). Additional support for this idea is provided by recent studies indicating that approximately 80% of infants known to be abused were classified as disorganized in their attachment behaviors (Cicchetti & Douglas, 1991; Lyons-Ruth, Connell, Grunebaum, & Botein, 1990; Lyons-Ruth, Repacholi, McLeod, & Silva, 1991).

Other evidence of reciprocity, in turn, is concerned with the internal representations of attachment relationships that infants and parents are believed to develop. These internalized "working models" or representations of self and others have been conceptualized for some time as a feature of infant development (Bowlby, 1988; Bretherton, 1990). Specifically, the future interpersonal associations of securely

attached infants are expected to be influenced by early caretaker–child relationships through the internalization of working models (or relationship templates) that represent the self as lovable and other people as trustworthy. Infants who have experienced difficulties with early attachment, on the other hand, are more likely to develop either pessimistic or hostile models of the social world and believe themselves to be incapable of maintaining effective connections with others. Consequently, internal working models provide individuals with an organizational format or template to use when providing meaning to the self in relation to others and when forming relationships with others in the future (Owens et al., 1995; Sroufe & Fleeson, 1986).

The reciprocal nature of attachment is apparent, therefore, with the increased recognition that parents bring their own working models to relationships with infants and young children (Bretherton et al., 1991; Seifer & Schiller, 1995). Consequently, the impact of adult working models on parent–child relations have begun to be studied by examining the relationships between parental working models and child attachment. This work has focused on the relationship histories of mothers (Main & Goldwyn, in press), with the result being that women who described their previous relationships as balanced and coherent tended to have infants and young children who were securely attached. In contrast, mothers who were either more dismissive of or preoccupied with their relationships tended to have youngsters who displayed insecure attachment relationships (Fonagy, Steele, & Steele, 1991; Main & Goldwyn, in press). Such findings suggest that working models may be important sources of influence on parental responsiveness that occurs during the ongoing process of reciprocity that occurs between parent and child.

An important outcome of these reciprocal attachment relationships is that infants who become securely attached as they mature will differ from their insecure counterparts in positive ways. These differences are believed to result from distinctive internal working models of the parent–child attachment relationship that have been incorporated by the young. Specifically, the securely attached seem to develop more positive feelings about self, greater security from the prototypic relationships that they have internalized, and basic relationship skills that are more adaptive (Sroufe & Fleeson, 1988). An overall characterization of these differences, therefore, is that infants who are securely attached tend to be more socially competent in a variety of ways at later stages of development. Such indicators of later social competence include problem-solving skills, frustration tolerance, peer relationship skills, curiosity about new things, self-confidence, self-direction, and less social withdrawal (Bretherton, 1990).

Longitudinal research also has indicated that greater social competence during childhood is predicted by key

elements of both sides of the "reciprocal parent–infant attachment model"—the secure attachment of infants and the associated responsiveness of mothers. For example, qualities such as greater sociability with unfamiliar adults and peers have been reported for children ranging in ages from 2–5 years old who were once classified as securely attached infants (Bretherton, 1990; La Freniere & Sroufe, 1985; Lutkenhaus, Grossman, & Grossman, 1985). Moreover, children with secure attachment histories were responded to more favorably by peers (Jacobsen & Willie, 1986; La Freniere & Sroufe, 1985) and were less likely to be identified as serious behavior problems (Erickson, Sroufe, & Egeland, 1985; Renken, Egeland, Marvinney, Mangelsdorf, & Sroufe, 1989). Closely related are findings that early maternal responsiveness, an important covariate of secure attachment, is predictive of fewer behavior problems at age 4 (Pettit & Bates, 1989) and higher levels of being considerate to others at age 10 (Bradley, Caldwell, & Rock, 1988).

An overall assessment of this literature, therefore, is that the early infant-to-parent attachment is best conceptualized in terms of its bidirectional qualities. Secure attachment, for example, tends to be associated with competent parents who are both responsive in a sensitive manner and have internalized working models from past relationships that are positive. Finally, early reciprocal relationships characterized by caretaker responsiveness and secure attachment predict that children at later stages of development will demonstrate social-emotional qualities characterized here as social competence.

Parent–Child Reciprocity as an Antecedent of Antisocial Behavior

Another program of research that uses a reciprocal or bidirectional perspective is the work of Gerald Patterson and colleagues (Patterson, 1982; Patterson & Bank, 1989; Patterson & Capaldi, 1991; Patterson, DeBaryshe, & Ramsey, 1989; Patterson, Reid, & Dishion, 1991), which examines the development of antisocial behavior in children. The specific focus of this work is concerned with families with children and preadolescents who are classified by parents, school authorities, and court systems as aggressive, antisocial, or "out of control." According to this perspective, parents who use inadequate socialization strategies often foster several forms of deviant (or socially incompetent) behavior, such as antisocial and aggressive behavior within families, peer groups, and school environments as well as deficient social, academic, and work skills.

The Patterson group rejects the idea that parents, peers, and other socialization agents have unidirectional effects on children in favor of a more complicated bidirectional model. Conceptualized as positive feedback loops, inept parenting

fosters antisocial child behavior and skill deficits (i.e., child characteristics) that, in turn, serve as further irritations contributing to additional parenting deficiencies. Similarly, aggressive behavior and poor social skills in the peer group often lead children to failure in school and rejection by prosocial agemates, which, in turn, contribute to more aggressive behavior and to further social skill deficiencies. Rejection by prosocial peers often fosters the additional tendency for youth to affiliate with deviant contemporaries who socialize them further for antisocial behavior and inept social skills. The key aspect of Patterson's work, however, has been the idea that inept family socialization practices are the primary contributors to children's antisocial behavior. Specifically, an important feature of inadequate family socialization is parental discipline that consists of failures to adequately label, track, and manage child behavior. Of particular importance is the use of harsh and inconsistent methods by parents who are seeking to inhibit undesirable child behavior.

Problematic family socialization also involves the lack of positive parenting that fosters effective interpersonal, academic, and work skills in children as well as ineffective monitoring or supervision—a construct referring to parents' awareness of their children's peer associates, free time activities, and physical whereabouts. Families that are "training grounds" for children's deviant behavior also are characterized as having poor problem-solving and conflict-management skills (Patterson, 1982; Patterson & Bank, 1989; Patterson & Capaldi, 1991; Patterson et al., 1989).

Perhaps the central contribution of the Patterson group for understanding the bidirectional nature of the parent–child relationship, however, is their description of coercive processes within families. Home environments that foster antisocial behavior in children often involve constant struggles among the family members. Individuals in these families are reluctant to initiate conversations, but when they do, inclinations to needle, threaten, and irritate each other often result. Consequently, interaction within these coercive home environments often centers around efforts by individuals in families to force other members to stop irritating them (Patterson & Capaldi, 1991; Patterson et al., 1989, 1991). Several elements contributing to the onset of coercive processes include unskilled parenting, children or adolescents with difficult temperaments, stressful or disruptive events, and substance abuse by parents. Of special importance is a process of escalation that occurs within the parent–youth relationship as adverse behaviors of a trivial nature provide an initial learning base for the later development of high-amplitude aggressive exchanges (Patterson, 1982; Patterson et al., 1989). The central assumption of Patterson's work is that parents who fail to punish "everyday" or minor coercive behavior actually foster interaction sequences that train children for more

serious forms of aggression. Family members engage in patterned coercive exchanges of behaviors that escalate progressively and become more aversive.

For older children and younger adolescents, the escalation of coercion is enhanced most commonly through a three-step process of escape–avoidance conditioning (i.e., negative reinforcement) that consists of (1) an attack episode, (2) a counterattack episode, and (3) a positive outcome. An important element in the maintenance and escalation of coercion is the role of negative reinforcement—or the removal of an aversive stimulus that functions to reinforce or increase behavior (Patterson & Capaldi, 1991; Patterson et al., 1989). This is illustrated by a situation in which a father is badgering and yelling at his son for wandering off with neighborhood friends and missing dinner. The son responds to this badgering by whining, followed by a barrage of yelling back—which, in turn, causes the father to back off (or discontinue his aversive behavior) and negatively reinforce the son.

Patterson further reports that parents of these problematic youngsters rarely use social reinforcement or social approval to control their offsprings' behaviors, but instead rely heavily on coercive techniques. An ironic aspect of such reciprocal processes is that youth who are raised in these troubled environments often become resistant to punishment—frequently by defying or fighting parents' coercion with countercoercive behavior reflecting the very acts that their elders are trying to suppress. Moreover, the young often enact such countercoercive behavior as a means of gaining the attention of parents. While parents in noncoercive families are likely to reciprocate with positive attention, more affection, and greater tendencies to stand firm in the face of youthful coercion, troubled or coercive families are more inclined to use coercive tactics with children as the only means of dealing with such circumstances.

The overall result of these coercive family environments is that children become trained for social incompetence by showing regular progressions from learning simple noncompliance to the acquisition of behavior that is physically assaultive. The consequences of such coercive interchanges within distressed families contribute, in turn, to deficits in important aspects of social competence, such as lower self-esteem, frequent antisocial behavior, problematic peer relationships, and poorer academic performance (Patterson, 1982; Patterson et al., 1989).

Critique of Reciprocal Socialization

An overall assessment of the previous sections on bidirectional or reciprocal interaction, therefore, indicates that socially competent children tend to be involved in mutually influential relationships with competent parents. Specifically, parents who seem attuned to the capabilities and devel-

opmental tasks of children (i.e., competent parenting) appear to have offspring who reciprocate with a variety of valued social qualities in the young (i.e., social competence). Parents who in different stages of development may follow in order to lead, respond in a sensitive manner, and provide an affectionate atmosphere tend to have children of different ages who synchronize their behaviors with parents during infancy, exhibit proximity-seeking, and demonstrate exploratory behavior as part of attachment. The work of Patterson on bidirectional influences, in turn, reminds us that both parents and children who lack social competence in reference to each other tend to engage in mutually reinforcing coercive cycles that lead to serious problems within the parent–youth relationship.

Although the work on reciprocity reveals important patterns of interaction, several complications and problems have also become evident in this research. Of special importance is "tyranny of the data," a problem caused by the staggering amount of sequential information generated on only a few cases. The complexity of such data and the required analytical procedures often lead to preoccupations with unlimited detail, use of small, nonrepresentative samples, and little attention to the theoretical significance of micro-level interaction (Peterson & Rollins, 1987; Stafford & Bayer, 1993). Such research requires funding that (1) is beyond the reach of most parent–child investigators, (2) may have problems with subject reactivity in observational settings, and (3) may have limited ecological validity (and limited generalizability) when older children and parents are involved. Of particular concern is that much of the work on reciprocity and attachment has been conducted in settings that lack generalizability to everyday environments. Specifically, the parent and, with increasing age, the child, are both aware of being observed and may act differently in calculated efforts to "manage an impression" (Copeland & White, 1991). Parents and children may hide what they consider to be private activities (e.g., conflict), make one person appear more or less problematic than is actually the case, or respond in more nonspecific manners with nervousness, shyness, and obviously self-monitored (artificial) responses.

While computer technology has provided the capacity to analyze reciprocal interaction at microscopic levels, it is still doubtful whether information acquired at a more macroscopic level will soon be replaced by these newer emphases on immediately specific behaviors. That is, as children develop, parent–youth interaction may be less a function of events occurring in immediately preceding time intervals, but instead may become increasingly a function of events that are remembered, summarized, and responded to over longer periods of time. Microanalyses, therefore, reveal almost nothing about the meaning of behaviors in terms of relationship histories, either to the observers or the participants of interaction (Clarke-Stewart, 1988). Data gathered through microanalytic techniques offer detailed descriptions of face-to-face relationships and the immediate effects of one person's behavior or another's. Despite assumptions to the contrary, however, very limited evidence exists that such data can be linked to important issues in the long-term development of children. Given that microanalyses are expensive and time-consuming, some researchers may find it preferable to use other strategies involving macro-level variables, which have proven to be more successful in predicting consequences that occur later in development (Clarke-Stewart, 1988; Copeland & White, 1991).

As indicated in previous sections of this chapter, the nature of parent–child relations may be shaped, in part, not by immediately contingent behaviors, but by more global perceptions that parents and children have formulated about each other. Children and adolescents often respond to parents in terms of their perceived legitimacy, their resources, or how they have been disciplined in the past. Likewise, parents often respond to children based on perceptions of their temperament or the history of their children's patterns of compliance. Consequently, important aspects of the parent–child relationship may be shaped not by immediately contingent behaviors, but by reciprocal meanings and expectations that are accumulated across the history of their association. Family (or parent–child) relationships may be largely a function of accumulated perceptions and long-term investments, rather than experiences of the moment.

Finally, recent insights from the new perspective of *chaos theory* also suggests that microanalytic analyses may be limited in the accuracy of predictions that result (Gleick, 1987; Gottman, 1991). According to this viewpoint, predictability, especially at the microanalytic level, is nonlinear and difficult to accomplish. As such, conventional approaches for prediction are inadequate because the specifics of any particular parent–child relationship can always deviate from expectations, with better prediction being possible only in a more general sense across many situations or families. Although accurate prediction of behavior is thought to be possible in the social sciences, the best predictions may occur as overall systemic patterns, rather than as specific events that may reflect only idiosyncratic sequences of interaction.

The Systemic-Ecological Perspective

An important contemporary recognition has been the idea that the parent–child relationship is not an isolated dyadic relationship, but at least a three-person relationship between mothers, fathers, and children (Bodman & Peterson, 1995). Moreover, beyond immediate family members, parent–child relationships are found within the context of many social relationships that impinge upon and set parameters for the way that parents and children socialize each other. Such a conception implies that a systems perspective is best suited to understand how social phenomena beyond the dyad redefine both the processes and outcomes that emerge between parents and children (Bodman & Peterson, 1995). The essential implications of this perspective is that both parental competence and children's social competence are, at least in part, a function of social phenomena beyond the parent–child relationship.

Stripped of much of its complexities, therefore, a systems perspective provides the view that all aspects of families are interrelated through dynamic, mutual, and circular mechanisms. Moreover, the family system and its subcomponents have substantial interconnections with other social environments, such as immediate social networks, the workplace, neighborhood, community, school, socioeconomic circumstances, and the ethnic-minority context (Bodman & Peterson, 1995; Broderick, 1993; Bronfenbrenner, 1979; Kantor & Lehr, 1978; Peterson, 1995b; Stafford & Bayer, 1993; Steinglass, 1987). Special properties of social systems (e.g., the family) include the condition of "wholeness"—or the quality that defines groups as being greater than the additive sums of their parts. The result of such a "wholistic" quality is that every element or phenomenon within the system may have implications for other components throughout the immediate family or the larger social system. These interconnections among the elements of a system, in turn, have mutual consequences and are conveyed either directly or indirectly throughout the family (Broderick, 1990; Peterson, 1986a).

Social systems such as families also tend to be organized hierarchically (i.e., individual, dyadic, and whole system levels) (Broderick, 1993; Bronfenbrenner, 1979; Stafford & Bayer, 1993; Steinglass, 1978), where each system is composed of smaller component subsystems that, in turn, like a series of Russian dolls, are elements of larger suprasystems (i.e., the larger family system). Although all subsystems of families are complex and different from other components, each level maintains its own boundaries that are variably permeable to input from the outside. The result is that individual, dyadic, and systemic levels of families occur in hierarchical fashion and are simultaneously interdependent and distinct.

The individual, from this perspective, is a biological and psychological system conceptualized as the basic component or level of the larger family system. Although partially explainable with biological and psychological models, individuals cannot be adequately understood without reference to the social context (e.g., the family) or without examining how their behavior has consequences for their interpersonal environment (i.e., part of which is the family). Next, the more encompassing dyadic level consists of the marital, parent–child, and sibling subsystems, in which mutual social processes are of primary concern between pairs of family members. Finally, the family unit level is the more general social context that circumscribes the marital, parent–child, and sibling subsystems. Each of these levels of the family system has some unique elements and some that are held in common with other levels of the system. The family unit or systemic level that immediately encompasses the parent–child relationship must be conceived in terms of multiple levels of analysis. Specifically, the larger family system consists of several subsystems, which are reciprocally interrelated so that a larger entity is produced that is not reducible to the sum of its parts (Broderick, 1993).

The concept of "boundary" is a key idea that is used to differentiate one family subsystem from another. Of special importance is the "permeability" of a boundary, or the extent to which a particular subsystem (e.g., the parental subsystem) is open to information and influence from larger systems and other subsystems (e.g., the child subsystem). As applied to the parent–child relationship, for example, authoritarian parents probably maintain a boundary between themselves and other subsystems that is largely closed to external information both from children and other sources of influence. Permissive parents, on the other hand, barely maintain boundaries and are extensively receptive to influence and information from other subsystems. Parents who are classified as authoritative, in turn, seem to maintain semipermeable boundaries that are selectively open to some information, but resist other forms of influence. Finally, overprotective parents often manipulate or obscure their subsystem boundaries to foster dependency in children by being open to some information, but by screening out any influence that contributes to autonomy (Bodman & Peterson, 1995). The family system is best understood, therefore, by attending to relationships within subsystems that are created by interacting individuals. More specifically, such a perspective demands that attention be paid to marital as well as parent–child relationships and to triadic relationships (i.e., three-person relationships) as well as parent–child and spousal dyads (Broderick, 1993; Steinglass, 1987).

The Marital Relationship and Divorce

An aspect of the family system that has received increasing research attention for its impact on the parent–child relationship and a variety of child outcomes is the quality of the marital relationship (Barber, 1990; Belsky, 1981, 1990; Belsky et al., 1989; Emery & Tuer, 1993; Erel & Burman, 1995). A wide variety of investigations on marital quality and divorce have either directly or indirectly addressed this issue. Research on this topic illustrates the basic proposition from

systems theory that boundaries between subsystems are variably open to mutual influences from each other, with the implication being that effective parent–child relationships may, in part, be a function of the extent to which marital difficulties are prevalent.

One approach to examining the role of marriage within the parent–child relationship involved the earlier efforts of researchers to conceptualize fathers roles in parenting compared to those of mothers. A frequent finding was that much of the fathers' influences on children are "indirectly" conveyed through mothers. That is, paternal influence resulted from various forms of psychological and economic support that functioned to fortify and sustain the quality of care that mothers provided to the young (Belsky, 1981; Lewis, Feiring & Weinraub, 1981; Pedersen, 1980).

The most common proposal with the strongest empirical support is the perspective that contends that the quality of parent–child relationships is sustained by the quality of the marriage. The model suggests that feelings of satisfaction and support in marriage often "spillover" into the parent–child relationship and predispose parents to respond in a sensitive manner to their children (Belsky et al., 1989; Erel & Burman, 1995; Stafford & Bayer, 1993). The corresponding logic is that negative or conflictual marital relationships stimulate feelings of irritability and emotional drain in parents, which, in turn, predispose them to be less responsive to their children. It is important to emphasize, however, that the "causal" direction of influence has not been defined, and it could just as easily be the case that adverse parent–child relationships may have detrimental consequences for marital quality (Erel & Burman, 1995; Stafford & Bayer, 1993).

Another perspective with limited empirical support predicts that a negative relationship will exist between the quality of marriage and the quality of parent–child relationships. That is, a stressful or conflictual marriage may increase parents' attention to the child as a means of compensating for unmet affectional needs between husbands and wives (Belsky, Youngblade, Rovine, & Volling, 1991; Engfer, 1988; Erel & Burman, 1995). This perspective also proposes that in families where prebirth marital quality is high, a child's birth may be viewed as a hindrance within the marital relationship, which, in turn, creates strain between parent and child.

Several investigators also have focused on the extent to which husbands and wives agree on a variety of parenting attitudes, values, and behaviors in reference to the children (Belsky et al., 1989; Deal, Halverson, & Wampler, 1989). Although some investigators have examined parental agreement as an aspect of high-quality marriages, others have examined the extent to which parental agreement on childrearing strategies (or behavior) may have consequences for socially competent outcomes in children. Specifically, consistency between parents on competent forms of childrearing (e.g., parental agreement on authoritative and supportive childrearing) has been reported to predict such positive outcomes in children and adolescents as high self-esteem, school adaptation, school achievement, intellectual functioning, empathy, social skills, and independence (Johnson et al., 1991; Vaughan et al., 1988). Many of these attributes of children and adolescents were described earlier as dimensions of social competence.

The interrelationships between marital and parent–child relationships also are illustrated when parental marriages become dissolved during the process of divorce. Despite the termination of the marriage, many of the same relationship issues continue to operate in reference to the children. As divorce rates have risen in recent decades concern has grown that children and adolescents from single-parent families are more likely to develop greater psychological and interpersonal problems than youth from intact families (Amato, 1993; Amato & Keith, 1991a,b; Hetherington, Stanley-Hagan, & Anderson, 19889; Seltzer, 1994; Wallerstein & Kelly, 1980). Although some observers tend to find that children sustain adverse consequences from the experience of divorce (Amato, 1993; Wallerstein & Kelly, 1980; Wallerstein, Corbin, & Lewis, 1988), others diminish the empirical consistency or social significance of these findings (Allen, 1993; Demo, 1993; Demo & Acock, 1988).

The trauma of divorce may contribute to escalating coercive exchanges between parents and children and less competent childrearing in the form of increased punitiveness, decreased support, less reasoning, and greater inconsistency. This decline in the quality of parent–child relationships corresponds with the high degree of discord that often characterizes the relationship between parents shortly before and after the divorce (Hetherington et al., 1989). Although parents may feel anger and resentment, those ex-spouses who control their hostility, engage in cooperative joint parenting, negotiate differences, and refrain from exposing their children to quarrels or violence have the best chances of sheltering children from the emotional and social problems commonly associated with divorce (Amato, 1993; Hetherington et al., 1989). Most children, in fact, wish to maintain positive relations with both parents and continue to benefit from this circumstance, even after their custodial parents have remarried (Hetherington et al., 1978, 1985; Zill, 1988).

Parental divorce is associated (albeit inconsistently and in modest degrees) with negative outcomes for such aspects of children's social competence as deficient academic achievement, conduct problems, psychological adjustment, self-esteem, and social relations (Amato & Keith, 1991b). For adults who experienced divorce as children, long-term tendencies exist for these individuals to experience diminished psychological adjustment, self-esteem, and social relations (Amato & Keith, 1991a; Wallerstein et al., 1989). The worst

short-term effects of divorce seem most evident for boys who are in the custody of single-parent mothers, whereas girls seem to adjust more readily to the immediate circumstances of marital dissolution (i.e., the first 2 years after divorce) (Guidubaldi & Cleminshaw, 1985; Guidubaldi & Perry, 1985; Guidubaldi, Perry, & Cleminshaw, 1984; Hetherington et al., 1985). Although some evidence exists that girls may subsequently experience long-term adjustment problems that appear later in adolescence or early adulthood (Hetherington, 1972; Wallerstein et al., 1988), such consequences (i.e., sometimes referred to as "sleeper effects") are disputed by recent investigators (Dunlop & Burns, 1995; MacDonald & DeMaris, 1995).

Results also have indicated that support systems outside families (e.g., peers and other adults besides parents) seem to help adolescents become more capable than younger children of coping with parental divorce and of developing greater autonomy, responsibility, and maturity (Brooks-Gunn, Warren, & Russo, in press; Hetherington, 1984; Steinberg & Silverberg, 1986; Wallerstein & Kelly, 1980). Additional evidence indicates that the worst trauma and effects of divorce occur during the period 1–2 years following the separation and that many parents and children eventually recover from these disturbances (Hetherington et al., 1978). Several reviewers have concluded that changes in marital status (or family structure) per se seem to have little separate influence on children, without considering the critical psychological and relationship factors that will greatly qualify the impact of divorce on the young (Allen, 1993; Amato, 1993; Demo, 1993; Hetherington et al., 1989) Included among these are the coping skills of parents and youth, the self-esteem of the young, and the quality of children's relationships with both parents, as well as the level of marital and postdivorce conflict between parents (Amato, 1993; Hetherington et al., 1989).

In contrast to the direct influence of structural change, therefore, the best explanations revolve around the combined influences of five central concepts: (1) the psychological loss of the noncustodial parent, (2) the effective adjustment of the custodial parent, (3) the extent of continued interparental conflict, (4) divorce-induced economic hardship, and (5) stressful life changes associated with divorce (e.g., moving to a new residence) (Amato, 1993). Compensating factors include the fact that the essential differences in the outcomes between children from intact and divorced homes have not proven to be very large or consistent across studies (Amato, 1993; MacDonald & DeMaris, 1995). Moreover, the key to children's successful adjustment to divorce (i.e., the maintenance of attributes defined earlier as social competence) appears to be parents who maintain a high level of competence in their childrearing (i.e., rational, supportive, and nonpunitive), maintain positive ties with the young, and diminish conflicts with their former spouse. Consequently, an important point is that, regardless of whether children are from divorced or intact homes, an important source of social competence is the quality of the parents' adult relationship (i.e., marital or postdivorce).

Family Cohesion and Adaptability

Besides the connections between one family subsystem (e.g., marital) and another (e.g., parent–child), some scholars have also identified dimensions of the entire family system that provide a context for the parent–child relationship. Scholars from various family systems orientations have focused on the patterns and interrelationships between children, parents, and other family members on a wide range of systemic variables, with the most prominent conception being the Circumplex Model of Family Functioning developed by Olson and associates (Olson, 1986, 1995; Olson, McCubbin, et al., 1983; Olson, Sprenkle & Russell, 1979; Olson, Russell, & Sprenkle, 1983). The central proposal of this model is that different families can be characterized in terms of the dimensions of cohesion and adaptability. The first of these constructs, family cohesion, refers to the emotional bonding (closeness versus distance) among members and the degree to which individual autonomy is experienced in the family system (Olson et al., 1979). According to Olson, families vary along the cohesion dimension in terms of disengaged, separated, connected, and enmeshed categories.

Family adaptability, in turn, refers to the ability of family systems to change their power structures, role relationships, and rules in response to situational and developmental stress (Olson, 1995; Olson et al., 1979). Specifically, this concept refers to the diverse means through which families deal with rules, roles, negotiation processes, discipline, and leadership. The categories rigid, structured, flexible, and chaotic are used to capture variation in the family adaptability concept. The Circumplex Model also includes the dimension of communication, which is conceptualized as a mediating factor that contributes to the levels of both cohesion and adaptability within families (Olson, 1986).

A central idea of Olson's Circumplex Model is that families with children will function best when they are balanced (or have mid-range scores) on both the adaptability and cohesion dimensions. Families with children who are balanced on these dimensions have been reported to be more satisfied and less stressed than other families having scores that vary from the moderate range on these dimensions (Olson et al., 1983). In the case of cohesion, for example, moderate levels of this dimension are supposed to be the most conducive environment for the development of adolescent social competence (Grotevant & Cooper, 1986). Families with moderate connectedness often provide environments in

which the young demonstrate more socially competent qualities such as negotiation, effective communication, responsibility for self, cooperation, identity formation, role-taking skills, and positive goals (Grotevant & Cooper, 1986; Olson, 1986).

In a similar fashion, Olson and colleagues conclude that moderate levels of adaptability, or a balance between rigid styles (i.e., overly structured, little change) and chaotic styles (i.e., little structure, possibly constant change), provide the best environment for adolescent development (Olson, 1986). This familial environment is also consistent with authoritative childrearing approaches in which parents outline rules, use firm control, and provide rationales, which socializes the young for social competence (Baumrind, 1978, 1991). Such family environments allow individuals to have sufficient psychological autonomy, while being emotionally close to families so that optimal conditions are prevalent to foster individuality within the context of connections with (or responsibility to) others.

The Circumplex Model, therefore, suggests how parental competence and children's social competence may be either accommodated or hindered by certain patterns of cohesion and adaptability at the overall system level of families. The most important implication of this model is that children and other family members are proposed to function most effectively (and demonstrate social competence) when moderate levels of cohesion and adaptability are prevalent.

Although the dimensions of cohesion and adaptability continue to be useful in research and the family environment of children (Burr & Lowe, 1987), the cumulative evidence on the Circumplex Model has been somewhat mixed. Contrasting results indicate, for example, that cohesion and adaptability may be either linear predictors or unrelated to various qualities of families (Green, Kolevon, & Vosler, 1985; Miller, Epstein, Bishop, & Keitner, 1985; Walker, McLaughlin, & Green, 1988). Some of the studies have reported divergent patterns of prediction for cohesion and the methodological soundness of the FACES III instrument (Barber & Buehler, 1996; Farrell & Barnes, 1993; Green, Harris, Forte, & Robinson, 1991).

Connections between the Family and Other Social Contexts

Although versions of systems theory applied to families have become increasingly important, awareness has also grown of the need to comprehend how social agents and contexts beyond family boundaries have connections with the parent–child relationship (Luster & Okagi, 1993; Stafford & Bayer, 1993). Perhaps the most comprehensive effort to conceptualize the broader social context is through the ecological systems perspective developed by Urie Bronfenbrenner (1979, 1986; Bronfenbrenner & Crouter, 1983). Because there is growing recognition of the constant interplay between person and environment in human development, Bronfenbrenner has argued that any understanding of human development must consider the context in which socialization occurs. The primary message is that parent–child relationships that either foster or hinder social competence cannot be understood separate from immediate and more distant social contexts. Consequently, research that is limited to parent effects, child effects, or the parent–child dyad will provide only partial information about developmental processes.

Besides a focus on reciprocal relationships between person and environment, the ecological systems perspective conceptualizes the environment quite differently from other frameworks. Specifically, the environment is conceptualized as a series of four concentric levels that vary in terms of proximity to the developing child. The most proximal level to the child, the microsystem, involves settings of day-to-day living, such as the home, school, and the peer group. Each of these immediate environments provides a context in which children are actively engaged in reciprocal interactions with others and are either directly influencing or are directly affected by the actions of others. The next level of the environment, the mesosystem, involves the amount and degree of linkage that exists between the various microsystems, or settings that directly involve children. An example of a mesosystem level of analysis would be to examine how the amount and degree of involvement between the parent–child setting and the child–school setting affect the competence of the young.

The micro and mesosystems, in turn, are embedded within exosystems, or those contexts that do not directly involve children, but are indirectly connected to the young. A commonly used example of an exosystem having implications for the parent–child relationship is the work setting of mothers and fathers. Although parental work does not directly involve the child, this context can have considerable impact on children by affecting the physical and emotional well-being of parents, as well as through family economic resources. Similarly, the parent–child relationship can impact the physical and emotional availability of parents in regard to the work environment. Another example of exosystemic contexts include parental social networks.

The final level, and the one in which all of the others are embedded, is the macrosystem. This level involves the basic "blueprints" of a particular society, inclusive of its cultural, economic, and political norms, values, and attitudes (Bronfenbrenner, 1979). Macrosystem issues are often the most difficult to research objectively because they form the basis for fundamental social philosophies and the everyday meanings of life.

Overall, the significant features of the ecological-system perspective are: (1) the focus on reciprocal interactions between children and their environment, (2) the recognition and inclusion of both direct and indirect sources of influence, and (3) the systemic organization of the environment. This orientation has become prominent in scholarship that examines the connections between the parent–child relationship and parents' marriage (Emergy & Tuer, 1993), social networks (Cochran, 1993), work environments (Crouter & McHale, 1993), and neighborhood and community influences (Garbarino & Kostelny, 1993; Klebanov, Brooks-Gunn, & Duncan, 1994). Other areas of theoretical application are child maltreatment (Belsky, 1980; Garbarino, 1977) and risk and resiliency in families (Belsky, 1980; Belsky et al., 1989).

Sources of Ecological Support or Vulnerability

An obvious conclusion that many researchers and scholars have reached rather belatedly is that the parent–child relationship can be understood systematically only in terms of its surrounding social context (Ambert, 1992; Belsky, 1990; Bronfenbrenner, 1979, 19886; Luster & Okagi, 1993; Stafford & Bayer, 1993). What is particularly important, then, is the nature of the social environment that either impinges directly upon or has indirect connections with families and parent–child relationships. A notable feature of these contexts is the extent to which they provide either "societal or ecological support" to (and help to enhance both parental competence and the social competence of children) or further enhance the vulnerabilities of the parent–child relationship to serious problems (e.g., incompetent parenting and socially incompetent children). Such a comprehensive view of societal or ecological support systems is concerned with the resources that a society provides (or the lack thereof) to parents and children to foster the development of their mutual relationship (Ambert, 1992).

A conception of this kind (i.e., societal or ecological support systems) includes a vast array of social circumstances that influence parent–child experiences, such as the immediate social network (e.g., extended family members, neighbors, friends, peers), socioeconomic factors (e.g., adequate housing, income, and income supplements), the quality of childcare and schools for children of all ages, the nature of health care, the provision of psychiatric and mental health support, the characteristics of parents' work environments, and the extent to which the larger society accepts and does not discriminate based on cultural or ethnic-minority status. Because the complexities of the social context are impossible to deal with in a single chapter, we have chosen to illustrate its importance by focusing on three elements: (1) the immediate social network (i.e., kin, friends, and peers); (2) the socioeconomic circumstances of parents with special attention to the workplace; and (3) the implications of ethnic minority status for the parent–child relationship.

The Parent–Child Relationship and Immediate Social Networks.

Some of the most immediate systemic connections are parental social networks and, to some extent, the relationship of child–peer networks to parent–child relationships. Parents' social networks refer to interactions and relationships with relatives, friends, neighbors, and other acquaintances (Cochran, 1993; Crnic, Greenberg, Ragozin, Robinson, & Busham, 1983; Unger & Powell, 1980). The relevance of social networks to parent–child relations typically has involved an appraisal of the amount of emotional, instrumental, and informational support provided to parents by these interconnections. During the early parenting years, research on social support has been quite consistent, with higher levels of social support being associated with secure infant attachment relationships (Crockenberg, 1981); higher quality mother–infant interaction (Crnic et al., 1983; Hann, 1989; Powell, 1980); warmer, less intrusive, and more accepting mother–toddler interactions (Crockenberg, 1987; Jennings, Stagg, & Connors, 1991); and greater satisfaction and less distress with parenting in early childhood (Koeske & Koeske, 1990).

Although the beneficial effects of parental social support have been documented, determining the most effective types of social support and the mechanisms by which support influences parenting is less clear. Social support has been measured in previous research as the structural components of the social network (e.g., size, density, frequency of contact, source of support), the functional aspects of support (e.g., financial assistance, caretaking, affiliation, emotional support), and perceived satisfaction with either the structural or functional aspects of support (Cochran, 1993). Although each type of support seems to be relevant and important, the perceived satisfaction with support has been the most consistent predictor of more competent parenting (Jennings et al., 1991).

Similarly, several models have sought to describe the mechanisms by which social support affects parenting. In one model, social support is conceptualized as having a direct effect on parenting through the provision of substitute care or when parents receive information about or praise for their parenting skills (Belsky, 1990). Social support also has been conceptualized as indirectly affecting parenting by either moderating (Crnic & Greenberg, 1987; Koeske & Koeske, 1990) or mediating the impact of stressful life events for the parents (Quittner et al., 1990). It is likely, then, that social support from friends, kin, and neighborhoods may assist in maintaining high-quality parenting, which, in turn, contributes to social competence in children. Taken together, research on social support suggests that it is an important

variable to consider when examining parent–child relations. Further research, however, is needed to identify exactly what types of social support are important for the different phases of parenting, with the important tasks being to test for direct, indirect, and interactive effects of social support.

Although a substantial body of literature exists on the relationship between parental social networks and parent–child relations, comparatively little research has been devoted to the relationship between child–peer networks and parent–child relations. This is particularly interesting in light of the common belief that, except for the powerful influence of families, peer relationships provide one of the most efficacious contexts for the socialization of children (Ladd, Hart, Wadsworth, & Golter, 1988). In conceptualizing associations between the parent–child and child–peer systems, researchers traditionally have focused on how relationships within the family indirectly effect child–peer relations via the impact of parenting on child social competency (Lewis & Feiring, 1989; Parke et al., 1989). The focus of such research has been to identify aspects of parental competence that promote social competency in the child, which, in turn, affects the child's relations with peers.

An example of scholarship that supports this indirect effects proposal is research on the developmental course of infant attachment. Specifically, warm, sensitive, and responsive caregiving has been associated with the development of secure infant attachment (Ainsworth et al., 1978), which, in turn, has been found to predict social competency and more effective peer relations during early and middle childhood (Elicker, England, & Sroufe, in press; Sroufe & Fleeson, 1986). Similarly, the work of Diana Baumrind (1978, 1990), which links styles of parenting to child social competence and peer competency, is another exemplary line of research supporting an indirect effects conceptualization between the family and peers environments. More recent research in this area has indicated several direct ways in which parents effect child–peer relations (e.g., by providing opportunities for encouragement of peer interactions) (Ladd et al., 1988; Lewis & Feiring, 1989; Parke et al., 1989). Moreover, in a study of the preschool years, Parke et al. (1989) found that parental supervision enhanced the quality of child–peer play in terms of children's abilities to take turns and play cooperatively.

The linkage between the parent–child and peer associations also continues during adolescence. That is, recent studies have indicated that specific parental behaviors (monitoring, encouragement of achievement, joint decision-making) are associated with specific adolescent behaviors (academic achievement, drug use, self-reliance), which, in turn, were significantly related to membership in either prosocial or antisocial peer groups ("populars," "jocks," "brains," "druggies," or "outcasts") (Brown, Mounts, Lamborn, & Steinberg, 1993; Dishion, Patterson, Stoolmiller, & Skinner,

1991). Parental encouragement of achievement, for example, may promote higher academic performance, which fosters association with peer groups characterized as the "populars" or the "brains" (Brown et al., 1993). Further research is needed that examines interactions between the characteristics of children, families, and peer networks to more fully understand how these important contexts are interconnected (Durbin et al., 1993).

Social Class and the Parent–Child Relationship. Social class membership is an important circumstance of life that provides experiences for the parent–child socialization process and the development of social competence by the young (Gecas, 1979; Peterson & Rollins, 1987; Smith & Graham, 1996). The root of these systemic influences lies in the different conditions of life, varied conceptions of social reality, different priorities, and distinct goals that parents of various socioeconomic levels (e.g., upper, middle, and lower classes) bring to the parent–child relationship. Such variable life experiences (e.g., in the workplace, school, or neighborhood) and priorities foster the tendency for parents and other socializing agents to value and place demands on the young for different forms of social competence so that adaptation can take place in distinctive social environments (Gecas, 1979; Kohn, 1977; Kohn & Schooler, 1983; Okagaki & Divecha, 1993; Peterson & Rollins, 1987; Wilson, Peterson, & Wilson, 1993). Several researchers have indicated, for example, that parents and other members of the lower class are more likely than occupants of the middle class to emphasize conformity and obedience as part of social competence. In contrast, members of the middle class tend to emphasize self-expression, achievement, autonomy, and self-control (Gecas, 1979; Kohn, 1977; Kohn & Schooler, 1983; Peterson & Rollins, 1987).

Similar to the manner that SES redefines the nature of social competence, a family's social class membership (e.g., occupational or educational attainment) also helps to explain why parents differ in their childrearing approaches (Gecas, 1979; Kohn, 1977; Peterson & Rollins, 1987). Melvin Kohn, for example, has proposed that parents from different socioeconomic levels vary in terms of the characteristics they value in children, which, in turn, may influence them to use different kinds of childrearing behavior. The occupational setting of parents, for example, is often identified as a key aspect of social class membership (some also identify school settings and other environments) that serves as a major source of childrearing values. Blue collar parents, for example, whose jobs are highly supervised by management and lacking in substantive complexity, tend to value obedience from their children. Consequently, such parents are more likely to believe in conformity to external authority and to emphasize obedience, good manners, neatness, and cleanliness in children. Such value orientations are expected to foster the frequent use of coercive and punitive behavior, coupled with a diminished emphasis on reasoning and nurturance by blue collar parents (Gecas, 1979; Okagaki & Divecha, 1993; Peterson & Rollins, 1987). Other research that is supportive of these findings about social class indicates that stresses on parents associated with economic deprivation due to sudden loss of employment (or sudden decline in class status) often translate into emotional distress, declines in parental efficacy, and the use of more authoritarian and less supportive behaviors by parents (Conger & Elder, 1994; Elder, Eccles, Ardelt, & Lord, 1995; Lempers, Clark-Lempers, & Simons, 1989).

In contrast, white collar parents who are more highly educated and work in settings where self-direction is rewarded tend to value self-governance and self-responsibility for themselves and their children. Placing emphasis on these value orientations is more likely to foster the use of reason, rational control, and supportiveness as well as to discourage authoritarian strategies by white collar parents. In general, the existing scholarship on social class and childrearing describes how parents from distinctive socioeconomic levels face very different problems, have different goals, and often choose different childrearing approaches for raising their young.

Work and the Parent–Child Relationship. Beyond consideration as part of family socioeconomic status, the connection between the parent's work environment and the parent–child relationship is a growing area of research concern. Much of the work on both paternal and maternal employment indicate that fathers, mothers, and children derive benefits from parental job experiences. It is certainly true, for example, that work experience (and occupational attainment) is a major predictor of higher personal morale for mothers and fathers as well as a great socioeconomic advantage for the quality of parents' and children's lives (Crouter & McHale, 1993; Hoffman, 1989; McLoyd, 1989; Menaghan & Parcel, 1990; Voydanoff, 1990). Besides these obvious realities, however, a gender bias has often motivated research on maternal employment through the assumption (without much empirical support) that mothers who work outside the home are often at odds with the maintenance of a high-quality relationship with their children. Paternal employment, on the other hand, is often viewed as a problematic issue only when fathers are either unemployed or are employed in low-wage occupations (Menaghan & Parcel, 1990). Despite some persistence of this bias, current scholarship on parental employment is beginning to strike a better balance in conceptualizing how the work settings of mothers and fathers have consequence for the parent–child relationship and the psychosocial outcomes of children (Menaghan & Parcel, 1990).

Instead of value-laden suppositions, then, the primary effect of parental employment on the parent–child relationship is a product of the workers' psychological orientations and personal well-being within their occupational contexts. Research on work socialization, for example, has examined how the substantive complexity of the workplace, involving the degrees of self-direction, diversity of stimuli, flexibility in work patterns, and the number of decisions to be made, has impact on parental values and childrearing strategies. The general trend of these findings indicates that greater substantive complexity in work settings predicts that parents will place greater emphasis on self-direction, autonomy, and nurturance in their childrearing approaches, whereas lower substantive complexity leads to a more conservative emphasis on obedience to authority (Crouter, 1984; Crouter & McHale, 1993; Kohn & Schooler, 1983; Mortimer, Lorence, & Kumka, 1986; Schooler, 1987).

Other influences of the workplace on parent–child relationships include the sources of job stress in the employment conditions of mothers and fathers. The origins of such stress include depersonalization, low wages, poor job conditions, limited advancement opportunities, long hours, job demands, poor social climate, and low job satisfaction (Crouter & McHale, 1993; Hibbard & Pope, 1987; Repetti, 1988). Increased parental stress, therefore, often has impact on the quality of parent–child interaction and the degree of parental involvement with the young (Piotrkowski, Rapoport, & Rapoport, 1987; Voydanoff, 1987).

Closely related to research on the sources and consequences of job stress is the scholarship indicating that loss of employment by fathers and the economic deprivation that often results has adverse consequences for the parent–child relationship (Conger & Elder, 1994; Elder et al., 1995; McLoyd, 1989). It is not surprising to learn, for example, that unemployed compared to employed men tend to be more depressed, anxious, and hostile and to have higher feelings of victimization and dissatisfaction with themselves and their lives (McLoyd, 1989; Voydanoff, 1990). Because such dispositions of unemployed men correspond with being gloomy and hostile, fathers who have experienced job and income loss are more likely to be less supportive, more punitive, and more arbitrary in their interactions with children (i.e., less competent parents) (Elder et al., 1985; Lempers et al., 1989). The embarrassment, economic deprivation, and declines in the quality of parenting that often result from parental job loss seem to predict that children will demonstrate somewhat greater tendencies to become more depressed, distrustful, lonely, emotionally sensitive, involved in socially disapproved acts, and inclined to violate school rules (i.e., become more socially incompetent). The psychosocial outcomes of children who experience deprivation of this kind often include such dimensions of social competence as lower self-esteem, less peer acceptance, and diminished ability to cope with stress (Elder et al., 1985; Lempers et al., 1989; McLoyd, 1989). Both the socioemotional consequences for children and declines in parenting are not solely a function of employment loss, but also are subject to such factors as youthful temperament, the physical attributes of children, and the personal resources of parents (Elder et al., 1985; Elder, Caspi, & Van Nguyen, 1986).

In reference to women in the workplace, on the other hand, most research indicates that the occupational participation of mothers has few adverse effects on children, with some evidence indicating that positive effects can result (Menaghan & Parcel, 1990; Spitze, 1988). This is true despite mixed results for the influence of maternal employment on mother–infant attachment, in which some research suggests no effects (Chase-Lamedale & Owen, 1987; Easterbrooks & Goldberg, 1988; Owen & Cox, 1988), while other work indicates that insecure attachment is somewhat more prevalent for infants of employed mothers (Barglow, Vaughn, & Molitor, 1987; Belsky & Rovine, 1988).

An overall view is that maternal employment expands the role models that are available for children, prevents dependency, encourages egalitarian gender role attitudes, and promotes more positive attitudes toward women and their employment (Hoffman, 1989; Kiecolt & Acock, 1988). Employed mothers also derive personal benefits from employment in the form of self-esteem, personal efficacy, and overall well-being (Mirowsky & Ross, 1986; Rosenfield, 1989), which, in turn, seem to mediate greater efforts by parents to foster (or allow) greater independence, maturity, and self-reliance by children (Amato & Ochiltree, 1986; Hoffman, 1989). Evidence is also increasingly apparent that fathers in dual-earner as compared to single-earner families become more involved in childcare (Crouter & McHale, 1993).

The most accurate assessment of the current knowledge about parental employment, therefore, is that, despite preoccupations with the supposed consequences of work involvement on the parent–child relationship, issues such as substantive job complexity, levels of supervision, work stress, parental resources, parental involvement, and role accumulation will greatly modify the impact of both maternal and paternal employment. Many of the commonly identified employment effects are actually mediated by (1) the specific attributes of the workplace and degree of parental satisfaction or dissatisfaction with job circumstances; (2) children's age, gender, social class, and personality characteristics; and (3) the quality of substitute childcare and other sources of social support that parents have available (Belsky, 1990; Crouter & McHale, 1993; Hoffman, 1989).

Ethnic-Minority Membership. Another important source of influence from the larger social context on the parent–child relationship is membership in a particular ethnic minority or cultural group. Although often acknowledged as an essential area of focus, much of the developmental and parent–child research remains focused on middle-class, Euro-American samples that implicitly create ethnocentric norms about processes within the parent–child relationships (Ambert, 1992; Hui & Triandis, 1985; Knight, Tein, Shell, & Roosa, 1992; Rogoff & Morelli, 1989). Scholars must become increasingly cognizant of such myopic views so that more accurate images of the cultural landscape characterized by ethnic diversity can become more prevalent (Dillworth-Anderson, Burton, & Turner, 1993).

The impact of ethnic-minority membership on the parent–child relationship includes culturally linked ways of thinking, valuing, feeling, and acting that the young are encouraged to acquire through socialization (Harrison, Wilson, Pine, Chan, & Buriel, 1990; Whiting & Whiting, 1975). Children who are members of ethnic groups are exposed to the particular group's shared identity, common ancestry, and common cultural lifeways that shape different conceptions of competent parenting and social competence in children. Through the socialization process, the young become exposed to the unique values, meanings, and goals of each ethnic (cultural) group that are conveyed by a distinct historical heritage, language, religion, customs, and common experience. Parents and other social agents pass on to children not only language, customs, and rituals, but also implicit assumptions regarding the nature of social relationships and the roles that youth must fulfill as they progress toward adulthood (Ogbu, 1981, 1985, 1987).

One consequence of such experiences is that children are faced with somewhat different definitions and expectations for social competence in various ethnic environments (Ogbu, 1981, 1987). That is, societies and ethnic groups vary in the extent to which specific aspects of social competence are valued and encouraged in the young (Arnett, 1995; Baumrind, 1978). For example, there is greater emphasis on conformity to parents' expectations, stronger reliance on family connections, and less emphasis on individual autonomy within Hispanic, Asian, and black ethnic groups than in the Anglo culture of the United States (Dillworth-Anderson et al., 1993; Giordano, Cernovich, & DeMaris, 1993; Harrison et al., 1990). Moreover, Mexican American and Asian youth are often thought to be more affiliative, cooperative, and responsive to the commands of authority figures than is the case for children and adolescents from the dominate, Anglo mainstream (Buriel, 1993; Rotheram & Phinney, 1987; Staples & Mirande, 1980; Vega, 1990).

According to Harrison et al. (1990), for example, common themes in ethnic-minority socialization (i.e., African-American, Asian American, Hispanic, and Native American families) include greater emphases on familism, collectivism, interdependence, cooperation, obligation, and reciprocity than is true within the dominant Euro-American culture (Delgado-Gaitan, 1987; Gutierrez, Sameroff, & Karrer, 1988; Serafica, 1989). Generally, it is argued that ethnic-minority children are socialized within families to think, feel, and act more extensively in ways that involve a cooperative rather than a competitive view of life. Contrasting with emphases on self-contained individualism and autonomy in the dominant culture, therefore, is the encouragement within several ethnic-minority communities of the conception that the "self" is not an isolated entity, but a component that is attached to systems such as families, households, communities, and the larger group (Harrison et al., 1990; Peterson, 1995).

Another central aspect of ethnic-minority socialization is on the process of acculturation and the recognition that many ethnic-minority parents and children are faced with issues related to being members of two worlds (i.e., the dominant and original cultures) in various degrees (Berry, 1990). The process of acculturation, which is especially relevant to immigrant populations, is a more complex process than simply accommodating to the culture of immigration while relinquishing characteristics of the original culture (Balcazar & Peterson, 1996; Szopocznik & Kurtines, 1980). Instead, there are a variety of ways that parents and children accommodate to the new culture, remain tied to their origins, or strike a balance between the two cultures in terms of cultural knowledge, emotional reactions, and behavioral practices (Balcazar & Peterson, 1996). Ethnic minority children are often faced, therefore, with the challenge of dealing with at least two worlds—the dominant culture and the lifeways of the particular ethnic-minority or cultural community of which they are original members. Both immigrant and native-born children are often socialized within ethnic-minority families to function in more than one culture by switching repertoires of behavior appropriately as called for by the circumstances. Some researchers have also suggested, in turn, that differential acculturation rates between parents and children lead to intergenerational conflict (Szapocznik & Hernandez, 1988). Others have found that the childrearing values and behaviors of successive generations of ethnic-minority parents may change as the acculturation process progresses and assimilation occurs (Buriel, 1993).

An important aspect of ethnic-minority socialization that differs from the dominant culture is the emphasis on racial or ethnic socialization. Black parents, on the one hand, play a critical role in socializing their children to accept the values and participate successfully as members of the larger, "mainstream" society (Taylor, Chatters, Tucker, & Lewis, 1990; Thornton, Chatters, Taylor, & Allen, 1990). An important complicating issue for ethnic-minority families, however, is the fact that racial prejudice and discrimination are important intervening aspects that complicate the socialization process faced by African-American and other ethnic-minority families. Consequently, a second task for ethnic-minority parents is to use socialization strategies that promote favorable orientations toward their own subcultural group as a means of fostering positive ethnic identities and abilities to function in a bicultural world (Harrison et al., 1990). A part of this objective is the requirement to foster attitudes, beliefs, and skills that buffer ethnic-minority children from a hostile social environment characterized by discrimination (Harrison et al., 1990; Jackson, McCullough, & Gurin, 1988; Peters, 1985). Although ethnic-minority families vary in the extent to which racial-ethnic socialization is practiced (Thornton et al., 1990; Vega, 1990), many of these efforts are designed to prepare their offspring for social inequalities by forewarning them about hostile aspects of the broader social environment. The overall result, then, is that the ethnic-minority context may have substantial consequences for parents' socialization strategies and the specific cultural definition of social competence that they seek to instill in the young.

Critique of Systemic Models

Systemic models are probably the most conceptually accurate of all the approaches used to examine the complexities of parent–child socialization. In support of this position is the growing consensus among scholars that human social relationships must be understood in terms of both multidirectional family processes and connections beyond family boundaries with many aspects of the surrounding social context. The most obvious negative side of systemic models is the incredible complexity required in research that attempts to accurately reflect the "true complexity" of the social world. Such models must account simultaneously for variables that are part of the parent–child relationship, the larger family system, and social-contextual variables, such as SES, ethnicity, and many others. As a result, the complicated nature of these models makes them appear to be "soft" or almost anti-scientific. Unfortunately, social science methodology may never (or at least for the foreseeable future) be able to capture the necessary complexity of systems models.

Research strategies for systemic models will greatly benefit, however, from the use of structural equation modeling that accommodates both complex theory-testing efforts with many variables and allows for the inclusion of reciprocal effects. Further work should be conducted to examine parent–child dyads in terms of "relationship scores," similar to the need for "family scores" that characterize overall family processes. This is contrary to much of the research on parent–child relationships that examines either perceptions or observations of an individual's (i.e., parent's or child's)

behavior, rather than characterizing the processes that occur between both parties simultaneously.

If parent–child relationships are to be understood within the context of families, future investigators must use a variety of research strategies intended to examine the processes between parents and children within the context of the larger family system. Although research on triadic and more complex relationships will have countless direct and indirect connections, researchers must continue to explore these complexities so that "realistic" aspects of relationships are investigated. Moreover, researchers should examine how aspects of the parent–child relationship (or an aspect of the parent–child subsystem) are either related to or reflect constructs used to conceptualize phenomena at the larger, family system level of analysis. Specifically, the authoritative parent, for example, a concept used to describe a style of childrearing within the parent–child subsystem, seems to have much in common with (and perhaps is reflective of) concepts used to describe constructs at the larger system level (see Bodman & Peterson, 1995). Indeed, one can easily find a large number of family system level concepts that seem conceptually analogous to characterizations of authoritative parenting as rational, firmly controlling, open to negotiation, fostering communication, and highly supportive. Systemic ideas of this kind include the concept that competent parents structure a "united coalition" with a "semipermeable boundary" in reference to children. Such attributes of "open family systems" are also portrayed as healthy environments for fostering a balance between autonomy and connectedness among family members (Bodman & Peterson, 1995; Peterson, 1995b).

Finally, a problem with virtually all of the approaches to research on parent–child relationships (including the systemic-ecological perspective) is the disproportionate emphasis on middle-class, Euro-American samples, with the result being that deficient attention is devoted to samples of diverse ethnic and socioeconomic origins (Harrison et al., 1990; Hui & Triandis, 1985; Knight et al., 1992; Rogoff & Merelli, 1989). Although some progress is being made (Hui & Triandis, 1985; Knight et al., 1992), there are few studies that effectively deal with such issues as the cross-ethnic equivalence of measures and the need to examine the role of acculturation in ethnic and immigrant populations. The changing ethnic composition of the U.S. population makes such research a substantial imperative for the future.

Conclusions

The purpose of this chapter has been to examine and make sense of the current status of parent–child research classified as the traditions of parent effects, child effects, reciprocal socialization, and systemic-ecological perspectives. Although these literatures are extremely diverse in substance and methodology, there are a number of common themes that appear in a variety of ways throughout this vast body of work.

1. *Responsiveness* tends to be a central characteristic of family systems and parent–child relationships that foster social competence in children. That is, parental responsiveness and warmth are key elements of reciprocal relationships (i.e., effective synchrony) leading to secure attachment. As development proceeds, parental supportiveness and responsive communication are important elements that predict the development of several aspects of social competence in the young. Furthermore, parent–child relationships must also be viewed in terms of the larger family system, which must have sufficient levels of connectedness or cohesion to function effectively. Finally, it is increasingly recognized that parent–child relationships are the most responsive when supported by social networks, neighborhoods, school systems, childcare institutions, work environments, communities, and the sociocultural values of the larger social context.

2. *Firm control* consists of moderately demanding, rational control that is consistently enforced and provides an alternative to either harsh, punitive, or psychologically intrusive approaches. Consistent with this theme, parents take charge through control attempts that are rule-based and where the authority of parents becomes less restrictive as children develop. Such ideas are conveyed through concepts like authoritative childrearing, inductive control, and parental monitoring as childrearing strategies that contribute to social competence in the young. Systems concepts that correspond with these ideas are family environments characterized by parental coalitions having semipermeable boundaries and moderate levels of cohesion and adaptability. The parents of such families engage in open communication with the young, which contributes to effective negotiation and problem solving. A common result is the development of social competence in children, which involves reasonable autonomy, at least moderate cooperativeness with (or conformity to) adults, high self-esteem, and effective achievement orientations.

3. *Excessive control* are those forms that are either too authoritarian or too intrusive into the psychological experience of children. Authoritarian, coercive, or punitive behavior inhibits social competence and appears to foster either problematic external conformity or "externalizing behavior" in the form of antisocial involvements by children who "act out" against society. Such arbitrary forms of control tend to "separate" the young from parents and other agents of socialization. Systems concepts that correspond with these ideas are parental subsystems with rigid boundaries and little receptivity to information from the child subsystem. Intrusive control, on the other hand, is overly protective in the

sense of fostering "internalizing attributes" such as excessive dependency. Parents who use intrusive control often manipulate their subsystem boundary to inhibit individuality and progress toward adulthood, with the result being excessive connectedness within family systems that inhibits the development of sufficient individuality by the young.

4. Another important theme in the parent–child literature is concerned with the *sources of parental authority*. Specifically, parental authority derives, in part, from perceptions by the young that mothers and fathers have valued resources, "power," or "authority" in their relationship. Specifically, the young make attributions that parents have capacities to establish their legitimacy and serve as objects of identification, as well as provide expertise, rewards, and punishments. Parents also are viewed as having authority when they model prosocial attributes and behavior, even when they are not aware of being observed. Finally, a major resource for parental authority is provided by the extent to which other social systems, such as socioeconomic, work, school, neighborhood, community, and ethnic contexts, either provide support or contradict effective childrearing.

5. It is also increasingly evident that socialization and interaction processes within the parent–child subsystem of the family must be understood as *bidirectional phenomena*. From infant temperament to efforts by adolescents to assert their autonomy, parents are affected by the presence, actions, and qualities of the young. The most fundamental aspects of an adult's identity are influenced when he or she makes the transition to parenthood. Increased evidence also indicates that parents and infants engage in synchronous interactions much like a dialogue or waltz. Perhaps this reciprocity contributes to attachment bonds, which, in turn, form the basis for later bidirectional relationships in childhood, adolescence, and adulthood.

6. A more comprehensive theme is that the parent–child relationship must be viewed within a complex array of *systemic-ecological relationships*. Specifically, the parent–child relationship is conceptualized as nested within a hierarchy of successively larger and mutually influential social contexts, consisting of the family, community, and larger sociocultural context. The larger social context includes such influences as general socioeconomic conditions and larger cultural influences as well as ethnic influences. The community context includes the interrelationships that families and parent–child relationships have with more immediate social contexts, such as the workplace, schools, peer groups, churches, and neighborhoods. A third level that immediately encompasses the parent–child relationship is the family environment, which recognizes the importance of other subsystems (i.e., marital and sibling subsystems) for parents and their young. Finally, the innermost relationship level designates the parent–child subsystem and recognizes that parent

effects, child effects, and reciprocal exchanges play important roles in socializing parents and children within families.

A compelling implication of such systemic conceptions is that the study of parent–child relationships has come a long way from the simplistic idea that socialization consists only of parents shaping or molding children. This progress becomes very clear through the complicated interconnections that have consequences either directly or indirectly within the parent–child relationship. Consistent with such a "panoramic" view of parent–child relationships, it is very difficult to retain the antiquated belief that children are simply a product of their own parents' talents or deficiencies in child-drearing. Instead, the essential message of a systemic model is that parenting is both a function and a responsibility shared by virtually all elements of a society (i.e., "it takes a village to raise a child"). As a result, we must systematically rethink how employers, teachers, religious leaders, human service professionals, government officials, and the resulting social policies (to name only a few) either share in or have important consequences for the parenting process. Moreover, we must fully appreciate the extent to which children socialize their parents and other adults and eventually reshape the social institutions that compose their social environment.

The overall meaning of such complexities, then, is that face-to-face relationships between parents and children are important, but they are only a portion of the total picture. This conception of parenting as a broader social function (or cooperative effort among many social agents) is a necessary but difficult realization for a society that values individualism, the sanctity of family privacy, and parental rights (Peterson, 1995b). Unfortunately, we are only beginning to realize that some of our basic cultural assumptions (e.g., the myth of family self-reliance or "family values") may be placing many children at risk for forms of socialization that are terribly deficient (Bellah, Madsen, Sullivan, Swidler, & Tipton, 1985; Peterson, 1995b). If the worth of a society is measured in terms of how it treats its children, we must do a better job of comprehending and taking responsibility for the fact that all of us are at least partially responsible for the social environments that structure the lives of children and their parents. The ultimate measure of our civilization's historic worth may well be defined by the extent to which parents, political leaders, and social institutions either grappled with or failed to deal with the fundamental issue of caring for and socializing our society's children.

References

Acock, A., & Schumm, W. R. (1993). Analysis covariance structure applied to family research and theory. In P. G. Boss, W. J. Doherty, R. LaRossa, W. R. Schumm, & S. Steinmetz (Eds.), *Sourcebook of family theories and methods: A contextual approach* (pp. 451–469). New York: Plenum.

Ainsworth, M. D. S. (1985). Patterns of attachment. *Clinical Psychologist, 38,* 27–29.

Ainsworth, M. D. S. (1989). Attachments beyond infancy. *American Psychologist, 44,* 709–716.

Ainsworth, M. D. S., Blehar, M. C., Waters, E., & Wall, S. (1978). *Patterns of attachment: A psychological study of the strange situation.* Hillsdale, NJ: Erlbaum.

Allen, K. R. (1993). The dispassionate discourse of children's adjustment to divorce. *Journal of Marriage and the Family, 55*(1), 46–50.

Amato, P. R. (1993). Children's adjustment to divorce: Theories, hypotheses, and empirical support. *Journal of Marriage and the Family, 55*(1), 23–38.

Amato, P. R., & Keith, B. (1991a). Parental divorce and adult well-being: A meta-analysis. *Journal of Marriage and the Family, 53,* 43–58.

Amato, P. R., & Keith, B. (1991b). Parental divorce and the well-being of children: A meta-analysis. *Psychological Bulletin, 110,* 26–46.

Amato, P. R., & Ochiltree, G. (1986). Family resources and the development of child competence. *Journal of Marriage and the Family, 48,* 47–56.

Ambert, A. (1992). *The effects of children on parents.* Binghamton, NY: Haworth.

Ambert, A. (1997). *Parents, children, and adolescents: Interactive relationships and development in context.* Binghamton, NY: Haworth.

Arnett, J. J. (1995). Broad and narrow socialization: The family in the context of a cultural theory. *Journal of Marriage and the Family, 57*(3), 617–628.

Bachman, J., O'Malley, P., & Johnson, J. (1978). *Adolescence to adulthood: Change and stability in the lives of young men.* Ann Arbor, MI: Institute for Social Research.

Balcazar, H., & Peterson, G. W. (1996, February). *Acculturative accommodation: A new perspective on acculturation and mental health among Mexican-American adolescents.* Paper presented at the national conference for the National Association of African-American and Latino Studies, Houston, TX.

Bandura, A. (1976). *Social learning theory.* Englewood Cliffs, NJ: Prentice-Hall.

Bandura, A., & Huston, A. (1961). Identification as a process of incidental learning. *Journal of Abnormal and Social Psychology, 63,* 311–318.

Bandura, A., Ross, D., & Ross, L. A. (1963). Vicarious reinforcement and imitative learning. *Journal of Abnormal and Social Psychology, 67,* 601–607.

Barber, B. K. (1990). Marital quality, parental behaviors, and adolescent self-esteem. In B. K. Barber & B. C. Rollins (Eds.), *Parent–adolescent relationships* (pp. 49–74). Baltimore: University Press of America.

Barber, B. (1992). Family, personality, and adolescent problem behaviors. *Journal of Marriage and the Family, 54,* 69–79.

Barber, B. K., & Buehler, C. (1996). Family cohesion and enmeshment: Different constructs, different effects. *Journal of Marriage and the Family, 58,* 433–441.

Barber, B. K., & Thomas, D. L. (1986). Dimensions of fathers' and mothers' supportive behavior: The case for physical affection. *Journal of Marriage and the Family, 48,* 783–794.

Barber, B. K., Olsen, J. E., & Shagle, S. C. (1994). Associations between parental psychological and behavioral control and youth internalized and externalized behaviors. *Child Development, 65,* 1120–1136.

Barglow, P., Vaughan, B., & Molitor, N. (1987). Effects of maternal absence due to employment on the quality of infant–mother attachment in a low-risk sample. *Child Development, 58*(4), 945–954.

Bates, J. E. (1987). Temperament in infancy. In J. D. Osofsky (Ed.), *Handbook of infant development* (2nd ed., pp. 1101–1149). New York: Wiley.

Bates, J. E. (1990). Conceptual and empirical linkages between temperament and behavior problems: A commentary on Sanson, Prior, and Kyrios. *Merrill-Palmer Quarterly, 36,* 193–199.

Baumrind, D. (1971). Current patterns of parental authority. *Developmental Psychology Monograph, 4*(1, Pt.2), 1–103.

Baumrind, D. (1972). Socialization and instrumental competence in young children. In E. Hartup (Ed.), *The young child: Reviews of research* (pp. 202–224). Washington, DC: Hemisphere.

Baumrind, D. (1978). Parental disciplinary patterns and social competence in children. *Youth and Society, 9*(3), 239–276.

Baumrind, D. (1980). New directions in socialization research. *American Psychologist, 35,* 639–652.

Baumrind, D. (1991). Effective parenting during the early adolescent transition. In P. A. Cowan & M. Hetherington (Eds.), *Family transitions* (pp. 111–163). Hillsdale, NJ: Erlbaum.

Becker, W. C. (1964). Consequences of different kinds of parental discipline. In M. L. Hoffman & L. Hoffman (Eds.), *Review of child development research* (Vol. 1, pp. 169–208). Chicago: University of Chicago Press.

Beebe, B., Alson, D., Jaffe, J., Feldstein, S., & Crown, C. (1988). Vocal congruence in mother–infant play. *Journal of Psycholinguistic Research, 17,* 245–259.

Bell, R. Q. (1968). A reinterpretation of the direction of effects in studies of socialization. *Psychological Review, 75,* 81–95.

Bell, R. Q., & Chapman, M. (1986). Child effects in studies using experimental or brief longitudinal approaches to socialization. *Developmental Psychology, 22*(5), 595–603.

Bell, R. Q., & Harper, L. V. (1977). *Child effects on adults.* Hillsdale, NJ: Erlbaum.

Bellah, R. N., Madsen, R., Sullivan, W. M., Swidler, A., & Tipton, J. M. (1985). *Habits of the heart: individualism and commitment in American life.* Berkeley: University of California Press.

Belsky, J. (1980). Child maltreatment: An ecological integration. *American Psychologist, 35,* 320–335.

Belsky, J. (1981). Early human experiences: A family perspective. *Developmental Psychology, 17,* 3–23.

Belsky, J. (1990). Child care and children's socioemotional development. *Journal of Marriage and the Family, 52,* 866–884.

Belsky, J., & Rovine, M. J. (1988). Nonmaternal care in the first year of life and the security of infant–parent attachment. *Child Development, 59,* 157–167.

Belsky, J., & Rovine, M. (1990). Patterns of marital change across the transition to parenthood: Pregnancy to three years postpartum. *Journal of Marriage and the Family, 52*(1), 5–20.

Belsky, J., Lang, M. E., & Rovine, M. (1985). Stability and change in marriage across the transition to parenthood: A second study. *Journal of Marriage and the Family, 47,* 855–865.

Belsky, J., Rovine, M., & Fish, M. (1989). The developing family system. In M. R. Gunnar & E. Thelen (Eds.), *Systems and development: The Minnesota Symposium on Child Psychology* (Vol. 22, pp. 167–209). Hillsdale, NJ: Erlbaum.

Belsky, J., Youngblade, L., Rovine, M., & Volling, B. (1991). Patterns of marital change and parent–child interaction. *Journal of Marriage and the Family, 53,* 487–498.

Berry, J. (1990). *Psychology of acculturation* (Nebraska Symposium on Motivation). Lincoln: University of Nebraska Press.

Bloch, M. N. (1987). The development of sex differences in young children's activities at home: The effect of social context. *Sex Roles, 16,* 279–301.

Block, J. H. (1976). Issues, problems, and pitfalls in assessing sex differences. A critical review. *Merrill-Palmer Quarterly, 22,* 285–308.

Bodman, D., & Peterson, G. W. (1995). Parenting processes. In R. D. Day, K. Gilbert, B. Settles, & W. R. Burr (Eds.), *Research and theory in family science* (pp. 205–225). Pacific Grove, CA: Brooks/Cole.

Bowlby, J. A. (1988). *A secure base: Parent–child attachment and healthy human development.* New York: Basic Books.

Bradley, R. H., Caldwell, B. M., & Rock, S. L. (1988). Home environment and school performance: A ten-year follow-up and examination of three models of environmental action. *Child Development, 59,* 852–867.

Brazelton, T. B., Koslowski, B., & Main, M. (1974). The origins of reciprocity: The early mother–infant interaction. In M. Lewis & L. A. Rosenblum (Eds.), *The effect of the infant on its caregiver* (pp. 49–76). New York: Wiley.

Bretherton, I. (1990). Open communication and internal working models: Their role in the development of attachment relationships. In R. A. Thompson (Ed.), *Socioemotional development* (pp. 57–113). Lincoln: University of Nebraska Press.

Bretherton, I., Biringen, Z., & Ridgeway, D. (1991). The parental side of attachment. In K. Pillemer & K. McCartney (Eds.), *Parent–child relations throughout life* (pp. 1–24). Hillsdale, NJ: Erlbaum.

Broderick, C. (1993). *Understanding family process: Basics of family systems theory.* Newbury Park, CA: Sage.

Bronfenbrenner, U. (1979). *The ecology of human development.* Cambridge, MA: Harvard University Press.

Bronfenbrenner, U. (1986). Ecology of the family as a context for human development: Research perspectives. *Developmental Psychology, 22*(6), 723–742.

Bronfenbrenner, U., & Crouter, A. C. (1983). The evolution of environmental models in developmental research. In W. Kessen (Ed.), *History, theory, and methods,* Volume I, *Handbook of child psychology* (4th ed., pp. 357–414). New York: Wiley.

Brooks-Gunn, J., Warren, M. M., & Russo, J. T. (in press). The impact of pubertal and social events upon girls' problem behavior. *Child Development.*

Brown, R. T., Borden, K. A., Clingerman, S. R., & Jenkins, P. (1988). Depression in attention deficit-disordered and normal children and their parents. *Child Psychiatry and Human Development, 18,* 119–132.

Brown, B. B., Mounts, N., Lamborn, S. D., & Steinberg, L. (1993). Parenting practices and peer group affiliation. *Child Development, 64,* 467–482.

Buri, J. R., Louiselle, P. A., Misukanis, T. M., & Mueller, R. A. (1988). Effects of parental authoritarianism and authoritiveness on self-esteem. *Personality and Social Psychology Bulletin, 14,* 271–282.

Buriel, R. (1993). Childrearing orientations in Mexican American families: The influence of generation and sociocultural factors. *Journal of Marriage and the Family, 55,* 987–1000.

Burns, G. L., & Farina, A. (1984). Social competence and adjustment. *Journal of Social and Personal Relationships, 1,* 99–113.

Burr, W. R., & Lowe, T. A. (1987). Olson's circumplex model: A review and extension. *Family Science Review, 1,* 5–22.

Caldera, Y. M., Huston, A. C., & O'Brien, M. (1989). Social interactions and play patterns of parents and toddlers with feminine, masculine, and neutral toys. *Child Development, 60,* 70–76.

Campbell, D. T., & Fiske, D. W. (1959). Convergent and discriminant validation by the multi-trait matrix. *Psychological Bulletin, 56,* 81–105.

Campbell, S. B. G. (1979). Mother–infant interactions as a function of maternal ratings of temperament. *Child Psychiatry and Human Development, 10,* 67–76.

Cassidy, J. (1994). Emotion regulation: Influences of attachment relationships. In N. A. Fox (Ed.), *The development of emotion regulation: Biological and behavioral considerations (Monographs of the Society for Research in Child Development, 59,* 2-3, serial no. 240, pp. 228–283). Chicago: University of Chicago Press.

Cassidy, J., & Berlin, L. J. (1993). The insecure/ambivalent pattern of attachment: Theory and research. *Child Development, 65,* 971–991.

Chase-Lansdale, P. L., & Owen, M. T. (1987). Maternal employment in a family context: Effects on infant–mother and infant–father attachments. *Child Development, 58*, 1505–1512.

Cicchetti, D., & Douglas, B. (1991). Attachment organization in maltreated preschoolers. *Development and Psychopathology, 3*, 397–411.

Clarke-Stewart, K. A. (1973). *Interactions between mothers and their young children: Characteristics and consequences* (Monographs of the Society for Research and Child Development, 38, 6, serial no. 153). Chicago: University of Chicago Press.

Clarke-Stewart, K. A. (1978). And Daddy makes three: The father's impact on mother and young child. *Child Development, 49*, 466–478.

Clarke-Stewart, K. A. (1988). Parents' effects on children's development: A decade of progress? *Journal of Applied Developmental Psychology, 9*, 41–84.

Cochran, M. (1993). Parenting and personal social networks. In T. Luster & L. O. Okagi (Eds.), *Parenting: An ecological perspective* (pp. 149–178). Hillsdale, NJ: Erlbaum.

Collins, W. A., & Repinski, D. J. (1994). Relationships during adolescence: Continuity and change in interpersonal perspective. In R. Montemayor, G. R. Adams, & T. P. Gullotta (Eds.), *Personal relationships during adolescence: Advances in adolescent development* (Vol. 6, pp. 7–36). Thousand Oaks, CA: Sage.

Conger, R. D., & Elder, G. H., Jr. (1994). *Families in troubled times: Adapting to change in rural America*. Hawthorne, NY: Aldine de Gruyter.

Coopersmith, S. (1967). *The antecedents of self-esteem*. San Francisco: Freeman.

Copeland, A. P., & White, K. M. (1991). *Studying families*. Newbury Park, CA: Sage.

Crnic, K., & Greenberg, M. (1987). Maternal stress, social support, and coping: Influences on the early mother–infant relationship. In C. F. Z. Boukydis (Ed.), *Research on support for parents and infants in the postnatal period* (pp. 25–40). Norwood, NJ: Ablex.

Crnic, K. A., & Greenberg, M. T. (1990). Minor parenting stress with children. *Child Development, 61*, 1628–1637.

Crnic, K. A., Greenberg, M. T., Ragozin, A. S., Robinson, N. ., & Busham, R. (1983). Effects of stress and social support on mothers and premature and full-term infants. *Child Development, 54*, 209–217.

Crockenberg, S. B. (1981). Infant instability, mother responsiveness, and social support influences on the security of infant–mother attachment. *Child Development, 52*, 857–865.

Crockenberg, S. B. (1987). Predictors and correlates of anger toward and punitive control of toddlers by adolescent mothers. *Child Development, 52*, 857–865.

Crouter, A. C. (1984). Participative work as an influence on human development. *Journal of Applied Developmental Psychology, 5*, 71–90.

Crouter, A. C., & McHale, L. M. (1993). The long arms of the job: Influences of parental work on childrearing. In T. Luster, & L. O. Okagi (Eds.), *Parenting: An ecological perspective* (pp. 179–202). Hillsdale, NJ: Erlbaum.

Darling, N., & Steinberg, L. (1993). Parenting style as context: An integrative model. *Psychological Bulletin, 113*(3), 487–496.

Deal, J. E, Halverson, C. F., & Wampler, K. S. (1989). Parental agreement on child-rearing orientations: Relations to parental, marital, family, and child characteristics. *Child Development, 60*, 1025–1034.

deArmas, A., & Kelly, J. A. (1989). Social relationships in adolescence: Skill development and training. In J. Morrell & F. Danner (Eds.), *The adolescent as decision maker: Applications in development and education* (pp. 48–63). New York: Academic Press.

Delgado-Gaitan, C. (1987). Tradition and transitions in the learning process of Mexican children: An ethnographic view. In G. Spindler & L. Spindler (Eds.), *Interpretive ethnography of education: At home and abroad* (pp. 333–359). Hillsdale, NJ: Erlbaum.

Demo, D. (1992). Parent–child relations: Assessing recent changes. *Journal of Marriage and the Family, 54*, 104–117.

Demo, D. H. (1993). The relentless search for effects of divorce: Forging new trails or tumbling down the beaten path. *Journal of Marriage and the Family, 55*(1), 42–45.

Demo, D. H., & Acock, A. C. (1988). The impact of divorce on children. *Journal of Marriage and the Family, 50*, 619–648.

Dillworth-Anderson, P., Burton, L. M, & Turner, W. L. (1993). The importance of values in the study of culturally diverse families. *Family Relations, 42*, 238–242.

Dishion, T. J., & Loeber, R. (1985). Male adolescent marijuana and alcohol use: The role of parents and peers revisited. *American Journal of Drug and Alcohol Abuse, 11*, 11–25.

Dishion, T. J., Patterson, B. R., Stoolmiller, M., & Skinner, M. L. (1991). Family, school, and behavioral antecedents to early adolescent involvement with antisocial peers. *Developmental Psychology, 27*, 172–180.

Dix, T. (1991). The affective organization of parenting: Adaptive and maladaptive processes. *Psychological Bulletin, 110*(1), 3–25.

Dix, T. (in press). Parenting on behalf of the child: Empathic goals in the regulation of responsive parenting. In I. E. Sigel, A. V. McGillicuddy-DaLisi, & J. J. Goodnow (Eds.), *Parental belief systems: The psychological consequences for children* (Vol. 2). Hillsdale, NJ: Erlbaum.

Dix, T., & Grusec, J. E. (1985). Parental attribution processes in the socialization of children. In I. E. Sigel (Ed.), *Parental belief systems: The psychological consequences for children* (pp. 201–234). Hillsdale, NJ: Erlbaum.

Dix, T., Ruble, D. N., Grusec, J. E., & Nixon, E. (1986). Social cognition in parents: Inferential and affective reactions to children of three age levels. *Child Development, 58*, 879–894.

Dix, T., Ruble, D. N., & Zambarano, R. J. (1989). Mother's implicit theories of discipline: Child effects, parent effects, and the attribution process. *Child Development, 60*, 1373–1391.

Dornbusch, S. M., Ritter, P. L., Leiderman, P. H., Roberts, D. F., & Fraleigh, M. J. (1987). The relation of parenting style to adolescent school performance. *Child Development, 59*, 1244–1257.

Dunlop, R., & Burns, A. (1995). The sleeper effect—myth or reality? *Journal of Marriage and the Family, 57*(2), 375–386.

Durbin, D. D., Darling, N., Steinberg, L., & Brown, B. B. (1993). Parenting style and peer group orientation among European-American adolescents. *Journal of Research on Adolescence, 3*, 87–100.

Easterbrooks, M. A., & Goldberg, W. A. (1988). Security of toddler–parent attachment: Relation to children's socio-personality functioning during kindergarten. In M. Greenberg, D. Cicchetti, & M. Cummings (Eds.), *Attachment in the preschool years: Theory, research, and intervention* (pp. 55–77). Chicago: University of Chicago Press.

Eckenrode, J., Laird, M., & Doris, J. (1993). School performance and disciplinary problems among abused and neglected children. *Developmental Psychology, 29*, 53–62.

Egeland, B., & Farber, E. (1984). Infant–mother attachment: Factors related to its development over time. *Child Development, 55*, 753–771.

Eisenberg, N. (1989). Prosocial development in early and mid-adolescence. In R. Montemayor, G. R. Adams, & T. P. Gullotta (Eds.), *Advances in adolescent development, from childhood to adolescence: A transitional period?* (pp. 240–268). Newbury Park, CA: Sage.

Elder, G. H., Caspi, A., & Van Nguyen, T. (1986). Resourceful and vulnerable children: Family influences in stressful times. In R. K. Silberstein, K. Eyforth, & G. Rudinger (Eds.), *Development as action in context* (pp. 167–186). New York: Springer-Verlag.

Elder, G. H., Van Nguyen, T., & Caspi, A. (1985). Linking family hardship to children's lives. *Child Development, 56*, 361–375.

Elder, G. H., Jr., Eccles, J. S., Ardelt, M., & Lord, S. (1995). Inner-city parents under economic pressure: Perspectives of the strategies of parenting. *Journal of Marriage and the Family, 57,* 771–784.

Elicker, J., England, M., & Sroufe, L. A. (in press). Predicting peer competence and peer relationships in childhood from early parent–child relationships. In R. Parke & G. Ladd (Eds.), *Family peer relationships: modes of linkage* (pp. 99–113). Hillsdale, NJ: Erlbaum.

Elliott, D. S., Huizinga, D., & Ageton, B. (1985). *Explaining delinquency and drug use.* Beverly Hills, CA: Sage.

Emde, R. N., Plomin, R., Robinson, J., Corley, R., DeFries, J., Fulker, D. W., Reznick, J. S., Campos, J., Kagan, J., & Zahn-Walker, C. (1992). Temperament, emotion, and cognition at fourteen months: The MacArthur longitudinal twin study. *Child Development, 63,* 1437–1455.

Emery, R. E., & Tuer, M. (1993). Parenting and the marital relationship. In T. Luster & L. Okagi (Eds.), *Parenting: An ecological perspective* (pp. 121–148). Hillsdale, NJ: Erlbaum.

Engfer, A. (1988). The interrelatedness of marriage and the mother–child relationship. In R. Hinde & I. Stevenson-Hinde (Eds.), *Relationships within families* (pp. 104–118). Oxford, England: Oxford University Press.

Erel, O., & Burman, B. (1995). Interrelatedness of marital relations and parent–child relations: A meta-analytic review. *Psychological Bulletin, 118*(1), 108–132.

Erickson, M. F., Sroufe, L. A., & Egeland, B. (1985). The relationship between quality of attachment and behavior problems in preschool in a high-risk sample. In I. Bretherton & E. Waters (Eds.), *Growing points of attachment theory and research (Monographs of the Society for Research in Child Development, 50,* 1-2, Serial No. 209, pp. 147–193). Chicago: University Chicago Press.

Fagot, B. I., & Leinbach, M. D. (1989). The young child's gender schema: Environmental input, internal organization. *Child Development, 60,* 663–672.

Farrel, M. P., & Barnes, G. M. (1993). Family systems and social support: A test of the effects of cohesion and adaptability on the functioning of parents and adolescents. *Journal of Marriage and the Family, 55,* 119–132.

Farrington, D. P. (1986). Stepping stones to adult criminal careers. In D. Olwens, J. Block, & M. R. Yarrow (Eds.), *Development of antisocial and prosocial behavior* (pp. 47–72). New York: Academic Press.

Felner, R. D., Lease, A. M., & Phillips, R. S. C. (1990). Social competence and the language of adequacy as a subject matter of psychology: A quadripartite framework. In T. P. Gullotta, G. R. Adams, & R. Montemayor (Eds.), *Developing social competency in adolescence: Advances in adolescent development* (pp. 245–264). Newbury Park, CA: Sage.

Felson, R. B., & Reed, M. (1986). The effect of parents on the self-appraisals of children. *Social Psychology Quarterly, 69,* 302–308.

Felson, R. B., & Zielinski, M. A. (1989). Children's self-esteem and parental support. *Journal of Marriage and the Family, 51,* 727–735.

Field, F., Greenwald, P., Morrow, C., Healy, B., Foster, T., Gutherz, M., & Frost, A. (1992). Behavior state matching during interaction of pre-adolescent friends versus acquaintances. *Developmental Psychology, 26*(2), 242–250.

Field, T., Healy, B., & LeBlanc, W. G. (1989). Sharing and synchrony of behavior states and heart rate in nondepressed versus depressed mother–infant interactions. *Infant Behavior and Development, 12,* 357–376.

Field, T., Healy, B., Goldstein, S., & Guthertz, M. (1990). Behavior-state matching and synchrony in mother–infant interactions of nondepressed versus depressed dyads. *Developmental Psychology, 26*(1), 7–14.

Fishbein, D. H. (1990). Biological perspectives in criminology. *Criminology, 28,* 27–57.

Fonagy, P., Steele, H., & Steele, M. (1991). Intergenerational patterns of attachment: Maternal representations of attachment during pregnancy and subsequent infant–mother attachment. *Child Development, 62,* 891–905.

Foote, N., & Cottrell, B. (1955). *Identify and interpersonal competence.* Chicago: University of Chicago Press.

Frodi, A. M., & Senchak, M. (1990). Verbal and behavioral responsiveness to the cries of atypical infants. *Child Development, 61,* 76–84.

Ganong, L. H., & Coleman, M. (1987). Effects of children on parental sex-role orientation. *Journal of Family Issues, 8,* 278–290.

Garbarino, J. (1977). The human ecology of child maltreatment: A conceptual model for research. *Journal of Marriage and the Family, 39,* 721–735.

Garbarino, J., & Kostelny, K. (1993). Neighborhood and community influences on parenting. In T. Luster & L. O. Okagi (Eds.), *Parenting: An ecological perspective* (pp. 203–226). Hillsdale, NJ: Erlbaum.

Gecas, V. (1979). The influence of social class on socialization. In W. R. Burr, R. Hill, F. J. Nye, & I. L. Reiss (Eds.), *Contemporary theories about the family* (Vol. 1, pp. 365–404). New York: Free Press.

Gecas, V., & Schwalbe, M. L. (1986). Parental behavior and adolescent self-esteem. *Journal of Marriage and the Family, 48,* 37–46.

Gecas, V., & Seff, M. A. (1990). Adolescents and families: A review of the 1980s. *Journal of Marriage and the Family, 52,* 941–958.

Giordano, F. C., Cernkovich, S. A., & DeMaris, A. (1993). The family and peer relations of black adolescents. *Journal of Marriage and the Family, 55,* 277–287.

Gleick, J. (1987). *Chaos: Making a new science.* New York: Penguin.

Goetting, A. (1986). Parental satisfaction: A review of research. *Journal of Family Issues, 7,* 83–109.

Goldberg, S., Perrota, M., & Minde, K. (1986). Maternal behavior and attachment in low birthweight twins and singletons. *Child Development, 57,* 34–46.

Goldfried, M. R., & d' Zurillia, T. J. (1969). A behavioral-analytic model for assessing competence. In C. D. Spielberger (Ed.), *Current topics in clinical and community psychology* (Vol. 1, pp. 44–59). New York: Academic Press.

Goldsmith, H. H., & Campos, J. J. (1986). Fundamental issues in the study of early temperament: The Denver Twin Temperament Study. In M. E. Lamb & A. Brown (Eds.), *Advances in developmental psychology* (pp. 231–283). Hillsdale, NJ: Erlbaum.

Gottman, J. M. (1991). Chaos and regulated change in families: A metaphor for the study of transitions. In P. A. Cowan & M. Hetherington (Eds.), *Family transitions.* Hillsdale, NJ: Erlbaum.

Green, R. G. (1989). Choosing family measurement devices for practice and research: SFI and FACES III. *Social Service Review, 63,* 304–320.

Green, R. G., Kolevon, M. F., & Vosler, N. R. (1985). The Beavers-Timberlawn model of family competence and the Circumplex Model of family adaptability and cohesion: Separate, but equal? *Family Process, 24,* 385–398.

Green, R. G., Harris, R. N., Forte, J. A., & Robinson, M. (1991). Evaluating FACES III and the Circumplex Model: 2,440 families. *Family Process, 30,* 55–73.

Grossman, K., & Grossman, K. E. (1986). Newborn behavior, early parenting quality and labor toddler-parent relationships in a group of German infants. In J. K. Nugent, B. M. Lester, & T. B. Brazelton (Eds.), *The cultural context of infancy* (pp. 83–101). Norwood, NJ: Ablex.

Grotevant, H. D., & Cooper, C. R. (1986). Individuation in family relationships: A perspective on individual differences in the development of identity and role-taking skill in adolescence. *Human Development, 29,* 82–100.

Grotevant, H. D., Cooper, C. R., & Condon, S. M. (1983). Individuality and connectedness in the family as a context for adolescent identity formation and role-taking skill. In H. D. Grotevant & C. R. Cooper (Eds.), *Adolescent development in the family* (pp. 43–59). San Francisco: Jossey-Bass.

Grusec, J. E., & Goodnow, J. G. (1994). Impact of parental discipline methods on the child's internalization of values: A reconceptualization of current points of view. *Developmental Psychology, 30*(1), 4–19.

Guidubaldi, J., & Cleminshaw, H. (1985). Divorce, family health, and child adjustment. *Family Relations, 34*, 35–41.

Guidubaldi, J., & Perry, J. D. (1985). Divorce and mental health sequelae for children: A two-year follow-up of a nationwide sample. *Journal of the American Academy of Child Psychiatry, 24*, 531–537.

Guidubaldi, J., Perry, J. D., & Cleminshaw, H. K. (1984). The legacy of parental divorce: A nationwide study of family status and selected mediating variables on children's academic and social competencies. In B. B. Lahey & A. E. Kazdin (Eds.), *Advances in clinical child psychology* (Vol. 7, pp. 109–151). New York: Plenum Press.

Gutierrez, J., Sameroff, A. J., & Karrer, B. M. (1988). Acculturation and SES effects on Mexican American parents' concepts of development. *Child Development, 59*, 250–255.

Hann, D. M. (1989). A systems conceptualization of the quality of mother–infant interaction. *Infant Behavior and Development, 12*, 251–264.

Harre, R. (1980). *A theory for social psychology.* Totowa, NJ: Rowan & Littlefield.

Harrison, A. O., Wilson, M. N., Pine, C. J., Chan, S. Q., & Buriel, R. (1990). Family ecologies of ethnic minority children. *Child Development, 61*, 347–362.

Hauser, S. T., Powers, S. I., Noam, G. G., & Jacobson, A. M. (1984). Familial contexts of adolescent ego development. *Child Development, 55*, 195–213.

Henry, C. S., & Peterson, G. W. (1995). Adolescent social competence, parental qualities, and parental satisfaction. *American Journal of Orthopsychiatry, 65*(2), 249–262.

Henry, C. S., Wilson, S. M., & Peterson, G. W. (1989). Parental power bases and processes as predictors of adolescent conformity. *Journal of Adolescent Research, 4*(1), 15–32.

Hetherington, E. M. (1972). Effects of father absence on personality development in adolescent daughters. *Developmental Psychology, 7*, 313–326.

Hetherington, E. M. (1984). Stress and coping in children and families. In A. Doyle, D. Gold, & D. S. Moskowitz (Eds.), *Children in families under stress: No. 24. New directions in child development* (pp. 7–33). San Francisco: Jossey-Bass.

Hetherington, E. M., Cox, M., & Cox, R. (1978). The aftermath of divorce. In J. H. Stevens & M. Matthews (Eds.), *Mother–child, father–child relations* (pp. 110–155). Washington, DC: National Association for the Education of Young Children.

Hetherington, E. M., Cox, M., & Cox, R. (1985). Long-term effects of divorce and remarriage on the adjustment of children. *Journal of the American Academy of Child Psychiatry, 24*, 518–530.

Hetherington, E. M., Stanley-Hagan, M., & Anderson, E. (1989). Marital transitions: A child's perspective. *American Psychologist, 44*(2), 303–312.

Hibbard, J. H., & Pope, C. R. (1987). Employment characteristics and health status among men and women. *Women and Health, 12*, 85–102.

Higgins, E. T. (1991). Development of self-regulatory and self-evaluative processes: Costs, benefits, and tradeoffs. In M. R. Gunnar & L. A. Sroufe (Eds.), *The Minnesota symposia on child development: Vol. 23. Self processes and development* (pp. 125–165). Hillsdale, NJ: Erlbaum.

Hoffman, L. W. (1989). Effects of maternal employment in the two-parent family. *American Psychologist, 44*, 283–292.

Hoffman, M. L. (1970). Moral development. In P. H. Mussen (Ed.), *Carmichael's manual of child psychology: Vol. 2* (pp. 261–359). New York: Wiley.

Hoffman, M. L. (1980). Moral development in adolescence. In J. Adelson (Ed.), *Handbook of adolescent psychology* (pp. 295–343). New York: Wiley.

Hoffman, M. L. (1982). Development of prosocial motivation: Empathy and guilt. In N. Eisenberg (Ed.), *The development of prosocial behavior* (pp. 281–313). New York: Academic Press.

Hoffman, M. L. (1994). Discipline and internalization. *Developmental Psychology, 30*(1), 26–28.

Holden, G. W., & Edwards, L. A. (1989). Parental attitudes toward childrearing: Instruments, issues, and implications. *Psychological Bulletin, 106*(1), 29–58.

Hui, C. H., & Triandis, H. C. (1985). Measurement in cross-cultural psychology: A review and comparison of strategies. *Journal of Cross-Cultural Psychology, 16*, 131–152.

Inkeles, A. (1968). Society, social structure, and child socialization. In J. A. Clausen (Ed.), *Socialization and society*, (73–129). Boston: Little, Brown.

Isabella, R. A. (1993). Origins of attachment: Maternal interactive behavior across the first year. *Child Development, 64*, 605–621.

Isabella, R. A., & Belsky, J. (1991). Interactional synchrony and the origins of infant–mother attachment: A replication study. *Child Development, 62*, 373–384.

Isabella, R. A., Belsky, J., & Von Eye, A. (1989). Origins of infant–mother attachment: An examination of interactional synchrony during the infant's first year. *Developmental Psychology, 25*, 12–21.

Jackson, J., McCullough, W., & Gurin, G. (1988). Family, socialization environment, and identity development in black Americans. In H. McAdoo (Ed.), *Black families* (2nd ed., pp. 242–256). Beverly Hills, CA: Sage.

Jacobson, J. L., & Willie, D. E. (1986). The influence of attachment patterns on developmental changes in peer interaction from the toddler to the preschool period. *Child Development, 57*, 338–339.

Jennings, K. D., Stagg, V., & Connors, R. E. (1991). Social networks and mothers' interactions with their preschool children. *Child Development, 62*, 966–978.

Jessor, R. (1992). Risk behavior in adolescence: A psychosocial framework for understanding and action. In D. E. Rogers & E. Ginzburg (Eds.), *Adolescents at risk: Medical and social perspectives* (pp. 19–34). Boulder, CO: Westview.

Johnson, B., Shulman, S., & Collins, W. (1991). Systemic patterns of parenting as reported by adolescents. *Journal of Adolescent Research, 6*, 235–252.

Jones, W. H., Freeman, J. E., & Goswick, R. A. (1981). The persistence of loneliness: Self and other determinants. *Journal of Personality, 49*, 27–28.

Jones, W. H., Hobbs, S. A., & Hockenbury, D. (1982). Loneliness and social skill deficits. *Journal of Personality and Social Psychology, 42*, 682–689.

Joreskog, K. G., & Sorbom, D. (1988). *LISREL* (2nd ed.). Mooresville, IN: Scientific Software.

Kagan, J. (1989). Temperamental contribution to social behavior. *American Psychologist, 44*, 66–74.

Kagan, J., Reznick, J. S., & Snidman, N. (1989). Issues in the study of temperament. In G. A. Kohnstamm, J. E. Bates, & M. K. Rothbart (Eds.), *Temperament in childhood* (pp. 147–168). New York: Wiley.

Kantor, D., & Lehr, W. (1975). *Inside the family.* San Francisco: Jossey-Bass.

Kazdin, A. F. (1987). *Conduct disorders in childhood and adolescence.* Newbury Park, CA: Sage.

Kiecolt, K. J., & Acock, A. C. (1988). The long-term effects of family structure on gender-role attitudes. *Journal of Marriage and the Family, 50*, 709–717.

Klebanov, P. K., Brooks-Gunn, J., & Duncan, G. J. (1994). Does neighborhood and family poverty affect mother's parenting, mental health and social support? *Journal of Marriage and the Family, 56*, 441–455.

Knight, G., Tein, J. Y., Shell, R., & Roosa, M. (1992). The cross-ethnic equivalence of parenting and family interaction measures among Hispanic and Anglo-American families. *Child Development, 23,* 1392–1403.

Kobak, H. R., & Sceery, W. (1988). Attachment in late adolescence: Working models, affect regulation, and representations of self and others. *Child Development, 59,* 135–146.

Koeske, G. F., & Koeske, R. D. (1990). The buffering effect of social support on parental stress. *American Journal of Orthopsychiatry, 60,* 440–451.

Koester, L. S., Papousek, H., & Papousek, M. (1989). Patterns of rhythmic stimulation by mothers with three-month-olds: A cross-model comparison. *International Journal of Behavioral Development, 12,* 143–154.

Kohn, M. L. (1977). *Class and conformity: A study in values* (2nd ed.). Chicago: University of Chicago Press.

Kohn, M. (1983). On the transmission of values in the family: A preliminary formulation. In A. C. Kerkoff (Ed.), *Research in sociology of education and socialization: A research annual* (pp. 3–12). Greenwich, CT: JAI Press.

Kohn, M. L., & Schooler, C. (1983). *Work and personality: An inquiry into the impact of social stratification.* Norwood, NJ: Ablex.

Korner, A. F. (1974). The effect of the infant's state, level of arousal, sex and ontogenetic stage on the caregiver. In M. Lewis & L. A. Rosenblum (Eds.), *The effect of the infant on its caregiver* (pp. 105–121). New York: Wiley.

Kuczynski, L., Kochanska, G., Radke-Yarrow, M., & Girnius-Brown, O. G. (1987). A developmental interpretation of young children's noncompliance. *Developmental Psychology, 23*(6), 799–806.

Lackey, P. N. (1989). Adults' attitudes about assignments of household chores to male and female children. *Sex Roles, 20,* 271–281.

Ladd, G. W., Hart, C. H., Wadsworth, E. M., & Golter, B. S. (1988). Preschooler's peer networks in nonschool settings: Relationship to family characteristics and school adjustment. In S. Salsinger, J. Antrobus, & M. Hammer (Eds.), *Social networks of children, adolescents, and college students* (pp. 61–92). Hillsdale, NJ: Erlbaum.

La Frenier, P. J., & Sroufe, L. A. (1985). Profiles of peer competence in the preschool: Interrelations between measures, influence of social ecology, and relation to attachment history. *Developmental Psychology, 21,* 56–69.

Lamb, M. (1977). Father–infant and mother–infant interaction in the first year of life. *Child Development, 48,* 167–191.

Larzelere, R. W., & Klein, D. M. (1987). Methodology. In M. B. Sussman & S. K. Steinmetz (Eds.), *Handbook of marriage and the family* (pp. 125–155). New York: Plenum.

Lee, C., & Bates, J. E. (1985). Mother–child interaction at age two years and perceived difficult temperament. *Child Development, 56,* 1314–1325.

Lempers, J. D., Clark-Lempers, D., & Simons, R. L. (1989). Economic hardship, parenting, and distress in adolescence. *Child Development, 60,* 25–39.

Lepper, M. R. (1981). Social control processes, attributions of motivation, and the internalization of social values. In E. T. Higgins, D. N. Ruble, & W. W. Hartup (Eds.), *Social cognition and social behavior: Developmental perspectives* (pp. 294–330). Cambridge, MA: Cambridge University Press.

Lerner, J. V. (1993). The influence of child temperamental characteristics on parent behavior. In T. Luster & L. Okagi (Eds.), *Parenting: An ecological perspective* (pp. 101–120). Hillsdale, NJ: Erlbaum.

Lerner, J. V., & Lerner, R. M. (1986). *Temperament and social interaction in infants and children.* San Francisco: Jossey-Bass.

Lester, B. M., Hoffman, J., & Brazelton, T. B. (1985). The rhythmic structure of mother–infant interaction in term and preterm infants. *Child Development, 56,* 15–27.

Lewis, C. C. (1981). The effects of firm control: A reinterpretation of findings. *Psychological Bulletin, 90,* 547–563.

Lewis, M. (1972). State as an infant–environment interaction: An analysis of mother–infant interactions function of sex. *Merrill-Palmer Quarterly, 18,* 95–122.

Lewis, M., & Feiring, C. (1989). Early predictors of childhood friendship. In T. J. Berndt & G. W. Ladd (Eds.), *Peer relationships in child development* (pp. 246–273). New York: Wiley.

Lewis, M., Feiring, C., & Weinraub, M. (1981). The father as a member of the child's social network. In M. Lamb (Ed.), *The role of the father in child development* (pp. 259–294). New York: Wiley.

Loeber, R., & Stouthamer-Loeber, M. (1986). Family factors as correlates and predictors of juvenile conduct problems and delinquency. In M. Torry & Norval Morris (Eds.), *Crime and justice* (Vol. 7, pp. 259–294). Chicago: University Chicago Press.

Luster, T., & Okagaki, L. (1993). Multiple influences on parenting: Ecological and life-course perspectives. In T. Luster & L. Okagaki (Eds.), *Parenting an ecological perspective* (pp. 227–250). Hillsdale, NJ: Erlbaum.

Lutkenhaus, P., Grossman, K. E., & Grossman, K. (1985). Infant–mother attachment at twelve months and style of interaction with a stranger at the age of three years. *Child Development, 56,* 1538–1542.

Lyons-Ruth, K., Connell, D. B., Grunebaum, H., & Botein, S. (1990). Infants at social risk: Maternal depression and family support services as mediators of infant development and security of attachment. *Child Development, 61,* 85–98.

Lyons-Ruth, K., Repacholi, B., McLeod, S., & Silva, E. (1991). Disorganized attachment behavior in infancy: Short-term stability, maternal and infant correlates and risk-related subtypes. *Development and Psychopathology, 3,* 377–396.

Lytton, H. (1990). Child and parent effects in boys' conduct disorder: A reinterpretation. *Developmental Psychology, 26,* 683–697.

Lytton, H., & Romney, D. M. (1991). Parent's differential socialization of boys and girls: A meta-analysis. *Psychological Bulletin, 109,* 267–296.

Maccoby, E. E. (1992). The role of parents in the socialization of children: A historical overview. *Developmental Psychology, 28*(6), 1006–1017.

Maccoby, E. E., & Martin, J. A. (1983). Socialization in the context of the family: Parent–child interaction. In E. M. Hetherington (Ed.), *Handbook of child psychology: Socialization, personality, and social development: Vol. 4* (pp. 1–101). New York: Wiley.

MacDonald, W. L., & DeMaris, A. (1995). Remarriage, stepchildren, and marital conflict: Challenges to the incomplete institutionalization hypothesis. *Journal of Marriage and the Family, 57,* 387–398.

Main, M., & Cassidy, J. (1988). Categories of response to reunion with a parent at age six: Predictable from infant attachment classifications and stable over a one-month period. *Developmental Psychology, 24,* 415–426.

Main, M., & Goldwyn, R. (in press). Interview-based adult attachment classifications: Related to infant–mother and infant–father attachment. *Developmental Psychology.*

Main, M., & Hesse, E. (1990a). The insecure disorganized/disoriented attachment pattern in infancy: Precursors and sequelae. In M. Greenberg, D. Cicchetti, & E. M. Cummings (Eds.), *Attachment in the preschool years: Theory, research, and intervention* (pp. 161–182). Chicago: University of Chicago Press.

Main, M., & Hesse, E. (1990b). Parents' unresolved traumatic experiences are related to infant disorganized attachment states. In M. T. Greenberg, D. Cicchetti, & E. M. Cummings (Eds.), *Attachment in the preschool years: Theory, research, and intervention* (pp. 183–199). Chicago: University of Chicago Press.

Main, M., & Solomon, J. (1990). Procedure for identifying infants as disorganized/disoriented during the Ainsworth Strange Situation. In M. Greenberg, D. Cicchetti, & E. M. Cummings (Eds.), *Attachment in the preschool years: Theory, research, and intervention* (pp. 89–103). Chicago: University of Chicago Press.

Mattesich, P., & Hill, R. (1987). Life cycle and family development. In M. B. Sussman & S. K. Steinmetz (Eds.), *Handbook of marriage and the family* (pp. 437–469). New York: Plenum.

McCord, J. (1990). Crime in moral and social contexts—The American Society of Criminology, 1989 Presidential Address. *Criminology, 28,* 1–26.

McDonald, G. W. (1977). Parental identification by the adolescent: A social power approach. *Journal of Marriage and the Family, 39,* 705–719.

McDonald, G. W. (1979). Determinants of adolescent perceptions of maternal and paternal power in the family. *Journal of Marriage and the Family, 41,* 757–770.

McDonald, G. W. (1980). Parental power and adolescents' parental identifications: A reexamination. *Journal of Marriage and the Family, 42,* 289–296.

McGillicuddy-DeLisi, A. V. (1985). The relationship between parental beliefs and children's cognitive level. In I. E. Sigel (Ed.), *Parental beliefs systems: The psychological consequences for children* (pp. 7–24). Hillsdale, NJ: Erlbaum.

McLoyd, V. C. (1989). Socialization and development in a changing economy. *American Psychologist, 44,* 292–302.

Menaghan, E. G., & Godwin, D. D. (1993). Longitudinal research methods and family theories. In P. G. Boss, W. J. Doherty, R. LaRossa, W. R. Schumm, & S. K. Steinmetz (Eds.), *Sourcebook of family theories and methods: A contextual approach* (pp. 259–273). New York: Plenum.

Menaghan, E. G., & Parcel, E. G. (1990). Parental employment and family life: Research in the 1980s. *Journal of Marriage and the Family, 52,* 1079–1098.

Miller, I. W., Epstein, N. B., Bishop, D. L., & Keitner, G. I. (1985). The McMaster family assessment devise: Reliability and validity. *Journal of Marital and Family Therapy, 11,* 345–356.

Miller, B. C., McCoy, J. K., Olson, T. D., & Wallace, C. M. (1986). Parental discipline and control attempts in relation to adolescent sexual attitudes and behavior. *Journal of Marriage and the Family, 48,* 503–512.

Mirowsky, J., & Ross, C. E. (1986). Social patterns of distress. *Annual Review of Sociology, 12,* 23–45.

Mortimer, J. T., Lorence, J., & Kumka, D. A. (1986). *Work, family, and personality: Transition to adulthood.* Norwood, NJ: Ablex.

Moss, H. A. (1974). Early sex differences and mother–infant interaction. In R. C. Friedman, R. M. Richart, & R. L. Vaude Wiele (Eds.), *Sex differences in behavior* (pp. 33–55). New York: Wiley.

Noller, P. (1994). Relationships with parents in adolescence: Process and outcome. In R. Montemayor, G. R. Adams, & T. P. Gullotta (Eds.), *Personal relationships during adolescence: Advances in adolescent development* (Vol. 6, pp. 37–77). Thousand Oaks, CA: Sage.

O'Brien, M., & Huston, A. C. (1985). Development of sex-typed play behavior in toddlers. *Developmental Psychology, 21,* 866–871.

Ogbu, J. (1981). Origins of human competence: A cultural-ecological perspective. *Child Development, 52,* 413–429.

Ogbu, J. (1985). A cultural ecology of competence among inner-city blacks. In M. B. Spencer, G. Kerse-Brookins, & W. R. Allen (Eds.), *Beginnings: The social and affective development of black* (pp. 45–66). Hillsdale, NJ: Erlbaum.

Ogbu, J. (1987). Cultural influence on plasticity in human development. In J. J. Gallagher & C. T. Ramsey (Eds.), *The malleability of children* (pp. 19–48). Baltimore: Paul H. Brookes.

Okagaki, L., & Divecha, D. L. (1993). Development of parental beliefs. In T. Luster & L. Okagi (Eds.), *Parenting: An ecological perspective* (pp. 35–67). Hillsdale, NJ: Erlbaum.

Olson, D. H. (1986). Circumplex model VII: Validation studies and FACES 111. *Family Process, 25,* 337–352.

Olson, D. H. (1995). Family systems: Understanding your roots. In R. D. Day, K. F. Gilbert, B. H. Settles, & W. R. Burr (Eds.), *Research and theory in family science* (pp. 131–153). Pacific Grove, CA: Brooks/Cole.

Olson, D. H., Sprenkle, D. H., & Russell, C. S. (1979). Circumplex model of marital and family systems: I. Cohesion and adaptability dimensions, family types, and clinical applications. *Family Process, 18,* 3–29.

Olson, D. H., McCubbin, H. A., Barnes, H., Unen, M., Maxen, M., & Wilson, M. (1983). *Families: What makes them work.* Los Angeles: Sage.

Olson, D. H., Russell, C. S., & Sprenkle, D. H. (1983). Circumplex model of marital and family systems: VI. Theoretical update. *Family Process, 22,* 69–83.

Openshaw, D. K., & Thomas, D. L. (1986). The adolescent self and the family. In G. K. Leigh & G. W. Peterson (Eds.), *Adolescents in families* (pp. 104–129). Cincinnati, OH: South-Western Publishing Co.

Openshaw, D. K., Thomas, D. L., & Rollins, B. C. (1983). Socialization and adolescent self-esteem: Symbolic interaction and social learning explanations. *Adolescence, 18,* 317–329.

Owen, M. T., & Cox, M. J. (1988). Maternal employment and the transition to parenthood. In A. E. Gottfried & A. W. Gottfried (Eds.), *Maternal employment and children's development: Longitudinal research* (pp. 85–119). New York: Plenum.

Owens, G., Croswell, J. A., Pan, H., Treboux, D., O'Connor, E., & Waters, E. (1995). The prototype hypothesis and the origins of attachment working models: Adult relationships with parents and romantic partners. In E. Waters, B. E. Vaughn, G. Posada, & K. Kondo-Hemura (Eds.), *Caregiving, cultural, and cognitive perspectives on secure-base behavior and working models* (*Monographs of the Society for Research in Child Development, 244, 60*(2-3), pp. 216–233). Chicago: University of Chicago Press.

Papousek, H., & Papousek, M. (1991a). Innate and cultural guidance of infants' integrative competencies: China, the United States, and Germany. In M. H. Bornstein (Ed.), *Cultural approaches to parenting* (pp.77–99). Hillsdale, NJ: Erlbaum.

Papousek, M., & Papousek, H. (1991b). Early verbalizations as precursors of language development. In M. E. Lamb & H. Keller (Eds.), *Infant development: Perspectives from German-speaking countries* (pp. 141–168). Hillsdale, NJ: Erlbaum.

Parke, R. D., & O'Leary, S. (1975). Father–mother–infant interaction in the newborn period: Some feelings, some observations and some issues. In K. Riegel & J. Meacham (Eds.), *The developing individual in a changing world: Social and environmental issues, Vol. 2* (pp. 112–128). The Hague: Mouton.

Parke, R. D., MacDonald, K. B., Burks, V. M., Bhamagri, N., Barth, J. M., & Beitel, A. (1989). Families and peer systems: In search of linkages. In K. Keppner & R. Lerner (Eds.), *Family systems and life-span development* (pp. 65–92). Hillsdale, NJ: Erlbaum.

Patterson, G. R. (1982). *A social learning approach: 3. Coercive family process.* Eugene, OR: Castalia.

Patterson, G. R. (1986). Performance models for antisocial boys. *American Psychologist, 41,* 432–444.

Patterson, G. R., & Bank, L. (1989). Some amplifying mechanisms for pathologic processes in families. In M. R. Gunnar & E. Thelen (Eds.), *Systems and development: The Minnesota symposium on child psychology* (Vol. 22, pp. 167–209). Hillsdale, NJ: Erlbaum.

Patterson, G. R., & Capaldi, D. M. (1991). Antisocial parents: Unskilled & vulnerable. In P. A. Cowan & E. M. Hetherington (Eds.), *Family transitions* (pp. 195–218). Hillsdale, NJ: Erlbaum.

Patterson, G. R., & Dishion, T. J. (1985). Contributions of families and peers to delinquency. *Criminology, 23*(1), 63–79.

Patterson, G. R., DeBaryshe, K., & Ramsey, E. (1989). A developmental perspective on antisocial behavior. *American Psychologist, 44*(2), 329–335.

Patterson, G. R., Reid, J. B., & Dishion, T. J. (1991). *A social learning approach: Vol. 4. Antisocial boys.* Eugene, OR: Castalia.

Pederson, D. R., & Moran, G. (1995). A categorical description of infant–mother relationships in the home and its relation to Q-sort measures of infant–mother interaction. In E. Waters, B. E. Vaughn, G. Posada, & K. Kondo-Ikemura (Eds.), *Caregiving cultural and cognitive perspectives on secure-base behavior and working models (Monographs of the Society for Research in Child Development, 244, 60*(2–3, pp. 111–132). Chicago: University of Chicago Press.

Pedersen, F. A. (1980). *The father–infant relationship: Observational studies in the family setting.* New York: Praeger.

Peters, M. (1985). Racial socialization of young black children. In H. McAdoo & J. McAdoo (Eds.), *Black children* (pp. 159–173). Beverly Hills, CA: Sage.

Peterson, G. W. (1986). Parent–youth power dimensions and the behavioral autonomy of adolescents. *Journal of Adolescent Research, 1,* 231–249.

Peterson, G. W. (1987). Role transitions and role identities during adolescence: A symbolic interactionist view. *Journal of Adolescent Research, 2,* 237–254.

Peterson, G. W. (1995a). Autonomy and connectedness in families. In R. Day, K. Gilbert, B. H. Settles, & W. R. Burr (Eds.), *Research and theory in family science* (pp. 20–41). Pacific Grove, CA: Brooks/Cole.

Peterson, G. W. (1995b). The need for common principles in prevention programs for children, adolescents, and families: *Journal of Adolescent Research, 10*(4), 470–485.

Peterson, G., Bush, K., & Supple, A. (in press). Predicting adolescent autonomous behavior. *Sociological Inquiry.*

Peterson, G. W., & Day, R. D. (1994, April). *Family connectedness and separateness as predictors of adolescent autonomy.* Paper presented at the annual meeting of the International Sociological Association, London, England.

Peterson, G. W., & Leigh, G. K. (1990). The family and social competence in adolescence. In T. P. Gullotta, G. R. Adams, & R. Montemayor (Eds.), *Developing social competency in adolescence: Advances in adolescent development* (Vol. 3, pp. 97–138). Newbury Park, CA: Sage.

Peterson, G. W., & Rollins, B. C. (1987). Parent–child socialization. In M. B. Sussman & S. K. Steinmetz (Eds.), *Handbook of marriage and the family* (pp. 471–507). New York: Plenum.

Peterson, G. W., & Stivers, M. E. (1986). Adolescents' behaviorist autonomy and family connectedness in rural Appalachia. *Family Perspective, 20*(4), 307–322.

Peterson, G. W., Rollins, B. C., & Thomas, D. L. (1985). Parental influence and adolescent conformity: Compliance and internalization. *Youth and Society, 16,* 397–420.

Pettit, G. S., & Bates, J. E. (1989). Family interaction patterns and children's behavior problems from infancy to 4 years. *Developmental Psychology, 25,* 413–420.

Piotrokowski, C. S., & Rapoport, R. N., & Rapoport, R. (1987). Families and work. In M. B. Sussman & S. K. Steinmetz (Eds.), *Handbook of marriage and the family* (pp. 251–283). New York: Plenum.

Plomin, R., & Dunn, J. (1986). *The study of temperament: Changes, continuities and challenges.* Hillsdale, NJ: Erlbaum.

Pomerleau, A., Bolduc, D., Malcuit, G., & Cossette, L. (1990). Pink or blue: Environmental gender stereotypes in the first two years of life. *Sex Roles, 22,* 359–367.

Posada, G., Gao, Y., Wu, F., Posada, R., Tascon, M., Schoelmerich, A., Sagi, A., Kondo-Ikemura, K., Haaland, Wenche, & Lynnevaag, B. (1995). The secure-base phenomenon across cultures: Children's behavior, mothers' preferences and experts concepts. In E. Waters, B. E. Vaughan, G. Posada, & K. Kondo-Ikemura (Eds.), *Caregiving, cultural, and cognitive perspectives on secure-base behavior and work-*

ing models (Monographs of the Society for Research in Child Development 244, 60(2–3), pp. 27–48). Chicago: University of Chicago Press.

Powell, D. R. (1980). Personal social networks as a focus for primary prevention of child maltreatment. *Infant Mental Health Journal, 1,* 232–239.

Putallaz, M., & Heflin, A. H. (1990). Parent–child interaction. In S. R. Asher & J. D. Coie (Eds.), *Peer rejection in childhood* (pp. 189–216). Cambridge, MA: Cambridge University Press.

Quittner, A. L., Glueckauf, R. L., & Jackson, D. N. (1990). Chronic parenting stress: Moderating versus mediating effects of social support. *Journal of Personality and Social Psychology, 59,* 1266–1278.

Radke-Yarrow, M., Zahn-Waxler, C., & Chapman, M. (1983). Children's prosocial dispositions and behavior. In E. M. Hetherington (Ed.), *Handbook of child psychology* (Vol. 4, pp. 469–545). New York: Wiley.

Renken, B., Egeland, B., Marvinney, D., Mangelsdorf, S., & Sroufe, L. A. (1989). Early childhood antecedents of aggressive and passive withdrawal in early elementary school. *Journal of Personality, 57,* 257–282.

Repetti, R. L. (1988). Family and occupational roles and women's mental health. In R. M. Schwartz (Ed.), *Women at work* (pp. 97–129). Los Angeles: UCLA Institute of Industrial Relations.

Rocissano, L., Slade, A., & Lynch, V. (1987). Dyadic synchrony and toddler compliance. *Developmental Psychology, 23*(5), 698–704.

Rodgers, R., & White, J. M. (1993). Family development theory. In P. G. Boss, W. J. Doherty, R. LaRossa, W. R. Schumm, & S. K. Steinmetz (Eds.), *Sourcebook of family theories and methods: A contextual approach* (pp. 225–254). New York: Plenum.

Rogoff, B., & Morelli, G. (1989). Perspectives on children's development from cultural psychology. *American Psychologist, 44,* 343–348.

Rohner, R. P. (1986). *The warmth dimension: Foundation of parental acceptance-rejection theory.* Beverly Hills, CA: Sage.

Rollins, B. C., & Thomas, D. L. (1975). A theory of parental power and child compliance. In R. E. Cromwell & D. H. Olson (Eds.), *Power in families* (pp. 38–60). Beverly Hills, CA: Sage.

Rollins, B. C., & Thomas, D. L. (1979). Parental support, power, and control techniques in the socialization of children. In W. R. Burr, R. Hill, F. I. Nye, & I. R. Reiss (Eds.), *Contemporary theories about the family: Vol. I* (pp. 317–364). New York: Free Press.

Rosenberg, M. (1965). *Society and the adolescent self-image.* Princeton, NJ: Princeton University Press.

Rosenblatt, P. C., & Fisher, L. R. (1993). Qualitative family research. In P. Boss, W. J. Doherty, R. LaRossa, W. R. Schumm, & S. K. Steinmetz (Eds.), *Sourcebook of family theories and methods: A contextual approach* (pp. 161–177). New York: Plenum.

Rosenfield, S. (1989). The effects of women's employment: Personal control and sex differences in mental health. *Journal of Health and Social Behavior, 30,* 77–91.

Rotheram, M. & Phinney, J. (1987). Definitions and perspectives in the study of children's ethnic socialization. In J. Phinney & M. Rotheram (Eds.), *Children's ethnic socialization: Pluralism and development.* Newbury Park, CA: Sage.

Rubin, J. Z., Provenzano, R. J., & Luria, Z. (1974). The eye of the beholder: Parents' view on sex of newborns. *American Journal of Orthopsychiatry, 43,* 518–519.

Sabatelli, R. M., & Waldron, R. J. (1995). Measurement issues in the assessment of the experiences of parenthood. *Journal of Marriage and the Family, 57,* 969–980.

Sanson, A., Oberklaid, F., Pedlow, R., & Prior, M. (1991). Risk indicators: Assessment of infancy predictors of pre-school behavior maladjustment. *Journal of Child Psychology and Psychiatry and Allied Disciplines, 32,* 609–626.

Schaefer, E. S. (1959). A circumplex model for maternal behavior. *Journal of Abnormal and Social Psychology, 59*, 226–235.

Schaefer, E. S. (1965). Children's reports of parental behavior. *Child Development, 36*, 552–557.

Schaffer, H. R. (1977). *Mothering*. Cambridge, MA: Harvard University Press.

Schmitt, N., & Stults, D. M. (1986). Methodology review: Analysis of multitrait-multimethod matrices. *Applied Psychological measurement, 10*, 1–22.

Schooler, C. (1987). Psychological effects of complex environments during the life span: A review and theory. In C. Schooler & K. Warner Schaie (Eds.), *Cognitive functioning and social structure over the life course* (pp. 24–29). Norwood, NJ: Ablex.

Schwartz, R., & Gottman, J. M. (1976). Toward a task analysis of assertive behavior. *Journal of Consulting and Clinical Psychology, 44*, 910–920.

Seifer, R., & Sameroff, A. J. (1986). The concept, measurement, and interpretation of temperament in young children: A survey of research issues. *Advances in Developmental and Behavioral Pediatrics, 7*, 143.

Seifer, R., & Schiller, F. (1995). The role of parenting sensitivity, infant temperament, and dyadic interaction in attachment theory and assessment. In E. Waters, B. E. Vaughan, G. Posada, & K. Kondo-Ikemura (Eds.), *Caregiving, cultural, and cognitive perspectives on secure-base behavior and working models* (*Monographs of the Society for Research in Child Development, 244, 60*(2–3), pp. 146–174). Chicago: University of Chicago Press.

Seltzer, J. A. (1994). Consequences of marital dissolution for children. *Annual Review of Sociology, 20*, 235–266.

Serafica, F. C. (1989). Counseling Asian-American parents: A cultural-developmental framework. In F. C. Serafica & A. I. Schwabel (Eds.), *Mental health of ethnic minorities* (pp. 235–259). New York: Praeger.

Siegelman, E. (1965). College student personality correlates of early parent-child relationships. *Journal of Consulting Psychology, 29*, 558–564.

Sigafoos, A., Reiss, D., Rich, J., & Douglas, E. (1985). Pragmatics in the measurement of family functioning. An interpretive framework for methodology. *Family Process, 24*, 189–203.

Simons, R. L., Johnson, C., & Conger, R. D. (1994). Harsh corporal punishment versus quality of parental involvement as an explanation of adolescent maladjustment. *Journal of Marriage and the Family, 56*, 591–607.

Small, S. (1990). *Preventive programs that support families with adolescents*. Working paper: Carnegie Council on Adolescent Development. Carnegie Corporation, Washington, DC.

Smetana, J. G., & Asquith, P. (1994). Adolescents' and parents' conceptions of parental authority and personal autonomy. *Child Development, 65*, 1147–1162.

Smith, T. E. (1983). Parental influence: A review of the evidence of influence and a theoretical model of parental influence process. In A. C. Kerckhoff (Ed.), *Research in sociology of education and socialization: Personal change over the life cycle* (pp. 13–45). Greenwich, CT: JAI Press.

Smith, T. E. (1986). Influence in parent-adolescent relationships. In G. K. Leigh & G. W. Peterson (Eds.), *Adolescents in families* (pp. 130–154). Cincinnati, OH: South-Western Publishing Co.

Smith, T. E., & Graham, P. B. (1996). Socioeconomic stratification in family research. *Journal of Marriage and the Family, 75*, 930–940.

Spitze, G. (1988). Women's employment and family relations: A review. *Journal of Marriage and the Family, 50*, 595–618.

Sroufe, L. A., & Fleeson, J. (1986). Attachment and the construction of relationships. In W. W. Hartup & Z. Rubin (Eds.), *Relationships and development* (pp. 51–71). Hillsdale, NJ: Erlbaum.

Sroufe, L. A., & Fleeson, J. (1988). The coherence of family relationships. In R. A. Hinde & J. Stevenson-Hinde (Eds.), *Relationships within families: Mutual influences* (pp. 27–47). Oxford: Oxford University Press.

Stafford, L., & Bayer, C. L. (1993). *Interaction between parents and children*. Newbury Park, CA: Sage.

Staples, R., & Mirande, A. (1980). Racial and cultural variations among American families: A decennial review of the literature on minority families. *Journal of Marriage and the Family, 42*, 887–903.

Steinberg, L. (1989). Pubertal maturation and parent–adolescent distance: An evolutionary perspective. In G. R. Adams, R. Montemayor, & T. P. Gullotta (Eds.), *Biology of adolescent behavior and development: Advances in adolescent development* (pp. 71–97). Newbury Park, CA: Sage.

Steinberg, L. (1990). Autonomy, conflict, and harmony in the family relationship. In S. S. Feldman & G. R. Elliot (Eds.), *At the threshold: The developing adolescent* (pp. 255–276). Cambridge, MA: Harvard University Press.

Steinberg, L., & Silverberg, S. B. (1986). The vicissitudes of autonomy in early adolescence. *Child Development, 57*, 841–851.

Steinberg, L., Lamborn, S., Dombusch, S., & Darling, N. (1992). Impact of parenting practices on adolescent achievement: Authoritative parenting, school involvement, and encouragement to succeed. *Developmental Psychology, 63*, 1266–1281.

Steinglass, P. (1987). A systems view of family interaction and psychopathology. In T. Jacob (Ed.), *Family interaction and psychopathology* (pp. 25–65). New York: Plenum.

Steinmetz, L. (1987). Family violence, past, present, and future. In M. Sussman & L. Steinmetz (Eds.), *Handbook of marriage and the family* (pp. 725–765). New York: Plenum.

Stierlin, H. (1974). *Separating parents and adolescents: A perspective on running away, schizophrenia, and waywardness*. New York: Quadrangle.

Straus, M. A. (1994). *Beating the devil out of them: Corporal punishment in American families*. New York: Lexington Books.

Symonds, P. (1939). *The psychopathology of parent–child relationships*. New York: Appleton-Century Crofts.

Szopocznik, J., & Hernandez, R. (1988). The Cuban American family. In C. H. Mindel, R. W. Habenstein, & R. Wright (Eds.), *Ethnic families in America* (pp. 198–214). New York: Elsevier.

Szopocznik, J., & Kurtines, W. (1980). Acculturation, biculturalism, and adjustment among Cuban Americans. In A. M. Padilla (Eds.), *Acculturation: Theory, models and some new findings* (pp. 139–161). Boulder, CO: Westview.

Taylor, R. J., Chatters, R. J., Tucker, M. B., & Lewis, E. (1990). Developments in research on black families: A decade review. *Journal of Marriage and the Family, 52*, 993–1014.

Teglasi, H., & MacMahon, B. H. (1990). Temperament and common problem behaviors of children. *Journal of Applied Developmental Psychology, 11*, 331–349.

Thomas, A. (1982). The study of difficult temperament: A reply to Kagan, Rothbart and Plomin. *Merrill-Palmer Quarterly, 28*, 313–315.

Thomas, A., & Chess, S. (1977). *Temperament and development*. New York: Brunner/Mazel.

Thomas, A., Chess, S., & Korn, S. J. (1982). The reality of difficult temperament. *Merrill-Palmer Quarterly, 28*, 1–20.

Thomas, E. B. (1990). Sleeping and waking states in infants: A functional perspective. *Neuroscience and Biobehavioral Reviews, 14*, 93–107.

Thomas, W. I., & Thomas, P. S. (1928). *The child in America*. New York: Knopf.

Thornton, M., Chatters, L. M., Taylor, R. J., & Allen, W. R. (1990). Sociodemographic and environmental influences on racial socialization by black parents. *Child Development, 61*, 401–409.

Tronick, E. Z. (1989). Emotions and emotional communication in infants. *American Psychologist, 44*, 112–119.

Turner, H. A., & Finkelhor, D. (1996). Corporal punishment as stressor among youth. *Journal of Marriage and the Family, 58,* 155–166.

Unger, D. O., & Powell, D. R. (1980). Supporting families under stress: The role of social networks. *Family Relations, 29,* 566–574.

Vaughn, B. E., Block, J. H., & Block, J. (1988). Parental agreement on child-rearing during early childhood and the psychological characteristics of adolescents. *Child Development, 59,* 1020–1033.

Vega, W. A. (1990). Hispanic families in the 1980s. A decade of research. *Journal of Marriage and the Family, 52,* 1015–1024.

Voydanoff, P. (1987). *Work and family life.* Beverly Hills, CA: Sage.

Voydanoff, P. (1990). Economic stress and family relations: A review of the eighties. *Journal of Marriage and the Family, 52,* 1099–1115.

Walker, L. S., McLaughlin, F. J., & Green, J. W. (1988). Functional illness and family functioning: A comparison of healthy and somaticizing adolescents. *Family Process, 27,* 317–325.

Wallerstein, J. S., & Kelly, J. (1980). *Surviving the breakup: How children and parents cope with divorce.* New York: Basic Books.

Wallerstein, J. W., Corbin, S. B., & Lewis, J. M. (1988). Children of divorce: A ten-year study. In E. M. Hetherington & J. D. Arasteh (Eds.), *Impact of divorce, single-parenting, and step-parenting on children* (pp. 197–214). Hillsdale, NJ: Erlbaum.

Waters, E., & Sroufe, L. A. (1983). Social competence as a developmental construct. *Developmental Review, 3,* 79–97.

Waters, E., Vaughn, B. E., Posada, G., & Kondo-Ikemuro, K. (1995). *Caregiving, cultural, and cognitive perspectives on secure-base behavior and working models* (*Monographs of the Society for Research in Child Development, 244, 60*(2-3). Chicago: University of Chicago Press.

White, R. W. (1959). Motivation reconsidered: The concept of competence. *Psychological Review, 66,* 297–323.

Whiting, B. B., & Whiting, J. W. M. (1975). *Children of sex cultures.* Cambridge, MA: Harvard University Press.

Widaman, K. F. (1985). Hierarchically nested covariance structure models for multitrait-multimethod data. *Applied Psychological Measurement, 9,* 1–26.

Wilson, S. W., Peterson, G. W., & Wilson, P. (1993). The process of educational and occupational attainment of adolescent females from low-income, rural families. *Journal of Marriage and the Family, 55,* 158–175.

Young, M. H., Miller, B. C., Norton, M. C., & Hill, E. J. (1995). The effect of parental supportive behaviors on life satisfaction of adolescent offspring. *Journal of Marriage and the Family, 57,* 813–822.

Zigler, E., & Trickett, P. K. (1978). IQ, social competence, and evaluation of early childhood intervention programs. *American Psychologist, 33,* 789–798.

Zill, N. (1988). Behavior, achievement, and health problems among children in stepfamilies: Findings from a national survey of child health. In E. M. Hetherington & J. D. Arasteh (Eds.), *Impact of divorce, single parenting, and stepparenting on children,* (pp. 325–368). Hillsdale, NJ: Erlbaum.

CHAPTER 14

Adolescence in Contemporary Families

Suzanne K. Steinmetz

Introduction

Adolescence, that unique period of age between childhood and adulthood, has been defined as the period of "stress and storm," or the "awkward age." Identifying the years encompassing the period defined as adolescence is beset with conceptual problems. Puberty, for example, may not be a good indicator because increased standards of health care and nutrition have caused the onset to occur earlier in successive generations of adolescents (i.e., referred to as the secular trend). Another problem in defining the parameters of adolescence results from the increased length of compulsory education and the increased number of youth who continue their education beyond high school. The result is that many young people delay their transition into full-time employment and marital and family roles, with the period of adolescence being extended and lasting longer than it did in the past.

Overview of the Chapter

In this introduction I will first review the history, definitions, and characteristics of and values held by adolescents, followed by a brief survey of major theories of adolescent socialization. Since a large portion of the literature on adolescence focuses on risky behavior and the lack of appropriate interactions with family, school, and community, theoretical approaches grounded in sociological and family studies theory appear more fruitful than ones focusing entirely on the

Suzanne K. Steinmetz • Department of Sociology, Indiana University–Purdue University at Indianapolis, Indianapolis, Indiana 46236.

Handbook of Marriage and the Family, 2nd edition, edited by Marvin Sussman, Suzanne K. Steinmetz, and Gary W. Peterson. Plenum Press, New York, 1999.

individual's physical, cognitive, and social development. A third section will examine developmental tasks and contemporary adolescents' ability to fulfill them. Autonomy, volunteer activities, paid employment, and helping parents with housekeeping and the care of siblings and elderly relatives will be discussed. Adolescent sexuality will be discussed in this section under intimacy.

A final section will provide a review of adolescents' risky behaviors and outcomes—substance abuse, teen pregnancy, sexually transmitted infections, violence, delinquency, truancy, and school dropouts. There will also be an examination of a number of behavior disorders, such as eating, learning, and conduct disorders and mood disorders such as depression, bipolar, and dissociative disorders.

Defining Adolescence

The term *adolescence* first appeared in G. Stanley Hall's work, *Adolescence: Its Psychology and Its Relations to Physiology, Anthropology, Sociology, Sex, Crime, Religion and Education* (1904), in which he posited the idea of "sturm und drang" or storm and stress (Smith, 1975). Hall's psychological theory of recapitulation was greatly influenced by Darwin's belief that ontogeny recapitulates phylogeny, that is, that individual development parallels the evolutionary development of the species. Thus Muuss (1988) suggests that early animal-like primitivism characterizes infancy and early childhood; periods of savagery characterize late childhood and adolescence; and more recent civilized ways of life characterize maturity.

The concept of adolescence as a period in the life cycle in which the young were no longer children but were not yet adults has been noted in classical literature. Plato suggested that youth in this age group were prone to argument for it own sake. They tended to leave no stone unturned, now that they viewed themselves as possessing wisdom, and would annoy everyone with their arguments (Conger, 1991). Over 2300 years ago, Aristotle noted that

> they are passionate, irascible, and apt to be carried away by their impulses.... They carry everything too far, whether it be their love or hatred or anything else. They regard themselves as omniscient and are positive in their assertions. (quoted in Kiell, 1967, pp. 18–19)

The Office of Christian Parents, written in 1616, divided the life span into six stages: infancy (birth to seven), childhood (7–14), youth (14–28), manhood (28–50), gravity (50–70), and old age (over 70) (Smith, 1975). Overlooking the fact that the age groups overlapped and were clearly designed for males, this schema reflected the social and economic circumstance that male youth faced in the early seventeenth century.

Youth were typically apprenticed to and lived with a master who taught them his craft, a practice advocated by Benjamin Franklin as a way that parents could remain friends with their adolescent-aged children. After serving their apprenticeship, most males would be in their late 20s before they were financially able to marry and establish an independent household. Therefore, the period of manhood (ages 28–50) noted earlier reflected the ages during which men married and raised children. Although adolescent women were not mentioned in this schema, it can be assumed that their life-course transitions were somewhat parallel to that of the adolescent male. Girls remained at home to help with family and childbearing chores, or they might be sent to live with a family who needed assistance with these chores.

Typically, adolescence was considered to be the teenage years but was often extended to 21 to be consistent with the age of majority. However, age of majority also varies by activity (e.g., one can vote at 18, but not drink until 21 years of age) and by state. The 1994 crime bill permits children as young as 13 to be tried as adults for some offenses (Children's Defense Fund, 1995). Baumrind (1987) has suggested that contemporary adolescence could be considered to span the ages of 10–25 years—which is remarkably consistent with that stage called "youth" identified in *The Offices of Christian Parents* (Smith, 1975).

While extending the age of adolescence to 25 years or older might make some sense for pediatricians defining their patient load or for social scientists attempting to define developmental tasks, it is not consistent with laws defining adult status. It is also inconsistent with life-cycle stages because a large number of individuals have completed their schooling, been engaged in full-time employment for a number of years, married, and started families by 25 years of age. For purposes of this chapter, I will designate the ages of 11–18 to be considered adolescence, although for certain sets of data such as teen pregnancy, where the data typically include youth up to 19 years of age, this age range will be expanded.

Demographic Characteristics

How would we describe adolescents as we enter the twenty-first century? As of 1995, approximately 14.1% of the U.S. population, just under 37 million young people, were between the ages of 10 and 19 years of age (U.S. Bureau of the Census, 1996). A majority of adolescents were Euro-American; 14% were African Americans, 12% were Hispanic; 3.4% were Asian or Pacific Islanders, and 1% were Native American, Eskimo, or Aleut (Hollman, 1993).

Although just under 22% of all children in the United States under the age of 18 live in poverty, minority children are at greater risk of experiencing poverty: 47% of African American children, 40% of Hispanic children, but only 17% of white children lived in poverty. Children and families living in poverty have increased dramatically in the past 2 decades, and even when controlling for race, 42% of single-parent families lived in poverty compared to 8% of two-parent families. There are over 4 million youth between the ages of 16 and 24 in the United States who are seeking employment but are unable to find jobs. Unemployment rates for African American youth are more than two and a half times the rate for white adolescents. In all areas examined in this chapter, minority status and living in a female-headed family increased the negative impact on children; when both conditions are present, the effect is considerable.

The National Health Survey (Collins & LeClere, 1996) found that income, education, and marital status of the parents and families has substantial impact on youth in several ways. Not only does higher income and education provide family members with more knowledge regarding good health habits, it also enables them greater access to better health and preventive services. A two-parent family is likely to have a higher income, as well as the availability of another parent to share in childrearing and household or family decision making.

Children under 18 years of age whose families had an annual income under $10,000 or who lived with a single parent had poorer health status, more limitations in activities, and a higher percentage of hospitalizations during the past year than children in households with higher incomes or two-parent households. Children and adolescents in single-parent homes also had higher levels of disability.

The educational level of parents also was an important factor, with lower levels of education contributing to a poorer health status for adolescents. Youth whose parent or guardian had less than 12 years of education reported higher rates of hospitalization than children in families where the responsible adult was better educated.

Although there are various age ranges used to describe the period of development called adolescence, there is equal confusion when legally defining adolescents for judicial purposes or for the provision of services. For example, in the case of certain criminal acts, a youth of 15 or 16 years of age or younger may be defined as an adult. In other states, female adolescents under the age of 18 have to seek parental consent to obtain reproductive health services such as contraceptives and abortions. Such practices preclude adolescent females from having responsibility for and control of their bodies in the same manner as those 18 or older who seek these services. The under 15-year-old who needs parental permission to seek her own medical care, however, is granted adult status and considered responsible to give permission for the medical care and social service assistance for her baby.

Values

The Allan Guttmacher Institute, in its report *Sex and America's Teenagers* (Alan Guttmacher Institute, 1994), found that most teenagers value responsibility, honesty, self-respect, and religious commitment. Having a good marriage and family life (8 out of 10 expect to marry), giving their children (7 out of 10 want children) better opportunities than they had, and finding meaning and purpose in life were important. Despite the vast differences in educational attainment, nearly all adolescents believed that education was important.

While these values are shared, the ability to achieve the goals embodied in these values differs by race, parents' education, social class, gender, and individual characteristics. In order to examine the impact of the twenty-first century on adolescents, we need to examine the developmental tasks of adolescence and how these tasks are being fulfilled in today's society.

Socialization of Youth

In societies with lower levels of technological development and a less complex division of labor, most children can learn their expected roles through direct observation of adults and on-the-job training. In more technologically complex societies, parents are limited in how much of the culture and specific knowledge they possess and can pass on to their children—hence the need for a long period of formal education.

Socialization techniques also vary by the society's concept of the nature of children. During the colonial period of United States, children were treated very harshly because parents believed that humans were born evil and had to have sinfulness beaten out of them (deMause, 1974). In the nineteenth century, child neglect was commonly justified by the belief that an all-controlling God would save those who were already in a "state of grace"; consequently, children didn't need their parents' help and protection. An entirely different conception of children has emerged in the twentieth century, one that recognizes the importance of parents in the socialization process and emphasizes the importance of affection and autonomy (self-direction) in the development of mental health and well-being.

During the first half of this century, the study of socialization tended to be centered in the field of child development and was focused on specific parental behaviors (i.e., the type of discipline strategy that produced certain characteristics in the child or adolescent) (see Steinmetz, 1979, for a review of these early studies). More recently, an entirely different conception of children has emerged that recognizes the importance of parents in the socialization process and emphasizes the importance of affection and autonomy (self-direction) in the development of mental health and well-being. During the past few decades, socialization has been increasingly defined as a lifelong process. A systems approach, which recognizes the impact of family, peer groups, and other social influences, as well as the direct interaction between parents and child, has been a major theoretical framework (see Peterson & Hann, Chapter 13, this volume).

Adolescence is a period characterized by considerable exploration. For most youth, entry into this new status of adolescence, with accompanying roles, is often a period characterized by trial-and-error attempts to adjust. Risky behavior, in many instances, occurs when adolescents experiment with or adopt adult behavior, such as drinking and sexual activity, yet lack the social maturity to handle these activities responsibly.

Major Theories of Adolescent Socialization

Many scholars have implicitly or explicitly used sociological or family studies theories to explain socialization in general and adolescent behavior more specifically. A social-psychological analysis of socialization, developed by E. Burgess (1926), conceptualized socialization as an interactive process—an outcome of the interplay between socializers and socializees, both of whom have needs and capacities. For Burgess, socialization had two dimensions: that of the group and that of the individual, and both were equally important.

Socialization in general can be viewed as a four-step process: (1) learning the content of the roles, (2) rehearsing roles, (3) receiving feedback from others about one's performance, and (4) adjustment and full acceptance of the new role. While this process in early childhood has been the primary focus of much research, we should recognize that socialization occurs throughout one's life and that peers, especially during adolescence, are formidable socialization agents.

In this section several theories used in the social sciences to explain adolescent development are explored: cognitive development, developmental/life cycle theory, symbolic interaction, resource/exchange theories, and structural/ functional/systems theory.

Cognitive Development Theory of Socialization

Freud's psychosexual theory tended to focus exclusively on the individual as an organism, but provided an early formulation of how humans develop from birth to death. A different stage theory, cognitive development, developed by psychologists, built on Freud's work and examined age-related changes in the individual's capacity for processing information. Following the pioneering work of Jean Piaget, a Swiss psychologist, researchers have found that children, under appropriate environmental conditions, gradually expand their ability to think in abstract terms. Contrary to the general belief that children's cognitive processes are the same as those of adults, Piaget and his colleagues discovered basic differences in the cognitive strategies of children and adolescents at various ages. The youngest see the world in absolute terms, slightly older children are able to perceive ambiguities, and by later adolescence, individuals can think in abstractions. Adolescents' cognitive development had been defined in terms of the construct *formal operations*. These include the ability to conceptualize the possible outcomes of behaviors, to think in a hypothetical-deductive manner (i.e., develop hypothesis), to think about one's own thoughts and the self, and to consider the self as an object of thought. Adolescents can also think abstractly about reference groups and used these generalized others to evaluate the self.

Socialization, from this perspective, refers to opportunities for expanding mental processes and for guided learning in a supportive environment. Without such assistance, the mind does not automatically develop the ability for abstract thinking. We all know adults who think like 8-year-olds and view things as either good or bad, right or wrong, true or false, with few shadings or ambiguities. Piaget's model has also influenced research on moral development. For example, Kohlberg (1969) built on Piaget's work in suggesting that moral or ethical judgment follow a stagelike course of growth from simple to ever more complex ways of thinking. Although the sequence of stages through which youth develop appear to be fixed, the age at which youth will pass through each stage is influenced by the level of development of the society and cultural, ethnic, and geographic circumstances, as well as individual and family attributes. This is helpful for understanding cross-cultural influences. These variables may enhance or limit the individual's ability to process complex information and thus influences their progress through each stage.

Developmental/Life-Cycle Theories of Development

These theoretical approaches were developed predominantly within the fields of child development and family studies. These approaches view socialization as a lifelong process in which individuals are continually required to learn new roles (and discard old ones) as they move from one stage to another (Baldwin, 1968; Duvall, 1957; Hill & Rodgers, 1964; Kohlberg, 1969).

Erikson (1968) identified eight stages of development and theorized that at each stage, the psychosocial task was aimed at solidifying the various elements of childhood identity into a consolidated identity of self. Failure to complete this task can result in role confusion. The major conflict that must be resolved in puberty and adolescence is to resolve the conflict between identity formation and role confusion. Families that encourage individuality and independence foster the process of identity exploration and formation in adolescents (Grotevant & Cooper, 1985). Kohn (1963) suggests that working-class parents emphasize obedience and following rules whereas middle-class parents emphasize independence and thinking for oneself because they are important characteristics for middle-class jobs. Therefore, it appears that middle-class youth would have an easier time with the formation of role identity than would working-class youth because the socialization that middle-class youth experience fosters the development of identity exploration and formation.

There are many similarities to Erikson's concept of resolving the psychosocial conflict for tasks within each stage and the concepts utilized by family development theorists. One major difference, however, is that development and life-cycle family theorists focus on how the individual family members master behavioral tasks required by each stage, while cognitive theorists are concerned with individuals developing an adequate self-concept based on resolving internal conflicts.

Theorists using a life-cycle "stage" approach examine the roles, responsibilities, and tasks required by families and individuals in each stage. Thus beginning families, those with no children, will be concerned with learning the roles of husband and wife and fulfilling occupational roles. Childbearing families, those who have started to have children, will be concentrating on learning to be parents while their children are learning to interact with parents, siblings, and peers. As children adapt to the role of schoolchild, teenager, and part-time employee, parents will have to adjust to the expectation that they will be relinquishing their control over their children. When these children enter college or join the workforce, the parents, who are now at the "launching" or empty nest stage, are learning to redefine themselves in ways that no longer focus on their parenting roles.

Each of these perspectives is somewhat helpful in understanding human behavior, but neither deals with the basic question raised by the concept of socialization: How are social roles learned? For the answer to this question, we must turn to another theory that addresses the "social self."

Symbolic Interaction Theory of Socialization: The Social Self

The symbolic interaction approach is concerned not only with externally observable or measurable circumstances, such as age, body appearance, social class, behavior, and values, but also with the symbolic meaning human beings attach to these concepts. As first noted by W. I. Thomas in his concept of the "definition of the situation," if individuals define situations as real then they are real in their consequences (paraphrased from Thomas & Thomas, 1937, p. 572).

From a sociological perspective, learning is an interactive process. That is, learning takes place in a particular society and culture, is mediated by specific social relationships, and involves symbolic interaction through spoken symbols or nonverbal gestures and facial and body language. The information that is exchanged between socializer and socializee is coded in symbols—the meanings given to particular words and gestures in a specific society. Because humans are capable of giving any meaning to a word or object ("symbolizing"), they are also able to invent and create rules for behavior. Therefore, what a child learns as the appropriate behavior ("role") for a given social position is whatever the socializers have defined as appropriate.

Furthermore, we are not born with a sense of who we are, but must develop a sense of "self" through symbolic communication with other people. In other words, the self is a social product, arising from social interaction. For an understanding of this process we turn to the theories of Charles Horton Cooley (1902–1956) and George Herbert Mead (1934–1962), whose early work laid the foundation for the theoretical perspective called symbolic interaction.

Cooley introduced the concept of the "looking glass self," a concept using the metaphor of the social mirror to convey the idea that we never see ourselves objectively, but rather as images reflected from the reactions of other people. The looking glass self has three elements: how we imagine other people see us, how we think they judge us, and how we feel about that judgment. Note that the possibility exists of making errors both in the way that others see us and in how we interpret their reactions, but there is no other material from which we can construct an identity. In other words, we are who we think other people think we are! Adolescents, with particular sensitivities to fitting in, are under substantial pressure to make sure that other people think they are appearing and acting in peer-approved ways.

Clearly, some people will have greater power than others to define us. The ones on whom we depend most for physical survival, approval, and affection will be those whom we most wish to please. These people, whom Mead calls "significant others," have a powerful impact on our socialization. Collectively, these significant others are our reference groups because their behaviors, attitudes, roles, values, and activities serve as reference points for shaping our own behaviors, attitudes, roles, values, and activities. Mead also speaks of the "generalized other" to refer to cultural standards of conduct for a particular status, that is, how everyone who occupies a given status (student, parent, worker, etc.) ought to behave. In the process of socialization, we learn both what we ought to do in the role according to cultural ideals (the generalized other) and what the people closest to us expect (significant other).

For Mead, socialization is essentially a process whereby we learn to "take the role of the other toward ourselves." By this, he means that it is the human capacity to put oneself in the place of another that is essential to becoming a member of society. It is because we have the ability to imagine how other people see us that we can guide our own behavior. It is this ability to take the roles of others toward oneself as well as learning one's own role toward others that symbolic interactionists consider to be the basic social process. Unless we are able to put ourselves in the place of others, to see ourselves as others see us, and to shape or modify our behavior according to expectations of generalized others, we are not fully socialized.

One problem adolescents face is that the behavior they deem appropriate because they have received the approval of their peers may be the very behaviors that parents and other adults consider inappropriate, socially unacceptable, and possibly delinquent. Peterson (1986) reminds us that youth's conception of self, which is based on interactions and the expectations of peers, may differ from parental expectations for youth. Parents' expectations for youth also change over time as they anticipate more independent decisions and behaviors from their children. Youth likewise anticipate being permitted more independent actions and more autonomy. He suggests that parent–adolescent interaction is based, to a large degree, on "role-making, the process of improvising, exploring and judging what is appropriate on the basis of the situation and the responses of others at the moment" (p. 23).

Roles provide a general "gestalt" that sets general parameters for social behavior, but leaves much for situational negotiation and individual creativity.

Resource and Exchange Theories

The social exchange framework is based on the assumption that individuals engage in rational decision making with the goal of initiating, continuing, or terminating a relationship (an investment) based on the greatest profits or smallest number of losses possible.

Two major resources adolescents can use to gain a more favorable position in family decision making are financial and interpersonal. Financially, they gain power through unpaid labor by performing household chores and caregiving tasks, through direct financial contributions, or indirectly by assuming the costs of their personal needs. An example of this power can be observed when adolescents state that having a job or caring for younger siblings or an older relative is an indication of their ability to be responsible and thus they should be allowed greater independence, for example, later curfews and more privileges. Adolescents can also gain power by forming a coalition with a parent that can result in a readjustment of marital power, for example encouraging and supporting a parent's decision to leave an abusive relationship, return to school, or take a particular vacation.

Families are enduring institutions, and decisions made at one point in time remain part of the family history. This encourages family members to operate through norms of reciprocity that make them feel morally obligated to interact in ways that benefit the members. The quality of a parent–child relationship, from a social exchange perspective, is based on the costs and rewards to each member as a result of this relationship. Peterson (1986) notes that parents will perceive the relationship as rewarding when adolescents "provide parents with affection, comply with parental expectations, agree with parental opinions, achieve effectively in areas valued by parents, function as companions, and represent the family favorably in public settings" (p. 29). However, parents perceive the parent–adolescent relationships as costly when youths "deplete their economic resources, are noncompliant, fail to agree with parents, lack achievement in areas that are valued by parents, affiliate with the "wrong" friends (as defined by parental values), and behave in a manner, e.g., delinquency, that publicly embarrasses their family" (p. 20).

Functional Analysis and Systems Theory

Structural-functional analysis, with its emphasis on structural components of the family and their roles or functions, can be somewhat limiting when attempting to examine adolescence within a contemporary context. The conservative aspects of functionalism (Chapter 7 by Vargus, this volume) do not allow us to see some of the changes in contemporary adolescents' lifestyle as positive. For example, functional theorists are alarmed over the early independence of adolescents and lack of direct supervision of their activities, which they view as contributing to delinquency, school failures, and teen pregnancy and thus threatening the stability of the social system.

However, for many adolescents, the increased independence is a reward because they have demonstrated maturity and responsibility by having a job, helping with household chores, or taking care of younger siblings. Functional analysis' conservativism and emphasis on correlational relationships, which tend to view the increasing number of employed mothers as a "cause" of the increasing rates of adolescent problems, has only limited usefulness. Systems theory, which developed from and uses many of the concepts of functional theory, places more emphasis on the interactional processes and thus can better facilitate an understanding of change.

Systems theory is especially valuable because it recognizes that adolescents, like all family members, do not operate as isolated individuals. They are part of a family system in which the actions of a parent or sibling have a direct impact on their own attitudes and behaviors. The effect of the systemness is best demonstrated in the sections that follow, in which risk-taking behaviors and the relationship of these behaviors to family variables are addressed.

One cannot overlook the importance of the interrelated behaviors and holistic context of the family when attempting to understand adolescent behavior. Other concepts in a family systems approach are the existence of patterned relationships in which each individual functions as a part of the system, hierarchical structures such as parent–child dyads, and boundaries, which serve to define information and actions that are permitted into or out of the family. Coalitions between parents are the norm, with parents being expected to present a united front in terms of expected adolescent behaviors. Coalitions between a parent and a child can be used to change the marital power system when, as discussed in the resource theory section, an adolescent forms a coalition with a parent. Boundary ambiguity, resulting from inappropriate coalitions between parent and child, is evidenced when a parent inappropriately elevates a child to the role of "parent" both in terms of responsibility and privileged communication with the parent or sexual behavior (i.e., molest and incest). Family Systems Theory focuses on maintaining a balance between cohesion and adaptability and change and stability over time (Olson, Russell, & Sprenkle, 1983; and see Peterson & Hann, Chapter 13, this volume, for an elaboration on Olson and colleagues' work).

Theoretical Applications

One of the major variables to be linked to socialization is social class, specifically as it influences disciplinary techniques. Melvin Kohn, in his classic work *Class and Conformity* (1969), utilized a structural-functional approach to explain socialization. Kohn demonstrated that parents who had jobs requiring that they follow rules and orders without question in order to be successful, a primary condition of working-class jobs, stressed obedience as an important socialization value for their children to possess. Parents in the middle class, on the other hand, who held jobs requiring independence and thinking for oneself, often emphasized that children should become autonomous and self-directing.

In his monograph *Children of the Great Depression* (1972), Glen Elder expanded his interpretations of the relationship between children and their families to include generational differences that reflected historical events such as the Great Depression, World War II, the postwar Baby Boom, and the hippie generation of the 60s that protested the Vietnam War. Although there are components of a structural-functional theoretical approach in his analysis, for example, an emphasis on performing highly structured roles, a symbolic interaction perspective permits greater understanding of the way that these historical events influence not only the behavior used to perform these roles, but also the meaning attached to such behavior. We gain insights into the reason by working- and lower-middle-class parents, who struggled to give their children the material symbols and values of the middle class, were dismayed to see their children reject these material advantages, symbols, and values as defective and immoral.

Susan Littwin in her book *The Postponed Generation* (1986) noted that individuals reaching adulthood in the 80s had been raised in an era of permissiveness and feelings of privilege and entitlement. These were the special youth, the youth that Robert Coles in *Children of Crisis, a Study of Courage and Fear* (1967), used to describe upper-class youth who exhibited "narcissistic entitlement." Resource and exchange theory provides a framework for understanding the problems that youth in the 1980s may have faced.

We need to consider how these adolescents, who have been reared in relative luxury and often have completed more education than their parents, will cope when they are unable to find that dream job. Furthermore, they may discover that those jobs that are available may not be personally fulfilling and may not pay wages that will enable these youth to maintain the middle-class standards of their parents.

As Littwin notes, most of these college-educated youth were middle class, not of the "privileged class," and thus were shocked to face the real world—one in which they were expected to work hard to achieve a standard of living that fell considerably short of that in which they were raised. Members of this generation, raised to believe that "how they felt" was more important than "what they did," chose to exchange their independent adult status for a dependent status in which they resided with their parents to maintain their outward appearance of upper-middle class status and the accouterments associated with this lifestyle. They were simply extending adolescence into their late 20s, early 30s, or later.

Developmental Tasks and Contemporary Adolescents' Ability to Fulfill Them

A Society of Extremes

Today we are a society of extremes. Only first place counts, and those who do not place first are left to consider their worth. Even those youth who are successful are often unable to face reality when their moment of stardom dims. This has been amply documented in terms of children who are television or movie stars who make millions and grace the covers of our popular magazines as long as their TV series continue or the movie roles keep coming. However, when they are unable to adapt to the not-so-cute adolescent or young adult roles and success comes to a halt, these childhood stars succumb to substance abuse, failed relationships, mental illness, and criminal behavior.

The problem of "poststardom depression" also is faced by athletes who train for Olympic gold, but have few other venues for their skill once they are no longer competitive. The child genius who enters college as a preteen may continue in a successful career, but may never regain the glory attained during childhood.

Attempts to have one's young child become a star start early with programs on how to build a better baby. Prenatal programs instruct parents to play classical music and foreign languages so that their children will have a head start in life. Parents have also been instructed in ways to teach their infants reading, foreign languages, and mathematics. How does the parent whose child can read at 3 years of age deal with "failure" when their child, as an adolescent, is simply an average student? More recently, with the much publicized murder of JonBenet Ramsey, a 6-year-old beauty contest winner, we have begun to question the wisdom of beauty contests for young children. More consideration is needed about the potential harm that may result for young girls of 5 or 6 when their clothes, makeup, behavior, and demeanor are more consistent with those of a 20-year-old than a preschool child.

What is the impact on the average teen or family with a special needs child when we focus only on "stars?" Although throughout history there have been youth who possessed special talents at a very young age, the pervasive visibility of a vast array of talented youth with adultlike careers in athletics, music, art, the theater, and academics is conveyed to impressionable youth through television and youth-oriented magazines.

This has implications not only for parents of gifted children, but also for parents of special needs children. Youth with chronic illnesses are living longer, and the trend is for children and youth to remain in their families rather than be placed in institutions. As a result, parenting may encompass a lifetime with few if any guideposts for parents. The literature suggests that the period encompassing adolescence has become exceedingly complicated and problematic not only for the youth themselves but also for parents, who are attempting to provide structure and guidance in an era dissimilar to that in which they were raised and without updated roadmaps for guidance.

Autonomy: Preparation for Adult Roles: Helping at Home, Teen Employment, and Volunteer Work

A psychosocial task associated with adolescence is autonomy, that is, the ability to assert individuality and become a productive member of society. Autonomy refers to the ability of the individual to meet his or her own basic needs, which had been met previously by parents or other adults. This is the preferred term because unlike the concept of independence, which suggests a rejection of one's parents, autonomy is a transitional stage during which individuals are able to physically distance themselves from, but not reject, their family and assume responsibility for their own affairs while maintaining emotional connection to parents and family members (Baumrind, 1991; Hill & Holmbeck, 1986; Steinberg, 1990).

Recent research on autonomy indicates that competent forms of autonomy for most adolescents develop with continuing bonds of relationship connectedness, harmony, and only moderate conflict with parents (Silverburg & Gondoli, 1996; Steinberg, 1990). Contemporary perspectives view this process as being subject to forces in the social environment that can greatly define this experience as varying widely from quite manageable to difficult, depending on the circumstances.

This contrasts with the classic view of adolescent autonomy proposed by psychoanalytic theorists that has dominated much of the twentieth century: Autonomy was achieved as an outgrowth of a separation process from parents, the rejection of childhood dependencies on parents, and within the context of inevitable "storm" and "stress." Psychoanalytic theorists viewed this turbulence leading to autonomy as virtually inevitable because its origins were supposed to be rooted in biological factors, the physiological changes of puberty, and

unconscious forces residing within the human psyche (A. Freud, 1958; Blos, 1979).

Muuss (1988) suggests that family influences are particularly important in the areas of autonomy, fostering self-esteem and self-confidence and stimulating the achievement of identity. He further notes that there are three domains of autonomy: behavioral, cognitive, and emotional. Of these, behavioral transitions are the most problematic because substantial differences often exist between adolescents and parents in the timing of these expectancies for greater autonomy (Collins & Luebker, 1994).

Researchers have suggested that developing emotional autonomy during adolescence, characterized by the ability of youth to make independent decisions and disagree with parental opinion, involves an increasing individuation form and decreasing emotional dependency on their parents. Emotional autonomy is acquired, however, within the context of parental support and acceptance (Grotevant & Cooper, 1985; Steinberg & Silverberg, 1986). This is different from detachment, in which adolescents have a negative perception of their parents and their parents have low acceptance of youth and do not support their attempts at gaining independence (Ryan & Lynch, 1989).

Cognitive autonomy, or value autonomy (Douvan & Adelson, 1966), refers to the adolescent's ability to make decisions without needing to seek the approval of others. According to Erikson (1968), to avoid foreclosure, which is simply adopting the opinions and values or roles of others without reflections, adolescents must develop autonomous commitment to specific values. The lack of cognitive autonomy has been linked to authoritarian family experiences and appears to produce adolescents who are excessively dependent (Allaman, Joyce, & Crandall, 1972) and rely on external locus of control (Harter, 1990). Muuss (1988) believes that the three domains are most likely interrelated, and parent–child relationships that foster cognitive autonomy are also likely to foster emotional autonomy resulting in self-governed, independent behavior, that is, behavioral autonomy.

Individuation, an aspect of autonomy, is the ability to see oneself as separate and distinct from one's family of origin, with clear boundaries existing between the daily life of the young person and the parent. For most individuals in Western countries this occurs in later adolescence when young adults leave the parental home to maintain their own residence.

The timing of individuation has received considerable attention. A number of studies have pointed to the disadvantages of early disengagement from parents in terms of youth demonstrating increased insecurity, increased concern for parental approval of their behavior and decisions, higher levels of moratorium and diffusions, and lower levels of identity achievement (Benson, Harris, & Rogers, 1992; Berman & Sperling, 1991; Frank, Pirsch, & Wright, 1990).

In contrast, other studies have found that late adolescents who lived apart from parents reported greater feelings of mutual respect and support between parents and youth and greater feelings of independence (Flanagan, Schulenberg, & Fuligni, 1992; Sullivan & Sullivan, 1980). There were differences observed by family structure; in single-parent families there were mutually shared expectations that the youth would reside in the home for a longer period of time; in stepfamilies the mutually shared expectations were that the youth would leave earlier (Goldscheider & Goldscheider, 1989; Mitchell, Wister, & Burch, 1989). Although leaving at a later age may be viewed as an indication of more difficult individuation, continued residence in the parental home may also reflect financial considerations. The young adult may live at home in order to financially afford postsecondary education or may feel obligated to remain at home for a period of time to help with finances or the care of a family member (Steinmetz, 1988).

Autonomy not only involves youth becoming prepared to take on work roles, but also includes the ability to separate from parents and succeed in school, part-time employment, and other skills and activities that prepare youth for their roles as adults. In today's society we also need to ponder the impact of mothers in the work force or workaholic dads: Does this create early independence or a longing for nurturance and being taken care of that may be played out during adult relationships and parenting? We also need to examine the effect of learning disabilities and physical, emotional, or mental handicaps on adolescents' ability to achieve independence. Finally, we need to look at dropout rates as well as the number of adolescents attending postsecondary academic or vocational programs to see if our educational systems are meeting the needs of our youth.

Teenage Employment. Childhood labor was so critical that Quakers in Colonial America prohibited their sons from marrying until they were 21 years of age in order that the parents might benefit from their labor and be reimbursed for the costs of rearing them (Frost, 1973). The end of the Depression ushered in the Fair Labor Standards Act, which dealt with child labor and extended compulsory school attendance to 16 years of age (Wrigley, 1986).

In earlier eras, adolescent employment was primarily through apprenticeship programs and factory and farm work and provided a major contribution to the family's economic security. Even in more recent decades, the employment of youth, especially part-time and during the summer, has been part of the social fabric in the United States. Today the growth of malls and the fast food industry has provided a major source of employment for adolescents, primarily in fast food and sales, as teens are more able to accommodate the flexible work schedules required in these fields.

Contrary to the advice of childrearing experts of the past who advocated work because "idle hands are the devil's workshop," contemporary experts are divided on the value of adolescents being employed. Receiving pay in the paid labor force reduces age-based segregation and provides adolescents with an opportunity to learn adult work roles while still in school—which is especially important to compensate for the welfare experience among lower socioeconomic youth.

Greenberger and Steinberg (1986) found that over 33% of sophomores worked 15 or more hours per week, over 20% worked 22 or more hours, and 6% worked 35 hours or more. One in four worked a half-time job while attending school full-time. For seniors, the average number of hours worked while in school was just over 20 hours and nearly 10% worked 35 hours or more. Most interesting was that the pattern of the number of hours worked by teenagers was unrelated to socioeconomic status (SES), parent's education, or occupation. Furthermore, economically disadvantaged students were less likely to work than middle-class students, who used their earnings primarily as discretionary income for clothes, cars, and leisure-time activities.

Finch and Mortimer (1985) found limited support for a relationship between poorer school performance in the 9th grade and working in the 10th, 11th, and 12th grades. Although Greenberger and Steinberg (1986) also found that working over 20 hours per week had only a slightly detrimental effect on grades and behavior among sophomores, employed students tended to take less demanding courses, and 60% of the employed students noted that work interfered with required reading. Employment was found to increase self-reliance among girls, but slightly decrease self-reliance among boys. The authors note that youth who have less interest in school and do poorly may elect to work longer hours because the paycheck provides a positive reward.

The key appears to be working in excess of 20 hours per week. D'Amico (1984), using data from the National Longitudinal Surveys, found that less time was spent on studies as the number of work hours grew in excess of 20 hours per week. Ruggerio, Greenberger, and Steinberg (1982) found that student workers were more likely to engage in deviant acts, and Johnston, Bachman, and O'Malley (1982) found a positive association with alcohol, marijuana, and tobacco. Greenberger and Steinberg (1986) found that middle-class (as compared to working-class) youth showed the greatest gains in delinquency.

Not only was teen employment in excess of 20 hours a week detrimental to health, development, and academic success, but Greenberger and Steinberg (1986) also found that teens typically work in age-segregated employment ghettos where the skills acquired did not serve as apprenticeships for future occupations or long-term movement up career ladders. Only 7% of students are employed in the skilled trades and other jobs. They suggest that there are psychosocial costs associated with teenage employment because it interferes with identity formation, peer groups, and academic success, which are the major developmental tasks of this age group.

We need to reexamine this "occupational elitism," that is, the belief that only certain types of jobs or work settings are acceptable for middle-class youth. With changing technology and workforce needs, it is unrealistic to assume that all, or even most, youth will find employment in intellectually challenging, highly skilled jobs. The skills, behaviors, and attitudes learned during an adolescent's employment in fast food or sales may be entirely consistent with those that will be required in adult employment.

There have been other negative outcomes related to teenage employment. Bachman and Schulenberg (1993) studied more than 70,000 respondents from the "Monitoring the Future" project and found that adolescents typically worked long hours that resulted in unhealthy lifestyles, especially loss of sleep and insufficient exercise, and opportunity costs (i.e., reduction in their ability to engage in other social and academic pursuits).

Longer hours of work for teens are associated with higher rates of tardiness (Greenberger & Steinberg, 1986), more conduct problems (Steinberg & Dornbusch, 1991), and lower grades (Finch & Mortimer, 1985). Longitudinal data (Steinberg, Fegley, & Dornbusch, 1993) revealed that employed students, when compared to nonemployed students, had lower grades, spent less time on homework, had lower educational expectations, and expressed more disengagement from school in the second year of the study. Mortimer and Finch (1996) caution that these studies have tended to focus exclusively on the detrimental effects of hours of employment and have overlooked the indirect contributions to the school life resulting from teen employment, such as paying for school and school-related social activities, an integral part of school life that parents might not be able to afford.

The ways in which the students' earnings are spent can also produce positive or negative effects. Marsh (1993) found, for example, that employment had a positive effect on grades when the earnings were used to save for college. Bachman (1983), however, raised the problems associated with "premature affluence," which results because youth have large amount of disposable income because their basic needs are still being met by their parents.

Data from the Youth Development Study (Mortimer, Finch, Ryn, & Shanahan, 1996; Shanahan, Finch, Mortimer, & Ryn, 1991) indicated that employed students did not have fewer close social relationships with friends but did experience depressed moods. Students who worked fewer hours did not invest their extra hours in homework; those who worked longer hours did not receive lower grades. Most employed students believed that their job provided them with the oppor-

tunity to learn new skills and the opportunity to help others and enhanced their status within the peer group. Their data indicate that 10th and 11th grade students who worked long hours experienced an increased use of alcohol, even when controlling for prior employment and alcohol use (Mortimer et al., 1996). However, they found that students who worked less than 20 hours or less a week had higher grades than either nonworking students or those who worked longer hours. Longer hours of teen employment result in a greater independence from parents (Mortimer & Shanahan, 1994; Steinberg et al., 1993), with interpretations differing as to whether this is a positive or negative trend. D'Amico (1984) suggested that employment in moderate amounts may foster perseverance and diligence, traits conducive to staying in school. It is also possible that it provides youth with a picture of the limited types of jobs available to them if they do not complete their education.

Historically, adolescents have always engaged in work. Zelizer (1985) reported that during the eighteenth and mid-nineteenth centuries, the value of children was based on their economic worth. Between 1870 and 1930 children became sentimentalized; they were no longer viewed as economically useful but were valued for their intrinsic worth—they were emotionally priceless. Thus, the current pattern of adolescents in the workforce is not a new trend, but rather a return to the centuries-old patterns in which youth had economic value. This current practice of adolescents being in the paid labor force may do better in teaching the work ethic than requiring household tasks, such as cleaning one's room, in return for an allowance, which characterized adolescence in the 1940s to 1960s.

Housework and Caretaking Responsibilities. The increased number of women in the workforce has meant that adolescents often have considerable responsibility in terms of housework and care for younger siblings and elderly relatives. Mortimer and Finch (1996) report that when compared with their mothers, teenage daughters report spending 14.2 hours each week on household chores, whereas their mothers spent just under 9.9 hours each week when they were teens; sons report spending 12.2 hours each week doing household chores compared to the 7.3 hours per week that fathers spent when they were teens.

In addition, girls averaged about 5.4 hours per week taking care of children or an elderly relative, whereas boys averaged 1.7 hours per week in these responsibilities. However, an average probably does not reflect the actual level of responsibility. For those girls having responsibility for the care of younger siblings (a task performed by 37.5% of girls), they spent nearly 14 hours per week performing this chore. Additionally, nearly 5% reported that they had to care for an elderly relative; these girls provided 4.6 hours of care per week. Twenty-three percent of boys had to care for younger siblings, and they spent 6 hours per week providing this care. Just over 3% of the boys provided care to an elderly person, and they spent just over 3 hours per week providing this care (Aronson, Mortimer, Zeirman, & Hacker, 1996).

Children contribute directly and indirectly to the family's economic well-being. Twelve percent of employed daughters and 16% of employed sons directly contributed at least some of their earnings to their parents. Indirectly, teens contribute to the family by using their earnings to buy clothes, food, car-related expenses, entertainment, and savings toward college, which relieves parents of having to purchase these items, thus enhancing the family's economic status.

Keith, Nelson, Schlabach, and Thompson (1990) examined the relationship between changing parental employment patterns and the development of responsibility in 174 early adolescents (10–14 years old). Parental employment status and gender of the child were not related to personal responsibility, but gender effects were significant for family responsibilities, with boys and girls assuming traditionally male and female roles. Compared to youth from single-parent families, adolescents from two-parent families in which one parent was not employed participated in more socially responsible volunteer activities.

Volunteer Activities. Volunteer activities are an important way that adolescents can achieve a sense of work and develop good citizenship attitudes. About three-fifths (61%) of youth ages 12–17 volunteered an average of 3.2 hours per week. Over one-fourth of those who volunteered performed 5 or more hours per week, and nearly half volunteered 2 or more hours (Hodgkinson, Weitzman, & Kirsch, 1992). While 51% of adults volunteered and 48% of young adults ages 18–24 volunteered, 61% of teens 12–17 participated in volunteer activities. Although the Gallup study found no gender differences, Keith et al. (1990) found that girls were more likely than boys to participate in volunteer activities. In 1991, teenage volunteers spent about 2.1 billion hours in formal volunteer activities (i.e., participation in activities without monetary or material gain to nonprofit groups) and informal volunteer activities (e.g., helping friends and others without pay, such as by babysitting and helping in community and school functions). The estimated value of the formal volunteer activities was $7 billion.

Involvement in religious organization is the most frequent type of volunteer activity, with 48% of teens reporting that they participated in these endeavors. Forty-four percent and 43%, respectively, engaged in informal volunteering and volunteer activities associated with youth development organizations, 36% volunteered in school and educational activities, 30% volunteered in environmental groups, and 18% did

volunteer work for the arts and humanities (Hodgkinson et al., 1992).

What predicts volunteer activities? First, the typical teen volunteer begins volunteering at an early age. In fact, 44% of teens volunteered before the age of 11 and one-third were engaged in volunteer activities before 10 years of age. Belonging to a youth group and raising money for a cause or organization was a typical pattern of involvement. Most important, parents who provided youth experiences and/or a role model of volunteering for their children were major predictors of volunteer activities as an adult (Hodgkinson, Weitzman, Crutchfield, Heffron, & Kirsch, 1996).

Social responsibility is another characteristic that is prevalent among youth who volunteer. Shapira and Ariella (1979) compared the altruistic and egotistic social responsibility of 5th grade Israeli children who lived in either the city or a kibbutz. This comparison was made by asking these youth to donate some or all of a valued reward they had earned earlier for the benefit of poor children. They found that kibbutz children scored higher on the social responsibility scale and were more generous than city children. Gender differences were prevalent, with females in both groups exhibiting higher social responsibility than boys.

Development of Identity, Self-Esteem, and Competence

The major psychosocial task of early and middle adolescence, according to Erikson (1964, 1958) is identity development, which has its origins in individual, sociocultural, and historical experiences. Erikson believed that a sense of identity required psychosocial reciprocity or a consistency "between that which he conceives himself to be and that which he perceives others to see in him and expect of him" (1956, 1994), which is similar in many ways to Cooley's (1956) "looking glass self" originally published in 1902.

The concept of identity is multidimensional and includes not only the literature on identity but also the related components of self-esteem, ego development, self-concept, self-perception, and self-efficacy. The sheer volume of literature, as well as conceptual, definitional, and methodological diversity in research on identity or the self, makes it one of the most complicated and contradictory bodies of work in the social sciences (Côté, 1996). A major part of this problem results from the various ways in which these terms have been defined, measured, and related to other variables. Further exacerbating the problem is the practice of many authors using these terms that designate aspects of the self interchangeably in the same article, program or research (see Adams, Gullotta, & Montemayor, 1992; Côté, 1996; Gecas & Frank, 1992; Gecas & Seff, 1990; Marcia, Waterman, Mattesson, Archer, & Orlofsky, 1993, for extensive reviews of this literature). Identity consists of several components, while self-concept, self-esteem, and self-efficacy or competence are closely related concepts that require separate consideration.

Erikson (1963, 1968), who is identified as first developing this concept, noted two problems that can inhibit the development of identity: identify confusion and identity foreclosure. Identity confused adolescents are characterized by the lack of a clear sense of identity, having difficulty in achieving consistent commitments and taking responsibility, have low self-esteem and immature moral reasoning, are impulsive, and tend to be focused on themselves (Adams, Abraham, & Markstrom, 1987; Marcia, 1980; Orlofsky, 1978; Waterman & Waterman, 1974). For adolescents in identity foreclosure, their sense of self-identification is prematurely fixed, and these adolescents are likely to be highly approval-oriented, be less autonomous, base their self-esteem on recognition by others, have more traditional religious values, be less reflective, and have less intimate personal relationships (Marcia, 1980; Orlofsky, 1978; Waterman & Waterman, 1974).

Marcia (1966) built on Erikson's concept of identity by expanding his two categories to a four-category paradigm of identity, moratorium, foreclosure, and identity diffusion to examine ego identity development. These categories are based on the presence or absence of a crisis and commitment in career and ideology domains.

Those youth who have achieved identity have gone through a period of exploration and have made commitments. Youth who are in the moratorium status are currently engaged in exploration. They are struggling with identity issues and are currently experiencing an identity crisis. Youth characterized as being in foreclosure have made commitments to identity issues, but have not seriously explored alternatives and thus may have reached commitment prematurely. Adolescents who are classified as being in the identify diffusion status have neither explored identity issues nor become committed to any.

A major trend observed between the 1960s and the 1980s was a tendency for adolescents to define themselves less in terms of socially defined status—for example, "I am a college student; I am a mother"—and more in terms of affect, desires, and styles of behavior—consistent with the "me" generation philosophy (Snow & Phillips, 1982). Whether or not this trend will remain is an important issue for future investigations.

Facilitators and Inhibitors of Identity Development.
Parental styles have been linked to the development of identity. Adolescents in families where mutual support and agreement were emphasized and individuality was not encouraged tended to score lower on a measure of identity exploration. However, adolescents in families that encouraged self-

assertion, permitted disagreement, and were responsive to and respected others' views tended to be those who scored higher on identity exploration (Grotevant & Cooper, 1985).

Peterson (1986) suggests that parental induction, which is based on the use of reason to influence adolescents, is less likely to result in hostile and resistant adolescent behavior and more likely to facilitate the prosocial behavior, moral development, and self-concept through internalizing the parent's rationale. Parental support and affectionate interaction with the adolescent predicts identification with and conformity to parents' expectations and a higher self-esteem in a positive manner (Gecas & Schwalbe, 1986). Coercive or punitive behaviors and verbal or physical control attempts without rational explanation, on the other hand, tend to discourage the development of social competence, which includes self-esteem as one of its components (Hoffman, 1980; Rollins & Thomas, 1979).

Higher identity commitment is found among adolescents who attend church more frequently (Markstom-Adams, 1994). A fairly large self-concept disparity, based on ethnic identity, was observed by Furnham and Kirris (1983) and considered to be a sign of healthy adjustment and development. The authors suggest that in-group favoritism indicates satisfaction with one's ethnic identity rather than a reflection of prejudice. African American parents more frequently reported discussing prejudice with their child; Japanese American and African American parents emphasized adaptation to society more than Mexican American parents; and Japanese American parents stressed achievement more than the other two groups (Phinney & Chavira, 1995).

Self-Esteem. A review of the literature by Blyth and Traeger (1983) suggests that there are probably no clear-cut age trends for self-esteem development that have been proven beyond a shadow of a doubt. However, it seems likely that there is a slight increase in the self-esteem of youth as they move from early into later adolescence. According to Margolin, Blyth, and Carbone (1988), a symbolic interactions perspective would predict that individuals learn who they are by observing how significant others respond to them. In a survey of 7th and 9th graders and their mothers, comparisons were made between the effects of parents' global appraisals and family members' reports of the kinds of interaction they shared (e.g., reports of attachment, family participation, intimacy, authoritarian control). Results indicated that mothers' global appraisals of their early adolescents' competency was the best predictor of adolescent self-esteem.

Walker and Green (1986) found that the quality of relationship with one's parents continued to influence self-esteem beyond the period of adolescence for both boys and girls, with an additional contribution resulting from self-evaluation or popularity for girls and evaluation of school performance for boys. The quality of the relationship with one's parents continues to influence self-esteem after the child becomes an adolescent.

A significant but moderate difference in self-esteem levels was observed to favor boys, and the reported levels of self-esteem also rose very significantly and commensurately with higher academic achievement for both genders (Robinson-Awana, Kehle, & Jenson, 1986). Although above-average girls tended to rate boys as lower in self-esteem, boys and average girls rate boys as higher in self-esteem.

Gender and race differentially influence on adolescents' self-esteem, with African Americans tending to score higher than white adolescents (Richman, Clark, & Brown, 1985; Simmons, Brown, Bush, & Blyth, 1978), males scoring higher than females (Richman et al., 1985; Simmons et al., 1978), and lower-class adolescents scoring lower than adolescents whose origins are in higher social classes (Richman et al., 1985). African American males and white females were less confident in their school ability than were African American females and white males (Richman et al., 1985).

Low self-esteem was linked to juvenile delinquency, poor academic performance, and depression in Rosenberg, Schooler, and Schoenbach's (1989) panel of 1886 adolescent boys for the second wave of the Youth in Transition study. Their results also indicate that not only does low self-esteem foster delinquency, but delinquency may, among some youth, enhance self-esteem.

Self-Concept, Self-Image, Self-Perception. The terms self-concept, self-image, and self-perception tend to be used interchangeably and are facilitated by cognitive enabling interactions, that is, those interactions that encourage the expression of independent thoughts and communication that enables acceptance and empathy (Hauser, Powers, Noam, & Bowlds, 1987). Thus, families who demonstrate clear, consistent, legitimate forms of parental control; low levels of conflict; and high amounts of noncompetitive sharing, affections, and support are providing an environment that enhances adolescent ego development, one aspect of which is gaining a more definitive self-conception (Coopersmith, 1967; Lewis, 1981; Openshaw & Thomas, 1986; Powers, Hauser, Schwartz, Noam, & Jacobson, 1983).

Bybee, Glick, and Zigler (1990) asked 5th, 8th, and 11th grade students to describe their ideal self-image. They found that a greater proportion of females than males mentioned two of the categories related to family life: marriage and improving relations with their family of origin. Males were more likely to mention categories surrounding athletics. References to athletic abilities and social acceptance peaked at the 8th grade, while mentions of college, marriage, and having children rose during higher grade levels. Fewer students mentioned physical appearance at higher grade levels.

The development and stability of self-concept over time reveled that self-esteem did not change during the elementary years, but decreased following the junior high transition (Notelman, 1987; Wigfield & Eccles, 1994). Mortimer and Lorence (1996) measured the stability of self-concept several times during high school and 10 years after graduating. A major finding of their study was that identity development occurs prior to adulthood and thereafter remains quite stable. The authors found that family support was important, but the variables measuring achievement had no significant influence on well-being at any of the time periods. Similar results were found for adolescents in New Zealand (Paterson, Pryor, & Field, 1995).

Several studies examined gender difference in the development of self-concept and self-esteem. In general, girls were more interpersonally oriented and more affiliative and tended to be more affected by the quality of relationships with others (Jackson, Hodge, & Ingram, 1994; Mboya, 1995). The influence of parental styles differed by gender, with both male and female adolescents viewing their fathers as authoritarian and less authoritative than mothers. The authoritative style was generally correlated with positive self-perceptions and the authoritarian style with negative self-perceptions. Maternal authoritativeness was particularly important for women (Klein, O'Bryant, & Hopkins, 1996). Jackson, Hodge, and Ingram's (1994) examination of gender differences in self-concept among high school and college students revealed differences in overall self-evaluation that favored males.

Other researchers, however, found no gender stereotypic differences (Marsh, 1993; Mboya, 1995; Roberts, Sariginani, Peterson, & Newman, 1990). Marsh (1993) studied 4000 adolescents (ages 12–16) and found no gender differences in self-concept across four age groups. However, gender differences in identity formation for resolving the issue of trust, initiative, and intimacy were independent of individual differences in age, educational level, vocabulary, and SES (Mellor, 1989).

Eskilson and Wiley (1987) and Streitmatter (1993) found support for traditional perspectives on sex-differentiated self-esteem based on family approval that changed from junior to senior high school. Females' identify concerns, according to Streitmatter (1993), are less focused on identify achievement. She suggests that gender differences in identity development may be linked to distinctive male–female trends in the use of relational self-definitions, which is consistent with Gilligan's (1982) views. Both genders were found to use similar process in the domains of vocational choice, religious beliefs, and sex-role orientation (Archer, 1989). However, males were significantly more likely to be foreclosed, whereas females were more likely to be diffused, in the area of political ideology. Females were significantly more likely to be in the moratorium or identity achieved statuses in regard to family roles.

Although gender differences were not found for math achievement, Skaalvik and Rankin (1994) noted that boys had higher mathematics self-concept and self-perceived math skill than did girls. Girls had higher verbal achievement than boys, but significant differences in verbal self-concept or self-perceived verbal skills were absent. Moreover, boys had higher math motivation and lower verbal motivation than girls. None of the gender differences in self-perceptions of ability or motivation could be explained by differences in achievement.

Self-Efficacy or Social Competence. Peterson and Leigh (1990) state that self-efficacy or social competence refers to the individual's ability to use environmental and personal resources to achieve desirable developmental outcomes. Competent individuals are neither passive recipients nor passive reactors to stimuli, but remain flexible and able to engage in reciprocal interactions between other individuals and the surrounding social environment.

Competency is composed of three components: development of internal or cognitive capacities, maintaining a balance between sociability and individuality (togetherness vs. autonomy), and development of age-appropriate social skills (Peterson & Leigh, 1990). These researchers alert us to the need to recognize gender and cultural differences, developmental expectations, and the context of the interaction. Social competence is influenced by parenting, which, in turn, is influenced by SES. Middle-class parents use reasoning, negotiation, and independent thinking skills in their jobs and encourage these skills in their children. Working-class parents, whose jobs demand conformity and obedience to rules, will tend to be more authoritarian and expect their children to obey rules and follow directions.

Four parental styles that can enhance or hinder the development of adolescent social competence have been noted by Baumrind (1975, 1980). Arbitrary and punitive imposition of parental authority with low amounts of nurturance characterizes the authoritarian style. This is quite different from the permissive style, in which the parent is available as a resource, but places little emphasis on controlling or shaping the behavior of youth. The harmonious parent style relies on democratic techniques and effective communication. Baumrind (1978) has observed that "authoritative" parenting, in which parents use a combination of discipline, reasoning, and autonomy-granting in an atmosphere of high nurturance, is most likely to result in successful adolescent competence defined as being responsible, independent, achievement-oriented, cooperative and friendly and possessing high levels of self-esteem.

Osborne (1990) investigated the nature of resilience and how it related to vulnerability and competence in an analysis of resilient children in a 1970 British birth cohort. The data set included measures of children's attainment and behavioral adjustment that were used to assess their general level of competence at 10 years of age and a range of social background factors at 5 and 10 years. Children whose mothers were not depressed were three and a half times more likely to be exceptional at 10 years of age compared with their peers with depressed mothers. The attitudes and behavior of the parents contributed most to the probability that a socially disadvantaged child achieved competence.

Amato (1989) found that high levels of competence during adolescence was associated with high levels of parental support, use of parental induction, high-quality sibling relationships, family cohesion, household responsibilities, and low levels of parental control and punishment. To be a competent adult, according to John Clausen (1991), one must successfully master this component by being able to recognize their strengths and weaknesses and take action to build or overcome them, as well as to accurately assess the aims of others in order to interact responsibly with them.

Maccoby and Martin (1983) revised Baumrind's (1967) three patterns of childrearing into four patterns of parenting styles: authoritative, authoritarian, indulgent, and neglectful, in their study of 14- to 18-year-olds in Wisconsin and California. They found that adolescents who characterized their parents as authoritative score highest on measures of psychosocial competence and lowest on measures of psychological and behavioral dysfunction; the reverse was true for adolescents who described their parents as neglectful. Adolescents whose parents are characterized as authoritarian scored reasonably well on measures indexing obedience and conformity to adult standards, but have relatively poorer self-concepts when compared to other youth. In contrast, adolescents from indulgent homes evidence a strong sense of self-confidence but report a higher frequency of substance abuse and school misconduct and are less engaged in school. Based on this study, the authors note the need to distinguish between two types of "permissive" families: those that are indulgent and those that are neglectful. Steinberg, Lamborn, Darling, Mounts, and Dornbusch (1994), in a follow-up study, noted that while there were observed benefits of authoritative parenting resulting from the continuance of prior levels of high adjustment, the deleterious consequences of neglectful parenting also tended to be accentuated.

Development of Intimacy and Adolescent Sexuality

According to Erikson (1968), the psychosocial crisis during early adolescence is identity versus identity diffusion; during late adolescence and young adulthood the issue or concern for psychosocial exploration or crisis is intimacy versus isolation. Erikson broadens the definition of intimacy to include close nonsexual relationships. He defines intimacy as the ability to have mutual relationships with other individuals in which the individuals' identities become fused but without loss of either's identity. Thus, adolescents must develop a sense of identity before they are capable of intimacy rather than pseudointimacy, which typically characterizes adolescent love relationships. Successful identity formation during adolescence is the prerequisite for resolution of the tension between intimacy and self-absorption in early adulthood.

Failure to achieve intimacy results in psychological distance characterized by the individual becoming centered entirely within himself or herself and leading to exploitation of others. Adolescents who have achieved identity formation, compared with adolescents who are in the foreclosure or the diffusion status, are more likely to have developed intimate relationships (Fitch & Adams, 1983; Marcia, 1976; Orlofsky, Marcia, & Lesser, 1973).

Therefore, the ability to develop close intimate relationships as preparation for the adult roles as partners and spouses is one of the primary tasks of adolescence. Erickson (1968) suggested that identity precedes intimacy for males, but identity follows intimacy or is developed simultaneously for females, presumably to enable them to be more flexible to meet the needs of their partners and children. Other scholars suggest that only assertive females develop according to the male pattern (Dyk & Adams, 1989; Matteson, 1993), and among females with a predominately masculine orientation, identity precedes intimacy, a pattern evidenced by both masculine- and feminine-oriented males (Dyk & Adams, 1990). Females with a more feminine orientation displayed a merging of identity and intimacy, suggesting a simultaneous rather than sequential pattern of development. However, both Dyk and Adams (1990) and Matteson (1993) report that intimacy may precede identity for females if they exhibit feminine orientation.

Gilligan (1982) argues that men and women exhibit contrasting patterns of identity and intimacy and for many females, identity and intimacy are actually fused. She proposes that male identity develops in terms of themes about individuality, agency, and independence, whereas female identity is more a product of intimacy, relationships with others, and connectedness. The research has either been mixed or unsupportive of Gilligan's position. Given societal definition of female adulthood, which is usually centered around marriage and children, it is understandable why a woman's sense of identity, that is, who she is, might be intricately tied with her ability to attract a mate.

Adolescent Sexuality. Because research has tended to focus on the negative consequence of adolescent sexuality,

we lack an understanding of the positive contribution of sexual behaviors to formation of adolescent sexual identity (Herold & Marshall, 1996). These researchers note that adolescent sexual behavior has been defined by two paradigms. The first, generated by Freudian psychoanalytic theory (S. Freud, 1933, 1953), is based on sexuality in adolescence as a biological imperative that needs to be controlled by individual and societal forces. The second, according to Miller and Fox (1987), suggests that sexuality is the outcome of "sexual pedagogy" rather than being internally driven. This sexual pedagogy, according to Gagnon and colleagues (Gagnon, 1990; Gagnon & Simon, 1973) is influenced by culture, social experiences, and time. Although sexual information and misinformation is present in all forms of the media, our youth are among the most uninformed and engage in the highest levels of risk-taking behaviors when compared to youth from other Western countries. An important aspect of risk-taking is the increasing number of youth engaging in premarital sex at younger ages when they do not possess the cognitive maturity to avoid the risks associated with unprotected sexual activity.

In a review of the literature, Herold and Marshall (1996) state that the research on sexual behavior tends to be embedded within a relational context and limited to heterosexual couples. Different sequences of behaviors leading to coitus were observed for European American and African American youth (Smith & Udry, 1985), suggesting different normative expectations. The behavioral sequence followed by European American youth consisted of embracing and fondling above and below the waist, both clothed and undressed. Among African American adolescents petting behaviors while unclothed did not lead to coitus.

A survey of a representative sample of 10,904 high school students in grades 9–12 conducted for the Centers for Disease Control and Prevention, Youth Risk Behavior Surveillance System (1996) found that 53.1% of students had experienced sexual intercourse during their lifetimes; African American students were significantly more likely than white and Hispanic students to have ever had sexual intercourse, with the numbers at 73.4%, 48.9%, and 57.6%, respectively. Of this group, 9% had initiated sexual intercourse before the age of 13, with males (12.7%) more likely than females (14.9%) and African American students (24.2%) more likely than white (5.7%) or Hispanic (8.8%) students.

In addition to age, gender, and race, early initiation into dating as well as the extent of dating predicted sexual behaviors. Those who began to date at about the age of 13, developed steady relationships earlier, and dated more frequently increased their likelihood of having more partners and of having intercourse more frequently at age 18 than those youth who began dating later and were less involved in these activities. Adolescent females reported that the motivation to engage in sexual relations was love within a romantic relationship (Carroll, Volk, & Hyde, 1985; Zelnik & Shah, 1983), but they were more likely to have experienced guilt (Sprecher, Barbee, & Schwartz, 1995). Adolescent males were motivated by physical desire (Carroll et al., 1985), experienced more satisfaction, and reported less emotional attachment, commitment, and guilt (Miller & Simon, 1974; Sorenson, 1973; Sprecher et al., 1995).

The sexual behaviors of adolescents have increasingly occurred separately from marriage or the mate-selection process (Gagnon, 1990). Two trends were found to have contributed to the increasing number of youth engaging in premarital sex and doing so at younger ages. First, females are experiencing puberty at an earlier age, with menarche occurring at an average age of 12.5 years of age, and marriage is occurring at a later age of about 24.3 years. Comparable ages for women a century ago, in 1890, were 14.8 years of age for menarche and 22.0 years of age at marriage. Thus, in 1890 there was an average interval of 7.2 years between menarche and marriage while in 1988 there were 11.8 years between menarche and marriage for women (Alan Gutmacher Institute, 1994). This provides a larger "window of opportunity" for nonmarital sexual activity to occur. In addition to this larger gap between puberty and marriage, other factors have contributed to a greater number of adolescents engaging in premarital sex. These include more reliable and easy to obtain contraception, more permissive attitudes regarding premarital sexual activity, more permissive role models portrayed in the media as well as in real life, and a greater amount of unsupervised time providing more opportunities for sexual activity to occur.

Over the past 3 decades, greater numbers of adolescents have become sexually active at increasingly younger ages. This increase can be attributed to the likelihood that 95% of white teenage women in the mid-1980s had their sexual debut premaritally; in the late 1950s only about 60% of white teenage women had a premarital sexual experience (Sonenstein, Pleck, & Ku, 1989). Because there were already high levels of premarital intercourse and marriage was less common among African American women, the increase in premarital sex among African American women during this same period was less than 10%. A similar trend was noted between 1979 and 1988 for men, ages 17–19, living in metropolitan areas, with an increase from 65% to 73% for white never-married men and an increase from 71% to 88% of African American, never-married males (Sonenstein et al., 1989).

The concern exists, however, that youth may be reporting sexual activity simply because of peer pressure and the belief that this behavior is common for virtually all other youth. One 3-year longitudinal study (Alexander, Somerfield, Ensminger, Johnson, & Kim, 1993) found that the

consistency in reporting sexual activity ranged from 89% to 94% for students in the 8th, 9th, and 10th grades, but that age at first intercourse was inconsistently reported by 67% of the students. Rodgers et al. (1982) found that African American males were more likely to be inconsistent; Newcomer and Udry (1984) found that females and whites were more likely to say they were honest. Alexander suggests that double standards in terms of sexual behavior, minority status, and peer group norms exist that may differentially influence the reporting of socially disapproved behaviors.

Various factors contribute to the likelihood of a teen engaging in sex, with age being the primary factor. In general, older teens are more likely to have sex, but pubertal development appears to be a major predictor for men and is the strongest predictor for African American women (Alan Gutmacher Institute, 1994; Udry, Billy, Morris, Groff, & Raj, 1985). The influence of parents and friends and living with both parents decreased the likelihood of an early sexual debut; having girlfriends or boyfriends who are sexually experienced increased the likelihood of an early sexual debut. Engaging in other risky behavior, such as smoking cigarettes, drinking alcohol, and taking drugs, also tended to be associated with an early sexual debut (Alan Gutmacher Institute, 1994). This occurs because risk behaviors tend to develop together or co-occur for many adolescents (Irwin & Millstein, 1986; Jessor & Jessor, 1977).

For women, factors such as race, income, religion, and geography show few differences (Forest & Singh, 1990). There were no differences by urban/rural location, with 53% of each group of women 15–19 years of age acknowledging sexual experience. About 60% of poor women, 53% of low income, and 50% of higher income women had sexual experience (Forest & Singh, 1990). Other research suggested that rates of premarital sexual activity increases as SES decreases (Hogan & Kitagawa, 1985; Moore, Simms, & Betsey, 1986), and adolescents in communities that are economically disadvantaged may find sexual activity to be a highly valued symbol of adult status (Moore, Morrison, & Glen, 1995; Stanton, Black, Kaljee, & Ricardo, 1993). Likewise, communities that have greater neighborhood economic resources and employment opportunities can have a positive influence (i.e., later first coitus among women and lower risk of impregnation for males) on sexual activity (Brewster, 1994; Brewster, Billy, & Grady, 1993; Ku et al., 1993).

Religious affiliation showed an interesting trend. Roman Catholic women reported the lowest percentage of premarital sexual experience (48%). Fundamentalist Protestants had the second highest percentage (55%), with other religious affiliations reporting 54% and other Protestant groups reporting 60%. Adolescents who belong to and participate in the activities of religious institutions that teach sexual abstinence tend to have a delay in the initiation of coitus (Miller &

Olson, 1988; Thornton & Camburn, 1987; Studh & Thornton, 1987).

Close parental supervision (Benda & Corwin, 1996; Benda & DiBlasio, 1994; Jessor & Jessor, 1977) and adolescents' perceptions of parental supervision (Hanson, Myers, & Ginsburg, 1987) also postponed the initiation of coitus. No parent control and extreme parental control predicted adolescent sexual activity; moderate parental control inhibited initiation into sexual activity (Miller, McCoy, Olson, & Wallace, 1986). When parents discuss sexual issues, more permissive parental values tend to be associated with earlier age at first coitus for the adolescents, while traditional values tend to result in postponing initial coitus (Miller, McCoy, Olson, & Wallace, 1986).

However, association with peers whom the adolescent believes are sexually active is a greater predictor of sexual behavior than either parental attitudes toward sexual behavior or the bond with parents (DiBlasio & Benda, 1992, 1993). Billy and Udry (1985) found gender differences whereby girls were influenced by their friends' sexual experiences; boys, however, specifically selected friends on the basis of the friends' prior sexual experience. It is clear that sexual attitudes, values, and behavior are shaped by a variety of influences.

Although this discussion provides insights into the rationale for premarital sex among older adolescents, in some instances, early sexual debut and sexually acting-out behavior are the result of being molested (Boyer & Fine, 1992; Everstine & Everstine, 1989). Discussions with counselors who work with adolescents as well as my own experiences working with adolescents suggest that some youth engage in sex to become pregnant like their peers and obtain the attention that is given by parents, peers, and school personnel. Others become pregnant because they believe it will enable them to leave an abusive or neglectful home. Given that for a small segment of society adolescent parenthood does occur, what should society be doing to support these young parents or providing them with the skills to become responsible adults?

From a number of perspectives, the research indicates that for optimum childbearing, parenthood should be deferred to those older than 18 years of age. However, this raises the issue of class-related values. Do all segments of society believe that parenthood for adolescents is undesirable? For some families, the birth of a child, regardless of the age of the mother, brings much joy. Our social policies and programs must resolve the conflict between not wanting to stigmatize adolescent women and their babies (e.g., the terms "bastard" or "illegitimate" no longer appear on the child's birth certificate) and instilling norms that encourage responsible parenthood at an older age. (See the section "Risky Sexual Behavior" later in this chapter for a more comprehen-sive discussion of the negative consequences of risky sexual activity.)

Variables That Impact on Adolescent Decision Making, Risky Behavior, and Outcomes

Not Making It

Sells and Blum (1996) note that the major cause of mortality and morbidity among adolescents is no longer infectious disease but rather behavioral etiologies. Many adolescents are engaging in risky behaviors that have serious and often fatal outcomes. This issue becomes more problematic for adolescents struggling to maintain their identity while faced with competing pressure and definitions of success. One can ask: How do adolescents achieve an adequate self-esteem or self-concept in a society that values only the top achievers? What are the tasks or activities that help or hinder adolescents' ability to develop adequate self-esteem, and what happens when youth are not able to fulfill the developmental tasks of adolescents? What happens to youth who are marginalized by poverty and lack of adequate individual, family, and community resources? Do these youth, when they are unable to fulfill traditionally valued goals of success, resort to alternative ways to fulfill societal goals when they are unable to make it in the mainstream, as claimed by Merton (1938)?

Much of the literature on adolescence tends to be viewed from a problems perspective. For example, sexuality is discussed in terms of social concerns over premature pregnancies and education is often discussed in terms of youth who are failing in school. Because the United States lacks a comprehensive family policy that includes health and education in the broadest terms, we tend to allocate money to study and remedy problems only after they have become catastrophic. For example, we overlooked the need to reduce family violence by allocating adequate resources to assist young families facing adversity until the number of abused children and women could no longer be ignored.

Today, families in poverty, especially minority families, have unbelievably high preteen and teenage pregnancy rates and increasingly high rates of school dropout, juvenile crime, and unemployment. For many of these youth, violence has also become a way of life, beginning with the physical and sexual abuse they experienced as young children and leading to exploitive behavior from peers and gangs and participating in street violence (Steinmetz, 1990, 1999). By the 1990s, many of the experiences of adolescents who were raised in poverty also were being observed in middle-class families. Teen pregnancy, substance abuse, delinquency, gangs, and school-related problems were no longer limited to adolescents in lower-class or minority families (Korem, 1995; Steinmetz, 1999).

Resources such as higher social class; good health status; pleasant appearance, demeanor, or personality; and supportive, stable families can reduce the likelihood of youth engaging in risky behavior, intervene when risky behavior occurs, and modify negative outcomes. Resources accord youth more leeway to experiment with adult roles while mitigating the more serious negative consequences. Because violence, drug use, sexually transmitted infections, and serious criminal behavior are occurring at an earlier age, society and parents are more likely to consider behaviors once labeled as mischievous as precursors to criminal behavior.

Adolescents are often unable to appreciate the interrelationships between psychological issues and behaviors. They lack a future-time perspective and are poorly equipped to plan ahead. Brown (1990) suggests that increased peer influence is selective, for example, in lifestyle issues, whereas parental influence continues in the areas of basic values, education, and occupational plans. Unfortunately, it is in those areas in which parental influence is lessened and allegiance to peers increases that may cause parents great concern. Peer pressure, with the expectations for risky behaviors such as sexual intercourse and drug experimentation, may override parental influence in shaping immediate behavior. In addition, it appears that some amount of risk-taking behavior is the norm and serves an important function.

Unfortunately, teens who are less cognitively mature are at increased risk for participating in health-damaging activities (Holmbeck, Crossman, Wandrei, & Gasiewski, 1994; Irwin & Millstein, 1986), thus increasing their risk for contracting sexually transmitted diseases (STDs) and AIDS. Because their understanding of health, illness, and medical care is less sophisticated than that of adults (Millstein, Adler, & Irwin, 1981), they have fewer emotional resources with which to cope when faced with serious consequences such as an unplanned pregnancy, incarceration, or AIDS.

It appears that the motivations to engage in risky behaviors, however, differ for middle- and lower-class adolescents. A symbolic interaction approach examining not only the behaviors but also the meaning attached to the behavior provides some interesting insights. The research suggests that middle-class youth often engage in risk-taking behavior because of a sense of invulnerability—"It won't happen to me." However, for youth living in poverty, experiencing a lack of opportunities, limited access to services, and (if they are a minority) racism, the motivation to engage in risk-taking results from apathy and a realization that for them life is precarious and short (*Adolescent Health*, 1991).

For many inner-city youth, planning their funeral has replaced planning their wedding. With life expectancy so truncated, risk-taking activities such as sexual activity,

drugs, and gang membership are a source of instant gratification, which is more enticing to these youth than are future-oriented sources of gratification resulting from years of education and skill-building.

Defining Risky Behavior

We need to ask: What is risky behavior? When is it defined as a "problem?" What resources provide a cushion enabling this behavior to result in less negative consequences? Many risky behaviors are youths' attempts to try on adult roles without the legal ability or experience to do so. For example, smoking, drinking, premarital sexual intercourse, and staying out late (beyond curfew) have far more serious consequences for adolescents than they do for adults who may engage in comparable behaviors.

Adolescents not only engage in risky behaviors, but they are also the victims of others' deliberate or accidental behaviors. The research suggests that family connections, in terms of intergenerational patterns, are important for most aspects of risky behaviors. For example, youth with family histories of depression, substance abuse, physical violence, or sexual abuse are much more likely to experience depression, have a substance abuse problem, engage in violence, or molest their own children than youth whose families do not have these problems.

The research discussed here provides evidence that risky behaviors tend to occur in clusters. Thus youth who are experiencing a mood disorder are often diagnosed with other emotional or behavioral disorders, frequently are using alcohol or drugs, and are experiencing problems in school and in their families. In the following sections, literature on mood disorders, behavior disorders, educational issues, family issues, sexual behavior, street violence, and substance abuse will be addressed.

Mood Disorders: Bipolar, Depression, and Dissociative Disorders

Mood disorders, according to the DSM-IV (American Psychiatric Association, 1994), include depressive disorders (unipolar major depression and dysthymic), bipolar disorders (manic-depressive), and cyclothymic disorders. These disorders can impact on an adolescent's ability to form an adequate self-concept as well as impair an adolescent's ability to make good decisions. The symptoms of mood disorders are often mistaken to be typical mood swings associated with the hormonal influence during adolescence. When mood disorders are not identified and treated, the adolescent's ability to perform in school, maintain appropriate peer relationship, and obey rules and laws deteriorates.

The recent literature has documented increasing levels

of depression, including clinical depression and dysphoric mood (Craighead, 1991; Rutter, 1995), which have been related to numerous problem behaviors in children and adolescents. In *The State of America's Children* (Children's Defense Fund, 1995) an estimated 7.7 million youth in the United States were reported to suffer from serious emotional disorders. Not only do 48% of these youth drop out of high school compared with 30% of youth with other disabilities, but 73% are arrested within 5 years of leaving school (Children's Defense Fund, 1995).

Adolescent problem behaviors are dichotomized into internalizing and externalizing disorders. Internalizing disorders include cognitive affect, anxiety, depression, suicidal ideation, and eating disorders. Externalizing disorders include delinquency, aggressions, drug use, high-risk sexual activity, and school-related problems. Both internalized and externalized disorders correlate with general depressive symptoms in community-based studies (Colten, Gore, & Asetine, 1991; Horowitz & White, 1987; Reinherz, Frost, Stewart-Berghaver, Kennedy, & Schille, 1990). Females tend to demonstrate internalized behavior; males tend to demonstrate externalized behavior.

Depression. In a study of 600 high school students, Blatt, Hart, Quinlan, Leadbeater, and Auerbach (1993) found that 48% of females and 21% of males exceeded the scores used to define clinical depression using an adaptation of the Community Epidemiological Survey for Depression in Children. Females had higher interpersonal dependency factors, but no sex-related differences on the self-critical factor were observed. These researchers state, "Interpersonal dysphoria and stress may lead to internalizing problems, whereas self-critical dysphoria and threats to competence may lead to externalizing problems" (p. 265).

The effects of ethnicity, gender, and SES on the relationship between four parenting styles and depression were investigated in a survey of nearly 4000 white, Hispanic, African American, and Asian 15-year-olds (Radziszewska, Richardson, Dent, & Flay, 1996). The authors found that authoritative parenting yielded the best, and unengaged parenting yielded the worst outcomes, in terms of depression, whereas permissive and autocratic styles produced intermediate results. This pattern generally held across ethnic and sociodemographic subgroups.

When the Children's Depression Inventory was administered to a group of 304 students in grades 3–12 (Worchel, Nolan, & Wilson, 1987), 21% of the students reported mild to moderate levels and 7% reported severe levels of depression. Consistent with other studies, females tended to internalize problems and reported more depression than did males, who were more likely to externalize problems. There were no age differences associated with depression.

Angold and Rutter (1992) examined the relationship between biological changes of puberty and depression in a sample of 3510 psychiatric patients 8–26 years of age. Although there were no sex-linked differences in the rates of depression before the age of 11, the rates for girls increased more quickly. By the age of 16, girls were twice as likely as boys to have significant depressive symptomatology. However, it appears that the biological changes associated with puberty had no effect on depression when age was controlled for.

Petersen, Sarigiani, and Kennedy (1991) collected longitudinal data from 169 students in grades 6 to 12 and found that females were at greater risk than males for developing depressed affect by 12th grade because they experienced more challenges in early adolescence than did boys. However, sex difference in depressed affect at 12th grade disappears once early adolescent challenges are considered. Although female high school students may be more likely to report a variety of depressive symptoms and receive higher depression scores than males, both males and females present symptoms that are congruent with their socially prescribed gender roles (Campbell, Byrne, & Baron, 1992).

Males, for example, tend to externalize depression and demonstrate aggressive, acting-out behaviors whereas women tend to internalize depression and present as withdrawn, melancholy, and expressing hopelessness and suicidal ideation. Rey (1995) found that adolescents ages 12–18 who were suffering from major depression were statistically more likely to perceive that their parents were less caring and more controlling than adolescents with other diagnoses. The findings of Nolen-Hoeksema and Girgus (1994) were consistent with other studies on the relationship between gender and depression, but only among those over age 15. No gender differences in depression rates were observed in prepubescent children who were under the age of 15.

Racial differences also were found in a number of studies. Kim and Chun (1993) examined racial differences between Asian-American and Caucasian adolescents in a sample of 529 male and 425 female Asian Americans and 576 male, and 471 female white students. The Asian-American males were less likely to be diagnosed with affective disorders than were European-American males; Asian females were more frequently diagnosed with major depression and nonpsychiatric disorders than were European-American females. No significant differences in depressive affect were found between African-American and white females (Lubin & McCollum, 1994).

Bipolar Disorder. Carlson and Weintraub (1993) evaluated youth with a parent who met one of three conditions: bipolar disorder (N = 134); other types of affect disorders (N = 240); and no psychiatric disorder (N = 108).

Behavior and attention problems in childhood and psychopathology and social/occupational impairment in young adulthood were higher in the bipolar risk group than in the control group, but no higher in the group with other types of affect disorders.

Although childhood behavior and attention problems were significantly associated with other psychopathology in all three groups, a unique relationship between childhood problems and young adult mood disorder was found only in the bipolar risk group.

Kashani, Burk, and Reid (1985) assessed the mental health status of 50 children (ages 7–17) who had a parent with unipolar or bipolar affective disorder. The parents, predominantly mothers, were administered a similar interview about their children. Findings indicate that 14% of the children were found to be depressed, and, compared to the remaining children, they showed significantly more symptoms of attention deficit disorder, oppositional disorder, mania, overanxious disorder, phobia, and bulimia. Furthermore, depressed children were abused significantly more than children who were not depressed.

Comorbidity. It also appears that a youth diagnosed with one form of a psychiatric disorder is likely to be diagnosed with other disorders. Borchardt and Bernstein (1995) examined comorbid psychiatric disorders in adolescents with bipolar disorder, hospitalized adolescents with unipolar depression, and adolescents with nonaffective psychiatric disorders. Results show that conduct disorder, attention-deficit hyperactivity disorder (ADHD), and psychosis were all significantly more common in the bipolar (manic-depressive) group than in the unipolar (major depressive or dysthymic) depressed group. Anxiety disorder was present in 40–45% of the adolescents in the unipolar and bipolar groups, but was not present in any of the adolescents in the control group.

Lewinsohn, Hops, Roberts, and Seeley (1993) collected data on the comorbidity of 1508 students at point of entry and 1 year later. They found that 9.6% met criteria for a current disorder, more than 33% had experienced a disorder over their lifetimes, and 31.7% of the latter had experienced a second disorder. High relapse rates were found for all disorders, especially for unipolar depression (18.4%) and substance use (15.0%). Female adolescents had significantly higher rates at all age levels for unipolar depression, anxiety disorders, eating disorders, and adjustment disorders; male adolescents had higher rates of disruptive behavior disorders.

Harrington, Bredenkamp, Groothues, and Rutter (1994) reexamined a group of youth first diagnosed with depression and age-matched controls first studied in 1978. Eighteen years later they found that depression in childhood was a strong predictor of attempted suicide in adulthood. Twenty-one percent of the depressed also had conduct disorder. However, as adults, youth who had been diagnosed with both depression and conduct disorder had a worse short-term outcome and a higher risk of adult criminality, but lower risk or depression in adulthood than depressed youth without conduct problems (Harrington, Fudge, Rutter, & Pickles, 1991).

Dissociative Disorder. This diagnosis, which was formerly called multiple personality disorder, is not considered a mood disorder in the DSM-IV (American Psychiatric Association, 1994), where it has a separate classification. However, adolescents with dissociative identity disorders (DID) will often appear to have severe change in affect. Dissociative disorder is also being included in this chapter because DID and its less severe form, Dissociative Disorder No Other Symptoms (DDNOS), tend to be misdiagnosed as depression, oppositional defiant disorder, conduct disorder, and attention-deficit disorder/attention-deficit hyperactivity disorder—four diagnoses that account for a considerable amount of family-related problems, school suspensions, school expulsions, and juvenile delinquency among adolescents. To provide more appropriate treatment, it is critical that researchers and service providers become more knowledgeable about this diagnosis.

My own experience working with an 11-year-old girl who was on numerous medications and had spent most of her life in residential facilities because of out-of-control, aggressive behavior is illustrative. My role was to assess the likelihood of reunification of this youth with her family. If this was not possible, long-term institutionalization appeared to be the only recourse. The case was a puzzle because this child had tested as highly intelligent, and she was very eager to please. During therapy, especially when addressing certain subjects, this calm, pleasant child's face and body were transformed into a raging whirlwind with unbelievably offensive and violent verbal language and actions. Yet within a few minutes, she would again become a sweet, pleasant child who wanted to please. I was fortunate to have two colleagues, Kathy Maxey and Sue Weiner, with considerable experience working with children diagnosed with DID. After staffing the case, they raised the possibility that this might be my client's diagnosis. With the parents' permission, Kathy Maxey joined me in a therapeutic session and after some general questions about daydreaming, not remembering things, and being blamed for things that she did not do, the child was asked, "Do you sometimes feel like there are other people or other voices in you?" She looked surprised, responded "How did you know?" and proceeded to describe and draw her internal system including an explanation of how all her parts (alters) communicated with each other.

Although my assignment was short-term assessment

and therapy, I was able to provide this adolescent with suggestions on how she could communicate with her parts, especially those parts that got her in trouble, and require that they all cooperate and help her behave appropriately. She will require long-term therapy to resolve the issue producing this diagnosis. However, in a handful of therapy sessions, I was able to help her get better control over her behavior and thus avoid long-term institutionalization.

There is a growing consensus that dissociative disorders, a psychological defense mechanism against traumatic experiences, begin in childhood although they are usually first diagnosed in the late 20s or early 30s with about 7 years between initial presentation to mental health services and accurate diagnosis (Putman, 1993). According to Peterson (1990), dissociative phenomena are normal occurrences throughout the child's development, peaking during latency (around 10 years of age) and typically declining with age. However, only about 10% of DID cases are diagnosed prior to age 20. Because DID has been considered to be rare and is often viewed with skepticism or sensationalism, epidemiological studies have not been conducted.

Nancy Hornstein (1994), a leading expert in diagnosing and treating dissociative disorders in children, has found that childhood trauma and dissociation have been associated with documented histories of sexual abuse (80%), combined sexual and physical abuse (60%), and witnessing family violence (70%).

Braun (1985) suggests that there is evidence that DID is familial, and Kluft (1986) considers it to be a cross-generational disorder because life as an offspring of a DID parent may be experienced as chaotic as the child tries to accommodate to the constantly changing roles and perception of the DID parents. In reviewing the research, Shirar (1996) reports that while a majority of adults with DID experienced physical, sexual, and emotional abuse as a child, this does not predict that they will abuse their own children. Coons (1985) found that only 9% of the children of DID parents were abused by this parent.

Because of the lack of awareness regarding this diagnosis, Hornstein (1994) reports that the average child has received close to three psychiatric diagnoses prior to being diagnosed with dissociative disorder, with the most common prior diagnosis being major depression or depressive psychosis (45.3%), posttraumatic stress disorder (29.6%), oppositional defiant disorder (17%), conduct disorder (14%), and attention-deficit hyperactivity disorder (12.5%). The conflicts around autonomy, identity, separation, and individuation that are focal during adolescence make working with adolescent patients with dissociative disorders challenging in terms of differentiating acting-out behavior from dissociative behavior.

Behavior Disorders: Eating, Conduct, Oppositional Defiant, and Attention-Deficit Disorders

The behavior disorders discussed in this section are primarily classified as disorders of infancy, childhood, and adolescence in the *Diagnostic and Statistical Manual of Mental Disorders, 4th Edition* (American Psychiatric Association, 1994), which is commonly referred to as the DSM-IV. The disorders include conduct disorder, oppositional defiant disorder, and attention-deficit (with or without hyperactivity) disorder. Eating disorders such as anorexia and bulimia, which are included in the discussion that follows, are a separate classification in the DSM-IV, but have been included in this section because they are major behavioral disorders that affect adolescents.

Eating Disorders. Obesity is not included under eating disorders. Although it is a general medical condition and can produce a negative definition of self, obesity can result from a number of sources, including genetic conditions, medication, and an imbalance in eating and exercise. Furthermore, according to the DSM-IV obesity has not been consistently associated with a psychological or behavioral syndrome (American Psychiatric Association, 1994).

Anorexia nervosa is defined as self-starvation; individuals who develop this disorder experience distorted perceptions of their own shape or size and are 15–20% below normal weight. The DSM-IV states that the onset of this disorder, which is often associated with a stressful life event, occurs at a mean age of 17 with data suggesting bimodal peaks at 14 and 18 years of age (American Psychiatric Association, 1994).

Bulimia is characterized by frequent binge eating followed by some form of purging, such as vomiting and/or the use of laxatives or diuretics. Bulimics are usually within the normal weight range and frequently experience depressive disorders. Bulimia typically begins in late adolescence or early adulthood, is often associated with an episode of dieting, and, as in anorexia, is considerably more likely to be experienced by females (American Psychiatric Association, 1994).

Consistent with other research, when adolescents were surveyed, males were generally pleased with their body proportions, but females preferred a figure that was significantly thinner than their current status; their dissatisfaction increased with age (Phelps, Johnson, Jiminex, Wilczenski, Andrea, & Healy, 1993). A survey of high school students in the 9th to 12th grades found that 59.8% of female students and 24.3% of male students were attempting to lose weight (Centers for Disease Control and Prevention, 1996). Hispanic and white students (45.4% and 43.1%, respectively) were significantly more likely than African-American students (33.2%) to report attempts at weight loss. While attempting to keep one's weight within normal limits is a worthwhile cause, 4.8% of these students took laxatives or vomited and 5.2% used diet pills to lose weight or to keep from gaining weight during the 30 days preceding the survey. Dieting and exercise were reported to have been used during the 30 days preceding the survey by 31.2% and 51.0% of the students, respectively.

A 1995 survey of seniors in 20 high schools in 18 states found that 12% of the adolescents surveyed suffered from either anorexia nervosa or bulimia; about 90% of these students were women (ANAD Ten Year Study, n.d.). Projecting the 12% of this group nationally suggests that 716,000 students may have serious forms of these illnesses that need to be recognized and treated. Ten percent report onset at 10 years of age or younger and 86% report onset by 20 years or age (ANAD–Facts about Eating Disorders, n.d.). These eating disorders affect 7 million women and 1 million men in the United States today (Meehan, 1990). Individuals who develop anorexia or bulimia are found in all economic, social, cultural and age groups. Of those who develop these disorders, 6% will die.

Freedman (1984) notes that children are socialized to believe that for males, the body is to be developed, strengthened, and made more functional; for females, the body is to be preserved, protected, and made more beautiful. Girls suffer psychologically from negative body image, lowered self-esteem, and achievement conflicts that result in depression (Sykes, Leuser, Melia, & Gross, 1988) and eating disorders. Chronic feelings of loneliness have been linked to anorexia nervosa (Gilbert & DeBlassie, 1984) and bulimia (Muuss, 1986). Freedman (1984) notes that the physical health of adolescents is constantly being undermined because of the increasing power of the media to define standards of appearance that exacerbate adolescents' problems.

Conduct and Oppositional Defiant Disorders. Conduct disorders, defined as repetitive and persistent patterns of behavior in which the basic right of others or major age-appropriate societal norms or rules are violated, fall into four main groupings: aggressive behavior that causes or threatens physical harm, property loss or damage, deceitfulness or theft, and serious violation of rules (American Psychiatric Association, 1994, p. 85).

Oppositional Defiant Disorder is defined as "a recurrent pattern of negativistic, defiant, disobedient and hostile behavior towards authority figures that persists for at least 6 months" (American Psychiatric Association, 1994, p. 91). A description of the four behaviors that characterize oppositional defiant disorder appear to be quite similar to normative behavior for adolescents: losing temper; arguing with adults;

defying or refusing to comply with requests or rules; being deliberately annoying; blaming others, being touchy, angry, or resentful; and being spiteful or vindictive. To be classified with this disorder, an adolescent must have at least four of these characteristics, which have persisted for at least 6 months. The labeling of an adolescent as oppositional defiant and to a lesser degree, as having a conduct disorder, tends to differ by gender, social class, race, and residential area as well as the tolerance of the parents, school, and community. Conduct disorder and oppositional defiant disorder are most always limited to youth under 18 years of age.

In a retrospective study of childhood problems, Windle (1993) found that externalizing problems occurring during childhood were predictive both of internalizing and externalizing adolescent problem behaviors and of an earlier age of onset for substance use. Avoidance behaviors in childhood were associated with depressive symptoms in adolescence.

Meyers, Burket, and Otto (1993) compared adolescents who were hospitalized for conduct disorders with adolescents who were hospitalized for other disorders. Over half met the criteria for conduct disorders and a majority of these also were diagnosed with substance abuse, attention-deficit hyperactivity disorder, and major depression. Those adolescents diagnosed as conduct disordered had an average of three disorders, while those who were diagnosed as not having conduct disorder were found to have an average of just over one diagnosis. The males and females in this sample were similar in their likelihood of being diagnosed as conduct disordered, whereas other research by Eme and Kavanaugh (1995) found that a number of factors contributed to the markedly greater tendency for males to develop conduct disorder.

Attention-Deficit Disorder. Attention-deficit disorder with or without hyperactivity is experienced by 3%–5% of all American children. Boys are disproportionally represented in this population, which is estimated to be up to 3.5 million children. This neurobiologically based disability is often accompanied by poor self-esteem and behavioral difficulties and is a leading cause of school failure and underachievement (American Psychiatric Association, 1994).

Two subtypes of attention-deficit hyperactivity disorder have been identified: A cognitive form, which included about 20% of those identified as having attention-deficit hyperactivity disorder, and a behavioral form, which included about 80% of those identified, were found in a sample of 1038 children ages 5–14 (August & Garfinkel, 1989). The behavioral subtypes were inattention, impulsivity, and hyperactivity, with a continuum of severity in which the most severe were indistinguishable from the conduct disordered. The cognitive subtype demonstrated severe academic underachievement along with inattention, impulsivity, and deficits in overactivity and processing that involved inadequate encoding and retrieval of linguistic information.

Gittelman, Mannuzza, Shenker, and Bonagura (1985) assessed late adolescent adjustment in a sample of 15- to 23-year-olds (N = 101) who had been diagnosed as hyperactive when they were 6–12 years of age. Analysis showed that in comparison to a control group the most common diagnoses for hyperactive adolescents at follow-up were attention-deficit disorder with hyperactivity, conduct disorder, and substance use disorders. Furthermore, they reported that adolescents who continued to be diagnosed with attention-deficit disorder (about 5%) were significantly more likely than those who no longer had their original symptoms to have an antisocial or substance use disorder. Conduct disorders were reported to have preceded or coincided with the onset of substance use disorders.

A similar study conducted by Klein and Mannuzza (1991) investigated the outcomes of adolescents who had been diagnosed with attention-deficit hyperactivity disorder. They found that an early diagnosis of the disorder predicted uniformly high rates of behavioral problems including cognitive impairment. Contrary to other studies, the negative outcomes for boys were only slightly more detrimental than those for girls. Although dysfunctions characterized by antisocial personality and drug use in adulthood are reduced, this dysfunction is associated with later criminality. Mannuzza, Klein, Bonagura, and Konig (1988) conducted a follow-up study of 16- to 23-year-old males who had been initially evaluated between ages 6 and 12. Although this study did not find differences between the males with initial diagnoses and the control group for conduct problems, substance use, temper outbursts, and attention-deficit disorder with hyperactivity, the control group did exhibit better overall functioning in school both behaviorally and academically.

Marshall, Longwell, and Goldstein (1990) tested whether parents' and children's affective attitudes and interactional behavior covaried with aggressive symptoms for families in which a child exhibited attention-deficit hyperactivity disorder. Affective attitudes of both parents and disordered sons were studied using a modified measure of expressed emotion and the 5-minute speech sample. Although a child's and his or her parent's emotional status were highly correlated and the child's behavior toward the parents was highly correlated with the child's aggressiveness, the child's behavior was not correlated with the child's expressed emotional feelings toward the parents. The authors suggest that the child's aggressiveness and a negative family climate may independently determine the long-term course of these children.

Persistence of Disorders over Time. A number of studies have found that psychiatric or personality disorders

tend to persist over time (Achenback, Howell, McConaughy, & Stanger, 1995; Angold & Costello, 1993; Cantwell & Baker, 1990; Lewis-Abney, 1993; Rey, Singe, Andrews, & Andrews, 1995). Cantwell and Baker (1990) in a follow-up study found high stability for only three diagnoses: infantile autism, attention-deficit disorder with hyperactivity, and oppositional defiant disorder. Another longitudinal study of youth previously diagnosed with attention-deficit disorder, both with and without hyperactivity, found similar results (Lewis-Abney, 1993). This study also found that parenting competence was negatively related to parental perceptions of the child's behavior. Older age of the child in combination with higher levels of impulsivity and/or hyperactivity were significant in predicting family functioning.

The developmental paths from adolescent to young adult syndromes were tested by reassessing individuals at ages 19–22 who participated in a national study where they had originally been assessed at ages 13–16 and 16–19 (Achenbach et al., 1995). Six syndromes were empirically derived from parent and self-reports, and several young adult syndromes were similar to, and predicted by, the syndromes observed during adolescence. Lambert, Hartsough, Sassone, and Sandoval (1987) examined the persistence of hyperactivity symptoms from childhood to adolescence by comparing 59 hyperactive boys and 58 matched male controls using assessment from parent, teacher, and youth. Results indicated that although 20% of these youth were free of problems, adolescents who were hyperactive as children were more likely to (1) become delinquent, (2) be suspended from school, and (3) evidence serious social and mental health outcomes. Similar results were found by Hechtman (1991), who noted that ADHD children continue to have symptoms of restlessness and attentional and cognitive difficulties, often resulting in serious academic, social, and emotional problems in adolescence.

Angold and Costello (1993) found that adolescents with major depressive disorders or dysthymia also tended to exhibit conduct disorder and oppositional defiant disorder. Bird, Gould, and Staghezza (1993), using a sample from the Puerto Rico child psychiatry epidemiological study, found a high level of comorbidity of four major diagnostic domains (attention-deficit disorders, conduct/oppositional disorders, depression, and anxiety).

Loeber, Green, Keenan, and Lahey (1995), in a longitudinal (6-year) study of the demographic and psychiatric predictors of the onset of conduct disorder, investigated whether physical fighting played a role in the transition from oppositional defiant disorder to conduct disorder in a sample of preadolescent boys (ages 7–12). Results indicated that physical fighting, lower social class status of the parent, oppositional defiant disorder, and parental substance use best predicted the onset of conduct disorder. The early onset of conduct disorder, on the other hand, was best predicted by attention-deficit hyperactivity disorder.

Educational Issues: Truancy, Drop-Outs, and Special Needs Youth

Education, a critical component in every youth's life, can provide the opportunity to overcome many obstacles, such as racial or gender discrimination, chronic illnesses, or handicapping conditions. Unfortunately, for many youth the educational experience exacerbates rather than ameliorates adversity. As a means of illustrating these points, youth with special school-related needs, truants, and school drop-outs are discussed in this section.

Youth with Special Needs. This category consists of youth identified as having learning disabilities as well as those youth labeled as gifted, both of whom have special school-related needs. *The Digest of Educational Statistics* (Snyder, Hoffman, & Geddes, 1996, Table 103) listed 4,736,338 youth ages 5–21 who were provided with educational services under the Individuals with Disabilities Education Act and related legislation during the 1992–1993 school year. Because the period of adolescence provides many challenges, the experiences of the learning-disabled youth may be even more stressful and lead to a higher incidence of behavioral dysfunction. Students with learning disabilities often have other problems, such as ADHD, further complicating their learning disability. Wayment and Zetlin's (1989) study using sentence completion found that handicapped and nonhandicapped youth identified similar stressors such as issues concerned with individuation and independence, but the learning-handicapped youth were less able to take control of situations or attempt to actively resolve the conflict.

Zetlin (1993) noted that learning-disabled students faced the additional tasks of trying to fit the norms of achievement exhibited by peers and siblings, while attempting to overcome their parents' overprotective behavior. Zetlin proposes the need to examine the cultural norms and the learning handicapped youth's inability to meet expectations.

Until recently, federal legislation protected these youth from being expelled from school without considerable legal obstacles. The Americans with Disabilities Act (ADA) protects these youth and mandates that schools make arrangements for students to attend mainstream classes as much as possible; their parents have become vocal advocates, backed with threats of lawsuits, to ensure that their children have these opportunities. Because of disruptive influences, threats of bodily injury, and actual physical violence perpetrated by some youth classified as having special needs, school systems and lawmakers are reevaluating this legislation. This reevaluation of ADA regulations as they apply to disruptive

youth has received additional support from the parents of children who must attend classes in which aggressive and disruptive students take a disproportionate amount of the teacher's time. These parents are now becoming vocal in their insistence that their children also have the right to attend class without major disruptions and fear of violence. State and federal legislation is under consideration that would enable school systems to expel these children. Although the argument has been made that these children, above all other children, need to be in school, an opposing argument states that at some point the needs (and costs) of a few students should not jeopardize the schooling of a vast majority of students.

Because "fitting in" is a major goal of adolescence, when teenagers differ in either a positive or negative direction, they may develop feelings of inferiority. Such is the case with gifted children, who may feel pressure to live up to parental and school expectations at the same time they experience peer pressure to fit in with other adolescents (Steinmetz, Clavan, and Stein, 1994). Swiatek (1993) examined the effect of academic acceleration on three cohorts of gifted adolescents and a control group consisting of gifted students who were not in academically accelerated programs. Youth in the academically accelerated programs did not suffer academically as a result of the decision, and did gain speed in their educational preparation. Furthermore, there was no evidence that youth suffer gaps or weaknesses in what they learn when they enter accelerated programs or that they "burn out" on academics. There also were no differences between the two groups in locus of control and only very small differences in self-esteem.

Manaster, Chan, Watts, and Wiehe's (1994) study of 144 gifted and talented 15- to 16-year-olds found that 79% of these youth thought that being gifted was a positive experience. Sixty-one percent of the youth thought that their classmates threatened them differently, and 35% considered their classmates' treatment to be negative.

Truancy and Drop-Outs. There are numerous obstacles to achieving independence today. Unlike earlier eras when youth dropped out of school to supplement the family income—an indication of a sense of responsibility and maturity—today's youth tend to drop out of school because they lack the ability or maturity to complete the tasks required in school or behave in an acceptable way.

Each day 6.3% of over 10 million youth enrolled in middle school (10,270,146) and 8% of just under 10 million youth enrolled in high school (9,726,514) are absent (Snyder et al., 1996, Table 40). The absentee rate is considerably higher in urban schools, up to 12% each day, and among low-income students and lower in rural areas and among higher-income students (U.S. Department of Education, 1996). A total of 14.25 million youth are absent from school each day and although illness and family crisis accounts for some of this absenteeism, the relationship between truancy and delinquency cannot be ignored. The *Manual to Combat Truancy* (U.S. Department of Justice, 1996) estimates that 80% of individuals currently incarcerated started out as truants; an even higher rate is observed among juvenile offenders. The *Manual to Combat Truancy* (1996) reports that truancy is clearly the gateway to crime; daytime burglary, vandalism, and violent juvenile crime have been linked to truancy. Statistics cited included: 71% of youth between 13 and 16 years of age prosecuted for criminal violations in Miami had been truant, 44% of violent juvenile crime occurred between 8:30 AM and 1:30 PM in San Diego, and daytime crime in Minneapolis dropped 68% when police began citing truant students. Truancy also predicted many psychiatric symptoms in adult life including depression, anxiety, and antisocial behavior (Robins & Robertson, 1996).

Sommer and Nagel (1991) assessed personal, family, and setting characteristics associated with truancy for 25 junior high school truants during the 8th grade and 25 nontruants matched for age, grade, gender, and SES. They found that truants were less likely to live with both parents, had more siblings, scored lower in academic ability and achievement, and were more likely to have been referred for disciplinary problems. They did not differ from nontruants, however, in attitudes toward school, interests, friendship patterns, or self-esteem.

Each day 13,076 high school students are suspended and 2217 drop out of high school (Sherman, 1994). These data only reflect the official drop-out rate because those youth who are not officially registered at the beginning of the school year are not likely to be recorded as drop-outs. As of October 1995, 5.4% of 16- and 17-year-olds and 14.6% of 18- and 19-year-olds had dropped out of school (Snyder et al., 1996, Table 102).

When all races were combined, males and females dropped out at about the same rates. However, white students ages 18–19 were considerably less likely to drop out (11.4%) than were African American (15.7%) or Hispanic students (30.8%). A similar trend was observed for students who were 16 and 17 years of age, with white students having a lower drop-out rate (4.7%) when compared to African American (5.6%) and Hispanic students (10.7%). Katsinas (1989) analyzed characteristics of drop-outs in Illinois and found that the Hispanic dropout rate was over 60%. This researcher also noted that the disproportionate underrepresentation of Hispanics in higher education, which resulted in a lack of Hispanic role models, might be contributing to this high drop-out rate.

The graduation rate for 1995–1996 was 71.5%, suggesting that just under 30% of our youth, attending both public and private schools, do not graduate from high school (Snyder et al., 1996, Table 98). Since the mid-1960s when rates of 75–76% for high school graduation were observed, there has been a continual decrease in the percentage of students graduating. Those graduating from high school not only have advantages in terms of occupational opportunities, but they are also extremely likely to continue their education.

There were 3,597,000 adolescents graduating from public and private high schools in the 1995–1996 school year, of which approximately 35% graduated from private high schools (Snyder et al., 1996, Tables 98 and 99). In 1992, 92.4% of all seniors in both public and private school reported that they planned to attend college (Snyder et al., 1996, Table 142), and in 1993, 62.6% of individuals 16 to 24 who had graduated from high school or obtained their GED during the preceding 12 months were actually enrolled in college (Snyder et al., 1996, Table 180). A slight decrease was observed for 1995, with 61.9% of students enrolled in college.

Economically disadvantaged adolescents are frequently unprepared for academic work when they enter elementary school, and the discrepancy tends to increase during the elementary school years, producing youth who have poor self-concepts, are less motivated, and have lower educational aspirations than middle-class youth (Applebee, Langer, & Mullis, 1986). Youth from economically disadvantaged homes are twice as likely as middle-income youth and nearly 11 times more likely than high-income youth to drop out of school (Sherman, 1994). Homelessness and numerous moves to other housing also contribute to truancy and dropping out of school (Donahue & Tuber, 1995; Horowitz, Springer, & Kose, 1988; Winborne & Murray, 1992). Although the national drop-out rate is just above 28%, this rate ranges between 40% and 70% in some of large urban school districts, with the percentages increasing annually (Snyder et al., 1996; Sherman, 1994).

The impact of traumatic events on dropping out was investigated by Harris (1983), in a comparison of 67 drop-out-prone, middle-class high school students (ages 15–19) with a group of age-matched successfully functioning students. In each of a wide range of areas, including delinquency, running away, suicidal behavior, loss, and victimization, the experiences of drop-out-prone youth were significantly different from controls. For example, 67% of the drop-out sample but only 27% of the controls had been victimized by physical abuse, incest, or sexual assault; 15% of the drop-out prone youth had lost a parent by death as compared with 2% of control group; and 36% of the drop-out-prone students had divorced parents as compared with 19% of the control group. The authors also suggest that in a middle-class community, becoming an "in-school drop-out" or actually quitting high school may result from emotional turmoil rather than boredom.

There are early warning signals predicting students who are at risk for dropping out, with significant differences being evident in behavior, grades, retention, and achievement scores of 3rd grade youth who eventually drop out as compared to those who graduate (Finn, 1989). Based on characteristics such as SES, age, number of grades repeated, and scores on achievement and IQ scores, it is possible to identify with 75% accuracy which 3rd graders will later drop out of high school. By 9th grade, predictions about who will drop out can be over 90% accurate (Lloyd, 1978). Dropping out is the end point of a long history that sets the stage for a lack of interest in education or lack of concern for academic failure. What is most disturbing is that such trends are prevalent at the same time that the percentage of adolescents entering and completing college is increasing. As a result, the gap between the haves and have-nots in our society is growing at an ominous rate.

This represents serious consequences for both these youth and our scientific, technologically oriented society with a labor force that requires workers to have both a basic education and specialized skills. Youth who drop out of school will find it more difficult to locate employment because employers, even for minimum wage jobs, prefer to hire high school graduates or youth who have received a GED. As a society, we are losing the potential skills and talents that these youth might provide were they to continue and complete their education.

In reviewing the research on factors relating to dropping out of school, Dryfoos (1990) notes that school quality is highly related to whether or not a student drops out, with segregated schools, schools with low teacher-pupil ratios, large schools with large classes, and schools with an emphasis on tracking and testing having larger drop-out rates. Given the extremely negative social consequences besides the educational losses that result from being a drop-out, it appears that "social" passing may have important latent effects on reducing the likelihood of youth engaging in other risky behaviors.

Unfortunately, the educational trend appears to be going in the opposite direction with the establishment of annual testing and more stringent academic and behavioral requirements for promotion to a higher grade or for remaining in school. As a result, students are often "warned out" of school, much like poor, elderly, or disabled citizens were warned out of towns in the eighteenth and nineteenth centuries so as not to become a responsibility for taxpayers (Steinmetz, 1988). These students include the less motivated, the emotionally or cognitively handicapped, and those living with extreme poverty, inadequate adult supervision, unplanned pregnancy, or chronic illness. This encouragement to leave often occurs because our school systems frequently do not have the resources or are unwilling to commit resources to provide programs that would meet these students' needs.

Family Issues: Divorce, Criminal Behavior, Family Violence, Sexual Abuse, and Runaways

The family serves as the primary socialization agency and can provide a zone of comfort against a hostile world, or it be an area of additional conflict, violence, and neglect. In this section, divorce, parental criminal behavior, physical and sexual abuse, courtship violence, and runaway or throwaway adolescents will be examined. Although these topics have been divided into separate subsections, the issues discussed are intricately intertwined.

Divorce. Allison and Furstenberg (1989) suggest that there are few serious effects of divorce during adolescence because of adolescents' better coping skills and their network of friends. Although research suggests that establishing one parent as custodial and one house as home (Preston & Madison, 1984) and residing with the same-sex parent facilitates adolescent adjustment (Camara & Resnick, 1988; Peterson & Zill, 1986), Buchanan, Maccoby, and Dornbusch's (1992) research did not support these findings. Their interviews with adolescents 4.5 years after divorce found no differences in adolescent depression, family decision-making practices, or household organization, based on whether custody was awarded to the mother, father, or both. Boys had a slightly better adjustment when living with their mothers; both boys and girls, because of poorer monitoring, had slightly poorer adjustments when living with their fathers, and dual-residency, when parents were cooperative, were the most positive arrangements.

Lower levels of social competency in areas such as interpersonal relationships, independence, achievement, and self-esteem have been identified as hindering adolescent adjustment postdivorce (Hetherington, Cox, & Cox, 1985; Peterson, Leigh, & Day, 1984), and self-esteem did not increase with the passage of time. Unfortunately, as a result of the multiple roles that the custodial parent assumes, the quality of parenting, in general, tended to decline.

However, other research (Hetherington & Arasten, 1984; Steinberg & Silverberg, 1986; Wallerstein & Kelly, 1979) suggests that the peer group as well as other significant adults facilitate adjustment and that the coping skills of the parents and youth, the quality of the relationship with the parents, and the adolescent's self-esteem seem to be mediating factors (Peterson & Leigh, 1990).

For a variety of reasons, experiencing one's parents' divorce can contribute to adolescents engaging in risky behavior. Needle, Su, and Doherty (1990) found that the relationship between divorce and adult criminality and delinquency were based on the age of the youth at the time of divorce. Although they reported that adolescents from intact homes were less likely to use marijuana than those from nonintact homes, this relationship was small, and other studies did not find such a relationship.

Ellwood and Stolberg (1993), in a comparison of youth (ages 8–11) whose parents remained married, were divorced, or who divorced and subsequently remarried, found that family composition had a significant effect on occurrence of stressful events and change in income, but not on children's adjustment. The most powerful predictors of positive child adjustment were parental consistency, appropriate discipline, low parental hostility, and accepting behaviors.

Parental Criminal Behavior. One of the more consistent findings in the literature is the relationship between parental criminal behavior and youth who engage in delinquent and criminal behavior (Farrington, Lambert, & West, 1998; Farrington & West, 1993; Henggeler, 1989; Loeber & Dishion, 1983; Steinmetz, 1996). Loeber and Dishion (1983) found that criminal behavior by parents and family members was a significant predictor of adolescent criminal behavior. Hawkins (1995), in reviewing the research, identified three risk factors for violence associated with the family. First was a lack of clear expectations and standards of behavior, excessively severe or inconsistent punishment, and parental failure to monitor children's activities. The second risk factor was family conflict between parents and/or between parents and child. The third was a family environment in which violence occurred or was favorably viewed.

A study of male adolescents with criminal backgrounds (Steinmetz, 1996) found that in 40% of the families, the father had a criminal record and of this group 65% were currently or had been incarcerated in the past. Mothers had criminal records in about one-fourth of the sample (half of this group has been incarcerated) and in 14% of these families both parents had criminal records. Furthermore, 44% had one or more siblings who had been involved with the criminal justice system. Moreover, adolescents whose mothers and fathers had criminal scores that reflected the frequency and severity of their acts above the midpoint had considerably higher criminal scores than youths whose parents had scores below the midpoint.

Family Violence. Research has related child abuse to a variety of negative outcomes, including violence to peers and siblings, juvenile delinquency, engaging in street violence as adults, and continuing the pattern of family violence by abusing their partners and children. (See Steinmetz, 1987,

for a review on the earlier research and Miller, Knudsen, and Copenhaver, Chapter 26, this volume, for a more recent update of this literature.)

Straus, Gelles, and Steinmetz (1980), in the first national study of family violence, reported that parents' use of violence on their adolescent children was extensive, 54% of youth 10–14 years of age and about 33% of children 15–17 years of age were hit by their parents. This data is consistent with Gil's (1970) report that 28% of abuse incidents involved youths over 12 years of age and the American Humane Association's (1978) report that 36% of abuse and neglect cases involved 10- to 18-year-olds. Gelles and Straus (1988), in the second national study of family violence noted that teenagers are as likely to be victims of abuse as are children under 3 years of age.

Numerous studies over the past 4 decades have found evidence for the long-term effects of exposure to family violence (Conger, 1984; Hawkins, 1995; Hotaling, Straus, & Lincoln, 1989; Palmer, 1962; Smith & Thornberry, 1995; Steinmetz, 1977, 1996; Strasburg, 1978; Widom, 1992). Widom (1992) found that childhood abuse increased the odds of future delinquency and adult criminality by 40%, the likelihood of being arrested as a juvenile by 53%, and the likelihood of committing a violent crime in the future by 38%. The relationship between experiencing severe child abuse and committing murder as an adult has also been observed (Palmer, 1962; Lewis, Moy, Jackson, Aaronson, Restifo, Serra, & Simos, 1985). However, other research found little relationship between these variables (Elmer, Evans, & Reinhart, 1977; Zingraff & Belyea, 1986), and some research suggests that assaulted children who witness and/or experience family violence become withdrawn rather than aggressive (Carlson, 1991; George & Main, 1979; Martin & Beezley, 1974; Prino & Peyrot, 1994; Rogosch & Cicchetti, 1994). There is evidence that the family's role in promoting aggression and delinquency is but one part of the picture.

It has been suggested that estimates of the relative influence of peers and parents on adolescent delinquency and aggression underestimate the influence of parents and inflate the importance of peers (Aseltine, 1995; Kandel, 1996). Yet, Aseltine (1995) reports that friends were the dominant source of influence on youths' delinquent and aggressive behavior, and peers accounted for as much as a two- to fourfold increase in the likelihood of delinquent behavior in one study (Keenan, Loeber, & Zhang, 1995).

The school environment was also a contributor to aggression and delinquency, with family processes and school variables accounting for about 40% of the total variance explained in early adolescent delinquent behavior in one study (Vazsonyi & Flannery, 1997). Violence in the media (Viemeroe, 1996; Palermo, 1995) as well as a host of other socializing and environmental influences have also been linked to aggression and delinquency in adolescence (Avakame, 1997; Benda & Corwyn, 1997; Bischof, Stith, & Whitney, 1995; Fagan & Wexler, 1987; Hawkins, 1995; Henggeler, 1989).

Being abused as a child was a major predictor of an adolescent's violence toward a parent and other family members (Corder, Ball, Haizlip, Rollins, & Beaumont, 1976; Kratcoski, 1982, 1985; Steinmetz, 1988) and parricide (Dutton & Yamini, 1995; Heide, 1994, 1995; Marleau & Webanck, 1997; Mones, 1991; Post, 1982). Monane, Leichter, and Lewis (1984) found that abused delinquents committed a disproportionate amount of violent crime as compared with nonabused delinquents, but other studies (Alfaro, 1978; Guttierres & Rich, 1981; Kratcoski & Kratcoski, 1982) found few differences between the type of crime (violent versus nonviolent) committed by delinquents who were abused.

Sexual Abuse, Molestation, and Incest. In a review of the research, Reppucci and Haugaard (1993) observed that because of differences in definition and reporting, sexual abuse rates vary from a conservative rate of 10% of American female youth (Haugaard & Reppucci, 1988), to Finkelhor's (1979) report of 19% of college females and 9% of college males reporting that they had experienced unwanted sexual touching, to the findings that 27% of college women had experienced rape or attempted rape since their fourteenth birthday (Koss, Gidycz, & Wisneiwski, 1987). Estimates suggest that about 25–30% of these youth are under the age of 7 (Finkelhor, 1986; Nibert, Cooper, Ford, Fitch, & Robinson, 1989) with a modal age of 10 (Melton, 1992). Russell (1982) reported that 28% of 930 women she interviewed had been sexually victimized before the age of 14.

Hussey and Singer (1993) compared 87 sexually abused adolescent psychiatric inpatients with 87 matched inpatient counterparts without a known history of sexual abuse on measures of social competence, self-esteem, depression, substance abuse, and perceptions of family characteristics and functioning. Both groups were similar on standardized measures of psychological distress and family functioning, but the sexually abused adolescents were significantly more likely to report substance abuse and problem behaviors. Another comparison of sexually abused youth receiving outpatient care with a matched sample of nonabused youth found similarities in both groups with attention-deficit hyperactivity disorder being the most frequent diagnosis (McLeer, Callaghan, Henry, & Wallen, 1994). One major difference was that posttraumatic stress disorder was the most prevalent psychiatric outcome, with 42.3% of sexually abused compared with 8.7% of nonabused youth receiving this diagnosis.

When youth have experienced both physical and sexual abuse, the problem outcomes appear to intensify. An analysis of the data on 42,568 adolescents found that those who had been both physically and sexually abused tended to exhibit more binge drinking and suicide ideation than those who experienced only one type of abuse (Luster & Small, 1997). These authors noted that high levels of supervision and support from at least one parent, as well as success in school, decreased the risk of problem outcomes.

Although earlier research tended to focus on sexual abuse of females, sexual abuse of males has been amply documented (Bolton, Morris, & MacEachron, 1989; Chandy, Blum, & Resnick, 1997; Finkelhor, 1979, 1984; Prendergast, 1993). Prendergast (1993) estimates that 1 in 6 boys has been abused before reaching 18 years of age. The research also indicates that sexually abused boys are at risk of developing sexually inappropriate behaviors including repeating the behavior they experienced by molesting younger children (Finkelhor, 1984; Grayston & DeLuca, 1995; Romano & DeLuca, 1997). Unfortunately, sexual abuse appears to continue intergenerationally.

Females who experienced sexual abuse as youth were significantly more likely than nonabused controls to have psychiatric disorders, self-harm and suicide attempts, and adolescent pregnancy (Romans, Martin, & Mullen, 1997). Male teenagers who had experienced sexual abuse were considerably more likely to have histories of suicidal involvement, eating disorder, substance abuse, risky sexual behavior, and delinquency (Chandy et al., 1997). A comparison of over 3000 male and female adolescents with histories of sexual abuse revealed that males were at higher risk than females for poor school performance and sexual risk-taking and more extreme use of alcohol and marijuana. Females were at higher risk for suicidal involvement, eating disorders, and more frequent use, but at lower levels of alcohol, than were males (Chandy et al., 1997).

Runaway and Throwaway Teens. A U.S. Department of Justice survey (1990) reported that there were 446,700 "broad scope runaways" (i.e., children who left home without permission and stayed away overnight), and an estimated 127,100 "broad scope throwaways" (i.e., a child has been out of the home for at least one night because [1] the child had been directly told to leave the household; [2] the child had been away from home and a caretaker refused to allow the child back; [3] the child had run away, but the caretaker made no effort to recover the child or did not care whether or not the child returned; or [4] the child had been abandoned or deserted). In the course of a year, an estimated 500,000 to 1.5 million young people run away from or are forced out of their homes, and an estimated 200,000 are homeless and living on the streets (U.S. Department of Justice, 1990). Although their ages range from younger than 11 to over 18, over half are between the ages of 15 and 16.

Throwaway youth who are encouraged or asked to leave home are in a particularly difficult situation. They are frequently too young to hold a job, and if their parents no longer live in the school district, they may not be permitted to remain in school. Furthermore, the juvenile court system does not have jurisdiction when the youth is not delinquent, mental and physical health services may be difficult to obtain without parental consent, and shelters for runaways have strict limits on the time that they will provide shelter to a minor.

In their study of runaways, Powers, Echenrode, and Jaklitch (1990) found that fewer than 25% came from intact families and one-third were born to single mothers. Forty-nine percent of the youths were classified as runaways—17% as homeless, 13% as contemplating running away, and 21% as in crisis but not on the run. Sixty percent had allegedly experienced physical abuse; 42% emotional abuse; 48% neglect; and 21% sexual abuse. Over one-third were "pushed out" of their homes by their families, and biological mothers were the most frequently cited perpetrators of maltreatment (63%), followed by biological fathers (45%).

Rotheram-Borus (1993), in studying suicide behavior among predominantly African-American and Hispanic youth recruited from four runaway programs (260 male and 316 female), reported that 37% had previously attempted suicide and 12% reported suicidal ideation four or more times; 47% reported never having serious suicidal ideation. No gender or ethnic differences in risk factors were observed.

Two distinct groups were identified by Kufeldt and Nimmor (1987) in their study of 489 runaway and homeless youth in Canada: true "runners," who leave home for extended time with no intention of returning, and "in and outers," who use running away as a temporary coping mechanism. A significant proportion of the youths interviewed had run from substitute care arrangements. Running away can be viewed as a rebellious response to powerlessness motivated by feelings of anger, resentment, disappointment, and the need to reduce tension (Schaffner, 1995).

DeMan, Dolan, Pelletier, and Reid (1994) investigated whether adolescent running-away behaviors are expressions of passive (internalization) or active (externalization) avoidance in 117 male and 149 female youth (ages 11–18). Males who ran away were characterized as demonstrating passive avoidance and internalization, as well as being associated with suicidal ideation, depression, and theft. Females' running-away behaviors were characterized as both withdrawal and overt deviancy, while being associated with vandalism, theft, drug and alcohol use, sexual activity, depression, and suicidal ideation.

Sexual and physical abuse were found to be major factors contributing to runaway behavior in numerous studies (Janus, Archambault, Brown, & Welsh, 1995; Janus, Burgess,

& McCormack, 1987; Gutierres & Reich, 1981; Kurtz, Kurtz, & Jarvis, 1991; McCormack, Burgess, & Guaccione, 1986; McCormack, Janus, & Burgess, 1986; Rotheram-Borus, Mahler, Koopman, & Langabeerm, 1996), and runaways were more likely to engage in other risky behavior when compared to their nonabused, runaway peers (Kurtz, Kurtz, & Jarvis, 1991; Whitbeck & Simons, 1990). Farber, Kinast, McCord, and Falkner (1984) found that 78% of the adolescents self-reported significant physical violence one year prior to their running away. McCormack et al. (1986) reported that 38% of male and 73% of female runaways had been sexually abused, and Gary, Moorhead, and Warren (1996) reported that 47% of 78 youths residing in a runaway shelter had reported physical abuse and 34% reported being sexually abused. It appears that the more abuse a runaway adolescent has experienced in the home, the more at risk he or she will be on the streets. A comparison of 43 habitual runaways with 39 nonrunaway adolescent males in a residential treatment center noted that runners had a greater number of prior placements and a history of abuse victimization and perpetration (Abbey, Nicholas, & Bieber, 1979).

Substance abuse was prevalent among adolescent runaways (Fors & Rojek, 1991; Yates, MacKenzie, Pennbridge, & Cohen, 1988; Windle, 1989). Yates et al. (1988) found that homeless youth have a greater incidence of drug and alcohol abuse, higher unemployment, and are five times more likely to drop out of school. Fors and Rojek (1991) noted that drug use is two to three times more prevalent for runaways, and they have more accepting attitudes toward selected illicit behavior (e.g., using beer and cocaine/crack, getting really drunk, and selling drugs) when compared with adolescents who remain in school.

Runaways also have severe emotional problems. Feitel, Margetson, Chamas, and Lipman (1992) found that 59% of youth in the shelter had conduct disorder, 75% were depressed, 41% had considered suicide, and more than 25% had attempted suicide. Booth and Zhang (1997) reported that 50% of male and 60% of female adolescents residing in a shelter were diagnosed with conduct disorder. Adlaf, Zdanowics, and Smart (1996) reported high rates of substance abuse, attempted suicide, loneliness, and depression in a study of 217 Toronto street youth. Homeless adolescents who are pregnant, when compared to pregnant adolescents who are living with their families were more likely to be diagnosed as depressed, to have previously attempted suicide, to have histories of sexual and physical abuse, and to be abusing drugs (Pennbridge, Mackenzie, & Swofford, 1991).

Survival sex was reported as a way of life, especially for those who had experienced sexual abuse (Simons & Whitbeck, 1991a), and was associated with high risk of STDs and AIDS in studies of the homeless and runaways (Hersch, 1988; Rotheram-Borus, Meyer-Bahlburg, & Rosario, 1992;

Yates et al., 1988). Over 7% of 446 male street youth in a California study had been involved in prostitution during the past 3 months (Pennbridge, Freese, & Mackenzie, 1992). Yates et al. (1991) noted that although prostitution-involved youth comprised only 25% of their study population, they accounted for 37% of the recorded medical diagnoses. A comparison of adolescents in a shelter for runaways with adolescents utilizing a community agency for gay and bisexual youth found that 29% of runaways and 23% of gay and bisexual youth had received or gave money or drugs for sexual acts. Simons and Whitbeck (1991b) suggest that early sexual abuse had an indirect affect on street youth's victimization because running from home increases the likelihood of a lifestyle based on participation in risky activities.

In addition to substance abuse and prostitution as an adult, other outcomes of adolescent runaway behavior and homelessness include intergenerational transmission of running (Plass & Hotaling, 1995) and homelessness as an adult (Simons & Whitbeck, 1991b).

Risky Sexual Behavior: Contraception, Pregnancy, STDs, Sexual Orientation, Prostitution, Sexual Harassment, and Date Rape

The material reviewed in this section deals with risky sexual intercourse among adolescents and its outcomes. Included are discussions of contraceptive knowledge and behavior, adolescent pregnancy, sexually transmitted infections, prostitution, sexual harassment, and sexual orientation. Because risky sexual intercourse often results in a next generation of children born to undereducated and unprepared parents as well as exposing youth to life-threatening STDs and AIDS, risky sexual behaviors are particularly problematic for our society.

Contraceptive Knowledge and Behavior. The good news is that two-thirds of adolescents currently report contraceptive use at first sexual intercourse; between 1982 and 1988 the percentage of adolescents who reported using condoms at sexual debut doubled (Sells & Blum, 1996). The bad news is that nearly a quarter of current sexually active students (24.8%) reported that they had used drugs or alcohol at the time of last sexual intercourse, and the percentage who used a condom at last intercourse (44%–60%) indicates that roughly 40%–56% of youth were unprotected against sexually transmitted infections. In addition to unplanned pregnancy, the presence of HIV necessitates that all sexually active adolescents use condoms in addition to other forms of birth control.

Data from the *Risk Behavior Surveillance System—1995* (Centers for Disease Control and Prevention, 1996) indicated that 54.4% of currently active students in grades 9–12

reported that they or their partner had used a condom during last sexual intercourse. Male students (60.5%) were significantly more likely than female students (48.6%), and African American students (66.1%) were significantly more likely than white (52.2%) or Hispanic (44.4%) students to report condom use during last intercourse. White students were more likely to use birth control pills (21.4%) than African American (10.2%) or Hispanic (11.4%) students.

Although parents were the preferred source of information about pregnancy and birth control (L. Harris & Associates, 1986), friend were mentioned as the most common source of this information (Handelsman, Cabral, & Weisfeld, 1987; Sanders & Mullis, 1988). Postrado & Nicholson (1992) reported that sexually active adolescents who talked with their parents about sex were more likely to use birth control; this was most effective with youth 9–11 years of age. In their review of interventions aimed at decreasing sexual activity and increasing contraceptive use, Voydanoff and Donnelly (1990) concluded that multifaceted programs composed of educational and vocational information and assistance, counseling, and health care services appeared to be the most effective.

Gordon (1990) reminds us that one contributing factor of premature pregnancy is the adolescent's lack of cognitive skills such as envisioning alternatives, evaluating alternatives, perspective-taking, and the ability to reason about chance and probability. These cognitive skills are relevant to adolescent decision making about contraception and the risks associated with risky sexual practices. Two manifestations of adolescent egocentrism—the imaginary audience and the personal fable—result in adolescents being able to differentiate their feelings and experiences from reality. From this perspective, Elkind (1967) suggests that adolescents see themselves as unique and not governed by the laws that affect the lives of other people. Harter (1990) suggests that self-worth and perceived self-concept become increasingly differentiated with age and linked to self-concept and level of perspective-taking and formal operational thought.

A study of high school and college freshman students (Holmbeck, Crossman, Wandrei, & Gasiewski, 1994) found that adolescents who had higher cognitive development and self-esteem scores not only had more knowledge about sexuality and contraception but also were more likely to report using contraception during sexual intercourse. High self-esteem was predictive of contraceptive use for females and sexual activity for males. The level of psychological, emotional, and social maturity was found to predict contraceptive compliance in another study (Miller & Moore, 1990).

Several studies have indicated that over one-third of adolescents who obtain medical contraception are noncompliant and up to 10% become pregnant even while enrolled in teen-oriented family-planning programs (Furstenberg, Lincoln, & Menken, 1981; Jorgesen, 1993; Namerow & Philliker, 1982). A review of studies on contraceptive compliance revealed that only 10–20% of youth reported consistent and appropriate use of contraception (Sells & Blum, 1996); substance use and other antisocial behaviors were found to be associated with poor contraceptive use among adolescents (Brooks-Gunn & Furstenberg, 1989; Voydanoff & Donnelly, 1990).

Even among compliant adolescents, pregnancy can occur when contraceptives fail. In a review of the literature, Dias and O'Mara (1998) note that the failure rate for oral contraceptives during the first year of use among adults was 3–8.7%; failure rate for intrauterine devices (IUD) was 2.4–4.5%. Contraceptive failure with Norplant, considered to be one of the more desirable forms of contraceptives for adolescents, is 0.2% for women weighing less than 50 kg (110 lbs.) to 2.4–9.3% for women whose weight exceeds 70 kg (154.3 lbs.). They note that the risk of pregnancy increases among women who continue to have regular menstrual cycles while using Norplant and among women below the age of 25. The researchers suggest that women in countries such as China, India, Bangladesh, and Nigeria, where Norplant was tested and received international success, tend to weigh considerably less than 154 pounds.

Adolescent Pregnancy. Jones, Forest, Goldman, Henshaw, Lincoln, Rosoff, Westoff, and Wulf (1996) note that although similar rates of sexual activity among adolescents are observed in France, Canada, Sweden, England, Wales, and the Netherlands, U.S. adolescents continue to have among the highest rates of pregnancy of all developed countries. Although the pregnancy rate among older adolescents has continue to declined since 1991, the proportion of births that were to unmarried teens in 1992 "reached the highest level ever recorded" (Children's Defense Fund, 1995, p. 81). This increasing percentage of unmarried teen mothers (70%) results, in part, from a decline in the number of marriages among teens, at the same time as there are decreasing birth rates among married teens. Evidence of increasing numbers of sexually active adolescents, combined with a decreasing pregnancy rate, suggests that sexually active teens are becoming more effective contraceptors (Alan Guttmacher Institute, 1994).

Nationally, the birth rate for persons 15–19 years of age has continued to decline. By 1996, the rate had fallen by 12% when compared to the 1991 rates (54.4 vs. 62.1) births per 1000 women in this age group (Centers for Disease Control and Prevention, 1998b). Between 1995 and 1996, the pregnancy rate for females ages 10–14 declined (1.3 vs. 1.2) births per 1000 females, demonstrating a similar trend of declining rates observed among 15–19 year old males and females. The rate for mothers ages 15–19 varied considerably by race and

ethnicity: 48.4 for whites, 91.7 for African Americans, 75.1 for American Indians, 25.4 for Asian/Pacific Islanders, and 101.6, the highest rate of all groups, for Hispanics. In 1995, not only were there nearly twice as many first births to teenage mothers among African Americans than whites (42% vs. 21%), but African-American births are considerably more likely to be nonmarital than white births (74% vs. 26%) (National Center for Health Statistics, 1996).

The total rate of parenthood among males 15–19 years of age declined by 3% from 1994–1995. This is a continuation of a 5-year decline from a high of 24.8 per 1000 live births in 1991 to 24.3 per 1000 live births in 1995 (Ventura, Martin, Curtin, & Mathews, 1997). African-American males have over two-and-a-half times the rate of teenage fatherhood then do white males (50.5 per 1000 vs. 19.7 per 1000 live births). These figures can be somewhat misleading because men tend to be older than their partners; thus, only 26% of young males involved in teen pregnancies were under the age of 18 (Alan Guttmacher Institute, 1994).

Based on a representative sample of youth in grades 9–12, 6.9% reported that they had been pregnant or gotten someone pregnant. African-American and Hispanic students (14.8% and 12.5%, respectively) were significantly more likely than white students (4.0%) to report having been pregnant or having gotten someone pregnant (Centers for Disease Control and Prevention, 1996b). This relatively low rate must be viewed with caution since dropping out of school is a major outcome of pregnancy for both male and female students. Therefore, students who had already been involved with a pregnancy are less likely to have remained in school and been available to participate in these surveys.

Forced early sexual activity appears to be a precursor to teen pregnancy. Boyer and Fine (1992), in their sample of 535 pregnant and parenting adolescents located in 35 program sites, reported that 62% had been victims of sexual molestation, attempted rape, or rape prior to their first pregnancy. Of the 55% who had been molested, the average age of the girl was 9.7 years at first molestation, with 24% reporting that the first experience occurred at 5 years of age or younger. Of those molested, over half (54%) had been victimized by family members and 77% had experienced molestation more than once. Furthermore, 44% had been raped (half had been raped more than once) and 42% had at least one attempted rape. These researchers observed that the major difference between pregnant adolescents who had been sexually victimized and those not victimized was that sexually victimized women had begun consensual sexual relations earlier, were more likely to have used drugs and alcohol, and were more likely to have an abusive partner. Finally, these women were more likely to have abused their children, had been contacted by protective services, and have had children removed.

Premature pregnancy is only one of several serious

consequences of adolescent sexual activity. Adolescents who are sexually active are more likely to have experience with a variety of potentially dangerous drugs, and to have school difficulties, legal difficulties, and multiple social problems (Dryfoos, 1990; Irwin & Millstein, 1986; Jessor & Jessor, 1977; Resnick & Burt, 1996). Premature parenthood has serious psychosocial consequences because young parents are more likely to quit school, remain dependent on public welfare, and have more subsequent illegitimate pregnancies (Furstenberg et al., 1981). Rauch-Elnekave (1994) reported that teen mothers who scored one or more years below grade level in reading and in language skills had infants with similar delays in language and social development, thus contributing to the next generation of youth facing educational limitations. Teen fathers do not escape; like teen mothers, they remain forever educationally behind their peers who defer parenthood until later (Furstenberg et al., 1981). The economic costs to society were estimated in 1985 to be $16.6 billion in public funds for Aid to Families with Dependent Children (AFDC), Medicaid, and food stamps to support families begun by teenage mothers (Voydanoff & Donnelly, 1990).

Pregnant adolescents and their partners are at considerable risks for poor medical, social, and economic outcomes (Elster & Hendricks, 1986; Jorgensen, 1993). Approximately 43% of unintended adolescent pregnancies among girls 15–17 years of age or younger, resulted in induced abortions, low birth weight, and prematurity; and birth defects and associated morbidity, and infant mortality characterize adolescent pregnancies that were continued (Furstenberg, 1991; Hoffert & Hayes, 1987; Jorgensen, 1993; Makinson, 1985). Children born to teen mothers are also at increased risk of being abused and of dying in the first year of life (Steinmetz, 1987).

While this accurately describes the birth outcomes for white youth, Geronimus (1996, 1997) suggests that among economically disadvantaged African Americans, 15-year-old mothers are one-half as likely to have low birthweight babies as those whose mothers are 25, and one-third as likely as those whose mothers are 35. She notes that low birthweights increased fourfold over these maternal ages and calls this effect "weathering" to indicate that cumulative exposure to social inequality may produce a more rapid decline in health status over time among low-income African Americans. Geronimus notes that for "first-born black American children, but not white, those with teen mothers are *less* likely to be born with low birth weights or to die as infants than those with older mothers" (1997, p. 8), a finding supported by other research (Ahmed, 1989; Geronimus, 1986, 1996; McCarthy & Hardy, 1993; Wolpin & Rosenweig, 1995).

Sexually Transmitted Infections: STDs and AIDS. Because young adults 20–24 years of age and adolescents

10–19 years of age are more likely to have multiple sexual partners (both sequential or concurrent), engage in unprotected intercourse, and select partners at high risk, they are at higher risk for acquiring sexually transmitted infections than are older adults (Centers for Disease Control and Prevention, 1997). In reviewing the research on sexually transmitted diseases, Sells and Blum (1996) observed that youth under 25 account for two-thirds of all sexually transmitted disease, with human papilloma virus and chlamydia being the most common. The rates of chlamydia range from 10% to 37% depending on the population studied; a similarly large range of rates, 13–38%, were reported for human papilloma virus in females (Centers for Disease Control and Prevention, 1996; Martinez, Smith, & Farmer, 1988).

During 1996, gonorrhea was particularly prevalent among youth ages 15–19. Women in this age group had the highest rates, 218.8 per 100,000; males in this age group had the second highest rate among males, 45.9 per 100,000 (Ventura, Peters, Martin, & Mauer, 1997). African-American youth accounted for 82% of the reported cases of gonorrhea followed by white (13%) and Hispanic (4%) youth (Sells & Blum, 1996). These authors also noted that youth between 10 and 24 years of age accounted for 34% of reported infections for primary and secondary syphilis; of this group, 57% of the reported cases occurred in females, and over 88% were reported for African Americans. The age- and gender-specific rates for primary and secondary syphilis for 1996 were 0.1 for male and 0.5 for female per 100,000 youth, ages 10–14; and 4.3 for male and 8.66 per 100,000 for female youth ages 15–19 years (Centers for Disease Control and Prevention, 1997). In general, the rates for STD have shown a decline over the past few years.

Because a greater proportion of African-American youth are sexually experienced at all ages, this increases their risks for becoming infected with sexually transmitted infections. These youth, especially males, tend to have multiple sexual partners, and individuals with multiple partners were consistently less likely to use condoms (Johnson, Jackson, Hinkle, & Gilbert, 1994; Smith & Udry, 1985; Sonenstein, Pleck, & Ku, 1991).

AIDS is the sixth leading cause of death among those 15–24 years of age (Ventura et al., 1997). *The State of America's Children Yearbook* (Children's Defense Fund, 1995) reports that one white and three African-American youth ranging from newborn to age under 25 die every day from AIDS. Individuals between the ages of 20 and 29 account for about 25% of the documented cases of AIDS. An analysis of the data through June 1996 indicated that there were 2574 reported cases of AIDS among youth 13–19 years of age. The gender differences in this age group (1647 for males vs. 927 for females) was considerably narrowed when those youth infected as a result of hemophilia (N = 678), an exclusively male disorder, were excluded. For the 20–24 group, however, major gender-based differences were observed: 15,061 for males (approximately 63% resulting from homosexual contact) and 4936 for females (Centers for Disease Control and Prevention, 1996).

Analysis of the data from January 1994 through June 1997 from the 25 states that had both HIV infection and AIDS case reporting indicates that among young people 13–24 years of age, 44% (N = 3203) were females, 63% (N = 4566) were African Americans, and 5% (394) were Hispanic (Centers for Disease Control and Prevention, 1998c, 1998d). African Americans of all ages are disproportionately affected by HIV/AIDS. Although they constitute an estimated 13% of the U.S. population, they make up 36% of all AIDS cases reported to CDC through 1997 (Centers for Disease Control and Prevention, 1998d). Approximately 2000 young people are infected each year, a number that has remained fairly stable since 1994 (Centers for Disease Control and Prevention, 1998c).

American Indians and Alaskan Natives also appear to be at a somewhat greater risk than the white population. This population, less than 1% of the total U.S. population, represented 0.3% of the AIDS cases reported to CDC through December 1997 (Centers for Disease Control and Prevention, 1998a). However, more disturbing for future trends is the HIV status of adolescents (5.2% of those diagnosed with HIV are 13–19 years of age; 39.7% are 20–29 years of age), suggesting that this population was more recently infected. This population is also at high risk for other sexually transmitted diseases with twice the average rate of gonorrhea and syphilis cases reported in 13 states surveyed during 1984–1988 (Centers for Disease Control and Prevention, 1998a).

Because of the estimated 7-year latency between the acquisition of HIV and the appearance of AIDS-related symptoms, it is clear that the majority of these individuals became infected as adolescents (Hein, 1989; Gayle, Rogers, Manorr, & Starcher, 1988). Joseph (1991) recalculated the AIDS infection rate in New York City and observed a higher rate than had been reported. Those infected were clustered in certain areas and tended to be heterosexual, poor, and minority adolescents. Therefore, the low number of diagnosed cases of AIDS in adolescents may be deceptive since early exposure to HIV may not emerge as AIDS until young adulthood. The seroprevalence of HIV in this age group is unknown, but certain data suggest that adolescent HIV infection truly represents an epidemic (Koop, 1989).

Analysis of 1990 data from the Centers for Disease Control indicates that adolescents at highest risk are gay youth, intravenous (IV) drug users, homeless and runaway youth, members of racial and ethnic minority groups, and youth in inner cities (Millstein, 1990). Zimet, Sobo, and Zimmerman (1995) warn that assumptions regarding run-

away youths' risky behaviors need to be accepted cautiously. Their study of runaway youth in two shelters suggests that youth were knowledgeable about behavioral risks for HIV infection, reported less frequent health-compromising sexual behaviors, and were less inclined to use drugs as compared with runaways described in other studies. The authors reported that adolescents with AIDS have a higher rate of heterosexual transmission, are more often asymptomatic, have a greater number of members from minority groups (African Americans and Hispanics), and are more likely to be overrepresented in risk categories.

Sexual Orientation. Adolescence is characterized as a time for sexual experimentation. Herold and Marshall (1996) report that a majority of youth who engage in homoerotic behavior in adolescence do not continue this behavior into adulthood. Others note that the majority of lesbians and gay men have engaged in heterosexual sex during adolescence or young adulthood (Bell & Weinberg, 1978; Savin-Williams, 1990). Thus, for some youth, sexual identity may be a process characterized by experimentation until one's sexual attractions, impulses, and behaviors merge into a heterosexual, homosexual, or bisexual identity—possibly a lifelong process (Savin-Williams & Rodriguez, 1993).

For males, the self-designation as gay occurs between 14 and 21 years of age, although awareness of being attracted to someone of the same gender occurs at about 13 years of age (Remafedi, 1987). For females, the age of awareness of being attracted to another female occurs at about 16 years of age, with self-description as a lesbian occurring at around age 21 (D'Augelli, Collins, & Hart, 1987). Fontaine (1998) found that 93% of junior or senior high school counselors and 21% of elementary school counselors reported contact with students who were dealing with sexual identity issues. Thirty-seven percent of these counselors reported that the gay and lesbian students they had counseled had contemplated or attempted suicide.

In addition to the typical issues revolving around sexuality, such as sexual development, development of intimate relationships, and self awareness, bisexual, gay, and lesbian youth face the additional hurdles as a result of the need to keep their identity secret for fear of retribution. Approximately three-quarters of gay and lesbian youth report being verbally or physically abused because of their sexuality, and about one-fourth report threats of physical violence (Savin-Williams, 1994). Pilkington and D'Augelli (1995), in their study of gay and lesbian youth (ages 15–21), reported that 80% had experienced verbal insults, 44% had been threatened with violence, 33% had objects thrown at them, 31% reported being chased or followed, and 17% reported being physically assaulted (i.e., punched, kicked, or beaten). Sears (1992) found that 80% of prospective teachers and 66% of guidance counselors reported negative feelings toward gays and lesbians. Schools, which should be teaching tolerance, are in some cases perpetuating intolerance (McFarland, 1998).

Savin-Williams (1990) observed that gay and lesbian youth must struggle with the same issues of fidelity and intimacy faced by heterosexual youth. Our society, however, devalues the existence of same-sex relationships and discourages and punishes youth for engaging in these activities. Thus, the need to be secretive and to live a double life places additional stress on lesbian and gay youth and impairs their ability to cope.

Issues regarding sexual orientation are further complicated by the sexual debut occurring earlier for both heterosexual and homosexual youth. In the past, this might have occurred in the last years of high school or later—at an age where a youth might more easily conceal his or her sexual identity and select friends who might be more tolerant. However, when an adolescent's sexual debut occurs during the middle school or early years of high school, family and peer pressure can become unbearable. Not only are homosexual male youth at higher risk for HIV/AIDS, gay and lesbian youth are also at a higher risk than heterosexual youth for committing suicide, running away, or being cast out by their family (Dempsey, 1994; Hershberger, Pilkington, & D'Augelli, 1997; Proctor & Gioze, 1994; Rotheram-Borus, Hunter, & Rosario, 1994).

Analysis of intake and case data on homeless and runaway youth collected through a consortium of agencies revealed that gay and bisexual adolescent youth appeared to be at increased risk for both homelessness and suicide (Kruks, 1991). Because gay males may have been forced out of their homes because of their sexual orientation, they are more likely to engage in survival sex (prostitution) than heterosexual male street youth, many of whom still live with their families. They also found that over half (53%) of their sample of 53 gay-identified street youths had attempted suicide compared with 30% of the 291 runaway youths studied by Stiffman (1989). Approximately 30% of gay and bisexual adolescent males have attempted suicide at least once (Remafedi, Farrow, & Deischer, 1991), and gay and lesbian youth represent 30% of all completed teen suicides (Gibson, 1989). These findings have been questioned, however, on methodological grounds (Mucker, 1995), and Shaffer, Fischer, Hicks, Paides, & Gould (1995), in their psychological autopsy of suicides of persons under age 20, did not support for Gibson's (1989) findings.

Prostitution. There appear to be different pathways into prostitution for male and female adolescents. Females are more likely to be introduced to prostitution by pimps who provided parental-like support as well as drugs and alcohol to

lower their resistance (Ennew, 1986; Rickel & Hendren, 1993). Peers on the street are the pathway for adolescent males' introduction into prostitution. There are considerable risks to adolescents who engage in prostitution, and young women have the additional risk of violence by pimps (Ennew, 1996). A comparison of the health status of 620 homeless youths, 153 of whom identified themselves as prostitutes, indicated that although prostitution-involved youths comprised only 25% of the study population, they accounted for 37% of the recorded medical diagnoses, which included pelvic inflammatory and other sex-related diseases, infectious disease, uncontrolled asthma, and drug and alcohol dependency, and they were twice as likely to have suicidal ideation or previous suicide attempts (Yates, MacKenzie, & Pennbridge, 1991).

Although much of the literature portrays adolescent male prostitution as primarily survival sex, a 3-year study of adolescent male prostitution (Cates, 1989) identified four main types: full-time street and bar hustlers, full-time call boys, part-time hustlers, and peer-delinquents. Cates observed that low self-esteem, not financial need, was the major contributing factor in the decision to become a male prostitute, as most of the youth had their basic needs (e.g., food, shelter, and clothing) met and many still lived with their families. Prostitution was not the result of adult coercion, but a mechanism to ameliorate these youths' feelings of inferiority, insecurity, and other emotional experiences.

Beyond feelings of alienation from family, school, and work, which leave youth free to engage in unconventional behavior (Gray, 1973), gender and sexual orientation are important factors. Simons and Whitbeck (1991) interviewed female adolescent runaways and adult homeless women and noted that early sexual abuse experiences directly increased the likelihood of engaging in prostitution. Moreover, sexual abuse was an indirect contributor to prostitution through such behaviors as running away, substance abuse, and other deviant activities.

Sexual orientation was the most significant variable distinguishing a control group of delinquent males from males who engaged in prostitution in Boyer's (1989) 2-year study of adolescent homosexual identity and prostitution. A similar relationship was found in Maiuro, Trupin, and James' (1983) comparison of female juvenile delinquents with histories of prostitution to a similar group who were not engaged in prostitution. They found that most females who were engaged in prostitution were androgynous or undifferentiated in their sex-role orientation, as measured by the Bem Sex-Role Inventory. Female adolescents with a masculine sex-role orientation had a relatively higher incidence of prostitution.

Sexual Harassment and Date Rape. A study based on 4200 responses of girls ages 9–19 to a questionnaire in the September 1992 issue of *Seventeen* magazine (Stein, 1995) revealed that 39% reported being harassed at school every day, 29% were harassed once a week, 89% reported sexual comments and gestures, and 83% reported that they were touched or grabbed. Four percent of the respondents reported being harassed by teachers, administrators, or school staff members. More than three-quarters of the girls stated that they told someone about the harassment, but when school officials were notified the school did nothing in 4% of the cases.

The study *Hostile Hallways: the AAUW Survey on Sexual Harassment in America's School* (Bryant, 1993) included findings that 84% of African American females, 82% of Hispanic females, and 87% of white females reported experiencing unwanted sexual comment or actions. Similar findings were reported for males: 81% of African American, 69% of Hispanic, and 75% of white males reported unwanted sexual comments or actions. Moore, Nord, and Peterson (1989) found that 13% of women 13 years of age or younger; 17% of 14-year-old women; 14% of 15- to 16-year-old women; 13% and 12% of 17- and 18-year-olds, respectively; and 14% of 19-year-olds reported both voluntary and involuntary sex.

Boyfriends, dates, friends, and acquaintance are the most common offenders of unwanted peer sexual contact (Small & Kerns, 1993). Although both males and females tend to consider consensual sexual activity justified when the women initiated the date, went to the man's apartment, or allowed the male to pay for the date (Muehlenhard, 1988), males tend to justify forced sex more frequently than do females (Davis, Peck, & Storment, 1993; Muehlenhard, 1988). Female adolescents were at greater risk for unwanted sexual activity among peers when they reported high peer conformity, previous sexual abuse by an adult, excessive alcohol use, and a lack of parental supervision (Small & Kerns, 1993).

Street Violence: Bullies, Gangs, Homicide, Accidental Death, and Motor Fatalities

Adolescents are the victims of violence in the streets and in the family (Steinmetz, 1990). However, they are also the perpetrators of violence in the form of bullying, gang-related violence, homicide, accidental death, and vehicular violence. These aspects of risk-taking or externalizing behaviors are examined in this section.

Bullying Behavior. Oleweus (1993) considers bullying to occur when a person is repeatedly exposed to negative actions on the part of one or more persons for a period of time. Three types of bullying behaviors were described by Title (1994); physical bullying, in which another person's body or property is harmed; emotional bullying, which harms

one's self-esteem; and social bullying, which harms an individual's acceptance by the peer group.

Espleage, Bosworth, Karageorge, and Daytner's (1996) study of bullying behaviors among 6th to 8th graders found that those youth who reported the highest bullying behavior were most likely to report significantly greater levels of forceful parental discipline, extensive viewing of TV violence, a history of problems at home and in school, and a record of fighting. Just under one-third of these youth lived in stepfamily households and 36% lived in single-parent homes. Exposure to higher levels of gang activity and access to guns were additional factors that differentiated this group from youth who did not engage in bullying behavior.

Research on bullying behavior conducted at Brandeis University suggests that youth who engage in severe bullying behaviors are significantly more likely to experience alcoholism, violent crime, family abuse, and failed relationships and to have difficulty keeping a job as an adult (Bernstein, n.d.). The victims also carry the bullying experience into adulthood by manifesting evidence of low self-esteem (Bernstein, n.d.), and an estimated 13% drop out of school because of the fear of violence (Mabe, 1995).

Slee and Rigby (1993) investigated the extent and nature of bullying among 211 female and 201 male children (ages 7–13) and their self-appraisals of peer relations. Ten percent of the boys and 6% of the girls reported that they were the victim of peer group bullying; for 8% of the youth, the bullying episodes lasted 6 months or more. Three independent factors were identified: a tendency to bully, a tendency to be victimized, and a tendency to act in a prosocial manner. The tendency to be victimized correlated negatively with self-appraisals of the number of friends, popularity, happiness, and feelings of safety at school.

A recent study of bullying behavior revealed that 10% of a sample of boys ages 10–16 had experienced nonsexual assault to the groin; 40% of the perpetrators were girls who were the same age as the victim. It is suggested that the girls may have been violent in retaliation against boys who harassed them (Reimer, 1996).

Gangs: Urban and Suburban. In 1991, there were an estimated 4881 gangs with 249,324 members in the United States; the 1995 National Youth Gang Study provided estimates that there were over 650,000 youth who were members of over 25,000 gangs (Curry, 1996; Curry, Ball, & Decker, 1996). An analysis of the 1989 and 1995 school crime supplements to the National Crime Victimization Survey of students ages 12–19 found that students reporting street gangs in their schools rose from 15% in 1989 to 28% in 1995 (Chandler, Chapman, Rand, & Taylor, 1998). The researchers found distinct racial differences, with 50% of Hispanic students, 35% of African-American students, and 23% of white students reporting gang activity that most likely reflected the neighborhood where the schools were located. The presence of street gangs increased the likelihood of a student experiencing violent victimization (e.g., a physical attack or a robbery by force, weapons, or threats). In 1995, 2.7% of students who reported no street gang presence at school were victimized compared with 7.5% of students who reported street gang presence (Chandler et al., 1998).

Despite the high profile of gangs in the media, relatively few young people join gangs. Even in highly impacted areas, the degree of participation has rarely exceeded 10%, and less than 2% of all juvenile crime is gang related (Bodinger-deUriarte, 1993). Korem (1995) has identified three types of gangs: delinquent gangs with a major desire for profit and thuggery; ideological gangs attached to a specific ideology that may or may not be political; and occult gangs that have an attachment to beliefs in occult powers. Cromwell, Taylor, and Palacios (1992) and Sanchez-Jankowski (1991) describe gangs as formal, rational organizations with established leadership structures, roles, rules, and the ability to maintain control over their members. Taylor (1988) suggests that some gangs have the ability to engage in entrepreneurial activities such as drug trafficking. This trend has been identified among some large youth gangs such as the Crips and Bloods in Los Angeles (Skolnick, 1990), Chicago's Vice Lords (Dawley, 1992) and Black Gangsters Disciples Nation (Block & Block, 1993). Sanders (1994) reported an increase from 3 per 100,000 to 11 per 100,000 in gang-related homicides in San Diego between 1985 and 1988 and suggests that this is the result of competition for money and turf in drug trafficking. (See Howell [1998] for a comprehensive review of this research.)

Block, Christakos, Jacob, and Przybylski (1996) report that two ongoing gun wars over the drug market in Chicago were responsible for more than 100 homicides during 1987–1994, which is 11% of all gang-related homicides in Chicago. Black gangs are relatively more involved in drug trafficking; Hispanic gangs, in turf-related violence; Asian and white gangs, in property crimes (Spergel, 1990)—observations that have been confirmed in an examination of 30 years of Chicago arrest data (Block et al., 1996). Analysis of Los Angeles data on arrests from 1979–1994 (Hutson, Anglin, Kyriacou, Hart, & Spears, 1995), and similar data from Boston for 1984–1994 (Miller, 1994) found that drug trafficking was not a major factor in youth homicides. Others have suggested that the street gang's structures lack the organizational skills to conduct drug-trafficking operations (Decker & Van Winkle, 1996; Klein & Maxson, 1994; Klein, Maxson, & Cunningham, 1991).

Although the media has suggested that the growth of gangs and gang violence is the result of drug trafficking, the data to support this is lacking. Maxson (1993) found that

social reasons, including family moves to improve quality of life and to be near relatives and friends to be the most common reason for migration. Block et al. (1996) found that only 3% of gang-motivated homicides were drug related. Furthermore, drive-by shootings appear to be acts of retaliation or spontaneous responses to turf violations or disrespecting gang colors, not drug trafficking (Decker & Van Winkle, 1996; Hutson et al., 1995). There is also evidence that the increase in lethality of weapons, rather than an increase in street gang assaults, accounted for the increase in homicides (Hutson et al., 1995; Block et al., 1996; Blumstein & Cork, 1996; Zimring, 1996).

Gangs provide the same fundamental needs of other social groups: recreation, a sense of belonging, companionship, protection, and training. In fact, most of the research reviewed indicated that gangs develop to meet the needs of youth that are not being met by the family, school, and community. For example, research utilizing life histories, participant observation, and questionnaires conducted in urban, suburban, and rural barrios of southern California during 1976–1981 demonstrated how a youth's self-identification with a gang is reinforced (Virgil, 1988). Virgil suggests that roles the group members represent provide the adolescent with the ingredients for self-identification; the symbols and rituals by which these roles are enacted reinforce this identity.

However, this source of identification for some youth is not without costs to other youth. Students who attend schools where gangs are present are twice as likely to report that they fear becoming victims of violence than students at schools without gangs (Trump, 1993). Schools themselves are rapidly becoming centers of gang activities, functioning as sites for recruitment and socializing (Arthur & Erickson, 1992; Bodinger-deUriarte, 1993). Even when gang members are suspended, they continue to use the school as a gang hangout—a base of operation—rather than as an educational institution (Boyle, 1992).

Korem (1995) provides documentation that gang activity is no longer limited to urban areas, but has been reported in increasing numbers in upscale communities since the mid-1980s. Although these gangs do not appear to be as dangerous as inner-city gangs, homicides and other acts of violence are increasing in frequency. Korem notes that it is common for anywhere from 50 up to 250 gang members to be present in a middle- or upper-middle-class community. In addition to exclusively female gangs, female membership can range from a high of 25% in urban gangs to between 5–10% in suburban gangs (Taylor, 1993; Korem, 1995). Korem (1995) proposes a typical flow of events that leads to gang formation in affluent communities: (1) chronic family breakdown in at least a segment of the community; (2) dress, hair styles, music, and graffiti indicative of the gang subculture;

(3) alcohol and drug abuse; and (4) unexpected eruption of violence producing a setting conducive for the formation of gangs. Initially, these characteristics tended to be confined to the inner city, but since the mid-to-late 1980s, the number of at-risk youth in affluent communities hit a critical mass resulting in the formation of affluent gangs. Gang subculture, with its dress, slang, and symbols, has become a visible part of the lifestyles of all American youth. Not only has gang membership and activity increased, but the population of gang "wannabes" and those who affect gang-related fashions and listen to music with gang-related themes have also increased.

Homicide, Suicide, and Accidental Death. Every day in America, 35 youths and children die by accident. Native American youth are at highest risk for accidental death, followed closely by white youth; African Americans have a slight risk of accidental death (Fingerhut & Kleinmen, 1990).

The United States has the highest firearm-related homicide rate of any industrialized society (Fingerhut & Kleinmen, 1990), and homicides were the second leading cause of death for individuals 15–24 years of age and the third leading cause of death among youth ages 5–14 during 1996 (Ventura, Peters, Martin, & Mauer, 1977). In 1996, homicides account for 18.1% of all deaths for youth ages 15–25 (Ventura et al., 1997). There are considerable differences in rates for homicide when examined by race. For African-American youth, ages 15–24, homicide is the leading cause of death, with 114.9 deaths per 100,000 males. This rate is over ten times higher than the rate of 11.7 per 100,000 for white youth (Bastian & Taylor, 1994). African-American males ages 12–24 were almost 14 times more likely to be homicide victims when compared to the general population (Bastian & Taylor, 1994). African-American women have a homicide rate that is four times higher than their white counterpart (Fingerhut & Kleinmen, 1990). Native American youth are at particular risk. Youth between the ages of 15 and 24 constituted 31% of homicide victims; males were the victims in 78% of incidents (Wallace, Calhoun, Powell, O'Neil, & James, 1996).

The risk of suicide is increasing among adolescents. In 1996, suicide was the sixth leading cause of death among youth 5–14 years of age and the third leading cause of death, accounting for 12.1% of deaths, among persons 15–24 years of age (Ventura et al., 1997). One estimate suggested that as many as 500,000 adolescents attempt suicide each year (Runyan & Gerken, 1989) and over 4600 suicides occurred in 1996 (Venture et al., 1997). In 1995, more than 90% of all suicides occurring in the United States were among whites (Kachur, Potter, James, & Powell, 1995). However, during the period from 1979–1992, suicide rates for Native Americans (a category that includes American Indians and Alaska Natives)

were about 1.5 times the national rates, and a disproportionate amount of suicides (64%) occurred among young male Native Americans during this period (Wallace et al., 1996).

Windle and Windle (1997) analyzed data from a 4-wave panel design of 975 adolescents and found that high levels of problem drinking and depressive symptoms were associated with higher levels of suicidal ideation and attempts. Adolescents who attempted suicide tended to have lower levels of family support, exhibited a greater use of substances to cope with stressors, and had peers who used substances. Parental loss through separation or divorce or repeated threats of parental separation (Adam, Bouckoms, & Streiner, 1982), family instability and chaotic home life (Kosky, Silburn, & Subrick, 1986), and a compromised process of individuation (Pfeffer, 1981; Heillig, 1983) were also found to be related to suicide ideation and attempts. However other research suggests that it is interpersonal conflict rather than separation or divorce that is predictive of suicidal ideation (deJong, 1992; Emery, 1982; Slater & Haber, 1984). As discussed in an earlier section, gay and lesbian youth are at particularly high risk for suicide ideation, attempts, and completed suicide.

Weapons and Violence. National victimization survey data indicate that over 2 million teenagers are the victims of violent crime annually (U.S. Department of Justice, 1992). During the 30 days preceding the 1995 Youth Risk Behavior Surveillance System survey, based on 10,904 high school students, grades 9–12, 20% of students had carried a gun, knife, or club. Male students were significantly more likely than female students to carry a weapon (31.1% and 8.3%, respectively) and African-American and Hispanic students (10.6% and 10.5%, respectively) were significantly more likely than white students (6.2%) to have carried a gun (Centers for Disease Control and Prevention, 1996).

Several studies concluded that carrying and threatening with a weapon have become major problems among adolescents. In Washington, D.C., 11% of 9th- and 10th-grade students had used a weapon to threaten someone (Altschuler & Brounstein, 1991); 6% of 11th-grade students in Seattle had carried a gun to school sometime in the past (Callahan & Rivara, 1992). A survey of 10th-, 11th-, and 12th-graders in a midwestern urban public school found that 16% of the students (25% of male students) reported carrying a weapon to school, and 6% did so more than six times (Asmussen, 1992); 3% of males in a survey of 11,000 students in 8th and 10th grades from 20 states reported bringing a handgun to school (National School Safety Center, 1989). Finally, 55% of incarcerated juvenile offenders reported that they carried guns all or most of the time prior to incarceration, and another 28% reported that they did so at least occasionally (Sheley & Wright, 1993).

Youth are not just carrying weapons, they are also using

them more frequently. During 1992, homicide data were reported on 20,738 offenders; of this group, 32% were between the ages of 15 and 24 (Ventura et al., 1997). Additionally, juveniles were responsible for 119,678 acts of violent crime during 1993, which included homicide and nonnegligent manslaughter (3284), forcible rape (5303), robbery (43,340), and aggravated assault (67,751) (U.S. Department of Justice, 1994). Unfortunately, it appears that carrying and using weapons have become a normal part of daily life for many adolescents.

Adolescents are also more likely to be the victims of violent crime. In 1996, persons ages 12–24 comprised 22% of the population but represented 35% of murder victims and 49% of victims of serious violent crime; 52% of rape/sexual assault victims were females younger than 25 (Perkins, 1997). Furthermore, 1 in 11 persons ages 12–15 (compared to 1 in 200 age 65 or older), 1 in 19 African-American youth (compared to 1 in 25 white youth), and 1 in 20 males (compared to 1 in 29 females) experienced violent crime (Perkins, 1997).

Motor Vehicle Fatalities. Possibly one of the most dangerous weapons, in terms of its potential for property damage, injury, and fatality, is the automobile. Yet every teen has the legal right to drive a car, usually by age 16. The National Safety Council (1993) reports that 78% of all unintentional injuries among youth are the result of motor vehicle accidents. Most fatal accidents occur at night and in rural areas, and males account for about 75% of these deaths (Sells & Blum, 1996). Passive restraints, reduced speed limits, and, most important, raising the legal age of drinking have resulted in a 38% decrease in auto fatalities between 1979 and 1992. The alcohol-related traffic fatality ratio decreased by greater than one-third. However, drivers between 16 and 20 years of age involved in an auto fatality were more likely than any other age group to have blood alcohol levels indicating impairment.

Substance Abuse: Tobacco, Marijuana, Alcohol, and Other Illegal Drugs

In the *State of America's Children Yearbook* (Children's Defense Fund, 1995), the arrest records for alcohol- and drug-related offenses indicate that substance use occurs at very early ages with clear racial differences. For example, African-American youth are more likely to be arrested for drug use (108 youth arrested each day) than for alcohol-related offenses (19 each day). White youth were more likely to be arrested for alcohol offenses; 144 youth were arrested each day for drug offenses, but more than double this number, or 290 arrests each day, were reported for alcohol-related offenses. Native American children and youth under the age of 20 are at extremely high risk, with 255 youth under 18

being arrested each day for drug offenses and 318 youth under 18 arrested for alcohol-related offenses. Asian and Hispanic youth, on the other hand, have relatively small rates of these offenses.

Drug use among youth develops in a predictable pattern in which experimentation with gateway drugs (cigarettes, alcohol, or marijuana) is followed by other drugs (Kandel, 1996). Individuals who being smoking in childhood are more inclined toward heavy smoking or drinking at an earlier age than those who start later. Furthermore, the use of cigarettes, alcohol, and marijuana is correlated with adolescent suicide, homicide, dropping out of school, motor vehicle crashes, delinquency, early sexual activity, STDs, and problem pregnancies (Adcock, Nagy, & Simpson, 1991; Irwin & Millstein, 1986; Jessor & Jessor, 1977). Havey and Dodd (1992) found that children of alcoholics had higher levels of depression and anxiety, were more likely to come from broken families, and had more abusive and stressful home environments than their peers from nonalcoholic families.

The 22nd annual Monitoring the Future Survey was administered in the spring of 1996 to a national probability sample of 14,824 high school seniors, 15,873 10th graders, and 18,368 8th graders in public and private schools. The data provided here must be viewed with caution since a large number of students drop out by 10th grade, resulting in students in 10th and 12th grade representing the more committed students with fewer emotional, physical, school, and delinquency-related problems.

Tobacco. The Monitoring the Future Survey (Mathias, 1996) reported that cigarette smoking continued to rise among 8th and 10th grade students and remained high among seniors, although there were no statistically significant changes in the high school seniors' cigarette use. In 1996, 21.0% of 8th graders, 30.4% of 10th graders, and 34% of seniors reported that they smoked cigarettes during the past month. The survey also indicated that for 9.4% of 10th grade students, smoking was an already a well established half-a-pack or more per day habit.

Landrine, Richardson, Klonoff, and Flay's (1994) investigation of predictors of smoking among adolescents reported that white adolescents smoked more than African Americans, Asians, and less acculturated Latinos, but not more than highly acculturated Latinos. Smoking among peers was the best predictor of smoking for white youth but had less predictive value for Hispanics and Asian youth and none for African-American youth.

Marijuana. There were increases in lifetime, annual, past 30 days, and daily use of marijuana by 8th and 10th graders, which continued a trend beginning in the early 1990s. The study indicated that 32.1% of 8th graders, 39.8% of 10th graders, and 44.9% of seniors had used marijuana at least once. Moreover, 9.1% of 8th and 20.4% of 10th graders reported current use (Mathias, 1996).

Unfortunately, the use of gateway drugs not only appears to predict greater involvement with alcohol and other drugs, but it also predicts less likelihood of staying alcohol and drug free (National Institute on Drug Abuse, 1987). It is particularly important to prevent initiation into gateway drug use and provide intense treatment to cease drug use among youth already using drugs.

Alcohol. The Monitoring the Future Survey (1996) indicated an increase in the daily use of alcohol by students in the 8th grade from 0.7% to 1.0% between 1995 and 1996; those reporting having "been drunk" in the past month increased from 8.3% to 9.6% during the same time. During the past month 21.3% of 10th graders and 31% of 12th graders reported having been drunk.

Flannery, Vazsonyi, Torquati, and Fridrich (1994) found no difference in their examination of the gender and ethnic influence on Caucasian and Hispanic adolescents at risk for substance use. Susceptibility to peer pressure and peer alcohol use were the best predictors of individual substance use.

Other Drugs. Decreases were observed between 1995 and 1996 in the current use of hallucinogens for seniors, from 4.4% to 3.5%; LSD use for 10th and 12th grade students dropped from 3.0% to 2.4% and 4.0% to 2.5%, respectively; and use of inhalants declined among 12th graders from 3.2% to 2.5% (Mathias, 1996). However, increases were reported in the use of PCP among 12th graders (0.6% to 1.3%) and cocaine (including crack, 4.0% to 4.9%) among 12th-grade students. Use of MDMA (Ecstasy) was added to the survey for all three grades for the first time with rates of 6%, 5.6%, and 3.4% among 12th, 10th, and 8th graders, respectively.

The Impact of Substance Abuse. Alcohol and other drug abuse is a contributing factor in 38% of child abuse and neglect cases, 50% of domestic violence disputes, 30% of juvenile delinquency cases, 62% of aggravated assaults, 50% of automobile accidents, 50% of homicides, and 80% of fire deaths (Children's Defense Fund, 1995). Pursley (1991) suggests that pathological gambling is closely associated with a broad spectrum of addictions, including chemical dependencies, utilized to escape the pain of failure in life resulting from dysfunctional parents and dropping out of school.

Substance use, which is highly related to early sexual activity, endangers not only young women, but also the fetus if they are pregnant. An article in *JAMA* (Phibbs, Batemen, & Schwartz, 1991) estimated the hospital costs of the 158,000 crack babies to be approximately $500 million a year. The total cost of medical care, education, and loss of human capital far exceeds this cost.

Several authors (Donovan & Jessor, 1985; Dryfoos,

1990) have demonstrated that behaviors that place adolescents at risk (sexual activity, drug use, delinquency) are closely interrelated. When 50 chemically dependent adolescent patients (mean age 15.8 years) in a residential program were compared with 50 nonchemically dependent high school students, the chemically dependent group had significantly more suicide attempts, early childhood abuse incidents, previous psychiatric interventions, special education classifications, familial divorce, and familial alcoholism than the nonchemical dependency group (Schiff & Cavaiola, 1990). Furthermore, the chemically dependent group was characterized by dual diagnoses of attention-deficit disorder, dyslexia, depression, and child abuse.

Since use of tobacco has been identified as the gateway drug and drug use has been identified as being intricately linked to a substantial number of other risky behaviors, it would appear that programs to prevent the initiation of smoking might be the most efficient way to proceed. Although the data suggest that the habitual use of illicit drugs is primarily confined to the last 3 years of high school, experimentation begins earlier, with about half of the students who used marijuana and an even greater percentage who used alcohol having experimented prior to entering high school (Robins & Przybeck, 1985).

Conclusions

Adolescence has become an especially difficult time in recent history because of the time lag between physical and social/cognitive maturity. It is also a difficult time because while adolescents, especially those in the later years of adolescence, might be physically and socially mature, they may not be considered legally mature and accorded adult rights. Exacerbating the situation are inconsistent laws defining adulthood in different ways. At 18 years of age, an individual is legally able to sign a contract and be held liable for fulfilling the conditions of the contract as well as enter the armed services and protect our country. Adolescents as young as 13 may be tried as an adult in a court of law for some offenses. Eighteen-year-olds, however, are not old enough to drink alcoholic beverages, rent a car, and, in some states, marry without parental consent.

Levels of poverty, especially among minority populations, continue to rise and play a major role in all risky behaviors. *Wasting America's Future*, a publication sponsored by the Children's Defense Fund (Sherman, 1994) indicated that every year of child poverty (at current levels) will cost the economy between $36 billion and $177 billion in lower future productivity and employment among those who grow up poor. In the Children's Defense Fund publication *The State of America's Children Yearbook* (1995), it is noted that these are direct losses in terms of human capital and do not include the cost of special education, foster care, crime, and teenage childbearing that result from child poverty.

This same publication noted that an estimated 7.7 million youth in the United States suffer from serious emotional disorders. Not only do 48% of these youth drop out of high school compared with 30% of youth with other disabilities, but 73% are arrested within 5 years of leaving school. The amount of education and training required to adequately prepare youth for adult roles is no longer reasonable for undermotivated youth or those with limited cognitive abilities and/or inadequate role models. The dwindling employment opportunities available for youth without a high school diploma do not pay an adequate salary—certainly not adequate enough to support a family.

We provide little or no mental health services for youth, and we watch them suffer from depression and other mood disorders and attempt suicide. Our policies on child abuse and child sexual abuse guarantee that only infants and toddlers will be protected from physical abuse and only those adolescents who are able to repeatedly tell a convincing story regarding sexual abuse will be believed and provided some assistance.

Although a segment of our adolescent population is achieving honors in school, on the athletic field, and in music, art, and other endeavors, a larger segment is falling further behind. Society has not addressed its responsibility to provide assistance for youth with lower levels of cognitive abilities. Just how we can prepare a youth with an IQ of 45 to be a productive citizen in today's society remains an unanswered question. How do we prepare a mother with an IQ of 50 to raise her children in an emotionally healthy, and socially and academically stimulating, environment? We defend the right of the mentally handicapped to have children, yet we provide few if any resources to help ensure that their children are given adequate care.

We are not permitted to mandate birth control for addicted women and have only limited treatment facilities for addicted mothers and their children. As a result, we are forced to sequentially remove the children from the home rather than provide treatment for the mother's addiction. We must develop appropriate social policies that balance individual rights such as the right to reproduce with our ability to provide comprehensive assistance to these parents and their children. We must more carefully monitor those children defined as "at risk" so that we may provide services to the families before these children reach adolescence.

Social policies regarding adolescent reproductive issues are inconsistent and often contradictory. We fail to provide adequate education or contraceptive and abortion information and resources, yet we penalize teen mothers by condemning them to lives of poverty when they do conceive. The recently passed legislation limiting Welfare benefits to 2 years raises questions about the long-term well-being of adolescent mothers and their children when their 2 years of benefits have expired.

The research reviewed in this chapter provides some insights. Inadequate preparation for parenthood and the lack of resources to care for the children of teen mothers are likely to result in child abuse and neglect. Such adverse consequences, in turn, will dramatically increase in the number of children being placed in foster homes and other institutional settings. This research indicates that children who lack family stability and adequate parenting and who live in poverty are more at risk of developing emotional problems, dropping out of school, accumulating a history of delinquency and substance abuse, and repeating the cycle of early sexual debut and premature parenthood. In all areas examined, children in poverty are at far greater risks. Without dramatic changes in our policies for children and families, institutional care of children will become the growth industry of the first decades of the twenty-first century.

Finally, we must find ways to bridge the expanding gap between adolescents growing up in stable, loving families with parents who have the knowledge and resources to help their children successfully meet the demands of the twenty-first century and those adolescent being raised in unstable, multiproblem, poor families who are unable to help their children successfully fulfill society's demands.

ACKNOWLEDGMENTS: I wish to thank Jessie Dias, Rose Mays, and Gary Peterson for comments and suggestions that were extremely helpful in developing and revising early drafts of this chapter and Tom Pickett for assistance with the literature review and proofreading the manuscript.

References

Abbey, A. A., Nicholas, K. B., & Bieber, S. L. (1997). Predicting runaways upon admission to an adolescent treatment center. *Residential Treatment for Children and Youth, 15*(2), 73–86.

Achenbach, T. M., Howell, C. T., McConaughy, S. H., & Stanger, C. (1995). Six-year predictors of problems in a national sample: III. Transitions to young adult syndromes. *Journal of the American Academy of Child and Adolescent Psychiatry, 34*(5), 658–669.

Adams, G. R., Abraham, K. G., & Markstrom, C. A. (1987). The relations among identity development, self-consciousness, and self-focusing during middle and late adolescence. *Developmental Psychology, 23*, 292–297.

Adam, K. S., Bouckoms, A., & Streiner, D. (1982). Parental loss and family instability in attempted suicide. *Archives of General Psychiatry, 39*, 1081–1085.

Adams, G. R., Gullotta, T. P., & Montemayor, R. (Eds.) (1992). *Adolescent identity formation.* Newbury Park, CA: Sage.

Adcock, A. G., Nagy, S., & Simpson, J. A. (1991). Selected risk factors in adolescent suicide attempts. *Adolescence, 26*(104), 817–828.

Adlaf, E. M., Zdanowicz, Y. M., & Smart, R. G. (1996). Alcohol and other drug use among street-involved youth in Toronto. *Addiction Research, 4*(1), 11–24.

Adolescent health volume III: Crosscutting issues in the delivery of health and related services. (1991). U.S. Congress, Office of Technology Assessment, Washington, DC: U.S. Government Printing Office (OTA-H-467).

Ahmed, F. (1989). Urban-suburban differences in the incidence of low birthweights in a metropolitan black population. *Journal of the National Medical Association, 81*, 849–855.

Alan Guttmacher Institute. (1994). *Sex and America's teenagers.* Washington, DC: Author.

Alexander, C. S., Somerfield, M. R., Ensminger, M. E., Johnson, K. E., & Kim, Y. J. (1993). Consistency of adolescents' self-report of sexual behavior in a longitudinal study. *Journal of Youth and Adolescence, 22*(5), 455–471.

Alfaro, J. (1978). *Child abuse and subsequent delinquent behavior.* New York: Select Committee on Child Abuse.

Allison, P. D., & Furstenberg, F. F. (1989). How marital dissolution affects children: Variations by age and sex. *Developmental Psychology, 25*(4), 540–549.

Allaman, J., Joyce, C., & Crandall, V. (1972). The antecedents of social desirability response tendencies of children and young adults. *Child Development, 43*, 1135–1160.

Altschuler, D., & Brounstein, P. (1991). Patterns of drug use, drug trafficking and other delinquency among inner-city adolescent males in Washington, D.C. *Criminology, 29*, 589–622.

Amato, P. R. (1989). Family processes and the competence of adolescents and primary school children. *Journal of Youth and Adolescence, 18*(1), 39–53.

American Association of University Women. (1993). *Hostile hallways: The AAUW survey on sexual harassment in America's schools.*

American Humane Association. (1978). *National analysis of official child neglect and abuse report.* Denver, CO.

American Psychiatric Association. (1994). *Diagnostic and statistical manual of mental disorders, (4th Ed.).* Washington, DC: Author.

ANAD ten year study. (n.d.). Highland Park, IL: National Association of Anorexia Nervosa and Associated Disorders.

ANAD—facts about eating disorder. (n.d.). Highland Park, IL: National Association of Anorexia Nervosa and Associated Disorders.

Anderson, J. E., Freese, T. E., & Pennbridge, J. N. (1994). Sexual risk behavior and condom use among street youth in Hollywood. *Family Planning Perspectives, 26*(1), 22–25.

Angold, A., & Costello, E. J. (1993). Depressive comorbidity in children and adolescents: Empirical, theoretical, and methodological issues. *American Journal of Psychiatry, 150*(12), 1779–1791.

Angold, A., & Rutter, M. (1992). Effects of age and pubertal status on depression in a large clinical sample. *Development and Psychopathology, 4*(1), 5–28.

Applebee, A. N., Langer, J. A., & Mullis, I. V. S. (1986). *The writing report card: Writing achievement in American schools.* Princeton, NJ: National Assessment of Educational Progress. Educational Testing Service.

Archer, S. L. (1989). Gender differences in identity development: Issues of process, domain and timing. *Journal of Adolescence, 12*(2), 117–138.

Aries, E., & Moorehead, K. (1989). The importance of ethnicity in the development of identity of Black adolescents. *Psychological Reports, 65*(1), 75–82.

Armistead, L., Forehand, R., Beach, S. R., & Brody, G. H. (1995). Predicting interpersonal competence in young adulthood: The roles of family, self, and peer systems during adolescence. *Journal of Child and Family Studies, 4*(4), 445–460.

Aronson, P. J., Mortimer, J. T., Zeirman, C., & Hacker, M. (1996). Generational differences in early work experiences and evaluation. In J. T. Mortimer & Finch. *Adolescents, work, and the family* (pp. 25–62). Thousand Oaks, CA: Sage.

Arthur, R., & Erickson, E. (1992). *Gangs and schools.* Holmes Beach, FL: Learning Publications.

Asmussen, K. (1992). Weapon possession in public high schools. *School Safety, Fall*, 28–30.

August, G. J., & Garfinkel, B. D. (1989). Behavioral and cognitive subtypes of ADHD. *Journal of the American Academy of Child and Adolescent Psychiatry, 28*(5), 739–748.

Aseltine, R. H. (1995). A reconsideration of parental and peer influences on adolescent deviance. *Journal of Health and Social Behavior, 36*, 103–121.

Avakame, E. F. (1997). Modeling the patriarchal factor in juvenile delinquency: Is there room for peers, church, and television? *Criminal Justice and Behavior, 24*(4), 477–494.

Bachman, J. G. (1983). Do high school students earn too much? *Economic Outlook USA, Summer*, 64–67.

Bachman, J. G., & Schulenberg, J. (1993). How part-time work intensity relates to drug use, problem behavior, time use, and satisfaction among high school seniors: Are these consequences or merely correlates? *Developmental Psychology, 29*, 220–235.

Baldwin, A. (1968). *Theories of child development.* New York: Wiley.

Bastian, L. D., & Taylor, B. M. (1994). *Young black male victims.* Bureau of Justice Statistics Crime Data Brief. National Crime Victimization Survey, U.S. Department of Justice.

Baumrind, D. (1967). Child care practices anteceding three patterns of preschool behavior. *Genetic Psychology Monographs, 75*, 43–88.

Baumrind, D. (1975). Early socialization and adolescent competence. In S. E. Dragastin & G. Elder (Eds.), *Adolescence in the life cycle* (pp. 117–143). Washington, DC: Hemisphere.

Baumrind, D. (1978). Parental disciplinary patterns and social competence in children. *Youth and Society, 9*(3), 239–276.

Baumrind, D. (1980). New directions in socialization research. *American Psychologist, 35*, 639–652.

Baumrind, D. (1991). Effective parenting during the early adolescent transition. In P. A. Cowan & E. M. Hetherington (Eds.), *Family transitions* (pp. 111–163). Hillsdale, NJ: Erlbaum.

Bell, A. P., & Weinberg, M. S. (1978). *Homosexualities: A study of diversity among men and women.* New York: Simon & Schuster.

Benda, B. B., & Corwyn, R. F. (1996). Testing a theoretical model of adolescent sexual behavior among rural families in poverty. *Child and Adolescent Social Work Journal, 13*(6), 469–494.

Benda, B. B., & Corwyn, R. F. (1997). Religion and delinquency: The relationship after considering family and peer influences. *Journal for the Scientific Study of Religion, 36*(1), 81–92.

Benda, B. B., & DiBlasio, F. A. (1994). An integration of theory: Adolescent sexual contacts. *Journal of Youth and Adolescence, 23*(3), 403–420.

Benson, M. J., Harris, P. B., & Rogers, C. S. (1992). Identity consequences of attachment to mothers and fathers among late adolescents. *Journal of Research on Adolescence, 2*(3), 187–204.

Berman, W. H., & Sperling, M. B. (1991). Parental attachment and emotional distress in the transition to college. *Journal of Youth and Adolescence, 20*(4), 427–440.

Bernstein, J. Y. (n.d.). *Bullies and victims: More similar than they think?* (press release). Boston, MA: Brandeis University.

Billy, J. O. G., & Udry, J. R. (1985). Adolescent sexual behavior and friendship choice. *Adolescence, 20*, 21–32.

Bird, H. R., Gould, M. S., & Staghezza, B. M. (1993). Patterns of diagnostic comorbidity in a community sample of children aged 9 through 16 years. *Journal of the American Academy of Child and Adolescent Psychiatry, 32*(2), 361–368.

Bischof, G. P., Stith, S. M., & Whitney, M. L. (1995). Family environments of adolescent sex offenders and other juvenile delinquents. *Adolescence, 30*(117), 157–170.

Blatt, S. J., Hart, B., Quinlan, D. M., Leadbeater, B., & Auerbach, J. (1993). Interpersonal and self-critical dysphoria and behavioral problems in adolescents. *Journal of Youth and Adolescence*, 22(3), 253–270.

Block, R., & Block, C. R. (1993). *Street gang crime in Chicago: Research in brief*. Washington, DC: U.S. Department of Justice, National Institute of Justice.

Block, C. R., Christakos, A., Jacob, A., & Przybylski, R. (1996). *Street gangs and crime: Patterns and trends in Chicago*. Research Bulletin. Chicago, IL: Illinois Criminal Justice Information Authority.

Blos, P. (1979). *The adolescent passage*. New York: International Universities Press.

Blumstein, A., & Cork, D. (1996). Linking Gun Availability to Youth Gun Violence. *Law and Contemporary Problems*, 59(1), 5–24.

Blyth, D. A., & Traeger, C. M. (1983). The self-concept and self-esteem of early adolescents. *Theory into Practice*, 22(2), 91–97.

Bodinger-deUriarte, C. (1993). *Membership in violent gangs fed by suspicion, deterred through respect*. Los Alamitos, CA: Southwest Regional Educational Laboratory.

Bolton, F. G., Jr., Morris, L. A., & MacEachron, A. E. (1989). *Males at risk*. Newbury Park, CA: Sage.

Booth, R. E., & Zhang, Y. (1997). Conduct disorder and HIV risk behaviors among runaway and homeless adolescents. *Drug and Alcohol Dependence*, 48(2), 69–76.

Borchardt, C. M., & Bernstein, G. A. (1995). Comorbid disorders in hospitalized bipolar adolescents compared with unipolar depressed adolescents. *Child Psychiatry and Human Development*, 26(1), 11–18.

Boyer, D. (1989). Male prostitution and homosexual identity. *Journal of Homosexuality*, 17(1–2), 151–184.

Boyer, D., & Fine, D. (1992). Sexual abuse as a factor in adolescent pregnancy and child maltreatment. *Family Planning Perspectives*, 24(1), 4–11.

Boyle, K. (1992). *School's a rough place: Youth gangs, drug users, and family life in Los Angeles*. Washington, DC: Department of Education, Office of Educational Research and Improvement.

Braun, B. (1985). The transgenerational incidence of dissociation and multiple personality disorder: A preliminary report. In R. Kluft (Ed.), *Childhood antecedents of multiple personality disorder* (pp. 127–150). Washington, DC: American Psychiatric Press.

Brewster, K. L. (1994). Race differences in sexual activity among adolescent women: The role of neighborhood characteristics. *American Sociological Review*, 59, 408–424.

Brewster, K. L., Billy, J. O. G., & Grady, W. R. (1993). Social context and adolescent behavior: The impact of community on the transition to sexual activity. *Social Forces*, 71, 713–740.

Bromley, M. A. (1988). Identity as a central adjustment issue for the Southeast Asian unaccompanied refugee minor. *Child and Youth Care Quarterly*, 17(2), 104–114.

Brooks-Gunn, J., & Furstenberg, F. F. (1989). Adolescent sexual behavior. *American Psychologist*, 44(2), 249–257.

Brown, B. (1990). Peer groups. In S. Feldman & B. Elliot (Eds.), *At the threshold: The development adolescent* (pp. 171–196). Cambridge, MA: Harvard University Press.

Browne, A., & Finkelhor, D. (1986). Impact of child sexual abuse: A review of research. *Psychological Bulletin*, 99(1), 66–77.

Bryant, A. L. (1993). Hostile hallways: The AAUW survey on sexual harassment in America's schools. *Journal of School Health*, 63(Oct.), 355–357.

Buchanan, C. M., Maccoby, E. E., & Dornbusch, S. M. (1992). Adolescents and their families after divorce: Three residential arrangements compared. *Journal of Research on Adolescence*, 2(3), 261–291.

Buehler, C., & Legg, B. H. (1992). Selected aspects of parenting and children's social competence post-separation: The moderating effects of child's sex, age, and family economic hardship. *Journal of Divorce and Remarriage*, 18(3–4), 177–195.

Burgess, E. W. (1926). The family as a unity of interacting personalities. *The Family*, 7(March), 3–9.

Bybee, J., Glick, M., & Zigler, E. (1990). Differences across gender, grade level, and academic track in the content of the ideal self-image. *Sex Roles*, 22(5–6), 349–358.

Cairns, E., & Mercer, G. W. (1984). Social identity in Northern Ireland. *Human Relations*, 37(12), 1095–1102.

Callahan, C., & Rivera, F. (1992). Urban high school youth and handguns. *Journal of the American Medical Association*, 267, 3038–3042.

Camara, K. A., & Resnick, G. (1988). Interparental conflict and cooperation: Factors moderating children's post-divorce adjustment. In E. M. Hetherington & J. D. Arasteh (Eds.), *Impact of divorce, single parenting, and stepparenting on children* (pp. 169–195). Hillsdale, NJ: Erlbaum.

Campbell, T. L., Byrne, B. M., & Baron, P. (1992). Adolescent depressed mood and young adult functioning: A longitudinal study. *Journal of Early Adolescence*, 12(3), 326–338.

Cantwell, D. P., & Baker, L. (1989). Stability and natural history of DSM-III childhood diagnoses. *Journal of the American Academy of Child and Adolescent Psychiatry*, 28(5), 691–700.

Carlson, B. E. (1991). Outcomes of physical abuse and observation of marital violence among adolescents in placement. *Journal of Interpersonal Violence*, 6(4), 526–534.

Carlson, G. A., & Weintraub, S. (1993). Childhood behavior problems and bipolar disorder: Relationship or coincidence? *Journal of Affective Disorders*, 28(3), 143–153.

Carroll, J. L., Volk, K. D., & Hyde, J. S. (1985). Differences in males and females in motives for engaging in sexual intercourse. *Archives of Sexual Behavior*, 14, 131–139.

Cates, J. A. (1989). Adolescent male prostitution by choice. *Child and Adolescent Social Work Journal*, 6(2), 151–156.

Centers for Disease Control and Prevention. (1996). Youth risk behavior surveillance. *Morbidity Monthly and Weekly Report*, 45(SS-4), 1–86.

Centers for Disease Control and Prevention. (1997). *Sexually transmitted disease surveillance, 1996*. Division of STD Prevention. U.S. Department of Health and Human Services, Public Health Service.

Centers for Disease Control and Prevention. (1998a). HIV/AIDS among American Indians and Alaskan Natives-United States, 1981–1997. *Morbidity and Mortality Weekly Report*, 47(8), 154–160.

Centers for Disease Control and Prevention. (1998b). Teenage births in the United States: State trends, 1991–96, an update. National Center for Health Statistics. *Monthly Vital Statistics Reports Summaries and Supplements*, 46, 11.

Centers for Disease Control and Prevention. (1998c, June). Trends: HIV infections increasing among women and minorities. *CDC HIV/AIDS Prevention Newsletter*, Public Health Service.

Centers for Disease Control and Prevention. (1998d, June). Work group meets on African-American initiative for HIV prevention. *CDC HIV/AIDS Prevention Newsletter*, Public Health Service.

Chandler, K. A., Chapman, C. D., Rand, M. R., & Taylor, B. M. (1998). *Students' reports of school crime: 1989 and 1995*. U.S. Departments of Education and Justice. NCES 98-241/NCJ-169607. Washington, DC.

Chandy, J. M., Blum, R. W., & Resnick, M. D. (1996). Gender-specific outcomes for sexually abused adolescents. *Child Abuse and Neglect*, 20(12), 121–123.

Chandy, J. M., Blum, R. W., & Resnick, M. D. (1997). Sexually abused male adolescents: How vulnerable are they? *Journal of Child Sexual Abuse*, 6(2), 1–16.

Children's Defense Fund. (1995). *State of America's children yearbook*. Washington, DC: Author.

Clausen, J. A. (1991). Adolescent competence and the life course, or why one social psychologist needed a concept of personality. *Social Psychology Quarterly, 54*(1), 4–14.

Colby, I. C. (1990). The throw-away teen. *The Journal of Applied Social Science, 14*(2), 277–294.

Coles, R. (1967). Children of crisis: A study of courage and fear. Boston: Little, Brown.

Collins, J. G., & LeClere, F. B. (1996). *Health and selected socioeconomic characteristics of the family: United States 1988–90.* National Center for Health Statistics. Washington, DC: U.S. Government Printing Office.

Collins, W. A., & Luebker, C. (1994). Parent and adolescent expectancies: Individual and relational significance. In J. G. Smetana (Ed.), *Beliefs about parenting: Origins and developmental implications* (pp. 65–80). San Francisco: Jossey-Bass.

Colten, E., Gore, S., & Asetine, R. H. (1991). The patterning of distress and disorder in a community sample of high school aged youth. In M. E. Colten & S. Gore (Eds.), *Adolescent stress causes and consequences* (pp. 157–180). New York: Aldine de Gruyter.

Conger, R. (1984). Family profiles of serious juvenile offenders. Paper presented at the second national conference for family violence researchers, Durham, NH.

Conger, J. J. (1991). *Adolescence and youth.* New York: HarperCollins.

Cooley, C. H. (1956). *Human nature and the social order.* Glencoe, Ill: Free Press. (Original work published in 1902)

Coons, P. (1985). Children of parents with multiple personality disorder. In R. Kluft (Ed.), *Childhood antecedents of multiple personality* (pp. 151–166). Washington, DC: American Psychiatric Press.

Cooper, C. R., Grotevant, H. D., & Condon, S. M. (1983). Individuality and connectedness in the family as a context for adolescent identity formation and role-taking skill. *New Directions for Child Development, 22*(Dec), 43–59.

Coopersmith, S. (1967). *The antecedents of self-esteem.* San Francisco: Freeman.

Corder, B. F., Ball, B. C., Haizlip, T. M., Rollins, R., & Beaumont, R. (1976). Adolescent parricide: A comparison with other adolescent murder. *American Journal of Psychiatry, 133*(Aug. 8), 957–961.

Cornell, C. P., & Gelles, R. J. (1982). Adolescent to parent violence. *The Urban Social Change Review, 15*, 8–14.

Côté, J. E. (1996). Identity: A multidimensional analysis. In G. R. Adams, R. Montemayor, & T. P. Gullotta (Eds.), *Psychosocial development during adolescence: Progress in development during adolescence* (pp. 130–180). Thousand Oaks, CA: Sage.

Craighead, W. E. (1991). Cognitive factors and classification issues in adolescent depression. *Journal of Youth and Adolescence, 20*, 311–315.

Cromwell, P., Taylor, D., & Palacios, W. (1992). Youth gangs: A 1990s perspective. *Juvenile and Family Court Journal, 43*, 25–31.

Current Population Reports. (1993a). *U.S. populations estimates by age, sex, race and hispanic origin: 1980 to 1991.* Washington, DC: U.S. Bureau of the Census.

Current Population Reports. (1993b). *Poverty in the United States: 1992 consumer incomes series,* P-60, *185,* Washington, DC: U.S. Bureau of the Census.

Curry, G. D. (1996). *National youth gang surveys: A review of methods and findings.* Office of Juvenile Justice and Delinquency Prevention. Washington, DC: U.S. Department of Justice.

Curry, G. D., Ball, R. A., & Decker, S. H. (1996). Estimating the national scope of gang crime from law enforcement data. In C. R. Huff (Ed.), *Gangs in America,* 2nd Ed. (pp. 21–36). Thousand Oaks, CA: Sage.

D'Amico, R. (1984). Does working in high school impair academic progress? *Sociology of Education, 57*, 157–164.

D'Augelli, A. R., Collins, C., & Hart, M. M. (1987). Social support patterns of lesbian women in a rural helping network. *Journal of Rural Community Psychology, 8*, 12–22.

Davis, T. C., Peck, G. Q., & Storment, J. M. (1993). Acquaintance rape and the high school student. *Journal of Adolescent Health, 14*, 220–224.

Dawley, D. (1992). *A nation of lords: The autobiography of the Vice Lords.* Second Edition. Prospect Heights, IL: Waveland.

Decker, S. H., & Van Winkle, B. (1996). *Life in the gang: Family, friends, and violence.* New York: Cambridge University Press.

deJong, M. L. (1992). Attachment, individuation, and risk of suicide in late adolescence. *Journal of Youth and Adolescence, 21*(3), 357–373.

DeMan, A., Dolan, D., Pelletier, R., & Reid, C. (1994). Adolescent running away behavior: Active or passive avoidance? *Journal of Genetic Psychology, 155*(1), 59–64.

deMause, L. (1974). *A history of childhood.* New York: Psycho-History Press.

Dembe, R., Williams, L., & Schmeidles, J. (1992). A structural model examining the relationship between physical child abuse, sexual victimization, and marijuana/hashish use in delinquent youth. *Violence and Victims, 7*(1), 41–62.

Dempsey, C. (1994). Health and social issues of gay, lesbian, and bisexual adolescents. *Families in Societies, 75*(3), 160–167.

Dias, P. J., & O'Mara, N. (1998). Norplant failure: An adolescent case study and review of the literature. *Journal of Pediatric and Adolescent Gynecology, 11*, 33–37.

DiBlasio, F. A., & Benda, B. B. (1992). Gender differences in theories of adolescent sexual activity. *Sex Roles, 27*(5–6), 221–239.

DiBlasio, F. A., & Benda, B. B. (1993). A conceptual model of sexually active peer association. *Youth and Society, 25*(3), 351–367.

Donovan, J. E., & Jessor, R. (1985). Structure of problem behavior in adolescence and young adulthood. *Journal of Consulting and Clinical Psychology, 53*, 890–904.

Douvan, E. A., & Adelson, J. (1966). *The adolescent experience.* New York: Wiley.

Donahue, R. J., & Tuber, S. B. (1995). The impact of homelessness on children's level of aspiration. *Bulletin of the Menninger Clinic, 59*(2), 249–255.

Dryfoos, J. G. (1990). *Adolescents at risk: Prevalence and prevention.* New York: Oxford University Press.

Dyk, P. A., & Adams, G. R. (1987). The association between identity development and intimacy during adolescence. *Journal of Research in Science Tracking, 29*, 441–451.

Dyk, P. H., & Adams, G. R. (1989). The association between identity development and intimacy during adolescence: A theoretical treatise. *Journal of Adolescent Research, 2*(3), 223–235.

Dyk, P. H., & Adams, G. R. (1990). Identity and intimacy: An initial investigation of three theoretical models using cross-lag panel correlations. *Journal of Youth and Adolescence, 19*(2), 91–110.

Dutton, D. G., & Yamini, S. (1995). Adolescent parricide: An integration of social cognitive theory and clinical views of projective-introjective cycling. *American Journal of Orthopsychiatry, 65*(1), 39–47.

Duvall, E. M. (1957). *Family development.* Philadelphia: Lippincott.

Elder, G. H. (1972). *Children of the great depression.* Chicago: University of Chicago Press.

Elkind, D. (1967). Egocentrism in adolescence. *Child Development, 38*(4), 1025–1034.

Ellwood, M. S., & Stolberg, A. L. (1993). The effects of family composition, family health, parenting behavior and environmental stress on children's divorce adjustment. *Journal of Child and Family Studies, 2*(1), 23–36.

Elmer, E. S., Evans, S., & Reinhard (1977). *Fragile families, troubled children.* Pittsburgh, PA: Pittsburgh University Press.

Elster, A. B., & Hendricks, L. (1986). Stress and coping strategies of adolescent fathers. In A. B. Elster & M. E. Lamb (Eds.), *Adolescent fatherhood* (pp. 55–65). Hillsdale, NJ: Erlbaum.

Eme, R. F., & Kavanaugh, L. (1995). Sex differences in conduct disorder. *Journal of Clinical Child Psychology, 24*(4), 406–426.

Emery, R. (1982). Parental conflict and the children of discord and divorce. *Psychological Bulletin, 92,* 310–330.

Ennew, J. (1986). *The sexual exploitation of children.* New York: St. Martin's.

Erikson, E. H. (1956). The problem of ego identity. *Journal of the American Psychoanalytic Association, 4,* 56–121.

Erikson, E. H. (1963). *Childhood and society.* New York: Norton.

Erikson, E. H. (1968). *Identity, youth, and crisis.* New York: Norton.

Everstine, D. S., & Everstine, L. (1989). *Sexual trauma in children and adolescents: Dynamics and treatment.* New York: Brunner/Mazel.

Ernst, C., & Angst, J. (1983). *Birth order: Its influence on personality.* New York: Springer-Verlag.

Eskilson, A., & Wiley, M. G. (1987). Parents, peers, perceived pressure, and adolescent self-concept: Is a daughter a daughter all of her life. *Sociological Quarterly, 28*(1), 135–145.

Espleage, D., Bosworth, M. A., Karageorge, K., & Daytner, G. (1996, August). Family environments and bullying behaviors: Interrelationships and treatment implications. Paper presented at the annual meeting of the American Psychological Association, Toronto, Canada.

Fagan, J., & Wexler, S. (1987). Family origins of violent delinquents. *Criminology, 25*(3), 643–669.

Farber, E. D., Kinast, C., McCord, W. D., & Falkner, D. (1984). Violence in families of adolescent runaways. *Child Abuse and Neglect, 8*(3), 295–299.

Farrington, D. P., Lambert, S., & West, D. J. (1998). Criminal careers of two generations of family members in the Cambridge study in delinquent development. *Studies on Crime and Crime Prevention, 7*(1), 85–106.

Farrington, D. P., & West, D. J. (1993). Criminal, penal and life histories of chronic offenders: Risk and protective factors and early identification. *Criminal Behaviour and Mental Health, 3*(4), 492–523.

Feitel, B., Margetson, N., Chamas, J., & Lipman, C. (1992). Psychosocial background and behavioral and emotional disorders of homeless and runaway youth. *Hospital and Community Psychiatry, 43*(2), 155–159.

Feldman, S. S., & Rosenthal, D. D. (1991). Age expectations of behavioural autonomy in Hong Kong, Australian and American youth: The influence of family variables and adolescents' values. *International Journal of Psychology, 26*(1), 1–23.

Finch, M. D., & Mortimer, J. T. (1985). Adolescent work hours and the process of achievement. In A. C. Kerchoff (Ed.), *Research in sociology of education and socialization* (Vol. 5, pp. 171–196). Greenwich, CT: JAI Press.

Fingerhut, L. A., & Kleinmen, J. C. (1990). International and interstate comparisons of homicide among young males. *Journal of American Medical Association, 263,* 3292–3295.

Finkelhor, D. (1979). *Sexually victimized children.* New York: Free Press.

Finkelhor, D. (1984). *Child sexual abuse: New theory and research.* New York: Free Press.

Finkelhor, D. (1986). Prevention: A review of programs and research. In D. Finkelhor & Associates (Eds.), *A sourcebook on child sexual abuse* (pp. 224–254). Beverly Hills, CA: Sage.

Finn, J. D. (1989). Withdrawing from school. *Review of Educational Research, 59*(2), 117–142.

Fitch, S. A., & Adams, G. R. (1983). Ego identity and intimacy status: Replication and extension. *Developmental Psychology, 19*(6), 839–845.

Flanagan, C., Schulenberg, J., & Fuligni, A. (1992). Residential setting and parent-adolescent relationships during the college years. *Journal of Youth and Adolescence, 22*(2), 171–189.

Flannery, D. J., Vazsonyi, A. T., Torquati, J., & Fridrich, A. (1994). Ethnic and gender differences in risk for early adolescent substance use. *Journal of Youth and Adolescence, 23*(2), 195–213.

Fontaine, J. R. (1998). Evidencing a need: School counselors' experiences with gay and lesbian students. *Professional School Counseling, 1*(3), 8–14.

Forest, J., & Singh, S. (1990). The sexual and reproductive behavior of American women, 1982–1988. *Family Planning Perspectives, 22,* 206–214.

Fors, S. W., & Rojek, D. G. (1991). A comparison of drug involvement between runaways and school youths. *Journal of Drug Education, 21*(1), 13–25.

Frank, S. J., Pirsch, L. A., & Wright, V. C. (1990). Adolescents' perceptions of their relationships with their parents: Relationships among deidealization, autonomy, relatedness, and insecurity and implications for adolescent adjustment and ego identity status. *Journal of Youth and Adolescence, 19*(6), 571–588.

Freedman, R. J., (1984). Reflections on beauty as it relates to health in adolescent females. *Women and Health, 9*(2–3), 29–45.

Freud, S. (1933). *New introductory lectures on psychoanalysis.* London: Hogarth.

Freud, S. (1953). *A general introduction of psychoanalysis.* New York: Permabooks.

Freud, A. (1958). Adolescence. *Psychoanalytic Study of the Child, 13,* 255–278.

Frost, W. J. (1973). *The Quaker family in colonial America.* New York: St. Martin's.

Furnham, A., & Kirris, R. (1983). Self-image disparity, ethnic identity and sex-role stereotypes in British and Cypriot adolescents. *Journal of Adolescence, 6*(3), 275–292.

Furstenberg, F. F., Lincoln, R., & Menken, J. (Eds.). (1981). *Teenage sexuality, pregnancy and childbearing.* Philadelphia: University of Pennsylvania Press.

Furstenberg, F. F. (1991). As the pendulum swings: Teenage childbearing and social concerns. *Family Relations, 40,* 27–138.

Gagnon, J. H. (1990). The explicit and implicit use of the scripting perspective in sex research. *Annual Review of Sex Research, 1,* 1–43.

Gagnon, J. H., & Simon, W. (1973). *Sexual conduct: The social sources of human sexuality.* Chicago: Aldine.

Garsarelli, P., Everhart, B., & Lester, D. (1993). Self-concept and academic performance in gifted and academically weak students. *Adolescence, 28*(109), 235–242.

Gary, F., Moorhead, J., & Warren, J. (1996). Characteristics of troubled youths in a shelter. *Archives of Psychiatric Nursing, 10*(1), 38–41.

Gayle, H., Rogers, M., Manoff, S., & Starcher, E. (1988, June). Demographic and sexual transmission differences between adolescents and adult AIDS patients. Paper presented at the IV International Conference on AIDS, Stockholm, Sweden.

Gecas, V., & Franks, D. D. (1992). *Social perspectives on emotion, Vol. 1.* Greenwich, CT: JAI Press.

Gecas, V., & Seff, M. A. (1990). Families and adolescents: A review of the 1980s. *Journal of Marriage and the Family, 52*(4), 941–958.

Gecas, V., & Schwalbe, M. L. (1986). Parental behavior and adolescent self-esteem. *Journal of Marriage and the Family, 48,* 37–46.

Gelles, R. J., & Straus, M. A. (1988). *Intimate violence.* New York: Simon & Schuster.

George, C., & Main, M. (1979). Social interactions of young abused children: Approach, avoidance and aggression. *Child Development, 50,* 306–318.

Geronimus, A. T. (1986). The effects of race, residence, and prenatal care on the relationship of maternal age to neonatal mortality. *American Journal of Public Health, 76,* 1416–1421.

Geronimus, A. T. (1996). Black/white difference in the relationship of maternal age to birthweight: A population-based test of the weathering hypothesis. *Social Science and Medicine, 42*(4), 589–597.

Geronimus, A. T. (1997, July). Race, socioeconomic group, and weathering. Paper presented at the joint meeting of the Public Health Conference on Records and Statistics, Washington, DC.

Gibson, P. (1989). Gay male and lesbian youth suicide. *Report of the secretary's task force report on youth suicide, Vol. 3.* (pp. 110–142). DHHS Pub. No. (ADM) 89-1622. ADAMHA. Washington, DC: Department of Health and Human Services.

Gil, D. (1970). *Violence against children: Physical child abuse in the United States.* Cambridge, MA: Harvard University Press.

Gilbert, E., & DeBlassie, R. (1984). Anorexia nervosa: Adolescent starvation by choice. *Adolescence, 19,* 839–846.

Gilligan, C. (1982). *In a different voice: Psychological theory and women's development.* Cambridge, MA: Harvard University Press.

Gittelman, R., Mannuzza, S., Shenker, R., & Bonagura, N. (1985). Hyperactive boys almost grown up: I. Psychiatric status. *Archives of General Psychiatry, 42*(10), 937–947.

Goldscheider, F. K., & Goldscheider, C. (1989). Family structure and conflicts: Nest-leaving expectations of young adults and their parents. *Journal of Marriage and the Family, 51,* 87–97.

Gordon, D. E. (1990). Formal operational thinking: The role of cognitive developmental processes in adolescent decision-making about pregnancy and contraception. *American Journal of Orthopsychiatry, 60*(3), 436–456.

Gray, D. (1973). Turning-out: A study of teenage prostitution. *Urban Life and Culture, 1*(4), 401–425.

Grayston, A. D., & DeLuca, R. V. (1995). Group therapy for boys who have experienced sexual abuse: Is it the treatment of choice? *Journal of Child and Adolescent Group Therapy, 5,* 57–82.

Greenberger, E., & Steinberg, L. D. (1986). *When teenagers work: The psychological and social costs of adolescent employment.* New York: Basic Books.

Grotevant, H. D., & Cooper, C. R. (1985). Patterns of interaction in family relationships and the development of identity exploration in adolescence. *Child Development, 56,* 415–428.

Grotevant, H. D., & Cooper, C. R. (1986). Individuation in family relationships: A perspective on individual differences in the development of identity and role-taking skill in adolescence. *Human Development, 29*(2), 82–100.

Gutierres, S. E., & Reich, J. W. (1981). A developmental perspective on runaway behavior: Its relationship to child abuse. *Child Welfare, 60*(2), 89–94.

Hall, S. (1904). *Adolescence: Its psychology and its relations to physiology, anthropology, sociology, sex, crime, religion and education, Vol. 1.* Englewood Cliffs, NJ: Prentice-Hall.

Hamburg, D. (1986). *Preparing for life: The critical transitions of adolescence.* New York: Carnegie Corporation of New York.

Handelsman, C. D., Cabral, R. J., & Weisfeld, G. E. (1987). Sources of information and adolescent sexual knowledge and behavior. *Journal of Adolescent Research, 2,* 455–463.

Hanson, S. L., Myers, D. E., & Ginsburg, A. L. (1987). The role of responsibility and knowledge in reducing teenage out-of-wedlock childbearing. *Journal of Marriage and the Family, 49*(2), 241–256.

Harrington, R., Fudge, H., Rutter, M., & Pickles, A. (1991). Adult outcomes of childhood and adolescent depression: II. Links with antisocial disorders. *Journal of the American Academy of Child and Adolescent Psychiatry, 39*(3), 434–439.

Harrington, R., Bredenkamp, D., Groothues, C., & Rutter, M. (1994). Adult outcomes of childhood and adolescent depression: III. Links with suicidal behaviours. *Journal of Child Psychology and Psychiatry and Allied Disciplines, 35*(7), 1309–1319.

Harris, L., & Associates. (1986). *American teens speak: Sex myths, TV and birth control: The Planned Parenthood poll.* New York: Planned Parenthood Federation of America.

Harris, L. H. (1983). Role of trauma in the lives of high school dropouts. *Social Work in Education, 5*(2), 77–88.

Harter, S. (1990). Self and identity development. In S. S. Feldman & G. R. Elliot (Eds.), *At the threshold: The developing adolescent* (pp. 352–387). Cambridge, MA: Harvard University Press.

Haugaard, J. J., & Reppucci, N. D. (1988). *The sexual abuse of children: A comprehensive guide to current knowledge and intervention strategies.* San Francisco: Jossey-Bass.

Hauser, S. R., Powers, S. I., Noam, G. G., & Bowlds, M. K. (1987). Family interiors or adolescent ego development trajectories. *Family Perspective, 21*(4), 263–282.

Hauser, S. R., Powers, S. I., Noam, G. G., & Jacobson, A. M. (1984). Familial contexts of adolescent ego development. *Child Development, 55,* 195–213.

Havey, J. M., & Dodd, D. K. (1992). Environmental and personality differences between children of alcoholics and their peers. *Journal of Drug Education, 22*(3), 215–222.

Hawkins, J. D. (1995). Controlling crime before it happens: Risk-focused prevention. *National Institute of Justice Journal, 229*(August), 10–18.

Hechtman, L. (1991). Resilience and vulnerability in long term outcome of attention deficit hyperactive disorder. *Canadian Journal of Psychiatry, 36*(6), 415–421.

Heide, K. M. (1994). Evidence of child maltreatment among adolescent parricide offenders. *International Journal of Offender Therapy and Comparative Criminology, 38*(2), 151–162.

Heide, K. M. (1995). *Why kids kill parents: Child abuse and adolescent homicide.* Thousand Oaks, CA: Sage.

Heillig, R. J. (1983). *Adolescent suicidal behavior: A family systems model.* Ann Arbor, MI: UMI Research Press.

Hein, K. (1989). AIDS in adolescence: Exploring the challenge. *Journal of Adolescence Health Care, 10*(3), 10–35.

Heineken, E., & Windemuth, D. (1988). The relevance of homo- and hetero-national reference groups on the development of German and Turkish pupils' ego identity in an integrated class: A case study. *Psychologie in Erziehung und Unterricht, 35*(4), 289–298.

Henggeler, S. W. (1989). *Delinquency in adolescence.* Newbury Park: Sage.

Herold, E. S., & Marshall, S. K. (1996). Adolescent sexual development. In G. R. Adams & R. Montemayor (Eds.), *Psychosocial development during adolescence* (pp. 62–94). Thousand Oaks, CA: Sage.

Hersch, P. (1988). Coming of age on city streets. *Psychology Today, 22,* 28–37.

Hershberger, S. L., Pilkington, N. W., & D'Augelli, A. R. (1997). Predictors of suicide attempts among gay, lesbian, and bisexual youth. *Journal of Adolescent Research, 12*(4), 477–497.

Hetherington, E. M., & Arasteh, J. D. (Eds.). (1988). *Impact of divorce, single parenting, and stepparenting on children.* Hillsdale, NJ: Erlbaum.

Hetherington, E. M., Cox, M., & Cox, R. (1985). Long-term effects of divorce and remarriage on the adjustment of children. *Journal of the American Academy of Child and Adolescent Psychiatry, 24*(5), 518–530.

Hill, J. P., & Holmbeck, G. N. (1986). Attachment and autonomy during adolescence. In G. Whitehurst (Ed.). *Annals of Child Development—Vol. 3* (pp. 145–189). Greenwich, CT: JAI Press.

Hill, R., & Rodgers, R. (1964). Toward a theory of family development. *Journal of Marriage and the Family, 26*(August), 262–270.

Hodgskinson, V. A., Weitzman, M. S., & Kirsch, A. D. (1992). *Giving and volunteering among American teenagers 12–17 years of age in the United States.* Gallup Survey. Washington, DC: Independent Sector.

Hodgskinson, V. A., Weitzman, M. S., Crutchfield, E. A., Heffron, A. J., & Kirsch, A. D. (1996). *Giving and volunteering in the United States.* Gallup Survey. Washington, DC: Independent Sector.

Hoffert, S. L., & Hayes, C. D. (Eds.) (1987). *Risking the future: Adolescent sexuality pregnancy and childbearing—Vol. 2.* Washington, DC: National Academy Press.

Hoffman, M. L. (1980). Moral development in adolescence. In J. Adelson (Ed.), *Handbook of adolescent psychology* (pp. 295–343). New York: Wiley.

Hofman, J. E., & Shahin, E. (1989). Arab communal identity in Israel and Lebanon. *Journal of Social Psychology, 129*(1), 27–35.

Hogan, D. P., & Kitagawa, E. M. (1985). The impact of social status, family structure, and neighborhood on the fertility of black adolescents. *American Journal of Sociology, 90,* 825–855.

Hollmann, F. W. (1993). U.S. populations estimates by age, sex, race and hispanic origin: 1900 to 1992. *Current Population Reports,* pp. 25–1095. Washington, DC: U.S. Bureau of the Census.

Holmbeck, G. N., Crossman, R. E., Wandrei, M. L., & Gasiewski, E. (1994). Cognitive development, egocentrism, self-esteem, and adolescent contraceptive knowledge, attitudes, and behavior. *Journal of Adolescence, 23*(2), 169–193.

Hornstein, N. L. (1993). Recognition and differential diagnosis of dissociative disorders in children and adolescents. *Dissociation, 6*(2–3), 136–144.

Horowitz, S. V., Springer, C. M., & Kose, G. (1988). Stress in hotel children: The effects of homelessness on attitudes towards school. *Children's Environments Quarterly, 5*(1), 34–36.

Horowitz, S. V., & White, H. R. (1987). Gender role orientations and styles of pathology among adolescents. *Journal of Health and Social Behavior, 28,* 259–271.

Hotaling, G. T., Straus, M. A., & Lincoln, A. J. (1989). Violence in the family and violence and other crimes outside the family. In M. Tonry & L. Ohlin, *Crime and justice: An annual review of research* (pp. 315–375). Chicago: University of Chicago Press.

Howell, J. C. (1998). *Youth gang drug trafficking and homicide: Policy and program implications.* Report prepared for the Office of Juvenile Justice and Delinquency Prevention (OJJDP), National Youth Gang Center, Institute for Intergovernmental Research.

Huff, C. R. (Ed.) (1990). *Gangs in America.* Newbury Park, CA: Sage.

Hussey, D. L., & Singer, M. (1993). Psychological distress, problem behaviors, and family functioning of sexually abused adolescent inpatients. *Journal of the American Academy of Child and Adolescent Psychiatry, 32*(5), 954–961.

Hutson, H. R., Anglin, D., Kyriacou, N., Hart, J., & Spears, K. (1995). The epidemic of gang-related homicides in Los Angeles County from 1979 through 1994. *The Journal of the American Medical Association, 274,* 1031–1036.

Irwin, C., & Millstein, S. (1986). Biopsychosocial correlates of risk-taking in adolescence. *Journal of Adolescent Health Care, 7*(supplement), 82–96.

Iverson, T. J., & Segal, M. (1990). *Child abuse and neglect: An information and reference guide.* New York: Garland.

Jackson, L. A., Hodge, C. N., & Ingram, J. M. (1994). Gender and self-concept: A reexamination of stereotypic differences and the role of gender attitudes. *Sex-Roles, 30*(9–10), 615–630.

Janus, M. D., Archambault, F. X., Brown, S. W., & Welsh, L. A. (1995). Physical abuse in Canadian runaway adolescents. *Child Abuse and Neglect, 19*(4), 433–447.

Janus, M. D., Burgess, A. W., & McCormack, A. (1987). Histories of sexual abuse in adolescent male runaways. *Adolescence, 22*(86), 405–417.

Jessor, R., & Jessor, S. (1977). *Problem behavior and psychosocial development: A longitudinal study of youth.* New York: Academic Press.

Johnson, E. H., Jackson, L. A., Hinkle, Y., & Gilbert, D. (1994). What is the significance of black white differences in risky sexual behavior? *Journal of the National Medical Association, 86*(10), 745–759.

Johnston, L. D., O'Malley, P. M., & Bachman, J. G. (1989). Drug use, drinking, and smoking: National survey results from high school, college and young adults 1975–1988. Washington, DC: National Institute on Drug Abuse.

Johnston, L. D., Bachman, J. G., & O'Malley, P. M. (1987). *Monitoring the future.* Institute for Social Research, University of Michigan. Washington, DC: U.S. Government Printing Office.

Jones, E. F., Forrest, J. D., Goldman, N., Henshaw, S. K., Lincoln, R., Rosoff, J. L., Westoff, C. F., & Wulf, D. (1986). *Teenage pregnancy in industrialized countries.* New Haven, CT: Yale University Press.

Jorgesen, S. R. (1993). Adolescent pregnancy and parenting. In T. P. Gullotta, G. R. Adams, & T. Montemayor (Eds.), *Adolescent sexuality* (pp. 103–140). Newbury Park, CA: Sage.

Joseph, S. C. (1991). AIDS and adolescence: A challenge to both treatment and prevention. *Journal of Adolescent Health, 12*(8), 614–618.

Jurick, A. J., & Jones, W. C. (1986). Divorce and the experience of adolescents. In G. K. Leigh & G. W. Peterson (Eds.), *Adolescents in families* (pp. 308–336). Cincinnati, OH: South-Western.

Kachur, S. P., Potter, L. B., James, S. P., & Powell, K. E. (1995). Suicide in the United States, 1980–1992. *Violence Surveillance Summary, No. 1.* National Center for Injury Prevention and Control.

Kandel, D. B. (1996). The parental and peer contexts of adolescent deviance: An algebra of interpersonal influences. *Journal of Drug Issues, 26*(2), 289–315.

Kndel, D. B., Raveis, V. H., & Davies, M. (1991). Suicidal ideation in adolescence: Depression, substance use, and other risk factors. *Journal of Youth and Adolescence, 20*(2), 289–309.

Kashani, J. H., Burk, J. P., & Reid, J. C. (1985). Depressed children of depressed parents. *Canadian Journal of Psychiatry, 30*(4), 265–269.

Katsinas, S. G. (1989). Educational arrears: Addressing the underenrollment of Hispanics in Illinois higher education. *Urban Review, 21*(1), 35–50.

Keenan, K., Loeber, R., & Zhang, Q. (1995). The influence of deviant peers on the development of boys' disruptive and delinquent behavior: A temporal analysis. *Development and Psychopathology, 7,* 715–726.

Kiell, N. (1967). *The universal experience of adolescence.* Boston: Beacon Press.

Keith, J. G., Nelson, C. S., Schlabach, J. H., & Thompson, C. J. (1990). The relationship between parental employment and three measures of early adolescent responsibility: Family-related, personal, and social. *Journal of Early Adolescence, 10*(3), 399–415.

Kim, L. S., & Chun, C. (1993). Ethnic differences in psychiatric diagnosis among Asian American adolescents. *Journal of Nervous and Mental Disease, 181*(10), 612–617.

Kinder, D., & Sears, D. (1981). Prejudice and politics: Symbolic racism versus threats to a good life. *Journal of Personality and Social Psychology, 40,* 414–431.

Klein, M. W., & Maxson, C. L. (1994). Gangs and cocaine trafficking. In D. MacKenzie & C. Uchida (Eds.), *Drugs and crime: Evaluating public policy initiatives* (pp. 42–58). Thousand Oaks, CA: Sage.

Klein, M. W., Maxson, C. L., & Cunningham, L. C. (1991). Crack, street gangs, and violence. *Criminology, 29,* 23–650.

Klein, R. G., & Mannuzza, S. (1991). Long-term outcome of hyperactive children: A review. *Journal of the American Academy of Child and Adolescent Psychiatry, 30*(3), 383–387.

Klein, H. A., O'Bryant, K., & Hopkins, H. R. (1996). Recalled parental authority style and self-perception in college men and women. *Journal of Genetic Psychology, 157*(1), 5–17.

Kluft, R. (1986). Treating children who have multiple personality disorder. In B. Braun (Ed.), *Treatment of multiple personality disorder* (pp. 81–105). Washington, DC: American Psychiatric Press.

Kohlberg, L. (1969). *Stages in the Development of Moral Thought and Action.* New York: Holt, Rinehart & Winston.

Kohn, M. L. (1969). *Class and conformity: A study in values.* Chicago: University of Chicago Press.

Koop, C. (1989). Introduction in AIDS and adolescents. *Journal of Adolescent Health Care, 10*(suppl), 35.

Koopman, C., Rosario, M., Exner, T., Henderson, R., Matthiew, M., & Gruen, R. S. (1992). Lifetime sexual behaviors among runaway males and females. *Journal of Sex Research, 29*(1), 15–29.

Korem, D. (1995). *Suburban gangs: The affluent rebels.* Richardson, TX: International Focus Press.

Kosky, R., Silburn, S., & Zubrick, S. (1986). Symptomatic depression and suicidal ideation: A comparative study with 628 children. *Journal of Nervous and Mental Disorders, 174,* 523–528.

Koss, M. P., Gidycz, C. A., & Wisniewski, N. (1987). The scope of rape: Incidence and prevalence of sexual aggression and victimization in a national sample of higher education students. *Journal of Consulting and Clinical Psychology, 55,* 162–170.

Kratcoski, P. C. (1982). Child abuse and violence against the family. *Child Welfare, 61*(7), 435–444.

Kratcoski, P. C. (1985). Youth violence directed toward significant others. *Journal of Adolescence, 8*(2), 145–157.

Kratcoski, P. C., & Kratcoski, L. D. (1982). The relationship of victimization through child abuse to aggressive delinquent behavior. *Victimology, 7*(1–4), 199–203.

Kruks, G. (1991). Gay and lesbian homeless/street youth: Special issues and concerns. *Journal of Adolescent Health, 12*(7), 515–518.

Ku, L., Sonenstein, F. L., & Peck, J. H. (1993). Young men's risk for behaviors for HIV infection and sexually transmitted diseases, 1988 through 1991. *American Journal of Public Health, 83,* 1609–1615.

Kufeldt, K., & Nimmor, M. (1987). Youth on the street: Abuse and neglect in the eighties. *Journal of Child Abuse and Neglect, 11*(4), 531–543.

Kurtz, P. D., Kurtz, G. L., & Jarvis, S. V. (1991). Problems of maltreated runaway youth. *Adolescence, 26*(103), 543–555.

Lambert, N. M., Hartsough, C. S., Sassone, D., & Sandoval, J. (1987). Persistence of hyperactivity symptoms from childhood to adolescence and associated outcomes. *American Journal of Orthopsychiatry, 57*(1), 22–32.

Lamborn, S. D., Mounts, N. S., Steinberg, L., & Dornbusch, S. M. (1991). *Child Development, 62*(5), 1049–1065.

Landrine, H., Richardson, J. L., Klonoff, E. A., & Flay, B. R. (1994). Cultural diversity in the predictors of adolescent cigarette smoking: The relative influence of peers. *Journal of Behavioral Medicine, 17*(3), 331–346.

Leukefeld, C. G., & Haverkos, H. W. (1993). Adolescent sexual development. In T. P. Gullotta, G. R. Adams, & R. Montemayor (Eds.), *Adolescent sexuality* (pp. 161–180). Newbury Park, CA: Sage.

Lewis-Abney, K. (1993). Correlates of family functioning when a child has attention deficit disorder. *Issues in Comprehensive Pediatric Nursing, 16*(3), 175–190.

Lewis, C. C. (1981). The effects of firm control: A reinterpretation of findings. *Psychological Bulletin, 90,* 547–563.

Lewis, D. O., Moy, E., Jackson, L. D., Aaronson, R., Restifo, N., Serra, S., & Simos, A. (1985). Biopsychosocial characteristics of children who later murder: A prospective study. *American Journal of Psychiatry, 1142* (10), 1161–1167.

Lewinsohn, P. M., Hops, H., Roberts, R. E., & Seeley, J. R. (1993). Adolescent psycho-pathology: I. Prevalence and incidence of depression and other DSM-III-R disorders in high school students. *Journal of Abnormal Psychology, 102*(4), 133–144.

Lewinsohn, P. M., Rohde, P., & Seeley, J. R. (1994). Psychosocial risk factors for future adolescent suicide attempts. *Journal of Consulting and Clinical Psychology, 1962*(2), 297–305.

Lincoln, A., & Straus, M. (Eds.) (1985). *Crime and the family.* Springfield, IL: Charles C Thomas.

Lloyd, D. (1978). Prediction on school failure from third-grade data. *Educational Psychological Measurement, 38,* 1193–1200.

Loeber, R., & Dishion, T. J. (1984). Boys who fight at home and school: Family conditions influencing cross-setting consistency. *Journal of Consulting and Clinical Psychology, 52,* 759–768.

Littwin, S. (1986). *The postponed generation.* New York: Morrow.

Loeber, R., Green, S. M., Keenan, K., & Lahey, B. B. (1995). Which boys will fare worse? Early predictors of the onset of conduct disorder in a six-year longitudinal study. *Journal of the American Academy of Child and Adolescent Psychiatry, 34*(4), 499–509.

Lubin, B., & McCullum, K. L. (1994). Depressive mood in black and white female adolescents. *Adolescence, 29*(113), 241–245.

Luster, T., & Small, S. A. (1997). Sexual abuse history and problems in adolescence: Exploring the effects of moderating. *Journal of Marriage and the Family, 59*(1), 131–142.

Mabe, A. (1995). Tips can put breaks on bullying behavior. *Feature stories.* Medical College of Georgia, September 21.

Maccoby, E., & Martin, J. (1983). Socialization in the context of the family: Parent-child interaction. In M. E. Hetherington (Ed.), *Handbook of child psychology, Vol. 4: Socialization, personality, and social development* (pp. 1–101). New York: Wiley.

Maggs, J. L., Almeida, D. M., & Galambos, N. L. (1995). Risky business: The paradoxical meaning of problem behavior for young adolescents. *Journal of Early Adolescence, 15*(3), 44–362.

Makinson, C. (1985). The health consequences of teenage fertility. *Family Planning Perspectives, 17,* 132–139.

Maiuro, R. D., Trupin, E., & James, J. (1983). Sex-role differentiation in a female juvenile delinquent population: Prostitute vs. control samples. *American Journal of Orthopsychiatry, 53*(2), 345–352.

Manaster, G. J., Chan, J. C., Watts, C., & Wiehe, J. (1994). Gifted adolescents' attitudes toward their giftedness: A partial replication. *Gifted Child Quarterly, 38*(4), 176–178.

Mannuzza, S., Klein, R. G., Bonagura, N., & Konig, P. H. (1988). Hyperactive boys almost grown up. II. Status of subjects without a mental disorder. *Archives of General Psychiatry, 45*(1), 13–18.

Marcia, J. E. (1966). Determination and construct validation of ego identity status. *Journal of Personality and Social Psychology, 3,* 551–558.

Marcia, J. E. (1976). Identity six years after: A followup study. *Journal of Youth and Adolescence, 5,* 145–160.

Marcia, J. E. (1980). Identity in adolescence. In J. Adelson (Ed.), *Handbook of adolescent psychology* (pp. 159–187). New York: Wiley.

Marcia, J. E., Waterman, A. S., Mattesson, D. R., Archer, S. L., & Orlofsky, J. L. (1993). *Ego identity: A handbook for psychosocial research.* New York: Springer-Verlag.

Margolin, L., Blyth, D., & Carbone, D. (1988). The family as a looking glass: Interpreting family influences on adolescent self-esteem from a symbolic interaction perspective. *Journal of Early Adolescence, 8*(3), 211–224.

Markstrom-Adams, C. (1994). A consideration of intervening factors in adolescent identity formation. In G. R. Adams, T. P. Gullotta, & R. Montemayor (Eds.), *Adolescent identity formation* (pp. 173–192). Newbury Park, CA: Sage.

Marleau, J. D., & Webanck, T. (1997). Parricide and violent crimes: A Canadian study. *Adolescence, 32,* 126.

Marsh, H. W. (1991). Employment during high school: Character building or a subversion of academic goals? *Sociology of Education, 64*(3), 172–189.

Marsh, H. W. (1993). The multidimensional structure of academic self-concept: Invariance over gender and age. *American Educational Research Journal, 30*(4), 841–860.

Marshall, V. G., Longwell, L., & Goldstein, M. J. (1990). Family factors associated with aggressive symptomatology in boys with attention deficit hyperactivity disorder: A research note. *Journal of Child Psychology and Psychiatry and Allied Disciplines, 31*(4), 629–636.

Martin, H. P., & Beezley, P. (1974). Prevention and consequences of abuse. *Journal of Operational Psychiatry, 6,* 68–77.

Mathias, R. (1997, March/April). Study takes a closer look at "ecstasy" use. *NIDA Notes.* Monitoring the future, 1996. National Institute on Drug Abuse, Centers for Disease Control and Prevention, Washington, DC.

Martinez, J., Smith, R., & Farmer, M. (1988). High prevalence of genital tract papillomavirus infection in female adolescents. *Pediatrics, 82,* 604–608.

Matteson, D. R. (1993). Sex differences in identity formation: A challenge to the theory. In J. E. Marcia, D. R. Matteson, A. S. Waterman, S. A. Archer, & J. L. Orlofsky (Eds.), *Ego identity: A handbook for psychosocial research.* New York: Springer-Verlag.

Maxson, C. L. (1993). Investigating gang migration: Contextual issues for intervention. *Gang Journal, 1*(2), 1–8.

May, P. A., & Van Winkle, N. (1994). Indian adolescent suicide: The epidemiologic picture in New Mexico. *American Indian and Alaska Native Mental Health Research, 4,* 5–34.

Mboya, M. M. (1995). Gender differences in teachers' behaviors in relation to adolescents' self-concepts. *Psychological Reports, 77*(3), 831–839.

McCarthy, J., & Hardy, H. (1993). Age at first birth and birth outcomes. *Journal of Adolescence, 3,* 373–392.

McCormack, A., Burgess, A. W., & Gaccione, P. (1986). Influence of family structure and financial stability on physical and sexual abuse among a runaway population. *International Journal of Sociology of the Family, 16*(2), 51–262.

McCormack, A., Janus, M. D., & Burgess, A. W. (1986). Runaway youths and sexual victimization: Gender differences in an adolescent runaway population. *Child Abuse and Neglect, 10*(3), 387–395.

McFarland, W. P. (1998). Gay, lesbian, and bisexual student suicide. *Professional School Counseling, 1*(3), 26–29.

McLeer, S. V., Callaghan, M., Henry, R., & Wallen, J. (1994). Psychiatric disorders in sexually abused children. *Journal of the American Academy of Child and Adolescent Psychiatry, 33*(3), 313–319.

Mead, G. H. (1962). *Mind, self and society.* Chicago: University of Chicago Press, 1962. (Original work published in 1934)

Meehan, V. (1990). Dangers of teenage dieting and diet products. Testimony presented at the September 24th Congressional Hearing on "Dangers of Adolescent Dieting and Dangerous Diet Products." Washington, DC.

Mellor, S. (1989). Gender differences in identity formation as a function of self-other relationships. *Journal of Youth and Adolescence, 18*(4), 361–375.

Melton, G. (1992). The improbability of prevention of sexual abuse. In D. J. Willis, E. Holden, & M. Rosenberg (Eds.), *Prevention of child maltreatment: Developmental and ecological perspectives* (pp. 168–189). New York: Wiley.

Miller, B. C., & Simon, W. (1974). Adolescent sexual behavior: Context and change. *Social Problems, 22,* 58–75.

Miller, B. C., & Fox, G. L. (1987). Theories of heterosexual behavior. *Journal of Adolescent Research, 2,* 269–282.

Miller, B. C., McCoy, J. K., Olson, T. D., & Wallace, C. M. (1986). Parental discipline and control attempts in relation to adolescent sexual attitudes and behavior. *Journal of Marriage and the Family, 48*(3), 503–512.

Miller, B. C., & Moore, K. A. (1990). Adolescent sexual behavior, pregnancy and parenting: Research through the 1980s. *Journal of Marriage and the Family, 52,* 1025–1044.

Miller, B. C., & Olson, T. D. (1988). Sexual attitudes and behavior of high school students in relation to background and contextual factors. *Journal of Sex Research, 24,* 194–200.

Miller, W. B. (1994). Boston assaultive crime. Cited in J. C. Howell (1997), *Juvenile justice and youth violence* (p. 120). Thousand Oaks, CA: Sage.

Millstein, S., Adler, N., & Irwin, C. (1981). Conceptions of illness in young adolescents. *Pediatrics, 68,* 834–839.

Millstein, S. G. (1990). Risk factors for AIDS among adolescents. *New Directions for Child Development, 50,* 3–15.

Mitchell, B. A., Wister, A. V., & Burch, T. K. (1989). The family environment and leaving the parental home. *Journal of Marriage and the Family, 51,* 605–613.

Monane, M., Leichter, D., & Lewis, D. O. (1984). Physical abuse in psychiatrically hospitalized children and adolescents. *Journal of the American Academy of Child Psychiatry, 23*(6), 653–658.

Mones, P. (1991). *When a child kills: Abused children who kill their parents.* New York: Pocket Books.

Moore, K. A., Nord, C. W., & Peterson, J. L. (1989). Nonvoluntary sexual activity among adolescents. *Family Planning Perspectives, 211,* 1100–1114.

Moore, K. A., Simms, M. C., & Betsey, C. L. (1986). *Choice and circumstances: Racial differences in adolescent sexuality and fertility.* New Brunswick, NJ: Transaction Books.

Moore, K. A., Morrison, D. R., & Glei, D. A. (1995). Welfare and adolescent sex: The effects of family history, benefit levels, and community. *Journal of Family and Economic Issues, 16*(2–3), 207–237.

Mortimer, J. T., Finch, M. D., Ryu, S., & Shanahan, M. J. (1996). The effects of work intensity on adolescent mental health, achievement, and behavioral adjustment: New evidence from a prospective study. *Child Development, 67*(3), 1243–1261.

Mortimer, J. T., & Lorence, J. (1996). Self-concept stability and change from late adolescence to early adulthood. *Research in Community and Mental Health, 2,* 5–42.

Mortimer, J. T., & Finch, M. D. (1996). *Adolescents, work, and family: An intergenerational developmental analysis.* Thousand Oaks, CA: Sage.

Meyers, W. C., Burket, R. C., & Otto, T. A. (1993). Conduct disorder and personality disorders in hospitalized adolescents. *Journal of Clinical Psychology, 54*(1), 21–26.

Muehlenhard, C. L. (1988). Misinterpreting dating behaviors and the risk of date rape. *Journal of Social and Clinical Psychology, 6,* 20–37.

Merton, R. K. (1938). Social structure and anomie. *American Sociological Review, 3,* 672–682.

Mueher, P. (1995). Suicide and sexual orientation: A critical summary of recent research and directions for future research. *Suicide and Life-Threatening Behavior, 25*(supplement), 72–81.

Muuss, R. E. (1986). Adolescent eating disorders: Bulimia. *Adolescence, 21,* 257–267.

Muuss, R. E. (1988). *Theories of adolescence* (5th ed.). New York: Random House.

Namerow, P., & Philliker, S. (1982). The effectiveness of contraceptive programs for teenagers. *Journal of Adolescence Health Care, 2,* 189–198.

Nathanson, C. A., & Becker, M. H. (1985). The influence of client-provider relationships on teenage women's subsequent use of contraception. *American Journal of Public Health, 75,* 33–38.

National Center for Health Statistics. (1996). *Vital statistics of the United States, 1992, Vol. 1, Natality.* DHHS Publication (PHS) 96-1100. Washington, DC: Government Printing Office.

National Safety Council. (1993). *Accident Facts.* Itasca, IL: Author.

National School Safety Center. (1989). *Safe schools overview.* Malibu, CA: National School Safety Center, Pepperdine University.

Needle, R. H., Su, S. S., & Doherty, W. J. (1990). Divorce, remarriage and adolescent substance use: A prospective longitudinal study. *Journal of Marriage and the Family, 52*(1), 157–169.

Newcomer, S. J., & Udry, J. R. (1984). Mothers' influence on the sexual behavior of their teenage children. *Journal of Marriage and the Family, 46,* 477–485.

Nibert, D., Cooper, S., Ford, J., Fitch, L. K., & Robinson, J. (1989). The ability of young children to learn abuse prevention. *Response to the Victimization of Women and Children, 12*(4), 14–21.

Nolen-Hoeksema, S., & Girgus, J. S. (1994). The emergence of gender differences in depression during adolescence. *Psychological Bulletin, 115*(3), 424–443.

Nottelmann, E. D. (1987). Competence and self-esteem during transition from childhood to adolescence. *Developmental Psychology, 23*(3), 441–450.

Nottelmann, E., & Jensen, P. S. (1995). Comorbidity of disorders in children and adolescents: Developmental perspectives. *Advances in Clinical Child Psychology, 17,* 109–155.

O'Brien, K. M., & Fassinger, R. E. (1993). A causal model of the career orientation and career choice of adolescent women. *Journal of Counseling Psychology, 40*(4), 456–469.

Olson, D., Russell, C. S., & Sprenkle, D. H. (1983). Circumplex model: Theoretical update. *Family Process, 22,* 69–83.

Olweus, D. (1993). *Bullying at school: What we know and what we can do.* Oxford: Blackwell.

O'Reilly, J. P., Tokuno, K. A, & Ebata, A. T. (1986). Cultural differences between Americans of Japanese and European ancestry in parental valuing of social competence. *Journal of Comparative Family Studies, 17*(1), 87–97.

Orlofsky, J. L. (1978). Identity formations, achievement and fear of success in college men and women. *Journal of Youth and Adolescence, 7,* 49–62.

Orlofsky, J., Marcia, J., & Lesser, I. (1973). Ego identity status and the intimacy versus isolation crisis of young adulthood. *Journal of Personality and Social Psychology, 27,* 211–219.

Openshaw, D. K., & Thomas, D. L. (1986). The adolescent self and the family. In G. K. Leigh & G. W. Peterson (Eds.), *Adolescents in families* (pp. 104–129). Cincinnati, OH: South-Western.

Osborne, A. F. (1990). Resilient children: A longitudinal study of high achieving socially disadvantaged children. *Early Child Development and Care, 62,* 23–47.

Overholser, J. C., Adams, D. M., Lehnert, K. L., & Brinkman, D. C. (1995). Self-esteem deficits and suicidal tendencies among adolescents. *Journal of the American Academy of Child and Adolescent Psychiatry, 34*(7), 919–928.

Palermo, G. B. (1995). Adolescent criminal behavior: Is TV violence one of the culprits? *International Journal of Offender Therapy and Comparative Criminology, 39*(1), 11–12.

Palmer, S. (1962). *The psychology of murder.* New York: Thomas Y. Crowell.

Parish, T. S. (1991). Ratings of self and parents by youth: Are they affected by family status, gender, and birth order? *Adolescence, 26*(101), 105–112.

Paterson, J., Pryor, J., & Field, J. (1995). Adolescent attachment to parents and friends in relation to aspects of self-esteem. *Journal of Youth and Adolescence, 24*(3), 365–376.

Pennbridge, J. N., Freese, T. E., & MacKenzie, R. G. (1992). High-risk behaviors among male street youth in Hollywood, California. *AIDS Education and Prevention, 4*(3), 24–33.

Pennbridge, J. N., MacKenzie, R. G., & Swofford, A. (1991). Risk profile of homeless pregnant adolescents and youth. *Journal of Adolescent Health, 12*(7), 534–538.

Perkins, C. A. (1997, September). Age patterns of victims of serious violent crime. (NCJ-162031). Washington, DC: U.S. Department of Justice, Office of Justice Programs, Bureau of Justice Statistics.

Petersen, A. C., Sarigiani, P. A., & Kennedy, R. E. (1991). Adolescent depression: Why more girls? *Journal of Youth and Adolescence, 20*(2), 247–271.

Peterson, G. (1990). Diagnosis of childhood multiple personality. *Dissociation, 3*(1), 3–9.

Peterson, G. W. (1986). Family conceptual frameworks and adolescent development. In G. K. Leigh & G. W. Peterson (Eds.), *Adolescents in families.* Cincinnati, OH: South-Western.

Peterson, G. W., & Leigh, G. K. (1990). The family and social competence in adolescence. In T. P. Gullotta, G. R. Adams, & R. Montemayor (Eds.), *Developing social competency in adolescence: Advances in adolescent development* (pp. 97–138). Thousand Oaks, CA: Sage.

Peterson, G. W., Leigh, G K., & Day, R. (1984). Family stress theory and the impact of divorce on children. *Journal of Divorce, 7,* 1–20.

Peterson, G. W., & Rollins, B. C. (1987). Parent-child socialization. In M. B. Sussman & S. K. Steinmetz (Eds.), *Handbook of marriage and the family* (pp. 471–534). New York: Plenum.

Peterson, J. L., & Zill, N. (1986). Marital disruption, parent-child relationships, and behavior problems in children. *Journal of Marriage and the Family, 48,* 295–307.

Pfeffer, C. R. (1981). The family system of suicidal children. *American Journal of Psychotherapy, 35,* 330–341.

Phelps, L., Johnson, L. S., Jimenez, D. P., Wilczenski, F. L., Andrea, R. K., & Healy, R. W. (1993). Figure reference, body dissatisfaction, and body distortion in adolescence. *Journal of Adolescent Research, 8*(3), 297–310.

Phibbs, C. S., Bateman, D. A., & Schwartz, R. M. (1991). The neonatal costs of maternal cocaine use. *Journal of the American Medical Association, 266,* 1521–1526.

Phinney, J. S., & Chavira, V. (1995). Parental ethnic socialization and adolescent coping with problems related to ethnicity. *Journal of Research on Adolescence, 5*(1), 31–53.

Pilkington, N. W., & D'Augelli, A. R. (1995). Victimization of lesbian, gay, and bisexual youth in community settings. *Journal of Community Psychology, 23,* 34–56.

Plass, R. S., & Hotaling, G. T. (1995). The intergenerational transmission of running away: Childhood experiences of the parents of runaways. *Journal of Youth and Adolescence, 24*(3), 335–348.

Powers, J. L., Eckenrode, J., & Jaklitsch, B. (1990). Maltreatment among runaway and homeless youth. *Child Abuse and Neglect, 14*(1), 87–98.

Post, S. (1982). Adolescent parricide in abusive families. *Child Welfare, 61*(7), 445–455.

Postrado, L., & Nicholson, H. (1992). Effectiveness in delaying the initiation of sexual intercourse of girls aged 12–14. *Youth & Society, 12,* 356–378.

Prino, C. T., & Peyrot, M. (1994). The effect of child physical abuse and neglect on aggressive, withdrawn, and prosocial behavior. *Child Abuse and Neglect, 18*(10), 871–884.

Prendergast, W. E. (1993). *The merry-go-round of sexual abuse: Identifying and treating survivors.* Binghamton, NY: Haworth.

Preston, G., & Madison, M. (1984). Access disputes in the context of the family structure after separation. *Australian Journal of Sex, Marriage, and the Family, 5,* 37–45.

Proctor, C. D., & Groze, V. K. (1994). Risk factors for suicide among gay, lesbian, and bisexual youths. *Social Work, 39*(5), 504–513.

Pursley, W. L. (1991). Adolescence, chemical dependency and pathological gambling. *Journal of Adolescent Chemical Dependency, 1*(4), 25–47.

Putman, F. (1993). *Diagnosis and treatment of multiple personality disorder.* New York: Guilford.

Rauch-Elnekave, H. (1994). Teenage motherhood: Its relationship to undetected learning problems. *Adolescence, 29*(113), 91–103.

Radziszewska, B., Richardson, J. L., Dent, C. W., & Flay, B R. (1996). Parenting style and adolescent depressive symptoms, smoking, and academic achievement: Ethnic, gender, and ses differences. *Journal of Behavioral Medicine, 19*(3), 289–305.

Rech, J. F. (1994). A comparison of the mathematics attitudes of black students according to grade level, gender, and academic achievement. *Journal of Negro Education, 63*(2), 212–220.

Reimer, A. (1996). Girls need to learn the ABCs of standing up to school bullies. *The Detroit News Home Page,* February 6, 1996. http://detnews.com/menu/s.

Remafedi, G. (1987). The healthy sexual development of gay and lesbian adolescents. *SIECUS Report, 17,* 7–8.

Remafedi, G., Farrow, J. A., & Deisher, R. W. (1991). Risk factors for attempted suicide in gay and bisexual youth. *Pediatrics, 87,* 869–875.

Reppucci, N. D., & Haugaard, J. J. (1993). Problems with child sexual abuse prevention programs. In R. J. Gelles & D. R. Loseke (Eds.), *Current controversies on family violence* (pp. 306–322). Newbury Park, CA: Sage.

Resnick, G., & Burt, M. (1996). Youth at risk: Definitions and implications for service delivery. *American Journal of Orthopsychiatry, 66*(2), 172–188.

Rey, J. M. (1995). Perceptions of poor maternal care are associated with adolescent depression. *Journal of Affective Disorders, 34*(2), 95–100.

Rey, J. M., Singh, M., Andrews, G., & Andrews, G. (1995). Continuities between psychiatric disorders in adolescents and personality disorders in young adults. *American Journal of Psychiatry, 152*(6), 895–900.

Reinherz, H. Z., Frost, A. K., Stewart-Berghaver, G., Kennedy, K., & Schille, C. (1990). The many faces of correlates of depressive symptoms in adolescents. *Journal of Early Adolescents, 10,* 455–471.

Richman, C. L., Clark, M. L., & Brown, K. P. (1985). General and specific self-esteem in late adolescent students: Race * gender * ses effects. *Adolescence, 20*(79), 555–566.

Rickel, A. U., & Hendren, M. C. (1993). Aberrant sexual experiences in adolescence. In T. P. Gullotta, G. R. Adams, & R. Montemayor (Eds.), *Adolescent sexuality* (pp. 141–160). Newbury Park, CA: Sage.

Roberts, L., Sariginani, P. A., Petersen, A. C., & Newman, J. L. (1990). Gender differences in the relationship between achievement and self-image during early adolescence. *Journal of Early Adolescence, 10*(2), 159–175.

Robins, L. N., & Przybeck, T. R. (1985). Age of onset of drug use as a factor in drug and other disorders. *National Institute on Drug Abuse: Research Monograph Series, 56,* 178–192. Washington, DC: National Institute on Drug Abuse.

Robinson-Awana, P., Kehle, T. J., & Jenson, W. R. (1986). But what about smart girls? Adolescent self-esteem and sex role perceptions as a function of academic achievement. *Journal of Educational Psychology, 78*(3), 179–183.

Rodgers, J. L., Billy, J. O. G., & Udry, J. R. (1982). The rescission of behaviors: Inconsistent responses in adolescent sexuality data. *Social Science Research, 11,* 280–296.

Rogosch, F. A., & Cicchetti, D. (1994). Illustrating the interface of family and peer relations through the study of child maltreatment. *Social Development, 3*(3), 291–308.

Rollins, B. C., & Thomas, D. L. (1979). Parental support, power, and control techniques in the socialization of children. In W. R. Burr, R. Hill, F. I. Nye, & I. R. Reiss (Eds.), *Contemporary theories about the family: Vol. 1* (pp. 317–364). New York: Free Press.

Romano, E., & De Luca, R. V. (1997). Exploring the relationship between childhood sexual abuse and adult sexual perpetration. *Journal of Family Violence, 12*(1), 85–98.

Romans, S., Martin, J., & Mullen, P. (1997). Childhood sexual abuse and later psychological problems: Neither necessary, sufficient nor acting alone. *Criminal Behaviour and Mental Health, 7*(4), 327–338.

Rosenberg, M., Schooler, C., & Schoenbach, C. (1989). Self-esteem and adolescent problems: Modeling reciprocal effects. *American Sociological Review, 54*(6), 1004–1018.

Rotheram-Borus, M. J. (1993). Suicidal behavior and risk factors among runaway youths. *American Journal of Psychiatry, 150*(1), 103–107.

Rotheram-Borus, M. J., Hunter, J., & Rosario, M. (1994). Suicidal behavior and gay-related stress among gay and bisexual male adolescents. *Journal of Adolescent Research, 9*(4), 498–508.

Rotheram-Borus, M. J., Mahler, K. A., Koopman, C., & Langabeerm, K. (1996). Sexual abuse history and associated multiple risk behavior in adolescent runaways. *American Journal of Orthopsychiatry, 66*(3), 390–400.

Rotheram-Borus, M. J., Meyer-Bahlburg, H. F., & Rosario, M. (1992). Lifetime sexual behaviors among predominantly minority male runaways and gay/bisexual adolescents in New York City. *AIDS Education and Prevention,* Fall Supplement, 34–42.

Ruggerio, M., Greenberger, E., & Steinberg, L. (1982). Occupational deviance among first-time workers. *Youth and Society, 13,* 423–448.

Runyan, C., & Gerken, F. (1989). Epidemiology and prevention of adolescent injury. *Journal of the American Medical Association, 262,* 2273–2279.

Russell, D. E. H. (1982). *Rape in marriage.* New York: Macmillan.

Rutter, M. (Ed.) (1995). *Psychosocial disturbances in young people: Challenges for prevention.* New York: Cambridge University Press.

Sadoff, R. L. (1971). Clinical observations on parricide. *Psychiatric Quarterly, 45,* 65–69.

Sanchez-Jankowski, M. S. (1991). *Islands in the street: Gangs and American urban society.* Berkeley: University of California Press.

Sanders, W. (1994). *Gangbangs and drive-bys: Grounded culture and juvenile gang violence.* New York: Aldin de Gruyter.

Sanders, G. F., & Mullis, R. L. (1988). Family influences on sexual attitudes and knowledge as reported by college students. *Adolescence, 23*(92), 837–846.

Savin-Williams, R. C. (1990). *Gay and lesbian youth: Expressions of identity.* Washington, DC: Hemisphere.

Savin-Williams, R. C., & Rodriguez, R. G. (1993). A developmental, clinical perspective on lesbian, gay male, and bisexual youths. In R. Montemajor, G. R. Adams, & T. P. Gullotta (Eds.), *Adolescent sexuality* (pp. 77–101). Newbury Park, CA: Sage.

Savin-Williams, R., & Cohen, K. M. (1994). Verbal and physical abuse as stressors in the lives of lesbian, gay male, and bisexual youths. *Journal of Consulting and Clinical Psychology, 62*(2), 261–269.

Shaffer, D., Fisher, R., Hicks, R. H., Parides, M., & Gould, M. (1995). Sexual orientation in adolescents who commit suicide. *Suicide and Life-Threatening Behavior, 25,* 64–71.

Schaffner, L. (1995, August). Runaway teenagers and emotional capital: A new look at rebellion and bad attitude. Paper presented at the annual meeting of the American Sociological Association, Washington, DC.

Schiff, M. M., & Cavaiola, A. A. (1990). Teenage chemical dependence and the prevalence of psychiatric disorders: Issues for prevention. *Journal of Adolescent Chemical Dependency, 1*(2), 35–46.

Schonpflug, U., & Jansen, X. (1995). Self-concept and coping with developmental demands in German and Polish adolescents. *International Journal of Behavioral Development, 18*(3), 385–405.

Sears, J. T. (1991). Educators, homosexuality, and homosexual students: Are personal feelings related to professional beliefs? *Journal of Homosexuality, 22*(2–3), 29–79.

Sells, C. W., & Blum, R. W. (1996). Morbidity and mortality among U.S. adolescents: An overview of data and trends. *American Journal of Public Health, 86*(4), 513–519.

Shanahan, M. J., Fince, M. D., Mortimer, J. T., & Ryu, S. (1991). Adolescent work experience and depressive affect. *Social Psychology Quarterly, 54*(4), 299–317.

Shapira, F., & Ariella, N. (1979). Giving in the kibbutz: Pro-social behavior of city and kibbutz children as affected by social responsibility and social pressure. *Journal of Cross Cultural Psychology, 10*(1), 57–72.

Sherman, A. (1994). *Wasting America's future: Children's Defense Fund report on the costs of child poverty.* Boston: Beacon Press.

Sheley, J., & Wright, J. (1993). *Gun acquisition and possession in selected juvenile samples.* National Institute of Justice, Research in Brief (December). Washington, DC: U.S. Department of Justice.

Shirar, L. (1996). *Dissociative children bridging the inner and outer world.* New York: Norton.

Sigelman, L., & Welch, S. (1993). The contact hypothesis revisited: Black-white interaction and positive racial attitudes. *Social Forces, 71,* 781–795.

Silverberg, L. B., & Gondoli, D. M. (1996). Autonomy in adolescence: A contextualized perspective. In G. R. Adams, R. Montemayor, & T. P. Gullota (Eds.), *Psychosocial development during adolescence: Progress in development during adolescence* (pp. 12–61). Thousand Oaks, CA: Sage.

Simmons, R. G., Brown, L., Bush, D. M., & Blyth, D. A. (1978). Self-esteem and achievement of black and white adolescents. *Social Problems, 26*(1), 86–96.

Simonds, J. F., McMahon, T., & Armstrong, D. (1991). Young suicide attempters compared with a control group: Psychological, affective, and attitudinal variables. *Suicide and Life Threatening Behavior, 21*(2), 134–151.

Simons, R. L., & Whitbeck, L. B. (1991a). Sexual abuse as a precursor to prostitution and victimization among adolescent and adult homeless women. *Journal of Family Issues, 12*(3), 361–379.

Simons, R. L., & Whitbeck, L. B. (1991b). Running away during adolescence as a precursor to adult homelessness. *Social Service Review, 65*(2), 224–247.

Skaalvik, E. M., & Rankin, R. J. (1994). Gender differences in mathematics and verbal achievement, self-perception and motivation. *British Journal of Educational Psychology, 64*(3), 419–428.

Skolnick, J. H. (1990). The social structure of street drug dealing. *American Journal of Police, 9,* 1–41.

Slater, E., & Haber, J. (1984). Adolescent adjustment following divorce as a function of familial conflict. *Journal of Consulting and Clinical Psychology, 52,* 920–921.

Slee, P. T., & Rigby, K. (1993). Australian school children's self appraisal of interpersonal relations: The bullying experience. *Child Psychiatry and Human Development, 23*(4), 273–282.

Snow, D. A., & Phillips, C. L. (1982). The changing self-orientations of college students: From institutions to impulse. *Social Science Quarterly, 63,* 462–476.

Small, S. A., & Kerns, D. (1993). Unwanted sexual activity among peers during early and middle adolescence. *Journal of Marriage and the Family, 55,* 941–952.

Smith, C., & Thornberry, T. P. (1995). The relationship between childhood maltreatment and adolescent involvement in delinquency. *Criminology, 33*(4), 451–481.

Smith, D. E., & Muenchen, R. A. (1995). Gender and age variations in the self-image of Jamaican adolescents. *Adolescence, 30,* 119, 643–654.

Smith, E. A, & Udry, J. R. (1985). Coital and non-coital sexual behaviors of white and black adolescents. *American Journal of Public Health, 75,* 1200–1203.

Smith, S. R. (1975). Religion and the conception of youth in seventeenth century England. *History of Childhood Quarterly: The Journal of Psychohistory, 2,* 493–516.

Snyder, T. D., Hoffman, C. M., & Geddes, C. M. (1996). *Digest of educational statistics.* National Center for Educational Statistics. (GPO #065-000-00904-8). Washington, DC: Government Printing Office.

Sonenstein, F. L., Pleck, J. H., & Ku, L. C. (1991). Levels of sexual activity among adolescent males in the United States. *Family Planning Perspectives, 23*(4), 162–167.

Sommer, B., & Nagel, S. (1991). Ecological and typological characteristics in early adolescent truancy. *Journal of Early Adolescence, 11*(3), 379–392.

Sonenstein, F., Pleck, J., & Ku, L. (1989, March). At risk of AIDS: Behaviors, knowledge nd attitudes among a national sample of adolescent males. Presented at the Annual Meeting of the Population Association of America, Baltimore, MD.

Sorenson, R. (1973). *Adolescent sexuality in contemporary America.* New York: World.

Sprecher, S., Barbee, A., & Schwartz, P. (1995). Was it good for you, too? Gender differences in first sexual intercourse experiences. *Journal of Sex Research, 32,* 3–15.

Spergel, I. A. (1995). *The youth gang problem.* New York: Oxford University Press.

Stanton, B. F., Black, M., Kaljee, L., & Ricardo, I. (1993). *Journal of Early Adolescence, 13*(1), 44–66.

Stein, N. (1995). Sexual harassment in school: The public performance of gendered violence. *Harvard Educational Review, 65*(2), 145–162.

Steinberg, L. (1990). Autonomy, conflict and harmony in family relationships. In S. Feldman and G. Elliot (Eds.), *At the threshold: The developing adolescent* (pp. 255–276). Cambridge, MA: Harvard University Press.

Steinberg, L. (1989). Maturation and parent-adolescent distance: An evolutionary perspective. In T. P. Gullotta, G. R. Adams, & R. Montemayor (Eds.), *Biology of adolescent behavior and development* (pp. 71–97). Newbury Park: Sage.

Steinberg, L., Lamborn, S., Darling, N., Mounts, N. S., & Dornbusch, S. M. (1994). Over-time changes in adjustment and competence among adolescents from authoritative, authoritarian, indulgent, and neglectful families. *Child Development, 65*(3), 754–770.

Steinberg, L., & Dornbusch, S. M. (1991). Negative correlates of part-time employment during adolescence: Replication and elaboration. *Developmental Psychology, 27,* 304–313.

Steinberg, L., Fegley, S., & Dornbusch, S. M. (1993). Negative impact of part-time work on adolescent adjustment: Evidence from a longitudinal study. *Developmental Psychology, 29,* 171–180.

Steinberg, L. D., & Silverberg, S. B. (1986). The vicissitudes of autonomy in early adolescence. *Child Development, 57,* 975–985.

Steinmetz, S. K. (1977). *The cycle of violence: Assertive, aggressive and abusive family interaction.* New York: Praeger.

Steinmetz, S. K. (1979). Disciplinary techniques and their relationship to aggressiveness, dependency and conscience (pp. 405–438). In W. R. Burr, R. Hill, F. I. Nye, & I. Reiss (Eds.), *Contemporary theories about the family,* Vol. I. New York: Free Press.

Steinmetz, S. K. (1987). Violence in the family: Past present and future. In M. B. Sussman & S. K. Steinmetz (Eds.), *Handbook of marriage and the family* (pp. 725–765). New York: Plenum.

Steinmetz, S. K. (1988). *Duty bound: Elder abuse and family care.* Newbury Park, CA: Sage.

Steinmetz, S. K. (1990). Confronting violence in the 1980s: In the streets, schools and home. In L. J. Hertzberg, G. F. Ostrum, & J. R. Fields (Eds.), *Violent behavior, Vol. 1: Assessment and intervention* (pp. 167–180). Great Neck, NY: PMA Publishing Corp.

Steinmetz, S. K. (1996). *Marion County residents of Boys' School: A demographic analysis.* Final report to the Marion County Community Corrections, Indiana Department of Corrections. Indianapolis, IN.

Steinmetz, S. K. (1999). Sociological theories of violence. In V. B. Van Hasselt & M. Hersen (Eds.), *Handbook of psychological approaches with violent offenders: Contemporary strategies and issues* (pp. 13–38). New York: Plenum.

Steinmetz, S. K., Clavan, S., & Stein, K. F. (1994). *Marriage and family realities: Historical and contemporary perspectives.* New York: HarperCollins.

Strasburg, P. A. (1978). *Violent delinquents: A report to the Ford Foundation from the Vera Institute of Justice.* Rochester, WA.

Stiffman, A. R. (1989). Suicide attempts in runaway youths. *Suicide and Life Threatening Behavior, 19*(2), 147–159.

Stoutjesdyk, D., & Jevne, R. (1993). Eating disorders among high performance athletes. *Journal of Youth and Adolescence, 22*(3), 271–282.

Streitmatter, J. L. (1988). Ethnicity as a mediating variable of early adolescent identity development. *Journal of Adolescence, 11*(4), 335–346.

Streitmatter, J. L. (1993). Gender differences in identity development: An examination of longitudinal data. *Adolescence, 28,* 55–66.

Straus, M. S., Gelles, R. J., & Steinmetz, S. K. (1980). *Behind closed doors: Violence in the American family.* Newbury Park, CA: Sage.

Studer, M., & Thornton, A. (1987). Adolescent religiosity and contraceptive usage. *Journal of Marriage and the Family, 49*(1), 117–128.

Sullivan, K., & Sullivan, A. (1982). Adolescent-parent separation. *Developmental Psychology, 16,* 93–100.

Sweet, R. (1982). Chlamydia salpingitis and infertility. *Fertility and Sterility, 38,* 530–533.

Swiatek, M. S. (1993). A decade of longitudinal research on academic acceleration through the study of mathematically precocious youth. *Roeper Review, 15*(3), 120–124.

Sykes, D. K., Leuser, B., Melia, M., & Gross, M. (1988). A demographic analysis of 252 patients with anorexia nervosa and bulimia. *International Journal of Psychosomatics, 35,* 1–9.

Taub, D. E., & Blinde, E. M. (1992). Eating disorders among adolescent female athletes: Influence of athletic participation and sport team membership. *Adolescence, 27*(108), 833–848.

Taub, D. E., & Blinde, E. M. (1994). Disordered eating and weight control among adolescent female athletes and performance squad members. *Journal of Adolescent Research, 9*(4), 483–497.

Taylor, C. S. (1988). Youth gangs organize for power, money. *School Safety,* Spring, 26–27.

Taylor, C. S. (1993). *Girls, gangs, women, and drugs.* East Lansing, MI: Michigan State University Press.

Thomas, W. I., & Thomas, D. S. (1937). *The child in America.* New York: McGraw-Hill.

Thornton, A., & Camburn, D. (1989). Religious participation and adolescent sexual behavior and attitudes. *Journal of Marriage and the Family, 51*(3), 641–653.

Title, B. B. (1994). No-bullying program. St. Vrain Valley School District. Longmont, CO.

Trump, K. S. (1993). *Youth gangs and schools: The need for intervention and prevention strategies.* Cleveland: Urban Child Research Center.

Tzuriel, D. (1984). Sex role typing and ego identity in Israeli, oriental, and western adolescents. *Journal of Personality and Social Psychology, 46*(2), 440–457.

Udry, J. R., Billy, J. O. G., Morris, N., Groff, T., & Raj, M. (1985). Serum androgenic hormones motivate sexual behaviors in boys. *Fertility and Sterility, 43,* 90–94.

U.S. Bureau of the Census. (1996). *Statistical Abstract of the United States.* No. 14, p. 15.

U.S. Department of Education. (1996). The Condition of Education—1996, Indicator 42. National Center for Education Statistics, Schools and Staffing Survey, 1993–94 (Teacher and School Questionnaires). Washington, DC: U.S. Government Printing Office.

U.S. Department of Health and Human Services. (1998). *Fact sheet.* Runaways and Homeless Youth Program, Administration on Children, Youth and Families. Washington, DC.

U.S. Department of Justice. (1990). *Missing, abducted, runaway, and thrownaway children in America, first report: Numbers and characteristics.* National Incidence Studies, Office of Juvenile Justice and Delinquency Prevention, Washington, DC.

U.S. Department of Justice. (1992). *Criminal victimization in the United States, 1991.* Washington, DC.

U.S. Department of Justice. (1994). Federal Bureau of Investigation, *Crime in the United States, 1993: Uniform Crime Reports,* December.

U.S. Office of Juvenile Justice and Delinquency Prevention. (1996). *Child victimizers: Violent offenders and their victims.* Washington, DC: U.S. Government Printing Office.

U.S. Department of Justice. (1996). Office of Elementary and Secondary Education, Safe and Drug Free Schools Program. *Manual to combat truancy.* Washington, DC: U.S. Government Printing Office.

Van-Riper, M., Ryff, C., & Pridham, K. (1992). Parental and family well-being in families of children with downs syndrome: A comparative study. *Research in Nursing and Health, 15*(3), 227–235.

Vazsonyi, A. T., & Flannery, D. J. (1997). Early adolescent delinquent behaviors: Associations with family and school domains. *Journal of Early Adolescence, 17*(3), 271–293.

Ventura, S. J., Martin, J. A., Curtin, S. C., & Mathews, T. J. (1997). Report of final natality statistics, 1995. *Monthly Vital Statistics Report, 45*(11), Supplement. Washington, DC: Centers for Disease Control and Prevention.

Ventura, S. J., Peters, K. D., Martin, J. A., & Mauer, J. D. (1997). Births and deaths: United States, 1996. *Monthly Vital Statistics Report, 46*(1), Supplement 2. Washington, DC: Centers for Disease Control and Prevention.

Viemeroe, V. (1996). Factors in childhood that predict later criminal behavior. *Aggressive Behavior, 22*(2), 87–97.

Vigil, J. D. (1988). Group processes and street identity: Adolescent Chicano gang members. *Ethos, 16*(4), 421–444.

Voydanoff, P., & Donnelly, B. W. (1990). *Adolescent sexuality and pregnancy.* Newbury Park, CA: Sage.

Walker, L. S., & Greene, J. W. (1986). The social context of adolescent self-esteem. *Journal of Youth and Adolescence, 15*(4), 315–322.

Wallace, L. J. D., Calhoun, A. D., Powell, K. E., O'Neil, J., & James, S. P. (1996). Homicide and suicide among Native Americans, 1979–1992. *Violence Surveillance Summary Series, No. 2.* Centers for Disease Control and Prevention, National Center for Injury Prevention and Control.

Wallerstein, J. S., & Kelly, J. B. (1979). Children and divorce, A review. *Social Work, 24*(6), 468–475.

Warr, M. (1993). Parents, peers, and delinquency. *Social Forces, 72*(1), 247–264.

Waterman, C. K., & Waterman, A. S. (1974). Ego identity status and decision styles. *Journal of Youth and Adolescence, 3,* 1–6.

Wayment, H. A., & Zeitlin, A. G. (1989). Coping responses of mildly learning handicapped and nonhandicapped adolescents. *Mental Retardation, 27,* 311–316.

Whitbeck, L. B., & Simons, R. L. (1990). Life on the streets: The victimization of runaway and homeless adolescents. *Youth and Society, 22*(1), 108–125.

Widom, C. (1992). *The cycle of violence.* U.S. Department of Justice, National Institute of Justice, Washington, DC.

Wigfield, A., & Eccles, J. S. (1994). Children's competence beliefs, achievement values, and general self-esteem: Change across elementary and middle school. *Journal of Early Adolescence, 14*(2), 107–138.

Winborne, D. G., & Murray, G. J. (1992). Address unknown: An exploration of the educational and social attitudes of homeless adolescents. *High School Journal, 75*(3), 144–149.

Windle, M. (1989). Substance use and abuse among adolescent runaways: A four-year follow-up study. *Journal of Youth and Adolescence, 18*(4), 331–344.

Windle, M. (1993). A retrospective measure of childhood behavior problems and its use in predicting adolescent problem behaviors. *Journal of Studies on Alcohol, 54*(4), 422–431.

Windle, R. C., & Windle, M. (1997). An investigation of adolescents' substance use behaviors, depressed affect, and suicidal behaviors. *Journal of Child Psychology and Psychiatry and Allied Disciplines, 38*(8), 921–929.

Whitbeck, L. B., & Simons, R. (1990). Life on the streets: The victimization of runaway and homeless adolescents. *Youth and Society, 22*(1), 108–125.

Wrigley, J. (1986). Compulsory school laws: A dilemma with a history. In J. Simon & D. Stipek (Eds.), *Reconsidering compulsory schooling for adolescents: Studies in social science, education and law.* New York: Academic Press.

Wolpin, K., & Rosenweig, M. (1995). Sisters, siblings and mothers: The effects of teenage childbearing on birth outcomes in a dynamic family context. *Econometrica, 63*, 303–326.

Wood, P. B., & Sonleitner, N. (1996). The effect of childhood interracial contact on adult antiblack prejudice. *International Journal of Intercultural Relations, 19*, 4.

Worchel, F., Nolan, B., & Wilson, V. (1987). New perspectives on child and adolescent depression. *Journal of School Psychology, 25*(4), 411–414.

Yablonsky, L., & Haskell, M. (1988). *Juvenile delinquency* (4th ed.). New York: Harper & Row.

Yates, G. L., MacKenzie, R., Pennbridge, J., & Cohen. (1988). A risk profile comparison of runaway and non-runaway youth. *American Journal of Public Health, 78*(37), 820–821.

Yates, G. L., MacKenzie, R., Pennbridge, J., Swofford, A. (1991). A risk profile comparison of homeless youth involved in prostitution and homeless youth not involved. *Journal of Adolescent Health, 12*, 545–548.

Yong, F. L., & McIntyre, J. D. (1991). Comparison of self-concepts of students identified as gifted and regular students. *Perceptual and Motor Skills, 73*(2), 443–446.

Zabin, L. S., Kantner, J. F., & Selnik, M. (1979). Risk of adolescent pregnancy in the first months of intercourse. *Family Planning Perspectives, 11*, 215–226.

Zelnik, M., & Shah, F. K. (1993). First intercourse among young Americans. *Family Planning Perspectives, 25*, 64–72.

Zetlin, A. G. (1993). Everyday stressors in the lives of anglo and Hispanic learning handicapped adolescents. *Journal of Youth and Adolescence, 22*(3), 327–335.

Zimet, G. D., Sobo, E. J., & Zimmerman, T. (1995). Sexual behavior, drug use, and AIDS knowledge among midwestern runaways. *Youth and Society, 26*(4), 450–462.

Zimring, F. E. (1996). Kids, guns, and homicide: Policy notes on an age-specific epidemic. *Law and Contemporary Problems, 59*, 25–38.

Zelizer, V. (1985). *Pricing the priceless child: The changing social value of children.* New York: Basic Books.

Zingraff, M. T., & Belyea, M. J. (1986). Child abuse and violent crime. In K. C. Haas & G. P. Alpert (Eds.), *The dilemmas of punishment: Readings on contemporary corrections* (pp. 49–63). Prospect Heights, IL: Waveland Press.

CHAPTER 15

Family Relations in Adulthood

Judith Treas and Leora Lawton

Until recently, the family of procreation, not the family of origin, was the focus of research on the family. Increasingly, scholarly attention has shifted from relations with one's spouse and dependent children to relations with adult siblings, aging parents, grown children, and other kin. Because members of recent cohorts have married later and later (if at all), the principal family relations of early and middle adulthood are very frequently with parents and siblings. The development of a life-course perspective on the family has contributed to the appreciation that relationships begun in childhood also have a place in adulthood.

Before family scholars began to chafe at the notion of an all-too-predictable family life cycle, much thinking about family life in adulthood was organized about family reproductive functions. Thus, young people were portrayed as readily swapping childhood dependency in their families of origin for adult responsibility to their own families of procreation. Singles were on the road to marriage, and young marrieds were on the road to parenthood. Adults who did not fit this portrait (i.e., life-long singles, divorcees, empty-nest mothers) were often dismissed as social problems, their family lives defined not by their existing family ties, but rather by whatever normatively prescribed relationships they lacked.

Various demographic developments and intellectual currents made this view of adult family relations increasingly untenable. Such trends as rising age at marriage, falling marital fertility, soaring divorce, and lengthening life expectancies meant that less and less of adulthood was spent procreating and parenting within marriages. Dependent chil-

dren and even spouses figured less prominently in the life course, particularly in early and late adulthood.

Social scientists have united changes in demographic behavior under the life-course approach. That is, the experience of an individual within a family at any given point in time is part of a process, rather than simply the outcome of a family status. Several dimensions of the life-course approach guide our discussion of contemporary family life in adulthood. Each dimension is essentially a context in which the individual and family exist.

The first dimension involves the recognition that family experiences reverberate across the life course. Thus, adults never quite leave behind their families of origin (or orientation) because formative family influences continue to have effects throughout adulthood. Parental divorce, for example, often weakens ties to noncustodial fathers, whose children, even in adulthood, feel less obligation for their fathers' welfare than do children from intact marriages.

Second is the appreciation that career contingencies and interdependencies shape family life. Adults face a constellation of competing and complementary roles, relationships, and obligations. Consider how being a daughter and a sister complement one another. Filial obligations to parents almost inevitably bring adults into closer contact with siblings, if only because parents share sibling news, orchestrate family gatherings, or require coordinated assistance. Work roles, on the other hand, are typically viewed as competing with family relations. The issue, of course, is not merely how people make trade-offs between obligations or package their family roles for more efficient execution. The situation of intimates also impinges. When one's spouse is sick or disabled, one's own social world may contract.

Third is the notion that family patterns are socially and historically situated. They vary across time and across social groups. In the case of female family headship, for example, families headed by women have certainly grown more common since mid-century, with African American families re-

Judith Treas • Department of Sociology, University of California, Irvine, Irvine, California 92697. Leora Lawton • TechSociety Research, 2342 Shattuck Avenue, #362, Berkeley, California, 94704.

Handbook of Marriage and the Family, 2nd edition, edited by Marvin Sussman, Suzanne K. Steinmetz, and Gary W. Peterson. Plenum Press, New York, 1999.

maining more likely than white families to be headed by women.

In addressing family relations in adulthood, this chapter first examines the contemporary influences that have delayed entry into marriage in early adulthood. These changes have in turn highlighted the importance of parents and siblings in adult life. These kin ties are the second focus of early and middle adulthood presented here. Today's "normal" transition into adulthood does not demand early marriage. Marriage has been increasingly delayed, while longer life expectancies increase the availability of parents and siblings across the life course. When no family of procreation—partner and children—arises, the family of origin—parents and siblings—continues to be a central focus into adulthood. The salience of spouse and/or children in the daily lives of most adults is undeniable, yet changes in North American family formation patterns mean that other family relationships loom larger in facilitating or inhibiting a successful trajectory through adulthood. The safety net provided by the family of origin increases in importance when resources elsewhere are inadequate. These ties recede as other family and career responsibilities create cross-pressures. Even for those who are married, of course, parents and siblings continue to be significant features of adult life. Consequently, the family of origin is a strategic locus that aptly demonstrates key features of family relations in adulthood—how they persist over the life course, how they are determined by other roles and relationships, and how they are shaped by macrosocial influences.

Trends in Family Formation

Marriage remains a highly central and meaningful status in an adult's life. Americans readily see obligations to spouse as more compelling than those to any other kin (Rossi & Rossi, 1990). Although marriage has been one of the most common markers of autonomous adulthood, it is becoming less dominant in the lives of American adults. The last 2 decades have seen an increasing proportion of young adults in the United States who do not marry young. The median age at first marriage for females has risen from 20.6 in 1970 to 24.0 in 1990; for males, it has increased from 22.5 to 25.9 (U.S. Bureau of the Census, 1997). In 1991, 52% of males ages 25–29 had never been married; among their female counterparts, 38% were never married. Even among 30- to 34-year-olds, about a third of men and women (38% and 31%, respectively) were not currently married (U.S. Bureau of the Census, 1997). Clearly, for a large percentage of young adults, family relationships are outside the personal context of marriage.

Several sources of nuptiality changes have been identified. One explanation emphasizes economic impediments to marriage as conditioned by high material aspirations that arise from individualistic values. Another explanation emphasizes not voluntary delays, but rather the social and demographic forces that make it harder to find a suitable spouse.

A demographic imbalance of men and women, especially within racial and socioeconomic marriage markets, confound the likelihood of finding a spouse (Guttentag & Second, 1983). Dramatic shifts in birth rates first gave a marriage market advantage to men in birth cohorts from the mid-1940s to the 1960s, as rising fertility ensured an ample supply of slightly younger women who constituted age-appropriate partners. When fertility began to decline, however, the advantage shifted to women.

Unfavorable sex ratios facing African American women are particularly striking. Black women outnumber black men in the 20–24 age group, although their white counterparts do not experience a shortfall of men until the 40–44 age cohort (U.S. Bureau of the Census, 1992). This reflects, in part, the higher mortality experienced by young African American men, especially from homicide (Keith & Smith, 1988). Also removing black men from the marriage market are higher rates of incarceration (Rogers, 1992). Although national data have not supported the notion that the composition of the population depresses marriage (Schoen & Kluegel, 1988), analyses of local "marriage markets" do support the notion of a marriage squeeze for African American women (Lichter, LeClere, & McLaughlin, 1990).

While it is possible that the census undercount for prime-age black men overstates the marriage squeeze for women in the African American community, the very individuals most apt to be missed in the census are the least desirable marriage partners—namely, the poor and the homeless. Overall, the uneven economic opportunities confronting black men undermine their attractiveness as marriage partners (Wilson, 1987). Black men tend to have lower educational attainments than do black women; thus, black women have more trouble than other women in finding men whose educations measure up to their own (South, 1991; South & Lloyd, 1992).

Although some demographic accounts of nuptiality declines point to supply-side shortages in potential marriage partners, other evidence suggests that the very demand for married life has declined. Widespread marriage delays are consistent with cultural values, attitudes, and preferences. De Tocqueville observed the strong individualist tendencies of Americans—tendencies owing to a particular form of market economy that rewards the actor but not his or her social support system (Marini, 1990). There is certainly evidence that preferences for age at marriage have been changing. Focusing on material aspirations at the expense of family commitments, high school seniors in 1986 reported that they favored later marriage and childbearing than did the cohort 10 years earlier (Crimmins, Easterlin, & Saito, 1991). Some question whether younger cohorts are being raised with the social skills necessary to negotiate a family household (Goldscheider & Waite, 1991). Lacking is not only housekeeping expertise, but also communication skills necessary to forge compromises between the needs of the individual and those of other family members. Changing social roles make compromises even more necessary as working wives confront the persistently gendered division of household labor. When men seek women to take care of the house and women seek men to share in that care, marriages face new challenges.

Cohabitation has also been interpreted as evidence of declining taste for marriage. Losing much of its stigma, cohabitation has certainly become more common. Because cohabitants are comparable to single people in terms of their childbearing, finances, employment, schooling, and self-identification as single persons, Rindfuss and Vandenheuval (1990) conclude that cohabitants do have individualistic tendencies that lead them to prefer independence to familism. Although cohabitation is a pathway to marriage for many couples (Booth & Johnson, 1988), many cohabiting unions do not lead to marriage, and many resulting marriages are of short duration. In fact, cohabitants are selected from those who are less approving of marriage and more accepting of divorce (Axinn & Thornton, 1992).

Not everyone agrees that cohabitation is a retreat from familism; indeed, some researchers emphasize that cohabitation is much like being married (Bumpass, Sweet, & Cherlin, 1991). Many cohabitants expect to marry; they may even have children without legal marriage. Since cohabitation has offset declining marriage rates, what has declined is *legal* unions, not unions per se. These unions may be unstable, but so are marriages. Cohabitation is not likely to overtake marriage in popularity, however. Despite the rise of new pathways into adulthood, many cohabitants endorse marriage (Ganong, Coleman, & Mapes, 1990).

Americans are marrying later when they marry at all. Some explanations of this nuptiality trend suggest that individualism has triumphed over familism. Others emphasize economic uncertainty or demographic obstacles to making a good match—factors that tend to leave young adults more dependent on their families of origin. Lacking a spouse to turn to for emotional comfort and material support, parents and siblings offer an essential safety net well into adulthood.

Adult Children and Their Parents

Until recently, researchers had taken for granted the quality and nature of family-of-origin ties in adulthood. Family ties emanating from the parental home had been seen as important to the support of elderly parents, but continuities in family roles across the broad sweep of the life course had been largely ignored. Hagestad (1987) called the discontinuity in attention to family of origin relationships the "al-

pha and omega" approach to intergenerational relationships. In other words, the study of intergenerational family relationships centered on young children or elderly adults while virtually ignoring parent–child relationships in the middle portion of life.

More and more research, however, is focusing on what parent–child relations mean for the adult child, rather than just for the aging, and perhaps dependent, parent. The life-course perspective offers a theoretical context for the evolution of parent–child relations over time and life stages. Adult relationships are now recognized as a function, in part, of childhood relations. The literature, for example, increasingly documents a link between childhood family structure, particularly parental divorce, and family relations in later life. As the child ages, however, the nature of intergenerational interaction changes with the changes in the child's own marital, financial, and occupational status.

If studies of adult child–parent relationships have emphasized the needs of the aging parent and the ability of grown children to meet them, children continue to benefit from their relationship with their parents in varied and important ways. Children receive financial help in the form of college tuition, loans for home-buying or other major purchases, plus smaller and more frequent contributions such as clothes for grandchildren. Social support takes a variety of forms—from listening sympathetically to problems to guaranteeing a place to go for holidays. Instrumental support includes babysitting grandchildren and providing housing after divorce or during unemployment. Parent–child relations in adulthood are manifest in shared living arrangements, helping behavior, and social support. We consider each of these sorts of intergenerational exchange in turn before reviewing the ways in which exchanges are affected by the events of childhood.

Coresidence: Leaving and Returning to the Nest

Despite the resolute neolocality of American marriage patterns, multigenerational living arrangements make a strategic site for investigating the continuing and contingent nature of parent–child relationships in adulthood. Living arrangements also demonstrate the historical changes and cultural variation in a significant mechanism of intergenerational support.

One of the earliest transitions into adulthood involves leaving the parental home to establish residential independence. With the rise in personal income, more and more people have been able to set up households apart from their parents (Kobrin, 1976). Moving out of the home has ceased to be merely a step toward marriage, but has become a step toward independence in its own right (Goldscheider & Waite, 1991). Leaving the nest does not signify the end of the parent–child relationship, but it seems to be associated with better parental well-being (White & Edwards, 1990)—an outcome that may well have a positive effect on the parent–child relationship. Although independent living is popular, there are variations by ethnicity, parental income and education, and education of the child. Parents' higher income and education and child's college plans increase the likelihood of leaving home early. When socioeconomic status (SES) is controlled, Hispanic and black families are less likely to see children leave home early (Goldscheider & DaVanzo, 1989).

Although 50% of children ages 18–24 are still living at home with their parents, this figure falls to less than 5% by age 30 (Lawton, Silverstein, & Bengtson, 1994b). Children tend to stay in the parental home longer when the situation works well for them. Harmonious parent–child relationships, particularly where the child's income is not a source of conflict, encourage coresidence. Parental divorce and other disruptions tend to push children out of the nest sooner (Aquilino, 1991). Early departures associated with divorce are not necessarily indicative of problems, however, since autonomy and self-reliance, some of the documented benefits of growing up in a divorced family, may encourage nest-leaving (Weiss, 1979).

Some intergenerational coresidence comes about not because of delays in nest-leaving, but rather because of nest-returning (Aquilino, 1990). Despite stereotypes of older dependent parents relocating to their children's homes, coresidence often benefits the middle-aged child (Speare & Avery, 1991). Being able to move back to the parents' home is one of the most important safety nets a child can enjoy (Ward, Logan, & Spitze, 1992). Cross-sectional studies reveal that divorced children are more likely to coreside than either married children or older, never-married children (Lawton, Silverstein, & Bengtson, 1994a). The incidence of temporary coresidence following divorce or lengthy unemployment is likely to be much higher than prevalence rates reveal. Indeed, studies of homelessness in the United States show that many homeless individuals and families lack the secure family relationships that ensure a roof over one's head (Weitzman, Knickman & Shinn, 1990).

Although most coresiding parents and children are content with their living arrangements (Aquilino & Supple, 1991), coresidence sometimes means conflict. When children have been unsuccessful either moving into or sustaining autonomous adult roles, conflict between parents and children is higher. Disagreements about coresidence also arise, on the other hand, if the child is prepared to leave home before the parent wishes (Goldscheider & Goldscheider, 1989). Young adults have higher expectations for residential independence than did previous cohorts, and they expect to achieve independence sooner than their parents anticipate. Thus, young adults and their parents may disagree over the "normal" progress to adulthood. Because of their generational stake in offspring (Bengtson & Kuypers, 1971), parents

view parent–child coresidence more positively than does the child (Suitor & Pillemer, 1988). However, parents, particularly mothers, sometimes resent the continuing burden of housework generated by grown offspring. Unfortunately, surveys on coresidence seldom identify whose household is being extended—a factor that may affect the observed harmony of intergenerational living arrangements.

Helping Behavior

One aspect of the parent–child relationship is exchanging help in the form of money, goods, and time. From a comparative perspective, this research emphasis on instrumental assistance is in some ways misplaced. Although Americans have higher rates of kin contact, they are less likely than those in other Western countries to expect to rely on assistance from their family members (Farkas & Hogan, 1994). Because help from kin tends to be episodic, cross-sectional studies have been inclined to underestimate the importance of family assistance at critical junctures in the life course.

Although resource flows in Western countries are from parents to children over most of the life course, most studies of intergenerational helping behavior have stressed what parents receive. The research focus is typically on the child's helping behavior and the stress that such help places on the caregiving child and his or her family. This ignores, on the one hand, the burdens that grown children may impose on the older generation, while a focus on elder care recasts what are often unproblematic exchanges as troublesome. Aside from the caregiver role, children have incentives to foster good relations with parents and in-laws for their own sake and the sake of grandchildren. When parents are healthy, parent–child relationships are perhaps less critical than in a crisis of parental disability, but they are still important.

Little financial help is provided by children to their parents today (Hogan & Eggebeen, 1991). Parents who receive help from their adult children are most likely to do so when they are physically dependent, financially at risk, and no longer married. Financial help comes from children who are most able to provide it, that is, offspring who are married, better educated, and with higher incomes (Eggebeen & Hogan, 1990; Goldscheider & Goldscheider, 1991; Hofferth, 1984). The effect of education on support apparently depends on how support is defined. Mutran and Reitzes (1984) find that education has a negative effect on helping behavior when such behavior is defined as money, advice, and other assistance; Crimmins and Ingegneri (1990), on the other hand, find that education has a positive effect on frequency of interaction after controlling for geographic distance.

Grown children with flexible work schedules and family commitments are most likely to provide the instrumental help particularly salient during a parent's disability. Typically the care provider has been a daughter (Brody & Schoonover,

1986), likely reflecting norms concerning the gendered division of labor. Married children tend to be more stable sources of support, but married children are also more likely to have other family members in the child's immediate household who compete for the caregiver's energy. Given career commitment and/or the financial need to work, employed daughters may feel especially strained by the conflicting demands of several generations. As work and family pose more and more obstacles, some women may give caregiving less priority than was the case in earlier generations (Brody & Schoonover, 1986; Merrill, 1993).

Help flowing from parents to children depends on some of the same considerations affecting children's assistance to parents. Marital status, of course, impacts helping behavior between generations (Eggebeen, 1992), because different family statuses are associated with different sets of needs, resources, and attachments. Because intergenerational transfers are from those with the most resources to those with the least, married parents are generally able to help their children with gifts, home loans, and services like babysitting and home maintenance. Divorced parents, especially divorced fathers, are less likely to help or want to help their children (Cooney & Uhlenberg, 1990; Uhlenberg & Cooney, 1990). Widowed parents, usually mothers, also provide less help—most likely because they have fewer monetary resources and may be in poor health (Crimmins & Ingegneri, 1990). Never-married children, particularly daughters, tend to receive more assistance from parents than do married children (Rossi & Rossi, 1990). Thus, marital status seems to define the needs, ability, and competing claims determining assistance between generations.

The kind of help offered depends on the gender of parents and offspring. Sons tend to help mothers in certain instrumental tasks. Daughters tend to help fathers in terms of personal care and comfort (Rossi & Rossi, 1990). Sons receive more household help, but less advice and childcare assistance, than do daughters (Eggebeen & Hogan, 1990). Sons give less help of all types to parents than do daughters.

Social Support in Parent–Adult Relationships

While many studies have examined the effect of children's social support on the well-being of the elderly, little research has investigated the impact of parental support on the well-being of younger adults. For example, the quality and nature of relationships between parents and children affect the outcomes of the younger generation in many ways. The quality of the mother–child relationship has been shown to be positively related to the daughter's self-esteem. When the daughter has few other social roles (e.g., as spouse or parent), the quality of her relationship with her mother is even more important (Baruch & Barnett, 1983).

Other research also underscores the significance of par-

ental ties for women. While both men and women expand their nonkin social ties through higher education and the workplace, marriage and parenthood lead to a decrease in nonkin ties for women, whereas men experience an increase (Moore, 1990). Thus, the importance of ties to the family of origin is contingent on other social roles. These roles are sometimes alternatives to kin ties and are sometimes in direct competition with them.

Parents also influence whether, how, and with whom social ties are formed. They may try to influence their children's mate selections, and some even introduce their children to prospective suitors (Whyte, 1990). Parental approval of one's choice of spouse is associated with better prospects for a high-quality marital relationship and an enduring union (Sprecher & Felmlee, 1992). While parental approval is undoubtedly correlated with predictors of marital success, it is possible that an ordered, supportive childhood leads children to follow a path more consistent with the parents' views of success. Besides influencing marriage, relations with one's parents also influence one's childbearing motivations (Miller, 1992). Good mothering in childhood and good current relations with parents lead to more positive (or less negative) views of children.

As seen in the issue of coresidence, parental support becomes more important when a child's social ties are severed by divorce. Both sons and daughters rely on parents for social support immediately after a divorce (Johnson, 1988). Gender of child affects the duration, extent, and kind of support received after divorce. Men are more likely to seek out kin for emotional support, drawing away from nonkin when they feel despondent. Women maintain kin networks long after the divorce and after depression passes (Gerstel, 1988). Given women's income loss following divorce, ties with parents may be even more necessary for women than men. Divorced fathers, however, often combine visits with their children and visits with their own parents, giving grandparents access to children and sharing the responsibility for supervising and entertaining offspring. Although daughters develop a reciprocally supportive relation with parents more often than do sons, both sons and daughters reorganize parent–child relationships in other ways (Johnson, 1988). Some children maintain private lives as much as possible given their resources. Others maintain ties between generations without developing particularly companionate relationships with parents.

Related to social support is physical access: How far away do generations live from each other, and how much contact do they maintain? Distance was found to be the most important factor in determining the nature and extent of instrumental and social support between parents and children (Dewit, Wister, & Burch, 1988; Litwak & Kulis, 1987; Mercier, Paulson, & Morris, 1989; Taylor & Chatters, 1991). While the majority of children do live within an hour of their parents (Lawton et al., 1994a), certain life contingencies—particularly marriage and higher education—are associated with greater distance. Closer proximity between parents and adult children is more likely when children are not married (Kulis, 1991), when parents are married, when offspring are daughters (Lawton et al., 1994a), and when parents are disabled (Kulis, 1991). When children do buy a home and begin to raise their own children, they live closer to parents than do renters and the childless. Greater distance between parents and children is more likely among those children with higher education and SES (Kulis, 1991).

Whether they live close by or far away, the affectual quality of the parent–child relationship is also important, if only because social and instrumental support is more available when affection is high (Silverstein, Lawton, & Bengtson, 1994). Most adult children and their parents report affectionate relations; over 80% state that feelings are close or very close (Lawton et al., 1994a,b; Rossi & Rossi, 1990). Variations exist among families, however; African American families report higher levels of affection than do white families (Lawton et al., 1994a,b; Mutran, 1985). Older adults tend to report better relationships than younger adults, perhaps reflecting maturation and convergence of roles (Umberson, 1992).

These overall dimensions of intergenerational relationships—living arrangements and geographic space, social support and contact, and affection—have modifying affects on one another. Distance obviously structures the amount and type of social contact and helping behavior feasible: It also indirectly impacts the levels of affection. Children who have greater contact with their mothers tend to have greater affection for them; in turn, greater affection leads to more frequent contact (Lawton et al., 1994b). In the case of fathers, greater contact leads to greater affection, but the relationship is not reciprocal.

Children of Divorce: Lasting Effects of Family of Origin

One extraordinary revelation in adult family life is the persisting influence of experiences in the family of origin. The long-term effects of parental divorce on adult children and parent–child relationships in adulthood illustrate this persistence over the life course. Fewer and fewer young people bring to adulthood a personal legacy of a childhood lived out in a household with two birth parents. During the last 2 decades, high rates of divorce have produced many children of divorce who, on some counts, appear to be making less successful progress in adulthood. Trouble forming families of procreation has been noted in several studies. Age at marriage tends to be younger as children leave troubled households, divorce rates tend to be higher (Bumpass, Sweet, & Martin, 1989; Glenn & Kramer, 1987; Kobrin & Waite, 1984; McLanahan & Bumpass, 1988), and marital happiness tends to be lower (Amato & Booth, 1991). In the lower socioeconomic classes, the likelihood of marrying at all appears to be lower for those from troubled families (Keith & Finlay, 1988).

Mancini and Blieszner's (1989) review of the parent–child literature urged an examination of negative as well as positive aspects of this relationship. The study of divorce in childhood has been in keeping with that mandate. The emotional well-being of adult children of divorce does not compare favorably to children from intact families (Glenn & Kramer, 1985; Kulka & Weingarten, 1979; McLanahan, 1988). Amato (1988) investigated the long-term implications of parental divorce on adult self-concept and self-esteem. Although divorce did not itself reduce self-esteem, parental divorce lowered the child's sense of power in adulthood. Amato stressed the sense of vulnerability reinforced by the associated traumas of moving, lower income, and school disruptions. Following divorce, the parent–child relationship itself did not fare as well even into adulthood (Lawton et al., 1994b; Umberson, 1992; Wallerstein & Blakeslee, 1989). It is not clear how much emotional distance results from children's severing attachment bonds (Umberson, 1992) as opposed to parents' withdrawing. Fathers, in particular, have much less to do with their children following divorce (Cooney & Uhlenberg, 1990; Spitze & Miner, 1992).

Even when controlling for SES, children of divorce have less successful entries into their adult life (Acock & Kiecolt, 1989). Some of the disadvantage results from lack of parental investment. Divorce brings financial hardship exacerbated by the fact that many fathers do not meet their legal obligation to provide for their children and ex-wives. The resources of a custodial parent may be strained if there is no mutually supporting adult relationship in the household and no one to share day-to-day responsibility for childrearing. In general, poor marital quality leads to less investment in children, lowering reciprocity to parents (Booth et al., 1994).

While divorce is not destiny—relatively few children suffer severe setbacks from parental divorce—there are ramifications for all areas of parent–child relations. For example, adult children are less likely to help divorced parents (Hamon, 1992), and children of divorce are less likely to receive help from their parents (White, 1992). The emotional costs are apparent in other ways. Children of divorce are less likely to state that they have high levels of affection for their parents, have frequent contact with them, or live in close proximity (Aquilino, 1994; Lawton et al., 1994a,b). This is particularly true for divorced fathers who were not the custodial parents (Aquilino, 1994; Lawton, 1990). The fact that divorced fathers tend to be geographically remote from their children leads to reduced contact, in turn diminishing the emotional attachment and ultimately leading to less affection in later life (Lawton et al., 1994b). Thus, intergenerational ties in adulthood bear the lasting influence of experience in the family of origin.

Parent–Child Relations in Life-Course Perspective

Due to longer life expectancies, bonds with parents persist through early and middle adulthood and sometimes to the threshold of old age itself. To be sure, the nature of the relationship may be renegotiated as children establish their independence and as the needs of aging parents reverse net flows of assistance and social support. Parent–child relations in adulthood exemplify key features of the life-course approach to family life.

First, families have lasting influences. Childhood experiences in the family of origin influence the family lives of adults. Being raised in a family where parents divorce, for example, poses some impediments to successful family formation and colors relations with parents in adulthood.

Second, the relations between parents and adult children are influenced by career contingencies and by other competing or complementary social roles. Intergenerational relations are recast when grown children divorce or suffer financial setbacks. The security of, and obligations to, a spouse influence not only what grown offspring receive from parents, but also what children contribute to parental well-being.

Third, these relations are culturally patterned and shaped by historical forces. Coresidence of parents and their grown children, for example, ebbs and flows in response to macroeconomic and demographic factors that make it more or less difficult for children to establish and maintain their own households. Even when socioeconomic factors are taken into account, however, children in African American and Hispanic families leave home later than do other young adults.

Siblings

Brothers and sisters are important people populating the world of children. As siblings grow up and leave the parental home, sibling ties are loosened. Sibs are seldom the most significant social relationships in adulthood. Confidences and social activities come to be shared with friends and coworkers. Intense emotional attachments focus on lovers. The business of making a living and maintaining a home binds husbands and wives. Children's baths, soccer games, and homework take precedence over less obligatory family interactions, and aging parents introduce a new set of responsibilities. Although there is high normative consensus about what is owed to parents and children, there is less consensus

about obligations to siblings (Rossi & Rossi, 1990). Sibling interaction in adulthood is largely discretionary. Competing social relationships, geographical separation, and the demands of jobs and parenting readily divert attention from siblings.

While parents, children, and spouses all invoke stronger commitments in adulthood, sibling relations are of singular interest, if only because no close family relationships are as enduring. Siblings welcome the newborn to the family, but they may also live to mourn the passing of brothers and sisters in old age. Thus, siblings surely count among what Antonucci and Akiyama (1987) have described as the "convoy" of lifelong intimates whose social support can be counted on to ease the passage through the life course.

The significance of siblings comes not merely from the fact that their life spans largely overlap. Sibling relations are *intragenerational* ones. Brothers and sisters can claim membership in a common generation within the family lineage and usually within the broader society as well. Historical changes have intensified this bond. Because families have come to have fewer children spaced closer together, siblings have increasingly been agemates. Born just a few years apart, they are not called on to bridge big developmental chasms. By contrast, 2 decades sometimes separated the earlier and later born siblings in historically large families; today this pattern of wide age disparities is largely limited to half siblings born into different marital unions. Siblings of similar ages and shared generation undoubtedly have more in common. Whatever their differences, they are more likely to share interests, schools, friends, and fashions as they move into adulthood. College women, for example, have more interaction with closely spaced siblings (Cicirelli, 1980). Closely spaced siblings probably follow one another's progress through the life course with greater interest because the age-related challenges facing a sibling are also their own.

The opportunities and demands of new roles ensure that sibling relations in adulthood will be colored by differences in experience. Siblings typically diverge in adulthood as they take on other roles. They acquire new interests and abandon customs from their family of origin in favor of those shared with spouses. They relocate to different parts of the country as well as achieve fame and fortune while some siblings encounter only failure. Despite these experiential differences, siblings bring to their relationship not only generational and age-related similarities, but also a common social and genetic heritage. The genetic legacy is told in similar physical features, talents, and medical risks. The social legacy reflects their common ethnic background, religious tradition, class origins, regional roots, and unique family ways of doing things. Their common legacy offers a common ground and understanding for maintenance of sibling bonds over the life course and in response to changing contingencies of life.

Sibling Effects in Early Adulthood

Sib networks of childhood reverberate through the life course. In no small measure, adults have been shaped by the demands and privileges of sibling membership in their families of origin. Some sibling influences with long-lasting consequences may be direct and largely unmediated by parents. For example, siblings' behavior is known to influence the sexual activity of adolescents (Hogan & Kitagawa, 1985; Rodgers & Rose, 1990). The number of siblings and their spacing, their gender and one's own, and one's place in the birth order also have long-lasting consequences.

In a society where schooling largely determines socioeconomic fortunes in adulthood, those born into larger families stand at a decided disadvantage. The educational attainments of individuals from larger families are lower than those from smaller families. Even when parental background characteristics are taken into account, individuals with four siblings achieve over a year less schooling than do those with two siblings (Blake, 1989, p. 44). Presumably, the deleterious effects of siblings result because parental resources must be spread thinner. If there is less money to support each child's schooling, there is also less time to interact with each child— the likely cause of lower verbal ability in big families (Blake, 1989, pp. 110–119). Of course, even children born into the same family encounter somewhat different circumstances. Because they must share parental resources throughout childhood and adolescence, for example, the middle siblings in big families fare worse educationally than do the youngest and oldest offspring.

Sibling Effects on Intergenerational Exchange

Even in adulthood, siblings must share parental attention. Controlling for parents' education and other factors, adults with more living siblings are less likely to get help from their parents (Cooney & Uhlenberg, 1992). This finding holds for many kinds of assistance—advice, money or gifts, childcare, help with transportation, car or home repairs, and work around the house. Of course, the characteristics of siblings affect how much help each receives because parents tend to concentrate their resources on offspring who need the most help (Aldous, 1987).

After controlling for the age of the parent, younger people and students still get more material assistance from parents than their better established siblings (Cooney & Uhlenberg, 1990). When parents share housing with grown children, it is more likely to be with never-married offspring than with their married brothers and sisters (Aquilino, 1990; Crimmins & Ingegneri, 1990). The never-married are also more likely to be the beneficiaries of parents' wills and life insurance policies (Rossi & Rossi, 1990). Thus, how much

assistance an adult gets from a parent is determined not merely by the adult child's needs, but also by the numbers and needs of other offspring.

Sibling structure also affects what adult children do on behalf of their parents. Whether number of siblings affects feelings of closeness between parents and children is a disputed point (Lawton, 1990; Spitze & Logan, 1991). In bigger families with more siblings to take on filial roles, individual adults do have less interaction with their parents and provide them with less support. The more siblings, the less frequently do adults visit or phone parents (Rossi & Rossi, 1990; Spitze & Logan, 1991). When parents grow older and require assistance, individual offspring from larger sibships assume less responsibility than do those with few brothers and sisters. In families where a parent reported some impairment, 47% of women who were only children helped with activities of daily living as compared with 27% of all daughters; 25% of men who were only children gave care as compared with only 9% of all sons (Coward & Dwyer, 1990). Thus, where there are other siblings to do the work, the chances one will have to help out are considerably lower, especially for men.

In keeping with their traditional roles as kinkeepers, women provide more support to aging parents than do men. Exactly how much women and men do for aging parents, however, seems to depend not only on the size of the sibling network, but also on its gender composition. Given the gendered division of labor in parent care, one would expect men with sisters to more readily offload parent care than men without sisters. Indeed, when men are picked as the primary caregiver, it is typically because they have no sisters (Lee, Dwyer, & Coward, 1993) or at least few sisters living nearby (Stoller, Forster, & Duniho, 1992). This lesser involvement of brothers does not simply reflect widowed mothers' preference for care by daughters; it holds even when gender and marital status of the parent are taken into account (Dwyer & Coward, 1991; Stoller et al., 1992).

Comparisons of single-gender and mixed-gender sibships have not provided a definitive test of the hypothesis that gender composition affects male involvement in parent care, in part because gender composition is confounded by sibship size. Single-gender sibships are apt to be smaller than those with both brothers and sisters. Since having fewer sibs is associated with taking greater responsibility for aging parents, the confounding of sibship size and gender composition could explain why both sons and daughters in single-gender sibships are somewhat more likely to be named as the "primary caregiver" than are their counterparts in mixed-gender sibling networks (Coward & Dwyer, 1990). Whatever the effect of single-gender sibships, it is apparently confined to *instrumental* activities of daily living (IADLs, such as household work, money management, or help going outside); no increase in the probability of parent care is found for other activities of daily living (ADLs, such as eating, getting in or out of bed, or toileting) (Dwyer & Coward, 1991). Interestingly, a study that controlled for both sibling numbers and gender composition found gender effects to be sensitive to whether the child or parent generation reported on intergenerational interaction (Spitze & Logan, 1991).

Research on parent care focusing on a single "responsible person" typically portrays filial responsibilities falling squarely on the shoulders of one sister (Abel, 1991). Studies focused on the sibling network paint a different picture of parental needs met through the coordinated action of several siblings (Matthews & Rosner, 1988; Matthews, Werkner, & Delaney, 1989). In fact, siblings often perceive the poor health or death of parents as a life event strengthening the sibling bond (Connidis, 1992). As a parent's ability to manage independently becomes compromised, siblings are drawn together because they must develop common understandings about the nature of the problem, what is needed, and who will do what. Indeed, these sibling agreements about what is to be done seem to be a critical part of initiating care for older parents. Even controlling for changes in parents' health, having siblings who begin helping out is a significant predictor that an adult will begin to assist the parent with ADL limitations (Dwyer, Henretta, Coward, & Barton, 1992).

According to Matthews and Rosner (1988), divisions of labor evolve between siblings, typically sisters, who provide "routine" assistance and those who are available for "backup" help. Larger sibling networks also permit other roles, especially for brothers: the "circumscribed" stance of reliable, but very delimited, interaction; the useful, if unpredictable, "sporadic" help; and even complete "dissociation" from filial obligations. Although birth order, affinities, longstanding grudges, and ascribed personality traits affect sibling interaction and assignment of parent care roles, Matthews and Rosner (1988) report that siblings seldom permit these factors to dominate the more important business of organizing to meet parental needs.

Employed and nonemployed sisters demonstrate an impressive orchestration of sibling roles (Matthews et al., 1989). Except when parents were in very poor health, sisters with paid jobs provided no less support to parents than did their sisters who were homemakers. Instead, employed sisters took on tasks compatible with their work schedules (e.g., paying bills) while their at-home sisters handled daytime emergencies and appointments. It remains to be seen how the Baby Boomers will negotiate parent care given the greater propensity of these women to be employed.

Sibling Relationships

Although the strongest kinship ties in American society are between spouses and between parents and children (Rossi & Rossi, 1990), siblings remain a significant kinship bond in adulthood. In a large national sample of Americans, half of adults with living siblings reported seeing a sibling at least once a month; almost two-thirds reported a sibling to be among their closest friends (White & Riedmann, 1992a). Not surprisingly, those with more sibling contact were more likely to name a sib as a friend. Sibling interaction in adulthood, however, is largely voluntary. After children leave the parental home, sibling interaction is shaped not merely by affinities, but also by situational constraints and opportunities posed by the life-course careers of the individual and his or her siblings (Cicirelli, 1982). Sibling relations are highly gendered, and their salience depends, in part, on the availability of siblings and closer kin.

As one might expect, individuals with more sibling contact have more surviving siblings and live closer to them (Lee, Mancini, & Maxwell, 1990; Suggs, 1989; White & Riedmann, 1992a,b). Those with high sibling contact are better educated and have higher incomes; they have greater resources to employ in overcoming geographic separation. All things being equal, African Americans have more contact with siblings while Asian Americans have less. Catholics also have more contact. Women have more contact than men. Having living sisters also increases contact, particularly for women.

The closest and most affectionate sibling ties are typically those between sisters (Gold, 1989; Lee et al., 1990; White & Riedmann, 1992a). Indeed, older widows' emotional well-being is enhanced by having more living sisters, while brothers have no such effect (McGhee, 1985; O'Bryant, 1988). Women seem generally more aware of their underlying feelings toward a same-sex sibling than are men (Bedford, 1989). Sister–sister dyads in late adulthood are often associated with "intimate" sibling relationships characterized by high psychological involvement, instrumental support, and total acceptance as well as by an absence of resentment and envy (Gold, Woodbury, & George, 1990). Brother–sister pairs are most likely to demonstrate "congenial" relationships—as reflected in moderate levels of psychological involvement, closeness, and instrumental and emotional support. By contrast, brother–brother dyads are more likely than other pairs to report relationships with lower levels of closeness and support and higher levels of envy and resentment. Regardless of gender composition, African American sibs are more likely to conform to positive relationship types and are less likely to be characterized by "hostile" or "apathetic" relations in later life (Gold, 1990).

As indicated by frequency of contact, ties to full siblings are closer than those to half or step brothers or sisters (White & Riedmann, 1992b). A hierarchy of sibling bonds is suggested by the fact that contact with half or step sibs is greater when there are fewer full siblings. Although full siblings are favored, individuals with half and step siblings see less of full sibs, too, perhaps because such families have lower overall cohesion. Growing up in an "intact," two-parent family fosters sibling contact. Leaving home later has a similar effect, presumably because extra time in the parental home cements sibling attachments or because happy, cohesive families do not prompt early nest-leaving. In any case, the distinctions between full and other siblings suggest that parental relations may affect sibling relations even in adulthood.

Contingent Careers: Life-Course Influences of Sibling Relations

Contact with siblings seems to decline as children grow up, siblings grow older, and parents die (White & Riedmann, 1992a). Life-course events, especially those that add to or subtract from one's network of intimates, have significant implications for sibling relations. Siblings are drawn together by responsibilities to young children or aging parents (Connidis, 1992; White & Riedmann, 1992a). Grown-up children, however, can offer adult companionship and services. Thus, siblings with adult children report less contact with brothers and sisters, fewer exchanges with siblings, and less reliance on siblings for help with troubles. A parent's death may be recalled as drawing siblings closer emotionally (Connidis, 1992), but it also removes a link forging friendship between siblings (White & Riedmann, 1992a).

Marriage clearly loosens sibling bonds. Married people are less likely to count siblings among their closest friends than are single adults (White & Riedmann, 1992a). Assessing the effects of marriage on relations with a sibling, adults are as likely to say they became closer emotionally as they are to say they grew more distant (Connidis, 1992). No other life event, however, generates as many mentions of reduced closeness and contact, presumably because married couples form a "closed subsystem" to which sibs have less access. Widowhood and divorce often reactivate sibling ties. Closer ties after a marital disruption reflect a number of considerations—the needs of the newly single; siblings' close, if dormant, emotional bonds; and/or the simple fact that a spouse no longer requires attention or shapes sibling interaction (Connidis, 1992).

Sibling Support in Adulthood

Responsibilities to adult siblings are less keenly felt than those to parents and children, but they rank well ahead of perceived obligations to friends and distant relations. A duty to comfort siblings in a crisis is generally recognized, although kin by marriage (i.e., children-in-law and parents-in-law) have stronger claims on monetary help in crisis or celebration gifts and visits (Rossi & Rossi, 1990, p. 173). In fact, only about 15% of American adults name a brother or sister as the one person they would call in an emergency, for a loan, or for advice (White & Riedmann, 1992a). African Americans and Hispanics, however, are more likely than non-Hispanic whites to name a sibling as someone they might turn to in an emergency (Taylor, Chatters, & Mays, 1988). Although siblings are not usually seen as the first bastion against troubles, they are more likely to be named as an emergency resource when there are no living parents to turn to.

In adulthood, siblings exchange gifts, services, and social support—albeit at lower levels than exchanges between generations. When a national sample of adults was asked about childcare, transportation, home repairs, housework, advice, and loans, 37% reported giving such help to a sibling and 26% reported receiving it recently (White & Riedmann, 1992a). Of course, sibling support takes many other forms. Numerous studies have documented actual support to siblings in later adulthood (Avioli, 1989). Some support is in the form of instrumental assistance, including financial support, temporary sick care, home maintenance, transportation, shopping, and legal or financial advice. Expressive support between siblings ranges even more broadly: Siblings bolster one another by providing companionship and social visits, celebrating special occasions, combatting loneliness, sharing problems and advice, giving a sense of belonging, relating family history and sharing reminiscences, creating reliable alliances and a family attachment, validating perceptions and self-worth, providing an opportunity for nurturance, cheering spirits, offering security and emotional support, and serving as role models.

Obligations to siblings, however, loom larger for those who have never married or had children—as evidenced by their tendency to name siblings as the beneficiaries of their wills (Rossi & Rossi, 1990, p. 477). As declining marriage rates swell the ranks of lifelong singles, adults with strong loyalties to brothers and sisters may become more commonplace. Older, never-married, childless women often report high involvement with siblings and their families—even establishing parentlike relationships with some nieces and nephews (Rubenstein, Alexander, Goodman, & Luborsky, 1991). These relations are characterized by some asymmetry because aunts cannot be certain that their siblings' adult children will feel obliged to support them.

Siblings do seem to offer extra support to those who cannot turn readily to spouse or children. Siblings are more likely to serve, for example, as confidants to older people who have fewer children (Connidis & Davies, 1992). Being never-married significantly increases the likelihood that African Americans name a sibling as a primary source of emergency assistance (Taylor et al., 1988). The impaired elderly who get help from siblings have fewer children and are more likely to be divorced or never-married than counterparts who not getting such help (Cicirelli, Coward, & Dwyer, 1992). Sibling support has also been identified as especially important in the community care of adults with serious mental illnesses because they are not likely to have married and because they often outlive parents (Horwitz, Tessler, Fisher, & Gamache, 1992). While needs of the disabled determine care by a parent, sibling assistance is not a given. It is influenced positively by the quality of the sibling relationship as well as negatively by the competition that the potential caretaker's work, marriage, and young children pose.

Sibling Relations in Life-Course Perspective

For siblings, the relation between feelings for siblings (e.g., affection, perceived closeness) and behavior (e.g., contact, support) is a complex one. Affect toward siblings is sometimes characterized by considerable ambivalence, and "true" feelings revealed by projective measures may not square with respondent's direct statements concerning closeness, good feelings, or antipathy regarding a given sib (Bedford, 1989). Indeed, a given behavior (e.g., interaction) may be associated with both positive and negative feelings. To be sure, friendly feelings toward sibs are associated with greater contact, reliance on sibs for support, and actual exchanges (White & Riedmann, 1992a). Greater contact, however, may provide more opportunities for sibling conflict—as evidenced by the positive association between these two variables (Lee, Mancini, & Maxwell, 1990). Although interaction and exchange are sometimes assumed to measure emotional solidary between sibs, they are imperfect indicators because so many situational variables (e.g., proximity) shape sibling interaction. Contact declines with advancing years, but this does not necessarily imply a decline in affection between siblings. Siblings may even come to feel closer to one another with the passing of time because feelings of envy, anger, and resentment once separating siblings appear to diminish by old age (Gold, 1989).

A life-course perspective on family relations in adulthood stresses that these relations generate lifelong influences, are shaped by career contingencies of the life course, and are socially and historically situated. Sibling relations manifest all these life-course characteristics.

Consider siblings' lasting consequences. They are formative influences on childhood development, as evidenced by the effects of sibling numbers on schooling. In adulthood, sibset membership continues to influence experience. The sibship, for example, affects both resource flows and contact between adult children and their parents.

Because no strong normative prescriptions require sibling solidarity in North American culture, the demands of life-course careers exercise a profound influence over sibling

associations. Contact, exchanges, and emotional closeness to brothers and sisters ebb and flow throughout adulthood in response to the opportunities, constraints, and needs posed by growing up and growing older. Sibling ties constitute a resource that, if often untapped, stands ready to be activated when a spouse dies, when parents need help, or when life events reunite sibs in the same community.

To be sure, the structure of adult sibships (e.g., numbers, gender, spacing, full–step–half relations) reflects cultural and historical patterns of family formation together with mortality regimes. Other factors that influence sibling interaction in adulthood are also subject to cultural variation and historical change (e.g., geographic mobility, educational attainment, lifelong singlehood, childlessness).

Conclusion

In many ways, the study of parent–child and sibling relationships in adulthood is, like air conditioning in the South, a former luxury but now a necessity. By isolating mortality to specific segments of our population—primarily the very old—and problematic fertility primarily to the unmarried teen population, the study of family is now focused not on the endpoints of demographic behavior, but on the life course in between. Comparing children of divorce to children from "intact" families with respect to their family and career outcomes demonstrates that family relationships at one point in life can be best understood with knowledge of earlier family experience.

It is, of course, misleading to generalize the process of family relations over the life course from the experience of one cohort, especially when the population structure is in flux, thereby altering availability of kin. Older persons are now likely to be parents of Baby Boomers, and, therefore, their children have siblings to share the responsibility of their parents' declining years. Having experienced delayed marriage and childbearing and low fertility, these same Baby Boomers are not apt to have the "wealth" of adult children that their parents had (Himes, 1992). They may have to rely more on their siblings.

Fortunately, new longitudinal studies (e.g., the National Survey of Families and Households) promise to address the dynamics of the dyadic relationship over the life course and the uniqueness of cohort experience. Much more remains to be known about the distinct experiences of significant subgroups of the population—social classes, ethnic and racial minorities, homosexuals, and the disabled. Categorical variables in quantitative models have been more successful at identifying ethnic differences in family life than in explaining them. The impact of extraordinary macroeconomic changes on family processes are even less well understood.

What is clear is the richness and complexity of family life in adulthood. The lives of parents and children, brothers and sisters, are woven together over many decades by past experience and present contingencies. Far from being a phenomenon of childhood and adolescence, the family of origin is a significant resource for most adults throughout their lives.

References

Abel, E. K. (1991). *Who cares for the elderly: Public policy and experiences of adult daughters.* Philadelphia, PA: Temple University Press.

Acock, A., & Kiecolt, K. J. (1989). Is it family structure or SES? Family structure during adolescence and adult adjustment. *Social Forces, 68,* 553–571.

Aldous, J. (1987). New views on the family life of the elderly and the near-elderly. *Journal of Marriage and the Family, 49,* 227–233.

Amato, P. (1988). Long-term implications of parental divorce for adult self-concept. *Journal of Family Issues, 9,* 201–213.

Amato, P., & Booth, A. (1991). Consequences of parental divorce and marital unhappiness for adult well-being. *Social Forces, 69,* 895–914.

Antonucci, T. C., & Akiyama, H. (1987). Social networks in adult life and a preliminary examination of the convoy model. *Journal of Gerontology, 42,* 519–527.

Aquilino, W. (1990). The likelihood of parent–child co-residence: Effects of family structure and parental characteristics. *Journal of Marriage and the Family, 52,* 405–419.

Aquilino, W. (1991). Predicting parents' experiences with coresident adult children. *Journal of Family Issues, 12,* 323–342.

Aquilino, W. (1994). Family disruption and young adults' relationships with parents. *Journal of Marriage and the Family, 56,* 295–313.

Aquilino, W., & Supple, K. (1991). Parent–child relations and parent's satisfaction with living arrangements. *Journal of Marriage and the Family, 53,* 13–27.

Avioli, P. S. (1989). The social support functions of siblings in later life. *American Behavioral Scientist, 33,* 45–57.

Axinn, W., & Thornton, A. (1992). The relationship between cohabitation and divorce: Selectivity or causal influence? *Demography, 29,* 357–374.

Axinn, W., & Thornton, A. (1993). Mothers, children and cohabitation: The intergenerational effects of attitudes and behavior. *American Sociological Review, 58,* 233–246.

Baruch, G., & Barnett, R. (1983). Adult daughter's relationships with their mothers. *Journal of Marriage and the Family, 45,* 601–606.

Bedford, V. H. (1989). Ambivalence in adult sibling relationships. *Journal of Family Issues, 10,* 211–224.

Bengtson, V. L., & Kuypers, J. A. (1971). Generational differences in the developmental stake. *Aging and Human Development, 2,* 249–260.

Blake, J. (1989). *Family size and achievement.* Berkeley: University of California Press.

Booth, A., & Amato, P. (1994). Parental marital quality, parental divorce and relations with parents. *Journal of Marriage and the Family, 56,* 21–34.

Booth, A., & Johnson, D. (1988). Premarital cohabitation and marital success. *Journal of Family Issues, 9,* 255–272.

Brody, E., & Schoonover, C. (1986). Patterns of parent care when adult daughters work and when they do not. *The Gerontologist, 26,* 372–381.

Bumpass, L., Sweet, J., & Martin, T. (1989). *Background and early marital factors in marital disruption* (NSFH Working Paper #14). Madison: University of Wisconsin.

Bumpass, L., Sweet, J., & Cherlin, A. (1991). Role of cohabitation in declining rates of marriage. *Journal of Marriage and the Family, 53,* 913–927.

Cicirelli, V. G. (1980). A comparison of college women's feelings toward their siblings and parents. *Journal of Marriage and the Family, 42,* 111–118.

Cicirelli, V. G. (1982). Sibling influence throughout the lifespan. In M. E. Lamb & B. Sutton-Smith (Eds.), *Sibling relationships: Their nature and significance across the lifespan.* Hillsdale, NJ: Erlbaum.

Cicirelli, V. G., Coward, R. T., & Dwyer, J. W. (1992). Siblings as caregivers for impaired elders. *Research on Aging, 14,* 331–350.

Connidis, I. A. (1992). Life transitions and the adult sibling tie: A qualitative study. *Journal of Marriage and the Family, 54,* 972–982.

Connidis, I. A., & Davies, L. (1992). Confidants and companions: Choices in later life. *Journal of Gerontology, 47,* S115–122.

Cooney, T. (1994). Young adults' relations with parents: The influence of recent parental divorce. *Journal of Marriage and the Family, 56,* 45–56.

Cooney, T., & Uhlenberg, P. (1990). The role of divorce in men's relations with their adult children after mid-life. *Journal of Marriage and the Family, 52,* 677–688.

Cooney, T. M., & Uhlenberg, P. (1992). Support from parents over the life course: The adult child's perspective. *Social Forces, 71,* 63–84.

Coward, R. T., & Dwyer, J. W. (1990). The association of gender, sibling network composition, and patterns of parent care by adult children. *Research on Aging, 12,* 158–181.

Crimmins, E., & Ingegneri, D. (1990). Interaction and living arrangements of older parents and their children: Past trends, present determinants, future implications. *Research on Aging, 12,* 3–35.

Crimmins, E., Easterlin, R., & Saito, Y. (1991). Preference changes among American youth: Family, work and goods aspirations, 1976–1986. *Population and Development Review, 17,* 115–133.

Dewit, D., Wister, A., & Burch, T. (1988). Physical distance and social contact between elders and their adult children. *Research on Aging, 10,* 56–80.

Dwyer, J. W., & Coward, R. T. (1991). A multivariate comparison of the involvement of adult sons versus daughters in the care of impaired parents. *Journal of Gerontology, 46,* S259–269.

Dwyer, J. W., Henretta, J. C., Coward, R. T., & Barton, A. J. (1992). Changes in helping behaviors of adult children as caregivers. *Research on Aging, 14,* 351–375.

Eggebeen, D. (1992). Family structure and intergenerational exchanges. *Research on Aging, 14,* 427–447.

Eggebeen, D., & Hogan, D. (1990). Giving between generations in American families. *Human Nature, 1,* 211–232.

Farkas, J., & Hogan, D. (1994). The demography of changing intergenerational relationships. In V. L. Bengtson, K. W. Schaie, & L. Burton (Eds.), *Intergenerational issues in aging* (pp. 1–18). New York: Springer.

Farley, R. (1988). After the starting line: Blacks and women in an uphill race. *Demography, 25,* 477–496.

Fein, D. (1990). Racial and ethnic differentials in U.S. Census omission rates. *Demography, 27,* 285–302.

Ganong, L., Coleman, M., & Mapes, D. (1990). A meta-analytic review of family structure and stereotypes. *Journal of Marriage and the Family, 52,* 287–297.

Gerstel, N. (1988). Divorce and kin ties: The importance of gender. *Journal of Marriage and the Family, 50,* 209–219.

Glenn, N. M., & Kramer, K. (1985). The psychological well-being of adult children of divorce. *Journal of Marriage and the Family, 47,* 905–912.

Glenn, N. M., & Kramer, K. (1987). The marriages and divorces of the children of divorce. *Journal of Marriage and the Family, 49,* 811–825.

Gold, D. T., (1989). Generational solidarity: Conceptual antecedents and consequences. *American Behavioral Scientist, 33,* 19–32.

Gold, D. T. (1990). Late-life sibling relationships: Does race affect typological distribution? *The Gerontologist, 30,* 741–748.

Gold, D. T., Woodbury, M. A., & George, L. K. (1990). Relationship classification using grade of membership analysis: A typology of sibling relationships in later life. *Journal of Gerontology, 45,* S43–51.

Goldscheider, F., & DaVanzo, J. (1989). Pathways to independent living in early adulthood: Marriage, semiautonomy and premarital residential independence. *Demography, 26,* 597–614.

Goldscheider, F., & Goldscheider, C. (1989). Family structure and conflict: Nest-leaving expectations of young adults and their parents. *Journal of Marriage and the Family, 51,* 87–98.

Goldscheider, F., & Goldsscheider, C. (1991). The intergenerational flows of income: Family structure and the status of black Americans. *Journal of Marriage and the Family, 53,* 499–508.

Goldscheider, F., & Waite, L. (1991). *New families, no families.* Berkeley: University of California Press.

Guttentag, M., & Secord, P. (1983). *Too many women? The sex ratio question.* Newbury Park, CA: Sage.

Hagestad, G. (1987). Parent–child relations in later life: Trends and gaps in past research. In J. Lancaster, J. Altmann, A. Rossi, & L. Sherrod (Eds.), *Parenting across the life span: Biosocial dimensions.* New York: Aldine de Gruyter.

Hamon, R. (1992). Filial role enactment by adult children. *Family Relations, 41,* 91–96.

Himes, C. (1992). Future caregivers: Projected family structures of older persons. *Journal of Gerontology, 47,* S17–26.

Hofferth, S. (1984). Updating children's life course. *Journal of Marriage and the Family, 47,* 93–116.

Hogan, D. P., & Eggebeen, D. (1995). Sources of emergency help and routine assistance in old age. *Social Forces, 73,* 917–936.

Hogan, D., & Kitagawa, E. (1985). The impact of social status, family structure, and neighborhood on the fertility of black adolescents. *American Journal of Sociology, 90,* 825–839.

Horwitz, A. V., Tessler, R. C., Fisher, G. A., & Gamache, G. M. (1992). The role of adult siblings in providing social support to the severely mentally ill. *Journal of Marriage and the Family, 54,* 233–241.

Johnson, C. (1988). Post-divorce reorganization of relationships between divorcing children and their parents. *Journal of Marriage and the Family, 50,* 221–231.

Keith, V., & Finlay, B. (1988). Impact of parental divorce on children's educational attainment, marital timing and likelihood of divorce. *Journal of Marriage and the Family, 50,* 797–810.

Keith, V., & Smith, D. (1988). The current differential in black and white life expectancy. *Demography, 25,* 625–640.

Kobrin, F. (1976). The fall of household size and the rise of the primary individual in the United States. *Demography, 13,* 127–138.

Kobrin, F., & Waite, L. (1984). Effects of childhood family structure on transition to marriage. *Journal of Marriage and the Family, 46,* 807–816.

Kulis, S. (1991). *Why honor thy Father and mother? Class, mobility, and family ties in later life.* New York: Garland.

Kulka, R., & Weingarten, H. (1979). The long-term effects of parental divorce in childhood on adult adjustment. *Journal of Social Issues, 35,* 50–78.

Lawton, L. (1990). *The quality of the parent and adult–child relationship.* Unpublished doctoral dissertation, Brown University, Providence, RI.

Lawton, L., Silverstein, M., & Bengtson, V. L. (1994a). Solidarity between generations in families. In V. L. Bengtson & R. A. Harootzan (Eds.), *Hidden connections: A national survey of intergenerational linkages in American society* (pp. 19–42). New York: Springer.

Lawton, L., Silverstein, M., & Bengtson, V. (1994b). Affection, social contact, and geographic distance between adult children and their parents. *Journal of Marriage and the Family, 56,* 57–68.

Lee, T. R., Mancini, J. A., & Maxwell, J. W. (1990). Sibling relationships in adulthood: Contact patterns and motivations. *Journal of Marriage and the Family, 52,* 431–440.

Lee, G.R., Dwyer, J. W., & Coward, R. T. (1993). Gender differences in parent care: Demographic factors and same-gender preferences. *Journal of Gerontology, 48,* S9–S16.

Lichter, D., LeClere, F., & McLaughlin, D. (1990). Local marriage markets and marital behavior of black and white women. *American Journal of Sociology, 96,* 843–867.

Litwak, E., & Kulis, S. (1987). Technology, proximity and measures of support. *Journal of Marriage and the Family, 49,* 649–661.

Mancini, J., & Blieszner, R. (1989). Aging parents and adult child: Research themes in intergenerational relations. *Journal of Marriage and the Family, 49,* 811–825.

Marini, M. M. (1990), *The rise in individualism in advanced industrial societies.* Paper presented at the Annual Meetings of the Population Association of America, Toronto, Canada.

Matthews, S. H., & Rosner, T. T. (1988). Shared filial responsibility: The family as the primary caregiver. *Journal of Marriage and the Family, 50,* 185–195.

Matthews, S. H., Werkner, J. E., & Delaney, P. (1989). Relative contributions of help by employed and nonemployed sisters to their elderly parents. *Journal of Gerontology, 44,* S36–S44.

McGhee, J. L. (1985). The effects of siblings on the life satisfaction of the rural elderly. *Journal of Marriage and the Family, 47,* 85–91.

McLanahan, S. (1988). The consequences of single parenthood for subsequent generations. *Focus, 11,* 16–21.

McLanahan, S., & Bumpass, L. (1988). Intergenerational consequences of family disruption. *American Journal of Sociology, 94,* 130–152.

Mercier, J., Paulson, L., & Morris, E. (1989). Proximity as a mediating influence on the perceived aging parent–adult child relationship. *The Gerontologist, 29,* 785–791.

Merrill, D. (1993). Daughters-in-laws as caregivers and the elderly: Defining the in-law relationship. *Research on Aging, 15,* 70–91.

Miller, W. B. (1992). Developmental experiences as antecedents of childbearing motivation. *Demography, 29,* 265–285.

Moen, P., Dempster-McCain, D., & Williams, R. (1992). Successful aging: A life course perspective on women's multiple roles and health. *American Journal of Sociology, 97,* 1612–1638.

Moore, G. (1990). Structural determinants of men's and women's personal networks. *American Sociological Review, 55,* 726–735.

Mutran, E. (1985). Intergenerational family support among blacks and whites: Response to culture or to socioeconomic differences. *Journal of Gerontology, 40,* 382–389.

Mutran, E., & Reitzes, D. (1984). Intergenerational support activities and well-being among the elderly: A convergence of exchange and symbolic interaction perspectives. *American Sociological Review, 49,* 117–130

O'Bryant, S. L. (1988). Sibling support and older widows' well-being. *Journal of Marriage and the Family, 50,* 173–183.

Preston, S., & Qian, Z. (1993). Changes in American marriage 1972–1987: Availability and forces of attraction by age and education. *American Sociological Review, 58,* 482–495.

Rindfuss, R., & Vandenheuval, A. (1990). Cohabitation: Precursor to marriage or an alternative to being single? *Population and Development Review, 16,* 703–726.

Rodgers, J. L., & Rowe, D. C. (1990). Adolescent sexual activity and mildly deviant behavior. *Journal of Family Issues, 11,* 274–293.

Rogers, R. (1992). Living and dying in the U.S.A.: Sociodemographic determinants of death among blacks and whites. *Demography, 29,* 287–304.

Rossi, A. S., & Rossi, P. H. (1990). *Of human bonding: Parent–child relations across the life course.* New York: Aldine de Gruyter.

Rubinstein, R. L., Alexander, B. B., Goodman, M., & Luborsky, M. (1991). Key relationships of never-married, childless older women: A cultural analysis. *Journal of Gerontology, 46*, 270–277.

Schoen, R., & Kluegel, J. (1988). The widening gap in black and white marriage rates: The impact of population and differential marriage propensities. *American Sociological Review, 53*, 895–904.

Silverstein, M., Lawton, L., & Bengtson, V. (1994). Types of relations between parents and adult children. In V. Bengtson & R. Harootyan (Eds.), *Intergenerational linkages: Hidden connections* (pp. 43–76). New York: Springer, 1994.

South, S. (1991). Sociodemographic differentials in mate selection preferences. *Journal of Marriage and the Family, 53*, 928–940.

South, S., & Lloyd, K. (1992). Marriage opportunities and family formation: Further implications of imbalanced sex ratios. *Journal of Marriage and the Family, 54*, 440–451.

Speare, A., & Avery, R. (1991). *Who helps whom in older parent–child families?* (PSTC Working Paper Series 91-03). Providence, RI: Brown University, Population Studies and Training Center.

Spitze, G., & Logan, J. R. (1991). Sibling structure and intergenerational relations. *Journal of Marriage and the Family, 53*, 871–884.

Spitze, G., & Milner, S. (1992). Gender differences in adult child contact among black elderly parents. *The Gerontologist, 32*, 213–218.

Spitze, G., Logan, J., Deane, G., & Zerger, S. (1984). Adult children's divorce and intergenerational relationships. *Journal of Marriage and the Family, 58*, 279–294.

Sprecher, S., & Felmlee, D. (1992). The influence of parents and friends on the quality and stability of romantic relationships: A three-wave longitudinal study. *Journal of Marriage and the Family, 54*, 888–900.

Stoller, E. P., Forster, L. E., & Duniho, T. S. (1992). Systems of parent care within sibling networks. *Research on Aging, 14*, 28–49.

Suggs, P. K. (1989). Predictors of association among older siblings: A black–white comparison. *American Behavioral Scientist, 33*, 70–80.

Suitor, J. J., & Pillemer, K. (1988). Explaining intergenerational conflict when adult children and elderly parents live together. *Journal of Marriage and the Family, 50*, 1037–1047.

Taylor, R., & Chatters, L. (1991). Extended family networks of older black adults. *The Journal of Gerontology, 46*, S210–S217.

Taylor, R. J., Chatters, L. M., & Mays, V. M. (1988). Parents, children, siblings, in-laws, and non-kin as sources of emergency assistance to black Americans. *Family Relations, 37*, 298–304.

Uhlenberg, P., & Cooney, T. (1990). Family size and mother–child relations in later life. *The Gerontologist, 30*, 618–625.

Umberson, D. (1992). Relationships between adult children and their parents: Psychological consequences for both generations. *Journal of Marriage and the Family, 54*, 664–674.

United States Bureau of the Census. (1997). *Statistical abstract of the United States, 1997.* Washington, DC: U.S. Government Printing Office.

Waite, L., & Harrison, S. (1992). Keeping in touch: How women in midlife allocate social contacts among kith and kin. *Social Forces, 70*, 637–654.

Walker, A., & Allen, K. (1991). Relationships between caregiving daughters and their elderly mothers. *The Gerontologist, 31*, 389–396.

Wallerstein, J., & Blakeslee, S. (1989). *Second chances: Men, women, and children a decade after divorce.* New York: Ticknor and Fields.

Ward, R., Logan, J., & Spitze, G. (1992). The influence of parent and child needs on coresidence in middle and later life. *Journal of Marriage and the Family, 54*, 209–221.

Weiss, R. (1979). Growing up a little faster: The experience of growing up in a single-parent household. *Journal of Social Issues, 35*, 97–111.

Weitzman, B., Knickman, J., & Shinn, M. (1990). Pathways to homelessness among New York City families. *Journal of Social Issues, 46*, 125–140.

Whitbeck, L., Simons, R., & Conger, R. (1991). The effects of early family relationships on contemporary relationships and assistance patterns between adult children and their parents. *Journal of Gerontology, 46*, S330–337.

White, L. (1992). The effect of parental divorce and remarriage on parental support for adult children. *Journal of Marriage and the Family, 13*, 234–250.

White, L., & Edwards, J. (1990). Emptying the nest and parental well-being. *American Sociological Review, 55*, 235–242.

White, L. K., & Riedmann, A. (1992a). Ties among adult siblings. *Social Forces, 71*, 85–102.

White, L. K., & Riedmann, A. (1992b). When the Brady Bunch grows up: Step/half- and full sibling relationships in adulthood. *Journal of Marriage and the Family, 54*, 197–208.

Whyte, M. K. (1990). *Dating, mating, and marriage.* New York: Aldine de Gruyter.

Wilson, W. J. (1987). *The truly disadvantaged: The inner city, the underclass, and public policy.* Chicago: University of Chicago Press.

CHAPTER 16

Gender and Family Relationships

Alexis J. Walker

For over 25 years, researchers have focused on gender as an important dimension of family relationships. The nature of that focus has changed significantly, however. Early research highlighted gender as an independent variable, that is, as a way to explain differences between women and men in marital satisfaction, power in decision making, and so forth. Gender was viewed as an unchangeable, unmalleable given. It was assumed that family life was inherently different for women and men. This approach was consistent with a focus on gender roles in families—differential obligations women and men were believed to incur, appropriately, because of their gender and their socialization into adulthood. In other words, women and men were seen as engaging in certain behaviors and occupying specific roles because they were female or male (Osmond & Thorne, 1993; Thompson, 1993; West & Zimmerman, 1987).

As demonstrated by Myra Ferree (1990), over the past 25 years feminist theory has informed the research on gender and family relationships. Briefly summarized, feminists reject the notion that families are separate, private institutions in society, believing instead that families can only be understood in relation to the broader social context or what is considered to be the public domain (Ferree, 1990). In other words, feminists rejected the notion of two separate, distinct spheres, public and private. Furthermore, rather than considering each family to be a unitary whole, feminists recognized that each family member experiences a unique life reflecting the fundamental conflicts of interest associated with gender and generation.

Feminist scholars began their study of families using a sex-role perspective, but rejected this approach after it was

Alexis J. Walker • Human Development and Family Sciences, Oregon State University, Corvallis, Oregon 97331-5102.

Handbook of Marriage and the Family, 2nd edition, edited by Marvin Sussman, Suzanne K. Steinmetz, and Gary W. Peterson. Plenum Press, New York, 1999.

shown to be reflective of the particular sociohistorical context in which it emerged and upon realization that it obscured the importance of the social structure. The term *sex* itself was rejected as implying a biological origin to perceived differences between women and men that ignored the influence of social structure evident in the term *gender*. Furthermore, feminists found that sex-role theory was unable to account for the tremendous variability evident in both women and men (see Osmond & Thorne, 1993; West & Zimmerman, 1987).

Employing different approaches, feminist researchers brought a variety of new perspectives to the study of gender and families. Feminist empiricists revised traditional scientific methodologies, addressing issues of significance to women while attempting to eliminate biases that prevent a more accurate understanding of reality (Baber & Allen, 1992). Empiricism is the dominant feminist approach evident in mainstream family journals, and it typifies the literature reviewed here. It is problematic to the extent that alternative approaches may be required to eliminate biases that marginalize women's experiences (Baber & Allen, 1992). A second feminist approach is standpoint theory, which postulates that knowledge depends on one's position in the social hierarchy (Hawkesworth, 1989). Standpoint theories acknowledge the difficulty individuals with privilege and power have in seeing the world from the point of view of people who are oppressed. Individuals with less power must know their own world and that of those who have power over them, thus giving them a more complete view of reality (e.g., Hill Collins, 1990). Standpoint theory runs the risk of privileging women's experience over that of men. Furthermore, both feminist empiricists and standpoint theorists run the risk of minimizing or ignoring variability among women (Baber & Allen, 1992). A third approach, postmodern feminism, argues that factors in addition to gender, such as race, class, age, sexual orientation, physical attractiveness, and family status, mediate each person's understanding of reality (Harding, 1987). The postmodern approach runs the risks of fragmenting the experiences of members of particular social categories and accepting every approach to discovering reality as valid (Baber & Allen, 1992). Its advantage lies in its potential to identify the ambiguity and contradiction in individual lives.

Recently, feminist theorists have modified perceptions of gender consistent with a social constructionist view, that is, that women and men are differentially placed in the social structure and help to create and reinforce it in systematic ways. Women and men are categorized and stratified such that their resulting perceptions, expectations, behavior, and experiences differ (Ferree, 1990; Mednick, 1989). These variations reflect beliefs and values about gender and simultaneously reinforce the privilege of one gender over another. This *gender perspective* has called old ways of examining gender into question. It specifically rejects the notion of families as separate from other social institutions and processes. Indeed, it acknowledges that broader social systems and structures impinge on everyday family life, reproducing inside families the divisions that exist outside of them (Barrett & McIntosh, 1982).

According to the gender perspective, individual behaviors and roles have "gendered meanings" (Ferree, 1990, p. 869); that is, what people do comes to symbolize gender. Instead of examining the behaviors and roles believed to be associated with gender, the focus is on how certain structures, behaviors, and attitudes come to be linked (see also Eagly, 1983; Eagly & Steffan, 1984). To understand the experiences of women and men, therefore, one must examine structure and symbol, resources and beliefs, institutions and interactions (Ferree, 1990; Smith, 1987; Thompson, 1993). Together, these processes account for the construction of female and male as different and male as better. According to Ferree:

> The fundamental question is how the illusion of a gender dichotomy is constructed and maintained in the face of between-sex similarity and within-sex difference, and the answer is found in the constant and contentious process of engendering behavior as separate and unequal. (pp. 868–869)

In effect, women and men create gender in their social interaction (Bohan, 1993; West & Zimmerman, 1987). Gender is not an individual property but a fundamental basis of social order (West & Zimmerman, 1987). (See also Ferree, 1990; Osmond & Thorne, 1993; Thompson, 1993; and West & Zimmerman, 1987, for explications of the gender framework.)

Families are ideal social institutions to examine gender because "[g]ender hierarchy is created, reproduced, and maintained on a day-to-day basis through interaction among members of a household" (Glenn, 1987, p. 348). Through everyday interactions, people negotiate gender, confirm and disconfirm each other as women and men, sustain or change

gender meanings, and create gender strategies (Ferree, 1990; Hochschild, 1989; Thompson, 1993; West & Zimmerman, 1987). Unfortunately, little research published in the study of families examines gender from this perspective (Thompson & Walker, 1995). In fact, a significant portion of the literature fails even to search for gender differences. Nevertheless, students of families increasingly attend to the role of gender in family life.

This chapter concentrates on literature published since 1989 as well as a few areas (e.g., kinship) absent from an earlier review. (See Thompson & Walker, 1989, for a comprehensive review of earlier research.) The chapter also highlights feminist approaches to the study of gender and families (see Thompson & Walker, 1995), with a focus on adults in families primarily in the United States, examining the gendered development of children in only the most cursory way. Specifically, I attend to gender as constructed in partnerships, in parenthood, in work, and in kinship.

Partnership

Few researchers study the construction and maintenance of gendered patterns in interpersonal relationships. Instead, they study courtship, the integration of partners into each other's social worlds, processes of relationship change and commitment, and couple interaction (see Surra, 1990, for a review). When included, gender is considered primarily as an individual property. For example, researchers study differential patterns of negativity in interaction between wives and husbands. Rather than considering the broader social structure, attention is given to the more immediate social network and relationship contexts. Sometimes, relationships themselves are the unit of analysis, reflecting an implicit assumption that relationship processes and patterns may be identical for women and men. Recent research that considers gender as an integral component in the way relationships are developed and maintained, and of gendered patterns in relationships as contributors to social structures, institutions, resources, beliefs, and interactions, is highlighted. I consider the timing and incidence of marriage, the connection between couple interaction and marital quality, power in marriage, and husbands' violence toward wives. I also briefly review research on gender as a component of nonmarital, romantic relationships.

Marriage

Timing and Incidence. Marriage rates are changing. First marriages now occur later, particularly for highly educated women and for Japanese American and Chinese American women (Ferguson, 1995). Furthermore, more women than men, especially African Americans, will never marry (Norton & Moorman, 1987). Remarriage after divorce is less frequent as well, particularly for the more educated (Norton & Moorman, 1987) and for women who receive child support (Folk, Graham, & Ballar, 1992). Remarriage rates are slightly higher for divorced men, and men remarry more quickly than women (Wilson & Clarke, 1992).

Declines in the rate of marriage appear to be due to a lessening preference for it rather than an increase in barriers to it (Goldscheider & Waite, 1986; Stacey, 1993). Declines have been greater for women than for men, yet men's rates are down as well. There is a reduced willingness of women to marry, in part because of their increased ability to support themselves as well as declines in the ability of men to be "good providers" (Lichter, Anderson, & Hayward, 1995). Furthermore, women with higher self-esteem have marriages of shorter duration (Esterberg, Moen, & Dempster-McClain, 1994). As Ross (1995) demonstrated, being in an unhappy marriage is worse for psychological well-being than living alone. Men, too, have more options outside of marriage, and there has been a decline in their relative preference for it. Goldscheider and Waite (1986) argued that the effects of women's reduced willingness and men's reduced preference to marry will weaken if men increase their home involvement and women increase their nonfamily involvement. In fact, men now choose as wives women who can share economic responsibility. These patterns demonstrate a transformation of the role of marriage in adult transitions. That is, marriage may now be discretionary for adult status (Lye & Biblarz, 1993).

Older black women relative to older black men have a disincentive to marry (Tucker, Taylor, & Mitchell-Kernan, 1993). African American men are more likely to desire marriage because of a need for care and/or a need for money. Having to provide care, however, is a disincentive for women. Thus marriage rates among older African Americans are low. Among all racial and ethnic groups, remarriage after widowhood is also low. Two-thirds never consider remarriage (Gentry & Shulman, 1988). They like being single and enjoy the independence of widowhood. This is especially true for those ages 36–65, but remarriage is low in all age groups.

Marital Quality and Interaction. Glenn and Weaver (1988) reported a systematic decline from 1972 to 1986 in the positive association between being married and reported happiness. They attribute this finding to an increase in the happiness of never-married men and a corresponding decrease in the happiness of married women. Others (Blair, 1993; McRae & Brody, 1989; but see Johnson, Amoloza, & Booth, 1992) also have shown that wives' experience of marriage is more negative than husbands'. This may be why

being married is more beneficial to men's well-being than women's and why the association between well-being and marriage is stronger for women (McRae & Brody, 1989). Being married, according to Ross (1995), does not guarantee social support. Furthermore, roles in addition to the wife role do not diminish the effect of negative marital experience for women (McRae & Brody, 1989).

Wives have higher marital satisfaction when they see their husbands as being more sensitive to them, when they share spiritual activities and physical affection, when they join in their husbands' activities, and when they see honesty and sincerity in their relationships (Bell, Daly, & Conzalez, 1987). African Americans are less likely than whites to see their marriages as harmonious, and the difference resides primarily in the lower scores of black women relative to white women (Broman, 1993). Broman argued that African American marriages face more stress and that African Americans may stay in lower-quality marriages more often than whites.

Early in a marriage, when husbands are satisfied, both spouses are affectionate and wives maintain high levels of affectional expression (Huston & Vangelisti, 1991). When wives are less satisfied, however, both husbands and wives are more negative and husbands are increasingly so over time. In other words, wives' satisfaction encourages husbands' positive socioemotional behavior while wives' dissatisfaction encourages husbands' negative behavior. Huston and Vangelisti propose two possible explanations: (1) husbands' negativity results in wives' dissatisfaction, which leads to husbands' greater negativity; or (2) wives' early dissatisfaction leads to husbands' negativity, which leads to wives' greater dissatisfaction. Both wives' dissatisfaction and husbands' negative behavior play an important role in the course of marital satisfaction (see also Vannoy & Philliber, 1992.)

Reports of marriage vary by outcome measures, however. Husbands and wives may report similar marital quality, but wives report more disagreement and more troubled marriages (Blair, 1993). Husbands are more traditional in their gender and family ideology, and their marital evaluations reflect their views. For example, husbands consider divorce more likely if their wives do less family work and if their wives have a different status job from their own, but wives consider divorce more likely if their husbands work long hours for pay. For both wives and husbands, wives' assessments of fairness have stronger effects on marital quality than husbands' assessments (Blair, 1993). Couples who agree on family ideology are more satisfied, especially if their attitudes are traditional. If they disagree, their satisfaction scores are lowest if the wife is nontraditional and the husband is traditional (Lye & Biblarz, 1993).

Religion plays a supportive role for African American

women, who are happier when their marriages have religious themes (Veroff, Sutherland, Chadiha, & Ortega, 1993). Themes of financial problems and children lead to unhappy feelings about the marriage for African American husbands. Money is very important to black men's views of marital tension. Veroff and colleagues (1993) suggested that black men may be concerned about their adequacy as husbands or fathers, a reasonable position given economic demands in the context of a racist society.

Middle-aged and older wives provide and receive less social support in marriage than husbands, although the data show considerable conjugal support in later life. Depner and Ingersoll-Dayton (1985) suggested that limits to personal resources or nurturance skills erode the bases of respect, affection, and compatibility among older persons; women alternatively may differentiate between support that is required by role obligations and that given freely. Others (Oggins, Veroff, & Leber, 1993; Rich, 1983) confirm that elderly wives, and to a lesser degree husbands, do not name their spouses as their most important confidants, although both, especially husbands, name them as companions (Connidis & Davies, 1990). Confiding is more common in black than in white couples and is particularly low among white husbands (Oggins et al., 1993).

After 20 years of marriage, wives report that resolving disagreements becomes more difficult over time (Vaillant & Vaillant, 1993). Also over time, wives report lower marital adjustment whereas husbands report greater declines in sexual satisfaction (see also Heaton & Albrecht, 1991). Among elderly couples, older wives are more likely to consider separating than older husbands (Levenson, Carstensten, & Gottman, 1993). In middle age, wives report greater enjoyment of children and grandchildren but more financial conflict and poorer physical health than husbands. Because middle-aged women with poorer-quality marriages are in poorer health, the authors suggested that dissatisfied marriages actually may make wives ill (see also Gottman & Levenson, 1992; Levenson, Carstensen, & Gottman, 1994).

Power. Except for work by Komter (1989), few studies focus directly on marital power (Thompson & Walker, 1995). In her view, because ideology favors equal power in marriage, individuals are rarely vocal about marital inequality; they may even be unaware of intracouple power discrepancies. She studied husbands' latent marital power, which was reflected in women being less likely than men to get what they wanted out of marriage. For example, more women than men wanted change in the distribution of family work. Women reported impediments to changing family labor and felt guilty for wanting these changes. Even women who expressed no desire for change reported being more resigned in their marriages than men. The anticipated negative re-

sponses of husbands was viewed as a major obstacle to change. Similarly, in sexual interaction, although both women and men wanted change, wives tended to settle for husbands' wishes more than husbands satisfied theirs. Finally, wives were more disssatisfied than husbands about the way couples handled money. Wives felt their husbands should participate more in financial decisions and should be more aware of their struggles to make ends meet. In leisure activities, women gave up hobbies and friends in accordance with their husbands' wishes.

Women were more cautious than men in their strategies for change. The same strategies (e.g., sanctioning, waiting) were more effective when used by men than by women. Women said their direct strategies to bring about change, such as leaving the kitchen messy or serving a cold meal, were ineffective. These strategies did not seem to bother their husbands. Furthermore, husbands tended to legitimate situations with which their wives were unhappy by describing them as natural or inevitable. In Komter's (1989) view, husbands' negative responses or attitudes toward their wives' proposals for change and wives' anticipation of their husbands' needs give advantages to husbands and solidify gendered patterns in ideology, attitudes, and behavior.

Power differences also are evident in patterns of conflict among mostly white, middle-class couples (Christensen & Heavey, 1990; Heavey, Layne, & Christensen, 1993). The pattern of wife demands, husband withdraws, is common in couples only when discussing something wives want. From a structural perspective, Christensen and Heavey argued that men's position in society means that relationships are already structured as they wish while women's position in society leads to wives seeking change. To avoid change sought by wives, husbands withdraw. This demand–withdraw pattern is destructive to marital quality and stability (Heavey et al., 1993).

Pyke (1994) studied the marital power of white women in second marriages. Wives' employment was not seen as a resource in marriages where husbands had lower status jobs or were chronically unemployed. Instead, wives' paid work was a burden to their husbands. In other couples, where husbands forbade or restricted their wives' paid work and took their wives' family labor for granted, wives' lack of commitment to paid work did not necessarily result in a loss of marital power. Wives limited in education and in dead-end jobs were able to focus on domestic work and to share power. A third group of wives had been restricted in paid employment in their first marriages, but had expanded paid work in their second marriages. These wives insisted that their husbands accept and support their wage labor, thus exercising marital power. Pyke demonstrated that marital power is not directly tied to labor force participation, but instead reflects individual and couple histories and patterns.

Lorber and Bandlamudi (1993) studied white couples who were in infertility treatment because of husbands' low fertility. The wives took medication with painful side effects and underwent painful procedures and repeated often unpleasant interactions with health-care personnel to conceive and carry a fetus to term. The husbands were tested and asked to produce sperm on demand. The infertile husbands exercised veto power over the couples' involvement in infertility treatment, but the burden of the daily decisions and actions was on the wives, who also bore most of the social stigma attached to childlessness.

Not all couples in this situation are alike, however. In one group, the wives also have physical conditions that, in combination with their husbands' condition, decrease their likelihood of conception. These wives see themselves as potentially benefiting from infertility treatment. They have little ambivalence about pursuing treatment, and they describe close or improved marriages as a result. These wives gain bargaining power from the physical and emotion work they do to support their husbands and the marriage. In another group of couples, where the wives already have children but their current husbands want very much to be fathers, wives are giving a gift to their grateful husbands. The couple is involved in treatment together, and wives get sympathy and support from their husbands. These marriages also are seen as close or improved since treatment began. These wives minimize their sacrifices, but their husbands' awareness and acknowledgment of them give them powerful credit in the marriage.

In a third group, husbands maintained their power by pressuring their wives to undergo treatment but distancing themselves from the experience. Wives benefited from their husbands' distancing by avoiding additional marital strain, but resented the extra emotion work they had to do on their own. In this third group of couples, there was less agreement about the quality and stability of the marriage. Lorber and Bandlamudi (1993) concluded that wives' marital power depends on their sense of agency. Women in the first group are in control. There are high costs in taking on their husbands' burdens, but they simultaneously validate themselves as women and protect their husbands' identity, thus strengthening their marriages. Women in the second group get support and gratitude from their husbands. Women in the third group have less agency, but gain credit they can use later. These women are in relationships that are the most vulnerable to negative outcomes from the process of seeking and receiving infertility treatment.

Violence

Most data on spousal violence is from whites (Browne, 1993). Among blacks, rates are higher in blue-collar than in white-collar couples, but, in both groups, rates are higher among blacks than among whites (Uzell & Peebles-Wilkins, 1994). For African Americans income is negatively related to spousal violence. Among middle-income couples, rates are lower when wives are employed. There are some data indicating that black wives are more likely than white wives to respond to their husbands' violent behavior with violence and that black husbands are more likely than white husbands to continue the violent pattern of behavior over time. Most data from non-whites are based on small, nonrandom samples, however, with little attention to contextual factors such as employment history and experience of discrimination.

Recent observational data (Babcock, Waltz, Jacobson, & Gottman, 1993) obtained from married couples (race and ethnicity not reported) in which some evidenced severe husband-to-wife violence revealed that husbands with less power in the marriage are more likely to be abusive toward their wives. Indeed, a communication pattern of husband demanding and wife withdrawing—withdrawing reflecting a more powerful position—is related to both husbands' physical violence and psychological abuse. The authors speculated that husbands compensate for their reduced marital power with violence. Self-report data from these same couples revealed that husbands escalate their violent behavior in response to both violent and nonviolent behaviors on the part of wives (Jacobson et al., 1994). That is, both wives and husbands agree that wives are unable to stop their husbands' violence. Furthermore, wives' violent behaviors, according to both wives and husbands, occur when husbands are emotionally or physically abusive, and both spouses agree that only wives are fearful during marital arguments. Jacobson et al. argue that the ability of husband violence to produce fear in wives makes violence an effective control mechanism for husbands.

Frieze (1983) found that wife rape was correlated strongly with other violent acts by husbands. Rape was not a result of wives refusing sex or being unfaithful. Instead, husbands who raped their wives appeared to enjoy violent sex, to desire it often, and to feel it was their right to demand it. Herbert, Silver, and Ellard (1991) discovered that, in comparison with those who left an abusive partner, women who remained in abusive relationships used cognitive strategies to view their relationships more positively. Similarly, in earlier rather than later shelter stays, women gave accounts that minimized their partner's violence (Wolf-Smith & LaRossa, 1992).

In a review of the literature, Browne (1993) concluded that violence against women is perpetuated primarily by male partners. Most studies of couple violence are problematic because they exclude intent and outcomes and they focus almost solely on incidence. Such data understate the higher rates of injury suffered by women and the perpetration of multiple aggressive acts in a single incident by men. Furthermore, the disproportionate focus on why women stay draws attention from the conditions that lead to and maintain violence.

Recently, Michael Johnson (1995) clarified our understanding of men's violence toward women by distinguishing between *common couple violence* and *patriarchal terrorism.* The former, usually minor in form and an occasional occurrence, is perpetuated by both wives and husbands in their everyday conflicts. Information on this form is obtained from large-scale survey research. In the latter, husbands escalate violence as they strive to exert and maintain control over their wives (see also Feazell, Mayers, & Deschner, 1984). Information on this form is obtained from studies of women seeking assistance. The delineation of these two patterns explains the relatively low rates of severe spousal violence identified in the survey literature, as well as the higher rates of violence toward and injury of women identified in smaller studies.

A second recent contribution comes from Gilgun (1995), whose research on incest perpetrators, mostly men, uncovered contradictions between behavior and sociocultural mores of which the perpetrators were unaware. Despite coercing children, refusing children's pleas that they stop, and helping others to see children who disclose the incest as lying, incest perpetrators saw their behavior as reflecting love and care. In her important contribution, Gilgun called for a public discourse on the moral dimensions of family relationships to reduce the incidence of incest, one that would place responsibility, appropriately, on the incest perpetrators themselves (see also Lackey & Williams, 1995).

Nonmarital Romantic Relationships

Kurdek and Schmitt (1986b) compared the relationships of 44 married, 35 heterosexual cohabiting, 50 gay, and 56 lesbian monogamous pairs, all of whom lived together and had no children living with them. Shared decision making was highest in lesbian couples, but support from families was highest among married persons. Partners in all relationship types, however, were similar to each other in the patterns of association among love, liking, attachment, and relationship satisfaction (see also Kurdek, 1994; Kurdek & Schmitt, 1986a). Other data (Lewis, Kozac, Milardo, & Grosnick, 1981) comparing lesbian and gay couples suggested that women partners confide in each other and talk things over more than men partners do. Verifying notions that women attend to the caring aspects of relationships, Schullo and Alperson (1984) found that individuals with women partners, both lesbians and heterosexual men, had higher expectations of being validated and of receiving credit for insight, and were more accurate in these expectations, than were those with men partners.

Summary of Gender and Partnerships

Marriages benefit men more than women, and this difference is reflected in a decreasing likelihood that women will marry or remarry. In both heterosexual and lesbian partnerships, women attend more to relationship quality, and their relationship attitudes and physical health are affected negatively by poor relationship quality and unfairness. Perhaps because of their lesser social power in heterosexual pairings, women have little inclination to make demands of their male partners and little likelihood of changing marriage so that it benefits them more. Participation in the paid labor force is not sufficient to increase marital power for women, but wives gain power relative to their husbands when their husbands are infertile or when wives have demonstrated their fertility by bearing children in the context of an earlier marriage. When wives have more power relative to husbands, however, husbands are more likely to be physically and psychologically abusive, and wives seem unable to stop this violence.

Outside of the small amount of literature reviewed here and that described in previous reviews (Thompson & Walker, 1989, 1995), the vast majority of research on partnerships is tied to notions of gender as an individual property with little consideration for the social context. The literature would benefit by attention to questions such as those posed by Thompson (1993): How does one's social location (i.e., gender, race, class, and sexual preference) construct gendered behavior? How do everyday situations contribute to the creation of women and men as separate and unequal? How do partners in interaction develop gender strategies capable of accommodating beliefs about gender, emotional needs, behavior, and existing structural conditions? In addition, Johnson (1995), in his analysis of the literature on intracouple violence, identified research questions that, if answered, would explicate the connections between structure and relationship behavior. Moreover, methodologies designed to attend directly to gender must separate the effects of beliefs, behaviors, and social structures. We also need to be attentive to the ways in which the social construction of gender shapes our theoretical perspectives (see Watkins, 1993).

Parenthood

The literature on children in families is preoccupied with their socialization into "gender roles." As noted earlier, the socialization perspective fails to recognize that definitions of "appropriately" gendered behavior reflect particular sociohistorical contexts, ignoring the role of social structure in shaping beliefs, attitudes, and actions. It is able to explain neither the similarities between women and men, and girls and boys, nor the tremendous variability within genders (see Ferree, 1990; Osmond & Thorne, 1993; West & Zimmerman, 1987). Furthermore, as noted by Barrie Thorne (1986) children are incorporated into the research literature primarily in ways that reflect adult concerns. In family studies, children are considered primarily as targets of socialization or as "learners of adult culture" (p. 85).

Here I attend to the literature on parenthood that has gender as a central concern. I examine the ideologies of motherhood and fatherhood as well as the research that describes the interaction and involvement of mothers and fathers with their children. Relationships between parents and their young children also are examined, as is responsibility for children and childcare. Finally, I consider the new research on fatherhood. Throughout, I highlight research affirming that parenthood is gendered in beliefs, behaviors, experiences, and consequences (Ganong, Coleman, & Mistina, 1995; Thompson & Walker, 1989). For relevant literature focused primarily on child outcomes, see Peterson and Hann, Chapter 13, this volume.

Motherhood and Fatherhood

New research on infertility confirms that motherhood continues to be seen as essential for women, while fatherhood is seen as desirable for men. Women are more pressured by family members to have children than are men (Marciano, 1978), and wives but not husbands experience infertility as an overwhelming failure (Greil, Leitko, & Porter, 1988). Women who desire to bear children but are unable to do so withdraw from contact with the "fertile world" and focus on the "problem" of their infertility because they feel they cannot lead a normal life. Men whose wives are unable to conceive are disconcerted, but they do not view infertility as a tragedy; they simply wish to return to a normal life. Both wives and husbands see infertility as a problem for wives. Yet, studies of elderly persons without children raise concerns about the narrowness of samples focused on persons seeking infertility treatment: Elderly women and men who are childfree by choice have levels of psychological well-being equal to that of parents who feel emotionally close to their children (Connidis & McMullin, 1993).

Besides the essential nature of parenthood, particularly for women, parental ideologies enshrine a narrow and gendered view of what makes a positive home environment for children: one with white, middle-class, heterosexual parents; an employed father; and a homemaking mother (Patterson, 1992). In theories, research, and everyday life, we assume that fathers and mothers each make necessary and unique contributions to their children's development. The courts also privilege the traditional nuclear family, strengthen fathers' rights more than mothers' rights, and value fathers'

biological contributions over mothers' biological contributions, ignoring the social aspects of bearing and rearing children and reflecting traditional assumptions about the proper activities of mothers and fathers (Barrett & McIntosh, 1982; Blankenship, Rushing, Onorato, & White, 1993; Patterson, 1992). Although some recent judicial decisions have given paternity rights to sperm donors and to unmarried mothers, in general, unmarried women are restricted in developing alternatives to traditional parenting arrangements.

Controlling for socioeconomic status, African American, Hispanic American, Asian American, and white married parents have similar attitudes toward parenting and report similar parental behavior (Julian, McKenry, & McKelvey, 1994). Persons in non-white racial and ethnic groups, however, place slightly more value on self-control and on doing well in school. Within each ethnic group, there are consistent but small differences between mothers and fathers. For example, Hispanic fathers value obedience, self-control, independence, and getting along with others more than Hispanic mothers; black mothers value independence and control of temper more, whereas black fathers value obedience and getting along with others more.

For African Americans in particular, parenthood is constrained by their knowledge of the inevitability of racism's impact on their children and their lack of power to prevent it. This is why, according to Hill Collins (1992), motherhood is a "fundamentally contradictory institution" for black women (p. 234). It may also be why black mothers are highly devoted to their children, but not always affectionate in their behavior (Hill Collins, 1992). For similar reasons, Tatum (1987) argued that middle-class African American parents stress respect from their children and emphasize discipline and racial identity in their parenting.

Parents in Interaction with Children. In their review, Thompson and Walker (1989) concluded that mothers are more involved and invested in their children than are fathers and that each has a unique style of parent–child interaction. Recently, researchers have attended to variability among mothers and among fathers in parent–child interaction. This search for variability is no longer exclusively tied to women's labor force participation. There continues to be little attention, however, to motherhood as a way in which women gain power (see Kranichfeld, 1987).

Generally, parents and children, especially absent fathers, spend little time together, except for homemaking mothers and their children (Demo, 1992; Nock & Kingston, 1988). A decreasing proportion of children live with two parents, and an increasing proportion of children, especially those who are African American or Hispanic, live with never-married parents, mostly mothers. Demo (1992) argued that assumptions about the impact of these structural changes on children overstate the reality, particularly for relationships between children and biological mothers. They are especially problematic in the case of African American and Hispanic families (see also Haurin, 1992), which demonstrate a long tradition of community-based care (Hill Collins, 1992; Jones, 1985; Stack, 1974). In other words, children who live with single mothers often have routine and stable contact with adults other than their mothers (see also Siegel, 1995).

What Mothers Do. Women vary in time spent with children. Homemaking mothers spend more time with children and are more involved in childcare (Ahrentzen, Levine, & Michelson, 1989; Nock & Kingston, 1988). Employed mothers spend less time, especially with preschoolers, particularly while doing chores (Moen, 1992), but mothers' employment has only a small impact on their time with children. Employment at night has no impact on mothers' time (Nock & Kingston, 1988). Mothers also have been shown to confide in or talk with their daughters and sons more than fathers do (Starrels, 1994). Mothers' nurturance toward their children is enhanced when their husbands are closer to their daughters and when mothers are less satisfied in their marriages (Starrels, 1994). Some (Grossman, Pollack, Golding, & Fedele, 1987) suggest that homemaking wives, by spending more one-on-one time with children than fathers, interfere with the development of a close relationship between fathers and their first-born preschoolers.

Recently, family scholars have begun to study lesbian parents. Hare and Richards (1993) found that two-mother families differed according to whether children came to the family through prior heterosexual relationships or were born in the context of a lesbian relationship. Families in the former were similar to stepfamilies in that the nonbiological mother was less involved with the children than the biological mother and less involved than coresidential biological fathers. Families in the latter were unique. The partners most likely made a joint decision to conceive or to adopt children, and both think of themselves and behave toward the children as mothers. The involvement of men in both types of families varied from absent—including unknown fathers—to highly involved, although there was more father involvement in families of the first type. Clearly, lesbian families are as diverse as heterosexual families.

What Fathers Do. In comparison with mothers, fathers perform little childcare and even less infant care, although during pregnancy both they and their wives expect that they will do things such as get up at night with, soothe, and feed their babies (Deutsch, Lussier, & Servis, 1993; Russell & Russell, 1987). Simons, Beaman, Conger, and Chas (1993) suggested that women are viewed as knowledgeable about parenting, so their husbands defer to them about how they should be involved in childcare. For example,

fathers' supportiveness as parents is related to their wives' beliefs about the impact of parents on children, and wives' dissatisfaction with their children is strongly tied to husbands' use of harsh discipline.

Fathers are involved more with boy than girl children, leading to the mothers of sons seeing less disadvantage in the marriage (Katzev, Warner, & Acock, 1994; Starrels, 1994; but see Abbott & Brody, 1985). Having a son increases marital stability (Morgan, Lye, & Condran, 1988) and fathers' involvement with any daughters (Harris & Morgan, 1991). Not all outcomes of greater paternal involvement are positive for mothers, however. A longitudinal study of preschoolers in Sweden (Cochran & Gunnarsson, 1985) revealed that boys are moved more often from center-based to home-based care and less often from home-based to center-based care than girls. The authors suggested that fathers are more concerned about sons' adjustment than daughters' adjustment, leading them to push for a return to home care when there are difficulties in center-based care. Abbott and Brody (1985) also suggested that fathers of boys may monitor their wives' mothering more than fathers of girls. Compared to fathers, mothers see less distinction between parenting daughters and parenting sons (Gilbert, Hanson, & Davis, 1982).

Much attention has been devoted to explaining the involvement of fathers with their children. Fathers are more affectionate and responsive when they have less difficult infants, when they are in better marriages, when they have high self-esteem, when they are sensitive to the feelings of others (Harris & Morgan, 1991; Volling & Belsky, 1991), when they believe they will be able caregivers to infants prior to becoming fathers (McHale & Huston, 1984), and when they have feminist views (Deutsch, Lussier, & Servis, 1993). More educated white and black fathers are more involved as fathers, although, because they generally come to fatherhood later, age may play as much a role as education (Cooney, Pedersen, Indelicato, & Palkovitz, 1993; Marsiglio, 1991; Starrels, 1994). Fathers also are more involved when their children are older and biological rather than stepchildren and when their wives are more involved as parents (Marsiglio, 1991; Starrels, 1994). Marsiglio (1991) concluded that mothers facilitate child–father relationships, but others (Hawkins & Roberts, 1992) say that fathers' involvement is restricted by mothers' gatekeeping activities.

Fathers' involvement with children is not particularly responsive to wives' paid work schedule, the number of hours they themselves engage in paid labor, their occupational prestige, the proportion of the family income they earn, or their attitudes about gender (Brayfield, 1995; Marsiglio, 1991). Nock and Kingston (1988) reported that fathers' time in paid work has a small negative impact on their time with children and that fathers with employed wives spend more time with children on Sundays. Fathers whose wives are employed in the evenings spend more evening time with children, usually watching television with them (see also Clarke, Allen, & Salinas, 1986; Deutsch, Lussier, & Servis, 1993; Floge, 1985). Presser (1988) found that men do more when they are the only adults in the household to do it, that is, when their wives are at paid work and they are at home with children (see also Brayfield, 1995). This is more likely in the evening, when young children spend a significant proportion of time sleeping.

Being African American enhances paternal involvement. Black fathers of preschoolers spend about one-third as much time caring for their children as their wives do; this is more time than white fathers spend (Ahmeduzzaman & Roopnarine, 1992). Relative to less involved black fathers, more involved black fathers are more educated; have higher incomes and longer marriages; have more support from friends, kin, coworkers, and church; and share their feelings more often. African American fathers from both urban and rural areas across marital statuses report high levels of involvement with their children (Hyde & Texidor, 1994). Four-fifths report bathing, diapering, feeding, and dressing their young children, and nearly 3 in 5 feel these tasks should be shared with mothers. They say they are more active in play and somewhat more active in childcare than their own fathers were with them. They believe that children need fathering most between the ages of 12 and 15 (see also Taylor, Chatters, Tucker, & Lewis, 1991), yet only 4 in 10 say that mothers are more important than fathers as child caregivers.

Amato (1989) observed adults with preschoolers on beaches, at a shopping center, in restaurants, and in other public settings. Two-fifths of the children were carried by, pushed in their stroller by, or had their hand held by a man, and half of the children were watched by men. Men were observed more often helping boy than girl children, in recreational settings relative to restaurants, in mixed-gender dyads relative to single adults or other groups, and for whites relative to African Americans or Asian Americans. The contextual data are consistent with the ways in which gender is constructed. In public settings, men display their concern for children, consistent with the new cultural imperative of the involved father (LaRossa, 1988; but see LaRossa & Reitzes, 1995). Moreover, involved men were more commonly observed in playlike rather than childcare settings. Other data (Asmussen & Larson, 1991) confirm that fathers spend a greater proportion of their time with children in play than mothers, who spend a greater proportion of their time with children in instrumental tasks. At home, and relative to mothers, fathers are rarely alone with their children (see also Amato, 1989).

Relationships with Children. Wenk, Hardesty, Morgan, and Blair (1994) reported that the well-being of boys is improved by the emotional and behavioral involvement of mothers and fathers, whereas the well-being of girls is im-

proved more by emotional involvement. As is true for men, activities, or "doing things," play an important role in the development of boys. Starrels (1994) found greater variabilty in father–daughter than in father–son relationships. Generally, however, fathers were not particularly supportive in their style of parenting, and they had very limited involvement with their daughters.

Data from children confirm the differential involvement of mothers and fathers in parenting, even though children report similar quality relationships with both parents (Asmussen & Larson, 1991; but see Wright & Keple, 1981). In both middle childhood and adolescence, children, especially daughters, see fathers as much less involved with them than mothers and as less nurturant and supportive, although fathers are seen as providing more instrumental support, such as buying things and giving money (Starrels, 1994). Daughters actually see mothers as more involved in discipline than fathers. Boys in middle childhood have less affection for their fathers than for their mothers, but they are more satisfied with time they spend with fathers. Preadolescent and adolescent boys confide less in their fathers but identify with them more and are more satisfied with time spent with them than time spent with mothers. Sons actually report more similar relationships between fathers and mothers than daughters do, perhaps because mothers do not differentiate in relationships with their children and because fathers are more involved with sons than with daughters. Fathers are seen by children as disciplining less than mothers in terms of enforcing rules and talking with them, but as being firmer and threatening to hit more often.

Parenting is a gendered activity, and it is seen that way by children as well as parents (Starrels, 1994; but see Russell & Russell, 1987). Both sons and daughters are closer to their fathers if wives have more decision-making authority in their marriages and if wives are more satisfied with their marriages. Having a close relationship with one's father and a less close and exclusive relationship with one's mother, then, involves having a happily married mother who has more power in the marriage.

Parental Divorce and Relationships with Children

Divorce disrupts the connection between fathers and their biological children (Furstenberg & Nord, 1985; Seltzer, 1991). Most children have little contact with their noncoresidential fathers, although this is less true of black fathers (Seltzer, 1991). Father–child relations after divorce demonstrate that fatherhood in the United States is orchestrated through mothers, thus making fatherhood sequential for those who remarry and have children in a second or later marriage (e.g., Seltzer & Brandreth, 1994).

Despite attempts to do so, researchers have been unable

to demonstrate much evidence that father visits or relationships with children after divorce improve children's well-being (e.g., Furstenberg, Morgan, & Allison, 1987; Hawkins & Eggebeen, 1991). Regardless of the child's gender, mother's marital status, mother's income, or time since divorce, there is little connection between visits by divorced, noncustodial fathers and child well-being, although payment of child support improves both children's educational achievement and their behavioral adjustment (King, 1994a,b). Although there is some variation in fathers' involvement among subgroups of the population, there is little evidence that such involvement benefits children.

Arendell (1992) asked why fathers lose contact with their biological children following divorce. She discovered that father absence is a way men control conflict with their former wives and sometimes with their children. Father absence comes about over time, usually after longer and longer periods between visits with children. Although not all fathers were absent, even those who had contact with their children saw absence as a viable strategy for dealing with the loss of rights they believed had occurred through divorce (see also Bertoia & Drakich, 1993). These rights included authority over their family, control of their earnings, and access to their children. Failure to comply with court orders for child support payments was described as legitimate given their perceived unfair treatment by the legal system. Despite evidence that absent fathers are much more likely to provide child support than to provide any other type of aid (Paasch & Teachman, 1991), fathers in Arendell's study felt this other aid was discounted by the courts. Failure to provide support also was a way to punish the children's mother for actions such as making visitation contingent on support receipt. Absence also helped fathers cope with the strong emotional reactions they had to the end of the marriage, to seeing children only occasionally, or in response to rejection by or resistance from the child.

To Arendell (1992), absent fathers consider fatherhood to be an ascribed status rather than an outcome of a process of interaction with their children. Being a father then is closely tied to being a husband. It is difficult for fathers to negotiate fatherhood without the mediation of their former wives, whom absent fathers saw as actively interfering with their attempts to visit their children. Furthermore, the small number of men who maintained custody and/or extensive involvement with their children and cooperative relationships with their former wives were criticized by others, especially men, and they struggled with the lack of concordance between paid work and family life that employed women negotiate routinely.

Responsibility for Children. Whether in dual-job, dual-career, or career-job couples, women plan childcare and implement those plans (Leslie, Anderson, & Branson, 1991). Women with more hours in paid employment, however, spend less time being responsible for childcare. Women make all of the arrangements for preschoolers in 79% of families and none of the arrangements in 1%; men make all the arrangements in 20% of families and none of the arrangements in 19% (Peterson & Gerson, 1992). Although there is little variability in responsibility for childcare, Peterson and Gerson explained the variability that exists by situational constraints, which differ by gender. Husbands are more responsible for childcare arrangements when there are more children, but number of children has no impact on wives' responsibility. Husbands increase and wives decrease their responsibility when wives spend more hours in paid work. So, men have more responsibility when family demands are high and when wives are unable to meet these demands on their own. Both women and men reduce responsibility for childcare arrangements as the percentage of women in their specific occupations increases. Women do less when they are satisfied with their advancement opportunities in paid work; that is, women are responsive to employment incentives. To Peterson and Gerson, these data confirmed that structural opportunity leads both women and men to minimize responsibility at home. They argued that responsibility for childcare arrangements arises from structural patterns that produce both differences between genders and variation within gender.

A different type of responsibility is the care of children with intense needs. Compared to a sample of matched families with healthy children, mothers but not fathers of children with myelomeningocele (spina bifida) had high parental stress. Kazak and Marvin (1984) argued that the efficient and easy solution to handling the daily demands of a disabled child was to rely on mothers, who then became frustrated and overwhelmed. Some (Vadasy, Fewell, Meyer, & Schell, 1984) see the presence of a disabled child as increasing demands on siblings as well, especially sisters. Hill and Zimmerman (1995) studied low-income, African American mothers caring for children with sickle cell disease (SCD). They endeavored to protect their sons, even refraining from paid employment to care for them, but saw a need to help their daughters be independent and learn how to deal with their circumstances.

Traustadottir (1991) found multiple strategies for dealing with increased family responsibilities due to the presence of a child with a disability, all of which relied heavily on mothers. Middle-class mothers involved in advocacy for disabled children tended to be empowered by their caregiving, seeing it as a source of pride and satisfaction and defining their activities as more fulfilling than paid work. Other mostly white, middle- or upper-middle-class women who felt they had little choice but to carry out their responsibilities as mothers saw caring for a child with a disability as disruptive, but the right thing to do. Working-class and poor mothers tended to see such caring as a part of life and to approach it in matter-of-fact ways. Rarely did mothers combine with caregiving to children with disabilities with careers. They were able to do so only when they had an ideological commitment to themselves and the value of their paid work, the financial resources to hire caregiving help, and a socially valued occupation. Such resources made it possible for mothers to violate social expectations and face the resulting sanctions from health-care and caregiving professionals and other caregiving mothers.

Fathers with disabled children were seen by mothers as supportive when they helped financially and when they encouraged mothers' dedication to their children (Traustadottir, 1991). They were seen as *exceptionally* supportive if they supported the mothers' advocacy work, if they were involved actively in discussions and decisions about the children, or if they helped at home. Fathers who did all of these things had wives who described their marriages more positively. Fathers who did none of these things had disappointed and resentful wives who said that their nagging hurt their marriages. Similarly, mothers of children with cancer saw their husbands as supportive if they were involved with the care of the child, but their husbands saw them as supportive if they were available at home (Barbarin, Hughes, & Chesler, 1985). To Traustadottir (1991), women's foray into the public world is a tenuous one, dependent on minimal demands for family work. When those demands increase, women are pressured to assume their preordained position as family laborers. This is evident also in the way mothers increase their involvement with children during the summer, when children are not in school (Crouter & McHale, 1993).

The New Research on Fatherhood. In the past 10 years, there has been an explosion of research on fatherhood (Thompson & Walker, 1995). LaRossa (1988) argued that there is a new expectation for involvement on the part of fathers, but others (Atkinson & Blackwelder, 1993) report that the popular literature has emphasized both the instrumental and the expressive aspects of fathering for at least 100 years. Silverstein (1991) found that government policy and research reflect an idealized view of motherhood and do not acknowledge the importance of fathers' involvement in children's development.

In spite profound problems recruiting participants, Daly (1993) studied how men with preschool children construct and define fatherhood. The 32 married fathers he enlisted could not identify fatherhood models. Although they respected them, none saw their own fathers as models. Typically, they saw their fathers as having had to emphasize paid work over family life. Without models, these fathers were anxious about whom to be and how to act. They created frag-

mented models of fatherhood by watching what their mothers and their wives did. Despite rejecting their own fathers as models, they emphasized that children should respect them, and they focused on setting standards of behavior, as their fathers had. Cohen (1993) affirmed Daly's (1993) findings. Men do not wish to be the type of fathers their fathers were to them; only one-third mentioned economic provision as a main responsibility of fathers, for example. Most agreed that they want to be role models, although many also described themselves as companions, playmates, or nurturers.

Parenthood, Marriage, and Well-Being. In their review of the literature, Thompson and Walker (1989) reported a more traditional division of family work with parenthood as well as reduced marital happiness. Both motherhood and marriage are enhanced when fathers respect and appreciate their wives as mothers, even if men do little childcare. They argued that, together, mothers and fathers create an illusion of involved fathers who share in childcare. They do so by perceiving fathers' accessibility to their children as actual involvement; by accepting fathers' justifications for limited involvement, such as the demands of paid work and a lack of patience; and by noting that fathers express a willingness to help if it is *really* needed.

Besides gender, the experiences of motherhood and fatherhood vary by race and ethnicity, social class, the numbers and ages of children, and employment status. Hispanic women with young children are less satisfied than those without children or than those with older children (Amaro, Russo, & Johnson, 1987). African American mothers have significantly more difficulty than fathers adjusting to an infant. Black fathers have better adjustment if they report high marital satisfaction, a planned pregnancy, and the desire for more children (Hobbs & Wimbish, 1977).

Although women experience fewer strains as mothers than they encounter in housework or paid work, such strains have a stronger impact on their psychological well-being (Kandel, Davies, & Raveis, 1985). Being a mother leads to both role overload and role conflict for white women, but having better quality experiences as a mother also reduces role conflict and anxiety when women are employed (Barnett & Baruch, 1985).

Middle-class women maintain their self-evaluations as mothers following the birth of a first child, but working-class women change their self-evaluations, particularly if they have difficult infants (Reilly, Entwisle, & Doering, 1987). In the child's first year, women in both groups are similar, reporting declines in self-evaluations as mothers shortly after the birth, but increases by 1 year postpartum. Reilly et al. suggested that motherhood is more difficult for working-class women because they have more life stress and because they are more likely to say the infant is the most important thing in their lives, yet middle-class white mothers also report less competence as parents when their children are present than when only adults are present (Wells, 1988).

Mothers and fathers with more young children are more depressed, an effect that operates through their more precarious financial circumstances, but children also directly increase women's depression (Ross & Huber, 1985). So, children directly affect women but not men both positively and negatively. Women and men with more children have less shared time in activities; this is especially so among African American and Hispanic couples (White, 1983).

Longitudinal data confirm that marital quality for white parents of infants declines significantly over the first 9 months of the child's life, especially for women and especially for parents of a first child (Belsky, Lang, & Rovine, 1985; Belsky, Spanier, & Rovine, 1983). Both wives and husbands report less love, less marital satisfaction, less frequent activities with the spouse, more conflict, and less positive spousal interactions after a child's birth (Hackel & Ruble, 1992; MacDermid, Huston, & McHale, 1990). McHale and Huston (1988), however, reported parallel declines in love and marital satisfaction for a matched group of nonparents.

Husbands who report declines in love and increases in conflict are more negative in interactions with infants (Belsky, Youngblade, Rovine, & Volling, 1991). Their children also show more negative affect and are more disobedient, and their wives report more marital conflict. When wives report less love, they are more supportive in their interactions with their children. Belsky et al. suggested that children's negative behavior may precipitate declines in the marriage and that women may be better able than men to keep their relationship with their children and their relationship with their spouse separate. Alternatively, wives may seek closer ties to their children when their marriages are poorer, or wives' involvement with children may precipitate marital distress and negativity in fathers. Generally, mothers have more positive interactions with children than fathers.

Belsky and Rovine (1990) called attention to the tremendous variability among couples in adjustment to parenthood. About half of all new parents show no change or even a slight increase in marital satisfaction with parenthood, and 40% show no change in feelings of love for their spouse. In couples with higher incomes, wives report more love with parenthood and husbands report less ambivalence. Conflict declines for nearly one-third of couples, but open communication declines for a similar percentage. Declines in marital quality are more likely for younger husbands and wives, the less educated, those married for fewer years, those with low self-esteem, and couples where husbands are less interpersonally sensitive. Wives also report more declines in marital quality with planned pregnancies. The authors suggest that

wives' declines are due to the contrast between their expectations and the reality of postpartum life.

Hackel and Ruble (1992) also recognized variability in the adjustment to parenthood. In general, new mothers and new fathers report poorer quality marriages when their prebirth expectations are disconfirmed. This is especially true for wives who report frequent discussions about family work during pregnancy; it is not true for women with traditional beliefs. Traditional women have fewer negative outcomes when they do more housework and childcare after the birth than they had expected, and they are less satisfied if they expected to do more childcare than they are doing. The authors suggested that such women may find extensive involvement with children to be satisfying. Nontraditional women are more satisfied if they do less childcare than they expected. Generally, women do more and men do less than they expected during pregnancy. Over one-third of men say their marriage is their most negative experience during pregnancy because of declines in sexual interaction, their wives' mood swings, the difficulty of providing increased emotional support to their wives, and the threat of the loss to their children of their position with their wives.

Kalmuss and her colleagues (Kalmuss, Davidson, & Cushman, 1992) also reported that violated expectancies play a role in the adjustment to parenthood for white, mostly high-income mothers. From pregnancy to postbirth, expectations slightly but significantly exceeded reality in the marital relationship, friendships, physical well-being, maternal competence, and the amount of childcare by husbands, and women overestimated their interest in employment. Women whose marriage, physical well-being, maternal satisfaction, and maternal competence were better than they anticipated were better adjusted. Women who received far more support from their husbands and relatives than they anticipated were less well adjusted. The authors suggested that such women may be more difficult to please, but another possibility may be that others see them as less competent mothers than they should be. Women who expected a great deal of help from their husbands also were less satisfied.

The Gendered Behavior of Children in Families. In her review of the literature, Goodnow (1988) confirmed that children's family work is increasingly gendered with age. Furthermore, she argued that, through the gendered allocation of labor, children are taught that men earn money for work and that women work as a way of showing love. Tasks assigned to boys (e.g., mowing lawns) may earn money when done for others. This is less true of tasks assigned to girls.

Benin and Edwards (1990) reported that children do less family work in dual-earner than in single-earner families. Sons spend less than 3 hours each week in family work, about one-third of the time spent by sons in single-earner families, and daughters spend just over 10 hours each week, nearly 25% more time than spent by daughters in single-earner families. In single-earner families, daughters spend only a half hour more per week than sons, but their family work is allocated in a gendered way. Children do the least amount of family work when their fathers are employed full-time and their mothers are employed part-time. Both daughters and sons in these families do 2.5 hours of family work per week. Benin and Edwards suggested that employed parents are too busy to involve their children more in family life. Berk (1985) reported that, if tasks are important to women, they are less likely to ask children to do them. That is, employed mothers may strive to demonstrate that their socially valued homemaker role is not affected negatively by their paid work. Demo and Acock (1993) found that children do very little in the way of household tasks, averaging between 3 and 6 hours per week, with more time spent by children in never-married, step-, and especially single-mother families. Finally, meta-analyses (Lytton & Romney, 1991) revealed that mothers and fathers encourage sex-typed activities in daughters and sons and fathers differentiate between girls and boys more than do mothers (Siegal, 1987).

Summary of Parenthood and Gender

Mothers and fathers do gender in the way they connect to each other as parents and to their girl and boy children. Mothers reaffirm the essential nature of motherhood to womanhood by becoming mothers and by their reaction to their inability to bear children. The centrality of motherhood to women is reflected also in their allocation of time in childcare and in interaction with children, time that is affected in only a limited way by their employment. Mothers have more responsibility for children, but high family demands coupled with mothers' paid work help fathers take more responsibility. Mothers' connection to the labor force is a tenuous one, however, that rarely withstands exceptional family demands.

Men feel economic responsibility primarily for their children who live with them, but their involvement with children is mediated through their wives. In public and recreational settings, however, in accordance with the cultural imperative of the involved father, men are more closely tied to their children. At home, fathers rarely interact with children when mothers are not also present. Fathers are more comfortable interacting with older children and with sons than with infants and daughters, and they prefer playlike to caretaking activities with children.

The division of labor becomes more traditional after the birth of a child, and marital happiness typically declines.

New mothers find that they overestimated their interest in paid work and what their husbands would do around the house. Their well-being declines if they are unable to see themselves as competent mothers. Children in less traditional families do less family work, enabling mothers to satisfy the requirements of the homemaker role and confirming for girls and boys that women and men are different and unequal. Mothers see marriages as better when they have sons, in part because they value fathers' involvement with their children. Women are able to combine less satisfying marriages and positive relationships with their children, but men unhappy in marriage are negative in father–child interaction. Being a husband and a father seem to be all of a piece for men; for women, motherhood and being a wife are separate.

Little research on parenthood reflects a gender perspective. We do not yet know how paid labor, beliefs about motherhood and fatherhood, and mothers' and fathers' behavior interact. Our research reflects the view that mothers and fathers should relate to children differently. Furthermore, the view that it is desirable for children to be raised in a traditional, heterosexual family and that they require interaction with both mothers and fathers is reflected in the search for negative outcomes in children in nontraditional families and positive outcomes in children who maintain contact with their noncoresidential fathers.

Family Work

Work, paid and unpaid, is at the center of gender-based inequality because the misalliance between wage labor and family life hinders the development of equality (Ferree, 1990, 1991; Hochschild, 1989; Osmond & Thorne, 1993). In Chapter 21 of this volume, Haas addresses the connections among gender, paid work, and family life. Here, I focus exclusively on gender and unpaid or family work, but with full recognition that the gendered patterns of wage labor are connected systematically to gendered patterns inside families (Ferree, 1990, 1991; Hochschild, 1989; Moen, 1992; Moen & Dempster-McClain, 1987; Potucheck, 1992; Spitze, 1988; Thompson & Walker, 1989).

Housework is the area of study within families that is most reflective of a gender perspective, so it receives significant attention here. I examine the housework women do and the housework men do, as well as how that work is affected by paid labor, the presence of children, and other factors. I look at the social context of housework, housework standards, the definition of tasks, and methodological issues in this area. Finally, I review childcare, the brief but heuristic literature on emotion work, and the connection between family work and marriage.

Housework

Regardless of age, race, ethnicity, or marital status, women spend more time in unpaid family work than men (Bergen, 1991; Blair, 1993; Blair & Johnson, 1992; Brayfield, 1992; Coltrane & Ishii-Kuntz, 1992; Danigelis & McIntosh, 1993; Demo & Acock, 1993; Deutsch, Lussier, & Servis, 1993; Ferree, 1991; Ishii-Kuntz & Coltrane, 1992; Perry-Jenkins & Folk, 1994; Shelton & John, 1993b; South & Spitze, 1994; Szinovacz & Harpster, 1994; Ward, 1993; Wright, Shire, Hwang, Dolan, & Baxter, 1992). On average, as Thompson and Walker noted (1989), wives do two to three times more family work than husbands. In the past 10 years, there have been many large-scale studies on representative samples describing the division of household labor in hetero-sexual families, exclusive of childcare. Across reports, wives do far more household work than husbands. Among first-married couples with children, nearly half of all husbands spend fewer than 6 hours per week, or less than 1 hour per day, in family labor (Coltrane & Ishii-Kuntz, 1992). Another 25% of husbands average between 6 and 11 hours a week, or a little over 1 hour a day. Fewer than 10% spent more than 20 hours a week. Over four-fifths of the wives, however, reported at least that much, a minimum of 3 hours a day. One third of the wives spend at least 40 hours per week on female tasks, nearly 6 hours a day.

Among white, dual-earner couples, 18% of husbands report spending more than 20 hours per week, and 10% say the division of labor is equal (Blair & Johnson, 1992; Ferree, 1991). Among couples age 50 and older, 1 in 5 husbands (18.9%) but few (.6%) wives report *no* hours in female tasks, and more husbands (4.5%) than wives (1.8%) report *no* hours in male tasks (Szinovacz & Harpster, 1994). Although two-thirds of wives and three-fourths of husbands disagree that housework is the wife's responsibility and three-quarters of both agree that it is important to share family work, husbands do little and their contributions are relatively invariable, even though, compared to wives, they say housework is more enjoyable (Ferree, 1991).

Men's Household Work. Considerable attention has been directed at determining the conditions under which men do more family work, attempting to explain an outcome with minimal variability. Although, in general, men do little family work, they do more when they are divorced or widowed (Danigelis & McIntosh, 1993; South & Spitze, 1994) and when both partners are working-class (Perry-Jenkins & Folk, 1994). Men do proportionately more, relative to their wives, when their wives are employed, although they do not actually spend more time in household labor than the husbands of nonemployed wives (Blair & Johnson, 1992; Coltrane & Ishii-Kuntz, 1992; Ishii-Kuntz & Coltrane, 1992; but see

Brayfield, 1992; Ward, 1993). Husbands also do more household work when their wives earn more income than they do (Brayfield, 1992; Coltrane & Ishii-Kuntz, 1992; Ishii-Kuntz & Coltrane, 1992; Shelton & John, 1993a) and when they see their employed wives' income as secondary to their own (Perry-Jenkins & Folk, 1994). When wives are employed or homemakers and husbands are retired, husbands do more "male" tasks (Szinovacz & Harpster, 1994). Younger husbands do more (Brayfield, 1992), as do those in first marriages (Coltrane & Ishii-Kuntz, 1992; Demo & Acock, 1993). Husbands do more when their families live in single- versus extended-family households (Szinovacz & Harpster, 1994) and when their households are larger (Danigelis & McIntosh, 1993). More educated husbands do more family work (Brayfield, 1992; Hardesty & Bokemeier, 1989), as do those whose attitudes are more egalitarian (Coltrane& Ishii-Kuntz, 1992; Ferree, 1991; Ishii-Kuntz & Coltrane, 1992; Shelton & John, 1993b; Szinovacz & Harpster, 1994; but see Brayfield, 1992; McHale & Crouter, 1992), whose wives' attitudes are less traditional, and whose wives demand sharing (Coltrane & Ishii-Kuntz, 1992; Hardesty & Bokemeier, 1989; Ishii-Kuntz & Coltrane, 1992). Husbands do more household labor when their wives care about having a clean house, when their wives care about having a proper dinner on the table, and when they say they cannot meet their wives' family work standards (Ferree, 1991). White men do more work when their wives are in higher status occupations and when they are employed for fewer hours (Coltrane & Ishii-Kuntz, 1992; Coltrane & Valdez, 1993; Deutsch, Lussier, & Servis, 1993; Shelton & John, 1993b), but black men do more family work when they are employed full-time (Shelton & John, 1993b). The more black and white men depend on their wives for income, however, especially in low-income households, the less family work they do (Brines, 1994). Non-white men do more family labor than white men. Indeed, the highest reported average rates and percentages are for black men, who spend about 25 hours per week and do about 40% of the family work (Shelton & John, 1993b). African American men also are less likely than white men to say the division of labor is unfair (John, Shelton, & Luschen, 1995). Hispanic men also report more weekly hours (23 vs. 20) than white men, but they do the same proportion (35%). Mexican American men do more family work when their wives earn as much or more than they do (Coltrane & Valdez, 1993), when their wives are in high-status occupations, when both wives and husbands agree that the husbands have not achieved as they had hoped, and if their wives demand their help and make lists or remind them of tasks that need doing, although their wives resent having to do these things (Coltrane & Valdez, 1993). Smaller-scale studies suggest that men do more when wives are viewed as coproviders (Perry-Jenkins & Crouter, 1990).

Having children has a minimal impact on men's family

work (Brayfield, 1992)—men actually do less housework when they have more children—but it has a profound impact on women's family work (Ishii-Kuntz & Coltrane, 1992; Shelton & John, 1993a). Both Brayfield (1992) and Coltrane and Ishii-Kuntz (1992) found that men do more when they have younger children, but Ishii-Kuntz and Coltrane (1992) found that they do less. Men do more, however, when their children do more (Ishii-Kuntz & Coltrane, 1992). Hawkins and Roberts (1992) wrote that men are motivated to do more when they want to be close to their wives, when their wives ask for their help, when their children need their help, and when they wish to compensate for lack of involvement.

Only 60% of the 20 dual-earner couples with school-aged children in Coltrane's (1989) study shared family labor with their wives, even though all said they assumed major responsibility for childcare and household work. What distinguished fathers in households where labor was shared was high education, delayed childbearing, and father's involvement in child care from the child's infancy. Coltrane argued that extensive involvement in childcare actually led to fathers sharing family labor. Across studies, however, the amount of explained variance in husbands' family work is rarely above 15%, less when trying to explain absolute hours, even with large, nationally representative samples and with impressive numbers of control variables.

Women's Household Work. Although mothers spend a similar amount of time in household work across family structures (Demo & Acock, 1993; Ishii-Kuntz & Coltrane, 1992), women do more when they are married as opposed to cohabiting (Danigelis & McIntosh, 1993; Shelton & John, 1993a; South & Spitze, 1994). Older women (Brayfield, 1992; Shelton & John, 1993a), women whose income is low, and those whose husbands' income is low do more family work (Bergen, 1991; Shelton & John, 1993a). Wives do more family work when they have preschoolers and when they have more children (Bergen, 1991; Ferree, 1991; Shelton & John, 1993a). Employed wives do less household work than homemakers (Brayfield, 1992; Shelton, 1990; Szinovacz & Harpster, 1994; Wright et al., 1992), retired wives do more than employed wives (Szinovacz & Harpster, 1994), and part-time workers do more than full time workers (Brayfield, 1992; Ferree, 1991; Shelton, 1990; Shelton & John, 1993a). Working-class women do more family labor (Perry-Jenkins & Folk, 1994), as do women when either spouse has traditional attitudes (Brayfield, 1992; Shelton & John, 1993a; but see Wright et al., 1992). Education, race, and ethnicity also influence wives' family labor. Lower education for either wives or husbands is related to more family work for women (Shelton & John, 1993a; but see Brayfield, 1992). Hispanic wives do more family work than black or white wives (Shelton & John, 1993b). Women who have more authority at work than their

husbands do less family work also, but this occurrence is rare (Brayfield, 1992). Brayfield (1992) also found that wives who earn more income than their husbands spend almost as much time in female tasks as wives whose husbands earn more than they earn.

Overall, context is more influential in predicting white women's than white men's family work; that is, more of the variance is predictable in women's family work. Shelton and John (1993a) argued that social norms, particularly those about marriage but also those for motherhood, shape the construction of gender in family labor. Married women, mothers and nonmothers, do more, but marriage has little impact on men's family work. There is a cultural presumption of family work for wives and mothers, but not for husbands or fathers (Hochschild, 1989). The presumption of responsibility leads to wives' control of their husbands' family work, as they control husbands' interaction and involvement with children (Hochschild, 1989). Such control, in part, may restrict men's involvement (Hawkins & Roberts, 1992), but it also increases wives' responsibility and work load. Wives expect little from husbands, although some say this is because women are reluctant to give up control of family labor. When both wives and husbands say wives are responsible for family work, wives do more and husbands do less (Ferree, 1991).

Contextual Factors. For Chicano couples, the division of labor is influenced by the migration process. Hondagneu-Sotelo (1992) found that the long marital separation of couples where husbands migrated prior to 1965 subsequently fostered a shared division of labor. In the United States, these husbands learned household chores because they lived in mostly male communities while their wives learned to support a household. Both developed pride in their skills and continued to use them when reunited. Couples where husbands migrated after 1965 had shorter periods of separation. After migration, they lived in mixed-gender communities where women were responsible for household chores. They maintained a relatively traditional division of labor when reunited. Other data reveal that women's entry into paid labor leads to more gender flexibility for Hispanic Americans (see Vega, 1991, for a review).

Surprisingly, social class (Wright et al., 1992) and wives' chronic illness or disability (Hafstrom & Schram, 1984; Szinovacz & Harpster, 1994) have a minimal impact on the distribution of family work. Similarly, the presence of a man (i.e., husband or partner) neither increases nor decreases time spent on household tasks by mothers (Demo & Acock, 1993). That is, men seem to do about as much housework as they create (see Hartmann, 1981).

Kurdek (1993) reported that gay and especially lesbian couples are more likely to share household work than heterosexual couples. The way they carry out tasks differs, however. Unlike heterosexual couples in which women do most of the household work on their own, lesbian and gay couples are more likely to balance tasks; that is, they divide tasks so that an equal number are performed by each partner. Only in lesbian couples are tasks likely to be shared; that is, both partners do tasks together.

Standards. Standards for family labor among dual-earner couples are high: Over 90% of wives and husbands want to have a clean house, and most husbands (71%) and wives (86%) want a "proper" dinner on the table (Ferree, 1991). Despite a widely held view that husbands cannot meet their wives' standards for family work (see for example Hawkins & Roberts, 1992), only one-third of dual-earner husbands report this as a problem (Ferree, 1991; see also Coleman, 1991). Indeed, Ferree (1991) demonstrated that husbands' expectations are more strongly related than wives' expectations to the division of family work. To Ferree, husbands' preferences are demands that women meet, although wives respond to their own preferences as well. In her view, reducing the standards of both will be necessary to obtain equality in family labor.

Compared with homemaking wives, full-time employed wives are less comfortable with a dirty house, like to cook less, are less attached to the kitchen, and are more likely to believe that meal preparation should not take long (Oropesa, 1993). They also use cleaning services more and eat out more. Oropesa argued that wives' *personal* income enables them to negotiate the purchase of cleaning services with husbands who are reluctant to help. They eat out more with their families, however, because they are less attached to the kitchen and because they have more *family* income. Employed wives get relief from eating out, but other family members enjoy it as well. Their joint enjoyment reduces the need for employed wives to rely on personal resources to relieve the obligation of meal preparation. Because full-time employed wives are purchasing homemaking services, "[t]he market is ... postponing the inevitable confrontation within families over what it means to do market work, to do housework, and to do gender" (p. 469).

Tasks. Researchers focus attention on who does what, and recent studies using newer (1980s and 1990s) data from large, representative samples have increased confidence in these findings. The results (Demo & Acock, 1993; Ferree, 1991; Mederer, 1993; Shelton & John, 1993b; Wright et al., 1992), summarized in this section, are convincing: Family tasks are gendered.

1. Meal preparation: Three-quarters of wives usually or always prepare meals, averaging 10–11 hours per week or 80%–89% of the combined total household time on this task, compared to 2 hours for husbands. Among the unemployed, Hispanic men do more meal preparation than men in other racial or ethnic groups (see DeVault, 1987, 1991, and Beoku-Betts, 1995, for discussions of how meal preparation can foster a sense of group identity and preserve cultural traditions).

2. House cleaning: Two-thirds to 75% of wives usually or always clean house, spending an average of 9–10 hours per week or 78%–84% of the combined total household time on this task, compared to 1 hour for husbands, only 3% of whom usually or always clean house. Among full-time employed men, black husbands clean house more than white husbands; among part-time employed men, black and Hispanic husbands spend more time on this task than white husbands do. Among the unemployed, Hispanic men do more than men in other racial or ethnic groups.

3. Washing dishes: 56%–75% of wives usually or always wash dishes, averaging 6–8 hours per week, or 70%–84% of the combined, total household time on this task, compared to 1 hour for husbands, only 7% of whom usually wash dishes. Among the unemployed, Hispanic men do more meal clean-up than men in other racial or ethnic groups.

4. Laundry: 69%–75% of wives usually or always do the laundry, averaging 5 hours per week or 84%–90% of the combined, total household time on this task, compared to negligible hours for husbands, only 7% of whom usually or always do laundry. Among full-time employed men, white husbands do laundry more often than blacks husbands.

5. Shopping: Two-thirds of wives usually or always do the shopping, spending 3 hours per week or 76%–95% of the combined total household shopping time, compared to 1 hour for husbands, only 12% of whom usually or always shop. Among full-time employed men, black husbands shop more than white husbands.

6. Driving: Wives spend 2–3 hours per week or 68%–94% of the total, combined household time driving family members, compared to 1 hour for husbands.

7. Financial tasks: 55% of wives usually or always pay bills, averaging 2 hours per week or 71%–95% of the combined, total household time on this task, compared to 1 hour for husbands. Just over one-quarter (27%) of husbands usually or always pay bills. Among full-time employed men, both black and Hispanic husbands spend more time than white husbands on this task.

8. Automobile-related tasks: Although women without live-in male partners spend 85% of the combined,

total household time on auto upkeep, women with live-in male partners spend only 7%–10%. On average, husbands spend 1–2 hours per week on automobile activities. Among full-time employed men, black husbands spend more time on these tasks than white husbands.

9. Outdoor tasks: Although women without live-in male partners spend 77% of the combined, total household time on outdoor tasks, women with live-in male partners spend only 30%–31%. On average, husbands spend 3–4 hours per week in outdoor tasks. Full-time employed black and white husbands spend more time in outdoor tasks than do Hispanic husbands.

Excluding the last two nonroutine, "masculine" tasks, wives spend a minimum of 68% and up to 95% of the household time in family work, an average of 37–42 hours per week. Husbands average 11–13 hours per week, as do the cohabiting partners of divorced and never-married mothers. Husbands do a little more, up to 15–16 hours per week, if their wives are employed, and a little less, 10–11 hours per week, if their wives are homemakers. Note also that, even when couples report a commitment to fairness and an equal division of labor, objective indicators suggest that wives do more than husbands (Blaisure & Allen, 1995; Coltrane, 1989).

Methodological Issues. Demo and Acock (1993) noted that household labor data underestimate women's family work because both childcare and responsibility for it are excluded. Other tasks are excluded as well. For example, Mederer (1993) reported on the tasks of cleaning the kitchen (56% of wives usually do it versus 12% of husbands) and pet care. The latter truly is a shared activity: 66% of wives say that wives and husbands take care of pets equally. When only one partner does it, however, 27% of wives usually or always do it themselves versus 8% of husbands.

Only the first five tasks listed above are typically included in measures of "female" or women's work, which is characterized by the absence of a clear start and end point, lack of discretion as to when to complete it, and little opportunity for leisure while doing it (e.g., Blair & Johnson, 1992). Coleman (1991) cautioned that asking people who does what task is not revealing about the nature of individual contributions. For example, husbands may discharge their responsibility for family dinners once each week by taking the family out. Alternatively, when their wives are not at home, they may heat meals their wives prepared and not clean up. Men and women differ in how family labor is conceptualized, something others have referred to as standards but what Coleman described as the difference between the absolute minimum and something beyond that. For example, hus-

bands may serve canned soup and peanut butter sandwiches for dinner or send their children to sleep in unmade beds. Coleman argued for more attention to what husbands actually do, when they do it, and whether they feel responsible.

Rarely has anyone focused on *responsibility* for tasks, although responsibility is described as critical by nearly all family work researchers (e.g., Demo & Acock, 1993). Helen Mederer (1993), in a notable exception, found that dual-earner wives, in addition to doing most (68%) of the tasks, also do most of the management: 77% usually or always plan dinner, 72% usually or always set standards for cleanliness, 71% usually or always make the grocery list, 63% usually or always are responsible for doctor's appointments, and 62% usually or always get ready for the next day. Fewer than 4% of these tasks are usually or always the responsibility of husbands. At least 60% of the time, men are usually responsible for car care, household repairs, and snow and lawn care. Three management responsibilities are less obviously skewed in either direction: making financial decisions, which is seen as shared equally by 71% of wives; assigning chores, which is viewed as shared equally by 51% of wives; and arranging repairs, which is believed to be shared equally by 33%.

Studies of household labor usually rely on data from wives, partly because wives have less missing data (e.g., Szinovacz & Harpster, 1994), but also because wives are more likely to agree to be interviewed. Wives and husbands disagree, however, on what husbands do: Husbands say they do more than wives say they do (Ferree, 1991; Oggins et al., 1993; Wright et al., 1992). Generally, researchers assume wives' data are more accurate, reasoning that family work is more visible to them, in part, because of their overwhelming responsibility for it (Komter, 1989; but see Ferree, 1991). Couples generally agree on who does the laundry, the cooking, and the shopping (Ferree, 1991; but see Brayfield, 1992; Wright et al., 1992), but they disagree by as much as 15% over who does dishes and cleans the house. Ferree describes these latter two areas as contested domains because they show considerable variability across couples. That is, where husbands take on more household tasks, they are more likely to do so in these two areas. Some (Brayfield, 1992; Wright et al., 1992) say shopping also is amenable to change.

Since its initial release, the National Survey of Families and Households (NSFH) has been the source for much of the work on the division of family labor. In addition to a 26% nonresponse rate for main respondents, however, it has a high rate of missing data for household labor items, particularly among secondary respondents and men who have characteristics associated with doing less family work (e.g., older, more traditional ideology, less education, older children). Thus, NSFH data probably overestimate men's contributions (Ishii-Kuntz & Coltrane, 1992; Szinovacz & Harpster, 1994; but see Marini & Shelton, 1993).

Childcare

As noted, most studies of family work exclude childcare. This is particularly problematic because the presence of children is associated with increased traditionalization of family work (MacDermid et al., 1990; Oggins et al., 1993). Although childcare is somewhat less segregated than household tasks, it, too, is gender specialized. Neither mothers nor fathers estimate fathers' contributions to childcare at more than half (Deutsch, Lozy, & Saxon, 1993). Fathers report between two-fifths and half of total parental time playing with children, helping them learn, making decisions, taking them to outings, disciplining them, setting limits, supervising them with other adults present, giving attention, putting them to bed, and worrying about them. Less than one-third of the time, fathers buy clothes, arrange children's social lives, and take them to the doctor. Fathers are most unlikely to feed their babies, soothe them, or get up with them at night, arguably the least pleasant of childcare tasks. They appear to do more childcare in public settings (Amato, 1989), if they have feminist attitudes (Deutsch, Lussier, & Servis, 1993), and when they have older children (Ferree, 1991). In Chicano families, childcare is less segregated than household work, although wives continue to have more responsibility for both (Coltrane & Valdez, 1993).

As with household tasks, the way in which childcare is conceptualized differs by gender. Hochschild (1989) gives as an example a father who responded to his son's request to play cards by saying that he didn't know how and to wait for his mom to return. This same father made popcorn for himself and his son when he was responsible for cooking dinner. This distracted and disengaged childcare results, in part, from the way in which mothers help to shape fathers' involvement with their children. According to Hochschild (1989), mothers sometimes are uncomfortable leaving children with fathers, who are rougher with the children than mothers are. Not leaving children with fathers is one way in which mothers become increasingly involved with children. Simultaneously, uninvolved fathers play the role of disciplinarian, indirectly shifting their children's focus to their mothers. Behavior is gendered even in one-parent families (Hall, Walker, & Acock, 1995). Controlling for demographic factors, single mothers spend more time in private interaction with children while single fathers spend more time in play. Single mothers also spend more time than single fathers in household tasks, although single fathers spend much more time than do fathers in two-parent households.

Emotion Work

A notable development in the literature is the inclusion of caring or emotion work—work to meet the emotional and psychological needs of family members—in studies of family labor (Daniels, 1987; Erickson, 1993; Hochschild, 1983, 1989). Dressel and Clark (1990) included both housework and emotion work in their study of care. Surprisingly, many of their respondents, especially men and especially the more relative to the less powerful (e.g., husbands to wives, parents to children), described *being there* as a caring act. When asked to generate their own list of caring activities, men were more likely than women to report routine, ordinary acts. Dressel and Clark concluded that women underestimate their care. They also noted that, for women, positive acts often occurred simultaneously with negative feelings, indicative of emotive dissonance.

Women were more likely to report acts to solicit connection to others, what the authors described as self-directed care. Men were more likely to mention acts that led to personal benefits of reflection, such as wanting to *show off* their wives. Women often described complex, multiple, and changing motives for caring acts and also were more likely to report acts undertaken in anticipation of another's preferences or needs, as well as services to others that individuals, without difficulty, could do for themselves. Dressel and Clark imputed coercion to these motives in that the acts were intended to influence others. The consequences of care differed by gender as well: Men were more likely than women to be rewarded for caring acts, perhaps because caring acts were not expected of them.

Erickson (1993), too, argued that relationships require effort and that caring is work. Couples construct a division of emotion work as they construct a division of household tasks. White, dual-earner wives have better marriages if their husbands do more emotion work, but husbands' relative contributions to housework have no impact on marriage. Wives also report less marital burnout (e.g., feeling emotionally drained) if they and their husbands do more emotion work, and, again, husbands' relative contributions to housework have no effect. An alternative interpretation, consistent with Hochschild's (1989) view of an economy of gratitude (also see Piña & Bengtson, 1995; Thompson, 1991), is that wives interpret husbands' housework as emotionally supportive.

Family Work and Marriage

In a noteworthy contribution to the family work literature, Thompson (1991) applied a distributive justice framework to the idea of fairness in the division of family labor (see also Hawkins, Marshall, & Meiners, 1995; Major, 1993). She noted that women do more than two-thirds of the family work, but less than one third feel it is unfair (see also DeVault, 1990). Husbands also see this unfair division as reasonable (Lennon & Rosenfield, 1994). Even though wives are less satisfied with the division of labor than their husbands, especially when they are in a stage of the family life cycle in which more family work is required (Suitor, 1991), most women do not see the division of labor as unfair. She asked, "How do women come to interpret the objectively lopsided distribution as fair?"

Thompson (1991) suggested that women value relationship outcomes, "down time," and responsive and attentive husbands. These outcomes are more important to women than time in family work and doing or not doing particular tasks, which is why time and tasks have little impact on wives' perceptions of fairness. She indicated also that, rather than comparing themselves to their husbands, they compare themselves to other women, thus undermining their sense of entitlement. Furthermore, they compare their husbands to other husbands or to their fathers or grandfathers. They also value their husbands' paid work more than their own, an orientation that further undermines their sense of entitlement. For Thompson, a 50-50 standard is too impersonal for women. Finally, there are many justifications for why men do less family work (e.g., fathers' paid work keeps them from greater involvement with their children, women have more time, women get more pleasure from family work, women want a cleaner house). True or not, these justifications are accepted. Thompson argued that women will sense injustice only if they lack desired outcomes, have high standards for comparison, and see no acceptable justification for being deprived of desired outcomes (see also Greenstein, 1995).

Lennon and Rosenfield (1994) demonstrated that women with few alternatives to marriage and who would end up in poverty without it are more likely to see the division of family labor as fair. The authors agree with Hochschild (1989), who demonstrated that women's perceptions of fairness are influenced by their dependence on men.

Hochschild (1989) also suggested that women more often than men see family work as love. This is why wives feel guilty when their families' needs are not met. In contrast, husbands' family work is viewed as a gift to their wives. This economy of gratitude helps to sustain an inequitable division of family labor. To Hochschild, the division of family labor, rather than being explained by resources (e.g., income, paid work hours) or individual factors (e.g., attitudes about gender; see also McHale & Crouter, 1992), reflects gendered strategies, that is, actions through which married persons try to solve problems in the context of cultural beliefs about gender. Furthermore, DeVault (1990) suggested that women are limited in their freedom to demand change in the distribution of family work because doing so challenges "powerful consensual understandings about male and female activity in the family setting" (p. 199). Conflict over family work, in her view, is silenced through a combination of its invisibility, the presumption that family work is chosen, and beliefs about the nexus between family work and the essential nature of women as wives and mothers. Finally, Kane and Sanchez (1994) demonstrated that women's economic dependence on men and men's gender interests (i.e., that they benefit from

women's greater family work and men's greater status in paid work) contribute to an acceptance of gender inequality by both women and men.

Summary of Family Work and Gender

Resources, attitudes, family structure, and context do not alter the fact that gender is the best predictor of who in families does which tasks as well as how much time people spend on family work. For women, being married leads to responsibility for and involvement in family labor. Although women and men believe that family work should be shared, it is not, and most women and men are unconcerned that it is not.

Rather than focus on the conditions that create and maintain a gendered division of household labor, researchers, with limited success, attempt to predict men's family work. Yet most such studies exclude childcare and pay little attention to responsibility. They fail to examine the way in which tasks are carried out. They focus little attention on how desired relationship outcomes, a husband's attentiveness to his wife, and the primacy of breadwinning for men but not for women maintain family labor as women's domain. They do not attend to the absence of conflict around family labor. Although research on household labor has dominated the study of gender and families over the past 25 years, we continue to know very little about it.

Kinship

As with other aspects of family life, connections with kin are gendered, although kin relations are usually described in gender-neutral terms. As well, they are portrayed as almost exclusively positive. Nydegger (1983) argued that this positive view results from our exclusive focus on personal relationships and the exclusion of the system of obligation inherent in kin ties. Here, I consider the connections among kin generally and the relationships among adult siblings. I review the literature on mothers, fathers, and their adult children; intergenerational aid exchange; how the child's marital status influences the parent–child tie; and coresidence. I also examine the research on grandparents and grandchildren. Finally, I consider caregiving to aging family members with particular attention to spouse and adult child caregivers. I discuss who gives care, what they do, and how caregiving influences them.

Ties among Kin

The role of kinkeeper is usually occupied by a woman and is often transferred overtime from mother to daughter (Rosenthal, 1985). Families with kinkeepers, in comparison to those without them, have more interaction (Rosenthal, 1985; Stueve, 1982), demonstrating the central role they play in solidifying family ties. Women have more contact with kin than men, and they receive more help from kin (Chatters, Taylor, & Jackson, 1985; Gerstel & Gallagher, 1993; Huston, McHale & Crouter, 1986; Kohen, 1983; Spitze & Logan, 1989). This is especially true of African Americans relative to whites and Hispanics (Silverstein & Waite, 1993; Taylor, Chatters, & Jackson, 1993; Taylor, Chatters, & Mays, 1988; Uhlenberg & Cooney, 1990), in part, because of strong traditions of shared responsibility among mothers, daughters, sisters, and fictive kin (Hill Collins, 1992; Jones, 1985). Scott and Black (1994) contend that African American families are better conceptualized as kin networks than as nuclear families, particularly the families of single mothers, but also those of unmarried black men who rely on male-centered networks when they are no longer primary in social networks dominated by women. Adults in upwardly mobile black families who reside in white neighborhoods also maintain kin contact, but their children are more dependent on nuclear family members than on other kin (Tatum, 1987).

Kin ties are stronger among women of the working than the middle class in both black and white families (Coke, 1992; Mutran & Reitzes, 1984). This may be because kin help is responsive to need (Heinemann, 1985). Women also need more assistance than men, consistent with their lesser access to financial resources. Among Chicanos, women give more health-related help and men help more with repairs, but advice and help with financial and personal problems are given along woman-to-woman and man-to-man lines (Markides, Boldt, & Ray, 1986). Among whites and African Americans, however, women provide more of every type of help to relatives than men except for repairs and financial aid (Gerstel & Gallagher, 1993; but see Marks & McLanahan, 1993).

Kin ties are stronger within gender lines, particularly among women and between mothers and daughters (Thompson & Heller, 1990; Umberson, 1992) and especially among unmarried women (Allen & Pickett, 1987; Marks & McLanahan, 1993). Relationships of young adult children with both their mothers and fathers, particularly unmarried children, are important to children's well-being (Amato, 1994). Although men do considerable kin work and have increased life satisfaction when they help their adult children and their parents (Spitze, Logan, Joseph, & Lee, 1994), married and widowed black and white women do more, averaging an extra paid work week each month helping members of their social network, predominantly kin (Gerstel & Gallagher, 1993).

Kin are expected to help when help is needed (Scott & Black, 1994), but support from kin is not without costs. Kin support buffered the effects of negative life events for men, but not for young women, in a southern black community. Dressler (1985) found that close connection with kin resulted in more careful examination of the behavior of young women who were expected to follow their relatives' advice. Close kin ties also increased the potential for women to have nonreciprocal connections. Belle (1982) contended that giving support without receiving it is itself stressful and that close connections to others, kin included, may increase women's vulnerability to the stress experienced when negative events occur in the lives of loved ones.

Relationships with Siblings

Among the rural elderly, having a sister has a strong positive influence on the life satisfaction of women, but having a brother has no influence on life satisfaction either for women or for men (McGhee, 1985). Both women and men who feel close to a sister are less depressed than those who do not (Cicirelli, 1989). Sisters have more frequent contact with each other than brothers, or than brothers and sisters, and women seem to want more sibling contact than men do (Connidis & Campbell, 1995; Lee, Mancini, & Maxwell, 1990). As kinkeepers, married sisters involve their husbands in such a way as to contribute to their sisters' well-being. For younger adults, having a married sister and positive ties with parents leads to better well-being for married sons (Barnett, Marshall, & Pleck, 1993). Thus, sisters keep their siblings emotionally tied to other family members.

Relationships between Parents and Adult Children

Parents and their adult children share high levels of contact and aid and positive emotional ties. This is especially true for mothers relative to fathers, African Americans relative to whites, and those who live closer, have fewer siblings, and are less educated (Atkinson, Kivett, & Campbell, 1986; Greenberg & Becker, 1988; Kulis, 1992; Lawton, Silverstein, & Bengtson, 1994; Spitze & Logan, 1990; Spitze, Logan, Deane, & Zerger, 1994; Thornton, Orbuch, & Axinn, 1995; Uhlenberg & Cooney, 1990; Umberson, 1992; but see Barnett et al., 1993). Some families have high levels of contact with parents, siblings, children, and in-laws, reflecting a "predisposition to family contact" (Waite & Harrison, 1992, p. 637). Parenthood continues to be important after children are grown: Adults who are dissatisfied as parents and who report strained ties with children, especially mothers, have lower psychological well-being (Umberson, 1992), but contact with children has little impact on the morale of the elderly (Lee & Ishii-Kuntz, 1987).

Both mothers and fathers experience stress when their sons but not their daughters are still dependent in adulthood (Greenberg & Becker, 1988). Divorced children, however, report more strain in their relationships with their mothers than with their fathers (Umberson, 1992). Parental divorce also affects ties with adult children. Children report the least affection for unmarried divorced fathers and less affection for remarried parents than parents in other marital statuses. Aid exchange is also lower between fathers and adult children than between mothers and adult children when parents are divorced (Amato, Rezac, & Booth, 1995). Relationships with fathers are more negatively affected than those with mothers by parents' divorce, no matter when the divorce occurs (Aquilino, 1994; Cooney, 1994; Cooney & Uhlenberg, 1990; Webster & Herzog, 1995). Similarly, divorced parents have lower parental satisfaction, are less happy with the way their children are, and are less satisfied with how they get along with their children than ever-married parents (Umberson, 1989).

Mothers. Mothers receive more help from children than fathers, have more contact with children, and are happier with the help their children give than fathers are (Umberson, 1992). African American mothers are more dissatisfied as parents, but they provide more and receive less support than their non-black counterparts. Parent–child ties are complex. Widows mention relationships with children most frequently of all relationships as making widowhood both easier and more difficult (Morgan, 1989). Mothers in particular find some of their children to be disappointing (Aldous, 1987), and mothers report being stressed by their adult children's problems, particularly when a daughter is out of touch with the family (Greenberg & Becker, 1988). Typically, however, elderly women see their adult daughters as confidants (Thompson & Heller, 1990), and daughters with good relationships with their mothers have higher well-being (Barnett, Kibria, Baruch, & Pleck, 1991). For mothers, relationships with children are a central concern and have a major impact on well-being (Umberson, 1989).

Fathers. Umberson (1992) found minimal effects of ties with fathers on psychological well-being, but those whose ties with their fathers were strained were more distressed. Supportive ties with fathers were more important to well-being for African Americans than whites, however. In a random, stratified sample of women social workers and licensed practical nurses in Boston, relationships with fathers were unrelated to well-being unless mothers were deceased (Barnett et al., 1991). This was true regardless of race (African American or white) or socioeconomic status.

Rural elderly men, 91% of whom were white, had more contact with a son than with a daughter. Although fathers reported positive emotional feelings for these maximum-contact sons, the sons provided minimal help to and received little help from their fathers. Only 5% of these fathers named

their sons as confidants; most named their wives (Kivett, 1988). For fathers, then, relationships with children are not as prominent as spousal ties and have less of an influence on well-being (Greenberg & Becker, 1988; Troll, 1987; Umberson, 1989). Children who themselves are parents have more contact with their fathers. Lawton et al. (1994) suggested that such contact is motivated by obligation or activity and controlled by the child rather than the parent.

Aid Exchange. Most parents and adult children maintain high levels of interaction throughout adulthood: They are in contact with each other, they exchange aid and gifts, and they help out in times of need. Women across generations have more contact and exchange more aid, instrumental and socioemotional, than men or than cross-gender pairs (Dean, Kolody, Wood, & Ensel, 1989; Marks & McLanahan, 1993; Silverstein & Litwak, 1993; Spitze, Logan, Deane et al., 1994; Spitze, Logan, Joseph et al., 1994). How we think about gender, about families, and about relationships creates a nexus of obligation for women. For example, elderly parents report that daughters, not sons, will be relied on in times of need (Silverstein & Litwak, 1993).

Among racial and ethnic groups, elderly persons of Hispanic descent are more likely than others to receive both household and socioemotional help from their adult children (Silverstein & Litwak, 1993). Employed African American mothers of young children receive more family support than comparable white mothers (Benin & Keith, 1995). A majority of African American mothers with minor children live close to family, and about 20% of those who are never-married or divorced and in poverty receive financial aid from kin (Jayakody, Chatters, & Taylor, 1993). Black mothers who live near kin also get more childcare aid from family than do other black mothers, but those who get this assistance are less happy with kin relations. Nearly 8 in 10 black mothers report emotional support from kin, however, particularly those who live near and feel close to them (Jayakody et al., 1993). Furthermore, African American mothers play a variety of roles in socializing their unmarried, adolescent daughters into motherhood (Apfel & Seitz, 1991).

Aid from parents is structured along gender lines. Fathers give advice to children about money, remodeling, and major purchases; mothers give advice to children about childrearing, chores, small purchases, and relationships (Greenberg & Becker, 1988). Married sons and especially married daughters get babysitting help from parents, especially from mothers (Spitze, Logan, Deane, et al., 1994). Adult children who receive more help, such as parents with young children, also give more help to their parents, suggestive of both intergenerational responsiveness and intergenerational reciprocity. Similarly, aging parents who need more help receive more help. Both never-married sons and especially never-married daughters help their parents more than divorced or married children, however. Spitze, Logan, Joseph, and Lee (1994) reported that middle-aged women and men both are stressed by helping their parents.

Aid Exchange and Adult Child's Marital Status. Half of parents in their 60s or older with at least one ever-married child have a child who has been divorced (Spitze, Logan, Deane et al., 1994). These parents are responsive to their adult child's need for help (Gerstel, 1988; Johnson, 1988b). Divorced mothers get more help from and have more contact with parents (and other kin) than either never-married (Marks & McLanahan, 1993) or married mothers (Spitze, Logan, Deane, et al., 1994). Single fathers also have extensive aid exchange with their parents (Marks & McLanahan, 1993), but they get less help with babysitting than married sons (Spitze, Logan, Deane, et al., 1994). Marks and McLanahan (1993) reported that nontraditional family structure is associated with greater aid exchange, but others (Spitze, Logan, Deane et al., 1994) found that remarried children get slightly less help than married children.

Conflicting reports may reflect variations by gender. Sons appear to rely on kin for practical help more in the early stages of divorce, especially from their mothers (Johnson, 1988a), but divorced daughters receive stable amounts of help from parents over time (Gerstel, 1988). Divorced sons with children and high incomes rely on kin for social interaction and to discuss personal issues. Their mothers help care for and entertain children on the weekends. Divorced daughters with children and low incomes rely on kin to provide help with household tasks and financial aid. Daughters who rely on kin are less distressed, but sons who rely on kin are more distressed, which is consistent with the gendered nature of autonomy in adulthood. Grandchildren bring adult children and their parents together, enabling divorced fathers to receive emotional support and divorced mothers to receive practical help (Gerstel, 1988). This help is not without costs to grandmothers, however, who are increasingly unhappy over time when compelled to be substitute mothers and more and more unlikely to provide that help (Johnson, 1988b). Satisfied grandmothers are those whose relationships with their children and grandchildren are characterized by few problems and few demands.

Divorced daughters equal married daughters in their help to parents, but divorced sons have slightly weaker ties to their parents than married sons (Spitze, Logan, Deane, et al., 1994). Spitze and her colleagues concluded that divorce has a relatively small impact on ties with parents. The former mother-in-law–former daughter-in-law bond, however, is very fragile, and does not always survive the divorce. Overall, there is tremendous variability among parent–child ties, even when children are divorced, and that variability is

minimized here (see Johnson, 1988b). For example, patterns of aid exchange are different with gay and lesbian couples and their family members. They are far more likely to report assistance from friends than from family, with only 13.5% reporting the receipt of aid from kin (Kurdek, 1988).

Coresidence. Adult daughters who live with their mothers report especially high quality relationships with them (Uhlenberg & Cooney, 1990), and mothers who live with daughters confirm these reports (Aquilino & Supple, 1991). Men who live with their adult children report higher home satisfaction than women (Umberson & Gove, 1989). This satisfaction is reduced if the child is separated or divorced (Aquilino & Supple, 1991) and enhanced if the men also help other adult children (Spitze, Logan, Joseph, et al., 1994).

Coresidence for short periods is common in the United States for both African Americans and whites. At least some time over a 15-year period, up to one-third of middle-aged white women and two-thirds of middle-aged black women live in an extended household (Beck & Beck, 1989; Taylor et al., 1991). Asian Americans have an even higher rate of inter-generational coresidence (Speare & Avery, 1993). Among African Americans, coresidence is more likely for never-married mothers with minor children than for married, divorced, or widowed mothers (Jayakody et al., 1993). Whites more often form intergenerational households with parents; blacks more often form intergenerational households with children (Beck & Beck, 1984; Glick & Lin, 1986).

Why do adult children and their parents coreside? For aging women, coresidence is related to off-time marital transitions: Elderly women who are recently divorced are likely to coreside with adult children, especially daughters, as are middle-aged women who are recently widowed. Data from the 1985 Current Population Survey showed that elderly women reside more commonly with sons than daughters, yet recently divorced middle-aged and elderly women and long-term widows more commonly reside with daughters (Cooney, 1989). Unmarried parents and unmarried children are the major beneficiaries of coresidence (Aquilino & Supple, 1991; Speare & Avery, 1993). African American adult childcare-givers are more likely than whites to live with their aging parents (Soldo, Wolf, & Agree, 1990).

Grandparents and Grandchildren

Grandparenthood is another social connection in which women have expertise, but which also gives men the chance to be nurturant in later life (Thomas, 1986). Grandmothers are more satisfied as grandparents than grandfathers (Thomas, 1986), however, and relationships with maternal grandmothers are closer than those with maternal grandfathers and either paternal grandparent (Matthews & Sprey, 1985). Kivett (1993) found that both African American and white rural, elderly grandmothers have the most frequent contact with the grandchild who is a child of the adult offspring they see most often. Black and white grandmothers are similar in closeness to grandchildren, agreement with grandchildren on life views, and expectations of help from grandchildren. Relative to white grandmothers, however, black grandmothers are more likely to live with grandchildren, to have more grandchildren, and to give more help to and receive more help from grandchildren (see also Taylor et al., 1991).

Rural white grandfathers have little interaction with grandchildren and see grandparenting as a low priority, although they expect their grandchildren to help them in times of need (Kivett, 1985). There is tremendous variability in grandparenting among urban African Americans, despite a long-standing tradition of surrogate parenting (Taylor et al., 1991). Maternal grandmothers more often serve as surrogate parents, although maternal grandfathers and maternal great-grandmothers occupy this role as well (Burton, 1992). Across racial groups, preschool children with employed mothers, when cared for by a relative, are most often cared for by a grandmother, particularly if their mothers are unmarried (Presser, 1989). Recently, researchers have attended to the phenomenon of grandparents raising grandchildren, which appears to have increased over the past decade, particularly among people of color (e.g., Solomon, 1995).

Caregiving to Aging Family Members

Women more often than men care for aging family members: wives more than husbands, daughters more than sons, and among the never-married, sisters more than brothers (Coward, Horne, & Dwyer, 1992; Stone, Cafferata, & Sangl, 1987). This is despite the fact that both women and men feel a sense of obligation to their aging parents (Finley, 1989). Affection is a stronger motivation for daughters' caregiving; obligation is a stronger motivation for sons' (Silverstein, Parrott, & Bengtson, 1995). Unmarried women have been shown to make life choices so that they are able to carry out responsibilities to middle-aged and aging parents (Allen & Pickett, 1987). Some argue that women have training in caregiving tasks and/or are used to doing tasks that are unskilled, repetitive, monotonous, have no boundaries, and lead to few tangible rewards (Finley, 1989; Stoller, 1990). Others say that society is structured and age is stratified in such a way that women are available to care because, relative to men, they live longer (Gerstel & Gallagher, 1994; Lee, Dwyer, & Coward, 1993), are less likely to be employed, are employed more in seasonal and part-time work, and contribute less income. That few adequate alternatives to family or informal care are available no doubt also plays a role (Abel,

1986; Aronson, 1985; Finch & Groves, 1983; Stoller, 1990; Walker, 1983). Views that women excel in such "female" tasks are contradicted with evidence that women provide caregiving aid even in "male" tasks (Finley, 1989). In addition, most women do not leave paid employment to give care, but employment does seem to excuse men from caregiving (Stoller, 1990), just as it excuses them from household labor.

Glazer (1990) argued convincingly that formalized health care relies increasingly on women to provide care that, in recent history, was provided by health-care workers, thus reducing the cost to providers, both public and private, and increasing the costs to women (see also Walker, 1983). Such costs are disproportionately borne by low-income and African American women and women without health insurance (Glazer, 1990). Caregiving is synonymous with home and with women (Graham, 1983; Walker, 1983). Caregiving tasks have low value (Finley, 1989), yet formal or paid care is seen as inferior to that provided by a loving wife, mother, or daughter. Caregiving contributes to women's lower status, but, for many women, it is a positive, fulfilling, meaningful, reciprocity-based activity (Abel, 1986, 1990a,b; Abel & Nelson, 1990). Caregiving has economic costs to women, including reduced income and Social Security benefits (Finch & Groves, 1983; Kingson & O'Grady-Leshane, 1993; Ungerson, 1983). It is unpaid work, yet it provides potential satisfaction that may not be available to women through paid work. Through both caregiving and kinkeeping, women have the opportunity to create obligation and accumulate power over others (DiLeonardo, 1987).

Who Helps?   A principle of substitution operates in caregiving: Spouses care first, but, when unavailable, daughters, then sons, provide care (Chappel, 1991; Johnson, 1983; Stoller & Earl, 1983). African Americans have fewer spouses and more siblings and friends as caregivers than do whites (Burton et al., 1995; Lawton, Rajagopal, Brody, & Kleban, 1992; White-Means & Thornton, 1990). Women and non-whites have more family helpers than do men and whites (Miller & McFall, 1991). African American caregiving networks in particular show increases in size and in activity as the need for help increases (Mui & Burnette, 1994; but see Burton et al., 1995). Both African Americans and Hispanics receive more informal and less formal (paid) care than whites (Muit & Burnette, 1994). Blacks are less likely to use in-home, formal services; Hispanics use more community services; and whites use more nursing home services (see also Hinrichsen & Ramirez, 1992; Montgomery & Kosloski, 1994; Wolinsky, Callahan, Fitzgerald, & Johnson, 1992). Men are more likely than women to use formal services (McFall & Miller, 1992).

Although studies tend to focus on primary caregivers, it is not uncommon for needy aging persons to receive aid from more than one person (Matthews & Rosner, 1988; Penrod, Kane, Kane, & Finch, 1995; Tennstedt, McKinlay, & Sullivan, 1989; but see Brody, Hoffman, Kleban, & Schoonover, 1989). Women predominate among both primary and secondary caregivers (Penrod et al., 1995; Tennstedt et al., 1989), but men are more likely to be secondary than primary caregivers. Most secondary caregiving men are husbands caring for their wives (Tennstedt et al., 1989).

What Do Women and Men Caregivers Do? Caregiving women and men perform different tasks. Women perform more activities of daily living (ADLs) or personal care (Hooyman, Gonyea, & Montgomery, 1985) and more instrumental activities of daily living (IADLs) or cooking, laundry, and routine household chores than men, but they do not differ in shopping, heavy chores, or financial management (also IADLs) (Miller & Cafasso, 1992; Stoller, 1990). Secondary caregivers help less in all aid categories and spend less time helping. Some (Tennstedt et al., 1989) report that, among secondary caregivers, men spend more time than women, but Stoller (1990) found that secondary caregivers give intermittent help and only infrequently do household tasks. Generally, as needs for assistance increase, helping shifts toward greater involvement by women, despite paid employment (Stoller, 1990; but see Gerstel & Gallagher, 1994). Caregiving is gendered in approach as well. Even with late-stage Alzheimer's patients, women, particularly wives, are more likely than men to continue to define themselves in relation to the care receiver and to think of the care receiver as reciprocating in the relationship (Chesla, Martinson, & Muwaswes, 1994).

How Does Caregiving Affect Women and Men? Black women report less strain and burden from caregiving than white women, perhaps because of a lengthy history of coping with stress (Fredman, Daly, & Lazur, 1995; Mui, 1992). They also report more mastery, more caregiving satisfaction and affirmation of beliefs, and less depression (Lawton et al., 1992; but see Young & Kahana, 1995). This is despite their poorer health, the greater caregiving demands they face, and more conflict between caregiving and other social responsibilities for African American caregivers (Fredman et al., 1995; Mui, 1992). African American caregivers, however, do report receiving more support with their caregiving activities than do white caregivers (Fredman et al., 1995). Blacks with more income and whites with less income report more burden (Lawton et al., 1992). The potential threat of caregiving to financial resources, particularly the fragile nature of financial stability for African Americans, must be particularly unsettling (Hartung, 1993).

Women say they receive more support as caregivers than do men (Thompson, Futterman, Gallagher-Thompson, Rose, & Lovett, 1993), but they also are more burdened by caregiving (Miller & Cafasso, 1992; Thompson et al., 1993). Men seem to protect themselves, in part, by remaining emotionally detached (Hinrichsen, 1991). Women also may be more stressed because they carry out more and more intensive caregiving tasks, report more conflicts between caregiving and paid work, and have fewer resources (Kramer & Kipnis, 1995; Pratt, Schmall, & Wright, 1987). Longitudinal data indicate that, in caring for persons with Alzheimer's disease, women have stable, high rates of depression, while men's depression increases over time (Schulz & Williamson, 1991). Women may experience a sense of entrapment in an unfulfilling role, while men more often become increasingly dissatisfied with their lack of social contacts. Women also report more conflicts between caregiving and their families and their personal well-being, perhaps because it is difficult for them to set limits (Pratt et al., 1987; see also Abel, 1986, 1990a). Caregivers who give personal care, mostly women, experience more caregiving burden (Hooyman et al., 1985), and caregivers who report more hassles, also typically women, report lower psychological well-being (Kinney & Stephens, 1989).

Caregiving Spouses

Although many studies, particularly those prior to the mid-1980s, analyzed data across caregivers, more recently researchers have focused specifically on wives versus husbands. These studies find both similarities and differences in caregiving by spouses.

What Do Spouse Caregivers Do? Generally, caregiving wives give more help and more types of help—both ADLs and IADLs—than husbands give (Miller, 1990b; Young & Kahana, 1989), although husbands report spending more time giving care (Miller, 1990b). Dwyer and Seccombe (1991) found that husbands report both more time and more tasks. They suggested that caregivers do not report tasks for which they have been responsible throughout their married lives, so wives may not report housework and laundry, but husbands who do these tasks always report them. Much of caregiving is normative activity for wives, so they may not define these tasks as caregiving (see also Sankar, 1993; Walker, Pratt, & Eddy, 1995). Husbands do more handiwork than wives (Young & Kahana, 1989).

Miller (1990b) reported that husbands, not wives, occasionally leave their cognitively impaired spouses at home alone. They recognize the potential danger in doing so, but are not worried, consistent with a view of women as passive. In seeking support from others, wife caregivers look for activities that would also involve their husbands, whereas husband caregivers seek activities for themselves. Both are equally committed to caregiving, but they think about it differently: Women focus on tasks and emotional support; men focus on their own activities and maintaining emotional distance. Wife caregivers are more concerned with their spouses' needs, feel more responsible for meeting those needs, and give more help (Williamson & Schulz, 1990).

How Does Caregiving Affect Wives and Husbands?
Wives are more negatively affected by caregiving than husbands (Fitting, Rabins, Lucas, & Eastham, 1986; Kosberg, Cairl, & Keller, 1990; Pruchno & Resch, 1989; Schulz, Visintainer, & Williamson, 1990; U.S. Select Committee on Aging, 1987; but see Mui, 1995b), and wives also report poorer past relationship quality with their impaired spouses. Williamson and Schulz (1990) found that when husbands report less close relationships, they, too, are more depressed. Miller (1990b) indicated that wives caring for cognitively impaired husbands feel compelled to give care even when they are not well themselves, find caregiving to be difficult emotionally, are particularly distressed when their care-received husbands are upset and holler at them, and fear their husbands' violent behavior.

For wives, assuming authority over a husband is difficult (Miller, 1987, 1990b; see also Pruchno & Resch, 1989). Wives worry about how their husbands will feel when told what to do or how to act. Exercising such authority makes wives feel angry and unkind (Miller, 1987), but for husbands, assuming authority is seen as natural (Miller, 1990b). Wives also feel a loss of control over the home environment, their traditional domain, because they give priority to their husbands' needs (Miller, 1987, 1990b). Husbands see caregiving as a job, a set of tasks and activities; they do not focus on the changed relationship with their wives (Miller, 1990b). They also do not feel a need to change their other home activities (e.g., gardening). Because they see their wives as compassionate and acquiescent, they do not expect them to interfere. Miller (1990a) also reported that caregiving wives have less access to social supports, although they do not differ from their husbands in emotional strain. The options of both are similarly restricted when caring for an impaired spouse, although wives care for spouses with greater impairment.

Husbands may experience less burden because they approach caregiving differently from wives. Other data indicate that wife caregivers are more burdened because they feel trapped; they must provide care, as they did when raising children, at a time when they expected to be free (Pruchno & Resch, 1989; Zarit, Todd, & Zarit, 1986). Alternatively, husbands may be less burdened because they are more likely than wives to supplement their care with formal services (Barusch & Speid, 1989; Pruchno & Resch, 1989). Husbands also appear better able than wives to cope with interpersonal problems with their spouses and to maintain emotional distance (Barusch & Speid, 1989; Zarit et al., 1986). Wives are more likely to report loss of identity with caregiving, especially those with limited social activities, although such loss is rare (Skaff & Pearlin, 1992). Relative to wives, husband caregivers are more depressed when they see financial support from kin and friends as inadequate (Moritz, Kasl, & Berkman, 1989). Greater burden for wives also may be an artifact of sample selection. Williamson and Schulz (1990) suggested that two types of spouse caregivers are recruited in research: wives with little choice but to provide care and husbands who are able and willing to do so and thus are less prone to depression.

Caregiving Children

It is understood that spouses will take care of each other should the need arise. It is less clear that adult children will care for aging parents. Most children, however, especially African Americans, feel obligated to help both parents, but daughters more to help mothers and sons more to help fathers (Finley, Roberts, & Banahan, 1988). When levels of impairment are low, daughters and sons are equally likely to be caregivers (Stoller & Pugliesi, 1989). Otherwise, daughters are far more likely to be caregivers than sons. Sons serve more often as secondary than as primary caregivers, but are primary caregivers when sisters are unavailable (Blenkner, 1965; Diemling & Bass, 1986; Horowitz, 1985; Stone et al., 1987).

When sons are primary caregivers, many tasks are carried out by their wives (Birkel & Jones, 1989). Daughters and daughters-in-law care for aging parents, in part, because it is acceptable for sons and husbands to limit their contributions. Men have primary and women secondary responsibility as breadwinners, so women, not men, are expected to change their paid work schedules to help their aging parents (see also Brody, Johnsen, & Fulcomer, 1984; Matthews, 1995). Men also are seen as unable to be responsive to or to anticipate an aging parent's needs. Caregiving women neither expect nor demand much help from men.

Some women caregivers are bothered by the limited help they receive from their brothers (Matthews, 1995; Matthews & Rosner, 1988). They feel responsible for caregiving, but they set limits on what they will do and rank other family obligations over those to their parents, even though they feel guilty doing so. An area of concern is where to rank their own needs. Anxious though they are to help, they are reluctant to meet excessive demands (Abel, 1989). As do homemaking women, they want others—parents, husbands, and siblings—to acknowledge and to appreciate what they do.

What Do Caregiving Daughters and Sons Do?
Daughters provide more help than sons in all forms of care-

giving activities, but they are similar to sons in "male" tasks, "neutral" (e.g., financial aid, health care) tasks, and the provision of emotional support (Horowitz, 1985). Women say their brothers do less, but brothers do not say the same of sisters (Lerner, Somers, Reid, Chiriboga, & Tierney, 1991). More than sons, daughters help their parents, especially their mothers, with ADLs and with IADLs (Dwyer & Coward, 1991; Dwyer & Seccombe, 1991; Lee et al., 1993). Overall, women across age groups do not think it is appropriate for men to give personal care (Brody et al., 1984), although sons are more comfortable giving personal care to fathers (Matthews, 1995). Daughters provide more personal care to parents even when they live farther away than sons. Caregiving sons also are more likely to supplement their caregiving with formal services (Gallagher, Rose, Rivera, Lovett, & Thompson, 1989; Montgomery & Kosloski, 1994; Soldo et al., 1990). Even secondary caregiving daughters give more help than secondary caregiving sons (Brody et al., 1989).

How do adult children approach caregiving? Matthews and Rosner (1988) say they operate on a principle of least involvement, not giving more care than is needed so as to maintain their own independence and that of their aging parents. When there are both daughters and sons, daughters are more likely than sons to provide routine caregiving in which regular and predictable assistance is required. They also are more likely than sons to serve as backup caregivers to primary caregiving sisters. Backup caregivers also offer predictable help. Circumscribed caregiving, more common among sons, is predictable yet constrained (e.g., helping with finances). Sporadic caregiving is also more common among sons, although sons will provide help when the need is minimal and when it is at their own convenience. Routine and backup caregivers see sporadic help as important but not significant in meeting parents' needs. Some siblings, more commonly sons but also daughters who have at least four brothers and/or sisters, cannot be counted on to help. Routine and backup caregivers see their noninvolved brothers as a sad fact, but they are angry at their noninvolved sisters or offer elaborate explanations to justify their lack of involvement. When there is only one sister and at least one brother, brothers may be more involved, but their assistance continues to be orchestrated by the sister (Matthews, 1995).

Employed women spend as much time caregiving as nonemployed women (Body & Schoonover, 1986; Finley, 1989; Matthews, Werkner, & Delaney, 1989; Stoller, 1983). In contrast, employed sons give much less help than nonemployed sons (Stoller, 1983). Employed caregiving daughters alter the times when they help rather than how much actual help they give (Matthews & Rosner, 1988). Brody and Schoonover (1986), however, found that employed caregiving daughters give less personal care, do less cooking, and

spend more time arranging for supplemental help so that their parents' needs are met. Matthews et al. (1989) reported that these daughters give less help with household chores and emotional support and regret not having enough time to spend with their parents socially. Generally, daughters but not sons make decisions about their paid work with their aging parents in mind (Matthews et al., 1989; Schulz et al., 1990; U.S. Select Committee on Aging, 1987; Williamson & Schulz, 1990; Young & Kahana, 1989). Daughters' help also appears to be unaffected by the number of children they have, but sons with more preschool children give more help (Stoller, 1983), perhaps because their wives are less able to help. Sons but not daughters indicate that the distance in residence from their parents makes it hard for them to help (Brody et al., 1989).

How Does Caregiving Affect Daughters and Sons?
Daughters report more conflict between caregiving and other obligations than do sons (Finley, 1989). Daughters also report more conflict with other family members, usually sisters and brothers, than do caregiving sons (Strawbridge & Wallhagen, 1991). Caregiving sons say their wives support them, but caregiving daughters are appreciative when their husbands have neutral attitudes toward their caregiving (Horowitz, 1985).

As do wives, daughters find caregiving to be stressful. Compared to sons, they give more help, go beyond minimum expectations, experience more problems, say they have to give up other things to give care, feel they are neglecting other family responsibilities, experience more time pressures, have to sacrifice leisure time, feel guilty when they are angry with their care-receiving parents, feel guilty about not helping more, experience emotional strain, are in poorer health, say that their emotional state and/or their future plans are affected by caregiving, and wait longer to institutionalize an aging parent (Brody et al., 1989; Brody, Dempsey, & Pruchno, 1990; Horowitz, 1985; Mui, 1995a; Schulz et al., 1990; U.S. Select Committee on Aging, 1987; Williamson & Schulz, 1990; Young & Kahana, 1989). Brody et al (1990) suggested that daughters are troubled by the contrast between what they think they should do as caregivers and what they actually do. Caregiving daughters also are bothered more than caregiving sons by poor quality relationships with their care-receiving parents (Mui, 1995a).

Relative to daughters, caregiving sons say they do not take enough time to talk with their mothers (Brody et al., 1989). Sons also are more bothered by their parents' disruptive behaviors than daughters are (Mui, 1995a). Most husbands of caregiving daughters report strains in their marriage due to their wives' caregiving. Thirty percent say it interferes with their time with their wives, but a greater percentage of wives report such interference (Kleban, Brody, Schoonover, & Hoffman, 1989). Nearly half of the husbands who live with their wives and mothers-in-law report intrusions on their privacy, and 20% say that their wives are sometimes caught between them and their mothers-in-law.

Matthews and Rosner (1988) identified several styles of husbands' responses to their wives' caregiving (Abel, 1989). Some are supportive, either directly caregiving themselves or actively supporting their caregiving wives. These husbands make it easier for their wives to give routine help. Other spouses are indifferent; they see their wives' caregiving as unrelated to them, and their views have no influence on their wives' caregiving. A third group is antagonistic; they make providing routine or backup caregiving an experience of conflict-laden choices. Generally, women have low expectations for help from their husbands, to whom they believe their primary obligations reside, so they are grateful when husbands neither resent nor interfere with caregiving (Abel, 1989; Matthews & Rosner, 1988). Similarly, they emphasize their duties *to* their children rather than any help they might get *from* them. Besides reporting more problems with their spouses, caregiving daughters more often than sons report family-related issues around their interactions with siblings (Smith, Smith, & Toseland, 1991). Expectations for help from siblings are high, but such help also brings with it potential conflict (Abel, 1989; Suitor & Pillemer, 1993).

Summary of Kinship and Gender

Connections among kin are orchestrated by and through women—grandmothers, mothers, and daughters—so it is not surprising that women give and receive more help from family members than men do. Kin ties are particularly strong among African Americans and Hispanics, as evident in higher levels of interaction, coresidence, and aid exchange. Not surprisingly, women are affected more than men by kin interaction and by problematic kin relations.

Being a woman brings with it responsibility and desirability for kin contact and their subsequent consequences. Women and men both benefit from and incur costs from kin interaction, but how those costs and benefits relate to the broader social structure, ideology, and behavior have not been examined systematically, nor have researchers investigated the ways in which responsibility for kin connections contributes to women's social power. Rather than focus on the conditions that create and maintain these gendered patterns, researchers focus on gender differences. With few exceptions, they pay little attention to the way in which intergenerational activities are carried out and the way in which the primacy of breadwinning for men but not for women maintains kin relations as a province of women.

Conclusion

Gender is a pervasive aspect of family life in all of its dimensions (Thompson & Walker, 1989). Men have privilege and power in society at large as well as in marriages and families, and they have the responsibility of providing for family members. Women have limited power and less privilege and they bear the responsibility for and involvement with children and kin. These patterns strengthen women's family connections—from which they derive considerable pleasure—and weaken their ties to paid labor—which has the potential to enhance their well-being. They also weaken men's family connections and strengthen men's ties to the labor market. As a result, men struggle to relate to their children, especially their daughters. It is now normative for fathers to lose contact with their biological children and to forego responsibility for supporting them after the dissolution of the relationship with the children's mother. As feminists have noted for 2 decades (e.g., Ferree, 1991), families are a location of struggle and support for both women and men. For women, however, and much less so for men, they are also a location of work. Gender continues to be the best predictor of who does what in families, a fact that receives surprisingly limited attention even in studies in which both women and men are included.

What are the conditions that create and maintain these gendered patterns? How do women and men in interaction help to establish and sustain these conditions? How do they come to see their gendered patterns as appropriate and fair? How do they sustain these beliefs of fairness in spite of stark evidence to the contrary? How do they avoid, minimize, and ignore conflicts that emerge from these gendered patterns? How do women obtain power and control through their social connections? Little of the related literature connects the everyday processes and patterns in marriage, parenthood, family labor, and kin ties to gendered social structures and ideologies. Such research is necessary to understand the connection between gender and families.

Over the past 2 decades, feminist research using a gender perspective has provided much insight into the nexus of gender and family life. Most of the research on gender, however, operationalizes it as a sex category or as an individual property. In applying a gender approach to the study of marital care, Thompson (1993) demonstrated how to consider the institutional and interactional context of gender in research. She applied a gender perspective to four levels of analysis: the broader sociohistorical context, the immediate context, interactional processes, and individual outcomes. She identified research questions to examine how gender is constructed at each level of analysis and through the interplay among them. I refer researchers who wish to "think about gender in new ways" (p. 567) to her work.

As Thompson and Walker (1989) noted, the question of why gendered patterns are so stubbornly resistant to change merits our attention. Research from the gender perspective has the potential to address fundamental questions about the experiences of women and men in families because it recognizes explicitly the connections between social structures and everyday family life. Indeed, it has the ability to revolutionize family studies. Its concurrent commitment to social change may also lead to changes in families that we have awaited for far too long.

References

Abbott, D. A., & Brody, G. H. (1985). The relation of child age, gender, and number of children to the marital adjustment of wives. *Journal of Marriage and the Family, 47,* 77–84.

Abel, E. K. (1986). Adult daughters and care for the elderly. *Feminist Studies, 12,* 479–497.

Abel, E. K. (1989). The ambiguities of social support: Adult daughters caring for frail elderly parents. *Journal of Aging Studies, 3,* 211–230.

Abel, E. K. (1990a). Family care of the frail elderly. In E. K. Abel & M. K. Nelson (Eds.), *Circles of care: Work and identity in women's lives* (pp. 65–91). Albany: State University of New York Press.

Abel, E. K. (1990b). Informal care for the disabled elderly: A critique of recent literature. *Research on Aging, 12,* 139–157.

Abel, E. K., & Nelson, M. K. (1990). Circles of care: An introductory essay. In E. K. Abel & M. K. Nelson (Eds.), *Circles of care: Work and identity in women's lives* (pp. 1–34). Albany: State University of New York Press.

Ahmeduzzaman, M., & Roopnarine, J. L. (1992). Sociodemographic factors, functioning style, social support, and fathers' involvement with preschoolers in African American families. *Journal of Marriage and the Family, 54,* 699–707.

Ahrentzen, S., Levine, D. W., & Michelson, W. (1989). Space, time, and activity in the home: A gender analysis. *Journal of Environmental Psychology, 9,* 89–101.

Aldous, J. (1987). New views on the family life of the elderly and the near-elderly. *Journal of Marriage and the Family, 49,* 227–234.

Allen, K. R., & Pickett, R. S. (1987). Forgotten streams in the family life course: Utilization of qualitative retrospective interviews in the analysis of lifelong single women's family careers. *Journal of Marriage and the Family, 49,* 517–526.

Amaro, H., Russo, N. F., & Johnson, J. (1987). Family and work predictors of psychological well-being among Hispanic women professionals. *Psychology of Women Quarterly, 11,* 505–521.

Amato, P. R. (1989). Who care for children in public places? Naturalistic observation of male and female caretakers. *Journal of Marriage and the Family, 51,* 981–990.

Amato, P. R. (1994). Father–child relations, mother–child relations, and offspring psychological well-being in early adulthood. *Journal of Marriage and the Family, 56,* 1031–1042.

Amato, P. R., Rezac, S. J., & Booth, A. (1995). Helping between parents and young adult offspring: The role of parental marital quality, divorce, and remarriage. *Journal of Marriage and the Family, 57,* 363–374.

Apfel, N. H., & Seitz, V. (1991). Four models of adolescent mother–grandmother relationships in black inner-city families. *Family Relations, 40,* 421–429.

Aquilino, W. S. (1994). Later-life parental divorce and widowhood: Impact on young adults' assessment of parent–child relations. *Journal of Marriage and the Family, 56,* 908–922.

Aquilino, W. S., & Supple, K. R. (1991). Parent–child relations and parent's satisfaction with living arrangements when adult children live at home. *Journal of Marriage and the Family, 53,* 13–27.

Arendell, T. (1992). After divorce: Investigations into father absence. *Gender and Society, 6,* 562–586.

Aronson, J. (1985). Family care of the elderly: Underlying assumptions and their consequences. *Canadian Journal of Aging, 4,* 115–125.

Asmussen, L., & Larson, R. (1991). The quality of family time among young adolescents in single-parent and married-parent families. *Journal of Marriage and the Family, 53,* 1021–1030.

Atkinson, M. P., & Blackwelder, S. P. (1993). Fathering in the 20th century. *Journal of Marriage and the Family, 14,* 975–986.

Atkinson, M. P., Kivett, V. R., & Campbell, R. T. (1986). Intergenerational solidarity: An examination of a theoretical model. *Journal of Gerontology, 41,* 408–416.

Babcock, J. C., Waltz, J., Jacobson, N. S., & Gottman, J. M. (1993). Power and violence: The relation between communication patterns, power discrepancies, and domestic violence. *Journal of Consulting and Clinical Psychology, 61,* 40–50.

Baber, K. M., & Allen, K. R. (1992). *Women and families: Feminist reconstructions.* New York: Guilford.

Barbarin, O. A., Hughes, D., & Chesler, M. A. (1985). Stress, coping, and marital functioning among parents of children with cancer. *Journal of Marriage and the Family, 47,* 473–480.

Barnett, R. C., & Baruch, G. K. (1985). Women's involvement in multiple roles and psychological distress. *Journal of Personality and Social Psychology, 49,* 135–145.

Barnett, R. C., Kibria, N., Baruch, G. K., & Pleck, J. H. (1991). Adult daughter–parent relationships and their associations with daughters' subjective well-being and psychological distress. *Journal of Marriage and the Family, 53,* 29–42.

Barnett, R. C., Marshall, N. L., & Pleck, J. H. (1993). Adult son–parent relationships and their associations with sons' psychological distress. *Journal of Family Issues, 13,* 505–525.

Barrett, M., & McIntosh, M. (1982). *The anti-social family.* London: Verso.

Barusch, A. S., & Speid, W. M. (1989). Gender differences in caregiving: Why do wives report greater burden? *The Gerontologist, 29,* 667–676.

Beck, R. W., & Beck, S. H. (1989). The incidence of extended households among middle-aged black and white women: Estimates from a 15-year panel study. *Journal of Family Issues, 10,* 147–168.

Beck, S., & Beck, R. W. (1984). The formation of extended households during middle age. *Journal of Marriage and the Family, 46,* 277–287.

Bell, R. A., Daly, J. A., & Conzalez, M. C. (1987). Affinity-maintenance in marriage and its relationship to women's marital satisfaction. *Journal of Marriage and the Family, 49,* 445–454.

Belle, D. (1982). The stress of caring: Women as providers of social support. In L. Goldberger & S. Breznitz (Eds.), *Handbook of stress: Theoretical and clinical aspects* (pp. 496–505). New York: Free Press.

Belsky, J., Lang, M., & Rovine, M. (1985). Stability and change in marriage across the transition to parenthood: A second study. *Journal of Marriage and the Family, 47,* 855–865.

Belsky, J., & Rovine, M. (1990). Patterns of marital change across the transition to parenthood: Pregnancy to three years postpartum. *Journal of Marriage and the Family, 52,* 5–19.

Belsky, J., Spanier, G. B., & Rovine, M. (1983). Stability and change in marriage across the transition to parenthood. *Journal of Marriage and the Family, 45,* 567–577.

Belsky, J., Youngblade, L., Rovine, M., & Volling, B. (1991). Patterns of marital change and parent–child interaction. *Journal of Marriage and the Family, 53,* 487–498.

Benin, M. H., & Edwards, D. A. (1990). Adolescents' chores: The difference between dual- and single-earner families. *Journal of Marriage and the Family, 52,* 361–373.

Benin, M., & Keith, V. M. (1995). The social support of employed African American and Anglo mothers. *Journal of Family Issues, 16,* 275–297.

Beoku-Betts, J. A. (1995). We got our way of cooking things: Women, food, and preservation of cultural identity among the Gullah. *Gender and Society, 9,* 535–555.

Bergen, E. (1991). The economic context of labor allocation: Implications for gender stratification. *Journal of Family Issues, 12,* 140–157.

Berk, S. F. (1985). *The gender factory.* New York: Plenum.

Bertoia, C., & Drakich, J. (1993). The fathers' rights movement: Contradictions in rhetoric and practice. *Journal of Family Issues, 14,* 592–615.

Birkel, R. C., & Jones, C. J. (1989). A comparison of the caregiving networks of dependent elderly individuals who are lucid and those who are demented. *The Gerontologist, 29,* 114–119.

Blair, S. L. (1993). Employment, family, and perceptions of marital quality among husbands and wives. *Journal of Family Issues, 14,* 189–212.

Blair, S. L., & Johnson, M. P. (1992). Wives' perceptions of the fairness of the division of household labor: The intersection of housework and ideology. *Journal of Marriage and the Family, 54,* 570–581.

Blaisure, K. R., & Allen, K. R. (1995). Feminists and the ideology and practice of marital equality. *Journal of Marriage and the Family, 57,* 5–19.

Blankenship, K. M., Rushing, B., Onorato, S. A., & White, R. (1993). Reproductive technologies and the U.S. courts. *Gender and Society, 7,* 8–31.

Blenkner, M. (1965). Social work and family relationships in later life with some thoughts on filial maturity. In E. Shanas & G. Streib (Eds.), *Social structure and the family: Generational relationships* (pp. 46–59). Englewood Cliffs, NJ: Prentice-Hall.

Bohan, J. S. (1993). Regarding gender: Essentialism, constructionism, and feminist psychology. *Psychology of Women Quarterly, 17,* 5–21.

Brayfield, A. (1992). Employment resources and housework in Canada. *Journal of Marriage and the Family, 54,* 19–30.

Brayfield, A. (1995). Juggling jobs and kids: The impact of employment schedules on fathers' caring for children. *Journal of Marriage and the Family, 57,* 321–332.

Brines, J. (1994). Economic dependency, gender, and the division of labor at home. *American Journal of Sociology, 100,* 652–688.

Brody, E. M., Dempsey, N. P., & Purchno, R. A. (1990). Mental health of sons and daughters of the institutionalized aged. *The Gerontologist, 30,* 212–219.

Brody, E. M., Hoffman, C., Kleban, M. H., & Schoonover, C. B. (1989). Caregiving daughters and their local siblings: Perceptions, strains, and interactions. *The Gerontologist, 29,* 529–538.

Brody, E. M., Johnsen, P. T., & Fulcomer, M. C. (1984). What should adult children do for elderly parents? Opinions and preferences of three generations of women. *Journal of Gerontology, 39,* 736–746.

Brody, E. M., & Schoonover, C. B. (1986). Patterns of parent-care when adult daughters work and when they do not. *The Gerontologist, 26,* 372–381.

Broman, C. L. (1993). Race differences in marital well-being. *Journal of Marriage and the Family, 55,* 724–732.

Browne, A. (1993). Violence against women by male partners: Prevalence, outcomes, and policy implications. *American Psychologist, 48,* 1077–1087.

Burton, L. M. (1992). Black grandparents rearing children of drug-addicted parents: Stressors, outcomes, and social service needs. *The Gerontologist, 32,* 744–751.

Burton, L. M., Kasper, J., Shore, A., Cagney, K., LaVeist, T., Cubbin, C., & German, P. (1995). The structure of informal care: Are there differences by race? *The Gerontologist, 35,* 744–752.

Chappell, N. L. (1991). Living arrangements and sources of caregiving. *Journal of Gerontology: Social Sciences, 46,* S1–S8.

Chatters, L. M., Taylor, R. J., & Jackson, J. S. (1985). Size and composition of the informal helper networks of elderly blacks. *Journal of Gerontology, 40,* 605–614.

Chesla, C., Martinson, I., & Muwaswes, M. (1994). Continuities and discontinuities in family members' relationships with Alzheimer's disease patients. *Family Relations, 43,* 3–9.

Christensen, A., & Heavey, C. L. (1990). Gender and social structure in the demand/withdraw pattern of marital conflict. *Journal of Personality and Social Psychology, 59,* 73–81.

Cicirelli, V. C. (1989). Feelings of attachment to siblings and well-being in later life. *Psychology and Aging, 4,* 211–216.

Clarke, D. D., Allen, C. M. B., & Salinas, M. (1986). Conjoint time-budgeting: Investigating behavioral accommodation in marriage. *Journal of Social and Personal Relationships, 3,* 53–69.

Cochran, M. M., & Gunnarsson, L. (1985). A follow-up study of group day care and family-based childrearing patterns. *Journal of Marriage and the Family, 47,* 297–309.

Cohen, T. F. (1993). What do fathers provide? Reconsidering the economic and nurturant dimensions of men as parents. In J. C. Hood (Ed.), *Men, work, and family* (pp. 1–22). Newbury Park, CA: Sage.

Coke, M. M. (1992). Correlates of life satisfaction among elderly African Americans. *Journal of Gerontology: Psychological Sciences, 47,* P316–P320.

Coleman, M. T. (1991). The division of household labor: Suggestions for future empirical consideration and theoretical development. In R. L. Blumberg (Ed.), *Gender, family, and economy: The triple overlap* (pp. 245–260). Newbury Park, CA: Sage.

Coltrane, S. (1989). Household labor and the routine production of gender. *Social Problems, 36,* 473–490.

Coltrane, S., & Ishii-Kuntz, M. (1992). Men's housework: A life course perspective. *Journal of Marriage and the Family, 54,* 43–57.

Coltrane, S., & Valdez, E. O. (1993). Reluctant compliance: Work–family role allocation in dual-earner Chicano families; In J. C. Hood (Ed.), *Men, work, and family* (pp. 151–175). Newbury Park, CA: Sage.

Connidis, I. A., & Campbell, L. D. (1995). Closeness, confiding, and contact among siblings in middle and late adulthood. *Journal of Family Issues, 16,* 722–745.

Connidis, I. A., & Davies, L. (1990). Confidants and companions in later life: The place of family and friends. *Journal of Gerontology: Social Sciences, 45,* S141–S149.

Connidis, I. A., & McMullin, J. A. (1993). To have or have not: Parent status and the subjective well-being of older men and women. *The Gerontologist, 33,* 630–636.

Cooney, T. M. (1989). Co-residence with adult children: A comparison of divorced and widowed women. *The Gerontologist, 29,* 779–784.

Cooney, T. M. (1994). Young adults' relations with parents: The influence of recent parental divorce. *Journal of Marriage and the Family, 56,* 45–56.

Cooney, T. M., Pedersen, F. A., Indelicato, S., & Palkovitz, R. (1993). Timing of fatherhood: Is "on-time" optimal? *Journal of Marriage and the Family, 55,* 205–215.

Cooney, T. M., & Uhlenberg, P. (1990). The role of divorce in men's relations with their adult children after mid-life. *Journal of Marriage and the Family, 52,* 677–688.

Coward, R. T., Horne, C., & Dwyer, J. W. (1992). Demographic perspectives on gender and family caregiving. In J. W. Dwyer & R. T. Coward (Eds.), *Gender, families, and elder care* (pp. 18–33). Newbury Park, CA: Sage.

Crouter, A. C., & McHale, S. M. (1993). Temporal rhythms in family life: Seasonal variation in the relation between parental work and family processes. *Developmental Psychology, 29,* 198–205.

Daly, K. (1993). Reshaping fatherhood. *Journal of Family Issues, 14,* 510–530.

Daniels, A. K. (1987). Invisible work. *Social Problems, 34,* 403–415.

Danigelis, N. L., & McIntosh, B. R. (1993). Resources and the productive activity of elders: Race and gender as contexts. *Journal of Gerontology: Social Sciences, 48,* S192–S203.

Dean, A., Kolody, B., Wood, P., & Ensel, W. M. (1989). Measuring the communication of social support from adult children. *Journal of Gerontology: Social Sciences, 44,* 371–379.

Deimling, G. T., & Bass, D. M. (1986). Symptoms of mental impairment among elderly adults and their effects on family caregivers. *Journal of Gerontology, 41,* 778–784.

Demo, D. H. (1992). Parent–child relations: Assessing recent changes. *Journal of Marriage and the Family, 54,* 104–117.

Demo, D. H., & Acock, A. C. (1993). Family diversity and the division of labor: How much have things really changed? *Family Relations, 42,* 323–331.

Depner, C. E., & Ingersoll-Dayton, B. (1985). Conjugal social support: Patterns in later life. *Journal of Gerontology, 40,* 761–766.

Deutsch, F. M., Lozy, J. L., & Saxon, S. (1993). Taking credit: Couples' reports of contributions to child care. *Journal of Family Issues, 14,* 421–437.

Deutsch, F. M., Lussier, J. B., & Servis, L. J. (1993). Husbands at home: Predictors of paternal participation in childcare and housework. *Journal of Personality and Social Psychology, 65,* 1154–1166.

DeVault, M. (1987). Doing housework: Feeding and family life. In N. Gerstel & H. E. Gross (Eds.), *Families and work* (pp. 178–191). Philadelphia: Temple University Press.

DeVault, M. (1990). Conflict over housework: A problem that (still) has no name. *Research in Social Movements, Conflict and Change, 12,* 189–202.

DeVault, M. (1991). *Feeding the family: The social organization of caring as gendered work.* Chicago: University of Chicago Press.

DiLeonardo, M. (1987). The female world of cards and holidays: Women, families and the work of kinship. *Signs, 12,* 440–453.

Dressel, P. L., & Clark, A. (1990). A critical look at family care. *Journal of Marriage and the Family, 52,* 769–782.

Dressler, W. W. (1985). Extended family relationships, social support, and mental health in a southern black community. *Journal of Health and Social Behavior, 26,* 39–48.

Dwyer, J. W., & Coward, R. T. (1991). A multivariate comparison of the involvement of adult sons versus daughters in the care of impaired parents. *Journal of Gerontology: Social Sciences, 46,* S259–S269.

Dwyer, J. W., & Seccombe, K. (1991). Elder care as family labor: The influence of gender and family position. *Journal of Family Issues, 12,* 229–247.

Eagly, A. H. (1983). Gender and social influence: A social psychological analysis. *American Psychologist, 38,* 971–981.

Eagly, A. H., & Steffan, V. J. (1984). Gender stereotypes stem from the distribution of women and men into social roles. *Journal of Personality and Social Psychology, 46,* 735–754.

Erickson, R. J. (1993). Reconceptualizing family work: The effect of emotion work on perceptions of marital quality. *Journal of Marriage and the Family, 55,* 888–900.

Esterberg, K. G., Moen, P., & Dempster-McClain, D. (1994). Transition to divorce: A life-course approach to women's marital duration and dissolution. *The Sociological Quarterly, 35,* 289–307.

Feazell, C. S., Mayers, R. S., & Deschner, J. (1984). Services for men who batter: Implications for programs and policies. *Family Relations, 33,* 217–223.

Ferguson, S. J. (1995). Marriage timing of Chinese American and Japanese American women. *Journal of Family Issues, 16,* 314–343.

Ferree, M. M. (1990). Beyond separate spheres; Feminism and family research. *Journal of Marriage and the Family, 52,* 866–884.

Ferree, M. M. (1991). The gender division of labor in two-earner marriages: Dimensions of variability and change. *Journal of Family Issues, 12,* 158–180.

Finch, J., & Groves, D. (1983). Introduction. In J. Finch and D. Groves (Eds.), *A labour of love: Women, work and caring* (pp. 1–10). London: Routledge & Kegan Paul.

Finley, N. J. (1989). Theories of family labor as applied to gender differences in caregiving for elderly parents. *Journal of Marriage and the Family, 51,* 79–86.

Finley, N. J., Roberts, M. D., & Banahan, B. F., III. (1988). Motivators and inhibitors of attitudes of filial obligation toward aging parents. *The Gerontologist, 28,* 73–78.

Fitting, M., Rabins, P., Lucas, M. J., & Eastham, J. (1986). Caregivers for dementia patients: A comparison of husbands and wives. *The Gerontologist, 26,* 248–252.

Floge, L. (1985). The dynamics of child-care use and some implications for women's employment. *Journal of Marriage and the Family, 47,* 143–154.

Folk, K. F., Graham, J. W., & Ballar, A. H. (1992). Child support and remarriage: Implications for the economic well-being of children. *Journal of Family Issues, 13,* 142–157.

Fredman, L., Daly, M. P., & Lazur, A. M. (1995). Burden among white and black caregivers to elderly adults. *Journal of Gerontology: Social Sciences, 50B,* S110–S118.

Frieze, I. H. (1983). Investigating the causes and consequences of marital rape. *Signs: Journal of Women in Culture and Society, 8,* 532–553.

Furstenberg, F. F., Jr., Morgan, S. P., & Allison, P. D. (1987). Parental participation and child's well-being after marital dissolution. *American Sociological Review, 52,* 695–701.

Furstenberg, F. F., Jr., & Nord, C. W. (1985). Parenting apart: Patterns of childrearing after marital disruption. *Journal of Marriage and the Family, 47,* 893–904.

Gallagher, D., Rose, J., Rivera, P., Lovett, S., & Thompson, L. W. (1989). Prevalence of depression in family caregivers. *The Gerontologist, 29,* 449–456.

Ganong, L. H., Coleman, M., & Mistina, D. (1995). Home is where they have to let you in: Beliefs regarding physical custody changes of children following divorce. *Journal of Family Issues, 16,* 466–487.

Gentry, M., & Shulman, A. D. (1988). Remarriage as a coping response for widowhood. *Psychology and Aging, 3,* 191–196.

Gerstel, N. (1988). Divorce and kin ties: The importance of gender. *Journal of Marriage and the Family, 50,* 209–219.

Gerstel, N., & Gallagher, S. K. (1993). Kinkeeping and distress: Gender, recipients of care, and work–family conflict. *Journal of Marriage and the Family, 55,* 598–607.

Gerstel, N., & Gallagher, S. (1994). Caring for kith and kin: Gender, employment, and the privatization of care. *Social Problems, 41,* 519–539.

Gilbert, L. A., Hanson, G. R., & Davis, B. (1982). Perceptions of parental role responsibilities: Differences between mothers and fathers. *Family Relations, 31,* 261–269.

Gilgun, J. F. (1995). We shared something special: The moral discourse of incest perpetrators. *Journal of Marriage and the Family, 57,* 265–281.

Glazer, N. Y. (1990). The home as workshop: Women as amateur nurses and medical care providers. *Gender and Society, 4,* 479–499.

Glenn, E. N. (1987). Gender and the family. In B. B. Hess & M. M. Ferree (Eds.), *Analyzing gender: A handbook of social science research* (pp. 348–380). Newbury Park, CA: Sage.

Glenn, E. N., & Weaver, C. N. (1988). The changing relationship of marital status to reported happiness. *Journal of Marriage and the Family, 50,* 317–324.

Glick, P. C., & Lin, S. (1986). More young adults are living with their parents: Who are they? *Journal of Marriage and the Family, 48,* 107–112.

Goldscheider, F. K., & Waite, L. J. (1986). Sex differences in the entry into marriage. *American Journal of Sociology, 92,* 91–109.

Goodnow, J. J. (1988). Children's household work: Its nature and functions. *Psychological Bulletin, 103,* 5–26.

Gottman, J. M., & Levenson, R. W. (1992). Marital processes predictive of later dissolution: Behavior, physiology, and health. *Journal of Personality and Social Psychology, 63,* 221–233.

Graham, H. (1983). Caring: A labour of love. In J. Finch & D. Groves (Eds.), *A labour of love: Women, work and caring* (pp. 13–30). London: Routledge & Kegan Paul

Greenberg, J. S., & Becker, M. (1988). Aging parents as family resources. *The Gerontologist, 28,* 787–791.

Greenstein, T. N. (1995). Gender ideology, marital disruption, and the employment of married women. *Journal of Marriage and the Family, 57,* 31–42.

Greil, A. L., Leitko, T. A., & Porter, K. L. (1988). Infertility: His and hers. *Gender and Society, 2,* 172–199.

Grossman, F. K., Pollack, W. S., Golding, E. R., & Fedele, N. M. (1987). Affiliation and autonomy in the transition to parenthood. *Family Relations, 36,* 263–269.

Hackel, L. S., & Ruble, D. N. (1992). Changes in the marital relationship after the first baby is born: Predicting the impact of expectancy disconfirmation. *Journal of Personality and Social Psychology, 62,* 944–957.

Hafstrom, J. L., & Schram, V. R. (1984). Chronic illness in couples: Selected characteristics including wife's satisfaction with and perception of marital relationship. *Family Relations, 33,* 195–203.

Hall, L. D., Walker, A. J., & Acock, A. C. (1995). Gender and family work in one-parent households. *Journal of Marriage and the Family, 57,* 685–692.

Hardesty, C., & Bokemeier, J. (1989). Finding time and making do: Distribution of household labor in nonmetropolitan marriages. *Journal of Marriage and the Family, 51,* 253–267.

Harding, S. (1987). Conclusion: Epistemological questions. In S. Harding (Ed.), *Feminism and methodology: Social science issues* (pp. 181–190). Bloomington: Indiana University Press.

Hare, J., & Richards, L. N. (1993). Children raised by lesbian couples: Does context of birth affect father and partner involvement? *Family Relations, 42,* 249–255.

Harris, K. M., & Morgan, S. P. (1991). Fathers, sons, and daughters: Differential paternal involvement in parenting. *Journal of Marriage and the Family, 58,* 531–544.

Hartmann, H. I. (1981). The family as the locus of gender, class, and political struggle: The example of housework. *Signs: Journal of Women in Culture and Society, 6,* 366–394.

Hartung, R. (1993). On black burden and becoming *nouveau poor. Journal of Gerontology: Social Sciences, 48,* S33–S34.

Haurin, R. J. (1992). Patterns of childhood residence and the relationship to young adult outcomes. *Journal of Marriage and the Family, 54,* 846–860.

Hawkesworth, M. E. (1989). Knowers, knowing, known: Feminist theory and claims of truth. *Signs, 14,* 533–557.

Hawkins, A. J., & Eggebeen, D. J. (1991). Are fathers fungible? Patterns of coresident adult men in maritally disrupted families and young children's well-being. *Journal of Marriage and the Family, 53,* 958–972.

Hawkins, A. J., Marshall, C. M., & Meiners, K. M. (1995). Exploring wives' sense of fairness about family work. *Journal of Family Issues, 16,* 693–721.

Hawkins, A. J., & Roberts, T. (1992). Designing a primary intervention to help dual-earner couples share housework and child care. *Family Relations, 41,* 169–177.

Heaton, T. B., & Albrecht, S. L. (1991). Stable unhappy marriages. *Journal of Marriage and the Family, 53,* 747–758.

Heavey, C. L., Layne, C., & Christensen, A. (1993). Gender and conflict structure in marital interaction: A replication and extension. *Journal of Consulting and Clinical Psychology, 61,* 16–27.

Heinemann, G. D. (1985). Interdependence in informal support systems: The case of elderly, urban widows. In W. A. Peterson & J. Quadagno (Eds.), *Social bonds in later life: Aging and interdependence* (pp. 165–186). Beverly Hills, CA: Sage.

Herbert, T. B., Silver, R. C., & Ellard, J. H. (1991). Coping with an abusive relationship: 1. How and why do women stay? *Journal of Marriage and the Family, 53,* 311–325.

Hill, S. A., & Zimmermann, M. K. (1995). Valiant girls and vulnerable boys: The impact of gender and race on mothers' caregiving for chronically ill children. *Journal of Marriage and the Family, 57,* 43–53.

Hill Collins, P. (1990). *Black feminist thought: Knowledge, consciousness, and the politics of empowerment.* Boston: Unwin Hyman.

Hill Collins, P. (1992). Black women and motherhood. In B. Thorne & M. Yalom (Eds.), *Rethinking the family: Some feminist questions* (2nd ed., pp. 215–245). Boston: Northeastern University Press.

Hinrichsen, G. A. (1991). Adjustment of caregivers to depressed older adults. *Psychology and Aging, 6,* 631–639.

Hinrichsen, G. A., & Ramirez, M. (1992). Black and white dementia caregivers: A comparison of their adaptation, adjustment, and service utilization. *The Gerontologist, 32,* 375–381.

Hobbs, D. F., Jr., & Wimbish, J. M. (1977). Transition to parenthood by black couples. *Journal of Marriage and the Family, 39,* 677–689.

Hochschild, A. (1983). *The managed heart: Commercialization of human feeling.* Berkeley: University of California Press.

Hochschild, A., with Machung, A. (1989). *The second shift: Working parents and the revolution at home.* New York: Viking.

Hondagneu-Sotelo, P. (1992). Overcoming patriarchal constraints: The reconstruction of gender relations among Mexican immigrant women and men. *Gender and Society, 6,* 393–415.

Hooyman, N., Gonyea, J., & Montgomery, R. (1985). The impact of in-home services termination on family caregivers. *The Gerontologist, 25,* 141–145.

Horowitz, A. (1985). Sons and daughters are caregivers to older parents: Differences in role performance and consequences. *The Gerontologist, 25,* 612–617.

Huston, T. L., McHale, S. M., & Crouter, A. C. (1986). When the honeymoon's over: Changes in the marriage relationship over the first year. In S. Duck & R. Gilmour (Eds.), *The emerging field of personal relationships* (pp. 109–132). Hillsdale, NJ: Erlbaum.

Huston, T. L., & Vangelisti, A. L. (1991). Socioemotional behavior and satisfaction in marital relationships: A longitudinal study. *Journal of Personality and Social Psychology, 61,* 721–733.

Hyde, B. L., & Texidor, M. (1994). A description of the fathering experience among black fathers. In R. Staples (Ed.), *The black family* (5th ed., pp. 157–164). Belmont, CA: Wadsworth.

Ishii-Kuntz, M., & Coltrane, S. (1992). Remarriage, stepparenting, and household labor. *Journal of Family Issues, 13,* 215–233.

Jacobson, N. S., Gottman, J. M., Waltz, J., Rushe, R., Babcock, J., & Holtzworth-Munroe, A. (1994). Affect, verbal content, and psychophysiology in the arguments of couples with a violent husband. *Journal of Consulting and Clinical Psychology, 62,* 982–988.

Jayakody, R., Chatters, L. M., & Taylor, R. J. (1993). Family support to single and married African American mothers: The provision of financial, emotional, and childcare assistance. *Journal of Marriage and the Family, 55,* 261–276.

John, D., Shelton, B. A., & Luschen, K. (1995). Race, ethnicity, gender, and perceptions of fairness. *Journal of Family Issues, 16,* 357–379.

Johnson, C. L. (1983). Dyadic family relationships and social support. *The Gerontologist, 23,* 377–383.

Johnson, C. L. (1988a). Active and latent functions of grandparenting during the divorce process. *The Gerontologist, 28,* 185–191.

Johnson, C. L. (1988b). Postdivorce reorganization of relationships between divorcing children and their parents. *Journal of Marriage and the Family, 50,* 221–231.

Johnson, D. R., Amoloza, T. O., & Booth, A. (1992). Stability and developmental change in marital quality: A three-wave panel analysis. *Journal of Marriage and the Family, 54,* 582–594.

Johnson, M. P. (1995). Patriarchal terrorism and common couple violence: Two forms of violence against women. *Journal of Marriage and the Family, 57,* 284–294.

Jones, J. (1985). *Labor of love, labor of sorrow: Black women, work, and the family from slavery to the present.* New York: Basic Books.

Julian, T. W., McKenry, P. C., & McKelvey, M. W. (1994). Cultural variations in parenting: Perceptions of Caucasian, African-American, Hispanic, and Asian-American parents. *Family Relations, 43,* 30–37.

Kalmuss, D., Davidson, A., & Cushman, L. (1992). Parenting expectations, experiences, and adjustment to parenthood: A test of the violated expectations framework. *Journal of Marriage and the Family, 54,* 516–526.

Kandel, D. B., Davies, M., & Raveis, V. (1985). The stressfulness of daily social roles for women: Marital, occupational and household roles. *Journal of Health and Social Behavior, 26,* 64–78.

Kane, E. W., & Sanchez, L. (1994). Family status and criticism of gender inequality at home and at work. *Social Forces, 72,* 1079–1102.

Katzev, A. R., Warner, R. L., & Acock, A. C. (1994). Girls or boys? Relationship of child gender to marital instability. *Journal of Marriage and the Family, 56,* 89–100.

Kazak, A. E., & Marvin, R. S. (1984). Differences, difficulties and adaptation: Stress and social networks in families with a handicapped child. *Family Relations, 33,* 67–77.

King, V. (1994a). Nonresident father involvement and child well-being: Can dads make a difference? *Journal of Family Issues, 15,* 78–96.

King, V. (1994b). Variation in the consequences of nonresident father involvement for children's well-being. *Journal of Marriage and the Family, 56,* 963–972.

Kingson, E. R., & O'Grady-Leshane, R. (1993). The effects of caregiving on women's social security benefits. *The Gerontologist, 33,* 230–239.

Kinney, J. M., & Stephens, M. A. P. (1989). Hassles and uplifts of giving care to a family member with dementia. *Psychology and Aging, 4,* 402–408.

Kivett, V. R. (1985). Grandfathers and grandchildren: Patterns of association, helping, and psychological closeness. *Family Relations, 34,* 565–571.

Kivett, V. R. (1988). Older rural fathers and sons: Patterns of association and helping. *Family Relations, 37,* 62–67.

Kivett, V. R. (1993). Racial comparisons of the grandmother role: Implications for strengthening the family support system of older black women. *Family Relations, 42,* 165–172.

Kleban, M. H., Brody, E. M., Schoonover, C. B., & Hoffman, C. (1989). Family help to the elderly: Perceptions of sons-in-law regarding parent care. *Journal of Marriage and the Family, 51,* 303–312.

Kohen, J. A. (1983). Old but not alone: Informal social supports among the elderly by marital status and sex. *The Gerontologist, 23,* 57–63.

Komter, A. (1989). Hidden power in marriage. *Gender and Society, 3,* 187–216.

Kosberg, J. I., Cairl, R. E., & Keller, D. M. (1990). Components of burden: Interventive implications. *The Gerontologist, 30,* 236–242.

Kramer, B. J., & Kipnis, S. (1995). Eldercare and work-role conflict: Toward an understanding of gender differences in caregiving burden. *The Gerontologist, 35,* 340–348.

Kranichfeld, M. L. (1987). Rethinking family power. *Journal of Family Issues, 8,* 42–56.

Kulis, S. S. (1992). Social class and the locus of reciprocity in relationships with adult children. *Journal of Family Issues, 13,* 482–504.

Kurdek, L. A. (1988). Perceived social support in gays and lesbians in cohabiting relationships. *Journal of Personality and Social Psychology, 54,* 504–509.

Kurdek, L. A. (1993). The allocation of household labor in gay, lesbian, and heterosexual married couples. *Journal of Social Issues, 49,* 127–139.

Kurdek, L. A. (1994). Areas of conflict for gay, lesbian, and heterosexual couples: What couples argue about influences relationship satisfaction. *Journal of Marriage and the Family, 56,* 923–934.

Kurdek, L. A., & Schmitt, J. P. (1986a). Early development of relationship quality in heterosexual married, heterosexual cohabiting, gay, and lesbian couples. *Developmental Psychology, 22,* 305–309.

Kurdek, L. A., & Schmitt, J. P. (1986b). Relationship quality of partners in heterosexual married, heterosexual cohabiting, and gay and lesbian relationships. *Journal of Personality and Social Psychology, 51,* 711–720.

Lackey, C., & Williams, K. R. (1995). Social bonding and the cessation of partner violence across generations. *Journal of Marriage and the Family, 57,* 295–305.

LaRossa, R. (1988). Fatherhood and social change. *Family Relations, 37,* 451–457.

LaRossa, R., & Reitzes, D. C. (1995). Gendered perceptions of father involvement in early 20th century America. *Journal of Marriage and the Family, 57,* 223–229.

Lawton, L., Silverstein, M., & Bengtson, V. (1994). Affection, social contact, and geographic distance between adult children and their parents. *Journal of Marriage and the Family, 56,* 57–68.

Lawton, M. P., Rajagopal, D., Brody, E., & Kleban, M. H. (1992). The dynamics of caregiving for a demented elder among black and white families. *Journal of Gerontology: Psychological Sciences, 47,* S156–S164.

Lee, G. R., Dwyer, J. W., & Coward, R. T. (1993). Gender differences in parent care: Demographic factors and same-gender preferences. *Journal of Gerontology: Social Sciences, 48,* S9–S16.

Lee, G. R., & Ishii-Kuntz, M. (1987). Social interaction, loneliness, and emotional well-being among the elderly. *Research on Aging, 9,* 459–482.

Lee, T. R., Mancini, J. A., & Maxwell, J. W. (1990). Sibling relationships in adulthood: Contact, patterns, and motivations. *Journal of Marriage and the Family, 52,* 431–440.

Lennon, M. C., & Rosenfield, S. (1994). Relative fairness and the division of housework: The importance of options. *American Journal of Sociology, 100,* 506–531.

Lerner, M. J., Somers, D. G., Reid, D., Chiriboga, D., & Tierney, M. (1991). Adult children as caregivers: Egocentric biases in judgments of sibling contributions. *The Gerontologist, 31,* 746–755.

Leslie, L. A., Anderson, E. A., & Branson, M. P. (1991). Responsibility for children: The role of gender and employment. *Journal of Family Issues, 12,* 197–210.

Levenson, R. W., Carstensten, L. L., & Gottman, J. M. (1993). Long-term marriage: Age, gender, and satisfaction. *Psychology and Aging, 8,* 301–313.

Levenson, R. W., Carstensten, L. L., & Gottman, J. M. (1994). The influence of age and gender on affect, physiology, and their interrelations: A study of long-term marriages. *Journal of Personality and Social Psychology, 67,* 56–68.

Lewis, R. A., Kozac, E. B., Milardo, R. M., & Grosnick, W. A. (1981). Commitment in same-sex love relationships. *Alternative Lifestyles, 4,* 22–42.

Lichter, D. T., Anderson, R. N., & Hayward, M. D. (1995). Marriage markets and marital choice. *Journal of Family Issues, 16,* 412–431.

Lorber, J., & Bandlamudi, L. (1993). The dynamics of marital bargaining in male infertility. *Gender and Society, 7,* 32–49.

Lye, D. N., & Biblarz, T. J. (1993). The effects of attitudes toward family life and gender roles on marital satisfaction. *Journal of Family Issues, 14,* 157–188.

Lytton, H., & Romney, D. M. (1991). Parents' differential socialization of boys and girls: A meta-analysis. *Psychological Bulletin, 109,* 267–296.

MacDermid, S. M., Huston, T. L., & McHale, S. M. (1990). Changes in marriage associated with the transition to parenthood: Individual differences as a function of sex-role attitudes and changes in the division of household labor. *Journal of Marriage and the Family, 52,* 475–486.

Major, B. (1993). Gender, entitlement, and the distribution of family labor. *Journal of Social Issues, 49,* 141–159.

Marciano, T. D. (1978). Male pressure in the decision to remain childfree. *Alternative Lifestyles, 1,* 95–112.

Marini, M. M., & Shelton, B. A. (1993). Measuring household work: Recent experience in the United States. *Social Science Research, 22,* 361–382.

Markides, K. S., Boldt, J. S., & Ray, L. A. (1986). Sources of helping and intergenerational solidarity: A three-generations study of Mexican Americans. *Journal of Gerontology, 41,* 506–511.

Marks, N. F., & McLanahan, S. S. (1993). Gender, family structure, and social support among parents. *Journal of Marriage and the Family, 55,* 481–493.

Marsiglio, W. (1991). Paternal engagement activities with minor children. *Journal of Marriage and the Family, 53,* 973–986.

Matthews, S. H. (1995). Gender and the division of filial responsibility between lone sisters and their brothers. *Journal of Gerontology: Social Sciences, 50,* S312–S320.

Matthews, S. H., & Rosner, T. T. (1988). Shared filial responsibility: The family as the primary caregiver. *Journal of Marriage and the Family, 50,* 185–195.

Matthews, S. H., & Sprey, J. (1985). Adolescents' relationships with grandparents: An empirical contribution to conceptual clarification. *Journal of Gerontology, 40,* 621–626.

Matthews, S. H., Werkner, J. E., & Delaney, P. J. (1989). Relative contributions of help by employed and nonemployed sisters to their elderly parents. *Journal of Gerontology: Social Sciences, 44,* S36–S44.

McFall, S., & Miller, B. H. (1992). Caregiver burden and nursing home admission of frail elderly persons. *Journal of Gerontology: Social Sciences, 47,* S73–S79.

McGhee, J. L. (1985). The effects of siblings on the life satisfaction of the rural elderly. *Journal of Marriage and the Family, 47,* 85–91.

McHale, S. M., & Crouter, A. C. (1992). You can't always get what you want: Incongruence between sex-role attitudes and family work roles and its implications for marriage. *Journal of Marriage and the Family, 54,* 537–547.

McHale, S. M., & Huston, T. L. (1984). Men and women as parents: Sex role orientations, employment, and parental roles. *Child Development, 55,* 1349–1361.

McHale, S. M., & Huston, T. L. (1988). The effect of the transition to parenthood on the marriage relationship. *Journal of Family Issues, 6,* 409–433.

McRae, J. A., & Brody, C. J. (1989). The differential importance of marital experiences for the well-being of women and men: A research note. *Social Science Research, 18,* 237–248.

Mederer, H. (1993). Division of labor in two-earner homes: Task accomplishment versus household management as critical variables in perceptions about family work. *Journal of Marriage and the Family, 55,* 133–145.

Mednick, M. T. (1989). On the politics of psychological constructs: Stop the bandwagon, I want to get off. *American Psychologist, 44,* 1118–1123.

Miller, B. (1987). Gender and control among spouses of the cognitively impaired: A research note. *The Gerontologist, 27,* 447–453.

Miller, B. (1990a). Gender differences in spouse caregiver strain: Socialization and role expectations. *Journal of Marriage and the Family, 52,* 311–321.

Miller, B. (1990b). Gender differences in spouse management of the caregiving role. In E. K. Abel & M. K. Nelson (Eds.), *Circles of care: Work and identity in women's lives* (pp. 92–104). Albany: State University of New York Press.

Miller, B., & Cafasso, L. (1992). Gender differences in caregiving: Fact or artifact? *The Gerontologist, 32,* 498–507.

Miller, B., & McFall, S. (1991). Stability and change in the informal task support network of frail older persons. *The Gerontologist, 31,* 735–745.

Moen, P. (1992). *Women's two roles: A contemporary dilemma.* New York: Auburn House.

Moen, P., & Dempster-McClain, D. I. (1987). Employed parents: Role strain, work time, and preference for working less. *Journal of Marriage and the Family, 49,* 579–590.

Montgomery, R. J. V., & Kosloski, K. (1994). A longitudinal analysis of nursing home placement for dependent elders cared for by spouses vs. adult children. *Journal of Gerontology: Social Sciences, 49,* S62–S74.

Morgan, D. L. (1989). Adjusting to widowhood: Do social networks really make it easier? *The Gerontologist, 29,* 101–107.

Morgan, S. P., Lye, D. N., & Condran, G. A. (1988). Sons, daughters, and the risk of marital disruption. *American Journal of Sociology, 94,* 110–129.

Moritz, D. J., Kasl, S. V., & Berkman, L. F. (1989). The health impact of living with a cognitively impaired elderly spouse: Depressive symptoms and social functioning. *Journal of Gerontology: Social Sciences, 44,* S17–S27.

Mui, A. D. (1992). Caregiver strain among black and white daughter caregivers: A role theory perspective. *The Gerontologist, 32,* 203–212.

Mui, A. D. (1995a). Caring for frail elderly parents: A comparison of adult sons and daughters. *The Gerontologist, 35,* 86–93.

Mui, A. D. (1995b). Multidimensional predictors of caregiver strain among older persons caring for frail spouses. *Journal of Marriage and the Family, 57,* 733–740.

Mui, A. D., & Burnette, D. (1994). Long-term care service use by frail elders: Is ethnicity a factor? *The Gerontologist, 34,* 190–198.

Mutran, E., & Reitzes, D. C. (1984). Intergenerational support activities and well-being among the elderly: A comparison of exchange and symbolic interaction perspectives. *American Sociological Review, 49,* 117–130.

Nock, S. L., & Kingston, P. W. (1988). Time with children: The impact of couples' work-time commitments. *Social Forces, 67,* 59–85.

Norton, A. J., & Moorman, J. E. (1987). Current trends in marriage and divorce among American women. *Journal of Marriage and the Family, 49,* 3–14.

Nydegger, C. (1983). Family ties of the aged: A cross-cultural perspective. *The Gerontologist, 23,* 26–32.

Oggins, J., Veroff, J., & Leber, D. (1993). Perceptions of marital interaction among black and white newlyweds. *Journal of Personality and Social Psychology, 65,* 494–511.

Oropesa, R. S. (1993). Using the service economy to relieve the double burden: Female labor force participation and service purchases. *Journal of Family Issues, 14,* 438–473.

Osmond, M. W., & Thorne, B. (1993). Feminist theories: The social construction of gender in families and society. In P. G. Boss, W. J. Doherty, R. W. LaRossa, W. R. Schumm, & S. K. Steinmetz (Eds.), *Sourcebook of family theories and methods: A contextual approach* (pp. 591–623). New York: Plenum.

Paasch, K. M., & Teachman, J. D. (1991). Gender of children and receipt of assistance from absent fathers. *Journal of Family Issues, 12,* 450–466.

Patterson, C. J. (1992). Children of lesbian and gay parents. *Child Development, 63,* 1025–1042.

Penrod, J. D., Kane, R. A., Kane, R. L., & Finch, M. D. (1995). Who cares? The size, scope, and composition of the caregiver support system. *The Gerontologist, 35,* 489–497.

Perry-Jenkins, M., & Crouter, A. C. (1990). Men's provider-role attitudes. *Journal of Family Issues, 11*, 136–156.

Perry-Jenkins, M., & Folk, K. (1994). Class, couples, and conflict: Effects of the division of labor on assessments of marriage in dual-earner families. *Journal of Marriage and the Family, 56*, 165–180.

Peterson, R. R., & Gerson, K. (1992). Determinants of responsibility for childcare arrangements among dual-earner couples. *Journal of Marriage and the Family, 54*, 527–536.

Piña, D. L., & Bengtson, V. L. (1995). Division of household labor and the well-being of retirement-aged wives. *The Gerontologist, 35*, 308–317.

Potucheck, J. L. (1992). Employed wives' orientations to breadwinning: A gender theory analysis. *Journal of Marriage and the Family, 54*, 548–558.

Pratt, C., Schmall, V., & Wright, S. (1987). Ethical concerns of family caregivers to dementia patients. *The Gerontologist, 27*, 632–638.

Presser, H. B. (1988). Shift work and child care among young dual-earner American parents. *Journal of Marriage and the Family, 50*, 133–148.

Presser, H. B. (1989). Some economic complexities of child care provided by grandmothers. *Journal of Marriage and the Family, 51*, 581–591.

Pruchno, R. A., & Resch, N. L. (1989). Husbands and wives as caregivers: Antecedents of depression and burden. *The Gerontologist, 29*, 159–165.

Pyke, K. D. (1994). Women's employment as a gift of burden? Marital power across marriage, divorce, and remarriage. *Gender and Society, 8*, 73–91.

Reilly, T. W., Entwisle, D. R., & Doering, S. G. (1987). Socialization into parenthood: A longitudinal study of the development of self-evaluations. *Journal of Marriage and the Family, 49*, 295–308.

Rich, A. (1983). Compulsory heterosexuality and lesbian existence. In E. Abel & E. K. Abel (Eds.), *The signs reader: Women, gender and scholarship* (pp. 139–168). Chicago: University of Chicago Press.

Rosenthal, C. J. (1985). Kinkeeping in the familial division of labor. *Journal of Marriage and the Family, 47*, 965–974.

Ross, C. E. (1995). Reconceptualizing marital status as a continuum of social attachment. *Journal of Marriage and the Family, 57*, 129–140.

Ross, C. E., & Huber, J. (1985). Hardship and depression. *Journal of Health and Social Behavior, 26*, 312–327.

Russell, G., & Russell, A. (1987). Mother–child and father–child relationships in middle childhood. *Child Development, 58*, 1573–1585.

Sankar, A. (1993). Culture, research, and policy. *The Gerontologist, 33*, 437–438.

Schullo, S. A., & Alperson, B. L. (1984). Interpersonal phenomenology as a function of sexual orientation, sex, sentiment, and trait categories in long-term dyadic relationships. *Journal of Personality and Social Psychology, 47*, 983–1002.

Schulz, R., Visintainer, P., & Williamson, G. M. (1990). Psychiatric and physical morbidity effects of caregiving. *Journal of Gerontology: Psychological Sciences, 45*, P181–P191.

Schulz, R., & Williamson, G. M. (1991). A 2-year longitudinal study of depression among Alzheimer's caregivers. *Psychology and Aging, 6*, 569–578.

Scott, J. W., & Black, A. (1994). Deep structures of African American family life: Female and male kin networks. In R. Staples (Ed.), *The black family* (5th ed., pp. 204–213). Belmont, CA: Wadsworth.

Seltzer, J. A. (1991). Relationships between fathers and children who live apart: The children's role after separation. *Journal of Marriage and the Family, 53*, 79–101.

Seltzer, J. A., & Brandreth, Y. (1994). What fathers say about involvement with children after separation. *Journal of Family Issues, 15*, 49–77.

Shelton, B. A. (1990). The distribution of household tasks: Does wife's employment status make a difference? *Journal of Family Issues, 11*, 115–135.

Shelton, B. A., & John, D. (1993a). Does marital status make a difference? Housework among married and cohabiting men and women. *Journal of Family Issues, 14*, 401–420.

Shelton, B. A., & John, D. (1993b). Ethnicity, race, and difference: A comparison of white, black, and Hispanic men's household labor time. In J. C. Hood (Ed:), *Men, work, and family* (pp. 131–150). Newbury Park, CA: Sage.

Siegel, J. M. (1995). Looking for Mr. Right? Older single women who become mothers. *Journal of Family Issues, 16*, 194–211.

Siegal, M. (1987). Are sons and daughters treated more differently by fathers than by mothers? *Developmental Review, 7*, 183–209.

Silverstein, L. B. (1991). Transforming the debate about child care and maternal employment. *American Psychologist, 46*, 1025–1032.

Silverstein, M., & Litwak, E. (1993). A task-specific typology of intergenerational family structure in later life. *The Gerontologist, 33*, 258–264.

Silverstein, M., Parrott, T. M., & Bengtson, V. L. (1995). Factors that predispose middle-aged sons and daughters to provide social support to older parents. *Journal of Marriage and the Family, 57*, 465–475.

Silverstein, M., & Waite, L. J. (1993). Are blacks more likely than whites to receive and provide social support in middle and old age? Yes, no, and maybe so. *Journal of Gerontology: Social Sciences, 48*, S212–S222.

Simons, R. L., Beaman, J., Conger, R. D., & Chas, W. (1993). Childhood experience, conceptions of parenting, and attitudes of spouse as determinants of parental behavior. *Journal of Marriage and the Family, 55*, 91–106.

Skaff, M. M., & Pearlin, L. I. (1992). Caregiving: Role engulfment and the loss of self. *The Gerontologist, 32*, 656–664.

Smith, D. (1987). *The everyday world as problematic*. Boston: Northeastern University Press.

Smith, G. C., Smith, M. F., & Toseland, R. W. (1991). Problems identified by family caregivers in counseling. *The Gerontologist, 31*, 15–22.

Soldo, B. J., Wolf, D. A., & Agree, E. M. (1990). Family, households, and care arrangements of frail older women: A structural analysis. *Journal of Gerontology: Social Sciences, 45*, S238–S249.

Solomon, J. C. (1995). "To grandmother's house we go": Health and school adjustment of children raised solely by grandparents. *The Gerontologist, 35*, 386–394.

South, S. J., & Spitze, G. (1994). Housework in marital and nonmarital households. *American Sociological Review, 59*, 327–347.

Speare, A., Jr., & Avery, R. (1993). Who helps whom in older parent–child families. *Journal of Gerontology: Social Sciences, 48*, S64–S73.

Spitze, G. (1988). Women's employment and family relations: A review. *Journal of Marriage and the Family, 50*, 595–618.

Spitze, G., & Logan, J. (1989). Gender differences in family support: Is there a payoff? *The Gerontologist, 29*, 108–113.

Spitze, G., & Logan, J. (1990). Sons, daughters, and intergenerational social support. *Journal of Marriage and the Family, 52*, 420–430.

Spitze, G., Logan, J., Deane, G., & Zerger, S. (1994). Adult children's divorce and intergenerational relationships. *Journal of Marriage and the Family, 56*, 279–293.

Spitze, G., Logan, J. R., Joseph, G., & Lee, E. (1994). Middle generation roles and the well-being of men and women. *Journal of Gerontology: Social Sciences, 49*, S107–S116.

Stacey, J. (1993). Good riddance to "The Family": A response. *Journal of Marriage and the Family, 55*, 545–547.

Stack, C. (1974). *All our kin: Strategies for survival in a black community*. New York: Harper & Row.

Starrels, M. E. (1994). Gender differences in parent–child relations. *Journal of Family Issues, 15*, 148–165.

Stoller, E. P. (1983). Parental caregiving by adult children. *Journal of Marriage and the Family, 45*, 851–858.

Stoller, E. P. (1990). Males as helpers: The role of sons, relatives, and friends. *The Gerontologist, 30*, 228–235.

Stoller, E. P., & Earl, L. L. (1983). Help with activities of everyday life: Sources of support for the noninstitutionalized elderly. *The Gerontologist, 23,* 64–70.

Stoller, E. P., & Pugliesi, K. L. (1989). Other roles of caregivers: Competing responsibilities or supportive resources. *Journal of Gerontology: Social Sciences, 44,* S231–S238.

Stone, R., Cafferata, G. L., & Sangl, J. (1987). Caregivers of the frail elderly: A national profile. *The Gerontologist, 27,* 616–626.

Strawbridge, W. J., & Wallhagen, M. I. (1991). Impact of family conflict on adult child caregivers. *The Gerontologist, 31,* 770–777.

Stueve, A. (1982). The elderly as network members. *Marriage and Family Review, 5,* 59–87.

Suitor, J. J. (1991). Marital quality and satisfaction with the division of household labor across the family life cycle. *Journal of Marriage and the Family, 53,* 221–230.

Suitor, J. J., & Pillemer, K. (1993). Support and interpersonal stress in the social networks of married daughters caring for parents with dementia. *Journal of Gerontology: Social Sciences, 48,* S1–S8.

Surra, C. A. (1990). Research and theory on mate selection and premarital relationships in the 1980s. *Journal of Marriage and the Family, 52,* 844–865.

Szinovacz, M., & Harpster, P. (1994). Couples' employment/retirement status and the division of household labor. *Journal of Gerontology: Social Sciences, 49,* S125–S136.

Tatum, B. D. (1987). *Assimilation blues: Black families in a white community.* Northampton, MA: Hazel-Maxwell Publishing.

Taylor, R. J., Chatters, L. M., & Jackson, J. S. (1993). A profile of familial relations among three-generation black families. *Family Relations, 43,* 332–341.

Taylor, R. J., Chatters, L. M., & Mays, V. M. (1988). Parents, children, siblings, in-laws, and nonkin as sources of emergency assistance to black Americans. *Family Relations, 37,* 298–304.

Taylor, R. J., Chatters, L. M., Tucker, N. B., & Lewis, E. (1991). Developments in research on black families: A decade review. In A. Booth (Ed.), *Contemporary families: Looking forward, looking back* (pp. 275–296). Minneapolis, MN: National Council on Family Relations.

Tennstedt, S. L., McKinlay, J. B., & Sullivan, L. M. (1989). Informal care for frail elders: The role of secondary caregivers. *The Gerontologist, 29,* 677–683.

Thomas, J. L. (1986). Gender differences in satisfaction with grandparenting. *Psychology and Aging, 1,* 215–219.

Thompson, E. H., Jr., Futterman, A. M., Gallagher-Thompson, D., Rose, J. M., & Lovett, S. B. (1993). Social support and caregiving burden in family caregivers of frail elders. *Journal of Gerontology: Social Sciences, 48,* S245–S254.

Thompson, L. (1991). Family work: Women's sense of fairness. *Journal of Family Issues, 12,* 181–196.

Thompson, L. (1993). Conceptualizing gender in marriage: The case of marital care. *Journal of Marriage and the Family, 55,* 557–569.

Thompson, L., & Walker, A. J. (1989). Gender in families: Women and men in marriage, work, and parenthood. *Journal of Marriage and the Family, 51,* 845–871.

Thompson, L., & Walker, A. J. (1995). The place of feminism in family studies. *Journal of Marriage and the Family, 57,* 847–865.

Thompson, M. G., & Heller, K. (1990). Effects of support related to well-being: Quantitative social isolation and perceived family support in a sample of elderly women. *Psychology and Aging, 5,* 535–544.

Thorne, B. (1986). Re-visioning women and social change: Where are the children? *Gender and Society, 1,* 85–109.

Thornton, A., Orbuch, T. L., & Axinn, W. G. (1995). Parent–child relationships during the transition to adulthood. *Journal of Family Issues, 16,* 538–564.

Traustadottir, R. (1991). Mothers who care: Gender, disability, and family life. *Journal of Family Issues, 12,* 211–228.

Troll, L. E. (1987). Mother–daughter relationships through the life span. In S. Oskamp (Ed.), *Applied social psychology annual: Vol. 7. Family processes and problems: Social psychological aspects* (pp. 284–305). Newbury Park, CA: Sage.

Tucker, M. B., Taylor, R. J., & Mitchell-Kernan, C. (1993). Marriage and romantic involvement among aged African Americans. *Journal of Gerontology: Social Sciences, 48,* S123–132.

Uhlenberg, P., & Cooney, T. M. (1990). Family size and mother–child relations in later life. *The Gerontologist, 30,* 618–625.

Umberson, D. (1989). Relationships with children: Explaining parents' psychological well-being. *Journal of Marriage and the Family, 51,* 999–1012.

Umberson, D. (1992). Relationships between adult children and their parents: Psychological consequences for both generations. *Journal of Marriage and the Family, 54,* 664–674.

Umberson, D., & Gove, W. R. (1989). Parenthood and psychological well-being: Theory, measurement, and stage in the family life course. *Journal of Family Issues, 10,* 440–462.

Ungerson, C. (1983). Why do women care? In J. Finch & D. Groves (Eds.), *A labour of love: Women, work and caring* (pp. 31–49). London: Routledge & Kegan Paul.

U.S. Select Committee on Aging. (1987). *Exploring the myths: Caregiving in America* (Comm. Publication No. 99-611). Washington, DC: U.S. Government Printing Office.

Uzell, O., & Peebles-Wilkins, W. (1994). Black spouse abuse: A focus on relational factors and intervention strategies. In R. Staples (Ed.), *The black family: Essays and studies* (5th ed., pp. 104–111). Belmont, CA: Wadsworth.

Vadasy, P. F., Fewell, R. R., Meyer, D. J., & Schell, G. (1984). Siblings of handicapped children: A developmental perspective on family interventions. *Family Relations, 33,* 155–167.

Vaillant, C. O., & Vaillant, G. E. (1993). Is the u-curve of marital satisfaction an illusion? A 40-year study of marriage. *Journal of Marriage and the Family, 55,* 230–239.

Vannoy, D., & Philliber, W. W. (1992). Wife's employment and quality of marriage. *Journal of Marriage and the Family, 54,* 387–398.

Vega, W. A. (1991). Hispanic families in the 1980s: A decade of research. In A. Booth (Ed.), *Contemporary families: Looking forward, looking back* (pp. 297–306). Minneapolis, MN: National Council on Family Relations.

Veroff, J., Sutherland, L., Chadiha, L. A., & Ortega, R. M. (1993). Predicting marital quality with narrative assessments of marital experience. *Journal of Marriage and the Family, 55,* 326–337.

Volling, B. L., & Belsky, J. (1991). Multiple determinants of father involvement during infancy in dual-earner and single-earner families. *Journal of Marriage and the Family, 53,* 461–474.

Waite, L. J., & Harrison, S. C. (1992). Keeping in touch: How women in midlife allocate social contacts among kith and kin. *Social Forces, 70,* 637–655.

Walker, A. (1983). Care for elderly people: A conflict between women and the state. In J. Finch & D. Groves (Eds.), *A labour of love: Women, work and caring* (pp. 106–128). London: Routledge & Kegan Paul.

Walker, A. J., Pratt, C. C., & Eddy, L. (1995). Informal caregiving to aging family members: A critical review. *Family Relations, 44,* 402–411.

Ward, R. A. (1993). Marital happiness and household equity in later-life. *Journal of Marriage and the Family, 55,* 427–438.

Watkins, S. C. (1993). If all we knew about women was what we read in *Demography*, what would we know? *Demography, 30,* 551–577.

Webster, P. S., & Herzog, A. R. (1995). Effects of parental divorce and memories of family problems on relationships between adult children and their parents. *Journal of Gerontology: Social Sciences, 50B*, S24–S34.

Wells, A. J. (1988). Variations in mothers' self-esteem in daily life. *Journal of Personality and Social Psychology, 55*, 661–668.

Wenk, D., Hardesty, C. L., Morgan, C. S., & Blair, S. L. (1994). The influence of parental involvement on the well-being of sons and daughters. *Journal of Marriage and the Family, 56*, 229–234.

West, C., & Zimmerman, D. (1987). Doing gender. *Gender and Society, 1*, 125–151.

Wharton, C. S. (1994). Finding time for the "second shift": The impact of flexible work schedules on women's double days. *Gender and Society, 8*, 189–205.

White, L. K. (1983). Determinants of spousal interaction: Marital structures or marital happiness. *Journal of Marriage and the Family, 45*, 511–519.

White-Means, S. I., & Thornton, M. C. (1990). Labor market choices and home health care provision among employed ethnic caregivers. *The Gerontologist, 30*, 769–775.

Williamson, G. M., & Schulz, R. (1990). Relationship orientation, quality of prior relationship, and distress among caregivers of Alzheimer's patients. *Psychology and Aging, 5*, 502–509.

Wilson, B. F., & Clarke, S. C. (1992). Remarriages: A demographic profile. *Journal of Family Issues, 13*, 123–141.

Wolf-Smith, J. H., & LaRossa, R. (1992). After he hits her. *Family Relations, 41*, 324–329.

Wolinsky, F. D., Callahan, C. M., Fitzgerald, J. F., & Johnson, R. J. (1992). The risk of nursing home placement and subsequent death among older adults. *Journal of Gerontology: Social Sciences, 47*, S173–S182.

Wright, E. O., Shire, K., Hwang, S., Dolan, M., & Baxter, J. (1992). The non-effects of class on the gender division of labor in the home: A comparative study of Sweden in the United States. *Gender and Society, 6*, 252–282.

Wright, P. H., & Keple, T. W. (1981). Friends and parents of a sample of high school juniors: An exploratory study of relationship intensity and interpersonal rewards. *Journal of Marriage and the Family, 43*, 559–570.

Young, R. F., & Kahana, E. (1989). Specifying caregiver outcomes: Gender and relationship aspects of caregiver stress. *The Gerontologist, 29*, 660–666.

Young, R. F., & Kahana, E. (1995). The context of caregiving and well-being outcomes among African and Caucasian Americans. *The Gerontologist, 35*, 225–232.

Zarit, S. H., Todd, P. A., & Zarit, J. M. (1986). Subjective burden of husbands and wives as caregivers: A longitudinal study. *The Gerontologist, 26*, 260–266.

Marital Dissolution

Divorce, Separation, Annulment, and Widowhood

Kimberly A. Faust and Jerome N. McKibben

Introduction

In the past, most marriages ended with the death of a spouse. Today, the majority of marriages will end with a divorce. Although marriage continues to be important, recent changes in the American lifestyle, such as cohabitation, later age at marriage, increased out-of-wedlock childbearing, divorce, and remarriage, have changed the institution of marriage. For many people, marriage is no longer seen as a lifetime commitment.

This chapter examines the ways in which marriages can end. Because researchers project that approximately half of all of today's marriages will end in divorce, we begin with a lengthy discussion of divorce. Marital dissolution by separation is discussed next, followed by annulments and, finally, death of a spouse. There are similarities in all of these types of marital dissolution. In all cases, family routines are interrupted, family lives change, parenting roles must be redefined, and emotional upheavals are inevitable. These issues, along with the societal trends associated with marital dissolution, are addressed.

Kimberly A. Faust and Jerome N. McKibben • Department of Behavioral Science, Fitchburg State College, Fitchburg, Massachusetts 01420-2697.

Handbook of Marriage and the Family, 2nd edition, edited by Marvin Sussman, Suzanne K. Steinmetz, and Gary W. Peterson. Plenum Press, New York, 1999.

Dissolution and Divorce Rates

Statistics and numbers reporting the current state of marital dissolution seem to be everywhere. Unfortunately, dissolution statistics can be somewhat deceptive. The main problems are reporting of the numbers and their interpretation. While all states provide the actual number of divorces, only about half of them include characteristics of the divorced population. Likewise, it is very difficult to ascertain the number of desertions per year as there is no formal reporting of desertion. Annulments are usually calculated as part of the divorce rate so it is hard to tease out any information about that type of dissolution. Dissolution due to the death of a spouse is easier to track because of the information presented on the death certificates.

Dissolution numbers are easily misinterpreted because they can be calculated or presented in several ways. The statistic that is most frequently cited is the absolute number of divorces granted each year. This is not an accurate measure since it does not take into account the changes in population or the age structure of that population. Increases or decreases in the number of divorces may be due to factors such as fewer people in their 20s or an overall rise in population. Since a rise in the number of divorces can sometimes be partially due to a rapid increase in population, there can be instances where the number of divorces rise quickly, but a divorce rate tied to the population will be increasing at a slower rate.

A simple calculation, often used by the media, is to compare the number of marriage licenses per year with the number of divorce decrees per year. While this is a convenient method, it is misleading because it compares two different populations. Marriage licenses are only granted to people who are currently single, while divorce decrees are only granted to people who are currently married. If the size of one population should change in relation to the other, the rates can rise or fall without any real change in behavior.

Another widely used method is the crude divorce rate. This is the number of divorces per 1000 population. While this measure takes into account changes in the size of the population, it also includes segments of the population that are not at risk of divorce, such as the unmarried and children. Furthermore, this measure also does not account for differences and changes in the age structure of the population.

A better way to report dissolution statistics is with the use of the refined divorce rate, calculated by comparing the number of divorces granted with the number of married women over the age of 15. Since this statistic compares the number of divorces with the total number of women at risk—adult married women—it tends to be a much more valid and reliable measurement of divorce trends. However, it does not predict a woman's chance of divorcing at any particular age or the odds of obtaining a divorce any time in her lifetime.

Historical Perspectives of Divorce

Rates of Change. Although desertion, not legal divorce, was the primary mode of marital dissolution prior to the 1900s, from 1865 to 1900 the number of legal divorces increased by 550%, while the divorce rate increased by only 133% (see Figures 1 and 2). The reasons for this differential were the rapid population growth due to immigration and a high level of natural increase (National Center for Health Statistics, 1973). Over time, the number of divorces and the divorce rate continued their slow but steady increase. A small spike in the divorce rate occurred from 1918 to 1920, an increase that coincided with the end of World War I (National Center for Health Statistics, 1973).

While the divorce rate fluctuated throughout the 1920s, the number of divorces continued to increase at a moderate pace due to the increase in total population. By 1930, 2 in every 6 marriages ended in divorce (National Center for Health Statistics, 1973). In the early 1930s both the number of divorces and the divorce rate had a short but steep drop. However, in the last half of the decade, both resumed their

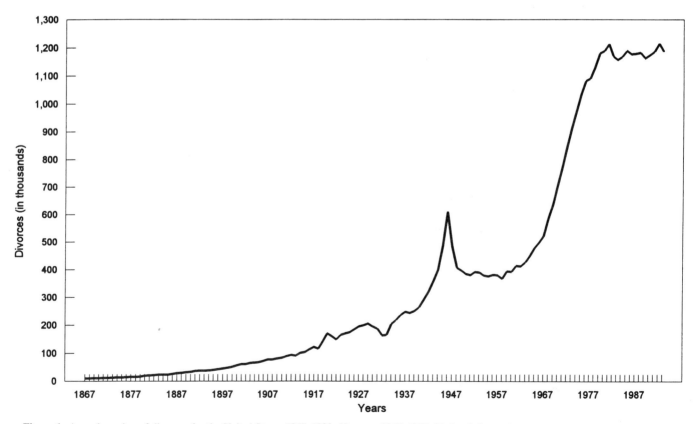

Figure 1. Annual number of divorces for the United States, 1867–1993. (*Sources*: 1867–1967, National Center for Health Statistics, 1973; 1968–1986, National Center for Health Statistics, 1990; 1987–1993, U.S. Bureau of the Census, 1995.)

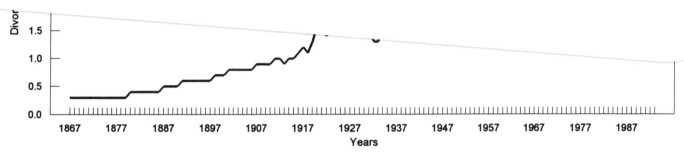

Figure 2. Annual divorce rate for the United States, 1867–1993. (*Sources*: 1867–1967, National Center for Health Statistics, 1973; 1968–1986, National Center for Health Statistics, 1990; 1987–1993, U.S. Bureau of the Census, 1995.)

upward trend (National Center for Health Statistics, 1973). The early 1930s' decline was not caused by a backlash of public opinions on divorce or any new civil restrictions enacted by political or religious leaders; rather, the primary cause was the Great Depression. Families simply could not afford to divorce. At this point desertion, without a legal divorce, once again became the primary mode of marital dissolution (Allen, 1968).

Divorce trends in the 1940s were dominated by the huge spike in the number of divorces and the divorce rates in the years from 1944 to 1948. In 1940 there were 264,000 divorces granted in the United States. In 1946, that number had more than doubled to 610,000. By the end of the decade, the number of divorces had dropped back to 397,000. This spike in divorces granted and its subsequent decline has been attributed to the large number of hasty marriages followed by long periods of separation due to military service in World War II. Thus, this fluctuation in the divorce rate was not caused by any fundamental change in the public attitude toward divorce but was rather a one-time social phenomenon (Garraty, 1979).

Starting in 1960, both the number of divorces and the divorce rate began to rise. These increases accelerated rapidly in the 1970s, dwarfing all previous records by 1980

(National Center for Health Statistics, 1973). In 1960, the divorce rate stood at 2.2 per 1000 population. By 1970 it had increased to 3.5 and by 1980 had reached a record of 5.3 per 1000 population.

One of the primary reasons for the dramatic 20-year increase was demographic change. During the mid-1960s the first of the Baby Boom generation reached the ages when they began to marry. The presence of a large and growing population at risk increased the number of divorces. However, due to population growth, the effect was more pronounced in the number of divorces as opposed to the divorce rate. Figure 1 shows that the 1946 peak in divorces was surpassed in 1969 but the 1946 record divorce rate was not broken until 1973.

The number of divorces peaked at 1,213,000 in 1981, and the number stayed fairly level for the nest 13 years. The divorce rate also peaked in 1981 at 5.3 per 1000 population. The divorce rate has been in a slow decline since that time because of the growth in the U.S. population and a decline in the number of marriages (National Center for Health Statistics, 1991). By 1993, the divorce rate was 4.6 per 1000 population (Guttman, 1996). Recent research has suggested that the number of divorces should start a decline in the late 1990s (Norton & Miller, 1992; Norton & Moorman, 1987).

Societal Attitudes. Historically, the increase in the divorce rate was seen as an indication of the declining social morals (Garraty, 1979). At the turn of the century (1900s), a coalition of prominent church groups joined forces to control divorce by making the divorce code more conservative. While they achieved some successes, they were faced with a slowly growing acceptance of divorce as a social disorder, as opposed to an individual transgression. The religious and political forces of the day tried to prevent the "moral decay" caused by divorce, but they failed to realize that this trend was just one aspect of a greater social transformation.

O'Neill (1973) argues that during the early 1900s women were beginning to realize greater economic and social freedoms. This was the start of a "new morality" that began to challenge the dominant Victorian thinking. One of the by-products of this change was a slow but steady increase in the number of divorces. Other factors, such as increases in industrialization and urbanization, weaker family and kinship ties, less influence on children by parents and community, and the growing suffragette movement, led women to reevaluate the benefits and costs of marriages (O'Neill, 1973).

These widespread societal trends also led to changes in the primary functions of the family. Prior to this period, families had to provide for all of the needs of their members. As society continued to industrialize and develop, families lost responsibility for many of their previous functions. Schools began to educate children, factories provided jobs and household goods, and hospitals provided health care. Families no longer occupied their former high status; they were left with only the core functions of emotional support and childcare (Ogburn, 1953).

With these changes in society, the level of acceptability for divorced persons continued to increase, particularly in the urban areas. Indeed, in the free-wheeling, rebellious 1920s a divorced man was seen in some circles as dashing and desirable. Divorce was gaining such acceptance that, in some circles, being divorced was viewed as a better alternative to never being married at all (Allen, 1959).

The spike in divorces after World War II did have a lingering effect on family formation in the 1950s. Because of the large number of divorces, there was now a unprecedented number of divorced people in the American population (Halem, 1980). This led to a record increase in the number of remarriages. Prior to World War II, the majority of remarriages were between widows and widowers. A growing proportion of the remarriages in late 1940s and the 1950s were between the divorced and involved stepchildren. As a result, the nation began to experience a new type of family unit, the blended family. While the number of families involved was small by today's standards, it represented a monumental increase compared to any previous period.

The resurgence of the women's movement in the 1960s; the increased number of women in the paid labor force, enrolled in colleges, and obtaining degrees; and the emphasis on careers for women as opposed to work all contributed to the rise in divorce. This fundamental restructuring of society, along with the rapid increase in divorce, led to the decline of the social stigma of being divorced. Indeed, being divorced was rapidly becoming acceptable, particularly during the 1970s (Halem, 1980).

While societal pressures were no longer against the divorced adult, children of divorced families were still of great interest and concern. Child support programs were in place, but few steps had been taken to ensure compliance with court-ordered child support. During the 1970s the standard of living for children in single-parent households continued to decline (Furstenberg & Cherlin, 1991).

The tolerant attitude toward divorce begun in previous decades continues today. The main difference is that now children are no longer seen as a deterrent to divorce. This change in acceptance is reflected in a 1985 survey in which 82% of the respondents disagreed with the statement, "When there are children in the family, parents should stay together even if they don't get along" (Thornton, 1989). Regardless of this tolerant attitude toward divorce much of the country is grappling with the many transformations in American society caused by the continued high rate of divorce. While there are a wide range of issues that need to be addressed, Riley (1991) suggests six areas that demand immediate attention:

1. Educators and counselors can support the ideal of lifetime marriages.
2. Stress on contemporary marriages must be reduced.
3. The mechanism of divorce needs attention and refinement, or perhaps, replacement.
4. Alimony, property, and child support awards must be equitable to all parties involved and must be effectively enforced.
5. Divorced families need expanded counseling and other services.
6. Children of divorce need and deserve more study and more counseling services.

Legal Issues. By the early 1910s many of the movements undertaken to make divorce more difficult to obtain had slowed, and their influence was waning. The focus on divorce began to shift toward setting specific criteria (grounds) for divorce and the possibility of creating divorce laws that were uniform across all states. However, by 1920, the individual states were left to create their own legal codes, eventually leading to the wide disparity of divorce codes in the United States (O'Neill, 1973). The lack of a uniform divorce states with lenient divorce laws.

This movement to unify the divorce laws started in the early 1900s and once again enjoyed wide support among people who wanted to protect the American family, but there was also substantial opposition to the movement. State leaders and legislators resented the attempt to regulate state laws. Feminists feared a uniform divorce code would take away the protection that divorce provided for women. Moderates wondered how a uniform divorce code could be agreed upon given the diversity of the United States population. In the end, the Uniform Divorce Law Proposal failed to clear Congress, and the movement to place greater restrictions on divorce began to fade (Riley, 1991).

During the 1930s there was no move to return to the old moral code of 40 years earlier, but there was a growing disposition to protect ongoing marriages. This change of emphasis was the result of a widespread sense of the damage done to children and spouses during a divorce (Allen, 1968). Indeed, given the fact that the percentage of divorces involving children had increased to 40% by 1935 (Jacobson, 1978), proponents of divorce reform argued that the children of divorced families were rapidly becoming the most severely damaged victims of the divorce process. An additional concern was that in the tough economic times of the 1930s, broken families were especially susceptible to falling below the poverty line. The poor economic climate also pushed the questions of child support and alimony into the forefront. While both of these programs had been in existence for many years, a civil code had never been established to set specific policy regarding the transfer of monies between ex-spouses (Halem, 1980).

As the economic situation in the United States began to improve in the second half of the 1930s, the divorce rate once again began to increase. By this time, few states had restrictive divorce laws, with New York and South Carolina being

make divorce laws more lenient gained momentum in the 1960s, cummulating with the advent of no-fault divorce.

The trend in no-fault divorce began in California in 1970. The authors of the no-fault legislation believed the new provision would help end adversarial divorces. Iowa followed the next year and by 1977 all states, with the exception of Pennsylvania, Illinois, and South Dakota, had some form of no-fault divorce laws (Riley, 1991). With divorce now relatively easy to obtain and the cost greatly reduced, the number of divorces almost tripled between 1970 and 1980.

Societal Factors of Divorce

As discussed in the preceeding section, a great many changes have occurred in American society that, in turn, have affected our attitudes toward divorce, our ability to obtain a divorce, our accepted roles within marriage, and our financial and emotional alternatives to marriage. This section explores, in more detail, specific institutions within the American society directly or indirectly related to divorce.

The Economy. The postindustrialized economy of the United States has led to tremendous changes in the labor force. Because of the changing nature of jobs, the shift from manufacturing to service jobs, and the increasing rates of college attendance, women have been entering the labor force in ever-increasing numbers (Bachu, 1993; Smith & Ward, 1985; Waldrop, 1994). Many studies have shown that married women who are employed are more likely to contemplate divorce (Huber & Spitze, 1980) and to divorce (Ross & Sawhill, 1975). The probability of divorce increases as the wife's income rises, both in absolute terms (Booth & White, 1980; Cherlin, 1979) and relative to her husband's income (Mott & Moore, 1979).

Not only does women's entry into the paid labor force increase their self-esteem and ability to support a family after divorce, it also allows them to encounter spousal alternatives. Increased labor force participation among women and men has been shown to increase the risk of divorce when employment circumstances increase an individual's opportunities for meeting possible new spouses (South & Lloyd, 1995).

Moreover, there have been many changes in the economy that can ease the time constraints on a single-parent family. Recent years have seen an explosion of services geared toward families with limited time resources. Grocery and department stores welcome shoppers 24 hours a day, doctors and dentists have extended their office hours to accommodate evening and weekend patients, and banks have extended their hours and have opened branches in local stores in a quest to lure more customers. These "user-friendly" services do increase sales, but they also make life easier for the single-parent family. Couples contemplating divorce need not worry about laundry, car care, or cooking skills; the service sector can address most needs. Whereas this change in the service industry may not have caused the increasing divorce rate, it exerts an indirect influence by reducing the time constraints of being a single parent.

Cultural Attitudes. The growing emphasis on individualism, self-fulfillment, and women's and men's rights in American society has changed social attitudes, cultural values, and ideology regarding the family. It has also led to a change in our expectations of marriage (Rice & Rice, 1986). We no longer view the American family as a unit of production, but rather a unit of consumption. To that end, we choose our marriage partners based on emotional feelings instead of economic reasons. Given this change in attitudes, romantic love and spousal emotional support are seen as integral to a successful marriage. Weitzman (1985) suggests that these emotional criteria for marital success are more difficult to meet, while Rice and Rice (1986) suggest that the American values of immediate gratification, mobility, and replacement further undermine the stability of marriage.

Furthermore, societal constraints against divorce have weakened over the years, as reflected in the increased divorce rates. No longer is the embarrassment and social stigma associated with a divorce as great as it used to be in the past. In fact, 40% of all marriages are a remarriage for at least one of the partners (National Center for Health Statistics, 1991a). Critics of divorce have suggested that the change in American attitudes concerning the acceptability of divorce caused the upswing in the number of divorces. Analysis by Cherlin (1981), however, showed that the change in attitudes toward divorce occurred only after the number of divorces was already high. Yet divorced or "broken" families are still viewed as different, deviant, and a possible threat to the

traditional two-parent family and to the stability of society as a whole (Popenoe, 1988; Thompson & Gonzola, 1983).

Life Expectancy and Health Status. The expectation of life at birth is currently 79 years for females and 73 years for males. The "oldest old" age group (over 85 years) is one of the fastest growing categories of the aging population (Weeks, 1994). Not only are Americans living longer, but we are also maintaining high levels of health. This will have an effect on divorce in that it will allow couples the opportunity for very long marriages. Children born in 1996 could possibly attain marriages 60 years or more of duration. Such long lifespans will enable people to have a great deal of time in which to divorce and remarry. The longer lifespans have greatly increased the number of years marriages can survive without being disrupted by the death of a spouse (Uhlenberg, 1983).

Children's health status can also have an indirect influence on the divorce rate by reducing the amount of time required to care for sick children and thus making single parenthood a more viable option. When children commonly contracted serious diseases such as diphtheria, scarlet fever, or polio, mothers had a difficult time joining the paid labor force because they needed to be at home caring for their ill, possibly quarantined, children (Weeks, 1994). Today, the most common childhood diseases are no more serious than chicken pox or measles. Working parents may only be required to stay at home for a few days caring for an ill child as opposed to devoting months of care. Fewer serious childhood illnesses combined with the widespread over-the-counter children's medications and after-hours medical clinics afford parents the ability to combine labor force employment and single parenthood.

Legal Issues. The "Divorce Revolution" (Weitzman, 1985) began in the 1970s with the introduction of the no-fault divorce laws in California. By 1991, all 50 states had adopted some form of no-fault laws. Although the individual state laws vary to some degree, all states now allow divorces to be granted without proof of wrongdoing.

Prior to the California no-fault laws, married couples could not get divorced without proving some type of marital fault. The majority of divorces were based on the legal categories of desertion, nonsupport, cruelty, or adultery. The successful divorce litigant was rewarded with the bulk of the monies and properties owned by the couple. In this way, divorce settlements could be used to reward or punish individuals. This adversarial system reflected the social norms and accepted beliefs of the time that marriage should be a lifelong commitment.

Today, the usual grounds to obtain a divorce are (Benokraitis, 1996):

length of time required apart is 6 months and longest is 6 years.

5. No-fault. No formal proof is necessary in this case. The only requirement is that both parties agree to the petition of the court.

Guttman (1993) suggests that these sweeping changes in the divorce laws reflect societal changes such as the women's movement, greater participation of women in the paid labor force, greater sexual freedom, the individualistic theme of the 1960s and 1970s, and, finally, the rising divorce rate. Lawmakers came to realize that the traditional fault-based laws were no longer appropriate in a changing society. The new divorce laws not only reflected a change in the legal code, but they also eliminated the moral issue of divorce (Guttman, 1993). In the new laws, the concept of fault has been removed as a basic premise of a failed marriage (Weitzman & Dixon, 1986). No longer must one spouse accuse the other of behaviors such as desertion, nonsupport, cruelty, adultery, impotence, or insanity. Instead, the couple needs only to agree that the marriage is no longer desirable. By removing the wrongdoing or fault aspect of divorce, there no longer needs to be a guilty or innocent party.

Second, the adversarial process of divorce has been diminished. Couples may now complete the legal divorce proceedings by simply filing the proper paperwork and paying a filing fee. Couples with little property or no child custody decisions can bypass attorneys and complete their own paperwork.

Third, the new laws redefined familial roles and parental responsibilities by suggesting that mothers and fathers should be equally responsible for their children's financial and overall well-being. In most cases, the "child's best interest" custody guidelines no longer automatically favor the mother.

Last, no-fault laws ended the practice of rewarding the each spouse equal rights to the accumulated wealth of the family. Some states divide a family's assets equally, while other states continue to take each family's circumstances and financial needs into account (Halem, 1980). Spousal support payments are awarded in less than 15% of all divorces and are usually for a limited time period. These payments are used to support the ex-spouse until employment can be attained. Older women and displaced homemakers (i.e., older full-time homemakers without adequate spousal support) are particularly disadvantaged, especially if they do not possess marketable job skills. In these cases, rehabilitative alimony may be awarded in which the ex-husband pays maintenance and education costs in order for the ex-wife to receive training that will enable her to find employment (Lamanna & Reidmann, 1994). The rationale is that, once the ex-wife finds employment, she will be able to support herself, but this ruling ignores the lower earning power of women compared to men. Benefits for many women, on the other hand, have included recent changes in Social Security provisions that now allow ex-spouses to claim one-half of their former spouse's retirement benefits if the marriage was at least 10 years in duration (Choi, 1992).

Although the no-fault divorce laws have reduced levels of bitterness and suffering, eliminated the need for collusion or perjury, and moved toward fairer financial settlements (Guttman, 1993), many states are looking for ways in which to ease the overall divorce process. Divorce mediation is one idea that seems to be gaining in popularity. It usually involves one or two professional mediators who meet with both the husband and the wife to negotiate a settlement and resolve conflicts inherent in the divorce process. Topics usually covered include child custody and property settlements. The main purpose in divorce mediation is to reduce time and money spent in divorce courts, but mediation is also helpful in reducing the conflict between spouses. Without the adversarial climate of the divorce court, couples, especially fathers, perceive higher levels of fairness in child custody decisions (Emery, Matthews, & Wyer, 1991). The job of the mediator is to keep interactions and negotiations balanced so that settlements will benefit both parties equally (Everett & Everett, 1994).

Many states also are implementing divorce counseling aimed at divorcing parents. The purpose of these programs is to teach and instruct parents how to reduce the trauma experienced by their children and how to work within the custody agreements mandated by the courts (Guttman, 1996).

Individual Risk Factors of Divorce

Widespread changes in the economy, women's and men's roles, the legal system, and societal values have coincided with the changing divorce rate. While these changes help explain divorce on a societal level, an in-depth discussion of personal factors is needed to explore divorce on an individual level. This section discusses individual demographic characteristics most commonly thought to be associated with divorce.

Age at Marriage. The inverse relationship between age at marriage and probability of divorce is among one of the strongest: The younger the age at marriage, the higher the likelihood of divorce (Kurdek, 1993; Morgan & Rindfuss, 1985; Thornton & Rodgers, 1987). Analysis by Martin and Bumpuss (1989) shows a high rate of disruption for teen marriages, with women who married as teens being twice as likely to divorce as those who married after the age of 22. However, Martin and Bumpass (1989) also found an increase of divorce for women who first married at ages 20 through 22. They found a 40% increase in the probability of separation in this age group from the late 1970s through the early 1980s. Because separation rates do not increase for the other age groups during this time period, Martin and Bumpuss (1989) theorize that "young" or teen marriages now actually extend into the early 20s.

In many cases, young couples lack the competence for marital roles. Immaturity is often coupled with lower income and education levels in early marriages to produce less stable unions. Frequently, couples who marry early are inadequately prepared for the emotional responsibilities of marriage nor do they have adequate financial support (Booth & Edwards, 1985). Young husbands and wives often have unrealistic expectations for marriage that are gleaned from the media or may feel overwhelmed by the new and challenging roles they are forced to assume. Young couples have had less time to gain social experience and understand adult roles within a marriage (Heaton, 1991). Early marriage may stunt adolescent development so that the skills necessary to de-

velop a marital culture, resolve personal crises, and adjust to changes in the marriage may not have yet been learned (Benokraitis, 1996).

An early marriage may cut short the period of mate selection, while an abbreviated mate selection process can result in hasty decisions. Teens may have a more difficult time choosing an appropriate partner because it is hard to predict what kind of spouse a teenager will mature into over the life of the marriage (Cherlin, 1996).

Conversely, there is some question about the relationship of a later age at marriage and the likelihood of divorce. Various studies have reported conflicting results for a late age at first marriage. Sweet and Bumpuss (1987) found a higher divorce rate for people who marry for the first time over the age of 35, a consequence that may result from the restricted pool of eligibles at later ages (Cherlin, 1996). Other contributing factors include tendencies to be "set" in a single lifestyle as well as the financial or emotional ability to easily resume an independent life outside of marriage. In contrast, a later study by Martin and Bumpass (1989) failed to find higher divorce rates for women who married at a later age.

Premarital Pregnancy and Births. Premarital pregnancies and births can greatly increase the risk of divorce, with a premarital birth exerting the greatest influence on the likelihood of divorce, especially for whites (Martin & Bumpass, 1989; Morgan & Rindfuss, 1985; Norton & Miller, 1992; Teachman, 1983; Waite & Lillard, 1991). The majority of these premarital pregnancies and births are thought to be unplanned, thus contributing to marital problems. An unplanned birth or pregnancy that leads the couple to quickly marry may truncate the mate selection process. Likewise, pressure from parents and peers to legitimize a child can result in a hurried marriage in which the marrying couple feels as if they have little choice in the process. Moreover, having children "out of order" (i.e., a birth before marriage) is thought to result in a greater degree of role conflict (Billy, Landale, & McLaughlin, 1986). Newlyweds require sufficient time to adapt to married life, while simultaneous demands for adaptation from both newly married and parental roles may place extremely high levels of pressure on couples. Premarital births are also a deviation from the expected sequencing and timing of American life-cycle events (Rindfuss & MacDonald, 1980; Teachman, 1983), which can lead to other negative effects such as limited career possibilities, lower income levels, and family disapproval (Guttman, 1993).

Women who experience premarital pregnancy or birth often are teenagers who are prone to increased risk of social and economic disadvantages throughout their lives. They are less likely to complete their educations, be in the labor force, and be economically self-supporting (Hays, 1987; Hoffman, ages and to have pr... ...

& Spain, 1986). As discussed earlier, a young age at marriage and premarital pregnancies and births are more likely to lead to divorce. Compared to whites, blacks are at greater risk for teenage pregnancy, premarital pregnancy, early marriage, and divorce (Garfinkel, McLanahan, & Robins, 1994).

Poverty is often a reason cited for variation between black and white divorce rates. Cherlin (1992) has suggested that the economic changes associated with a postindustrialized economy have placed blacks at a disadvantage. Specifically, blacks are more likely to experience economic hardships and insecurities that lead to divorce. Yet Bianchi and Spain (1986) found that divorce is less of an economic hardship for black women than it is for white women because black women are more likely to have entered the labor force. Moreover, more blacks are in living arrangements with other earners, a circumstance that allows them an alternative source of economic support after a divorce. In fact, after a divorce, blacks tend to recoup nearly all of their former income, while whites only recoup about half of their former income levels.

There are thus many complicated interactions between race and other factors of divorce such as income levels, completed education, premarital births, and age at marriage. For this reason, Martin and Bumpuss (1989) suggest that black/white divorce differentials be viewed in terms of expected rates. Their study divided women into groups according to their likelihood of marital dissolution as predicted by specific factors associated with divorce. They found, in turn, that various groups of blacks were still more likely to divorce than were whites.

The rate of divorce among Hispanics is about the same as it is for whites (Zinn & Eitzen, 1996), despite the fact that Hispanics share many characteristics with blacks such as low economic status, lower education levels, and a younger average age at marriage. Hispanics are less likely to divorce than are blacks, with the most common explanation being the

an extent that m... ...

parent's marriage at least through the preschool years. Additional children only decrease the likelihood of divorce to a very small degree, while the presence of older children and/or children born prior to the marriage significantly increase the probability of divorce (Morgan & Rindfuss, 1985; Waite & Lillard, 1991). These findings have lead Lillard and Waite (1993) to propose a feedback effect in which the rising divorce rate operates to increase the number of second marriages that include stepchildren. The presence of stepchildren, in turn, increases the risk of divorce within second marriages while subsequently lowering the probability that the new couples will have children of their own—a development that often contributes to the stability of second marriages.

Not only does the age of children affect the likelihood of divorce, but the gender of children is also found to play a large part in marital stability. Morgan (1988) found that families whose children were exclusively daughters had a higher divorce rate than families whose children were limited to sons. Likewise, analysis by Morgan, Lye, and Condran (1988) showed that sons compared to daughters significantly decrease the risk of marital dissolution by 9%. They attributed this to fathers' greater role in raising sons, a deeper involvement in the family, and fathers' decreased desire to seek a divorce. For families with sons present, fathers appear more likely to take an active role in childcare and family activities, with fathers being more involved with sons than daughters during playtime, discipline, and supervision activities (Katzev, Warner, & Acock, 1994; Lamb, Pleck, & Levine, 1987). Harris and Morgan (1991) report that, when boys are present in a family, children receive more attention from and report closer relationships with their fathers.

Women report fewer problems in marriages and fewer disadvantages from marriage when men assume a greater share of family activities (Barnett & Baruch, 1987; Blair &

Johnson, 1992). Families with male children, in turn, result in men assuming a greater share of childcare activities, and marriages with sons tend to be more stable (Baruch & Barnett, 1986; Heaton & Albrecht, 1991).

Premarital Cohabitation. Although it is commonly assumed that cohabitation before marriage will increase the stability of later marriages for those couples who do marry, research has indicated that just the opposite happens. Couples who cohabit before marriage have higher rates of marital dissolution or divorce (DeMaris & Rao, 1992; Lillard, Brien, & Waite, 1995; Nock, 1995; Teachman & Polonko, 1990). Bennett, Blanc, & Bloom (1988), for example, suggest that couples who cohabit are a select group in the sense of having less commitment to marriage as an institution, being more willing to end unhappy unions, and perhaps being less committed to working on relationships. In fact, researchers continue to show that cohabitators are indeed a select group who differ from noncohabitators in many ways. Cohabitators seem to be less likely to adapt to traditional marital expectations (Axinn & Thornton, 1993; Booth & Johnson, 1988; Thomson & Colella, 1992), and in fact may have higher expectations for marriage and are more likely to believe that marriage should be ended if either partner is unhappy (Cherlin, 1992).

Individuals who engage in cohabitation often tend to be more approving of divorce as an answer to marital problems. Cohabitors are also more likely to have divorced parents (Axinn & Thornton, 1993), which leads to a lower commitment to marriage and higher risks of divorce (Amato & Keith, 1991). Another difference between the two groups is that cohabitators are more likely to have stepchildren in their relationships (Bumpass, Sweet, & Cherlin, 1991). Questions as to the discipline of children, financial support, and relationships with former spouses can cause many problems and may lead to higher rates of dissolution in cohabitational unions. Nett (1988) identifies relationships with the children from previous unions as one of the chief problems facing a marriage. Religious differences are also found between cohabitors and noncohabitators. The lack of religious belief or religiosity may be linked to fewer sanctions against divorce, while those with a low degree of religiosity and irregular church attendance are more likely to cohabit (Newcomb, 1979).

The experience of cohabitation itself may have a negative impact on the future marriage. If finances were not pooled in the union or if the couple experienced a high degree of autonomy within the cohabiting union, they may have difficulty in adapting to changes inherent with the advent of marriage. Couples who are used to greater freedom within the context of cohabitation may be more likely to end a subsequent marriage (DeMaris & MacDonald, 1993). Other researchers suggest that cohabitation undermines the legitimacy and institution of marriage, while making divorce a reasonable option in the face of problems (Thomson & Colella, 1992). If the cohabitors devalue the legitimacy of marriage, prior experience with cohabitation could provide viable alternatives to an unhappy marriage.

Intergenerational Transmission of Divorce. Many adults who experienced the divorce of their parents often desire to avoid a divorce at all costs. However, adult children of divorce are more likely to experience divorce than are adult children from intact families (Amato, 1993; Bumpuss, Martin, & Sweet, 1991; McLanahan & Bumpuss, 1988; Webster, Orbuch, & House, 1995). Several causes have been put forth to explain the relationship between parental divorce and adult children's subsequent divorce. The first cited cause is concerned with the amount of economic hardship experienced by the custodial parent and children (Amato & Partridge, 1987; Choi, 1992; Duncan & Rodgers, 1991). Weitzman (1985) reports a 73% decrease in the standard of living for custodial mothers and children in the first year following a divorce. The decline in standard of living is thought to lead to a reduction in the well-being of children that can predispose children to long-term personal problems. Economic disadvantages for children of divorced parents explain a large portion of lower education levels and increases in a young woman's chances of a premarital pregnancy or birth (McLanahan, 1988; McLanahan & Sandefur, 1994), all of which are characteristics associated with a higher likelihood of divorce. Saluter (1994) suggests that a lower family income leads successively to a lower likelihood of college attendance, earlier entry into sexual unions, earlier age at marriage, and higher rates of divorce. Cherlin, Kurman, and Chase-Lansdale (1995) propose that early sexual intercourse leading to increased cohabitation and a higher likelihood of a premarital birth may be the central mechanism by which parental divorce produces an increased incidence of divorce for the children of divorced parents.

The second explanation focuses on the stress associated with divorce. The changes in routine, loss of daily conflict with one parent, changes in childcare routines, and loss of income can result in feelings of anxiety, loneliness, or disruptive behavior in children (Chase-Lansdale & Hetherington, 1990; Kurdeck, 1991; Stack, 1989; Zill, Morrison, & Coiro, 1993). Researchers have found evidence that young children of divorced parents are especially prone to feelings of depression and anxiety and are torn by feelings of loyalty to both parents (Wallerstein & Kelly, 1980). High stress levels can be reflected in low achievement in school work, thereby reducing rates of high school graduation or years of schooling completed (McLanahan & Sandefur, 1994). The overwhelming stresses associated with divorce may have long-term effects on the emotional and social adjustments of children, leading to young adults who are poorly prepared for marriage.

A third suggestion for the relationship between parental divorce and adult children's increased likelihood to experience their own divorce is the interparental conflict that often precedes divorce. That conflict between parents harms children is well established (Camara & Resnick, 1988; Depner, Leino, & Chun, 1993; Devall, Stoneman, & Brody, 1986). Children may react negatively to the conflict or they may be drawn into the conflict between the parents (Webster et al., 1995). Caspi and Elder (1988) theorize that parental conflict influences the personality and interactional style of children. Children residing in a home with high levels of parental conflict may never learn appropriate methods of arguing or fighting within a marriage. A lack of role models who can successfully disagree or solve problems could lead to adult children who are ill-equipped to survive disagreements or crises in their own marriages.

The socialization process within a divorced family is the fourth suggestion for higher rates of divorce for children of divorced parents. Children who were raised in a divorced household may internalize feelings of acceptance of divorce as a viable option for a troubled marriage. If children learned in the past to view divorce as an acceptable alternative to marriage then the tendency may follow for the young (who are now adults) to view their own divorce as acceptable. Another interpretation of the socialization process of divorced families concerns the lack of parental control exhibited by divorced parents. Keith and Finlay (1988) hypothesize that girls may choose high-risk husbands because of lack of control exercised over their dating and mate selection behavior. Others (Baydar, 1988; Block, Block, & Gjerde, 1988) propose that prior to and after a divorce, parents tend to be preoccupied with their own needs and emotions. The result of such self-preoccupation, in turn, is that children's needs may be ignored, leaving them at risk for greater degree of trauma. Recent research supports this claim. Keirnan and Chase-Lansdale (1993) and Cherlin et al. (1991), for example, found that children whose parents would eventually divorce showed more behavior problems and did less well in school long before their parents separated. The adults' trauma associated with the divorce process and aftermath often leads to higher rates of depression and suicide (Broman, 1988). It can also lead to lower levels of children's well-being and higher levels of behavioral and educational problems.

Finally, Pope and Mueller (1976) hypothesize that the sex and marital roles learned by children determine future marital success for white males and females and for black females. Children in divorced families will not learn appropriate marital roles as well as children from intact families will. However, Pope and Mueller (1976) do concede that

economic circum...
roles learned with...

Socioeconomic

of the most importan...
higher the socioeconom...
divorce. As levels of co...
ployment status increase...
Bumpuss, 1989; South &...

In general, the highe...
lower the probability of c...
effect of completed educat...
Divorce rates are lower for...
completed education but are...
graduate education (Houseeknecht, Vaughn, & Macke, 1984). These findings are thought to reflect the interaction of education level and women's earning power.

In a national survey, Glick (1984) found people with a college degree to be less likely to divorce than people with only a high school degree. Tzeng (1992) found that couples with homogamous education levels and traditional employment patterns had higher levels of marital stability. It is theorized that college graduates have access to better paying jobs and more traditional employment patterns, leading to fewer financial strains on the marriage. A second feature of a college education involves increases in the average age at marriage. Most students postpone marriage until after completing their college degrees, thereby resulting in an later age at marriage (Benokraitis, 1996). College experience also may augment a couple's ability to communicate and compromise. Communication skills learned in the college classroom maybe translated into better communication within marriage.

In general, a higher divorce rate is linked to lower status jobs and lower income levels (Martin & Bumpuss, 1989). Research on income levels shows that divorce is more likely if the husband is unemployed or if his income is erratic (Cherlin, 1992). Lack of employment or a low income can place a strain on marriage leading to depression, feelings of inadequacy, anger, and disappointment. The fear of financial instability or the failure to reach economic or educational goals contribute to marital dissolution (White, 1990). Conversely, a high income couple has much more to lose from a divorce as each may experience a significant drop in total income (Weiss, 1984). These couples may view their combined income level as a barrier to divorce (Cutright, 1971).

Some conflict exists, however, in reference to the effect of women's employment status. The employment of a wife, for example, may add to the family income level and reduce financial strain but at the same time may lead to disagreement over the traditional division of labor in the home. An employed wife who is still responsible for the bulk of housework and childcare could develop feelings of dissatisfaction with her husband's efforts at home (Goldscheider & Waite, 1991; White, 1991). The ability to earn an income in the paid labor force also may present an alternative to marriage for employed women while at the same time increasing her sense of self worth. In the absence of economic dependence on a husband, therefore, a wife may visualize more options for herself such as divorce, being single, or finding alternative partners (Booth, Johnson, & White, 1984; Greenstein, 1990).

Remarriage. Approximately 70% of separated and divorced men and women will remarry at some point in the future. However, these remarriages are more likely to end in divorce than are first marriages. The individual demographic characteristics that influence a first divorce, such as age at marriage, premarital birth, race, income, and education levels, also work to affect the probability of a second divorce. Researchers suggest, however, that inherent within second marriages are situations that can place additional strains on subsequent marriages. Cherlin (1996) hypothesizes that the lack of accepted roles and ambiguous legal rights of stepparents has led to more conflict in remarriages. Questions of financial responsibility, discipline, adoption, and visitation schedules certainly can lead to conflict and stress within a remarriage. Conversely, Furstenberg and Spanier (1984) argue that remarriages are self-selecting for people who consider divorce an acceptable alternative. Other researchers (Booth & Edwards, 1992; Martin & Bumpass, 1989) found that a majority of remarried people had begun their first marriages at young ages and were more prone to a second divorce. More recent work concerning remarriages proposes that cohabiting couples with children should be considered as being similar to stepfamilies (Bumpass, Raley, & Sweet, 1995). Obviously, these cohabiting stepfamilies would be concerned with many of the same problems such as finance, discipline, and child custody.

Religion. Religious influences regarding divorce have declined in the recent past. For example, the Catholic Church still prohibits divorce but no longer excommunicates Catholics who do divorce. Churches and clergy of all denominations accept divorced parishioners into their congregations. Although religious institutions are more accepting of divorce, it is still discouraged by the majority of religions. Not surprisingly, people who report strong religious beliefs and high levels of religiosity are less likely to divorce (Colasanto & Shriver, 1989; Glenn & Supancic, 1984). Perhaps higher levels of involvement in a organized religion serve to strengthen family relationships or, at the minimum, reinforce traditional family roles. The shared sense of values, beliefs, and community inherent in religious beliefs may lead to greater levels of marital stability. Couples sharing the same religion are more likely to reconcile after a separation and

are less likely to experience divorce (Lehrer & Chiswick, 1993; Wineberg, 1994).

The divorce rate for interfaith marriages, on the other hand, continues to remain high (Chan & Heaton, 1989). Marriages between Protestants and Catholics and between Gentiles and Jews are consistently less stable than are same-faith marriages (Bumpuss & Sweet, 1972). The lack of shared values and beliefs is thought to lead to more conflict within family roles, children's socialization, and religious traditions. In fact, the highest rates of divorce have been found in families where only one spouse is of the Mormon faith (Bahr, 1982).

Divorce rates do vary according to religious preference (Heaton, Albrecht, & Martin, 1985). Protestants have the highest divorce rate, Catholics are next, and Jews have the lowest rate. Within the Protestant religious category, Presbyterians have the lowest rate of divorce followed by Episcopalians, Methodists, and, finally, Baptists (Glenn & Supancic, 1984). It remains to be seen what the affect of the growing religious fundamentalist movement will have on divorce rates in the United States. The strong emphasis on family life and marriage as espoused by the fundamentalist movement has the potential to lower the divorce rates for its followers (Cohen, 1990). Yet, Baptists and other denominations usually categorized as fundamentalist currently have higher divorce rates than do nonfundamentalist Protestant denominations (Chan &Heaton, 1989). Readers should be aware that most studies using fundamentalist status as a variable do so by simply assigning the term "fundamentalist" to a list of specific conservative Protestant denominations like Baptist or Pentecostal (Ellison & Musick, 1993). By using denomination as proxy for fundamentalism, many individuals who do not consider themselves as fundamentalist are nevertheless assigned to that group by virtue of their membership in a conservative denomination. Others, such as Catholics who may consider themselves to be fundamentalist, are not assigned to the fundamentalist category when such proxy variables are used (Faust, 1995).

Theoretical Models of the Divorce Process

Inherent in the development of theoretical models of divorce is the belief that divorce is a series of common stages and experiences for couples. Not all couples will experience all of the various stages, nor will they necessarily experience them in a particular order, but the various stages can help explain the divorce experience for the majority of Americans.

The models presented here are a representation of the various models that have been developed over the recent past. These models were chosen for their orientation and levels of analysis. For a more thorough examination of the theoretical models of divorce, see Salts (1979).

Model 1: The Six Stations of Divorce.   Paul Bohannan (1970) has developed a schematic for the contemporary divorce process. Within his discussion of divorce he has identified six levels or stations of divorce.

The *Emotional Divorce* is the first step in the divorce process and is the phase during which emotions and feelings begin to change. As the marriage begins to fail, spouses become distant and withdraw from each other. Spouses often turn to work, family, friends, or substance abuse to ease the pain accompanying the emotional divorce. Some couples may seek counseling at this point in the hope of saving the marriage, while others may begin to accept the inevitability of ending the marriage. Often referred to as "separation distress," the emotional distancing between marital partners can be extremely emotional and painful. Most divorced people report symptoms of depression, anxiety, unhappiness, and loneliness resulting in higher suicide rates for the divorced (Stack, 1989). Women tend to respond better to separation distress than do men. Diedrick (1991) suggests that women have stronger social networks and, as a result, may receive more support after the divorce than do men. Moreover, men are more likely to leave the family home and spend a decreased amount of time with their children (Dudley, 1991). These two factors may account for the higher degree of separation distress experienced by men.

The *Legal Divorce*, the second step or phase, involves, the formal, legal dissolution of the marriage. The couple must decide grounds for the divorce, child custody issues, and property settlements. This can be a lengthy stage if the spouses do not readily agree on specific issues or if they are determined to punish each other. No-fault divorce laws, on the other hand, have enabled legal divorce to become more streamlined, less adversarial, and less likely to include alimony as a component. In 1994, of the 15% of women who were awarded alimony, only 3% actually received any payments (Benokraitis, 1996).

Although Bohannan (1970) lists the *Economic Divorce* as a separate station, couples almost always experience this phase simultaneously with the legal divorce. Although no-fault divorce laws were meant to end unequal financial settlements and create a more equal division of property, less than half of all women receive property settlements. In 1990, only 32% of all divorced women received any property settlements. Fathers who were awarded custody of the children received 47% of family assets, while mothers who were awarded custody received only 28% of family assets (Benokraitis, 1996). Many families are forced to sell property and liquidate family assets to address the debts owed by the family. To the uninitiated, economic issues of divorce are often thought to end with the division of real property. In reality, economic divorce covers much more than property to include the division of future earnings, retirement and pension benefits, payment of debts, educational expenses for the ex-spouse and/or children, and income tax issues such as joint tax returns and rights to claim children as dependents. The economic divorce has the potential to continue for years in the case of ex-spouses who fail to make required child support payments and requests for changes in the amount of child support.

The *Co-parental Divorce* is a station that involves the settlement of legal responsibility in reference to any children produced by the marriage. Legal custody and physical custody must be decided at this point as well as the arrangement for child support payments. The most recent trends within this station include the movement toward joint legal custody and joint physical custody (Meyer & Garasky, 1993). Joint legal custody refers to the sharing by both parents of the legal responsibilities involved in childrearing, while joint physical custody refers to the sharing of living arrangements for children. The idea of grandparents' rights has also been a recent trend to such an extent that some states have passed bills that allow grandparents to seek visitation rights against a custodial parent (Marcus, 1991).

The *Community Divorce* refers to the point at which coworkers, family, and friends are informed about the divorce. Divorcing couples often find that their relationships with others change at this point, and many still feel stigmatized by family, friends, and coworkers (Gasser & Taylor, 1990). Some people may feel threatened to have a newly single person in their midst, while others may feel awkward and withdraw from the relationship. Sides are chosen because rarely do people remain on friendly terms with both partners in the divorce. Just as property is divided in a divorce, so are friends and acquaintances. Divorce can be particularly stressful on in-law relationships because regardless of the nature of in-law relationship, there is an expectation to remain loyal to kin.

Finally, the *Psychic Divorce* is usually the culminating stage of a divorce process and is often the most difficult one. This station involves the ability to psychologically end and separate oneself from the marriage. Such change in thinking about oneself as a single person instead of a marital partner can be a long, painful process. Unlike the death of a spouse, a divorce may not provide a sense of closure to the marriage, a circumstance that is especially apparent when children and custody issues are involved. If the divorced couple is forced to remain in contact with each other, it may be very difficult to complete this station. Feelings of loneliness, doubt, loss, and fear are common in this stage of the divorce process.

Divorce as a Process of Mourning.   This theoretical framework developed by Wiseman (1975) is based on an application of crisis theory. Wiseman (1975) identified five stages of the divorce process. The first stage is *denial*. In this stage of the divorce process, couples either deny problems and/or they admit to having problems but attribute those problems to outside influences such as jobs or the economy. Eventually, the stress of the marital problems upset the balance of the relationship and the couple will move to the next stage, *loss and depression*. At this point, the couple finally admits to the problems in the relationship. For many couples this is the first time that the seriousness of the marital problems are acknowledged, which often results in feelings of grief, depression, and loneliness. In the next stage, *anger and ambivalence*, feelings of anger and depression become stronger as the couple progresses through the formal legal stages of the divorce. As couples confront the economic and custody issues of their divorce, they may also wonder if the marriage could have been saved—could they have tried harder to keep the marriage intact? The uncertainty associated with divorce can increase the feelings of ambivalence at this stage. *Reorientation of lifestyle and identity* is the next stage. When the divorce is proceeding through the legal system, the couple must find or develop a new identity. They are forced to revise their self-images and to reevaluate their professional, social, and sexual relationships with others. Of course, this reorientation will vary greatly among individuals, some finding the process fairly easy and others contending with a great deal of self-examination and struggle. The final stage of Wiseman's framework, acceptance, is characterized by an acceptance of the end of the marriage and the couple relationship. New coping mechanisms are now in place and the individuals are able to move forward into new relationships.

Divorce as a Psychological Process. This framework of divorce is based on clinical research by Kessler (1975) and has as its basis seven emotional stages of divorce which couples must go through. First is *disillusionment*. In this stage, the differences and difficulties in the marriage are discovered. All marriages must experience this to some degree, a period that Kessler views as one of discovery and as a turning point. Some couples will acknowledge the differences and work to minimize them, thereby strengthening their marriages. Those couples who accentuate the differences and difficulties will most likely move on to the second stage of the divorce process, termed *erosion*. Couples who cannot or will not work to minimize the problems of the marriage will eventually face feelings of anger, disappointment, and frustration as their marriage deteriorates. In the third stage, *detachment*, the couple distances themselves from each other, losing interest in the marital relationship. This stage is marked by a significant reduction of investment in the marriage, resulting in an emotional separation of the partners. Often seen as the most traumatic aspect of the divorce process, the next stage, *physical separation* of the

couple, usually leads to intense feelings of loneliness, anxiety, and confusion. The spouse who initiated the separation may experience additional feelings of guilt, while the spouse who was not the initiator may experience feelings of rejection or loss. Once the physical separation has been completed, the individuals must free themselves from the psychological presence of each other and move on to *mourning*, the next stage. It is at this stage that the couple must learn to think of themselves as individuals independent of each other and, in a sense, mourn the loss of the marriage. The next stage, *second adolescence*, is unique to the various theoretical frameworks. Kessler categorizes it as a time of excitement, in which individuals are able to look toward the future without pain and anger and allow themselves to begin to formulate plans of their own. In the final stage, *exploration and hard work*, goals and plans initiated in the previous stage are defined and reevaluated. Plans become more realistic and individuals exert more control over their actions.

Divorce as a Psychosocial Process. This theoretical framework is based on social exchange theory, which states that people seek to maximize benefits while minimizing costs through rational decision making. The social exchange theory is used to understand the divorce process as a function of evaluating the costs and benefits of marital relationships. Guttman (1993) developed four stages of the psychosocial process.

Deciding: As problems and changes occur in marriages, couples either work through such issues or eventually decide that the costs of marriage outweigh the benefits and thus initiate the process of divorce.

Separation: This second stage is characterized by the physical separation of the couple. Guttman (1993) emphasizes the timing of the separation, with a longer time period between the decision to separate and the actual date of separation being associated with less trauma and depression for both individuals.

Struggling: After the physical separation, the individuals must reorganize their lives into two separate households. Adjustment can be frustrating and painful, especially as the family proceeds through the formalized legal stages, including financial and custody issues.

Winning: The final stage of the psychosocial process is marked by the realization that the benefits of the postdivorce life outweigh the costs of the divorce.

Consequences of Divorce on Children and Adults

Amato (1993) proposes there are five explanations to account for children's adjustment to a divorce. Loss of the noncustodial parent, adjustment of the custodial parent, interparental conflict, economic hardship, and stress associated with divorce all affect children's ability to adjust to the changes in the family structure. Adults must also cope with these changes in regard to themselves and their children. Although children and adults will react differently in each individual case, adjustment often involves some combination of Amato's explanations, which are implicit in the following topics.

Emotional and Psychological Effects on Children and Adults. Although marital conflict can have a significant negative impact on children and adults, the overriding public opinion is that divorce is both harmful and difficult. Little research has been conducted on the positive benefits of ending unhappy marriages. Most research to date has focused on the negative emotional and psychological effects of divorce.

Kitson and Morgan (1991) have suggested that as divorce becomes more prevalent, adjustment difficulties for both adults and children should decrease. This does not seem to be the case, as most divorced adults and children report some amount of anxiety, unhappiness, and loneliness (Song, 1991). Several studies have shown that adult children of divorce report lower levels of satisfaction in friendships, family life, and happiness (Glenn, 1991). Children from divorced families have been shown to be more likely to partake of deviant behavior such as truancy, burglary, and drug use (Demo & Acock, 1991). Also, children can experience the indirect effects of divorce when teachers, social workers, and family members expect different behavior from children of divorced parents. Amato (1991) suggests that children of divorce are treated negatively by their teachers, but it is not clear if this is due to behavioral problems exhibited by the children or to a bias on the part of the teachers. Other studies of divorce (Gasser & Taylor, 1990; Gerstel, 1987) report that separated and divorced adults are often stigmatized by families, friends, and coworkers. Likewise, single-parent families are frequently viewed as deviant partial families that threaten the future of the traditional nuclear family.

Living Arrangements of Children and Parents. Current increases in rates of divorce are predicted to lead to a growing number of children spending time in single-parent households. As a result of divorce, marital dissolution, and nonmarital childbearing, it is expected that approximately 50% of the children born in recent birth cohorts will spend some time in single-parent households (Bumpass & Raley, 1993). Although recent trends in child custody arrangements have been in the direction of more joint physical custody and fathers having sole physical custody (Figure 3), it is still the case that the great majority of children live primarily with their mothers after a divorce (Seltzer, 1991). Only about 15% of all single-parent families are headed by men (U.S. Bureau of the Census, 1993b).

Studies of parent–child relations do show long-term effects as a result of divorce and the loss of the noncustodial parent. Peterson and Zill (1986) found that divorce was not greatly harmful to children's relations with custodial mothers but was a negative influence on the relationship with noncustodial fathers. Interestingly, divorce seems to harm the relationship between noncustodial fathers and children to a greater degree than the relationship between noncustodial mothers and children (Aquilino, 1994; Cooney & Uhlenberg, 1990; Rossi & Rossi, 1990).

Whereas few women are noncustodial mothers, a strong negative stereotype is believed to be associated with women who relinquish or lose custody of their children (Paskowicz, 1982). Although Greif (1995) did not find support for this negative stereotype, he found that the majority of noncustodial mothers visited with their children at least once a month. Additional studies (Furstenberg, Nord, Peterson, & Zill, 1983; Seltzer & Bianchi, 1988) have found that noncustodial mothers are less likely to lose contact with their children and more likely to have greater contact with their children than noncustodial fathers. Such higher levels of maternal–child contact may account for the stronger relationship between noncustodial mothers and children.

Although the number of custodial fathers raising children alone has tripled from 1970 to 1990, such relationships still account for only a small percentage of the living arrangements of children after divorce (Greif, 1995). Most children in these situations do report positive relationships with their custodial fathers (Risman & Park, 1988), while other studies report that girls who live with their fathers are less competent socially and are more depressed than boys who live with their fathers (Camara & Resnick, 1988; Peterson & Zill, 1986). Likewise, girls living with their custodial fathers have lower school grades and more adjustment problems than boys who live with their custodial mothers (Maccoby, Buchannan, Mnookin, & Dornbusch, 1993). From the fathers' perspective, the primary problems with raising their children consist of balancing childcare and work, reestablishing a social life, and interacting with the court system (Greif, 1995).

The relationship between children and their noncustodial fathers is often tenuous. Fathers with higher completed education levels remain more involved with their children (Cooney & Uhlenberg, 1990; Furstenberg et al., 1983; Seltzer & Bianchi, 1988). Likewise, when parents postpone divorce until the children are young adults, the ties between fathers and their children remain unaffected (Furstenberg, Hoffman, & Shrestha, 1995). However, numerous national surveys show a steady decrease in the relationship over time (Furstenberg, 1988; Seltzer, 1991; Wallerstein & Kelly, 1980). Bianchi (1990) found more than 60% of noncustodial fathers either did not visit their children or had no contact with them for over 1 year. In cases when fathers did visit their children after

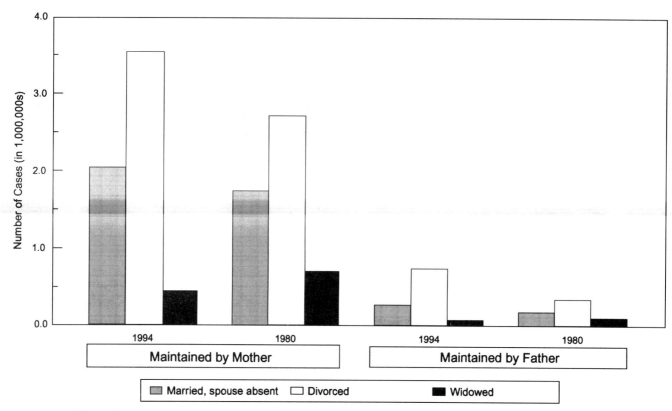

Figure 3. One-parent family groups by gender and marital status, 1980 and 1994. (*Source*: Rawlings and Saluter, 1995.)

the divorce, the frequency of those visits seriously declined after about 2 years (Loewen, 1988), a development that may be linked to the roles that fathers commonly play within the family unit. Furstenberg and Cherlin (1991) suggest that men view wives and children as a singular entity. Because their responsibilities to children are viewed as being firmly linked to responsibilities to their wives, the severing of bonds between husbands and wives automatically results in diminishing the bonds between fathers and children. An alternative view by Seltzer (1991) proposes that parents do not know what noncustodial fathers' roles ought to be, and that uncertainty may account for the limited and sporadic relationships with fathers and children. Other researchers propose various reasons as to why noncustodial fathers fail to maintain relationships with their children. For example, by limiting contact with children after a divorce, the fathers face fewer reminders of the loss and pain involved in their divorce (Hetherington, Cox, & Cox, 1978; Lund, 1987). Conflict with the former spouse is another reason suggested for the week relationships between fathers and children (Wright & Price, 1986). Finally, Cooksey and Craig, 1998 suggest that noncustodial fathers who remarry find themselves more involved with their new families in terms of time and finances.

Noncustodial fathers report little influence over childrearing decisions (Seltzer, 1991; Fox, 1995), while tending to pursue recreational activities with their children. Mothers are more likely to take over the more routine childrearing tasks such as medical care and organization of children's activities (Furstenberg & Nord, 1985; Maccoby & Mnookin, 1992; Marsiglio, 1991). Estrangement from fathers that often begins in childhood continues to decline through adolescence and into adulthood to an extent that contact with and probability of coresidence with fathers is reduced. Being a noncustodial father also reduces the odds that men see their adult children as sources of support in times of possible need (Cooney & Uhlenberg, 1990; Rossi & Rossi, 1990). Noncustodial fathers tend to stay more involved with their daughters than with their sons (Seltzer, 1991), yet daughters of divorce report less intimacy with their fathers than do daughters from intact families (Cooney, 1994; Cooksey & Craig, 1998).

Child Custody Arrangements. There are two main types of custody for children after a divorce, sole custody and joint custody. The first of these, sole custody, occurs when one parent is assigned complete control of a child's legal and physical needs. The second, joint custody, occurs when both parents share the responsibility of childrearing. Joint custody can further be divided into joint legal custody, wherein parents share the legal responsibilities of the child's needs, and joint physical custody, wherein parents share the day-to-day living arrangements. Although the majority of states now allow, or in many cases encourage, joint custody, in actuality the incidence of joint custody remains low (Donnelly & Finkelhor, 1993; Ferreiro, 1990). It is usually those parents with higher incomes, higher completed education levels, and those in urban areas, and nonwhites who are most likely to be awarded joint custody (Donnelly & Finkelhor, 1993).

The arguments in favor of joint legal and/or joint physical custody focus on the ways in which it benefits parents and children (Ferreiro, 1990; Glazer, 1989; Pearson & Thoennes, 1990). Joint custody is thought to relieve the stress of custody battles by avoiding a "winning" and a "losing" parent. By sharing the responsibilities of childrearing, it allows both parents to be actively involved in all aspects of the child's life and eases the strain of being a single parent. Finally, joint custody is thought to improve children's adjustment to divorce by maintaining the active involvement of both parents in childrearing and by making the children feel more secure and less harmed by the fear of losing the noncustodial parent.

Arguments against joint custody focus on the problems encountered by families trying to share children (Ferreiro, 1990; Schulman & Pitt, 1982; Steinmen, 1981). Children in joint physical custody must split their time between the mother's home and the father's home, a circumstance having the potential for two separate sets of rules, the complications of stepsiblings, and disruption of daily routines. Mothers may sense their authority over their children to be reduced in the case of joint custody (Weitzman, 1985), and the children may also feel a divided sense of loyalty between the parents. Finances could pose a problem through such requirements as the need to maintain larger homes with extra room to accommodate the visiting children. Both joint legal and joint physical custody can be very difficult to abide if the parents cannot work together. Conflict or anger over past behavior may influence the ability of the joint decision-making process. Donnelly and Finkelhor (1992), for example, found no evidence that children in joint custody arrangements had less conflict or better relations with their parents. Conversely, children in sole custody arrangements were found to give their parents more support than those in shared custody. In fact, Luepnitz (1986) reports that it is not the type of custody arrangement that is of importance, but the amount of interparental conflict present that shapes the experience of children whose parents divorce.

Interparental Conflict. Conflict between parents that occurs before and after the divorce can have long-term effects on children. High levels of conflict prior to the divorce may create a hostile atmosphere in the home and may contribute to parental neglect of children's needs (Seltzer, 1993). In a longitudinal study of the effects of children and divorce, Cherlin et al. (1991) discovered that children exhibited predivorce behavioral and academic problems prior to the divorce, with the trauma of divorce beginning well before the actual separation of the parents.

Parental conflict after the divorce may force children to take sides (Cooney, 1994) and may lead to a greater likelihood of children being close to only one parent (Peterson & Zill, 1986). Children in two-parent families with high levels of conflict are more depressed and show more signs of behavioral problems than children in divorced families with lower levels of conflict. Consistent with such findings, other studies have shown that high levels of conflict after the divorce may harm the father–child relationship to a greater degree than the mother–child relationship (Amato & Booth, 1991; Rossi & Rossi, 1990).

Money and childrearing practices are the problems cited most often as causing conflict after the divorce (Hanson, 1993). If the issues that caused conflict prior to the divorce are still of concern to the parents, the addition of money and childrearing conflicts only serve to exacerbate the overall conflict level. This can be especially troublesome in the cases of joint custody. Adolescents in joint custody arrangements with a high level of parental conflict report feeling caught between their parents. They may be drawn into the disagreements or they may feel as if they must be mediators between the parents, both situations resulting in higher levels of depression and behavioral problems (Buchanan, Maccoby, & Dornbusch, 1991). Often, high levels of conflict after the divorce lead to a disruption in the relationship between parents and children (Maccoby et al., 1993).

Economic Difficulties. It is commonly understood that divorce leads to changes in the financial circumstances of parents and children. The loss of the husband's income, in addition to the lack of child support payments, combine to substantially lower a family's standard of living. On average, the custodial mother's and children's standard of living is reduced by 30% while the noncustodial father's standard of living increases by 15% (Hoffman & Duncan, 1988). In 1994, 53% of single-mother families fell below the poverty line (Saluter, 1994). Mothers, who overwhelmingly have custody of their children, respond to the financial constraints by increasing their involvement in the paid labor force or by turning to government sources such as Aid to Families with Dependent Children (Bianchi & McArthur, 1991). Stepfathers are also significant sources of income within remarried families (Aquilino, 1994).

Parents who separate and divorce begin with lower incomes and fewer assets prior to the divorce than parents who do not divorce (Bianchi & McArthur, 1991). The expense of maintaining two homes may result in a higher percentage of income being used for the necessities and a lower percentage of income used for the "extras" such as music lessons, vacations, or membership in organized sports programs. Economic difficulties are known to be closely linked to lower levels of educational achievement for children of divorce (Guidubaldi, 1988; Krein & Beller, 1988; McLanahan & Sandefur, 1994), with perhaps the lack of money for "extras" being reflected in such attainment outcomes.

Child Support. The Child Support Amendments of 1984 and the Family Support Acts of 1988 and 1994 combined to standardize and formalize regulations concerning child support. States are now required to use set formulas for calculating child support, with courts having a choice of two formulas. The first is a cost-sharing method based on the costs of raising a child, and the second is based on parents' incomes and ability to pay (Garfinkel, Oellerich, & Robins, 1991). When a custodial parent is better able to support the children, child support from the noncustodial parent will be set at a lower rate. Noncustodial mothers are usually ordered to pay lower child support awards because custodial fathers tend to have higher incomes (Bianchi, 1994).

Child support awards are to be periodically reviewed to account for inflation and other changes in the economy or in the circumstances of the child's needs. If the noncustodial parent does not willingly make the payments, the monies are to be withheld from wages or tax refunds (Garfinkel et al., 1991). Teachman (1991) found that automatic deductions from wages accounted for a 15–25% increase in compliance with child support awards. However, if a parent changes jobs frequently or is self-employed, it is very difficult to withhold child support payments from the parent's wages.

Noncustodial fathers with higher incomes who visit regularly, live close to the children, and are not remarried are the most likely to pay their court-ordered child support (Teachman, 1991). Payment of child support, however, does not result in a closer relationship when the children reach adulthood (Furstenberg, Hoffman, & Shrestha, 1995). Fathers were equally likely to pay child support to daughters as to sons, indicating that sex of the child does not influence fathers' compliance in paying child support (Paasch & Teachman, 1991).

Despite changes in the law, many children do not receive the support payments to which they are entitled. In 1990, 77% of mothers with children under age 21 were awarded child support. Of these mothers, only three-fourths actually received any payments, with the average total amount being $3300 per year (Benokraitis, 1996). The longer the parents are separated, the less likely fathers are to pay child support and the smaller are the payments (Bellar & Graham, 1993).

Fathers may fail to pay their court-ordered child support, in part, because when they leave the family household, the time spent with children declines. Fathers who live apart from their children question the use of the child support monies. This inability to monitor the expenditures can lower the compliance with the child support orders (Weiss & Willis, 1985). Moreover, fathers must usually arrange the children's finances through the custodial mother, a difficult task if high levels of conflict and mistrust exist between parents.

Part of the problem with noncompliance of child support awards is that states vary a great deal in the enforcement of child support laws. Recent legislation to increase compliance rates has focused on forcing parents to pay either by placing liens on properties (Meyer & Bartfeld, 1996) or by withholding official licensing such as real estate or driver's licenses. Other researchers (Braver, Fitzpatrick, & Bay, 1991) suggest that unemployment is the principal reason for noncompliance with child support orders. To date, little has been done to enhance the earnings capacity of noncustodial parents (Meyer & Bartfeld, 1996).

Beyond the obvious financial benefits of receiving child support payments, children's well-being does seem to be enhanced by the receipt of the payments. Fathers who comply with the child support orders also are more likely to visit the children (Furstenberg et al., 1983; Seltzer, 1998). Perhaps it is the combination of the willingness to make the payments and the visits that create a stronger relationship between the child and the noncustodial father.

Gender Differences. As noted earlier, males and females may face differing consequences of divorce. "Her divorce" is often characterized by a loss of status associated with the husband's identity. This can be especially difficult for older women who may have fewer resources for career development and limited opportunities to remarry (Choi, 1992). Likewise, economic difficulties tend to be greater for women than for men, with custodial mothers' and children's standards of living being reduced by 30% while the noncustodial fathers' standards of living increase by 15% (Hoffman & Duncan, 1988). As a result, many divorced mothers must turn to government sources such as Aid to Families with Dependent Children (Bianchi & McArthur, 1991).

Compared to men, women tend to have stronger family and friendship networks upon which to draw during a divorce. For this reason, in part, women fare better emotionally after separation and divorce than do men (Diedrick, 1991). Women are also more likely to receive custody of their children after a divorce, and there is a strong negative stereotype associated with women who relinquish or lose custody of children (Paskowicz, 1982). Additionally, divorce has not been found to greatly harm children's relations with their custodial mothers, but it can negatively influence the relationship with the noncustodial fathers (Peterson & Zill,

1986). Interestingly, divorce seems to harm the relationship between noncustodial fathers and children to a greater degree than the relationship between noncustodial mothers and children (Aquilino, 1994; Cooney & Uhlenberg, 1990; Rossi & Rossi, 1990).

"His divorce" is often characterized by loneliness and loss of family status as a result of being the noncustodial parent. As noted earlier, divorce harms the relationship between noncustodial fathers and children to a greater degree than the relationship between noncustodial mothers and children (Aquilino, 1994; Cooney & Uhlenberg, 1990; Rossi & Rossi, 1990). Furthermore, contact with children after a divorce can be a reminder of the loss and pain involved in the divorce (Hetherington et al., 1978; Lund, 1987) and may also be confounded with conflict with the former spouse. Frequently, noncustodial fathers feel as if they retain the financial obligations of fatherhood while having little influence in the rearing of their children (Lamanna & Riedmann, 1994).

Beyond having fewer emotional outlets and networks to rely upon in dealing with these feelings of loss, loneliness, and absence from their children's lives (Diedrick, 1991), men are restricted by the traditional male gender role, which discourages them from seeking help with their emotional needs after a divorce.

Marital Separation

Another type of marital dissolution is legal separation, an option granted by courts in some states. These are instances in which the couple remains legally married but has a formalized, legal agreement that covers child support, visitation rights, separate living arrangements, and economic responsibilities. Other states have decreed legal separation to be unnecessary and have abolished it from their legal codes (Lamanna & Reidmann, 1994).

More common is informal marital separation, in which couples merely stop living together but never proceed with the legal separation or a formal divorce decree. Many low-income couples use informal marital separation instead of divorce because of their inability to pay legal fees associated with divorce (Watkins, Menken, & Vaughan, 1981). Morgan (1988) found that being nonwhite and of lower income significantly increased the likelihood of remaining separated for long periods of time.

Not all copies who are separated do so by choice. Rindfuss and Stephen (1990) report that involuntary marital separation is more likely to end in divorce. Couples who do not live together because of military service or incarceration in prisons are more likely to divorce than are couples who are able to live together. A study of military wives (Wood, Scarville, & Gravino, 1995) showed that many wives, particularly the younger wives, reported both the separation period

and the reunion with their husbands to be stressful. Because blacks are more likely to be incarcerated and are three times more likely to be in the military than are whites, they are more likely to have high rates of involuntary marital separation (Rindfuss & Stephen, 1990). These higher rates of marital separation may help explain the higher divorce rates for blacks.

Marital separation does not always end in divorce regardless of the ability to pay the divorce fees or the circumstances of the separation. In a recent national study addressing the outcomes of marital separations, Wineberg (1994, 1995) found that approximately one-third of attempted reconciliations are successful. The probability of success depends on education levels, religious similarity, religious conversion at the time of marriage, age homogamy, and cohabitation prior to marriage. Couples who initially share the same religion or couples in which one of the partners converted to other's religion at the time of marriage are significantly more likely to reconcile after a marital separation. Wineberg (1994) proposes that commitment to religion, shared religious values, traditions, or sense of religious community help keep the reconciliation intact. Couples who are the same age or who have higher education levels may be more likely to have a successful reconciliation because of the similar life expectancies. The finding that cohabitation prior to marriage is significantly related to a successful reconciliation is surprising given the well-established finding that cohabitation prior to marriage is related to a higher divorce rate. Wineberg explains this apparently contradictory finding by suggesting that a subgroup of cohabitors exists who are quite committed to marriage, know their partners better through the experience of cohabitation, and, therefore, are more successful at reconciliation.

Annulments

Although annulments have their origin in the Roman Catholic Church, most are currently civil rather than religious in nature. The two forms should not be confused; civil annulments involve the fulfillment of legal requirements for the termination of a marriage, while religious annulments are concerned with religious requirements specific to Church doctrine. In the case of a religious annulment, a legal divorce or a civil annulment also must be obtained to satisfy the legal requirements of the state.

For annulled marriages, the courts find causes that existed prior to the marriage that render it either void or voidable. A void marriage is one that never existed and therefore does not require a court decree to declare it invalid. An example of a void marriage would be a case of bigamy where a previous legal marriage currently in existence prevents the second marriage from being legal and binding. A second example is a consanguineous marriage, which occurs when biologically related couples marry. The similarity between both cases is that the participants were not originally free or legally able to marry, with the result being that the marriage never existed and requires termination.

A voidable marriage does require a court decree to render it invalid, with grounds for annulment involving fraud or misrepresentation of self, a partner under the legal age of consent, impotence, and insanity (Rice, 1996). The insanity guideline also includes people who are not able to grasp the meaning of the marriage premise, but does not include being inebriated to the point of not remembering the marriage ceremony (Knox & Schacht, 1994).

In a civil annulment proceeding only one spouse needs to take action, but it must be initiated within the lifetime of both the husband and the wife within a reasonable period of time. If the injured party willingly chooses to cohabit after the fraud or some other reason for the annulment is known, he or she may have waived the right to an annulment (Rice, 1996).

Once a marriage has been voided through a civil annulment, both parties are returned to their premarital status, with all properties and monies being returned to original owners and no spousal support available. A common myth about annulments is that children from the union are considered illegitimate after an annulment. This is not the case, however, because children from annulled (civil or religious) unions are considered legitimate and are eligible for child support payments.

Currently, about 3% of all legal divorces are actually annulments (Lamanna & Reidmann, 1994). Given a choice, many people choose divorce rather than annulment because community property rules apply in the former but not in the latter. Moreover, with the liberalization of divorce laws and the declining stigma of divorce, many couples see no-fault divorce as being easier than proving cause for a voidable marriage.

Widowhood

While only 10% of the marriages begun in 1900 ended in divorce, the majority of marital relationships ended with the death of a spouse, a trend that has not been prevalent since the mid-1970s. Today more marriages per year end in divorce than in the death of a spouse (Cherlin, 1996). Because women live longer and men are more likely to remarry, widowhood is more likely than widowerhood (Gass-Sternas, 1995). Currently, 49% of all women over the age of 65 have experienced the death of a spouse as compared to only 14% of men (U.S. Bureau of the Census, 1993b). The average age for a woman to lose her husband is 70 years, while men are 72.3 years old on the average when the lose their wives. A woman will spend 15 years as a widow on the average, and the typical man will spend 8 years as a widower (Treas, 1995).

The adjustment to the loss of a spouse usually begins with the bereavement period, a time of mourning the death of the marital partner. This gives way to a time of adjustment when the remaining spouse learns to cope with the new, unmarried status. In the case of a prolonged illness, the adjustment period may begin before the death of the spouse; in the case of a sudden death, the adjustment process can be more difficult because it is unexpected.

The end of a marriage because of death affects men and women differently. Women are more likely to experience financial problems if they did not play an active role in the household finances prior to their husband's death. Another financial problem that widows may face is "Widow's Gap." Unless disabled, a woman without labor force experience is not eligible for Social Security payments until the age of 60 (Choi, 1992). If her husband dies when she is only 57 years old and she never worked outside the home for pay, she must wait 3 years to collect Social Security funds. Fortunately, women tend to have larger social networks that can offer help, advice, and companionship. Men, on the other hand, do not tend to have the extensive social networks and are less likely to find solace after the death of a wife (Brubaker, 1991). They experience greater health problems and higher rates of suicide than do widows (Li, 1995).

The problems of young widows and widowers tend to be much different from those of older widows and widowers. The most obvious is the presence of dependent children, with the combination of widowhood and single parenthood being a double stressor on families (Gass-Sternas, 1995). Nevertheless, younger widows and widowers are much more likely to remarry and create blended families, while only 2% of elderly widows and 4% of elderly widowers will eventually remarry (U.S. Bureau of the Census, 1993b). Of the elderly who do remarry, most report high levels of marital satisfaction (Sheehy, 1995).

Conclusion

Although divorce is the leading cause of marital dissolution, widowhood, separation, and annulments still account for a significant portion of marriages that are terminated. Historically, divorce did not play a large role in marital dissolution, with death of a spouse being the most common way that marriages ended in the past. As Americans began living longer and healthier lives, they began to end their marriages through divorce instead of waiting for the death of a spouse. Currently, the divorce rate stands at 4.3 per 1000 population, but researchers predict a slight slowing of the divorce rate in the immediate future.

The divorce rate increased within a changing atmosphere of acceptance. Over time, as Americans became more accepting of divorce, the numbers of divorces increased, which, in turn, led to divorce becoming more commonplace and more frequent. Not only did divorce become more acceptable, but American society also changed and developed in such a way that divorce became a viable alternative for many people. Industrialization, the women's movement, legal changes, and the focus on individualism have led many people to reevaluate the institution of marriage.

Not only have widespread societal changes played a part in the growth of marital dissolution, but individual factors are also known to influence the likelihood of divorce and marital separation. Some of the most common factors include, but are not limited to, an early age at marriage, premarital births, intergenerational transmission of divorce resulting from having divorced parents, lower income and completed educational levels, and religious differences.

In the future, divorce will most likely become an increasingly accepted alternative family experience and will no longer be seen as deviant or detrimental to the traditional family. Marital separation will continue to be an alternative to formal divorce as the cost of divorce litigation increases, thereby making a legal divorce prohibitive to many who cannot afford legal counsel. Annulments will probably remain at their current low level (3% of all dissolutions) as most people find divorce to be less legally complex than annulment. Finally, the number of marriages ended by the death of a spouse will more than likely increase due to the aging of the Baby Boom generation. Despite the high divorce rate of Baby Boomers, however, most will be married as they enter their later years. The sheer size of this generation will produce a significant increase in the number of widows and widowers.

The future of research on marital dissolution should focus not only on the indicators and consequences of divorce but also on the positive aspects of dissolution. To date, very little emphasis has been placed on the positive outcomes of ending unhappy marriages. As the Baby Boom generation marries, divorces, and remarries, future research considerations should include the sequential decision-making process of multiple marriages as well as family changes brought about by the death of a spouse, ex-spouse, parent, and stepparent.

References

Allen, F. L. (1959). *Only yesterday*. New York: Harper & Row.

Allen, F. L. (1968). *Since yesterday*. New York: Harper & Row.

Amato, P. R. (1991). The "child of divorce" as a person prototype: Bias in the recall of information about children in divorced families. *Journal of Marriage and the Family, 53*, 59–69.

Amato, P. R. (1993). Children's adjustment to divorce: Theories, hypotheses, and empirical support. *Journal of Marriage and the Family, 55*, 23–38.

Amato, P. R. & Booth, A. (1991). Consequences of parental divorce and marital unhappiness for adult well-being. *Social Forces, 69*, 905–914.

Amato, P. R., & Keith, B. (1991). Parental divorce and adult well-being: A meta-analysis. *Journal of Marriage and the Family, 53*, 43–58.

Amato, P. R., & Partridge, S. (1987). Women and divorce with dependent children: Material, personal, family, and social well-being. *Family Relations, 36*, 316–320.

Aquilino, W. S. (1994). Impact of childhood family disruption of young adults' relationships with parents. *Journal of Marriage and the Family, 56*, 295–313.

Axinn, W. G., & Thornton, A. (1993). Mothers, children, and cohabitation: The intergenerational effects of attitudes and behavior. *American Sociological Review, 58*, 233–246.

Bachu, A. (1993). *Fertility of American women: June 1992* (U.S. Bureau of the Census, Current Population Reports P20-470). Washington, DC: U.S. Government Printing Office.

Bahr, S. J. (1982). The pains and joys of divorce: A survey of Mormons. *Family Perspective, 16*, 191–200.

Barnett, R. C., & Baruch, G. K. (1987). Determinants of fathers' participation in family work. *Journal of Marriage and the Family, 49*, 29–40.

Baruch, G. K., & Barnett, R. C. (1986). Consequences of fathers' participation in family work: Parents' role strain and well-being. *Journal of Personality and Social Psychology, 51*, 983–992.

Baydar, N. (1988). Effects of parental separation and reentry into union on the emotional well-being of children. *Journal of Marriage and the Family, 50*, 967–981.

Becker, G. S., Landes, E., & Michael, R. T. (1977). An economic analysis of marital instability. *Journal of Political Economy, 85*, 1141–1187.

Bellar, A. H., & Graham, J. W. (1993). *The economics of child support*. New Haven, CT: Yale University Press.

Bennett, N. G., Blanc, A. K., & Bloom, D. E. (1988). Commitment and the modern union: Assessing the link between premarital cohabitation and subsequent marital stability. *American Sociological Review, 53*, 127–138.

Benokraitis, N. V. (1996). *Marriages and families* (2nd ed.). Upper Saddle River, NJ: Prentice-Hall.

Bianchi, S. M. (1994). The changing demographic and socioeconomic characteristics of single-parent families. *Marriage and Family Review, 56*, 500–515.

Bianchi, S. M., & McArthur, E. (1991). *Family disruption and economic hardship: The shortrun picture for children* (U.S. Bureau of the Census, Current Population Reports, Series P-70, No. 23). Washington, DC: U.S. Government Printing Office.

Bianchi, S. M., & Spain, D. (1986). *American women in transition*. New York: Russell Sage Foundation.

Billy, J., Landale, N., & McLaughlin, S. (1986). The effects of marital status and first birth or marital dissolution among adolescent mothers. *Demography, 23*, 329–349.

Bird, G., & Melville, K. (1994). *Families and intimate relationships*. New York: McGraw-Hill.

Blair, S. L., & Johnson, M. P. (1992). Wives' perception of the fairness of the division of household labor: The intersection of housework and ideology. *Journal of Marriage and the Family, 54*, 570–581.

Block, J., Block, J. H., & Gjerde, P. F. (1988). Parental functioning and the home environment in families of divorce: Prospective and concurrent analyses. *Journal of Children and Adolescent Psychiatry, 23*, 207–213.

Bohannon, P. (1971). *Divorce and after*. New York: Doubleday.

Booth, A., & Edwards, J. N. (1985). Starting over: Why remarriages are more unstable. *Journal of Family Issues, 13*, 179–194.

Booth, A., & Johnson, D. (1988). Premarital cohabitation and marital success. *Journal of Marriage and the Family, 9*, 255–272.

Booth, A., & White, L. K. (1980). Thinking about divorce. *Journal of Marriage and the Family, 92,* 605–616.

Booth, A., Johnson, D., & White, L. K. (1984). Women, outside employment, and marital instability. *American Journal of Sociology, 90,* 567–583.

Braver, S., Fitzpatrick, P., & Bay, C. (1991). Noncustodial parent's report of child support payments. *Family Relations, 40,* 180–185.

Broman, C. L. (1988). Household work and family life satisfaction of blacks. *Journal of Marriage and the Family, 50,* 743–748.

Brubaker, T. (1991). Families in later life: A burgeoning research area. In A. Booth (Ed.), *Contemporary families: Looking forward, looking back* (pp. 226–248). Minneapolis, MN: National Council on Family Relations.

Buchannan, C., Maccoby, E., & Dornbusch, S. (1991). Caught between parents: Adolescents' experience in divorced homes. *Child Development, 62,* 1008–1029.

Bumpass, L., & Raley, R. K. (1993). *Trends in the duration of single-parent families* (National Survey of Households and Families working paper No. 58). Madison: Center for Demography and Ecology, University of Wisconsin.

Bumpass, L., & Sweet, J. (1989). National estimates of cohabitation. *Demography, 26,* 615–625.

Bumpass, L., Martin, T. C., & Sweet, J. (1991). The impact of family background and early marital factors on marital disruption. *Journal of Family Issues, 12,* 22–42.

Bumpass, L., & Sweet, J. (1972). Differentials in marital instability: 1970. *American Sociological Review, 37,* 756–766.

Bumpass, L., Sweet, J., & Cherlin, A. (1991). The role of cohabitation in declining rates of marriage. *Journal of Marriage and the Family, 53,* 913–927.

Bumpass, L., Raley, R. K., & Sweet, J. (1995). The changing character of stepfamilies: Implications of cohabitation and nonmarital childbearing. *Demography, 32,* 425–436.

Camara, K. A., & Resnick, G. (1988). Interparental conflict and cooperation: Factors moderating children's post-divorce adjustment. In E. M. Hetherington & J. D. Arasteh (Eds.), *Impact of divorce, single parenting, and stepparenting on children* (pp. 129–134). Hillsdale, NJ: Erlbaum.

Caspi, A., & Elder, G. H. (1988). Emergent family patterns: The intergenerational construction of problem behavior and relationships. In R. A. Hinde & J. Stevenson-Hinde (Eds.), *Relationships within families* (pp. 215–235). Oxford, New York: University Press.

Chan, L., & Heaton, T. B. (1989). Demographic determinants of delayed divorce. *Journal of Divorce, 13,* 97–112.

Chase-Lansdale, P. L., & Hetherington, E. M. (1990). The impact of divorce on life-span development: Short and long-term effects. In P. B. Baltes, D. L. Featherman, & R. M. Lerner (Eds.), *Life span development and behavior* (pp. 105–150). Hillsdale, NJ: Erlbaum.

Cherlin, A. (1977). The effect of children on marital dissolution. *Demography, 14,* 265–272.

Cherlin, A. J. (1979). Work life and marital dissolution. In G. Levinger & O. Moles (Eds.), *Divorce and separation: Context, causes, and consequences* (pp. 123–132). New York: Basic Books.

Cherlin, A. J. (1981). *Marriage, divorce, remarriage.* Cambridge, MA: Harvard University Press.

Cherlin, A. J. (1996). *Public and private families.* New York: McGraw-Hill.

Cherlin, A., Furstenberg, F., Chase-Lansdale, P., Kiernan, K., Robins, P., Morrison, D., & Teitler, J. (1991). Longitudinal studies of the effects of divorce on children in Great Britain and the Untied States. *Science, 252,* 1386–1389.

Cherlin, A., Keirman, K. J., & Chase-Lansdale, P. (1995). Parental divorce in childhood and demographic outcomes in young adulthood. *Demography, 32,* 299–318.

Choi, N. G. (1992). Correlates of the economic status of widowed and divorced elderly women. *Journal of Family Issues, 13,* 38–54.

Cohen, N. J. (1990). *The fundamentalist perspective.* Grand Rapids, MN: Eerdmans.

Colsanto, D., & Shriver, J. (1989). Middle-aged face marital crisis. *Gallup Report, 284,* 34–38.

Cooksey, E., & Craig, P. (1998). Parenting from a distance: The effects of parental characteristics on contact between nonresidential fathers and their children. *Demography, 35,* 187–200.

Cooney, T. M. (1994). Young adults' relations with parents: The influence of recent parental divorce. *Journal of Marriage and the Family, 56,* 45–56.

Cooney, T. M., & Uhlenberg, P. (1990). The role of divorce in men's relations with their adult children after mid-life. *Journal of Marriage and the Family, 52,* 677–688.

Cutright, P. (1971). Income and family events: Marital stability. *Journal of Marriage and the Family, 33,* 291–306.

DeMaris, A., & MacDonald, W. (1993). Premarital cohabitation and marital instability: A test of the unconventionality hypothesis. *Journal of Marriage and the Family, 55,* 399–407.

DeMaris, A., & Rao, K. V. (1992). Premarital cohabitation and subsequent marital stability in the United States: A re-assessment. *Journal of Marriage and the Family, 54,* 178–190.

Demo, D. H., & Acock, A. C. (1991). The impact of divorce on children. In A. Booth (Ed.), *Contemporary families: Looking forward, looking back* (pp. 162–191). Minneapolis, MN: National Council on Family Relations.

Depner, C. E., Leino, E. V., & Chun, A. (1993). Interparental conflict and child adjustment: A decade review and meta-analysis. *Family Council Courts Review, 30,* 323–341.

Devall, E., Stoneman, Z., & Brody, G. (1986). The impact of divorce and maternal employment of pre-adolescent children. *Journal of Marriage and the Family, 35,* 153–160.

Diedrick, P. (1991). Gender differences in divorce adjustment. *Journal of Divorce and Remarriage, 14,* 33–46.

Donnelly, D., & Finkelhor, D. (1992). Does equality in custody arrangement improve the parent–child relationship? *Journal of Marriage and the Family, 54,* 837–845.

Donnelly, D., & Finkelhor, D. (1993). Who has joint custody? Class differences in the determination of custody arrangements. *Family Relations, 42,* 57–60.

Dudley, J. (1991). Increasing our understanding of divorced fathers who have infrequent contact with their children. *Family Relations, 40,* 279–285.

Duncan, G. J., & Rodgers, W. (1991). Has children's poverty become more persistent? *American Sociological Review, 6,* 538–550.

Ellison, C. G., & Musnick, M. A. (1993). Southern intolerance: A fundamentalist effect? *Social Forces, 72,* 379–398.

Emery, R., Matthews, S., & Wyer, M. (1991). Child custody mediation and litigation: Further evidence on the differing views of mothers and fathers. *Journal of Consulting and Clinical Psychology, 59,* 410–418.

Espenshade, T. (1985). Marriage trends in America: Estimates, implications, and underlying causes. *Population and Development Review, 11,* 193–245.

Everett, C., & Everett, S. (1994). *Healthy divorce.* San Francisco, CA: Jossey-Bass.

Faust, K. A. (1995, October). *Comparisons of definitions of religious fundamentalism and their effects on fertility measures.* Paper presented at the Annual meeting of the Southern Demographic Association, Richmond, VA.

Ferreiro, B. W. (1990). Presumption of joint custody: A family policy dilemma. *Family Relations, 39,* 420–425.

Fox, G. L. (1995). Noncustodial fathers following divorce. (Single parent families: Diversity, myths, and realities, part I). *Marriage and Family Review, 20,* 257–282.

Furstenberg, F. F., Jr. (1988). Good dads-bad dads: The two faces of fatherhood. In A. J. Cherlin (Ed.), *The Changing American Family and Public Policy* (pp. 193–218). Washington, DC: Urban Institute Press.

Furstenberg, F., & Cherlin, A. (1991). *Divided families: What happens to children when parents part.* Cambridge, MA: Harvard University Press.

Furstenberg, F., & Spanier, G. (1984). Recycling the family: Remarriage after divorce. Beverly Hills, CA: Sage.

Furstenberg, F., Nord, C. W., Peterson, J. L., & Zill, N. (1983). The life course of children of divorce. *American Sociological Review, 8,* 656–668.

Furstenberg, F., Hoffman, S., & Shrestha, L. (1995). The effect of divorce on intergenerational transfers: New evidence. *Demography, 32,* 319–334.

Garfinkel, I. S. (1992). *Assuring child support: An extension of social security.* New York: Russell Sage.

Garfinkel, I. S., Oellerich, D., & Robins, P. K. (1991). Child support guidelines: Will they make a difference? *Journal of Family Issues, 12,* 404, 429.

Garfinkel, I. S., McLanahan, S., & Robins, P. K. (Eds.). (1994). *Child support and child well-being.* Washington, DC: Urban Institute Press.

Garraty, J. A. (1979). *The American nation* (4th ed.). New York: Harper & Row.

Gass-Sternas, K. A. (1995). Single parent widows: Stressors, appraisal, coping, resources, grieving responses, and health. *Marriage and Family Review, 20,* 411–445.

Gasser, R. D., & Taylor, C. M. (1990). Role adjustment of single parent fathers with dependent children. *Family Relations, 40,* 397–400.

Gerstel, N. (1987). Divorce and stigma. *Social Problems, 34,* 172–186.

Glazer, S. (1989). Joint custody: Is it good for the children? *Editorial Research Reports, 39,* 58–69.

Glenn, N. D. (1991). Quantitative research on marital quality in the 1980s. In A. Booth (Ed.), *Contemporary families: Looking forward, looking back* (pp. 28–41). Minneapolis, MN: National Council on Family Relations.

Glenn, N. D., & Supancic, M. (1984). The social and demographic correlates of divorce and separation in the United States: An update and reconsideration. *Journal of Marriage and the Family, 46,* 563–575.

Glick, P. C. (1984). Marriage, divorce, and living arrangements: Prospective changes. *Journal of Family Issues, 5,* 7–26.

Goldscheider, F. K., & Waite, L. J. (1991). *New families, no families? The transformation of the American home.* Berkeley: University of California Press.

Greenstein, T. N. (1990). Marital disruption and the employment of married women. *Journal of Marriage and the Family, 52,* 657–676.

Greif, G. (1995). Single fathers with custody following separation and divorce. *Marriage and Family Review, 20,* 213–232.

Guidubaldi, J. (1988). Differences in children's divorce adjustment across grade level and gender: A report from the NASP-Kent State Nationwide Project. In S. Wolchik and P. Karoly (Eds.), *Children of divorce: Empirical perspectives on adjustment* (pp. 215–238). New York: Gardner.

Guttman, J. (1993). *Divorce in psychosocial perspective: Theory and research.* Hillsdale, NJ: Erlbaum.

Guttman, M. (1996, June 21–23). The split over divorce. *USA Weekend Magazine,* pp. 5–7.

Halem, L. C. (1989). *Divorce reform.* New York: Free Press.

Hanson, T. L. (1993). *Family structure, parental conflict, and child well-being.* Ph.D. thesis, Department of Sociology, University of Wisconsin, Madison.

Harris, K. M., & Morgan, S. P. (1991). Fathers' involvement in parenting sons and daughters. *Journal of Marriage and the Family, 53,* 531–544.

Hays, C. D. (Ed.). (1987). *Risking the future: Adolescent sexuality, pregnancy, and childbearing, Vol. 1.* Washington, DC: National Academy Press.

Heaton, T. B. (1990). Marital stability through the child-rearing years. *Demography, 27,* 55–63.

Heaton, T. B. (1991). Time-related determinants of marital dissolution. *Journal of Marriage and the Family, 53,* 285–295.

Heaton, T. B., Albrecht, S. L. (1991). Stable unhappy marriages. *Journal of Marriage and the Family, 53,* 747–758.

Heaton, T. B., & Albrecht, S. L., & Martin, T. K. (1985). The timing of divorce. *Journal of Marriage and the Family, 47,* 631–639.

Hetherington, E. M., Cox, M., & Cox, R. (1978). The aftermath of divorce. In J. H. Stevens & M. Matthews (Eds.), *Mother–child, father–child relations* (pp. 146–176). Washington, DC: National Association for the Education of Young People.

Hoffman, S. D., & Duncan, G. J. (1988). What are the economic costs of divorce? *Demography, 25,* 641–645.

Hoffman, S. D., Foster, E. M., & Furstenberg, F. F. (1993). Re-evaluating the costs of teenage childbearing. *Demography, 30,* 1–14.

Houseknert, S. K., Vaugn, S., & Marken, A. S. (1984). Marital disruption among professional women: The timing of career and family events. *Social Problems, 31,* 273–284.

Huber, J., & Spitze, G. (1980). Considering divorce: An expansion of Becker's theory of marital instability. *American Journal of Sociology, 86,* 75–89.

Jacobson, D. S. (1978). The impact of marital separation/divorce on children: I. Parent–child separation and child adjustment. *Journal of Divorce,* 341–360.

Katzev, A., Warner, R., & Acock, A. (1994). Girls or boys? Relationship of child gender to marital instability. *Journal of Marriage and the Family, 56,* 89–100.

Keirnan, K. E., & Chase-Lansdale, P. L. (1993). Children and marital breakdown: Short- and Long-term consequences. In A. Blum & J. Rallu (Eds.), *European population, Vol. II: Demographic dynamics* (pp. 312–319). London: John Libby.

Keith, V. M., & Finlay, B. (1988). The impact of parental divorce on children's educational attainment, marital timings, and likelihood of divorce. *Journal of Marriage and the Family, 50,* 797–809.

Kessler, S. (1975). *The American way of divorce: prescription for change.* Chicago: Nelson Hall.

Kitson, G. C., Babri, K. B., & Roach, M. J. (1985). Who divorces and why: A review. *Journal of Family Issues, 6,* 255–293.

Kitson, G. C., & Morgan, L. A. (1991). The multiple consequences of divorce. In A. Booth (Ed.), *Contemporary families: Looking forward, looking back* (pp. 113–119). Minneapolis, MN: National Council on Family Relations.

Knox, D., & Schacht, C. (1994). *Choices in relationships* (4th ed.). St. Paul, MN: West.

Krein, S. F., & Beller, A. H. (1988). Educational attainment of children from single-parent families: Differences by exposure, gender, and race. *Demography, 25,* 221–234.

Kurdek, L. A. (1991). The relations between reported well-being and divorce history, availability of a proximate adult, and gender. *Journal of Marriage and the Family, 53,* 71–78.

Kurdek, L. A. (1993). Predicting marital dissolution: A 5-year prospective longitudinal study of newlywed couples. *Journal of Personality and Social Psychology, 64,* 221–242.

Lamanna, M., & Reidmann, A. (1997). *Marriages and families.* Belmont, CA: Wadsworth.

Lamb, M. E., Pleck, J. H., & Levine, J. A. (1987). Effects of increased paternal involvement on fathers and mothers. In C. Lewis & M. O'Brien (Eds.), *Reassessing fatherhood: New observations on fathers and the modern family* (pp. 208–218). Beverly Hills, CA: Sage.

Lehrer, E. L., & Chiswick, C. U. (1993). Religion as a determinant of marital stability. *Demography, 30,* 385–404.

Li, G. (1995). The interaction effects of bereavement and sex on the risk of suicide in the elderly: An historical cohort study. *Social Science and Medicine, 40,* 825–828.

Lillard, L. A., & Waite, L. J. (1993). A joint model of marital childbearing and marital disruption. *Demography, 30,* 653–681.

Lillard, L. A., Brien, M. J., & Waite, L. J. (1995). Pre-marital cohabitation and subsequent marital dissolution: Is it self-selection? *Demography, 32,* 437–458.

Loewen, J. W. (1988). Visitation fatherhood. In P. Bronstein & C. Cowan (Eds.), *Men's changing role in the family* (pp. 194–213). New York: Wiley.

Luepnitz, D. (1986). A comparison of maternal, paternal, and joint custody: Understanding the varieties of post-divorce family life. *Journal of Divorce, 9,* 1–12.

Lund, M. (1987). The non-custodial father: Common challenges in parenting after divorce. In C. Lewis & L. O'Brien (Eds.), *Reassessing fatherhood: New observations on fathers and the modern family* (pp. 108–115). London: Sage.

Lye, D. N., & Biblarz, T. J. (1993). The effects of attitudes toward family life and gender roles on marital satisfaction. *Journal of Family Issues, 14,* 157–188.

Maccoby, E., & Mnookin, R. H. (1992). *Dividing the child: Social and legal dilemmas of custody.* Cambridge, MA: Harvard University Press.

Maccoby, E., Buchannan, C. M., Mnookin, R. H., & Dornbusch, S. M. (1993). Postdivorce roles of mothers and fathers in the lives of their children. *Journal of Family Psychology, 7,* 24–38.

Marcus, A. D. (1991, June 5). Grandparents turn to the courts to seek permission to visit their grandchildren. *The Wall Street Journal,* p. B1.

Marsiglio, W. (1991). Paternal engagement activities with minor children. *Journal of Marriage and the Family, 53,* 973–986.

Martin, T. C., & Bumpass, L. L. (1989). Recent trends in marital disruption. *Demography, 26,* 37–51.

McLanahan, S. (1988). Family structure and dependency: Early transitions to female household headship. *Demography, 25,* 1–16.

McLanahan, S., & Bumpass, L. (1988). Intergenerational consequences of family disruption. *American Journal of Sociology, 94,* 130–152.

McLanahan, S., & Sandefur, G. (1994). *Growing up with a single parent: What hurts, what helps.* Cambridge, MA: Harvard University Press.

Meyer, D. R., & Bartfeld, J. (1996). Compliance with child support orders in divorce cases. *Journal of Marriage and the Family, 58,* 201–212.

Meyer, D. R., & Garasky, S. (1993). *Custodial fathers: Myths, realities, and child support policy* (Institute for Research on Poverty Discussion paper 982-92). Madison: University of Wisconsin.

Morgan, L. A. (1988). Outcomes of marital separation: A longitudinal test of predictors. *Journal of Marriage and the Family, 50,* 493–498.

Morgan, S., & Rindfuss, R. R. (1985). Marital disruption: Structural and temporal dimensions. *American Journal of Sociology, 90,* 1055–1057.

Morgan, S. P., Lye, D. N., & Condran, G. A. (1988). Sons, daughters, and the risk of marital disruption. *American Journal of Sociology, 94,* 110–129.

Mott, F. L., & Moore, S. F. (1979). The causes of marital disruption among young American women: An interdisciplinary perspective. *Journal of Marriage and the Family, 41,* 355–365.

National Center for Health Statistics. (1973). *100 years of marriage and divorce statistics: United States, 1867–1967.* Washington, DC: U.S. Government Printing Office.

National Center for Health Statistics. (1991a). *Cohabitation, marriage, marital dissolution, and remarriage: United States, 1988* (Advance data no. 194). Washington, DC: U.S. Government Printing Office.

National Center for Health Statistics. (1991b). *Final divorce statistics* (Monthly Vital Statistics report 39, supplement 2). Washington, DC: U.S. Government Printing Office.

Nett, E. M. (1988). *Canadian families: Past and present.* Toronto: Butterworths.

Newcomb, M. (1979). Cohabitation in America: An assessment of consequences. *Journal of Marriage and the Family, 41,* 597–603.

Nock, S. (1995). A comparison of marriages and cohabiting relationships. *Journal of Marriage and the Family, 16,* 53–76.

Norton, A. J., & Miller, I. F. (1992). *Marriage, divorce, and remarriage in the 1990s* (U.S. Bureau of the Census, Current Population Reports, series P23-180). Washington, DC: Government Printing Office.

Norton, A. J., & Moorman, J. E. (1987). Current trends in marriage and divorce among American women. *Journal of Marriage and the Family, 49,* 3–14.

Ogburn, W. F. (1953). The changing functions of the family. In R. Winch & R. McGinnis (Eds.), *Selected studies in marriage and the family* (pp. 27–31). New York: Henry Holt.

O'Neill, W. L. (1973). *Divorce in the progressive ear.* New York: New Viewpoints.

O'Neill, W. L. (1975). *The progressive years.* New York: Harper & Row.

Paasch, K. M., & Teachman, J. D. (1991). Gender of children and receipt of assistance from absent fathers. *Journal of Family Issues, 12,* 450–466.

Parkman, A. (1992). *No-fault divorce: What went wrong?* Boulder, CO: Westview.

Paskowicz, P. (1982). *Absentee mothers.* Totowa, NJ: Allanheld, Osmun, and Co.

Pearson, J., & Thoennes, N. (1990). Custody after divorce: Demographic and attitudinal patterns. *American Journal of Orthopsychiatry, 60,* 233–249.

Peterson, J., & Nord, C. W. (1990). The regular receipt of child support: A multistep process. *Journal of Marriage and the Family, 52,* 539–551.

Peterson, J., & Zill, N. (1986). Marital disruption, parent–child relationships, and behavior problems in children. *Journal of Marriage and the Family, 48,* 295–307.

Pope, H., & Mueller, C. W. (1976). The intergenerational transmission of marital instability: Comparisons by race and sex. *The Journal of Social Issues, 32,* 49–66.

Popenoe, D. (1988). *Disturbing the nest: Family change and decline in modern societies.* New York: Aldine de Gruyter.

Rankin, R. P., & Maneker, J. S. (1985). The duration of marriage in a divorce population: The impact of children. *Journal of Marriage and the Family, 47,* 15–20.

Rawlins, S. W., & Saluter, A. F. (1995). *Household and family characteristics: March 1994* (U.S. Bureau of the Census, Current population Reports, series P20-483). Washington, DC: U.S. Government Printing Office.

Rice, F. P. (1996). *Intimate relationships, marriages, and families (3rd ed.).* Mountain View, CA: Mayfield.

Rice, J. K., & Rice, D. G. (1986). *Living through divorce: A developmental approach to divorce therapy.* New York: Guilford.

Riley, G. (1991). *Divorce: An American tradition.* New York: Oxford University Press.

Rindfuss, R. R., & MacDonald, M. (1980). *Earnings, relative income, and family formation, part II: Fertility* (Institute for Research on Poverty Discussion Paper). Madison: University of Wisconsin.

Rindfuss, R. R., & Stephen, E. (1990). Marital noncohabitation: Absence does not make the heart grow fonder. *Journal of Marriage and the Family, 52,* 259–270.

Risman, B. J., & Park, K. (1988). Just the two of us: Parent–child relationships in single-parent homes. *Journal of Marriage and the Family, 50,* 1049–1062.

Ross, H. L., & Sawhill, I. V. (1975). *Time of transition: The growth of families headed by women.* Washington, DC: Urban Institute Press.

Rossi, A. S., & Rossi, P. H. (1990). *Of human bonding: Parent–child relations across the life course.* Hawthorne, NY: Aldine.

Salts, C. J. (1979). Divorce process: Integration of theory. *Journal of Divorce, 2,* 233–240.

Saluter, A. (1994). Marital status and living arrangements: March 1993 (U.S. Bureau of the Census, Current Population Reports, series P20-478). Washington, DC: U.S. Government Printing Office.

Schulman, J., & Pitt, V. (1982). Second thoughts on joint child custody: Analysis of legislation and its implications for women and children. *Women's Law Forum, 12,* 538–571.

Seltzer, J. A. (1991). Relationships between fathers and children who live apart: The father's role after separation. *Journal of Marriage and the Family, 53,* 79–101.

Seltzer, J. A. (1998). Father by law: Effects of joint legal custody on non-resident fathers' involvement with children. *Demography, 35,* 135–146.

Seltzer, J. A., & Bianchi, S. (1988). Children's contact with absent parents. *Journal of Marriage and the Family, 50,* 663–677.

Sheehy, G. (1995). *New passages: Mapping your life across time.* New York: Random House.

Smith, J., & Ward, M. (1985). Time series growth in the female labor force. *Journal of Labor Economics, 3,* S59–S90.

Song, Y. I. (1991). Single Asian American women as a result of divorce: Depressive affect and changes in social support. *Journal of Divorce and Remarriage, 14,* 219–230.

South, S., & Lloyd, K. (1995). Spousal alternatives and marital dissolution. *American Sociological Review, 60,* 21–35.

South, S., & Spitze, G. (1986). Determinants of divorce over the marital life course. *American Sociological Review, 51,* 583–590.

Stack, S. (1989). The impact of divorce on suicide in Norway, 1951–1980. *Journal of Marriage and the Family, 51,* 229–238.

Steinman, S. (1981). The experience of children in a joint-custody arrangement: A report of a study. *American Journal of Orthopsychiatry, 51,* 403–414.

Sweet, J., & Bumpass, L. (1987). *American families and households.* New York: Russell Sage Foundation.

Teachman, J. D. (1983). Early marriage, Premarital fertility, and marital dissolution. *Journal of Family Issues, 4,* 105–126.

Teachman, J. D. (1991). Contributions to children by divorced fathers. *Social Problem, 38,* 358–371.

Teachman, J., & Polonko, K. (1990). Cohabitation and marital stability in the United States. *Social Forces, 69,* 207–220.

Thompson, E. H., & Gonzola, P. A. (1983). Single parent families: In the mainstream of American society. In E. Macklin & R. Rubin (Eds.), *Contemporary families and alternative lifestyles* (pp. 112–139). Beverly Hills, CA: Sage.

Thomson, E., & Colella, U. (1992). Cohabitation and marital stability: Quality or commitment? *Journal of Marriage and the Family, 54,* 259–267.

Thorton, A. (1989). Changing attitudes toward family issues in the United States. *Journal of Marriage and the Family, 51,* 873–898.

Thorton, A., & Rodgers, W. (1987). The influence of individual and historical time on marital dissolution. *Demography, 24,* 1–22.

Treas, J. (1995). *Older Americans in the 1990s and beyond: Population bulletin.* Washington, DC: Population Reference Bureau.

Tzeng, M. S. (1992). The effects of socioeconomic heterogamy and changes on marital dissolution for first marriages. *Journal of Marriage and the Family, 54,* 609–619.

Uhlenberg, P. (1983). Death and the family. In M. Gordon (Ed.), *The American family in social-historical perspective* (pp. 168–177). New York: St. Martin's.

U.S. Bureau of the Census. (1993a). *Household and family characteristics: March 1992* (Current Population Reports, series P20-467). Washington, DC: U.S. Government Printing Office.

U.S. Bureau of the Census. (1993b). *Sixty five plus in America* (Current Population Reports, series P23-178RV). Washington, DC: U.S. Government Printing Office.

U.S. Bureau of the Census. (1995). *Statistical abstract of the United States.* Washington, DC: U.S. Government Printing Office.

Waite, L. J., & Lillard, L. A. (1991). Children and marital disruption. *American Journal of Sociology, 96,* 930–953.

Waldrop, J. (1994, September). Change is good, unless it happens. *American Demographics,* 12–13.

Wallerstein, J. S., & Kelly, J. B. (1980). *Surviving the breakup: How children and parents cope with divorce.* New York: Basic Books.

Watkins, S. C., Menken, J., & Vaughn, B. (1981, March). *The fertility of the formerly married.* Paper presented at the annual meeting of the Population Association of America, Washington, DC.

Webster, P. S., Orbuch, T. L., & House, J. S. (1995). Effects of childhood family background on adult marital quality and perceived stability. *American Journal of Sociology, 101,* 404–432.

Weeks, J. R. (1994). *Population* (5th ed.). Belmont, CA: Wadsworth.

Weiss, R. S. (1984). The impact of marital dissolution on income and consumption in single-parent households. *Journal of Marriage and the Family, 46,* 155–167.

Weiss, Y., & Willis, R. J. (1985). Children as collective goods and divorce settlements. *Journal of Labor Economics, 3,* 268–292.

Weitzman, L. J. (1985). *The divorce revolution: The unexpected social and economic consequences for women and their children in America.* New York: Free Press.

Weitzman, L. J., & Dixon, R. (1986). The transformation of legal marriage through no-fault divorce. In A. Skolnick & J. Skolnick (Eds.), *Family in transition* (pp. 169–195). Little, Brown.

White, L. K. (1990). Determinants of divorce: A review of research in the eighties. *Journal of Marriage and the Family, 52,* 904–912.

White, L. K. (1991). Determinants of divorce. In A. Booth (Ed.), *Contemporary families: Looking forward, looking back* (pp. 150–161). Minneapolis, MN: National Council on Family Relations.

Wineberg, H. (1994). Marital reconciliation in the United States: Which couples are successful? *Journal of Marriage and the Family, 56,* 80–88.

Wineberg, H. (1995). An examination of ever-divorced women who attempted a marital reconciliation before becoming divorced. *Journal of Divorce and Remarriage, 22,* 3–4.

Wiseman, R. (1975). Crisis theory and the process of divorce. *Social Casework, 56,* 205–212.

Wood, S., Scarville, J., & Gravino, K. (1995). Waiting wives: Separation and reunion among Army wives. *Armed Forces and Society, 21,* 217–236.

Wright, D. W., & Price, S. J. (1986). Court-ordered child support payment: The effect of the former spouse relationship on compliance. *Journal of Marriage and the Family, 48,* 869–874.

Zill, N., Morrison, D. R., & Coiro, M. J. (1993). Long-term effects of parental divorce on parent–child relationships, adjustment, and achievement in young adulthood. *Journal of Family Psychology, 7,* 91–103.

Zinn, M. B., & Eitzen, D. S. (1996). *Diversity in families (4th ed.).* New York: HarperCollins.

The Family and Other Institutions

The chapters in Part IV examine the interface between families and other institutions such as religion, law, work, health, policy, and the economy. An overall theme is that most families are not isolated from other institutions, but are extensively integrated with and influenced by the components of the larger society. At the same time, however, families should not be viewed simply as passive recipients of influence from other social institutions. Instead, changes in families that occur across time have considerable impact on other institutions.

Chapter 18, "Families and Religions" by Patricia Wittberg, begins by suggesting that the current popular image of families who participate in religious activities is that of traditional nuclear families sitting in church pews on Sunday. Wittberg argues, however, that this conception is not only an idea of fairly recent origins but also one that has already become seriously out-of-date. An important focus is the author's exploration of historical and cultural variations that shape the interrelationships between religion and family. More specific issues include the changing roles of church and family, the impact of changes in families on religion, the influence of religion on family, doctrinal changes, and alienation of nonnormative families. Wittberg reminds us that a long history of tension has existed between churches and families in areas such as who has primary authority over its members and the principal placement of a person's duty and responsibility. She further notes that both institutions currently appear to be flexible and vibrant.

Chapter 19, "Economics and the Family," by Paul Carlin, reveals that only three decades have past since modern economic analysis was initially applied to family issues. Many topics of current concern involve (1) economic factors and their consequences for marriage and marital dissolution, (2) time allocation in paid labor and household tasks, (3) the wage inequality between men and women, (4) the economic status of children and the elderly, (5) poverty and welfare reform, and (6) the intergenerational transfers of wealth and human capital. An important perspective conveyed by the author is that individuals rationally pursue self-interest except in cases where altruism and caring is invoked within families. In his conclusion, Carlin provides concise summary statements of the research in several areas concerned with economics and the family.

Chapter 20, "American Families and American Law," by David Rosen, provides an overview of family law and notes that except for criminal acts between family members (e.g., domestic violence), most family law comprises civil laws governing the foundation and dissolution of family and kinship relationships. Much of this body of law defines the legally imposed rights and duties governing these relationships. Rosen examines various aspects of marriage and divorce, child support, custody, and visitation, as well as the legal issues involving adoption, surrogacy, and sperm donation. An important conclusion he makes is that changes in the legal system reflect redefinitions of the privileged legal status of nuclear families in a direction that recognizes a greater multiplicity of claims and relationships—a continuing transformation from status to contract.

Linda Haas, in Chapter 21, "Families and Work," examines the impact of unpaid family work, labor force participation, and company policies on family life. She discussed the reciprocal effects of family and work with attention to research on families that tends to be overlooked: minority, rural, working-class, remarried, and single-parent families. She concludes by suggesting that future research is beginning to consider the nongendered interdependence between work and family systems. She also reports that social beliefs about work, parenting, and gender influence marital dynamics and the participation of family members in unpaid family work (e.g., domestic work). Haas suggests that this scholarship needs to be extended to a wider variety of families that are more representative of contemporary U.S. society.

Douglas Crews and Hector Balcazar, in Chapter 22, "Exploring Family and Health Relationships: The Role of Genetics, Environment, and Culture," examine the concept of health and well-being and the genetic factors that influence family members' health status throughout life. They present a biological foundation for understanding family genetic patterns (e.g., inherited disease) as well as a discussion of lifestyle factors such as obesity and smoking on health status. The authors describe several models that add to our understanding of the relationships between family and health. Crews and Balcazar conclude, in turn, that even when equality exists in access to health care, environment and genetics continue to play a very important role in health status.

Chapter 23, by Phyllis Moen and Kay Forest, "Strengthening Families: Policy Issues for the Twenty-First Century," discusses recent governmental legislation, including the Family and Medical Leave Act of 1993, the Child Care and Development Block Grant of 1990, the Family Support Act of 1988, and the recently passed Personal Responsibility Act that places a 2-year lifetime limitation on welfare except in extraordinary circumstances. The authors also examine tacit family policy regarding new reproductive technologies and family formation. Moen and Forest conclude with a discussion on the role of government in bridging the gaps between family needs and family resources. A key point is that government should provide support for families without promoting dependency and work in partnership to promote well-being without constraining families' options and opportunities.

CHAPTER 18

Families and Religions

Patricia Wittberg

Introduction

The respective roles of religion and the family—and the relationships between these roles—have been redefined several times throughout history. The current popular image of a father, a mother, and two small children praying together in a church pew on Sunday is a relatively recent formulation—and is already seriously out-of-date. In this chapter, we first survey the roles for religion and the family that have been devised in other societies and during other historical epochs. We then explore how the rise of Protestantism led to our current stereotype of Church and family. Finally, we survey research on how contemporary developments in each institution are affecting the other.

Historical and Cultural Variations

Throughout most of humanity's existence, and still today in many parts of the world, religious beliefs and practices have largely coincided with the daily life of the family. One's religion, like one's parentage and clan affiliation, was an essential part of one's very identity, no more subject to personal choice than the act of breathing (Casanova, 1994, p. 45). As one study of Latino Catholicism put it:

> [A]ll the members of the pueblo were conscious of being members of a community, and the community of necessity was Catholic. When a Latin American said he was *catolico*, or, more commonly, *muy catolico*, very Catholic, he did not necessarily mean he had been at Mass or the sacraments; he simply meant that he was a member of a pueblo, which was Catholic.... Practice of the faith in the United States is not a

Patricia Wittberg • Department of Sociology, Indiana University–Purdue University at Indianapolis, Indianapolis, Indiana 46202.

Handbook of Marriage and the Family, 2nd edition, edited by Marvin Sussman, Suzanne K. Steinmetz, and Gary W. Peterson. Plenum Press, New York, 1999.

> community manifestation; it is a matter of personal choice or commitment. The Latins, on the other hand, are "Catholic" because they belong to a Catholic people. (Fitzpatrick, 1983, p. 238, see also Espin, 1994, p. 317)

In such a relatively undifferentiated social structure, one's religion did *not*, necessarily, imply regular attendance at church services, or even completely orthodox beliefs: "Indeed, precisely because the official Christian structure of society guaranteed that everybody was leading Christian lives, it was not so necessary to stress personal devotion. It was the structure itself that was religious, not necessarily the personal lives that people lived within it" (Casanova, 1994, p. 16; see also Carroll, 1989, pp. 31–37).

Religious affiliation, therefore, did not involve personal choice. One was a Catholic because one was Mexican (or Italian); Orthodox because one was Serbian or Greek; Jewish because one was born into the Jewish community. Once members of these nationalities migrated to religiously pluralistic U.S. cities, their traditional, family-centered faith worlds enabled them to retain—or even intensify—their ethnic identity (Diaz-Stevens, 1994; Hargrove, 1983a; Orsi, 1985; Tomasi, 1975). One Detroit study concluded that urban religious groups should be thought of as "not only as associations, but as subcommunities as well; not merely as carriers of religious norms in any narrow sense, but as the carriers of complex subcultures relevant to almost all phases of human existence" (Lenski, 1963, p. 334). Urban religious groups helped new and second-generation immigrants retain their unique identity in a heterogeneous urban environment.

Of course, these family and clan-centered faith worlds often interacted with professional religious "specialists." Various wandering holy men or solitary hermits might serve as sacred talismens to whom petitioners might have recourse. An organized priesthood might exist as well. Some of these priests maintained the shrines that served as focal points for popular pilgrimages or festivals. In many societies, however, the priestly caste was either tied to, or identical with, the ruling elite. The rulers of ancient Egypt and Mesopotamia, of pre-Columbian Mesoamerica and medieval Japan, for example, were semidivine priest-kings whose role it was to represent the nation as a whole to its god. This separately organized professional religion, however, did not relate in any significant way to the daily lives of families. Families had their own gods and protective spirits, whom they honored in their own rituals.

Attempts of separately organized religions such as Christianity to influence family life were often fiercely resisted—both by the state and by the family. Several historians have pointed out, for example, that the early Christians' claims of a right to *choose* whether and whom to marry struck at the very foundations of the state's—and the family's—authority (Brown, 1988; Pagels, 1988). Christianity per se wasn't illegal in the Roman empire, but virginity certainly was (McNamara, 1985). Third- and fourth-century Roman women, however, were especially attracted to the new faith, since its option of virginity freed them from onerous family demands and arranged childhood marriages (Brown, 1988; McNamara, 1985; Pagels, 1988). The early Christian Church, therefore, wielded great influence over the family lives of its female converts. Their unconverted parents and other relatives, meanwhile, viewed the Church hierarchy as an unwanted interloper, luring children from their familial responsibilities.

The conflict between Church and family—and between Church and state—was short-lived. With the collapse of the Western Roman Empire, medieval Christianity became a collection of "community cults" in which local community membership and religion were again coextensive. "Within this structure, there was much room for fusion as well as fission between Christian and pagan, official and popular forms of religiosity" (Casanova, 1994, p. 16). The Church also advanced an alternate, pseudofamily model—that of celibate monks and nuns in monasteries—which it claimed was superior to earthly familial relations. By and large, throughout the Middle Ages, Church and family left each other alone.

Not until after the Reformation did the Catholic Church attempt to reassert its authority over family-centered religion (D'Antonio & Cavanaugh, 1983; Hargrove, 1983). But the long-established "popular Christianity" of families and village communities usually resisted these newfangled clerical attempts to impose a more officially-sanctioned set of beliefs and practices (Bretell, 1990; Carroll, 1989; Orsi, 1985; Tomasi, 1975). Over the centuries and all across Europe, clergy and families engaged in complex negotiations and compromises over the relative realms of family-centered and church-centered Catholicism (Bretell, 1990; Hynes, 1989).

The simmering hostility between the professional clergy and the familial practitioners of "folk" Catholicism has been noted by several historians and anthropologists. According to Orsi (1985), the *domus* or family household, *was* the religion of Italian Harlem between 1880 and 1950. Unattached individuals outside the domus—primarily unmarried women and priests—were targets of suspicion and ridicule. It was widely assumed that the priests were not *really* celibate, but were violating the sanctity of the domus by illicit sexual liaisons with its female members. A similar folk suspicion has been reported for rural Portugal (Bretell, 1990), Spain (Behar, 1990), and Brittany (Badone, 1990a) in the twentieth century. Interestingly, Orsi notes, religious order priests such as Dominicans or Franciscans were less suspect than diocesan priests, perhaps because the familylike structure of their orders resembled the domus. Also, order priests often supported the popular desire for family- and village-centered ceremonies when the diocesan clergy opposed them (Badone, 1990a; Engh, 1992; McCrea & Markle, 1992).

In their role as the custodians of the family, women played key roles in the domus-centered religion—roles often denied them in the male-dominated, institutionalized Church. Latina women have traditionally constructed and maintained the home altars that remain a prominent feature even in urban apartments (Diaz-Stevens, 1994). Kaufman (1991) theorizes that Orthodox Judaism is so appealing to ba'alat teshuvah—the women who return to orthodoxy from less observant traditions—precisely because it provides them with a sacralized family role:

> Orthodoxy is appealing ... because, as a woman, she claims she brings spirituality into the world: "You know, since the destruction of the second temple, the family is like the 'holy tabernacle' on earth. Each week I bring divine presence into this household by preparing for Shabbos, I *make* Shabbos.... When I separate and burn a portion of the challah [Sabbath bread], when I light the candles to welcome the Shabbos queen, I am like a high priestess. When I went to Bais Chana, we learned that women create the middot [character] formation of the Jewish people. (p. 41; see also Jacobs, 1996)

Individual women may also have a special, public status in the local community's folk religion. Diaz-Stevens (1994) speaks of the *rezadora*, a pious, elderly woman known for her wisdom and the efficacy of her prayers. In the New York Puerto Rican community which Diaz-Stevens studied, twice as many would go to a rezadora for prayers or advice as would go to a priest. In rural Puerto Rico, "la rezadora ... is often asked to lead the petitions or thanksgiving prayers for a good crop, just as her prayerful guidance is sought in times of drought or floods, at weddings, baptisms, in the commemoration of the final departure of a friend or relative, and for special feastdays, such as the patron saint of the nation, region, or town" (Diaz-Stevens, 1994, p. 250). Other sacralized ritual roles for women included the *santiguo*, in which the *comadrona* (midwife) prayed over the expectant mother and blessed her unborn child, and *el perdon y el ajuste de cuentas* (the settling of accounts), in which the *curandera* or faith healer called together the friends and family members of a dying person. Eastern Jewish immigrant women perform similar ritual functions in modern Israel (Sered, 1991).

By far the more common pattern, therefore—both historically and today—is for the family, clan, and village to be the loci in which the most significant "religious" activities are carried out and for the clan, family, or village members to be the principal organizers and participants in them. If a professional clergy or an organized church exists, it maintains a dialectical and negotiated relationship with its putative flock, permitting some practices to continue unchecked, actively encouraging folk religion when it suits institutional interests, and not *really* expecting the laity to be regular participants at formal church services.* Rarely, if ever, is it successful in imposing formal Church doctrine and practices on the domus-centered religion.†

If this pattern, common as it is, appears strange and unfamiliar to the American reader, there is a reason. The archetypical American stereotype of Church and family is based, not on the dialectic between a domus-centered religion and an often celibate and *non*-family-attached clergy, but rather on a new model developed by the Protestant Reformation.‡ It is to this model that we now turn.

The Reformation and "Voluntaryism"

The Protestant Reformation ushered in a new pattern—an "axial shift"—for the relationship between the family and religion (Casanova, 1994, pp. 51, 69). Instead of being considered part of a religion simply because of one's membership in a certain family, village, or ethnic group, one was expected to make a voluntary and personal decision to accept the official doctrines of a specific church and to participate in its formal rituals (Hargrove, 1983a). With the arrival of Protestantism, therefore, a shift took place from the "community cult" to which all automatically belonged by birth to "religious communities," which are constituted "in and through the association and congregation of individuals in response to a religious message" (Casanova, 1994, p. 46).

This new associational model implied risks, both for the

church and for the family: "The world of voluntary associations is ... dynamic, as people take up and put down group loyalties" (Sandomirsky & Wilson, 1990, p. 1211). Individuals might choose *not* to join the church, which would then lose members or split into sects (Hargrove, 1983a). And the family lost the assurance that its children would automatically be part of the same religious system as their parents and other adult relatives. Both institutions thus devised a mutually beneficial role-sharing. The role of parents was to socialize their children so that they would someday make their personal decision for Christ and also to encourage each other in living out their own religious commitment (Hargrove, 1983b). The role of the church was to supply structures and activities to assist the family in its God-given task.*

Protestant voluntaryism was thus filtered through the nuclear family, *not* through some larger clan or ethnic group. As Vidich and Bensman (1968) reported of one small town in the 1950s:

> Children, with few exceptions, adopt the church of their parents. However, affiliation by kinship does not assure family continuity in a given church. In the Protestant churches, unless the husband is without a church, the wife upon marriage affiliates with the church of her spouse and any children who are products of this mating do likewise. Siblings and first cousins who all trace their descent to a common maternal grandfather can belong to different churches.... Beyond the nuclear family, kinship groups are not identified with a particular church. (p. 230).

In Protestant Christianity, therefore, a sort of "mutual backscratching" existed between home and church (Ammerman & Roof, 1995, p. 6). Churches were to help families have healthy relationships and rear well-disciplined, religious children.† Families, in their turn, were urged to inculcate in their children the doctrines and values of the church.

The Changing Roles of Church and Family

The mutual relationship that developed between church and family in Protestant America was formalized during the 1950s in the theories of Talcott Parsons. According to Parsons, modern society has become more institutionally differentiated, with many functions formerly fulfilled by the family having been moved to the public sphere. The primary role of the family is now expressive: fulfilling its members' emotional needs, "binding up the wounds" received in the public arena, and training the next generation in needed values and

---

*Espin (1994) recounts incidents in which popular religious symbols and practices were invoked by the lower clergy in the Mexican Catholic Church in their struggles against the pro-Spanish hierarchy, and by all Latin American church leaders later in the nineteenth century in their struggles against the Enlightenment.

†See Brettel (1990) and Orsi (1985) for unsuccessful attempts by the clergy to gain control over Portuguese and Italian feste.

‡One could argue that even Catholicism has adopted the Protestant model for the relationship between church and family in recent decades, at least since Vatican II (see Badone, 1990b; Behar, 1990; D'Antonio & Cavanaugh, 1983; A. J. Perrez, 1994).

---

*For example, Pevey et al. (1996) report that motherhood and family concerns were the chief topics that regularly surfaced in the bible study group they observed.

†A recurring topic of church-sponsored research is whether churches are successful in doing this. See, for example, Burkett's (1993) study on whether a family's church membership helps discourage teens from drinking.

discipline (Parsons, 1960; see also Wright, 1995, p. 273). The childrearing practices of the family provide the "plausibility structure" (Berger, 1969) or the "mental model" (Kirkpatrick & Shaver, 1990), which, then internalized by the children, enables them to become productive members of society.

"The place modernity assigns to religion is 'home,'" understood not as the physical space of the household but as 'the abiding place of one's affections (Webster's).' Home is the sphere of love, expression, intimacy, subjectivity, sentimentality, emotions, irrationality, morality, spirituality, and religion" (Casanova, 1994, p. 64). Parsons did not believe that the Church any longer had much *direct* influence on the larger society's values, but that it could exercise *indirect* influence in "assisting parents to socialize their children and to achieve emotional satisfaction with each other" (Parsons, 1960, p. 16). Such a role is vitally necessary in modern society, with its large, impersonal government and industrial bureaucracies. The function of the family and the Church is to serve as the major remaining structures that mediate intimacy and community in the modern world (Berger, 1977; Hargrove, 1983a).

Recently, however, social scientists have begun to question these theories. They doubt whether the Church, through the family, really transmits values and valued behavior to the next generation and also whether churches and families together can, or should, mediate community and intimacy in an ever-changing and increasingly large-scale society. The idea of Church and family as havens from modern society

> lead[s] to three powerful, if misleading, conclusions: one, that modernity is necessarily destructive of community; two, that larger, cultural re-organizing processes have not already permeated these sectors; and three, that the family and the church provide sanctuary—if not protection—from the negative consequences of change. (Marler, 1995, p. 24)

For these critics, the Church and the family have already changed—dramatically. And it is an open question to what extent they an continue to fulfill their mutual bargain of protecting and passing on religious beliefs and values—or whether it is even necessary that they do so.

Changes in the Family

As has been amply documented in the other chapters in this volume, the family has changed dramatically during the past few decades. Whereas the percentage of American households consisting of married persons with children was 40% in 1970, it was barely 26% in 1990 (Marler, 1995). The percentage of marriages ending in divorce is about 40%; more than half of all children spend at least some time in a single-parent family before reaching adulthood. About 6% of all U.S. couples are living together without being married.

Perhaps the most striking figure is the increase in persons living alone: From 1 in 10 in 1950 to 1 in 4 in 1992. Those individuals who do marry are waiting until later ages before they "tie the knot": In 1960, only 28% of women ages 20–24 were single; now two-thirds are. The median age at marriage rose 3 years between 1970 and 1990 (Kosmin & Lachman, 1993). Couples are having fewer children, if indeed they have any at all: In 1960 almost 90% of married women in their late 20s had had at least one child, but by 1991, only 71% had done so. Married women with small children are also much more likely to be working outside the home, and some 54% of preschool children are cared for outside the home (Chadwick & Garrett, 1995).

For some subpopulations, the figures are even more striking. Over 50% of all African American families are headed by a single parent, usually the mother (Ingrassia, 1994). African American women are far less likely than white or Latina women ever to marry (25% as compared to fewer than 10% have never married). Among Latinos, Puerto Ricans have the highest rate of single-parent families: 35.3% as compared to 16.4% for Mexican Americans and 14.9% for Cuban Americans (L. Perez, 1994). According to many researchers, this is due to the devastating effects of U.S. deindustrialization on these vulnerable populations (Gilkes, 1995).

To sum up, therefore, "the family" of the 1990s often looks quite different than "the family" of the 1950s—which, in turn, was different from "the family" of earlier decades. To what extent, if at all, have churches adapted to these changes?

Changes in the Churches

To complicate matters, churches have also been changing. Among the causes of these changes have been the increased institutional segmentation of American society and the rise in "expressive individualism" in U.S. culture (Bellah, Madsen, Sullivan, Swidler, & Tipton, 1986). A "second disestablishment" has occurred, so that each institutional sphere—education, industry, government—has begun to generate its own separate normative system (Casanova, 1994). Isolated from any significant political, moral, or economic role in the public arena, religion has become "the vehicle, in the individual realm, of personal fulfillment and integration" (Marciano, 1988, p. 287). "The church has lost authority and power over society, over persons in the society, and even over persons in the church itself, many of whom might be described as *in* the church but not *of* it. The church has become a service institution, functioning to help *individuals* attain authenticity and transcendental subjectivity" (Reiff, 1995, p. 201; emphasis in original).

"Of all the recent religious changes in America, few

are more significant, or more subtle, than the enhanced religious individualism of our time" (Roof & McKinney, 1987, p. 40). For the overwhelming majority of Americans, religion has now become a thoroughly privatized choice (Roof & Gesch, 1995). For almost half of the respondents in one study, even one's family has no authority to influence one's personal religious preference—a striking change from the familial role in faith transmission that had been envisioned in traditional Protestantism (Roof & Gesch, 1995). One-third of all Americans change their religious affiliation at least once in their lives (Sandomirsky & Wilson, 1990).

Once they become church members, individuals often feel no special obligation to defer to church authority on either doctrine or morality. This can lead, on the one hand, to religious syncretism—a "cafeteria" Presbyterianism or Catholicism—in which "individuals are on their own in their private efforts to patch together the fragments into a subjectively meaningful whole" (Casanova, 1994, p. 37). It can also result in a resistance to *any* church attempts to impose behavioral standards:

> Questions of authority, discipline, practice, and common life often seem foreign, or at least secondary. Foremost is the individual's choice of whether to pursue a "religious matter;" then come whatever commitments of a personal or communal sort, if any, a person may choose to make. (Roof & McKinney, 1987, p. 40)

Such lay independence erodes the power of the clergy. Americans

> increasingly question all authority, hierarchy and domination.... This is a particular problem for those hierarchically organized Protestant denominations, such as the Episcopalians, Lutherans, and Methodists, who can no longer expect their laity, as the old adage says, to "shut up, sit up, and pay up." The clergy have responded by dispensing as far as possible with their clerical collars and other robes of office, opening up their ranks to women, and adapting their once-powerful role as pastors into that of enablers, facilitators, and managers of communities of the faithful. (Kosmin & Lachman, 1993, p. 233)

In the resulting "buyers' market" for church affiliation, individuals "shop around" for a local church that fulfills their personal preferences and needs—and, secondarily, the needs of their minor children, should they happen to have any (Berger, 1969; Casanova, 1994; Finke & Stark, 1992; Kosmin & Lachman, 1993). Most Americans have never had an "absolute allegiance" to a particular denomination (Casanova, 1994, p. 54). It is relatively easy to leave one that fails to satisfy or that challenges one's personal lifestyle:

> The erosion of church's ability to enforce sanctions has been widely discussed in recent literature.... If church leaders choose to maintain adherence to traditional teachings, then they are left with two alternatives when they face dissention. They can withhold strong negative sanctions, look the other way, and accommodate dissenting members, or they can impose strict sanctions and face the prospect of losing members to other churches. (Demmitt, 1992, p. 5)

Especially with regard to deviations in family patterns—working mothers, divorce and remarraige, premarital pregnancy—church officials are now more constrained to accommodate to these changes rather than challenge them.

To summarize these changes, one might cite the new church–family pattern observed by Marciano (1988):

> One or both spouses, having chosen a set of religious beliefs suitable to their personal needs, transmit them to their children. Children enter the same religious market and are subject to the various competing normative systems offered by religious and secular culture. As they grow older, children synthesize their own beliefs, which may involve changes in religious affiliation by intensity, or by denomination, or it may involve disaffiliation. (p. 288)

The effects of this new, individualized ethos on churches have become increasingly evident in recent decades. Denominational structures and identities are weakened to the point of irrelevance. Parachurch movements with familial foci–Promise Keepers, the Million Man March, Teens for Christ—flourish alongside churches, often drawing greater loyalty and participation from church members, and even from the clergy, than their putative denominational affiliation does. A new restructuring of church boundaries—or lack of boundaries—seems to be taking place. What familial role can religion play in this new environment?

Family Surrogates and Family Residues

As has already been noted, the traditional sociological theory concerning the relationship between family and religion in modern Western society has been Parsons' formulation that religion is a private affair relegated to the sphere of the home. Recently, the disintegration of the family and the expansion of religious individualism have called into question the Church's relevance and future in this model.

A competing theory does exist, however. According to the Family Surrogate Theory advanced by Glock, Ringer, and Babbie (1967), churches are most attractive to those *deprived* of family ties. A similar hypothesis is referred to, and partially supported, by Kirkpatrick and Shaver (1990), who argue that belief in a loving god is a compensation, among some individuals, for a lack of family closeness while they were growing up (see Taylor & Chatters, 1988, for a similar finding among African Americans). If true, this would imply that family disintegration and stress would lead to an *increased* role and influence for churches. Christiano (1986), however, failed to replicate Glock and colleagues' findings and concluded that churches did not fulfill a surrogate family role for those deprived of natural family ties.

Marler (1995) has further argued that any involvement in church activities and worship by isolated individuals not currently in "two-parent-with-children" families is a "family residue" effect: These are widows and elderly couples who had begun to be active in their church as young parents and who continue this involvement after their children are grown. Young singles, "dinks" (double income no kids), and single mothers with small children generally do not participate in church-based religious activities. Further research remains to be done to clarify exactly how, if at all, churches function as substitutes for family ties.

What, then, is the relationship between religion and the family today? How is it changing, as church and domestic patterns change? Subsequent sections of this chapter outline the recent research that attempts to answer these questions.

The Impact of Family Changes on Religion

As has already been noted, few American Protestants have an "absolute allegiance" to a particular denomination (Casanova, 1994, p. 54). To what extent does an individual's family exacerbate or mitigate his or her propensity to "shop around" for a religious affiliation? A number of studies have found that persons who marry and have children are more likely to increase their religious participation, less likely to apostasize, and more likely to return to the Church after dropping out (Chaves, 1991; Roof, 1990; Sherkat & Wilson, 1995; Stoltzenberg, Blair-Loy, & Waite, 1995). Marriage can even neutralize other factors that might otherwise lead to disaffiliation. Peterson (1994) found that, while increased education normally resulted in a decline of conservative religious beliefs, this was not the case if the conservative was married to an equally conservative and equally educated spouse. The religiously beneficial effect of marriage holds true for African Americans as well as for whites (Taylor, 1988b); however, there are some indications that the relationship between marriage/parenthood and religious participation is less strong for Catholics than it is for Protestants (Mueller & Cooper, 1986). There are other differences as well. Getting married and having children before the age of 25 reduces the likelihood of apostasy and increases the likelihood of return to the faith for men, but is a much less significant factor for women (Sandomirsky & Wilson, 1990; Wilson & Sherkat, 1994). The beneficial impact of children on their parents' church attendance seems to hold only up to the age of 12 (Stoltzenberg et al., 1995).

Does marriage ever *reduce* religious affiliation? Kosmin and Lachman (1993) found that the single strongest factor in determining whether an adult will withdraw from religious participation or move to another denomination is the religious indifference or denominational affiliation of his or her spouse. Some researchers have argued that family ties are a primary factor in bringing about conversion to another religion (Sherkat & Wilson, 1995). Cult conversions, for example, have been found to spread through networks of family members (Robbins, 1983; Snow, Zurcher, & Elkand-Olson, 1980). Davidman (1991) found, however, that Orthodox Jewish synagogues grew more through individual conversions than through the affiliation of families, while both Lofland (1966) and Cohen (1975) found that the cults they studied drew members primarily from isolated individuals (see also Marciano, 1988). In some cases, therefore, marriage and family formation seem to encourage religious affiliation or reaffiliation. In other cases, however, family ties may compete with or attenuate religious participation.

Faith Transmission across Generations

How well do families still fulfill their role of passing on religious beliefs and values to the next generation? At first glance, the many recent changes in family patterns would appear to have eroded such a cross-generational link. Several authors hold that the higher age of first marriage and the postponement of childbearing serve to lengthen the interim between one's religious affiliation as a child and one's adult affiliation as a parent—the time when many young singles and married couples are least tied to formal church structures. This reduces "the sense of continuity that would 'automatically' re-affiliate young families with the religion of their childhood" (Marciano, 1988, p. 291; see also Johnson, 1976). Improved life expectancies and the relative rarity of death in a family's experience might also lessen the perceived need for religious consolation (Aldous, 1983). Increased geographic mobility may further attenuate ties to a faith community (Dashefsky & Levine, 1983). Finally, there is evidence that members of any given religious tradition are increasingly likely to marry outside of it (Glenn, 1982). What effect do these changes, and the changes noted earlier, have on the ability of families to hand on their faith?

Several studies indicate that, if the family ever fulfilled its role of faith transmission, it has much greater difficulty doing so today. Weak to nonexistent relationships have been found between parental values or practices and those of their teenage children (Cornwall & Thomas, 1990; Francis & Brown, 1991; Hoge, Petrillo, & Smith, 1982; Potvin & Sloane, 1985). There is an overall decline in religious practice as adolescents get older, and this decline appears unaffected by parents' own religiosity or their attempts to control the behavior of their children (McNamara, 1992; Potvin & Sloane, 1985). At the most, home religious observances might influence the private religious behaviors of teens, but whether or not a parent attends church has little independent impact (Cornwall, 1988; Cornwall & Thomas, 1990; Erickson, 1992). According to this research, any parental influence on the later religiosity of adult children is mediated primarily through the friendship networks that parents encouraged their offspring to develop as teenagers—possibly because they had sent them to a religious school (Cornwall, 1988; Spilka, Hood, & Gorsuch, 1985).

Other researchers have found, however, that parents' values and practices *do* influence their teenage children. Although youth are less traditional than their parents, their values resemble each other (Dudley & Dudley, 1986). Children who came from close and loving families were less likely to renounce their religion and more likely to return if they had done so (Hoge, 1988; Hunsberger & Brown, 1984; Rossi & Rossi, 1990; Sherkat & Wilson, 1995; Wilson & Sherkat, 1994). The values of the mother had more impact than those of the father, and parents who were in agreement on their own religious values had a greater impact than those who disagreed (Dudley & Dudley, 1989; Sandomirsky & Wilson, 1990).* Among Catholics, D'Antonio (1988) found that continued affiliation depended on how "joyous" the mother's approach to religion was and how close the young Catholic felt to his or her family (see also Fee & Greeley, 1981). In the 1950s and 1960s, at least, attending a parochial school had a greater effect on Catholic children who came from "devout" families (Greeley & Rossi, 1966).

The varying conclusions of this research indicate that, while all parents may *want* to pass their religious affiliation and level of practice on to their children, not all families are equally able to do so (Wilson & Sherkat, 1994). The most successful are those parents who are able to establish their child's familiarity with and preference for a certain kind of religious practice as an integral part of their early family environment. Bible-based conservative Protestant parents are especially likely to be able to do this, according to one study (Sherkat & Wilson, 1995); Catholic, Mormon, and Lutheran families, according to another (Sandomirsky & Wilson, 1990).

Recent research also indicates that parents' images of God can influence how they relate to their children—which in turn affects how their children perceive God. The more parents viewed God as loving, the more their children viewed *them* as loving, and the more loving the children perceived their parents to be, the more likely they were to image God as loving (Hertel & Donahue, 1995; see also Potvin, Hoge, & Nelsen, 1976). Conversely, "harsh punishment delivered on a regular basis by a distant, cold parent is all too likely to translate into a perception of God as harsh, uncaring, and perhaps irrational" (Ratcliff, 1995, p. 70).

To sum up, Kirkpatrick and Shaver (1990) suggest that

*Sandomirsky and Wilson (1990), however, found that parents' religious homogamy decreased the odds of apostasy only for female children.

whether or not a relationship exists between the religious values and practices of parents and their adult offspring depends on several interacting factors: how religious the parents (especially the mother) were, whether the parent–child relationship was close and secure or "avoidant" and distant, and exactly how "religiousness" was measured:

> For several measures of religiousness, and particularly those concerning theistic beliefs focusing on a personal God and on one's personal relationship with God, insecure (avoidant) parental attachments were associated with high levels of adult religiousness, and secure attachments with lower levels. However ... this relationship was observed only for respondents who had grown up with relatively non-religious mothers. (p. 329)

It will be noted that Kirkpatrick and Shaver's research postulates a relationship that is the *opposite* of that hypothesized by Parsons and that seems to support the Family Surrogate model. Conversely, Hertel and Donahue's (1995) research on God images seems more congruent with Parsons' and Berger's theories.

Doctrine Changes

The changes in the family have affected not only *whether* religious faith is transmitted to the younger generation but also the *content* of the doctrine. One of these doctrinal changes has been in the very concept of the Divinity. There has been a general decline in Americans' tendency to see God as authoritarian and punitive and an increase in the image of God as loving and indulgent (Nelsen, Potvin, & Shields, 1977; Potvin et al., 1976). Neitz (1995) noted that the Catholic charismatics she studied had "new images of God that were very different from those I had grown up with in the pre-Vatican II Roman Catholic church.... The God the Father, with whom they spoke on a regular basis, was Daddy-god, not a powerful creator and stern judge, but an affectionate parent who 'loves you just the way you are' " (p. 289). Compare this image with Capps' (1992) account of God as a stern and punishing parental figure. Hertel and Donahue (1995) postulate that this shift is at least partially due to a shift in American childrearing practices.

The Church's moral doctrines, of course, are the most frequently challenged and most frequently changed—particularly those that have to do with the family. Beginning with the Anglicans in the 1930s, mainline Protestant denominations quietly dropped their prohibition of birth control (Thornton, 1988).

> By the mid-twentieth century, nearly all Protestant denominations had approved the practice of contraception. Official acceptance of family planning was endorsed, for instance, in the 1930's by the Federal Council of Churches of Christ in America, the Connecticut Council of Churches, the American Unitarian Association, the General Council of Con-

gregational and Christian Churches, and the Protestant Episcopal Church. In the 1950's, endorsement came from the Synod of the Augustana Lutheran Church, the Methodist Church, and the Lutheran Church, Missouri Synod. (Goodson, 1996, p. 48)

By the end of the 1950s, the members of the major Protestant denominations displayed "no significant difference" in their universal approval of family planning (Goodson, 1996, p. 51).* Later, the churches' positions on homosexuality and abortion were also modified—although much less quietly (Hargrove, 1983b; Kosmin & Lachman, 1993).

The Catholic Church, on the other hand, attempted to resist the pressures for doctrinal change. In 1968, Paul VI issued Humanae Vitae, the encyclical reaffirming the ban on contraception. This action, however, "seems to have done more damage to the formal teaching authority of the pope than any other action in this century" (D'Antonio, 1988, p. 91). The Church's teachings were widely ignored, and today, young Catholic adults mirror the attitudes and practices of the American population as a whole on family issues. Only a very small minority of Catholics in any age group were willing to concede Church officials authority over contraceptive practices (D'Antonio, Davidson, Hoge, & Wallace, 1996). Similarly small was the minority of Catholics granting the Church final say in issues of divorce and remarriage or premarital sex (D'Antonio et al., 1996). "These data reveal that the Roman Catholic Church, as represented by the Vatican, has lost its moral authority as teacher on matters of family and sexual morality" (D'Antonio, 1988, p. 96).

The growing independence of their flocks leaves conservative churches in a dilemma. Demmitt (1992) found, for example, that Southern Baptist pastors continued to give verbal support to traditional family patterns, but looked the other way and did not penalize those families who deviated: "Leaders of conservative churches have responded to changes in family norms by limiting their role in the family decision-making process to that of an advisor. They clearly endorse the traditional family model, but they leave the final decision on the enactment of family roles up to the family" (pp. 16–17). Similarly, although African American churches profess the strong Christian taboo against premarital and extramarital sex, ministers' preaching on the subject was "sometimes accompanied by sly remarks akin to 'a shoe should not be bought unless it fits.' ... Most black churches probably condemn promiscuity. They probably tolerate extramarital sex conducted discretely, but condemn it if a scandal erupts" (Jackson, 1983, p. 204). African American churches, like white denominations, have also opposed divorce. But

ministers have shifted their emphasis from outright condemnation to urging couples who are considering divorce to seek pastoral counseling.

The Family Emphasis

Despite often reluctant doctrinal adaptations to changing marital patterns, the traditional nuclear family remains central to the Protestant model of religion—family relations. This is especially true for conservative Protestants: For them, the family is the "master issue," (Hanson, 1989, p. 349) an ideal, "an icon that has become endangered and is in crisis" (Hadden, 1983, p. 253). The most powerful message of these churches is one of solid, secure, and changeless familial relationships ordained by Divine fiat (Hawley, 1994). The forces of evil are seen as being actively involved in attacking the family, and, by so doing, they are attacking the basic foundations of our well-being and the very existence of our country (Hadden, 1983). To protect the family, conservative Protestant groups have gone beyond attempting to regulate sexual morality and divorce. They also oppose the entry of women into the labor force and the disruption of the "natural" authority of the husband over his wife or of parents over their children (Hall, 1995). "A major point of contention for Christian fundamentalism is the perception that the traditionally strong rights of parents are being challenged and undermined. More and more, rights of parents are either being replaced by other agents of socialization or being taken away through government intervention" (Hanson, 1989, p. 349).

Why this continued emphasis on the traditional family in such a time of change? Many analysts think that the increased family emphasis of fundamentalist writers is their defensive reaction to larger, uncontrollable societal change (Brown & Hawley, 1994; Hadden, 1983). Relatively little space in their articles and sermons is devoted to elaborating on the positive benefits of family life, such as nurturance, love, and support. "The overwhelming message that comes across ... is that the family is an institution for which the primary function is the exercise of control over the base impulses of human beings. And, at this moment in history, it stands in perilous danger of losing the battle" (Hadden, 1983, p. 254). Antifamily forces are everywhere: in a hostile Supreme Court that allows abortion and promotes the right of unmarried teens to make their own decisions about contraceptive use, in an educational system controlled by secular humanists, in an atheistic and corrupt mass media that ridicules family values. But, most of all, it is demonic in origin:

> The changes occurring in society and to the family are seen by fundamentalists NOT as a cluster of closely related cultural changes, but as a finely tuned conspiracy "coordinated

---

*Although, according to Goodson (1996), a growing minority of conservative Protestants have begun again to oppose contraception and family planning. This attitude is beginning to be reflected in seminarians at conservative Protestant seminaries.

by a master blueprint of international scope.... It is so perfectly orchestrated that it could not be anything except the handiwork of the Antichrist." (quoted in Hanson, 1989, p. 350)

The beleagured family, therefore, is an icon for all of the modern cultural changes that seem to be eroding the influence of the Church.

The family emphasis of the Catholic Church may have a similar origin and function. D'Antonio and Cavanaugh (1983) note that the nineteenth-century immigration of Catholics to the United States created severe disruptions in families, and they speculate that the Church developed its central focus of "strengthening the family and of [maintaining] a social discipline grounded in family life" precisely to meet this challenge (pp. 148–149). According to Burns (1992), once the Vatican's ability to influence political affairs was eroded by the liberal revolutions and nation-building movements of the nineteenth century, the Church began to concentrate on the one area about which it could still freely speak: family morality. In both conservative Protestantism and Roman Catholicism, therefore, a heightened family emphasis appears to be, at least in part, a reaction of Church officials to adverse social and cultural changes that they—and their flocks—could not otherwise control (Brinkerhoff & Mackie, 1988).

Mainline Protestant churches, on the other hand, have tended to adapt to changes in the family, both doctrinally and pastorally. The most common response of many churches to the increased number of married women in the workforce, for example, has been to start daycare centers (Ammerman & Roof, 1995). Books and articles offer suggestions for how religious education can address issues of importance to non-traditional families (Neff, 1995; Ratcliff, 1995; Stellway, 1995). Different relationship configurations are increasingly being accepted as natural and legitimate familial patterns: The Unitarian-Universalists, for example, have redefined the family as simply "a unit of two or more people who interact physically and emotionally in a mutually beneficial manner" (Hargrove, 1983b, p. 121). Some critics, however, worry that the openness of mainline churches to these new family types might appear *too* permissive and might neglect the ideological needs of traditional families. Conservative literature and seminars would then fill this vacuum, luring intact nuclear families away from mainline denominations (Scanzoni, 1988).

Moreover, adapting to a more diverse family population poses additional challenges that even mainline churches have difficulty meeting (Aldous, 1983; Marler, 1995). Male clergy may be ambivalent about ministering to the divorced, to single parents, or to "the sexually unhappy" (Aldous, 1983, p. 75). Several studies found that even mainline clergy felt that they had had inadequate preparation for roles as pastoral counselors in such cases (Goodson, 1996; Summers & Cunningham, 1989; White, 1995). An additional problem arises because the less traditional members—singles, working women, feminists—are less active in Church affairs than the Church's traditional population of married couples with children had been. Including too many such members in one's denomination can therefore lead to a loss of vitality (Gesch, 1995; see also Gee, 1991; DeVaus, 1984). Since the unmarried are more likely to drop out of churches altogether, denominations that concentrate on attracting and serving married couples will have fewer apostates (Sandomirsky & Wilson, 1990). Even the more liberal denominations, therefore, attract a proportionately larger percentage of traditional families than exists in the American populations as a whole (Marler, 1995).

The Alienation of "Anomalous" Families

Whether it springs from a reactive condemnation of disruptive social change or a simple difficulty in knowing how to meet the diverse needs of families in flux, there is evidence that the traditional family focus of churches may alienate those whose families or lifestyle do not conform to the standard model. Thus, while membership in a conventional family *increases* religious participation, "unconventional" families are much less well served—and less likely to participate as a result (Stoltzenberg et al., 1995). Parents who have children at extremely young ages (e.g., before age 20) do not show increased church attendance (Stoltzenberg et al., 1995). Single and divorced women with children are much less likely to participate in church activities.* Divorced, single, and separated men and women are, in fact, more likely to profess *no* religion at all (Hadaway & Roof, 1988; Kosmin, 1993). Cohabiting couples, even those who formerly attended church regularly, are less likely to attend after entering into their current stigmatized relationship (Stoltzenberg et al., 1995; Thornton, Axinn, & Hill, 1992). So are married women employed full-time outside the home (Hertel, 1995). One survey of Mormon women showed that those who worked outside the home saw their jobs as drastically decreasing their opportunity to engage in religious activities (Chadwick & Garrett, 1995). In general, nontraditional family status and egalitarian sex-role attitudes are powerful—and negative—predictors of religious involvement (Gesch, 1995).

Not only are individuals in nontraditional family lifestyles less religiously active, but they are also less likely to

*Taylor and Chatters (1988) found that being divorced was associated with reduced church support among blacks as well as among whites. Stoltzenberg, Blair-Loy, and Waite (1995), however, found that the divorce/religious participation relationship held true for men, but that divorce actually *increased* older women's religious participation.

pass the faith on to subsequent generations. They are more likely to support individual choice in whether or not their children attend church and are less likely to stress religion in general (Dudley & Dudley, 1989; Robinson, 1994; Roof & Gesch, 1995). This relationship holds for Jews as well as Christians (Brodbar-Nemzer, 1986; Dashefsky & Levine, 1983).

In general, African Americans have higher levels of church participation and religious practice than do whites (Levin, Taylor, & Chatters, 1994; Taylor, 1988b; Taylor & Chatters, 1986). But African American churches have also begun to have difficulty attracting individuals who are in less than traditional families, especially in the urbanized areas of the northeast, north central, and western United States (Ellison, 1997; Ellison & Gay, 1990; Taylor, 1988a,b). Male participation overall is low: 75% of black churchgoers are women, and this figure rises to 90% in many Holiness and Pentecostal congregations (Kosmin & Lachman, 1993; Taylor, 1988a). "This absence of black men has been explained alternatively and concurrently by their overinvolvement with the criminal justice system, their higher mortality rates, their shame at unemployment and impoverishment, and their alienation from the historic relationship between black women and the pastor" (Gilkes, 1995, pp. 186–187). Black churches are also relatively disconnected from the "matriarchal proletariat" in many inner cities (Jackson, 1983, p. 206). Outside of the South, other organizations and lifestyles compete with the churches for the allegiance of young blacks, which dilutes the traditional influence that religion has had on the African American family (Ellison & Gay, 1990). Many African American churches have therefore made aggressive attempts to attract more male members, a campaign they link explicitly to the needs of black families. As one pastor stated, "When you build black men, you build strong families and strong communities [and] you can't complain about that" (Goldman, 1990; p. B2; see also Youngblood, 1990). But while researchers have found most African American churches to be actively involved in family support and community outreach programs, there is less data available on how successful these efforts are at reaching the poorest and most alienated segments of the black community (Caldwell, Greene, & Billingsley, 1992; Ellison, 1997).

There is some evidence, in fact, that the increasing isolation of African Americans in poverty-impacted inner cities continues to pose a major challenge to black churches. Their middle- and working-class members—the majority of whom are elderly women—are often at a loss in addressing the systemic issues that lie at the root of family and community ills:

> Thus, the ministry of the church to the local community and the ministry of the church to the congregation become increasingly divergent. The family emergencies that are representative of the current problems facing poor black families may occur in the members' family networks, but these do not confront the congregation regularly and directly. The nephew who is arrested, or the grandson who is shot, or the granddaughter who is pregnant, is not present to confront the congregation immediately. The pastor knows about the situation and responds—conducting the funeral, visiting the hospital with his or her parishioner, dedicating or christening the infant with AIDS, or going to the detention center on grandmother's behalf. However, the hard-won respectability of this older and more sedate congregation is maintained at the price of secrecy and denial about the actual proximity of social problems to their own lives (Gilkes, 1995, p. 185; see also Baer, 1988; Lincoln & Mamiya, 1990).

At least one study indicates that many churches do not have even this minimal level of involvement in the needs and lives of the poorest and most disrupted families: "Whereas the beneficiaries of the *ideal* church's purpose are the poor and unchurched as well as the current [more middle-class] members, in actuality, the members' needs take precedence over those of the other two groups" (Mukenge, 1983, p. 165). The church Mukenge studied actually refused opportunities to reach out to the poor of the area because such efforts would not help the current members and would be too much trouble to supervise adequately.

Since mainstream African American denominations have been "somewhat reluctant to address directly the issues of the underclass" (Kosmin & Lachman, 1993, p. 135), this has left a vacuum into which others have moved (Singer, 1988; Taylor, 1988a). The Nation of Islam, mainstream Sunni Moslems, and other Islamic groups have active prison ministries. As a result, it is estimated that several hundred thousand black prison inmates are Muslim, and blacks comprise some 40% of all Muslims in the United States (Kosmin & Lachman, 1993). Although most prison conversions are temporary, Muslim churches remain the only African American religious bodies that are predominantly male in membership. The strong Muslim emphasis on traditional family values is, nevertheless, attractive to many African American women as well (McCloud, 1995).

Recently, a "back to church" movement has been attracting young, middle-class black adults back to mainstream African American denominations. The returnees are concerned "with providing faith for their children, as well as finding meaning and a support system for themselves"—reasons similar to those given by returning white families (Cimino, 1996, p. 1). A few of the black mainline denominations have borrowed from the Muslims in designing special, quasimilitary programs to attract young underclass men as well. Whether these initiatives will be sufficient to overcome the alienation of those who see the Church as concerned primarily with traditional, "respectable" families, and not with persons like themselves, remains to be seen.

Changes in U.S. families have had wide-ranging impacts on churches and on the practice of religion. While some families are successful in maintaining religious commitment among their members, others—especially nontraditional families—are not. Some churches have responded by quietly changing their doctrines, adopting new pastoral practices, or ignoring the situation altogether. Other churches have militantly reaffirmed traditional sexual morality and/or familial roles, with varying success. Despite these efforts, a growing population, both in the black and white communities, appears to have become alienated from established churches altogether. Some of these disaffiliated reconnect, if only temporarily, to new sectarian movements. Whether they embrace, resist, or ignore them, no churches have been unaffected by changes in the American family.

The Impact of Religion on the Family

As several authors have pointed out, the links between religious ideology and familial behavior "might more accurately be thought of as meaning interdependence between institutions than as a causal relationship" (Heaton & Goodman, 1985, p. 344). Family patterns influence religion, but the reverse is also true. An extensive literature documents the ways in which individuals' religious affiliation/commitment may influence their sexual/familial attitudes and their behavior.*

Premarital Sex and Cohabitation

Several studies have indicated that at least some types of religious affiliation continue to have a significant impact on reducing the incidence of teenage premarital sex. Heaton (1988) reported that active Mormon college students were less likely to engage in or approve of premarital sex than were either inactive Mormons or students from other denominations. McNamara (1991) found similar results for actively religious Catholic teens, as compared to less active ones at the same high school. Beck, Cole, and Hammond (1991) found that white adolescents belonging to "institutionalized sects"—Pentecostals, Mormons, and Jehovah's Witnesses— were less likely than those in other religious groups to engage in premarital sex. Teens from Baptist, other fundamentalist, or Catholic traditions, however, did not engage in premarital sex any less often than mainline Protestants.† This relationship was independent of the level of church attendance

*For a list of some of the most recent studies in addition to those reviewed here, see Thornton et al. (1992).
†A study by Ritchey and Dietz (1990) contradicts this assertion, at least for religiously active Catholics, whom Ritchey and Dietz argue do engage in premarital sex less often than do religiously active mainline Protestants.

among the teens. Beck et al. theorized that, since Baptist, Catholic, and mainline Protestant theologies all condemn premarital sexual behavior, the mere teaching of a denomination is not enough: "More likely, what appears to distinguish institutionalized sects ... is the level of commitment and social integration engendered by experiences, expectations, and involvement that may generally create higher levels of adherence to principles of faith" (p. 179).

It is interesting that the relationship between church activity and premarital sex appears to hold for white teens only. For African Americans, the effects of denominational affiliation on such practices was muted or nonexistent, although black teenage girls with no affiliation at all were significantly more likely to engage in premarital sex than either religiously affiliated blacks or religiously nonaffiliated whites (Beck et al., 1991; Brewster, 1994).

Religiosity also affects the likelihood of cohabitation. Thornton et al. (1992) found that young adults who said that their religion was important to them and those who reported frequent church attendance were less likely to live together before being married. Several other studies found that religious "nones" were less likely to marry at all (Bock & Radelet, 1988; Heaton & Goodman, 1985). Catholics, too, are less likely than Protestants ever to marry, and the more religiously committed the respondents are, the stronger this Catholic–Protestant difference becomes (Ritchey & Dietz, 1990). While these findings were based on a 1982 survey, more recent research indicates that Catholic women are slower to enter unions—both marriage and cohabitation— than Protestants, with white conservative denominations having the highest rates of marriage (Heaton & Goodman, 1985; Kosmin & Lachman, 1993; Thornton et al., 1992).

Age at Marriage

Most research has found that religious affiliation also affects the age at which people marry for the first time. Whites from fundamentalist and sectarian backgrounds are more likely to marry before the age of 20, while Catholics and non-Christians are more likely to postpone marriage (Hammond, Cole, & Beck, 1993; Thomas, 1983; Thornton et al., 1992). Again, affiliation with a fundamentalist or sectarian church did not similarly affect whether or not African Americans married at a young age (Hammond et al., 1993).

Fertility, Contraception, Abortion

Religious affiliation and commitment also impacts family size—albeit in changing ways. Although earlier studies (e.g., Westoff & Potvin, 1966) indicated that Catholics had higher rates of fertility than Protestants, the two groups appear to have converged in recent years, so that current Catholic family size mirrors the national average (Bahr & Chadwick, 1988). While Catholic family patterns are becoming less distinct, however, Conservative Protestant patterns are becoming more distinct. Several studies found that conservative religious groups have higher fertility rates, with religiously observant Mormons having the highest of all (Ammerman & Roof, 1995; Goodson, 1996; Heaton, 1988; Heaton & Goodman, 1985; Kosmin & Lachman, 1993; Marcum, 1981; Mosher & Hendershot, 1984; Thomas, 1983; Thornton, 1988). Jews, on the other hand, have traditionally had lower fertility rates, as have religious "nones" (Dashefsky & Levine, 1983). Mixed Catholic-Protestant marriages have varied effects, reducing fertility for Catholic wives, but not affecting the fertility of Protestant wives (Lehrer, 1996).

Although, as has already been mentioned, those churches that continue to oppose abortion and contraception have found their teaching widely ignored, there is nevertheless some indication that these proscriptions have had at least an initial impact. In Europe, the most rapid and earliest declines in fertility occurred in those countries where the churches were weakest (Thornton, 1988). Still, the widespread convergence of fertility rates across Catholic and mainline Protestant denominations indicates that their adherents are making their own decisions on this issue. On abortion, Catholics and white Baptists are most similar in their attitudes, supporting abortion in cases of health, birth defects, and rape (D'Antonio & Cavanaugh, 1983; D'Antonio et al., 1996). While black churches oppose abortion, incidence of this procedure has also risen among African Americans. And, unlike white fundamentalist ministers and Catholic clergy, black pastors have rarely been involved in the "pro-life" movement (Jackson, 1983).

Sex Roles

It is by now widely known that conservative Protestant denominations prescribe more traditional gender roles for married couples than do other denominations (Ammerman & Roof, 1995; Hertel & Hughes, 1987). This mirrors a tendency among conservative groups to express patriarchal images of God (Roof & Roof, 1984). Theologians, female clergy, and feminist members of mainline churches, on the other hand, have been more likely to press for a reinterpretation of the scriptural passages that appear to mandate a subordinate role for women:

> Where the feminists deal with biblical injunctions against full female participation (in New Testament books such as Acts and St. Paul's epistles), they call into question culture bound translations of scriptures and point out that, in their original languages, these books showed women occupying leadership roles in early Christianity.
>
> Jewish feminists tend to emphasize the sexually non-exclusive appeal of the Law (Torah) and the sociohistorical forces creating patriarchal rather than androgynous leadership and practices. (Marciano, 1988, p. 305)

Recently, there has been a new tendency in evangelical literature to emphasize the *mutual* submission of both marriage partners to each other, rather than to concentrate on the wife's submission alone. Conservative Protestant writers appear to be divided on this issue (Bartkowski, 1996a,b; Wilson & Musick, 1995).

Research evidence shows that the theological interpretations of these denominations are reflected in their family sex roles. Women from conservative denominations are the least likely to work outside the home (Ammerman & Roof, 1995; Heaton & Goodman, 1985), a pattern that becomes stronger the more religious the woman is (Chadwick & Garrett, 1995). Mormon women are the most likely to say that women should not work outside the home at all, but should rather help her husband's career. Mormon couples are also much less likely to divide household chores equally (Heaton, 1988). In one study, the best predictor of conservative gender attitudes was belonging to the Moral Majority (Brinkerhoff & Mackie, 1988).

Although black churches show, by and large, the same male domination of the ministry as white churches do, African American denominations do not appear to have an official position on prescribed gender roles in the family. Clearly, one reason for this is that black women have usually had to work outside the home due to the pervasive labor market discrimination against black men. At the same time, however, many African Americans continue to hold conservative theological views on family values. As a result of these conflicting pressures, one church within a denomination may support, for example, the Equal Rights Amendment, while an adjacent church may not (Jackson, 1983). An exception is the various Muslim groups:

> Perhaps the World Community of Al-Islam is the largest black religious body in the United States today to prescribe and proscribe familial behavior. In addition to segregated seating by sex during worship, the prescribed sex roles within the family are typically segregated by specific tasks. (Jackson, 1983, p. 209)

Orthodox Jewish groups, too, show a strictly traditional division of family gender roles (Davidman, 1991; Kaufman, 1991).

Why are these unequal sex roles so attractive to women? One school of thought cites the reduction in anomie that follows upon the clear delimitation of gender boundaries. Other researchers found that adhering to traditional female gender roles was considered a small price to pay if one's husband also adhered to *his* roles—supporting the family, being faithful to his spouse, becoming actively involved with raising his children, and so on:

> Some of the women said they would have been described [before their conversion to a fundamentalist Protestant sect] as "liberated women;" the only trouble was, they didn't feel liberated or happy. Something major was missing. They wanted intimate relationships with strong, sensitive men—

not an uncommon desire—but they couldn't find any. These women were interested in exploring alternative means to finding happiness and fulfillment. They expressed the sentiment of the T.V. commercial, "If you want him to be more of a man, be more of a woman" (Rose, 1987, p. 252; see also Pevey, Williams, & Ellison, 1996).

Or, as one Orthodox Jewish woman put it:

> I am a child of the liberated generation.... For all the sexual freedom I felt in my late adolescence and early adulthood, I can tell you that it was more like sexual exploitation. I felt there were no longer any rules; on what grounds did one decide to say no? If the rule was casual sex and you engaged in it, on what grounds did you say no.... What rules did you use? If you see what I'm saying, without overriding rules, or without protection of some sort, the sexual liberation meant that women were free to be exploited more by men ... the laws of *tabarat hamishpacha* [family purity laws, regulating sexuality and requiring about a two-week abstinence each month during the woman's menstrual cycle] make so much sense. For instance I am not a sex object to my husband; he respects me and respects my sexuality. Because he does not have access to me anytime he wishes, he cannot take me for granted. The separation restores our passion and places the control of it in my hands (Kaufman, 1991, pp. 9–10).

Nevertheless, evidence indicates that these women do feel several tensions: between the American ideology of equality and their church's prescribed female subordination, between the ideal of an intact marriage and staying in an insupportable one, between the economic necessity of paid work and the church's preference for stay-at-home motherhood. Ammerman (1987) found that, in the suburban fundamentalist church she studied, "the disjuncture between Fundamentalist norms and family realities is the primary cause of psychological disturbance in the ... congregation" (p. 145). And, in response to Rose's (1987) comment to her respondents that, "You have a number of strong men in this fellowship," one elder's wife quickly and passionately responded, "But it's not been without a cost—the death of women" (p. 250).

In general, most women, and their husbands, quietly make their own decisions:

> While their ideals may lead them in one direction, the reality of their family and economic situations may lead them in another.... Ideals have to be weighed alongside more mundane factors such as income, education, and family structure. In other words, one cannot necessarily predict that strong, conservative religious beliefs about a woman's role will keep her out of the labor force. (Hall, 1995, pp. 147–148; see also Stacey, 1990)

A similar disjuncture between theological prescriptions and actual practice has been found to occur in family decision making: Fundamentalist women often report making decisions with their husbands, despite the latter's official position as head of the family (Pevey et al., 1996). In all cases, gender roles are an area of negotiation and compromise—between husband and wife, and between the couple and the Church (Pevey et al., 1996).

These conflicts and negotiations are most evident in religious (and secular) communes. Aidala (1985) reported that "lack of agreement about the status, duties, and 'proper' attributes of women and men was a source of conflict and schism within secular communes" (pp. 295–296) and that the presence of children made the disagreements worse. In reaction, the members of many communal groups in New Religious Movements (NRMs) devised strongly atypical family roles for men and women: compulsory celibacy, group-controlled marriage, promiscuity, communal childrearing, and the like (Aidala, 1985; Chmielewski, Kern, & Klee-Hartzell, 1993; Robbins & Bromley, 1992; Wagner, 1982). Some groups strongly reaffirmed traditional sex role complementarities; others were self-consciously committed to enforcing equality between the sexes.

Many researchers who study communal religious groups have argued that strong dyadic marriage bonds are actually detrimental to their overall unity and that all successful communes must regulate them in some way (Coser, 1974; Kanter, 1972; Shenker, 1986; Zablocki, 1980). For most of these researchers, a high drop-out rate or actual communal dissolution would signal a failure to come to terms with marital and family roles. Several have noted that the cults that prescribed a more subordinate role for women had lower percentages of women members than those NRMs that offered more equal gender roles (Galanter et al., 1979; Harder, 1972; Harder, Richardson, & Simmonds, 1976).

At least one more recent researcher, however, has taken a more sanguine view. Palmer (1993) argues that NRMs are more diverse and fluid in their patterns of gender and authority and thus serve as a "spiritual supermarket" to women "seeking alternative spiritual, sexual and social experiences":

> She can be celibate "sister," a devoted "wife," a domineering "lover," a veiled "Nubian bride," an immortal "Yin-Yang Unit," a "breeder" of the perfect race, an ageless, celibate "daughter" with magical powers, a "quadrasexual playmate," or an asexual shaman. (p. 345)

After a "liminal period" experimenting with these roles—usually for less than 3 years—between 80% and 90% of the women leave for more mainstream adult roles (Palmer, 1993). Thus, their brief group participation serves as a rite of passage to adult sexuality.

Childrearing

If religious affiliation and commitment so profoundly affect gender roles within a marriage, it is logical to expect that childrearing practices would also be affected. While previous literature reported that Catholics were more authoritarian than Protestants in their childrearing practices and that Jews were less authoritarian (Dashefsky & Levine, 1983; Westoff, 1979), more recent research has found that Conservative Protestants have begun to surpass Catholics in this area (D'Antonio et al., 1996; Ellison & Sherkat, 1993a; Wiehe, 1990). Although Conservative Protestants and Catholics both value obedience more than mainline Protestants and Jews do, Catholics are now no more likely than the latter two groups to support corporal punishment (Ellison & Sherkat, 1993a). Ellison and Sherkat (1993b) argue that Conservative Protestants endorse corporal punishment for three reasons:

> *First*, literalists tend to take seriously (more so than other persons) the doctrine of original sin, which is partly rooted in a literal interpretation of Genesis. This doctrine holds that all persons are born sinful, tending toward egocentrism and selfishness. *Second*, literalists generally view the punishment of sin as appropriate and necessary. This basic preoccupation with themes of sin and judgment makes "shaping the will" of youngsters an especially urgent task for many conservative Protestant parents. *Third*, the Bible explicitly underscores the importance of parental discipline, and both the Old and New Testaments contain *specific* passages that appear to recommend the use of physical punishment by parents. (p. 141; see also Ellison & Sherkat, 1993a)

Similarly, another study found that parents who view human nature as basically bad are more authoritarian in their child-rearing practices (Clayton, 1988).

The darker side to this is the assertion by Capps (1992) and Greven (1991) that religiously based authoritarian discipline readily shades over into child abuse:

> Greven explores the religious legitimations that support parents' and other adults' physical abuse of children, focusing especially on the widely held religious conviction that the child enters this world with a distorted or wayward will. It is therefore the responsibility of parents to break, or at the least, so successfully to challenge and frustrate the child's natural will that he or she will then be able to respond to parental guidance and live in conformity with the superior will of God. Weak or permissive parents who fail to carry out this responsibility are abdicating their God-given obligations (Capps, 1992, p. 3)

This passage is followed by a quote from Billy Graham's biography describing the excessive physical punishment his father inflicted on him for "fretfully squirming" in church— "indicating that religion was as much the cause as it was the putative cure for his sinful temperament" (Capps, 1992, p. 3). Another author compares excessive religiosity to an "addiction" that can destroy families and traumatize children (Roberts, 1989).

Religiosity does not have an unalloyed bad effect on childrearing. One study postulates that corporal punishment may not be damaging if it is an accepted part of a close-knit community that strictly regulates its use (Ellison, Bartkowski, & Segal, 1996; see also Bartkowski, 1995; Ellison, 1996). Capps (1992) notes that religious leaders have also been in the forefront in denouncing child abuse. A new evangelical literature is surfacing among Conservative Protestants that discourages corporal punishment in favor of a more loving

approach (Bartkowski, 1996a), and one study (Weisner, Beizer, & Stolze, 1991) found that religious parents were more likely than nonreligious ones to accept the responsibility for caring for their developmentally handicapped children.

Accusations of child abuse have become a major weapon of the anti-cult movement, and so should be carefully scrutinized before being accepted at face value. Charges that "babies were being beaten" were cited by Janet Reno as a major reason for her decision to authorize the ill-fated FBI raid on the Branch Davidian compound (Ellison & Bartkowski, 1995). While some of the charges against David Koresh appear to have been true, others seem to have been the result of a pervading "moral panic" about the evil influence of cults. Research is currently underway to explore in greater depth the role of children in new religions.*

The Quality of a Marriage

Although research by Kinsey in the 1950s and by Masters and Johnson in the 1970s, showed a positive correlation between active religiosity and "sexual dysfunction, guilt, and conflict" (Marciano, 1988, p. 309), more recent studies indicate otherwise. One in-depth study of 15 couples in long-lasting marriages found that those with above-average religious practice and commitment experienced greater satisfaction in their lives and greater support in the inevitable family crises that occurred (Robinson, 1994; see also Hatch, James, & Schumm, 1986; Stinnett, 1983; Thomas & Roghaar, 1990). A study of Seventh-Day Adventists found similarly positive results, as did research on African American churchgoers (Dudley & Dudley, 1989; Dudley & Kosinski, 1990; Ellison, 1997). Of 17 studies conducted between 1938 and 1980 that were reviewed by Bahr and Chadwick (1988), 13 reported a direct and positive relationship between religiosity and marital satisfaction (see also Spilka, Hood, & Gorsuch, 1987). Greeley (1993) claims that an active prayer life and closeness to God is actually associated with a more satisfying sex life among married couples (see also Tavris & Sadd, 1977). In contrast, men who describe themselves as religious independents typically report less marital satisfaction (Bock & Radelet, 1988), and there is a statistically significant chance that persons in religiously heterogamous marriages or in a marriage with an irreligious partner will be less likely to describe their unions as "very happy" (Glenn, 1982, p. 562).

*Susan Palmer has a forthcoming edited volume, with pieces by James Richardson (assessing the evidence of child abuse against the family), Burke Rochford (second-generation Hare Krishna children), Helen Berger (on "witchlings"), and more. A few of these will be presented at the Association for the Sociology of Religion meetings in August [1996]. In fact, much of this emerging work moves well beyond the important issue of abuse/nonabuse, exploring the successes and failures of these groups in (re)defining the concept of "family," and transmitting faith across generation.

How does this tale of marital bliss among the most religious fit with the tendency of Conservative Protestants both to be more religiously involved and to expect subordinate marital roles of women? Scanzoni (1988), for example, charges that male dominance in a family fosters wife-beating and incest. Cornwall and Thomas (1990), on the other hand, asserted that, among Mormons, a feeling of belonging to the institutional church was associated with a *reduction* in family violence. McNamara (1988) argues that, because social scientists have relied on the more polemical literature and sermons of the new Christian Right, they have a biased view of these groups' family practices that neglects the more pastoral services that they also provide to married couples. The officially subordinate role of the wife does *not* mean that her opinions are not listened to: "The highest form of love will emerge in a relationship in which *each* one willingly submits to true values held by the other" (p. 295; see also Bartkowski, 1996a,b).

The relationship between religiosity and marital satisfaction is probably a complex one, depending on how both of these variables are measured. Several researchers have found indications that creedal assent, involvement in church activities, and spiritual growth are positively related to marital happiness, while biblical literalism is negatively related (Hunt & King, 1978; McIntosh & Spilka, 1995).

Divorce

It is well known that religious participation and affiliation are negatively related to divorce. In general, Conservative Protestant groups, Mormons, and Catholics have the lowest divorce rates, religious "nones" the highest (Ammerman & Roof, 1995; Bock & Radelet, 1988; Heaton & Goodman, 1985; Kosmin & Lachman, 1993; Larson, 1989). Mormons and other Protestants are the most likely to remarry after divorce; Catholics and religious "nones" are the least likely (Heaton & Goodman, 1985). Divorce rates are lower among active religious participants than among their inactive coreligionists (Heaton & Goodman, 1985; Thomas, 1983). Among Jews, the divorce rate is generally lower than among Catholics and Protestants, and Jews with greater group commitment are less likely to divorce than are noncommitted Jews (Brodbar-Nemzer, 1986, 1988; Dashefsky & Levine, 1983).

Religious intermarriage also poses problems for marital stability. As several researchers have noted, rates of intermarriage are rising for most mainline Protestant groups, for Catholics, and for Jews (Hendrickx, Lammers, & Ultee, 1991; McCutcheon, 1988), while intermarriage rates of Conservative Protestants have not changed. This appears to be due to declining cultural barriers that once separated the former groups and to the fact that "marriage in the United States has become very largely a secular institution, with religious institutions exerting only weak influences on marital choice" (Glenn, 1982, p. 564). Partners in religiously heterogamous marriages, as has already been noted, are less likely to express marital satisfaction. It stands to reason, then, that they would be more likely to divorce (Glenn, 1982; Thomas, 1983).

Religion thus continues to have a wide range of impacts on family life, at least among some populations: reducing the likelihood of premarital sex and cohabitation, raising (or lowering) the age of marriage, affecting family size, prescribing sex roles and childrearing practices, raising marital satisfaction, and reducing the likelihood of divorce. Not every denomination is able to exert these effects (although perhaps all would like to do so), and not all races, genders, or ages are subject to them. As researchers who study churches and religion cannot discount the influence of the changing family, those who study the family cannot discount that of the changing Church.

Religion against the Family

Although we tend to assume that religion is naturally supportive of family life, such is not always the case. Both institutions claim ultimate authority over their members. What happens if they disagree?

There is a long history, beginning with the story of Abraham and Isaac in Genesis (22:1–19), of the demands of religion superseding the familial responsibilities of individuals. To be sure, Abraham ultimately did not have to offer his son as a sacrifice, but Jephthah did (Judges 11:29–40). And Christ's own opinion of the subject is almost as severe: "I have come to set a man against his father, a daughter against her mother" (Matthew 10:35); "If anyone comes to me without hating his father, mother, wife, children, brothers, sisters ... he cannot be my disciple' (Luke 14:25–26). Adherents of early Christianity were expected to neglect even the most basic familial responsibilities:

> Another to whom [Jesus] said, "Follow me," replied, "let me go and bury my father first." But [Jesus] answered "leave the dead to bury their dead; your duty is to go and spread the news of the Kingdom of God." (Luke 9:59–60)

Most Christian denominations, of course, do not attempt to exercise such demanding jurisdiction over their members today. But the underlying tension between religious and parental authority remains, and to the extent that a church or sect exercises its jurisdiction, it will elicit intense opposition from the unconverted families of its members (Cornwall & Thomas, 1990; Marciano, 1988; see also Conway & Seligman, 1979; Cohen, 1975; Rudin & Rudin, 1980; Shupe & Bromley, 1979).

Many sects and cults* promote themselves as their members' "true family" and attempt to foster cathetic bonds that supersede those of their biological families (Marciano, 1988; Robbins, 1983). New converts find a sense of belonging and speak of their conversion as "coming home." Many who join such groups report that they came from emotionally distant families or had recently experienced a divorce or other familial disruption (Kirkpatrick & Shaver, 1990), but other members had loving, close biological ties. Sects tend to look with disfavor on external family obligations because members with such outside ties are less controllable (Coser, 1974; Kanter, 1972). This is especially true if the "unsaved" relatives are considered a danger to the convert's own faith (Marciano, 1988; Singer, 1988). According to Galanter (1989), such "xenophobic" fearfulness of outsiders—even *family* outsiders—is a common characteristic of cults. The new convert must then become an active agent of the cult's boundary control, breaking off all contact with his or her relatives and friends.

Such attitudes naturally cause dismay, fear, and anger in the convert's family, with potentially disastrous results for both sides. Often families unite in avowedly anti-cult groups such as Free Our Children from the Children of God, and many employ professional "deprogrammers" to abduct their child and persuade him or her to leave the cult (Marciano, 1988; Shupe, Spielmann, & Stigall, 1977). However, the more the parents assault the religious group's boundaries, the more defensive and closed the group is likely to become. Marciano (1988) and Galanter (1989) both note that many cults would *like* to establish courteous relationships with their members' families, if only as a way of attracting further recruits to the group. A more effective course of action for worried parents, Galanter found, is to adopt a "benign and accommodating attitude" to their child's newfound religion (p. 115).

Conclusions

As society changes, religion and the family change. "Not only the churches, but families, too, have become voluntary associations" in which one can *choose* to participate—

*The definitions of "sect" and "cult" have been hotly contested in sociological literature. This chapter follows Roberts (1995) in applying both terms to spiritually demanding religious groups with strong boundaries against outsiders. Sects are groups that break off from an established denomination and claim to be a more pure return to the basic faith tradition that the denomination has compromised. Examples would be Jehovah's Witnesses, various black Holiness sects, and storefront Christian churches in general. Cults are groups that claim some *new* revelation that distinguishes them from older denominations. The Unification Church, the Nation of Islam, and the Followers of the Bhagwan Rajneesh would be examples.

or not (Marciano, 1988, p. 312). As these two once powerful social institutions change, the relationships between them also change. Marriage, Glenn (1988) argues, is now a secular institution, only weakly, if at all, influenced by religion. Vast segments of the American population—the divorced, young singles, homosexual couples, single parents—confront churches that seem to be fixated on the vanished ideal of a nuclear family with a stay-at-home mother, an ideal that has less and less relevance to their actual lives. For them, churches are outmoded relics that they ignore or actively avoid. Church leaders may issue pronouncements on marital and familial issues, but few pay attention.

Religious affiliation, in its turn, has become a "thoroughly privatized choice" over which one's family has little or no control (Roof & Gesch, 1995, pp. 62–63). Parents attempt in vain to instill religious belief and practice in their offspring, only to watch their sons and daughters drift into nonobservance, apostasy, or (perhaps worst of all from a parental viewpoint) cultic alternatives that usurp familial ties.

And yet some of the fastest-growing churches and parachurch movements are those that focus on the family. Persistent patterns continue to exist between religious affiliation, belief, and practice, on the one hand, and marital happiness, familial roles, and childrearing, on the other. Even home rituals are enjoying a resurgence. To paraphrase Mark Twain's famous aphorism, the reports of the death of either institution may have been greatly exaggerated.

References

Aidala, A. A. (1985). Social change, gender roles and new religious movements. *Sociological Analysis, 46,* 287–314.

Aldous, J. (1983). Problematic elements in relationships between churches and families. In W. V. D'Antonio & J. Aldous (Eds.), *Families and religions: Conflict and change in modern society* (pp. 67–80). Beverly Hills, CA: Sage.

Ammerman, N. T. (1987). *Bible believers: Fundamentalists in the modern world.* New Brunswick, NJ: Rutgers University Press.

Ammerman, N. T., & Roof, W. C. (1995). Old patterns, new trends, fragile experiments. In N. T. Ammerman & W. C. Roof (Eds.), *Work, family and religion in contemporary society* (pp. 1–20). New York: Routledge.

Badone, E. (1990a). Breton folklore of anticlericalism. In E. Badone (Ed.), *Religious orthodoxy and popular faith in European society* (pp. 140–162). Princeton, NJ: Princeton University Press.

Badone, E. (1990b). Introduction. In E. Badone (Ed.), *Religious orthodoxy and popular faith in European society* (pp. 1–23). Princeton, NJ: Princeton University Press.

Baer, H. A. (1988). The metropolitan spiritual churches of Christ: The socio-religious evolution of the largest of the black spiritual associations. *Review of Religious Research, 30:*140–150.

Bahr, H. M., & Chadwick, B. A. (1988). Religion and family in Middletown, U.S.A. In D. L. Thomas (Ed.), *The religion and family connection: Social Science perspectives* (Religious Studies Center Specialized Monograph Series, Vol. III, pp. 51–65). Provo, UT: Brigham Young University.

Bartkowski, J. P. (1995). Spare the rod ... or spare the child? Divergent perspectives on Conservative Protestant child discipline. *Review of Religious Research, 37,* 97–116.

Bartkowski, J. P. (1996a). *Beyond biblical literalism and inerrancy: Conservative Protestants and the hermeneutic interpretation of scripture.* Unpublished paper, University of Texas at Austin.

Bartkowski, J. P. (1996b). *Debating the merits of patriarchy: Discursive disputes over spousal authority among evangelical family commentators.* Unpublished paper, University of Texas at Austin.

Beck, S. H., Cole, B. S., & Hammond, J. P. (1991). Religious heritage and premarital sex: Evidence from a national sample of young adults. *Journal for the Scientific Study of Religion, 30,* 173–180.

Behar, R. (1990). The struggle for the church: Popular anticlericalism and religiosity in post-Franco Spain. In E. Badone (Ed.), *Religious orthodoxy and popular faith in European society* (pp. 76–112). Princeton, NJ: Princeton University Press.

Bellah, R. N., Madsen, R., Sullivan, W. M., Swidler, A., & Tipton, S. M. (1986). *Habits of the heart: Individualism and commitment in American life.* New York: Harper & Row.

Berger, P. (1969). *The sacred canopy.* New York: Doubleday Anchor.

Berger. P. (1977). In praise of particularity: The concept of mediating structures. In P. Berger, *Facing up to modernity: Excursions in society, politics and religion* (pp. 130–147). New York: Basic Books.

Bock, E. W., & Radelet, M. L. (1988). Marital integration of religious independents: A reevaluation of its significance. *Review of Religious Research, 29,* 228–241.

Bretell, C. B. (1990). The priest and his people: The contractual basis for religious practice in rural Portugal. In E. Badone (Ed.), *Religious orthodoxy and popular faith in European society* (pp. 55–75). Princeton, NJ: Princeton University Press.

Brewster, K. L. (1994). Race differences in sexual activity among adolescent women: The role of neighborhood characteristics. *American Sociological Review, 59,* 408–424.

Brinkerhoff, M. B., & Mackie, M. (1988). Religious sources of gender traditionalism. In D. L. Thomas (Ed.), *The religion and family connection: Social science perspectives* (Religious Studies Center Specialized Monograph Series, vol. III, pp. 232–257). Provo, UT: Brigham Young University.

Broadbar-Nemzer, J. Y. (1986). Divorce and group commitment: The case of Jews. *Journal of Marriage and the Family, 48,* 329–340.

Broadbar-Nemzer, J. Y. (1988). The contemporary American Jewish family. In D. L. Thomas (Ed.), *The religion and family connection: Social science perspectives* (Religious Studies Center Specialized Monographs Series, vol. III, pp. 66–87). Provo, UT: Brigham Young University.

Brown, K. M. (1994). Fundamentalism and the control of women. In J. S. Hawley (Ed.), *Fundamentalism and gender* (pp. 175–202). Oxford: Oxford University Press.

Brown, P. (1988). *The body and society: Men, women and sexual renunciation in early Christianity.* New York: Columbia University Press.

Burkett, S. R. (1993). Perceived parents' religiosity, friends drinking and hellfire: A panel study of adolescent drinking. *Review of Religious Research, 35,* 134–153.

Burns, G. (1992). *The frontiers of Catholicism: The politics of ideology in a liberal world.* Berkeley: University of California Press.

Caldwell, C. H., Greene, A. D., & Billingsley, H. (1992). The black church as a family support system: Instrumental and expressive functions. *National Journal of Sociology, 6,* 21–40.

Capps, D. (1992). Religion and child abuse: Perfect together. *Journal for the Scientific Study of Religion, 31,* 1–14.

Carroll, M. P. (1989). Italian Catholicism: Making direct contact with the sacred. In R. O'Toole (Ed.), *Sociological studies in Roman Catholicism* (pp. 27–44). New York: Mellen.

Casanova, J. (1994). *Public religions in the modern world.* Chicago: University of Chicago Press.

Chadwick, B. S., & Garrett, D. H. (1995). Women's religiosity and employment: The LDS experience. *Review of Religious Research, 36,* 277–293.

Chaves, M. (1991). Family structure and Protestant church attendance: The sociological basis of cohort and age effects. *Journal for the Scientific Study of Religion, 39,* 329–340.

Chmielewski, W. E., Kern, L. J., & Klee-Hartzell, M. (Eds.). (1993). *Women in spiritual and communitarian societies in the United States.* Syracuse, NY: Syracuse University Press.

Christiano, K. (1986). Church as family surrogate: Another look at family ties and church involvement. *Journal for the Scientific Study of Religion, 25,* 339–354.

Cimino, R. P. (1996, February). Black baby boomers reshaping churches. *Religion Watch, 11*(4), 1.

Clayton, L. O. (1988). The impact of parental views of the nature of humankind upon child-rearing attitudes. In D. L. Thomas (Ed.), *The religion and family connection: Social science perspectives* (Religious Studies Center Specialized Monograph Series, Vol. III, pp. 272–282). Provo, UT: Brigham Young University.

Cohen, D. (1975). *The new believers.* New York: Ballantine.

Conway, F., & Seligman, J. (1979). *Snapping.* New York: Delta.

Cornwall, M. (1988). The influence of three aspects of religious socialization: Family, church and peers. In D. L. Thomas (Ed.), *The religion and family connection: Social science perspectives* (Religious Studies Center Specialized Monograph Series, Vol. III, pp. 207–231). Provo, UT: Brigham Young University.

Cornwall, M., & Thomas, D. L. (1990). Family, religion and personal communities: Examples from Mormonism. *Marriage and Family Review, 15,* 229–252.

Coser, L. (1974). *Greedy institutions: Patterns in undivided commitment.* New York: Free Press.

D'Antonio, W. V. (1980). The family and religion: Exploring a changing relationship. *Journal for the Scientific Study of Religion, 19,* 89–104.

D'Antonio, W. V. (1988). The American Catholic family: Signs of cohesion and polarization. In D. L. Thomas (Ed.), *The religion and family connection: Social science perspectives* (Religious Studies Center Specialized Monograph Series, vol. III, pp. 88–106). Provo, UT: Brigham Young University.

D'Antonio, W. V., & Aldous, J. (1983). *Families and religions: Conflict and change in modern society.* Beverly Hills, CA: Sage.

D'Antonio, W. V., & Cavanaugh, M. J. (1983). Roman Catholicism and the family. In W. V. D'Antonio & J. Aldous (Eds.), *Families and religions: Conflict and change in modern society* (pp. 141–162). Beverly Hills, CA: Sage.

D'Antonio, W. V., Davidson, J. D., Hoge, D. R., & Wallace, R. A. (1996). *Laity, American and Catholic: Transforming the Church.* Kansas City: Sheed and Ward.

Dashefsky, A., & Levine, I. M. (1983). The Jewish family: Continuing challenges. In W. V. D'Antonio & J. Aldous (Eds.), *Families and religions: Conflict and change in modern society* (pp. 163–190). Beverly Hills, CA: Sage.

Davidman, L. (1991). *Tradition in a rootless world.* Berkeley: University of California Press.

DeLamater, J., & MacCorquodale, P. (1979). *Premarital sexuality: Attitudes, relationships, behaviors.* Madison: University of Wisconsin Press.

Demmitt, K. P. (1992). Loosening the ties that bind: The accommodation of dual earner families in a conservative Protestant church. *Review of Religious Research, 34,* 3–19.

DeVaus, D. (1984). Work force participation and sex differences in church attendance. *Review of Religious Research, 25,* 247–286.

Diaz-Stevens, A. M. (1994). Latinas and the church. In J. P. Dolan & A.

Figueroa-Deck (Eds.), *Hispanic Catholic culture in the U.S.* (pp. 240–277). South Bend, IN: University of Notre Dame Press.

Dudley, M. G., & Kosinski, F. A. (1990). Religiosity and marital satisfaction: A research note. *Review of Religious Research, 32,* 77–86.

Dudley, R. L., & Dudley, M. G. (1986). Transmission of religious values from parents to adolescents. *Review of Religious Research, 28,* 3–15.

Dudley, R. L., & Dudley, M. G. (1989). Religion and family life among Seventh Day Adventists. *Family Science Review, 2,* 359–372.

Ellison, C. G. (1996). Conservative Protestantism and the corporal punishment of children: Clarifying the issues. *Journal for the Scientific Study of Religion, 35,* 1–16.

Ellison, C. G. (1997). Religious involvement and the subjective quality of family life among African-Americans. In R. J. Taylor, L. M. Chatters, & J. S. Jackson (Eds.), *Family life in black America* (pp. 186–209). Newbury Park, CA: Sage.

Ellison, C. G., & Bartkowski, J. P. (1995). Babies were being beaten: Exploring child abuse allegations at Ranch Apocalypse. In S. A. Wright (Ed.), *Armageddon in Waco: Critical perspectives on the Branch Davidian conflict* (pp. 111–149). Chicago: University of Chicago Press.

Ellison, C. G., & Gay, D. A. (1990). Region, religious commitment and life satisfaction among black Americans. *The Sociological Quarterly, 31,* 123–147.

Ellison, C. G., & Sherkat, D. E. (1993a). Conservative Protestantism and support for corporal punishment. *American Sociological Review, 58,* 131–144.

Ellison, C. G., & Sherkat, D. E. (1993b). Obedience and autonomy: Religion and parental values reconsidered. *Journal for the Scientific Study of Religion, 32,* 313–329.

Ellison, C. G., Bartkowski, J. P., & Segal, M. L. (1996). Conservative Protestantism and the parental use of corporal punishment. *Social Forces, 74,* 1003–1028.

Engh, M. E. (1992). *Frontier faiths: Church, temple, and synagogue in Los Angeles, 1846–1888.* Albuquerque: University of New Mexico Press.

Erickson, J. A. (1992). Adolescent religious development and commitment. *Journal for the Scientific Study of Religion, 31,* 131–152.

Espin, O. O. (1994). Popular Catholicism among Latinos. In J. P. Dolan & A. Figueroa-Deck (Eds.), *Hispanic Catholic culture in the U.S.* (pp. 308–359). South Bend, IN: University of Notre Dame Press.

Fee, J. L., & Greeley, A. (1981). *Young Catholics in the United States and Canada: A report to the Knights of Columbus.* Los Angeles: Sadlier.

Finke, R., & Stark, R. (1992). *The churching of America, 1776–1990.* New Brunswick, NJ: Rutgers University Press.

Fitzpatrick, J. P. (1983). Faith and stability among Hispanic families: The role of religion in cultural transition. In W. V. D'Antonio & J. Aldous (Eds.), *Families and religions: Conflict and change in modern society* (pp. 221–242). Beverly Hills, CA: Sage.

Francis, L. J., & Brown, L. B. (1991). The influence of home, church and school on prayer among sixteen-year-old adolescents in England. *Review of Religious Research, 33,* 112–123.

Galanter, M. (1989). *Cults: Faith, healing, and charisma.* New York: Oxford University Press.

Galanter, M., Rabkin, R., Rabkin, J., & Deutsch, A. (1979). The "Moonies": A psychological study of conversion and membership in a contemporary religious sect. *American Journal of Psychiatry, 1363,* 165–170.

Gee, E. M. (1991). Gender differences in church attendance in Canada: The role of labour force participation. *Review of Religious Research, 32,* 267–273.

Gesch, L. (1995). Responses to changing lifestyles: "Feminists" and "traditionalists" in mainstream religion. In N. T. Ammerman & W. C. Roof (Eds.), *Work, family and religion in contemporary society* (pp. 123–136). New York: Routledge.

Gilkes, C. T. (1995). The storm and the light: Church, family, work and social crisis in the African-American experience. In N. T. Ammerman & W. C. Roof (Eds.), *Work, family and religion in contemporary society* (pp. 177–198). New York: Routledge.

Glenn, N. D. (1982). Interreligious marriage in the U.S.: Patterns and recent trends. *Journal of Marriage and the Family, 44,* 555–566.

Glock, C., Ringer, B., & Babbie, E. (1967). *To comfort and to challenge: A dilemma of the contemporary church.* Berkeley: University of California Press.

Goldman, A. L. (1990, July 5). Black minister recruits more men for the church. *New York Times,* p. B2.

Goodson, P. (1996). *Protestant seminary students' views of family planning and intention to promote family planning through education.* Ph.D. dissertation, University of Texas at Austin.

Grasmick, H. G., Bursik, R. J., & Kimpel, M. L. (1991). Protestant fundamentalism and attitudes toward corporal punishment of children. *Violence and Victims, 6,* 283–297.

Grasmick, H. G., Morgan, C. S., & Kennedy, M. B. (1992). Support for corporal punishment in the schools: A comparison of the effects of socioeconomic status and religion. *Social Science Quarterly, 73,* 179–189.

Greeley, A. M. (1993). *Faithful attraction.* New York: TOR.

Greeley, A. M., & Rossi, P. (1966). *The education of American Catholics.* Chicago: Aldine.

Greven, P. (1991). *Spare the child: The religious roots of punishment and the psychological impact of physical abuse.* New York: Knopf.

Hadaway, C. K., & Roof, W. C. (1988). Disaffiliation from mainline churches. In D. G. Bromley (Ed.), *Falling from the faith* (pp. 29–46). Newbury Park, CA: Sage.

Hadden, J. K. (1983). Televangelism and the mobilization of a new Christian Right family policy. In W. V. D'Antonio & J. Aldous (Eds.), *Families and religions: Conflict and change in modern society* (pp. 247–266). Beverly Hills, CA: Sage.

Hall, C. (1995). Entering the labor force: Ideals and realities among evangelical women. In N. T. Ammerman & W. C. Roof (Eds.), *Work, family and religion in contemporary society* (pp. 137–154). New York: Routledge.

Hammond, J. A., Cole, B. S., & Beck, S. H. (1993). Religious heritage and teenage marriage. *Review of Religious Research, 35,* 117–133.

Hanson, R. A. (1989). Religion and the family: The case of Christian fundamentalism. *Family Science Review, 2,* 347–358.

Harder, M. (1972). Jesus people. *Psychology Today, 6,* 37–43.

Harder, M. W., Richardson, J. T., & Simmonds, R. (1976). Life style: Courtship, marriage and family in a changing Jesus Movement organization. *International Review of Modern Sociology, 6,* 155–172.

Hargrove, B. (1983a). The church, the family and the modernization process. In W. V. D'Antonio & J. Aldous (Eds.), *Families and religions: Conflict and change in modern society* (pp. 21–48). Beverly Hills, CA: Sage.

Hargrove, B. (1983b). Family in the white American Protestant experience. In W. V. D'Antonio & J. Aldous (Eds.), *Families and religions: Conflict and change in modern society* (pp. 113–140). Beverly Hills, CA: Sage.

Hatch, R. C., James, D. E., & Schumm, W. R. (1986). Spiritual intimacy and marital satisfaction. *Family Relations, 35,* 539–545.

Hawley, J. S. (Ed.). (1994). *Fundamentalism and gender.* New York: Oxford University Press.

Heaton, T. B. (1988). The four C's of the Mormon family: Chastity, conjugality, children and chauvinism. In D. L. Thomas (Ed.), *The religion and family connection: Social science perspectives* (Religious Studies Center Specialized Monograph Series, vol. III, pp. 107–124). Provo, UT: Brigham Young University.

Heaton, T. B., & Goodman, K. L. (1985). Religion and family formation. *Review of Religious Research, 26,* 343–359.

Hendrickx, J., Lammers, J., & Ultee, W. (1991). Religious assortive marriage in the Netherlands. *Review for Religious Research, 33*, 123–145.

Hertel, B. R. (1995). Work, family and faith: Recent trends. In N. T. Ammerman & W. C. Roof (Eds.), *Work, family and religion in contemporary society* (pp. 81–121). New York: Routledge.

Hertel, B. R., & Donahue, M. J. (1995). Parental influences on God images among children: Testing Durkheim's metaphoric parallelism. *Journal for the Scientific Study of Religion, 34*, 186–199.

Hertel, B. R., & Hughes, M. (1987). Religious affiliation, attendance, and support for "pro-family" issues in the U.S. *Social Forces, 65*, 858–882.

Hoge, D. R. (1988). Why Catholics drop out. In D. R. Bromley (Ed.), *Falling from the faith* (pp. 81–99). Newbury Park, CA: Sage.

Hoge, D. R., Petrillo, G. H., & Smith, E. I. (1982). Transmission of religious and social values from parents to teenage children. *Journal of Marriage and the Family, 44*, 569–580.

Hunsberger, B. E., & Brown, L. B. (1984). Religious socialization and apostasy. *Journal for the Scientific Study of Religion, 23*, 239–251.

Hunt, R. A., & King, M. B. (1978). Religiosity and marriage. *Journal for the Scientific Study of Religion, 17*, 399–406.

Hynes, E. (1989). Nineteenth century Irish Catholicism, farmers' ideology, and national religion: Explorations in cultural explanation. In R. O'Toole (Ed.), *Sociological studies in Roman Catholicism* (pp. 45–69). New York: Mellen.

Ingrassia, M. (1994, August 30). Endangered family. *Newsweek*, 17–26.

Jackson, J. J. (1983). Contemporary relations between black families and black churches in the United States. In W. V. D'Antonio & J. Aldous (Eds.), *Families and religions: Conflict and change in modern society* (pp. 191–220). Beverly Hills, CA: Sage.

Jacobs, J. L. (1996). Women, ritual and secrecy: The creation of crypto-Jewish culture. *Journal for the Scientific Study of Religion, 35*, 97–108.

Johnson, G. E. (1976). The impact of family formation patterns on Jewish community involvement. *Analysis, 60*, 1–5.

Kanter, R. M. (1972). *Commitment and community: Communes and utopias in sociological perspective*. Cambridge, MA: Harvard University Press.

Kaufman, D. (1991). *Rachel's daughters: Newly orthodox Jewish women*. New Brunswick, NJ: Rutgers University Press.

Kirkpatrick, L. A., & Shaver, P. R. (1990). Attachment theory and religion: Childhood attachments, religious beliefs, and conversion. *Journal for the Scientific Study of Religion, 29*, 315–334.

Kosmin, B. A., & Lachman, S. P. (1993). *One nation under God: Religion in contemporary American society*. New York: Harmony Books.

Larson, L. E. (1989). Religiosity and marital commitment: "Until death do us part" revisited. *Family Science Review, 2*, 285–302.

Lehrer, E. L. (1996). The role of the husband's religious attitudes in the economic and demographic behavior of families. *Journal for the Scientific Study of Religion, 35*, 145–155.

Lenski, G. (1963). *The religious factor: A sociological inquiry*. Garden City, NY: Anchor Books.

Levin, J. S., Taylor, R. J., & Chatters, L. M. (1994). Race and gender differences among older adults: Findings from four national surveys. *Journal of Gerontology: Social Sciences, 49*, S137–S145.

Lincoln, C. E., & Mamiya, L. (1990). *The black church in the African-American experience*. Chapel Hill, NC: Duke University Press.

Lofland, J. (1966). *Doomsday cult*. Englewood Cliffs, NJ: Prentice-Hall.

Marciano, T. D. (1988). Families and religions. In M. Sussman (Ed.), *Handbook of marriage and the family* (pp. 288–315). New York: Plenum.

Marcum, J. P. (1981). Explaining fertility differences among U.S. Protestants. *Social Forces, 60*, 532–543.

Marler, P. L. (1995). Lost in the fifties: The changing family and the nostalgic church. In N. T. Ammerman & W. C. Roof (Eds.), *Work, family and religion in contemporary society* (pp. 23–60). New York: Routledge.

Masters, W. H., & Johnson, V. E. (1970). *Human sexual inadequacy*. Boston: Little, Brown.

McCloud, A. B. (1995). *African American Islam*. New York: Routledge.

McCrea, F. B., & Markle, G. (1992, August 21). *Medjugorje and the crisis in Yugoslavia*. Paper presented at the American Sociological Association, Pittsburgh, PA.

McCutcheon, A. L. (1988). Denominations and religious intermarriage: Trends among white Americans in the twentieth century. *Review of Religious Research, 29*, 213–227.

McIntosh, D. N., & Spilka, B. (1995). Religion and the family. In B. J. Neff & D. Ratcliff (Eds.), *Handbook of family religious education* (pp. 36–60). Birmingham, AL: Religious Education Press.

McNamara, J. A. (1985). *A new song: Celibate women in the first three Christian centuries*. New York: Harrington Park Press.

McNamara, P. H. (1988). The New Christian Right's view of the family and its social science critics: A study in differing presuppositions. In D. L. Thomas (Ed.), *The religion and family connection: Social science perspectives* (Religious Studies Center Specialized Monograph Series, vol. III, pp. 285–302). Provo, UT: Brigham Young University.

McNamara, P. H. (1992). *Conscience first, tradition second*. Albany: State University of New York Press.

Mosher, W. D., & Hendershot, G. E. (1984). Religious affiliation and the fertility of married couples. *Journal of Marriage and the Family, 46*, 671–678.

Mueller, D. P., & Cooper, P. (1986). Religious interest and involvement of young adults: A research note. *Review of Religious Research, 27*, 245–254.

Mukenge, I. R. (1983). *The black church in urban America: A case study in political economy*. New York: University Press of America.

Neff, B. J. (1995). The diverse traditional family. In B. J. Neff & D. Ratcliff (Eds.), *Handbook of family religious education* (pp. 115–136). Birmingham, AL: Religious Education Press.

Neitz, M. J. (1995). Constructing women's rituals. In N. T. Ammerman & W. C. Roof (Eds.), *Work, family and religion in contemporary society* (pp. 283–304). New York: Routledge.

Nelsen, H. M., Potvin, R. H., & Shields, J. (1977). *The religion of children*. Washington, DC: U.S. Catholic Conference.

Nelsen, H. M., & Kroliczak, A. (1984). Paternal use of the threat of "God will punish." *Journal for the Scientific Study of Religion, 23*, 267–271.

Orsi, P. A. (1985). *The madonna of 115th street: Faith and community in Italian Harlem, 1880–1950*. New Haven, CT: Yale University Press.

Pagels, E. (1988). *Adam, Eve and the serpent*. New York: Random House.

Palmer, S. J. (1993). Women's "cocoon work" in new religious movements: Sexual experimentation and feminine rites of passage. *Journal for the Scientific Study of Religion, 32*, 343–355.

Parsons, T. (1960). The American family: Its relationship to personality and to the social structure. In T. Parsons & R. F. Bales (Eds.), *Family, socialization and interaction processes* (pp. 3–33). New York: Free Press.

Perez, A. J. (1994). The history of Hispanic liturgy since 1965. In J. P. Dolan & A. Figueroa-Deck (Eds.), *Hispanic Catholic culture in the U.S.* (pp. 360–408). South Bend, IN: University of Notre Dame Press.

Perez, L. (1994). Cuban families in the U.S. In R. L. Taylor (Ed.), *Minority families in the United States* (pp. 95–112). Englewood Cliffs, NJ: Prentice-Hall.

Peterson, L. R. (1994). Education, homogamy and religious commitment. *Journal for the Scientific Study of Religion, 33*, 122–134.

Pevey, C., Williams, C. L., & Ellison, C. G. (1996). Male god imagery and female submission: Lessons from a Southern Baptist ladies' bible class. *Qualitative Sociology, 19*, 173–193.

Potvin, R. H., Hoge, D. R., & Nelsen, H. M. (1976). *Religion and American youth: With emphasis on Catholic adolescents and young adults.* Washington, DC: U.S. Catholic Conference.

Potvin, R. H., & Sloane, D. M. (1985). Parental control, age, and religious practice. *Review of Religious Research, 27,* 3–14.

Ratcliff, C. (1995). Parenting and religious education. In B. J. Neff & D. Ratcliff (Eds.), *Handbook of family religious education* (pp. 61–86). Birmingham, AL: Religious Education Press.

Reiff, J. T. (1995). Nurturing and equipping children in the "public church." In N. T. Ammerman & W. C. Roof (Eds.), *Work, family and religion in contemporary society,* (pp. 199–218). New York: Routledge.

Ritchey, P. N., & Dietz, B. (1990). Catholic/Protestant differences in marital status. *Review of Religious Research, 32,* 65–77.

Robbins, T. (1983). *Cults, converts and charisma: The sociology of New Religious Movements.* Thousand Oaks, CA: Sage.

Robbins, T., & Bromley, D. (1992). Social experimentation and the significance of American new religions: A focused review essay. In T. Robbins & D. Bromley (Eds.), *Research in the social scientific study of religion* (Vol. 4, pp. 1–28). Greenwich, CT: JAI Press.

Roberts, K. A. (1995). *Religion in sociological perspective.* Belmont, CA: Wadsworth.

Roberts, T. W. (1989). Religious addiction and the family system: Implications for the family clinician. *Family Science Review, 2,* 317–326.

Robinson, L. C. (1994). Religious orientation in enduring marriage: An exploratory study. *Review of Religious Research, 35,* 207–218.

Roof, W. C. (1990). Return of the baby boomers to organized religion. In C. Jacquet (Ed.), *Yearbook of American and Canadian churches* (pp. 284–291). Nashville, TN: Abingdon Press.

Roof, W. C., & Gesch, L. (1995). Boomers and the culture of choice. In N. T. Ammerman & W. C. Roof (Eds.), *Work, family and religion in contemporary society* (pp. 61–79). New York: Routledge.

Roof, W. C., & McKinney, W. (1987). *American mainline religion.* New Brunswick, NJ: Rutgers University Press.

Roof, W. C., & Roof, J. L. (1984). Review of the polls: Images of God among Americans. *Journal for the Scientific Study of Religion, 23,* 201–205.

Rose, S. D. (1987). Women warriors: The negotiation of gender in a charismatic community. *Sociological Analysis, 48,* 245–258.

Rossi, A., & Rossi, P. (1990). *Of human bonding: Parent–child relations across the life course.* New York: deGruyter.

Rudin, J., & Rudin, R. (1980). *Prison or paradise? The new religious cults.* Philadelphia: Fortress Press.

Sandomirsky, S., & Wilson, J. (1990). Processes of disaffiliation: Religious mobility among men and women. *Social Forces, 68,* 1211–1229.

Scanzoni, L. D. (1988). Contemporary challenges for religion and the family from a Protestant woman's point of view. In D. L. Thomas (Ed.), *The religion and family connection: Social science perspectives* (Religious Studies Center Specialized Monograph Series, vol. III, pp. 125–142). Provo, UT: Brigham Young University.

Sered, S. S. (1991). Conflict, complement, and control: Family and religion among eastern Jewish women in Jerusalem. *Gender & Society, 5,* 10–29.

Shenker, B. (1986). *Intentional communities: Ideology and alienation in communal societies.* London: Routledge.

Sherkat, D. E., & Wilson, J. (1995). Preferences, constraints and choices in religious markets: An examination of religious switching and apostasy. *Social Forces, 73,* 993–1026.

Shupe, A. D., Spielmann, R., & Stigall, S. (1977). Deprogramming: The new exorcism. *American Behavioral Scientist, 20,* 941–956.

Shupe, A. D., & Bromley, D. G. (1979). The moonies and the anti-cultists: Movement and countermovement in conflict. *Sociological Analysis, 40,* 325–334.

Singer, M. (1988). The social context of conversion to a black religious sect. *Review of Religious Research, 30,* 177–192.

Snow, D. A., Zurcher, L. A., & Elkand-Olson, S. (1980). Social networks and social movements: A microstructural approach to differential recruitment. *American Sociological Review, 45,* 787–801.

Spilka, B., Hood, R. W., & Gorsuch, R. L. (1985). *The psychology of religion: An empirical approach.* Englewood Cliffs, NJ: Prentice-Hall.

Stacey, J. (1990). *Brave new families.* New York: Basic.

Stellway, R. J. (1995). The family redefined. In B. J. Neff & D. Ratcliff (Eds.), *Handbook of family religious education* (pp. 87–114). Birmingham, AL: Religious Education Press.

Stinnett, N. (1983). Strong families: A portrait. In D. R. Mace (Ed.), *Prevention in family services* (pp. 79–123). Beverly Hills, CA: Sage.

Stoltzenberg, R. M., Blair-Loy, M., & Waite, L. J. (1995). Religious participation in early adulthood: Age and family life cycle effects on church membership. *American Sociological Review, 60,* 84–103.

Summers, J. R., & Cunningham, J. L. (1989). Premarital counseling by clergy: A key link between church and family. *Family Science Review, 2,* 327–336.

Tavris, C., & Sadd, S. (1977). *The Redbook report on female sexuality.* New York: Dell.

Taylor, R. J. (1988a). Correlates of religious non-involvement among black Americans. *Review of Religious Research, 30,* 126–138.

Taylor, R. J. (1988b). Structural determinants of religious participation among Black Americans. *Review of Religious Research, 30,* 114–125.

Taylor, R. J., & Chatters, L. M. (1986). Patterns of informal support to elderly black adults: Family, friends and church members. *Social Work, 31,* 432–440.

Taylor, R. J., & Chatters, L. M. (1988). Church members as a source of informal social support. *Review of Religious Research, 30,* 193–203.

Thomas, D. L. (1983). Family in the Mormon experience. In W. V. D'Antonio & J. Aldous (Eds.), *Families and religions: Conflict and change in modern society* (pp. 267–288). Beverly Hills, CA: Sage.

Thomas, D. L., & Roghaar, H. B. (1990). Postpositivist theorizing: The case of religion and the family. In J. Sprey (Ed.), *Fashioning family theory: New approaches* (pp. 186–230). Newbury Park, CA: Sage.

Thornton, A. (1988). Reciprocal influences of family and religion in a changing world. In D. L. Thomas (Ed.), *The religion and family connection: Social science perspectives* (Religious Studies Center Specialized Monograph Series, vol. III, pp. 27–50). Provo, UT: Brigham Young University.

Thornton, A., & Camburn, D. (1987). The influence of the family on premarital sexual attitudes and behavior. *Demography, 24,* 323–340.

Thornton, A., Axinn, W. G., & Hill, D. H. (1992). Reciprocal effects of religiosity, cohabitation, and marriage. *American Journal of Sociology, 98,* 628–651.

Tomasi, S. M. (1975). *Piety and power: The role of Italian parishes in the New York metropolitan area.* New York: Center for Migration Studies.

Vidich, A. J., & Bensman, J. (1968). *Small town in mass society* (rev. ed). Princeton, NJ: Princeton University Press.

Wagner, J. (Ed.). (1982). *Sex roles in contemporary American communes.* Bloomington: Indiana University Press.

Weisner, T. S., Beizer, L., & Stolze, L. (1991). Religion and families of children with developmental delays. *American Journal on Mental Retardation, 95,* 647–662.

Westoff, C. F. (1979). The blending of Catholic reproductive behavior. In R. Wuthnow (Ed.), *The religious dimension* (pp. 91–113). New York: Academic Press.

Westoff, C. F., & Potvin, R. H. (1966). Higher education, religion, and women's family-size orientations. *American Sociological Review, 31,* 489–496.

White, J. W. (1995). Family ministry methods. In B. J. Neff & D. Ratcliff (Eds.), *Handbook of family religious education* (pp. 207–226). Birmingham, AL: Religious Education Press.

Wiehe, V. R. (1990). Religious influence on parental attitudes toward the use of corporal punishment. *Journal of Family Violence, 5,* 173–186.

Wilson, J., & Musick, M. (1995). Personal autonomy in religion and marriage: Is there a link? *Review of Religious Research, 37,* 3–18.

Wilson, J., & Sherkat, D. E. (1994). Returning to the fold. *Journal for the Scientific Study of Religion, 33,* 148–161.

Wright, S. A. (1995). Religious innovation in the mainline church: House churches, home cells, and small groups. In N. T. Ammerman & W. C. Roof (Eds.), *Work, family and religion in contemporary society* (pp. 261–281). New York: Routledge.

Youngblood, J. R. (1990). *The conspicuous absence and the controversial presence of the black male in the local church.* Unpublished D. Min thesis, United Theological Seminary, Dayton, OH.

Zablocki, B. (1980). *The joyful community.* Chicago: University of Chicago Press.

CHAPTER 19

Economics and the Family

Paul S. Carlin

Introduction

It has only been in the last 30 years that modern economic analysis has been brought to bear on the family. The pioneering work in this area was done by Nobel laureate Gary Becker in the 1960s and 1970s as has since been consolidated into his monograph, *A Treatise on the Family* (1981, 1991). Since that time some of the primary areas of interest for economists have been: (1) factors influencing marriage formation and dissolution; (2) economic consequences of divorce and separation; (3) time allocation within the family, including changing patterns of labor supply for married women and time devoted to household tasks by married men and women; (4) trends in earnings inequality; (5) trends in wage inequality between women and men; (6) poverty, welfare reform, and the interactions between income maintenance, dependency, and family stability; (7) altruism and intergenerational transfers of wealth and human capital (educational and learning abilities); (8) the economic status of the elderly; and (9) the economic status of children. All of these issues are addressed in this chapter, but time allocation and issues relating to poverty and welfare receive disproportionate weight.

This chapter focuses primarily on the United States, although some evidence from other countries is introduced for the sake of comparison. Unless otherwise indicated, data and statistics are for the United States. I also give some idea of the insights that emerge from theoretical economic analysis and provide and analyze important empirical evidence that has appeared in the economics literature.*

It is worth noting that economic analysis has been applied to a variety of other issues not addressed in this chapter. Grossbard (1980) and Grossbard-Shechtman (1982) have applied economic analysis to issues addressed more customarily by anthropology, including polygamy and marriage formality in Guatemala. Tauchen, Witte, and Long (1991) provided a first look at domestic violence by economists. Monographs that provide a general introduction to economic analysis of families and related issues, in addition to Becker (1991), discussed later, include Blau and Ferber (1992) and Grossbard-Shechtman (1992); Ferber and Nelson (1993) have provided a good sampling of feminist thought on a variety of economic issues including the family. This chapter focuses on contributions from the economics literature; perspectives from other fields are ignored here for the sake of brevity and focus.

Modern Economic Theories of the Family

Theories of Gary Becker

Modern economic theories of the family start with *A Theory of the Allocation of Time* (Becker, 1965), in which Becker analyzed the family as a production unit that produces broadly defined *commodities* such as mental and physical health, children of varying levels of quality, prestige, esteem, and so on. Time and purchased goods are combined by individuals within the family to produce these commodities. Gronau (1977) introduced the distinction between home time

Paul S. Carlin • Department of Economics, Indiana University–Purdue University at Indianapolis, Indianapolis, Indiana 46202.

Handbook of Marriage and the Family, 2nd edition, edited by Marvin Sussman, Suzanne K. Steinmetz, and Gary W. Peterson. Plenum Press, New York, 1999.

*The theme and direction of this chapter were determined in 1993. There was an opportunity to update some of the references in 1996. In a rapidly evolving field, much can appear in a 2- to 3-year period that would suggest substantial modification to what is written here. Interested readers should consult Rosenzweig and Stark (1997) for the most current, comprehensive view of economics and the family.

that is production oriented (e.g., washing dishes), and time that is consumption oriented (e.g., reading a work of fiction). Viewed this way, the goods that are used to produce commodities may be produced at home (e.g., raising a vegetable garden, providing a home-cooked meal or caring for one's own children in the home) or may be purchased in the market with funds earned by working for pay (e.g., purchasing vegetables at a supermarket, eating out at a restaurant, or sending one's child to a daycare center).

This theory receives its fullest expression in *A Treatise on the Family* (Becker, 1981, 1991). Although the mathematical notation can be intimidating, the work provides the best insight into the economic approach to the theoretical analysis of the family. The second, enlarged edition represents a substantial improvement over the first edition because it includes much new work of the author from the 1980s; Becker also clarifies some of his earlier arguments in the light of the criticism they generated. The underlying assumption is that individuals rationally pursue their self-interest, except in cases where altruism or caring within the family is invoked. Applying the logic of formal economic analysis leads to a number of inferences, some of which have proven controversial, including:

1. A husband and wife can gain from division of labor, with one spouse specializing in work for pay and the other specializing in work at home. Small differences between men and women, related to childbearing by women or market discrimination of women, can be sufficient to induce wives to specialize in home production and husbands to specialize in market work.

2. Positive assortative mating should be observed for most traits other than wages. Negative assortative mating should be observed for wages due the specialization argument in (1).

3. Increases in income may lead to increased investment in children and tend to reduce the number of children per family to facilitate such investment.

4. Increasing transfer payments to the elderly in the form of Social Security, Medicare, and so on tend to reduce the demand for one's own children. Families become more dispersed and perform fewer functions because of the rise of market and governmental institutions for the education and training of young people and for the protection of individuals and, especially, the elderly from economic disaster.

5. Compensatory education and public health programs will lead to some reduction in private familial resources devoted to these needs. Hence, despite the intention, the main effect of such programs is to reallocate funds to low-income families, which may

improve health and education by a much smaller amount than would be anticipated based on the size of the public expenditure. This was advanced as a partial explanation for the empirical finding that Head Start and other such programs appeared to have no lasting effects on the children who participated.

6. The "rotten kid" theorem asserts that, if a parent is altruistic toward the children in the family, even a selfish child will act to maximize the income of the family because that will increase the transfers from the altruist to the selfish child.

7. Reductions in fertility and increases in divorce are due primarily to changes in underlying economic and social conditions rather than to changes in birth control techniques and divorce laws, respectively; fertility would have fallen and divorces increased even if there had been no advances in birth control technology and no liberalization of divorce laws.

Becker's work has inspired numerous empirical studies designed to test some of his propositions and has provided the theoretical framework for most of the work investigating various elements of family economics. Nevertheless, some economists have tried to develop alternative models of family decision making.

Alternative Models of Family Decision Making

Economists Manser and Brown (1980) and McElroy and Horney (1981) independently developed a model of household decision making that embodied the idea of two adults, a man and a woman, bargaining over the allocation of time and goods in the household. Using the tools of cooperative game theory, they showed that, for certain purposes, Becker's model can be considered a special case of their model. Apart from technical predictions that are of interest primarily to economists, there is a new emphasis on bargaining power within the marriage. Anything that enhances a spouse's welfare if the marriage were to end tends to increase that spouse's bargaining power in a continuing marriage and should result in a redistribution of goods and/or leisure from the other spouse. For example, if a wife brings wealth into a marriage and would expect to control that wealth in the event of divorce, that should enhance her bargaining position and leave her with more consumption of material goods and leisure than other similar wives without control over such wealth. Changes in divorce laws that would result in divorce settlements more generous to wives should have similar effects. Reductions in the availability of marriageable men should enhance the bargaining position of husbands. These anticipated postmarriage effects should alter the allocation of time and goods in intact households.

Despite the claimed advantages of the bargaining model, it has attracted relatively few adherents for three reasons. First, it is less tractable than Becker's model in terms of its mathematics. Second, many implications of the bargaining power approach can be generated as well from a Beckerian model. (For example, Grossbard-Shechtman [1984] used a Beckerian perspective to argue that changes in the ratio of marriageable men to women should affect the labor force participation of married women. That directly alters the allocation of time and indirectly alters the allocation of goods.) Finally, Chiappori (1988a, 1991) has effectively criticized some of the technical aspects of the cooperative bargaining model of the family and has suggested (1988b, 1992) an alternative model that can accommodate both the Beckerian model and the simple bargaining model as special cases. As yet, however, little empirical work based on Chiappori's model has appeared (see Browning et al. 1994, for an early empirical study of household clothing expenditures using the Chiappori framework).

A small body of empirical work based on bargaining models has begun to take shape. The standard model of family labor supply received formal testing and empirical support in Ashenfelter and Heckman (1974). Schultz (1990) has shown, using data from a socioeconomic survey in Thailand, that one of the implications of their model is not supported, namely that the nonearned (property) income of husband and wife has identical effects on labor supply and family consumption decisions. Thomas (1990) found, for Brazilian data from the mid-1970s, that unearned income under control of the wife has a larger effect on family health outcomes than wealth under control of the husband. These examples show that bargaining analysis of family interactions has the potential to bring new insights into empirical work. Where the data make it possible, empirical work should distinguish between forms of income belonging to the wife and those belonging to the husband.

Carlin (1991a) and Ott (1992) have suggested ways of extending the bargaining model. Both rely on the notion of considering marriage as a two-stage enterprise. In the initial stage spouses bargain over time allocation, with increased allocation of time to consumption activities (consumption of goods and leisure) as positive first-period outcomes and with human capital investment activities (education or work*) as negative outcomes (because they require time and other resources) in the first period which lead to positive outcomes in

the second period. The human capital investment leads to higher wages and better job security in the future, which translates into increased bargaining power and therefore more desirable outcomes in the second stage. In the section on "Economic Consequences of Divorce and Separation" later in this chapter, Carlin's bargaining implications for time allocation within the family are considered.

Marriage Formation and Dissolution

Let us consider two issues under the heading of marriage formation and dissolution. The first is the question raised by Becker's model, which suggests that positive assortative mating should be observed for most traits, but not for earning power. Do women and men with high earning power marry each other, or do men with high earning power marry women with low earning power but high household skills? The second is the question raised by changing marital and divorce patterns. What is causing the decline in the marriage rate and the increase in the divorce rate?

Negative or Positive Assortative Mating for Earning Power?

First, consider the prediction of Becker's model that for most traits except earning power there should be positive assortative mating; negative assortative mating should be observed for the trait earning power. High-wage men marry low-wage women. Not all economists agree with Becker. Lam (1988) has shown, in a theoretical paper, that if the primary source of gains to marriage is due to a kind of complementarity from the joint consumption of goods purchased in the market, then it is possible that there would be positive assortative mating on wages. Weiss and Willis (1993) argued that we may find high-wage men marrying high-wage women if (1) the payoff to coordinating work and investment activities is high for both (the husband may work while the wife studies and vice versa) or if (2) having a spouse with a similar income leads to greater conformity in the demand for joint consumption activities (attending movies, parties, etc.) and in the strategies for raising children.

It is also true that the Becker hypothesis is dependent on the notion that there is a clear separation between traits that contribute to the effective management of the home and to success in the marketplace. With the advent of modern home technology, however, it is less clear that there is a *sharp* distinction between home and market skills, although gains from specialization still exist. Two further questions may be asked. First, even if specialization between home and market human capital produces a greater household product, are there negative outcomes for those working exclusively in the

*In this article, the terms *work* and *market work* are used to represent work for pay outside the home. The terms *household tasks* and *home production* are used to represent work that directly benefits one's own family and is typically not for remuneration. Household tasks include household maintenance and chores, childcare, shopping, and so forth. This work/tasks dichotomy is observed for reasons of convenience in exposition and not because of any presumed difference in the value of work as opposed to tasks.

home, such as alienation and increased risk of financial insecurity should the marriage dissolve? Second, does it make sense to ask the division of labor question at the level of home and market? Even if there are gains to specialization that are not offset by alienation or risk factors, perhaps that would involve division of labor among household tasks rather than specialization at the level of work versus family.

There has been little effective empirical testing of assortative mating on wages. Smith (1979) presented the earliest careful statistical analysis, which suggests that partial correlations between spouses' wages (where wages for nonworking wives are predicted on the basis of education, past work experience, and other socioeconomic variables) are positive, but low (0.035 for white couples). Also, in an indirect test of the proposition, Carlin (1991b) examined data collected from a national survey in the mid-1970s and found that wives of husbands with managerial careers were significantly more likely to work than wives of husbands with other kinds of careers. As the probability of working is positively related to the wage offer, this suggests positive assortative mating on wages. However, women married to men with professional occupations (physician, dentist, architect, scientists, judge, or lawyer) were significantly less likely to work, consistent with negative assortative mating on wages. Shaw (1989), using panel data from 1968 to 1981, found a weak positive correlation between actual lifetime incomes of spouses (0.016) but a much higher correlation between the potential lifetime income of spouses (0.363). The difference is due to the discontinuous labor force participation of women. Her study suggests there is positive assortative mating on the traits that can produce earnings if both spouses devote themselves to those goals. However, it was still true, for the period studied, that women married to men with high earnings took more time away from the labor market so that there was relatively little correlation between actual incomes of spouses. None of these empirical studies conclusively refute Becker's hypothesis on assortative mating, but the hypothesis does not receive much support. It seems reasonable to conclude that Becker's hypothesis does a better job of describing traditional patterns of marriage in industrialized countries in the past or in developing nations at the present. For now, there seems to be gathering evidence in the United States that positive assortative mating for earning power is more and more likely to be observed.

Marriage Rates

The marriage rate for both men and women in the United States has been declining over the past 20 years. For example, among women 15 years old and older, the marriage rate per 1000 women fell from 28.4 in 1970 to 23.9 in 1988.

During the same period the rate for men fell from 31.1 to 25.9 per 1000. At the same time, the divorce rate has been rising. For married women 15 years and older, the rate rose from 14.9 per 1000 to a high of 22.6 in 1980, with the rate falling to 20.9 by 1990.* In 1960, 80% of black women ages 20–34 and 66% of black men in the same age group had married one or more times. By 1990 the comparable figures were 46% for women and 38% for men (Wood, 1995). These trends have contributed to the feminization of poverty. The falling marriage rate and rising divorce rate, higher for black Americans, have been associated with a rising black female headship rate and an even sharper rise in the nonwhite illegitimacy rate.† The feminization of poverty is considered in the section, "Trends in Wage Inequality between Men and Women," later in this chapter; economic explanations for other trends are considered here.

One explanation for the falling marriage rates (Becker, 1991) is that rising wages for women make gender-based division of labor within the family less efficient, a trend that lowers the gains to marriage and so lowers marriage rates. Apart from observing the strong movements of women's wages and marriage rates in opposite directions over the last 20 years there is little direct empirical evidence for this hypothesis.

If there are fewer gains to specialization, does that mean that *divorce* rates should rise with increases in women's wage rates? The answer is not necessarily, because it is *unanticipated* changes that would cause divorce. If a women expects to earn a high wage, then she would either marry a different husband or not marry at all. Conditional upon finding an appropriate mate, there is no reason to expect an increased likelihood of divorce. In a time of changing expectations the probability of unanticipated realizations rises, however, making divorce more likely. Hoffman and Duncan (1995) found that Aid to Families with Dependent Children (AFDC) benefit levels are positively related to marital dissolution but that higher earnings for husbands and higher wage rates for the wives actually reduce the probability of divorce or separation. Their examination of 1098 first marriages begun between 1968 and 1983 and observed for 1–17 years provides no support for the notion that rising wage rates for women have resulted in higher divorce rates, so either the gains to marriage have not declined, or at the least, unanticipated declines in the gains to marriage have not resulted from rising wages for women.

There has been substantial discussion in the literature of

*The source for marriage and divorce rates in 1980 and 1988 is U.S. Bureau of the Census (1992, Table 127, p. 90). The source for the divorce rate in 1990 is U.S. Bureau of the Census (1995, Table 142, p. 102).
†The source for headship and illegitimacy rates is Moffitt (1992, Figure 4, p. 28).

the hypothesis of Wilson (1987). Wilson claimed that the falling marriage rate for blacks is due primarily to the decline in employment among young black males. Constructing a male marriageable pool index (MMPI), he shows that declines in the MMPI are associated with declines in marriage rates in the 1960s and 1970s. The hypothesis has been questioned by Ellwood and Crane (1990), who found that the rates moved in opposite directions in the 1980s with the percent married continuing down and the MMPI turning up. Furthermore, the decline in the percentage of black males ages 25–34 was more drastic for the employed than the unemployed from 1970 to 1988. Robert Wood (1995) tested the Wilson hypothesis using both the MMPI and a revised MMPI based on income rather than employment. Although the revised MMPI does a better job than the employment-based MMPI, changes in it still can account for only about 3%–4% of the declines in marriage rates for young black women from 1970 to 1980. It seems that the Wilson hypothesis will have to be joined with other hypotheses to gain a comprehensive insight into the phenomenon of falling marriage rates among blacks. Becker's work suggests that rising employment and income among young black women must surely play a role, although feedback effects make it difficult to isolate the effects of any one variable.

"No-Fault" Divorce Laws and the Tendency to Divorce

Has the movement to adopt "no-fault" divorce laws accelerated the tendency to divorce? The basic issue is whether the change that made obtaining a divorce easier increased the number of divorces or simply accommodated the increased desire to divorce. The latter trend, of course, would have been felt even if the laws had not changed. Becker (1991) noted that in California, the first state to adopt no-fault divorce, there was a surge in divorces in the first 2 years after its implementation, but a return to the long-term upward trend in divorce became prevalent after the first 2 years. He concluded that there was little long-term effect on divorce rates. His evidence is only indicative, however, because some of the states in the comparison group also moved to adopt some form of no-fault divorce shortly after California, thus California is compared to a moving target, not a fixed one. Peters (1986) also failed to find any appreciable effect of no-fault divorce on divorce probabilities. In a careful subsequent study, however, Weiss and Willis (1993) found that the movement to the new legal regime did increase the hazard of divorce for marriages, whether children were present or not. Becker (1991) argued that even the Weiss and Willis results would only explain a small portion of the increase in divorce rates after 1970. Becker remains con-

vinced that the increased divorce rate is due primarily to changing economic and social factors. Another possible contributor to the increased divorce rates of the 1970s is demographic.

It is well known that divorces are more likely to occur early in marriage. For example, Becker (1991) cited Public Health Service statistics to the effect that 40% of divorces happen in the first 5 years of marriage. Economic explanations of this phenomenon emphasize two factors: (1) the uncertain information, at time of marriage, about many traits of the new spouse makes it likely that there will be substantial surprises in the first few years of marriage and (2) the accumulation of partner-specific capital such as children makes divorce less likely later in marriage. When contraception is fairly effective, partners who view divorce probability as high will be less likely to have children (Lillard, 1993). This is also an example of the self-fulfilling nature of doubts about a marriage. Because a given marriage is viewed by the partners as rather unlikely to succeed, they are less likely to acquire marriage-specific capital, and so make the eventual divorce all the more likely.

The Baby Boom generation was, to a great extent, experiencing the first few years of marriage during the 1970s and 1980s. As these years have a higher incidence of divorce, the divorce rate per 1000 marriages would rise strictly because of the "Boomer" composition effect. Recent marriages would comprise a higher percentage of all marriages than is typical. To the extent that there are feedback effects the divorce rate would rise in a multiplicative way. Married women, seeing their friends' marriages ending in divorce, would be more likely to seek work outside the home as insurance against divorce. By Becker's comparative advantage argument, therefore, such actions would make it more likely that divorce would ensue. By the same token, if divorce is thought to be likely, the couple is more likely to delay having children; this too increases the probability of divorce. To the extent that the increased divorce rate of the 1970s and early 1980s is linked to the Baby Boom generation we should see some declines in divorce rates or at least a decline in the upward trend through the rest of the 1990s. The small declines in the divorce rate and the rising birth rate in the early 1990s is consistent with this demographic interpretation.

Lillard (1993) has identified additional economic causes of divorce. Using pooled cross-sectional and time series data for 1968–1985 from the Panel Study of Income Dynamics, he finds that the hazard of marital disruption is higher in states and times where the cost of lawyers is lower and the aggregate divorces per capita is higher. This suggests price and feedback effects for the period studied. If it is cheaper to get a divorce, the hazard of divorce is higher. If there have been more divorces in the recent past, existing marriages are at greater risk. The presence of children from a previous marriage also increases the hazard of divorce.

Economic Consequences of Divorce and Separation

Along with the rise in divorce rates has come an increased concern about the economic consequences of divorce on the family. How do the children, former wife, and former husband fare after divorce? It has been suggested that the rise in divorce, coupled with a failure on the part of former husbands to pay court-mandated child support, has led directly to the feminization of poverty. It is well established that the immediate effect of divorce, on average, is primarily to lower the living standard of the former wife and any children if she is the custodial parent.

Living Standards of Divorced Parents and Children

Duncan and Hoffman (1991) found for national data from the early 1980s that family income for divorced women fell by 34% (25% if adjusted for the smaller family size after divorce); family income fell by only 15% for divorced men (a 3% increase if adjusted for smaller family size). Burkhauser, Duncan, Hauser, and Berntsen (1991), using survey data from 1986 found that, after taxes and public transfers (such as AFDC, food stamps, etc.), the median woman's living standards fell by 24% from the year prior to the year after divorce, and 22% of the women had large drops of 50% or more in living standards. The median divorced man's living standard after taxes and transfers dropped by only 6%. Interestingly they find that German women fared even worse than American women after divorce, while German men fared the same as American men, with a 44% loss for women compared to a 6% loss for men.

The longer term negative effect of divorce on women is not so drastic. Duncan and Hoffman (1991) found that 5 years after divorce the woman and her children are, on average, better off than they were before the divorce, but not as well off as they would have been had the marriage remained intact. In most cases the improvement was due to remarriage, although retraining and increased work experience had a modest effect. Remarriage prospects are substantially lower for black than white women, suggesting that they are likely to suffer more from divorce over a longer period.

Peters (1993) analyzed the National Longitudinal Survey of Work Experience of Young Women to obtain information on 1326 young women (between the ages of 19 and 29 in 1973) who were in their first marriage in 1973. All but 123 of these were married continuously from 1973 to 1982; 123 had been divorced by 1978. The economic outcomes for all the 1326 women were compared for the period from 1978 to 1982. Peters confirmed the importance of remarriage, finding that, on average, by the end of a 5-year period, real family income was 9% lower than before divorce if there was no remarriage, but 5% higher than before the divorce if the woman did remarry. This rise in real family income upon remarriage supports the notion of Becker and others that divorce is often the result of an unexpectedly low realization from the original match. Peters also inferred, however, that this slightly better outcome for those who remarry has little impact on the divorce decision of married women. The more negative, short-term outcomes apparently have more predictive power in terms of explaining the divorce decision. The typical woman must, necessarily, view remarriage prospects as risky and not to be relied upon.

Child Support Nonpayment

Certainly one important cause of the differential effect of divorce on men and women has been the nonpayment of child support. According to Beller and Graham (1989), in the mid-1980s only about one divorced woman in three living with her own children under the age of 21 received any child support payments. Of those who received any child support payments, the average was only a little over $2000 and represented less than 20% of the family income. Consistent with widespread evidence on the effects of nonwage income, Beller and Graham found that, controlling for other factors, child support awards reduce the annual hours of work of a divorced woman, but not by as much as nonwage income from other sources such as AFDC. As the receipt of child support payments is problematic, it cannot be considered as full nonwage income. It seems likely that only those who are receiving such payments steadily would come to rely on them, hence the relatively small effect. Part of the nonpayment of child support is due to the low earnings of many divorced men. However, this is not the complete story, as many divorced men who can afford child support payments do not make them.

Weiss and Willis (1985) explained the tendency of divorced fathers to avoid child support payments as a monitoring problem. They argued that the noncustodial parent (typically the father) cannot perfectly monitor the expenditure of the child support monies and so is likely to see them as contributing disproportionately to the welfare of the former wife rather than the children. They note that this is a classic economic example of a collective good problem with costly monitoring of resource allocation. Whether the collective good is public roads, street lights, national defense or expenditures on children, unless there is legal compulsion of one form or another (taxes for example), there tends to be under provision of the collective good. The collective good problem is alleviated while the couple is married because there is (relatively) costless monitoring of the resource allocation within the family. In an analysis of survey data from the mid-1980s, Weiss and Willis (1993) inferred from statistical work that to have 1 dollar's worth of impact on the welfare of the children, the ex-husband must transfer about 4 dollars to the ex-wife. This seems high, but if it should prove to be a robust finding, it would certainly explain much of the reluctance of fathers to support children who are in the custody of the mother.

Since child support payments have been an uncertain income source for divorced women, other more regular sources have been sought: regular jobs, AFDC, and remarriage. Lester (1991) indicated that, in 1989, child support, when received, typically made up no more than 15%–20% of household income. To the extent that the actual receipt of a child support obligation is viewed by many divorced women as an unreliable "windfall," it would not be surprising that other sources of income are relied upon to take care of the necessary expenses related to the children. When a child support payment is received, relatively little of it might be expended directly on children, as their needs may already have been taken care of out of other sources of income. Still, Del Boca and Flinn (1994) showed that the larger the proportion of custodial mothers' income received as child support, the greater her share of spending on child-related goods. It seems that ex-wives and ex-husbands are locked in a "prisoner's dilemma," where the ex-husband fulfills his child support obligation only sporadically because he believes (and observes) that relatively little of his payment is spent directly on his children; the ex-wife spends relatively little of the child support payments received directly on the children because she believes (and observes) that child support cannot be relied upon for the needs of her children. In such a situation there is a clear role for government to step in with child support enforcement to create a situation where everyone's welfare can be unambiguously improved.

If the payment of child support obligations becomes a reliable source of income for the custodial parent, those funds can be directed more toward the needs of the children. The children benefit because more funds are directed toward their needs; the father gains because he contributes more to the direct ongoing welfare of his children and hence should have a better relationship with them, including more frequent visitation (see Veum, 1992) as well as increased satisfaction from higher-quality children; the mother gains because there is increased probability that she will not have to seek support from the government in the form of public welfare transfer programs; society gains because fewer resources need be devoted to public transfers to support custodial parents and their children.

The federal government has taken steps to make the collection of child support more routine. The Child Support Enforcement Amendments of 1984 to the Social Security Act provide for mandatory wage withholding of child support when payments are delinquent, and the 1988 Family Support Act provides for wage withholding in new child support cases, effective in 1994, and requires that child support awards be updated more frequently (Garfinkel, Robins, Wong, & Meyer, 1990). Evidence from Lester (1991) suggests that this legislation has had an effect on the collection of child support, although there is still a significant shortfall. In 1989, of the 4.95 million women with children under the age of 21 who were due child support payments, 51% received the full amount awarded, 24% received less than the full amount, and 25% received no payment.

This leaves the difficulty with divorced fathers with low earnings. Withholding child support from wages is ineffective if there are low or no wages. The Wisconsin Child Support Assurance System (CSAS) was designed, in part, to address this problem of low-income families with only a custodial parent present. It provides a minimum guaranteed level of child support regardless of whether the child support can be collected from the noncustodial parent and was field-tested in selected counties of Wisconsin. Its designers hoped that it could become the model for national child support legislation, but political developments in Wisconsin prevented its implementation there (Garfinkel et al., 1990). See the section "Does AFDC Lead to Welfare Dependence?" later in this chapter, for additional discussion of the CSAS.

Time Allocation within the Family: Labor Supply and Household Tasks

The labor supply (time allocation to work outside the home) of married women and men has been extensively analyzed by economists both theoretically and empirically. The allocation of time to productive uses in the home has received less attention, in part because of the difficulty of obtaining accurate data.

Labor Supply of Married Women

The empirical economics literature on the labor supply of married women is extensive (see Killingsworth & Heckman, 1986, for a survey of studies through the mid-1980s). A special issue of the *Journal of Human Resources* (Nakamura & Shaw, 1994) provides more recent evidence. We know that the labor supply of married women responds positively to their own wage and inversely to their husbands' and that most of this effect is centered on the participation decision rather than on the decision of how many hours to work (part-time versus full-time, for example). Additional years of schooling and added years of prior work experience, while controlling for other factors, tend to increase hours of work; the presence of young children (especially under 6 years of age) still tends to depress hours of work for married women, at least for data through the mid-1980s (Zabel, 1993). There is heterogeneity and persistence among women workers. There are women who work and continue to work after interruptions for childbirth and there are women who do not work. Most of the increased labor supply of women has involved the increase in workers and a decrease in non-workers, not in an increase in the hours of the workers. What about male labor supply?

The husband's own wage typically has a very small negative impact on his hours of work (often not statistically significant), while wife's wage has no impact. Schooling and experience have the same positive effect for men; the effect of young children is different and has apparently changed in recent years. For data up through the 1970s, most studies of male labor supply found that the presence of young children had a significant positive effect on hours worked (see Ham, 1982; Johnson & Pencavel, 1984; Pencavel, 1986; Triest, 1992). The conventional interpretation was that fathers worked more hours after children were born to generate more income to cover the increased present and future expenses. This explanation took the traditional division of labor within the family as a given. In work using data from the 1980s, Triest (1990) found that young children now have no statistically significant impact on male labor supply. Although preliminary, this suggests that the traditional patterns of division of labor may be starting to break down.

In the standard pre-Becker theory of household decision making, the decisions to work for pay outside the home and of how many hours to work were assumed to depend on the size of the wage offer available and the reservation wage of the husband or wife. The reservation wage is the implicit return, measured in dollars, for nonmarket uses of time. The higher the wage offer and the lower the reservation wage, the more likely the given individual works. The greater the income available to the individual from nonwage sources, the lower the probability of working. The most common sources of nonwage income are (1) income from assets, (2) funds transferred from an income maintenance program, and (3) spouse's earnings. A rise in any of these three sources tends to reduce the probability of working and, among those working, to reduce the hours of work. Indeed, virtually every empirical study that has examined this issue in the last 25 years, and there have been dozens, possibly hundreds, finds evidence to confirm these effects. When combined with the Becker insight that even a small difference in either productivity at home or in the wage offer (whether due to discrimination or any other factor) can provide strong incentives for

specialization, these findings tended, at least initially, to form the basis of a defense of the status quo in specialization by gender. Married women would tend to specialize in the home because of low wage offers for women and high wage offers for their husbands.

Nevertheless, Becker (1991) conceded that, in this century, married women have been specializing less in the home and men have been devoting more time to the home. He explained this in terms of complementarity in many home activities, most notably in sexual and other enjoyment and in the raising of children. If such complementarities are important, then only partial rather than complete household specialization would be observed. Willis (1987) also pointed out that household division of labor may become less extreme as economic development leads to the substitution of market-produced commodities for home-produced commodities and as discrimination against working women lessens. Economic development can lead to a self-perpetuating cycle for women. Rising wages for women reduce the specialization of married women in household production and reduce the family's demand for children. Both effects reinforce the greater involvement of women in the labor market, which leads women to acquire more human capital both in formal education and on-the-job work experience and, in turn, leads to higher wages for women.

In any case, the increasing participation of married women in the labor force continues, both in the United States and in other Western industrialized countries. Mincer (1985) reported that, in the United States, the labor force participation of married women had increased from 30.5% in 1960 to 40.8% in 1970 to 50.1% in 1980 for a growth rate of almost 2½% per year. By 1980 the labor force participation rate for married women was above 50% in Australia, Britain, France, Germany, Sweden, and the United States. It was highest in Sweden, at 75.6%, but Mincer pointed out that most of their recent growth has been in part-time work, suggesting that the greater than proportional involvement of married women with the home and children has not been completely reversed, even there. Indeed, a recent study by Flood and Klevmarken (1992) reveals that, according to a time diary study from 1984, Swedish husbands spent about 1.75 times as many hours per week at market work as their wives, while Swedish wives spent about 1.80 times as many hours on housework as their husbands.

In the United States, the labor force participation of married women continues to grow. Shank (1988) reported that by March 1987, 68.1% of married women, ages 25–54, with husband present, were in the labor force; when the husband is not present, the number rises to 70.9%. Even more significantly, the labor force participation of married women with young children has risen precipitously, in part because of rising divorce rates; 55% of women with children under

3 years of age were in the labor force in 1987. According to Hayghe (1986), this figure is up from 25.8% in 1970 and 41.5% as recently as 1980. Two-thirds of mothers of children under 3 years old are now in the labor force. Hayghe and Bianchi (1994) reported that married mothers of older children (ages 6–17 and none under 6) had a participation rate of 78.4% by 1992.

Of course, not all of this participation is in full-time, year-round work. Still, Hayghe and Bianchi documented that more than 1 in 4 married mothers with children under the age of 3 worked full-time, year-round. For African American families the participation rates are higher; 72% of married mothers with children under 3 are in the workforce, and almost 83% of African American mothers of older children work in the market. While the participation rates for full-time, year-round work are lower in level, they are growing faster than the overall labor force participation rate. The participation rate for full-time, year-round work has risen for married mothers of children under 6 from 9.6% in 1970 to 17.7% in 1980 and finally to 30.6% in 1992. Williams (1995) reported that the participation rate for part-time employment has grown from about 12% in 1957 to 20.6% in 1982 and then fell to 18.5% by 1990. The recent decline is apparently connected to women holding on to full-time jobs. Although they are still almost twice as likely as men to leave full-time for part-time work, women's rates of leaving full-time jobs have been falling. Still, it is clear that part-time and/or part-year work for the mother is an important component of family labor supply, especially when children are young.

Self-employment can also provide some flexibility for married women. Devine (1994) reported that 1 of 4 women was self-employed in 1975 and that by 1990 the ratio had increased to 1 in 3. There seem to be two primary groups of self-employed women. One group (about 55%) works part-time or part-year, obtaining added income in a way that emphasizes flexibility; the other group works long hours year-round, as is the case for the typical entrepreneur. The latter group has grown from about 33% of self-employed women in 1975 to about 45% in 1990. The typical self-employed woman is older, more likely to have a spouse present, and more likely to be covered by a spouse's health-care policy than her counterparts who are employed by others.

Time Allocation to Household Tasks

Can a family life of reasonable quality be obtained with both parents working full-time when children are young? If one of the parents must accept part-time work or a temporary absence from the labor market, which will it be? While the tradition has been for the wife to opt for part-time work and the husband to work full-time, there appear to be increasing instances of the husband taking on either part-time or no

work, especially during the early years of the children's lives. The tendency to provide parental leave for either the mother or father following a birth recognizes and tends to encourage an increased involvement of the father in the family. Is there any statistical evidence that fathers are taking an increasing role in the family? Economists tend to emphasize time diary data from national surveys. Such data are collected in a series of interviews covering both weekdays and weekends in various seasons and require the individual to completely allocate the previous 24-hour day. Consequently, this information is much more reliable than other time use data, which often relies on reports of typical days or weeks reconstructed by respondents on the basis of imperfect memory.

The largest such survey for the United States is the University of Michigan's Time Use in Economic and Social Accounts, collected for the years 1975–1976 with a small follow-up for 1981. Juster and Stafford (1991) summarized the principal findings of this study and made reference to similar studies from other countries (Botswana, Denmark, Finland, Hungary, Japan, Nepal, Norway, Sweden, and the U.S.S.R.). The main findings from their survey of cross-country time use data from the 1960s through the early 1980s include: (1) total work (work for an employer plus home production) is higher for men than women only in countries with high income levels (United States, Sweden, Norway, and Denmark); (2) housework (routine chores, home projects and childcare) time for men is typically around 11 to 12 hours per week, rising to the upper teens for Norway and Sweden and falling to the low single digits for Japan; (3) husbands in Sweden do the most housework, but as of 1984, women still did 1.76 times as much housework. In other countries this ratio ranged from Norway and Denmark (a bit below 2) to the United States and U.S.S.R. (2.2), to Hungary (2.7), to Botswana and Nepal (almost 4) to Japan (8.9).

Clearly, among these countries, Japan would represent the most inegalitarian time use patterns between married men and women. Denmark has made rapid progress in altering this ratio from 1964, when women provided 8 times as much housework as men, to 1987, when women provided only 1.8 times as much housework. In the United States the ratio fell from 3.7 in 1965 to 2.2 in 1981—less dramatic than Denmark but a substantial change nonetheless. In Denmark the change coupled a large increase (9 hours per week) for men with a large decrease (7 hours per week) for women; in the United States the change was due to a small increase for men (2.3 hours per week) and a much larger decrease for women (11.3 hours per week). In the United States, total work time for men (57.8 hours per week) remained above that for women (54.4 hours per week) because the decline in men's average hours of work was not as steep as the decline in women's hours of house work. Moreover, the increase in average hours of work for married women was not as steep as suggested by the popular press (5 hours from 1965 to 1981, a rise from 18.9 to 23.9 hours per week).

Juster and Stafford (1991) argued, convincingly, that their picture is different from that in the popular press because the figures reported there are almost always based on long-term memory concerning the typical number of hours worked rather than adjusted for many periods when the actual hours worked are fewer than scheduled hours or for periods when work is not scheduled. Because married women have been more likely to have intermittent attachment to the labor force and have been more likely to take jobs that accommodate time away from work for household duties (especially child-related ones), this problem of biased reporting is more likely to affect their reported work hours.

Have women benefitted from these changes in time use patterns? Fuchs (1988) concluded that the ratio of women's total work hours to men's total work hours increased substantially. Fuchs argued that the lot of women had not improved much from 1965 to 1981, in part because the increase in their market work was only partly compensated by a (smaller) reduction in home work so that total work hours increased. Manchester and Stapleton (1991) argued that Fuchs' conclusion that the ratio of women's total work hours to men's total work hours increased substantially is in error. By carefully constructing comparable subsamples for 1965–1966, 1975–1976, and 1981 time use surveys, Manchester and Stapleton concluded that the women's total work hours to men's total work hours ratio was quite stable over this time period; in fact, the ratio declined although not by a statistically significant amount. Like Juster and Stafford, they find that married women's increased work hours (+4.3) from 1965 to 1981 are more than offset by the decrease in housework hours (−9.7); the decrease in married men's paid work hours (−5.9) is partially offset by increased housework hours (+2.8). Married women spend 1 hour per week, on average, less with childcare while husbands spend a half-hour more. Manchester and Stapleton concluded that Fuchs' pessimism about the possibility of women increasing their well-being by entering the labor market is unfounded and that increases in job opportunities should increase the well-being of married women. The Manchester and Stapleton article also opens up the possibility that children may lose, at least in terms of total time spent with parents. In their sample, parents spent, on average, one-half hour per week less with their children in 1981 as compared to 1964.

Carlin (1991a) explored this issue, among others, using a cross-sectional approach on the 1975–1976 time use data. He found evidence that wives in states that moved to various forms of no-fault divorce (which, according to Weiss and Willis [1993], made divorce settlements more generous to wives) tended to reduce their hours devoted to home tasks and/or consumption activities to increase time spent at work and education activities. Although these changes tended to

increase the wives' well-being, the quality time that children spent with parents decreased. Defining quality time as child-care time spent on helping/teaching, reading/talking, indoor playing, and outdoor playing, Carlin found a significant decrease of about a half-hour per week in these activities by women in most of the states that moved toward no-fault divorce in either grounds or division of property. This was not matched by a concomitant increase in quality time with the fathers, and the extent to which purchased childcare or childcare by other relatives compensated for all or part of the difference cannot be determined from these data.

No-Fault Divorce and the Labor Force Participation of Married Women

Have changes in divorce laws increased the labor force participation of married women? Parkman (1992) confirms the statistical work of Peters (1986) on 1979 data from the Current Population Survey. Residence in a no-fault divorce state led to significant increases in labor force participation for married women. Parkman argued, persuasively, that this increased participation is due to divorce courts not recognizing the reduced human capital of married women who increase their specialization in home production. This was of less importance prior to no-fault divorce because the courts were less often involved in financial settlements. One spouse could not easily get a divorce; hence the spouse who wanted the divorce (the husband, for example) had to "bribe" the other party (the wife) in the form of a negotiated settlement that was independent of the laws governing the distribution of property and alimony. Recognizing that this would no longer be the case with no-fault provisions that rely more heavily on court determination, married women who would face substantial deterioration of human capital in the form of labor market skills had a strong incentive to maintain labor force participation even when young children were present in the family. Parkman's empirical results are consistent with this interpretation but the data set he uses is not rich enough to view this as a critical test of his hypothesis. If his hypothesis can be confirmed, it would provide an argument for either repealing no-fault divorce or encouraging marriage contracts that spell out clearly the rights of a spouse who specializes disproportionately in home production should the marriage end in divorce. Without either of these policy changes, the incentive remains for two-career marriages to grow as a form of divorce insurance for wives.

Childcare and the Labor Force Participation of Married Women

Another variable of importance in considering the labor force participation of married women is the availability of high-quality childcare. Leibowitz, Klerman, and Waite (1992) used National Longitudinal Survey of Youth data from 1979 to 1986 to analyze the differences in employment and childcare choice for new mothers as their children age from birth to 2 years old. They provided some preliminary evidence verifying that these decisions do vary with the age of the child. Nearly one-third of the mothers in this sample returned to work within 3 months of giving birth; of these, more than half used a relative to provide childcare. More than 40% of the mothers were working by the time the child was 2; of these slightly fewer than half used a relative for childcare. If a grandmother lived in the household, the mother was more likely to return to work by the time the child was 24 months old, but the presence of a grandmother had no significant impact on the labor force participation decision when the child was 3 months old. Furthermore, the size of the maximum federal plus state childcare tax credit had a significantly positive effect on the likelihood that the mother returns to work when the child is 3 months old but apparently had no impact on the decision at 24 months of age.

Ribar (1992) analyzed data for 1985 from the Survey of Income Program Participation (SIPP) and found that the cost of private childcare has a large negative effect on the likelihood of a married woman with young children participating in the labor force. His findings imply that a 10% reduction in the hourly cost of child care (e.g., due to a government subsidy) would tend to increase the hours of work of such mothers by more than 7%. Larger subsidies would, of course, have larger effects. Gustafsson and Stafford (1992) analyzed Swedish data for 1984 and found that lower prices for public daycare encourage use when those spaces are not rationed. Furthermore, they found that the high quality of public childcare in Sweden encourages its use by married women with preschoolers even when income is high. Not all of this increased use shows up in the form of increased labor force participation, as some of the use represents a switch from private to public daycare by mothers who are already working. In a subsequent study, Ribar (1995) improved on his empirical methodology and revisited the 1985 SIPP data. He now concludes that married women's labor supply is fairly insensitive to changes in childcare subsidy rates. Marginal subsidy reductions would apparently encourage women to shift to lower cost kinds of childcare but would have little impact on their employment and hours decisions. Further work needs to be done before we can be sure of this conclusion. What kind of subsidization should be undertaken if we are interested either in better childcare or more labor force participation?

Michalopoulos, Robins, and Garfinkel (1992) considered the current federal childcare tax credit and the effect of making it refundable so that low-income families with little tax liability would nevertheless be able to get some benefit from childcare subsidies. They estimated their structural model on a sample from the SIPP and then performed simula-tions to gauge the effect of changes in subsidy rates, wage rates, and nonlabor income. Making the tax credit refundable would significantly increase the share of the subsidy going to low-income women but would not change the quality of childcare very much. Low-income women would increase their hours of work and many would switch from high-quality free childcare to slightly higher-quality purchased childcare.

All of this suggests, of course, that decisions about labor force participation are intertwined with decisions about fertility and family size. While economists have made some headway in considering fertility, there are many unanswered questions. Hotz and Miller (1988) provided an example of an ambitious attempt to interrelate these objectives in a substantive empirical study. Montgomery and Trussell (1986) and Olsen (1994) provide overviews of the interaction between economic and demographic studies of fertility and population. Schultz (1994) examines connections between welfare generosity and labor market opportunities for women on marital rates and fertility.

The Consequences of Mothers' Labor Force Participation on Children

Does this increased labor force participation of married women with children have negative effects on the children? Stafford (1987) analyzed time diary data on 77 two-parent families with preschool-age children in 1975–1976 who were successfully reinterviewed in 1981–1982. Although the sample is small, the time diary data enables Stafford to have very complete and accurate measures of maternal time use. The follow-up survey asked teachers of the grade school children to rate the child's cognitive development in seven areas, including ability to concentrate, comprehension of class discussions, and so on. Mother's education, father's time in childcare, age, and sex of the child all had minor statistical impacts on the ratings. Family income had a positive and highly significant effect on the ratings; the presence of male siblings, especially those 3–4 years old when the child in question was a preschooler, had a significant negative impact on the ratings. Mother's time spent talking and reading and time spent helping and teaching had a positive impact on the ratings, but was barely significant at conventional levels. Finally, the amount of time a mother spent on market work in 1975–1976 had a negative impact on the ratings that was highly significant. However, because mothers' work also increases family income and therefore raised the ratings, the overall effect of mothers working is ambiguous.

Blau and Grossberg (1992) have presented more recent evidence on this issue. Using a sample of 874 3- and 4-year-olds from the 1986 National Longitudinal Surveys Youth Cohort, they examine factors that affect the cognitive development of children, as measured by their age-standardized scores on the Peabody Picture Vocabulary Test. They found that a woman who works all of the weeks during the first year of a child's life lowers the child's standardized score by about 5.8 points, but that a woman who works throughout the second and later years raises the child's standardized score by 4.2 points. Hence, the children whose mothers worked throughout their first 3–4 years of life have scores that cannot be distinguished statistically from children whose mothers did not work at all. Blau and Grossberg's findings are complementary to those of Stafford. As their findings are based on a much larger sample of children, this suggests putting more weight on their study. However, their outcome measure is narrower and their measure of the extent of mothers' labor force participation is cruder, so their results are not clearly superior to Stafford's. Also, Barnett (1992) noted that studies of preschool programs that relied only on intelligence effects missed many of the (positive) effects on other outcome measures such as cognitive achievement, eventual high school graduation, and so on. The Blau and Grossberg results are subject to this same criticism. As these longitudinal surveys stretch out over time it should be possible to analyze these other effects as well. A survey article by Haveman and Wolfe (1995) and research by Hill and O'Neill (1994) suggested that the added income effect is smaller than the reduced parental time effect so that children of working mothers have lower cognitive achievement. Resolution of this issue has important implications for the continued movement by married women toward continuous work histories. These results constitute initial evidence in favor of some parental leave during the first year after a child's birth. From an economic perspective, this is only valid if the leave increases the educational attainment of children of working mothers more than it increases the number of working mothers.

Will fathers increase their participation in childcare and other household activities? Let us look at Sweden for some evidence. Sweden has a number of policies designed to increase fathers' involvement in childcare. In the early 1980s these included (1) a cash benefit (90% of gross earnings) for 12 months in connection with childbirth that could be used by either parent or shared between them; (2) 10 days leave of absence for the father when the child is born; (3) up to 120 days annually to care for a sick child up to the age of 12 for either parent; and an additional 2 days off per child (ages 4–12) per year for parent education or visiting the child's preschool or school (Sundström, 1994). It is rather surprising therefore that studies of male labor supply in Sweden mirror the studies in the United States. Before 1980 there is a positive effect of children on male labor supply (Blomquist, 1983); after 1980, there is no statistically significant effect (Blomquist & Hansson-Brusewitz, 1990). However, Carlin and Flood (1997) have recently analyzed Swedish time diary data for 1984 and find that men with children under the age of 12 do tend to have significantly more days away from work even though their reported "normal" annual working hours are unaffected by the presence of children. It thus appears that Swedish policies are having an effect on the behavior of fathers and may serve as a model for other countries interested in promoting greater involvement of fathers in the care of children. This research does not investigate the question of whether the increased participation of fathers in childcare is worth the cost in terms of lost hours of market work for the Swedish economy.

In summary we observe that, at least in Western industrialized countries, married women are devoting more time to market work and married men more time to household chores and childcare. The total time allocated to market work, household tasks, and childcare is fairly comparable across gender. Nevertheless women still devote much more time than men to home and family and men devote more time than women to market work. There is some evidence that public policy can influence the degree of gender specialization.

The next two sections consider issues closely related to the labor force participation of women and trends in earnings inequality and the wage gap between women and men. If real wages for men are declining, economic theory suggests (1) that more married women will work and will work longer hours and (2) there will be fewer potential gains from marriage for women and less specialization of married women to household tasks. If wage discrimination is lessened and women's real wages are rising, the second effect is reinforced. As long as the empirical evidence is still right about women's labor supply being positively related to their own wage rate, the first effect is reinforced as well.

Contemporary Trends in Earnings Inequality

Earnings Inequality among Men

There has been a growing perception that earnings became less equal in the 1980s, that the working rich grew richer and the working poor grew poorer. Economic research confirms that perception, especially for male workers. In an excellent review article, Levy and Murnane (1992) indicated that, corrected for inflation, from 1979 to 1988 the proportion of working men earning more than $40,000 increased and the percentage of men earning less than $20,000 increased. Combined with relatively slow growth in average earnings, this means that many young, less educated men today have lower real earnings than their fathers at comparable stages in the life cycle.

The trend in inequality is no longer disputed; research has focused on finding the causes of the growing inequality. Harrison, Tilly, and Bluestone (1986) argued that the loss of high-wage manufacturing jobs to foreign competition was the primary source of the trend. Murphy and Welch (1992) found that there was also less demand for poorly educated workers in those manufacturing sectors that were not losing jobs to foreign competition. One of the ways firms can defend themselves from foreign competition is to modernize and substitute capital equipment for labor. So this source of inequality is, at least indirectly, related to heightened worldwide competition for markets. A demographic element is supplied by Blackburn (1990), who pointed out that the proportion of unmarried men in the labor force doubled from 1967 to 1985. As unmarried men have higher variation in their earnings, this demographic factor contributes to the growth in male earnings inequality. Burtless (1995) surveyed a number of studies of the impact of foreign trade on employment and pay of the less skilled in the United States and Europe. He concluded that liberal trade policies have apparently affected a broad class of low-skilled workers, not just those directly impacted by the inability to meet foreign competition. Nevertheless, he also notes that changes in technology may have played a more important role and that trade protection would be very deleterious if technical change (e.g., computers) is leading to the greater inequality.

Karoly (1992) found that the increased inequality of earnings cannot be attributed to increased labor force participation by women. The increased inequality among men and among women was partially offset by the narrowing of the male–female wage gap, which contributed to lower inequality between men and women. Changes in age and schooling patterns since 1975 have tended to reduce inequality, while changes in industry shares have tended to increase inequality. One cannot say that the increased inequality is due solely to changes in gender, age, education, or industry shares in the labor force. Nevertheless, while the increased supply of women is not implicated in the increased inequality of earnings, Katz and Murphy (1992) concluded that this increased inequality is due to increases in the demand for women as well as better-educated workers generally and, within occupations, the high-skill end of the occupation. They suggest that part of the within-occupation demand shift likely reflects changes, such as computers, that tend to require more skill and more education.

Earnings Inequality among Women

Women have also seen growing hourly wage inequality and slow growth in hourly wages. However, increases in hours of work per year has overwhelmed the hourly effect. A large reduction in the variance of number of hours worked per year has greater weight than the small increase in hourly wage inequality when we look at annual earnings. There is less inequality in annual earnings among working women today; the percentage of women earning less than $20,000 annually has shrunk, while the percentage earning over $20,000 annually has grown (Levy & Murnane, 1992).

Effect of Married Women's Earnings on Family Inequality

Shaw (1989) addressed the question of the effect of married women's earnings on inequality of family earnings. Because of positive assortative mating for many characteristics, there is a concern that the increased participation of married women in the labor force will increase inequality in family earnings. Using Panel Study of Income Dynamics data for 1968–1981, Shaw found that the participation of wives has a small equalizing tendency for lifetime family earnings. That is because, during that period, women with high-earning spouses tended to have higher earnings than average both before and after childrearing years but substantially lower than average earnings during the child rearing years. Of course, if married women start to have more continuous labor force participation during the childrearing ages, this finding will have to be reexamined. Shaw also acknowledged that if increased labor force participation is associated with a greater incidence of female-headed households, household inequality would tend to increase. Behrman, Rosenzweig, and Taubman (1994) studied the effect of the marriage market on household inequality by examining the outcomes for two samples of twins born between 1917–1927 and 1935–1955, respectively. Twin studies allow the researchers to have better controls for individual variation in unobserved characteristics. Their studies reinforce the findings of Shaw in that positive assortative mating for educational outcomes is partially offset by negative assortative mating for labor force participation. We await a study based on more recent data to determine if the increased labor force participation of married women is changing and exacerbating household earnings inequality.

Trends in Wage Inequality between Men and Women

The Gross Wage Gap

Because the level of women's wages has feedback effects on the division of labor in the family and influences a married woman's decision to participate in the labor force, the progress of women's wages has a definite impact on family well-being. Furthermore, the narrowing of the wage gap between women and men, other things equal, decreases earnings inequality.

Blau (1992) reported that, for white women, the ratio of average hourly earnings for women to average hourly earnings for men increased from 60% in 1971 to 74% in 1988. The wage gap fell from 40% to 26%. Among blacks, the ratio of women's to men's wages rose from 68% to 86% over the same period, a fall in the wage gap from 32% to 14%. The earnings gap between men and women has been attributed by economists to either differences in human capital or wage and employment discrimination.

The human capital argument builds on the traditional role model of the wife who has primary responsibility for the home and the husband who has the responsibility to work. Because married women have had primary responsibility for home and children they are less likely to invest in human capital that is appropriate to uninterrupted careers. In this view, married women were more likely, as verified by the data, to interrupt careers for childcare responsibilities or to switch jobs when the husband was transferred or moved voluntarily to another geographic area. The wife would also, it was argued, search for jobs over a narrower geographical area as she would be called upon to leave work if a child needed to be picked up from school and so on. For all of these reasons, any woman who anticipated being married and raising a family would have been reluctant to invest in human capital for jobs where such interruptions were detrimental to one's career.

The wage and employment discrimination argument is that women have been systematically excluded from a variety of high-paying jobs and careers because of male prejudice. In this view, early antidiscrimination laws that prohibited unequal pay for equal work were not sufficient and much of the earnings gap was due to occupational segregation of women into relatively low-paying jobs.

The differences between the two arguments are actually subtle and difficult to untangle using statistical methods. The human capital argument emphasizes a woman's *choice* of training, education, and career, taking societal attitudes as given; the discrimination argument emphasizes *restrictions* on a woman's choice because of societal attitudes. The approach that has been used in economics to disentangle these two effects is to estimate earnings functions for men and women. Such studies see how much of the earnings gap can be explained by human capital factors such as education, work experience, and other related factors. The unexplained portion of the gap, in the minds of some, can be attributed to labor market discrimination. Others argue that it simply puts an upper bound on the amount of discrimination. Arguing from statistical theory the unexplained portion of any regression is a measure of our ignorance. To argue that the entire gap is due to discrimination is to argue that the regression in question has controlled for all other possible sources of a wage gap. Some examples of such unobserved sources might include drive, motivation, willingness to place job over family, and choice of subfield (4 years of college-level engineering is worth more in the market than 4 years of college-level education in nursing, and there are differences within engineering and nursing specialties as well).

Economists who argue that the unexplained gap represents an upper bound tend to be working with a narrow interpretation of discrimination. These economists are interested in discriminatory actions by an employer. Does the employer pay lower wages for a subgroup that is actually just as productive as others who get higher pay? If so, then there is labor market discrimination. However, if a subgroup gets lower pay because of *societal* attitudes about sex and family roles or because of choices made because of perceptions of past discrimination then there is no current labor market discrimination. It is important to distinguish between current employer discrimination and other more general forms of discrimination in order to know whether we need either better laws, better enforcement of laws directed at employer discrimination, or broader initiatives.

Those who take a broader view of discrimination argue that the unexplained portion of the wage gap may underestimate the true extent of discrimination because all choices that lead to particular fields of study, careers, years of work experience, and so on are influenced by past as well as current discrimination. Perhaps surprisingly, Becker, who is generally considered one of the more conservative analysts of the family, fits in this second group. Becker (1991, p. 63) has argued that *all* of the earnings gap should be attributed to discrimination and other causes of any gender-based division of labor within the family. The broad view of discrimination argues that all of these forms of discrimination are interrelated and wound up together. Consequently, they cannot be attacked piecemeal.

Without resolving this disagreement, let us look briefly at the evidence economists have found for the existence of the wage gap, the extent to which it has shrunk, and whether it is likely to shrink further in the future.

Cain (1986) observed that the median earnings ratio (women to men) for year-round, full-time workers remained at about 0.6 from 1939 to 1982, for a gross wage gap of 40%. O'Neill and Polachek (1993) updated the series and found a significant narrowing of the gap. The ratio was 0.62 in 1982, rising to 0.64 in 1987, 0.69 in 1989, and 0.72 in 1990 for a gross wage gap of 28%. Orazem, Mattila, and Yu (1990) argued that we should look at the earnings ratios within individual labor markets rather than across the economy as a whole. When they break down the information across 37 occupations and then reaggregate to get an overall measure weighted by the presence of women in various occupations, they find that the earnings ratio rose from about 0.62 in 1967 to 0.74 in 1986. They concluded that gains have been made but that a gap of 26% still remained as of 1986. Their controlling for occupation thus reduces the unexplained gap by 10 percentage points (one-third). Smith and Ward (1989) have argued that this slow observed progress is tied to the rapid entry (or reentry) into the labor force during the 1970s and early 1980s of women with relatively low levels of work experience. They present evidence suggesting that, even without any further gains in opening up new occupations to women, the gap should shrink further from 1985 to 1995 than it did in the 10 previous years (because the average work experience of women will now rise rapidly relative to the work experience of men). Evidence from Wellington (1993) tended to support Smith and Ward. She found that half of the reduction in the gender wage gap from 1976 to 1985 was due to changes in women's work histories including job tenure with a given employer.

Some other recent work has examined the prospects of women in a particular field where overt discrimination should be least in evidence, the legal profession. A woman lawyer should be able to file suit to overturn any such discrimination. Using the American Bar Association's Survey of Career Satisfaction/Dissatisfaction, Laband and Lentz (1993) found no evidence of discrimination against women lawyers on earnings or promotion. They do find evidence of perceptions of less overt forms of discrimination. Women lawyers expressed significantly less satisfaction than their male counterparts on items such as "chance to advance is good," "advancement is determined by the work one does," and "I have control over matters I handle." Working with surveys of graduates of the University of Michigan Law School, Wood, Corcoran, and Courant (1993) estimated a wage gap regression for male and female lawyers. The unadjusted gap in average annual earnings between a sample of male and female graduates 15 years after graduation is 39%. Controlling for law school performance, marital and fertility history, experience, and job setting (business vs. government lawyer, size of firm, and so on) this still leaves as much as one-third of the gap (13%) unexplained. It is clear that a major portion of the gap is, even for this highly paid group, related to the different commitment of men and women to parenting. This is not overt labor market discrimination but, as Becker has observed, due to discrimination and/or other causes of the gender-based division of labor in the family.

The Unexplained Wage Gap

A number of economists (see Cain, 1986, pp. 749–759 for a survey of efforts through 1985) have attempted to explain the earnings gap by examining large national samples of men and women that report not only earnings but a number of human capital measures such as education and labor market experience. Recent examples include Baldwin and Johnson (1992), Barron et al. (1993). Even and Macpherson (1993), and Fields and Wolff (1995). These studies explained between 30% and 60% of the gap by controlling for some of the following factors: occupation, industry, union status, education, prior work experience, and turnover; that leaves 40% or more unexplained that could be attributed to discrimination. If a single study could control for all of these

factors at once, the unexplained gap might shrink to 20% or below.

Those who argue that remaining discrimination is small emphasize that in general the unexplained residual from a regression is simply a measure of our ignorance. To attribute it entirely to discrimination requires that the *only* unobserved factor that can affect wages is discrimination. Bergmann (1989), on the other hand, who argued that most of the wage gap is due to women being denied equal access to well-paying jobs, would view controlling for occupation and industry as clearly inappropriate because that would validate any occupational or industry-based discrimination that has resulted in differential representation of women in different occupations and industries. She would argue that part of the *explained* portion of the wage gap is not independent of discrimination either. There seems little reason to hope that these different views of discrimination will be reconciled by additional empirical evidence from wage discrimination studies.

Wage gap studies can also document whether wages of men and women are moving closer over time or not. Blau and Kahn (1994) found that the unadjusted ratio of women's to men's wages rose from about 60% to almost 70% from 1975 to 1987. If adjusted for human capital differences (education, work experience, and race) the ratio rose from about 72% to about 78%. The gap thus continued to close over this period. Rise in women's work experience relative to men's accounted for about half of the closing, with the rising relative wage in women's occupations contributing more than a quarter of the closing; deunionization accounted for 13%, mostly by shrinking male wages.

These techniques can also be applied to examine the wage gap between black and white women. Anderson and Shapiro (1996) find, from a study of 2007 white and black women ages 33–44 (the National longitudinal Study of the Labor Market Experience of Young Women for 1968–1988), that this wage gap fell from about 50% in 1940 to about 0 in 1980, when controlling for age, education, and labor market characteristics. Unfortunately these gains eroded in the 1980s so that by 1988 there was again an unexplained gap of 12% between the wages of white and black women.

Poverty and Welfare Reform: Interactions between Income Maintenance, Dependency, and Family Stability

Does AFDC Lead to Welfare Dependence?

The major response of the government to poverty has been in the form of income maintenance programs such as AFDC and targeted assistance such as food stamps, Medicaid, and public housing. Economists have considered the effects of such programs on the incentive to work, long-term welfare dependency, family structure, and the transmission of dependency from one generation to the next.

In an excellent survey of the economics literature in these areas, Moffitt (1992) noted that numerous studies document a statistically significant reduction in the labor supply of female heads of families due to the AFDC and food stamp programs. While there may be some legitimate concern about such a reduction, the estimates of the effect are not large. The midpoint estimate of the effect for female heads on AFDC would imply a reduction in weekly hours of work from about 14 to the actual average of 9. This implies reduced earnings, at the minimum wage, of about $1000 a year. Even if the work disincentive effects could be reduced to none, there would be a substantial shortfall in earnings. Nevertheless, in a society where most nonpoor women with young children work there is a growing concern about programs that appear to reduce the incentives of poor mothers to work.

Of special importance for public policy is the question of whether the welfare system contributes to the rise in the number of households headed by women with no spouse present. In over 90% of AFDC caseloads, benefits are paid to families that consist of a mother and her children, with no spouse present. The Becker model would suggest that the state displaces the role of the husband as primary wage earner and hence encourages either nonmarriage, divorce, or abandonment in the event of prolonged unemployment. Others, such as Wilson and Neckerman (1986), have suggested that the decline is primarily related to the worsening economic opportunities for young black men in the 1970s and 1980s as jobs have moved out of the inner cities and skill requirements have risen.

A first approach looks at the broad evidence on rates and AFDC benefit levels to see if there is an association between the two trends. Evidence presented in Moffitt (1992) indicated that the real (i.e., adjusted for inflation) value of AFDC benefits rose steadily from 1960 to 1975, leveled off and then fell in the late 1970s and early 1980s, leveling off again in the mid-1980s. Hence for the early period there is a positive correlation between rises in real benefit levels and indicators like nonwhite female headship rates, divorce rates, and illegitimacy rates. On the other hand, there is no particular relationship between those rates for the period 1975–1986. This latter evidence leads Moffitt to conclude there is little support for the hypothesis that the welfare system is a determinant of the growth in households headed by women and in illegitimacy. Existing evidence, however, does not allow us to reject the notion that the welfare system was one of the causes of the early rise in these indicators. Furthermore, if behavior adjusts only gradually to changes in incentive structure, the relatively modest drop-off in the real value

of AFDC benefits might be too small to reverse a pattern of behavior built up over 15 years that saw a substantial rise in the real value of the AFDC benefit. Is there other evidence that can be brought to bear on the question of welfare dependency?

A second approach looks at the evidence from careful statistical analysis of cross-sectional or panel data on the characteristics of large numbers of households. Multiple regression techniques are used to control for other observable factors that influence family structure. A number of recent economic studies examine welfare effects on family structure and welfare dependency. Hoffman and Duncan (1988) considered the remarriage decisions of women who were divorced or separated between 1969 and 1982. They found that changes in benefit levels positively affect the utilization of AFDC by these women but do not have any appreciable effect on their probability of remarriage. As remarriage is one of the primary means by which female-headed families move from welfare to nonwelfare status, this finding suggests that AFDC does not supplant the goal of an intact family with earned income. Hoffman and Duncan (1995) find that more generous AFDC benefits do slightly increase the risk of marital dissolution. As divorce and separation lead typically to the creation of a female-headed household that is at greater risk of poverty and welfare dependence, their evidence suggests the possibility of a causal link between welfare generosity and welfare dependency.

Hutchens, Jakubson, and Schwartz (1989) examined the question of welfare dependency in considering whether a single mother establishes her own independent household or resides in the home of another, presumably that of her own mother or grandmother. The implication is that if the mother is not establishing her own household the risk of welfare dependency across generations is greater. For this reason, some states have reduced the benefits paid to single mothers who reside as a subfamily. Hutchens et al. found a small positive effect of these benefit reduction provisions on the propensity to establish an independent household but found little relationship between the overall level of AFDC benefits and the propensity to establish an independent household.

A related issue is whether the public assistance displaces intergenerational family assistance. Rosenzweig and Wolpin (1994b) studied nearly 3000 matched parent–daughter pairs in the National Longitudinal Survey of Youth from 1968 to 1985. They found that public assistance for the poor slightly substitutes for parental assistance, but the effect is very small. A $1000 increase in public aid reduces the incidence of parental aid by about 3%. However, their data do not allow them to identify reductions in the amount of aid short of reducing it to zero. Hence more work is needed to firmly establish this tentative conclusion.

Although there is still much research to be done in this

area, none of the recent empirical findings from the economics literature suggest that reducing AFDC benefit levels alone would have anything more than a very modest effect on marriage rates, divorce rates, or illegitimacy. Other forms of intervention, such as encouraging the completion of high school, generating economic opportunities, and reducing the incidence of high stress events during childhood, hold more promise for the long-term reduction of welfare dependency across generations. The evidence clearly suggests that reducing the incidence of welfare receipt in a given generation should have multiplied effects through successive generations.

Early work experience is associated with women leaving AFDC rolls faster. Petersen (1995) examined the Census Bureau's SIPP to determine the rate of leaving AFDC for 502 female-headed families that began receiving AFDC between June 1987 and August 1991. If a woman held a job at the time of enrolling in AFDC and/or worked for at least 6 consecutive months during the 18-month period before the survey, then she was much more likely to leave AFDC during any given month. It may be that prior work experience enables women to become self-sufficient through better employment and earnings, but it may also be that women with early experience are the ones with more drive and determination. That is, their drive and determination get them early jobs and also, should they fall into welfare, make it less likely they will stay there. Whether the work experience causes the early exit from AFDC or personal qualities influence both the tendency to have work experience and the short stay on AFDC cannot be determined from this study.

Another issue receiving increased attention is recidivism. If an exit from welfare is followed by a return to welfare the goal of a transition to permanent independence is not achieved. Stevens (1994) studied data on poverty and non-poverty spells from 1968 to 1988. She found that half of those who rise above the poverty line fall below it again within a 5-year period. She also found that the recidivism rate has been rising for white female-headed households. With regard to specific antipoverty programs, Blank and Ruggles (1994) found that about 20% of all spells off of AFDC and food stamps end with a return to those programs within a 6- to 9-month period. This suggests that targeting antirecidivism efforts at the period around 6 to 8 months after leaving AFDC or food stamps would be effective.

One policy reform that would, if implemented, substantially reduce the receipt of welfare in the current generation is the Child Support Assurance System (CSAS) described by Garfinkel, Robins, Wong, and Meyer (1990). The CSAS is designed to sharply reduce the reliance on the welfare system by divorced or abandoned women who should be, but are not, receiving child support payments from the fathers of their children. A minimum child support benefit is guaranteed, along with automatic wage-withholding of the child support payment from the wages of the father. The system makes up any difference between child support collections from the father and the minimum guarantee. This system was to be field-tested in Wisconsin but political opposition prevented its full implementation (Garfinkel, 1994). Computer-generated microsimulations suggest that the system has the potential to reduce poverty, lower welfare caseloads, and reduce the overall cost of income maintenance. However, it is a relatively expensive anti-poverty program because it is not narrowly targeted on the poor. If the program helps all families who are eligible for child support, it will help more nonpoor than poor families (Sorensen & Clark, 1994). Support for the program must be sought in terms of a broader impact than simply reducing poverty. We do not know yet whether we could expect reductions in long-term welfare dependency as a result of CSAS. Nevertheless, the following studies suggest that any reduction in current welfare dependency should tend to reduce the intergenerational transmission of dependency.

Welfare Dependence across Generations

Is welfare dependency transmitted across generations? Antel (1992) examined data on 2430 women ages 14–19 in 1979 (and their mothers) from the National Longitudinal Survey of Youth 1979–1988. He found that, controlling for a number of other socioeconomic variables, if a mother was receiving AFDC during 1979, the probability of her daughter participating in welfare in 1987 was raised from about 1 in 14 to nearly 1 in 3. The data do not allow Antel to distinguish between long-term and short-term stays on welfare, but they seem to provide striking evidence of the incidence of welfare being related across generations.

Several studies examine the connection between AFDC and out-of-wedlock births among black teenage females. Duncan and Hoffman (1990) found, consistent with the Wilson (1987) hypothesis, that marital and career opportunities play a much larger role in out-of-wedlock births to teenage mothers than does the level of AFDC benefits available. AFDC benefit levels have a positive effect on the likelihood of experiencing an out-of-wedlock birth, but the effect is not statistically significant; variables related to economic opportunities in terms of geography and family characteristics had a significant impact on the likelihood of out-of-wedlock births. Those with the least to lose in terms of economic prospects are most likely to experience out-of-wedlock birth.

Haveman and Wolfe (1993) examined 20 years of longitudinal data on 892 young women followed from when they were 6 and under to when they were between the ages of 19 and 25. This is the richest and most appropriate data set utilized yet for considering the issue of welfare dependency across generations. They consider both the likelihood of an out-of-wedlock birth during the teen years and, conditional on having had an out-of-wedlock birth, the likelihood of applying for AFDC benefits. Results indicated, in turn, that if the child's mother graduated from high school or if the family reported membership in some religion, an out-of-wedlock birth was significantly less likely. Moreover, an increase in the number of parental separations made out-of-wedlock births more likely, while the number of remarriages was negatively associated with the likelihood of out-of-wedlock births. The welfare status of parents also had no significant impact on the likelihood of an out-of-wedlock birth. However, if the child's parents received welfare or if the household had relatively low income during the childhood years, then teenage mothers were significantly more likely to apply for welfare benefits when an out-of-wedlock birth occurred. More frequent childhood moves was another variable that increased the likelihood of seeking AFDC benefits. Community economic indicators and state welfare generosity variables also were found to have small effects that were not statistically significant. Finally, the increased tendency for daughters of AFDC mothers to *apply* for welfare benefits may be due either to reduced feelings of stigma or simply to better knowledge of the welfare system.

Lundberg and Plotnick (1995) examined premarital childbearing among nearly 2000 14- to 16-year-old women in 1979. The results of this study revealed that decisions of white teenagers concerning marriage after conception, abortion, and pregnancy appear to be related to state policies on welfare, abortion, and family planning. No such relationship, however, could be established for black teenage women. Even among the white women, in turn, it was not clear whether the relationship was causal or whether the state policies are simply indicators of state-specific attitudes about abortion, premarital birth, and so on. Consequently, it was concluded that a policy change due to national directives would have no effect on teenage decisions when the policies were merely indicators. However, if the policies actually change the costs of various behaviors, then such changes would be more likely to have an impact on white teenage women.

Effects of Teen Birthing on Mother

A related but separate question concerns the ill effects of giving birth while still a teenager. This event could have negative consequences, potentially for both mother and child. Geronimus and Korenman (1992) presented evidence that suggests earlier studies overestimated the negative effects of teen birth on the future socioeconomic outcomes for the mother. By appropriately controlling for family background heterogeneity (in mother's and father's education,

number of siblings, and parental family arrangement) they found the association of teen birth with socioeconomic variables less severe but still deleterious. When they use a sample of sisters, they find, with two or three data sets, that the effects are still weaker. Nevertheless, they do not completely overturn the findings of earlier studies indicating that teen births continue to have a significantly negative impact on the socioeconomic status of the mother.

Related to such results, Ribar (1994) found indirect evidence of success for Title IX of the Educational Amendments of 1972, which outlawed discrimination on the basis of pregnancy and parenthood in the public schools. In a study of 4658 women from the 1979–1985 panels of the National Longitudinal Study of Youth, Ribar found that teenage parenthood and failure to complete school are no longer tightly linked, with the implication being that policies to prevent teen births might now have little effect on high school completion. Instead, Ribar concluded that policies and programs directed at the shared determinants of teen births and school drop-out are likely to have higher payoff. Efforts to keep families together and increase parental education have the potential to reduce teen births and improve high school completion. For black women, however, McElroy (1996) finds evidence that it is not having a birth before age 18 that reduces 4-year college enrollment, but rather that early birth after age 17 (including ages 18, 19, and 20) is the primary contributor. Simply getting out of high school, therefore, may not be the answer or a guarantor of success.

Effects of Teenage Childbirth on the Children of Teen Mothers

These findings may be contrasted with findings on the outcomes for *children* of teenage mothers (reported in Geronimus, Korenman & Hillemeier, 1994, and Geronimus & Korenman, 1993). Evidence was presented in these studies suggesting that, once family background characteristics are properly controlled, having a teenage mother (rather than an older mother) has no significant negative effect on infant health or early child development. Rosenzweig and Wolpin (1995) echo this finding in a careful study of 6900 births to 3710 mothers from the National Longitudinal Surveys Youth Cohort. They control for mother's weight prior to pregnancy, mother's net of birthweight weight gain per week, whether the mother obtains prenatal care, number of cigarettes smoked, consumption of alcohol, and spacing between births if not the first birth. After controlling for various behaviors that are more likely to occur among low-income mothers, having a birth at younger ages, if anything, increases birthweight. Furthermore, Bronars and Grogger (1994) found no evidence of negative effects of unplanned births on the educational progress of the resulting children. The results of these studies call into question whether interventions to reduce teen childbearing will, by themselves, have a significant impact on the well-being of poor children. Merely delaying the birth of children is unlikely to improve birth outcomes much. A strategy that focuses on reducing detrimental behavior appears more likely to improve health problems of newborns than simply getting teenage girls to delay motherhood. Consequently, if the delayed motherhood also brings with it increased maturity that reduces the incidence of negative behaviors, then delaying motherhood may still have some payoff.

Altruism and Intergenerational Transfers of Wealth and Human Capital

Correlations of Fathers' and Sons' Earnings

Becker and Tomes (1979, 1986) suggested that intergenerational mobility among income classes will depend on (1) the investment in children of both time and money, (2) the inheritability of characteristics, and (3) the presence of any capital market imperfections that may make it more difficult for the children of low-income parents to borrow for purposes of human capital investment. Becker (1991) noted that, if ability is inheritable and if wealthier parents also invest more in the human capital of their offspring, there could be relatively little intergenerational mobility. He noted further, however, that most studies of intergenerational mobility in earnings completed through the mid-1980s show very low correlations of father and son earnings. Most of these studies have focused on the earnings of fathers and sons or on the family incomes of parents and daughters because of the intermittent labor market participation of many women. Based on these data, Becker concluded that a substantial regression to the mean in earnings exists so that any worry about cultures of poverty or wealth being persistent would seem to be unnecessary. Recently, however, studies have appeared that suggest less intergenerational mobility in the United States than had been previously suspected.

Before examining the overall measures of intergenerational mobility in earnings, consider some of the factors involved in the transmission of human capital. For example, Peters (1992) has pulled together some data from the National Longitudinal Surveys of Labor Market Experience on parents and their adult children. The mothers were between the ages of 30 and 44 in 1967 and the fathers between the ages of 45 and 59 in 1966; the children were between the ages of 26 and 30 at the time of the interview. Although results indicated that a positive association existed between parent and child incomes, there also was evidence of substantial mobility for both sons and daughters. However, because the adult children are still in the relatively early years of their work lives, these data must be viewed as early indicators rather than as definitive. (The same caveat applies to the studies by Solon and Zimmerman discussed later.)

Solon (1992) noted that most prior studies of intergenerational mobility by sociologists and by economists such as Behrman and Taubman (1985) estimated the correlation in the logarithm of fathers' and sons' earnings to be 0.2 or less. He argues that these studies tended to underestimate the correlation because (1) they used one-time measures of income like annual earnings rather than looking at earnings over a more significant portion of the career, and (2) they have tended to use data from relatively homogeneous samples rather than random samples. Solon avoided these problems in analyzing 384 father–son pairs from the Panel Study on Income Dynamics, a national probability sample. Because of attrition from 1968 to 1984 the final sample probably includes fewer low-income people than a true random sample but is still more heterogeneous than previous samples. Solon found correlations in family income, long-run earnings, and hourly wages that are 0.4 or higher—more than twice as high as previous studies. Moreover, Zimmerman (1992) corroborated these findings using a sample of 876 father–son pairs from the National Longitudinal Survey from 1966 to 1981. He found the elasticity of sons' earnings to fathers' earnings to be 0.4 or higher and that measures of intergenerational mobility such as wages, earnings, and a socioeconomic status index all show similar amounts of intergenerational mobility. This suggests considerably less mobility in earnings than previously thought. Note, however, that even a correlation among fathers and sons earnings of 0.5 would not be grossly inconsistent with the notion of *shirtsleeves to shirtsleeves in three (or four) generations*. Fathers earning 200% more than the mean would, on average, have sons earning 100% more, grandsons earning 50% more and greatgrandsons earning 25% more than the mean. Similarly, greatgrandsons of men earning 50% less than the mean would, on average, earn only 6% less than the mean. Consequently, the position of one's parents and grandparents in the income distribution means a lot, even in the United States, but does not mean everything. Thus, relative position alone cannot explain a culture of poverty (or of wealth) extending over more than a few generations. This is perfectly consistent, of course, with the notion of a culture of relative poverty extending over 40 to 60 years, which many would argue is a high price to exact from the descendants of an unsuccessful family.

The Quantity/Quality Trade-off in Children and the Transmission of Wealth

The family planning decisions of parents influence the success of their children, with such observers as Becker

(1991) emphasizing that parents face a quantity/quality trade-off. The more children a family has, other things being equal, the fewer resources of time and money available for investment in the children's human capital. Some recent evidence in favor of the quantity/quality trade-off for children, for example, is provided by Hanushek (1992) who examined a sample of low-income families from the Gary Income Maintenance Experiment 1971–1975. Evidence indicated that larger family size significantly reduces children's achievement in grades 2 through 6 as measured by scores on Iowa reading comprehension and vocabulary tests. In contrast, birth order has no significant effect on such achievement apart from the higher probability of being in a smaller family if you are the first- rather than the second- or later-born child. Indeed, for families with four or more children, being born later is an advantage in terms of achievement scores. Such results may be due to the low-income sample and the relative prevalence of births before finishing schooling; Hanushek is unable to control for mother's schooling. Rosenzweig and Wolpin (1994a) examined the educational outcomes of siblings where mothers sometimes continued schooling between births and at other times did not. They found that schooling of the mother at the time of giving birth increases the educational achievement of the child. Neither divorce nor market work by the mothers had any apparent impact on measured achievement. We cannot generalize from this sample to the country as a whole, but the results are suggestive.

On the quantity/quality trade-off, Peters (1992) found that having more siblings lowered the earnings of sons but not daughters. Controlling for income level, the mother's work status had a positive impact on the income of daughters. If the father attended college, the income and earnings of sons was raised, while only a small positive effect was apparent for daughters. Among high-income parents, however, fathers who attended college functioned to raise the income of daughters as well.

Government Programs and the Transfer of Wealth and Poverty across Generations

What about government attempts to influence either income distribution or the intergenerational transmission of wealth and poverty? Can government programs reduce either the transmission of wealth or poverty across generations? Barro (1974) and Barro and Becker (1988) have suggested that altruistic linkages between generations of a given family tend to render any targeted government redistribution among those members ineffective. Government spending on Social Security for the elderly may be offset by reduced transfers from children to their elderly parents; increased spending on children's education and libraries may be offset by lower parental expenditures on such items. However, capital con-

straints on the poor may make these offsetting effects smaller for low-income families than for the rich.

Becker (1991) has also suggested that even government-supported efforts to provide greater opportunities for children from low-income families may be offset partially or in full by parents transferring family expenditures away from the favored (by the government program) children toward other children and/or themselves. This effect would be especially troublesome for measuring the results of field studies where some children within a family are in the experimental group and others are in the control group. Even if a program were fairly successful, the tendency of parents to reallocate family resources to those outside the program (and hence in the control group) could mitigate the positive effects of a program. Even if all children in a family are recipients of a given service, the parents may reduce the amount they would otherwise have spent on these items in favor of other consumption items.

Becker pointed to evidence on compensatory education programs for the disadvantaged as partial support for his arguments. Most research has indicated that preschool enrichment programs have produced short-term gains in IQ but no long-term gains. However, Barnett (1992) has reviewed the data from a number of early preschool projects from the 1960s, especially the Perry Preschool Study, and found that, although these programs had no permanent effect on IQ, they did improve the long-term success of the children in school. Specifically, participants were less likely to be retained in a grade or require special education, and they had consistently higher achievement test scores from age 7 through 19.

One cannot generalize from these relatively small projects to a national program like Head Start, but Barnett's findings do suggest that the benefits of compensatory preschool education programs may not be entirely offset by smaller parental investment. Currie and Thomas (1995), for example, considered the effect of Head Start enrollment on 5000 children and found substantial benefits (persisting through adolescence) to white children who attended Head Start in terms of rising scores on tests measuring academic performance. Furthermore, they were 47% less likely to repeat a grade than other white children. Overall, their study confirms the earlier findings of no lasting effect of Head Start on the educational attainment of black children.

More complete follow-through and analysis of outcomes for children in Head Start programs seems necessary before a firm conclusion can be reached. Family and neighborhood environment may be simply too deleterious for the early advantages from Head Start enrollment to be maintained. In any case, this evidence questions Becker's conjecture about the transfer of family resources being sufficient to fully offset governmental expenditures on these programs. It seems unlikely that black families would act to offset public expenditures, while it seems even more certain that white families would not.

Altonji, Hayashi, and Kotlikoff (1992) have found evidence against the extreme version of the hypothesis that families will offset government expenditures in favor of the young or the old. Using data on families over the past 22 years in the Panel Study of Income Dynamics, they found that, at a given point in time, the consumption of parents and children depends on their own income, not on the combined income of parents and children. Furthermore, changes in consumption expenditures over time are highly dependent upon changes in one's personal income, not on changes in the total income of parents and children. Finally, the resources of the extended family have only a modest effect on household consumption. Altonji et al. suggested, for example, that their findings merely rule out the idea that extended families completely pool their resources over generations and across time, but does not serve as evidence against all transfers between generations. It certainly does not rule out the notion that parents will assist children or children assist elderly parents to offset an unexpected income shortfall. It might also be instructive to partition their sample and look only at families with relatively substantial wealth to determine if there is greater or lesser tendency to pool income across generations for families that are unconstrained by capital markets.

Becker and Tomes (1986) argued that wealthy families will always invest the efficient amount in their children's human capital but that poorer families may not because they are constrained from borrowing to finance such investment. If there is an effective implicit contract between parents and children, enforced perhaps by guilt and social pressure, that parents will invest more in children's human capital in return for support when they are elderly, this problem is diminished. Nevertheless, they concluded that government taxes and transfers that shift funds from the relatively wealthy to the relatively poor for the purposes of human capital investment (e.g., publicly supported education) will enhance efficiency as well as equity.

What about governmental provision of Social Security? Because of the financing mechanism, Social Security in the United States can be thought of as a wealth transfer from children to parents. If the altruism of children toward parents when they are old is certain, Nerlove et al. (1988) concluded that such a redistribution of wealth should increase human capital investment of lower-income families closer to efficient levels. In a recent paper, however, Chakrabarti, Lord, and Rangazas (1993) argued that if the altruism of the children to the parents is uncertain, where some risk exists that the children will contribute nothing to the parents, then this redistribution lowers human capital investment in children. Because Social Security increases the probability that chil-

dren (especially from poor families) will provide no support when the parents are old, the parents have less incentive to invest in their children's human capital. Low-income parents in a society without Social Security have an incentive to "oversacrifice" current consumption to raise investment in children's human capital closer to the efficient level. When they are recipients of adequate support from public funds as they become older, less private incentive exists to undergo extensive sacrifice. In a related way, Becker and Murphy (1988) have argued that public support of education, *together with* public support of the elderly in retirement, can be efficiency-enhancing in overcoming the difficulties that lower-income families have in obtaining funds for both kinds of support.

Laurence Kotlikoff, as reported in the National Bureau of Economic Research (1992), worried that such public support is one of the reasons for the relatively low savings rate in the United States compared to other industrialized countries. He argued that economic exchanges and support within families are substantially lower than in the past. He worried, consistent with Becker, that the tendency to bequeath may be falling because of the deterioration of family ties, coupled with the increased provision of annuities; this would tend to reduce U.S. savings at a time when it is generally felt that national savings rates ought to increase. Of course part of the low savings rate of the 1970s and 1980s was due to demographic effects. Because the Baby Boom generation was slow to marry and have children, traditional patterns of low or no savings before marriage, dissaving during the early years of family formation, and saving once the children become older were prevalent. These patterns were probably smoothed somewhat for the typical middle- and upper-income "Boomer." Saving was probably a bit higher when single, especially the last few years of being single. Dissaving was lower, on the other hand, during the first years of family formation because of some accumulated assets, with savings rising rapidly as children age and moderate- and upper-income parents often save for both children's college educations and their own retirement. Despite Kotlikoff's worries, therefore, savings rates may rise in the 1990s and the first decade or two of the next century.

Wealth is not perfectly transferred across generations although there is a higher correlation between the earnings of fathers and sons as well as parents' family incomes and those of daughters than had previously been thought. It would appear to take at least four generations for the advantages of wealth or the disadvantages of poverty to dissipate. Nevertheless, the great-grandchildren of a wealthy family are only slightly higher in income distribution, on average, than someone whose great-grandparents had an average income. Moreover, on the average, the great-grandchildren of poor families are only slightly below average on income distribution. The quantity/quality trade-off is important, as those from larger families appear to have lower achievement levels in school and may have lower earnings as well. Controlling for income, market work by mothers appears to have either no effect or a small negative effect overall on the achievement and earnings of children. It also appears that government programs can contribute to this process, with evidence being absent that intrafmaily altruism can fully offset the effects of programs like Social Security, public support for education, and compensatory education. Indeed, such programs probably enhance efficiency, although side effects include increases in intergenerational independence (loosening family ties) and, with other things being equal, diminished savings rates.

The Economic Status of the Elderly

Because the elderly constitute the fastest growing segment of society and the front edge of the Baby Boom cohort is now within 15 years of traditional retirement age, enormous concern exists about the current and future well-being of the elderly and the burden that aging Boomers will place on their children and grandchildren. Hurd (1990) presents an extensive and insightful survey of research results concerning the economic status of the elderly up through the late 1980s. The expected number of years retired for elderly men increased by about 4 years or 31% from 1970 to 1986. Nevertheless, in the absence of an unanticipated decrease in productivity (e.g., due to an economic depression), Social Security, savings, and pensions appear sufficient for the needs of current elderly and those now approaching retirement. Whether they will still be sufficient by the second or third decade of the next century is an open question.

There is now a large number of workers compared to retirees, but this demographic pattern will change soon. Should transfers to the elderly in the form of Social Security, Medicaid, and Medicare be made less generous? Hurd finds that, on average, the elderly are at least as well as well off, on average, as the nonelderly, a finding that favors the reduction of transfers, especially as the burden on the working generations grows. Elderly widows, on the other hand, have a very high poverty rate and certainly need continued support. Furthermore, Rendall and Speare (1995) find that if elderly women did not reside with their extended families, their poverty rates would jump by more than 40%. Although some may argue that the state should make it possible for elderly women to live independently of their families, it seems more likely that economic constraints will result in increased numbers of elderly women residing with their immediate relatives as the working age population shrinks relative to the retired. If economies are to be achieved, therefore, better targeted support for the elderly seems in order.

Another option is to change provisions of Social Security to encourage longer labor market participation by the elderly. Ruhm (1995) finds with recent data that the early retirement provisions of Social Security have continued to be an important determinant of early retirement. Reimers and Honig (1996) find that increases in the Social Security credit for delaying retirement would be effective in encouraging the continued labor supply of older women, while increasing the limit on allowed earnings before Social Security benefits are taxed would encourage older men to continue their participation.

As the health and longevity of the elderly improve, we need to revisit the notion of early and normal retirement ages. An idea worth considering is for the Social Security Administration to index (with adjustment every 10 years or so, not annually) the early and normal retirement ages to some percentage of the expected age at death for those who have reached the age of 60. This could initially be set at the average rate of the last 30 years, based on the appropriate mortality tables and the ages of 62 and 65, respectively. That way, as longevity increases, the expected normal work life would increase as well.

The Economic Status of Children

The Current Economic Status of Children

Although a full consideration of the current economic status of children is beyond the scope of this work, a good entry point is the work of Haveman and Wolfe (1993, 1995). The evidence they presented (Haveman & Wolfe, 1993) suggests that children, overall, are no worse off than in past years, except for children at the low end of the income distribution. More than 20% of our children are living in poor families compared with only 15% in 1973. This is due partly to the increased incidence of female-headed families, partly to the increased prevalence of low earnings among male family heads, and partly to the drop in the real value of per-family cash transfers such as AFDC, food stamps, and Supplemental Security Income. Does this represent a failure of the "Great Society" programs of the 1960s? Demographic evidence that challenges such a belief is the fact that the percentage of children in poverty was much higher before those programs—over 25% overall and over 60% for African Americans (Haveman & Wolfe, 1993).

The rising health-care costs and the accompanying tendency to eliminate or reduce employer-paid health benefits have resulted in worsening health care for children of the working poor and near-poor. The percentage of children not covered by health insurance has increased from under 13% in 1980 to almost 16% in 1989. Educational outcomes, on the other hand, have generally improved, with a much reduced high school drop-out rate, especially for African Americans, and average SAT scores that rose substantially in the 1980s (Haveman & Wolfe, 1993).

Determinants of the Success or Failure of Children

In another article, Haveman and Wolfe (1995) reviewed and critiqued research that has attempted to uncover the determinants of children's success or failure, with a special look at the bottom of the income distribution. The following are the chief findings they report: (1) Growing up in a poor family reduces education and earnings; (2) growing up in a household where the mother works when the child is young appears to reduce educational attainment but has no effect on experiencing out-of-wedlock births or becoming a welfare recipient; (3) growing up in a family that has received welfare increases the probability of a single mother enrolling in welfare programs but does not increase the probability of an out-of-wedlock birth; (4) government policies can have a significant impact on various outcomes but their effect is smaller than parental impacts; (5) experiencing a parental divorce worsens educational outcomes and increases the probability that daughters will experience an out-of-wedlock birth and/or suffer from divorce; and (6) there appear to be some positive neighborhood effects, controlling for family characteristics—neighborhoods with multiple problems appear to have especially deleterious effects on children. While few of these conclusions are surprising and some are foreshadowed in earlier sections, Haveman and Wolfe also suggest a research agenda that can sharpen our understanding of some of these effects.

In work appearing since their survey, Hill and O'Neill (1994) studied the effects of family and neighborhood on the cognitive achievement of young children (ages 3–8 in the late 1980s). Their evidence reinforces that surveyed by Haveman and Wolfe (1995): (1) When mothers work during their children's early years, the increased income does not fully offset the negative effects from loss of parental time and (2) neighborhood effects, after controlling for a variety of other possible causes, are terribly important for the achievement of young children. Better family leave policies may be needed to overcome the first effect. More importantly, it seems clear that policies that have tried to address racial segregation in schools without addressing geographic segregation and isolation have left too many children growing up in dysfunctional neighborhoods. Policies that can lead to greater geographic integration across income and racial lines have the potential to provide substantial direct benefits to children of the poor and to reduce the acrimonious "we versus them" nature of much of the debate over welfare reform.

Concluding Remarks

The past 20 years have seen an increasing involvement of economists in research on the family. Economics has contributed a number of provocative hypotheses. A summary of these hypotheses and other issues of concern to those studying the family follows.

Bargaining Effects

The nonlabor income of husband and wife has differing effects on labor supply and child health. This is inconsistent with the traditional economic model of the family and suggests that empirical models should consider bargaining effects on family allocations of time and goods.

Marriage

In the United States there is a growing tendency to observe positive assortative mating for the trait of earning power, although this may not show up as clearly in annual earnings as in lifetime earnings.

Divorce and Its Consequences

Ease of divorce (through no-fault provisions or low cost of lawyers) appears to increase the hazard of divorce, although the rise in divorce rates in the 1970s was also due to demographic, economic, and social factors.

Adjusted for family size, the income of women falls substantially after divorce, while for men there is little or no fall in living standards. After 5 years women's incomes have largely recovered, most often due to remarriage.

The irregular payment of child support by divorced fathers in the 1970s and 1980s is linked either to low income or, when income is adequate, to a "prisoners' dilemma" problem. Programs like the Wisconsin Child Support Assurance System may have the potential to alleviate this problem when the cause is low income of the father, but it is an expensive remedy. In other cases, mandatory wage-withholding of child support can change the incentives facing divorced fathers and mothers so that the payments become regular and are devoted directly or indirectly to the children.

Family Time Allocation to Market and Home

The labor force participation of women has grown in all Western societies. Married women and married women with young children have recently been making the largest gains. Even in the Scandinavian countries, which have had the largest gains, married women still spend almost twice as much time as their husbands on housework, and the husbands spend almost twice as much time on market work. Although the distribution of time is not egalitarian, there is no reason to think that women have lost as a result of the increased labor force participation. Time diary evidence from the United States suggests that the total time allocated to market and household work has declined for both men and women, with women experiencing at least as great a decline as men. Evidence from Sweden suggests that government policies can promote some reallocation of fathers' time from market work to childcare.

The increased labor force participation of married women has somewhat reduced the time devoted by families to the direct nurture and care of their children. Nevertheless, there is no evidence that this has caused substantial lasting harm to the children. Evidence on school achievement and intelligence tests finds that scores are lower because the mother spends less time with the children, but higher because of the greater ability to purchase child-enhancing products from the market (due to the increased family income because the mother works). Overall, it appears that the former effect outweighs the latter, as cognitive achievement of the children of working mothers is somewhat lower. There is stronger evidence of negative effects on children, however, if the mother returns to work immediately after a child is born; this argues in favor of more generous parental leave policies, especially for the first year after a child is born.

The finding that mother's work reduces the total amount of quality time spent with children suggests the importance of high-quality childcare. Proposals have been made to increase government subsidies for childcare and to make them refundable. The evidence suggests that the first proposal would increase the use of childcare and may increase labor force participation; the second proposal would increase the proportion of the subsidy going to low-income women. Some would increase their hours of work and others would switch from public to higher quality private childcare. Marginal increases in childcare subsidies would mainly improve the quality of childcare; there would be little impact on the number of hours worked. Children should benefit from such an increase.

Earnings Inequalities

There has been increased inequality in annual and hourly earnings among men and in hourly wages for women. Annual earnings for women are more equal because of the substantial increase in the percentage of women working in the market. Earnings inequality between men and women has been falling slowly. The increased inequality among men is attributed mainly to the decline in the manufacturing sector due, in part, to foreign competition and increased skill requirements in all sectors. The increased percentage of single men apparently also contributed to the growing inequality.

The gross wage gap between white men and women (full-time workers) has fallen from 40% to 26% over the past 18 years, while it has fallen from 32% to 14% for black men and women. It appears that somewhere between 75% and 80% of this gap can be explained by various observable productivity-related characteristics. One perspective argues that the unexplained residual gap of 5%–10% is simply a measure of our ignorance; we do not know what to attribute it to. An alternative view takes the position that the entire unexplained gap is due to discrimination, as is a portion of the explained gap. Attributing part of the differential to differing years of education, experience, occupation, or industry are all suspect because women's choices are constrained by past discrimination and the expectation of current discrimination.

Transmission of Wealth and Human Capital across Generations

There is some evidence that the generosity of welfare benefits has a small positive effect on the likelihood of a divorced woman applying for AFDC benefits. Having a mother who received AFDC appears to increase the probability that a woman will seek AFDC benefits herself. Out-of-wedlock births, however, seem to be determined more by economic and social conditions rather than the generosity of welfare benefits or the welfare dependency of one's mother. Once a child is born out of wedlock, the woman who is the daughter of a woman who received AFDC is much more likely to apply for AFDC benefits than women whose mothers never received welfare benefits.

The correlation of parent–child income in the United States may be as high as 0.4. Nevertheless the advantages or disadvantages of a family's high or low income will be largely dissipated typically within four generations or so.

The quantity/quality trade-off for children is important; those from larger families appear to have lower achievement levels in school and may have lower earnings as well.

Controlling for income, market work by mothers appears to have either no effect or a slight negative effect overall on the achievement and earnings of children.

Intrafamily altruism does not fully offset the effects of programs like Social Security, public support of education, and compensatory education. The latter two decrease the transmission of income inequality across generations.

Economic Status of the Elderly

With the exception of widows, the elderly are as well or better off than most other age groups. Although the Social Security fund is adequate for the current elderly and those approaching retirement, the system will be strained in the next century as the ratio of retirees to those between the ages of 18 and 65 shrinks. As the health and longevity of the elderly continue to improve, the normal working age for retirement benefits should be adjusted so that the normal working years are a fixed percentage of a normal healthy life.

Economic Status of Children

Children of low-income parents are worse off than their counterparts 25 years ago but are better off than poor children before the "War on Poverty" programs of the 1960s were initiated. The rising percentage of children not covered by health insurance is one of the most serious hardships facing children at the current time. The rising educational attainment of African American children, evidenced by lower drop-out rates and rising SAT scores, gives reason for hope.

The main determinants of children's success appear to be growing up in a stable family that does not experience welfare, the mother not working (full-time) during the child's early years, residing in a neighborhood that does not have high crime rates and low educational attainment.

Many of the conclusions listed here are based on preliminary evidence. Additional research to verify and extend these findings is needed. Furthermore, there are unanswered questions, and, as always, new findings lead to new questions. We still do not understand long-term welfare dependency as well as we should, nor do we have effective strategies to alleviate the suffering it implies. We need to sharpen our understanding of how to help children of poor parents succeed. We need to do a better job of disentangling the effects of discrimination and other factors on the wage gap between men and women. The methods employed by Wood, Corcoran, and Courant (1993) to study graduates of the University of Michigan Law School should be replicated for graduates of other fields. More long-term evidence of the effects of mother's workforce participation on the achievement and earnings of her children is needed before we can be fully confident about the preliminary results. We need to know more about the determinants of family time allocation to market work, household work, and childcare. Can we move toward a completely egalitarian division of labor, or are there some limits? If there are limits, what determines them? Data from national studies should prove important for finding the answers to these questions.

ACKNOWLEDGMENTS. Part of the work for this project was completed while the author was the Erik Malmsten Visiting Professor of Economics at Göteborg University, Göteborg, Sweden. I thank Anders Klevmarken for his generous help in arranging the visit and support. Tim Phillips and Eda Cetinok provided very able research assistance on this project.

References

Altonji, J., Hayashi, F., & Kotlikoff, L. J. (1992). Is the extended family altruistically linked? Direct tests using micro data. *American Economic Review, 82,* 1177–1198.

An, C. B., Haveman, R., & Wolfe, B. (1993). Teen out-of-wedlock births and welfare receipt: The role of childhood events and economic circumstances. *Review of Economics and Statistics, 75,* 195–208.

Anderson, D., & Shapiro, D. (1996). Racial differences in access to high-paying jobs and the wage gap between black and white women. *Industrial and Labor Relations Review, 49,* 273–286.

Antel, J. J. (1992). The intergenerational transfer of welfare dependency: Some statistical evidence. *Review of Economics and Statistics, 74,* 467–473.

Ashenfelter, O., & Heckman, J. J. (1974). The estimation of income and substitution effects in a model of family labor supply. *Econometrica, 42,* 73–85.

Baldwin, M., & Johnson, W. G. (1992). Estimating the employment effect of wage discrimination. *Review of Economics and Statistics, 74,* 446–455.

Barnett, W. S. (1992). Benefits of compensatory preschool education. *Journal of Human Resources, 27,* 279–312.

Barro, R. J. (1974). Are government bonds net wealth? *Journal of Political Economy, 82,* 1095–1117.

Barron, J. M., Black, D. A., & Loewenstein, M. A. (1993). Gender differences in training, capital and wages. *Journal of Human Resources, 28,* 343–364.

Becker, G. S. (1965). A theory of the allocation of time. *Economic Journal, 75,* 493–517.

Becker, G. S. (1973). A theory of marriage: Part I. *Journal of Political Economy, 81,* 813–846.

Becker, G. S. (1979). An equilibrium theory of the distribution of income and intergenerational mobility. *Journal of Political Economy, 87,* 1153–1189.

Becker, G. S. (1981). *A treatise on the family.* Cambridge, MA: Harvard University Press.

Becker, G. S. (1991). *A treatise on the family: Enlarged edition.* Cambridge, MA: Harvard University Press.

Becker, G. S., & Barro, R. J. (1988). A reformulation of the economic theory of fertility. *Quarterly Journal of Economics, 103,* 1–25.

Becker, G. S., & Murphy, K. M. (1988). The family and the state. *Journal of Law and Economics, 31,* 1–18.

Becker, G. S., & Tomes, N. (1979). An equilibrium theory of the distribution of income and intergenerational mobility. *Journal of Political Economy, 87,* 1153–1189.

Becker, G. S., & Tomes, N. (1986). Human capital and the rise and fall of families. *Journal of Labor Economics, 4,* S1–S39.

Behrman, J. R., & Taubman, P. (1985). Intergenerational earnings mobility in the United States: Some estimates and a test of Becker's intergenerational endowment's model. *Review of Economics and Statistics, 67,* 144–151.

Behrman, J. R., Rosenzweig, M. R., & Taubman, P. (1994). Endowments and the allocation of schooling in the family and in the marriage market: The twins experiment. *Journal of Political Economy, 102,* 1131–1174.

Beller, A., & Graham, J. (1989). The effect of child support payments on the labor supply of female family heads. *Journal of Human Resources, 24,* 664–688.

Bergmann, B. (1989). Does the market for women's labor need fixing? *Journal of Economic Perspectives, 3,* 43–60.

Blackburn, M. L. (1990). What can explain the increase in earnings inequality among males? *Industrial Relations, 29,* 441–456.

Blank, R. M., & Ruggles, P. (1994). Short-term recidivism among public assistance recipients. *American Economic Review* (Papers and Proceedings), *84*, 49–53.

Blau, F. D. (1992, Spring). Gender and economic outcomes. *NBER Reporter*, 4–7.

Blau, F. D., & Ferber, M. (1992). *The economics of women, men and work* (2nd ed.). Englewood Cliffs, NJ: Prentice-Hall.

Blau, F. D., & Grossberg, A. J. (1992). Maternal labor supply and children's cognitive development. *Review of Economics and Statistics*, *74*, 474–481.

Blau, F. D., & Kahn, L. M. (1994). Rising wage inequality and the U.S. gender gap. *American Economic Review* (Papers and Proceedings), *84*, 23–28.

Blomquist, N. S. (1983). The effect of income taxation on the labor supply of married men in Sweden. *Journal of Public Economics*, *22*, 169–197.

Blomquist, N. S., & Hansson-Brusewitz, U. (1990). The effect of taxes on male and female labor supply in Sweden. *Journal of Human Resources*, *25*, 317–357.

Bronars, S. G., & Grogger, J. (1994). The economic consequences of unwed motherhood: Using twin births as a natural experiment. *American Economic Review*, *84*, 1141–1156.

Browning, M., Bourguignon, F., Chiappori, P.-A., & Lechene, V. (1994). Income and outcomes: A structural model of intrahousehold allocation. *Journal of Political Economy*, *102*, 1067–1096.

Burkhauser, R. V., Duncan, G., Hauser, R., & Berntsen, R. (1991). Wife or frau, women do worse: A comparison of men and women in the United States and Germany following marital dissolution. *Demography*, *28*, 353–360.

Burtless, G. (1995). International trade and the rise in earnings inequality. *Journal of Economic Literature*, *33*, 800–816.

Cain, G. G. (1986). The economic analysis of labor market discrimination: A survey. In O. C. Ashenfelter & R. Layard (Eds.), *Handbook of labor economics* (Vol. 1, pp. 693–785). Amsterdam: North-Holland.

Carlin, P. S. (1991a). Intrafamily bargaining and time allocation. In T. P. Schultz (Ed.), *Research in population economics* (Vol. 7, pp. 215–243). Greenwich, CT: JAI Press.

Carlin, P. S. (1991b). Home investment in husband's human capital and married women's labor supply. *Journal of Population Economics*, *4*, 71–86.

Carlin, P. S., & Flood, L. (1997). Do children affect the labor supply of Swedish men? Time diary vs. survey data. *Labour Economics*, *4*, 167–183.

Chakrabarti, S., Lord, W., & Rangazas, P. (1993). Uncertain altruism and investment in children. *American Economic Review*, *83*, 994–1002.

Chiappori, P. A. (1988a). Nash-bargained household decisions: A comment. *International Economic Review*, *29*, 791–796.

Chiappori, P. A. (1988b). Rational household labor supply. *Econometrica*, *56*, 63–90.

Chiappori, P. A. (1991). Nash-bargained household decisions: A rejoinder. *International Economic Review*, *32*, 761–762.

Chiappori, P. A. (1992). Collective labor supply and welfare. *Journal of Political Economy*, *100*, 437–467.

Connelly, R. (1992). The effect of child care costs on married women's labor force participation. *Review of Economics and Statistics*, *74*, 83–90.

Currie, J., & Thomas, D. (1995). Does Head Start make a difference? *American Economic Review*, *85*, 341–364.

Del Boca, D., & Flinn, C. J. (1994). Expenditure decisions of divorced mothers and income composition. *Journal of Human Resources*, *29*, 742–761.

Devine, T. J. (1994). Characteristics of self-employed women in the U.S. *Monthly Labor Review*, *117*, 20–34.

Duncan, G., & Hoffman, S. (1990). Welfare benefits, economic opportunities and, out-of-wedlock births among black teenage girls. *Demography*, *27*, 519–535.

Duncan, G., & Hoffman, S. (1991). Economic consequences of marital instability. In M. David & T. Smeeding (Eds.), *Horizontal equity, uncertainty and well-being* (pp. 427–467). Chicago: University of Chicago Press.

Ellwood, D. T., & Crane, J. (1990). Family change among black americans: What do we know? *Journal of Economic Perspectives*, *4*, 65–84.

Even, W. E., & Macpherson, D. A. (1993). The decline of private sector unionism and the gender wage gap. *Journal of Human Resources*, *28*, 279–296.

Ferber, M. A., & Nelson, J. A. (Eds.). (1993). *Beyond economic man, feminist theory and economics*. Chicago: University of Chicago Press.

Fields, J., & Wolff, E. N. (1995). Interindustry wage differentials and the gender wage gap. *Industrial and Labor Relations Review*, *49*, 105–120.

Flood, L., & Klevmarken, N. A. (1992). *Market work, household work and leisure: An analysis of time-use in Sweden*. Memorandum No. 172, Department of Economics, Göteborg University, Göteborg, Sweden.

Fuchs, V. (1988). *Women's quest for economic equality*. Cambridge, MA: Harvard University Press.

Garfinkel, I. (1994). The child support revolution. *American Economic Review* (Papers and Proceedings), *84*, 81–85.

Garfinkel, I., Robins, P. K., Wong, P., & Meyer, D. R. (1990). The Wisconsin Child Support Assurance System. *Journal of Human Resources*, *25*, 1–31.

Geronimus, A. T., & Korenman, S. (1992). The socioeconomic consequences of teen childbearing reconsidered. *Quarterly Journal of Economics*, *107*, 1187–1214.

Geronimus, A. T., & Korenman, S. (1993). Maternal youth or family background? On the health disadvantages of infants with teenage mothers. *American Journal of Epidemiology*, *137*, 213–225.

Geronimus, A. T., Korenman, S., & Hillemeier, M. (1994). Does young maternal age adversely affect child development? *Population and Development Review*, *20*, 585–609.

Gronau, R. (1977). Leisure, home production and work—the theory of the allocation of time revisited. *Journal of Political Economy*, *85*, 1099–1123.

Grossbard, A. (1980). The economics of polygamy. In J. Simon & J. DaVanzo (Eds.), *Research in population economics* (Vol. 2, pp. 1321–1350). Greenwich, CT: JAI Press.

Grossbard-Shechtman, A. (1982). A theory of marriage formality—the case of Guatemala. *Economic Development and Cultural Change*, *30*, 813–830.

Grossbard-Shechtman, A. (1984). A theory of allocation of time in markets for labor and marriage. *The Economic Journal*, *94*, 863–882.

Grossbard-Shechtman, S. A. (1992). *On the economics of marriage*. Boulder, Co: Westview.

Gustafsson, S., & Stafford, F. (1992). Child care subsidies and labor supply in Sweden. *Journal of Human Resources*, *27*, 204–230.

Ham, J. C. (1982). Estimation of a labour supply model with censoring due to unemployment and underemployment. *Review of Economic Studies*, *49*, 335–354.

Hanushek, E. A. (1992). The trade-off between child quantity and quality. *Journal of Political Economy*, *100*, 84–117.

Harrison, B., Tilly, C., & Bluestone, B. (1986). Wage inequality takes a great U-turn. *Challenge*, *29*, 26–32.

Haveman, R., & Wolfe, B. (1993). Children's prospects and children's policy. *Journal of Economic Perspectives*, *7*, 153–174.

Haveman, R., & Wolfe, B. (1995). The determinants of children's attainments: A review of methods and findings. *Journal of Economic Literature*, *33*, 1829–1878.

Hayghe, H. V. (1986). Rise in mother's labor force activity includes those with infants. *Monthly Labor Review*, *109*, 43–45.

Hayghe, H. V., & Bianchi, S. M. (1994). Married mothers' work patterns. *Monthly Labor Review, 117*, 24–30.

Hill, M. A., & O'Neill, J. (1994). Family endowments and the achievement of young children with special reference to the underclass. *Journal of Human Resources, 29*, 1064–1100.

Hoffman, S. D., & Duncan, G. (1988). A comparison of choice-based multinomial and nested logit models: The family structure and welfare use decisions of divorced or separated women. *Journal of Human Resources, 23*, 550–562.

Hoffman, S. D., & Duncan, G. (1995). The effect of incomes, wages, and AFDC benefits on marital disruption. *Journal of Human Resources, 30*, 19–41.

Hotz, V. J., & Miller, R. A. (1988). An empirical analysis of life cycle fertility and female labor supply. *Econometrica, 56*, 91–118.

Howell, D. R., & Wolff, E. N. (1991). Trends in the growth and distribution of skills in the U.S. workplace, 1960–85. *Industrial and Labor Relations Review, 44*, 486–502.

Hurd, M. D. (1990). Research on the elderly: Economic status, retirement, and consumption and saving. *Journal of Economic Literature, 28*, 565–637.

Hutchens, R., Jakubson, G., & Schwartz, S. (1989). AFDC and the formation of subfamilies. *Journal of Human Resources, 24*, 599–628.

Johnson, T. R., & Pencavel, J. H. (1984). Dynamic hours of work functions for husbands, wives and single females. *Econometrica, 52*, 363–389.

Juster, F. T., & Stafford, F. P. (1991). The allocation of time: Empirical findings, behavioral models and problems of measurement. *Journal of Economic Literature, 29*, 471–522.

Karoly, L. A. (1992). Changes in the distribution of individual earnings in the United States: 1967–1986. *Review of Economics and Statistics, 74*, 107–115.

Katz, L., & Murphy, K. (1992). Changes in relative wages, 1963–1987: Supply and demand factors. *Quarterly Journal of Economics, 107*, 35–78.

Killingsworth, M., & Heckman, J. J. (1986). Female labor supply: A survey. In O. Ashenfelter & R. Layard (Eds.), *Handbook of labor economics* (Vol. 1, pp. 103–204). Amsterdam: North-Holland.

Laband, D. M., & Lentz, B. F. (1993). Is there sex discrimination in the legal profession? *Journal of Human Resources, 28*, 230–258.

Lam, D. (1988). Marriage markets and assortative mating with household public goods. *Journal of Human Resources, 23*, 462–487.

Leibowitz, A., Klerman, J. A., & Waite, L. J. (1992). Employment of new mothers and child care choice. *Journal of Human Resources, 27*, 112–133.

Lester, G. H. (1991). Child support and alimony: 1989. *Current Population Reports, Consumer Income* (Series P-60, No. 173, U.S. Department of Commerce, Bureau of the Census).

Levy, F., & Murnane, R. J. (1992). U.S. earnings levels and earnings inequality: A review of recent trends and proposed explanations. *Journal of Economic Literature, 30*, 1333–1381.

Lillard, L. A. (1993). Simultaneous equations for hazards: Marriage duration and fertility timing. *Journal of Econometrics, 56*, 189–217.

Lundberg, S. (1988). Labor supply of husbands and wives: A simultaneous equations approach. *Review of Economics and Statistics, 70*, 224–235.

Lundberg, S., & Plotnick, R. D. (1995). Adolescent premarital childbearing: Do economic incentives matter? *Journal of Labor Economics, 13*, 177–200.

Manchester, J., & Stapleton, D. (1991). On measuring the progress of women's quest for economic equality. *Journal of Human Resources, 26*, 562–580.

Manser, M., & Brown, M. (1980). Marriage and household decision-making: A bargaining analysis. *International Economic Review, 21*, 31–44.

McElroy, M., & Horney, M. J. (1981). Nash-bargained household decisions: Toward a generalization of the theory of demand. *International Economic Review, 22*, 333–349.

McElroy, S. W. (1996). *Early childbearing, high school completion, and college enrollment: Evidence from 1980 high school sophomores.* (Heinz School of Public Policy and Management Working Paper No. 96-10). Pittsburgh, PA: Carnegie Mellon University.

Michael, R. T., & Becker, G. S. (1973). On the new theory of consumer behavior. *Swedish Journal of Economics, 75*, 378–396.

Michalopoulos, C., Robins, P. K., & Garfinkel, I. (1992). A structural model of labor supply and child care demand. *Journal of Human Resources, 27*, 166–203.

Mincer, J. (1985). Intercountry comparisons of labor force trends and of related developments: An overview. *Journal of Labor Economics, 3*, S1–S32.

Moffitt, R. (1992). Incentive effects of the U.S. welfare system: A review. *Journal of Economic Literature, 30*, 1–61.

Montgomery, M., & Trussell, J. (1986). Models of marital status and childbearing. In O. C. Ashenfelter & R. Layard (Eds.), *Handbook of labor economics* (Vol. 1, pp. 205–271). Amsterdam: North-Holland.

Murphy, K., & Welch, F. (1992). The structure of wages. *Quarterly Journal of Economics, 107*, 285–326.

Nakamura, A., & Shaw, K. (1994). Overview for special issue on women's work, wages and well-being. *Journal of Human Resources, 29*, 203–222.

National Bureau of Economic Research. (1992, Spring). Conference report on economics of the family. *NBER Reporter*, 12–13.

Nerlove, M., Razin, A., & Sadka, E. (1988). A bequest-constrained economy: Welfare analysis. *Journal of Political Economy, 37*, 203–220.

Olsen, R. J. (1994). Fertility and the size of the U.S. labor force. *Journal of Economic Literature, 32*, 60–100.

O'Neill, J., & Polachek, S. (1993). Why the gender gap in wages narrowed in the 1980s. *Journal of Labor Economics, 11*, 205–228.

Orazem, P. F., Mattila, J. P., & Yu, R. C. (1990). An index number approach to the measurement of wage differentials by sex. *Journal of Human Resources, 25*, 125–136.

Ott, N. (1992). *Intrafamily bargaining and household decisions.* New York: Springer-Verlag.

Parkman, A. M. (1992). Unilateral divorce and the labor-force participation rate of married women, revisited. *American Economic Review, 82*, 671–678.

Pencavel, J. (1986). Labor supply of men: A survey. In O. Ashenfelter & R. Layard (Eds.), *Handbook of labor economics* (Vol. 1, pp. 3–102). Amsterdam: North-Holland.

Peters, H. E. (1986). Marriage and divorce: Informational constraints and private contracting. *American Economic Review, 76*, 437–454.

Peters, H. E. (1992). Patterns of intergenerational mobility in income and earnings. *Review of Economics and Statistics, 74*, 456–466.

Peters, H. E. (1993). The importance of financial considerations in divorce decisions. *Economic Inquiry, 31*, 71–86.

Petersen, C. D. (1995). Female-headed families on AFDC: Who leaves welfare and who doesn't? *Journal of Economic Issues, 29*, 619–628.

Reimers, C., & Honig, M. (1996). Responses to Social Security by men and women. *Journal of Human Resources, 31*, 359–382.

Rendall, M. S., & Speare, A., Jr. (1995). Elderly poverty alleviation through living with family. *Journal of Population Economics, 8*, 383–405.

Ribar, D. C. (1992). Child care and the labor supply of married women. *Journal of Human Resources, 27*, 134–165.

Ribar, D. C. (1994). Teenage fertility and high school completion. *Review of Economics and Statistics, 76*, 413–424.

Ribar, D. C. (1995). A structural model of child care and the labor supply of married women. *Journal of Labor Economics, 13*, 558–597.

Rosenzweig, M. R., & Stark, O. (Eds.). (1977). *Handbook of population and family economics.* Amsterdam: Elsevier Science.

Rosenzweig, M. R., & Wolpin, K. I. (1994a). Are there increasing returns to the intergenerational production of human capital? *Journal of Human Resources, 29,* 670–693.

Rosenzweig, M. R., & Wolpin, K. I. (1994b). Parental and public transfers to young women and their children. *American Economic Review, 84,* 1195–1212.

Rosenzweig, M. R., & Wolpin, K. I. (1995). Sisters, siblings and mothers: The effect of childbearing on birth outcomes in a dynamic family context. *Econometrica, 63,* 303–326.

Ruhm, C. J. (1995). Secular changes in the work and retirement patterns of older men. *Journal of Human Resources, 30,* 362–385.

Schultz, T. P. (1990). Testing the neoclassical model of family labor supply and fertility. *Journal of Human Resources, 25,* 599–634.

Schultz, T. P. (1994). Marital status and fertility in the United States. *Journal of Human Resources, 29,* 637–669.

Shank, S. E. (1988). Women and the labor market: The link grows stronger. *Monthly Labor Review, 111,* 3–8.

Shaw, K. L. (1989). Intertemporal labor supply and the distribution of family income. *Review of Economics and Statistics, 71,* 196–205.

Smith, J. P. (1979). The distribution of family earnings. *Journal of Political Economy, 87,* S163–S192.

Smith, J. P., & Ward, M. (1989). Women in the labor market and women in the family. *Journal of Economic Perspectives, 3,* 9–23.

Solon, G. R. (1992). Intergenerational income mobility in the United States. *American Economic Review, 82,* 393–408.

Sorensen, E., & Clark, S. (1994). A child-support assurance program: How much will it reduce child poverty and at what cost? *American Economic Review* (Papers and Proceedings), *84,* 114–119.

Stafford, F. P. (1987). Women's work, sibling competition, and children's school performance. *American Economic Review, 77,* 972–980.

Stevens, A. H. (1994). The dynamics of poverty spells: Updating Bane and Ellwood. *American Economic Review* (Papers and Proceedings), *84,* 34–37.

Sundström, M. (1994, June). *Does family leave reduce the gender wage gap? Evidence on wage effects of usage of family leave benefits among male and female employees of the Swedish Telephone Company.* Paper presented at the eighth annual meeting of the European Society for Population Economics, Tilburg, The Netherlands.

Sundström, M. (1994). Does family leave reduce the gender wage gap? Paper presented at the Eighth Meeting of the European Society for Population Economics, Tilburg, The Netherlands.

Tauchen, H. V., Witte, A. D., & Long, S. K. (1991). Domestic violence: A nonrandom affair. *International Economic Review, 32,* 491–511.

Thomas, D. (1990). Intra-household resource allocation: An inferential approach. *Journal of Human Resources, 25,* 635–644.

Triest, R. K. (1990). The effect of income taxation on labor supply in the United States. *Journal of Human Resources, 25,* 491–516.

Triest, R. K. (1992). The effect of income taxation on labor supply when deductions are endogenous. *Review of Economics and Statistics., 74,* 91–99.

U.S. Bureau of the Census. (1992). *Statistical abstract of the United States: 1992* (112th ed.). Washington, DC: U.S. Government Printing Office.

U.S. Bureau of the Census. (1995). *Statistical abstract of the United States: 1995* (115th ed.). Washington, DC: U.S. Government Printing Office.

Veum, J. R. (1992). Interrelation of child support, visitation, and hours of work. *Monthly Labor Review, 115,* 40–47.

Weiss, Y., & Willis, R. (1985). Children as collective goods and divorce settlements. *Journal of Labor Economics, 3,* 268–292.

Weiss, Y., & Willis, R. (1993). Transfers among divorced couples: Evidence and interpretation. *Journal of Labor Economics, 11,* 629–679.

Wellington, A. J. (1993). Changes in the male/female wage gap, 1976–1985. *Journal of Human Resources, 27,* 383–411.

Williams, D. R. (1995). Women's part-time employment: A gross flows analysis. *Monthly Labor Review, 118,* 36–44.

Willis, R. (1987). What have we learned from the economics of the family? *American Economic Review* (Papers and Proceedings), *77,* 68–81.

Wilson, W. J. (1987). *The truly disadvantaged.* Chicago: University of Chicago Press.

Wilson, W. J., & Neckerman, K. M. (1986). Poverty and family structure: The widening gap between evidence and public policy issues. In S. H. Danziger & D. H. Weinberg (Eds.), *Fighting poverty* (pp. 232–259). Cambridge, MA: Harvard University Press.

Wood, R. G. (1995). Marriage rates and marriageable men. *Journal of Human Resources, 30,* 163–193.

Wood, R. G., Corcoran, M. E., & Courant, P. N. (1993). Pay differences among the highly paid: The male–female earnings gap in lawyers' salaries. *Journal of Labor Economics, 11,* 417–441.

Zabel, J. E. (1993). The relationship between hours of work and labor force participation in four models of labor supply behavior. *Journal of Labor Economics, 11,* 387–416.

Zimmerman, D. J. (1992). Regression toward mediocrity in economic stature. *American Economic Review, 82,* 409–429.

CHAPTER 20

American Families and American Law

David M. Rosen

Introduction

This chapter presents an overview of American family law. Obviously, there are many laws that affect family life, ranging from the laws governing inheritance and the intergenerational transfer of property to the laws of taxation and zoning. In addition, there are some aspects of family law that are of profound importance but that are really part of the criminal law, including laws dealing with the national problem of domestic violence and abuse, which affects both women and children. Through most of this century, however, family law has come to mean the civil laws governing the foundation and dissolution of family and kinship relationships and the legally imposed rights and duties that govern these relationships. These are the laws of marriage, divorce, custody, visitation, child support, paternity, and adoption. These areas of law are the focus of this chapter, although from time to time issues from other areas of the law necessarily enter the discussion.

Sources of Family Law

Family law, like most law, is very much a craft of place, a normative regime that works by the light of local knowledge (Geertz, 1983). It is probably impossible to fully understand American family law except in the context of how it is practiced in actual communities and as part of the shared discourse of those communities (Greenhouse, Yngvesson, &

David M. Rosen • Department of Social Sciences and History, Fairleigh Dickinson University, Madison, New Jersey 07940.

Handbook of Marriage and the Family, 2nd edition, edited by Marvin Sussman, Suzanne K. Steinmetz, and Gary W. Peterson. Plenum Press, New York, 1999.

Engle, 1994). It is nevertheless important to see the development of the law in its own right, for it is a major element in the symbolic representation of American family life.

Family law is primarily state law, which means that, for the most part, it is the legislative enactments and judicial decisions of the several states that control this symbolic domain. There are, however, three significant exceptions to this. First, United States Supreme Court decisions, especially but not exclusively dealing with right of privacy and procedural due process, have profoundly affected the ways courts and legislatures in every state may dictate family law and policy. Second, Congressional legislation in such areas as child support and parental kidnapping have preempted state law and have required states to develop uniform standards in these areas. Third, since 1892, the National Conference of Commissioners for the development of the Uniform State Law have created model codes in all areas of law, including family law, parts of which have been voluntarily adopted by many states. Accordingly, the general trend has been to see greater uniformity in family law throughout the United States.

The Development of Family Law

How does the law conceptualize the family, and how has this conceptualization changed over time? Four broad trends should be noted.

First, beginning with Sir Henry Maine in the nineteenth century, students of the law have seen legal obligations as a whole, and family relations in particular, as moving from being functions of status to have the characteristics of a contract. In the context of family law, this means that the rights and duties of family members with respect to one another have shifted from being clearly imposed by law and society as a result of the social status of marriage to a situation in which these rights and duties are increasingly subject to contractual agreements negotiated by the parties. Marriage and family relations in this sense are becoming much more like commercial relations. This shift characterizes much of the legal relationship between husband and wife; it is markedly less clear with respect to the duties owed by parents toward their children. It is also true that most people do not merely wish to live together under a self-created contractual arrangement. Instead, people still seek the status of marriage and the moral recognition bestowed upon this status. Indeed, as we shall see later in this chapter, much of the current controversy over the legal standing of gay and lesbian marriages has nothing to do with whether individuals may live together and everything to do with whether such arrangements have the legal and moral standing of heterosexual marriages. Thus despite the fact that family and kinship relations often give off the odor of the marketplace, there is no evidence that such relationships are disappearing in favor of some commerce-based substitute (Trautmann, 1987).

Second, the family unit per se, and especially the idea of the nuclear family, is increasingly losing its privileged position in society. Some time ago, Shorter (1975) observed that "the nuclear family is a state of mind rather than a particular kind of structure or set of household arrangements. What really distinguishes the nuclear family ... is a special sense of solidarity that separates the domestic unit from the surrounding community" (p. 205). Likewise, Farber (1966) observed that "natural family" paradigm (by which he primarily meant the "nuclear family") was giving way to the "legal family," a significantly more decentered construct. The nuclear family, of course, is hardly universal and has had a checkered history in much of American life (Zaretsky, 1976). Nevertheless, it was the reigning family model in America during the Cold War era and the current generation has inherited much of its form, psychology, and sentiment (May, 1988). It is also clear that for some time the law recognized the privileged status of this type of family. This model is, nevertheless, fading in favor of one that emphasizes the rights of individuals within the family unit rather than the significance of an ideal type of family unit. The law stands less as the guardian of a specific type of family than as the definer of the rights and duties of people involved in a social network in which they contest their individual rights.

Third, the focus upon individual rights rather than the defense of a particular social form has converted the legal concept of the family into a gloss for a wide variety of family arrangements. In some respects, this is quite positive, since historically the legal concept of the family rarely captured the full diversity of American family life and kinship. Instead, the legal definition of family was and still is, in many respects, openly hostile to the family arrangements of the poor

and working class (Stack, 1974, 1984). But it is also true that current patterns of marriage and divorce throughout society have resulted in the reconstitution of family and kinship relations that link partners, former partners, households, children, and property in an array of complex social relationships (Lewin, 1993; Stacey, 1990; Weston, 1991). Sometimes dubbed "the unclear family" (Simpson, 1990), these arrangements more closely approximate a social network in which legally imposed rights and duties cut across the temporal boundaries of household and domestic life.

Fourth, the law is now clearly struggling to develop concepts with which to frame the emergence of new family forms and the ways individual rights can be articulated within these forms. The new models are tentative, sometimes ordering human relationships in rather modern contract terms, sometimes giving legal recognition to new forms of social relationships, and sometimes falling back on very basic concepts of blood and biology. It is the very indeterminacy of law that appears most striking in this era. Indeed, while it can be argued that culturally constituted ideas about contract can and should replace culturally constituted ideas of birth and blood as the basis for family and kinship, it is by no means certain in contemporary family law. Instead, like its object, the family, family law remains a highly contested domain in which the "facts" of birth and blood have been decentered but not eliminated (Scheffler, 1991).

Marriage and Divorce

In the Anglo-American legal system, marriage traditionally has been considered the bedrock of family life, although courts are increasingly treating issues of family life as separate from those of marriage. From a constitutional perspective, marriage is a highly privileged institution; the United States Supreme Court in *Griswold v. Connecticut* (1965) determined that the right to marry is a fundamental right, similar to that of freedom of speech or the free exercise of religion. Accordingly, the right of any state to regulate marriage is extremely limited and subject to strict scrutiny by the courts.

The kinds of regulation that states are allowed to impose include laws that make marriages automatically void if they involve incest or bigamy. States vary in the degree of blood relation prohibited. The Uniform Marriage Law and Divorce Law of 1970 prohibits marriage between ascending or descending relatives—brothers and sisters and nieces and nephews. Many states follow this model. Bigamy was harshly treated under the common law, and there are reports of women having been burned at the stake in colonial Maryland and Massachusetts for this crime. Although bigamy is outlawed, there appear to be extremely few cases of bigamy being prosecuted in the United States now compared to the nineteenth century. Bigamy seems to be a crime rooted in the morality of a social system in which men were very mobile and women were still confined to the domestic sphere where their chastity required legal protection (Friedman, 1993).

Polygamous marriages have not been permitted in the United States since the Supreme Court, in *United States v. Reynolds* (1878), upheld Utah's prohibition against polygamy practiced by members of the Mormon church. However, polygamy is still practiced by breakaway sects of Mormons in both Utah and Idaho. States may also permit marriages to be voidable by a party on a number of grounds, such as a partner being under the age of legal consent, being physically incapable of having sexual relations, lacking mental capacity or suffering from an incurable mental illness, or instances in which the consent by a party was obtained by fraud or duress.

Marriage and the Right of Privacy

The idea of marriage as a fundamental right was first laid down in 1965 in *Griswold v. Connecticut*, in which the Supreme Court determined that marital relations are a constitutionally protected right of privacy protected against unjustified state interference. Two years later, in *Loving v. Virginia* (1967), the Supreme Court categorized marriage as a "civil right," striking down as unconstitutional Virginia's ban on interracial marriage. In 1978, in *Zablocki v. Redhail*, the Court held that the right of marriage is protected under the due process provisions of the Fifth and Fourteenth Amendments. Because of these decisions, states may impose only reasonable regulations that do not unduly interfere with decisions to enter into marital relationships.

These cases point to a quiet but significant shift in the paradigm of marriage used by the Supreme Court in making its decisions. In *Griswold* the Supreme Court declared unconstitutional a Connecticut statute that criminalized the use of contraceptives by married persons. The thrust of *Griswold* was that the marital relationship per se was a constitutionally protected sphere of human relationships in which the right of privacy prevailed over government intrusion. In 1972, in the case of *Eisenstadt v. Baird*, the Supreme Court overturned a state law banning the distribution of contraceptive foam to an unmarried person. In his opinion, Justice Brennan wrote, "It is true that in *Griswold* the right of privacy in question inhered in the marital relationship. Yet the marital couple is not an independent entity with a mind and heart of its own, but an association of two individuals each with a separate intellectual and emotional makeup. If the right of privacy means anything it is the right of the individual, married or single to be free of governmental intrusion." What has sometimes been characterized as Justice Brennan's "passing remark" ultimately became enshrined as the principle underlying a woman's right to an abortion in *Roe v. Wade*

(1973) and its progeny. For our purposes, however, the shift in the Court's thinking about where the right of privacy resides marks a further shift in the view of whether marriage as a separate status was especially protected and privileged apart from the rights of the individuals who make up the marital relationship (Dolgin, 1994; Gunther, 1972, 1980). It is hard to know what this might mean in practical terms, but it is consistent as we shall see later, with state court decisions that have teased away the special legal prerogatives of the marital relationship in a variety of contexts.

What Is a Marriage?

While modern American law has only a limited ability to regulate the right to marry, it has an enormous impact upon the rights and duties of the partners to each other and their children once the marriage has been created in law. Legally, marriage has two often contradictory qualities: It is a contract and a status. Put another way, it is a social position created by contract. Marriage is a contract in the sense that the rights and duties of marriage are the result of an agreement. The eighteenth-century jurist William Blackstone, whose commentaries written between 1765 and 1769 provided a comprehensive but conservative summary of the common law of England, boldly asserted, "Our law considers marriage in no other light than as a civil contract" (p. 433). Marriage is a status in the social sense that membership in that institution involves the allocation of prestige, power, and esteem. It is a status in the legal sense that the rights and duties of marriage are not freely bargained for, but flow from the social position created by the contract. In reality, if marriage were a pure contract, the parties to the marriage would, within relatively broad legal parameters, have the right to set the terms and conditions of the marriage as well as to determine the remedies available to either party as a result of the breach. For most of recent history, however, this has not been the case.

Instead, the status characteristics of marriage have been amplified by its ascriptive qualities. Divorce did not become possible in England until 1857, and up to the time of the American Revolution divorce was virtually impossible in the United States. The traditional legal definition of marriage was the voluntary union of one man and one woman for life. Under this definition the social position created by marriage is as rigid as those assigned to age, race, and sex. Once brought into being, the law imposed obligations that the parties could not change. Even today, under American law, marriage is not an ordinary contract governed by Article 1, Section 10, of the Constitution, which prohibits the states from impairing contractual and legal obligations of the parties to one another. The obligations and rights inherent in a marriage, unlike those in other kinds of contracts, can be modified by state law without violating this section of the Constitution.

A Redefinition of Marriage

The traditional definition of marriage regards it as a heterosexual union. Indeed, as of the date of this chapter, the only type of marriage recognized in the United States is between opposite-sex partners. A few states, such as California, Florida, and Texas, specifically prohibit the granting of marriage licenses to any other than a heterosexual couple. But most states have assumed that the heterosexual nature of marriage is self-evident and have not therefore included specific prohibitions of other types of unions. In the last 20 years there have been numerous challenges to the heterosexual definition of marriage. In *Baker v. Nelson* (1971), a Minnesota court turned back a challenge to this assumption by a gay couple who argued that the absence of specific language in Minnesota law entitled them to marry. Similar challenges have been launched in Kentucky, Washington, Colorado, and Ohio. The most recent case upholding the prohibition against gay and lesbian marriage is *Dean v. District of Columbia* (1995), in which the District of Columbia Court of Appeals ruled that the District of Columbia Human Rights Act, which otherwise banned discrimination against gays and lesbians, did not compel the District to grant them a marriage license. The court held that there is no fundamental constitutional right of same-sex couples to marry.

The most successful challenge to the exclusion of gay and lesbian marriage to date is the current Hawaiian case of *Baehr v. Lewin* (1993). In *Baehr*, Hawaii's Supreme Court found that the state's exclusionary marriage policy was in violation of Hawaii's constitutional guarantee of equal protection on the basis of gender. The court, however, remanded the case back to the trial court to give the state the opportunity to demonstrate a compelling reason for the policy. At trial, the circuit court found no compelling reasons for the policy. Most legal observers believed that if the matter was revisited by the Hawaii Supreme Court it would have found the ban on same-sex marriage to be unconstitutional. However in the election of November 1998 the voters of Hawaii authorized the legislature to amend the constitution to prohibit same-sex marriage. As a result the entire issue may be on the back-burner for years to come.

In the future if any state does recognize same-sex marriage other states may be required to recognize these marriages under Article IV of the United States Constitution, which requires that "full faith and credit be given in each State to the public acts, records and judicial proceedings of every other State." Just as is the case of opposite-sex marriages, any same-sex marriage taking place one state will be deemed a legal marriage in any state where the couple resides following the marriage.

In anticipation of the Hawaii decision, several states, most recently Illinois, enacted legislation barring the grant-ing of full faith to gay and lesbian marriages. Moreover, in May 1996 the Defense of Marriage Act came into law. This bill defines "marriage" under federal law as the legal union between one man and one woman and defines a "spouse" as a husband or wife of the opposite sex. The proposed bill denies same-sex partners who are lawfully married under any state law from all benefits, rights, or privileges extended by the federal government. Equally important, the bill specifically exempts states from the Constitutional requirement to give "full faith and credit" to same-sex marriages.

The impact of this law is significant. For example, it would deny same-sex marriage partners and their children protection under the Parental Kidnapping Act of 1980. This legislation requires that states enforce the child custody determinations made by another state. It would also abrogate a state's duty to enforce child support orders under the Child Support Orders Act of 1994.

If the issue of same-sex marriage ever comes before the U.S. Supreme Court it is by no means clear how the Court will deal with this matter. In the 1986 case of *Bowers v. Hardwick*, the Court upheld as constitutional a Georgia statute criminalizing sodomy among gay men. More recently, however, in the 1996 case of *Romer v. Evans*, the Court declared unconstitutional and a violation of the Equal Protection Clause of the Fourteenth Amendment an amendment to the Colorado State Constitution that precluded the enactment of any law designed to protect the status of persons based on their homosexual, lesbian, or bisexual orientation, conduct, practices, or relationships. The Court determined that the law did not have a rational relationship to legitimate state interests but was motivated by animus and designed to make gay and lesbian persons unequal to everyone else by specifically withdrawing their legal protections against discrimination. It is hard to see how *Bowers v. Hardwick* could still be deemed good law under this analysis since if a state cannot lawfully discriminate against homosexual conduct it can hardly be permitted to criminalize such conduct. But it is by no means clear that the *Romer* decision means that the Court will ultimately determine that same-sex marriage is a fundamental right.

Marriage and the Status of Women

The First Property Revolution: Married Women's Property Acts

Nineteenth-century marriage imposed severe civil liabilities upon women. Particularly repugnant by modern standards was the doctrine of *coverture*, which placed a woman under her husband's so-called "wing, protection, and cover." Under coverture, the husband and wife were regarded as "one person." This meant that the legal existence of the woman, the *femme couvert*, was suspended during the course of the marriage, and her legal rights were consolidated with those of her husband. Under the doctrine of coverture, a woman could not independently enter into a contract, carry out a trade or business except as an agent of the husband, or sue or be sued in a civil court of law. The property rights of married women were also severely limited under the common law, which gave husbands absolute right to the personal property of wives as well as the right to any rent or profit from their real property. A wife had no similar rights in reference to her husband's property. Blackstone, explaining such marital disabilities imposed upon women, concluded, without irony, that "the disabilities which the wife lies under are for the most part designed for her protection and benefit, so great a favorite is the female sex under the laws of England" (p. 445).

It is important to note that even under coverture it was possible for parties to a marriage to regulate some of their economic relationships by contract. Under coverture, antenuptial agreements became a staple of middle- and upper-class marriages in nineteenth-century America, in an attempt to avoid the disabilities imposed by marriage. But it was crucial that such agreements be prenuptial, since the common law decreed that once they were married the husband and wife were a single legal person and therefore could not contract with one another. The law simply did not permit them to legally shape the terms and conditions of their marriage independently of the rights granted by legislative enactment. Nowadays, virtually any kind of property right that accrues by virtue of marriage can be waived by an antenuptial contract. But there are still some exceptions. For example, spouses cannot generally waive the sharing of expenses during the marriage because this would negate the statutory duty of spouses to support one another.

Even without antenuptial agreements, coverture began to wither away during the nineteenth century. Many states passed married women's property acts, which placed married women in the same position they would have been in if they had been single. In 1840, New York permitted a married woman to insure her husband for her own benefit. By 1854, a married woman was entitled to hold property of her own as if she were single, and by 1880 a husband and wife who held lands as tenants in common, joint tenants, or tenants by the entirety were empowered to partition or divide the property between themselves and become independent owners. Thus by the beginning of the nineteenth century, both statute and premarital contracts began to lay out a more equitable economic environment for marriage. The separate property that women owned prior to their marriage was no longer under the control of their husbands upon marriage, nor were women's civil rights under the control of their spouses. There were various forces moving for these changes, with some of the

impetus being attributable to the action of nineteenth-century feminists. Equally important, however, was the emergence of mass ownership of property and the need for a free and economically rational market in land unencumbered by the common law rules that originally had served to protect the interests of a small elite. Thus, as Friedman (1983) has pointed out, the law seemed to ratify a revolution in the family economy in which men and women now stood on equal footing with reference to the legal status of property individually owned by the parties.

The Second Property Revolution: Equitable Distribution

The married women's property acts dealt with the issue of the separate property owned by men and women, but there still remained the issue of determining the status of property acquired by the parties during the marriage. In an era when few women worked outside the home, formal title to the property of a marriage was often vested in men. When the incidence of divorce was low, the formal determinants of title had little or no impact upon the partners to a marriage. But as divorce rates began to rise in the middle of this century, and more women entered the workplace and achieved increasing personal autonomy and control of property, society seemed to take a new look at the legal status of property acquired during a marriage.

In some states, the legal status of property was less of a problem; California, for instance, is a "community property" state in which the basic legal rule is that the property accumulated in marriage from the earnings of husband and wife is community property to be equally divided by the parties upon divorce. In community property states, the post-divorce issues focus on how marital property is to be divided.

In most other states, however, upon divorce formal title to property was often determinative; a divorced woman's lifetime right to alimony was designed in part to compensate her for the fact that formal ownership of property, real and personal, remained in her husband's hands. The concept of equitable distribution refers to a variety of statutory schemes adopted by state legislatures in the 1970s and 1980s that addressed the issue of how to distribute the property of a marriage upon its dissolution.

Equitable distribution laws were framed primarily to deal with the distribution of property upon the dissolution of a marriage, which will be treated later in this chapter in the section on divorce. What concerns us here are the basic assumptions made in these laws about the legal status of property held by the parties during the course of the marriage. Equitable distribution laws treat all property acquired during the course of a marriage as part of a single marital estate to be divided equitably in the event of divorce.

Equitable distribution laws also have developed a very liberal view of the scope of this property. Importantly, formal title is irrelevant. All "property," including houses, cars, bank accounts, business interests, equities, insurance policies, pension plans, and the value of professional licenses, are deemed part of the marital estate regardless of which of the parties has formal title. Thus, a husband has a legal interest in the economic value of a license to practice dentistry that his wife acquired during the course of the marriage. He may not be licensed to practice dentistry, but his economic stake in the license is legally vested as part of the marital estate. In theory, the married couple are treated as virtual business partners. Upon divorce, just as in the dissolution of a partnership, the property of the marriage is to be divided equitably between the partners. Equitable distribution, however, does not mean a 50–50 split, and, as discussed later in the section on divorce, there are a variety of factors that come into play in determining how the estate is distributed among the partners.

Equitable distribution laws formally come into play only when the marriage partners have been unable to resolve the property issues by contract. But even where most issues are resolved privately by the parties using a separation agreement, the legal rules still have an enormous impact upon negotiations. Tax law affects bargaining over issues such as lump sum versus periodic payments in the distribution of property. Moreover, court preference with respect to custody may determine how the noncustodial parent may desire to structure child support payments (Mnookin & Kornhauser, 1979).

The laws of equitable distribution assume that the parties can contract with one another either before or during a marriage to achieve any economic arrangements that they see fit. Indeed, the law encourages the parties to waive the statutory scheme by framing a contract that is mutually acceptable to the parties (i.e., a prenuptial agreement or separation agreement). The laws assume that marital partners have the absolute right to frame virtually any economic relationship they wish, as long as it is consented to voluntarily. Only in the absence of such a contract do the laws of equitable distribution apply. Equitable distribution laws encourage freedom of contract in the economic relationship between spouses. This can be accomplished by both antenuptial and postnuptial agreements. Equitable distribution laws ordinarily encourage marital partners to settle their economic relations by themselves outside of any statutory scheme that might otherwise be imposed by law. On the whole, the bargain struck by the parties will govern after the dissolution of the marriage.

In this context, it is important to know that the modern law of contracts itself only began to develop in the nineteenth- century. Before the nineteenth century, the validity of a contract was evaluated in terms of whether the exchange between the contracting parties was inherently just or fair. It was only in the nineteenth century that the validity of a contract was judged largely in terms of whether it embodied the wills of the contracting parties, regardless of its inherent fairness (Horowitz, 1977). Unlike most modern commercial contracts, marital contracts still partake of a residue of justice and fairness. Accordingly, extreme hardship usually allows a former spouse to sue for support despite the existence of an agreement in which no support is provided. Unlike those in the commercial world, contracts reached by married partners must be fair and reasonable. Moreover, each party is required to provide the other with a complete disclosure of income and assets. As a rule, states impose requirements that are designed to ensure that the parties to the contract have equal power at the bargaining table. Accordingly, states impose disclosure rules so that each party is required to disclose financial conditions to the other as a prerequisite for reaching an agreement. The commercial doctrine of "caveat emptor" has no place in marital contracts. Obviously, the main application and importance of the idea of equitable distribution lies in the area of divorce, but the economic aspects of divorce are predicated upon the ideas about property acquired during the marriage.

The existence of such rules has not eliminated unfairness between spouses. The emotional and psychological strength of the parties, the desire or ability to gain custody of children, and the economic opportunities available to the partners postdivorce often mean that agreements that seem fair on their face can be intentionally or unintentionally unfair in practice. In such situations the economic power of the parties can mean that one former spouse may not be able to enforce an agreement. Equality under the law does not necessarily translate into equality in fact. There is no doubt that continuing differences in economic power between men and women can have a profound effect upon the consequences of an agreement. Indeed, many observers are convinced that as a practical matter the modern system of divorce has economically penalized women and children, although the degree of their loss has been the subject of sharp debate (Cherlin, 1992; Faludi, 1996).

In a widely disseminated study, Weitzman (1985) claimed that after a no-fault divorce a woman's standard of living dropped an average of 72%, while a man's increased by 42%. These figures were extraordinary, since most other research suggested that a woman's standard of living dropped by about 30% and a man's rose by about 10% (Hoffman & Duncan, 1988; Hoffman & Holmes, 1976). Weitzman, however, argued that these dire economic consequences of divorce were a direct result of no-fault divorce. It is now clear that Weitzman's data were misinterpreted and that her original data actually show a change in the standard of living between men and women that is similar to that of other studies. More importantly, the data actually show that no-fault divorce has no greater economic impact upon the economic status of women than fault-based divorce does (Peterson, 1996a,b; Weitzman, 1996). Despite these findings, it still remains clear that women experience a significant post-divorce economic decline in their standard of living. Still others see the legal and family systems as so characterized by unfairness that formal rule of equality under the law only serves to mask inequity. These people call for a complete rethinking of the economics of marriage and divorce in the light of ideas about justice and fairness (Fineman, 1991, 1995; Okin, 1989; Walzer, 1983).

Divorce

The common law did not permit divorce, which it termed "absolute" divorce. It did permit divorce from "bed and board," the predecessor of a current decree of separation, which did not permit the parties to remarry. Until recently, modern divorce law, although it permitted divorce, still harbored the common law's hostility to divorce. Divorce law was an instrument designed to preserve marriage by ensuring that the person found responsible for the dissolution of a marriage was punished. Historically, divorce was an adversarial procedure in which the law required the finding of "fault" and the declaration that one party was "innocent" and the other "guilty." Until recently, many states required evidence of adultery, desertion, or extreme cruelty. Some states, such as New York until 1967, restricted the grounds of divorce to adultery, in essence restricting divorce to situations in which one spouse was shown to be guilty of criminal conduct.

Traditionally, a finding of fault had serious implications for the parties, especially for women. In some states the "guilty" party was forbidden to remarry without the permission of the court. More importantly, there was a direct relation between fault and the awarding of postdivorce relief. Before equitable distribution statutes were enacted, the property of a marriage was divided upon the basis of legal title. This meant that the formal indicia of title determined who obtained the property after divorce. If there was joint title the property was divided evenly. If the husband held title to the car, the car was his. If the wife held title to bank accounts, the accounts were hers. As a practical matter, in a world where men dominated the workplace and women were frequently assigned to the domestic sphere, formal title to property was frequently held by men. Upon divorce, the wife usually received not property but alimony until she died or remarried. Alimony was only awarded, however, to an "innocent" spouse. Typically, if the wife was found liable for misconduct upon which a divorce could be granted then she would be permanently deprived of alimony. Thus alimony was granted based upon a judicial determination of innocence.

The laws governing divorces have also become increasingly flexible. Nowadays "fault" grounds have been greatly expanded to include drug addiction and alcoholism, imprisonment, sexual conduct other than adultery, or institutionalization for mental illness. In addition, beginning with California in 1969 all states now provide for no-fault grounds such as the continuous separation of the parties for a specified period or time or for irreconcilable differences, incompatibility, or irretrievable breakdown of the marriage. The idea of no-fault divorce was at least partly a result of the recognition that the finding of fault was often a legal fiction at best. In addition, courts and legislatures became concerned with the fact that people living in marriages that were otherwise "dead" were forced to perjure themselves in court as a means of obtaining a divorce where no legal fault actually existed. At the same time that no-fault divorce was developing, the concept of fault began to be stripped of its impact after divorce. In the vast majority of states, fault has been swept away from having bearing in the distribution of marital property or alimony.

There are, however, some states, including Alabama, Connecticut, Florida, and New Hampshire, where fault still has some bearing upon both issues. Some states, such as Michigan, are interested in reintroducing more fault-based divorce. There is also some case law that considers marital fault a factor in child custody and visitation decisions, but only if it has a direct impact on the child. If the conduct has no direct bearing on the child, most courts will not use it as a factor in deciding custody and visitation.

The finding of fault may still play a major role in the area of child custody and visitation. Fault is also reemerging in the form of tort claims, such as the intentional infliction of emotional distress or assault and battery at the time of divorce or afterwards. This is possible because the traditional common law tort immunities prohibiting tort litigation between spouses has disappeared. Some courts, however, are concerned that coupling tort actions with divorce actions improperly injects fault into no-fault proceedings any may undermine the efforts of a court to mediate property and custody issues. Thus if the tort claim is pursued a court may be inclined to try the issues separately so as to isolate the divorce proceedings from the tort claim. *Hakkila v. Hakkila* (1991).

Equitable Distribution and the Division of Marital Property

Marital property is usually thought of as anything of economic value resulting from the individual or combined efforts of both spouses during the marriage. Marital property includes items such as real property, personal property, gifts between spouses, wedding gifts, vested and nonvested pension rights, profit sharing, retirement and savings plans, bank accounts, interests in corporations, partnerships and businesses, and professional licenses. Marital property must be acquired during the marriage. Property acquired before the marriage is deemed to be separate property, but even separate property can become marital property in some circumstances. For example, if separate property is placed into a joint bank account or otherwise placed in the name of the married couple, a presumption arises that the separate property has been given as a gift to the other spouse.

In the event of divorce, marital property that is not divided according to the terms of a written contractual agreement will become subject to equitable distribution. Equitable distribution does not mean an equal split of marital property, although courts dealing with a long-term marriage will often aim for an equal division. State law provides a number of factors that are to be taken into account in reaching a division of the property. Typically, an equitable distribution statute will require the court to examine factors such as the income and property of the marital couple at the time of the marriage, the length of the marriage, the age and health of the parties, the need of the custodial parent to occupy or own the marital residence, as well as the loss of inheritance and pension rights. This statute also includes any equitable claim or interest in or direct or indirect contribution made to the acquisition of marital property by the person not having title to the property. Such interests or claims include joint efforts, expenditures, and contributions as a spouse-parent, wage-earner, and homemaker. Further considered in these claims are contributions to the career potential of the other partner and the probable future financial circumstances of each partner. In theory, the factors considered in equitable distribution are designed to recognize the economic contribution of the spouse who raised children and did not work outside the domestic sphere by valuing intangible contributions equally with those of the income-earning spouse.

The Concept of Maintenance

The concept of maintenance is a derivative of the older concept of alimony, a practice that dates back to the time before absolute divorce was available and was coupled with the limited concept of divorce from bed and board. Because limited divorce did not terminate the marriage and the parties could not remarry, alimony represented the continuation of the husband's marital obligations once cohabitation was terminated. When absolute divorce became available and remarriage became possible, the concept of alimony was continued. In recent years alimony has been relabeled as maintenance. Although historically only the husband was obligated to pay alimony, the gender limitation was eliminated in 1979 by the

United States Supreme Court decision in *Orr v. Orr*. A host of rationales have been advanced to explain the continued existence of alimony/maintenance. These include the husband's continuing obligation of support, the desire to reward virtue and punish misconduct, and financial need, as well as the support of an especially needy spouse who is disabled or in custodial care.

Most equitable distribution statues have retained the concept of alimony, now recast as maintenance, with some important differences. First, unlike traditional alimony, maintenance is not necessarily permanent and, in fact, is more likely to be temporary. Court-ordered maintenance often takes into account the length of the marriage and the standard of living enjoyed by the couple during the marriage. A court that awards maintenance is able to review the entire financial character of the marital relationship, including the tangible and nontangible contributions of each spouse. The court examines such factors as (1) the present and future earning capacities of both parties; (2) the ability of the parties to become self supporting; (3) the period of time and training necessary to make parties self-supporting; (4) the reduced or lost earning capacities of spouses who delayed, deferred, or reduced their incomes or career opportunities for the benefit of the other spouses; and (5) the contribution that spouses may have made to the careers or career potentials of the other parties. Courts may also see maintenance as a homemaker's "pension" or as a form of rehabilitation. Finally, courts may take into account excessive or abnormal expenditures, destruction, concealment, or fraudulent disposition of property held in common. This is not an exhaustive list, but it indicates the degree to which such statutory schemes are designed to promote equity in the economic dissolution of the marriage.

Child Support

Child support is one major area in which status rather than contract still rules supreme. Indeed, in contrast to equitable distribution, which promotes the contract model in the ordering of economic relations between spouses, the national trend in child support issues has been to limit the discretion of the parties and to make child support and the enforcement of child support subject to increasingly rigorous statutory schemes. When equitable distribution laws first appeared, it was clearly articulated that no agreement between the partners could free up either parent from their legally imposed duty to support the child. The law always required courts to maintain a supervisory role over the support and maintenance of children. In the last 10 years, however, many states established fixed standards of support for children, usually requiring the noncustodial parent to pay a specific percentage of his or her income to the custodial parent in the form of support. Couples who entered into an agreement for the provision of child support were often exempt from the standards, but in 1988 the Family Support Act required all states to adopt mandatory support guidelines that would serve as rebuttable presumptions in the awarding of child support.

In 1991, regulations adopted by the United States Department of Health and Human Services required all child support orders to conform with the states' child support guidelines. This has been interpreted by the federal government as including any agreements reached by the parties for the provision of child support. While federal regulations still allow for some deviation from state guidelines, the regulations limit the circumstances under which deviations from the guidelines are permitted. Federal regulations require that state courts take into account the "best interest of the child" before permitting any deviation, and judges are required to justify any deviations from the requirements.

Part of the drive to impose statutory duties of child support comes from increasing attention paid to nonmarital children (i.e., children born out of wedlock), where none of the issues addressed by equitable distribution apply. Indeed, in the absence of marriage virtually the only legal duties fathers and mothers have with respect to children are statutorily defined. Nevertheless, in two rulings in 1968 (*Levy v. Louisiana*; *Glona v. American Guarantee and Liability Ins. Co.*) the United States Supreme Court determined that legal discrimination against illegitimate children violated the equal protection clause of the United States Constitution. As a result, both marital children and nonmarital children stand in the same legal relationship to their parents with respect to all the rights and duties of parenthood.

States have been driven by two broad considerations: the protection of children by imposing economic duties upon noncustodial parents and the drive to reduce the levels of government economic support for children. All state child support guidelines apply to the parents of children regardless of whether the parents are married to one another, and courts are required to order support within the framework of these guidelines. Most states use a model that combines the income of both custodial and noncustodial parents, with a percentage allocated by the number of children and the relative income of the spouses. Other states base support only on the income of the noncustodial parent (Munsterman, 1990). Some states now permit courts to order the father of a nonmarital child to pay part of the mother's expenses related to pregnancy and childbirth. One lower court in New York recently required an underage unwed father to pay child support, even though the father was technically a victim of statutory rape by the older mother. In *Mercer County Department of Social Services v. Alf M* (1992), the couple had sexual intercourse when the father was 16 years old and the mother was 21. The father claimed he was a victim of statutory rape but the court determined that father's remedy lay in a criminal charge against the mother and that the child should not be penalized because of the mother's actions.

Most states require that all applicants for Aid to Families with Dependent Children assign their rights to uncollected child support to the state and must cooperate in its enforcement. New York's Family Court Act requires that where a child has been on public assistance, the awarding of support must be made retroactive to the date the child became eligible for public assistance. One idea behind this law is to require noncustodial parents to reimburse child support paid by the state in the form of public assistance, but for low-income people it may be an attempt to squeeze blood from a stone, as the noncustodial parent may never have had the means to pay adequate child support to begin with.

Enforcement of Child Support

One of the most pressing problems in the area of child support has been the problem of interstate enforcement of child support orders. Such issues become prevalent when parents reside in separate states or when the noncustodial parent simply abandons his or her family obligations and moves to another state. The first attempt to deal with this problem was the Uniform Reciprocal Enforcement of Support Act (URESA), which was adopted by the National Commissioners on State Laws in 1950; a revised form (RURESA) was adopted in 1968. URESA or RURESA has been adopted by every state legislature in the United States and provides, by an application in the home or originating state, for an order of support to be enforced in the state of the noncustodial parent. RURESA was an attempt to provide a relatively simple method for interstate enforcement of child support obligations. The parties each appear separately in the courts of their home states, rather than having to appear jointly in one of the states. In 1992 the National Commissioners approved the Uniform Interstate Family Support Act (UIFA), which has now been adopted by 25 states. The UIFA, designed to supersede URESA and RURESA, also provides home state courts with jurisdiction over nonresident noncustodial parents as well as with the interstate establishment of parentage, even if not connected to a support proceeding.

Portions of the Child Support Act of 1994 also provide that states must give full faith and credit to the child support orders of other states. This prevents another state from modifying the child support orders of the original state. Accordingly, if a noncustodial parent moves to another state, he or she may apply for modification only in the state that originally issued the order. The result is that custodial parents will have both notice and opportunity to oppose the application for modification.

Custody

When a child is born, both parents have equal rights to the custody of the child, and determination of custody is usually made by the agreement of the divorcing parties. When such an agreement is not possible, the child becomes a ward of the court. The court must then make a custody determination based upon the best interests of the child. In making a custody determination, courts are to be guided by the best interests of the child rather than by the merits of any dispute between the parties. However, because the idea of the best interests of the child is very vague, it actually offers no practical set of guidelines for courts to follow.

Under the common law the father usually retained custody. Since absolute divorce was rare under the common law, however, this was almost always in the context of "divorce from bed and board," in which the parties could not remarry. As divorce became more common, new laws tended to favor the awarding of the custody of young children to the mother. This was widely known as the "tender years doctrine"; a father contesting the custody of young children was required to show that the mother was unfit. The tender years doctrine is now deemed to be unconstitutional and a form of gender-based discrimination. Under modern law there is no presumption of custody for either parent. At face, decisions about custody should be gender neutral.

Gender Discrimination in Custody

There is considerable controversy as to whether gender neutrality is in fact neutral. Many observers continue to believe that the tender years doctrine remained an unwritten presumption despite legal lip service to its demise, but their biggest fear was that the assumptions underlying the tender years doctrine, namely the primacy of care at home by full-time mothers, would actually undermine the custody claims of working women. Indeed, in a leading case in 1986, the California Supreme Court in *Burchard v. Garay* ruled that parents' work status could not be used against them in custody disputes. In her concurring opinion, Chief Justice Rose Bird wrote that "to force women into the marketplace and then to penalize them would be cruel." But these words appear to be the harbinger of problems working women face in contested custody cases. In fact, recent scholarship argues that although the tender years doctrine been formally been jettisoned, in fact, women may have to bargain away their economic rights to retain custody (Bartlett & Stack, 1986).

Some recent and well-publicized cases show that some courts are discriminating against working mothers. A Michigan circuit court, in *Ireland v. Smith* (1996), recently awarded custody of a child to a father who claimed that his mother (the paternal grandmother) would provide daycare of his daughter if he were awarded custody of the child. His wife, by contrast, intended to put the daughter in daycare while she attended the University of Michigan. The court determined that the child should be placed with "blood relatives" rather than with strangers. The decision in this case was remanded by higher Michigan courts, which rejected the notion that daycare at the university was inferior per se to the care provided by the grandmother. Some states, such as Minnesota and West Virginia, have adopted a "primary caretaker standard" for awarding custody. This standard would give preference in custody to the spouse who actually took care of the children during the course of the marriage. In theory, this should protect many working mothers who both work and assume the primary care of children.

Despite the fiery debates over custody, there are very few empirical studies of custody decisions. In the one major empirical study, Maccoby and Mnookin (1992) found in California that in 80% of the cases they studied there was no conflict in the custody request by the parents. In California, parents can request sole physical custody or joint physical custody. In 500 of the 705 cases studied, the request was for physical custody by the mother, and the court granted 90% of these requests. In the 47 cases where sole physical custody was requested for the father the court granted 75% of these requests. In 198 cases where the custody was uncontested, the mother was granted custody in 117, the father in 52, and a compromise reached in the remaining cases. This study is a reminder that the vast majority of custody cases are either uncontested or settled without judicial intervention and that the physical custody is still primarily in the hands of mothers.

Custody takes three basic forms: physical custody by the father or the mother, legal custody, and joint or shared custody. Physical custody means that the child physically resides with a parent who has complete control over the daily affairs of the child. Legal custody involves the right to make legal decisions with respect to the education, health, and welfare of the child. Although one parent may have physical custody, legal custody may be given to both parents. Joint or shared custody covers a range of custody arrangements in which legal custody and physical custody are invested in both parents. Some states, like California, have specifically enacted legislation defining these terms. Many states implicitly incorporate these distinctions in legal proceedings. Parents may share legal custody in that they agree to joint decision making about major issues in the child's life.

Attitudes towards joint custody vary from state to state. New York courts usually do not award joint custody on the grounds that it is impractical and breaks down in practice. As a result, in New York joint custody is almost always achieved through formal agreement by the parties rather than by order of the courts. California, in contrast, encourages joint custody, while in Arizona the courts are authorized to award joint custody even over the objections of the parties.

Visitation

When one parent is awarded custody, the other is almost invariably awarded visitation rights. The awarding of visitation is typically seen as part of the child's right to have a right to associate with both parents. In fact, however, the child does not have an enforceable right to visitation and in practice noncustodial parents can choose not to exercise visitation rights. There has been some progress in enforcing visitation when it is wrongfully denied by the custodial parent.

In the past courts made it extremely difficult for the custodial parent to relocate. Given the primacy of the right of visitation, wrongful relocation has sometimes resulted in a custodial parent losing custody. The underlying assumption behind this view was that it was in the child's interest that the postdivorce family have some resemblance to the predivorce family. In many states this view has relaxed, with the trend being for more and more states to uphold the relocation rights of custodial parents even if this poses difficulties for the visitation rights of noncustodial parents. Although not every state has taken this view, many appear to have decided that the best interests of the child may be consistent with the desire of the custodial parent to remarry or obtain better employment, so relocation will be more routinely be permitted. Finally, it should be noted that the Uniform Interstate Child Visitation Act is currently being drafted by the National Law Commissioners.

Grandparental Visitation

The common law placed a wall of protection around the nuclear family and gave parents an absolute right as gatekeepers to determine who among kin or friends could have access to the children of the family. Under the common law grandparents had absolutely no right of visitation or even communication if it was forbidden by the parents.

The modern concept of a grandparental "right of visitation" developed out of situations in which the nuclear family was deemed "impaired" by death, divorce, or lack of parental fitness. Grandparental visitation emerged as a functional substitute designed to shore up a damaged family. Increasingly, however, grandparental visitation is conceptualized as an independent right of the child regardless of the status of the family or the wishes of the parents. In the 1991 case of *Emanual S. v. Joseph E.*, the parents of the child denied visitation to the grandparents, arguing that a court order to the contrary would be a denial of the parental right to determine

who a child associates with. In *Emanual*, however, the court indicated that, in evaluating grandparental rights, the best interest of the child and the equities of the situation would govern rather than an absolute rule in favor of parental authority. Accordingly, where a good relationship between grandparents and grandchildren exists and there is no reason to believe that grandchildren would be adversely affected by visitation, the courts will be increasingly likely to award visitation regardless of parental objections.

National Unification of Custody Procedures

Child custody is another legal area where there is increasing uniformity throughout the United States. Child custody cases are among the most difficult cases that courts must face. Custody decisions made by courts are never "final" because under the principle of the "best interest of the child," custody cases may be relitigated until the child reaches legal adulthood. Until the early 1980s, custody litigation throughout the United States was chaotic. Many states permitted relitigation of custody matters merely if the child were physically present in the state. As a result, interstate child snatching by embittered parents was widespread. To remedy this the National Conferences of Commissioners on Uniform State Laws drafted the Uniform Child Custody Jurisdiction Act (UCCJA), which has now been adopted by every state in the country. The act provides a national basis for determining which courts will assert jurisdiction in child custody cases. In parallel, Congress passed the Parental Kidnapping Prevention Act (PKPA), which was signed into law in 1980. The UCCJA and the PKPA are very similar, but federal law provides additional remedies, perhaps most importantly the requirement that custody and visitation decrees in one state receive full faith and credit in another.

In 1985 the United States Senate ratified the Hague Convention on the Civil Aspects of International Child Abduction. The implementing legislation in the United States is the International Child Abduction Remedies Act of 1988, which has been supplemented by the International Parental Kidnapping Act of 1993. Because of the worldwide problem of parental kidnapping, there are hundreds of cases each year. The Hague Convention established legal rights and procedures for the prompt return of children who have been wrongfully removed from one country to another. The aim of the convention is to restore the preabduction situation by restoring the child to the habitual residence for the purpose of adjudicating the dispute. But because most countries are not signatories to the Hague Convention, the United States has strengthened its position against parental kidnapping by making it a felony to remove a child from the United States with the intent to obstruct parental rights.

What Is a Family?

While much of law is involved in coining definitions, the law has rarely paid attention to the basic definitions that underlie legal thought. Thus the law has rarely been asked to define the meaning of family. The codification of family law throughout the United States has largely proceeded with the fiction that the concept of family used by the law was widely accepted and uncontested throughout the culture. This essentially meant that the law presumed that the family was fundamentally a nuclear family formed through a heterosexual marriage. But recent changes in American life have caused courts to rethink the entire legal and cultural basis of family and kinship in America. Several challenges to the traditional concepts of the family have emerged. Among these are new forms of domestic relations arising from divorce and remarriage that create complex networks of family relationship that cut across traditional domestic and household boundaries; widespread networks of relationships of kin and family formed without marriage, especially among the poor; the public emergence of domestic relationships between gay and lesbian partners; and the development of new reproductive technologies such as *in vitro* fertilization, sperm donation, and egg donation, which have made possible numerous and sometimes mindboggling combinations of egg, sperm, and womb. The widespread emergence and public recognition of these new families, which, like traditional families, have problems that require the intervention of the courts, have challenged courts to decide whether traditional legal concepts of family relations should be extended to include these new relationships.

The Supreme Court and the Family

At the national level, the U.S. Supreme Court has occasionally ventured into the domain of defining the family. In *Village of Belle Terre v. Borass* (1974), the court upheld a village ordinance that prohibited more than three persons unrelated by blood or marriage from sharing the same household. The arrangement did not prohibit unmarried couples, but it did exclude various forms of group living. In *United States Department of Agriculture v. Moreno* (1973), the court ruled that the government could not deny food stamps to households containing unrelated families. In *New Jersey Welfare Rights Organization v. Cahill* (1973) the court ruled that the government could not deny welfare to families with illegitimate children. In *Moore v. City of East Cleveland* (1977), the court ruled against a single family zoning ordinance that defined family so narrowly that a grandmother was prevented from having her two grandchildren live with her. Indeed, if these cases stand for anything, it is for the fundamental right to live in an extended family rather than a nuclear family (Tribe, 1978). *Moore* placed severe limitations upon government interference in precisely those kinds of kin and family arrangements likely to be prevalent within poor and working-class communities.

New Legal Definitions of the Family

Some of the most interesting decisions relating to the definition of the family have resulted from the housing crisis in New York City. New York City has a very low rental vacancy rate and a complex system of laws involving rent control and rent stabilization that are designed to make housing affordable to middle-income people. The right to live in a rent-controlled or rent-stabilized apartment was often dependent upon whether a person qualified as a member of the "family" of a current leaseholder. Beginning in the 1980s, New York courts began to examine the concept of family in this context. In *Yorkshire House Associates v. Lulkin* (1982), a New York court ruled that the eviction of an unmarried couple was in violation of the city's human rights law, which banned discrimination on the basis of marital status. In *420 East 80th Company v. Chin* (1982), the court ruled against the attempted eviction of a gay couple, holding that the "immediate family" term in the lease did not require a traditional nuclear family.

An important case in New York was the 1989 case of *Braschi v. Stahl Associates, Co.*, decided by the Court of Appeals, New York's highest court. Here the question was whether Miguel Braschi, a gay man, would be able to remain as a tenant in the apartment he had shared with his domestic partner, Leslie Blanchard, for more than 10 years. At issue was the court's interpretation of New York City rent and eviction regulations, which provided that upon the death of a tenant in a rent-controlled apartment, the landlord may not dispossess "either the surviving spouse of the deceased tenant or some other family member of the deceased tenant's family who has been living with the tenant." The Court of Appeals specifically focused on the meaning of the term "family."

The court rejected the idea that the term "family member" should be construed consistently with New York's intestacy laws, which regulate the inheritance of property, to mean relationships of blood, consanguinity, or adoption. Instead, the court argued that the noneviction provisions are not designed to govern succession to property, but to protect certain occupants from the loss of their homes. In light of this, the court argued that the term "family" should not be "rigidly restricted to those people who have formalized their relationship by obtaining, for instance, a marriage certificate or adoption order. The intended protection against sudden eviction should not rest on fictitious legal distinctions or genetic history, but instead should find its foundation in the reality of family life." The court proceeded to provide a distinctly cultural view of family as "a group of people united by certain convictions or common affiliation" or as a "collective body of persons who live in one house under one head or management." Finally, the court added that in using the term "family" the legislature had "intended to extend protection to those who reside in households having all of the normal familial characteristics." Indeed, the court went on at length to describe how much the relationship between Braschi and Blanchard fit the facts of family life:

> Appellant and Blanchard lived together as permanent life partners for more than 10 years. They regarded one another, and were regarded by friends and family, as spouses. The two men's families were aware of the nature of the relationship, and they regularly visited each other's families and attended family functions together, as a couple. Even today, Appellant continues to maintain a relationship with Blanchard's niece, who considers him an uncle.

The court, in upholding the right of the surviving partner, declared that protection against eviction "should find its foundation in the reality of family life. In the context of eviction, a ... realistic, and certainly valid, view of a family includes two adult lifetime partners whose relationship is long-term and characterized by an emotional and financial commitment and interdependence." This decision of the court prompted major changes in the rent control and rent stabilization codes in New York. Although lesbian and gay couples will benefit greatly by these actions, the greatest beneficiaries are expected to be a wide range of nontraditional families, especially families of the poor. Outside the domain of housing, however, it has been far more difficult to obtain statutory redefinitions of family. To be sure, some states permit gay and lesbian couples to register as domestic partners and many corporations are extending benefits to such partnerships, but in the key areas of family law such recognition has involved significant struggle. This is exemplified by the case of *Alison D. v. Virginia M.* (1991), in which a New York Appellate Division ruled that the term "parent" applied solely to biological relationships and denied a former lesbian partner visitation rights to a child whom she and the biological mother of the child had parented together. In this case, the two women began living with each other in 1978. In 1980, they decided to raise a family, and Virginia M. was artificially inseminated. A boy was born, and the two women shared in the care of the child and jointly assumed all parenting responsibilities. In 1983, the relationship between the women ended, and Alison D. moved out of their home. Initially, she enjoyed regular visitation, but her former partner cut off all visitation in 1987.

The court's decision of May 1990 left Alison D. without any legal rights to see the child. In *Alison D. v. Virginia M.*, the court was called upon to define the legal meaning of parent. At issue in this case was whether Alison D. had visitation rights to a child she and her former lesbian lover had parented together. Her basic claim was that she stood *in loco parentis* to the child, that is, that the relationship the partners created gave her all the rights, duties, and responsibilities of a parent. As in the previous cases, the language of the law does not specifically define the term parent. Thus, the court was asked to adopt the concept of parent as one standing *in loco parentis*.

The court admitted that Alison D. and the child had a close and loving relationship, but defined the issue as solely a dispute between a parent and a nonparent with respect to visitation of the child. Pronouncing Alison D. a "biological stranger," it chose to follow a line of cases that grant rights to nonparents only under extraordinary circumstances such as the unfitness of the biological parent. In her dissent, Justice Kooper rejected the court's reliance upon biology. She argued for a cultural definition of parenthood. In particular, she asserted that like the term "family," the term "parent" should be subject to a "frank inquiry into the realities of the relationship involved." As we shall see in the next section, some of the difficulties that arose in this case have not been resolved in some states in which unmarried couples, both homosexual and heterosexual, have been permitted to adopt children. As a result, in some states adoption has become a process of family formation in situations where adults are unable or unwilling to marry.

Adoption

Adoption did not exist under the common law and is strictly a statutory creation. The first adoption laws were enacted in Alabama in 1850 and in Massachusetts in 1851 and quickly spread throughout the country (Friedman, 1983). Traditionally, adoption is a legal mechanism whereby the biological or "natural" parent or parents surrendered their legal rights and duties to a child and transferred them to another person or persons. Adoption legally cuts off the biological parents from the child. Following adoption, the biological parents no longer have any duty to support the child. In addition, the contemporary laws of adoption, with some exceptions, provide that inheritance rights traced through the biological parents are terminated and are transferred to the adopting parents; thus the adopted child's rights are equivalent to those of a biological child.

Adoption is an area of family law that has undergone considerable transformation during the last decade. When adoption laws were first enacted, cultural considerations triumphed over biological ties to former relatives. Admittedly some early courts and legislatures were somewhat uneasy about the absolute dismissal of blood relationships through adoption, but the predominant view rapidly spread throughout the United States.

Recently, ideas about biological relations have reentered the issue of adoption, particularly in three key areas. The first area is the expansion of the rights of the unmarried biological father in the adoption away of his nonmarital child. Second is the rapidly developing concept of "open adoptions," which permit and/or encourage the maintenance of a relationship between the adopted children and their biological parents. (Notwithstanding this trend, there are no states in which biological parents retain the legal status as parents.) Third is the right of the adopted child's biological grandparents or siblings to maintain a legally enforceable relationship with their adopted-away biological kin. The general trend has been to weaken the absolute legal control that the adopting parents have over their adopted children in favor of an approach that focuses on the children's rights to a relationship with biological kin. It is also clear that modern adoption trends point to the creation of families in which the social network of the family encompasses multiple claims of original natal families and adopting families (Model, 1994).

As a legal procedure, adoptions require the consent of the biological parents. Where a marital child is involved, the consent of both parents is required. Traditionally, where a nonmarital child was involved, adoption statutes usually required only the biological mother's consent to the adoption. The rights of the biological father were irrelevant to the process regardless of the kin ties or degree of parental relationship he had with the child. Thus even if the father were supporting the child, or living together with the mother and the child, the child could be adopted away without his consent. The legal and cultural reasoning that served as the basis for this law was that the possibility of placing a child within a functional nuclear family overrode all other considerations. Accordingly, when the mother made the decision to place the child in this highly idealized family context, the mere fact of biology was forced to bow to culture. Through a number of constitutional rulings based on procedural due process and equal protection, the United States Supreme Court has now altered the rights of nonmarital biological fathers. The right of fathers to veto the adoption away of their biological children has emerged as a conditional right dependent upon the strength of the contact that fathers have created with the child.

The issue of notification of a nonmarital biological father to the existence of adoption proceedings was at least partly settled in *Lehr v. Robinson* (1983). Here the court ruled provisions that required notice to the father if the father's name was present on the birth certificate to be constitutional. In *Caban v. Muhammed* (1979), the Supreme Court ruled unconstitutional the adoption away of a child without the consent of a nonmarital father who had a substantial relationship with his children. These two rulings have required a retooling of state legislative schemes to give biological fathers veto power over the adoption of children with whom they have a substantive relationship. There has been a significant amount of judicial and legislative effort to define criteria that would meet the standard established by the court.

Courts have also recently ruled that both siblings and grandparents are not barred from seeking visitation rights with children who have been adopted away. In the past the judicial presumption was that once a child was adopted, the adoption process cut off not only the relationship between the child and his biological parents but also, by extension, the legal relationship between the child and his or her biological siblings and grandparents. Increasingly, however, the rights of biological parents and those of other kin are being understood to be separate issues. To be sure, the primacy of the adopting family is still the main element in adoption, but there has been an erosion of the common law rule that parents are the absolute gatekeepers to the nuclear family and their decisions as to who can visit their children not subject to any interference by the courts. In this respect, the adopting family is no different from the nonadopting family, which has similarly lost absolute control over blocking visitation of children by grandparents and siblings. The driving ideology behind this is the focus on the child's independent rights to have relationships with siblings and grandparents (Felder, 1995; Galasso, 1994).

A second major shift in adoption has been the expansion of the right to adopt. Traditionally, most courts favored married couples as potential adoptive parents. As a general rule adoption proceedings, like custody proceedings, were governed by the "best interests of the child" standard. Courts have felt that much of the rationale behind adoption was to give the child a functioning family based upon the ideal model of the nuclear family. In most states today, however, it is not only families who can adopt, but single people as well. Historically, many states have discriminated against gays and lesbians in both adoption and custody, but such discrimination is disappearing. Moreover higher courts in both New York and Vermont have recently addressed the larger issue of whether couples need be married or of the opposite sex to adopt. Most state statutes do not directly address the issue of whether gay and lesbian couples may adopt but Florida and New Hampshire specifically prohibit adoption by gays and lesbians. Lower courts in a dozen states, however, have approved adoption by these groups.

In the 1995 cases *In the Matter of Dana* and *In the Matter of Jacob*, New York's Court of Appeals decided that an unmarried partner of a child's biological mother, whether heterosexual or homosexual, who is raising the child together with the biological parent, can become the child's second parent through adoption. In *Jacob*, the child's biological father and mother were divorced, and the mother had custody and was living with a new partner when they filed for adoption. The biological father had given his permission for adoption. *In the Matter of Dana* involved a lesbian couple had had lived together for 19 years. One of the partners was artificially inseminated and gave birth to a child. The partners were sharing full parental responsibilities when they filed a petition for adoption. Relying on the policy that adoption must be construed in light of the best interests of the child, the court focused on the broad policy matters that support the idea that functional parents in this situation should be entitled to become legal parents.

First, the court noted that the children would benefit from Social Security, life insurance, health insurance, and the right to inherit from both parents. The children would also benefit from the fact that both parents would be legally entitled to make medical decisions. Equally importantly, the court noted that it would promote the security of parental ties for the children should one of the parents die, become disabled, or should the coparents separate. The court specifically noted that it wanted to avoid the disruptive type of visitation battle described earlier in *Alison D. v. Virginia M.*

A major technical hurdle in these cases is that the adoption laws of both New York and Vermont, like the adoption laws of most states, cut off the rights of the biological parents in adoption proceedings. Strictly interpreted, it would have meant that the biological parent would have lost her rights to the child in favor of the adopting copartner. The law usually has carved out an exception to this in the case of so-called stepparent adoptions, in which a stepparent may adopt the child of his or her spouse. But the stepparent exception required the stepparent to be married to the biological parent. These cases called for an extension of the stepparent model to situations where the adopting partner is unmarried to the biological parent. In deciding that second-parent adoptions fit into the stepparent model, the court determined that cutting off the legal relationship between the biological parent and the child only applied when there is an adoption between strangers and there is a need to promote the stability of the new adopted family by blocking intrusion by the child's former biological parents. The court reasoned that severance of ties is not required when the adopted child remains in the "natural" family unit. In the Vermont case of *Adoption of B.L.V.B. and E.L.V.B.*, the court determined that in a family unit composed of a natural mother and her partner and where the adoption is in the best interest of the child, the termination of the natural mother's rights was unreasonable and unnecessary. Interestingly, in order to affirm these adoptions, the court had to further soften the traditional hard line between the biological family of origin and the new legal family. In these new situations where the biological father had given consent to adoption in one case or was apparently an un-

known sperm donor in the other, the adopting family was labeled the "natural family unit."

Surrogacy

In recent years, new reproductive technologies have challenged family law in radical ways. Issues relating to the custody and control of frozen embryos upon divorce and the legal status of children conceived by artificial insemination after the death of the father are part of a medical revolution that is driving a legal revolution. Among the most significant issues that have arisen in the last decade is the idea of surrogate parenting. Surrogacy, or surrogate parenthood, involves a woman (the surrogate) intentionally bearing a child for someone else. Usually the woman has entered into a contract or intends to surrender the child to someone else, usually through adoption. Surrogacy has a brief but complex legal history (Field, 1990). Typically, surrogacy involves two possible scenarios. The first is so-called "traditional surrogacy," where a woman is impregnated by the sperm of a man (usually through artificial insemination) who is not her husband, with the intent of transferring custody to him or perhaps to him and his wife for adoption. The birth mother or gestational mother is also the genetic mother of the child.

The celebrated New Jersey case *In the Matter of Baby M* (1988) involved traditional surrogacy. In *Baby M*, Mary Beth Whitehead (the surrogate) entered into a commercial contract for $10,000 with William Stern and his wife, in which she agreed to artificial insemination by Stern. She gave birth to a baby, but decided not to go forward with the agreement. The New Jersey Supreme Court ultimately voided the surrogacy agreement as against public policy, and the Stern's adoption of Baby M was vacated. In the end, however, custody was awarded to Stern on a "best interest of the child" basis. Mrs. Whitehead was awarded visitation.

The second type of surrogacy, termed "gestational surrogacy," involves the implantation of a fertilized ovum in the womb of a woman who is not the genetic mother of the child. This is illustrated by the California case *Calvert v. Johnson* (1993), involving a commercial contract between Mark and Crispina Calvert and Anna Johnson. Under the terms of the contract, Mark Calvert's sperm was mixed with Crispina Calvert's eggs and the resulting embryo was implanted in the uterus of Anna Johnson (the surrogate). The Calverts were the genetic parents, but Anna Johnson carried the child to term and gave birth to the baby. The trial court in California declared that the Calverts were the legal parents of the baby because they were the genetic parents. On appeal, the California Supreme Court affirmed the award but based its decision upon its reading of the intent of the contract.

Surrogacy usually involves a commercial contract in

which money is paid to the surrogate for the promise to surrender the child at birth, but it need not be a commercial agreement. States differ significantly in their treatment of surrogacy. It has been banned in several states, including New York and New Jersey, as contrary to public policy. New York imposes fines and criminal penalties for commercial surrogacy while making a noncommercial contract unenforceable. Some states such as Nevada and West Virginia explicitly permit surrogacy; still others have taken no position on surrogacy. The Uniform Status of Children of Assisted Conception Act provides two options. Where jurisdictions recognize surrogacy, the intended mother is the legal mother; where surrogacy is not recognized, the act provides that the birth mother is the legal mother.

But even if surrogacy agreements are unenforceable, the question remains as to how the law will treat the child born of such a contract. Once the agreement is deemed unenforceable, there is virtually nothing that government can actually do to prevent a birth mother from going ahead with an adoption. Indeed, the state cannot legally impose the care and custody of a child upon a mother who does not want such a child.

More problematic is the situation in which the surrogate does not wish to relinquish the child for adoption. Here the Uniform Act and state legislation are designed to ensure that there is only one mother. The New York statute denies the genetic mother any standing in initiating a custody action. As Kandel (1994) has pointed out, current legislation as well as court rulings appear to privilege the ideology of the nuclear family even in the face of the fact that there actually are two mothers. Indeed, Kandel advances the view that surrogacy laws should recognize both mothers. Similarly, Dolgin (1993, 1995) argues that the court decisions in both *Baby M* and *Calvert* support the traditional notions of the nuclear family. Perhaps it is the very novelty of the arrangements in the reproductive context, which most dramatically calls the traditional family into question, that has prompted a defense of the nuclear family.

The practical outcome of current law in this area hardly promotes nuclear families. In the case of "traditional" surrogacy, a breach of contract both in states that recognize surrogacy and those that do not will invariably lead to a custody battle between the genetic father and the surrogate (the gestation/genetic mother). Under gestational surrogacy (assuming the intent of most gestational surrogacy agreements is to provide a child for the genetic mother), a breach of contract in a state that recognizes surrogacy will usually lead to the awarding of the child to the genetic mother and genetic father. Where a state does not recognize surrogacy, a breach will lead to a custody fight between the genetic father and the birth mother. To be sure, the genetic mother will be legally cut off but to the extent that she remains married to the genetic father she may construct a relationship with her offspring. As a result, the only case in which one of the mothers will absolutely be cut off from involvement with the child is that of the birth mother in a state that recognizes surrogacy. It is ironic that laws that at first blush appear to preserve the ideology of the traditional family are so dependent upon contract principles and yield such unhappy results.

Sperm Donors

The dramatic rise in the use of artificial insemination to achieve pregnancy has also created dramatic legal problems. In the past, courts frequently distinguished between two types of artificial insemination: artificial insemination with the husband's semen (homologous insemination) and artificial insemination with the sperm of a third-party donor, usually anonymous (heterologous insemination). Cases where the living husband is the donor present no legal problems, as artificial insemination is treated exactly like sexual intercourse. Cases where the donor is anonymous also present few problems. In some states the possible parental rights of an anonymous donor have been blocked by statute and by case law in others. California's statute, which is applicable to both married and unmarried women, bars a sperm donor from asserting parental rights where the sperm is provided by a licensed physician. New York has a similar law that by statute applied only to married women but has been extended to unmarried women by the courts. In the case of a married couple, the child conceived by heterologous artificial insemination is deemed to be the child of the husband. The general view, expressed in the 1968 California case *People v. Sorenson*, is that a child conceived by an anonymous donor has no natural father. The sperm donor was analogized to the blood donor or kidney donor.

Several recent cases, however, involve artificial insemination of unmarried women by known donors. In the 1994 case *Thomas S. v. Robin Y.*, a New York court entered an order of filiation recognizing the paternity of a sperm donor who was known to his child as her father and who had considerable contact with the child. The court ordered the case remanded to the family court for a hearing on visitation. In this case, Robin Y. was artificially inseminated by Thomas S. in San Francisco and gave birth to a daughter while living with a lesbian life partner. The partners then relocated to New York. There was an oral agreement between the parties that Thomas S. would have no parental rights, but when the child was about 3½ years old, the mother contacted Thomas S., a relationship began to develop, and the child began to refer to him as "Dad." The relationship continued even though the father and child resided in different parts of the country. The court's decision suggests that the rights of known sperm donors will be treated very much like that of unwed fathers. To the extent that the sperm donor creates a substantial relationship with a child he will be deemed to have some level of parental rights. Whether the existence of a written agreement between parties would have changed the court's view of the matter is unknown.

Conclusion

In this chapter I have attempted to demonstrate some of the major changes in family law over the second half of this century. These changes are characterized by the fading away of the privileged legal concept of the nuclear family in favor of one that recognizes a multiplicity of claims and relationships in the formation of family and kin ties. These changes illustrate that the American law of the family is still part of the long march from status to contract that was first observed by Sir Henry Maine in the nineteenth century.

Family and kinship are not only about contracts; American law and American society continue to recognize other principles at work in the formation of family and kinship ties. These principles include the idea that people who have come together and shared the trials and tribulations of domestic life have created economic, emotional, and moral ties that deserve recognition under the law. In addition, ideas about blood, biology, and nature still permeate much language of life and the law, not merely because these are old familiar ideas, but because people still search for connections that somehow seem to transcend temporal social arrangements. It is irrelevant that these "natural" connections may themselves be shaped by underlying cultural assumptions. In varying combinations, these ideas of nature and culture will continue to be part of the texture of the issues surrounding the relationship between law and the family.

ACKNOWLEDGMENTS: The author thanks Tori Rosen, Myra Bluebond-Langner, Carol Stack, Randy Kandel, and the anonymous reviewers for their helpful comments and criticism of the ideas contained in earlier versions of this chapter.

References

Adoptions of B.L.V.B. and E.L.V.B., 169 Vt. 368 (1993).

Alison D. v. Virginia M., 77 N.Y.2d 651 (1991).

Augustine C. v. Michael B. 84 A.D.2d 740 (N.Y. App. Div., 1981).

Baehr v. Lewin, 852 P.2d 44 (Haw. 1993).

Baker v. Nelson, 291 Minn 310 (1971).

Bartlett, K., & Stack, C. (1986). Joint custody, feminism, and the dependency dilemma. *Berkeley Women's Law Journal, 2*, 941.

Blackstone, W. (1899). *Commentaries on the laws of England (additional commentaries by Thomas M. Cooley)* (4th ed.). Chicago: Calagan & Co.

Bowers v. Hardwick, 487 U.S. 186 (1986).

Braschi v. Stahl Associates, 74 N.Y.2d 201 (1989).

Burchad v. Garay, 724 P.2d 486 (Cal 1986).

Caban v. Muhammed, 441 U.S. 380 (1979).

Calvert v. Johnson, 5 Cal Rptr. 4th 88 (1993).

Cherlin, A. (1992). *Marriage, divorce, remarriage.* Cambridge, MA: Harvard University Press.

Child Support Orders Act, 108 Stat. 4064 (1994).

Dean v. District of Columbia, 653 A.2d 307 (D.C. 1995).

Defense of Marriage Act 110 Stat. 2419 (1996).

Dolgin, J. (1993). Just a gene: Judicial assumptions about parenthood. *UCLA Law Review, 40*, 637–642.

Dolgin, J. (1994). The family in transition: From Griswold to Eisenstadt and beyond. *Georgetown Law Review, 82*, 1519–1571.

Dolgin, J. (1995). Family law and the facts of family. In S. Yanagisako & C. Delancy (Eds.), *Naturalizing power* (pp. XX). New York: Routledge.

Eisenstadt v. Baird, 405 U.S. 438 (1972).

Emanual S. v. Joseph E., 161 A.D.2d 83 (N.Y. App. Div., 1990).

Ettore I. v. Angela D., 127 A.D.2d 6 (N.Y. App. Div., 1987).

Faludi, S. (1996). Statistically challenged. *The Nation, 262*, 10.

Family Support Act, 102 Stat. 2743 (1988).

Farber, B. (1966). *Kinship and family organization.* New York: Wiley.

Felder, M. (1995, February 6). Visitation for grandparents and greatgrandparents. *New York Law Journal*, p. 3.

Field, M. (1990). *Surrogate motherhood.* Cambridge, MA: Harvard University Press.

Fineman, M. (1991). *The illusion of inequality.* Chicago: University of Chicago Press.

Fineman, M. (1995). *The neutered mother, the sexual family.* New York: Routledge.

420 East 80th Company v. Chin, 97 A.D. 2d 390 (N.Y. App. Div., 1983).

Friedman, L. (1983). *A history of American law.* New York: Simon & Shuster.

Friedman, L. (1993). *Crime and punishment in American history.* New York: Basic Books.

Galasso, P. (1994, April 29). Whose children are they anyway? *New York Law Journal*, p. 1.

Geertz, C. (1983). *Local knowledge.* New York: Basic Books.

Glona v. American Guarantee Co., 391 U.S. 73 (1968).

Greenhouse, C., Yngvesson, B., & Engle, D. (1994). *Law & community in three American towns.* Ithaca, NY: Cornell University Press.

Griswold v. Connecticut, 381 U.S. 479 (1965).

Gunther, G. (1972). Forward: A model for a new equal protection. *Harvard Law Review, 86*, 110.

Gunther, G. (1980). *Cases and material on constitutional law.* New York: Foundation Press.

Hakkila v. Hakkila, 112 N.M. 172 (1991).

Hoffman, S., & Duncan, J. (1988). What are the economic consequences of divorce? *Demography, 25*, 641–645.

Hoffman, S., & Holmes, J. (1976). Husbands, wives and divorce. In G. Duncan and J. Morgan (Eds.), *Five thousand American families patterns of economics program* (pp. 23–62). Ann Arbor, MI: Institute for Sound Research.

Horowitz, M. (1977). *The transformation of American law.* Cambridge, MA: Harvard University Press.

In the Matter of Baby M., 109 N.J. 396 (1988).

In the Matter of Dana, 86 N.Y.2d 651 (N.Y. Ct. App., 1995).

In the Matter of Jacob, 86 N.Y.2d 651 (N.Y. Ct. App., 1995).

Ireland v. Smith, 451 Mich. 457 (1996).

Kandel, R. (1994). Which came first: The mother or the egg? A kinship situation in gestational surrogacy. *Rutgers Law Review, 47*, 165.

Lehr v. Robinson, 463 U.S. 248 (1983).

Levy v. Louisiana, 39 U.S. 68 (1968).

Lewin, E (1993). *Lesbian mothers*. Ithaca, NY: Cornell University Press.

Loving v. Virginia, 388 U.S. 1 (1967).

Maccoby, E., & Mnookin, R. (1992). *Dividing the child*. Cambridge, MA: Harvard University Press.

Main, H. (1963). *Ancient law*. Boston: Beacon.

Matter of Sharon GG v. Duane HH, 98 A.D.2d 466 *aff'd* 63 NY 859 (1983).

May, E. (1988). *Homeward bound*. New York: Basic Books.

Mercer County Department of Social Services v. Alf M., 155 Misc. 2d 703, 589 N.Y.S.2d 288 (1992).

Michael H. v. Gerald D., 491 U.S. 10 (1989).

Mnookin, R. H., & Kornhauser, L. (1979). Bargaining in the shadow of the law: The case of divorce. *The Yale Law Journal, 88*, 950–997.

Model, J. (1994). *Kinship with strangers*. Berkeley: University of California Press.

Moore v. City of East Cleveland, 431 U.S. 494 (1977).

Munsterman, X. (1990). *A guide to child support payments guidelines*, Williamsburg, VA: National Center for State Courts.

New Jersey Welfare Rights Organization v. Cahill, 411 U.S. 619 (1973).

Okin, S. (1989). *Justice, gender, and the family*, New York: Basic Books.

Orr v. Orr, 440 U.S. 268 (1979).

Parental Kidnapping Act, 94 Stat. 3568 (1980).

People v. Sorensen, 68 Cal. 2d 280, 437 P.2d. 465 (1968).

Peterson, R. (1996a). A reevaluation of the economic consequences of divorce. *American Sociological Review, 61*, 528–536.

Peterson, R. (1996b). Statistical errors, faulty conclusions, misguided policy: Reply to Weitzman. *American Sociological Review, 61*, 539–549.

Revised Uniform Reciprocal Support Act, 9B U.L.A. 381 (1968).

Roe v. Wade, 410 U.S. 113 (1973).

Romer v. Evans, 116 S. Ct 1620 (1996).

Scheffler, H. (1991). Sexism and naturalism in the study of kinship. In M. di Leonardo (Ed.), *Gender at the crossroads of knowledge* (pp. 361–382). Berkeley: University of California Press.

Shorter, E. (1975). *The making of the American family*. New York: Basic Books.

Stacey, J. (1990). *Brave new families*. New York: Basic Books.

Stack, C. (1974). *All our kin*. New York: Harper.

Stack, C. (1984). Cultural perspectives on child welfare. *Review of Law and Social Change, 12*, 539–547.

Thomas S. v. Robin Y., 618 N.Y.S. 356 (1994).

Trautmann, T. (1987). *Lewis Henry Morgan and the invention of kinship*. Berkeley: University of California Press.

Tribe, L. (1978). *American constitutional law*. Mineola, NY: Foundation Press.

Uniform Child Custody Jurisdiction Act.

Uniform Interstate Family Support Act, 9B ULA Sections 101 905 (West Supp. 1996).

Uniform Marriage and Divorce Act 9A U.L.A. 201 (1987 and West Supp. 1996).

Uniform Reciprocal Enforcement Support Act, 9B ULA Section 553 (1958).

Uniform Status of Children of Assisted Conception Act, 9B U.L.A. 163 (West Supp. 1994).

United States Department of Agriculture v. Moreno, 413 U.S. 528 (1973).

U.S. v. Reynolds, 98 U.S. 145 (1878).

Village of Belle Terre v. Borass, 416 U.S. 1 (1974).

Walzer, M. (1983). *Spheres of justice*. New York: Basic Books.

Weitzman, L. (1985). *The divorce revolution*. New York: Free Press.

Weitzman, L. (1996). The economic consequences of divorce are still unequal. *American Sociological Review, 61*, 537–538.

Weston, K. (1991). *Families we choose*. New York: Columbia University Press.

Yorkshire House Associates v. Lulkin, 114 Misc 2d 40, 450 N.Y.2d 962 (1982).

Zaretsky, E. (1976). *Capitalism, the family, and personal life*. New York: Harper and Row.

Zeblock v. Redhail, 434, U.S. 374 (1978).

CHAPTER 21

Families and Work

Linda Haas

Introduction

For most adults, family and work roles are the most significant sources of identity. Historically, social scientists investigated work and family roles as if they were separate from one another; the family and the economy were studied as distinct social institutions. As more women have entered the paid labor force, researchers have paid increasing attention to linkages between family and work (Bielby & Bielby, 1988b). We can no longer ignore that most individuals are trying to balance work and family roles—87% of American adults live with other family members and 47% are responsible for the care of a dependent family member (children, ill partner, or ill parent) (Galinsky, Bond, & Friedman, 1993).

This review summarizes recent research studies concerning linkages between families and work. It first considers the social context of this research and then examines theoretical perspectives on family–work linkages. The third section describes research on the gender-based division of labor for unpaid family work. The fourth section examines the impact of men's and women's paid employment on family relationships, and the fifth part looks at the impact of family responsibilities on individuals' labor force participation, work performance, and employment attitudes. Next, research analyzing the consequences of individuals' simultaneous membership in both family and work systems is reviewed, followed by suggestions for future study.

Most of the work reviewed here has appeared in the last

10 years, since the last *Handbook* was published. Excellent reviews of the literature on families and work published before 1987 can be found in Menaghan and Parcel (1991); Piotrowski, Rapoport, and Rapoport (1987); Spitze (1991); and Voydanoff (1987, 1988a). This review is also limited to investigations of families in the United States. American and foreign scholars are becoming more interested in family–work linkages worldwide (e.g., Björnberg, 1992; Higgins & Duxbury, 1992; Holt & Thaulow, 1995; Wolcott & Glezer, 1995), but substantial bodies of literature on other countries are still lacking. Because social structure and culture affect dramatically the nature of family and work in ways that cannot be adequately explored here (see Lewis, Izraeli, & Hootsmans, 1992), this review is restricted to a single cultural setting. Although most American research is still conducted on white, urban, middle-class, husband–wife households based on first marriages, a special effort was undertaken to review studies of minority, rural, working-class, remarried, and single-parent families.

The family is an emotional unit, based on love and affection, that provides psychological security and nurturance to its members. In addition, the family is also a work unit. Family members must be active in the formal economy for an income ("paid work"), and they must also care for the household and family members ("unpaid family work"). Following the example of Gerstel and Gross (1987), therefore, work is defined broadly as an activity that produces something of value for others.

Finally, research on families and work must necessarily examine gender roles. Gender inequality exists in both paid work and unpaid family work, and inequality in one area reinforces inequality in the other (Chafetz, 1990). Consequently (following the example of Ferree, 1991a), this review makes a point of analyzing rather than taking for granted the gendered nature of work–family linkages.

Linda Haas • Department of Sociology, Indiana University–Purdue University at Indianapolis, Indianapolis, Indiana 46202.

Handbook of Marriage and the Family, 2nd edition, edited by Marvin Sussman, Suzanne K. Steinmetz, and Gary W. Peterson. Plenum Press, New York, 1999.

The Social Context of Research on Families and Work

In the 1990s, linkages between work and family systems have become stronger and more important to study than ever before because of several social trends. These trends involve employment patterns, family demographics, ideologies regarding gender and marital roles, and changes in workplace policies and practices.

Employment Patterns

Women participate in the labor force in increasing numbers, and a greater proportion exhibit a permanent attachment to the labor force. The most dramatic change has been in the percentage of mothers who are employed. In 1960, only 28% of married women with children under 18 were in the labor market, compared to 68% in 1994 (Chow & Bertheide, 1988; Herz & Wootton, 1996). Women no longer leave the labor market for long periods, even when their children are small. In 1994, 60% of mothers with preschool-aged children were employed, compared to only 19% in 1960 (Herz & Wootton, 1996; U.S. Bureau of the Census, 1990). The figures for minority mothers and women heading households are quite similar (Hayghe, 1990; Herz & Wootton, 1996).

Meanwhile, the percentage of men who are in the labor force has decreased slightly (Hayghe & Haugen, 1987; Wilkie, 1991). Early retirement has become more common, due to poor health or job loss, combined with improved retirement and disability benefits (Hayghe & Haugen, 1987; Wilkie, 1991). Problems obtaining permanent employment are partially to blame for African American men's lessened labor force participation (Menaghan & Parcel, 1991).

These changes in women's and men's employment patterns reflect changes in the overall structure of the American labor market. A continued decline in real earnings since the 1970s has made two incomes crucial for the maintenance of families' standard of living (Wilkie, 1991). This decline seems to be associated with the elimination of many formerly well-paying manufacturing jobs, wage concessions in several unionized industries, and the establishment of a two-tier wage system that offers lower wages and slower pay increases to new entrants into the labor market. These developments are reflected in the relatively low wages of young men. In 1993, for example, one-third (32%) of men ages 20 and 34 had incomes below the official poverty level, up from 14% in 1969 (Sidel, 1996). The incomes of young African American men have decreased even more: Over half (56%) had wages below poverty level by 1987, compared to 42% in the mid-1960s (Wilkie, 1991). Cyclical unemployment and permanent job loss due to takeovers, plant closing, and layoffs also create an atmosphere of economic uncertainty in families, which encourages women's labor force participation (Menaghan & Parcel, 1991).

The necessity of two incomes in the family is not the only factor to boost female numbers in the workforce. Traditionally male jobs (e.g., in manufacturing) are disappearing, and the types of jobs women traditionally have held (e.g., in services) are increasing. In 1961, for example, 30% of jobs were in manufacturing, compared to only 18% by 1988. During the same period, the percentage of jobs in service areas increased from 14% to 24% (Howe & Parks, 1989). The increase in typically women's jobs helps encourage more women to enter the labor market.

Despite the widespread entrance of women into the labor force, their employment patterns remain quite different from those of men. Women are still more likely than men to work part-time or part-year (one-fourth at the time involuntarily) and to quit work to care for young, ill, or elderly family members (Barker, 1993; Galinsky et al., 1993; Menaghan & Parcel, 1991). This may be because women can expect fewer rewards from their employment than men can. The gender wage gap *has* lessened in recent years—full-time employed women's median weekly wages were 76% of men's in 1994, up from 63% in 1976 (Herz & Wootton, 1996). However, this change appears to be related as much to a decline in men's wages as to an improvement in women's (Glass, 1992).

Women are still not given the opportunity to take on the challenges of as wide a variety of jobs as men are. While occupational segregation seems to have declined significantly in recent years, task segregation has not. For example, although there are more women physicians, particular jobs within that occupation (e.g., pediatrician, surgeon) tend to be overwhelmingly dominated by one sex or the other. Moreover, women still get a lower return for their education and training than do men: In 1994, women with a bachelor's degree who worked full-time earned only $41 more a week than men with only a high school diploma (Herz & Wootton, 1996). Using 1980 census data, Cooney and Uhlenberg (1991) found that only 42% of highly educated women occupied careers (full-time positions as managers or professionals with above-average pay), in comparison to 68% of men. Job segregation and employment discrimination may negatively affect women's motivation to seek employment, as well as their earning potential.

Another change in employment patterns that has implications for family life is the tendency for substantial numbers of Americans to work evening, night, and weekend schedules. In 1985, one-sixth of working mothers and one-fifth of fathers worked fixed non-daytime shifts. Almost one-fourth (24%) of mothers worked weekends, along with 30% of fathers. This is partly due to a growing demand for services after 5 PM and on weekends, which is in turn a result of women being less available to shop or be home to let in service workers during the day. Nonstandard work schedules can alter patterns in family work and influence couples' choices regarding childcare (Presser, 1989).

Home-based work is an increasingly popular option for employment, and the home-based labor force is growing at a much faster pace than the traditional workforce (Masuo, Walker, & Furry, 1992). A recent nine-state study found that 6% of households contained a home-based worker, either working at piece rates for a company, doing sales or clerical work, or as a business owner. The majority (58%) of home-based workers are men, but women often become home-based workers because they want to stay at home with their children or find it difficult to arrange for adequate childcare. Companies often find it profitable to use home-based workers to avoid paying employee benefits and to increase their flexibility; the portability and low cost of computers and communications software also make it feasible for some employees to work from home (Masuo et al., 1992; Rowe, Stafford, & Owen, 1992; Stafford, Duncan, & Genalo, 1992).

Changes in the labor market and fluctuating economic cycles have made unemployment a common occurrence in recent years (Perrucci, Perrucci, Targ, & Targ, 1988). Although the official unemployment rate is well below 10%, this figure underestimates the real rate in several ways. First, the figure reflects unemployment at only a given time. The percentage of people unemployed *sometime* during a given year is often double (Mellor & Parks, 1988). Official statistics do not include "discouraged workers" (those who have given up looking for work) or part-time workers who would prefer full-time jobs. If accounted for in the official percentages, these groups would raise the number of unemployed by several million. Even in periods of economic recovery, large numbers of families are hit by the unemployment or underemployment of one or more family members (Voydanoff, 1991).

Changing employment patterns, then, have led and promise to continue to lead to both employment uncertainty and pressure on women to enter the labor market. Dual-earner families are therefore likely to become more common. In 1994, 66% of married couples with children were in this category, up from 42% in 1975 (Herz & Wootton, 1996). At the same time, women remain occupationally and financially disadvantaged in comparison to men, and these differences can influence the dynamics of family relationships.

Changing Family Demographics

In addition to changes in employment patterns, there are important changes in family structure that need to be taken into account when considering work–family linkages. The United States continues to have one of the highest rates of marriage in the world, but Americans are marrying later. In

1993, the average age of first marriage stood at 26.5 for men and 24.5 for women (up from 23.2 and 20.8, respectively, in 1970) (Costello & Krimgold, 1996). The increase in marriage age is accompanied by a tendency for a greater proportion of people to remain unmarried their entire lives. The proportion of adult white women who never married was 19% in 1993, up from 11% in 1975. The rate for African Americans was substantially higher, at 35% in 1993 (up from 20% in 1975) (Costello & Krimgold, 1996; Sorrentino, 1990). These rising ages of marriage and higher numbers of permanently single people are tied to changes in the economy. Individuals need more education to compete successfully for better paying jobs, and marriage is often postponed until this further training is completed (Roos, 1985). The inability of men to obtain a decent paying job has also been named as a deterrent to marriage, especially among African Americans. For every three unmarried black women in their 20s, there is roughly only one unmarried black male with earnings above the poverty threshold (Lichter, McLaughlin, Kephart, & Landry, 1992; Taylor, Chatters, Tucker, & Lewis, 1991).

The United States experienced a "Baby Boomlet" between 1977 and 1988 (Exter, 1988). Despite this boomlet, fertility rates remain low. In 1994, the average was 2.08 children per woman, which is slightly below replacement level (U.S. Department of Commerce, 1995). Low fertility rates are generally associated with women's increased participation in the labor market (Sorrentino, 1990). However, research by White and Kim (1987) shows that employment discourages women from having large families, not from becoming parents in the first place. Many European countries have developed social policies to increase birth rates, fearing the economic consequences of an aging population. Such policies (e.g., paid parental leave and subsidized daycare) are designed to make it easier for workers to bear and raise children without losing their position in the labor market (Haas, 1992). So far, the United States has not reacted similarly.

Following a later age of marriage, the average age at which women have their first child has also increased. Teachman and Schollaert (1989) have found that early first births are associated with higher future earnings for men, while later first births are associated with higher future earnings for women. Since men participate more in housework and childcare if they wait to have children until their late 20s (Coltrane & Ishii-Kuntz, 1992; Daniels & Weingarten, 1988), a continued pattern of later births might help to equalize some of the gender inequities in pay and the division of household labor.

Another trend in fertility has been a rising number of children born outside wedlock. The number of children born to unmarried women tripled between 1970 and 1992. The percentage of all births occurring outside wedlock was 11% in 1970; by 1992, it was 30%. While the rate of out-of-wedlock births for African Americans has gone up from 38% in 1970 to 68% in 1992, the rate of increase for whites was actually much greater, going from only 6% in 1970 to 23% in 1992 (U.S. Department of Commerce, 1995).

While the divorce rate has apparently leveled off, it remains among the highest in the world (Costello & Krimgold, 1996; Sorrentino, 1990). Experts estimate that as many as two-thirds of all first marriages may eventually end in separation or divorce (Martin & Bumpass, 1989). High expectations for self-fulfillment and economic stress contribute to the high divorce rate.

A high rate of out-of-wedlock births and a high divorce rate have both led to the formation of a large number of single-parent families in the United States. It has been estimated that one-third of all employees will be single parents sometime during their lifetimes (Casey & Pitt-Catsouphes, 1994). Over one-fourth of children (27%) lived with a single parent in 1993, twice the percentage in 1970 (Costello & Krimgold, 1996). The rate of single parenthood is rising faster in African American families than among whites. The main reason for this is the increasing tendency for blacks to remain unmarried, which in turn is a consequence of the high rates of unemployment and low earnings of black men (Taylor et al., 1991).

Most single-parent families are headed by women, and female-headed households have high rates of poverty. Almost half (46%) of female-headed households had incomes below the poverty line in 1993, compared to less than one-fourth (22%) of households headed by single men. Minority female-headed families are particularly likely to live in poverty, with 60% of Hispanic and 58% of African American female-headed households living under the official poverty threshold, compared to 40% of white female-headed households (Costello & Krimgold, 1996). Women's greater likelihood of heading a family living in poverty is mainly due to their lower earnings (Baca Zinn, 1989; Starrells, Bould, & Nicholas, 1994).

Another type of family that is gaining in numbers is stepfamilies, households with a married couple and at least one child from a former relationship. It is estimated that there are at least 4.3 million stepfamilies in the United States and that one-sixth of children under age 18 live in such households (Eshleman, 1994). Recognizing the existence of this type of family structure is important for the study of linkages between families and work because these linkages may be different than they are for families based on first marriages. For example, maternal employment is more common in mother–stepfather families than it is in first marriages (Thomson, 1994; U.S. Bureau of the Census, 1992a). And as we will see later, stepfamilies seem less governed by traditional notions of gender roles and are more likely to share household labor.

The last demographic trend of importance in the study of family and work is the aging of the population. The combination of a relatively low birth rate and medical advances has led to an increasing life expectancy and an aging population. In 1960, the American life expectancy at birth was 70; by 1991, life expectancy at birth had risen to 76 (Costello & Krimgold, 1996). In 1991, individuals who had reached 65 could expect to live 17 years longer, compared to 14 years in 1960 (Costello & Krimgold, 1996). While most of those over 65 are healthy and able to live independently, many rely upon extended family members for support. A national survey of middle-aged persons found that 15% had "significant obligations" to parents or parents-in-law in 1992, up from 7% in 1988 (Loomis & Booth, 1995). Workplace surveys indicate that 20%–30% of all workers at any given time are involved in giving assistance to an older person, usually a parent (Anastas, Gibeau, & Larson, 1990; Galinsky & Stein, 1990). The drive to reduce health-care costs limits elders' eligibility for certain services, which means greater reliance on family members to provide primary medical care (Glazer, 1988; Osterbusch, Keigher, Miller, & Linsk, 1987; Pyke & Bengtson, 1996).

Changing Gender Ideologies

Since the 1960s, attitudes toward gender and marital roles have become more egalitarian, with more support for women's employment and men's participation in family work (Thornton, 1989). One longitudinal study suggests that structural change in the economy is a major force behind changing gender-role attitudes. Wilkie (1993) found men's support for married women's employment had increased from a 68% approval rating in 1972 to 79% by 1989. A 1990 Gallup poll found that over half (57%) of Americans preferred a marriage where both husband and wife have jobs and share childrearing and housework. This percentage had increased somewhat, from 48% in 1977. Another question in the 1990 poll asked if it was better for everyone involved if the man was the achiever outside the home while the woman takes care of home and family, and one-half disagreed with this (DeStefano & Colasanto, 1990).

Most Americans believe that women and men are capable of taking on work responsibilities traditionally assigned to the other sex. Almost all of those surveyed in the Gallup Poll (91%) said that women were as capable of success in the workplace as men, while over three-fourths (78%) said that men were as capable as women of being good parents. A majority of those questioned (59%) said that working mothers can establish as good relations with children as nonemployed mothers. Americans are less enthusiastic about couples equally sharing roles traditionally the province of one sex. A national survey conducted in 1987–1988 revealed that both men and women think that women should do about two-thirds of the housework, even if they are employed (Lennon & Rosenfield, 1994).

The trend toward egalitarian attitudes regarding family and work roles is more evident among some groups than others. Women hold more liberal attitudes than men, while women with labor force experience are more egalitarian than women who have always been housewives (Blair, 1993; DeStefano & Colasanto, 1990; Glass, 1992; Hoffman & Kloska, 1995; Kane & Sanchez, 1994; Thornton, 1989). Substantial differences between generations also exist. For example, almost three-fourths of people under the age of 30 in the Gallup poll wanted to have a marriage with two jobs and the sharing of domestic responsibilities, compared to 52% of those over 50 years old (DeStefano & Colasanto, 1990). The relationship between race and gender role attitudes is less clear, with studies reporting mixed findings (Blee & Tickamyer, 1995; Wilkie, 1993).

Organizational Responsiveness to Work and Family Issues

American governmental units and private companies have been slow to recognize the linkages between work and family and to respond by developing supportive programs and policies. The U.S. government, in particular, is far behind that of almost all industrial nations in enacting programs to help working parents (Aldous & Dumon, 1991; Haas, 1992). The problems individuals have in managing work and family responsibilities simultaneously have been regarded as their own personal problems, not responsibilities that government or the employer should share. Senior officials and managers have lacked sensitivity toward family issues, often because they have not had to deal with them personally. Both government and company officials tend to have a short-term orientation toward the economic benefits to be obtained from providing more supports to working parents. The cost of potential programs is judged prohibitive, without considering the long-term consequences of not providing such programs (Greenhaus, 1988; Hall & Richter, 1988).

Recently, the federal government has made modest efforts to help working families cope, with childcare tax credits, a tax-savings plan to pay for childcare with pre-tax dollars, special funds for subsidizing the childcare costs of low-income working parents, and the Family and Medical Leave Act of 1993, which grants up to 12 weeks of unpaid leave to certain categories of employees (Hofferth & Deich, 1994; Lamb, Sternberg, & Ketterlinus, 1992). Some companies have developed policies and programs to help working families. Most commonly provided are flextime and unpaid leave (Hayghe, 1988). Employers increasingly offer help with childcare—assistance in locating childcare, sub-

sidies for childcare, and, in a few cases, on-site childcare at reasonable cost (Galinsky, Hughes, & David, 1990; Hayghe, 1988). Some companies provide relocation assistance, family counseling, paid personal days, educational programs, family leave, resource clearinghouses, and respite programs for elder care (Kola & Dunkle, 1988; Voydanoff, 1988a). Company responsiveness to families will be discussed in more detail later under the topic of public strategies to help individuals cope with multiple roles.

Theoretical Perspectives on Family and Work

The government and most companies have tended to base their policies toward work and family on what Chow and Bertheide (1988) call a "separate spheres model." Social scientists also traditionally regarded family and work as static, separate and independent social systems, with little effects on one another. According to this model, the family is seen as women's special sphere, but their domestic labor remains largely invisible and is assumed to be distinct from and unrelated to economic activities performed in the public sphere. Men's identities and activities are assumed to revolve around participation in the paid labor market outside the home; involvement in this more prestigious sphere justifies male dominance within the home as well as outside it. In this model, the benefits of women's employment for society and for families are downplayed, while men's lack of active involvement in family life is taken for granted. Work organizations are expected to be organized as if employees had no other responsibilities or allegiances that would affect their devotion to their jobs (e.g., childcare or a partner with a job). The effects of family on men's work performance and satisfaction are not considered to be important to examine. Presumed biological and psychological differences between the sexes, along with sex-typed socialization practices, are used as explanations for the gender-based division of labor for paid and unpaid work.

According to Chow and Bertheide (1988), the model of separate spheres is rarely used by social scientists today, although it is still popular among policymakers. It has been called into question by research that suggests that family and work systems have permeable boundaries, with events in one domain affecting attitudes, behavior, and well-being in the other (Greenberger & O'Neil, 1990). The more common approach to looking at work–family linkages is to consider how family and work systems may have "spillover" effects on each other (Bowen, 1988; Lambert, 1990). Since most people are members of both systems, it has become increasingly important to examine how participation in one setting influences a person's ability to perform responsibilities in the other setting.

Chow and Bertheide (1988) maintain that the spillover model is based on some unsound assumptions. Most work–family research in this tradition has concentrated on the effects of work on family rather than vice versa (Bowen, 1988; Ishii-Kuntz, 1994). Proponents of the model tend to assume that the work system has more impact on the family system because industrial societies value productive activities outside the home over reproductive and domestic activities inside the home. Women's and men's participation in work and family systems is also examined differently. Women's employment is assumed to be secondary to their domestic responsibilities and inevitably problematic for family well-being. On the other hand, employment is regarded as men's primary family responsibility, and the impact of family life on men's work continues to receive little attention. Spillover is assumed generally to be negative, for example, when a frustrated worker becomes angry at family members. Potentially positive consequences of simultaneous membership in work and family systems are not often considered. Researchers using the spillover model also tend to focus on how work–family role conflict and strain can be reduced by individual coping activities, rather than on how changes in social institutions may be required.

Some work–family scholars have tried to redefine the spillover model to consider the impact of family on employment as well as positive consequences of multiple roles (e.g., Bowe, 1988; Lambert, 1990). Chow and Bertheide (1988), however, prefer an entirely new approach to examining family and work relationships, "the interactive model of system interdependence." This model "recognizes the mutual interdependence between family and work systems, taking into account the reciprocal influences of work and family and acknowledging their independent as well as their joint effects" (p. 25). This model recognizes that combining work and family is not simply a women's issue, because research shows that men's interest in an active family life is growing and that their greater involvement has positive benefits for children. Finally, researchers in this tradition take into account the economic, social, and political context of work and family. Some emphasize how changes in work–family roles are motivated by changes in the national economy (England & Farkas, 1986). Others examine workplace policies designed to help individuals balance family and work roles (Galinsky, Friedman, & Hernandez, 1991). Chow and Bertheide maintain that this model is beginning to affect research and policy making.

The interactive model is influenced by the development of gender theory by feminist family scholars. According to Ferree (1991a), feminism challenges the view that the family is a private sphere where women "are held responsible for everything." Instead, families are regarded as "fully integrated into wider systems of economic and political power"

(p. 104). Feminists prefer to consider family and work together as "a single, historically variable, gendered system" (p. 108). Both men and women are recognized as workers and family members, and paid and unpaid work are studied in terms of their "gendered meanings." Rather than view individuals' work and family roles as stable, with roots in childhood sex-role socialization, feminist theorists emphasize how roles are dynamic and socially constructed by daily experience and reinforced by political and economic institutions (Ferree & Hess, 1987; Thompson, 1993). Perhaps the most influence gender theory has had is on the study of family members' participation in unpaid family work.

Unpaid Family Work

Unpaid family work consists of activities that maintain the household and meet the physical and emotional needs of family members. Such work also makes participation of family members in paid employment possible (Ferree, 1991b). The unpaid work performed in family settings has been to a large extent undervalued and invisible; even those who perform most of it tend to downplay its significance (DeVault, 1987). It has only recently been regarded by social scientists and others as a form of work. Usually researchers imply that household work is a form of drudgery, something to be avoided or at best spread around to as many family members as possible. Some social scientists question this assumption and adopt a more positive approach, one that involves examining the division of labor for household work as an outcome of individuals moral principles and orientations (e.g., Ahlander & Bahr, 1995; Stohs, 1994).

Many studies have focused on the extent to which household work is shared by husbands and wives, particularly in the context of the growing number of two-earner households, and on the factors associated with men's participating more in unpaid family work. (Coleman, 1991, reviews the literature on this topic from the 1970s and 1980s). While research on these topics continues, studies are also focusing on the meanings family work has for women and men, the process by which the division of domestic labor becomes engendered, individuals' satisfaction with the division of labor in their own families, and the ideological and structural conditions under which equal sharing of domestic labor becomes possible.

Sharing of Unpaid Family Work

Studies published since 1986 suggest that there have been some changes in the domestic division of labor, but that women still remain more responsible than men for domestic work. Two types of studies have generally been conducted:

One focuses on the amount of time each spouse devotes to unpaid family work, and the other relies on perceptions regarding which spouse generally does particular tasks.

Housework. Findings from the two largest time studies conducted since 1985 (the 1988 National Survey of Families and Households and the 1985 Americans' Use of Time project) suggest that women are responsible for about 70% of all the time spent in housework (Blair & Lichter, 1991; Lennon & Rosenfield, 1994; Robinson, 1988). The 1988 survey found that women on the average spent about 33 hours a week on household tasks, while men spent 14 (Blair & Lichter, 1991). Smaller national studies as well as research based on regional samples have found women's share of housework hours to range between 61% and 74% of all the time spent by the couple on domestic work (Googins, 1991; Lawrence, Draugh, Tasker, & Wozniak, 1987; Manke, Seery, Crouter, & McHale, 1994; Perkins & DeMeis, 1996; Zick & McCullough, 1991). Women even spend more time doing housework in single-parent families than do men who head such families (Hall, Walker, & Acock, 1995).

The types of household chores that women do tend to be distinctly different from what men do. The 1985 study found that women spent 16.1 hours and men 4.1 hours per week in activities considered traditionally female (e.g., cooking, dishwashing, cleaning, clothing care) (Robinson, 1988). Men were more likely to spend time at activities considered traditionally male (e.g., repairs, gardening, bill-paying), but these were far less time-consuming. Men spent an average of 5.9 hours a week on these activities, compared to women's average of 3.4. Blair and Lichter (1991) estimated that 60% of men's family work time would have to be reallocated to different tasks before the pattern of sex segregation in unpaid family work now present in U.S. households would be eliminated.

Research studies that ask respondents who does what task in the household also reveal that housework remains a gendered activity. A 1990 Gallup poll found that two-thirds or more of respondents said women did "all or most" of the laundry, meal preparation, grocery shopping, dishwashing, and cleaning in their households, while 60% or more said minor household repairs and car maintenance were male activities (DeStefano & Colasanto, 1990). Similar patterns of gender specialization have been reported in other studies of family life, regardless of couples' age, race, marital status, urban or rural residence, occupational status, and marital status (Carlisle, 1994; Dancer & Gilbert, 1993; Ferree, 1991b; Galinsky & Bond, 1996; Gjerdingen & Chaloner, 1994; Hall et al., 1995; Hardesty & Bokemeier, 1989; Herrea & Del-Campo, 1995; Hilton & Haldeman, 1991; John, Shelton, & Luschen, 1995; Lawrence et al., 1987; MacDermid, Huston, & McHale, 1990; Wilson, Tolson, Hinton, & Kiernan, 1990).

A controversy still exists in the recent research literature regarding whether or not men's participation in housework has increased to coincide with women's increased participation in the labor force. (Spitze, 1991, reports this same state of affairs for research published between 1975 and 1986.) Some researchers maintain that there is little evidence that men's contribution to unpaid family work has increased (Blair & Lichter, 1991; Leslie, Anderson, & Branson, 1991). Robinson (1988), on the other hand, using national time budget data, states that men's participation in housework has increased absolutely (albeit modestly), from 2.1 hours a week for traditionally female tasks in 1965 to 4.1 hours in 1985. Because women's housework time has decreased even more dramatically (from 24.3 hours per week in 1965 to 16.1 in 1985), men's proportion of housework time has increased from 8% to 20% in the 20 years between studies. Zick and McCullough's (1991) longitudinal study of Utah couples found the same patterns as Robinson for the years 1977–1978 to 1987–1988. We might not expect a further trend toward equity in household labor time unless men participate much more in housework. There is a limit to how much employed women can reduce time spent on housework, and it may have already been reached (Shelton, 1990).

Childcare. Most of the research on the domestic division of labor has focused on housework, but there is growing interest in researching the gendered nature of parenting activities as well. Moreover, some research studies suggest that there has been more progress made in sharing of childcare (Leslie et al., 1991), but that mothers remain more involved in childcare than fathers. The 1981 Study of Time Use found that American fathers in dual-earner households were responsible for about 40% of all the childcare time spent by parents on workdays, and somewhat more on Sundays (Nock & Kingston, 1988). Some smaller scale studies have found similar percentages (Barnett & Baruch, 1987a), although others have found less (Cowan & Cowan, 1987; Leslie et al., 1989).

Some research studies have not asked parents about hours spent in childcare but instead have measured the respondent's (usually the mother's) perceptions of the extent to which their partners share responsibility for or generally participate in childcare. These studies also find that mothers are much more active than fathers in childcare (Galinsky & Bond, 1996; Gjerdingen & Chaloner, 1994; Hossain & Roopnarine, 1993; Wille, 1995; Wilson et al., 1990).

In recent years, researchers interested in the subject of men's participation in childcare have considered childcare as a multidimensional phenomenon and have found that there are distinct differences in the types of childcare mothers and fathers are likely to do. Three main types of childcare have been distinguished: engagement in activities designed to meet children's basic physical needs; participation in activities designed to meet children's emotional, recreational, and educational needs; and overall taking of responsibility for children's well-being.

Research studies generally find that fathers are significantly more likely to engage in play and enrichment activities than they are in physical caretaking. Most of the time fathers report spending with children is spent in recreational activities (Darling-Fisher & Tiedje, 1990; Grossman, Pollack, & Golding, 1988; Leslie et al., 1989). The 1981 Study of Time Use found that men were responsible for 51% of the time parents spent playing or having fun with preschool-aged children in dual-earner households on a Sunday, but only for 28% of time spent in physical caretaking (Nock & Kingston, 1988). Studies that ask parents what types of activities they engage in with their children or which use observational techniques report similar patterns (Herrera & DelCampo, 1995; Hochschild, 1989; Marsiglio, 1991; Rustia & Abbott, 1990). A 1990 Gallup poll found that three-fourths of mothers said they did all or most of the caring for children on a daily basis and taking care of them when they were sick (DeStefano & Colasanto, 1990). When single mothers and single fathers are examined separately, however, no significant differences are found in time parents spend playing, helping with homework, or reading. Single dads do spend more time outdoors with their children in leisure activities, while single moms spend more time in private talks (Hall et al., 1995).

Less research has been conducted on men's feelings of responsibility for children (Coleman, 1991), but a review of the literature suggests that there is growing interest in this topic. Barnett and Baruch (1987a) asked couples who was responsible for "remembering, planning and scheduling" various specific childcare tasks and found that most fathers (71%) were responsible for none. Two other studies have examined men's participation in making childcare arrangements. A 1986 national survey of the high school class of 1972 found that women in dual-earner households were significantly more likely than their partners to be responsible for making childcare arrangements for preschool-aged and younger school-age children (Peterson & Gerson, 1992). Leslie et al. (1991) also found women more responsible for making childcare arrangements. Qualitative studies of parents attempting shared parenting arrangements reveal that even fathers who participate actively in routine childcare do not often assume equal responsibility for planning and initiating childcare tasks (Coltrane, 1989; Ehrensaft, 1987; Jump & Haas, 1987).

Leslie et al. (1991) have defined responsibility for childcare as an "ongoing perceptual state as opposed to behavior." Time parents spend supervising and watching over their children without directly interacting with them seems to fit in here. Fathers appear to be more involved in this type of re-

sponsibility than in the kind that involves planning (Lamb, 1987, calls this availability or access). Leslie et al. (1991) found that men's share of time spent being responsible for children in this way was one-third compared to women's two-thirds. A 1984–1985 national survey of childcare arrangements of dual-earner couples showed that almost one in five (19%) fathers cared for children under age 5 while mothers were working (U.S. Bureau of the Census, 1992b). Brayfield (1995) reported on a national survey that showed that fathers were the sole caretakers of children an average of 10 hours a week in households where mothers were employed.

For both housework and childcare, substantially more couples say they believe the work should be shared equally by men and women than actually practice such an arrangement (Ferree, 1991b; Hilton & Haldeman, 1991). LaRossa (1988) writes, for example, of a big difference between the "culture of fatherhood" and the "conduct of fatherhood." A gap between attitudes and practice also exists for the third type of unpaid family work considered here, elder care.

Elder Care. Care of elderly parents is increasingly regarded as a form of family work (Finley, 1989; Stoller, 1990). Research indicates a growing trend for people to believe that care of aging parents should be shared by sons and daughters (Mancini & Blieszner, 1991). Men and women also report similar feelings of filial obligation, but do not behave consistently with that attitude (Finley, Roberts, & Banahan, 1988).

Spouses are the most likely persons to care for frail elderly persons, but when a spouse is not available, an adult daughter usually becomes responsible for caregiving (Dwyer & Coward, 1992; Noelker & Townsend, 1987; Witt, 1994). A national survey found that only 17% of elders requiring assistance from adult children named sons as their primary caregiver (Dwyer & Secombe, 1991). Matthews and Rosner (1988) found that daughters reported more routine involvement, while sons were only sporadically involved in elder caregiving. Sons tend to become involved only if no daughter exists or if she lives too far away. Even in these circumstances, men often rely upon their spouses for assistance and limit their involvement in physical caretaking activities, much as they do for children (Dwyer & Secombe, 1991).

Nursing Family Members. An additional type of domestic work that has increased in importance in recent years is caring for a relative or family member who is recovering from an illness or operation and has been released from the hospital much sooner than once they may have been. Americans are now called upon to provide medical and after-surgical care for family members that formerly would have been provided in institutional settings (e.g., intravenous medications, catheterization, bandage replacement). This is in addition to the help that may be needed to move the recovering person around the house, bathe them, provide special meals, supervise medications, and generally make them comfortable. While not much research has been conducted on this type of family work to date, it appears that women are more likely to participate in this type of domestic labor than are men. Allen (1994) found that husbands were less likely than wives to spend time providing such care to sick spouses and were also less likely than wives to do housework tasks that came up during the sick person's recovery.

Spousal Career Support. A last type of unpaid family work does not yet have a recognized name that parallels terms like housework, childcare, or elder care, although it is associated with what has been called "two-person careers" or "organization families" (Orthner, Bowen, & Beare, 1990; Papanek, 1973). I label this work "spousal career support," the practical and emotional work individuals do that makes valuable contributions to their partners' careers or jobs. So far, research attention has focused only on the work some *wives* do to help their husbands in certain careers, which typically are traditionally dominated by men (e.g., upper management, politics, religion, military, or medicine). Husbands of successful women undoubtedly also participate in this work, but to date this seems not to have interested social scientists.

Pavalko and Elder's (1993) study of women born in 1910 allowed them to distinguish three levels of involvement women can have in their husbands' occupations. The work they outline corresponds with the descriptions of spousal career support uncovered in other studies (Daniels, 1987; Fowlkes, 1987; Orthner et al., 1990; Zussman, 1987). Women might be "unpaid partners" in their husbands' careers, highly involved in doing a good portion of the same work their husbands are responsible for, as in religion or politics. Wives might also be "auxiliary workers," working for husbands involved in self-employment or creative endeavors without pay as researchers, receptionists, office managers, office decorators, and campaign workers. A third category of spousal career support, according to Pavalko and Elder, is that of "enabler"; these spouses work more indirectly to enhance their husbands' reputation, through entertaining employees, bosses, or clients; participating in community philanthropic organizations; and maintaining an elaborate home.

Providing spousal career support also involves "emotional work." A wife is often expected to provide sympathy, encouragement, recognition, and appreciation to spur her husband on to greater achievement. At the same time, she is expected to accept that her husband's job is his "first love"

and that she must "submerge her own emotions and needs in the service of his" (Fowlkes, 1987, p. 351).

Explanations for the Gender-Based Division of Labor

Several research studies have considered why women remain overwhelmingly more responsible for unpaid family labor than men. Three main factors have been identified as worthy of research: time availability, differences in economic resources, and gender ideology (Blair & Lichter, 1991; Dwyer & Secombe, 1991; Kamo, 1988; Ross, 1987; Spitze, 1991; Thompson & Walker, 1991). Coltrane and Ishii-Kuntz (1992) call these "models of household labor allocation." Most of the tests of these models concern housework, although some examine childcare; whether these models may adequately explain gender variations in other types of unpaid family work has been insufficiently explored.

Time Availability Model. According to this model, spouses will divide the responsibility for family work based on the time it takes and the amount of time they have available. Variables of interest include amount of work hours, scheduling of work hours, and numbers and age of children.

The time availability model predicts that women will have less time to do family work when they enter the labor force and that their husbands will therefore have to pick up the slack. The model also predicts that women who work full-time are more likely to share domestic work with their spouses than women who work part-time. Studies testing these predictions have yielded mixed results. On the one hand, research shows fairly consistently that employed wives spend less time in household labor than unemployed wives and full-time women workers spend less time than part-timers (Barnett & Baruch, 1987b; Berardo, Shehan, & Leslie, 1987; Ferree, 1991b; Kallenberg & Rosenfeld, 1990; Leslie et al., 1989; Manke et al., 1994; Moen & Dempster-McClain, 1987; Nock & Kingston, 1988; Ross, 1987). What is not clear is whether husbands pick up the slack.

In this regard, it is important to distinguish research studies that look at men's *absolute* participation in domestic work (measured by number of hours or frequency of doing a particular task) from studies that look at men's *relative* participation in comparison to their wives (measured by the percentage of family work men do or questions about which spouse usually does a particular task). Findings are mixed when it comes to looking at the effects of women's employment on men's *absolute* amount of participation. Some studies have found that husbands in dual-earner households do participate significantly more in household labor than husbands in single-earner households, but the differences tend to be modest and more evident for childcare than for housework (Atkinson, 1992; Barnett & Baruch, 1988; Blair & Lichter, 1991; Darling-Fisher & Tiedje, 1990; Gjerdingen & Chaloner, 1994; Hossain & Roopnarine, 1993; Rexroat & Shehan, 1987; Ross, 1987). Other studies show that men participate no more in domestic labor if their wives are employed (Hardesty & Bokemeier, 1989; Marsiglio, 1991; Nock & Kingston, 1988; Shelton, 1990). Most studies reveal that men's absolute participation in domestic labor does *not* vary relative to wives' work hours (Brayfield, 1995; Ferree, 1991b; Kalleberg & Rosenfeld, 1990; Leslie et al., 1989; Rexroat & Shehan, 1987; Starrells, 1994), although others have found a difference (Atkinson, 1992; Barnett & Baruch, 1988). One study has found that husbands do more unpaid family work when their wives have longer employment histories (Pittman & Blanchard, 1996).

Research that looks particularly at the *proportion* or *relative* share of housework and childcare done by husbands in comparison to wives does tend to find that men's share is greater when wives are employed (Barnett & Baruch, 1988; Berardo et al., 1987; Blair & Lichter, 1991; Coltrane & Ishii-Kuntz, 1992; Dancer & Gilbert, 1993; Kamo, 1988; Rexroat & Shehan, 1987). Lennon and Rosenfield's (1994) analysis of the 1987–1988 National Survey of Families and Households' data set found men in dual-earner households were responsible for 23% of the time couples spent in traditionally female household tasks. Men's relative participation in domestic work has also been found to be related to the amount of wives' work hours (Barnett & Baruch, 1988; Cowan & Cowan, 1987; Darling-Fisher & Tiedje, 1990; Ferree, 1991b). Since men's absolute participation in domestic work has changed very little, it seems safe to assume that these findings are due mostly to women cutting back on their domestic work. Furthermore, the extent of task segregation by gender has been found to remain unaffected by women's labor force participation, according to a 1988 national survey (Blair & Lichter, 1991).

The impact of men's work hours on their participation in family work has also been examined as a test of the time availability model. Men who work a greater number of hours in paid employment are predicted to be less available to spend time at family work and therefore less likely to participate in it. Most studies find support for this, although the effects of men's work hours on family work are modest (Coltrane & Ishii-Kuntz, 1992; Cowan & Cowan, 1987; Crouter, Perry-Jenkins, Huston, & McHale, 1987; Ferree, 1991b; Guelkow, Bird, & Koball, 1991; Hardesty & Bokemeier, 1989; Marsiglio, 1991; Rexroat & Shehan, 1987; South & Spitze, 1994). Some studies, however, have found no relationship (Barnett & Baruch, 1987a; Leslie et al., 1989; Moen & Dempster-McClain, 1987; Perkins & DeMeis, 1996; Peterson & Gerson, 1992). Pittman and Blanchard (1994) found

only the discrepancy between husbands' and wives' work hours significantly predicted men's housework time, with husbands doing more housework when the discrepancy was less.

Scheduling of work hours could also affect individuals' opportunity to perform domestic tasks. The U.S. Census Bureau (1992b) reported that sharing of childcare is least likely when both parents work day shifts. This is in accordance with other studies that have found that husbands are more likely to participate in housework and childcare when their wives work evening, night, or weekend shifts (Brayfield, 1995; Presser, 1988, 1994). Blair and Lichter (1991) found that there was less task segregation by sex when men work a shift work schedule, but this was due mostly to women spending less time in housework, rather than men spending more. Brayfield (1995) found that fathers who work evening or night shifts were more likely to care for their preschool-aged children than fathers who worked day shifts. When men have a flexible work schedule it tends to increase the amount of time they spend in domestic work (Gerson, 1993; Guelkow et al., 1991; Wharton, 1994). However, when women have a flexible work schedule, it also increases the amount of time they spend in unpaid family work (Silver & Goldscheider, 1994). Lechner (1991) found that full-time workers who frequently adjusted their work schedules to accommodate elder care responsibilities were unable to maintain their level of caregiving commitment over time.

Another way to look at the impact of time availability on men's participation in family work is to consider men's participation over the life course. Rexroat and Shehan (1987) considered how husbands' participation in domestic work is related to adult life stages and found that men spend more time in housework during stages that demand the least occupational involvement—early career and postretirement. Other studies have found that older or retired men do more domestic work than employed husbands (Coverman & Sheley, 1986; Dorfman, 1992; Dorfman & Heckert, 1988). Studies also show, however, that these men's increased time spent in domestic work is often devoted to traditionally masculine tasks rather than housework and that the time they spend is still relatively short (as little as 8 hours a week), even when their wives remain employed (Rexroat & Shehan, 1987).

The presence and age of children have been examined as possible determinants of the gender-based division of labor, according to the time availability model. Having more children and younger children is presumed to increase the domestic workload and consequently add to the pressure for men to share. Here again, findings are mixed. Some studies find that men's *relative* share of family work is greater when there are more children in the family (Barnett & Baruch, 1987a; Blair & Lichter, 1991; Coltrane & Ishii-Kuntz, 1992;

Ferree, 1991b; Gunter & Gunter, 1991; Nock & Kingston, 1988; Peterson & Gerson, 1992), while other studies find no (or curvilinear) effects of family size (Kamo, 1991; Marsiglio, 1991; Presser, 1994; Ross, 1987; Sanchez, 1994b). Some studies find that men do proportionately more when there are younger children present in the household (Barnett & Baruch, 1987a; Bergen, 1991; Marsiglio, 1991; Rexroat & Shehan, 1987), while others find no effect (Hardesty & Bokemeier, 1989; Ishii-Kuntz & Coltrane, 1992a; Peterson & Gerson, 1992). Moreover, some studies show no effects of family structure on men's *absolute* amount of participation in family work (Blair & Lichter, 1991; Brayfield, 1995; Ferree, 1991b; Pittman & Blanchard, 1996; Rexroat & Shehan, 1987), while others do (Barnett & Baruch, 1987a; Bergen, 1991; Nock & Kingston, 1988; Perkins & DeMeis, 1996).

Resource Model.   Another explanation for the gender-based division of labor also relates to the effects of employment. According to the resource model, women's employment provides them with earnings, which they can use as a resource to gain power within marriage. This power can be used to push husbands to share domestic work, either to relieve women of a heavy workload, help them escape certain onerous tasks, or gain the privilege of more leisure time. The more money women bring into the marriage, especially in comparison to their husbands, the more likely domestic labor will be shared. Studies that test this prediction look at the proportion of family income brought in by wives and its effects on men's participation in housework and childcare.

Research findings give only partial support to this prediction. Several studies have found that men do a bigger share of domestic work when women earn a higher proportion of family income (Coltrane & Ishii-Kuntz, 1992a; Ferree, 1991b; Gerson, 1993; Jump & Haas, 1987; Kamo, 1988; Lennon, Wasserman, & Allen, 1991; Presser, 1994; Rexroat & Shehan, 1987; Ross, 1987; Steil & Weltman, 1991; Wharton, 1994). Other studies find no relationship (Hardesty & Bokemeier, 1989; Hochschild, 1989; Leslie et al., 1991). Here again, it appears that increased sharing is more likely due to women doing less domestic work rather than men doing more. Studies that look at the effects of women's relative income on men's *absolute* amount of domestic work tend to find no relationships (Blumstein & Schwartz, 1991; Ferree, 1991b; Pittman & Blanchard, 1996; Rexroat & Shehan, 1987). Moreover, research suggests that relatively high income reduces *women's* time spent in domestic work (Berardo et al., 1987; Blumstein & Schwartz, 1991; Ferree, 1991b).

Ideology Model.   The third main model used for understanding the gender-based division of labor relates to the persistence of traditional gender-role attitudes. Holding traditional attitudes toward men's and women's family roles is

seen as decreasing couples' motivations to share domestic work.

Men's and women's attitudes have usually been considered separately as possible determinants of the domestic division of labor. Some researchers have found men's attitudes to be related to sharing of unpaid family work (Blair & Johnson, 1992; Blair & Lichter, 1991; Coltrane & Ishii-Kuntz, 1992; Ferree, 1991b; Gunter & Gunter, 1991; Hochschild, 1989; Kamo, 1988; Pittman & Blanchard, 1996; Presser, 1994; Ross, 1987), while others have not (Barnett & Baruch, 1987a; Crouter et al., 1987; Finley, 1989; Marsiglio, 1991). Most studies have discovered that when women hold egalitarian gender attitudes, family work is shared more evenly (Barnett & Baruch, 1988; Blair & Lichter, 1991; Coltrane & Ishii-Kuntz, 1992; Ferree, 1991b; Gunter & Gunter, 1991; Hardesty & Bokemeier, 1989; Pittman & Blanchard, 1996), but again, some studies have not discovered a significant relationship (Barnett & Baruch, 1987a; Finley, 1989; Marsiglio, 1991; Ross, 1987). Greenstein (1996) maintains that the interaction between husbands' and wives' gender ideologies is important to consider in predicting the domestic division of labor. He found that husbands do proportionately more housework when both partners share egalitarian gender attitudes. The importance of marital interaction on the domestic division of labor is discussed in more detail later.

In summary, we can say that recent research indicates only limited support for all three models. These models usually explain only a modest amount of variance in the domestic division of labor (9% for the National Survey of Families and Households—Pittman & Blanchard, 1996). In addition, there remains a striking persistence of the gender-based division of labor even among couples most likely to practice equality–dual-career couples (according to the models) (Berardo et al., 1987; Dancer & Gilbert, 1993; Hertz, 1986; Jump & Haas, 1987; Leslie et al., 1989, 1991; Ozer, 1995; Steil & Weltman, 1991). This suggests that we need to look further if we want to explain the persistence of what Hochschild (1989) calls employed wives "second shift." Recent research offers promising directions for future work in this area, through directing our attention to the importance of interactional patterns within marriage, the gendered construction of parenthood, and institutional constraints on equal sharing of family work.

Marital Dynamics.   An alternative approach to the study of men's participation in domestic work focuses on the interpersonal dynamics between husbands and wives. This approach has alternately been called "the microstructural perspective" (Risman & Schwartz, 1989), "the social constructionist approach" (Kimmel, 1987), and the "relational approach" (Thompson & Walker, 1991). It presumes that the division of labor in the family is a result of dynamic roles and relationships individuals negotiate with one another. It is consonant with symbolic interactionist and gender theories in the emphasis on how family roles are created within each family, rather than just a given aspect of family life (Ferree, 1991a; Perry-Jenkins & Crouter, 1990). According to Backett (1987), researchers have neglected the interactive effects of family members on each other's behavior.

Before outlining some of the aspects of marital dynamics that can affect decision making about family and work roles, it is important to point out that husband–wife interaction regarding domestic roles takes place within a cultural institution, "marriage," which has until recently stressed separate roles for men and women. Some research studies suggest that this cultural institution still reproduces the traditional division of domestic labor. For example, two studies have found that married women spent significantly more time doing housework than do cohabiting women (although men's hours did not vary by marital status) (Shelton & John, 1993; South & Spitze, 1994). Perkins and DeMeis (1996) discovered no significant difference in the amount of time spent in housework by single men and single women, but did find that married men spent significantly less time doing traditionally female household tasks than did single men. Ishii-Kuntz and Coltrane (1992b) reported that remarried couples are more likely to share household work than are couples in a first marriage, presumably because remarriage is an "incomplete institution" with less scripted roles.

Within marriage, couples have some latitude in negotiating the division of labor for family work, especially nowadays when gender-role attitudes are less traditional than ever before. They are also often pressed to negotiate by the fact that both partners are in the labor force, and outside social support for working parents is generally lacking. Recent research gives us many insights into this negotiation process.

One facet of a couple's negotiations about the division of labor is consideration of the significance of each spouse's employment and earnings for the relationship. Researchers have assumed that as women enter the labor force, responsibility for family work will become more shared. As was indicated earlier, this is hardly the case. Hood's (1986) study showed that wives can be employed without taking *responsibility* for providing family income (just as men often participate in specific housework or childcare tasks without taking on overall responsibility). The *meaning* of wives' labor force participation in terms of its importance as breadwinning is a matter of negotiation within families (Potuchek, 1992). In most families, women's income-earning is not regarded as being as important for the family's economy as men's income-earning is, and women are not regarded as equally obligated to provide family income. For example, in 1989, only about half of men thought wives should share responsibility for

providing income, while the vast majority (80%) approved of wives' working (Wilkie, 1993). This pattern has been found to be true in blue-collar, white-collar, and dual-career families (Haas, 1986; Hood, 1986; Perry-Jenkins & Crouter, 1990; Rosen, 1987; Weiss, 1987; Zavella, 1987). In Potuchek's study (1992), only 15% of employed women considered themselves to be "co-breadwinners"; that is, income-earning was an important reason for their employment, their incomes were considered critical for meeting family expenses, their jobs were considered as important as their husbands', and they were defined as equal providers. When couples define men as more responsible for breadwinning, this allows men to remain relatively uninvolved in family work (Perry-Jenkins & Crouter, 1990).

The meaning and significance of the *husband's* employment also affects negotiations concerning the division of unpaid work in the family. When couples decide that the husband's identity (i.e., masculinity) is tied up more with employment than the wife's, he is permitted to do less family work at home so that family responsibilities will not interfere with his commitment to and energy for paid employment (Hochschild, 1989). Women become defined as supplementary earners and are thus free to assume greater responsibility for family work (Ferree, 1991a).

Another important aspect of marital dynamics that affects the familial division of labor concerns commitment to the relationship (Coleman, 1991). For many women, maintaining a satisfactory marriage, with love, emotional closeness, and companionship, is more important than having an equal marriage. Women negotiate work contracts inside the household on this basis (Brannen, 1992). Hochschild's (1989) qualitative study of dual-earner couples with preschool-aged children showed that many women were reluctant to press husbands to do more domestic work because they feared divorce. Keeping peace at home was more important to them than getting their husbands to do more domestic chores.

Some research studies suggest women may be right to be worried. Men who share in domestic work usually report less love for their wives, more negative marital interaction, lower levels of marital satisfaction, greater marital conflict, and fewer benefits of marriage than do men who do not share (Benin & Agostinelli, 1988; Broman, 1991; Crouter et al., 1987; McHale & Crouter, 1992; Voydanoff, Fine, & Donnelly, 1994). Vannoy-Hiller and Philliber (1989) found that women's assertiveness regarding the division of labor negatively affected husbands' perceptions of marital quality. Some researchers have found exceptions to this pattern, however. Willoughby and Glidden (1995) found that marital satisfaction for both partners was higher when fathers participated more in the care of children with disabilities. Herrera and DelCampo (1995) found higher levels of positive family functioning in middle-aged Mexican American working-class families when husbands participated more in domestic work. Blair's (1993) analysis of data from the National Survey of Families and Households revealed that husband's participation in domestic labor had no impact on their feeling that divorce was likely.

Not surprisingly, women adjust their expectations for the division of labor in light of their husbands' resistance to sharing (Hochschild, 1989). Studies find that the majority of employed wives are satisfied with an inequitable division of unpaid work, although a considerable range of satisfaction has been reported in different studies (50%–94%) (Dancer & Gilbert, 1993; DeVault, 1990; Hochschild, 1989; Lennon & Rosenfield, 1994; Rosen, 1987; Suitor, 1991).

Recently, several published studies have considered factors related to spouses' feeling that the division of labor is "fair." Not unexpectedly, women are found to be more dissatisfied with the division of labor than men are (John et al., 1995; Lennon & Rosenfield, 1994; Sanchez, 1994a; Sanchez & Kane, 1996). It is important to note, however, that the majority of both sexes report the sharing of household work as "fair" (Sanchez & Kane, 1996). The less housework their husbands do, the more likely women are to perceive the situation as unfair (Gjerdingen & Chaloner, 1994; Hawkins, Marshall, & Meiners, 1995; Lennon & Rosenfield, 1994; Mederer, 1993; Sanchez, 1994a; Sanchez & Kane, 1996). For husbands, the opposite is the case—the more housework they do, the more they see the situation as unfair (Lennon & Rosenfield, 1994; Sanchez, 1994a; Sanchez & Kane, 1996). The relationship between feelings of unfairness and race is unclear. One study found that black and Hispanic men were more likely than white men to see the division as unfair (John et al., 1995), while another found African American men were less likely than other ethnic groups to do so (Sanchez & Kane, 1996).

Women are more likely to feel the division is unfair if they are in a dual-earner household than if it is just the husband who is employed; women in dual-career marriages tend to be even more dissatisfied than women in marriages where partners are not both in careers (Dancer & Gilbert, 1993; Gjerdingen & Chaloner, 1994; Lennon & Rosenfield, 1994; Mederer, 1993). One study found no relation between wives' number of employment hours and feelings of unfairness (Sanchez, 1994b), while a more comprehensive national survey did find a relationship (Sanchez & Kane, 1996). A feeling of role strain or overload might therefore prompt women's sense of unfairness. Alternatively, women with higher status jobs and who work more hours may become more incensed because they can afford to be—they probably make enough money that they can exert some influence over the marriage or even leave it if need be. So far, research is inconclusive about which of these two possible explanations is the most plausible. Although two studies have not found any relationship between women's economic dependency on men and their sense of unfairness (Lennon & Rosenfield, 1994; Sanchez & Kane, 1996), Lennon and Rosenfield's (1994) analysis of national survey data revealed that women who believed their lives would be worse off outside marriage were more likely to view the division of housework as fair, as were women who earned poverty-level wages.

The impact of gender role attitudes on individuals' sense of fairness about the division of domestic work is still also a clouded issue. Contrary to what we might expect, women's gender role attitudes have not been strong predictors of their sense of fairness. Men with more liberal attitudes, however, are more likely to view an inequitable division of labor as unjust (Blair & Johnson, 1992; Sanchez & Kane, 1996).

Some attention has been paid to studying the *consequences* of women's sense of fairness about the division of labor, as well as to the determinants (described earlier). When women feel satisfied with the division of labor, they report more love in the marriage, greater marital happiness, more marital adjustment, and more positive marital interaction (Blair, 1993; Burley, 1995; Crouter et al., 1987; Lennon & Rosenfield, 1994; Pina & Bengtson, 1993). They also report less symptoms of depression (Glass & Fujimoto, 1994; Lennon & Rosenfield, 1994; Voydanoff et al., 1994).

Meantime, women develop various ways of accommodating themselves to an inequitable division of labor in order to help them feel it is basically a fair one. These include saying that they actually enjoy doing domestic tasks, relishing a "supermom" role, claiming that they can count on receiving help from husbands when they *really* need it, being grateful that their husbands are occasionally willing to cross gender boundaries to do traditionally female tasks, accepting their husbands' moral support for their employment in lieu of practical domestic support, and believing that their husbands really appreciate their domestic efforts (Backett, 1987; Benin & Agostinelli, 1988; Blair & Johnson, 1992; DeVault, 1990; Hochschild, 1989; Thompson, 1991). Women also take practical steps to reduce dissonance and inner conflict by lowering their paid work hours and standards for housekeeping and childcare. (Coping strategies for dealing with multiple roles will be discussed in more detail later.)

Case studies of couples involved in more equal sharing of domestic work emphasize the importance of negotiation and marital dynamics in altering the division of labor (Blaisure & Allen, 1995; Ehrensaft, 1987; Hertz, 1986). Coltrane's (1989) study of couples who shared childcare found that men's growing competence as parents was heavily dependent on wives' attitudes. Lamb (1987) also suggests that support from mothers is crucial for men's ability to become active fathers. Several studies show that women's characteristics correlate more with husbands' level of participation in domestic work than husbands' own traits, suggesting that women play an important role in encouraging or discouraging men's participation in domestic work (Barnett & Baruch, 1987a; Grossman et al., 1988; Yogman, Cooley, & Kindlon, 1988).

The Gendered Construction of Parenthood. As mentioned earlier, belief in the inevitability of a gender-based division of labor is declining in popularity. However, according to Coleman (1991), gender ideologies still reinforce the gender-based division of labor in the family. Of particular importance is the gendered construction of parenthood (Brannen, 1992). Parental attitudes and behaviors inside households are shaped by ideologies concerning motherhood, childhood, and childcare that are developed and promulgated outside households by experts, the mass media, popular culture, and the medical establishment. These ideologies contribute not only to a gender segregation of childcare but also to gender specialization in the rest of the marriage (Thompson & Walker, 1991).

One belief about parenthood is that a woman's main purpose in life is to be a carer and nurturer (Thompson & Walker, 1991). Her identity and status presumably derives from her relation to the children and husband for whom she cares. Without this identity, women are presumed to be less than whole persons. A related belief is that women are more capable of affiliation than men, which helps qualify them to be the primary parent (Crosby, 1991). A 1990 Gallup poll found that 60% of men and women believed that "women get a greater sense of satisfaction from caring for their family than from a job well done at work" (DeStefano & Colasanto, 1990). These beliefs persist despite evidence that single women and childless women have the same levels of psychological well-being as other women (Callan, 1987; Coleman, Antonucci, Adelmann, & Crohan, 1987). In addition, there is evidence that the father role is very important to men and that men obtain much satisfaction from it (Altergott, 1988; Cohen, 1987; Marsiglio, 1991).

Another belief is that women know instinctively how to care for children, and therefore are the ones best suited to be responsible for their daily care (Daniels & Weingarten, 1988). Wille's (1995) intensive study of 70 families found that parents believed mothers were better able to care for infants than were fathers, and that belief in turn influenced parenting roles. Research shows, however, that fathers and mothers display similar behaviors when interacting with newborns and that both are capable of forming intimate relationships with infants (Yogman et al., 1988). After childbirth, women have more opportunity to learn appropriate parenting behaviors than men do because they take maternity leave and often reduce their involvement in paid employ-

ment. However, when men have opportunities to learn, their competency in parenting grows likewise (Coltrane, 1989).

Perhaps most importantly, there is a heavy emphasis on the significance of the mother–child relationship for child well-being. After World War II, research on institutionalized war orphans found that such children suffered serious emotional and physical problems. This research was used to convince women that their children needed their full-time care to avoid a similar fate (Brannen, 1992). Since the 1950s, this concern has been heightened by a call from experts to maximize children's potential. Mothers are regarded as particularly well suited to provide special enriching activities and experiences to children: "Abiding, attentive, active, hands-on parenting is seen as imperative for mothers but optional for fathers" (Thompson & Walker, 1991, p. 91). National surveys in the mid-1980s found that about half of women and between two-thirds and three-fourths of men believed that preschool-aged children suffer when their mothers are employed (Thornton, 1989). Full-time employed mothers are widely viewed as less concerned with the welfare of others and less nurturant than other mothers (Bridges & Orza, 1992). These beliefs persist despite evidence that fathers' interaction with children is also important for child development, that full-time absorption in mothering can be very stressful for women, and that children with employed mothers generally suffer no negative consequences (Crosby, 1991; Lamb, 1987; Scarr, Philips, & McCartney, 1989; Thompson & Walker, 1991).

A new version of this cultural ideal, "supermom," has arisen to deal with the reality that the majority of mothers are in the labor force, in opposition to expert advice and popular opinion. According to this ideal, employed mothers must compensate children for their absence (and thereby reduce their own guilt feelings) by devoting themselves to their children as much as possible when they are home. Women are expected to do this without compromising their careers or lowering their standards (Ferree, 1987b). There are two images of supermoms in the popular culture. One overly positive image portrays working mothers as glamorous, competent, and well-organized (Crosby, 1991; Hochschild, 1989). According to Crosby (1991), this image "can make a perfectly normal woman feel grossly inadequate" (p. 67). The second image is overly negative, portraying a "bedraggled Mrs. Juggler whose supermom cape has become badly tattered" (p. 66). This image warns women that they will suffer negative consequences if they combine parenting and work.

The social construction of parenting as a gendered activity helps legitimate the gender-based division of labor in the household and gender differences in employment patterns and opportunities. These structures in turn help to legitimate ideology (Moss & Brannen, 1987). While this cycle may be difficult to break, Hertz (1986) maintains that couples trying to establish more egalitarian sharing of domestic work help create new ideologies of masculinity and femininity.

Institutional Constraints on Equal Sharing. Another set of influences on the division of unpaid work lies outside the family—in the gendered nature of economic and political institutions and their policies and practices. Coleman (1991) calls this the "male-dominated political economy."

According to Cowan and Cowan (1987), the labor market is structured to keep men at work and women at home. Men tend to hold higher-paid and higher-status jobs in the "primary sector," where family commitments are not expected to influence or interfere with work. Women, on the other hand, hold jobs in the "secondary sector," where opportunities to advance are few and earnings and status are low (Moss & Brannen, 1987). Thus it becomes easy for women to retain a greater commitment to family life than work and to agree that their husbands are family breadwinners who can be excused from family work. According to microeconomic theory, it is more "efficient" and beneficial to the family if women rather than men reduce their involvement in employment to do family work, since women face labor market discrimination (Menaghan & Parcel, 1991). Research shows that women's and men's commitments to work and family are influenced by the opportunities both have for remunerative, meaningful employment and the extent to which their employers provide support programs for workers with families (Bielby & Bielby, 1988b; Galinsky & Stein, 1990; Gerson, 1987, 1993; Lorence, 1987; Marsiglio, 1993; Pittman & Orthner, 1988; Rosen, 1987). According to Lamb (1987), workplace inflexibility and families' reliance on men for economic support are among the most important reasons for men's low levels of involvement in family life.

Political obstacles to men and women sharing responsibility for family work also exist. These take the form of limited enforcement of equal employment opportunity legislation, low subsidies for childcare facilities, tax disincentives for dual-earner households, and a lack of legislated employment benefits such as flextime, paid time off to care for sick family members, and paid parental leave (Scarr et al., 1989). Such policies exist in countries like Sweden, which seriously advocates an egalitarian sharing of breadwinning and family work by men and women (Haas, 1992, 1996). Availability of childcare affects women's labor force participation. Many homemakers say they would look for employment if qualified, affordable daycare were available (O'Connell & Bloom, 1987).

There are many reasons why American politicians have chosen not to prioritize the provision of assistance to working parents. Gerson (1993) notes that one of the most important

is the lack of cultural interest in the well-being of children and the low value that is placed on their care. As long as taking care of children is undervalued, isolated, and invisible, we cannot expect substantial change in political institutions or greater interest among men in being involved in their care.

Impact of Employment on Families

The previous section described research concerning the impact of employment on the division of labor for unpaid family work. There is an expanding research literature on how family members' jobs have effects on other aspects of family life (Lambert, 1990; Menaghan, 1991). In the past, the starting point for much of this research was the separate spheres model. Most studies focused on the potential negative effects of women's employment on families and the anticipated positive effects of men's employment. A review of recent research shows that the separate spheres model still inspires some of the research questions being investigated, but findings often help dispel the myth of separate spheres, supporting the "spillover" model. Topics considered have included the impact of employment on marital stability and satisfaction, as well as parent–child relations. There is also a growing literature on the impact of parental employment on children's participation in household work and on child poverty, which is reviewed here. Workplaces in general influence the quality of family relationships through existing policies and practices that reinforce the myth that work and family are separate spheres and that men and women should be responsible for these separate spheres. This section ends, therefore, with a review of this literature.

Marital Stability and Satisfaction

The rate of women's labor force participation and the divorce rate have increased dramatically since the 1950s, and this has led researchers to assume that women's employment contributes to marital instability (Ferber & O'Farrell, 1991). Several reasons for this have been offered. As we have seen, women's absence from the home reduces the time they have for doing unpaid family work, and this could reduce men's quality of life so much that divorce would ensue. Most explanations, however, focus on the impact of women's income-earning. An independent income might enable a woman in an unsatisfactory marriage to leave the marriage and support herself. Women's income-earning might violate traditional gender-role expectations and thus destroy the foundation of some marriages and some men's self-esteem.

Recent research does not support these hypotheses. It is true that women's economic dependence on men has substantially lessened over the past few decades (Sorenson & McLanahan, 1987). However, women's income-earning has been found to stabilize marriage rather than destroy it (Greenstein, 1990). Economic studies show that wives' earnings keep many families out of poverty, and the slight improvement in family income in the past few decades is largely attributable to women's entrance into the labor market. Even after taking into account work-related costs like childcare, dual-earner couples are economically advantaged in comparison to single-earner couples, with more disposable income and higher rates of home ownership (Hanson & Ooms, 1991). The relationship between family income and divorce is well documented, with poorer families being more likely to divorce than ones who are better off. Research shows that men's unemployment increases financial hardship, and hardship contributes to divorce (Broman, Hamilton, & Hoffman, 1990; Liem & Liem, 1988). Women's unemployment is presumed to have a similar effect.

While economic rewards accompanying employment seem to improve marital stability, the scheduling of work can undermine it. Working a job with a nonstandard shift (i.e., evenings, nights, or weekends) has been found to increase a couple's chances of divorce (White & Keith, 1990). Researchers have also discovered that the more hours women work, the greater a couple's chances are for divorce (Greenstein, 1990; Hill, 1988). Greenstein (1995), however, noticed that women's hours of employment are negatively related to marital stability only for women holding nontraditional gender attitudes. He suggests that women who work more hours and have more feminist views are more likely to perceive the domestic division of labor as unfair and consequently are more likely to seek a divorce, while women with more traditional views find ways of justifying unfairness in overall workloads.

Researchers have examined the effects of employment on other aspects of the marriage, in addition to the propensity for divorce. Several researchers have investigated how involuntary unemployment affects marital satisfaction and levels of conflict. Most studies find that the unemployment of either spouse is accompanied by negative changes in the quality of marital relationships (Broman et al., 1990; Conger et al., 1990; Kopasci, 1991; Voydanoff & Donnelly, 1989). (An exception is Perrucci & Targ, 1988). Couples deal with unemployment better if they employ internal coping strategies (e.g., reframe the problem), external coping strategies (e.g., use community resources), and can depend upon spousal support (Perrucci & Targ, 1988). Research suggests that the financial hardship that accompanies unemployment is what causes harm to marital relationships (Broman et al., 1990; Perrucci & Targ, 1988).

Job insecurity appears to take a toll on marital relationships as well. A recent study of university faculty and staff found that individuals who reported stress due to university budget problems reported lower scores on the Locke-Wallace Marital Adjustment Test and a greater number of marital problems (Larson, Wilson, & Beley, 1994).

Little research has been conducted on the impact of *voluntary* unemployment on marriage. Myers and Booth (1996), however, used a national longitudinal survey conducted between 1980 and 1992 to examine the effects of men's retirement on several aspects of marital well-being, including happiness, interaction, disagreements, problems, and stability. They found that only one aspect of men's preretirement employment affected marital quality: Men who had unsatisfactory jobs experienced an improvement in marital quality after retirement. Age of retirement, occupational status, and preretirement income had no effects. Wife's employment and the division of household labor, however, were important factors in postretirement marital quality. Marital quality was lower when wives' worked more hours, earned more money, and were more responsible for family work. Marital quality improved after retirement if men began participating more in household chores.

Research has also examined the impact of women's employment status on marital quality. Vannoy and Philliber (1992) found that wives' employment status and hours had only minor effects on perceptions of marital quality. Blair (1993) found no significant effects of women's work hours on reports of marital happiness of husbands and wives. Rogers (1996) also discovered no significant effect of women's employment on marital happiness in a sample of families with older children, but she did find that employment significantly decreased marital happiness in stepfamilies where the mother was employed. When the mother brought more children into the marriage, however, wives' employment had positive impacts on marital happiness. She concludes that under these circumstances husbands may view wives' employment as "fair" and "just," so the typical negative results would not occur.

Some researchers have examined the impact of women's occupational prestige on marital quality. Results from the National Survey of Families and Households show that husbands are *less* likely to be considering divorce if their wives have prestigious jobs, although marital happiness reports were not affected (Blair, 1993). Orbuch and Custer's (1995) study emphasizes the importance of taking race into account in studies of work–family linkages. They found that African American men who were married to professional women reported lower marital well-being than men married to women in nonprofessional employment; meanwhile, wives' occupational prestige had no effect on white husbands' marital well-being. They speculate that the poor job outlook for black males makes wives' success a sensitive issue in black families.

While employment itself does not seem to have a strong adverse effect on marital interaction, structural characteristics of jobs may cause harm. Shift workers report lower levels of marital quality in one study (White & Keith, 1990), but not in another (Blair, 1993). Workers with "extended job time" (e.g., weekend work, job-related travel, extensive overtime) report more marital tension in two studies (Hoffman, 1989; Hughes, Galinsky, & Morris, 1992), although spouses' absolute number of work hours did not affect marital happiness in another (Blair, 1993).

Psychological characteristics of jobs can also negatively affect family relationships. Men who report a substantial degree of stress or arguments at work report higher levels of negative marital interaction (Bolger, DeLongis, Kessler, & Wethington, 1989; Crouter et al., 1987). Marital companionship is also reduced when employees experience job stress or pressure at the workplace (Hughes et al., 1992; Repetti, 1989). Women who reported more stress at work were more likely to report lower levels of marital adjustment (Sears & Galambos, 1992).

Another psychological aspect of work is job commitment. Blair (1993) found no effect of individuals' level of job commitment on various measures of marital adjustment. Perry-Jenkins and Crouter (1992), however, found that women who were ambivalent about their provider responsibilities reported lower marital satisfaction.

Two other aspects of marriage have been examined in terms of their relationship to partners' employment—leisure time patterns and power. Hill (1988) found that women's employment resulted in couples spending less time in shared activities. Kingston and Nock (1989), however, uncovered no significant differences in time together between single-earner and dual-earner couples. Recent work suggests that wives' employment and wives' income levels positively affect women's power in marriage (Blumstein & Schwartz, 1991; Spitze, 1991; Steil & Weltman, 1991). Pyke's (1994) qualitative research, however, shows how the meanings husbands attach to women's employment can affect whether or not employment leads to women's increased power within marriage. When husbands disapprove of wives' working or see wives' employment as a threat (more likely when men themselves are in low-status jobs or are chronically unemployed), then working does not increase women's power in marriage. Pyke found that women were more likely to gain power benefits from employment in second marriages, after leaving male-dominated first marriages.

Parent–Child Relations and Child Outcomes

An earlier section in this chapter described research on the effects of employment on parents' *time* spent with children. Past research on the impact of work on parents' *rela-*

tionships with children mostly focused on two topics: the impact of mothers' employment on young children's well-being and how child socialization varies by parents' job experiences. While these topics continue to receive researchers' attention, this chapter also covers studies that look at the impact of parental employment on children's participation in household work and likelihood of growing up in poverty.

Impact of Mother's Employment on Children's Well-Being. Several decades of research have mostly laid to rest the concern that mothers' employment per se has serious negative impacts on children, although, as we have seen, the general public still believes this to be true (Spitze, 1991, reviews the latest of this literature). Researchers are still interested, however, in knowing if some specific conditions might lead to women's jobs having especially negative or positive impacts on children's well-being.

One of the factors that has recently been considered is *continuity* of women's employment. Greenstein's (1993) study looked at a large sample of young children whose mothers were disproportionately likely to be young, minority, and unmarried, and found that children of mothers who had been continuously employed were less likely to exhibit problem behaviors than children whose mothers had not been employed. Menaghan and Parcel (1995) also discovered that children whose mothers stayed in stable jobs over a 2-year period experienced improvements in home environments, in terms of stimulation and support. Wolfer and Moen (1996) found that the more years a mother had been employed, the more likely black daughters were to stay in school. No impact of work continuity on white daughters was found.

Another factor that has been investigated as an influence on children's well-being is mothers' *hours* of employment. Greenstein (1993) found no significant effect of mothers' work hours on behavior problems in children's first year, but did find that hours correlated positively with behavioral problems during the children's second and third years of life. He suggests that programs and policies that support working parents might help to eliminate these negative effects and urged researchers to study this subject within an ecological framework that takes into account structural effects on individual outcomes.

Two studies that looked at the impact of mothers' work hours on children's achievement found that children with part-time employed mothers had higher achievement than children of unemployed or full-time employed mothers (Muller, 1995; Williams & Radin, 1993). Muller (1995) notes, however, that this result could be explained by a third variable, amount of time unsupervised after school, with full-time unemployed mothers being more likely to have unsupervised children and unsupervised children performing at a lower level than supervised children. Availability of adequate supervision might be one of the structural factors that Greenstein (1993) reminds us to take into account when assessing the impact of maternal employment on child academic outcomes. Wolfer and Moen's (1996) study of daughters staying in school also found positive effects of part-time employment for black young women (although not whites), which they interpret as the consequence of mothers' experiencing less role overload and role strain. A large study of adolescents in two-parent families in California and Wisconsin found that full-time maternal employment had a negative impact on the grades of middle- and upper-middle-class boys, but not on girls (Bogenschneider & Steinberg, 1994).

Relatively little attention has been paid to the impact of fathers' employment on parent–child relations. Call (1996a) found no important effects of fathers' unemployment on adolescents' relations with parents. One study of business students in a southern public university found that students reported being closer to fathers who were more family versus career oriented; fathers' work hours had no impact on perceived closeness (Goldsmith, Hoffman, & Hofacker, 1993).

Impact of Job Experiences on Child Socialization. Early on, researchers examined the impact of men's job experiences on their childrearing style. Researchers are still interested in the impact of job experience on socialization, but are now increasingly looking at mothers as well as fathers. In general, having a "complex" job with opportunities for self-direction has been found to be related to parents of both sexes valuing self-direction and autonomy in their children (Gottfried & Gottfried, 1988; Grossman et al., 1988; Menaghan & Parcel, 1991; Spade, 1991). Mothers with such jobs have also been found to provide more cognitive stimulation and affective warmth to their children, while mothers who start jobs low in complexity tend to offer home environments that offer less stimulation and warmth (Menaghan & Parcel, 1991, 1995). Ryu and Mortimer's (1996) study found that same-sex parents' employment situations had more impact on adolescent values than opposite-sex parents' jobs.

Work conditions can also influence parenting style. One study of employed parents and their 5- to 7-year-olds found that positive features of parents' work (complexity of work with people, challenge, and stimulation) were significantly associated with positive parenting practices that involved more warmth and responsiveness and less harsh punishment (Greenberger, O'Neil, & Nagel, 1994). Grimm-Thomas and Perry-Jenkins' (1994) study of working-class fathers suggests that this connection occurs through the effects work has on self-esteem. They found that men who reported more positive job conditions (involving autonomy, work clarity, innovation, involvement, supervisor support, peer cohesion,

and physical comfort) had higher self-esteem; when men had higher self-esteem, they were more likely to display warmth and positive regard to their children and engage less in negative techniques of psychological control. The researchers speculate that fathers with less satisfying jobs are less sure of themselves and in turn become less accepting of children and more threatened by their behavior. One recent study of African American families found that fathers who felt overcontrolled as workers engaged in parental behaviors of "overcontrol," which in turn led to children exhibiting problem behaviors (Mason, Cauce, Gonzales, Hiraga, & Grove, 1994).

A lack of work can also influence men's parenting. Studies show that unemployment gives men increased opportunities for contact with their children, but that the quality of the interaction tends to become more negative. Unemployed fathers tend to be more irritable and more likely to engage in arbitrary and physical punishment, even physical abuse (Broman et al., 1990; McLoyd, 1989; Rayman, 1988). Job stress has also been found to negatively affect men's evaluation of the father role (Altergott, 1988).

Parental Employment and Children's Participation in Family Work. Several studies conducted before 1987 on the effects of mother's employment on children's participation in household work tended to find no significant impact of living in a dual-earner family on children's likelihood of doing chores (see Benin & Edwards, 1990, for a review of this literature). Some studies conducted since that time have also come up with the same conclusion (Peters & Haldeman, 1987).

Researchers have begun to explore this mystery in more depth, looking particularly at the influence of mothers' work hours and gender of the child. Benin and Edwards' (1990) analysis of time diaries found that adolescents did more household chores in families where mothers worked full-time, and did the least amount in families where mothers worked part-time (adolescents in one-earner families fell in between). Girls with full-time employed mothers did almost 10 hours of household work per week, compared to only 3 hours for boys. Manke et al. (1994) also found girls to do more household work in households where mothers worked full-time, although in their study of 4th and 5th graders in central Pennsylvania, children in families where mothers worked part-time worked more at chores than did children in one-earner families. Benin and Edwards speculate that full-time working mothers reduce their role overload by delegating their traditional work to daughters rather than to sons because they feel that girls are more capable of performing it. While the amount of time spent on household chores was similar for adolescent girls and boys in one-earner households in the Benin and Edwards study, gender segregation in task allocation was significantly greater in these types of households in comparison to households where both parents were employed.

Parental Employment and Child Poverty. Although the U.S. economy is typically regarded as being in good shape, the median income of families with young children has fallen 34% (adjusted for inflation) since the early 1970s and the child poverty rate has risen during the 1990s. By 1993, the child poverty rate was higher than it had been since 1964, with 23%, or 16 million, children under age 18 now living under the official poverty line. This state of affairs is extremely serious. Sixteen million American children experience problems with hunger, dangerous or unhealthy housing conditions, and even homelessness. Poor children are more likely to die from birth defects, infectious diseases, house fires, and domestic violence. Poor children are more likely to suffer severe problems with self-esteem, self-identity, and motivation, which in turn affect school performance, academic achievement, and occupational status (Sidel, 1986).

The latest round of debates about changing the welfare system shows that most Americans think poverty will end if women stop having children outside wedlock and mothers go to work, instead of relying on public handouts. Poor children are indeed more likely to live in mother-only families, but these are more likely to be created by divorce than by illegitimacy. And as was discovered earlier, many women have children without getting married because their potential marriage partners have poor job prospects. Labor market opportunities help to determine family structure, probably more than family structure determines labor market opportunities.

The idea that mothers going to work will end poverty is also misguided. *Two-thirds* (61%) of poor children live in households with at least one wage-earner. Astonishingly, analysis of national survey data shows that parental employment status is not a significant predictor of whether or not a household is in poverty (Lichter & Eggebeen, 1994). The presence of a wage-earner brings the least economic return to Latino families (Lichter & Landale, 1995). Parental employment, therefore, does not result necessarily in children's economic well-being (Sidel, 1996) because frequently the wage-earner is a woman, and women earn far less than men.

Alessandri's (1992) research suggests that even low-income employment can have positive impacts on children—10- to 12-year-olds with employed single mothers were more likely to report better family cohesion, self-esteem, and grades than children of nonemployed low-income single mothers. Yet living in a single-parent family will likely have more positive outcomes for children when their parents have a chance for decent-paying work. Menaghan and Parcel (1995) found that single mothers with high-wage jobs had children who experienced positive home environments with adequate stimulation and supportiveness.

Changes in state and federal welfare regulations do not seem likely to end child poverty. While these regulations may open up some job opportunities, they typically force women to take jobs that are unlikely to accrue wages that will get their families out of poverty. The answer lies in dramatically improving women's wage rates (Lichter and Landale, 1995).

Impact of the Organization of Work Life on Families

So far this section has described research analyzing how individuals' employment status and job characteristics affect family relationships. A new topic in work–family studies is how the organization of work life in general influences family life. Bowen and his associates maintain that work organizations possess cultures—assumptions, values, norms, and expectations—that not only can prevent individuals from realizing the values and goals they have for their marriages and relationships with children, but can also shape workers' orientations to family life (Bowen, 1988, 1991; Bowen & Orthner, 1991; Orthner et al., 1990).

One assumption of the "traditional organizational model" is that work comes first for men, before family, and that men fully meet their responsibilities to their families through income-earning (Bowen & Orthner, 1991; Orthner et al., 1990). Women workers, in turn, are viewed as secondary earners and are assumed to be primarily oriented to their marital and parental roles, not to career advancement (Orthner et al., 1991). Another assumption is that work and family must be kept separate for the smooth and efficient functioning of each, so family-oriented women (and men) must deal with the challenges of combining work and family roles without assistance from employers (Friedman, 1987). Workplace values include efficiency, rationality, short-term thinking, and above all economic profit; values more consonant with consideration of employees' family lives (e.g., collaborativeness, long-term orientation, social responsibility) are usually absent (Bowen, 1988).

Organizational norms and expectations reflect organizational values and affect employees' family lives through work structure (expectations for amount and scheduling of work time, travel, relocation) and work environment dynamics (supervisor flexibility, appropriate career paths, and criteria for rewards) (Bowen, 1988). Formal and informal recruitment policies are often designed to produce a good "fit" between the individuals' and the organization's values. Company values and norms are also communicated through policy statements, personnel policies, training programs, and deliberate coaching of newer employees by older ones. Operational criteria for status and rewards within the organization as well as the behavior of leader figures teach employees about organizational expectations (Schein, 1990).

Increasing numbers of work organizations have become more sensitive to the family responsibilities of employees and have developed policies and programs to help individuals combine work and family (Galinsky et al., 1991; Orthner et al., 1990). However, most organizations lag behind. Almost all the firms that do provide programs direct them to women, who are still assumed to be more family-oriented than men (Bowen, 1988; Galinsky et al., 1990; Kamerman & Kahn, 1987; Raabe & Gessner, 1988). The dominance of women among the users of such programs reinforces the notion that women are in charge of family life. It thereby becomes easier to justify limiting women's employment opportunities and income (Voydanoff, 1991). Women who take advantage of company maternity leave, for example, have more restricted job opportunities after childbirth than before (Cowan & Cowan, 1987).

Some men struggle against the organizational constraints imposed on them and seek opportunities to modify their labor force involvement for family reasons. Cowan and Cowan (1987) found, however, that fathers of infants were faced with increased work demands and hostile attitudes if they suggested to employers that they would like more time with their children. Hunt and Hunt (1987) maintain that individuals of both sexes need to continue to challenge the structure of contemporary workplaces, rather than settle for "losses in the social sphere" (p. 199). Kessler-Harris (1987) says that if *men* put a greater emphasis on their family roles, there "would no longer be negative attributes in the work force, but simply part of the baggage all workers brought with them to the workplace" (p. 523). This in turn would lead to employers being more amenable to accommodating workers' family roles.

There is still little empirical work on the effects of workplace culture on families. Bowen (1988) has outlined a conceptual model that could be used in such research. An increasing number of researchers are examining the effects of family-friendly workplace policies on individuals, but the focus is more on work-related attitudes and behavior rather than on family variables (Gonyea, 1993; Greenberger, Goldberg, Hamill, O'Neil, & Payne, 1989). One recent exception is a study by Volling and Belsky (1991) that found that working at a supportive workplace improved men's quality of interaction with infants.

In an attempt to speak the language that company officials understand, researchers are encouraged to examine the effects of progressive company policies on economic productivity, rather than on marital or parent–child relations. Positive attitudes toward work and more time spent at the job are assumed to enhance worker productivity through reducing the strain employees feel in having to combine work and family roles (Friedman, 1987). Although research on this topic is still sparse (Kingston, 1990), the studies that have been done suggest that family-friendly company policies do improve work attitudes (job satisfaction, organizational commitment, and morale) as well as work behavior (retention, attendance, and lowered tardiness) (Galinsky & Stein, 1990; Gonyea & Googins, 1992; Greenberger et al., 1989; National Council of Jewish Women, 1987; Pittman & Orthner, 1988; Zedeck & Mosier, 1990).

Effects of Family on Work

Employers' growing interest in developing family-friendly company policies is evidence of an increased recognition that family life affects work behavior and attitudes. Much of the early research on the effects of family on work was influenced by "gendered" theoretical models: Women's work behavior and attitudes were assumed to be determined by their predisposition to be oriented to marital and parenting roles, while men's work attitudes and behavior were hypothesized to be affected by characteristics of their jobs (e.g., extent of autonomy allowed, rewards given) (Ferree, 1991a). More recently, researchers have discovered evidence that supports a more gender-neutral model explaining work behavior and attachment. This section examines the impact of family responsibilities on the labor market behavior, work attitudes, and work rewards of men and women.

Effects of Family Responsibilities on Labor Market Behavior

Impact of Dependent Care Responsibilities. Most research on the effects of family on work deals with how responsibility for children affects women's labor force participation. A quick glance at statistics shows that parenthood no longer substantially reduces women's likelihood of being employed. In 1975, about half of women with children under age 18 were in the paid labor force; by 1994, 70% were. Even having preschool-aged children has much less impact on women's employment status than formerly. In 1975, only 4 out of 10 mothers with children under age 6 worked outside the home; by 1994, the figure was 6 out of 10. Half of all women with an infant under 1 year of age are in the labor force (Herz & Wootton, 1996).

Parenthood does affect certain groups of women's labor force participation more than others. Women who earn a high proportion of family income before childbirth or who have high-status jobs have been found to be more likely to return to work sooner after childbirth than other women (Garrett, Luebeck, & Wenk, 1992; Wenk & Garrett, 1992; Yoon & Waite, 1994). Having a longer work history before childbirth and having access to maternity leave also increases women's chances of returning to work sooner (Joesch, 1994; O'Connell, 1990). Surprisingly, having more than one preschool-aged child in the home already has not been found to keep women home longer (Garrett et al., 1992; Glass, 1988; Spenner & Rosenfeld, 1989). Over time, racial differences in return-to-work patterns have virtually disappeared (Yoon & Waite, 1994).

The number of hours women are likely to work when employed has not changed substantially in the last two decades; in 1970 and in 1993 about 70% of employed women worked 35 hours or more per week (i.e., "full-time"). Mothers with children under age 14 have been found to work fewer hours than other women, while fathers with children of the same age work more hours than other men (Hayghe & Haugen, 1987). Having a preschool-aged child is particularly likely to lead to women working part-time; in 1993, 43% of all mothers of preschool-aged children worked full-time year-round, in comparison to 56% of mothers of school-aged children (Herz & Wootton, 1996). Even mothers working in high-status, demanding careers in science, engineering and medicine tend to work part-time (Grant, Simpson, Rong, & Peters-Golden, 1990; Zukerman, 1987). Although there is some evidence that mothers often prefer part-time work as a way to reduce overload (Moen & Dempster-McClain, 1987), Mutchler's (1987) research suggests that parenthood actually increases women's chances of being "underemployed"—that is, working part-time involuntarily. Unmarried and divorced mothers seem to be particularly likely to work part-time involuntarily, and this involuntary part-time employment is usually associated with poverty-level earnings (McLanahan & Booth, 1991; Mutchler, 1987).

Involvement in family roles also seems to reduce women's tendency to be involved in careers (defined as managerial or professional positions requiring higher education). Cooney and Uhlenberg (1991) found that highly educated women with children were significantly less likely to be in a career than were highly educated women without children or men with or without children. They discovered, however, that highly educated women with children were significantly more likely to be on a career track in 1980 than were such women in 1970; only 25% of highly educated women with children had careers (according to census data) in 1970, compared to 42% in 1980. No significant changes in fathers' likelihood of being in a career were noticed. Madamba and DeJong (1994) found that delayed childbearing, and having children 5 years of age and over, significantly increased Puerto Rican women's chances of being in a white-collar job.

There are some additional respects in which women's labor market behavior seems to be affected by responsibility for children. Mothers are more likely than fathers or other women to miss days of work, and research suggests that up to 40% of parents miss work because of childcare responsibilities (Ferber & O'Farrell, 1991; Friedman, 1987). Women are also more likely to spend unproductive time on the job because of phone calls or concern about what is happening at home and to come in late or leave early to care for children (Ferber & O'Farrell, 1991; Fernandez, 1986; Friedman, 1987; Zambrana & Frith, 1988). Women are more likely than men to stay at home with sick children (Googins, 1991).

Research suggests that gender differences in labor force participation, work hours, absenteeism, and productive time on the job are not primarily due to women's lower commitment or attachment to work, but to problems locating and sustaining reliable, affordable, high-quality childcare. Childcare problems affect women's labor market status more because most couples still hold mothers more responsible for childcare than fathers. When men take more responsibility for childcare they are just as likely as women to be absent from work (Ferber & O'Farrell, 1991; Galinsky et al., 1991). One-fourth of working parents of preschoolers (and one-third of working parents with infants and toddlers) find it difficult to find childcare. One-fourth of parents have had breakdowns in regular arrangements, leading to tardiness, leaving early, or absenteeism (Galinsky & Stein, 1990). A 1988 national survey of human resource professionals in over 1000 companies found that childcare problems led to absenteeism and tardiness in 90% of companies and to low productivity in one-third (Society for Human Resource Management, 1992). Sick children cause particular problems for parents; Googins (1991) found that if they couldn't stay home from work, parents would check in by phone or bring the child to work. Single parents and low-income married women have the most difficulty establishing and maintaining good childcare arrangements, primarily because they have less income for purchasing good substitute care (Ferber & O'Farrell, 1991; McLanahan & Booth, 1991).

Responsibilities for ailing, elderly parents also affect women's labor force behavior. Women experience more interruptions in their work due to elder care responsibilities than do men (Neal, Chapman, Ingersoll-Dayton, Emlen, & Boise, 1990). Surveys have found that one-fifth of all caregivers of elderly parents cut back on their work hours, 29% are forced to rearrange their work schedules, about one-fifth take unpaid leave, one-third have been late or left work early because of elder care problems, and about one-third work less efficiently because of stress (Galinsky et al., 1991; Stone, Cafferata, & Sang, 1987). Franklin, Ames and King (1994) found that employed female caregivers made "short-term" and "long-term" adjustments in their work behavior to adapt to their responsibilities for elder care. Short-term adjustments were more likely when the elder to be cared for was a spouse and when hours of care required were occasional or fewer in number; the adaptations included arriving late or leaving work early, taking days off without pay, taking personal sick days, changing hours, and refusing a promotion. The long-term adjustments made involved leaves of absence, which were more likely to occur when elders needed more medical care, help with daily living, or supervision. Daughters of elders who require substantial assistance with daily living are often forced to quit work entirely (Barnes, Given, & Given, 1995). Ettner (1995) found that coresidence with an ailing parent was significantly associated with women's withdrawal from the labor force, while caring for a disabled parent who still lived outside the home reduced work hours only if such care involved 10 hours or more per week.

Here again, evidence suggests that an inability to make satisfactory care arrangements, rather than a weak commitment to work, explains the cutbacks in employment women make (Ferber & O'Farrell, 1991). An Oregon study found that over one-half of workers with responsibilities for elders had difficulty locating appropriate care (Galinsky et al., 1991).

Concern for the care of dependents causes some women to elect to work evening or weekend shifts (when husbands can care for children) or even leave the workplace entirely for home-based employment (Christensen, 1987; Presser, 1987). However, there is little evidence that most women limit their occupational choices to jobs that would help them cope with their responsibilities for children or elders, for example, by picking jobs requiring less effort (to save energy for unpaid family work) and offering greater flexibility. Bielby and Bielby's (1988a) analyses of national survey data revealed that while women were more involved in unpaid family work, their jobs required slightly more mental and physical effort than did men's. Glass and Camarigg (1992) also investigated if full-time employed mothers occupied jobs that would be compatible with their family responsibilities, that is, jobs involving less effort and greater flexibility. They found that in fact women were significantly less likely than men to occupy jobs that were easy and flexible. Moreover, being married, having children, and having younger children did not increase women's likelihood of holding jobs with these characteristics. They conclude that jobs with characteristics that would help women manage work and family roles are hard for them to obtain, for such rewards tend to be linked to jobs men typically hold. The workers with the easiest and most flexible jobs were men without children; Glass and Camarigg suggest that it is easier for employers to offer these benefits to this group because they won't need to take much advantage of them. Other studies have also found that jobs held predominantly by women are not more likely than other jobs to offer flexibility and how requirements for exertion (Barry, 1987; Glass, 1990).

Impact of Marital Dynamics. While dependent care affects women's work patterns, marital dynamics can also influence work behavior and performance. Women's employment and work hours have been found to be significantly affected by the extent to which their husbands approve of their working (Ulbrich, 1988; Zavella, 1987). Husbands tend to be more positive when the family really needs extra income or when wives have a strong career orientation (Burris, 1991). In addition, having a lower-earning husband and being in a unstable marital relationship increases women's chance of being in the labor force (Gerson, 1987; McLanahan & Booth, 1991).

The requirements of the husbands' job, or their desire for occupational achievement, can also affect women's involvement in the paid labor force (Fowlkes, 1987). According to Hochschild (1989), women's "backstage support" (including domestic work) enhances husbands' job performance more than husbands' support enhances wives' performance. Frequent moves because of husbands' job transfers have been found to undermine women's participation in paid work (Morrison & Lichter, 1988). On the positive side, husbands can give their wives instrumental support, especially in the professions, by providing contacts, mentoring, and protection against sexual harassment (Epstein, 1987; Weiss, 1987).

In a national study of over 1000 U.S. companies, human resource professionals named marital stress as the main cause of low productivity (Society for Human Resource Management, 1992). The effects of marital stress on productivity may be stronger for men than for women. Bolger et al. (1989) found that men who reported arguments at home noted that this led to more arguments at work. A 1992 national survey found that marital distress had important negative effects on men's work (including absences), especially for those who had been married less than 10 years. Marital distress, however, was not associated with women's work loss (Forthofer, Markman, Cox, Stanley, & Kessler, 1996). Bowen (1991) has posited that a poor fit between the individual's marital values (e.g., time together) and the organization's values and norms (e.g., overtime requirements) can have an impact on worker productivity.

Effects of Family on Work Attitudes

Realizing that work behavior and work attitudes are correlated (though not always highly), researchers have looked at the effects of family responsibilities on individuals' attitudes toward work. It has been assumed that because of gender socialization and family responsibilities, women will be less interested in and satisfied with paid employment than men. Lorence (1987) calls this the "gender model of sex differences in job involvement." Research suggests that this is not the case, lending support for what Lorence calls the "job model of sex differences in job involvement."

Various measures of work attitudes have been used. Lorence (1987) measures "job involvement" by how often respondents did nonrequired work, felt time dragged on the job, and felt involved in their jobs. Others have investigated "job satisfaction," asking respondents how well their present job matches their ideal job in specific respects or overall (Hanson & Sloane, 1992; Hodson, 1989; Zambrana & Frith, 1988). Bielby and Bielby's (1989) measure of "work identity" examined how much life satisfaction comes from work. Pittman and Orthner's (1988) "job commitment" scale asked about satisfaction with their work organization and current assignment and certainty about remaining with the organization. Lobel and St. Clair (1992) measured willingness to put in a great deal of effort. Lambert (1991) looked at job satisfaction, intrinsic interest in the job, and the importance workers attach to work.

The results of these studies refute the validity of the gender model of job involvement. Using a wide variety of measures, they found no or only small gender differences in work orientation. In examining what predicts women's and men's work orientations, they typically find that family variables—like marital status, number of children, and spouse's job characteristics—play no or little role in women's (or men's) work attitudes. Instead, differences in *job* characteristics explained differences in attitudes toward work for both women and men. Although varying from study to study, the list of influential job variables includes autonomy, skill utilization, significance, variety, pay level, prestige, and how interesting the job is (Bielby & Bielby, 1989; Hanson & Sloane, 1992; Hodson, 1989; Lambert, 1991; Lorence, 1987).

Research suggests that work commitment and job satisfaction are also affected by characteristics of work organizations, particularly whether the organization is supportive and responsive to family needs (Greenberger et al., 1989; Lambert, 1991; Pittman & Orthner, 1988). Another structural determinant of work commitment is childcare availability. Burris (1991) found women more likely to prioritize family roles over work roles if they were single parents or had low income, which made it harder to locate and pay for adequate childcare. Feelings about work are more negative for single parents and for married workers when they are concerned about the quality of their childcare arrangements (Greenberger & O'Neil, 1990).

Effects of Family on Work Rewards, Economic Success, and Achievement

Mothers are more likely to work part-time and occupy lower-status jobs, which explains their low earnings. However, even controlling for hours and occupational status, women still earn less than men. Looking only at individuals who were in full-time careers requiring higher education, Cooney and Uhlenberg (1991) found mothers' earnings to be only 59% of fathers' for the 35- to 39-year-old age group.

This difference in earnings might be related to differences in the levels of support women and men give each other in pursuing their careers. Bellas' (1992) national survey of male faculty found that married men were more likely than unmarried men to have higher degrees and higher ranks and to have published more books and articles; these achievements in turn earned married men higher salaries. Even controlling for these achievement factors, Bellas found married men to earn higher income, and married men with nonemployed wives to earn the highest incomes of all.

Landau and Arthur (1992) also found that being a married man was associated with higher earnings and that having a nonemployed wife increased earnings even more. Their study of managerial and professional employees of a Fortune 500 company, however, also included women, and found no gender differences in the relationship between marital status and earnings or between having a nonemployed spouse and higher earnings. Still, married men earned higher incomes than married women, and the researchers suggest that companies are set up so that they "tend to detect and invest in human capital of married men more than women or single men" (p. 678).

Loscocco and Leicht's (1993) study of small business owners also examined the impact of family variables on individuals' economic success. They found that men's businesses were more profitable than women's but this was due to the fact that their businesses had been around longer, employed more people, and were often in the computer field. Although women business owners were primarily responsible for domestic work in their families, this had no effect on their business earnings, and women's commitment to getting their businesses to succeed was not significantly different than men's. These results are consistent with the findings described earlier that suggest that gender differences in work orientation are insignificant and that gender differences in work patterns are related more to job characteristics and gender discrimination than to women's primary identification with their family role.

Impact of Simultaneous Membership in Work and Family Systems

Most research on the linkages between family and work looks at the effects of membership in one system on membership in the other. It has become increasingly popular, however, to look at men and women as simultaneous members of both systems and to study more directly how employment and family environments jointly affect individuals' well-being (Bolger et al., 1989; Kline & Cowan, 1988). Resources and strategies that help individuals successfully combine work and family roles have also been investigated.

This research has been stimulated by the increased tendency for women, particularly wives and mothers, to be in the labor force, and most studies center on the consequences of women's dual roles. Given the solid body of evidence that women remain more responsible for domestic life than men and that organizations remains on the whole unresponsive to employees' family demands, employed women (especially wives and mothers) are expected to experience lower levels of well-being than men and other women. Aspects of well-being that have been looked at include emotional well-being, role stress, and role strain.

Emotional Well-Being, Role Stress, and Role Strain

Emotional Well-Being. Although some studies have found small differences between employed men's and women's psychological well-being, recent work by Ensminger and Celentano (1990) suggests that these may be disappearing. Research has also shown that employed women do not suffer lower levels of emotional well-being (e.g., low self-esteem, anxiety, depression) in comparison to other women. Some researchers have found that employed women exhibit more well-being than housewives (Rosenfield, 1989; Spitze, 1991), while other researchers have found no significant difference (Anshensel & Pearlin, 1987; Atkinson, 1992; Schwartzberg & Dytell, 1988). An increase in employment hours has been found to improve women's psychological well-being (Wetherington & Kessler, 1989), although Glass and Fujimoto's (1994) results suggest that there is an upper threshold for work hours at which point work becomes associated with less well-being. Baruch, Biener, and Barnett (1987) argue that employment enhances women's well-being because the "workplace appears more often than not to offer such benefits as challenge, control, structure, positive feedback, and self-esteem and to provide a valued set of social ties" (p. 132).

Research consistently shows that psychological distress is lower for individuals occupying multiple roles (worker, spouse, parent) than for individuals occupying only one or two (Coleman et al., 1987; Epstein, 1987; Gove & Zeiss, 1987; Voydanoff & Donnelly, 1989). This is true for men as well as women (Barnett, Marshall, & Pleck, 1992; Loomis & Booth, 1995; Robinson & Spitze, 1992). One hypothesis is that "multiple roles protect individuals by providing alternative sources of gratification" (Schwartzberg & Dytell, 1988, p. 188). We now have more details about the many types of gratification individuals gain by participating in multiple roles. These include a sense of accomplishment, improved interpersonal relationships, enhanced opportunities to develop talents and abilities, clarified goals and priorities, development of time management skills, and having a greater variety of experiences (Marshall & Barnett, 1993; Scharlach,

1994). Marshall and Barnett (1993) found that women were significantly more likely to recognize these "work-family gains" than were men.

Role Stress. Another aspect of well-being that is often examined in relation to work–family linkages is role stress. Researchers ask individuals how much worry, tension, conflicting demands, ambiguity, work overload, and problems they are experiencing *within* each specific domain—work, marriage, and parenthood. (Some researchers label this "role conflict," but this is a confusing term that could mean conflict within a role or conflict between roles. Therefore, the experience of stress in regard to a particular role is termed "role stress" here.) According to Crosby's (1991) review of the literature, stress within roles is more common than stress between roles (described later as role strain).

Studies that have compared employed women and homemakers in terms of parenting stress have not found significant differences (Killien & Brown, 1987; Scott & Alwin, 1989). Some studies have found no gender differences in role stress for either family or work roles (Bolger et al., 1989; Phelan, Bromet, Schwartz, Dew, & Curtis, 1993; Voydanoff & Donnelly, 1989), but others have (Anderson and Leslie, 1991; Scott & Alwin, 1989; Wanamaker & Bird, 1990). This discrepancy may be related to the extent to which researchers control for objective job characteristics (e.g., safety, access to flextime), which have been found to be gender linked and which in turn can affect perception of role stress (Phelan et al., 1993).

Researchers also have looked at the impact of marriage and parenthood on employees' reports of role stress in their occupational roles. Phelan et al. (1993) found no significant effect of marriage or parenthood on professional men's or women's sense of role stress at work (measured in terms of conflicting demands and ambiguity). Women with children, however, were more likely than other groups to report conflicting demands at work.

Role Strain. Role strain can be defined as the level of perceived conflict *between* work and family roles and the degree of reported overload or stress experienced trying to meet multiple role demands (Guelzow et al., 1991). Role conflict and role overload have been found to have negative impact on psychological well-being (Paden & Buehler, 1995).

This conflict has many dimensions; it can mean not having enough time and energy to meet the demands of all roles, guilt about not meeting the demands of all roles, and concerns about the consequences of not meeting the demands of all roles (Marshall & Barnett, 1993; Scharlach, 1994). Individuals can obtain positive benefits ("work–family gains") at the same time as they experience role strain ("work–family strains") (Marshall & Barnett, 1993; Scharlach, 1994).

Between one-fifth and two-thirds of workers experience role strain as it is defined here (Casey & Pitt-Catsouphes, 1994; Cournoyer & Mahalik, 1995; Ferber & O'Farrell, 1991; Friedman, 1987; Googins, 1991; Herrera & DelCampo, 1995; Stone et al., 1987). More employees complain that work interferes with their family life than vice versa (Ferber & O'Farrell, 1991; Frone, Russell, & Cooper, 1992). Workers are more likely to report work–family conflict if they have dependents to care for, or when those dependents require higher than ordinary levels of care (Friedman, 1987; Gottleib, Kelloway, & Fraboni, 1994). Certain job characteristics are also positively associated with role strain, including extended work hours and work pressure (Hughes et al., 1992; Voydanoff, 1988b).

Attitudes toward employment can also contribute to role strain. Jackson's (1993) study of African American employed mothers found that role strain was less when women's employment status was consistent with their preference. O'Neil and Greenberger (1994) found that fathers with low work commitment experienced less role strain than those with high commitment; work commitment had no effect on women's role strain, however.

Women have been found to exhibit higher levels of role strain than men in most studies (Anshensel & Pearlin, 1987; Baruch & Barnett, 1987a; Bolger et al., 1989; Ferber & O'Farrell, 1991; Friedman, 1987; Frone et al., 1992; Googins, 1991; Gottlieb et al., 1994; Greenberger et al., 1989; Marshall & Barnett, 1993; Moen & Dempster-McClain, 1987). (An exception is a study by Burke, 1988.) It is possible that gender differences in strain may be due to women's likelihood of being responsible for children rather than the consequences of occupying multiple roles. In support of this, Schwartzberg and Dytell (1988) found that employed married mothers reported the same levels of role overload and conflict as nonemployed married mothers. Greenberger et al. (1989) found similar levels of role strain among employed married mothers of preschool-aged children and employed single mothers. On the other hand, Marshall and Barnett (1993) found that employed mothers reported more role strain than did employed women without children.

Guelkow et al. (1991) have developed a model that connects emotional well-being, role stress, and role strain. Findings from a study of professional couples showed that work and family demands affect the amount of strain (conflict and overload) individuals experience, which in turn has an impact on emotional stress, role stress, and physical stress (in that order). Other researchers have also found empirical connections between role stress or role strain and psychological well-being (Burke, 1988; Googins, 1991; Schwartzberg & Dytell, 1988; Voydanoff & Donnelly, 1989). Guelkow et al. (1991) emphasize, however, that the impact of role strain on emotional well-being is mediated by individual's coping responses. These responses can help prevent or minimize a decline in well-being. This explains why levels of stress and strain are usually reported to be moderate, rather than high.

Individual Coping Strategies

Researchers have uncovered many strategies individuals and couples use to reduce role stress and strain produced by combining work and family roles. Most people rely on several (Carlisle, 1994; Hochschild, 1989; Schnittger & Bird, 1990).

Cutting Back on Work. One main approach is to cut back on the work involved in one or both roles. Mothers of preschoolers are particularly likely to use the strategy of cutting back on hours of paid work, although this in turn usually has a negative effect on family finances and women's self-esteem (Brett & Yogev, 1988; Burris, 1991; Folk & Beller, 1993; Hochschild, 1989; Moen & Dempster-McClain, 1987; Wanamaker & Bird, 1990). Only some categories of women can afford to reduce work–family conflict by working part-time; a national survey found that mothers of preschoolers who worked part-time were disproportionately white, married, and in a white-collar occupation (Folk & Beller, 1993).

Cutting Back on Housework. Some women cope with role stress or role strain by cutting back on their housework time. They usually accomplish this by lowering their housekeeping standards, hiring outside help, or recruiting children to do work (Hochschild, 1989; Wanamaker & Bird, 1990). These strategies have their limits. Standards can only be cut back so far before health and comfort are threatened. Hiring help is an option only for people who can afford it.

Women's willingness to delegate household chores to children has more potential, but interestingly there is evidence that children do no more housework in households where both parents work than when the mother is a housewife (Benin & Edwards, 1990; Call, 1996b). Moreover, while adolescents start out doing a substantial amount of domestic work in 9th grade (16.5 hours a week), by the time they reach 12th grade, girls do an average of 13 and boys an average of 8 hours of work a week (Call, 1996b). Most domestic work involves chores traditionally defined as female (cooking, cleaning, dishwashing, and laundry), and boys are typically not assigned these responsibilities (Benin & Edwards, 1990; Call, 1996b; Manke et al., 1994). Children help out more with housework when families are larger, when they have a low income, and when they are headed by a single parent (Call, 1996b). Adolescents seem more likely to participate in care of younger siblings than they are to do housework; 49% of girls and 39% of boys in 9th grade report being actively involved in this activity, but this, too, decreases over time. Children seldom participate in care of elders—only 8% did so in 9th grade and only 4% did so by 12th grade (Call, 1996b).

Psychological Approaches. The aforementioned coping strategies require taking some type of action (or inaction). Other coping strategies described in the research literature involve a more psychological approach. For example, individuals can choose to prioritize one role over others to reduce feelings of guilt and pressure. It is common for women to prioritize their family role over their role as worker; when one role becomes less salient, less role conflict ensues (Bielby & Bielby, 1989; Burris, 1991; Greenhaus, 1988; Wanamaker & Bird, 1990; Zambrana & Frith, 1988). Such prioritizing, however, can reduce women's job opportunities and motivation to achieve in the labor market, which in turn can have a negative effect on their income and social status. Women also often resort to "supermoming," which involves maintaining high standards for housework, childcare, and work performance, at the cost of rest and meeting personal needs (Ferree, 1987b; Hochschild, 1989). Other negative approaches include passive acceptance and avoiding responsibility (Anderson & Leslie, 1991; Hochschild, 1989; Wanamaker & Bird, 1990).

A somewhat more positive psychological coping strategy involves developing organizational skills (time management, compartmentalization) (Carlisle, 1994; Wanamaker & Bird, 1990). Another positive strategy used by women and men alike is "cognitive restructuring" (also known as "positive appraisal" and "reframing the problem"). This involves focusing on the benefits to be gained from combining work and family roles (e.g., more income), rather than on the problems associated with it (Compas & Williams, 1990; Crosby, 1991; Wanamaker & Bird, 1990). Cognitive restructuring has been found to decrease women's role strain and increase marital adjustment (Anderson & Leslie, 1991; Hochschild, 1989; Wanamaker & Bird, 1990).

Noticeably missing in this list of strategies typically employed by women in dual-earner marriages is holding the husband equally responsible for housework and childcare (Menaghan & Parcel, 1991). As we have seen in an earlier section, husbands are much less involved in the domestic sphere, and the majority of wives have up to now tolerated this. Research suggests that employment yields the most psychological benefits to women when their husbands are active in family work (Hoffman, 1989; Lennon et al., 1991; Ozer, 1995; Spitze, 1995). There is also some evidence that women may be considering this as an option more than before. One study of Mexican American women in working-class occupations found that they preferred their husbands to spend more time in family work rather than play the role of "supermom" themselves (Herrera & DelCampo, 1995).

Institutional Change

The list of coping responses just cited only includes what Hochschild (1989) calls "personal strategies." Personal coping strategies do not help much with the amount of overload and conflict experienced by women in dual-earner households (Ferree, 1987b; Shinn, Wong, Simko, & Ortiz-Torres, 1989). "Public strategies" are needed; these involve dramatic restructuring of the workplace along with the development of government programs that would support working parents.

The Mommy Track. There have already been some changes made in workplaces to accommodate the influx of working mothers into the labor market. Some of these attempts to restructure work to reduce role strain seem likely to reinforce gender inequality, however. One of these is establishment of separate career ladders for mothers, which allow more interruptions and flexibility than traditional ladders (Schwartz, 1989). While this helps companies with recruitment and retention of qualified workers, it perpetuates the gender-based division of labor for domestic work and keeps the organization itself from becoming more nurturing (Ferber & O'Farrell, 1991; Googins, 1991).

Part-Time and Contingent Work. Another change in workplace structure that might have limited impact on working parents' experience of work–family conflict is the spread of part-time and "contingent" work (contingent workers are temporarily employed by an organization). One out of five U.S. workers in 1990 worked less than 35 hours a week, and another 25%–30% of workers fall into the category of doing "contingent" work (Barker, 1993). Most women still work full-time and most are still not contingent workers; still, more women find themselves in these categories than men (Barker, 1993).

Some people choose part-time or contingent jobs to spend more time at home, and others benefit from the extra time at home such jobs grant. For example, Barker (1993) found that part-time professional women were more satisfied with their jobs and with their families than full-time working women. Such jobs also have their drawbacks. Part-timers in Barker's study reported they were excluded from organizational activities and lacked opportunities for skill development. Workers with less education could expect to be even more disadvantaged, since part-time jobs are typically paid at a lower rate than full-time jobs, yield little job security or opportunity for promotion, and offer few if any insurance or retirement benefits (Pleck, 1992).

The trend toward part-time and contingent work appears to be accelerating, more at the instigation of employers than employees. One-fourth of part-time employees wish they could work full-time (Pleck, 1992). Companies can save substantial amounts of money and increase their flexibility through hiring workers who do not retain the same rights and privileges as full-time workers.

Home-Based Employment. Home-based employment for women is another policy that has been proposed as a solution to women's work–family role strain, but it also tends to maintain gender differences by not challenging women's traditional responsibility for domestic work. While women doing home-based work often appreciate the independence of home-based employment and report lower levels of work–family role strain, they also report social isolation, reduced career opportunities, and loss of credibility as wage earners (Christensen, 1987; Silver, 1993; Silver & Goldscheider, 1994). They earn lower incomes, have less income stability, and enjoy fewer employee benefits than other women workers and men in home-based employment (Gringeri, 1995; Rowe et al., 1992).

Women who work out of their homes adapt their employment to family demands more than men do—working fewer hours and not claiming separate work space in the home (Rowe & Bentley, 1992). They also perform more housework and childcare than other women workers or male home-based workers (Silver, 1993; Silver & Goldscheider, 1994). While women often enter home-based employment so they can remain responsible for housework and care for their own children, home-based employment does not always allow them to do that. Over one-third (38%) of female home-based workers report depending on others to care for their children, and the remainder say they are forced to restrict their work time to hours when children are asleep or in school (Heck, 1992; Rowe et al., 1992). When stressed, one-fourth of female full-time home-based workers hire help with housework (Winter, Puspitawati, Heck, & Stafford, 1993).

Flextime. Many employers offer workers the opportunity to arrive at and depart from work according to their own needs within a 2-hour band, as long as they still put in the requisite number of hours (referred to as "flextime"). Between 31% and 57% of companies offer this option (Christensen & Staines, 1990; Galinsky et al., 1991; McNeely & Fogarty, 1988; Raabe & Gessner, 1988; Seyler, Monroe, & Garland, 1995; Society for Human Resource Management, 1992). In 1985, 12% of employees had a formal right to flextime (Mellor, 1986). The Families and Work Institute's 1992 survey of employees found that 44% of employed

parents could work less 1 day and make it up later and 27% could set their own start and end times (Galinsky & Bond, 1996). There are gender differences in access to and use of flextime. Some studies have found that men have greater flexibility in scheduling (Galinsky & Bond, 1996; Mellor, 1996), but it is women who tend to use flextime for the purposes of meeting family responsibilities, particularly childcare (Rothman & Marks, 1987).

Although there is evidence that flextime improves worker morale, productivity, and performance (by reducing tardiness, absenteeism, and turnover) (Christensen & Staines, 1990; Gonyea & Googins, 1992; Rothman & Marks, 1987), recent studies suggest that flextime does not significantly reduce work–family role strain (Nelson, Quick, Hitt, & Moesel, 1990; Shinn et al., 1989). It has been suggested that flextime by itself is not a dramatic enough change in workplace policy to substantially help individuals balance family and work roles (Presser, 1989; Rothman & Marks, 1987).

Unpaid Family Leave. Other workplace programs that are often mentioned as helping individuals balance work and family roles also promise to have limited impact in their present form. One example is unpaid family leave at childbirth. Government statistics indicate that in 1989–1990, 31% of women workers in private companies had access to unpaid maternity leave, while 16% of men had access to unpaid paternity leave (Grossman, 1992). The 1993 Family and Medical Leave Act increased this coverage substantially, but exclusions in the legislation prevent all parents from being covered. For example, almost one-third of American women and over one-fourth of men work for companies with fewer than 25 employees, and these companies can prohibit workers from taking leave, according to the law. Workers in larger companies may not be covered if their work is considered crucial to the organization's functioning or if they are contingent workers (Trzcinski, 1994). Moreover, while it is clearly an improvement to have the right to take time off at childbirth or in a family health crisis without worrying about losing one's job, most workers cannot take such leave without suffering severe financial hardship (Burris, 1991; Zedeck & Mosier, 1990).

Dependent Care Assistance. There are changes in employment policy that are more likely than those listed here to have strong positive effects on individuals' ability to combine work and family roles.

One major area of needed policy is assistance to employees in locating and obtaining high-quality, affordable care for children and elders. Concern about dependent care increases workers' stress, and there is evidence that corporate childcare programs reduce absenteeism and tardiness (Galinsky et al., 1991; Goldberg, Greenberger, Hamill, & O'Neil, 1992; Gonyea & Googins, 1992; Lennon et al., 1991).

The numbers of companies offering some type of child-care assistance has risen sharply, from 600 companies in 1982 to 5600 companies in 1990 (Galinsky et al., 1991). Help in locating dependent care may simply take the form of providing information on local openings (Auerbach, 1990), which Galinsky and others (1991) found happened in 54% of the large companies they surveyed. About half of employers participate in the government-sponsored pretax savings plan that allows workers to put aside tax-exempt money for child-care expenses (Society for Human Resource Management, 1992). Some companies go further by helping increase the quality of childcare through financially supporting training of daycare providers and sponsoring their own on-site or near-site facilities, but this involved only 13% of companies in the Families and Work Institute survey (Galinsky et al., 1991). A few employers (an estimated 6%) provide more direct assistance with the expenses of childcare by offering vouchers or discounts that can be used to defray childcare costs (Auerbach, 1990; Galinsky et al., 1991).

The studies reported here tend to include America's largest companies, yet many American workers work for small businesses. When we look at individual's access to childcare benefits, the numbers are quite low. Government surveys from 1989–1990 show that only 1% of workers in companies with fewer than 100 employees and 5% of workers in companies with more than 100 employees had some type of childcare assistance as a company benefit. These numbers are up slightly from 1985 (U.S. Department of Labor, 1989a, 1990).

Evidence suggests that corporate interest in providing dependent care assistance to employees is not dramatically increasing. One study found that human resource professionals, the individuals most in change of developing and implementing corporate policy on this issue, are not strongly supportive of corporate involvement in childcare (Covin & Brush, 1993).

Dramatic improvements in the supply and affordability of childcare for working parents will probably require increased governmental assistance. Childcare is still in short supply—for example, in 1990, there were 9.3 million preschoolers with working parents and only childcare centers slots for one-fourth of them (Hofferth & Deich, 1994). Childcare costs now take up 10%–25% of family budgets in working families, one-third in families below the poverty line (Galinsky et al., 1991). About one-fourth of workers with elder care responsibilities report that paying for elder care causes problems for them (Galinsky & Stein, 1990). It is hard to imagine families being able to afford to pay more for dependent care, yet often the quality of dependent care is not up to the standards professionals recommend. In Sweden, where the quality of childcare is high, parents pay only a small percentage of total costs (13%), while the government pays for the rest (Haas, 1996).

Paid Family Leave. Another major area of workplace policy involves allowing workers paid time off to care for family members when regular arrangements fail or when they otherwise need to be at home (Auerbach, 1990; Galinsky et al., 1991; Raabe & Gessner, 1988). Only about 20% of all private employees, according to a 1989–1990 national survey, are entitled to take personal days off with pay to help with family responsibilities (Grossman, 1992). Paid leave at childbirth is even more rare, with only 2% of women having access to paid maternity leave and only 1% of men having access to paid paternity leave (Grossman, 1992). At least one state (New Jersey) has found a way to offer paid benefits during maternity leave through considering this a temporary disability. Research shows that the availability of outside income allows women to stay home longer on unpaid family leave. Right now, women often return to work after only 6 weeks at home because they cannot afford to forego more wages. Many child experts think this is too soon and recommend paid maternity leave that would eliminate the difficult choices women must make after childbirth about when to return to work (Hyde, 1995; Joesch, 1994).

Research suggests that employers may be amenable to increasing the availability of paid personal leave days (Nelson & Couch, 1990), but the vast majority oppose the concept of voluntarily providing longer paid parental leave, just as they once vigorously opposed government-mandated unpaid family leave (Society for Human Resource Management, 1992). Government mandates may be the only way to bring about paid family leave (Aldous, 1990).

Shorter Standard Work Weeks. Research shows that the likelihood of role strain increases with work hours (Galinsky et al., 1991; Goldberg et al., 1992). Work time in the United States has increased 15% since the mid-1970s (Bailyn, 1993). Many employees regularly work overtime—37% of men and 13% of women work 50 or more hours a week (Galinsky et al., 1991). Workers who have to work extended hours are more likely to report work–family interference than other workers (Hughes et al., 1992). Elimination of overtime would therefore likely help employees balance family and work roles.

Even a regular 40-hour week can cause stress. One half of full-time working mothers and two-thirds of working fathers say they would prefer working fewer hours so they could spend more time with their families (Moen & Dempster-McClain, 1987). A 30-hour work week would probably significantly reduce role strain and improve family life, since the studies cited here often show that part-time employment has positive benefits for individuals and families. A shorter work week, however, would not help families in the long run if workers' future chances for advancement, pay levels, and benefit levels were shortchanged. The only way to ensure that working less than a 40-hour work week will not hurt an individual's job chances is to make a 30-hour work week the standard for all workers, regardless of family status.

Supervisor Training. One of the most important sources of work–family problems is an unsympathetic supervisor (Galinsky & Stein, 1990; Hoffman, 1989; National Council of Jewish Women, 1987; Nelson & Couch, 1990; Spitze, 1991). Unsupportive supervisors can keep employees from taking advantage of the family benefits that exist (Kamerman & Kahn, 1987; Piotrowski, Hughes, Kessler-Sklar, Pleck, & Staines, 1993; Raabe & Gessner, 1988). Glass and Estes (1996) found that an unsupportive supervisor was associated with women exiting the labor force after childbirth. Over one-fourth of employees responsible for elder care said their supervisors made it more difficult for them (Scharlach, 1994). One worker explained how this was: "All the boss cares about is work, work, work; he never cares about how tired I am from taking care of my mother and how hard it is for me" (Scharlach, 1994, p. 30). When a national sample of two-parent working families were asked what workplace changes would improve their quality of life while maintaining or improving their productivity, the majority mentioned training supervisors to be more responsive to workers' family needs (Galinsky & Stein, 1990).

Supervisor support for workers' family responsibilities involves realizing that family issues can affect job performance, being knowledgeable about company policies that help families, and being flexible when family problems occur (Galinsky & Stein, 1990). Only a few corporations provide training to managers and supervisors on work and family issues (Galinsky et al., 1991).

Counseling and Educational Programs. The last major category of work–family support involves helping workers deal with work–family stress through counseling services, support groups, newsletters, and educational seminars (Galinsky et al., 1991; McNeely & Fogarty, 1988; Raabe & Gessner, 1988). Employees often wish they had more educational opportunities at work. One study of employees responsible for elder care found that 40% or more wanted workshops, lectures, articles, and counseling; 93% were even willing to pay all or some of the costs involved (Scharlach, 1994).

A large number of companies offer family counseling that can be used to help resolve work–family problems, but fewer companies confront work–family issues more directly, for example, in the form of seminars (McNeely & Fogarty, 1988; Nelson & Couch, 1990). The Family and Work Institute's study of large Fortune 1000 companies found that one-fourth offered work–family seminars, 5% offered work–family support groups, and 3% published work–family handbooks (Galinsky et al., 1991).

Improvement in Job Conditions, Including Pay. While specific work–family programs would probably reduce the incidence of stress and role strain for workers, Galinsky and others (1993) conclude from their national study of workers that improvements in work quality and work conditions would likely have as much or more positive affects on individuals' ability to balance work and family roles. Parents themselves are aware of this connection, as revealed in Googin's (1991) study where parents named improved job conditions as the most popular solution for solving work–family balancing problems.

Job conditions that are relevant to workers' balancing work and family roles include workload, job autonomy, work schedule control, social relationships at work, pay, adequate health coverage, and job security (Galinsky et al., 1991, 1993; MacDermid & Targ, 1995). Of these conditions, parents themselves are most likely to single out higher pay as the one aspect of their jobs that would improve quality of family life while maintaining or improving their work productivity (Galinsky & Stein, 1990). Aldous (1990) suggests that higher wages would reduce stress and help families pay for the kinds of services that would help them balance work and family roles.

Determinants of Companies' Adoption of Family-Friendly Policies

Several studies explore under what circumstances companies develop work–family policies. Some focus on organizational characteristics associated with "family-friendliness." Others look at companies' motivations for developing family benefits, which include responding to pressure put on them by external agents of change (e.g., unions and government). The process by which company culture is changed to become more supportive of workers' family lives is also beginning to come under researchers' scrutiny.

Organizational Characteristics. Companies are more likely to develop family benefits for employees when there are a large number of women employees and when employees are younger—in both cases there is a large population of employees at risk for role strain (Auerbach, 1990; Bowen & Orthner, 1991; Galinsky et al., 1991; Seyler et al., 1995). Family-friendly companies also tend to have a high-level "champion" who pushes for change, sometimes even a woman in management (Galinsky et al., 1991; Kamerman & Kahn, 1987). Companies that already offer fairly generous benefits to their employees are more likely to confirm their greater sense of social responsibility by extending this list to include work and family programs (Auerbach, 1990; Galinsky et al., 1991; Kamerman & Kahn, 1987). There also seems to be a tendency for larger corporations to be interested in work and family issues (Fogarty & McNeely, 1988; Galinsky et al., 1991; Kamerman & Kahn, 1987; Liebig, 1993). This may be because larger companies can better absorb program costs or because they have larger human resource departments to help the company keep in touch with demographic trends and employee needs.

Motivations for Change. When asked more specifically why they developed work-family programs and policies, family-friendly companies' motivations tend to reflect a concern for economic profit, rather than a more general regard for the quality of workers' family lives. A desire to recruit and retain valued employees usually is named as the primary motivation (Galinsky et al., 1991; Kamerman & Kahn, 1987; Nelson & Couch, 1990). Improvement in morale and job satisfaction that carries over to enhanced productivity is also often mentioned, as is a desire to reduce tardiness, absenteeism, and unproductive work time spent worrying about dependents (Galinsky et al., 1991).

Companies are sometimes motivated to change because of pressures put on them by external agents, like unions. The U.S. Department of Labor's (1992) study of collective bargaining agreements covering 1000 or more workers in 1990 found that half included one or more work-family provisions, with maternity leave being the most common. McNeely and Fogarty (1988) found that the extent of unionization was positively related to company receptiveness to work–family programs, and York (1993) presents evidence that unionized workers are more likely than the nonunionized to have access to parental leave. Unions seem more likely to put work–family issues on the bargaining agenda if they serve workers in the public sector or in service jobs and if they have significant numbers of female leaders and staff at both local and national levels (Morgan & Milliken, 1982; York, 1993).

American unions appear to be increasingly active in the work–family area, especially in trying to win more family leave and dependent care benefits (York, 1993). York (1993) maintains, however, that unions' efforts reflect pragmatic rather than ideological motives. Union membership has decreased, as big manufacturing concerns have scaled down workforces or moved abroad. Labor organizers have attempted to reach more female employees by offering them contracts that feature family benefits. Evidence that women are the target for union efforts in bargaining for work–family

benefits is shown by the fact that only 8% of collective bargaining contracts contain any provisions that make parental leave available to men (U.S. Department of Labor, 1992). Male labor union leaders are usually not interested in challenging the notion of women's and men's domination of separate spheres and typically oppose substantial changes in the scheduling of work. Such changes, in turn, would acknowledge the permeability of the boundaries between work and family and would make combining work and family roles easier for men as well as women (e.g., home-based work and reductions in work hours) (Cook, 1993; Martin, Courage, Godbey, Seymour, & Tate, 1993).

American labor unions have played important leadership roles in political coalitions that have organized to change government policy in the area of work and family (Cowell, 1993). The policies they have most visibly argued for include federally and state-mandated parental leave and increased childcare subsidies for working parents (Michaels, 1995; York, 1993). A cross-national study of nine industrialized nations (including the United States) found that countries with strong unions were more likely to have government-mandated programs that forced companies to adopt policies that would allow individuals to combine work and family roles (Rosenfeld & Birkelund, 1995).

Most European countries have government-mandated programs that force companies to take into account the family responsibilities of employees (Wolcott & Glezer, 1995). The most common type of government involvement mandates employees' rights to take family leave with pay. Sweden's policy is one of the most generous, granting parents up to a full year of paid leave after childbirth with substantial pay compensation, as well as 60 days off per year with pay to take care of sick child and 10 days off for fathers immediately after childbirth (Haas, 1996). Most European countries offer paid family leave and require that men be given access and encouragement to take advantage of leave policies (Ditch, Barnes, Bradshaw, Commaille, & Eardley, 1994). Some company officials in the United States have suggested that they could offer more programs of this type if the government would provide them tax incentives or grants for doing so (Society for Human Resource Management, 1992). Such incentives might work better than mandates in a country like the United States, where resentment against government intrusion is strong. Government policies to promote work–family linkages promise to have positive effects on company attitudes. A cross-national study by Hogg and Harker (1992) found that "government commitment to work–family issues positively encourages employers to become more involved" (p. v).

Another important way governments can help promote work–family well-being is through the passage and vigorous enforcement of legislation that grants women higher pay, particularly equal pay for comparable worth. Sweden's unions and government have been strong advocates of pay equity for women, and this has resulted in women's earnings being closer to men's than anywhere else in the world and to the elimination of poverty among single mother-headed households (Haas, 1996).

Governments can promote positive work–family linkages in other ways, without encroaching on the traditional rights of employers to dictate the conditions of work. European governments are very actively involved in increasing the supply of childcare places, reducing the costs of childcare to parents by subsidizing childcare and early preschools, and improving the quality of childcare through provider training and regulation (Ditch et al., 1994). Some countries have made efforts to help families with elder care as well, in the form of subsidizing home-based care and offering high-quality residential care for those who cannot live at home (Ditch et al., 1994).

Dynamics of Organizational Change. Recognition of work–family issues as an economic issue is typically the first step in companies' evolution toward being considerate of their workers' family lives (Galinsky et al., 1991; Gonyea & Googins, 1992). Research by the Families and Work Institute suggests that companies go through four stages on their way to becoming family-friendly (Galinsky et al., 1991).

In *pre-stage I*, companies are barely aware of work–family issues and have few programs. The programs that might help families, like flextime or part-time work, are actually designed to help companies deal with energy or commuting problems or are used to scale down the labor force. About one-third of American Fortune 500 companies fit in this stage.

Almost half (46%) of the companies in the Families and Work Institute survey were in the first stage of development toward being more family-friendly, with childcare policies aimed at women. In *stage I*, companies become concerned about childcare because they see problems with childcare having a negative impact on female employees' productivity. A self-study is conducted to investigate these problems in more depth, engineered by management or an appointed task force. An on-site daycare center is often found to be the obvious solution to workers' problems with childcare, but this is usually rejected by most employers as too expensive and disruptive. They then elect to offer some assistance, like information and referral or perhaps greater flextime, so parents can use outside childcare providers with less difficulty.

In *stage II*, companies begin to consider a broader range of work–family issues in addition to childcare, usually because they have become more aware of the shrinking size of the male labor force and the need to recruit and retain more women workers. Companies' awareness of these issues comes about when work–family concerns achieve a high level of visibility outside the company (e.g., through the mass media) (Milliken, Dutton, & Beyer, 1990). About one-fifth (19%) of companies are in *stage II* (Galinsky et al., 1991). At this point, work–family issues have the attention of senior level decision makers, and work–family programs and new initiatives usually come under the responsibility of an individual or office on a part-time or full-time basis. A more integrated approach to work and family issues is developed, which might involve a review and reformulation of existing policies and the establishment of new programs. Managers receive special training so programs will be implemented successfully.

By *stage III*, companies are in the process of transforming their entire company culture to be more responsive to workers' family responsibilities, through changing the overall goal and mission of the company. Only 2% of companies were found to be in this stage in the Families and Work Institute study. At this point, managers realize that every employee at some time during their lives will experience work–family conflict. Such companies also understand how family-friendly policies, if used mainly by women, can reinforce gender inequity. They link work–family programs with efforts to improve women's potential for advancement within the organization and actively demonstrate to employees that use of family programs will not have harmful effects on promotion or job security. Managers play a crucial role in this process—they receive special training and are encouraged to be role models in their own use of work–family benefits. Stage III companies also become active in the larger community in helping to promote work–family issues and improve the supply of services for dependent care (Galinsky et al., 1991).

Management expert Lotte Bailyn (1993) explores in more detail what life in a stage III company would be like, and she makes a strong case that workplace practices and policies need to be totally transformed in three fundamental ways. First, companies must highly prioritize sensitivity to the personal and family needs of individual employees and be willing to adapt work to this new perspective. The sensitivity that Bailyn advocates is of a different character than is seen now in work organizations, which either offer ad hoc accommodations to a few valued workers who need some slack temporarily to manage family responsibilities or formal programs that no one dares take advantage of because to do so would send the wrong message about the worker's commitment to the company. The sensitivity Bailyn advocates gives more consideration to the needs of the family than to the needs of the workplace. Lambert (1993) maintains that most companies prefer to adopt work–family policies that give more consideration to the workplace than the family—for example, flextime and childcare subsidies ensure that parents spend more time at work than at home. Instead, companies could be looking at policies that have a different focus—how to maximize the amount of time parents spend at home rather than at work (e.g., with paid leave or home-based work). Both Bailyn and Lambert emphasize that companies must be more actively involved in identifying how job and organizational conditions create or exacerbate employees' difficulties in combining work and family life. Bailyn maintains that family issues can be viewed as opportunities for rethinking how work can be restructured, for the benefit of both the employee *and* the employer.

Individuals often dare not take advantage of formal work–family support programs because corporations are based on the assumption that "visible time at work" (Bailyn, 1993, p. 68) and "intense and sustained involvement in work" (Lambert, 1993, p. 240) guarantee productivity and profitability. Lambert (1993) cites research that shows little correlation between hours of work and quality of work performed. This relates to Bailyn's second recommendation for change, which is to completely abolish the idea that visible time at work is necessary for productivity within work organizations. Many companies do not trust workers to do their work unless supervisors can keep an eye on them, when in fact most workers have a high amount of commitment and loyalty to their organizations (Galinsky et al., 1993). Bailyn recommends that management set goals for workers, as well as benchmarks of accountability, but leave how to accomplish these goals up to the workers themselves. She believes that increased autonomy at work will improve motivation, productivity, psychological well-being, and family well-being.

This recommendation for enhancement of worker autonomy seems to fit in with an ongoing trend in corporations to rely on "high involvement team approaches to managing work" (Crouter & Manke, 1994, p. 122). Crouter and Manke are not so sure that this approach has only positive benefits; they point out that such work is more complex and challenging but that this can cause stress that might spillover to families. Lambert (1993), however, maintains that if work group norms follow the company's lead in terms of prioritizing personal and family concerns, coworkers will help individual workers in balancing work and family roles. The importance of the work group for supporting working parents has been found in research in Sweden, where men are more likely to take parental leave when their workmates are positive toward the concept (Haas, 1992).

The third basic change Bailyn (1993) feels is essential for workers to maintain a harmonious balance between employment and family roles is for work organizations to develop multiple career paths and ways of defining what it means to be a "success." Currently, to do well in an organization (in terms of acquiring higher wages, greater prestige,

and better fringe benefits), individuals must move up a management ladder, even if their interests and strengths lie in doing more of the basic work of the organization. The Families and Work Institute surveyed employees in several companies and found that between one-fourth to two-thirds believe there was only one path for success within their corporate cultures (Schwartz, 1994). Bailyn (1993) maintains organizations would benefit if they would place value on individuals working up to the potential of their strengths, rather than placing value only on hierarchical advancement into management. Individuals and families would benefit through enhanced psychological well-being and the enjoyment of intrinsic and extrinsic job rewards.

Gerson (1993) maintains that such fundamental changes in work organization are necessary if we are to see a more even balance between men's and women's responsibility for income-earning and family: "Effective social supports could transform men's family involvement from a latent, incipient possibility to expected, unremarkable behavior" (p. 286). As it stands now, work organizations can powerfully shape men's interest in and opportunities to be involved in family life (Bowen & Orthner, 1991; Haas & Hwang, 1995).

These changes may sound utopian, but Bailyn (1993), Gerson (1993), and Lambert (1993) assert that organizations must pay closer attention to economic, demographic, and social trends and adapt themselves to those trends. If they fail to do so, they will suffer economically through lost productivity, and individuals will suffer emotionally and interpersonally through role stress and role strain.

Future Directions

The study of work–family linkages is now past its infancy. Although research was focused initially on the impact of male unemployment on families, the effects of mothers' employment on children, and the stresses and coping strategies of dual-career couples (Voydanoff, 1988a), current empirical efforts have expanded dramatically beyond these topics. There is a rich and interesting body of literature on how individuals' participation in employment affects family life as well as how their membership in a family influences their job behavior and attitudes. Activities surrounding home maintenance and the care of children and elders are now studied as a form of work, and considerable attention has been paid to the conditions under which such work is shared by family members. The psychological impact of individuals' simultaneous membership in work and family systems has received close scrutiny, and the efficacy of personal and public strategies for coping with multiple roles is beginning to be investigated.

There are several other important trends evident in the

research literature reviewed in this chapter that are worth mentioning. They may be portents of the future or simply characteristic of the most recent era of work–family research.

Researchers have begun to move beyond focusing entirely on individuals' attitudes and behavior and the internal dynamics of families to examining the larger social context of work–family linkages. Changes in society have been found to have a significant impact on individuals' participation in and attitudes toward paid employment and family work. These changes concern labor market structure and employment patterns, as well as trends in marriage, childbearing, divorce, and aging. Researchers are also beginning to study how social beliefs about work, parenting, and gender influence marital dynamics and individuals' involvement in paid and unpaid family work. In addition, company and government policy is increasingly considered as playing an important role in individuals' ability to combine work and family roles. The challenge for the future is to develop and empirically test theoretical models that link individuals' work attitudes and behavior, family dynamics, and changes in social institutions.

Another trend in social science research on families and work is to consider the mutual interdependence between work and family systems. A growing number of investigations look at the effects of family (particularly responsibilities for children and ailing elderly parents) on individuals' employment performance and commitment. It has also become more popular to consider how traditional expectations at work can reduce individuals' opportunities to have satisfactory family lives. The challenge for the future is to design studies and present results in a way that can be used by policy makers interested in developing programs that would help employees achieve their family and work goals.

Social scientists now almost take for granted that the linkages between work and family systems have become gendered. At the societal level, men and women are still expected to have different orientations toward work and family, and the impact of each system on the other is expected to vary depending on the person's sex. Researchers who have tested these assumptions find that gender differences in paid employment and work orientations are actually not substantial and that the gender differences that persist are usually related to structural barriers to equality (e.g., job discrimination, lack of childcare) rather than to biological or psychological predispositions. The challenge for the future is to explore in more detail how structural features of jobs and society influence individuals' family and work roles, regardless of gender.

Researchers have determined that gender differences in attitudes toward and participation in unpaid family work persist and are highly resistant to change. The reasons for this lie in the structure of jobs and in women's disadvantaged labor market position, as well as in the retention of traditional attitudes toward men's and women's roles. But research also suggests that a complete understanding of the domestic division of labor requires study of marital dynamics, including the meanings attached to wives' and husbands' employment, the importance given to role equity in comparison to other marital values, and the negotiations involved in the development of the marital contract for paid and unpaid work. Attention needs to also be paid to how the entire culture and structure of work organizations influence individuals' role preferences and opportunities. The challenge for the future is to develop both quantitative and qualitative research designs that increase understanding of how the division of unpaid family work is constructed by domestic partners and how negotiations are affected by the demands and supports at the workplace.

The research reviewed here suggests that individuals' occupancy of multiple roles (spouse, parent, elder caretaker, employee) has surprisingly positive consequences for psychological well-being. Role overload and conflict between roles certainly exists, but they appear to be due less to multiple role commitments than to the lack of structural supports for what Faye Crosby (1991) calls "juggling." The challenge for the future is to transmit these findings to larger lay audiences, which could help jugglers realize the benefits of their lifestyle and inspire them to work for needed changes in social institutions. We could also pay more attention to learning how better to teach about the practical aspects of managing work and family roles in high school and college (Way & Rossman, 1994).

Early research on families and work focused on white, upper-middle class couples, who had adopted a dual-career lifestyle. In the past 5 years, researchers have begun to study more varied types of families, including those in rural settings and from various ethnic communities. Special attention has also been paid in some studies to the work and family roles of single parents. Some types of families are more likely to be economically disadvantaged, and research suggests that a lack of economic resources and employment in jobs with less attractive rewards and benefits have dramatic impacts on individuals' work behavior and attitudes, their ability to combine work and family roles, and their children's wellbeing. The challenge in the future is for a greater number of researchers to study work and family linkages among all the different types of families that make up the United States to help document the consequences of social and economic conditions on the quality of family life.

Finally, the study of work and family in recent years has been influenced by the development of social theory, particularly gender theory. Specific models have also been proposed, for example, Chow and Bertheide's (1988) "interactive model of system interdependence," Bowen's (1988) "conceptual model of work and family linkages," and Guelkow et al.'s (1991) "model of the stress process for dual-career men and women." A challenge for researchers in the future is to continue the conceptual development, testing, and building of theoretical models of work–family linkages.

References

Ahlander, N. R., & Bahr, K. S. (1995). Beyond drudgery, power, and equity: Toward an expanded discourse on the moral dimensions of housework in families. *Journal of Marriage and the Family, 57,* 54–68.

Aldous, J. (1990). Specification and speculation concerning the politics of workplace family policies. *Journal of Family Issues, 11,* 355–367.

Aldous, J., & Dumon, W. (1991). Family policy in the 80s. In A. Booth (Ed.), *Contemporary families* (pp. 466–481). Minneapolis, MN: National Council on Family Relations.

Alessandri, S. M. (1992). Effects of maternal work status in single-parent families on children's perception of self and family and school achievement. *Journal of Experimental Child Psychology, 54,* 417–433.

Allen, S. M. (1994). Gender differences in spousal caregiving and unmet need for care. *Journal of Gerontology, 94,* 187–195.

Altergott, K. (1988). Work and family: Understanding men's role evaluations. *Lifestyles: Family and Economic Issues, 8,* 181–198.

Anastas, J. W., Gibeau, J. L., & Larson, P. J. (1990). Working families and eldercare: A national perspective on an aging America. *Social Work, 35,* 405–411.

Anderson, E. A., & Leslie, L. A. (1991). Coping with employment and family stress: Employment arrangement and gender differences. *Sex Roles, 24,* 233–237.

Anshensel, C. S., & Pearlin, L. I. (1987). Structural contexts of sex differences in stress. In R. C. Barnett, L. Biener, & G. K. Baruch (Eds.), *Gender and stress* (pp. 75–95). New York: Free Press.

Atkinson, A. M. (1992). Stress levels of family day care providers, mothers employed outside the home, and mothers at home. *Journal of Marriage and the Family, 54,* 379–386.

Auerbach, J. D. (1990). Employer-supported child care as a women-responsive policy. *Journal of Family Issues, 11,* 384–400.

Baca Zinn, M. (1989). Family, race and poverty in the 80s. *Signs–Journal of Women in Culture and Society, 14,* 856–874.

Backett, K. (1987). The negotiation of fatherhood. In C. Lewis & M. O'Brien (Eds.), *Reassessing fatherhood* (pp. 74–90). London: Sage.

Bailyn, L. (1993). *Breaking the mold—women, men, and time in the new corporate world.* New York: Free Press.

Barker, K. (1993). Changing assumptions and contingent solutions: The costs and benefits of women working full- and part-time. *Sex Roles, 28,* 47–71.

Barnes, C. L., Given, B. A., & Given, C. W. (1995). Parent caregivers: A comparison of employed and not employed daughters. *Social Work, 40,* 375–381.

Barnett, R. C., & Baruch, G. K. (1987a). Determinants of fathers' participation in family work. *Journal of Marriage and the Family, 49,* 29–40.

Barnett, R. C., & Baruch, G. K. (1987b). Mother's participation in child care: Patterns and consequences. In F. C. Crosby (Ed.), *Spouse, parent, worker: On gender and multiple roles* (pp. 63–73). New Haven, CT: Yale University Press.

Barnett, R. C., & Baruch, G. K. (1988). Correlates of fathers' participation in family work. In P. Bronstein & C. P. Cowan (Eds.), *Fatherhood today* (pp. 66–78). New York: Wiley.

Barnett, R. C., Marshall, N. L., & Pleck, J. H. (1992). Men's multiple roles and their relation to men's psychological distress. *Journal of Marriage and the Family, 54,* 358–367.

Barry, J. (1987). Women production workers. *American Economic Review, 75,* 262–265.

Baruch, G. K., & Barnett, R. C. (1987). Role quality and psychological well-being. In F. J. Crosby (Ed.), *Spouse, parent, worker* (pp. 63–73). New Haven, CT: Yale University Press.

Baruch, G. K., Beiner, L., & Barnett, R. C. (1987). Women and gender in research on work and family stress. *American Psychologist, 42,* 130–136.

Bellas, M. L. (1992). The effects of marital status and wives' employment on the salaries of faculty men: The (house) wife bonus. *Gender and Society, 6,* 609–622.

Benin, M. H., & Agostinelli, J. (1988). Husbands' and wives' satisfaction with the division of labor. *Journal of Marriage and the Family, 50,* 349–361.

Benin, M. H., & Edwards, D. A. (1990). Adolescents' chores: The difference between dual-earner and single-earner families. *Journal of Marriage and the Family, 52,* 361–373.

Berardo, D. H., Shehan, C. L., & Leslie, G. R. (1987). A residue of tradition: Jobs, careers, and spouses' time in housework. *Journal of Marriage and the Family, 49,* 381–390.

Bergen, E. (1991). The economic context of labor allocation: Implications for gender stratification. *Journal of Family Issues, 12,* 140–158.

Bielby, D. D., & Bielby, W. T. (1988a). She works hard for the money: Household responsibilities and the allocation of work effort. *American Journal of Sociology, 93,* 1031–1059.

Bielby, D. D., & Bielby, W. T. (1988b). Women's and men's commitment to paid work and family—theories, models, and hypotheses. *Women and Work, 3,* 249–263.

Bielby, W. T., & Bielby, D. D. (1989). Family ties: Balancing commitments to work and family in dual earner households. *American Sociological Review, 54,* 776–789.

Björnberg, U. (Ed.). (1992). *European parents in the 1990s.* New Brunswick, NJ: Transaction.

Blair, S. L. (1993). Employment, family, and perceptions of marital quality among husbands and wives. *Journal of Family Issues, 14,* 189–212.

Blair, S. L., & Johnson, M. P. (1992). Wives' perceptions of the fairness of the division of household labor: The intersection of housework and ideology. *Journal of Marriage and the Family, 54,* 57–58.

Blair, S. L., & Lichter, D. T. (1991). Measuring the division of household labor. *Journal of Family Issues, 12,* 91–113.

Blaisure, K. R., & Allen, K. R. (1995). Feminists and the ideology and practice of marital equality. *Journal of Marriage and the Family, 57,* 5–19.

Blee, K. M., & Tickamyer, A. R. (1995). Racial differences in men's attitudes about women's gender roles. *Journal of Marriage and the Family, 57,* 21–30.

Blumstein, P., & Schwartz, P. (1991). Money and ideology—their impact on power and the division of household labor. In R. L. Blumberg (Ed.), *Gender, family and economy* (pp. 261–288). Newbury Park, CA: Sage.

Bogenschneider, K., & Steinberg, L. (1994). Maternal employment and adolescents' academic achievement. *Sociology of Education, 67,* 60–77.

Bolger, N., DeLongis, A., Kessler, R. C., & Wethington, E. (1989). The contagion of stress across multiple roles. *Journal of Marriage and the Family, 51,* 175–183.

Bowen, G. L. (1988). Corporate supports for the family lives of employees. *Family Relations, 37,* 183–188.

Bowen, G. L. (1991). *Navigating the marital journey.* New York: Praeger.

Bowen, G. L., & Orthner, D. K. (1991). Effects of organizational culture on fatherhood. In F. Bozett & S. Hanson (Eds.), *Fatherhood and families in cultural context* (pp. 187–217). New York: Springer.

Brannen, J. (1992). Money, marriage and motherhood. In S. Arber & N. Gilbert (Eds.), *Women and working lives* (pp. 54–70). London: Macmillan.

Brayfield, A. (1995). Juggling jobs and kids. *Journal of Marriage and the Family, 57*, 321–332.

Brett, J. M., & Yogev, S. (1988). Restructuring work for family: How dual-earner couples with children manage. *Journal of Social Behavior and Personality, 3*, 159–174.

Bridges, J. S., & Orza, A. M. (1992). The effects of employment role and motive for employment on the perceptions of mothers. *Sex Roles, 27*, 331–343.

Broman, C. L. (1991). Gender, family roles, and the psychological well-being of blacks. *Journal of Marriage and the Family, 53*, 508–519.

Broman, C. L., Hamilton, V. L., & Hoffman, W. S. (1990). Unemployment and its effects on families: Evidence from a plant closing study. *American Journal of Community Psychology, 18*, 643–659.

Burke, R. J. (1988). Some antecedents and consequences of work-family conflict. *Journal of Social Behavior and Personality, 3*, 287–302.

Burley, K. A. (1995). Family variables as mediators of the relationship between work–family conflict and marital adjustment among dual-career men and women. *The Journal of Social Psychology, 135*, 483–497.

Burris, B. H. (1991). Employed mothers: The impact of class and marital status on the prioritizing of family work. *Social Science Quarterly, 72*, 50–66.

Call, K. T. (1996a). Adolescent work as an "arena of comfort" under conditions of family discomfort. In J. T. Mortimer & M. D. Finch (Eds.), *Adolescents, work, and family* (pp. 129–166). Thousand Oaks, CA: Sage.

Call, K. T. (1996b). The implications of helpfulness for possible selves. In J. T. Mortimer & M. D. Finch (Eds.), *Adolescents, work, and family* (pp. 63–96). Thousand Oaks, CA: Sage.

Callan, V. J. (1987). The personal and marital adjustment of mothers and of voluntarily and involuntarily childless wives. *Journal of Marriage and the Family, 49*, 847–856.

Carlisle, W. (1994). Sharing home responsibilities: Women in dual-career marriages. In C. W. Konek & S. L. Kitch (Eds.), *Women and careers* (pp. 138–152). Thousand Oaks, CA: Sage.

Casey, J. C. & Pitt-Catsouphes, M. (1994). Employed single mothers. *Employee Assistance Quarterly, 9*, 37–53.

Chafetz, J. (1990). *Gender equity.* Beverly Hills, CA: Sage.

Chow, E. N., & Bertheide, C. W. (1988). The interdependence of family and work: A framework for family life education, policy, and practice. *Family Relations, 37*, 23–28.

Christensen, K. E. (1987). Women, families, and home-based employment. In N. Gerstel & H. B. Gross (Eds.), *Families and work* (pp. 478–490). Philadelphia: Temple University Press.

Christensen, K. E., & Staines, G. L. (1990). Flextime: A viable solution to work/family conflict? *Journal of Family Issues, 11*, 455–476.

Cohen, T. (1987). Remaking men. *Journal of Family Issues, 8*, 57–77.

Coleman, L. M., Antonucci, T. C., Adelmann, P. K., & Crohan, S. E. (1987). Social roles in the lives of middle-aged and older black women. *Journal of Marriage and the Family, 49*, 761–771.

Coleman, M. T. (1991). The division of household labor. In R. L. Blumberg (Ed.), *Gender, family, and economy* (pp. 245–260). Newbury Park, CA: Sage.

Coltrane, S. (1989). Household labor and the routine production of gender. *Social Problems, 36*, 473–490.

Coltrane, S., & Ishii-Kuntz, M. (1992). Men's housework: A life course perspective. *Journal of Marriage and the Family, 54*, 43–57.

Compas, B. E., & Williams, R. A. (1990). Stress, coping, and adjustment in mothers and young adolescents in single- and two-parent families. *American Journal of Community Psychology, 18*, 525–545.

Conger, R. D., Elder, G.H., Lorenz, F. O., Conger, K. L., Simons, R. L., Whitbeck, L. B., Huck, S., & Melby, J. N. (1990). Linking economic hardship to marital quality and instability. *Journal of Marriage and the Family, 52*, 643–656.

Cook, A. H. (1993). Comments. In D. S. Cobble (Ed.), *Women and unions* (pp. 148–156). Ithaca, NY: ILR Press.

Cooney, T. M., & Uhlenberg, P. (1991). Changes in work–family connections among highly educated men and women. *Journal of Family Issues, 12*, 69–90.

Costello, C., & Krimgold, B. K. (1996). *The American woman 1996–97.* New York: Norton.

Cournoyer, R. J., & Mahalik, J. R. (1995). Cross-sectional study of gender role conflict examining college-aged and middle-aged men. *Journal of Consulting Psychology, 42*, 11–19.

Coverman, S., & Sheley, J. F. (1986). Change in men's housework and child care time, 1965–1975. *Journal of Marriage and the Family, 48*, 413–422.

Covin, T. J., & Brush, C. C. (1993). A comparison of student and human resource professional attitudes toward work and family issues. *Group and Organization Management, 18*, 29–49.

Cowan, C. P., & Cowan, P. A. (1987). Men's involvement in parenthood. In P. Berman & F. Pederson (Eds.), *Men's transitions to parenthood* (pp. 145–174). Hillsdale, NJ: Erlbaum.

Cowell, S. (1993). Family policy—a union approach. In D.S. Cobble (Ed.), *Women and unions* (pp. 115–128). Ithaca, NY: ILR Press.

Crosby, F. J. (1991). *Juggling—the unexpected advantages of balancing career and home for women and their families.* New York: Free Press.

Crouter, A. C., & Manke, G. (1994). The changing American workplace—implications for individuals and families. *Family Relations, 43*, 117–124.

Crouter, A. C., Perry-Jenkins, M., Huston, T. L., & McHale, S. M. (1987). Processes underlying father involvement in dual-earner and single-earner families. *Developmental Psychology, 23*, 431–440.

Dancer, L. S., & Gilbert, L. A. (1993). Spouses' family work participation and its relation to wives' occupational level. *Sex Roles, 28*, 127–145.

Daniels, A. K. (1987). The hidden work of constructing class and community: Women volunteer leaders in social philanthropy. In N. Gerstel & H. B. Gross (Eds.), *Families and work* (pp. 220–235). Philadelphia: Temple University Press.

Daniels, P., & Weingarten, K. (1988). The fatherhood clock. In P. Bronstein & C. P. Cowan (Eds.), *Fatherhood today* (pp. 36–52). New York: Wiley.

Darling-Fisher, C. S., & Tiedje, L. B. (1990). The impact of maternal employment characteristics on fathers' participation in child care. *Family Relations, 39*, 20–26.

DeStefano, L., & Colasanto, D. (1990, February). Unlike 1975, today most Americans think men have it better. *The Gallup Poll Monthly*, 25–36.

DeVault, M. L. (1987). Doing housework: Feeding and family life. In N. Gerstel & H. Gross (Eds.), *Families and Work* (pp. 178–191). Philadelphia: Temple University Press.

DeVault, M. L. (1990). Conflict over housework. *Research in Social Movements, Conflict and Change, 12*, 189–202.

Ditch, J., Barnes, H., Bradshaw, J., Commaille, J., & Eardley, T. (1994). *European observatory on national family policies: A synthesis of national family policies.* Keighley, England: University of York.

Dorfman, L. T. (1992). Couples in retirement. In M. Szinovaca, D. J. Ekerdt, & B. H. Vinick (Eds.), *Families and retirement* (pp. 159–173). Newbury Park, CA: Sage.

Dorfman, L. T., & Heckert, D. A. (1988). Egalitarianism in retired rural couples. *Family Relations, 37*, 73–78.

Dwyer, J. W., & Coward, R. T. (1992). Gender, family and long-term care of the elderly. In J. W. Dwyer & R. Coward (Eds.), *Gender, families, and elder care* (pp. 3–17). Newbury Park, CA: Sage.

Dwyer, J. W., & Secombe, K. (1991). Elder care as family labor: The influence of gender and family position. *Journal of Family Issues, 12,* 229–247.

Ehrensaft, D. (1987). *Parenting together.* New York: Free Press.

England, P., & Farkas, G. (1986). *Households, employment and gender.* New York: Aldine.

Ensminger, M. E., & Celentano, D. D. (1988). Unemployment and psychiatric distress. *Social Science Medicine, 27,* 239–247.

Epstein, C. F. (1987). Multiple demands and multiple roles: The conditions of successful management. In F. J. Crosby (Ed.), *Spouse, parent, work: On gender and multiple roles* (pp. 23–39). New Haven, CT: Yale University Press.

Eshleman, J. R. (1994). *The family.* Needham Heights, MA: Allyn & Bacon.

Ettner, S. L. (1995). The impact of "parent care" on female labor supply decisions. *Demography, 32,* 63–80.

Exter, T. (1988). Demographic forecasts: Peak-A-Boo. *Monthly Labor Review, 110,* 63.

Ferber, M. A., & O'Farrell, B. (1991). *Work and family—policies for a changing work force.* Washington, DC: National Academy Press.

Fernandez, J. P. (1989). *Child care and corporate productivity.* Lexington, MA: Health.

Ferree, M. M. (1987a). Family and job for working class women. In N. Gerstel & H. B. Gross (Eds.), *Families and Work* (pp. 289–301). Philadelphia: Temple University Press.

Ferree, M. M. (1987b). The struggles of superwoman. In C. Bose, R. Feldberg, & N. Sokloff (Eds.), *Hidden aspects of women's work* (pp. 161–180). New York: Praeger.

Ferree, M. M. (1991a). Feminism and family research. In A. Booth (Ed.), *Contemporary families* (pp. 103–121). Minneapolis, MN: National Council on Family Relations.

Ferree, M. M. (1991b). The gender division of labor in two-earner marriages: Dimensions of variability and change. *Journal of Family Issues, 12,* 158–180.

Ferree, M. M., & Hess, B. B. (1987). Introduction. In B. B. Hess & M. M. Ferree (Eds.), *Analyzing gender* (pp. 9–30). Newbury Park, CA: Sage.

Finley, N. J. (1989). Theories of family labor as applied to gender differences in caregiving for elderly parents. *Journal of Marriage and the Family, 51,* 79–86.

Finley, N. J., Roberts, D. M., & Banahan, B. (1988). Motivators and inhibitors of attitudes of filial obligation toward aging parents. *Gerontologist, 28,* 73–78.

Folk, K. F., & Beller, A. H. (1993). Part-time work and child care choices for mothers of preschool children. *Journal of Marriage and the Family, 55,* 146–157.

Forthofer, M. S., Markman, H. J., Cox, M., Scott, S., & Kessler, R. C. (1996). Associations between marital distress and work loss in a national sample. *Journal of Marriage and the Family, 58,* 597–605.

Fowlkes, M. R. (1987). The myth of merit and male professional careers: The roles of wives. In N. Gerstel & H. B. Gross (Eds.), *Families and work* (pp. 347–361). Philadelphia: Temple University Press.

Franklin, S. T., Ames, B. D., & King, S. (1994). Acquiring the family eldercare role: Influence on female employment adaptation. *Research on Aging, 16,* 27–42.

Friedman, D. (1987). *Family-supportive policies.* New York: Conference Board.

Frone, M. R., Russell, M., & Cooper, M. L. (1992). Prevalence of work–family conflict. *Journal of Organizational Behavior, 13,* 723–729.

Galinsky, E., & Bond, J. T. (1996). Work and family: The experiences of mothers and fathers in the U.S. labor force. In C. Costello & B. K.

Krimgold (Eds.), *The American woman, 1996–1997* (pp. 79–103). New York: Norton.

Galinsky, E., & Stein, P. (1990). The impact of human resource policies on employers. *Journal of Family Issues, 11,* 368–383.

Galinsky, E., Hughes, D., & David, J. (1990). Trends in corporate family-supportive policies. *Marriage and Family Review, 15,* 75–94.

Galinsky, E., Friedman, D. E., & Hernandez, C. A. (1991). *The corporate reference guide to work–family programs.* New York: Families and Work Institute.

Galinsky, E., Bond, J. T., & Friedman, D. E. (1993). *The changing work-force: Highlights of the national study.* New York: Families and Work Institute.

Garrett, P., Lubeck, S., & Wenk, D. A. (1992). Childbirth and maternal employment. In J. S. Hyde & M. J. Essex (Eds.), *Parental leave and child care* (pp. 24–38). Philadelphia: Temple University Press.

Gerson, K. (1987). How women choose between employment and family: A developmental perspective. In N. Gerstel & H. B. Gross (Eds.), *Families and Work* (pp. 270–288). Philadelphia: Temple University Press.

Gerson, K. (1993). *No man's land—men's changing commitments to family and work.* New York: Basic Books.

Gerstel, N., & Gross, H. B. (1987). Introduction and overview. In N. Gerstel & H. B. Gross (Eds.), *Families and work* (pp. 1–12). Philadelphia: Temple University Press.

Gjerdingen, D. K., & Chaloner, K. (1994). Mothers' experience with household roles and social support during the first post-partum year. *Women and Health, 21,* 57–74.

Glass, J. (1988). Job quits and job changes: The effects of young women's work conditions and family factors. *Gender and Society, 2,* 228–240.

Glass, J. (1990). Impact of occupational segregation on working conditions. *Social Forces, 90,* 779–796.

Glass, J. (1992). Housewives and employed wives: Demographic and attitudinal change, 1972–1986. *Journal of Marriage and the Family, 54,* 559–569.

Glass, J., & Camarigg, V. (1992). Gender, parenthood, and job–family compatibility. *American Journal of Sociology, 98,* 131–151.

Glass, J. L., & Estes, S. B. (1996). Workplace support, child care, and turnover intentions among employed mothers of infants. *Journal of Family Issues, 17,* 317–335.

Glass, J., & Fujimoto, T. (1994). Housework, paid work, and depression among husbands and wives. *Journal of Health and Social Behavior, 35,* 179–191.

Glazer, N. Y. (1988). Overlooked, overworked: Women's unpaid and paid work in the health services "cost crisis." *International Journal of Health Services, 18,* 119–137.

Goldberg, W. A., Greenberger, E., Hamill, S., & O'Neil, R. (1992). Role demands in the lives of employed single mothers with preschoolers. *Journal of Family Issues, 13,* 312–333.

Goldsmith, E. B., Hoffman, J. J., & Hofacker, C. F. (1993). Insights into the long-term effects of parents' careers on reported parent–offspring closeness. *Journal of Employment Counseling, 30,* 50–54.

Gonyea, J. G. (1993). Family responsibilities and family-oriented policies: Assessing the impact on the workplace. *Employee Assistance Quarterly, 9,* 1–29.

Gonyea, J. G., & Googins, B. K. (1992). Linking the worlds of work and family: Beyond the productivity trap. *Human Resource Management, 31,* 209–226.

Googins, B. K. (1991). *Work/family conflicts.* New York: Auburn House.

Gottfried, A. E., & Gottfried, A. W. (1988). *Maternal employment and child development.* New York: Plenum.

Gottlieb, B. H., Kelloway, E. K., & Fraboni, M. (1994). Aspects of eldercare that place employees at risk. *The Gerontologist, 34,* 815–821.

Gove, W., & Zeiss, C. (1987). Multiple roles and happiness. In F. J. Crosby

(Ed.), *Spouse, parent, worker* (pp. 125–137). New Haven, CT: Yale University Press.

Grant, L., Simpson, L. A., Rong, X. L., & Peters-Golden, H. (1990). Gender, parenthood, and work hours of physicians. *Journal of Marriage and the Family, 52,* 39–50.

Greenberger, E., & O'Neil, R. (1990). Parents' concerns about their child's development: Implications for fathers' and mothers' well-being and attitudes toward work. *Journal of Marriage and the Family, 52,* 621–635.

Greenberger, E., Goldberg, W. A., Hamill, S., O'Neil, R., & Payne, C. K. (1989). Contributions of a supportive work environment to parents' well-being and orientation to work. *American Journal of Community Psychology, 17,* 755–783.

Greenberger, E., Goldberg, W. A., Crawford, T., & Granger, J. (1992). Beliefs about the consequences of maternal employment for children. *Psychology of Women Quarterly, 12,* 35–59.

Greenberger, E., O'Neil, R., & Nagel, S. K. (1994). Linking workplace and homeplace: Relations between the nature of adults' work and their parenting behaviors. *Developmental Psychology, 30,* 990–1002.

Greenhaus, J. H. (1988). The intersection of work and family roles: Individual, interpersonal, and organizational issues. *Journal of Social Behavior and Personality, 3,* 23–44.

Greenstein, T. N. (1990). Marital disruption and the employment of married women. *Journal of Marriage and the Family, 52,* 657–676.

Greenstein, T. N. (1995). Gender ideology, marital disruption, and the employment of married women. *Journal of Marriage and the Family, 57,* 31–42.

Greenstein, T. N. (1996). Husbands' participation in domestic labor. *Journal of Marriage and the Family, 58,* 585–595.

Grimm-Thomas, K., & Perry-Jenkins, M. (1994). All in a day's work: Job experiences, self-esteem, and fathering in working-class families. *Family Relations, 43,* 174–181. Gringeri, C. E. (1995). Flexibility, the family ethic, and rural home-based work. *Affilia, 10,* 70–86.

Grossman, F. K., Pollack, W. S., & Golding, E. (1988). Fathers and children: Predicting the quality and quantity of fathering. *Developmental Psychology, 24,* 82–91.

Grossman, G. M. (1992). U.S. workers receive a wide range of employee benefits. *Monthly Labor Review, 115,* 36–39.

Guelkow, M. B., Bird, G. W., & Koball, E. H. (1991). An exploratory path analysis of the stress process of dual-career men and women. *Journal of Marriage and the Family, 53,* 151–164.

Gunter, B. G., & Gunter, N. C. (1991). Inequities in household labor. *Journal of Social Behavior and Personality, 6,* 559–572.

Haas, L. (1986). Wives' orientation toward breadwinning: Sweden and the United States. *Journal of Family Issues, 7,* 358–381.

Haas, L. (1992). *Equal parenthood and social policy.* Albany, NY: State University of New York Press.

Haas, L. (1996). Family policy in Sweden. *Journal of Family and Economic Issues, 17,* 47–92.

Haas, L., & Hwang, P. (1995). Company culture and men's usage of family leave benefits in Sweden. *Family Relations, 44,* 28–36.

Hall, D. T., & Richter, J. (1988). Balancing work life and home life: What can organizations do to help? *The Academy of Management Executive, 2,* 213–223.

Hall, L. D., Walker, A. J., & Acock, A. C. (1995). Gender and family work in one-parent households. *Journal of Marriage and the Family, 57,* 685–692.

Hanson, S.L., & Ooms, T. (1991). The economic costs and rewards of two-earner, two-parent families. *Journal of Marriage and the Family, 53,* 622–634.

Hanson, S. L., & Sloane, D. M. (1992). Young children and job satisfaction. *Journal of Marriage and the Family, 54,* 799–811.

Hardesty, C., & Bokemeier, J. (1989). Finding time and making do: Distribution of household labor in nonmetropolitan marriages. *Journal of Marriage and the Family, 51,* 253–267.

Hawkins, A. J., Marshall, C. M., & Meiners, K. M. (1995). Exploring wives' sense of fairness about family work. *Journal of Family Issues, 16,* 693–721.

Hayghe, H. V. (1988). Employers and child care. *Monthly Labor Review, 111,* 38–43.

Hayghe, H. V. (1990). Family members in the work force. *Monthly Labor Review, 113,* 14–19.

Hayghe, H. V., & Haugen, S. E. (1987). A profile of husbands in today's labor market. *Monthly Labor Review, 110,* 12–17.

Heck, R. K. Z. (1992). The effects of children on the major dimensions of home-based employment. *Journal of Family and Economic Issues, 13,* 315–346.

Herrera, E. S., & DelCampo, R. L. (1995). Beyond the superwoman syndrome: Work satisfaction and family functioning among working-class Mexican-American women. *Hispanic Journal of Behavioral Sciences, 17,* 49–60.

Hertz, R. (1986). *More equal than others—women and men in dual-career marriages.* Berkeley: University of California Press.

Herz, D. E., & Wootton, B. H. (1996). Women in the workforce. In C. Costello & B. K. Krimgold (Eds.), *The American woman 1996–97* (pp. 44–78). New York: Norton.

Higgins, C. A., & Duxbury, L. E. (1992). Work–family conflict: A comparison of dual-career and traditional-career men. *Journal of Organizational Behavior, 13,* 89–111.

Hill, M. (1988). Marital stability and spouses' shared time. *Journal of Family Issues, 9,* 427–451.

Hilton, J. M., & Haldeman, V. A. (1991). Gender differences in the performance of household tasks by adults and children in single-parent and two-parent, two-earner families. *Journal of Family Issues, 12,* 114–130.

Hochschild, A. (1989). *The second shift: Working parents and the revolution at home.* New York: Viking.

Hodson, R. (1989). Gender differences in job satisfaction. *Sociological Quarterly, 30,* 385–399.

Hofferth, S. L., & Deich, S. G. (1994). Recent U.S. child care and family legislation in comparative perspective. *Journal of Family Issues, 15,* 424–448.

Hoffman, L. W. (1989). Effects of maternal employment in the two-parent family. *American Psychologist, 44,* 283–292.

Hoffman, L. W., & Kloska, D. D. (1995). Parents' gender-based attitudes toward marital roles and child rearing. *Sex Roles, 32,* 273–295.

Hogg, C., & Harker, L. (1992). *The family friendly employer—examples from Europe.* New York: Families and Work Institute.

Holt, H., & Thaulow, I. (1995). *Family-friendly workplaces.* Copenhagen, Denmark: Ministry of Social Affairs.

Hood, J. C. (1986). The provider role: Its meaning and measurement. *Journal of Marriage and the Family, 48,* 349–359.

Hossain, Z., & Roppnarine, J. L. (1993). Division of household labor and child care in dual-earner African-American families with infants. *Sex Roles, 29,* 571–583.

Howe, W. J., & Parks, W. (1989). Labor market completes sixth year of expansion in 1988. *Monthly Labor Review, 110,* 3–12.

Hughes, D., Galinsky, E., & Morris, A. (1992). The effects of job characteristics on marital quality. *Journal of Marriage and the Family, 54,* 31–42.

Hunt, J. G., & Hunt, L. L. (1987). Male resistance to role symmetry in dual-earner households: Three alternative explanations. In N. Gerstel & H. B. Gross (Eds.), *Families and work* (pp. 192–203). Philadelphia: Temple University Press.

Hyde, J. S. (1995). Women and maternity leave: Empirical data and public policy. *Psychology of Women Quarterly, 19,* 299–313.

Ishii-Kuntz, M. (1994). Work and family life. *Journal of Family Issues, 15,* 490–506.

Ishii-Kuntz, M., & Coltrane, S. (1992a). Predicting the share of household labor. *Sociological Perspectives, 35,* 629–647.

Ishii-Kuntz, M., & Coltrane, S. (1992b). Stepparenting and household labor. *Journal of Family Issues, 13,* 215–233.

Jackson, A. P. (1993). Black, single, working mothers in poverty. *Social Work, 38,* 26–34.

Joesch, J. M. (1994). Children and the timing of women's paid work after childbirth. *Journal of Marriage and the Family, 56,* 429–440.

John, D., Shelton, B. A., & Luschen, K. (1995). Race, ethnicity, gender and perception of fairness. *Journal of Family Issues, 16,* 357–379.

Jump, T. L., & Haas, L. (1987). Fathers in transition: Dual-career fathers participating in child care. In M. Kimmel (Ed.), *Changing men—new directions in research on men and masculinity* (pp. 98–114). Newbury Park, CA: Sage.

Kalleberg, A. L., & Rosenfeld, R. A. (1990). Work in the family and in the labor market: A cross-national, reciprocal analysis. *Journal of Marriage and the Family, 52,* 331–346.

Kamerman, S. B., & Kahn, A. J. (1987). *The responsive workplace.* New York: Columbia University Press.

Kamo, Y. (1988). Determinants of the household division of labor. *Journal of Family Issues, 9,* 177–200.

Kamo, Y. (1991). A nonlinear effect of the number of children on the division of household labor. *Sociological Perspectives, 34,* 215–218.

Kane, E.W., & Sanchez, L. (1994). Family status and criticism of gender inequality at home and at work. *Social Forces, 72,* 1079–1102.

Kessler-Harris, A. (1987). The debate over women in the workplace. In N. Gerstel & H. B. Gross (Eds.), *Families and work* (pp. 520–539). Philadelphia: Temple University Press.

Killien, M., & Brown, M. A. (1987). Work and family roles of women: Sources of stress and coping strategies. *Health Care for Women International, 8,* 169–184.

Kimmel, M. (1987). Rethinking "masculinity." In M. Kimmel (Ed.), *Changing men—new directions in research on men and masculinity* (pp. 9–24). Newbury Park, CA: Sage.

Kingston, P. W. (1990). Illusions and ignorance about the family-responsive workplace. *Journal of Family Issues, 11,* 438–454.

Kingston, P. W., & Nock, S. L. (1987). Time together among dual-earner couples. *American Sociological Review, 52,* 391–400.

Kline, M., & Cowan, P. A. (1988). Re-thinking the connections among "work" and "family" and well-being. *Journal of Social Behavior and Personality, 3,* 61–90.

Kola, L. A., & Dunkle, R. E. (1988). Eldercare in the workplace. *Social Casework, 69,* 569–574.

Kopasci, R. C. (1991). Limited options for unemployed women. *International Journal of Sociology and Social Policy, 11,* 51–67.

Lamb, M. E. (1987). *The father's role: Cross-cultural perspectives.* Hillsdale, NJ: Erlbaum.

Lamb, M. E., Sternberg, K.L., & Ketterlinus, R. D. (1992). Child care in the United States: The modern era. In M. E. Lamb, K. J. Sternberg, C. P. Hwang, & A. G. Broberg (Eds.), *Child care in context—cross-cultural perspectives* (pp. 207–223). Hillsdale, NJ: Erlbaum.

Lambert, S. J. (1990). Processes linking work and family: A critical review and research agenda. *Human Relations, 43,* 239–257.

Lambert, S. J. (1991). The combined effects of job and family characteristics on the job satisfaction, job involvement, and intrinsic motivation of men and women workers. *Journal of Organizational Behavior, 12,* 341–363.

Lambert, S. J. (1993). Workplace policies as social policy. *Social Service Review, 67,* 237–260.

Landau, J., & Arthur, M. B. (1992). The relationship of marital status, spouse's career status, and gender to salary level. *Sex Roles, 27,* 665–681.

LaRossa, R. (1988). Fatherhood and social change. *Family Relations, 37,* 451–457.

Larson, J. H., Wilson, S. M., & Beley, R. (1994). The impact of job insecurity on marital and family relationships. *Family Relations, 43,* 138–143.

Lawrence, F. C., Draugh, P. S., Tasker, G. E., & Wozniak, P. H. (1987). Sex differentiation in household labor time—a comparison of rural and urban couples. *Sex Roles, 17,* 489–502.

Lechner, V. M. (1991). Predicting future commitment to care for frail parents among employed caregivers. *Journal of Gerontological Social Work, 18,* 69–84.

Lennon, M. C., & Rosenfield, S. (1992). Women and mental health: The interaction of job and family conditions. *Journal of Health and Social Behavior, 33,* 316–327.

Lennon, M. C., & Rosenfield, S. (1994). Relative fairness and the division of housework. *American Journal of Sociology, 100,* 506–531.

Lennon, M. C., Wasserman, G. A., & Allen, R. (1991). Infant care and wives' depressive symptoms. *Women and Health, 17,* 1–23.

Leslie, L. A., Branson, M. P., & Anderson, E. A. (1989). The impact of couples' work profile on husbands' and wives' performance on child-care tasks. *Family Perspective, 22,* 327–344.

Leslie, L. A., Anderson, E. A., & Branson, M. P. (1991). Responsibility for children: The role of gender and employment. *Journal of Family Issues, 12,* 197–210.

Lewis, S., Izraeli, D., & Hootsmans, H. (1992). Dual-earner families—international perspectives. London: Sage.

Lichter, D. T., & Eggebeen, D. J. (1994). The effect of parental employment on child poverty. *Journal of Marriage and the Family, 56,* 633–645.

Lichter, D. T., & Landale, N. S. (1995). Parental work, family structure, and poverty among Latino children. *Journal of Marriage and the Family, 57,* 346–354.

Lichter, D. T., McLaughlin, D. K., Kephart, G., & Landry, D. J. (1992). Race and the retreat from marriage. *American Sociological Review, 57,* 781–799.

Liebig, P. S. (1993). Factors affecting the development of employer-sponsored eldercare programs, implications for employed caregivers. *Journal of Women and Aging, 5,* 59–78.

Liem, R., & Liem, J. H. (1988). Psychological effects of unemployment on workers and their families. *Journal of Social Issues, 44,* 87–105.

Lobel, S. A., & St. Clair, L. (1992). Effects of family responsibilities, gender, and career identity salience on performance outcomes. *Academy of Management Journal, 35,* 1057–1069.

Loomis, L., & Booth, A. (1995). Multigenerational caregiving and well-being. *Journal of Family Issues, 16,* 131–148.

Lorence, J. (1987). A test of "gender" and "job" models of sex differences in job involvement. *Social Forces, 66,* 121–142.

Loscocco, K. A., & Leicht, K. T. (1993). Gender, work–family linkages, and economic success among small business owners. *Journal of Marriage and the Family, 55,* 875–887.

MacDermid, S. M., & Targ, D.H. (1995). A call for greater attention to the role of employers in developing, transforming, and implementing family policies. *Journal of Family and Economic Issues, 16,* 145–170.

MacDermid, S. M., Huston, T.L., & McHale, S. M. (1990). Changes in marriage associated with the transition to parenthood. *Journal of Marriage and the Family, 52,* 475–486.

Madamba, A. B., & DeJong, G. F. (1994). Determinants of white-collar employment: Puerto Rican women in metropolitan New York. *Social Science Quarterly, 75,* 53–66.

Mancini, J. A., & Blieszner, R. (1991). Aging parents and adult children. In A. Booth (Ed.), *Contemporary families* (pp. 249–264). Minneapolis, MN: National Council on Family Relations.

Manke, B., Seery, B. L., Crouter, A. C., & McHale, S. M. (1994). The three corners of domestic labor. *Journal of Marriage and the Family, 56,* 657–668.

Marshall, N. L., & Barnett, R. C. (1993). Work–family strains and gains among two-earner couples. *Journal of Community Psychology, 21,* 64–78.

Marsiglio, W. (1991). Paternal engagement activities with minor children. *Journal of Marriage and the Family, 53,* 973–986.

Marsiglio, W. (1993). Contemporary scholarship on fatherhood. *Journal of Family Issues, 14,* 484–509.

Martin, P. Y., Courage, M. M., Godbey, K. L., Seymour, S. P., & Tate, R. (1993). Status politics, labor-management status, and gender: Leaders' views on employers and workers' family obligations. *Research in Social Movements, Conflicts and Change, 15,* 83–112.

Martin, T. C., & Bumpass, L. L. (1989). Recent trends in marital disruption. *Demography, 26,* 37–51.

Mason, C. A., Cauce, A. M., Gonzales, N., Hiraga, Y., & Grove, K. (1994). An ecological model of externalizing behaviors in African-American adolescents. *Journal of Research on Adolescence, 4,* 639–655.

Masuo, D. M., Walker, R., & Furry, M. M. (1992). Home-based workers. *Journal of Family and Economic Issues, 13,* 245–262.

Matthews, S. H., & Rosner, T. T. (1988). Shared filial responsibility: The family as the primary caregiver. *Journal of Marriage and the Family, 50,* 185–195.

McHale, S. M., & Crouter, A. C. (1992). You can't always get what you want: Incongruence between sex-role attitudes and family work roles and its implications for marriage. *Journal of Marriage and the Family, 54,* 537–547.

McLanahan, S., & Booth, K. (1991). Mother-only families. In A. Booth (Ed.), *Contemporary families* (pp. 405–428). Minneapolis, MN: National Council on Family Relations.

McLoyd, V. C. (1990). The impact of economic hardship on black families and children: Psychological distress, parenting, and socioemotional development. *Child Development, 61,* 311–346.

McNeely, R. L., & Fogarty, B. A. (1988). Balancing parenthood and employment: Factors affecting company receptiveness to family-related innovations in the workplace. *Family Relations, 37,* 189–195.

Mederer, H. J. (1993). Division of labor in two-earner homes. *Journal of Marriage and the Family, 55,* 133–145.

Mellor, E. (1986). Shift work and flextime—how prevalent are they? *Monthly Labor Review, 109,* 14–21.

Mellor, E., & Parks, W. (1988). A year's work: Labor force activity from a different perspective. *Monthly Labor Review, 111,* 13–18.

Menaghan, E. G. (1991). Work experiences and family interaction processes: The long reach of the job? *Annual Review of Sociology, 17,* 419–444.

Menaghan, E. G., & Parcel, T. L. (1991). Parental employment and family life. In A. Booth (Ed.), *Contemporary families* (pp. 361–380). Minneapolis: National Council on Family Relations.

Menaghan, E. G., & Parcel, T. L. (1995). Social sources of change in children's home environments. *Journal of Marriage and the Family, 57,* 69–84.

Michaels, B. (1995). A global glance at work and family. *Personnel Journal, 74,* 85–93.

Milliken, F. J., Dutton, J. E., & Beyer, J. M. (1990). Understanding organizational adaptation to change: The case of work–family issues. *Human Resource Planning, 13,* 91–107.

Moen, P., & Dempster-McClain, D. (1987). Employed parents: Role strain, work time, and preferences for working less. *Journal of Marriage and the Family, 49,* 579–590.

Morrison, D. R., & Lichter, D. T. (1988). Family migration and female employment. *Journal of Marriage and the Family, 50,* 161–172.

Moss, P., & Brannen, J. (1987). Fathers and employment. In C. Lewis & M. O'Brien (Eds.), *Reassessing fatherhood* (pp. 36–53). London: Sage.

Muller, C. (1995). Maternal employment, parent involvement, and mathematics achievement among adolescents. *Journal of Marriage and the Family, 57,* 85–100.

Mutchler, J. E. (1987). Gender differences in the effects of family status on underemployment. *International Journal of Sociology and Social Policy, 7,* 5–18.

Myers, S. M., & Booth, A. (1996). Men's retirement and marital quality. *Journal of Family Issues, 17,* 336–357.

National Council for Jewish Women. (1987). *Accommodating pregnancy in the workplace.* New York: National Council for Jewish Women.

Neal, M., Chapman, N., Ingersoll-Dayton, B., Emlen, A., & Boise, L. (1990). Absenteeism and stress among employed caregivers the elderly, disabled adults, and children. In D.E. Biegel & A. Blum (Eds.), *Aging and caregiving* (pp. 160–183). Newbury Park, CA: Sage.

Nelson, D. L., Quick, J. C., Hitt, M. A., & Moesel, D. (1990). Politics, lack of career progress, and work/home conflict: Stress and strain for working women. *Sex Roles, 23,* 169–185.

Nelson, P. T., & Couch, S. (1990). The corporate perspective on family responsive policy. *Marriage and Family Review, 15,* 95–114.

Nock, S. L., & Kingston, P. W. (1988). Time with children: The impact of couples' work-time commitments. *Social Forces, 67,* 59–85.

Nock, S. L., & Kingston, P. W. (1989). The division of leisure and work. *Social Science Quarterly, 70,* 24–39.

Noelker, L. S., & Townsend, A. L. (1987). Perceived caregiving effectiveness. In T. H. Brubaker (Ed.), *Aging, health, and family* (pp. 58–79). Newbury Park, CA: Sage.

O'Connell, M., & Bloom, D. E. (1987). *Juggling jobs and babies: America's child care challenge.* Washington, DC: Population Reference Bureau.

O'Neil, R., & Greenberger, E. (1994). Patterns of commitment to work and parenting: Implications for role strain. *Journal of Marriage and the Family, 56,* 101–118.

Orbuch, T. L., & Custer, L. (1995). The social context of married women's work and its impact on black husbands and white husbands. *Journal of Marriage and the Family, 57,* 333–345.

Orthner, D. K., Bowen, G. L., & Beare, V. G. (1990). The organization family: A question of work and family boundaries. *Marriage and Family Review, 15,* 15–36.

Osterbusch, S. E., Keigher, S. M., Miller, B., & Linsk, N. L. (1987). Community care policies and gender justice. *International Journal of Health Services, 17,* 217–232.

Ozer, E. M. (1995). The impact of childcare responsibility and self-efficacy on the psychological health of professional working mothers. *Psychology of Women Quarterly, 19,* 315–335.

Paden, S. L., & Buehler, C. (1995). Coping with the dual-income lifestyle. *Journal of Marriage and the Family, 57,* 101–110.

Papanek, H. (1973). Men, women, and work: Reflections on the two-person career. *American Journal of Sociology, 78,* 852–872.

Pavalko, E. K., & Elder, G. H. (1993). Women behind the men: Variation in wives' support of husbands' careers. *Gender and Society, 7,* 548–567.

Perkins, H. W., & DeMeis, D. K. (1996). Gender and family effects on the "second shift" domestic activity of college-educated wives. *Gender and Society, 10,* 78–93.

Perrucci, C., Perrucci, R., Targ, D., & Targ, H. (1988). *Plant closings.* New York: Aldine de Gruyter.

Perrucci, D., & Targ, D. (1988). Effects of a plant closing on marriage and family life. In P. Voydanoff & L. Majka (Eds.), *Families and economic distress* (pp. 55–71). Beverly Hills, CA: Sage.

Perry-Jenkins, M., & Crouter, A. C. (1990). Men's provider-role attitudes. *Journal of Family Issues, 11,* 136–156.

Perry-Jenkins, M., & Crouter, A. C. (1992). Linkages between women's provider-role attitudes, psychological well-being, and family relationships. *Psychology of Women Quarterly, 16,* 311–329.

Peters, J. M., & Haldeman, V. A. (1987). Time used for household work. *Journal of Family Issues, 8,* 212–225.

Peterson, R. R., & Gerson, K. (1992). Determinants of responsibility for child care arrangements among dual-earner couples. *Journal of Marriage and the Family, 54,* 527–536.

Phelan, J., Bromet, E. J., Schwartz, J. E., Dew, M. A., & Curtis, E. C. (1993). The work environments of male and female professionals. *Work and Occupations, 20,* 68–89.

Pina, D. L., & Bengtson, V. L. (1993). The division of household labor and wives' happiness, ideology, employment, and perceptions of support. *Journal of Marriage and the Family, 55,* 901–912.

Piotrowski, C. S., Hughes, D., Pleck, J., Kessler-Sklar, S., & Staines, G.L. (1993). *The experience of childbearing women in the workplace.* New York: National Council of Jewish Women.

Piotrowski, C. S., Rapoport, R. N., & Rapoport, R. (1987). Families and work. In M. B. Sussman & S. K. Steinmetz (Eds.), *Handbook of marriage and the family* (pp. 251–284). New York: Plenum.

Pittman, J. F., & Blanchard, D. (1996). The effects of work history and timing of marriage on the division of household labor. *Journal of Family Issues, 58,* 78–90.

Pittman, J. F., & Orthner, D. K. (1988). Gender differences in the prediction of job commitment. *Journal of Social Behavior and Personality, 3,* 227–248.

Pleck, J. H. (1992). Work–family policies in the United States. In H. Kahne & J. Z. Giele (Eds.), *Women's work and women's lives* (pp. 248–275). Boulder, CO: Westview.

Potuchek, J. L. (1992). Employed wives' orientation to breadwinning: A gender theory analysis. *Journal of Marriage and the Family, 54,* 548–558.

Presser, H. B. (1987). Work shifts of full-time dual-career couples. *Demography, 24,* 99–112.

Presser, H. B. (1988). Shift work and child care among young dual-earner American parents. *Journal of Marriage and the Family, 50,* 133–148.

Presser, H. B. (1989). Can we make time for children? The economy, work schedules, and child care. *Demography, 26,* 523–543.

Presser, H. B. (1994). Employment schedules among dual-earner spouses and the division of household labor by gender. *American Sociological Review, 59,* 348–364.

Pyke, K. D. (1994). Women's employment as a gift or burden? Marital power across marriage, divorce, and remarriage. *Gender and Society, 8,* 73–91.

Raabe, P. H., & Gessner, J. C. (1988). Employer family-supportive policies: Diverse variations on the theme. *Family Relations, 37,* 196–202.

Rayman, P. (1988). Unemployment and family life. In P. Voydanoff & L. Majka (Eds.), *Families and economic stress* (pp. 119–134). Beverly Hills, CA: Sage.

Repetti, R. L. (1989). Effects of daily workload on subsequent behavior during marital interaction. *Journal of Personality and Social Psychology, 57,* 651–659.

Rexroat, C., & Shehan, C. (1987). The family life cycle and spouses' time in housework. *Journal of Marriage and the Family, 49,* 737–750.

Risman, B., & Schwartz, P. (1989). Being gendered: A microstructural view of intimate relationships. In B. Risman & P. Schwartz (Eds.), *Gender in intimate relationships—a microstructural approach* (pp. 1–9). Belmont, CA: Wadsworth.

Robinson, J. P. (1988). Who's doing the housework. *American Demographics, 10,* 24–28, 63.

Robinson, J., & Spitze, G. (1992). Whistle while you work? The effect of household task performance on women's men's well-being. *Social Science Quarterly, 73,* 844–861.

Rogers, S. J. (1996). Mothers' work hours and marital quality: Variations by family structure and family size. *Journal of Marriage and the Family, 58,* 606–617.

Roos, P. A. (1985). *Gender and work.* Albany: State University of New York Press.

Rosen, E. I. (1987). *Bitter choices: Blue-collar women in and out of work.* Chicago: University of Chicago Press.

Rosenfeld, R. A., & Birkelund, G. E. (1995). Women's part-time work: A cross-national comparison. *European Sociological Review, 11,* 111–134.

Rosenfield, S. (1989). The effects of women's employment: Personal control and sex differences in mental health. *Journal of Health and Social Behavior, 30,* 77–91.

Ross, C. E. (1987). The division of labor at home at home. *Social Forces, 65,* 817–833.

Rothman, S. M., & Marks, E. M. (1987). Adjusting work and family life: Flexible work schedules and family policy. In N. Gerstel & H. B. Gross (Eds.), *Families and work* (pp. 469–477). Philadelphia: Temple University Press.

Rowe, B. R., & Bentley, M. T. (1992). The impact of the family on home-based work. *Journal of Family and Economic Issues, 13,* 279–298.

Rose, B. R., Stafford, K., & Owen, A. J. (1992). Who's working at home. *Journal of Family and Economic Issues, 13,* 159–172.

Rustia, J., & Abbott, D. A. (1990). Predicting paternal role enactment. *Western Journal of Nursing Research, 12,* 145–160.

Ryu, S., & Mortimer, J. T. (1996). The "occupational linkage hypothesis" to occupational value formation in adolescents. In J. T. Mortner & M. D. Finch (Eds.), *Adolescents, work and family* (pp. 167–190). Thousand Oaks, CA: Sage.

Sanchez, L. (1994a). Gender, labor allocations, and the psychology of entitlement within the home. *Social Forces, 73,* 522–553.

Sanchez, L. (1994b). Material resources, family structure, resources and husbands' housework participation. *Journal of Family Issues, 15,* 379–402.

Sanchez, L., & Kane, E. W. (1996). Women's and men's constructions of perceptions of housework fairness. *Journal of Family Issues, 17,* 358–387.

Scarr, S., Philips, D., & McCartney, K. (1989). Working mothers and their families. *American Psychologist, 44,* 1402–1409.

Scharlach, A. E. (1994). Caregiving and employment: Competing or complementary roles? *The Gerontologist, 34,* 378–385.

Schein, E. H. (1990). Organizational culture. *American Psychologist, 45,* 109–119.

Schnittger, M. H., & Bird, G. W. (1990). Coping among dual-career men and women across the family life cycle. *Family Relations, 39,* 199–205.

Schwartz, D. (1994). *An examination of the impact of family-friendly policies on the glass ceiling.* New York: Families and Work Institute.

Schwartz, F. (1989). Management women and the new facts of life. *Harvard Business Review, 67,* 65–76.

Schwartzberg, N. S., & Dytell, R. S. (1988). Family stress and psychological well-being among employed and nonemployed mothers. *Journal of Social Behavior and Personality, 3,* 175–190.

Scott, J., & Alwin, D. F. (1989). Gender differences in parental strain: Parental role or gender role? *Journal of Family Issues, 10,* 482–503.

Sears, H. A., & Galambos, N. L. (1992). Women's work conditions and marital adjustment in two-earner couples: A structural model. *Journal of Marriage and the Family, 54,* 789–797.

Seyler, D. L., Monroe, P. A., & Garland, J. C. (1995). Balancing work and family: The role of employer-sponsored child care benefits. *Journal of Family Issues, 16,* 170–193.

Shelton, B. A. (1990). The distribution of household tasks—does wife's employment status make a difference. *Journal of Family Issues, 11,* 115–135.

Shelton, B. A., & John, D. (1993). Does marital status make a difference? *Journal of Family Issues, 14,* 401–420.

Shinn, M., Wong, N. W., Simko, P. A., & Ortiz-Torres, B. (1989). Promoting the well-being of working parents: Coping, social support, and flexible job schedules. *American Journal of Community Psychology, 17*, 31–55.

Sidel, R. (1996). *Keeping women and children last.* New York: Penguin.

Silver, H. (1993). Homework and domestic work. *Sociological Forum, 8*, 181–204.

Silver, H., & Goldscheider, R. (1994). Flexible work and housework. *Social Forces, 72*, 1103–1119.

Society for Human Resource Management. (1992). *Work and family survey report.* Alexandria, VA: Society for Human Resource Management.

Sorenson, A., & McLanahan, S. (1987). Married women's economic dependency, 1940–1980. *American Journal of Sociology, 93*, 659–687.

Sorrentino, C. (1990). The changing family in international perspective. *Monthly Labor Review, 113*, 41–58.

South, S. J., & Spitze, G. (1994). Housework in marital and nonmarital households. *American Sociological Review, 59*, 327–347.

Spade, J. Z. (1991). Occupational structure and men's and women's parental values. *Journal of Family Issues, 12*, 343–360.

Spenner, K. I., & Rosenfeld, R. A. (1990). Women, work, and identities. *Social Science Research, 19*, 266–299.

Spitze, G. (1991). Women's employment and family relations. In A. Booth (Eds.), *Contemporary families* (pp. 381–404). Minneapolis, MN: National Council on Family Relations.

Stafford, K., Winter, M., Duncan, K. A., & Genalo, M. A. (1992). Studying at home income generation. *Journal of Family and Economic Issues, 13*, 139–158.

Starrells, M. E. (1994). Husbands' involvement in female gender-typed household chores. *Sex Roles, 31*, 473–491.

Starrells, M. E., Bould, S., & Nicholas, L. J. (1994). The feminization of poverty in the United States. *Journal of Family Issues, 15*, 590–607.

Steil, J. M., & Weltman, K. (1991). Marital inequality: The importance of resources, personal attributes, and social norms on career valuing and the allocation of domestic responsibilities. *Sex Roles, 24*, 161–179.

Stohs, J. H. (1994). Alternative ethics in employed women's household labor. *Journal of Family Issues, 15*, 550–561.

Stoller, E. P. (1991a). Males as helpers: The role of sons, relatives and friends. *Gerontologist, 30*, 228–235.

Stone, R., Cafferata, G. L., & Sangl, J. (1987). Caregivers of the frail elderly: A national profile. *Gerontologist, 27*, 616–626.

Suitor, J. J. (1991). Marital quality and satisfaction with the division of household labor across the family-life cycle. *Journal of Marriage and the Family, 53*, 221–230.

Taylor, R.J., Chatters, L. M., Tucker, M. B., & Lewis, E. (1991). Developments in research on black families. In A. Booth (Ed.), *Contemporary families* (pp. 275–296). Minneapolis, MN: National Council on Family Relations.

Teachman, J. D., & Schollaert, P. T. (1989). Economic conditions, marital status, and the timing of first births. *Sociological Forum, 4*, 27–45.

Thomson, E. (1994). "Settings" and "development" from a demographic point of view. In A. Booth & J. Dunn (Eds.), *Stepfamilies: Who benefits? Who does not?* (pp. 89–96). Hillsdale, NJ: Erlbaum.

Thompson, L. (1991). Family work: Women's sense of fairness. *Journal of Family Issues, 12*, 181–191.

Thompson, L. (1993). Conceptualizing gender in marriage. *Journal of Marriage and the Family, 55*, 557–570.

Thompson, L., & Walker, A. J. (1991). Gender in families. In A. Booth (Ed.), *Contemporary Families* (pp. 76–102). Minneapolis, MN: National Council on Family Relations.

Thornton, A. (1989). Changing attitudes toward family issues in the United States. *Journal of Marriage and the Family, 51*, 873–893.

Trzcinski, E. (1994). Family and medical leave, contingent employment, and flexibility: A feminist critique of the U.S. approach to work and family policy. *The Journal of Applied Social Sciences, 18*, 71–87.

Ulbrich, P. M. (1988). The determinants of depression in two-income marriages. *Journal of Marriage and the Family, 50*, 121–131.

U.S. Department of Commerce. (1995). *Statistical abstract of the United States 1995.* Washington, DC: Government Printing Office.

U.S. Bureau of the Census. (1990). *Statistical abstract of the United States.* Washington, DC: Government Printing Office.

U.S. Bureau of the Census (1992a). *Households, families, and children: A thirty year perspective* (Current Population Reports, series P23, no. 181). Washington, DC: Government Printing Office.

U.S. Bureau of the Census. (1992b). *Who's minding the kids?* (Current Population Reports, series P-70, no. 20). Washington, DC: Government Printing Office.

U.S. Department of Labor. (1989a). *Employee benefits in medium and large firms, 1988* (Bulletin #2336). Washington, DC: Government Printing Office.

U.S. Department of Labor. (1989b). *News, April 4.* Washington, DC: Government Printing Office.

U.S. Department of Labor. (1990). *Employee benefits in small private establishments, 1990* (Bulletin #2388). Washington, DC: Government Printing Office.

U.S. Department of Labor. (1992). *Work and family provisions in major collective bargaining agreements* (Report #144). Washington, DC: Government Printing Office.

Vannoy, D., & Philliber, W. (1992). Wife's employment and quality of marriage. *Journal of Marriage and the Family, 54*, 387–398.

Vannoy-Hiller, D., & Philliber, W. (1989). *Equal partners.* Beverly Hills, CA: Sage.

Volling, B. L., & Belsky, J. (1991). Multivariate determinants of father involvement during infancy in dual-earner and single-earner families. *Journal of Marriage and the Family, 53*, 461–474.

Voydanoff, P. (1987). *Work and family life.* Beverly Hills, CA: Sage.

Voydanoff, P. (1988a). Work and family: A review and expanded conceptualization. *Journal of Social Behavior and Personality, 3*, 1–22.

Voydanoff, P. (1988b). Work role characteristics, family structure demands, and work/family conflict. *Journal of Marriage and the Family, 50*, 749–761.

Voydanoff, P. (1991). Economic distress and family relations. In A. Booth (Ed.), *Contemporary families* (pp. 429–445). Minneapolis, MN: National Council on Family Relations.

Voydanoff, P., & Donnelly, B. W. (1989). Work and family roles and psychological distress. *Journal of Marriage and the Family, 51*, 923–932.

Voydanoff, P., Fine, M. A., & Donnelly, B. W. (1994). Family structure, family organization, and quality of family life. *Journal of Family and Economic Issues, 15*, 175–200.

Wanamaker, N. J., & Bird, G. W. (1990). Coping with stress in dual-career marriages. *International Journal of Sociology of the Family, 20*, 199–212.

Way, W. L., & Rossmann, M. M. (1994). The interrelation of work and family: A missing piece of the vocational education research agenda. *Journal of Vocational Education Research, 2*, 1–24.

Weiss, R. S. (1987). Men and their wives' work. In F. J. Crosby (Ed.), *Spouse, parent, worker: On gender and multiple roles* (pp. 109–121). New Haven, CT: Yale University Press.

Wenk, D., & Garrett, P. (1992). Having a baby: Some predictions of maternal employment around childbirth. *Gender and Society, 6*, 49–65.

Wharton, C. S. (1994). Finding time for the "second shift": The impact of flexible work schedules on women's double days. *Gender and Society, 8*, 189–205.

White, L., & Keith, B. (1990). The effect of shift work on the quality and stability of marital relations. *Journal of Marriage and the Family, 52*, 453–462.

White, L. K., & Kim, H. (1987). The family-building process: Childbearing choices by parity. *Journal of Marriage and the Family, 49,* 271–279.

Wilkie, J. R. (1991). The decline in men's labor force participation and income and the changing structure of family economic support. *Journal of Marriage and the Family, 53,* 111–122.

Wilkie, J. R. (1993). Changes in U.S. men's attitudes toward the family provider role, 1972–1989. *Gender and Society, 7,* 261–279.

Wille, D. F. (1995). The 1990s: Gender differences in parenting roles. *Sex Roles, 33,* 803–817.

Williams, E., & Radin, N. (1993). Paternal involvement, maternal employment, and adolescents' academic achievement: An 11 year follow-up. *American Journal of Orthopsychiatry, 63,* 306–312.

Willoughby, J. C., & Glidden, L. J. (1995). Fathers helping out. *American Journal on Mental Retardation, 4,* 399–406.

Wilson, M. N., Tolson, T. F., Hinton, I. D., & Kiernan, M. (1990). Flexibility and sharing of childcare duties in black families. *Sex Roles, 22,* 409–425.

Winter, M., Puspitawati, H., Heck, R. K., & Stafford, K. (1993). Time-management strategies used by households with home-based work. *Journal of Family and Economic Issues, 14,* 69–92.

Witt, J. L. (1994). The gendered division of labor in parental caretaking. *Journal of Women and Aging, 6,* 65–89.

Wolcott, I., & Glezer, H. (1995). *Work and family life.* Melbourne, Australia: Australian Institute of Family Studies.

Wolfer, L. T., & Moen, P. (1996). Staying in school—maternal employment and the timing of black and white daughters' school exit. *Journal of Family Issues, 17,* 540–560.

Yogman, M., Cooley, J., & Kindlon, D. (1988). Fathers, infants, and toddlers. In P. Bronstein & C. Cowan (Eds.), *Fatherhood today* (pp. 53–65). New York: Wiley.

Yoon, Y.-H., & Waite, L. J. (1994). Converging employment patterns of black, white, and Hispanic women: Return to work after childbearing. *Journal of Marriage and the Family, 56,* 209–217.

York, C. (1993). Bargaining for work and family benefits. In D. S. Cobble (Ed.), *Women and unions* (pp. 130–143). Ithaca, NY: ILR Press.

Zambrana, R. E., & Frith, S. (1988). Mexican-American professional women: Role satisfaction differences in single and multiple role lifestyles. *Journal of Social Behavior and Personality, 3,* 347–361.

Zavella, P. (1987). *Women's work and Chicano families.* Ithaca, NY: Cornell University Press.

Zedeck, S., & Mosier, K. L. (1990). Work in the family and employing organization. *American Psychologist, 45,* 240–245.

Zick, C. D., & McCullough, J. L. (1991). Trends in married couples' time use. *Sex Roles, 24,* 7–18.

Zuckerman, H. (1987). Persistence and change in the careers of men and women scientists and engineers. In L. S. Dix (Ed.), *Women: Their underrepresentation and career differentials in science and engineering.* Washington, DC: National Academy Press.

Zussman, R. (1987). Work and family in the new middle class. In N. Gerstel & H. B. Gross (Eds.), *Families and Work* (pp. 338–346). Philadelphia: Temple University Press.

Zvonkovic, A. M., Greaves, K. M., Schmiege, C. J., & Hall, L. D. (1996). The marital construction of gender through work and family decisions: A qualitative analysis. *Journal of Marriage and the Family, 58,* 91–100.

CHAPTER 22

Exploring Family and Health Relationships

The Role of Genetics, Environment, and Culture

Douglas E. Crews and Hector Balcazar

Introduction

Concepts such as familial disease, familial aggregation, familial resemblance, family care, family violence, family therapy, family dynamics, and family history are increasingly bandied about by the media and popular news magazines of today. These ideas are used widely in the scientific literature, and several contributors to this volume make use of such concepts when describing areas of family scholarship. All are attempting to emphasize that the family is not only a unit of society useful for social analysis, but also a socioeconomic-emotional structure that cares for, interacts with, and sometimes harms its members. The purpose of this chapter is to explore family and familial factors that contribute either to healthy well-being or to its opposite, vulnerability to disease. To accomplish this goal several topics are described regarding family and health. An examination of family aggregations of disease is examined first. In this section emphasis is placed on chronic diseases and their risk factors. The concept of family inheritance and its interaction

Douglas E. Crews • Department of Anthropology and School of Public Health, The Ohio State University, Columbis, Ohio 43210. Hector Balcazar • Department of Family Resources and Human Development, Arizona State University, Tempe, Arizona 85287-2502.

Handbook of Marriage and the Family, 2nd edition, edited by Marvin Sussman, Suzanne K. Steinmetz, and Gary W. Peterson. Plenum Press, New York, 1999.

with environmental factors also is underscored. In a second section, contemporary issues of family and health are examined using several theoretical models as reference points to describe relationships between family and health and the factors contributing to these relationships. Finally, future research and policy implications are discussed.

Familial Aggregations: General Concepts

Health differences between individuals may originate at any point along life's continuum. One's family and familial inheritance are always in continuous interaction with individual health and well-being. Either the sperm or the egg, or both, that join to create one's zygote may carry potentially lethal or disabling *alleles* (alternative versions of a gene controlling the same trait, there are three major alleles at the ABO locus). In utero the developing fetus may be exposed to numerous environmental toxins that enter the mother's system—for example, alcohol, drugs, metabolites of tobacco smoke, polychlorinated biphenyls (PCBs), and mercury (see Marbury et al., 1983; Schell, 1991; Tennes & Blackard, 1980). Socioeconomic conditions may lead to poor maternal health, lack of prenatal care, and consequent poor health status at birth, perinatally, during infancy, or during childhood. During infancy, growth and development may be compromised by undernutrition, overnutrition, and malnutrition or by inadequate sunlight and ventilation (see Bogin, 1988; Martorell, 1989; Stinson, 1985). Throughout infancy and childhood the family may or may not buffer the developing child from environmental insults and personal injury and may or may not provide a safe and relatively danger-free environment. Occupational exposures may occur in parents, but become manifest in children (e.g., exposure to lead in battery manufacturing, radium dial painting in watch factories, power plant exposures). Any of these factors may initiate or exacerbate illness and disease at any point in an individual's life history.

Even as adults, our family continues to provide a social, economic, and cultural buffer or conduit for experiences with illness and disability throughout the life span. To understand these multiple influences, it is necessary to explore individual life histories and their associations with family factors. An important obstacle to such understanding, however, is the arbitrary and error-prone method of dividing a person's life history into periods such as intrauterine development, infancy, childhood, puberty, adolescence, young adult, mature adult, older adult, late life, senescence, terminal morbidity, and mortality. One reason is that life stages are not quite as easy to separate as such facile terms suggest. Instead, the life span is a continuum and, for those who survive, a gradual transition from fertilization through termination (see Garruto & Crews, 1994). The longer that individual life continues, the more patterns of transition between subsequent stages are likely to become variable. Almost everyone spends 9 months in utero, but puberty occurs at a wider range of ages, from as young as 7 to as old as 18 years (and even older), while old age senescence may occur as early as 40 or as late as 70 or more years.

Academicians and practitioners alike are interested in the processes by which disease shows a familial pattern. Such diseases may range from nearly complete genetic causation (e.g., cystic fibrosis and Huntington's disease) to almost completely environmental causation (e.g., lead poisoning). The majority of diseases, however, are more likely to represent complex gene–environment relationships, such as seen with phenylketonuria, insulin dependent and non-insulin dependent diabetes mellitus, and Alzheimer's and Parkinson's diseases.

Today, birth defects and congenital malformations have plateaued at about 5% of live births in the United States (see McConkey, 1993). While the etiologies of most birth defects, childhood and chronic degenerative diseases, and psychotic conditions remain unknown (see Crews & Gerber, 1994; Crews & James, 1991), the etiologies of most crippling and deadly childhood infections have been established.

It has also become clear that many persons in present-day populations are at high risk for developing chronic degenerative diseases and psychiatric disturbances as they grow older. Contributors to these trends include the increasing average age of many populations, with some of the most important factors being the increased proportions of people living beyond their fifth and sixth decades of life, as well as the corresponding altered circumstances of life that have accompanied this trend. Such changes in life history parameters result in exposure of alleles and *genotypes* (the two alleles that an individual carries at a particular locus, there are six different genotypes at the ABO locus: AA, AB, AO, BB, BO, OO) to new pressures of lifestyle and environment that have not been encountered previously by most of humankind. Consequently, these alterations in life history patterns expose a lack of fit between stone age physiology and phenotypes currently living in the fast lane of modern cosmopolitan life (Eaton, Konner, & Shostak, 1988; see also Crews & Gerber, 1994).

One of the main goals of epidemiology is the identification of health phenomena in time and space. When applied to genetic and chronic diseases, in turn, epidemiology attempts to identify disease clusters or the incidence of disease in a certain area at a particular time (see Khoury, Beaty, & Cohen, 1993). These clusters can involve varied spaces such as geographic areas and occupational domains or varied sites such as schools, other institutions (e.g., religions organizations or churches), and certain groups in a population. One of the more prominent groups or social institutions is the family.

When diseases cluster within a family, such clusters are referred to as familial aggregations. Such aggregations occur when the number of affected individuals occurring with the family of a *proband* (the individual in the family who first comes to the attention of health-care workers) who has the disease exceeds the expected number compared to the general population: "Traditionally, family aggregation of a disease is measured by comparing the number of affected relatives of cases to the number of affected relatives of controls, with an odds ratio greater than one serving as a measure of familial aggregation" (Masestri, Beaty, Liang, Boughman, & Ferencz, 1988, p. 351).

Familial Aggregations: Genetics and Genes

Men and women carry the same basic chromosome complements and genetic loci, except for the size differences in their sex chromosomes and the fact that men are hemizygous (having only one-half the normal chromosomal number) for the X-chromosome. The activity and function of these similar hereditary materials, however, may be quite different when found in a male or a female body. For example, on average compared to men, women show about 10% higher rates of *sister chromatid exchanges* (SCE) (the exchange of seemingly identical segments of DNA in duplicating cells without any known alteration of cell viability or function due to the breakage and rejoining of DNA strands) during cell cycles and show three different peaks of SCE during the menstrual cycle (see Wilcosky & Rynard, 1990). The exact significance of these findings for health and well-being may not be clear. Gender differences in hereditary materials, however, suggest the possibility that quantitative differences exist between men and women in DNA replication and associated factors. This also underscores the potential for diseases with primarily a genetic etiology to manifest gender differences.

A widely identified pattern is that daughters are more likely than sons to resemble their parents when their parents are subgrouped according to traits with a genetic basis (e.g., stature, fat placement, blood groups) (Wolanski, 1974). This may suggest that males have a wider latitude in phenotypic development and/or are more influenced by environmental factors than are females (see also Stinson, 1985). Sex differences in hereditary materials may also account, in part, for the greater loss of Y-bearing zygotes and embryos during intrauterine development. Genetic differences may also be the basis for the greater susceptibility of male infants, children, and adults to environmental and infectious causes of morbidity and mortality. The greater mortality rates of males at almost all ages in cosmopolitan settings may be another partial result of genetic differences.

As previously stated, genetic factors may account for as much as 5% of total childhood morbidity in cosmopolitan settings such as the United States, where almost one-third of pediatric hospital admissions are associated with some genetic etiology (McConkey, 1993). Khoury and colleagues (1993), for example, view differential genetic susceptibility as playing a key role in understanding the etiology and pathogenesis of many common diseases. Conditions such as coronary heart disease (CHD) (Rao et al., 1982), cancer (Cho & Vogelstein, 1992; Shields & Harris, 1991), congenital malformations (Moore, 1988; Spranger et al., 1982), diabetes (Cox, Epstein, & Speilman, 1989) and schizophrenia (Kidd, 1987) are the focus of numerous ongoing genetic investigations.

Besides these underlying genetic factors, such conditions and syndromes may be expressed differentially in males and females, even when they share the same genotypes. Sex differences appear because physiological factors determined by biological sex may result in variable responsiveness to the same or even somewhat different environments. Moreover, it is possible that phenotypic plasticity, which allows variable response patterns to the environment within a single genotype, may allow males to respond within a single lifetime to altered reproductive circumstances that provide more early or late reproductive opportunities. Thus, more flexible genetic control of phenotype may allow males to vary more from familial norms in their phenotypes than females and may represent a biological trade-off between reproductive success and optimal health and longevity.

Familial Aggregations: Risk Factors and Chronic Diseases

Many diseases and health-related phenomena can be described as family aggregations. These familial clusters include perinatal experiences such as genetic predispositions to short pregnancy periods, aggregations of congenital cardiovascular malformations in infants, and aggregations of chronic diseases such as diabetes mellitus, cardiovascular disease, and cancers.

Different modes of genetic inheritance show variations in their patterns of affected relatives. For example, it is more likely for siblings of unaffected parents to show concordance for recessive disorders than it is to find parent–offspring pairs concordant for these disorders. Conversely, sex-linked recessive disorders usually occur in a grandfather–grandson pair. As the degree of relationship declines, the fraction of shared genes decreases and disease incidence decreases as genetic distance from the proband increases. This pattern of declining disease incidence among more distant relatives may be the major indicator that a disease is familial (see Khoury et al., 1993; Weiss, Chakraborty, & Majumder, 1982).

The frequency of a disease-causing allele in a population influences the degree of risk in families, since an allele at high frequency allows inheritance from multiple individuals in a pedigree (see Weiss et al., 1982). In general, when the level of familial risk is small, "the probability that a relative of the proband is affected depends ... on the type of relationship, the affection state (disease state) of the proband, and the disease frequency in the population" (Weiss et al., 1982, p. 541).

To illustrate that such excess risk in families is anything but trivial, we need only review some data on hazard ratios for breast cancer in relatives of white probands from Claus, Risch, and Thompson (1989). Working with data from the Cancer and Steroid Hormone Study, 1980–1982, Claus et al. examined age at onset of cancer as a confounding variable in familial aggregations of breast cancer. For sisters of affected probands with disease onset at age 50, with neither other affected relatives nor an affected mother, the hazard ratio was estimated at 1.7 (1.4–2.0). If breast cancer occurred in the proband at 30 years, however, the estimated hazard ratio for sisters was 4.3 (3.3–5.6), a 2.5-fold increase (data from Table 5, Claus et al., 1989). In the most extreme cases of familial aggregation, where probands are affected at age 30+, have an affected mother, and have at least one affected sister, the hazard ratio for additional sisters is 44.2 (23.5–83.2). A three- to fourfold increased hazards of 15.1 (9.4–29.3) exists for sisters of probands affected at age 30 whose mothers also are affected but who have no affected sisters; this is almost 10 times the risk that exists for sisters of unaffected probands with no affected relatives (see Claus et al., 1989, for a more complete description). Relatively small risks or hazard ratios in families indicate that environmental factors may play a greater role than genetic factors, whereas large ratios indicate genetic factors (Weiss et al., 1982).

Determining genetic influence in chronic diseases is difficult since, by definition, degenerative or chronic diseases have extended and variable periods of onset and risk of onset increases with age. Weiss et al. (1982) state, "For many degenerative diseases the effect of familial factors seems to be to raise the risk at young adult ages, that is, to shift the age-onset curve toward younger years. Often, the clinical pathology of the disease is basically the same ... in both familial and sporadic cases and the only discernible effect of high-risk alleles is to lower the ages of onset" (p. 547). Studies in families also noted that, due to the relatively young ages of some of the members, the onset of chronic diseases has not yet occurred where it eventually may, so that family aggregations change with time. Moreover, although a genetic basis cannot be ruled out, shared lifestyles and culture patterns rather than genetic mechanisms may be responsible for apparent family aggregations (Khoury et al., 1993). Issues of culture and family are explored in a subsequent section.

Importantly, the familial aggregation of risk factors may also result from assortative mating of parents according to socioeconomic status (SES), ethnic group, religion, stature, body habitus, or other physical factors that are associated with disease outcomes. Most studies indicate that aggregation of environmental risk factors as well as genetic susceptibility may result in family aggregations of disease. One of the goals of family studies is to isolate environmental (confounding) risk factors in attempting to assess genetic effects (Ottman et al., 1991). Dorman et al. (1988) suggest that comparing concordance of risk factors among affected and unaffected pairs of family members could illuminate the role of environment.

Obesity and Fat Patterns

Although the association is not universal, obesity is commonly viewed as a risk factor for several chronic diseases (e.g., hypertension, cardiovascular disease, and diabetes). Numerous characteristics contribute to obesity's classification as both a genetic and an environmental risk factor (see Andres, 1978; Crews, 1989; McGarvey, Bindon, Crews, & Schendel, 1989). Body build is determined by genetics to a great degree, and anatomical morphology appears strongly canalized. Alterations in body habitus (aspects of morphology associated with disease onset or progression) in response

to environmental factors are usually minor (e.g., slightly increased height from improved diet), while build may be largely due to inborn factors. Conversely, obesity is one of the most environmentally labile of physical features, with overweight and obesity being influenced strongly by familial and cultural factors. Dietary patterns learned during childhood, for example, persist into adulthood (Sellers, Kushi, & Potter, 1991), regardless of whether there is growing awareness of diets that benefit health and well-being. The placement of fat on the body, on the other hand, appears to be in large part determined by constitutional factors and to result in a stronger risk factor for chronic disease than does level of obesity (Vague, 1956; Vague, Bjorntrap, Guy-Grand, Rebuffe-Scrue, & Vague, 1985).

Obesity is significantly associated with the relative incidence of several chronic diseases, including cardiovascular disease, hypertension, non-insulin-dependent diabetes mellitus (NIDDU), and cancer. For example, a longitudinal study of 284 white school children and their families (both parents, at least one sibling, a related aunt or uncle, and one first cousin) conducted over 4 years demonstrated that obesity in childhood predicts obesity in adulthood. This study also found that obesity in adulthood is a long-term indicator of cardiovascular disease (Burns, Moll, & Lauer, 1989).

Other findings from this study also indicated that children who weighed on average 20% more than the mean weight of their peers (adjusted for height differences) had lower HDL cholesterol levels and higher triglyceride levels (Burns et al., 1989). *Body mass index** (BMI) (a measure of weight relative to body size) clustered in these families, as did risk factors for cardiovascular disease. Findings from this study indicated that "overweight relatives had consistently higher blood pressure, total cholesterol, LDL-cholesterol, total triglyceride levels, and lower HDL-cholesterol levels" (Burns et al., 1989, p. 983).

A well-documented finding is that high blood cholesterol levels and low HDL cholesterol increase the risk for cardiovascular disease (see Savage et al., 1991). Estimates indicate that genetically determined differences in BMI account for 38% of the variability in both cardiovascular disease (CVD) and lipid levels, while 62% of the variation is attributable to environmental factors (Burns et al., 1989). Multivariate analysis revealed that, when indices of relative fat placement (waist/hip ratio, percent trunk, fat, relative fat pattern index) are included in the same model with overweight or obesity, no significant effect of obesity on the endpoint of cardiovascular disease or mortality is observed. Rather, the fat placement index usually shows a significant

---

*Body mass index = wt/ht^2 = Kg/m^2. A BMI greater than about 27 Kg/m^2 is considered overweight; over 30 Kg/m^2 is considered obese.

effect on morbid outcomes (see Gerber, Schnall, & Pickering, 1990; Stern & Haffner, 1986).

Available data suggest that the placement or patterning of subcutaneous fat on the torso is subject to much greater genetic control than is either the actual amount of fat or the degree of obesity (Bouchard, Perusse, LeBlanc, Tremblay, & Theriault, 1988; Hasstedt, Ramirez, & Kuida, & Williams, 1989). For example, Hasstedt et al. defined "a relative-fat-pattern index [RFPI] as the ratio of subscapular skinfold thickness to the sum of the subscapular and suprailiac skinfold thicknesses" (p. 917). Following a likelihood analysis, they reported recessive inheritance of an allele that elevated mean RFPI. Persons who were homozygous for this allele tended to have small superiliac skinfolds rather than large subscapular skinfolds (Hasstedt et al., 1989). Interestingly, this allele appeared to be homozygous significantly more frequently in younger rather than older cases of obesity, coronary heart disease, and hypertension. Such a finding may indicate earlier mortality of persons homozygous for this allele. Supporting a genetic/familial basis for fat placement is the additional suggestion that environment, diet, and socioeconomic factors appear to influence fat patterning much less than they do the amount of fat (see Mueller, 1983).

Obesity is known to be a risk factor for cardiovascular disease within certain ethnic groups. In studies of Japanese men living in Hawaii, Puerto Rican men, and American white men, for example, it was found that "heavier men were more likely to die from coronary disease" (Ramirez, 1991, p. 191). Obesity was not associated with CVD in Mexican Americans and Native Americans (Savage & Harlan, 1991), nor is it strongly associated with mortality in Samoan Americans, one of the most obese populations worldwide (Crews, 1988, 1989).

The relative importance of obesity for cardiovascular diseases also has been demonstrated in a large population study. Burns et al. (1989) concluded that there was 50% higher mortality from coronary heart disease among moderately heavy persons (35% overweight) compared to people who weighed within 10% of their respective age to height specific weight. Additionally, this mortality rate increased by 100% in persons with severe obesity (50% overweight) (Burns et al., 1989). This supports MacLean's (1988) theory that levels of disease severity are relative to the degree that associated risk factors are severe. A continuous pattern is suggested, which raises questions as to precisely what age is to be reported for the onset of a chronic disease that develops over decades.

Indisputable evidence now appears to exist that obesity is inherited through both family environment and genes and plays a major role in the development of several chronic diseases. The question that must now be posed, however, is whether obesity is in and of itself a chronic disease, or whether it is but a risk factor for other conditions. Given the fact that obesity is, to a large degree, controllable, a reduction in associated chronic diseases may follow as people become more aware of health risks posed by obesity. However, if morbid obesity is itself a genetically determined degenerative condition, perhaps it must be treated as aggressively as the other conditions frequently found in association with obesity, such as diabetes, hypertension, and CHD.

Lipids

Many studies have shown that high levels of blood cholesterol (>200 mg/dl total cholesterol) are predictive of cardiovascular diseases in adults and that children with high cholesterol levels are prone to have high levels as adults. Although evidence suggests that there is a degree of heritability for this risk, it also is clear that dietary intake and subsequent control of BMI alters genetic risks. The twin studies cited earlier provide evidence for the contribution of obesity to dyslipidemia, while research by Burns et al. (1989) on schoolchildren and their families showed that total cholesterol (total-c) and low-density lipoprotein (LDL-c) cholesterol levels of the heavy probands (children who weighted on average 20% more than the mean weight of their peers) were not elevated. However, their high-density lipoprotein cholesterol (HDL-c) levels were significantly lower and their total triglyceride levels were higher than the average or lean weight probands. Overweight relatives (BMI >75th percentile) of the heavy probands consistently showed higher levels of total triglycerides, LDL-c, and total-c and lower HDL-c levels (Burns et al., 1989).

Additional evidence for genetic effects on lipid metabolism come from the analysis of *restriction fragment length polymorphisms* (RFLPs) (DNA polymorphisms discovered with use of enzymes that cut DNA strands at highly specific points) of the AI-CIII-AIV locus on chromosome 11 (see Anderson et al., 1989). In this case, 11- to 14-year-old boys carrying any one of several minor RFLP alleles at this site tended to cluster in higher deciles of the triglyceride distribution and to have lower HDL-c levels (Anderson, Barnes, Lee, & Swenson, 1989).

In a study of 800 multiethnic children ages 10 to 13, a high positive correlation was found between BMI, skinfold measurements, high triglyceride levels, and low HDL cholesterol levels (Wong, Bassin, & Deitrich, 1991). Over 2880 7th graders participated in a lipid screening in 1972–1973; of these, 561 still living in 1981–1982 participated in a rescreening (Reed et al., 1986). Families of youths with persistently high total-c had statistically nonsignificant higher prevalences of ischemic heart disease (IHD). Families of youths with lower HDL-c showed higher prevalence of IHD, while those with high levels of HDL-c showed a deficit of IHD

(Reed et al., 1986). Interestingly, HDL-c and total-c showed an interaction, with the highest levels of IHD observed in families with high total-c and low HDL-c. Lower IHD prevalences occurred in families in which youths showed high total-c and high HDL-c levels (see Reed et al., 1986, for further discussion).

Strikingly similar results were reported in a study of 98 healthy school children from Rochester, Minnesota, by Moll et al. (1983). They reported that CHD in the grandfathers of the index children was associated with the index child's total-c and LDL-c level. However, CHD in the grandfathers was most strongly associated with the index child's HDL-c level as a fraction of total-c (Moll et al., 1983, p. 127). Such results suggest, in turn, that familial levels of lipids in individuals apparently are established early in life, with HDL-c and total-c levels being under some degree of genetic control. Moreover, the alleles affecting these HDL-c and total-c levels are apparently inherited independently, and even a single measure of lipid levels in elementary school children reveals aspects of family risk for heart disease (see Moll et al., 1983; Reed et al., 1986).

Smoking

The family can be viewed as a cultural unit with specific systems of social interactions and rewards. Many behavioral patterns, pathological as well as beneficial, develop within the context of these family systems. One of the most obvious of these is tobacco use in the form of cigarette smoking by family members. A child is more likely to smoke, for example, if both parents smoke than if only one or neither parent smokes. Moreover, sibling smoking behavior has various consequences in different ethnic groups. African American adolescents, for example, have been found to initiate smoking most often when a sister smoked and to continue to smoke most often when a brother was a smoker (Johnson & Gilbert, 1991). In contrast, European American adolescents tended to initiate smoking when an older brother smoked, while continuation was best predicted by a father who smoked (Johnson & Gilbert, 1991).

Evidence shows that smoking contributes to several chronic diseases. For example, although a lower incidence of cardiovascular diseases is generally prevalent among women, the risk of sudden death from coronary heart disease is equally a threat to men and women who smoke (Polednak, 1987). The incidence of hypertension also is positively correlated with smoking, especially among African American males (Livingston, Levine, & Moore, 1991). Smoking is also one of many factors hypothesized to predict bladder and pancreatic carcinomas, while the recent 50% increase in female lung cancer deaths is attributed to increased smoking by women (Polednak, 1987). Furthermore, tobacco use contributes to 25–35% of all cancer deaths in men, 5%–10% of cancer deaths in women, and as much as 80%–85% of all lung cancer deaths (Polednak, 1987).

Recent research has indicated that genetic factors may influence levels of metabolic enzymes for hydrocarbons or their receptors; that is, there may be a genetic predisposition for some types of lung cancer such as non-small cell carcinoma. Additionally, there is evidence that mucociliary transport of toxic agents and glycoproteins in respiratory tract mucus may be genetically influenced (Polednak, 1987).

Cigarette smoking, and the development of diseases such as lung cancer, represents cumulative exposure to environmental insults interacting with susceptible phenotypes. Development occurs over time and involves several "stages" ranging from initiation to promotion to autonomous progression. Malignancy does not suddenly appear; rather, it represents "a sequence of molecular and biochemical events occurring over a latency-induction period measured in years" (Schottenfeld, 1986). The familial nature of smoking-related morbidity may also be enhanced by second-hand smoke, a risk factor to which all family members are exposed.

Chronic Degenerative Diseases

Cardiovascular Disease. It is well established that CVD tends to run in families and that elevated levels of serum cholesterol, hypertension, and obesity place individuals at increased risk for CVD (Glueck et al., 1974; Morrison et al., 1983). The evidence is also clear that genetic variation is associated with lipid levels, blood pressure, obesity, and myocardial infarction (Bouchard et al., 1988; Brown & Goldstein, 1984, 1986; Jeuvemaitre et al., 1992). Estimates of the genetic contribution to total-c levels range as high as 50%–60% (Moll et al., 1983; Rao et al., 1982); evidence for within-family aggregation of lipid levels and ischemic heart disease is also extensive (see Reed et al., 1986). In fact, a specific genetic disease, familial hypercholesterolemia, has been identified in populations around the world.

Estimates based on RFLPs of the known apolipoprotein genes (AI, CIII, AIV) suggest that alleles at these loci, or at closely linked loci, also have major effects on lipid levels in the general population (see Anderson et al., 1989). Effects on both HDL-cholesterol and triglyceride levels have been hypothesized to occur in men and women, respectively, for different apolipoprotein alleles. Specifically, results indicate that differences in lipid metabolism appear related to genetic factors that produce different outcomes for men than for women. For example, in a study of diabetes, CHD, and other risk factors, the presence of diabetes and a family history of early CHD magnified the risk of CHD for both men and women relative to nondiabetics without a family history of early CHD (relative risk (RR) of 21.3; 95% confidence level (CI) of 91.0–50.0) (Schumacher, Hunt, & Williams, 1990). Interestingly, a large sex difference in these associations was observed, with a family history of diabetes being a risk factor for CHD in women (RR = 2.5; 95% CI: 1.0, 6.4), but not in men (RR = 0.4; 95% CI: 0.2, 1.1) (Schumacher et al., 1990). These data seem to indicate, in turn, that the familial nature of such conditions is to some degree sex dependent.

An additional well-documented sex differential in CHD risk is the protection of women from atherosclerosis (McGill & Stern, 1979). In their extensive review of sex and athero-sclerosis, McGill and Stern conclude that neither "circulating estrogens or androgens at physiologic levels either accelerate or inhibit atherogenesis" (p. 216). Furthermore, established cardiovascular risk factors do not explain this sex differential, and the sex difference "is concentrated in the coronary arteries of whites" (p. 217).

Diabetes. Obesity has been shown to be directly related to the incidence of Type 2 diabetes, or NIDDM, a disease that is highly familial as indicated by a nearly 100% concordance among monozygotic twins (Rich, 1990). Estimates that a child of one affected parents has a 20% lifetime chance of developing the disease suggests that NIDDM has a strong genetic basis (Weiss et al., 1982), but substantial evidence also exists that obesity plays a major role in the expression of NIDDM. Populations at greatest risk for developing NIDDM are those that have experienced rapid lifestyle changes, including changes in physical activity and diet, that have resulted in an increased incidence of obesity (O'Dea, 1991). For example, the high incidence of diabetes in Puerto Rico—the rate of diagnosed cases was 5.1% in 1986, double the United States' rate—is attributed to the fact that more than a quarter of the adult population is moderately (10%–20% > ideal weight) or seriously (20%+ > ideal weight) overweight. This change is attributed to increased fat in a diet that until recently included high starch from rice and beans (Ramirez, 1991). Similar examples include Hispanics, Australian aborigines, Native Americans, Asian Americans, and South Pacific Islanders, in whom the incidence of NIDDM has increased as the incidence of obesity has increased (Crews, Bindon, & Smith-Ozeran, 1991; Douglas & Milligan, 1991; O'Dea, 1991).

Obesity is associated with insulin resistance to the extent that the glucoregulatory action of insulin is impaired progressively as fatness increases. Ultimately, this level of impairment increases to a point where NIDDM is clinically manifest, while reduction in the degree of obesity can improve the metabolic abnormalities that occur in NIDDM. Such practices as weight loss, increased physical activity, and a low-fat, high-fiber diet lead to improved insulin sensitivity (O'Dea, 1991). Reversal of the effects of obesity show

that, while there is a genetic susceptibility to NIDDM, the lifestyle factor of diet, which is established within the family system early in life, directly influences expression of this chronic disease.

Substantial evidence indicates, therefore, that obesity plays a major role in the development of chronic diseases and is, to a large degree, controllable by lifestyle modification. As awareness of the risks posed by obesity disseminates, a reduction in obesity-related chronic diseases may occur. The early ages reported for the onset of most chronic eating disorders and obesity in cosmopolitan societies, however, suggest that early family influences on this major public health problem need to be addressed.

Hypertension. Reports persist of genetic factors contributing to blood pressure regulation (Cambien et al., 1992; Carter & Kannel, 1990; Crews, Barley, Harper, & Carter, 1993; Jeunemaitre et al., 1992), despite an equal number of hypothesized genetic markers that have failed to show any statistical associations with blood pressure in other samples (Barley et al., 1991; Carter et al., 1993; Morris & Griffiths, 1988). Based on results from the Framingham Heart Study, Carter and Kannel (1990) estimate that the majority of the transmissible component for systolic blood pressure is due to polygenic background. An alternative view, however, is provided by Jeunemaitre et al. (1992), whose data directly link the angiotensin gene with hypertension among both U.S. and French samples. Although knowledge that hypertension is a familial disease has been common for decades, these data are among the first indicators of a direct genetic basis for this linkage, besides those already reported for family and lifestyle factors, such as dietary intakes of salt and fats and smoking.

Obesity also is implicated in the incidence of hypertension, which contributes to the development of cardiovascular disease. In their study of school children and their families, Burns et al. (1989) showed that weight gain in children to a level of obvious obesity resulted in increased blood pressure levels. Moreover, overweight relatives from this sample consistently had higher blood pressure levels than nonoverweight adults (Burns et al., 1989). Similarly, a twin study found that "pairs that were concordant for dyslipidemic hypertension were significantly more obese than concordant-negative pairs ... in the analysis of discordant monozygotic pairs.... The twin with dyslipidemic hypertension, although genetically identical to his co-twin, had a significantly higher mean BMI" (Selby et al., 1991, p. 2083). That is, even among identical twins who share the same genes, the one who has a poor lipid profile and hypertension may be more overweight.

It has been estimated that 48% of hypertension in European Americans and 28% in African Americans would be eliminated with adequate control of obesity alone (Burns et al., 1989). These statistics suggest that, among African Americans, genes and familial aggregation may account for a greater percent of hypertension than in European Americans. Such results also underscore the need both for continued research efforts and public health interventions aimed at health promotion and disease prevention.

In a study of 1093 women ages 50–94, it was found that the only significant difference between the *normotensive* (persons with blood pressure in the normal range: systolic blood pressure [SBP] below 160 mmHg and diastolic blood pressure [DBP] below 90 mmHg) and *hypertensive* (persons with either SBP or DPB above 160 or 90 mmHG, respectively) subjects (41.5% of the sample) was the greater obesity of the latter (Kritz-Silverstein, Wingard, & Barrett-Corner, 1989). Additional data suggest that each of these conditions— diabetes, hypertension, CHD, and obesity—tend to co-occur in families (Schumacher et al., 1990). In their ongoing examination of Health Family Trees of Utah school children, diabetics with a family history of CHD had a relative risk for CHD of 21.3 (95% CI = 9.1–50.0), while nondiabetics without a family history of early CHD had a relative risk of 1 (Schumacher et al., 1990).

Cancer. Although the influence of obesity on cancer etiology is not clearly defined, research suggests that excess dietary fat consumption may influence the development of cancers of the colon, endometrium, breast, and gallbladder (Schottenfeld, 1986). This is again supportive of the likelihood that lifestyle factors learned early in life within families have either a positive or negative influence on a health outcome. More important for familial syndromes of cancer, such as familial breast cancer, may be the occurrence of mutations in *p53* (a protein known as the antioncogene gene that apparently prevents oncogenesis, e.g., the development of a cancer) or other tumor suppressor genes along with activation of *oncogenes* (genes that cause cancer) (see Hollstein, Sidransky, Vogelstein, & Harris, 1991; Kozah, Hall, & Baird, 1986; Malkin et al., 1990). This is an area of very active ongoing research that will likely lead to the identification of genetic factors in many familial aggregations of cancer.

Family and Health Relationships: Development of Conceptual Models

Familial aggregations of chronic disease conditions and risk factors are attributable to a combination of genetic susceptibility and the presence of environmental risk factors. The concept of family and the interplay of environmental factors affecting health status and the well-being of family members is explored more extensively in subsequent sections. The concept of health is further defined to include more

elements beyond chronic disease states and the risk factors associated with disease states.

When exploring how family and familial factors affect well-being and disease, it seems clear from the previous section that a need exists to incorporate a multidimensional perspective to understand whether causation exists between a set of predictor variables associated with family characteristics and health outcomes. In this multidimensional perspective, powerful psychosocial forces need to be accounted for as part of the environment when examining familial aggregations of well-being and disease. Several conceptual models are reviewed in this section that guide the study of family and health relationships toward a multidimensional perspective.

The Concept of Family: A Contemporary Perspective

The concept of the family is continuously changing and evolving. Families today represent a great variety of household structures, marital bonds, and family arrangements. Coinciding with dramatic changes in society, new family structures have increased, such as single-parent households (much more frequently headed by a woman than a man), new stepfamily arrangements, couples with no children, and many other variations (Frisbie & Bean, 1995). Some of these arrangements are a result of powerful societal trends, socioeconomic conditions, labor market forces, and values systems, as well as ideals for achieving individualism rather than collectivism as a way of family life. Although there is some controversy regarding the strength of the family as a social institution in America, what is clear is that family structures have changed (Frisbie & Bean, 1995). These changes include, among others, an increase in the proportion of persons who have never married and live alone and an increase in the rate of divorce or marital disruptions. Traditional nuclear families composed of a two-parent household are by no means the norm in American society today. New family systems are evolving as a result of divorce, the high rates of remarriage involving children, and the creation of stepfamily systems.

When addressing health outcomes from the perspective of human development issues, the role of families is best viewed from a family systems perspective (Ross, Mirowsky, & Goldsteen, 1990). A family systems perspective is useful for recognizing the great diversity of new family arrangements. In this regard, there is a need to understand the underlying mechanisms through which family arrangements and family systems affect the health conditions of members.

The Concept of Health and Well-Being

The concept of well-being and high levels of functioning is shaping the health field. Increasing emphasis is being placed on prevention and health promotion in a manner that moves beyond rehabilitation and treatment. The medical model, which has been used traditionally to combat infectious diseases, needs to be expanded to include behavioral and psychosocial factors that are related to chronic diseases, including CVD and cancer, the two leading causes of death among adults in the United States. The study of family and health relationships must incorporate examinations of the health–disease continuum and temporal issues relating to treatment, recovery, and prevention. How familial factors affect or shape these components is a subject of continuous investigation. Thus, a need exists for incorporating a biopsychosocial and cultural perspective when addressing family–health relationships. A model that incorporates the temporal relationships of health and disease statuses must explore how family characteristics (e.g., family support) may influence how individuals move from a diseased state to a healthy state. Moreover, it is important to understand how family arrangements and situations might increase the vulnerability or be protective of individual welfare in reference to detrimental health outcomes.

Models for Studying Family and Health Relationships

Several models are introduced in this section for understanding the complex relationships between family and health within the context of current societal trends and diverse socioeconomic conditions of families.

Structural Analysis Model

A general approach that has guided the empirical work on family and health relationships is the structural analysis model proposed by Ross et al. (1990). The study of family and its effect on health is explored in this model based on two types of patterns: causal chains and conditional and interaction effects. According to this approach, both causal and conditional effects are important for empirical testing of why and how the family affects well-being.

Four aspects of family arrangements are described under this structural analysis approach to explore various causal and conditional effects: marriage, parenthood, the wife's employment, and the family's social and economic status (Ross et al., 1990). The effects of marriage as a family system and their relationship to the well-being of individual family members have been the most widely explored component of family living arrangements. Several explanations have been given for observed health differences associated with marital status. The structural arrangements model provides the basis for incorporating a series of predictors or explanatory variables that account for health variations among family members that appear to be a function of marriage.

Sex Differences, Marriage, Longevity, and Health

A clear superiority of women in terms of survivorship and longevity has been established within all contemporary urbanized societies having modern health-care systems and in most developing nations (Haug & Folmar, 1986; Hazzard, 1986, 1989; Smith & Warner, 1989; Verbrugge, 1985; Waldron, 1983). Numerous mechanisms have been proposed to explain these gender differences, including the protective effects of female hormones and the menstrual cycle and differences in lipid metabolism and associated lipoproteins. Other explanations involve the lifestyle and social differences associated with risk factors (smoking, consumption of saturated fats, risk-taking behavior, male–male competition, hazardous occupations) for disease and early mortality as well as the genetic effects of X-linked recessive conditions, sex-limited traits, and DNA repair processes.

No clear frontrunner has become obvious to explain the greater longevity of women. Instead, the differential mortality rates and life spans of men and women are most likely a product of the biological complexity and multifactorial etiology of men and women. Other authorities continue to champion a genetic model associated with genotypic sex (see Smith & Warner, 1989), often based on the hypothesized influences of sex hormones on longevity, while others support a lifestyle and environmental model (see Hazzard, 1986, 1989). The best models, however, probably lie somewhere between or are combinations of these extremes (see Verbruegge, 1985).

A prominent pattern in our society, therefore, is that women outlive men. For every 100 women age 65 plus, there are 67 men, while for every 100 women age 85 plus, there are only 42 men (data cited in Haug & Folmar, 1986). Because married women tend to be younger than their spouses, their longer lives often are completed while they are bereft of spouses and experiencing greater social isolation. Haug and Folmar (1986) suggest that, due to these different experiences, women are more likely to lack the support of a spouse, live alone, and suffer emotional, cognitive, and health losses— factors that suggest a lower quality of life—yet women still live longer.

Physiological differences between men and women also may contribute to observed sex differences in longevity and survival. For example, it is widely accepted that menstruating women are protected from CHD. Although most early theories suggested that high levels of circulating estrogens in women were protective (see McGill & Stern, 1979; Sullivan, 1982; Waldron, 1983), recent analyses have provided conflicting results and theories. Some evidence suggests that, rather than estrogen, loss of iron stores during each menstrual cycle may be the protective mechanism (Sullivan, 1983). Based on findings that iron in catalytic amounts enhances the production of toxic oxygen metabolites, Sullivan (1983) suggested that higher levels of circulating ferritin may be capable of damaging heart tissues. Thus, iron deficiency following menstruation, rather than hormones, may be what protects menstruating women from CHD, a result indicating that women who take iron-fortified vitamin supplements are at increased risk of CHD compared to women who do not. In contrast, men, who do not possess any similar mechanism for reducing their iron stores and circulating ferritin levels (Sullivan, 1983), may show increased CHD secondary to their usually persistent higher levels of circulating ferritin.

Biological and cultural/environmental factors are likely to play important roles in producing sex differentials both in mortality rates resulting from specific causes and ultimately in longevity differences between the sexes (see Waldron, 1983). Wylie (1994) suggests, for example, that one strong inference from the accumulated data on sex differentials in longevity is that genes on "the X-chromosome contribute powerfully to improve female survival" (p. 674). For *hemizygous* (having only a single copy of a particular chromosome, in this case the X-chromosome) men, therefore, the idea that exposure of their X-linked genes to environmental and lifestyle stressors may result in reduced longevity cannot be refuted at present. Although some observers have suggested that greater female survivorship is a universal phenomena in both extant and extinct human and nonhuman populations, current evidence indicates that males experience and have experienced greater survivorship than females in some populations (data reviewed in Gravilov & Gavilova, 1993; Waldron, 1983). Thus, Gravilov and Gravilova (1993) suggest that the widely proposed inherent biological superiority in the longevity of women may be no more than a statistical artifact of sampling from particular human societies during specific decades. Thus, the question, "Why do women live longer than men?" posed by Hazzard (1989) and Hoden (1987), apparently remains to be answered.

In the general U.S. population, the average life span of women ranges between 75–80 years and that of men between 70–75 years across marital, racial ethnic, socioeconomic, and regional subgroupings (National Center for Health Statistics, 1986). Married men outlive their nonmarried peers, while married women do not live quite as long as their single peers. This finding has been interpreted by some as indicating that marriage somehow benefits men in survival potential, but reduces the survival of women. Most such comparisons, however, contain methodological flaws involving insufficient controls for educational, occupational, maternal, social, and cultural influences on the life span. Other common flaws include the failure to control for possible adverse behavioral, psychological, or health attributes that may be associated

with men remaining single or women marrying. Moreover, married women are exposed more frequently to physiological stresses and mortality associated with pregnancy, miscarriages, and childbirth than are nonmarried women.

Concepts of vitality and frailty are likely to be useful in understanding differences in longevity between married and single men and women. Vitality is associated with greater resilience to or lack of susceptibility to diseases and environmental stressors that are predictive of disease and death in persons with more average buffering mechanisms. Conversely, persons with below-average buffering mechanisms are described frequently as exhibiting frailty in the form of increased susceptibility to disease or risk of death from extraneous factors. Frail men may be buffered from stress by marriage, or those men who marry may tend to have greater vitality. Another possibility is that those with greater frailty may be less inclined to marry. Conversely, frail females may be more likely to marry or fail to benefit from marital buffering mechanisms, while females with greater vitality may be less likely to marry.

The concepts of vitality and frailty affecting mortality differentials by marital status (due to marriage protection) require further investigation. For example, current studies have yet to discern the extent to which mortality differentials are a result of marriage selection or arise from causal mechanisms associated with a protective effect of marriage (Fu & Goldman, 1996). A recent study using data from the National Longitudinal Study of Youth examined the marriage selection hypothesis (Fu & Goldman, 1996). In this study the authors examined health-related characteristics and behaviors affecting entry into marriage. The results of this study showed that health-related variables are, indeed, associated with the timing of first marriage. People with unhealthy behaviors such as high levels of alcohol consumption and use of hard drugs were less likely to be married than their healthier counterparts. Of particular interest in this study was the finding that the presence of health limitations was unrelated to entry into marriage (Fu & Goldman, 1996).

Another element of vitality to consider in a marriage bond is the fact that persons with long-term and/or late-life disabilities who reside in families may engage in more active lifestyles, receive more personalized care, or maintain better nutrition and lifestyles than similar individuals without family support. Married men also are more likely to benefit from these aspects of spousal caregiving than are married women, who are commonly younger, healthier, and less likely to engage in full-time employment than their spouses. Thus, married women are likely to have and invest more "time" and "vitality" on spousal care than do their older mates.

Survival and longevity variation by marital status have led to numerous explanatory theories of why married individuals might live longer. Married couples have more social support to combat stress and each partner has someone on whom to rely for care when ill. Moreover, the ability to find a spouse may be selective of certain physical, mental, and emotional characteristics associated with longer survival, as previously discussed (Fu & Goldman, 1996; Mott & Haurin, 1985). Most research, therefore, supports the better survival probabilities of married individuals (Kitagawa & Hauser, 1973; Mott & Haurin, 1981), with an example being Mott and Haurin's (1981) study in which multiple differences in overt health, employment, and "selection processes" involved in matrimony were controlled. Specifically, results indicated that married men, ages 45–59, were more likely to survive 15 years than nonmarried men, with respective adjusted survival probabilities (the likelihood of surviving until the end of a longitudinal study, in this case 15 years) of .712 and .632. After adjusting for mate selectivity phenomena, economic well-being, and overt health problems, respective survival probabilities of .812 versus .732 ($p < .01$), .692 versus .618 ($p < .05$), and .615 versus .544 at ages 45–49, 50–54, and 55–59, respectively, were reported. Significant residual differentials of this kind are interpreted as supporting social-psychological effects on survival (see Mott & Haurin, 1985, Figs. 2 and 3, pp. 43–45).

More recent studies have demonstrated that the relationship between mortality and marital status also is mediated by family income (Rogers, 1995; Ross et al., 1990). These results highlight the importance of incorporating socioeconomic indicators into the study of marriage and mortality. As Rogers pointed out in his study, income reflects people's current social circumstances and, together with other factors, helps explain their current life chances. Those people who were single and poor, for example, experienced the highest mortality, whereas married people with high incomes had the lowest mortality of all groups.

A variety of explanations have been postulated to explain how marriage may protect partners against mortality. Married people have greater social support and more social bonds; they are thus healthier because, as Rogers (1995) pointed out, "married individuals are more likely to comply with medical regimens, abstain from smoking, drink moderately, avoid risk-taking behavior, and lead stable, secure, and scheduled lifestyles" (p. 524). Higher incomes provide additional protection and access to resources for securing a more healthy lifestyle (Rogers, 1995). The effects of marriage on a healthy lifestyle also have been postulated to result from the support given a partner in avoiding the onset of disease, helping to catch and treat disease, and aiding in recovery (Ross et al., 1990). Such health protections that are part of marriage also appear to favor men's well-being more than they lead to more positive circumstances for women (Ross et al., 1990). It remains to be seen, however, what forms of health protection are developed within marriage bonds as

women's roles, values, attitudes, and behaviors change inside and outside the household, due to employment, income, and status (Rogers, 1995).

Another topic within structural analysis, economic marital acquisitions, is a conditional effect for explaining a possible positive effect of marriage on women's health. Using data from the 1987 National Medical Expenditure survey, Hahn (1993) examined this effect by testing the extent to which economic assets gained through marriage explained the inverse relationship between marriage and poor health of women. Hahn found that married women were rated healthier than women who were single primarily because the latter were divorced, separated or widowed or had never married. Factors included as marital acquisitions were owning a home, having income in excess of their own, having private insurance, and having a greater number of children in the home. The last factor (i.e., number of children) was unexpected, and age of the children, mother's employment, and childcare arrangements were not included as control variables (these variables can affect the nature of the relationship between having children and the well-being of parents). Consequently, these results should be interpreted with caution.

Controversy also exists regarding the effect that children have on the emotional and physical well-being of parents. These effects are complex and depend on many factors (type of family arrangement—single, divorce, married—family income, mother's paid employment, support from partner) (Ross et al., 1990). From an economic standpoint, increases in the economic well-being of families tend to reduce the negative effects of children on the health of parents (Ross et al., 1990). The most detrimental effects on parents' health are observed in single female-headed households in which children face economic deprivation, have insufficient social support and access to services, and have limited possibilities for improving their social conditions.

Health Effects on Family Systems

The study of family and health-related outcomes should not be confined only to explorations of health as a dependent variable. Reciprocal relationships associated with declines in health status and the effects of health on marital quality also need to be considered. Booth and Johnson (1994) examined the effects of health changes as shifts occurred in the quality of marital relationships longitudinally in a national sample of 1298 married persons. The authors used two measures of marital quality: an attitudinal assessment of marital happiness and a divorce proneness measure. Divorce proneness was defined as the propensity to divorce. Health status was assessed by the question: In general, would you say your own health is excellent, good, fair, or poor? The results of this study showed that decrements in health were associated with a negative influence on the quality of marital relationships. The effects on marital quality were explained by such factors as changes in financial circumstances, shifts in the division of household labor, declines in marital interaction, and problematic behavior by individuals whose health had declined (Booth & Johnson, 1994).

Even though the authors reported that changes in health status had a detrimental effect on marital quality, they also recognized that not all marriages seemed to be affected similarly. The authors recommended that future researchers should examine factors that differentiate those marriages in which the quality of marital relationships remains unaffected by decrements in health status from those marriages in which the quality of marital relationships is negatively affected by health problems. Differences in health behaviors that are associated with marriage selection are another example of reciprocal relationships between family and health (Fu & Goldman, 1996).

Integrative Models: A Biopsychosocial and Cultural Approach to the Study of Family and Health Relationships

The increase in the proportion of minority populations in the United States has brought a growing recognition of the diversity, philosophy, household structure, and family arrangements of ethnic/racial families (Jacobsen, 1995). Ethnic families and mixed racial families add new dimensions to the study of family and health. The study of ethnic variation as it pertains to family characteristics and arrangements provides an opportunity to identify how families from different ethnic backgrounds view health and respond to disease. With increased economic hardships, and societal changes, family systems have become very adaptive and responsive to day-to-day living conditions. Some families are able to cope and develop buffer mechanisms against conditions of poverty, unemployment, violence, and lack of health care. Other families, however, just "fall through the cracks," a possible result of racism, discrimination, or some form of social segregation associated with economic hardships and social ills. It is in the context of ethnicity, race, racism, and health that new empirical models of family and health need to be developed (Guralnik & Leveille, 1997).

The study of ethnic families and their structural characteristics and cultural expressions can provide important clues for understanding differential health outcomes among diverse populations. Of particular interest for the study of family and health relationships, therefore, is the extent to which issues of culture and ethnicity explain familial circumstances and arrangements. These contextual circumstances, in turn, may play a variety of roles in affecting either positively or negatively the health practices, attitudes, behaviors,

and overall health statuses of individual family members. Unfortunately, only limited attempts have been undertaken to develop empirical models in the area of family and health that include elements of culture and ethnicity. However, concepts of family have been incorporated in the context of cultural theory to explain, for example, how Anglo families differ from other ethnic families in terms of parenting styles and the role of extended families (Arnett, 1995). The theory developed by Arnett, for example, involving distinctions between broad and narrow socialization, places the socialization process of the family in a cultural context. Cultures that emphasize narrow socialization place obedience and conformity as their higher values, whereas cultures characterized by broad socialization promote independence, individualism, and self-expression (Arnett, 1995).

An important issue concerning the incorporation of culture and ethnicity into the study of family and health relationships is the need to measure directly elements of culture and their psychosocial components (Betancourt & Lopez, 1993; Hughes, Seidman, & Williams, 1993). Unfortunately, little emphasis has been placed on developing theories of family and health within a cultural context when addressing differences in health and disease statuses. One of the reasons for the limited analyses of ethnicity and culture within family and health relationships has been the complexity of factors that are directly or indirectly involved in these relationships (Guralnik & Leveille, 1997). Perhaps the one exception to this lack of theory-building has occurred within the profession of public health, in which several conceptual models have been developed that can be integrated into the study of family and health relationships (James, 1993; Krieger et al., 1993; La Veist, 1996). These conceptual models include a biopsychosocial and a cultural approach, both of which are beginning to be used in studies of ethnic differences in health outcomes. Family factors are included within these models as important mediators for explaining health outcome differences among various ethnic groups.

One of these models (James, 1993) was developed as an alternative explanation for documenting the psychosocial significance of race or ethnicity as a risk factor for the delivery of low-birth-weight infants among ethnic minority groups (e.g., African Americans). The high rate of low birth weight and infant mortality among children of African American women is one of the most pressing public health problems that remains unresolved today (Dean et al., 1995; James, 1993; Krieger et al., 1993). Emphasis in this model is placed on incorporation of structural factors such as economic and sociocultural forces, which have been neglected in the study of health problems such as low birth weight (James, 1993). According to the model proposed by James, high rates of low birth weight and infant mortality observed in African Americans can be explained through a biopsychosocial process.

Because African American women belong to one of the most socioeconomically disadvantaged groups in our society, they often are exposed to physical and social environmental stressors that generate psychosocial stress (James, 1993). Of interest is the fact that family and social networks can protect individuals from the negative effects of stress by acting as sources of social support. These sources of social support found within the family and other social networks are part of the cultural framework of these women. Protective cultural forces or culturally based strategies can serve to protect the psychological well-being of pregnant African American women within the context of family processes. If cultural traits that are expressed in family relationships are not present or are being overwhelmed by issues of poverty, isolation, and discrimination, then disadvantaged women are more inclined to engage in high-risk behavior (e.g., smoking, drinking, drug use) to cope with their situation (James, 1993). According to the model proposed by James, once behavioral risk factors begin to affect the health status of women, the standard biological risks will follow (e.g., low weight gain, anemia), causing an increase in the likelihood of delivering a low-birth-weight infant.

Adding another dimension to the cultural significance of family as a factor for explaining health–disease outcomes among ethnic minority women is the "so called Mexican/Hispanic-paradox, or family paradox" (Frisbie & Bean, 1995; Scribner, 1996). Despite similar socioeconomic circumstances between African American and Hispanics or Mexican Americans, the rates of low birth weight and infant mortality for Mexican Americans closely resemble the rates observed in the Anglo population (Krieger et al., 1993). This paradoxical combination of low mortality and diminished low birth weight despite sociodemographic risk factors has been interpreted as resulting from protections derived from traditional Hispanic or Mexican cultural orientations (Balcazar, Peterson, & Cobas, 1996; Balcazar, Peterson, & Krull, 1997; Scribner, 1996; Scribner & Dwyer, 1989; Sherraden & Barrera, 1996a,b). Family characteristics have been postulated as a central component of such cultural protection. Among the family characteristics and cultural values of interest are (1) the greater marital stability of Mexican American marriages, (2) a more familistic rather than individualistic orientation (similar to the concept of narrow socialization described by Arnett (1995)), (3) a cultural emphasis on interpersonal harmony in relationships, (4) the avoidance of conflict in relationships, (5) a strong attachment to nuclear and extended family members, (6) respect for authority figures, (7) a preference for closeness and warmth in interpersonal space, (8) a present time orientation valuing the here and now, and (9) strong gender roles providing for distinctive behavior by men and women (Castro, 1992; Marin & Marin, 1991; Ramirez, 1991; Zambrana, 1995).

The family paradox concept provides a good opportunity to explore further the extent to which family cultural characteristics help explain the health of individual members of minority groups. Many examples in the literature have described elements of Hispanic/Mexican family variables in relationship to health. These family variables can be used (1) as mediators of factors affecting health outcomes (Castro et al., 1996), (2) as promoters of positive change in health behaviors (Baranowski, Nader, Dunn, & Vanderpool, 1982; Cousins et al., 1992), (3) as factors for the identification of subgroups who have different risk factors for health outcomes (Balcazar, Castro, & Krull, 1995; Balcazar et al., 1997), and (4) as elements of interventions for delivering effective health promotion programs (Castro et al., 1995; Flores, Castor, & Fernandez-Esquer, 1995).

Of particular interest in the study of family and health relationships among Hispanics/Mexican Americans are issues of whether Mexican Americans have a limited sense of control over their lives, have a passive approach toward the recognition of health problems, or have a fatalistic acceptance of illness (Castro, Furth, & Karlow, 1984; Castro et al., 1996). Conflicting data exist regarding this pessimistic notion about health attitudes and beliefs among Mexican Americans despite strong familistic orientations observed in this group. Research is needed to discern the impact of these psychosocial influences on the health of Mexican Americans. In this regard, the concepts of control, self-efficacy, and how family characteristics might have an effect on either supporting or not supporting these individual traits require further examination. The social psychology of health and illness behaviors is a necessary area of focus to understand concepts such as a sense of control and self-efficacy within both cultural and familial social contexts (Kessler et al., 1995; Ross et al., 1990).

Contextual Models for Examining Family and Health Relationships

An important need exists for models that identify components of the complex contextual environment that have health implications for families. Such a contextual model would include indicators of social class, discrimination/oppression, social inequality, and complex social support systems available both within as well as outside family boundaries (Guralnik & Leveille, 1997; House, Landis, & Umberson, 1988; Krieger et al., 1993; McLean et al., 1993). The development of contextual models of family and health relationships must incorporate a wider range of intervening factors at the individual, family, neighborhood, and community levels. These new contextual models should reflect the interplay among family factors within the context of social, economic, and cultural systems that affect health and disease states of family members.

Existing psychosocial models such as the one proposed by McLean and coworkers (1993) can be used to guide the development of such contextual models. In the McLean model, stressors and buffer systems play both mediating and direct roles within a broader social, environmental, political, and historical context. Within this model, psychosocial factors are hypothesized to affect pregnancy outcomes directly through effects on behavior or indirectly through physiological (biological) responses. For example, in the context of pregnancy outcomes such as low birth weight, psychosocial factors represent behaviors associated with standard risk factors such as consumption of alcohol and illicit drugs, cigarette smoking, inadequate diet, and unprotected teenage sex (James, 1993). Alterations of physiological states such as changes in the immunological response due to stress and poor nutrition are examples of indirect effects. Social support systems both within and outside families as well as the nurturing effects of diverse cultural traits of family members can serve as important protective factors. Such familial/cultural support systems appear to prevent unhealthy behaviors and practices leading to various disease statuses (including unwanted pregnancy outcomes).

Research on the Mexican paradox described earlier strongly suggests that the worsening of birth outcomes among second-generation Mexican American women is associated with the role that acculturation plays in promoting "unhealthy practices" during pregnancy (Balcazar et al., 1996; Scribner & Dwyer, 1989). Among these "unhealthy" practices associated with the "acculturation hypothesis" are enhanced reproductive risks resulting from the increased use of toxic substances during pregnancy, such as tobacco, alcohol, and other illegal substances (e.g., marijuana). Another problematic consequence is the deterioration in diet found in pregnant Mexican American women who are highly acculturated versus those who are low in acculturation (Guendelman & Abrams, 1995). Although increased acculturation has been associated with negative health practices during pregnancy, positive protective factors also have been identified that appear to be a function of Mexican culture. For example, retention of a traditional Mexican cultural orientation has been postulated to provide "protective mechanisms" that shelter pregnant women from adverse health conditions, including the worst risk factors of pregnancy (Balcazar et al., 1996; Scribner & Dwyer, 1989). Among the cultural factors that have been postulated as "protective" during pregnancy are the role of the family and family support systems. There is supportive evidence that family functioning or family support has been linked to protection against negative pregnancy outcomes (Ramsey, Abell, & Baker, 1986; Sherraden & Barrera, 1996a,b).

The use of contextual models also means that minority group family systems (e.g., African Americans) may differ substantially from definitions associated with the traditional anglo- or Euro-American family (Dean et al., 1995). For example, in the African American culture, families tend to place great value on the wisdom of elders (including grandparents, uncles, and aunts). Thus, parents may not have final authority over their children with regard to provision of guidance, may not be their offsprings' main source of wisdom, or may not command their greatest respect. Obviously, a variety of support mechanisms from family networks are associated with elements of family functioning in African American families. According to Billingsley (1992), the African American family is best described as: "an intimate association of persons of African descent who are related to one another by a variety of means including blood, marriage, formal adoption, informal adoption or by appropriation sustained by a history of common residence in America and deeply imbedded in a network of social structures, both internal and external to itself. Numerous interlocking elements come together forming an extraordinarily resilient institution" (quoted in Dean et al., 1995, p. 21).

The African American experience with respect to the prevalence of hypertension and its potential for prevention (Krieger et al., 1993) can be used to illustrate the need for contextual models when exploring family and health relationships. As described in a previous section, genes and familial aggregation may account for a greater percent of hypertension in African Americans than in European Americans. However, a closer look at the research on hypertension among African Americans suggests that a variety of stressors, including responses to distressing social, economic, and environmental situations, may be important psychosocial risk factors for hypertension (Krieger et al., 1993).

Krieger and colleagues (1993) have underscored, for example, that measuring racism and discrimination as potential stressors leading to elevated blood pressure among African Americans has been a difficult task. This is one reason why it has been difficult to identify sources of stress and inequality as contributing factors in causal links that explain hypertension in African Americans. Development of contextual models, therefore, may facilitate our understanding of how buffer mechanisms (including family, cultural traits, and social support) may counteract the negative effects of stressors. In addition, these models may shed light on sources of stress that are linked to racism, discrimination, and cultural insensitivity. All these elements of the family's social context can have important health implications.

The development of contextual models using family and related social support variables also may help to understand how public health interventions may facilitate the control of hypertension in different cultures. This is particularly true in groups that are especially vulnerable to hypertension but for whom it has been difficult to design interventions, such as adult African American males. Family, social support groups and community network organizations, including religious institutions and churches, have been important avenues for intervention and control of hypertension among adult African American males. Through the power of their churches and the role of spirituality in their lives, significant others have a central role in encouraging adult African American males to comply with hypertension control programs (Eng, Hatch, & Callan, 1985). Understanding the significant effects of churches as units of practice will require new approaches to the assessment of social supports and social networks within the cultural and social context of African Americans. The role of families in their context with respect to control of hypertension control and limiting other disease conditions (e.g., diabetes) must be viewed as part of a complex cultural and social system in which the church frequently plays a mediating, and often primary, function (Eng et al., 1985).

Future Research and Policy Implications

Models of family and health relationships described in this chapter emphasize that a multidimensional approach should be used when examining reciprocal relationships between family and health. Previous and ongoing studies of familial aggregations of disease have facilitated the examination of the role of genetic causation and its complex relationships with the environment. They also have shown that family as a system and its reciprocal relationships with health and disease must be studied not in isolation, but in conjunction with the psychosocial, economic, and cultural contexts of families. Family systems are dynamic, and their structure and relationships will vary depending on the cultural and social context operating at a given time. The concept of family systems must be inclusive and must account for differential interpretations and definitions of the family within specific historical, social, and cultural contexts. In this regard, all Anglo families will not conform to a unified definition of the family system, and Anglo family forms do not provide a general template for families from other cultures.

Families are not static; they are part of a social, environmental, political, and historical context that is constantly changing. In addition, a variety of cultural norms, attitudes, and behaviors present in modern society affect how family members interact inside and outside the family system. These different interactions take the form of social support, psychological well-being, and other resources that may have important implications for the maintenance of health and prevention of disease within families.

Future research on families and health outcomes need to emphasize the development of integrative and contextual models and the measurement of many predictor variables at different levels of social organization. New statistical and methodological strategies are needed that include the analysis of family variables in conjunction with a variety of variables that incorporate elements of the social system (e.g., discrimination, racism, economic well-being, etc.) as well as elements of the psychosocial environment of family members.

Persistent problems exist in the current literature examining familial influences on health and disease. Much of our current knowledge is based on cross-sectional data; a great need exists for longitudinal designs. Greater attention is needed in the study of family and health issues to the selection of more representative samples, numbers of cases observed, and degree of statistical power attained. Questions of access to health care also influence most relationships between family and health.

Given equality of access to health care, family still appears to have a disproportionate effect on our health throughout our lives. Environmental exposures, as well as genetic contributions of our parents, may affect our predispositions to disease during uterine development, infancy, childhood, or periods of growth and development. Conversely, genetic heritage may not express its potential until later life, after problematic alleles are already passed to the next generation or have hindered our own attainment of marriage and reproductive success.

The study of family and health relationships should be expanded to include family systems that take into account the different members of any family. The health–disease continuum also must reflect those health outcomes associated with recovery, control, and management of disease conditions and how family systems and other contextual forces may play a role in affecting or modifying these outcomes.

Research in this area could be expanded to define global indicators of the health and well-being of families as an outcome measurement. These new definitions of family health could be used as a baseline to monitor the broader effects of environment, social segregation, racism, and other aspects of the social environment on the health of all family members. These global indicators could incorporate the parameters of health and disease for all members of a particular family system being studied (parents, children, other nuclear and extended family members living in the same household, etc.).

The family's role as a protective and nurturing element in the health process should not be underestimated. Patient–provider relationships within the medical system of health care could benefit from a better understanding of the powerful positive influences of families. In-depth studies of minority families and their strengths are needed to develop new approaches and systems of patient–provider relationships. Cultural sensitivity and cultural competence are important issues that could reduce barriers between health-care providers and members of minority and other families.

In summary, several implications for health policy can be derived from the family perspectives described in this chapter. Familial aggregations of disease conditions should be better monitored by the health-care system and by the family itself so that preventive approaches can be identified. The family should be treated as a unit when addressing these aggregations of disease conditions and when formulating preventive approaches. Health problems can, in part, be conceptualized as a family problem and, as such, can be addressed within the context of the family system.

The strengths of family systems should be viewed as part of the process of delivering health care and providing patient care education and managing disease conditions. Moreover, cultural diversity issues relating to family relationships, practices, and counseling services must be emphasized. In this regard, policies should be directed toward emphasizing the positive aspects/strengths of families by social service organizations, networks, and community agencies. A strategy of empowerment for families should be used to enhance elements to elicit positive changes in health and the prevention of disease. More community organizations and community health networks should be involved in the promotion of families as positive systems of change in association with the health-care system.

References

Abora, J. C., & Mott, F. (1991). Substance use and prenatal care during pregnancy among young women. *Family Planning Perspectives, 23*(3), 117–128.

Anderson, R. A., Barnes, T. L., Lee, J., & Swenson, D. (1989). Restriction fragment length polymorphisms associated with abnormal lipid levels in an adolescent population. *Atherosclerosis, 77,* 227–237.

Andres, R. (1978). Effect of obesity on total mortality. *International Journal of Obesity, 4*(4), 381.

Arnett, J. J. (1995). Broad and narrow socialization: The family in the context of a cultural theory. *Journal of Marriage and the Family, 57,* 617–628.

Balcazar, H., Castro, F. G., & Krull, J. L. (1995). Cancer risk reduction in Mexican American women: The role of acculturation, education, and health risk factors. *Health Education Quarterly, 22,* 61–84.

Balcazar, H., Peterson, G., & Cobas, J. (1996). Acculturation and health-related risk behaviors among Mexican American pregnant youth. *American Journal of Health Behavior, 20,* 425–433.

Balcazar, H., Peterson, G., & Krull, J. (1997). Acculturation and family cohesiveness in Mexican American pregnant women: Social and health implications. *Journal of Family & Community Health, 20,* 17–32.

Baranowski, T., Nader, P. R., Dunn, K., & Vanderpool, N. A. (1982). Family self-help: Promoting changes in health behavior. *Journal of Marriage and the Family,* 161–173.

Barley, J., Carter, N. D., Cruickshank, K., Jeffrey, S., Smith, A., Charlett, A., & Webb, D. J. (1991). Renin and atrial naturetic peptide restriction length polymorphisms: Association with ethnicity and blood pressure. *Journal of Hypertension, 9,* 993–996.

Betancourt, H., & López, S. R. (1993). The study of culture, ethnicity, and race in American psychology. *American Psychologist, 48,* 629–637.

Billingsley, A. (1992). *Climbing Jacob's ladder: The enduring legacy of African-American families.* New York: Simon & Shuster.

Bouchard, C., Perusse, L., LeBlanc, C., Tremblay, A., & Theriault, G. (1988). Inheritance of the amount and distribution of human body fat. *International Journal of Obesity, 12*(3), 205–215.

Bogin, B. (1988). *Patterns of human growth.* New York: Cambridge University Press.

Booth, A., & Johnson, D. R. (1994). Declining health and marital quality. *Journal of Marriage and the Family, 56,* 218–223.

Brown, M. S., & Goldstein, J. L. (1984). How LDL receptors influence cholesterol and atherosclerosis. *Scientific America, 251*(5), 58–66.

Brown, M. S., & Goldstein, J. L. (1986). A receptor-mediated pathway for cholesterol homeostasis. *Science, 232,* 34–47.

Burns, T. L., Moll, P. P., & Lauer, R. M. (1989). The relation between ponderosity and coronary risk factors in children and their relatives. *American Journal of Epidemiology, 129,* 973–987.

Cambien, F., Poirier, O., et al. (1992). Deletion polymorphism in the gene for angiotensin-converting enzyme is a potent risk factor for myocardial infarction. *Nature, 359,* 641–644.

Carter, C. L., & Kannel, W. B. (1990). Evidence of a rare gene for low systolic blood pressure in the Framingham heart study. *Human Heredity, 40,* 235–241.

Carter, N. D., Cooper, R., Crews, D. E., Cruickshank, K., Jeffery, S., Ozunlesi, A., Sagnella, G., & Barley, J. (1993). Angiotensin I-converting enzyme polymorphism in different populations: Associations with hypertension and plasma renin activity. *The Third International Symposium on ACE Inhibition* (abstract).

Castro, F. G. (1992). *Hispanic mental health: Issues for the year 2000 and beyond.* Washington, DC: National Coalition for Hispanic Health and Human Service Organizations.

Castro, F. G., Furth, P., & Karlow, H. (1984). The health beliefs of Mexican, Mexican American and Anglo American women. *Hispanic Journal of Behavioral Sciences, 6,* 365–383.

Castro, F. G., Elder, J., Elder, J., Coe, K., Tafoza-Barraza, H., Moratto, S., Campbell, N., & Talaneia, G. (1995) Mobilizing churches for health promotion in Latino communities: Compañeros en la Salud. *Journal of the National Cancer Institute Monographs, 18,* 127–135.

Castro, F. G., Coe, K., Gutierrez, S., & Saenz, D. (1996). Designing health promotion programs for Latinos. In P. M. Kato & T. Mann (Eds.), *Handbook of diversity issues in health psychology* (pp. 319–345). New York: Plenum.

Cho, K. R., & Vogelstein, B. (1991). Genetic alterations in the adenoma carcinoma sequence. *Cancer, 70,* 1727–1731.

Claus, E., Risch, N., & Thompson, W. (1989). Age at onset as an indicator of familial risk of breast cancer. *American Journal of Epidemiology, 131,* 961–972.

Cousins, J. H., Rubovits, D. S., Dunn, J., Reeves, R., Ramirez, A., & Forez, T. J. (1992). Family versus individually oriented intervention for weight loss in Mexican American women. *Public Health Reports, 107,* 549–555.

Cox, N. J., Epstein, P. A., & Spielman, R. S. (1989). Linkage studies on NIDDM and the insulin and insulin-receptor genes. *Diabetes, 38,* 653–658.

Crews, D. E. (1988). Body weight, blood pressure and the risk of total and cardiovascular diseases and diabetes mellitus in a modernizing population. *Social Science and Medicine, 16,* 175–181.

Crews, D. E. (1989). Cause specific mortality, life expectancy, and debilitation in aging Polynesians. *American Journal of Human Biology, 1*(3), 347–353.

Crews, D. E., & Gerber, L. (1993). Why are age and chronic degenerative diseases related? In D. E. Crews & R. Garruto (Eds.), *Biological anthropology and aging: An emerging synthesis.* New York: Oxford University Press.

Crews, D. E., & James, G. D. (1991). Human evolution and the genetic epidemiology of chronic degenerative diseases. In G. G. N. Mascie-Taylor & G. Lasker (Eds.), *Applications of biological anthropology to human affairs* (pp. 185–206). Cambridge, England: Cambridge Studies in Biological Anthropology.

Crews, D. E., Bindon, J. R., & Smith-Ozeran, J. E. (1991). Apolipoprotein polymorphisms and body habitus in American Samoans. *Diabetes, 40*(Suppl. 1), 433A.

Crews, D. E., Barley, J., Harper, G. J., & Carter, N. D. (1993). Renin and ANP RFLPs and ACE polymorphism in American Samoans: Associations with blood pressure. *American Journal of Human Biology, 5*(1), 134–135.

Dean, G., Mathis, M., Shaw, P., White, P., & Wingate, T. (1995). *The gap: Infant mortality rates. Recommendations for interventions to reduce the black–white infant mortality gap.* Atlanta: Georgia Division of Public Health, Family Health Branch, Women's Health Section.

Dorman, J. S., Trucco, M., LaPorte, R. E., & Kuller, L. H. (1988). Family studies: The key to understanding the genetic and environmental etiology of chronic disease? *Genetic Epidemiology, 5,* 305–319.

Douglas, J. G., & Milligan, S. E. (1991, Spring). Race, ethnicity, and health: Diabetes and hypertension. *Ethnicity and Disease, 1,* 152–153.

Eaton, S. B., Konner, M. J., & Shostak, K. (1988). Stone agers in the fast lane: Chronic diseases in evolutionary perspective. *American Journal of Medicine, 84,* 739–749.

Eng, E., Hatch, J., & Callan, A. (1985). Institutionalizing social support through the church and into the community. *Health Education Quarterly, 12,* 81–92.

Flores, E. T., Castro, F. G., & Fernandez-Esquer, M. E. (1995). Social theory, social action, and intervention research: Implications for cancer prevention among Latinos. *Journal of the National Cancer Institute Monographs, 18,* 101–108.

Frisbie, W. P. & Bean, F. D. (1995). The Latino family in comparative perspective: Trends and current conditions. In C. Jacobsen (Ed.), *Racial and ethnic families in the United States* (pp. 29–41). New York: Garland.

Fu, H., & Goldman, N. (1996). Incorporating health into models of marriage choice: Demographic and sociological perspectives. *Journal of Marriage and the Family, 58,* 740–758.

Garruto, J., & Crews, D. E. (1994). Epilogue: Human aging—the scientific relevance of transdisciplinary approaches. In D. E. Crews & R. Garruto (Eds.), *Biological anthropology and aging: An emerging synthesis* (pp. 434–436). New York: Oxford University Press.

Gerber, L. M., Schnall, P. L., & Pickering, T. (1990). Body fat and its distribution in relation to casual ambulatory blood pressure. *Hypertension, 15*(5), 508–513.

Gleuck, C. J., Fallat, R. W., & Tsang, R. (1974). Hyperlipidemia in progeny of parents with myocardial infarction before age 50. *American Journal of Diseases of Children, 127,* 70–75.

Gravilov, L. A., & Gravilova, N. S. (1991). *The biology of life span: A quantitative approach* (V. P. Skulachev, Ed.; J. Payne & L. Payne, Trans.). New York: Hardwood Academic.

Guendelman, S., & Abrams, B. (1995). Dietary intake among Mexican American women: Generational differences and a comparison with white non-Hispanic women. *American Journal of Public Health, 85,* 20–25.

Guralnik, J. M., & Leveille, S. G. (1997). Annotation: Race, ethnicity, and health outcomes—unraveling the mediating role of socioeconomic status. *American Journal of Public Health, 87,* 728–729.

Hahn, B. A. (1993). Marital status and women's health: The effect of economic marital acquisitions. *Journal of Marriage and the Family, 55,* 495–504.

Hasstedt, S. J., Ramirez, M. E., Kuida, H., & Williams, R. R. (1989). Recessive inheritance of a relative fat pattern. *American Journal of Human Genetics, 45,* 917–925.

Haug, M. R., & Folmar, S. J. (1986). Longevity, gender, and quality of life. *Journal of Health and Social Behavior, 27,* 332–345.

Hazzard, W. R. (1986). Biological basis of the sex differential in longevity. *Journal of the American Geriatrics Society, 34,* 455–471.

Hazzard, W. R. (1989). Why do women live longer than men? *Postgraduate Medicine, 85,* 271–283.

Holden, C. (1987). Why do women live longer than men? *Science, 238,* 158–160.

Hollstein, M., Sidransky, D., Vogelstein, B., & Harris, C. C. (1991). p53 mutations in human cancer. *Science, 253,* 49–53.

House, J. S., Landis, K. R., & Umberson, D. (1988). Social relationships and health. *Science, 241,* 540–545.

Hughes, D., Seidman, E., & Williams, N. (1993). Cultural phenomena and the research enterprise: Toward a culturally anchored methodology. *American Journal of Community Psychology, 21,* 687–703.

Hunt, S. C., Williams, R. R., & Barlow, G. K. (1986). A comparison of positive family history definitions for defining risk of future disease. *Disease, 39*(10), 809–821.

Jacobsen, C. (1995). *Racial and ethnic families in the United States.* New York: Garland.

James, S. A. (1993). Racial and ethnic differences in infant mortality and low birth weight. A psychosocial critique. *Annals of Epidemiology, 3,* 130–136.

Jeunemaitre, X., Soubrier, F., Kotelevlsev, Y. V., Lifton, R. P., Williams, C. S., Charru, A., Hunt, S. C., Hopkins, R. N., Williams, R. R., Lalouel, J. M., & Coroval, P. (1992). Molecular basis of human hypertension: Role of angiotensinogen. *Cell, 7,* 169–180.

Johnson, E. H., & Gilbert, D. (1991, Fall). Familial and psychological correlates of smoking in black and white adolescents. *Ethnicity and Disease, 1,* 320–334.

Kessler, R., House, J., Anspach, R., & Williams, D. (1995). Social psychology and health. In K. S. Cook, G. A. Fine, & J. S. House (Eds.), *Sociological perspectives on social psychology* (pp. 548–570). Boston: Allyn & Bacon.

Khoury, K., Beaty, T. H., & Cohen, B. H. (1993). *Fundamentals of genetic epidemiology.* New York: Oxford University Press.

Kidd, K. K. (1987). Searching for major genes for psychiatric disorders. In G. Brock & G. Collins (Eds.), *Molecular approaches to human polygenic disease* (pp. 84–193). New York: Wiley.

Kitagawa, E., & Hauser, P. (1973). *Differential morality in the United States.* Cambridge, MA: Harvard University Press.

Kozah, F. K., Hall, J. G., & Baird, P. A. (1986). Familial breast cancer in males. *Cancer, 58,* 2836–2839.

Krieger, N., Rowley, D. L., Herman, A. A., Avery, B., & Phillips, M. T. (1993). Racism, sexism, and social class: Implications for studies of health, disease, and well-being. *American Journal of Preventive Medicine, 9,* 82–122.

Kritz-Silverstein, D., Wingard, D., & Barrett-Corner, E. (1989). The relation of reproductive history and parenthood to subsequent parenthood. *American Journal of Epidemiology, 130,* 399–403.

Lancaster, J. B., & King, B. J. (1985). An evolutionary perspective on menopause. In J. K. Brown & V. Kerns (Eds.), *In her prime: A new view of middle-aged women* (pp. 7–15). South Hadley, MA: Bergin and Garvey.

LaVeist, T. A. (1996). Why we should continue to study race … but do a better job: An essay on race, racism and health. *Ethnicity and Disease, 6,* 21–29.

Livingston, I. L., Levine, D. M., & Moore, R. D. (1991). Social integration and black interracial variation in blood pressure. *Ethnicity and Disease, 1,* 135–151.

MacLean, C. J. (1988). Assessing changes in risk factor effect over multiple levels of severity. *American Journal of Epidemiology, 127,* 663–672.

Malkin, D., Li, F. P., Strong, L. C., Fraumeni, J. F., Nelson, C. E., Kim, D. H., Kassel, J., Gryka, M. A., Bischoff, F. Z., Tainsky, M. A., & Friend, S. H. (1990). Germ line p53 mutations in a familial syndrome of breast cancer, sarcomas, and other neoplasms. *Science, 250,* 1233–1238.

Marbury, M. C., Linn, S., Mason, R., Schoenbaum, S., Stubbfield, P. G., & Ryan, K. J. (1983). The association of alcohol consumption with outcome of pregnancy. *American Journal of Public Health, 73*(10), 1165–1168.

Marin, G., & Marin, B. V. (1991). *Research with Hispanic populations.* Newbury Park, CA: Sage.

Martorell, R. (1989). Body size, adaptation and function. *Human Organization, 48,* 15–20.

Masestri, N. E., Beaty, T. H., Liang, K., Boughman, J. A., & Ferencz, C. (1988). Assessing familial aggregation of congenital cardiovascular malformations in case-control studies. *Genetic Epidemiology, 5,* 343–354.

McConkey, E. H. (1993). *Human genetics: The molecular revolution.* New York: Jones and Bartlett.

McGarvey, S. T., Bindon, J. R., Crews, D. E., & Schendel, P. E. (1989). Modernization and human biology: Ecological and adaptive perspectives on adiposity and chronic disease. In M. A. Little & J. D. Haas (Eds.), *Human population biology: A transdisciplinary science* (pp. 263–279). Oxford, England: Oxford University Press.

McGill, H. C., & Stern, M. P. (1979). Sex and atherosclerosis. *Atherosclerosis Review, 4,* 157–242.

McLean, D. E., Hatfield-Timajchy, K., Wingo, P., & Floyd, R. (1993). Psychosocial measurement: Implications for the study of preterm delivery in black women. *American Journal of Preventive Medicine, 9,* 39–81.

Moll, P. P., Sing, C. F., Weidman, W. H., Gordon, H., Ellefson, R. D., Hedgson, P. A., & Kottke, B. A. (1983). Total cholesterol and lipoproteins in school children: Prediction of coronary heart disease in adult relatives. *Circulation, 67*(1), 127–134.

Moore, K. L. (1988). *The developing human: Clinically oriented embryology.* Philadelphia: W. B. Sanders.

Morris, B. J., & Griffiths, L. R. (1988). Frequency in hypertensives of alleles for a RFLP associated with the renin gene. *Biochemical and Biophysical Communications, 150*(1), 219–224.

Morrison, J. A., Namboodiri, K., Green, P., Martin, J., & Glueck, C. J. (1983). Familial aggregation of lipids and lipoproteins and early identification of dyslipoproteinemia. *Journal of the American Medical Association, 250,* 1860–1868.

Mott, F. L., & Haurin, J. R. (1985). Factors affecting mortality in the years surrounding retirement. In H. S. Parnes, J. E. Crowley, R. J. Haurin, L. J. Less, W. R. Morgan, F. L. Mott, & G. Nestel (Eds.), *Retirement among American men* (pp. 31–56). Lexington, MA: DC Heath and Company.

Mueller, W. A. (1983). The genetics of human fatness. *Yearbook of Physical Anthropology, 26,* 215–230.

National Center for Health Statistics. (1986). *Health statistics on older persons: United States 1986* (Analytical and Epidemiological Studies series 3, no. 25). Washington, DC: U.S. Government Printing Office.

O'Dea, K. (1991, Spring). Westernization and non-insulin-dependent diabetes in Australian Aborigines. *Ethnicity and Disease, 1,* 171–187.

Ottman, R., Susser, E., & Meisner, M. (1991). Control for environmental risk factors in assessing genetic effects on disease familial aggregation. *American Journal of Epidemiology, 134,* 298–309.

Polednak, P. (1987). *Host factors and disease.* Springfield, IL: Charles C. Thomas.

Rao, D. C., Laskarzewski, P. M., Morrison, J. A., Khoury, P., Kelly, K., Wetter, R., Russells, J., & Glueck, C. J. (1982). The Cincinnati lipid research clinic family study: Cultural and biological determinants of lipids and lipoprotein and lipoprotein concentrations. *American Journal of Human Genetics, 34,* 888–903.

Ramirez, E. A. (1991). Cardiovascular Health in Puerto Ricans Compared to Other Groups in the United States. *Ethnicity and Disease, 1*(Spring), 188–199.

Ramirez, M. (1991). *Psychotherapy and counseling with minorities.* New York: Pergamon.

Ramsey, C. N., Abell, T. D., & Baker, L. C. (1986). The relationship between family functioning, life events, family structure, and the outcomes of pregnancy. *Journal of Family Practice, 22,* 521–526.

Reed, T., Wagener, D. K., Donahue, R. P., & Kuller, L. H. (1986). Young adult cholesterol as a predictor of familial ischemic heart disease. *Preventive Medicine, 15,* 292–303.

Rich, S. (1990). Mapping genes in diabetes. *Diabetes, 39,* 1315–1319.

Rogers, R. G. (1995). Marriage, sex, and mortality. *Journal of Marriage and the Family, 57,* 515–526.

Ross, C. E., Mirowsky, J., & Goldsteen, K. (1990). The impact of the family on health: The decade in review. *Journal of Marriage and the Family, 52,* 1059–1078.

Savage, P. J., & Harlan, W. R. (1991). Racial and ethnic diversity in obesity and other risk factors. *Ethnicity and Disease, 1*(Spring), 200–211.

Schell, L. A. W. (1991). Pollution and human growth: Lead, noise, polychlorobiphenyl compounds and toxic wastes. In G. G. N. Mascie-Taylor & G. Lasker (Eds.), *Applications of Biological Anthropology to Human Affairs.* Cambridge: Cambridge Studies in Biological Anthropology.

Schottenfeld, D. (1986). Genetic and environmental factors in human carcinogenesis. *Journal of Chronic Disease, 39,* 1021–1030.

Schumacher, M. C., Hunt, S. C., & Williams, R. R. (1990). Interactions between diabetes and family history of coronary heart disease and other risk factors for coronary heart disease among adults with diabetes in Utah. *Epidemiology, 1,* 298–304.

Scribner, R. (1996). Paradox as paradigm. The health outcomes of Mexican Americans. *American Journal of Public Health, 86,* 303–305.

Scribner, R., & Dwyer, J. (1989). Acculturation and low birthweight among Latinos in the Hispanic HANES. *American Journal of Public Health, 79,* 1263–1267.

Selby, J. V., Newman, B., Quiroga, J., Christian, J. C., Austin, M. A., & Fabitz, R. R. (1991). Concordance for dyslipidemic hypertension in male twins. *Journal of the American Medical Association, 265*(16), 2079–2084.

Sellers, T. A., Kushi, L. H., & Potter, J. D. (1991). Can dietary intake patterns account for the familial aggregation of disease? *Genetic Epidemiology, 8,* 105–112.

Sherraden, M. S., & Barrera, R. E. (1996a). Poverty, family support, and well-being of infants: Mexican immigrant women and childbearing. *Journal of Sociology and Social Welfare, 23,* 27–54.

Sherraden, M. S., & Barrera, R. E. (1996b). Maternal support and cultural influences among Mexican immigrant mothers. *Families in Society, 2,* 298–313.

Shields, P., & Harris, C. C. (1991). Molecular epidemiology and the genetics of environmental cancer. *Journal of the American Medical Association, 266*(5), 681–687.

Smith, D. W. E., & Warner, H. R. (1989). Does genotypic sex have direct effect on longevity? *Experimental Gerontology, 24,* 277–288.

Spranger, J., Benirschke, K., Hall, J. G., Lenz, W., Lowry, R. B., Opitz, J. M., Pinsky, L., Schwarzacher, H. G., & Smith, D. W. (1982). Errors of morphogenesis: Concepts and terms. *Journal of Pediatrics, 100,* 160–165.

Stern, M. P., & Haffner, S. M. (1986). Body fat distribution and hyperinsulinemia as a factor for diabetes and cardiovascular disease. *Atherosclerosis, 6,* 123–130.

Stinson, S. (1985). Sex differences in environmental sensitivity during growth and development. *Yearbook of Physical Anthropology, 28,* 123–147.

Sullivan, J. L. (1982). The sex differences in ischemic heart disease. *Perspectives in Biology and Medicine, 24*(4), 657–671.

Tennes, K., & Blackard, C. (1980). Maternal alcohol consumption, birth weight, and minor physical anomalies. *American Journal of Obstetrics and Gynecology, 138,* 774–780.

Vague, J. (1956). The degree of masculine differentiation of obesities: A factor determining predisposition to diabetes, atherosclerosis, gout, and uric calculous disease. *American Journal of Clinical Nutrition, 4,* 20–34.

Vague, J., Bjorntrap, P., Guy-Grand, B., Rebuffe-Scrue, M., & Vague, P. (1985). *Metabolic complications of human obesities.* Amsterdam: Excerpta Medica.

Verbrugge, J. (1985). Gender and health: An update on hypothesis and evidence. *Journal of Health and Social Behavior, 26,* 156–182.

Waldron, I. (1983). Sex differences in human mortality: The role of genetic factors. *Social Sciences and Medicine, 17*(6), 321–322.

Weiss, K. M., Chakraborty, R., & Majumder, P. (1982). Problems in the assessment of relative risk of chronic disease among biological relatives of affected individuals. *Journal of Chronic Disease, 35,* 539–551.

Wilcosky, T. C., & Rynard, S. M. (1990). Sister chromatia exchanges. In B. S. Hulkay, T. C. Wilcosky, & J. D. Griffith (Eds.), *Biological markers in epidemiology* (pp. 105–124). New York: Oxford University Press.

Wolanski, N. (1974). The stature of offspring and the assortative mating of parents. *Human Biology, 46*(4), 613–619.

Wong, N. D., Bassin, S. L., & Deitrick, R. (1991, Fall). Relationship of blood lipids to anthropometric measures and family medical history in an ethnically diverse school-aged population. *Ethnicity and Disease, 1,* 351–363.

Wylie, C. M. (1984). Contrasts in the health of elderly men and women. Analysis of recent data for whites in the United States. *Journal of American Geriatrics, 32*(9), 670–675.

Zambrana, R. E. (1995). *Understanding Latino families: Scholarship, policy and practice.* Thousand Oaks, CA: Sage.

CHAPTER 23

Strengthening Families

Policy Issues for the Twenty-First Century

Phyllis Moen and Kay B. Forest

Introduction

Families are once again in the political spotlight in the United States at all levels of government. In the first edition of this *Handbook*, Moen and Schorr (1987) depicted the 1970s and the 1980s as a period of the politicization of the American family, stating that conservatives and liberals alike have couched political agendas in a family rhetoric (p. 795). This war with words escalated exponentially in the 1990s, such that family values took center stage in political campaigns. Democrats, Republicans, and Independents alike described the family as pivotal, both the source of the nation's capability and vitality and the locus of its deepest afflictions and frailties. Indeed, the 1990s represented a time of growing consensus that we as a nation are experiencing a profound crisis in the institution of the family. The declines and heightened vulnerabilities social scientists and observers have recounted over the last several decades are coming increasingly to inform, and shape, the policy agenda. At the same time, family and family values are polarizing Americans in a culture war over the role of the state in family life and indeed over competing visions of the fundamental nature of families— what they are and what they should be (Blankenhorn, Bayme, & Elshtain, 1990; Bronfenbrenner, McClelland, Wethington, Moen, & Ceci, 1996; Hewlett, 1991; Hunter, 1991; Whitehead, 1992).

Key trends in the 1990s have been the growing recognition of the economic plight of families, the movement of the Baby Boom cohort into parenting (with the apparent fostering of a new sense of familism), a shift in 1993 from 12 years of Republican leadership in the executive branch and a view of families as private spheres (requiring minimal governmental assistance and only as a last resort) to a Democratic administration with a strong interest in families and children (and the provision of governmental supports necessary to promote their optimal functioning) to an even more striking shift in 1995 from 40 years of Democratic domination of the House of Representatives to Republican control of both houses of Congress. But even before the 1992 and 1994 elections, policies and polemics were increasingly scripted in terms of family well-being, and the states and the courts played an expanding role in shaping policies affecting families.

In this chapter we build on the groundwork in Moen and Schorr (1987) to describe recent policy developments in the United States related to families. For a more in-depth treatment of the background of family policy formulation and the role of social research in defining or responding to the family policy arena, the reader is encouraged to refer to the first edition of this *Handbook* as well as other articles (cf. Moen & Firebaugh, 1994; Moen & Forest, 1990; Moen & Jull, 1995). This chapter is divided into four broad sections, including an overview of the conceptual and historical foundations behind family-related policies, three examples of recent relevant legislation, an example of emerging tacit family policy, and efforts toward developing a pro-family policy perspective.

Phyllis Moen • Bronfenbrenner Life Course Center, Cornell University, Ithaca, New York 14850-4401. **Kay B. Forest** • Department of Sociology, Northern Illinois University, DeKalb, Illinois 60115.

Handbook of Marriage and the Family, 2nd edition, edited by Marvin Sussman, Suzanne K. Steinmetz, and Gary W. Peterson. Plenum Press, New York, 1999.

Conceptual and Historical Foundations

What Is Meant by Family Policy?

Policy as Deliberative. Titmus (1974) defines policy as the principles that govern action directed toward given ends (p. 23). He points out that the underlying assumption of the term is one of being able to affect change; we do not have weather policies because we can't do much by way of changing it. "Family policy" can include a range of activities of governments and organizations, including private associations, aimed at transforming families and/or family well-being.

Hohn and Lüscher (1988) use the term to refer to "public activities, measures, and organizations that attempt to recognize, support, complement, and thus influence or even enforce specifically or generally defined achievements of the family" (p. 329). Their definition distinguishes family policies by the deliberate goal of improving family well-being (see also Lüscher, 1990 and Zimmerman, 1988). However, a broad view of *family policy* can include virtually all social and economic policies since they all touch the lives of family members (e.g., Myrdal, 1968). In fact, Kamerman and Kahn (1978) see family policy as everything that governments do to and for families. This is certainly a legitimate approach, but we prefer to distinguish between policies affecting families and family policies per se.

Like Moen and Schorr (1987) we choose a more narrow definition, defining family policy as a widely agreed-on set of objectives for families, toward the realization of which the state (and other institutions) deliberately shapes programs and policies. Thus explicit family policy refers to interventions intentionally aimed at families. Many political actions have unintentional family-related consequences; thus there exist tacit, as well as explicit, family policies, with a range of policies and programs affecting families, even though they weren't created with families, or family policy, in mind. Examples of explicit family policies include the Personal Responsibility and Work Opportunity Act of 1996 and the Family and Medical Leave Act. Implicit or tacit policies focusing on individuals but affecting families as well include such programs as Social Security, the G.I. Bill, and Head Start.

Families as Broadly Conceived. The notion of family policy really turns, of course, on what is meant by family. This was not a problem in earlier times, when there was a general consensus on depicting families as consisting of, broadly, kinship relations and/or domestic households (e.g., Robertson, 1991). But concomitant with shifts in the demography of, and life-course changes in, marriage and fertility (Bronfenbrenner et al., 1996; Bumpass, 1990; Cheal, 1993; Cherlin, 1988), public definitions of the family have been broadened by those on the political left to recognize a range of forms (see Macklin & Rubin, 1983; Scanzoni & Marsiglio, 1991, 1993). At the same time, others on the political right have embraced a more narrow definition, characterizing only married parents and their children as families (Skolnick, 1987). Both broad and narrow definitions often carry with them the freight and fervor of ideology; characterizing as much what families should be as what they are. This public discourse on the family typically takes the shape of emotional and polemic debates about morality, hinging, at least in part, on divergent definitions by some and the assignment by others of a privileged position to families with traditional marriages.

We take an ecumenical, inclusive view of the diversity of families, an approach we feel is necessary to fit with today's realities. This emphasis on family diversity also points to variations in families by ethnicity and class, as well as by life stage, with concomitant variations in values and vulnerabilities. Rather than a predictable life cycle, we need to consider life-course variations in household and kinship arrangements as men and women move in and out of various living arrangements and primary relationships (Cochran, Larner, Riley, Gunnarson, & Henderson, 1990; Scanzoni & Marsiglio, 1991, 1993). When we use the term the family we refer to the institution of the family, encompassing a range of forms.

Families and the Life Course. We draw on a life-course approach to families and family policies to appreciate the temporal aspects of family needs and the historical and cultural contexts in which first individuals, and now families, have become units of state concern (Elder, 1974, 1992; Heinz, 1996; Mayer & Mueller, 1986; Moen & Forest, 1990; Moen & Jull, 1995; Moen & Wethington, 1992; Weymann, 1996). Life-course issues include recognition of the dynamic nature of family roles and circumstances as families and individuals move through their life lines, the interdependence of lives and life choices among family members, the situational imperatives confronting families, the possibility for crisis and divergent paths, and the cumulation of advantage and disadvantage experienced by some (Elder & Caspi, 1990). We also consider why individuals, not families, have typically been the locus of governmental interest and action.

A life-course approach embraces the notion of a family career (e.g., Aldous, 1996; Moen & Wethington, 1992), consisting of shifts in roles, relationships, and responsibilities over time, with concomitant shifts in family needs, resources, and vulnerabilities. Thus it may well be the intersection of roles, such as that of worker and parent, that generates strains and challenges for families. Or unexpected crisis events—unemployment, war mobilization, illness, death—can place families in crisis. The life-course perspective also locates families as important mediators between large-scale social events and changes (such as economic downturns) and outcomes for individual lives (e.g., Conger & Elder, 1994; Elder,

1974; Moen, Kain, & Elder, 1983). The ways families respond, in terms of their adaptations to shifting social and economic circumstances, influence the lives of individual members in both the long and short term (Moen & Wethington, 1992).

A life-course approach can inform the study of family policies in at least two ways. First, social policies expanding or restricting the family's strategies of adaptation can have enduring, and possibly unanticipated, influences. And the timing of government programs and entitlements in the family's life course may be consequential in fostering the cumulation of advantage, or conversely, disadvantage, over time. Second is the location of families and policies in historical context. Policy-makers are frequently called upon to respond to the pressure of cohorts passing through the social service system, as when the large Baby Boom cohort moved through the educational system (Ryder, 1965). Increasing longevity is already pointing to the pressures on the retirement system as this cohort moves into their later years.

Why So Little Family Policy in The United States?

Family Policy in Other Countries. There are both similarities and differences between families in the United States and other advanced societies. European nations are also in a transitional phase, experiencing major shifts in gender roles and in the configuration of families (Kahn & Kamerman, 1988; Sorrentino, 1990). Thus, the United States is not alone in facing family problems and challenges. However, this country is unique in its reluctance to join the issue in the policy arena. European countries, unlike the United States, provide supports to women, parents, and families in the form of children's allowances, maternity benefits, and paid parental leaves of absence. These supports reflect both convictions about the importance of families and children's welfare along with pragmatic concerns about low birth rates (and, consequently, a diminishing labor force).*

Evidence of this pro-family policy commitment in other industrial countries lies in their systems of child allowance; that is, the provision of direct subsidies for children in each family, which exist to assist families, especially low-income families, in raising their children (Pressman, 1970; p. 53). For example, during 1989–1990, French parents could receive a means-tested family allowance of FF737 (approximately US$127) for one child under 3, with additional supplements available for second and later children, including those over

*European countries, unlike the United States, have had strict immigration policies and therefore rely on their own citizens to meet labor force demand. Thus, their investment in policies conducive to fertility and to the quality of the next generation relate not only to family well-being but also to the labor market (Gladstone, Williams, & Belous, 1985; Kamerman & Kahn, 1988; Kamerman, Kahn, & Kingston, 1983; Moen, 1989).

the age of 15 (Snyder, 1992). Single parents and parents of handicapped children received somewhat higher allowances, and all family payments were in addition to paid maternity leave and government provisions for childcare. As of midyear 1990, German parents received family benefits for each child until the age of 16. Parental leave was available for either parent at DM600 (approximately US$357) up to 18 months, with an additional later educational allowance and tax relief on childcare available. As of 1990, similar resources were also available in countries such as Norway, Spain, Portugal, Switzerland, Greece, and Denmark, among others (for a detailed summary of European family benefits, see Kahn & Kamerman, 1988; Snyder, 1992).

By contrast, the United States, while paying lip service to the importance of families and children, gives even higher regard to the ethic of individualism and the tenets of the free enterprise system, and has been notably reluctant to pay the costs of expanded government benefits for families. When services are provided, they are frequently piecemeal and often inadequate. For example, support for families raising children takes the form of an income tax exemption for children; however, those without incomes or with low earnings fail to benefit from such a program (Employee Benefit Research Institute, 1993).

We in the United States, individually and collectively, remain uncertain, if not divided, as to what families should be and what the role of government should be in supporting families. Prevailing attitudes about gender, sexuality, maternal employment, children, and families remain ambivalent and contradictory. This is of pivotal importance in seeking to understand the absence of any coherent political or private sector response to the changing family in this country. For example, because of the absence of any consensus about women's roles, or about the role of government in family matters, we are markedly reluctant to adopt social policies and institutional arrangements designed to reduce the inevitable conflicts and overloads of combining employment with family responsibilities. This is despite the fact that currently over half of American mothers of preschoolers, and even infants, are employed (Kingston, 1993; MacDermid & Targ, 1995; Moen & Jull, 1995; Pleck, 1992).

The roles of men and women are undergoing a progressive transformation in all advanced societies, but the rate of change among them varies considerably. Sweden is one country that has taken the lead in fashioning structural mechanisms to promote a reconciliation of work and family roles for both men and women (Moen, 1989). Still, citizens in some European countries, such as Germany and Great Britain, express ambivalence similar to that voiced in the United States about the employment of mothers of young children (Alwin, Braun, & Scott, 1990). And even in Sweden it is women who continue to have the primary responsibility for home and family (Haas, 1992; Moen, 1989; Popenoe, 1988).

Families, Individuals, and Government. Governments have always regulated families, especially in terms of family ties and transitions, such as who, when, and how a couple marries, ownership of property, and rights of inheritance. But the pervasive intervention of government in so many aspects of contemporary individual and family life is a relatively new phenomenon, concomitant with the rise of the modern welfare state (Mayer & Mueller, 1986; Weymann, 1996). Federal, state, and local governments touch the lives of families at virtually every life stage and in every aspect of decision-making—from marriage or cohabitation to fertility choices to child care and children's educational opportunities to jobs, housing, health care, income security and transfers, divorce, widowhood—the list is endless. However, this mounting body of public regulation and influence represents in the United States a series of incremental decisions focusing on individual lives, not families, and creates a tacit, often contradictory, rather than explicit family policy.

The increasing involvement of government in the welfare of citizens has meant that the modern state focuses on individuals qua individuals, not as members of collectives such as families. As Mayer and Mueller (1986; p. 223) point out, legal and bureaucratic rationality establishes the individual, not the family, as the object of state interest and intervention. This, in turn, promotes a view of individuals as separate, distinctive actors facing life choices and life chances on their on, and structures the individual life course in terms of movement in and out of various age-graded roles (Riley, Kahn, & Foner, 1994; Meyer, 1996; Riley, Johnson, & Foner, 1972). Thus governments almost invariably provide services and benefits to individuals, not families. The exception is in terms of some income transfers (such as the now defunct Aid to Families with Dependent Children and its replacement, the Personal Responsibility and Work Opportunity Act of 1996), which take into account household, as well as individual, assets and earnings. However, unemployment compensation, social security, and disability payments are based on an individual's prior earnings, not family need.* An emphasis on individualism militates against government intervention into family life and often gives birth to policies that are antithetical to the best interests of families and children.

Entrenched Ideologies and Cultural Diversity. We have long upheld a doctrine of two spheres which designates the home and family as a private arena, the place where children should be taught values and belief systems, and very much the special province of wives and mothers. The sanctity of the family means that it has been put off limits to govern-

ment intrusion, a position strongly endorsed in both the Reagan and Bush administrations (Aldous & Dumon, 1990; Jacobs & Davies, 1991; Palmer & Sawhill, 1984). Moreover, the traditional emphasis in the United States on free enterprise and on the supremacy of the individual, along with the pluralistic nature of our society, has long precluded the adoption of family goals on the political agenda. The laissez-faire orientation of our society has underscored the preeminence of economic interests, as illustrated by President Bush's 1990 and 1992 vetoes of the Family and Medical Leave Act, which established government mandates presumed injurious to the business community (subsequently signed by President Clinton).

Regional, ethnic, and religious differences in values have precluded a consensus on the meaning of family well-being, much less a common understanding of the proper roles of women and men within society. Similarly, the layered structure of government—city, county, state, and federal, as well as executive, legislative, and judicial—encourages a patchwork of often incompatible legislation and regulation in lieu of a national policy addressing the needs and well-being of families (Quadagno, 1990, 1994; Steiner, 1981; Strawn, 1993; Zigler & Frank, 1988; Zimmerman & Owens, 1989).

A case in point is the shifting conception of family law: what constitutes a proper family, the power and authority of the husband/father, the role of wives/and mothers, the nature of state in relation to children (Mintz, 1989; Mintz & Kellogg, 1988; Pleck, 1987).

We in the United States confront a true cultural dilemma, with the reality of family life today often at odds with ingrained values concerning the family. For example, while Americans of all ages increasingly endorse the notion of wives' employment, many remain uneasy about the employment of mothers of young children. There are inherent cultural contradictions in having mothers of young children employed, since women still have the principal responsibility for child care. While the federal government in the 1980s was noticeably reluctant to intervene in providing supports for working parents, it did promote women's equality of opportunity. The 1990s brought a new concern with the plight of working families (Newman, 1993; Spalter-Roth & Hartmann, 1995), as American society thus conveyed a mixed message that reinforced the primacy of domesticity in women's lives but stressed the increasing significance of their employment as well.*

---

*This, however, is not necessarily the case in Europe, where families are more often the unit of policy interest. This points to the need for comparative studies of family policy (see, e.g., Hohn & Lüscher, 1988; Moen, 1989).

*For a discussion of the doctrine of two spheres see Cott and Pleck (1979) and Degler (1980). A fuller discussion of the ambivalence concerning policies affecting family life is in Moen and Schorr (1987) and Klatch (1987). An important ingredient in the drive toward equality of employment opportunity for women was the Civil Rights Act of 1964.

Why Are Families Once Again on the Policy Agenda?

In the late 1980s and the 1990s, there was increasing demand for a governmental focus on families, not only on individuals. Former Congresswoman Patricia Schroeder (D-Colorado) reflected this new familism in government: "It's time for a 'New Deal' for American families" (1989, p. 1410). This concern with actions on behalf of families is a response to growing perceptions of structural lags between family realities and institutional supports (Riley et al., 1994). Demographic, cultural, and economic changes have increased the vulnerability and threatened the viability of a significant portion of American families; policy makers of all political persuasions are coming to recognize that fact. In addition to the fact that the nature of families and family life is undergoing a remarkable transformation, three situational imperatives have placed families at the forefront of the domestic policy debate: economic downturns, a renewed emphasis on familism, and the change from a Republican to a Democratic presidency, concomitant with a widespread consensus regarding the failure of existing policies.

The Family in Transition. There is considerable and growing diversity in American families, both in structure and behavior, and this diversity is overlaid with both class and race differences and divisions (Bronfenbrenner et al., 1996).

In contrast to their parents or grandparents, Americans now in their twenties and thirties are better educated, have fewer children, and bear them later in life. They are postponing marriage and are less likely to marry or to stay married. Women are more likely than ever to be employed, regardless of their race, marital status, or family responsibilities. Americans today face an array of choice about marriage and divorce, the number and timing of children, and the division of labor by gender. Reductions and delays in fertility and marriage, increases in single-parenthood and educational achievement—along with the women's movement, declining real wages, and the specter of poverty—all are producing greater variety in family forms and creating a new social dilemma in the form of the gender role revolution and the working family (Moen, 1992, 1998).

Economic Change. Despite the economic boom years of the late 1990s, two economic and temporal realities placed the plight of families once more on the policy agenda. The first is the growing vulnerability and time-squeeze experienced by working families across the economic spectrum, and the second is the increasing inequality between families at the top and at the bottom of the income distribution.

Broadening Vulnerabilities. By the 1990s, and unlike the 1960s, the dilemmas of families were no longer defined as the exclusive province of the poor—or single parents—or minority families. In fact, with the pressures experienced by the realities of declining wages and reduced occupational opportunities of the 1980s and early 1990s, and the rising number of two earner couples, middle-class families also came to be, and to see themselves as, increasingly vulnerable. Thus family issues cut across class and racial lines (Galston, 1992; Newman, 1993).

Part of this can be seen in the nature of the job market. In the 1980s the part-time workforce grew about twice as fast as total employment in the U.S. economy, increasing from 16.3 million workers in 1980 to 19.8 million in 1988. The growth of temporary jobs was even more striking, moving from a minuscule 0.4 million in 1980 to 1.1 million in 1988, a 175% increase (Employee Benefit Research Institute, 1993; Belous, 1989; Nine to Five, 1986). Despite the low employment rate, in the late 1990s, the whole notion of a contract between employees and employers that traded work investment and seniority for job security was no longer a reality for many workers (Moen, 1998).

Not surprisingly, given child care and other domestic responsibilities, women hold the majority of part-time and temporary jobs, and are the least likely to have an uninterrupted career (Han & Moen, 1998). In 1995 almost one job in three (29.4%) was a nonstandard work arrangement, with 34.3% of women workers and 25.3% of males working in nonstandard jobs (including contract work and self-employment) (see Kalleberg et al., 1997). But the proliferation of these jobs was far more a result of the changing economy than a response to the needs of women balancing work and family roles. Employers recruit such a "contingent workforce" because it is flexible and encumbers significantly lower labor costs. Still, these working arrangements do offer women more flexibility and discretionary time in reconciling their work and family obligations. But they also exact a heavy price: Part-time and temporary jobs tend to be low-wage jobs with few benefits, typically without security and providing little opportunity or advancement* (Christensen, 1995; Han & Moen, 1998; Spalter-Roth & Hartmann, 1995).

Growing Inequality. By the late 1990s, a number of scholars were documenting the time constraints experiences by contemporary working families (e.g., Hochschild, 1989, 1997; Schor, 1992; Clarkberg, 1998). Families as a unit are putting in more hours at work and experiencing concomitant strains and overloads. This has underscored the structural lags (Riley & Riley, 1994) in the way work and career paths

*For a discussion of part-time workers, see Belous (1989), International Labour Organization (1989), and Kahne (1985).

are organized. The breadwinner/homemaker template is increasingly out of date. The need for new public and private sector policies and practices that can support working families is becoming part of the contemporary discourse (Moen, 1998). In combination with the declining wages of the 1980s and early 1990s, there has also been an eroding of benefits for poor families, especially those with children (Bronfenbrenner et al., 1996). The principal safety net prior to 1996 was the AFDC, a program funded jointly by the federal and state governments. Because AFDC benefits were not indexed for inflation, the purchasing power of the AFDC benefit eroded steadily from 1970 and 1992 (National Commission on Children, 1991; Strawn, 1994). Moreover, structural changes in the economy, concomitant with the movement of middle-class black families out of the inner cities and to the suburbs, created a dismal economic climate for those without much education and skills (Wilson, 1987). In the latter half of the 1990s, new welfare policies, the Personal Responsibility and Work Opportunity Act of 1996, and a booming economy produced families who were better off as well as families that were worse off.

The effects of economic changes on families are perhaps most strikingly revealed in the growing poverty rates of preschool children. Throughout the 1970s the proportion of children in poverty stayed at between 17% and 18% it climbed rapidly in the 1980s, and by 1990 was leveling off at 23% (National Center for Children in Poverty, 1992). In fact, children under 6 are more likely to be poor than any age group, and the rates for minority groups are astounding: 50% for black and 40% for Hispanic children, compared to 14% for white children. Whether or not preschoolers are poor depends in large degree on whether or not they have employed parents: Only 8% of preschoolers with one or more parent holding a full-time job was poor in 1990, while 78% of those whose parents were not employed were poor. Still, over one in four poor children had a parent working full-time, but not earning enough to bring to the family out of poverty (Bronfenbrenner et al., 1996).

In social research and in the policy arena, we are seeing a renewed focus on the relationships between family structure and family well-being (e.g., Bronfenbrenner et al., 1996; Burkhauser & Duncan, 1989; Garfinkel & McClanahan, 1986; McLanahan & Sandefur, 1994; Moynihan, 1986; Wilson, 1987). The bottom line, in the focus on family structure, is children. Children in the United States are not only more likely to be poor than those who live in other industrialized nations, but they are also more likely to live in extreme poverty (Smeeding, 1990).

The United States has a policy to promote the welfare and well-being of its elderly, as exemplified in social security legislation and Medicare (Moen, 1996). As a consequence the poverty rate of older people is now much lower than in the middle of the twentieth century. In 1990 the federal government spent on average $11,350 per elderly person compared to $1,020 per child under age 18 (Strawn, 1994).

As economist Tim Smeeding (1990) points out:

> The major instruments of U.S. social policy were created more than one-half century ago, when widows, war veterans, and older people were society's at-risk groups. A fresh vision of social policy is needed to address the new realities of poverty in America: the economic plight and vulnerability of a large minority of our children and impoverished families. The political challenge is to convince the childless and childful that it is in their direct interest to rectify this situation. (p. 70)

Cohorts, Culture, and the New Familism. Social historian Barbara Dafoe Whitehead (1992) at the Institute for American Values describes three cultural periods: the traditional familism of the 1940s–1960s with its emphasis on marriage and parenting, the period of individualism (1960s–1980s) focusing more on the adult-centered self (a time of rising divorce rates and declining birth rates) and the new familism of the 1990s, with a reassessment of norms and a renewed interest in families. This emerging familism was documented in trends in attitudes and values as captured by opinion surveys (e.g., Glenn, 1992). It may well reflect the movement of the Baby Boom generation into parenthood and the shifts in perspective that are concomitant with the transition into parental responsibilities. The difficulty that so many Baby Boomers are facing is resolving the new realities of greater equality and opportunity for women in the workplace with the ongoing demands of parenthood. And this crisis of working parents hits the middle class as well as the working class, broadening the issue of government supports to families from simply one of welfare for the poor.

There is growing recognition of the possible deleterious long-term effects of divorce and single parenthood on children (Bronfenbrenner et al., 1996; Furstenberg, 1990; Garfinkel & McLanahan, 1986; McLanahan & Sanders, 1994). Social observers increasingly call for a new sense of community, responsibility, and commitment to family ties (Blankenhorn, Bayme, & Elshtain, 1990).

Perceived Failure of Existing Policies. There has been a widespread concern that, rather than supporting families, government policies have in fact been eroding their effectiveness. Glazer (1988) points out that governmental programs seek to take over roles that were previously the jurisdiction of the family: "In our social policies we are trying to deal with the breakdown of traditional ways of handling distress. These traditional ways are located in family, primarily, but also in the ethnic group, the neighborhood, the church" (p. 3).

In the 1980s the Reagan and then the Bush administrations adopted a hands-off approach to family policy. They believed that the War on Poverty, launched with the Economic Opportunity Act of 1964 under President Lyndon B.

Johnson, was a failure. President Ronald Reagan claimed that the federal government declared war on poverty, and poverty won (see Moynihan, 1989, p. 16). While others have challenged this thesis (Moynihan, 1989; Schram, 1991), the 12 years of Republican occupation of the White House reflected the conviction that government should play a minimal role in promoting family interests. This perspective remained dominant in the Republican-led Congress of the 1990s. The ideological orientation was that the private sector, voluntary organizations, and informal individual relationships should replace government in promoting family and individual well-being.

But just as some observers found fault with the government programs passed during the 1960's Great Society initiatives, researchers began to chronicle the impacts on families and individuals of the policies of the Reagan and Bush administrations. They found that, by both not keeping up with inflation and creating stricter eligibility requirements, government spending on welfare was reduced (e.g., Jacobs & Davies, 1991; Palmer & Sawhill, 1984). The result was an increase in the national poverty rate, which had fallen to 11% in 1973 and which rose to 15% in 1982 and 1983 (Pressman, 1990). Another consequence was a change in the composition of the poor. In the 1960s poverty was predominately found among the elderly and rural populations; today's poor are more likely to be members of young families and families headed by women (Bronfenbrenner et al., 1996; Presser, 1995).

Social observers increasingly view the changes in the composition and nature of poverty from a life-course perspective: looking at the movement of individuals and families in and out of economic difficulty over time (e.g., Burkhauser & Duncan, 1989; Mayer & Schoepflin, 1989; O'Rand, 1995) and the long-term consequences of childhood poverty for individuals, families, and society (e.g., Bronfenbrenner et al., 1996; Edelman, 1987; Moynihan, 1986). The adoption of the residual model of domestic policy meant a real curtailment or reduction in the social services provided at the federal level and greater attention to family policy at the state level of government (e.g., Wisensale, 1990; Wisensale & Allison, 1989; Zimmerman & Owens, 1989). This was exemplified in the push for welfare reform culminating in the Personal Responsibility and Work Opportunity Act of 1996, which dismantled the federal welfare program.

By the 1990s the plight of families and the issue of family values were increasingly issues that could not be ignored by either liberals or conservatives. For some, family values apparently embody the conventional two-parent, wife as homemaker, family of the 1950s (Dreyfous, 1992), which itself is something of a social aberration (Coontz, 1992). For others, family values involve ways to support and strengthen the capacities of families to manage for themselves. But no one claims that families are not undergoing tremendous challenges, or that effective families are not central to the well-being of both individuals and the nation.

Recent Relevant Legislation

The Family and Medical Leave Act of 1993

Background. In 1940, on the eve of World War II, only one in four (25%) workers was female. By 1945 women had become 29% of the labor force, falling slightly (to 27%) in 1947 following the war, but climbing back to 29% by 1950. Since 1950 the trend has been continuously upward. Women have accounted for 60% of the increase in the labor force over the last four decades, coming to represent 45% of the workforce by 1990. By the twenty-first century, labor force experts predict that almost half of all workers will be female, a sizable portion of whom will be women with young children (Hofferth & Phillips, 1987).

Almost 90% of the women entering the labor force are expected to become pregnant during the course of their work lives. However, this cannot be dismissed as merely a women's issue. Most men, too, become fathers, and about 60% of employed men have wives who are working. Growing numbers of men as well as women must coordinate their jobs with their spouses' jobs, along with several forms of childcare. In fact, half the work force now consists of workers married to an employed spouse (Han & Moen, 1998).

Employers as well as government officials and social observers are beginning to voice concern about the impacts of family exigencies on worker availability, stability, commitment and performance.*

Legislation affecting working women has typically focused on equality issues in the workplace. Legislators in the 1960s and early 1970s concentrated principally on the enactment of nondiscrimination and affirmative action laws. One such law, having wide repercussions, is the Pregnancy Discrimination Act of 1978 (Public Law 95-555). It states that women affected by pregnancy, childbirth, or related medical conditions shall be treated the same for all employment-related purposes, including receipt of benefits under fringe benefit programs, as other persons not so affected but similar in their inability to work. If an employer generally provides disability benefits, such benefits must also be available to pregnant women. Five states (California, Hawaii, New Jersey, New York, and Rhode Island) and Puerto Rico mandated the provision of temporary disability benefits to workers at the time of this writing. This means that approximately 40 percent of employed women in all the United States have the

---

*Employers and unions as well as workers are finding it difficult to continue partitioning the family and the workplace into two discrete domains (see reports by Bohen, 1983; Bureau of National Affairs, 1984, 1986; Catalyst, 1986; Friedman, 1986a,b; Galinsky, 1987).

right to a maternity leave with partial wage replacement—usually for six weeks—at the time of childbirth. Until the passage of the Family and Medical Leave Act in 1993, the Pregnancy Discrimination Act constituted the only federal policy enacted expressly to provide maternity or parental leave-related benefits.

We as a nation have yet to reach a clear consensus concerning the desirability or social utility of having both parents—and especially mothers of young children—work outside the home and what structural arrangements will make it possible for both parents to succeed at home and at work. But demographic trends in maternal employment have captured the public interest, and the dilemmas of working families became a major policy issue in the 1980s and 1990s. In 1987 the Supreme Court, in a landmark decision, upheld a California law requiring employers to give female workers an unpaid pregnancy disability leave of up to four months with a guarantee that their jobs will be available when they return to work. As a result the courts endorsed the provision of separate treatment on the basis of pregnancy or childbirth-related disabilities.

These issues have also been joined by a growing number of states. In the 1970s Montana, Connecticut, and Massachusetts, and in 1980 California passed maternity leave legislation. In 1987 Minnesota enacted the first parental leave law in the nation, enabling each parent to take up to six weeks of unpaid leave following the birth or adoption of a child. Many states had passed maternity or parental leave laws prior to the passage of the Family and Medical Leave Act of 1993.* Clearly, work-family concerns have become firmly established as public issues.

Employer Initiatives. Although the private sector has generally been slow to respond to the changes in the work force, private sector initiatives, at least among large corporations, are on the rise (Catalyst, 1993; Employment Benefit Research Institute, 1993; Galinsky, Friedman & Hernandez, 1991). Employers have been adopting new personnel policies and benefits for three reasons: (1) to attract and retain workers in a tight labor market, (2) to enhance productivity and reduce absenteeism, and (3) to be "socially responsible" in the eyes of the public. These work and family initiatives take a number of forms: creating or subsidizing childcare facilities

and services; providing information, counseling, and referral services; offering financial assistance for childcare; easing rigid time demands; contributing to community childcare programs; and facilitating the geographical relocation of workers and their families.*

Government encouragement in the form of tax incentives is no small inducement to act, as is the threat of government intervention through mandating benefits. Yet employers, individually and through their trade associations, argue that changes in employment conditions and benefits should remain voluntary and not be imposed by federal or state governments. For example, both the U.S. Chamber of Commerce and the National Association of Manufacturers vigorously attacked all parental leave bills introduced in Congress on grounds that, if enacted, such legislation would be excessively costly, prohibitively so to small businesses. Their opposition remained strident despite the fact that the Family and Medical Leave Act that was subsequently enacted applies to employers of more than 50 workers and provides a maximum leave of only 12 weeks. The employer position was well stated by Alexander B. Trowbridge, president of the National Association of Manufacturers:

> Employers, not government, are in the best position to decide the type and scope of benefits to be made available to employees. The economic feasibility of parental leave programs is different for each company. It is determined by a wide range of factors, including the type of business, competitive standards in the industry, the size and skill of the workforce, and the company's ability to assume costs. Such factors must be taken into account when planning benefits packages. (Bureau of National Affairs, 1987, p. A14)

Systematically gathered and nationally representative trend data on the number and type of firms offering flexible working hours, parental leave, and childcare assistance are only beginning to be collected (e.g., Catalyst, 1993; Christensen, 1995; Employee Benefit Research Institute, 1993; Galinsky et al., 1991). But the existing evidence suggests that it is the larger businesses that are taking the lead in adopting work–family policies, with these initiatives accelerating in the 1980s and 1990s. Moreover, family supportive personnel policies and benefits are most likely to be adopted by firms with larger numbers of young, female, skilled, nonunion workers, as well as those imbued with a sense of social responsibility.†

But the driving force impelling change typically is more pragmatic than philosophical. As John Bell, senior vice president of the Bank of America, said: "Corporations will

---

*For a discussion of the effects of state maternity leave statutes see Trzcinski (1990, 1989). States having maternity or parental leave law legislation as of this writing are Connecticut, Iowa, Louisiana, Maine, Minnesota, Oregon, Rhode Island, Tennessee, Washington, West Virginia, and Wisconsin (Finn-Stevenson & Trzcinski, 1990). A few local governments also have addressed the work/family predicament. In California, for example, the cities of Concord and San Francisco imposed in 1985 a small fee on commercial developments within the city, earmarking these funds for childcare (Lydenberg, 1986).

*Bureau of National Affairs (1984, 1986); Friedman (1986a,b); Axel (1985).
†See Axel (1985). Some national surveys of large corporations and select response rates suggest that there was about a fourfold increase (to 2500) in the first half of the 1980s in the number of companies helping with employees' childcare needs (Friedman, 1986a).

change when it is in their interest to do so" (Bohen, 1983; p. 33). It appears that this self-interest is beginning to surface. Growing numbers of firms are now in the process of re-examining and changing their employment practices. Large trend setting corporations, such as IBM, Kodak, Xerox, and Corning, are developing particularly comprehensive, wide-ranging, family-supportive policies for their employees. But these changes are themselves uneven, with most small companies and many large ones yet to adopt new policies. A 1988 survey by the Bureau of Labor Statistics found that only 2% of the full-time employees in mid-size to large firms had paid maternity leave and only 1% had paid paternity leave available. However, a third of those surveyed reported that they were able to take unpaid maternity leave and 16% could take unpaid paternity leave, each for an average of 4 months.*

Federal Legislation.   Legislation related to the provision of unpaid family and medical leaves of absence for workers was first introduced in the U.S. Congress by Patricia Schroeder and others in 1985. By the summer of 1990, and again in 1992, watered-down versions of the Family and Medical Leave Act were passed by Congress, then vetoed by President Bush. This act provided a job guarantee and health benefits for workers (taking time off to care for infants, newly adopted or sick children, ill parents/spouses). It was supported by most Democrats and the more liberal factions of Congress (Monroe & Garand, 1991), but the House of Representatives failed to override. Few politicians quarreled with the notion that parents—or at least new mothers—require some time off following the birth of a child or with the need for expanded and improved childcare arrangements. But still to be resolved by conservatives were such critical issues as whether parental leaves should be mandated by the federal government and, if so, how long such leaves should last, who should be eligible, whether they should be paid or unpaid, and how to apportion the costs that inevitably accrue to businesses offering these leaves.

Bill Clinton, in his first presidential campaign, endorsed the notion of family leave and was not persuaded that businesses would be harmed by such legislation, especially given that 95% of businesses, those with fewer than 50 employees,

*The trendline in the provision of maternal or parental leaves remains open to question. A 1980–1981 survey of various size firms found that about half offered some form of maternity disability leave (Kamerman, Kahn, & Kingston, 1983), and a 1984 survey of some of the nation's largest corporations found that fully 95% of the companies responding offered some form of paid disability leave. However, since only about one-fourth (26%) of the corporations contacted returned the questionnaire, it is likely that those responding were more apt to offer these benefits. But even within this select sample, employers were far less supportive of leaves for new fathers than for new mothers, with almost two-thirds considering it not reasonable for men to take any amount of parental leave (Catalyst, 1986). For a fuller discussion of parental leave policies at the state level see Trzcinski (1990).

would be exempt. Accordingly, another version of this bill was quickly passed by Congress in the early weeks of the Clinton administration and was signed by President Clinton on February 5, 1993.

The Act provides up to 12 weeks of unpaid, job-protected leave per year for the birth or adoption of a child or for the serious illness of the employee or an immediate family member. Health insurance coverage is continued during the leave, and the employer may substitute an employee's accrued paid leave for any part of the 12-week period. Eligibility is restricted to those employees who have worked 1250 hours (25 hours per week) over the previous 12 months and for at least 12 months. If the employee does not return to work following the leave they are required to pay back their health insurance premiums to their employer.

Employees are required to provide at least 30 days advance notice prior to taking the leave for foreseeable leaves (such as childbirth or adoption), and to provide medical certification justifying need for leave for their own or their family member's illness. Key employees in a firm (those in the highest 10% of the workforce) may be exempt from coverage. To date, the definition of family remains conservative in that domestic partners, either heterosexual or homosexual, are excluded from coverage.

A Swedish Comparison.   The parental leave debate in the United States stands in marked contrast to that of other advanced nations. Consider the case of Sweden, an exemplar with regard to policies for working parents (Haas, 1992; Moen, 1989; Moen & Forest, 1990). The attention in Sweden to work/family policies was grounded in a concern for declining births rates, the shortage of labor necessitating women's employment, and a deep commitment to gender equality. What was unique in Sweden was the early recognition that both women's and men's roles at work and at home needed changing in order to promote gender equality. And this was grounded in the notion that everyone has the right, even the obligation to work, women as well as men.

Important policy changes occurred in the 1970s. In 1974, Sweden's maternity leave policy was replaced with a parental insurance system providing parents with six months of leave to share, with 90% of one's wages paid while on leave. Moreover, men were entitled to 10 days off (with full pay) during the first month following childbirth, to assist in the care of both mother and child. Additionally, both mothers and fathers could take 10 days off (with pay) to care for a sick child or when the child's caregiver is ill. Throughout the 1970s and 1980s, these benefits were expanded, culminating in a year off (with 90% pay) and additional time off without pay, generous time off to care for a sick child, and the option of reducing one's workday to six hours a day while there are preschoolers at home.

Swedish fathers initially took little advantage of these

parental leave policies; however, fathers are increasingly using these benefits, especially the "daddy days" off with pay following childbirth. But it remains women, not men, who take the bulk of parental leave, and women, not men, who reduce their hours to part time (Haas, 1992; Moen, 1989).

Implications. The Family and Medical Leave Act was an important first step for the United States in recognizing that workers frequently have family responsibilities and in acknowledging the legitimacy of those responsibilities. The purpose of the act is an explicit statement of a policy to strengthen families:

1. To balance the demands of the workplace with the needs of families, to promote the stability and economic security of families, and to promote national interests in preserving family integrity.
2. To entitle employees to take reasonable leave for medical reasons, for the birth or adoption of a child, and for the care of a child, spouse, or parent who has a serious health condition.

However, parental leave in America remains for at most 12 weeks a year and includes no provision for salary replacement. Thus it provides support only for those families who can afford to have a wage earner take time off without pay. As the Swedish example suggests, women more than men are likely to take advantage of the Act, and the time off may be woefully inadequate for family needs. Above and beyond parental leave, the whole issue of the time squeeze experienced by working families remains very much on the public, if not the policy, agenda (e.g., Hochschild, 1997; Moen, 1998; Schor, 1992; Sapin and Bianchi, 1996).

The Childcare and Development Block Grant of 1990

Background. There has been little social consensus about childcare, a topic that historically has been seen as a private, family concern, and certainly not as a public, governmental issue. In fact, in 1990, the National Research Council's Panel on Child Care Policy noted that the only two points of general agreement about childcare in the United States was that (1) our current system is inadequate and (2) childcare should be conducive to the healthy development of children (Hayes et al., 1990).

The first federal legislation on childcare was precipitated by World War II and the spiraling need for women in the civilian workforce. The enactment of the Lanham Act in 1942 provided matching grants to states for daycare centers to foster the employment of women in war-production industries. But facilities never met the demand for daycare during the war, and support for daycare ceased shortly after the war's end and the return to "normalcy."*

Following the war, the only daycare subsidies available were provided by Head Start, a program begun in the 1960s offering nutritious meals and early education to low-income preschoolers, but one that in fact helped to resolve the childcare problems of some working mothers (see Zigler & Muenchow, 1992). Head Start is a center-based educational program for poor preschool children that focuses on family support as well as educational and social services for children. It was conceived during the civil rights movement and reform-oriented 1960s, based on the notion of environmental enrichment and studies of early intervention in promoting intellectual development. Two developmental psychologists, Urie Bronfenbrenner and Edward Zigler, were instrumental in pushing for a family focus, in the form of parental involvement, which became central to the Head Start program. This program points to the importance of the political and economic climate in implementing policies and the complex interplay between the findings of social research, political decision makers, the media, and interest groups, as well as public opinion (Valentine & Zigler, 1983; Zigler & Muenchow, 1992).

The political climate was less favorable when Congress passed the Comprehensive Child Development Act in 1971. It was vetoed by President Nixon, who saw it as harmful to the family-centered child rearing he preferred. This Act was meant to lay the groundwork for universally available childcare services, and would have brought together Head Start and other childcare and preschool programs (Zigler & Muenchow, 1992). However, President Nixon saw it as committing the government to the side of communal approaches to child rearing over against the family-centered approach (Zigler & Muenchow, 1992: 146). This framing of childcare legislation as antifamily meant that for 20 years no such legislation was passed.

Still, in 1967 Congress brought the various childcare programs located in departments of the federal government under one set of regulations (the Federal Interagency Day Care Requirement). And the passage of Title XX of the Social Security Amendments, adopted in 1974, did provide grants to states for daycare services in order to facilitate the employment of low-income women. A concern has been that child daycare programs, such as Head Start, preschools under Title I of the Elementary and Secondary Education Act, and Title XX daycare are all located in different agencies with separate funding and different goals (Morgan, 1994).

In 1976 a childcare tax credit for families was legislated, defining childcare as a legitimate work-related expense.

---

*See discussions of this period (Campbell, 1984; Kaledin, 1984; Margolis, 1984; Milkman, 1987; Tobias & Anderson, 1974).

However, childcare benefits for middle-income families, in the form of tax credits, were not widely available until the passage of the Economic Recovery Tax Act of 1981. The Dependent Care Tax Credit it established allows parents to deduct up to $2400 per year for the cost of caring for one child and $4800 for two or more children. The actual credit taken, however, depends on the amount of income earned, making it far more beneficial to middle- and upper-income families than to those with low incomes. Over 7 million families claimed the Dependent Care Tax Credit in 1984, establishing it as the largest single government subsidy for childcare.

Such tax credits are relatively meaningless for families with low earnings who pay little or no taxes. Moreover, the Title XX block grants to states earmarked for daycare for low-income families were reduced in 1981, along with a reduction in the income eligibility level necessary for families to qualify. As a result of these cutbacks, 35 states provided childcare services for fewer children in 1985 than in 1981 (AFL-CIO Executive Council, 1986).

Another important component of the FSA welfare package was the Earned Income Tax Credit. Under EITC, tax credit is available to families who have a child under the age of 19 or the age of 24 if a student (Chilman, 1994). In 1991, the program paid eligible employed families up to 14% of their annual earned income in the form of a "negative income tax." One-child families were paid a maximum of $1,192; families with two or more children received $1,235. This amount was to decline incrementally as family income increased, with a ceiling of $21,164 per year to still quality for benefits. The EITC continues to be available as a federal tax credit, although families may have their refunds count against their grants if they are combining welfare and work. In 1997, families with two or more children and annual earnings of less than $29,290 were eligible for an EITC of up to $3,656.

Childcare and Welfare.

Childcare has long been linked to social welfare programs. The Title XX Social Services Block Grant, for example, was targeted specifically to low-income families. However, along with the growing dissatisfaction with the federal welfare strategy came a recognition of the importance of maternal employment, culminating in welfare reform promoting paid work in 1996. Consequently, legislators increasingly came to see childcare responsibilities as impediments to the economic self-sufficiency of women raising children on their own. An early advocate of this view was Christopher Dodd (D-Connecticut), the Senate sponsor of a major daycare bill in the 1980s:

> We can afford to have childcare because the absence of it is costing so much. We're paying out $10 billion a year in (welfare) payments to start with, and any survey done that

> I've seen in the last decade or so indicates that the major reason why people do not get off welfare and go to work is the absence of any kind of childcare program (Noble, 1988, p. 4).

The 1990s saw a growing acceptance in the halls of Congress of some form of public support for childcare, at least for poor children whose parents lack the means to purchase care in the open market.

Defining the Issue.

Childcare bills providing grants to states and to the private sector to expand and improve childcare have been introduced and reintroduced, helping to spark a new debate on the federal role in childcare. In the 1980s childcare was very much on the front burner at both the federal and state levels, with coalitions of childcare advocates, women's and professional groups, and unions actively lobbying for their preferred bills. Both major party presidential candidates prominently featured childcare in their 1988 campaigns. The Republican and Democratic political parties actively wooed the TICKS, two income couples with kids. With over half the mothers of infants and over two-thirds of the mothers of dependent children now in the labor force, it was clear that working family concerns such as childcare were not going to disappear from the policy agenda.

The National Research Council's Panel on Child Care Policy concluded in 1990 that no single policy can address the childcare needs of all families and children; what is needed is an array of coordinated policies and programs responsive to the distinctive needs of families located in particular contexts and situations The panel also judged that responsibility for meeting childcare needs should be shared among individuals, families, voluntary organizations, employers, communities and government. Three issues are paramount in developing a comprehensive system: quality, accessibility, and affordability (Hayes et al., 1990).

Similarly, conservative and liberal legislators alike began to come to terms with the childcare dilemma. Increasingly, the issue became not whether affordable, quality childcare should be available but the role the federal government should play in its provision and regulation.

Recent Legislation.

In the 1990 Omnibus Budget Reconciliation Act, Congress included a new program of grants to states, the Childcare and Development Block Grant. This was the culmination of a number of proposals for federal legislation on childcare, including the Act for Better Child Care, proposed by Senator Dodd, and represents a series of compromises on the nature and purpose of childcare for young children.

The Act authorized $2.5 billion to states over a three year period, with 75% of the funds used for childcare services for low income families and 25 percent to improve the quality of childcare and the availability of early childhood development and before- and after-school care.

This Block Grant requires that states fund services both by grants or contracts to providers and by providing certificates or vouchers that parents may give to eligible providers. "Eligible" providers can include care provided by friends, relatives, neighbors, or church-based centers (Department of Health and Human Services, 1991). The goal of these alternative mechanisms of funding is to increase parental choice with regard to the type of care for their children. Some observers see parental choice as an effort to keep the family center stage in the care of children, but it also limits the ability of states to require higher standards of care (Hofferth, 1992). The Act also states that parents must have unlimited access to their children in provider care, that providers must keep records of parental complaints, and that states must provide parents with information on licensing and regulatory requirements and complain procedures. In addition, states are required to establish basic health and safety requirements related to disease prevention, building and physical safety standards, and minimum health and safety training. The Consortium of Family Organizations (COFO) assessed the "family impacts" of this Child Care and Development Block Grant Act and concluded that the Act did include a family perspective on childcare and provides "a welcome balance among the competing goals and principles that have been embedded in the national discussions and debates on child care policy" (1992, p. 10).

With the Personal Responsibility and Work Opportunity Act of 1996 (PRWOA), however, the childcare guarantee that was part of the FSA was repealed by Congress (Greenberg, 1998a). States are free to provide childcare but no longer obligated to do so. There are now Childcare and Development Funds (CCDF) in every state to be coordinated with Temporary Assistance for Needy Families (TANF) programs and welfare-to-work transitions.

In addition to the CCDF, the new welfare law does permit a range of alternative funding strategies for childcare needs (Greenberg, 1998b). A state can spend funds from TANF for childcare use; it can transfer up to 10% TANF funds to the Title XX Social Services Block Grant or up to 30% of TANF funds to the CCDF. There is also the option of using state funds from its "maintenance of effort" (MOE) requirement.* Different methods of funding childcare have different consequences for TANF recipients themselves. For example, if TANF funds are used for childcare, those months count against the recipient's federal time limit, even if no

*The TANF maintenance of effort (MOE) requirement stipulates that in order to receive a federal block grant, a state must meet its historic state expenditure level, which is the nonfederal spending previously needed for welfare programs such as AFDC, JOBS, Emergency Assistance, etc. (Greenberg, 1998b).

other assistance if provided. If childcare funds are received, the family will also be required to turn its child support over to the state, to be distributed according to the state's discretion. These same stipulations do not apply if the recipient receives childcare through the CDDF.

Other considerations also apply. Funding available for childcare is presently higher through TANF. In FY 1997, 30% of TANF was just under $5 billion (Greenberg, 1998b). The entire CCDF was only $3 billion. Moreover, funds that have been transferred out of TANF to other programs are no longer subject to TANF rules but will fall under the regulations of the receiving program. Currently, the federal eligibility guideline for CCDF for each state is 85% of the state's median income. TANF funds that are transferred to Title XX must be used for families at or below 200% of the poverty threshold. At the same time, TANF funds are primarily intended to provide cash assistance and employment and training services for needy families. States will have to balance the pros and cons of using different funding sources to meet childcare needs.

According to a report by the Children's Defense Fund (CDF) (1988), the current level of spending on childcare to support low-income families falls woefully short. The CDF report finds that only one child in 10 eligible under federal law is actually receiving needed childcare assistance. In response, President Clinton's proposed budget for FY 1999 included $20 billion over the next five years for childcare and the Head Start program (U.S. Department of Health and Human Services, 1998). The Historic Child Care Initiative would increase funding for the CCDBG by $7.5 billion over five years. The request for FY 1999 alone totaled $5.1 billion for childcare services. As part of this initiative, major efforts will be made to improve accreditation of federally sponsored childcare providers, including attention to both quality and safety, appropriate staff-to-child ratios, and affordability. The president also proposed a $150 million Research and Evaluation Fund to increase knowledge about the U.S. childcare system, with a particular focus on the needs of low-income families.

The Welfare Wars

Background. While adult pauperism has historically been considered a crime, if not an illness, poor children present a unique problem. On the one hand, they can hardly be held responsible for their plight. Yet, by extension, public assistance to children living in poverty also benefits their parents. For this reason, across more than 50 years of welfare policy in the United States, debate has persisted over the method of assistance, the meaning of entitlement, and the role of government in providing relief to poor families.

On the assumption that children could be saved from a

life of poverty, a majority of states had by 1931 instituted a Mother's Aid, Mother's Pension, or Aid to Dependent Children (ADC) program (Pearce, 1989; Quadagno, 1994; Trattner, 1979). In 1935 during the New Deal, ADC nationalized the state-based programs. Consistent with the ideology of separate spheres, the original ADC provided support for the children of single parents, with mothers designated as the main conduit of this support. Case workers closely monitored the capacity to care of the recipient-mothers, discouraging any employment that might interfere with child supervision and full-time domesticity (Nelson, 1990; Trattner, 1979). Until the 1950s and 1960s, welfare policies aimed at women continued to encourage economic dependence in exchange for care-giving services; moreover, this paternalism was generally reserved for white widowed mothers and their children, a reflection of the country's racial biases as well (Mink, 1990; Pearce, 1989; Quadagno, 1994). The more recent increase in divorced or unmarried (rather than widowed) recipients as well as the entry of black women into the welfare system fundamentally changed the program's purpose and challenged previous public notions of mothers and children as part of the "deserving poor" (Berrick, 1991; Quadagno, 1994).

The distinction between deserving and undeserving poor implies that the undeserving poor are categorically different from the rest of the population. Yet research indicates that the proportion of families permanently in poverty is relatively small, while the size of the population at risk of economic need is quite large. Longitudinal analysis of a nationwide sample of over 5000 families has documented the movement back and forth across the poverty line of a sizable proportion of families over time (Duncan, Coe, & Hill, 1981). Moreover, during the 1980s U.S. rates for poverty among children was shown to exceed those of other industrialized nations (Smeeding, 1990). Approximately one American child in five lives in poverty (U.S. Bureau of the Census, 1992). An overall growth rate in child poverty of over 11% since 1980 suggests that the original promise of ADC has somehow been derailed. Nevertheless, public resentment associated with welfare has ultimately served to politicize welfare reform, as evidenced in the pattern of policy initiatives since the 1960s.

The Great Society Programs. The first postwar wave of welfare reform occurred with the Great Society legislation of the 1960s, under the leadership of Presidents Kennedy and Johnson. Prior to this time, means-tested programs for the poor were limited, with the bulk of the welfare state aimed at the nonpoor in the form of New Deal social insurance programs, supplemented by union negotiations for healthcare, disability, and pension benefits (Brown, 1988; Quadagno, 1994; Trattner, 1979). The Great Society reforms,

however, targeted those overlooked in the existing system, those with intermittent attachment to the labor force and the working poor. Under this new War on Poverty, existing service programs were expanded and new programs were developed to support the poor into full-time employment. Beginning in 1964, Congress enacted the Food Stamp Program, based on a pilot program initiated by executive order by President Kennedy in 1961. During the same year, 10 other programs were authorized under President Johnson's Great Society program, including a Job Corps to provide work experience and training, a domestic peace corps (VISTA), a program of aid to small businesses, a training program for heads of families receiving public assistance, a work-study program to provide students from low-income families with part-time work, community action programs, legal services, Upward Bound, and Project Head Start (Quadagno, 1994; Trattner, 1979).

As far-sighted as the programs sound, they were not viewed by everyone as an optimal solution to the poverty problem. Herbert Hill, NAACP Labor Director, called the administration's antipoverty program inadequate and

> an extension of white welfare paternalism: We must rescue the anti-poverty program from the social work profession and from the politicians who want merely a sterile and ineffective program that will mean little or nothing for the Negro community. We must shed the illusion that this is a war on poverty—it is merely a BB shot against it. A real war on poverty would require fundamental alterations in our national economy and the mobilization of a significant portion of the national income for this purpose. ("Charges against anti-poverty program ...." 1996)

Late in 1966 the war on poverty stalled, primarily for three reasons: (1) skyrocking costs of the war in Vietnam; (2) eroded Congressional support in response to riots in some impoverished areas; (3) a lack of pressure from the White House for a strong program (Quadagno, 1994). While such projects as Head Start and the Neighborhood Youth Corps fared well and the Child Nutrition Act expanded the government's school food program, service programs such as the Job Corps program and community action had funding cut ("Job Corps program seen entering crucial period," 1966).

Aid to Families with Dependent Children (AFDC) became a permanent federal program in 1967, extending states' power, however, to deny federal assistance to families if an unemployed father was living at home. Although President Johnson took no position on this cutback, he noted that 12 million children in families below the poverty line received no benefits, 33 states did not meet their own minimum standards for subsistence in their AFDC payments, and only 12 states had community work and training programs for unemployed parents ("Text of President's message on children and youth," 1967). One year later, the Committee on

School Lunch Participation, in their report "Daily Bread," found that less than 4% of public school children were able to participate in the School Lunch Program, although 6 million were eligible. During the same year, a Presidential Commission on Hunger was established to study the extent of hunger and malnutrition in the United States ("Congress, Administration focus attention on hunger," 1968).

The Shift toward Retrenchment. Ironically, although major welfare legislation was passed during the Kennedy and Johnson administrations, many anti-poverty programs did not get into full operation until the Nixon administration (Brown, 1988; Gilbert & Kahl, 1987; Quadagno, 1994). By this time, the United States was on the edge of an economic downturn. Antipathy toward anti-poverty spending grew during the 1970s; in particular, public opinion turned against programs that were most likely to be associated with racial minorities.

Although President Reagan can be credited with the most clearly articulated legislative attack on welfare programs for the poor, the trend actually began earlier. In spite of his conservative stance on welfare, President Nixon in 1969 proposed the Family Assistance Plan (FAP), which would have extended welfare benefits to all working-poor families, including two-parent families (Brown, 1988; Quadagno, 1994; Trattner, 1979). The bill was defeated in Congress, which created instead the Supplemental Security Income (SSI) program, expanded cash and in-kind transfers, but trimmed back core service programs associated with the Great Society reforms. Again, in 1977, President Carter put forward his welfare reform Program for Better Jobs and Income (PBJI), which would have eliminated AFCD, SSI, and food stamps and replaced them with cash payments for about 32 million people, including the working poor (Rovner, 1987b; Trattner, 1979). Again, the reform was defeated by Congress. Not surprisingly, gains from the war on poverty began to erode, as the poverty rate jumped from 11.4% of the population in 1978 to 13.0% by 1980 (U.S. Bureau of the Census, 1990b).

The defeat of both the Nixon and Carter plans were early warning signs of the period of retrenchment to follow, in which the Reagan administration during the 1980s cut billions of dollars from most benefits associated with the Great Society programs, in particular, assistance to the working poor (Brown, 1988; Quadagno, 1994). Most vulnerable were the Work Incentives Program (WIN) (which was replaced with a workfare program at minimum wage), AFDC, food stamps and various school-based food programs for children, housing subsidies, energy assistance, Medicaid, and family planning services (Levitan, Belous, & Gallo, 1988). For example, due to tighter eligibility regulation, in 1982 alone 8% or approximately 250,000 families were removed from AFDC rolls. By 1983, there were almost as many people

living in poverty as there had been in 1963 (Gilbert & Kahl, 1987); in fact, one in every five American families lived at or below 125% of the poverty income level (U.S. Bureau of the Census, 1990b). Yet however blighted the war on poverty, these figures could have been higher without the Great Society reforms. The allocation retrenchment policies of the early Reagan administration eventually led to the first major legislative welfare reform movement since the Great Society, beginning with the Family Support Act (FSA) of 1988. In January 1987, in his State of the Union address, President Reagan promised again to "reform this outmoded social dinosaur [welfare] and finally break the poverty trap" (Rovner, 1987a, p. 206). His lack of clear direction, however, left open the opportunity for congressional initiatives and the possibility of bipartisan support, spurred on by the release of a March Congressional report, finding that 18 states currently provided benefits below 15% of the state's median income (Rovner, 1987b). After almost two years of debate, hearings, and compromises—a rocky course led to a great extent by Senator Daniel Patrick Moynihan (D-New York), lead sponsor of the Senate bill, and then-Governor Bill Clinton, chair of the National Governors Association—the FSA became law in October 1988.

The Family Support Act of 1988. By 1988, 20.4 percent of all children in the United States lived below the poverty line (U.S. Bureau of the Census, 1990b). The FSA attempted to reconcile the dilemma of how to provide for children and at the same time not reward parents who did not work. Based on the assumption that education, work experience, training, and support are the ways to reduce welfare dependency (Education Writers Association, 1988), the FSA was hailed as "the most significant overhaul of the welfare system in half a century" (Rovner, 1988b, p. 2699). The law required each state to establish and operate a Job Opportunities and Basic Skills program (JOBS), targeting families at risk of long-term welfare dependency, in particular, women who are high-school dropouts and/or who have little work experience. All able-bodied welfare recipients were required to enroll in the JOBS program, with the exception of mothers of preschoolers under age 3 (and at state's option, under age 1), those employed over 30 hours a week, mothers under age 16 attending school full time, and pregnant women. In addition, the bill required states to guarantee childcare and healthcare during the first 12 months of employment, as well as transportation and other work-related expenses needed to participate in the JOBS program (Chilman, 1991; Graham, 1988; Lurie & Sanger, 1991; Rovner, 1988b). Critics of the FSA argued that the bill maintained the Reagan myth of family self-sufficiency through low-wage employment (Graham, 1988). While the law prohibited states from requiring welfare recipients to work off their benefits at less than minimum wage, cash benefits were cut dollar for dollar as earnings increased, beginning after the first four months of the job. At the time the FSA was passed, minimum wage was still set at the 1983 level of $3.35 an hour. To bring a family of four out of poverty, a single mother would have had to earn wages at 60% above the minimum wage. The 1994 poverty level was set at $14,335, remaining an unreachable goal even with the subsequent minimum-wage increase to $4.25 an hour.

Critics also claimed that JOBS was little more than remedial education and job training that would only engulf long-term welfare recipients into a endless labyrinth of programs ("Editorial," 1988). For some, therefore, the FSA appeared to be an attempt to make "having a baby on welfare an even more unpleasant experience than it is now" ("Editorial," 1988, p. 24). Proponents of the policy, however, cited examples of successful workfare programs. A study by the Manpower Demonstration Research Corporation found that three JOBS programs in Georgia, Michigan, and California resulted in large increases in employed persons, with the greatest reduction in welfare spending to date (U.S. Department of Health and Human Services, 1995a). After two years, participants in the JOBS programs were receiving 22% fewer AFDC benefits, 14% fewer food stamp benefits, and were 24% more likely to be employed, although at low-wage jobs. The most successful JOBS programs in the study were those with an emphasis on immediate employment supports, at least in the short term.

Among the issues tackled by the FSA, the least controversial was that of enforcing child support from absent fathers (Rovner, 1988a). As of spring 1988, about 59% of single-parent mothers living with children under the age of 21 were awarded child support payments by agreement or by the courts (U.S. Bureau of the Census, 1990a). Of these, about half (51.3%) received the full amount due. The average annual amount was $2710. According to one estimate, the federal government would save a net of $403 million over 5 years in welfare and related costs if child-support provisions were enacted (Rovner, 1988a). Provisions of the FSA required all states to automatically withhold child-support payments from the absent parents' wages or salary by fiscal year 1994.

The automatic wage-withholding provision initially met opposition from divorced fathers' groups, who claimed that mandating that employers withhold child support payments could jeopardize a father's job security and that monthly support payments are sometimes the only leverage a father has to guarantee visitation rights. Nevertheless, nearly $10 billion was collected from non-custodial parents in 1994, and approximately $11 billion was collected in 1995 (U.S. Department of Health and Human Services, 1995b). Part of this increase was due to the establishment of 735,000 paternities, up from 554,205 in 1992.

Another important component of the FSA welfare package was the Earned Income Tax Credit. Under EITC, tax credit is available to families who have a child under the age of 19 or the age of 24 if a student (Chilman, 1994). In 1991, the program paid eligible employed families up to 14% of their annual earned income of $6,180 or less in the form of a "negative income tax." One-child families were paid a maximum of $1,192; families with two or more children received $1,235. This amount was to decline incrementally as family income increased, with a ceiling of $21,164 per year to still quality for benefits.

In spite of its sweeping reforms, the success of the Family Support Act was undercut by the recession of the early 1990s. From 1989 to 1992, the number of families receiving AFDC benefits rose 25%. States were unable to provide funds to match the federal education and job training programs, causing them to freeze or cut AFDC benefits. Moreover, accompanying these fiscal constraints was a lack of public support for welfare, heralding "discussions of behavioral poverty and ... government's right (and obligation) to do something about it," according to Douglas Besharov, an American Enterprise Institute scholar ("Clinton, Congress talk of welfare reform," 1993, p. 374).

In short, under the current controversy over welfare reform lies a fundamental disagreement about welfare recipients themselves, and thus the reasons for poverty in the United States. One camp argues that welfare policies in the past have served as a safety net to help most families avoid long-term poverty (e.g., Duncan, Coe & Hill, 1984; Duncan & Rodgers, 1991). In contrast, analysts from the other camp insist that welfare clients are responsible for their condition and thus in need of disciplinary if not punitive measures to discourage welfare use. The FSA reflected this philosophy. Its lack of success, however, only intensified the commitment among its supporters to hold welfare recipients accountable.

In mid-1994, President Clinton unveiled his plan to "end welfare as we know it," calling for more spending on job training and childcare but requiring that recipients find work within two years of accepting welfare benefits ("Welfare reform takes a back seat," 1994, p. 364). Arguing that the Clinton plan would treat welfare recipients more generously than working families, conservative Congressional leaders countered with legislation designed to dismantle the federal welfare system with the Personal Responsibility and Work Opportunity Act (PRWOA).

Personal Responsibility and Work Opportunity Act of 1996. As part of the conservative Contract with America, the PRWOA was specifically intended to "reduce government [welfare] dependency, attack illegitimacy, require welfare recipients to work, and cut welfare spending" (Gillespie & Schellhas, 1994, p. 66). Like the FSA, it is grounded in the assumption that the current welfare system "had the unintended consequence of making welfare more attractive than work to many families" by paying $3,000 more per year than a minimum-wage job (Gillespie & Schellhas, 1994, p. 67). It should be noted, however, at this time full-time year-around employment at minimum wage earned only an annual wage of $8,480, which was 27 percent below the 1995 poverty line for a family of three (National Organization for Women, 1996).

After two years of fierce bipartisan negotiations, the PRWOA became law in 1996. The legislation effectively ended over 50 years of federal welfare policy and created in its place the Temporary Assistance for Needy Families (TANF) Block Grant (Children's Defense Fund (CDF), 1997; Greenberg & Savner, 1996; Street, 1997), turning the responsibility for antipoverty efforts back to the states for the first time since 1936. In turn, each state was required to begin its own TANF program by July, 1997, based on federal rules accompanying the legislative reforms.

The PRWOA repealed the AFDC, JOBS, and Emergency Assistance to Families with Children Programs (Greenberg & Savner, 1996). In their place, federal funds in the form of a block grant are distributed to states to spend according to state welfare policies. The amount of this block grant is capped at a federal limit of $16.4 billion annually, with a $2 billion contingency fund in case of a recession. Although it appears to be substantial, critics argue that the $2 billion rainy-day fund is grossly inadequate: a recession comparable to the recession of 1989–1992 would require an additional $3 billion to be available at the current population level (CDF, 1997). This means that, in times of economic downturn, emergency public aid for needy families would not be available.

Under TANF, the states are obligated to operate a welfare program in all political subdivisions, but these programs do not have to be uniform nor must they include cash transfer payments (CDF, 1997; Street, 1997). States also have the option to subcontract the administration of welfare programs to religious organizations, private charities, and private corporations.

A central goal of all state programs must be the steady reduction of the number of welfare recipients. Unlike previous federal entitlement, TANF funds may not be used to assist a family that has received assistance for 60 months or more (CDF, 1977; Greenburg & Savner, 1996; Street, 1997). States have the option of granting hardship exceptions for up to 20% of their caseload. States may also impose shorter lifetime limits. For example, Ohio set a 36-month lifetime limit on assistance under their Ohio Works First program (Ohio Bureau of Employment Services, 1997). If a good cause exists, the family or assistance group can reapply for an additional 24 months, but only after a 24-month period of ineligibility. For those who continue to receive TANF assistance, the work requirements are increased dramatically over previous federal welfare legislation. Recipients who are not

otherwise exempt must participate in work activities within two months of receiving assistance, unless the state opts out (CDF, 1997; Greenberg & Savner, 1996; Street, 1997). In addition, the state must meet a progressive work participation rate, with 50% of all families by FY 2002 and 90% of two-parent families involved in work activities by FY 1999. To calculate the number of hours a TANF recipient will be required to work, states must divide the amount of TANF benefits by the minimum wage and may not require more hours of workfare than this equivalent amount. Under certain conditions, some TANF recipients will be exempt from the workfare requirements. For example, parents with a child under the age of one may be excluded (CDF, 1997). Unlike previous welfare laws, however, only 12 months of vocational education counts toward the work requirement, with no more than 30% of all of a state's workfare participants involved in vocational education (Street, 1997).

Minor parents can receive TANF funds only if they are living at home or in another adult-supervised setting (CDF, 1997; Greenberg & Savner, 1996). They must attend high school or an alternative educational or training program as soon as their child is at least three months old. Some states have also experimented with denying mothers additional funds if they have more children while on welfare. A recent four-year study in New Jersey found, however, that the family cap had *no* effect on the birth rate among welfare recipients ("New Jersey officials say birth rate drop not linked to welfare benefits," 1997).

As part of its emphasis on paternity and child support, the PRWOA strengthens state child support activities (Department of Health and Human Services, 1998). In FY 1997, noncustodial parents paid $13 billion, up from $8 billion in 1992 and representing an additional 1.4 million child support collection cases. Also in 1997, the Department of Health and Human Services (DHHS) awarded $1.5 million in demonstration grants to states for innovative projects to improve child support enforcement, most of which are linked to state welfare programs and low-income, young, and at-risk fathers. States must also meet federal mandates for a child support enforcement program to remain eligible for their TANF grants. As part of this effort, 1.1 million paternities were established in FY 1997 for out-of-wedlock births, more than double the number in 1992.

Because the main goal of current welfare reform is employment, several provisions are designed to facilitate welfare-to-work transitions. States may use up to 30% of their block grant funds for programs under the Child Care and Development Block Grant and the Title XX Social Service Block Grant, with certain stipulations (Greenberg & Savner, 1996). Moreover, the Balanced Budget Act of 1997 included a welfare-to-work grant. Yet, while childcare funds have increased, they fall about $2.4 billion short of the new need. In the event that a single parent of a child under 6 cannot find childcare, states may not reduce or terminate that family's TANF assistance.

As part of the PRWOA, Medicaid is still available to those families who would have been eligible under the old ADFC guidelines, even if they exceed the five-year time limit (CDF, 1997). This benefit is considered to be part of transitional support, as welfare recipients to move to employment that may lack health insurance (Brown, 1997). In addition, some state programs provide recipients with assistance for transportation and other work-related needs for up to two years after leaving welfare. The EITC continues to be available as a federal tax credit, although families may have their refunds count against their TANF grants if they are combining welfare and work. In 1997, families with two or more children and annual earnings of less than $29,290 were eligible for an EITC of up to $3656.

While the PRWOA addresses some of the limitations of the FSA, opponents cite several long-term consequences for the welfare overhaul policies. The central problem with block grants is that they replace entitlement to a minimum standard of living with different eligibility requirements across 50 different states (CDF, 1997; Street, 1997). States are encouraged to experiment with their own welfare programs, and there are small incentives available to states that keep welfare spending per person low and that demonstrate a net decrease in out-of-wedlock births. Critics argue that these incentives are not in the best interests of real welfare reform but may encourage draconian measures to cut state welfare rolls (Vobejda & Havemann, 1997). In addition, under the PRWOA, states will no longer receive matching federal funds for welfare spending. States will have to dig deeper into their own budgets to make up the shortage or further cut back welfare rolls.

Overall, the results of the new welfare law have been dramatic. Between January 1993 and January 1997, the number of welfare recipients in the United States fell by 20% or 2.75 million recipients (Council of Economic Advisors, 1997). (But note that the new welfare policies were enacted in a time of unprecedented economic prosperity with a sustained period of low unemployment.) Preliminary analysis from nine state reports suggests that between 50% and 60% of recipients leave welfare for employment, with average wages falling between $5.50 and $7.00 an hour (National Governors' Association, 1997). It is not clear, however, where the other 40% to 50% of former welfare recipients have gone. In Illinois, for example, the welfare caseload declined by 17% in the first year of implementation of the PRWOA. Yet more than half of the recipients were dropped from the rolls for missing a welfare program-related appointment ("Welfare's down; but what's up?" 1998).

Some states that reported large drops in welfare benefits were also those that requested waivers to narrow eligibility and strengthen sanctions through experimental policies (Council of Economic Advisors, 1997). According to the Midwest Job Gap Project, a provision of the PRWOA actually creates an incentive for states to avoid improving employment-related programs (Street, 1997). The "caseload reduction credit" reduces a state's work participation requirements by the number of percentage points that a state's welfare caseload fell since FY 1995. Simply terminating assistance through sanctions is cheaper and faster than finding that same person a job, but delivers the same credit to the state.

Policy analysts are also concerned that there are simply not enough low-skilled jobs available to employ those moving from welfare to work. For example, in the Midwest the regional worker-to-job ratio was 4 to 1, including both unemployed workers and welfare recipients among the jobseekers (Kleppner and Theodore, 1997). Moreover, surveys of state occupational employment and wages show that approximately 20% of all current jobs have median wages at or below 125% of the poverty threshold (U.S. Bureau of Labor Statistics, 1996), wages that are not likely to support financial self-sufficiency even with full-time year-round employment.

Finally, the end of "welfare as we know it" means the end of a way of thinking about public assistance for both caseworkers and recipients (Brown, 1997; Street, 1997). TANF-era reform requires extensive retraining of frontline staff, who must confront a host of new discretionary decisions, using their evaluation of recipients' personal circumstances to determine which welfare mothers must go to work and when, which will be allowed to attend college, which will be potentially sanctioned and at what level, which can receive only a one-time/diversionary payment, and which will receive ongoing assistance (Street, 1997, p. 57). With the twin priorities of "work first" and welfare-roll reduction, the PRWOA may be more of a "carrot and stick" approach to welfare reform than a genuine antipoverty effort (Street, 1997). Research based on prior trends in reducing welfare shows that decreases in welfare spending actually produce increases in the total poor population as well as the dependent poor (Schram, 1991). This stems, in part, from the tendency of recent mandatory workfare programs to channel welfare recipients into the low-wage market (Mann and Albelda, 1989; Rose, 1990) while reducing overall eligibility for benefits. Real welfare reform would require substantial government subsidies for training as well as jobs, while the present legislation is cost-cutting and thus doomed to failure. If there is a silver lining in the cloud of current welfare reform, however, it may be in the chance to test the magic of the American economy without the "liberal" welfare state to blame for the perpetuation of poor families (Street, 1997).

An Example of Tacit Family Policy in the Making

Ongoing and controversial family issues revolve around reproduction, childbearing, and childrearing (Faludi, 1991; Hofferth, 1992). Technological advancements have rendered reproduction both more voluntary and more varied than ever before and are producing an emerging body of family policy in the form of state legislation and court opinion. We define this as an example of tacit policy in that these frequently represent ad hoc decisions in light of individual cases, not a deliberate attempt to frame a policy agenda.

Reproductive Technologies and Family Formation

With the advance of the new reproductive technologies, the opportunity to parent has been extended to a range of individuals and couples who previously, due to infertility or the lack of an opposite-sex partner, would not have been able to produce their own biological offspring. These new ways of creating human life have been hailed by supporters as socially beneficial in that they create "ardently wanted life" (Schuck, 1990, p. 135). Opponents, however, have taken positions extending from the Vatican's complete opposition to any form of "artificial reproduction" that deviates from normal heterosexual intercourse within marriage (Macklin, 1988; Michalsky, 1989) to a particular contest with the legal and ethical considerations raised by surrogate motherhood as unique among the forms of technologically assisted reproduction (e.g., Annas, 1990; Corea, 1985; Macklin, 1988, 1990).

This section first summarizes the main arguments surrounding the each of the new reproductive techniques (NRTs), focusing on constitutional rights to reproduction, contractual versus family law, and ethical concerns. Within each of these debates also lie assumptions about what constitutes parenthood. In this respect, intentionally or not, the arena of family policy has been widened to include lawyers, judges, doctors, social workers, and a host of other experts and authorities who shape the final decision about who will and will not be allowed to lay legitimate claims to the children produced through NRTs and thus be included in their family formation. It is this tacit form of family policy making that is the main concern of this section.

Artificial Insemination.   The first NRT to be developed, over a century ago, was artificial insemination (AI). A simple procedure, AI involves the depositing of ejaculated sperm into women's uterus. First used among married couples to treat infertility, the technique has been employed to overcome conception difficulties by artificially inseminating the wife with the husband's sperm (AIH) (Lauritzen, 1990). In cases in which either the husband is sterile or a single woman wants to have a child, a third-party donor is involved (AID). If a doctor performs AID, the donor as well as the donee generally remain anonymous. The simplicity of AID, however, also permits private insemination, in which both parties involved are known to one another (Field, 1988; Wikler & Wikler, 1991).

Regulation of AID occurs in two policy arenas, legal and medical. In most states, artificial insemination statutes offer clear legal determination for the parties involved, conforming with the guidelines of the Uniform Parentage Act. When AID is performed by a doctor using an anonymous donor, the legal motherhood of the woman giving birth is thus recognized and no rights or obligations to the sperm donor are provided (Corea, 1985; Field, 1988; Wikler & Wikler, 1991). The case is clearest when a wife is inseminated with her husband's consent, in essence, legislating the extinguishing of the genetic father's traditional role in favor of the rearing father (Annas, 1988a).

The court has not been so clear when there is no husband in the picture. A 1977 New Jersey court ruling (*C.M. v. C.C.*) granted visitation rights and the duty of child support to a sperm donor who was known to the single AID mother. Although the donor originally intended to provide only sperm in the AID arrangement, the court's decision supported the donor's rights because the insemination was privately accomplished (Field, 1988) and because it was in the best interests of the child to have two parents whenever possible (Corea, 1985). In a third case involving a lesbian single AID mother (*Jourdan C. v. Mary K.*), the sperm donor appeared to have changed his feelings about donating sperm as the pregnancy continued. The court again ruled in the sperm donor's favor, because insemination had not been carried out in accordance with the state's statutory requirement of a physician's supervision (Field, 1988). *Jourdan C.* was treated by the court as a divorce case; the judge forbade the mother to leave the state with her child and ordered her and the donor to meet in conciliation court, despite the fact that the two were barely acquaintances and the mother was raising the child in a coparenting relationship with another women (Corea, 1985; Field, 1988).

Medical regulation of AID has been less consistent. Originally, AI as a technique in human reproduction was developed by physicians, who—along with their patients—believed that medical skills were necessary to perform the procedure (Wikler & Wikler, 1991). Infertility within marriage was understood as a medical problem, and physicians could thus serve as specialists who were protected by professional confidentiality. Wikler and Wikler argue that AI has remained medicalized, not because a physician was essential or even necessary to safely perform the insemination procedure, but because this arrangement met the needs of all involved and included an implicit element of social control.

In fact, 21 state statutes specifically require that AI be performed by a physician (Office of Technology Assessment, 1988).

In addition to administering the insemination procedure, the role of the physician is to serve as an extension of public morality and associated views about reproduction (Wikler & Wikler, 1991). Like legislation and judicial regulation, medical control of AID has shaped the options of prospective parents. Based on a number of considerations, physicians may refuse to inseminate a woman. The most widely practiced form of AID gatekeeping has been to deny services to unmarried women. Although many have relaxed this criterion, lesbians are still less likely to receive AID services from a physician; the emergence of sperm banks, however, has offered an alternative route, permitting lesbians to avoid moral medical confrontations (Office of Technology Assessment, 1988). Other physician criteria for the exclusion of certain women as candidates for AID have included such characteristics as low socioeconomic status, low intelligence, and physical disabilities (Wikler & Wikler, 1991). Sperm banks were also found to have screening criteria, including criminal record, drug and alcohol abuse, psychological immaturity, lack of a high school diploma, and evidence of child abuse (Office of Technology Assessment, 1988). While such criteria appear to be perfectly reasonable attempts to protect unborn children, we should ask not merely what screening guidelines are used but how stringently are they applied and how equitably across prospective parents. Physician selectivity also can extend to genetic paternity. One study found that over 90% of physicians surveyed did not allow the recipient to select her donor (Curie-Cohen & Shapiro, 1979). Evidence also suggests that physicians frequently use the sperm of medical school personnel, ostensibly due to their high levels of health and intelligence. In combination with the screening of recipients, AID practice can too easily resemble a policy of eugenics in which higher social class and other socially valued characteristics are selectively reproduced (Corea, 1985).

Tight legal and medical control of AI serve not only to selectively grant parenthood, however, but also to hold shut the flood gates of social change. Even in its most conservative form (AIH), artificial insemination interrupts the relationship between physical sex and conception. Donor insemination furthers the break between consanguineous and social kinship already begun by the reality of adoptive families. The extension of AID availability to unmarried women, however, pushes us to new questions about family formation. In response, as can be seen in both the legal and medical precedents discussed earlier, this step threatens an unraveling of a far greater tradition than that of the linkage of blood and kinship. Courts, judges, Congress, and medical practitioners are able to extend male authority into the changing procedures of family formation that appear to be eroding patriarchal control of the family unit.

It is precisely this point that has brought applause for artificial insemination from some sectors, as single heterosexual women and lesbians are now able to parent and establish families outside of the constraints and obligations of heterosexual marriage (Seligman, 1990; Corea, 1985). As the establishment of sperm banks has opened up channels for nontraditional AID parenting, women have also increasingly been circumventing both medical and legal complications by self-insemination, underscoring the need for reconsideration of the medicalization of AID and its inherent character of social control (Wikler & Wikler, 1991).

Despite its radical potential, AID has been perhaps the least controversial of the new reproductive technologies. Public discomfort with the procedure has focused in general on the risk of AIDS and hepatitis infection and other sexually transmitted diseases (e.g., Gaines, 1990), distress among AID offspring regarding their origins and/or a fear of disclosure among AID parents (Edwards, 1991), and alarm that AID reinforces if not encourages male reproductive irresponsibility (Callahan, 1991). Perhaps because the procedure itself is, in reality, very close to natural conception, related legal suits (custody and child support) have generally been settled through the provisions of family law (Corea, 1985; Field, 1988). Moreover, under artificial insemination state statutes, physician-administered AID legally prevents sperm donors from making paternal claims. Those women who have been denied access to AID have also been members of groups least likely to fight legal battles over constitutionally protected privacy rights to reproduction. And ultimately, the ethical and moral issues raised by artificial insemination have been overshadowed by the more complicated questions effected by other procedures among the new reproductive technologies, in particular, surrogate motherhood and in vitro fertilization.

Surrogate Motherhood

Mired in a host of objections and defenses, surrogate motherhood has emerged as a deeply controversial practice among the new reproductive technologies. Surrogate motherhood can take two forms. In the event of female infertility or a need/desire to avoid pregnancy, another woman, the surrogate, can serve as both the genetic and gestational mother, artificially inseminated with the sperm of the intended rearing father. A variation includes gamete intrafallopian transfer (GIFT), in which the intended rearing mother also makes a genetic contribution through a complicated process of egg retrieval, and in vitro fertilization, with the embryo then planted and carried to term in the uterus of a gestational mother. In either case, the surrogate is intended only as a substitute for the intended rearing mother; she is expected to sever her relationship with the child at birth, in accordance with the surrogacy contract. In the vast majority of cases, the plan goes according to design; the exceptions make headlines. In either case, however, the practice of surrogacy is still hotly debated on legal, social, and ethical grounds, with different priorities rising from different philosophical camps.

Support for the practice of surrogate motherhood is generally grounded in the belief of the constitutional right to marital procreation (Robertson, 1988) and the principles of contract and family law (Charo, 1990; Field, 1988; Schuck, 1990). Following, some proponents argue that antisurrogacy legislation violates equal protection because it treats infertile couples differently, allowing AID but forbidding surrogacy (Field, 1988). For others, the decisive factor in evaluating surrogate motherhood is that it brings children to parents who cherish them (Schuck, 1990). Because these parents are further willing to pay, the women who choose to become surrogates benefit in terms of both altruistic and economic rewards. Thus, the morality of surrogacy should rest on the greater social good rather than on the insignificant number of cases in which problems have arisen.

Another prosurrogacy perspective focuses on the women who become surrogates and holds that women have the ability and right to control their own bodies, including the ability to enter knowingly and competently into a contractual agreement (e.g., Gostin, 1990; Macklin, 1988). Set aside from the commercialization of surrogacy, one can claim that surrogate arrangements between consenting adults are no more objectionable than nonmarital sexual intercourse or volunteering for biomedical or behavioral research (Macklin, 1988). Because of the necessity of informed consent to the surrogate arrangement, requirements for surrogacy could also be compared to informed consent to medical treatment. Thus, a woman has the right to decide if and when she will participate in a surrogate arrangement, with the intention of participating in the family formation process for an infertile couple.

Following the underlying assumption of rights in these positions, when the surrogacy contract is challenged, legal resolution essentially centers on the contradictory rights of the genetic father and the surrogate mother (e.g., Allen, 1990; Field, 1988; Schneider, 1990), and the rights of the child involved, including her or his best interests (Annas, 1990; Gostin, 1990; Holder, 1990). At stake in the first instance is a man's right to reproduce genetically and to become the socially recognized parent of his biological offspring. At stake in the second instance is the woman's right to control her own body and to become the socially recognized parent of her biological offspring, regardless of previous contractual arrangements made with the genetic father. Moreover, control over her own body includes the right to loan or lease out

gestational services as well as the right to "have a change of heart" once the child is born (Annas, 1990; Capron & Radin, 1990). In the highly publicized case of *Baby M.*, a New Jersey Supreme Court ruled the surrogacy contract criminal and void and determined that both the genetic father, William Stern, and the genetic and surrogate mother, Mary Beth Whitehead, were the legal parents of the child (Chesler, 1989).

More recently, however, surrogate rights have become complicated by those cases in which the surrogate mother is the gestational mother but not the genetic mother, as in the case of *Anna J. v. Mark C.* In a decision that troubled many surrogate rights activists, a California appellate court decided in favor of the genetic parents (Pollitt, 1990) and determined the gestational mother to be a "genetic stranger" to the child (Tifft, 1990). Such a decision ignores the "sweat equity" involved in what is arguably the surrogate's greater biological and psychological investment: a nine-month contribution to the child's development, presence both at the birth and immediately thereafter (Annas, 1988b). Expert witnesses have also testified that giving up children causes permanent emotional damage, a finding that argues against the enforcement of surrogacy contracts against the wishes of the surrogate (Field, 1988).

Interestingly, the child's interests frequently are among the last considerations in the surrogacy debate (Annas, 1990) but are the least easily determined by presumption rather than by the individual circumstances in each case (Gostin, 1990). Moreover, critical questions remain about the best interests of contracted babies born with serious defects as well as the psychological well-being of the surrogate mother's other children, who may fear also being sold (Holder, 1990). Even so, child advocates are divided on the potential harm done to children of surrogacy. Because children may experience confusion about their genetic origins (Schneider, 1990), perhaps adult offspring should be allowed access to information about their genetic/biological patrents (Robertson, 1990). On the one hand, testimony suggests that children of surrogate mothers will experience lower self-esteem with the realization that their mothers never intended to love them or take responsibility for them (Ward, 1988, cited in Macklin, 1991). On the other hand, one adult AID child expressed gratitude to her family for going to such trouble to give her life (Field, 1988).

Surrogacy is not always a commercial venture. Some surrogates do donate their gestational services, even to perfect strangers (Field, 1988). Some women report that they enjoy being pregnant and experiencing birth but have no need for more children. Others are more altruistic and empathetic in their motives, wanting to stop the pain of infertility that they perceive in others (Corea, 1985; Field, 1988). Both cases echo the nineteenth-century ideal of the nurturing mother who gives freely of herself; however, this is hardly a move forward into the twenty-first century.

Opposition to surrogacy includes both specific charges against commercialization or paid surrogacy (Arditti, 1987), as well as broader attacks on the ideological, patriarchal base that underlies the motivation of virtually all NRTs (Corea, 1985). In fact, by mid-1992, 17 states had decided that contracted surrogate motherhood was harmful commerce (1992). Some contractual opponents are hesitant to outright condemn commercial surrogacy but suggest that the writing of surrogacy contracts be burdened with particularly strong procedural requirements (Schneider, 1990, fn130) or laden with constitutional privacy rights guaranteed to limit a surrogate's ability to alienate her procreative and parenting rights (Allen, 1990).

Bolder arguments claim that surrogacy is babyselling (Annas, 1990) and the exploitation of poor women as breeders (Corea, 1985). Arditti (1987) writes that commercial surrogacy can survive only because of these class differences. For example, based on the fee of $10,000 paid to many surrogate mothers, the calculated hourly wage for surrogate motherhood falls well below the minimum wage, at approximately $1.57 per hour. Furthermore, if the baby is stillborn or dies, the surrogate receives only a fee of $1,000. That the child is viewed by the genetic father as a "product" is further underscored by his right to refuse a child who is not as intended, that is, not genetically related (American Bar Association, cited in Gostin, 1990, pp. 279–280).

In turn, legal prohibition of payment for surrogacy would avoid the economic exploitation of poor women and would also underscore the value of human personhood and the unacceptability of commercial reproduction (Capron & Radin, 1990; Macklin, 1990).

Complete opposition to surrogacy is also voiced. One argument is that the surrogacy contract can be derailed at so many junctions as to suggest that it should be discouraged as an institution that is antithetical to human happiness and one that contradicts family law's expressive function of protecting children from abandonment (Schneider, 1990). George Annas (1990) challenges that "[t]he truth about surrogacy's family building is that it can create one parent–child relationship only by destroying another parent–child relationship" (p. 45). He argues that, unlike adoption, which places the child's interest first, surrogacy foremost represents the interests of the adult parties.

Still another opposition point of view holds that women in a patriarchal pronatalist society are never really free to make voluntary decisions about whether or not to use the NRTs (Corea, 1985). Thus, in addition to objections about the economic exploitation of poor women, surrogacy opponents view the infertile wife's decision to participate in a surrogacy contract as one of ideological cohesion and self-deception

(Corea, 1985; Annas, 1990), reinscribing the "supremacy of the sperm" (Arditti, 1987:43) and the primacy of the father's genetic contribution over both the risks and investments of pregnancy.*

We Are Family: Who Decides?

Clearly, the new reproductive technologies have forced us to rethink definitions of "the family" (Edwards, 1991; Macklin, 1991). They have expanded our reproductive options to include assisting heterosexual couples to safely delay childbirth; they have enabled infertile couples to achieve deeply desired parenthood; they have extended notions of family to gay men and lesbians. But beyond the surface of this brave new world, the NRTs are hardly democratic. In the remainder of this section, we will discuss the complex network of arbitrators involved in the normatively simple act of reproduction when it becomes linked with technological innovation. Thus the danger of the NRTs is perhaps less in how they contribute to a redefinition of "the family" and more in how they can legitimize who may and who may not form a legally and socially sanctioned family structure. As Edwards (1991) demonstrates, in combination, surrogacy and AID have the potential of creating five different parents for a single child: a genetic mother, a gestational mother, a social mother, a genetic father, and a social father. While such a scenario is unlikely to be common practice, this typology illustrates how legal (and thus custodial) parenthood may ultimately be dissected in the courts, the examining rooms, and the consultation chambers rather than held within the control of the individual or couple seeking to build a family.

Due to its noncoital methods of fertilization, parenting through the new reproductive technologies necessitates the cooperation of several parties beyond the intended rearing parents. Such an arrangement automatically takes the intimate decision for procreation at least one step beyond the sanctions of privacy. For women seeking AID to achieve pregnancy, gatekeeping practices by physicians have limited access only to those who have acceptable psychological, physical, and personal histories (Office of Technology Assessment, 1988; Wikler & Wikler, 1991). In general, custodial disputes are likely to occur only in the event of private AID, in which the courts tend to favor paternity rights of donors regardless of the mother's extenuating circumstances (Corea, 1985; Field, 1988).

In the case of surrogacy, the cast of players included in the process of creating a human being has the potential of

*We have not dealt with in vitro fertilization, cryopreservation, or gamete intrafallopian transfer. Of these, cryopreservation is the most interesting, in our opinion, because the legal "disposal" of frozen embryos may deny parenthood to one party while the implantation and gestation of those embryos can force another party into undesired parenthood.

resembling a Wagnerian opera, with the conferral of legitimate parenthood varying with the assumptions of any given ethical position. To date, most policy concerning surrogacy has been shaped by legal counsel, medical practitioners, state legislatures, and the court system. The subsequent lack of cohesive policy about surrogacy contracts makes generalizations difficult; however, a walk through the Model Surrogacy Act can give us a sense of the complexity of the conferral process.

Under the Family Law Section of its Model Surrogacy Act, the American Bar Association acts to provide for "the best interests of children" born from surrogacy arrangements, moving quickly to "overrule the common law presumption that she who bears a child is presumed to be its mother" (American Bar Association, cited in Gostin, 1990, pp. 270–271). In the text of the MSA, the surrogate is thereafter defined as "the gestational carrier of any embryo, a fetus, or a child," and as "a provider of genetic material," if her ovum is used (p. 271). The term "parent" is reserved for the individual or individuals who intend to assume legal parenthood; both married and unmarried persons may employ the services of a surrogate. Payment of the surrogate for her services is not prohibited, based on an assumption of noncoercion.

Full and informed consent of all parties is required. In addition to being apprised of all legal rights and liabilities, and medical and psychological risks, the contracting parties must undergo several examinations. These include certifications of acceptability by a physician, a mental health practitioner, and a social worker. Either the surrogate's attorney or the intended parents' attorney can also require mandatory counseling of any of the involved parties. Thus, at several points along the way, any one of several experts can interrupt and/or abort the parenting decision.

Once fertilization has occurred, the surrogate is not allowed to voluntarily terminate the pregnancy unless such a procedure is medically necessary and may be sued for breach of contract should she have a change of heart. After the child is born, custody of the child is enforceable by court order to the "intended parent or parents," provided that the child is certified as genetically related to them. In the event that the child is "not as intended," that is, not genetically related to one or both of the intended parents, the surrogate "may assume custody of the child if she chooses," unless the result is due to physician or laboratory error, in which case she may not assume custody (American Bar Association, cited in Gostin, 1990, pp. 279–280). In other words, by the provisions of the ABA Family Law Model Surrogacy Act, the case could occur in which, due to a mistake in the artificial fertilization procedure, a surrogate could carry and deliver a child not only genetically her own but also that of her husband or male partner and not be allowed to retain custody of that child.

In summary, according to the act, the "right" to parent, and by extension to form a family, is reserved only for those individuals who initially enter the surrogate agreement with the intention of becoming parents. Should they fail by expert opinion to be determined suitable, not only as parties in a surrogate agreement but also as future parents of a child born of a surrogate arrangement, they would be unable to exercise their parenting "rights." In other words, these rights are conditioned upon approval by state representatives. Only under the unusual circumstances of physician or laboratory error, however, can the surrogate, that is the woman who carried the child during gestation, exercise a "right" to motherhood.

The MSA is thus a blend of priorities, contractual and best interest. First and foremost is the priority of a contractual arrangement, even in the case of surrogacy in which the surrogate contributes both gestational service and genetic material, that is, in which she is the biological mother. The language of the MSA is careful to avoid a biological association in favor of a contractual one. The contractual priority occurs first in its provision for a court order to deliver the child to the "intended parents" immediately after its birth regardless of the surrogate's "change of heart," and again in the case of physician or laboratory error, in which the surrogate may not assume custody even though she may be both genetic and gestational mother. Although the best interests of the child are stated early in the text of the MSA, ultimately these interests are considered only in the examination of the "intended parents" by a social worker prior to the artificial fertilization of the surrogate and are suspended in the event that the child is "not as intended" because of defect. In the latter case, the consideration reverts back to the conditions of contractual obligations. In the final analysis, the child is a product; the surrogate a manufacturing plant; the surrogate agency, along with the legal, medical, and social experts, the producers; and the intended parents, the consumers. Rules of the market prevail, including the need for institutional approval and consumer protection.

Recognizing the potential for the commercialization of both surrogacy services and the children who are the "products," several alternatives to the strict enforcement of a surrogate contract are proposed. The first position concludes that surrogacy arrangements should neither be criminalized nor prohibited but that contractual provisions should allow for a "best interests" custody determination in the event that the gestational mother refuses to relinquish her parental rights (Gostin, 1990). Such an arrangement would respect both the unforeseen maternal bonding of the surrogate as well as the parental feelings and desires of the genetic father.

(Notice, however, that the priority here is still the genetic basis of legitimate claim, which does not include the maternal feelings and desires of the intended rearing mother, who generally remains invisible.)

As was made clear from the examples of actual court cases cited earlier, decisions in contested surrogacy contracts have reflected to different degrees the spirit of the MSA, in which the considerations of the gestational mother are rendered secondary to those of "father's rights." A comparison of the cases of surrogate Mary Beth Whitehead and Anna Johnson underscores the legal privileging of genetic inheritance over maternal bonding during gestation. Ironically, this position leaves feminists divided between the "ethic of care" (see Gilligan, 1982) and an interruption of the equation of womanhood with mandatory motherhood in favor of a nonrelational model of individual rights (Despreaux, 1989).

Furthermore, a significant nondemocratic feature of all of the NRTs is their cost, which selects out prospective parents who lack the financial means to overcome infertility; not surprisingly, for example, no attempt has been made to extend the benefits of NRTs to poor women on Medicaid (Annas, 1990). Thus, for those unlucky enough to be infertile, social class prohibits reproduction through a form of modern eugenics. The single exception is in the growing practice of self-insemination, which bypasses both higher costs and physician regulation. This so-called turkey-baster method, however, leaves AID mothers vulnerable to custody suits by acquaintance donors who have a "change of heart" (Wikler & Wikler, 1991).

Furthermore, virtually all state statutes require the screening of couples proposing to be the rearing parents for suitability, with the imposition of middle-class values (Field, 1988:63). And in spite of their higher rates of infertility, little effort has been made to make NRTs accessible to prospective black parents (Annas, 1990; Arditti, 1987).

Ultimately, NRTs raise some deep philosophical questions about how much the state should be able to regulate reproductive choices. The prochoice movement has made clear that women who do not seek motherhood should have access to safe, legal, and affordable abortion services. But by their very nature as innovative services within a capitalist economy, the NRTs pose very different types of problems concerning regulated reproduction. First, there is the issue of accessibility, determined to a great extent by the power of the pocketbook. While lower-income women, particularly women of color, are facing rising rates of infant mortality as well as coerced sterilization, acceptable upper-income couples are able to hire both men and women to supply their missing reproductive pieces and parts. It appears that, even in our pronatal society, some parents are considered more deserving than others. Second, the separation of gestation and

motherhood, even without genetic contribution, reinforces the ideology of genetic ownership and its primacy over human intimate relationships. Such a privileging runs the danger of reinforcing an antisocial individualistic model of social organization over one which sees the connectedness between human beings as critical for the health of human society. Finally, the commercialization of women's reproductive capabilities, while demonstrating women's "control over their bodies," serves to underscore the notion of women as breeders, as incubators, as reproductive machines (Corea, 1985). Rather than moving us forward into a society in which both men and women are involved in the ethics of care through mutual parenting, NRTs offer distinct possibilities for the reinforcement of patriarchal ownership of progeny, the state's further intervention into reproductive choice, and the conceptualization of the uterus as a place to be filled, separate and distinct from the woman of whom it is a living part.

Such an admonition, however, is not aimed at NRTs themselves but at a system of regulation and commerce that seeks to preserve the status quo at the expense of the greater social good. Ironically, the degree of public invasion into private life and the use of the NRTs is not dissimilar to that in contemporary abortion legislation. Today, a woman's choice to obtain a safe, legal, and affordable abortion is limited—depending on the state—by a range of conditions and restrictions. For example, federal funding for Medicaid abortions has been prohibited for over a decade (Merton, 1981). Until very recently, federally financed clinics were prohibited from counseling women on abortion, further limiting access for poor women, a ruling overturned during the early days of the Clinton administration (Roe's Momentous Anniversary, 1993). Some state abortion statutes require the husband's consent or parental consent if the women is under 18 (Abortion marches on, 1992). In particular, both parental consent laws and the prohibition of Medicaid funding for abortions have curtailed reproductive freedom for those women who may be most desperate to avoid an unwanted pregnancy. At the present time, states continue to aggressively chip away at the provisions of *Roe v. Wade*, such that Senator Paul Wellstone commented that "a right of a woman to decide, in theory, will not be a right in practice" (Panel backs abortion measure, 1992, p. A16).

Even in those cases where abortion is legal, the medicalization of abortion through the language of *Roe v. Wade* gives doctors absolute control of the shape its availability and procedures (Rothman, 1989). The salience of institutionalized control over abortion can be further measured in the debate over the legal distribution of the steroid analogue RU 486, effective both as a "morning-after" pill and as an abortifacient (New use, 1992). Antichoice activists fear that

RU 486 would mean the end of abortion clinics, depriving "prolife forces of their most visible enemy" (Heaney, 1991, p. 12). Hailed as less dangerous than surgical abortion by prochoice activists, RU 486 would likely nonetheless be strictly monitored by medical supervision (see Banwell & Paxman, 1992).

In either the case of abortion or NRTs, the individuals most personally involved are those least likely to have control over the availability of effective and safe procedures for their own reproductive choices. Political, medical, and legal practitioners increasingly serve as the arbiters of family formation as we move into the brave new world of the twenty-first century.

Toward a Family Perspective

Are Family Policies Necessary?

The demand for federal or state action on behalf of families or their individual members comes into play when there is a gap between family needs and the resources with which to meet these needs. For example, the social security system was predicated on the plight of older Americans in light of the economic exigencies of the Great Depression of the 1930s. And health insurance and care became a topic of the 1990s both because of spiraling costs and the fact that growing numbers of Americans were without health insurance.

Miller and Roby (1970) proposed six dimensions of well-being, and conversely "needs": income, assets, basic services, self-respect (status), opportunities for education and social mobility, and participation in many forms of decision making. Their point was that adequate income may be a necessary ingredient to well-being, but that *quality of life* is also critical (p. 186). To this list and in light of the "quality-of-life" criterion, we would also add another dimension that is key to family well-being and effectiveness: *time*. With the soaring numbers of single-parent and dual-earner families, time is increasingly a scarce resource in contemporary family life (Moen, 1992, 1998).

A life-course perspective, with its focus on change over the family cycle and across historical time, might offer fruitful insights on families and family policies (Moen & Forest, 1990; Moen & Jull, 1995). Consider the concept of *control cycles* (Elder, 1998; Elder & Caspi, 1990; Moen & Yu, 1998). Families move in and out of positions that make it possible to mobilize effectively in the face of external and internal threats. Their spheres of control, and corresponding repertoire of strategies, shift over the life course, along with shifts in household composition, family needs, and family resources, as well as external supports, demands, constraints, and opportunities.

Where and when should public policy act to support families? We suggest four broad areas of family performance where the state may well wish to adopt policies to enhance family life: family structure and formation, the family economy, the family as a socializing unit, and the family as a caregiving unit. We have presented an extensive discussion of one aspect of family formation in terms of NRTs in the preceding section. Clearly these developments call for the establishment of policies related to how we as a nation, or as individuals, reproduce ourselves. We turn now to three other functions of families.

The Household Economy. The family unit is also an economic unit, a household economy systematically allocating resources, both in the form of income and assets and in terms of the participation of family members in the labor force (Blossfeld & Huinink, 1991; Goode, 1960; Kertzer & Hogan, 1989; Moen & Wethington, 1992; Smelser & Halpern, 1978). Families as collective entities send their members out to work, assign household tasks, share wages and resources, move from city to city, or from country to country, and buy farms, homes, television sets, cars. Depicting families and households as role-allocating, income-pooling, and income-spending units is both intuitively compelling and empirically valid (e.g., Davis, 1976; Hareven, 1978; Hill, 1970; LePlay, 1877; Stack, 1974).

Intergenerational transfers are important strategies as families shift economic, emotional and human resources from one generation to the next in conjunction with shifts in the relative distribution of needs and responsibilities, abilities and assets (Hill, 1970). Sanders and Nee (1996) describe the immigrant family as possessing important social and cultural capital that affect work-related decisions such as self-employment. Human, social, and economic capital in the kinship network become strategic family assets that can be cultivated, tapped, and transmitted both within and across generations (Bott, 1957; Coleman, 1988; Hareven, 1982; Modell, 1978; Sanders & Nee, 1996).

The evidence suggests that increasingly the family economy is in trouble (Bronfenbrenner et al., 1996). Economic as well as time pressures are a fact of life for many American families, especially those with young children. Moreover, studies suggest that there was little prospect for upward mobility during the 1980s decade. While the economic upturn of the 1990s improved the prospects of many families, the United States continued to experience increasing income inequality between households (Bronfenbrenner et al., 1996). This same story of economic hardship not only makes it difficult for families to make ends meet; it also affects both short- and long-term decision making (Moen & Wethington, 1992). A case in point: Joblessness can preclude family formation and stability, leading to an increase in mother-only families (Clarkberg et al., 1995; Clarkberg, 1998; Garfinkel & McLanahan, 1986; Wilson, 1987). Social research has documented that the reality or specter of job or income loss has deep and profound implications for family life, as do the chronic strains of insufficient income (Conger & Elder, 1994; Conger et al., 1990; Conger et al., 1992; Elder, 1974; Liker & Elder, 1983; Moen, Kain, & Elder, 1983; Voydanoff & Majka, 1988; Wilson, 1987).

Families as Producers of the Next Generation. Families are not only income pooling, economic units, they are also, literally, the cradle of the next generation. The delicate balance of interaction between parent and child has enormous consequences for both and leaves an indelible imprint on the next generation (Bronfenbrenner, 1979, 1990, 1995; Parcel & Menaghan, 1994). It is this dimension of families that is increasingly seen as at risk (e.g., Hewlett, 1991). To build competence and character in children requires not only financial resources but also a certain stability in routine, and, of course, time. As more children are raised by single parents or dual-worker couples, time has become the new scarcity of American family life (Moen, 1992, 1998; Clarkberg & Moen, 1998; Schor, 1992; Hochschild, 1997). We as a society are managing only because of the makeshift accommodations of individual parents, typically mothers, and their families. But everyone suffers as a consequence: Women with young children are exhausted, family life is hectic, the workplace is often disrupted, and work at home and on the job continues to be defined and limited by gender. There appears to be a growing consensus that we must adopt, as a matter of national policy, basic structural changes in our institutions—modifying the time and timing of employment and providing available, affordable, and quality childcare (Moen, 1994, 1998; Pleck, 1992). The coupling of work and family roles is a major challenge that we, as a nation, have only begun to address, one that stands to be even more formidable in the coming years.

Families as Systems of Care. Families are not only the child-rearing systems of our society, but they also provide informal care for the infirm of society, with an estimated 80% to 90% of medical care provided by family members, especially wives, daughters, and daughters-in-law (Moen, Robison, & Dempster-McClain, 1995; Moen, Robison, & Fields, 1995; Robison, Moen, & Dempster-McClain, 1995; Stone, Cafferata, & Sangl, 1987; U.S. House of Representatives Select Committee on Aging, 1988). The role of kin in caring for family members has been—and remains—an important research topic for scholars of the family (Litwak, 1985; Litwak & Szelenyi, 1969; McCubbin, 1979; Mogey, 1990; Shanas & Sussman, 1977; Stack, 1974). Intergenerational transfers are also important strategies

as families shift economic, emotional, and human resources from one generation to the next in conjunction with shifts in the relative distribution of needs and responsibilities, and abilities and assets (Hill, 1970). Human, social, and economic capital in the kinship network are strategic family assets that can be cultivated, tapped, and transmitted both within and across generations (Coleman, 1988; Modell, 1978; Pillemer & Lüscher, 1998; Sanders & Nee, 1996).

Social policies and programs can strengthen the abilities of families and their kinship networks to help one another. The goal would be to support, not replace, family commitments and caring.

New Directions

The reality of the last decades of this century has been the dissonance engendered, individually and collectively, between our experiences and our values. Consider three examples:

- We want economically secure families that manage to make ends meet on their own, but unemployment is a fact or fear of families at all stages of the life course, and declining or stagnant wages and job security, along with the growing incidence of single parents, have swelled the ranks of the working poor.
- We want parents to raise their own children, but two-earner or employed single-parent families have become the rule, not the exception; childcare is a real need, and time for children has become a scarce commodity in families, regardless of their economic status.
- Growing numbers of families are faced with, and want to provide, caregiving for their elderly and infirm, but find it difficult, if not impossible, to do so.

The gaps between family needs and family resources are becoming increasingly apparent. The question is, what is the role of government in bridging these gaps?

Titmus (1974) describes three models of social policy: *residual*, to be implemented only as a last resort when the private market and the family as an institution are not effective in meeting needs; *achievement based*, responding to merit, work performance, and productivity; and *redistributive*, providing services on the principle of need. The two models most relevant to family policy are the residual model (assuming that families and the market manage best on their own and require a minimum of government intervention) and the redistributive model (based in part on the principle of social equality in providing families and their members with command over resources).

Charles Murray's book *Losing Ground* (1984) is an example of the residual notion of family policy. He argued that government interventions in welfare (prior to the 1996 welfare reform act) had done more harm than good, producing incentives to remain economically dependent, and that government should get out of the welfare business. In contrast, Moynihan (1986) suggested that a national family policy would establish that families are important to the functioning of society and that, accordingly, American government should promote the stability and well-being of the American family. From Moynihan's viewpoint, social programs of the federal government should be formulated and administered with this in mind.

We have moved from the 1960s, with its focus on redistribution, through the 1980s, where the residual notion held sway, through the 1990s, where the goal has been to strengthen both the capacities and the responsibilities of families. Moen and Schorr (1987) urged an agenda on issues that unite rather than issues that divide. Some scholars and advocates—across the political spectrum—have done just that (Aldous & Dumon, 1990; Blankenhorn, Bayme, & Elshtain, 1990; Bronfenbrenner et al., 1996; Edelman, 1987; Jacobs & Davies, 1991; Working Seminar on Family and American Welfare Policy, 1986), resulting in the passage of the Family Support Act of 1988, the Child Care and Development Block Grant of 1990, and, after three tries, the Family and Medical Leave Act of 1993. By contrast, welfare reform, the Personal Responsibility and Work Opportunity Act of 1996, produced deep divisions as to the role of the federal government as a safety net.

Former Congresswoman Pat Schroeder suggested that a national family policy should have three goals: to acknowledge the rich diversity of American families, to protect families' economic well-being, and to provide families with flexible ways to meet their economic and social needs (1989, p. 1413). As we move into the twenty-first century, we are not apt to see an explicit family policy; however, we can expect to see policies framed within a family perspective, one that considers the anticipated and unanticipated implications, for families, of proposed legislation.

Advocates for and against government involvement in family life are both profamily; they differ on how to help families be most effective. Ongoing dialogues and debates about intervention versus strengthening families showcase a fundamental difference about government's role. How can we as a nation provide supports for families without at the same time promoting dependence, rather than independence? How can government programs work in partnership with families in promoting well-being without constraining their options and opportunities? And how can profamily programs and policies be implemented in the face of constricted budgetary realities? These are the questions facing those—both in and out of government—concerned with family well-being, and they are being framed with increasing urgency.

ACKNOWLEDGMENTS: Support for the writing of this chapter was provided by grants from the National Institute on Aging (#IT50 AG11711) and the Alfred P. Sloan Foundation (#96-2-9).

References

Abortion marches on (1992, February 17). *National Review*, p. 15.

Aldous, J. (1996). *Family careers*. New York: Wiley.

Aldous, J., & Dumon, W. (1990). Family policy in the 1980s: Controversy and consensus. *Journal of Marriage and the Family, 52,* 1136–1151.

Allen, A. L. (1990). Surrogacy, slavery, and the ownership of life. *Harvard Journal of Law & Public Policy, 13,* 139–149.

Alwin, D. F., Braun, M., & Scott, J. (1990). *The separation of work and family: Gender differences on sex-role attitudes in Britain, Germany and the United States.* Paper presented at the meeting of the International Sociological Society, Madrid, Spain.

Annas, G. J. (1988a, October/November). Redefining parenthood and protecting embryos: Why we need laws. *Hastings Center Report,* 50–52.

Annas, G. J. (1988b). Death without dignity for commercial surrogacy: The case of Baby M. *Hastings Center Report, 18,* 21–24.

Annas, G. J. (1990). Fairy tales surrogate mothers tell. In L. Gostin (Ed.), *Surrogate motherhood: Politic and privacy* (pp. 43–55). Bloomington: Indiana University Press.

Arditti, R. (1987). The surrogacy business. *Social Policy, 18,* 42–46.

Axel, H. (1985). *Corporations and families: Changing practices and perspectives.* New York, NY: Conference Board.

Banwell, S. S., & Paxman, J. (1992). The search for meaning: Ru 486 and the law of abortion. *American Journal of Public Health, 82,* 1399–1406.

Belous, R. S. (1989). *The contingent economy: The growth of the temporary, part-time and subcontracted workforce.* Washington, DC: National Planning Association.

Berrick, J. D. (1992). Welfare and child care: The intricacies of competing social values. *Social Work, 36,* 345–351.

Blankenhorn, D., Bayme, S., & Elshtain, J. B. (1990). *Rebuilding the nest: A new commitment to the American family.* Milwaukee, WI: Family Service America.

Blossfeld, H. P., & Huinink, S. (1991). Human capital investments or norms of role transition? How women's schooling and career affect the process of family formation. *American Journal of Sociology, 94,* 300–334.

Bohen, H. (1983). *Corporate Employment Policies Affecting Families and Children: The United States and Europe.* New York: Aspen Institute for Humanistic Studies.

Bott, E. (1957). *Family and social network: Roles, norms, and external relationships in ordinary urban families.* London: Tavistock.

Bronfenbrenner, U. (1979). *The ecology of human development.* Cambridge, MA: Harvard University Press.

Bronfenbrenner, U. (1990). Discovering what families do. In D. Blankenhorn, S. Bayme, & J. B. Elshtain (Eds.), *Rebuilding the nest: A new commitment to the American family* (pp. 27–38). Milwaukee, WI: Family Service America.

Bronfenbrenner, U. (1995). Developmental ecology through space and time: A future perspective. In P. Moen, G. H. Elder, Jr., and K. Lüscher (Eds.), *Examining lives and context: Perspectives on the ecology of human development* (pp. 619–648). Washington, DC: American Psychological Association.

Bronfenbrenner, U., McClelland, P., Wethington, E., Moen, P., & Ceci, S. (1996). *The state of Americans: This generation and the next.* New York: Free Press.

Brown, A. (1997, March). *Reworking welfare: Technical assistance for states and localities*, Washington, DC: Department of Health and Human Services. [http://aspe.os.dhhs/hsp/isp/work1st/frontm.htm].

Brown, M. K. (1988). The segmented welfare system: Distributive conflict and retrenchment in the United States, 1968–1984. In M. K. Brown (Ed.), *Remaking the welfare state: Retrenchment and social policy in America and Europe* (pp. 182–210). Philadelphia: Temple University Press.

Bumpass, L. (1990). What's happening to the family? Interactions between demographic and institutional change. *Demography, 27*, 284–298.

Burkhauser, R. V., & Duncan, G. J. (1989). Economic risks of gender roles: Income loss and life events over the life course. *Social Science Quarterly, 70*(1), March.

Bureau of National Affairs. (1984). *Employers and Child Care: Development of a New Employee Benefit*. Washington, DC: Bureau of National Affairs.

Bureau of National Affairs. (1986). *Work and family: Walking the tightrope*. Rockville, MD: Bureau of National Affairs.

Bureau of National Affairs. (1987). *Employee assistance programs: Benefits, problems, and prospects*. Washington, DC: Bureau of National Affairs.

Callahan, D. (1991). Opening the debate? A response to the Wikler. *The Millbank Quarterly, 69*, 41–44.

Campbell, L. (1984). *Conflicts facing women in professional careers*. Linfield College. Photocopy of typescript.

Capron, A. M., & Radin, M. J. (1990). Choosing family law over contract law as a paradigm for surrogate motherhood. In L. Gostin (Ed.), *Surrogate motherhood: Politic and privacy* (pp. 59–76). Bloomington: Indiana University Press.

Catalyst. (1986). *Flexible benefits: How to set up a plan when your employees are complaining, your costs are rising, and you're too busy to think about it*. New York, NY: Catalyst.

Catalyst. (1993). Recommendations for employees. *Flexible work arrangements II: Succeeding with part-time options*. New York, NY: Catalyst.

Charges against anti-poverty programs range from paternalism to political pork barrel and undermining city hall. (1966). *Congressional Quarterly Almanac, XXII*, 408–409.

Charo, R. A. (1990). Legislative approaches to surrogate motherhood. In L. Gostin (Ed.), *Surrogate motherhood: Politic and privacy* (pp. 88–121). Bloomington: Indiana University Press.

Cheal, D. (1993). Unity and difference in postmodern families. *Journal of Family Issues, 14*, 5–20.

Cherlin, A. (1988). *The changing American family and public policy*. Washington, DC: Urban Institute.

Chesler, P. (1989). *Sacred bond: The legacy of Baby M*. New York: Harper & Row.

Children's Defense Fund. (1997). *Summary of current welfare legislation (Public Law 104-193)*. [http://www.childrensdefense.org/fairstart_welsum.html].

Children's Defense Fund. (1998, March 11). *New Children's Defense Report offers disturbing view of child care from the states*. [http://www.childrensdefense.org/release0311098.html].

Chilman, C. S. (1991). Public policies and family. In C. S. Chilman, E. W. Nunnally, & F. M. Cox (Eds.), *Variant family forms*. Newbury Park, CA: Sage Publishers.

Christensen, K. (1995). *Contingent work arrangements in family-sensitive corporations*. Boston University: Center on Work and Family.

Clarkberg, M. (1998). The price of partnering: The role of economic well-being in young adults' first union experiences. Forthcoming in *Social Forces*.

Clarkberg, M., & Moen, P. (1998). The time-squeeze: Married couples' work-hours patterns and preferences. Unpublished manuscript.

Clarkberg, M., Stolzenberg, R. M., & Waite, L. J. (1995). Attitudes, values, and entrance into cohabitational versus marital unions. *Social Forces, 74*(2), 609–634.

Clinton, Congress talk of welfare reform. (1993). *Congressional Quarterly Almanac, XLIX*, 373–375.

C.M. v. C.C., 152 N. J. Super. 160, 377 A.2d 821 (1977).

Cochran, M., Larner, M., Riley, D., Gunnarson, L., & Henderson, C. (1990). *Extending families: The social networks of parents and children*. New York: Cambridge University Press.

Coleman, J. S. (1988). Social capital in the creation of human capital. *American Journal of Sociology, 94*, S95–S120.

Congress, Administration focus attention on hunger. (1968). *Congressional Quarterly Almanac, XXIV*, 695–700.

Conger, R. D., Elder, G. H., Jr., Lorenz, F. R., Simons, R. L., Whitbeck, L. B., Huck, S., & Melby, J. N. (1990). Linking economic hardship to marital quality and instability. *Journal of Marriage and the Family, 52*, 643–656.

Conger, R. D., Elder, G. H., Jr., Foster, E. M., & Ardelt, M. (1992). Families under economic pressure. *Journal of Family Issues, 13*, 5–37.

Conger, R. D., & Elder, G. H., Jr. (1994). *Families in troubled times: Adapting to changes in rural America*. Hawthorne, NY: Aldine de Gruyter.

Consortium of Family Organizations. (1992). The Child Care and Development Block Grant Program: A family impact assessment. *Family Policy Report, 2*(1).

Coontz, S. (1992). *The way we never were: American families and the nostalgia trap*. New York, NY: Basic Books.

Corea, G. (1985). *The mother machine*. New York: Harper & Row.

Cott, N. F., & Pleck, E. H. (1979). *A heritage of her own: Toward a new social history of American women*. New York: Simon and Schuster.

Council of Economic Advisors. (1997, May). *Technical report: Explaining the decline in welfare receipt, 1993–1996*. [http://www.nab.com/econ/decline_in_welfare.html]

Curie-Cohen, L., & Shapiro, E. (1979). Current practice of artificial insemination by donor in the United States. *New England Journal of Medicine, 33*, 585–590.

Davis, H. L. (1976). Decision making within the household. *Journal of Consumer Research, 2*, 241–260.

Department of Health and Human Services. (1998, June 24). *Child support enforcement: A Clinton administration priority*. [http://www.hhs.gov/cgi-bin/waisgate]

Department of Health and Human Services. (1998, March 17). *HHS child care programs: Investing in our future*. [http://www.hhs.gov/cgi-bin/waisgate]

Department of Health and Human Services. (1991). Child Care and Development Block Grant. *Federal Register, 56*(26), 194–26240.

Degler, C. N. (1980). *At odds: Women and the family in America from the revolution to the present*. New York: Oxford University Press.

Despreaux, M. A. (1989). Surrogate motherhood: A feminist perspective. *Research in the Sociology of Health Care, 8*, 99–134.

Dreyfous, L. (1992, October 6). Family what? *The Ithaca Journal*, 10b.

Duncan, G. J., & Rodgers, W. (1991). Has children's poverty become more persistent? *American Sociological Review, 56*, 538–550.

Duncan, G. J., Coe, R. D., & Hill, M. S. (1984). The dynamics of poverty. In G. J. Duncan (Ed.), *Years of poverty, years of plenty* (pp. 33–69). Ann Arbor, MI: Institute for Social Research.

Edelman, M. W. (1987). *Families in peril: An agenda for social change*. Cambridge, MA: Harvard University Press.

Editorial. (1988, November 21). *New Republic*, 24.

Education Writers Association. (1988). *Myth #9: Literacy is the ticket out of welfare*. Washington, DC: Institute for Educational Leadership.

Edwards, J. N. (1991). New conceptions: Biosocial innovations and the family. *Journal of Marriage and the Family, 53*, 349–360.

Elder, G. H., Jr. (1974). *Children of the Great Depression: Social change in life experience.* Chicago: University of Chicago Press.

Elder, G. H., Jr. (1998). The Life Course as Developmental Theory. *Child Development, 69*(1), 1–12.

Elder, G. H., Jr., & Caspi, A. (1990). Studying lives in a changing society: Sociological and personological explorations. In A. Rabin (Ed.), *Studying persons and lives* (pp. 201–247). New York: Springer.

Employee Benefit Research Institute. (1993). The changing environment of work and family. *EBRI Issue Brief Newsletter, 138,* pg. #1-3.

Faludi, S. (1991). *Backlash: The undeclared war against American women.* New York: Crown.

Field, M. (1988). *Surrogate motherhood.* Cambridge, MA: Harvard University Press.

Finn-Stevenson, M., & Trzcinski, E. (1991). Mandated leave: An analysis of federal and state legislation. *American Journal of Orthopsychiatry, 61,* 4.

Friedman, D. E. (1986). *A briefing book on families and work: Managing related issues.* New York: Conference Board.

Furstenberg, F. F., Jr. (1990). Divorce and the American family. *Annual Review of Sociology, 16,* 379–403.

Galston, W. (1992). New familism, new politics. *Family Affairs, 5,* 7–9.

Gaines, J. (1990, October 7). A scandal of artificial insemination. *The New York Times Magazine,* 23–28.

Galinsky, E. (1987). *The Family Study.* New York: Bank Street College of Education, Division of Research, Demonstration, and Policy.

Galinsky, E., Friedman, D. E., & Hernandez, C. A. (1991). *The corporate reference guide to work family programs.* New York, NY: Families and Work Institute.

Galinsky, E., Friedman, D. E., & Hernandez, C. A. (Eds.). (1992). *Parental leave and productivity.* New York, NY: Families and Work Institute.

Galinsky, E., Friedman, D. E., & Hernandez, C. A. (1993). *The changing workforce.* New York, NY: Families and Work Institute.

Garfinkel, I., & McLanahan, S. (1986). *Single mothers and their children.* Washington, DC: Urban Institute Press.

Gilbert, D., & Kahl, J. A. (1987). *The American class structure: A new synthesis,* 3rd ed. Belmont, CA: Wadsworth Publishing.

Gillespie, E., & Schellhas, B. (1994). *Contract with America.* New York: Random House.

Gilligan, C. (1982). *In a different voice.* Cambridge, MA: Harvard University Press.

Gladstone, L. W., Williams, J. D., & Belous, R. S. (1985). *Maternity and parental leave policies: A comparative analysis.* Washington, DC: Congressional Research Service, Library of Congress.

Glazer, L. J. (1998). *Good paying occupations: A study of occupational wages in the great lake states: Updated and expanded.* Ann Arbor, MI: Michigan Future.

Glenn, N. D. (1992). What the numbers say. *Family Affairs, 5,* 5–7.

Goode, W. J. (1960). A theory of role strain. *American Sociological Review, 25,* 483–496.

Gostin, L. (1990). A civil liberties analysis of surrogacy arrangements. In L. Gostin (Ed.), *Surrogate motherhood: Politic and privacy* (pp. 3–23). Bloomington: Indiana University Press.

Graham, M. (1988). Good jobs at bad wages. *The New Republic, 21,* November: 27–29.

Greenberg, M. H. (1998a, January). *The child care protection under TANF.* Washington, DC: Center for Law and Social Policy. [http://epn.org/clasp/thechild.html].

Greenberg, M. H. (1998b, January). *Spend or transfer? Federal or state? Considerations for using TANF and TANF-related dollars for child care.* Washington, DC: Center for Law and Social Policy. [http://epn.org/clasp/spendort.html].

Greenberg, M. H., & Savner, S. (1996, August 13). *The Temporary Assistance for Needy Families block grant.* Washington, DC: Center for Law and Social Policy. [http://epn.org/clasp/clsmmry.html].

Han, S. K., & Moen, P. (1998). Work and family in temporal context: A life course approach. (Forthcoming in *The Annals of the American Academy of Political and Social Sciences*).

Haas, L. (1992). *Equal parenthood and social policy: A study of parental leave in Sweden.* Albany, NY: State University of New York Press.

Hareven, T. K. (1978). *Transitions: The family and the life course in historical perspective.* New York: Academic Press.

Hareven, T. K. (1982). *Family time and industrial time: The relationship between the family and work in a New England industrial community.* New York: Cambridge University Press.

Hayes, C. D., Palmer, J. L., & Zaslow, M. J. (1990). *Who cares for America's children: Child care policy for the 1990s.* Washington, DC: National Academy Press.

Heaney, R. P. (1991). RU-486 and abortion strategies: Pro-Life forces are mobilizing to block its importation and approval in the United States. *America, 164,* 12–13.

Heinz, W. R. (1996). Status passages as micro-macro linkages in life course research. In A. Weymann and W. R. Heinz (Eds.), *Sociology and Biography* (pp. 51–66). Weinheim: Duetscher Studien Verlag.

Hewlett, S. A. (1991). *When the bough breaks: The cost of neglecting our children.* New York: Basic Books.

Hill, R. (1970). *Family development in three generations.* Cambridge, MA: Schenkman.

Hochschild, A. (1989). *The second shift.* New York: Avon Books.

Hochschild, A. (1997). *The time bind: When work becomes home and home becomes work.* New York: Metropolitan Books.

Hofferth, S. L. (1992). *Who has the last word: Family policy research in the 1980s and 1990s.* Paper presented at the annual meeting of the Southern Sociological Society. New Orleans, LA.

Hofferth, S. L., & Phillips, D. A. (1987). Childcare in the United States, 1970–1995. *Journal of Marriage and the Family, 49*(3), 559–571.

Hohn, C., & Lüscher, K. (1988). The changing family in the Federal Republic of Germany. *Journal of Family Issues, 9,* 317–335.

Holder, A. R. (1990). Surrogate motherhood and the best interests of children. In L. Gostin (Ed.), *Surrogate motherhood: Politic and privacy* (p. 87). Bloomington: Indiana University Press.

Hunter, J. D. (1991). *Culture wars: The struggle to define America.* NY: Basic Books.

International Labour Organisation. (1989). *Working Time Issues in Industrialized Countries.* Geneva: International Labour Office.

Jacobs, F. H., & Davies, M. W. (1991). Rhetoric or reality? Child and family policy in the United States. *Social Policy Report, V,* (4).

Jourdan, C. v. Mary K., 179 Cal. App. 3d 386, 224 Cal Rptr. 530 (1986).

Kahn, A. J., & Kamerman, S. B. (1988). *Child support: From debt collection to social policy.* Newbury Park, CA: Sage.

Kahne, H. (1985). *Reconceiving part-time work: New perspectives for older workers and women.* Totowa, NJ: Rowman & Allanheld.

Kaledin, E. (1984). *Mothers and more: American women in the 1950s.* Boston: Twayne Publishers.

Kalleberg, A. L., Rosell, E., Hudson, K., Webster, D, Reskin, B. F., Cassier, N., & Applebaum, E. (1997). *Nonstandard work, nonstandard jobs.* Washington, DC: Economic Policy Institute.

Kamerman, S. B., Kahn, A. J., & Kingston, P. W. (1983). *Maternity policies and working women.* New York: Columbia University Press.

Kamerman, S. K., & Kahn, A. J. (1978). *Family policy: Government and families in fourteen countries.* New York: Columbia University Press.

Kertzer, D. I., & Hogan, D. P. (1988). Family structure, individual lives, and societal change. In M. W. Riley (Ed.), *Social change and the life course, Vol. I.* Newbury Park, CA: Sage.

Klatch, R. E. (1987). *Women of the new right*. Philadelphia: Temple University Press.

Kingston, P. W. (1993). Illusions and ignorance about the family-responsive workplace. *Journal of Family Issues, 11*, 438–454.

Kleppner, P., & Theodore, N. (1997). *Work after welfare: Is the Midwest's booming economy creating enough jobs?* DeKalb, IL: Midwest Job Gap Project, Office for Social Policy, Northern Illinois University.

Lauritzen, P. (1990), March/April). What price parenthood? *Hastings Center Report*, 38-46.

LePlay, F. (1877). *Les ouvriers europeens, 6*, Paris.

Levitan, S. A., Belous, R. S., & Gallo, F. (1988). *What's happening to the American family?: Tensions, hopes, realities*. Baltimore: Johns Hopkins University Press.

Liker, J. K., & Elder, G. H., Jr. (1983). Economic hardship and marital relations in the 1930s. *American Sociological Review*, 343–359.

Litwak, E. (1985). *Helping the elderly: The complementary roles of informal networks and formal systems*. New York: Guilford.

Litwak, E., & Szelenyi, I. (1969). Primary group structures and functions: Kin, neighbors and friends. *American Sociological Review, 34*, 465–481.

Lurie, I., & Sanger, M. B. (1991, March). The family support act: Defining the social contract in New York. *Social Service Review*, 43–67.

Lüscher, K. (1990, February). The social meaning of family policy. Paper presented at a colloquium of the Family Research Center, University of Minneapolis, MN.

Lydenberg, S. D. (1986). *Rating America's corporate conscience: A provocative guide to the companies behind the products you buy every day*. Reading, MA: Addison-Wesley.

MacDermid, S. M., & Targ, D. B. (1995). A call for greater attention to the role of employers in developing, transforming, and implementing family policies. *Journal of Family and Economic Issues, 16*, 145–170.

Macklin, R. (1988). Is there anything wrong with surrogate motherhood? An ethical analysis. *Law, medicine, and health care, 16*, 57–64.

Macklin, R. (1990). Is there anything wrong with surrogate motherhood? In L. Gostin (Ed.), *Surrogate motherhood: Politic and privacy* (pp. 136–150). Bloomington: Indiana University Press.

Macklin, R. (1991, January/February). Artificial means of reproduction and our understanding of the family. *Hastings Center Report, 21*, 5–11.

Macklin, R., & Rubin, R. (1983). *Contemporary families and alternative lifestyles: Handbook on research and theory*. Beverly Hills: Sage.

Mann, C., & Albelda, R. (1989). Eroding entitlements: Welfare's long downhill slide. *Dollars and Sense, 146*, 16–18.

Margolis, M. L. (1984). *Mothers and such: Views of American women and why they changed*. Berkeley: University of California Press.

Mayer, K. U., & Mueller, W. (1986). The state and the structure of the life course. In A. B. Sorensen, F. E. Weinert, & L. R. Sherrod (Eds.), *Human development and the life course: Multidisciplinary perspectives* (pp. 217–245). Hillsdale, NJ: Erlbaum.

Mayer, K. U., & Schoepflin, U. (1989). Litigation and society. *Annual Review of Sociology, 15*, 360–572.

McCubbin, H. I. (1979). Integrating coping behavior in family stress theory. *Journal of Marriage and Family, 41*, 237–244.

McLanahan, S. S., & Sandefur, G. (1994). *Growing Up With a Single Parent: What Hurts, What Helps*. Cambridge, MA: Harvard University Press.

Merton, A. H. (1981). *Enemies of choice: The right-to-life movement and its threat to abortion*. Boston: Beacon.

Meyer, M. H. (1996). Making Claims as Workers or Wives: The Distribution of Social Security Benefits. *American Sociological Review, 61*, 449–465.

Michalsky, W. (1989). The Vatican heresy. *The Humanist, 49*, 27–28.

Miller, S. M., & Roby, P. (1970). *Future of inequality*. New York: Basic Books.

Milkman, R. (1987). *Gender at Work: The Dynamics of Job Segregation by Sex During World War II*. Urbana: University of Illinois Press.

Mink, G. (1990). The lady and the tramp. In L. Gordon (Ed.), *Women, the state, and welfare* (pp. 92–122). Madison: University of Wisconsin Press.

Mintz, S. (1989). Regulating the American family. *Journal of Family History, 14*, 387–408.

Mintz, S., & Kellogg, S. (1988). *Domestic revolution: A social history of family life*. New York: Free Press.

Modell, J. (1978). Patterns of consumption, acculturation, and family income strategies in late nineteenth-century America. See Hareven, Vinovskis (1978), pp. 206–240.

Moen, P. (1989). *Working parents: Transformations in gender roles and public policies in Sweden*. Madison, WI: University Wisconsin Press.

Moen, P. (1992). *Women's two roles: A contemporary dilemma*. New York: Auburn House.

Moen, P. (1994). Women, work and family: A sociological perspective on changing roles. In M. W. Riley, R. L. Kahn, & A. Foner (Eds.), *Age and structural lag: Society's failure to provide meaningful opportunities in work, family, and leisure* (pp. 151–170). New York: Wiley.

Moen, P. (1996). Changing age trends: The pyramid upside down. In U. Bronfenbrenner, P. McClelland, E. Wethington, P. Moen, & S. Ceci (Eds.), *The state of the Americans: This generation and the next*. New York: Free Press.

Moen, P. (1998). Recasting Careers: Changing Reference Groups, Risks, and Realities. *Generations*, (Spring): 40–45.

Moen, P., Kain, E. L., & Elder, G. H., Jr. (1983). Economic conditions and family life: Contemporary and historical perspectives. In J. Nelson & F. Skidmore (Eds.), *American families and the economy: The high costs of living* (pp. 213–259). Washington, DC: National Academy Press.

Moen, P., & Schorr, A. E. (1987). Families and social policy. In M. B. Sussman & S. K. Steinmetz (Eds.), *Handbook of marriage and the family* (pp. 795–813). New York: Plenum.

Moen, P., & Forest, K. B. (1990). Working parents, workplace supports, and well-being: The Swedish experience. *Social Psychology Quarterly, 53*, 117–131.

Moen, P., & Wethington, E. (1992). Family adaptation strategies. *Annual Review of Sociology, 18*, 233–251.

Moen, P., & Firebaugh, F. (1994). Family policies and effective families: A life course perspective. *International Journal of Sociology and Social Policy* (special issue), *14*(1/2), 30–53.

Moen, P., Robison, J., & Fields, V. (1994). Women's work and caregiving roles: A life course approach. *Journal of Gerontology: Social Sciences, 49*(4), S176–186.

Moen, P., & Jull, P. (1995). Informing family policies: The uses of social research. *Journal of Family and Economic Issues, 16*(1), 79–107.

Moen, P., Robison, J., and Dempster-McClain, D. (1995). "Caregiving and Women's Well-Being: A Life Course Approach." *The Journal of Health and Social Behavior, 36*(3): 259–273.

Moen, P., & Yu, Y. (1998). *Cycles of control*. Unpublished Manuscript.

Mogey, J. (1990). *Aiding and aging: The coming crisis in support for the elderly by kin and state*. New York: Greenwood.

Monroe, P. A., & Garand, J. C. (1991). Parental leave legislation in the U.S. Senate: Toward a model of roll-call voting. *Family Relations, 40*, 208–218.

Morgan, D. (1994). A surrogacy issue: Who is the other mother? *International Journal of Law and the Family, 8*, 386–412.

Moynihan, D. P. (1986). *Family and nation*. San Diego: Harcourt Brace Jovanovich.

Moynihan, D. P. (1989). Toward a post-industrial social policy. *Public Interest, 96*, 16–27.

Myrdal, A. (1968). *The nation and the family*. Cambridge: Massachusetts Institute of Technology.

Murray, C. (1984). *Losing ground: American social policy, 1950–1980.* New York: Basic Books.

National Commission on Children. (1991). *Beyond rhetoric: A new American agenda for children and families.* Washington, DC: U.S. Government Printing Office.

National Governors' Association. (1998, April). Tracking recipients after they leave welfare: Summaries of state follow-up studies. [http://www.nga.org/Welfare/StateFollowUp.htm].

National Organization for Women. (1996). Increasing the minimum wage. [http://www.now.org].

National Center for Children in Poverty. (1992). *Five million children: 1992 update.* Newsletter published at School of Public Health, Columbia University. New York, NY.

Nelson, B. J. (1990). The origins of the two-channel welfare state: Workmen's compensation and mothers' aid. In L. Gordon (Ed.), *Women, the state, and welfare* (pp. 123–151). Madison: University of Wisconsin Press.

Newman, K. S. (1993). *Declining fortunes: The withering of the American dream.* New York: Basic Books.

New Jersey officials say birth rate drop not linked to welfare benefits. (1997, September 12). *The Washington Post,* 1611.

New use for the French 'abortion' pill. (1992, October 10). *Science,* 228–229.

Nine to Five, National Association of Working Women. (1986). *Working at the margins: Part-time and temporary workers in the United States.* Cleveland, OH: 9 to 5, National Association of Working Women, September.

Noble, K. B. (1988, May 1). Child care: The federal role grows in the '80s. *New York Times,* 4.

Office of Technology Assessment (U.S. Congress). (1988). *Artificial insemination practice in the United States: Medical and social issues.* Washington, DC.

Ohio Bureau of Employment Services. (1997). The core message of Ohio Works First. [http://www.state.oh.us/obes/html/welfare_to_work.htm].

O'Rand, A. (1995). The Cumulative Stratification of the Life Course. In R. H. Binstock and L. K. George (Eds.), *The Handbook of Aging and the Social Sciences, 4th edition.* San Diego, CA: Academic Press.

Palmer, J., & Sawhill, I. (1984). *The Reagan record: An assessment of America's changing domestic priorities.* Washington, DC: Urban Institute Press.

Panel backs abortion measure. (1992, July 2). *New York Times,* A16.

Parcel, T., & Menaghan, E. (1994). *Parents' jobs and children's lives.* New York: Aldine de Gruyter.

Pearce, D. M. (1989). Farewell to alms: Women's fare under welfare. In J. Freeman, *Women: A feminist perspective,* 4th Edition (pp. 493–504). Mountain View, CA: Mayfield Publications Company.

Pillemer, K., & Lüscher, K. (1998). Intergenerational ambivalence: A new approach to the study of parent-child relations in later life. *Journal of Marriage and the Family,* 60(2), 413–425.

Pleck, E. (1987). *Domestic tyranny: The making of American social policy against family violence from colonial times to the present.* New York: Oxford University Press.

Pleck, J. H. (1992). Work-family policies in the United States. In H. Kahne & J. Z. Giele (Eds.), *Women's work and women's lives* (pp. 248–275). Boulder, CO: Westview.

Pollitt, K. (1990). When is a mother not a mother? *The Nation, 31,* December: 840.

Popenoe, D. (1988). *Disturbing the nest: Family change and decline in modern societies.* New York: Aldine de Gruyter.

Presser, H. B. (1995). Are the interests of women inherently at odds with the interests of children or the family? A viewpoint. In K. O. Mason & A. Jensen (Eds.), *Gender and family change in industrialized worlds.* Oxford: Oxford University Press.

Pressman, S. (1970). *Job discrimination and the black woman.* Pittsburgh, PA: Know, Inc.

Pressman, S. (1990). America's new poverty crisis. *Forum for Applied Research and Public Policy,* 5, 47–55.

Quadagno, J. (1990). Race, class, and gender in the U.S. welfare state: Nixon's failed family assistance plan. *American Sociological Review,* 55, 11–28.

Quadagno, J. S. (1994). *The color of welfare: How racism undermined the war on poverty.* New York: Oxford University Press.

Reich, R. B. (1994). *Report on the American workforce.* Washington, DC: U.S. Department of Labor.

Riley, M. W., Johnson, M., & Foner, A. (1972). *Aging and society II: A sociology of age stratification.* New York: Sage.

Riley, M. W., Kahn, R. L., & Foner, A. (1994). *Age and structural lag.* New York: J. Wiley.

Riley, M. W., & Riley, J. W., Jr. (1994). Structural lag: Past and future. In M. W. Riley, R. L. Kahn, & A. Foner (Eds.), *Age and structural lag* (pp. 15–36). New York: Wiley.

Robison, J., Moen, P., & Dempster-McClain, D. (1995). "Women's Caregiving: Changing Profiles and Pathways." *Journal of Gerontology: Social Sciences,* 50B(6), S362–S373.

Robertson, J. A. (1988). Procreative liberty and the state's burden of proof in regulating noncoital reproduction. *Law, medicine, and health care, 16,* 18–26.

Robertson, J. A. (1990). Procreative liberty and the state's burden of proof in regulating noncoital reproduction. In L. Gotsin (Ed.), *Surrogate motherhood: Politic and privacy* (pp. 24–42). Bloomington: Indiana University Press.

Robertson, A. F. (1991). *Beyond the family: The social organization of human reproduction.* Berkeley: University of California Press.

Roe v. Wade, 410 U.S. 113, 35L. ed.2d 147 (1973).

Roe's Momentous Anniversary. (1993, January 24). *New York Times,* E4.

Rose, N. E. (1990). From the WPA to workfare: It's time for a truly progressive government work program. *Journal of Progressive Human Services, 1,* 17–42.

Rothman, B. K. (1989). *Recreating motherhood: Ideology and technology in a patriarchal society.* New York: Norton.

Rovner, J. (1987a, January). Congress takes ball and runs after state of the union punt. *Congressional Quarterly Weekly, 31,* 206–208.

Rovner, J. (1987b, March). Daniel Patrick Moynihan: Making welfare work. *Congressional Quarterly Weekly, 21,* 503–507.

Rovner, J. (1988a, July). Deep schisms Still imperil welfare overhaul. *Congressional Quarterly Weekly, 18,* 1647–1650.

Rovner, J. (1988b, October). Congress clears overhaul of welfare system. *Congressional Quarterly Weekly, 1,* 2699–2701.

Ryder, N. B. (1965). The cohort as a concept in the study of social change. *American Sociological Review, 30,* 843–861.

Spain, D., & Bianchi, S. (1996). *Balancing Act.* New York: Russell Sage Foundation.

Sanders, J. M., & Nee, V. (1996). Social capital, human capital, and immigrant self-employment. *American Sociological Review,* 61, 231–249.

Scanzoni, J., & Marsiglio, W. (1991). Wider families as primary relationships. *Marriage and Family Review, 17,* 117–133.

Scanzoni, J., & Marsiglio, W. (1993). New action theory and contemporary families. *Journal of Family Issues, 14,* 105–132.

Schneider, C. E. (1990). Surrogate motherhood from the perspective of family law. *Harvard Journal of Law & Public Policy, 13,* 125–131.

Schram, S. F. (1991). Welfare spending and poverty: Cutting back produces more poverty, not less. *The American Journal of Economics and Sociology, 50,* 129–141.

Schor, J. B. (1992). The overworked American: The unexpected decline of leisure. *Contemporary Sociology,* 21(6), 843–845.

Schroeder, P. (1989). Toward a national family policy. *American Psychologist, 44,* 1410–1413.

Schuck, P. H. (1990). The social utility of surrogacy. *Harvard Journal of Law and Public Policy, 13*, 132–138.

Shanas, E., & Sussman, M. B. (1977). *Family, bureaucracy, and the elderly.* Durham, NC: Duke University Press.

Skolnick, A. S. (1987). *The intimate environment: Exploring marriage and the family* (4th edition). Boston: Little, Brown.

Smeeding, T. M. (1990). Children and poverty: How the U.S. Stands. *Forum for Applied Research and Public Policy, 5*, 65–70.

Smelser, N. J., & Halpern, S. (1978). The historical triangulation of family, economy and education. *American Journal of Sociology, 89*, 288–315.

Snyder, P. (1992). *The European woman's almanac.* New York: Columbia University Press.

Sorrentino, C. (1990). The changing family in international perspective. *Monthly Labor Review, 113*, 41–58.

Spalter-Roth, R., & Hartmann, H. (1995). Contingent work: Its consequences for economic well-being, the gendered division of labor, and the welfare state. In K. Barker & K. Christensen (Eds.), *Contingent workers: From entitlement to privilege.* Washington, DC.

Stack, C. B. (1974). *All our kin: Strategies for survival in a black community.* New York: Harper & Row.

Steiner, G. (1981). *The futility of family policy.* Washington, DC: Brookings Institution.

Stone, R., Cafferata, G. L., & Sangl, J. (1987). Caregivers of the frail elderly: A national profile. *The Gerontologist, 17*, 486–491.

Strawn, J. (1994). *Final report: The national governors' association survey of state welfare reforms.* Washington, DC: National Governors' Association.

Strawn, J. (1993). *No way out: Low funding for welfare reform leaves many AFDC families in poverty.* Washington, DC: Center on Budget and Policy Priorities.

Street, P. (1997). *Find a job: The recent history and future of welfare reform in six midwestern states.* DeKalb, IL: Midwest Job Gap Project, Office for Social Policy, Northern Illinois University.

Text of President's message on children and youth. (1967). *Congressional Quarterly Almanac, Vol. XXIII*, 54a–58a.

Tifft, S. (1990). It's all in the (Parental) genes. *Time 5 November:* 77.

Titmus, R. M. (1974). *Social policy: An introduction.* NY: Pantheon.

Trattner, W. I. (1979). *From poor law to welfare state: A history of social welfare in America*, 2nd edition. New York: The Free Press.

Tobias, S., & Anderson, L. (1974). *What really happened to Rosie The Riveter?: Demobilization and the female labor force.* New York: MSS Modular Publications.

Trzcinski, E. (1990). *Leave policies in small business: Findings from the U.S. small business administration employee leave survey.* Washington, DC: U.S. Small Business Administration, Office of Advocacy.

Trzcinski, E., & Alpert, W. T. (1994). Pregnancy and parental leave benefits in the United States and Canada: Judicial decisions and legislation. *The Journal of Human Resources, 29*, 2.

U.S. Bureau of the Census. (1990a). Child support and alimony: 1987. *Current Population Reports,* Washington, DC: U.S. Department of the Census, Bureau of the Census. Series P-23, No. 167.

U.S. Bureau of the Census. (1990b). *Statistical Abstract of the United States: 1990* (110th edition). Washington, DC: U.S. Department of the Census, Bureau of the Census.

U.S. Bureau of the Census. (1992). *Statistical Abstract of the United States: 1992* (112th edition). Washington, DC: U.S. Department of Commerce, Bureau of the Census.

U.S. Bureau of Labor Statistics. (1996). *Job creation and employment opportunities: The United States labor market, 1993–1996.* Washington, DC: Bureau of Labor Statistics.

U.S. Department of Health and Human Services. (1995a). Study of jobs program shows largest savings in welfare costs. July. [http://www.handsnet.org/handsnet].

U.S. Department of Health and Human Services. (1995b). Child support collections up 40 percent since 1992. December. [http://www.handsnet.org/handsnet].

U.S. House of Representatives Select Committee on Aging. (1988). Exploding the myths: Caregiving in America. No. 100-665. Washington, DC: U.S. Government Printing Office.

Valentine, J., & Zigler, E. F. (1983). Head Start: A case study in the development of social policy for children and families. In E. F. Zigler, S. L. Kagan, & E. Klugman (Eds.), *Children, families and government: Perspectives on American social policy* (pp. 266–280). Cambridge: Cambridge University Press.

Vobejda, B., & Havermann, J. (1997, January 13). Success after welfare? Massachusetts provides a glimpse of the human toll behind the decline in caseloads. *The Washington Post National Weekly*, 6.

Voydanoff, P., & Majka, L. C. (1988). *Families and economic distress: Coping strategies and social policy.* Newbury Park, CA: Sage.

Welfare's down; but what's up? (1998, July 5). *Chicago Tribune*, A1.

Welfare reform takes a back seat. (1994). *Congressional Quarterly Almanac, L*, 364–365.

Weymann, A. (1996). Interrelating society and biography discourse markets and the welfare state's life course policy. In A. Weymann & W. R. Heinz (Eds.), *Society and Biography* (pp. 241–258). Weinheim: Deutscher Studien Verlag.

Whitehead, B. D. (1992). A new familism? *Family Affairs, 5*, 1–5.

Wilson, W. J. (1987). The truly disadvantaged: The inner city, the underclass, and public policy. Chicago: University of Chicago Press.

Wikler, D., & Wikler, N. J. (1991). Turkey-baster babies: The demedicalization of artificial insemination. *The Milbank Quarterly, 69*, 5–40.

Wisensale, S. K. (1990). Approaches to Family policy in state government: A report on five states. *Family Relations, 39*, 136–140.

Wisensale, S. K., & Allison, M. D. (1989). Family leave legislation: State and federal initiatives. *Family Relations, 38*, 189–192.

Working Seminar on Family and American Welfare Policy. (1986). American Enterprise Institute, Washington, DC.

Work and Family: Essentials of a Decent Life. (1986). AFL-CIO Executive Council. Washington, DC: AFL-CIO.

Zigler, E., & Muenchow, S. (1992). *Headstart: The inside story of America's most successful educational experiment.* New York: Basic Books/Harper.

Zigler, E. F., & Frank, M. (1988). *The Parental leave crisis: Toward a national policy.* New Haven, CT: Yale University Press.

Zimmerman, S. L. (1988). *Understanding family policy: Theoretical approaches.* Newbury Park, CA: Sage.

Zimmerman, S. L., & Owens, P. (1989). Comparing the family policies of three states: A content analysis. *Family Relations, 38*, 190–195.

PART V

Changing Family Patterns and Roles

The final part of the *Handbook* focuses on family dynamics and processes and consists of chapters on conflict and power, communication, family violence, sexuality, and marital therapy. These chapters focus on microlevel family concepts, the purpose being to identify and describe processes that (1) fall within a normal or adaptive range, (2) deviate from normality and become problematic, and (3) provide specific ways of intervening in families to help restore normal functioning.

In Chapter 24, "Family Dynamics: An Essay on Conflict and Power," Jetse Sprey pays particular attention to the dynamics of process, especially the interplay between the conflicts of interest and the reciprocal use of power in social interaction. He suggests that his goal is not to summarize the research on existing theory and research, but rather to reflect on the current knowledge in this area. The purpose of this reflection is to rethink and strengthen the explanatory capacity of the existing knowledge base. He concludes that recent social changes have not liberated females, males, or their minor children, but in contrast may have fostered competitive arrangements among them. An important result is that individual spouses, couples, and their networks must be sufficiently committed and knowledgeable to survive and prosper on the edge of chaos.

In Chapter 25, "Family Communication," Gail Whitchurch and Fran Dickson provide a historical overview of family communication and review basic research and applied research on family communication. The authors discuss the basic assumptions that provide a conceptual foundation for family communication and suggest that more attention be paid to the highly complex, subjective, and private nature of families. According to Whitchurch and Dickson, a communication perspective provides the view that families are defined through their intrafamilial interactions rather than through their structural arrangements.

In Chapter 26, "Family Abuse and Violence," JoAnn Langley Miller, Dean Knudsen, and Stacey Copenhaver remind the reader that perpetrators and survivors of one or more forms of family violence can be found in virtually any social group, social class, race, ethnicity, or gender. Several theoretical perspectives (individual, interactional, and sociocultural) and different types of domestic violence (child abuse, domestic violence, and elder abuse) are explored and analyzed. Explanations are provided as to why certain topics were not covered (date violence, hate crimes, and variation by class, race, ethnicity, and religion). The authors conclude with a discussion of the problems associated with mandatory reporting.

Robert Francoeur and Linda Hendrixson, in Chapter 27, "Human Sexuality," provide a biopsychosociocultural perspective to study human sexuality. In doing so, sexual development is conceptualized in terms of six critical stages in prenatal development (genetic, gonadal, hormonal, internal sexual anatomy, external sexual anatomy, and sexual brain encoding) and psychosexual development after birth. The authors also discuss the effect of somatosensory and affectional nurturance, religion's view of sexuality, sexual dysfunctions, and AIDS on the family. Reconceptualizing human sexuality so that new understandings about the nature, meaning, and social function of human sexuality are incorporated, the authors argue, will have definite consequences in clinical work for all age groups, martial statuses, sexual orientations, and mental and physical disabilities.

Chapter 28, "Theories and Techniques of Marital and Family Therapy," by Nadine Kaslow, Florence Kaslow, and Eugene Farber, begins with a history of the growth of family therapy in the past 2 decades.

Subsequently, the authors describe and assess a variety of conceptual therapy models, including psycho-analytic, Bowenian, contextual, structural, strategic, systemic, behavioral, and cognitive-behavioral. Faced with such a diverse array of therapies to select from, the authors applaud recent trends to move from adherence to either a unitary theoretical perspective or eclectic theoretical approaches to a more systematic integration. Consistent with this idea, the authors propose a three-stage process for integrating various theories of family therapy.

CHAPTER 24

Family Dynamics

An Essay on Conflict and Power

Jetse Sprey

Power is not an amulet possessed by one person and not by another; it is a structural characteristic of human relationships—of all human relationships. (Elias, 1978)

This chapter deals with the dynamics of process in contemporary marriages and families, while focusing especially on the ongoing interplay between the conflicts of interest and the reciprocal use of power that underlies the day-to-day existence of those involved in these social arrangements. It does not offer a comprehensive overview of the current state of theorizing and research on the phenomenon of conflict or the use of power. Competent recent treatments of such and related issues are available in the literature (cf. Boss, 1987; Farrington & Chertok, 1993; Steinmetz, 1987; Szinovacz, 1987). Instead, this chapter reflects on the current knowledge about conflict and power with the aim of rethinking and strengthening its explanatory capacity.

The rationale for this approach—one somewhat at variance with the usual handbook format—is twofold. First, yet another inventory of our knowledge about conflict and power in marriages and families following so closely on the heels of the recent reviews noted in the preceeding paragraph would be redundant. Second, "rethinking," as I see it, means more than just thinking things over again. Rather, it means to "think differently, to question dominant assumptions about what is supposed to be natural or necessary, to envisage new possibilities, to analyze and restructure experience" (Rorty,

Jetse Sprey • Department of Sociology, Case Western Reserve University, Cleveland, Ohio 44106.

Handbook of Marriage and the Family, 2nd edition, edited by Marvin Sussman, Suzanne K. Steinmetz, and Gary W. Peterson. Plenum Press, New York, 1999.

1991, p. 11). This chapter, then, has as much to say about the ways in which conflict and power are dealt with in family studies as it does about current findings in this area.

The discussion is also based on the premise that if conflict and power are not clearly construed, a real understanding and explanation of the actual nature of process in marriages and families are prevented. It assumes that our collective ability to think and reason about the dynamics of these processes depends on the availability of a relatively coherent conceptual vocabulary.

The chapter begins with a brief discussion of the concept of *process* as it currently is used in the family literature. Then follows a brief discussion of the key notions under consideration, to wit, *process*, *dynamics*, *conflict*, and *power*. Initially, each one is dealt with separately, but only for the sake of clarity. In the final sections of the chapter a deliberate effort is made to illustrate their interdependence. This is done through the use of examples taken from an array of important publications that—each in its own way—were successful in portraying the essence of marital and family realities.

Family Process

Of the ideas cited above, conflict and power have been subjected to repeated analytical dissection. Process and its associated dynamics often remain relatively unspecified. For example, the index to the *Sourcebook of Family Theories and Methods* (Boss, Doherty, LaRossa, Schumm & Steinmetz, 1993) does not include the term *process*, despite frequent use in the book. This is an omission that may be understandable in the case of a word considered self-explanatory to many students of the family. Rhetorically, as figures of speech, the terms *process* and *dynamics* attach the connotations of movement and change to marriage and family living. Naming a journal *Family Process*, for example, announces a concern with what is really happening in marriages and families. Similarly, the label "family process theory" suggests an approach designed to get to the bottom of things. Analytically, however, such labels promise more than they deliver, so that a closer look at these ideas is in order.

Thinking about Process

At this writing, process seems to be used primarily to identify a specific sequence of more or less related events. Such chains often are assumed, explicitly or implicitly, to be causally connected. This causality, however, often rests on the commonsense belief that antecedent events are a cause of those that follow in their wake. At times, this may be the case, of course, but it is something that must be demonstrated rather than simply assumed. This requires, as a first step, the transformation of what may have been a persuasive metaphor into an analytic tool or concept. This is not always easy, especially in the case of such elusive phenomena as marriage and family processes. One begins by asking, what exactly do we mean by process? Can its "reality" be captured conceptually? I think so, but something is likely to get lost in translation.

Process, as I see it, is all that happened, is happening, and may happen in marriages and families or, on the macro level, to the course of the institutions of marriage and family. In reality, it is analogous to the sound of music: When the band stops all that is left is silence, a memory, and the possibility that it will play again. Process, received as such, takes on substance only when it is experienced. As soon as we freeze it for the sake of measurement, it disappears. A river without a stream turns into a lake or a pond, systems that are characterized by different dynamics. A good study of lakes may help but does not suffice to explain the dynamics of a river's flow. In a similar vein, students of medicine who dissect human cadavers may discover a great deal about the workings of the human body. How much they learn about its life, however, remains to be seen.

Family process, on both micro and macro levels, presents a chain of probabilities, events that may or may not happen along the way. As soon as one does come "alive," it turns into a frozen accident. What matters, then, is not so much the fact that a given course of events can be seen as a process, but rather its origin, its intensity, and its direction. A storm, for example, is experienced through its force, but it may make sense to study its beginning to speculate about its duration and future path. There is no reason to believe that the dynamics of process of human marriages and families lie completely beyond the reach of our explanatory potential.

The conceptual tools used to describe its nature, however, likely are "stand-ins" for the real "thing" and should be interpreted in that capacity. Some of these substitutes are quite relevant to the focus of this chapter and warrant some discussion.

System as a Substitute for Process

In his book *Living Systems*, Miller (1978) defined process as "all change over time of matter-energy or information in a system" (p. 23). It stands for change and movement within a finite social setting and attaches the notion of "systemness" to all more or less enduring configurations of human and animal sociability. This allows *systems theory*, a powerful multidisciplinary approach, to enter the explanatory domain of family scholarship (cf. Whitchurch & Constantine, 1993, p. 325). With "system" as a setting and a substitute, the term "process" itself may remain relatively unspecified or, if deemed helpful, used only metaphorically.

No wonder, then, that over 2 decades ago Kantor and Lehr (1975), in their trendsetting study *Inside the Family*, pronounced process to be "virtually coterminous" with the notion of system (p. 9), a premise that has become very much a part of systems thinking in the family field. The title of Carlfred Broderick's recent book (1993), *Understanding Family Process: Basics of Family Systems Theory*, illustrates this quite well. Regrettably, the authors did not clarify the "almost-but-not-quite" of their "virtual" fit between system and process. This poses a problem for those scholars who, with or without the aid of systems theory, are trying to understand the exact dynamics of marriage and family living.

Undoubtedly, the *concepts* of system and systemness are basic tools in family studies. Their use as substitutes for the *totality* of process in marriages and families, however, may not suffice to grasp all that may be happening through their course, nor do they offer sufficient access to the institutional paths of marriage and family during their joint march to the twenty-first century. A brief illustration may help clarify this point.

Any system, real or abstract, is supposed to have a boundary. In Broderick's (1990) words, "family process theory begins ... with the basic premise that the family is an ongoing, open, social system" (p. 178). To *be* open, however, implies a degree of closure, so one may ask: How open must a boundary be before its enclosed space ceases to be "systemic?" How permanent must it be (and so on)? Of course, such questions are conceptual and can be dealt with as such. Actual choices depend on how individual scholars choose to *define* the extent to which it makes sense to match the system concept with a specific segment of the real world. As Whitchurch and Constantine (1993) put it, "[T]he very act of identifying several components as a system is equivalent to drawing a boundary between what is included within the system and what is not part of the system" (p. 333).

Such analytic choices are not completely arbitrary because they reflect the various ways in which scholars imagine the reality of what exists inside such boundaries. The starting images, then, may become unduly rigid and, as such, constrain the ability to question. One might ask, for example, whether it is feasible to imagine a finite but borderless system. In other words, can we conceive of the "insides" of Kantor and Lehr's (1975) families as spaces without boundaries? I doubt it, but in the real world such phenomena do exist. Our planet earth, for example, "has a definite area, wrapped around a roughly spherical volume, but it has no edges; travel far enough in any direction on the surface of the earth, and you get back to where you started ... the surface is closed, yet unbounded" (Davies & Gribbin, 1992, p. 89). Our search, then, presents a space that cannot be dealt with on a two-dimensional plane, a territory that one can leave by approaching and crossing its border. Leaving planet earth requires "getting-off" rather than "getting-out," a quite different procedure.

It would be interesting to rethink family systems analysis in a spherical perspective, but this would take us beyond the scope of this chapter. Suffice it to note that, at this point, multidimensional approaches are not completely absent from family studies (cf. Whitchurch & Constantine, 1993). It may be of interest to note, however, that Albert Einstein's seminal notion of a closed but unbounded universe gave rise to a new image of space, to the idea of curved space time, and eventually to a theory of relativity. In contrast, the images that still underlie most theorizing in the family field remain decidedly flat.

Process within a Process

One way to conceive of family or marital process is to equate either one with its clearly recognizable manifestations. This essentially reductionist strategy can be used on both the institutional and the interpersonal level of analysis. Mate selection, for example, often is treated as a macro process, while parenting, marital adjustment, and divorce tend to be seen as micro ones. Metaphorically speaking, this approach redirects questioning from the river to one identifiable current in its stream. This is not wrong, as long as it is understood that rivers are made up of more than just the sum of what floats along between their shores. Family scholars, at times, ignore this caveat.

Perhaps reductionist thinking is appealing when one is confronted with a complex social phenomenon. In the family field we find it embedded in more than just one explanatory approach. For example, the authors of a recent, thorough discussion of the use of qualitative research (Ambert, Adler,

Adler, & Detzner, 1995) argue that it "is particularly well suited to the study of family processes on several levels of analysis" and that it "emphasizes meanings, the multiplicity of realities in a family, and the general sociopsychological context" (pp. 880–881). Without disputing these claims, one may wonder what exactly is meant by a "multiplicity of realities." Do they conjointly constitute a complete social process? If so, how are they related? Randomly? Orderly? Does each reality demand its own kind of analysis. If so, how do these various approaches interrelate? In other words, after reducing Humpty Dumpty to a "multiplicity" of pieces, how do we put the little fellow back together again?

These concerns are far from frivolous. To put them in perspective a comparison with an example of holistic thinking is useful:

> [L]ife is not located in the property of any single molecule—in the details—but is a collective property of systems of interacting molecules. Life, in this view, emerged whole and has always remained whole. Life, in this view, is not to be located in its parts, but in the collective emergent properties of the whole they create. (Kauffman, 1995, p. 24)

Paraphrasing this quote, I suggest that we should conceive of process in marriages and families not as located in its members, or member categories, but rather in the collective *emergent* properties of the whole, or the system, they collectively create. As in the case of "life," marriages and families emerge as *wholes* and remain that way until they, for whatever reason, fall apart. Their process continues to "emerge" until that final event.

Divorce: A Current in the Stream

Of the earlier cited events, divorce especially is difficult to separate from the presence of conflicts of interest and the reciprocal use of power. Students of divorce tend to conceive of it as *the* process in those marriages or families that appear "destined" to dissolve (cf. Gottman, 1994, p. 88). Its course, then, originates in and evolves from an antecedent stage of maladjustment:

> [L]ooked at from a family dynamics and not a legal standpoint, divorce can best be regarded as a process. It has roots somewhere in the past, before the divorce event, and carries with it effects that extend into the future. Each family member will be profoundly affected by it. (Ahrons & Rogers, 1987, p. 25)

In a somewhat more recent study of divorce and its consequences, Kitson and Holmes (1992) wrote:

> For many couples, deciding to end their marriages is a process of escalating levels of discontent, including frighteningly fierce arguments that may become physically violent, or lengthy, increasingly alienating silences during which hurts and wrongs continue to pile up. (p. 4)

We see a picture of escalation, one implying a chain of events leading, almost inevitably, to a final outcome.

Underpinning these descriptions is the definition of a process that derives its identity from its outcome. In that sense it is analogous to the definition of an "accident" as something that occurred accidentally. To describe its emergent nature, however, the divorce process should be seen as a sequence that may or may not lead to marital dissolution. In the same vein, mate selection, as a process, must be described as a series of happenings that, at best, are a necessary but not a sufficient prelude to the selection of a marriage partner.

Most current research on divorce is not based on these definitions. Consequently, it only deals with the "whats" and the "hows" of what happened in systems that indeed dissolved. Such research data are worthwhile, especially when matched with control samples from the pool of not-yet-dissolved marriages and/or families. The questions that usually remain unanswered concern the circumstances surrounding the point at which mere probability began to approach actuality. At that stage existing periods of turbulence change into a dominant "cascade" (Gottman, 1994), and dissolution becomes a real possibility. Borrowing from the vocabulary of chaos theory, one might say that at such a stage the system has been caught in the gravitational field of its "attractor" (Casti, 1995).

To my knowledge, this crucial transitional stage has not been identified. It may never be, because its actual occurrences may well be outcomes of the unique interplay between contingencies, chance events, and the intrinsic instability of marital and/or family processes. After all, the decisive cascade in any process doomed to dissolve might be propelled by a "strange attractor" (Casti, 1995, pp. 29–30). It is the last of the aforementioned factors, the intrinsic instability, that seems most thoroughly investigated by students of the divorce process. This kind of research most often reduces the whole to a set of component levels, each of which is then studied in its own analytic context. A few examples of this form of research merit consideration here to illustrate the contributions but also the limitations of such explanatory strategies.

Andrew Cherlin's revised edition of *Marriage, Divorce, Remarriage* (1992) offers an informative demographic treatment of the course and dissolution of marriages in the United States during this century. Its explanatory approach is a macro one so that spouses, couples, and social trends are dealt with primarily as reactors to "social forces." Process itself, in that context, becomes a social trend. This is evident, for example, from the observation that "if prosperity had been the only engine driving the trends of the 1950s, then early marriage, high birth rates, and moderate divorce rates should have continued throughout the almost equally prosperous 1960s" (p. 43). On this level of analysis, what happens

between spouses in actual couples is not directly relevant. The terms process, power, and conflict remain relatively unspecified throughout the author's text. His focus is, correctly, on the fate of the institutional arrangements of marriage and family, all evoked causality remains strictly statistical.

In contrast to this, Vaughan's (1986) in-depth study of the erosion and ultimate dissolution of intimate bonds closely depicts the interpersonal realities of the "uncoupling" process:

> The patterns found in uncoupling ... grow out of the observation of many lives—of many people dealing with the loss of role and attempting to manage the consequences. Each experience defies absolute categorization, however. So fragile, so fluid, so idiosyncratic is the individual human situation, that we cannot foresee its course. (p. 190)

Vaughan recognizes patterns but also is aware of the essential unpredictability of what transpires between members of couples on their way to dissolution. The individual spouse, rather than the marital relationship, is the ultimate unit of her analysis. Her "initiators" invariably confront, directly or indirectly, "partners," who only seem free to react, although the logic of process allows for situations in which both parties act as initiators or reactors. Inevitably, therefore, Vaughan's discussion moves at times to a relational level, for example:

> [T]he balance of power between two people in an intimate relationship is often subject to sudden and subtle shifts. Even when both are prepared for separation, it does not always occur in egalitarian and harmonious ways. (p. 131–132)

The concepts "egalitarian," "harmony," and "balance" describes attributes of ties rather than individuals. Not surprisingly, the terms "confrontation" and "power" appear in the index of this book. Both are essential analytic tools in the explanation of the uncoupling as well as the continuity of marriage and family relationships.

Finally, a brief look at Gottman's important work (1994, 1995), which spanned a period of more than 20 years, is in order. His multilevel research efforts aim to explain and predict which couples decide to divorce and why they choose to do so. At this point, the author asserts that he can predict, with over 94% accuracy, which couples will dissolve over a period of 3–8 years. His claim reflects a theory of marital process and a research design that, over the years, incorporated systematic observation and controlled experimentation in addition to more conventional data-gathering strategies. He proposed "a simple cascade model: decline in marital satisfaction, which leads to consideration of separation or divorce, which leads to separation, which leads to divorce" (1994, p. 88). At a later stage, this "simple" model evolved into a sequence of "two cascade's" (1995, p. 106).

The model, however, does not explain when or why

dissatisfaction starts in the marital process or why it escalates to a point of no return in many but not all instances. Logically, it may have been present right from the beginning. In fact, chaos theorizing emphasizes the extreme sensitivity of nonlinear processes, such as marriages and families, to initial conditions. Somewhat surprisingly, in my view, Gottman (1994) seems pessimistic about the potential theoretical contributions of nonlinear thinking to family studies:

> We are discovering that we will never be able to predict tomorrow's weather any better than we can now, even if we have all the information in the world about weather patterns. Given this state of affairs about physical nature, how can be expect people's social relationships to be more orderly and predictable over time (p. 409)

It is, however, not the "orderliness" but the "predictability" of human processes that is at issue here. Chaos theorizing posits a state of *orderly* chaos as a predictable mode of most complex systems.

On the other hand, Gottman (1994) sounds optimistic about the predictive potential of his work:

> We are finding that if we observe behavior properly, people's closest relationships are predictable, even over a period of years.... Despite the riot of people's personal lives, when we study them scientifically, the social world appears to be quite lawful, predictable, and understandable. (p. 409)

His "predictability," however, resembles that of a object falling out of an airplane high up in the sky. Unless something quite out of the ordinary happens, one may safely predict that it will continue to "cascade" toward its final destination. In such a context, then, one's line of questioning shifts from the "why" to the "why not." Gottman and his coworkers are reaching the limits of what reasonably can be predicted about the fate of marriages and families. Our potential to *understand* the essentially "chaotic" order of marital and family processes, however, may well continue to improve. Chaos theory undoubtedly will be of help in that endeavor.

Considering the foregoing discussion, it is not startling to see that most research on the consequences of divorce follow a more or less reductionist path. Men, women, and children in dissolving marriages and families are treated as members of social categories and are studied as such. After all, individual lives are easier to map than relationships or networks. Of course, such a research strategy leaves some questions unasked. What does happen, for example, to the family and/or marital process after the decree is granted? Does it continue in bits and pieces? If so, what bits and what kind of pieces? We do know that divorced spouses frequently continue to argue, negotiate, or exert power in each other's lives (cf. Amato, 1993; Ambert, 1989; Booth & Amato, 1994; Demo, 1993; Ganong, Coleman, & Mistina, 1995; Johnson, 1988; Matthews & Sprey, 1984). New and renewed ties or networks may well evolve between former spouses, divorced

parents and their children or stepchildren, parents and stepparents, and children and stepchildren. These bonds are not likely to emerge at random. If we fail to think of them as a process, perhaps a loosely structured one, we may lose track of their systemic nature and be left only with an image of the lives of participants as uprooted, resembling tumbleweeds rolled about by the winds of chance.

Process Reconsidered

Reconsidering the idea of process, a comment by Ludwig Wittgenstein (1958) is apt:

> I want you to remember that words have those meanings which we have given them.... I may have given a definition of a word and used the word accordingly.... Or else we might, by the explanation of a word mean the explanation which, on being asked, we are ready to give.... Many words in this sense then don't have a strict meaning. But this is not a defect. To think it is would be like saying that the light of my reading lamp is no real light at all because it has no sharp boundary. (p. 27)

Marriage and family processes can be seen as systemic and finite but, like the light of Wittgenstein's lamp, not clearly demarcated. They begin at a given point in time but have no predetermined ending. Of course, this does not mean that marriages and families last forever but rather that during their existence the end always remains an expectation, perhaps a promise or perhaps a threat. Only historians, by the nature of their craft, can claim knowledge about how events came to an end. Those who are involved in a social process, on the other hand, only can plan, try, pray, and/or hope for the best.

Adopting a viewpoint of marital and family processes as nonlinear in nature allows for a better grasp of the distinction between "orderly chaos" and "noise" in the study of their course. In chaos theorizing "noise" denotes random fluctuations, while "chaos" refers to

> randomness or irregularity that arises in a deterministic system. In other words, chaos is observed even in the complete absence of environmental noise. An important aspect of chaos is that there is a sensitive dependence of the dynamics to the initial conditions. This means that although in principle it should be possible to predict future dynamics as a function of time, this is in reality impossible since any error in specifying the initial condition, no matter how small, leads to an erroneous prediction at some future time. (Glass & Mackey, 1988, pp. 6–7)

Chaos theory or, better, the realm of mathematics called "nonlinear dynamics" is used in disciplines as diverse as physiology, meteorology, and hydrology. I believe its message to be of considerable potential to students of marriage and family (cf. Sprey, 1995; Ward, 1995). It raises fundamental questions about the predictability of all processes in our field and alerts us to the many pitfalls associated with the use of "linear" thinking in our explanatory practice.

Dynamics

The concept of dynamics also may serve as a stand-in for that of process. *Webster's Dictionary* (1984) defines it as the "study of the relationship between motion and forces affecting motion," while "dynamic" denotes "energy, force, or motion in relation to force." These meanings come from the Greek words for powerful (*dunamikos*) and power (*dunamis*). In family studies both terms often are used to symbolize movement and change in family process, but also to stress the proper way to analyze it. The final part of the first edition of this *Handbook*, for example, was titled "Family Dynamics and Transformation." It contains chapters on power, stress, and domestic violence (Sussman & Steinmetz, 1987, p . 649), but it is not clear why only these topics deserve the label "dynamic." Methodologically, the "dynamic" label often serves to proclaim that an explanatory path is more than just "static." The author of a comprehensive chapter on family power, for example, argues that "for a descriptive analysis of power, a static model of control may suffice, but an explanation of power relations must reflect the complexity and dynamics of ongoing 'powering' processes" (Szinovacz, 1987, p. 659).

What, then, qualifies a concept as dynamic? Its definition? Its use? Its measurement? Or all of these? After all, words are basically arbitrary and static. Replacing "power" with "powering" and "structure" with "structuring" does not necessarily make their meanings more dynamic.

A quote from a volume about human reproductive behavior may be of some help at this point:

> Although we like to think of families and households as fixed social modules, at some level of consciousness we must know that they are bunches of interacting life processes which are continually being undermined by time, and which require constant management. We may take comfort in our family portraits secure in their frames, but the sort of static image we like to put on the mantelpiece has very limited use when it comes to analyzing the social dynamism of reproduction. (Robertson, 1991, p. 159)

Family portraits probably adorn the mantelpieces in many North American households. If a picture is removed because its image seems no longer interesting or relevant, what is there to take its place? A video perhaps? A video of a deceased uncle would not bring him back to life but it might make it easier to remember him as an active, living human being, which is, of course, the real issue here. Robertson's admonition—if I have properly interpreted it—is not about what is static or dynamic on our mantelpieces, but about what is "framed" in our minds. Terms such as static and dynamic identify conceptions that, by their design and use, allow but also constrain our ability to imagine and reason about what takes place in actual marriages and families. As the German sociologist Elias (1978) put it:

> We say, "The wind is blowing," as if the wind were actually a thing at rest which, at a given point in time, begins to move and blow. We speak as if the wind were separate from its blowing, as if a wind could exist which did not blow. (p. 112)

It is not unusual in the family field to see "family" analyzed as separate from its process, as if a family could exist apart from it. Regardless of their depth or scope, what makes specific concepts more or less dynamic than others depends on the ways in which they are used. The conception of divorce process, for example, remains a "static" one as long as it derives its meaning only from its outcome.

The change in focus from the individual to what exists between and among people constitutes a crucial step in the direction of a holistic analysis of marriage and family processes. Such a move does not necessarily require a complete removal of persons and their attributes from the analysis. People, in a relational context, derive their "individuality" from the social ties and networks of which they are a part. It leads to a conceptual vocabulary designed to describe the ongoing, forever emerging, and often unforeseeable course of process in marriages and families. It also serves as a reminder, however, that it is not completely possible to capture, let alone explain, a "reality" that becomes the past as soon as we finished experiencing it.

All things considered, then, it is clear that many concepts in our field indeed are static. They identify outcomes and label the processes that brought them about. This does not negate their analytic usefulness, but merely offers grounds for explanatory caution and precision. When a sports event is in progress, for example, it is unwise to proclaim a "winning game" for one team. Some final scores are more predictable than others but, as gamblers know, "the game ain't over till it's over." Getting married, becoming a parent, being divorced, and a death in the family all represent static events. Of course, depending on the circumstances, such events can be statistically predicted and, therefore, are crucial to the reliable mapping of the social processes they identify. However, such events are outcomes that should not be used to explain what "caused" them.

On Conflict

Although this chapter is not intended to restate or define conflict theory, it is rooted in a conflict perspective. Therefore, a brief overview of its basic premises and ideas is in order.

Scope and Depth

In their appraisal of the role of conflict theorizing in family studies, Farrington and Chertok (1993) concluded that after its emergence in the 1970s, it remained a relatively minor theoretical approach. They attribute this limited growth to an absence of "intellectual coherence" among the various brands of conflict theorizing that were put forward during the past quarter-century:

> [T]he social conflict approach to the study of the family ... is best seen as a curious amalgam, consisting of rather unlikely bedfellows, including Marxist thought, structural-functionalism, feminist theory, Weberian sociology, psychoanalytic theory, communication theory, phenomenological sociology, and sociobiology ... the combining of a number of different—and, at times, highly dissimilar—ideas under the single, general rubric of "family conflict theory." (p. 372)

Their point is well-taken, but among the "unlikely bedfellows" cited, I consider only Marxist thought, feminist theory, and, in a broader sense, sociobiology, as truly representative of conflict theorizing. The other approaches offer an assortment of theoretical explanations *of* conflict in and between marriages and families. Much of the confusion to which the authors refer stems from the fact that many family scholars do not distinguish clearly between "theories of conflict" and "conflict theory."

The conflict approach is a "perspective" rather than a single theory. It resembles Laudan's (1977) idea of a "research tradition" that represents a coherent set of "general assumptions about the entities and processes in a domain of study, and about the appropriate methods to be used in investigating the problems and constructing the theories in that domain" (p. 81; see also Wilson, 1983, pp. 6–7). Like "systems thinking," a term used by Whitchurch and Constatine (1993) to denote a "worldview" (p. 325), the conflict approach presents a focused way of looking a reality that allows for more than one specific line of reasoning. Its conceptual vocabulary is flexible enough to assimilate ideas from other related schemes, while the perspective stays intact to provide the initial images of what is to be questioned and explained.

Without doubt, such a perspective invites a degree of diversity reminiscent of Farrington and Chertok's (1993) "lack of intellectual coherence." I consider this an asset rather than a liability. Theorizing is an intentional, goal-oriented human activity and reflects the interests of scholars who, at times, may search for satisfactory rather than optimal solutions (Sprey, 1988). Consequently, a good deal of explanations in our field are rooted in the top soil of marital and family realities and have as their primary aim reliable description and, where possible, statistical prediction. They cover the ground, like a well-tended lawn, but do not reach deeply in search of hidden theoretical constructs. Conflict thinking, because of its history and philosophical heritage, digs deeper but, in a practice-oriented field, pays a price for this in popularity.

One further point remains to be made. Within a conflict perspective, randomness, rather than overt conflict or disorder, constitutes the counterpoint to order. Explanation, therefore, should account for *both* war and peace in marriages and families (Sprey, 1979). Hostile confrontations, appeasement moves, mutual exploitation, and cooperation are *all* considered integral components of process in marriages and families.

Presuppositions

Explanatory practice rests on ontological and epistemological premises about the nature of humans, their societies, and their ability to know about such matters. The family field is no exception. My basic assumptions were stated in earlier writings (Sprey, 1979, 1988) and are identified here only when they are directly relevant to the focus of this chapter.

The word "presuppositions" refers to the most general assumptions that a person makes, what one presupposes when confronting the real world (cf. Alexander, 1987, p. 10). To begin, my first assumption is that the ultimate questions about the "whys" of humans and their societies can be framed best in an evolutionary—not necessarily strictly Darwinian—frame of reference (Sprey, 1979, p. 133; 1988). In that context, conflicts of interest are considered to be pervasive:

> A world in which virtually every individual is genetically distinct is one in which substantial disagreements between individuals would be expected, with each selected for maximization of its *own* inclusive fitness. Therefore real possibilities exist for conflicts of interest between individuals of the same sex ... between mates.... and even between parents and offspring. (Barash, 1982, p. 337)

There is no reason to believe that the species *Homo sapiens* is an exception. We may expect selfishness, cheating, and coercion to be as much a possibility in human family life as they are in reproductive and caring processes among other social animals. At the same time, we can expect cultures, as cumulative systems of human survival, to contain scripts and rules that fashion and constrain phenomena such as cheating, selfishness, and other forms of abuse in marital and family settings. Of course, such prescriptions may vary both between and within human societies, but they profoundly influences the perception of conflicts of interest and the exercise of power. Cultures are not to be considered mere "uniform and integrated wholes," but rather systems of "conventional discourse whose coherence, however partial, problematic, and incomplete, enables recognition of connections among the things that people do." This makes human conduct "not just appropriate but intelligible and fraught with sense" (Rosaldo, 1980, p. 28). Structures, overt or latent, not necessarily impinge directly on human interaction in micro or macro processes. Culture, however, does, because it is an integral part of being human.

My second presupposition or assumption rests on Simmel's (1959) seminal observation that human societies are structures "composed of unequal elements," while the "equality toward which democratic or socialistic efforts are directed ... is actually an equivalence of people, functions, or positions (p. 351). Human interaction, be it in communities, networks, or families, always carries the burdens of inequality and necessity. As one famous conflict theorist, Karl Marx (1973), once put it, "the human being is in the most literal sense a social animal, not merely a gregarious animal, but an animal which can individuate itself only in the midst of society" (p. 84). Such societies and their institutional arrangements are made up of "unequals" who have no option but to exist jointly for the sake of survival. So far, during the pilgrimage of humanity, the arrangements of marriage and family, in many forms, seem to have served as crucial vehicles for collective survival.

My third basic assumption concerns not only human nature but also, by implication, the human condition because the two cannot be separated in our thinking. At the onset of *The Presentation of Self in Everyday Life*, Goffman (1959) writes:

> Regardless of the particular objective which the individual has in mind and his motive for having this objective, it will be to his interest to control the conduct of others, especially their responsive treatment of him. (p. 3)

Controlling the actions of others, especially strangers, is in one's interest, regardless of what one has in mind, because the human environment is both unsafe and uncertain. A similar message comes from Wilson (1978), a sociobiologist, when he suggests that humans—as an evolved species—tend to be predisposed to respond with unreasoning aversion to perceived external threats and are inclined to escalate their reactions sufficiently to neutralize the latter by a safe margin. They tend to distrust strangers and are inclined to solve conflicts by opting for aggressive rather than peaceful tactics (p. 119). Wilson sees this genetic propensity as selectively advantageous, a claim that, in view of what we know about human history and the present, seems reasonable. It is not necessary here to ask how much of human nature reflects genetic programming and how much of it reflects the accumulated "wisdom" of its past. The overly simple culture-versus-nature dichotomy is irrelevant to the argument presented in this chapter. What does matter is a view of "humanness" in which attack remains favored over retreat, suspicion over trust, and control over flexibility. This type of "inclination," in my view, is not caused by or anchored in human heredity alone but constitutes a presence that evolved during our

prehuman past and that, like the grin on the face of the Cheshire Cat, lingers on after the rest is gone.

Key Concepts

Central to a conflict perspective is the idea of competition or conflict of interest. It implies two preconditions, scarcity and interdependence. In the absence of real or perceived scarcity there is little to compete about, while a state of interdependence means the presence of others with whom potentially scarce resources may have to be shared. Perceived in this manner, competition identifies a condition of negative interdependence between those involved in a given social process. Gains for some inevitably are associated with losses for others.

The existence of a competitive state may be hidden, latent, and misunderstood by those involved. It may operate as a condition *and* a process. Traffic, for example, is competitive because each vehicle on the road competes, directly or indirectly, with every other one. It is during the rush hour, however, that stresses most likely are felt and actually may lead to hostile confrontations between drivers. By the same token, marriages and families, as arenas in which genders and generations coexist, harbor an ever-present competitive potential.

Resource scarcity may be permanent. Limited access to the other spouse, for example, constitutes a more or less continuous state of scarcity in contemporary marriages. Ensuring conflicts of interest must be managed rather than solved through continued negotiation and compromise. The resulting order is, at best, a negotiated one and open to renegotiation.

In this chapter the term "conflict" stands for competitive *behavior*, that is, action taken to gain or protect access to disputed means or ends. Such actions or tactics may be either direct or indirect. In the field of sports, individuals or groups directly confront one another, for example, in a tennis match. A track meet, on the other hand, illustrates indirect competitive behavior. In both cases, however, the winners gain at the expense of the losers.

Direct competition or overt conflict in marriages and families can range from "gamelike" orderly confrontations to episodes of physical violence. It may take the form of verbal battles, physical combat, passive aggression, or acts of sabotage, to mention just a few of its many manifestations. It is important to realize, however, that not all such tactics are, in and by themselves, destructive or dysfunctional. Threats and promises, for example, can be analyzed as tactics designed to avoid potentially harmful confrontations or to prevent the escalation of verbal confrontations into ones of physical violence (Sprey, 1979, pp. 138–139). All these encounters, however, involve the reciprocal exercise of power, a phenomenon to be dealt with in more detail in the following section.

On Power

The idea of power remains a contested one in the family literature, a situation that so far shows no sign of change. Szinovacz (1987) for example, observed that we "are all aware that there is, indeed, such a 'Thing,' and many of us 'agree to disagree' on the exact meaning of this Thing" (p. 651). Her point is well taken, but it is noteworthy that many disagreements concern the very essence of the "Thing." This lack of consensus may stimulate further dialogue, but conflicting positions also become polarized so that differences, rather than a search for common ground, become the focus.

To highlight the range of such possible disputes, some elementary questions about power and its uses in marriages and families are offered to illustrate the multifaceted and pervasive presence of power (cf. Lukes, 1978). How do we think about power? As vested in individuals or as an attribute of the ties that bind them? What exactly does it mean if we proclaim one family member as more powerful than others? Can we extend such a claim to social categories, such as gender or age? If so, what are we saying? How do we perceive the power of social institutions? Does it make sense to claim that "the" family is either gaining or losing its power in modern societies? Is a marriage between two powerful individuals by necessity a strong one? How do family members exert power over one another? Is all use of power intentional? Are its consequences always destructive? How is this decided, and by whom? Finally, how do we deal with the intentional avoidance of the use of power in a family? As a move in a power-game, or as a refusal to play the game?

In view of the wide range of these questions, it seems safe to suggest that power pervades most, if not all, aspects of marital and family processes. Ironically, this also allows its presence to be taken for granted and remain unexplored, except when its abuse makes it visible. The phenomenon of power, for example, does not feature prominently in the text of a comprehensive volume titled *Embattled Paradise; The American Family in an Age of Uncertainty* (Skolnick, 1991). The noise of battle and the fear of uncertainty, implied in this title, are effectively muted by the quiet tone of a narrative described as "insightful, thoughtful, and readable" by an admiring reviewer (Hansen, 1993). At its level of discourse, direct references to the many faces of power may have seemed irrelevant. A book that focuses on diversity in families (Zinn & Eitzen, 1993) does not cite conflict in its index and provides a limited, rather individualistic treatment of the role of power in marital decision making. It is hard to imagine diversity, cultural or social, without hearing echoes from the canyons of conflict and power. Hearing, however, requires listening, and the noises of power, seemingly coming out of nowhere, easily go unnoticed.

Preliminaries

Power is a dispositional concept because it describes a potential. So defined, its presence can precede emerging conflicts of interest and other contingencies that may lead to its actual use. The results of such usage, for instance, success or failure, cannot be foretold simply on the basis of what is known about available resources. Explaining power does require a choice of context and focus. Some scholars elect to focus on the "anonymous" power structures in society at large, while others decide to concentrate on its use in face-to-face settings, such as family interaction, sibling relations, marriage, and cohabitation. In the former instance, however, the dynamics of power may stay hidden, to be inferred from overtly more obvious phenomena. Foucault (1982), a master of this type of analysis, once suggested that the best way to recognize such hidden power structures is to take the resistance against them as a point of departure and to analyze their workings by focusing on the existing "antagonism of strategies":

> As a starting point, let us take a series of oppositions which have developed over the last few years: opposition to the power of men over women, of parents over children, of psychiatry over the mentally ill, of medicine over the population, of administration over the ways people live. (p. 211)

This type of power, then,

> mediate[s] everyday life which categorizes the individual, marks him by his own individuality, attaches him to his own identity, imposes a law of truth on him which he must recognize and which others have to recognize in him. It is a form of power which makes individuals ... subject to someone else by control and dependence, and tied to his own identity by a conscience or self-knowledge. (p. 212)

In other words, such "forces" transform women into wives, men into husbands, and their offspring into children. By the same token, such antagonisms may give rise to the very "oppositions" that confront and possibly restructure imbalances. Faced by such challenges, entrenched privilege and authority may lose their anonymity and become tied to the social position of a class or group. The label "patriarchy," for instance, removed the anonymity of those who are accused of benefitting from gender-based privileges (cf. Johnson, 1995). In this way, then, the "macro" penetrates the "micro" of human sociability.

Definitions

The idea of power is a systemic and contextual one. It pertains to relations between individuals and/or groups. The fact that someone happens to be physically strong only has meaning relative to others who are more, less, or equally strong. Despite this, many family scholars approach the analysis of its use within an individualistic frame of reference. Labels such as "female" and/or "male" power illustrate this point. Much research centers on the power of categories, such as "wives," "husbands," and "grandparents." In this explanatory approach, power is seen as the ability to influence or control the lives of others, even against their will, or, more broadly, as the ability "to define and control circumstances and events so that one can influence things to go in the direction of one's interests" (Rorty, 1992, p. 2). This kind of research does offer valuable information about the many ways in which husbands and wives, as categories, use their power resources. It shows *how* they negotiate, but does not tell us *why* negotiation is seen as desirable or perhaps inevitable. Nor does it show from whence the rules and values that structure such negotiations come. Are they themselves subject to negotiation or renegotiation? Why, for example, is it that what is considered fair by one spousal category is perceived as unfair by the other? (Hochschild, 1989; LaRossa, 1997; LaRossa & LaRossa, 1981).

The definition of power as a property of social ties or networks demands a shift in focus. The relationship itself becomes the unit of analysis, while people linked by it derive their identities from being part of it. "Friends," for example, are individuals who are involved in a bond called friendship, while an only child does not qualify as either a "sister" or a "brother."

Relations have attributes, such as the *balance* of their power. They may be symmetrical, asymmetrical, transitive, intransitive, reflexive, or irreflexive. Elias (1984) suggested that almost all sociologial treatments of power are inadequate simply because they do not consistently focus on power balances. As an intrinsic aspect of what ties individuals or groups together, power needs to be seen as more than just a "thing" belonging to one party to be used to control the lives of others. The "strong" do not have power in the absence of the "weak." For example, the mere potential of parental sanctions, be they physical or otherwise, may well suffice to "control" the behavior of their children.

Excessive use of alcohol and exposure to parental violence during early childhood are perennial favorites among explanations for all forms of domestic violence (Gelles & Conte, 1991; see also Flanzer, 1993). Statistically, these phenomena indeed are associated with the abusive use of physical force in marriages and families. Such statistics, however, do not provide sufficient access to the "why" of what happens between spouses, parents and children, or siblings in violence-prone households. Who hits first in such families may well be a chance event, but repeated physical violence is no accident and, therefore, is in need of explanation. Making

an inventory of first-hitters on the basis of traits such as gender, age, or income level, may provide grounds for disputes about which gender category or generation should be labeled "most violent" (cf. Straus, 1993). Such information, however, offers little insight into the actual dynamics of the reciprocal use of power in such households.

Using Power

As a potential, power is a presence in the lives of all marriages and families. It is there during negotiations and as part of solutions. As earlier suggested, even if not actually used it may lead to compliance. When a working-class wife in a classic study of contraceptive practices was asked about her husband's attitude, she had this to say:

> He thinks they [condoms] cost too much money and would rather spend it on beer. My husband was a boxer for a while and he is quite strong, so I don't argue with him too much. (Rainwater, 1960, p. 37)

I doubt that this message has lost much with age. it accentuates the crucial importance of the *balance* of power in marital and/or family relations and serves as a reminder of the relativity of all resources.

In fact, few social institutions exhibit such imbalances more than do marriage and family. As Hill (1965) observed many years ago:

> Compared with other associations in society the average family is badly handicapped organizationally. Its age composition is heavily weighted with dependents, and it cannot freely reject its weak members and recruit more competent team mates. Its members receive an unearned acceptance; there is no price for belonging. Because of its unusual age composition and its uncertain sex composition, it is intrinsically a puny work group and an awkward decision-making group. (p. 35)

Marriages, families, and other cohabitative arrangements all qualify as ongoing "networks of interdependent human beings, with shifting asymmetrical power balances" (Benthem van den Bergh, 1971, p. 19). Power is not added to their process, but is an integral part of it.

To understand the role of power in our society and its social institutions it should be kept in mind that the knowledge many people have about their world may be inadequate or even wrong. Because of this the expectations, attitudes, and decisions informed by such unreliable information can have unplanned and unforeseen results. These need not be random and may be collectively perceived and/or experienced as "forces" in their own right by people who may not know each other or recognize their shared fate. Many North American housewives, for example, appeared unaware of their collective experience until Friedan's *Feminine Mystique* (1963) opened their eyes.

Elias (1978) saw these "unintentional human interdependencies" as being "at the root of every intentional interaction" (p. 94). This led him to suggest that the initiatives and responses of such interdependent people may be analyzed as "moves" in social "games" that may serve as heuristic tools in the study of societal complexity (cf. Sprey, 1988). I will use such "models" in order to look more closely at the mutual exercise of power in marital and family relations.

Let us assume that in a two-person game, such as chess, one of the players has superior skills so that she or he usually controls the outcome and the course of each match. A parent playing with a child, for example, may dictate the duration and the outcome of any given game. If the players become more equally skilled the situation changes. Neither party controls either the outcome or the course of any given game. If, for whatever reason, the situation gets out of hand neither player has the power to restore the normal course of events. To accomplish this, voluntary cooperation of both parties is essential. Because it takes two to maintain a dyad, but only one to destroy it, the game's process is fragile, especially if the relative power of the partners approaches equality. If negotiations fail, coercive tactics, such as promises (bribes), threats (blackmail), or the use of force, become real possibilities.

The use of physical or nonviolent coercive tactics in marriages and families very much depends on relational attributes, such as the degree of symmetry between resources and the extent to which members depend on each other's contributions. This is a setting in which, to varying degrees, all members of the household are implicated (Sprey, 1991). In the interpretation of what is observed on the "surface" of marital and family living, it is easy to lose sight of the intrinsic logic of their respective processes. The following brief quote illustrates this important point:

> The greater the inequality, the more one person makes all the decisions and has all the power, the greater the risk of violence. Power, power confrontations, and perceived threats to domination, in fact, are underlying issues in almost all acts of family violence. (Gelles & Straus, 1988, p. 82)

The authors seem to argue that in a situation of severely imbalanced power relations those with "all the power" also will use it. This begs all questioning about the *reciprocal* exercise of power in such networks. Contrary to this assertion, I would expect that the greater the imbalance of power, the lower the likelihood of its deliberate instrumental use. After all, why *would* someone in total control resort to the use of power? Would it simply be for the fun of it? Or can it be that the "weak," even in quite uneven power settings, continue to pose a challenge to the "strong"? If so, what challenge? Does their power rest on their ability to leave the

"game?" In fact, we know very little about the power of the powerless, something that will continue to be so until we relinquish our thinglike notion of power.

One further comment on the reciprocity of the use of power is relevant to this point. Clearly, a pronounced discrepancy in physical strength allows for the calculated use of force as a means of control. However, this only tells part of the story and does not offer a sufficient explanation of its use. Consider, for example, a different quote from the previously cited work:

> My husband wanted to think of himself as the head of the household. He thought that the man should wear the pants in the family. Trouble was, he couldn't seem to get his pants on. He had trouble getting a job and almost never could keep one. If I didn't have my job as a waitress, we would have starved. Even though he didn't make no money, he still wanted to control the house and the kids. But it was my money, and I wasn't about to let him spend it on booze and gambling. (Gelles & Straus, 1988, p. 82)

What is really at issue in this dismal case—the husband's power or his lack of it? It appears to be both. The man is strong enough to abuse his wife and children but he also depends on his spouse's earnings. The key issue, therefore, is dependence rather than domination. This traditional but economically powerless husband wants to but cannot "think of himself as the head of the household" and, so, with the help of alcohol, becomes abusive in whatever ways he can. The imbalance of physical resources in this case merely allows for their abuse. It identifies a necessary but not a sufficient condition.

Dependency, especially on those with whom one's fate is shared, may lead to the use of coercive tactics, but at best addresses questions of necessity. Some husbands may be proud and grateful to live with an earning spouse. I do agree with Gelles and Strauss' (1988) contention that what *does* make relationships like the one described here intrinsically unstable is the pronounced asymmetry in the structuring of their processes. This continuously challenges and ultimately may defeat the negotiating efforts of not just one but *all* family members.

It is worth noting that when gender is absent as a source of inequality, dependency continues to be a source of conflict in close relationships. The author of a study of partner abuse in lesbian couples, for example, reports:

> It appears that violence in lesbian relationships occurs at about the same frequency as violence in heterosexual relationships. The abuse may be physical and/or psychological, ranging from verbal threats and insults to stabbings and shootings.... What emerged as significant in my research was not the forms of abuse inflicted, but, rather, the factors that appear to give rise to the abuse.... The factor that ... was most strongly associated with abuse was partner's relative dependency on one another. More specifically, batterers ap-

peared to be intensely dependent on the partners whom they victimized. (Renzetti, 1992, pp. 115–116)

Other studies of gay and lesbian couples support this conclusion (cf. Blumstein & Schwartz, 1983; Lie & Gentlewainer, 1991).

Referring to Elias (1978) once again, "when one person (or group of persons) lacks something which another person or group has the power to withhold, the latter has a function for the former. Thus men have a function for women and women for men, parents for children, and children for parents" (p. 78). and, one might add, the weak have a function for the strong.

Families, such as the ones described earlier, are marked by a type of interdependence that is primarily one of unfilled collective needs. They exist, therefore, in a state of perpetual conflict of interests that lead to confrontations whose roots those involved may not fully comprehend. Because their resources are so few, all members have the "power" to make each other's lives miserable by withholding whatever little they have to share. No wonder that such processes are prone to violence and disorder. By the same token it is possible to develop cooperative values and skills that encourage improvisation and collective survival (cf. Stacey, 1990), a phenomenon to be discussed in detail later in the chapter.

Power and Complexity

When two-person systems grow into larger ones, their processes rapidly become more complex. "Complexity" is seen here as the ratio between the size of a network and the number of its possible interpersonal ties. For example, a simple calculation shows that a triad allows for three dyadic relationships. A five-person group permits 10, while a size of eight allows for 28 different dyadic combinations. Of course, larger networks also have the potential for a growing number of traids, foursomes, and so on. In other words, while a group's size increases along a linear path its structuring potential grows exponentially. As alluded to earlier, under such conditions the ability of individuals and their group to control the course and the outcome of their joint fate decreases dramatically.

To survive as a viable process in the face of growing size a game's structure turns into that of a "team." In such a setting individual players may well be inclined to perceive their roles as "increasingly opaque and uncontrollable" (Elias, 1978, p. 85). Family process is not exempt from the logic of complexity, so that even small changes are likely to affect its existing balance of power, a point that warrants a further comment.

In terms of complexity, a marriage exhibits the simplest possible structure, two partners and one tie. As indicated previously, its vulnerability does not lie in its size, but in the

profound interdependence of its members. No wonder, then, that prominent researchers, such as Gottman (1994), consider its emotional quality as crucial to the well-being of its members and, therefore, to its stability. After all, there is little else that remains to support voluntary bonding in modern societies. The addition of a member to the marital dyad, for example, that of a child, complicates its structure and, as such, can be expected to challenge its negotiated order. The transformation of a marriage into a family, a small one numerically, thus represents a fundamental change in its process. Each further addition, regardless of its kind, contributes exponentially to its complexity. On the current social scene, increases in size also often reflect the ongoing reshaping of our households and/or kinship networks. Stepparents, stepchildren, and stepsiblings always have been a feature of such networks, but death traditionally provided vacancies. Currently, however, dissolution is the main source of supply. All this, in combination with declining mortality rates and increased life expectancy, has created a new complexity that demands coping skills and knowledge not yet available in the storehouse of our culture. Consequently, contemporary family living remains poorly understood, untried, and, in that capacity, "increasingly opaque and uncontrollable" to many of those involved in it.

Process, Conflict, and Power

Farrington and Chertok (1993) saw the idea of power "as central to many versions of family conflict theory as the notion of conflict itself" (p. 370). I would add that separate theories of family conflict or power, at best, offer only limited accounts of the dynamics of process in marriages or families. In line with this, power and conflict are approached "holistically" in this section, so that the presence of one implies that of the other.

For a start, I provide a brief anecdote on which to draw for further discussion. Years ago, I used to watch young boys play baseball on my street, five or six of them managing to field two opposing teams. One tiny boy was posted far away on someone's front lawn, where he would wait eagerly for an occasional ball to come his way. Once, when questioned, he told me that he liked to play but disliked always having to be "permanent outfielder." In response to my suggestion that he complain to the others, he said, "But then they won't let me play."

This story tells much of what this section is about, a lack of alternatives in people's lives—at play, at work, during mate selection, and throughout the course of their marital and family careers. This lack of options underlies and fashions many conflicting interests between spouses, siblings, and the generations within marriages and families. Individuals in face-to-face relationships tend to hold one another, rather than their joint fate, responsible for their problems. They have few options but to resort to bargaining or the use of coercive tactics to safeguard or improve what they see as their best interests.

How spouses negotiate and the consequences of their joint efforts for their family lives represent core questions in family studies. They often are dealt with in the explanatory context of "exchange theory", an approach that focuses "on how relationships develop, on how relationships are experienced, on the patterns and dynamics that emerge within ongoing relationships, and on the factors mediating the stability of relationships" (Sabatelli & Shehan, 1993, p. 385). Research on the "hows" of exchange has contributed much to our knowledge of the multiple uses of power in marriages and families, as well as in society at large (cf. Molm, Quist, & Wisely, 1994). Its main emphasis, however, is on what is happening and can be observed in day-to-day interactions. Consequently, the intrinsic logic of the exchange process and its linkages with outside social networks often remains somewhat obscure.

Nancy Hartsock, in her book *Money, Sex, and Power* (1985), reminds us of Marx's claim that "the social relations of capitalism generate two epistemological systems, the one at the level of appearance, and rooted in the activity of exchange, the other at the level of real social relations, and rooted in the activity of production" (p. 9). She then proposes an additional level to better understand domination based on gender as well as socioeconomic class:

> [T]he domination of one gender by the other can only be made visible at a still deeper level, an epistemological level defined by reproduction. Thus, rather than argue, with Marx, that reality must be understood as bi-leveled, I am suggesting that it must be understood as three-tiered. (pp. 9–10)

Her critique of Marx is to the point, but I prefer an image of our human world as one in which *all* forms of domination are underpinned by the asymmetries that characterize *all* potential ties between the weak and the strong. Such a view, reflecting so-called "theoretical realism" (cf. Wilson, 1983, pp. 167–175; Bhaskar, 1989), does posit a multilevel picture of human realities (Sprey, 1988, p. 881). In its context, then, both gender and age can be perceived as intrinsic aspects of all power exchanges in marriages and families.

Family Tales

The purpose of my baseball story is to bring out the power of the "game" itself and to illustrate the extent to which it influences its own rules and values. The story again draws our attention to the fact that most games people play offer few reasonable alternatives. It makes good sense for older boys to exile a younger one to the safety of someone's front yard. Playing ball on public streets is dangerous and young children are impulsive. In addition, small teams do need their more experienced players in key positions. The game itself prescribes many of the inequalities confronted by its players if it is to survive as a sanctioned endeavor in a competitive and uncertain social environment. Children's games, like others, have their own special realms of scarcity. If more playgrounds were available, for example, young children would not play on public streets and teams could be larger. More "talent" might be available and player deployment more flexible. The use of power, then, always is contextual and, as such, reflects the varied-and-often-hidden, competitive underpinnigs from which Foucault's "forms of power" emerge.

Hochschild's (1989) study of dual-worker families offers valuable insight into the conflicts of interest that appear to plague this growing addition to the American family scene. Many of these problems were fore-shadowed in an earlier publication, at a time when dual-work arrangements still were labeled "nontraditional":

> In the United States we view the difficulties faced by working couples (especially working parents) as essentially personal problems rather than public issues. Parents must, for the most part, manage their own problems of child care, shiftwork, geographical mobility, job security, and the rising cost of living. Working couples today deal with the strain between work and family essentially on their own. Their "coping" strategies include establishing priorities for work and family responsibilities, reducing involvement in one role … or seeking outside support. (Moen, 1982, p. 35)

And:

> The conflicts between work and family roles are seldom resolved, rather, they are "juggled" in a time-budgeting process that is often unsatisfactory. Because of the traditional division of labor within the family it is the woman who is seen as principally responsible for the domestic chores, including childcare. (p. 37)

Things did not change a great deal over the past decade. Current dual-earner couples, such as those described by Hochschild (1989), still constitute a process in which the balance of power remains uneven so that many wives work one shift at the factory or office and a second one at home.

The negotiated order described by Hochschild (1989) differs in content from a game children play but, as a social configuration, does share some of its characteristics. Both tend to be seen as "voluntary" in our culture, but in reality neither one is matched by truly equal alternatives. In both cases the "players" depend on each other but the balance of power in their networks is unequal and unstable. Moreover, the structuring of process in both instances limits the options available to individual participants and constrains what they collectively can achieve. Contrary to the worlds of children, however, many of the spouses in Hochschild's sample, wives as well as husbands, seem entangled in an institutional form that, on the face of it, appears to have lost its way. Because of this, established and familiar rules become meaningless to some spouses and confusing to others.

Hochschild (1989) believes the rapid move of married women into the "economy" to be responsible for the sharp increase in dual-worker families but does not see it as a proximate cause of all their problems:

> The exodus of women into the economy has not been accompanied by a cultural understanding of marriage and work that would make this transition smooth. The workforce has changed. Women have changed. But most workplaces have remained inflexible in the face of family demands of their workers and at home, most men have yet to really adapt to the changes in women. The strain between the change in women and the absence of change in much else leads me to speak of a "stalled revolution." (p. 12)

This claim strikes me as valid but also limited. The case materials presented in the book indicate that the problems of families reflect the genesis of new and yet unfamiliar ties, rather than mere discrepancies in the rates of change of male and female attitudes. The "strain" referred to seems symptomatic of a setting in which spouses, as well as generations, are confronting and expected to cope with a rapidly and haphazardly evolving culture. Like all evolution this change may appear "chaotic" to those involved, because it is uneven, largely unplanned, and, at this writing, far from finished. It is neither "revolutionary" or "stalled," but its final outcome, so far, remains uncertain and is thus a source of anxiety to all those caught in its process.

In contemporary culture, for example, the established "homemaker" role tends to be perceived with a mixture of ambiguity and disdain (Hochschild, 1989). The author herself refers to contemporary working wives as "modern-day urbanizing peasants" (p. 246) and suggests that their occupational gains are countered by an increased dependency at home:

> If women's work outside the home increases their need for male help inside it, two facts—that women earn less and that marriages have become less stable—inhibit many women from pressing men to help more. (p. 249)

The German sociologist Beck (1992), on the other hand, observes that the addition of a second income to the family earnings makes husbands less dependent on the whims of the labor market, which, in turn, increases *their* dependence on their working spouses (p. 173). On a deeper level, then, it is not the position of any one gender category, but rather the balance of power between them that is changing and becoming increasingly more unstable in modern marriages and families.

Hochschild's (1989) reference to "modern-day urbaniz-

ing peasants" also needs a comment. Two brief quotes from an authoritative study of French nineteenth-century farm families (Segalen, 1980), are relevant:

> Women's place in the rural family is unique, too ... though the law made her an inferior, she was, in fact, viewed as a producer, and as such, had a special relationship with the soil. Whatever the economic level of the farm, its future largely depended on the woman's labour. (p. 2)

While:

> [T]he man–wife relationship in peasant society is based not on the absolute authority of one over the other, but on the complementarity of the two. This relationship is determined by the particular nature of peasant sociability: before being a couple, the man and the wife form part of the male and female groups which make up the basic framework of human relationships. (p. 9)

The images of family process as portrayed by Segalen and Hochschild differ. The former paints a social and culturally sanctioned inequality in which each member—male, female, and child—is assigned a clear and presumably essential role. In the latter's narrative, we see a social arrangement in which the roles of males and females, at work and at home, are rapidly changing. They are becoming more similar but also increasingly competitive rather than complementary. It is a change in which any previous "relationship with the soil," or with any other "givens" from the past for that matter, is disappearing.

So far, as suggested in Moen's (1982) perceptive comments, we are witnessing changes that people living in marriages and families must deal with by themselves. Hochschild's (1989) data, and those reported by others (cf. Popenoe, 1993), seem to show that many families are not doing this to their own satisfaction. Using a game analogy once again, the balance of power between players is coming closer to equal, the game process is becoming less stable, and the potential of all players to control collectively their joint fate is waning. No wonder, then, that "dissolution" is becoming institutionalized as a "game event" on the sociocultural level of marriage and family.

All this does not suggest, however, that the survival of all marriages and families is becoming an impossible or even an unlikely event. It is noticeable that survival strategies, such as tinkering, improvising, and innovating, increasingly are accepted as a normal aspect of marriage and family living. Even more basic challenges to the established wisdom of our past are entering the realm of current discourse about the aims and meanings of the societal arrangements of marriage and family. To give a still controversial example, the legalization of gay and lesbian unions no longer is seen as harmful by everyone to the survival of these institutions. To the contrary, it is becoming clear that their most important social functions lies in their ordering capacity, regardless of what form this "order" takes. Who will opt to participate in such arrangements is a contextual matter and, as such, depends on the needs and inclinations of those involved. In the societal domain of childcare—the family's main function—continuing social improvisation is leading to an array of forms, ranging from the use of nannies to a growing variety of daycare facilities (cf. Jones, Tepperman, & Wilson, 1995, Chapter 7).

The ethnographic information provided in Stacey's (1990) in-depth study of two "new" families in California's Silicon Valley adds valuable insight into the dynamics of such coping strategies. Her focused description of process details the lives of families that

> were supplying the electronics industry with workers who occupied very different income and status positions. A given household at any moment was likely to be composed of individuals with diverse employment, income, and mobility histories. Sex, age, and family status structured some of these variations, and the complexity and fluidity of class positions appeared to reflect the marital and occupational instability endemic to the area. (p. 30)

The Silicon Valley, parenthetically, has one of the highest marital failure rates among U.S. metropolitan areas (p. 25).

The members of the author's two "extended" family networks stubbornly tried to manage the contingencies of their uncertain social environment and demonstrated a willingness to innovate to protect their collective familial and marital interests:

> Parental divorce, Silicon Valley drug culture, and turbulent employment conditions contributed to a troubled adolescence for Lanny and Jimmy and to inauspicious class mobility prospects for them and Katie. On the other hand, the material and emotional resources of their divorce-extended family spared Pamela's children the most severe effects of the recent burst in the Silicon Valley bubble. All lived in housing provided or subsidized by their multiple parents or other house mates. All received periodic family aid in securing job training, employment referrals, and multiple forms of practical assistance. (p. 112)

These and other reported events echo negotiated arrangements—some contested, others not. They differ from those described in Hochschild's (1989) study because these families have fewer resources and alternatives in their dealings with a risky and often exploitative outside world. They are, however, far from passive in confronting it and one another.

The behavior of the people described in the foregoing, innovative as it may be, is not new. Marital and family processes—analogous to different rivers making their way to final destinations—remain variations on a common theme. Their dynamics do not differ qualitatively from those described decades ago by researchers such as Oscar Lewis and Carol Stack. The slum families depicted in Lewis' book *La Vida* (1966), for example, and the black family networks in

Stack's book *All Our Kin* (1974) equally show the will and ability to survive through improvisation, innovation, and the manipulation of family ties and networks. What *did* change during the past 30 years is the degree of risk associated with life in severely disadvantaged social settings. The proliferation of hard drugs and sophisticated firearms significantly raise the odds against the survival of families and their individual members (Anderson, 1990).

The kinship networks studied by Stack (1974) and Lewis (1966) existed under conditions of extreme poverty and social deprivation. As a social condition, poverty has not changed much over the years. It helps create settings and contingencies in which power, on the average, tends to be used more spontaneously and physically than in more affluent social environments. As Lewis reports:

> In the Rios family, uncontrolled rage, aggression, violence and even bloodshed are not uncommon; their extreme impulsivity affects the whole tenor of their lives.... Sex is used to satisfy a great variety of needs—for children, for pleasure, for money, for revenge, for love, to express machismo and to compensate for all the emptiness in their lives. Even family unity, one of the most sacred values in this family-oriented culture, is sometimes threatened by the danger of seduction by stepfathers, the sexual rivalry between sisters, between mothers and daughters, and occasionally between grandmothers and granddaughters.... The women in this book show more aggressiveness and a greater violence of language and behavior than the men.... In the Rios family it is the women who take the initiative in breaking up the marriages. They call the police during family quarrels and take their husbands into court for nonsupport of the children. Indeed, a great deal of aggressiveness of the women is directed against men. The women teach children to depend upon the mother and to distrust men. (pp. xxvi–xxvii)

Stack's observations are similar and also provide insight into the ways in which the potential for violence, and the perpetual scarcity that often underlies it, are countered:

> Black families in the Flats and the non-kin they regard as kin have evolved patterns of co-residence, kinship-based exchange networks linking multiple domestic units, elastic household boundaries, life-long bonds to three-generation households, social controls against the formation of marriages that could endanger the network of kin, the domestic authority of women, and limitations on the role of the husband or male friend within a woman's kin network. (p. 124)

Family tales, like those here, offer information and insights but, of course, no systematic basis for representative quantitative generalizations.

In a theoretical perspective—that of conflict—these studies do suggest, however, that the stability of process in marriages and families is associated with their potential to manage collectively conflicts of interest and the reciprocal use of power. In practice, this requires a willingness and ability to negotiate, compromise, and cooperate. It does *not* require either the suppression or the total avoidance of competitive confrontations or the exercise of power. To quote Foucault (1980) once more:

> In defining the effects of power as repression, one adopts a purely juridical conception of such power, one identifies power with a law which says no ... what makes power hold good, what makes it accepted, is simply the fact that it doesn't only weigh on us as a force that says no, but that it traverses and produces things, it induces pleasure, forms knowledge, produces discourse. (p. 119)

In small face-to-face networks, such as marriages and families, the use of power to control may be balanced by motives to protect the type of solidarity needed to cope and to survive.

People in families, as I see them, function as strategists rather than theorists. Their plans and designs aim first and foremost to ensure their day-to-day joint survival. Theories, in that context, at best serve as recipes and are evaluated primarily on how well they have worked so far. In the words of the French sociologist Bourdieu (1990),

> There is an enormous difference between trying to understand the nature of matrimonial relations between two families so as to get your son or daughter married off ... and trying to understand these relations so as to construct a theoretical model of them. (p. 60)

What "works" for given families depends very much on the resources that are available to them. Hochschild's families, for example, could afford survival strategies that were not only unavailable but also of little help to those described by Lewis. The more severe are the problems of joint survival, the more likely it seems that situation-specific or unique ties move to the foreground as potential means of support. Wiseman (1991), for example, reports in her study of the wives of alcoholics that "when the wife of an alcoholic seeks help, she must consider if the relationship between herself and any member of her family or that of her husband is good enough to ask for such assistance, and further if that member is the right person to handle such aid" (p. 178). Theories, as formulated and shared by academics, may not be directly relevant or adequate to serve as guideposts in the face of such emergencies.

Conclusion

A few final comments must suffice to bring this chapter to a close. They serve to clarify the logic of its procedure and to highlight out the main issues touched on in the text.

First, a comment on a comment. The editors of the *Sourcebook of Family Theories and Methods* (Boss et al., 1993) expressed a concern about what they saw as emerging "postpositive trends" in the field of family studies:

> The contemporary focus on language, meaning, and constructionism can blind scholars to the "objective" social forces affecting families. Societal structures of discrimination are not reducible to socially created constructs; we believe that they have an independent reality and influence beyond the construction processes of those in disadvantaged positions. (p. 18)

Because their concern is pertinent to the theoretical stance and the substantive focus of this chapter, it deserves a brief comment. This quote echoes the uneasy fusion of an ontological issue with an epistemological one. It is quite possible to imagine the presence of a real world, but to assume also that its final "truth" lies beyond the limits of human knowing. If so, this means that only language, in its many forms, is available as a vehicle for the sharing of ideas, reasoning, and explanations. Because Nature does not speak for herself, all *we* can do is talk and listen to each other and ourselves. The explanations we share with our fellows are "negotiated" ones, claims that, by necessity, remain open to reconsideration.

I agree that it makes analytic sense to act as if there are independent social forces that influence the fate of marriages, families, and the social institutions they represent. The conceptualization of such "causal forces," however, should go beyond simple categorizations such as, "sex, age, position in the socio-economic structure, ... race, and ethnicity" (Gelles, 1993, p. 31). This dismantling of a seemingly "objective" social structure into the purely operational categories cited here only leads to descriptions that may be of use to practitioners and family living. The pursuit of relevant explanations cannot remain confined to what can be seen and measured in various realms of human sociability. It should include what reasonably can be imagined to "exist" below its surface.

Given this point of view, a major concern of this chapter *is* the impact of "hidden" power structures on the institutional and interpersonal realities of marriage and family. Such "forces" initially may be recognized, not necessarily completely, by those whom they oppress. In fact, the cited studies by Hochschild, Stacey, Stack, and Lewis serve as a reminder of the Marxian adage that humans do create their history, but not under conditions of their own choosing.

Contemporary marriages and families, regardless of their many forms, create processes fashioned by asymmetric bonding and shifting power balances. Depicted metaphorically, their "streams" are a composite of currents marked by quiet flow, turbulence, or rapids that together move toward an ultimate, but not necessarily certain, destination. Considering the course of marriages and families in such a context, one wonders *why* their members, especially under conditions described by Stacey, Stack, and Lewis, bother to negotiate at all. Why do reasonable adults continue to beget and care for offspring under hazardous and uncertain conditions? Why do they, at times, also add the care of elderly parents, relatives, or outsiders to their reproductive overload? It is in response to the call of human instinct? Of tradition? Of outside pressure? Or of some combinations of such? At this writing, we do not know the answers. In fact, questions of this nature are not asked very often in family studies.

Some of the sources cited in this chapter, each in its own way, bear witness that outside power sources invade and become integral components of marriage and family living. How this happens is an open question because the reciprocity between "modernity" and its many institutional forms remains poorly understood. Beck (1992), for one, comments that it is becoming fashionable to attach the prefix "post" to emerging social arrangements that confuse us. The formula "past-plus-post" then offers a way to camouflage a puzzling encounter with a reality that, on the fact of it, seems to have lost its bearings (p. 12). He proposes the concept of "risk society" to describe a new "modernity" that is emerging from within the contours of classical industrial society (p. 13). To elaborate on this provocative idea would lead beyond the scope of this chapter, but the recognition of "risk" as a fundamental attribute of contemporary society is very much in line with this chapter's theoretical approach.

In their remarkable book, *Order out of Chaos* (1984), Prigogine and Stengers reach back to the wisdom of an old Talmudic text:

> "Let's hope it works" ... exclaimed God as he created the World, and this hope, which has accompanied all the subsequent history of the world and humankind, has emphasized right from the outset that this history is branded with the mark of radical uncertainty. (p. 313)

It is this uncertainty and the many contingencies it brings with it that permeate the social environment of current marriages and families. Spouses and successive generations will have to learn to live with it, now and in years to come.

It bears repeating, at this point, that the distinction between the "in" and the "out" of marriages and families is a conceptual one. If unduly reified it creates the image of two interrelated but separate worlds, while in reality there is only one. A brief look at the world of nonhuman creatures underlines this important point. Tropical oceans are the home of tiny jellyfish, whose bodies consist of about 75% ocean water. They seem fragments of the sea around them. Other small polyps, by extracting matter from the sea, help build the coral reefs that, long after their "founders" are gone, continue to exist as dominant ecosystems. Would it be helpful, analytically, to view human families as "fragments" of their sociocultural environments? If so, which polyp species would offer the most appropriate analogy—the drifting jellyfish or the coral builders? In fact, it is irrelevant which one we

select as long as our analysis remains focused on how and why the "external" becomes an integral component of any process under consideration. Despite vast disparities, the interiors of small ocean creatures and those of human families do share one basic trait. Their boundaries connect them with, rather than just separate them from, their respective environments.

Let me end with a look at the institutional realms of marriage and family first with an observation and then with a suggestion. Past and even recent social changes did not "liberate" either female or male spouses, let alone their minor children. So far, they only set them adrift in a societal process from which many traditional props and guideposts are disappearing. During this transition the social "games" of marriage and family have been allowed to evolve into increasingly competitive arrangements. Traditionally, students of marriage and family perceived this kind of change as linear, that is, more or less continuous and somehow proportional to the impact of events in and around its course. If perceived as "constructive" or "functional" its outcome was, and still is, seen as a reconstructed equilibrium of sorts. These "roller coaster" models (cf. Hill, 1949; Boss, 1987), useful as they were in the past, no longer suffice. They should be augmented and eventually replaced by perceptions of change, macro as well as micro, derived from current "chaos" theorizing. In that perspective sociocultural change, as a process, moves along a path characterized by orderly disorder. Its course and final outcomes are quite sensitive to initial system states but are not necessarily continuous or predictable.

On the institutional level of marriage and family, this calls up a picture of reproductive and caring–giving social forms that increasingly incorporate and *depend* on realistic types of dissolution. Moreover, this institutional order may well derive its strength and durability from sanctioning intimate bonding between adults regardless of gender or age. In a similar vein, it may require—rather than just allow—a range of different rule-governed parenting practices. To grasp the realities of such changes, consider in the realm of physics the phase transitions through which a solid substance becomes a fluid, and ultimately a gas. Ice can be seen as a "frozen process," one in which the ties between the molecules are rigid in the extreme. Living systems may approach this phase but could not survive for long as such. When ice melts it changes to water, a flowing state, and it becomes an orderly process. The relations between molecules obey rules but are "capable of behavior so rich and unpredictable that it constantly flirts with becoming unfathomably intricate, or chaotic" (Johnson, 1995, p. 279). Finally, as steam, all traces of rigidity are vaporized into a seeming randomness of movement. The observed "complexity" in most marriages and families is analogous to that of a fluid state of affairs in which behavior that is varied and unpredictable must be considered "normal" rather than "surprising." On the institutional level, such a condition of fluidity not merely allows but also depends on a multitude of social and cultural alternatives.

Under such conditions, individual spouses, couples, and their networks must learn to be sufficiently committed and knowledgeable to survive and prosper on what some scholars call "the edge of chaos" (Kauffman, 1995). Whether they will succeed in doing this remains to be seen. Paraphrasing the words of Prigogine and Stenger's God, "Let's hope they will."

References

Ahrons, C. R., & Rogers, R. C. (1987). *Divorced families*. New York: Norton.

Alexander, J. C. (1987). *Twenty lectures: Sociological theory since World War II*. New York: Columbia University Press.

Amato, P. R. (1993). Children's adjustment to divorce: Theories, hypotheses, and empirical support. *Journal of Marriage and the Family, 55*, 23–39.

Ambert, A. (1989). *Ex-spouses and new spouses: A study of relationships*. Greenwich, CT: JAI Press.

Ambert, A., Adler, P. A., Adler, P., & Detzner, D. F. (1995). Understanding and evaluating qualitative research. *Journal of Marriage and the Family, 57*, 879–893.

Anderson, E. (1990). *Streetwise: Race, class, and change in an urban community*. Chicago: University of Chicago Press.

Barash, D. P. (1982). *Sociobiology and behavior* (2nd ed.). New York: Elsevier.

Beck, U. (1992). *Risk society: Towards a new modernity*. Newbury Park, CA: Sage.

Benthem van den Bergh, G. (1971). *The structure of development: An invitation to the sociology of Norbert Elias*. Den Haag, Netherlands: Institute of Social Studies.

Bhaskar, R. (1989). *Reclaiming reality*. London: Verso.

Blumstein, P., & Schwartz, P. (1983). *American couples: Money, work, sex*. New York: Morrow.

Booth, A., & Amato, P. R. (1994). Parental marital quality, parental divorce, and relations with parents. *Journal of Marriage and the Family, 56*, 21–34.

Boss, P. G. (1987). Family stress. In M. B. Sussman & S. K. Steinmetz (Eds.), *Handbook of marriage and the family* (pp. 695–723). New York: Plenum.

Boss, P. G., Doherty, W. J., LaRossa, R., Schumm, W. R., & Steinmetz, S. K. (Eds.). (1993). *Sourcebook of family theories and methods: A contextual approach*. New York: Plenum.

Bourdieu, P. (1990). *The logic of practice*. Stanford, CA: Stanford University Press.

Broderick, C. B. (1990). Family process theory. In J. Sprey (Ed.), *Fashioning Family Theory* (pp. 171–206). Newbury Park, CA: Sage.

Broderick, C. B. (1993). *Understanding family process*. Newbury Park, CA: Sage.

Casti, J. L. (1995). *Complexification*. New York: Harper Perennial.

Cherlin, A. J. (1992). *Marriage, divorce, remarriage* (rev., enlarged ed.). Cambridge, MA: Harvard University Press.

Davies, P., & Gribbin, J. (1992). *The matter myth: Beyond chaos and complexity*. London: Penguin.

Demo, D. H. (1993). The relentless search for effects of divorce: Forging new trails or tumbling down the beaten path. *Journal of Marriage and the Family, 55*, 42–46.

Elias, N. (1978). *What is sociology?* New York: Columbia University Press.

Elias, N. (1984). Knowledge and power. In N. Stehr & V. Meja (Eds.), *Society and knowledge* (pp. 259–291). New Brunswick, NJ: Transaction.

Farrington, K., & Chertok, E. (1993). Social conflict theories of the family. In P. G. Boss, W. J. Doherty, R. LaRossa, W. R. Schumm, & S. K. Steinmetz (Eds.), *Sourcebook of family theories and methods* (pp. 357–381). New York: Plenum.

Flanzer, J. P. (1993). Alcohol and other drugs are key causal agents of violence. In R. J. Gelles & D. R. Loseke (Eds.), *Current controversies on family violence* (pp. 171–181). Newbury Park, CA: Sage.

Foucault, M. (1980). *Power/knowledge: Selected interviews & other writings 1972–1977* (C. Gordon, Ed.). New York: Pantheon.

Foucault, M. (1983). The subject and power. In H. L. Dreyfus & P. Rabinow (Eds.), *Michel Foucault: Beyond structuralism and hermeneutics* (pp. 208–226). Chicago: University of Chicago Press.

Friedan, B. (1963). *The feminine mystique*. New York: Dell.

Ganong, L., Coleman, M., & Mistina, D. (1995). Home is where they have to let you in: Beliefs regarding physical custody changes of children following divorce. *Family Issues, 16*, 466–487.

Gelles, R. J. (1993). Through a sociological lens: Social structure and family violence. In R. J. Gelles & D. R. Loseke (Eds.), *Current controversies on family violence* (pp. 31–46). Newbury Park, CA: Sage.

Gelles, R. J., & Conte, J. R. (1991). Domestic violence and sexual abuse of children: A review of research in the eighties. In A. Booth (Ed.), *Contemporary families*. Minneapolis, MN: National Council on Family Relations.

Gelles, R. J., & Straus, M. A. (1988). *Intimate violence*. New York: Simon & Schuster.

Glass, L., & Mackey, M. C. (1988). *From clocks to chaos*. Princeton, NJ: Princeton University Press.

Goffman, E. (1959). *The presentation of self in everyday life*. New York: Doubleday.

Gottman, J. M. (1994). *What predicts divorce? The relationship between marital processes and marital outcomes*. Hillsdale, NJ: Erlbaum.

Gottman, J. M. (1995). The dissolution of the American family. In W. J. O'Neill, Jr. (Ed.), *Family: The first imperative* (pp. 103–115). Cleveland, OH: The William J. & Dorothy K. O'Neill Foundation.

Hansen, S. L. (1993). Review of *Embattled Paradise: The American family in an age of uncertainty*, by Arlene Skolnick. *Journal of Marriage and the Family, 55*, 244.

Hartsock, N. C. M. (1985). *Money, sex, and power*. Boston: Northeastern University Press.

Hill, R. (1949). *Families under stress*. New York: Harper & Row.

Hill, R. (1965). Generic features of families under stress. In H. J. Parad (Ed.), *Crisis intervention* (pp. 32–52). New York: Family Service Association of America.

Hochschild, A. (1989). *The second shift: working parents and the revolution at home*. New York: Viking Penguin.

Johnson, C. (1988). *Ex familia: Colleen Leahy Johnson*. New Brunswick, NJ: Rutgers University Press.

Johnson, G. (1995). *Fire in the mind; science, faith, and the search for order*. New York: Knopf.

Johnson, M. P. (1995). Patriarchal terrorism and common couple violence: Two forms of violence against women. *Journal of Marriage and the Family, 57*, 283–295.

Jones, C. L., Tepperman, L., & Wilson, S. J. (1995). *The futures of the family*. Englewood Cliffs, NJ: Prentice-Hall.

Kantor, D., & Lehr, W. (1975). *Inside the family: Toward a theory of family process*. San Francisco: Jossey-Bass.

Kauffman, S. (1995). *At home in the universe.* New York: Oxford University Press.

Kellert, S. H. (1993). *In the wake of chaos.* Chicago: University of Chicago Press.

Kitson, G. C., & Holmes, W. A. (1992). *Portrait of divorce.* New York: Guilford.

LaRossa, R. (1977). *Conflict and power in marriage.* Newbury Park, CA: Sage.

LaRossa, R., & LaRossa, M. M. (1981). *Transition of parenthood: How infants change families.* Newbury Park, CA: Sage.

Laudan, L. (1977). *Progress and its problems; towards a theory of scientific growth.* Berkeley: University of California Press.

Lewis, O. (1966). *La vida. A Puerto Rican family in the culture of poverty— San Juan and New York.* New York: Random House.

Lie, G., & Gentlewainer, S. (1991). Intimate violence in lesbian relationships: Discussion of survey findings and practice implications. *Journal of Social Service Research, 15,* 41–59.

Lukes, S. (1978). Power and authority. In T. Bottomore & R. Nisbet (Eds.), *A history of sociological analysis* (pp. 633–676). London: Heineman.

Marx, K. (1973). *Grundrisse.* London: Penguin.

Matthews, S. H., & Sprey, J. (1984). The impact of divorce on grandparenthood: An exploratory study. *The Gerontologist, 24,* 41–47.

Miller, J. G. (1978). *Living systems.* New York: McGraw-Hill.

Moen, P. (1982). The two-provider family: Problems and potentials. In M. E. Lamb (Ed.), *Nontraditional families: Parenting and child development* (pp. 13–43). Hillsdale, NJ: Erlbaum.

Molm, L. D., Quist, T. M., & Wisely, P. A. (1994). Imbalanced structures, unfair strategies: Power and justice in social exchange. *American Sociological Review, 59,* 98–121.

Popenoe, D. (1993). American family decline, 1960–1990: A review and appraisal. *Journal of Marriage and the Family, 55,* 527–542.

Prigogine, I., & Stengers, I. (1984). *Order out of chaos.* Boulder, CO: New Science Library.

Rainwater, L. (1960). *And the poor get children.* Chicago: Quadrangle Books.

Renzetti, C. M. (1992). *Violent betrayal: Partner abuse in lesbian relationships.* Newbury Park, CA: Sage.

Robertson, A. F. (1991). *Beyond the family.* Berkeley: University of California Press.

Rorty, A. O. (1992). Power and powers. In T. E. Wartenberg (Ed.), *Rethinking power* (pp. 1–13). Albany: State University of New York Press.

Rosaldo, M. Z. (1980). *Knowledge and passion: Ilongot notions of self and social life.* New York: Cambridge University Press.

Sabatelli, R. M., & Shehan, C. L. (1993). Exchange and resource theories. In P. G. Boss, W. J. Doherty, R. LaRossa, W. R. Schumm, & S. K. Steinmetz (Eds.), *Sourcebook of family theories and methods: A contextual approach* (pp. 385–411). New York: Plenum.

Segalen, M. (1983). *Love and power in the peasant family.* Chicago: University of Chicago Press.

Simmel, G. (1959). How is society possible? In K. H. Wolff (Ed.), *Essays on sociology, philosophy and aesthetics* (pp. 337–356). New York: Harper Torchbooks.

Skolnick, A. (1991). *Embattled paradise: The American family in an age of uncertainty.* New York: Basic Books.

Sprey, J. (1979). Conflict theory and the study of marriage and the family. In W. R. Burr, R. Hill, F. I. Nye, & I. L. Reiss (Eds.), *Contemporary theories about the family* (pp. 130–159). New York: Free Press.

Sprey, J. (1988). Sociobiology and the study of family conflict. In E. E. Filsinger (Ed.), *Biosocial perspectives on the family* (pp. 137–158). Newbury Park, CA: Sage.

Sprey, J. (1990). Theoretical practice in family studies. In J. Sprey (Ed.), *Fashioning family theory* (pp. 9–33). Newbury Park, CA: Sage.

Sprey, J. (1991). Studying adult children and their parents. In S. P. Pfeifer & M. B. Sussman (Eds.), *Families: Intergenerational and generational connections* (pp. 221–235). Binghamton, NY: Haworth.

Sprey, J. (1995). Explanatory practice in family studies. *Journal of Marriage and the Family, 57,* 867–878.

Stacey, J. (1990). *Brave new families.* New York: Basic Books.

Stack, C. B. (1974). *All our kin.* New York: Harper & Row.

Steinmetz, S. K. (1987). Family violence: Past, present, future. In M. B. Sussman & S. K. Steinmetz (Eds.), *Handbook of marriage and the family* (pp. 725–765). New York: Plenum.

Straus, M. A. (1993). Physical assaults by wives: A major social problem. In R. J. Gelles & D. R. Loseke (Eds.), *Current controversies on family violence* (pp. 67–87). Newbury Park, CA: Sage.

Sussman, M. B., & Steinmetz, S. K. (Eds.). (1987). *Handbook of marriage and the family.* New York: Plenum.

Szinovacz, M. (1987). Family power. In M. B. Sussman & S. K. Steinmetz (Eds.), *Handbook of marriage and the family* (pp. 651–693). New York: Plenum.

Vaughan, D. (1986). *Uncoupling.* New York: Oxford University Press.

Ward, M. (1995). Butterflies and bifurcations: Can chaos theory contribute to our understanding of family systems? *Journal of Marriage and the Family, 57,* 629–639.

Whitchurch, G. G., & Constantine, L. L. (1993). Systems theory. In P. G. Boss, W. J. Doherty, R. LaRossa, W. R. Schumm, & S. K. Steinmetz (Eds.), *Sourcebook of family theories and methods: A contextual approach* (pp. 329–352). New York: Plenum.

Wilson, E. O. (1978). *On human nature.* Cambridge, MA: Harvard University Press.

Wilson, J. W. (1983). *Social theory.* Englewood Cliffs, NJ: Prentice-Hall.

Wiseman, J. P. (1991). *The other half. Wives of alcoholics and their social-psychological situation.* New York: Aldine de Gruyter.

Wittgenstein, L. (1958). *The blue and brown books.* New York: Harper Torchbooks.

Zinn, M. B., & Eitzen, D. S. (1993). *Diversity in families* (3rd ed.). New York: HarperCollins.

CHAPTER 25

Family Communication

Gail G. Whitchurch and Fran C. Dickson

Introduction

This chapter provides an overview of a communication approach to families and highlights how this approach enriches overall understanding of micro-level family processes. We draw mainly from the communication discipline because, although scholarship on families with a communication approach occurs in a number of disciplines, it is often situated in the family communication specialty area of the communication discipline. Therefore, our overarching goal is to increase understanding of how family communication specialists in the communication discipline conceptualize and research communication patterns within the family.

First, we present a historical and topical overview of the communication discipline. Second, we trace the study of families in the communication discipline with focus on the theoretical heritage of this specialty area. Third, we present seven assumptions made about families when a communication approach is taken. Fourth, a discussion of family communication research and pedagogy milestones is presented to give an overview of basic and applied research in family communication. Finally, we conclude with a chapter summary and a discussion of future directions in family communication.

We are using the phrase *communication approach* to refer to a way of looking at families that entails three characteristics of seeking knowledge: ways of defining a family, focus, and the primary purpose for attention to communication and families. The first of these characteristics means that from a communication approach, a family is defined through

its communication—both verbal and nonverbal*—rather than solely through biological or legal kinship, as would be the case with a structural approach to families. In other words, when a communication approach is taken, it is axiomatic that a family unit† constitutes itself through a process in which people differentiate themselves from nonfamily members by interacting together as a family, thereby constructing a definition of themselves as "family."

With a communication approach, defining *family* structurally by biological or legal kinship ties also is accepted; however, this definition is expanded to include family units and subunits that are constructed only through interaction, such as foster children or long-time friends who are considered to "be family," unmarried couples who view themselves as committed partners, and other fictive kin. The axiom that family units and subunits are constructed through interaction and/or through structure is central to a communication approach to families.

This approach also differs dramatically from that of family scholars who take "communication" to be a variable to be measured along with other indicators of family functioning. That is, rather than viewing communication as a central process through which people construct and maintain

Gail G. Whitchurch • Department of Communication Studies, Indiana University–Purdue University at Indianapolis, Indianapolis, Indiana 46202.
Fran C. Dickson • Department of Human Communication Studies, University of Denver, Denver, Colorado 80208.

Handbook of Marriage and the Family, 2nd edition, edited by Marvin Sussman, Suzanne K. Steinmetz, and Gary W. Peterson. Plenum Press, New York, 1999.

*Research from a communication perspective takes a very broad view of what is meant by the terms *verbal communication* and especially *nonverbal communication*. Whereas verbal communication is considered to be the language (i.e., a shared symbol system) only, nonverbal communication often is taken to include all other forms of communication, even if they are unintentional (see Watzlawick, Beavin, & Jackson, 1967, for a discussion). This would include, but is not limited to, communication behaviors such as hand gestures and other body movements, eye contact and lack of contact, use of time (i.e., chronemics), aspects of physical appearance such as items of apparel (i.e., artifactual communication) and body shape, and paralinguistic cues made with the vocal cords, such as "hmmm" and "uh."
†The terms *family unit* and *family subunit* are used instead of the analogous, and more commonly used, terms *family system* and *family subsystem*. This is to avoid the possible implicaction that in this chapter a systems theory approach is emphasized over other theories.

themselves as a family, the *communication as a variable* approach treats communication as just one determinant of how well a family functions. For example, communication is just one dimension that contributes to overall marital satisfaction in Spanier's (1979) Dyadic Adjustment Scale. More recently, in a study of gender and conflict in marriage, Heavey, Layne, and Christensen (1993) studied pairs of spouses' demand–withdrawal patterns of communication as predictors of overall marital satisfaction. Both of these studies conceptualize communication as one aspect of marital functioning, rather than as the central focus of the research.

The second characteristic of a communication approach to families is that families are studied at the micro level: one or a few family units, family dyads (e.g., spouse/spouse, parent/dependent child, aging parent/adult child, or grandparent/grandchild), or larger family subunits (e.g., stepparent/stepchildren, child/biological parents/stepparents, or all the siblings in a family). That is, a communication approach to families does not focus on individual family members in isolation from other family members, nor does it focus on large numbers of family units at the macro level.

Third and finally, as we are using the term here, a communication approach is different from approaches to communication and families that are primarily intended to facilitate practice. For example, the term *family communication* carries heavy emphasis on communication skills training for many therapists (e.g., O'Donohue & Crouch, 1996; Williams & Jurich, 1995) and family life educators (e.g., Duncan & Brown, 1992; Kieren & Doherty-Poirier, 1993; Smith & Hawes, 1987). Although certainly family life education, couple/family therapy, and clinical social work are examples of disciplinary specialties that also have strong interest areas in communication and families, the literature from these disciplines often has as its primary purpose the providing of direct services with families in the form of training and/or therapy. Because therapy- and other intervention-oriented literature are not typically conducted by communication scholars, it is not emphasized in this chapter (see Chapter 28, by Kaslow and colleagues, on family therapy in this volume).

Scholarship Related to Families in the Communication Discipline: An Overview

The communication discipline has its most distant origins in more than 2000 years of the rhetorical tradition, even though the ancient Greek and Roman thinkers were not often aware that they were studying communication (Schramm, 1997). Even with its ancient origins, however, the modern communication discipline "is a New World discipline"; that is, with much of the discipline developed rapidly during U.S.

westward migration, as "people sought to better their lives through improved communication skills" (Osborn, 1990, p. B2). The modern communication discipline includes both rhetorical and social science traditions (with the latter rooted mostly in the twentieth century) and a variety of specializations (e.g., Anderson, Birkhead, Eason, & Strine, 1988; Delia, 1987). These specializations range widely in focus from areas such as interpersonal communication by one or two communicators to communication in small group, organizational, public, and mass communication contexts. Despite this variety, both the rhetorical and the social science traditions of the discipline share a common emphasis on the construction of meaning through the exchange of messages.

In the modern communication discipline, currently there are three major groups of communication discipline scholars who study families, described more fully later in this section: mass communication, interpersonal communication, and family communication. Each is located in a different specialty area of the discipline with widely varying guiding paradigms, theories, and methodologies. Although it might appear that either interpersonal communication or family communication would be a subcategory of the other, the roots in the communication discipline and the ways of studying families in these two specialty areas are actually quite different (as will be discussed later). Further, the contrast of the mass communication specialty area with the other two specialties is even greater than they have with each other.

The dissimilarity is so extensive because the literature based on mass communication and families and the literature on face-to-face interaction in family units and subunits have developed almost completely separately from one another. The origins of this separation are complex and occurred mainly because of the ways the communication discipline developed historically, rather than for philosophical reasons (Fitzpatrick & Ritchie, 1993; Meadowcroft & Fitzpatrick, 1988; Reardon & Rogers, 1988). The separation occurred primarily because, although all three areas are primarily based in the social science tradition of the discipline, mass communication historically was guided by a different set of assumptions about the nature of communication than the other two, as is discussed further in the subsection on mass communication later in this chapter. The study of mass media is often separated from the study of face-to-face interaction because its channels are mediated rather than direct, the potential number of message recipients is very large, and feedback to the messages is minimal (Reardon & Rogers, 1988).

In contrast, interpersonal communication specialists and family communication specialists are among communication discipline scholars who study face-to-face interaction. Their view of communication is that it is a central *process* in relationships; that is, communication is transactive (i.e., mutual, simultaneous, and ongoing), dynamic, and unique (Miller & Nicholson, 1976). Therefore, they use the term *communication* to denote this process, eschewing the term "communications." The term *communication* emphasizes the conceptualization of the nature of communication as a dynamic, ongoing process of communica*ting*, rather than as an exchange of communications, which, in this view, is a narrow term that is synonymous with the word "messages."

Scholarship Related to Families in the Communication Discipline: The Mass Communication Specialty Area

The mass communication specialty area is generally considered not to be part of the family communication specialty area. Therefore, only a brief sketch of this specialty area is included in this chapter, but see Bryant and Zillman (1986) and Bryant (1990) for further discussion of these and other topics related to the study of mass communication, children, and families.

In addition to the reasons enumerated earlier, one of the chief reasons for the differentiation of mass communication from interpersonal communication and from family communication is that literature on mass communication in general traditionally has usually been guided by a mechanistic perspective on communication (Fisher, 1978), with less influence from the meaning-centered interactional perspective and the communication behavior-focused pragmatic perspective (Fisher, 1978) that influence the other two specialty areas. (However, an increasing number of communication scholars who study family interaction and mass communication are influenced by symbolic interaction theory, especially with respect to the influence of family viewing of television on processes by which families create their social reality; Alexander, 1990.)

The mechanistic perspective emphasizes fidelity of messages that have been transmitted and then received through mediated channels (e.g., radio or television), rather than the simultaneous sending/receiving of messages that occurs during the process of face-to-face interaction. Given the focus on fidelity of mediated message transmission and reception emphasized in the mechanistic perspective, it is not surprising that the immense majority of research related to families in the mass communication specialty area of the communication discipline involves television *and* families and/or children. Examples include portrayals of the family on television (e.g., Heintz, 1992; Pingree & Thompson, 1990; Skill, Wallace, & Cassata, 1990); families' and family dyads' social uses of television (e.g., Brown, Childers, Bauman, & Koch, 1990); and media effects on families and family members, especially children (e.g., Austin, Roberts, & Nass, 1990).

One particularly influential line of research related to mass communication and families is the Family Communication Patterns (FCP) model (McLeod & Chaffee, 1972), which assumes that the communication environment of the family influences both children's socialization and their perceptions of reality. The FCP and the research it generated conceptualize families in terms of two kinds of family values and interactional styles that are thought to influence power and communication patterns. The socio-orientation examines obedience and harmony to determine the degree of conformity. The concept-orientation examines self-reliance. The two interactional styles are sometimes combined to form four family types: protective families (emphasize perceived agreement and respect for elders); pluralistic families (value the discussion of ideas over interpersonal harmony); consensual families (emphasize both harmony and idea exchange); and laissez-faire families (emphasize neither harmony nor idea exchange).

Even so, there is some mass communication literature on family interaction. The two areas of research that are most fully developed to date are studies of the family viewing situation, especially coviewing of programs (i.e., interaction during television viewing), and kinds of interaction that occur with respect to media. Alexander (1990) categorizes the latter into four areas. The areas are (1) control (i.e., how parents influence their children's viewing of television); (2) how family members, especially parents, influence the interpretation or evaluation of program content; (3) how television contributes to maintaining the family system by generating family interaction about programs watched; and (4) the impact on the family by television in the culture at large.

Scholarship Related to Families in the Communication Discipline: The Interpersonal Communication Specialty Area

The specialty area of interpersonal communication has evolved and changed greatly over the years. Initially, scholars borrowed terms and concepts from the mechanistic model (e.g., Berlo, 1960; Shannon & Weaver, 1949) for the early work in theory-building on face-to-face interaction that was burgeoning during the 1960s. That is, communication was conceptualized as, initially the one-way and subsequently as the two-way, sending and receiving of messages. This is in contrast with what is now termed a transactional or *transactive* view (Barnlund, 1970; Mortensen, 1972). The transactive view of communication, which now predominates in the discipline specialty areas where face-to-face interaction is studied, conceptualizes communication between dyad members as a constant, changing process in which the participants are mutually and simultaneously adapting their communication to that of the other member. Although this transactive conceptualization can seem simplistic in contemporary times, it was, and is, very important to the discipline of communication because it has profoundly changed the way in which scholars view the construction of social meaning through interaction with others.

Although both the interpersonal communication and the family communication specialty areas of the communication discipline view communication as a transactive process, there are identifiable differences between the two areas and between the kinds of research conducted by scholars in each area. Even so, these should be taken as general organizing categories rather than as rigid divisions; further, there is some overlap between the two specialty areas in that a few communication scholars publish in both specialty areas.

Interpersonal communication scholars' primary focus is on constructs such as compliance-gaining, uncertainty reduction, and self-disclosure, and on examining how those specific constructs operate in a variety of contexts, such as friendship, stranger, or family dyads. In other words, in interpersonal communication research the interpersonal communication construct is the central focus of the research, and families and family dyads are just one context in which the construct of interest can be examined. For example, Stafford has conducted programmatic research on the construct of conversational memory (e.g., Stafford & Daly, 1994; Stafford, Waldron, & Infield, 1989), also studying this construct in the context of marriage (e.g., Stafford, Burggraf, & Sharkey, 1987). Similarly, Canary has studied argument structures in both decision-making groups (Canary, Brossmann, & Seibold, 1987) and marriage (Canary, Weger, & Stafford, 1991). Sometimes comparisons of interpersonal communication constructs are made between family dyads and other kinds of dyads within the same study (e.g., Fitzpatrick & Dindia, 1986).

The focus of interpersonal communication scholars who study interpersonal communication in families is on various family dyads (i.e., as compared to research on entire family units). The marital dyad has received considerably more attention than other family dyads such as sibling dyads or even the parent–dependent child dyad. In fact, Knapp (1993) notes that this situation reflects the interpersonal communication literature in general, which has focused largely on interacting adults.

As noted earlier, the communication construct of interest takes precedence in interpersonal communication research related to family dyads. Constructs that have been studied include similarity and attraction in marriage (e.g., Burleson & Denton, 1992), compliance-gaining (e.g., Witteman & Fitzpatrick, 1986), conflict (e.g., Sillars, Pike, Jones, & Redmon, 1983), understanding (e.g., Sillars, Pike, Jones, & Murphy, 1984), self-disclosure (e.g, Petronio, 1991), conver-

sational complaints (e.g., Alberts, 1988), and conversational memory (Sillars, Weisberg, Burggraf, & Zeitlow, 1990; Stafford, Burggraf, & Sharkey, 1987).

An example of one of these areas of interpersonal communication research on marriage is that of the relationship of communication, understanding, and marital satisfaction. For example, interpersonal communication researchers such as Pike and Sillars (1985) found that couples who described themselves as dissatisfied with their marriages reciprocated more negative nonverbal affect (e.g., paralinguistic cues that included vocal tones indicating coldness, sarcasm, impatience, blaming) than did satisfied couples. Interestingly, when satisfied and dissatisfied couples were compared with respect to verbal communication and salience of conflict issues, dissatisfied couples actually had less negative reciprocity than did satisfied couples. The affect of satisfied couples was fairly consistent regardless of whether the conflict issue was salient or nonsalient; this finding could indicate that satisfied couples do not allow conflict to escalate.

In the literature on interpersonal communication and children, there is a tendency to focus on the individual (e.g., children's language acquisition and children's communication competence). Even so, one contribution of a communication perspective on families to the literature on children and communication is gradual movement toward studying the child as situated in a parent–child dyad (Stafford & Bayer, 1993). For example, scholars studying families from a communication perspective have begun to do research on such areas as children in interaction with their parent(s).

Scholarship Related to Families in the Communication Discipline: The Family Communication Specialty Area

For family communication specialists, the family is the central organizing construct of study, not a context for communication. In other words, family communication researchers are equally interested in how the family interacts, and in communication constructs; family communication researchers generally do not compare families to other kinds of social units. To reiterate, it is this orientation that differentiates interpersonal communication scholars from family communication scholars.

The family communication specialty area is considerably "younger" than both the mass communication and interpersonal communication specialty areas. For example, the interest group on family communication in the National Communication Association professional organization was founded as recently as 1989 (Whitchurch, 1993) and became large enough to become a division in 1995—the Family Communication Division.

In the 1990s, the term *family communication* in the communication discipline has come to refer generally to communication scholarship on family units and its various subunits. In addition to their focus on families as a central organizing concept, family communication specialists share a recognition that families have idiosyncratic characteristics that have no corollary in nonfamilial interpersonal communication or in ad hoc or standing small groups.* Thus, most communication scholars who define themselves as family communication specialists accept parent–child communication, sibling communication, marital communication, and family interaction and mass communication as being part of *family communication*. However, the reciprocal often is not the case; that is, not all communication scholars who specialize in studying communication and marriages or children, or in studying mass communication and families, would consider themselves also to be family communication scholars.

Theoretical Heritage of the Family Communication Specialty Area

Many, if not most, family communication specialists have a systems theory worldview. This worldview often is combined with one or both of two general perspectives on communication (i.e., ways of understanding communication; Fisher, 1978): the interactional perspective and the pragmatic perspective.

The first of these, the interactional perspective, focuses on the communicator as performing a role; accordingly, communication is viewed as a dialogue (as compared to a monologue) that facilitates the role-taking that is the locus of the perspective (Fisher, 1978). When this perspective guides family communication research, research on families and marriages has a theoretical heritage grounded in the pioneering work of the sociologist and symbolic interaction theorist Ernest W. Burgess. The primary reason for this theoretical heritage is that Burgess was the first to define the family in terms of its interaction: "a unity of interacting personalities," by which he meant a family as a living, changing, growing thing, "a unity of interacting persons," rather than "a mere collection of individuals" (Burgess, 1926, p. 5). Thus, Burgess was a catalyst for shifting focus from studying the family as an institution to conceptualizing the family as a unit created and maintained by its interaction.

Although Burgess proposed his definition of the family

in 1926, no data-based research using this definition had been conducted until Gerald Handel and Robert Hess undertook such a study in the early 1950s (Handel, 1994). In 1959, Hess and Handel published the first in-depth empirical study of family internal dynamics, a qualitative study of the family based on Burgess' definition. Hess and Handel's *Family Worlds* (1959) was arguably the first data-based work to study the family as a unit that constructs its reality through its interaction, departing from the psychological or psychiatric assessment of individual family members that had characterized much of earlier research on family interiors. Key findings were five essential processes of family life that are common to all families, regardless of structure: establishing a pattern of separateness and connectedness, establishing satisfactory congruence of images, evolving family themes, establishing the boundaries of the family's world of experience, and dealing with significant biosocial issues such as gender and age of family members.

Other theoretical cornerstones of the family communication specialty area include Berger and Kellner's classic (1964) article on marriage, and Kantor and Lehr's (1975) *Inside the Family*, which examined intrafamilial interaction to identify three* family types: closed families (which function predictably with fixed boundaries, emphasize authority, family values, and moderation, and prefer predictability in scheduling and planning); open families (which prefer flexible scheduling and extrafamilial boundaries and use persuasion rather than coercion to address family conflicts); and random families (which behave unpredictably with very permeable boundaries for both family members and outsiders, and spend time and energy irregularly because spontaneity is highly valued). As with the Hess and Handel (1959) study before it, in the Kantor and Lehr study separateness/connectedness and boundaries were found to be particularly important.

The second general perspective on communication that is influential in family communication, the pragmatic perspective, is outlined in the model of human communication described in the classic work *Pragmatics of Human Communication* (Watzlawick, Beavin, & Jackson, 1967). Essentially, the pragmatic perspective "concentrates on the behavior of the communicator as the fundamental component of human communication" rather than on the outcome or effect of a communicative act (Fisher, 1978, p. 195).

This perspective is an important source of theoretical guidance for both family communication and family therapy (Whitchurch & Rogers, 1993). Generally termed the Palo Alto Model in the communication discipline (Communica-

---

*Some early researchers attempted to extrapolate small group theories and findings to families. For example, findings about role differentiation from early reserach on small groups were extrapolated to families, most notably by Parsons and Bales (1955). However, by the early 1970s it was apparent that studies of families rarely produce results consistent with those of ad hoc small groups (Bochner, 1976). Most family scientists have now come to believe that the unique properties of a family differentiate them from any other small group (Whitchurch & Constantine, 1993).

*Constantine postulated a fourth family paradigm: synchronous-type families, which are thought to develop a consentience (nonintellectual sense of unity to avoid conflict), in which family members remain uninvolved, even disconnected, with one another, while maintaining relatively rigid behavior patterns (Constantine, 1986; Constantine & Israel, 1985).

tion School and similar terms in the family therapy discipline), the pragmatic perspective draws from four theory bases (Wilder, 1979): cybernetics/General Systems Theory/ information theory, the Theory of Logical Types (Whitehead & Russell, 1910–1913), mathematical Group Theory, and a "rules" orientation to communication behavior. Of these four theory bases, systems/cybernetics/information theory is particularly influential on the Palo Alto model of human communication.

All micro-level research on families with a communication approach (as well as some specific schools of therapy, for that matter) guided by the Palo Alto model are micro-level systems theories that are descended from General System Theory (GST) (see Whitchurch & Constantine, 1993, for a review of GST and related theories, including micro-level family systems theories). Family communication research guided by the pragmatic perspective makes the fundamental assumption that the interdependence of communicators' behaviors is what defines relationships. The influence of pragmatics, as well as its antecedents, systems/cybernetics/ information theory, is evident in two research milestones that helped give rise to the family communication specialty area.

Family Communication Research Milestones

Although there were a few other early works on families in the communication discipline (e.g., Chartier & Chartier, 1975; Crocker, 1951), we identify two dissertations completed in the early and mid-1970s as milestones that inaugurate the development of the family communication specialty area. We distinguish the dissertation of Rogers (1972) as a milestone for two reasons. First, it focuses on patterns of *interacts*, or message–response exchanges in dialogue between pairs of spouses; second, the marital couple was Rogers' initial focus (i.e., interpersonal communication research was not "translated" to the context of the marital dyad).

Rogers developed an empirical model of relational control, based directly on the theoretical work of the Palo Alto group (Whitchurch & Rogers, 1993), especially that of Watzlawick (1964), Sluzki and Beavin (1965), and Watzlawick et al. (1967). In her model, *control* is viewed as the process by which power comes about in a marital relationship; that is, spouses attempt to influence their partners' behavior through message exchange. Although both control and power are viewed as social codetermined phenomena, Rogers and her coauthors reserve the term "power" for power bases (Raven & French, 1956); thus, power is viewed as an outcome rather than as a dynamic process.

Similarly, we mark the Fitzpatrick dissertation (1976) as a milestone because marriage also was her primary focus, as she emphasized that each marriage is different from the next and demonstrated empirically that the unique characteristics of any given marriage emerge from the interaction of the two spouses. Fitzpatrick's work spans both the interactional and the pragmatic perspectives in that it is based on both perceptions and communication behaviors in developing an empirically based typology of marital relationships.

In her initial typology development, Fitzpatrick (1976) identified three marital couple types based on how couples define and experience their relationship through the pairs of individual spouses' perceptions of their marital relationship with respect to eight factors: ideology of traditionalism, ideology of uncertainty and change, sharing, autonomy, undifferentiated space, temporal regularity, conflict avoidance, and assertiveness. The types are Traditionals (exhibiting conventional values, stability, traditional roles, and a high degree of companionship and sharing in the marriage); Independents (those with nonconventional values about relationships and family life, autonomy, different personal and psychological space, and high levels of companionship and sharing in the marriage); and Separates (couples with conventional values but ambivalence about those values, unexpressed conflict, and low levels of companionship and sharing in the marriage). Fitzpatrick (1976, 1988) also differentiated between "pure" couple types (pairs of spouses' individual types are the same) and "mixed" couple types (pairs of spouses' individual types differ). Whereas the Rogers and Fitzpatrick dissertations were empirical, during the same time period (early to mid-1970s), family communication pedagogy also was beginning to develop.

Family Communication Pedagogy Milestones

The history of pedagogy in the family communication specialty area can be demarcated with Goldberg and Goldberg's (1976) syllabus that focused on children's language acquisition and on interpersonal communication research on children and marriages to conceptualize a course on family communication. Subsequently, Galvin and Wilkinson (1980) proposed family communication as a "forum for communication education" (p. 1), although they note that "this is not to say that [communication teachers] hold the panacea for curing all marital woes and familial heartaches" (p. 6).

Galvin continued this line of work with her colleague Bernard Brommel, publishing in 1982 the first textbook that identified family communication as a specialty area of the communication discipline. The Galvin and Brommel textbook also spans both the interactional and the pragmatics perspectives in that it was influenced both by Hess and Handel (1959) and by the adaptability, cohesion, and communication dimensions of the systems-based Circumplex Model (Olson, Sprenkle, & Russell, 1979).

Family communication pedagogy generally tends to be more descriptive than prescriptive (Berko, 1992; Whitchurch, 1992, 1993); that is, it emphasizes research and theory in family communication rather than communication skills. Even so, teachers of family communication courses have recently been engaging in considerable self-examination and discussion among themselves about the appropriate boundaries between pedagogy and practice in the family communication course. This discussion centers around having students analyze their own autobiographical narratives in the family communication course and is described in more detail later in the subsection on applied research on family communication. Before that, however, we turn to some assumptions about family from a communication approach.

Assumptions about Families from a Communication Approach

We turn now to seven assumptions about families that can be identified in the literature on families written with a communication approach. The assumptions are labeled with numbers for convenience only—no interpretation of ranking or hierarchy should be made. Taken together as a whole, these assumptions are a description of the unique ways that families and their communication are viewed with a communication approach. Further, these assumptions guide family researchers in their exploration of families using a communication approach.

Assumption 1: Relationships Are Constructed through Interaction

Scholars who take a communication approach to families believe that the construction of relationships through interaction is central to the process of creating a family's social reality, as family members create and sustain their family identity through their communication. In other words, the communication within the family is constitutive, that is, the communication itself creates the social world of the family. In this view, events do not have intrinsic, concrete meanings; rather, the process of creating meaning within the family is enacted through members' reaction to events and to each other's verbal and nonverbal communication behaviors in terms of what those behaviors mean in the family's social world. Thus, the meaning is constructed through communication among family members over time, and it influences their long-term, enduring interactional patterns.

The context in which the communication occurs is also crucial because messages within the family can be understood only if examined within the reality created by the family members. Shotter (1993) characterizes this relationship between communication and the experience of reality as a loop: Communication actions within the family determine how reality is experienced for family members, and the experience of reality affects the communication patterns within the family.

In previous research, the construction of relationships through interaction guided two early germinal studies on families: Hess and Handel (1959) and Kantor and Lehr (1975). (Both were described earlier in this chapter.) However, this assumption, and its attendant theoretical perspective, has more often been employed for examination of couples' communication. For example, Berger and Kellner (1964) introduced this notion to the literature on marriage in their discussion of how couples socially construct their reality and define themselves in and through their conversations with one another. Through communication, couples cocreate what Berger and Kellner call "private spheres" and a "private world view," constructing a private world that is the unique construction of the couple. Over time, this unique, private world view becomes "concrete" to the couple, a process that Berger and Kellner term *objectivation of reality*.

Dickson (1995) demonstrated these concepts and processes in data-based research when she asked couples married more than 50 years to tell their jointly constructed relational story. Analysis of the couples' stories revealed that the couples' themes of connectedness and separateness in their stories about each life stage had been cocreated and maintained in and through their communication; for example, it was common for couples in this study to finish each other's stories. The factual "truth" of the story was not important in terms of their couple identity; what mattered was what they had jointly coconstructed it and now believed it to be true. Davis' (1973) early work on marriage and intimacy identified this process as *coupling*; Knapp and Van- gelisti (1996) have a similar description of the process during which couples develop a joint identity through attempts to balance needs of individuality and mutuality within their relationship.

Assumption 2: The Family Is an Interacting System

Family research guided by a communication approach takes as a given that families are systems, or "set[s] of elements standing in interrelation among themselves and with the environment" (Bertalanffy, 1975, p. 159). This assumption is widely shared in many disciplines and approaches to family scholarship, but a communication approach to families focuses extensively on the *interactions* among the components of the system (i.e., the family members). In human systems, communication is much more complex than merely the exchange of literal content of information or reduction of uncertainty in interactions, largely because humans' actions in their various levels of systems are based on their socially coconstructed reality (Whitchurch & Constantine, 1993).

In scholarship on families using a communication approach, this assumption is manifested by family members always being viewed in relation to at least one other family member. For example, as noted earlier, the first textbook to identify family communication as a specialty area in the communication discipline (Galvin & Brommel, 1982) was guided in part by micro-level systems theory in the form of the Circumplex Model (Olson et al., 1989; Olson et al., 1979).

Data-based research on couples and families with a communication approach also has often been guided micro-level applications of GST. For example, the work of Edna Rogers and her colleagues (e.g., Rogers, 1972, 1989; Rogers & Farace, 1975; Rogers-Millar & Millar, 1979) shifts the focus from the individual communicator to the interaction patterns between communicators in analyzing relational control, which is the power dimension of relationships conceptualized in dynamic, rather than static, terms. That is, one spouse's utterance (termed an *act*) is coded as an attempt to take control (i.e., assert having power in the relationship), but it is not until the other spouse's reply is coded and the two utterances are considered together as a unit (termed an *interact*) that a full picture of control emerges (i.e., whether the first spouse gains power or not). The original Rogers model focuses on interaction of the marital couple; coding schemes based on the relational control model have been extended from dyads to family units and tested in family-related therapy settings (Friedlander & Heatherington, 1989; Gaul, Simon, Friedlander, & Cutler, 1991).

Micro-level systems theory has guided the research of other researchers who work with a communication approach to families (e.g., Bavelas & Segal, 1982). Further, some researchers have melded family systems theory approaches with symbolic interaction/social construction of relationships (e.g., Fitzpatrick, 1976, 1988; Kantor & Lehr, 1975; Reiss, 1981). What is paramount in this assumption is that every one of the studies cited in this subsection, and many other studies, share in common the focus on the communication behaviors that create patterns *between* communicators.

Assumption 3: Families Are Constantly Managing and Negotiating Dialectical Tensions throughout Their Family Life Cycle

Dialectical tensions in family life refer to the constant state of affairs for all families, in which they manage sets of two opposing, dynamic forces that are contradictory yet interdependent. These forces result in dialectical tensions that emerge from different human needs and generate change in the family over time (Baxter, 1988, 1990). Baxter (1993) notes that three primary dialectical tensions have emerged from this body of research: integration/separation (also called separateness/connectedness by Hess & Handel, 1959), stability/change, and expression/privacy.

The integration/separation dialectic highlights the tension between the need to be a part of a family while also needing to be autonomous and independent from the family. For example, marital partners often grapple with this tension when they feel a need to be an individual as well as an intimate marital partner (Scarf, 1987).

The tension of stability/change focuses on the need for spontaneity and unpredictability while also enjoying the comfort of familiarity (Baxter, 1988, 1990; Baxter & Simon, 1993). Different subunits within a family have different kinds of dialectical tensions and needs, which creates complicated management of these needs. For example, a marital dyad might have more need for spontaneity in their relationship, while the children in the family thrive on the stability of the family routines.

The third tension, expression/privacy, refers to family members' need to be open and express themselves to other family members, while simultaneously seeking some privacy and protection from feeling vulnerable through exposing the self to others (e.g., Petronio & Harriman, 1990). This dialectical tension accounts for how much family members want to reveal about themselves to each other and how much information they want to remain private. Again, different subunits within the family might have different relational norms for managing this tension. For example, adolescents in the family might want to share personal information on their sexual activity with a parent but simultaneously feel the need to keep sexual information private and out of the family arena. Similarly, this parent might feel that he or she should know everything about the child but realize that the child has a need to keep some information private.

Dialectical tensions within families have been explored by other communication scholars. For example, Bochner (1984) and his colleagues (Bochner & Eisenberg, 1987; Cissna, Cox, & Bochner, 1990) emphasize the partners' struggle with opposing forces of openness and closedness and how families grapple with tensions between differentiation and integration and between stability and change. The fluidity and complexity of these tensions as a family moves through its family life cycle is also stressed in this body of research (e.g., Ellis & Bochner, 1992). Baxter and Montgomery's (1996) book emphasizes the importance of examining from a communication perspective the dialectical processes that exist in relationships and families.

These dialectical tensions may involve different communication patterns and be more central during different life stages for a family (Baxter, 1990, 1993; Duck, 1990). For example, a family with adolescents may contend with the interdependent tensions of autonomy and connectedness, where a family with school-age children may struggle with the tension of stability and change.

It is through communication within the family that these tensions are negotiated over the family life cycle. For example, Stamp (1994) explored how couples manage tensions associated with role expectations, enactment, and negotiation during the transition to parenthood. Cissna et al. (1990) examined how stepfamilies manage and renegotiate dialectical tensions during the blending process. Sillars, Burggraf, Yost, and Zietlow (1992) found that couples manage different kinds of communication themes in different life stages, such that later-life couples were more likely to express themes of togetherness and younger couples were more likely to express themes of separateness.

Assumption 4: Families Must Manage and Renegotiate Their Relational Definitions throughout Their Family Life Cycle

Scholars who take a communication approach to families believe that families must constantly manage their definitions of their relationships with one another and must renegotiate these relational definitions from time to time. This process occurs in and through the communication exchanged among family members. For example, Fitzpatrick, Vangelisti, and Firman (1994) demonstrated this process in their examination of how couples expand their relational definition of each other from spouse to include coparent. These researchers found that it is the dialogue and information exchanged between the couple that allows them to manage the change of their relational definition. Similarly, Coleman and Ganong (1995) found that divorced parents redefine their relationship with each other so they can continue mutual coparenting of their children.

Another example of research that involves the renegotiating of relational definitions within the family is Lewis and Lin's (1996) discussion and analysis of the processes occurring between midlife parents and their adult children. The authors argue that midlife parents and their adult children manage many changes in their relationship around the areas of family intimacy and attachment, family residence, family power patterns, and the exchange of resources. Along the same lines, Cooney and Uhlenberg (1992) discuss how parents provide different kinds of support for their children throughout the life cycle. The authors imply that the various kinds of support may parallel various kinds of relational definitions that emerge for the parent and adult child.

A final example of relational redefinition comes from later in the family life cycle. When they become the caregiver to older family members, adult members of multigenerational families are required to renegotiate relational definitions with other adult family members. Taking on the caregiver role of an aged parent or parent-in-law requires communication about significant role redefinition for the caregiver and the entire family (Baum & Page, 1991; Pearlin, Mullan, Semple, & Skaff, 1990; Query & Flint, 1996).

Assumption 5: Communication Definitions of Family Subunits Are Privileged over Structural Definitions of Family Subunits

As noted earlier, with a communication approach, families are defined as created by both structure and interaction, as well as through interaction only. Even so, all researchers who study families with a communication approach eventually are forced to use structural definitions to talk about families, using terms such as parent–child, nuclear and extended family forms, and spouses and marriage. It is important to note, however, that although scholars taking a communication approach to families often use structural terms to discuss their work, they are not *defining* the family by its structure; rather, they are using structural terms to *label constructs*. Because, from a communication approach, interaction, rather than structure alone, is what defines family relationships, structural labels are of use for only part of the ways families are defined with a communication approach. That is, these labels only address the structural ways a family is defined, and ignore the ways a family is defined through interaction only. Because a corollary set of interactional labels does not exist, researchers taking a communication approach to families must rely on structural labels, despite these labels' limitations for this approach.

The use of structural labels can be misleading when reading research that has been conducted using a communication approach. Although researchers adopting this approach explore such relationships as parent–child, siblings, husband–wife, and many other family relationships, the researchers are focusing on interaction and meanings that arise from the interactions within these subunits, not on the structural characteristics of that particular family relationship. Examples of this research are communication research on dual-career couples (e.g., Rosenfeld, Bowen, & Richman, 1995; Wood, 1995), grandparent–grandchild dyads (Cryer-Downs, 1989), marital dyads (e.g., Markman & Notarius, 1987), and parent–dependent child dyads (Buerkel-Rothfuss, Fink, & Buerkel, 1995; Dixson, 1995; Stafford & Dainton, 1995).

Assumption 6: Understanding Communication during Family Transitions Is Critical to Understanding Family Life Cycles

Studying family life cycle transitions has been elusive in the family literature. Although it is typical for the stages of the family life cycle to be demarcated with the oldest child's age, we suggest that with a communication approach, exploring communication during the transitional processes as families move from one stage to another could be far more informative in terms of defining the nature of interaction within the family. For example, the few studies to date on structural stages of the family life cycle from a communication approach suggest that couples and families take on family roles and positions (i.e., clusters of roles) by "talking themselves" into their new roles (e.g., Baxter, 1988; Stamp, 1994). Specifically, Stamp demonstrated this process by examining dialogue between couples who were pregnant with their first child, and again shortly after the birth of the child. In the dialogue reported, this rich study illustrates how couples view their relationship differences and roles before and after the transition to parenthood.

There has been less research on how families mutually reconstruct their perceptions of life-cycle transitional events, even though the idea of demarcating family life-cycle stages through identifying changes in family interaction patterns during family life-cycle transitions has been in the literature since 1978 (Aldous, 1978, 1996). Even so, one clue comes from research by Dickson (1995), whose data on couples married for more than 50 years suggest that couples, regardless of whether they eventually have children or not, go through an identifiable transition to the stage Dickson calls the "family vision" stage, in which couples discuss having children and develop through their interaction their image of what they want their future family life cycle to be like. Another example of this assumption is Stamp's (1994) research on how couples manage this transition to parenthood, cited earlier in this section.

Assumption 7: Families Create and Maintain Their Own Unique Family Mini-Cultures

In 1982, Wood introduced the notion of *relational culture*, which refers to "processes, structure, and practices that create, express and sustain personal relationships and the identities of the partners" (Wood, 1995, p. 150). Relational cultures are comprised of several properties: They contain unique content, they develop and change over time, they are dialectical in nature, and they can be healthy or unhealthy. Relational culture emerges from the meanings that family members assign to events, rituals, activities, symbols, and interactions that comprise their family life (Wood, 1995).

The culture metaphor can also be applied to families (Baxter, 1987; Fitzpatrick & Ritchie, 1993; Montgomery, 1992) and to marriage. For example, Fitzpatrick (Fitzpatrick, 1988; Fitzpatrick & Ritchie, 1993) discusses how married couples create a "mini-culture" through the way in which they define their marital relationship. She also refers to the notion of marital ideology as the beliefs, values, and standards individuals hold when conceptualizing the marital relationship; these values, beliefs, and standards guide the communication patterns that emerge among the couple members. These ideologies tend to be unique to the couple partners; therefore, each couple's culture has unique characteristics that define the nature of their interactions. Although most of the research on relational culture has occurred among married couples, research evidence of the existence of family cultures is emerging as well (e.g., Baxter & Clark, 1996; M. Miller, 1995; Sillars, 1995).

Overview of Family Communication Research

There are a variety of ways to categorize family communication research; we use two main categories in this overview: basic or applied research. In this chapter, we use the term *basic research* (called *theoretical research* by some writers) to refer to either scientific or humanistic research that is intended primarily to explore theoretical relationships of phenomena (Carroll, 1968; Smith, 1988).

In so doing, basic research helps extend existing theories and/or contributes to development of new theories (Carroll, 1968); Craig (1995) notes that "its top priority is to address theoretical problems and controversies, fill gaps in knowledge, and in general, to advance the discipline [of the particular researchers]" (p. 148). Thus, basic research can be thought of as the "how" rather than the "how to" (Planalp, 1993). Although laboratory or field experiments are common methodologies for basic research in general (Carroll, 1968), they are not included in this chapter because historically this kind of research seldom has been conducted in the communication discipline; other research methods are generally considered to be more suitable for exploring the nature and quality of communication. Methodologies used in applied research emphasize situations similar or identical to those in which the findings are to be used (Carroll, 1968), or naturalistic inquiry.

Applied research can be distinguished from basic research on the basis of the kinds of questions asked and the nature of the work, as well as the kinds of research methodologies used (Carroll, 1968). Applied research has as its top priority the addressing of well-defined problems of the practical world (Carroll, 1968; Craig, 1995). Further, although the purpose of applied communication research is to use communication theory and research in practical ways to address real problems concerning human communication (Cissna, 1982; Eadie, 1990; O'Hair, Kreps, & Frey, 1990; Whitchurch & Webb, 1995), it is not intended to provide direct services to families—this is the domain of practice. It bears noting that applied communication research specifically about communication and families certainly can and does inform practice. Even so, it does not attempt interventions (Argyris, 1995), nor is it intended to disseminate techniques for conducting therapy or training (but see Chapter 28, by Kaslow and colleagues on family therapy in this volume).

The intent of basic research to develop, test, and/or extend theory sometimes has been used as a position from which to criticize, even belittle, applied research; from such a position, applied research is sometimes described as narrow and atheoretical (G. Miller, 1995). We concur with Miller's (1995) assessment of such a position as a limited vision of applied research. Applied research is not intrinsically atheoretical, even though its primary purpose is to address practical, real world problems. Even while addressing practical problems, applied research can be heavily grounded in the theoretical assumptions about families that emerge from basic research endeavors.

Definitions of basic research and of applied research vary from the view that these two are different forms of research that can benefit from each other to the view they overlap considerably (Argyris, 1995). Our literature review indicates not only that the latter of these two positions (i.e., that basic and applied research can overlap) is the more accurate characterization of literature on communication and families, but also that applied research sometimes overlaps with practice. Examples are research-based training programs, such as PREP™ (Prevention and Relationship Enhancement Program) (Markman, Duncan, Storaasli, & Howes, 1987; Markman, Floyd, Stanley, & Storaasli, 1988; Markman, Jamieson, & Floyd, 1983; Markman, Renick, Floyd, Stanley, & Clements, 1993). We turn now to discussions of basic research and applied research in family communication; the studies cited should be taken as exemplars rather than as exhaustive reviews.

Basic Research in Family Communication

The emphasis of the family communication specialty area is on interaction *among* communicators, so it is not surprising that only a few works related to families published in this discipline focus on individuals (e.g., Brennan & Wamboldt, 1990; Jorgenson, 1989; Krokoff, 1990; Ritchie & Fitzpatrick, 1990; Sillars et al., 1990). Even so, there has been some attempt to meld the intrapersonal (i.e., individual) and interpersonal levels of analysis to increase overall understanding of communication in families (Fitzpatrick & Wamboldt, 1990).

Despite a strong interest in families as units, family communication specialists in the communication discipline have done less basic research on entire family units than on family dyads and other family subunits. This tendency is not unique to the communication discipline; it seems to hold across disciplines and across family-related areas of study besides communication. There are only a few extant communication approach studies on family units that are based on data from more than two communicators; qualitative examples include Hess and Handel (1959) as well as Kantor and Lehr (1975), and a quantitative example is the research program of Olson and associates (1989).

In our review of the literature, basic family communication research is identifiable as different from applied family communication research because the former expands knowledge about communication in a particular kind of family relationship, but does not focus on a particular practical problem associated with that relationship. For example, the family dimension of power has been extensively explored in basic family communication research. An extensive research program on power and family communication is that of Rogers and her colleagues on relational control. In the original Rogers model, dyadic dialogue is coded using the Ericson and Rogers (1973) relational coding system.* An interact is said to be "complementary" when one spouse's message asserts control (a "one-up") and the other spouse's message accepts assertion of control (a "one-down"), or vice-versa. In a "transitory" interact, a spouse's response to a one-up message neither asserts control nor relinquishes it (a "one-across"). A "symmetrical" interact is coded when both spouses' messages assert control, when both spouses relinquish control, or when both spouses give one-across messages (Rogers-Millar & Millar, 1979).

Rogers-Millar and Millar (1979) found that couples in complementary relationships rated themselves as more satisfied than those in symmetrical relationships. Gage (1988) reported observational research on 25 violent couples during 5-minute conflict interactions about the cause of their most recent violent incident, finding that 89% of the exchanges between the spouses fit a pattern of competitive symmetry. That is, control directions were the same, with each spouse behaving toward the other the way the other behaved (Rogers-Millar & Millar, 1979). Gage also measured "domineeringness" (the more one-up messages people give, the more domineering they are said to be) and "dominance" (the resultant phenomenon of the spouse accepting the one-up messages by giving his or her own one-down messages), finding that one spouse's domineering behaviors were strongly associated with similar behaviors by the other.

Gage's (1988) work might appear to exacerbate the conflict over whether wives actually use violence against their husbands offensively. Indeed, a severe critic might state that Gage's results suggest that the wives "having it coming" when they are verbally aggressive with their husbands. Gelles' (1974) work some 15 years earlier might seem to point to the same conclusion: "[W]ives who have been hit or beaten by their husbands often explain that they provoked the attack by nagging their husbands" (p. 158). Further, the

*Other researchers have been expanding the relational communication control model beyond dyadic interaction to coding the interaction of larger family units (e.g., Friedlander & Heatherington, 1989; Heatherington & Friedlander, 1990). The Heatherington and Friedlander studies have found that speakers' multiple messages often seek to establish coalitions that challenge other speakers.

pattern of competitive symmetry that Gage found is in contradiction to the general view in family violence field that violent interspousal relationships are complementary. For example, Weitzman and Dreen (1982) suggest that violent couples assume complementary roles.

Perhaps this contradiction, as well as the high rate of female domineeringness found by Gage, can be explained by the possibility that she and Weitzman and Dreen were studying different kinds of violent interspousal relationships. This possibility was supported by the applied communication research of Whitchurch (1994), who examined violent critical incidents (i.e., interactions about which inferences can be made) in four types of violent couple relationships empirically derived from the couples' relationship characteristics. She found statistically significant differences in the couples' use of symbolic violence (e.g., swearing, insults), their severe physical violence (e.g., beating up the spouse), and their de-escalating conflict behaviors (e.g., trying to reason with the spouse).

Power is not the only family dimension explored through basic family communication research. For example, a large research program by Fitzpatrick (1988) and her colleagues has identified differences in various communication dimensions across the Traditional, Independent, and Separate couple types described earlier (Fitzpatrick, 1988; Fitzpatrick & Ritchie, 1993). For example, with respect to power and compliance-gaining, the Traditional type is characterized by the giving of orders, while the give-and-take of challenges and justifications marks the Independent and mixed couple types. With respect to self-disclosure in marriage, Traditional husbands were likely to have only their wives as confidants, with the wives apparently able to help husbands express feelings. In contrast and in keeping with their nonconventional ideas about sex roles, both husbands and wives in the Independent type were willing to disclose feelings. As would be expected from their emotional disengagement from one another and their reluctance to engage in conflict, Separate couples rarely experienced emotion in the relationship and rarely expressed emotion if they did experience it.

Other basic research in the family communication literature contributes considerable breadth to what is known about the interior of couple relationships with respect to the duration and content of communication (but no real world problems are specified). For example, Dickson-Markman and Markman (1988) found that spouses tend to report an average of 1.24 interactions per day, usually over the evening meal, lasting for an average of 2 hours. They also found that couples tend to discuss relational issues when communicating about other events such as conflict or making love.

Similarly, research efforts on conversational themes headed by Sillars (e.g., Sillars, Weisberg, Burggraf, & Wilson, 1987; Sillars et al., 1992) suggest that mature and satis-

fied couples are more likely to communicate with each other about relational issues (termed "communal themes" by Sillars et al.) such as togetherness, cooperation, and communication, than about individual themes such as individual differences and personality. The research of Noller and Feeney (1990) further expands knowledge about talk time and conversational topics; they found that both husbands and wives initiate conversations about their relationship and that these conversations are more likely to occur when the couple is alone rather than with others.

Applied Research in Family Communication

As discussed earlier, in applied research in family communication, communication discipline theories and research methods are used to *inform* the work of qualified clinicians (Whitchurch & Webb, 1995), but not to *be* their actual work. Admittedly, this distinction is sometimes hazy, but a recent trend in the communication discipline illustrates some differences between applied research on families and practice with families.

The applied aspects of the family communication specialty area initially were exclusively pedagogical (e.g., Galvin, 1979; Galvin & Wilkinson, 1980; Goldberg & Goldberg, 1976; Long & Grant, 1992; Vangelisti, 1991; Whitchurch, 1993). However, the practice of some writers on communication and families is classroom teaching (Whitchurch & Rogers, 1993); examples are evident in family communication textbooks (e.g., Arliss, 1993; Galvin & Brommel, 1996; Noller & Fitzpatrick, 1993; Pearson, 1993; Turner & West, 1998; Yerby, Buerkel-Rothfuss, & Bochner, 1995). Even though in such cases the practitioners of family communication pedagogy are qualified teachers, the transition from applied research to practice is not as clear-cut as it is in clinical disciplines. Since the 1980s, scholars in the communication discipline at large have been engaged in a long discussion over the appropriate place of communication skills in communication curricula (e.g., Katriel & Philipsen, 1981). Family communication scholars have examined this issue with respect to couples and families (e.g., Sillars & Weisberg, 1987; Whitchurch & Pace, 1993) and to individuals with communication problems (e.g., Booth-Butterfield & Cottone, 1991).

Intradisciplinary debate has been vigorous with respect to the family communication course. Some family communication scholars argue for use of postmodern theories, especially narrative analysis methods in the family communication course to teach students to deconstruct their own stories, reasoning that doing so makes the family communication course more meaningful (e.g., Bochner & Kiesinger, 1992; Rosenfeld, 1992, 1994; Wolff, 1990; Yerby et al., 1995). Other family communication scholars have argued against autobiographical self-analysis in the family communication classroom, arguing for a strong delineation between applied research and practice (e.g., Berko, 1992; Buerkel-Rothfuss, 1990; Galvin, 1992; Kelley, 1992; R. Long, 1992; Whitchurch, 1993; Whitchurch & Sharp, 1994).

Some other applied aspects of the family communication specialty area have emphasized data-based research that examines communication and problems that occur in real families (Whitchurch & Webb, 1995). For example, Ferguson and Dickson (1995) examined how children living in single-parent homes experience their mother's dating. This qualitative study found that children whose mothers are dating want to be included in the dating process by having information about the person their mother is with and where they are going and by being included in activities with their mother's dates, while having clear boundaries about how their mothers' dates relate to them. This study does not suggest interventions or recommendations about single mothers' dating, but it does increase understanding of how children experience and feel about their mothers' dating activities.

Some applied family communication studies are more directly intended to provide research findings that are of direct use by clinicians and other practitioners. For example, Steier, Stanton, and Todd (1982) compared patterns of turn-taking and alliance formation in families with one member who is addicted to drugs and "normal" families. Vangelisti studied counselors directly, exploring their perspectives on couple communication (Vangelisti, 1994). Vangelisti and Banski (1993) found higher marital satisfaction among couples who had debriefing conversations at the end of their respective day's work; this research finding is echoed in works on couple communication intended for the general reading public (Doherty, 1997a,b).

Other applied family communication studies follow the same pattern of the Ferguson and Dickson piece in studying real life social issues to increase understanding about complicated family processes with respect to these social issues, not to suggest interventions for these life events. Examples include Stamp's work on the transition to parenthood (Stamp, 1994; Stamp & Banski, 1992); Dickson's (1995) work on later-life, long-lasting marriages; and Huston and Vangelisti's (1995) study on the effects of parenthood on marriage. Examples of other lines of applied communication research include family violence (Infante, Sabourin, Rudd, & Shannon, 1990; Payne & Sabourin, 1990; Petronio, Reeder, Hecht, & Ros-Mendoza, 1996; Sabourin, 1995; Stamp & Sabourin, 1995; Varallo, Ray, & Ellis, 1998; Whitchurch & Pace, 1993); intergenerational traditions of suicide (M. Miller, 1995); and family social support (Gotcher, 1993; Leach & Braithwaite, 1996).

The comparatively large number of applied communi-

cation studies dated in the 1990s cited here represent the rapid increase in applied family communication research during this decade. From this increase, we conclude that the family communication specialty area is coming of age, as we discuss in the final section of the chapter.

Summary and Future Directions

In this chapter, we first explored what is meant by the general term *communication approach to families*. Second, we presented a historical and topical overview of the communication discipline. Third, we examined the study of families in the communication discipline with focus on the theoretical heritage of this specialty area. Fourth, we presented seven assumptions made about families when a communication approach is taken. Fifth, a discussion of family communication research and pedagogy milestones was presented to give an overview of basic and applied research in family communication. Finally, we conclude the chapter with a discussion of future directions in family communication.

We strongly believe that the specialty area of family communication research is coming of age. For example, based on findings from the few communication approach studies to date on family life stages, we believe that in the future the examination of the communication processes associated with dialectical tensions over the stages of the family life cycle will be an especially fruitful area of research. The theoretical orientations and methodological advances in the communication discipline offer the opportunity to examine complex processes that occur within family units.

Findings from communication approach research on families indicate the critical need for researchers to be aware of what Gilgun, Daly, and Handel (1992) and Larzelere and Klein (1987) refer to as the highly complex, subjective, and private nature of families. This chapter indicates that a communication approach to families has the potential to open family scholars to various methodologies that are not as often used to study families as are methodologies that emphasize family structure. We suggest that frequently, qualitative methodologies that focus on communication, such as narrative analysis, conversational analysis of family interaction, theme analysis of family stories and rituals, and quantitative methodologies such as interaction analysis, capture the meaning-centered, unique, and private nature of family interaction better than methodologies that emphasize family structure. Thus, we believe that a major contribution of a communication approach to families is to produce knowledge about families that is not visible with other approaches to studying families—insights and understanding on how families define themselves and live their everyday lives together.

References

Alberts, J. (1988). An analysis of couples' conversational complaints. *Communication Monographs, 55*, 184–197.

Aldous, J. (1978). *Family careers: Developmental change in families.* New York: Wiley.

Aldous, J. (1996). *Family careers: Rethinking the developmental perspective.* Thousand Oaks, CA: Sage.

Alexander, J. (1990). Television and family interaction. In J. Bryant (Ed.), *Television and the American family* (pp. 211–225). Hillsdale, NJ: Erlbaum.

Anderson, J. A., Birkhead, D., Eason, D. L., & Strine, M. S. (1988). The caravan of communication and its multiple histories: A dialogue. In R. P. Hawkins, J. M. Wiemann, & S. Pingree (Eds.), *Advancing communication science: Merging mass and interpersonal processes* (pp. 276–307). Newbury Park, CA: Sage.

Arliss, L. (1993). *Contemporary family communication: Messages and meanings.* New York: St. Martin's Press.

Argyris, C. (1995). Knowledge when used in practice tests theory: The case of applied communication research. In K. N. Cissna (Ed.), *Applied communication in the 21st century* (pp. 1–19). Mahwah, NJ: Erlbaum.

Austin, E. W., Roberts, D. F., & Nass, C. I. (1990). Influence of family communication on children's television-interpretation processes. *Communication Research, 17*, 545–564.

Barnlund, D. C. (1970). A transactional model of communication. In K. K. Sereno & C. D. Mortensen, *Foundations of communication theory* (pp. 83–102). New York: Harper and Row.

Bateson, G. (1971). Cybernetics of self. *Psychiatry, 34*, 1–18.

Baum, M., & Page, M. (1991). Caregiving and multigenerational families. *The Gerontologist, 31*, 762–769.

Bavelas, J. B., & Segal, L. (1982). Family systems theory: Background and implications. *Journal of Communication, 32*, 99–107.

Baxter, L. A. (1987). Symbols of relationship identity in relationship cultures. *Journal of Social and Personal Relationships, 4*, 261–279.

Baxter, L. A. (1988). A dialectical perspective on communication strategies in relationship development. In S. W. Duck, D. F. Hay, S. E. Hobfoll, W. Iches, & B. Montgomery (Eds.), *Handbook of personal relationships* (pp. 257–273). Chichester, England: Wiley.

Baxter, L. A. (1990). Dialectical contradictions in relationship development. *Journal of Social and Personal Relationships, 7*, 69–88.

Baxter, L. A. (1993). The social side of personal relationships: A dialectical perspective. In S. Duck (Ed.), *Understanding relationship processes, 3: Social context and relationships* (pp. 139–165). Newbury Park, CA: Sage.

Baxter, L. A., & Clark, C. L. (1996). Perceptions of family communication patterns and the enactment of family rituals. *Western Journal of Communication, 60*, 254–268.

Baxter, L. M., & Montgomery, B. M. (1996). Relating: Dialogues and dialectics. New York: Guilford.

Baxter, L. A., & Simon, E. P. (1993). Relationship maintenance strategies and dialectical contradictions in personal relationships. *Journal of Social and Personal Relationships, 10*, 225–242.

Berger, P., & Kellner, H. (1964). Marriage and the construction of reality. *Diogenes, 64*, 1–24.

Berko, R. M. (1992, October). *Teaching the family course: Ethical issues.* Paper presented at the annual meeting of the National Communication Association, Chicago.

Berlo, D. K. (1960). *The process of communication.* New York: Holt, Rinehart and Winston.

Bertalanffy, L. von. (1968). *General System Theory.* New York: George Braziller.

Bertalanffy, L. von. (1975). *Perspectives on General System Theory: Scientific-philosophical studies.* New York: George Braziller.

Bochner, A. P. (1976). Conceptual frontiers in the study of communication in families: An introduction to the literature. *Human Communication Research, 2*, 381–397.

Bochner, A. P. (1984). The functions of communication in interpersonal bonding. In C. Arnold & J. Bowers (Eds.), *Handbook of rhetorical and communication theory* (pp. 554–621). Boston: Allyn & Bacon.

Bochner, A. P., & Eisenberg, E. M. (1987). Family process: System perspectives. In C. R. Berger & S. H. Chaffee (Eds.), *Handbook of communication science* (pp. 540–563). Beverly Hills, CA: Sage.

Bochner, A. P., & Kiesinger, C. (1992, November). *Ordinary People and the call of stories.* Paper presented at the meeting of the National Communication Association, Chicago.

Booth-Butterfield, S., & Cottone, R. R. (1991). Ethical issues in the treatment of communication apprehension and avoidance. *Communication Education, 40*, 172–179.

Brennan, J. L., & Wamboldt, F. S. (1990). From the outside in: Examining how individuals define their experienced family. *Communication Research, 17*, 444–461.

Brown, J. D., Childers, K. W., Bauman, K. E., & Koch, G. G. (1990). The influence of new media and family structure on young adolescents' television and radio use. *Communication Research, 17*, 65–82.

Bryant, J. (Ed.). (1990). *Television and the American family.* Hillsdale, NJ: Erlbaum.

Bryant, J., & Zillman, D. (Eds.). (1986). *Perspectives on media effects.* Hillsdale, NJ: Erlbaum.

Buerkel-Rothfuss, N. (1990, November). *Teaching family communication: Keeping family skeletons in family closets.* Paper presented at the Preconvention Conference on Family Communication, National Communication Association annual convention, Chicago, IL.

Buerkel-Rothfuss, N. L., Fink, D. S., & Buerkel, R. A. (1995). Communication in the father-child dyad: The intergenerational transmission process. In T. J. Socha & G. H. Stamp (Eds.), *Parents, children, and communication: Frontiers of theory and research* (pp. 63–86). Mahwah, NJ: Erlbaum.

Burgess, E. W. (1926). The family as a unity of interacting personalities. *The Family, 7*(1), 3–9.

Burke, J. A., Becker, S. L., Arbogast, R. A., & Naughton, J. M. (1987). Problems and prospects of applied research: The development of an adolescent smoking prevention program. *Journal of Applied Communication Research, 15*, 1–18.

Burleson, B. R., & Denton, W. H. (1992). A new look at similarity and attraction in marriage: Similarities in social-cognitive and communication skills as predictors of attraction and satisfaction. *Communication Monographs, 59*, 268–287.

Canary, D. J., Brossmann, B. G., & Seibold, D. R. (1987). Argument structures in decision-making groups. *Southern Speech Communication Journal, 53*, 18–37.

Canary, D. J., Weger, H., Jr., & Stafford, L. (1991). Couples' argument sequences and their associations with relational characteristics. *Western Journal of Speech Communication, 55*, 159–179.

Carroll, J. B. (1968). Basic and applied research in education: Definitions, distinctions, and implications. *Harvard Educational Review, 38*, 263–276.

Chartier, J., & Chartier, M. R. (1975). Perceived parental communication and self-esteem: An exploratory study. *Western Journal of Speech Communication, 34*, 26–31.

Cissna, K. N. (1982). Editor's note: What is applied communication research? *Journal of Applied Communication Research, 10*(2), i–iii.

Cissna, K. N., Cox, D. E., & Bochner, A. P. (1990). A dialectic of marital and parental relationships within the stepfamily. *Communication Monographs, 57*, 44–61.

Coleman, M., & Ganong, L. (1995). Family reconfiguring following divorce. In S. W. Duck & J. T. Wood (Eds.), *Understanding relationship processes, 5: Relationship challenges* (pp. 73–108). Thousand Oaks, CA: Sage.

Cooney, T. M., & Uhlenberg, P. (1992). Support from parents over the life course: The adult child's perspective. *Social Forces, 71*, 63–84.

Constantine, L. L. (1986). *Family paradigms*. New York: Guilford.

Constantine, L. L., & Israel, J. T. (1985). The family void: Treatment and theoretical aspects of the synchronous family paradigm. *Family Process, 24*, 525–547.

Craig, R. T. (1989). Communication as a practical discipline. In B. Dervin, L. Grossberg, B. J. O'Keefe, & E. Wartella (Eds.), *Rethinking communication: Volume 1, paradigm issues* (pp. 97–122). Newbury Park, CA: Sage.

Craig, R. T. (1995). Applied communication research in a practical discipline. In K. N. Cissna (Ed.), *Applied communication in the 21st century* (pp. 147–155). Mahwah, NJ: Erlbaum.

Crocker, L. (1951). Communication and the family. *Journal of Communication, 1*, 63–66.

Cryer-Downs, V. (1989). The grandparent-grandchild relationship. In J. F. Nussbaum (Ed.), *Life-span communication: Normative processes* (pp. 257–281). Hillsdale, NJ: Erlbaum.

Davis, M. S. (1973). *Intimate relations*. New York: Free Press.

Delia, J. G. (1987). Communication research: A history. In C. R. Berger & S. H. Chaffee, *Handbook of Communication Science* (pp. 20–98). Newbury Park, CA: Sage.

Desmond, R. J., Singer, J. L., & Singer, D. G. (1990). Family mediation: Parental communication patterns and influences of television on children. In J. Bryant (Ed.), *Television and the American family* (pp. 293–309). Hillsdale, NJ: Erlbaum.

Dickson, F. C. (1995). The best is yet to be: Research on long-lasting marriages. In J. T. Wood & S. W. Duck (Eds.), *Understudied relationships: Off the beaten track* (pp. 22–50). Beverly Hills, CA: Sage.

Dickson-Markman, F., & Markman, H. J. (1988). The effects of others on marriage: Do they help or hurt? In P. Noller & M. A. Fitzpatrick (Eds.), *Perspectives on marital interaction* (pp. 294–322). Clevedon, England: Multilingual Matters, Ltd.

Dixson, M. D. (1995). Models and perspectives of parent-child communication. In T. J. Socha & G. H. Stamp (Eds.), *Parents, children, and communication: Frontiers of theory and research* (pp. 43–62). Mahwah, NJ: Erlbaum.

Doherty, W. J. (1997a). *The intentional family*. Reading, MA: Addison-Wesley.

Doherty, W. J. (1997b). Making time for your marriage. *Family Circle*, June 24, 1997 issue, pp. 34–37. (Reprinted section of *The intentional family*.)

Duck, S. W. (1990). Relationships as unfinished business: Out of the frying pan and into the 1990s. *Journal of Social and Personal Relationships, 7*, 5–24.

Duncan, S. F., & Brown, G. (1992). RENEW: A program for building remarried family strengths. *Families in Society, 73*, 149–158.

Eadie, W. F. (1990). Being applied: Communication research comes of age. *Journal of Applied Communication Research*, special issue (no volume number), p. 1–6.

Ellis, C., & Bochner, A. P. (1992). Telling and performing personal stories: The constraints of choice in abortion. In C. Ellis & M. Flaherty (Eds.), *Investigating subjectivity* (pp. 97–101). Newbury Park, CA: Sage.

Ericson, P. M., & Rogers, L. E. (1973). New procedures for analyzing relational communication. *Family Process, 12*, 244–267.

Ferguson, S. M., & Dickson, F. C. (1995). Children's expectations of their single parents' dating behaviors: A preliminary investigation of emergent themes relevant to single parent dating. *Journal of Applied Communication Research, 23*, 308–324.

Fisher, B. A. (1978). *Perspectives on human communication*. New York: Macmillan.

Fitzpatrick, M. A. T. (1976). A typological examination of communication in enduring relationships. Unpublished doctoral dissertation, Temple University.

Fitzpatrick, M. A. (1988). *Between husbands and wives: Communication in marriage*. Newbury Park, CA: Sage.

Fitzpatrick, M. A. (1990). *Ageing, health, and family communication: A theoretical perspective*. In H. Giles, H. Coupland, & J. M. Wiemann (Eds.), *Communication, health, and the elderly, Fulbright papers, vol. 8* (pp. 213–228). Manchester, England: Manchester University Press.

Fitzpatrick, M. A., & Dindia, K. (1986). Couples and other strangers: Talk time in spouse-spouse interaction. *Communication Research, 13*, 625–652.

Fitzpatrick, M. A., & Ritchie, L. D. (1993). Communication theories. In P. Boss, W. Doherty, R. LaRossa, W. Schumm, & S. Steinmetz (Eds.), *Sourcebook of family theories and methods: A contextual approach* (pp. 565–585). New York: Plenum.

Fitzpatrick, M. A., & Ritchie, L. D. (1994). Communication schemata within the family: Multiple perspectives on family interaction. *Human Communication Research, 20*, 275–301.

Fitzpatrick, M. A., Vangelisti, A. L., & Firman, S. M. (1994). Perceptions of marital interaction and change during pregnancy: A typology approach. *Personal Relationships, 1*, 101–122.

Fitzpatrick, M. A., & Wamboldt, F. S. (1990). Where is all said and done? Toward an integration of intrapersonal and interpersonal models of family communication. *Communication Research, 17*, 421–430.

Frentz, T. S. (1995). The unbearable darkness of seeing. Presidential address to the Southern States Communication Association, April 7, 1995, New Orleans, LA.

Friedlander, M., & Heatherington, L. (1989). Analyzing relational control in family therapy interviews. *Journal of Counseling Psychology, 37*, 261–268.

Gage, R. B. (1988). An analysis of relational control patterns in abusive couples. Unpublished doctoral dissertation, Seton Hall University, South Orange, NJ.

Galvin, K. M. (1979). Social simulation in the family communication course. *Communication Education, 28*, 68–72.

Galvin, K. M. (1992, October). *Teaching the family communication course: Ethical issues*. Paper presented at the meeting of the National Communication Association, Chicago, IL.

Galvin, K. M., & Brommel, B. J. (1982). *Family communication: Cohesion and change* (1st ed.). Glenview, IL: Scott, Foresman.

Galvin, K. M., & Brommel, B. J. (1996). *Family communication: Cohesion and change* (4th ed.). New York: HarperCollins.

Galvin, K., & Wilkinson, C. (1980). Family communication as an applied area. *Journal of the Illinois Speech and Theatre Association, 34*, 1–8.

Gaul, R., Simon, L., Friedlander, M. L., & Cutler, C. (1991). Correspondence of family therapists' perceptions with FRCCCS coding rules for triadic interactions. *Journal of Marital and Family Therapy, 17*, 379–393.

Gelles, R. J. (1974). *The violent home*. Beverly Hills, CA: Sage.

Gilgun, J. F., Daly, K., & Handel, G. (1992). *Qualitative methods in family research*. Newbury Park, CA: Sage.

Goldberg, J. H., & Goldberg, A. A. (1976). Family communication. *Western Speech Communication, 40*, 104–110.

Gotcher, J. M. (1993). The effects of family communication on psychological adjustment of cancer patients. *Journal of Applied Communication Research, 21*, 176–188.

Handel, G. (1994, November). *Family Worlds* and the qualitative tradition in family research. Paper presented on the panel, *Gerald Handel on Family Worlds and qualitative family research*. National Communication Association annual convention, New Orleans, LA.

Heatherington, L., & Friedlander, M. (1990). Complementarity and symmetry in family therapy communication. *Journal of Counseling Psychology, 37*, 261–268.

Heavey, C. L., & Layne, C., & Christensen, A. (1993). Gender and conflict structure in marital interaction: A replication and extension. *Journal of Consulting and Clinical Psychology, 61*, 16–27.

Heintz, K. E. (1992). Children's favorite television families: A descriptive analysis of role interactions. *Journal of Broadcasting and Electronic Media, 36*, 443–451.

Hess, R., & Handel, G. (1959). *Family worlds*. Chicago: University of Chicago Press.

Huston, T. L., & Vangelisti, A. L. (1995). How parenthood affects marriage. In M. A. Fitzpatrick & A. L. Vangelisti (Eds.), *Explaining family interactions* (pp. 147–176). Thousand Oaks, CA: Sage.

Infante, D. A., Sabourin, T. C., Rudd, J. E., & Shannon, E. A. (1990). Verbal aggression in violent and nonviolent marital disputes. *Communication Quarterly, 38*, 361–371.

Jorgenson, J. (1989). Where is the "family" in family communication?: Exploring families' self-definitions. *Journal of Applied Communication Research, 17*, 27–41.

Kantor, D., & Lehr, W. (1975). *Inside the family*. New York: Harper Colophon Books.

Katriel, T., & Philipsen, G. (1981). "What we need is communication": "Communication" as a cultural category in American speech. *Communication Monographs, 48*, 301–317.

Kelley, D. (1992, October). *Reflections on the ethics of teaching the family communication course*. Paper presented at the meeting of the National Communication Association, Chicago, IL.

Kieren, D. K., & Doherty-Poirier, M. (1993). Teaching about family communication and problem-solving: Issues and future directions. In M. E. Arcus, J. D. Schvaneveldt, & J. J. Moss (Eds.), *Handbook of family life education, vol. 2 Practice of family life education*, pp. 155–179. Newbury Park, CA: Sage.

Knapp, M. (1993). Editor's introduction to L. Stafford and C. L. Bayer, *Interaction between parents and children*. Newbury Park, CA: Sage.

Knapp, M. L., & Vangelisti, A. L. (1996). *Interpersonal communication and human relationships* (3rd ed.). Boston: Allyn & Bacon.

Krokoff, L. J. (1990). Hidden agendas in marriage: Affective and longitudinal dimensions. *Communication Research, 17*, 483–499.

Larzelere, R. E., & Klein, D. M. (1987). Methodology. In M. B. Sussman & S. K. Steinmetz (Eds.), *Handbook of marriage and the family* (pp. 125–155). New York: Plenum.

Leach, M. S., & Braithwaite, D. O. (1996). A binding tie: Supportive communication of family kinkeepers. *Journal of Applied Communication Research, 24*, 200–216.

Lewis, R. A., & Lin, L. (1996). Adults and their midlife parents. In N. Vanzetti & S. Duck (Eds.), *A lifetime of relationships* (pp. 364–382). Albany, NY: Brooks/Cole.

Long, B. W., & Grant, C. H. (1992). The "surprising range of the possible": Families communicating in fiction. *Communication Education, 41*, 89–107.

Long, R. (1992, October). *Teaching the family communication course: Ethical issues*. Paper presented at the meeting of the National Communication Association, Chicago, IL.

Markman, H. J., Duncan, W., Storaasli, R. D., & Howes, P. W. (1987). Understanding major mental disorder: The contribution of family interaction research. In K. Hahlweg & M. J. Goldstein (Eds.), *The Family Process Press Monograph Series* (pp. 266–289). New York: Family Process Press.

Markman, H. J., Floyd, F. J., Stanley, S. M., & Storaasli, R. D. (1988). Prevention of marital distress: A longitudinal investigation. *Journal of Consulting and Clinical Psychology, 56*, 210–217.

Markman, H. J., Jamieson, K. J., & Floyd, F. J. (1983). The assessment and modification of premarital relationships: Preliminary findings on the etiology and prevention of marital and family distress. *Advances in Family Intervention, Assessment, and Theory, 3*, 41–90.

Markman, H. J., & Notarius, C. I. (1987). Coding marital and family interaction: Current status. In T. Jacobs (Ed.), *Family interaction and psychopathology: Theories, methods, and findings*, pp. 396–428. New York: Plenum.

Markman, H. J., Renick, M. J., Floyd, F. J., Stanley, S. M., & Clements, M. (1993). Preventing marital distress through communication and conflict management training: A 4- and 5-year follow-up. *Journal of Consulting and Clinical Psychology, 61*, 1–80.

McLeod, J. M., & Chaffee, S. R. (1972). The construction of social reality. In J. T. Tedeschi (Ed.), *The social influence process*. Chicago, IL: Aldine Atherton.

Meadowcroft, J., & Fitzpatrick, M. A. (1988). Theories of family communication: Toward a merger of intersubjectivity and mutual influence processes. In R. P. Hawkins, J. M. Wiemann, & S. Pingree (Eds.), *Advancing communication science: Merging mass and interpersonal processes* (pp. 253–274). Newbury Park, CA: Sage.

Miller, G. R. (1995). "I think my schizophrenia is better today," said the communication researcher unanimously: Some thoughts on the dysfunctional dichotomy between pure and applied communication research. In K. N. Cissna (Ed.), *Applied communication in the 21st century* (pp. 47–55). Mahwah, NJ: Erlbaum.

Miller, G. R., & Nicholson, H. E. (1976). *Communication inquiry: A perspective on process*. Reading, MA: Addison-Wesley.

Miller, M. (1995). An intergenerational case study of suicidal tradition and mother-daughter communication. *Journal of Applied Communication Research, 23*, 247–270.

Montgomery, B. (1992). Communication as the interface between couples and culture. In S. A. Deetz (Ed.), *Communication yearbook vol. 15* (pp. 476–508). Newbury Park, CA: Sage.

Mortensen, C. D. (1972). *Communication: The study of human interaction*. New York: McGraw-Hill.

Noller, P., & Feeney, J. A. (1990). Attachment style and marital communication. *Proceedings of the 5th International Conference on Personal Relationships*. Oxford, UK.

Noller, P., & Fitzpatrick, M. A. (1993). *Communication in family relationships*. Englewood Cliffs, NJ: Prentice-Hall.

O'Donohue, W., & Crouch, J. L. (1996). Marital therapy and gender-linked factors in communication. *Journal of Marital and Family Therapy, 22*, 87–101.

O'Hair, D., Kreps, G. L., & Frey, L. R. (1990). Conceptual issues. In D. O'Hair & G. L. Kreps (Eds.), *Applied communication theory and research* (pp. 3–22). Hillsdale, NJ: Erlbaum.

Olson, D. H., McCubbin, H., Barnes, H. L., Larsen, A. S., Muxen, M. J., & Wilson, M. A. (1989). *Families: What makes them work* (2nd edition). Beverly Hills, CA: Sage.

Olson, D. H., Sprenkle, D., & Russell, C. (1979). Circumplex Model of Marital and Family Systems I: Cohesion and adaptability dimensions, family types and clinical applications. *Family Process, 18*, 3–28.

Osborn, M. (1990, January 17). The study of communication flourishes in a democratic environment. *Chronicle of Higher Education*, pp. B2–B3.

Parsons, T., & Bales, R. F. (1955). *Family, socialization, and interaction process*. Glencoe, IL: Free Press.

Pearlin, L. I., Mullan, J. T., Semple, S. J., & Skaff, M. M. (1990). Caregiving and the stress process: An overview of concepts and their measures. *The Gerontologist, 30*, 583–594.

Pearson, J. C. (1993). *Communication in the family: Seeking satisfaction in changing times* (2nd edition). New York: HarperCollins.

Petronio, S. (1991). Communication boundary management: A theoretical model of managing disclosure of private information between marital couples. *Communication Theory, 1*, 311–335.

Petronio, S., & Bradford, L. (1993). Issues interfering with the use of written communication as a means of relational bonding between absentee, divorced fathers and their children. *Journal of Applied Communication Research, 21*, 163–175.

Petronio, S., & Harriman, S. (1990, November). *Parental privacy invasion: The use of deceptive and direct strategies and the influence on the parent–child relationship*. Paper presented at the National Communication Association annual convention, Chicago, IL.

Petronio, S., Reeder, H. M., Hecht, M. L., and Ros-Mendoza, T. M. (1996). Disclosure of sexual abuse by children and adolescents. *Journal of Applied Communication Research, 24*, 181–199.

Pike, G. R., & Sillars, A. L. (1985). Reciprocity of marital communication. *Journal of Social and Personal Relationships, 2*, 303–324.

Pingree, S., & Thompson, M. E. (1990). The family in daytime serials. In J. Bryant (Ed.), *Television and the American family* (pp. 113–127). Hillsdale, NJ: Erlbaum.

Planalp, S. (1993). Communication, cognition, and emotion. *Communication Monographs, 60*, 3–9.

Query, J. L., & Flint, L. J. (1996). The caregiving relationship. In N. Vanzetti & S. Duck (Eds.), *A lifetime of relationships* (pp. 455–483). Albany, NJ: Brooks/Cole.

Raven, B. H., & French, J. R. P. Jr. (1956). A formal theory of social power. *Psychological Review, 63*, 181–194.

Reardon, K. K., & Rogers, E. M. (1988). Interpersonal versus mass media communication: A false dichotomy. *Human Communication Research, 15*, 284–303.

Reiss, D. (1981). *The family's construction of reality*. Cambridge, MA: Harvard University Press.

Ritchie, L. D., & Fitzpatrick, M. A. (1990). Family communication patterns: Measuring intrapersonal perceptions of interpersonal relationships. *Communication Research, 17*, 523–544.

Rogers, L. E. (1972). Dyadic systems and transactional communication in a family context (Doctoral dissertation, Michigan State University). *Dissertation Abstracts International, 33*, 11A. (University Microfilms No. 73-12, 810).

Rogers, L. E. (1989). Relational communication processes and patterns. In *Rethinking communication, Vol. 2* (pp. 280–290). In B. Dervin, L. Grossberg, B. O'Keefe, & E. Wartella (Eds.). Newbury Park, CA: Sage.

Rogers, L. E., & Farace, R. V. (1975). Analysis of relational communication in dyads: New measurement procedures. *Human Communication Research, 1*, 222–239.

Rogers-Millar, L. E., & Millar, F. E. (1979). Domineeringness and dominance: A transactional view. *Human Communication Research, 5*, 238–246.

Rosenblatt, P. C. (1994). *Metaphors of family systems theory: Toward new constructions*. New York, NY: Guilford.

Rosenfeld, L. B. (1992, October). *Teaching the family course: Ethical issues*. Paper presented at the meeting of the National Communication Association, Chicago.

Rosenfeld, L. B. (1994, November). *Ethical considerations in assigning students to write personal narratives in a family communication course*. Paper presented at the annual meeting of the National Communication Association, New Orleans, LA.

Rosenfled, L. B., Bowen, G. L., & Richman, J. M. (1995). Communication in three types of dual-career marriages. In M. A. Fitzpatrick & A. L. Vangelisti (Eds.), *Explaining family interaction* (pp. 257–289). Thousand Oaks, CA: Sage.

Sabourin, T. C. (1995). The role of negative reciprocity in spouse abuse: A relational control analysis. *Journal of Applied Communication Research, 23*, 271–283.

Scarf, M. (1987). *Intimate partners: Patterns in love and marriage*. New York: Random House.

Schramm, W. (1997). *The beginnings of communication study in America* (S. Chaffee & E. Rogers, Eds.). Thousand Oaks, CA: Sage.

Shotter, J. (1993). *Conversational realities: The construction of life through language*. Newbury Park, CA: Sage.

Shannon, C., & Weaver, W. (1949). *The mathematical theory of communication*. Urbana, IL: University of Illinois Press.

Sillars, A. L. (1995). Communication and family culture. In M. A. Fitzpatrick & A. L. Vangelisti (Eds.), *Explaining family interactions* (pp. 375–399). Thousand Oaks, CA: Sage.

Sillars, A. L., Burggraf, C. S., Yost, S., & Zietlow, P. H. (1992). Conversational themes and marital relationship definitions: Quantitative and qualitative investigations. *Human Communication Research, 19*, 124–154.

Sillars, A. L., Pike, G., Jones, T. R., & Murphy, M. A. (1984). Communication and understanding in marriage. *Human Communication Research, 10*, 317–350.

Sillars, A. L., Pike, G. R., Jones, T. S., & Redmon, K. (1983). Communication and conflict in marriage. *Communication Yearbook, 7*, 414–429.

Sillars, A. L., & Weisberg, J. (1987). Conflict as a social skill. In M. E. Roloff and G. R. Miller (Eds.), *Interpersonal processes: New directions in communication research* (pp. 140–171). Newbury Park, CA: Sage.

Sillars, A. L., Weisberg, J., Burggraf, C. S., & Wilson, E. A. (1987). Content themes in marital conversations. *Human Communication Research, 13*, 495–528.

Sillars, A. L., Weisberg, J., Burggraf, C. S., & Zietlow, P. H. (1990). Communication and understanding revisited: Married couples' understanding and recall of conversations. *Communication Research, 17*, 500–522.

Skill, T., Wallace, S., & Cassata, M. (1990). Families on prime-time television: Patterns of conflict escalation and resolution against intact, nonintact, and mixed-family settings. In J. Bryant (Ed.), *Television and the American family* (pp. 129–163). Hillsdale, NJ: Erlbaum.

Sluzki, C., & Beavin, J. (1965). Simetría y complementaridad: Una definición operacional y una tipología de parejas. *Acta Psiquiátrica y Psicológica de America Latina, 11*, 321–330.

Smith, M. J. (1988). *Contemporary communication research methods*. Belmont, CA: Wadsworth.

Smith, F. M., & Hawes, B. (1987). Early adolescents practice effective communication in the family setting: A curriculum unit. *Journal of Vocational Home Economics Education, 6*, 19–26.

Spanier, G. B. (1976). Measuring dyadic adjustment: New scales for assessing the quality of marriage and similar dyads. *Journal of Marriage and the Family, 38*, 15–28.

Stafford, L., & Bayer, C. L. (1993). *Interaction between parents and children*. Newbury Park, CA: Sage.

Stafford, L., & Daly, J. A. (1984). Conversational memory: The effects of recall mode and memory expectations on remembrances of natural conversations. *Human Communication Research, 10*, 379–402.

Stafford, L., Burggraf, C. S., & Sharkey, W. F. (1987). Conversational memory: The effects of time, recall mode, and memory expectancies on remembrances of natural conversations. *Human Communication Research, 14*, 203–229.

Stafford, L., & Dainton, M. (1995). Parent–child communication within the family system. In T. J. Socha & G. H. Stamp (Eds.), *Parents, children, and communication: Frontiers of theory and research* (pp. 3–22). Mahwah, NJ: Erlbaum.

Stafford, L., Waldron, V. R., & Infield, L. L. (1989). Actor-observer differences in conversational memory. *Human Communication Research, 15,* 590–611.

Stamp, G. H. (1994). The appropriation of the parental role through communication during the transition to parenthood. *Communication Monographs, 61,* 89–112.

Stamp, G. H., & Banski, M. A. (1992). The communicative management of constrained autonomy during the transition to parenthood. *Western Journal of Communication, 56,* 281–300.

Stamp, G. H., & Sabourin, T. C. (1995). Accounting for violence: An analysis of male spousal abuse narratives. *Journal of Applied Communication Research, 23,* 284–307.

Steier, F., Stanton, M. D., & Todd, T. C. (1982). Patterns of turn-taking and alliance formation in family communication. *Journal of Communication, 32,* 148–160.

Thomas, C. E., Booth-Butterfield, M., & Booth-Butterfield, S. (1995). Perceptions of deception, divorce disclosures, and communication satisfaction with parents. *Western Journal of Communication, 59,* 228–245.

Turner, L. H., & West, R. (1998). *Perspectives on family communication.* Mountain View, CA: Mayfield.

Vangelisti, A. L. (1991). The pedagogical use of family measures: "My, how you've grown!" *Communication Education, 40,* 187–201.

Vangelisti, A. L. (1994). Family secrets: Forms, functions, and correlates. *Journal of Social and Personal Relationships, 11,* 113–135.

Vangelisti, A. L., & Banski, M. (1993). Couples' debriefing conversations: The impact of gender, occupation, and demographic characteristics. *Family Relations, 42,* 149–157.

Varallo, S. M., Ray, E. B., & Ellis, B. H. (1998). Speaking of incest: The research interview as social justice. *Journal of Applied Communication Research, 26,* 254–271.

Wartella, E., & Reeves, B. (1987). Communication and children. In C. R. Berger & S. H. Chaffee (Eds.), *Handbook of communication science* (pp. 619–650). Newbury Park, CA: Sage.

Watzlawick, P. (Ed.). (1964). *An anthology of human communication: Text and tape.* Palo Alto, CA: Science and Behavior Books.

Watzlawick, P., Beavin, J., & Jackson, D. (1967). *The pragmatics of human communication.* New York: Norton.

Weitzman, J., & Dreen, K. (1982). Wife beating: A view of the marital dyad. *Social Casework, 63,* 259–265.

Whitchurch, G. G. (1992). Communication in marriages and families: A review essay of family communication textbooks. *Communication Education, 41,* 337–343.

Whitchurch, G. G. (1993). Designing a course in family communication. *Communication Education, 42*(3), 255–267.

Whitchurch, G. G. (1994, November). *Violent critical incidents in four types of violent interspousal relationships.* Paper presented at the National Communication Association annual convention, New Orleans, LA.

Whitchurch, G. G. (1995, November). *Overview of family communication research: Complexities and multi-faceted characteristics.* Paper presented at the Second Preconvention Conference on Family Communication, National Communication Association annual convention, San Antonio, TX.

Whitchurch, G. G., & Constantine, L. L. (1993). Systems theory. In P. Boss, W. Doherty, R. LaRossa, W. Schumm, and S. Steinmetz (Eds.), *Sourcebook of family theories and methods: A contextual approach* (pp. 325–352). New York: Plenum.

Whitchurch, G. G., & Pace, J. L. (1993). Communication skills training and interspousal violence. *Journal of Applied Communication Research, 21,* 96–102.

Whitchurch, G.G., & Rogers, L. E. (1993, November). *Applications of the "Communication Systems School"/Palo Alto Model in family therapy and family communication.* Paper presented at the National Communication Association annual convention, Miami, FL.

Whitchurch, G. G., & Sharp, J. F. (1994, November). *Student self-analysis of autobiographical narratives in the family communication course: An examination of the boundaries between family communication and therapy.* Paper presented at the National Communication Association annual convention, New Orleans, LA.

Whitchurch, G. G., & Webb, L. M. (1995). Applied family communication research: Casting light upon the demon. *Journal of Applied Communication Research, 23*(4), 239–246.

Whitehead, A. N., & Russell, B. (1910–1913). *Principia Mathematica,* 3 volumes. Cambridge: Cambridge University Press.

Wilder, C. (1979). The Palo Alto Group: Difficulties and directions of the interactional view for human communication research. *Human Communication Research, 5,* 171–186.

Williams, L., & Jurich, J. (1995). Predicting marital success after five years: Assessing the predictive validity of FOCCUS. *Journal of Marital and Family Therapy, 21,* 141–153.

Witteman, H., & Fitzpatrick, M. A. (1986). Compliance-gaining in marital interaction: Power bases, processes, and outcomes. *Communication Monographs, 53,* 130–143.

Wolff, L. O. (1990, November). *Stories that shape us: Family narrative in the family communication course.* Paper presented at the Preconvention Conference on Family Communication, National Communication Association annual convention, Chicago, IL.

Wood, J. T. (1982). Communication and relational culture: Basis for the study of human relationships. *Communication Quarterly, 30,* 75–84.

Wood, J. T. (1995). *Relational communication; Continuity and change in personal relationships.* Belmont, CA: Wadsworth.

Yerby, J., Buerkel-Rothfuss, N., & Bochner, A. P. (1995). *Understanding family communication* (2nd ed.). Scottsdale, AZ: Gorsuch Scarisbrick.

CHAPTER 26

Family Abuse and Violence

JoAnn Langley Miller and Dean D. Knudsen

with Stacey Copenhaver

"Do you know," my father said ... "there's only one person who could have given you the strength to leave me" ... I looked at him. "You?" I said, at last. "Yes," he said. (Harrison, 1997, p. 192)

At age 20 a thoughtful woman from a family with high social status began a lengthy period of enslavement to her father, a theologian. Claiming only that he loved his daughter, the father took possession of his daughter's body, her sexuality, her emotional well-being, her social and family relationships, and nearly her life itself. Now an acclaimed young novelist, Kathryn Harrison quietly writes about the years of her own father–daughter incest experiences in *The Kiss*. Her memoirs tell about an ordinary case of family abuse. There were no repressed memories recovered, no failed social service agency, no murdered victim, and no falsely accused offender. There are, however, permanent and emotional scars resulting from an especially insidious form of family abuse and perplexing questions that can never be answered. *The Kiss* compels its readers to acknowledge a well-known social fact: A family member characterized by any socioeconomic group, any age, either gender, or any race or ethnicity can experience one or several forms of family abuse and violence. A highly educated mother can neglect her newborn infant, a university professor can kill his partner, an older sister can batter a young brother, a middle-aged husband can rape his wife, and a mother can exploit financially and physically abuse her own elderly mother.

Family abuse and violence has a long, perhaps infinite, history. Infanticide, especially of girl babies, insufferable brutality toward children, the sexual exploitation of children

and adolescents, sibling violence and sexual assaults, and physical and emotional attacks on intimate partners have occurred in family relationships for much of human history. For the past 2 centuries the legitimacy of family abuse and violence has been seriously questioned, but only recently have the many forms of family abuse and violence become generally recognized social problems in the United States and other nations.

Introduction

This chapter examines some of the forms of family abuse and violence, defined generally as "act[s] carried out with the intention, or perceived as having the intention of physically hurting another person" (Gelles & Straus, 1979, p. 554). This general definition requires that one social actor, a family member, *intends* to hurt another family member. Further, it requires a *social act* or a behavior to occur. Accidents, wishes, or fantasies are not included. This definition excludes many acts of verbal or emotional abuse, behaviors that hurt, but not physically (Brassard, Hart, & Hardy, 1993; Daro, 1988; O'Hagan, 1995). According to most states' laws it excludes many forms of neglect or negligence. Negligence by a parent, because of a religious belief, to seek appropriate medical care for an ill child is not included in this definition, nor are the thousands of cases of neglect of the unborn that result in physical or emotional deficiencies at birth each year in the United States (Garrity-Rokous, 1994; McCurdy & Daro, 1994; Weise & Daro, 1995).

We begin this chapter with a general definition of family abuse, one that claims that the social actor's intention or state of mind, along with the actor's physical behaviors, must be scrutinized to study family violence. The general definition includes all possible family members: persons in traditional and nontraditional families; adults and children, including

JoAnn Langley Miller and Dean D. Knudsen • Department of Sociology and Anthropology, Purdue University, West Lafayette, Indiana 47907.

Handbook of Marriage and the Family, 2nd edition, edited by Marvin Sussman, Suzanne K. Steinmetz, and Gary W. Peterson. Plenum Press, New York, 1999.

706 • Part V • Changing Family Patterns and Roles

foster and stepchildren; domestic partners; and cohabiting or noncohabiting romantic and sexual partners. Throughout the chapter, we also provide more specific definitions for each form or type of family abuse and violence analyzed. By introducing both a general definition and specific definitions of family violence we raise a fundamental debate that concerns scholars and policy makers alike: Is family violence a singular phenomenon, a problem that requires a unified method of inquiry and an integrated set of social policies and organizations designed to respond to different forms of a single social problem? Or are the various forms and types of family violence unique, so different and so distant from each other that any attempt to study or remedy them as a single social problem is at best futile, and perhaps dangerous for the various types of victims and survivors of child abuse, partner abuse, and elder abuse?

This debate has critical conceptual and practical implications. At a conceptual level, the debate challenges the validity of two dominant system approaches, a gendered versus nongendered systems approach, for studying family violence problems. A gendered systems approach takes the position that "gender and the unequal distribution of power should be the organizing principle for understanding the [family violence or child abuse] phenomenon" (Berliner, 1990, p. 128). The dominance and power of men over women in a society or a culture, according to a gendered systems approach, explains why women are battered by their male partners or why acts of child sexual abuse tend to be perpetrated by males against female infants or children. A nongendered perspective that adopts a family systems approach (Downs, 1996; Straus, Gelles, & Steinmetz, 1980) explains the various forms of family abuse and violence as a function of family characteristics and interaction patterns. We contend that the dominant gendered and nongendered systems approaches have utility for studying family violence and abuse because they examine how the family, a social institution, and gender relations within the family and the larger society provide explanations for the causes and consequences of child abuse, partner abuse, and elder abuse. Nonetheless, a profound challenge for future scholars is the development of perspectives that can more completely explain the multiple problems subsumed by the umbrella term "family abuse and violence."

At the practical level, accepting that there are multiple problems of family abuse and violence poses severe challenges to many existing social policies and legal remedies. An extant and dominant social policy across many states and social service agencies is to preserve the family—a presumably vital social institution—while protecting individuals within the family. Programs are designed to minimize the need to place a child in a foster home or the amount of time an abused child spends apart from biological parents (Panel on

Research on Child Abuse and Neglect, 1993). Therapy or counseling programs for men who batter their partners, especially if mandated by the courts, aim at preserving families (Barnett, Miller-Perrin, & Perrin, 1997), and laws promulgated in response to elder abuse protect only the dependent, elderly family member (Penhale, 1993).

Rigorous social science evaluations of service and treatment programs offering help for parents, spouses, or children that are premised on the family preservation model do not find conclusive and positive outcomes (Azar & Wolfe, 1989; Barrera, Palmer, Brown, & Kalaher, 1994; Bath & Haapala, 1993; Berk, 1993; Rossi, 1992; Shepard, 1992; Tracy, Haapala, & Pecora, 1991). Family preservation programs may indeed be cost-efficient alternatives to foster care or the placement of an abused or neglected child or elder family member in a social institution, but there is not empirical evidence to support the contention these social programs are likely to have positive, long-term benefits. They may, in fact, cause irreparable harm.

Once a proponent of family preservation programs, Richard Gelles now argues strongly for the adoption of child-centered policies that, in response to child abuse incidents, will abandon the widespread "fantasy" that social service agencies can protect the abused child while preserving the family. Gelles (1996) presents a case study of a 15-month-old boy, David (a pseudonym), who was killed by his mother 3 months after a social service caseworker determined a lack of evidence sufficient to substantiate a child abuse claim. David was underweight for his age, and an X ray taken months before his death showed he had a chipped elbow. Although both parents were investigated in David's case, and they had abused their older child severely enough to lose custody of her, David remained for his 15 month life with his biological parents. Gelles says, "What haunts me about David is that we know enough about child abuse that we could have, and should have, saved his life" (p. ix). He shows empirically that "30 to 50 percent of the children killed by parents or caretakers are killed *after* they were identified by child welfare agencies, were involved in interventions, and were either left in their homes or returned home after a short-term placement" (p. 149).

Is there one, multidimensional social problem, aptly called family violence, that requires a singular but systematic explanation and social response? Or are there are there at least three different social problems—child abuse, partner abuse, and elder abuse—that require at least three explanations, three social policies, and three types of responses? We offer no answer to these questions, but instead invite readers to formulate their own conclusions. We do, however, offer a modest proposal for making sense of the pervasive theories and empirical studies we analyze in this chapter: Child abuse, partner abuse, and elder abuse are subject to "hairsplitting discussions" about what they are, how they are defined, and how common they are. We cannot let the discussions "obscure the fact that a significant number of [persons] are exposed to unacceptable forms of violence." To prevent child abuse, partner abuse, and elder abuse, social rules (attitudes, norms, public policies, and social programs) must be developed to guarantee safe *dependence* for old people and children, while promoting safe *independence* for adult women and men in contemporary society (Whittaker, 1996, p. 150).

In this chapter we discuss the history of child abuse, violence between adult family members, and elder abuse. We define each form of abuse and violence as distinctive problems, explore their emergence as social problems, assess their incidence and prevalence, and consider the consequences of such behaviors and social interventions for individuals and for society.

The term "family" has many definitions, as other contributors to this *Handbook* point out, but for our purposes it is a small social group, usually sharing a common residence, involving intimacy among members, with expectations of longevity or permanence, and often characterized by age and gender differentiation among members. This definition includes married and unmarried couples, heterosexuals, lesbians, and gays. It includes stepfamilies and families with members from as few as one generation or many as four generations. Because the focus of this chapter is on family abuse and violence, other forms of violence, such as violence between dating couples, attacks among members of social groups, hate crimes, or abuse or violence that occurs outside the family, are excluded. Similarly, research on some forms of child or adult neglect, or the failure to act in a way that protects another from harm, is not included.

The number of published studies on the family violence that harms children, adults, and elderly adults has increased dramatically over the past 2 decades. Our review and analysis is based on what we conclude is a concise yet accurate examination of the history of family violence, the current knowledge and empirical evidence, and the major theoretical perspectives that are most useful for researching family abuse and violence problems. We devote some attention to policy issues, specifically the consequences of changes in laws and the social services on the frequency and severity of violence and abuse within families, and we conclude with an overview of some of the recent controversies that dominate the fields of family violence.

History of Violence in Families

Childhood, the stage of life that is supposed to be carefree, safe, secure, and characterized by innocence and tenderness, is actually a period of insecurity, trauma, and threat for many social groups. The history of childhood is a history of infanticide, mutilation, beatings, forced labor, and gentleness. Maltreatment "has been justified for many centuries by the belief that severe physical punishment was necessary either to maintain discipline, to transmit educational ideas, to please certain gods, or to expel evil spirits" (Radbill, 1968, p. 3). These harsh behaviors, often associated with the perceived need to socialize children, appear to have existed and been tolerated until recently throughout the world.

Infanticide was outlawed in Rome in 374 AD because of a desire to increase the population. The killing of less socially "desirable" infants, however, persists. The killing of babies born outside of marriage and deformed or unwanted babies, especially girl babies, has continued to the present time in the United States and other nations (Finkelhor, 1997; Silverman & Kennedy, 1988). As late as the middle of the nineteenth century, infanticide victims were sealed in the structures of new buildings and bridges in Germany to make them stronger. Dead or dying infants were common sights on the dung heaps in the London streets (de Mause, 1974). Public concern about the well-being of children is a relatively new phenomenon and is arguably the result of cultural and psychoanalytic mechanisms (de Mause, 1974), the consequence of technological and social changes (Bakan, 1971; Pagelow, 1984), and other factors (e.g., Gartner, 1993; Shorter, 1975).

Changes brought by the Industrial Revolution, urbanization, the creation of schools, geographic mobility, and the intellectual and cultural developments that followed the Renaissance and Reformation produced new understandings and new legal definitions of parental obligations and custody in Western societies. By the 1670s, Puritans in the Massachusetts Bay Colony had enacted the first laws against "unnatural severity" to children and beating of spouses by either husbands or wives (Pleck, 1989, p. 22). By the mid-nineteenth century, a number of U.S. states began to prosecute parents for cruelty toward their children, but the 1893 Mary Ellen Wilson case in New York City crystallized efforts to deal with abuse (Costin, 1991; Ross, 1980). The Society for the Prevention of Cruelty to Children was founded, and "Child Savers" intervened to protect children from parental inattention, neglect, or violence (Bellingham, 1983; Zelizer, 1985). Despite the fact that by the beginning of the twentieth century child protective systems were already in place, industrial expansion, World War I, the Great Depression, and then World War II intervened to divert public attention from child maltreatment. It was not until the 1960s that child abuse was "discovered" by the medical profession, although evidence had been accumulating for decades from radiologists, social workers, and child advocates (e.g., Kempe, Silverman, Steele, Droegemueller, & Silver, 1962; Williams, 1994). The combination of several factors, including the elimination of a need for child labor, the conception of violence as unacceptable, leadership from high-status medical professionals, and media involvement, resulted in the identification of child abuse as a social problem (e.g., Pfohl, 1977), leading to the identification of other forms of family violence, especially spouse/partner abuse and attacks on elders (Loseke, 1992; Steinmetz, 1988).

Violence and abuse between adult intimates, especially partner abuse or "domestic violence," like child abuse, has a long history. There is considerable evidence that the patriarchal laws and customs that have existed for centuries are intimately associated with violence toward wives. The inferior social, economic, and political positions assigned to women and the claim of ownership of wives by husbands have been enforced by law, resulting in legitimated battering and rape (O'Donovan, 1993). In essence, the legal rights given to husbands by English common law allowed husbands to judge, control, punish, and even kill their wives for serious offenses (Pagelow, 1984; Sigler, 1989). Religious institutions further reinforced female subservience (e.g., Davidson, 1977; Fortune, 1995; Scarf, 1988; Steinmetz, 1987). The English jurist Blackstone viewed marriage as the merger of the wife's identity into that of her husband (Weitzman, 1981). Wives lost control of their property, their children, and even their own bodies, placing physical violence, including rape within the marriage, outside the purview of the law. By the late nineteenth century, several states had effected changes that prohibited husbands from such acts. Nevertheless, violence between spouses continued to be so common that Straus (1976), in one of his earliest studies of family violence, described the marriage license as a "hitting license." Social survey and government data show that social institutional efforts to diminish or eliminate all forms of spouse abuse appear to be only moderately effective (Bachman & Saltzman, 1996; Straus & Gelles, 1986).

Family systems perspectives argue that child abuse, violence between intimates, and elder abuse can only be understood by noting the distinctive features of families and the beliefs about them. Families, compared to other social groups, have several unique characteristics, for example, age and sex differences, a wide range of activities and interests, privacy, and long-term and intense involvement (Gelles & Straus, 1979; Steinmetz, 1987).

These structural features of the family are buttressed by a set of three related beliefs that Pleck (1987) describes as the "Family Ideal." First, there is the belief in privacy and separation from the public world, where strong emotions and qualitatively different relationships, characterized by more affection, a long-lasting or perceived permanence, and social binding are developed. Second, a belief exists that conjugal and parental rights, including the right to demand obedience

to maintain domestic order and harmony, rest with the head of the household, usually the husband. Third is the belief that the family must be preserved, as the agency through which women achieve happiness by the suppression of self-realization. Given these conditions, it is not surprising that attacks on child abuse and family violence have been seen by some as a challenge to family life itself.

As the media reported evidence of an increase in the level of domestic violence or partner abuse in the 1970s, a social concern about abuse of the elderly also emerged and became a dominant social problem in the 1980s. The discovery of elder abuse by the media (Steinmetz, 1981) was related to a variety of demographic and social changes in modern society. The extension of life and life expectancy and the long-term declining birth rate generated a relatively large senior population with fewer children to care for them. Further, elders are often perceived as a nonproductive or even dependent segment of society, making them subject to inattention, neglect, and control by family members and other caretakers.

Information about elder abuse was initially somewhat difficult to obtain, partly because of the elderly's dependence, isolation, and invisibility and the family beliefs noted earlier. In one review, the authors suggested that elder abuse is "a phenomenon (a) that we do not know how to define; (b) for which we have no reliable estimate of the number of persons affected; and (c) about which we know little regarding risk factors" (Pillemer & Suitor, 1988, p. 27). These problems affect our understanding of elder maltreatment especially, although information about all types of family violence is subject to severe limitations, both theoretically and methodologically.

To get past the limitation of relying on the elderly for information about how they are abused, Steinmetz (1988) conducted in-depth, face-to-face interviews with 104 middle-aged persons who care for their elder parents. In this first comprehensive self-report study, she finds that elder abuse is associated with the daily tasks and the resulting stress connected to caring for dependent parents. Thus, the prevention of abuse by reducing caretaker stress, increasing caretakers' knowledge of the possibility of abuse, and reducing the social isolation experienced by many elder parents and their caretakers is currently the preferred social response to this particular social problem (Deitch, 1993; Steinmetz, 1988).

Theories, Perspectives, and Research Methods

Family violence problems cannot be adequately explained or comprehensively studied with any single theory or particular research method. Contemporary publications show that health-care perspectives (Shornstein, 1997; Stark & Flitcraft, 1996), legal studies (Downs, 1996; Lemon, 1996), criminal justice theories (Buzawa, Buzawa, & Inciardi, 1996), a social work orientation (Mullender, 1996), and interdisciplinary approaches (Kaplan & Davidson, 1996; Wallace, 1996) all attempt to explain and document the problems of child abuse, partner abuse, and elder abuse. The social and behavioral sciences, especially psychology and sociology, have published more than 1000 journal articles on the different forms of family violence over the last decade.

Because family violence is indeed a complex social problem that seems to persist across time and across cultures, it resists the development of a definitive explanation that can be translated into social policy. Moreover, all the forms of family violence that are analyzed in this chapter have evoked strong emotional responses in society. As a result, advocate groups are formed whose members work, often without pay, to help abused children, battered partners, and the elderly. Advocates are often critical of academics and researchers, claiming that social scientists are too "technical," too focused on "esoteric notions," and too insensitive to the real life-and-death crises and the real ethical and safety issues that victims and survivors of family violence encounter in society (Gondolf, Yllo, & Campbell, 1997). Consequently, instead of the collaboration between researcher and advocate that is needed to develop effective programs, valid and reliable theory, and rigorous empirical studies, the supposedly "objective" explanation of family violence remains at odds with the "subjective" narratives of those millions of persons who experience the pain, the harm, and the threat of continued family violence. Evaluation studies are still centered on cost-benefit analyses and objective outcome measures, while "street theory" is still dismissed for its lack of testable research hypotheses.

Child abuse, a primary example, is a "highly charged emotional issue" (Azar, 1991, p. 31), and the attention it generated was first directed toward intervention and treatment of victims. As a result, theoretical concerns and the collection of high-quality data that would provide a basis for identifying the causes of abuse were delayed. Instead, diverse perspectives and epistemologies of those most directly associated with the problem shaped the explanations that emerged.

Medical professionals, the first to become involved, focused on the victim's injuries, placing a heavy emphasis on the psychopathology and mental problems of perpetrators as the primary causes of child abuse. As information accumulated, additional or competing explanations were sought. The legal and criminal justice professions defined abusive behaviors as criminal acts that must be punished with criminal sanctions. Intent, or the "guilty mind," a central tenet of criminal law, became the basic issue in response to child abuse. However, legal actions, including the prosecution and conviction of the criminal perpetrator, did not stop the abuse. Thus, social scientists began to offer new perspectives on maltreatment that focused on its context (Knudsen, 1988). By the mid-1960s, systematic research on family violence was initiated (Gelles, 1974; Straus, Gelles, & Steinmetz, 1980; see Steinmetz, 1987, for a review of the literature). As the volume and scientific sophistication of the research increased, questions extended beyond the incidence and prevalence of abuse cases to the social sources, proximate causes, and consequences of abuse. Unfortunately, despite efforts to provide comprehensive information about child maltreatment (e.g., Breire, Berliner, Bulkley, Jenny, & Reid, 1996), consensus about definitions, casual inferences, and appropriate methodologies remains an elusive goal. Reviews of various theories and studies of family violence and aggression provide abundant evidence of these problems.

Theoretical Issues

Efforts to apply theoretical models to explain family violence have had limited success, in part because of the diversity of academic disciplines involved and the lack of collaboration between advocates and social scientists. Numerous theoretical perspectives in the social sciences have been used and adapted to identify the concepts that explain various aspects of violent behavior: attributes of perpetrators, characteristics of victims, interaction patterns, cultural beliefs about the legitimacy of violence, ethnic or religious group norms, and features of social systems. For example, Gelles and Straus (1979) grouped 15 theories into three general categories or types: intraindividual theories, social-psychological theories, and sociocultural theories. Steinmetz (1987) modified the categories somewhat to organize 16 theories or models.

Typologies of classification schemes involve different conceptions of violence and make different assumptions about the origins or causes of violent behavior. They also represent different levels of analysis, and they range from simple single factor explanations of an individual's behaviors or personality traits to complex, multifactor explanatory or causal models (Azar, 1991).

In this chapter, we distinguish three broad types of theories or perspectives that inform and guide family violence researchers: (1) individualist perspectives, (2) interactional perspectives, and (3) sociocultural perspectives. Each of these types incorporates a variety of specific explanations of family violence that are similar in terms of their levels of analysis, their complexity, and the assumptions they share about social problems and society.

Individualist Theories. Individualist perspectives attempt to explain acts of family violence with characteristics of the person. What is *wrong* with the person, the individual, who sexually abuses a child? Which *personality trait* best explains the person who batters a marital partner? Why would an *adult child* harm an elderly parent? These individualistic questions focus on the individual and why a person with certain traits, characteristics, or problems acts violently or abusively toward another.

Violence, according to the individualist theory, is narrowly defined as acts of physical aggression. Although there is a focus on specific acts, these theories locate causality within the perpetrator. In general, single factors, such as a particular personality trait or psychiatric disorder, are identified to explain violent behavior directed at a family member. There are three distinctive subtypes of individualist level theories that drive contemporary family violence research: explanations based on (1) psychopathological factors, (2) perpetrator characteristics, and (3) victim characteristics.

1. Psychopathological explanations assume intraindividual causes for acts of aggression, such as a mental illness or a disease of the individual. Each theory in this subtype provides a simple, single factor explanation for acts of family violence.

To illustrate: DMS-IV (American Psychiatric Association, 1994) identifies Factitious Disorder by Proxy (FDP), popularly known as "Munchausen syndrome by proxy," as a form of child abuse. The perpetrator, often the mother of a young child, feigns a medical disease or illness in her child. The results can be severe or even fatal for the youngest and most vulnerable victims. Psychiatry treats FDP as a form of medical abuse of children and locates causality in the parent or caretaker as a "parent's pathologic wish for sympathy and attention" (Ostfeld & Feldman, 1996, p. 85).

2. Perpetrator characteristics perspectives identify the individual's defective personality trait or abnormality, such as poor impulse control or drug or alcohol addiction, as the cause of violence.

To illustrate: Hanson, Gizzarelli, and Scott (1994) report that child sexual abusers tend to suffer from extreme feelings of "vulnerability" or "inadequacy." Studies of chronic spouse abuse find that an "antisocial orientation" partly explains repeated acts of violence. Some researchers invoke an "antisocial personality disorder," an adult disorder that according to the American Psychiatric Association may have genetic or biological explanations, to explain the intergenerational transmission of family violence (DiLalla & Gottesman, 1991). Luntz and Widom (1994) used a rigorous, longitudinal research design to follow a sample of 416 abused children and 283 nonabused children from the same metropolitan area into young adulthood. These researchers report that the children who were abused, compared to their non-abused counterparts, were more likely to manifest antisocial personality problems and abusive behaviors as young adults. (Most of the abused children did not, however, abuse others as young adults.)

3. Victim characteristics perspectives locate the cause of violence in abnormal behavior or attributes of victims of family violence, such as a physical disability, a chronic illness, or a multiple birth, which precipitates a reaction by the abuser.

To illustrate: Psychiatric syndromes, such as "premenstrual syndrome" (Carney & Williams, 1983) or "posttraumatic stress syndrome" (Erlinder, 1984) are sometimes offered as legal explanations for acts of violence committed against ill victims within the family (Downs, 1996).

Individualist perspectives have some strengths, but they tend to have many weaknesses and limitations in their ability to explain family violence. All told, they provide simple, straightforward explanations for specific forms of violence that are perpetrated by individuals whose behaviors fit models of psychological or medical disorders or illnesses. In some cases, an appropriate diagnosis may lead to effective medical or psychiatric treatment. These perspectives, however, tend to be offer only post hoc explanations of behaviors and events. Only after a parent kills a family member is posttraumatic stress syndrome invoked to explain what otherwise is incomprehensible. Consequently, individualist theories have little predictive ability and even less utility for proposing strategies to ameliorate the family violence problem. These theories tend to explain only a small amount or part of the family violence problems (Pagelow, 1992). The most common and the most frequently occurring forms and incidents of family abuse cannot be explained with perspectives that focus on the unusual, individual case. Imagine the futility of a homicide prevention program that is designed to address the individualistic pathologies of Charles Manson. In addition, family violence explanations that are based on victim characteristics either tend to blame the victim of violence, for example the abused parent, or they render helpless the adult perpetrator. No effective remedy for family violence, a social problem, can be premised exclusively on an individual's illness or past trauma.

Interactional Theories. Interactional perspectives broadly identify family violence as patterns of violent acts or incidents of violence that are perpetrated by one social actor against another social actor. Causality is located in the interaction itself or in the relationship between or among social actors. Why are some marriages or some nonmarried couples characterized by *chronic acts* of physical violence? How is it possible for *a mother* to kill her *own children*? Why would a *son* abuse his elderly and frail *mother*? These questions center on repeated acts or patterns of family abuse or violence. Instead of explaining a problem with individualistic illnesses, disorders, or disabilities, social interactional perspectives focus on social relationships, such as a domestic partnership, parent–child bond, or perceptions of the self in relationship to another social actor. In this chapter we consider five distinctive subtypes of interactional theories that inform contemporary research on family violence: (1) social bonding, (2) exchange theory and deterrence, (3) interpersonal resource or power perspectives, (4) social learning theory, and (5) symbolic interaction perspectives.

1. Social bonding perspectives, derived partly from social control theory (Hirschi, 1969), argue that social interactions generate the formation of relationships and social bonds, including affective attachments, between actors that prescribe and proscribe certain behaviors. Parent–child relationships or domestic partner relationships induce social bonds that prescribe affection, care, and attention while they proscribe neglect, emotional abuse, or acts that will harm the other person in the relationship. Lacking affective attachments to family member(s) and lacking social bonds to family members as well as to the family as a conventional social institution, the individual member faces an increased likelihood of acting in abusive or violent ways toward the other in a familial relationship.

To illustrate: Lackey and Williams (1995) find that inadequate social bonding explains family violence, including violence across generations. The failure of a parent to bond with a child, and the corresponding lack of appropriate affective ties to a child, is offered as a single factor explanations for child homicide or infanticide, the leading cause of death for children under age 18 in the United States (Finkelhor, 1997).

2. Social exchange theories posit that violence, including acts of family violence, result from a pattern or period of negative social interaction that is evaluated by the social actor in cost-benefit terms. Research based on exchange perspectives tends to focus on dyads, especially the married or unmarried adult partnership or the caretaker and victim of elder abuse (Barnett, Miller-Perrin, & Perrin, 1997; Hinrichsen, Hernandez, & Pollack, 1992).

To illustrate: Johnson (1992) studied 426 women who resided in a battered women's shelter to explain why some of the women decided to return home to their abusive marriages. She found that being employed, rather than personal income, predicted a decision not to return to the violent home: "[A] battered woman with few or no marketable skills or access to employment … perceives that her alternatives inside the marriage [are] more rewarding and less costly than alternatives outside the relationship, even though she is being subjected to severe abuse" (p. 175). This empirical finding, Johnson argues, supports exchange theory because it

shows how a battered woman may compare the rewards and costs of her alternatives—to remain in an abusive relationship or to leave her marriage. Applications of exchange theory attempt to explain how the threat or use of police arrest can deter repeated acts of domestic violence (Berk & Newton, 1985; Miller & Krull, 1997; Sherman, 1992). A domestic partner, according to an exchange perspective, is deterred from battering episodes once she or he subjectively evaluates and compares the substantial financial, personal, and social "costs" of arrest with the lesser "benefits" of controlling the other partner with acts or threats of physical violence.

3. Resource and interpersonal power theories that explain family violence are derived from basic social exchange hypotheses. These perspectives identify and sometimes quantify the power and control one social actor has over another within the family as a function of the relative resources, such as income or occupational prestige, attributable to the social actor. If violence within the family occurs, it is likely to be perpetrated by the more dominant or powerful family member against the less dominant or less powerful family member. The intention is to use interpersonal power and force to obtain compliance from the less powerful family member. (Some theorists argue the opposite: The partner with higher relative resources and interpersonal power is *less likely* than the other to resort to the use of force to control the other.)

To illustrate: In an early publication, Gelles (1983) proposed that "people hit and abuse other family members because they can" (p. 274). In a more recent publication, the authors integrate social interaction theories to compare battered and nonbattered women who were using shelter, counseling, and support services in a central Virginia county. The researchers found that battered women, compared to the nonbattered women, perceived they had little or no interpersonal power over their abusers and were, therefore, dependent upon them, incapable of leaving the oppressive relationship (Forte, Franks, Forte, & Rigsby, 1996).

4. Social learning theories (Bandura, 1971) propose that violence, like all other social behaviors, is learned. A social actor may observe, model, or experience aggressive and violent behaviors. Children exposed to violence or children who experience abuse or violence within the family face an increased likelihood of perpetrating violence against another child or against a family member as a child or later on as an adult (Dutton, Van Ginkel, & Starzomski, 1995; Egeland, 1993; Fagin & Wexler, 1987).

To illustrate: Lenore Walker's *The Battered Woman* (1979) articulates a social learning theory that explains a "cycle" of repeated acts of violence perpetrated by men against women who learn "helplessness" in response. Walker derived her "learned helplessness" concept from behavioral research that was conducted by a psychologist, Martin Seligman. In his research Seligman administered electric shocks to caged dogs. After repeated shocks the dogs, even when their cage doors were opened, made no attempt to escape— they had learned to be helpless. In generalizing to human, adult women living in abusive relationships, Walker (1984) argued that a cycle of violence perpetrated against a woman generates a "battered woman syndrome," a form of post-traumatic stress disorder that can result in substance abuse, depression, learned helplessness, and low self-esteem.

There is perhaps no other perspective or theory in the field of family violence that has been more used, more challenged, or more empirically discredited than Walker's cycle of violence, her use of learned helplessness, and the development of the battered woman syndrome. Downs (1996) analyzes the empirical studies and the ineffective use of Walker's syndrome by attorneys who represent battered women. He concludes: "Learned helplessness reduces battered women to the status of dogs. It denies the very integrity and potential agency that women wish to attain.... [It] is so reductionist as to eliminate volition" (p. 155).

5. Symbolic interaction perspectives focus on the symbolic communication between social interaction partners and the construction and reconstruction of a socially defined "reality." These perspectives assume a social world in which the self and identity emerge through interaction. To understand family violence requires the researcher to understand the meanings or the definitions that family members attribute to interactions and interpersonal relationships.

To illustrate: An act of family violence may be a response to perceived negative evaluations of the self by others, especially in a culture that tolerates violent behavior. Interpersonal relationships marked by chronic aggression or violence involve interaction partners who try to "make sense" of violent episodes, the relationship, and the self. Stets (1988) argues that an individual who batters another is attempting to regain the self, lost through chronic violence, by the use of physical force. Finkelhor (1993) uses a symbolic interaction perspective to illustrate how a caretaker who is dependent on an elder parent may feel powerless and therefore abuse the elder. Another caretaker who, when interacting with the elder parent attributes negative meanings to the aging process, may neglect the elder.

Interactional level theories offer many insights for the study of family violence. Because they study the processes and patterns of social behavior and family relationships they have greater explanatory power than indiviualist theories. Family violence by definition involves social relationships and social behaviors, making an interactional level theory appropriate for explaining the types and forms of family violence that occur most frequently and most chronically in contemporary societies. Interaction theories that account for the multiple factors associated with family violence hold more promise than single factor theories for the development of appropriate social responses to child abuse, partner abuse, and elder abuse. Although the extant interactional perspectives are somewhat limited by their general lack of specificity or ability to offer comprehensive causal explanations, an integration of social bonding, social exchange, interpersonal power, social learning, and symbolic interaction perspectives could generate causal and empirically testable theories of family abuse and violence in the near future. Contemporary work that expounds power theory (Gondolf, 1995) for explaining spouse abuse is an exemplar of an integrative approach.

Sociocultural Theories. Do the social problems of family violence occur *across most societies* and cultures? Do the *norms* that define appropriate family relationships and behaviors vary across geographical regions of the United States, or across religious, ethnic, gender, and age groups in the United States? Are there explanations for certain types of family violence that are best informed by *socialization* perspectives that center on *cultural norms*? Does a sociocultural thesis of *patriarchy* explain why men dominate women in most cultures and societies? Is the *family* itself, a social institution characterized by distinctive features, the best explanation for all forms of family violence? These questions highlight the need for cultural or societal level theories of family violence. The premise is a simple one: Cultural and societal norms define, legitimate or invalidate, and encourage or punish the many forms of control, including the use of force, that family members use in their social relationships and interactions. In this chapter we appraise five types of sociocultural theories: (1) culture of violence perspectives, (2) a theory of patriarchy, (3) feminist theory, (4) functional perspectives, and (5) family systems theories.

1. Culture of violence theories assume broad support within a culture for certain values that tolerate or encourage the use of force, including physical violence, for settling disputes that arise within or outside of the family. These perspectives posit that violence is learned behavior that is perceived within the culture as the appropriate means for dispute resolutions and social control in many settings, from parents punishing children, to the social response to crime, to fighting wars with other nations.

To illustrate: In the United States, the emergence and proliferation of culture of violence theories can be attributed to the pioneering but inherently flawed work of Marvin Wolfgang (1958), who claims that certain "subcultures" in U.S. society, for example, the underclass, show a greater acceptance of violence. As a result, a "subculture of violence" develops, apart from the mainstream culture. Violent norms developed within the subculture of violence explain why violent crime rates and acceptance of violence are greater in the South than in other regions of the United States. This circular theory (the explanation for the subculture of violence is based exclusively on the definition of the concept) provided some family researchers simple and simply wrong explanations for why poor children and poor adults seem to dominate the ranks of family violence victims. Because all forms of family violence occur behind closed doors (see Straus et al., 1980), family violence researchers reject simplistic cultural theories and instead examine how culture helps explain the social constructions of acceptable identities and gender roles and acceptable social control mechanisms. Katz (1995) and Collier (1995) exemplify the development of perspectives that attend to cultural norms to examine models of the "successful male" and "masculinities" that condone the superior social position of men over women, which in turn lead to patterns of violence, perpetrated by male partners in intimate and familial relationships. These models are socially constructed and legitimated by social institutions, including professional sports, family law, and criminal law. In her exceptionally sophisticated research that is designed to explain violence in African American families in the United States, Ucko (1994) shows the need to study the interaction of African and American cultural norms. The African ideology of gender egalitarianism interacts with African American gender norms that result in part from a history and culture of slavery, discrimination, and poverty in the United States. Only the interaction of cultural norms can explain the rates and types of family violence experienced by black families in the United States.

2. Patriarchal theories draw on the history of patriarchy to explain family violence and especially domestic violence. Patriarchy means the "rule of the father," and theories based on this concept claim that male dominance across cultures, including the legal use of masculine force and violence to sell, control, exploit, or kill women and children, results in violent behavior within the family. The patriarchal perspective claims that an ideology of male dominance over women is uncontested in the larger society as well as in the family, resulting in the exploitation and oppression of women. Further, it is supported by various social institutions, especially the law and religion in contemporary Western societies (O'Donovan, 1993).

To illustrate: Some theorists explain how patriarchy, a cultural explanation of family violence, emerged. Fischer (1979) and Macionis (1989) examine how historical and technological shifts in the means of food production, from hunting and gathering to horticulture, and then to agriculture, resulted in the production of surplus food, population increases and the need for a political system. Men, the producers of surplus food, created specialized and highly re-

warded occupations to control the distribution of food and related resources and gained positions of power over women. Other theorists explain the consequences of patriarchy. Dobash and Dobash (1978) argue: "Wife beating ... has existed for centuries as an acceptable and a desirable part of a patriarchal family system within a patriarchal society" (p. 426).

Theories of family violence that are based on patriarchy are challenged with empirical research and by competing theories. In general, critics ask two questions: How can a patriarchal perspective explain why many cultures and many social groups lack male-against-female violence, and why do some women kill their children or abuse their lesbian partners or elder parents? Straus, Kaufman, Kantor and Moore (1997) implicitly examine the culture of patriarchy empirically and show a decline between 1968 and 1994 in the acceptance of cultural norms that tolerate husband-to-wife violence. Theoretically, Whittaker (1996) challenges the ability of patriarchy to explain female perpetrated elder abuse, while Spatt (1995) challenges the perspective to explain the California law that makes criminal acts of domestic violence committed within same-sex cohabiting relationships.

3. Feminist perspectives typically build on the traditional and historical understanding of patriarchy in their explanations of how and why power is used and abused against women and girls within the family. Contemporary feminist perspectives address the range of family violence problems in society, including elder abuse and domestic violence in gay and lesbian households. One characteristic that distinguishes a feminist perspective of family violence is the position it takes on social advocacy or activism.

To illustrate: Feminists and feminist theories vary extremely in their scholarship and their politics. Collectively, however, what unites them is a concern for the experiences lived by women and girls and how feminist work can improve the services delivered to victims and survivors of family violence. Feminists work in safe shelters, rape crisis centers, counseling offices, child or elder protective services organizations, and the political arena to improve the social status and conditions of individuals who have been abused and harmed by family members (see e.g., Ferraro, 1989; Pence & Paymar, 1986; Yllo, 1993). A feminist perspective is interdisciplinary, centered by questions pertaining to the oppression of women and girls and characterized by a world view that highly values methods of inquiry that represent women's and girl's subjective experiences (Mann & Kelley, 1997). Feminists, including feminist advocates who work collaboratively with academic or government researchers, are deliberately conscious of their own cultural biases, listen reflectively to understand the experiences of family violence, and act as negotiators between clients, service providers, and scientific researchers (Gondolf, Yllo, & Campbell, 1997).

4. Functional theories argue that the family functions to reproduce the population; protect members from emotional, physical, and economic hardships; socialize children and help them adjust to changing social circumstances; and support all family members in their activities in other social institutions, such as education, work, and religion. Functional theorists assume that family violence perpetrators fail to adhere to appropriate social roles and norms that preclude the use of force to maintain stability or order in parent–child or male–female relations. Ambiguity or confusion about norms or inadequate socialization may lead to deviance, including the use of physical force that exceeds normatively acceptable levels.

To illustrate: A theory that concentrates on the importance of preventing domestic violence argues that a preliminary but necessary step to prevention is the acknowledgment of the importance of gender role socialization that condones inequality of the sexes: "[M]ost young persons are socialized to act out … sex-based power … and responsibility 'scripts' and are therefore likely to encounter work and school arrangements that reinforce the reality and acceptability of battering behavior in intimate relationships" (Tifft, 1993, p.9). Gender role socialization "from birth," according to some functional orientations, explains why men batter and why women are battered. It is responsible for the man's desire to exert power and the woman's acceptance of a "subordinate" position in the family that values nurturance, conciliation, and deference (Birns, Cascardi, & Meyer, 1994).

5. Family systems theories (gender-neutral perspectives) emphasize the interaction of a bounded social system or social institution, for example, the family, with other social institutions and with its environment, such as the community. To explain family violence, the systems theorist must examine the structural and interactional features of the family and consider the social processes in which positive and negative feedback produce or encourage violence.

To illustrate: Rouse (1997), based on the early Gelles and Straus (1979) theoretical articulation, identifies ten distinctive characteristics of the family that contribute to family violence: (1) the privacy norm for family interactions; (2) involuntary membership of children in the family; (3) power differences between parents and children, as well as between domestic partners; (4) unrealistically high expectations for marriage and childrearing; (5) the diffuseness of family roles; (6) the intense, emotional involvement in family relationships; (7) the impinging or constraining activities that limit individual freedom of action within the family; (8) the extended time spent in family interactions; (9) changes in the family life cycle; and (10) a discontinuity or conflict between family and other social institutional roles. Systems theories also consider the stresses from the larger society, such as poverty or unemployment (Straus, 1980), that increase the likelihood of violence within the family.

Sociocultural theories of family violence have generated a tremendous amount of research in the United States and in other nations on the problems of child abuse, partner abuse, and elder abuse. Murray Straus, the most prominent family violence author, along with his collaborators from the University of New Hampshire Family Research Laboratory, are responsible for this early and continuing influence. The strengths of sociocultural level theories include their ability to edify how characteristics of family members, family relationships, family interactions, and features of the larger society concomitantly work to increase or decrease the likelihood and the severity of the various types of family abuse and violence in contemporary societies. These perspectives recognize the complexity of the problems and generate testable research hypotheses. However, a sociocultural level theory in its entirety defies empirical observation. No researcher can ever observe or collect sufficient data to represent the cultural and societal level features that influence the problems of family violence.

Gelles (1996) claims that a "one-size-fits-all" approach to theorizing family violence problems and their possible remedies is "unreasonable" (p. 113). Our concise and partial consideration of the various theories and perspectives that inform family violence researchers and policy makers illustrates his point well. Many theories, operating at different levels of analysis, are required to understand and research the various problems of family violence. Extant theories and perspectives guide research in family violence by defining the issues to be studied, by framing the questions to be asked, and by shaping the form of causal explanations.

Methodological Issues

Issues and questions facing those who study family violence problems are similar to those addressed by all social science researchers. In addition, family violence researchers face unique challenges and issues, especially ethical ones (Miller, 1991). Research designs for the study of child and adult victims and survivors that depend on the collection of new data (rather than the use of government statistics or already existing databases) include the traditional and quantitative survey methods and evaluation studies. Some of the more important decisions the researcher must make are about sampling designs, instrument design, data collection methods, and analysis methods.

Family violence researchers should expect to find relatively low estimates of abuse and violence when one type of respondent sample is used: samples of the general population. Researchers should expect relatively high estimates of abuse and violence when they sample workers or professionals in the field; or clinical populations, such as women in shelters, children or elders in protective care, or survivors of family violence.

Research instruments are critically important tools for measuring family violence and abuse. The social science challenge to use reliable and valid measures is heightened in evaluation studies and in studies that attempt to establish the extent of a social problem, the causes of the problem, and appropriate remedies for the problem. The Conflict Tactics Scale (CTS), both the original and the modified versions, are criticized for not providing information on the context or injury levels that occur when persons are abused by family members. In addition, the CTS is limited by the nature of self-report instruments; that is, respondents may underestimate or exaggerate their behaviors, or they may inaccurately recall them. Nonetheless, the numerous studies published that show high reliability and construct validity for the scale and its subscales (Straus & Gelles, 1990) help convince policy makers and social program administrators to rely on estimates of violence based on the CTS.

Data collection methods are as varied in studies of family violence as they are across the divergent fields of social science inquiry. Face-to-face interviews, phone surveys, and mail surveys are commonly used methods to collect data with the use of quantitative survey research instruments. Other data collection methods that are extremely valuable for understanding the experiences of violence from the victim's and survivor's perspectives include unstructured interviews, reflective listening methods to understand survivors' biographies and narratives, and the observations of persons who work in the field.

The appropriate analysis of data, whether numerical codes in a computer database or transcriptions of audiotaped narratives told to an activist-researcher, is determined largely by the research design, but more importantly by the purpose for the research. If a program administrator wants to know what "works," statistical analyses of data to test research hypotheses that are derived from the more scientific theories of violence or abuse in the family are necessary. However, if state legislators need to understand the process of surviving repeated acts of violence by a marital or domestic partner, appropriate analysis requires the researcher to represent adequately the distinctive voices of survivors with careful, inductive analysis that is not structured by research hypotheses. All family violence researchers need to recognize that their work can be consumed or used in ways that are unanticipated. How the media report and promote their own agenda, based on what scientists find and advocates profess, can misrepresent the intentions of any family violence study.

Family violence research, like all social science research, must be ethical, based on three basic principles. First, research must benefit participants or the larger society. Second, it must respect the autonomy of participants, generally by ensuring the informed and voluntary consent of all participants. Third, it must follow the principle of justice, or the maintenance of research procedures that do not exploit participants or negatively affect other members of society. Newman, Kaloupek, Keane, and Folstein (1997) argue that following these three basic principles requires a delicate balancing act for the family violence or trauma researcher, especially when studying vulnerable or dependent victims.

In addition to general ethical concerns, those who study family violence problems encounter unique ethical issues. Most important, the researcher must work to avoid the harm that can result from family violence research. It is obvious to any researcher that disclosing to abusive partners the location of a battered women's shelter would gravely threaten the residents' safety. The ethical problems faced by family violence researchers also include some less obvious and more subtle questions and dilemmas. For example, where should research findings be published? Which findings should be published? In "value-free" and "objective" science endeavors, these questions are either not relevant or, possibly, unethical. In the field of family violence research, however, even the best-intentioned but misguided intervention in response to family violence can cause harm to individuals or to large numbers of individuals in a community. In addition, the privacy and intimacy of family relations, the dependence of children and the elderly, the politics of lawmaking, the dilemma of including or excluding the abuser in couple research, and the ethical problems of conducting cross-cultural family violence research (Fontes, 1997) provide a partial list of considerations for the ethical researcher who works in the field of family violence.

The physical abuse of children was the first form of family violence brought to public attention, and it illustrates many of the methodological problems in this area of study. Concerns about the definitions of child abuse were complicated by problematic research designs, sampling problems, and measurement issues (Mash & Wolfe, 1991). The interrelationships among theories, definitions (both conceptual and operational), and methods are illustrated by a overview of studies on the incidence and prevalence of the physical abuse of children. Incidence refers to the frequency or the number of cases of abuse that occur within a specified time period, usually 1 year. Prevalence refers to the frequency or the number of times an individual is abused over the course of a relationship or a stage of life. Both incidence and prevalence measures are used to estimate levels of child abuse as well as other forms of family violence.

At least four approaches have been used to calculate the levels of child abuse: (1) surveys of defined populations that identify levels of violence from self-reports of perpetrators or victims, (2) surveys of professionals in agencies that work with children, (3) total reports made by anyone to child protective services, and (4) investigated and validated reports to child protective services. Other sources of data, not specifically oriented toward children but that provide information about child victims, include the FBI's Uniform Crime Reports and the Bureau of Justice Statistics (Whitcomb, 1992). These sources use varied definitions of abuse and distinctive methods for obtaining data and reach different conclusions regarding the incidence or prevalence of child abuse.

Survey research is best exemplified by the National Family Violence Surveys that were designed and conducted by Straus and his associates (Gelles & Straus, 1988; Straus & Gelles, 1986; Straus, Gelles, & Steinmetz, 1978). Interviews were conducted with representative samples of parents in the U.S. general population in 1975 and again in 1985. Parents were asked if they had taken specific actions directed toward a child during the past year. The Conflict Tactics Scale, used to measure all forms of family violence, included the following actions: (1) threw something at the child; (2) pushed, grabbed, or shoved; (3) slapped or spanked; (4) kicked, bit, or hit with fist; (5) hit or tried to hit with an object; (6) beat up the child; (7) threatened with knife or gun; and (8) used knife or gun (Straus & Gelles, 1986). Child physical abuse is measured with responses to items 4–8. Based on this subset of actions, the incidence rate (number of children ages 3–17 experiencing one or more of such actions per 1000 children) was 140 in 1975 and 107 in 1985. If only the most severe violent actions are counted, using responses to questions 4, 6, and 8, the incidence rates were 36 per 1000 children in 1975 and 19 per 1000 children in 1985.

Another general population survey in 1995 was conducted by the Gallup Organization, based on telephone interviews with a sample of 1000 parents age 18 or over, to question them about actions they had taken toward their children. Physical abuse was defined by a "yes" answer to any of the following: "Hit child on some other part of the body besides the bottom with something like a belt, hairbrush, stick, or some other hard object"; "Hit child with fist or kicked hard"; "Shook child (only if *under* age of 2)"; "Threw or knocked child down"; or "Beat child up, that is, you hit him or her over and over as hard as you could." Researchers reported physical abuse rates of 49 per 1000 children—10 times as high as official rates and over twice as high as the 1985 rate reported for the National Family Violence Survey (Straus & Gelles, 1990).

Surveys of professional respondents (workers or professionals in organizations that respond to child abuse) were used for the National Incidence Studies completed in 1980 and in 1986. Reports of maltreatment were collected from Child Protective Service (CPS) workers and from professionals in other community agencies (schools, hospitals, police, courts). Abuse involved "serious injuries that could have been avoided" for the first study, but abuse also included children "at risk" for the second study (NIS, 1981, 1988). Empirical findings regarding physical abuse indicated an incidence rate of 3.1 in 1980, counting only serious injuries, but 4.9 and 5.7 for 1980 and 1986, respectively, based on the broader "at risk" measure. Either estimate is much smaller than those provided by general population surveys.

Total CPS reports reflect community and professional standards for determining appropriate childcare. Thus, a report to CPS indicates that someone believes that a child has been abused and exercises discretion to report. Given the ambiguity of definitions, such beliefs challenge the validity of indications of abuse. In 1986, CPS agencies received about 2,086,000 reports (American Humane Association [AHA], 1988). Severe injuries, younger victims, and sexual abuse appear to be most likely reported (Ards & Harrell, 1993). Analysis of subsets of states suggests that 28% of the reports involved physical injury, for a total physical abuse rate of 9.2, also considerably lower than rates derived from general population surveys.

If only the investigated and substantiated CPS reports for 1986 are considered, the physical abuse rate is approximately 4.6 per 1000 children (AHA, 1988). The figure for 1993 was 3 incidents per 1000 children (U.S. Department of Health and Human Services, 1994). Such an approach rests on the assumption that CPS workers or police are likely to use more consistent judgments and discretion than reporters, thereby creating a standard operational definition. This incidence rate is lowest of all, and undoubtedly is an underestimate, due to failure of some persons to report, a lack of evidence caused by delayed investigations, conflicting definitions, and other factors.

All told, the disparity in rates and the number identified as physically abused based on those rates varies from 107, or a total of 6.5 million children in 1985 (Straus & Gelles, 1986) to 5.7, or over 358,000 children, in 1986 (NIS, 1988) to 4.6, or about 200,000 children (AHA, 1987, 1987). This disparity reflects differences in definitions, methodologies, and assumptions about causality. Which estimate should be used to document incidence rates of physical abuse? Clear conceptual and operational definitions of violence are essential if research is to answer this question and others about family violence.

Traditional research in the fields of child abuse, partner abuse, and elder abuse tends to be *ex post facto*, single group studies, with relatively few inquiries that use a control or comparison group or an experimental design. Samples are often drawn for convenience, without concern for representativeness, creating nongeneralizable results (e.g., Mash & Wolfe, 1991; Widom, 1988). Consequently, traditional social science-oriented research must be examined carefully, especially studies offering causal explanation or those that describe the effects of violence for providing evaluations of interventions or treatment programs.

Violence and Abuse toward Children

Following the publication of "The Battered Child Syndrome" (Kempe et al., 1962), media response and the involvement by medical professionals, advocacy groups, and legislatures produced a level of legal activity to protect children that was unmatched for any other social problem (Nelson, 1984). Medical, legal, and social services quickly developed, with each bringing a distinctive set of definitions, different causal approaches, and varied styles of interventions and prevention.

Violence and Definitions of Child Abuse

Public Law 93-247 initiated federally funded research, intervention, and treatment programs. It defined child abuse and neglect in general terms:

> the physical or mental injury, sexual abuse, negligent treatment or maltreatment of a child under the age of eighteen by a person who is responsible for the child's welfare under circumstances which indicate that the child's health or welfare is harmed or threatened thereby. (*Interdisciplinary Glossary*, 1978, pp. 8–9)

Considerable discretion is granted by this definition to parents and professionals in their identification of the injuries or the threats to a child's health or welfare. Efforts to provide more specific definitions have generally been unsuccessful (e.g., Besharov, 1985; Gelles, 1982; Hutchinson, 1990), despite the significance of both conceptual and operational definitions for research, practice, and policy.

Vignettes describing the many types of physical violence that are directed toward children, from spanking to severe acts of violence that result in serious injuries, evoke some agreement but also some disagreement in perceptions of seriousness and the reactions taken by physicians, nurses, police, lawyers, teachers and social workers. For cases that do not result in obvious harm only, perceptions and reactions differ widely. Only in extreme situations or in cases that are clearly injurious to the child do researchers find relative consensus in perceptions and judgments of appropriate actions to take (e.g., Giovannoni & Becerra, 1979; O'Toole, Turbett, Sargent, & O'Toole, 1987; Snyder & Newberger, 1986). Responses to child abuse vignettes vary across segments of the general population as well, especially according

to the race, gender, education, religiosity, marital status, occupation, or experience of parenthood, which influence respondents' definitions of appropriate actions (e.g., Garrett, 1982; Roscoe, 1990; Webster, 1991).

Vignettes and perceptions of appropriate responses to child abuse cases generate abstract conceptions regarding the severity of abuse and the appropriate social response to the social problem. However, conceptions of appropriate and inappropriate childcare are grounded in and shaped by cultural, social, and personal factors that influence how legal definitions of child abuse are applied. Laws mandate the reporting of suspected abuse cases to CPS, but many incidents are not reported. Empirical study shows that at least half of all child abuse cases are not reported, regardless of legal mandate (Hazzard & Rupp, 1986; Kalichman, Craig, & Follingstad, 1988; Osborne, Hinz, Rapppaport, & Williams, 1988; Warner & Hansen, 1994). Why? In addition to ambiguous definitions, a widespread fear of retaliation by the perpetrator, ignorance of the law, and beliefs that the child will not benefit from the report, as well as the perpetrator's, victim's, and observer's age and sex and their personal beliefs about families, also affect the likelihood of reporting a child abuse case.

Incidence and Prevalence

Despite these circumstances, about 3 million official reports of child maltreatment are now received by CPS and police departments in the United States each year. Any reported case requires an investigation. Based on earlier patterns, about 40% of the reported cases are validated, indicating that about 1.2 million children are victims of some form of physical, emotional, and sexual violence or neglect each year. Approximately half the validated cases are child neglect. Of the remaining 600,000, at least 250,000 are cases of physical violence, at least 150,000 cases are sexual abuse, and the remainder involve multiple types of maltreatment. All cases of child maltreatment involve a component of some form of emotional abuse (AHA, 1988). These figures indicate a growing public awareness of the problem, but the actual number of abused children remains unknown. A challenge to state intervention into families continues, making precise estimates even more difficult to achieve (Olafson, Corwin, & Summit, 1993).

A child's reaction to incidents and the child's conception of sexual behavior are critical for defining actions such as abuse, and thus in determining accurate levels of child sexual abuse (e.g., Lloyd, 1992; Wurtele & Miller, 1987). Official reports underestimate incidence rates, and surveys of children in the general or clinical populations are simply not available for calculating rates of sexual abuse. However, the National Incidence Studies (surveys of professionals) reported 2.5 children per 1000, or about 150,000 victims of molestation annually, based on the assumption of harm from intrusion, molestation with genital contact, other fondling, and inadequate supervision over sexual behavior (NIS, 1988). These figures are similar to those derived from official government agency reports.

Prevalence rates, the number of children per 1000 ever sexually abused from birth to age 18, offer some additional evidence of the frequency of sexual abuse. Based on surveys of adults and college students, prevalence rates range from 60 to 600 for women and 50 to 100 for men (e.g., Fromuth & Burkhart, 1987; Peters, Wyatt, & Finkelhor, 1986; Russell, 1983). Finkelhor (1993) concludes that "at least one in four girls and one in ten boys will suffer victimization" (p. 67). These estimates are based on retrospective accounts by adults, using respondent samples drawn from specific populations rather than randomly selected from the general population, and on definitions of sexual abuse that are induced from the responses to questions about childhood sexual activities and experiences. As a result, the conceptual and methodological limitations preclude definitive statements about the prevalence of child sexual abuse (e.g., Haugaard & Reppucci, 1988; Martin, Anderson, Romans, Mullen, & O'Shea, 1993; Morrison & Green, 1992), but the data do indeed support the claim that sexual abuse is a common experience for thousands of children each year in the United States.

Emotional abuse per se is extremely difficult to define, partly because some psychological harm results in all or most physical and sexual abuse cases. Independent actions, those that are intended to be rejecting, degrading, isolating, corrupting, and exploitive, have been defined as emotional abuse (Brassard, Germalin, & Hart, 1987; Garbarino, Guttman, & Seeley, 1986). The operationalization of emotional abuse is problematic, partly due to definition difficulties and partly due to an inability to distinguish emotional abuse apart from other forms of child abuse, resulting in no clear estimate of incidence or prevalence at this time (Hart & Brassard, 1991).

The National Incidence Studies (NIS) defined emotional abuse as close confinement, verbal assault, deprivation as punishment, or economic exploitation. In the 1980 NIS study, over 138,000 children were counted as actual victims. When the broader "at risk" criteria were applied for the 1986 study, researchers estimate that 211,000 children each year in the United States are victims of emotional abuse—more than the numbers of children victimized by sexual abuse (NIS, 1981, 1988). CPS reports of valid emotional abuse cases are much lower, less than 30,000 children in 1986. This discrepancy illustrates the difficulty in defining and documenting this particular form of child abuse and violence (AHA, 1988).

Causal Factors

Numerous social science studies that are designed to identify the unique characteristics of individual perpetrators of child abuse have produced, at best, ambiguous results. Psychopathology explains the actions of a relatively small number of abusers, and the reviews of studies on personality profiles indicate very limited success in identifying the underlying attributes or perpetrator characteristics that are associated with either physical or sexual abuse (e.g., Okami & Goldberg, 1992; Murphy & Peters, 1992; Milner & Chilamkurti, 1991; Wolfe, 1985). Studies of parents who are identified as physical abusers indicate that many have low self-esteem, poor self-concepts, poorly developed cognitive skills, and unrealistic expectations. Measurement problems, unclear definitions, and the lack of comparison or control groups make such findings tentative (e.g., Holden & Edwards, 1989; Knudsen, 1992).

Individualist explanations of sexual abuse that center on both perpetrator and child characteristics have not been very successful. Abnormal response patterns on personality tests are found to be typical of some abusers (Kalichman & Henderson, 1991; McIvor & Duthie, 1986) but have limited value for explaining sexual activities with children (Hall, 1989). Other factors such as inadequate social skills or inappropriate socialization (e.g., Knight, 1989; Muller, Caldwell, & Hunter, 1993; Parker & Parker, 1986), heightened responsiveness to sexually explicit materials (e.g., Marshall, Barbaree, & Butt, 1988), perpetrator self-centeredness (Gilgun & Connor, 1989), or special vulnerability, such as the "trusting" child or the "availability" of the child victim (Conte, Wolfe, & Smith, 1987), have been identified. Each of these factors offers some insight, but none by itself is sufficient to explain the high levels of sexual abuse. Interactional theories have been used to explain violence toward children. Abuse is the result of a failure in relationships, caused by the inadequate or unequal abilities of the parent and child. Attachment and bonding theories assume a uniqueness in the mother–infant experience that precludes or prevents abuse. Early clinical studies (e.g., Bowlby, 1980) supported this interpretation, but later nonclinical research (e.g., Birns, 1988; Chess & Thomas, 1982; Eyer, 1992) is not able to document the importance of mother–infant bonding for explaining physical violence directed against children in the family. Nevertheless, researchers do find that the risk of sexual abuse is higher in stepfamilies than it is in biologically related families (Alexander & Lupfer, 1987; Finkelhor & Baron, 1986; Gordon, 1989; Paveza, 1988), consistent with a bonding interpretation.

Social learning theories, especially those that explain the intergenerational transmission of violence as learned behavior, propose that children learn violence and its acceptability through experiences or observations that become major influences on their behavior as children and as adults. Despite the intuitive appeal and popularity of the intergenerational transmission thesis, the empirical data that are analyzed to test the thesis yield inconsistent and inadequate support for it (e.g., Benjamin, 1980; Burgess & Youngblood, 1988). The national surveys of family violence show that less than 20% of abused children become abusers as adults (Straus & Gelles, 1990; Straus, Gelles, & Steinmetz, 1980). A review of self-report studies concluded that less than one-third of abused children become abusive adults (Kaufman & Zigler, 1993). Further, after an extensive review of the research literature, Widom (1983) finds that the majority of abusive adults were not abusive children, concluding: "[E]mpirical evidence demonstrating that abuse leads to abuse is fairly sparse" (p. 23).

The theory and research on how the abused becomes the abuser also fails to explain incest or sexual abuse of children committed outside the family. Though most sexual abuse occurs within families, a significant proportion does not, especially sexual abuse perpetrated by children and adolescents. Further, the diagnosis of sexual abuse is severely hampered by the secrecy and shame that usually surrounds the abuse, by the various conceptions and interpretations of the experience by the charges associated with child custody decisions (e.g., Faller, 1991), and by age and knowledge of the child (Jackson & Nuttal, 1993). Several researchers have noted that some offenders have experienced sexual abuse as children (Benoit & Kennedy, 1992). However, a systematic review of the sexual abuse perpetrator studies that was completed by Hanson and Slater (1988) reports that less than 30% of sexual abusers report any prior victimization. While this figure is about three times the rate for the general population, at least two-thirds of perpetrators of sexual abuse were not sexually abused, suggesting that other factors are important in explaining their abusive behaviors (e.g., Breire, Henschel, & Smijanich, 1992; Hall & Hirschman, 1992; Pawlak, Boulet, & Bradford, 1991).

Undoubtedly, the etiology of incest is complex: Some children are groomed and courted, some are brutally attacked, some submit because family interactions have left them powerless, and some are socialized to believe that some forms of incest are appropriate (e.g., Aiosa-Karpas, Karpas, Pelcovitz, & Kaplan, 1991; deYoung & Lowry, 1992; Frude, 1989; Madonna, Van Scoyk, & Jones, 1991; Okami, 1991; Reis & Heppner, 1993).

Sociocultural theories emphasize the social context and cultural values that support violent acts. Normative support for the physical punishment of children in the United States is reflected by an emphasis on parental responsibility and family privacy and is rooted in religious and legal traditions (e.g., Ellison & Sherkat, 1993; Garbarino & Kostelny, 1992; Grasmick, Bursik, & Kimpel, 1991; Graziano, Lindquist, Kunce, & Munjal, 1992; Grevan, 1990; Pleck, 1987; Straus, 1991b). In combination with stress-producing events such as unwanted pregnancy, the loss of a job, divorce, and neighborhood instability, the social and cultural values that support or legitimate violence allow and encourage the physical and emotional abuse of children (Trickett, Aber, Carlson, & Cicchetti, 1991).

The findings and theories we present here are suggestive, and not conclusive. Most of the current research in the child abuse field is retrospective rather than prospective; it fails to use control or comparison groups, it lacks specificity in measuring abuse, it is cross-sectional in design rather than longitudinal, and it employs convenience rather than randomly drawn samples. All these limitations mean that caution should be used when any attempt is made to generalize or apply research findings. Further, studies of child abuse reflect the researcher's disciplinary training, experiences, personal values, and general perspectives of the children abused. Explanations of violence as a social level phenomenon typically rely on individual level data and a lack of adequate theoretical specification. These issues have serious implications for social policy decisions about intervention and prevention programs that intend to ameliorate the problem of child abuse.

Consequences of Violence

A large number of studies attempt to document the negative effects of physical, sexual, and emotional abuse on children. Unfortunately, most of the findings must be qualified due to the theoretical and methodological limitations identified earlier, making causal linkages between violence and specific behavioral conditions difficult (e.g., Breire, 1992; Haugaard & Emery, 1989; Rivera & Widom, 1990). Nevertheless, some consistent results have emerged from studies using different theoretical and methodological perspectives.

Recent research supports the earlier studies regarding the short-term effects of child abuse. Evidence indicates that physically abused children, compared to nonabused children, have lower self-esteem, ambition, social competence, and verbal and cognitive skills and are more likely to experience depression and respond to aggression with aggression (e.g., Eckenrode, Laird, & Doris, 1993; Fatout, 1990; Haskett & Kistner, 1991; Kaufman, 1991; Salzinger, Feldman, Hammer, & Rosario, 1991; Wolfe, 1987; Wolfe & Jaffe, 1991). These findings are important for the development of interpersonal skills and adult psychological health.

Long-term consequences are not easily documented. Efforts to show a direct relationship between violence and later criminality have generally been unsuccessful, largely due to methodological problems (e.g., Doerner, 1987; Gray, 1988; Kratcoski & Kratcoski, 1983; Rivera & Widom, 1990). Further, these effects may be mediated by a variety of factors, such as out-of-home placement, strong social support, or intervention and treatment (e.g., Downs, Miller, Testa, & Panek, 1992; Kurtz, Gaudin, Howling, & Wodarski, 1993; Martin & Elmer, 1992). However, despite the difficulties in making direct inferences, long-term consequences, including low self-esteem and social competence, exist for a significant proportion of adults who were physically abused as children (e.g., Breire & Runtz, 1987; Pollock et al., 1990).

Even nonabusive levels of violence (defined by state statutes) appear to have important, negative impacts on adult development. The most ambitious and careful study that examines the long-term effects of physical punishment of children is Straus' *Beating the Devil Out of Them: Corporal Punishment in American Families* (1994). Using a wide range of analytic techniques, statistics, and sources, Straus concludes that ending the hitting of children will reduce stress and trauma within families, result in more rewarding family relationships, and lower the levels of alienation, depression, and suicidal tendencies that exist, thus producing a society with less crime. In a recently published study, Straus, Sugarman, and Giles-Sims (1997) report the findings from research in which they asked a sample of mothers if they had spanked their 6- to 9-year-old children at least once during the prior week and, if so, how often they spanked their children. Based on a 2-year follow-up survey of the same 807 mothers, Straus reports that spanking is directly correlated with the increased likelihood of school children cheating, lying, bullying other children, and manifesting problems at school. If the elimination of spanking in the family can reduce personal, family, and social problems, imagine the future society in which corporal punishment in school, currently in use in some of the states, exists no longer (Straus & Mathur, 1996; Straus, Sugarman, et al., 1997).

Studies on the consequences of child sexual abuse demonstrate a wide range of possible psychological problems for the child and the adolescent victim. A comprehensive review of the initial and the long-term consequences of sexual abuse (Browne & Finkelhor, 1986) finds numerous negative effects that have been supported by subsequent research. The reviewers indicated that guilt, shame, somatic complaints, inappropriate sexual behavior, and poor social relations are frequently observed short-term sequelae. These findings generally have been bolstered by later research (e.g., Friedrich, 1993; Hotte & Rafman, 1992; Kalichman, 1991; Lanktree, Breire, & Zaidi, 1991; Shapiro, Leifer, Martone, & Kassem, 1992). However, one review of short-term effects noted that

the majority of such effects are symptoms of clinical child samples in general (Beitchman et al., 1992), illustrative of a sampling issue (general population vs. clinical population samples) that pertains to most child abuse studies. The psychological and social difficulties for victims of sexual abuse appear also to be related to the severity and the type of sexual abuse, the age of child victim, the length and intensity of the abuse, and the child's relationship to the perpetrator (e.g., Breire & Runtz, 1987; Conte & Schuerman, 1987; Nash, Zivney, & Hulsey, 1993). Negative, short-term consequences are found in children of all racial, ethnic, religious and socioeconomic groups, although the contexts and circumstances that may modify these effects remain obscure.

Long-term sequelae for sexual abuse have been identified by numerous studies, although it remains impossible to identify specific effects, independent of other factors, such as family problems, the use of force, and the individual's experiences. Still, the consistency of research findings suggest several serious long-term consequences of sexual abuse and the family circumstances associated with it. Sexual dysfunctions, anxiety and fear, depression, and higher levels of suicide are found among adult victims of child sexual abuse (e.g., Beitchman et al., 1991; Collings, 1995; Cutler & Nolen-Hoeksema, 1991; Johnson & Kendel, 1991; Saunders, Villeponteaux, Lipovsky, Kilpatrick, & Veronen, 1992; Tomlin, 1991). In addition, parenting problems, revictimization (battering and rape), and personality disorders have been found (e.g., Alexander & Lupfer, 1987; Cole, Woolger, Power, & Smith, 1992; Russell, 1986).

The emergence of HIV has produced additional concerns regarding forced sexual activities. No adequate data exist to estimate incidence or prevalence rates of HIV among children. However, there appears to be agreement that severe sexual abuse (forced sexual intercourse, oral sex, or sodomy) is associated with an increased risk of contracting the HIV virus (Allers, Benjack, White & Rousey, 1993; Jason, 1991) because of initial contact with an infected adult perpetrator as well as the increased sexual activity by the child or adolescent following abuse.

Despite the documented immediate and long-term effects of sexual violence toward children, one comprehensive review of the published studies finds that many researchers report that they find a substantial proportion of victims who are asymptomatic (Kendall-Tackett, Williams & Finkelhor, 1993). Estimates of those not affected range from 20%–50% of the children who are sexually abused. The wide range in estimates is perhaps due to the use of different measures, delayed reactions, or lack of actual impact. It is clear that many women and men who were once victims of incest have coped, survived, and succeeded despite their experiences, perhaps due to strong social support from family and friends, therapeutic intervention, or personal strengths (e.g., Reis &

Heppner, 1993). Additional research is needed to identify and document those factors that can protect and assist child victims of sexual violence.

Data from the National Family Violence Survey indicate that emotional or verbal violence directed at children is associated with social and psychological problems. Based on a nationally representative sample of 3346 children, verbal aggression by parents is related to physical aggression, delinquency, and interpersonal problems of children. This empirical relationship "applies for all age groups, and for both boys and girls, in both low and high socioeconomic status families" (Vissing, Straus, Gelles, & Harrop, 1991, p. 235).

Other research (e.g., Breire & Runtz, 1987) offers similar findings regarding the effects of emotional abuse per se, or emotional abuse in conjunction with other forms of violence. Unfortunately, more precise definitions and a better elaboration of concepts are needed to delineate these sequelae adequately.

Responses: Treatment and Prevention

Given the emphases on family privacy and parental control and the legitimacy of physical punishment of children, it is only natural that treatment programs for physical violence have been directed toward changing the behavior of parents and perpetrators, with relatively little attention to victims, except in cases of severe injury. Prenatal education of parents, psychotherapy, and crisis management programs are designed to provide knowledge of child needs and developmental processes, effect changes in pathological behaviors, and train parents in stress management. Few programs address many of the sources of stress, such as low income, isolation, poor education, young parenthood, family crises, and social incompetence that appear to contribute to physical abuse. While some multiservice programs have produced desired changes in parents and other abusers (e.g., Lutzker & Rice, 1987; Whiteman, Fanshel, & Grundy, 1987), there is little evidence that traditional therapeutic interventions with individuals are effective.

Two major studies that were designed to measure treatment effectiveness reported similar results. The first concluded that abusers receiving lay services, rather than professional services, were judged to have lower propensities to abuse in the future. A second study examined 46 different factors that were identified as contributors to neglect and emotional, sexual, and adolescent abuse. The length of time services were provided is an important correlate of treatment success. However, the researchers conclude that "treatment efforts in general are not very successful" (Daro, 1988, p. 121). Traditional services, notably one-to-one counseling and casework, were the least likely to produce positive results. A review of treatment program effectiveness studies

suggests that few programs have been subjected to rigorous evaluation despite the dramatic growth of intervention services (Oates & Bross, 1995).

Intervention on behalf of families and victims of sexual violence tends to use traditional approaches. One study assessing over 550 sexual abuse programs reports that individual counseling (93%) and family counseling (90%) are the most common services offered, but less than half of the programs regularly use standardized measures to evaluate clients (Cichetti & Barnett, 1991). These studies show that typically, therapeutic services for sexual abuse are unplanned, unsystematic, and often contradictory in their service characteristics. Treatment for victims and perpetrators may be selected on the basis of availability, cost, or ease of access.

Among the treatment programs available for offenders are biological or organic treatments (antiandrogens or hormonal treatments, including "chemical castration," and surgery), group therapy, family therapy, and behavioral treatments such as covert sensitization, cognitive restructuring, biofeedback, and arousal conditioning (Becker & Hunter, 1992; O'Donohue & Letourneau, 1993). Analysis of the effectiveness of these types of interventions suggest that a combination of treatments may reduce recidivism (e.g., Hall, Shondrick, & Hirschman, 1993; Marshall & Barbaree, 1988; Rice, Quinsey, & Harris, 1991).

One of the major problems for nonincarcerated offenders is the failure to complete treatment programs, making evaluation of the program or success in the program difficult. Unfortunately, many of those who fail to complete the process appear to be the most in need of therapy (e.g., Chaffin, 1992). Programs for victims of family sexual violence are diverse, but most involve a variety of treatments for both children and adult victims of incest, focused on low self-esteem, guilt, blame, and social relationships (e.g., Alexander, Neimeyer, Follette, Moore, & Harter, 1989; Clarke & Hornick, 1988; Friedrich, Luecke, Beilke, & Place, 1992; Singer, 1989).

Effectiveness of these programs is difficult to determine, and although some recent studies show promise in mediating negative consequences (Faller, 1988; Rust & Troupe, 1991), one review concludes that "to date there has been no study demonstrating definitely the efficacy of any treatment method" (O'Donohue & Elliott, 1992). There is some evidence to support the premise that family and friends are significant factors for minimizing the impact of violence on the victim and the victim's ability to complete the treatment programs (Edwards & Alexander, 1992; Follette, Alexander, & Follette, 1991).

Efforts to create prevention programs for physical abuse generally have been focused on "at-risk" populations identified through various tests (e.g., Browne & Saqi, 1988; Milner

& Robertson, 1989; Schneider, 1982). Screening is compromised by unacceptably low levels of predictability and negative consequences of labeling for "false positives." Consequently, the current focus is on primary prevention, including universal access to services such as prenatal medical care, parental education, increased peer involvement, childcare, support groups, and community organizations. In addition, advocacy programs and public education programs have been initiated (Donnelly, 1991). One study (Showers, 1992) examines the outcome of a "Don't Shake the Baby" program and reports that nearly half of the participants indicate that they are less likely to shake their babies because of the program, although no behavioral data are available to corroborate the participants' claims.

Sexual abuse prevention, because of the secrecy usually involved, often assumes that children must be prepared to protect themselves from sexual violence, through education programs by teachers, pediatricians, counselors, and others. Numerous approaches have been developed (e.g., Finkelhor & Dziuba-Leatherman, 1995; Tutty, 1990), although there is little solid empirical evidence of effectiveness (e.g., Daro, 1991). Further, family privacy and parental control over their children can only diminish the positive outcomes of any program designed to prevent incest.

Clearly, successful programs that prevent violence toward children have yet to be identified and documented, although some evidence suggests that programs are more successful in providing knowledge than in preventing injuries (Finkelhor, Asdigian, & Dziuba-Leatherman, 1995). Carefully conceptualized research, with appropriate, well-defined samples, is needed to allow the development of comprehensive policies to protect children (Melton & Flood, 1994).

Domestic Violence and Abuse

Domestic violence includes physical violence, sexual abuse, and emotional abuse and refers to the systematic use of force or the threat of force by an adult partner who has the intention to harm the other partner. Domestic violence often includes a motive of control or domination. Domestic partnerships, for the purposes of this chapter, include cohabiting heterosexual, lesbian, and gay couples. Although dissolved domestic partnerships (divorced or separated couples) are included, "dating" couples are not. In contrast to child abuse, some analysts claimed that the scholarly work on domestic violence is "newer, less developed, and less clearly divided into schools of thought" (Breines & Gordon, 1983, p. 507). By the end of the 1990s, such claims are suspect. The research is rich and varied, and clearly is divided into distinctive schools of thought, especially in consideration of the

gendered (feminist) and nongendered (family violence) systems approach for analyzing this particular social problem (Breines & Gordon, 1983; Brush, 1993; Kurz, 1993). Like the child abuse field, partner abuse studies examine offender characteristics, victim characteristics, social interaction patterns, and how families and family-like relationships influence the likelihood and severity of violent patterns. Some studies are conducted at the individual or interpersonal level of analysis; however, more recent work tends to depend on structural factors and the social contexts in which violence between intimates takes place to explain either the levels and consequences of domestic violence or the effectiveness of domestic violence intervention.

Similar to child abuse research, the history of the study of domestic violence shows definitional and operationalization problems (Frieze, 1983; Geffner, Rosenbaum, & Hughes, 1988; Straus, 1991a; Webster, 1991). For example, is the severity of abuse defined by the offender's acts or by injuries sustained by a partner? Must violence be repeated to be considered "abuse?" Do abusive acts include verbal threats, acts that cause emotional harm, and forced and nonconsensual sexual activity? Finally, can men and couples be victims of any or all forms of abuse?

Initial estimates of the levels of domestic violence in the United States (the 1975 National Family Violence Survey, for example) were based only on married couples, inevitably resulting in an underestimation of violence between cohabiting intimates (Miller, 1979). Most recent estimates now include heterosexual cohabiting couples and some include lesbian and gay couples.

Violence between Heterosexual Partners

Physical Abuse. Numerous studies have documented that too much physical violence occurs within intimate heterosexual relationships. The 1975 National Family Violence Survey, based on a large and representative sample of American families (Straus, Gelles, & Steinmetz, 1980), reported that over 16% of the 2143 couples interviewed had engaged in at least one of eight violent acts measured with the CTS. Furthermore, the most common type of incident reported is a situation in which both the husband and the wife engaged in some form of physically violent act.

In the 1985 National Family Violence Resurvey of 6002 currently married or cohabiting couples, 30% of the couples indicated that they experienced at least one violent altercation during the course of their marriage (Gelles & Straus, 1988; Straus, 1991a), and 16% of American couples, or one of every six, reported an incident involving violence during that year. Comparing findings from the two surveys, researchers found a 27% decline in reports of lesser and more severe violence against wives between 1975 and 1985.

Given the magnitude and rapidity of such a drop, the researchers offered three possible explanations: methodological differences between the two surveys, a reluctance to report severe violence due to media coverage of family violence, and an actual decline in violence against women due to changes in family structure, the economy, alternatives for battered women, treatment programs, and deterrence-oriented police intervention. Egley (1991) conducted a cohort analysis of the national studies and concluded that the reported reductions in levels of domestic violence probably do not represent actual decreases. Still, these studies provided a body of evidence "suggesting that the major causes of physical violence in the family are to be found in certain basic characteristics of the American family and American society," such as male dominance in the family and the larger society and levels of poverty in the U.S. (Straus, 1990b, pp. 6–7).

Relatively little attention has been directed toward documenting variations of violence patterns among racial or ethnic groups. Using data from the National Family Violence Surveys, Hampton, Gelles, and Harrop (1991) reported that the overall rate of violence in black male-to-female incidents remained the same, nearly 17 per 1000 couples, in both 1975 and 1985, while severe violence, a measure of wife-beating, decreased by 43% (from 113 in 1975 to 64 in 1985). Based on a sample of battered women obtained through references by family court, a battered women's shelter, and a homeless shelter, Joseph (1997) finds "there were no significant differences in the nature and extent of the abuse between Black and White women" (p. 167).

Simply presenting violence rates by race may obscure differences that may have been due to income level, employment status, different cultural expectations and values concerning violence, or access to social networks (Lockhart, 1991). Based on an analysis of data from three social experiments designed to assess the consequences of arrest on repeated acts of violence, controlling for education, family composition, and employment status, Miller and Krull (1997) conclude there is empirical evidence to "refute the contention that Blacks perpetrate more domestic violence than other racial or ethnic groups" (p. 246). Whites, compared to blacks, Hispanics, and Asians, perpetrated significantly *more* repeated acts of domestic violence in one city. When social class and social network embeddedness are controlled in the National Family Violence Survey data, virtually all of the race differences between blacks and whites disappeared (Cazenave & Straus, 1990). Even based on an earlier study of 307 black and white women of various social class positions, Lockhart (1987) found that there are no significant differences between the proportion of black and white women who experienced family violence, or in the number of times violence was experienced. The only significant differ-

ence found was that a larger proportion of black middle-class (45.6%) women reported that they experienced marital violence compared to white middle-class women (27.1%).

Most recently, several studies have examined physical violence against women of color, going beyond presenting rates of violence by race. These studies point to the necessity of taking culture(s) into account when researching physical violence (Campbell, Campbell, King, Parker, & Ryan, 1994; Chester, Robin, Koss, Lopez, & Goldman, 1994; Kantor, Jasinski, & Aldarondo, 1994; Perilla, Bakeman, & Norris, 1994; Urquiza, Wyatt, & Root, 1994). All told, one may safely conclude that racial and cultural stereotypes do not provide any useful or accurate information about the levels or severity of domestic violence experienced in contemporary American society.

Violence against male partners has been examined within the context of violence between intimates (Steinmetz, 1987; Steinmetz & Lucca, 1988; Stets & Straus, 1990; Straus et al., 1980). Researchers, using analysis of National Family Violence Survey data, have reported that in comparison to men, women initiate attacks just as often (Stets & Straus, 1990; Straus, 1991b), are more likely to use physical violence, and use it with greater frequency (Steinmetz, 1987). In their review of changes in family violence rates from 1975 to 1985, Straus and Gelles (1990a) remark that "the rates for violence by wives are remarkably similar to the rates for violence by husbands" (p. 96). Whereas rates of husband-to-wife incidents decreased over the decade, rates of woman-to-man incidents increased. Some contend that the CTS, because it does not adequately measure the context surrounding the violence or the degree of injury sustained, may result in the misrepresentation of "assaults" by women against their male partners. Perhaps acts of retaliation or self-defense explain female-to-male assaults. There is, however, no strong empirical study to support the contention.

Wife abuse and husband abuse research has been widely criticized (Breines & Gordon, 1983; Brush, 1993; Gelles, 1987; Kurz, 1993; Pagelow, 1984; Straton, 1994), usually based on arguments that inadequate measures of who was injured, who initiated the violence, or self-defense were used. Further, some suggest that the use of the CTS is problematic because the scale and its subscales do not "deal with the bias possibly resulting from the fact that 'violent' behaviors by a man may be ignored as nothing out of the ordinary, while similar behavior by a woman may be so out of character that it is well remembered" (Breines & Gordon, 1985, p. 512).

The causes of domestic violence remain elusive. Researchers have determined a long list of factors that are associated with higher or lower rates of physical violence between intimates. Risk factors include a previous history with family violence (Straus et al., 1980); the use or abuse of alcohol (Kantor & Straus, 1990); stress from poor economic circumstances (Straus, 1990b); gender inequality (Coleman & Straus, 1990; Gerber, 1991; Straus et al., 1980; Yllo, 1984); the status of women in the larger society (Yllo, 1984; Yllo & Straus, 1990); pregnancy and the postpartum period (Gelles, 1987, 1990b; Gielen, O'Campo, Faden, Kass, & Xue, 1994); wives' marital dependency (Kalmuss, 1982; Kalmuss & Straus, 1990); and social isolation, particularly among cohabiting couples (Stets, 1991). Additionally, some suggest that the physical abuse of women in a relationship is closely linked with sexual abuse (Frieze, 1983; Hanneke, Shields, & McCall, 1986).

Sexual Assault and Marital Rape. Until recently, rape within marriage was (and still is in a small number of states) considered legally impossible in the United States (Augustine, 1990–1991; Bidwell & White, 1986). Spousal immunity or husband exemption from rape charges is traced back to British Lord Matthew Hale's 1736 proclamation, in *Pleas of the Crown*: "[T]he husband cannot be guilty of a rape committed by himself upon his lawful wife, for by their mutual matrimonial consent and contract the wife hath given up herself in this kind unto her husband which she cannot retract" (cited in Augustine, 1990–1991). This proclamation was based on the notion that a wife was considered her husband's property, and that upon marriage, husband and wife united into a single legal being (a husband). Thus, a husband could not rape his wife any more than he could steal from or rape himself.

Spousal immunity from the charge of rape remained essentially unchanged until the 1970s, and it was only during the 1980s and 1990s that U.S. states displayed an open rejection of the marital exemption by eliminating certain or all aspects of the exemption in their criminal codes. Currently only three states retain explicit marital rape exemptions in their penal codes. The exemption has been eliminated in 24 states, and 23 states specify circumstances or conditions, such as living apart, for a woman to charge her spouse with rape (Barnett, Miller-Perrin, & Perrin, 1997). Although women's organizations have successfully persuaded legislators to abolish or change marital rape exemption laws, the marital rape problem persists and is well documented. The conviction of a husband for raping a wife remains one of the most unusual criminal convictions achieved in any and all U.S. courts.

Russell (1982), in pioneering research, defined sexual assault or rape within the marriage as any type of forced sex (vaginal, anal, and oral sex, as well as forced digital penetration). Other researchers broaden the definition of sexual abuse to include acts such as forced kissing and the forced fondling of genitals (Finkelhor & Yllo, 1985; Frieze, 1983). Researchers examining marital rape must be cautious in how they define and then operationalize sexual abuse, especially

because many women do not define sexual abuse by their husbands as "rape," even when intercourse has been forced on them. Therefore, without the appropriate questions or measures, many incidents of rape or sexual abuse go undetected.

Through her interviews with 930 women, Russell (1982) found that one of every seven women who had ever been married had reported one or more experiences of marital rape. Beyond the women in Russell's sample who met her definition, "Many women not included in this group saw it as their 'duty' to submit to sexual intercourse with their husbands even when they had no desire for sex or were repulsed by the idea" (p. 58). Similarly, Finkelhor and Yllo (1985), based on interviews with 323 Boston women, found that 10% of the women reported that they were forced into having sex with their husbands or male partners. Bidwell and White (1986) identify several factors in the marital dyad that are associated with the occurrence of marital rape: lower quality marriages, continuous disagreement, premarital pregnancies, and the occurrence of physical violence.

Emotional Abuse. A number of researchers study the emotional abuse of children by parents or other caretakers, but studies on adult intimate emotional abuse are still limited in number. Several terms to indicate emotional abuse are often used interchangeably: verbal abuse, verbal aggression, and psychological abuse. Sabourin (1991) notes that verbal abuse is often operationally defined by the occurrence and intensity of several verbal acts: insulting, accusing, rejecting, and disconfirming. Straus and Sweet (1992) define verbal or symbolic aggression as a communication, either verbal or nonverbal, intended to cause psychological pain to another person or perceived as having that intent. It includes threats of physical or sexual aggression and can include acts such as name-calling, door-slamming, and sulking. Using the 1985 National Family Violence Survey data, Straus and Sweet report that 74% of the men and 75% of the women in cohabiting couples engaged in one or more verbal attacks during the year.

The relationship between emotional abuse and physical abuse is complex, and it is usually examined only by research that is designed to study physical violence incidents. Most studies find that some form of verbal abuse is a precursor to physical violence (Miller & Krull, 1997). Gagne (1992) reports that Appalachian wives abused by their husbands are often socially isolated, left at home without transportation, and forced to have children against their own wishes. Tifft (1993) reports that some men who batter also use emotional, torturelike tactics to control their partners, such as the deprivation of sleep or enforced social isolation. In some studies, a decline in verbal aggression is found to be associated with an increase in age and the number of children in a family (Straus & Sweet, 1992).

The most comprehensive study of emotional abuse was conducted by Stacey, Hazelwood, and Shupe (1994) based on their interviews with violent couples who participated in a counseling program in Austin, Texas. These researchers identified 13 forms of emotional abuse, including denial of freedom, censoring phone calls, name-calling, and the use of verbal threats. For both men and women, name-calling or belittling is the most frequently occurring form of emotional behavior. Moreover, men and women are equally likely to deny rights of privacy to each other. There are also some gender differences in the ways adult partners emotionally abuse each other. Women who emotionally abuse are least likely to deny their male partners access to their family members or to withhold sex from their partners. Men who emotionally abuse are least likely to make verbal threats to use a weapon or to kill or to deny their partners access to jointly held money.

Violence between Gay or Lesbian Partners

The U.S. Department of Justice distributed nationwide a special report, *Murder in Families*, based on the analysis of a representative sample survey of state and county prosecutors' records. The report shows that 16% of all murder victims in the United States are killed by a family member, and it summarizes the several known correlates of family murder, including mental illness, the abuse of alcohol, and offender and victim race and gender. In their discussion of gender, the report's authors state, "[S]pousal murder ... *by definition includes a man and a woman*" (Dawson & Langan, 1995, p. 4, emphasis added). The authors also note that an analysis of the same data, excluding heterosexual spouses and including "other family members," shows "murderers and victims were of the same sex in 65 percent of family murders" (p. 4). If same-sex family homicides and assaults were included in all domestic violence research it is quite possible or even likely that researchers would find that rates of intrasex violence are similar to intersex violence rates of interpersonal violence.

The Department of Justice report serves to corroborate a claim that only domestic violence within heterosexual couples has received considerable research and political attention over the past 2 decades. Relatively few studies have been published on violence between intimates in same-sex relationships (e.g., Coleman, 1994; Letellier, 1994), and an even fewer number of states now recognize that adult family partnerships include lesbian and gay couples. There are, however, some recent and noteworthy changes in domestic violence statutes and documents that are written to encourage uniformity across state laws. *The Model Code on Domestic Violence* (1994) uses only gender-neutral language to define family violence and family or household members. Family

members, according to the Model Code, include adults who live together or have lived together and adults who are (or were) engaged in a sexual relationship. The California legislature amended its Penal Code in 1995 to eliminate any opposite-sex language in its domestic violence statues. It also defines cohabitants to include "unrelated adult persons ... having sexual relations" (Spatt, 1995). Plowman (1996) writes about a Massachusetts woman who approached the prosecutor's office to file a complaint of domestic violence:

> It was a difficult decision to make. She had braved days and nights of physical abuse.... It took her five tries before she was able to summon the courage to walk through the courthouse doors.... [S]he explained that she was a victim of domestic abuse and would like to seek protection under Chapter 209A of the Massachusetts abuse protection law. "Is this your boyfriend or your husband?" the clerk asked. "My girlfriend," she said. (pp. 3–4).

The silence about violence in same-sex relationships is diminishing. It occurs, nonetheless, for a number of reasons: (1) There is a lack of reporting and often a disbelief that same-sex violence can occur; (2) there is a fear among gay and lesbian organizations that publicizing intimate violence would destroy credibility and fuel homophobic attacks; (3) lesbian violence contradicts patriarchal and feminist explanations of family violence; and (4) lesbian violence destroys challenges the belief that a nonviolent, egalitarian lesbian community could emerge (Island & Letellier, 1991; Renzetti, 1988, 1992; Schilit, Lie, Montagne, & Reyes, 1992).

A silence on homosexual domestic violence does not mean that the problem does not exist, as the literature in this field attests. A scarcity of empirical studies is due not only to the sensitive nature of battering and sexual violence, but also to the problems of locating a representative sample of a generally hidden group in the larger society. Despite sampling difficulties, several studies can be examined to form an empirical base from which to estimate the level and severity of the problem (Brand & Kidd, 1986; Lie, Schilit, Bush, Montagne, & Reyes, 1991; Renzetti, 1988, 1992; Waterman, Dawson, & Bologna, 1989).

Estimated levels of domestic violence in gay and lesbian partnerships vary across studies depending on the types of violence examined, whether one or both partners were surveyed, and whether incidence or prevalence measures were used. Renzetti (1992) examines numerous studies of incidence and prevalence among lesbian and heterosexual domestic partnerships and estimates conservatively that at least 25% of lesbians in domestic partnerships experience domestic violence. Coleman (1994) finds that almost 47% of women in lesbian couples are violent, and, in a survey of 1109 lesbians, Lie and Gentlewarrior (1991) find that 52% of the sample reports being victims of aggression by their partners.

With respect to emotional or psychological abuse, a survey of 284 lesbians finds that 90% claim they had experienced psychological abuse and 31% of the women reported that they had been forced to have sex with their current or most recent partners (Waterman et al., 1989). In sum, lesbian couples experience the types and levels of domestic violence found in opposite-sex couples.

Gay domestic violence is also documented in the research literature. Island and Letellier (1991) estimate that between 330,000 and 650,000 gay men are victimized by domestic violence each year. Bourg and Stock (1994) report that valid estimates of the levels of gay partner violence range from 11% to 20%. When the CTS was used to measure and estimate levels of violence among gay couples (Renzetti, 1988, 1992), researchers found that 95% of the sample had verbally abused their partners at least once during the prior year, and 47% had physically abused their partners. Gay men tend to be more verbally and physically abusive toward their partners compared to gay women, but gay men tend to abuse sexually at a lower rate than gay women in their domestic partnerships. Waterman et al. (1989) studied sexual coercion among gay couples and found that 12% of the men reported being forced to have sex with their current or most recent partners. Men who reported being victims of forced sex also were significantly more likely to be either a victim or perpetrator of other forms of violence in their domestic relationship.

Several factors, such as dependency, jealousy, an imbalance of power between partners, personality characteristics (Coleman, 1994), being victimized in a past relationship, a history of family violence, and alcohol abuse, are associated with violence in homosexual domestic relationships. Empirical studies, even those limited by sampling design, clearly show that violence in same-sex relationships exists and poses serious consequences for a large number of persons.

Some of the social responses to gay domestic violence are similar to what is experienced by heterosexual partners who are physically, sexually, or emotionally abused. Gays and lesbians also face unique challenges when, as individual victims or as segments of the general population, they seek a medical, social service, or criminal justice responses to domestic violence. Police, due to homophobia, cultural stereotypes, or inappropriate training, respond ineffectively to domestic violence among gay couples, and prosecutors and judges are reluctant to grant or enforce protective orders. Gay communities are reluctant to acknowledge the problems of domestic violence in fear of contributing to the stereotypes and prejudices held about gay and lesbian relationships. "Outing" by a well-intentioned medical or social service provider can result in the loss of family relationships or work, and gays and lesbians feel ostracized by battered women

shelters or counseling programs that respond to "male" perpetrators and "female" victims (Letellier, 1994; Lockhart, White, & Causby, 1994; Plowman, 1996; Renzetti, 1992).

Consequences of Violence by Heterosexual and Homosexual Partners

Physical violence results in injury and, in the most severe cases, death. There is also evidence to suggest a link between battering and female suicide (Vitanza, Vogel, & Marshall, 1995), especially among black and pregnant women (Stark & Flitcraft, 1995). Physical abuse can cause low self-esteem, feelings of shame, and helplessness in victims (Pagelow, 1984). Many of the psychological consequences are related to common elements of the abusive relationship: betrayal of a trust, a sense of powerless to end the abuse, and isolation and social stigma that may be experienced as a result of the abuse (Finkelhor, Hotaling, & Yllo, 1988). While the effects of physical violence can be apparent in terms of physical injuries such as cuts and bruises, the consequences of verbal or emotional abuse are not as easily observable. However, verbal aggression may be as damaging or even more damaging than physical aggression (Straus & Sweet, 1992).

Women raped or sexually abused by their partners tend to experience a diminished sense of self-worth. They are also likely to feel guilt, depression, and an inability to resume sexual intimacy in subsequent relationships. Fear, a sense of betrayal, anger, humiliation, and degradation are common. Sexual dysfunctions and physical injuries can result (Bidwell & White, 1986; Finkelhor & Yllo, 1985; Pagelow, 1989; Russell, 1982). While there is only a limited empirical base on which to draw conclusions about the consequences of rape for a gay partner, some studies do show that men experience consequences that are very similar to those experienced by women who are marital rape victims (Island & Letellier, 1991).

Intimate violence poses grave consequences for the larger society. Victims of intimate violence face an increased risk of becoming a future victim or a future perpetrator compared to those not victimized by domestic violence (Finkelhor et al., 1988; Straus, 1990a). Straus proposes that the more violent husbands are toward their wives, the more violent the wives and mothers are toward their children. Taking into consideration the number of women who are battered, even if one accepts only the conservative estimates, the implications for children are staggering. Evidence is accumulating to show that the observation of family violence by children has serious consequences for them (e.g., Davis & Carlson, 1987; Kashani, Daniel, Dandoy, & Holcomb, 1992; O'Keefe, 1994; Sternberg et al., 1993; Wilson, Cameron,

Jaffe, & Wolfe, 1989). Experiencing violence firsthand or viewing violence as a legitimate or commonplace behavior may increase a tolerance of violence in other settings, thus contributing to the cultural approval of violence.

Responses to Domestic Violence and Abuse

Social responses to domestic violence, especially in the forms of legislative developments and the development of social, medical, and criminal justice intervention programs, may be aimed at the victim of violence, the perpetrator of violence, or the social agents who assist victims and punish perpetrators. Victim assistance programs include medical assistance to treat immediate physical injuries, legal assistance to file a complaint or file a restraining order, employment assistance, mental health services, and shelters for immediate separation from the batterer to provide a sense of psychological and physical safety (Brown & O'Leary, 1997; Goolkasian, 1986; Grad, 1997; Margolin, Sibner, & Gleberman, 1988; Miller & Krull, 1997; New York State Senate, 1996; Sedlak, 1988). Unfortunately, most shelters are understaffed and underfunded, and only the most unusual shelter provides any services designed specifically for older women, battered lesbians, gay men, or bisexual partners (Letellier, 1994; Margolies & Leeder, 1995; Vinton, 1992).

Intervention with batterers can take the form of therapy or education to change attitudes and stop abuse, or it may take the form of police intervention and arrest (Dunford, Huizinga, & Elliott, 1990; Ferraro, 1993; Gondolf & McFerron, 1989; Margolies & Leeder, 1995; Polsby, 1992). Evaluating the success of therapeutic or educational intervention with batterers is difficult, partly due to the chronic problems of high client attrition levels and low client motivation or commitment levels (Sedlak, 1988). Evaluation studies suggest only modest success for any batterer program, with some researchers concluding that only 50% of the men who complete programs refrain from physical assaults and only 40% refrain from terroristic threats for 6 months or a year (DeMaris & Jackson, 1992; Gondolf, 1995; Hamberger & Hastings, 1990; Tolman & Bhosley, 1991).

A large body of research, including field experimentation, has focused on the effectiveness of police arrest on reducing recidivistic domestic violence (Berk, Campbell, Klop, & Western, 1992; Dutton, Hart, Kennedy, & Williams, 1992; Sherman, 1992). Some researchers (Sherman & Berk, 1984; Syers & Edleson, 1992) argue that police arrest can substantially reduce recidivism of wife-battering, consistent with deterrent and social control perspectives. In other published statements, researchers warn that arrest can stop the violence only for certain types of offenders, usually those who have "stakes" or interests in following the conventional norms of the larger society (Hirschel, Hutchinson, & Dean,

1992; Pate & Hamilton, 1992; Sherman, 1992; Sherman & Smith, 1992). For others—unemployed men, for example—arrest is no more effective for preventing recidivistic violence than any other form of intervention.

In the majority of traditional domestic violence cases, women experience a lack of protection not only from the police, but also from the rest of the criminal justice system. Ferraro (1993) points out that there are very real limitations to the criminal justice approach to protecting women from their batterers because "it focuses on the control of specific incidents without attention to the complex social and economic problems of women" (p. 174). Based on an examination of the multiple factors associated with domestic violence, one author of the major arrest studies concludes that innovative treatment programs, for example, "hybrid programs," including drug and alcohol treatment as well as the more traditional counseling approach, are necessary to prevent recidivism among those domestic violence perpetrators who enter the criminal justice system (Goldkamp, 1996). In 1995, the National Institute of Justice released a report that summarized evaluations of 23 law enforcement training programs it sponsored for police and social service agents. The purpose of the programs was to help those who respond to domestic violence become better educated and more responsive to domestic violence victims. The evaluation report concludes that continued improvements are necessary, including the need "to protect victims better and to allow law enforcement agencies *wider discretion* in dealing with offenders" (Newmark, Harrell, & Adams, 1995, p. 3; emphasis added).

Despite programs that mandate arrest and grant temporary restraining orders, women continue to be abused, harassed, and threatened. Nevertheless, many manage to cope with persistent violence. The frequently asked but erroneous and ignorant question, "Why do victims stay?" fails to address the real problem: "Why do the abusers abuse, and continue to abuse?" It also fails to consider the social, contextual, financial, and relationship factors that can explain domestic partner abuse as well as the interpersonal relationships that can be formed between victim-survivors and social agents that can help stop the abuse (Bowker, 1983; Ford, 1991; Herbert, Silver, & Ellard, 1991; Johnson, 1992; Nurius, Furrey, & Berliner, 1992; Tifft, 1993).

Altogether, a thorough examination and a meta-analysis of the correlates and causes of violence between intimates is necessary to develop, implement, and evaluate effective intervention and prevention strategies. Methodologically, there are strong needs for survey research based on representative samples and longitudinal designs, and even stronger needs for interview studies with women and men who are willing to tell their stories of violence to researchers and advocates who are willing to listen. There is less need for any new law or any more law that mandates a single set of actions for a varied population and varied social problems. There is, however, a strong need for an understanding that *legal discretion* as well as the *victim's power* to use extant laws are imperatives for developing effective social responses to domestic violence. Domestic violence victims are independent adults who need services from programs, including criminal justice programs, that are designed to help stop the violence against domestic partners.

Elder Abuse

A Quiet Scandal

Elder abuse, according to a presidential press release, is this nation's "quiet scandal," although the American Medical Association (AMA) (1995) estimates that 1.8 million victims suffer some medical or psychological consequence annually in the United States. Only in 1992 did the federal government enact the Elder Abuse and Dependent Adult Civil Protection Act (EADACPA), permitting elder victims to file charges and to recover losses in civil courts for physical abuse or neglect, or for financial or fiduciary abuse (Hankin, 1996). In 1995, Wolf testified before a U.S. Senate Special Committee on Aging and identified the types, correlates, and consequences of elder abuse. Wolf (1996) testified that elder abuse cases are characterized by the type of abuse perpetrated, by the victim and perpetrator's relationship, and by the gender and race of the victim. The four major types of abuse are physical, psychological or emotional, financial, and neglect.

Physical and emotional abuse are also found when studying other major forms of family violence, child abuse and domestic violence. Two relatively distinctive types of elder abuse are neglect and financial abuse. Whereas the child neglect problem is well documented by researchers, the levels and consequences of elder neglect are less known. If a caretaker in an institution or at home neglects the elder, dehydration, malnourishment, skin conditions, hemorrhaging below the scalp, and other physical problems, including death, may result (AMA, 1995). The second distinctive form of elder abuse, financial abuse, can result in the loss of money, valued items, and control over one'e estate; the accumulation of unpaid bills; and an increased likelihood of state institutionalization.

Explanations

Elder abuse is now a focal concern of family violence research. The documentation of a substantial number of elderly victims was accomplished by the National Family Violence Surveys, conducted in 1975 and 1985, that have been discussed throughout this chapter. Elder abuse, in part, is explained by the major demographic shifts and changes that characterize the U.S. population over the last 50 years (Steinmetz, 1981). The average life expectancy of the average person in the United States has increased, the number of persons and the proportion of the population 60 years and older have increased, and the push toward deinstitutionalization and home care for the elderly have influenced the emotional and the financial resources families have and use to care for their elder members (Gelles & Cornell, 1990; Steinmetz, 1988).

Perceptions of child abuse and domestic violence have influenced the research and the reporting of elder abuse cases (Crystal, 1987; Utech & Garrett, 1992). Concerns for proving intentionality, injury, physical versus nonphysical maltreatment, and arbitrary age categorizations have posed problems for the development of a clear-cut, universally accepted definition of elder abuse. Little attention has been focused on how race and ethnicity shape definitions of elder abuse in the United States (for exceptions see Carson, 1995; Griffin, 1994), although extensive literature on elder abuse in other nations and cultures is available.

Levels and Types of Abuse

Given its recent "discovery" by the media, the research on elder abuse is somewhat less developed in the field of family violence research than it is in the field of gerontology. Family violence researchers form estimates of elder abuse and its correlates that are generally based on small, nonrandom, area samples. Early estimates of elder abuse and neglect ranged from 4.1% to 10% (see Steinmetz, 1987, 1988, for reviews of these early studies).

Many estimates of abuse come from service providers to the elderly or official reports made to adult protective services. Illinois service providers estimated incidence rates of verbal or emotional abuse at 11.2% and physical abuse at 2.8% (Poertner, 1986). South Carolina's Adult Protective Services substantiated 13,273 cases of elderly "maltreatment" between 1974 and 1984 (Cash & Valentine, 1987). Because determining the separate rates of abuse is difficult, abuse and neglect are often grouped together in elder maltreatment studies.

Harris (1996), rather than studying elder abuse cases perpetrated by caretakers, studied the problem of domestic violence among elderly couples. For this nationwide, representative study, she analyzed the 1985 National Family Violence Resurvey data and identified 842 married participants age 60 or older. Analytically, Harris compared violent and nonviolent elder couples to violent and nonviolent younger couples. She concludes that the risk factors identified to predict domestic violence generally—verbal abuse, marital conflict, and stress—also predict spouse abuse among the elderly. Also using the 1985 National Family Violence Resurvey data, Pillemer and Suitor (1988) studied 520 respondents age 65 or older and found that 4.2% of the husbands reported physical violence perpetrated by their wives, and 3.3% of the wives reported husband-to-wife physical violence during the year prior. These domestic violence studies show that elder men and women are often the victims of family abuse, but can also be the perpetrators of family abuse and violence (Utech & Garrett, 1992).

The elderly are not exempt from sexual abuse, although the extent of elder sexual abuse is unknown. In a study that examined cases of suspected sexual abuse, researchers found that most victims are women and had experienced a limited capacity for independent functioning and self-protection. Offenders tend to be sons or husbands (Ramsey-Klawsnik, 1991). Legal prohibitions of rape and sexual assault, although they vary widely across the states, uniformly require voluntary consent for lawful sexual relations. An elder who cannot give consent because of any mental or physical limitation faces an increased vulnerability to rape or sexual abuse by caretakers in institutions or in their private home.

Current research on elder abuse highlights both victim and abuse characteristics, as well as the social factors associated with elder abuse. Reports of elder abuse are most likely to find that most victims are women of very advanced ages with low incomes. Most studies suggest that victims with physical or mental impairments have a higher likelihood of abuse than those not suffering from these types of impairments.

In general, elder abuse is more likely to be perpetrated under conditions of a high degree of external stress and when elders are socially isolated from other relatives or friends. When victims are perceived as a source of stress to the abuser, they are more likely to be abused. The majority of the abusers live with their elderly relatives and are most likely the victim's children. These generalizations, replicated by other social science researchers, are based on a 2-year study titled *Duty Bound: Elder Abuse and Family Care*, in which the researcher-author interviewed elders as well as their caretakers (Steinmetz, 1988).

Some exploratory perpetrator-oriented studies find that the more severe abusers can suffer from mental illnesses, be financially dependent, and have drug and alcohol dependencies (Anetzberger, Korbin, & Austin, 1994; Godkin, Wold, & Pillemer, 1989; Greenberg, McKibben, & Raymond, 1990). Researchers have also reported that abusive relationships are characterized by a high level of conflict between the perpetrator and the elder.

Elder abuse studies clearly challenge patriarchal and feminist systems theories of family violence. In an unusual book based on their own empirical studies, Aitken and Griffin (1996) argue that elder abuse is a highly gendered so-

cial problem. They find, like other researchers, that most victims are women, especially the eldest victims; most perpetrators are women, whether the abuse occurs in an institution or in a home; a large number of elderly men are abused by their domestic partners or by their daughters; and a large number of older women are abused by their sons. These observations and descriptions have implications for understanding the consequences of elder abuse. They also pose questions regarding appropriate social responses to the various forms of elder abuse.

An overview of the literature on the consequences of other forms of family violence suggests strongly that elder victims may suffer from abuse in physical, emotional, or financial ways. Elders may sustain varying degrees of physical injuries from abuse or develop medical problems as a result of maltreatment, including neglect. Greenberg et al. (1990) studies 204 professionally confirmed cases of abuse and neglect and found substantial depression among the maltreated elders. In another study of elderly persons, researchers found that elder abuse victims were significantly more depressed than those elders who had not been abused (Pillemer & Prescott, 1989).

Responses to Elder Abuse

Current intervention and prevention strategies take the form of legal responses or political advocacy and social services. Although lacking any empirical justification, mandatory reporting statutes exist or are under active consideration in most U.S. states. For cases of financial abuse, legal action may take the form of revoking the abuser's power of attorney (Callahan, 1982). Criminal court intervention may result in the mandatory removal of elderly family members from their own homes, where they are in physical danger, and placement in the custody of guardians (Heisler, 1991). Guardianship is intended to safeguard the abused elder, but guardians may perpetrate further abuse, and therefore increase the dependency of elders on their adult (and abusive) children. Psychological abuse is generally not handled by the criminal justice system. Instead, it is likely addressed by social service programs, and referrals for professional assistance for victims and perpetrators are often made.

Adult protective services (APS) programs now operate in every state, but the legal, medical, and social services provided to abused elders vary widely across states (Mixon, 1995). In cases of abuse where the victim is impaired or dependent, housing, health, home maintenance, and financial management services can be extended (Pagelow, 1989; Pillemer & Suiter, 1988). Elder mediation is another method of social intervention available for resolving some types of elder conflicts (Craig, 1994). For elders who are independent of their abusers, self-help groups provide valuable services and emotional support. Individual assistance can also take the form of reassuring the elderly that abuse is unlawful and of educating them and their caretakers of their rights. Perpetrators of elder abuse may receive psychological counseling or use self-help groups. Those perpetrators who are financially dependent on the elders they abuse can receive assistance for finding housing and employment in some social programs (Pillemer & Suiter, 1988). While these approaches are used to intervene in some elder abuse cases, their effectiveness has not been systematically evaluated.

Preventive measures are the most important methods for ameliorating the elder abuse problems in the United States. They should focus on maintaining and building support systems that are needed by the elderly and their caretakers. Callahan (1982) suggests that to prevent elder abuse, the elderly must have economic security and more funds invested toward their needs. Finally, an informed awareness and sensitivity to the problems and needs of the elderly population are needed. Even with these suggestions, effective intervention and prevention strategies require an improved social science based understanding of the causes and correlates of elder abuse (Blakely & Dolon, 1991). Clear definitions that take into consideration the multiple dimensions of elder abuse are needed, additional research is needed to correct the current limitations and methodological weaknesses associated with elder abuse, and insightful and sophisticated theoretical models based on a blend of social science and victim explanations are needed (Hugman, 1995; Johnson, 1995; Steinmetz, 1988, 1991, 1993). We need no new studies, however, to confirm that people of all ages experience violence and abuse at the hands of a family member.

Omissions, Controversies, and Conclusions

Omissions

We conclude this chapter by first identifying the problems not covered in these pages. Second, we bring forward some current and emerging controversies in the field. We conclude without offering any resolutions for family violence problems. Instead we hope that the information we provided will encourage more work in the field that is designed to create comprehensive and socially useful explanations of family violence and abuse.

Dating Violence.   Not discussed in this chapter are the problems of violence and rape in dating but not cohabiting couples in the United States. An emerging research literature shows that the consequences of date rape and date violence can be severe and long-lasting. Established correlates of these forms of violence include alcohol and drug abuse,

conflicting expectations for intimate relationships, prior experiences with the forms of interpersonal violence, and asymmetrical power. Clearly needed are studies that examine couples *not* dating or living on college campuses.

Hate Crimes.   A second problem not discussed is often called "hate crime," or acts and expressions that intentionally cause emotional or physical harm to another because of sex, race, ethnicity, or religion. Since some types of hate crimes are directed at family members or at couples who dare challenge the cultural norms and stereotypes that delimit appropriate "coupling," these offenses fall within the boundaries of several conceptualizations of family abuse and violence.

Variation by Class, Race, Ethnicity, and Religion. Our third, and in our own estimation most important, omission is the systematic analysis of all forms of child abuse, domestic violence, and elder abuse that vary considerably across social classes, race, ethnicity, and religious groups in the United States. Not only are these factors associated with the likelihood of abuse, but they are also strongly associated with the social programs and the social policies that are developed and implemented in response to family violence across the states and by the federal government. Social class influences the supposedly mandatory reporting of child abuse, the supposedly mandated police arrest of domestic violence offenders, and the supposed mandatory reporting of suspected elder abuse victims. Definitions of abuse and violence and social responses to victims and perpetrators vary across ethnic groups, race groups, and religious groups.

Why did we omit these issues and the volumes of research literature devoted to them? The simple and straightforward response is that only limited space is available to summarize and discuss family violence problems. The more accurate response is that we contend that family violence problems are complex. Current laws provide simplistic responses, and existing social research is plentiful but too limited in scope or focus to assist policy makers effectively. Desperately needed are analyses of all the published and distributed studies that were designed to describe or explain a particular family violence problem or to evaluate the legislation and social programs that were established to ameliorate some of the family violence problems. The meta-analyses that are needed must attend to how social class, race, ethnicity, and religion interact with the other known correlates of family violence and how they influence the programs designed to respond to these social problems.

Controversies

Myths.   The study of family violence generates controversy and myth. Consider for example media attention to the "urban myths" associated with child abuse. A news headline or a book published by a respected press may conclude that ritualistic or satanic abuse of children—usually involving animal mutilations, torture, and sexual abuse of child victims—is a social problem that urgently needs documentation and treatment. But Gelles (1996) reports: "Although a small industry of seminars and training sessions on ritual and satanic abuse has developed over the past few years.... [N]ot a single case of satanic murder, human sacrifice, or cannibalism has been documented" (p. 15). Likewise, the "tens of thousands" of children who are abducted, raped, and killed each year is a grave exaggeration of a particular form of child abuse that helped only to create an industry—the National Center for Missing and Exploited Children (funded by the U.S. Department of Justice)—but does nothing to establish accurately the extent of the kidnapping problem in the United States.

These (and other) myths are not harmless. Myths and exaggerations generate fear, they ask for governments to misspend funds to sponsor the creation of unnecessary programs, and they distract citizens from paying attention to the social problems that effect hundreds of thousands of victims.

The Mandatory Response Flaw. The mandatory response flaw is based on a concept that we borrow from *The Book of David* (Gelles, 1996). We use the concept to generalize the most pervasive social responses to child abuse, domestic violence, and elder abuse. The mandatory response flaw refers to the mandatory reporting and investigation of child abuse cases, the mandatory arrest of suspected domestic violence offenders, and the mandatory reporting of elder abuse. To *mandate* a response eliminates any discretion or any choice in response. Gelles (1996) warns that "abandoning the three-decade-long commitment to mandatory reporting [of child abuse] is only slightly less heretical than arguing that family preservation programs are ineffective or even dangerous for some children" (p. 153). Gelles claims that mandatory reporting of child abuse fails in at least four ways: (1) reported cases disproportionately represent children from lower social classes and minority children; (2) it overworks child protection workers and makes them less capable of responding effectively to the severe cases; (3) it assumes professionals are either unwilling or incapable to treat cases; and (4) it gives only a false hope that cases of maltreatment can all be served.

Mandatory (or preferred) arrest policies for domestic violence suspects that have been adopted by more than 90% of metropolitan police departments in the United States fail for at least five reasons: (1) Arrest can increase the likelihood of physical violence following arrest, especially if the perpetrator was arrested for a verbal threat; (2) victims can be revictimized by police, courts, and programs that do not respond to victim needs; (3) the victim is unlikely to gain power-by-alliance with criminal justice actors under mandatory arrest conditions that eliminate all power, control, and discretion from the adult victim and from the police; (4) actual arrests are more likely in lower-class and minority neighborhoods; and (5) to avoid problems associated with arrest, police may not respond to reports of domestic violence.

Mandatory reporting of elder abuse fails for at least five reasons: (1) Victims and caretakers can be unnecessarily stigmatized; (2) an unacceptably high level of false accusations can result; (3) nonvoluntary and unnecessary institutionalization of the elder family member can occur; (4) an unnecessary loss of control over decision making, including financial decisions, by the elder and other family members may occur, and (5) social isolation and family abandonment of elders is possible.

The mandatory response flaw to family violence problems has, as yet, undocumented explanations. We attend to three related and problematic issues: (1) the family preservation ideal, (2) the "one-size-fits-all" theory and program approach, and (3) trust in the law-making process and the courts to resolve problems and protect U.S. citizenry.

First is the family preservation ideal, discussed earlier in the context of child abuse problems. To preserve the fiction that "the family" (whatever "the family" means) is the best social context for the child, a social worker may unwittingly return a battered child to the person or persons who will become the child's murderer (Gelles, 1996). The family preservation ideal also generates problematic responses to other forms of family violence and abuse. A pastor or a mental health counselor may encourage a battered wife to return to "the family," to her abuser, in order to forgive him, care for her children, and hope that the axe does not fall. A case worker who mandatorily investigates an allegation of elder neglect may encourage the overworked and financially stressed caretaker to provide more physical hygiene, leaving the elder within "the family" to suffer from wounds that will not heal or from an act of violence in response to the investigation.

Let our claim be clearly stated. Whenever it is in:

1. the *best interest of the child* to remain in the family
2. the *best interest of the spouse* to remain in the family
3. the *best interest of the elder* family member to remain in the family

the individual and his or her family should and must receive all the social, medical, and financial services that are necessary to thrive physically, psychologically, and spiritually. However, all laws and all programs that aim to ameliorate the family violence problems in the United States must recognize the necessity to abandon "the family" preservation ideal and recognize the need to develop remedies in the best interest of the child, the adult, and the elder person who have suffered from abuse and violence within the family. Likewise, social researchers and advocates for social reform need to direct efforts toward the development of multiple theories, multiple programs, and multiple ideals. They must abandon the "one-size-fits-all" theory approach (such as a "family systems theory" to parallel a "family preservation ideal") for explaining the complex problems of family violence and abuse.

Finally, the mandatory flaw in the field of family violence is perhaps due to a heavy reliance on law and legal agents to solve problems and protect the citizenry from harm. Laws are supposed to keep our streets clean, regulate the quality of air and water, prevent crime, guarantee parasite-free processed food, and maintain social control. Laws are intended to reflect our social and cultural norms. There is, quite candidly, no empirical evidence whatsoever to support any claim that law succeeds in regulating morality, behavior, interpersonal behaviors, or familial behaviors without oppressing all the freedoms U.S. citizens fight for and cherish. To rely on the law to stop child abuse, domestic violence, or elder abuse would naturally require "mandatory" practices. If the law cannot handle the problems, what can? Innovative and perhaps creative ideas are needed.

Conclusions

To conclude, we reiterate: Family violence problems are indeed serious social problems. Although theoretical and methodological questions and issues persist, the widespread abuse of children, adults, and elders in U.S. society is unequivocally established. The variety of perspectives to explain the problems is helpful for identifying a multitude of factors that lead to violence, but as yet, we are far from predicting specific incidents. The integration of different levels of theory and the development of theories that have use value for policy makers are necessary next steps in the development of a comprehensive explanation of the causes and consequences of child abuse, partner abuse, and elder abuse. We know, however, that all forms of family violence have severe, negative consequences for individuals, for families, and for the larger society. Unfortunately, the social response to family violence is still politicized, mandated, and legalized more than it is informed by social science research. Intervention programs appear to have limited effectiveness for stopping violence, in part because of inadequate resources and a lack of coordination among legal and social services and other organizations concerned with family violence. Prevention remains the best hope, but prevention requires support by state and federal governments and private organizations to educate and help rather than to mandate and institutionalize.

References

Aikten, L., & Griffin, G. (1996). *Gender issues in elder abuse.* Newbury Park, CA: Sage.

Aiosa-Karpas, C. J., Karpas, R., Pelcovitz, D., & Kaplan, S. (1991). Gender identification and sex role attribution in sexually abused adolescent females. *Journal of the American Academy of Child and Adolescent Psychiatry, 30,* 266–271.

Alexander, P. C., & Lupfer, S. A. (1987). Family characteristics and long-term consequences associated with sexual abuse. *Archives of Sexual Behavior, 16,* 235–245.

Alexander, P. C., Neimeyer, R. A., Follette, V. M., Moore, M. K., & Harter, S. (1989). A comparison of group treatments of women sexually abused as children. *Journal of Consulting and Clinical Psychology, 57,* 479–483.

Allers, C. T., Benjack, K. I., White, J. A., & Rousey, J. T. (1993). HIV vulnerability and the adult survivor of childhood sexual abuse. *Child Abuse and Neglect, 17,* 291–298.

American Humane Association (AHA). (1988). *Highlights of official child neglect and abuse reporting 1986.* Denver CO: Author.

American Medical Association. (1995). *Diagnostic and treatment guidelines on mental health effects of family violence.* Washington, DC: Author.

American Psychiatric Association. (1994). *Diagnostic and statistical manual of mental disorders* (4th ed.). Washington, DC: Author.

Anetzberger, G. J., Korbin, J. E., & Austin, C. (1994). Alcoholism and elder abuse. *Journal of Interpersonal Violence, 9,* 184–193.

Ards, S., & Harrell, A. (1993). Reporting of child maltreatment: A secondary analysis of the national incidence surveys. *Child Abuse and Neglect, 17,* 337–344.

Augustine, R. I. (1990–1991). Marriage: The safe haven for rapists. *Journal of Family Law, 29,* 559–590.

Azar, S. T. (1991). Models of child abuse: A meta-theoretical analysis. *Criminal Justice and Behavior, 18,* 30–46.

Azar, S. T., & Wolfe, D. A. (1989). Child abuse and neglect. In E. J. Mash & R. A. Barkely (Eds.), *Treatment of child disorders* (pp. 451–489). New York: Guilford.

Bachman, R., & Coker, A. L. (1994). Police involvement in domestic violence: The interactive effects of victim injury, offender's history of violence, and race. *Violence and Victims, 10,* 91–96.

Bachman, R., & Saltzman, L. E. (1996). *Violence against women: Estimates from the redesigned survey* (Bureau of Justice Statistics Special Report, NCJ no. 154348. Rockville, MD: US Department of Justice.

Bakan, D. (1971). *Slaughter of the innocents: A study of the battered child phenomenon.* Boston: Beacon.

Bandura, A. (1971). *Social learning theory.* Morristown, NJ: General Learning.

Barnett, I. W., Miller-Perrin, C., & Perrin, R. D. (1997). *Family violence across the lifespan.* Thousand Oaks, CA: Sage.

Barrera, M., Palmer, S., Brown, R., & Kalaher, S. (1994). Characteristics of court-involved men and non-court-involved men who abuse their wives. *Journal of Family Violence, 9,* 333–345.

Bath, H. I., & Haapala, D. A. (1993). Intensive family preservation services with abused and neglected children: An examination of group differences. *Child Abuse and Neglect, 17,* 213–225.

Becker, J. V., & Hunter, J. A., Jr. (1992). Evaluation of treatment outcome for adult perpetrators of child sexual abuse. *Criminal Justice and Behavior, 19,* 74–92.

Beitchman, J. H., Zucker, K. J., Hood, J. E., daCosta, G. A., & Akman, D. (1991). A review of the short-term effects of child sexual abuse. *Child Abuse and Neglect, 15,* 537–556.

Beitchman, J. H., Zucker, K. J., Hood, J. E., daCosta, G. A., Akman, D., & Cassavia, E. (1992). A review of the long-term effects of child sexual abuse. *Child Abuse and Neglect, 16,* 101–118.

Bellingham, B. (1983). The unspeakable blessing: Street children, reform rhetoric, and misery in early industrial capitalism. *Politics and Society*, *12*, 303–330.

Benjamin, M. (1980). Abused as a child, abusive as a parent: Practitioners beware. In R. Volpe, M. Breton, & J. Milton (Eds.), *The maltreatment of the school-aged child* (pp. 197–202). Lexington, MA: Lexington Books.

Benoit, J. L., & Kennedy, W. A. (1992). The abuse history of male adolescent sex offenders. *Journal of Interpersonal Violence*, *7*, 543–548.

Berk, R. A. (1993). What the scientific evidence shows: On average, we can do no better than arrest. In R. J. Gelles & D. R. Loseke (Eds.), *Current controversies on family violence* (pp. 323–336). Newbury Park, CA: Sage.

Berk, R. A., Campbell, A., Klap, R., & Western, B. (1992). The deterrent effect of arrest: A Bayesian analysis of four field experiments. *American Sociological Review*, *57*, 698–708.

Berk, R., & Newton, P. (1985). Does arrest really deter wife battery? An effort to replicate the findings of the Minneapolis spouse abuse experiment. *American Sociological Review*, *50*, 253–262.

Berkeley Planning Associates. (1978). *Evaluation of child abuse and neglect demonstration project, 1974–1977* (Vol. 1 & 2, Child Abuse and Neglect Treatment Programs: Final Report and Summary of Findings). Washington, DC: U.S. Department of Health, Education and Welfare.

Berliner, L. (1990). Domestic violence: A humanist of feminist issue? *Journal of Interpersonal Violence*, *9*, 209–228.

Besharov, D. (1985). Right versus rights: The dilemma of child protection, *Public Welfare*, *43*, 19–27.

Bidwell, L., & White, P. (1986). The family context of marital rape. *Journal of Family Violence*, *1*, 277–287.

Birns, B. (1988). The mother–infant tie: Of bonding and abuse. In M. B. Straus (Ed.), *Abuse and victimization across the life span* (pp. 9–31). Baltimore: Johns Hopkins University Press.

Birns, B., Cascardi, M., & Meyer, S. (1994). Sex role socialization: Developmental influences on wife abuse. *American Journal of Orthopsychiatry*, *64*, 50–59.

Blackman, J. (1989). *Intimate violence: A study of injustice*. New York: Columbia University Press.

Blakely, B. E., & Dolon, R. (1991). Area agencies on aging and the prevention of elder abuse: The results of a national study. *Journal of Elder Abuse and Neglect*, *3*, 21–40.

Bourg, S., & Stock, H. V. (1994). A review of domestic violence arrest statistics in a police department using a pro-arrest policy: Are pro-arrest policies enough? *Journal of Family Violence*, *9*, 177–192.

Bowker, L. H. (1983). *Beating wife-beating*. Lexington, MA: Heath.

Bowlby, J. (1980). *Attachment and loss: Loss, sadness and depression*. New York: Basic Books.

Brand, P. A., & Kidd, A. H. (1986). Frequency of physical aggression in heterosexual and female homosexual dyads. *Psychological Reports*, *59*, 1307–1313.

Brassard, M. R., Germain, R., & Hart, S. N. (Eds.). (1987). *Psychological maltreatment of children and youth*. New York: Pergamon.

Brassard, M. R., Hart, S. N., & Hardy, D. (1993). The psychological maltreatment rating scales. *Child Abuse and Neglect*, *17*, 715–729.

Breines, W., & Gordon, L. (1983). The new scholarship on family violence. *Signs*, *8*, 490–531.

Breire, J. (1992). Methodological issues in the study of sexual abuse. Effects. *Journal of Consulting and Clinical Psychology*, *60*, 196–203.

Beire, J. H., & Runtz, M. (1987). Post sexual abuse trauma: Data and implications for clinical practice. *Journal of Interpersonal Violence*, *2*, 367–379.

Breire, J., Henschel, D., & Smiljanich, K. (1992). Attitudes toward sexual abuse: Sex differences and construct validity. *Journal of Research in Personality*, *26*, 398–406.

Breire, J., Berliner, L., Bulkley, J., Jenny, C., & Reid, T. (1996). *The APSAC handbook on child maltreatment*. Thousand Oaks, CA: Sage.

Brown, P. D., & O'Leary, K. D. (1997). Wife abuse in intact couples: A review of couples treatment programs. In G. Kaufman Kantor & J. L. Jasinski (Eds.), *Out of the darkness: Contemporary perspectives on family violence* (pp. 194–207). Thousand Oaks, CA: Sage.

Browne, A., & Finkelhor, D. (1986). The impact of sexual abuse: A review of the research. *Psychological Bulletin*, *91*, 66–77.

Browne, K., & Saqi, S. (1988). Approaches to screening for child abuse and neglect. In K. Browne, C. Davies, & P. Stratton (Eds.), *Early prediction and prevention of child abuse* (pp. 57–85). New York: Wiley.

Brush, L. C. (1993). Violent acts and injurious outcomes in married couples: Methodological issues in the National Survey of Families and Households. In P. B. Bart & E. G. Moran (Eds.), *Violence against women: The bloody footprints* (pp. 240–251). Newbury Park, CA; Sage.

Burgess, R. L., & Youngblood, L. M. (1988). Social incompetence and the intergenerational transmission of abusive parental practices. In G. T. Hotaling, D. Finkelhor, J. T. Kirkpatrick, & M. A. Straus (Eds.), *Family abuse and its consequences* (pp. 38–60). Beverly Hills, CA: Sage.

Buzawa, E. S., Buzawa, C. G., & Inciardi, J. A. (Eds.). (1996). *Domestic violence: The criminal justice response (2nd ed.)*. Thousand Oaks, CA: Sage.

Callahan, J., Jr. (1982). Elder abuse programming: Will it help the elderly? *Urban and Social Change Review*, *15*, 15–16.

Campbell, D. W., Campbell, J., King, C., Parker, B., & Ryan, J. (1994). The reliability and factor structure of the Index of Spouse Abuse with Alllcan-American women. *Violence and Victims*, *9*, 259–274.

Carney, R. M., & Williams, B. D. (1983). Premenstrual syndrome: A criminal defense. *Notre Dame Law Review*, *252*, 2726.

Carson, D. K. (1995). American Indian elder abuse: Risk and protective factors among the oldest Americans. *Journal of Elder Abuse and Neglect*, *7*, 17–39.

Cash, T., & Valentine, D. (1987). A decade of adult protective services: Case characteristics. *Journal of Gerontological Work*, *10*, 7–60.

Cazenave, N. A., & Straus, M. A. (1990). Race, class, network embeddedness, and family violence. In M. A. Straus & R. J. Gelles (Eds.), *Physical violence in American families* (pp. 321–339). New Brunswick, NJ: Transaction Publishers.

Chaffin, M. (1992). Factors associated with treatment completion and progress among intrafamiliar sexual abusers. *Child Abuse and Neglect*, *16*, 257–264.

Chess, S., & Thomas, A. (1982). Infant bonding: Mystique and reality. *American Journal of Orthopsychiatry*, *52*, 213–222.

Chester, B., Robin, R. W., Koss, M. P., Lopez, J., & Goldman, D. (1994). Grandmother dishonored: Violence against women by male partners in American Indian communities. *Violence and Victims*, *9*, 249–258.

Cicchetti, D., & Barrett, D. (1991). Toward the development of a scientific nosology of child maltreatment. In D. Cicchetti & W. Grove (Eds.), *Thinking clearly about psychology* (pp. 346–377). Minneapolis: University of Minnesota Press.

Clarke, M. E., & Hornick, J. P. (1988). The child sexual abuse victim: Assessment and treatment issues and solutions. *Contemporary Family Therapy*, *10*, 235–242.

Cole, P., Woolger, C., Power, T. G., & Smith, K. D. (1992). Parenting difficulties among adult survivors of father–daughter incest. *Child Abuse and Neglect*, *16*, 249–249.

Coleman, D. H., & Straus, M. A. (1990). Marital power, conflict, and violence in a nationally representative sample of American couples. In M. S. Straus & R. J. Gelles (Eds.), *Physical violence in American families* (pp. 287–304). New Brunswick, NJ: Transaction Publishers.

Coleman, V. E. (1994). Lesbian battering: The relationship between personality and the perpetration of violence. *Violence and Victims, 9*, 139–152.

Collier, R. (1995). *Masculinity, law, and the family*. London: Routledge.

Collings, S. J. (1995). The long-term effects of contact and noncontact forms of child sexual abuse in a sample of university men. *Child Abuse and Neglect, 19*, 1–6.

Conte, J., & Schuerman, J. R. (1987). Factors associated with an increased impact of child sexual abuse. *Child Abuse and Neglect, 11*, 201–211.

Conte, J., Wolfe, S., & Smith, T. (1987, July). *What sexual offenders tell us about prevention: Preliminary findings*. Paper presented at the Family Violence Conference, University of New Hampshire, Durham.

Costin, L. B. (1991). Unraveling the Mary Ellen legend: Origins of the "cruelty" movement. *Social Service Review, 65*, 203–223.

Craig, Y. (1994). Elder mediation: Can it contribute to the prevention of elder abuse and the protection of the rights of elders and their careers? *Journal of Elder Abuse and Neglect, 6*, 83–96.

Crystal, S. (1987). Elder abuse: The latest crisis. *Public Interest, 88*, 56–66.

Cutler, S. E., & Nolen-Hoeksema, S. (1991). Accounting for sex difference in depression through female victimization: Childhood sexual abuse. *Sex Roles, 24*, 425–438.

Daro, D. (1988). *Confronting child abuse: Research for effective program design*. New York: Free Press.

Daro, D. (1991). Child sexual abuse prevention: Separating fact from fiction. *Child Abuse and Neglect, 15*, 1–4.

Davidson, T. (1977). Wifebeating: A recurring phenomenon throughout history. In M. Roy (Ed.), *Battered women: A psychosociological study of domestic violence* (pp. 2–23). New York: Van Nostrand Reinhold.

Davis, G. E., & Leitenberg, H. (1988). Adolescent sex offenders. *Psychological Bulletin, 101*, 417–427.

Davis, L. V., & Carlson, B. E. (1987). Observation of spouse abuse: What happens to the children? *Journal of Interpersonal Violence, 2*, 279–291.

Dawson, J. M., & Langan, P. A. (1994). *Murder in families* (Bureau of Justice Statistics, Special Report, NCJ no. 143498. Rockville, MD: Department of Justice.

Deitch, I. (1993, August). *Alone, abandoned, assaulted: Prevention and intervention of elder abuse*. Paper presented at the Annual Meeting of the American Psychological Association, Toronto.

DeMaris, A., & Jackson, J. K. (1987). Batterers' reports of recidivism after counseling. *Social Casework, 68*, 458–465.

de Mause, L. (1974). The evolution of childhood. In L. de Mause (Ed.), *The history of childhood* (pp. 1–73). New York: Psychohistory Press.

deYoung, M., & Lowry, J. A. (1992). Traumatic bonding: Clinical implications in incest. *Child Welfare, 71*, 165–175.

DiLalla, L. F., & Gottesman, I. (1991). Biological and genetic contributors to violence—Widom's untold tale. *Psychological Bulletin, 109*, 125–129.

Dobash, R. E., & Dobash, R. P. (1978). Wives: The "appropriate" victims of marital violence. *Victimology, 2*, 426–441.

Dobash, R. E., & Dobash, R. P. (1980). *Violence against wives: A case against the patriarchy*. London: Open Books.

Doerner, W. G. (1987). Child maltreatment seriousness and juvenile delinquency. *Youth and Society, 19*, 197–224.

Doll, L., Joy, D., Bartholow, B., Harrison, J., Bolan, G., Douglas, J., Saltzman, L., Moss, P., & Delgado, W. (1992). Self reported childhood and adolescent sexual abuse among adult homosexual and bisexual men. *Child Abuse and Neglect, 16*, 855–864.

Donnelly, A. H. C. (1991). What we have learned about prevention: What we should do about it. *Child Abuse and Neglect, 15*, 99–106.

Downs, D. L. (1996). *More than victims: Battered women, the syndrome society, and the law*. Chicago: University of Chicago Press.

Downs, W. R., Miller, B. A., Testa, M., & Panel, D. (1992). Long term effects of parent-to-child violence for women. *Journal of Interpersonal Violence, 7*, 365–382.

Dunford, F. W., Huizinga, W. D., & Elliott, D. S. (1990). The role of arrest in domestic assault: The Omaha police experiment. *Criminology, 28*, 183–206.

Dutton, D. G., Hart, S. D., Kennedy, L. W., & Williams, K. R. (1992). Arrest and the reduction of repeat wife assault. In E. S. Buzawa & C. G. Buzawa (Eds.), *Domestic violence: The changing criminal justice response* (pp. 11–128). Westport, CT: Auburn House.

Dutton, D. G., Van Ginkel, C., & Starzomski, A. (1995). The role of shame and guilt in the intergenerational transmission of abusiveness. *Violence and Victims, 10*, 121–131.

Eckenrode, J., Laird, M., & Doris, J. (1993). School performance and disciplinary problems among abused and neglected children. *Developmental Psychology, 29*, 53–62.

Edwards, J. J., & Alexander, P. C. (1992). The contribution of family background to the long-term adjustment of women sexually abused as children. *Journal of Interpersonal Violence, 7*, 306–320.

Egeland, B. (1993). A history of abuse is a major risk factor for abusing in the next generation. In R. J. Gelles & D. R. Loseke (Eds.), *Current controversies on family violence* (pp. 197–208). Newbury Park, CA: Sage.

Egley, L. C. (1991). What changes the societal prevalence of domestic violence? *Journal of Elder Abuse and Neglect, 3*, 65–69.

Ellison, C. G., & Sherkat, D. E. (1993). Conservative Protestantism and support for corporal punishment. *American Sociological Review, 58*, 131–144.

Erlinder, P. (1984). Paying the price for Vietnam: Post-traumatic stress disorder and criminal behavior. *Boston College Law Review, 305*, 308.

Eyer, D. (1992). *Infant bonding: A scientific fiction*. New Haven, CT: Yale University Press.

Faller, K. C. (1991). Possible explanations for child sexual abuse allegations in divorce. *Journal of Orthopsychiatry, 61*, 86–91.

Faller, K. C. (1988). *Child sexual abuse*. New York: Columbia University Press.

Fagin, J., & Wexler, S. (1987). Crime at home and in the streets: The relationship between family and stranger violence. *Violence and Victims, 2*, 5–23.

Fatout, M. F. (1990). Consequences of abuse on the relationships of children. *Families in Society, 71*, 76–78.

Ferraro, K. (1989). Policing woman battering. *Social Problems, 36*, 61–74.

Ferraro, K. (1993). Cops, courts and women battering. In P. B. Bar & E. G. Moran (Eds.), *Violence against women: The bloody footprints* (pp. 165–176). Newbury Park, CA: Sage.

Ferraro, K. J., & Johnson, J. M. (1983). How women experience battering: The process of victimization. *Social Problems, 30*, 325–339.

Finkelhor, D. (1993). Epidemiological factors in the clinical identification of child sexual abuse. *Child Abuse and Neglect, 17*, 67–70.

Finkelhor, D. (1997). The homicides of children and youth: A developmental perspective. In G. Kaufman Kantor & J. L. Jasinski (Eds.), *Out of the darkness: Contemporary perspectives on family violence* (pp. 17–34). Thousand Oaks, CA: Sage.

Finkelhor, D., & Baron, L. (1986). Risk factors for child sexual abuse. *Journal of Interpersonal Violence, 1*, 43–71.

Finkelhor, D., & Dziuba-Leatherman, D. (1995). Victimization prevention programs: A national survey of children's exposure and reactions. *Child Abuse and Neglect, 19*, 129–139.

Finkelhor, D., & Yllo, K. (1985). *License to rape: Sexual abuse of wives*. New York: Holt, Rinehart and Winston.

Finkelhor, D., Hotaling, G. T., & Yllo, K. (1988). *Stopping family violence*. Newbury Park, CA: Sage.

Finkelhor, D., Asdigian, N., & Dziuba-Leatherman, J. (1995). The effectiveness of victimization prevention instruction: An evaluation of children's responses to actual threats and assaults. *Child Abuse and Neglect, 19*, 141–153.

Fischer, E. (1979). *Woman's creation: Sexual evolution and the shaping of society.* New York: Doubleday.

Follette, V. M., Alexander, P. C., & Follette, W. C. (1991). Individual predictors of outcome in group treatment for incest survivors. *Journal of Consulting and Clinical Psychology, 59,* 150–155.

Fontes, L. A. (1997). Conducting ethical cross-cultural research on family violence. In G. Kaufman Kantor & J. L. Jasinski (Eds.), *Out of the darkness: Contemporary perspectives on family violence* (pp. 296–312). Thousand Oaks, CA: Sage.

Ford, D. A. (1991). Prosecution as a victim power resource: A note on empowering women in violent conjugal relationships. *Law and Society Review, 25,* 313–334.

Forte, J. A., Franks, D. D., Forte, J. A., & Rigsby, T. (1996). Asymmetrical role-taking: Comparing battered and nonbattered women. *Social Work, 41,* 59–73.

Fortune, M. M. (1995). The importance of religious issues: Roadblocks or resources? In Staff of Volcano Press (compilers). *Family violence and religion: An interfaith resource guide* (pp. 267–288). Volcano, CA: Volcano Press.

Friedrich, W. N. (1993). Sexual victimization and sexual behavior in children: A review of recent literature. *Child Abuse and Neglect, 17,* 59–66.

Friedrich, W. N., Luecke, W. J., Beilke, R. L., & Place, V. (1992). Psychotherapy outcome of sexually abused boys. *Journal of Interpersonal Violence, 7,* 396–409.

Frieze, I. H. (1983). Investigating the causes and consequence of marital rape. *Signs, 8,* 552–553.

Fromuth, M. E., & Burkhart, B. R. (1987). Childhood sexual victimization among college men: Definitional and methodological issues. *Violence and Victims, 2,* 244–253.

Frude, N. (1989). Sexual abuse: An overview. *Educational and Child Psychology, 6,* 34–44.

Gagne, P. L. (1992). Appalachian women: Violence and social control. *Journal of Contemporary Ethnography, 20,* 387–415.

Gallup Organization. (1996). *Disciplining children in America: A Gallup poll report.* Princeton, NJ: Author.

Garbarino, J., & Kostelny, K. (1992). Child maltreatment as a community problem. *Child Abuse and Neglect, 16,* 455–464.

Garbarino, J., Guttmann, E., & Seeley, J. W. (1986). *The psychologically battered child.* San Francisco, CA: Jossey-Bass.

Garrett, K. (1982). Child abuse: Problems of definition. In P. H. Rossi & S. L. Nock (Eds.), *Measuring social judgments: The factorial survey approach* (pp. 177–203). Beverly Hills, CA: Sage.

Garrity-Rokous, F. E. (1994). Punitive legal approaches to the problem of prenatal drug exposure. *Infant Mental Health Journal, 15,* 218–237.

Gartner, R. (1993). Methodological issues in cross-cultural large-survey research on violence. *Violence and Victims, 8,* 199–215.

Geffner, R., Rosenbaum, A., & Hughes, H. (1988). Research issues concerning family violence. In V. B. Van Hasselt, R. L. Morrison, A. S. Bellack, & M. Hersen (Eds.), *Handbook of family violence* (pp. 457–481). New York: Plenum.

Gelles, R. J. (1974). *The violent home.* Beverly Hills, CA: Sage.

Gelles, R. J. (1982). Problems in defining and labeling child abuse. In R. H. Starr, Jr. (Ed.), *Child abuse prediction: Policy implications* (pp. 1–30). Cambridge, MA: Ballinger.

Gelles, R. J. (1983). An exchange/social control theory. In D. Finkelhor, R. J. Gelles, G. T. Hotaling, & M. A. Straus (Eds.), *The dark side of families: Current family violence research* (pp. 151–165). Beverly Hills, CA: Sage.

Gelles, R. J. (1987). *Family violence.* Newbury Park, CA: Sage.

Gelles, R. J. (1990a). The medical and psychological costs of family violence. In M. A. Straus & R. S. Gelles (Eds.), *Physical violence in American families* (pp. 425–430). New Brunswick, NJ: Transaction Publishers.

Gelles, R. J. (1990b). Violence and pregnancy. In M. A. Straus & R. J. Gelles (Eds.), *Physical violence in American families* (pp. 279–286). New Brunswick, NJ: Transaction Publishers.

Gelles, R. J. (1996). *The book of David: How preserving families can cost children's lives.* New York: Basic Books.

Gelles, R. J., & Cornell, C. P. (1990). *Intimate violence in families.* Newbury Park, CA: Sage.

Gelles, R. J., & Straus, M. A. (1979). Determinants of violence in the family: Toward a theoretical integration. In W. R. Burr, R. Kill, F. I. Nye, & I. L. Reiss (Eds.), *Contemporary theories about the family* (pp. 549–581). New York: Free Press.

Gelles, R. J., & Straus, M. A. (1988). *Intimate violence.* New York: Simon & Schuster.

Gelles, R. J., & Cornell, C. P. (1987). Elder abuse: The status of current knowledge. In A. J. Gelles (Ed.), *Family violence* (pp. 168–182). Newbury Park, CA: Sage.

Gerber, G. L. (1991). Gender stereotypes and power: Perceptions of roles in violent marriages. *Sex Roles, 24,* 439–458.

Gielen, A. C., O'Campo, P. J., Faden, R. R., Kass, N. E., & Xue, X. (1994). Interpersonal conflict and physical violence during the childbearing year. *Social Science and Medicine, 39,* 781–787.

Gilgun, J. F., & Connor, T. M. (1989). How perpetrators view child sexual abuse. *Social Work, 361,* 249–251.

Giovannoni, J. M., & Becerra, R. M. (1979). *Defining child abuse.* New York: Free Press.

Godkin, M. A., Wolf, R. S., & Pillemer, K. A. (1989). A case comparison analysis of elder abuse and neglect. *International Journal of Aging and Human Development, 28,* 207–225.

Godkin, M. A., Wolf, R. S., & Pillemer, K. A. (1989). A case comparison analysis of elder abuse and neglect. *International Journal of Aging and Human Development, 28,* 207–225.

Goldkamp, J. S. (1996). *Role of drug and alcohol abuse in domestic violence treatment: Dade County's domestic violence court experiment: Final report.* Rockville, MD: Department of Justice.

Gondolf, E. W. (1995). Alcohol abuse, wife assault, and power needs. *Social Service Review, 69,* 274–284.

Gondolf, E. W. (1997). Expanding batterer program evaluation. In G. Kaufman Kantor & J. L. Jasinski (Eds.), *Out of the darkness: Contemporary perspectives on family violence* (pp. 208–218). Thousand Oaks, CA: Sage.

Gondolf, E. W., & McFerron, J. R. (1989). Handling battering men: Police action in wife abuse cases. *Criminal Justice and Behavior, 16,* 429–439.

Gondolf, E. W., Yllo, K., & Campbell, J. (1997). Collaboration between researchers and advocates. In G. Kaufman Kantor & J. L. Jasinski (Eds.), *Out of the darkness: Contemporary perspectives on family violence* (pp. 255–267). Thousand Oaks, CA: Sage.

Goode, W. J. (1971). Force and violence in the family. *Journal of Marriage and the Family, 33,* 624–636.

Goolkasian, G. A. (1986). *Confronting domestic violence: A guide for criminal justice agencies.* Washington, DC: U.S. Department of Justice.

Gordon, M. (1989). The family environment of sexual abuse: A comparison of natal and stepfather abuse. *Child Abuse and Neglect, 13,* 121–130.

Grad, S. (1997, August 29). Abuse case handling debated. *Los Angeles Times,* A3.

Grasmick, H. G., Bursik, R. J., & Kimpel, M. (1991). Protestant fundamentalism and attitudes toward corporal punishment of children. *Violence and Victims, 6,* 273–298.

Gray, E. (1988). The link between child abuse and juvenile delinquency: What we know and recommendations for policy and research. In G. Hotaling, D. Finkelhor, J. Kirkpatrick, & M. A. Straus (Eds.), *Family abuse and its consequences* (pp. 108–123). Beverly Hills, CA: Sage.

Graziano, A. M., Lindquist, C. M., Kunce, L. J., & Munjal, K. (1992).

Physical Punishment on Childhood and Current Attitudes. *Journal of the Interpersonal Violence, 7*, 147–155.

Greenberg, J. R., McKibben, M., & Raymond, J. A. (1990). Dependent adult children and elder abuse. *Journal of Elder Abuse and Neglect, 2*, 73–86.

Greven, P. (1990). *Spare the child: The religious roots of physical punishment and the psychological impact of physical abuse.* New York: Knopf.

Griffin, L. W. (1994). Elder maltreatment among rural African-Americans. *Journal of Elder Abuse and Neglect, 6*, 1–27.

Hall, G. C. (1989). WAIS-R and MMPI profiles of men who have sexually assaulted children: Evidence of limited utility. *Journal of Personalty Assessment, 53*, 404–412.

Hall, G. C., & Hirschman, R. (1992). Sexual aggression against children: A conceptual perspective of etiology. *Criminal Justice and Behavior, 19*, 8–23.

Hall, G. C. N., Shondrick, D. D., & Hirschman, R. (1993). Conceptually derived treatment for sexual aggressors. *Professional psychology: Research and practice, 24*, 62–69.

Hamberger, L., & Hastings, J. E. (1990). Recidivism following spouse abuse abatement counseling: Treatment program implications. *Violence and Victims, 5*, 157–170.

Hampton, R. L., Gelles, R. J., & Harrop, J. (1991). Is violence in black families increasing? A comparison of 1975 and 1985 national survey rates. In R. L. Hampton (Ed.), *Black family violence* (pp. 3–18). Lexington, MA: Lexington Books.

Hanneke, C. R., Shields, N. M., & McCall, G. J. (1986). Assessing the prevalence of marital rape. *Journal of Interpersonal Violence, 1*, 350–362.

Hanson, R. K., & Slater, S. (1988). Sexual victimization in the history of sexual abusers: A review. *Annals of Sex Research, 1*, 485–499.

Hanson, R. K., Gizzarelli, R., & Scott, H. (1994). The attitudes of incest offenders. *Criminal Justice and Behavior, 21*, 187–202.

Harris, S. B. (1996). For better or for worse: Spouse abuse grown old. *Journal of Elder Abuse and Neglect, 8*, 1–33.

Harrison, K. (1997). *The kiss: A memoir.* New York: Random House.

Hart, S. N., & Brassard, M. R. (1991). Psychological maltreatment: Progress achieved. *Development and Psychopathology, 3*, 61–70.

Haskett, M. E., & Kistner, J. A. (1991). Social interactions and peer perceptions of young physically abused children. *Child Development, 62*, 979–990.

Haugaard, J. J., & Emery, R. E. (1989). Methodological issues in child sexual abuse research. *Child Abuse and Neglect, 13*, 89–100.

Haugaard, J. J.,& Reppucci, N. D. (1988). *The sexual abuse of children.* San Francisco, CA: Jossey-Bass.

Hazzard, A., & Rupp, C. (1986). A note on the knowledge and attitudes of professional groups toward child abuse. *Journal of Community Psychology, 14*, 219–223.

Heisler, C. J. (1991). The role of the criminal justice system in elder abuse cases. *Journal of Elder Abuse and Neglect, 3*, 5–33.

Herbert, T., Silver, R. C., & Ellard, J. H. (1991). Coping with an abusive relationship: How and why do women stay? *Journal of Marriage and the Family, 53*, 311–325.

Hinrichsen, G. A., Hernandez, N. A.,& Pollack, S. (1992). Difficulties and rewards in family care of depressed older adults. *Gerontologist, 32*, 486–492.

Hirschel, J. D., Hutchinson, I. W. III, & Dean, C. W. (1992). The failure of arrest to deter spouse abuse. *Journal of Research in Crime and Delinquency, 29*, 7–33.

Hirschi, T. (1969). *Causes of delinquency.* Berkeley, CA: University of California Press.

Hoff, L. A. (1988). Collaborative feminist research and the myth of objectivity. In K. Yllo & M. Bograd (Eds.), *Feminist perspectives on wife abuse* (pp. 269–281). Newbury Park, CA: Sage.

Holden, W., & Edwards, L. E. (1989). Parental attitudes toward child rearing: Instruments, issues and implications. *Psychological Bulletin, 106*, 29–58.

Hotte, J., & Rafman, S. (1992). The specific effects of incest on prepubertal girls from dysfunctional families. *Child Abuse and Neglect, 16*, 273–283.

Hugman, R. (1995). The implications of the term "elder abuse" for problem definition and response in health and social welfare. *Journal of Social Policy, 24*, 493–507.

Hutchinson, E. D. (1990). Child maltreatment: Can it be defined? *Social Service Review, 64*, 60–78.

Interdisciplinary glossary on child abuse and neglect: Legal, medical, and social work terms. (1978). Washington, DC: U.S. Department of Health, Education and Welfare.

Island, D., & Letellier, P. (1991). *Men who beat the men who love them: Battered gay men and domestic violence.* New York: Haworth.

Jackson, H., & Nuttal, D. (1993). Clinician responses to sexual abuse allegations. *Child Abuse and Neglect, 17*, 127–143.

Jason, J. M. (1991). Abuse, neglect, and the HIV-infected child. *Child Abuse and Neglect, 15*, 79–88.

Johnson, B. K., & Kenkel, M. E. (1991). Stress, coping and adjustment in female adolescent incest victims. *Child Abuse and Neglect, 15*, 293–305.

Johnson, I. M. (1992). Economic, situational, and psychological correlates of the decision making process of battered women. *Families in Society, 73*, 168–176.

Johnson, I. M. (1995). Family members' perceptions of and attitudes towards elder abuse. *Families in Society: The Journal of Contemporary and Human Services, 76*, 220–229.

Joseph, J. (1997). Woman battering: A comparative analysis of black and white women. In G. Kaufman Kantor & J. L. Jasinski (Eds.), *Out of the darkness: Contemporary perspectives on family violence* (pp. 161–169). Thousand Oaks, CA: Sage.

Kalichman, S. C. (1991). Psychopathology and personality characteristics of criminal sexual offenders as a function of victim age. *Archives of Sexual Behavior, 20*, 187–197.

Kalichman, S. C., & Henderson, M. (1991). MMPI profile subtypes of nonincarcerated child molesters: A cross-validation study. *Criminal Justice and Behavior, 18*, 379–396.

Kalichman, S. C., Craig, M. E., & Follingstad, D. R. (1988). Mental health professionals and suspected cases of child abuse: An investigation of factors influencing reporting. *Community Mental Health Journal, 24*, 43–51.

Kalmuss, D. S. (1982). Wife's marital dependency and wife abuse. *Journal of Marriage and the Family, 44*, 227–286.

Kalmuss, D. S., & Straus, M. A. (1990). Wife's marital dependency and wife abuse. In M. A. Straus & R. J. Gelles (Eds.), *Physical violence in American families* (pp. 369–382). New Brunswick, NJ: Transaction Publishers.

Kantor, G. K., & Straus, M. A. (1990). The "drunken bum" theory of wife beating. In M. A. Straus & R. J. Gelles (Eds.), *Physical violence in American families* (pp. 203–224). New Brunswick, NJ: Transaction Publishers.

Kantor, G. K., Jasinski, J. L., & Aldarondo, E. (1994). Sociocultural status and incidence of marital violence in Hispanic families. *Violence and Victims, 9*, 207–222.

Kaplan, S. J., & Davidson, H. A. (Eds.). (1996). *Family violence: A clinical and legal guide.* Washington, DC: American Psychiatric Press.

Kashani, J. H., Daniel, A. E., Dandoy, A. C., & Holcomb, W. R. (1992). Family violence: Impact on children. *Journal of the American Academy of Child and Adolescent Psychiatry, 31*, 181–189.

Katz, J. (1995). Reconstructing masculinity in the locker room: The Mentors in Violence Prevention Project. *Harvard Educational Review, 65,* 163–174.

Kaufman, J. (1991). Depressive disorders in maltreated children. *Journal of the American Academy of Child and Adolescent Psychiatry, 30,* 257–265.

Kaufman, J., & Zigler, E. (1993). The intergenerational transmission of abuse is overstated. In R. J. Gelles & D. R. Loeske (Eds.), *Current controversies in family violence* (pp. 209–221). Newbury Park, CA: Sage.

Kempe, C. H., Silverman, F. N., Steele, B. F., Droegemueller, W., & Silver, H. K. (1962). The battered child syndrome. *Journal of the American Medical Association, 181,* 107–112.

Kendall-Tackett, K. A., Williams, L. M., & Finkelhor, D. (1993). Impact of sexual abuse on children. *Psychological Bulletin, 113,* 164–180.

Knudsen, D. D. (1988). *Child positive services: Discretion, decisions, dilemmas.* Springfield, IL: Charles C Thomas.

Knudsen, D. D. (1992). *Child maltreatment: Emerging perspectives.* Dix Hills, NY: General Hall.

Kratcoski, P. C., & Kratcoski, L. D. (1983). The relationship of victimization through child abuse to aggressive delinquent behavior. *Victimology, 7,* 199–203.

Kurz, P. D., Gaudin, J. M., Howling, P. T., & Wodarski, J. S. (1993). The consequences of physical abuse and neglect on the school age child: Mediating factors. *Children and Youth Services Review, 15,* 85–104.

Kurz, D. (1993). Social science perspectives on wife abuse. In P. B. Bart & E. G. Moran (Eds.), *Violence against women: The bloody footprints* (pp. 252–269). Newbury Park, CA: Sage.

Lackey, C., & Williams, K. R. (1995). Social bonding and the cessation of partner violence across generations. *Journal of Marriage and the Family, 57,* 295–305.

Lanktree, C., Briere, J., & Zaidi, L. (1991). Incidence and impact of sexual abuse in a child outpatient sample: The role of direct inquiry. *Child Abuse and Neglect, 15,* 447–453.

Laroritz, S. (1990). Whatever happened to Mary Ellen? *Child Abuse and Neglect, 14,* 143–149.

Leonard, K. E., & Jacob, T. (1988). Alcohol, alcoholism, and family violence. In V. B. Van Hasselt, R. L. Morrison, A. S. Bellack, & M. Hersen (Eds.), *Handbook of family violence* (pp. 383–406). New York: Plenum.

Lemon, N. K. D. (Ed.). (1996). *Domestic violence laws: A comprehensive overview of cases and sources.* Bethesda, MD: Austin & Winfield.

Letellier, P. (1994). Gay and bisexual male domestic violence victimization: Challenges to feminist theory and responses to violence. *Violence and Victims, 9,* 95–106.

Lie, G. Y., & Gentlewarrior, S. (1991). Intimate violence in lesbian relationships: Discussion of survey findings and practice implications. *Journal of Social Service Research, 15,* 41–49.

Lie, G. Y., Schilit, R., Bushy, J., Montague, M., & Reyes, L. (1991). Lesbians in currently aggressive relationships: How frequently do they report aggressive past relationships? *Violence and Victims, 6,* 121–135.

Lloyd, R. M. (1992). Negotiating child sexual abuse: The interactional character of investigative practices. *Social Problems, 39,* 109–124.

Lockhart, L. L. (1987). A reexamination of the effects of race and social class on the incidence of marital violence: A search for reliable differences. *Journal of Marriage and the Family, 49,* 603–610.

Lockhart, L. L. (1991). Spousal violence: A cross-racial perspective. In R. L. Hampton (Ed.), *Black family violence* (pp. 85–101). Lexington, MA: Lexington Books.

Lockhart, L. L., White, B. W., & Causby, V. (1994). Letting out the secret: Violence in lesbian relationships. *Journal of Interpersonal Violence, 9,* 469–492.

Loseke, D. R. (1991). Reply to Murray A. Straus: Readings on "Discipline and deviance." *Social Problems, 38,* 162–165.

Loseke, D. R. (1992). *The battered woman and shelters: The social construction of wife abuse.* Albany: State University of New York Press.

Luntz, B. K., & Widom, C. S. (1994). Antisocial personality disorder in abused and neglected children grown up. *American Journal of Psychiatry, 151,* 670–674.

Lutzker, J. R., & Rice, J. M. (1987). Using recidivision data to evaluate Project 12-Ways: An ecobehavioral approach to the treatment and prevention of child abuse and neglect. *Journal of Family Violence, 2,* 283–290.

Macionis, J. J. (1989). *Sociology.* Englewood Cliffs, NJ: Prentice-Hall.

Madonna, P. G., Van Scoyk, S., & Jones, D. P. H. (1991). Family interactions within incest and nonincest families. *American Journal of Psychiatry, 148,* 46–49.

Mann, S., & Kelley, L. R. (1997). Standing at the crossroads of modernist thought: Collins, Smith, and the new feminist epistemologies. *Gender and Society, 11,* 391–408.

Margolies, L. & Leeder, E. (1995). Violence at the door: Treatment of lesbian batterers. *Violence Against Women, 1,* 139–157.

Margolin, G., Sibner, L. G., & Gleberman, L. (1988). Wife battering. In V. B. Van Hasselt, R. L. Morrison, A. S. Bellack, & M. Hersen (Eds.), *Handbook of family violence* (pp. 89–117). New York: Plenum.

Marshall, W. W., & Barbaree, H. (1988). The long-term evaluation of a behavioral treatment program for child molesters. *Behavioral Research and Therapy, 26,* 499–511.

Marshall, W. W., Barbaree, H. E., & Butt, J. (1988). Sexual offenders against male children: Sexual preferences. *Behavioral Research and Therapy, 26,* 338–391.

Martin, J. A., & Elmer, E. (1992). Battered children grown up: A follow-up study of individuals severely maltreated as children. *Child Abuse and Neglect, 16,* 75–87.

Martin, J., Anderson, J., Romans, S., Mullen, P., & O'Shea, M. (1993). Asking about child sexual abuse: Methodological implications of a two stage survey. *Child Abuse and Neglect, 17,* 383–392.

Mash, E. J., & Wolfe, D. A. (1991). Methodological issues in research on physical child abuse. *Criminal Justice and Behavior, 18,* 8–29.

McCurdy, K., & Daro, D. (1994). Child maltreatment: A national survey of reports and fatalities. *Journal of Interpersonal Violence, 9,* 75–94.

McIvor, D. L., & Duthie, B. (1986). MMPI profiles of incest offenders: Men who molest younger children and men who molest older children. *Criminal Justice and Behavior, 13,* 450–452.

Melton, G. B., & Flood, M. F. (1994). Research policy and child maltreatment: Developing the scientific foundation for effective protection of children. *Child Abuse and Neglect, 18*(Suppl.), 1–27.

Miller, J. L. (1991). Family violence research: Some basic and applied questions. In D. D. Knudsen & J. L. Miller (Eds.), *Abused and battered: Social and legal responses to family violence* (pp. 3–16). New York: Aldine de Gruyter.

Miller, J. L., & Krull, A. C. (1977). Controlling domestic violence: Victimization resources and police intervention. In G. G. Cantor & J. L. Jasinki (Eds.), *Out of the darkness: Contemporary perspectives on family violence* (pp. 235–254). Thousand Oaks, CA: Sage.

Milner, J. S., & Chilamkurti, C. (1991). Physical child abuse perpetrator characteristics: A review of the literature. *Journal of Interpersonal Violence, 6,* 345–366.

Milner, J. S., & Robertson, K. R. (1989). Development of a random response scale for child abuse potential inventory. *Journal of Clinical Psychology, 41,* 639–643.

Mixon, P. M. (1995). An adult protective services perspective. *Journal of Elder Abuse and Neglect, 7,* 60–87.

Morrison, S., & Greene, E. (1992). Juror and expert knowledge of child sexual abuse. *Child Abuse and Neglect, 16,* 595–613.

Mullender, A. (1996). *Rethinking domestic violence: The social work and probation response.* London: Routledge.

Muller, R. T., Caldwell, R. A., & Hunter, J. E. (1993). Child provocativeness and gender as factors contributing to the blaming of victims of physical child abuse. *Child Abuse and Neglect, 17,* 249–260.

Murphy, W. D., & Peters, J. M. (1992). Profiling child sexual abusers: Psychological considerations. *Criminal Justice and Behavior, 19,* 24–37.

Nash, M. R., Zivney, O. A., & Hulsey, T. A. (1993). Characteristics of sexual abuse associated with greater psychological impairment among children. *Child Abuse and Neglect, 17,* 401–408.

National Council of Juvenile and Family Court Judges. (1994). *Model code on domestic and family violence.* Drafted by the Advisory Committee of the Conrad N. Hilton Foundation Model Code Project. San Diego, CA: National Council of Juvenile and Family Court Judges.

National Institute of Justice Research Preview Series. Rockville, MD: U.S. Department of Justice.

National Research Council, Panel on Research on Child Abuse and Neglect, Commission on Behavioral and Social Sciences and Education. (1993). *Understanding child abuse and neglect.* Washington, DC: National Academy Press.

Nelson, B. J. (1984). *Making an issue of child abuse: Political agenda setting for social problems.* Chicago: University of Chicago Press.

Newman, E., Kaloupek, D. G., Keane, T. M., & Folstein, S. F. (1997). Ethical issues in trauma research: The evolution of an empirical model for decision making. In G. Kaufman Kantor & J. L. Jasinski (Eds.), *Out of the darkness: Contemporary perspectives on family violence* (pp. 271–281). Thousand Oaks, CA: Sage.

Newmark, L., Harrell, A., & Adams, W. P. (1995). *Evaluation of police training conducted under the family violence prevention and services act.*

New York State Senate. (1996). Albany, NY: Senate Bill No. S06260. "Domestic Violence." Passed April 2, 1997.

NIS. (1981). *Executive summary: National Study of the Incidence and Severity of Child Abuse and Neglect.* Washington, DC: U.S. Government Printing Office.

NIS. (1988). *Study findings: Study of national incidence and prevalence of child abuse and neglect.* Washington, DC: U.S. Department of Health and Human Services.

Nurius, P., Furrey, I., & Berliner, L. (1992). Coping capacity among women with abusive partners. *Violence and Victims, 7,* 229–243.

Oates, R. K., & Bross, D. C. (1995). What have we learned about treating child physical abuse? A literature review of the last decade. *Child Abuse and Neglect, 19,* 463–473.

O'Donohue, W. T., & Elliott, A. N. (1992). Treatment of the sexually abused child: A review. *Journal of Clinical Child Psychology, 21,* 218–228.

O'Donohue, W., & Letourneau, E. (1993). A brief group treatment for the modification of denial in child sexual abusers: Outcome and follow-up. *Child Abuse and Neglect, 17,* 299–304.

O'Donovan, K. (1993). *Family law matters.* London: Pluto Press.

O'Hagan, K. P. (1995). Emotional and psychological abuse: Problems of definition. *Child Abuse and Neglect, 19,* 449–461.

Okami, P. (1991). Self-reports of "positive" childhood and adolescent sexual contacts with older persons: An exploratory study. *Archives of Sexual Behavior, 20,* 437–457.

Okami, P., & Goldberg, N. (1992). Personality correlates of pedophilia: Are they reliable indicators? *Journal of Sex Research, 29,* 297–328.

O'Keefe, M. (1994). Linking marital violence, mother–child/father–child aggression, and child behavior problems. *Journal of Family Violence, 9,* 63–78.

Olafson, E., Corwin, D. L., & Summit, R. C. (1993). Modern history of child sexual abuse awareness: Cycles of discovery and suppression. *Child Abuse and Neglect, 17,* 7–24.

Osborne, Y. H., Hinz, L. D., Rappaport, N., & Williams, H. (1988). Parent social attractiveness, parent sex, child temperament and socioeconomic status as predictors of the tendency to report child abuse. *Journal of Social and Clinical Psychology, 6,* 69–76.

Ostfeld, B. M., & Feldman, M. D. (1996). Factitious disorder by proxy: Clinical features, detection, and management. In M. D. Feldman & S. J. Eisendrath (Eds.), *The spectrum of factitious disorders* (pp. 83–108). Washington, DC: American Psychiatric Press.

O'Toole, R., Turbett, J. P., Sargent, J., & O'Toole, A. (1987, July). Recognizing and reacting to child abuse: Physicians, nurses, teachers, social workers, law enforcement officers, and community residents. Paper presented at the Family Violence Conference, University of new Hampshire, Durham.

Pagelow, M. D. (1984). *Family violence.* New York: Praeger.

Pagelow, M. D. (1989). The incidence and prevalence of criminal abuse of other family members. In L. Ohiin & M. Tonry (Eds.), *Family violence* (pp. 263–313). Chicago: The University of Chicago Press.

Pagelow, M. D. (1992). Adult victims of domestic violence. *Journal of Interpersonal Violence, 7,* 87–120.

Panel on Research on Child Abuse and Neglect. (1997). *Understanding child abuse and neglect.* Washington, DC: National Academy Press.

Parker, H., & Parker, S. (1986). Father–daughter sexual abuse: An emerging perspective. *American Journal of Orthopsychiatry, 56,* 531–549.

Pate, A. M., & Hamilton, E. E. (1992). Formal and informal deterrents to domestic violence: The Dade County spouse assault experiment. *American Sociological Review, 57,* 691–697.

Paveza, G. J. (1988). Risk factors in father–daughter child sexual abuse: A case-control study. *Journal of Interpersonal Violence, 3,* 290–306.

Pawlak, A. E., Boulet, J. R., & Bradford, J. M. W. (1991). Discriminant analysis of a sexual functioning inventory with intrafamilial and extrafamilial child molesters. *Archives of Sexual Behavior, 20,* 27–34.

Pence, E., & Paymar, M. (1986). *Power and control tactics of men who batter.* Duluth: Minnesota Program Development.

Penhale, B. (1993). The abuse of elderly people: Considerations for practice. *British Journal of Social Work, 23,* 95–112.

Perilla, J. L., Bakeman, R., & Norris, F. H. (1994). Culture and domestic violence: The ecology of abused Latinas. *Violence and Victims, 9,* 325–339.

Peters, S. D., Wyatt, G. E., & Finkelhor, D. (1986). Prevalence. In D. Finkelhor (Ed.), *Sourcebook on child sexual abuse* (pp. 15–59). Beverly Hills, CA: Sage.

Pfohl, S. J. (1977). The "discovery" of child abuse. *Social Problems, 24,* 310–323.

Pillemer, K., & Prescott, D. (1989). Psychological effects of elder abuse: A research note. *Journal of Elder Abuse and Neglect, 1,* 65–73.

Pillemer, K., & Suitor, J. (1988). Elder abuse. In V. B. Van Hasselt, R. L. Morrison, A. S. Bellack, & M. Hersen (Eds.), *Handbook of family violence* (pp. 247–270). New York: Plenum.

Pleck, E. (1987). *Domestic tyranny: The making of American social policy against family violence from colonial times to the present.* New York: Oxford University Press.

Pleck, E. (1989). Criminal approaches to family violence, 1640–1980. In L. Ohlin & M. Tonry (Eds.), *Family violence* (pp. 19–57). Chicago: University of Chicago Press.

Plowman, W. B. (1996). Domestic violence transcends social groups. *Domestic Violence Prevention, 2,* 3–5.

Poertner, J. (1986). Estimating the incidence of abused older persons. *Journal of Gerontological Social Work, 9,* 3–15.

Pollock, V. E., Briere, J., Schneider, L., Knop, J., Mednick, S. A., & Goodwin, D. W. (1990). Childhood antecedents of antisocial behavior: Parental alcoholism and physical abusiveness. *American Journal of Psychiatry, 147,* 1290–1293.

Polsby, D. D. (1992). Suppressing domestic violence with law reforms. *Journal of Criminal Law and Criminology, 83,* 250–253.

Radbill, S. X. (1968). A history of child abuse and infanticide. In R. E. Helfer & C. H. Kempe (Eds.), *The battered child* (pp. 3–17). Chicago: University of Chicago Press.

Ramsey-Klawsnik, H. (1991). Elder sexual abuse: Preliminary findings. *Journal of Elder Abuse and Neglect, 3,* 73–90.

Reis, S. D., & Heppner, P. P. (1993). Examination of coping resources and family adaptation in mothers and daughters of incestuous versus non-clinical families. *Journal of Counseling Psychology, 40,* 100–108.

Renzetti, C. (1988). Violence in lesbian relationships: A preliminary analysis of causal factors. *Journal of Interpersonal Violence, 3,* 381–399.

Renzetti, C. (1992). *Violent betrayal: partner abuse in lesbian relationships.* Newbury Park, CA: Sage.

Rice, M. E., Quinsey, V. L., & Harris, G. T. (1991). Sexual recidivism among child molesters released from a maximum security psychiatric institution. *Journal of Consulting and Clinical Psychology, 59,* 381–386.

Rivera, B., & Widom, C. S. (1990). Childhood victimization and violent offending. *Violence and Victims, 5,* 19–35.

Roscoe, B. (1990). Defining child maltreatment: Ratings of parental behavior. *Adolescence, 25,* 517–529.

Ross, C. J. (1980). The lessons of the past: Defining and controlling child abuse in the United States. In G. Gerbner, C. J. Ross, & E. Zigler (Eds.), *Child abuse: An agenda for action* (pp. 63–81). New York: Oxford University Press.

Rossi, P. H. (1992). Assessing family preservation programs. *Children and Youth Services Review, 14,* 75–95.

Rouse, L. P. (1997). Domestic violence: Hitting us where we live. In D. Dunn & D. V. Walker (Eds.), *Analyzing social problems: Essays and exercises* (pp. 17–22). Upper Saddle River, NJ: Prentice-Hall.

Russell, D. E. H. (1982). *Rape in marriage.* New York: Collier Books.

Russell, D. E. H. (1983). The incidence and prevalence of intrafamilial and extrafamilial sexual abuse of female children. *Child Abuse and Neglect, 7,* 133–146.

Russell, D. E. H. (1986). *The secret trauma: Incest in the lives of girls and women.* New York: Basic Books.

Rust, J. O., & Troupe, P. A. (1991). Relationship of treatment of child sexual abuse with school achievement and self concept. *Journal of Early Adolescence, 11,* 420–429.

Sabourin, T. C. (1991). Perceptions of verbal aggression in interspousal violence. In D. D. Knudsen & J. L. Miller (Eds.), *Abused and battered: Social and legal responses to family violence* (pp. 135–145). New York: Aldine de Gruyter.

Salzinger, S., Feldman, R. S., Hammer, M., & Rosario, M. (1991). Risk of physical child abuse and personal consequences for its victims. *Criminal Justice and Behavior, 18,* 64–81.

Saunders, B. E., Villeponteaux, L. A., Lipovsky, J. A., Kilpatrick, D. G., & Veronen, L. J. (1992). Child sexual assault as a risk factor for mental disorders among women. *Journal of Interpersonal Violence, 7,* 189–204.

Scarf, M. (1988). *Battered Jewish wives: Case studies in the response to rage.* Lexington, NY: Edwin Mellen Press.

Schilit, R., Lie, G. Y., & Montagne, M. (1990). Substance use as a correlate of violence in intimate lesbian relationships. *Journal of Homosexuality, 19,* 51–65.

Schilit, R., Lie, G. Y., Montagne, M. & Reyes, L. (1992). Intergenerational transmission of violence in lesbian relationships. *Affilia, 6,* 72–87.

Schneider, C. J. (1982). The Michigan screening profile of parenting. In R. H. Starr, Jr. (Ed.), *Child abuse prediction: Policy implications* (pp. 157–174). Cambridge, MA: Bellinger.

Seaver, C. (1996). Muted lives: Older battered women. *Journal of Elder Abuse and Neglect, 8,* 3–21.

Sedlak, A. J. (1988). Prevention of wife abuse. In V. B. Hasselt, R. L. Morrison, A. S. Bellack, & M. Hersen (Eds.), *Handbook of family violence* (pp. 319–358). New York: Plenum.

Shapiro, J. P., Leifer, M., Martone, M. W., & Kassem, L. (1992). Cognitive functioning and social competence as predictors of maladjustment in sexually abused girls. *Journal of Interpersonal Violence, 7,* 159–164.

Shepard, M. (1992). Predicting batterer recidivism five years after community intervention. *Journal of Family Violence, 7,* 167–178.

Sherman, L. W., & Berk, R. A. (1984). The specific deterrent effects of arrest for domestic assault. *American Sociological Review, 49,* 261–272.

Sherman, L. W. (1992). *Policing domestic violence: Experiments and dilemmas.* New York: Free Press.

Sherman, L. W., & Smith, D. A. (1992). Crime, punishment, and stake in conformity: Legal and informal control of domestic violence. *American Sociological Review, 57,* 680–690.

Shornstein, S. L. (1997). *Domestic violence and health care: What every professional needs to know.* Thousand Oaks, CA: Sage.

Shorter, E. (1975). *The making of the modern family.* New York: Basic Books.

Showers, J. (1992). "Don't Shake the Baby": The effectiveness of a prevention program. *Child Abuse and Neglect, 16,* 11–18.

Sigler, R. T. (1989). *Domestic violence in context: An assessment of community attitudes.* Lexington, MA: Lexington Books.

Silverman, R. A., & Kennedy, L. W. (1988). Women who kill their children. *Violence and Victims, 3,* 113–127.

Singer, K. I. (1989). Group work with men who experienced incest in childhood. *American Journal of Orthopsychiatry, 59,* 468–472.

Snyder, J. C., & Newberger, E. H. (1986). Consensus and differences among hospital professionals in evaluating child maltreatment. *Violence and Victims, 1,* 125–139.

Spatt, M. (1995, January 24). Same-sex domestic violence cases now covered by state law. *OutNOW,* 1–2.

Stacey, W. A., Hazelwood, L. R., & Shupe, A. (1994). *The violent couple.* Westport, CT: Praeger,

Stark, E., & Flitcraft, A. (1995). Killing the beast within: Woman battering and female suicidality. *International Journal of Health Services, 25,* 43–64.

Stark, E., & Flitcraft, A. (1996). *Women at risk: Domestic violence and women's health.* Thousand Oaks, CA: Sage.

Steinmetz, S. K. (1981, January/February). Elder abuse. *Aging,* 6–10.

Steinmetz, S. K. (1987). Family violence: past, present, and future. In M. B. Sussman & S. K. Steinmetz (Eds.), *Handbook of marriage and the family* (pp. 725–765). New York: Plenum.

Steinmetz, S. K. (1988a). *Duty bound: Elder abuse and family care.* Newbury Park, CA: Sage.

Steinmetz, S. K. (1988b). Elder abuse by family caretakers: Processes and intervention strategies. *Contemporary Family Therapy: An International Journal, 10,* 256–261.

Steinmetz, S. K. (1993). The abused elderly are dependent: Abuse is caused by the perception of stress associated with providing care. In R. J. Gelles & D. R. Loeske (Eds.), *Current controversies in family violence* (pp. 222–236). Newbury Park, CA: Sage.

Steinmetz, S. K., & Lucca, J. A. (1988). Husband battering. In V. B. Van Hasselt, R. L. Morrison, A. S. Bellack & M. Hersen (Eds.), *Handbook of family violence* (pp. 233–246). New York: Plenum.

Sternberg, K. J., Lamb, M. E., Greenbaum, C., Cicchetti, D., Dawud, S., Cortes, R. M., Knspin, O. & Lorey, F. (1993). Effects of domestic violence on children's behavior problems and depression. *Developmental Psychology, 29,* 44–52.

Stets, J. E. (1988). *Domestic violence and control.* New York: Springer.

Stets, J. E. (1991). Cohabiting and marital aggression: The role of social isolation. *Journal of Marriage and the Family, 53,* 669–680.

Stets, J. E., & Straus, M. A. (1990). Gender differences in reporting marital violence and its medical and psychological consequences. In M. A.

Straus & R. J. Gelles (Eds.), *Physical violence in American families* (pp. 151–165). New Brunswick, NJ: Transaction Publishers.

Straton, J. C. (1994). The myth of the "battered husband syndrome." *Masculinities, 9,* 70–82.

Straus, M. A. (1976). Social inequality, cultural norms, and wife beating. *Victimology, 1,* 54–76.

Straus, M. A. (1990). Societal stress and marital violence in a national sample of American families. In F. Wright, C. Bahn, & R. W. Rieber (Eds.), *Annals of the new York Academy of Sciences, Vol. 347: Forensic psychology and psychiatry* (pp. 229–250). New York: New York Academy of Sciences.

Straus, M. A. (1990a). How violent are American families? Estimates from the National Family Violence Resurvey and other studies. In M. A. Straus & R. J. Gelles (eds.), *Physical violence in American families* (pp. 95–112). New Brunswick, NJ: Transaction Press.

Straus, M. A. (1990b). Ordinary violence, child abuse, and wife beating: What do they have in common? In M. A. Straus & R. J. Gelles (Eds.), *Physical violence in American families* (pp. 403–424). New Brunswick, NJ: Transaction Publishers.

Straus, M. A. (1990c). Social stress and marital violence in a national sample of American families. In M. A. Straus & R. J. Gelles (Eds.), *Physical violence in American families* (pp. 181–201). New Brunswick, NJ: Transaction Publishers.

Straus, M. A. (1991a). Physical violence in American families: Incidence rates, causes, and trends. In D. D. Knudsen & J. L. Miller (Eds.), *Abused and battered: Social and legal responses to family violence* (pp. 17–34). New York: Aldine de Gruyter.

Straus, M. A. (1991b). Discipline and deviance: Physical punishment and violence and other crime in adulthood. *Social Problems, 38,* 180–197.

Straus, M. A. (1994). *Beating the devil out of them: Corporal punishment in American families.* New York: Lexington Books.

Straus, M. A., & Gelles, R. J. (1986). Societal change in family violence from 1975 to 1985 as revealed by two national surveys. *Journal of Marriage and the Family, 48,* 465–479.

Straus, M. A., & Gelles, R. J. (1990). *Physical violence in American Families: Risk Factors and adaptions to violence in 8,145 families.* New Brunswick, NJ: Transaction Publishers.

Straus, M. A., Gelles, R. J., & Steinmetz, S. K. (1980). *Behind closed doors: Violence in the American family.* Garden City, NY: Doubleday.

Straus, M. A., Kantor, G. G., & Moore, D. W. (1997). Change in cultural norms approving marital violence from 1968 to 1994. In G. G. Kantor and J. L. Jasinski, (Eds.), *Out of the darkness: Contemporary perspectives on family violence* (pp. 3–16). Thousand Oaks, CA: Sage.

Straus, M., & Mathur, A. K. (1996). Social change and trends in approval of corporal punishment by parents from 1968 to 1994. In D. Frehsee, W. Horn, & K. Bussman (Eds.), *Violence against children* (pp. 91–105). Berlin: Walter de Gruyter.

Straus, M. A., & Sweet, S. (1992). Verbal symbolic aggression in couples: Incidence rates and relationships to personal characteristics. *Journal of Marriage and the Family, 54,* 346–357.

Straus, M. A., Gelles, R. J., & Steinmetz, S. (1980). *Behind closed doors: Violence in the American family.* Garden City, NY: Anchor Press.

Straus, M. A., Kantor, G. K., & Moore, D. W. (1997). Change in cultural norms approving marital violence from 1968–1994. In G. Kaufman Kantor & J. L. Jasinski (Eds.), *Out of the darkness: Contemporary perspectives on family violence* (pp. 3–16). Thousand Oaks, CA: Sage.

Straus, M. A., Sugarman, D. B., & Giles-Sims, J. (1997). Spanking by parents in subsequent anti-social behavior of children. *Archives of Pediatric and Adolescent Medicine, 151,* 761–767.

Syers, M., & Edleson, J. L. (1992). The combined effects of coordinated criminal justice intervention in woman abuse. *Journal of Interpersonal Violence, 7,* 490–502.

Tifft, L. L. (1993). *Battering of women: The failure of intervention and the case for prevention.* Boulder, CO: Westview Press.

Tolman, R. M., & Bhosley, G. (1991). The outcome of participation in a shelter-sponsored program for men who batter. In D. Knudsen & J. Miller (Eds.), *Abused and battered* (pp. 113–122). New York: Aldine de Gruyter.

Tomlin, S. S. (1991). Stigma and incest survivors. *Child Abuse and Neglect, 15,* 557–566.

Trickett, P. K., Aber, J. L., Carlson, V., & Cicchetti, D. (1991). Relationship of socioeconomic status to the etiology and development sequelae of physical child abuse. *Developmental Psychology, 27,* 148–158.

Tracy, E. M., Haapala, D. A., & Pecora, J. (Eds.). (1991). *Intensive family preservation services: An instructional sourcebook.* Cleveland, OH: Case Western Reserve University.

Tutty, L. M. (1990). Preventing child sexual abuse: A review of current research and theory. In M. Rothery & G. Cameron (Eds.), *Child maltreatment: Expanding our concept of helping* (pp. 259–275). Hillsdale, NJ: Erlbaum.

Ucko, L. G. (1994). Culture and violence: The interaction of Africa and America. *Sex Roles, 31,* 185–204.

Urquiza, A. J., Wyatt, G. E., & Root, M. P. P. (1994). Introduction: Violence against women of color. *Violence and Victims, 9,* 203–206.

U.S. Department of Health and Human Services. (1994). *Child maltreatment 1993: Reports from the states to the National Center on Child Abuse and Neglect.*

Utech, M. R., & Garrett, R. R. (1992). Elder and child abuse: Conceptual and perceptual parallels. *Journal of Interpersonal Violence, 7,* 418–428.

Vinton, L. (1992). Battered women's shelters and older women: The Florida experience. *Journal of Family Violence, 7,* 63–72.

Vissing, Y. M., Straus, M. A., Gelles, R. J., & Harrop, J. W. (1991). Verbal aggression by parents and psychosocial problems of children. *Child Abuse and Neglect, 15,* 223–238.

Vitanza, S., Vogel, L. C. M., & Marshall, L. L. (1995). Distress and symptoms of posttraumatic stress disorder in abused women. *Violence and Victims, 10,* 23–34.

Walker, L. (1979). *The battered woman.* New York: Harper and Row.

Wallace, H. (1996). *Family violence: legal, medical, and social perspectives.* Lexington, MA: Allyn & Bacon.

Warner, I. E., & Hansen, D. J. (1994). The identification and reporting of physical abuse by physicians: A review and implications for research. *Child Abuse and Neglect, 18,* 11–25.

Waterman, C., Dawson, L., & Bologna, M. J. (1989). Sexual coercion in gay male and lesbian relationships: Predictors and implications for support services. *Journal of Sex Research, 26,* 118–124.

Webster, R. L., Goldstein, J., & Segall, A. (1985). A test of the explanatory value of alternative models of child abuse. *Journal of Comparative Family Studies, 16,* 295–317.

Webster, S. W. (1991). Variations in defining family mistreatment: A community survey. In D. D. Knudsen & J. Miller (Eds.), *Abused and battered: Social and legal responses to family violence* (pp. 49–61). new York: Aldine de Gruyter.

Weise, D., & Daro, D. (1995). *Current trends in child abuse reporting and fatalities: The results of the 1994 annual fifty state survey.* Chicago: National Committee to Prevent Child Abuse.

Weitzman, L. (1981). *The marriage contract: Spouses, lovers, and the law.* New York: Free Press.

Whitcomb, D. (1992). *When the victim is a child* (2nd ed.). Washington, DC: U.S. Department of Justice.

Whiteman, M., Fanshel, D., & Grundy, I. F. (1987). Cognitive-behavioral interventions aimed at anger of parents at risk of child abuse. *Social Work, 32,* 469–474.

Whittaker, T. (1996). Violence, gender, and elder abuse. In B. Fawcett, B. Featherstone, J. Hearn, & C. Toft (Eds.), *Violence and gender relations: Theories and interventions* (pp. 147–160). Thousand Oaks, CA: Sage.

Widom, C. S. (1988). Sampling biases and implications for child abuse research. *American Journal of Orthopsychiatry, 58*, 260–270.

Widom, C. S. (1989). Does violence beget violence? A critical examination of the literature. *Psychological Bulletin, 106*, 3–28.

Williams, L. M. (1994). Recall of childhood trauma. *Journal of Consulting and Clinical Psychology, 62*, 1167–1176.

Williamson, I. M., Borduin, C. M., & Howe, B. A. (1991). The ecology of adolescent maltreatment: A multilevel examination of adolescent physical abuse, sexual abuse, and neglect. *Journal of Consulting and Clinical Psychology, 59*, 449–457.

Wilson, S. K., Cameron, S., Jaffe, P., & Wolfe, D. (1989). Children exposed to wife abuse: An intervention model. *Social Casework, 70*, 180–184.

Wolfe, D. A. (1985). Child-abusive parents: An Empirical Review and Analysis. *Psychological Bulletin, 97*, 462–782.

Wolfe, D. A. (1987). *Child abuse: Implication for child development and psychopathology*. Beverly Hills, CA: Sage.

Wolfe, D. A., & Jaffe, P. (1991). Child abuse and family violence as determinants of child psychopathology. *Canadian Journal of Behavioral Science, 23*, 282–299.

Wolf, R. S. (1996). Elder abuse and family violence: Testimony presented before the U.S. Senate Special Committee on Aging. *Journal of Elder Abuse and Neglect, 8*, 81–96.

Wolfgang, M. E. (1958). *Patterns of criminal homicide*. Philadelphia: University of Pennsylvania Press.

Wurtele, S. K., & Miller, C. L. (1987). Children's conceptions of sexual abuse. *Journal of Clinical Child Psychology, 16*, 184–191.

Yllo, K. (1984). The status of women, marital equality, and violence against wives. *Journal of Family Issues, 5*, 307–320.

Yllo, K. (1993). Through a feminist lens: Gender, power, and violence. In R. J. Gelles & D. R. Loseke (Eds.), *Current controversies on family violence* (pp. 47–62). Newbury Park, CA: Sage.

Yllo, K., & Straus, M. A. (1990). Patriarchy and violence against wives: The impact of structural and normative factors. In M. A. Straus & R. J. Gelles (Eds.), *Physical violence in American families* (pp. 383–399). New Brunswick, NJ: Transaction Publishers.

Zelizer, V. (1985). *Pricing the priceless child: The changing social value of children*. New York: Basic Books.

CHAPTER 27

Human Sexuality

Robert T. Francoeur and Linda L. Hendrixson

Orientation

Sexology

The American College of Sexologists includes within the purview of sexology "all those aspects, anatomical, physiological, psychological, medical, sociological, anthropological, historical, legal, religious, literary and artistic, that contribute to our understanding of what it means to develop as healthy sexual persons with a positive image of our sexuality in a particular social milieu" (Francoeur, Cornog, Perper, & Scherzer, 1995, p. 588). In this chapter, our perspective is biopsychosociocultural, starting with the biological origins of psychosexual development—the effects of genetics on anatomy and hormones and of hormonally differentiated neural tendencies on behavior. Several aspects of the psychological, sociological, and cultural aspects of humans linked with this biological foundation are discussed here because they involve areas of great public concern and present fertile areas for researchers.

Sex and Gender Definitions

The term "sex" is often used without definition despite its variety of implied meanings. Alfred Kinsey defined sex as physical behavior that results in orgasm, even though many

Robert T. Francoeur • Biology and Allied Health Sciences, Fairleigh Dickinson University, Madison, New Jersey 07940. **Linda L. Hendrixson** • Department of Health, East Stroudsburg University, East Stroudsburg, Pennsylvania 18301.

Handbook of Marriage and the Family, 2nd edition, edited by Marvin Sussman, Suzanne K. Steinmetz, and Gary W. Peterson. Plenum Press, New York, 1999.

expressions of our sexuality and much of our sexual behavior do not result in orgasm. Sex is also used to refer to a person's sexual anatomy, or to any behavior involving the penis and vagina. Some distinguish between sexual organs that are primarily erotic in function, genital organs that are basically reproductive, and sexuogenital organs that serve both functions (Diamond & Karlen, 1980). However, because our anatomy, physiology, neural pathways, and behaviors are more or less feminized/defeminized and masculinized/not masculinized by the sex hormones from our testes, ovaries, and adrenal glands, from early gestation to death, sex can be seen as permeating every aspect of our body, mind, and personality (Francoeur, 1997; Francoeur et al., 1995).

The term sex is often misapplied to talk about gender. Gender is defined as "one's personal, social, and/or legal status as a male or a female or as a person of mixed gender" (Francoeur et al., 1995, p. 238). Gender (core) identity is the identification and awareness we have of ourselves as being either male or female. Gender role (behavior) is "everything that a person says or does to indicate to others or to the self the degree that one is male or female or ambivalent" (Money & Tucker, 1975, p. 9). Our response to all the expectations and social messages we get from others about how we should act as sexual persons produces our gender role behavior. These messages, or social scripting, often involve gender-role stereotyping, which forces the individual male or female person into certain roles and expectations delineated by society. These related concepts are included in the expression Gender Identity/Role (G-I/R) (Money, 1987, p. 15).

A recent elaboration of the GI-R concept adds gender orientation to gender identity and gender-role behavior. While common usage refers to sexual orientation, meaning homosexual, heterosexual, and bisexual, a more accurate usage is emerging that speaks of gender orientation, which includes three aspects: affectional (love) orientation, fantasy orientation, and erotic (sexual) orientation (Francoeur, 1991).

Sexual Development Before Birth

The Eve and Adam Plans

In mammals the general innate developmental tendency, termed the Eve Plan (or Eve Principle), produces a female infant with a reproductive potential without relying on any genetic and hormonal control factors beyond the basic requirement of two X chromosomes. Unless diverted by genetic or hormonal factors at critical times into the male developmental path, fetal sexual anatomy and neural encoding follow the feminizing developmental path. The Adam Plan (or Principle) requires

1. A Y chromosome and a testes-determining gene (Sex Region of Y chromosome [SRY] or Testes Determining Factor gene [TDF]) that set the stage for
2. A subsequent cascade of other masculinizing, particularly testosterone and dihydrotestosterone and male fertility genes; and
3. The defeminizing Mullerian inhibiting hormone

These genetic and hormonal factors operate at a variety of critical periods in fetal and postnatal development to produce a male who is more or less masculinized in his gender role (Money, 1980, 1988). Psychosexual development involves two concurrent processes operating from early pregnancy to death on two different axis: a feminizing/defeminizing axis and a masculinizing/not-masculinizing axis (Francoeur, 1991; Money & Ehrhardt, 1972; Reinisch, Rosenblum, & Sanders, 1987; Weinrich, 1987). Because this process of masculinization and defeminization involves many factors, each of which is seldom an all-or-nothing process, every human develops with his or her own unique combination as a sexual person. The result usually falls within the socially acknowledged domains of male or female, but this is not always a clear dichotomy. A significant percentage of infants are born "cross-coded" for a homosexual, lesbian, or bisexual orientation. Some infants are "cross-coded" for their gender identity (transsexuals) or gender roles (transvestites). Some infants may be more or less cross-coded for gender roles that society recognizes with terms such as "sissy boys," "effeminate males," and "tomboys." An estimated 2% of newborns experience some degree of cross-coding that leaves them with ambiguous genitals. These intersex individuals are technically known as true or pseudohermaphrodites. These variations can occur alone, or in any combination thereof, giving us a "rainbow" of flavors in our individual experience of gender and sex.

The question currently being raised by various cross-coded activists and advocacy organizations is whether their conditions should be viewed by parents, the medical community, and society as defects requiring intervention and treatment or as variations that should be recognized and accepted despite our discomfort with individuals who do not fit our standard of dichotomous male or female.

The Psychosexual Development Process

Psychosexual development has been described in terms of our passing through a series of "gates," "windows," or "critical periods" (Money & Tucker, 1975, p. 73). In this analogy, our passage through some developmental gate occurs at a very specific critical or sensitive period in time. At fertilization, for instance, the union of egg and sperm quickly and irreversibly determines our genetic sex, although the influence of sex-related genes continues throughout life. Between 6 to 12 weeks after fertilization the embryo develops either ovaries or testes, and then male or female internal and external anatomy. Some "gates" tend to have short critical periods, after which that aspect of our sexuality is "locked," irreversibly set. The windows for hormone actions, neural encoding, gender scripting, and gender roles are less well defined and last a lifetime (Money, 1987).

The human brain is much larger and more specialized than the brian of any other mammal. However, an upright posture keeps the pelvic girdle of human females (and most primates) relatively small, too small to allow the fetal brain to develop its neural control over survival behaviors to the maturity other higher mammals have at birth. The human infant is born premature, months before it can walk or talk. Humans experience a 9-month uterogestation, during which the brain stem develops reflexive neural control over survival behaviors (feeding, mating, flight, and fighting). During late uterogestation, development of the fetal limbic and neocortical systems allows some conscious neural control over reflexive behaviors. If the limbic midbrain and neocortical levels developed fully during uterogestation, the fetal head would be too large to pass through the birth canal. Consequently, the human is born premature, and completes its neural development during an exterogestation that lasts a year or more, doubling its brain capacity and making neural connections to allow a full range of emotional and conscious integrations (Walsh, 1991).

In what developmental scientists now term an *interactive model of psychosexual development*, nature—genes, hormones, and anatomical/neural developments—continually interact with nurture—the environment and learning—from conception to death. The 12 developmental gates or critical stages outlined here are landmarks in this interaction. This paradigm is commonly visualized in a linear form based on two pathways, male/masculine and female/feminine, with the possibility of cross-coding for various aspects of gender identity, gender role, and gender orientation. However, it helps to visualize this process in an alternative way, as a series of 12 concentric circles, starting with chromosomal/genetic sex (gate 1) and extending to gate 12, one's mature gender-identity/role/orientation (G-I/R/O) on the outside (Hendrixson, unpublished). Within each of the 12 circles, cross-coding variations can occur. In either paradigm, the most common outcome is individuals who more or less fit in with the clear sexual/gender dichotomy of male/female that dominates Euro-American cultures. However, as noted earlier, a significant minority of individuals are more or less cross-coded for variations in their G-I/R/O, including homosexual males and females, bisexually oriented persons, transsexuals, transvestites, true and pseudohermaphrodites, intersexual persons, ambiguously genitaled persons, and persons who identify themselves as "gender fluid." In many non-Euro-American cultures "third-gendered persons" are recognized and often valued. In American culture, third-gendered persons are only recently becoming visible.

Six Critical Stages in Prenatal Development

Gate 1: Genetic Sex. Fertilization, the union of a male- or female-determining sperm, with a Y or an X sex chromosome with 22 body chromosomes (autosomes), with an ovum containing one X chromosome and 22 autosomes, marks the start of an individual's psychosexual development. The resulting zygote has either 44 autosomes plus two X chromosomes (46,XX) for a female or 44 autosomes plus XY sex chromosomes (46,XY) for a male.

Variations result when the egg or sperm has an abnormal chromosome number. Males with two or more X chromosomes and one or more Y chromosomes are lanky and sterile but sexually potent—Klinefelter syndrome. The most common female variation usually with one instead of two X chromosomes (45,XO), is a sexually juvenile, sterile female with no ovaries who can with hormone replace lead a normal life as a mature female—Turner syndrome. A genetic male (46,XY) with a partially deleted Y may also show symptoms of Turner syndrome. Sexual mosaics with different chromosome complements in different cells of the body may result from two sperm fertilizing an ovum, from the fusion of two zygotes, or from unequal chromosome distribution (nondisjunction) in cell divisions after fertilization (Money, 1988; Moore, 1988).

Gates 2 and 3: Gonadal and Hormonal Sex. During weeks 4–6 of pregnancy, primordial undifferentiated gonads (reproductive glands) begin developing in the upper abdominal cavity. Embryos may develop with two testes, with two ovaries, with one ovary and one testis, with ovariotestes, or with no gonads (as in Turner syndrome). The presence or absence of a testes-determining factor (SRY or TDF) gene on the Y chromosome is the critical factor in testicular differentiation. If a SRY gene is present, the gonads become testes in the weeks 6 to 8. If no SRY gene is present, the primordial gonads develop into ovaries at about 12 weeks. Presence of an SRY gene does not, however, guarantee development of testes. A duplicated dose sensitive sex reversal (DSS) gene on the X chromosome can cancel the effect of a SRY gene and cause a 46,XY embryo to develop as a normal female. This phenomenon raises a question about the Eve Principle, the assumption that female sexual development occurs independent of fetal hormones.

The testes and ovaries quickly begin producing sex hormones, a predominance of androgenic hormones in males and estrogens in female fetuses. Small amounts of androgens are produced by the ovaries and the adrenal gland cortex in females and estrogenic hormones by the testes and adrenal glands of males.

The presence of threshold levels of androgenic or masculinizing hormones (testosterone and dihydrotestosterone, or DHT) and a defeminizing hormone (Mullerian inhibiting hormone, or MIH) (discussed later) is critical in the development of male sexual anatomy and neural encoding. The estrogens and androgenic hormones are critical in development of gender-specific secondary sexual characteristics at critical periods during childhood and at puberty.

Gate 4: Internal Sexual Anatomy. In weeks 4–6 of pregnancy, the fetus develops an ambisexual system of internal ducts with the capacity to follow either the male or female path, or both paths simultaneously. This ambisexual system includes a pair of Wolffian (mesonephric) ducts and a parallel set of Mullerian (paramesonephric) ducts.

In the male fetus (weeks 6–12), testosterone causes the Wolffian ducts to differentiate into the paired vas deferens, prostate, seminal vesicles, and associated male structures. At the same time, MIH causes the Mullerian ducts to degenerate, thereby defeminizing the internal sexual anatomy.

In the female fetus, the absence of a threshold level of testosterone allows the Wolffian ducts to degenerate. With no MIH to block their development, the Mullerian ducts form the paired fallopian tubes and fuse into a single vagina and single uterus (Francoeur, 1991; Moore, 1988).

Variations include genetic/gonadal males (46,XY) with a genetic mutation that prevents the production of the testosterone receptor protein that enables cells to transport testosterone from the blood stream into cells where it can have its masculinizing effects. Androgen-insensitive or testicular-feminized males have external female genitals and a female psyche. A much rarer condition is a genetic/gonadal male who lacks MIH and has both male and female internal sexual systems.

Gate 5: External Sexual Anatomy. In week 8, the external sexual anatomy is still ambisexual, with an undifferentiated genital tubercle, a pair of swellings, and a pair of folds reaching from the tubercle to just in front of the anus. In the third and fourth months, above-threshold levels of masculinizing DHT stimulate the tubercle to become a penis and the swellings and folds to fuse into the scrotal sac and lower shaft of the penis. The testes do not descend from the abdominal cavity into the scrotum until just before birth under the influence of MIH. In the female fetus, with a subliminal level of DHT, the tubercle develops as a clitoris. The swellings and folds remain separated to become the major and minor labia (Francoeur, 1991; Moore, 1988). Variations include a wide range of ambiguous or intersex external genitals.

Gate 6: Sexual Brain Encoding. In late pregnancy thresholds levels of masculinizing and defeminizing hormones cross the blood–brain barrier and encode a variety of neural tendencies in the limbic and hypothalamic regions of the cerebral hemispheres, both before and after birth.

Neural circuits in the hypothalamus are encoded for production of gonadotropic hormone-releasing hormone (Gn-RH) in a cyclic pattern for females and in an acyclic (tonic) pattern in males. After puberty, in both females and males, Gn-RH from the hypothalamus stimulates the anterior pituitary to produce follicle-stimulating hormone (FSH) and luteinizing hormone (LH). These two gonadotropic hormones from the anterior pituitary regulate continuous production of sperm and testosterone in the testes and cyclic egg maturation and the uterine/menstrual cycle (Barinaga, 1991; Gibbons, 1991; Holden, 1991; Money, 1986; Nash, 1992; Pool, 1994).

An as-yet-unidentified masculinizing or defeminizing hormone establishes a neural pattern for earlier puberty in women and later puberty in men. The difference between early and later puberty has a sexually dimorphic effect on the corpus collosum, a communications bridge connecting the right and left hemispheres. In males, a later puberty allows reduction in the size of the corpus callosum and more time for the right and left cerebral hemispheres to specialize. In females, earlier puberty prevents partial regression of the corpus callosum and maintains better communications between the cerebral hemispheres. Interpretation of this gender dimorphism is controversial. Hemispheric specialization appears to give males a general advantage in details and coordination—right hemispheric activities—while less specialization and better interhemispheric communications give females an advantage in intuition and pattern recognition (Barinaga, 1991; Gibbons, 1992; Holden, 1991; Nash, 1992; Pool, 1994; Tanner, 1990; Tavris, 1992).

Researchers are now trying to detect other results of prenatal neural encoding for gender dimorphism, gender identity, and orientations. These patterns include the dimorphism of female priority to touch and male priority to sight, female proceptivity, pheromone responses, the possibility of an ideal lover template, and the interstitial nucleus of the anterior hypothalamus–region 3 (INAH-3) are which appears to control sexual attraction to women (LeVay, 1991; Money, 1986, 1988; Perper, 1985; Walsh, 1991). Research on genetic- and hormone-based, gender-dimorphic "tendencies," "flavorings," "neural encoding," or "brain templates" related to sexuality is complemented by considerable research on the "genetics of personality" with studies of identical and fraternal twins raised apart from birth (Holden, 1987).

In summary, the six prenatal gates of human psychosexual development are:

1. Chromosomal/genetic sex—established at fertilization
2. Gonadal sex—established at 6–12 weeks
3. Hormonal sex—begins at about 8 weeks and continues more or less fluid throughout life
4. Internal sexual anatomy—8–16 weeks.
5. External sexual anatomy—8–12 weeks.
6. Neural pathways and tendencies encoded—second trimester on through age 3; and perhaps later

Psychosexual Development after Birth

Critical Periods in Exterogestation

Neural and functional maturation of the limbic and neocortical systems of the triune human brain are particularly evident in the year or 2 after our premature birth, during exterogestation, and during childhood and preadolescence. The psychosexual aspects of this maturation are marked by six postnatal gates:

7. Gender assignment—at birth, or prenatal sex ascertainment
8. Gender scripting—begins at birth and continues throughout life; may begin prenatally
9. Gender role behavior—begins developing in first year
10. Gender identity—irreversibly finalized at birth or shortly thereafter, even though not consciously recognized until about age 2 or 3; continues to develop in response to scripting and expanding, maturing self-image
11. Gender orientation—prenatal tendencies elaborated on after birth, consciously recognized and acknowledged in adolescence or adult life
12. Pubertal and adult G-I/R

Gates 7 and 10: Gender of Assignment and Gender Identity. When parents and family encounter the newborn's external sexual anatomy, at birth or after a prenatal chromosomal test, they react by assigning it a gender status, male or female. This immediately sets in motion a whole tapestry of sexual role expectations or scripting to which the infant gradually learns to respond in rewarding ways.

We tend to think our gender roles are all learned from scripting, forgetting that basic elements of the newborn's gender identity and gender orientation have already been laid down in the fetal neural pathways. Two unusual cases support the hypothesis that gender identity is encoded in the brain before birth and elaborated on and finalized soon after birth.

In 1965, identical twin boys were circumcised at the age of 7 months. One of the twins was accidentally castrated by a severe circumcision trauma. At 17 months, this twin was given plastic surgery and gender reassigned as a female. Despite intensive efforts to script and rear the twin as a female, the twin's prenatal neural encoding for a male gender identity persisted. At age 18, after discovering the facts about her accidental castration, "she" sought and obtained sex reassignment surgery with phalloplasty and gender reassignment as a male. He was later reported to be living successfully as a heterosexual male (Colapinto, 1997; Diamond, 1998; Lebacqz, 1997; Money & Ehrhardt, 1975; Money & Tucker, 1972). Two other cases of cross-reared twins with similar outcomes have been reported by Diamond (1998).

The case for a prenatal gender identity encoding is strengthened by the outcome of children in the Dominican Republic studied by Imperato-McGinley and colleagues (1979). Seven generations of individuals, all descended from one woman in a rural village, have a mutation in the gene regulating the synthesis of DHT. As a result of intermarriage, over three dozen children were conceived with two mutant genes. Without sufficient DHT in the second trimester of pregnancy, the external anatomy of these infants developed in the female track, although their chromosomes, gonads, and internal structures were male. Raised from births as girls, these children experienced an unusual puberty. The burst of testosterone at puberty induced the external female anatomy of these children to change into male anatomy. As their external genitals shifted in the male direction, these children gave give up their imposed female gender identity and adopted a male gender identity that conformed with their prenatal neural encoding (Diamond, 1994; Money & Ehrhardt, 1972; Reinisch et al., 1987; Weinrich, 1987).

Diamond (1998) sums up the evidence for a prenatal neural encoding of gender identity, noting that:

> Despite the writings of some on the power of upbringing, role modeling, and learning, there is no known case anywhere in which an otherwise normal individual has accepted rearing or life status in an imposed role of the sex opposite to that of his or her natural genetic and endocrine history. The removal of penis and testes and imposition of a female rearing has never proven sufficient to overcome the inherent bias of the normal male [or female] nervous system. (p. 67)

The infant's sexual anatomy also molds its own growing awareness of its body self-image as male or female. Identifying with the same-sex parent and countermodeling with the other-sex parent also aid in the development of a secure gender identity. The use of sexually dimorphic language, with the basic distinctions of mommy versus daddy and he versus she, reinforces this gender awareness in the child's second year. This personal conviction about one's maleness or femaleness and one's growing gender identity is gradually integrated, irreversibly, into one's personality and gender role as a sexual, gendered person.

Gates 8 and 9: Gender Scripting and Gender Roles. The traditional pattern of psychosexual development as it relates to what we call masculine and feminine behavior pictures two opposing gradients or currents. A truly feminine female suppresses or has no masculine traits at all; a truly masculine male never exhibits any trait that we see as feminine. In reality, every gendered person expresses a basic mixture of what we call masculine and feminine behavioral patterns (Reinisch & Sanders, 1984). Masculinity and femininity are independent but related trends on a general axis rather than as opposing currents. Our sexual potential as male or female is expressed to its fullest when our personalities express a rich and balanced blend of masculine and feminine traits. This androgynous blend expresses a dynamic balance of the yin and yang, poetic and rational, left-handed and right-handed, emotional and intellectual energies that exist as potentials in every gendered human (Holden, 1987; Nash, 1992; Reinisch et al., 1987; Singer, 1972).

Efforts to promote gender equality and acceptance of androgyny must, however, recognize the influence and importance of hormone-induced, gender-related behavioral tendencies and innate patterning of neural encoding. In her 1983 Presidential Address to the American Sociological Association, Alice Rossi (1984) warned that theories that neglect the fundamental biological and neural differences between the sexes "carry a high risk of eventual irrelevance against the mounting evidence of sexual dimorphism from the biological and neural sciences.... Diversity is a biological fact, while equality is a political, ethical, and social precept" (p. 4). Recent research in the neurosciences give added weight to this warning (Gorman, 1992; Holden, 1987, 1992).

While brain development during uterogestation establishes a foundation for gender roles, the human brain is subject to important conditioning and scripting during the following 3 years of exterogestation. In the first year after birth the human brain triples its birth weight, and this development continues until age 3 (Walsh, 1991).

In developmental, sociological terms, a script is a personally internalized set of behaviors, attitudes, values, and expectations accepted as appropriate by an individual. Originally developed by Eric Berne in 1970 as part of transactional analysis, scripting is currently applied by sociologists to psychosexual development (Gagnon, 1990).

A sexual script has five key variables that specify, on a personal or cultural level, with whom one has sex, what one does sexually, when sex is appropriate, the proper setting for sex, and why one has sex. This appears to overlap the concept of a lovemap. However, there is a major difference between the sociological construct of a sexual script and the developmental construct of a lovemap. Scripting theory denies the existence of a biologically based sexual drive and claims that sexual learning and social contingencies almost completely account for what we do sexually. A lovemap, as described by Money (1986) and others, starts with a biologically based sexual drive and prenatal neural encoding, which are then elaborated on by learning, conditioning, and scripting to form adolescent and adult normophilic or vandalized paraphilic lovemaps. Lovemaps resist change because they are based in neural pathways.

Recognizing the existence of gender dimorphic encoding or "flavorings" in the brain can be used by society and individuals to legitimize sexist gender-based stereotypes and inequalities. Tavris (1992) rightly warns that feminist battles for equality, including the late 1880s' suffragist movement and the 1960–1970s' women's movement, have always elicited reactionary attempts to establish the immutability of certain gender differences. However, recognition of gender differences can also be used to adapt educational processes and the functioning of the business world and society in general to take advantage of different gender skills (Tanner, 1990). A reasonable course in this controversial area would be to not deny but accept real gender differences without exaggerating them, and at the same time continue the struggle to eliminate the unequal social consequences that flow from them (Tavris, 1992).

Early Sexual Explorations and Rehearsal Play. Ultrasound scans have documented the functioning of the erection reflex in 17-week-old male fetuses. Female fetuses have a similar sexual capacity, although not as early since female sexual anatomy begins its development later in gestation than does the male (Calderone, 1985; Colonna & Solnit, 1981). Newborn males as young as 3 weeks and females as young as 7 months have been observed experiencing spontaneous or induced erections and orgasms (Bakwin, 1974; Conn & Kanner, 1940; Kinsey, Pomeroy, Martin, & Gebhard, 1953).

Sooner or later, most children learn to masturbate. Most children seem to forget their early autoerotic experiences. Boys generally rediscover this experience or learn about it from peers in their preadolescent or early adolescent years.

Girls frequently do not rediscover masturbation until after they are sexually active with a partner (Martinson, 1980).

Sociosexual play and explorations among same-aged children and preadolescents, both among siblings and nonsiblings, are emotionally charged issues for most parents in our culture because adults tend to read their own sexual and erotic meanings into such explorative play. Such childhood play is prompted more by the need to explore, learn, and confirm their sexual identities than it is by satisfying sexual urges. Many researchers today contend that early sexual exploration and rehearsal play is positive, growth-promoting, and contributes to both normal physical and psychological development (Borneman, 1983; Goldman & Goldman, 1982; Kirkpatrick, 1986; Martinson, 1980). Money (1986) claims that many adult forms of paraphilic behavior are the result of vandalized lovemaps caused by traumas inflicted by adults on children in response to discovery of their normal and spontaneous sexual rehearsal play.

Gender Orientations (Gate 11).

The Gender/Gender Orientations Rainbow. Our understanding of the complexities of psychosexual development has moved from a simplistic, black-and-white construct of male versus female, heterosexual and homosexual, to a sensitivity for the broad spectrum of a "gender rainbow." The gender continuum or rainbow includes all kinds of variations in the paths taken by individuals through the six prenatal and six postnatal gates of psychosexual development. The continuum includes a variety of males, females, and intersexes, genetic-gonadal males raised as females because of androgen-insensitivity or DHT deficiency, and persons with Turner, Klinefelter, and other conditions. It also includes a wide range of gender-cross-codings in neural pathways and tendencies both before and after birth, with the episodic cross-gender behaviors of transvestites and the chronic cross-coded conditions of transsexuals, transgenderists, and "he-she" or "she-males." It includes a continuum with a variety of normophilic, hyperphilic, hypophilic, and vandalized paraphilic lovemaps.

Similarly, a once-simplistic, dichotomous view of a normal, homogeneous heterosexual majority and a small minority of equally homogeneous homosexual persons has been replaced with an awareness of the rich varieties of heterosexualities, bisexualities, and homosexualities: "To be aware of the place each of us occupies on the gender continuum, to know our unique color on the gender rainbow, and to better integrate these special attitudes, talents, and ideas into our lives, is to know a more enhanced and enriched sense of being" (Schaefer & Wheeler, cited in Francoeur, 1991, p. 524; see also Fausto-Sterling, 1993).

Kinsey's Research. By the early 1990s, evidence from genetic studies of human families and twins, preliminary evidence of neuroanatomical differences in the limbic systems of heterosexual and homosexual men and heterosexual women, and cases of cross-sex rearing strongly indicated that a basic, seemingly irreversible gender orientation tendency is encoded in neural pathways before birth. This tendency is elaborated on by postnatal social and familial factors. Thus, an individual may take many years to recognize his or her gender orientation and accept her or his lesbian or gay identity (Green, 1987).

In any discussion of gender orientations—gay, lesbian, bisexual, and heterosexual identities—one must be aware of the changing operational definitions researchers have articulated and used over the years. In taking over 11,000 sexual histories in the 1940s, Kinsey used two quantifiable criteria: sexual behavior to orgasm with persons of the same and/or other gender and sexual attraction to persons of the same and/or other gender. He also warned that the terms homosexual, heterosexual, and ambisexual should be used as adjectives to describe stimuli and behaviors, but not as substantive nouns for persons (Kinsey, Pomeroy, & Martin, 1948).

Despite this warning, we commonly refer to persons as homosexuals, heterosexuals, and bisexuals, implying that a "-sexual" term is an appropriate substantive term for a person's identity, lifestyle, and gendered relationships. Currently there is a growing shift away from the substantive term "sexual orientations" to "gender orientations," although we have no equivalent gender substantive for homosexual, heterosexual, and bisexual.

In terms of overt behavior and sexual attraction, Kinsey's data showed that half of American males were "0" on a scale where 0 indicates an exclusively heterosexual experience and attraction and 6 an exclusive homosexual experience and attraction. Four percent of the men fell in the 6 category of the Kinsey Six Scale. The remaining 46% were distributed in five categories between 1 and 5 to indicate the ratio of their experience and attraction with both men and women.

In understanding the Kinsey data, it is obvious that a woman or man who has experienced one or more orgasms with partners of the same gender more than likely does not identify him or herself as having a homosexual or bisexual orientation. Men and women in prison, in the military, or in other environments where other-gender partners are few or nonexistent may engage in sexual activities with a same-gender partner or even be attracted to such for sexual release. When other-gender partners are available, these same persons quickly revert to heterosexual relations. Kinsey's research included a disproportionate number of prisoners. He also did not deal with what are now known as gay, lesbian, bisexual identities or with the awareness individuals have of themselves as living a gay, lesbian, or bisexual lifestyle and identity. Finally, Kinsey's research did not deal with the developmental or temporal variations for persons who shift back and forth across the Kinsey Six Scale during their lifetimes.

A Sexual Orientation Grid. Emergence of a self-identified gay community in the late 1970s allowed more in-depth research on gender orientations. Klein and colleagues (1985) expanded the Kinsey research into the developmental dimension, adding five aspects to the original criteria of sexual behavior and attraction. Klein's model of sexual orientation and affectional preference includes:

1. Sexual attraction, answering the question of whom we find attractive as a potential or real sexual partner
2. Sexual behavior, answering the question of who our actual sexual partners have been
3. Sexual fantasies
4. Emotional or affectional preference
5. Social preferences, answering the question of which sex we are more comfortable with in our leisure and social life
6. Lifestyle, answering the questions of the dominant sexual orientation (of the Kinsey Six Scale) of the people with whom we spend most of our time.
7. Self-identification, the way we view ourselves on the Kinsey Six Scale, from 0 to 6.

In Klein's research, the subject rates himself or herself in these seven areas using the 0–6 Kinsey Six Scale. The rating in each aspect is done on the longitudinal basis of 5 years ago, the current year, and one's ideal state or future goal. The result is 21 subratings, which can be totaled up and divided by 21 to give an inclusive Kinsey Six Scale rating.

Developmental, longitudinal studies using the Klein Sexual Orientation Grid are just beginning and will not provide a more realistic picture of sexual orientation and affectional preference until a sufficiently large random sample has been followed for some years. However, common sense suggests that few persons rating themselves honestly on this 21 category grid would find themselves a pure Kinsey 0, exclusively heterosexual, or a pure Kinsey 6, exclusively homosexual. This raises a question about the relevance of trying to force men and women into dichotomous or tripartite pigeon holes of gay, straight, or inbetween. Such labeling may be politically important for sexual minorities seeking recognition and civil rights and for persons concerned about the harmful influence of those labeled as "deviant," "sinner," "criminal," "sexual invert," "psychologically unbalanced," or "sick" on our society. Labeling persons according to their gender orientations, however, is becoming more and more difficult as we gain new insights into the rainbow of gender orientations.

A Panerotic Potential. Kinsey and Klein focused on the interpersonal dimension of gender orientation, ignoring erotic reactions and relations not involving persons. Picking up Freud's concept of the infant being born with a "polymorphic perversity," Stayton (1980, 1992) maintains that we are born with a "panerotic potential.... Nature's intention seems to be to produce persons who are sexual in the fullest sense of the word" (1992, p. 14). Noting that humans satisfy their need for sensual/erotic nurturance in many different ways, Stayton addresses four dimensions or outlets:

1. Autoerotic orientations
2. Animal and inanimate sexual objects
3. Interpersonal relationships
4. The erotic potential of mysticism and transcendence

Stayton sees the development of a healthy sexual orientation as having two elements: (1) achieving a creative balance between serving one's own needs and being able to delay or substitute (sensual/erotic) gratification, and (2) integrating and resolving the natural tensions between one's own personal erotic preferences and those approved of by society.

In adjusting to the sensual-erotic potential of one's own body, we find a balance between an extreme of total self-serving narcissistic (autoerotic) pleasuring and the other extreme of complete denial of the sensual self. In exploring and developing our erotic potential in the animate and inanimate areas of our world, a healthy sexual orientation balances and integrates the sensual and erotic potentials of the animal world, nature, and the universe. In the interpersonal area of our eroticism, Stayton cites the cross-cultural work of Ford and Beach (1951) to support the hypothesis that most people are, by nature, basically bisexual but predominantly heterosexual, somewhere in the Kinsey 1 or 2 categories. Only our particular Western cultural values and social scripting dictate that this interpersonal erotic potential be narrowed down to a single heterosexual monogamous pairing for adults.

The transcendent dimension of our erotic potential is the most controversial and the least documented in human experience. Eastern religions, particularly Taoism, commonly see an intimate connection between sexual relations, human sexuality, and the transcendent goal of mysticism (Francoeur, 1992; Sannella, 1987). Western culture has a few scattered examples: the eroticism of the biblical Solomon's Song of Songs, the erotic poetry of the Spanish medieval mystics John of the Cross and Theresa of Avila, the pre-Raphaelite Dante Gabriel Rossetti (1828–1882), and the romantic visionary William Blake (1757–1827).

For centuries Western Christian traditions have sought to constrict the range of acceptable sexual/erotic outlets, while ancient Eastern traditions have embraced the spiritual dimensions of sex and extolled the role of women as sexual teachers. However, it is the Western analytical, rational Apollonian tradition, with its emphasis on the value of the individual, its dichotomy of body-soul, doctrine of an original

sin, and manipulation of nature, that has allowed women to move toward equality with men and celebrate the spiritual dimensions of erotic-sensual pleasure (Francoeur, 1992; Gardella, 1986; Paglia, 1990).

Biological Theories. The strongest evidence that gender orientation begins with a biological basis comes from genetic studies of human families and twins. Forty years ago Kallmann (1952a,b; 1963) reported 100% concordance in 40 monozygotic twin pairs when one twin admitted to homosexual behavior. Concordance for homosexuality among 45 dizygotic twin pairs was essentially similar to the general population rate. Although some researchers found similar genetic evidence (Schlegel, 1962), subsequent studies reported no monozygotic concordance for homosexuality. This latter finding fit the mood of the 1960s and 1970s, which preferred to have homosexual orientation result from a free will choice or social conditioning rather than a biological predisposition (Diamond, 1994; Gellman, 1992).

In the 1980s, new studies of familial tendencies and comparisons of concordances figures for gender orientations of siblings and identical and fraternal twins found strong evidence for a major genetic component in sexual orientation (Allen & Gorski, 1991, 1992; Bailey et al., 1991, 1993; Diamond, 1994; Green, 1987; Pillard & Weinrich, 1986; Pillard, Poumadere, & Carretta, 1982; Weinrich, 1987; Whitam & Mathy, 1986).

Attempts to find differences in the ratio or amounts of androgenic and estrogenic hormones in gay men, lesbians, and heterosexual-oriented persons have not yielded significant data (Dorner, 1988; Gooren, Fliers, & Courtney, 1990; Meyer-Bahlburg, 1987; Weinrich, 1987). Provocative preliminary work by LeVay (1991) suggests that a specific region in the hypothalamus may explain or be related to the gender orientation of gay men. This center appears to regulate sexual attraction to women. LeVay found that the third interstitial nucleus of anterior hypothalamic region (INAH-3) is well developed in heterosexual men. However, the INAH-3 of gay men studied by LeVay matched the undeveloped state and size of heterosexual women (Barinaga, 1991; Gellman, 1992). Genetic studies include discovery of a set of marker genes on the X chromosome (Xq28) in 33 of 40 pairs of homosexual brothers (Hamer et al., 1993), indicating a genetic factor for at least some gay men, inherited through the maternal line (Byne & Parsons, 1993). McFadden (1998) has reported finding a difference in the development of the inner ear that suggests that the cochlea of lesbian women and heterosexual males are similarly poorly developed and lacking in the sensitivity to soft sounds easily detected by heterosexual women. McFadden has hypothesized that the prenatal hormones that masculinize the auditory centers of lesbians and heterosexual men also activate the neural circuit (INAH-3) that controls sexual attraction to women while inhibiting whatever neural circuit stimulate sexual attraction to males.

Other Hypotheses. Attempts to explain homosexual orientation as an arrested oral/anal stage promoted by a castration anxiety (Freud); the lack of a strong male role image and a domineering, seductive mother reinforcing a son's effeminate behavior; or the linking of a male's earliest erotic experiences with masturbation fantasies are not supported by current evidence.

Cross-Cultural Studies. Ford and Beach (1951) reported that nearly two-thirds of the 190 societies they analyzed sanctioned some form of homosexual activity and relationship. In these cultures, the majority of men and often also women fit into the Kinsey 1–2 categories. Although homosexual behavior is often strongly disapproved of or severely punished in more sexually restrictive cultures, exclusively homosexual and other unconventional behaviors are more common in these cultures than in more permissive cultures.

Recent Surveys. According to Kinsey's statistics, half of all American men were exclusively heterosexual—Kinsey 0—in both their experiences and attraction. Four percent were exclusively homosexual—Kinsey 6—with no experience or attraction to women. The remaining 46%, with varying proportions of sexual experiences and attraction to both sexes, were bisexual.

Recent surveys suggest a reevaluation of the bisexual range in Kinsey's 40-year-old nonrandom data. Weinberg and Williams (1974) found that only one in five self-identified gay American men and one in ten Dutch and Danish gay men put themselves in Kinsey's 2/3/4 bisexual category. Bell and Weinberg (1978), McWhirter and Mattison (1984), and others found that over three-quarters of thousands of males who have experienced homosexual behavior identified themselves as exclusively gay. Less than one in ten of these men said they have had more than incidental sex with a female.

There is also a question about the actual numbers of men in the Kinsey 5–6 category. In 1991 probability sample of Dallas households, only 7.3% of males reported any same-sex contact between 1978 and 1989. Diamond (1998) found less than 3% of males and 1.2% of females reported same-sex or bisexual activity in his random sample of 2000 Hawaiians.

In a 1989 national random sample of male and female sexual behavior, Dutch researchers found only 13% of the males admitted to having had at least one homosexual experience. Of this 13%, only 3.3% identified themselves as homosexual while an additional 4.5% identified as bisexual. Among the Danish women surveyed, only 10% reported ever having a homosexual experience. Only 3% considered

themselves bisexual, while less than 1 in 200 considered herself lesbian (summarized in Diamond, 1998). These and other recent studies in Britain, Denmark, and the United States appear fairly consistent.

These new data suggest that the percentage of predominantly heterosexual American males may be more like 90%, with 5% exclusively or predominantly homosexual and another 5% bisexual. But without careful definitions and reliable, large-scale, random sample studies in different cultures, we still cannot answer the intriguing question Alfred Kinsey asked 40 years ago about the frequency distributions of gender orientations (Diamond, 1998).

Unconventional Sexual Expressions. Since the mid-1960s, restrictive attitudes toward unconventional sexual behavior have changed considerably in the direction of tolerance, and even acceptance, in some areas. The prevalent obsession of Victorians with the debilitating evil of self-pollution has changed to a general acceptance of masturbation as a common and normal sexual outlet for adolescents, single persons of all ages, and even within marriage. Nationwide polls show that the percentage of Americans approving responsible premarital sexual relations, accepting oral sex, and enjoying contraceptive—nonprocreative—sexual relations is now a solid majority. By 1990, the number of American households of unmarried couples was approaching 3 million, five times higher than it was in 1970.

The growing tolerance of homosexuality includes the 1974 decision of the American Psychiatric Association to remove "unconventional sexual orientation" from its list of "mental disorders, diseases and abnormalities"; annual Gay Pride demonstrations across the nation commemorating the 1969 Stonewall Inn riot in Greenwich Village; the growing number of businesses and urban jurisdictions granting recognition and marital benefits to "domestic partners"; and the growing number of schools teaching a "family rainbow curriculum" (Celis, 1993). Although tolerance for other less conventional sexual objects and roles is less evident in American society, the open discussion of these patterns of behavior in the printed media and on television has contributed to more understanding and a less judgmental view.

Applying the social scripting and panerotic potential models to unconventional behavior gives us a new understanding of these sexual expressions. While the individual is born with a panerotic potential biased by its prenatal gender identity and gender orientation tendencies, the randomness of postnatal scripting and developmental vulnerability can play a major role in developing each person's own unique flavoring after birth. The "psychological linking" that ties specific objects, roles, behavior, or stimuli with sexual pleasure and sets up patterns of behavior appears to be random and unpredictable. A male may develop a fetishistic scripting that links a particular item of clothing or body part with sexual stimuli and pleasure because of some adolescent experience(s). Another male, exposed to a seemingly identical experience, may not be scripted for a fetish. A boy may link the wearing of feminine apparel with an erotic turn-on as his erotic and sexual behavior develops in adolescence and may become an adult transvestite. The roles of dominance and submission, linking pain with sexual arousal and pleasure, can result in sadomasochistic patterns or in the role-playing sexual games of bondage and discipline (Gagnon & Simon, 1973; Money, 1985, 1986, 1988). An unanswered question is why many more males than females develop vandalized love-maps for fetishes and socially deviant sexual orientations.

Unconventional gender expressions occur in the transvestite, the transgenderist, and the transsexual. Prenatal cross-gender neural encoding can result in a transvestite who experiences a compulsive episodic need to dress as the other gender. In other individuals, prenatal cross-gender neural encoding results in a chronic need to adopt the gender role and behaviors of the other sex. In the case of an anatomical male transgenderist, this means expressing himself as a male in heterosexual relations and marriage but being compelled to play the feminine social role in all other aspects of his life. The transsexual, on the other hand, may be either an anatomical male or female, with a gender identity that is in open conflict with his or her chromosomes and sexual anatomy (Bolin, 1988; Docter, 1988). In 1995, neurobiologists at the Netherlands Institute for Brain Research in Amsterdam reported found that a tiny region in the hypothalamus known as BSTc was 50% larger in gay and heterosexual men than it was in heterosexual women and male-to-female transsexuals. In rates, the hypothalamic BSTc plays a key role in male sexual behavior.

As one's gender identity and some aspects of one's gender role are irreversibly fixed before or soon after birth, psychotherapy alone has proved of little or no help to transvestites, transgenderists, and transsexuals.

For transvestites, the usual treatment has been counseling and support groups to help the individual and his(her) partner cope with an unalterable need. Recently, however, a new approach has been developed that uses neurotransmitter (serotonin) antagonists to lower the anxiety level of transvestites (and other paraphilics) enough to allow them to understand their behavior and alter it (Coleman & Cesnik, 1989, 1990; Francoeur, Koch, & Weis, 1998).

For the transgenderist, counseling and support groups are also useful. Since transgenderists are not interested in changing their sexual anatomy to conform with their gender identity and role, sex change surgery is not an option. For transsexuals, the most common solution today involves psychological screening and counseling coupled with surgery to allow their anatomy to conform with their gender identity.

Because of their deep-seated gender conflict and the social problems this triggers, many transsexuals suffer personality disorders that can only be relieved by sex change surgery (Bolin, 1988; Docter, 1988). A recent development, the publication of *Hermaphrodites with Attitudes*, a quarterly newsletter of the Intersex Society of North America, suggests a new awareness emerging among transsexuals who celebrate their intersex status and refuse sex reassignment surgery (Francoeur et al., 1998).

Gate 12: Puberty and Juvenile/Adult Gender Identity/Role. In Western societies, sexual orientation, romanticism, and erotic responses are linked together in our consciousness during puberty, when the surge of hormones trigger dramatic changes in secondary sexual characteristics and the maturation of the reproductive capacity.

The psychological effects of puberty are as dramatic as the more obvious physical changes. Forty years ago, Sullivan (1953) highlighted the preadolescent need for intimacy with persons of the same gender. With puberty, a new need for intimacy, reinforced by a lusty dynamism usually oriented toward persons of the other gender, emerges to conflict with the preadolescent same-sex need for intimacy. Building on this juvenile G-I/R with its natural, neural encoded sexual orientation, the maturation of puberty and adolescence leads to one's adult identification as a sexual person, a male or a female, with a definite more or less fixed gender role and a sexual orientation and affectional preference. Throughout this development, familial and social influences are crucial in the scripting and development of a healthy, positive sexual self-identity, as will be evident in subsequent sections of this chapter.

The concept of sexual scripting emphasizes the impact of life experiences, especially during adolescence, when our erotic and sexual behaviors are taking shape. Sexual scripting begins at birth and continues throughout one's life, although some stages are more susceptible to influence and others are fairly resistant to change. In the next section, we examine several aspects of scripting, in the birth process, childhood, and adolescence, with an emphasis on healthy and antisocial consequences.

Somatosensory/Affectional Nurturance

Our current understanding of the interaction of nature (genes, chromosomes, hormones, neural anatomy) with nurture (learning and scripting) at critical periods in our psychosexual development, outlined earlier, provides a framework in which we can examine several elementary and fundamental factors that deeply affect the wellness of our individual psychosexual development.

Birthing Nurturance

After World War II, European concepts in health care and childbirth found a fertile and receptive audience in America. Hospitals and schools promoted workshops in the Lamaze and Lebouyer methods of childbirth for prospective parents. The LaLeche League promoted breast-feeding (Arms, 1975; Wertz & Wertz, 1979).

In breaking with the traditional American obstetrical practice of delivery, including a heavy reliance on induced delivery and general anesthesia, the emphasis and concern shifted from the physician and the mother to making the birth of the new human as natural and comfortable as possible. The Leboyer "gentle birthing" emphasizes a delivery environment designed to reduce stress on the newborn and to provide a gentle transition from the warm quiet nurturing womb to the nurturing caresses of the parents. Mother and father handle the actual delivery, maintaining physical contact, and touching and stroking the infant from its first emergence from the vagina until it is comfortably nursing at the breast. The physician becomes a resource person in the background. Specialists in child development now recognize the long-term importance of the initial bonding between parents and infant that can be facilitated by more natural forms of delivery. The initial bonding between mother and child is mediated by nurturing touch, setting the stage for the child's expanding integration into society and its development of intimacy skills. An aphorism neatly sums up the process, as we move from "Skin Love to Kin Love to In Love" (Walsh, 1991).

Body Pleasure and the Origins of Violence

The recognition of the importance of nurturance in childbirth takes on added significance for the wholesome development of our sexual self-image when linked on the effects of touch and motion on the child and adolescent.

Harry and Margaret Harlow's pioneering laboratory experiments with monkeys have been extended by others to show how somatosensory affectional and kinesthetic stimuli (nurture-learning) directly affect specific neural circuits and pathways (nature) that regulate adult human behavior (Harlow, 1971; Harlow & Harlow, 1965; Mitchell, 1975). The specific neural system involved centers in the reciprocal relationship between the pleasure-processing system (the septum pellucidum or septal hippocampal circuits) and the violence and aggression-processing system (amygdala) in the limbic system, and in the kinesthetic-processing center in the vestibular-cerebellar system and frontal/temporal lobes of the mammalian brain (Prescott, 1975, 1989). Stimulation of one circuit system inhibits the activity and neural development of the other center. When the brain's somatosensory

pleasure is "turned on," the violence circuits are somehow "turned off": "The reciprocal relationship of pleasure and violence is highly significant, because certain sensory experiences during the formative periods of development will create a neuropsychological predisposition for either violence-seeking or pleasure-seeking behavior later in life" (Prescott, 1975, p. 65).

On the behavioral level, using the Textor Cross-Cultural Summary, Prescott (1989) found a strong correlation linking low levels of adult violence with high scores on the infant physical affection scale in specific societies. Similarly, in other societies, high levels of adult violence correlated with low physical affection scores. This correlation in 39 of 49 societies clearly indicates a very strong causal connection between the two variables.

The hypothesis becomes inescapable when the remaining 10 societies that did not fit the initial correlation were examined. In the six societies characterized by low infant physical affection and low adult physical violence, one finds a consistently permissive view of adolescent and premarital sex: "Thus, the detrimental effects of infant physical affectional deprivation seem to be compensated for later in life by sexual body pleasure experiences during adolescence" (Prescott, 1975, p. 67). Each of the four remaining societies, characterized by high infant nurturance and high adult violence, have strong taboos against premarital sexual behavior and place a very high value on premarital virginity: "It appears that the beneficial effects of infant physical affection can be negated by repression of physical pleasure later in life" (Prescott, 1975, p. 67). When the statistical analysis includes nurturance and body pleasuring during both infancy and adolescence, the reciprocal causal relation of nurturance and violent behavior holds for all 49 cultures.

In subsequent analyses using both contemporary American and other Western cultures, Prescott (1989, 1996) found that correlates of adult physical violence include negative attitudes toward gun control, abortion, nudity, sexual pleasure, premarital and extramarital sex, breast-feeding, and women, along with a glorification of war and usage of both drugs and alcohol. The correlates of high infant nurturance include such social factors as low class stratification, prolonged breast-feeding, a high sense of human dignity and the individual person, acceptance of abortion, acceptance of premarital and extramarital sex, low sex anxiety and dysfunction, deemphasis of private property and war, few children within an extended family structure, and peer relationships between women and men.

The importance of touch and kinesthetic stimuli is rooted in their ability to trigger the production and release of neuropeptides that are largely concentrated in the limbic system, the emotional center of the brain. The most interesting neuropeptides are the endorphins—endogenous, morphinelike substances that kill pain, cause euophoria, and sedate the individual. While the effects of endorphines vary, depending on where in the brain circuitry they are operating and the type of receptor with which they bind, these natural opiods combine with the hormone oxytocin released in the nursing mother to promote the bonding that occurs between the child and its mother or other adult during breast-feeding and other nurturing activities (Walsh, 1991).

Sketching the result of inadequate nurturance and kinesthetic stimuli during critical developmental stages, Prescott (1996) suggests a Somatosensory Affectional Deprivation (SAD) Syndrome. The SAD Syndrome is characterized by autisticlike, ritual rocking that may stimulate opioid production to compensate in part for kinesthetic deprivation, a lack of emotional development, limited self-awareness, self-directed violence, and a difficulty or inability to relate to others through touch, cuddling, and body pleasuring. Environmental factors can also contribute to the SAD Syndrome and its consequences. Poverty, crowding, and drugs in urban ghettos and the social acceptance or even celebration of violence in the media can promote somatosensory affectional deprivation. Sensory receptors and neural afferent tracts in these systems can be damaged during prenatal and/or postnatal development by alcohol, drugs, stress, illness, disease, anoxia, neurotoxins, and malnutrition.

The Sexual Assaulter

Complementing the insights of postnatal bonding and the SAD Syndrome, our understanding of the developmental processes that lead to antisocial and sexually violent personalities can deepen our understanding of the conditions and environment that may promote a balanced, healthy sexual maturation and the ability to enter into and maintain mature, rewarding intimate relationships.

In the 1970s, rehabilitative specialists gained insight into two questions. First, why do some men and women become obsessive-compulsive in their need to control other persons through assault, abuse, or seduction? Second, why do some persons use sex for this control while others turn to nonsexual antisocial behavior to achieve control? Among the main reasons that have been uncovered are:

1. A breakdown or failure in the development of an individual's ability to communicate with others as equals
2. A failure to see oneself as different but equal
3. A failure to develop the skills needed to relate in an intimate way with another person
4. A socialization process that reduces other people to sexual objects to be used at will (Groth, 1979; McCombie, 1980; Prendergast, 1991)

Socially deviant behavior often has its roots in an inadequate personality. An inadequate personality is not an inadequate person, but rather a person who perceives himself or herself as never being equal to his or her peers. A person with an inadequate personality is never satisfied that he or she has done the best that he or she could have done. Parental praise is not taken as earned or deserved, but only as given by the parent out of duty. This personality type can only see others as being better than he or she is. They always see themselves at the bottom of any comparison or ranking (Prendergast, 1991).

A child with an inadequate personality has a natural but exaggerated need to please parents and adults. In adolescence, this need shift to a wanting to please one's peers and be accepted as an equal by them. But the feelings of inadequacy block this goal.

In the developmental-descriptive profile proposed by Prendergast (1991, 1993, 1996), the child with an inadequate personality takes one of three directions:

1. Into a middle-of-the-road, healthy personal adjustment and socialization: the adjust-er
2. Into denial path, where refusal to deal with one's perceived inadequacy drives the individual to compensate with maladaptive but socially tolerated behavior, or with antisocial behavior of various types: the deny-er
3. Into the acceptance path where the individual is resigned to her or his inadequacy and compensates with a variety of maladaptive but socially tolerated or antisocial behaviors: the accept-er

The Path of Social/Personal Adjustment. A child with an inadequate personality may work through his or her feelings of inadequacy and to become relatively adjusted and balanced with the help of friends, parents, a teacher, a coach, or others.

When a child cannot resolve his or her perceived inadequacy, he or she will compensate for perceptions of inadequacy by either denial or acceptance. Denial and acceptance can be expressed in maladaptive but socially accepted or tolerated behavior, or in antisocial behavior.

The Path of Denial and Overcompensation Some people who have not resolved their feelings of inadequacy react by denial and overcompensation. The deny-er spends much time and energy trying to outdo others in sports, academics, or sexual activities. The socially acceptable deny-er may become the superior, the corporate executive controlling the lives of thousands of employees and millions of dollars. The male deny-er may also become the super stud, or

Don Juan. No matter how the deny-er tries to compensate, he or she is seldom content or satisfied (Prendergast, 1991).

When the denial of inadequacy takes a criminal or antisocial path, the deny-er may use physical force and terror to gain control, for example, by mugging, robbing, spouse or child abuse, or murder. In denying their feelings of inadequacy, some may use sex in an antisocial way, trying to gain control in compulsive, repetitive acts of sexual assault.

The Path of Acceptance and Seduction. The adolescent who takes the accept-er path simply "gives up." The accept-er views gaining the recognition of peers and seeing oneself as equal to them as impossible. Socially integrated accept-ers tend to find a comfortable niche. They become the clerk or secretary at the fiftieth desk who hardly ever considers the possibility of moving up to the forty-ninth desk.

Accept-ers generally enjoy their dependent role. They need protection and want a certain amount of direction from others. Unless a catastrophe hits, the accept-er will not try to change. The accept-er interprets verbal and physical abuse from a partner as evidence that he or she is "really loved and accepted."

Socially deviant accept-ers compensate for their accepted feelings of inadequacy by controlling others in seductive ways, for example, as embezzlers, forgers, or arsonists. When the accept-er seeks to compensate by gaining control through sexual seduction, she or he becomes a pedophile, hebophile, exhibitionist, voyeur, or obscene phone caller. Male accept-ers may also use seduction in seeking acceptance in passive homosexual behavior or with young children who want to please adults.

The obvious questions raised by this developmental-descriptive profile is why some persons with an inadequate personality use nonsexual behavior to gain control through violence or seduction, whereas others use sexual assault or seduction to gain the same end. In nine out of ten cases, the crucial factor appears to be an unresolved sexual trauma suffered at an early age, usually between ages 5 and 7. Although this trauma occurs early in development, it is usually not confronted until puberty and adolescence, when the child experiences an erotic/sexual awakening (Prendergast, 1991).

Rehabilitative therapies for convicted compulsive-repetitive sex offenders, like the Reeducation of Attitudes and Repressed Emotions (ROARE) technique, have a success rate of about 90% (Prendergast, 1991). In dealing with the whole developmental process that was diverted from a healthy path, ROARE reeducation, for instance, includes a thorough sex-education course using explicit films, a rage-induced regression designed to deal with the early sexual trauma when repressed, training in emotional expression, and reeducation of the self for a positive but reality-oriented body image and for a comfortableness with body pleasuring through masturbation and massage.

Religion and Sexual Values

While many societies use shame and an individual's responsibility for protecting the family reputation to regulate sexual behavior, Judaic and Christian traditions, and societies based on these value systems, have used personal guilt, the concept of sin, and the threat of eternal damnation to control sexual behavior. In the history of Christianity, the dominant theme has been a pervasive, negative attitude toward sexuality, sexual pleasure, and sexual expressions, particularly when the parties are not married, heterosexual, and open to reproduction (Lawrence, 1990; Ranke-Heinemann, 1990). (For a discussion of specific religious influences on sexual attitudes and values in 32 different contemporary cultures/countries, see Francoeur, 1997.)

Although religious value systems and attitudes vary, recent analyses indicate the existence of two distinct, underlying moral systems, each supported by its own unique philosophy and cosmology (weltanschauung). These two moral systems and their cosmologies represent the two ends of a continuum that encompasses a wide range of approaches to sexual behavior and relationships. At the cosmological end of the continuum is a fixed philosophy of nature, belief in a universe and human nature created in finished form by God "in the beginning." Supporting the evolving world or cosmogenic end of the continuum is a belief in a universe and human nature (including our sexuality) that is always changing and struggling to become what God intends it to become (Francoeur, 1983, 1988, 1989; Francoeur et al., 1998). Out of these two weltanschauungs come distinctly opposing views of human nature, the origin of evil, and the nature and purpose of human sex and sexuality.

In the fixed cosmos, humans were created perfect and evil results from a primeval "fall." Redemption, a return to paradise, depends on a savior, asceticism, and the avoidance of sensual pleasure. Religions rooted in a fixed philosophy of nature tend to stress a patriarchal, exclusively male clergy, literal interpretations of sacred texts, clear gender roles for men and women, a supernatural life hereafter as a reward for suffering here, and a legalistic, act-oriented, unchanging morality. Sexual activity is more often viewed as a demonic force that must be restrained lest it destroy the family and society. Sexual morality is based on marriage and reproduction, on "proper use" of the sexual (genital) organs in exclusive heterosexual coitus. Noncoital sex (autoerotic, oral, and anal), nonmarital sex, and homosexual activity are often considered unnatural and immoral, along with marital contraceptive (nonreproductive) intercourse.

In the evolving world perspective, physical and moral evil are inevitable, a natural part of the growth pains that humans experience in exploring and developing their potential as sexual persons. The focus shifts from the nature of genital acts to the human quality of relationships. Religious traditions that accept an evolving or process perspective tend to share authority between male and female clergy and blur the distinction between clergy and laity. More tolerant of the truths that other religions may express, these churches do not interpret their sacred texts literally and accept revelation as an ongoing reality. Gender roles are flexible, and morality emphasizes persons in their environment rather than acts and their conformity to unchanging laws. Human sexuality is viewed as a positive, natural, nurturing, and creative sensual energy. Sexual relations are seen as an important aspect of our growth and maturation as loving, fully human persons. Sex and marriage are linked together, but in a way that allows nonreproductive, nonmarital, and even nonheterosexual expressions as possible vehicles of expressions of love and creativity. This approach is much more tolerant of alternate lifestyles than fundamentalist religions are (Francoeur, 1983, 1988).

These two perspectives are expressed in sexual values derived from fundamentalist creationism (natural law), biblical covenant, and situation-humanistic traditions.

Fundamentalist Creationist Values

This perspective is clearly expressed in the teachings of the Southern Baptist Church, Church of the Latter-Day Saints, various evangelical groups, Roman Catholic Vatican statements, Hasidic and orthodox Jewish groups, Eastern Orthodox Christians, and statements by several lead speakers at the 1992 Republican National Convention.

A 1986 letter to the Bishops of the Catholic Church on the pastoral care of homosexual persons is typical: "The entire discussion of homosexuality is [based on] the theology of creation we find in Genesis.... Although the particular inclination of the homosexual person is not a sin, it is a more or less strong tendency ordered toward an intrinsic moral evil; and thus the inclination itself must be seen as an objective disorder" (Gramick & Furey, 1988, pp. 1–10). All homosexual acts and relationships "are condemned as a serious depravity and even presented in the Bible as the sad consequences of rejecting God" (Kosnick et al., 1977, p. 201). In his 1968 encyclical Humanae Vitae, Pope Paul VI claimed that Christian doctrine requires that all sexual and genital activity must occur only within the framework of heterosexually monogamous marriage. In its guide on premarital sex, the minority report from the General Assembly of the Presbyterian Church (United Presbyterian Church, 1991, Part 2, p. 53), urges discussion of the loneliness and difficulty of the single state in the context of "God's providential will" and the clear wisdom and moral necessity of "Just say no!"

Within this divine order perspective, various positions on contraception, masturbation, and divorce exist, with some Protestant fundamentalists accepting contraception and the Eastern Orthodox Christians accepting divorce and remarriage (Marty & Appleby, 1992). Advocates of this perspective are often strongly opposed to sex education that includes safer sex education, distribution of free condoms in public schools and church-related hospitals, and the "Children of the Rainbow" elementary school curricula, with a reading list that includes books, like *Heather Has Two Mommies* and *Daddy's Roommate*, that present homosexuality and gay and lesbian families as acceptable.

Covenantal Process Values

Most evident in Protestantism, this value system was clearly expressed in the United Presbyterian Church U.S.A. (1970) document on sexuality and the human community and repeated in the 1991 majority report of the General Assembly's Special Committee on Sexuality. The 1970 document lists four goals or values for all interpersonal relationships, whether or not they include sexual intimacy:

1. Enhancing rater than limiting one's spiritual freedom
2. Expressing a compassionate and consistent concern for the well-being of the partner
3. Strengthening the creative potential of persons called to stewardship in God's world
4. Expressing joy and opening to persons the flow of grace that enables them to live without despair

Recognizing that "the Christian community encompasses a wide diversity of racial, ethnic, and cultural groups, and therefore a wide variety of assessments of sexuality and sexual-behavior" (p. 7), the covenantal approach emphasizes God's promise of "creating, forgiving and healing love" without attempting to categorize specific sexual acts or relationships as either inherently good or inherently bad.

Supporting the covenantal approach is a view of divine revelation quite different from that endorsed by the fundamentalist creationist natural law approach, evident in this Episcopalian statement:

> The Judaeo-Christian tradition is a tradition precisely because, in every historical and social circumstance, the thinking faithful have brought to bear their best interpretation of the current realities in correlation with their interpretation of the tradition as they have inherited it. Thus, the truth in the Judaeo-Christian tradition is a dynamic process to be discerned and formulated rather than a static structure to be received. (Thayer et al., 1987, p. 10)

The Bible is misunderstood and misused when approached as a book of moral prescriptions directly applicable to all moral dilemmas. Rather, the Bible is the record of the response to the Word of God addressed to Israel and to the Church throughout centuries of changing social, historical, and cultural conditions. The faithful responded within the realities of their particular situation, guided by the direction of previous revelation, but not captive to it (Thayer, 1987, p. 9). Other statements and study documents in this perspective are found in Kosnick et al. (1977), United Church of Christ (1977), and the 1991 majority report of the United Presbyterian Church Special Committee on Human Sexuality.

Situation Ethics and Humanistic Values

According to Joseph Fletcher, author of *Situation Ethics: The New Morality* (1966), "sexual behavior is morally acceptable in any form—heterosexual, homosexual, bisexual, autosexual (masturbation), or polysexual. What makes any act right or wrong is what it is intended to accomplish—its foreseeable consequences. Sex is a means to an end beyond the sexual act itself. No sexual act is intrinsically right or wrong. No sexual act, in and of itself, should be either blamed or praised apart from whatever human values motivated and guided it" (personal communication; see also Kirkendall, 1976, pp. 4–6).

The Reproductive–Relational Dichotomy

A major shift in our image and understanding of human sexuality came with the reproductive technologies of the 1960s. While some rank the contraceptive pill among the most influential of human revolutions, Reiss (1990) points out that if women's social programming, restrictive sexual upbringing, and the taboo against premarital sex or at least sex without a serious commitment had not already been undermined, the pill would not have gained wide acceptance. Before women could embrace the pill, they had to become convinced of their right to sexual equality with men and their right to sexual pleasure and fulfillment. In addition society had to accept the sexual equality and rights of women.

Although the contraceptive pill was not the trigger for the 1960s' sexual revolution, it did promote a psychological and cultural separation of human reproduction from sexual intercourse. This message has been reinforced by the birth of the world's first test tube baby in 1978. In recent years, the media have documented our revolution in reproductive technologies. The media carry stories about why tens of thousands of American women conceive each year by artificial insemination, about clinics specializing in embryo transplants, and about surrogate mothers paid by women unable to carry their own child. After 2 or more million years of experiencing sex and reproduction as inseparable realities, men and women today engage in relational or recreational sex as a form of interpersonal pleasure and communication without the fear of pregnancy.

This reality has forced every church to recognize the reality that most sexual activities today are not engaged in for procreation and that a significant proportion of sexual relations occurs before, after, or outside the marital union. In the 1990s every church is confronted by a growing tension between traditional heterosexual-marital-procreative sexual ethics and the need for recognizing, accommodating, and integrating men and women who are living a wide variety of sexual lifestyles and relationships that do not fit into the traditional morality. In many denominations, a battle rages over the ordination of sexually active gay men and lesbians to ministry as clergy, priests, or rabbis.

In analyzing the current conflict and prospect for a devastating "civil war" within the churches, the Minority Report to the Presbyterian General Assembly (1991) compared today's situation with the debate among early Christians over the extent to which Gentile converts would be required to accept circumcision and the tenets of Judaism before becoming Christians. The outcome of recent church debates cannot be predicted, but accommodating the consequences of the evolution of relational sex will not be without major stress (Thayer et al., 1987; United Presbyterian Church, 1991).

Negative Learning and Sexual Dysfunctions

Intimacy Skills

Achieving sexual maturity and health is a lifelong process that each of us experiences within a particular sociocultural milieu. Crucial in our development of intimacy skills is the presence of physical nurturance in infancy, childhood, and adolescence (see Prescott's research discussed earlier in this chapter).

A complementary view by Lorna and Philip Sarrel (1980) highlights the nine aspects of this development as:

1. An evolving positive sense of one's body image and gender
2. Learning to deal with, overcome, or moderate the guilt, shame, and childhood inhibitions associated with sexual thoughts and behavior
3. A gradual loosening of libidinal ties with parents and family
4. Learning what is erotically pleasurable
5. Achieving a comfortableness with and understanding of our sexual orientation
6. Achieving an increasingly satisfying and rich sexual life, free of compulsions and dysfunctions

7. A growing awareness of being a sexual person and of the place and value of sexual intimacy, communications, and pleasuring in whatever lifestyle we choose

8. Accepting the responsibility for ourselves and our part in the sexual unfolding of our partner

9. A gradually increasing ability to experience eroticism as one aspect of intimacy with another person

Achieving sexual maturity means developing one's self image as a socially integrated and healthy sexual person capable of self-fulfilling and other enriching intimacy. This lifelong challenge is a process filled with risks. These include a variety of internal and external barriers, roadblocks, mistakes, misadventures, traumas, misinformation, and social scripting by parents, family, and the subculture and society in which we grow up. Each of us reacts to these influences in our own unique way, even as we experience our own unique combination of these factors.

The Sexual Response Cycle, Dysfunctions, and Therapies

Sexual Responses. The behavioral research of Masters and Johnson (1966, 1970) gave us some important insights into the physiological stages of sexual functioning, dividing the sexual response cycle into excitement, plateau, orgasm, and resolution stages. After some sex therapists criticized the physiological exclusivity of the Master's and Johnson model, David Reed (Stayton, 1989) proposed a psychological overlay in what he termed the Erotic Stimulus Pathway mode. In Reed's model, (1) seduction (being sexually turned on and sexually turning on the potential partner) occurs during the Desire and early Excitement stages, (2) a focus on sensations dominates during the late excitement and plateau stages, (3) psychological surrender coincides with organism, and (4) reflection on the encounter during resolution and afterward leads to the decision of whether or not to continue the relationship (Stayton, 1989). Masters and Johnson have also been criticized for labeling their sexual response cycle model as "the human sexual response," implying that all normal human sexual responses must fit this phallic, coitus, and organism-oriented model (Tiefer, 1991).

Masters and Johnson used their response cycle model to classify the types of sexual dysfunctions during the sexual arousal stage as (1) inhibited sexual arousal (erectile problems in males and inhibited vaginal lubrication in females, (2) painful intercourse (dyspareunia) in both men and women, and (3) vaginal spasms (vaginismus). They also classified orgasmic dysfunctions as (1) early ejaculation, (2) inhibited ejaculation in men, and (3) inhibited orgasm in women. Concurrently, Masters and Johnson devised behavioral exercises that would be useful in treating these dysfunctions. In 1974 and 1979, Helen Singer Kaplan expanded our understanding of the "new sex therapy" by integrating the new behavioral therapies with more traditional psychotherapy.

Desire Phase Dysfunctions. Kaplan also added a new dimension to the classification of arousal and orgasmic dysfunctions by dealing with antecedent problems in the desire phase, focusing on (1) inhibited sexual desire (ISD) or lack of sexual desire (LSD), (2) desire phase conflicts in which a couple experience conflicting levels of desire for sexual intimacy and intercourse, and (3) sexual aversion, which includes a phobic reaction and negative physical responses.

Inhibited sexual desire and desire conflicts may be due to psychological, organic, or a combination of psychological and organic causes. Sexual aversion is due solely to psychological causes. (Psychological and organic causes for sexual dysfunctions are discussed later.)

Excitement/Plateau Phase Dysfunctions. Inhibited sexual arousal (male ISA), formerly labeled impotence, is the inability of a male to have and maintain an erection sufficient for coitus. Female ISA, formerly referred to as frigidity, is the inability of a female to become aroused and experience labial and clitoral erection and concurrently vaginal lubrication to facilitate coitus.

Orgasm Phase Dysfunctions. A male may experience inhibited male orgasm (IMO) during coitus, but not during masturbation and/or oral sex. Early (premature) ejaculation is surrounded by considerable debate about what constitutes early or premature ejaculation, since the term depends very much on the female partner and what she considers "too early" relative to her own orgasm and pleasure needs. Inhibited female orgasm also raises questions about whether a woman can be said to experience IFO if she does not experience orgasm as a result of penile thrusting during coitus but has an orgasm before or after intercourse as a result of manual, digital, or oral stimulation.

Other Sexual Difficulties. Painful intercourse (dyspareunia) is due to physical deformities in the genitals, genital infections, or lack of vaginal lubrication. Vaginal spasms (vaginismus) prevent or interfere with vaginal intercourse.

Primary and Secondary Sexual Dysfunctions. A sexual dysfunction is termed primary when the person has always experienced it in sexual encounters, regardless of the situation or partner involved. A sexual dysfunction is said to be secondary when it occurs only with a certain partner or partners, or in certain situations. The term situational dysfunction is also sometimes used for a secondary dysfunction.

Organic and Psychological Causes. Organic factors such as medications, tranquilizers, poor nutrition, antihypertensive drugs, alcohol, narcotics, physical impairments, diabetes, spinal cord traumas, kidney dialysis, and hormone imbalances may be the primary cause in an estimated 20%–30% of the cases of sexual dysfunctions (Bullard, 1988; Francoeur & Leyson, 1991; Seagrave, 1988). The psychosocial and relational origins underlying the majority of sexual dysfunctions have taken on new importance with our growing knowledge of the developmental aspects of our sexual unfolding. A healthy sexual development depends on both normal biological development and a positive social scripting from our family, ethnic and cultural background, religious training, and societal roots, as well as an adequate nurturance. Yet, because every human experiences a mixture of positive and negative inputs into their sexual development (there is no such thing as a perfectly normal and absolutely healthy social and biological environment), every human encounters an occasional or persistent sexual dysfunction.

Sexual aversion is exclusively due to psychological causes: a poor body image and self-image, strong feelings of sexual inadequacy, a traumatic sexual experience in the past, performance anxiety, strong guilt feelings about sex, overwhelming fears of pregnancy or sexually transmitted diseases, strong negative messages from family or society, and fears of becoming involved, vulnerable, or intimate. The lack of sexual desire is much more often due to psychological factors, although organic causes can certainly be factors. Again, the psychological factors may echo those noted for the anxiety reactions of sexual aversion, but one can add others, such as hostility toward the other sex or the need for "the lure of forbidden fruit," which can reduce sexual desire in a legitimate relationship (Seagrave, 1988).

The same organic and psychological factors that may lead to sexual aversion and the lack of sexual desire can also come into play in dysfunctions that affect sexual arousal and orgasm. To those listed here, we can add others: inability to relate to another person as a peer, lack of a positive sexual self image leading to "spectatoring" or constant attempts to "observe" and evaluate one's own performance, misinformation and lack of understanding of what sexual relations may involve, and guilt and anxiety messages about sex in general or about specific sexual behaviors. Questions about what is "normal" or "natural" in sexual relations and behaviors can be based on a variety of criteria—social, religious, legal, statistical, medical, psychological, and personal. Conflicts between what the individual believes is normal and what his or her partner or society views as normal can result in different sexual dysfunctions, depending on the individual's reaction (Haeberle, 1978).

The long-standing American dedication to psychotherapy, the emergence of behavioral therapies for sexual dysfunctions in the 1960s, and their popularity based on simplicity led most sex therapists, until recently, to the belief that 90% or more of all cases of sexual dysfunction are primarily psychological in origin. That belief, however, was never supported with research data. Wagner and Metz (1980), Wagner and Green (1981), Schumacher and Lloyd (1981), and others seriously challenged this belief. Schumacher, for instance, found that 72% of impotent men had an organic disease, compared with only 12% of men with no erectile problem. Wagner created the first casts of the penile arteries and veins, documenting in men with erectile problems not uncommon anatomical causes of impotence. These include abnormal arteries incapable of bringing a blood supply sufficient for erection, insufficient cavernous tissue, and faulty vein valves, which reduce erection by allowing blood to leak out instead of being retained.

Four factors must be present for normal sexual arousal; for vasocongestion, which results in penile, clitoral, and labial erection; and for vaginal lubrication in women. These factors are (1) for men, a proper blood supply to the penis; (2) intact pelvic nerves, which tell the arteries and veins when to open and close; (3) normal erectile tissue capable of engorgement; and (4) a reasonable emotional milieu. Until recently, most sex research and therapy focused on the last of these four factors, the psychological. The new awareness stresses the importance of a variety of anatomical and physiological disorders as the main cause in perhaps 30% of all sexual dysfunctions and as a significant contributing factor in another 30%–50% of dysfunctions.

"Impotence can be caused by virtually every drug listed in the *Physician's Desk Reference*," according to Richard Spark (Brody, 1983, p. C8), an endocrinologist at Harvard Medical School. Antihypertensive medication for high blood pressure, antiasthmatics, narcotics, antidepressants, and tranquilizers are among the more common offending medications. Low testosterone or high prolactin levels, vascular anomalies including those associated with atherosclerosis, and neuropathies (nerve dysfunctions) associated with diabetes, arthritis, and multiple sclerosis are also now part of the etiological picture. However, this research is only starting, and our knowledge of the anatomical and physiological basis of sexual function, especially in the female, is still quite primitive and limited (Whipple, 1991). In 1998, several pharmaceutical companies began marketing prescription and over-the-counter oral and transdermal medications that hold promise of aiding four out of five of the 30 million American males estimated to be suffering from erectile problems (Stipp & Whitaker, 1998).

Sexual Therapies. Short-term, task-oriented behavioral therapies may be useful in treating many simpler sexual dysfunctions, but many sexual therapists are finding it helpful to use a broader based, multimodal therapy. The new therapies combine behavioral exercises with counseling and psychotherapy to focus on both the current dysfunction and its origins in deficiencies in the individual's sexual unfolding, numerous examples of which have been cited in earlier sections of this chapter. Few therapists today who deal with sexual dysfunctions see themselves as pure sex therapists. More and more, the term sex therapy refers to a focus of intervention used by psychologists, marriage counselors, family therapists, and psychotherapists rather than to a distinctive and exclusive technique (Kaplan, 1974, 1979, 1983; Leiblum & Pervin, 1989; Leiblum & Rosen, 1988; Messer, 1986). Informal self-help and support groups also provide opportunities for dealing with sexual problems and difficulties with gender-conflicted persons and troubled, recovering, or dysfunctional individuals and their partners.

As with the extensive rehabilitation and reeducation of the compulsive repetitive sexual assaulter mentioned earlier, restoring the person with a sexual dysfunction to a healthy state means dealing with and remedying whatever deficiencies may exist in his or her early psychosexual development. Obviously, this therapy and remedial reeducation have different meanings in different times and settings, depending on what is considered "normal"–statistically, religiously, socially, or legally—in one's particular subculture and milieu. The precise meaning of sexual health and maturity is dynamic and ever-changing as our culture and subcultures change.

AIDS and the Family

As the AIDS pandemic continues through its second decade in the United States, unforseen issues have emerged as important considerations in attempts to meet the needs of people living with AIDS (PLWAs). What began as a disease syndrome affecting individuals has become a problem that confronts whole families in America. Researchers, health providers, and policy makers have had to rework their approaches to take into account the impact that AIDS has on family members, both immediate and extended. Our definition of "family" has undergone much change throughout this pandemic. As we consider the people who care for PLWAs, and those who care about them, family has come to be defined much more broadly than before. The family of origin has been replaced or extended to include non-blood-related friends, lovers, AIDS buddies, and others who provide emotional and instrumental support (Giaquinta, 1989).

For many PLWAs, estrangement from birth families is a way of life. AIDS exacerbates those earlier problems. Others become estranged after their diagnosis is discovered. Families who have not disclosed the illness of their family member live with fear of ostracism and discrimination. If an AIDS

diagnosis is kept secret within the family, social isolation becomes a continuing problem. Family pressures escalate if children are involved, especially if those children are infected (Glaser, 1991; Tasker, 1992). The financial strain of caring for adults and/or children with AIDS can be considerable. Finding competent doctors is an additional serious challenge throughout the country. Medical costs, health insurance, adequate health care and social support, caregiving, child custody, disclosure, stigma, discrimination, loss, and grieving are among the troubling issues facing families and others living with AIDS (Macklin, 1989; McDonell, Abell, & Miller, 1991; Younge, 1989).

Emerging Populations and Changing Locales

AIDS is no longer found in what were originally perceived to be the only affected American AIDS populations—white, middle-class gay men and minority intravenous drug users in the inner cities (Voeller, 1991; Wiener, 1991). AIDS is now found in:

- People who live in rural locations
- Middle- and upper-class women, many of whom do not misuse drugs or alcohol
- Women who have only vaginal sex with men
- Women who have rectal sex with men, but do not report this behavior
- Women who have received contaminated donor semen
- Women who have had oral sex with other women
- Middle- and upper-class men
- Men who have only vaginal sex with women, and do not have sex with other men
- Black, Hispanic, and Asian gay/bisexual men
- Teenagers who have been sexually abused as children
- People who use drugs, such as heroin, but do not use needles
- Athletes who use contaminated needles while injecting illegal steroids
- Women with blood-clotting disorders
- People who have received contaminated organ transplants and other body tissues
- Senior citizens
- Babies who nurse from infected mothers

There is no longer a statistically precise AIDS profile or pattern. To a great extent, epidemiological categories have become meaningless.

The spread of AIDS to rural and small-town locations is worth noting. Most people still equate AIDS with major urban areas, and, true, the numbers of cases are highest there. However, the pandemic has diffused from urban epicenters past suburbia and into small, rural enclaves in the United

States (Cleveland & Davenport, 1989). The spread of AIDS in Africa along truck routes as men seek sex away from home is not unlike the spread of AIDS along major highways in the United States, as people travel in and out of metropolitan AIDS epicenters. The government is paying little attention to rural AIDS in America; it is the least understood and least researched part of our national epidemic, with numbers of infected rising dramatically.

Limited research shows that some PLWAs who left their rural birthplaces for life in the city are now returning to their rural families to be cared for. Many PLWAs who grew up in cities are leaving their urban birthplaces and moving to the country, where they believe it is healthier for them, mentally and physically. This is especially true for recovering addicts whose city friends have died of AIDS and who hope to escape a similar fate.

Besides the "in-migration" of people with AIDS to rural locations, there are many indigenous people in small towns who are infected as well. The numbers of cases of HIV/AIDS is increasing rapidly in rural America, where social services are inadequate, medical care is generally poor, and community denial is a reality. Federal and state monies continue to be channeled to inner-city agencies, leaving rural and small-town providers with scant resources to ease increasing caseloads (Hendrixson, 1996/1997).

Complexion of the Pandemic

The face of AIDS is changing in other ways, as well. There is now a considerable number of infected people who have outlived medical predictions about their morbidity and mortality. These are divided into two groups: asymptomatic nonprogressors and long-term survivors. Both groups test HIV antibody-positive, indicating past infection with HIV.

Despite being HIV antibody-positive, the first group shows no other laboratory or clinical symptoms of HIV. The second group has experienced immune suppression and some opportunistic infections and is diagnosed as having AIDS, but continues to live beyond its expected life span (Laurence, 1994). In addition, there are others who are inexplicably uncharacteristic:

- People who have been diagnosed with AIDS, but who do not test HIV-antibody-positive, meaning that there is no indication of previous exposure to the virus, despite their illnesses
- People who have "retro-converted" from testing HIV antibody-positive to now testing HIV antibody-negative
- People who are repeatedly exposed to HIV through sex or contaminated blood and who do not become infected

Scientists have no explanation for these anomalies. Little research has been done on people who do not fit the accustomed pattern physicians look for. Yet, the very fact that they challenge medical expectations is a clue that they hold answers that may help thousands of others in this country.

In many ways, some new drug treatments have helped infected people forestall serious illnesses, turning AIDS into more of a chronic than an acute illness syndrome. Yet many PLWAs have renounced azidothymidine (AZT) and other toxic antiretroviral drugs because of their serious side effects. Increasing numbers of patients are embracing alternative therapies—physical, mental, and spiritual—rather than taking potent AIDS drugs. Others are combining the best of conventional and unconventional medicine in their own self-styled treatment plans. The new protease inhibitors offer much promise, but it is too early to know what long-term side effects they may produce. The bottom line is that AIDS no longer automatically equates with death.

HIV-Positive Children Coming of Age

As life is extended, more and more children born with the virus are moving through late childhood and early adolescence in relatively good physical health. New challenges await them and their families. Some children may know they are infected with HIV; others may not. They continue to grow socially, with sexual feelings beginning to emerge. How do we help them fit in with their uninfected peers? How do we teach them about their sexuality? How do we prepare them for dating situations? What do we say when they speak of marriage hopes? How do we teach them about safer sex? What new approaches in HIV/AIDS education should health teachers consider as these children enter their classes? Parents, teachers, and youth leaders are wrestling with new questions that were unanticipated 10 years ago when we believed that HIV antibody-positive children would not live much beyond toddlerhood.

Conclusion

In the years of the AIDS pandemic, we have no cure and no vaccine for this disease. Thousands have died in our country, most of them young people. Thousands more have died in other countries. New advances in drug treatments and alternative/holistic modalities have helped some American PLWAs, but many families continue to silently mourn the death of their loved ones. The stigma of AIDS is ever-present; the fear continues. Yet, compassion and love have emerged, as well, as caring people reach out to help those who are suffering. AIDS appears to have "dug in" for the long term while science looks for answers. In the meanwhile, we need to ask two questions. First, as scientists search for the truth of AIDS, are they asking the right questions? Second, as the disease shifts from its former pattern of early, premature death to a more manageable long-term chronic illness, are we meeting the needs of all the people infected and affected by this disease—PLWAs, their families, and their loved ones?

Trends and Projections

Several major social developments in this century appear to be forcing a major paradigm shift in our understanding of human sexuality: feminism and a continuing shift toward gender equality, the contraceptive and reproductive technologies, a recognition of the biological roots of the gender and gender orientation rainbows, the efforts of churches to develop a new sexual morality for the twenty-first century, the election of President Clinton and the increasing split between the conservative fundamentalist religious right and the secular and mainstream religious left, increasing pressure on government and the workplace to recognize the civil rights of homosexual persons, and, of course, the impact of AIDS on human relations. The combined effect of these developments appears likely to be a break in the ancient cycle of liberal–conservative pendulum swings (Ehrenreich, 1986; Francoeur, 1996; Jaspers, 1953). We appear to be on the verge of a major paradigm shift, projecting the evolution of human sexuality and lifestyles into a quite new orbit. In this paradigm shift, seven trends may be projected for the future of American sexuality:

1. An increasing need to understand human sexuality as the lifelong interaction of nature (genes, hormones, sexual anatomy, and neural templates) and nurture (social environment, ethnic and cultural learning). This includes efforts to understand better (1) the evolutionary pressures of natural selection that underlie our patterns of monogamy, polygamy, adultery, and divorce (Fisher, 1992); (2) the neurotransmitters and hormonal factors (natural endorphines, amphetamines, and oxytocin) that affect our falling in love and bonding; and (3) genes, familial tendencies, and neuroanatomical circuits possibly associated with gender orientations.

2. "Desexing" our sexual behavior, with less emphasis on coital and performance pressures; a growing appreciation of the panerotic, nurturing character of all our senses; and a comfortable diffusion of sexuality throughout the whole body spirit that makes us the sexual persons we are. Three factors promoting this trend are: (1) growing pressure from women for men to break out of their phallic/coital obsessions,

(2) the increasing number of sexually active men in their later years when erectile/coital performance naturally declines, and (3) the continuing threat of AIDS (Francoeur, 1996b).

3. "Demaritalizing," with an increasing breakdown of the social, legal, and moral limitations of sexual behavior and intercourse to married couples and a growing acceptance of sexual intimacy among single adolescents and adults. Recent data indicate a significant shift toward earlier puberty with half of African-American girls and one in six white girls beginning puberty by age 8 while the average onset of menses has remained steady about age 12. This earlier onset of puberty and the increasing trend to delay marriage increases the pressure on society and parents to deal with adolescent sexuality (Herman-Giddens et al., 1997). One aspect of this will be society's need to deal with the increasing number of adolescent and adult women who, for a variety of immature and mature reasons, choose to be sexually active with the risk of becoming single mothers. As life expectancies continue to rise, along with social mobility and women in the workforce, society and individuals will need to deal with the functional values of sexual exclusivity and lifelong pair bonding (Chapman, 1986; Fisher, 1992; Francoeur, 1996; Richardson, 1985).

4. "Degenderizing" sexual behavior and values, with increasing attention to the quality of the intimacy shared by two or more persons, regardless of their genders and sexual anatomies. This will include recognition of homosexual unions and domestic partners of all types.

5. "Degenitalizing" human reproduction, making pregnancy by coitus or the growing resources of genetic and reproductive technologies a conscious, if less frequent, choice that maximizes the health of the offspring.

6. An accelerated "decriminalizing" and "normalizing" of variant sexual behaviors and relationships. Civil and criminal law will continue to regulate the sexual behavior where preadolescent minors are involved or where physical harm or public disorder result.

7. "Spiritualizing" our human sexuality, focusing on sexual intimacy as a way of transcending the limits of the individual and relating intimately and reverently to other persons and, through them, with the cosmos. In recognizing our persistent need for nurturance, the "pluralism" and "relationalizing" of sex will cut across many traditional boundaries of age differences, handicaps, marital status, and gen-

der, replacing patriarchal, phallocentric concerns for coital performance and controlling female sexuality with a new more holistic, sensual erotic awareness and expression that recognizes gender differences in sexual intimacy while affirming gender equality (Francoeur, 1996).

The increasing pluralism of human sexuality will create problems and tensions of adaptation. Many people will retreat into the security of traditional values, denying the changes that are occurring all around them. Others, educated for and comfortable with change, decision making, and flexibility, will adapt and grow. But for the majority of Americans, the most common path is likely to be one of stumbling, tension-filled attempts to accept inevitable changes over which they will have little control.

Clinical Implications and Research Suggestions

In this review of human sexual development as we know it today, several implications can be highlighted for clinical practice (Bullough, 1994). The first implication involves reconceptualizing human sexuality to incorporate our new understanding of the nature, meaning, and social functions of human sexuality. This sex-affirming reconceptualization will have definite consequences in clinical work with women, children, teenagers, the aged, gay men and women, single persons, the physically handicapped, and the mentally retarded. Our changing concepts of what is "healthy," "normal," "abnormal," "conventional," "unconventional," and "dysfunctional" will greatly modify clinical practice.

A second consequence with clinical significance is the social restructuring that will have to occur as we adjust to these new meanings and functions of human sexuality and a variety of domestic and family forms. As the range of conventional and socially acceptable sexual behavior and relations expands, new social and emotional support systems will be needed for sexually active single persons of all ages, for men and women in flexible, nonexclusive relationships, for new family forms, and for persons with a gay or bisexual orientation. An important element in this social restructuring will be the legal recognition of these new meanings and functions. Each of these restructurings will impact clinical practice and education.

A third clinical implication is our obvious need to develop new value systems to guide us in sexual or intimate relations and in reproduction. Although the main focus here will be the articulation of two distinct, general value systems (one for intimacy and the other for reproduction), clinical practice will at the same time require a new sensitivity to the diversity of people's sexual and familial value systems,

which stem from their religious, economic, ethnic, and racial diversity. The as-yet-little-studied variations in American ethnic values will very likely become much more important in clinical practice as we expand our knowledge and appreciation of sexuality and erotic pleasure beyond the middle-class, white, educated criteria that have dominated our clinical practice (Francoeur et al., 1998). In 1997, Eng and Butler reported that the incidence rates of curable sexually transmissible diseases (excluding HIV) in the United States are the highest in the developed world, with rates that are 50 to 100 times higher than other industrialized nations. For example, the reported incidence of gonorrhea in 1995 was 150 cases per 100,000 persons in the United States versus 3 cases per 100,000 in Sweden. The long-standing inability of American society to deal with sexual behavior and its consequent STDs continues to have a disproportionate impact on women, infants, young people, and racial/ethnic minorities.

The fourth clinical implication is our need to develop a commonly accepted nomenclature and basic models of human sexual response, dysfunctions, and therapy, emphasizing the overriding similarities and differences of male and female patterns. As we develop new nomenclature and new models, we will need to incorporate and integrate the sexual, erotic, and nurturance dimensions outlined in this chapter. As this new holistic view emerges and becomes part of clinical practice, human sexuality will again become an integral part of human development, resolving the Platonic-Kantian dualism of past Western civilization.

Each of the four clinical implications mentioned here contains a variety of obvious issues and problems for productive and promising research in the years ahead. We will need research on each of the four developments. Research will also be needed to ascertain how each of these new developments can be used to improve diagnosis and treatment, as well as to provide an improved social climate for personal development.

References

Allen, L. S., & Gorski, R. A. (1991). Sexual dimorphism of the anterior commissure and massa intermedia of the human brain. *Journal of Comparative Neurobiology, 312,* 97–104.

Allen, L. S., & Gorski, R. A. (1992). Sexual orientation and the size of the anterior commissure in the human brain. *Proceedings National Academy of Sciences U.S.A. Neurobiology, 89,* 7199–7202.

Arms, S. (1975). *Immaculate deception: A new look at women and childbirth in America.* Boston: Houghton Mifflin.

Bailey, J. M., & Pillard, R. C. (1991). A genetic study of male sexual orientation. *Archives of General Psychiatry, 48,* 1089–1096.

Bailey, J. M., Pillard, R. C., Neale, C., & Agyei, Y. (1993). Heritable factors influence sexual orientation in women. *Archives of General Psychiatry, 50,* 217–223.

Bakwin, H. (1974). Erotic feelings in infants and young children. *Medical Aspects of Human Sexuality, 8*(10), 200–215.

Barinaga, M. (1991, August 30). Is homosexuality biological? *Science, 253,* 956–957.

Bell, A., & Weinberg, M. (1978). *Homosexualities: A study of diversity among men and women.* New York: Simon & Schuster.

Bell, A., Weinberg, M. S., & Hammersmith, S. K. (1981). *Sexual preference: Its development in men and women.* Bloomington: Indiana University Press.

Bolin, A. (1988). *In search of Eve: Transsexual rites of passage.* South Hadley, MA: Bergin & Garvey.

Borneman, E. (1983). Progress in empirical research on children's sexuality. *SIECUS Report, 12*(2), 1–5.

Boswell, J. (1980). *Christianity, social tolerance, and homosexuality.* Chicago: University of Chicago Press.

Brody, J. E. (1983, September 28). How drugs can cause decreased sexuality. *New York Times,* C1, C10.

Bullard, D. (1988). Treatment of desire disorders in the medically ill and physically disabled. In S. R. Leiblum & R. C. Rosen (Eds.), *Sexual desire disorders* (pp. 348–385). New York: Guilford.

Bullough, V. L. (1994). *Science in the bedroom: A history of sex research.* New York: Basic Books.

Calderone, M. (1985). Adolescent sexuality: Elements and genesis. *Pediatrics* (Suppl.), 699–703.

Califia, P. (1997). *Sex changes: The politics of transgenderism.* San Francisco: Cleis.

Celis, W. (1993, January 6). Schools across U.S. cautiously adding lessons on gay life. *New York Times.*

Chapman, A. B. (1986). *Man-sharing: Dilemma or choice.* New York: Morrow.

Colapinto, J. (1997, December 11). The true story of John-Joan. *Rolling Stone,* 55ff.

Coleman, E., & Cesnik, J. (1989). Use of lithium carbonate in the treatment of autoerotic asphixia. *American Journal of Psychotherapy, 43*(2), 277–286.

Coleman, E., & Cesnik, J. (1990). Skoptic syndrome: The treatment of an obsessional gender dysphoria with lithium carbonate and psychotherapy. *American Journal of Psychotherapy, 44*(2), 204–217.

Colonna, A. B., & Solnit, A. J. (1981). Infant sexuality. *SIECUS Report, 9*(4), 1–2.

Conn, J., & Kanner, L. (1940). Spontaneous erections in childhood. *Journal of Pediatrics, 16,* 337–340.

Diamond, M. (1998). Bisexualities: A biological perspective. In: E. Haeberle & R. Gindorf (eds.), *Bisexualities: The ideology and practice of sexual contact with both men and women* (pp. 53–80). New York: Continuum.

Diamond, M., & Karlen, A. (1980). *Sexual decisions.* Boston: Little, Brown.

Docter, R. F. (1988). *Trasvestites and transsexuals: Toward a theory of cross-gender behavior,* New York: Plenum.

Dorner, G. (1988). Neuroendocrine response to estrogen and brain differentiation in heterosexuals, homosexuals, and transsexuals. *Archives of Sexual Behavior, 17,* 57–75.

Ehrenreich, B., Hass, G., & Jacobs, E. (1987). *Remaking Love: The Feminization of Sex.* New York: Doubleday/Anchor.

Ehrhardt, A., & Meyer-Bahlburg, H. (1981). Effects of prenatal sex hormones on gender-related behavior. *Science, 211,* 1312–1317.

Eng, T. R., & Butler, W. T. (1997). *The hidden epidemic: Confronting sexually transmitted diseases.* Washington, DC: National Academy Press.

Fausto-Sterling, A. (1993, March/April). The five sexes: Why male and female are not enough. *The Sciences (New York Academy of Science),* 20–25.

Fisher, H. (1992). *Anatomy of love: The natural history of monogamy, adultery, and divorce.* New York: W. W. Norton.

Fletcher, J. (1966). *Situation ethics: The new morality.* Philadelphia: Westminster Press.

Ford, C., & Beach, F. (1951). *Patterns of sexual behavior.* New York: Harper & Row.

Francoeur, R. T. (1983). Religious reactions to alternative lifestyles. In E. D. Macklin & R. H. Rubin (Eds.), *Contemporary families and alternative lifestyles: A handbook on research and theory* (pp. 379–399). Beverly Hills, CA: Sage.

Francoeur, R. T. (1988). Two different worlds, Two different moralities. In J. Gramick & P. Furey (Eds.), *The Vatican and homosexuality* (pp. 189–200). New York: Crossroads.

Francoeur, R. T. (1989). Thinking about sexual ethics: New dimensions in human sexuality. In R. H. Iles (Ed.), *The Gospel imperative in the midst of AIDS: Towards a prophetic pastoral theology.* Wilton, CT: Morehouse.

Francoeur, R. T. (1991). *Becoming a sexual person* (2nd ed.). New York: Macmillan.

Francoeur, R. T. (1992, April–May). Sex and spirituality: The relevance of eastern experiences. *SIECUS Report, 20*(4), 1–8.

Francoeur, R. T. (1996). Sexual codes. In G. T. Kurian & G. T. T. Molitor (Eds.), *Encyclopedia of the future* (pp. 830–834). New York: Simon & Shuster.

Francoeur, R. T. (Ed.). (1997). *International encyclopedia of sexuality.* New York: Continuum.

Francoeur, R. T., & Leyson, J. F. L. (1991). Pharmacosexology: Sexual side effects of medications and other drugs. In J. F. J. Leyson (Ed.), *Sexual rehabilitation of the spinal-cord-injured patient* (pp. 445–464). Clifton, NJ: Humana Press.

Francoeur, R. T., Cornog, M., Perper, T., & Scherzer, N. A. (1995). *A complete dictionary of sexology.* New York: Continuum.

Francoeur, R. T., Koch, P. B., & Weis, D. L. (1998). *Sexuality in America: Understanding our sexual values and behavior.* New York: Continuum.

Gagnon, J. (1990). The explicit and implicit use of scripting perspectives in sex research. *Annual Review of Sex Research, 1,* 1–44.

Gagnon, J., & Simon, W. (1973). *Sexual conduct: The social origins of human sexuality.* Chicago: Aldine.

Gardella, P. (1986). *Innocent ecstasy: How Christianity gave America an ethic of sexual pleasure.* New York: Oxford University Press.

Gellman, D. (1992, February 24). Born or bred? *Newsweek,* 46–53.

Giaquinta, B. S. (1989, May/June). Researching the effects of AIDS on families. *American Journal of Hospice Care,* 31–36.

Gibbons, A. (1991, August 30). The brain as "sexual organ." *Science, 253,* 957–959.

Glaser, E. (1991). *In the absence of angels: A Hollywood family's courageous story.* New York: Putnam.

Goldman, R., & Goldman, J. (1982). *Children's sexual thinking.* Boston: Routledge & Kegan Paul.

Gooren, L., Fliers, E., & Courtney, K. (1990). Biological determinants of sexual orientation. In J. Bancroft (Ed.), *Annual Review of Sex Research* (vol. 1, pp. 175–196). Lake Mills, IA: Society for the Scientific Study of Sex.

Gorman, C. (1992, January 20). Sizing up the sexes. *Time,* 42–51.

Gramick, J., & Furey, P. (1988). *The Vatican and homosexuality.* New York: Crossroads.

Green, R. (1987). *The "sissy boy" syndrome and the development of homosexuality.* New Haven, CT: Yale University Press.

Groth, A. N. (1979). *Men who rape: The psychology of the offender.* New York: Plenum.

Haeberle, E. (1978). *The sex atlas.* New York: Seabury Press.

Hamer, D. H., Hu, S., Magnuson, V. L., Hu, N., & Pattatucci, A. M. L. (1993). A linkage between DNA markers on the X chromosome and male sexual orientation. *Science, 261,* 321–327.

Harlow, H. (1971). *Learning to love.* New York: Ballantine.

Harlow, H., & Harlow, M. (1965). The effect of rearing conditions on behavior. In J. Money (Ed.), *Sex research: New developments* (pp. 161–175). New York: Holt.

Hendrixson, L. L. (1997). The psychosocial and psychosexual impact of HIV/AIDS disease on rural women: A qualitative study (2 vols.). Doctoral dissertation, New York University, 1996. *Dissertation Abstracts International,* vol. 57, A5312.

Herman-Giddens, M. E. (1997, April). Secondary sexual characteristics and menses in young girls seen in office practice: A study from the pediatric Research in Office Settings network. *Pediatrics, 99*(4), 505–512.

Holden, C. (1987, August 7). The genetics of personality. *Science, 237,* 598–601.

Holden, C. (1991, August 30). Is the "gender gap" narrowing? *Science, 253,* 959–960.

Imperato-McGinley, J., Peterson, R., Gautier, T., & Sturla, W. (1979). Androgens and the evolution of male-gender identity among male pseudohermaphrodites and 5-alpha-reductase deficiency. *New England Journal of Medicine, 300,* 1233–1237.

Jaspers, K. (1953). *The origin and goal of history.* New Haven, CT: Yale University Press.

Kallmann, F. (1952a). Comparative twin study on the genetic aspects of male homosexuality. *Journal of Nervous and Mental Disease, 115,* 283–298.

Kallmann, F. (1952b). Twin and sibship study of overt male homosexuality. *American Journal of Human Genetics, 4,* 136–146.

Kallmann, F. J. (1963). Genetic aspects of sex determination and sexual maturation potentials in man. In G. Winokur (Eds.), *Determinants of human sexual behavior.* Springfield, IL: Charles C Thomas.

Kaplan, H. S. (1974). *The new sex therapy.* New York: Brunner/Mazel.

Kaplan, H. S. (1979). *Disorders of sexual desire.* New York: Brunner/Mazel.

Kaplan, H. S. (1983). *The evaluation of sexual disorders.* New York: Brunner/Mazel.

Kinsey, A., Pomeroy, W., & Martin, C. (1948). *Sexual behavior in the human male.* Philadelphia: Saunders.

Kinsey, A., Pomeroy, W., Martin, C., & Gebhard, P. (1953). *Sexual behavior in the human female.* Philadelphia: Saunders.

Kirkendall, L. (1976). A new bill of sexual rights and responsibilities. *The Humanist, 36*(1), 4–6.

Kirkpatrick, A. C. (1986). Some correlates of women's childhood sexual experiences: A retrospective study. *Journal of Sex Research, 22*(2), 221–242.

Klein, F., Sepekoff, B., & Wolf, T. J. (1985). Sexual orientations: A multivariable dynamic process. In F. Klein & T. J. Wolf (Eds.), *Bisexuality: Theory and research* (pp. 35–49). Binghamton, NY: Haworth.

Kohlberg, L. (1969). Stage and sequence: The cognitive-developmental approach to socialization. in D. Goslin (Ed.), *Handbook of socialization theory and research.* Chicago: Rand McNally.

Kosnick, A., Carroll, W., Cunningham, A., Modras, R., & Schulte, J. (1977). *Human sexuality: New dimensions in American Catholic thought.* New York: Paulist Press.

Lawrence, R. (1989). *The poisoning of eros: Sexual values in conflict.* New York: Augustine Moore Press.

Lebacqz, K. (1997). Difference or defect? Intersexuality and the politics of difference. *The Annual: Society of Christian Ethics, 17,* 213–229.

Leiblum, S., & Pervin, L. (1989). *Principles and practice of sex therapy* (2nd ed.). New York: Guilford.

Leiblum, S. R., & Rosen, R. C. (Eds.). (1988). *Sexual desire disorders.* New York: Guilford.

LeVay, S. (1991, August 30). A difference in hypothalamic structure between heterosexual and homosexual men. *Science, 253,* 1034–1037.

Leyson, J. F. (Ed.). (1991). *Sexual rehabilitation of the spinal cord injured patient.* Clifton, NJ: Humana Press.

Macklin, E. (Ed.). (1989). *AIDS and families: Report of the AIDS Task Force, Groves Conference on Marriage and the Family.* New York: Harrington Park Press.

Martinson, F. M. (1980). Childhood sexuality. In B. B. Wolman (Ed.), *Handbook of human sexuality* (pp. 29–60). Englewood Cliffs, NJ: Prentice-Hall.

Marty, M. E., & Applyby, R. S. (Eds.). (1992). *Fundamentalisms observed.* Chicago: University of Chicago Press.

Masters, W., & Johnson, V. (1966). *Human sexual response.* Boston: Little, Brown.

Masters, W., & Johnson, V. (1970). *Human sexual inadequacy.* Boston: Little, Brown.

McCombie, S. (Ed.). (1980). *The rape crisis intervention handbook: A guide for victim care.* New York: Plenum.

McDonell, J., Abell, N., & Miller, J. (1991, January). Family members' willingness to care for people with AIDS: A psychosocial assessment model. *Social Work, 36*(1), 43–53.

McFadden, D. (1998, March 3). Inner ear development in lesbian women. *Proceedings of National Academy of Sciences.*

McWhirter, D., & Mattison, A. M. (1984). *The male couple: How relationships develop.* Englewood Cliffs, NJ: Prentice-Hall.

Messer, S. B. (1986). Behavioral and psychoanalytic perspectives in therapeutic choice points. *American Psychologist, 41*(11), 1261–1272.

Meyer-Bahlburg, H. F. L. (1987). Psychoendocrine research and the societal status of homosexuals. *Journal of Sex Research, 23*(1), 114–120.

Mitchell, G. (1975, April). What monkeys can tell us about human violence. *The Futurist, 9*(2), 75–80.

Money, J. (1980). *Love and love sickness: The science of sex, gender differences, and pair bonding.* Baltimore: Johns Hopkins University Press.

Money, J. (1985). *The destroying angel: Sex, fitness & food in the legacy of degeneracy theory, Graham crackers, Kellogg's corn flakes & American health history.* Buffalo, NY: Prometheus Press.

Money, J. (1986). *Lovemaps: Clinical concepts of sexual/erotic health and pathology, paraphilia, and gender transposition in childhood, adolescence, and maturity.* New York: Irvington Press.

Money, J. (1987). Propaedeutics of diecious G-I/R: Theoretical foundations for understanding dimorphic gender-identity role. In J. M. Reinisch, L. A. Rosenblum, & S. A. Sanders (Eds.), *Masculinity/femininity: Basic perspectives* (pp. 13–28). New York: Oxford University Press.

Money, J. (1988). *Gay, straight, and in-between: The sexology of erotic orientation.* New York: Oxford University Press.

Money, J., & Ehrhardt, A. (1972). *Man & woman boy & girl.* Baltimore: Johns Hopkins University Press.

Money, J., & Tucker, P. (1975). *Sexual signatures: On being a man or woman.* Boston: Little, Brown.

Moore, K. L. (1988). *The developing human: Clinically oriented embryology* (4th ed.). Philadelphia: Saunders.

Nash, J. M. (1992, January 22). Sizing up the sexes. *Time,* 42–51.

Paglia, C. (1990). *Sexual personae: Art and decadence from Nefertiti to Emily Dickinson.* New York: Random House Vintage.

Perper, T. (1985). *Sex signals: The biology of love.* Philadelphia: iSi Press.

Piaget, J. (1965). *The moral judgment of the child.* New York: Free Press.

Pillard, R., Poumadere, J., & Carretta, R. (1982). A family study of sexual orientation. *Archives of Sexual Behavior, 11*(6), 511–520.

Pillard, R., & Weinrich, J. (1986). Evidence of familial nature of male homosexuality. *Archives of General Psychiatry, 43,* 808–812.

Pool, R. (1994). *Eve's rib: Searching for the biological roots of sex differences.* New York: Crown.

Prendergast, W. (1991). *Treating sex offenders in correctional institutions and outpatient clinics: A guide to clinical practice.* Binghamton, NY: Haworth.

Prendergast, W. E. (1993). *The merry-go-round of sexual abuse: Identifying and treating survivors.* Binghamton, NY: Haworth.

Prendergast, W. E. (1996). *Sexual abuse of children and adolescents: A preventive guide for parents, teachers, and counselors.* New York: Continuum.

Prescott, J. W. (1975). Body pleasure and the origins of violence. *The Futurist, 9*(2), 64–74.

Prescott, J. W. (1989). Affectional bonding for the prevention of violent behaviors: Neurobiological, psychological and religious/spiritual determinants. In: L. J. Hertzberg et al. (Eds.), *Violent behavior. Volume 1: Assessment and intervention.* New York: PMA Publishing.

Prescott, J. W. (1996). The origins of human love and violence. *Pre- and Perinatal Psychology Journal, 10*(3), 143–187.

Ranke-Heinemann, U. (1990). *Eunuchs for the kingdom of heaven: Women, sexuality, and the Catholic church.* New York: Doubleday.

Reinisch, J. M., & Sanders, S. A. (1984). Hormonal influences on sexual development and behavior. In A. Moraczewski (Ed.), *Sex and gender: A theological and scientific inquiry.* St. Louis: Pope John Center.

Reinisch, J. M., Rosenblum, P., & Sanders, S. (1987). *Masculinity/femininity: Basic perspectives.* New York: Oxford University Press.

Reiss, I. L. (1990). *An end to shame: Shaping our next sexual revolution.* Buffalo, NY: Prometheus Press.

Richardson, L. (1985). *The new other woman: Contemporary single women in affairs with married men.* New York: Free Press.

Rossi, A. (1984). Gender and parenthood: American Sociological Association, 1983 Presidential address. *American Sociological Review, 49.*

Sannella, L. (1987). *The Kundalinin experience.* Lower Lake, CA: Integral Publishing.

Sarrel, L., & Sarrel, P. (1980). *Sexual unfolding.* Boston: Little, Brown.

Schlegel, W. S. (1962). Die Konstitutionbiologischen Grundlagen der Homosexualitat. *Z. Menschl. Vererb. Konstitutionslehre., 36*, 341–364.

Schumacher, S., & Lloyd, C. W. (1981). Physiological and psychological factors in impotence. *Journal of Sex Research, 11*(1), 40–53.

Seagrave, R. T. (1988). Drugs and desire. In S. R. Leiblum & R. C. Rosen (Eds.), *Sexual desire disorders* (pp. 314–347). New York: Guilford.

Singer, J. (1972). *Androgyny: Toward a new theory of sexuality.* New York: Anchor Doubleday.

Stayton, W. R. (1980). A theory of sexual orientation: The universe as a turn-on. *Topics in Clinical Nursing, 1*(4), 1–7.

Stayton, W. (1989). A theology for sexual pleasure. *American Baptist Quarterly, 8*(2), 94–108.

Stayton, W. R. (1992). A theology of sexual pleasure. *SIECUS Report, 20*(4), 9–15.

Stipp, D., & Whitaker, R. (1998, March 16). The selling of impotence. *Fortune,* 114–124.

Sullivan, H. S. (1953). *Interpersonal theory of psychiatry.* New York: Norton.

Tanner, D. (1990). *You just don't understand: Women and men in conversation.* New York: Ballantine.

Tasker, M. (1992). *How can I tell you? Secrecy and disclosure with children when a family member has AIDS.* Bethesda, MD: Association for the Care of Children's Health (ACCH) Publications Center.

Tavris, C. (1992). *The mismeasure of woman.* New York: Simon & Schuster.

Thayer, N. S. T., Black, C., DuBose, E., Hamilton, A., et al. (1987, March). Family life and sexuality report. *The Voice* (The Episcopal Diocese of Newark, New Jersey), 9–11.

Tiefer, L. (1991). Historical, scientific, clinical and feminist criticisms of "The Human Sexual Response Cycle" model. *Annual Review of Sex Research, 2*, 1–24.

United Church of Christ, Board of Homeland Ministers. (1977). *Human sexuality: A preliminary study.* Eleventh General Synod. New York and Philadelphia.

United Presbyterian Church in the U.S.A. (1970). *Sexuality and the human community.* Philadelphia: Author.

United Presbyterian Church in the U.S.A. General Assembly Special Committee on Human Sexuality. (1991). *Part 1: Keeping body and soul together: sexuality, spirituality, and social justice. Part 2: Minority report of the Special Committee on Human Sexuality* (Report to the 203rd General Assembly). Baltimore, MD: Presbyterian Church (U.S.A.).

Voller, B. (1991). AIDS and heterosexual anal intercourse. *Archives of Sexual Behavior, 20*(3), 233–276.

Wagner, G., & Green, R. (1981). *Impotence: physiological, psychological, surgical diagnosis and treatment.* New York: Plenum.

Wagner, G., & Metz, P. (1980). Impotence (erectile dysfunction) due to vascular disorders: An overview. *Journal of Sex Research, 6*(4), 223–233.

Walsh, A. (1991). *The science of love: Understanding love and its effects on mind and body.* Buffalo: Prometheus.

Weinberg, M., & Williams, C. (1974). *Male homosexuals: Their problems and adaptations.* New York: Oxford University Press.

Weinrich, J. (1987). *Sexual landscapes: Why we are what we are, why we love whom we love.* New York: Scribners.

Wertz, R., & Wertz, D. (1979). *Lying-in: A history of childbirth in America.* New York: Schocken.

Whipple, B. (1991). Female sexuality. In J. F. J. Leyson (Ed.), *Sexual rehabilitation of the spinal-cord-injured patient* (pp. 19–38). Clifton, NJ: Humana Press.

Whitam, F. L., & Mathy, R. M. (1986). *Male homosexuality in four societies: Brazil, Guatamala, the Philippines, and the United States.* New York: Praeger.

Wiener, L. S. (1991). Women and human immunodeficiency virus: A historical and personal psychosocial perspective. *Social Work, 36*(5), 375–378.

Younge, R. (1989, Winter). Report from the frontlines: Unsung heroines of the AIDS epidemic. *Health/PAC Bulletin,* 16–18.

CHAPTER 28

Theories and Techniques of Marital and Family Therapy

Nadine J. Kaslow, Florence W. Kaslow, and Eugene W. Farber

Historical Overview

Histories of the intertwined fields of marriage and family therapy have appeared during the past 2 decades (e.g., Broderick & Schrader, 1991; Guerin, 1976; F. Kaslow, 1982, 1987; Thomas, 1992). Elaborating upon an earlier version of this material (F. Kaslow, 1987), this chapter concentrates on developments in the past decade, a time during which the convergence of the marital and family therapy fields has been accepted.

Trends

A number of trends have emerged during the past decade that have altered the field of marital and family therapy (Broderick & Schrader, 1991; F. Kaslow, 1990; N. Kaslow & Celano, 1993).

Organizations. The 1980s witnessed the growth in membership of the two major organizations, the American Association for Marriage and Family Therapy (AAMFT) and the American Family Therapy Academy (AFTA). Both organizations develop and disseminate standards of practice, of-

Nadine J. Kaslow • Departments of Psychiatry and Behavioral Sciences and Pediatrics and Psychology, Emory University, and Grady Health System, Atlanta, Georgia 30335-3801. **Florence W. Kaslow** • Florida Couples and Family Institute, Palm Beach Gardens, Florida 33418; Department of Medical Psychology in Psychiatry, Duke University, Durham, North Carolina 27708-001; and School of Professional Psychology, Florida Institute of Technology, Melbourne, Florida 32901-6988. **Eugene W. Farber** • Department of Psychiatry and Behavioral Sciences, Emory University, Atlanta, Georgia 30335-3801.

Handbook of Marriage and the Family, 2nd edition, edited by Marvin Sussman, Suzanne K. Steinmetz, and Gary W. Peterson. Plenum Press, New York, 1999.

fer continuing education opportunities, and support the implementation of research and the development of effective intervention strategies. AAMFT also is involved in licensure and promulgating codes of ethics regarding families, accreditation of training programs, and public policy. The American Association of Sex Educators, Counselors, and Therapists (AASECT), American Orthopsychiatric Association (AOA/ Ortho), the National Association of Social Workers (NASW), and National Council of Family Relations (NCFR) offer family therapy-oriented presentations at conferences and publish related articles in their journals. The Group for the Advancement of Psychiatry (GAP) Task Force on the Family, which publishes monographs and articles on family diagnosis and treatment, keeps the psychiatric profession informed about salient issues in family therapy and family psychiatry. The Academy of Psychologists in Marital, Family, and Sex Therapy reconstituted itself and became the Division of Family Psychology in the American Psychological Association (APA) in 1985 (Division 43). This division includes family psychologists who identify themselves as scientists and practitioners.

Ethical Guidelines. The establishment, teaching, and enforcement of ethical guidelines for the practice of family therapy (e.g., AAMFT, 1988) and family research (N. Kaslow & Gurman, 1985) have been a major priority (for review see Patten, Barnett, & Houlihan, 1991). One overriding and unique concern refers to how to handle confidentiality when the therapist or researcher has contact with family subsystems and receives information (e.g., affairs, financial data, medical status) not consciously known to all family members. A corollary trend is the increased consistency between ethical guidelines and legal mandates for reporting such behaviors as abuse of minors, or imminent risk in a family member of suicide or homicide. This latter trend has precipitated controversy in the field regarding identified patient status in the case of suicidality and homicidality and culpability in instances of abuse. To pure systems theorists, these problems reflect family dysfunction and the idea that there is a perpetrator, a victim, or a psychiatrically disabled family member is antithetical to a systems perspective. Conversely, to therapists who are nonpurists, the idea that the dysfunctional behavior (e.g., parent–child incest) may need to be addressed in both individual members and the transactional system is logical and even essential (e.g., Trepper & Barrett, 1989).

Licensure and Certification Laws.   The number of states that have licensure or certification laws has increased. This emanates from an effort to ensure consumer protection through enhancing the recognition of marriage and family therapy as a distinct mental health specialty whose practitioners are eligible for insurance reimbursement. This emphasis on ethics, law, and licensure/certification also augments the level of accountability of members of the profession.

Gender-Sensitive Paradigms.   Feminist family therapists underscore the power imbalances between men and women and highlight gender differences in various domains of functioning, with particular attention to marital, parent–child, and larger family relationships (e.g., Goodrich, Rampage, Ellman, & Halstead, 1988; Luepnitz, 1988; McGoldrick, Anderson, & Walsh, 1989; Walters, Carter, Papp, & Silverstein, 1988). Feminist family therapy seeks to modify the social conditions contributing to the maintenance of gender-prescribed behaviors and to alter the social structures that perpetuate an oppressive and hierarchical society to the detriment of women's well-being. They posit that emphasizing egalitarian relationships between men and women enables individuals to reach their fullest potential with regard to power and intimacy and to enjoy the multiplicity of roles they play. The *Journal of Feminist Family Therapy* gives voice to these issues.

More recently, the men's movement has mushroomed (e.g., Meth & Pasick, 1990; Pittman, 1993). Overriding concerns have been to validate a multitude of images and behaviors of male figures and to support men in valuing feelings and relationships with their partners, children, and family of origin, particularly their fathers. The pursuits of work and money, in competitive and power-driven ways, have been deemphasized.

The advent of these two movements has caused upheaval and controversy. This has prompted a reevaluation of family therapy tenets and the creation of gender-sensitive paradigms of assessment and intervention.

Diversity.   There has been increased recognition of ethnic, racial, religious, and socioeconomic diversity. Thus, family therapists now more readily take into account and treat respectfully the myriad traditions and values represented in families (e.g., Boyd-Franklin, 1989; McGoldrick, Pearce, & Giordano, 1982). This reflects an increased acceptance of cultural diversity and multiculturalism.

Multiplicity of Family Forms.   As the composition of families in American society has become more varied, clinicians have expanded their repertoire for dealing with the multiplicity of family forms. Major family types include single-parent families, partners living together, married heterosexual and gay and lesbian couples, married couples with children, three- and four-generation families living together, divorced binuclear families, remarried and step families, foster and adoptive families, and groups of individuals living together as a family unit (e.g., Carl, 1990; F. Kaslow & Schwartz, 1987; Sager et al., 1983; Schwartz & Kaslow, 1977; Visher & Visher, 1987; Wallerstein & Kelly, 1980). Within any of these family types, there can be members from different racial, religious, and ethnic backgrounds.

Internationalization of the Field.   Another trend has been the internationalization of the field (e.g., F. Kaslow, 1982). This phenomena has been expressed in the formation of the International Family Therapy Association (IFTA) and the International Academy of Family Psychologists. There has been a proliferation of journals in many countries and languages. Family therapists throughout the world look to leading teachers, theoreticians, and practitioners from such countries as the United States, Australia, Belgium, Canada, England, Germany, Israel, Italy, and Norway.

Family Assessment Devices.   The past 2 decades have witnessed the development of increasing numbers of family assessment devices, including self-report measures, observational coding schemas for family interaction, and projective techniques (e.g., Markman & Notarius, 1987). Self-report measures assess overall marital and family adjustment, marital communication and intimacy, quality of family life, and family life-cycle events.

Direct observational methods for coding interaction patterns have become more sophisticated, complex, scientifically validated, and frequently employed. Many coding schemas evaluate interpersonal dimensions that differentiate healthy and dysfunctional families: dominance, affect, communication, information exchange, conflict and support/validation (Markman & Notarius, 1987). One commonly used microanalytic coding schema, the Family Interaction Coding System (Patterson, Ray, Shaw, & Cobb, 1969), sequentially analyzes aversive and prosocial behaviors in family transactions to ascertain the family's level of coerciveness. The Marital Interaction Coding System (Hops, Wills, Patterson, & Weiss, 1972), which recently has been revised

(MICS III), is a microanalytic coding schema that evaluates marital interaction in terms of problem description, blame, proposal for change, validation, invalidation, irrelevance, and nonverbal affect.

Another microanalytic coding schema emerged from researchers' attempts to capture the high levels of emotional reactivity and overinvolvement characteristic of some families with a symptomatic loved one. Based upon research that identified high levels of expressed emotion (EE) as precipitating relapse in schizophrenic individuals (e.g., Brown, Birley, & Wing, 1972), Doane and colleagues (Doane, West, Goldstein, Rodnick, & Jones, 1981) developed a schema that examines the affective style characterizing the direct interactions of parents and patients. This method has revealed that psychologically disturbed individuals in families with negative affective styles have a comparatively poorer course than do persons in families with benign affective styles (e.g., Doane, Falloon, Goldstein, & Mintz, 1985).

Macroanalytic analyses of family interactions typically are applied to observational data obtained in relatively unstructured interactions. A frequently used macroanalytic coding system is the Beavers Timberlawn Family Evaluation Scale (Beavers, 1977), a Likert-type clinician's rating scale of structure, mythology, goal-directed negotiation, autonomy, and affect.

Microanalytic coding schemas provide rich data about complex interactions that are ecologically valid. However, garnering, coding, and analyzing these data is costly and labor intensive. Macroanalytic coding schemas are easier and less expensive to use. Even though they capture the interactional gestalt, they fail to capture the discrete behaviors of the individuals involved, and thus lack the depth and breadth characteristic of the microanalytic schemas. The overall result, however, has been that the development of self-report measures and observational coding schemas has contributed to the generation of more valid and reliable research.

Classification of Healthy, Midrange, and Dysfunctional Families

Divergent perspectives on what constitutes healthy, midrange, and dysfunctional family dynamics and interactional processes have emerged (Walsh, 1993). Several schemas have been developed for measuring family characteristics and patterns that determine the classification of families. Such schemas offer a portrait of healthy functioning that serves as the foundation from which clinicians can help distressed families move in the direction of healthier patterns and processes.

Taken together, the various portraits of healthy families (e.g., F. Kaslow, 1981a; F. Kaslow & Hammerschmidt, 1992; Satir & Baldwin, 1983; Whitaker & Bumberry, 1988) and the classification schemas proposed (e.g., Epstein, Bishop, Ryan,

Miller, & Keitner, 1993; Beavers, 1977, 1990; Lewis, Beavers, Gossett, & Phillips, 1976; Olson, Sprenkle, & Russell, 1979; Olson et al., 1983; Reiss, 1981) indicate that the characteristics of healthy family functioning also are contingent upon the family's life cycle stage and sociocultural context. Key dimensions along which family functioning are characterized include cohesion, change, and communication. Optimal families are cohesive, with a clear, yet flexible structure, allowing for both closeness and age-appropriate autonomy. They adapt their power structure, role relationships, and rules in response to situational and developmental demands and new information from the environment. Relatively equal power is the norm for the marital dyad and a clear power hierarchy exists between the parental subsystem and the children that is modified according to the developmental stage of the children. There is ample opportunity to alter standards for behavior control using negotiation and problem solving. All family functions are performed so that members are not overburdened with too many roles, and there is flexibility in the roles played. Communication vis-à-vis affective and instrumental concerns is clear and effective, and there is congruence between the content and process.

Research. Only during the past 15 years have family therapy practitioners and theorists given much credence to the importance of quantitative and qualitative research to describe family processes and to ascertain the efficacy of various family intervention approaches for various types of problems and families (e.g., Hazelrigg, Cooper, & Borduin, 1987). The proliferation of devices for evaluating family functioning and change has made possible the evolution and replication of clinically meaningful studies. Members of the major organizations are involved in this endeavor, and professional conferences and publications are devoted to the integration of family research, theory, and practice.

Expansion of the Field. The field of marital and family therapy has been expanded to include such subspecialties as sex therapy, divorce therapy, and divorce mediation. Family therapists increasingly have turned their attention to families with members who abuse alcohol and drugs; have a psychosomatic, learning, or personality disorder or another internalizing or externalizing disorder; and families characterized by sexual abuse and/or other forms of physical violence (e.g., Everett, Halperin, Volgy, & Wissler, 1989; Minuchin, Rosman, & Baker, 1978; Stanton & Todd, 1982; Trepper & Barrett, 1989). This trend toward increased inclusivity in patient populations is likely to continue.

Integrative Perspective. The final and perhaps overarching trend is a movement away from a purist family systems approach to a more integrative, comprehensive theoretical and treatment perspective. This is manifested in numerous spheres of activity. For example, many family clinicians integrate a range of theoretical models and the intervention techniques associated with the different schools of family therapy. Another indicator of this trend is the resurgence of the importance of the individual in the family system and of the mutual and reciprocal impact of the individual on the family and the family on the individual. A corollary of this is concern for promoting coevolution of the individual and the family, such that individual and family needs are balanced. Given the reemergence of concern for the individuals within the family system (e.g., Feldman, 1992; Wachtel & Wachtel, 1986), it has become more acceptable to conduct psychological testing, pharmacological interventions, and individual or couples therapy concurrent or sequential with family therapy or to hospitalize a family member with severe symptoms and impairments that do not respond to outpatient interventions.

Overview of Conceptual Models

As the trend toward an integrationist perspective suggests, theories of family therapy are not monolithic. Rather, this rubric subsumes approaches ranging from traditional psychoanalytic and learning theories to systems and communications theories. Further, family theories are not totally distinct; they share common elements and there is much overlap between the different schools of family therapy. First, the majority of schools view the family as a system whose members are interdependent. The family is comprised of subsystems with generational links and boundaries, communication networks, coalitions and alliances, rules, secrets, myths, and rituals. Second, the three key dimensions of family functioning (i.e., cohesion, adaptability, communication) are the focus of multiple approaches (Olson et al., 1979). Third, most family therapists concur that a paramount goal of therapy is to change the family systems' interactional patterns, with individual change occurring as a product of systems change (Sander, 1979). Additional goals include developing role flexibility and adaptability, balancing power, establishing individuality within the family collectively, and increasing the clarity and specificity of communication. The main areas of divergence between schools of thought relate to the definition of family composition (e.g., nuclear, extended), who must be present at the therapy session, the importance of history versus the centrality of the here-and-now, focus on intrapsychic versus interpersonal dynamics, the nature and meaning of the presenting problem, the role of assessment, the importance of mediating goals, the ultimate goals of therapy, the notion of problem and solution, and the personality and role of the therapist (Beels & Ferber, 1972; Gurman, 1979; F. Kaslow, 1987).

The major family theories detailed are (1) psychoanalytic, (2) Bowenian/multigenerational, (3) contextual, (4) symbolic-experiential, (5) communication, (6) strategic, (7) systemic, (8) structural, (9) behavioral and cognitive-behavioral, and (10) psychoeducational (F. Kaslow, 1987; N. Kaslow & Celano, 1993). Integrative family therapy perspectives also will be articulated. Each theory offers a different view of the family "reality" and a perspective on family health and dysfunction. Techniques and terminology are similar among the theories, though not identical because each perspective exists within the context of a different epistemology.

Psychoanalytic Family Therapy

History and Theoretical Development. Psychoanalytic family therapy, the nearest descendant of individual psychoanalytically oriented psychotherapy, is one of the only family models that acknowledges its ties to psychoanalytic thinking. This approach emphasizes the role of the unconscious and past history in determining behavior and motivations, the necessity of insight for behavioral change, and the importance of transference and countertransference dynamics.

One early proponent of psychoanalytic family therapy was Nathan Ackerman (e.g., Ackerman, 1938), who founded the Family Institute of New York to train therapists in psychoanalytic family therapy and treat troubled families (Guerin, 1976; F. Kaslow, 1980; LaPerriere, 1979). Following Ackerman's death, this facility was renamed the Ackerman Institute. Other key figures who developed variants of a psychoanalytic family therapy approach include James Framo, Ivan Boszormenyi-Nagy, Robin Skynner, Norman Paul, and John Bell. Recently, a number of writers have integrated object relations and family systems theories (Scharff, 1989; Scharff & Scharff, 1987; Slipp, 1988). Since object relations family therapy now is the dominant psychoanalytically oriented approach, the following comments are devoted to this model.

Basic Structure and Goals. Object relations family therapy, a long-term treatment approach, addresses unresolved intrapsychic conflicts that are reenacted in one's current life, causing interpersonal and intrapsychic difficulties. Session membership depends on the presenting problem and the goals of each treatment phase. Goals typically include delineating and redefining problems so that they are more accessible to resolution; clarifying boundary issues; explicating individual needs and desires and how these can be fulfilled within the marital–family system; modifying narcissistic or inappropriate demands; increasing expressive and listening skills; diminishing coercive and blaming statements; facilitating problem solving and conflict resolution; modifying dysfunctional rules and communication patterns; helping family members achieve increased insight; strengthening ego functioning; acknowledging and reworking defensive projective identifications; attaining more mature internal self and object representations; developing more satisfying interpersonal relationships that support one's needs for attachment, individuation, and psychological growth; reducing interlocking pathologies among family members; and resolving spousal and therapist–patient transferences. When these goals are achieved, they make possible the attainment of more ultimate goals, including trust and closeness, role flexibility, appreciation of uniqueness, comfort with and enjoyment of one's sexuality, an egalitarian power relationship between the couple as parents and spouses, a balance between the cognitive and affective realms of living, positive self-image for each and family esteem for all, clear communication, and the resolution of neurotic conflicts (Gurman, 1979). These goals are concordant with the healthy family portraits discussed earlier.

Techniques and Process of Therapy. During the initial phase, the therapist provides a holding environment (e.g., time, space, and structure for therapy) that enables family members to feel safe and secure enough to express their feelings and beliefs, feel intimate, and maintain a sense of self. The therapist reparents the family by providing consistent nurturance and structure to enhance the development of individual members and the family unit.

Given the importance of the past as it contributes to and shapes the present, assessment plays a central role. Thus, during the initial phase, a history of each family member is conducted, focusing on family of origin dynamics, early experiences, presenting problems, and treatment history. The clinician observes family interaction during an open-ended interview to ascertain family members' level of object relations, predominant defense mechanisms, and the relationship between current interactional patterns and family of origin dynamics. Because the marital dyad creates the family unit, the psychotherapist explores the unconscious and conscious reasons for the couple's choice of mate, the evolution of the marital relationship, the conflicts and experiences that predated the marriage, and the influences of these on the current marital and family interactions and affective quality. The underlying meaning of presenting problems and the interactional themes constitute the central foci of the evaluation.

Once a therapeutic alliance is established and a thorough history is obtained, the therapist empathically interprets conflicts, resistances, negative transference, defenses, and patterns of interaction indicative of unresolved intrapsychic and interpersonal conflicts. Effective interpretations link an individual's and family's history with current feelings,

thoughts, behaviors, and transactions, permitting more adaptive family interactional patterns and intrapsychic changes. The clinician encourages and supports affective communication and increased demonstration of affectionate feelings, clarifies the nature of the family's communication, challenges assumptions and beliefs and tries to dislodge constricting and rigidly adhered to outdated patterns, and facilitates the development of insight into the self and deeper awareness of other family members. Technical errors occur when a safe holding environment has not been established, interpretations are poorly timed and do not attend to significant intrapsychic or interpersonal dynamics, or when therapist comments reflect unarticulated and unresolved countertransference issues.

Object relations family therapists address transference and countertransference dynamics to facilitate the therapeutic endeavor. They use their own reactions to the family's interaction patterns (objective countertransference) to understand empathically the shared, yet unspoken, experiences of each family member regarding family interactional patterns (unconscious family system of object relations). They employ their objective countertransference reactions to interpret interpersonal patterns in which one family member is induced to behave in a circumscribed and maladaptive fashion (projective identification).

Issues of loss and separation are attended to during each session and toward the end of the treatment process. During the termination phase, salient conflicts are reviewed and reworked. There is an opportunity for mourning the loss of the therapist, who has become an important attachment figure.

Although there are specific techniques associated with object relations family therapy, techniques are considered secondary to the alliance between therapist and family, and thus do not define the practice of object relations family therapy. Rather, the defining characteristic is the therapist's joining with the family and creating a safe holding environment within which family members rediscover each other and the lost parts of the self projected onto one another. These family therapists focus on the therapeutic alliance as a curative factor and use transference interpretations as the cornerstone of the treatment. Additional attention is paid to countertransference dynamics as these influence the work between therapist and family. Thus, the therapist's clinical supervision and personal therapy needs to address those unresolved intrapsychic and interpersonal conflicts related to family of origin issues affecting their clinical work with families.

Treatment Applicability. Clinicians typically use object relations family therapy with high-functioning families whose members are psychologically oriented, well educated, interested in gaining insight, and possess the resources necessary to engage in long-term treatment. Some clinicians also have advocated its use with families with a schizophrenic, borderline, or narcissistic member (Scharff, 1989); families with children and adolescents; families who divorce and remarry; and families coping with trauma and loss (e.g., Scharff & Scharff, 1987).

Bowenian/Multigenerational Family Therapy

History and Theoretical Development. Murray Bowen, who did his early work with schizophrenics at the Menninger Clinic and the National Institute of Mental Health (NIMH), subsequently joined the faculty in the Department of Psychiatry, Georgetown University Medical School in Washington, DC, and founded the Georgetown University Family Center. Bowen, the first president of the American Family Therapy Academy, died in 1990, and his death was mourned by family therapists throughout the world.

A pivotal point in Bowen's career was his presentation of his own process of differentiation from his family of origin. This laid the groundwork for his emphasis on the awareness of, and disengagement from, toxic triangles within one's family of origin. This emphasis also was applied to supervision of trainees, as Bowen believed that therapists who engaged in personal family of origin work became more effective psychotherapists and had more satisfying personal relationships (Roberto, 1992).

Guerin (1976) and Fogarty (1976) extended Bowen's work on genograms, dimensions of self, and the multigenerational model of family therapy. McGoldrick and Gerson (1986) illuminated further the language and technique of genograms.

Bowenian family therapy, also referred to as multigenerational or family of origin therapy, views mental illness as a product of disturbed interpersonal relationships. However, unlike the psychoanalytic approach, the Bowenian approach holds that it is one's degree of unmodulated anxiety and level of differentiation from the family of origin that influences one's interpersonal relationships; thus change must occur at the level of the relationship system.

A number of fundamental characteristics of Bowen theory deserve note. First, Bowen envisioned his theory as applicable to the human condition in general and to all life. Second, he emphasized viewing phenomena (e.g., psychiatric disorders) along a continuum. Third, Bowen focused on the person of the therapist and argued that a therapist's capacity to be therapeutic was a function of his or her level of differentiation. Fourth, he asserted that chronic anxiety, a pervasive experience characteristic of all living systems, is the primary source of psychological dysfunctions and that differentiation is the remedy for chronic anxiety (Friedman, 1991).

Bowen (1988) offered eight interlocking constructs to elucidate his theory (Friedman, 1991): differentiation of self, emotional cut-off, family emotional system, family projection process, triangulation, sibling position, multigenerational transmission process, and societal regression. Differentiation of self, the cornerstone of the theory, refers to the extent to which individuals distinguish between emotional and intellectual processes. Highly differentiated individuals are capable of decision making and problem solving without responding to internal emotional influences. They are neither invested overly in the emotional climate of their family of origin nor totally withdrawn from it and impervious to its importance. Conversely, when a person's intellectual functioning is dominated by emotions and there is a fusion between thinking and feeling functions, the person is low on the differentiation continuum. Bowen (1988) spoke of families with schizophrenic members as characterized by an "undifferentiated family ego mass."

Some individuals who have trouble differentiating attempt to distinguish themselves from their family of origin by withdrawing and denying their importance. They may insulate themselves through geographic separation or severing virtually all contact. This pseudodifferentiation has been referred to as emotional cut-off. Fewer symptoms of distress are noted in multiple generations of a family when there is emotional contact present between individuals in different generations and family members strive toward high degrees of self-differentiation.

The family emotional system refers to emotionally interdependent individuals, comprising a system with its own organizational principles and including the members' individual and collective thoughts, feelings, fantasies, associations, and past relationship history. A nuclear family emotional system typically is formed by marital partners with equivalent levels of self-differentiation. Their patterns of interaction are based upon their level of differentiation from their families of origin. When two highly self-differentiated individuals marry, they typically forge a healthy and stable relationship. Conversely, low levels of differentiation in one or both marital partners may be associated with a familial system characterized by emotional fusion, marital conflict, and dysfunction in one or both spouse. Such circumstances also occur in conjunction with triangulation of a third party (child, friend, relative, lover, issue, symptom) or projection of anxiety and lack of self-differentiation from the family of origin onto one or more of the children.

Bowen referred to this latter phenomenon as the family projection process. Parents project their difficulties onto their most vulnerable child, the child with the lowest level of self-differentiation, who is the most fusion-prone offspring. This child experiences difficulty in attaining adaptive age-appropriate emotional separation. The less differentiated the parents are from their families of origin, the greater the reliance on the family projection process to stabilize the system and the more likely that more than one child will evidence emotional impairments.

Triangles, the basic building blocks of any emotional (relational) system, represent the smallest stable relationship system (Bowen, 1988). Triangulation is another mechanism by which marital dyads attempt to stabilize the tension in their relationship secondary to high levels of anxiety. When anxiety is low and external conditions are calm, the marital dyad is relatively stable and triangulation is less apt to occur. As anxiety, stress, and fusion within the family system increase, the stability of the marital dyad may be threatened, and a vulnerable third party is involved to form a triangle. If this triangle fails to stabilize the situation, additional individuals are recruited to form interlocking triangles.

Other key concepts include the multigenerational transmission process, wherein severe dysfunction is hypothesized to be transmitted through the family emotional system over several generations; sibling position, which reflects Bowen's assertion that interactions between marital partners may be influenced by each partner's birth order; and societal regression, where societal dynamics involve a dialectic between the opposing forces of symbiosis and individuation. The result of such a dialectic, in turn, is that, when the society faces chronic stress, its functional level of differentiation decreases.

Basic Structure and Goals. Bowenian family therapy is a relatively structured and long-term approach, typically conducted by a single therapist with a marital dyad or individual adults. Individuals and the relational system are the patient unit. Greater differentiation of self within one's family of origin constitutes the core objective. A second related goal is to detriangulate each individual from maladaptive three-party systems by resolving dyadic tensions and becoming emotionally disentangled from the interpersonal conflicts that generated the triangulation.

Techniques and Process of Therapy. Family of origin sessions are structured to enable each individual to speak rationally as a means of decreasing emotionality. To accomplish this, the therapist alternately asks each partner about themselves, their responses to each others' comments, the presenting problem, and their nuclear and extended families. The therapist educates participants about Bowenian theory by encouraging and coaching visits to one's family of origin, with the intent being to work through unresolved emotional attachments and foster increased differentiation. In marital therapy, the focus alternates between the spouses, with the therapist deliberately serving as the third point of the triangle. As the marital pair becomes aware of this triangula-

tion process during therapy, they often gain insight into the patterned relational maneuvers they use to triangulate vulnerable family members (e.g., child). As the therapist works with the marital dyad toward detriangulation, the couple often acts differently at home, and the fusion of the family decreases.

Bowenian therapists highlight the importance of ascertaining multigenerational historical information. Presenting problems are interpreted in the context of manifestations of fusion and differentiation. Problems are reframed, needs and desires are clarified, increased reciprocity and cooperation are fostered, nonfunctional relational system rules are modified, and transference is avoided to keep the intensity of the relationship on the original family members. This avoidance of transference, a major departure from psychoanalytic practice, is a core element of Bowen's systems model.

A featured technique used to facilitate family of origin work is constructing genograms, or visual graphs that depict a family genealogy or family tree (Bowen, 1988; McGoldrick & Gerson, 1986). Genograms provide information about individual family members, the family's structure, and interrelationships over generations. Genograms, useful in engaging the family, offer a rich source of systemic hypotheses about behavior, beliefs, values, and legacies inherent in a family's functioning. Genograms enable the therapist to use a systemic perspective in conceptualizing, reframing, and detoxifying current and past family problems to unblock the relational system and foster increased differentiation of self. As genograms are not driven by a given theoretical approach, they are used by clinicians from diverse theoretical orientations (Roberto, 1992).

Treatment Applicability. Family of origin therapy is practiced most commonly with individuals and couples in whom the capacity to move toward differentiation and objective processing of emotions is relatively high. Therapists espousing this orientation typically work with the most differentiated family members, given that these individuals are assumed to be the most capable of change. However, many family of origin therapists, including Bowen himself, use these techniques in working with dysfunctional couples and families. Usually, a family of origin approach is inappropriate for individuals and couples in acute crisis, but rather is valid for those persons interested in engaging in long-term work that focuses on core relational issues. Few empirical studies could be located evaluating the efficacy of family of origin therapy.

Contextual Therapy

History and Theoretical Development. The originator of contextual family therapy, Ivan Boszormenyi-Nagy, established his reputation through his work with families at Eastern Pennsylvania Psychiatric Institute (EPPI) in Philadelphia. His experiences with intensive psychotherapy and research with schizophrenic inpatients and their families laid the groundwork for his model. His colleagues at EPPI included James Framo, with whom he coedited *Intensive Family Therapy* (1965), a book that reflects his efforts to integrate British object relations theory, existentialism, and the interpersonal model of psychiatry (Roberto, 1992). In 1973, he and Geraldine Spark wrote *Invisible Loyalties: Reciprocity in Intergenerational Family Therapy* (Boszormenyi-Nagy & Spark, 1973). Following the publication of this classic, Boszormenyi-Nagy renamed his approach contextual therapy, a shift reflecting an emphasis on multigenerational relational dynamics and individual personality dynamics. Like Bowen, Boszormenyi-Nagy was a founder of AFTA. A professor at Hahnemann Medical University in Philadelphia, he currently directs an institute in suburban Philadelphia.

Boszormenyi-Nagy outlined four relationship dimensions that serve as the basis for the relational context and dynamics of family functioning (Boszormenyi-Nagy & Krasner, 1986). The first dimension, facts, refers to what is provided by one's destiny. Facts may be unavoidable and due to chance and fate (e.g., ethnicity, gender, physical health) or avoidable reflecting an individual's or family's construction of reality (e.g., family historical context, social context). Psychology, the second dimension, refers to the individual's emotional experience, behavior patterns, aspirations, and motivations. These intrapersonal processes are indicative of interpersonal patterns and familial dynamics. The third dimension, transactions, refers to family organizational patterns regarding roles, communication styles and sequences, power, and intimacy. The fourth dimension focuses on relational ethics, the cornerstone of contextual therapy. Relational ethics refers to fair and trustworthy interpersonal interactions in which the welfare and entitlements of oneself and all other family members are acknowledged, valued, and respected.

Boszormenyi-Nagy and Spark's (1973) theory of contextual family therapy emphasizes legacy, loyalty, indebtedness to one's family of origin, and the influence of one's biological roots. Legacy is "the universal injunction of parental accountability, including the human mandate to reverse the injustices of the past for the benefit of the next generation" (Boszormenyi-Nagy et al., 1991, p. 205). This legacy engenders family loyalties, expressed as unconscious (and thus invisible) repetition of familial expectations, roles, alliances and coalitions, and modes of behavior and communication. The terms "legacy" and "loyalty" refer to the inevitable acquisition of expectations and responsibilities by each individual to the family as a whole. These legacies and

loyalties lead each family member to develop and maintain an invisible ledger of merit and indebtedness, a multigenerational account system of investments and obligations in each relationship. This ledger varies depending upon family members' contributions (e.g., providing support and affirmation) and withdrawals (e.g., exploiting others). When family members mutually give due credit to one another for their contributions to enhancing their life, there is an equal distribution of family emotional resources and more adaptive individual and family functioning. When individuals or families experience themselves as possessing an imbalance in their ledger of merit and indebtedness, trust is diminished, deprived family members manifest destructive entitlement or overindebtedness, and a family scapegoat often emerges.

Basic Structure and Goals. Contextual therapy, a long-term and intensive approach, may be conducted with individuals, family units, or multigenerational systems. This approach is most efficacious when conducted by a cotherapy team, as two therapists provide a balanced and complementary model of give-and-take in human interactions. Including as many family members as possible from the outset is considered optimal, especially when family members are willing and able to work together for a mutually beneficial outcome. Whether therapy involves individuals, the marital dyad, the nuclear family, or the multigenerational family system depends on family members' optimal resource potential for enhancing mutual trust and self-validation, a key component of an individual's self-esteem (Boszormenyi-Nagy et al., 1991). Although the cotherapists serve as catalysts for change, between-session family meetings and rituals are the arenas in which change is consolidated. Additional homework may assist family members in developing more positive and trusting relationships.

The goal of contextual therapy is "rejunction," or the rebalancing of one's obligations in family relationships (Boszormenyi-Nagy et al., 1991). The rejunction process includes acknowledging equitable multilaterality, resolving problems by making invisible loyalties conscious and explicit, repairing ruptured or strained relationships, committing to a fair balance of give-and-take (relational mutuality), and reengaging in living mutuality. The therapist encourages exploration by family members of their own capacities for correcting imbalances in the ledger of merit and indebtedness through increased availability toward others and the redefined use of others as resources. This promotes reliance on self-validation or validation derived from fair consideration of others' needs. Although insight into one's family of origin dynamics is a necessary component of the change and healing process and thus a goal of the work, lasting change requires efforts at rejunction. Finally, contextual therapy, rather than emphasizing symptom reduction, focuses on enhancing positive relational resources.

Techniques and Process of Therapy. Contextual family therapy involves creating an environment within which family members feel safe to make conscious their unconscious ledger of merit and indebtedness, make visible their invisible loyalties, and engage in the rejunction process. The therapist's assumption of the role of advocate for all family members, across multiple generations, whether present or absent, fosters a safe therapeutic climate in which trust in relationships may be rebuilt. This technique, in which the therapist empathically acknowledges each individual's perspective in a nonjudgmental fashion, has been referred to as multidirectional partiality. Once people know that they will be given the opportunity to speak and be listened to sensitively, they are more likely to hear and acknowledge the other side(s) of an issue. Then, the process of give-and-take begins to function within the family, forming the basis for trustworthiness in the relationship. Within this multidirectional partiality, the therapist may take sides to involve a distant or exploited member, always realizing that a rebalancing must take place at some point.

The assessment process is ongoing and includes evaluation of the family's competencies and vulnerabilities, current status, and relational patterns through a three-generation genogram. The therapist appraises the relational ethics of the family unit, emphasizing facts, individual members' personalities, and transactional patterns (e.g., scapegoating, power alignments, hierarchy). The therapist ascertains family members' capacities for empathy, reliability and trustworthiness, the multigenerational legacies and loyalties, interpersonal conflicts based on competing needs and motives, and the nature and quality of attachments. The inclusion of history-taking serves as an additional vehicle for building trust between the therapist and the family.

In the working-through phase, the therapist addresses the presenting problem and allows all the family members present to express their opinion concerning the difficulty. A shift away from the presenting problem takes place quickly thereafter, with a redirection of focus toward the more basic dynamic issues and associated defenses and resistances. The presenting problem is reframed as reflecting underlying concerns regarding loyalty to one's family of origin and the concomitant imbalance in the family relationships. Exploration of family legacies, invisible loyalties, and ledger balances are focal.

Major therapeutic techniques used to enhance the rejunction process include: (1) siding with each family member at different times to maintain multidirectional partiality, while simultaneously holding family members accountable for their views and actions vis-à-vis the ledger of merit and indebtedness; (2) crediting each family member for his or her efforts and contributions to the family, usually beginning with the most vulnerable family member who has been hurt the most (i.e., the scapegoat); (3) eliciting family members' spontaneous overtures to address constructively their own difficulties in an effort to balance fairness between individuals rather than on a systemic level; (4) implementing a moratorium wherein family members are encouraged to consider the benefits of making changes and choosing if and when changes will be made, without feeling pressured by the therapist to change; (5) utilizing the rejunction process to facilitate family members' making relational changes, reconnecting with members of one's immediate and extended family, and rebalancing accounts; (6) loyalty framing in an effort to examine disloyalties and foster appreciation of existing, albeit invisible, loyalties; and (7) helping family members engage in the process of fair exoneration for the choices and behaviors of one's parents, with the goal of establishing more adaptive communication between children and their parents.

Although transference reactions may be manifested between family members or between family members and a therapist, transference work is not considered focal. Rather, the therapists help family members understand and modify their relationships, underscore the importance of family roles, and provide the necessary reparenting to support the rejunction process. When family members acknowledge invisible loyalties, rebalance unsettled accounts, and exonerate their parents, the termination phase commences. Successful termination entails addressing and working through issues of loss, separation, and abandonment.

Treatment Applicability. This approach has been criticized as too intellectual and inappropriate for treating families from the lower economic classes and those who are not highly articulate. Yet, Boszormenyi-Nagy and colleagues (1991) assert that their approach is applicable to most human problems, as the theory is built on basic principles relevant to a cross-section of families regardless of race, ethnicity, or socioeconomic status. They further argue that the concepts of trust, fairness, and reciprocity are basic relational concepts pertinent to the treatment of individuals from all sociocultural backgrounds, manifesting a broad range of symptoms and relational difficulties. The contextual approach not only is applicable to present problems, but also emphasizes the preventive aspect anchored in the rebalancing of present relationships for the benefit of future offspring. A number of writers have addressed the appropriateness of contextual therapy for work with children and their families (Goldenthal, 1991). To date, there is minimal empirical validation for the efficacy of this approach.

Symbolic-Experiential Therapy

Carl Whitaker, another family therapy pioneer, used clinical experiences with children and severely disturbed adults to gain insight into the nature and utility of primary process ("craziness"), the importance of regression in fostering growth, the value of entering a patient's world intuitively by allowing one's own unconscious to comprehend the metacommunication of the patient's unconscious, and the importance of the therapist fashioning a style harmonious with his or her own nature. At Emory University Department of Psychiatry in Atlanta, Whitaker and colleagues experimented with cotherapy and focused on deciphering the symbolic meaning of psychotic communications. A feature of this approach was to treat inpatients in conjunction with family members and significant others, with the purpose being to foster positive growth by increasing insight into family dynamics and the identified patients' symptomatology. Later, at the University of Wisconsin Medical School, Whitaker articulated the symbolic-experiential model of family therapy (Whitaker & Keith, 1981), which while influenced by the work of communication theorists at the Mental Research Institute (MRI) in Palo Alto, is rooted primarily in affective experiences that are evident during the process of change. Implicit in his writings and teachings is a clarion call for the experience of therapy to be an authentic encounter for all involved, a position similar to that espoused by humanists and existentialists.

Whitaker (1976) asserted that theory hinders clinical practice and posited that his symbolic-experiential approach is largely atheoretical. Despite this contention, however, some basic tenets and key concepts are associated with this approach: symbolic experience, growth, psychotherapy of the absurd, battles for structure and initiative, psychotherapeutic impasse, and playing (Napier & Whitaker, 1978). Symbolic-experiential therapy deals "with the representation system underneath what's actually being said" (Whitaker & Bumberry, 1988, p. 78). This approach deemphasizes conscious thinking about problems, while stressing increased awareness of unconscious and affective experiences to help individuals expand their range of life experience and live a freer and more creative life (Whitaker & Bumberry, 1988). To do so, individuals must grapple with universal life issues, including sexuality, "craziness," loving and hating, and death. Whitaker also is known for his writings on the healthy family (e.g., Whitaker & Bumberry, 1988) and for providing guidelines to help keep the therapist alive and avoid therapist burn-out (Whitaker, 1976).

Other theorists identified with the experiential and humanistic schools include Satir (1967, 1972), Duhl and Duhl (1981), Kempler (1981), and Kantor and Lehr (1975). Due to space considerations, only Whitaker's approach is detailed.

Incorporated in this discussion is a delineation of Satir's central experiential family therapy techniques.

Basic Structure and Goals. The course of symbolic-experiential family therapy typically is of intermediate duration, conducted at variable frequency. Sessions optimally include the symptomatic family member, the nuclear and extended family, and the index person's social support network. The structure of therapy is built on a "therapeutic suprasystem" (Roberto, 1991), consisting of the family or couple in treatment and a cotherapy team or therapist and consultant. Whitaker recommends a cotherapy team to increase the clinician's potency and give each therapist support and a partner to bail him or her out when ensnared by family dynamics. This approach enables the therapists to play more roles and alternate functions consistent with the idea that "members of the family should be able to play all positions on the family team," and go beyond stereotypical roles. The cotherapy team exhibits a pattern of caring that enables the family to risk becoming more anxious, instead of relying on defensive and self-protective interactional patterns. When cotherapy is not possible, a consultant or consultation group provides a systemic view of the family, supports the therapist, and enhances problem-solving potential (Roberto, 1992).

Symbolic-experiential therapy enables individuals to develop an increased tolerance for the absurdity of life and to balance interpersonal connectedness with expressions of individuation (Whitaker & Bumberry, 1988). The work aims to increase family members' sense of cohesion, help them support individual family members' needs in the process of individuation and negotiation of developmental tasks, and foster creativity, spontaneity, and accessibility of affective experience in the family unit and in individual members. Operationalization of these goals is developed by members of the therapeutic suprasystem, based on the unique family system and its relational patterns.

Techniques and Process of Therapy. In symbolic-experiential family therapy, a strong therapeutic alliance is essential, and the personality of the therapist encompasses absurdity, humor, and personal authenticity. While engaged actively in the therapeutic process, the therapists do not direct the therapy. Rather, they listen, observe, reflect upon their own emotional responses, and challenge maladaptive familial interactional patterns without focusing on their etiology. The role of the therapist is akin to that of a "coach" or surrogate grandparent, roles requiring a balance of nurturance and caring with structure and discipline. Keith and Whitaker (1981) drew an analogy between play therapy and family therapy, depicting the importance of playing with the entire family, actually, symbolically, or metaphorically. In so doing, the therapists convey permission to play, freeing the patients to have fun together, thereby making family life less serious and constrained.

During the beginning phase, the therapists join with the family to build sufficient trust and credibility that the family is willing to invest in treatment. This process is facilitated by the practitioners' use of self, play, humor, metaphors, and reframing to expand the family's perspective about problems and present symptoms as attempts to grow. The use of self refers to the therapist's modeling through sharing metaphorical allegories and teaching stories, free associations, memories, and fantasies aimed at offering alternative problem-solving strategies and supporting the family members' initiatives for change. This enables families to trust the therapist enough to share their idiosyncratic inner world (Whitaker, 1976).

The battles for structure and initiative must be waged before a solid therapeutic alliance is developed, enabling the family to reorganize to cure the symptomatic (scapegoated) member and heighten differentiation (Whitaker & Keith, 1981). The battle for structure refers to a battle over ground rules regarding treatment structure, session membership, scheduling, and fees (Napier & Whitaker, 1978). Its aim is to establish the cotherapists as consultants for change. This battle is completed when a minimum of a two-generation structure to the therapy is established, with the therapists in charge and having optimal flexibility in working with the family. When this battle is resolved successfully, family regression occurs, engendering an intense transference relationship and underscoring the seriousness of the therapeutic endeavor. This battle for initiative is then undertaken, with the cotherapy team encouraging family members to take responsibility for their own growth and life choices. This struggle is resolved when the family takes control of the direction of the sessions and initiates changes *and* when the cotherapy dyad establishes an existential I–thou relationship with each family member. During this phase, information is obtained regarding the presenting problem, families of origin, and family interactional patterns.

In the middle phase, interventions create an "interpersonal expansion of the symptom" and the family addresses their life problems. Techniques used to facilitate this process include redefining symptoms as efforts toward growth, explicating covert conflict, separating interpersonal and internal stress and modeling fantasized alternatives to stress, reversing roles, and involving grandparents and other extended family members in the treatment process (e.g., Roberto, 1991). Techniques endorsed by Satir (1967, 1972) also may be employed during this phase. Family members may be encouraged to enact scenes in their lives (drama, family reconstruction) and create static (family sculpture) or dynamic (stress ballet) nonverbal presentations that express their perceptions of family relationships. The use of experi-

ential techniques, in conjunction with the therapists' use of self, helps the family develop alternative interactional patterns that facilitate change and growth (Whitaker & Keith, 1981).

Many families effectively negotiate the middle phase of the therapy endeavor, evidencing improvements and handling problems in a more competent manner. However, for some families, the work may lead to an "impotence impasse," in which the family does not take responsibility for their own problems and thus does not change (Whitaker & Keith, 1981). This impasse is resolved when the family and cotherapy team mutually agree upon treatment decisions.

Throughout the therapy, and particularly in the middle phase, Whitaker cautions against engaging in symptom relief, arguing that symptoms develop as adaptations to pathological family or societal situations. The implication of this assertion is that symptom relief could precipitate the emergence of symptoms in other family members or disintegration of the family unit. Thus, he recommends the use of paradoxical reframing, which involves prescribing the symptom until it becomes so exaggerated that it is abandoned. Whitaker practiced "psychotherapy of the absurd" before others described the use of paradox in family therapy. He underscored the importance of using paradoxical reframing with wisdom, warmth, and humor, and not as a gimmick.

In the end phase, the cotherapy team disengages from the family systems, restricting their interventions to problematic situations that the family is unable to manage on its own. This permits the family to reflect on its own functioning and assume increasing responsibility for decision making and problem solving. The result is that the relationship between the cotherapy team and family moves from that of consultant–patient to a partnership. To promote this relational shift, the cotherapists spontaneously self-disclose, express grief regarding termination, and request feedback. The termination of therapy occurs when family members demonstrate sufficient self-confidence and competencies in managing life events. Termination is accompanied by the family system's and cotherapy dyad's acknowledgment of mutual interdependence and loss of a meaningful relationship.

Treatment Applicability. Symbolic-experiential family therapy has been used with families with a range of difficulties, including those in which the identified patient carries a schizophrenia spectrum disorder diagnosis. It has been argued that this approach may have limited efficacy with families in which a member evidences an antisocial or narcissistic personality disorder or for families coping with a trauma (e.g., divorce, abuse). While empirical studies have not been presented, the efficacy of the model is suggested in detailed case descriptions (e.g., Bumberry & Whitaker, 1988; Napier & Whitaker, 1978).

Communication Model

History and Theoretical Development. The communication model of family therapy, including the Mental Research Institute (MRI) interactional approach and the work at the Brief Family Therapy Center in Milwaukee, has helped shape the form and nature of family therapy. Communication theorists posit that because actors in a system are interdependent, the behavior of any one member affects all other members, and the important time and relational dimension is the here and now. Given that the family is more than the sum of the individual personalities and includes their interactions, it is nonsummative (Olson, 1970). Whether an action makes a temporary impact or leads to lasting change depends on the sources (society or external system, family's history and tradition of power allocation, family unit's equilibrium and need for survival and system maintenance at the time) from which power is derived (Stanton, 1981). Thus, the communications model reconceptualizes symptoms as reflecting interactional and situation dynamics, underscoring the importance of the social context in shaping behavior.

The MRI interactional school of family therapy was conceived in Palo Alto, California, in the 1950s by Gregory Bateson, Don Jackson, John Weakland, and Jay Haley, who shared an interest in the nature of the communication process. They applied anthropological methods of participant observation and objective scrutiny and social systems theory to their work with families of schizophrenics. Virginia Satir later joined the MRI group and moved into the foreground of the dynamic band of family therapy pioneers. Her family therapy primer, *Conjoint Family Therapy* (1967) outlined the core ideas of the communications wing of family systems theory and therapy. Today, her followers are loosely banded together in the Avanta Network formed in the 1980s.

The Palo Alto group, based on their research regarding communication patterns in schizophrenic families, asserted that all behavior is communication, occurring at the surface or content level and the metacommunication or intent level (a communication that adds meaning to the surface or content level communication). In "Toward a theory of schizophrenia" (1956), Bateson, Jackson, Haley, and Weakland conceptualized double-bind communications, a form of paradoxical communication in which contradictory messages are communicated concurrent with a third message that the receiver not make explicit the logical inconsistencies in the message received. Once the recipient perceives the world in these contradictory "damned-if-you-do," "damned-if-you-don't" messages, any portion of the sequence is sufficient to activate confusion.

Other concepts that have contributed to family systems theory by members of this group merit inclusion. Jackson's (1957) notion of family homeostasis refers to the family unit's attempts to maintain the status quo and resist internal or external threat to that equilibrium. As such, the therapist's efforts at change may activate family mistrust, making imperative deft strategies and an accurate understanding of the family's dynamics as revealed in their verbal and nonverbal messages. Satir (1967) demonstrated that if one family member is troubled, then all members are in pain. Leverage for gaining entrance can be found in recognizing this shared, reciprocal pain and indicating that all can improve family functioning and find ways of having their own needs met and the pain reduced through conjoint family therapy. Because of her sensitivity to the importance of nonverbal communication, Satir developed such techniques as family sculpting, a means of depicting each member's view of the family, without using words filtered through secondary-process thinking. Sculpting has been further developed and elaborated by others (e.g., Duhl, 1983; Papp, 1976).

Weakland and the others now at the MRI, including Jules Riskin, Paul Watzlawick, and Arthur Bodin, developed brief family intervention and crisis techniques, combining communications, strategic, and structural theory and techniques. Rapid problem resolution conducive to positive change is pursued (e.g., Watzlawick, Weakland, & Fisch, 1974).

Steve deShazer, Insoo Berg, and colleagues established the Brief Family Therapy Center in Milwaukee, in which solution-focused brief therapy was developed and practiced (deShazer, 1985). This approach assumes that family dysfunction reflects ineffective problem-solving efforts and that families possess the knowledge and motivation necessary for problem resolution. Thus, therapy helps families initiate the solution process. The therapist works with the family to develop blueprints for change, referred to as "skeleton keys," enabling the family to unlock doors to enhanced problem resolution and associated family satisfaction. This approach draws heavily from the Ericksonian tradition and is similar to the systemic therapy practiced by Selvini Palazolli and colleagues.

For purposes of illustration, the discussion that follows focuses on the MRI brief therapy approach.

Basic Structure and Goals. Therapies based in the communications model typically are time-limited interventions. Sessions are scheduled weekly or biweekly, with a maximum of 10 meetings. This structured approach employs active interventions. Sessions are conducted by a single clinician or cotherapy pair, often with consultant(s) positioned behind a one-way mirror to provide objective input and recommend interventions. The primary goal is problem resolution aimed at reducing or eliminating suffering. It is not expected that families will understand how the change occurred, nor is the development of a strong therapeutic alliance fostered.

Techniques and Process of Therapy. Adherents of the communications school are pragmatic and problem focused. The approach is primarily behaviorally oriented and insight is not deemed essential for change. Because repetitive, dysfunctional behavioral sequences and transactions occur in the present and are perpetuated by ongoing behavior, their modification dictates intervention in the present system and not consideration of past events and emotions (Stanton, 1981). The therapist must take deliberate, forceful steps to change enough facets of the repetitive problem-maintaining behavior patterns that the symptom no longer is needed. Repetitious, dysfunctional behavior and communication patterns are replaced with new, healthier ways of communicating and acting. Communication therapists differentiate between first-order change, allowable by families because it entails only superficial modification that does not alter significantly the system or its members, and second-order change, which results from major alterations in the interaction and transaction patterns. Second-order change is deemed essential to a successful therapeutic outcome (Watzlawick et al., 1974).

The MRI brief therapy approach is conducted in the following sequence (Segal, 1991): (1) identification of family members motivated for the intervention; (2) data collection regarding problem behaviors and prior problem-solving efforts; (3) establishment of a defined and operationalized goal; (4) formulation of a plan to promote change; (5) implementation of therapeutic techniques aimed at disrupting maladaptive problem-solving attempts and enhancing the use of more effective strategies; (6) evaluation of treatment efficacy; and (7) termination when a small, but significant and apparently durable change is noted and the family conveys a capacity to manage problems effectively without the therapist's help.

Paradoxical injunctions, commonly employed by adherents to the MRI brief therapy approach, are shared by strategic and systemic therapists. Two classes of paradoxical directives may be used to change the family's attempted solutions. The family may be instructed to change the problem behavior or to increase the frequency and/or intensity of the symptomatic behavior (symptom prescription). Symptom prescription, a therapeutic double bind, facilitates second-order change by placing family members in an untenable position vis-à-vis the problem so that any action taken produces changes in the problem behavior. That is, a symptomatic family member who is instructed not to change the problem-behavior is caught in a dilemma. If he or she complies with the therapeutic instruction, it demonstrates that the

person is able to control the symptom and thus can no longer claim to be exhibiting the symptomatic behavior. If the family member defies the directive, the symptom is ameliorated and change results.

Treatment Applicability. The efficacy of the MRI brief therapy approach has been documented in case reports of families in which an individual member evidences a range of symptomatic behaviors (e.g., depression, sexual dysfunction, child and adolescent behavior problems) that decrease following treatment. However, few systematic treatment outcome studies have been conducted focusing on the model's effectiveness. Proponents assert that the general systems theory underlying the communication model of family therapy may be applied to larger social organizations (Bodin, 1981).

Structural Family Therapy

History and Theoretical Development. The structural model of family therapy, which serves as the basis for much of family therapy practice today, was developed primarily by Salvador Minuchin and colleagues (Minuchin, 1974; Minuchin, Montalvo, Guerney, Rosman, & Schumer, 1967; Minuchin et al., 1978), notably Harry Aponte, Edgar Auerswald, H. Charles Fishman, Jay Haley, Lynn Hoffman, Braulio Montalvo, and Bernice Rosman.

Structural family theory and therapy evolved to its present form at the Philadelphia Child Guidance Clinic, where Minuchin served as director from 1965 to 1981. This clinic, which services low-income families as its major clientele, is an internationally recognized center for training professionals and paraprofessionals. Since Minuchin and his wife, Patricia, moved to New York City, where they train structural family therapists, the Philadelphia Child Guidance Clinic has continued to flourish under Alberto Serrano until 1996. The structural family therapy model has been expanded for use with African American populations by incorporating an eco-structural perspective wherein family transactions with external social systems are a focus of concern (Boyd-Franklin, 1987).

This model has achieved great popularity, fostered, in part, by theory and therapeutic techniques that are explicit and lend themselves to being taught systematically. To use this approach effectively, the therapist must be comfortable being a conductor (Beels & Ferber, 1972), an active and powerful therapist who conveys expertise and a belief in his or her abilities to assist the family to mobilize their capacity to change. As the stage director or producer of the family drama, the therapist expects family members to accommodate to his or her directives, and therefore communicates his or her expertise in facilitating change.

This theory-based approach conceptualizes adaptive and maladaptive functioning in terms of the organized patterns of interaction between individuals, their families, and the social context (for reviews, see Colapinto, 1991; Minuchin, 1974; Minuchin & Fishman, 1981; Minuchin et al., 1967). A central tenet is the notion of a hierarchial organization within the family based upon appropriate boundaries and the delineation between subsystems. Family systems are comprised of subsystems, including the spouse subsystem (marital dyad), parental subsystem (which may include a grandparent or other adult in a central role and/or a parentified child), parent–child dyads, and the sibling subsystem (the child's first peer group) (Minuchin et al., 1976).

Alignment refers to the "joining or opposition of one member of a system to another in carrying out an operation" (Aponte, 1976, p. 434). Coalitions, covert alliances between two family members against a third, and alliances, the sharing by two individuals of a common interest not held by a third person, are two primary forms of alignments in families. Boundaries and alignments depend on power or force, "the relative influence of each [family] member on the outcome of an activity" (Aponte, 1976, p. 434).

Families experience transitions as their members develop and the family system proceeds through a family developmental life cycle (Haley, 1973). The family structure must adapt to these changes to foster continued growth, while providing a stable environment. When a family cannot adapt, rigid interaction patterns develop that resist alteration, even when perceived by family members as dysfunctional. Such inflexible patterns prevent the family from exploring new alternatives and progressing effectively through the family life cycle.

Impairments in boundaries, inappropriate alignments, and/or power imbalances are hallmarks of dysfunctional families. These families are often classified as enmeshed or disengaged, terms referring to the characteristic way in which family members establish contact with each other (Minuchin et al., 1978). In one form of maladaptive family structure, disengaged families, the members do not seem to be involved with, care about, or react to one another. Enmeshed families, on the other hand, lie at the opposite end of the spectrum concerned with maladaptive family involvement and exhibit excessive interconnections among members and immediate reactivity to each others' moods and behaviors to an extent that change initiated by one person is met with immediate resistance by others.

Dysfunctional family alignments require at least three participants and circumstances where two members consistently agree with each other in the form of a stable coalition against a third member. When two family members mutually identify a third member as the source of the problem, a detouring coalition emerges to give the impression of har-mony and reduce stress in the dyad. Triangulation occurs when two opposing family members both insist that a third member side with him or her against the opposing party. The third person, often a child, feels conflicted about such a split allegiance, resulting in symptomatic behavior. Dysfunctional family transactions, reflecting the inability of family members to use their authority in implementing assigned roles, are indicative of problems in the family's balance of power.

From a structural family therapy perspective, healthy families have well-defined structures and are flexible and relatively cohesive. They accommodate to the changing functions and roles of individuals, subsystems, the family unit as a whole, and the sociocultural context.

Basic Structure and Goals. Structural family therapy, a brief therapy approach, is flexible regarding the number of therapists involved, which family members participate in a given interview, and the location, length, and frequency of interviews. Typically, however, a single therapist is employed, the family members who interact on a daily basis are involved in the sessions, and treatment consists of weekly sessions of 5 to 7 months' duration. When the presenting problem is serious (e.g., an anorexic adolescent in medical danger), the index person may be hospitalized, while the family receives intensive family therapy (Minuchin et al., 1978).

The primary goal is the resolution of the presenting problem through the restructuring of the family unit so that more adaptive interactional patterns prevail. An additional goal is the alteration of the family's construction of reality, by facilitating the development of alternative explanatory schemas for conceptualizing the problem. This enables the family to develop more adaptive transactions.

Techniques and Process of Therapy. According to structural family therapists, families enter therapy when stress has overloaded the system and the family continues to maintain its homeostatic balance by repeating the same pathological behaviors. The task of therapy is to restructure the family by introducing alternate ways of interacting. The family is presumed to have the capacity to adopt new patterns; thus structural therapists search for competence within the family, rather than exploring the roots of dysfunctional behavior.

This approach incorporates three cyclical and overlapping stages: joining, assessing, and restructuring. The therapist joins the family rapidly and in a position of leadership to collect data and diagnose the problem. By entering the system, the therapist learns how the family experiences reality and gains awareness of family rules, myths, and themes. Maintenance (supporting the existing structure of the family or subsystem), tracking (following the content of the family's communication with minimal intervention), and mimesis (adopting the behavior and affective style of the family) facilitate the joining process. The presenting problem initially is accepted as the real problem, and interventions are designed to relieve the symptom and improve the system's functioning. Once this occurs, the family may decide to work on other problems. This is a more symptom-oriented approach than psychoanalytic therapies, yet not as symptom-focused as the strategic therapies discussed later in this chapter.

Six domains of family functioning are assessed during the evaluation phase: structure, boundary quality, and resonance; flexibility and capacity for change; interactional patterns of the various subsystems; role of the index person and how the symptomatic behavior maintains family homeostasis; the ecological context within which the presenting problem emerges and is maintained; and the developmental stage of individual family members and the family unit as a whole. This results in the formulation of a family map and diagnosis in which relationships between structural problems and current symptoms are explicated.

The restructuring phase redresses the structural difficulties identified previously. The stance is taken that, within the hierarchy, the parents should have the power, and when necessary, they are supported by the therapist in asserting it. Process (how the family interacts) rather than content (what is said) is the key to therapy. Nonverbal aspects of the communication process are important data.

A number of therapeutic techniques have been associated with the restructuring process. Spatial interventions may entail rearranging seating in a session, removing members temporarily, or having certain members observe the session from behind a one-way mirror, taking them out of the action for a while and forcing others to relate. These spatial interventions facilitate change in interpersonal boundaries in an effort to alter the perspectives of the family members. Enactments, designed to induce the family to act out dysfunctional and habitual transactional patterns in the session, provide the therapist opportunities to intervene directly to facilitate structural change. Another means of altering embedded family patterns involves the therapist's use of self to unbalance the maladaptive homeostasis of the system. The clinician temporarily supports particular family members to modify the usual hierarchical organization and introduce the possibility of new combinations or options. To change family members' constructions of reality vis-à-vis the presenting problem, the therapist attempts to transform the family's linear view of the problem to one of complementarity. Education may be provided in an effort to restructure the family. Paradox can be used to confuse family members, disrupt entrenched thinking, and prompt a search for alternatives.

Additional techniques include escalating stress, boundary marking (modifying transactional patterns such that appropriate boundaries are reinforced), and assigning homework tasks (for a review, see Colapinto, 1991). The therapist may encourage the family to reenact a dysfunctional transaction and then intervene by increasing the intensity and escalating stress via prolonging the occurrence of the enactment, introducing new variables (new family members), or indicating alternate transactions. Then, by having the family enact a changed pattern of transaction that may include boundary marking, the session serves as a viable model for interaction outside the therapy room. An example is the family lunch with the anorexic and her family, in which the symptom and the family's interactions are confronted *in vivo* and then are reenacted differently (Minuchin et al., 1978). The assignment of homework serves as a diagnostic probe to determine familial openness to change and as a mechanism to enable the maladaptive communication patterns and structures to be altered.

In sum, Minuchin (1974) posits that therapy induces a more optimal family organization that enables family members to realize their own growth potential. This is accomplished by a therapeutic process in which the family's perception of reality is challenged, alternate ways of interacting are presented, and new self-reinforcing transactional patterns are developed that eventuate in more satisfying relationships amongst family members.

Treatment Applicability. Empirically based treatment outcome studies reveal that the structural family therapy approach can be applied successfully to a range of problems and symptoms (e.g., psychosomatic illnesses, externalizing behavior disorders, substance abuse) in families from all economic levels and with various family structures. This approach commonly is used when the identified patient is a child and the treatment of choice is family therapy.

Strategic Family Therapy

Strategic family therapy gained considerable prominence during the 1970s and 1980s (Haley, 1963, 1973, 1976, 1984; Madanes, 1984). Haley first explicated the strategic family therapy model in Palo Alto and elaborated it later at the Philadelphia Child Guidance Clinic with Minuchin and subsequently at the Family Therapy Institute of Washington, DC, which he cofounded with Cloe Madanes. Haley (1971) and Madanes (1981), like Whitaker, became intrigued with the potency inherent in the use of paradox to disrupt rigid relational and communication patterns. They personified the communication theorists' interest in strategic interventions, based on evaluation of the current structure and functioning of the family system. Haley became the first editor of *Family Process* in 1962, the first journal devoted to family theory and therapy.

The strategic therapies of Haley, Madanes, and Lynn Hoffman, influenced by Bateson's communication theory and Ericksonian hypnosis, view problems as metaphors for family dysfunction maintained by faulty and incongruent hierarchies and malfunctioning triangles and have behavior change as their main objective. Symptom formation usually occurs during family life-cycle transitions, when a developmental task is not mastered adequately, thus precipitating a crisis. Under such conditions, an individual's development becomes fixated and symptoms evolve as expressions of the unresolved crisis. The complex and circular behavioral sequences that comprise a family's problem-solving attempts perpetuate the presenting problem (Haley, 1976) and thus family system change is necessary for individual change.

Another early bastion of strategic family therapy was in Texas, where Robert MacGregor, Harry Goolishian, Alberto Serrano, and colleagues devised multiple-impact family therapy (Beels & Ferber, 1972), which involved bringing families in for several days of marathon treatment (MacGregor, 1990). They recognized that potent strategic maneuvers were necessary to dislodge existing rigid patterns and structures. Later Goolishian and colleagues were attracted to the use of paradoxes and metaphors. In the late 1970s, the Galveston Family Institute emerged as a training and treatment site for this theory and methodology (Goolishian & Anderson, 1990). During the 1970s and 1980s, the Galveston group became involved in epistemology, cybernetics, recursiveness, and the work of Humberto Maturana (Dell, 1981).

More recently, members of the Galveston group have focused their attention upon a social constructionist perspective (e.g., Goolishian & Anderson, 1990), a view shared by other family therapy leaders (e.g., Hoffman, 1992). According to the social constructionist model, meanings are developed through social interaction and social consensus (Gergen, 1985). Understandings are arrived at through mutual co-construction of events, negotiated through social interactions. These understandings are associated with the context within which they emerge, and thus meanings constantly evolve in relation to the social context of a given interaction. To the extent that new explanatory narratives of meaning can be co-constructed, individuals possess more flexibility in approaching life events and social interactions.

Another stronghold of social construction is in Norway, with Tom Andersen's (1991) work with a reflecting team. The reflecting team joins the interviewer and family and shares their observations. The team's reflections are tied to the content of the conversation and do not use negative connotations in describing events. The reflecting process provides the participants with the flexibility to shift between listening and talking about the issues at hand. This work assumes that there is no one right way to construe a given situation or problem. As such, language is a vehicle through which the clinician and family cocreate a description and understanding of the presenting issues.

The following discussion focuses on Haley and Madanes' problem-solving therapy as illustrative of strategic approaches. Given the overlap between some of the strategic family therapies and the communications and systemic models, relevant therapeutic structures and techniques discussed previously are noted briefly.

Basic Structure and Goals. Strategic therapy, typically a brief intervention, may include the entire family or only one or two members of a family system, for weekly or biweekly sessions. Strategic family work is structured, with the therapist directing the questions, giving directives, and intervening actively. Teaching skills, imparting knowledge, and giving practical advice are not priorities. Sessions are conducted by a single therapist, while consultant(s) provide objective input and recommend strategic interventions from behind a one-way mirror.

The major goal is resolving the family's presenting problem within the social context, by replacing stereotypical behaviors with greater flexibility, redistributing power for a more equitable balance, and enabling participants to communicate more clearly and accurately. To accomplish this, small and specific subgoals related to the resolution of the presenting problems are identified collaboratively. These subgoals are conceptualized as increases in positive behaviors. This strategy enhances family motivation by engendering a sense that change is possible. The ultimate aim of the work is to alter interactional sequences that maintain problem behaviors, thereby facilitating resolution of family crisis and progression to the next phase of life-cycle development. These changes are consistent with achieving second-order change.

Techniques and Process of Therapy. Adherents of this school are pragmatic and symptom focused. The approach is behaviorally oriented and insight is not deemed essential for change. Because repetitive, dysfunctional behavioral sequences and transactions occur in the present and are perpetuated by continuing, current behavior, modification of these patterns dictates intervention in the present system and not consideration of past events and emotions (Stanton, 1981). The therapist must take deliberate, forceful steps to change enough facets of the repetitive pattern so that the symptom will no longer be needed. The practitioner endeavors to replace repetitive, dysfunctional behavior and communication patterns with new, healthier ways of communicating and acting. Strategic therapists are active and authoritative, exercising their persuasive powers to convince a family to follow a precise straightforward or paradoxical directive.

The first stage of problem-solving therapy consists of an

initial interview in which the presenting problem and its context are ascertained (Haley, 1976). This interview includes the social stage, problem stage, interaction stage, goal-setting stage, and task-setting stage. This assessment culminates in the first set of therapeutic directives based upon the therapist's understanding of the family diagnosis and the presenting problem.

In the middle phase, these tactical interventions are implemented as strategies for addressing each problem (Madanes, 1981). The directives, which may be straight or paradoxical, provide information about the family (including resistances to change), intensify the therapeutic relationship, and facilitate structural change in interactional sequences maintaining the problem. Straight directives enlist family cooperation with requests of the therapist and may help in times of family crisis. There is frequent use of paradoxical directives and the framing of therapeutic double binds or split messages. Whichever half of the contradictory message the family chooses to follow will engage them in some aspect of improvement. A directive that appears to contradict the desired goals actually serves to propel the family toward change. In effect, once the problem is clearly defined, definite goals have been set, and the paradoxical instructions have been given, the responses are observed and the therapist continues to encourage the customary behavior (symptom prescription), thus ruling out "rebellious improvement." The therapist then expresses bewilderment at the changes that occur, refusing to take credit for them.

Key techniques employed to challenge the family's homeostasis and create change in existing behavioral sequences include paradox, reframing, creating ordeals, pretending, and unbalancing. Major paradoxical techniques are therapeutic double-bind communications (described earlier), positioning (accept and exaggerate family communications, underscoring the absurdity of the situation and thereby prompting the family to reevaluate and potentially modify their stance), restraining (discourage change by outlining associated dangers), and symptom prescription. In symptom prescription, it is suggested that the symptom be increased, thereby giving the appearance of sanctioning the undesirable behaviors. The therapist's efforts do not arouse resistance from the identified patient, who no longer needs to defend his or her right to maintain the problem behavior. By recommending exacerbation of the symptom, the therapist intends to intensify the symptom such that it no longer serves a useful function in the system, and thus the symptom is ameliorated (Haley, 1963). Additionally, if the person can deliberately make the symptom more severe, the therapist acquires leverage to point out that, as he or she can control the behavior by increasing it, then control also can be exercised to decrease it.

Reframing is a technique in which behaviors that have been criticized as disturbed are relabeled positive (positive connotation), thereby introducing a new view of reality. An acting-out, belligerent adolescent may be relabeled the family savior; his or her behavior is interpreted as a sacrifice in the service of holding the parents' marriage together, since the only time they are united is when the adolescent gets into trouble. This new perspective enables the family to be grateful rather than critical, thus facilitating resolution of the marital conflict and forcing confrontation with the reality of the burden the scapegoat bears. Thus, reframing redefines the situation in a manner that suggests new solutions to old problems.

Other techniques used by strategic therapists are elaborated briefly in the following paragraph. Ordeals are therapeutic maneuvers in which family members are asked to engage in behaviors that they dislike, but that would improve family relationships. Pretending involves a request by the therapist that the symptomatic person feign his or her symptom. This voluntary manifestation of the symptom alters perceptions of the symptomatic individual and the function of the problem behavior in the system. Unbalancing involves the strategic support of one family member as a means of interfering with the equilibrium that maintains the problem, oftentimes through the prescription of homework.

Termination is initiated when significant improvements in the presenting problem have occurred and the family reveals a capacity to manage problems without the therapist. In the termination phase, the family is credited for having made the changes, yet cautioned against developing a sense of false optimism about a problem-free existence.

Treatment Applicability. Strategic family therapy has been applied in work with couples and families presenting with myriad symptoms, including schizophrenia spectrum disorders, substance abuse, anxiety disorders, family violence, incest, and child and adolescent behavior problems (e.g., Madanes, 1990; Stanton, 1981; Szykula, Morris, & Sudweeks, 1987). There is a paucity of empirical data regarding the efficacy of this approach.

Systemic Family Therapy

Systemic family therapy was elucidated by the Milan group in Italy. Influenced by Bateson's writing on circular epistemology, family systems theory was incorporated in the development of brief systemic therapy. The systemic approach focuses on process, viewing the family and therapist as an ecosystem wherein each member affects the psychological well-being of all other members. According to this perspective, problem behavior is maintained by rule-governed transactional patterns, with the symptom sustaining the family homeostasis. The family is conceptualized as a nonlinear and complex cybernetic system, with interlocking feedback mechanisms and repetitive behavioral sequence patterns. Systemic family therapists emphasize the importance of illuminating the meaning of second-order cybernetics, namely the cybernetics of cybernetics, using these efforts as a foundation for family interventions.

The Milan approach was initially applied to disturbed children and their parents (Selvini Palazzoli, Boscolo, Cecchin, & Prata, 1978), including families with an anorexic member (Selvini Palazzoli, 1974). The work also focused on the role of the referring person in the therapy and the use of paradox and counterparadox (Selvini Palazzoli et al., 1978). In 1980 the Milan group divided into two autonomous groups. Mara Selvini Palazzoli and Guiliana Prata turned their attention to finding an invariant prescription applicable to all families. Selvini Palazolli and her research collaborators articulated a systemic model of psychotic processes in families (Selvini Palazolli, Cirillo, Selvini, & Sorrentino, 1989). Luigi Boscolo and Gianfranco Cecchin formed their own treatment and training center (Milan Associates) and asserted that interventions should be tailored to specific family dynamics.

The treatment methods practiced by the Milan group (e.g., use of therapeutic team as consultants, symptom prescription, ritualized prescriptions, and circular questioning) influenced many European (e.g., Andolfi, 1979), Canadian (Tomm, 1984a,b), and American family therapists, including staff at the Ackerman Institute, among them Lynn Hoffman, Peggy Papp, and Olga Silverstein. Hoffman subsequently founded her own family institute in Amherst, Massachusetts.

Basic Structure and Goals. Systemic family therapy sessions are typically few in number (ranging from 3–20), spaced at monthly intervals to permit time for interventions to take root and elicit systemic change. The number of sessions determined at the outset of treatment is adhered to strictly. Sessions are conducted by a single therapist or cotherapy pair, and consultant(s) may be positioned behind a one-way mirror to recommend systemic interventions. Selvini Palazzoli and colleagues (Selvini Palazzoli et al., 1978) generally use the "Greek chorus," observers in an adjoining room and behind a one-way mirror who may call the therapist out and make suggestions, "take sides," and participate in postsession deliberations regarding the written prescription.

The overarching goal is to create an environment for exploring the family's belief systems, providing new conceptualizations of family difficulties (cognitive maps), and facilitating change. To this end, the treatment team maintains a systemic perspective to resolve the presenting problem within the family context. Specific goals are articulated by the family members, and the therapy team holds that it is the family's responsibility to make changes. In instances in which the therapist disagrees with the family's goals, family wishes are respected except in cases where their decisions may be harmful to one or more family members (e.g., abuse or incest). It is not expected that families will come to understand how the change occurred, nor is the development of a strong therapeutic alliance fostered.

Techniques and Process of Therapy. Incorporating a more evolutionary viewpoint than their strategic colleagues, systemic family therapists posit that when the family's rules and conceptual framework for understanding reality (i.e., epistemology) are no longer adaptive, problematic behaviors emerge. Using a framework that introduces new information to foster the family's development of an alternative epistemology and spontaneous change, sessions are organized according to a relatively standard treatment format. During the presession, information is gathered by the consulting team. Then, the therapist(s) meets with the family, provides the information gleaned from the presession, and facilitates discussion allowing for observation of the family's transactional patterns. Next, the therapist–cotherapy dyad and the "Greek chorus" meet in a separate room to share observations, opinions, and suggestions. A systemic hypothesis and associated interventions are then formulated. The therapist or cotherapy pair then rejoin the family, provide feedback from the meeting with the consultants, and offer a directive for a task to be completed outside of the session. This directive typically takes the form of a paradoxical suggestion, symptom prescription, or ritual and may be offered in a letter or telegram, which is sometimes sent to the family following the session. These prescriptions are designed to produce information regarding family connectedness, rather than to elicit resistance. The final stage of each session consists of a postsession discussion among team members of family responses to the intervention and the development of a written summary of the session.

In addition to using techniques from the model delineated here, a number of intervention strategies are associated with systemic approaches, including circular questioning (asking one family member to comment on transactions between two other members), positive connotation (reframing all behavior as positive to preserve family homeostasis and cohesion), rituals (prescribing an individualized action or series of actions aimed at altering family roles by addressing the conflict between unspoken and spoken family rules), and counterparadoxical interventions (presenting a therapeutic double bind in which the overt communication is for the family not to change). These techniques elucidate family games (specific repetitive patterns of family interaction) (Prata, 1990), introduce a new conceptualization of family problems, and encourage discovery of new solutions to problems through systemic change.

Termination occurs at the predetermined time. Typically, the problem behavior has been resolved, or at least ameliorated. The therapist may suggest that the family return for a review session at a later date.

Systemic therapists, unlike their strategic colleagues, historically have adopted a relatively neutral and nonreactive stance, avoiding entanglement in family alliances or coalitions. These clinicians hold that this position provides maximal leverage for creating change, as the therapist may attend to the entire system without being inducted into family games (Selvini Palazzoli et al., 1989). More recently, systemic family therapists have been encouraged to share their systemic hypotheses with the family and minimize the use of paradoxical interventions.

Treatment Applicability. The systemic approach has been used with couples and families experiencing a variety of behavior problems, including psychotic, mood, and personality disorders; alcohol abuse; and psychosomatic illnesses (Carr, 1991; Selvini Palazolli, 1974; Selvini Palazolli et al. 1978). In a review of 10 empirical investigations of systemic family therapy, Carr (1991) reported symptomatic relief in two-thirds to three-quarters of cases and systemic change in half of the cases. Families completing systemic treatment also develop a broader systemic perspective (Bennun, 1986).

Behavioral and Cognitive-Behavioral Therapies

History and Theoretical Development. Behavioral and cognitive-behavioral marital and family therapies encompass a spectrum of techniques and treatment models (for a review, see Goldenberg & Goldenberg, 1991; Holtzworth-Munroe & Jacobson, 1991). Behavioral therapists treating couples or families acknowledge the systems concept, emphasizing the interdependent nature of the behavior patterns between members of a couple or family (Fay & Lazarus, 1984). According to this perspective, people maintain each others' behavior through reinforcement; behavioral control is thus a circular or reciprocal process. Behavioral therapists stress the importance of family members' learning or relearning more adaptive ways of relating. Behavioral marital therapy (BMT), originating with Richard Stuart (e.g., Stuart, 1980) and Robert Liberman (1970), has been articulated in detail by Jacobson and Margolin (1979). BMT, incorporating principles from social learning theory and social exchange theory, teaches couples to use skills that enhance their relationship and thereby increase marital satisfaction. BMT identifies and increases potentially reinforcing events and minimizes the occurrence of aversive marital interactions to balance the reward/cost ratio in a reinforcing manner for each member of the dyad. Behavioral marital therapists en-

hance the marital dyad's capacity to recognize, initiate, and acknowledge positive interactions; decrease aversive interchanges; develop and utilize more adaptive communication skills and problem-solving strategies; and negotiate problem resolution via contingency contracting (Liberman, Wheeler, deVisser, Kuehnel, & Kuehnel, 1980). Cognitive processes associated with marital dysfunction and behavioral sequences maintaining problem behaviors are examined (Jacobson & Margolin, 1979).

Behavioral techniques also have been applied to the treatment of sexual dysfunction in couples (for a review, see Heiman, LoPiccolo, & LoPiccolo, 1981; Kaplan, 1974; Masters, Johnson, & Kolodny, 1986). Sex therapists assume that sexual dysfunction may be a primary contributor to relationship problems, and thus conjoint sex therapy focuses on alleviating sexual difficulties. Although there are variations in sex therapy approaches, they share common elements, including sex education and reeducation, communication and skills training in sexual technique, reduction of performance anxiety, and attitude change strategies.

Literature has accumulated pertaining to the efficacy of behavioral parent-training techniques and programs for children. Parent training (e.g., Gordon & Davidson, 1981; Patterson, 1971), drawing upon principles of social learning theory, instructs parents about behavioral concepts and techniques that may be applied to problematic child behavior. The goal of behavioral parent-skills training is to change parents' responses to undesirable child behaviors to reduce and control such behaviors (for a review, see Gordon & Davidson, 1981). After establishing a baseline of the problem behavior and conducting a functional analysis, the therapist helps the family develop an alternative set of reinforcement contingencies that will lead to more adaptive child behaviors. Techniques such as time-out procedures and contingency contracts are employed. Parent training programs have become popular because they empower parents, the individuals with the potential to be the most significant change agents in their child's life.

Behavioral interventions have been developed for families (e.g., Alexander & Parsons, 1982; Epstein, Bishop, & Levin, 1978). Alexander and colleagues (e.g., Alexander & Parsons, 1982; Barton & Alexander, 1981), for example, developed functional family therapy (FFT), an approach in which all behavior is viewed as adaptive and thus functional. The interpersonal functions of each family members' behavior are determined prior to instituting change. Efforts are directed toward modifying family members' cognitions and emotional responses to help the family conceptualize difficulties in a systemic fashion and share responsibility for behavior change. Education is provided, and new skills needed to maintain positive behavior change are taught.

Epstein and colleagues (1978) developed the McMaster

Model of Family Functioning, now known as problem-centered systems therapy (Epstein & Bishop, 1981), using general system theory to describe the structure, organization, and transactional patterns of the family unit within the following domains of family functioning: problem solving, communication, roles, affective responsiveness, affective involvement, and behavioral control. This treatment approach defines and prioritizes problems, outlines available treatment options, negotiates expectations for change, implements tasks relevant to addressing the problems, evaluates task completion, summarizes treatment progress, and develops future plans for problem management.

Finally, methods have been devised for treating couples and families based upon an integration of cognitive and behavioral psychology (e.g., Beck, 1988; Epstein, Schlesinger, & Dryden, 1988). Cognitive-behavioral family treatment assumes that cognitive mediation of events influences family interactional patterns and family members' emotions and actions. Problems arise from family members' distorted beliefs about one another and from dysfunctional transactional patterns. Assessment focuses on examining cognitive processes and behaviors. Commonly used cognitive intervention techniques include cognitive restructuring procedures and self-instructional training. The behavioral strategies include communication, assertiveness, and problem-solving training, as well as behavior exchange procedures.

For purposes of illustration of behavioral and cognitive-behavioral therapies, the FFT model is detailed. This model integrates cognitive and behavioral approaches, is based upon a well-articulated set of principles, and has received strong empirical support (Goldenberg & Goldenberg, 1991).

Basic Structure and Goals. Most behavioral and cognitive-behavioral marital and family therapies, including FFT, are brief, time limited, structured, and conducted by a single therapist. Treatment fosters changes in cognition and behavior of each individual person and the family unit. The family is offered alternative conceptualizations of events, enabling individuals to behave more adaptively and family members to interact more harmoniously.

Techniques and Process of Therapy. FFT proceeds in stages. In the assessment phase, three levels of family functioning are evaluated: relationship (interactional patterns and processes), functional (adaptive functions of behavioral sequences), and individual (identification of behavioral, cognitive, and affective changes required for each family member to modify problem behavior).

Family interventions are divided into therapeutic and educational strategies designed to modify family members' cognitions and affects. Therapy refers to interventions that address family resistances, mobilize and motivate family members to change, and prepare the family to benefit from educational interventions. Adherents to this approach assume that behavior change requires alterations in family members' self-perceptions and construals regarding other family members, and thus, family members are helped to question their understanding of family patterns and the presenting problem. This reattribution strategy is reflected in the process, style, and content of therapist–family communications.

Relabeling, the reattribution technique used frequently by functional family therapists to facilitate change, is similar to positive reframing. It refers to a message that recasts roles, behaviors, and emotions perceived in negative terms by family members more positively (revalencing) and sensitizes family members to the functional properties or interpersonal effects of each others' behaviors and emotions. Revalencing facilitates alternative understanding and affective responses that are more consistent with family members' expectations. The relabeling of behavior implicitly communicates that the dissatisfied individual actually has greater control over the problematic interactional pattern than he or she recognizes.

In the educational component of the intervention, instruction is offered in a manner consistent with the functional outcomes of family members' behavior and the therapeutic reattributions that the therapist has created within the family unit: "The functions of behavior are not changed through education, but the form of process that generates or controls these outcomes is changed" (Barton & Alexander, 1981, p. 425). Functional family therapists use an array of overt behavior change interventions (e.g., contingency contracting and management, modeling, systematic desensitization, time-out procedures, and training in communication skills, assertiveness, and problem solving) to promote change. The techniques employed are chosen based upon goodness of fit with the functions and processes of family life.

In behavioral and cognitive-behavioral marital and family treatment, therapists adopt a directive stance and function as scientists, role models, teachers, and educators. These clinicians acknowledge that a collaborative working alliance is essential for behavior change. Functional family therapists are noted for their explications of strategies for developing such a working alliance. To create the optimal environment and prepare the family for change, adherents to this orientation present as warm and empathic, integrate emotions and behavior, adopt a nonjudgmental stance, employ humor to reduce tension, and use selective self-disclosure to provide information to the family. Functional family therapists employ structuring skills to assist the family in implementing change. Structuring skills, typically associated with the education phase, encompass directiveness, self-confidence, and clarity. Practitioners of this approach continually evaluate their impact on family members and calibrate their style of interaction to maximize their fit with the family's functional characteristics.

Treatment Applicability. Behavioral and cognitive-behavioral approaches to marital and family therapy have addressed a range of behavioral, emotional, and relational problems. Research with FFT has demonstrated that modifying dysfunctional family processes is associated with a dramatic reduction in recidivism rates for juvenile delinquents whose families comply with treatment (Alexander & Parsons, 1982). These interventions are associated with long-term maintenance of treatment gains and increased familial capacity to cope with developmental transitions.

Since behavioral and cognitive-behavioral approaches have been the object of more empirical investigation than the other family therapy treatment models, findings from this work are mentioned briefly here. In a recent review of the literature (Holtzworth-Monroe & Jacobson, 1991), it was asserted that behavioral marital therapy is more efficacious than control conditions in relieving marital discord and promoting marital satisfaction. Variables associated with positive treatment outcome include the development of a collaborative therapist–couple partnership, active client engagement in the intervention process, and compliance with assigned tasks. Empirical evaluation of behavioral parent training has demonstrated its effectiveness in managing disruptive behavior disorders, elimination disorders, and anxiety disorders. Child-focused behavioral family therapy has been efficacious in ameliorating the presenting problem in a heterogenous sample of children (Szykula et al., 1987). Treatment outcome research focusing on sexual dysfunctions has yielded high rates of success for behavioral treatments (Heiman et al., 1981). The effectiveness of cognitive-behavioral family therapy has been demonstrated for remarried families and families with older adults, substance abusers, and depressed and suicidal individuals (for a review, see Thomas, 1992). Client variables associated with good prognosis include at least average intellectual functioning and capacity for abstraction of all participants, children who are school-aged or older, and family members who demonstrate relative acceptance of one another (Epstein et al., 1988).

Psychoeducational Family Therapy

Psychoeducational approaches to family therapy and counseling are designed to remediate individual and family difficulties and enhance functioning (Levant, 1986; McFarlane, 1991). To enhance family life, these models train family members to be helpers to their loved ones and teach communication and problem-solving skills to prevent the emergence of problems (Levant, 1986). These approaches have been developed based upon a multitude of theoretical perspec-

tives, and some are atheoretical in orientation. Psychoeducational programs have been developed for parent training (e.g., Berkowitz & Graziano, 1972; Gordon, 1976; Levant, 1986), marriage enhancement (e.g., Jacobson & Margolin, 1979), and family skills training and enrichment (e.g., Guerney, 1977; L'Abate & Weinstein, 1987). The family psychoeducation work that has gained the most prominence focuses on working with families in whom one member manifests severe psychopathology, such as schizophrenia (e.g., Anderson, Reiss, & Hogarty, 1986; Falloon, Boyd, & McGill, 1984; McFarlane, 1983) or affective disorders (e.g., Clarkin, Haas, & Glick, 1988).

Family therapists from a variety of perspectives devised clinical interventions for families with schizophrenic members based on systems theory. These strategies became less commonly practiced in the last decade as the economic realities of deinstitutionalization precluded widespread funding for family therapy and neuroscientists using pharmacological treatments challenged the need for psychosocial interventions. In response to these challenges, many psychosocial researchers turned their attention to understanding those communication patterns and social processes that influence the course of schizophrenia spectrum disorders (e.g., Brown et al., 1972; Doane et al., 1981, 1985; Leff & Vaughn, 1981; Mikowitz, Goldstein, Falloon, & Doane, 1984). Findings from this research led to the development of a family-based treatment aimed at preventing relapse (e.g., Anderson et al., 1986). Adherents utilize a medical model, conceptualizing schizophrenia as a severely debilitating functional brain impairment. Accordingly, a central assumption is that families can be educated to create a familial milieu that minimizes stressors exacerbating the patient's psychiatric condition and enhances the schizophrenic family member's adaptive functioning (McFarlane, 1991). Psychoeducational family interventions for schizophrenia spectrum disorders are presented as illustrative of psychoeducational approaches to family therapy and counseling.

Basic Structure and Goals. Family psychoeducation, a structured treatment approach that can be conducted with an individual family or in a multiple family group format, usually is provided by two clinicians. Session frequency depends on the patient's psychiatric condition and the stage of the family education process. The treatment is generally long-term. Sessions are frequent in the early phases, and the intervals between sessions increase during the latter phases.

The long-term goals include relapse prevention and reintegration of the patient into the community. To accomplish these goals, short-term and intermediate goals are defined, including stabilization of symptoms, enlistment of family members in the education process, provision of education regarding psychotic conditions and pharmacological interventions, establishment of a treatment team that includes family members and emphasizes continuity of care, encouragement of the development and use of a social support system, and assistance to the family in managing the stress associated with caring for a family member with a prolonged psychiatric condition. Throughout treatment, goals are discussed and negotiated.

Techniques and Process of Therapy. Individual and multiple family psychoeducation approaches include four phases. The first phase coincides with the family member's first psychotic episode or subsequent relapse. A collaborative relationship is established with all significant family members and the patient. An evaluation of the crisis is conducted, during which family members' reactions to the patient's symptoms and the treatment environment are elicited. The family's structure, coping strategies, and social support system are assessed. At the close of this phase, a contract specifying the structure of the intervention is delineated.

In the second phase, educational information is provided via a day or weekend workshop or a series of brief, ongoing informational sessions interspersed across family meetings. Educational workshops are presented in a lecture and discussion format designed for family members and friends of the patient. Sometimes, concurrent education is presented to the patient in a group format. In addition to presenting material on the nature, symptoms, and management of schizophrenia spectrum disorders, the educational component addresses risk factors associated with relapse and effective coping strategies.

The third phase, the reentry period, begins when the patient returns to the community and lasts approximately 1 year. Emphasis is placed on stabilization of the patient outside the hospital milieu. In the fourth and final phase, rehabilitation, therapists and family members collaborate to enhance the adaptive functioning of the patient. Termination depends upon the patient's clinical status and the family's desire for continued treatment and/or social support.

Techniques employed in psychoeducation sessions include (1) informal socializing at the initiation of the session, (2) reviewing homework assignments, (3) examining between-session events, (4) reframing stressors in a fashion consistent with the information provided during the educational components, (5) teaching problem-solving and communication skills, and (6) emphasizing medication compliance. The therapists offer advice, guidance, and information, communicating their own expertise and acknowledging the value of the family's experience in helping their loved one.

Treatment Applicability. Psychoeducational approaches have proven efficacious in work with families with

a schizophrenic member or a mood disorder (e.g., Anderson et al., 1986). Additionally, psychoeducational parent training, marriage enhancement, and family skills training and enrichment programs have received modest empirical support for their general value (Levant, 1986).

Integrative Family Therapy

The recent trend within the psychotherapy field is a move from adherence to either a unitary or eclectic theoretical approach to systemic integration of models (Norcross & Goldfried, 1992). One example of the rapidly growing pursuits of psychotherapy integration is reflected in the newly founded *Journal of Psychotherapy Integration*, the publication of the Society for the Exploration of Psychotherapy Integration. As part of this trend, efforts to create an integrative bridge between individual and family approaches have emerged (e.g., Feldman, 1992; Pinsof, 1983; Sander, 1979; Scharff & Scharff, 1987; Slipp, 1988; Sugarman, 1986; Wachtel & Wachtel, 1986). Within the marital and family therapy field, some theoreticians selectively have combined a limited number of perspectives (e.g., Alexander & Parsons, 1982; Anderson et al., 1986; Epstein et al., 1988; Falloon et al., 1984; Greenberg & Johnson, 1988; L'Abate, 1986; Liddle, 1985; Pinsof, 1983; Stanton, 1981). Others have advocated integration of a range of models (e.g., Duhl & Duhl, 1981; Gurman, 1981; Kaslow, 1981b; Kirschner & Kirschner, 1986; Lebow, 1987; Moultrup, 1986; Pinsof, 1995; Textor, 1988).

Integrative models unify previously divergent theories and techniques into a supraordinate structure, with an appreciation of the similarities and differences of the perspectives being combined. Integrative approaches to marital and family therapy synthesize general systems theory and at least one additional approach (Lebow, 1987). These models may differ in their reliance on the amalgamation of intervention strategies from distinct models into a particular approach, integration of two or more approaches into a unitary theoretical and clinical entity, and use of intervention strategies from different approaches chosen because of their appropriateness for addressing specific problems (Johnson & Greenberg, 1987). Theory integration aims toward developing more broadly useful models for understanding and treating dysfunction, models that accommodate flexibly therapist differences in personality and skill level and the unique characteristics of each family unit (Aradi & F. Kaslow, 1987).

F. Kaslow and colleagues (e.g., Aradi & Kaslow, 1987; Kaslow, 1991) proposed a three-stage process of family therapy theory integration. Stage 1 offers six criteria as the basis for systematic theory examination, including the explanatory, diagnostic, therapeutic, prognostic, evaluative, and preventive power of the theory. Theories are evaluated according to their usefulness in conceptualizing and assessing family strengths and dysfunction, generating a treatment approach, predicting course of dysfunction and treatment outcome, offering an approach for process and outcome research, and addressing prevention.

Stage 2 addresses key therapist variables, underscoring the view that theory integration involves an interaction between the therapist's predilections and personality style and his or her scientific assessment of the available theories. The goodness of fit between a therapist's belief systems and the components of different treatment approaches provides a context for evaluating a theory's integrative potential for the given therapist. Similarly, family variables, the focus of Stage 3 in theory integration, represent an important contextual dimension for ascertaining the utility of a model. Thus, the therapist must incorporate the family's construction of reality (Reiss, 1981) in developing a conceptual model most suited for the family's interactional patterns and style.

Comprehensive theory integration provides a framework for the synthesis of discrete theories and their components into a more holistic approach, specifically adapted to account for unique contextual and symptom variables, allowing for selecting that approach or combination of approaches most likely to help this family with this problem/symptom at this moment in time. As such, many integrative models are possible, making implausible the explication of a specific framework according to the dimensions of basic structure and goals of treatment, and intervention techniques and process. Given that integrative models of marital and family therapy have emerged only recently, there is little empirical process or outcome data from which to evaluate their efficacy.

Concluding Comments

This chapter has provided a conceptual roadmap of differing theories of marital and family therapy, with the hope of stimulating the reader toward increased awareness of the multitude of theories and therapies, as well as a personal integration of one's own theories of choice. Although it is intended to be as inclusive as possible, not all significant leaders could be mentioned, and specific categorizations are those of the current authors.

Not surprisingly, no school of thought contains all of the elements integral to a conceptual schema that merits consideration as a complete theory. Yet, all schools contribute sufficiently to the development of the field to warrant inclusion. It is anticipated that during the late 1990s the field will exhibit more intellectual and scientific rigor in the pursuit of a refined understanding of the processes and outcomes of marital and family therapy.

The future of practice, research, and training in marital and family therapy will incorporate the trends and theoretical approaches presented in this chapter and will evolve in response to the emergence of new academic, clinical, professional, sociocultural, and political influences. Gurman and Kniskern (1992), in an effort to anticipate the shape of this evolution, postulated that the practice of marital and family therapy will be influenced increasingly by insurance reimbursement policies. This has come to pass. Additionally, consistent with the emergence of integrative family therapy approaches, the field of family therapy has witnessed a decreasing emphasis on adherence to particular schools of thought and a simultaneous increasing flexibility in combining treatment models and associated techniques. As a result, marital and family therapists have become more flexible and effective in treating couples and families presenting with the entire spectrum of psychological dysfunction, and are doing so in a manner that attends more to the therapist–family relationship.

Although there has been a proliferation of research on family interactional processes, there are limited empirical data regarding marital and family therapy processes and outcomes. Future research will be enhanced by increased cooperation between clinicians and researchers and strengthened by attention to theory-based evaluations and the integration of quantitative and qualitative research endeavors. Hopefully, as we move toward the twenty-first century, advancements in empirical investigation, combined with the trend toward theory integration, will influence the nature of clinical practice and enhance its efficacy.

References

Ackerman, N. (1938). The unity of the family. *Archives of Pediatrics, 55,* 51–62.

Alexander, J., & Parsons, B. V. (1982). *Functional family therapy.* Monterey, CA: Brooks/Cole.

American Association for Marriage and Family Therapy (1982, rev. 1988). *AAMFT code of ethical principles for marriage and family therapists.* Washington, DC: Author.

Andersen, T. (Ed.). (1991). *The reflecting team: Dialogues and dialogues about the dialogues.* New York: Norton.

Anderson, C. M., Griffin, S., Rossi, A., Pagonis, I., Holder, D. P., & Treiber, R. (1986). A comparative study of the impact of education versus process groups for families of patients with affective disorders. *Family Process, 25,* 185–206.

Anderson, C. M., Reiss, D. J., & Hogarty, G. E. (1986). *Schizophrenia and the family.* New York: Guilford.

Andolfi, M. (1979). *Family therapy: An interactional approach.* New York: Plenum.

Aponte, H. J. (1976). Underorganization in the poor family. In P. J. Guerin (Ed.), *Family therapy: Theory and practice* (pp. 432–448). New York: Gardner.

Aradi, N. S., & Kaslow, F. W. (1987). Theory integration in family therapy: Definition, rationale, content and process. *Psychotherapy: Theory, Research, and Practice, 25,* 598–608.

Barton, C., & Alexander, J. (1981). Functional family therapy. In A. S. Gurman & D. P. Kniskern (Eds.), *Handbook of family therapy* (pp. 403–443). New York: Brunner/Mazel.

Bateson, G. (1972). *Toward an ecology of mind.* New York: Ballantine Books.

Bateson, G., Jackson, D. D., Haley, J. E., & Weakland, J. (1956). Toward a theory of schizophrenia. *Behavioral Science, 1,* 251–264.

Beavers, W. R. (1977). *Psychotherapy and growth: Family systems perspective.* New York: Brunner/Mazel.

Beavers, W. R. (1985). *Manual of Beavers-Timberlawn Family Evaluation Scale and Family Style Evaluation.* Dallas, TX: Southwest Family Institute.

Beavers, W. R., & Hampson, B. B. (1990). *Successful families: Assessment and intervention.* New York: Norton.

Beck, A. T. (1988). *Love is never enough.* New York: Harper & Row.

Beels, C., & Ferber, A. (1972). What family therapists do. In A. Ferber, M. Mendelsohn, & A. Napier (Eds.), *The book of family therapy* (pp. 168–232). New York: Science House.

Bennun, I. (1986). Evaluating family therapy: A comparison of the Milan and problem solving approaches. *Journal of Family Therapy, 8,* 235–242.

Berkowitz, B. P., & Graziano, A. M. (1972). Training parents as behavior therapists: A review. *Behavioral Research and Therapy, 10,* 297–317.

Bodin, A. M. (1981). The interactional view. Family therapy approaches of the Mental Research Institute. In A. S. Gurman & D. P. Kniskern (Eds.), *Handbook of family therapy* (pp. 267–309). New York: Brunner/Mazel.

Boszormenyi-Nagy, I., & Framo, J. L. (1965). *Intensive family therapy.* New York: Harper & Row.

Boszormenyi-Nagy, I., & Krasner, B. R. (1986). *Between give and take: A critical guide to contextual therapy.* New York: Brunner/Mazel.

Boszormenyi-Nagy, I., & Spark, G. (1973). *Invisible loyalties: Reciprocity in intergenerational family therapy.* New York: Harper & Row.

Boszormenyi-Nagy, I., Grunebaum, J., & Ulrich, D. (1991). Contextual therapy. In A. S. Gurman & D. P. Kniskern (Eds.), *Handbook of family therapy* (Vol. II) (pp. 200–238). New York: Brunner/Mazel.

Bowen, M. (1988). *Family therapy in clinical practice* (2nd ed.). Northvale, NJ: Jason Aronson.

Boyd-Franklin, N. (1989). *Black families in therapy: A multi-systems approach.* New York: Guilford.

Broderick, C. B., & Schrader, S. S. (1991). The history of professional marriage and family therapy. In A. S. Gurman & D. P. Kniskern (Eds.), *Handbook of family therapy* (Vol. II, pp. 3–40). New York: Brunner/Mazel.

Brown, G. W., Birley, J. L. T., & Wing, J. F. (1972). Influence of family life on the course of schizophrenic disorders: A replication. *British Journal of Psychiatry, 121,* 241–258.

Carl, D. (1990). *Counseling same-sex couples.* New York: Norton.

Carr, A. (1991). Milan systemic family therapy: A review of ten empirical investigations. *Journal of Family Therapy, 13,* 237–263.

Clarkin, J. K., Haas, G. L., & Glick, I. D. (Eds.). (1988). *Affective disorders and the family: Assessment and treatment.* New York; Guilford.

Colapinto, J. (1991). Structural family therapy. In A. S. Gurman & D. P. Kniskern (Eds.), *Handbook of family therapy* (Vol.-II, pp. 417–443). New York: Brunner/Mazel.

Dell, P. (1981). Paradox redux. *Journal of Marital and Family Therapy, 7,* 127–134.

deShazer, S. (1985). *Keys to solution in brief therapy.* New York: Norton.

Doane, J. A., West, K. L., Goldstein, M. J., Rodnick, E. H., & Jones, J. E. (1981). Parental communication deviance and affective style: Predictors of subsequent schizophrenia spectrum disorders in vulnerable adolescents. *Archives of General Psychiatry, 38,* 679–685.

Doane, J. A., Falloon, I., Goldstein, M. J., & Mintz, J. (1985). Parental affective style and the treatment of schizophrenia: Predicting course of illness and social functioning. *Archives of General Psychiatry, 43,* 34–42.

Duhl, B. (1983). *From the inside out and other metaphors: Creative and integrative approaches to training in systems thinking.* New York: Brunner/Mazel.

Duhl, B. S., & Duhl, F. J. (1981). Integrative family therapy. In A. S. Gurman & D. P. Kniskern (Eds.), *Handbook of family therapy* (pp. 483–516). New York: Brunner/Mazel.

Epstein, N. B., & Bishop, D. S. (1981). Problem-centered systems therapy of the family. In A. S. Gurman & D. P. Kniskern (Eds.), *Handbook of family therapy* (pp. 444–482). New York: Brunner/Mazel.

Epstein, N. B., Bishop, D. S., & Levin, S. (1978). The McMaster model of family functioning. *Journal of Marital and Family Counseling, 4,* 19–31.

Epstein, N., Schlesinger, S. E., & Dryden, W. (Eds.). (1988). *Cognitive-behavioral therapy with families.* New York: Brunner/Mazel.

Epstein, N., Bishop, D. S., Ryan, C., Miller, I., & Keitner, G. (1993). The McMaster model: View of healthy family functioning. In F. Walsh (Ed.), *Normal family processes* (2nd ed., pp. 138–160). New York: Guilford.

Everett, C., Halperin, S., Volgy, S., & Wissler, A. (1989). *Treating the borderline family: A systemic approach.* Boston: Allyn & Bacon.

Falloon, I., Boyd, J., & McGill, C. (1984). *Family care of schizophrenia.* New York: Guilford.

Fay, A., & Lazarus, A. A. (1984). The therapist in behavioral and multi-modal therapy. In F. W. Kaslow (Ed.), *Psychotherapy with psycho-therapists* (pp. 1–18). New York: Haworth.

Feldman, L. B. (1992). *Integrating individual and family therapy.* New York: Brunner/Mazel.

Fogarty, T. (1976). Systems concepts and the dimensions of self. In P. J. Guerin (Ed.), *Family therapy: Theory and practice* (pp. 144–153). New York: Gardner Press.

Friedman, E. H. (1991). Bowen theory and therapy. In A. S. Gurman & D. P. Kniskern (Eds.), *Handbook of family therapy* (Vol. II, pp. 134–170). New York: Brunner/Mazel.

Gergen, K. (1985). The social constructionist movement in modern psychology. *American Psychologist, 40,* 266–275.

Goldenberg, I., & Goldenberg, H. (1991). *Family therapy: An overview* (3rd ed.). Pacific Grove, CA: Brooks/Cole.

Goldenthal, P. (1991). Contextual therapy with children and families. *Innovations in clinical practice: A source book, 10,* 85–97.

Goodrich, T. J., Rampage, C., Ellman, B., & Halstead, K. (1988). *Feminist family therapy: A casebook.* New York: Norton.

Goolishian, H. A., & Anderson, H. (1990). Understanding the therapeutic process: From individuals and families to systems and language. In F. W. Kaslow (Ed.), *Voices in family psychology* (Vol. 1, pp. 91–113). Newbury Park, CA: Sage.

Gordon, S. B., & Davidson, N. (1981). Behavioral parent training. In A. S. Gurman & D. P. Kniskern (Eds.), *Handbook of family therapy* (pp. 517–555). New York: Brunner/Mazel.

Gordon, T. (1976). *P.E.T. in action.* New York: Peter H. Wyden.

Greenberg, L. S., & Johnson, S. M. (1988). *Emotionally focused therapy for couples.* New York: Guilford.

Guerin, P. J. (Ed.). (1976). *Family therapy: Theory and practice.* New York: Gardner.

Guerney, B. G., Jr. (Ed.). (1977). *Relationship enhancement.* San Francisco: Jossey-Bass.

Gurman, A. S. (1979). Dimensions of marital therapy: A comparative analysis. *Journal of Marital and Family Therapy, 5,* 5–18.

Gurman, A. S. (1981). Integrative marital therapy: Toward the development of an interpersonal approach. In S. Budman (Ed.), *Forms of brief psychotherapy* (pp. 415–457). New York: Guilford.

Gurman, A. S., & Kniskern, D. P. (1992). The future of marital and family therapy. *Psychotherapy: Theory, Research, Practice, and Training, 29*, 65–71.

Haley, J. (1963). *Strategies of psychotherapy.* New York: Grune & Stratton.

Haley, J. (1971). *Changing families.* New York: Grune & Stratton.

Haley, J. (1973). *Uncommon therapy: The psychiatric techniques of Milton H. Erickson, M.D.*. New York: Norton.

Haley, J. (1976). *Problem-solving therapy.* San Francisco: Jossey-Bass.

Haley, J. (1984). *Ordeal therapy: Unusual ways to change behavior.* San Francisco: Jossey-Bass.

Hazelrigg, M. D., Cooper, H. M., & Borduin, C. M. (1987). Evaluating the effectiveness of family therapies: An integrative review and analysis. *Psychological Bulletin, 101*, 428–442.

Heiman, J. R., LoPiccolo, L., & LoPiccolo, J. (1981). The treatment of sexual dysfunction. In A. S. Gurman & D. P. Kniskern (Eds.), *Handbook of family therapy* (pp. 592–630). New York: Brunner/Mazel.

Hoffman, L. (1992). A reflective stance for family therapy. In S. McNamee & K. J. Gergen (Eds.), *Therapy as social construction* (pp. 7–24). London: Sage.

Holtzworth-Munroe, A., & Jacobson, N. S. (1991). Behavioral marital therapy. In A. S. Gurman & D. P. Kniskern (Eds.), *Handbook of family therapy* (Vol. II, pp. 96–133). New York: Brunner/Mazel.

Hops, H., Wills, T. A., Patterson, G. R., & Weiss, R. L. (1972). *Marital interaction coding system.* Eugene: University of Oregon Research Institute.

Jackson, D. D. (1957). The question of family homeostasis. *Psychiatric Quarterly Supplement, 31*, 79–90.

Jacobson, N. S., & Margolin, G. (1979). *Marital therapy: Strategies based on social learning and behavior exchange principles.* New York: Brunner/Mazel.

Johnson, S. M., & Greenberg, L. S. (1987). Integration in marital therapy: Issues and progress. *The International Journal of Eclectic Psychotherapy, 6*, 202–215.

Kantor, D., & Lehr, W. (1975). *Inside the family: Toward a theory of family process.* San Francisco: Jossey-Bass.

Kaplan, H. S. (1974). *The new sex therapy: Active treatment of sexual dysfunction.* New York: Brunner/Mazel.

Kaslow, F. W. (1980). History of family therapy in the United States: A kaleidoscopic overview. *Marriage and Family Review, 3*, 77–111.

Kaslow, F. W. (1981a). Profile of the healthy family. *Interaction, 4*, 1–15.

Kaslow, F. W. (1981b). A dialectic approach to family therapy and practice: Selectivity and synthesis. *Journal of Marital and Family Therapy, 7*, 345–351.

Kaslow, F. W. (Ed.). (1982). *The international book of family therapy.* New York: Brunner/Mazel.

Kaslow, F. W. (1987). Marital and family therapy. In M. B. Sussman & S. K. Steinmetz (Eds.), *Handbook of marriage and the family* (pp. 835–859). New York: Plenum.

Kaslow, F. (Ed.). (1990). *Voices in family psychology* (Vols. 1 and 2). Newbury Park: Sage.

Kaslow, F. W. (1991). The art and science of family psychology: Retrospective and perspective. *American Psychologist, 46*, 621–626.

Kaslow, F. W., & Hammerschmidt, H. (1992). Long term "good" marriages: The seemingly essential ingredients. In B. J. Brothers (Ed.), *Couples therapy: Multiple perspectives* (pp. 15–38). Binghamton, NY: Haworth.

Kaslow, F. W., & Schwartz, L. (1987). *The dynamics of divorce: A life cycle perspective.* New York: Brunner/Mazel.

Kaslow, N. J., & Celano, M. (1993). Family therapy. In A. S. Gurman & S. B. Messer (Eds.), *Modern psychotherapies: Theory and practice* (pp. 343–402). New York: Guilford.

Kaslow, N. J., & Gurman, A. S. (1985). Ethical considerations in family therapy research. *Counseling and Values, 30*, 47–61.

Keith, D., & Whitaker, C. (1981). Play therapy: A paradigm for work with families. *Journal of Marital and Family Therapy, 6*, 243–254.

Kempler, W. (1981). *Experiential psychotherapy within families.* New York: Brunner/Mazel.

Kirschner, D. A., & Kirschner, S. (1986). *Comprehensive family therapy: An integration of systemic and psychodynamic treatment models.* New York: Brunner/Mazel.

L'Abate, L. (1986). *Systematic approach to family therapy.* New York: Brunner/Mazel.

L'Abate, L., & Weinstein, S. E. (1987). *Structured enrichment programs for couples and families.* New York: Brunner/Mazel.

LaPerriere, K. (1979). Family therapy training at the Ackerman Institute: Thoughts of form and substance. *Journal of Marital and Family Therapy, 5*, 53–58.

Lebow, J. L. (1987). Integrative family therapy: An overview of major issues. *Psychotherapy: Theory, Research and Practice, 24*, 584–594.

Leff, J., & Vaughn, C. (1981). The role of maintenance therapy and relatives' expressed emotion in relapse of schizophrenia: A two-year follow-up. *British Journal of Psychiatry, 139*, 102–104.

Levant, R. F. (Ed.). (1986). *Psychoeducational approaches to family therapy and counseling.* New York: Springer.

Lewis, J. M., Beavers, W. R., Gossatt, J. T., & Phillips, V. A. (1976). *No single thread: Psychological health in family systems.* New York: Brunner/Mazel.

Liberman, R. (1970). Behavioral approaches to family and couple therapy. *American Journal of Orthopsychiatry, 40*, 106–118.

Liberman, R. P., Wheeler, E., deVisser, L. A. J. M., Kuehnel, J., & Kuehnel, T. (1980). *Handbook of marital therapy: A positive approach to helping troubled relationships.* New York: Plenum.

Liddle, H. (1985). Five factors of failure in structural/strategic family therapy: A contextual construction. In S. Coleman (Ed.), *Failures in family therapy* (pp. 151–189). New York: Guilford.

Luepnitz, D. A. (1988). *The family interpreted: Feminist theory in clinical practice.* New York: Basic Books.

MacGregor, R. (1990). Team family methods in the public sector. In F. W. Kaslow (Ed.), *Voices in family psychology* (Vol. 1, pp. 156–170). Newbury Park, CA: Sage.

Madanes, C. (1981). *Strategic family therapy.* San Francisco: Jossey-Bass.

Madanes, C. (1990). *Sex, love, and violence.* New York: Norton.

Markham, H. J., & Notarius, C. I. (1987). Coding marital and family interaction: Current status. In T. Jacob (Ed.), *Family interaction and psychopathology: Theories, methods, and findings* (pp. 329–390). New York: Plenum.

Masters, W., Johnson, V., & Kolodny, R. (1986). *On sex and human loving.* Boston: Little, Brown.

McFarlane, W. R. (Ed.). (1983). *Family therapy in schizophrenia.* New York: Guilford.

McFarlane, W. R. (1991). Family psychoeducational treatment. In A. S. Gurman & D. P. Kniskern (Eds.), *Handbook of family therapy* (Vol. II, pp. 363–395). New York: Brunner/Mazel.

McGoldrick, M., & Gerson, R. (1985). *Genograms in family assessment.* New York: Norton.

McGoldrick, M., Anderson, C. M., & Walsh, F. (Eds.). (1989). *Women in families: A framework for family therapy.* New York: W. W. Norton.

McGoldrick, M., Pearce, J. K., & Giordano, J. (Eds.). (1982). *Ethnicity and family therapy.* New York: Guilford.

Meth, R. L., & Pasick, R. S. (1990). *Men in therapy: The challenge of change.* New York: Guilford.

Miklowitz, D. J., Goldstein, M. J., Falloon, I. R. H., & Doane, J. A. (1984).

Interactional correlates of expressed emotion in the families of schizophrenics. *British Journal of Psychiatry, 144*, 482–487.

Minuchin, S. (1974). *Families and family therapy.* Cambridge, MA: Harvard University Press.

Minuchin, S., & Fishman, H. C. (1981). *Family therapy techniques.* Cambridge, MA: Harvard University Press.

Minuchin, S., Montalvo, B., Guerney, B., Rosman, B., & Schumer, F. (1967). *Families of the slums.* New York: Basic Books.

Minuchin, S., Rosman, B. L., & Baker, L. (1978). *Psychosomatic families: Anorexia nervosa in context.* Cambridge, MA: Harvard University Press.

Moultrup, D. (1986). Integration: A coming of age. *Contemporary Family Therapy: An International Journal, 8*, 157– 167.

Napier, A. Y., & Whitaker, C. A. (1978). *The family crucible.* New York: Harper & Row.

Neill, J. R., & Kniskern, D. P. (Eds.). (1982). *From psyche to system: The evolving therapy of Carl Whitaker.* New York: Guilford.

Norcross, J. C., & Goldfried, M. R. (Eds.). (1992). *Handbook of psychotherapy integration.* New York: Basic Books.

Olson, D. H. (1970). Marital and family therapy: Integrative review and critique. *Journal of Marriage and the Family, 32*, 501–538.

Olson, D., Sprenkle, D., & Russell, C. (1979). Circumplex model of marital and family systems: Cohesion and adaptability dimensions, family types, and clinical applications. *Family Process, 18*, 3–28.

Olson, D. H., McCubbin, H. I., Barnes, H., Larsen, A., Muxen, M., & Wilson, M. (1983). *Families: What makes them work.* Beverly Hills, CA: Sage.

Papp, P. (1976). Family choreography. In P. J. Guerin (Ed.), *Family therapy: Theory and practice* (pp. 465–479).

Patten, C., Barnett, T., & Houlihan, D. (1991). Ethics in marital and family therapy: A review of the literature. *Professional Psychology: Research and Practice, 22*, 171–175.

Patterson, G. R. (1971). *Families: Application of social learning to family life.* Champaign, IL: Research Press.

Patterson, G. R., Ray, R. S., Shaw, D. A., & Cobb, J. A. (1969). *Manual for coding of family interactions* (rev. ed.). New York: Microfiche Publications.

Pinsof, W. M. (1983). Integrative problem-centered therapy: Toward the synthesis of family and individual psychotherapies. *Journal of Marital and Family Therapy, 9*, 19–35.

Pinsof, W. M. (1995). *Integrative problem centered therapy.* New York: Basic Books.

Pittman, F. (1993). *Man enough: Fathers, sons, and the search for masculinity.* East Rutherford, NJ: Putnam.

Prata, G. (1990). *A systemic harpoon into family games.* New York: Brunner/ Mazel.

Reiss, D. (1981). *The family's construction of reality.* Cambridge, MA: Harvard University Press.

Roberto, L. G. (1991). Symbolic-experiential family therapy. In A. S. Gurman & D. P. Kniskern (Eds.), *Handbook of family therapy* (Vol. II, pp. 444–476). New York: Brunner/Mazel.

Roberto, L. G. (1992). *Transgenerational family therapies.* New York: Guilford.

Sager, C. J., Brown, H. S., Crohn, H., Engel, T., Rodstein, E., & Walker, L. (1983). *Treating the remarried family.* New York: Brunner/Mazel.

Sander, F. M. (1979). *Individual and family therapy: Toward an integration.* Northvale, NJ: Jason Aronson.

Satir, V. (1967). *Conjoint family therapy.* Palo Alto, CA: Science and Behavior Books.

Satir, V. (1972). *Peoplemaking.* Palo Alto, CA: Science and Behavior Books.

Satir, V., & Baldwin, M. (1983). *Satir step by step: A guide to creating change in families.* Palo Alto, CA: Science and Behavior Books.

Scharff, J. S. (Ed.). (1989). *Foundations of object relations family therapy.* Northvale, NJ: Jason Aronson.

Scharff, D. E., & Scharff, J. S. (1987). *Object relations family therapy.* Northvale, NJ: Jason Aronson.

Schwartz, L. S., & Kaslow, F. W. (1997). *Painful partings: Divorce and its aftermath.* New York: Wiley.

Segal, L. (1991). Brief therapy: The MRI approach. In A. S. Gurman & D. P. Kniskern (Eds.), *Handbook of family therapy* (Vol. II, pp. 171–199). New York: Brunner/Mazel.

Selvini Palazzoli, M. (1974). *Self starvation.* London: Human Context Books.

Selvini Palazzoli, M., Boscolo, L., Cecchin, G., & Prata, G. (1978). *Paradox and counterparadox.* Northvale, NJ: Jason Aronson.

Selvini Palazzoli, M., Cirillo, S., Selvini, M., & Sorrentino, A. M. (1989). *Family games: General models of psychotic processes in the family.* New York: Norton.

Slipp, S. (1988). *The technique and practice of object relations family therapy.* Northvale, NJ: Jason Aronson.

Stanton, M. D. (1981). Strategic approaches to family therapy. In A. S. Gurman & D. P. Kniskern (Eds.), *Handbook of family therapy* (pp. 361– 402). New York: Brunner/Mazel.

Stanton, M. D., & Todd, T. (1982). *The family therapy of drug abuse and addiction.* New York: Guilford.

Stuart, R. B. (1980). *Helping couples change: A social learning approach to marital therapy.* New York: Guilford.

Sugarman, S. (Ed.). (1986). *The interface of individual and family therapy.* Rockville, MD: Aspen Publishers.

Szykula, S. A., Morris, S. B., & Sudweeks, C. (1987). Child-focused behavior and strategic therapies: Outcome comparisons. *Psychotherapy: Theory, Research, and Practice, 24*, 546–551.

Textor, M. R. (1988). Integrative family therapy. *International Journal of Family Psychiatry, 9*, 93–105.

Thomas, M. B. (1992). *An introduction to marital and family therapy: Counseling toward healthier family systems across the lifespan.* New York: Macmillan.

Tomm, K. M. (1984a). One perspective on the Milan approach: Part I. Overview of development, theory and practice. *Journal of Marital and Family Therapy, 10*, 113–125.

Tomm, K. M. (1984b). One perspective on the Milan approach: Part II. Description of session format, interviewing style, and interventions. *Journal of Marital and Family Therapy, 10*, 253–271.

Trepper, T. S., & Barrett, M. J. (1989). *Systemic family treatment of incest.* New York: Brunner/Mazel.

Visher, E., & Visher, J. (1987). *Old loyalties, new ties: Therapeutic strategies with stepfamilies.* New York: Brunner/Mazel.

Wachtel, E. F., & Wachtel, P. L. (1986). *Family dynamics in individual psychotherapy: A guide to clinical strategies.* New York: Guilford.

Wallerstein, J. S., & Kelly, J. B. (1980). *Surviving the breakup: How children and parents cope with divorce.* New York: Basic Books.

Walsh, F. (Ed.). (1993). *Normal family processes* (2nd ed.). New York: Guilford.

Walters, M., Carter, B., Papp, P., & Silverstein, O. (1988). *The invisible web: Gender patterns in family relationships.* New York: Guilford.

Watzlawick, P., Weakland, J., & Fisch, R. (1974). *Change: Principles of problem formation and problem resolution.* New York: Norton.

Whitaker, C. (1976). The hindrance of theory in clinical work. In P. J. Guerin, Jr. (Ed.), *Family therapy: Theory and practice* (pp. 154–164). New York: Gardner.

Whitaker, C. A., & Bumberry, W. M. (1988). *Dancing with the family: A symbolic-experiential approach.* New York: Brunner/Mazel.

Whitaker, C. A., & Keith, D. V. (1981). Symbolic-experiential family therapy. In A. S. Gurman & D. P. Kniskern (Eds.), *Handbook of family therapy* (pp. 187–225). New York: Brunner/Mazel.

Index

Divorce (*cont.*)
  in China, 119
  cohabitation as risk factor for, 314
  community, 487
  comparative studies of, 94
  co-parental, 487
  cross-societal research on, 95
  differentials in, 56–58
  economic, 487
  economic consequences of, 6, 59, 352, 491–492; *see also* Alimony
  educational factors in, 56
  emotional, 487
  as family reorganization cause, 316
  father–child relationship after, 425, 447–448
  as female-headed household cause, 62
  historical perspective on, 31, 476–479
  intergenerational transmission of, 56, 484–485
  among Japanese Americans, 120–121
  kinship relationships and, 89
  legal, 487
  legal issues in, 478–479, 480–482
  marriage age and, 311
  in military families, 493
  as mourning process, 487–488
  no-fault, 479, 480, 481, 487
  parent–adult child relationship, 86
  parent–child relationship and, 459
  prediction of, 670–671
  prevention of, 207
  process of, 486–488, 669–671
  psychic, 487
  as psychological process, 488
  as psychosocial process, 488
  reforms in, 146
  risk factors for, 482–486
  in sixteenth-century Germany, 23
  social attitudes toward, 478
  societal factors in, 479–480
Divorced persons
  parental relationships of, 429
  stigmatization of, 489
Divorce mediation, 481–482, 769
Divorce rate, ix–x, 3, 65, 318, 494–495
  Amish, 136
  calculation of, 475–47
  Chinese, 119
  Chinese-American, 120
  current (1998), 494
  factors affecting, 55–56
  female employment and, 46
  historical perspective on, 476–477
  increase, 47
  in Japan, 120
  Japanese-American, 120–121
  marriage age and, 51
  Mexican-American, 122, 123
  1965–1990, 55–56
  Puerto Rican, 126, 127
  religious affiliation and, 486
  in second marriages, 318–319
  in Silicon Valley, 681
Divorce therapy, 481–482, 769

DNA (deoxyribonucleic acid) replication, 614–615
Dodd, Christopher, 643
Dollard, J., 226
Domestic Discord (Mourer and Mourer), 224
Domesticity, as women's primary role, 636
Domestic violence, 443–444, 706–707
  causes of, 723–724
  common couple, 444
  complementary roles in, 697–698
  consequences of, 726–727
  decrease in, 722
  definition of, 722
  among the elderly, 728–729
  emotional: *see* Emotional abuse
  between heterosexual couples, 722–725
  historical perspective on, 708
  intervention and prevention strategies for, 727–728
  marital rape, 724
  measurement of, 278
  men's apologetic behavior following, 156
  physical abuse, 722–724
  rate of, 6
  among same-sex couples, 725–726
  sexual assault, 724
  by women, 723, 729
Dominance, 293
  male, 769, 706, 714, 723
    in Amish families, 135
    in Chinese families, 117–118, 119
    in Japanese families, 120
    patriarchy and, 712, 713–714
    sexual, 752
  theoretical realism concept of, 679
Domineering behavior
  of homosexuals' mothers, 751
  in marriage, 697, 698
Dominican Republic, 747
Dominicans, intermarriage by, 127
"Don't Shake the Baby" program, 722
Door-slamming, as emotional abuse, 724
Downsizing, of workforce, 4–5, 168
Down's syndrome, 159, 343
Drive-by shootings, 406
Dropping out, of school, 394, 395–396, 401, 410
Drug abuse
  by adolescents, 399
  as elder abuse risk factor, 729
  family communication and, 699
  opium addiction, 234, 235, 236
  during pregnancy, 613
Drugs
  gateway, 409
  as sexual dysfunction cause, 759
Drug trafficking, 8
  by gangs, 406
Dual-income families, 65
  balance of power in, 680
  conflicts of interest in, 679
  household division of labor by, 46, 322, 452, 453
  middle-class, 5–6

Dual-income families, (*cont.*)
  paternal childcare in, 357
  as TICKS (two income couples with kids), 643
Duby, Georges, 14
Duquense Studies in Phenomenological Psychology, 242
Dyadic Adjustment Scale, 292, 296–297, 299, 688
Dyadic Parent–Child Interactional Coding System, 298
Dyadic relationships, future trends in, 167
Dyads, 145
  caregiving, 147
  familial, 264
  interpersonal communication in, 690
  marital
    in Bowenian therapy, 773
    in contextual therapy, 774
    as family subsystems, 780
Dying patients, nurses' relationships with, 236
Dynamics, familial, 2
  conflict and, 156–157
  intimacy and, 156
  of process, 667–684
    conflict theory of, 672–675, 683–684
    power in, 675–682, 683–684

Earned Income Tax Credit, 643, 647, 649
Eastern Europe, marriage and household patterns in, 17
Eastern Orthodox Christians, position on divorce and remarriage, 756
Eastern Pennsylvania Psychiatric Institute, 774
Eating disorders, of adolescents, 391–392
  sexual abuse-related, 398
Eclecticism
  of family research, 214
  postmodernist concept of, 208
Ecole des Hautes Etudes, Sixieme Section de l', 15
Ecological fallacy, 264
Ecological systems perspective, on parent–child relationship, 353–359
Ecological theory, 263
Economic development, 97
Economic factors, *see also* Income
  in child custody, 484, 487
  in divorce, 479–480, 483, 484, 487, 491–492
  in domestic violence, 443
  in family policy, 637–638, 637–638
  in female labor force participation, 45
  in marital dissolution, 57, 58
  in marital satisfaction, 442
  in marriage age, 48
  in marriage patterns, 17
  in retirement, 168
Economic interdependence, 41
Economic marital acquisitions, 623
Economic mobility, 113
Economic Recovery Act, 643
Economics, supply-side, 7

ISBN 0-306-45754-7

90000

9 780306 457548

DATE DUE

ILL			
4613298			
3/20/02			
FE 27 '06			
GAYLORD			PRINTED IN U.S.A.